PEARSON

COMMON CORE

Literature

GRADE 7

PEARSON

HOBOKEN, NEW JERSEY • BOSTON, MASSACHUSETTS
CHANDLER, ARIZONA • GLENVIEW, ILLINOIS

ISBN-13:   978-0-13-326818-8
ISBN-10:   0-13-326818-7
6 7 8 9 10 11 12 V057 18 17 16 15 14

PEARSON
COMMON CORE
Literature

GRADE 7

PEARSON

HOBOKEN, NEW JERSEY • BOSTON, MASSACHUSETTS
CHANDLER, ARIZONA • GLENVIEW, ILLINOIS

Contributing Authors

The contributing authors guided the direction and philosophy of Pearson Common Core Literature. They helped to build the pedagogical integrity of the program by contributing content expertise, knowledge of the Common Core State Standards, and support for the shifts in instruction the Common Core will bring. Their knowledge, combined with classroom and professional experience, ensures Pearson Common Core Literature is relevant for both teachers and students.

William G. Brozo, Ph.D., is a Professor of Literacy in the Graduate School of Education at George Mason University in Fairfax, Virginia. He earned his bachelor's degree from the University of North Carolina and his master's and doctorate from the University of South Carolina. He has taught reading and language arts in the Carolinas and is the author of numerous articles on literacy development for children and young adults. His books include *To Be a Boy, To Be a Reader: Engaging Teen and Preteen Boys in Active Literacy; Readers, Teachers, Learners: Expanding Literacy Across the Content Areas; Content Literacy for Today's Adolescents: Honoring Diversity and Building Competence; Supporting Content Area Literacy with Technology* (Pearson); and *Setting the Pace: A Speed, Comprehension, and Study Skills Program*. His newest book is *RTI and the Adolescent Reader: Responsive Literacy Instruction in Secondary Schools*. As an international consultant, Dr. Brozo has provided technical support to teachers from the Balkans to the Middle East, and he is currently a member of a European Union research grant team developing curriculum and providing adolescent literacy professional development for teachers across Europe.

Diane Fettrow spent the majority of her teaching career in Broward County, Florida, teaching high school English courses and serving as department chair. She also worked as an adjunct instructor at Broward College, Nova Southeastern University, and Florida Atlantic University. After she left the classroom, she served as Secondary Language Arts Curriculum Supervisor for several years, working with more than 50 of the district's high schools, centers, and charter schools. During her time as curriculum supervisor, she served on numerous local and state committees; she also served as Florida's K–12 ELA content representative to the PARCC Model Content Frameworks Rapid Response Feedback Group and the PARCC K–12 and Upper Education Engagement Group. Currently she presents workshops on the Common Core State Standards and is working with Pearson on aligning materials to the CCSS.

Kelly Gallagher is a full-time English teacher at Magnolia High School in Anaheim, California, where he has taught for twenty-seven years. He is the former co-director of the South Basin Writing Project at California State University, Long Beach, and the author of *Reading Reasons: Motivational Mini-Lessons for Middle and High School; Deeper Reading: Comprehending Challenging Texts, 4–12; Teaching Adolescent Writers;* and *Readicide: How Schools Are Killing Reading and What You Can Do About It*. He is also a principal author of *Prentice Hall Writing Coach* (Pearson, 2012). Kelly's latest book is *Write Like This* (Stenhouse). Follow Kelly on Twitter @KellyGToGo, and visit him at www.kellygallagher.org.

Elfrieda "Freddy' Hiebert, Ph.D., is President and CEO of TextProject, a nonprofit organization that provides resources to support higher reading levels. She is also a research associate at the University of California, Santa Cruz. Dr. Hiebert received her Ph.D. in Educational Psychology from the University of Wisconsin-Madison. She has worked in the field of early reading acquisition for 45 years, first as a teacher's aide and teacher of primary-level students in California and, subsequently, as a teacher educator and researcher at the universities of Kentucky, Colorado-Boulder, Michigan, and California-Berkeley. Her research addresses how fluency, vocabulary, and knowledge can be fostered through appropriate texts. Professor Hiebert's research has been published in numerous scholarly journals, and she has authored or edited nine books. Professor Hiebert's model of accessible texts for beginning and struggling readers—TExT—has been used to develop numerous reading programs that are widely used in schools. Dr. Hiebert is the 2008 recipient of the William S. Gray Citation of Merit, awarded by the International Reading Association; is a member of the Reading Hall of Fame; and has chaired a group of early childhood literacy experts who served in an advisory capacity to the CCSS writers.

Donald J. Leu, Ph.D., is the John and Maria Neag Endowed Chair in Literacy and Technology and holds a joint appointment in Curriculum and Instruction and Educational Psychology in the Neag School of Education at the University of Connecticut. Don is an international authority on literacy education, especially the new skills and strategies required to read, write, and learn with Internet technologies and the best instructional practices that prepare students for these new literacies. He is a member of the Reading Hall of Fame, a Past President of the National Reading Conference, and a former member of the Board of Directors of the International Reading Association. Don is a Principal Investigator on a number of federal research grants, and his work has been funded by the U.S. Department of Education, the National Science Foundation, and the Bill and Melinda Gates Foundation, among others. He recently edited the *Handbook of Research on New Literacies* (Erlbaum, 2008).

Ernest Morrell, Ph.D., is a professor of English Education at Teachers College, Columbia University, and the president-elect of the National Council of Teachers of English (NCTE). He is also the Director of Teachers College's Harlem-based Institute for Urban and Minority Education (IUME). Dr. Morrell was an award-winning high school English teacher in California, and he now works with teachers and schools across the country to infuse multicultural literature, youth popular culture, and media production into standards-based literacy curricula and after-school programs. He is the author of nearly 100 articles and book chapters as well as five books, including *Critical Media Pedagogy: Achievement, Production, and Justice in City Schools* and *Linking Literacy and Popular Culture*. In his spare time he coaches youth sports and writes poems and plays.

Karen Wixson, Ph.D., is Dean of the School of Education at the University of North Carolina, Greensboro. She has published widely in the areas of literacy curriculum, instruction, and assessment. Dr. Wixson has been an advisor to the National Research Council and helped develop the National Assessment of Educational Progress (NAEP) reading tests. She is a former member of the IRA Board of Directors and co-chair of the IRA Commission on RTI. Recently, Dr. Wixson served on the English Language Arts Work Team that was part of the Common Core State Standards Initiative.

Grant Wiggins, Ed.D., is the President of Authentic Education in Hopewell, New Jersey. He earned his Ed.D. from Harvard University and his B.A. from St. John's College in Annapolis. Grant consults with schools, districts, and state education departments on a variety of reform matters; organizes conferences and workshops; and develops print materials and Web resources on curricular change. He is perhaps best known for being the co-author, with Jay McTighe, of *Understanding by Design* and *The Understanding by Design Handbook,* the award-winning and highly successful materials on curriculum published by ASCD.

INTRODUCTORY UNIT Contents

COMMON CORE FOUNDATIONS

COMMON CORE STATE STANDARDS

The following standards are introduced in this unit and revisited throughout the program.

Reading Literature

2. Determine a theme or central idea of a text and analyze in detail its development over the course of the text; provide an objective summary of the text.

10. By the end of the year, read and comprehend literature, including stories, dramas, and poems, in the grades 6–8 text complexity band proficiently, with scaffolding as needed at the high end of the range.

Reading Informational Text

2. Determine a central idea on a text and analyze its development over the course of the text; provide an objective summary of the text.

8. Trace and evaluate the argument and specific claims in a text, assessing whether the reasoning is sound and the evidence is relevant and sufficient to support the claims.

Writing

1. Write arguments to support claims with clear reasons and relevant evidence.

2. Write informative/explanatory texts to examine a topic and convey ideas, concepts, and information through the selection, organization, and analysis of relevant content.

5. With some guidance and support from peers and adults, develop and strengthen writing as needed by planning, revising, editing, rewriting, or trying a new approach, focusing on how well purpose and audience have been addressed.

7. Conduct short research projects to answer a question, drawing on several sources and generating additional related, focused questions for further research and investigation.

8. Gather relevant information from multiple print and digital sources, using search terms effectively; assess the credibility and accuracy of each source; and quote or paraphrase the data and conclusions of others while avoiding plagiarism and following a standard format for citation.

9. Draw evidence from literary or informational texts to support analysis, reflection, and research.

Additional standards addressed in these workshops:
Writing
1.a, 1.b, 1.e, 2.a-c, 2.f
Language
1, 2, 6

DIGITAL ASSETS KEY

These digital resources, as well as audio and the Online Writer's Notebook, can be found at **pearsonrealize.com**.

- Interactive Whiteboard Activities
- Virtual Tour
- Close Reading Notebook
- Video
- Close Reading Tool for Annotating Texts
- Grammar Tutorials
- Online Text Set

UNIT 1 Unit at a Glance

■ UNIT VOCABULARY

Academic Vocabulary appears in *blue*.

Introducing the Big Question   *attitude, challenge, communication, competition, compromise, conflict, danger, desire, disagreement, misunderstanding, obstacle, opposition, outcome, resolution, struggle, understanding*

Rikki-tikki-tavi   *revived, immensely, veranda, mourning, consolation, cunningly*

Two Kinds *from* The Joy Luck Club   *reproach, conspired, devastated, nonchalantly, expectations, sentimental*

The Third Wish   *verge, dabbling, presumptuous, rash, remote, malicious*

Ribbons   *sensitive, meek, coax, laborious, exertion, furrowed*

The Night the Bed Fell; Stolen Day   *ominous, perilous, culprit, solemn, assumption, common, discover, perspective*

Amigo Brothers   *devastating, perpetual, evading, effective, literally, communication*

Get More From Competition   *maximize, optimal, deteriorates, attitude, sufficient, resolution*

Forget Fun, Embrace Enjoyment   *advocacy, trivialness, endeavors, perceive, explain, cite*

Video Game Competitiveness, Not Violence, Spurs Aggression, Study Suggests   *aggressive, spur, blunt, experiment, insight*

Win Some, Lose Some   *aversion, imposters, emerged, attitude, convince*

Orlando Magic   *illustrate, debate*

■ COMMON CORE STATE STANDARDS

For the full wording of the standards, see the standards chart following the Contents pages.

Reading Literature
RL.7.1, RL.7.2, RL.7.3, RL.7.4, RL.7.6, RL.7.10

Reading Informational Text
RI.7.1, RI.7.2, RI.7.3, RI.7.4, RI.7.5, RI.7.6, RI.7.7, RI.7.8, RI.7.10

Writing
W.7.1, W.7.1.a, W.7.1.b, W.7.1.c, W.7.1.d, W.7.1.e, W.7.2, W.7.2.a, W.7.2.c, W.7.2.d, W.7.2.e, W.7.3, W.7.3.a, W.7.3.b, W.7.3.c, W.7.3.d, W.7.3.e, W.7.5, W.7.7, W.7.8, W.7.9, W.7.9.a

Speaking and Listening
SL.7.1, SL.7.1.a, SL.7.1.b, SL.7.1.c, SL.7.1.d, SL.7.2, SL.7.3, SL.7.4, SL.7.5, SL.7.6

Language
L.7.1, L.7.2, L.7.2.a, L.7.3.a, L.7.4.a, L.7.4.b, L.7.4.c, L.7.4.d, L.7.5.a, L.7.5.b, L.7.5.c, L.7.6

UNIT 2 What should we learn?

DIGITAL ASSETS KEY

These digital resources, as well as audio and the Online Writer's Notebook, can be found at **pearsonrealize.com**.

🖵 Interactive Whiteboard Activities

🌐 Virtual Tour

📋 Close Reading Notebook

▶️ Video

🔍 Close Reading Tool for Annotating Texts

G Grammar Tutorials

📚 Online Text Set

■ UNIT VOCABULARY

Academic Vocabulary appears in *blue*.

Introducing the Big Question   *analyze, curiosity, discover, evaluate, examine, experiment, explore, facts, information, inquire, interview, investigate, knowledge, question, understand*

Life Without Gravity   *manned, spines, feeble, blander, globules, readapted*

I Am a Native of North America   *distinct, communal, justifies, promote, hoarding, integration*

All Together Now   *legislation, tolerant, culminated, fundamental, equality, optimist*

Rattlesnake Hunt   *adequate, desolate, forage, translucent, arid, mortality*

***from* Barrio Boy; A Day's Wait**   *reassuring, contraption, formidable, epidemic, flushed, evidently, adaptation, culture, diversity, tradition*

No Gumption   *gumption, crucial, aptitude, identify, insight, purpose*

Intrinsic Motivation Doesn't Exist, Researcher Says   *psychologists, tout, fosters, perceptions, investigate, acknowledge*

The Cremation of Sam McGee   *cremated, whimper, loathed, images, contribute, outcome*

A Special Gift—The Legacy of "Snowflake" Bentley   *hexagons, evaporated, negatives, observe, focus, inquiry*

All Stories Are Anansi's   *dispute, opinion, acknowledge, communicate, contribute, tradition*

Maslow's Theory of Motivation and Human Needs   *diagram, explain, theory*

■ COMMON CORE STATE STANDARDS

For the full wording of the standards, see the standards chart following the Contents pages.

Reading Literature
RL.7.1, RL.7.2, RL.7.3, RL.7.4, RL.7.6, RL.7.10

Reading Informational Text
RI.7.1, RI.7.2, RI.7.3, RI.7.4, RI.7.5, RI.7.6, RI.7.7, RI.7.8, RI.7.9, RI.7.10

Writing
W.7.1, W.7.1.a, W.7.1.b, W.7.1.c, W.7.1.d, W.7.1.e, W.7.2, W.7.2.a, W.7.2.b, W.7.2.d, W.7.3, W.7.3.a, W.7.3.b, W.7.3.d, W.7.3.e, W.7.4, W.7.5, W.7.6, W.7.7, W.7.8, W.7.9, W.7.9.b, W.7.10

Speaking and Listening
SL.7.1, SL.7.1.a, SL.7.1.b, SL.7.1.c, SL.7.1.d, SL.7.2, SL.7.3, SL.7.4

Language
L.7.1, L.7.2, L.7.2.b, L.7.3, L.7.3.a, L.7.4, L.7.4.b, L.7.4.c, L.7.4.d, L.7.5.a, L.7.5.b, L.7.6

UNIT 3   What is the best way to communicate?

DIGITAL ASSETS KEY

These digital resources, as well as audio and the Online Writer's Notebook, can be found at **pearsonrealize.com**.

🖥 Interactive Whiteboard Activities

🌐 Virtual Tour

📋 Close Reading Notebook

📹 Video

🔍 Close Reading Tool for Annotating Texts

G Grammar Tutorials

📚 Online Text Set

UNIT 3 Unit at a Glance

UNIT VOCABULARY

Academic Vocabulary appears in *blue*.

Introducing the Big Question *communicate, contribute, enrich, entertain, express, inform, learn, listen, media, produce, react, speak, teach, technology, transmit*

Poetry Collection 1 *translates, luminous, minnow, swerve, utter, fragrant*

Poetry Collection 2 *fascinated, granite, crystal, haunches*

Poetry Collection 3 *groves, fathom, withered, curdled, sputters, smattering*

Poetry Collection 4 *downy, coveted, envying, incessantly, uncommonly, supple*

Miracles; in Just— *exquisite, distinct, appreciate, insight, perceive, unique*

The Highwayman *torrent, bound, strove, contrast, identify, opposing*

Carnegie Hero Fund Commission *commemorated, prompted, eligible, explain, definition, characteristic*

The Myth of the Outlaw *nondescript, repulsive, commissioned, attitude, reflect, viewpoint*

The Real Story of a Cowboy's Life *discipline, gauge, emphatic, challenge, attitude, evaluate*

After Twenty Years *spectators, intricate, simultaneously, communicate, contradiction, contribute*

Harriet Tubman *subjected, feigned, conferred, media, solve, reactions*

Wanted: Harriet Tubman, Abolitionist *convincing, facts, conclude*

COMMON CORE STATE STANDARDS

For the full wording of the standards, see the standards chart following the Contents pages.

Reading Literature
RL.7.1, RL.7.2, RL.7.3, RL.7.4, RL.7.5, RL.7.6, RL.7.7, RL.7.10

Reading Informational Text
RI.7.1, RI.7.2, RI.7.3, RI.7.4, RI.7.5, RI.7.6, RI.7.9, RI.7.10

Writing
W.7.1, W.7.1.d, W.7.2, W.7.2.a, W.7.2.b, W.7.2.c, W.7.2.d, W.7.2.e, W.7.3, W.7.3.a, W.7.3.b, W.7.3.d, W.7.3.e, W.7.4, W.7.5, W.7.6, W.7.7, W.7.8, W.7.9, W.7.9.a, W.7.10

Speaking and Listening
SL.7.1, SL.7.1.a, SL.7.1.b, SL.7.1.c, SL.7.1.d, SL.7.2, SL.7.3, SL.7.4, SL.7.5, SL.7.6

Language
L.7.1, L.7.1.a, L.7.1.b, L.7.1.c, L.7.2, L.7.3, L.7.3.a, L.7.4, L.7.4.a, L.7.4.c, L.7.4.d, L.7.5, L.7.5.b, L.7.5.c, L.7.6

UNIT 4　Do others see us more clearly than we see ourselves?

DIGITAL ASSETS KEY

These digital resources, as well as audio and the Online Writer's Notebook, can be found at **pearsonrealize.com**.

- Interactive Whiteboard Activities
- Virtual Tour
- Close Reading Notebook
- Video
- Close Reading Tool for Annotating Texts
- Grammar Tutorials
- Online Text Set

UNIT 4 · Unit at a Glance

■ READ

Text Analysis
Dialogue
Stage Directions
Characters' Motives
Setting
Main Idea
Tone
Author's Argument
Expository Writing

Comprehension
Purpose for Reading
Analyze Point of View

Language Study
Latin root *-grat-*
Latin prefix *inter-*

Conventions
Prepositions and Prepositional Phrases
Appositives and Appositive Phrases

Language Study Workshop
Connotation and Denotation

■ DISCUSS

Presentation of Ideas
Dramatic Monologue

Responding to Text
Panel Discussion
Partner Discussion
Debate
Group Discussion

Speaking and Listening Workshop
Conducting an Interview

■ RESEARCH

Research and Technology
Costume Plans

Investigate the Topic:
Leaders and Followers
Crowds and Their Actions
Bullying
McCarthyism
Mass Hysteria
Herd Mentality
Wisdom of the Crowd
Memorial to a Leader

■ WRITE

Writing to Sources
Letter
Tribute
Editorial
Argumentative Essay
News Report
Argument
Expository Essay
Autobiographical Narrative

Writing Process Workshop
Argument: Review of a Short Story
Word Choice: Finding the Perfect Word
Sentence Fluency: Revising Sentences Using Participles

■ **UNIT VOCABULARY**

Academic Vocabulary appears in *blue*.

Introducing the Big Question   *appearance, appreciate, assumption, bias, characteristic, define, focus, identify, ignore, image, perception, perspective, reaction, reflect, reveal*

A Christmas Carol: Scrooge and Marley, Act I   *implored, morose, destitute, void, conveyed, gratitude*

A Christmas Carol: Scrooge and Marley, Act II   *astonish, compulsion, severe, meager, audible, intercedes*

Zoos: Joys or Jails?; Kid Territory: Why Do We Need Zoos?   *habitats, vulnerable, resources*

The Monsters Are Due on Maple Street   *flustered, persistently, defiant, affect, identify, convince*

All Summer in a Day   *slackening, vital, resilient, environment, awareness, incident*

Joseph R. McCarthy   *unscrupulous, furor, riveted, evaluations, debate, investigations*

The Salem Witch Trials of 1692   *accusations, successive, disbanded, established, determination, formal, simultaneously*

Herd Mentality? The Freakonomics of Boarding a Bus   *investment, muster, succumb, behavior, contribute, assumptions*

Follow the Leader: Democracy in Herd Mentality   *pertinent, explicit, inherent, transmitting, complex, refute*

Martin Luther King, Jr., Memorial   *understand, materials, significance*

■ **COMMON CORE STATE STANDARDS**

For the full wording of the standards, see the standards chart following the Contents pages.

Reading Literature
RL.7.1, RL.7.2, RL.7.3, RL.7.4', RL.7.5, RL.7.7, RL.7.9, RL.7.10

Reading Informational Text
RI.7.1, RI.7.2, RI.7.3, RI.7.4, RI.7.5, RI.7.6, RI.7.9, RI.7.10

Writing
W.7.1, W.7.1.a, W.7.1.b, W.7.1.c, W.7.1.d, W.7.1.e, W.7.2, W.7.2.a, W.7.2.b, W.7.3, W.7.3.a, W.7.3.b, W.7.3.d, W.7.3.e, W.7.4, W.7.5, W.7.7, W.7.8, W.7.9, W.7.9.a, W.7.10

Speaking and Listening
SL.7.1, SL.7.1.a, SL.7.1.b, SL.7.1.c, SL.7.1.d, SL.7.2, SL.7.4, SL.7.5, SL.7.6

Language
L.7.1, L.7.1.a, L.7.1.c, L.7.2, L.7.2.b, L.7.3, L.7.3.a, L.7.4.a, L.7.4.b, L.7.4.c, L.7.5.b, L.7.5.c, L.7.6

UNIT 5 Community or individual—which is more important?

PART 3
TEXT SET DEVELOPING INSIGHT 🌐

BECOMING AMERICAN

PART 4
DEMONSTRATING INDEPENDENCE

Independent Reading

ONLINE TEXT SET 📚

DIGITAL ASSETS KEY

These digital resources, as well as audio and the Online Writer's Notebook, can be found at **pearsonrealize.com**.

🖥 Interactive Whiteboard Activities

🌐 Virtual Tour

📋 Close Reading Notebook

▶️ Video

🔍 Close Reading Tool for Annotating Texts

Ⓖ Grammar Tutorials

📚 Online Text Set

■ **READ**

Text Analysis
Myth
Legend and Fact
Cultural Context
Folk Tales
Comparing Universal Themes
Symbolism
Narrative Poem
Narration
Direct Quotation
Dialogue
Idiom

Comprehension
Cause and Effect
Compare and Contrast

Language Study
Latin root -dom-
Latin prefix uni-
Latin suffix -ity
Greek root -myst-

Conventions
Infinitive Phrases and Gerund Phrases
Punctuation Marks
Commas
Capitalization

Language Study Workshop
Figurative Language

■ **DISCUSS**

Presentation of Ideas
Persuasive Speech
Television News Report

Comprehension and Collaboration
Debate
Retelling

Responding to Text
Group Discussion
Partner Discussion
Debate
Write and Discuss

Speaking and Listening Workshop
Research Presentation

■ **RESEARCH**

Investigate the Topic: Becoming American
Politics and Becoming American
Help in "Becoming American"
American Literature
The Chinese Exclusion Act
"The New Colossus"
Urban "Melting Pots"
Immigration to the United States

■ **WRITE**

Writing to Sources
Myth
Description
Plot Summary
Review
Comparison-and-Contrast Essay
Autobiographical Narrative
Expository Essay
Explanatory Essay
Problem-and-Solution Essay
Short Story
Informative Essay

Writing Process Workshop
Explanatory Text: Cause-and-Effect Essay
Organization: Organize Logically
Conventions: Revising Incorrect Use of Commas

■ UNIT VOCABULARY

Academic Vocabulary appears in *blue*.

Introducing the Big Question *common, community, culture, custom, diversity, duty, environment, ethnicity, family, group, individual, team, tradition, unify, unique*

Demeter and Persephone *defies, monarch, dominions, intervene, realm, abode*

Popocatepetl and Ixtlaccihuatl *shortsightedness, routed, decreed, relished, unanimous, feebleness*

Sun and Moon in a Box *regretted, reliable, curiosity, pestering, relented, cunning*

The People Could Fly *shed, scorned, hoed, croon, mystery, shuffle*

The Voyage; To the Top of Everest *impervious, inflicted, designated, saturation, attitude, challenge, environment, outcome*

My First Free Summer *vowed, summoned, contradiction, explain, perspective, strategy*

How I learned English *notions, transfixed, writhing, relationship, outcome, explain*

mk *adequate, deceive, ignorant, communicate, predict, process*

Byron Yee: Discovering a Paper Son *decipher, interrogations, scrutiny, discover, enhance, cites*

from **Grandpa and the Statue** *subscribed, peeved, swindle, characterize, debate, discover*

Melting Pot *fluent, bigots, dolefully, community, attitude, compose*

United States Immigration Statistics *legal, approximately, individual*

■ COMMON CORE STATE STANDARDS

For the full wording of the standards, see the standards chart following the Contents pages.

Reading Literature
RL.7.1, RL.7.2, RL.7.3, RL.7.4, RL.7.5, RL.7.6, RL.7.9, RL.7.10

Reading Informational Text
RI.7.1, RI.7.2, RI.7.3, RI.7.4, RI.7.5, RI.7.6, RI.7.9, RI.7.10

Writing
W.7.1, W.7.1.a, W.7.1.b, W.7.2, W.7.2.a, W.7.2.b, W.7.2.c, W.7.2.d, W.7.2.e, W.7.2.f, W.7.3, W.7.3.a, W.7.3.b, W.7.3.d, W.7.3.e, W.7.4, W.7.5, W.7.7, W.7.8, W.7.9, W.7.9.a

Speaking and Listening
SL.7.1, SL.7.1.a, SL.7.1.b, SL.7.1.c, SL.7.1.d, SL.7.2, SL.7.4, SL.7.5, SL.7.6

Language
L.7.1, L.7.1.a, L.7.2, L.7.2.a, L.7.2.b, L.7.3, L.7.3.a, L.7.4, L.7.4.b, L.7.5, L.7.5.a, L.7.5.b, L.7.6

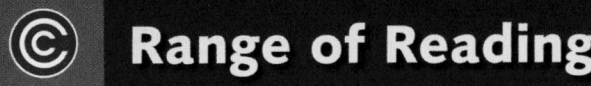

Literature

ONLINE LITERATURE LIBRARY

Highlighted selections are found in the **Online Literature Library (OLL)** in the Online Student Edition.

Range of Reading

Informational Text—Literary Nonfiction

ONLINE LITERATURE LIBRARY

Highlighted selections are found in the
Online Literature Library (OLL) in the
Online Student Edition.

Features and Workshops

ONLINE TEXT SETS

These selections can be found in the **Online Literature Library** in the Online Student Edition.

The Common Core State Standards will prepare you to succeed in college and your future career. They are separated into four sections—Reading (Literature and Informational Text), Writing, Speaking and Listening, and Language. Beginning each section, the College and Career Readiness Anchor Standards define what you need to achieve by the end of high school. The grade-specific standards that follow define what you need to know by the end of your current grade level.

Common Core Reading Standards

College and Career Readiness Anchor Standards

Key Ideas and Details

1. Read closely to determine what the text says explicitly and to make logical inferences from it; cite specific textual evidence when writing or speaking to support conclusions drawn from the text.

2. Determine central ideas or themes of a text and analyze their development; summarize the key supporting details and ideas.

3. Analyze how and why individuals, events, and ideas develop and interact over the course of a text.

Craft and Structure

4. Interpret words and phrases as they are used in a text, including determining technical, connotative, and figurative meanings, and analyze how specific word choices shape meaning or tone.

5. Analyze the structure of texts, including how specific sentences, paragraphs, and larger portions of the text (e.g., a section, chapter, scene, or stanza) relate to each other and the whole.

6. Assess how point of view or purpose shapes the content and style of a text.

Integration of Knowledge and Ideas

7. Integrate and evaluate content presented in diverse formats and media, including visually and quantitatively, as well as in words.

8. Delineate and evaluate the argument and specific claims in a text, including the validity of the reasoning as well as the relevance and sufficiency of the evidence.

9. Analyze how two or more texts address similar themes or topics in order to build knowledge or to compare the approaches the authors take.

Range of Reading and Level of Text Complexity

10. Read and comprehend complex literary and informational texts independently and proficiently.

Grade 7 Reading Standards for Literature

Key Ideas and Details

1. Cite textual evidence to support analysis of what the text says explicitly as well as inferences drawn from the text.

2. Determine a theme or central idea of a text and analyze its development over the course of the text; provide an objective summary of the text.

3. Analyze how particular elements of a story or drama interact (e.g., how setting shapes the characters or plot).

Craft and Structure

4. Determine the meaning of words and phrases as they are used in a text, including figurative and connotative meanings; analyze the impact of rhymes and other repetitions of sounds (e.g., alliteration) on a specific verse or stanza of a poem or section of a story or drama.

5. Analyze how a drama's or poem's form or structure (e.g., soliloquy, sonnet) contributes to its meaning.

6. Analyze how an author develops and contrasts the points of view of different characters or narrators in a text.

Integration of Knowledge and Ideas

7. Compare and contrast a written story, drama, or poem to its audio, filmed, staged, or multimedia version, analyzing the effects of techniques unique to each medium (e.g., lighting, sound, color, or camera focus and angles in a film).

8. (Not applicable to literature)

9. Compare and contrast a fictional portrayal of a time, place, or character and a historical account of the same period as a means of understanding how authors of fiction use or alter history.

Range of Reading and Level of Text Complexity

10. By the end of the year, read and comprehend literature, including stories, dramas, and poems, in the grades 6–8 text complexity band proficiently, with scaffolding as needed at the high end of the range.

Grade 7 Reading Standards for Informational Text

Key Ideas and Details

1. Cite several pieces of textual evidence to support analysis of what the text says explicitly as well as inferences drawn from the text.

2. Determine two or more central ideas in a text and analyze their development over the course of the text; provide an objective summary of the text.

3. Analyze the interactions between individuals, events, and ideas in a text (e.g., how ideas influence individuals or events, or how individuals influence ideas or events).

Craft and Structure

4. Determine the meaning of words and phrases as they are used in a text, including figurative, connotative, and technical meanings; analyze the impact of a specific word choice on meaning and tone.

5. Analyze the structure an author uses to organize a text, including how the major sections contribute to the whole and to the development of the ideas.

6. Determine an author's point of view or purpose in a text and analyze how the author distinguishes his or her position from that of others.

Integration of Knowledge and Ideas

7. Compare and contrast a text to an audio, video, or multimedia version of the text, analyzing each medium's portrayal of the subject (e.g., how the delivery of a speech affects the impact of the words).

8. Trace and evaluate the argument and specific claims in a text, assessing whether the reasoning is sound and the evidence is relevant and sufficient to support the claims.

9. Analyze how two or more authors writing about the same topic shape their presentations of key information by emphasizing different evidence or advancing different interpretations of facts.

Range of Reading and Level of Text Complexity

10. By the end of the year, read and comprehend literary nonfiction in the grades 6–8 text complexity band proficiently, with scaffolding as needed at the high end of the range.

Common Core Writing Standards

College and Career Readiness Anchor Standards

Text Types and Purposes

1. Write arguments to support claims in an analysis of substantive topics or texts, using valid reasoning and relevant and sufficient evidence.

2. Write informative/explanatory texts to examine and convey complex ideas and information clearly and accurately through the effective selection, organization, and analysis of content.

3. Write narratives to develop real or imagined experiences or events using effective technique, well-chosen details, and well-structured event sequences.

Production and Distribution of Writing

4. Produce clear and coherent writing in which the development, organization, and style are appropriate to task, purpose, and audience.

5. Develop and strengthen writing as needed by planning, revising, editing, rewriting, or trying a new approach.

6. Use technology, including the Internet, to produce and publish writing and to interact and collaborate with others.

Research to Build and Present Knowledge

7. Conduct short as well as more sustained research projects based on focused questions, demonstrating understanding of the subject under investigation.

8. Gather relevant information from multiple print and digital sources, assess the credibility and accuracy of each source, and integrate the information while avoiding plagiarism.

9. Draw evidence from literary or informational texts to support analysis, reflection, and research.

Range of Writing

10. Write routinely over extended time frames (time for research, reflection, and revision) and shorter time frames (a single sitting or a day or two) for a range of tasks, purposes, and audiences.

Grade 7 Writing Standards

Text Types and Purposes

1. Write arguments to support claims with clear reasons and relevant evidence.

    a. Introduce claim(s), acknowledge alternate or opposing claims, and organize the reasons and evidence logically.

    b. Support claim(s) with logical reasoning and relevant evidence, using accurate, credible sources and demonstrating an understanding of the topic or text.

    c. Use words, phrases, and clauses to create cohesion and clarify the relationships among claim(s), reasons, and evidence.

    d. Establish and maintain a formal style.

    e. Provide a concluding statement or section that follows from and supports the argument presented.

2. Write informative/explanatory texts to examine a topic and convey ideas, concepts, and information through the selection, organization, and analysis of relevant content.

    a. Introduce a topic clearly, previewing what is to follow; organize ideas, concepts, and information, using strategies such as definition, classification, comparison/contrast, and cause/effect; include formatting (e.g., headings), graphics (e.g., charts, tables), and multimedia when useful to aiding comprehension.

    b. Develop the topic with relevant facts, definitions, concrete details, quotations, or other information and examples.

    c. Use appropriate transitions to create cohesion and clarify the relationships among ideas and concepts.

    d. Use precise language and domain-specific vocabulary to inform about or explain the topic.

    e. Establish and maintain a formal style.

    f. Provide a concluding statement or section that follows from and supports the information or explanation presented.

3. Write narratives to develop real or imagined experiences or events using effective technique, relevant descriptive details, and well-structured event sequences.

    a. Engage and orient the reader by establishing a context and point of view and introducing a narrator and/or characters; organize an event sequence that unfolds naturally and logically.

    b. Use narrative techniques, such as dialogue, pacing, and description, to develop experiences, events, and/or characters.

    c. Use a variety of transition words, phrases, and clauses to convey sequence and signal shifts from one time frame or setting to another.

    d. Use precise words and phrases, relevant descriptive details, and sensory language to capture the action and convey experiences and events.

    e. Provide a conclusion that follows from and reflects on the narrated experiences or events.

Production and Distribution of Writing

4. Produce clear and coherent writing in which the development, organization, and style are appropriate to task, purpose, and audience.

5. With some guidance and support from peers and adults, develop and strengthen writing as needed by planning, revising, editing, rewriting, or trying a new approach, focusing on how well purpose and audience have been addressed.

6. Use technology, including the Internet, to produce and publish writing and link to and cite sources as well as to interact and collaborate with others, including linking to and citing sources.

Research to Build and Present Knowledge

7. Conduct short research projects to answer a question, drawing on several sources and generating additional related, focused questions for further research and investigation.

8. Gather relevant information from multiple print and digital sources, using search terms effectively; assess the credibility and accuracy of each source; and quote or paraphrase the data and conclusions of others while avoiding plagiarism and following a standard format for citation.

9. Draw evidence from literary or informational texts to support analysis, reflection, and research.

   a. Apply *grade 7 Reading standards* to literature (e.g., "Compare and contrast a fictional portrayal of a time, place, or character and a historical account of the same period as a means of understanding how authors of fiction use or alter history").

   b. Apply *grade 7 Reading standards* to literary nonfiction (e.g., "Trace and evaluate the argument and specific claims in a text, assessing whether the reasoning is sound and the evidence is relevant and sufficient to support the claims").

Range of Writing

10. Write routinely over extended time frames (time for research, reflection, and revision) and shorter time frames (a single sitting or a day or two) for a range of discipline-specific tasks, purposes, and audiences.

Common Core State Standards Overview

Common Core Speaking and Listening Standards

College and Career Readiness Anchor Standards

Comprehension and Collaboration

1. Prepare for and participate effectively in a range of conversations and collaborations with diverse partners, building on others' ideas and expressing their own clearly and persuasively.

2. Integrate and evaluate information presented in diverse media and formats, including visually, quantitatively, and orally.

3. Evaluate a speaker's point of view, reasoning, and use of evidence and rhetoric.

Presentation of Knowledge and Ideas

4. Present information, findings, and supporting evidence such that listeners can follow the line of reasoning and the organization, development, and style are appropriate to task, purpose, and audience.

5. Make strategic use of digital media and visual displays of data to express information and enhance understanding of presentations.

6. Adapt speech to a variety of contexts and communicative tasks, demonstrating command of formal English when indicated or appropriate.

Grade 7 Speaking and Listening Standards

Comprehension and Collaboration

1. Engage effectively in a range of collaborative discussions (one-on-one, in groups, and teacher-led) with diverse partners on *grade 7 topics, texts, and issues,* building on others' ideas and expressing their own clearly.

   a. Come to discussions prepared, having read or researched material under study; explicitly draw on that preparation by referring to evidence on the topic, text, or issue to probe and reflect on ideas under discussion.

   b. Follow rules for collegial discussions, track progress toward specific goals and deadlines, and define individual roles as needed.

   c. Pose questions that elicit elaboration and respond to others' questions and comments with relevant observations and ideas that bring the discussion back on topic as needed.

   d. Acknowledge new information expressed by others and, when warranted, modify their own views.

2. Analyze the main ideas and supporting details presented in diverse media and formats (e.g., visually, quantitatively, orally) and explain how the ideas clarify a topic, text, or issue under study.

3. Delineate a speaker's argument and specific claims, evaluating the soundness of the reasoning and the relevance and sufficiency of the evidence.

Presentation of Knowledge and Ideas

4. Present claims and findings, emphasizing salient points in a focused, coherent manner with pertinent descriptions, facts, details, and examples; use appropriate eye contact, adequate volume, and clear pronunciation.

5. Include multimedia components and visual displays in presentations to clarify claims and findings and emphasize salient points.

6. Adapt speech to a variety of contexts and tasks, demonstrating command of formal English when indicated or appropriate. (See grade 7 Language standards 1 and 3 for specific expectations.)

Common Core State Standards Overview

Common Core Language Standards

Conventions of Standard English

1. Demonstrate command of the conventions of standard English grammar and usage when writing or speaking.

2. Demonstrate command of the conventions of standard English capitalization, punctuation, and spelling when writing.

Knowledge of Language

3. Apply knowledge of language to understand how language functions in different contexts, to make effective choices for meaning or style, and to comprehend more fully when reading or listening.

Vocabulary Acquisition and Use

4. Determine or clarify the meaning of unknown and multiple-meaning words and phrases by using context clues, analyzing meaningful word parts, and consulting general and specialized reference materials, as appropriate.

5. Demonstrate understanding of word relationships, and nuances in word meanings.

6. Acquire and use accurately a range of general academic and domain-specific words and phrases sufficient for reading, writing, speaking, and listening at the college and career readiness level; demonstrate independence in gathering vocabulary knowledge when considering a word or phrase important to comprehension or expression.

Grade 7 Language Standards

Conventions of Standard English

1. Demonstrate command of the conventions of standard English grammar and usage when writing or speaking.

   a. Explain the function of phrases and clauses in general and their function in specific sentences.
   b. Choose among simple, compound, complex, and compound-complex sentences to signal differing relationships among ideas.
   c. Place phrases and clauses within a sentence, recognizing and correcting misplaced and dangling modifiers.

2. Demonstrate command of the conventions of standard English capitalization, punctuation, and spelling when writing.

   a. Use a comma to separate coordinate adjectives (e.g., *It was a fascinating, enjoyable movie but not He wore an old[,] green shirt*).

   b. Spell correctly.

Knowledge of Language

3. Use knowledge of language and its conventions when writing, speaking, reading, or listening.

   a. Choose language that expresses ideas precisely and concisely, recognizing and eliminating wordiness and redundancy.

Vocabulary Acquisition and Use

4. Determine or clarify the meaning of unknown and multiple-meaning words and phrases based on *grade 7 reading and content,* choosing flexibly from a range of strategies.

   a. Use context (e.g., the overall meaning of a sentence or paragraph; a word's position or function in a sentence) as a clue to the meaning of a word or phrase.

   b. Use common, grade-appropriate Greek or Latin affixes and roots as clues to the meaning of a word (e.g., *belligerent, bellicose, rebel*).

   c. Consult general and specialized reference materials (e.g., dictionaries, glossaries, thesauruses), both print and digital, to find the pronunciation of a word or determine or clarify its precise meaning or its part of speech.

   d. Verify the preliminary determination of the meaning of a word or phrase (e.g., by checking the inferred meaning in context or in a dictionary).

5. Demonstrate understanding of figurative language, word relationships, and nuances in word meanings.

   a. Interpret figures of speech (e.g., literary, biblical, and mythological allusions) in context.

   b. Use the relationship between particular words (e.g., synonym/antonym, analogy) to better understand each of the words.

   c. Distinguish among the connotations (associations) of words with similar denotations (definitions) (e.g., *refined, respectful, polite, diplomatic, condescending*).

6. Acquire and use accurately grade-appropriate general academic and domain-specific words and phrases; gather vocabulary knowledge when considering a word or phrase important to comprehension or expression.

COMMON CORE WORKSHOPS

- BUILDING ACADEMIC VOCABULARY

- WRITING AN OBJECTIVE SUMMARY

- COMPREHENDING COMPLEX TEXTS

- ANALYZING ARGUMENTS

- CONDUCTING RESEARCH

Common Core State Standards

Literature 2, 10
Informational Text 2, 8
Writing 1a, 1b, 1e, 2, 2a, 2b, 2c, 2f, 5, 7, 8, 9
Language 1, 2, 6

BUILDING ACADEMIC VOCABULARY

Academic vocabulary is the language you encounter in textbooks and on standardized tests and other assessments. Understanding these words and using them in your classroom discussions and writing will help you communicate your ideas clearly and effectively.

There are two basic types of academic vocabulary: general and domain-specific. **General academic vocabulary** includes words that are not specific to any single course of study. For example, the general academic vocabulary word *analyze* is used in language arts, math, social studies, art, and so on.

Domain-specific academic vocabulary includes words that are usually encountered in the study of a specific discipline. For example, the words *factor* and *remainder* are most often used in mathematics classrooms and texts.

 **Common Core State Standards**

Language

6. Acquire and use accurately grade-appropriate general academic and domain-specific words and phrases; gather vocabulary knowledge when considering a word or phrase important to comprehension or expression.

General Academic Vocabulary

Word	Definition	Related Words	Word in Context
analyze (AN uh lyz) *v.*	break down into parts and examine carefully	analytical analysis	Our assignment is to **analyze** the story's ending.
appreciate (uh PREE shee ayt) *v.*	recognize the value of; be thankful for	appreciative appreciating	Once I read Frost's poem, I learned to **appreciate** his use of symbols.
assumption (uh SUMP shuhn) *n.*	belief or acceptance that something is true	assume assuming	The **assumption** in the essay is well supported by facts.
attitude (AT uh tood) *n.*	mental state involving beliefs, feelings, and values		The writer's **attitude** toward his subject was respectful and full of admiration.
awareness (uh WAYR nihs) *n.*	knowledge gained from one's own perceptions or from information	aware unaware	It is important to develop an **awareness** of the writer's message.
bias (BY uhs) *n.*	tendency to see things from a slanted or prejudiced viewpoint	biased unbiased	You must consider if an advertisement contains **bias** or tries to mislead the reader.
challenge (CHAL uhnj) *v.*	act of calling into question; dare	challenging challenged	Ted invited me to **challenge** him to a debate.

Ordinary Language:
I **like** poems with strong rhymes and rhythms.

Academic Language:
I **appreciate** poems with strong rhymes and rhythms.

Word	Definition	Related Words	Word in Context
characteristic (kar ihk tuh RIHS tihk) *n.*	trait; feature	character characteristically	One **characteristic** of poetry is figurative language.
common (KOM uhn) *adj.*	ordinary; expected	commonality uncommon	It is **common** for an essay to contain humor.
communicate (kuh MYOO nuh kayt) *v.*	share thoughts or feelings, usually in words	communication communicating	It is important to be able to **communicate** thoughts and feelings in writing.
communication (kuh myoo nuh KAY shuhn) *n.*	activity of sharing information or speaking	communicate communicated	There seemed to be a lack of **communication** between the mother and daughter.
community (kuh MYOO nuh tee) *n.*	group of people who share an interest or who live near each other	commune	Local newspapers serve the **community** where the paper is published.
conclude (kuhn KLOOD) *v.*	bring to a close; end	concluding conclusion	The writer was able to **conclude** the essay with a positive memory.
contribute (kuhn TRIHB yoot) *v.*	add to; enrich	contribution contributing	Editorials **contribute** to a public discussion about an issue.
convince (kuhn VIHNS) *v.*	persuade; cause to accept a point of view	convincing convinced	It is important to **convince** readers of the character's dream.
culture (KUL chuhr) *n.*	collected customs of a group or community	cultural culturally	Folk tales reveal the values of a **culture** and teach a lesson.
debate (dih BAYT) *v.*	argue in an attempt to convince	debated debating	The two students tried to **debate** whether or not the new Web site was helpful.
define (dih FYN) *v.*	determine the nature of or give the meaning of	defined definition	I was able to **define** the story's plot quickly.
discover (dihs KUV uhr) *v.*	find or explore	discovering discovery	The reader tries to **discover** the reasons for the character's behavior.
diversity (duh VUR suh tee) *n.*	variety, as of groups or cultures	diverse diversify	Reading works from different writers provides **diversity**.
environment (ehn VY ruhn muhnt) *n.*	surroundings; the natural world	environs environmentally	The essay described the beautiful **environment** where the writer lived.

Ordinary Language: In this essay, I will **tell the meaning** of key terms.

Academic Language: In this essay, I will **define** key terms.

Word	Definition	Related Words	Word in Context
evaluate (ih VAL yoo ayt) v.	judge; determine the value or quality of	evaluated evaluation	The girl was unable to evaluate her friend's work without bias.
examine (ehg ZAM uhn) v.	study in depth; look at closely	examining examination	In order to examine the evidence, it was necessary to research the subject.
explain (ehk SPLAYN) v.	make plain or clear	explaining explanation	I will explain three key factors in the story's success.
explore (ehk SPLAWR) v.	investigate; look into	explored exploration	I wrote a research report to explore my ideas.
facts (fakts) n.	accepted truths or reality	factual nonfactual	I supported my statement with facts and details.
focus (FOH kuhs) n.	central point or topic of investigation	focused focusing	The focus of the essay was to provide information about water safety.
generate (JEHN uhr ayt) v.	create	generated generating	Before researching, I tried to generate a list of topics to explore.
identify (Y DEHN tuh fy) v.	recognize as being; name	identification identity	How do you identify the meaning of this poem?
ignore (ihg NAWR) v.	refuse to notice; disregard	ignored ignoring	If we ignore the message, we miss the purpose of the writing.
image (IHM ihj) n.	picture; representation	imagery imaging	The image in the book helped me to visualize the story.
individual (ihn duh VIHJ oo uhl) n.	single person or thing	individuality individualism	The story is told from the perspective of one individual.
inform (ihn FAWRM) v.	tell; give information about	information informative	The purpose of the research paper was to inform the reader about whales.
inquire (ihn KWYR) v.	ask in order to learn about	inquiring inquired	We were assigned to inquire about weather patterns and present our findings.
insight (IHN syt) n.	ability to see the truth; understanding	insightful insightfully	My teacher shared her insight about the characters with us.

Word	Definition	Related Words	Word in Context
investigate (ihn VEHS tuh gayt) v.	examine thoroughly	investigated investigation	As a team, we were able to investigate each aspect of the problem.
media (MEE dee uh) n.	collected sources of information, including newspapers, television, and the Internet		The media are an everyday source of information and entertainment for the public.
opposition (op uh ZIHSH uhn) n.	state of being against	oppose opposing	The villain in the story provided opposition to the hero's happiness.
outcome (OWT kuhm) n.	way something turns out		We found the outcome of the problem to be a favorable solution.
perceive (puhr SEEV) v.	be aware of; see	perceived perception	I was able to perceive Jenny's character through her actions and words.
perception (puhr SEHP shuhn) n.	act of becoming aware of through one or more of the senses	perceive perceptive	My perception of the character changed over the course of the story.
perspective (puhr SPEHK tihv) n.	point of view		I did not agree with the writer's perspective.
produce (pruh DOOS) v.	make; create	produced producing	In order to produce a new show, the writing team must provide a script.
reaction (ree AK shuhn) n.	response to an influence, action, or statement	react reactor	I had a strong reaction to the claims made in the commercial.
reflect (rih FLEHKT) v.	think about; consider	reflected reflection	In order to reflect on what had been said, I took some quiet time.
resolution (rehz uh LOO shuhn) n.	end of a conflict in which one or both parties is satisfied	resolve resolving	The resolution of the story helped me to see how a compromise can help many people.
team (teem) n.	group united in a common goal	team v.	Our team prepared a report, and each member presented a part of it.

Word	Definition	Related Words	Word in Context
technology (tehk NOL uh jee) n.	practical application of science to business or industry	technological technologically	At one time, the computer was considered a new **technology**.
tradition (truh DIHSH uhn) n.	custom, as of a social group or culture	traditional traditionally	A **tradition** is often handed down to a new generation though storytelling.
transmit (trans MIHT) v.	send or give out	transmitted transmission	We were able to **transmit** our message over the school's radio station.
understanding (uhn duhr STAN dihng) n.	agreement; end of conflict	understand understandable	The students came to an **understanding** of how best to organize the club.
unify (YOO nuh fy) v.	bring together as one	unified unifying	It is important to **unify** details so that they support the central idea.
unique (yoo NEEK) adj.	one of a kind	uniqueness uniquely	Each writer has a **unique** way of telling a story.

Practice

Examples of various kinds of domain-specific academic vocabulary appear in the charts below. Some chart rows are not filled in. In your notebook, look up the definitions of the remaining words, provide one or two related words, and use each word in context.

Social Studies: Domain-Specific Academic Vocabulary

Word	Definition	Related Words	Word in Context
communism (KOM yuh nihz uhm) *n.*	economic and social system where the land and all products of industry belong to the government as a whole	commune communist	**Communism** failed in Eastern Europe.
dissent (dih SEHNT) *n.*	difference of feeling or opinion	dissention dissenter	There was much **dissent** and disagreement in the government.
neutrality (noo TRAL uh tee) *n.*	state of being neutral, or not taking sides in a conflict	neutral	Switzerland kept its **neutrality** during World War II.
segregation (sehg ruh GAY shuhn) *n.*	separation of people because of race, color, or gender	segregate segregated	The civil rights movement helped to end **segregation** in the South.
socialism (SOH shuh lihz uhm) *n.*	theory or system of organization in which major sources of production are owned or controlled by the community or government	social socialist	**Socialism** stresses the community rather than the individual.
adaptation (ad uhp TAY shuhn) *n.*			
emigration (ehm uh GRAY shuhn) *n.*			
colonization (KOL uh nih ZAY shuhn) *n.*			
nobility (noh BIHL uh tee) *n.*			
urbanization (UR buh nih ZAY shuhn) *n.*			

Mathematics: Domain-Specific Academic Vocabulary

Word	Definition	Related Words	Word in Context
negative number (NEHG uh tihv NUM buhr) *n.*	number below zero on a number line; indicated by a minus sign	positive number	The number −4 is a **negative number,** while 4 is a positive number.
odds (odz) *n.*	probability that something will happen	odd oddity	What are the **odds** that I will win the lottery?
proportion (pruh PAWR shuhn) *n.*	statement of the equality of two ratios, or the mathematical relationship of a part to the whole	proportionate proportional	The teacher said that the **proportion** should be written as 4/2 = 10/5.
range (RAYNJ) *n.*	difference between the largest and smallest values in a group of numbers	range *v.* ranging	Find the **range** in the following number set: 2, 3, 4, 5, and 6.
ratio (RAY shee oh) *n.*	proportionate relationship between two numbers		The **ratio** of 5 to 2 is written as 5:2.
minimum (MIHN uh muhm) *n.*			
property (PROP uhr tee) *n.*			
rate (rayt) *n.*			
reliability (rih LY uh bihl uh tee) *n.*			
sequence (SEE kwuhns) *n.*			

Science: Domain-Specific Academic Vocabulary

Word	Definition	Related Words	Word in Context
hypothesis (hy POTH uh sihs) *n.*	something not proved but assumed to be true for the purpose of further study or argument	hypothesize hypothetical	The **hypothesis** that the earth was flat was later proven to be false.
erosion (ih ROH zhuhn) *n.*	process by which the surface of the earth is worn away by the action of water and other natural events	erode eroded	The hurricane caused beach **erosion.**
metamorphic (meht uh MAWR fihk) *adj.*	changing in form or structure	metamorphosis	**Metamorphic** rock is formed by heat and pressure within the earth.
solubility (sol yuh BIHL uh tee) *n.*	ability of a substance to dissolve	soluble insoluble	We tested the **solubility** of salt in a science lab.
synthesize (SIHN thuh syz) *v.*	form by combining parts or elements	synthetic synthesis	Scientists **synthesize** compounds by combining two or more substances.

Science: Domain-Specific Academic Vocabulary *(continued)*

Word	Definition	Related Words	Word in Context
energy (EHN uhr jee) *n.*			
evidence (EHV uh duns) *n.*			
gene (jeen) *n.*			
heredity (huh REHD ih tee) *n.*			
substance (SUB stuhns) *n.*			

Art: Domain-Specific Academic Vocabulary

Word	Definition	Related Words	Word in Context
intensity (ihn TEHN suh tee) *n.*	quality of a color's brightness and purity	intense intensify	The intensity of the red paint was stronger than the artist wanted.
linear (LIHN ee uhr) *adj.*	having to do with a line	line nonlinear	The sculpture of the building was linear and rigid.
saturation (sach uh RAY shuhn) *n.*	degree of purity of a color	saturate saturated	The saturation of the pink paint gave the room a lively feel.
texture (TEHKS chuhr) *n.*	way things feel, or look as if they might feel, when touched	textured	The carpet had a thick and fluffy texture.
unity (YOO nuh tee) *n.*	look and feel of wholeness in a work of art	unite unified	The mural had good balance and unity.
definition (dehf uh NIHSH uhn) *n.*			
form (fawrm) *n.*			
motion (MOH shuhn) *n.*			
space (spays) *n.*			
value (VAL yoo) *n.*			

Technology: Domain-Specific Academic Vocabulary

Word	Definition	Related Words	Word in Context
database (DAY tuh bays) *n.*	collection of related information stored in a computerized format	data	The library has a **database** of all its books.
digital (DIHJ ih tuhl) *adj.*	available in an electronic format	digit digitize	I have a **digital** version of that book on my computer.
login (LOG ihn) *n.*	information related to an electronic account name and its password	logging in	I use my **login** to access my account on a secure Web site.
network (NEHT wuhrk) *n.*	group of computers connected together to share information	network *v.* networking	The Internet is the largest **network** in the world.
platform (PLAT fawrm) *n.*	group of compatible computers that can share software	platform *adj.*	PC is the computer **platform** used in our school.
bookmark (BOOK mahrk) *n.*			
copy (KOP ee) *n.*, v.			
download (DOWN lohd) *v.*			
input (IHN poot) *n.*, v.			
output (OWT poot) *n.*, v.			

Increasing Your Word Knowledge

Increase your word knowledge and chances of success by taking an active role in developing your vocabulary. Here are some tips for you.

To own a word, follow these steps:

Steps to Follow	Model
1. Learn to identify the word and its basic meaning.	The word *examine* means "to look at closely."
2. Take note of the word's spelling.	*Examine* begins and ends with an *e*.
3. Practice pronouncing the word so that you can use it in conversation.	The *e* on the end of the word is silent. Its second syllable gets the most stress.
4. Visualize the word and illustrate its key meaning.	When I think of the word *examine*, I visualize a doctor checking a patient's health.
5. Learn the various forms of the word and its related words.	*Examination* and *exam* are forms of the word *examine*.
6. Compare the word with similar words.	*Examine*, *peruse*, and *study* are synonyms.
7. Contrast the word with similar words.	*Examine* suggests a more detailed study than *read* or *look* at.
8. Use the word in various contexts.	"I'd like to *examine* the footprints more closely." "I will *examine* the use of imagery in this poem."

Building Your Speaking Vocabulary

Language gives us the ability to express ourselves. The more words you know, the better able you will be to get your points across. There are two main aspects of language: reading and speaking. Using the steps above will help you to acquire a rich vocabulary. Follow these steps to help you learn to use this rich vocabulary in discussions, speeches, and conversations.

Steps to Follow	Tip
1. Practice pronouncing the word.	Become familiar with pronunciation guides, which will help you to sound out unfamiliar words. Listening to audiobooks as you read the text will help you learn pronunciations of words.
2. Learn word forms.	Dictionaries often list forms of words following the main word entry. Practice saying word families aloud: "generate," "generated," "generation," "regenerate," "generator."
3. Translate your thoughts.	Restate your own thoughts and ideas in a variety of ways, to inject formality or to change your tone, for example.
4. Hold discussions.	With a classmate, practice using academic vocabulary words in discussions about the text. Choose one term to practice at a time, and see how many statements you can create using that term.
5. Tape-record yourself.	Analyze your word choices by listening to yourself objectively. Note where your word choice could be strengthened or changed.

WRITING AN OBJECTIVE SUMMARY

The ability to write objective summaries is key to success in college and in many careers. Writing an effective objective summary involves recording the key ideas of a text while demonstrating your understanding.

What is an Objective Summary?

An effective objective summary is a concise, complete, accurate, and objective overview of a text. The following are key characteristics of an objective summary:

- A good summary focuses on the main theme, or central idea, of a text and specific, relevant details that support that theme, or central idea. Unnecessary supporting details are left out.

- An effective summary is usually brief. However, the writer must be careful not to misrepresent the text by leaving out key elements.

- A successful summary accurately captures the essence of the longer text it is describing.

- An effective summary remains objective—the writer refrains from inserting his or her own opinions, reactions, or personal connections into the summary.

What to Avoid in an Objective Summary

- An objective summary is not a collection of sentences or paragraphs copied from the original source.

- It is not a long recounting of every event, detail, or point in the original text.

- A good summary does not include evaluative words or comments, such as the reader's overall opinion of or reaction to the piece. An objective summary is not the reader's interpretation or critical analysis of the work.

 **Common Core State Standards**

Literature
2. Determine a theme or central idea of a text and analyze its development over the course of the text; provide an objective summary of the text.

Informational Text
2. Determine two or more central ideas in a text and analyze their development over the course of the text; provide an objective summary of the text.

Model Objective Summary

Review the elements of an effective objective summary, which are pointed out in the sidenotes that appear next to the summary. Then, write an objective summary of a selection you recently read. Review your summary, and delete any unnecessary details, personal opinions, or evaluations of the text.

Summary of "Mowgli's Brothers"

"Mowgli's Brothers" is one of the stories in *The Jungle Book*, written by Rudyard Kipling. The setting of the story is a jungle in India, and the ~~enchanting~~ story tells the tale of Mowgli, a young boy who is raised by wolves.

A one-sentence synopsis, or brief overview, highlighting the theme, or central idea, of the story can be an effective start to a summary.

One night Mother and Father Wolf woke from their rest to find Tabaqui, a jackal, at the mouth of their cave, begging for food. No one in the jungle liked Tabaqui. However, the wolves gave him a bone to eat in spite of the fact that he upset Mother Wolf ~~by complimenting her on her four young cubs. The wolves thought it was unlucky to compliment children to their faces~~. Tabaqui further upset the wolves by bringing the news that Shere Khan, a tiger, was moving into their hunting grounds.

The adjective *enchanting* indicates an opinion and should not be included in an objective summary.

Unnecessary details should be eliminated.

After Tabaqui left, Father Wolf set out on his hunt. He heard Shere Khan's roar and then saw him rolling around on the ground. The tiger had landed in a woodcutter's fire while trying to catch his prey.

Soon after that, something approached the wolves' cave. Father Wolf was ready to pounce until he saw what it was—a smiling, happy baby boy. Father Wolf gently picked up the man's cub and brought him to Mother Wolf. The man's cub was not at all afraid, and he snuggled right up with the wolf cubs.

Transition words and phrases show chronological order and enable readers to easily follow the order of events.

Before long, Shere Khan stuck his big head into the cave. He wanted the man's cub, which had been his prey. The wolves wouldn't give him up, which angered the tiger. But Mother Wolf was even angrier. She said, "The man's cub is mine... He shall not be killed. He shall live to run with the Pack and to hunt with the Pack; and in the end. . .he shall hunt thee."

If actual sentences from the story are used to show the essence of a text, they must be placed within quotation marks.

Mother Wolf named the man's cub Mowgli, and he was brought before the Wolf Pack for approval. With the help of Baloo the bear and Bagheera the black panther, Mowgli was accepted into the Pack. Shere Khan slinked away into the night, roaring his disapproval.

COMPREHENDING COMPLEX TEXTS

Over the course of your school years, you will be required to read increasingly complex texts as preparation for college and a career. A complex text is a text that contains challenging vocabulary; long, complex sentences; figurative language; multiple levels of meaning; or unfamiliar settings and situations.

The selections in this textbook provide you with a range of readings, from short stories to autobiographies, poetry, drama, myths, and even science and social studies texts. Some of these texts will fall within your comfort zone; others will most likely be more challenging.

Strategy 1: **Multidraft Reading**

Most successful readers know that to fully understand a text, you must reread it several times. Get in the habit of reading a text or portions of a text two to three times in order to ensure that you get the most out of your reading experience. To fully understand a text, try this multidraft reading strategy:

1st Reading
On your first reading, look for the basics. If, for example, you are reading a story, look for who does what to whom, what conflicts arise, and how conflicts are resolved. If the text is nonfiction, look for the main ideas and the ways they are presented. If you are reading a lyric poem, read first to get a sense of who the speaker is. Also take note of the poem's setting and main focus.

2nd Reading
During your second reading of a text, focus on the artistry or the effectiveness of the writing. Look for text structures and think about why the author chose those organizational patterns. Then, examine the author's creative uses of language and the effects of that language. For example, has the author used metaphor, simile, or hyperbole? If so, what effect did that use of figurative language create?

3rd Reading
After your third reading, compare and contrast the text with other similar selections you have read. For example, if you read a haiku, think of other haiku you have read and ways the poems are alike or different. Evaluate the text's overall effectiveness and its central idea, or theme.

 **Common Core State Standards**

Literature
10. By the end of the year, read and comprehend literature, including stories, dramas, and poems, in the grades 6–8 text complexity band proficiently, with scaffolding as needed at the high end of the range.

Independent Practice

As you read this poem, practice the multidraft reading strategy by completing a chart like the one below. Use a separate piece of paper.

"Prayers of Steel" by Carl Sandburg

Lay me on an anvil, O God.
Beat me and hammer me into a crowbar.
Let me pry loose old walls;
Let me lift and loosen old foundations.

Lay me on an anvil, O God.
Beat me and hammer me into a steel spike.
Drive me into the girders that hold a skyscraper together.
Take red-hot rivets and fasten me into the central girders.
Let me be the great nail holding a skyscraper through blue
      nights into white stars.

Multidraft Reading Chart

	My Understanding
1st Reading Look for key ideas and details that unlock basic meaning.	
2nd Reading Read for deeper meanings. Look for ways in which the author used text structures and language to create effects.	
3rd Reading Read to integrate your knowledge and ideas. Connect the text to others of its kind and to your own experience.	

Strategy 2: **Close Read the Text**

To comprehend a complex text, perform a close reading—a careful analysis of the words, phrases, and sentences within the text. As you close read, use the following tips to comprehend the text:

Tips for Close Reading
1. **Break down long sentences** into parts. Look for the subject of the sentence and its verb. Then, identify which parts of the sentence modify, or give more information about, the subject.
2. **Reread difficult passages** to confirm that you understand their meaning.

3. **Look for context clues,** such as
 	
   a. restatement of an idea. For example, in this sentence, "defeated" restates the verb *vanquished*.
     The army **vanquished,** or <u>defeated</u>, its enemy.
 	
   b. definition of sophisticated words. In this sentence, the underlined information defines the word *girder*.
     A **girder's** <u>long beam provides support for the floor above.</u>
 	
   c. examples of concepts and topics. In the following passage, the underlined text provides an example of the adjective *voracious*.
     <u>Eating his entire dinner, two apples, and a banana</u> finally satisfied Rob's **voracious** appetite.
 	
   d. contrasts of ideas and topics. The following sentence points out a difference between Lori and Ellen.
     Lori was **vivacious,** <u>unlike her shy, quiet</u> sister Ellen.

4. **Identify pronoun antecedents.** If long sentences or passages contain pronouns, reread the text to make sure you know to whom or what the pronouns refer. In the following passage, the underlined pronouns all have the antecedent *freedom*.   **Freedom** is precious. Through <u>it</u> we prosper. In <u>its</u> absence we doubt, quake, rage, and suffer; <u>it</u> is just as necessary to life as is the air we breathe. For, without <u>it</u>, we surely perish.
5. **Look for conjunctions,** such as *and, or,* and *yet,* to help understand relationships between ideas.
6. **Paraphrase,** or restate in your own words, passages of difficult text in order to check your understanding. Remember that a paraphrase is a word-for-word restatement of an original text; it is not a summary.

Close Reading Model

As you read this document, take note of the sidenotes that model ways to unlock meaning in the text.

from "Speech to the Constitutional Convention" by Benjamin Franklin

To the People of the State of New York:

I confess that I do not entirely approve of this Constitution at present; but, sir, I am not sure I shall never approve of it, for, having lived long, I have experienced many instances of being obliged, by better information or fuller consideration, to change opinions even on important subjects, which I once thought right, but found to be otherwise. It is therefore that, the older I grow, the more apt I am to doubt my own judgment of others. Most men, indeed, as well as most sects in religion think themselves in possession of all truth, and that wherever others differ with them, it is so far error. . . . .

In these sentiments, sir, I agree to this Constitution with all its faults—if they are such—because I think a general government necessary for us, and there is no form of government but what may be a blessing to the people if well administered; and I believe, further, that this is likely to be well administered for a course of years, and can only end in despotism, as other forms have done before it, when the people shall become so corrupted as to need a despotic government, being incapable of any other. I doubt, too, whether any other convention we can obtain may be able to make a better Constitution; for, when you assemble a number of men, to have the advantage of their joint wisdom, you inevitably assemble with those men all their prejudices, their passions, their errors of opinion, their local interests, and their selfish views. From such an assembly can a perfect production be expected?

It therefore astonishes me, sir, to find this system approaching so near to perfection as it does. . . .

Break down this long sentence into parts. The text highlighted in yellow conveys the basic meaning of the sentence. The text highlighted in blue provides additional information.

Look for antecedents. In this sentence, the noun *faults* is replaced by the pronoun *they*. The conjunction *because*, highlighted in blue, indicates a cause-and-effect relationship.

Search for context clues. The words in blue are context clues that help you figure out the meaning of the word that appears in yellow.

Strategy 3: **Ask Questions**

Be an attentive reader by asking questions as you read. Throughout this textbook, we have provided questions for you following each selection. These questions are sorted into three basic categories that build in sophistication and lead you to a deeper understanding of the texts you read.

Here is an example from this text:

Some questions are about **Key Ideas and Details** in the text. To answer these questions, you will need to locate and cite explicit information in the text or draw inferences from what you have read.

Some questions are about **Craft and Structure** in the text. To answer these questions, you will need to analyze how the author developed and structured the text. You will also look for ways in which the author artfully used language and how those word choices impacted the meaning and tone of the work.

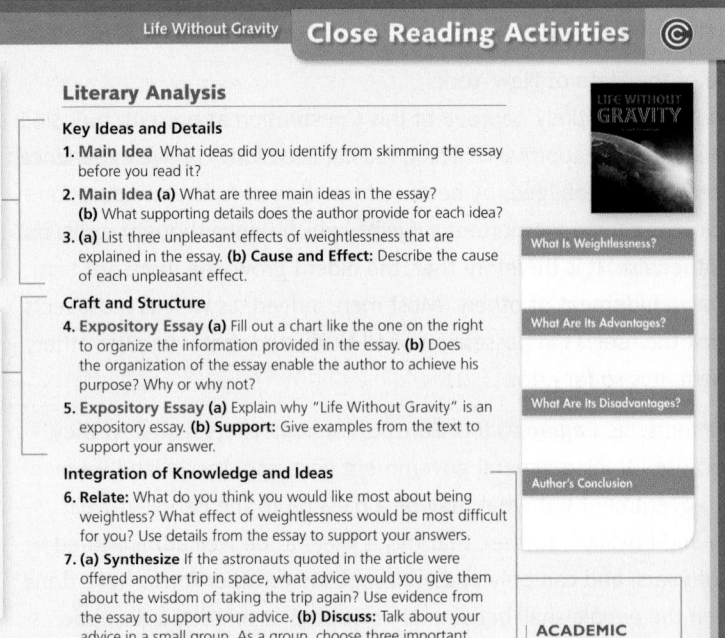

Some questions are about the **Integration of Knowledge and Ideas** in the text. These questions ask you to evaluate a text in many different ways, such as comparing texts, looking at arguments in the text, and many other methods of analyzing a text's ideas.

As you read independently, ask similar types of questions to ensure that you fully enjoy and comprehend texts you read for school and for pleasure. We have provided sets of questions for you on the Independent Reading pages at the end of each unit.

Model

Following is an example of a complex text. The sidenotes show sample questions that an attentive reader might ask while reading.

Sample questions:

from "Owning Books" by William Lyon Phelps

in a radio broadcast on April 6, 1933:

The habit of reading is one of the greatest resources of mankind; and we enjoy reading books that belong to us much more than if they are borrowed. . . your own books belong to you; you treat them with that affectionate intimacy that annihilates formality. Books are for use, not for show; you should own no book that you are afraid to mark up, or afraid to place on the table wide open and face down. A good reason for marking favorite passages in books is that this practice enables you to remember more easily the significant sayings, to refer to them quickly, and then in later years, it is like visiting a forest where you once blazed a trail. You have the pleasure of going over the old ground, and recalling both the intellectual scenery and your own earlier self.

Key Ideas and Details Does the first sentence state facts or express an opinion? Who is meant by *we* and *us*?

Craft and Structure What parallel structures does the writer use in this passage? What effect does that use have on readers?

Integration of Knowledge and Ideas To what extent do you agree with the author's viewpoint? Explain.

INFORMATIONAL TEXT

Independent Practice

Write three to five questions you might ask yourself as you read this passage from a speech delivered by Theodore Roosevelt at the Grand Canyon in 1903.

from "Speech at the Grand Canyon" by Theodore Roosevelt

. . . In the Grand Canyon, Arizona has a natural wonder which, so far as I know, is, in kind, absolutely unparalleled throughout the rest of the world. I want to ask you to do one thing in connection with it, in your own interest and in the interest of the country—to keep this great wonder of nature as it now is. I was delighted to learn of the wisdom of the Santa Fe railroad people in deciding not to build their hotel on the brink of the canyon. I hope you will not have a building of any kind, not a summer cottage, a hotel, or anything else, to mar the wonderful grandeur, the sublimity, the great loneliness and beauty of the canyon. Leave it as it is. You cannot improve on it. The ages have been at work on it, and man can only mar it. What you can do is to keep it for your children, your children's children and for all who come after you, as one of the great sights which every American, if he can travel at all, should see. . . .

ANALYZING ARGUMENTS

The ability to evaluate an argument, as well as to make one, is an important skill for success in college and in the workplace.

What Is an Argument?

Chances are, you have used the word *argument* to refer to a disagreement between people. This type of argument involves trading opinions and evidence in a conversational way, with both sides contributing to the discussion. A formal argument, however, presents one side of a controversial or debatable issue. Through this type of argument, the writer logically supports a particular belief, conclusion, or point of view. A good argument is supported with reasoning and evidence.

Purposes of Argument

There are three main purposes for writing a formal argument:

- to change the reader's mind about an issue
- to convince the reader to accept what is written
- to motivate the reader to take action, based on what is written

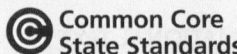 **Common Core State Standards**

Language
6. Acquire and use accurately general academic and domain-specific words and phrases.

Informational Text
8. Trace and evaluate the argument and specific claims in a text, assessing whether the reasoning is sound and the evidence is relevant and sufficient to support the claims.

Elements of an Argument
Claim (assertion)—what the writer is trying to prove Example: *Sports programs should be funded by private individuals, not schools.*
Grounds (evidence)—the support used to convince the reader Example: *Because students who participate in sports get the benefits of that activity, the students should do fund-raising to pay for the use of equipment and training.*
Justification—the link between the grounds and the claim; why the grounds are credible Example: *For example, participants in sports often get college scholarships—money that is paid to them. Since those students benefit personally from the sports experience, they should help fund the cost of the sports activities.*

Evaluating Claims

When reading or listening to an argument, critically assess the claims that are made. Analyze the argument to identify claims that are based on fact or that can be proved true. Also evaluate evidence that supports the claims. If there is little or no reasoning or evidence provided to support the claims, the argument may not be sound or valid.

Model Argument

from "Speech Supporting Women's Suffrage"
by Robert L. Owen

Women compose one-half of the human race. . . A full half of the work of the world is done by women. A careful study of the matter has demonstrated the vital fact that these working women receive a smaller wage for equal work than men do, and that the smaller wage and harder conditions imposed on the woman worker are due to the lack of the ballot. . . . Equal pay for equal work is the first great reason justifying this change of governmental policy.

Claim: Smaller wages and poor working conditions for women are caused by the fact that women cannot vote.

Grounds: Equal pay should be given for equal work.

There are other reasons which are persuasive: First, women, take it all in all, are the equals of men in intelligence, and no man has the hardihood to assert the contrary. . . .

Grounds: Women are just as intelligent as men.

Every evil prophecy against granting the suffrage has failed. The public men of Colorado, Wyoming, Utah, and Idaho give it a cordial support.

The testimony is universal:

First, it has not made women mannish; they. . .are better able to protect themselves and their children because of the ballot.

An opposing argument is acknowledged and refuted.

Second, they have not become office-seekers. . . It [suffrage] has made women broader and greatly increased the understanding of the community at large of the problems of good government. . . .

It has not absolutely regenerated society, but it has improved it. It has raised the . . .moral standard of the suffrage, because there are more criminal men than criminal women. . . .

Justification: Women should have the right to vote because government derives its powers from the consent of the governed, and women are half of the governed population. Also, taxation without representation is against U.S. principles. If women are to be taxed, they should have a vote.

The great doctrine of the American Republic that "all governments derive their just powers from the consent of the governed" justifies the plea on one-half of the people, the women, to exercise the suffrage. The doctrine of the American Revolutionary War that taxation without representation is unendurable justifies women in exercising the suffrage.

A strong conclusion does more than simply restate the claim.

THE ART OF ARGUMENT: RHETORICAL DEVICES AND PERSUASIVE TECHNIQUES

Rhetorical Devices

Rhetoric is the art of using language in order to make a point or to persuade listeners. Rhetorical devices such as the ones listed below are accepted elements of argument. Their use does not weaken an argument. Rather, the use of rhetorical devices is regarded as a key part of an effective argument.

Rhetorical Devices	Examples
Repetition The repeated use of words, phrases, or sentences	It is not **fair** to expect this treatment. Nor is it **fair** to pay for this decision.
Parallelism The repeated use of similar grammatical structures	Good students learn to read, <u>to question, and to respond</u>.
Rhetorical Question Calls attention to the issue by implying an obvious answer	Shouldn't consumers get what they pay for?
Sound Device The use of alliteration, assonance, rhyme, or rhythm	The invention is both **p**ractical and **p**rofitable.
Simile and Metaphor Compares two seemingly unlike things or asserting that one thing *is* another	**Teachers** are <u>like sparks</u> igniting the curiosity of their students.

Persuasive Techniques

Persuasive techniques are often found in advertisements and in other forms of informal persuasion. Although techniques like the ones below are sometimes found in informal arguments, they should be avoided in formal arguments.

Persuasive Techniques	Examples
Bandwagon Approach/Anti-Bandwagon Approach Appeals to a person's desire to belong; encourages or celebrates individuality	Anyone with any sense will vote for Richard Rock. Vote your conscience; an election is not a popularity contest.
Emotional Appeal Evokes people's fear, anger, or desire	Without working smoke detectors, your family is in danger.
Endorsement/Testimony Employs a well-known person to promote a product or idea	"I use this toothpaste, and it brightens my movie-star smile."
Loaded Language The use of words that are charged with emotion	The heroic firefighters bravely battled the raging inferno.
Hyperbole Exaggeration to make a point	Our candidate does the work of ten people.

Model Speech

The excerpted speech below includes examples of rhetorical devices and persuasive techniques.

from "Inaugural Address" by Dwight D. Eisenhower

My fellow citizens:

. . . Since this century's beginning, a time of tempest has seemed to come upon the continents of the earth. Masses of Asia have awakened to strike off shackles of the past. Great nations of Europe have fought their bloodiest wars. Thrones have toppled and their vast empires have disappeared. New nations have been born.

> The use of alliteration makes these phrases memorable.

For our own country, it has been a time of recurring trial. We have grown in power and in responsibility. We have passed through the anxieties of depression and of war to a summit unmatched in man's history. Seeking to secure peace in the world, we have had to fight through the forests of the Argonne, to the shores of Iwo Jima, and to the cold mountains of Korea. . .

> Eisenhower uses parallelism and repetition to emphasize his main points.

How far have we come in man's long pilgrimage from darkness toward light? Are we nearing the light—a day of freedom and of peace for all mankind? Or are the shadows of another night closing in upon us?. . .

> Rhetorical questions call attention to the speaker's point.

. . . we know that the virtues most cherished by free people—love of truth, pride of work, devotion to country—all are treasures equally precious in the lives of the most humble and of the most exalted. The men who mine coal and fire furnaces and balance ledgers and turn lathes and pick cotton and heal the sick and plant corn—all serve as proudly, and as profitably, for America as the statesmen who draft treaties and the legislators who enact laws.

> Additional examples of parallel structure enable the audience to follow Eisenhower's ideas and to be moved by his words.

. . . We must be willing, individually and as a Nation, to accept whatever sacrifices may be required of us. A people that values its privileges above its principles soon loses both.

> Sound devices, such as alliteration, are a way to emphasize a phrase.

These basic precepts are not lofty abstractions, far removed from matters of daily living. . . Patriotism means equipped forces and a prepared citizenry. Moral stamina means more energy and more productivity. . .Love of liberty means the guarding of every resource that makes freedom possible. . .

No person, no home, no community can be beyond the reach of this call. We are summoned to act in wisdom and in conscience, to work with industry, to teach with persuasion, to preach with conviction, to weigh our every deed with care and with compassion. For this truth must be clear before us: whatever America hopes to bring to pass in the world must first come to pass in the heart of America.

> The parallelism created by repeated grammatical structures gives the speech rhythm.

COMPOSING AN ARGUMENT

 **Common Core
State Standards**

Choosing a Topic

You should choose a topic that matters to people—and to you. Brainstorm topics you would like to write about, and then choose the topic that most interests you.

Once you have chosen a topic, check to be sure you can make an arguable claim. Ask yourself:

1. What am I trying to prove? What ideas do I need to get across?

2. Are there people that would disagree with my claim? What alternate, or opposing, opinions might they have?

3. Do I have evidence to support my claim? Is my evidence sufficient or relevant?

If you are able to put into words what you want to prove and answered "yes" to numbers 2 and 3, you have an arguable claim.

Introducing the Claim and Establishing Its Significance

Before you begin writing, think about your audience and what they probably know about the topic. Then, provide only as much background information as necessary. Remember that you are not writing a summary of the issue—you are crafting an argument. Once you have provided context for your argument, clearly state your claim, or thesis. A written argument's claim often, but not always, appears in the first paragraph.

Developing Your Claim with Reasoning and Evidence

Now that you have made your claim, you must support it with evidence, or grounds. A good argument should have at least three solid pieces of evidence to support the claim. Evidence can range from personal experience to researched data or expert opinion. Knowing your audience's knowledge level, concerns, values, and possible biases can help you decide what kind of evidence will have the strongest impact. Make sure your evidence is up to date and comes from a credible source. Don't forget to credit your sources and address the opposing counterclaim.

Writing a Concluding Statement or Section

Restate your claim in the conclusion of your argument, and synthesize, or pull together, the evidence you have provided. Make your conclusion strong enough to be memorable to the reader; leave him or her with something to think about.

Writing

1.a. Introduce claim(s), acknowledge alternate or opposing claims, and organize the reasons and evidence logically.

1.b. Support claim(s) with logical reasoning and relevant evidence, using accurate, credible sources and demonstrating an understanding of the topic or text.

1.e. Provide a concluding statement or section that follows from and supports the argument presented.

Practice

Complete an outline like the one below to help you plan your own argument.

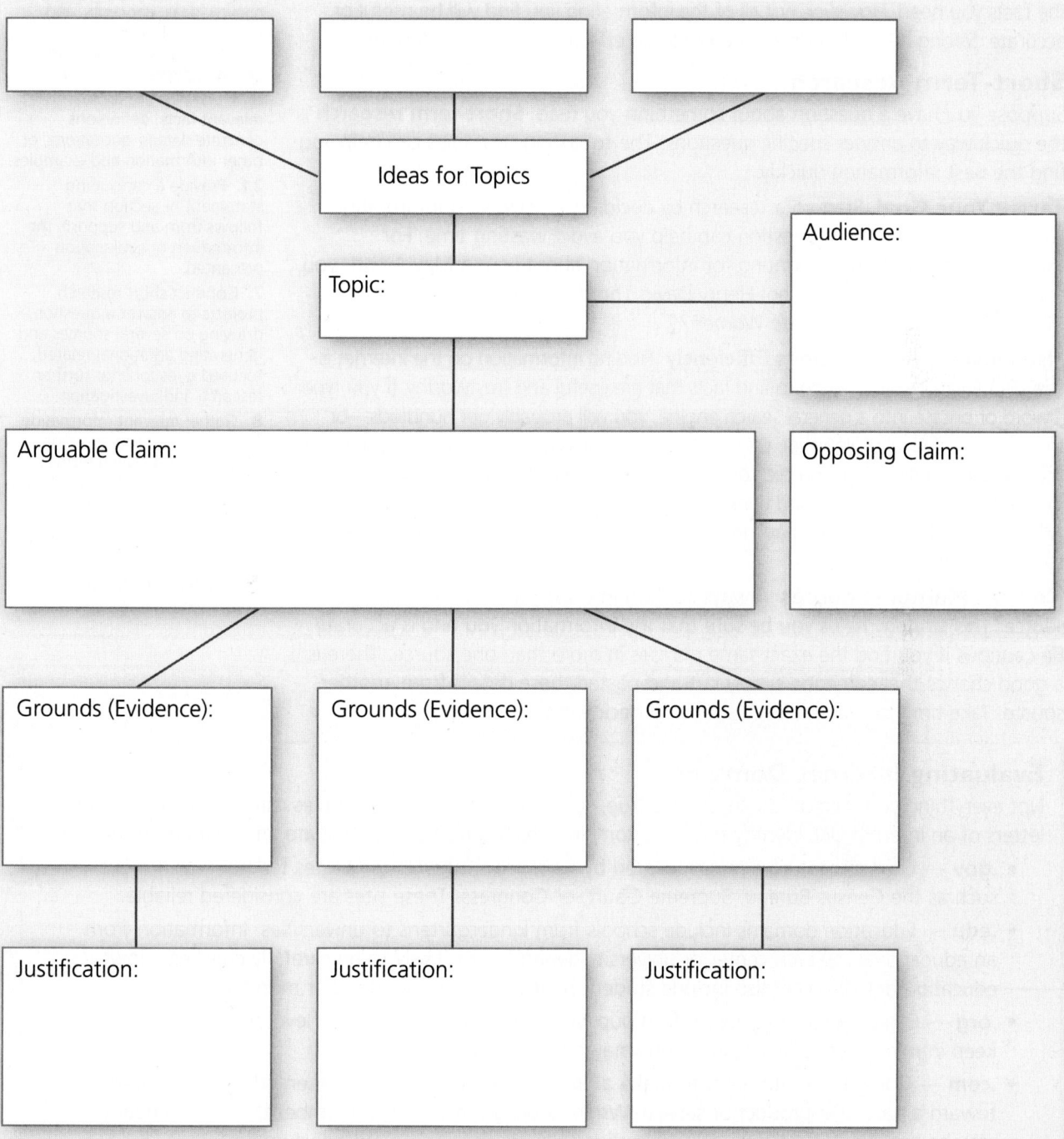

Ideas for Topics

Audience:

Topic:

Arguable Claim:

Opposing Claim:

Grounds (Evidence):

Grounds (Evidence):

Grounds (Evidence):

Justification:

Justification:

Justification:

Common Core Workshop — INTRODUCTORY UNIT

CONDUCTING RESEARCH

Research is an organized search for information. Do you want to answer a question or explore a topic? Books, the Internet, or other reference sources will likely have the facts you need. However, not all of the information you find will be useful or accurate. Strong research skills are the key to an effective search for information.

Short-Term Research

Suppose you have a question about something you read. **Short-term research** is the quick way to answer specific questions. The following strategies can help you find the best information quickly.

Target Your Goal Start your research by deciding exactly what information you need. Writing a focus question can help you avoid wasting time. For example, instead of simply hunting for information about Louisa May Alcott, you might ask "How did Alcott meet Henry David Thoreau?" or "How was Louisa May Alcott similar to Jo in *Little Women?*"

Use Online Search Engines Efficiently Finding information on the Internet is easy. But it can be a challenge to find facts that are useful and trustworthy. If you type a word or phrase into a general search engine, you will probably get hundreds—or thousands—of results. However, those results may not lead you to the facts you need. Scan search results before you click on one of them. The first result is not always the most relevant. Read the text and think about the source before making a choice as to which result is best. Open the page in a new window or tab so that you can return easily to your search results.

Consult Multiple Sources Always confirm information in more than one source. This strategy helps you be sure that the information you find is accurate. Be cautious if you find the exact same phrases in more than one source. There is a good chance that someone simply cut-and-pasted these details from another source. Take time to evaluate each source to decide if it is trustworthy.

Common Core State Standards

Writing

2. Write informative/explanatory texts to examine a topic and convey ideas, concepts, and information through the selection, organization, and analysis of relevant content.

2.b. Develop the topic with relevant facts, definitions, concrete details, quotations, or other information and examples.

2.f. Provide a concluding statement or section that follows from and supports the information or explanation presented.

7. Conduct short research projects to answer a question, drawing on several sources and generating additional related, focused questions for further research and investigation.

8. Gather relevant information from multiple print and digital sources, using search terms effectively; assess the credibility and accuracy of each source; and quote or paraphrase the data and conclusions of others while avoiding plagiarism and following a standard format for citation.

Evaluating Internet Domains

Not everything you read on the Internet is true, so you have to evaluate sources carefully. The last three letters of an Internet URL identify the site's domain, which can help you evaluate information on the site.

- **.gov** — Government sites are sponsored by a branch of the United States federal government, such as the Census Bureau, Supreme Court, or Congress. These sites are considered reliable.
- **.edu** — Education domains include schools from kindergartens to universities. Information from an educational research center or university department is likely to be carefully checked. However, education domains can also include student pages that are not edited or monitored.
- **.org** — Organizations are nonprofit groups and usually maintain a high level of credibility. But, keep in mind that some organizations may reflect strong biases.
- **.com** — Commercial sites exist to make a profit, so the information presented may be biased toward a particular product or service. When viewing these sites, remember that the company may be providing information to encourage sales or to promote a positive image.

Long-Term Research

If you want to explore a topic in depth, **long-term research** allows you to carry out a detailed, comprehensive investigation. Whether your final goal is a formal research report or a media presentation, you will need to consult multiple sources for information. An organized research plan will help you gather and synthesize information from multiple sources.

As the flowchart on this page shows, long-term research is a flexible process. You will regularly adjust your approach based on what you learn about the topic in the research process. Throughout your research, you may need to adjust your approach to refocus your thesis, gather more information, or reflect on what you have learned.

The Research Process

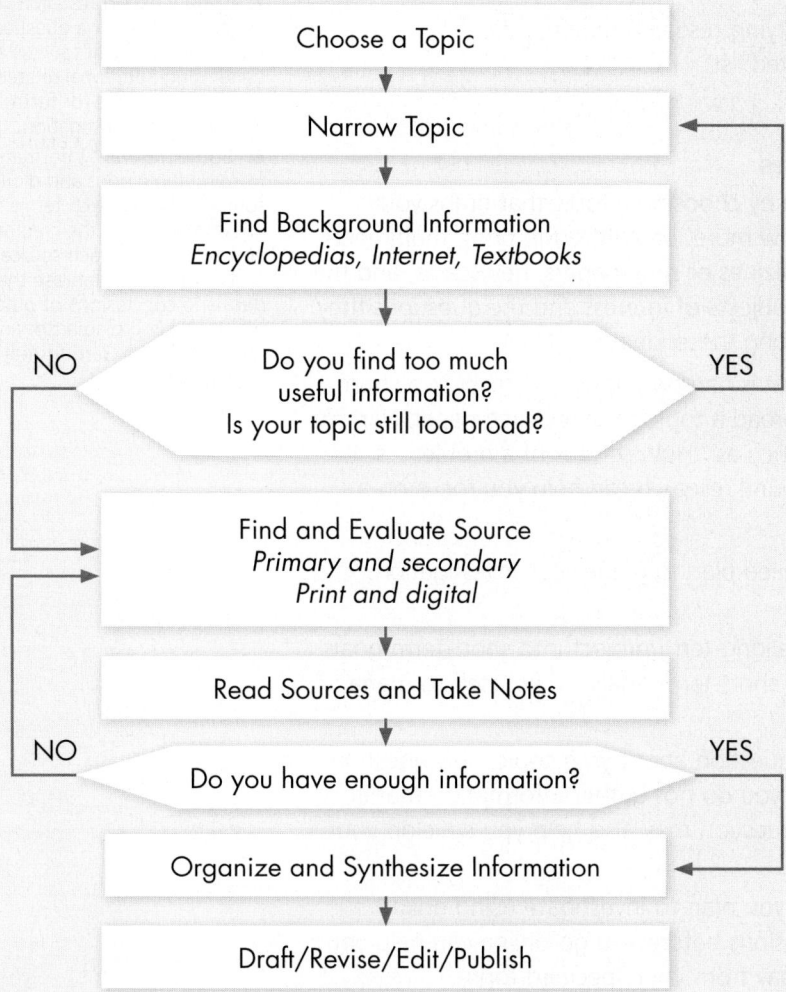

Refer to the Research Process Workshop (pages lxxii–lxxix) for more details about the steps in this flowchart.

RESEARCH PROCESS WORKSHOP

Research Writing: Research Report

A **research report** analyzes information gathered from reference materials, observations, interviews, or other sources to present a clear and accurate picture of a topic or answer to a question.

Elements of a Research Report

- an overall focused topic or main idea to be analyzed
- relevant and tightly drawn questions on the topic
- a thesis statement with a clear and accurate perspective
- a clear organization and smooth transitions
- appropriate facts and relevant details to support main point
- visuals or media to support key ideas
- accurate, complete citations identifying research materials by means of footnotes or a Works Cited list
- a strong concluding statement

Prewriting/Planning Strategies

Choose and narrow a topic. Begin by choosing a topic that grabs your attention and makes you curious to know more. Look through print, multimedia, and digital sources, such as recent magazines or newspapers, newscasts, and the Internet. List current events, issues, or subjects of interest and the questions they spark in you. Select your topic from among these ideas.

After you choose your topic, make sure it is narrow enough to cover in a short report. For example, "illiteracy" is too broad a topic for a research paper. Narrow the topic by asking focused questions such as "How serious of a problem is illiteracy in the United States?" Background research can help you focus on a more specific topic.

Create a research plan. Use a detailed plan to guide your investigation. Your plan may include these parts:

- **Set Short-Term Goals** Breaking a long-term project into short-term goals can prevent last-minute stress. Set short-term goals for yourself to manage your workload efficiently.
- **Research Question** Compose a question about your topic. This question will help you stay on track so that you do not gather information that is too broad for your purpose. This question may also help you develop your thesis statement.
- **Search Terms** Write down terms you plan to investigate using online search engines. Making these decisions before you go online can help you avoid digressions that take you away from your specified topic.
- **Source List** As you research, create a list of sources you will consult. Add sources to your list as you discover them. Place a check next to sources you have located and then underline sources you have explored thoroughly.

© **Common Core State Standards**

Writing

2. Write informative/explanatory texts to examine a topic and convey ideas, concepts, and information through the selection, organization, and analysis of relevant content.

2.b. Develop the topic with relevant facts, definitions, concrete details, quotations, or other information and examples.

2.f. Provide a concluding statement or section that follows from and supports the information or explanation presented.

7. Conduct short research projects to answer a question, drawing on several sources and generating additional related, focused questions for further research and investigation.

8. Gather relevant information from multiple print and digital sources, using search terms effectively; assess the credibility and accuracy of each source; and quote or paraphrase the data and conclusions of others while avoiding plagiarism and following a standard format for citation.

Gathering Details Through Research

Use multiple sources. An effective research project combines information from several sources. It is important not to rely too heavily on a single source. The creativity and originality of your research depends on how you combine ideas from many places. Plan to include a variety of these types of resources:

- **Primary and Secondary Resources** Use both primary sources (firsthand or original accounts, such as interview transcripts and newspaper articles) and secondary sources (accounts that are not original, such as encyclopedia entries or an online library catalog) in your research.

- **Print and Digital Resources** The Internet allows fast access to data, but print resources are often edited more carefully. Plan to include both print and digital resources in order to guarantee that your work is accurate.

- **Media Resources** You can find valuable information in media resources such as documentaries, television programs, podcasts, and museum exhibitions. Public lectures by experts also offer an opportunity to hear an expert's thoughts on a topic.

- **Original Research** Depending on your topic, you may wish to conduct original research to include among your sources. For example, you might interview experts or eyewitnesses or conduct a survey to analyze opinions in your own community.

Take clear notes on sources. Listed below are different strategies you may use to take notes:

- Use index cards to create **notecards** and **source cards**. Write one note per card and note the source of the information and the page number on which it is found.

- Photocopy articles and copyright pages from print sources; then, highlight relevant information.

- Print articles from the Internet or copy them directly into a folder on your computer. Remember to record the Web addresses of printouts from online sources.

You will use these notes to help you properly cite your sources in your report.

Credit your sources. Copying from sources without citing them is **plagiarism**, an act that has serious academic and legal consequences. Without giving credit to a source, you are stealing another person's words. It is important to use ethical practices when conducting research.

Whether you are paraphrasing, summarizing, or using a direct quotation, you must credit the source. You can give credit by writing a *Works Cited list*, a list of the print and nonprint sources you have used.

Review pages lxxx–lxxxi to see the appropriate format for citing sources in a Works Cited list.

Notecard

> **Education**
> Papp, p.5
>
> Only the upper classes could read.
>
> Most of the common people in Shakespeare's time could not read.

Source Card

> Papp, Joseph
> and Kirkland, Elizabeth
>
> **Shakespeare Alive!**
>
> New York: Bantam Books, 1988

Drafting Strategies

Develop a main idea or thesis. Review your prewriting notes to determine the overall focus of your report. Then, write a sentence that expresses your main idea. This sentence is called a **thesis statement**. As you draft, refer to your thesis statement to help keep your report focused. **Example:** *Whales are among the most intelligent mammals on Earth.*

Pose relevant questions. When you research, you may come up with more questions about your topic. The questions you ask yourself should be relevant to your thesis and tightly drawn. This means you should not stray too far from the perspective you convey in your report.

Make an outline. Group your prewriting notes by category. Use Roman numerals (I, II, III) to number your most important points. Under each Roman numeral, use capital letters (A, B, C) for the supporting details. Use your outline as a guide for developing your draft by turning your outline notes into complete sentences. As you outline, review the data you have collected.

- Refer to the notes you made on index cards in the prewriting and researching stage.
- Confirm that the supporting details you include directly relate to the thesis statement.
- Delete any irrelevant information or research you have gathered.

Include visuals to support key ideas. Using charts or other visual aids allows you to present detailed information that might otherwise interrupt the flow of your report. In your writing, introduce the visual and explain its purpose. Direct readers to reference these aids as needed. To create visual aids, carry out these steps:

- Use databases and spreadsheets to organize, manage, and prepare information for your report.
- Clarify your charts, graphs, and tables by using headings and adding appropriate spacing.
- Vary the color and design of your visual aids as you display different types of information.

Common Core State Standards

Writing

2.a. Include formatting, graphics, and multimedia when useful to aiding comprehension.

2.c. Use appropriate transitions to create cohesion and clarify the relationships among ideas and concepts.

5. With some guidance and support from peers and adults, develop and strengthen writing as needed by revising, focusing on how well purpose and audience have been addressed.

7. Conduct short research projects to answer a question, drawing on several sources and generating additional related, focused questions for further research and investigation.

8. Assess the credibility and accuracy of each source; and quote or paraphrase the data and conclusions of others while avoiding plagiarism and following a standard format for citation.

9. Draw evidence from literary or informational texts to support analysis, reflection, and research.

PLAN YOUR CITATIONS

As you draft, remember to use quotation marks around any words that you pick-up directly from a source. You should also give credit for ideas or facts that are unique to one source.

Revising Strategies

Analyze your organization. Look over your draft and analyze your organization to see if it matches your outline. Stop at the end of each paragraph and refer to your outline. Follow these steps:

1. Mark each paragraph with the Roman numeral and capital letter from your outline and write a key word or phrase to identify the subject of the paragraph.

2. If all the paragraphs with the same Roman numeral are not next to each other, decide whether the change is an improvement. If it is not, correct it.

Check your facts. Read through your draft to verify that the facts, statistics, and quotations you cite are accurate. Don't rely on your memory—refer to the original source material as you work. With the exception of direct quotations, be sure you have written the information in your own words.

Vary sentence length. To add interest to your writing, vary the length of your sentences. Underline or highlight sentences in your draft in alternating colors so you can easily see differences in length. Then, review your color coding. Combine short, choppy sentences or break up longer sentences if there are too many of either.

Model: Revising to Vary Sentence Length

Basketball has been played in various forms for hundreds of years. The modern sport was introduced in 1891. An instructor at a YMCA was looking to keep his students active during the long New England winters.

The basketball hoop was made from a peach basket ~~. The basket had~~ with a closed bottom. Soon, the players realized that if they removed the bottom, the game could be played quicker.

Review. Ask a classmate, your teacher, or another adult to read your report to determine if the organization of your draft is clear. If your reader finds areas that require transitions, consider revising your draft by adding a word, phrase, or sentence that shows the connection between your paragraphs. Use transitions such as *at first, finally,* or *as a result* to show relationships between ideas.

Ask the reader for feedback as to whether or not you have supported your thesis statement adequately. Revise your report as needed based on your reviewer's comments.

EDITING AND PROOFREADING

During the editing process, you will focus on giving credit to the sources you used. You will also look for mistakes in formatting, grammar, and spelling in your work.

Focus on citations. Cite the sources for quotations, factual information, and any ideas that are not your own. Some word-processing programs have features that allow you to create footnotes and endnotes. If you are using MLA style, citations should appear in parentheses directly after the information cited. Include the author's last name and the relevant page number.

Example: *In the last 50 years, one third of tropical rainforests have been destroyed (Warburton 455).*

Create a reference list. Following the format your teacher assigns, create a Works Cited list of the information you used to write your research report. (For more information, see Citing Sources, pp. lxxx–lxxxi).

Focus on format. Present your research formally by including the following formatting features: an appropriate title page, pagination, spacing and margins, and citations. Make sure you have used the assigned system for crediting sources in your paper and for listing them at the end.

Proofread. Carefully reread your draft and correct spelling and grammar errors. Check to be sure that you have used quotation marks correctly and that each opening quotation mark has a corresponding closing quotation mark.

Publishing and Presenting

In addition to submitting your research report to your teacher, you might decide to use one of these strategies to share your findings with classmates.

Give an oral report. Use your research report as the basis for an oral presentation on your topic. Keep your audience in mind and revise accordingly as you prepare your presentation.

Create a multimedia presentation. Computer software makes it easy to combine text and images in an engaging way. You might record yourself reading your finished report and then add appropriate images to be viewed during playback. Or you can create a more elaborate presentation that integrates text, images, sound, and video.

Organize a panel discussion. If several of your classmates have written about a similar topic, plan a discussion to compare and contrast your findings. Speakers can summarize their research before opening the panel to questions from the class.

 **Common Core State Standards**

Language
1. Demonstrate command of the conventions of standard English grammar and usage when writing and speaking.
2. Demonstrate command of the conventions of standard English capitalization, punctuation, and spelling when writing.

MODEL: RESEARCH PAPER

This model research paper shows how one student developed a thesis statement by analyzing information. Notice how the writer integrates facts and details and uses parentheses to give credit for ideas taken from research sources. The Works Cited list at the end of the report gives more details about the works she used in her research.

Hatching Chirpers: Laura Agajanian, Santa Clara, CA

Hatching Chirpers

A hen's egg is an amazing thing. Sitting in the nest, it seems as if it is an inanimate, or lifeless, object, but it contains everything that is needed to make a chick. In order for the chick to grow inside the egg, however, the right external conditions are needed. Under normal circumstances, these conditions are provided by the hen. They can also be reproduced and regulated in an incubator. My investigation was to discover whether the hen or the incubator would more efficiently and effectively provide the right external conditions. My hypothesis is that an incubator can provide the right external conditions more effectively and efficiently. Let's find out.

A chicken egg should take about twenty-one days to incubate, or take form. During that time, the eggs must be kept warm. The ideal temperature is between 99 and 100 degrees Fahrenheit. In addition, the eggs must be rotated, or turned, every eight to twelve hours. If they remain in one position for longer than that, the chick can become stuck to one side of the egg and may not form properly (Johnson 14–16).

Usually, the temperature and the turning are handled by the hen that sits on the nest. She regulates the temperature of the eggs by getting off the nest or standing above the eggs if the eggs begin to get too warm. When they have had some time to cool, she gets back on the nest. The hen turns the eggs by poking at them with her beak until each egg rolls a little to one side, eventually turning from its original position (Scott).

An incubator performs these same functions. The temperature inside the incubator is measured and regulated by a thermostat that tells the heater when to turn on and when to turn off. In this way, the temperature of the eggs is kept at a constant 99 degrees. The eggs sit on a device that rolls them every eight hours. This device is controlled by an electronic timer. It is dependable because it is automatic and does not require a person to push a button for the eggs to turn. It is more efficient than a hen, because all the eggs get turned equally and consistently (Little Giant 2–6).

In the first paragraph, Laura identifies her main topic, the question she is investigating. In this science report, she provides a hypothesis—a proposition that the research will prove or disprove. This statement gives her perspective or viewpoint on the topic.

Accurate facts and details gathered through the formal research process are presented. Since these are specific statistics that a reader might want to check, the writer gives the source.

The report is organized to give balanced information about both methods being investigated—natural hatching and incubation.

Based on the fact that conditions in the incubator are more consistent and controlled, I concluded that an incubator sets the ideal conditions more efficiently, and I hypothesized that it would hatch eggs more effectively. To test my hypothesis, I observed four hens sitting on a total of twenty-four eggs and placed twenty-four eggs in an incubator. Each egg was marked with a small x so that I could observe how frequently and completely each egg was turned. Chart A shows specific observations over a twenty-five-day period.

Detailed information that would interrupt the flow of the report is presented in a separate chart for readers to reference as needed.

Chart A

Day	Incubator Observations	Nest Observations
Day 1	**6:45 AM:** After placing the turner in the incubator, I put the 24 eggs on the turner. The temperature leveled off at 100 degrees. The eggs have warmed up quickly. **5:33 PM:** The turner is working efficiently—eggs are tilted appropriately.	**7:10 AM:** After placing the 24 eggs on the nests in the cage, I put food and water in the cage. Then, I placed the hens in the cage. **6:01 PM:** All hens are on the eggs.
Day 5	X marks on the eggs show that eggs have made a complete turn.	X marks on the eggs show that the eggs were not turned completely since I last checked.
Day 10	The turner seems to be tilting the eggs efficiently—X marks show a complete turn.	X marks show that 18 eggs were turned, but 6 were not.
Day 15	The temperature of the eggs is at a steady 100 degrees. Ideal temperature is 100–101 degrees (Hamre).	Two hens have moved off the nest for a brief time. Temperature of the eggs right now is 97 degrees.
Day 25	The incubator has hatched 13 out of the 24 eggs.	The hens have hatched 10 out of the 24 eggs.

In general, the incubator eggs received much more consistent attention to their condition. The machine did not need to stop to eat or exercise, as the hens did. The marks on the eggs showed that the eggs under the hens did not always get completely turned. Sometimes, some of the eggs were turned and some were not. In addition, the hens sometimes left the nest for as long as an hour. When the temperature of the eggs was measured after a hen had been gone a long time, the egg temperature was sometimes as low as 97 degrees.

After twenty-five days, the hens had hatched ten out of the twenty-four eggs, and the incubator had hatched thirteen. The difference between the two numbers is not great enough to say that one way of incubating is more effective than the other. The incubator is definitely more efficient at delivering ideal conditions than the hens were. However, since the increased efficiency does not result in a higher number of hatches, maybe "ideal" conditions are not required for a successful hatch.

Laura concludes by explaining whether the research did or did not support her original hypothesis.

Works Cited

Hamre, Melvin L. "Hatching and Brooding Small Numbers of Chicks." *University of Minnesota Extension,* 2013. Web. 3 December 2015.

Johnson, Sylvia A. *Inside an Egg.* Minneapolis: Lerner Publications Company, 1982. Print.

Little Giant Instruction Manual for Still Air Incubator and Automatic Egg Turner. Miller Mfg. Co., So. St. Paul, MN, 1998. Print.

Scott, Wyatt. Personal Interview. 1 Dec. 2015.

In her "Works Cited" list, Laura provides information on the sources she cites, or notes, in her research report.

CITING SOURCES AND PREPARING MANUSCRIPT

Proofreading and Preparing Manuscript

Before preparing a final copy, proofread your manuscript. The chart shows the standard symbols for marking corrections to be made.

Proofreading Symbols	
Insert	∧
delete	ℒ
close space	⊂⊃
new paragraph	¶
add comma	⌃
add period	⊙
transpose (switch)	∩
change to cap	a̲
change to lowercase	ℓ

- Choose a standard, easy-to-read font.
- Type or print on one side of unlined 8 1/2" × 11" paper.
- Set the margins for the side, top, and bottom of your paper at approximately one inch. Most word-processing programs have a default setting that is appropriate.
- Double-space the document.
- Indent the first line of each paragraph.
- Number the pages in the upper right corner.

Follow your teacher's directions for formatting formal research papers. Most papers will have the following features:

- Title Page
- Table of Contents or Outline
- Works Cited List

Avoiding Plagiarism

Whether you are presenting a formal research paper or an opinion paper on a current event, you must be careful to give credit for any ideas or opinions that are not your own. Presenting someone else's ideas, research, or opinion as your own—even if you have phrased it in different words—is *plagiarism*, the equivalent of academic stealing, or fraud.

Do not use the ideas or research of others in place of your own. Read from several sources to draw your own conclusions and form your own opinions. Incorporate the ideas and research of others to support your points. Credit the source of the following types of support:

- Statistics
- Direct quotations
- Indirectly quoted statements of opinions
- Conclusions presented by an expert
- Facts available in only one or two sources

Crediting Sources

When you credit a source, you acknowledge where you found your information and you give your readers the details necessary for locating the source themselves. Within the body of the paper, you provide a short citation, a footnote number linked to a footnote, or an endnote number linked to an endnote reference. These brief references show the page numbers on which you found the information. Prepare a reference list at the end of the paper to provide full bibliographic information on your sources. These are two common types of reference lists:

- A bibliography provides a listing of all the resources you consulted during your research.
- A Works Cited list indicates the works you have referenced in your paper.

The chart on the next page shows the Modern Language Association format for crediting sources. This is the most common format for papers written in the content areas in middle school and high school. Unless instructed otherwise by your teacher, use this format for crediting sources.

MLA Style for Listing Sources

Book with one author	Pyles, Thomas. *The Origins and Development of the English Language.* 2nd ed. New York: Harcourt, 1971. Print.
Book with two or three authors	McCrum, Robert, William Cran, and Robert MacNeil. *The Story of English.* New York: Penguin, 1987. Print.
Book with an editor	Truth, Sojourner. *Narrative of Sojourner Truth.* Ed. Margaret Washington. New York: Vintage, 1993. Print.
Book with more than three authors or editors	Donald, Robert B., et al. *Writing Clear Essays.* Upper Saddle River: Prentice, 1996. Print.
Single work in an anthology	Hawthorne, Nathaniel. "Young Goodman Brown." *Literature: An Introduction to Reading and Writing.* Ed. Edgar V. Roberts and H. E. Jacobs. Upper Saddle River: Prentice, 1998. 376–385. Print. [Indicate pages for the entire selection.]
Introduction to a work in a published edition	Washington, Margaret. Introduction. *Narrative of Sojourner Truth.* By Sojourner Truth. Ed. Washington. New York: Vintage, 1993. v–xi. Print.
Signed article from an encyclopedia	Askeland, Donald R. "Welding." *World Book Encyclopedia.* 1991 ed. Print.
Signed article in a weekly magazine	Wallace, Charles. "A Vodacious Deal." *Time* 14 Feb. 2000: 63. Print.
Signed article in a monthly magazine	Gustaitis, Joseph. "The Sticky History of Chewing Gum." *American History* Oct. 1998: 30–38. Print.
Newspaper	Thurow, Roger. "South Africans Who Fought for Sanctions Now Scrap for Investors." *Wall Street Journal* 11 Feb. 2000: A1+. Print. [For a multipage article that does not appear on consecutive pages, write only the first page number on which it appears, followed by the plus sign.]
Unsigned editorial or story	"Selective Silence." Editorial. *Wall Street Journal* 11 Feb. 2000: A14. Print. [If the editorial or story is signed, begin with the author's name.]
Signed pamphlet or brochure	[Treat the pamphlet as though it were a book.]
Work from a library subscription service	Ertman, Earl L. "Nefertiti's Eyes." *Archaeology* Mar.–Apr. 2008: 28–32. *Kids Search.* EBSCO. New York Public Library. Web. 18 June 2008 [Indicate the date you accessed the information.]
Filmstrips, slide programs, videocassettes, DVDs, and other audiovisual media	*The Diary of Anne Frank.* Dir. George Stevens. Perf. Millie Perkins, Shelley Winters, Joseph Schildkraut, Lou Jacobi, and Richard Beymer. 1959. Twentieth Century Fox, 2004. DVD.
CD-ROM (with multiple publishers)	Simms, James, ed. *Romeo and Juliet.* By William Shakespeare. Oxford: Attica Cybernetics; London: BBC Education; London: Harper, 1995. CD-ROM.
Radio or television program transcript	"Washington's Crossing of the Delaware." *Weekend Edition Sunday.* Natl. Public Radio. WNYC, New York. 23 Dec. 2003. Television transcript.
Internet Web page	"Fun Facts About Gum." NACGM site. 1999. National Association of Chewing Gum Manufacturers. Web. 19 Dec. 1999 [Indicate the date you accessed the information.]
Personal interview	Smith, Jane. Personal interview. 10 Feb. 2000.

All examples follow the style given in the *MLA Handbook for Writers of Research Papers,* seventh edition, by Joseph Gibaldi.

Does every conflict have a winner?

UNIT PATHWAY

PART 1
SETTING EXPECTATIONS

- INTRODUCING THE BIG QUESTION
- CLOSE READING WORKSHOP

PART 2
TEXT ANALYSIS
GUIDED EXPLORATION

DIFFERENT PERSPECTIVES

PART 3
TEXT SET
DEVELOPING INSIGHT

COMPETITION

PART 4
DEMONSTRATING INDEPENDENCE

- INDEPENDENT READING
- ONLINE TEXT SET

CLOSE READING TOOL

Use this tool to practice the close reading strategies you learn.

STUDENT eTEXT

Bring learning to life with audio, video, and interactive tools.

ONLINE WRITER'S NOTEBOOK

Easily capture notes and complete assignments online.

Find all Digital Resources at **pearsonrealize.com.**

Does every conflict have a winner?

A conflict is a struggle between opposing forces. A conflict can be as small as a disagreement between friends about what movie to see. On the other hand, it can be as large as a civil war. When you struggle with a decision, you have a conflict within yourself. There are many kinds of conflict. Some can be dangerous. Others, like a sports competition, can be exciting. When a conflict is worked out, it is resolved. Different kinds of conflicts are resolved in different ways.

Exploring the Big Question

Collaboration: One-on-One Discussion Start thinking about the Big Question by making a list of different conflicts you have experienced or heard about. Describe one specific example of each of the following types of conflict.

- An argument or disagreement between friends
- A misunderstanding between two people
- A competition between teams or in a contest
- A struggle to make a decision
- A struggle to overcome a challenge or an obstacle

Share your examples with a partner. Talk about the cause of each conflict and the way the conflict worked out. As you exchange ideas, build upon each other's comments. You may want to use the conflict-related words on the next page in the course of your discussion.

Connecting to the Literature Each reading in this unit will give you additional insight into the Big Question. After you read each text, pause to consider ways in which the characters handled conflict.

Vocabulary

Acquire and Use Academic Vocabulary The term "academic vocabulary" refers to words you typically encounter in scholarly and literary texts and in technical and business writing. Review the definitions of these academic vocabulary words.

attitude (at′ ə tōōd′) *n.* person's opinions and feelings about someone or something

challenge (chal′ ənj) *n.* something that tests your skills and abilities

communication (kə myōō′ni kā′shən) *n.* process of sharing information or expressing thoughts and feelings

conflict (kän′ flikt′) *n.* struggle between opposing forces

opposition (äp′ə zish′ən) *n.* person, group, or force that tries to prevent you from accomplishing something

outcome (out′kum′) *n.* way a situation turns out; result or consequence

resolution (rez′ə lōō′shən) *n.* working out of a problem or conflict

understanding (un′dər stan′ diŋ) *n.* agreement

Gather Vocabulary Knowledge Additional words related to conflict are listed below. Categorize the words by deciding whether you know each one well, know it a little bit, or do not know it at all.

competition	desire	obstacle
compromise	disagreement	struggle
danger	misunderstanding	

Then, do the following:

1. Work with a partner to say each word and explain what you think each word means.
2. Consult a print or online dictionary to confirm each word's pronunciation and meaning.
3. Then, use at least four of the words in a brief paragraph about a conflict you experienced or heard about.
4. Take turns reading your paragraphs aloud.

Common Core State Standards

Speaking and Listening
1. Engage effectively in a range of collaborative discussions with diverse partners on grade 7 topics, texts, and issues, building on others' ideas and expressing their own clearly.

Language
6. Acquire and use accurately grade-appropriate general academic and domain-specific words and phrases; gather vocabulary knowledge when considering a word or phrase important to comprehension or expression.

Close Reading Workshop

In this workshop you will learn an approach to reading that will deepen your understanding of literature and will help you better appreciate the author's craft. The workshop includes models for close reading, discussion, research, and writing. After you have reviewed the strategies and models, practice your skills with the Independent Practice selection.

Common Core State Standards

RL.7.1, RL.7.2, RL.7.3, RL.7.6; W.7.2, W.7.7, W.7.9; SL.7.1
[For full standards wording, see the chart in the front of this book.]

CLOSE READING: SHORT STORY

In Part 2 of this unit you will focus on reading various short stories. Use these strategies as you read the texts.

Comprehension: Key Ideas and Details

- Read first to unlock basic meaning.
- Use context clues to help you determine the meanings of unfamiliar words. Consult a dictionary, if necessary.
- Identify unfamiliar details that you might need to clarify through research.

- Distinguish between what is stated directly and what must be inferred.

Ask yourself questions such as these:
- Who are the main characters?
- What conflict drives the main events?
- What is the story's setting?

Text Analysis: Craft and Structure

- Think about the genre of the work and how the author presents ideas.
- Analyze the author's choice of words and the impact of those words.
- Note how the setting, characters, and events work together to build suspense and establish theme.

Ask yourself questions such as these:
- From whose point of view, or perspective, is the story told? How does this perspective influence what the reader does and does not know?
- What do I learn about the characters from the story's dialogue and narration?

Connections: Integration of Knowledge and Ideas

- Look for relationships among key ideas. Identify causes and effects and comparisons and contrasts.
- Look for key ideas, symbolic images, or repetition. Then, connect ideas to identify the theme of the story.

- Compare and contrast this work with other works you have read.

Ask yourself questions such as these:
- How has this work increased my knowledge of a subject or an author?
- What lessons have I learned that I can apply to my life?

Read

As you read this short story, take note of the annotations that model ways to closely read the text.

Reading Model

"The Dinner Party" by Mona Gardner

The country is India. A colonial official[1] and his wife are giving a large dinner party. They are seated with their guests—army officers, and government attachés with their wives, and a visiting American naturalist—in their spacious dining room. It has a bare marble floor, open rafters, and wide glass doors opening onto a veranda.

A spirited discussion springs up between a young girl who insists that women have outgrown the jumping-on-a-chair-at-the-sight-of-a-mouse era and a colonel who says that they haven't.[2]

"A woman's unfailing reaction in any crisis," the colonel says, "is to scream. And while a man may feel like it, he has that ounce more of nerve control than a woman has. And that last ounce more is what counts."

The American does not join in the argument but watches the other guests. As he looks, he sees a strange expression come over the face of the hostess. She is staring straight ahead, her muscles contracting slightly.[3] With a slight gesture, she summons the native boy standing behind her chair and whispers to him. The boy's eyes widen, and he quickly leaves the room.

Of the guests, none except the American notices this or sees the boy place a bowl of milk on the veranda just outside the open doors.

The American comes to with a start. In India, milk in a bowl means only one thing—bait for a snake. He realizes there must be a cobra in the room. He looks up at the rafters—the likeliest place—but they are bare. Three corners of the room are empty, and in the fourth the servants are waiting to serve the next course. There is only one place left—under the table.[4]

Key Ideas and Details

1 An Internet search will reveal that India was part of the British Empire until 1947. The "colonial official" is British.

Craft and Structure

2 In this passage, a small argument breaks out between a young girl and a colonel, who believes that women lack self-control. Characters' beliefs may be clues to theme.

Craft and Structure

3 The narrator's point of view is limited to what the American notices. By leaving the cause of the hostess's expression unknown, the author creates suspense.

Craft and Structure

4 The dashes in this passage help convey the sense that the American's thoughts are racing as he takes in details and comes to conclusions about the snake.

His first impulse is to jump back and warn the others, but he knows the commotion would frighten the cobra into striking.[5] He speaks quickly, the tone of his voice so arresting that it sobers everyone.

"I want to know just what control everyone at this table has. I will count to three hundred—that's five minutes—and not one of you is to move a muscle. Those who move will forfeit fifty rupees. Ready!"

The twenty people sit like stone images while he counts. He is saying "two hundred and eighty" when, out of the corner of his eye, he sees the cobra emerge and make for the bowl of milk. Screams ring out as he jumps to slam the veranda doors safely shut.[6]

"You were right, Colonel!" the host exclaims. "A man has just shown us an example of perfect control."[7]

"Just a minute," the American says, turning to his hostess. "Mrs. Wynnes, how did you know the cobra was in the room?"

A faint smile lights up the woman's face as she replies, "Because it was crawling across my foot."[8]

Integration of Knowledge and Ideas
5 Again, the idea of self-control surfaces as the American fights off panic.

Craft and Structure
6 The climax occurs as the snake leaves and the dinner guests scream in fear.

Integration of Knowledge and Ideas
7 The host's statement recalls the argument from the beginning of the story: self-control is a male trait. So far, the story seems to prove the colonel right.

Craft and Structure
8 The hostess's remark shows that she has more self-control than any other character. This twist reveals the theme: Courage and self-control are not specific to a gender.

Discuss

Sharing your own ideas and listening to the ideas of others can deepen your understanding of a text and help you look at a topic in a whole new way. As you participate in collaborative discussions, work to have a genuine exchange in which classmates build upon one another's ideas. Support your points with evidence and ask meaningful questions.

Discussion Model

Student 1: The author makes sure that we know the setting of the story. In the first sentence, she says: "The country is India." That makes sense, since you'd never have a cobra at a dinner party in Great Britain.

Student 2: I think it's about more than just the snake. The author describes a "spacious dining room," " bare marble floor," and "wide glass doors opening onto a veranda." So the story is not only set in India, it seems like the characters are rich people in India.

Student 3: I agree. I wonder how Gardner's ideas about women fit into this setting. The women only get one sentence of dialogue, and the men don't seem to respect them since they don't think women have "nerve control." Is the setting important because women were not equal in colonial India?

Research

Targeted research can clarify unfamiliar details and shed light on various aspects of a text. Consider questions that arise in your mind as you read, and use those questions as the basis for research.

Research Model

Questions: *What was life like for British women in colonial India?*

Key Words for Internet Search: British women and colonial India

Result: Women in World History: British Empire, George Mason University

What I Learned: British women who went to India with their husbands mostly stayed at home and lived in luxury, but had few rights. Some women worked at jobs outside the home, such as teaching local women or participating in missionary work.

Write

Writing about a text will deepen your understanding of it and will also allow you to share your ideas more formally with others. The following model essay analyzes the role that characters, setting, and plot have in establishing theme and cites evidence to support the main ideas.

Writing Model: Argument

Real Courage

"The Dinner Party," by Mona Gardner, appears on first reading to be a simple story with a surprise ending. Upon closer reading, however, it is clear that Gardner carefully crafted this story in order to develop a powerful theme: That both women and men are capable of great bravery and self-control. Plot events, character development, and the story's setting all work together to reveal this theme.

> The writer presents the essay's thesis in the first paragraph, preparing readers for the claims and evidence that will follow.

As the story begins, a "spirited discussion" takes place between a young woman and a colonel. The two disagree about whether or not women are capable of self-control. This minor conflict sets the stage for the story events that are to come.

The story is told from a third-person limited point of view. The narrator focuses on the observations of an American naturalist, sharing with us his viewpoint of the action taking place at a small dinner party. Suspense builds as the narrator watches his hostess's "strange expression," contracting muscles, and whispered instructions to a servant. As more of the American's observations are revealed, the reader realizes the seriousness of the situation: There is a deadly snake in the room full of guests. The American, a man, controls his feelings of panic and manages to trick the guests into sitting still until the snake is successfully removed from the room.

> The writer identifies elements of the author's craft and explains their significance in the story.

Following these tense events, the host of the party makes a comment about the self-control exhibited by the American, saying, "A man has just shown us an example of perfect control." It becomes apparent, however, that although the American did show bravery and control, it is the hostess herself who exhibited the most self-control. She had been aware the entire time of the snake's presence because it was resting on her foot, and she quietly took the first steps to having it removed.

> Direct quotations from the story support claims.

The story's theme is made all the more powerful when you consider the story's setting of colonial India. British women in colonial India were not granted the rights and respect of British males. In fact, British women were typically regarded as fragile and needing protection. Given this context, the story's theme takes on even more power.

> Evidence from research can also be used to support claims, as in this example about the story's setting.

As you read the following story, apply the close reading strategies you have learned. You may need to read the short story multiple times in order to grasp key ideas and details, appreciate its craft and structure, and integrate knowledge and ideas.

"The Treasure of Lemon Brown"
by Walter Dean Myers

The dark sky, filled with angry, swirling clouds, reflected Greg Ridley's mood as he sat on the stoop of his building. His father's voice came to him again, first reading the letter the principal had sent to the house, then lecturing endlessly about his poor efforts in math.

"I had to leave school when I was thirteen," his father had said, "that's a year younger than you are now. If I'd had half the chances that you have, I'd . . ."

Greg had sat in the small, pale green kitchen listening, knowing the lecture would end with his father saying he couldn't play ball with the Scorpions. He had asked his father the week before, and his father had said it depended on his next report card. It wasn't often the Scorpions took on new players, especially fourteen-year-olds, and this was a chance of a lifetime for Greg. He hadn't been allowed to play high school ball, which he had really wanted to do, but playing for the Community Center team was the next best thing. Report cards were due in a week, and Greg had been hoping for the best. But the principal had ended the suspense early when she sent that letter saying Greg would probably fail math if he didn't spend more time studying.

"And you want to play *basketball*?" His father's brows knitted over deep brown eyes. "That must be some kind of a joke. Now you just get into your room and hit those books."

That had been two nights before. His father's words, like the distant thunder that now echoed through the streets of Harlem, still rumbled softly in his ears.

It was beginning to cool. Gusts of wind made bits of paper dance between the parked cars. There was a flash of nearby lightning, and soon large drops of rain splashed onto his jeans. He stood to go upstairs, thought of the lecture that probably awaited him if he did anything except shut himself in his room with his math book, and started walking down the street instead. Down the block there was an old tenement that had

Meet the Author

Best-selling author **Walter Dean Myers** (b. 1937) writes about what he calls "the most difficult period of my life, the teen years." He dropped out of high school and joined the army when he was 17, but he did not give up on writing. He is a three-time finalist for the National Book Award. Myers bases much of his work on his childhood experiences growing up in Harlem.

CLOSE READING TOOL

Read and respond to this selection online using the **Close Reading Tool**.

impromptu (im
prämp´tōō´) *adj.*
unscheduled; unplanned

ajar (ə jär´) *adj.*
slightly open

tentatively (ten´ tə
tiv lē) *adj.* hesitantly;
with uncertainty

been abandoned for some months. Some of the guys had held an impromptu checker tournament there the week before, and Greg had noticed that the door, once boarded over, had been slightly ajar.

Pulling his collar up as high as he could, he checked for traffic and made a dash across the street. He reached the house just as another flash of lightning changed the night to day for an instant, then returned the graffiti-scarred building to the grim shadows. He vaulted over the outer stairs and pushed tentatively on the door. It was open, and he let himself in.

The inside of the building was dark except for the dim light that filtered through the dirty windows from the streetlamps. There was a room a few feet from the door, and from where he stood at the entrance, Greg could see a squarish patch of light on the floor. He entered the room, frowning at the musty smell. It was a large room that might have been someone's parlor at one time. Squinting, Greg could see an old table on its side against one wall, what looked like a pile of rags or a torn mattress in the corner, and a couch, with one side broken, in front of the window.

He went to the couch. The side that wasn't broken was comfortable enough, though a little creaky. From the spot he could see the blinking neon sign over the bodega on the corner. He sat awhile, watching the sign blink first green then red, allowing his mind to drift to the Scorpions, then to his father. His father had been a postal worker for all Greg's life, and was proud of it, often telling Greg how hard he had worked to pass the test. Greg had heard the story too many times to be interested now.

For a moment Greg thought he heard something that sounded like a scraping against the wall. He listened carefully, but it was gone.

Outside the wind had picked up, sending the rain against the window with a force that shook the glass in its frame. A car passed, its tires hissing over the wet street and its red taillights glowing in the darkness.

Greg thought he heard the noise again. His stomach tightened as he held himself still and listened intently. There weren't any more scraping noises, but he was sure he had heard something in the darkness—something breathing!

He tried to figure out just where the breathing was coming from; he knew it was in the room with him. Slowly he stood, tensing. As he turned, a flash of lightning lit up the room, frightening him with its sudden brilliance. He saw nothing, just the overturned table, the pile of rags and an old newspaper on the floor. Could he have been imagining the sounds? He continued listening, but heard nothing and thought that it might have just been rats. Still, he thought, as soon as the rain let up he would leave. He went to the window and was about to look when he heard a voice behind him.

"Don't try nothin' 'cause I got a razor here sharp enough to cut a week into nine days!"

Greg, except for an involuntary tremor in his knees, stood stock still. The voice was high and brittle, like dry twigs being broken, surely not one he had ever heard before. There was a shuffling sound as the person who had been speaking moved a step closer. Greg turned, holding his breath, his eyes straining to see in the dark room.

The upper part of the figure before him was still in darkness. The lower half was in the dim rectangle of light that fell unevenly from the window. There were two feet, in cracked, dirty shoes from which rose legs that were wrapped in rags.

"Who are you?" Greg hardly recognized his own voice.

"I'm Lemon Brown," came the answer. "Who're you?"

"Greg Ridley."

"What you doing here?" The figure shuffled forward again, and Greg took a small step backward.

"It's raining," Greg said.

"I can see that," the figure said.

The person who called himself Lemon Brown peered forward, and Greg could see him clearly. He was an old man.

His black, heavily wrinkled face was surrounded by a halo of crinkly white hair and whiskers that seemed to separate his head from the layers of dirty coats piled on his smallish frame. His pants were bagged to the knee, where they were met with rags that went down to the old shoes. The rags were held on with strings, and there was a rope around his middle. Greg relaxed. He had seen the man before, picking through the trash on the corner and pulling clothes out of a Salvation Army box. There was no sign of the razor that could "cut a week into nine days."

"What are you doing here?" Greg asked.

"This is where I'm staying," Lemon Brown said. "What you here for?"

"Told you it was raining out," Greg said, leaning against the back of the couch until he felt it give slightly.

"Ain't you got no home?"

"I got a home," Greg answered.

"You ain't one of them bad boys looking for my treasure, is you?" Lemon Brown cocked his head to one side and squinted one eye. "Because I told you I got me a razor."

"I'm not looking for your treasure," Greg answered, smiling. "If you have one."

"What you mean, if I have one," Lemon Brown said. "Every man got a treasure. You don't know that, you must be a fool!"

"Sure," Greg said as he sat on the sofa and put one leg over the back. "What do you have, gold coins?"

"Don't worry none about what I got," Lemon Brown said. "You know who I am?"

"You told me your name was orange or lemon or something like that."

"Lemon Brown," the old man said, pulling back his shoulders as he did so, "they used to call me Sweet Lemon Brown."

"Sweet Lemon?" Greg asked.

"Yessir. Sweet Lemon Brown. They used to say I sung the blues so sweet that if I sang at a funeral, the dead would commence to rocking with the beat. Used to travel all over Mississippi and as far as Monroe, Louisiana, and east on over to Macon, Georgia. You mean you ain't never heard of Sweet Lemon Brown?"

"Afraid not," Greg said. "What . . . what happened to you?"

"Hard times, boy. Hard times always after a poor man. One day I got tired, sat down to rest a spell and felt a tap on my shoulder. Hard times caught up with me."

"Sorry about that."

"What you doing here? How come you didn't go on home when the rain come? Rain don't bother you young folks none."

"Just didn't." Greg looked away.

"I used to have a knotty-headed boy just like you." Lemon Brown had half walked, half shuffled back to the corner and sat down against the wall. "Had them big eyes like you got, I used to call them moon eyes. Look into them moon eyes and see anything you want."

"How come you gave up singing the blues?" Greg asked.

"Didn't give it up," Lemon Brown said. "You don't give up the blues; they give you up. After a while you do good for yourself, and it ain't nothing but foolishness singing about how hard you got it. Ain't that right?"

"I guess so."

"What's that noise?" Lemon Brown asked, suddenly sitting upright.

Greg listened, and he heard a noise outside. He looked at Lemon Brown and saw the old man pointing toward the window.

Greg went to the window and saw three men, neighborhood thugs, on the stoop. One was carrying a length of pipe. Greg looked back toward Lemon Brown, who moved quietly across the room to the window. The old man looked out, then beckoned frantically for Greg to follow him. For a moment Greg couldn't move. Then he found himself following Lemon Brown into the hallway and up darkened stairs. Greg followed as closely as he could. They reached the top of the stairs, and Greg felt Lemon Brown's hand first lying on his shoulder, then probing down his arm until he finally took Greg's hand into his own as they crouched in the darkness.

"They's bad men," Lemon Brown whispered. His breath was warm against Greg's skin.

"Hey! Rag man!" A voice called. "We know you in here. What you got up under them rags? You got any money?"

Silence.

"We don't want to have to come in and hurt you, old man, but we don't mind if we have to."

Lemon Brown squeezed Greg's hand in his own hard, gnarled fist.

There was a banging downstairs and a light as the men entered. They banged around noisily, calling for the rag man.

"We heard you talking about your treasure." The voice was slurred.

"We just want to see it, that's all."

"You sure he's here?" One voice seemed to come from the room with the sofa.

"Yeah, he stays here every night."

"There's another room over there; I'm going to take a look. You got that flashlight?"

"Yeah, here, take the pipe too."

Greg opened his mouth to quiet the sound of his breath as he sucked it in uneasily. A beam of light hit the wall a few feet opposite him, then went out.

"Ain't nobody in that room," a voice said. "You think he gone or something?"

"I don't know," came the answer. "All I know is that I heard him talking about some kind of treasure. You know they found that shopping bag lady with that money in her bags."

"Yeah. You think he's upstairs?"

"Hey, old man, are you up there?"

Silence.

"Watch my back, I'm going up."

There was a footstep on the stairs, and the beam from the flashlight danced crazily along the peeling wallpaper. Greg held his breath. There was another step and a loud crashing noise as the man banged the pipe against the wooden banister. Greg could feel his temples throb as the man slowly neared them. Greg thought about the pipe, wondering what he would do when the man reached them—what he *could* do.

Then Lemon Brown released his hand and moved toward the top of the stairs. Greg looked around and saw stairs going up to the next floor. He tried waving to Lemon Brown, hoping the old man would see him in the dim light and follow him to the next floor. Maybe, Greg thought, the man wouldn't follow them up there. Suddenly, though, Lemon Brown stood at the top of the stairs, both arms raised high above his head.

"There he is!" A voice cried from below.

"Throw down your money, old man, so I won't have to bash your head in!"

Lemon Brown didn't move. Greg felt himself near panic. The steps came closer, and still Lemon Brown didn't move. He was an eerie sight, a bundle of rags standing at the top of the stairs, his shadow on the wall looming over him. Maybe, the thought came to Greg, the scene could be even eerier.

Greg wet his lips, put his hands to his mouth and tried to make a sound. Nothing came out. He swallowed hard, wet his lips once more and howled as evenly as he could.

"What's that?"

As Greg howled, the light moved away from Lemon Brown, but not before Greg saw him hurl his body down the stairs at the men who had come to take his treasure. There was a crashing noise, and then footsteps. A rush of warm air came in as the downstairs door opened, then there was only an ominous silence.

Greg stood on the landing. He listened, and after a while there was another sound on the staircase.

"Mr. Brown?" he called.

"Yeah, it's me," came the answer. "I got their flashlight."

Greg exhaled in relief as Lemon Brown made his way slowly back up the stairs.

"You OK?"

"Few bumps and bruises," Lemon Brown said.

"I think I'd better be going," Greg said, his breath returning to normal. "You'd better leave, too, before they come back."

"They may hang around outside for a while," Lemon Brown said, "but they ain't getting their nerve up to come in here again. Not with crazy old rag men and howling spooks. Best you stay a while till the coast is clear. I'm heading out west tomorrow, out to East St. Louis."

"They were talking about treasures," Greg said. "You *really* have a treasure?"

"What I tell you? Didn't I tell you every man got a treasure?" Lemon Brown said. "You want to see mine?"

"If you want to show it to me," Greg shrugged.

"Let's look out the window first, see what them scoundrels be doing," Lemon Brown said.

They followed the oval beam of the flashlight into one of the rooms and looked out the window. They saw the men who had tried to take the treasure sitting on the curb near the corner. One of them had his pants leg up, looking at his knee.

"You sure you're not hurt?" Greg asked Lemon Brown.

"Nothing that ain't been hurt before," Lemon Brown said. "When you get as old as me all you say when something hurts is, 'Howdy, Mr. Pain, sees you back again.' Then when Mr. Pain see he can't worry you none, he go on mess with somebody else."

Greg smiled.

"Here, you hold this." Lemon Brown gave Greg the flashlight.

He sat on the floor near Greg and carefully untied the strings that held the rags on his right leg. When he took the rags away, Greg saw a piece of plastic. The old man carefully took off the plastic and unfolded it. He revealed some yellowed newspaper clippings and a battered harmonica.

"There it be," he said, nodding his head. "There it be."

Greg looked at the old man, saw the distant look in his eye, then turned to the clippings. They told of Sweet Lemon Brown, a blues singer and harmonica player who was appearing at different theaters in the South. One of the clippings said he had been the hit of the show, although not the headliner. All of the clippings were reviews of shows Lemon Brown had been in more than 50 years ago. Greg looked at the harmonica. It was dented badly on one side, with the reed holes on one end nearly closed.

"I used to travel around and make money for to feed my wife and Jesse—that's my boy's name. Used to feed them good, too. Then his mama died, and he stayed with his mama's sister. He growed up to be a man, and when the war come he saw fit to go off and fight in it. I didn't have nothing to give him except these things that told him who I was, and what he come from. If you know your pappy did something, you know you can do something too.

"Anyway, he went off to war, and I went off still playing and singing. 'Course by then I wasn't as much as I used to be, not without somebody to make it worth the while. You know what I mean?"

"Yeah," Greg nodded, not quite really knowing.

"I traveled around, and one time I come home, and there was this letter saying Jesse got killed in the war. Broke my heart, it truly did.

"They sent back what he had with him over there, and what it was is this old mouth fiddle and these clippings. Him carrying it around with him like that told me it meant something to him. That was my treasure, and when I give it to him he treated it just like that, a treasure. Ain't that something?"

"Yeah, I guess so," Greg said.

"You *guess* so?" Lemon Brown's voice rose an octave as he started to put his treasure back into the plastic. "Well, you got to guess 'cause you sure don't know nothing. Don't know enough to get home when it's raining."

"I guess . . . I mean, you're right."

"You OK for a youngster," the old man said as he tied the strings around his leg, "better than those scalawags what come here looking for my treasure. That's for sure."

"You really think that treasure of yours was worth fighting for?" Greg asked. "Against a pipe?"

"What else a man got 'cepting what he can pass on to his son, or his daughter, if she be his oldest?" Lemon Brown said. "For a big-headed boy you sure do ask the foolishest questions."

Lemon Brown got up after patting his rags in place and looked out the window again.

"Looks like they're gone. You get on out of here and get yourself home. I'll be watching from the window so you'll be all right."

Lemon Brown went down the stairs behind Greg. When they reached the front door the old man looked out first, saw the street was clear and told Greg to scoot on home.

"You sure you'll be OK?" Greg asked.

"Now didn't I tell you I was going to East St. Louis in the morning?" Lemon Brown asked. "Don't that sound OK to you?"

"Sure it does," Greg said. "Sure it does. And you take care of that treasure of yours."

"That I'll do," Lemon said, the wrinkles about his eyes suggesting a smile. "That I'll do."

The night had warmed and the rain had stopped, leaving puddles at the curbs. Greg didn't even want to think how late it was. He thought ahead of what his father would say and wondered if he should tell him about Lemon Brown. He thought about it until he reached his stoop, and decided against it. Lemon Brown would be OK, Greg thought, with his memories and his treasure.

Greg pushed the button over the bell marked Ridley, thought of the lecture he knew his father would give him, and smiled.

Close Reading Activities

Read

Comprehension: Key Ideas and Details

1. (a) Who are the main characters in "The Treasure of Lemon Brown"? **(b) Analyze:** What is one thing you learn about each main character from his actions? Cite specific details in your answer.

2. (a) Where does the story take place? **(b) Synthesize:** How does the setting help advance the plot?

3. Summarize: Write a brief, objective summary of the story, citing story details.

Text Analysis: Craft and Structure

4. (a) Generalize: What do you learn about Lemon Brown through the way he talks? **(b) Evaluate:** Using details from the text, explain how the author's use of dialogue strengthens his characterization.

5. (a) Describe two key conflicts in the story. **(b) Interpret:** How are these key conflicts resolved?

6. (a) Deduce: At the story's end, what has Greg learned that causes him to smile? **(b) Predict:** How will Greg's relationship with his father change in the future? Cite evidence to support your prediction.

7. (a) Interpret: What is the story's theme? **(b) Support:** Which story elements provide the most significant clues to its theme?

Connections: Integration of Knowledge and Ideas

Discuss
Conduct a **small-group discussion** about the setting of the story and how it contributes to the story's *mood,* or the feeling it creates in the reader. Discuss the ways in which the setting reflects Greg's personal dilemma.

Research
Walter Dean Myers was appointed Ambassador for Young People's Literature. Briefly research some of the work he has done in this role, considering the following:

a. the messages he shares with his audiences

b. the ways he inspires young authors

Take notes as you perform your research. Then, write a brief **explanation** of the work Walter Dean Myers does in this role and his influence on young adult readers. In your explanation, explain the message in "The Treasure of Lemon Brown," and tell why that message is inspirational.

Write
In this story, Walter Dean Myers plays with the meaning of the word "treasure." Think about the typical ideas associated with treasures and whether or not Myers uses the traditional definition in his story. Write an **essay** in which you discuss the value of Lemon Brown's treasure and why it is important to him. Cite details from the story to support your analysis.

 Does every conflict have a winner?

How do Greg and his father become "winners" as a result of Greg's experience with Lemon Brown? Explain your answer.

"It takes a **thousand voices**
to tell a **single story**."

—**Native American proverb**

DIFFERENT PERSPECTIVES

As you read the stories in this section, notice each character's unique point of view. Then, consider how characters' perspectives change as they gain new knowledge, face challenging situations, and interact with others. The quotation on the opposite page will help you start thinking about the ways in which considering others' perspectives can broaden our view of the world.

◀ **CRITICAL VIEWING** How does this image reflect the meaning of the quotation on the opposite page?

READINGS IN PART 2

SHORT STORY
Rikki-tikki-tavi
Rudyard Kipling (p. 26)

EXEMPLAR TEXT Ⓖ
SHORT STORY
Two Kinds from *The Joy Luck Club*
Amy Tan (p. 48)

SHORT STORY
The Third Wish
Joan Aiken (p. 70)

SHORT STORY
Ribbons
Laurence Yep (p. 82)

CLOSE READING TOOL

Use the **Close Reading Tool** to practice the strategies you learn in this unit.

Elements of a Short Story

A short story is a brief work of fiction. No two stories are identical, but they all share some common elements.

A **short story** takes readers on a quick, focused journey. Authors use the following elements of fiction to make the trip interesting.

Characters are the people or animals that take part in a story's action. They are driven by **motivation,** their reasons for acting as they do.

Conflict is the central problem or struggle that the characters face. A short story typically has one central conflict.

Plot is the sequence of events in a story. Events are often presented in chronological order, though they may be told out of sequence.

Setting is the time and place of a story. The setting can create a **mood,** or atmosphere.

Point of view is the perspective from which a story is told.

Theme is the central message expressed in a story. A theme is a general truth or observation about life or human nature.

Characters: the people or animals in a story
- In **direct characterization**, the author describes a character.
- In **indirect characterization**, the author reveals a character through speech and actions.

Conflict: a problem the characters face
- An **external conflict** is a struggle between a character and an outside force.
- An **internal conflict** takes place within a character's mind.

Plot: the sequence of events in a story
- **Exposition** introduces the situation.
- **Rising action** introduces the **conflict**.
- **Climax** is the turning point.
- **Falling action** is when the conflict eases.
- **Resolution** is the conclusion.

Short Story Elements

Setting: the time and place of the action, including
- historical period;
- physical location;
- season of year and time of day;
- climate and weather;
- culture and social systems or traditions.

Theme: a central message or insight
- **Stated themes** are expressed directly.
- **Implied themes** are suggested by the author.
- **Universal themes** recur in different cultures and time periods.

Point of View

The perspective from which a short story is told, or narrated, affects the kinds of information readers receive. When a story is told from the **first-person** point of view, the narrator is a character in the story. Readers learn only what that character knows, thinks, or feels.

When a story is told from the **third-person** point of view, the narrator is not a character, but a voice outside the story. A third-person narrator may be either **omniscient** or **limited**. An omniscient narrator is able to relate the inner thoughts and feelings of all the characters. A narrator with a limited point of view reveals the thoughts and feelings of only one character.

Example: Points of View

First Person
I could hear the footsteps, but I couldn't see a thing. Where was the light switch?

Third-Person Omniscient
Ted heard someone approaching, but in the darkness, he had no idea it was a burglar.

Another difference among types of narrators is that some narrators are objective, while others are subjective. An **objective narrator** is a neutral observer who reports on story events without adding personal comments. A **subjective narrator,** however, participates in the story and offers opinions about what takes place. This type of narrator can influence the way readers understand events and characters.

Some subjective narrators are unreliable, which means that readers cannot trust everything they say. For example, a story might be narrated from the perspective of a small child who is too young to understand certain story events. In this case, readers may have to piece together clues to fully grasp what is happening in the story.

Comparing Narrators

Objective	Subjective
At the news conference, Max responded to each question in a careful, measured tone. It was over in less than ten minutes.	Like every good politician, Max knew how to hide his feelings. In front of the camera, he became a slick advertisement for himself.

A narrator is a filter through which readers get information. However, the narrator does not reflect the only point of view in a story. Each character has his or her perspective as well. Two characters in a story may have very different perspectives on the same event. Readers can make inferences about a character's point of view based on the information and details the narrator provides.

Common Core State Standards

Reading Literature
3. Analyze how particular elements of a story or drama interact (e.g., how setting shapes the characters or plot).

6. Analyze how an author develops and contrasts the points of view of different characters or narrators in a text.

Analyzing How Elements Interact

The interaction of key story elements reveals the **theme** of a story.

In the best short stories, story elements interact to convey a meaningful **theme,** or insight about life or human nature.

Inferring a Theme Most authors do not simply state a story's theme. Instead, they develop it over the course of the story through elements such as character, conflict, and plot. Readers must infer, or figure out, the theme by analyzing story clues and thinking about how they add up to a central message or insight.

Characters and Theme To determine the theme of a story, notice the words, thoughts, and actions of the characters. Characters' **motivations,** or reasons for doing what they do, may also contribute to the theme. Note the **dialogue,** or what the characters say, as well as the narrator's observations and descriptions.

Narrator's Observations	Theme
Dee grinned at me as she left the stage. My shy, timid friend was standing tall and proud.	A friend can help you overcome fears and develop your potential.
Dialogue	
"I made it!" Dee shouted to Carla in the hall. "Thanks for talking me into trying out for the play!"	

Conflict and Theme Most stories focus on a **conflict,** or struggle between opposing forces. When the conflict is **external,** a character struggles with an outside force. When the conflict is **internal,** a character struggles with himself or herself. A story's central conflict often ties directly to its theme. Look at these examples:

External Conflict	Possible Theme
Character versus a force of nature	Humans should not underestimate the power of nature.
Character versus society	Individuals must carve out their own paths in life.
Internal Conflict	**Possible Theme**
Character versus his or her fears	People may be stronger than they realize.
Character facing a difficult decision	People should trust their instincts.

The ways that characters respond to a story's conflict can provide clues to the story's theme. In particular, pay attention to how the main character changes during the story and what he or she may have learned by the end.

Plot and Theme Events in the plot help develop a story's theme. The **exposition** and **rising action** develop the focus of the story. The **climax,** or turning point, often reveals a shift that points to an underlying message. As the story winds down to its **resolution,** that message becomes clearer.

Remember that story events may not flow in chronological order. An author may interrupt the sequence of events with a **flashback**—a scene from the past—or by **foreshadowing,** giving clues that hint at events to come. Such devices can move the story along while conveying the author's message.

Point of View and Theme A story may be told from the point of view of a character in the story or of an outside narrator. The narrator's point of view is crucial to the message of the story because readers know only what the narrator knows or chooses to tell. Use point of view to help you determine theme. Consider who is telling the story and what message the narrator seems to think is important.

Setting and Theme The place and time in which a story occurs can affect everything from the characters' motivations to the central conflict. Therefore, setting may have a strong influence on a story's message. In some cases, the setting is so important that the events of the story could not take place in any other time or location.

Symbols and Theme A **symbol** is a person, a place, or an object that represents something else. A dove, for example, is often a symbol for peace. Authors may use symbols to highlight or emphasize key concepts. As you read, pay attention to objects that seem to represent important ideas. Understanding the deeper meaning of a symbol can help you determine a story's theme.

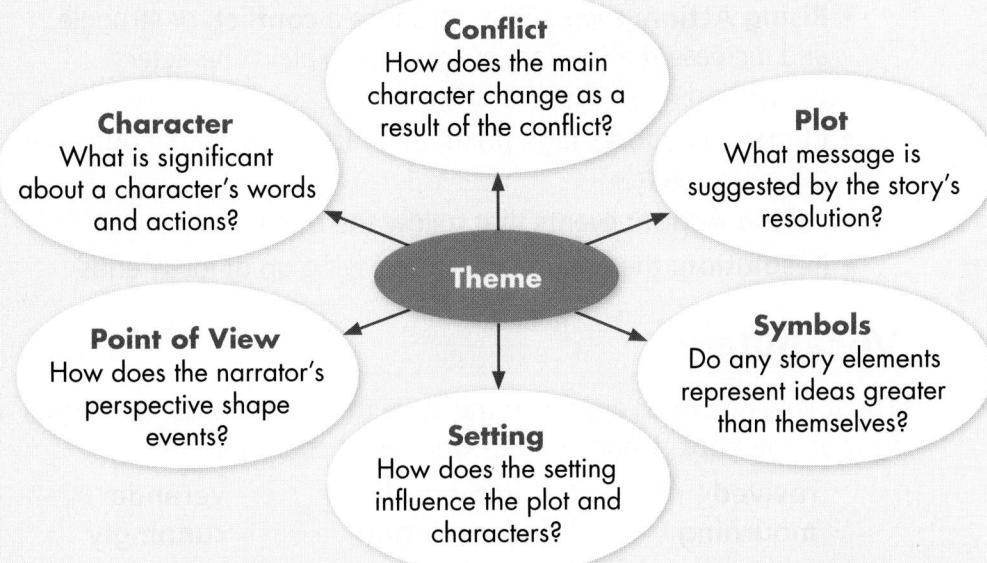

Conflict
How does the main character change as a result of the conflict?

Character
What is significant about a character's words and actions?

Plot
What message is suggested by the story's resolution?

Point of View
How does the narrator's perspective shape events?

Theme

Symbols
Do any story elements represent ideas greater than themselves?

Setting
How does the setting influence the plot and characters?

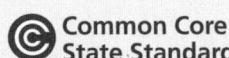
Meet the Author

Rudyard Kipling (1865–1936) was born in Bombay, India, to English parents. Although he moved to England when he was five, Kipling remained attached to the land of his birth. In 1882, he returned to India and began writing the stories that would make him famous. His many popular books of stories and poems include *The Jungle Book* and *Kim*. In 1907, Kipling became the first English writer to win the Nobel Prize in Literature.

Ⓒ **Common Core State Standards**

**Reading Literature
3.** Analyze how particular elements of a story or drama interact.

**Language
4.b.** Use common, grade-appropriate Greek or Latin affixes and roots as clues to the meaning of a word.

6. Acquire and use accurately grade-appropriate general academic and domain-specific words and phrases; gather vocabulary knowledge when considering a word or phrase important to comprehension or expression.

? Does every conflict have a winner?

Think about the Big Question as you read "Rikki-tikki-tavi." Take notes on how characters triumph or suffer as a result of conflicts.

CLOSE READING FOCUS

Key Ideas and Details: **Make Predictions**

Predicting means making an intelligent judgment about what will happen next in a story based on text details. You can also use prior knowledge to make predictions. For example, if a character sees dark clouds, you can predict that a storm is coming. That is because your prior knowledge tells you that dark clouds often mean stormy weather.

As you read, use details from the story and your prior knowledge to make predictions about what characters will do.

Craft and Structure: **Plot**

Plot is the related sequence of events in a story. Each event moves the story forward. Some plot events hint at what might happen next. Such events create **foreshadowing.** A plot has the following elements:

- **Exposition:** introduction of the setting, the characters, and the basic situation
- **Rising Action:** events that introduce a **conflict,** or struggle, and increase the tension; events that explain characters' past actions
- **Climax:** the story's high point, at which the eventual outcome becomes clear
- **Falling Action:** events that follow the climax
- **Resolution:** the final outcome and tying up of loose ends

Vocabulary

The following words appear in the story that follows. List the words in your notebook. Underline the words that share a suffix.

revived	immensely	veranda
mourning	consolation	cunningly

CLOSE READING MODEL

The passage below is from Rudyard Kipling's short story "Rikki-tikki-tavi." The notes to the right of the passage show ways in which you can use close reading skills to make predictions and analyze plot.

from "Rikki-tikki-tavi"

Then Rikki-tikki went out into the garden to see what was to be seen. It was a large garden, only half cultivated, with bushes as big as summerhouses of Marshal Niel roses, lime and orange trees, clumps of bamboos, and thickets of high grass.[1]

Rikki-tikki licked his lips. "This is splendid hunting-ground," he said, and his tail grew bottlebrushy at the thought of it,[2] and he scuttled up and down the garden, snuffing here and there till he heard very sorrowful voices in a thorn-bush.

It was Darzee, the tailorbird, and his wife. They had made a beautiful nest by pulling two big leaves together and stitching them up the edges with fibers, and had filled the hollow with cotton and downy fluff. The nest swayed to and fro, as they sat on the rim and cried.[3]

"What is the matter?" asked Rikki-tikki.

"We are very miserable," said Darzee. "One of our babies fell out of the nest yesterday, and Nag ate him."[4]

Plot

1 Kipling describes the garden in great detail. Because he is introducing the setting, you know that this is the exposition stage of the plot. You can expect to learn more about the characters and the basic situation soon.

Make Predictions

2 Rikki-tikki is excited that the garden is "splendid hunting-ground." His tail grows large and bushy with excitement. These details reveal that he is a hunter who has confidence in his skills. You may predict that he will have a chance to use those skills before long.

Plot

3 New characters, Darzee and his wife, are introduced here. You might ask yourself, "What earlier event made these birds unhappy?"

Make Predictions

4 Even without knowing who or what Nag is, you may predict that the conflict in the story will involve this character.

Rikki-tikki-tavi

Rudyard Kipling

This is the story of the great war that Rikki-tikki-tavi fought, single-handed, through the bathrooms of the big bungalow in Segowlee cantonment.[1] Darzee, the tailorbird bird, helped him, and Chuchundra (chōō chun´ drə) the muskrat, who never comes out into the middle of the floor, but always creeps round by the wall, gave him advice; but Rikki-tikki did the real fighting.

He was a mongoose, rather like a little cat in his fur and his tail, but quite like a weasel in his head and his habits. His eyes and the end of his restless nose were pink; he could scratch himself anywhere he pleased, with any leg, front or back, that he chose to use; he could fluff up his tail till it looked like a bottle brush, and his war cry as he scuttled through the long grass, was: *"Rikk-tikk-tikki-tikki-tchk!"*

One day, a high summer flood washed him out of the burrow where he lived with his father and mother, and carried him, kicking and clucking,

---

1. Segowlee cantonment (sē gou´ lē kan tän´ mənt) *n.* living quarters for British troops in Segowlee, India.

down a roadside ditch. He found a little wisp of grass floating there, and clung to it till he lost his senses. When he revived, he was lying in the hot sun on the middle of a garden path, very draggled² indeed, and a small boy was saying: "Here's a dead mongoose. Let's have a funeral."

"No," said his mother; "let's take him in and dry him. Perhaps he isn't really dead."

They took him into the house, and a big man picked him up between his finger and thumb and said he was not dead but half choked; so they wrapped him in cotton wool, and warmed him, and he opened his eyes and sneezed.

"Now," said the big man (he was an Englishman who had just moved into the bungalow); "don't frighten him, and we'll see what he'll do."

It is the hardest thing in the world to frighten a mongoose, because he is eaten up from nose to tail with curiosity. The motto of all the mongoose family is, "Run and find out"; and Rikki-tikki was a true mongoose. He looked at the cotton wool, decided that it was not good to eat, ran all round the table, sat up and put his fur in order, scratched himself, and jumped on the small boy's shoulder.

"Don't be frightened, Teddy," said his father. "That's his way of making friends."

"Ouch! He's tickling under my chin," said Teddy.

Rikki-tikki looked down between the boy's collar and neck, snuffed at his ear, and climbed down to the floor, where he sat rubbing his nose.

"Good gracious," said Teddy's mother, "and that's a wild creature! I suppose he's so tame because we've been kind to him."

"All mongooses are like that," said her husband. "If Teddy

---

2. **draggled** (drag´ əld) *adj.* wet and dirty.

◀ **Vocabulary**
revived (ri vīvd´)
v. came back to life or consciousness

Plot
What important details about the mongoose are revealed in the exposition on the previous page?

Comprehension
Who is Rikki-tikki-tavi, and how does he meet Teddy?

Vocabulary ▶

immensely
(i mens′ lē) *adv.* a
great deal; very much

veranda (və ran′də) *n.*
an open porch, usually
with a roof

doesn't pick him up by the tail, or try to put him in a cage,
he'll run in and out of the house all day long. Let's give him
something to eat."

They gave him a little piece of raw meat. Rikki-tikki liked
it immensely, and when it was finished he went out into the
veranda and sat in the sunshine and fluffed up his fur to
make it dry to the roots. Then he felt better.

"There are more things to find out about in this house," he
said to himself, "than all my family could find out in all their
lives. I shall certainly stay and find out."

He spent all that day roaming over the house. He nearly
drowned himself in the bathtubs, put his nose into the ink
on a writing table, and burned it on the end of the big man's
cigar, for he climbed up in the big man's lap to see how
writing was done. At nightfall he ran into Teddy's nursery
to watch how kerosene lamps were lighted, and when Teddy
went to bed Rikki-tikki climbed up too; but he was a restless
companion, because he had to get up and attend to every
noise all through the night, and find out what made it. Teddy's
mother and father came in, the last thing, to look at their boy,
and Rikki-tikki was awake on the pillow. "I don't like that,"
said Teddy's mother; "he may bite the child." "He'll do no such
thing," said the father. "Teddy's safer with that little beast
than if he had a bloodhound to watch him. If a snake came
into the nursery now—"

But Teddy's mother wouldn't think of anything so awful.

Early in the morning Rikki-tikki came to early breakfast in
the veranda riding on Teddy's shoulder, and they gave him
banana and some boiled egg; and he sat on all their laps one
after the other, because every well-brought-up mongoose
always hopes to be a house mongoose some day and have
rooms to run about in, and Rikki-tikki's mother (she used
to live in the General's house at Segowlee) had carefully told
Rikki what to do if ever he came across Englishmen.

Then Rikki-tikki went out into the garden to see what
was to be seen. It was a large garden, only half cultivated,
with bushes as big as summer houses of Marshal Niel roses,
lime and orange trees, clumps of bamboos, and thickets of
high grass. Rikki-tikki licked his lips. "This is a splendid
hunting ground," he said, and his tail grew bottlebrushy at
the thought of it, and he scuttled up and down the garden,

Make Predictions
Based on the parents'
thoughts about Rikki,
what do you predict
will happen in the
story?

snuffing here and there till he heard very sorrowful voices in a thornbush.

It was Darzee, the tailorbird, and his wife. They had made a beautiful nest by pulling two big leaves together and stitching them up the edges with fibers, and had filled the hollow with cotton and downy fluff. The nest swayed to and fro, as they sat on the rim and cried.

"What is the matter?" asked Rikki-tikki.

"We are very miserable," said Darzee. "One of our babies fell out of the nest yesterday and Nag ate him."

"H'm!" said Rikki-tikki, "that is very sad—but I am a stranger here. Who is Nag?"

Darzee and his wife only cowered down in the nest without answering, for from the thick grass at the foot of the bush there came a low hiss—a horrid cold sound that made Rikki-tikki jump back two clear feet. Then inch by inch out of the grass rose up the head and spread hood of Nag, the big black cobra, and he was five feet long from tongue to tail. When he had lifted one third of himself clear of the ground, he stayed balancing to and fro exactly as a dandelion tuft balances in the wind, and he looked at Rikki-tikki with the wicked snake's eyes that never change their expression, whatever the snake may be thinking of.

"Who is Nag?" he said. "*I* am Nag. The great god Brahm[3] put his mark upon all our people when the first cobra spread his hood to keep the sun off Brahm as he slept. Look, and be afraid!"

He spread out his hood more than ever, and Rikki-tikki saw the spectacle mark on the back of it that looks exactly like the eye part of a hook-and-eye fastening. He was afraid for the minute; but it is impossible for a mongoose to stay frightened for any length of time, and though Rikki-tikki had never met a live cobra

Rikki-tikki licked his lips. "This is a splendid hunting ground," he said . . .

Comprehension
How do Teddy's parent's feel about Rikki-tikki-tavi's staying at their house?

---

3. Brahm (bräm) short for Brahma, the name of the chief god in the Hindu religion.

before, his mother had fed him on dead ones, and he knew that all a grown mongoose's business in life was to fight and eat snakes. Nag knew that too, and at the bottom of his cold heart he was afraid.

"Well," said Rikki-tikki, and his tail began to fluff up again, "marks or no marks, do you think it is right for you to eat fledglings out of a nest?"

Nag was thinking to himself, and watching the least little movement in the grass behind Rikki-tikki. He knew that mongooses in the garden meant death sooner or later for him and his family; but he wanted to get Rikki-tikki off his guard. So he dropped his head a little, and put it on one side.

"Let us talk," he said. "You eat eggs. Why should not I eat birds?"

"Behind you! Look behind you!" sang Darzee.

Rikki-tikki knew better than to waste time in staring. He jumped up in the air as high as he could go, and just under him whizzed by the head of Nagaina (nə gī´nə), Nag's wicked wife. She had crept up behind him as he was talking, to make an end of him; and he heard her savage hiss as the stroke missed. He came down almost across her back, and if he had been an old mongoose he would have known that then was the time to break her back with one bite; but he was afraid of the terrible lashing return stroke of the cobra. He bit, indeed, but did not bite long enough, and he jumped clear of the whisking tail, leaving Nagaina torn and angry.

"Wicked, wicked Darzee!" said Nag, lashing up high as he could reach toward the nest in the thornbush; but Darzee had built it out of reach of snakes; and it only swayed to and fro.

Plot
What details intensify the conflict here?

▼ **Critical Viewing**
Based on this photograph, which animal would you expect to win a match to the death—the cobra or the mongoose? Why?

Rikki-tikki felt his eyes growing red and hot (when a mongoose's eyes grow red, he is angry), and he sat back on his tail and hind legs like a little kangaroo, and looked all around him, and chattered with rage. But Nag and Nagaina had disappeared into the grass. When a snake misses its stroke, it never says anything or gives any sign of what it means to do next. Rikki-tikki did not care to follow them, for he did not feel sure that he could manage two snakes at once. So he trotted off to the gravel path near the house, and sat down to think. It was a serious matter for him.

If you read the old books of natural history, you will find they say that when the mongoose fights the snake and happens to get bitten, he runs off and eats some herb that cures him. That is not true. The victory is only a matter of quickness of eye and quickness of foot—snake's blow against mongoose's jump—and as no eye can follow the motion of a snake's head when it strikes, that makes things much more wonderful than any magic herb. Rikki-tikki knew he was a young mongoose, and it made him all the more pleased to think that he had managed to escape a blow from behind. It gave him confidence in himself, and when Teddy came running down the path, Rikki-tikki was ready to be petted.

Make Predictions
What do you predict will be the outcome of the conflict? What prior knowledge helps you make that prediction?

Comprehension
Who is Nagaina, and what does she do to Rikki-tikki-tavi?

Science Connection

Cobra Fact and Fiction

Although the snakes in this story have fictional abilities and characteristics, many of their qualities are accurately based on those of real animals.

- Cobras do have spectacle-shaped markings on their hood, as shown in the picture below.

- Cobras are known to enter houses, just as Nag and Nagaina do in the story.

- A female cobra is extremely dangerous and vicious after laying eggs.

- Unlike the snakes in the story, however, real cobras do not travel in pairs or work together to hatch their eggs.

Connect to the Literature

What fictional characteristics and qualities does Kipling give to the cobras in this story?

But just as Teddy was stooping, something flinched a little in the dust, and a tiny voice said: "Be careful. I am death!" It was Karait (kə rīt′), the dusty brown snakeling that lies for choice on the dusty earth; and his bite is as dangerous as the cobra's. But he is so small that nobody thinks of him, and so he does the more harm to people. ●

Rikki-tikki's eyes grew red again, and he danced up to Karait with the peculiar rocking, swaying motion that he had inherited from his family. It looks very funny, but it is so perfectly balanced a gait that you can fly off from it at any angle you please; and in dealing with snakes this is an advantage. If Rikki-tikki had only known, he was doing a much more dangerous thing than fighting Nag, for Karait is so small, and can turn so quickly, that unless Rikki bit him close to the back of the head, he would get the return stroke in his eye or lip. But Rikki did not know: his eyes were all red, and he rocked back and forth, looking for a good place to hold. Karait struck out. Rikki jumped sideways and tried to run in, but the wicked little dusty gray head lashed within a fraction of his shoulder, and he had to jump over the body, and the head followed his heels close.

Teddy shouted to the house: "Oh, look here! Our mongoose is killing a snake"; and Rikki-tikki heard a scream from Teddy's mother. His father ran out with a stick, but by the time he came up, Karait had lunged out once too far, and Rikki-tikki had sprung, jumped on the snake's back, dropped his head far between his fore legs, bitten as high up the back as he could get hold, and rolled away. That bite paralyzed Karait, and Rikki-tikki was just going to eat him up from the tail, after the custom of his family at dinner, when he remembered that a full meal makes a slow mongoose, and if he wanted all his strength and quickness ready, he must keep himself thin.

He went away for a dust bath under the castor-oil bushes, while Teddy's father beat the dead Karait. "What is the use of that?" thought Rikki-tikki. "I have settled it all"; and then Teddy's mother picked him up from the dust and hugged him, crying that he had saved Teddy from death, and Teddy's father said that he was a providence,[4] and Teddy looked on with big scared eyes. Rikki-tikki was rather amused at all the fuss, which, of course, he did not understand. Teddy's mother might just as well have petted Teddy for playing in the dust. Rikki was thoroughly enjoying himself.

That night, at dinner, walking to and fro among the wineglasses on the table, he could have stuffed himself three times over with nice things; but he remembered Nag and Nagaina, and though it was very pleasant to be patted and petted by Teddy's mother, and to sit on Teddy's shoulder, his eyes would get red from time to time, and he would go off into his long war cry of "*Rikk-tikk-tikki-tikki-tchk!*"

Plot
What details in this paragraph show that the tension is over?

Teddy carried him off to bed, and insisted on Rikki-tikki sleeping under his chin. Rikki-tikki was too well bred to bite or scratch, but as soon as Teddy was asleep he went off for his nightly walk round the house, and in the dark he ran up against Chuchundra the muskrat, creeping round by the wall. Chuchundra is a brokenhearted little beast. He whimpers and cheeps all the night, trying to make up his mind to run into the middle of the room, but he never gets there.

Chuchundra is a brokenhearted little beast.

"Don't kill me," said Chuchundra, almost weeping. "Rikki-tikki don't kill me."

"Do you think a snake-killer kills muskrats?" said Rikki-tikki scornfully.

"Those who kill snakes get killed by snakes," said Chuchundra, more sorrowfully than ever. "And how am I to be sure that Nag won't mistake me for you some dark night?"

"There's not the least danger," said Rikki-tikki; "but Nag is in the garden, and I know you don't go there."

Comprehension
What happens when Rikki meets Karait?

---

4. **a providence** (präv′ ə dəns) *n.* a godsend; a valuable gift.

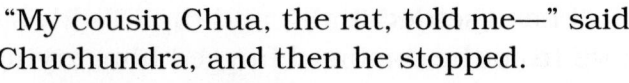

"My cousin Chua, the rat, told me—" said Chuchundra, and then he stopped.

"Told you what?"

"H'sh! Nag is everywhere, Rikki-tikki. You should have talked to Chua in the garden."

"I didn't—so you must tell me. Quick, Chuchundra, or I'll bite you!"

Chuchundra sat down and cried till the tears rolled off his whiskers. "I am a very poor man," he sobbed. "I never had spirit enough to run out into the middle of the room. H'sh! I mustn't tell you anything. Can't you *hear,* Rikki-tikki?"

Rikki-tikki listened. The house was as still as still, but he thought he could just catch the faintest *scratch-scratch* in the world—a noise as faint as that of a wasp walking on a windowpane—the dry scratch of a snake's scales on brickwork.

"That's Nag or Nagaina," he said to himself; "and he is crawling into the bathroom sluice.[5] You're right, Chuchundra; I should have talked to Chua."

He stole off to Teddy's bathroom, but there was nothing there, and then to Teddy's mother's bathroom. At the bottom of the smooth plaster wall there was a brick pulled out to make a sluice for the bath water, and as Rikki-tikki stole in by the masonry curb where the bath is put, he heard Nag and Nagaina whispering together outside in the moonlight.

"When the house is emptied of people," said Nagaina to her husband, "*he* will have to go away, and then the garden will be our own again. Go in quietly, and remember that the big man who killed Karait is the first one to bite. Then come out and tell me, and we will hunt for Rikki-tikki together."

"But are you sure that there is anything to be gained by killing the people?" said Nag.

"Everything. When there were no people in the bungalow, did we have any mongoose in the garden? So long as the bungalow is empty, we are king and queen of the garden; and remember that as soon as our eggs in the melon bed hatch (as they may tomorrow), our children will need room and quiet."

Plot

What details add to the conflict as Rikki overhears this conversation?

---

5. sluice (slōōs) *n.* drain.

"I had not thought of that," said Nag. "I will go, but there is no need that we should hunt for Rikki-tikki afterward. I will kill the big man and his wife, and the child if I can, and come away quietly. Then the bungalow will be empty, and Rikki-tikki will go."

Rikki-tikki tingled all over with rage and hatred at this, and then Nag's head came through the sluice, and his five feet of cold body followed it. Angry as he was, Rikki-tikki was very frightened as he saw the size of the big cobra. Nag coiled himself up, raised his head, and looked into the bathroom in the dark, and Rikki could see his eyes glitter.

"Now, if I kill him here, Nagaina will know;—and if I fight him on the open floor, the odds are in his favor. What am I to do?" said Rikki-tikki-tavi.

Nag waved to and fro, and then Rikki-tikki heard him drinking from the biggest water jar that was used to fill the bath. "That is good," said the snake. "Now, when Karait was killed, the big man had a stick. He may have that stick still, but when he comes in to bathe in the morning he will not have a stick. I shall wait here till he comes. Nagaina—do you hear me?—I shall wait here in the cool till daytime."

There was no answer from outside, so Rikki-tikki knew Nagaina had gone away. Nag coiled himself down, coil by coil, round the bulge at the bottom of the water jar, and Rikki-tikki stayed still as death. After an hour he began to move, muscle by muscle, toward the jar. Nag was asleep, and Rikki-tikki looked at his big back, wondering which would be the best place for a good hold. "If I don't break his back at the first jump," said Rikki, "he can still fight; and if he fights—O Rikki!" He looked at the thickness of the neck below the hood, but that was too much for him; and a bite near the tail would only make Nag savage.

"It must be the head," he said at last; "the head above the hood; and, when I am once there, I must not let go."

Then he jumped. The head was lying a little clear of the water jar, under the curve of it; and, as his teeth met, Rikki braced his back against the bulge of the red earthenware to hold down the head. This gave him just one second's purchase,[6] and he made the most of it. Then he was battered

---

6. **purchase** (pu̇r´ chəs) *n.* firm hold.

Comprehension
Where are Nag and Nagaina, and what are they planning?

to and fro as a rat is shaken by a dog—to and fro on the floor, up and down, and round in great circles: but his eyes were red, and he held on as the body cart-whipped over the floor, upsetting the tin dipper and the soap dish and the fleshbrush, and banged against the tin side of the bath. As he held he closed his jaws tighter and tighter, for he made sure he would be banged to death, and, for the honor of his family, he preferred to be found with his teeth locked. He was dizzy, aching, and felt shaken to pieces when something went off like a thunderclap just behind him; a hot wind knocked him senseless and red fire singed his fur. The big man had been wakened by the noise, and had fired both barrels of a shotgun into Nag just behind the hood.

Rikki-tikki held on with his eyes shut, for now he was quite sure he was dead; but the head did not move, and the big man picked him up and said: "It's the mongoose again, Alice; the little chap has saved *our* lives now." Then Teddy's mother came in with a very white face, and saw what was left of Nag, and Rikki-tikki dragged himself to Teddy's bedroom and spent half the rest of the night shaking himself tenderly to find out whether he really was broken into forty pieces, as he fancied. ●

When morning came he was very stiff, but well pleased with his doings. "Now I have Nagaina to settle with, and she will be worse than five Nags, and there's no knowing when the eggs she spoke of will hatch. Goodness! I must go and see Darzee," he said.

Without waiting for breakfast, Rikki-tikki ran to the thornbush where Darzee was singing a song of triumph at the top of his voice. The news of Nag's death was all over the garden, for the sweeper had thrown the body on the rubbish heap.

"Oh, you stupid tuft of feathers!" said Rikki-tikki angrily. "Is this the time to sing?"

"Nag is dead—is dead—is dead!" sang Darzee. "The valiant Rikki-tikki caught him by the head and held fast. The big man brought the bang-stick and Nag fell in two pieces! He will never eat my babies again."

"All that's true enough; but where's Nagaina?" said Rikki-tikki, looking carefully round him.

▲ Critical Viewing
What role does Darzee, the tailor-bird, play in the conflict between Rikki-tikki-tavi and the cobras?

Plot
Why is the death of Nag part of the rising action rather than the resolution?

"Nagaina came to the bathroom sluice and called for Nag," Darzee went on; "and Nag came out on the end of a stick—the sweeper picked him up on the end of a stick and threw him upon the rubbish heap. Let us sing about the great, the red-eyed Rikki-tikki!" and Darzee filled his throat and sang.

"If I could get up to your nest, I'd roll all your babies out!" said Rikki-tikki. "You don't know when to do the right thing at the right time. You're safe enough in your nest there, but it's war for me down here. Stop singing a minute, Darzee."

"For the great, the beautiful Rikki-tikki's sake, I will stop," said Darzee. "What is it, O Killer of the terrible Nag!"

"Where is Nagaina, for the third time?"

"On the rubbish heap by the stables, mourning for Nag. Great is Rikki-tikki with the white teeth."

"Bother my white teeth! Have you ever heard where she keeps her eggs?"

"In the melon bed, on the end nearest the wall, where the sun strikes nearly all day. She had them there weeks ago."

"And you never thought it worthwhile to tell me? The end nearest the wall, you said?"

"Rikki-tikki, you are not going to eat her eggs?"

"Not eat exactly; no. Darzee, if you have a grain of sense you will fly off to the stables and pretend that your wing is broken, and let Nagaina chase you away to this bush! I must get to the melon bed, and if I went there now she'd see me."

Darzee was a featherbrained little fellow who could never hold more than one idea at a time in his head; and just because he knew that Nagaina's children were born in eggs like his own, he didn't think at first that it was fair to kill them. But his wife was a sensible bird, and she knew that cobra's eggs meant young cobras later on; so she flew off from the nest, and left Darzee to keep the babies warm, and continue his song about the death of Nag. Darzee was very like a man in some ways.

She fluttered in front of Nagaina by the rubbish heap, and cried out, "Oh, my wing is broken! The boy in the house threw a stone at me and broke it." Then she fluttered more desperately than ever.

Nagaina lifted up her head and hissed, "You warned Rikki-tikki when I would have killed him. Indeed and truly, you've chosen a bad place to be lame in." And she moved toward

◀ **Vocabulary**
mourning (môr´nin̄) *adj.* expressing grief, especially after someone dies

Make Predictions
What do you think Rikki is going to do with Nagaina's eggs? What details in the story make you think so?

Comprehension
What prevents Rikki from celebrating Nag's death?

"The boy broke it with a stone!" shrieked Darzee's wife.

"Well! It may be some **consolation** to you when you're dead to know that I shall settle accounts with the boy. My husband lies on the rubbish heap this morning, but before night the boy in the house will lie very still. What is the use of running away? I am sure to catch you. Little fool, look at me!"

Darzee's wife knew better than to do *that, for* a bird who looks at a snake's eyes gets so frightened that she cannot move. Darzee's wife fluttered on, piping sorrowfully, and never leaving the ground, and Nagaina quickened her pace.

Rikki-tikki heard them going up the path from the stables, and he raced for the end of the melon patch near the wall. There, in the warm litter about the melons, very **cunningly** hidden, he found twenty-five eggs, about the size of a bantam's eggs,[7] but with whitish skin instead of shell.

"I was not a day too soon," he said; for he could see the baby cobras curled up inside the skin, and he knew that the minute they were hatched they could each kill a man or a mongoose. He bit off the tops of the eggs as fast as he could, taking care to crush the young cobras, and turned over the litter from time to time to see whether he had missed any. At last there were only three eggs left, and Rikki-tikki began to chuckle to himself, when he heard Darzee's wife screaming:

"Rikki-tikki, I led Nagaina toward the house, and she has gone into the veranda, and—oh, come quickly—she means killing!"

Rikki-tikki smashed two eggs, and tumbled backward down the melon bed with the third egg in his mouth, and scuttled to the veranda as hard as he could put foot to the ground. Teddy and his mother and father were there at early breakfast; but Rikki-tikki saw that they were not eating anything. They sat stone-still, and their faces were white. Nagaina was coiled up on the matting by Teddy's chair, within easy striking distance of Teddy's bare leg, and she was swaying to and fro singing a song of triumph.

"Son of the big man that killed Nag," she hissed, "stay still. I am not ready yet. Wait a little. Keep very still, all you three. If you move I strike, and if you do not move I strike, Oh, foolish

---

7. **bantam's** (ban´ təmz) **eggs** n. eggs of a small chicken.

Vocabulary ▶
consolation
(kän´ sə lā´ shən) *n.*
something that
comforts a
disappointed person

cunningly (kun´ iŋ
lē) *adv.* cleverly

Plot
Do you think this scene
is the climax or part
of the rising action?
Why?

people, who killed my Nag!"

Teddy's eyes were fixed on his father, and all his father could do was to whisper, "Sit still, Teddy. You mustn't move. Teddy, keep still."

Then Rikki-tikki came up and cried: "Turn round, Nagaina; turn and fight!"

"All in good time," said she, without moving her eyes. "I will settle my account with *you* presently. Look at your friends, Rikki-tikki. They are still and white; they are afraid. They dare not move, and if you come a step nearer I strike."

"Look at your eggs," said Rikki-tikki, "in the melon bed near the wall. Go and look, Nagaina."

The big snake turned half round, and saw the egg on the veranda. "Ah-h! Give it to me," she said.

Rikki-tikki put his paws one on each side of the egg, and his eyes were blood-red. "What price for a snake's egg? For a young cobra? For a young king cobra? For the last—the very last of the brood? The ants are eating all the others down by the melon bed."

Nagaina spun clear round, forgetting everything for the sake of the one egg; and Rikki-tikki saw Teddy's father shoot out a big hand, catch Teddy by the shoulder, and drag him across the little table with the teacups, safe and out of reach of Nagaina.

"Tricked! Tricked! Tricked! *Rikk-tck-tck!*" chuckled Rikki-tikki. "The boy is safe, and it was I—I—I that caught Nag by the hood last night in the bathroom." Then he began to jump up and down, all four feet together, his head close to the floor. "He threw me to and fro, but he could not shake me off. He was dead before the big man blew him in two. I did it. *Rikki-tikki-tck-tck!* Come then, Nagaina. Come and fight with me. You shall not be a widow long."

Nagaina saw that she had lost her chance of killing Teddy, and the egg lay between Rikki-tikki's paws. "Give me the egg, Rikki-tikki. Give me the last of my eggs, and I will go away and never come back," she said, lowering her hood.

"Yes, you will go away, and you will never come back; for you will go to the rubbish heap with Nag. Fight, widow! The big man has gone for his gun! Fight!"

Rikki-tikki was bounding all round Nagaina, keeping just out of reach of her stroke, his little eyes like hot coals.

Spiral Review

SETTING How would a fight with Nagaina in an open space like the veranda be different from Rikki-tikki's fight with Nag?

Plot

What details increase the tension in the story at this point?

Comprehension

What does Rikki bring with him to the veranda?

Nagaina gathered herself together, and flung out at him. Rikki-tikki jumped up and backward. Again and again and again she struck, and each time her head came with a whack on the matting of the veranda and she gathered herself together like a watchspring. Then Rikki-tikki danced in a circle to get behind her, and Nagaina spun round to keep her head to his head, so that the rustle of her tail on the matting sounded like dry leaves blown along by the wind.

He had forgotten the egg. It still lay on the veranda, and Nagaina came nearer and nearer to it, till at last, while Rikki-tikki was drawing breath, she caught it in her mouth, turned to the veranda steps, and flew like an arrow down the path, with Rikki-tikki behind her. When the cobra runs for her life, she goes like a whiplash flicked across a horse's neck.

Rikki-tikki knew that he must catch her, or all the trouble would begin again. She headed straight for the long grass by the thornbush, and as he was running Rikki-tikki heard Darzee still singing his foolish little song of triumph. But Darzee's wife was wiser. She flew off her nest as Nagaina came along, and flapped her wings about Nagaina's head. If Darzee had helped they might have turned her; but Nagaina only lowered her hood and went on. Still, the instant's delay brought Rikki-tikki up to her, and as she plunged into the rat hole where she and Nag used to live, his little white teeth were clenched on her tail, and he went down with her—and very few mongooses, however wise and old they may be, care to follow a cobra into its hole. It was dark in the hole; and Rikki-tikki never knew when it might open out and give Nagaina room to turn and strike at him. He held on savagely, and struck out his feet to act as brakes on the dark slope of the hot, moist earth.

Then the grass by the mouth of the hole stopped waving, and Darzee said: "It is all over with Rikki-tikki! We must sing his death song. Valiant Rikki-tikki is dead! For Nagaina will surely kill him underground."

So he sang a very mournful song that he made up all on the spur of the

Spiral Review
SETTING How does the setting of the cobra's hole introduce uncertainty into the plot?

Plot
How does Darzee's comment in this passage add to the tension?

minute, and just as he got to the most touching part the grass quivered again, and Rikki-tikki, covered with dirt, dragged himself out of the hole leg by leg, licking his whiskers. Darzee stopped with a little shout. Rikki-tikki shook some of the dust out of his fur and sneezed. "It is all over," he said. "The widow will never come out again." And the red ants that live between the grass stems heard him, and began to troop down one after another to see if he had spoken the truth.

Rikki-tikki curled himself up in the grass and slept where he was—slept and slept till it was late in the afternoon, for he had done a hard day's work.

"Now," he said, when he awoke, "I will go back to the house. Tell the Coppersmith, Darzee, and he will tell the garden that Nagaina is dead."

The Coppersmith is a bird who makes a noise exactly like the beating of a little hammer on a copper pot; and the reason he is always making it is because he is the town crier to every Indian garden, and tells all the news to everybody who cares to listen. As Rikki-tikki went up the path, he heard his "attention" notes like a tiny dinner gong; and then the steady *"Ding-dong-tock!* Nag is dead—*dong!* Nagaina is dead! *Ding-dong-tock!"* That set all the birds in the garden singing, and the frogs croaking; for Nag and Nagaina used to eat frogs as well as little birds. When Rikki got to the house, Teddy and Teddy's mother and Teddy's father came out and almost cried over him; and that night he ate all that was given him till he could eat no more, and went

Plot
What part of the plot does Rikki's comment illustrate?

Comprehension
What happens when Nagaina goes down the snake hole?

to bed Teddy's shoulder, where Teddy's mother saw him when she came to look late at night.

"He saved our lives and Teddy's life," she said to her husband. "Just think, he saved all our lives."

Rikki-tikki woke up with a jump, for all the mongooses are light sleepers.

"Oh, it's you," said he. "What are you bothering for? All the cobras are dead; and if they weren't, I'm here."

Rikki-tikki had a right to be proud of himself; but he did not grow too proud, and he kept that garden as a mongoose should keep it, with tooth and jump and spring and bite, till never a cobra dared show its head inside the walls.

Language Study

Vocabulary The words listed below appear in "Rikki-tikki-tavi." Answer each question below. Then, explain your response.

revived   immensely   veranda   mourning   cunningly

1. Is someone who has just been *revived* ready to run a race?

2. If you like someone *immensely,* how do you feel about him or her?

3. When you sit on a *veranda,* are you inside the house?

4. Would a *mourning* widow be likely to smile?

5. If you are *cunningly* disguised, can you be recognized?

Word Study

Part A Explain how the **Latin suffix -*tion*** contributes to the meanings of the words *infection, creation,* and *restoration.* Consult a dictionary if necessary.

Part B Use the context of the sentences and your knowledge of the Latin suffix -*tion* to explain your answer to each question.

1. If a painting is an *imitation,* is it the original?

2. If someone offers a *suggestion,* is he being helpful?

WORD STUDY

The **Latin suffix -*tion*** is an ending that turns a verb into a noun meaning "the thing that is."

In this story, Nagaina suggests that Teddy's death will be a **consolation**, or something that is consoling, or comforting, for Darzee's wife.

Close Reading Activities

Literary Analysis

Key Ideas and Details

1. (a) How does Rikki feel about the cobras? How do the cobras feel about Rikki? **(b) Compare:** Using details from the story, compare Rikki's and the cobras' personalities.

2. (a) What is the relationship between Nag and Nagaina? **(b) Analyze:** What does Nagaina do to make matters worse for Nag and herself? **(c) Draw Conclusions:** In what way does this plan make Nagaina a villain?

3. Make Predictions What information in the early part of the story might have led you to predict that Rikki would defeat the cobras?

4. Make Predictions (a) What is another prediction you made as you read this story? **(b)** Use a graphic organizer like the one on the right to show how you made your prediction.

Craft and Structure

5. Plot (a) Identify two plot events that increase the tension between Rikki and Nag. **(b)** How do Rikki's and Nag's attitudes toward Teddy's family differ? Cite details to support your response.

6. Plot (a) Identify two or three events that move the plot toward the climax, when Rikki and Nagaina battle. **(b)** What textual evidence supports the idea that Rikki is a hero?

Integration of Knowledge and Ideas

7. (a) Analyze: What role does Darzee play in the story? **(b) Compare and Contrast:** Whose approach to life, Darzee's or Rikki's, is more effective? Explain your answer, citing evidence from the text.

8. (a) Analyze: "Rikki-tikki-tavi" is among the most widely read short stories ever written. Why do you think it is so popular? Use details from the story to support your position. **(b) Evaluate:** Do you think the story deserves this standing? Explain.

9. **Does every conflict have a winner?** With a small group, discuss the following questions: **(a)** In what way are Nagaina's eggs innocent victims of the conflict? **(b)** How do Teddy and his family suffer? **(c)** What does this story suggest about how conflict in the natural world relates to human conflict?

Story Details

+

My Prior Knowledge

=

Prediction

ACADEMIC VOCABULARY

As you write and speak about "Rikki-tikki-tavi," use the words related to conflict that you explored on page 3 of this textbook.

Conventions: Common, Proper, and Possessive Nouns

A **common noun** names a person, place, or thing. A **proper noun** names a specific person, place, or thing. A **possessive noun** shows ownership.

Common nouns are not capitalized unless they begin a sentence or are in a title. **Proper nouns** are always capitalized.

- Examples of common nouns include *singer, city,* and *boy.*
- Examples of proper nouns include *Abraham Lincoln, London,* and *Selena.*

Possessive nouns show ownership. They are formed in different ways for plural and singular nouns. Study the chart below.

Type of Noun	Rule	Example
Singular: player	Add apostrophe -s.	The player's bat
Singular ending in -s: Lucas	Add apostrophe -s.	Lucas's room
Plural that ends in -s: bees	Add apostrophe.	The bees' buzzing
Plural not ending in -s: children	Add apostrophe -s.	The children's toys

Practice A

Underline the nouns in each sentence. Then, label each as a common or proper noun. Finally, identify which ones are possessive.

1. Teddy found Rikki-tikki-tavi in the middle of a path.
2. Teddy's mother took the mongoose inside.
3. The animal jumped onto the boy's shoulders.
4. Darzee and his wife cried for their baby.

Reading Application In "Rikki-tikki-tavi," find a sentence containing a common noun, a sentence containing a proper noun, and a sentence containing a possessive noun.

Practice B

Complete each sentence with a noun, using the form in parentheses.

1. It was (singular possessive) idea to destroy the cobras' eggs.
2. The female cobra, (proper), wanted the last egg.
3. Teddy's (common) told his son not to be afraid.
4. The muskrat's name is (proper).

Writing Application Choose one of the scenes of conflict in the story. Write three sentences about it, using at least one common, proper, or possessive noun in each.

Writing to Sources

Informative Text In "Rikki-tikki-tavi," a mongoose and two cobras interact in ways that are natural to the two species. Write an **informative article** that explains this interaction.

An informative article teaches readers about a topic and contains these elements:

- an introduction, a body, and a conclusion
- details that tell *when, how much, how often,* and *to what extent*
- a formal style that contains no slang or incomplete sentences
- terms specific to your topic, such as *den, venom,* and *predator*

As you write, support your ideas with specific details from the story. Cite passages precisely, weaving them smoothly into your article.

Grammar Application As you write, use common, proper, and possessive nouns correctly.

Speaking and Listening

Comprehension and Collaboration With a partner, engage in an **informal debate** based on "Rikki-tikki-tavi." Each of you should choose an opposing viewpoint to present, defending the actions of either the mongoose or the cobras in the story. As you prepare your arguments, reread parts of the story to examine the characters' actions.

Follow these steps to complete the assignment:

- Support your ideas with valid arguments based on credible research and on story details.
- Respect your partner's time to talk. Do not interrupt. Listen carefully.
- As you listen to your partner, take note of his or her argument. When it is your turn to talk, do one of three things: (1) Explain why your partner's argument is not sufficiently supported. (2) Explain why the evidence offered contradicts your partner's argument. (3) Explain why one of your partner's arguments is illogical or inconsistent.

Common Core State Standards

Writing
2.d. Use precise language and domain-specific vocabulary to inform about or explain the topic.
2.e. Establish and maintain a formal style.

Speaking and Listening
1.a. Come to discussions prepared, having read or researched material under study; explicitly draw on that preparation by referring to evidence on the topic, text, or issue to probe and reflect on ideas under discussion.
3. Delineate a speaker's argument and specific claims, evaluating the soundness of the reasoning and the relevance and sufficiency of the evidence.

Language
2. Demonstrate command of the conventions of standard English capitalization, punctuation, and spelling when writing.

Meet the Author

If **Amy Tan's** mother had gotten her way, Tan (b. 1952) would have two professions—doctor and concert pianist. Although Tan showed early promise in music, at thirty-seven she became a successful fiction writer instead. Tan has written many books— most for adults, and some for children. Writing is sometimes tough, Tan admits, but she keeps this in mind: "A story should be a gift." That thought propels Tan to keep creating memorable characters and events.

 Common Core State Standards

Reading Literature
6. Analyze how an author develops and contrasts the points of view of different characters or narrators in a text.

Language
6. Acquire and use accurately grade-appropriate general academic and domain-specific words and phrases; gather vocabulary knowledge when considering a word or phrase important to comprehension or expression.

? Does every conflict have a winner?

Think about the Big Question as you read "Two Kinds." Take notes about the conflicts that arise between the main characters.

CLOSE READING FOCUS

Key Ideas and Details: **Make Predictions**

A **prediction** is an informed judgment about what will happen. Use details in the text to make predictions as you read. Then, read ahead to verify predictions—to check whether your predictions are correct.

- As you read, ask yourself if new details support your predictions. If they do not, revise your predictions based on the new information.
- If the predictions you make turn out to be wrong, reread to look for details you might have missed.

Craft and Structure: **Character and Point of View**

A **character** is a person or animal in a literary work.

- A **character's motives** are the emotions or goals that drive him or her to act in a certain way.
- **Character traits** are the individual qualities that make each character unique. You can identify character traits by noticing how characters think, act, and speak.

A character's **point of view** is his or her unique perspective.

- When a story is told from the **first-person point of view,** the narrator is a character who participates in the action and uses the first-person pronoun *I.*
- When a story is told from the **third-person point of view,** the narrator is not a character in the story. He or she uses third-person pronouns such as *he* and *she* to refer to the characters.

Vocabulary

The following words are critical to the meaning of the story that follows. Copy the words into your notebook. As you read, record each word's definition.

reproach	conspired	devastated
nonchalantly	expectations	sentimental

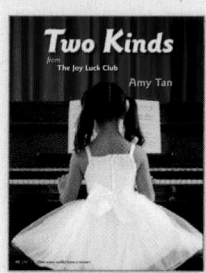

CLOSE READING MODEL

The passage below is from Amy Tan's story "Two Kinds." The annotations to the right of the passage show ways in which you can use close reading skills to make predictions and analyze character and point of view.

from "Two Kinds"

And after seeing my mother's disappointed face once again, something inside of me began to die. I hated the tests, the raised hopes and failed expectations.[1] Before going to bed that night, I looked in the mirror above the bathroom sink and when I saw only my face staring back—and that it would always be this ordinary face—I began to cry. Such a sad, ugly girl! I made high-pitched noises like a crazed animal, trying to scratch out the face in the mirror.

And then I saw what seemed to be the prodigy side of me—because I had never seen that face before. I looked at my reflection, blinking so I could see more clearly. The girl staring back at me was angry, powerful.[2] This girl and I were the same. I had new thoughts, willful thoughts, or rather thoughts filled with lots of won'ts. I won't let her change me, I promised myself. I won't be what I'm not.[3]

So now on nights when my mother presented her tests, I performed listlessly, my head propped on one arm. I pretended to be bored. And I was.[4] I got so bored I started counting the bellows of the foghorns out on the bay while my mother drilled me in other areas.

Character and Point of View
1 The narrator uses the first-person pronouns *my, me,* and *I* and shares her innermost thoughts and emotions. These details reveal that the story is written in the first-person point of view.

Character and Point of View
2 As the narrator gains new insights into her own personality, she reveals new character traits. Despite her feelings of failure and frustration, she realizes that she is "powerful."

Make Predictions
3 The narrator promises to be true to herself. Since a *promise* implies commitment, you may predict that she is determined to resist her mother's attempts to change her.

Make Predictions
4 The narrator describes her performance as *listless,* or lacking energy and effort. Her obvious boredom might lead you to predict that the mother will become frustrated and give up on the "tests."

Two Kinds

from
The Joy Luck Club

Amy Tan

My mother believed you could be anything you wanted to be in America. You could open a restaurant. You could work for the government and get good retirement. You could buy a house with almost no money down. You could become rich. You could become instantly famous.

"Of course you can be prodigy,[1] too," my mother told me when I was nine. "You can be best anything. What does Auntie Lindo know? Her daughter, she is only best tricky."

America was where all my mother's hopes lay. She had come here in 1949 after losing everything in China: her mother and father, her family home, her first husband, and two daughters, twin baby girls. But she never looked back with regret. There were so many ways for things to get better.

老師

We didn't immediately pick the right kind of prodigy. At first my mother thought I could be a Chinese Shirley Temple.[2] We'd watch Shirley's old movies on TV as though they were training films. My mother would poke my arm and say, *"Ni kan"* [nē kän]—You watch. And I would see Shirley tapping her feet, or singing a sailor song, or pursing her lips into a very round O while saying, "Oh my goodness."

"Ni kan," said my mother as Shirley's eyes flooded with tears. "You already know how. Don't need talent for crying!"

Soon after my mother got this idea about Shirley Temple, she took me to a beauty training school in the Mission district and put me in the hands of a student who could barely hold the scissors without shaking. Instead of getting big fat curls, I emerged with an uneven mass of crinkly black fuzz. My mother dragged me off to the bathroom and tried to wet down my hair.

"You look like Negro Chinese," she lamented, as if I had done this on purpose.

Character
In what ways might the details in this paragraph contribute to the mother's motives?

Character
What are the mother's motives for taking her daughter to beauty training school?

Comprehension
Whom does the narrator's mother want her to be like?

---

1. **prodigy** (präd´ ə jē) *n.* child of unusually high talent.
2. **Shirley Temple** American child star of the 1930s. She starred in her first movie at age three and won an Academy Award at age six.

The instructor of the beauty training school had to lop off these soggy clumps to make my hair even again. "Peter Pan is very popular these days," the instructor assured my mother. I now had hair the length of a boy's, with straight-across bangs that hung at a slant two inches above my eyebrows. I liked the haircut and it made me actually look forward to my future fame.

In fact, in the beginning, I was just as excited as my mother, maybe even more so. I pictured this prodigy part of me as many different images, trying each one on for size. I was a dainty ballerina girl standing by the curtains, waiting to hear the right music that would send me floating on my tiptoes. I was like the Christ child lifted out of the straw manger, crying with holy indignity. I was Cinderella stepping from her pumpkin carriage with sparkly cartoon music filling the air.

In all of my imaginings, I was filled with a sense that I would soon become *perfect*. My mother and father would adore me. I would be beyond reproach. I would never feel the need to sulk for anything.

But sometimes the prodigy in me became impatient. "If you don't hurry up and get me out of here, I'm disappearing for good," it warned. "And then you'll always be nothing." •

老師

Every night after dinner, my mother and I would sit at the Formica kitchen table. She would present new tests, taking her examples from stories of amazing children she had read in *Ripley's Believe It or Not,* or *Good Housekeeping, Reader's Digest,* and a dozen other magazines she kept in a pile in our bathroom. My mother got these magazines from people whose houses she cleaned. And since she cleaned many houses each week, we had a great assortment. She would look through them all, searching for stories about remarkable children.

The first night she brought out a story about a three-year-old boy who knew the capitals of all the states and even most of the European countries. A teacher was quoted as

Character
Why is the mother interested in stories about remarkable children?

saying the little boy could also pronounce the names of the foreign cities correctly.

"What's the capital of Finland?" my mother asked me, looking at the magazine story.

All I knew was the capital of California, because Sacramento was the name of the street we lived on in Chinatown. "Nairobi!"[3] I guessed, saying the most foreign word I could think of. She checked to see if that was possibly one way to pronounce "Helsinki" [hel siṇ′ kē] before showing me the answer.

Predict
How do you think the narrator will do on the harder tests? Read on to verify your prediction.

The tests got harder—multiplying numbers in my head, finding the queen of hearts in a deck of cards, trying to stand on my head without using my hands, predicting the daily temperatures in Los Angeles, New York, and London.

One night I had to look at a page from the Bible for three minutes and then report everything I could remember. "Now Jehoshaphat had riches and honor in abundance and . . . that's all I remember, Ma," I said.

And after seeing my mother's disappointed face once again, something inside of me began to die. I hated the tests, the raised hopes and failed expectations. Before going to bed that night, I looked in the mirror above the bathroom sink and when I saw only my face staring back—and that it would always be this ordinary face—I began to cry. Such a sad, ugly girl! I made high-pitched noises like a crazed animal, trying to scratch out the face in the mirror.

And then I saw what seemed to be the prodigy side of me—because I had never seen that face before. I looked at my reflection, blinking so I could see more clearly. The girl staring back at me was angry, powerful. This girl and I were the same. I had new thoughts, willful thoughts, or rather thoughts filled with lots of won'ts. I won't let her change me, I promised myself. I won't be what I'm not.

Predict
What is your prediction about the mother's reaction when the girl performs poorly on the tests? Why?

So now on nights when my mother presented her tests, I performed listlessly, my head propped on one arm. I pretended to be bored. And I was. I got so bored I started counting the bellows of the foghorns out on the bay while my mother drilled me in other areas. The sound was comforting and reminded me of the cow jumping over the

Comprehension
What would the narrator and her mother do every night after dinner?

---

3. Nairobi (nī rō′ bē) *n.* capital of Kenya, a country in east central Africa.

moon. And the next day, I played a game with myself, seeing if my mother would give up on me before eight bellows. After a while I usually counted only one, maybe two bellows at most. At last she was beginning to give up hope.

Two or three months had gone by without any mention of my being a prodigy again. And then one day my mother was watching *The Ed Sullivan Show*[4] on TV. The TV was old and the sound kept shorting out. Every time my mother got halfway up from the sofa to adjust the set, the sound would go back on and Ed would be talking. As soon as she sat down, Ed would go silent again. She got up, the TV broke into loud piano music. She sat down. Silence. Up and down, back and forth, quiet and loud. It was like a stiff embraceless dance between her and the TV set. Finally she stood by the set with her hand on the sound dial.

She seemed entranced by the music, a little frenzied piano piece with this mesmerizing[5] quality, sort of quick passages and then teasing lilting ones before it returned to the quick playful parts.

"*Ni kan,*" my mother said, calling me over with hurried hand gestures. "Look here."

I could see why my mother was fascinated by the music. It was being pounded out by a little Chinese girl, about nine years old, with a Peter Pan haircut. The girl had the sauciness[6] of a Shirley Temple. She was proudly modest like a

▼ **Critical Viewing**
How does the girl in this photograph compare with your image of the story's narrator?

4. *The Ed Sullivan Show* popular variety show, hosted by Ed Sullivan, that ran from 1948 to 1971.
5. **mesmerizing** (mez´ mər īz iŋ) *adj.* hypnotizing.
6. **sauciness** (sô´ sē nəs) *n.* liveliness; boldness; spirit.

proper Chinese child. And she also did this fancy sweep of a curtsy, so that the fluffy skirt of her white dress cascaded slowly to the floor like the petals of a large carnation.

In spite of these warning signs, I wasn't worried. Our family had no piano and we couldn't afford to buy one, let alone reams of sheet music and piano lessons. So I could be generous in my comments when my mother bad-mouthed the little girl on TV.

"Play note right, but doesn't sound good! No singing sound," complained my mother.

"What are you picking on her for?" I said carelessly. "She's pretty good. Maybe she's not the best, but she's trying hard." I knew almost immediately I would be sorry I said that.

"Just like you," she said. "Not the best. Because you not trying." She gave a little huff as she let go of the sound dial and sat down on the sofa.

The little Chinese girl sat down also to play an encore of "Anitra's Dance" by Grieg.[7] I remember the song, because later on I had to learn how to play it.

Three days after watching *The Ed Sullivan Show*, my mother told me what my schedule would be for piano lessons and piano practice. She had talked to Mr. Chong, who lived on the first floor of our apartment building. Mr. Chong was a retired piano teacher and my mother had traded housecleaning services for weekly lessons and a piano for me to practice on every day, two hours a day, from four until six.

When my mother told me this, I felt as though I had been sent to hell. I whined and then kicked my foot a little when I couldn't stand it anymore.

"Why don't you like me the way I am? I'm *not* a genius! I can't play the piano. And even if I could, I wouldn't go on TV if you paid me a million dollars!" I cried.

My mother slapped me. "Who ask you be genius?" she shouted. "Only ask you be your best. For you sake. You think I want you be genius? Hnnh! What for! Who ask you!"

"So ungrateful," I heard her mutter in Chinese. "If she

7. **Grieg** (grēg) *n.* Edvard Grieg (1843–1907), Norwegian composer.

Character
What does this conversation indicate about the difference between the mother's and daughter's traits and motives?

▲ **Critical Viewing**
This television stood four feet tall. How have television and technology changed over the years?

Comprehension
Why does the mother decide that the narrator should play the piano?

had as much talent as she has temper, she would be famous now."

Mr. Chong, whom I secretly nicknamed Old Chong, was very strange, always tapping his fingers to the silent music of an invisible orchestra. He looked ancient in my eyes. He had lost most of the hair on top of his head and he wore thick glasses and had eyes that always looked tired and sleepy. But he must have been younger than I thought, since he lived with his mother and was not yet married.

I met Old Lady Chong once and that was enough. She had this peculiar smell like a baby that had done something in its pants. And her fingers felt like a dead person's, like an old peach I once found in the back of the refrigerator; the skin just slid off the meat when I picked it up.

> *He looked ancient...and had eyes that always looked tired and sleepy.*

I soon found out why Old Chong had retired from teaching piano. He was deaf. "Like Beethoven!"[8] he shouted to me. "We're both listening only in our head!" And he would start to conduct his frantic silent sonatas.

Our lessons went like this. He would open the book and point to different things, explaining their purpose: "Key! Treble! Bass! No sharps or flats! So this is C major! Listen now and play after me!"

And then he would play the C scale a few times, a simple chord, and then, as if inspired by an old, unreachable itch, he gradually added more notes and running trills and a pounding bass until the music was really something quite grand.

I would play after him, the simple scale, the simple chord, and then I just played some nonsense that sounded like a cat running up and down on top of garbage cans. Old Chong smiled and applauded and then said, "Very good! But now you must learn to keep time!"

So that's how I discovered that Old Chong's eyes were too

Predict
How do you think the narrator will react to Old Chong's piano lessons? Read on to verify your prediction.

---

8. **Beethoven** (bā′ tō′ vən) *n.* Ludwig van Beethoven (1770–1827), German composer who began to lose his hearing in 1801. Some of his greatest pieces were written when he was completely deaf.

slow to keep up with the wrong notes I was playing. He went through the motions in half-time. To help me keep rhythm, he stood behind me, pushing down on my right shoulder for every beat. He balanced pennies on top of my wrists so I would keep them still as I slowly played scales and arpeggios.[9] He had me curve my hand around an apple and keep that shape when playing chords. He marched stiffly to show me how to make each finger dance up and down, staccato[10] like an obedient little soldier.

He taught me all these things, and that was how I also learned I could be lazy and get away with mistakes, lots of mistakes. If I hit the wrong notes because I hadn't practiced enough, I never corrected myself. I just kept playing in rhythm. And Old Chong kept conducting his own private reverie.

So maybe I never really gave myself a fair chance. I did pick up the basics pretty quickly, and I might have become a good pianist at that young age. But I was so determined not to try, not to be anybody different that I learned to play only the most ear-splitting preludes, the most discordant hymns.

Over the next year, I practiced like this, dutifully in my own way. And then one day I heard my mother and her friend Lindo Jong both talking in a loud bragging tone of voice so others could hear. It was after church, and I was leaning against the brick wall wearing a dress with stiff white petticoats. Auntie Lindo's daughter, Waverly, who was about my age, was standing farther down the wall about five feet away. We had grown up together and shared all the closeness of two sisters squabbling over crayons and dolls. In other words, for the most part, we hated each other. I thought she was snotty. Waverly Jong had gained a certain amount of fame as "Chinatown's Littlest Chinese Chess Champion."

Character
What motivates the daughter to play piano badly?

Comprehension
What useful information does the narrator learn about her piano teacher?

---

9. **arpeggios** (är pej´ ē ōz) *n.* notes in a chord played separately in quick succession.
10. **staccato** (stə kät´ ō) *adv.* played crisply, with clear breaks between notes.

"She bring home too many trophy," lamented Auntie Lindo that Sunday. "All day she play chess. All day I have no time do nothing but dust off her winnings." She threw a scolding look at Waverly, who pretended not to see her.

"You lucky you don't have this problem," said Auntie Lindo with a sigh to my mother.

And my mother squared her shoulders and bragged: "Our problem worser than yours. If we ask Jing-mei wash dish, she hear nothing but music. It's like you can't stop this natural talent."

And right then, I was determined to put a stop to her foolish pride.

老師

A few weeks later, Old Chong and my mother **conspired** to have me play in a talent show which would be held in the church hall. By then, my parents had saved up enough to buy me a secondhand piano, a black Wurlitzer spinet with a scarred bench. It was the showpiece of our living room.

For the talent show, I was to play a piece called "Pleading Child" from Schumann's[11] *Scenes from Childhood*. It was a simple, moody piece that sounded more difficult than it was. I was supposed to memorize the whole thing, playing the repeat parts twice to make the piece sound longer. But I dawdled over it, playing a few bars and then cheating, looking up to see what notes followed. I never really listened to what I was playing. I daydreamed about being somewhere else, about being someone else.

The part I liked to practice best was the fancy curtsy: right foot out, touch the rose on the carpet with a pointed foot, sweep to the side, left leg bends, look up and smile.

My parents invited all the couples from the Joy Luck Club[12] to witness my debut. Auntie Lindo and Uncle Tin were there. Waverly and her two older brothers had also come. The first two rows were filled with children both younger and older than I was. The littlest ones got to go first. They recited simple nursery rhymes, squawked out tunes on miniature violins, twirled Hula Hoops, pranced in pink ballet tutus, and when they bowed or curtsied, the audience would sigh in unison, "Awww," and then clap enthusiastically.

When my turn came, I was very confident. I remember

◄ **Vocabulary**
conspired (kən spīrd´) *v.* planned together secretly

And right then, I was determined to put a stop to her foolish pride.

Comprehension
What do the narrator's mother and Auntie Lindo discuss?

---

11. **Schumann** (shōō´ män) Robert Alexander Schumann (1810–1856), German composer.
12. **Joy Luck Club** four Chinese women who have been meeting for years to socialize.

my childish excitement. It was as if I knew, without a doubt, that the prodigy side of me really did exist. I had no fear whatsoever, no nervousness. I remember thinking to myself, This is it! This is it! I looked out over the audience, at my mother's blank face, my father's yawn, Auntie Lindo's stiff-lipped smile, Waverly's sulky expression. I had on a white dress layered with sheets of lace, and a pink bow in my Peter Pan haircut. As I sat down I envisioned people jumping to their feet and Ed Sullivan rushing up to introduce me to everyone on TV.

And I started to play. It was so beautiful. I was so caught up in how lovely I looked that at first I didn't worry how I would sound. So it was a surprise to me when I hit the first wrong note and I realized something didn't sound quite right. And then I hit another and another followed that. A chill started at the top of my head and began to trickle down. Yet I couldn't stop playing, as though my hands were bewitched. I kept thinking my fingers would adjust themselves back, like a train switching to the right track. I played this strange jumble through two repeats, the sour notes staying with me all the way to the end.

When I stood up, I discovered my legs were shaking. Maybe I had just been nervous and the audience, like Old Chong, had seen me go through the right motions and had not heard anything wrong at all. I swept my right foot out, went down on my knee, looked up and smiled. The room was quiet, except for Old Chong, who was beaming and shouting, "Bravo! Bravo! Well done!" But then I saw my mother's face, her stricken face. The audience clapped weakly, and as I walked back to my chair, with my whole face quivering as I tried not to cry, I heard a little boy whisper loudly to his mother, "That was awful," and the mother whispered back, "Well, she certainly tried."

And now I realized how many people were in the audience, the whole world it seemed. I was aware of eyes burning into my back. I felt the shame of my mother and father as they sat stiffly throughout the rest of the show.

We could have escaped during intermission. Pride and some strange sense of honor must have anchored my parents to their chairs. And so we watched it all: the

Predict
How do you predict the mother will react to her daughter's poor piano playing?

Spiral Review
PLOT Do you think the narrator's poor performance will inspire a change in her actions and attitude as the story progresses? Why or why not?

eighteen-year-old boy with a fake mustache who did a magic show and juggled flaming hoops while riding a unicycle. The breasted girl with white makeup who sang from *Madama Butterfly* and got honorable mention. And the eleven-year-old boy who won first prize playing a tricky violin song that sounded like a busy bee.

After the show, the Hsus, the Jongs, and the St. Clairs from the Joy Luck Club came up to my mother and father.

"Lots of talented kids," Auntie Lindo said vaguely, smiling broadly.

"That was somethin' else," said my father, and I wondered if he was referring to me in a humorous way, or whether he even remembered what I had done.

Waverly looked at me and shrugged her shoulders. "You aren't a genius like me," she said matter-of-factly. And if I hadn't felt so bad, I would have pulled her braids and punched her stomach.

I felt the shame of my mother and father as they sat stiffly throughout the rest of the show.

Comprehension
What happens at the talent show?

◀ **Critical Viewing**
How do you think the narrator felt watching the other children perform?

devastated (dev´ ə stāt´ əd) *v.* destroyed; completely upset

nonchalantly (nän´ shə länt´ lē) *adv.* seemingly uninterested

Predict
What do you predict the mother will say to her daughter now that the piano recital is over?

But my mother's expression was what **devastated** me: a quiet, blank look that said she had lost everything. I felt the same way, and it seemed as if everybody were now coming up, like gawkers at the scene of an accident, to see what parts were actually missing. When we got on the bus to go home, my father was humming the busy-bee tune and my mother was silent. I kept thinking she wanted to wait until we got home before shouting at me. But when my father unlocked the door to our apartment, my mother walked in and then went to the back, into the bedroom. No accusations. No blame. And in a way, I felt disappointed. I had been waiting for her to start shouting, so I could shout back and cry and blame her for all my misery. ●

老師

I assumed my talent-show fiasco meant I never had to play the piano again. But two days later, after school, my mother came out of the kitchen and saw me watching TV.

"Four clock," she reminded me as if it were any other day. I was stunned, as though she were asking me to go through the talent-show torture again. I wedged myself more tightly in front of the TV.

"Turn off TV," she called from the kitchen five minutes later.

I didn't budge. And then I decided. I didn't have to do what my mother said anymore. I wasn't her slave. This wasn't China. I had listened to her before and look what happened. She was the stupid one.

She came out from the kitchen and stood in the arched entryway of the living room. "Four clock," she said once again, louder.

"I'm not going to play anymore," I said **nonchalantly**. "Why should I? I'm not a genius."

She walked over and stood in front of the TV. I saw her chest was heaving up and down in an angry way.

"No!" I said, and I now felt stronger, as if my true self had finally emerged. So this was what had been inside me all along.

"No! I won't!" I screamed.

She yanked me by the arm, pulled me off the floor, snapped off the TV. She was frighteningly strong, half pulling, half carrying me toward the piano as I kicked the throw rugs under my feet. She lifted me up and onto the hard bench. I was sobbing by now, looking at her bitterly. Her chest was heaving even more and her mouth was open, smiling crazily as if she were pleased I was crying.

"You want me to be someone that I'm not!" I sobbed. "I'll never be the kind of daughter you want me to be!"

"Only two kinds of daughters," she shouted in Chinese. "Those who are obedient and those who follow their own mind! Only one kind of daughter can live in this house. Obedient daughter!"

"Then I wish I wasn't your daughter. I wish you weren't my mother," I shouted. As I said these things I got scared. It felt like worms and toads and slimy things crawling out of my chest, but it also felt good, as if this awful side of me had surfaced, at last.

"Too late change this," said my mother shrilly.

And I could sense her anger rising to its breaking point. I wanted to see it spill over. And that's when I remembered the babies she had lost in China, the ones we never talked about. "Then I wish I'd never been born!" I shouted. "I wish I were dead! Like them."

It was as if I had said the magic words. Alakazam!—and her face went blank, her mouth closed, her arms went slack, and she backed out of the room, stunned, as if she were blowing away like a small brown leaf, thin, brittle, lifeless.

It was not the only disappointment my mother felt in me. In the years that followed, I failed her so many times,

" You want me to be someone that I'm not!" I sobbed. "I'll never be the kind of daughter you want me to be!"

Comprehension
How does the narrator feel about her performance at the talent show?

Vocabulary ▶
expectations (ek′
spekt tā′ shənz) *n.* things
looked forward to

each time asserting my own will, my right to fall short of **expectations**. I didn't get straight A's. I didn't become class president. I didn't get into Stanford. I dropped out of college.

For unlike my mother, I did not believe I could be anything I wanted to be. I could only be me.

And for all those years, we never talked about the disaster at the recital or my terrible accusations afterward at the piano bench. All that remained unchecked, like a betrayal that was now unspeakable. So I never found a way to ask her why she had hoped for something so large that failure was inevitable.

And even worse, I never asked her what frightened me the most: Why had she given up hope?

For after our struggle at the piano, she never mentioned my playing again. The lessons stopped. The lid to the piano was closed, shutting out the dust, my misery, and her dreams.

So she surprised me. A few years ago, she offered to give me the piano, for my thirtieth birthday. I had not played in all those years. I saw the offer as a sign of forgiveness, a tremendous burden removed.

"Are you sure?" I asked shyly. "I mean, won't you and Dad miss it?"

"No, this your piano," she said firmly. "Always your piano. You only one can play."

"Well, I probably can't play anymore," I said. "It's been years."

"You pick up fast," said my mother, as if she knew this was certain. "You have natural talent. You could been genius if you want to."

"No I couldn't."

"You just not trying," said my mother. And she was neither angry nor sad. She said it as if to announce a fact that could never be disproved. "Take it," she said.

But I didn't at first. It was enough that she had offered it to me. And after that, every time I saw it in my parents'

> *For unlike my mother,*
>
> *I did not believe I could be*
>
> *anything I wanted to be.*
>
> *I could only be me.*

Predict
How do you predict the narrator will respond to the gift of the piano?

living room, standing in front of the bay windows, it made me feel proud, as if it were a shiny trophy I had won back. ●

Last week I sent a tuner over to my parents' apartment and had the piano reconditioned, for purely sentimental reasons. My mother had died a few months before and I had been getting things in order for my father, a little bit at a time. I put the jewelry in special silk pouches. The sweaters she had knitted in yellow, pink, bright orange—all the colors I hated—I put those in moth-proof boxes. I found some old Chinese silk dresses, the kind with little slits up the sides. I rubbed the old silk against my skin, then wrapped them in tissue and decided to take them home with me.

After I had the piano tuned, I opened the lid and touched the keys. It sounded even richer than I remembered. Really, it was a very good piano. Inside the bench were the same exercise notes with handwritten scales, the same secondhand music books with their covers held together with yellow tape.

I opened up the Schumann book to the dark little piece I had played at the recital. It was on the left-hand side of

◄ **Vocabulary**
sentimental (sen tə ment´ əl) *adj.* emotional; showing tender feeling

Predict
What do you think the narrator will do now that the piano has been tuned after so many years?

Comprehension
What gift does the narrator receive for her 30th birthday? Why?

the page, "Pleading Child." It looked more difficult than I remembered. I played a few bars, surprised at how easily the notes came back to me.

And for the first time, or so it seemed, I noticed the piece on the right-hand side. It was called "Perfectly Contented." I tried to play this one as well. It had a lighter melody but the same flowing rhythm and turned out to be quite easy. "Pleading Child" was shorter but slower; "Perfectly Contented" was longer, but faster. And after I played them both a few times, I realized they were two halves of the same song.

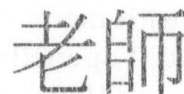

Language Study

Vocabulary The words listed below appear in "Two Kinds." Make up an answer to each numbered question. Use a complete sentence that includes the italicized vocabulary word.

> **reproach devastated nonchalantly expectations sentimental**

1. Why did the *reproach* bother him?

2. What kind of weather *devastated* the crops?

3. Why did he behave *nonchalantly* toward the girls?

4. Why don't the team's new uniforms meet your *expectations*?

5. Why are movies about pets often *sentimental*?

Word Study

Part A Explain how the **Latin root -*spir*-** contributes to the meaning of the words *perspire* and *respiration*. Consult a dictionary if necessary.

Part B Use the context of the sentences and your knowledge of the Latin root -*spir*- to explain your answer to each question.

1. Is a *spirited* person lively or dull?

2. If something *inspires* you, does it make you feel excitement?

WORD STUDY

The **Latin root -*spir*-** means "breath."

If you say something "under your breath," you say it in secret. In this story, two characters **conspire**, or secretly plan, to have the narrator play piano in a talent show.

Close Reading Activities

Literary Analysis

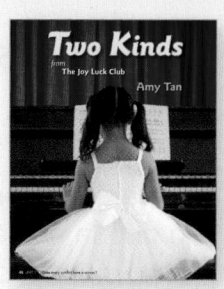

Key Ideas and Details

1. (a) In what ways does the mother pressure her daughter for change? **(b) Draw Conclusions:** How does the difference in their attitudes create problems? Support your answer with details from the text.

2. Make Predictions (a) What predictions did you make about how well the narrator would play at the recital? **(b)** On what details did you base each prediction? **(c)** Did reading ahead cause you to change your prediction?

3. Make Predictions (a) At what point in the story were you able to predict that the daughter would eventually refuse to play the piano? **(b)** What details in the text led you to make this prediction? **(c)** Did your prediction change as you read? Explain.

Craft and Structure

4. Character and Point of View Using a diagram like the one shown, list the daughter's character traits, supporting your answers with story details.

5. Character and Point of View (a) What motives does the daughter have to rebel against her mother? Cite details from the text that reveal these motives. **(b)** What are the mother's character traits and motives that cause her to keep pushing her daughter? Cite textual evidence to support your answers.

6. Character and Point of View How might the story be different if it were told from the mother's point of view? Support your answer with details from the story.

Integration of Knowledge and Ideas

7. (a) What are the titles of the two pieces in the Schumann book that the daughter plays at the end of the story? **(b) Connect:** In what ways do the titles and pieces reflect the daughter's feelings about herself?

8. Make a Judgment: Should the narrator's mother have pushed the daughter as she did? Explain, using examples from the text to support your opinion.

9. **Does every conflict have a winner?** In this story, conflict results when a mother pushes her daughter to become a success. Is there a winner in this conflict? Explain.

ACADEMIC VOCABULARY

As you write and speak about "Two Kinds," use the words related to conflict that you explored on page 3 of this textbook.

Conventions: **Personal and Possessive Pronouns**

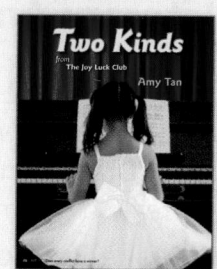

A **personal pronoun** takes the place of a noun or another pronoun named elsewhere in the text. A **possessive pronoun** shows possession or ownership.

Pronouns are used every day in conversation. Writers use pronouns to avoid the awkwardness of repeating the same noun over and over.

Personal Pronouns	I, me, we, us, you, he, him, she, her, it, they, them
Possessive Pronouns	my, mine, our, ours, your, yours, his, her, hers, its, their, theirs

Personal and possessive pronouns must agree in number and in gender with the nouns or pronouns to which they refer.

Singular: Read this *book*. *It* is my favorite.
Plural: These are *the ranchers'* horses. The horses are *theirs*.
Feminine: Where is *Mary*? Here are *her* gloves.
Masculine: *Al's* dog was hungry. *His* dog ate the food.

Practice A

Identify the personal pronoun in each item. Then, identify the noun it replaces.

1. When the daughter practices piano, she makes mistakes.

2. The mother has many magazines and enjoys reading them.

3. A three-year-old boy knows all the state capitals. He can also pronounce the names of foreign cities.

Speaking Application In "Two Kinds," find three sentences with personal pronouns. Recite these sentences to a partner and identify the personal pronouns.

Practice B

Rewrite each sentence, using a possessive pronoun in place of each underlined word or words. Be sure the pronoun agrees with the noun it replaces in number and gender.

1. The mother's daily tests are boring.

2. The mother's and father's disappointment at the recital is clear.

3. Mr. Chong's piano lessons are useless.

4. The daughter does not take the piano, even though it is the daughter's.

Writing Application Write two sentences about the mother and daughter in "Two Kinds." Use possessive pronouns.

Writing to Sources

 **Common Core**
State Standards

Narrative Text Write a **journal entry** from the point of view of a character from "Two Kinds."

- Choose a character and a specific situation from the story.
- Write from the character's point of view, using the word *I*. Refer to details from the story to accurately represent the character's traits and motives.
- Describe the situation by presenting a clear sequence of events that unfolds naturally and logically.
- Use dialogue and descriptive details to convey the character's thoughts and feelings.

Grammar Application As you write, be sure to use personal and possessive pronouns correctly. Make sure your possessive pronouns agree in number and gender with the nouns or pronouns to which they refer.

Writing
W.3.a. Engage and orient the reader by establishing a context and introducing a narrator and/or characters; organize an event sequence that unfolds naturally and logically.

W.3.b. Use narrative techniques, such as dialogue, pacing, and description, to develop experiences, events, and/or characters.

W.7. Conduct short research projects to answer a question, drawing on several sources and generating additional related, focused questions for further research and investigation.

Language
L.1. Demonstrate command of the conventions of standard English grammar and usage when writing or speaking.

Research and Technology

Build and Present Knowledge Research traditional Chinese beliefs and customs about the relationship between parents and children. Then, write an **outline** that provides background information.

Follow these steps to complete the assignment:

- Generate a list of questions on your topic to guide your research.
- Consult a variety of library or Internet resources to answer your questions.
- Organize your thoughts by jotting down notes.
- In outline form, state briefly and in your own words the main points and key details of what you learned.
- Group your notes by category. Use Roman numerals (I, II, III) to number your most important points. Under each Roman numeral, use capital letters for each supporting detail.
- Share your findings with other students. Then, in small groups, discuss whether or not the traditional beliefs and customs are reflected in "Two Kinds."

As a child, **Joan Aiken** (1924–2004) often walked in the fields near her home in England and created stories to amuse herself. She was inspired by her father, stepfather, and mother, who were all writers. She was also inspired by the classic novels her mother read to her when Aiken was young. By age five, Aiken was writing her own tales. Her stories, whether written for children or adults, often contain elements of horror, fantasy, and mystery.

© **Common Core State Standards**

Reading Literature
1. Cite several pieces of textual evidence to support analysis of what the text says explicitly as well as inferences drawn from the text.

Language
4.b. Use common, grade-appropriate Greek or Latin affixes and roots as clues to the meaning of a word.

? Does every conflict have a winner?

Think about the Big Question as you read "The Third Wish." Take notes on ways in which the story explores the nature of conflict.

CLOSE READING FOCUS

Key Ideas and Details: **Make Inferences**

Authors usually do not directly tell you everything about a story's characters, setting, and events. Instead, readers must **make inferences,** or develop logical ideas about unstated information.

- To form inferences, you must recognize details that the author states explicitly, or directly, in the story. Next, connect those details with what you know about life.
- Then, develop an informed idea, or inference, about the story's characters, setting, and events, based on that information.

Craft and Structure: **Conflict and Resolution**

In most fictional stories, the plot centers on a **conflict**—a struggle between opposing forces. There are two kinds of conflict:

- When there is **external conflict,** a character struggles with an outside force, such as another character or nature.
- When there is **internal conflict,** a character struggles with himself or herself to overcome opposing feelings, beliefs, needs, or desires.

A story can have a series of small conflicts that contribute to the main conflict. The **resolution,** or outcome, often comes toward the end of the story, when the problem is settled in some way.

Vocabulary

Copy the following words from "The Third Wish" into your notebook. Which two words share the same suffix? What part of speech is created when that suffix is used?

verge	dabbling	presumptuous
rash	remote	malicious

CLOSE READING MODEL

The passage below is from Joan Aiken's story "The Third Wish." The annotations to the right of the passage show ways in which you can use close reading skills to make inferences and analyze conflict and resolution.

from "The Third Wish"

Leita made him a good wife. But as time went by Mr. Peters began to feel that she was not happy. She seemed restless,[1] wandered much in the garden, and sometimes when he came back from the fields he would find the house empty and she would return after half an hour or so with no explanation of where she had been. On these occasions she was always especially tender and would put out his slippers to warm and cook his favorite dish[2]—Welsh rarebit with wild strawberries—for supper.

One evening he was returning home along the river path when he saw Leita in front of him, down by the water. A swan had sailed up to the verge and she had her arms round its neck and the swan's head rested against her check.[3] She was weeping, and as he came nearer he saw that tears were rolling, too, from the swan's eyes.

"Leita, what is it?" he asked, very troubled.

"This is my sister," she answered. "I can't bear being separated from her."[4]

Conflict and Resolution

1 Aiken describes Leita as "not happy" and "restless," feelings that suggest a possible internal conflict. You may expect that the story will explore the cause of Leita's conflict.

Make Inferences

2 Leita's actions may lead you to infer that although she is sad, she cares deeply for her husband and wants him to be happy.

Make Inferences

3 These physical gestures are tender and trusting. From them, you can infer that Leita and the swan have a close relationship. You might ask yourself how this relationship is related to Leita's sadness.

Conflict and Resolution

4 Here readers learn the reason for Leita's unhappiness. You might wonder if Leita's internal conflict will begin to be resolved through a reunion with her sister.

The Third Wish

Joan Aiken

ONCE THERE WAS A MAN WHO WAS DRIVING IN HIS CAR AT DUSK ON A SPRING EVENING THROUGH PART OF THE FOREST OF SAVERNAKE. HIS NAME WAS MR. PETERS. THE PRIMROSES WERE JUST BEGINNING BUT THE TREES WERE STILL BARE, AND IT WAS COLD; THE BIRDS HAD STOPPED SINGING AN HOUR AGO.

As Mr. Peters entered a straight, empty stretch of road he seemed to hear a faint crying, and a struggling and thrashing, as if somebody was in trouble far away in the trees. He left his car and climbed the mossy bank beside the road. Beyond the bank was an open slope of beech trees leading down to thorn bushes through which he saw the gleam of water. He stood a moment waiting to try and discover where the noise was coming from, and presently heard a rustling and some strange cries in a voice which was almost human—and yet there was something too hoarse about it at one time and too clear and sweet at another. Mr. Peters ran down the hill and as he neared the bushes he saw something white among them which was trying to extricate[1] itself; coming closer he found that it was a swan that had become entangled in the thorns growing on the bank of the canal.

The bird struggled all the more frantically as he approached, looking at him with hate in its yellow eyes, and when he took hold of it to free it, it hissed at him, pecked him, and thrashed dangerously with its wings which were powerful enough to break his arm. Nevertheless he managed to release it from the thorns, and carrying it tightly with one arm, holding the snaky head well away with

◄ **Critical Viewing**
What details of this picture could help you predict that this story has elements of fantasy?

Conflict and Resolution
What external conflict does Mr. Peters face after he finds the swan?

---

1. **extricate** (eks´ tri kāt´) v. set free.

Vocabulary ▶

verge (vʉrj)
n. edge; brink

dabbling (dab´ lin) *v.*
wetting by dipping,
splashing, or paddling
in the water

presumptuous
(prē zump´ chŏŏ əs)
adj. overconfident;
lacking respect

Spiral Review
PLOT The King of the
Forest grants Mr. Peters
three wishes, but not
without a warning.
How does granting
the wishes advance the
plot? How does the
warning hint at how
the plot might develop?

the other hand (for he did not wish his eyes pecked out), he took it to the **verge** of the canal and dropped it in.

The swan instantly assumed great dignity and sailed out to the middle of the water, where it put itself to rights with much **dabbling** and preening, smoothing its feathers with little showers of drops. Mr. Peters waited, to make sure that it was all right and had suffered no damage in its struggles. Presently the swan, when it was satisfied with its appearance, floated in to the bank once more, and in a moment, instead of the great white bird, there was a little man all in green with a golden crown and long beard, standing by the water. He had fierce glittering eyes and looked by no means friendly.

"Well, Sir," he said threateningly, "I see you are **presumptuous** enough to know some of the laws of magic. You think that because you have rescued—by pure good fortune—the King of the Forest from a difficulty, you should have some fabulous reward."

"I expect three wishes, no more and no less," answered Mr. Peters, looking at him steadily and with composure.[2]

"Three wishes, he wants, the clever man! Well, I have yet to hear of the human being who made any good use of his three wishes—they mostly end up worse off than they started. Take your three wishes then"—he flung three dead leaves in the air—"don't blame me if you spend the last wish in undoing the work of the other two."

Mr. Peters caught the leaves and put two of them carefully in his briefcase. When he looked up, the swan was sailing about in the middle of the water again, flicking the drops angrily down its long neck.

Mr. Peters stood for some minutes reflecting on how he should use his reward. He knew very well that the gift of three magic wishes was one which brought trouble more often than not, and he had no intention of being like the forester who first wished by mistake for a sausage, and then in a rage wished it on the end of his wife's nose, and then had to use his last wish in getting it off again. Mr. Peters had most of the things which he wanted and was very content with his life. The only thing that troubled him was that he was a little lonely, and had no companion for his old age. He decided to use his first wish and to keep the other two in case of an emergency. Taking a thorn he pricked his tongue with

---

2. **composure** (kəm pō´ zhər) *n.* calmness of mind.

it, to remind himself not to utter **rash** wishes aloud. Then holding the third leaf and gazing round him at the dusky undergrowth, the primroses, great beeches and the blue-green water of the canal, he said:

"I wish I had a wife as beautiful as the forest."

A tremendous quacking and splashing broke out on the surface of the water. He thought that it was the swan laughing at him. Taking no notice he made his way through the darkening woods to his car, wrapped himself up in the rug and went to sleep.

When he awoke it was morning and the birds were beginning to call. Coming along the track towards him was the most beautiful creature he had ever seen, with eyes as blue-green as the canal, hair as dusky as the bushes, and skin as white as the feathers of swans.

"Are you the wife that I wished for?" asked Mr. Peters.

"Yes, I am," she replied. "My name is Leita."

She stepped into the car beside him and they drove off to the church on the outskirts of the forest, where they were married. Then he took her to his house in a **remote** and lovely valley and showed her all his treasures—the bees in their white hives, the Jersey cows, the hyacinths, the silver candlesticks, the blue cups and the luster bowl for putting primroses in. She admired everything, but what pleased her most was the river which ran by the foot of his garden.

"Do swans come up there?" she asked.

"Yes, I have often seen swans there on the river," he told her, and she smiled.

Leita made him a good wife. But as time went by Mr. Peters began to feel that she was not happy. She seemed restless, wandered much in the garden, and sometimes when he came back from the fields he would find the house empty and she would return after half an hour or so with no explanation of where she had been. On these occasions she was always especially tender and would put out his slippers to warm and cook his favorite dish—Welsh rarebit[3] with wild strawberries—for supper.

One evening he was returning home along the river path when he saw Leita in front of him, down by the water. A swan had sailed up to the verge and she had her arms round its neck and the swan's head rested against her cheek. She was

---

3. **Welsh rarebit** a dish of melted cheese served on crackers or toast.

◀ **Vocabulary**
rash (rash) *adj.*
too hasty

remote (ri mōt´) *adj.* far away from anything else

Conflict and Resolution
What inner conflict is resolved for Mr. Peters when he gets a wife?

Make Inferences
On what details does Mr. Peters base his inference that Leita is not happy?

Comprehension
What happens after Mr. Peters makes his first wish?

Mythology Connection

A Star Is Born

The graceful, noble swan has been celebrated in the myths and literature of many cultures. It is also visible in the skies as a constellation, Cygnus the Swan.

In one version of how the constellation came to be, Phaethon, a human son of Apollo the sun god, borrowed his father's chariot. Phaethon drove dangerously, and to stop him, Zeus hurled a thunderbolt at him. It killed him instantly, and he fell from the sky.

Phaethon's friend Cygnus searched the river for him. As Apollo watched him dive in, he thought Cygnus resembled a swan. When Cygnus died of grief, Apollo took pity and changed him into a swan, placing him forever among the stars.

Connect to the Literature

What similarities can you find between the story of Cygnus and "The Third Wish"?

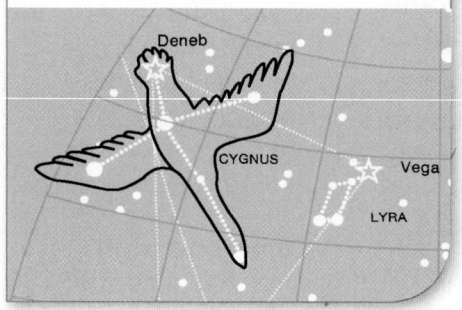

weeping, and as he came nearer he saw that tears were rolling, too, from the swan's eyes.

"Leita, what is it?" he asked, very troubled.

"This is my sister," she answered. "I can't bear being separated from her."

Now he understood that Leita was really a swan from the forest, and this made him very sad because when a human being marries a bird it always leads to sorrow.

"I could use my second wish to give your sister human shape, so that she could be a companion to you," he suggested.

"No, no," she cried, "I couldn't ask that of her."

"Is it so very hard to be a human being?" asked Mr. Peters sadly.

"Very, very hard," she answered.

"Don't you love me at all, Leita?"

"Yes, I do, I do love you," she said, and there were tears in her eyes again. "But I miss the old life in the forest, the cool grass and the mist rising off the river at sunrise and the feel of the water sliding over my feathers as my sister and I drifted along the stream."

"Then shall I use my second wish to turn you back into a swan again?" he asked, and his tongue pricked to remind him of the old King's words, and his heart swelled with grief inside him.

"Who will take care of you?"

"I'd do it myself as I did before I married you," he said, trying to sound cheerful.

She shook her head. "No, I could not be as unkind to you as that. I am partly a swan, but I am also partly a human being now. I will stay with you."

Poor Mr. Peters was very distressed on his wife's account and did his best to make her life happier, taking her for drives in the car, finding beautiful music for her to listen to on the radio, buying clothes for her and even suggesting a trip round the world. But she said no to that; she would prefer to stay in their own house near the river.

He noticed that she spent more and more time baking wonderful cakes—jam puffs, petits fours, éclairs and meringues. One day he saw her take a basketful down to the river and he guessed that she was giving them to her sister.

He built a seat for her by the river, and the two sisters spent hours together there, communicating in some wordless manner. For a time he thought that all would be well, but then he saw how thin and pale she was growing.

One night when he had been late doing the accounts he came up to bed and found her weeping in her sleep and calling:

"Rhea! Rhea! I can't understand what you say! Oh, wait for me, take me with you!"

Then he knew that it was hopeless and she would never be happy as a human. He stooped down and kissed her goodbye, then took another leaf from his notecase, blew it out of the window, and used up his second wish.

Next moment instead of Leita there was a sleeping swan lying across the bed with its head under its wing. He carried it out of the house and down to the brink of the river, and then he said, "Leita! Leita!" to waken her, and gently put her into the water. She gazed round her in astonishment for a moment, and then came up to him and rested her head lightly against his hand; next instant she was flying away over the trees towards the heart of the forest.

He heard a harsh laugh behind him, and turning round saw the old King looking at him with a **malicious** expression.

"Well, my friend! You don't seem to have managed so wonderfully with your first two wishes, do you? What will you do with the last? Turn yourself into a swan? Or turn Leita back into a girl?"

"I shall do neither," said Mr. Peters calmly. "Human beings and swans are better in their own shapes."

But for all that he looked sadly over towards the forest where Leita had flown, and walked slowly back to his house.

Next day he saw two swans swimming at the bottom of the garden, and one of them wore the gold chain he had given Leita after their marriage; she came up and rubbed her head against his hand.

Mr. Peters and his two swans came to be well known in that part of the country; people used to say that he talked to swans and they understood him as well as his neighbors. Many people were a little frightened of him. There was a story that once when thieves tried to break into his house they were set upon by two huge white birds which carried them off bodily and dropped them in the river.

Conflict and Resolution
Beyond what he has already done to resolve his wife's conflict, what else do you suggest Mr. Peters could do?

◄ **Vocabulary**
malicious (mə lish´ əs) *adj.* hateful; spiteful

Comprehension
Why does Leita want to be a swan again?

As Mr. Peters grew old everyone wondered at his contentment. Even when he was bent with rheumatism[4] he would not think of moving to a drier spot, but went slowly about his work, with the two swans always somewhere close at hand.

Sometimes people who knew his story would say to him: "Mr. Peters, why don't you wish for another wife?"

"Not likely," he would answer serenely. "Two wishes were enough for me, I reckon. I've learned that even if your wishes are granted they don't always better you. I'll stay faithful to Leita."

One autumn night, passers-by along the road heard the mournful sound of two swans singing. All night the song went on, sweet and harsh, sharp and clear. In the morning Mr. Peters was found peacefully dead in his bed with a smile of great happiness on his face. In his hands, which lay clasped on his breast, were a withered leaf and a white feather.

Make Inferences
What inferences can you make from knowing what Mr. Peters held in his hands when he died?

---

4. **rheumatism** (roo´ mə tiz´ əm) *n.* pain and stiffness of the joints and muscles.

Language Study

Vocabulary The words listed below appear in "The Third Wish." Each word is used in a question. Answer each question, and then explain your response.

verge	presumptuous	dabbling	remote	rash

1. Does Australia seem *remote* to people who live in the U.S.?

2. Does it take a long time to make a *rash* decision?

3. Is it safe to stand on the *verge* of a steep cliff?

4. Is it *presumptuous* of a host to invite guests to a party?

5. If you see someone *dabbling* in a pool, is he in danger?

WORD STUDY
The **Latin prefix *mal-*** means "bad." In this story, the old King looks at Mr. Peters with a **malicious**, or hateful, look that shows a desire to cause him harm.

Word Study

Part A Explain how the **Latin prefix *mal-*** contributes to the meanings of these words: *malfunction, maladjusted, malnutrition.* Consult a dictionary if necessary.

Part B Use the context of the sentences and your knowledge of the Latin prefix *mal-* to explain your answer to each question.

1. If something is *malodorous,* does it smell good?

2. What kind of physical *malady* might a player have after a football game?

Close Reading Activities

Literary Analysis

Key Ideas and Details

1. **(a)** How does Mr. Peters get the opportunity to ask for three wishes? **(b) Connect:** Based on the King of the Forest's words, how did you think Mr. Peters's wishing would turn out? Was your prediction correct?

2. **(a)** How does Mr. Peters use his first wish? **(b) Speculate:** Why do you think he does not wish for riches? Cite textual support for your answer.

3. **Make Inferences** List details that support the inference that Mr. Peters loves Leita more than he loves himself.

4. **Make Inferences** List details that support the inference that Leita still loves Mr. Peters even after she changes back to a swan.

5. **Make Inferences (a)** Is Mr. Peters afraid to die? **(b)** What details from the text support your inference?

Craft and Structure

6. **Conflict and Resolution (a)** What conflict does Mr. Peters's first wish introduce? **(b)** What resolution does Mr. Peters find for the conflict?

7. **Conflict and Resolution** In a chart like the one shown, identify two smaller conflicts that build toward Mr. Peters's main conflict, and tell how each is resolved.

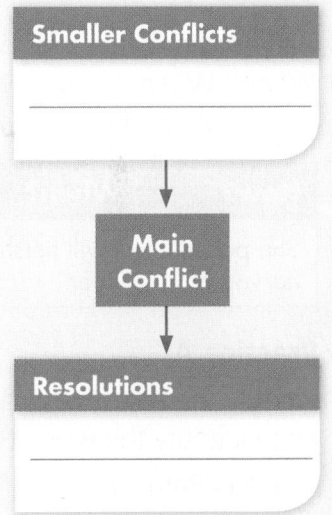

Integration of Knowledge and Ideas

8. **(a) Make a Judgment:** Do you think Mr. Peters used his wishes wisely? **(b) Support:** What evidence from the story supports your opinion?

9. **Apply:** Many cultures have traditional tales about wishes that do not work out. Why might this kind of story be so common?

10. **?** **Does every conflict have a winner? (a)** Think about the decision Mr. Peters made to resolve his internal conflict. Was his decision wise? **(b)** What story details support your response? **(c)** Who were the "winners" in this story?

ACADEMIC VOCABULARY

As you write and speak about "The Third Wish," use the words related to conflict that you explored on page 3 of this textbook.

Conventions: **Adjectives and Adverbs**

An **adjective** is a word that modifies or describes a noun or pronoun. An **adverb** is a word that modifies or describes a verb, an adjective, or another adverb.

Adjectives may answer the questions *What kind? How many? Which one?* or *Whose?* Possessive nouns and pronouns are used as adjectives to answer the question *Whose?*

Coordinate adjectives are two or more adjectives that modify the same noun and are separated by a comma. You can tell if adjectives are coordinate if the word *and* could be used in place of the comma.

What kind?	Dan ate a <u>hot</u>, <u>crusty</u> roll.	**How many?**	We sold <u>fifty</u> tickets.
Which one?	Hand me <u>that</u> one.	**Whose?**	We saw <u>Kathy's</u> play.

Adverbs provide information by answering the question *How? When? Where? How often?* or *To what extent?* Many adverbs end in the suffix *-ly.* This chart shows examples:

How?	When?	Where?	How often?	To what extent?
She paced *nervously.*	I will finish it *later.*	The robins flew *away.*	Linda *always* laughs.	Luke moved *slightly.* Jo is *very* sad.

Practice A

Identify the adjective or adverb in each sentence. Then identify the word it modifies or describes.

1. Mr. Peters heard a faint cry.
2. The swan struggled frantically in the water.
3. Mr. Peters wished for a beautiful wife.
4. Mr. Peters used his second wish to please Leita.

Reading Application In "The Third Wish," find one sentence with two or more adjectives and one sentence with two or more adverbs. Then, identify the adjectives and adverbs.

Practice B

Add adjectives or adverbs to each sentence based on the question in parentheses.

1. Mr. Peters was driving a car down a stretch of the road. (What kind of road?)
2. The swan was struggling in the canal. (How was it struggling?)
3. Leita was pleased by the river near the garden. (To what extent was she pleased?)

Writing Application Write two sentences in which you use coordinate adjectives to describe the relationship between Mr. Peters and Leita.

Writing to Sources

Narrative Text Write an **anecdote**, or brief story, that tells what might have happened if Mr. Peters had not turned Leita back into a swan. Follow these steps:

- First, think of how the story would unfold with the new ending. Review "The Third Wish" to find details about Mr. Peters and Leita that indicate how each may have behaved if Leita had remained human.

- Then, jot down your ideas for a conflict that could have arisen. Is the conflict internal or external? Include descriptive details that vividly present the situation.

- Next, decide on a resolution to the conflict. As you draft your story, make sure that the resolution logically follows the event presented in the climax.

- Finally, conclude by describing how the characters grow or change as a result of their experiences.

Grammar Application Check your writing to be sure you have used adjectives and adverbs correctly. Include some coordinate adjectives in your anecdote.

Speaking and Listening

Presentation of Ideas Write a **news story** based on "The Third Wish." In your story, announce the death of Mr. Peters and hail him as a local hero.

Follow these steps to complete the assignment:

- Reread the story, noting important details about Mr. Peters to include in your news story.

- Organize the story to present your details in the most effective order. For instance, you might present events in the order in which they occurred or in order of importance.

- Review your word choice to ensure that you have brought the news events to life and that you have maintained a formal tone.

- Practice reading your news story aloud, using proper grammar and a formal style, before presenting it to the class.

 **Common Core State Standards**

Writing
2.a. Introduce a topic clearly, previewing what is to follow; organize ideas, concepts, and information, using strategies such as definition, classification, comparison/contrast, and cause/effect; include formatting, graphics, and multimedia when useful to aiding comprehension.

2.e. Establish and maintain a formal style.

3. Write narratives to develop real or imagined experiences or events using effective technique, relevant descriptive details, and well-structured event sequences.

3.e. Provide a conclusion that follows from and reflects on the narrated experiences or events.

Speaking and Listening
6. Adapt speech to a variety of contexts and tasks, demonstrating command of formal English when indicated or appropriate.

Language
2.a. Use a comma to separate coordinate adjectives.

Meet the Author

Laurence Yep (b. 1948) was born in San Francisco. He grew up in an apartment above his family's grocery store in an African American neighborhood. As a child, Yep rode a bus to a bilingual school in Chinatown. He feels that these experiences with different cultures led him to write science fiction and fantasy stories in which characters face new worlds and learn new languages and customs. Yep was 18 when he sold his first story to a magazine for a penny a word.

© **Common Core State Standards**

Reading Literature
1. Cite several pieces of textual evidence to support analysis of what the text says explicitly as well as inferences drawn from the text.
2. Determine a theme or central idea of a text and analyze its development over the course of the text.

Language
4.b. Use common, grade-appropriate Greek or Latin affixes and roots as clues to the meaning of a word (e.g., *belligerent, bellicose, rebel*).

Does every conflict have a winner?

Think about the Big Question as you read "Ribbons." Take notes on how characters in the story work to resolve conflicts.

CLOSE READING FOCUS

Key Ideas and Details: **Make Inferences**

Stories present a wealth of details. Some details are stated explicitly; other details are unstated, or implied. An **inference** is a conclusion you draw about something that is not directly stated. Use details in the text to make inferences about a story. For example, if a story opens with a man running down a dark alley while looking over his shoulder, you might infer that the man is trying to get away from someone or something.

One way to make inferences is to read between the lines by asking questions, such as, "Who is the character running from?" and "Has the character done something wrong?"

Craft and Structure: **Theme**

A story's **theme** is its central idea, message, or insight into life. Occasionally, the author states the theme directly. More often, however, the theme is implied.

As you read, look at what the characters say and do, where the story takes place, and what objects in the story seem important. These details will help you determine the theme—what the author wants to teach you about life.

Vocabulary

You will encounter the following words in this story. Copy the words into your notebook. Circle the words that are adjectives. After you read, see how your knowledge of each word has increased.

sensitive	meek	coax
laborious	exertion	furrowed

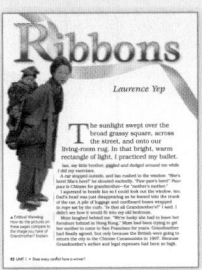

CLOSE READING MODEL

The passage below is from Laurence Yep's story "Ribbons." The annotations to the right of the passage show ways in which you can use close reading skills to make inferences and determine theme.

from "**Ribbons**"

Mom bowed formally as Grandmother reached the porch. "I'm so glad you're here," she said. Grandmother gazed past us to the stairway leading up to our second-floor apartment. "Why do you have to have so many steps?" she said.
Mom sounded as meek as a child. "I'm sorry, Mother," she said.[1]

Dad tried to change the subject. "That's Stacy, and this little monster is Ian." "*Joe sun, Paw-paw,*" I said. "Good morning, Grandmother." It was afternoon, but that was the only Chinese I knew, and I had been practicing it.[2]
Mother had coached us on a proper Chinese greeting for the last two months, but I thought Grandmother also deserved an American-style bear hug. However, when I tried to put my arms around her and kiss her, she stiffened in surprise. "Nice children don't drool on people," she snapped at me.[3]
To Ian, anything worth doing was worth repeating, so he bowed again. "*Joe sun, Pawpaw.*" Grandmother brightened in an instant. "He has your eyes," she said to Mom.
Mom bent and hefted Ian into her arms. "Let me show you our apartment. You'll be in Stacy's room."
Grandmother didn't even thank me.[4]

Make Inferences
1 The narrator describes Mom as "meek as a child." Since *meek* means "unwilling to argue," you might infer that Mom is respectful and obedient toward Grandmother.

Make Inferences
2 From this greeting, you may infer that Grandmother is from China. Since the narrator has been practicing the greeting, you may also infer that she wants to impress Grandmother.

Theme
3 Grandmother rejects a gesture of affection that is typical in western culture. Her reaction hints at a possible theme: the cultural differences between eastern and western traditions.

Make Inferences
4 The first-person pronoun *me* tells you that the narrator is Stacy. Her words may lead you to infer that although she wants to impress Grandmother, she finds her grandmother to be a little rude.

Ribbons

Laurence Yep

T he sunlight swept over the broad grassy square, across the street, and onto our living-room rug. In that bright, warm rectangle of light, I practiced my ballet.

Ian, my little brother, giggled and dodged around me while I did my exercises.

A car stopped outside, and Ian rushed to the window. "She's here! She's here!" he shouted excitedly. "Paw-paw's here!" *Paw-paw* is Chinese for grandmother—for "mother's mother."

I squeezed in beside Ian so I could look out the window, too. Dad's head was just disappearing as he leaned into the trunk of the car. A pile of luggage and cardboard boxes wrapped in rope sat by the curb. "Is that all Grandmother's?" I said. I didn't see how it would fit into my old bedroom.

Mom laughed behind me. "We're lucky she had to leave her furniture behind in Hong Kong." Mom had been trying to get her mother to come to San Francisco for years. Grandmother had finally agreed, but only because the British were going to return the city to the Chinese Communists in 1997. Because Grandmother's airfare and legal expenses had been so high,

▲ **Critical Viewing**
How do the pictures on these pages compare to the image you have of Grandmother? Explain.

there wasn't room in the family budget for Madame Oblomov's ballet school. I'd had to stop my daily lessons.

The rear car door opened, and a pair of carved black canes poked out like six-shooters. "Wait, Paw-paw," Dad said, and slammed the trunk shut. He looked sweaty and harassed.

Grandmother, however, was already using her canes to get to her feet. "I'm not helpless," she insisted to Dad.

Ian was relieved. "She speaks English," he said.

"She worked for a British family for years," Mom explained.

Turning, Ian ran toward the stairs. "I've got the door," he cried. Mom and I caught up with him at the front door and made him wait on the porch. "You don't want to knock her over," I said. For weeks, Mom had been rehearsing us for just this moment. Ian was supposed to wait, but in his excitement he began bowing to Grandmother as she struggled up the outside staircase.

Grandmother was a small woman in a padded silk jacket and black slacks. Her hair was pulled back into a bun behind her head. On her small feet she wore a pair of quilted cotton slippers

Comprehension
Why does the narrator have to stop her daily ballet lessons?

"Paw-paw's here!" Paw-paw is Chinese for grandmother—for "mother's mother."

Make Inferences
Why might Grandmother have complained about "so many steps"?

Vocabulary ▶
sensitive (sen´ sə tiv) *adj.* easily hurt or affected

meek (mēk) *adj.* timid; not willing to argue

coax (kōks) *v.* use gentle persuasion

laborious (lə bôr´ ē əs) *adj.* taking much work or effort

shaped like boots, with furred tops that hid her ankles.

"What's wrong with her feet?" I whispered to Mom.

"They've always been that way. And don't mention it," she said. "She's **sensitive** about them."

I was instantly curious. "But what happened to them?"

"Wise grandchildren wouldn't ask," Mom warned.

Mom bowed formally as Grandmother reached the porch. "I'm so glad you're here," she said.

Grandmother gazed past us to the stairway leading up to our second-floor apartment. "Why do you have to have so many steps?" she said.

Mom sounded as **meek** as a child. "I'm sorry, Mother," she said.

Dad tried to change the subject. "That's Stacy, and this little monster is Ian."

"*Joe sun, Paw-paw,*" I said. "Good morning, Grandmother." It was afternoon, but that was the only Chinese I knew, and I had been practicing it.

Mother had coached us on a proper Chinese greeting for the last two months, but I thought Grandmother also deserved an American-style bear hug. However, when I tried to put my arms around her and kiss her, she stiffened in surprise. "Nice children don't drool on people," she snapped at me.

To Ian, anything worth doing was worth repeating, so he bowed again. "*Joe sun, Paw-paw.*"

Grandmother brightened in an instant. "He has your eyes," she said to Mom.

Mom bent and hefted Ian into her arms. "Let me show you our apartment. You'll be in Stacy's room."

Grandmother didn't even thank me. Instead, she stumped up the stairs after Mom, trying to **coax** a smile from Ian, who was staring at her over Mom's shoulder.

Grandmother's climb was long, slow, **laborious**. *Thump, thump, thump.* Her canes struck the boards as she slowly mounted the steps. It sounded like the slow, steady beat of a mechanical heart.

Mom had told us her mother's story often enough. When Mom's

father died, Grandmother had strapped my mother to her back and walked across China to Hong Kong to escape the Communists who had taken over her country. I had always thought her trek was heroic, but it seemed even braver when I realized how wobbly she was on her feet.

I was going to follow Grandmother, but Dad waved me down to the sidewalk. "I need you to watch your grandmother's things until I finish bringing them up," he said. He took a suitcase in either hand and set off, catching up with Grandmother at the foot of the first staircase.

While I waited for him to come back, I inspected Grandmother's pile of belongings. The boxes, webbed with tight cords, were covered with words in Chinese and English. I could almost smell their exotic scent, and in my imagination I pictured sunlit waters lapping at picturesque docks. Hong Kong was probably as exotic to me as America was to Grandmother. Almost without thinking, I began to dance.

Dad came back out, his face red from exertion. "I wish I had half your energy," he said. Crouching, he used the cords to lift a box in each hand.

I pirouetted,[1] and the world spun round and round. "Madame Oblomov said I should still practice every day." I had waited for this day not only for Grandmother's sake but for my own. "Now that Grandmother's here, can I begin my ballet lessons again?" I asked.

Dad turned toward the house. "We'll see, hon."

Disappointment made me protest. "But you said I had to give up the lessons so we could bring her from Hong Kong," I said. "Well, she's here."

Dad hesitated and then set the boxes down. "Try to understand, hon. We've got to set your grandmother up in her own apartment. That's going to take even more money. Don't you want your room back?"

Poor Dad. He looked tired and worried. I should have shut up, but I loved ballet almost as much as I loved him. "Madame put me in the fifth division even though I'm only eleven. If I'm absent much longer, she might make me start over again with the beginners."

"It'll be soon. I promise." He looked guilty as he picked up the boxes and struggled toward the stairs.

◀ Vocabulary
exertion (eg zur′ shən)
n. physical work

Make Inferences
What can you infer about Stacy from her dancing and her talk with Dad?

Comprehension
In whose room will Grandmother stay?

---

1. pirouetted (pir′ o͞o et′ əd) *v.* whirled around on one foot.

▲ **Critical Viewing**
The shoes on the right are similar to the ones that Grandmother wore in China. How old do you think Grandmother was when she wore these shoes?

Dad had taken away the one hope that had kept me going during my exile[2] from Madame. Suddenly I felt lost, and the following weeks only made me more confused. Mom started laying down all sorts of new rules. First, we couldn't run around or make noise because Grandmother had to rest. Then we couldn't watch our favorite TV shows because Grandmother couldn't understand them. Instead, we had to watch Westerns on one of the cable stations because it was easier for her to figure out who was the good guy and who was the bad one.

Worst of all, Ian got all of her attention—and her candy and anything else she could bribe him with. It finally got to me on a warm Sunday afternoon a month after she had arrived. I'd just returned home from a long walk in the park with some friends. I was looking forward to something cool and sweet, when I found her giving Ian an ice cream bar I'd bought for

2. **exile** (eg´ zīl) *n.* a forced absence.

myself. "But that was *my* ice cream bar," I complained as he gulped it down.

"Big sisters need to share with little brothers," Grandmother said, and she patted him on the head to encourage him to go on eating.

When I complained to Mom about how Grandmother was spoiling Ian, she only sighed. "He's a boy, Stacy. Back in China, boys are everything."

It wasn't until I saw Grandmother and Ian together the next day that I thought I really understood why she treated him so much better. She was sitting on a kitchen chair with her head bent over next to his. She had taught Ian enough Chinese so that they could hold short, simple conversations. With their faces so close, I could see how much alike they were.

Ian and I both have the same brown eyes, but his hair is black, while mine is brown, like Dad's. In fact, everything about Ian looks more Chinese. Except for the shape of my eyes, I look as Caucasian as Dad. And yet people sometimes stare at me as if I were a freak. I've always told myself that it's because they're ignorant and never learned manners, but it was really hard to have my own grandmother make me feel that way. •

Even so, I kept telling myself: Grandmother is a hero. She saved my mother. She'll like me just as much as she likes Ian once she gets to know me. And, I thought in a flash, the best way to know a person is to know what she loves. For me, that was the ballet.

Ever since Grandmother had arrived, I'd been practicing my ballet privately in the room I now shared with Ian. Now I got out the special box that held my satin toe shoes. I had been so proud when Madame said I was ready to use them. I was the youngest girl on pointe[3] at Madame's school. As I lifted them out, the satin ribbons fluttered down around my wrists as if in a welcoming caress. I slipped one of the shoes onto my foot, but when I tried to tie the ribbons around my ankles, the ribbons came off in my hands.

---

3. on pointe (pwänt) dancing on the tip of the toe (of the ballet shoe).

Theme
What does Mom's comment tell you about the treatment of boys in China? What message about life do these details suggest?

Comprehension
How do things change when Grandmother moves into the house?

I could have asked Mom to help me reattach them, but then I remembered that at one time Grandmother had supported her family by being a seamstress. •

Grandmother was sitting in the big recliner in the living room. She stared uneasily out the window as if she were gazing not upon the broad, green lawn of the square but upon a Martian desert.

"Paw-paw," I said, "can you help me?"

Grandmother gave a start when she turned around and saw the ribbons dangling from my hand. Then she looked down at my bare feet, which were callused from three years of daily lessons. When she looked back at the satin ribbons, it was with a hate and disgust that I had never seen before. "Give those to me." She held out her hand.

I clutched the ribbons tightly against my stomach. "Why?"

"They'll ruin your feet." She lunged toward me and tried to snatch them away.

Angry and bewildered, I retreated a few steps and showed her the shoe. "No, they're for dancing!"

All Grandmother could see, though, was the ribbons. She managed to totter to her feet without the canes and almost fell forward on her face. Somehow, she regained her balance. Arms reaching out, she stumbled clumsily after me. "Lies!" she said.

"It's the truth!" I backed up so fast that I bumped into Mom as she came running from the kitchen.

Mom immediately assumed it was my fault. "Stop yelling at your grandmother!" she said.

By this point, I was in tears. "She's taken everything else. Now she wants my toe-shoe ribbons."

Grandmother panted as she leaned on Mom. "How could you do that to your own daughter?"

"It's not like you think," Mom tried to explain.

However, Grandmother was too upset to listen. "Take them away!"

Make Inferences
What can you infer about Grandmother based on her reaction to the ribbons?

Grandmother gave a start when she turned around and saw the ribbons dangling from my hand.

Mom helped Grandmother back to her easy chair. "You don't understand," Mom said.

All Grandmother did was stare at the ribbons as she sat back down in the chair. "Take them away. Burn them. Bury them."

Mom sighed. "Yes, Mother."

As Mom came over to me, I stared at her in amazement. "Aren't you going to stand up for me?"

But she acted as if she wanted to break any ties between us. "Can't you see how worked up Paw-paw is?" she whispered. "She won't listen to reason. Give her some time. Let her cool off." She worked the ribbons away from my stunned fingers. Then she also took the shoe.

For the rest of the day, Grandmother just turned away every time Mom and I tried to raise the subject. It was as if she didn't want to even think about satin ribbons.

That evening, after the dozenth attempt, I finally said to Mom, "She's so weird. What's so bad about satin ribbons?"

"She associates them with something awful that happened to her," Mom said.

That puzzled me even more. "What was that?"

She shook her head. "I'm sorry. She made me promise never to talk about it to anyone." •

The next morning, I decided that if Grandmother was

Spiral Review
CHARACTER Based on the scene with the ribbons, list one detail you learn about each of these characters: Grandmother, Mom, and Stacy.

Comprehension
How does Grandmother react when she sees the ribbons from the ballet shoes?

going to be mean to me, then I would be mean to her. I began to ignore her. When she entered a room I was in, I would deliberately turn around and leave.

For the rest of the day, things got more and more tense. Then I happened to go into the bathroom early that evening. The door wasn't locked, so I thought it was unoccupied, but Grandmother was sitting fully clothed on the edge of the bathtub. Her slacks were rolled up to her knees and she had her feet soaking in a pan of water.

"Don't you know how to knock?" she snapped, and dropped a towel over her feet.

However, she wasn't quick enough, because I saw her bare feet for the first time. Her feet were like taffy that someone had stretched out and twisted. Each foot bent downward in a way that feet were not meant to, and her toes stuck out at odd angles, more like lumps than toes. I didn't think she had all ten of them, either.

"What happened to your feet?" I whispered in shock.

Looking ashamed, Grandmother flapped a hand in the air for me to go. "None of your business. Now get out."

"Don't you know how to knock?" she snapped, and dropped a towel over her feet.

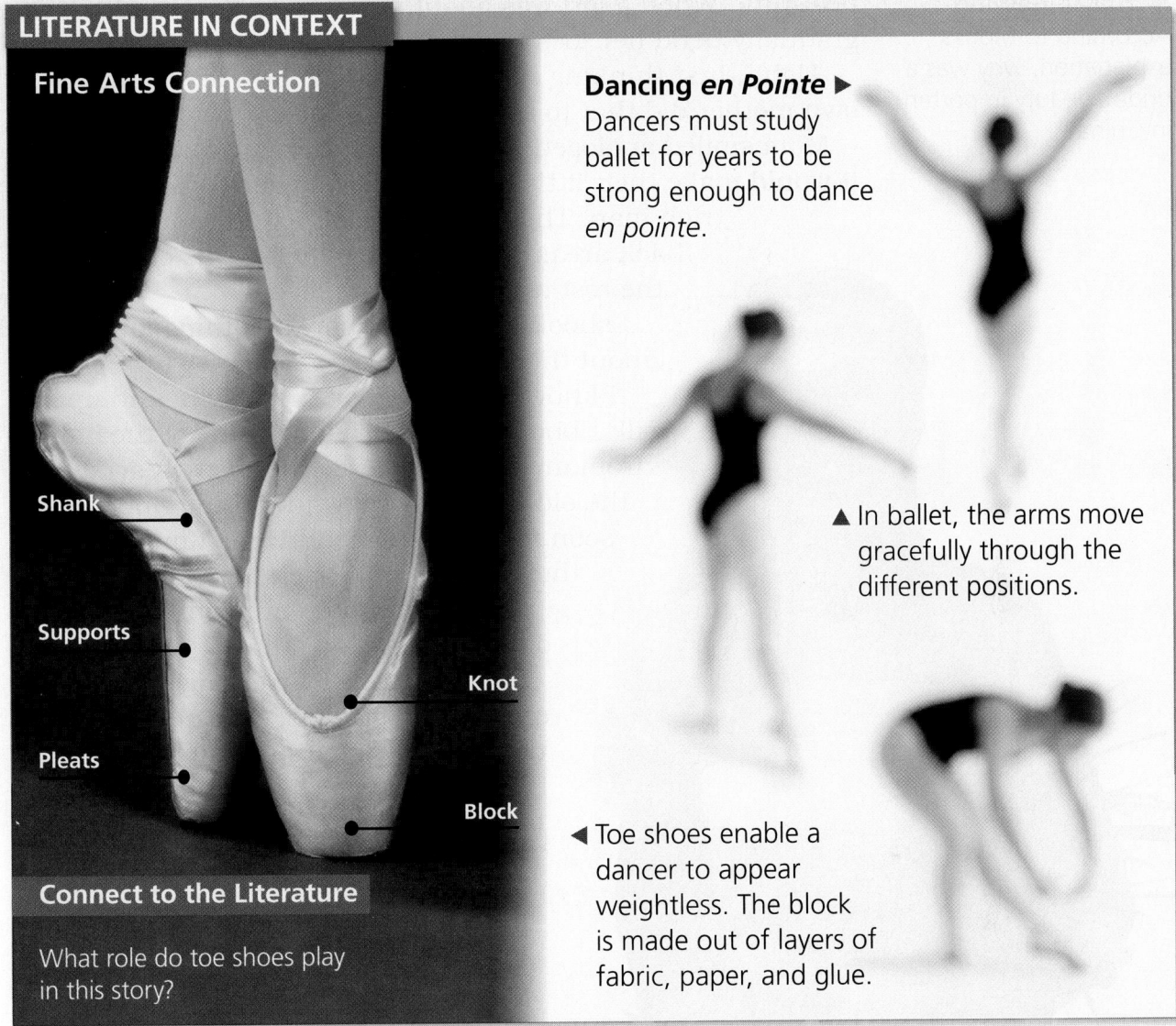

Fine Arts Connection

Dancing *en Pointe* ▶
Dancers must study ballet for years to be strong enough to dance *en pointe*.

Shank

Supports

Pleats

Knot

Block

▲ In ballet, the arms move gracefully through the different positions.

◀ Toe shoes enable a dancer to appear weightless. The block is made out of layers of fabric, paper, and glue.

Connect to the Literature

What role do toe shoes play in this story?

She must have said something to Mom, though, because that night Mom came in and sat on my bed. Ian was outside playing with Grandmother. "Your grandmother's very upset, Stacy," Mom said.

"I didn't mean to look," I said. "It was horrible." Even when I closed my eyes, I could see her mangled feet.

I opened my eyes when I felt Mom's hand on my shoulder. "She was so ashamed of them that she didn't like even me to see them," she said.

"What happened to them?" I wondered.

Mom's forehead **furrowed** as if she wasn't sure how to explain things. "There was a time back in China when people thought women's feet had to be shaped a certain way to look

◀ **Vocabulary**
furrowed (fur´ōd) v.
wrinkled

Comprehension
What did Stacy see that made Grandmother upset?

▼**Critical Viewing**
According to Mom's
explanation, why was a
bride's beauty important
in China?

beautiful. When a girl was about five, her mother would gradually bend her toes under the sole of her foot."

"Ugh." Just thinking about it made my own feet ache. "Her own mother did that to her?"

Mom smiled apologetically. "Her mother and father thought it would make their little girl attractive so she could marry a rich man. They were still doing it in some of the back areas of China long after it was outlawed in the rest of the country."

I shook my head. "There's nothing lovely about those feet."

"I know. But they were usually bound up in silk ribbons." Mom brushed some of the hair from my eyes. "Because they were a symbol of the old days, Paw-paw undid the ribbons as soon as we were free in Hong Kong—even though they kept back the pain."

I was even more puzzled now. "How did the ribbons do that?"

Mom began to brush my hair with quick, light strokes. "The ribbons kept the blood from circulating freely and bringing more feeling to her feet. Once the ribbons were gone, her feet ached. They probably still do."

I rubbed my own foot in sympathy. "But she doesn't complain."

"That's how tough she is," Mom said.

Finally the truth dawned on me. "And she mistook my toe-shoe ribbons for her old ones."

Mom lowered the brush and nodded solemnly. "And she didn't want you to go through the same pain she had."

I guess Grandmother loved me in her own way. When she came into the bedroom with Ian later that evening, I didn't leave. However, she tried to ignore me—as if I had become tainted by her secret.

When Ian demanded a story, I sighed. "All right. But only one."

Naturally, Ian chose the fattest story he could, which was my old collection of fairy tales by Hans Christian Andersen. Years of reading had cracked the spine so that the book fell open automatically in his hands to the story that had been my favorite when I was small. It was the original story of "The Little Mermaid"—not the cartoon. The picture illustrating the tale showed the mermaid posed like a ballerina in the middle of the throne room.

"This one," Ian said, and pointed to the picture of the Little Mermaid.

When Grandmother and Ian sat down on my bed, I began to read. However, when I got to the part where the Little Mermaid could walk on land, I stopped.

Ian was impatient. "Come on, read," he ordered, patting the page.

"After that," I went on, "each step hurt her as if she were walking on a knife." I couldn't help looking up at Grandmother.

This time she was the one to pat the page. "Go on. Tell me more about the mermaid."

So I went on reading to the very end, where the Little Mermaid changes into sea foam. "That's a dumb ending," Ian said. "Who wants to be pollution?"

"Sea foam isn't pollution. It's just bubbles," I explained. "The important thing was that she wanted to walk even though it hurt."

"I would rather have gone on swimming," Ian insisted.

"But maybe she wanted to see new places and people by going on the land," Grandmother said softly. "If she had kept her tail, the land people would have thought she was odd. They might even have made fun of her."

When she glanced at her own feet, I thought she might be talking about herself—so I seized my chance. "My satin ribbons aren't like your old silk ones. I use them to tie my toe shoes on when I dance." Setting the book down, I got out my other shoe. "Look."

Grandmother fingered the dangling ribbons and then pointed at my bare feet. "But you already have calluses there."

I began to dance before Grandmother could stop me. After a minute, I struck a pose on half-toe. "See? I can move fine."

She took my hand and patted it clumsily. I think it was the first time she had showed me any sign of affection. "When I

Theme
What details in this paragraph support a theme of understanding cultural differences?

Comprehension
What happened to Grandmother's feet when she was a child?

saw those ribbons, I didn't want you feeling pain like I do."

I covered her hands with mine. "I just wanted to show you what I love best—dancing."

"And I love my children," she said. I could hear the ache in her voice. "And my grandchildren. I don't want anything bad to happen to you."

Suddenly I felt as if there were an invisible ribbon binding us, tougher than silk and satin, stronger even than steel; and it joined her to Mom and Mom to me.

I wanted to hug her so badly that I just did. Though she was stiff at first, she gradually softened in my arms.

"'Let me have my ribbons and my shoes," I said in a low voice. "Let me dance."

"Yes, yes," she whispered fiercely.

I felt something on my cheek and realized she was crying, and then I began crying, too.

"So much to learn," she said, and began hugging me back. "So much to learn."

Make Inferences
Why do you think the narrator and her grandmother are crying?

Language Study

Vocabulary The words below appear in "Ribbons." Use your knowledge of the words to answer each numbered question. Explain your responses.

sensitive **meek** **coax** **exertion** **furrowed**

1. If a girl is *meek,* how might she answer questions in class?

2. How would you *coax* someone to go somewhere with you?

3. What is your least favorite type of *exertion?*

4. If your forehead is *furrowed,* how might you feel?

5. If someone is *sensitive,* is it a good idea to tease him?

WORD STUDY
The **Latin suffix** ***-ious*** means "full of." In this story, the grandmother's walking is **laborious**, requiring much labor, or work, as she climbs the stairs.

Word Study

Part A Explain how the **Latin suffix** ***-ious*** contributes to the meaning of the words *glorious, gracious,* and *harmonious.* Consult a dictionary if necessary.

Part B Use the context of the sentences and your knowledge of the Latin suffix *-ious* to explain your answer to each question.

1. If a meal is *nutritious,* what kinds of foods does it include?

2. Whom do you know with *ambitious* goals?

Close Reading Activities

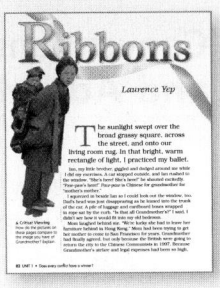

Literary Analysis

Key Ideas and Details

1. **Make Inferences** The author describes Grandmother's arrival by saying, "The rear car door opened, and a pair of carved black canes poked out like six-shooters." **(a)** What first impression of Grandmother do these details create? **(b)** Why do you think the author includes these details instead of simply introducing the character by name?

2. **Make Inferences** Grandmother carried her daughter on her back to Hong Kong to escape her enemy. What questions might you ask to help you make an inference about Grandmother's life?

3. **(a)** Identify two examples from the story that show how Stacy's life changes when Grandmother arrives. **(b) Analyze Causes and Effects:** For each example, tell how you would expect Stacy to feel about these changes.

4. **(a)** How does Stacy learn the secret of Grandmother's feet? **(b) Connect:** How does Stacy's attitude change after her mother explains older Chinese customs? Support your response.

Craft and Structure

5. **Theme** What theme does the story convey about understanding between grandparents and grandchildren? In a graphic organizer like the one shown, list details about the setting and characters that support the theme.

6. **(a) Deduce:** How does the author reveal differences between generations and cultures in this story? **(b) Support:** Support your answer with details from the story.

Integration of Knowledge and Ideas

7. **Evaluate:** Discuss with a partner whether or not you sympathize with Stacy. Provide evidence from the text to support your view. Then, discuss how hearing your partner's responses and examples from the text did or did not change your view.

8. **Does every conflict have a winner? (a)** How do Grandmother and Stacy finally overcome their conflict and begin to understand and appreciate one another? **(b)** What lessons does each character learn? What story details support your response?

Setting

↓

Theme

↑

Character

ACADEMIC VOCABULARY

As you write and speak about "Ribbons," use the words related to conflict that you explored on page 3 of this textbook.

Conventions: **Comparison of Adjectives and Adverbs**

Most adjectives and adverbs have three degrees of comparison: the *positive*, the *comparative,* and the *superlative.*

The **positive** is used when no comparison is made: Hannah is a *fast* runner.

The **comparative** is used when two things are being compared: Eva is a *faster* runner than Hannah.

The **superlative** is used when three or more things are being compared: Emmy is the *fastest* runner on the team.

Forming Comparative and Superlative Degrees	
Use *-er* or *more* to form the comparative degree.	faster, taller, more intelligent, more expressive
Use *-est* or *most* to form the superlative degree.	brightest, biggest, most nutritious, most sorrowful
Use *more* and *most* with modifiers of three or more syllables.	more popular, more intelligently, most popular, most intelligently

Practice A

Identify the adjective or adverb in each sentence. Then, identify the degree of comparison it indicates: *positive, comparative,* or *superlative.*

1. Ian was happy when Grandmother arrived.

2. The stairs were more dangerous for Grandmother than they were for Stacy.

3. Westerns were easier than comedies for Grandmother to understand.

4. The most difficult days in Grandmother's life were in the past.

Reading Application Find five adjectives and adverbs in "Ribbons," and indicate the degree of comparison each reflects: positive, comparative, or superlative.

Practice B

Complete each sentence with the adjective or adverb described in parentheses.

1. For Stacy, the _____ activity is ballet dancing. (superlative form of *enjoyable*)

2. Grandmother and Ian have _____ conversations. (positive form of *simple*)

3. The more Grandmother favors Ian, the _____ Stacy gets. (comparative form of *angry*)

Writing Application Write at least three sentences about the relationship between Stacy and her grandmother. Use positive, comparative, and superlative adjectives and adverbs in your sentences.

Writing to Sources

Response to Literature Write a **letter to the author** in which you tell whether or not you liked the story, making specific references to the text to support your opinion. As you draft, follow these steps:

- Begin with your overall reaction to "Ribbons."
- In several paragraphs, state and support your ideas about the story by referring to the text. You may wish to connect events in the story with your own experiences to demonstrate your understanding of the story.
- Draft your letter using correct business letter format. Refer to the Writing Handbook at the back of this textbook if you need help. Establish and maintain a formal writing style throughout your letter.
- End with a brief conclusion that summarizes the ideas you have presented in the body of your letter.

Grammar Application As you write, use positive, comparative, and superlative forms of adjectives and adverbs properly.

Research and Technology

Build and Present Knowledge Create a **poster** based on "Ribbons." In your poster, give information about the basic arm and foot positions used in ballet and the benefits of learning to dance. Follow these steps to complete the assignment:

- Identify the topic of your poster. Then, jot down questions to guide your research.
- Develop a research plan. Then, use the Internet and library resources to conduct your research.
- Use photos, drawings, and diagrams to illustrate your poster.
- Include information about the ballet terms that appear in the story, such as *pirouette* and *en pointe*.
- Present your poster and research to the class. You may want to add music or sound effects to emphasize key points.

 **Common Core State Standards**

Writing
1.d. Establish and maintain a formal style.
1.e. Provide a concluding statement or section that follows from and supports the argument presented.
7. Conduct short research projects to answer a question, drawing on several sources and generating additional related, focused questions for further research and investigation.

Speaking and Listening
5. Include multimedia components and visual displays in presentations to clarify claims and findings and emphasize salient points.

Language
1. Demonstrate command of the conventions of standard English grammar and usage when writing or speaking.

Does every conflict have a winner?

Explore the Big Question as you read these stories. Take notes to compare the ways that the main characters deal with the conflicts they face.

READING TO COMPARE CHARACTERS

Authors James Thurber and Sherwood Anderson use many different techniques to portray the characters in their stories. After reading both stories, compare and contrast how the two authors bring their main characters to life.

ESSAY

THE NIGHT THE BED FELL

JAMES THURBER

SHORT STORY

Stolen Day

Sherwood Anderson

"The Night the Bed Fell"

James Thurber (1894–1961)
According to James Thurber, if you had lived in his Ohio home, you would have witnessed absurd events. While writing of such events, he always showed affection for his quirky relatives. Thurber's literary home was *The New Yorker* magazine, where he wrote essays that gently poked fun at the world. He often did line drawings to accompany his essays, even when his eyesight began to fail him.

"Stolen Day"

Sherwood Anderson (1876–1941)
As a teenager, Sherwood Anderson worked as a newsboy, a housepainter, and a stable groom. Later, he fought in Cuba in the Spanish-American War. Even though Anderson did not begin to write professionally until he was forty years old, he is considered an important writer. His novel *Winesburg, Ohio* was published in 1919. In it, Anderson used simple, everyday language to capture the loneliness and hopelessness of characters living in a small town.

Comparing Characters

A **character** is a person, animal, or being that takes part in the action of a literary work. In literature, you will find characters with a range of personalities and attitudes. For example, a character might be dependable and smart but also stubborn. The qualities that make each character unique are called **character traits.** Writers use the process of **characterization** to create and develop characters. There are two types of characterization:

- **Direct characterization:** The writer directly states or describes the character's traits.

- **Indirect characterization:** The writer reveals a character's personality through his or her words and actions and through the thoughts, words, and actions of others.

A character's responses may be internal or external. An **internal response** reveals a character's thoughts, while an **external response** consists of a character's actions or deeds. Writers use the internal and external responses of characters to develop the plot of a literary work. For example, the characters' responses can strongly influence the conflict—the problem or struggle that increases the tension in a story.

As you read the texts that follow, look for character traits that show each narrator's qualities, attitudes, and values. Use a chart like the one below to analyze how the writer of each text develops the narrator's character.

	"The Night the Bed Fell"	"Stolen Day"
Main character		
Direct description		
Character's words and actions		
What others say about character		

Common Core State Standards

Reading Literature
3. Analyze how particular elements of a story or drama interact.

Reading Informational Texts
3. Analyze the interactions between individuals, events, and ideas in a text.

Writing
2.a. Introduce a topic clearly, previewing what is to follow; organize ideas, concepts, and information, using strategies such as definition, classification, comparison/contrast, and cause/effect.

THE NIGHT THE BED FELL

JAMES THURBER

I suppose that the high-water mark of my youth in Columbus, Ohio, was the night the bed fell on my father. It makes a better recitation (unless, as some friends of mine have said, one has heard it five or six times) than it does a piece of writing, for it is almost necessary to throw furniture around, shake doors, and bark like a dog, to lend the proper atmosphere and verisimilitude[1] to what is admittedly a somewhat incredible tale. Still, it did take place.

It happened, then, that my father had decided to sleep in the attic one night, to be away where he could think. My mother opposed the notion strongly because, she said, the old wooden bed up there was unsafe: it was wobbly and the heavy headboard would crash down on father's head in case the bed fell, and kill him. There was no dissuading him, however, and at a quarter past ten he closed the attic door behind him and went up the narrow twisting stairs. We later heard ominous creakings as he crawled into bed. Grandfather, who usually slept in the attic bed when he was with us, had disappeared some days before. On these occasions he was usually gone six or eight days and returned growling and out of temper, with the news that the

---

1. **verisimilitude** (ver′ ə si mil′ ə tōod) *n.* appearance of truth or reality.

Federal Union[2] was run by a passel of blockheads and that the Army of the Potomac[3] didn't have a chance.

We had visiting us at this time a nervous first cousin of mine named Briggs Beall, who believed that he was likely to cease breathing when he was asleep. It was his feeling that if he were not awakened every hour during the night, he might die of suffocation. He had been accustomed to setting an alarm clock to ring at intervals until morning, but I persuaded him to abandon this. He slept in my room and I told him that I was such a light sleeper that if anybody quit breathing in the same room with me, I would wake instantly. He tested me the first night—which I had suspected he would—by holding his breath after my regular breathing had convinced him I was asleep. I was not asleep, however, and called to him. This seemed to allay his fears a little, but he took the precaution of putting a glass of spirits of camphor[4] on a little table at the head of his bed. In case I didn't arouse him until he was almost gone, he said, he would sniff the camphor, a powerful reviver. Briggs was not the only member of his family who had his crotchets.[5] Old Aunt Melissa Beall (who could whistle like a man, with two fingers in her mouth) suffered under the premonition that she was destined to die on South High Street, because she had been born on South High Street and married on South High Street. Then there was Aunt Sarah Shoaf, who never went to bed at night without the fear that a burglar was going to get in and blow chloroform[6] under her door through a tube. To avert this calamity—for she was in greater dread of anesthetics than of losing her household goods—she always piled her money, silverware, and other valuables in a neat stack just outside her bedroom, with a note reading: "This is all I have. Please take it and do not use your chloroform, as this is all I have." Aunt Gracie Shoaf also had a burglar phobia, but she met it with more fortitude. She was confident that burglars had been getting into her house every night for forty years. The fact that she never missed any thing was to her no proof to the contrary. She always claimed that she scared them off before they could take anything, by throwing shoes down the hallway. When she went to bed she piled, where she could get at them handily, all the shoes

◄ **Vocabulary**
ominous (äm´ ə nəs)
adj. threatening

Character
What details about this character are probably exaggerated?

Character
What are the contrasts between the aunts' beliefs and reality?

Comprehension
What kind of a story does the narrator say he is going to tell?

---

2. **Federal Union** northern side during the Civil War of the 1860s. He is under the illusion that the Civil War has not yet ended.
3. **Army of the Potomac** one of the northern armies during the Civil War.
4. **spirits of camphor** liquid with a powerful odor.
5. **crotchets** (kräch´ its) *n.* peculiar ideas.
6. **chloroform** (klôr´ ə fôrm´) *n.* substance used at one time as an anesthetic.

Some nights she threw them all. by James Thurber

there were about her house. Five minutes after she had turned off the light, she would sit up in bed and say "Hark!" Her husband, who had learned to ignore the whole situation as long ago as 1903, would either be sound asleep or pretend to be sound asleep. In either case he would not respond to her tugging and pulling, so that presently she would arise, tiptoe to the door, open it slightly and heave a shoe down the hall in one direction, and its mate down the hall in the other direction. Some nights she threw them all, some nights only a couple of pair.

But I am straying from the remarkable incidents that took place during the night that the bed fell on father. By midnight we were all in bed. The layout of the rooms and the disposition[7] of their occupants is important to an understanding of what later occurred. In the front room upstairs (just under father's attic bedroom) were my mother and my brother Herman, who sometimes sang in his sleep, usually "Marching Through Georgia" or "Onward, Christian Soldiers." Briggs Beall and myself were in a room adjoining this one. My brother Roy was in a room across the hall from ours. Our bull terrier, Rex, slept in the hall.

My bed was an army cot, one of those affairs which are made wide enough to sleep on comfortably only by putting up, flat with the middle section, the two sides which ordinarily hang down like the sideboards of a drop-leaf table. When these sides are up, it is **perilous** to roll too far toward the edge, for then the cot is likely to tip completely over, bringing the whole bed down on top of one, with a tremendous banging crash. This, in fact, is precisely what happened about two o'clock in the morning. (It was my mother who, in recalling the scene later, first referred to it as "the night the bed fell on your father.")

▲ Critical Viewing
How would Gracie Shoaf defend the actions shown in this drawing?

Vocabulary ▶
perilous (per´ ə ləs) *adj.* dangerous

7. **disposition** (dis´ pə zish´ ən) *n.* arrangement.

Always a deep sleeper, slow to arouse (I had lied to Briggs), I was at first unconscious of what had happened when the iron cot rolled me onto the floor and toppled over on me. It left me still warmly bundled up and unhurt, for the bed rested above me like a canopy. Hence I did not wake up, only reached the edge of consciousness and went back. The racket, however, instantly awakened my mother, in the next room, who came to the immediate conclusion that her worst dread was realized: the big wooden bed upstairs had fallen on father. She therefore screamed, "Let's go to your poor father!" It was this shout, rather than the noise of my cot falling, that awakened Herman, in the same room with her. He thought that mother had become, for no apparent reason, hysterical. "You're all right, Mamma!" he shouted, trying to calm her. They exchanged shout for shout for perhaps ten seconds: "Let's go to your poor father!" and "You're all right!" That woke up Briggs. By this time I was conscious of what was going on, in a vague way, but did not yet realize that I was under my bed instead of on it. Briggs, awakening in the midst of loud shouts of fear and apprehension, came to the

▼ **Critical Viewing**
What part of the story does this picture show?

Character
How does the mother's reaction make this situation humorous?

Comprehension
On what type of bed is the narrator sleeping?

He came to the conclusion that he was suffocating. by James Thurber

quick conclusion that he was suffocating and that we were all trying to "bring him out." With a low moan, he grasped the glass of camphor at the head of his bed and instead of sniffing it poured it over himself. The room reeked of camphor. "Ugf, ahfg," choked Briggs, like a drowning man, for he had almost succeeded in stopping his breath under the deluge of pungent spirits. He leaped out of bed and groped toward the open window, but he came up against one that was closed. With his hand, he beat out the glass, and I could hear it crash and tinkle on the alleyway below. It was at this juncture that I, in trying to get up, had the uncanny sensation of feeling my bed above me! Foggy with sleep, I now suspected, in my turn, that the whole uproar was being made in a frantic endeavor to extricate me from what must be an unheard-of and perilous situation. "Get me out of this!" I bawled. "Get me out!" I think I had the nightmarish belief that I was entombed in a mine. "Gugh," gasped Briggs, floundering in his camphor.

By this time my mother, still shouting, pursued by Herman, still shouting, was trying to open the door to the attic, in order to go up and get my father's body out of the wreckage. The door was stuck, however, and wouldn't yield. Her frantic pulls on it only added to the general banging and confusion. Roy and the dog were now up, the one shouting questions, the other barking.

Father, farthest away and soundest sleeper of all, had by this time been awakened by the battering on the attic door. He decided that the house was on fire. "I'm coming, I'm coming!" he wailed in a slow, sleepy voice—it took him many minutes to regain full consciousness. My mother,

Character
What action does Briggs perform that helps to reveal his nervous personality?

▶ **Critical Viewing**
How does the action in this drawing capture the mood of the story?

Roy had to throw Rex. by James Thurber

still believing he was caught under the bed, detected in his "I'm coming!" the mournful, resigned note of one who is preparing to meet his Maker. "He's dying!" she shouted.

"I'm all right!" Briggs yelled to reassure her. "I'm all right!" He still believed that it was his own closeness to death that was worrying mother. I found at last the light switch in my room, unlocked the door, and Briggs and I joined the others at the attic door. The dog, who never did like Briggs, jumped for him—assuming that he was the culprit in whatever was going on—and Roy had to throw Rex and hold him. We could hear father crawling out of bed upstairs. Roy pulled the attic door open, with a mighty jerk, and father came down the stairs, sleepy and irritable but safe and sound. My mother began to weep when she saw him. Rex began to howl. "What in the name of heaven is going on here?" asked father.

The situation was finally put together like a gigantic jigsaw puzzle. Father caught a cold from prowling around in his bare feet but there were no other bad results. "I'm glad," said mother, who always looked on the bright side of things, "that your grandfather wasn't here."

Character
What characteristics make the mother amusing?

◄ **Vocabulary**
culprit (kul´prit)
n. guilty person

Critical Thinking

1. **Key Ideas and Details (a)** Who is in the house on the night Thurber describes? **(b) Compare:** What quality or qualities do these characters share? **(c) Support:** What examples from the text illustrate the shared qualities?

2. **Key Ideas and Details (a)** Describe the layout of the rooms. **(b) Analyze:** Why is the placement of the rooms in the house important to the events?

3. **Key Ideas and Details (a)** What do Briggs, Aunt Sarah Shoaf, and Aunt Gracie Shoaf do before going to bed? **(b) Infer:** What do you suppose the author, looking back, thinks of this behavior? **(c) Make a Judgment:** Do you think the author treats his relatives fairly in the essay? Cite textual details in your response.

4. **Integration of Knowledge and Ideas (a)** Why do each of the people in the household have a different idea of what has happened? **(b)** How is the conflict among these ideas resolved? *[Connect to the Big Question: Does every conflict have a winner?]*

Stolen Day

Sherwood Anderson

It must be that all children are actors. The whole thing started with a boy on our street named Walter, who had inflammatory rheumatism.[1] That's what they called it. He didn't have to go to school.

Still he could walk about. He could go fishing in the creek or the waterworks pond. There was a place up at the pond where in the spring the water came tumbling over the dam and formed a deep pool. It was a good place. Sometimes you could get some big ones there.

I went down that way on my way to school one spring morning. It was out of my way but I wanted to see if Walter was there.

He was, inflammatory rheumatism and all. There he was, sitting with a fish pole in his hand. He had been able to walk down there all right.

It was then that my own legs began to hurt. My back too. I went on to school but, at the recess time, I began to cry. I did it when the teacher, Sarah Suggett, had come out into the schoolhouse yard.

She came right over to me.

"I ache all over," I said. I did, too.

Character
What can you tell about the narrator based on the pain he experiences?

I kept on crying and it worked all right.

"You'd better go on home," she said.

So I went. I limped painfully away. I kept on limping until I got out of the schoolhouse street.

Then I felt better. I still had inflammatory rheumatism pretty bad but I could get along better.

I must have done some thinking on the way home.

"I'd better not say I have inflammatory rheumatism," I decided. "Maybe if you've got that you swell up."

I thought I'd better go around to where Walter was and ask him about that, so I did—but he wasn't there.

"They must not be biting today," I thought.

I had a feeling that, if I said I had inflammatory rheumatism, Mother or my brothers and my sister Stella might laugh. They did laugh at me pretty often and I didn't like it at all.

"Just the same," I said to myself, "I have got it." I began to hurt and ache again.

I went home and sat on the front steps of our house. I sat there a long time. There wasn't anyone at home but Mother and the two little ones. Ray would have been four or five then and Earl might have been three.

It was Earl who saw me there. I had got tired sitting and was lying on the porch. Earl was always a quiet, **solemn** little fellow.

He must have said something to Mother for presently she came.

"What's the matter with you? Why aren't you in school?" she asked.

I came pretty near telling her right out that I had inflammatory rheumatism but I thought I'd better not. Mother and Father had been speaking of Walter's case at the table just the day before. "It affects the heart," Father had said. That frightened me when I thought of it. "I might die," I thought. "I might just suddenly die right here; my heart might stop beating."

Character
Why does the narrator's pain suddenly disappear?

Spiral Review
THEME How might the narrator's so-called pain relate to a possible theme?

Vocabulary ▶
solemn (säl´ əm) *adj.*
serious; somber

I kept on crying and it worked all right.

On the day before I had been running a race with my brother Irve. We were up at the fairgrounds after school and there was a half-mile track.

"I'll bet you can't run a half-mile," he said. "I bet you I could beat you running clear around the track."

And so we did it and I beat him, but afterwards my heart did seem to beat pretty hard. I remembered that lying there on the porch. "It's a wonder, with my inflammatory rheumatism and all, I didn't just drop down dead," I thought. The thought frightened me a lot. I ached worse than ever.

"I ache, Ma," I said. "I just ache."

She made me go in the house and upstairs and get into bed.

It wasn't so good. It was spring. I was up there for perhaps an hour, maybe two, and then I felt better.

I got up and went downstairs. "I feel better, Ma," I said.

Mother said she was glad. She was pretty busy that day and hadn't paid much attention to me. She had made me get into bed upstairs and then hadn't even come up to see how I was.

I didn't think much of that when I was up there but when I got downstairs where she was, and when, after I had said I felt better and she only said she was glad and went right on with her work, I began to ache again.

I thought, "I'll bet I die of it. I bet I do."

I went out to the front porch and sat down. I was pretty sore at Mother.

"If she really knew the truth, that I have the inflammatory rheumatism and I may just drop down dead any time, I'll bet

▲ **Critical Viewing**
Does this boy look genuinely upset, or do you think he is making himself cry, as the story's narrator does? Explain.

Character
What character trait do the narrator's thoughts suggest?

Comprehension
What does the narrator believe is wrong with him?

she wouldn't care about that either," I thought.

I was getting more and more angry the more thinking I did.

"I know what I'm going to do," I thought; "I'm going to go fishing."

I thought that, feeling the way I did, I might be sitting on the high bank just above the deep pool where the water went over the dam, and suddenly my heart would stop beating.

And then, of course, I'd pitch forward, over the bank into the pool and, if I wasn't dead when I hit the water, I'd drown sure.

They would all come home to supper and they'd miss me.

"But where is he?"

Then Mother would remember that I'd come home from school aching.

Character
Based on this imaginary scene, what words would you use to describe the narrator?

She'd go upstairs and I wouldn't be there. One day during the year before, there was a child got drowned in a spring. It was one of the Wyatt children.

Right down at the end of the street there was a spring under a birch tree and there had been a barrel sunk in the ground.

Everyone had always been saying the spring ought to be kept covered, but it wasn't.

So the Wyatt child went down there, played around alone, and fell in and got drowned.

Mother was the one who had found the drowned child. She had gone to get a pail of water and there the child was, drowned and dead.

This had been in the evening when we were all at home, and Mother had come running up the street with the dead, dripping child in her arms. She was making for the Wyatt house as hard as she could run, and she was pale.

She had a terrible look on her face, I remembered then.

"So," I thought, "they'll miss me and there'll be a search made. Very likely there'll be someone who has seen me sitting by the pond fishing, and there'll be a big alarm and all the town will turn out and they'll drag the pond."

I was having a grand time, having died. Maybe, after they found me and had got me out of the deep pool, Mother would grab me up in her arms and run home with me as she had run with the Wyatt child.

I got up from the porch and went around the house. I got my fishing pole and lit out for the pool below the dam. Mother was busy—she always was—and didn't see me go. When I got there I thought I'd better not sit too near the edge of the high bank.

By this time I didn't ache hardly at all, but I thought.

"With inflammatory rheumatism you can't tell," I thought.

"It probably comes and goes," I thought.

"Walter has it and he goes fishing," I thought.

I had got my line into the pool and suddenly I got a bite. It was a regular whopper. I knew that. I'd never had a bite like that.

I knew what it was. It was one of Mr. Fenn's big carp.

Mr. Fenn was a man who had a big pond of his own. He sold ice in the summer and the pond was to make the ice. He had bought some big carp and put them into his pond and then, earlier in the spring when there was a freshet,[2] his dam had gone out.

So the carp had got into our creek and one or two big ones had been caught—but none of them by a boy like me.

The carp was pulling and I was pulling and I was afraid he'd break my line, so I just tumbled down the high bank holding onto the line and got right into the pool. We had it out, there in the pool. We struggled. We wrestled. Then I got a hand under his gills and got him out.

He was a big one all right. He was nearly half as big as I was myself. I had him on the bank and I kept one hand under his gills and I ran.

I never ran so hard in my life. He was slippery, and now and then he wriggled out of my arms; once I stumbled and fell on him, but I got him home.

So there it was. I was a big hero that day. Mother got a washtub and filled it with water. She put the fish in it and all the neighbors came to look. I got into dry clothes and went down to supper—and then I made a break that spoiled my day.

Character
What do the narrator's actions with the carp reveal about his physical condition?

Comprehension
What happened to the Wyatt child?

---

2. **freshet** (fresh´ it) a great rise or overflowing of a stream caused by heavy rains or melted snow.

I was a BIG hero that day.

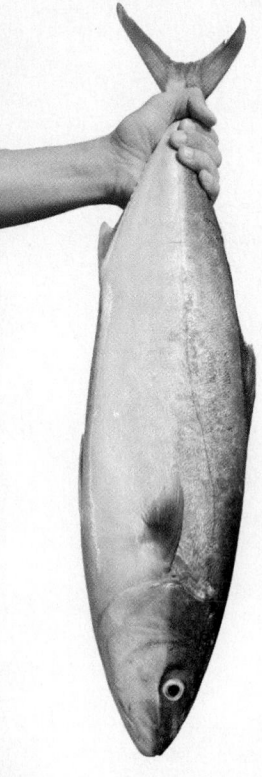

There we were, all of us, at the table, and suddenly Father asked what had been the matter with me at school. He had met the teacher, Sarah Suggett, on the street and she had told him how I had become ill.

"What was the matter with you?" Father asked, and before I thought what I was saying I let it out.

"I had the inflammatory rheumatism," I said—and a shout went up. It made me sick to hear them, the way they all laughed.

It brought back all the aching again, and like a fool I began to cry.

"Well, I *have* got it—I *have*, I *have*," I cried, and I got up from the table and ran upstairs.

I stayed there until Mother came up. I knew it would be a long time before I heard the last of the inflammatory rheumatism. I was sick all right, but the aching I now had wasn't in my legs or in my back.

Critical Thinking

1. **Key Ideas and Details (a)** What inspires the narrator to think he has inflammatory rheumatism? **(b) Infer:** Why does the narrator think this would be an appealing disease to have? Support your response with textual evidence.

2. **Key Ideas and Details (a)** What does the narrator do after he gets home? **(b) Infer:** Why does his mother pay him little attention?

3. **Integration of Knowledge and Ideas (a)** How does his family respond when the narrator says he has inflammatory rheumatism? **(b) Defend:** Do you think the narrator's family should have been more understanding? Why or why not?

4. **Integration of Knowledge and Ideas** Does the story's ending resolve the conflict between what is true and what the narrator thinks is true? Explain, citing details from the story to support your response. *[Connect to the Big Question: Does every conflict have a winner?]*

Writing to Sources

Comparing Characters

1. **Key Ideas and Details** Identify one example of direct characterization and one example of indirect characterization in each selection.

2. **Key Ideas and Details (a)** What happens to the narrator's army cot in "The Night the Bed Fell"? **(b)** What does his mother think happened?

3. **Key Ideas and Details (a)** What does the narrator of "Stolen Day" do that causes his teacher to send him home? **(b)** Why does he do this?

4. **Integration of Knowledge and Ideas** Use a chart like the one below to compare and contrast the narrators of both texts.

	How similar?	How different?
Narrator: "Stolen Day"	A boy	Believes he is sick
Narrator: "The Night the Bed Fell"		

 Timed Writing

Explanatory Text: Essay

In an essay, compare and contrast the narrators in these selections. Describe ways in which the narrators' internal and external responses to conflict affect the development of the plot. Cite evidence from the texts to support your analysis. **(30 minutes)**

5-Minute Planner

1. Read the prompt carefully and completely.

2. Answer these questions to help you gather your ideas.

   • How does each narrator respond to conflict? To what extent do the narrators' responses affect the plot of each selection?

   • Which narrator do you think will learn the most from his experiences? Why?

3. Create an outline in which you organize the details of your essay.

4. Reread the prompt, and then use your outline to draft your essay.

USE ACADEMIC VOCABULARY

As you write, use academic language, including the following words or their related forms:

assumption

common

discover

perspective

For more information about academic vocabulary, see pages xlvi-l.

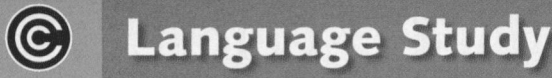

Using a Dictionary and Thesaurus

If you need to know the meaning, the pronunciation, or the part of speech of a word, you can find that information in a **dictionary.** In addition, a dictionary can show you a word's **etymology,** or origin. Etymologies explain how words come into the English language and how they change over time. Check the front or back of a dictionary for a guide to the symbols and abbreviations used in etymologies.

Here is an example of a dictionary entry. Notice what it tells you about the word *anthology.*

Dictionary

> **anthology** (an thäl′ ə jē) *n., pl.* **-gies** [Gr. *anthologia,* a garland, collection of short poems < *anthologos,* gathering flowers < *anthos,* flower + *legein,* to gather] a collection of poems, stories, songs, excerpts, etc., chosen by the compiler

In a **thesaurus,** you will find a list of a word's synonyms, or words with similar meanings. You can use a thesaurus when you are looking for alternate word choices in your writing. Look at this example of a thesaurus entry.

Thesaurus

> **clarify** *v.* interpret, define, elucidate, see EXPLAIN.

Note that a thesaurus does not provide definitions of words. Before you use a word you find in a thesaurus, check a dictionary to be sure you understand the word's meaning.

Where To Find a Dictionary and Thesaurus You can find these resources in book form at your school or library. You can also use *digital tools,* such as *online dictionaries* and *thesauruses,* to find the most precise words to express your ideas. Ask your teacher to recommend the best online word study resources.

 **Common Core State Standards**

Language

4.c. Consult general and specialized reference materials, both print and digital, to find the pronunciation of a word or determine or clarify its precise meaning or its part of speech.

4.d. Verify the preliminary determination of the meaning of a word or phrase.

5.c. Distinguish among the connotations (associations) of words with similar denotations (definitions) (e.g., *refined, respectful, polite, diplomatic, condescending*).

Practice A Find each of the following words in a print or online dictionary. Write down the first pronunciation, part of speech, and definition of each word. Then, use each word in a sentence that shows its meaning.

  1. voyage   **2.** robust   **3.** engulf   **4.** intricate

Practice B Use a print or online thesaurus to find an alternate word for the italicized word in each sentence. Choose a more expressive word that means the same thing as the original. Verify the meaning of the word you choose in a dictionary.

  1. I had to *run* down the street to catch the school bus on time.

  2. After soccer practice, all we wanted to do was *sit* on the couch.

  3. On our class trip to the nature trail, our assignment was to *find* as many bugs as possible.

  4. After the storm, Damian had to *make* his storage shed again.

  5. We had to *push* the trash down to make it fit in the can.

Activity Create a quick-reference thesaurus of some commonly used words. Make notecards like the one shown for the words *big, nice,* and *interesting.* Share your notecards with classmates and collect more synonyms. Then, with a partner, distinguish the shades of meaning that each word conveys. Use cards like these to help you find precise words when you write.

Word:
Part of speech:
Definition:
Synonym 1:
Synonym 1 Definition:
Shades of Meaning:
Synonym 2:
Synonym 2 Definition:
Shades of Meaning:

Comprehension and Collaboration

With a partner, look up the meanings of the words *bolt* and *preserve*. Note that each word can be used as both a noun and a verb. For each word, write one sentence using the word as a noun and another sentence using the word as a verb.

Delivering an Oral Summary

 **Common Core State Standards**

Speaking and Listening
4. Present claims and findings, emphasizing salient points in a focused, coherent manner with pertinent descriptions, facts, details, and examples; use appropriate eye contact, adequate volume, and clear pronunciation.

An **oral summary** shares many of the characteristics of a written summary. The guidelines below will help you plan what you want to say and help you say it with confidence.

Learn the Skills

Summarize. Like its written counterpart, an oral summary should briefly state the main idea of a work, with only as many details as needed to give a complete, but concise, picture of the work.

Organize your points in sequence. To create a summary to use in an oral presentation, organize your ideas and record them on notecards.

Write the "main idea"—the overall statement of the work's content—on your first notecard. Include one or two key details that support the main idea. Make additional cards to present points from the beginning, middle, and end of the work. Write your conclusion on a separate card. Refer to your notecards as you deliver your presentation.

Show a comprehensive understanding. As you prepare your presentation, do not just string together fact after fact. Ask yourself, "What does all this mean?" Try to convey a genuine understanding of what you have seen or read, not just the surface details.

Consider your audience. Include enough information so that your audience can follow the summary accurately.

Plan your delivery. Try to project confidence and a positive attitude. Plan and practice your delivery so that you stay focused when presenting.

- **Vary your sentence structure.** To add interest, vary your sentence structure just as you do when you write. Listen to your words and monitor yourself for errors in grammar.

- **Use your voice well.** Be energetic, but speak clearly and precisely. Enunciate every word. Vary the pitch and speed of your voice to keep your listeners engaged. Make sure that you are speaking loudly enough to be heard clearly.

- **Make eye contact.** Memorize as much of your summary as you can to enable you to make eye contact with listeners.

Main Idea
Giant pandas have become rare because hunters kill them.
Facts: There are only about 2,500 living in the wild. There are only about 150 in zoos.

Conclusion
If we can support the efforts to save pandas, maybe there will be more pandas in the world of our children and grandchildren.

Practice the Skills

Presentation of Knowledge and Ideas Use what you have learned in this workshop to complete the following activity.

ACTIVITY: **Prepare and Deliver an Oral Summary**

Choose an article, at least three pages long, from a magazine or Web site. Present an oral summary of the article to your class. Use the instruction on the previous page and the following steps to guide you:

- Begin with a strong opening statement. You might use a rhetorical question—a question asked for effect: *Does anyone wonder what happened to the plans for the new park?* You might use an impressive fact contained in the article: *It has been two years since the plans were first approved.*
- Use formal English, and vary the structure of your sentences.
- When presenting, project your voice so that everyone can hear you. Pronounce words clearly and make eye contact with your audience.
- End with a strong closing statement that relates to your opening statement. *So, that is what has happened to the park plans: repeated budget cuts.*

While your classmates give their presentations, use a checklist like the one below to rate their work.

Presentation Evaluation Checklist

Presentation Content	**Presentation Delivery**
Was the summary clear and easy to follow? Check all that apply. ❑ It has a strong beginning and ending. ❑ It includes all key points. ❑ I understood the main points of the work based on this summary.	Did the speaker deliver the summary effectively? Check all that apply. ❑ The speaker established good eye contact. ❑ The speaker enunciated clearly and maintained good volume. ❑ The speaker varied rate and pitch of voice. ❑ The speaker used formal English and varied sentence structure.

Comprehension and Collaboration Ask your classmates to give you feedback by saying how they rated you on the Presentation Evaluation Checklist.

Write a Narrative

Autobiographical Narrative

Defining the Form Stories that tell of real events in a writer's life are called **autobiographical narratives.**

Assignment Write an autobiographical narrative about an event in your life that helped you grow or changed your outlook. Include

- ✓ a clear *sequence of events* involving you, the writer
- ✓ a problem or *conflict,* or a clear contrast between past and present viewpoints
- ✓ a *plot* line that includes a beginning, rising action, climax, and resolution, or *denouement*
- ✓ *pacing* that effectively builds the action
- ✓ *specific details and quotations*
- ✓ well-developed *major and minor characters*
- ✓ error-free writing, including *correct use of pronouns*

To preview the criteria on which your autobiographical narrative may be judged, see the rubric on page 125.

© **Common Core State Standards**

Writing

3. Write narratives to develop real or imagined experiences or events using effective technique, relevant descriptive details, and well-structured event sequences.

3.a. Engage and orient the reader by establishing a context and point of view and introducing a narrator and/or characters; organize an event sequence that unfolds naturally and logically.

FOCUS ON RESEARCH

When you write an autobiographical narrative, you might perform research to

- jog your memory about the event you are describing.
- discover other people's memories of the event.
- give your writing authenticity, or a true-to-life feel.

Research for an autobiographical work is more personal than other kinds of research. To gather information, interview people who were involved in the event; reread journal entries, letters, or emails from that time; and examine keepsakes and other objects that remind you of the event.

READING-WRITING CONNECTION

To get a feel for narrative nonfiction, read the excerpt from *Barrio Boy* by Ernesto Galarza on page 234.

Prewriting/Planning Strategies

Choose a topic. To choose the right event from your life to narrate, use one of the following strategies:

- **Freewriting** Write for five minutes about whatever comes to mind on these general topics: *funny times, sad times,* and *lessons I have learned.* When you are finished, review what you have written and circle any ideas that could make a good topic for your purpose and audience.

- **Listing** Fill in a chart like the one below. In each column, list names or descriptions of memorable people and things that you know or have a particular viewpoint about from home, school, or travel. Review your chart to find connections between the items. For each connection you find, circle the two items and draw an arrow between them. Finally, review the connections you have found, and jot down ideas for engaging stories that they suggest.

People	Places	Things	Events

Make a timeline. Once you have decided on a topic, begin to gather the details that you will use in your narrative. Fill out a timeline like the one shown to organize your details in time order.

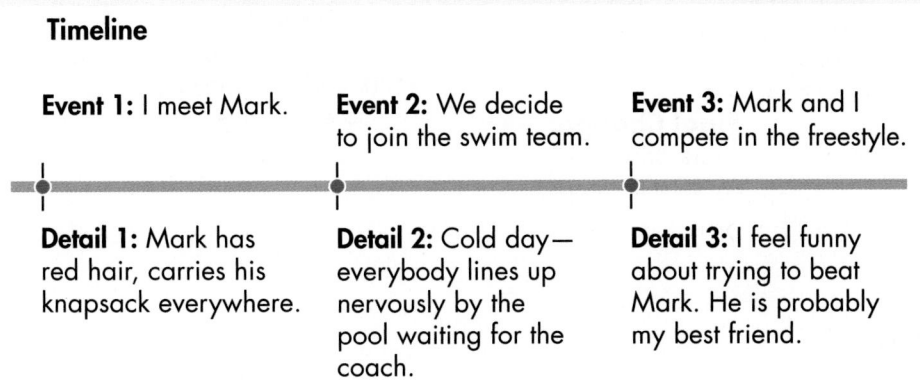

Timeline

Event 1: I meet Mark.

Event 2: We decide to join the swim team.

Event 3: Mark and I compete in the freestyle.

Detail 1: Mark has red hair, carries his knapsack everywhere.

Detail 2: Cold day—everybody lines up nervously by the pool waiting for the coach.

Detail 3: I feel funny about trying to beat Mark. He is probably my best friend.

Drafting Strategies

Common Core State Standards

Writing

3. Write narratives to develop real or imagined experiences or events using effective technique, relevant descriptive details, and well-structured event sequences.

3.a. Engage and orient the reader by establishing a context and point of view and introducing a narrator and/or characters; organize an event sequence that unfolds naturally and logically.

3.d. Use precise words and phrases, relevant descriptive details, and sensory language to capture the action and convey experiences and events.

3.e. Provide a conclusion that follows from and reflects on the narrated experiences or events.

Map out your story. Make a conflict chart like the one below. In the center, write a brief description of the conflict. Fill in linked circles with specific narrative action related to the conflict. Number the circles to help put the events of your story in order. As you draft, refer to your chart to help connect details to your central conflict.

Develop the plot line. Once you have mapped out the plot, make sure that you arrange the pace in the story so that the conflict intensifies during the **rising action.** The climax should be the highest point of interest in your story. **The resolution,** or **denouement,** should be the conclusion in which your conflict is resolved.

Develop a setting. A vivid setting can bring your story to life and help readers understand your characters. When describing a setting, try to appeal to several of your readers' senses. Draw a word picture of the place with precise and colorful nouns, adjectives, verbs, and adverbs.

Vague Description: We lived in a small town.

Vivid Description: Main Street smelled like pine trees because the woods were only steps away.

Develop characters through dialogue. Bring people to life by using dialogue—quoting what people said as they said it. Do not report everything a character says. Instead, create conversations that vividly show the character's feelings, gestures, and expressions as he or she reacts to events.

Provide a conclusion. Bring your narrative to a satisfying close by resolving conflicts and sharing insights or reflections with your readers.

Background
Mark and I were best friends.

Event 1:
Mark and I are matched in an important race.

Central Conflict
My friendship with Mark vs. my desire to win.

Event 2:
As the race approaches, Mark and I stop talking to each other.

Final Change:
Mark and I tied! We're still friends.

Finding Your Voice

Voice describes a writer's distinctive style and can be influenced by word choice, sentence structure, and tone—the writer's attitude toward his or her subject. A professional writer usually has a distinct voice that makes his or her writing instantly recognizable. For example, think of how a jazz musician and a hip-hop artist might play "The Star-Spangled Banner" completely differently. Developing a unique voice can take time. These tips and activities will help get you started.

Learning from the Professionals Next time you read a passage that you enjoy in a literary work, think about the writer's voice. Filling in a chart like the one shown will help you analyze voice. The examples in this chart refer to Ernesto Galarza's *Barrio Boy*, which appears on pages 234–239, but you can use a similar chart for any text.

Word Choice	*A new building, painted yellow; a straight sharp nose; her blond radiant face*
Sentence Structure	Long sentences that link together descriptive phrases
Tone	Observant, interested, and admiring, but not overly emotional

Refining Your Voice As you write your autobiographical narrative, review your draft for word choice, sentence structure, and tone. Remember to consider your purpose and audience. Decide if your style of writing should be formal or informal. Are you happy with the voice you are using? If not, try revising some of these elements to adjust your voice. Ask yourself these questions:

- *Word Choice:* What kinds of words have I chosen? Have I used precise language to create a strong impression?

- *Sentence Structure:* How did I arrange the words in my sentences? What type of sentences do I typically create?

- *Tone:* How do I feel about my subject? Has my word choice helped convey my intended tone?

Ask a partner to read your draft and give feedback. By adjusting the elements above, you can adjust your voice. Many writers refer to this process as "finding their voice."

Revising Strategies

Review sequence of events. Read through your narrative to make sure that the events you describe flow logically and are in chronological order. Add transition words, such as *first, next, later,* and *finally,* to clarify the sequence of events.

Check your pacing. A good story builds to a single most exciting moment, called the **climax.** The secret of building to a climax is **pacing**—the speed at which your story moves along. Pace your story to build suspense. To improve the pacing of your story, use the following strategies:

- Cut details and events that do not build suspense or heighten readers' interest.
- Revise or delete any paragraph that is not clearly connected to the central conflict.
- Make clear connections between other events to show readers how events relate to each other.

Use specific, precise nouns. Look for nouns that are vague or general and might leave the reader wondering *what kind.* Replace general and vague nouns with specific and precise ones. Review your draft, circling any nouns that do not answer the questions *What exactly?* and *What kind?* Replace these nouns with specific, precise nouns that convey a lively picture. Use a dictionary to confirm the precise meaning of the words you are using.

Vague	**Precise**
stuff ——————⟶	souvenirs

General	**Specific**
decorations ——————⟶	party streamers and balloons

Peer Review

Give your draft to one or two classmates to read. Ask them to highlight details that slow the story down or ideas that are unconnected to the central conflict. Use the feedback to eliminate any unnecessary details from your draft. As you review comments and revise your draft, adjust your writing to suit your purpose and audience as needed.

Writing

3.a. Engage and orient the reader by establishing a context and point of view and introducing a narrator and/or characters; organize an event sequence that unfolds naturally and logically.

3.b. Use narrative techniques, such as dialogue, pacing, and description, to develop experiences, events, and/or characters.

3.c. Use a variety of transition words, phrases, and clauses to convey sequence and signal shifts from one time frame or setting to another.

3.d. Use precise words and phrases, relevant descriptive details, and sensory language to capture the action and convey experiences and events.

5. With some guidance and support from peers and adults, develop and strengthen writing as needed by planning, revising, editing, rewriting, or trying a new approach, focusing on how well purpose and audience have been addressed.

Language

3.a. Choose language that expresses ideas precisely and concisely, recognizing and eliminating wordiness and redundancy.

Checking Pronoun-Antecedent Agreement

Incorrect pronoun-antecedent agreement occurs when a personal pronoun disagrees with its antecedent in person, number, or gender.

Identifying Incorrect Pronoun-Antecedent Agreement An **antecedent** is the word or words for which a pronoun stands. A pronoun's antecedent may be a noun, a group of words acting as a noun, or another pronoun.

| Antecedent | Pronoun |

Example: I told <u>Alexis</u> to bring a bathing suit with <u>her</u>.

In this example, the pronoun *her* is third person and singular. It agrees with its feminine antecedent, *Alexis,* which is also third person (the person spoken about) and singular.

Fixing Agreement Errors To fix an incorrect pronoun-antecedent agreement, identify both the pronoun and the antecedent for which it stands. Then use one of the following methods.

1. **Identify the person of the antecedent** as first, second, or third. Choose a pronoun that matches the antecedent in person.

2. **Identify the number of the antecedent** as singular or plural. Choose a pronoun that matches the antecedent in number.

3. **Identify the gender of the antecedent** as masculine or feminine. Choose a pronoun that matches the antecedent in gender.

Personal Pronouns		
	Singular	**Plural**
First Person	I, me, my, mine	we, us, our, ours
Second Person	you, your, yours	you, your, yours
Third Person	**Feminine:** she, her, hers **Masculine:** he, him, his **Neutral:** it, its	they, them, their, theirs

Grammar in Your Writing

Read your draft. Draw an arrow from each personal pronoun to its antecedent. If the agreement is incorrect, fix it using one of the methods above.

Bicycle Braking Blues

Crash! Once again, I found myself flying off my bike and toward the grass. At age eight, crashes were an everyday occurrence, and I reminded myself that it was better to practice braking here by the lawn than to risk another episode like "The Club Hill Clobbering."

> With this hint, Alexander clearly connects his introduction to the central conflict of his story.

It all started when I arrived at my grandparents' house in Galesburg to spend the summer. I made many friends in their neighborhood, but they spent most of their time riding bikes, and I didn't have one. Then, my step-grandmother gave me the almost new, metallic green bike that her grandson had outgrown. I was overjoyed to have a bike. . . . I learned to ride it well enough—what I didn't learn was how to use the brakes. On the flat ground near my grandparents' house, I just let the bike slow down until I could put my feet down.

> Adding this detail helps move the story along—it shows why a bike is so important to Alexander.

One day my babysitter took me for lunch at the club grill. She rode my grandfather's golf cart while I rode my bike. When we had to climb the big hill leading up to the club, I walked my bike alongside the cart. After lunch, I mounted my bike while Erika drove Grandpa's golf cart. As we headed toward home, neither of us gave a thought to . . . the HILL.

> Alexander narrates events in clear sequence.

As we came around the corner of the bike path, I started picking up speed. By the time I realized what was happening, it was too late. "The hill!" I yelled to Erika. "Your brakes! Use your brakes!" she shouted. With the wind rushing in my ears, I could hardly hear her. Looking down the hill, I saw a golf cart was blocking the path. It seemed to be getting bigger and closer by the second. "Well," I thought to myself, "it's now or never." I steered my speeding bike toward the grass alongside the path and jumped off sideways. I leapt off and BAM! The world turned upside down and inside out. The next sound I heard was the grumbling of a golf cart engine. It sounded annoyed about the jumble of parts in its path. The next thing I saw was Erika's face. She was so scared that her face was stiff and pale. I stood up to show Erika that I was fine. The only damage I sustained was some dirt on my jeans, and the bike survived without too many scratches too. Also, my pride was hurt. How can you ride a bike if you can never go down hill? So every day, Erika took me to the hill and we'd go a little further up. That way, I learned to brake on a hill, little by little, rather than getting clobbered again!

> Using this precise noun helps vividly convey the scene to readers.

> Details such as *stiff* and *pale* help readers vividly imagine Erika's expression.

Editing and Proofreading

Review your draft to correct errors in spelling, grammar, and punctuation.

Focus on the Dialogue: As you proofread your story, pay close attention to the correct punctuation of dialogue—the actual words spoken by a character. Use the examples as a guide. All dialogue should be enclosed in quotation marks. A split dialogue is when a quotation is split up with additional information in the middle, such as identifying the speaker.

"She went home," I said.

"Wow!" I yelled. "I love it."

Publishing and Presenting

Consider one of the following ways to share your writing:

Present an oral narrative. Practice telling your story, using notes rather than reading from your draft, until you can deliver it smoothly and naturally. Practice using gestures to emphasize key points. Tell your story to the class.

Make a poster. Arrange photos, artwork, or small souvenirs, along with a neat copy of your narrative, on posterboard to display in class.

Reflecting on Your Writing

Writer's Journal Jot down your answer to this question:

As you wrote, what new insights into your story did you have?

Spiral Review
Earlier in the unit, you learned about **adjectives and adverbs** (p. 78). Check the use of these modifiers in your autobiographical narrative. Review your work to be sure you have used adjectives to describe nouns, and adverbs to describe verbs.

Rubric for Self-Assessment

Find evidence in your writing to address each category. Then, use the rating scale to grade your work.

Criteria	Rating Scale
Purpose/Focus Clearly presents a narrative that develops real experiences and events	*not very .... very* 1 2 3 4
Organization Organizes events clearly and logically; presents a strong conclusion that follows from and reflects on events in the narrative	1 2 3 4
Development of Ideas/Elaboration Establishes a clear context and point of view; effectively uses narrative techniques, such as dialogue, pacing, and description	1 2 3 4
Language Uses precise words, descriptive details, and sensory language to convey experiences and events.	1 2 3 4
Conventions Uses proper grammar, including correct use of pronouns and antecedents	1 2 3 4

SELECTED RESPONSE

I. Reading Literature

Directions: *Read this passage from "The Three Century Woman"
by Richard Peck. Then, answer each question that follows.*

Ⓒ **Common Core
State Standards**

RL.7.2, RL.7.3, RL.7.6;
W.7.10
[For full standards wording,
see the chart in the front of
this book.]

"I guess if you live long enough," my mom said to Aunt Gloria, "you get your
fifteen minutes of fame."

Mom was on the car phone to Aunt Gloria. The minute Mom rolls out of the
garage, she's on her car phone. It's state-of-the-art and better than her car.

We were heading for Whispering Oaks to see my great-grandmother
Breckenridge, who's lived there since I was a little girl. They call it an Elder Care
Facility. Needless to say, I hated going.

The reason for Great-grandmother's fame is that she was born in 1899. Now
it's January 2001. If you're one of those people who claim the new century
begins in 2001, not 2000, even you have to agree that Great-grandmother
Breckenridge has lived in three centuries. This is her claim to fame.

We waited for a light to change along by Northbrook Mall, and I gazed <u>fondly</u>
over at it. Except for the Multiplex, it was closed because of New Year's Day.
I have a severe mall habit. But I'm fourteen, and the mall is a place without
homework. Aunt Gloria's voice filled the car.

"If you take my advice," she told Mom, "you'll keep those Whispering Oaks
people from letting the media in to interview Grandma. Interview her my foot!
Honestly. She doesn't know where she is, let alone how many centuries she's
lived in. The poor old soul. Leave her in peace. She's already got one foot in
the—"

"Gloria, your trouble is you have no sense of history." Mom gunned across
the intersection. "You got a C in history."

"I was sick a lot that year," Aunt Gloria said.

"Sick of history," Mom mumbled.

"I heard that," Aunt Gloria said.

They bickered on, but I tuned them out. Then when we turned in at
Whispering Pines, a sound truck from IBC-TV was blocking the drive.

"Good grief," Mom murmured. "TV."

"I told you," Aunt Gloria said, but Mom switched her off. She parked in a
frozen rut.

"I'll wait in the car," I said. "I have homework."

"Get out of the car," Mom said.

1. **Part A** Which of the following **character traits** best describes Aunt Gloria?

   A. bored   **C.** shy

   B. silly   **D.** concerned

   Part B Which detail from the passage best supports the answer to Part A?

   A. "Aunt Gloria's voice filled the car."

   B. "'I was sick a lot that year,' . . ."

   C. "'The poor old soul. Leave her in peace.'"

   D. "This is her claim to fame."

2. Which sentence from the passage shows the **first-person point of view?**

   A. "They call it an Elder Care Facility."

   B. "Now it's January 2001."

   C. "Needless to say, I hated going."

   D. "The minute mom rolls out of the garage, she's on her car phone."

3. What **conflict** does the narrator in the story face?

   A. She wants to go to the mall, but she has to do homework.

   B. She must visit her great-grandmother at the nursing home, but she hates going.

   C. She tries to tune out her mom and aunt bickering on the phone, but she can't.

   D. She has homework to do, but she forgot it at home.

4. Which of the following details from the passage is not part of the story's **plot?**

   A. "'She doesn't know where she is, let alone how many centuries she has lived in.'"

   B. "It's state-of-the-art and better than her car."

   C. "We were heading for Whispering Oaks to see my great-grandmother Breckenridge, who's lived there since I was a little girl."

   D. "'I guess if you live long enough,' my mom said to Aunt Gloria, 'you get your fifteen minutes of fame.'"

5. Which sentence best conveys a **theme** of the story?

   A. "Then when we turned in at Whispering Pines, a sound truck from IBC-TV was blocking the drive."

   B. "The reason for Great-grandmother's fame is that she was born in 1899."

   C. "Mom was on the car phone to Aunt Gloria."

   D. "'Gloria, your trouble is you have no sense of history.'"

6. Which of the following answer choices is an example of **direct characterization?**

   A. "Mom was on the car phone to Aunt Gloria."

   B. "They bickered on, but I tuned them out."

   C. "'I'll wait in the car.'"

   D. "I have a severe mall habit."

7. **Part A** Which answer choice is the best definition of the underlined word *fondly?*

   A. with affection

   B. tiredly

   C. with disgust

   D. uncaringly

   Part B Which context clue helps you determine the meaning of *fondly?*

   A. "along by Northbrook Mall"

   B. "I gazed"

   C. "it was closed because of New Year's Day"

   D. "I have a severe mall habit."

⏱ Timed Writing

8. In a paragraph, explain how the writer uses **indirect characterization** to describe Mom. Support your ideas with at least three specific examples from the passage.

GO ON

II. Reading Informational Text

Directions: *Read the passage. Then, answer each question that follows.*

Common Core State Standards

RI.7.1, RI.7.5; L.7.1, L.7.2, L.7.2.a
[For full standards wording, see the chart in the front of this book.]

The American Alligator

Appearance

Alligators look like large lizards with thick bodies and tails. They have strong jaws and many sharp teeth. An alligator's eyes stick up above its skull, allowing it to see above the water while its body is beneath the surface. It swims by moving its powerful tail from side to side.

Average Size				
Length when hatched	**Length for adult male**	**Length for adult female**	**Weight for adult male**	**Weight for adult female**
9 inches	11–12 feet	9 feet or less	450–550 pounds	160 pounds

Diet

Alligators are meat-eating reptiles that eat birds, fish, snakes, turtles, frogs, and mammals. Alligators are good hunters, partly because they are not easily seen by their prey. That is because they swim with only their eyes and tough, scaly backs visible above the surface. To an unsuspecting creature, an alligator can look like a dead log floating in the water.

1. If you wanted to write a physical description of an American alligator, in which sections of this encyclopedia entry would you look for information?

   A. Appearance *and* Length When Hatched
   B. Appearance *and* Average Size
   C. Appearance *and* Diet
   D. Average Size *and* Diet

2. What are the subheads in this encyclopedia entry?

   A. The American Alligator *and* Appearance
   B. Appearance *and* Average Size
   C. Appearance *and* Diet
   D. Average Size *and* Diet

3. Which generalization is *not* supported by information in the encyclopedia entry?

   A. Male alligators are bigger than females.
   B. Alligators spend much of their time in the water.
   C. Alligators do not live in the ocean.
   D. Alligators use their sense of sight for hunting.

4. What can you infer from the information in the encyclopedia entry?

   A. Alligators are dangerous.
   B. Alligators are found in the South.
   C. Alligators are easy to train.
   D. Alligators live a long time.

III. Writing and Language Conventions

Directions: *Read the passage. Then, answer each question that follows.*

(1) The Robert Johnson swimming Pool can be a flurry of activity in the summer. (2) Swimming pools have been around for centuries. (3) The squealing children jump repeatedly and excited into the turquoise water. (4) Across the pool is the sound of happy voices engaged in a "Marco Polo" game. (5) Childrens beach balls fly across the pool. (6) You can tell they are all having a great time swimming. (7) When the swimmers finally get out, the scorching pavement burns their feet. (8) Everyone is laughing and running for the towel. (9) Labor Day comes. (10) That unique feeling of summer ends when the lifeguard locks the gate, closing the pool until next year.

1. Which revision to sentence 8 shows correct **pronoun-antecedent agreement**?
   A. Everyone is laughing and running for its towel.
   B. Everyone is laughing and running for their towel.
   C. Everyone is laughing and running for our towel.
   D. Everyone is laughing and running for his or her towel.

2. Which sentence includes at least one **personal pronoun**?
   A. sentence 9
   B. sentence 5
   C. sentence 6
   D. sentence 4

3. Which revision shows the *best* way to correct the use of **adverbs** in sentence 3?
   A. The squealing children jump repeatedly and excitedly into the turquoise water.
   B. The squealing children jump repeated and excitedly into the turquoise water.
   C. The squealing children repeated jump and excited into the turquoise water.
   D. The squealing children jump repeatedly and excited into the turquoise water.

4. What is the correct way to capitalize the **proper nouns** in sentence 1?
   A. The Robert Johnson swimming pool can be a flurry of activity in the Summer.
   B. The Robert Johnson Swimming Pool can be a flurry of activity in the summer.
   C. The Robert Johnson Swimming pool can be a flurry of activity in the summer.
   D. The Robert johnson swimming pool can be a flurry of activity in the summer.

5. What is the correct way to punctuate the **possessive noun** in sentence 5?
   A. Childrens beach ball's fly across the pool.
   B. Childrens' beach ball fly across the pool.
   C. Children's beach balls' fly across the pool.
   D. Children's beach balls fly across the pool.

6. Which answer choice identifies the **adjectives** in sentence 10?
   A. unique, summer
   B. summer, next
   C. unique, next
   D. next, year

CONSTRUCTED RESPONSE

 **Common Core State Standards**

RL.7.1, RL.7.2, RL.7.3, RL.7.6; W.7.7, W.7.8, W.7.9.a; SL.7.5, SL.7.6
[For full standards wording, see the chart in the front of this book.]

Directions: *Follow the instructions to complete the tasks below as required by your teacher.*

As you work on each task, incorporate both general academic vocabulary and literary terms you learned in Parts 1 and 2 of this unit.

Writing

TASK 1 ▶ Literature [RL.7.3; W.7.9.a]

Analyze Conflict and Character

Write an essay in which you analyze how conflict shapes the main characters in two stories from Part 2.

- Choose two stories and briefly summarize a conflict that the main character faces in each story.

- Analyze how the conflict and its resolution affects each main character's beliefs, thoughts, feelings, actions, and reactions. Tell whether or not each character changes or grows as a result of the conflict.

- Provide examples from both texts to support your analysis.

- Use appropriate transitions to clarify the relationships between ideas in your essay.

TASK 2 ▶ Literature [RL.7.6; W.7.9.a]

Analyze Characters' Points of View

Write an essay in which you identify two characters' points of view from a story in Part 2. Analyze how the author develops and contrasts the points of view of these characters.

- Identify two characters with distinct points of view in a story from Part 2. Describe what the characters believe and how they feel. Discuss their motives.

- Analyze how the author develops each character's point of view through narration, dialogue, and action. Include concrete details from the story to develop and support your analysis.

- Then, discuss how the author contrasts the points of view of your chosen characters through their dialogue, actions, and reactions.

- As you revise, check your writing for correct spelling and punctuation.

TASK 3 ▶ Literature [RL.7.1; W.7.9.a]

Evaluate Plot

Write an essay in which you evaluate the plot in one of the stories in Part 2.

Part 1

- Choose a story with a plot that you feel is developed in a particularly effective way.

- Reread the story, taking notes on the plot.

- Evaluate how effectively the parts of the plot work together to move the story forward. Focus on the exposition, rising action and conflict, climax, falling action, and resolution.

Part 2

- Write an essay in which you explain your evaluation of the plot. Cite specific examples of effective narrative techniques such as the use of foreshadowing, descriptive language, or specific details that build tension or suspense.

- Maintain a consistent style and tone in your writing.

Speaking and Listening

TASK 4 Literature [RL.7.2; SL.7.6]

Analyze and Develop Theme

Write a brief narrative in which you develop the theme of a story from Part 2 in a different way. Read your story aloud to a group of classmates.

- Choose a story from Part 2 with a theme that interests you. Note how the author develops the theme over the course of the story.

- Then, write a brief narrative in which you express the same theme in a new way. Consider using characters' words and actions, setting, symbols, or conflict to develop the theme.

- As you write, choose language that expresses your ideas clearly and effectively.

- Read your story aloud to a group of classmates.

TASK 5 Literature [RL.7.3; SL.7.5]

Analyze Conflict Development

Give a presentation in which you use multimedia or visual displays to clarify your analysis of how particular story elements interact to develop the conflict in a story from Part 2.

- Prepare a presentation in which you identify the internal or external conflict faced by the main character in a story of your choice.

- Analyze how particular story elements, such as setting, plot, and other characters, interact to develop the conflict.

- Create a story map, a cause-and-effect chart, a slide show, or another graphic display to visually present the conflict's development.

- Accurately use appropriate vocabulary and content-area words as you present your display to the class.

Research

TASK 6 Literature [RL.7.2; W.7.7, W.7.8]

 ## Does every conflict have a winner?

In Part 2, you have read literature about different types of conflicts. Now you will conduct a short research project on a conflict that is happening in your community or in our country. Use both the literature you have read and your research to help reflect on this unit's Big Question. Review the following guidelines before you begin your research:

- Focus your research on one conflict.
- Gather relevant information from at least two reliable print or digital sources.
- Take careful notes as you conduct your research.
- Cite your sources accurately.

When you have completed your research, write a response to the Big Question. Discuss how your initial ideas about conflict have changed or been reinforced. Support your response with an example from the literature you read and an example from your research.

"Live daringly, boldly, fearlessly. Taste the relish to be found in **competition**—in having put forth the best within you."

—Henry J. Kaiser

PART 3
TEXT SET DEVELOPING INSIGHT

COMPETITION

The selections in this unit all relate to the Big Question: **Does every conflict have a winner?** Conflicts often arise from various competitive situations, ranging from sports to musical performances to academic achievements. The texts that follow offer different perspectives on competition. As you read, consider insights the authors present about the conflicts that can arise as a result of competition.

◄ **CRITICAL VIEWING** Do you think Henry J. Kaiser's quotation relates only to athletic competition, such as the competition between the two fencers in this photo? Explain.

CLOSE READING TOOL

Use the **Close Reading Tool** to practice the strategies you learn in this unit.

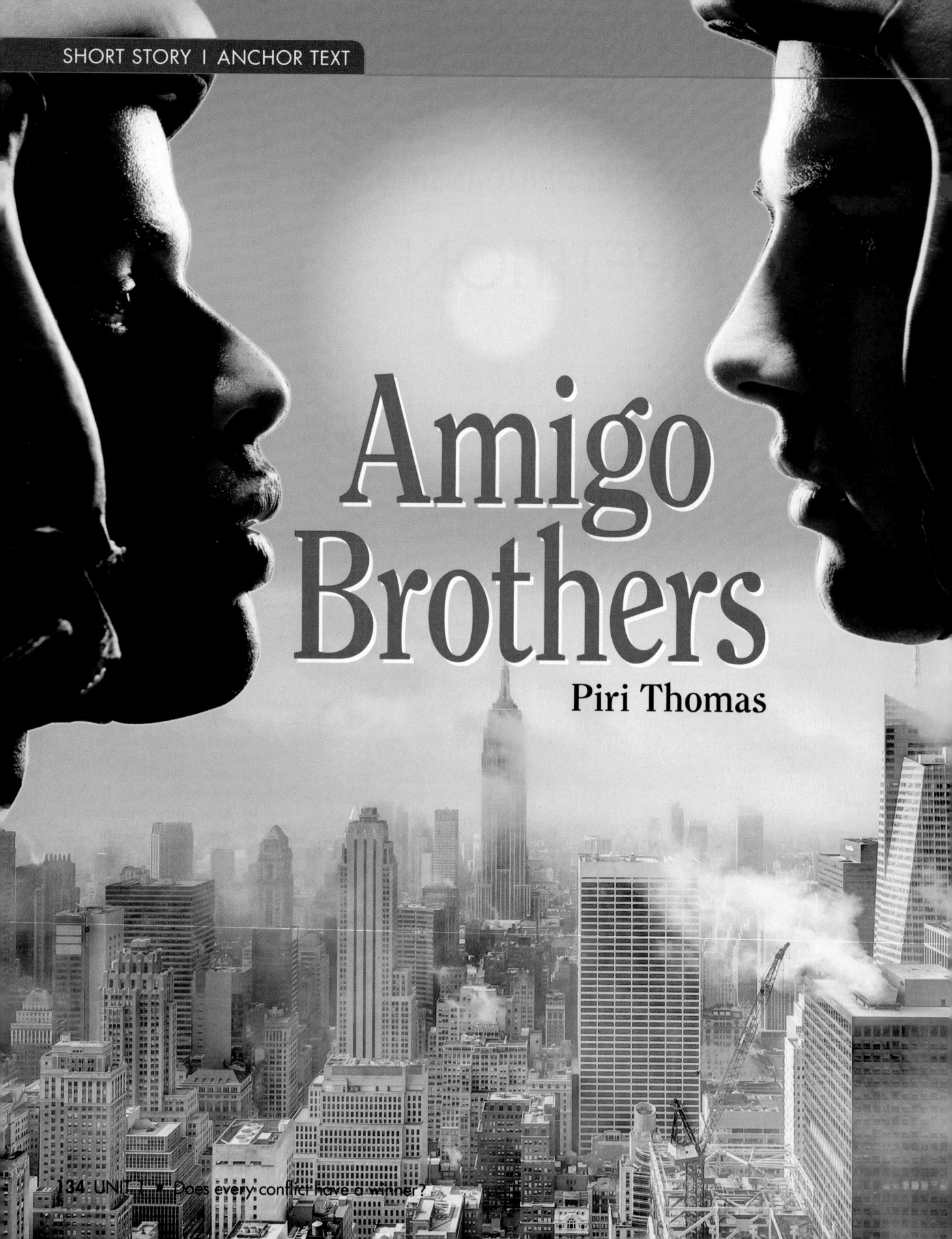

Amigo Brothers

Piri Thomas

Antonio Cruz and Felix Vargas were both seventeen years old. They were so together in friendship that they felt themselves to be brothers. They had known each other since childhood, growing up on the lower east side of Manhattan in the same tenement building on Fifth Street between Avenue A and Avenue B.

Antonio was fair, lean, and lanky, while Felix was dark, short, and husky. Antonio's hair was always falling over his eyes, while Felix wore his black hair in a natural Afro style.

Each youngster had a dream of someday becoming lightweight champion of the world. Every chance they had the boys worked out, sometimes at the Boys Club on 10th Street and Avenue A and sometimes at the pro's gym on 14th Street. Early morning sunrises would find them running along the East River Drive, wrapped in sweat shirts, short towels around their necks, and handkerchiefs Apache style around their foreheads.

While some youngsters were into street negatives, Antonio and Felix slept, ate, rapped, and dreamt positive. Between them, they had a collection of *Fight* magazines second to none, plus a scrapbook filled with torn tickets to every boxing match they had ever attended, and some clippings of their own. If asked a question about any given fighter, they would immediately zip out from their memory banks divisions, weights, records of fights, knock-outs, technical knock-outs, and draws or losses.

Each had fought many bouts representing their community and had won two gold-plated medals plus a silver and bronze medallion. The difference was in their style. Antonio's lean form and long reach made him the better boxer, while Felix's short and muscular frame made him the better slugger. Whenever they had met in the ring for sparring sessions, it had always been hot and heavy.

Now, after a series of elimination bouts, they had been informed that they were to meet each other in the division finals that were scheduled for the seventh of August, two weeks away—the winner to represent the Boys Club in the Golden Gloves Championship Tournament.

The two boys continued to run together along the East River Drive. But even when joking with each other, they both sensed a wall rising between them.

devastating ▶
(dev´ ə stāt´ iŋ) *adj.*
destructive;
overwhelming

One morning less than a week before their bout, they met as usual for their daily work-out. They fooled around with a few jabs at the air, slapped skin, and then took off, running lightly along the dirty East River's edge.

Antonio glanced at Felix who kept his eyes purposely straight ahead, pausing from time to time to do some fancy leg work while throwing one-twos followed by upper cuts to an imaginary jaw. Antonio then beat the air with a barrage of body blows and short **devastating** lefts with an overhand jaw-breaking right. After a mile or so, Felix puffed and said, "Let's stop a while, bro. I think we both got something to say to each other."

Antonio nodded. It was not natural to be acting as though nothing unusual was happening when two ace-boon buddies were going to be blasting each other within a few short days.

They rested their elbows on the railing separating them from the river. Antonio wiped his face with his short towel. The sunrise was now creating day.

Felix leaned heavily on the river's railing and stared across to the shores of Brooklyn. Finally, he broke the silence.

"Man, I don't know how to come out with it."

Antonio helped. "It's about our fight, right?"

"Yeah, right." Felix's eyes squinted at the rising orange sun.

"I've been thinking about it too, *panín*. In fact, since we found out it was going to be me and you, I've been awake at night, pulling punches on you, trying not to hurt you."

"Same here. It ain't natural not to think about the fight. I mean, we both are *cheverote* fighters and we both want to win. But only one of us can win. There ain't no draws in the eliminations."

Felix tapped Antonio gently on the shoulder. "I don't mean to sound like I'm bragging, bro. But I wanna win, fair and square."

Antonio nodded quietly. "Yeah. We both know that in the ring the better man wins. Friend or no friend, brother or no . . ."

Felix finished it for him. "Brother. Tony, let's promise something right here. Okay?"

"If it's fair, *hermano*, I'm for it." Antonio admired the courage of a tugboat pulling a barge five times its welterweight size.

"It's fair, Tony. When we get into the ring, it's gotta be like we never met. We gotta be like two heavy strangers that want the same thing and only one can have it. You understand, don'tcha?"

"Sí, I know." Tony smiled. "No pulling punches. We go all the way."

"Yeah, that's right. Listen, Tony. Don't you think it's a good idea if we don't see each other until the day of the fight? I'm going to stay with my Aunt Lucy in the Bronx. I can use Gleason's Gym for working out. My manager says he got some sparring partners with more or less your style."

Tony scratched his nose pensively. "Yeah, it would be better for our heads." He held out his hand, palm upward. "Deal?"

"Deal." Felix lightly slapped open skin.

"Ready for some more running?" Tony asked lamely.

"Naw, bro. Let's cut it here. You go on. I kinda like to get things together in my head."

"You ain't worried, are you?" Tony asked.

"No way, man." Felix laughed out loud. "I got too much smarts for that. I just think it's cooler if we split right here. After the fight, we can get it together again like nothing ever happened."

The amigo brothers were not ashamed to hug each other tightly.

"Guess you're right. Watch yourself, Felix. I hear there's some pretty heavy dudes up in the Bronx. *Suavecito*, okay?"

"Okay. You watch yourself too, *sabe*?"

Tony jogged away. Felix watched his friend disappear from view, throwing rights and lefts. Both fighters had a lot of psyching up to do before the big fight.

The days in training passed much too slowly. Although they kept out of each other's way, they were aware of each other's progress via the ghetto grapevine.

The evening before the big fight, Tony made his way to the roof of his tenement. In the quiet early dark, he peered over the ledge. Six stories below the lights of the city blinked and the sounds of cars mingled with the curses and the laughter of children in the street. He tried not to think of Felix, feeling he had succeeded in psyching his mind. But only in the ring would he really know. To spare Felix hurt, he would have to knock him out, early and quick.

Up in the South Bronx, Felix decided to take in a movie in an effort to keep Antonio's face away from his fists. The flick was *The Champion* with Kirk Douglas, the third time Felix was seeing it.

The champion was getting hit hard. He was saved only by the sound of the bell.

Felix became the champ and Tony the challenger.

The movie audience was going out of its head. The challenger, confident that he had the championship in the bag, threw a left. The champ countered with a dynamite right.

Felix's right arm felt the shock. Antonio's face, superimposed[1] on the screen, was hit by the awesome blow. Felix saw himself in the ring, blasting Antonio against the ropes. The champ had to be forcibly restrained. The challenger was allowed to crumble slowly to the canvas.

When Felix finally left the theatre, he had figured out how to psyche himself for tomorrow's fight. It was Felix the Champion vs. Antonio the Challenger.

He walked up some dark streets, deserted except for small pockets of wary-looking kids wearing gang colors. Despite the fact that he was Puerto Rican like them, they eyed him as a stranger to their turf. Felix did a fast shuffle, bobbing and weaving, while letting loose a torrent of blows that would demolish whatever got in its way. It seemed to impress the brothers, who went about their own business.

Finding no takers, Felix decided to split to his aunt's. Walking the streets had not relaxed him, neither had the fight flick. All it had done was to stir him up. He let himself quietly into his Aunt Lucy's apartment and went straight to bed, falling into a fitful sleep with sounds of the gong for Round One.

Antonio was passing some heavy time on his rooftop. How would the fight tomorrow affect his relationship with Felix? After all, fighting was like any other profession. Friendship had nothing to do with it. A gnawing doubt crept in. He cut negative thinking real quick by doing some speedy fancy dance steps, bobbing and weaving like mercury.[2] The night air was blurred with **perpetual** motions of left hooks and right crosses. Felix, his *amigo* brother, was not going to be Felix at all in the ring. Just an opponent with another face. Antonio went to sleep, hearing the opening bell for the first round. Like his friend in the South Bronx, he prayed for victory, via a quick clean knock-out in the first round.

Large posters plastered all over the walls of local shops announced the fight between Antonio Cruz and Felix Vargas as the main bout.

The fight had created great interest in the neighborhood. Antonio and Felix were well liked and respected. Each had his own loyal following. Antonio's fans counted on his boxing skills. On the other side, Felix's admirers trusted in his dynamite-packed fists.

Felix had returned to his apartment early in the morning of August 7th and stayed there, hoping to avoid seeing Antonio. He turned the radio on to salsa music sounds and then tried to read while waiting for word from his manager.

perpetual ▶
(pər pech′ oo əl) *adj.*
constant; unending

---

1. **superimposed** (soo′ pər im pōzd′) *adj.* put or stacked on top of something else.
2. **mercury** (mur′ kyoor ē) *n.* the element mercury, also known as quicksilver because it is so quick and fluid.

The fight was scheduled to take place in Tompkins Square Park. It had been decided that the gymnasium of the Boys Club was not large enough to hold all the people who were sure to attend. In Tompkins Square Park, everyone who wanted could view the fight, whether from ringside or window fire escapes or tenement rooftops.

The morning of the fight Tompkins Square was a beehive of activity with numerous workers setting up the ring, the seats, and the guest speakers' stand. The scheduled bouts began shortly after noon and the park had begun filling up even earlier.

The local junior high school across from Tompkins Square Park served as the dressing room for all the fighters. Each was given a separate classroom with desk tops, covered with mats, serving as resting tables. Antonio thought he caught a glimpse of Felix waving to him from a room at the far end of the corridor. He waved back just in case it had been him.

The fighters changed from their street clothes into fighting gear. Antonio wore white trunks, black socks, and black shoes. Felix wore sky blue trunks, red socks, and white boxing shoes. Each had dressing gowns to match their fighting trunks with their names neatly stitched on the back.

The loudspeakers blared into the open windows of the school. There were speeches by dignitaries, community leaders, and great boxers of yesteryear. Some were well prepared, some improvised on the spot. They all carried the same message of great pleasure and honor at being part of such a historic event. This great day was in the tradition of champions emerging from the streets of the lower east side.

Interwoven with the speeches were the sounds of the other boxing events. After the sixth bout, Felix was much relieved when his trainer Charlie said, "Time change. Quick knock-out. This is it. We're on."

Waiting time was over. Felix was escorted from the classroom by a dozen fans in white T-shirts with the word FELIX across their fronts.

Antonio was escorted down a different stairwell and guided through a roped-off path.

As the two climbed into the ring, the crowd exploded with a roar. Antonio and Felix both bowed gracefully and then raised their arms in acknowledgment.

Antonio tried to be cool, but even as the roar was in its first birth, he turned slowly to meet Felix's eyes looking directly into his. Felix nodded his head and Antonio responded. And both as one, just as quickly, turned away to face his own corner.

Bong—bong—bong. The roar turned to stillness.

"Ladies and Gentlemen. *Señores y Señoras.*"

The announcer spoke slowly, pleased at his bilingual efforts.

"Now the moment we have all been waiting for—the main event between two fine young Puerto Rican fighters, products of our lower east side. In this corner, weighing 134 pounds, Felix Vargas. And in this corner, weighing 133 pounds, Antonio Cruz. The winner will represent the Boys Club in the tournament of champions, the Golden Gloves. There will be no draw. May the best man win."

The cheering of the crowd shook the window panes of the old buildings surrounding Tompkins Square Park. At the center of the ring, the referee was giving instructions to the youngsters.

"Keep your punches up. No low blows. No punching on the back of the head. Keep your heads up. Understand. Let's have a clean fight. Now shake hands and come out fighting."

Both youngsters touched gloves and nodded. They turned and danced quickly to their corners. Their head towels and dressing gowns were lifted neatly from their shoulders by their trainers' nimble fingers. Antonio crossed himself. Felix did the same.

BONG! BONG! ROUND ONE. Felix and Antonio turned and faced each other squarely in a fighting pose. Felix wasted no time. He came in fast, head low, half hunched toward his right shoulder, and lashed out with a straight left. He missed a right cross as Antonio slipped the punch and countered with one-two-three lefts that snapped Felix's head back, sending a mild shock coursing through him. If Felix had any small doubt about their friendship affecting their fight, it was being neatly dispelled.

Antonio danced, a joy to behold. His left hand was like a piston pumping jabs one right after another with seeming ease. Felix bobbed and weaved and never stopped boring in. He knew that at long range he was at a disadvantage. Antonio had too much reach on him. Only by coming in close could Felix hope to achieve the dreamed-of knockout.

Antonio knew the dynamite that was stored in his *amigo* brother's fist. He ducked a short right and missed a left hook. Felix trapped him against the ropes just long enough to pour some punishing rights and lefts to Antonio's hard midsection. Antonio slipped away from Felix, crashing two lefts to his head, which set Felix's right ear to ringing.

Bong! Both *amigos* froze a punch well on its way, sending up a roar of approval for good sportsmanship.

Felix walked briskly back to his corner. His right ear had not stopped ringing. Antonio gracefully danced his way toward his stool none the worse, except for glowing glove burns, showing angry red against the whiteness of his midribs.

"Watch that right, Tony." His trainer talked into his ear. "Remember Felix always goes to the body. He'll want you to drop your hands for his overhand left or right. Got it?"

Antonio nodded, spraying water out between his teeth. He felt better as his sore midsection was being firmly rubbed.

Felix's corner was also busy.

"You gotta get in there, fella." Felix's trainer poured water over his curly Afro locks. "Get in there or he's gonna chop you up from way back."

Bong! Bong! Round two. Felix was off his stool and rushed Antonio like a bull, sending a hard right to his head. Beads of water exploded from Antonio's long hair.

Antonio, hurt, sent back a blurring barrage of lefts and rights that only meant pain to Felix, who returned with a short left to the head followed by a looping right to the body. Antonio countered with his own flurry, forcing Felix to give ground. But not for long.

Felix bobbed and weaved, bobbed and weaved, occasionally punching his two gloves together.

Antonio waited for the rush that was sure to come. Felix closed in and feinted[3] with his left shoulder and threw his right instead. Lights suddenly exploded inside Felix's head as Antonio slipped the blow and hit him with a pistonlike left catching him flush on the point of his chin.

Bedlam[4] broke loose as Felix's legs momentarily buckled. He fought off a series of rights and lefts and came back with a strong right that taught Antonio respect.

Antonio danced in carefully. He knew Felix had the habit of playing possum when hurt, to sucker an opponent within reach of the powerful bombs he carried in each fist.

A right to the head slowed Antonio's pretty dancing. He answered with his own left at Felix's right eye that began puffing up within three seconds.

Antonio, a bit too eager, moved in too close and Felix had him entangled into a rip-roaring, punching toe-to-toe slugfest that brought the whole Tompkins Square Park screaming to its feet.

---

3. feinted (fānt′ əd) *v.* pretended to make a blow.
4. Bedlam (bed′ ləm) *n.* condition of noise and confusion.

Rights to the body. Lefts to the head. Neither fighter was giving an inch. Suddenly a short right caught Antonio squarely on the chin. His long legs turned to jelly and his arms flailed out desperately. Felix, grunting like a bull, threw wild punches from every direction. Antonio, groggy, bobbed and weaved, **evading** most of the blows. Suddenly his head cleared. His left flashed out hard and straight catching Felix on the bridge of his nose.

Felix lashed back with a haymaker,[5] right off the ghetto streets. At the same instant, his eye caught another left hook from Antonio. Felix swung out trying to clear the pain. Only the frenzied screaming of those along ringside let him know that he had dropped Antonio. Fighting off the growing haze, Antonio struggled to his feet, got up, ducked, and threw a smashing right that dropped Felix flat on his back.

Felix got up as fast as he could in his own corner, groggy but still game. He didn't even hear the count. In a fog, he heard the roaring of the crowd, who seemed to have gone insane. His head cleared to hear the bell sound at the end of the round. He was very glad. His trainer sat him down on the stool.

In his corner, Antonio was doing what all fighters do when they are hurt. They sit and smile at everyone.

The referee signaled the ring doctor to check the fighters out. He did so and then gave his okay. The cold water sponges brought clarity to both *amigo* brothers. They were rubbed until their circulation ran free.

Bong! Round three—the final round. Up to now it had been tic-tac-toe, pretty much even. But everyone knew there could be no draw and this round would decide the winner.

This time, to Felix's surprise, it was Antonio who came out fast, charging across the ring. Felix braced himself but couldn't ward off the barrage of punches. Antonio drove Felix hard against the ropes.

The crowd ate it up. Thus far the two had fought with *mucho corazón*. Felix tapped his gloves and commenced his attack anew. Antonio, throwing boxer's caution to the winds, jumped in to meet him.

Both pounded away. Neither gave an inch and neither fell to the canvas. Felix's left eye was tightly closed. Claret red blood poured from Antonio's nose. They fought toe-to-toe.

The sounds of their blows were loud in contrast to the silence of a crowd gone completely mute. The referee was stunned by their savagery.

---

5. **haymaker** punch thrown with full force.

Bong! Bong! Bong! The bell sounded over and over again. Felix and Antonio were past hearing. Their blows continued to pound on each other like hailstones.

Finally the referee and the two trainers pried Felix and Antonio apart. Cold water was poured over them to bring them back to their senses.

They looked around and then rushed toward each other. A cry of alarm surged through Tompkins Square Park. Was this a fight to the death instead of a boxing match?

The fear soon gave way to wave upon wave of cheering as the two *amigos* embraced.

No matter what the decision, they knew they would always be champions to each other.

BONG! BONG! BONG! "Ladies and Gentlemen. *Señores* and *Señoras*. The winner and representative to the Golden Gloves Tournament of Champions is . . ."

The announcer turned to point to the winner and found himself alone. Arm in arm the champions had already left the ring.

ABOUT THE AUTHOR

Piri Thomas (1928–2011)

Growing up on the streets of New York City's Spanish Harlem, Piri Thomas faced tough challenges like poverty, gangs, and racism. He later related those struggles in his best-selling auto-biographical novel, *Down These Mean Streets*. The book introduced many non-Hispanics to the world of *el barrio*—"the neighborhood."

When he was young, Thomas tried to avoid the difficult world around him by surrounding himself with books. "My one island of refuge in *el barrio* was the public library," Thomas has recalled. "I gorged myself on books. . . . Reading helped me to realize that there was a world out there far vaster than the narrow confines of *el barrio*."

Close Reading Activities

READ

Comprehension

Reread all or part of the text to help you answer the following questions.

1. What dream do Antonio and Felix share?

2. What deal do Antonio and Felix make?

3. What do Antonio and Felix do during their time apart?

4. Why are so many people in the neighborhood interested in the fight?

5. Who wins the fight? Explain.

Language Study

Selection Vocabulary The following passages are from the story. Identify synonyms for each boldfaced word. Then, use each word in a sentence.

- Antonio then beat the air with … short **devastating** lefts. . . .
- The night air was blurred with **perpetual** motions of left hooks and right crosses.
- Antonio, groggy, bobbed and weaved, **evading** most of the blows.

Diction and Style Study this sentence from the story and answer the questions that follow.

> If asked a question about any given fighter, they would immediately zip out from their memory banks divisions, weights, records of fights, knock-outs, technical knock-outs, and draws or losses.

1. (a) Use context to define *zip*. **(b)** Why does the author use *zip* instead of a synonym?

2. (a) To what does the term *memory banks* refer? **(b)** What is the connotation, or connected image or emotion, of the phrase in context?

Research: Clarify Details Choose at least one detail in this story that is unfamiliar to you and briefly research it. Explain how your research sheds light on an aspect of the story.

Summarize Write an objective summary of the story. Remember that an objective summary is free from opinion and evaluation.

Conventions Read this passage from the story. Identify the proper nouns in the passage. Explain what effect their use adds to the story.

> Up in the South Bronx, Felix decided to take in a movie in an effort to keep Antonio's face away from his fists. The flick was *The Champion* with Kirk Douglas, the third time Felix was seeing it.

Academic Vocabulary

The following academic vocabulary words appear in blue in the questions on the facing page.

effective   **literally**   **communication**

Categorize the words. Decide whether you know each one well, a little, or not at all. Look up definitions of the words you are unsure of or do not know.

Literary Analysis

Reread the passages and answer the questions:

Focus Passage 1 *(p. 136)*

Antonio helped. "It's about our fight, right?" … We go all the way."

Focus Passage 2 *(p. 141)*

Antonio waited for the rush … screaming to its feet.

Key Ideas and Details

1. (a) What does Felix want to discuss with Antonio? **(b)** How does Antonio respond? **(c)** What understanding do the boys reach?

Craft and Structure

2. (a) Interpret: Why does the author choose to use Spanish words in passages of dialogue? **(b) Evaluate:** Would the story be as **effective** without the use of Spanish? Explain.

3. (a) What does Antonio mean, **literally** and figuratively, by "not pulling punches"? **(b) Interpret:** In what way is this whole passage about "not pulling punches"?

Integration of Knowledge and Ideas

4. (a) Compare: How are the boys alike in their worries, their **communication,** and their hopes? **(b) Synthesize:** In what way might the boys' similarities lead to fierce competition?

Key Ideas and Details

1. (a) What is happening in this passage? **(b)** What details bring these events to life?

Craft and Structure

2. (a) From what point of view is this sequence narrated? **(b) Evaluate:** How does this point of view affect reader sympathies?

3. Analyze: The fight is described as a "rip-roaring, punching, toe-to-toe slugfest." In what way does the author's word choice enhance the pacing and suspense of the passage? Cite details to support your response.

Integration of Knowledge and Ideas

4. (a) Analyze: How does this characterization, or description, of the friends differ from the beginning of the story? **(b) Evaluate:** What does this change indicate about the nature of competition?

Conflict

A conflict is a struggle between opposing forces. An **internal conflict** takes place within a character's mind. In an **external conflict,** a character struggles against some outside force, such as another person. Reread the story, taking notes on conflict.

1. (a) What external conflict do the boys face? **(b)** What internal conflict do they face? **(c)** In what ways are the two conflicts similar and different?

2. Competition How does the author develop the idea of competition and cooperation? Cite details from the story in your answer.

 **Common Core State Standards**

RL.7.1, RL.7.2, RL.7.3, RL.7.4, RL.7.6; L.7.4.a, L.7.5.a, L.7.5.b, L.7.5.c, L.7.6
[For full standards wording, see the chart in the front of this book.]

DISCUSS

From Text to Topic **Group Discussion**

Discuss the following passage with a group of classmates. Take notes. Contribute your own ideas, and support them with examples from the text.

> "Ladies and Gentlemen. *Señores* and *Señoras*. The winner and representative to the Golden Glove Tournament of Champions is..." The announcer turned to point to the winner and found himself alone. Arm in arm, the champions had already left the ring.

QUESTIONS FOR DISCUSSION

1. Why does the story not name the winner?
2. What makes both boys "champions"?
3. What insight about competition does this story reveal?

WRITE

Writing to Sources **Explanatory Text**

Assignment

Write an **analytical essay** in which you identify a theme of "Amigo Brothers" and explore its development.

Prewriting and Planning Reread the story, noting details that describe the two friends and the conflicts they face. Analyze the story's title for clues to theme, and look for ways in which the characters' words and actions reveal growth. Then, formulate a statement about the theme, or insight about life revealed in the story.

Drafting Begin your draft by introducing your overall analysis of theme. Then, support your analysis by describing ways in which the story's title, plot, and characters' actions reveal theme. Support your ideas by citing specific textual evidence. Conclude your essay by summarizing your findings.

Revising Review your draft and rearrange details, where necessary, to strengthen your argument. Use transitions to help readers make connections between your ideas. Add supporting details where needed, and delete details that detract from your main points.

Editing and Proofreading Review your word choice, and replace informal or imprecise words with more formal, specific words. Take note of your use of pronouns to be sure that each is used correctly and has a clear antecedent. Proofread carefully to ensure your writing is free from errors in spelling and grammar.

CONVENTIONS

Check the pronouns in your essay to ensure they agree in number with their subjects.

RESEARCH

Research **Investigate the Topic**

Healthy and Unhealthy Competition Although Felix and Antonio fight hard, many readers may view their competition as a healthy one. However, not all competitions are viewed this way.

> ### Assignment
>
> Conduct research to find a variety of opinions on competition. Use the Internet, library databases, and the library catalog. Take notes by paraphrasing and summarizing ideas, and be sure your notes include your sources. Share your findings in a **visual presentation** for the class.

Formulate a Plan Before you begin, create a research plan. Jot down specific questions that will guide your exploration.

Gather Sources Once you have completed a research plan, consult a variety of credible sources. For example, you may use library databases to locate journal or magazine articles. Use the Internet to find up-to-date information from a variety of experts on competition.

Take Notes Take notes on each source. Jot down what each source says about competition—healthy or unhealthy, positive or negative. Use an organized note-taking strategy:

- Make a source card or spreadsheet column for each source. Number each source 1, 2, 3, and so on.

- As you create each notecard, put the number of the source in the corner of the card or enter the note into the appropriate spreadsheet column.

- Remember to take notes using your own words, and clearly identify direct quotations.

Synthesize Multiple Sources Pull together your findings by creating a poster. Draw a line horizontally across a large sheet of poster board. Label the ends *Negative* and *Positive*. Draw points on the line to show the relative attitudes of your different sources toward competition. Briefly label the source's stance, or attitude, above each point and identify the source below.

Present Ideas When your poster is complete, display it and present the ideas from negative to positive, expanding on what the labels show. Then, sum up for the class what your diagram reveals about attitudes toward competition.

PREPARATION FOR ESSAY

You may use the knowledge you gain during this research assignment to support your claims in an essay you will write at the end of this section.

Common Core State Standards

RL.7.2; W.7.2, W.7.2.c, W.7.5, W.7.7, W.7.8, W.7.9, W.7.9.a; SL.7.1, SL.7.4, SL.7.5; L.7.1, L.7.2, L.7.3.a
[For full standards wording, see the chart in the front of this book.]

Get More From Competition

Christopher Funk

Whether you are in sports or business, whether you compete for fun or profit, there are hidden strategies both to boost your performance and find more enjoyment in the process. Here are five such strategies.

First, to maximize your likelihood of winning (whether a game or a contract), forget about winning!

The more that you think about the outcome, the more mental focus is drained away from the process of getting there. To do your best, all your mental energy needs to be concentrated in the present. If you stay focused on the immediate demands that are right in front of you, winning will take care of itself. A bit cliché, but true.

Second, think of the contest as an opportunity to stretch yourself. Focus on how you can gain.

This is particularly valuable when you can think of how you can benefit, even if you end up losing. Perhaps you can gain new insights that will help you compete better the next time around. The attitude that "nothing is gained in a losing effort" not only robs you of potential gains, but makes losing more likely.

Third, find the middle ground between stress and relaxation. You cannot "force" optimal performance by putting yourself under increased pressure.

Performance **deteriorates** under high stress. On the other hand, you need a certain amount of stress to shift your mind and body into full gear. So if you tend to be rather lax, fire yourself up. Kick yourself in the pants. Tell yourself that it really does matter and that you must do well. But if you tend to get too serious or worried, take the opposite approach. Bring a dimension of play to your competing. Even when the consequences are important (in fact, especially when they are very important), relax and have some fun. People handle serious situations best when they lighten up. Take this strategy and you'll enjoy yourself more, and you'll perform better.

maximize ▶
(mak´sə mīz´) *v.*
make the most of

optimal ▶
(äp´tə məl) *adj.* best or most favorable; optimum

deteriorates ▶
(dē tir´ē ə rāts) *v.*
gets worse

Fourth, think of your opponent as your partner. To do your best, you need the opponent to push you. You gain the most when you have tough competitors. Good competition comes about when all competitors are doing well. So appreciate your opponents; without them, you would not be able to reach the same heights of performance. While you want to defeat your opponents, opponents are not enemies.

Fifth, compete with a sense of deep purpose. If you are simply competing to gain personal benefit (whether material benefit or ego), you are going to perform less well than if you are dedicated to values, goals, and ideals that are beyond yourself. So know what is important to you and find your center of gravity beyond yourself. . . . Find your mission and you'll perform at your peak. Just as important, you'll have an enduring sense of satisfaction.

READ

Comprehension

Reread all or part of the text to help you answer these questions.

1. What is the purpose of this article?

2. On what does the author advise readers to focus?

3. According to the author, what is better than competing for personal gain?

Research: Clarify Details Choose one unfamiliar detail in this article to research. Then, explain how your research sheds light on the article.

Summarize Write an objective summary of the article. Remember to leave out opinions and judgements.

Language Study

Selection Vocabulary The following sentences appear in the selection. Define each boldfaced word, and then use the word in a sentence of your own.

• First, to **maximize** your likelihood of winning

(whether a game or a contract), forget about winning!

• You cannot "force" **optimal** performance by putting yourself under increased pressure.

• Performance **deteriorates** under high stress.

Literary Analysis

Reread to answer the questions.

> **Focus Passage** *(p. 148)*
> Performance deteriorates … and you'll perform better.

Key Ideas and Details

1. (a) According to the author, what should you do if you are too relaxed? What should you do if you are too worried? **(b)** What is the benefit of having the right **attitude**?

Craft and Structure

2. The author uses repetition and parallel structures: "Kick yourself...," and "Tell

yourself..." **Analyze:** Explain the effect of these language choices on readers.

3. (a) Is the author's tone in this passage formal or informal? **(b) Analyze:** What is the overall effect of the author's tone?

Integration of Knowledge and Ideas

4. (a) What is the author's overall advice on the challenge of competing? **(b) Evaluate:** Does the author provide **sufficient** support for his main points? Cite details from the text in your response.

Structure

Structure refers to the organization of a text. Elements that contribute to a text's structure include formatting and the order in which ideas are presented.

1. What is the relationship between the boldfaced headings and the text that follows?

2. How does the structure of this article contribute to its effectiveness?

DISCUSS • RESEARCH • WRITE

From Text to Topic **Partner Discussion**

Discuss the following passage with a partner. Contribute your own ideas, and support them with examples from the text.

> So know what is important to you and find your center of gravity beyond yourself.... Find your mission and you'll perform at your peak. Just as important, you'll have an enduring sense of satisfaction.

Research **Investigate the Topic**

Mind and Body The mind-body connection is a big topic in sports. It may be that some sports are best played by "mind first" athletes, while others are best played by "body first" athletes.

Assignment

Conduct research to define the mind-body connection. Then define and cite examples of athletes who might be considered "mind first" or "body first." Consult Web sites or magazine articles. Take clear notes and identify your sources so that you can easily access the information later. Share your findings in an **informal speech** to the class. Draw a conclusion about which athletes tend to be stronger competitors—those who are "mind first" or those who are "body first."

Writing to Sources **Narrative**

Funk's article gives some specific recommendations for success.

Assignment

Write a **fictional narrative** in which a character follows some or all of Funk's advice. Make sure your story has a **resolution,** which may or may not include winning a contest. Follow these steps:

- Introduce characters, setting, and conflict in the exposition.
- Create a smooth progression of plot events that build on one another and lead to a climax.
- Use dialogue and description to develop the character and events.
- Bring events to a satisfying conclusion in the story's resolution.

QUESTIONS FOR DISCUSSION

1. What does Funk mean by "center of gravity beyond yourself"?

2. For Funk, what is more important in competition, the mind or the body? Explain.

PREPARATION FOR ESSAY

You may use the results of your research to support your claims in an essay you will write at the end of this section.

ACADEMIC VOCABULARY

Academic terms appear in blue on these pages. If these words are not familiar to you, use a dictionary to find their definitions. Then, use the words as you speak and write about the text.

 **Common Core State Standards**

RI.7.2, RI.7.4, RI.7.5, RI.7.8; W.7.3, W.7.3.b, W.7.3.c, W.7.7; SL.7.1, SL.7.1.a; L.7.4.a, L.7.6
[For full standards wording, see the chart in the front of this book.]

Forget Fun, Embrace Enjoyment

Adam Naylor, EdD

After years of sitting and listening to competitive coaches, I am struck by their relationship with fun. They will talk at length about offense, defense, discipline, and effort … and a bit after the fact say, "and yeah, it needs to be fun." Sometimes a shrug of the shoulder accompanies this afterthought. Ultimately, a rather unconvincing **advocacy** for fun. Coaches get regularly called to task by more politically correct sects[1] for being out of touch and borderline abusive … and sometimes rightfully so. Yet, not in this case, the shrug and "well sure I guess it's important," approach to fun is onto something.

There is a problem with fun. It is the wrong word that creates the wrong idea … especially at more adult levels of competition (teenage years on). Words matter. They create cognitive schemas[2] and shape behaviors. Fun is the right idea, but the wrong mental message.

Fun sends a message of **trivialness** and purposeless living. Fun, in the pleasurable sense, is hedonistic.[3] This is why

advocacy ▶
(ad´və kə sē) *n.* support for a particular idea or mission

trivialness ▶
(triv´ē əl nes) *n.* state of having little importance

---

1. **more politically correct sects** groups that focus more on ways in which certain ideas or practice might be unjust or give offense to certain groups.
2. **cognitive schemas** (skē´məz) *n.* mental networks of ideas, beliefs, knowledge, and associations.
3. **hedonistic** (hē də nis´ tik) *adj.* pleasure loving.

it does not seem to sit right with many people who are engaged in competitive sport. Fun is a lazy tropical vacation, not an early morning row on the river. Fun is dinner with friends and a movie, not racing around a soccer pitch on a rainy afternoon. The word "fun" occupies space in many minds that does not fit the emotion of striving on the playing field.

So abandon the idea altogether? Certainly not. Refine thinking and reword things a bit.

At the foundation of play is "enjoyment." An activity that engages interest and challenges the individual appropriately. Mihaly Csikszentmihalyi, father of Flow,[4] articulates this concept so well: "[competitive sport] that stretches one's ability is enjoyable"; "after an enjoyable event, we know that we have changed"; "enjoyment happens only as a result of unusual investments of attention" (Csikszentmihalyi and Csikszentmihalyi, 1998). Enjoyment involves effort, both mental and physical. It does not occur during trivial **endeavors,** but rather as part of a purpose driven life. Effortful and purpose driven … sounds like sports.

Sports at all levels ought to be enjoyable. This comes from embracing the many challenges of competition. It also comes from abandoning the juvenile concept of fun. The youngest athletes get enjoyment—they experiment with new techniques, they dare opponents to strike them out, they relish the brisk fall afternoons of play, and they strive with healthy grimaces on their faces. To a casual observer, it would look like they are having fun … sure maybe, but truly they have mastered the enjoyment necessary for success at all stages and ages of sport.

◄ **endeavors**
(en dev´ərz) *n.*
attempts; efforts

---

4. **Flow** (flō) *n.* a mental state defined by psychologist Mihaly Csikszentmihalyi of being completely absorbed in what you are doing.

ABOUT THE AUTHOR

Adam Naylor (b. 1974)

A professor at Boston University, Adam Naylor does not just teach college students. He has also educated Olympic medalists, US Open players, and Stanley Cup champions by using sports psychology as a means to inner and outer success. On the subject of competition, Naylor says that the "hard stuff"—things like diving for the goal and running at full tilt through the finish line—is most meaningful. He adds that "the black and white stuff on the scoreboard or stat sheet" just does not compare.

Close Reading Activities

READ

Comprehension

Reread the text as needed to answer these questions.

1. What is the topic of this article?
2. What main point does the author make about the topic?

Language Study

Selection Vocabulary Create a word map for each boldfaced word from the selection. Then, use each word in a sentence of your own.

• . . . a rather unconvincing **advocacy** for fun.

Literary Analysis

Reread the passage and answer the following questions.

> **Focus Passage** (pp. 152–153)
> Funs sends a message … striving on the playing field.

Key Ideas and Details

1. (a) According to Naylor, what message does the word *fun* send? (b) How do some athletes **perceive** the word *fun*?

Craft and Structure

2. (a) How does the author use repetition in

Persuasive Techniques

A **persuasive technique** is a strategy an author uses to persuade readers. Two common persuasive techniques are the use of **loaded language**—or highly-charged emotional words—and the use of **expert opinions**.

1. (a) What do *hedonistic* and *striving* mean?

Research: Clarify Details Research at least one unfamiliar detail in this article. Explain how your research clarified your understanding.

Summarize Write an objective summary of the text to confirm your comprehension.

• Fun sends a message of **trivialness** and purposeless living.
• It does not occur during trivial **endeavors**....

this paragraph? (b) **Evaluate:** What is the effect of this repetition?

3. (a) What descriptive examples does Naylor use in this paragraph? (b) **Draw Conclusions:** What message about fun does Naylor convey through these examples?

Integration of Knowledge and Ideas

4. (a) **Generalize:** What is the author's claim, or main argument? (b) **Evaluate: Explain** how elements of word choice and style help support the claim.

(b) How does this loaded language create a contrast?

2. Why does the author **cite** the testimony of Csikszentmihalyi?

3. **Competition** For the author, is competition "fun" or "enjoyment"? Explain how persuasive techniques contrast the two ideas.

DISCUSS • RESEARCH • WRITE

From Text to Topic **Debate**

With a partner, informally debate the ideas in the following passage. Support your ideas with details from the text as well as examples drawn from real life.

> Words matter. They create cognitive schemas and shape behaviors. Fun is the right idea, but the wrong mental message.

Research **Investigate the Topic**

Coaching and Competition Adam Naylor begins his argument by mentioning athletic coaches' attitude toward fun.

Assignment

Conduct research to find out how professional coaches regard the notion of fun in competitive sports. Use a library database to find journal articles about the topic, or use a variety of online sources to find web articles and media clips. Take clear notes and carefully identify your sources so that you can easily access the information later. Record your findings in an **annotated listing**.

Writing to Sources **Argument**

In the article, Naylor makes the claim that even young athletes know how to get enjoyment from competition.

Assignment

Write an **argument** in which you agree or disagree with Naylor about young athletes and competition. Follow these steps as you write your argument:

- State your claim telling whether you agree or disagree with Naylor.
- In the body of your essay, state your reasons, supporting them with examples from the text and from your own research.
- Organize your details logically, using transitions to connect your ideas.
- Use a formal style.
- Sum up your argument in a concluding paragraph or section.

QUESTIONS FOR DISCUSSION

1. In contrast to *fun*, what ideas does the word *enjoyment* inspire?

2. Can words really shape behavior by making a difference in how and why we compete? Cite evidence from the text in your discussion.

PREPARATION FOR ESSAY

You may use the results of your research to support your ideas in the essay you will write at the end of this section.

ACADEMIC VOCABULARY

Academic terms appear in blue on these pages. Use the words as you speak and write about the text.

 **Common Core State Standards**

RI.7.1, RI.7.2, RI.7.3, RI.7.4, RI.7.8; W.7.1.a–e, W.7.7, W.7.8; SL.7.1, SL.7.1.a; L.7.4.a, L.7.6
[For full standards wording, see the chart in the front of this book.]

Video Game Competitiveness, Not Violence, Spurs Aggression, Study Suggests

Jennifer LaRue Huget

aggressive ▶
(ə gresˊiv) *adj.*
forceful, especially
in a destructive
or mean way

spur ▶
(spur) *v.* cause

For years, researchers having been trying to tease out the relationship between video game violence and **aggressive** behavior on the part of people who play such games. So far, it's seemed that violence in video games may **spur** aggression in players, at least in the first few minutes after the game is played.

A study published Aug. 17 in the American Psychological Association journal "Psychology of Violence" adds the useful insight that it might not be the games' violent content itself that sparks aggression but instead their level of competitiveness.

In a series of small experiments involving college undergraduates, researchers had participants play one of two games that were equally matched for competitiveness, difficulty and pace of action. One of the games had been determined to be substantially more violent than the other. When the games ended, participants took part in a second task they thought to be unrelated to the game-playing experiment (which they had been told was about eye movement, not aggressive behavior): They were asked to prepare a hot-sauce mixture for a taster who they knew had reported a dislike for hot and spicy food. Those who played the violent video game were no more likely to create a large quantity of spicy food—an act that has been established in the realm of psychological research as an aggressive act—than those who played the nonviolent game.

But in a second experiment, games were selected on the basis of how competitive they were. After the game playing, participants again took part in the "hot sauce paradigm"[1] portion of the research. Those whose games had been determined to be more competitive were far more likely to create large quantities of very spicy sauce for their poor tasters. They also had significantly higher heart rates.

The authors point out that many violent video games also tend to be extremely competitive. So separating out the effect of the level of competitiveness could open new channels for both understanding the link between video games and aggressive behavior and also, perhaps, figuring out how to **blunt** that effect.

blunt ▶
(blunt) *v.* lessen;
make less forceful

---

1. paradigm (parˊə dīmˊ) *n.* approach based on a theory.

READ • WRITE

Comprehension

Reread the text as needed to answer these questions.

1. What does the article say about video games?

2. (a) What happened in the first **experiment**? **(b)** How did the second experiment vary from the first one?

Language Study

Selection Vocabulary Define each boldfaced word from the selection, and use the word in a sentence of your own.

- **aggressive**
- **spur**
- **blunt**

Literary Analysis

Reread the selection to answer the following questions.

Key Ideas and Details

1. (a) In the past, what did researchers believe caused aggressive behavior in people who play violent video games? **(b)** What new information on this topic appeared in the study published in "Psychology of Violence"?

Craft and Structure

2. (a) What word or phrase most clearly shows the relationship between the two experiments in the study? **(b) Draw Conclusions:** What type of relationship does this word convey?

3. Deduce: Why does the author use the words *could* and *perhaps* in the last sentence?

Integration of Knowledge and Ideas

4. (a) What is the main **insight** in this article? **(b) Speculate:** How might video game developers respond to this article? Explain.

Writing to Sources **Informative Text**

This article reports on the relationship between aggression and competition.

> **Assignment**
> Write an **essay** in which you evaluate the author's conclusion. Introduce your main idea, and then support it using details from the text and outside research. Choose precise details to make your ideas clear, and strive to achieve a formal tone.

ACADEMIC VOCABULARY

Academic terms appear in blue on these pages. If these words are not familiar to you, use a dictionary to find their definitions. Then, use the words as you speak and write about the text.

 Common Core State Standards

RI.7.2, RI.7.4; W.7.2, W.7.2.d–e; L.7.4.a, L.7.4.d, L.7.6
[For full standards wording, see the chart in the front of this book.]

Win Some, Lose Some

Charles Osgood

aversion ▶
(ə vʉr´zhən) *n.*
intense dislike

The victor may get the spoils,[1] but the true rewards go to those who are good sports. We all have little victories and defeats in our lives, and some big ones too. Rare is the day that we don't add to both our "Win" and "Loss" columns. Obviously we would like the Ws to outweigh the Ls, but our appetite for victory and our **aversion** to defeat seem to have sharpened in recent years. We don't handle either one very well anymore.

---

1. the victor may get the spoils person who wins not only has the pleasure of winning but gets additional benefits.

The role models we get from the worlds of entertainment, sports and politics have not been terribly helpful. You'd think that these public individuals, who must deal with winning and losing on a regular basis, would set a sportsmanlike example for the rest of us.

Whatever happened to the old gladiator mantra[2] "We who are about to die salute you"? It gets me to thinking about that Joe Raposo song "(Here's to the) Winners." Is it any surprise that he never bothered to write a song called "Here's to the Losers"? (Truth be told, some-one else did.)

It feels wonderful to win, but how should winners express their satisfaction in the moment of victory? How should they comport themselves in the presence of those they've vanquished? As if they had just conquered Nazi Germany or found a cure for cancer? Conversely, how should the losers express their frustration and disappointment in moments of defeat? A sense of perspective is difficult to come by in hard-fought contests.

For their part, today's sports fans haven't come that far from the days of the gladiator. They know that their teams can't win 'em all, but they do want to see the thrill of victory and the agony of defeat acted out. And so the players, who are also players in the theatrical sense, celebrate not only game victories but completely routine plays as well. You'll see some NFL players doing a little dance to taunt the opposition every time they catch a pass or make a tackle. It's a far cry from the days when Tom Landry of the Dallas Cowboys would tell Hollywood Henderson to try to look as if he'd done it before. Landry himself used to stand stoically on the sidelines like a man waiting for a bus. You could not tell from his facial expression or bearing whether his team was ahead or behind.

In the poem "If," his famous litany[3] of what it takes to "be a man, my son," Rudyard Kipling observes, "If you can meet with triumph and disaster,/And treat those two **impostors** just the same...." They are impostors, you know. A musician friend of mine has a sign on his studio wall that reads "Show Me a Good Loser and I'll Show You a Loser!" Do musicians think in terms of winners and losers too? Are they that competitive?

◀ **impostors**
(im päs′tərz) *n.*
people or things pretending to be someone or something else

---

2. **mantra** (man′trə) *n.* statement repeated often, much like or as a chant or song refrain.
3. **litany** (lit′ 'n ē) *n.* list.

Many of them are. For in the arts, as in virtually every kind of human endeavor, there is an element of competition.

There's a story, apocryphal[4] perhaps, about Fritz Kreisler, the virtuoso violinist, sitting in the audience at a Berlin Philharmonic concert next to pianist Josef Hofmann. The twelve-year-old prodigy Jascha Heifetz was performing a solo in Tchaikovsky's Violin Concerto in D Major.

"It's very hot in here, isn't it?" Kreisler is supposed to have whispered to Hofmann between movements.

Without a moment's hesitation, Hofmann is said to have whispered back, "Not for pianists."

Artists may not like to admit it, but in the arts, as in virtually every endeavor, there is an element of competition. It's human nature to want to do better than somebody else. Victory is better than defeat, just as surely as health, wealth and wisdom are better than sickness, poverty and ignorance. With winning comes not only the thrill of victory but also the gold medal, the job, the Oscar, the Nobel, the presidency or the Lombardi Trophy—the prize that goes to the winner of the Super Bowl.

That coveted award is named for Vince Lombardi, the legendary football coach often credited (if "credit" is the appropriate word here) with saying "Winning isn't everything. It's the only thing!" In fact, he never said it. It may have been another coach, UCLA's Red Sanders, who uttered those words.

While he was in college, Lombardi was one of Fordham University's "Seven Blocks of Granite." (Fordham is my alma mater.[5]) After graduation, he taught Latin and chemistry and coached at St. Cecilia High School (also my alma mater) in Englewood, New Jersey. What he said, according to people there who knew him well, was "Winning isn't everything, but wanting to win is."

Later, as a coach for the Green Bay Packers, he pushed his players to work hard. And you bet he wanted to imbue[6] them with a strong desire to win—but not at all costs. That would have been inconsistent with character. And to Lombardi, character was what counted most—on the field and in life.

In the end, we do seem to save our respect for the individuals who show the most character when faced with situations of triumph or loss. We admire

Nobel Peace Prize Medal

---

4. **apocryphal** (ə päk′rə fəl) *adj.* most likely not true but repeated as if true nevertheless.
5. **alma mater** (al′mə mät′ər) school, university, or college that someone attended.
6. **imbue** (im byōō′) *v.* to convey in a way that causes someone or something to become filled with or saturated by what is conveyed.

people like Joe DiMaggio, Jacqueline Kennedy, Billie Jean King, Michael Jordan and Christopher Reeve[7]—a partial list, but you get the idea.

For all of its melodrama and legal wrangling, even our drawn-out presidential election last fall may have taught us some valuable lessons. When he ultimately conceded the contest, Vice-President Gore[8] made a statement that was sportsmanlike and unequivocal. He called on those who had voted for him to join him in supporting President Bush and wishing him well.

At his inauguration a month later, Bush publicly thanked President Clinton for his years of service and acknowledged Gore as a worthy opponent. It was an election campaign "conducted with spirit and ended with grace," Bush said. That was graceful on his part.

I recently took my seventeen-year-old son, Jamie, a high school senior, to the campus of a college to which he was applying on an early decision basis. I waited with other parents as our children went in for their interviews. In most cases, as each one **emerged**, you could tell right away whether the outcome was a W or an L. Some of the kids came running out grinning and with thumbs up. Others came out looking crushed or in tears. A few parents of the latter seemed angry and berated their offspring for not having done well enough. When Jamie came through the door, I caught his eye across the room, and he smiled. I swear there was no way to tell from his face or manner how things had gone. I could not have been more proud.

◀ **emerged**
(ē mʉrjd') v. came out

---

7. **Christopher Reeve** actor who became paralyzed but went on to become a spokesperson for those with spinal cord injuries.
8. **Vice-President Gore** candidate who lost to George W. Bush in the presidential election of 2000.

ABOUT THE AUTHOR

Charles Osgood (b. 1933)

Known for his witty comments and signature bow tie, Charles Osgood has entertained radio listeners and television watchers for decades. Osgood, who writes his own stories, gets up each morning at 2:30 so that he can arrive in the office by 3:30 and get started on the morning news cycle. An economist by training, Osgood says he just fell into radio. He developed his own unique style by adding "little rhymes" to his reports. This habit earned him the title of "poet in residence" and eventually helped lead to jobs in television. In addition to broadcasting, Osgood has appeared on screen as the narrator of Dr. Seuss's *Horton Hears a Who*. He is also the author of six books and the winner of many prizes and awards for journalism.

READ

Comprehension

Reread to answer these questions.

1. How has sportsmanship decreased, according to Osgood?

2. What qualities should both winners and losers have?

3. What did Osgood's son do that made the author proud?

Research: Clarify Details Choose at least one unfamiliar detail in this article, and research it. Then, explain how your research clarifies your understanding of the article.

Summarize Write an objective summary of the article. Do not include your opinions or evaluations.

Language Study

Selection Vocabulary Define each boldfaced word from the text, and then write a synonym for each.

- …our **aversion** to defeat…
- …treat those two **impostors** just the same. …
- As each one **emerged,** you could tell…

Literary Analysis

Reread the focus passage and answer the following questions.

> **Focus Passage** (p. 160)
>
> Artists may not like to admit it… the winner of the Super Bowl.

Key Ideas and Details

1. According to Osgood, what desire is "just human nature"?

Craft and Structure

2. **(a)** What sound devices are present in the phrase "health, wealth, and wisdom"?

What effect is created? **(b) Contrast:** What effect is created by the phrase "sickness, poverty, and ignorance"? **(c) Analyze:** Why do you think Osgood chose these phrases to present his ideas?

3. **(a)** Find examples of hyperbole, or exaggeration, in this passage. **(b) Connect:** In what way does the use of hyperbole help Osgood make his point?

Integration of Knowledge and Ideas

4. **(a) Generalize:** What is the main idea of this passage? **(b) Interpret:** What is the author's **attitude** toward winning?

Rhetorical Devices

A **rhetorical device** is the use of language to persuade or **convince** a reader. Take notes on the author's use of rhetorical devices.

1. **(a)** Cite two examples of *rhetorical questions,* or questions the author uses to make a point. **(b)** What ideas do the implied answers convey?

2. **Competition (a)** Why are the words *winners* and *losers* repeated so often in this article? **(b) Infer:** What larger insight about competition does Osgood convey? Explain.

DISCUSS • RESEARCH • WRITE

From Text to Topic **Panel Discussion**

Discuss the following passage with a group of classmates. Take notes as you listen. When you speak, contribute your own ideas and support them with examples from the text.

> "For their part, today's sports fans haven't come far from the days of the gladiator. They know that their teams can't win 'em all, but they do want to see the thrill of victory and the agony of defeat acted out. And so the players, who are also players in the theatrical sense, celebrate not only game victories but completely routine plays as well."

Research **Investigate the Topic**

A Model of Character Osgood cites examples from Vince Lombardi's life in his arguments.

Assignment

Conduct research to learn more about Lombardi's views on triumph and loss in competition. Find a biography in your library's online database or a good online encyclopedia. Take clear notes and carefully identify your sources so that you can easily access the information later. Share your findings in an **informal presentation** for the class.

Writing to Sources **Argument**

Osgood argues that "true rewards go to those who are good sports."

Assignment

Write an **argument** in which you either agree or disagree with Osgood's claim. Follow these steps:

- State your own claim clearly and introduce opposing claims.
- Support your claims with relevant evidence from the text and from additional research. Refute opposing claims.
- Logically organize your argument, and use transitional words, phrases, and clauses to create cohesion.
- Establish and maintain a formal style through word choice and tone.

QUESTIONS FOR DISCUSSION

1. What comparisons does Osgood make in the passage?

2. What insights about competitive sports does the passage reveal?

PREPARATION FOR ESSAY

You may use the results of your research to support your ideas in the essay you will write at the end of this section.

ACADEMIC VOCABULARY

Academic terms appear in blue on these pages. If these words are unfamiliar, look up their definitions in a dictionary. Then, use the words as you to speak and write about the text.

 **Common Core State Standards**

RI.7.1, RI.7.2, RI.7.4, RI.7.6, RI.7.8; W.7.1.a–d, W.7.7, W.7.9; SL.7.1; L.7.4.a, L.7.5.b, L.7.6
[For full standards wording, see the chart in the front of this book.]

Orlando Magic
Leroy Neiman

READ • DISCUSS • WRITE

Comprehension

Study the painting to answer the following questions.

1. Where does the action in this painting take place?

2. Describe what is happening in the painting.

Critical Analysis

Key Ideas and Details

1. **(a)** Which player is identified by name? **(b) Speculate:** Why might the artist have chosen to identify only one player?

Craft and Structure

2. **(a) Distinguish:** Describe the qualities of the colors the artist uses in this painting. **(b) Analyze:** Which colors draw the eye? **(c) Evaluate:** Why do they do so?

3. **(a) Analyze:** Which images in the painting are in focus? Which images are out of focus? **(b) Evaluate:** What effect does the contrast between clear and blurry images have upon the viewer?

Integration of Knowledge and Ideas

4. **Synthesize:** What ideas about competition does this painting **illustrate**? Explain, using details from the painting to support your response.

From Text to Topic **Debate**

Form teams to **debate** this question: Is this painting mainly about competition, or is it mainly about a specific player? Discuss the painting with your team to prepare.

Writing to Sources **Argument**

Write a brief **argument** in which you compare and contrast the depiction of competition in this painting with the depiction of competition in another nonfiction selection in this section. Explain and support reasons why one of the two selections is a more accurate, meaningful, or exciting way to show competition. As you incorporate specific details from the painting and from the other selection, be sure to use words, phrases, and clauses to clarify the relationships between your ideas.

Common Core State Standards

RI.7.7; W.7.1, W.7.1.c; SL.7.1, SL.7.2
[For full standards wording, see the chart in the front of this book.]

ACADEMIC VOCABULARY

Academic terms appear in blue on these pages. If these words are not familiar to you, use a dictionary to find their definitions. Then, use them as you speak and write about the text.

Speaking and Listening: Group Discussion

Competition and Conflict The texts in this section vary in genre, length, style, and perspective. However, all of the texts explore ideas about competition and conflict. The ways in which we view competition, and the things we gain and lose as we compete, are related to the Big Question addressed in this unit: **Does every conflict have a winner?**

▲ Refer to the selections you read in Part 3 as you complete the activities on this assessment.

Assignment

Conduct discussions. With a small group of classmates, conduct a discussion about the issues of competition and conflict. Refer to the texts in this section, other texts you have read, and your personal experience and knowledge to support your ideas. Begin your discussion by addressing the following questions:

- How does competition create conflict?
- How can our attitudes toward competing change our experiences?
- How do competition and conflict bring out the best and the worst in us?
- How can we compete in positive ways?

Summarize and present your ideas. After you have fully explored the topic, summarize your discussion and present your findings to the class as a whole.

Criteria for Success

✓ **Organizes the group effectively**
Appoint a group leader and a timekeeper. The group leader should present the discussion questions. The timekeeper should make sure the discussion takes no longer than 20 minutes.

✓ **Maintains focus of discussion**
As a group, stay on topic and avoid straying into other subject areas.

✓ **Involves all participants equally and fully**
No one person should monopolize the conversation. Rather, everyone should take turns speaking and contributing ideas.

✓ **Follows the rules for collegial discussion**
As each group member speaks, others should listen carefully. Build on one another's ideas, and support viewpoints and opinions with sound reasoning and evidence. Express disagreement respectfully.

USE NEW VOCABULARY

As you speak and share ideas, work to use the vocabulary words you have learned in this section. The more you use new words, the more you will "own" them.

Writing: **Narrative**

Competition and Conflict We all face conflicts. Some of these conflicts relate to competition in sports, in school, and even in friendships. Often, such conflicts change how we think or behave, in big or little ways.

© **Common Core State Standards**

W.7.3.a–b, W.7.3.d–e; SL.7.1.a–d
[For full standards wording, see the chart in the front of this book.]

Assignment

Write a **personal narrative,** or a true story of events from your life. Begin by introducing a conflict you have experienced that is related to competition. Tell what happened to increase the conflict and describe if and how you resolved it. In your conclusion, reflect on what you learned or how you changed as a result of your experience.

Criteria for Success

Purpose/Focus
✓ **Connects specific incidents with larger ideas**
Make meaningful connections between your experiences and the texts you have read in this section.

✓ **Clearly conveys the significance of the story**
Provide a conclusion in which you reflect on what you experienced.

Organization
✓ **Sequences events logically**
Structure your narrative so that individual events build on one another to create a coherent whole.

Development of Ideas/Elaboration
✓ **Supports insights**
Include both personal examples and details from the texts you have read in this section.

✓ **Uses narrative techniques effectively**
Although a personal narrative is a work of nonfiction, it may include storytelling elements like those found in fiction. Consider using dialogue to help readers "hear" how characters sound.

Language
✓ **Uses description effectively**
Use vivid descriptive details to help readers picture settings and characters.

Conventions
✓ **Does not have errors**
Check your narrative to eliminate errors in grammar, spelling, and punctuation.

WRITE TO EXPLORE

Writing is a way to explore what you feel and think: You may change your mind or get new ideas as you work. As you write your personal narrative, explore your ideas on the topic of competition and conflict.

Writing to Sources: **Argument**

Competition and Conflict The readings in this section present many ideas about competition and conflict. They raise questions, such as the following, about various aspects of competition and conflict.

- How can competition help us become better people?
- How can communication change our experience of conflict and competition?
- What is the relationship between competition and aggression?
- Can we learn to win and lose with grace and dignity?

Focus on the question that intrigues you the most, and then complete the following assignment.

> ### Assignment
> Write an **argumentative essay** in which you state and defend a claim about values, problems, or advice related to competition and conflict. Build evidence for your claim by analyzing the presentation of competition and conflict in two or more texts from this section. Clearly present, develop, and support your ideas with examples and details from the texts.

Prewriting and Planning

Choose texts. Review the texts in the section to determine which ones you will cite in your essay. Select at least two texts that will provide strong material to support your argument.

Gather details and craft a working thesis, or claim. Use a chart like the one shown to develop your claim.

Focus Question: How can communication change our experience of conflict and competition?

Text	Passage	Notes
"Amigo Brothers"	"No pulling punches. We go all the way."	Tony and Felix talk about their competition and how they will deal with it.
"Forget Fun, Embrace Enjoyment"	"Words matter. They create cognitive schemas and shape behaviors."	Author argues that good competition is enjoyable and brings out our best.
Example Claim: Communicating our ideas can help us understand and benefit from competition and conflict.		

Prepare counterarguments. Note possible objections to your claim and evidence. Plan to include and address the strongest of these counterclaims in your essay.

INCORPORATE RESEARCH

As you write your argument, refer to the research you conducted as you read the texts in this section. Choose appropriate details from your research to support your claims and build your argument.

Drafting

Structure your ideas and evidence. Create an informal outline or list of ideas you want to present. Decide where you will include evidence and which evidence you will use to support each of your main points.

Address counterclaims. Strong argumentation takes differing ideas into account and addresses them directly. As you organize your ideas, build in sections in which you explain opposing opinions or differing interpretations. Then, write a reasoned, well-supported response to those counterclaims.

Frame and connect ideas. Write an introduction that will grab readers' attention. Consider beginning with a compelling quotation or a surprising detail. Use words, phrases, and clauses to link the major sections of your essay and to clarify the relationships between your claims and the evidence that supports them. Finally, sum up your ideas in a strong concluding paragraph.

Revising and Editing

Review content. Make sure that your claim is clearly stated and that you have supported it with convincing evidence from the texts in this section. Underline main ideas in your paper and confirm that each one is supported. Add more proof as needed.

Review style. Revise to cut wordy passages. Check to be sure you have found the clearest, simplest way to communicate your ideas. Review your word choice to ensure your tone is objective and your style is formal.

Common Core State Standards

W.7.1.a–e; L.7.3.a
[For full standards wording, see the chart in the front of this book.]

CITE RESEARCH CORRECTLY

Take note of the evidence from outside sources you have included in your argument. Follow accepted conventions to cite your sources. See the Citing Sources pages in the Introductory Unit of this textbook for additional guidance.

Self-Evaluation Rubric

Use the following criteria to evaluate the effectiveness of your essay.

Criteria	Rating Scale
Purpose/Focus Introduces a precise claim and distinguishes the claim from alternative or opposing claims; provides a concluding section that follows from and supports the argument presented	*not very ... very* 1 2 3 4
Organization Establishes a logical organization; uses words, phrases and clauses to link the major sections of the text, create cohesion, and clarify relationships among claims, reasons, and evidence, and between claims and counterclaims	1 2 3 4
Development of Ideas/Elaboration Develops the claim and counterclaims fairly, supplying evidence for each while pointing out the strengths and limitations of both	1 2 3 4
Language Establishes and maintains a formal style and objective tone	1 2 3 4
Conventions Attends to the norms and conventions of the discipline	1 2 3 4

Titles for Extended Reading

In this unit, you have read texts in a variety of genres. Continue to read on your own. Select works that you enjoy, but challenge yourself to explore new authors and works of increasing depth and complexity. The titles suggested below will help you get started.

INFORMATIONAL TEXT

Geeks: How Two Lost Boys Rode the Internet out of Idaho
by Jon Katz   EXEMPLAR TEXT ©
Villard Books, 2000

In this **nonfiction** book, Jesse and Eric, two computer "geeks" with few social skills or future prospects, meet the reporter Jon Katz, who convinces them that they can use their computer savvy to create a better life.

Discoveries: Working It Out

What role does conflict play in social studies, science, music, and mathematics? The **essays** and **stories** in this book explore different types of conflicts and how they are worked out.

The Emperor's Silent Army
by Jane O'Connor

In 1974, farmers digging in China uncovered an army of life-sized clay soldiers buried for over 2,000 years. This work of **historical nonfiction** tells that story.

LITERATURE

The Devil's Arithmetic
by Jane Yolen

In this **historical novel,** a girl finds herself whisked back in time to a Polish village to experience firsthand the horrors her relatives experienced during the Holocaust.

The Collected Poems of Langston Hughes
by Langston Hughes   EXEMPLAR TEXT ©
Vintage, 1994

Langston Hughes was just nineteen when his first poem, "The Negro Speaks of Rivers," was published. This collection of **poetry** spans Hughes's long and brilliant career.

White Fang and The Call of the Wild
by Jack London

White Fang tells the story of a wild wolf who suffers hardships and cruelty until a man adopts him. In *The Call of the Wild*, a pampered dog is stolen from his home and forced to become a sled dog in the Yukon. In both novels, animals rely on instinct to survive in brutal environments.

Heat
by Mike Lupica
Philomel, 2006

Michael Arroyo is such a skilled pitcher that coaches of rival baseball teams demand proof of his age. In this **novel,** Michael must struggle to find a way to play the game that he loves and to cope with his difficult home life.

ONLINE TEXT SET

ARTICLE
The Fall of the Hindenburg
Michael Morrison

NOVEL EXCERPT
from Letters from Rifka Karen Hesse

EDITORIAL
Veteran Returns, Becomes Symbol Minneapolis Star and Tribune

Preparing to Read Complex Texts

Attentive Reading As you read on your own, ask yourself questions like these to enrich your reading experience.

When reading narratives, ask yourself...

Comprehension: **Key Ideas and Details**

- Can I clearly picture the setting of the story? Which details help me do so?
- Can I picture the characters clearly in my mind? Why or why not?
- Do the characters speak and act like real people? Why or why not?
- Which characters do I like? Why? Which characters do I dislike? Why?
- Do I understand why the characters act as they do? Why or why not?
- What does the story mean to me? Does it express a meaning or an insight I find important and true?

Text Analysis: **Craft and Structure**

- Does the story grab my attention right from the beginning? Why or why not?
- Do I want to keep reading? Why or why not?
- Can I follow the sequence of events in the story? Am I confused at any point? If so, what information would make the sequence clearer?
- Do the characters change as the story progresses? If so, do their changes seem believable?
- Are there any passages that I find especially moving, interesting, or well written? If so, why?

Connections: **Integration of Knowledge and Ideas**

- How is this story similar to and different from other stories I have read?
- Do I care what happens to the characters? Do I sympathize with them? Why or why not?
- How do my feelings toward the characters affect my experience of reading the story?
- Did the story teach me something new or cause me to look at something in a new way? If so, what did I learn?
- Would I recommend this story to others? Why or why not?
- Would I like to read other works by this author? Why or why not?

Common Core State Standards

Reading Literature/ Informational Text

10. By the end of the year, read and comprehend literature, including stories, dramas, and poems, and literary nonfiction in the grades 6–8 text complexity band proficiently, with scaffolding as needed at the high end of the range.

What should we learn?

THE BIG ?

UNIT PATHWAY

PART 1
SETTING EXPECTATIONS

- INTRODUCING THE BIG QUESTION
- CLOSE READING WORKSHOP

PART 2
TEXT ANALYSIS
GUIDED EXPLORATION

EXPLORING IDEAS

PART 3
TEXT SET
DEVELOPING INSIGHT

MOTIVATION

PART 4
DEMONSTRATING INDEPENDENCE

- INDEPENDENT READING
- ONLINE TEXT SET

CLOSE READING TOOL

Use this tool to practice the close reading strategies you learn.

STUDENT eTEXT

Bring learning to life with audio, video, and interactive tools.

ONLINE WRITER'S NOTEBOOK

Easily capture notes and complete assignments online.

Find all Digital Resources at **pearsonrealize.com.**

 THE BIG **?**

What should we learn?

Everyone has their own ideas about what is important to learn. Some people believe we should learn information that helps us develop practical skills. Others believe we should explore topics driven by our curiosity and talents.

When you think about what we should learn, remember that knowledge includes skills you learn in school and lessons you learn from others. It also includes information that helps you understand other cultures, and ideas that inspire you to investigate the world around you. No matter what is most important to you, the drive to discover new things is something we all have in common.

Exploring the Big Question

Collaboration: Group Discussion Start thinking about the Big Question by making a list of things you believe are important to learn. Describe an example for each of the following:

- A skill that could save someone's life
- A subject you would like to study in school
- A job that requires specific knowledge
- An idea that might make the world a better place
- A personal interest of yours

With a small group, discuss why you think some of these items are more important to learn than others. During your discussion, speak when it is your turn and listen to others without interrupting. Assign a discussion leader to keep ideas moving forward and a group recorder to list the items in the order of importance the group agrees to support. Ask a timekeeper to monitor your discussion and limit it to fifteen minutes. Finally, choose a speaker to present your group's ideas to the class.

Connecting to the Literature The texts in this unit explore the different ways we learn—from experience, from others, and from ourselves. Each reading will give you additional insight into the Big Question.

Vocabulary

Acquire and Use Academic Vocabulary The term "academic vocabulary" refers to words you typically encounter in scholarly and literary texts and in technical and business writing. Review the definitions of these academic vocabulary words. Then, practice using these words in your writing and academic discussions.

**Common Core
State Standards**

Speaking and Listening
1.b. Follow rules for collegial discussions, track progress toward specific goals and deadlines, and define individual roles as needed.

Language
4.d. Verify the preliminary determination of the meaning of a word or phrase.
6. Acquire and use accurately grade-appropriate general academic and domain-specific words and phrases; gather vocabulary knowledge when considering a word or phrase important to comprehension or expression.

analyze (an´ə līz´) *v.* break into parts in order to study closely

discover (di skuv´ər) *v.* find something hidden or previously unknown; find out

evaluate (ē val´yoo āt´) *v.* judge or rate

examine (eg zam´ ən) *v.* study in depth in order to find or check something

explore (ek splôr´) *v.* travel through an unfamiliar area to find out what it is like; thoroughly discuss a topic

facts (fakts) *n.* true information about a topic

inquire (in kwīr´) *v.* ask someone for information

investigate (in ves´tə gāt´) *v.* examine thoroughly

Gather Vocabulary Knowledge Additional words related to learning are listed below. Categorize the words by deciding whether you know each one well, know it a little bit, or do not know it at all.

curiosity	interview	question
experiment	knowledge	understand
information		

Then, do the following:

1. Write the definitions of the words you know.
2. Verify the definitions by looking up each word in a print or online dictionary. Revise your definitions as needed.
3. Continue to use the dictionary to look up the meanings and pronunciations of the unknown words.
4. Then, write a paragraph, using all the vocabulary words, about the types of things you think are important to learn.

Close Reading Workshop

In this workshop, you will learn an approach to reading that will deepen your understanding of literature and will help you better appreciate the author's craft. The workshop includes models for close reading, discussion, research, and writing. After you have reviewed the strategies and models, practice your skills with the Independent Practice selection.

 **Common Core State Standards**

RI.7.1, RI.7.2, RI.7.5, RI.7.6, RI.7.9; W.7.2, W.7.7; SL.7.1
[For full standards wording, see the chart in the front of this book.]

CLOSE READING: NONFICTION

In Part 2 of this unit you will focus on reading various types of nonfiction. Use these strategies as you read the texts.

Comprehension: Key Ideas and Details

- Read first to unlock basic meaning.
- Use context clues to help you determine the meanings of unfamiliar words.
- Identify unfamiliar details that you might need to clarify through research.
- Distinguish between what is stated directly and what must be inferred.

Ask yourself questions such as these:
- What is the author's central idea or thesis?
- What evidence does the author present to explain or support the central idea?

Text Analysis: Craft and Structure

- Think about the genre of the work and how the author presents ideas.
- Analyze the overall structure and organization of the work.
- Consider how the author's word choice expresses his or her attitude toward the subject or audience.

Ask yourself questions such as these:
- What is the author's point of view or opinion? How does the author's point of view affect my understanding of the topic?
- What is the author's purpose in writing this piece?

Connections: Integration of Knowledge and Ideas

- Look for relationships among key ideas. Identify causes and effects, and comparisons and contrasts.
- Analyze the author's arguments and evaluate the supporting evidence.
- Compare and contrast this work with other nonfiction texts you have read.

Ask yourself questions such as these:
- How has this work increased my knowledge of a subject, issue, or event?
- Have I changed my attitude or beliefs based on the information in the selection? Why or why not?

Read

As you read this excerpt, take note of the annotations that model ways to closely read the text.

Reading Model

from *Freedom Walkers: The Story of the Montgomery Bus Boycott* by Russell Freedman

Not so long ago in Montgomery, Alabama, the color of your skin determined where you could sit on a public bus.[1] If you happened to be an African American, you had to sit in the back of the bus, even if there were empty seats up front.

Back then, racial segregation was the rule throughout the American South. Strict laws—called "Jim Crow" laws—enforced a system of white supremacy that discriminated against blacks and kept them in their place as second-class citizens.[2]

People were separated by race from the moment they were born in segregated hospitals until the day they were buried in segregated cemeteries. Blacks and whites did not attend the same schools, worship in the same churches, eat in the same restaurants, sleep in the same hotels, drink from the same water fountains, or sit together in the same movie theaters.

In Montgomery, it was against the law for a white person and a Negro to play checkers on public property or ride together in a taxi.[3]

Most southern blacks were denied their right to vote. The biggest obstacle was the poll tax, a special tax that was required of all voters but was too costly for many blacks and for poor whites as well. Voters also had to pass a literacy test to prove that they could read, write, and understand the U.S. Constitution. These tests were often rigged to disqualify even highly educated blacks. Those who overcame the obstacles and insisted on registering as voters faced threats, harassment, and even physical violence. As a result, African Americans in the South could not express their grievances in the voting booth, which, for the most part, was closed to them. But there were other ways to protest, and one day a half century ago, the black citizens in Montgomery rose up in protest and united to demand their rights—by walking peacefully.[4]

It all started on a bus.[5]

Key Ideas and Details
1 Quick research reveals that Freedman's book was published in 2006; by using the phrase "Not so long ago," the author emphasizes that segregation is part of our recent history.

Craft and Structure
2 The author uses highly charged language such as "white supremacy" and "kept them in their place" to reveal his negative attitude toward segregation.

Key Ideas and Details
3 These examples vividly show how "Jim Crow" laws affected people's lives.

Integration of Knowledge and Ideas
4 This paragraph builds to its main idea—African Americans finally "rose up in protest."

Craft and Structure
5 The author uses *foreshadowing* by hinting at events to come. This sentence engages readers and makes them curious about what "started on a bus."

Jo Ann Robinson

Looking back, she remembered it as the most humiliating experience of her life, "a deep hurt that would not heal."[6] It had happened just before Christmas in 1949. She was about to visit relatives in Cleveland, Ohio, where she would spend the holidays.

Earlier that day she had driven out to Dannelly Field, the Montgomery, Alabama, airport, and checked her luggage for the flight to Cleveland. Then she drove back to the campus of Alabama State, an all-black college where she had been hired that fall as a professor of English. After parking her car in the campus garage, she took her armful of Christmas gifts, walked to the nearest bus stop, and waited for a ride back to the airport.[7]

Soon a Montgomery City Lines bus rolled into view and pulled up at the stop. Balancing her packages, Jo Ann Robinson stepped aboard and dropped her dime into the fare box. She saw that the bus was nearly empty. Only two other passengers were aboard—a black man in a seat near the back and a white woman in the third seat from the front. Without thinking, Robinson took a seat two rows behind the white woman.

"I took the fifth-row seat from the front and sat down," she recalled, "immediately closing my eyes and envisioning, in my mind's eye, the wonderful two-week vacation I would have with my family and friends in Ohio."[8]

Jolted out of her reverie by an angry voice, she opened her eyes and sat upright. The bus driver had come to a full stop and turned in his seat. He was speaking to her. "If you can sit in the fifth row from the front seat of the other buses in Montgomery," he said, "suppose you get off and ride in one of them."

The driver's message didn't register at first. Robinson was still thinking about her holiday trip. Suddenly the driver rose from his seat, went over to her, and stood with his arm drawn back, as if to strike her. "Get up from there!" he yelled. "Get up from there!"[8]

Shaken and alarmed, Robinson bolted to her feet and stumbled off the bus in tears, packages falling from her arms. She had made the mistake of sitting in one of the front ten seats, which were reserved for white riders only.

"I felt like a dog," she wrote later. "And I got mad, after this was over, and I realized I was a human being, and just as intelligent and far more [educationally] trained than that bus driver was.[9] But I think he wanted to hurt me, and he did. I cried all the way to Cleveland."

Key Ideas and Details
6 Detailed recollections and quotations emphasize a key idea: Jo Ann Robinson suffered a "humiliating experience."

Key Ideas and Details
7 The author establishes Robinson's status as a valued member of her community and describes the innocent nature of her trip.

Craft and Structure
8 The harsh threats from the bus driver sharply contrast with the earlier image of Robinson envisioning her Christmas vacation.

Integration of Knowledge and Ideas
9 The title of the book and textual details suggest that the author's purpose is to inform readers about the Montgomery bus boycott while also giving the human side of the story.

Discuss

Sharing your own ideas and listening to the ideas of others can deepen your understanding of a text and help you look at a topic in a whole new way. As you participate in collaborative discussions, work to have a genuine exchange in which classmates build upon one another's ideas. Support your points with evidence and ask meaningful questions.

Discussion Model

Student 1: This author gives so many examples of how people were segregated "from the moment they were born . . . until the day they were buried." This was everyday life in the United States!

Student 2: What struck me was the image of the woman with an armful of packages being treated "like a dog" by the bus driver. I could really picture that scene in my mind.

Student 3: The author chose words that really show you segregation's cruelty. The idea that people were thought of as "second-class citizens" and kept "in their place" is terrible.

Student 2: The story ended before describing the Montgomery bus boycott. I wonder if Robinson was involved in the protest.

Research

Targeted research can clarify unfamiliar details and shed light on various aspects of a text. Consider questions that arise in your mind as you read, and use those questions as the basis for research.

Research Model

Questions: *What was the Montgomery bus boycott? Was Jo Ann Robinson involved?*

Key Words for Internet Search: "Montgomery bus boycott" AND "Jo Ann Robinson"

Result: Encyclopedia of Alabama: Montgomery Bus Boycott; Encyclopedia of Alabama: Jo Ann Robinson

What I Learned: The Montgomery bus boycott was an important protest in the civil rights movement. It led to the United States Supreme Court barring segregation on public transportation. Robinson helped start the boycott after Rosa Parks, an African American, was arrested for refusing to give up her bus seat to a white man. Martin Luther King, Jr., was heavily involved in the protest.

Write

Writing about a text will deepen your understanding of it and will also allow you to share your ideas more formally with others. The following model essay evaluates Russell Freedman's use of powerful language and descriptive details, and cites evidence to support the main ideas.

Writing Model: Informative Text

Language and Description in *Freedom Walkers: The Story of the Montgomery Bus Boycott*

The early 1950s was a difficult time for African Americans in Montgomery, Alabama. They were commonly denied their rights, and segregation on public buses was the law. In this passage from his book, Russell Freedman uses expressive language and descriptive details to make the terrible effects of segregation in Montgomery real for readers.

The writer establishes the essay's thesis in the opening paragraph.

In the first section, Freedman's choice of highly charged words and phrases paints a grim picture of everyday life in Alabama. African Americans were "kept … in their place as second-class citizens" by a "system of white supremacy" and were separated "from the moment they were born … until the day they were buried." These details create an image of a society that was so unfair that it had to change. The section ends by foreshadowing an event on a bus that would lead to a protest against this injustice.

The writer supports claims with specific examples of "highly charged" words and phrases.

The second section describes what happened on a Montgomery bus in 1949. The author portrays Jo Ann Robinson as a busy professional woman cheerfully boarding a bus at the beginning of a holiday trip to visit relatives. Her statement that she was "envisioning, in my mind's eye, the wonderful two-week vacation I would have with my family and friends in Ohio" strengthens the image of Robinson as an innocent victim. That peaceful moment is shattered, however, when the bus driver "with his arm drawn back, as if to strike her" yells at her to "Get up from there!" She had taken a seat reserved for whites. The contrast between the two images effectively expresses the cruelty of the incident. The additional description that "shaken and alarmed, Robinson bolted to her feet and stumbled off the bus in tears, packages falling from her arms" further emphasizes this contrast. The selection ends with Robinson's comment that "I cried all the way to Cleveland."

The writer uses direct quotations to support the analysis.

Although the excerpt ends before discussion of the Montgomery bus boycott itself, the author's detailed description of Robinson's fear, anger, and outrage at the injustice of segregation makes it clear why, years later, she became one of the leaders of the Montgomery bus boycott.

Details from outside research can be used to fill in gaps in information.

As you read the following text, apply the close reading strategies you have learned. You may need to read the article multiple times.

from *What Makes a Rembrandt a Rembrandt?*
by Richard Mühlberger

*Meet the Author*

Richard Mühlberger (b. 1938) has been an author, an art critic, and an educator at art museums. Many of his books—including *What Makes a Van Gogh a Van Gogh?* and *What Makes a Leonardo a Leonardo?*—bring to life the works of the world's greatest artists.

Citizen Soldiers

A Dutch poet of Rembrandt's day wrote, "When the country is in danger, every citizen is a soldier." That was the idea behind the militia, or civic guard companies, which trained citizens how to fight and shoot in case their city was attacked. Each company drilled in archery, the crossbow, or the musket. By Rembrandt's time, militia companies were as much social clubs as military organizations.

Captain Frans Banning Cocq, out to impress everyone, chose Rembrandt to paint his militia company, with members of the company paying the artist to have their portraits included in the painting. The huge canvas was to be hung in the new hall of the militia headquarters, where it would be seen at receptions and celebrations along with other militia paintings.

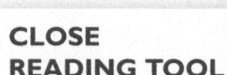

CLOSE READING TOOL

Read and respond to this selection online using the **Close Reading Tool**.

By the mid-seventeenth century, there were more than one hundred big militia paintings hanging in public halls in the important cities of the Netherlands. In all of these group portraits, the men were evenly lined up so that each face got equal attention, just as they had been in traditional anatomy lesson paintings. Rembrandt did not like this way of presenting the scene. He had seen militia companies in action, and there were always people milling about who were not militiamen but who took part in their exercises and parades. To add realism to the piece, he decided to include some of these people, as well as a dog. There was room on the wall for a canvas about sixteen feet wide, large enough for Rembrandt to do what no other painter had ever done before. His idea was to show the exciting commotion before a parade began.

Two Handsome Officers

Everywhere in the painting, Rembrandt used sharp contrasts of dark and light. Everything that honors the citizen soldiers and their work is illuminated; everything else is in shadow. Captain Frans Banning Cocq is the man dressed in black with a red sash under his arm, striding forward in the center. Standing next to him is the most brightly lighted man in the painting, Lieutenant Willem van Ruytenburgh, attired in a glorious gold and yellow uniform, silk sash, soft leather cavalry boots, and a high hat with white ostrich plumes. His lancelike weapon, called a partisan, and the steel gorget[1] around his neck—a leftover from the days when soldiers wore full suits of armor—are the only hints that he is a military man. Rembrandt links him to Banning Cocq by contrasting the colors of their clothing and by painting the shadow of Banning Cocq's hand on the front of van Ruytenburgh's coat. The captain is giving orders to his lieutenant for the militia company to march off.

Banning Cocq is dressed in a black suit against a dark background, yet he does not disappear. Rembrandt made him the most important person in the composition. Van Ruytenburgh turns to listen to him, which shows his respect for his commander. Banning Cocq's face stands out above his bright red sash and white collar. How well Rembrandt knew that darkness makes faces shine! The captain's self-assured pace, the movement of the tassels at his knees, and the angle of his walking staff are proof of the energy and dignity of his stride.

---

1. **gorget** (gôr´ jit) *n.* a piece of armor for the throat.

Muskets and Mascots

On either side of these two handsome officers, broad paths lead back into the painting

Rembrandt knew that when the huge group scene was placed above eye level on the wall of the militia headquarters, these empty areas would be the first to be seen. He wanted them to lead the eyes of viewers to figures in the painting who did not have the advantage of being placed in the foreground. In the middle of one of these paths is a man in red pouring gunpowder into the barrel of his musket. Behind the captain, only partially seen, another man shoots his gun into the air, and a third militiaman, to the right of van Ruytenburgh, blows on his weapon to clean it. Loading, shooting, and cleaning were part of the standard drill for musketeers, and so they were included in the painting to demonstrate the men's mastery of their weapons.

Walking in a stream of bright light down the path on the left is a blond girl dressed in yellow with a dead chicken tied to her waist. She has a friend in blue behind her. In their public shows, the militia would choose two young girls to carry the emblems[2] of their company, here the claws of a bird. The yellow and blue of the girls' costumes are the militia's colors. In the parade that is being organized, these mascots will take a prominent place, the fair-haired girl holding aloft the chicken's claws.

Many of the background figures stand on stairs so that their faces can be seen. The man above the girl in yellow is Jan Corneliszoon Visscher, after Banning Cocq and van Ruytenburgh the highest-ranking person in the militia company. He waves a flag that combines the colors of the militia company with the three black crosses of Amsterdam. While Rembrandt did not pose him in bright light, he made him important by placing him high up on the stairs, by showing the sheen in his costume, and by giving him the large flag to unfurl.

---

2. emblems *n.* objects that stand for something else; symbols.

A Red Ribbon and Fine Old Clothes

In spite of his partial appearance, the drummer on the right seems ready to come forward to lead a march with his staccato beat. The sound seems to bother the dusty dog below. Behind the drummer, two men appear to be figuring out their places in the formation. The one in the white collar and black hat outranks many of the others in the scene. His prestige is signaled in an unusual way: A red ribbon dangles over his head, tied to the lance of the man in armor behind van Ruytenburgh. Additional lances can be counted in the darkness, some leaning against the wall, others carried by militiamen. Their crisscross patterns add to the feeling of commotion that Rembrandt has captured everywhere on the huge canvas.

The costumes worn in this group portrait are much more ornate and colorful than what Dutchmen ordinarily wore every day. Some, like the breeches and helmet of the man shooting his musket behind Banning Cocq, go back a hundred years to the beginnings of the militia company. In the eyes of many Dutchmen, clothing associated with a glorious past brought special dignity to the company. What an opportunity for Rembrandt, perhaps the greatest lover of old clothes in Amsterdam!

Not a Night Watch

Night Watch is a mistaken title that was given to the painting over a hundred years after Rembrandt died, but it has stuck, and is what the painting is almost universally called. Although the exaggerated chiaroscuro[3] does give an impression of night-time, there is daylight in the scene. It comes from the left, as the shadows under Banning Cocq's feet prove. And it is clear that no one in the painting is on watch, alert to the approach of an enemy. The official title of the painting is *Officers and Men of the Company of Captain Frans Banning Cocq and Lieutenant Willem van Ruytenburgh.*

Rembrandt completed the painting in 1642, when he was thirty-six years old. He probably had no idea that it would be the most famous Dutch painting of all time. In 1678, one of his former students wrote that it would "outlive all its rivals," and within another century the painting was considered one of the wonders of the world.

---

3. **chiaroscuro** (kē är′ ə skoor′ ō) *n.* a dramatic style of light and shade in a painting or drawing.

Close Reading Activities

Read

Comprehension: Key Ideas and Details

1. (a) Why was Rembrandt hired to paint the militia company? **(b) Analyze:** How did Rembrandt change the way military group portraits were painted?

2. (a) Interpret: According to the article, what techniques does Rembrandt use to emphasize higher-ranking figures? **(b) Support:** How does the painter make the background figures visible?

3. (a) Classify: Which two people in the painting are not actual militia members? **(b) Hypothesize:** Would these people have been included in a more traditional militia portrait? Explain.

4. Summarize: What details in the painting suggest that a parade is being organized?

Text Analysis: Craft and Structure

5. (a) Analyze: What are two possible purposes the author had for writing this article? **(b) Support:** Cite details from the text that support each purpose.

6. (a) Distinguish: What organizational pattern does the author use to describe "Two Handsome Officers"? **(b) Assess:** Is this organization appropriate for the section? Explain.

Connections: Integration of Knowledge and Ideas

Discuss

In this article, the author mixes historical details with details about the painting he describes. In a **small-group discussion,** share your ideas about whether or not this technique is effective. Use evidence from the text to support your main points.

Research

Night Watch is one of Rembrandt's most famous works. Find a larger reproduction of the painting. Then, conduct research to find an article about it. Compare this new article to Mühlberger's, considering the ways the authors describe and evaluate Rembrandt's painting techniques, including his use of color, light, and shadow.

Take notes as you perform your research. Then, write a brief **explanation** comparing and contrasting the articles' discussions of Rembrandt's painting techniques.

Write

Good literary nonfiction typically presents key ideas in a logical order. Write an **essay** in which you evaluate the organization of key ideas in this selection. Cite details from the article to support your analysis.

THE BIG ? What should we learn?

Consider how reading about art helps you learn more about it. What might Rembrandt be trying to teach through his artwork? Explain.

"The **mind**, once **expanded**
to the dimensions of larger ideas,
never returns to its original size."

—Oliver Wendell Holmes

EXPLORING IDEAS

The authors in this section introduce and explore ideas through different forms of nonfiction. As you read, think about whether the information in each text is new to you, or whether it helps you explore a familiar topic in a new way. The quotation on the opposite page will help you start thinking about the ways in which learning new information and reexamining familiar ideas can alter our perception and broaden our understanding.

◄ **CRITICAL VIEWING** Explain your interpretation of the picture on the opposite page. How does the image relate to the concept of exploring ideas?

READINGS IN PART 2

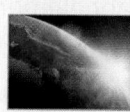
EXPOSITORY ESSAY
Life Without Gravity
Robert Zimmerman
(p. 194)

REFLECTIVE ESSAY
I Am a Native of North America
Chief Dan George
(p. 204)

PERSUASIVE SPEECH
All Together Now
Barbara Jordan (p. 214)

NARRATIVE ESSAY
Rattlesnake Hunt
Marjorie Kinnan Rawlings (p. 222)

CLOSE READING TOOL

Use the **Close Reading Tool** to practice the strategies you learn in this unit.

Elements of Nonfiction

Nonfiction is writing about actual people, ideas, and events.

Nonfiction writing presents information that is true or thought to be true. Two broad categories of nonfiction are **functional texts,** which are practical documents that help readers perform everyday tasks, and **literary nonfiction,** which features some of the same literary elements and techniques as fiction.

Authors of nonfiction write with one or more **purposes,** or goals, in mind. Usually, these are to inform, describe, or persuade. To fulfill his or her purpose, the writer organizes information in a logical **structure,** or arrangement of parts, using patterns of organization such as these:

- **Chronological,** which presents events in the order in which they happened

- **Spatial,** which describes items as they appear in space—for example, left to right

- **Comparison-and-contrast,** which groups ideas based on their similarities and differences

- **Cause-and-effect,** which explains how one event causes another

- **Problem-and-solution,** which examines a problem and proposes ways to solve it

Literary Nonfiction In addition to informing, describing, or persuading, literary nonfiction may have an additional purpose: to entertain. When a work of literary nonfiction tells a story, it is called **narrative nonfiction.** It may include the elements listed in the right-hand column of the chart below.

Storytelling Elements in Narrative Nonfiction

In Fiction	In Narrative Nonfiction
Characters are developed through • **direct characterization,** or statements about what the characters are like; • **indirect characterization,** or descriptions of what the characters do, say, and think.	**Direct** and **indirect characterization** reveal the personalities of **real people.**
Setting is revealed through • **vivid descriptions** of **time, place,** and **customs;** • **figurative language,** or unusual comparisons, such as similes.	**Vivid descriptions** and **figurative language** describe **real places, real historical eras,** and **real customs.**
Plot, or the sequence of fictional events in a story, is **artfully paced and organized** to sustain readers' interest.	**Artful pacing and organization** describe **actual events.**

Forms of Literary Nonfiction

In addition to narrative nonfiction, three common forms of literary nonfiction are articles, essays, and speeches.

Articles are short prose works that present facts about a subject. They may appear in print sources, such as newspapers, or in online sources, such as Web sites.

Essays are also short prose works that focus on a particular subject. They may be more personal than articles, however. The author of an essay often has a deep emotional connection to the subject.

Speeches are written texts that are delivered orally to an audience. Like an essay, a speech expresses the speaker's point of view, or perspective, on a topic.

Types of Nonfiction

Just as there are different *forms* of nonfiction, there are also different *types*—each with its own general purpose. The chart below shows the most common types of nonfiction and gives examples of ways that a work of each type might address the same general subject: pets.

Common Core State Standards

Reading Informational Text

3. Analyze the interactions between individuals, events, and ideas in a text (e.g., how ideas influence individuals or events).

4. Determine the meaning of words and phrases as they are used in a text, including figurative, connotative, and technical meanings; analyze the impact of a specific word choice on meaning and tone.

5. Analyze the structure an author uses to organize a text, including how the major sections contribute to the whole and to the development of the ideas.

6. Determine an author's point of view or purpose in a text and analyze how the author distinguishes his or her position from that of others.

Types and Purposes of Nonfiction

Type	Purpose	Examples
Expository	to present facts and ideas or to explain a process	an online article that explores ways to keep your dog healthy
Persuasive	to convince readers to take an action or to adopt a point of view	a speech urging the audience to adopt a pet
Narrative	to tell the story of a real-life experience	an essay about a dog who saved a person's life
Descriptive	to provide a vivid picture of something	an essay about the writer's favorite pet
Reflective	to explain the writer's insights about an event or experience	an essay describing lessons about life the writer learned from owning a pet
Humorous	to entertain and amuse	an article about the challenges of training a very frisky puppy
Analytical	to break a large idea into parts to show how the parts work as a whole	an article that discusses the criteria used for judging champion show dogs

Analyzing Structure and Relationships in Literary Nonfiction

The **structure** of a nonfiction work provides clues to the **author's purpose.**

Writers of nonfiction deliberately arrange their words, sentences, paragraphs, and sections in ways that clearly develop their key ideas.

Text Features You can often tell how a nonfiction work is organized by looking at its arrangement on the page. **Text features,** such as subheads and charts, can provide clues about the author's purpose.

If a text has . . .	It is probably organized . . .	Its purpose may be . . .
steps or dates	in time order	• to tell a story • to explain a process
section headings	by topic	• to inform • to describe

Key Ideas All nonfiction works communicate one or more key ideas. The opening sentences of a work usually state or suggest the key idea and hint at the author's purpose:

> I was only three when I first smelled the fresh, damp soil of Grandma's garden. Somewhere inside me, a seed of love sprouted and began to grow.

These sentences convey the key idea that the writer began gardening at a very young age. The author's purpose might be to reflect on a personal experience.

Point of View The author's **point of view** is his or her basic beliefs about a subject. The opening sentences in the previous example tell you that the author has a passion for gardening. Her point of view is that gardening is a worthwhile pursuit.

Major Sections Nonfiction may be organized into **sections** arranged under headings. Each section supports a key idea and helps fulfill the author's purpose. Consider the section headings in an article about New York City:

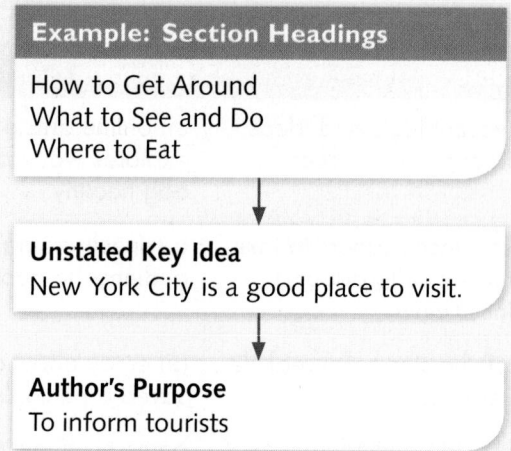

Example: Section Headings
How to Get Around
What to See and Do
Where to Eat

Unstated Key Idea
New York City is a good place to visit.

Author's Purpose
To inform tourists

The structure, key idea, and purpose of a text are interrelated. The headings suggest that there are a lot of things to do in New York City. The information presented indicates that the article is meant for visitors. These elements combine to express the author's purpose to offer guidance to tourists.

Logical Relationships Nonfiction works show their subjects in relationship to the larger world. For instance, they may show cause-and-effect relationships, such as ways in which people are affected by events and ideas—and vice versa. Here are some specific examples.

If a text is about . . .	It might show . . .
the Civil War	• what events and ideas caused the war • who suffered during the war
the author's life as a spy	• what caused her career choice • how her actions affected others
social networks	• how they have impacted users' lives • why they have become so popular

People do not always agree about the causes or effects of an event. Two writers, given the same facts, may express different opinions. Each writer's point of view affects his or her interpretation of information. In some nonfiction works, the writer may be *biased,* expressing a one-sided opinion. However, a writer is not necessarily biased just because he or she has a particular point of view.

Word Choice Looking closely at an author's choice of words can help you detect his or her point of view. Word choice can also help reveal an author's **tone,** or attitude toward his or her subject and audience. In particular, notice words with positive or negative **connotations,** or emotional associations. For example, the words *curious* and *nosy* have the same basic meaning. However, calling someone "curious" conveys positive connotations, while calling that same person "nosy" conveys negative connotations.

Figurative Language In literary nonfiction, writers often use figurative language, or unusual comparisons, to bring an idea to life and to create a certain tone. Look at the example below, in which a girl is described in three very different ways.

Example	Lily is compared to . . .	Tone
"Cyclone Lily" strikes again.	a cyclone	sarcastic
Lily sheds her things like a tree sheds leaves.	a tree	matter-of-fact
Lily is bursting with life. She can't help but drop petals along the way.	a flower	adoring

Meet the Author

As a boy, **Robert Zimmerman** (b. 1953) loved science-fiction books. They appealed to him because "the time was the early 1960s, when the first humans were going into space, and these books had an optimistic and hopeful view of that endeavor, as well as the future." As a child, Zimmerman viewed the blastoff of NASA's first manned spacecraft. He recalls thinking, "This is the United States. We can do anything if we put our minds to it!"

 **Common Core State Standards**

Reading Informational Text
2. Determine two or more central ideas in a text and analyze their development over the course of the text; provide an objective summary of the text.
5. Analyze the structure an author uses to organize a text, including how the major sections contribute to the whole and to the development of the ideas.

 What should we learn?

Think about the Big Question as you read "Life Without Gravity." Take note of how a lack of gravity can affect the human body.

CLOSE READING FOCUS

Key Ideas and Details: **Main Idea**

The **main idea** is the central point of a nonfiction text. While most texts focus on one main idea, some may address two or more closely related central ideas. The main idea of a paragraph is often stated in a topic sentence. The rest of the paragraph presents **supporting details** that give examples, explanations, or reasons.

When you read nonfiction, adjust your reading rate to recognize main ideas.

- **Skim,** or look over the text quickly, to get a sense of the main ideas before you begin reading.
- **Read closely** to learn what the central ideas are.
- **Scan,** or run your eyes over the text, to find answers to questions, to clarify, or to find supporting details.

Craft and Structure: **Expository Essay**

An **expository essay** is a short piece of nonfiction in which an author explains, defines, or interprets ideas, events, or processes. The organization, or structure, of the information depends on the topic and on the author's purpose, or reason for writing. Ideas may be developed in sections or in related paragraphs. Transitional words, such as *finally* and *since,* may clarify the development of ideas. As you read, analyze the structure the author uses to present ideas.

Vocabulary

You will encounter the following words in "Life Without Gravity." Copy the words into your notebook. If there are words you do not know, circle the part of each word that seems familiar and might be a clue to its meaning.

manned	**spines**	**feeble**
blander	**globules**	**readapted**

CLOSE READING MODEL

The passage below is from Robert Zimmerman's expository essay "Life Without Gravity." The annotations to the right of the passage show ways in which you can use close reading skills to identify main ideas and supporting details and to understand an expository essay.

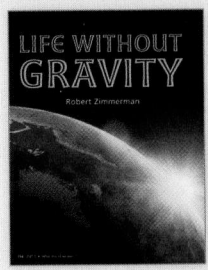

from "Life Without Gravity"

Being weightless in space seems so exciting.[1] Astronauts bounce about from wall to wall, flying! They float, they weave, they do somersaults and acrobatics without effort. Heavy objects can be lifted like feathers, and no one ever gets tired because nothing weighs anything.[2] In fact, everything is fun, nothing is hard.

NOT! Since the first manned space missions in the 1960s, scientists have discovered that being weightless in space isn't just flying around like Superman.[3] Zero gravity is alien stuff. As space tourist Dennis Tito said when he visited the international space station, "Living in space is like having a different life, living in a different world."

Worse, weightlessness can sometimes be downright unpleasant. Your body gets upset and confused. Your face puffs up, your nose gets stuffy, your back hurts, your stomach gets upset, and you throw up.[4] If astronauts are to survive a one-year journey to Mars—the shortest possible trip to the Red Planet—they will have to learn how to deal with this weird environment.

Main Idea

1 In the topic sentence, the author clearly states the main idea of this paragraph: Weightlessness in space seems exciting.

Main Idea

2 In the body of the paragraph, the author supports the main idea. He provides specific examples that show why weightlessness is exciting.

Expository Essay

3 The author emphasizes the word *NOT!* to grab your attention and introduce a contrasting view— the view he actually holds. Now you may guess that the purpose of this essay is to explain why weightlessness is not actually fun.

Main Idea

4 In this paragraph, the author uses vivid and surprising examples to support the idea that weightlessness can be "downright unpleasant."

LIFE WITHOUT GRAVITY

Robert Zimmerman

Being weightless in space seems so exciting. Astronauts bounce about from wall to wall, flying! They float, they weave, they do somersaults and acrobatics without effort. Heavy objects can be lifted like feathers, and no one ever gets tired because nothing weighs anything. In fact, everything is fun, nothing is hard.

NOT! Since the first **manned** space missions in the 1960s, scientists have discovered that being weightless in space isn't just flying around like Superman. Zero gravity is alien stuff. As space tourist Dennis Tito said when he visited the international space station, "Living in space is like having a different life, living in a different world."

Worse, weightlessness can sometimes be downright unpleasant. Your body gets upset and confused. Your face puffs up, your nose gets stuffy, your back hurts, your stomach gets upset, and you throw up. If astronauts are to survive a one-year journey to Mars—the shortest possible trip to the Red Planet—they will have to learn how to deal with this weird environment.

Our bodies are adapted to Earth's gravity. Our muscles are strong in order to overcome gravity as we walk and run. Our inner ears[1] use gravity to keep us upright. And because gravity wants to pull all our blood down into our legs, our hearts are designed to pump hard to get blood up to our brains.

In space, the much weaker gravity makes the human body change in many unexpected ways. In microgravity,[2] your blood is rerouted, flowing from the legs, which become thin and sticklike, to the head, which swells up. The extra liquid in your head also makes you feel like you're hanging upside down or have a stuffed-up nose.

The lack of gravity causes astronauts to routinely "grow" between one and three inches taller. Their **spines** straighten

◀ **Vocabulary**
manned (mand) *adj.* having human operators on board

spines (spīnz) *n.* backbones

Expository Essay
What information do you learn about the human body in these paragraphs?

Spiral Review
AUTHOR'S POINT OF VIEW How does the author regard space travel? Explain your answer.

Comprehension
What are some disadvantages of weightlessness?

---

1. **inner ears** (in´ ər irz) *n.* internal parts of the ears that give people a sense of balance.
2. **microgravity** (mī´ krō grav´ i tē) *n.* state of near-weightlessness that astronauts experience as their spacecraft orbits Earth.

Vocabulary ▶
feeble (fē′ bəl)
adj. weak

blander (bland′ ər)
adj. more tasteless

globules (gläb′ yo͞olz)
n. drops of liquid

out. The bones in the spine and the disks between them spread apart and relax.

But their bones also get thin and spongy. The body decides that if the muscles aren't going to push and pull on the bones, it doesn't need to lay down as much bone as it normally does. Astronauts who have been in space for several months can lose 10 percent or more of their bone tissue. If their bones got much weaker, they would snap once the astronauts returned to Earth.

And their muscles get weak and flabby. Floating about in space is too easy. If astronauts don't force themselves to exercise, their muscles become so **feeble** that when they return to Earth they can't even walk.

Worst of all is how their stomachs feel. During the first few days in space, the inner ear—which gives people their sense of balance—gets confused. Many astronauts become nauseous. They lose their appetites. Many throw up. Many throw up a lot!

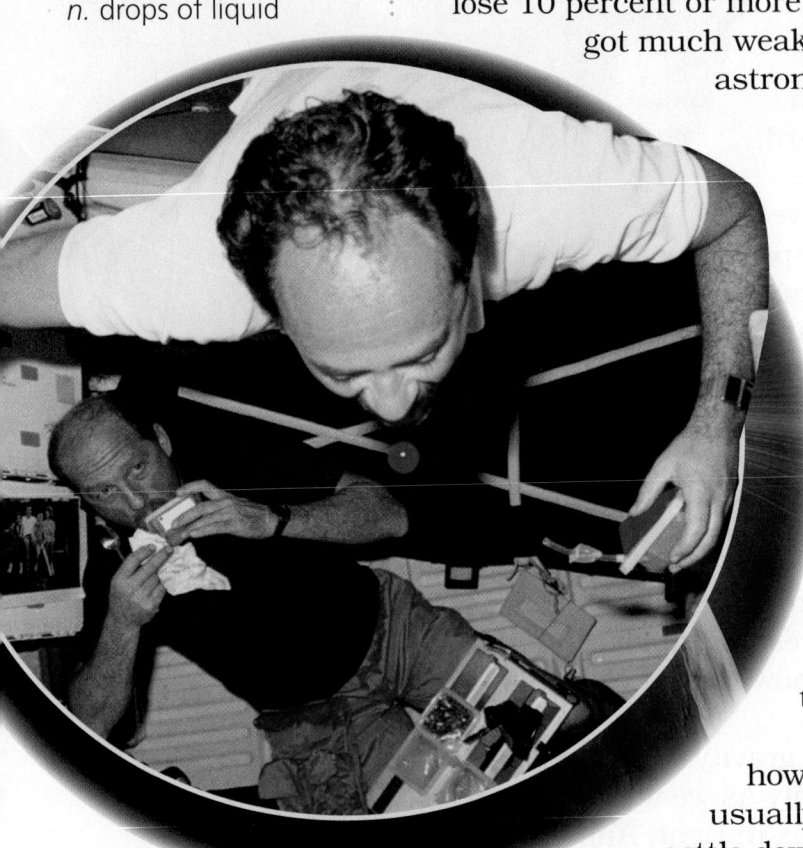

Weightlessness isn't all bad, however. After about a week people usually get used to it. Their stomachs settle down. Appetites return (though astronauts always say that food tastes **blander** in space). The heart and spine adjust.

Then, flying around like a bird becomes fun! Rooms suddenly seem much bigger. Look around you: The space above your head is pretty useless on Earth. You can't get up there to work, and anything you attach to the ceiling is simply something you'll bump your head on.

In space, however, that area is useful. In fact, equipment can be installed on every inch of every wall. In weightlessness you choose to move up or down and left or right simply by

▲
Critical Viewing
Why do you think the red liquid in this picture is floating around? Explain.

Main Idea
What is the main idea in this paragraph?

pointing your head. If you turn yourself upside down, the ceiling becomes the floor.

And you can't drop anything! As you work you can let your tools float around you. But you'd better be organized and neat. If you don't put things back where they belong when you are finished, tying them down securely, they will float away. Air currents will then blow them into nooks and crannies, and it might take you days to find them again.

In microgravity, you have to learn new ways to eat. Don't try pouring a bowl of cornflakes. Not only will the flakes float all over the place, the milk won't pour. Instead, big balls of milk will form. You can drink these by taking big bites out of them, but you'd better finish them before they slam into a wall, splattering apart and covering everything with little tiny milk **globules**.

Some meals on the space station are eaten with forks and knives, but scooping food with a spoon doesn't work. If the food isn't gooey enough to stick to the spoon, it will float away.

Everyone in space drinks through a straw, since liquid simply refuses to stay in a glass. The straw has to have a clamp at one end, or else when you stop drinking, the liquid will continue to flow out, spilling everywhere.

To prevent their muscles and bones from becoming too weak for life on Earth, astronauts have to follow a boring two-hour exercise routine every single day. Imagine having to run on a treadmill for one hour in the morning and then ride an exercise bicycle another hour before dinner. As Russian astronaut Valeri Ryumin once said, "Ye-ech!"

Even after all this exercise, astronauts who spend more than two months in space are usually weak and uncomfortable when they get back to Earth. Jerry Linenger, who spent more than four months on the Russian space station, *Mir*, struggled to walk after he returned. "My

LITERATURE IN CONTEXT

Science Connection

Weighted Down Your weight in pounds is actually the measure of the downward force of gravity upon your body. How much force gravity puts on you depends on the size and mass of the planet on which you are standing.

Imagine that on Earth you weigh 100 pounds. Because the surface gravity of Jupiter is 2.64 times that of Earth, you would weigh 264 pounds on Jupiter without eating a forkful more. On the other hand, surface gravity on the moon is one-sixth of Earth's gravity. That means your moon weight would be just under 17 pounds, though you would look exactly the same.

Of course, when you are not on a planet or moon, you are out of gravity's pull, so you weigh nothing at all.

Connect to the Literature

Is weightlessness as described in "Life Without Gravity" something you would like to experience? Why or why not?

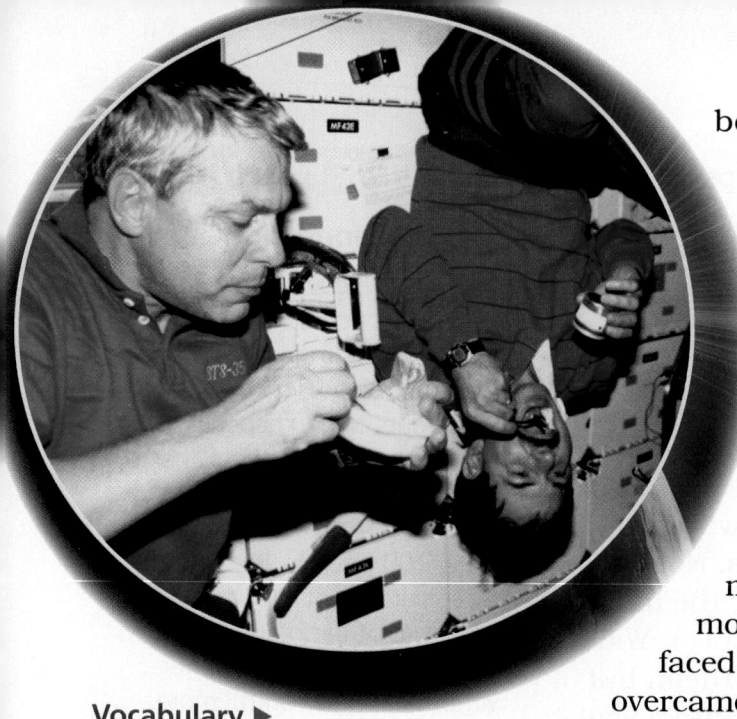

Vocabulary ▶
readapted (rē ə
dapt′ əd) *v.* gradually
adjusted again

body felt like a 500 pound barbell," he said. He even had trouble lifting and holding his fifteen-month-old son, John.

When Linenger went to bed that first night, his body felt like it was being smashed into the mattress. He was constantly afraid that if he moved too much, he would float away and out of control.

And yet, Linenger recovered quickly. In fact, almost two dozen astronauts have lived in space for more than six months, and four have stayed in orbit for more than a year. These men and women faced the discomforts of weightlessness and overcame them. And they all **readapted** to Earth gravity without problems, proving that voyages to Mars are possible . . . even if it feels like you are hanging upside down the whole time!

Language Study

Vocabulary The words in blue appear in "Life Without Gravity." Rewrite each sentence so that it includes a word from the list that conveys the same basic meaning as the italicized word or phrase.

| manned | spines | blander | globules | readapted |

1. My cold makes this food seem *less tasty.*

2. Space flights *with humans aboard* took place in the 1960s.

3. When the thermometer broke, *tiny drops* of mercury spilled out.

4. With no *bones in our backs,* we would not be able to stand.

5. After being away on vacation, we have *gotten used to* being home.

Word Study

Part A Explain how the **Old English suffix -ness** contributes to the meanings of the words *dreariness, togetherness,* and *greatness.* Consult a dictionary if necessary.

Part B Use what you know about the Old English suffix -ness to explain your answer to each question.

1. If Sara is known for her *nastiness,* does she treat people well?

2. Could *laziness* prevent someone from being productive?

WORD STUDY
The **Old English suffix -ness** means "the condition or quality of being." It usually indicates that the word is a noun. In this essay, the author explains that **feebleness,** a weakened condition, can be brought on by a lack of gravity.

Literary Analysis

Key Ideas and Details

1. Main Idea What ideas did you identify from skimming the essay before you read it?

2. Main Idea (a) What are three main ideas in the essay? **(b)** What supporting details does the author provide for each idea?

3. (a) List three unpleasant effects of weightlessness that are explained in the essay. **(b) Cause and Effect:** Describe the cause of each unpleasant effect.

Craft and Structure

4. Expository Essay (a) Fill out a chart like the one on the right to organize the information provided in the essay. **(b)** Does the organization of the essay enable the author to achieve his purpose? Why or why not?

5. Expository Essay (a) Explain why "Life Without Gravity" is an expository essay. **(b) Support:** Give examples from the text to support your answer.

Integration of Knowledge and Ideas

6. Relate: What do you think you would like most about being weightless? What effect of weightlessness would be most difficult for you? Use details from the essay to support your answers.

7. (a) Synthesize If the astronauts quoted in the article were offered another trip in space, what advice would you give them about the wisdom of taking the trip again? Use evidence from the essay to support your advice. **(b) Discuss:** Talk about your advice in a small group. As a group, choose three important pieces of advice to share with the class.

8. **THE BIG** **?** **What should we learn? (a)** How do the experiences of other people—such as those of the astronauts in this essay—help us to learn about the world? **(b)** What can we learn from people who experiment with something new? Explain.

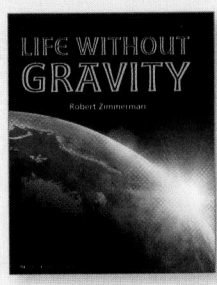

What Is Weightlessness?
What Are Its Advantages?
What Are Its Disadvantages?
Author's Conclusion

ACADEMIC VOCABULARY

As you write and speak about "Life Without Gravity," use the words related to learning that you explored on page 175 of this textbook.

Conventions: Action Verbs and Linking Verbs

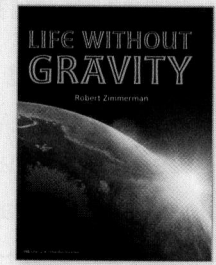

A **verb** is a word that expresses an action or a state of being. Every complete sentence must have at least one verb.

- An **action verb** tells what action someone or something is doing.
- A **linking verb** joins the subject of a sentence with a word or phrase that describes or renames the subject. The most common linking verbs are forms of *be*, such as *am, is, are, was, were, has been,* and *will be*. Other linking verbs include *seem, become, stay, feel, taste,* and *look*. Several of these verbs can also be used as action verbs.

Action Verbs	Linking Verbs
I *smelled* the roses.	The roses *smelled* fresh.
He *tastes* the apples.	The apple *tastes* sour.
The farmers *grow* corn.	The corn *grows* tall.
She *felt* the turtle's shell.	The shell *felt* hard.

Practice A
Identify the verb or verbs in each sentence, and indicate whether they are action verbs or linking verbs.

1. Weightlessness is sometimes unpleasant.
2. A weightless person experiences back pain.
3. Our muscles are strong because of gravity.
4. Astronauts learn new ways to eat.

Reading Application In "Life Without Gravity," find one sentence with a linking verb and one with an action verb.

Practice B
Write a sentence for each item, using the subject indicated and a form of the linking verb in parentheses.

1. astronaut (seem)
2. space camp (be)
3. equipment (stay)
4. gravity (become)

Writing Application Choose a photo from the essay and write two sentences about it, one using a linking verb, and one using an action verb.

Writing to Sources

Explanatory Text An **analogy** makes a comparison between two or more things that are alike in some ways but otherwise different. For example: *A follower without a leader is like a planet without a sun.*

- Use this sentence starter to write a basic analogy based on what you learned from the essay: "Life without gravity is like _____."

- Then, write several sentences to develop your analogy. Support your statements with details from the essay. You may also use anecdotes (personal stories), examples from real life, and facts or statistics to explain your ideas.

Grammar Application Reread your analogy to make sure you have used action verbs and linking verbs correctly.

Speaking and Listening

Presentation of Ideas Listen to the audio version of "Life Without Gravity," which is available in the eText version of your textbook. As you listen, take notes on the main ideas and supporting details in the essay. Then, in a small group, compare and contrast the audio and text versions. Discuss the elements that make each version compelling. Finally, use your notes to help you prepare and deliver an **oral summary** of your findings.

- Be objective. In your own words, outline the main ideas and supporting details of the essay. Compare ways in which the text and audio version present key ideas. Then, provide points of contrast between the two versions.

- Gather your notes and organize them logically.

- Assign presentation roles. Rehearse your presentation, adjusting the volume of your voice and perfecting your pronunciation of words.

- Present your summary to the class. Strive to maintain eye contact as you speak.

- After your presentation, invite comments and feedback from the class.

Common Core State Standards

Reading Informational Text
7. Compare and contrast a text to an audio, video, or multimedia version of the text, analyzing each medium's portrayal of the subject (e.g., how the delivery of a speech affects the impact of the words).

Writing
9. Draw evidence from literary or informational texts to support analysis, reflection, and research.
9.b. Apply grade 7 Reading standards to literary nonfiction.

Speaking and Listening
2. Analyze the main ideas and supporting details presented in diverse media and formats and explain how the ideas clarify a topic, text, or issue under study.
4. Present claims and findings, emphasizing salient points in a focused, coherent manner with pertinent descriptions, facts, details, and examples; use appropriate eye contact, adequate volume, and clear pronunciation.

Language
1. Demonstrate command of the conventions of standard English grammar and usage when writing or speaking.

Chief Dan George
(1899–1981), the son of
a tribal chief, was named
Geswanouth Slahoot but
was also known as Dan
Slaholt. At age five, he was
sent to a mission boarding
school, where his last name
was changed to George.
Years later, George won the
role of an aging Indian in
a TV series. He won acting
awards and earned parts
in major motion pictures.
With fame, George became
a spokesperson for Native
Americans.

**© Common Core
State Standards**

Reading Informational Text
1. Cite several pieces of textual
evidence to support analysis of
what the text says explicitly as well
as inferences drawn from the text.
2. Determine two or more central
ideas in a text and analyze their
development over the course of
the text.
3. Analyze the interactions
between individuals, events, and
ideas in a text.
6. Determine an author's point
of view or purpose in a text
and analyze how the author
distinguishes his or her position
from that of others.

? What should we learn?

Explore the Big Question as you read "I Am a Native of North
America." Take notes on what can be learned from the values and
lifestyle of Native Americans.

CLOSE READING FOCUS

Key Ideas and Details: **Main Idea**

The **main** or **central idea** is the most important idea in a literary
work or a passage of text. A single main idea may grow out of
two or more important ideas that the author develops throughout
the text. Sometimes the author directly states the main idea and
then provides the key points that support it. These key points are
supported in turn by details such as examples and descriptions.

Other times, the main idea is unstated. Readers must make
inferences from the text in order to determine the main idea. To
do this, notice how the writer groups details, and then look for
sentences that pull details together.

Craft and Structure: **Reflective Essay**

A **reflective essay** is a brief prose work that presents a writer's
thoughts and feelings—or reflections—about an experience or
idea. The purpose is to communicate these thoughts and feelings
so that readers will respond with thoughts and feelings of their
own. As you read a reflective essay, think about the ideas the
writer is sharing and analyze the interactions between individuals,
events, and ideas in the text.

Vocabulary

You will encounter the following words in this reflective essay. Copy
the words into your notebook, noting which ones you know, which
ones you know a little bit, and which ones you do not know at all.
After reading the essay, see how your knowledge of each word has
increased.

distinct	**communal**	**justifies**
promote	**hoarding**	**integration**

CLOSE READING MODEL

The passage below is from "I Am a Native of North America." The annotations to the right of the passage show ways in which you can use close reading skills to identify and make inferences about main ideas and to understand a reflective essay.

from "I Am a Native of North America"

Love is something you and I must have.[1] We must have it because our spirit feeds upon it. We must have it because without it we become weak and faint. Without love our self-esteem weakens. Without it our courage fails. Without love we can no longer look out confidently at the world. Instead we turn inwardly and begin to feed upon our own personalities and little by little we destroy ourselves.[2]

You and I need the strength and joy that comes from knowing that we are loved. With it we are creative. With it we march tirelessly. With it, and with it alone, we are able to sacrifice for others.[3]

There have been times when we all wanted so desperately to feel a reassuring hand upon us . . . there have been lonely times when we so wanted a strong arm around us . . . I cannot tell you how deeply I miss my wife's presence when I return from a trip. Her love was my greatest joy, my strength, my greatest blessing.[4]

Main Idea

1 This paragraph begins with a topic sentence that directly states a main idea. You can expect to find support for this idea in the sentences to come.

Main Idea

2 The author provides supporting details that focus on the universal human need for love. These details explain why love is so important.

Reflective Essay

3 The author uses emotionally-charged language to express his thoughts and feelings about love. As you explore these ideas, you may respond with your own thoughts and feelings on the subject.

Reflective Essay

4 Here, the author offers an example from his own experience. The power and emotion of this personal detail may prompt you to consider who is important in your own life.

I Am a Native of North America

Chief Dan George

Vocabulary ▶
distinct (di stiŋkt´) *adj.*
separate and different

communal (kə myo͞on´
əl) *adj.* shared by all

I n the course of my lifetime I have lived in two **distinct** cultures. I was born into a culture that lived in **communal** houses. My grandfather's house was eighty feet long. It was called a smoke house, and it stood down by the beach along the inlet.[1] All my grandfather's sons and their families lived in this large dwelling. Their sleeping apartments were separated by blankets made of bull rush reeds, but one open fire in the middle served the cooking needs of all. In houses like these, throughout the tribe, people learned to live with one another; learned to serve one another; learned to respect the rights of one another. And children shared the thoughts of the adult world and found themselves surrounded by aunts and uncles and cousins who loved them and did not threaten them. My father was born in such a house and learned from infancy how to love people and be at home with them.

And beyond this acceptance of one another there was a deep respect for everything in nature that surrounded them. My father loved the earth and all its creatures. The earth was his second mother. The earth and everything it contained was a gift from See-see-am[2] . . . and the way to thank this great spirit was to use his gifts with respect. ●

Reflective Essay
What experience or idea is the author reflecting on here?

---

1. **inlet** (in´ let) *n.* narrow strip of water jutting into a body of land from a river, a lake, or an ocean.
2. **See-see-am** the name of the Great Spirit, or "The Chief Above," in the Salishan language of Chief George's people.

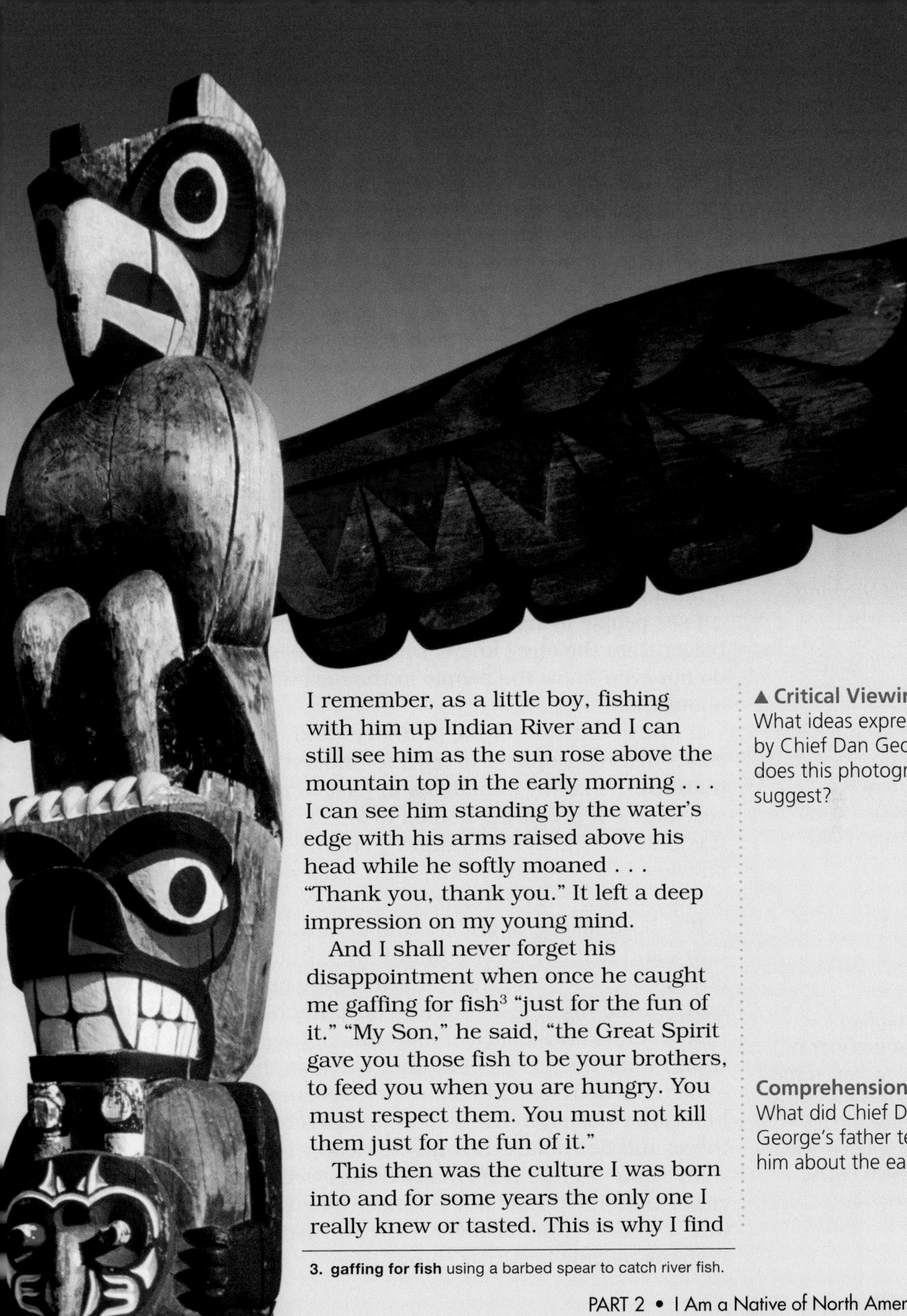

I remember, as a little boy, fishing with him up Indian River and I can still see him as the sun rose above the mountain top in the early morning . . . I can see him standing by the water's edge with his arms raised above his head while he softly moaned . . . "Thank you, thank you." It left a deep impression on my young mind.

And I shall never forget his disappointment when once he caught me gaffing for fish[3] "just for the fun of it." "My Son," he said, "the Great Spirit gave you those fish to be your brothers, to feed you when you are hungry. You must respect them. You must not kill them just for the fun of it."

This then was the culture I was born into and for some years the only one I really knew or tasted. This is why I find

3. **gaffing for fish** using a barbed spear to catch river fish.

▲ **Critical Viewing**
What ideas expressed by Chief Dan George does this photograph suggest?

Comprehension
What did Chief Dan George's father teach him about the earth?

▲ **Critical Viewing**
Based on what you have read, describe what the people in these boats might be doing.

Vocabulary ▶
justifies (jus´ tə fiz´)
v. excuses; explains

Spiral Review
AUTHOR'S POINT OF VIEW How would you describe the author's attitude toward his subject? Support your answer with details from the essay.

it hard to accept many of the things I see around me.

I see people living in smoke houses hundreds of times bigger than the one I knew. But the people in one apartment do not even know the people in the next and care less about them.

It is also difficult for me to understand the deep hate that exists among people. It is hard to understand a culture that justifies the killing of millions in past wars, and is at this very moment preparing bombs to kill even greater numbers. It is hard for me to understand a culture that spends more on wars and weapons to kill, than it does on education and welfare to help and develop.

It is hard for me to understand a culture that not only hates and fights its brothers but even attacks nature and abuses her. I see my white brother going about blotting out nature from his cities. I see him strip the hills bare, leaving ugly wounds on the face of mountains. I see him tearing things from the bosom of mother earth as though she were a monster, who refused to share her treasures with him. I see him throw poison in the waters, indifferent to the life he kills there; and he chokes the air with deadly fumes.

My white brother does many things well for he is more clever than my people but I wonder if he knows how to love well. I wonder if he has ever really learned to love at all. Perhaps he only loves the things that are his own but never learned to love the things that are outside and beyond him. And this is, of course, not love at all, for man must love all creation or he will love none of it. Man must love fully or he will become the lowest of the animals. It is the power to love that makes him the greatest of them all . . . for he alone of all animals is capable of love.

Love is something you and I must have. We must have it because our spirit feeds upon it. We must have it because without it we become weak and faint. Without love our self-esteem weakens. Without it our courage fails. Without love we can no longer look out confidently at the world. Instead we turn inwardly and begin to feed upon our own personalities and little by little we destroy ourselves.

You and I need the strength and joy that comes from knowing that we are loved. With it we are creative. With it we march tirelessly. With it, and with it alone, we are able to sacrifice for others.

There have been times when we all wanted so desperately to feel a reassuring hand upon us . . . there have been lonely times when we so wanted a strong arm around us . . . I cannot tell you how deeply I miss my wife's presence when I return from a trip. Her love was my greatest joy, my strength, my greatest blessing.

I am afraid my culture has little to offer yours. But my culture did prize friendship and companionship. It did not look on privacy as a thing to be clung to, for privacy builds up walls and walls promote distrust. My culture lived in big family communities, and from infancy people learned to live with others.

My culture did not prize the hoarding of private possessions; in fact, to hoard was a shameful thing to do among my people. The Indian looked on all things in nature as belonging to him and he expected to share them with others and to take only what he needed.

Everyone likes to give as well as receive. No one wishes only to receive all the time. We have taken much from your culture . . . I wish you had taken something from our culture . . . for there were some beautiful and good things in it.

Main Idea
What key words or sentences so far have helped you determine the essay's main idea?

Reflective Essay
What experiences does the author reflect on here?

◄ **Vocabulary**
promote (prə mōt´) v. encourage; contribute to the growth of

hoarding (hôr´ diŋ) n. accumulation and storage of items or supplies

Vocabulary ▶
integration (in´ tə grā´
shən) *n.* the end of
separation of cultural
or racial groups

Soon it will be too late to know my culture, for **integration** is upon us and soon we will have no values but yours. Already many of our young people have forgotten the old ways. And many have been shamed of their Indian ways by scorn and ridicule. My culture is like a wounded deer that has crawled away into the forest to bleed and die alone.

The only thing that can truly help us is genuine love. You must truly love us, be patient with us and share with us. And we must love you—with a genuine love that forgives and forgets . . . a love that forgives the terrible sufferings your culture brought ours when it swept over us like a wave crashing along a beach . . . with a love that forgets and lifts up its head and sees in your eyes an answering love of trust and acceptance.

This is brotherhood . . . anything less is not worthy of the name.

I have spoken.

Language Study

Vocabulary The words boldfaced below appear in "I Am a Native of North America." For each, choose its **antonym,** or word that is opposite in meaning, from among the three choices given. Explain your answers.

1. distinct: (a) similar **(b)** different **(c)** decided

2. communal: (a) busy **(b)** private **(c)** organized

3. promote: (a) encourage **(b)** advance **(c)** prevent

4. hoarding: (a) storing **(b)** distributing **(c)** saving

5. integration: (a) segregation **(b)** assimilation **(c)** mixing

WORD STUDY

The **Latin root -*just*-** means "law" or "fair and right." In this essay, Chief Dan George cannot understand a culture that **justifies**, or defends as right, the killing of others in a war.

Word Study

Part A Explain how the **Latin root -*just*-** contributes to the meanings of the words *justice, adjust,* and *injustice.* Consult a dictionary if necessary.

Part B Use the context of the sentences and your knowledge of the Latin root *-just-* to explain your answer to each question.

1. If a decision is *unjust,* is it fair?

2. If there is no *justification* for your error, are you to blame?

Close Reading Activities

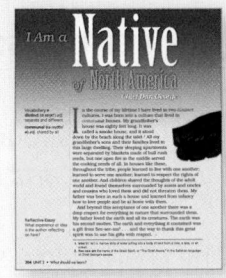

Literary Analysis

Key Ideas and Details

1. (a) What details does Chief Dan George provide about his father's relationship with nature? **(b)** Find a sentence from the essay that pulls these details together.

2. (a) Name three things that people learn from growing up in communal homes. Use examples from the essay to support your answer. **(b) Compare and Contrast:** Identify several differences between the "two distinct cultures" in which Chief Dan George lived.

3. Main Idea (a) What is the main idea of the essay? **(b)** Is the main idea stated directly, or do you have to determine it by making inferences? **(c)** What key points and supporting details contribute most to the development of the main idea?

Craft and Structure

4. Reflective Essay Analyze the reflective essay in a chart like the one on the right. In the top box, write George's reflections on three points. In the middle box, write your response to each point. Trade charts with a partner and discuss your responses. Then, in the last box, explain whether your responses changed based on your discussion.

5. Reflective Essay (a) What three things puzzle Chief Dan George about his "white brother"? **(b) Interpret:** When Chief Dan George says, "My white brother . . . is more clever than my people," what does he mean by *clever*? **(c) Support:** What details in the text support your interpretation?

> | George's Reflections |
> | --- |
> | |
> | **My Responses** |
> | |
> | **After Discussion** |
> | |

Integration of Knowledge and Ideas

6. (a) Analyze: What is the "brotherhood" that Chief Dan George talks about in the essay? **(b) Evaluate:** Is this brotherhood important? Why or why not?

7. Make a Judgment: Can people maintain a sense of cultural identity while interacting with members of another group that does not have the same culture? Explain your answer, using evidence from the text to support your ideas.

8. **What should we learn? (a)** Why is it important to know the beliefs and traditions of those who came before us? **(b)** What could happen if we ignore the past?

ACADEMIC VOCABULARY

As you write and speak about "I Am a Native of North America," use words related to learning that you explored on page 175 of this textbook.

Conventions: **The Principal Parts of Verbs**

A verb has four **principal parts**: *present, present participle, past,* and *past participle.*

The chart below shows the four principal parts of *talk,* a regular verb, as well as the principal parts of several commonly misused irregular verbs. Notice that when you use the present participle or the past participle, you include a helping verb. Common helping verbs include *has, have, had, am, is, are, was,* and *were.* A verb combined with its helping verb is called a *verb phrase.*

	Present	**Present Participle**	**Past**	**Past Participle**
Regular	talk	(is) talking	talked	(has) talked
Irregular	sit	(is) sitting	sat	(has) sat
Irregular	am, is, are	(is) being	was	(has) been
Irregular	has, have	(is) having	had	(has) had
Irregular	begin	(is) beginning	began	(has) begun

Practice A

Identify the verb or verb phrase in each sentence. Then identify its principal part.

1. Chief Dan George's family lived in a large communal house.
2. He had learned much from his grandfather.
3. He is yearning for greater tolerance in America.
4. Chief Dan George believes in love.

Reading Application In "I Am a Native of North America," locate at least three of the principal parts of verbs.

Practice B

Complete each sentence, using a principal part of the verb in parentheses. Identify the principal part you have used.

1. People once (know) Chief Dan George as Dan Slaholt.
2. By the age of 17, he (work) at different jobs.
3. Before appearing in movies, he (act) in TV shows.
4. Chief Dan George (call) on his readers to love one another.

Writing Application Choose an idea or image mentioned in the essay and write four sentences about it, using each of the four principal parts of verbs.

Writing to Sources

Informative Text Make an **outline** to show the main idea and supporting details in "I Am a Native of North America." Build your outline using this format:

At the top of your outline, write a sentence that states the main ideas of the essay in your own words. Then, list subtopics for each main idea, and finally, list details. Refer back to the text to find and confirm specific details.

- Use Roman numerals to identify each key point.
- Use capital letters to identify supporting details.

Once you have completed your outline, write a brief summary of the essay.

Grammar Application Check your writing to be sure you have used the principal parts of verbs correctly.

Speaking and Listening

Presentation of Ideas In a small group, present a **response** to an audio version of "I Am a Native of North America." Access the audio recording, which is available in the eText version of your textbook. Follow these steps to complete your response.

- Listen to the audio version as a group, taking notes on the impact of the selection as it is read aloud. For example, note whether the audio version brings certain words and phrases to life, or if it conveys a certain tone that is not evident in the print version.
- Next, discuss with the group ways in which the audio version enhanced or detracted from the meaning and tone of the printed version. Replay the audio and reread the print version to find specific examples that support your group's ideas.
- After your discussion, plan a presentation to the class in which you share your response.
- Assign presenter roles, and rehearse your presentation.
- At the conclusion of your presentation, invite questions and comments from your audience.

Common Core State Standards

Reading Informational Text
7. Compare and contrast a text to an audio, video, or multimedia version of the text, analyzing each medium's portrayal of the subject.

Writing
2.a. Introduce a topic clearly, previewing what is to follow; organize ideas, concepts, and information, using strategies such as definition, classification, comparison/contrast, and cause/effect; include formatting (e.g., headings), graphics (e.g., charts, tables), and multimedia when useful to aiding comprehension.

Language
1. Demonstrate command of the conventions of standard English grammar and usage when writing or speaking.
5.b. Use the relationship between particular words (e.g., synonym/antonym) to better understand each of the words.

Meet the Author

Barbara Jordan (1936–1996) inherited her skill at public speaking from her father, a Baptist minister. As a high school student in Houston, Texas, Jordan won public speaking competitions. In 1966, Jordan was elected to the Texas Senate, and she became a member of Congress in 1972. During the 1976 Democratic National Convention, she became the first African American to deliver the keynote speech at a major party's political convention. In 1990, the National Women's Hall of Fame voted Jordan one of the most influential women of the twentieth century.

Ⓒ **Common Core State Standards**

Reading Informational Text
8. Trace and evaluate the argument and specific claims in a text, assessing whether the reasoning is sound and the evidence is relevant and sufficient to support the claims.

Language
4.b. Use common, grade-appropriate Greek or Latin affixes and roots as clues to the meaning of a word.

? **What should we learn?**

Think about the Big Question as you read "All Together Now." Note ways in which the persuasive essay can help you learn about tolerance.

CLOSE READING FOCUS

Key Ideas and Details: **Classifying Fact and Opinion**

When you read nonfiction, it is important to classify types of information. Distinguishing between fact and opinion is a key skill.

- A **fact** is something that can be proved.
- An **opinion** is a person's judgment or belief. It may be supported by factual evidence, but it cannot be proved.

As you read, recognize clues that indicate an opinion, such as the phrases *I believe* or *in my opinion*. Also look for words such as *always, never, must, cannot, best, worst,* and *all,* which may be part of broad statements that reveal personal judgments.

Craft and Structure: **Persuasive Essay**

A **persuasive essay** is a work of nonfiction that presents a series of arguments to convince readers to believe or act in a certain way. When you read persuasive essays, be alert for the use of persuasive techniques. Then, decide whether a particular technique represents reasonable and relevant support that convinces you to accept or act on the author's ideas. As you read, identify and analyze the persuasive techniques defined below.

- **Appeals to authority** use the statements of experts and well-known people.
- **Appeals to emotion** use words that convey strong feelings.
- **Appeals to reason** use logical arguments backed by facts.

Vocabulary

You will encounter the following words in this persuasive essay. Copy the words into your notebook. Write antonyms—words with opposite meanings—for as many words as you can.

legislation	tolerant	culminated
fundamental	equality	optimist

CLOSE READING MODEL

The passage below is from Barbara Jordan's persuasive essay "All Together Now." The annotations to the right of the passage show ways in which you can use close reading skills to classify fact and opinion and to understand a persuasive essay.

from "All Together Now"

When I look at race relations today I can see that some positive changes have come about. But much remains to be done, and the answer does not lie in more legislation. We *have* the legislation we need; we have the laws. Frankly, I don't believe that the task of bringing us all together can be accomplished by government.[1] What we need now is soul force—the efforts of people working on a small scale to build a truly tolerant, harmonious society. And parents can do a great deal to create that tolerant society.[2]

We all know that race relations in America have had a very rocky history. Think about the 1960s when Dr. Martin Luther King, Jr., was in his heyday and there were marches and protests against segregation and discrimination. The movement culminated in 1963 with the March on Washington.[3]

Following that event, race relations reached an all-time peak. . . . At last, black people and white people seemed ready to live together in peace.

But that is not what happened. By the 1990's the good feelings had diminished. Today the nation seems to be suffering from compassion fatigue, and issues such as race relations and civil rights have never regained momentum.[4]

Fact and Opinion

1 The phrase, "I don't believe" indicates that the author is expressing an opinion.

Persuasive Essay

2 In this sentence, Jordan introduces the cornerstone of her argument by appealing to readers' sense of community. She uses the term "soul force" to stir and empower readers to take action on the issue.

Fact and Opinion

3 The author strengthens her argument with facts. She mentions actual dates, people, and events— the 1960s, Martin Luther King, Jr., and the March on Washington.

Persuasive Essay

4 Here Jordan changes her tone. She uses the words "diminished," "suffering," and "compassion fatigue" to develop an emotional appeal. Jordan's message is that past gains in race relations are in danger of slipping away due to inaction.

All Together Now

Barbara Jordan

Vocabulary ▶

legislation (lej´ is lā´ shən) *n.* law-making

tolerant (täl´ ər ənt) *adj.* accepting; free from bigotry or prejudice

culminated (kul´ mə nāt´ əd) *v.* reached its highest point, or climax

fundamental (fun´ də ment´ ´l) *adj.* basic; forming a foundation

When I look at race relations today I can see that some positive changes have come about. But much remains to be done, and the answer does not lie in more legislation. We *have* the legislation we need; we have the laws. Frankly, I don't believe that the task of bringing us all together can be accomplished by government. What we need now is soul force—the efforts of people working on a small scale to build a truly tolerant, harmonious society. And parents can do a great deal to create that tolerant society.

We all know that race relations in America have had a very rocky history. Think about the 1960s when Dr. Martin Luther King, Jr., was in his heyday and there were marches and protests against segregation[1] and discrimination. The movement culminated in 1963 with the March on Washington.

Following that event, race relations reached an all-time peak. President Lyndon B. Johnson pushed through the Civil Rights Act of 1964, which remains the fundamental piece of civil rights legislation in this century. The Voting Rights Act of 1965 ensured that everyone in our country could vote. At last, black people and white people seemed ready to live together in peace.

▼ Critical Viewing
Based on this photo and the title, what do you think this essay will be about?

---

1. **segregation** (seg´ rə gā´ shən) *n.* the practice of forcing racial groups to live apart from each other.

But that is not what happened. By the 1990's the good feelings had diminished. Today the nation seems to be suffering from compassion fatigue, and issues such as race relations and civil rights have never regained momentum.

Those issues, however, remain crucial. As our society becomes more diverse, people of all races and backgrounds will have to learn to live together. If we don't think this is important, all we have to do is look at the situation in Bosnia[2] today.

How do we create a harmonious society out of so many kinds of people? The key is tolerance—the one value that is indispensable in creating community.

If we are concerned about community, if it is important to us that people not feel excluded, then we have to do something. Each of us can decide to have one friend of a different race or background in our mix of friends. If we do this, we'll be working together to push things forward.

One thing is clear to me: We, as human beings, must be willing to accept people who are different from ourselves. I must be willing to accept people who don't look as I do and don't talk as I do. It is crucial that I am open to their feelings, their inner reality.

What can parents do? We can put our faith in young people as a positive force. I have yet to find a racist baby. Babies come into the world as blank slates and, with their beautiful innocence, see others not as different but as enjoyable companions. Children learn ideas and attitudes from the adults who nurture them. I absolutely believe that children do not adopt prejudices unless they absorb them from their parents or teachers.

The best way to get this country faithful to the American dream of tolerance and equality is to start small. Parents can actively encourage their children to be in the company of people who are of other racial and ethnic backgrounds. If a child thinks, "Well, that person's color is not the same as mine, but she must be okay because she likes to play with the same things I like to play with," that child will grow up with a broader view of humanity.

I'm an incurable optimist. For the rest of the time that I have left on this planet I want to bring people together. You

Persuasive Essay
Which persuasive technique does Jordan use with this reference to Bosnia?

Spiral Review
STRUCTURE The author organizes her ideas by asking and then answering a question. Do you think this structure is effective? Explain.

◄ Vocabulary
equality (ē kwôl´ə tē) n. social state in which all people are treated the same

optimist (äp´ tə mist) n. someone who takes the most hopeful view of matters

Fact and Opinion
What clue words in this paragraph show that the author is expressing an opinion?

Comprehension
What did the Voting Rights Act of 1965 do?

---

2. **Bosnia** (bäz´ nē ə) n. country, located on the Balkan Peninsula in Europe, that was the site of a bloody civil war between different ethnic and religious groups during the 1990s.

might think of this as a labor of love. Now, I know that love means different things to different people. But what *I* mean is this: I care about you because you are a fellow human being and I find it okay in my mind, in my heart, to simply say to you, I love you. And maybe that would encourage you to love me in return.

It is possible for all of us to work on this—at home, in our schools, at our jobs. It is possible to work on human relationships in every area of our lives.

▲ **Critical Viewing**
Does this photograph reflect the attitude Jordan conveys in the essay? Explain.

Language Study

Vocabulary The words listed below appear in "All Together Now." Answer each numbered question by writing a complete sentence that includes the italicized vocabulary word. Explain your answers.

> **tolerant   culminated   fundamental   equality   optimist**

1. Is reading a *fundamental* part of education?

2. If Joan is an *optimist,* does she believe things will end well?

3. If people are *tolerant,* are they likely to accept others?

4. If a soccer team's season *culminated* in victory, what happened?

5. If a country is founded on *equality,* are some people treated differently than others?

WORD STUDY

The **Latin root -*leg-*** means "law." In this essay, Barbara Jordan argues that we need more than just **legislation**, or the act of making laws, to improve race relations.

Word Study

Part A Explain how the **Latin root -*leg-*** contributes to the meanings of the words *allegation, legacy,* and *privilege.* Consult a dictionary if necessary.

Part B Use your knowledge of the Latin root -*leg-* to explain your answer to each question.

1. Is a thief likely to give a *legitimate* account of his actions?

2. Would you expect an honest person to do something *illegal*?

Literary Analysis

Key Ideas and Details

1. **Classifying Fact and Opinion** List two facts Jordan uses to support her ideas.

2. **Classifying Fact and Opinion** In a chart like the one on the right, record three opinions Jordan expresses, and list the clues from the text that helped you identify each opinion.

3. **(a)** How does Jordan summarize the history of race relations from the 1960s to the 1990s? Use examples from the essay to support your answer. **(b) Interpret:** In your own words, describe what Jordan means by "compassion fatigue."

Opinion

Clues

Craft and Structure

4. **Persuasive Essay** Identify one appeal to authority, one appeal to emotion, and one appeal to reason that Jordan uses in this persuasive essay.

5. **(a)** According to Jordan, how do children learn ideas and attitudes? Support your answer with a quotation from the essay. **(b) Interpret:** What does Jordan mean when she says "I have yet to find a racist baby"?

6. **Persuasive Essay (a)** What is the most convincing argument Jordan makes? **(b)** Why is it convincing?

Integration of Knowledge and Ideas

7. **(a)** What "one value" is necessary to create "a harmonious society"? **(b) Analyze:** Why does Jordan suggest Americans "start small" to promote this value? **(c) Apply:** What types of behavior might help reduce the problems Jordan describes?

8. **(a)** What does Jordan suggest parents do to foster a sense of community? **(b) Evaluate:** Do you think that Jordan's ideas could work to promote tolerance? Explain your answer using textual details.

9. **THE BIG ?** **What should we learn?** Discuss the following questions in a small group. **(a)** How can learning about the history of race relations help us in the future? **(b)** What can this knowledge teach us?

ACADEMIC VOCABULARY

As you write and speak about "All Together Now," use the words related to learning that you explored on page 175 of this textbook.

Conventions: **Conjunctions and Interjections**

All Together Now
Barbara Jordan

> **Conjunctions** connect words or groups of words. **Coordinating conjunctions,** such as *but* and *so,* connect words or groups of words of the same kind, such as two or more nouns or verbs.

In the following examples, the coordinating conjunctions are boldfaced. The words or groups of words they connect are italicized.

Nouns: The *pen* **and** *paper* contained fingerprints.

Verbs: Shall we *walk* **or** *ride* our bicycles?

Groups of words: *He ran out the door,* **but** *the bus had already left.*

> An **interjection** is a part of speech that expresses a feeling, such as pain or excitement. An interjection may be set off with a comma or an exclamation point. Interjections can add emphasis and are especially useful for writing realistic dialogue.

In these examples, notice how the interjections are punctuated and how they make the writing sound more realistic.

Pain: Ouch! I hit my toe.

Excitement: Wow, Melissa can run really fast!

Coordinating Conjunctions		
and	nor	so
but	or	yet
for		

Common Interjections	
Wow	Hey
Whew	Boy
Well	Yikes
Oh	Oops

Practice A

In each sentence, identify the coordinating conjunction and the words or groups of words connected by the conjunction.

1. My great-grandmother and great-grandfather grew up during segregation.

2. As young kids they attended all-black schools, but their high school was integrated.

3. Great-grandma had to work to help the family, so she waited tables after school.

4. Great-grandpa wrote and edited articles for the African-American newspaper.

Reading Application In "All Together Now," find two coordinating conjunctions, and identify the words they connect.

Practice B

Rewrite each sentence, adding an interjection and the appropriate punctuation.

1. Many brave people put their lives on the line in the 1960s.

2. Did you know that some people actually died while fighting for civil rights?

3. Dr. Martin Luther King, Jr., inspired many people.

4. Do you know of any books I should read about the Civil Rights Movement?

Writing Application Write a paragraph about the ways that people can work together to bring about positive change. Use at least two coordinating conjunctions and two interjections.

Writing to Sources

Argument Write a brief **persuasive letter** to community leaders advising them how people in the community can promote tolerance. Use examples from Jordan's essay to support your ideas and arguments. Demonstrate understanding of your topic as you draft.

- Clearly state your claim, or position. For example, "Promoting tolerance in our community would . . . ."
- Identify your goals. Then, use details from the text and other reliable sources to explain how to meet those goals.
- Defend your claims with logical reasoning and relevant evidence. Be sure to address alternate or opposing claims.
- Review your letter to ensure you have used correct formatting and that your tone is respectful and formal.

Grammar Application Check your writing to make sure you have used and punctuated conjunctions properly. To maintain a formal tone, you may decide not to use interjections in your letter.

Speaking and Listening

Comprehension and Collaboration In a small group, write a **public service announcement** (PSA) on promoting the fair treatment of all people. Follow these steps to complete the assignment.

- Begin by brainstorming for ideas. Give all group members a chance to speak. Record everyone's ideas, and then as a group decide which ideas you will use in your PSA.
- Identify your audience, then draft your PSA. Support your claims with examples from "All Together Now." You may wish to include other relevant information that supports your main idea and appeals to your audience.
- Make your PSA memorable by using persuasive techniques such as those Jordan used in her essay.
- Present your PSA to the class. After your presentation, ask for feedback from your classmates.

 **Common Core State Standards**

Writing
1.a. Introduce claim(s), acknowledge alternate or opposing claims, and organize the reasons and evidence logically.
1.b. Support claim(s) with logical reasoning and relevant evidence, using accurate, credible sources and demonstrating an understanding of the topic or text.

Speaking and Listening
4. Present claims and findings, emphasizing salient points in a focused, coherent manner with pertinent descriptions, facts, details, and examples.

Language
1. Demonstrate command of the conventions of standard English grammar and usage when writing or speaking.
2. Demonstrate command of the conventions of standard English capitalization, punctuation, and spelling when writing.

Meet the Author

After starting out as a journalist, **Marjorie Kinnan Rawlings** (1896–1953) quit and moved to a farm she bought in northern Florida. There, her experiences and close exposure to nature inspired her to write several novels, including the 1939 Pulitzer Prize–winning book, *The Yearling*. While working on *The Yearling*, Rawlings prepared for key scenes by participating in bear hunts. Her writing reflects an intimate understanding and appreciation of the outdoors.

© **Common Core State Standards**

Reading Informational Text
4. Determine the meaning of words and phrases as they are used in a text, including figurative, connotative, and technical meanings; analyze the impact of a specific word choice on meaning and tone.

Language
6. Acquire and use accurately grade-appropriate general academic and domain-specific words and phrases.

? What should we learn?

Explore the Big Question as you read "Rattlesnake Hunt." Take notes on the ways that learning about rattlesnakes helps the author learn about herself.

CLOSE READING FOCUS

Key Ideas and Details: **Classifying Fact and Opinion**

As you read nonfiction, note details a writer uses to support an idea. You can classify these details into two basic categories. A **fact** is information you can prove. An **opinion** is a judgment.

- **Fact:** The room measures ten feet by twelve feet.
- **Opinion:** Green is the best color for the room.

Be aware that some writers present opinions or beliefs as facts. To get to the truth, use resources to check facts.

Craft and Structure: **Word Choice, or Diction**

A writer's **word choice,** or **diction,** can make writing seem difficult or easy, formal or informal. Diction includes not only individual words but also the phrases and expressions the writer uses. The answers to these questions shape a writer's diction:

- *What does the audience already know about the topic?* The writer may have to define terms or use simpler language.
- *What feeling will this work convey?* The use of casual or formal language can make a work serious or funny, academic or personal. The type of language and the length and style of the sentences can make a work seem simple or complex.

As you read, notice how the author's word choice affects the way you respond to a text.

Vocabulary

You will encounter the following words in this essay. Write the words in your notebook, circling the one that has an opposite meaning from *life*. Explain how you arrived at your answer.

adequate	desolate	forage
translucent	arid	mortality

CLOSE READING MODEL

The passage below is from Marjorie Kinnan Rawlings's essay "Rattlesnake Hunt." The annotations to the right of the passage show ways in which you can use close reading skills to classify fact and opinion and to analyze the author's word choice, or diction.

from "Rattlesnake Hunt"

I hope never in my life to be so frightened as I was in those first few hours. I kept on Ross' footsteps, I moved when he moved, sometimes jolting into him when I thought he might leave me behind. He does not use the forked stick of conventional snake hunting, but a steel prong, shaped like an L, at the end of a long stout stick.[1] He hunted casually, calling my attention to the varying vegetation, to hawks overhead, to a pair of the rare whooping cranes that flapped over us. In mid-morning he stopped short, dropped his stick, and brought up a five-foot rattlesnake draped limply over the steel L. It seemed to me that I should drop in my tracks.[2]

"They're not active at this season," he said quietly. "A snake takes on the temperature of its surroundings.[3] They can't stand too much heat for that reason, and when the weather is cool, as now, they're sluggish."[4]

The sun was bright overhead, the sky a translucent blue, and it seemed to me that it was warm enough for any snake to do as it willed.

Word Choice, or Diction
1 Rawlings knows that many of her readers may be unfamiliar with snake-hunting tools. She defines her terms clearly and uses simple comparisons to help you visualize the prong that Ross uses.

Word Choice, or Diction
2 Rawlings creates a conversational tone with the use of informal language and a detail about her intense personal reaction to the sight of the snake.

Fact and Opinion
3 Here Rawlings provides facts that explain the snake's behavior. These facts help her—and her readers—feel less intimidated by the snake.

Word Choice, or Diction
4 *Sluggish* means "slow to respond or react." This informal but vivid word is effective in helping you understand the snake's current state.

Rattlesnake Hunt

Marjorie Kinnan Rawlings

Ross Allen, a young Florida herpetologist,[1] invited me to join him on a hunt in the upper Everglades[2]—for rattlesnakes. Ross and I drove to Arcadia in his coupé[3] on a warm January day.

I said, "How will you bring back the rattlesnakes?"

"In the back of my car."

My courage was not adequate to inquire whether they were thrown in loose and might be expected to appear between our feet. Actually, a large portable box of heavy close-meshed wire made a safe cage. Ross wanted me to

---

1. **herpetologist** (hʉr´ pə täl´ ə jist) *n.* someone who studies reptiles and amphibians.
2. **Everglades** large region of marshes in southern Florida, about one hundred miles long and averaging fifty miles in width.
3. **coupé** (kōō pā´) *n.* small two-door automobile.

write an article about his work and on our way to the unhappy hunting grounds I took notes on a mass of data that he had accumulated in years of herpetological research. The scientific and dispassionate detachment of the material and the man made a desirable approach to rattlesnake territory. As I had discovered with the insects and varmints,[4] it is difficult to be afraid of anything about which enough is known, and Ross' facts were fresh from the laboratory.

The hunting ground was Big Prairie, south of Arcadia and west of the northern tip of Lake Okeechobee. Big Prairie is a **desolate** cattle country, half marsh, half pasture, with islands of palm trees and cypress and oaks. At that time of year the cattlemen and Indians were burning the country, on the theory that the young fresh wire grass that springs up from the roots after a fire is the best cattle **forage**. Ross planned to hunt his rattlers in the forefront of the fires. They lived in winter, he said, in gopher holes, coming out in the midday warmth to forage, and would move ahead of the flames and be easily taken. We joined forces with a big man named Will, his snake-hunting companion of the territory, and set out in early morning, after a long rough drive over deep-rutted roads into the open wilds.

I hope never in my life to be so frightened as I was in those first few hours. I kept on Ross' footsteps, I moved when he moved, sometimes jolting into him when I thought he might leave me behind. He does not use the forked stick of conventional snake hunting, but a steel prong, shaped like an L, at the end of a long stout stick. He hunted casually, calling my attention to the varying vegetation, to hawks overhead, to a pair of the rare whooping cranes that flapped over us. In mid-morning he stopped short, dropped his stick, and brought up a five-foot rattlesnake draped limply over the steel L. It seemed to me that I should drop in my tracks.

"They're not active at this season," he said quietly. "A snake takes on the temperature of its surroundings. They can't stand too much heat for that reason, and when the weather is cool, as now, they're sluggish."

---

4. **varmints** (vär´ mənts) *n.* animals regarded as troublesome.

◄ **Vocabulary**
desolate (des´ ə lit) *adj.* lonely; solitary

forage (fôr´ ij) *n.* food for domestic animals

Fact and Opinion
What reference source could confirm the fact in the last paragraph about a snake's temperature?

Comprehension
Why is the narrator going on a rattlesnake hunt?

Vocabulary ▶
translucent (trans
lōo´ sənt) *adj.* allowing
some light through

arid (ar´id) *adj.*
getting little rain, and
therefore very dry

The sun was bright overhead, the sky a **translucent** blue, and it seemed to me that it was warm enough for any snake to do as it willed. The sweat poured down my back. Ross dropped the rattler in a crocus sack and Will carried it. By noon, he had caught four. I felt faint and ill. We stopped by a pond and went swimming. The region was flat, the horizon limitless, and as I came out of the cool blue water I expected to find myself surrounded by a ring of rattlers. There were only Ross and Will, opening the lunch basket. I could not eat. Will went back and drove his truck closer, for Ross expected the hunting to be better in the afternoon. The hunting was much better. When we went back to the truck to deposit two more rattlers in the wire cage, there was a rattlesnake lying under the truck.

Ross said, "Whenever I leave my car or truck with snakes already in it, other rattlers always appear. I don't know whether this is because they scent or sense the presence of other snakes, or whether in this **arid** area they come to the car for shade in the heat of the day."

The problem was scientific, but I had no interest. •

That night Ross and Will and I camped out in the vast spaces of the Everglades prairies.

▼ Critical Viewing
What makes the snake
in this photograph
appear dangerous?

We got water from an abandoned well and cooked supper under buttonwood bushes by a flowing stream. The camp fire blazed cheerfully under the stars and a new moon lifted in the sky. Will told tall tales of the cattlemen and the Indians and we were at peace.

Ross said, "We couldn't have a better night for catching water snakes."

After the rattlers, water snakes seemed innocuous[6] enough. We worked along the edge of the stream and here Ross did not use his L-shaped steel. He reached under rocks and along the edge of the water and brought out harmless reptiles with his hands. I had said nothing to him of my fears, but he understood them. He brought a small dark snake from under a willow root.

"Wouldn't you like to hold it?" he asked. "People think snakes are cold and clammy, but they aren't. Take it in your hands. You'll see that it is warm."

Again, because I was ashamed, I took the snake in my hands. It was not cold, it was not clammy, and it lay trustingly in my hands, a thing that lived and breathed and had mortality like the rest of us. I felt an upsurgence of spirit.

The next day was magnificent. The air was crystal, the sky was aquamarine, and the far horizon of palms and oaks lay against the sky. I felt a new boldness and followed Ross bravely. He was making the rounds of the gopher holes. The rattlers came out in the mid-morning warmth and were never far away. He could tell by their trails whether one had come out or was still in the hole. Sometimes the two men dug the snake out. At times it was down so long and winding a tunnel that the digging was hopeless. Then they blocked the entrance and went on to other holes. In an hour or so they made the original rounds, unblocking the holes. The rattler in every case came out hurriedly, as though anything were preferable to being shut in. All the time Ross talked to me, telling me the scientific facts he had discovered about the habits of the rattlers. ●

"They pay no attention to a man standing perfectly still," he said, and proved it by letting Will unblock a hole while he stood at the entrance as the snake came out. It was exciting to

▲ **Critical Viewing**
Snakes are often pictured in art and on artifacts such as this Native American basket. Why do you think that is so?

◄ **Vocabulary**
mortality (môr tal′ ə tē) *n.* the condition of being mortal, or having to die eventually

Comprehension
How are the narrator's feelings changing?

6. **innocuous** (in näk′ yoo əs) *adj.* harmless.

watch the snake crawl slowly beside and past the man's legs. When it was at a safe distance he walked within its range of vision, which he had proved to be no higher than a man's knee, and the snake whirled and drew back in an attitude[7] of fighting defense. The rattler strikes only for paralyzing and killing its food, and for defense.

"It is a slow and heavy snake," Ross said. "It lies in wait on a small game trail and strikes the rat or rabbit passing by. It waits a few minutes, then follows along the trail, coming to the small animal, now dead or dying. It noses it from all sides, making sure that it is its own kill, and that it is dead and ready for swallowing."

A rattler will lie quietly without revealing itself if a man passes by and it thinks it is not seen. It slips away without fighting if given the chance. Only Ross' sharp eyes sometimes picked out the gray and yellow diamond pattern, camouflaged among the grasses. In the cool of the morning, chilled by the January air, the snakes showed no fight. They could be looped up limply over the steel L and dropped in a sack or up into the wire cage on the back of Will's truck. As the sun mounted in the sky and warmed the moist Everglades earth, the snakes were warmed too, and Ross warned that it was time to go more cautiously. Yet having learned that it was we who were the aggressors; that immobility meant complete safety; that the snakes, for all their lightning flash

---

7. **attitude** (at´ ə to͞od´) *n.* a position or posture of the body.

Fact and Opinion
Is Ross stating fact or opinion in this paragraph? How do you know?

Word Choice, or Diction
How would you rephrase "as the sun mounted in the sky and warmed the moist Everglades" in less formal language?

in striking, were inaccurate in their aim, with limited vision; having watched again and again the liquid grace of movement, the beauty of pattern, suddenly I understood that I was drinking in freely the magnificent sweep of the horizon, with no fear of what might be at the moment under my feet. I went off hunting by myself, and though I found no snakes, I should have known what to do.

The sun was dropping low in the west. Masses of white cloud hung above the flat marshy plain and seemed to be tangled in the tops of distant palms and cypresses. The sky turned orange, then saffron. I walked leisurely back toward the truck. In the distance I could see Ross and Will making their way in too. The season was more advanced than at the Creek, two hundred miles to the north, and I noticed that spring flowers were blooming among the lumpy hummocks. I leaned over to pick a white violet. There was a rattlesnake under the violet.

If this had happened the week before, if it had happened the day before, I think I should have lain down and died on top of the rattlesnake, with no need of being struck and poisoned. The snake did not coil, but lifted its head and whirred its rattles lightly. I stepped back slowly and put the violet in a buttonhole. I reached forward and laid the steel L across the snake's neck, just back of the blunt head. I called to Ross:

"I've got one."

He strolled toward me.

"Well, pick it up," he said.

I released it and slipped the L under the middle of the thick body.

"Go put it in the box."

He went ahead of me and lifted the top of the wire cage. I made the truck with the rattler, but when I reached up the six feet to drop it in the cage, it slipped off the stick and dropped on Ross' feet. It made no effort to strike.

"Pick it up again," he said. "If you'll pin it down lightly and reach just back of its head with your hand, as you've seen me do, you can drop it in more easily."

I pinned it and leaned over. •

"I'm awfully sorry," I said, "but you're pushing me a little too fast."

He grinned. I lifted it on the stick and again as I had it at head height, it slipped off, down Ross' boots and on top of his feet. He stood as still as a stump. I dropped the snake on his feet for the third time. It seemed to me that the most patient of rattlers might in time resent being hauled up and down, and for all the man's quiet certainty that in standing motionless there was no danger, would strike at whatever was nearest, and that would be Ross.

I said, "I'm just not man enough to keep this up any longer," and he laughed and reached down with his smooth quickness and lifted the snake back of the head and dropped it in the cage. It slid in among its mates and settled in a corner. The hunt was over and we drove back over the uneven trail to Will's village and left him and went on to Arcadia and home. Our catch for the two days was thirty-two rattlers.

I said to Ross, "I believe that tomorrow I could have picked up that snake."

Back at the Creek, I felt a new lightness. I had done battle with a great fear, and the victory was mine.

Language Study

Vocabulary The words listed below appear in "Rattlesnake Hunt." For each item, write a single sentence correctly using the words indicated.

adequate forage translucent arid mortality

1. arid, farmer

2. mortality, medicine

3. adequate, light

4. forage, horse

5. translucent, marbles

WORD STUDY

The **Latin root -sol-** means "alone." Rawlings's hunting trip takes her into **desolate**, or lonely, territory.

Word Study

Part A Explain how the **Latin root -sol-** contributes to the meaning of the words *soliloquy, consolidate,* and *soloist.* Consult a dictionary if necessary.

Part B Use the sentence context and your knowledge of the Latin root -sol- to explain your answer to each question.

1. How many people can play a game of *solitaire?*

2. If you seek *solitude,* do you want others around?

Close Reading Activities

Literary Analysis

Key Ideas and Details

1. **Classifying Fact and Opinion** Identify one fact and one opinion in the essay.

2. **(a)** Why does Rawlings go on the hunt? **(b) Infer:** Why do Rawlings's feelings about snakes change when she holds one? Support your inference using details from the text.

3. **Classifying Fact and Opinion** What resource would you use to check the facts about a rattlesnake's vision?

4. **Classifying Fact and Opinion** How do both facts and opinions help Rawlings explain her experience with snakes? Cite details from the text in your response.

Craft and Structure

5. **Word Choice, or Diction** Review the author's word choice, or diction, by completing a chart like the one on the right. Then, summarize the effect of the writer's word choice, or diction.

6. **Word Choice, or Diction** Reread the top of page 227. How do phrases like "the liquid grace of movement, the beauty of pattern" reflect the author's new attitude toward snakes?

7. **(a)** Note two ways in which Rawlings shows that she has partly overcome her fears. **(b) Infer:** Why does the author announce at the end of the hunt that she has won a "victory"?

Technical Vocabulary
_____

Formal Language
_____

Informal Language
_____

Integration of Knowledge and Ideas

8. **Analyze:** How is the information presented about snakes the same as or different from information found in works of fiction, popular media, or textbooks? Support your answer with specific examples from the essay.

9. **Evaluate:** How successful was the author in sharing her experiences with readers? Explain.

10. **THE BIG ?** **What should we learn? (a)** In what ways does the hunt change how Rawlings thinks about nature and herself? **(b)** How does conquering our fears allow us greater freedom to learn about the world? Support your response with examples.

ACADEMIC VOCABULARY

As you write and speak about "Rattlesnake Hunt," use the words related to learning that you explored on page 175 of this textbook.

Close Reading Activities Continued

Conventions: Simple and Compound Subjects and Predicates

Every sentence has a **subject** and a **predicate,** which together express a complete thought. The subject describes whom or what the sentence is about. The predicate is a verb that tells what the subject does, what is done to the subject, or what the condition of the subject is.

- A **simple subject** is the main noun or pronoun. A **complete subject** is a simple subject and all the words that modify it.
- A **simple predicate** is the main verb or verb phrase. A **complete predicate** is a simple predicate and all the words that modify or complete it.

- A **compound subject** contains two or more subjects that share the same verb. The subjects are joined by a conjunction such as *and* or *or*.
- A **compound predicate** contains two or more verbs that share the same subject. The predicates are joined by a conjunction.

Simple Subject/ Simple Predicate	Complete Subject/ Complete Predicate	Compound Subject	Compound Predicate
The well-known <u>author</u> <u><u>wrote</u></u> many stories.	<u>The talented writer</u> <u>described her life in Florida.</u>	<u>Rawlings and the hunter</u> walked carefully.	Snakes <u>sleep or wake</u> on their own schedules.

Practice A

Rewrite these sentences. Underline the simple subjects, double underline the simple predicates, and circle any compound subjects and compound predicates.

1. The author follows a snake hunter.
2. He and the author hunt snakes in the upper Everglades.
3. The man knows the area well.
4. The snake hunter finds and captures rattlesnakes.

Reading Application In "Rattlesnake Hunt," identify the subjects and predicates in three different sentences.

Practice B

Write sentences using the subjects and predicates listed.

1. snake; slithers
2. herons, whooping cranes; fly
3. gopher; hid
4. Ross, Will; hiked, hunted
5. hawk; waits, watches

Writing Application Write three sentences about snakes. Then, circle the simple subjects and the predicates. Finally, draw a line between the complete subjects and complete predicates.

Writing to Sources

Informative Text Write an **adaptation** of an incident described in "Rattlesnake Hunt." Retell the incident for a new audience, such as a group of kindergarteners or a class of students learning English. Follow these steps:

- Review the essay, and choose an incident to retell. Then, decide on an audience.
- Draft to reflect the needs and interests of your audience.
- Use precise words and sensory language to add life and immediacy to your description. Include quotations from the selection to highlight important parts of the incident.
- Finally, revise to organize ideas logically, making sure you have met both your purpose and the needs of your audience.

Grammar Application Make sure to use subjects and predicates correctly in your essay. Compound subjects joined with *and* share the same verb and take the plural form. Compound subjects joined with *or* take the form of the verb that agrees with the subject closest to the verb.

Research and Technology

Build and Present Knowledge Write a **help-wanted ad** for a person to work with Ross Allen, the herpetologist. Before you write, use online search terms, such as *herpetologist, experience required,* and *scientist* to find related help-wanted ads to use as models. To determine the necessary qualifications to describe in your ad, refer to details in the essay.

- Notice the concise writing style of ads, and review what the ads cover, including job responsibilities, education, experience, skills, and personal traits the employer seeks.
- Use language that is appropriate for a business ad, including correct grammar and tone.
- Type your ad on a computer and use the spell-check feature.
- Add clip art or other visual displays to enhance key ideas, clarify a point, or add interest.
- Experiment with typefaces to emphasize main ideas.

**Common Core
State Standards**

Writing

3.d. Use precise words and phrases, relevant descriptive details, and sensory language to capture the action and convey experiences and events.

4. Produce clear and coherent writing in which the development, organization, and style are appropriate to task, purpose, and audience.

5. Develop and strengthen writing as needed by planning, revising, editing, rewriting, or trying a new approach, focusing on how well purpose and audience have been addressed.

6. Use technology, including the Internet, to produce and publish writing and link to and cite sources as well as to interact and collaborate with others, including linking to and citing sources.

8. Gather relevant information from multiple print and digital sources, using search terms effectively.

Language

1. Demonstrate command of the conventions of standard English grammar and usage when writing or speaking.

4.b. Use common, grade-appropriate Greek or Latin affixes and roots as clues to the meaning of a word.

Comparing Texts

 ## What should we learn?

Explore the Big Question as you read these selections. Take notes on what the main characters learn and how that knowledge helps them face their situations.

READING TO COMPARE FICTION AND NONFICTION

As you read a short story by Ernest Hemingway and an autobiographical narrative by Ernesto Galarza, compare and contrast the ways that these authors use elements of fiction and nonfiction.

from *Barrio Boy*

Ernesto Galarza (1905–1984)
When he was a young child, Ernesto Galarza moved with his family from Mexico to California. There, his family harvested crops and struggled to make ends meet. Galarza learned English quickly and won a scholarship for college. From 1936 to 1947, Galarza worked to improve education and workers' lives in Latin America. When he returned to California, he worked to gain rights for farm workers.

"A Day's Wait"

Ernest Hemingway (1899–1961)
A true adventurer, Ernest Hemingway based much of his writing on his own experiences. He served as an ambulance driver in World War I, worked as a journalist, traveled the world, and enjoyed outdoor sports. Hemingway's fiction celebrates his spirit of adventure. Among his most famous works are *A Farewell to Arms, For Whom the Bell Tolls,* and *The Old Man and the Sea.*

Comparing Fiction and Nonfiction

Fiction is prose writing that tells about imaginary characters and events. Novels, novellas, and short stories are types of fiction. **Literary nonfiction** is prose writing that tells about real people, places, objects, or events. Biographies, memoirs, and historical accounts are types of nonfiction.

While one is fiction and the other nonfiction, the selections that follow are both examples of **narrative writing** that include the following elements:

- a *narrator* who tells the story
- *characters*, or people living the story
- *dialogue*, or the conversations that the characters have
- story *events* that make up the action
- a *theme* or *central idea*

These elements work together to develop the narratives. For example, both writers use dialogue to convey the impact that a specific event or situation has upon the characters.

The use of a narrator is another important element of fiction and literary nonfiction. The narrator in the excerpt from *Barrio Boy* tells about an important real event in the writer's life. In contrast, the narrator in "A Day's Wait" tells the story of an imagined boy on a single day. As you read, use a chart like the one shown to note ways in which the elements and features of the works are similar and different.

Barrio Boy   **A Day's Wait**

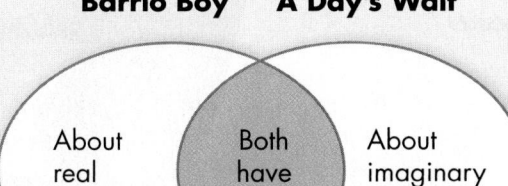

About real people | Both have characters | About imaginary characters

 Common Core State Standards

Reading Literature
3. Analyze how particular elements of a story or drama interact.

Reading Informational Texts
3. Analyze the interactions between individuals, events, and ideas in a text.

Writing
2.a. Introduce a topic clearly, previewing what is to follow; organize ideas, concepts, and information, using strategies such as definition, classification, comparison/contrast, and cause/effect; include formatting, graphics, and multimedia when useful to aiding comprehension.

from

Barrio Boy

Ernesto Galarza

My mother and I walked south

on Fifth Street one morning to the corner of Q Street and turned right. Half of the block was occupied by the Lincoln School. It was a three-story wooden building, with two wings that gave it the shape of a double-T connected by a central hall. It was a new building, painted yellow, with a shingled roof that was not like the red tile of the school in Mazatlán. I noticed other differences, none of them very reassuring.

We walked up the wide staircase hand in hand and through the door, which closed by itself. A mechanical contraption screwed to the top shut it behind us quietly.

Up to this point the adventure of enrolling me in the school had been carefully rehearsed. Mrs. Dodson had told us how to find it and we had circled it several times on our walks. Friends in the *barrio*[1] explained that the director was called a principal, and that it was a lady and not a man. They assured us that there was always a person at the school who could speak Spanish.

Exactly as we had been told, there was a sign on the door in both Spanish and English: "Principal." We crossed the hall and entered the office of Miss Nettie Hopley.

Miss Hopley was at a roll-top desk to one side, sitting in a swivel chair that moved on wheels. There was a sofa against the opposite wall, flanked by two windows and a door that opened on a small balcony. Chairs were set around a table and framed pictures hung on the walls of a man with long white hair and another with a sad face and a black beard.

The principal half turned in the swivel chair to look at us

◄ **Critical Viewing**
Does this picture convey the emotions that a child might feel as he enrolls in a new school? Explain.

◄ **Vocabulary**
reassuring
(rē ə shoor′ iŋ)
adj. having the effect of restoring confidence

contraption
(kən trap′ shən)
n. strange device or machine

Nonfiction
Who is the narrator of this work? How can you tell?

---

1. barrio (bär′ ē ō) *n.* part of a town or city where most of the people are Hispanic.

◄ Critical Viewing
Do you think the narrator would feel comfortable in a classroom like this one? Why or why not?

over the pinch glasses crossed on the ridge of her nose. To do this she had to duck her head slightly as if she were about to step through a low doorway.

What Miss Hopley said to us we did not know but we saw in her eyes a warm welcome and when she took off her glasses and straightened up she smiled wholeheartedly, like Mrs. Dodson. We were, of course, saying nothing, only catching the friendliness of her voice and the sparkle in her eyes while she said words we did not understand. She signaled us to the table. Almost tiptoeing across the office, I maneuvered myself to keep my mother between me and the gringo lady. In a matter of seconds I had to decide whether she was a possible friend or a menace.[2] We sat down.

Then Miss Hopley did a **formidable** thing. She stood up. Had she been standing when we entered she would have seemed tall. But rising from her chair she soared. And what she carried up and up with her was a buxom superstructure,[3] firm shoulders, a straight sharp nose, full cheeks slightly molded by a curved line along the nostrils, thin lips that moved like steel springs, and a high forehead topped by hair gathered in a bun. Miss Hopley was not a giant in body but when she mobilized[4] it to a standing position she seemed

Vocabulary ►
formidable
(fôr´ mə də bəl) *adj.*
impressive

---

2. **menace** (men´ əs) *n.* danger; threat.
3. **buxom superstructure** full figure.
4. **mobilized** (mō´ bə līzd´) *v.* put into motion.

a match for giants. I decided I liked her.

She strode to a door in the far corner of the office, opened it and called a name. A boy of about ten years appeared in the doorway. He sat down at one end of the table. He was brown like us, a plump kid with shiny black hair combed straight back, neat, cool, and faintly obnoxious.

Miss Hopley joined us with a large book and some papers in her hand. She, too, sat down and the questions and answers began by way of our interpreter. My name was Ernesto. My mother's name was Henriqueta. My birth certificate was in San Blas. Here was my last report card from the Escuela Municipal Numero 3 para Varones of Mazatlán,[5] and so forth. Miss Hopley put things down in the book and my mother signed a card.

As long as the questions continued, Doña[6] Henriqueta could stay and I was secure. Now that they were over, Miss Hopley saw her to the door, dismissed our interpreter and without further ado took me by the hand and strode down the hall to Miss Ryan's first grade.

Miss Ryan took me to a seat at the front of the room, into which I shrank—the better to survey her. She was, to skinny, somewhat runty me, of a withering height when she patrolled the class. And when I least expected it, there she was, crouching by my desk, her blond radiant face level with mine, her voice patiently maneuvering me over the awful idiocies of the English language.

During the next few weeks Miss Ryan overcame my fears of tall, energetic teachers as she bent over my desk to help me with a word in the pre-primer. Step by step, she loosened me and my classmates from the safe anchorage of the desks for recitations at the blackboard and consultations at her desk. Frequently she burst into happy announcements to the whole class. "Ito can read a sentence," and small Japanese Ito, squint-eyed and shy, slowly read aloud while the class listened in wonder: "Come, Skipper, come. Come and run." The Korean, Portuguese, Italian, and

> My name was Ernesto.
> My mother's name was
> Henriqueta. My birth
> certificate was in
> San Blas.

Comprehension
How did the principal welcome the narrator and his mother?

---

5. **Escuela Municipal Numero 3 para Varones of Mazatlán** (es kwä lä mōō nē sē päl′ nōō′ me rō träs pä′ rä bä rō′ nesuv mä sät län′) Municipal School Number 3 for Boys of Mazatlán.
6. **Doña** (dō′ nyä) Spanish title of respect meaning "lady" or "madam."

Polish first graders had similar moments of glory, no less shining than mine the day I conquered "butterfly," which I had been persistently pronouncing in standard Spanish as boo-ter-flee. "Children," Miss Ryan called for attention. "Ernesto has learned how to pronounce *butterfly*!" And I proved it with a perfect imitation of Miss Ryan. From that celebrated success, I was soon able to match Ito's progress as a sentence reader with "Come, butterfly, come fly with me."

Like Ito and several other first graders who did not know English, I received private lessons from Miss Ryan in the closet, a narrow hall off the classroom with a door at each end. Next to one of these doors Miss Ryan placed a large chair for herself and a small one for me. Keeping an eye on the class through the open door she read with me about sheep in the meadow and a frightened chicken going to see the king, coaching me out of my phonetic ruts in words like *pasture, bow-wow-wow, hay,* and *pretty,* which to my Mexican ear and eye had so many unnecessary sounds and letters. She made me watch her lips and then close my eyes as she repeated words I found hard to read. When we came to know each other better, I tried interrupting to tell Miss Ryan how we said it in Spanish. It didn't work. She only said "oh" and went on with *pasture, bow-wow-wow,* and *pretty.* It was as if in that closet we were both discovering together the secrets of the English language and grieving together over the tragedies of Bo-Peep. The main reason I was graduated with honors from the first grade was that I had fallen in love with Miss Ryan. Her radiant, no-nonsense character made us either afraid not to love her or love her so we would not be afraid, I am not sure which. It was not only that we sensed she was with it, but also that she was with us. Like the first grade, the rest of the Lincoln School was a sampling of the lower part of town where many races made their home. My pals in the second grade were Kazushi, whose parents spoke only Japanese; Matti, a skinny Italian boy; and Manuel, a fat Portuguese who would never get into a fight but wrestled you to the ground and just sat on you. Our assortment of nationalities included Koreans, Yugoslavs, Poles, Irish, and home-grown Americans.

At Lincoln, making us into Americans did not mean scrubbing away what made us originally foreign. The teachers called us as our parents did, or as close as they could pronounce our names in Spanish or Japanese. No one was ever scolded or punished for speaking in his native tongue on

Nonfiction
What details in this passage tell about each character in the narrative?

Spiral Review
CENTRAL IDEA How do Galarza's memories of Lincoln School relate to a central idea?

the playground. Matti told the class about his mother's down quilt, which she had made in Italy with the fine feathers of a thousand geese. Encarnación acted out how boys learned to fish in the Philippines. I astounded the third grade with the story of my travels on a stagecoach, which nobody else in the class had seen except in the museum at Sutter's Fort. After a visit to the Crocker Art Gallery and its collection of heroic paintings of the golden age of California, someone showed a silk scroll with a Chinese painting. Miss Hopley herself had a way of expressing wonder over these matters before a class, her eyes wide open until they popped slightly. It was easy for me to feel that becoming a proud American, as she said we should, did not mean feeling ashamed of being a Mexican.

▲ **Critical Viewing**
What do you think it would be like to travel in a stagecoach like the one in this picture?

Critical Thinking

1. **Key Ideas and Details** Describe Galarza's experiences as a newcomer in school. Provide specific textual details in your summary.

2. **Key Ideas and Details (a)** Why is Galarza afraid of Miss Ryan at first? **(b) Interpret:** What does Galarza mean when he says Miss Ryan "was with it" and "with us"?

3. **Integration of Knowledge and Ideas** What experiences in Lincoln School help Galarza realize his dream of "becoming a proud American"? Cite details to support your analysis.

4. **Integration of Knowledge and Ideas (a)** What is the unknown that frightens Galarza in this story? **(b)** What does Galarza learn about himself and those around him from his experiences at school? **(c)** Why is this learning process important? *[Connect to the Big Question: What should we learn?]*

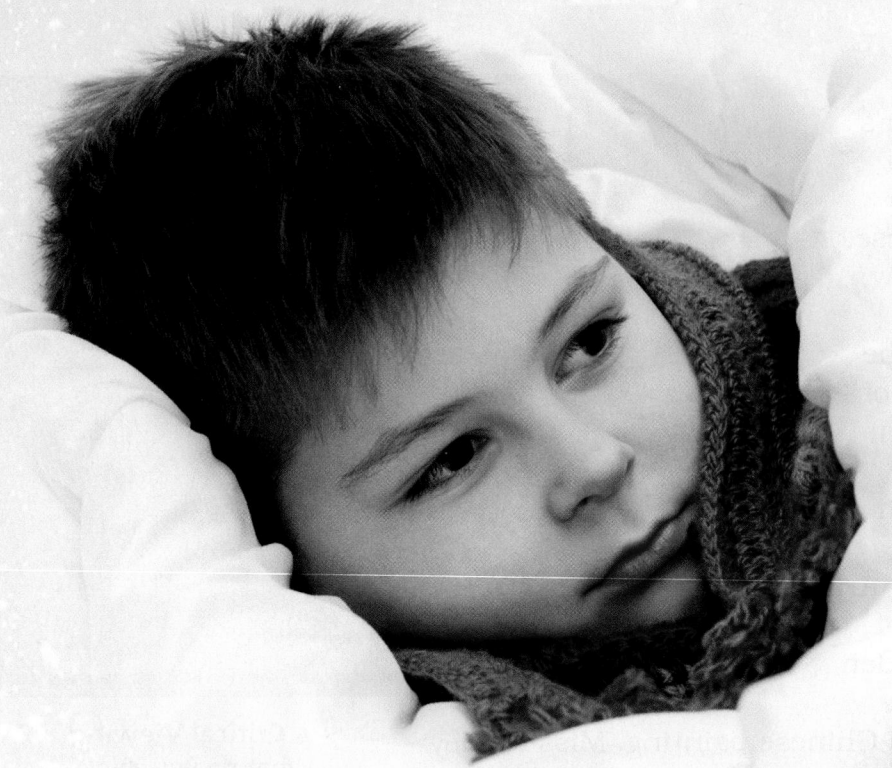

A Day's Wait

Ernest Hemingway

▲ **Critical Viewing**
Describe how you think the boy in this picture might feel.

He came into the room to shut the windows while we were still in bed and I saw he looked ill. He was shivering, his face was white, and he walked slowly as though it ached to move.

"What's the matter, Schatz?"[1]

"I've got a headache."

"You better go back to bed."

"No. I'm all right."

"You go to bed. I'll see you when I'm dressed."

But when I came downstairs he was dressed, sitting by the fire, looking a very sick and miserable boy of nine years. When I put my hand on his forehead I knew he had a fever.

"You go up to bed," I said, "you're sick."

"I'm all right," he said.

When the doctor came he took the boy's temperature.

---

1. Schatz (shäts) German term of affection, used here as a loving nickname.

"What is it?" I asked him.

"One hundred and two."

Downstairs, the doctor left three different medicines in different colored capsules with instructions for giving them. One was to bring down the fever, another a purgative, the third to overcome an acid condition. The germs of influenza can only exist in an acid condition, he explained. He seemed to know all about influenza and said there was nothing to worry about if the fever did not go above one hundred and four degrees. This was a light **epidemic** of flu and there was no danger if you avoided pneumonia.

Back in the room I wrote the boy's temperature down and made a note of the time to give the various capsules.

"Do you want me to read to you?"

"All right. If you want to," said the boy. His face was very white and there were dark areas under his eyes. He lay still in the bed and seemed very detached from what was going on.

I read aloud from Howard Pyle's *Book of Pirates*; but I could see he was not following what I was reading.

"How do you feel, Schatz?" I asked him.

"Just the same, so far," he said.

I sat at the foot of the bed and read to myself while I waited for it to be time to give another capsule. It would have been natural for him to go to sleep, but when I looked up he was looking at the foot of the bed, looking very strangely.

"Why don't you try to go to sleep? I'll wake you up for the medicine."

◄ **Vocabulary**
epidemic (ep′ ə dem′ ik) *n.* outbreak of a contagious disease

"I'd rather stay awake."

After a while he said to me, "You don't have to stay in here with me, Papa, if it bothers you."

"It doesn't bother me."

"No. I mean you don't have to stay if it's going to bother you."

I thought perhaps he was a little lightheaded and after giving him the prescribed capsules at eleven o'clock I went out for a while.

It was a bright, cold day, the ground covered with a sleet that had frozen so that it seemed as if all the bare trees, the bushes, the cut brush and all the grass and the bare ground had been varnished with ice. I took the young Irish setter for a little walk up the road and along a frozen creek, but it was difficult to stand or walk on the glassy surface and the red dog slipped and slithered and I fell twice, hard, once dropping my gun and having it slide away over the ice.

We **flushed** a covey of quail under a high clay bank with overhanging brush and I killed two as they went out of sight

Vocabulary ▶
flushed (flusht) *v.*
drove from hiding

Fiction
Who is the narrator of this work? How do you know?

"You don't have to stay in here with me, Papa, if it bothers you."

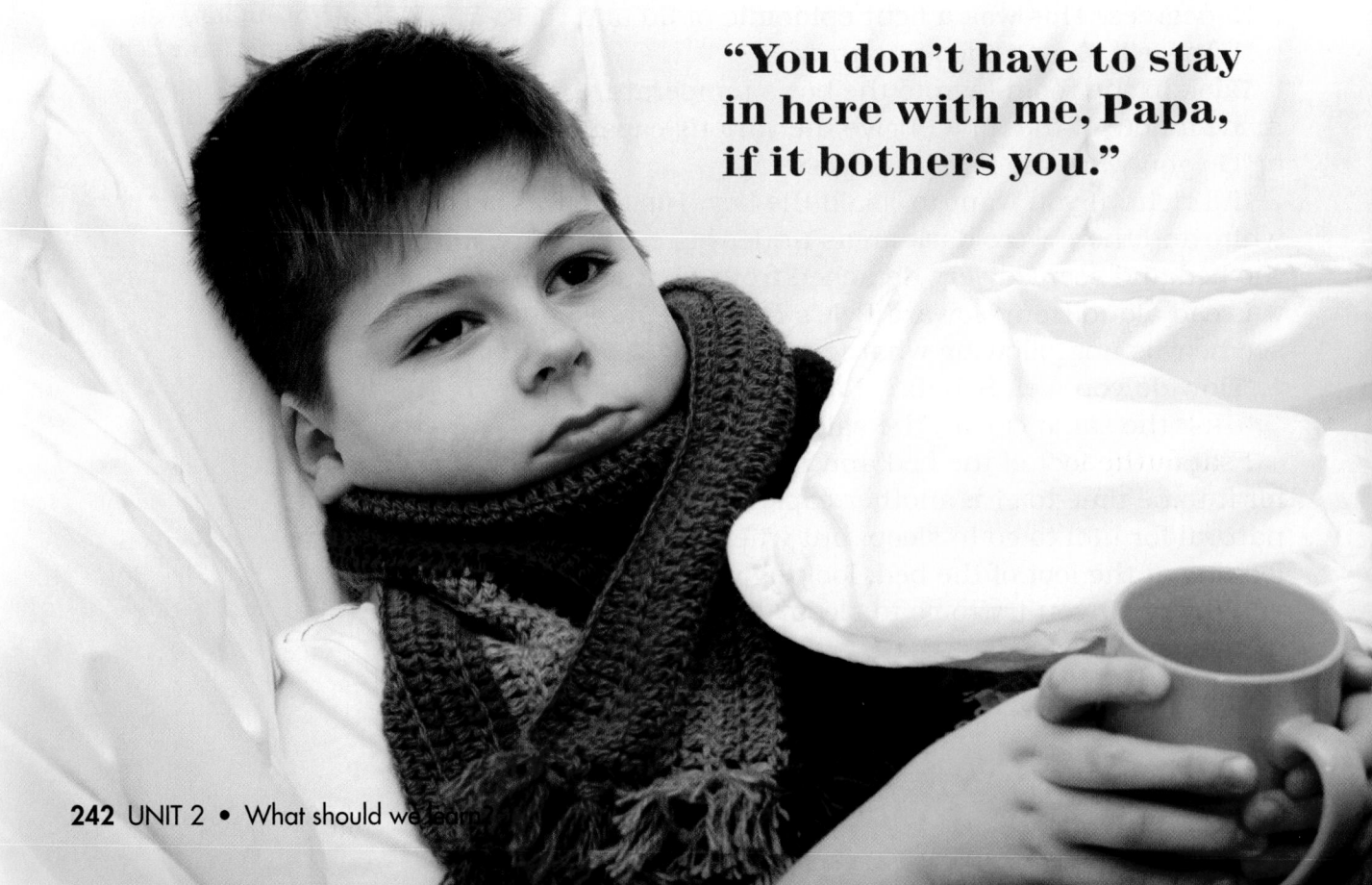

over the top of the bank. Some of the covey lit in trees but most of them scattered into brush piles and it was necessary to jump on the ice-coated mounds of brush several times before they would flush. Coming out while you were poised unsteadily on the icy, springy brush they made difficult shooting, and I killed two, missed five, and started back pleased to have found a covey close to the house and happy there were so many left to find on another day.

At the house they said the boy had refused to let anyone come into the room.

"You can't come in," he said. "You mustn't get what I have."

I went up to him and found him in exactly the position I had left him, white-faced, but with the tops of his cheeks flushed by the fever, staring still, as he had stared at the foot of the bed.

I took his temperature.

"What is it?"

"Something like a hundred," I said. It was one hundred and two and four tenths.

"It was a hundred and two," he said.

"Who said so?"

"The doctor."

"Your temperature is all right," I said. "It's nothing to worry about."

"I don't worry," he said, "but I can't keep from thinking."

"Don't think," I said. "Just take it easy."

"I'm taking it easy," he said and looked straight ahead. He was evidently holding tight on to himself about something.

"Take this with water."

"Do you think it will do any good?"

"Of course it will."

I sat down and opened the *Pirate* book and commenced to read, but I could see he was not following, so I stopped.

"About what time do you think I'm going to die?" he asked.

"What?"

"About how long will it be before I die?"

"You aren't going to die. What's the matter with you?"

"Oh, yes, I am. I heard him say a hundred and two."

Spiral Review

THEME What critical information has the boy learned from this conversation with his father? How does his reaction relate to a possible theme?

"People don't die with a fever of one hundred and two. That's a silly way to talk."

"I know they do. At school in France the boys told me you can't live with forty-four degrees. I've got a hundred and two."

He had been waiting to die all day, ever since nine o'clock in the morning.

"You poor Schatz," I said. "Poor old Schatz. It's like miles and kilometers. You aren't going to die. That's a different thermometer. On that thermometer thirty-seven is normal. On this kind it's ninety-eight."

"Are you sure?"

"Absolutely," I said. "It's like miles and kilometers. You know, like how many kilometers we make when we do seventy miles in the car?"

"Oh," he said.

But his gaze at the foot of the bed relaxed slowly. The hold over himself relaxed too, finally, and the next day it was very slack and he cried very easily at little things that were of no importance.

Critical Thinking

1. **Key Ideas and Details (a)** Why does the boy tell his father to leave the sickroom? **(b) Infer:** What does this action reveal about the boy?

2. **Key Ideas and Details (a)** Why does the boy think he will die? Use details from the story to support your response. **(b) Interpret:** What is the meaning of the story's title?

3. **Key Ideas and Details (a) Analyze:** Which of the boy's words and actions give clues that he believes something terrible is wrong? **(b) Evaluate:** Do you think the story is about the boy's bravery or about the boy's fear? Explain. **(c) Speculate:** What might have happened if the boy had shared his fears?

4. **Integration of Knowledge and Ideas** When the truth of the boy's illness is explained to him, what has he learned about his own character? *[Connect to the Big Question: What should we learn?]*

Comparing Fiction and Nonfiction

1. Craft and Structure (a) For each selection, tell whether the narrator and events are real or imagined. **(b)** Based on your answer, what rules about truth and accuracy did each writer follow for writing these selections?

2. Key Ideas and Details Complete a chart like the one shown to help you analyze one character in each story.

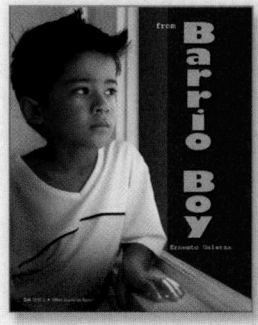

Character	Detail	Fiction or Nonfiction?
The boy in "A Day's Wait"		
Miss Ryan in *Barrio Boy*		

3. Integration of Knowledge and Ideas (a) How might "A Day's Wait" be different if it were nonfiction? **(b)** How might *Barrio Boy* change if it were fiction?

Timed Writing

Explanatory Text: Essay

In a brief essay, compare and contrast the narrators of *Barrio Boy* and "A Day's Wait." State your topic in the introduction and discuss how the narrator presents the events in each work. Consider adding a chart to show what is the same and different. **(40 minutes)**

5-Minute Planner

1. Gather your ideas by jotting down answers to these questions:

   - Which work includes more personal details about the narrator?
   - Do the narrator's thoughts and actions build toward a specific theme or insight? Why or why not?
   - Which narrator is central to the narrative's action?

2. Choose an organizational strategy. If you use the block method, present all the details about one narrator, then all the details about the other narrator. If you use the point-by-point method, discuss one aspect of both narrators, then another aspect of both narrators, and so on.

3. Reread the prompt and then draft your essay.

USE ACADEMIC VOCABULARY

As you write, use academic language, including the following words or their related forms:

adaptation

culture

diversity

tradition

For more information about academic vocabulary, see pp. xlvi-l.

Word Origins

A word's **origin,** or **etymology,** tells the history of the word. Knowing the history of a word or word part can help you understand its meaning. This chart gives the meanings of several Latin, Greek, Old English, and Middle English word parts.

 **Common Core State Standards**

Language

4.b. Use common, grade-appropriate Greek or Latin affixes and roots as clues to the meaning of a word.

4.c. Consult general and specialized reference materials, both print and digital, to find the pronunciation of a word or determine or clarify its precise meaning or its part of speech.

5.a. Interpret figures of speech (e.g., literary, biblical, and mythological allusions) in context.

Latin and Greek Word Parts			
Roots	**Origin**	**Meaning**	**Examples**
-aud-	Latin	to hear	audio, audience
-struct-	Latin	to build	structure, instruct
-port-	Latin	to carry	portable, transport
Prefixes	**Origin**	**Meaning**	**Examples**
inter-	Latin	among, between	Internet, international
mis-	Old English	wrong, not	misbehave, misfortune
tele-	Greek	distant	telephone, telescope
Suffixes	**Origin**	**Meaning**	**Examples**
-ful	Middle English	full of	joyful, fearful
-less	Middle English	without	careless, thoughtless

Practice A

For each word in italics, underline the root, prefix, or suffix. Then, explain how the meaning of the word part contributes to the meaning of the word. If necessary, consult a print or online dictionary.

1. The *construction* of the new bank building is on schedule.
2. When Samuel *interrupts* me, I can't remember what I have been saying.
3. When the roads are slick, electronic signs alert drivers to be *careful*.
4. The *auditorium* was full of people eager to hear the new symphony.
5. The losing candidate suspected that the votes had been *miscounted*.

Many words and phrases in English come from **Latin, Greek, and Anglo-Saxon mythology.** Study the chart below to learn the origins of some of these words and phrases.

Words and Phrases From Mythology		
Word or Phrase	**Origin**	**Meaning**
January	Janus, a Roman god, had two faces— one looking forward and one looking backward.	The first month of our calendar year
Achilles heel	Achilles, a great Greek warrior, was known to be weak only in his foot.	A weakness or weak point
herculean effort	The Greek hero Hercules was known for his strength and for completing twelve difficult tasks.	A difficult task requiring great strength
high horse	In medieval England, nobles were given tall horses to show their importance. The phrase "get off your high horse" developed from this practice.	A superior attitude

Comprehension and Collaboration

Trade your odyssey story (see Activity below) with a partner. Rewrite your partner's story to include three new words based on word parts from the chart on the previous page. You may use words that appear in this Language Study, other words you know, or new words you find in a dictionary.

Practice B

Identify the word or phrase from the chart that is associated with each sentence.

1. When Byron bragged about his new car we told him <u>not to be too proud of himself</u>.

2. It is always good to have a fresh start in <u>the new year</u>.

3. I can usually stick to a healthy diet, but my <u>weakness</u> is brownies.

4. Beating the other team will require <u>us to be stronger than ever</u>.

Activity An **allusion** is a reference to a well-known person, event, literary work, or work of art. Many works of literature contain allusions. For example, a writer might describe a long or difficult journey as an "odyssey." This is an allusion to the Odyssey, a long epic poem that was written sometime between 600 and 800 B.C. In the poem, the ancient Greek hero Odysseus takes a long, difficult voyage to reach his home. Another ancient Greek hero is Hercules, who was famous for completing amazingly difficult tasks. Write a short tale about an odyssey in which the hero must make a herculean effort. Your story can be set in either the past or the present.

Evaluating a Persuasive Presentation

A **persuasive presentation** is similar to a persuasive composition. Its purpose is to persuade the listener to do, buy, or believe something. Use these strategies to assess persuasive presentations.

Learn the Skills

Evaluate content. Like its written counterpart, an effective persuasive presentation includes a clear statement of the speaker's position and relevant supporting evidence. Listen to every word of a persuasive presentation in order to explain the speaker's purpose. Evaluate the speaker's claims, and identify whether the speaker is appealing to your emotions or using facts, statistics, and other information that can be proved.

Determine the speaker's attitude. Ask yourself these questions to determine how the speaker feels about his or her subject:

- Does the speaker appeal to emotion or to reason?
- Does he or she use words that convey strong images or associations?
- What do the speaker's body language and facial expressions suggest?
- What is the speaker's tone of voice?

Listen for a logical organization. Follow the argument from point to point. Listen for the connections between ideas. Also, listen for a convincing introduction and conclusion.

Listen for strong evidence. Think about the anecdotes, descriptions, facts, statistics, and specific examples that support the speaker's position. Is the reasoning sound? Does the speaker provide sufficient and convincing evidence? Why or why not?

Ask questions. Never be afraid to ask questions. You will discover how well the speaker has researched the topic by seeing how he or she responds to questions about the evidence.

Challenge bias or faulty logic. If you disagree with something the presenter has said, express your opinion. Respect the speaker's viewpoints if you identify bias or faulty logic. If you suspect a piece of evidence is wrong, ask the speaker to cite its source.

Clarify and contribute. Paraphrase a speaker's key points to clarify what you have heard. You might also share a personal anecdote or observation that affirms the speaker's position.

 **Common Core State Standards**

Speaking and Listening

2. Analyze the main ideas and supporting details presented in diverse media and formats and explain how the ideas clarify a topic, text, or issue under study.

3. Delineate a speaker's argument and specific claims, evaluating the soundness of the reasoning and the relevance and sufficiency of the evidence.

Practice the Skills

Presentation of Knowledge and Ideas Use what you have learned in this workshop to complete the following activity.

ACTIVITY: Evaluating a Persuasive Presentation

Watch a persuasive sales pitch, either live or on videotape or television.
- Identify the speaker's message.
- Determine if the speaker's purpose is to inform or to influence the audience.
- Explain how you felt listening to the message.
- List questions that the speaker's claims raise for you.
- Jot down notes about the presentation, such as the speaker's tone of voice, body language, and facial expressions.
- Draw conclusions about the speaker's message by considering verbal and nonverbal cues.

Use the Assessment Guide below to interpret the content and delivery of the persuasive presentation you watched.

Assessment Guide
What is the speaker's message?
Is the speaker's purpose to inform or to influence the audience?
Is the speaker's reasoning sound?
Does the speaker provide sufficient and relevant evidence to support his or her claims?
How could you research the speaker's claims?
What does the speaker hope you will do after hearing the message?
On what points would you challenge the speaker?
How effective was the delivery of the presentation?
What can you conclude about the speaker's verbal and nonverbal communication, including tone of voice, gestures, and facial expressions?

Comprehension and Collaboration Compare your findings with those of your classmates. As a group, discuss how you can use the strategies above to evaluate other messages, such as advertisements, commercials, and other persuasive presentations.

Write an Argumentative Text

Argumentative Essay

Defining the Form In an **argumentative essay,** the writer states and supports a claim based on factual evidence. You might use elements of this form in writing editorials or reviews.

Assignment Write an argumentative essay in which you use logic and reasoning to convince readers to agree with your claim. Your essay should feature the following elements:

✓ a *clear statement of your position* on an issue that has more than one side

✓ the *context* surrounding the issue

✓ *persuasive evidence* and *logical reasoning* that support your claims

✓ statements that *acknowledge opposing views and offer counterarguments*

✓ an *appropriate organizational structure* for an argument

✓ formal language that appeals *mainly to reason*

✓ error-free writing, including *effectively combined sentences*

To preview the criteria on which your argumentative essay may be judged, see the rubric on page 257.

FOCUS ON RESEARCH

When you write an argumentative essay, be sure to use strong evidence to support your claim.

- Evidence should be credible, or come from a trustworthy source. Generally, the most reliable Web sites are those from government organizations, major museums, and academic institutions.

- As you gather information, make sure that sources agree on basic facts. If you find one source with facts that are contradicted by other sources, that source is probably inaccurate.

- Cite your sources properly in your essay. The Research Workshop in the Introductory Unit provides useful information on citations.

Common Core State Standards

Writing

1. Write arguments to support claims with clear reasons and relevant evidence.

1.a. Introduce claim(s), acknowledge alternate or opposing claims, and organize the reasons and evidence logically.

1.b. Support claim(s) with logical reasoning and relevant evidence, using accurate, credible sources and demonstrating an understanding of the topic or text.

READING-WRITING CONNECTION

To get the feel for argumentative writing, read "All Together Now" by Barbara Jordan, on page 214.

Prewriting/Planning Strategies

Hold a roundtable. With a group, hold a roundtable discussion of problems in your school. Raise as many different issues as possible. Jot down topics that spark strong feelings in you. Choose from these subjects for your essay topic.

Make a quick list. Fold a piece of paper in thirds lengthwise. In the first column, write issues and ideas that interest you. In the second column, write a descriptive word for each idea. In the third column, give an example that supports your description. Make sure each issue has an opposing side. Choose the issue or idea that interests you most.

Issues and Ideas	Descriptive Word	Examples
Cafeteria food	tasteless	macaroni and cheese
Water pollution	scary	streams polluted by fertilizer runoff
New playground	needed	child hurt on slide

Narrow your focus. Evaluate your topic to be sure you can fully and effectively discuss it. For example, the topic "violence in the media" would cover violence on news reports, in movies, in video games, and on television. To write an effective argumentative essay, you should consider focusing on violence in one medium, not all four.

Gather evidence to support your position. Conduct research either in the library, on the Internet, or by interviewing experts on your topic. Gather the following types of support from accurate, credible sources:

Facts: statements that can be proved true

Statistics: facts presented in the form of numbers

Anecdotes: brief stories that illustrate a point

Quotations from Authorities: statements from leading experts

Examples: facts, ideas, or events that support a general idea

Anticipate counterarguments. Make a list of the arguments people might have against your position. For each, identify a response that you can use to address the issues in your essay.

Drafting Strategies

Ⓒ Common Core State Standards

Writing

1.c. Use words, phrases, and clauses to create cohesion and clarify the relationships among claim(s), reasons, and evidence.

1.d. Establish and maintain a formal style.

1.e. Provide a concluding statement or section that follows from and supports the argument presented.

Language

1. Demonstrate command of the conventions of standard English grammar and usage when writing or speaking.

3. Use knowledge of language and its conventions when writing, speaking, reading, or listening.

Develop and support your claim. To make your position clear to your readers, review your notes and develop a *thesis statement*— one strong sentence that states your claim. Include this statement in your introduction.

Organize to emphasize your arguments and address counterarguments. As you draft, present the supporting evidence you have gathered, starting with your least important points and building toward your most important ones. Use transitional words and phrases to unify your writing and show the relationships among your ideas. Address opposing concerns and counterarguments directly—do not avoid them. Delete information that does not support or add anything to your argument. Write a powerful conclusion that follows the logic of the evidence and supports your argument. Consider the method shown in the pyramid.

Introduction and claim

- First set of arguments
- Supporting details

- Concerns and counterarguments
- Statements proving opposition is weak or incorrect

- Strongest argument
- Supporting details

Conclusions

Choose precise words. Forceful language helps convey your point and builds support for your position. Create a speaker's voice by using precise, lively words that will appeal to readers' sense of reason and stir their emotions.

> **Vague:** a *good* candidate
>
> **Precise:** a *trustworthy* candidate
> an *intelligent* candidate

Appeal to your audience. Use words that your audience will understand. If you are writing for teenagers, use informal language, but avoid slang and maintain standard English. If you are writing to a government official, use a formal style and serious language. Also, choose words that add interest and encourage readers to continue reading.

Revising for Correct Verb Tense

A verb expresses an action or a state of being. Verbs have tenses, or different forms, that tell when something happens or exists.

Identifying Verb Tense In standard English, verbs have six tenses: present, past, future, present perfect, past perfect, and future perfect.

Present indicates an action that happens regularly or states a general truth: *I walk my dog Squeegee every morning. He is happy.*

Past indicates an action that has already happened: *We walked earlier than usual yesterday. It was sunny.*

Future indicates an action that will happen: *We will walk on the beach this summer. The sand will feel hot.*

Present perfect indicates an action that happened some time in the past or an action that happened in the past and is still happening now: *We have walked here every day for two years.*

Past perfect indicates an action that was completed before another action in the past: *We had walked around the corner before Squeegee barked.*

Future perfect indicates an action that will have been completed before another: *We will have walked two hundred miles before I need new shoes.*

Fixing Incorrect Verb Tense To fix an incorrect form of a verb, first identify any questionable verbs in your essay. Then, verify the correct form using one of the following methods.

1. **Review the basic forms of the six tenses.** First, identify the time—present, past, or future—in which the action occurs. Then, review the examples above to determine which form corresponds with that time. Avoid shifting tenses needlessly.

2. **Rewrite the sentence.** Consider which verb tense will make your ideas as precise as possible. Revise using that tense.

Grammar in Your Writing

Choose a paragraph in your draft. Underline the verbs in each sentence of the paragraph. If the tense for any verb is faulty or shifts needlessly, fix it using one of the methods described above.

Revising Strategies

Highlight your main points. To check your organization, highlight each main point. Then, use one or more of these strategies:

- If a reader needs to know one main point in order to understand a second one, make sure the first main point comes *before* the second.

- If one main point means the same as another, combine them, or combine the paragraphs in which they appear.

- If one main point is stronger than the others, move it to the end of your essay.

Writing

1.c. Use words, phrases, and clauses to create cohesion and clarify the relationships among claim(s), reasons, and evidence.

Language

3. Use knowledge of language and its conventions when writing, speaking, reading, or listening.

3.a. Choose language that expresses ideas precisely and concisely, recognizing and eliminating wordiness and redundancy.

Model: Revising to Highlight Main Points

The best way a person can make his or her voice heard is by voting on Election Day! In the United States, the government is elected by each and every voting citizen. In some other countries, people do not have the right to vote. Their leaders are in power, and the people sometimes do not have a way to make their opinion heard. Their voices are silent, and they must listen to what their leaders tell them to do. Our system is not always perfect, but it does give us the chance to keep trying to make things better.

Combine sentences to show connections. To improve your writing, combine short, choppy sentences to stress the connections between ideas.

Similar Ideas: The town permits skating on the lake. We don't have the money to open a rink.

Combined: The town permits skating on the lake **because** we don't have the money to open a rink.

Opposing Ideas: The food is better heated. Most classrooms do not have microwave ovens.

Combined: The food is better heated, **but** most classrooms do not have microwave ovens.

Peer Review

Read your draft to a group of peers. Ask if the order of your main points is logical. Consider their responses as you revise.

Revising to Combine Sentences Using Conjunctions

Too many short sentences in a row can make your writing choppy—that is, your writing will seem to have a repetitive stop-start quality. Using conjunctions to combine sentences will help you create a smoother, more varied writing style. It will also create cohesion and clarify the relationships among claims, reasons, and evidence.

Identifying Sentences to Combine Combine sentences that express similar ideas by using words that clarify the relationship between the ideas. Here are two common ways to combine sentences:

Use a coordinating conjunction, such as *and* or *but*.

CHOPPY: I really wanted to sleep. I had to walk my dogs.

COMBINED: I really wanted to sleep, **but** I had to walk my dogs.

Add a subordinating conjunction, such as *after* or *until*.

CHOPPY: You cannot read the book. I want a chance.

COMBINED: You cannot read the book **until** I get a chance.

Fixing Choppy Sentences To fix choppy sentences, rewrite them using the following method.

1. **Identify relationships between sentences.** Look for a series of related short sentences. Identify whether the ideas in the sentences are of equal importance or unequal importance.

2. **Combine sentences.** Combine sentences showing equal importance by using coordinating conjunctions. Use subordinating conjunctions to combine sentences of unequal importance.

Coordinating Conjunctions	Common Subordinating Conjunctions
and, or, so, for, but, nor, yet	after, although, as, as if, as long as, because, before, even though, if, in order that, since, so that, than, though, unless, until, when, whenever, where, wherever, while

Grammar in Your Writing

Read your draft aloud, highlighting any passages that sound choppy. Then, revise by combining sentences using the method described.

Common Core State Standards

Language
2.b. Spell correctly.

Decide the Future

To you, voting may seem like just a waste of time, just a mere piece of paper with boxes on it, that you have to go through to mark which person you want for that particular job. But to me, it's something more, much more. . . it's your chance to decide the future. Everyone who is eligible should take advantage of the right to vote.

I'm not the only one who thinks voting should be a top priority for people. For years, companies and organizations have supplied numerous reminders and reasons to explain when and why you vote. You've seen the commercials; they've all told us about it. Voting is important for a number of reasons. Politicians decide how much government support we will get for college tuition, how many jobs will be available, and who will pay more taxes.

Eenie, meenie, miney mo, . . . maybe you don't want to vote because you feel as if you don't know enough about the candidates to make an informed decision. However, newspapers, television broadcasts, performance records—all these fact-based sources of information are available to the interested voter who wants to make a responsible choice. Find out what the candidates have been doing and what they plan to do. Make your decision based on information.

In many countries, voting is not an option. In countries with kings and queens, leaders are born into their positions. In other countries, the leaders take control rather than being voted into a leadership role. Often leaders who are not elected can be corrupt or tyrannical, because the people can't remove them from power. We are citizens of a free country in which we have the right to vote. Whether or not the system works perfectly, it is better than a system with no voting. Vote because you can. Remind yourself that not everyone is as lucky.

If you don't vote, you have less control over your own life. Voting is your chance to make your voice heard. It's your chance to decide the future.

In the opening paragraph, Amanda points out the two "sides" to the voting issue. She follows with her thesis statement.

This evidence supports the statement that others think voting is a top priority.

This evidence supports the idea that voting matters.

Here, Amanda identifies and addresses readers' concerns and counterarguments.

Here, Amanda gives two examples of types of countries where voting is not an option. She also discusses the negative results of this fact.

Amanda reminds readers that not everyone has the right to vote. She uses language that appeals to both reason and emotion.

Editing and Proofreading

Review your draft to correct errors in spelling, grammar, and punctuation errors.

Focus on Spelling Irregular Plurals

- Change the *y* to *i* and add *-es* to nouns that end in a consonant and *y* (*memory/memories*).
- Do not change the *y* but add *-s* to nouns that end in a vowel and *y* (*play/plays, key/keys*).
- For most nouns ending in *fe,* change the *fe* to *ve* and and *-s* (*elf/elves, wife/wives*).

Publishing and Presenting

Consider one of the following ways to share your writing:

Deliver a speech. Use your argumentative essay as the basis for a speech that you give to your classmates.

Post your essay. Many local newspapers will publish well-written argumentative essays if they appeal to the newspaper's audience. Submit your composition and see what happens.

Reflecting on Your Writing

Writer's Journal Jot down your answer to this question:

What part of the writing process was most challenging? Explain.

Spiral Review
Earlier in the unit, you learned about **principal parts of verbs** (p. 210) and **conjunctions** (p. 218). Review your essay to be sure that you have used verbs and coordinating conjunctions correctly.

Rubric for Self-Assessment

Find evidence in your writing to address each category. Then, use the rating scale to grade your work.

Criteria	Rating Scale			
Purpose/Focus Clearly presents a position on an issue that has at least two sides	*not very* .... *very* 1	2	3	4
Organization Introduces the topic and make a clear claim; organizes reasons and evidence logically; provides a concluding section that follows from the argument presented	1	2	3	4
Development of Ideas/Elaboration Supports the claim with clear reasons and relevant evidence, using credible sources; addresses counterarguments; establishes and maintains a formal style	1	2	3	4
Language Uses precise language to strengthen the argument; uses words, phrases, and clauses to clarify the relationships among claims and reasons	1	2	3	4
Conventions Uses proper grammar, including correct use of conjunctions	1	2	3	4

SELECTED RESPONSE

I. Reading Literature/Informational Text

Directions: *Read the excerpt from "The Eternal Frontier" by Louis L'Amour. Then, answer each question that follows.*

Common Core State Standards

RI.7.1, RI.7.2, RI.7.3, RI.7.4, RI.7.8; W.7.10
[For full standards wording, see the chart in the front of this book.]

The question I am most often asked is, "Where is the frontier now?"

The answer should be obvious. Our frontier lies in outer space. The moon, the asteroids, the planets, these are mere stepping stones, where we will test ourselves, learn needful lessons, and grow in knowledge before we attempt those frontiers beyond our solar system. Outer space is a frontier without end, the eternal frontier, an everlasting challenge to explorers not [only] of other planets and other solar systems but also of the mind of man.

All that has gone before was <u>preliminary</u>. We have been preparing ourselves mentally for what lies ahead. Many problems remain, but if we can avoid a devastating war we shall move with a rapidity scarcely to be believed. In the past seventy years we have developed the automobile, radio, television, transcontinental and transoceanic flight, and the electrification of the country, among a multitude of other such developments. In 1900 there were 144 miles of surfaced road in the United States. Now there are over 3,000,000. Paved roads and the development of the automobile have gone hand in hand, the automobile being civilized man's antidote to overpopulation.

What is needed now is leaders with perspective; we need leadership on a thousand fronts, but they must be men and women who can take the long view and help to shape the outlines of our future. There will always be the nay-sayers, those who cling to our lovely green planet as a baby clings to its mother, but there will be others like those who have taken us this far along the path to a limitless future. We are a people born to the frontier. It has been a part of our thinking, waking, and sleeping since men first landed on this continent. The frontier is the line that separates the known from the unknown wherever it may be, and we have a driving need to see what lies beyond . . .

1. Which answer choice most clearly identifies the passage as an example of a **persuasive essay?**
   A. the author clearly defines an unfamiliar topic
   B. the author attempts to convince readers by presenting well-supported claims
   C. the author shares personal reflections and insights
   D. the author uses vivid language to describe a person, place, or thing

2. What is the author's main **argument** in this passage?
   A. We should be concerned about the problem of overpopulation.
   B. We should explore outer space beyond what has already been discovered.
   C. We should prepare ourselves mentally for the future.
   D. We should cling to our planet.

3. Which answer choice states the most likely reason for L'Amour's **word choice** in referring to outer space as "the eternal frontier"?
   A. A frontier is an unknown or unexplored area.
   B. The frontier is a popular setting for movies.
   C. Books about frontiers are often bestsellers.
   D. Many readers will think the frontier is an interesting topic.

4. Which claim from the passage appeals most strongly to readers' emotions?
   A. "Outer space is a frontier without end, the eternal frontier"
   B. "We have developed the automobile, radio, television, transcontinental and transoceanic flight"
   C. "We are a people born to the frontier. It has been part of our thinking, waking, and sleeping"
   D. "The frontier is the line that separates the known from the unknown wherever it may be"

5. Which phrase from the passage is an example of a **fact?**
   A. "if we can avoid a devastating war"
   B. "we shall move with a rapidity scarcely to be believed"
   C. "In 1900 there were 144 miles of surfaced road in the United States"
   D. "The automobile being civilized man's antidote to overpopulation"

6. Which phrase from the passage is an example of an **opinion?**
   A. "'Where is the frontier now?'"
   B. "The answer should be obvious."
   C. "We have developed the automobile, radio, television, transcontinental and transoceanic flight"
   D. "Paved roads and the development of the automobile have gone hand in hand."

7. **Part A** Which answer choice states the best definition of the underlined word *preliminary?*
   A. logical
   B. leading up to
   C. historic
   D. concluding

   Part B Which context clue in the passage helps you define *preliminary?*
   A. "beyond our solar system"
   B. "also of the mind of man"
   C. "All that has gone before"
   D. "preparing ourselves mentally"

Timed Writing

8. Make a list of the **author's main arguments.** In an essay, evaluate whether the author supports each **argument** with **facts** or only offers **opinions** to persuade readers to accept his ideas. Cite evidence from the text to support your analysis.

GO ON

II. Reading Informational Text

Directions: *Read the passage. Then, answer each question that follows.*

Common Core State Standards

RI.7.1, RI.7.3, RI.7.6; L.7.1, L.7.2, L.7.3
[For full standards wording, see the chart in the front of this book.]

Salamander Population at Risk in Oasis Springs

The Agency for Natural Habitats recently discovered a rare species of salamander living in Oasis Springs, a popular spring-fed pool. We have found that the process used for cleaning the pool is endangering these creatures. To keep the water safe for swimmers, the pool staff currently uses a combination of bleach and brushing to treat algae. This treatment kills the salamanders. Today, we are announcing to the public the steps we will take to preserve the salamander population in Oasis Springs.

Our most important solution involves a new cleaning process. The pool will be cleaned without brushes or bleach. Divers will wipe the rocky bottom with special cloths. No soap products will be used.

We will also participate in a special breeding program to foster the growth of the salamander population. Ten salamanders will be taken from the pool each month to reproduce. They will then be reintroduced into the pool. This program has been successful in other locations with endangered salamander populations.

Finally, specialists will visit the pool each week to monitor the salamander population. An expert committee will then review the results and report on the program's success.

These crucial steps will allow both salamanders and people to enjoy Oasis Springs for many years to come.

1. Part A What is the main purpose of the passage?

A. to persuade the public to help save the salamanders

B. to explain how to clean the spring-fed pool without harming people

C. to inform the public about the proposed steps to save the salamander population

D. to explore the life of a salamander

Part B Which of the following answer choices *best* shows the author's purpose?

A. "Today, we are announcing to the public the steps we will take to preserve the salamander population in Oasis Springs."

B. "An expert committee will then review the results"

C. "The Agency for Natural Habitats recently discovered a rare species of salamander"

D. "This program has been successful in other locations"

2. Which answer choice is a proposed solution to the problem?

A. Ban swimming in the pool.

B. Clean the pool without bleach or brushes.

C. Close the pool to the public.

D. Bring divers in to clean the salamanders.

III. Writing and Language Conventions

Directions: *Read the passage below. Then, answer each question that follows.*

(1) "Seventh Grade" is a funny and believable story. (2) In it, a boy named Victor likes a girl named Teresa. (3) To impress her, Victor pretends to speak French in class. (4) Although he seems smart, he did not really know French. (5) Victor's teacher knows Victor is faking. (6) However, the teacher is very cool. (7) He does not tell the class that Victor has answered incorrectly. (8) That is because he will remember his own life as a teenager.

1. Which of the following sentences contains a **linking verb?**
   A. sentence 2
   B. sentence 3
   C. sentence 4
   D. sentence 7

2. Identify the **complete subject** and **complete predicate** of sentence 1.
   A. "Seventh Grade" is / a funny and believable story.
   B. "Seventh Grade" / is
   C. "Seventh Grade" is a / funny and believable story.
   D. "Seventh Grade" / is a funny and believable story.

3. Which revision of sentence 6 uses an **action verb?**
   A. However, the teacher seems very cool.
   B. However, the teacher was very cool.
   C. However, the teacher has a very cool attitude.
   D. However, the teacher will be very cool.

4. What is the best way to revise the **tenses** of the verbs in sentence 8?
   A. Change *will remember* to the present tense.
   B. Change *is* to the past tense.
   C. Change *is* to the present perfect tense.
   D. Change *is* to the past perfect tense.

5. What **principal part** of the verb *tell* appears in sentence 7?
   A. present
   B. present participle
   C. past
   D. past participle

6. Which revision to sentence 4 creates agreement by presenting all verbs in the **present tense?**
   A. Although he was smart, he did not really know French.
   B. Although he seemed smart, he does not really know French.
   C. Although he seems smart, he does not really know French.
   D. All the verbs are already in the present tense.

CONSTRUCTED RESPONSE

Common Core State Standards

RI.7.1, RI.7.2, RI.7.4, RI.7.5, RI.7.6, RI.7.8, RI.7.9; W.7.2, W.7.2.c, W.7.7, W.7.8, W.7.9.b; SL.7.3, SL.7.4; L.7.3.a, L.7.5

[For full standards wording, see the chart in the front of this book.]

Directions: *Follow the instructions to complete the tasks below as assigned by your teacher.*

As you work on each task, incorporate both general academic vocabulary and literary terms you learned in Part 2.

Writing

TASK 1 Informational Text [RI.7.5, RI.7.6, RI.7.9; W.7.9.b; L.7.3.a]

Analyze Structure and Purpose

Write an essay in which you compare the characteristics of two different types of nonfiction selections from Part 2.

- Choose two selections that represent different types of nonfiction.
- Describe how information is organized in each selection.
- Analyze the author's purpose for writing each selection, and evaluate the connection between that purpose and the selection's organization.
- Discuss the similarities and differences in purpose and structure.
- Each paragraph should have a central idea supported by details from the selections.
- Revise your essay to eliminate unnecessary information and to correct any errors.

TASK 2 Informational Text [RI.7.1, RI.7.5; W.7.2.c, W.7.9.b; L.7.3.a]

Analyze Text Structure

Write an essay in which you analyze the structure an author uses to organize a work of literary nonfiction in Part 2.

- Identify and describe the structure the author uses to organize the text you chose.
- Explain how the major sections contribute to the text as a whole and to the development of the author's ideas.
- Cite evidence from the text to support your analysis while presenting your ideas in an organized manner.

- Review your essay to ensure that each sentence has a subject and a predicate. Revise your essay using transitions, such as conjunctions, to combine choppy sentences.

TASK 3 Informational Text [RI.7.1, RI.7.6; W.7.2.c, W.7.9.b]

Determine an Author's Point of View

Write an essay in which you identify and analyze the author's point of view in a selection from Part 2.

Part 1

- Choose a selection in which the author establishes a clear point of view on a topic. Begin by stating the topic and describing the author's perspective on it.
- Analyze how the author presents his or her perspective: Is some evidence emphasized more than other evidence? Does the author include facts or just an interpretation of facts?
- Make notes on the author's perspective and use of supporting facts. Answer the following question: Do you think the author conveys his or her point of view effectively?

Part 2

- Write an essay in which you explain the author's point of view and describe how the author uses facts and evidence to support his or her perspective.
- In your conclusion, state whether you think the author conveys his or her point of view effectively. Support your opinion with examples from the text.
- Revise your essay, adding transitions to create cohesion and clarify the relationships among ideas.

Speaking and Listening

TASK 4 ▶ Informational Text [RI.7.8; W.7.2; SL.7.3; L.7.3.a]

Evaluate Arguments

With a small group of classmates, decide on a text from Part 2 that will be the basis for individual oral presentations. Work independently to evaluate the author's argument. Then, present your ideas to the group and evaluate the presentations of other members.

- As the basis for your presentation, write an essay in which you trace and evaluate the author's argument and specific claims. Include your assessment of the author's reasoning and evidence.
- Use precise language to express your ideas and appeal to your audience.
- Take turns presenting your evaluations.
- Evaluate your classmates' presentations by assessing their use of clear reasoning and relevant and sufficient evidence.

TASK 5 ▶ Informational Text [RI.7.1, RI.7.4; SL.7.4; L.7.5]

Analyze the Impact of Word Choice

Give an oral presentation in which you analyze how word choice and diction impact the meaning and tone of a text from Part 2.

- Select a work from Part 2 and explain why you chose it. Then, choose a specific passage to use as the focus of your analysis.
- Describe the tone of the selection (for example, formal or informal, serious or funny)
- Analyze how the author's word choice affects your response to the text. Consider specific words, sentence length and style, and the overall feeling conveyed. Include supporting examples and quotations from the text.
- Consider whether the author could have achieved a completely different effect by using different words or by changing the structure.
- During your presentation, establish eye contact, speak with appropriate volume, and pronounce words clearly.

Research

TASK 6 ▶ Informational Text [RI.7.2; W.7.7, W.7.8]

 ## What should we learn?

In Part 2, you have read literary nonfiction about ideas and subjects that are important to learn. Now, conduct a short research project about something you believe is important to learn. Perhaps it is a specific skill, a subject you would like to study, or an interesting career. Use the literary nonfiction you have read in Part 2 and your research to reflect on this unit's Big Question. Review the following guidelines before you begin:

- Focus your research on one specific topic.
- Gather relevant information from at least two reliable print or digital sources.
- Take notes as you research your topic.
- Cite your sources according to accepted conventions.

When you have completed your research, write a response to the Big Question. Discuss whether your initial ideas have changed or been reinforced. Support your response with examples from the Part 2 selections as well as examples from your research.

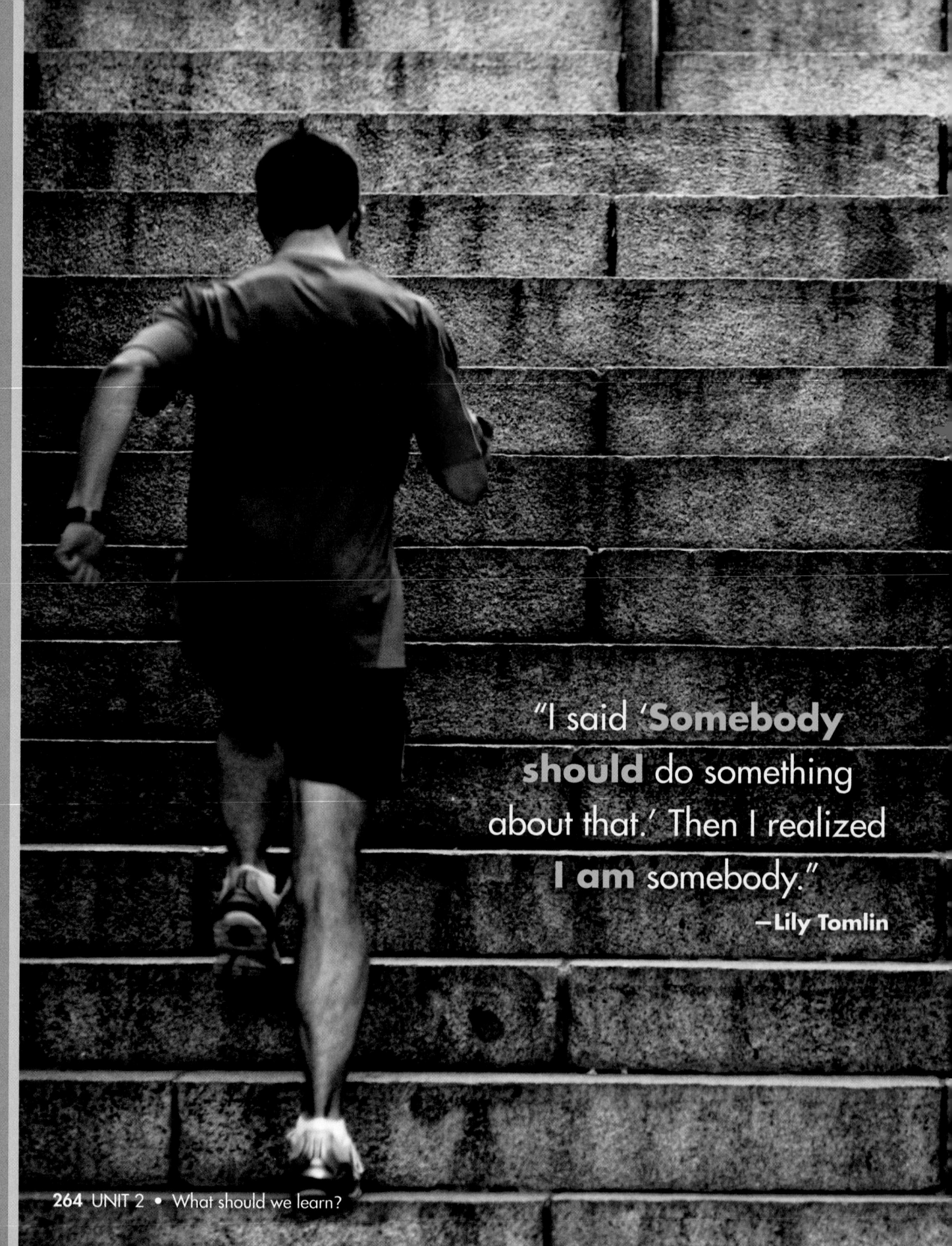

"I said 'Somebody should do something about that.' Then I realized I am somebody."

—Lily Tomlin

MOTIVATION

The selections in this unit all deal with the Big Question: **What should we learn?** In this section, texts in various genres explore ideas about human behavior and motivation. As you read, consider whether motivation comes from within or is learned from others, and think about the ways that a person's goals and behavior may change as a result of learning.

◀ **CRITICAL VIEWING** Does this photograph make you feel motivated? Why or why not?

READINGS IN PART 3

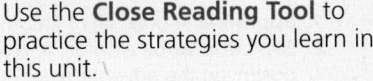

CLOSE READING TOOL

Use the **Close Reading Tool** to practice the strategies you learn in this unit.

NO GUMPTION

RUSSELL BAKER

I began working in journalism when I was eight years old. It was my mother's idea. She wanted me to "make something" of myself and, after a level-headed appraisal[1] of my strengths, decided I had better start young if I was to have any chance of keeping up with the competition.

The flaw in my character which she had already spotted was lack of "gumption." My idea of a perfect afternoon was lying in front of the radio rereading my favorite Big Little Book,[2] *Dick Tracy Meets Stooge Viller.* My mother despised inactivity. Seeing me having a good time in repose, she was powerless to hide her disgust. "You've got no more gumption than a bump on a log," she said. "Get out in the kitchen and help Doris do those dirty dishes."

My sister Doris, though two years younger than I, had enough gumption for a dozen people. She positively enjoyed washing dishes, making beds, and cleaning the house. When she was only seven she could carry a piece of short-weighted cheese back to the A&P, threaten the manager with legal action, and come back triumphantly with the full quarter-pound we'd paid for and a few ounces extra thrown in for forgiveness. Doris could have made something of herself if she hadn't been a girl. Because of this defect, however, the best she could hope for was a career as a

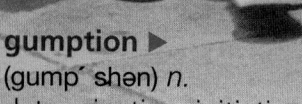

gumption ▶
(gump´ shən) *n.*
determination; initiative

---

1. **appraisal** (ə prāz´ əl) *n.* judgment; evaluation.
2. **Big Little Book** a small, inexpensive picture book that often portrayed the adventures of comic-strip heroes like Dick Tracy.

nurse or schoolteacher, the only work that capable females were considered up to in those days.

This must have saddened my mother, this twist of fate that had allocated all the gumption to the daughter and left her with a son who was content with Dick Tracy and Stooge Viller. If disappointed, though, she wasted no energy on self-pity. She would make me make something of myself whether I wanted to or not. "The Lord helps those who help themselves," she said. That was the way her mind worked.

She was realistic about the difficulty. Having sized up the material the Lord had given her to mold, she didn't overestimate what she could do with it. She didn't insist that I grow up to be President of the United States.

Fifty years ago parents still asked boys if they wanted to grow up to be President, and asked it not jokingly but seriously. Many parents who were hardly more than paupers still believed their sons could do it. Abraham Lincoln had done it. We were only sixty-five years from Lincoln. Many a grandfather who walked among us could remember Lincoln's time. Men of grandfatherly age were the worst for asking if you wanted to grow up to be President. A surprising number of little boys said yes and meant it.

I was asked many times myself. No, I would say, I didn't want to grow up to be President. My mother was present during one of these interrogations.[3] An elderly uncle, having posed the usual question and exposed my lack of interest in the Presidency, asked, "Well, what do you want to be when you grow up?"

I loved to pick through trash piles and collect empty bottles, tin cans with pretty labels, and discarded magazines. The most desirable job on earth sprang instantly to mind. "I want to be a garbage man," I said.

My uncle smiled, but my mother had seen the first distressing evidence of a bump budding on a log. "Have a little gumption, Russell," she said. Her calling me Russell was a signal of unhappiness. When she approved of me I was always "Buddy."

When I turned eight years old she decided that the job of starting me on the road toward making something of myself

---

3. **interrogations** (in ter ə´ gā´ shənz) *n.* situations in which a person is formally questioned.

could no longer be safely delayed. "Buddy," she said one day, "I want you to come home right after school this afternoon. Somebody's coming and I want you to meet him."

When I burst in that afternoon she was in conference in the parlor with an executive of the Curtis Publishing Company. She introduced me. He bent low from the waist and shook my hand. Was it true as my mother had told him, he asked, that I longed for the opportunity to conquer the world of business?

My mother replied that I was blessed with a rare determination to make something of myself.

"That's right," I whispered.

"But have you got the grit, the character, the never-say-quit spirit it takes to succeed in business?"

My mother said I certainly did.

"That's right," I said.

He eyed me silently for a long pause, as though weighing whether I could be trusted to keep his confidence, then spoke man-to-man. Before taking a **crucial** step, he said, he wanted to advise me that working for the Curtis Publishing Company placed enormous responsibility on a young man. It was one of the great companies of America. Perhaps the greatest publishing house in the world. I had heard, no doubt, of the *Saturday Evening Post*?

Heard of it? My mother said that everyone in our house had heard of the *Saturday Post* and that I, in fact, read it with religious devotion.

Then doubtless, he said, we were also familiar with those two monthly pillars of the magazine world, the *Ladies Home Journal* and the *Country Gentleman.*

Indeed we were familiar with them, said my mother.

Representing the *Saturday Evening Post* was one of the weightiest honors that could be bestowed in the world of business, he said. He was personally proud of being a part of that great corporation.

My mother said he had every right to be.

Again he studied me as though debating whether I was worthy of a knighthood. Finally: "Are you trustworthy?"

My mother said I was the soul of honesty.

"That's right," I said.

The caller smiled for the first time. He told me I was a lucky young man. He admired my spunk. Too many young men thought life was all play. Those young men would not go far

crucial ▶
(krōō′ shəl) *adj.*
important; critical

in this world. Only a young man willing to work and save and keep his face washed and his hair neatly combed could hope to come out on top in a world such as ours. Did I truly and sincerely believe that I was such a young man?

"He certainly does," said my mother.

"That's right," I said.

He said he had been so impressed by what he had seen of me that he was going to make me a representative of the Curtis Publishing Company. On the following Tuesday, he said, thirty freshly printed copies of the *Saturday Evening Post* would be delivered at our door. I would place these magazines, still damp with the ink of the presses, in a handsome canvas bag, sling it over my shoulder, and set forth through the streets to bring the best in journalism, fiction, and cartoons to the American public.

He had brought the canvas bag with him. He presented it with reverence fit for a chasuble.[4] He showed me how to drape the sling over my left shoulder and across the chest so that the pouch lay easily accessible[5] to my right hand, allowing the best in journalism, fiction, and cartoons to be swiftly extracted and sold to a citizenry whose happiness and security depended upon us soldiers of the free press.

The following Tuesday I raced home from school, put the canvas bag over my shoulder, dumped the magazines in, and, tilting to the left to balance their weight on my right hip, embarked on the highway of journalism.

We lived in Belleville, New Jersey, a commuter town at the northern fringe of Newark. It was 1932, the bleakest year of the Depression. My father had died two years before, leaving us with a few pieces of Sears, Roebuck furniture and not much else, and my mother had taken Doris and me to live with one of her younger brothers. This was my Uncle Allen. Uncle Allen had made something of himself by 1932. As salesman for a soft-drink bottler in Newark, he had an income of $30 a week; wore pearl-gray spats,[6] detachable collars, and a three-piece suit; was happily married; and took in threadbare relatives.

With my load of magazines I headed toward Belleville Avenue. That's where the people were. There were two filling stations at the intersection with Union Avenue, as well as an A&P, a fruit stand, a bakery, a barber shop, Zuccarelli's

---

4. **chasuble** (chaz´ ə bəl) *n.* sleeveless outer garment worn by priests.
5. **accessible** (ak ses´ ə bəl) *adj.* available.
6. **spats** (spats) *n.* cloth or leather material that covers the upper part of shoes or ankles.

drugstore, and a diner shaped like a railroad car. For several hours I made myself highly visible, shifting position now and then from corner to corner, from shop window to shop window, to make sure everyone could see the heavy black lettering on the canvas bag that said *The Saturday Evening Post*. When the angle of the light indicated it was suppertime, I walked back to the house.

"How many did you sell, Buddy?" my mother asked.

"None."

"Where did you go?"

"The corner of Belleville and Union Avenues."

"What did you do?"

"Stood on the corner waiting for somebody to buy a *Saturday Evening Post*."

"You just stood there?"

"Didn't sell a single one."

"For God's sake, Russell!"

Uncle Allen intervened. "I've been thinking about it for some time," he said, "and I've about decided to take the *Post* regularly. Put me down as a regular customer." I handed him a magazine and he paid me a nickel. It was the first nickel I earned.

Afterwards my mother instructed me in salesmanship. I would have to ring doorbells, address adults with charming self-confidence, and break down resistance with a sales talk pointing out that no one, no matter how poor, could afford to be without the *Saturday Evening Post* in the home.

I told my mother I'd changed my mind about wanting to succeed in the magazine business.

"If you think I'm going to raise a good-for-nothing," she replied, "you've got another think coming." She told me to hit the streets with the canvas bag and start ringing doorbells the instant school was out next day. When I objected that I didn't feel any aptitude for salesmanship, she asked how I'd like to lend her my leather belt so she could whack some sense into me. I bowed to superior will and entered journalism with a heavy heart.

My mother and I had fought this battle almost as long as I could remember. It probably started even before memory began, when I was a country child in northern Virginia and my mother, dissatisfied with my father's plain workman's life, determined that I would not grow up like him and his people,

aptitude ▶
(ap′ tə to͞od) *n.*
talent; ability

with calluses on their hands, overalls on their backs, and fourth-grade educations in their heads. She had fancier ideas of life's possibilities. Introducing me to the *Saturday Evening Post*, she was trying to wean me as early as possible from my father's world where men left with lunch pails at sunup, worked with their hands until the grime ate into the pores, and died with a few sticks of mail-order furniture as their legacy. In my mother's vision of the better life there were desks and white collars, well-pressed suits, evenings of reading and lively talk, and perhaps—if a man were very, very lucky and hit the jackpot, really made something important of himself—perhaps there might be a fantastic salary of $5,000 a year to support a big house and a Buick with a rumble seat[7] and a vacation in Atlantic City.

And so I set forth with my sack of magazines. I was afraid of the dogs that snarled behind the doors of potential buyers. I was timid about ringing the doorbells of strangers, relieved when no one came to the door, and scared when someone did. Despite my mother's instructions, I could not deliver an engaging sales pitch. When a door opened I simply asked, "Want to buy a *Saturday Evening Post*?" In Belleville few persons did. It was a town of 30,000 people, and most weeks I rang a fair majority of its doorbells. But I rarely sold my thirty copies. Some weeks I canvassed the entire town for six days and still had four or five unsold magazines on Monday evening; then I dreaded the coming of Tuesday morning, when a batch of thirty fresh *Saturday Evening Posts* was due at the front door.

"Better get out there and sell the rest of those magazines tonight," my mother would say.

I usually posted myself then at a busy intersection where a traffic light controlled commuter flow from Newark. When the light turned red I stood on the curb and shouted my sales pitch at the motorists.

"Want to buy a *Saturday Evening Post*?"

One rainy night when car windows were sealed against me I came back soaked and with not a single sale to report. My mother beckoned to Doris.

"Go back down there with Buddy and show him how to sell these magazines," she said.

---

7. **rumble seat** in the rear of early automobiles, a seat that could be folded shut.

Brimming with zest, Doris, who was then seven years old, returned with me to the corner. She took a magazine from the bag, and when the light turned red she strode to the nearest car and banged her small fist against the closed window. The driver, probably startled at what he took to be a midget assaulting his car, lowered the window to stare, and Doris thrust a *Saturday Evening Post* at him.

"You need this magazine," she piped, "and it only costs a nickel."

Her salesmanship was irresistible. Before the light changed half a dozen times she disposed of the entire batch. I didn't feel humiliated. To the contrary. I was so happy I decided to give her a treat. Leading her to the vegetable store on Belleville Avenue, I bought three apples, which cost a nickel, and gave her one.

"You shouldn't waste money," she said.

"Eat your apple." I bit into mine.

"You shouldn't eat before supper," she said. "It'll spoil your appetite."

Back at the house that evening, she dutifully reported me for wasting a nickel. Instead of a scolding, I was rewarded with a pat on the back for having the good sense to buy fruit instead of candy. My mother reached into her bottomless supply of maxims[8] and told Doris, "An apple a day keeps the doctor away."

By the time I was ten I had learned all my mother's maxims by heart. Asking to stay up past normal bedtime, I knew that a refusal would be explained with, "Early to bed and early to rise, makes a man healthy, wealthy, and wise." If I whimpered about having to get up early in the morning, I could depend on her to say, "The early bird gets the worm."

The one I most despised was, "If at first you don't succeed, try, try again." This was the battle cry with which she constantly sent me back into the hopeless struggle whenever I moaned that I had rung every doorbell in town and knew there wasn't a single potential buyer left in Belleville that week. After listening to my explanation, she handed me the canvas bag and said, "If at first you don't succeed . . ."

Three years in that job, which I would gladly have quit after the first day except for her insistence, produced at least one valuable result. My mother finally concluded that I would never

---

8. maxims (mak´ simz) *n.* wise sayings.

make something of myself by pursuing a life in business and started considering careers that demanded less competitive zeal.

One evening when I was eleven I brought home a short "composition" on my summer vacation which the teacher had graded with an A. Reading it with her own schoolteacher's eye, my mother agreed that it was top-drawer seventh grade prose and complimented me. Nothing more was said about it immediately, but a new idea had taken life in her mind. Halfway through supper she suddenly interrupted the conversation.

"Buddy," she said, "maybe you could be a writer."

I clasped the idea to my heart. I had never met a writer, had shown no previous urge to write, and hadn't a notion how to become a writer, but I loved stories and thought that making up stories must surely be almost as much fun as reading them. Best of all, though, and what really gladdened my heart, was the ease of the writer's life. Writers did not have to trudge through the town peddling from canvas bags, defending themselves against angry dogs, being rejected by surly strangers. Writers did not have to ring doorbells. So far as I could make out, what writers did couldn't even be classified as work.

I was enchanted. Writers didn't have to have any gumption at all. I did not dare tell anybody for fear of being laughed at in the schoolyard, but secretly I decided that what I'd like to be when I grew up was a writer.

ABOUT THE AUTHOR

Russell Baker (b. 1925)

Newspaper columnist, author, and humorist Russell Baker grew up during the Great Depression, a period in the 1930s of poor business conditions and major unemployment. Baker began his career as a journalist for *The Baltimore Sun* and *The New York Times.* He later won a Pulitzer Prize for his "Observer" column that was published for more than thirty years in the *Times*. He won a second Pulitzer Prize for his autobiography *Growing Up*, from which "No Gumption" comes.

READ

Comprehension

Reread all or part of the text to help you answer the following questions.

1. What is young Russell Baker's problem?

2. What job does Baker get?

3. What skill does Doris have that Baker does not have?

Language Study

Selection Vocabulary The following passages are from the autobiography. Define each boldfaced word, and then use the word in a sentence.

- The flaw in my character which she had already spotted was lack of **"gumption."**
- Before taking a **crucial** step, he said, he wanted to advise me that working for the Curtis Publishing Company . . .
- When I objected that I didn't feel any **aptitude** for salesmanship, she asked how I'd like to lend her my leather belt . . .

Diction and Style Study the following sentence from the autobiography. Then, answer the questions that follow.

> She wanted me to "make something" of myself and, after a level-headed appraisal of my strengths, decided I had better start young if I was to have any chance of keeping up with the competition.

1. (a) What is a synonym for *strengths* in this sentence? **(b)** What other meaning does *strength* have?

2. (a) Who is "the competition"? **(b)** In what other context is the word *competition* often used? **(c)** Why do you think the author

chose to use "the competition" rather than another term?

Conventions Read this passage from the autobiography. Identify the verbs in the compound predicate in the passage. Then, explain what idea is emphasized in the compound predicate.

> The following Tuesday I raced home from school, put the canvas bag over my shoulder, dumped the magazines in, and, tilting to the left to balance their weight on my right hip, embarked on the highway of journalism.

Research: Clarify Details Choose at least one unfamiliar detail from the text and briefly research it. Then, explain how the information sheds light on an aspect of the autobiography.

Summarize Write an objective summary of the autobiography. Remember that an objective summary does not contain opinions.

Academic Vocabulary

The following words appear in blue in the instructions and questions on the facing page.

identify   **insight**   **purpose**

Categorize the words by deciding whether you know each one well, know it a little bit, or do not know it at all. Then, use a print or online dictionary to look up the definitions of the words you are unsure of or do not know at all.

Literary Analysis

Reread the identified passages. Then, respond to the questions.

> **Focus Passage 1** *(pp. 266–267)*
>
> The flaw in my character which she had already spotted…were considered up to in those days.

> **Focus Passage 2** *(p. 272)*
>
> Brimming with zest, Doris, who was then seven…which cost a nickel, and gave her one.

Key Ideas and Details

1. Interpret: What does Baker's mother mean when she says he has no "gumption"?

2. Define: Citing details from the passage, explain why Doris has gumption.

Craft and Structure

3. (a) In this passage, point out one example of direct characterization and one example of indirect characterization. **(b) Evaluate:** Which type of characterization is more effective? Explain.

4. (a) Identify details that show this autobiography is set in the past. **(b) Analyze Cause and Effect:** How will the time period in which she grows up affect Doris's work choices in the future?

Integration of Knowledge and Ideas

5. Draw Conclusions: Infer what makes Baker happy and what makes Doris happy. Then, draw a conclusion about happiness.

Key Ideas and Details

1. (a) What is the driver's response to Doris's actions? **(b) Contrast:** How does Doris's approach to selling differ from Baker's approach?

2. Interpret: What is Baker's reaction to his sister's salesmanship?

Craft and Structure

3. (a) What words does the author use to describe Doris? **(b) Analyze:** How do these words show why she is successful?

4. Evaluate: How does the author use exaggeration to create humor in this passage? Cite details from the text in your answer.

Integration of Knowledge and Ideas

5. Connect: The author's mother has said he has "no gumption." What **insight** does this passage provide into the meaning of *gumption*?

. . . .

Autobiography

In an **autobiography,** the writer communicates details about his or her own life. Autobiographical writing may tell about a person's whole life or only a part of it.

1. What does Baker's humorous tone suggest about his **purpose** for writing?

2. Motivation What might Baker want to communicate about himself, his mother, and Doris?

3. Cite textual examples that show how Baker uses conflict, suspense, and resolution to develop the plot.

Common Core State Standards

RI.7.1, RI.7.2, RI.7.4, RI.7.6; L.7.4.c, L.7.5.b, L.7.6
[For full standards wording, see the chart in the front of this book.]

DISCUSS

From Text to Topic **Group Discussion**

Discuss the following passage with a group of classmates. Take notes during the discussion. Contribute your own ideas, and support them with examples from the text.

> "Buddy," she said, "maybe you could be a writer."…
> So far as I could make out, what writers did couldn't even be classified as work. (p. 273)

QUESTIONS FOR DISCUSSION:

1. How does this passage show Baker's sense of humor?

2. What idea about a writing career does Baker find motivating? What makes this observation humorous?

WRITE

Writing to Sources **Argument**

Assignment

Write a **persuasive essay** in which you agree or disagree with the following statement: *Money provides the best motivation for success.* Consider both Baker's goals for himself and his mother's goals for him.

Prewriting and Planning Choose your position. Then, reread the autobiography, looking for details that support your claim. Record your notes in a web diagram. Put your claim and counterclaim(s) in the center and supporting details in the outer circles.

Drafting Draft a strong introduction, body, and conclusion.

- **Introduction** State your claim, or your position on the issue.
- **Body** Acknowledge opposing opinions, or counterclaims. Present facts, reasons and examples to support your position and refute counterclaims. Cite specific details from the text and other relevant evidence.
- **Conclusion** Sum up your argument in a strong concluding statement.

Revising Reread your essay, making sure you have strongly supported your claim and addressed counterclaims. Make clear connections between your claim and the evidence that supports it by using transitional words and phrases, such as those below.

for example	*specifically*	*in particular*
because	*such as*	*for this reason*

Editing and Proofreading Double-check your essay for commonly confused words, such as *accept/except, than/then,* and *are/our.* Make any necessary corrections.

CONVENTIONS

Check your use of pronouns to ensure each pronoun has a clear antecedent, and that all antecedents agree with their pronouns in gender and number.

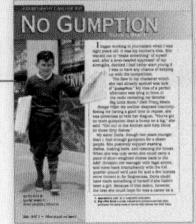

RESEARCH

Research **Investigate the Topic**

Goals and Motivation In this autobiography, Baker's own aims in life differ from his mother's goals for him. Many people believe there is a clear link between motivation and goals. For example, some people believe success depends on setting achievable goals.

Assignment

Conduct research to learn what experts say about the relationship between goals and motivation. Consult a dictionary for definitions and search print and online sources using key words such as *goals* and *motivation*. Take clear notes and carefully identify your sources so that you can easily access the information later. Share your findings in an **oral presentation** for the class.

Gather Sources Locate a variety of print and electronic sources. For example, you might consult a published study by experts that explains the findings of a study or research project. You may also look for information in news articles and reference books. Choose sources that feature expert authors and up-to-date information.

Take Notes Take notes on each source, either electronically or on notecards. Use an organized note-taking strategy.

- Use key words like *incentives* and abbreviations such as *e.g.* (for example).

- Use separate notecards to organize subtopics.

- If you plan to include a direct quotation, use the exact words of the source and place the words inside quotation marks. Otherwise, paraphrase by putting the information in your own words.

Synthesize Multiple Sources Assemble data from your sources and organize it into a cohesive presentation. Draw conclusions about the relationship between goals and motivation. Use your notes to construct an outline for your presentation. Create a Works Cited list as described in the Research Workshop in the Introductory Unit of your textbook.

Organize and Present Ideas Review your outline and practice delivering your presentation. Be prepared to answer questions from your audience.

PREPARATION FOR ESSAY

You may use the knowledge you gain during this research assignment to support your claims in an essay you will write at the end of this section.

Common Core State Standards

W.7.1.a, W.7.1.b, W.7.1.c, W.7.1.e, W.7.5, W.7.6, W.7.7, W.7.8; SL.7.1.a, SL.7.1.c; L.7.2.b
[For full standards wording, see the chart in the front of this book.]

Intrinsic Motivation Doesn't Exist, Researcher Says

Jeff Grabmeier

COLUMBUS, Ohio—While some **psychologists** still argue that people perform better when they do something because they want to—rather than for some kind of reward, such as money—Steven Reiss suggests we shouldn't even make that distinction.

Reiss, a professor of psychology at Ohio State University, argues that a diverse range of human motivations can't be forced into these categories of intrinsic and extrinsic motivations. Psychologists say intrinsic motivations are those that arise from within—doing something because you want to—while extrinsic motivations mean people are seeking a reward, such as money, a good grade in class, or a trophy at a sporting event.

"They are taking many diverse human needs and motivations, putting them into just two categories, and then saying one type of motivation is better than another," said Reiss, who outlines his argument in the current issue of the journal *Behavior Analyst*.

"But there is no real evidence that intrinsic motivation even exists."

The issue is more than academic, Reiss said. Many sports psychology books, and books advising how to motivate students and business people, **tout** the value of intrinsic motivation and warn that extrinsic rewards can undermine people's performance.

The argument is that people should do something because they enjoy it, and that rewards only sabotage natural desire.

Reiss disagrees.

"There is no reason that money can't be an effective motivator, or that grades can't motivate students in school," he said. "It's all a matter of individual differences. Different people are motivated in different ways."

Reiss has developed and tested a theory of motivation that states there are 16 basic desires that guide nearly all meaningful behavior, including power, independence, curiosity, and acceptance. Whether you agree there are 16 desires or not, he said there is not any way to reduce all of these desires to just two types.

In addition to trying to fit all motivations into two types, Reiss said proponents of intrinsic motivation are also making value judgments by saying some types of motivation are better than others.

"For example, some people have said that wealth and materialism lead to inferior quality happiness, but there is no real proof of that," he said.

"Individuals differ enormously in what makes them happy—for some competition, winning and wealth are the greatest sources of happiness, but for others, feeling competent or socializing may be more satisfying. The point is that you can't say some motivations, like money, are inherently inferior."

In the article, Reiss points to some of the problems he sees with the theories and studies connected to intrinsic motivation. One problem is that people who tout the value of intrinsic motivation have several different definitions for what that means, and these definitions change depending on circumstances.

One common definition, for example, is that intrinsic motivation is that which is inherently pleasurable, while extrinsic motivation is not. For example, the argument is that children are naturally curious and enjoy learning for the joy it brings them. Grades, they argue, are an extrinsic reward that **fosters** competition and makes learning less pleasurable.

◄ **psychologists**
(sī käl′ ə jists) *n.* experts who study the human mind and behavior

◄ **tout**
(tout) *v.* promote

◄ **fosters**
(fôs′tərz) *v.* promotes the growth or development of

However, Reiss said his research has found people show a wide range of curiosity—some people are very curious and enjoy spending a great deal of time learning on their own. However, many people are not very curious and don't enjoy learning for its own sake.

"There are many children for whom the important reward to them is the grades they get, the competition among classmates," Reiss said. "This goes against what some psychologists say, who think competition is bad and a non-competitive attitude is good, and that learning and curiosity are intrinsic values that everyone shares. They are pushing their own value system on to everybody."

> **"There are many children for whom the important reward to them is the grades they get, the competition among classmates. . ."**

Another way of defining intrinsic motivation is the means-end definition, which says intrinsic motivation is doing what we want, whereas extrinsic motivation is doing something to get something else. For example, some might argue that children playing baseball are intrinsically motivated by the joy of playing, while a professional baseball player is extrinsically motivated, by money and championships.

But Reiss said this definition confuses means and ends. A child playing baseball may be satisfying his need for physical exercise, while the professional player is satisfying his parental instinct by providing a good income for his family.

For children and professionals, baseball is a means to two different ends.

Reiss also criticized many of the studies, which proponents say prove the existence of intrinsic motivation, and how it can be undermined by extrinsic rewards.

For example, many studies have purportedly shown how people who enjoy doing a specific activity—such as children who enjoy drawing—do that activity less after they are offered rewards. But when the results show the subjects continue the activity even after the rewards are offered, the researchers have argued that this just shows the subjects expect to get a reward and no longer are intrinsically motivated.

"The results are always turned around to prove their hypothesis."

Also, researchers have assumed that rewards simply make people

less interested in the intrinsic joys of an activity. But Reiss said many of these studies haven't considered the possibility that the negative effect of rewards has nothing to do with intrinsic or extrinsic motivations. Instead, rewards may cause some people to pursue an activity less because of the negative feelings they cause, such as performance anxiety.[1] Avoiding an activity because of performance anxiety related to a reward is not the same as avoiding it simply because the reward undermines intrinsic motivation.

"Too many studies that supposedly prove intrinsic motivation have serious flaws in logic, or too many important uncontrolled variables,"[2] he said. "There needs to be more scientific rigor."

---

1. **performance anxiety** fear of performing for an audience.
2. **uncontrolled variables** things in an experiment that could give false results.

ABOUT THE AUTHOR

Jeff Grabmeier

Jeff Grabmeier serves as Senior Director of Research and Innovation Communications at Ohio State University, where he writes about research in social sciences, business, and humanities. He is also co-chair of the Education Committee of the National Association of Science Writers. This organization supports teachers of science writing and people who want to become science writers by sponsoring workshops and fellowships.

READ

Comprehension

Reread all or part of the text to help you answer the following questions.

1. How do psychologists define *intrinsic* and *extrinsic* motivation?

2. What does Reiss say is wrong about many studies on intrinsic motivation?

Research: Clarify Details Choose at least one unfamiliar detail from the text and briefly research it. Then, explain how your research clarifies the article.

Summarize Write an objective summary of the article that is free from opinions.

Language Study

Selection Vocabulary Define each boldfaced word from the article, then use it in a sentence of your own.

• …some **psychologists** still argue that people perform better when they do something because they want to…

• Many sports psychology books, and books advising how to motivate students and business people, **tout** the value of intrinsic motivation…

• Grades, they argue, are an extrinsic reward that **fosters** competition…

Literary Analysis

Reread the identified passage. Then, respond to the following questions.

Focus Passage *(pp. 279–280)*

One common definition…don't enjoy learning for its own sake.

Key Ideas and Details

1. (a) What is an example of each type of motivation? **(b)** Which is more pleasurable according to common definitions? **(c) Connect:** What evidence contradicts these **perceptions**?

Craft and Structure

2. (a) What transition words does the author use to connect ideas in the passage? **(b) Connect:** What relationship do the words show? **(c) Analyze:** Why are transitions especially important in informational texts such as this one?

Integration of Knowledge and Ideas

3. Speculate: Based on this passage, what might people find if they **investigate** the connection between grades and motivation?

Expository Writing

Expository writing explains or informs. In an expository article, the author provides information that supports the main idea and his or her purpose for writing.

1. (a) What is the main idea of the article? **(b)** What types of details does the author provide to support the main idea?

2. (a) What is the author's most likely purpose for writing this article? **(b)** What is a possible secondary purpose?

DISCUSS • RESEARCH • WRITE

From Text to Topic **Group Discussion**

Discuss the following passage with a group of classmates. Take notes during the discussion. Contribute your own ideas and support them with examples from the text.

> "There is no reason that money can't be an effective motivator, or that grades can't motivate students in school," he said. "It's all a matter of individual differences. Different people are motivated in different ways."

Research **Investigate the Topic**

Money and Grades According Steven Reiss, money can be an effective motivator. Some people think it is a good idea to give students financial rewards for getting good grades. Others disagree.

Assignment

Conduct research to find out what experts say about the idea of motivating students to get good grades by offering them money. Consult print and digital sources for information about studies on the pros and cons of this practice. Take clear notes and carefully identify your sources so that you can easily access the information later. Share your findings in an **informal speech** for the class.

Writing to Sources **Argument**

This article introduces the idea that people are motivated by a variety of factors and that extrinsic rewards, such as money, may be good motivators. Do you agree or disagree?

Assignment

Write an **argument** in which you take a position for or against the practice of rewarding good grades with money. Follow these steps:
- Introduce your claim and **acknowledge** an opposing claim.
- Support your claim with evidence from your research.
- Use words and phrases that clearly show the relationships between your claims and the evidence that supports them.
- Establish and maintain a formal style.

QUESTIONS FOR DISCUSSION

1. How does Reiss feel about money as a motivator?
2. What does Reiss believe about the ways in which people are motivated?

PREPARATION FOR ESSAY

You may use the results of your research to support your ideas in the essay you will write at the end of this section.

ACADEMIC VOCABULARY

Academic terms appear in blue on these pages. If these words are not familiar to you, use a dictionary to find their definitions. Then, use the words as you speak and write about the text.

 **Common Core State Standards**

RI.7.1, RI.7.2, RI.7.6; W.7.1, W.7.1.c, W.7.1.d; SL.7.1; L.7.4
[For full standards wording, see the chart in the front of this book.]

The Cremation of Sam McGee

Robert Service

There are strange things done in the midnight sun
  By the men who moil[1] for gold;
The Arctic trails have their secret tales
  That would make your blood run cold;
5 The Northern Lights have seen queer sights,
  But the queerest they ever did see
Was that night on the marge[2] of Lake Lebarge
  I **cremated** Sam McGee.

Now Sam McGee was from Tennessee,
  where the cotton blooms and blows.
10 Why he left his home in the South to roam
  'round the Pole, God only knows.
He was always cold, but the land of gold
  seemed to hold him like a spell;
Though he'd often say in his homely way
  that "he'd sooner live in hell."

On a Christmas Day we were mushing our way
  over the Dawson trail.
Talk of your cold! through the parka's fold
  it stabbed like a driven nail.
15 If our eyes we'd close, then the lashes froze
  til sometimes we couldn't see;
It wasn't much fun, but the only one
  to **whimper** was Sam McGee.

cremated ▶
(krē'māt' id) v. burned a dead body to ashes

whimper ▶
(hwim' pər) v. make low, crying sounds

1. **moil** (moil) v. toil and slave.
2. **marge** (märj) n. poetic word for the shore of the lake.

And that very night, as we lay packed tight
    in our robes beneath the snow,
And the dogs were fed, and the stars o'erhead
    were dancing heel and toe,
He turned to me, and "Cap," says he,
    "I'll cash in this trip, I guess;
20 And if I do, I'm asking that you
    won't refuse my last request."
Well, he seemed so low that I couldn't say no;
    then he says with a sort of moan:
"It's the cursed cold, and it's got right hold
    till I'm chilled clean through to the bone.
Yet 'tain't being dead—it's my awful dread
    of the icy grave that pains;
So I want you to swear that, foul or fair,
    you'll cremate my last remains."

25 A pal's last need is a thing to heed,
    so I swore I would not fail;
And we started on at the streak of dawn;
    but God! he looked ghastly pale.
He crouched on the sleigh, and he raved all day
    of his home in Tennessee;
And before nightfall a corpse was all
    that was left of Sam McGee.

There wasn't a breath in that land of death,
    and I hurried, horror-driven,
30 With a corpse half hid that I couldn't get rid,
    because of a promise given;
It was lashed to the sleigh, and it seemed to say:
    "You may tax your brawn[3] and brains,
But you promised true, and it's up to you
    to cremate those last remains."

---

3. brawn (brôn) *n.* physical strength.

Now a promise made is a debt unpaid,
    and the trail has its own stern code.
In the days to come, though my lips were dumb,
    in my heart how I cursed that load.
35 In the long, long night, by the lone firelight,
    while the huskies, round in a ring,
Howled out their woes to the homeless snows—
    O God! how I **loathed** the thing.
And every day that quiet clay
    seemed to heavy and heavier grow;
And on I went, though the dogs were spent
    and the grub was getting low;
The trail was bad, and I felt half mad,
    but I swore I would not give in;
40 And I'd often sing to the hateful thing,
    and it hearkened with a grin.

loathed ▶
(lō*th*d) *v.* hated

Till I came to the marge of Lake Lebarge,
    and a derelict[4] there lay;
It was jammed in the ice, but I saw in a trice
    it was called the "Alice May."
And I looked at it, and I thought a bit,
    and I looked at my frozen chum;
Then "Here," said I, with a sudden cry,
    "is my cre-ma-tor-eum."

45 Some planks I tore from the cabin floor,
    and I lit the boiler fire;
Some coal I found that was lying around,
    and I heaped the fuel higher;
The flames just soared, and the furnace roared—
    such a blaze you seldom see;
And I burrowed a hole in the glowing coal,
    and I stuffed in Sam McGee.

Then I made a hike, for I didn't like
    to hear him sizzle so;
50 And the heavens scowled, and the huskies howled,
    and the wind began to blow.
It was icy cold, but the hot sweat rolled
    down my cheeks, and I don't know why;

---

4. **derelict** (der′ ə likt′) *n.* abandoned ship.

And the greasy smoke in an inky cloak
    went streaking down the sky.

I do not know how long in the snow
    I wrestled with grisly fear;
But the stars came out and they danced about
    ere again I ventured near;
55 I was sick with dread, but I bravely said:
    "I'll just take a peep inside.
I guess he's cooked, and it's time I looked"; . . .
    then the door I opened wide.

And there sat Sam, looking cool and calm,
    in the heart of the furnace roar;
And he wore a smile you could see a mile,
    and he said: "Please close that door.
It's fine in here, but I greatly fear
    you'll let in the cold and storm—
60 Since I left Plumtree, down in Tennessee,
    it's the first time I've been warm."

There are strange things done in the midnight sun
    By the men who moil for gold;
The Arctic trails have their secret tales
    That would make your blood run cold;
65 *The Northern Lights have seen queer sights,*
    But the queerest they ever did see
Was that night on the marge of Lake Lebarge
    I cremated Sam McGee.

ABOUT THE AUTHOR

Robert Service (1874–1958)

A writer of novels, poetry, and ballads, Robert Service was born in England and raised in Scotland. At age twenty he went to work for a bank in Vancouver, British Columbia, in Canada. After two years, he was assigned to a Yukon branch of the bank. While in the Yukon Territory, he met fur trappers and gold prospectors. After leaving the bank, Service traveled in the Arctic, where he observed the people living there and recorded his adventures.

READ

Comprehension

Reread all or part of the text to help you answer the following questions.

1. Why is Sam McGee in the Arctic?

2. What promise does the speaker make to Sam?

3. What is surprising about the poem's conclusion?

Research: Clarify Details Choose at least one unfamiliar detail in the poem and briefly research it. Then, explain how your research sheds light on the poem.

Summarize Write an objective summary of the poem. Remember that an objective summary is free from opinion and evaluation.

Language Study

Selection Vocabulary Define each boldfaced word. Then, identify the part of speech that the three words share. Finally, use the words in sentences of your own.

- … I **cremated** Sam McGee.
- … the only one to **whimper** was Sam McGee.
- … O God! How I **loathed** the thing.

Literary Analysis

Reread the identified passage. Then, respond to the following questions.

> **Focus Passage** *(p. 286)*
>
> Now a promise made…and it hearkened with a grin.

Key Ideas and Details

1. (a) What is the speaker's struggle in this passage? **(b) Analyze:** Why does he refuse to give in?

2. Deduce: Why is the speaker's task so difficult?

Craft and Structure

3. Interpret: How do the rhyming words in the middle and ends of lines affect the sound of the poem?

4. (a) What are two vivid **images** in this stanza? **(b) Evaluate:** What specific words make these images vivid? Why?

Integration of Knowledge and Ideas

5. Connect: How does the setting **contribute** to the action?

Characters

A **character** is a person or an animal that takes part in the action in a literary work. Reread the poem, and take notes on ways in which the author develops characters to show their motivations.

1. Motivation What motivates Sam McGee to stay in the Arctic?

2. (a) Why does McGee want to be cremated? **(b)** Why does the speaker agree to McGee's request?

3. Motivation How does the **outcome** relate to McGee's character and motivation?

DISCUSS • RESEARCH • WRITE

From Text to Topic **Partner Discussion**

Discuss the following passage with a partner. Contribute your own ideas, support them with examples from the text, and respond to your partner's ideas.

> I do not know how long in the snow
>   I wrestled with grisly fear;
> But the stars came out and they danced about
>   ere again I ventured near;
> I was sick with dread, but I bravely said:
>   "I'll just take a peep inside.
> I guess he's cooked, and it's time I looked"; …
>   then the door I opened wide.

QUESTIONS FOR DISCUSSION

1. What words in this passage create a tense mood?

2. How do the words *cooked* and *looked* break the tense mood and create humor?

Research **Investigate the Topic**

Klondike Gold Rush In "The Cremation of Sam McGee," poet Robert Service captures the excitement and danger that prospectors faced during the Klondike Gold Rush of the 1890s.

Assignment
Conduct research to learn what motivated prospectors to join the Klondike Gold Rush. Consult print and electronic sources. Take clear notes and carefully identify your sources. Share your findings in a **brief research paper.**

PREPARATION FOR ESSAY

You may use the results of your research assignment to support your ideas in the essay you will write at the end of this section.

Writing to Sources **Narrative**

"The Cremation of Sam McGee" describes the adventures of two gold prospectors during the Klondike Gold Rush.

Assignment
Write a **fictional narrative** in which you imagine you are searching for gold during the Klondike Gold Rush. Describe your adventures.
- Write from the first-person point of view.
- Use time-order words, such as *first, next,* and *last,* to show a clear sequence of events.
- Use precise words and sensory language to capture the action.
- Provide a satisfying conclusion that follows from the narrated experience.

ACADEMIC VOCABULARY

Academic terms appear in blue on these pages. If these words are not familiar to you, use a dictionary to find their definitions. Then, use the words as you speak and write about the text.

 **Common Core State Standards**

RL.7.1, RL.7.2, RL.7.3, RL.7.4, RL.7.6; W.7.3, W.7.3.c, W.7.3.d, W.7.7, W.7.10; SL.7.1
[For full standards wording, see the chart in the front of this book.]

A Special Gift—
The Legacy of "Snowflake" Bentley

Barbara Eaglesham

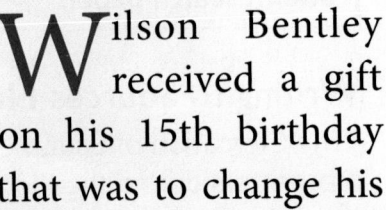

Wilson Bentley received a gift on his 15th birthday that was to change his life—an old microscope his mother had once used in teaching. As birthday gifts go, it might not have seemed like much, but to this 1880s Vermont farm boy it was special indeed.

"When the other boys of my age were playing with popguns and sling-shots, I was absorbed in studying things under this microscope," he later wrote.

And nothing fascinated him more than snowflakes. It would become a passion that would last a lifetime, earn him the nickname "Snowflake Bentley," and make him known around the world.

Focused on Beauty

If you have ever seen a snowflake design on a mug, or on jewelry, or maybe on a tote bag, chances are it was based on one of Bentley's more than 5,000 photomicrographs[1] of snow crystals (snow crystals are the building blocks of snowflakes).

At first, though, Bentley did not own a camera. He had only his eyes and his microscope, and no way to share his enjoyment of the delicate **hexagons** other than to draw them. As soon as the snow started to fly (and if his chores were done), he would collect some snow crystals on a board painted black. He'd spend hours inside his woodshed, where he had his microscope, picking up the most perfect ones on the end of a piece of straw from a broom and transferring them to a microscope slide. There, he would flatten them with a bird feather. Then, holding his breath, he would observe the crystal and hurry to draw what he saw before it **evaporated** into thin air. It was a frustrating business to try to capture all the details in a drawing while simultaneously being in a race against time.

Eventually, a few years later, Bentley noticed an advertisement for a microscope and camera that he knew was the answer to his dreams. The problem was, the equipment cost $100—equal to a whopping $2,000 today. His father, being a serious, hard-working farmer, felt that looking through a microscope was a waste of time. "Somehow my mother got him to spend the money," Bentley wrote, "but he

◄ **evaporated**
(ē vap´ ə rāt əd) v.
changed from a liquid to a gas

◄ **hexagons**
(hek´ sə gänz´) n.
six-sided figures

---

1. **photomicrographs** photographs made through a microscope.

never came to believe it had been worthwhile." That was probably a feeling shared by the locals of Jericho, who nicknamed him "Snowflake" Bentley.

Undeterred, he began his quest to photograph a snow crystal. Once he attached the microscope to the camera and rigged up a way to focus it without running back and forth (he couldn't reach the focus knob from behind the camera), he began experimenting with photography. In the 1880s, few people owned a camera, so Bentley had no one to ask for help. Time after frustrating time, his **negatives** appeared blank. Not until the following winter did he figure out that too much light was reaching the camera lens. His solution was to place a metal plate with a pinhole in the center beneath the stage of the microscope, to cut down the stray light and allow only the light waves carrying the image to reach the camera.

This was the key, and on January 15, 1885, at the age of 19, Bentley finally photographed a snowflake! Many hours over the next 45 years were spent in his tiny darkroom beneath the stairs developing negatives that he then carried, often by lantern-light, to the brook for washing. In all that time, he never saw two snow crystals that were exactly alike, although he realized that if he were able to collect two crystals side-by-side from the same cloud, there was a good chance that they might look the same. (Scientist Nancy Knight did just that in 1988, and indeed found two identical snow crystals!)

An artist as well as a scientist, Bentley wanted to find a way to make the shape of the crystal stand out more from the white background of the photo paper. He couldn't bring himself to alter his original glass plate negatives, so he began making copies of them and scraping the photographic emulsion away from the edges of the images with a knife, a time-consuming trick that allowed sunlight through, turning the background black when printed by sunlight.

Bentley's book, *Snow Crystals,* containing 2,453 of his photographs, was finally published and delivered to his house just weeks before his death in 1931.

negatives ▶
(neg´ə tivz) *n.* photograhic images in which the light and dark areas are reversed

Bentley was pleased. He never made more than a few thousand dollars from his work, but it had been a labor of love and he was satisfied to know that he would finally be able to share the beauty of his snow crystals with the world.

He is remembered primarily for this accomplishment, but to his friends and family, he was kind, gentle, and funny "Willie." He was the man who would sometimes tie an insect to a blade of grass to photograph it covered with dew the next morning, and who always chewed every bite 36 times. He was a gifted pianist who also played the violin and clarinet. He was the bachelor farmer who lived in the same farmhouse all his life. To scientists, he was the untrained researcher who not only photographed snow crystals, but also kept a detailed daily log of local weather conditions throughout his life and developed a method to measure the size of raindrops. To the people of Jericho, he is remembered as the not-so-flaky-after-all "Snowflake" Bentley.

ABOUT THE AUTHOR

Barbara Eaglesham (b. 1957)

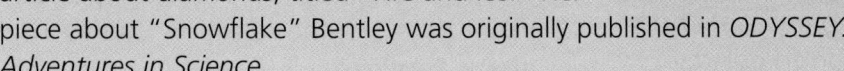

A lab instructor in microbiology at Cornell University, Barbara Eaglesham loves looking through a microscope. "I get very jazzed about science," Eaglesham confesses. "I love to attempt to communicate complicated subjects to young people." Eaglesham has written an article about diamonds, titled "Fire and Ice." Her piece about "Snowflake" Bentley was originally published in *ODYSSEY: Adventures in Science.*

READ

Comprehension

Reread all or part of the text to help you answer the following questions.

1. What gift changed Wilson Bentley's life?

2. Before he had a camera, how did Bentley capture the shapes of snowflakes?

3. Why did Bentley's first photographs appear blank?

Research: Clarify Details Choose at least one unfamiliar detail from this article and briefly research it. Then, explain how your research sheds light on an aspect of the article.

Summarize Write an objective summary of the article. Remember that an objective summary is free from opinion and evaluation.

Language Study

Selection Vocabulary Define each boldfaced word from the article, and then use the word in a sentence of your own.

- … and no way to share his enjoyment of the delicate **hexagons** other than to draw them.

- … he would observe the crystal and hurry to draw what he saw before it **evaporated** into thin air.

- Time after frustrating time his **negatives** appeared blank.

Literary Analysis

Reread the identified passage. Then, respond to the following questions.

> **Focus Passage** *(p. 292)*
> This was the key, and on January 15… when printed by sunlight.

Key Ideas and Details

1. **Interpret:** What did Bentley **observe** that makes each snow crystal special?

2. **Analyze:** How did Bentley make the shape of the crystals more visible in his photographs?

Craft and Structure

3. **(a)** List two details that show the writer conducted research in order to write this article. **(b) Speculate:** What sources might she have consulted in her research?

4. **(a) Interpret:** What is the tone of this passage? **(b) Support:** What details convey the tone?

Integration of Knowledge and Ideas

5. **Relate:** In what ways was Bentley's work beneficial to science?

Biography

A **biography** is a form of nonfiction in which a writer tells the life story of another person. Reread this biographical article, and note how the author uses characterization to portray Bentley and show his motivation.

1. **Motivation** How did Bentley's curiosity give his life **focus**?

2. What details in the selection lead to insights about Bentley?

DISCUSS • RESEARCH • WRITE

From Text to Topic **Partner Discussion**

Discuss the following passage with a partner. Take notes during the discussion. Share your own ideas, and support them with examples from the text.

> Bentley's book, *Snow Crystals*, containing 2,453 of his photographs, was finally published and delivered to his house just weeks before his death in 1931. Bentley was pleased. He never made more than a few thousand dollars from his work, but it had been a labor of love and he was satisfied to know that he would finally be able to share the beauty of his snow crystals with the world.

Research **Investigate the Topic**

Snow Crystals Snow crystals fascinated Wilson Bentley, and they continue to fascinate people today.

Assignment

Conduct research to learn more about snow crystals. Consult print and Internet sources. Take clear notes and carefully identify your sources. Share your findings in an **annotated poster.** Include a paragraph in which you explain what motivated Wilson Bentley to devote his life's work to the study of snow crystals.

Writing to Sources **Informative Text**

"The Legacy of 'Snowflake' Bentley" focuses on one man's study of snow crystals. Consider what you learned about scientific **inquiry** from his method of study.

Assignment

Write an **informative essay** in which you explain how curiosity motivated Wilson Bentley to make a lasting contribution to science.

- Introduce the topic clearly, and briefly preview what your essay will cover.
- Develop the topic with facts and details, using science terms such as *evidence* and *hypothesis* when appropriate.
- Organize your ideas in a logical sequence.
- Maintain a formal style and tone.

QUESTIONS FOR DISCUSSION

1. What idea is emphasized by the words *finally* and *just weeks* in the first sentence?

2. What is Bentley's "labor of love"? What does this phrase reveal about Bentley's motivation for his work?

PREPARATION FOR ESSAY

You may use the results of your research to support your ideas in the essay you will write at the end of this section.

ACADEMIC VOCABULARY

Academic terms appear in blue on these pages. If these words are not familiar to you, use a dictionary to find their definitions. Then, use the words as you speak and write about the text.

 **Common Core State Standards**

RI.7.1, RI.7.3; W.7.2, W.7.2.e, W.7.7; SL.7.1
[For full standards wording, see the chart in the front of this book.]

All Stories Are Anansi's

African Folk Tale ◆ Harold Courlander

I n the beginning, all tales and stories belonged to Nyame (nē ä′ mē), the Sky God. But Kwaku Anansi (kwä′ kōo ə nän′ sē), the spider, yearned to be the owner of all the stories known in the world, and he went to Nyame and offered to buy them.

The Sky God said: "I am willing to sell the stories, but the price is high. Many people have come to me offering to buy, but the price was too high for them. Rich and powerful families have not been able to pay. Do you think you can do it?"

Anansi replied to the Sky God: "I can do it. What is the price?"

"My price is three things," the Sky God said. "I must first have Mmoboro (mō bô′ rō), the hornets. I must then have Onini (ō nē′ nē), the great python. I must then have Osebo (ō sä′ bō), the leopard. For these things I will sell you the right to tell all stories."

Anansi said: "I will bring them."

He went home and made his plans. He first cut a gourd from a vine and made a small hole in it. He took a large calabash[1] and filled it with water. He went to the tree where the hornets lived. He poured some of the water over himself, so that he was dripping. He threw some water over the hornets, so that they too were dripping. Then he put the calabash on his head, as though to protect himself from a storm, and called out to the hornets: "Are you foolish people? Why do you stay in the rain that is falling?"

The hornets answered: "Where shall we go?"

"Go here, in this dry gourd," Anansi told them.

The hornets thanked him and flew into the gourd through the small hole. When the last of them had entered, Anansi plugged the hole with a ball of grass, saying: "Oh, yes, but you are really foolish people!"

He took his gourd full of hornets to Nyame, the Sky God. The Sky God accepted them. He said: "There are two more things."

Anansi returned to the forest and cut a long bamboo pole and some strong vines. Then he walked toward the house of

---

1. **calabash** (kal′ ə bash′) *n.* large fruit that is dried and made into a bowl or cup.

Onini, the python, talking to himself. He said: "My wife is stupid. I say he is longer and stronger. My wife says he is shorter and weaker. I give him more respect. She gives him less respect. Is she right or am I right? I am right, he is longer. I am right, he is stronger."

When Onini, the python, heard Anansi talking to himself, he said: "Why are you arguing this way with yourself?"

The spider replied: "Ah, I have had a **dispute** with my wife. She says you are shorter and weaker than this bamboo pole. I say you are longer and stronger."

Onini said: "It's useless and silly to argue when you can find out the truth. Bring the pole and we will measure."

So Anansi laid the pole on the ground, and the python came and stretched himself out beside it.

"You seem a little short," Anansi said.

The python stretched further.

"A little more," Anansi said.

"I can stretch no more," Onini said.

"When you stretch at one end, you get shorter at the other end," Anansi said. "Let me tie you at the front so you don't slip."

He tied Onini's head to the pole. Then he went to the other end and tied the tail to the pole. He wrapped the vine all around Onini, until the python couldn't move.

"Onini," Anansi said, "it turns out that my wife was right and I was wrong. You are shorter than the pole and weaker. My **opinion** wasn't as good as my wife's. But you were even more foolish than I, and you are now my prisoner."

Anansi carried the python to Nyame, the Sky God, who said: "There is one thing more."

Osebo, the leopard, was next. Anansi went into the forest and dug a deep pit where the leopard was accustomed to walk. He covered it with small branches and leaves and put dust on it, so that it was impossible to tell where the pit was. Anansi went away and hid. When Osebo came prowling in the black of night, he stepped into the trap Anansi had prepared and fell to the bottom. Anansi heard the sound of the leopard falling, and he said: "Ah, Osebo, you are half-foolish!"

When morning came, Anansi went to the pit and saw the leopard there.

"Osebo," he asked, "what are you doing in this hole?"

"I have fallen into a trap," Osebo said. "Help me out."

"I would gladly help you," Anansi said. "But I'm sure that if I

dispute ▶
(di spyo͞ot´) *n.* disagreement

opinion ▶
(ə pin´ yən) *n.* belief based on what seems true or probable to one's own mind

bring you out, I will have no thanks for it. You will get hungry, and later on you will be wanting to eat me and my children."

"I swear it won't happen!" Osebo said.

"Very well. Since you swear it, I will take you out," Anansi said.

He bent a tall green tree toward the ground, so that its top was over the pit, and he tied it that way. Then he tied a rope to the top of the tree and dropped the other end of it into the pit.

"Tie this to your tail," he said.

Osebo tied the rope to his tail.

"Is it well tied?" Anansi asked.

"Yes, it is well tied," the leopard said.

"In that case," Anansi said, "you are not merely half-foolish, you are all-foolish."

And he took his knife and cut the other rope, the one that held the tree bowed to the ground. The tree straightened up with a snap, pulling Osebo out of the hole. He hung in the air head downward, twisting and turning. And while he hung this way, Anansi killed him with his weapons.

Then he took the body of the leopard and carried it to Nyame, the Sky God, saying: "Here is the third thing. Now I have paid the price."

Nyame said to him: "Kwaku Anansi, great warriors and chiefs have tried, but they have been unable to do it. You have done it. Therefore, I will give you the stories. From this day onward, all stories belong to you. Whenever a man tells a story, he must **acknowledge** that it is Anansi's tale."

In this way Anansi, the spider, became the owner of all stories that are told. To Anansi all these tales belong.

◀ **acknowledge**
(ak näl´ ij) v. recognize and admit

ABOUT THE AUTHOR

Harold Courlander (1908–1996)

Harold Courlander is best known for his collections of folk tales from around the world. He once told an interviewer that his interest in folk tales arose from the rich multicultural environment in his hometown of Detroit, Michigan. During Courlander's career, he published more than thirty-five books. As he traveled around the world, he made sound recordings of the music and stories of African, African American, and Native American cultures. When asked about his work, Courlander has said, "I think of myself primarily as a narrator. I have always had a special interest in using fiction and nonfiction narration to bridge communication between other cultures and our own."

READ

Comprehension

Reread all or part of the text to help you answer the following questions.

1. What price does the Sky God ask for his stories?

2. What is Anansi's attitude toward the other animals?

3. Why does Anansi succeed when warriors and chiefs have failed?

Research: Clarify Details Choose at least one unfamiliar detail from the story and briefly research it. Then, explain how the information sheds light on an aspect of the folk tale.

Summarize Write an objective summary of the folk tale. Remember that an objective summary is free from opinion and evaluation.

Language Study

Selection Vocabulary Identify at least one synonym for each boldfaced word from the selection. Then, use each word in a sentence of your own.

- "Ah, I have had a **dispute** with my wife."
- My **opinion** wasn't as good as my wife's.
- Whenever a man tells a story, he must **acknowledge** that it is Anansi's tale.

Literary Analysis

Reread the identified passage. Then, respond to the following questions.

> **Focus Passage** (p. 298)
>
> The spider replied: "Ah, I have had a dispute … and you are now my prisoner."

Key Ideas and Details

1. **(a)** How does Anansi gain Onini's trust? **(b) Analyze:** How does Anansi convince the python to let himself be tied to the bamboo pole?

2. **Infer:** What is Anansi's opinion of Onini? Cite evidence from the text to support your answer.

Craft and Structure

3. **Infer:** Based on this passage, what is one possible theme, or lesson, of the folk tale?

Integration of Knowledge and Ideas

4. **(a) Interpret:** What characteristics of Anansi are revealed in his encounter with Onini? **(b) Apply:** How does Onini's behavior resemble that of a human?

Folk Tales

A **folk tale** is a story composed orally and then passed from person to person by word of mouth. Reread the folk tale, and take notes on ways in which the author uses animal characters to **communicate** a lesson about human motivation.

1. In what ways are the animal characters like humans?

2. **Motivation (a)** What motivates the hornets, the python, and the leopard to listen to Anansi? **(b)** What motivates Anansi to succeed?

DISCUSS • RESEARCH • WRITE

From Text to Topic **Small Group Discussion**

Discuss the following passage with three or four classmates. Take notes during the discussion. **Contribute** your own ideas, and support them with examples from the text.

> The Sky God said: "I am willing to sell the stories, but the price is high. Many people have come to me offering to buy, but the price was too high for them. Rich and powerful families have not been able to pay. Do you think you can do it?"
> Anansi replied to the Sky God: "I can do it. What is the price?"

Research **Investigate the Topic**

Tricksters in Folk Tales Trickster characters are common in the **tradition** of folk literature. These characters use their cleverness to try to trick others. The coyote, the fox, and the rabbit are common trickster animals in folk literature.

Assignment

Conduct research to find out about common trickster characters and to learn what types of feelings and desires typically motivate their actions. Consult print and digital sources. Take clear notes and carefully identify your sources. Share your findings in an **informal presentation** for the class.

Writing to Sources **Narrative**

This folk tale tells about a trickster spider that outsmarts other characters and succeeds in owning all the stories in the world.

Assignment

Write your own **folk tale** about the trickster character of your choice.

- Introduce your trickster character and explain his or her motivation.
- Describe the main events in the story using vivid verbs and descriptive language.
- Conclude by telling whether or not the trickster got what he or she wanted, and why.

QUESTIONS FOR DISCUSSION

1. What idea is emphasized by the Sky God's statements about payment? Why do you think he does not simply name a price?

2. What do you learn about Anansi when he says "I can do it" before he knows the Sky God's price?

PREPARATION FOR ESSAY

You may use the results of your research assignment to support your ideas in the essay you will write at the end of this section.

ACADEMIC VOCABULARY

Academic terms appear in blue on these pages. If necessary, use a dictionary to find their definitions. Then, use the words as you speak and write about the text.

 **Common Core State Standards**

RL.7.1, RL.7.2, RL.7.6; W.7.3; SL.7.1; L.7.5.b, L.7.6 [For full standards wording, see the chart in the front of this book.]

Maslow's Theory of Motivation and Human Needs

LEVELS OF NEEDS   MOTIVATION & BEHAVIOR

LEVEL 5 = Self-Actualization

FULFILLMENT OF GOALS & DREAMS
Need for self-fulfillment. Desire to realize your full potential and become the best you are capable of becoming.

CREATIVITY
Be a self-starter, have enthusiasm, be creative, be dedicated, enjoy challenges, love to accomplish results!

LEVEL 4 = Self-Esteem

SELF RESPECT & ACCEPTANCE
Need for reputation, prestige, and recognition from others. Contains the desire to feel important, strong and significant.

BRAINPOWER
Display your talents and skills, have self-confidence, appreciate attention and recognition from others.

LEVEL 3 = Love & Relationships

COMMUNICATION & RESPONSE
Need to be loved and to love. Includes the desire for affection and belonging.

VALIDATION
Join and be active in clubs and groups, be able to talk to others, contribute to society, marry and have a family.

LEVEL 2 = Your Family & Work

SOCIAL SAFETY & SECURITY
Need to be safe from physical and psychological harm in the present and future, and trust in a predictable future.

SURVIVAL SKILLS
Work, save for future, improve skills and talents, be responsible, and want an organized predictable world.

LEVEL 1 = Your Body

PHYSICAL SAFETY & SECURITY
Need to stay alive! Biological and cultural imperatives to live. Includes having enough healthy food, air, and water to survive.

SURVIVAL SKILLS
Eat, sleep, and take care of your bodily needs, provide for clothing, shelter, comfort, be free from pain.

READ • RESEARCH

Comprehension

Review the infographic to answer the following questions.

1. **(a)** What is the subject of the chart? **(b)** What is the relationship between the two columns in the chart?

2. **(a)** What information about the chart does the pyramid **diagram** show? **(b)** Which level of needs and motivations is the highest?

Critical Analysis

Key Ideas and Details

1. **(a) Compare and Contrast:** How are the two columns in the chart for Level 1 alike and different? **(b) Draw Conclusions:** Who do you think experiences Level 1 needs, motivation, and behavior? **Explain** your reasoning.

2. **Analyze:** Explain the focus of Level 4.

Craft and Structure

3. **(a) Interpret:** What are the fundamental differences between the levels at the top of the pyramid and the levels at the bottom? **(b) Hypothesize:** Maslow's **theory** is always shown in a pyramid diagram. Why do you think he chose this shape in which to visually represent his theory?

Integration of Knowledge and Ideas

4. **Draw Conclusions:** Based on the pyramid diagram, does Maslow think most adults achieve self-actualization, or is this group a small percentage of the population? Explain your reasoning.

Research **Investigate the Topic**

Abraham Maslow Abraham Maslow pioneered a branch of psychology called humanistic psychology. Maslow's ideas are illustrated in this chart.

Assignment

Conduct research to find out more about Abraham Maslow, Maslow's Theory of Morivation, and the focus of humanistic psychology. Take careful notes and identify your sources. Share your findings in a **brief research report.**

Common Core State Standards

RI.7.1, RI.7.3, RI.7.5, RI.7.6; W.7.7; L.7.6
[For full standards wording, see the chart in the front of this book.]

ACADEMIC VOCABULARY

Academic terms appear in blue on these pages. If these words are not familiar to you, use a dictionary to find their definitions. Then, use the words as you speak and write about the chart.

Speaking and Listening: **Group Discussion**

Motivation and Learning The texts in this section vary in genre, length, style, and perspective. However, all of the texts present ideas related to human behavior and the factors that motivate us. The issue of motivation, and whether it comes from within or is learned from others, is fundamentally related to the Big Question addressed in this unit: **What should we learn?**

▲ Refer to the selections you read in Part 3 as you complete the activities on this assessment.

Assignment

Conduct discussions. With a small group of classmates, conduct a discussion about the issues of motivation and learning. Refer to the texts in this section, other texts you have read, and your personal experience and knowledge to support your ideas. Begin your discussion by addressing the following questions:

- What are some factors that motivate people? Does every action have a motivation?
- To what extent can goals and behavior change as a result of learning?
- Why are some people more motivated than others? Can we learn to be more motivated?
- What effects can time and place have on motivation and learning?

Summarize and present your ideas. After you have fully explored the topic, summarize your discussion and present your findings to the class as a whole.

Criteria for Success

✓ **Organizes the group effectively**
Appoint a group leader and a timekeeper. The group leader should present the discussion questions. The timekeeper should make sure the discussion takes no longer than 20 minutes.

✓ **Maintains focus of discussion**
As a group, stay on topic and avoid straying into other subject areas.

✓ **Involves all participants equally and fully**
No one person should monopolize the conversation. Rather, everyone should take turns speaking and contributing ideas.

✓ **Follows the rules for collegial discussion**
As each group member speaks, others should listen carefully. Build on one another's ideas and support viewpoints and opinions with sound reasoning and evidence. Express disagreement respectfully.

USE NEW VOCABULARY

As you speak and share ideas, work to use the vocabulary words you have learned in this unit. The more you use new words, the more you will "own" them.

Writing: **Narrative**

Motivation and Learning The texts in this section portray different individuals who learned important lessons when they came to understand the factors that motivated themselves or others.

Common Core State Standards

W.7.3.a–b, W.7.3.d–e; SL.7.1.a–d
[For full standards wording, see the chart in the front of this book.]

Assignment

Write an **autobiographical narrative,** or a true story about your own life, in which you discuss a time when you were motivated by a goal that was at odds with the expectations of your family, a friend, or your community. Describe what you wanted and what the other person or group wanted. Tell about the conflict that resulted and how the conflict was resolved. In your conclusion, explain what you learned from the experience.

Criteria for Success

Purpose/Focus

✓ **Connects specific incidents with larger ideas**

Make meaningful connections between your experiences and the texts you have read in this section.

✓ **Clearly conveys the significance of the story**

Provide a conclusion in which you reflect upon what you experienced.

Organization

✓ **Sequences events logically**

Structure your narrative so that individual events build on one another to create a coherent whole.

Development of Ideas/Elaboration

✓ **Supports insights**

Include both personal examples and details from the texts you have read in this section.

✓ **Uses narrative techniques effectively**

Even though an autobiographical narrative is nonfiction, it may include storytelling elements like those found in fiction. Consider using dialogue to help readers "hear" how characters sound.

Language

✓ **Uses description effectively**

Use descriptive details to bring settings and characters to life.

Conventions

✓ **Does not have errors**

Check your narrative to eliminate errors in grammar, spelling, and punctuation.

WRITE TO EXPLORE

Writing is a way to explore what you feel and think: You may change your mind or get new ideas as you work. As you write your autobiographical narrative, explore your ideas on motivation and learning.

Writing to Sources: **Informative Text**

Motivation and Learning The related readings in this section present a range of ideas about what motivates people to take action. The selections raise questions, such as the following, about whether motivation comes from within or is a result of an outside factor or experience:

- What can we learn when a goal conflicts with a promise or commitment?
- When is it important to reconsider our motivations?
- Can a goal that comes from an inner motivation be beneficial to society?

Focus on the question that intrigues you the most, and then complete the following assignment.

Assignment

Write an **informative essay** in which you explore the connection between learning and motivation. Develop your essay by analyzing relevant ideas and information in two or more texts from this section. Choose a strategy for organizing your essay. For example, you might compare and contrast the motivations of characters in the selections. Clearly present, develop, and support your ideas with examples, details, and quotations from the texts.

Prewriting and Planning

Choose texts. Review the texts in this section to determine which ones you will cite in your essay. Select at least two texts that will provide strong material to support your examination of motivation and learning.

Gather details and craft a working topic. Use a chart like the one shown to develop your topic. Though you may refine or change your ideas as you write, details in your chart can help you establish a clear direction.

Focus Question: What effect does motivation have on learning?

Text	Passage	Notes
"The Legacy of 'Snowflake' Bentley"	"When the other boys of my age were playing…I was absorbed in studying things under this micro-scope," he later wrote.	At a young age, Bentley was curious and motivated by learning
"Intrinsic Motivation Doesn't Exist, Researcher Says"	"Individuals differ enormously in what makes them happy—for some competition, winning and wealth are the greatest sources of happiness…"	Researcher says competi-tion, winning, and wealth motivate some people

Example Topic: Some people are motivated by an inner desire to learn, but others are motivated to learn by a desire for recognition or a reward.

INCORPORATE RESEARCH

As you write your informative essay, refer to the research you conducted as you read the texts in this section. Choose appropriate ideas and details from your research to support your thesis statement.

Drafting

Develop a thesis statement. Review your notes to help you develop a thesis statement—one strong sentence that sums up your main idea about motivation. Include this statement in your introduction.

Organize to connect supporting ideas and details. Create an informal outline or list of ideas you want to present. Decide which facts, definitions, details, quotations, or examples best support each idea. Then, as you draft, make sure the relationships among your ideas are clear. For example, you might explore comparisons and contrasts by noting similarities and differences in the motivations of two characters. You might analyze cause and effect by showing the relationship between the setting and achievement of a goal.

Use topic-related terms. Give your essay a scholarly tone by using terms you have learned from your reading and research. Review the definitions of terms such as *intrinsic motivation,* and *Maslow's Theory,* and use them where appropriate in your essay.

Revising and Editing

Review content. Make sure your thesis is clearly stated and that you have supported it with facts, details, and examples from the texts you read. Underline main ideas in your essay and confirm that each one is supported.

Review style. Revise rambling sentences that are hard to follow, and omit unnecessary words. Check that you have found the clearest, simplest way to communicate your ideas.

Common Core State Standards

W.7.2.a–b, W.7.2.d
[For full standards wording, see the chart in the front of this book.]

CITE RESEARCH CORRECTLY

Take note of the evidence from outside sources that you have included in your informative essay. Be sure to cite those sources in your final draft. Refer to the Citing Sources pages in the Introductory Unit of this textbook for additional guidance.

Self-Evaluation Rubric

Use the following criteria to evaluate the effectiveness of your essay.

Criteria	Rating Scale
	not very .... very
Purpose/Focus Introduces a specific topic; provides a concluding section that follows from and supports the information or explanation presented	1 2 3 4
Organization Organizes complex ideas, concepts, and information to make important connections and distinctions; uses appropriate and varied transitions to link the major sections, create cohesion, and clarify relationships among ideas	1 2 3 4
Development of Ideas/Elaboration Develops the topic with well-chosen, relevant and sufficient facts, extended definitions, concrete details, quotations or other information and examples appropriate to the audience's knowledge of the topic	1 2 3 4
Language Uses precise language and domain-specific vocabulary to clearly convey ideas	1 2 3 4
Conventions Uses correct conventions of grammar, spelling, and punctuation	1 2 3 4

Titles for Extended Reading

In this unit, you have read texts in a variety of genres, including literary nonfiction. Continue to read on your own. Select books that you enjoy, but challenge yourself to explore new topics, new authors, and works of increasing depth and complexity. The titles suggested below will help you get started.

INFORMATIONAL TEXT

Barrio Boy
by Ernesto Galarza

As a young boy in the early twentieth century, Galarza moved from a tiny Mexican village to a bustling Latino neighborhood in Sacramento, California. Follow him on his journey in this **memoir** of his early life.

Astronomy & Space   EXEMPLAR TEXT ©
Edited by Phillis Engelbert

Explore outer space in this three-volume **encyclopedia,** which includes a timeline, photographs, biographies, and a glossary of important words to know.

Discoveries: Finding Our Place in the World

This collection of **essays** explores four subject areas. In it, you will find "Stonehenge: Groundbreaking Discoveries," "Where on Earth Are You?" "From Bricks to Mortar to Cyberspace: Art Museums Online," and "Testing the Market."

Nonfiction Readings Across the Curriculum

This collection of **essays** and **stories** features writers such as Beverly Cleary, Gary Paulsen, Joe Namath, and more. Delve into its pages to find interesting observations about sports, literature, science, and social studies.

Green Lantern's Book of Inventions
by Clare Hibbert

With a comic book superhero as your guide, learn about great inventions through the ages—from the wheel to the Internet—in this **nonfiction** book.

LITERATURE

Child of the Owl
by Laurence Yep

When her father is hospitalized, twelve-year-old Casey is sent to live with her grandmother in the strange and unfamiliar world of Chinatown. This **novel** follows Casey as she learns to accept her new situation, drawing strength from family history and Chinese legend.

Slow Dance Heart Break Blues
by Arnold Adoff

In this collection of **poetry,** Adoff uses a hip-hop style and modern imagery to explore issues important to teenagers, such as love, loss, and identity.

ONLINE TEXT SET

SHORT STORY
Suzy and Leah Jane Yolen

EXPOSITORY ESSAY
Conversational Ballgames
Nancy Masterson Sakamoto

DRAMATIC MONOLOGUE
My Head Is Full of Starshine
Peg Kehret

Preparing to Read Complex Texts

Attentive Reading As you read on your own, ask yourself questions like these to enrich your reading experience.

When reading literary nonfiction, ask yourself...

Comprehension: **Key Ideas and Details**

- Is the author writing about a personal experience or a topic he or she has studied? In either case, what are my expectations about the work?
- Are the ideas the author expresses important? Why or why not?
- Did the author live at a different time and place than the present? If so, how does that affect his or her choice of topic and attitude?
- Does the author express beliefs that are very different from mine? If so, how does that affect what I understand and feel about the text?
- Does any one idea seem more important than the others? Why?
- What can I learn from this work?

Text Analysis: **Craft and Structure**

- Does the author organize ideas so that I can understand them? If not, what is unclear?
- Is the work interesting right from the start? If so, what has the author done to capture my interest? If not, why?
- Does the author give me a new way of looking at a topic? If so, how? If not, why?
- Is the author an expert on the topic? How do I know?
- Does the author use a variety of evidence that makes sense? If not, what is weak?
- Does the author use words in ways that are both interesting and clear? If so, are there any sections that I enjoy more than others?

Connections: **Integration of Knowledge and Ideas**

- Does the work seem believable? Why or why not?
- Do I agree or disagree with the author's arguments or ideas? Why?
- Does this work remind me of others I have read? If so, in what ways?
- Does this work make me want to read more about this topic? Does it make me want to explore a related topic? Why or why not?

Common Core State Standards

Reading Literature/ Informational Text
10. By the end of the year, read and comprehend literature, including stories, dramas, and poems, and literary nonfiction in the grades 6–8 text complexity band proficiently, with scaffolding as needed at the high end of the range.

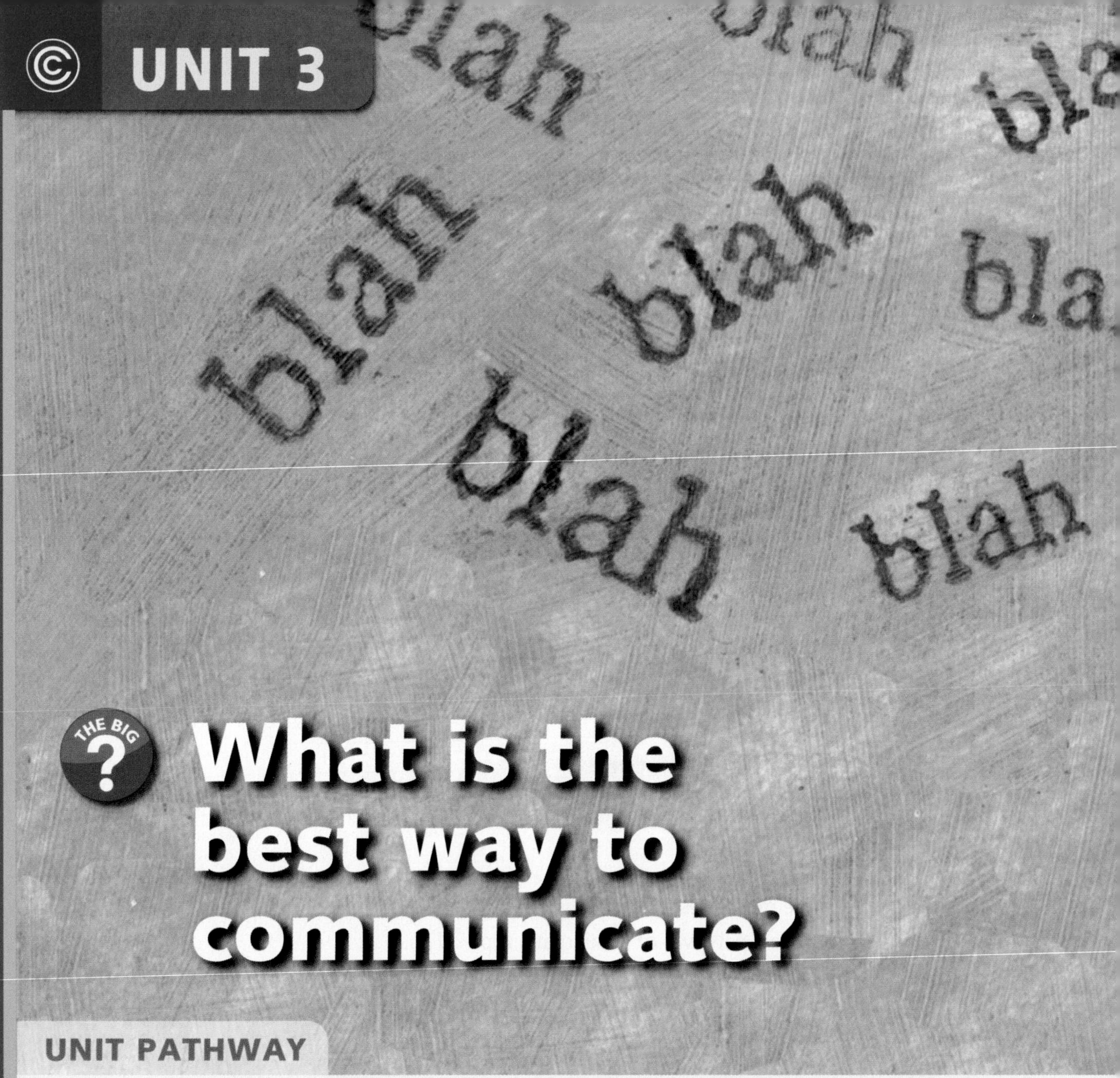

THE BIG ? What is the best way to communicate?

UNIT PATHWAY

PART 1 SETTING EXPECTATIONS	PART 2 TEXT ANALYSIS GUIDED EXPLORATION	PART 3 TEXT SET DEVELOPING INSIGHT	PART 4 DEMONSTRATING INDEPENDENCE
• INTRODUCING THE BIG QUESTION	SOUNDS AND IMAGES	HEROES AND OUTLAWS	• INDEPENDENT READING
• CLOSE READING WORKSHOP			• ONLINE TEXT SET 

CLOSE READING TOOL

Use this tool to practice the close reading strategies you learn.

STUDENT eTEXT

Bring learning to life with audio, video, and interactive tools.

ONLINE WRITER'S NOTEBOOK

Easily capture notes and complete assignments online.

Find all Digital Resources at **pearsonrealize.com.**

What is the best way to communicate?

We communicate for different reasons and in different ways. Through communication, we can send a message to another person. The message may entertain or inform, and it may be made in person or transmitted through technology. We use telephones, television, and the Internet to send messages, videos, and music to many people or to those far away. We can also express ourselves through art, music, and photography. Sometimes, we read, or watch, or listen to communication created by someone else. With so many reasons and ways to communicate, we often have to choose the *best* way to express ourselves.

Exploring the Big Question

Collaboration: One-on-One Discussion Start thinking about the Big Question by making a list of ways that people communicate. Describe one specific example of each of these types of communication:

- telling stories
- transmitting messages through technology
- talking to friends or family members
- filming an event
- speaking in public
- creating music or art

Share your examples with a partner. With your partner, discuss which items on your lists are the best ways to communicate and why. Build on your partner's ideas, responding to each with related ideas of your own. Ask questions to make sure you have understood each other's points, and clarify your meaning as needed. As you exchange ideas, build upon each other's comments. You may want to use the vocabulary words on the next page in your discussion.

Connecting to the Literature The texts in this unit explore the different ways we communicate our thoughts and ideas. Each reading will give you additional insight into the Big Question.

Vocabulary

Acquire and Use Academic Vocabulary The term "academic vocabulary" refers to words you typically encounter in scholarly and literary texts and in technical and business writing. Review the definitions of these academic vocabulary words. Then, practice using these words in your writing and academic discussions.

Common Core State Standards

Speaking and Listening
1. Engage effectively in a range of collaborative discussions with diverse partners on grade 7 topics, texts, and issues, building on others' ideas and expressing their own clearly.

Language
6. Acquire and use accurately grade-appropriate general academic and domain-specific words and phrases; gather vocabulary knowledge when considering a word or phrase important to comprehension or expression.

communicate (kə myo͞o′ ni kāt′) *v.* share ideas, thoughts, or feelings; make known to others

contribute (kən trib′ yo͞ot) *v.* add to; enrich

inform (in fôrm′) *v.* tell; give information about

media (mē′ dē ə) *n. pl.* sources of information, such as newspapers, television, and the Internet

produce (prə do͞os′) *v.* make; create

react (rē akt′) *v.* respond to

speak (spēk′) *v.* use oral language

technology (tek näl′ ə jē) *n.* machines, equipment, and ways of doing things that are based on modern knowledge about science

transmit (trans mit′) *v.* send or give out

Gather Vocabulary Knowledge Additional words related to communication are listed below. Categorize the words by deciding whether you know each one well, know it a little bit, or do not know it at all.

enrich	express	listen
entertain	learn	teach

Then, do the following:

1. Work with a partner to write each word on one side of an index card and its definition on the other side.
2. Verify the definitions by looking them up in a print or online dictionary and revising your cards as needed.
3. Place the cards with the words facing up in a pile.
4. Take turns drawing a word card, pronouncing the word and then using it in an original sentence.

Close Reading Workshop

In this workshop, you will learn an approach to reading that will deepen your understanding of literature and will help you better appreciate the author's craft. The workshop includes models for close reading, discussion, research, and writing. After you have reviewed the models, practice your skills with the Independent Practice selection.

 **Common Core State Standards**

RL.7.1, RL.7.2, RL.7.4, RL.7.5; W.7.2, W.7.4, W.7.7, W.7.9.a; SL.7.1
[For full standards wording, see the standards chart in the front of this book.]

CLOSE READING: POETRY

In Part 2 of this unit you will focus on reading various poems. Use these strategies as you read the texts.

Comprehension: Key Ideas and Details

- Read first to unlock basic meaning.
- Use context clues to help you determine the meanings of unfamiliar words.
- Identify unfamiliar details that you might need to clarify through research.
- Distinguish between what is stated directly and what must be inferred.

Ask yourself questions such as these:
- What is this poem about?
- Who is the speaker of the poem?
- To which senses do the poem's images appeal?
- How does the speaker feel about the topic?

Text Analysis: Craft and Structure

- Notice the poet's creative and unusual use of language.
- Consider how rhythm, repetition, and other sound devices develop the poem's meaning.
- Consider how the poem's structure relates to its meaning.

Ask yourself questions such as these:
- How does the poet's word choice create vivid images?
- What ideas do those images convey?
- How do the poem's sounds and structure affect meaning?

Connections: Integration of Knowledge and Ideas

- Look for relationships among key ideas. Identify causes and effects, and comparisons and contrasts.
- Look for imagery and analyze its deeper meaning.
- Synthesize to determine the poem's theme.

Ask yourself questions such as these:
- How has this work increased my knowledge of a subject, author, or genre?
- What theme, or insight about life, does this poem express?

Read

As you read this poem, take note of the annotations that model ways to closely read the text.

Reading Model

"The Railway Train" by Emily Dickinson

I like to see it lap the miles,
And lick[1] the valleys up,
And stop to feed itself at tanks;
And then, prodigious, step

5   Around a pile of mountains,[2]
And supercilious, peer
In shanties by the sides of roads;
And then a quarry pare

To fit its sides, and crawl between,
10 Complaining all the while
In horrid, hooting stanza;
Then chase itself down hill

And neigh[3] like Boanerges;[4]
Then, punctual as a star,
15 Stop—docile and omnipotent[5]—
At its own stable door.

Craft and Structure
1 The repeated *l* sounds at the beginnings of the words *lap* and *lick* help build a playful image of a speeding train.

Key Ideas and Details
2 The context clue "step/ Around a pile of mountains" can help you infer that *prodigious* means "very big." This image supports the idea that the train is powerful.

Craft and Structure
3 Throughout the poem, the speaker compares the train to an animal. The word *neigh*, which imitates a horse's whinny, reinforces this comparison.

Key Ideas and Details
4 Research can help you determine that *Boanerges* is a Biblical reference to a loud, fiery speaker. This line repeats the idea of the train's power.

Integration of Knowledge and Ideas
5 *Docile* means "easily managed," and *omnipotent* means "all-powerful." The contrast between these words implies that the speaker has conflicting ideas about the train.

Discuss

Sharing your own ideas and listening to the ideas of others can deepen your understanding of a text and help you look at a topic in a whole new way. As you participate in collaborative discussions, work to have a genuine exchange in which classmates build upon one another's ideas. Support your points with evidence and ask meaningful questions.

Discussion Model

Student 1: It's interesting that Emily Dickinson talks about the train as if it were alive. The words *lap, lick, feed,* and *stable* make me think of a giant workhorse.

Student 2: That's what I picture, too. I notice that every stanza has words that make the train seem like a living thing. She builds on that idea throughout the poem by including more lifelike features, such as the train "peering," "crawling," "complaining," and "hooting."

Student 3: The thing I find most interesting is that the speaker says she enjoys watching the train in line 1, but a lot of the descriptions are not very positive. She claims that the train is proud and she says it complains. I wonder what Dickinson thought of trains, which were just becoming popular in her time.

Research

Targeted research can clarify unfamiliar details and shed light on various aspects of a text. Consider questions that arise in your mind as you read, and use those questions as the basis for research.

Research Model

Question: *How did the growth of the railroad affect Americans in the late 1800s?*

Key Words for Internet Search: expansion AND railroad AND 1800s

Result: U.S. History.org, Early American Railroads; How Stuff Works, Railroad Expansion

What I Learned: The railroad's introduction and expansion in the United States during the 1800s had an enormous impact. On one hand, trains made shipping and travel easier than ever before. However, railroads threatened small businesses, railroad owners took advantage of workers, and some protestors were so strongly opposed to the railway that they turned to violence to stop its expansion.

Write

Writing about a text will deepen your understanding of it and will also allow you to share your ideas more formally with others. The following model essay analyzes the use of poetic elements to express the speaker's point of view, and cites evidence to support its main ideas.

Writing Model: Informative Text

"The Railway Train"—Good, Bad, or Both?

Emily Dickinson compares a train to a horse in her poem "The Railway Train." Her word choice and use of poetic elements create vivid images of the powerful train while expressing the speaker's conflicting feelings.

> The writer clearly states the essay's thesis in the first paragraph, preparing readers for the ideas to follow.

The poem begins by setting up the comparison between the train and a horse, using descriptions, such as "lap the miles," as if the train was going to race around a track and then "stop to feed itself at tanks." Dickinson builds the comparison and imagery by continuing sentences across stanzas. The poem ends with a sense of completion as the train/horse returns to "its own stable door."

> Direct quotations and examples support the writer's claims.

Within this image of the horse running its course and returning home, Dickinson uses sound devices that allow readers to "hear" the train and its "horrid, hooting." Word choice, sound devices, and extended comparisons end in an image of power with the stopped train "docile and omnipotent / At its own stable door." Given this description, the speaker obviously respects the "beast's" power but seems to hold some negative sentiment toward it as well.

> The writer makes a direct connection between the quotation and the thesis.

In line 1, the speaker declares, "I like to see it." However, it becomes apparent that the speaker's feelings about the train are complicated: She likes and dislikes it at the same time. By the second stanza, the train is described as snobbish and looking down on the shanties. In the third stanza, there are more negative descriptions—*complaining* and *horrid.* By the end, though, positive feelings return with words like *punctual* and *docile.* The speaker is uncertain, showing both her appreciation of and her hesitation regarding the train. She likes to watch it, but thinks it is loud and out of place.

The speaker of the poem shares the mixed feelings people of the time had about the railroad and its expansion. Through comparisons, descriptions, sound devices, and word choice, Dickinson paints a vivid picture of the train and expresses the speaker's doubt about the new invention that would soon take over transportation in the United States.

> By including information gathered during research, the writer connects the poem to a real historical event: the birth and expansion of the railroad.

As you read the following poems, apply the close reading strategies you have learned. You may need to read the poems multiple times.

Maestro

by Pat Mora

Meet the Author

Born in El Paso, Texas, in 1942, **Pat Mora** enjoys writing about the Mexican-American heritage of the Southwest. Bilingual and bicultural, she writes poetry in English and Spanish and often includes Spanish words and phrases in her English-language poems.

Vocabulary ▶
maestro (mīs´ trō) *n.* great musician

snare (sner) *v.* catch; capture

> He hears her
> when he bows.
> Rows of hands clap
> again and again he bows
> 5 to stage lights and upturned faces
> but he hears only his mother's voice
>
> years ago in their small home
> singing Mexican songs
> one phrase at a time
> 10 while his father strummed the guitar
> or picked the melody with quick fingertips.
> Both cast their music in the air
> for him to *snare* with his strings,
> songs of *lunas*[1] and *amor*[2]
> 15 learned bit by bit.
> She'd nod, smile, as his bow slid
> note to note, then the trio
>   *voz,*[3] *guitarra,*[4] *violín*[5]
> would blend again and again
> 20 to the last pure note
> sweet on the tongue.

---

1. lunas (lōō´ näs) *n.* Spanish for "moons."
2. amor (ä´ môr´) *n.* Spanish for "love."
3. voz (vōs) *n.* Spanish for "voice."
4. guitarra (gē tär´ rä) *n.* Spanish for "guitar."
5. violín (vē ō lēn´) *n.* Spanish for "violin."

The Desert Is My Mother
by Pat Mora

I say feed me.
She serves red prickly pear[1] on a spiked cactus.

I say tease me.
She sprinkles raindrops in my face on a sunny day.

5　I say frighten me.
She shouts thunder, flashes lightning.

I say hold me.
She whispers, "Lie in my arms."

I say heal me.
10　She gives me chamomile, oregano, peppermint.

I say caress me.
She strokes my skin with her warm breath.

I say make me beautiful.
She offers turquoise for my fingers,
15　a pink blossom for my hair.

I say sing to me.
She chants her windy songs.

I say teach me.
She blooms in the sun's glare,
20　the snow's silence,
the driest sand.

The desert is my mother.
El desierto es mi madre.
The desert is my strong mother.

---

1. prickly pear *n.* a species of cactus with sharp spines and an edible fruit.

Bailando[1]
by Pat Mora

I will remember you dancing,
spinning round and round
a young girl in Mexico,
your long, black hair free in the wind,
5 spinning round and round
a young woman at village dances
your long, blue dress swaying
to the beat of *La Varsoviana*,[2]
smiling into the eyes of your partners,
10 years later smiling into my eyes
when I'd reach up to dance with you,
my dear aunt, who years later
danced with my children,
you, white-haired but still young
15 waltzing on your ninetieth birthday,
more beautiful than the orchid
pinned on your shoulder,
tottering now when you walk
but saying to me, *"Estoy*[3] *bailando,"*
20 and laughing.

---

1. **Bailando** (bī län´ dō) *v.* Spanish for "dancing."
2. **La Varsoviana** (lä bär´ sō byä´ nä) *n.* a lively folk dance.
3. **Estoy** (es toï´) *v.* Spanish for "I am."

Close Reading Activities

Read

Comprehension: **Key Ideas and Details**

1. (a) What scene is described in lines 1–5 of "Maestro"? **(b) Interpret:** What does the speaker mean by "he hears only his mother's voice" (line 6)? **(c) Infer:** Which means more to the maestro—his present audience or his childhood memories? Explain.

2. Interpret: What does the speaker mean by saying "The Desert Is My Mother"?

3. (a) Describe three of the times the aunt dances in "Bailando." **(b) Connect:** What key idea do these images convey?

4. Summarize: Write a brief, objective summary of each poem. Cite details from the poems in your writing, but do not include your opinions or evaluations.

Text Analysis: **Craft and Structure**

5. (a) Find one image that appeals to the sense of touch, one that appeals to sight, and one that appeals to hearing in "The Desert Is My Mother." **(b) Analyze:** Do these images help paint an effective picture of the desert? Explain.

6. Analyze: How does the one-sentence, one-stanza structure of "Bailando" reinforce the poem's key ideas?

7. (a) Identify one example of repetition in each poem. **(b) Analyze:** Explain how each example conveys an idea or helps structure the poem.

Connections: **Integration of Knowledge and Ideas**

Discuss
Conduct a **small-group discussion** in which you analyze how the poet uses imagery and figurative language to express the theme of each poem.

Research
Briefly research the effect Mora's culture has had on her work. Consider the following:
a. Mora's use of Spanish words in her poetry
b. the melding of American and Mexican cultures
c. the geography of Mora's childhood
Take notes as you research. Then, write a brief **analysis** of how Mora's cultural background influences one of the poems you read.

Write
Choose one of the poems and identify a lesson it suggests about life. In an **essay,** explain how well this lesson applies to life in general. Give examples to support your evaluation.

 ### What is the best way to communicate?

Consider how people communicate without using words. Why do you think Mora uses poetry to describe these wordless ways of communicating? Explain.

"To **read a poem** is to **hear** it with our eyes; to hear it is to **see** it with our ears."

—Octavio Paz

SOUNDS AND IMAGES

As you read the poetry in this section, analyze how the poets use the written word to create distinct images and sounds. The quotation on the opposite page will help you start thinking about the ways in which poetic sounds and images can communicate unique ideas and important themes.

◀ **CRITICAL VIEWING** What ideas about sounds and images does this picture communicate to you?

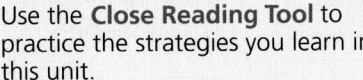

CLOSE READING TOOL

Use the **Close Reading Tool** to practice the strategies you learn in this unit.

Focus on Craft and Structure

Elements of Poetry

Poetry uses the rhythms and sounds of words as well as their meanings to set the imagination in motion.

Poetry is a type of literature that uses the sounds, rhythms, and meanings of words to describe the world in striking and imaginative ways. Poetry comes in many forms, from structured traditional verse to contemporary poems that follow few rules. However varied their forms may be, many poems are made up of the same elements.

Lines and Stanzas Poetry is divided into **lines,** or groups of words. In some poems, the first word of each line is capitalized, even if it is not the beginning of a sentence. A sentence in a poem may stretch over several lines. The first one or two lines may *break,* or end, before the sentence is finished. However, good readers of poetry know that they should read the sentence as a whole, without pausing at the end of every line.

In many poems, lines are organized in units of meaning called **stanzas.** The lines in a stanza work together to express one key idea. A blank line, called a **stanza break,** signals that one stanza has ended and a new stanza is beginning.

As you read the poem below, think about the key idea in each stanza, and identify the relationship between ideas.

Refrains and Repetition Like a catchy song, a poem may repeat lines, either identically or with variations. A line or group of lines that is repeated at regular intervals in a poem is called a **refrain.** In a refrain, a poet reminds readers and listeners of a key idea, image, or event. Often, a refrain is repeated at the end of each stanza. A poet may also repeat lines with **variations**—changing one or more words with each repetition.

As you read the poem at the bottom of the page, notice how the poet uses repetition, including a refrain, to emphasize his key ideas.

"Life"
by Paul Laurence Dunbar

A crust of bread and a corner to sleep in,
A minute to smile and an hour to weep in,
A pint of joy to a peck of trouble,
And never a laugh but the moans come double;
    And that is life!

> This five-line **stanza** compares life's joys to its sorrows. Together, the lines **focus on one key idea:** Life has more sorrow than joy.

A crust and a corner that love makes precious,
With a smile to warm and the tears to refresh us;
And joy seems sweeter when cares come after,
And a moan is the finest of foils for laughter;
    And that is life!

> The **focus changes,** and a **new stanza** starts. Here, the speaker describes life's joys. **The key idea** is that sorrow intensifies joy.

Sound Devices

Rhythm and Meter Most poems have **rhythm,** or a beat, created by the stressed and unstressed syllables in words. To sustain a pattern of rhythm, or **meter,** a poet may arrange words and break lines at certain points.

Meter is measured in **feet,** or units of stressed and unstressed syllables. As you read the following lines, look for the pattern in the arrangement of stressed syllables (´) and unstressed syllables (˘). Feet are divided by slashes (/).

> Whĕn Í / sĕe bírch / ĕs beńd /
>   tŏ le´ft / ańd right
> Ăcroś´s / thĕ lińes / ŏf straíght / ĕr
>   dárk / ĕr trées,
> Ĭ lik´e / tŏ thińk / sŏme bóy's /
>   bĕen swíng / iňg thém.
> (from "Birches," Robert Frost)

In this example, each foot consists of one unstressed syllable followed by one stressed syllable. This down-up, down-up rhythmic pattern fits the subject of an imagined boy swinging on the branches of trees.

Poets may break a metrical pattern for effect. For example, Frost shifts the accent to the first syllable in this line from "Birches": "Kicking his way down through the air to the ground." The shift emphasizes the boy's movement.

Rhyme Some poems also contain **rhyme,** or the repetition of vowel and consonant sounds at the ends of words, as in _tin_ and _pin_. In many poems, the **rhymes** follow a particular pattern, or rhyme **scheme.** In the following example, the first line rhymes with the third line, and the second line rhymes with the fourth line. This rhyme scheme is indicated by using a different letter for each rhyme sound: _abab_.

Rhyme Scheme	
How doth the little crocodile	a
Improve his shining tail,	b
And pour the waters of the Nile	a
On every golden scale!	b

(from "How Doth the Little Crocodile," Lewis Carroll)

Additional Sound Devices

Poets may also use other sound devices to enhance mood and meaning in their poems.

- **Alliteration** is the repetition of consonant sounds in the beginnings of words, as in _slippery slope._
- **Repetition** is the use of any element of language—a sound, word, or phrase—more than once.
- **Onomatopoeia** is the use of words that imitate sounds. _Splat, hiss,_ and _gurgle_ are all examples of onomatopoeia.

Common Core State Standards

Reading Literature

4. Determine the meaning of words and phrases as they are used in a text, including figurative and connotative meanings; analyze the impact of rhymes and other repetitions of sounds (e.g., alliteration) on a specific verse or stanza of a poem or section of a story or drama.

5. Analyze how a drama's or poem's form or structure (e.g., soliloquy, sonnet) contributes to its meaning.

Analyzing Language, Form, and Structure in Poetry

Poetic language is specific, imaginative, and rich with emotion. Every **form** of poetry has its own **structure**.

Poetic language begins when a writer weaves together the images and associations called up by words and says something unique that could not be said in different words.

Shade of Meaning The **denotation** of a word is its literal, dictionary definition. The **connotation** consists of the ideas and feelings that the word brings to mind. The chart below lists several words that refer to dogs. Consider the differences in the words' connotations (printed in darker type).

Denotative and Connotative Meanings
canine ——→ dog
pooch ——→ **friendly, lovable** dog
mongrel ——→ **mean, ugly** mixed-breed dog

The technical term *canine* has a neutral connotation, neither positive nor negative. By contrast, the word *pooch* conveys positive feelings, while *mongrel* conveys negative feelings.

Imagery To create vivid word pictures, poets use **imagery,** or descriptions that appeal to the five senses. Imagery helps poets convey what they see, hear, smell, taste, or touch.

The example below appeals to the senses of taste, hearing, and smell.

> **Example: Imagery**
>
> Taste the green in the lettuce,
> Hear the crunch of its freshness,
> Smell its earth perfume.

Figurative Language To help readers share their perceptions and insights, poets may also use **figurative language,** or language that is not meant to be taken literally. Many types of figurative language are comparisons that show how things are alike in surprising ways. Three common types of figurative language are similes, metaphors, and personification.

A **simile** uses the word *like* or *as* to compare two seemingly unlike things.
- *His hands were as cold as steel.*

A **metaphor** describes one thing as if it were something else.
- *My chores were a mountain waiting to be climbed.*

In **personification,** the writer gives human qualities to a nonhuman subject.
- *The fingertips of the rain tapped a steady beat on the windowpane.*

There are many different forms of poetry. A poet chooses the form that best suits his or her intended meaning.

Narrative poetry tells a story in verse. Narrative poems have elements similar to those in short stories, such as plot and characters.

Haiku is a three-line Japanese form that describes something in nature. The first and third lines each have five syllables, and the second line has seven.

Free Verse poetry is defined by its lack of structure. It has no regular meter, rhyme, fixed line length, or specific stanza pattern.

Lyric poetry expresses the thoughts and feelings of a single speaker, often in highly musical verse.

Ballads are songlike poems that tell stories. They often deal with adventure or romance.

Concrete poems are shaped to look like their subjects. The poet arranges the lines to create a picture on the page.

Limericks are humorous, rhyming five-line poems with a specific rhythm pattern and rhyme scheme.

Look at the lyric poem below to see how the structural elements of rhythm, rhyme, and imagery help reinforce the poet's meaning.

Analysis of Lines from "Tiare Tahiti," Rupert Brooke		
Taü here, Mamua!	a	• The poem's meter emphasizes the commands "crown" and "come."
Crown the hair, and come away!	b	
Hear the calling of the moon,	c	• The *b* rhyme sound ties lines 3–5 together, reflecting their focus on the night's beauty. This focus is developed with **imagery**.
And the whispering scents that stray	b	
5 About the idle warm lagoon.	c	
Hasten, hand in human hand,	d	• The new *c* rhyme sound in lines 6–7 introduces a new idea: the speaker urges Mamua to come to the lagoon. The **alliteration** of the *h, w,* and *d* sounds reinforces this idea.
Down the dark, the flowered way,	b	
Along the whiteness of the sand,	d	
And in the water's soft caress,	e	• Lines 9–10 rhyme, interrupting the pattern of alternating rhymes. The interruption shows that these lines express a key idea: Nature can ease the mind.
10 Wash the mind of foolishness,	e	
Mamua, until the day.	b	

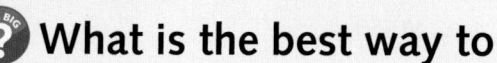 **What is the best way to communicate?**

Explore the Big Question as you read Poetry Collection 1. Take notes on how each poet arranges words to communicate meaning.

CLOSE READING FOCUS

Key Ideas and Details: **Draw Conclusions**

The techniques a poet uses may require readers to think critically to determine a poem's meaning. When you **draw conclusions,** you arrive at an overall meaning or understanding by pulling together various details. Drawing conclusions helps you recognize ideas that are not directly stated.

Asking questions like the ones that follow can help you identify details and make connections that enable you to draw conclusions.

- What details does the writer include and emphasize?
- How are the details related? Is there a pattern?
- What do the details mean all together?

Craft and Structure: **Forms of Poetry**

There are many different **forms of poetry**. Each form has specific rules that guide the structure and content.

- A **lyric poem** expresses the poet's thoughts and feelings about a single image or idea in vivid, musical language.
- In a **concrete poem,** the poet arranges the letters and lines to create a visual image that suggests the poem's subject.
- **Haiku** is a traditional form of Japanese poetry that is often about nature. The first and third lines always have five syllables, and the second line always has seven syllables.

Vocabulary

You will encounter the following words in Poetry Collection 1. In your notebook, make three columns: *verbs, nouns,* and *adjectives.* Write each word in the appropriate column.

translates	luminous	minnow
swerve	utter	fragrant

CLOSE READING MODEL

The passages below are from William Jay Smith's "Seal" and Bashō's "Haiku." The annotations to the right of the passages show ways in which you can use close reading skills to draw conclusions and recognize forms of poetry.

---

from "Seal"

See how he dives
From the rocks with a zoom!
See how he darts[1]
Through his watery room

Draw Conclusions

1 The words *dives*, *zoom*, and *darts* suggest grace and speed. These details may help you conclude that seals are able to move through the water quickly and easily.

---

from "Haiku"

On sweet plum blossoms[2]
The sun rises suddenly.
Look, a mountain path![3]

Draw Conclusions

2 From this detail, you might draw the conclusion that this scene takes place in the springtime, when flowers "blossom," or bloom.

Forms of Poetry

3 The five-syllable, seven-syllable, five-syllable structure tells you immediately that this poem is haiku.

Meet the Poets

"Winter"

Nikki Giovanni (b. 1943) is not only a poet but also a college professor who teaches both English literature and African American studies. She has won numerous awards for her poetry, including three NAACP Image Awards for Literature.

"The Rider"

When **Naomi Shihab Nye** (b. 1952) was fourteen, her family moved from Missouri to the Middle East. Though she now values learning about her Arab heritage, the move was not easy for her. Nye has published volumes of poetry as well as books for children.

"Seal"

William Jay Smith (b. 1918) was born in Winnfield, Louisiana. He has taught college students, written poetry and essays, translated Russian and French poetry, and even served in the Vermont State Legislature.

"Haiku"

Matsuo Bashō (1644–1694) was born in Japan and began studying poetry at an early age. He wrote poetry, taught poetry, served as a noble in the court, and lived in a monastery. He remains one of Japan's most famous poets.

Winter

Nikki Giovanni

Frogs burrow the mud
snails bury themselves
and I air my quilts
preparing for the cold

5   Dogs grow more hair
mothers make oatmeal
and little boys and girls
take Father John's Medicine[1]

Bears store fat
10 chipmunks gather nuts
and I collect books
For the coming winter

---

1. **Father John's Medicine** old-fashioned cough syrup.

Draw Conclusions
Why are all the activities described in the poem necessary?

THE Rider

Naomi Shihab Nye

Vocabulary ▶
translates (trans´ lāts)
v. expresses the same
thing in another form

luminous (loo´ mə nəs)
adj. giving off light

Forms of Poetry
Whose feelings does
the poem express—"a
boy's" or the speaker's?
Explain.

A boy told me
if he rollerskated fast enough
his loneliness couldn't catch up to him,

the best reason I ever heard
5 for trying to be a champion.

What I wonder tonight
pedaling hard down King William Street
is if it translates to bicycles.

A victory! To leave your loneliness
10 panting behind you on some street corner
while you float free into a cloud of sudden azaleas,
luminous pink petals that have
    never felt loneliness,
no matter how slowly they fell.

◄ **Critical Viewing**
What details in this photograph convey the feelings the poem describes?

Seal

William Jay Smith

See how he dives
  From the rocks with a zoom!
    See how he darts
      Through his watery room
5   Past crabs and eels
    And green seaweed,
    Past fluffs of sandy
    Minnow feed![1]
    See how he swims
10 With a swerve and a twist,
   A flip of the flipper,
   A flick of the wrist!
   Quicksilver-quick,
   Softer than spray,
15 Down he plunges
  And sweeps away;
 Before you can think,
Before you can utter
Words like "Dill pickle"
20 Or "Apple butter,"
Back up he swims
Past Sting Ray and Shark,
Out with a zoom,
A whoop, a bark;
25 Before you can say
  Whatever you wish,
    He plops at your side
      With a mouthful of fish!

---

1. **feed** (fēd) *n.* tiny particles that minnows feed on.

Forms of Poetry
Why might the poet have arranged the lines of the poem this way?

◄ **Vocabulary**
minnow (min ō)
n. small fish

swerve (swʉrv) *n.*
curving motion

◄ **Vocabulary**
utter (ut´ ər) *v.* speak

◄ **Critical Viewing**
What details in this photograph remind you of the poem?

Haiku
Bashō

On sweet plum blossoms
The sun rises suddenly.
Look, a mountain path!

Forms of Poetry
How are these three poems similar?

Has spring come indeed?
On that nameless mountain lie
Thin layers of mist.

Vocabulary ▶
fragrant (frā´ grənt)
adj. sweet smelling

Temple bells die out.
The fragrant blossoms remain.
A perfect evening!

Language Study

Vocabulary The words listed below appear in Poetry Collection 1. Rewrite each numbered sentence using one of the vocabulary words.

translates   minnow   swerve   utter   fragrant

1. The sleds make turning movements at the bottom of the hill.
2. Frozen by stage fright, the actor could not speak a word.
3. Dan speaks the English word in Spanish.
4. John saw hundreds of tiny silver fish in the pond.
5. The sweet-smelling lilac bushes are my favorite.

WORD STUDY

The **Latin root -*lum*-** means "light." In "The Rider," the speaker sees flowers with **luminous**, or brightly lit, petals.

Word Study

Part A Explain how the **Latin root -*lum*-** contributes to the meanings of the words *lumen* and *luminescence*. Consult a dictionary if necessary.

Part B Use the context of the sentences and your knowledge of the Latin root -*lum*- to explain your answer to each question.

1. Is a *luminary* someone who is unknown?
2. When you switch on a light, does it *illuminate* the room?

Literary Analysis

Key Ideas and Details

1. **Draw Conclusions** For each poem, ask a question that helps you draw the conclusion given. **(a)** The speaker in "Winter" accepts the changing seasons as part of the natural cycle of life. **(b)** The speaker in "The Rider" values speed. **(c)** The seal in "Seal" zooms around quickly. **(d)** The speakers in the three haiku value nature.

2. **(a)** What two sports are discussed in "The Rider"? **(b) Compare:** What do the two sports have in common? Include details from the poem to support your answer.

Craft and Structure

3. **Forms of Poetry** In a chart like the one on the right, write the name of the poems from this collection that have the characteristics described in the left column.

4. **Forms of Poetry** How is the form of each poem suited to the ideas it conveys? Cite specific textual evidence to support your claims.

5. **Forms of Poetry** Based on the three haiku, how would you describe Bashō's attitude toward nature? Use specific details from the poems to support your answer.

6. **(a)** Identify six words that describe the movement of the seal in "Seal." **(b) Infer:** How would you describe the mood or feeling that these words create?

Characteristics of Poem	Poem
Three lines; 17 syllables	
Lines shaped like subject	
Thoughts of one speaker	
Single image or idea	
Musical language	

Integration of Knowledge and Ideas

7. **(a)** What actions do the animals and people take in "Winter"? **(b) Connect:** How do these actions reflect winter in your experience? Explain.

8. **(a) Relate:** Which poem in this collection did you enjoy the most? Why? **(b) Speculate:** Do you think these poems are meaningful for people your age? Explain.

9. **What is the best way to communicate? (a)** Which techniques or words convey ideas, pictures, or feelings most effectively in these poems? **(b)** How does form or structure help communicate a poem's meaning? Explain your answer, citing evidence from the poems.

ACADEMIC VOCABULARY

As you write and speak about Poetry Collection 1, use the words related to communication that you explored on page 313 of this textbook.

Conventions: **Sentence Functions and End Marks**

Sentences are classified into four categories based on their **functions**. Each type of sentence calls for its own specific punctuation mark(s).

Category	Function	End Marks	Example
Declarative	to make statements	. period	Our cat chased a squirrel up a tree.
Interrogative	to ask questions	? question mark	Where did I put my jacket?
Imperative	to give commands	. *or* ! period or exclamation point	Put your books away. *or* Don't touch that stove!
Exclamatory	to call out or exclaim	! exclamation point	That's a great idea!

Practice A

Identify the function of each sentence.

1. How fast can that boy rollerskate?
2. The bike rider noticed some pink azaleas.
3. That seal is so sleek and graceful!
4. What do seals like to eat?
5. Smell the fragrant flowers.
6. Has spring come at last?
7. Prepare your house for winter.
8. It is so cozy here by the fire!

Reading Application In Poetry Collection 1, find one declarative sentence, one interrogative sentence, one imperative sentence, and one exclamatory sentence.

Practice B

Follow the directions to write a sentence that performs the indicated function.

1. Make a statement about bike riding.
2. Ask a question about winter.
3. Issue a command that one of the haiku speakers might give.
4. Make an exclamation about a seal.

Writing Application Write four sentences about the poems in this collection. Use one declarative sentence, one interrogative sentence, one imperative sentence, and one exclamatory sentence.

Writing to Sources

Poetry Write a **lyric poem, concrete poem,** or **haiku** to share your thoughts in new, creative ways.

- Choose a subject that interests you. Write the subject in the center of a piece of paper, and create a cluster diagram around it.
- Brainstorm by listing vivid descriptions, action words, thoughts, and feelings in the cluster diagram.
- Review the characteristics of each poetic form and decide which form is best suited to your topic. Next, review the poem or poems in Poetry Collection 1 that have the form you have chosen. Note techniques the poet uses that you could replicate in your own work. Then, use your notes to draft your poem. Add a creative title to capture your readers' interest.
- Use one or more computer programs, such as a word-processing or drawing program, to write and format your poem. Use punctuation, line length, and word arrangement to create the desired effect. Publish your poem by posting it on an approved Web site or in your classroom.

Grammar Application Check to be sure you have correctly punctuated your writing.

Speaking and Listening

Presentation of Ideas In the library or online, find a recording of a poet reading his or her own lyric poetry. Listen to one or more of the poems with a small group of classmates as you read the written version of each poem. Then, in a brief **presentation** to your group, compare the experience of reading a poem to the experience of hearing it read aloud. Follow these steps:

- Analyze the effects of hearing the words in comparison with reading them. Support your opinion with specific reasons and examples from the recording and the text.
- Listen carefully to each person's opinions and weigh them against your own.
- With your group, acknowledge new information expressed by others and discuss whether or not your opinion changed after listening to other responses.

 **Common Core State Standards**

Reading Literature
7. Compare and contrast a written story, drama, or poem to its audio, filmed, staged, or multimedia version, analyzing the effects of techniques unique to each medium.

Writing
4. Produce clear and coherent writing in which the development, organization, and style are appropriate to task, purpose, and audience.
6. Use technology, including the Internet, to produce and publish writing.

Language
2. Demonstrate command of the conventions of standard English capitalization, punctuation, and spelling when writing.

Speaking and Listening
1.d. Acknowledge new information expressed by others and, when warranted, modify their own views.

What is the best way to communicate?

Explore the Big Question as you read Poetry Collection 2. Take notes on the ways in which the poems explore ways of communicating.

CLOSE READING FOCUS

Key Ideas and Details: **Draw Conclusions**

To interpret meaning in poetry, **draw conclusions** by connecting important details. For example, if the speaker in a poem describes beautiful flowers, bright sunshine, and happy children, you might conclude that he or she has a positive outlook. As you read, identify important details. Then, look at the details together to draw a conclusion about the poem's meaning.

Craft and Structure: **Figurative Language**

Figurative language is language that is not meant to be taken literally. Writers use figures of speech, or figurative language, to express ideas in vivid and imaginative ways. Common figures of speech include the following:

- A **simile** compares two unlike things by using the word *like* or *as: My love is like a red, red rose.*
- A **metaphor** compares two unlike things by saying that one thing *is* another: *Life is a bowl of cherries.*
- In **personification,** a nonhuman subject is given human characteristics: *The stars were dancing.*
- A **symbol** is a thing that represents something other than itself. For example, a dove may symbolize peace.

Vocabulary

You will encounter the following words in Poetry Collection 2. Decide whether you know each word well, know it a little bit, or do not know it at all. After you read, use each word in a sentence that shows the word's meaning.

fascinated	granite
crystal	haunches

ⓒ **Common Core State Standards**

Reading Literature
4. Determine the meaning of words and phrases as they are used in a text, including figurative and connotative meanings; analyze the impact of rhymes and other repetitions of sounds on a specific verse or stanza of a poem or section of a story or drama.

Language
6. Acquire and use accurately grade-appropriate general academic and domain-specific words and phrases; gather vocabulary knowledge when considering a word or phrase important to comprehension or expression.

CLOSE READING MODEL

The passages below are from Naomi Long Madgett's "Life" and Langston Hughes's "Mother to Son." The annotations to the right of the passages show ways in which you can use close reading skills to draw conclusions and analyze figurative language.

---

from "Life"

Life is but a toy that swings on a bright gold chain[1]
Ticking for a little while[2]
To amuse a fascinated infant,

Figurative Language
1 The speaker says life *is* a toy. This metaphor creates a strong opening image for the poem.

Draw Conclusions
2 When you connect the phrase *ticking for a little while* with the image of a gold chain, you may visualize a pocket watch. From this image, you may conclude that the speaker believes life passes swiftly.

---

from "Mother to Son"

Well, son, I'll tell you:
Life for me ain't been no crystal stair.[3]
It's had tacks in it,
And splinters,

Draw Conclusions
3 The speaker uses informal language to describe life's struggles. You may conclude that she has little formal education, but her life experience has given her great wisdom.

Meet the Poets

"Life"

Naomi Long Madgett (b. 1923) first discovered poetry at the age of seven or eight, while reading in her father's study. She was most inspired by the poets Alfred, Lord Tennyson and Langston Hughes, though their styles are quite different. Madgett once said, "I would rather be a good poet than anything else." Her ambition to create good poetry has led her to write more than seven collections of poems.

"The Courage That My Mother Had"

Edna St. Vincent Millay (1892–1950) was the daughter of a hard-working nurse who encouraged her daughters to be independent and to love reading. Millay's mother had a powerful influence on young Edna, who grew up to be a widely published writer and political activist. Born in Rockland, Maine, Millay published her first poem at the age of fourteen. In 1923, she became the first woman to win the Pulitzer Prize for poetry.

"Mother to Son"

Langston Hughes (1902–1967) published his first work just a year after his high school graduation. Though he wrote in many genres, Hughes is best known for his poetry. He was one of the main figures in the Harlem Renaissance, a creative movement among African Americans that took place in the 1920s in New York City.

"Fog"

Carl Sandburg (1878–1967) was born in Illinois to Swedish immigrant parents. Although he won the Pulitzer Prize in both poetry and history, he was not a typical scholar. By the time his first book appeared, he had tried many different occupations, including farm worker, stagehand, railroad worker, soldier, and cook.

Life

Naomi Long Madgett

Life is but a toy that swings on a bright gold chain
Ticking for a little while
To amuse a fascinated infant,
Until the keeper, a very old man,
5   Becomes tired of the game
And lets the watch run down.

◄ **Vocabulary**
fascinated (fas´ ə nāt´
əd) *adj.* very interested

The Courage That My Mother Had

Edna St. Vincent Millay

The courage that my mother had
Went with her, and is with her still:
Rock from New England quarried;[1]
Now granite in a granite hill.

5   The golden brooch[2] my mother wore
She left behind for me to wear;
I have no thing I treasure more:
Yet, it is something I could spare.

   Oh, if instead she'd left to me
10   The thing she took into the grave!—
That courage like a rock, which she
Has no more need of, and I have.

Vocabulary ▶
granite (gran´ it) *n.*
hard, gray rock

Draw Conclusions
What detail in the third
stanza shows how the
speaker feels about her
mother?

---

1. **quarried** (kwôr´ ēd) *adj.* carved out of the ground.
2. **brooch** (brōch) *n.* large ornamental pin.

Mother to Son

Langston Hughes

Well, son, I'll tell you:
Life for me ain't been no **crystal** stair.
It's had tacks in it,
And splinters,
5 And boards torn up,
And places with no carpet on the floor—
Bare.
But all the time
I'se been a-climbin' on,
10 And reachin' landin's,
And turnin' corners,
And sometimes goin' in the dark
Where there ain't been no light.
So boy, don't you turn back.
15 Don't you set down on the steps
'Cause you finds it's kinder hard.
Don't you fall now—
For I'se still goin', honey,
I'se still climbin',
20 And life for me ain't been no crystal stair.

◀ **Vocabulary**
crystal (kris′ təl)
adj. made of clear,
brilliant glass

Figurative Language
What does the staircase
symbolize?

Draw Conclusions
What details in the
poem support the
conclusion that life has
not been easy for the
mother?

FOG
Carl Sandburg

The fog comes
on little cat feet.

It sits looking
over harbor and city
5   on silent **haunches**
and then moves on.

Vocabulary ▶
haunches (hônch´
əz) *n.* upper legs and
hips of an animal

Language Study

Vocabulary The words listed below appear in Poetry Collection 2. Explain your answer to each numbered question.

fascinated   granite   crystal   haunches

1. If Michael is *fascinated* by the show, is he bored?

2. If something is made of *granite,* will it break easily?

3. If a glass is made of *crystal,* is it fragile?

4. Is it possible for a dog to sit on its *haunches*?

WORD STUDY

The **suffix -er,** means "one who." The watch in "Life" has a **keeper,** someone who winds the watch to keep it going.

Word Study

Part A Explain how the **suffix -er** contributes to the meanings of the words *writer, climber,* and *thinker.* Consult a dictionary if necessary.

Part B Use the context of the sentences and your knowledge of the suffix *-er* to explain your answer to each question.

1. Is a champion *swimmer* likely to win a prize in running?

2. What does a *photographer* enjoy doing?

Close Reading Activities

Literary Analysis

Key Ideas and Details

1. **(a)** In "Life," what image does Naomi Long Madgett use to describe life? **(b) Evaluate:** Is it an effective image? Why or why not?

2. **Draw Conclusions** Use a graphic organizer like the one on the right to connect details from the poem "Life" to reach the conclusion given.

3. **Draw Conclusions** Which details from "The Courage That My Mother Had" support the conclusion that the speaker admires her mother?

4. **Draw Conclusions (a)** What qualities does the mother in "Mother to Son" demonstrate through her words and actions? Cite specific examples from the poem. **(b)** Why does the mother need these qualities?

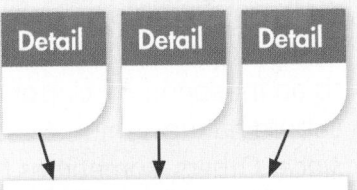

Conclusion: The speaker believes that people lose interest in life as they grow older.

Craft and Structure

5. **Figurative Language (a)** In "Fog," to what is fog compared? **(b)** How are these two things alike? **(c)** What type of figurative language does the author use? How can you tell?

6. **Figurative Language (a)** What is a symbol of hardship in "Mother to Son"? What is a symbol of ease and luxury? **(b)** How are these things alike and different?

7. **Figurative Language (a)** What is a symbol for strength in "The Courage That My Mother Had"? **(b)** How do you know?

Integration of Knowledge and Ideas

8. **Interpret:** In "The Courage That My Mother Had," why would the speaker rather have her mother's character than the physical item her mother left her?

9. **(a)** What three things does the fog do in "Fog"? **(b) Connect:** What qualities of fog make it a good subject for a poem?

10. **What is the best way to communicate?** How can a poet use figures of speech to communicate ideas in new and different ways?

ACADEMIC VOCABULARY

As you write and speak about Poetry Collection 2, use the words related to communication that you explored on page 313 of this textbook.

Conventions: Independent and Dependent Clauses

A **clause** is a group of words with its own subject and verb. The two major types of clauses are independent clauses and dependent clauses.

An **independent clause** can stand by itself as a complete sentence. A **dependent clause** (also called a **subordinate clause**) cannot stand alone as a complete sentence but instead adds information to an independent clause. Some dependent clauses begin with subordinating conjunctions, such as *if, when, because, where,* and *since.* Others (sometimes called **relative clauses**) begin with relative pronouns, such as *who, whom, whose, which,* and *that.*

Comparing Two Kinds of Clauses	
Independent	**Dependent**
S V The mosque has a golden dome.	S V *since* the mosque has a dome
S V I planted the heirloom tomatoes in May.	S V *that* I planted in May

Practice A

Identify the independent and dependent clauses in each sentence.

1. The infant was amused when the watch was swinging back and forth.
2. She had courage that was like granite.
3. When the fog came in, we could not see ten feet ahead.
4. The mother climbed stairs where there was no light.

Reading Application In Poetry Collection 2, find a sentence with an independent and a dependent clause. Explain the role of each clause.

Practice B

Identify the dependent clause in each sentence. Then, use the dependent clause to write a new sentence.

1. When we were driving, the fog made it difficult to see.
2. If these stairs were repaired, they would be safer.
3. This watch, which is made of gold, is quite valuable.

Writing Application Write two sentences about poetry that both include dependent clauses. Label each independent and dependent clause.

Writing to Sources

Explanatory Text Create a **metaphor** using one of the following topics from the poems in this collection as inspiration:

- life
- a quality, such as courage
- an idea, such as nature

Before you write, review the poems in Poetry Collection 2, and note techniques the authors use to create effective metaphors. Use precise language to compare your topic to something else, such as an object, an idea, or an animal. Then, extend the metaphor by making several connected comparisons. Use vivid images and descriptive language to develop your metaphor.

Grammar Application Check your writing to make sure it is free from grammatical errors.

Research and Technology

Build and Present Knowledge Working with a partner, write a **scientific explanation** of fog. Present your findings to the class in an oral report.

- Use library resources to research the natural phenomenon of fog. If you are using a reference book, scan the table of contents to see if your topic is addressed. Then, review the index for key words.
- Look up unfamiliar or scientific terms in a glossary or dictionary.
- Find out how, why, and when fog forms, and why it disappears. As you write your explanation, support it with factual details.
- Use diagrams, illustrations, photographs, maps, or other visuals to clarify your findings and emphasize key points.
- Conclude your report by briefly analyzing Carl Sandburg's poem and evaluating the effectiveness of his comparison between fog and a cat. Support your claims with details from your research and from the poem. Be sure to communicate information in your own words.

Common Core State Standards

Writing

2. Write informative/explanatory texts to examine a topic and convey ideas, concepts, and information through the selection, organization, and analysis of relevant content.

2.d. Use precise language and domain-specific vocabulary to inform about or explain the topic.

7. Conduct short research projects to answer a question, drawing on several sources.

Speaking and Listening

5. Include multimedia components and visual displays in presentations to clarify claims and findings and emphasize salient points.

Language

1.a. Explain the function of phrases and clauses in general and their function in specific sentences.

 **What is the best way to communicate?**

Think about the Big Question as you read Poetry Collection 3. Note ways in which the poets use sound devices to communicate ideas.

CLOSE READING FOCUS

Key Ideas and Details: **Paraphrase**

When you **paraphrase**, you restate something in your own words. To paraphrase a poem, you must first understand its meaning. Begin by looking for the poem's main idea and the details that support it. Reading aloud according to punctuation can help you identify complete thoughts in a poem. Observe these rules:

- Keep reading when a line has no end punctuation.
- Pause at commas; pause slightly longer at dashes and semicolons.
- Stop at periods, question marks, or exclamation points.

Craft and Structure: **Sound Devices**

Sound devices use the sounds of words to create musical effects that appeal to the ear. These sound devices are used in poetry:

- **Onomatopoeia** is the use of words with sounds that suggest their meanings: the *shooshing* of skis
- **Alliteration** is the repetition of sounds at the beginnings of words: *maggie* and *millie* and *mollie* and *may*
- **Repetition** is the repeated use of words, phrases, or rhythms: To the swinging and the ringing / *of the bells, bells, bells* *Of the bells, bells, bells, bells*

© **Common Core State Standards**

Reading Literature
4. Determine the meaning of words and phrases as they are used in a text, including figurative and connotative meanings; analyze the impact of rhymes and other repetitions of sounds (e.g., alliteration) on a specific verse or stanza of a poem or section of a story or drama.

Vocabulary

You will encounter the following words in Poetry Collection 3. Write the words in your notebook and circle the word that you associate with a sound. Then, use the word in a sentence.

groves	fathom	withered
curdled	sputters	smattering

CLOSE READING MODEL

The passages below are from Shel Silverstein's "Sarah Cynthia Sylvia Stout Would Not Take the Garbage Out" and William Shakespeare's "Full Fathom Five." The annotations to the right of the passages show ways in which you can use close reading skills to paraphrase as you read and analyze sound devices.

from "Sarah Cynthia Sylvia Stout Would Not Take the Garbage Out"

It filled the can, it covered the floor,

It cracked the window and blocked the door[1]

With bacon rinds and chicken bones,

Drippy ends of ice cream cones,

Prune pits, peach pits, orange peel,

Gloppy glumps of cold oatmeal,...[2]

Sound Devices

1 By repeating the phrase, "It ___ the ___," the poet creates a strong rhythm and a sense of the unstoppable force of the garbage.

Sound Devices

2 The nonsense phrase *gloppy glumps* calls to mind the real words *sloppy lumps,* which can help you understand its meaning. Alliteration makes the phrase sound silly, which adds to the poem's bouncy rhythm and humorous tone.

from "Full Fathom Five"

Full fathom five thy father lies;

Of his bones are coral made;

Those are pearls that were his eyes;[3]

Nothing of him that doth fade....

Paraphrase

3 When you encounter unfamiliar or difficult language, slow down, reread, and then try to paraphrase the lines. You might paraphrase these lines like this: "Your father lies under five fathoms of water. His bones are now made of coral, and his eyes are made of pearls."

Meet the Poets

"Train Tune"

Louise Bogan (1897–1970) grew up in Maine and attended the Girls' Latin School in Boston, where she developed an interest in poetry. During her writing career, she became known for her compact use of language and for the traditional form of her poems. A very private person, Bogan struggled with her fame as a highly respected poet, critic, and lecturer.

"Full Fathom Five"

William Shakespeare (1564–1616) is widely regarded as the greatest writer in the English language. He wrote thirty-seven plays, many of which are still performed frequently today. They include *Romeo and Juliet*, *Hamlet*, and *A Midsummer Night's Dream*.

"Sarah Cynthia Sylvia Stout Would Not Take the Garbage Out"

Shel Silverstein (1932–1999) was a cartoonist, composer, folk singer, and writer. He began writing poetry at an early age, before he had a chance to study any of the great poets. "I was so lucky that I didn't have anyone to copy," he once said.

"Onomatopoeia"

Eve Merriam (1916–1992) became fascinated with words when she was quite young. "I remember being enthralled by the sound of words," she said. This fascination led her to write poetry, fiction, nonfiction, and drama.

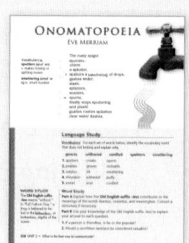

Train Tune

Louise Bogan

Back through clouds
Back through clearing
Back through distance
Back through silence

5　Back through groves
Back through garlands
Back by rivers
Back below mountains

Back through lightning
10　Back through cities
Back through stars
Back through hours

Back through plains
Back through flowers
15　Back through birds
Back through rain

Back through smoke
Back through noon
Back along love
20　Back through midnight

◀ **Vocabulary**
groves (grōvz) *n.*
small groups of trees

FULL FATHOM FIVE

WILLIAM SHAKESPEARE

Vocabulary ▶
fathom (fath´ əm)
n. unit of length
used to measure the
depth of water

Paraphrase
After which lines do you
come to a complete
stop when reading?

Full **fathom** five thy father lies;
   Of his bones are coral made;
Those are pearls that were his eyes;
   Nothing of him that doth fade
5   But doth suffer a sea change
Into something rich and strange.
Sea nymphs hourly ring his knell;[1]
                 Ding-dong.
Hark! Now I hear them—Ding-dong bell.

---

1. knell (nel) *n.* funeral bell.

Sarah Cynthia Sylvia Stout Would Not Take the Garbage Out

Shel Silverstein

Sarah Cynthia Sylvia Stout
Would not take the garbage out!
She'd scour[1] the pots and scrape the pans,
Candy[2] the yams and spice the hams,
5 And though her daddy would scream and shout,
She simply would not take the garbage out.
And so it piled up to the ceilings:
Coffee grounds, potato peelings,
Brown bananas, rotten peas,
10 Chunks of sour cottage cheese.
It filled the can, it covered the floor,
It cracked the window and blocked the door
With bacon rinds[3] and chicken bones,
Drippy ends of ice cream cones,
15 Prune pits, peach pits, orange peel,
Gloppy glumps of cold oatmeal,
Pizza crusts and withered greens,
Soggy beans and tangerines,
Crusts of black burned buttered toast,

---

1. scour (skour) *v.* clean by rubbing vigorously.
2. candy (kan´ dē) *v.* coat with sugar.
3. rinds (rīndz) *n.* tough outer layers or skins.

20 Gristly bits of beefy roasts . . .
   The garbage rolled on down the hall,
   It raised the roof, it broke the wall . . .
   Greasy napkins, cookie crumbs,
   Globs of gooey bubble gum,
25 Cellophane from green baloney,
   Rubbery blubbery macaroni,
   Peanut butter, caked and dry,
   Curdled milk and crusts of pie,
   Moldy melons, dried-up mustard,
30 Eggshells mixed with lemon custard,
   Cold french fries and rancid meat,
   Yellow lumps of Cream of Wheat.
   At last the garbage reached so high
   That finally it touched the sky.
35 And all the neighbors moved away,
   And none of her friends would come to play.
   And finally Sarah Cynthia Stout said,
   "OK, I'll take the garbage out!"
   But then, of course, it was too late . . .
40 The garbage reached across the state,
   From New York to the Golden Gate.
   And there, in the garbage she did hate,
   Poor Sarah met an awful fate,
   That I cannot right now relate⁴
45 Because the hour is much too late.
   But children, remember Sarah Stout
   And always take the garbage out!

---

4. **relate** (ri lāt´) *v.* tell.

◀ **Vocabulary**
withered (with´
ərd) *adj.* dried up

Sound Devices
Which sound device
does the poet use in
line 24? Explain.

◀ **Vocabulary**
curdled (kurd´
'ld) *adj.* rotten

Spiral Review
TONE Which words
and phrases on this
page contribute to a
humorous, lighthearted
tone? Explain.

◀ **Critical Viewing**
The author drew
the cartoons that
accompany the poem.
How does the art add
to the poem's humor?

ONOMATOPOEIA

EVE MERRIAM

Vocabulary ▶
sputters (sput´ ərz)
v. makes hissing or
spitting noises

smattering (smat´ ər
iŋ) *n.* small number

The rusty spigot
sputters,
utters
a splutter,
5 spatters a smattering of drops,
gashes wider;
slash,
splatters,
scatters,
10 spurts,
finally stops sputtering
and plash!
gushes rushes splashes
clear water dashes.

Language Study

Vocabulary For each set of words below, identify the vocabulary word
that does not belong and explain why.

groves	withered	curdled	sputters	smattering
1. sputters	creaks	opens		
2. prairies	groves	orchards		
3. surplus	bit	smattering		
4. shrunken	withered	puffy		
5. sweet	sour	curdled		

WORD STUDY
The **Old English suffix**
-less means "without."
In "Full Fathom Five," a
king is believed to be
lost in the **fathomless**, or
bottomless, depths of the
ocean.

Word Study

Part A Explain how the **Old English suffix -less** contributes to the
meanings of the words *fearless, ceaseless,* and *meaningless.* Consult a
dictionary if necessary.

Part B Use your knowledge of the Old English suffix *-less* to explain
your answer to each question.

1. If a person is *friendless,* is he or she popular?

2. Would a *worthless* necklace be considered valuable?

Literary Analysis

Key Ideas and Details

1. **Paraphrase** In a chart like the one on the right, write an example from each poem in which you read according to punctuation rather than stopping at the end of a line. Then, paraphrase each example.

2. **(a)** What emotion does the speaker mention in "Train Tune"? **(b) Speculate:** Why do you think the poet includes this detail? Support your answer.

3. **(a)** Name two changes that the speaker describes happening to the father in "Full Fathom Five." **(b) Interpret:** Why does the poet call these changes "rich and strange"?

Poem Title and Example	Paraphrase

Craft and Structure

4. **Sound Devices (a)** Find two examples of alliteration in "Sarah Cynthia…" **(b)** How does alliteration add to the humor of the poem?

5. **Sound Devices (a)** Identify the repetition in "Train Tune." **(b)** What effect does this sound device have when you read the poem out loud?

6. **Sound Devices (a)** Identify three words from "Onomatopoeia" that sound like falling water. **(b) Analyze:** How do the sounds of the words help convey the author's meaning?

7. **Sound Devices (a)** What sound device is used in the title "Full Fathom Five"? **(b)** Find an example of another sound device in the poem.

Integration of Knowledge and Ideas

8. **Evaluate:** Which of these poems has the most musical quality? Give examples from the poem to support your answer.

9. **(a) Infer:** What lesson might readers learn from "Sarah Cynthia . . ."? **(b) Analyze:** Do you think the poet intended to teach a lesson? Why or why not?

10. **What is the best way to communicate? (a)** Which poem evokes the strongest response in you? Explain. **(b)** How do the sounds of the poem contribute to your response? Cite specific examples from the poem.

ACADEMIC VOCABULARY

As you write and speak about Poetry Collection 3, use the words related to communication that you explored on page 313 of this textbook.

Conventions: **Sentence Structures**

A **simple sentence** consists of one independent clause—a group of words that has a subject and a verb and can stand by itself as a complete thought. A **compound sentence** consists of two or more independent clauses linked by a word such as *and, but,* or *or.* A **complex sentence** contains one independent clause and one or more dependent clauses—a group of words that has a subject and verb but is not a complete thought. A **compound-complex sentence** consists of two or more independent clauses and one or more dependent clauses.

Simple sentence: We planned a picnic.
Compound sentence: We planned a picnic, but it rained.   (ind. clause) (ind. clause)
Complex sentence: Because there is rain, which has lasted all day, we are indoors.   (dep. clause) (dep. clause) (ind. clause)
Compound-complex sentence: Because it rained, we are indoors, but it is still a fun time.   (dep. clause) (ind. clause) (ind. clause)

Practice A

Identify each sentence as simple, compound, complex, or compound-complex.

1. The garbage piled up to the ceiling.
2. The man, who lies beneath the sea, has pearls for eyes.
3. The train that chugs along the tracks passes by a river, but it does not go through a tunnel.
4. The spigot is rusty, and its handle does not turn easily.

Reading Application In Poetry Collection 3, find a simple sentence, a compound sentence, a complex sentence, and a compound-complex sentence.

Practice B

For each item, write a sentence and then identify its structure. Use at least three different sentence structures.

1. Tell why a poet would use humor.
2. Describe why a poet would use onomatopoeia.
3. Explain why a poet would choose to express himself or herself through poetry.
4. Describe a scene from one of the poems you have read.

Writing Application Write a paragraph from the perspective of Sarah Cynthia Sylvia Stout. Use all four sentence structures.

Writing to Sources

Informative Text Write a **paraphrase** of one of the poems you read in Poetry Collection 3.

- Carefully reread each stanza of the poem to identify the poet's main idea.
- Use a dictionary to define words you do not know. Replace these words with familiar synonyms, or words that have the same meaning.
- Restate the entire poem in your own words.
- Reread your paraphrase to make sure it has the same meaning as the original. Make revisions as necessary.

Grammar Application Check your writing to be sure your sentence structures are effective.

Speaking and Listening

Presentation of Ideas Present a **poetry reading** of one of the poems from Poetry Collection 3.

Follow these guidelines as you prepare:

- Rehearse your reading with a small group.
- Be sure you are pronouncing each word correctly, and reading according to punctuation.
- To help you read with the appropriate expression, consider the poet's intentions in writing the poem. Did the poet mean to convey a serious tone or a silly tone? What type of rhythm did the poet want the poem to have?
- Practice reading slowly and expressively. You may decide to emphasize certain words or ideas by raising or lowering the volume of your voice. Do not read with a singsong tone. Be sure that your reading sounds natural.
- Speak clearly, and make eye contact periodically with your audience.
- Ask a partner for feedback on your reading, and make changes based on his or her suggestions.

After you have finished rehearsing, hold a reading for the class.

 **Common Core State Standards**

Writing

9.a. Apply *grade 7 Reading standards* to literature.

Speaking and Listening

4. Use appropriate eye contact, adequate volume, and clear pronunciation.

6. Adapt speech to a variety of contexts and tasks, demonstrating command of formal English when indicated or appropriate.

Language

1.b. Choose among simple, compound, complex, and compound-complex sentences to signal differing relationships among ideas.

4.c. Consult general or specialized reference materials, both print and digital, to find the pronunciation of a word or determine or clarify its precise meaning or its part of speech.

5.b. Use the relationship between particular words to better understand each of the words.

 What is the best way to communicate?

Think about the Big Question as you read Poetry Collection 4. Take notes on how each poet uses sound devices to explore the nature of communication.

CLOSE READING FOCUS

Key Ideas and Details: **Paraphrase**

When you **paraphrase**, you restate something in your own words to make the meaning clear to yourself. If you are unsure of a poem's meaning, reread the poem to clarify ideas.

- First, look up the definitions of unfamiliar words in the original passage and replace them with words you know.
- Identify the poet's main ideas. Restate the passage, using your own everyday words.
- Reread the passage to make sure your version makes sense.

Craft and Structure: **Sound Devices**

Rhythm and rhyme are two techniques poets use to give poems a musical quality. Rhythm is a poem's pattern of stressed (´) and unstressed (˘) syllables. Rhyme is the repetition of sounds at the ends of words. A poem's rhythmical pattern is called **meter.** Meter is measured in *feet,* or units of stressed and unstressed syllables. A **rhyme scheme** is a pattern of rhymes. In this example, the words *sire* and *fire* create a rhyme. Each metrical foot is set off by slashes.

Hálf / ĭn dreáms / hĕ sáw / hĭs síre /
Wíth / hĭs gréat / hănds fúll / ŏf fíre.

Vocabulary

You will encounter the following words in Poetry Collection 4. In your notebook, write two words that have both prefixes and suffixes. How do these affixes affect the meaning of each word?

incessantly	uncommonly	supple
downy	coveted	envying

CLOSE READING MODEL

The passage below is from Edgar Allan Poe's poem "Annabel Lee." The annotations to the right of the passage show ways in which you can use close reading skills to paraphrase and to analyze sound devices.

from "Annabel Lee"

It was many and many a year ago,
   In a kingdom by the sea,[1]
That a maiden there lived whom you may know
   By the name of Annabel Lee;
And this maiden she lived with no other thought
   Than to love and be loved by me.[2]

I was a child and *she* was a child,
   In this kingdom by the sea.
But we loved with a love that was more than love—
   I and my Annabel Lee—
With a love that the wingèd seraphs of Heaven
   Coveted her and me.[3]

Sound Devices

1 Poe establishes a strong pattern of stressed and unstressed syllables. Notice how this rhythm suggests the ebb and flow of ocean waves.

Paraphrase

2 You may need to clarify the meaning of these lines to fully understand Poe's language. First, reread the lines, then restate them in your own words. For example, "Annabel Lee was a young woman who was deeply in love with the speaker, who was also deeply in love with her."

Sound Devices

3 The repetition of the long *e* sound at the ends of the words *sea*, *Lee*, and *me* creates a rhyme scheme that reinforces the poem's musical quality.

Meet the Poets

"Stopping by Woods on a Snowy Evening"

Robert Frost (1874–1963) was born in San Francisco but moved to New England when he was eleven. That region of the country proved to be inspirational for him as a writer. His most popular poems describe New England country life and landscapes. Frost won the Pulitzer Prize four times—more than any other poet.

"Annabel Lee"

Edgar Allan Poe (1809–1849) won great literary success but suffered much personal loss in his life. His mother died when he was just two years old. Later in life, he also suffered the loss of his beloved wife, Virginia. After her death, Poe became depressed and antisocial. Much of his writing reflects this loss of an ideal love.

"Father William"

Lewis Carroll (1832–1898) is the pen name of Charles Dodgson, a mathematics professor who was born in England. Under his pen name, Dodgson wrote *Alice's Adventures in Wonderland* and *Through the Looking Glass*. Like these classic novels, his poems are noted for their clever wordplay, nonsensical meanings, and delightfully zany words.

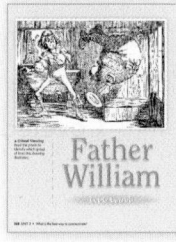

"Jim"

Gwendolyn Brooks (1917–2000) began writing at the age of seven and published her first poem, "Eventide," at age thirteen. As an adult, Brooks wrote hundreds of poems, many of which focus on the African American experience. In 1950, she became the first African American to win a Pulitzer Prize.

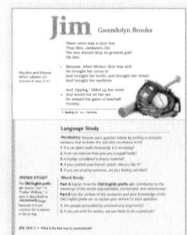

Stopping by Woods on a Snowy Evening
Robert Frost

Whose woods these are I think I know.
His house is in the village, though;
He will not see me stopping here
To watch his woods fill up with snow.

5 My little horse must think it queer
To stop without a farmhouse near
Between the woods and frozen lake
The darkest evening of the year.

He gives his harness bells a shake
10 To ask if there is some mistake.
The only other sound's the sweep
Of easy wind and downy flake.

The woods are lovely, dark, and deep,
But I have promises to keep,
15 And miles to go before I sleep,
And miles to go before I sleep.

Rhythm and Rhyme
In lines 1–8, which lines end with rhyming words?

◄ **Vocabulary**
downy (dou′ nē)
adj. soft and fluffy

Annabel Lee

Edgar Allan Poe

Rhythm and Rhyme
Which syllables are stressed in the first two lines?

It was many and many a year ago,
    In a kingdom by the sea,
That a maiden there lived whom you may know
    By the name of Annabel Lee;
And this maiden she lived with no other thought
    Than to love and be loved by me.

I was a child and *she* was a child,
    In this kingdom by the sea.
5 But we loved with a love that was more than love—
    I and my Annabel Lee—
With a love that the wingèd seraphs[1] of Heaven
    Coveted her and me.

And this was the reason that, long ago,
    In this kingdom by the sea,
A wind blew out of a cloud, chilling
    My beautiful Annabel Lee;
So that her highborn kinsmen came
    And bore her away from me,
10 To shut her up in a sepulcher[2]
    In this kingdom by the sea.

Vocabulary ▶
coveted (kuv´ it əd)
v. wanted; desired

---

1. **wingèd seraphs** (ser´ efs) *n.* angels.
2. **sepulcher** (sep´ əl kər) *n.* vault or chamber for burial; tomb.

The angels, not half so happy in Heaven,
    Went **envying** her and me:—
Yes! that was the reason (as all men know,
    In this kingdom by the sea)
That the wind came out of a cloud by night,
    Chilling and killing my Annabel Lee.

But our love it was stronger by far than the love
    Of those who were older than we—
    Of many far wiser than we—
15 And neither the angels in Heaven above
    Nor the demons down under the sea
Can ever dissever[3] my soul from the soul
    Of the beautiful Annabel Lee;

For the moon never beams, without bringing
    me dreams
Of the beautiful Annabel Lee;
And the stars never rise, but I feel the bright eyes
    Of the beautiful Annabel Lee;
20 And so, all the night-tide, I lie down by the side
Of my darling—my darling—my life and my bride,
    In her sepulcher there by the sea—
    In her tomb by the sounding sea.

◀ **Vocabulary**
envying (en´ vē iŋ) *v.*
wanting something
that someone else has

Paraphrase
How would you
paraphrase lines 15–18?

---

3. dissever (di sev ´ ər) *v.* separate; divide.

▲ **Critical Viewing**
Read the poem to
identify which group
of lines this drawing
illustrates.

Father William

Lewis Carroll

"You are old, Father William," the young man said,
　　"And your hair has become very white;
And yet you **incessantly** stand on your head—
　　Do you think, at your age, it is right?"

5　"In my youth," Father William replied to his son,
　　"I feared it might injure the brain;
But, now that I'm perfectly sure I have none,
　　Why, I do it again and again."

　"You are old," said the youth, "as I mentioned before.
10　　And have grown most **uncommonly** fat;
Yet you turned a back-somersault in at the door—
　　Pray, what is the reason of that?"

　"In my youth," said the sage, as he shook his gray locks,
　　"I kept all my limbs very **supple**
15 By the use of this ointment—one shilling[1] the box—
　　Allow me to sell you a couple?"

　"You are old," said the youth, "and your jaws are too weak
　　For anything tougher than suet;[2]
Yet you finished the goose, with the bones and the beak—
20　　Pray, how did you manage to do it?"

　"In my youth," said his father, "I took to the law,
　　And argued each case with my wife;
And the muscular strength, which it gave to my jaw,
　　Has lasted the rest of my life."

25　"You are old," said the youth, "one would hardly suppose
　　That your eye was as steady as ever;
Yet you balanced an eel on the end of your nose—
　　What made you so awfully clever?"

　"I have answered three questions, and that is enough,"
30　　Said his father; "don't give yourself airs!
Do you think I can listen all day to such stuff?
　　Be off, or I'll kick you downstairs!"

---

1. shilling (shil´iŋ) *n.* British coin.
2. suet (soo´it) *n.* fat used in cooking.

◀ **Vocabulary**

incessantly (in ses´ ənt lē) *adv.* without stopping

uncommonly (un käm´ ən lē) *adv.* remarkably

supple (sup´ əl) *adj.* able to bend easily; flexible

Paraphrase
How would you paraphrase "Don't give yourself airs!"?

Jim

Gwendolyn Brooks

There never was a nicer boy
Than Mrs. Jackson's Jim.
The sun should drop its greatest gold
On him.

Rhythm and Rhyme
Which syllables are
stressed in lines 5–6?

5 Because, when Mother-dear was sick,
   He brought her cocoa in.
   And brought her broth, and brought her bread.
   And brought her medicine.

   And, tipping,¹ tidied up her room.
10 And would not let her see
   He missed his game of baseball
   Terribly.

___

1. tipping (tip´ iŋ) *v.* tiptoeing.

Language Study

Vocabulary Answer each question below by writing a complete sentence that includes the italicized vocabulary word.

1. If a car alarm wails *incessantly,* is it annoying?

2. How can exercise help give you a *supple* body?

3. Is burlap considered a *downy* material?

4. If you *coveted* your friend's jacket, did you like it?

5. If you are *envying* someone, are you feeling satisfied?

WORD STUDY

The **Old English prefix un-** means "not." In "Father William," a man is described as **uncommonly** large because it is not common for a person to be so big.

Word Study

Part A Explain how the **Old English prefix un-** contributes to the meanings of the words *unpredictable, unintended,* and *uninformed.*

Part B Use the context of the sentences and your knowledge of the Old English prefix *un-* to explain your answer to each question.

1. Are people persuaded by *unconvincing* arguments?

2. If you are *unfit* for service, are you likely to do a good job?

Close Reading Activities

Literary Analysis

Key Ideas and Details

1. **Paraphrase** Paraphrase the following lines:
   (a) lines 11–12 of "Stopping by Woods on a Snowy Evening"
   (b) lines 9–10 of "Annabel Lee"
   (c) lines 13–16 of "Father William"
   (d) lines 3–4 of "Jim"

2. **Paraphrase** Identify two words in these poems that you might look up in a dictionary to help you paraphrase meaning.

3. **(a)** In "Jim," what tasks does the boy perform for his mother? **(b) Infer:** What detail tells you that Jim is not selfish?

4. **(a)** In "Annabel Lee," how does the speaker react to Annabel Lee's death? Provide a quotation from the poem to support your answer. **(b) Infer:** What will prevent the separation of the speaker's soul from Annabel Lee's soul? Support your answer.

Craft and Structure

5. **Sound Devices (a)** Do all the poems have rhythmic patterns? Explain. **(b)** Which poem has the most interesting rhythm? Support your opinion with examples from the text.

6. **Sound Devices** Use a chart like the one on the right to analyze rhyme in each poem.

7. **Sound Devices (a)** What words in Frost's poem describe sights and sounds? **(b)** What is the mood, or feeling, of the poem?

Poem	Rhyming Words
Father William	
Stopping by Woods . . .	
Jim	
Annabel Lee	

Integration of Knowledge and Ideas

8. **(a)** In "Stopping by Woods on a Snowy Evening," why has the speaker stopped? **(b) Infer:** What about the place captures his attention? **(c) Speculate:** Why do you think Frost uses the image of a snowy night to communicate the idea of the journey through life?

9. **(a)** Identify two misconceptions about older people that Carroll pokes fun at in "Father William." **(b) Synthesize:** What misconceptions do you think people have today about older people? Explain why they are misconceptions.

10. **What is the best way to communicate? (a)** Which of these poems do you think expresses the most emotion toward its subject? **(b)** How is emotion most clearly communicated in the poem? Explain, citing textual details.

ACADEMIC VOCABULARY

As you write and speak about Poetry Collection 4, use the words related to communication that you explored on page 313 of this textbook.

Conventions: **Subject-Verb Agreement**

> To maintain correct **subject-verb agreement,** subjects and verbs must agree in number.

To check subject-verb agreement, determine whether the subject is singular or plural and then make sure the verb matches.

Singular subject and verb: Sarah enjoys swimming.
Plural subject and verb: They enjoy bowling.

A compound subject consists of two subjects joined by a conjunction such as *and, or,* or *nor.* When the subjects joined are plural, they take a plural verb. When the subjects joined are singular, refer to the rules in the chart below.

Two or more singular subjects joined by *and* take a plural verb.	*Running* **and** *tennis* **are** both fun sports.
Singular subjects joined by *or* or *nor* take a singular verb.	*Running* **or** *walking* **is** good exercise. Neither *running* **nor** *walking* **is** a waste of time.
When singular and plural subjects are joined by *or* or *nor,* the verb must agree with the closer subject.	Neither the *roast* **nor** the *potatoes* **are** cooking. Concert *tickets* **or** a fancy *dinner* **is** a great gift.

Practice A

Complete each sentence with one of the verbs in parentheses.

1. Mrs. Jackson's son Jim (were/was) a very nice boy.
2. The man and his horse (stop/stops) by the woods.
3. Neither Father William nor his son (play/plays) baseball.
4. Annabel Lee and her kinsmen (go/goes) away from the speaker.

Reading Application In Poetry Collection 4, find three subjects and verbs that illustrate subject-verb agreement.

Practice B

Complete each sentence with a subject that agrees with the verb.

1. Neither _____ nor his _____ feels well.
2. Either the _____ or the _____ has filled up with snow.
3. _____ and _____ have a conversation about getting old.

Writing Application Write three sentences about poetry. Include one sentence with a singular subject, one with a plural subject, and one with a compound subject. Make sure subjects and verbs agree.

Writing to Sources

Poetry Write a **poem** about a person you know.

- Review the poems in this collection and note techniques and words the poets use to effectively portray a person.

- Then, choose someone to whom you would like to pay tribute or who evokes a strong emotion in you.

- Collect your thoughts by taking notes that describe the person and convey your feelings about him or her.

- Draft your lines. After you have expressed your ideas and feelings, revise your poem using rhythm to add a musical quality.

- Type your poem on a computer using a word-processing or publishing program. Use text-editing features such as the thesaurus and spell-check as you revise and edit your poem. Post your poem on the classroom Web site.

Grammar Application Check your writing to make sure your subjects and verbs agree.

Research and Technology

Build and Present Knowledge Conduct a **survey** in which you ask classmates to rate the poems from Poetry Collection 4 according to specific categories. These categories may include best character description, best use of language, or best rhythm, rhyme, and meter.

- Formulate the survey questions. Evaluate your questions to be sure they are clear and answerable.

- Count the number of votes that each poem receives in each category. Then, note which poems received the most votes in each category.

- With a small group, discuss the survey results. Generate questions to evaluate whether the survey was or was not effective and why. Refer to specific examples and details from the poems to support your evaluations.

 **Common Core State Standards**

Writing

6. Use technology, including the Internet, to produce and publish writing and link to and cite sources as well as to interact and collaborate with others, including linking to and citing sources.

7. Conduct short research projects to answer a question, drawing on several sources and generating additional related, focused questions for further research and investigation.

Speaking and Listening

1.c. Pose questions that elicit elaboration and respond to others' questions and comments with relevant observations and ideas that bring the discussion back on topic as needed.

2. Analyze the main ideas and supporting details presented in diverse media and formats (e.g., visually, quantitatively, orally) and explain how the ideas clarify a topic, text, or issue under study.

Language

1. Demonstrate command of the conventions of standard English grammar and usage when writing or speaking.

What is the best way to communicate?

Explore the Big Question as you read these poems. Take notes on the ways in which each poem communicates a particular view of the world.

READING TO COMPARE IMAGERY

Poets Walt Whitman and E. E. Cummings use imagery to paint vivid pictures in the minds of readers. As you read the poems, consider how descriptive language can make the reader "see" exactly what the writer sees. Compare the role imagery plays in each poem.

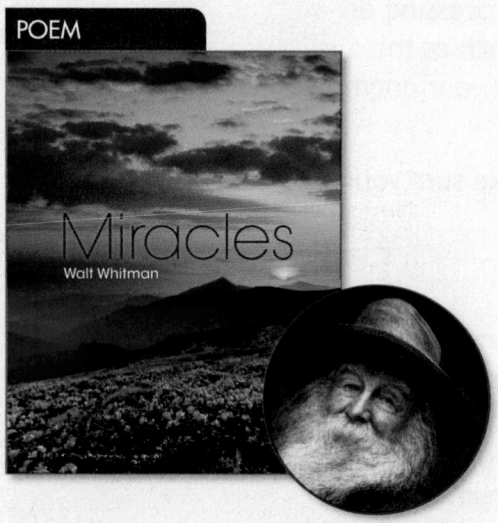

"Miracles"

Walt Whitman (1819–1892)
Walt Whitman worked at many occupations during his life. He was a printer, a teacher, and a newspaper reporter. In 1855, Whitman first published *Leaves of Grass*. In this book, he abandoned regular rhyme and rhythm in favor of free verse, which followed no set pattern. Now considered a masterpiece, the book led critics to regard Whitman as the father of American poetry.

"in Just—"

E. E. Cummings (1894–1962)
Edward Estlin Cummings published his first collection of poetry in the early 1920s. The work stood out for many reasons, including Cummings's original use of language and unusual punctuation, capitalization, and spacing. Cummings often wrote poems that were playful and humorous. These poems reflected his attitude that "the most wasted of all days is one without laughter."

Comparing Imagery

In poetry, an **image** is a word or phrase that appeals to one or more of the five senses. Poets use **imagery** to bring their poems to life with descriptions of how their subjects look, sound, feel, taste, and smell. Here are two examples:

- The phrase "the sweet, slippery mango slices" appeals to the senses of taste and touch.
- The phrase "glaring lights and wailing sirens" appeals to the senses of sight and hearing.

Writers also create **mood** through their use of images, words, and descriptive details. Mood is the feeling created in the reader by a literary work or passage. The mood of a work may be described with adjectives such as *joyous, gloomy, cozy,* or *frightening.*

To fully appreciate images and experience the mood in a poem, determine the meanings of any unfamiliar words the poet uses—including words the poet has made up. Also, pay close attention to the *connotations*—or emotional associations—of words, as well as to their figurative, or nonliteral, meanings.

Both "Miracles" and "in Just—" contain images that appeal to the senses. In a chart like the one below, keep track of the images in the two poems. Note the sense that an image appeals to and write the image in the appropriate box. Keep in mind that some images may appeal to more than one sense, so you may put an image into more than one box. After you read, use your chart to help you compare and contrast the authors' use of imagery.

Common Core State Standards

Reading Literature

4. Determine the meaning of words and phrases as they are used in a text, including figurative and connotative meanings; analyze the impact of rhymes and other repetitions of sounds on a specific verse or stanza of a poem or section of a story or drama.

Writing

1. Write arguments to support claims with clear reasons and relevant evidence.

Language

5.c. Distinguish among the connotations (associations) of words with similar denotations (definitions) (e.g., *refined, respectful, polite, diplomatic, condescending*).

Sense	Images	
	"Miracles"	"in Just—"
Sight		
Hearing		
Touch/Movement		
Taste		
Smell		

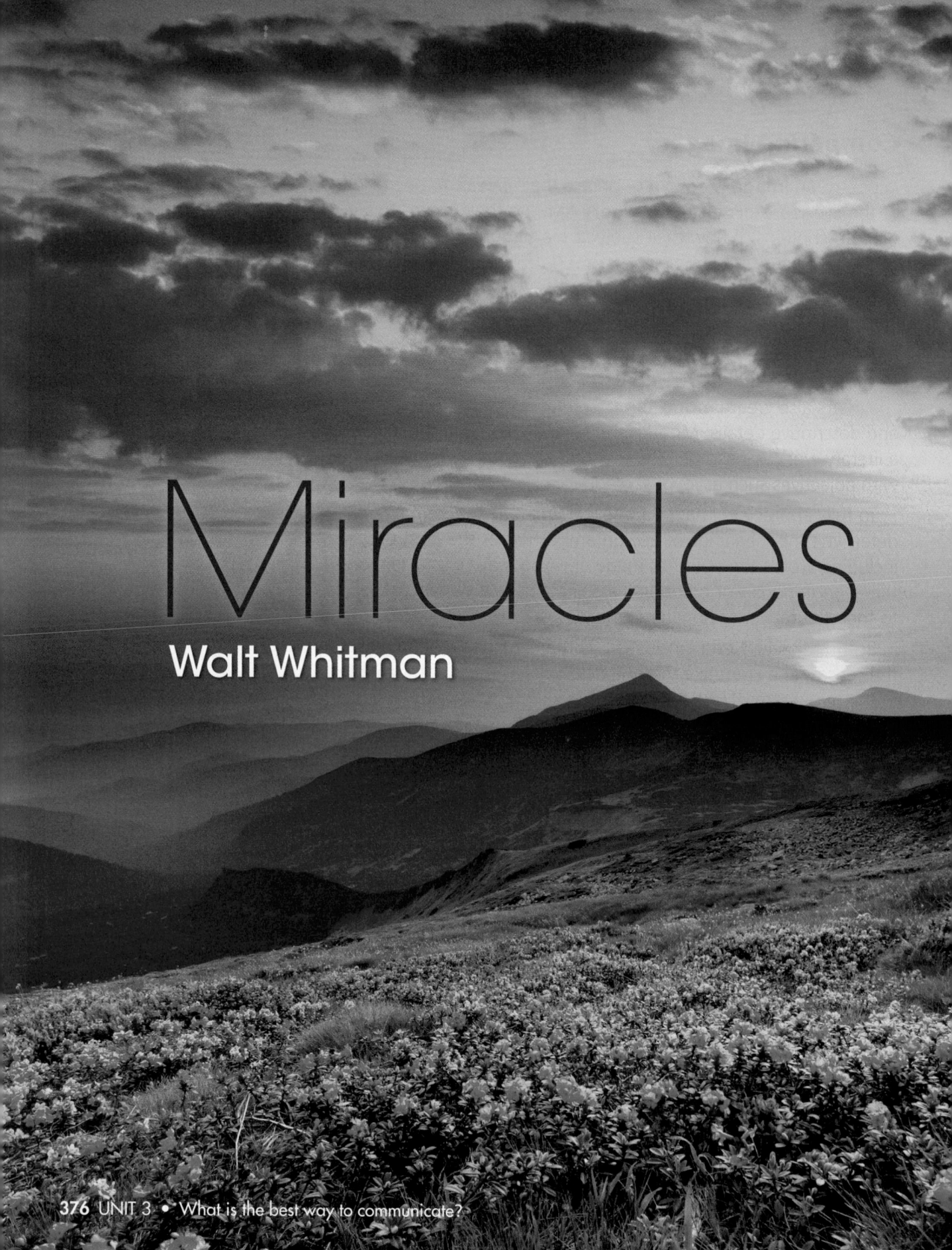

Miracles

Walt Whitman

Why, who makes much of a miracle?
As to me I know of nothing else but miracles,
Whether I walk the streets of Manhattan,
Or dart my sight over the roofs of houses toward the sky,
5 Or wade with naked feet along the beach just in the edge
       of the water,
Or stand under trees in the woods,
Or talk by day with any one I love . . .
Or sit at table at dinner with the rest,
Or look at strangers opposite me riding in the car,
10 Or watch honey-bees busy around the hive of a summer
       forenoon,
Or animals feeding in the fields,
Or birds, or the wonderfulness of insects in the air,
Or the wonderfulness of the sundown, or of stars shining
       so quiet and bright,
Or the exquisite delicate thin curve of the new moon in
       spring;
15 These with the rest, one and all, are to me miracles,
The whole referring, yet each distinct and in its place.

To me every hour of the light and dark is a miracle,
Every cubic inch of space is a miracle,
Every square yard of the surface of the earth is spread
       with the same,
20 Every foot of the interior swarms with the same.

To me the sea is a continual miracle,
The fishes that swim—the rocks—the motion of the
       waves—the ships with men in them,
What stranger miracles are there?

◄ **Critical Viewing**
Does this photograph convey the feelings expressed by the speaker in the poem? Explain.

Imagery
Which image in the first seven lines appeals to the sense of touch?

◄ **Vocabulary**
exquisite
(eks´ kwiz it) *adj.*
beautiful in a delicate way

distinct (di stiŋkt´)
adj. separate and different

Critical Thinking

1. **Key Ideas and Details (a) Classify:** List events that the speaker calls miracles. **(b) Infer:** Why is the sea a "continual miracle"?

2. **Integration of Knowledge and Ideas** Why do you think Whitman decided to use poetry to describe the beauty around him? [Connect to the Big Question: *What is the best way to communicate?*]

in Just–

E.E. Cummings

in Just—
spring   when the world is mud-
luscious the little
lame balloonman

5 whistles   far   and wee

and eddieandbill come
running from marbles and
piracies and it's
spring

10 when the world is puddle-wonderful

the queer
old balloonman whistles
far   and   wee
and bettyandisbel come dancing

15 from hop-scotch and jump-rope and

it's
spring
and
     the

20   goat-footed

balloonMan   whistles
far
and
wee

Critical Thinking

1. **Key Ideas and Details** **(a)** What scene does the speaker describe? **(b) Analyze:** Why do you think he uses unusual words such as "mud-luscious"?

2. **Craft and Structure** Cummings breaks many language conventions. When do you think a writer should be allowed to break grammatical rules? *[Connect to the Big Question: What is the best way to communicate?]*

Comparing Imagery

1. **Craft and Structure** Give an example from each poem of an image that appeals to the senses listed below. Then, explain the meaning, including the connotations, of key words in each image. **(a)** hearing **(b)** touch

2. **Craft and Structure (a)** Using a chart like the one shown, identify and explain sight images in each poem. Explain the meaning, including the connotations, of key words in each image. **(b)** Which poem has more vivid sight images? Why?

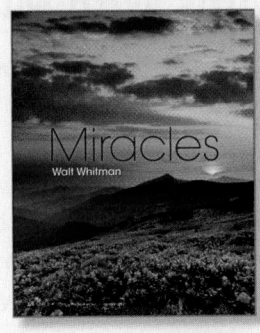

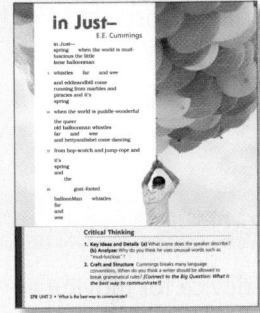

Miracles	in Just—
Image:	Image:
Effect:	Effect:

 Timed Writing

Argument: Recommendation
Write an essay in which you recommend one of the two poems to someone your age. Choose the poem that you believe provides more effective examples of imagery. Include details from the text to support your claim. **(40 minutes)**

5-Minute Planner
1. Read the prompt carefully and completely.

2. Gather your ideas by jotting down answers to these questions:
   - What do you find fascinating or distinctive about the imagery in the poem you recommend?
   - Which images are most meaningful to you?
   - In what ways is the imagery in your chosen poem more effective than the imagery in the other poem?

3. To help you address the questions above, review the graphic organizer you completed as you read the poems.

4. Reread the prompt, and then draft your essay. Remember to support your argument with clear reasons and relevant textual evidence.

USE ACADEMIC VOCABULARY

As you write, use academic language, including the following words or their related forms:

appreciate

insight

perceive

unique

For more information about academic vocabulary, see pages xlvi–l.

Words With Multiple Meanings

A **multiple-meaning word** is a word that has more than one definition. Many words in English have multiple meanings; for example, *peach* can be defined as a color or a fruit. To determine the meaning intended in a sentence, you must consider the context, or the overall meaning of the sentence or paragraph in which the word appears. You also need to look at the function of the word in the sentence. Some words with multiple meanings can be used as different parts of speech. The following chart shows a multiple-meaning word used in two different sentences.

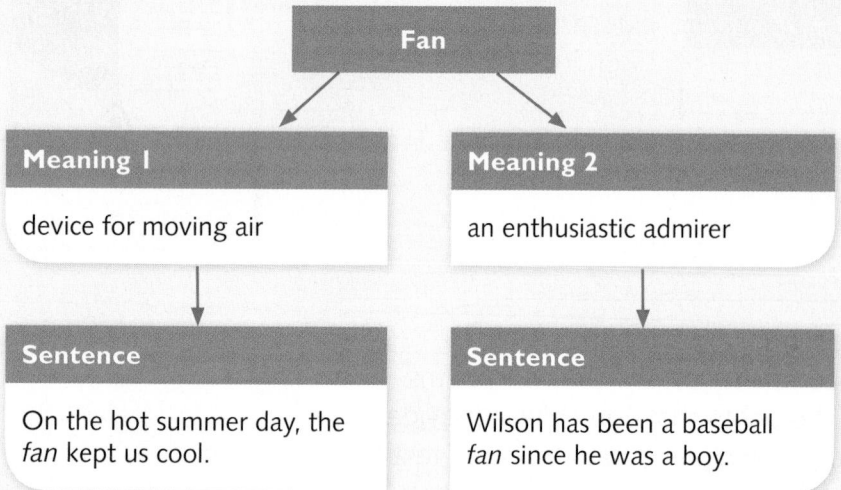

Fan

Meaning 1	Meaning 2
device for moving air	an enthusiastic admirer

Sentence	Sentence
On the hot summer day, the *fan* kept us cool.	Wilson has been a baseball *fan* since he was a boy.

© **Common Core State Standards**

Language

4. Determine or clarify the meaning of unknown and multiple-meaning words and phrases based on *grade 7 reading and content,* choosing flexibly from a range of strategies.

4.a. Use context (e.g., the overall meaning of a sentence or paragraph; a word's position or function in a sentence) as a clue to the meaning of a word or phrase.

4.c. Consult general and specialized reference materials (e.g., dictionaries, glossaries, thesauruses), both print and digital, to find the pronunciation of a word or determine or clarify its precise meaning or its part of speech.

4.d. Verify the preliminary determination of the meaning of a word or phrase (e.g., by checking the inferred meaning in context or in a dictionary).

Practice A

Write the meaning of each italicized word. Verify the meaning in a dictionary.

1. a. When the *bats* swooped down on my head, I let out a scream.

  b. I wish we could get new *bats* for our softball team this year.

2. a. Julian was not *present* to collect the prize he won.

  b. I decided to make my sister's birthday *present* this year.

3. a. The *second* hand on the clock ticked loudly.

  b. Liliana won *second* prize at the science fair.

4. a. We saved the *rest* of the cake for the next class.

  b. After running a mile in track, we all needed a *rest*.

Practice B

For each word listed, write two sentences that use different meanings of the word. If necessary, look up the meanings in a dictionary.

1. kind

2. object

3. express

4. ring

5. dash

6. season

7. desert

8. seal

Activity Use a print or digital dictionary to learn about the following multiple-meaning words: *power, degree, dynamite, file,* and *patient*. Write each word on a separate notecard like the one shown. Fill in the left column of the notecard with one of the word's meanings. Fill in the right column with another of the word's meanings. Then, trade notecards with a partner, and discuss the different meanings and uses of the words that each of you found.

Word: _____	
Part of Speech:	**Part of Speech:**
Definition:	**Definition:**
Example Sentence:	**Example Sentence:**

Comprehension and Collaboration

Work with two or three classmates to write a sentence that uses two different meanings of each of the following words. For example: *While we sat in a traffic jam, I was able to eat my breakfast of toast and jam.*

- **fair**
- **long**
- **last**

Evaluating Media Messages and Advertisements

Media messages and advertisements appear on television, the radio, and the Internet. To ensure you understand and respond appropriately to these messages, critically evaluate them using the strategies in this lesson.

Learn the Skills

Determine the purpose. Identify the purpose, or goal, of the message. Some messages are meant to inform, to persuade, or to entertain. Some messages are attempts to sell you something or to convince you to do something.

Analyze images and sounds. Think critically about what you see and hear. Notice how the mood created by music and sounds influences your response to the message. Analyze the differences between images and sounds used in messages designed to sell and those used in messages designed to inform.

Challenge the claims and evidence. Analyze the accuracy of the claims. Consider whether the reasoning is logical and whether sufficient and relevant evidence supports the claims.

Identify propaganda techniques. To effectively analyze the logic of the messages, be alert to techniques involving faulty reasoning.

- **Slant and Bias:** Beware of any message that presents only one side of a many-sided issue.

- **Bandwagon Appeal:** Beware of messages that suggest you will feel left out if you do not do or buy something.

- **Spokespersons:** Ask yourself whether the spokesperson for the message has the knowledge to back up his or her claims.

Analyze the use of language. Advertisers use language to appeal to certain groups of people. For example, formal language can make messages seem more accurate. While informal language and popular slang are often used to appeal to a younger audience.

Interpret visual techniques. Lighting can draw attention to specific parts of an image or create a certain mood. Camera angles can influence the way you view an image. For instance, a close-up shot can focus your attention on a single subject, whereas a panoramic shot will show you the larger context but with few details. Special visual effects can change or enhance an existing image to increase audience appeal or interest.

 **Common Core State Standards**

Speaking and Listening

2. Analyze the main ideas and supporting details presented in diverse media and formats and explain how the ideas clarify a topic, text, or issue under study.

3. Delineate a speaker's argument and specific claims, evaluating the soundness of the reasoning and the relevance and sufficiency of the evidence.

Practice the Skills

Presentation of Knowledge and Ideas Use what you have learned in this workshop to complete the following activity.

ACTIVITY: Evaluate Media Advertisements

Watch three television commercials. Then, follow these steps:

- Identify the message and interpret the purpose of each commercial.

- Ask questions that help you evaluate the evidence that supports the claims in each commercial.

- Explain how each commercial makes you feel.

- List memorable details from each commercial, such as special effects, camera angles, lighting, and music. Explain how these elements support the purpose of the commercial.

- Use the Interpretation Guide to interpret the advertisements.

Use the Interpretation Guide to analyze the content of each commercial.

Interpretation Guide

Visual Techniques
Which visual techniques are evident in the advertisement? Briefly explain each.

- ❏ camera angles   ❏ special effects
- ❏ special lighting   ❏ other visual

Sound Techniques
Which sound techniques are evident in the advertisement? Briefly explain each.

- ❏ music   ❏ special effects   ❏ other visual techniques

Messages
What is the ad's message? How can you tell?

Claims and Evidence
Does the advertisement conatin claims about a product? If so, what are they? What evidence is provided to support the claims? Is the evidence relevant? Is there enough reasonable evidence to support the claims? Explain.

Purpose
What is the purpose of the advertisement?

Comprehension and Collaboration Compare your findings with those of your classmates. As a group, interpret how visual and sound techniques influence the message in an advertisement.

Write an Explanatory Text

Comparison-and-Contrast Essay

Defining the Form In a **comparison-and-contrast essay,** the writer analyzes the similarities and differences between two or more related subjects. You might use elements of this form in persuasive essays, journals, and reviews.

Assignment Write a comparison-and-contrast essay that helps readers make a decision or see old things in a fresh way. Your essay should feature these elements:

✓ A *topic involving two or more things* that are neither nearly identical nor extremely different

✓ *Relevant facts, descriptions and examples* that illustrate *both similarities and differences*

✓ A *clear organization* that highlights the points of comparison

✓ An *introduction* that grabs readers' interest, and a strong, memorable *conclusion*

✓ error-free writing, including the correct use of *sentence structures that clarify relationships*

To preview the criteria on which your comparison-and-contrast essay may be judged, see the rubric on page 391.

FOCUS ON RESEARCH

When you write a comparison-and-contrast essay, you might conduct research to

• learn background information about each subject.

• locate facts, statistics, or other details that describe each subject.

• find quotations that highlight key details about each subject.

When presenting your research, be sure to cite your sources properly. The Research Workshop in the Introductory Unit contains information on how to cite sources.

Common Core State Standards

Writing
2. Write informative/explanatory texts to examine a topic and convey ideas, concepts, and information through the selection, organization, and analysis of relevant content.
2.a. Introduce a topic clearly, previewing what is to follow; organize ideas, concepts, and information, using strategies such as definition, classification, comparison/contrast, and cause/effect.
2.b. Develop the topic and relevant facts, definitions, concrete details, quotations, or other information and examples.
2.d. Use precise language and domain-specific vocabulary to inform about or explain the topic.
2.e. Establish and maintain a formal style.

Prewriting/Planning Strategies

Choose a topic. To choose a topic for your essay, use one of these strategies:

- **Quicklist** Fold a piece of paper in thirds lengthwise. In the first column, list recent choices you have made—for instance, products you have bought or activities you have completed. In the second column, next to each choice, write a precise descriptive phrase. In the third column, give an alternative to your choice.

  Example: polka-dot sweatshirt / playful, silly / team jacket
  Review your list, and choose the most interesting pairing to compare and contrast.

- **BUT Chart** Write the word BUT down the center of a piece of paper. On the left, list items with something in common. List differences among them on the right. Then, choose your topic from this list.

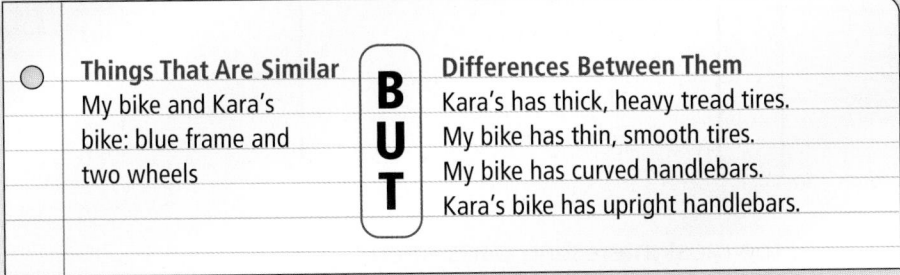

Get specific. You may find that your topic is too broad to cover in a brief essay. Use the following strategies to narrow your topic.

- **Describe it** to someone who is not familiar with it.
- **Apply it,** explaining what you can do with it, on it, or to it.
- **Analyze it** by breaking it into parts.
- **Argue for or against it,** explaining good and bad points, while maintaining a formal style.

Examine the specific details from your notes and circle those that can be connected to create a focused topic.

Show similarities and differences. Focus on gathering details that show similarities and differences between your subjects. Use a Venn diagram to organize your details. Fill in details about one subject on the left side of the diagram and details about the other on the right side. Use the middle section to list common features.

Drafting Strategies

Organize the body of your draft. Your essay should be easy for readers to follow and understand. There are two main ways to organize a comparison-and-contrast essay. Choose the organization that is most appropriate to your topic and purpose.

- **Block Method** Present all the details about one of your subjects, and then present all the details about your next subject. This method works well if you are writing about more than two subjects or if your topic is complex.

- **Point-by-Point Method** Discuss one aspect of both subjects, then another aspect of both subjects, and so on.

Methods of Organization

Block Method
A. Theater
1. Amount of variety
2. Intensity
3. Realism
B. Television
1. Amount of variety
2. Intensity
3. Realism

Point-by-Point Comparison
A. Amount of Variety
1. Theater
2. Television
B. Intensity
1. Theater
2. Television
C. Realism
1. Theater
2. Television

Layer ideas using SEE. Often, the most interesting parts of an essay are the details you offer to support your main ideas. Use the SEE method to ensure that your main ideas are supported with strong elaboration.

- *State* your main idea in every paragraph to stay on topic.
- *Extend* the idea with an example that proves the main idea.
- *Elaborate* by offering further details to describe your example.

Include formatting, graphics, and multimedia. Use headings to highlight the main sections in your paper. Graphics, such as charts and tables, or multimedia, such as a tape recording or slide show, can strengthen your ideas and further audience comprehension.

Clarify relationships. Use words and phrases to show relationships between ideas. Transitions that show comparisons include *also, just as, like,* and *similarly.* Transitions that show contrasts include *although, but, however, on the other hand, whereas,* and *while.*

Common Core State Standards

Writing

2.a. Organize ideas, concepts, and information, using strategies such as definition, classification, comparison/contrast, and cause/effect; include formatting, graphics, and multimedia when useful to aiding comprehension.

2.b. Develop the topic and relevant facts, definitions, concrete details, quotations, or other information and examples.

2.c. Use appropriate transitions to create cohesion and clarify the relationships among ideas and concepts.

4. Produce clear and coherent writing in which the development, organization, and style are appropriate to task, purpose, and audience.

Developing Your Ideas

Ideas make up the content of any piece of writing. In your comparison-and-contrast essay, you may have several thoughts about your subjects that are based on your own experience. Other ideas may come from your research. Follow these tips to develop your ideas.

Focus on important features. Begin by listing all the features you can think of for each subject. Then, review your list to identify features that are very important and those that are less important. Write "key" next to the important features. These are the ideas you should focus on as you write your essay.

Choose relevant details. Make sure that the details you include are relevant. For example, in an essay comparing Walt Whitman's free verse to rhyming poetry, the lives of Whitman or another poet are probably not relevant. Instead, you should focus on the characteristics of each kind of poetry.

Make comparisons complete. To make your comparisons effective, provide similar information on each subject. For example, suppose you are writing to compare the cities of New York and London. If you write about the size, diversity, and industries of New York, you should write about the same features of London in order to present a balanced comparison. Of course, you may describe a feature found in one subject but not in the other to show an important difference between your subjects. For example, if you are comparing two kinds of birds, the fact that penguins can swim but eagles cannot may be a significant detail. Use a chart similar to the one below to organize your points of comparison.

Feature	Subject 1	Subject 2
Feature 1		
Feature 2		
Feature 3		
Feature 4		

Revising Strategies

Heighten interest. Check your essay to make sure it grabs and holds your readers' attention. Use the following strategies:

- Sharpen your introduction to intrigue readers, and encourage them to read further. Consider including a strong image, a surprising comparison, or a thought-provoking question or quotation.
- Add details that are surprising, colorful, and important.
- Add headings, relevant graphics, or multimedia.
- Add language, such as transitions, to emphasize similarities or differences.
- Rework your conclusion to add impact or leave readers with a lingering question. Be sure your conclusion makes the value of the comparison and contrast clear.

Writing
2.e. Provide a concluding statement or section that follows from and supports the information or explanation presented.
4. Produce clear and coherent writing in which the development, organization, and style are appropriate to task, purpose, and audience.
5. With some guidance and support from peers and adults, develop and strengthen writing as needed by planning, revising, editing, rewriting, or trying a new approach, focusing on how well purpose and audience have been addressed.

Language
1.b. Choose among simple, compound, complex, and compound-complex sentences to signal differing relationships among ideas.
1.c. Place phrases and clauses within a sentence, recognizing and correcting misplaced and dangling modifiers.
3.a. Choose language that expresses ideas precisely and concisely, recognizing and eliminating wordiness and redundancy.

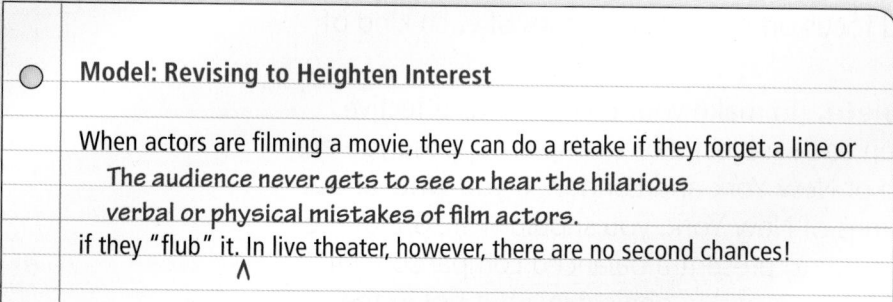

Model: Revising to Heighten Interest

When actors are filming a movie, they can do a retake if they forget a line or
The audience never gets to see or hear the hilarious
verbal or physical mistakes of film actors.
if they "flub" it. In live theater, however, there are no second chances!

Avoid repetition. Check your writing for unnecessary repetition. Sometimes writers will repeat a point but add something slightly different the second time. You can avoid repetition by combining the two sentences to include the additional information while increasing interest with sentence variety.

Repetitive: Lastly, the best thing about theater is it's real. What I mean is you see when people make mistakes. You see people being human by making mistakes every so often.

Combined: Lastly, the best thing about theater is it's human and real. You can see when people make mistakes.

Peer Review

Read your revised draft to a teacher or classmate. Ask whether you repeated information. Together, look for ways to make your writing clearer and less repetitive.

Revising Sentence Structures to Clarify Relationships

Coordination relates two clauses of equal importance. **Subordination** relates a less important clause to a more important clause. Choosing the correct word to link these clauses will clarify the relationships.

Revising Sentences to Clarify Coordination If two clauses are related and of equal weight, use **coordinating conjunctions.** *And* can be used to join related clauses. Often, though, the conjunctions *or, but,* or *so* can make the relationship between the clauses clearer, as in this example:

> **Original sentence:** It was raining, *and we* took the car.

> **Revised sentence:** It was raining, *so we* took the car.

Revising Sentences to Clarify Subordination If the clauses are not equal, you must use a **subordinating conjunction** or a **relative pronoun.** Conjunctions such as *after, before,* and *when* indicate time. *Because* or *since* show cause and effect, as in this example:

> *When* the curtain fell, the audience burst into applause.

Avoiding Dangling and Misplaced Modifiers Be careful to avoid dangling and misplaced modifiers. A **dangling modifier** does not modify any word in the sentence; a **misplaced modifier** modifies the wrong word. Revise your writing to fix these problems.

> **Fixing a Dangling Modifier**
> **Incorrect:** After beginning to boil, we turned the heat off.
> **Correct:** After the water began to boil, we turned the heat off.

> **Fixing a Misplaced Modifier**
> **Incorrect:** I viewed a video on my computer that I had never seen before.
> **Correct:** On my computer, I viewed a video that I had never seen before.

Grammar in Your Writing

Review your draft, looking for relationships between ideas that you can clarify by using coordination or subordination. In addition, look for dangling or misplaced modifiers. Revise your comparison-and-contrast essay to fix these issues.

Stage vs. Set

Theater or television? If you are under eighteen, you more than likely said "television." Have you ever stopped to consider what the magical world of theater has to offer?

Anyone who has been to the theater can tell you that there is nothing like the feeling of sitting and watching people perform. Actors get something special out of theater, too. Knowing that hundreds of people are watching your every move creates a special kind of excitement.

There's also variety. In live theater, every show is different. When you watch a rerun on television, it's the exact same thing every time. With theater, you get a different experience every night. You can go to see the same show with a different cast or director and the performance will be totally different. Even if you go to a show with the same cast and director, it will be different. An actor might forget a line and improvise or suddenly decide to change the way he or she is playing a character in a scene. The audience never knows exactly what will happen.

Theater is also larger than the drama you see on television. I don't care how big a screen your television has, theater will always be BIGGER—the emotion more passionate, the voices louder, and the effect more profound. In theater, you have to project your voice and movements so that they carry to the back rows of the audience. In television, actors just need to be seen and heard by the cameras and microphones.

Lastly, the best thing about theater is it's human and real. You see when people make mistakes. On television, everything has to be perfect or they do a retake. You never see television actors miss a line or trip over their feet. Since there is no second chance in theater, everything is more spontaneous. When a performance takes an unexpected turn, the audience gets to see the professionalism of the actors as they respond to something new.

Next time you're channel surfing and there's nothing good on, why not take some time to check out what's playing in your community playhouse? Who knows? Maybe you'll discover a rising talent. Even better, maybe you'll decide you want to become an actor or actress after you see how thrilling a live production really is.

In the first paragraph, Mackenzie introduces the comparison in a way that grabs the reader's attention. She compares things that are alike, yet different.

Mackenzie develops her argument by including examples and explanations, using the point-by-point method of organization.

Mackenzie uses elaboration to support her main points.

In the final paragraph, Mackenzie offers a strong conclusion that challenges the reader to accept her point of view.

Editing and Proofreading

Review your draft to correct errors in grammar, spelling, and punctuation.

Focus on empty language. Review your work to delete words that do not add value or meaning. Consider cutting words such as *very* and *really* and clauses such as *I think, as I said,* and *you know.*

Publishing and Presenting

Consider one of the following ways to share your writing.

Be a consumer watchdog. If your essay contains information that is useful to consumers, form a Consumer Information Panel. Post your essays to a class blog or school Web site. Include links to reliable, related sites, such as government Web sites that focus on health and safety or consumer issues.

Submit it to a magazine. Submit your essay to a magazine that specializes in the subject you have chosen. You can find publishing information and an address in a recent edition of the magazine.

Reflecting on Your Writing

Writer's Journal Jot down your answer to this question:

What was the most important improvement you made when revising?

Spiral Review
Earlier in the unit, you learned about **independent and dependent clauses** (p. 348) and about **sentence structures** (p. 360). Review your essay to be sure that subjects and verbs agree in number and that you have a variety of sentence structures to add interest to your essay.

Rubric for Self-Assessment

Find evidence in your writing to address each category. Then, use the rating scale to grade your work.

Criteria	Rating Scale
Purpose/Focus Clearly analyzes the similarities and differences between two or more related subjects	*not very* .... *very* 1　　2　　3　　4
Organization Introduces the topic in a way that grabs the reader's interest; provides clear organization that highlights the major points of comparison; uses appropriate transitions to create cohesion and clarify relationships among ideas; provides a strong, memorable conclusion	1　　2　　3　　4
Development of Ideas/Elaboration Creates an informative and explanatory text that examines a topic using a comparison/contrast organization; develops the topic with concrete details that illustrate both similarities and differences between the subjects; provides relevant facts, definitions, quotations, and examples; establishes and maintains a formal style	1　　2　　3　　4
Language Uses variety of sentence structures; uses precise language and domain-specific vocabulary to compare and contrast a topic	1　　2　　3　　4
Conventions Uses proper grammar, including correct use of coordination and subordination to clarify relationships	1　　2　　3　　4

SELECTED RESPONSE

 **Common Core State Standards**

RL.7.4, RL.7.5; W.7.2
[For full standards wording, see the chart in the front of this book.]

I. Reading Literature

Directions: *Read "The Village Blacksmith" by Henry Wadsworth Longfellow. Then, answer each question that follows.*

Under a spreading chestnut tree
    The village smithy stands;
The smith, a mighty man is he,
    With large and sinewy hands;
5 And the muscles of his brawny arms
Are strong as iron bands.

His hair is crisp, and black, and long,
    His face is like the tan;
His brow is wet with honest sweat,
10   He earns whate'er he can,
And looks the whole world in the face,
    For he owes not any man.

Week in, week out, from morn till night,
    You can hear his bellows blow;
15 You can hear him swing his heavy sledge
    With measured beat and slow,
Like a sexton ringing the village bell,
    When the evening sun is low.

And children coming home from school
20   Look in at the open door;
They love to see the flaming forge,
    And hear the bellows roar,
And catch the burning sparks that fly
    Like chaff from a threshing-floor.

25 He goes on Sunday to the church,
    And sits among his boys;
He hears the parson pray and preach,
    He hears his daughter's voice,
Singing in the village choir,
30   And it makes his heart rejoice.
It sounds to him like her mother's voice,
    Singing in Paradise!
He needs must think of her once more,
    How in the grave she lies;
35 And with his hard, rough hand he wipes
    A tear out of his eyes.

Toiling—rejoicing—sorrowing,
    Onward through life he goes;
Each morning sees some task begin,
40   Each evening sees it close;
Something attempted, something done,
    Has earned a night's <u>repose</u>.

Thanks, thanks to thee, my worthy friend,
    For the lesson thou hast taught!
45 Thus at the flaming forge of life
    Our fortunes must be wrought;
Thus on its sounding anvil shaped
    Each burning deed and thought.

1. **Part A** "The Village Blacksmith" is an example of which **form of poetry?**

   A. haiku

   B. free verse

   C. narrative poem

   D. limerick

   Part B Which answer choice best supports your answer to Part A?

   A. The lines of the poem have a particular number of syllables.

   B. The poem is humorous.

   C. The poem has a rhyme scheme.

   D. The poem tells a story.

2. **Part A** Which line from the poem contains an example of **imagery?**

   A. "His brow is wet with honest sweat"

   B. "The village smithy stands"

   C. "And children coming home from school"

   D. "Has earned a night's repose"

   Part B The imagery from Part A appeals to which of the following senses?

   A. sight and hearing

   B. touch and hearing

   C. sight and touch

   D. taste and smell

3. Which lines from the poem contain the best example of the sound device **rhyme**?

   A. "And children coming home from school / Look in at the open door"

   B. "It sounds like his mother's voice / Singing in Paradise!"

   C. "With measured beat and slow / Like a sexton ringing the village bell / When the evening sun is low"

   D. "Thus on its sounding anvil shaped / Each burning deed and thought"

4. Which lines contain an example of a **simile?**

   A. lines 47–48

   B. lines 3–5

   C. lines 15–17

   D. lines 29–30

5. Which line contains the **sound device** of allieration?

   A. "He hears the parson pray and preach"

   B. "A tear out of his eyes"

   C. "With measured beat and slow"

   D. "It sounds to him like her mother's voice"

6. Identify the type of **figurative langauge** contained in the following lines:

   "They love to see the flaming forge, / And hear the bellows roar"

   A. simile

   B. metaphor

   C. symbol

   D. personification

7. Which answer choice states the best definition of the underlined word *repose?*

   A. work

   B. rest

   C. worry

   D. entertainment

🕐 Timed Writing

8. Identify one **simile,** one **metaphor,** and one example of **personification** in the poem. In an essay, explain how this **figurative language** contributes to the poem's overall meaning.

GO ON

II. Reading Informational Text

Common Core State Standards

RI.7.5; L.7.1.a, L.7.1.b, L.7.2
[For full standards wording, see the chart in the front of this book.]

Directions: *Read the passage below. Then, answer each question that follows.*

How to Set up an E-mail Filter

An e-mail filter sorts your e-mail, deletes unwanted junk mail, and helps you avoid e-mail scams. Follow these steps to make your e-mail inbox easier to navigate and to avoid annoying junk e-mails.

Step 1 Open your e-mail account and locate the "Tools," "Filters," or "Options" menu items. Usually, these are listed at the top of the screen.

Step 2 Once you have found the Filters option, click on "New" to create a new folder. **TIP:** Name the folder "Junk Mail" so it is easy to find.

Step 3 Set up the rules, or conditions, for the filter. The rules enable you to control what happens to e-mail that is delivered to your account. **TIP:** One rule you can set is to send e-mails from unknown senders to your new folder. This means that any message from a sender who is not listed in your address book will be sent to the Junk Mail folder.

Step 4 Specify the action you want the filter to execute. Filters can sort e-mails into a folder, delete e-mails, or take other actions your e-mail provider offers. **TIP:** If your filter sends unwanted e-mails to a folder, be sure to check the folder periodically to see if a *wanted* e-mail has been sent there by mistake.

Step 5 Click "OK" or "Save" to save your new folder. **TIP:** You can add new filters for different uses, such as organizing e-mail correspondence related to school, work, or family.

1. **Part A** Which of the following is a key step in setting up an e-mail filter?

   A. open your junk mail first
   B. avoid e-mail scams
   C. check your junk mail folder for wanted e-mails
   D. set up the conditions of the filter

   Part B Which action is part of the key step you identified in Part A?

   A. Add new filters for different uses.
   B. Click "OK" or "save" to save to your new folder.
   C. Make a rule to send e-mails from unknown senders to a folder.
   D. Name the folder "Junk Mail" so it is easy to find.

2. What is the purpose of the tips that follow each step?

   A. They provide additional information and advice.
   B. They summarize the main points of the steps.
   C. They provide definitions for technical terms.
   D. They clarify difficult concepts.

III. Writing and Language Conventions

Directions: *Read the script for the multimedia report. Then, answer each question that follows.*

Slide 1 (1) Visual: Title Slide: Stick Insects (2) *Script:* There is 2,000 species of stick insects, including 41 that exist in North America. (3) They are the coolest bugs in your backyard!

Slide 2 (4) *Visual:* Walking Stick (5) *Script:* Adults look like sticks, and their eggs resemble seeds. (6) This is called camouflage. (7) Birds cannot eat bugs that they cannot see.

Slide 3 (8) *Visual:* Huge walking stick on man's face (9) *Script:* India is home to some of the world's biggest stick insects (10) Some are over twelve inches long. (11) There are not any this large in the United States.

---

1. Which of the following revisions changes sentence 9 to a **interrogative sentence?**

   A. India is home to some of the world's biggest stick insects!
   B. India is home to some of the world's biggest stick insects.
   C. Did you know that India is home to some of the world's biggest stick insects?
   D. You might not know that India is home to some of the world's biggest stick insects.

2. Which of these sentences contains a **dependent clause?**

   A. sentence 3
   B. sentence 5
   C. sentence 6
   D. sentence 7

3. What is the **function** of sentence 10?

   A. to ask a question
   B. to call out or exclaim
   C. to make a statement
   D. to give a command

4. Which is the *best* way to combine sentences 10 and 11 to make a **compound sentence?**

   A. Some are over twelve inches long, but there are not any this large in the United States.
   B. Some are over twelve inches long there are not any this large in the United States.
   C. Some are over twelve inches long, there are not any that large in the United States.
   D. Some are over twelve inches long, so there are not any that large in the United States.

5. How should sentence 2 be revised to fix incorrect **subject-verb agreement?**

   A. There are 2,000 species of stick insects, including 41 that exists in North America.
   B. There are 2,000 species of stick insects, including 41 that exist in North America.
   C. There is 2,000 species of stick insects, including 41 that exists in North America.
   D. The sentence contains no error in subject-verb agreement.

CONSTRUCTED RESPONSE

 **Common Core State Standards**

RL.7.4, RL.7.5; W.7.7, W.7.8, W.7.9.a; SL.7.1, SL.7.1.c, SL.7.1.d, SL.7.4; L.7.1
[For full standards wording, see the chart in the front of this book.]

Directions: *Follow the instructions to complete the tasks below as required by your teacher.*

As you work on each task, incorporate both general academic vocabulary and literary terms you learned in Parts 1 and 2.

Writing

TASK 1 Informational Text [RL.7.5; W.7.9.a]

Compare and Contrast Forms of Poetry

Write an essay in which you compare and contrast two poetic forms.

- Review the specific rules that guide the structure of each of these poetic forms: lyric poetry, concrete poetry, and haiku. Choose two forms to compare and contrast in your essay.

- Select one or more poems of each form from Part 2 of this unit.

- In your essay, compare and contrast the characteristics of each poetic form. Support your analysis with specific examples from the poems you have chosen.

- Explain how each characteristic you discuss contributes to the meaning of the poem.

- Include your topic sentence in the introductory paragraph. Organize the body of your comparison-and-contrast essay to clearly show comparisons and contrasts.

TASK 2 Literature [RL.7.4; W.7.9.a; L.7.1]

Analyze Word Choice

Write an essay in which you use the literal and implied meanings of words to help you interpret a poem in Part 2.

- Choose a poem that features powerful words and images.

- Note examples of figurative language—such as similes, metaphors, and personification—and imagery that appeals to the five senses. Analyze the impact of each example.

- Cite evidence from the poem to support your analysis.

- As you edit, make sure you have used correct punctuation, including commas to separate items in a series.

TASK 3 Literature [RL.7.5; W.7.9.a]

Analyze a Poem's Form and Structure

Write an essay in which you analyze the form and structure of a poem in Part 2.

Part 1

- Choose a poem from Part 2 to use as the basis of your analysis.

- Read the poem several times, taking notes on these elements of form and structure: rhyme, rhythm and meter, line length, stanza divisions, punctuation, capitalization, and spacing. Explain how these elements, both individually and together, contribute to the poem's meaning and effect.

Part 2

- Write an essay in which you analyze the form and structure of your chosen poem. Include the elements listed above in Part 1.

- Revise your work to correct any run-on sentences or sentence fragments. Place phrases and clauses within sentences to clarify the relationships among ideas.

- Publish your finished essay in the classroom library. Include a copy of the original text of the poem.

Speaking and Listening

TASK 4 Literature [RL.7.4; SL.7.4]

Analyze the Impact of Sound Devices

Give an oral presentation of an essay in which you analyze the impact of sound devices in a poem in Part 2.

- Analyze the impact of rhyme and other sound devices, such as repetition or alliteration, in a poem from Part 2. Consider how the sound devices affect the poem's mood, meaning, and tone.

- Organize your key points and support them with examples from the poem.

- Before your presentation, consult a print or online dictionary to find the pronunciations of unknown words.

- Deliver your presentation to the class. Use appropriate eye contact, adequate volume, and clear pronunciation.

TASK 5 Literature [RL.7.4; SL.7.1]

Lead a Discussion About Word Choice

Lead a small-group discussion about the effects of word choice in a poem from Part 2.

- Choose a poem with powerful language to use as the basis for your discussion. Prepare by jotting down words from the poem that you find particularly effective. Note the figurative or connotative meanings of these words.

- Ask someone in your group to read the poem aloud. Then, allow group members to share their opinions and ideas about word choice in the poem. Follow general rules for discussion, taking turns speaking.

- Pose questions and respond to others' questions. Acknowledge new information and adjust your own ideas in response if necessary.

- Use formal English and academic vocabulary as you discuss the poem.

Research

TASK 6 Literature [RL.7.4; W.7.7, W.7.8]

 ## What is the best way to communicate?

In Part 2 of this unit, you have read literature about ways people communicate. Now you will conduct a short research project on one type of communication. Use both the literature you have read and your research to reflect on this unit's Big Question. Review the following guidelines before you begin:

- Focus your research on one type of communication.

- Gather relevant information from at least two reliable print or digital sources.

- Take notes as you research your topic.

- Cite your sources accurately.

When you have completed your research, write a response to the Big Question. Discuss how your initial ideas have been either changed or reinforced. Support your response with an example from literature and an example from your research.

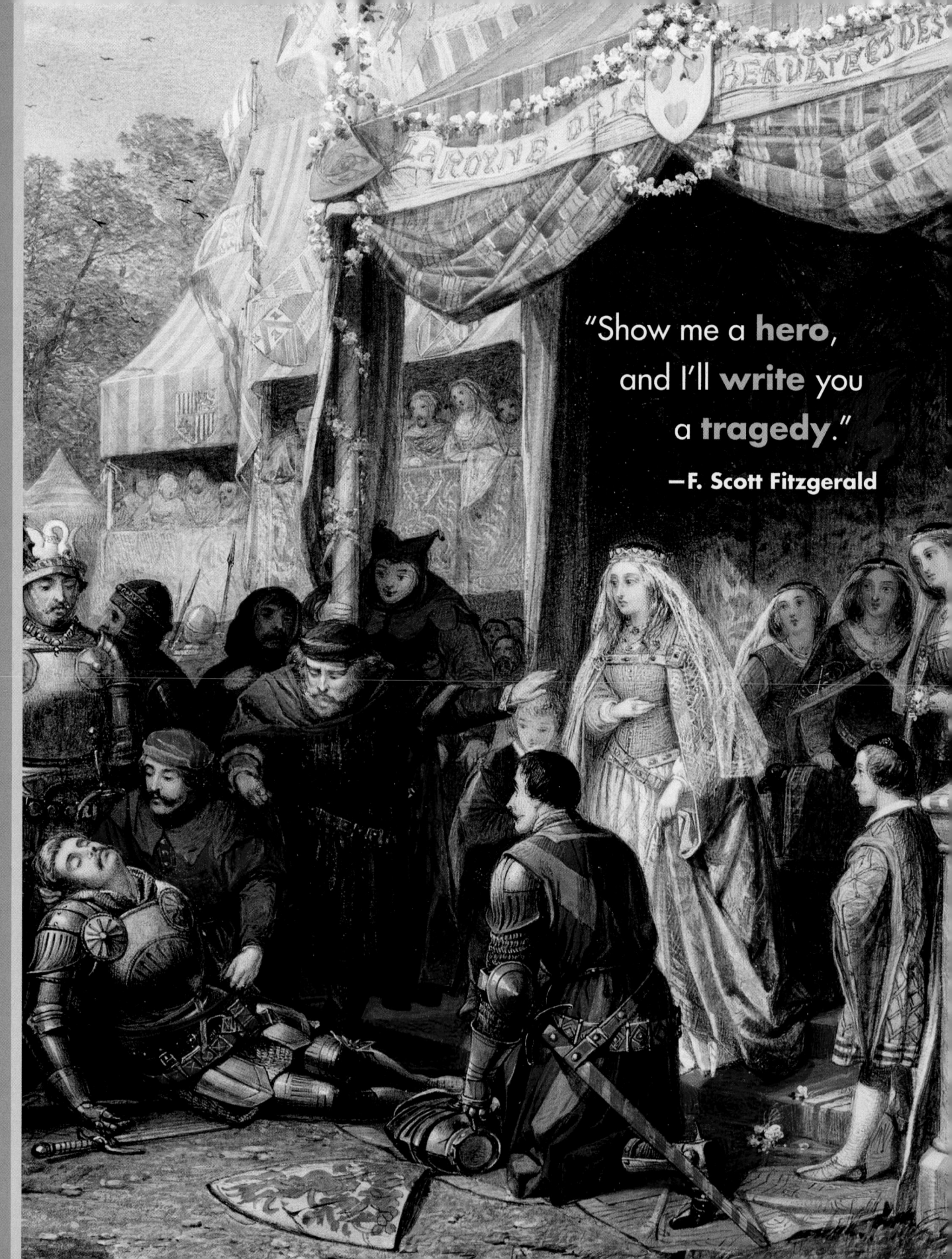

"Show me a **hero**, and I'll **write** you a **tragedy**."

—**F. Scott Fitzgerald**

HEROES AND OUTLAWS

The selections in this unit all deal with the Big Question: **What is the best way to communicate?** Often, the information that is communicated about a person shapes our ideas about whether that person is a hero or an outlaw. As you read the texts in this section, analyze how the authors depict heroes and outlaws, and notice how the difference between the two can sometimes blur.

◄ **CRITICAL VIEWING** How does the scene depicted in this painting connect to the idea of heroes and outlaws?

CLOSE READING TOOL

Use the **Close Reading Tool** to practice the strategies you learn in this unit.

THE HIGHWAYMAN

Alfred Noyes

PART ONE

The wind was a **torrent** of darkness among the gusty trees.
The moon was a ghostly galleon[1] tossed upon cloudy seas.
The road was a ribbon of moonlight over the purple moor,[2]
And the highwayman came riding—
5   Riding—riding—
The highwayman came riding, up to the old inn door.

He'd a French cocked-hat on his forehead, a bunch of lace at his chin,
A coat of the claret velvet, and breeches of brown doeskin.
They fitted with never a wrinkle. His boots were up to the thigh.
10 And he rode with a jeweled twinkle,
         His pistol butts a-twinkle,
His rapier hilt[3] a-twinkle, under the jeweled sky.

Over the cobbles he clattered and clashed in the dark innyard.
He tapped with his whip on the shutters, but all was locked and barred.
15 He whistled a tune to the window, and who should be waiting there
But the landlord's black-eyed daughter,
         Bess, the landlord's daughter,
Plaiting a dark red love knot into her long black hair.

And dark in the dark old innyard a stable wicket creaked
20 Where Tim the ostler[4] listened. His face was white and peaked.

◀ **torrent**
(tôr´ ənt) *n.* flood

---

1. galleon (gal´ ē ən) *n.* large Spanish sailing ship.
2. moor (moor) *n.* open, rolling land with swamps.
3. rapier (rā´ pē ər) **hilt** large cup-shaped handle of a rapier, which is a type of sword.
4. ostler (äs´ lər) *n.* stable worker.

His eyes were hollows of madness, his hair like moldy
hay,
But he loved the landlord's daughter,
The landlord's red-lipped daughter.
Dumb as a dog he listened, and he heard the robber
say—
25 "One kiss, my bonny[5] sweetheart, I'm after a prize
tonight,
But I shall be back with the yellow gold before the
morning light;
Yet, if they press me sharply, and harry me through the
day,
Then look for me by moonlight,
Watch for me by moonlight,
30 I'll come to thee by moonlight, though hell should bar the
way."

He rose upright in the stirrups. He scarce could reach her
hand,
But she loosened her hair in the casement.[6] His face
burnt like a brand[7]
As the black cascade of perfume came tumbling over his
breast;
And he kissed its waves in the moonlight,
35 (O, sweet black waves in the moonlight!)
Then he tugged at his rein in the moonlight, and galloped
away to the west.

PART TWO

He did not come in the dawning. He did not come at
noon;
And out of the tawny sunset, before the rise of the moon,
When the road was a gypsy's ribbon, looping the purple
moor,
40 A redcoat troop came marching—
Marching—marching—
King George's men[8] came marching, up to the old inn
door.

---

5. **bonny** (bän´ ē) *adj.* Scottish for "pretty."
6. **casement** (kās´ mənt) *n.* window frame that opens on hinges.
7. **brand** (brand) *n.* piece of burning wood.
8. **King George's men** soldiers serving King George of Great Britain.

They said no word to the landlord. They drank his ale
    instead
But they gagged his daughter, and **bound** her, to the foot
    of her narrow bed.

◀ **bound**
(bound) *v.* tied

45 Two of them knelt at her casement, with muskets at their
    side!
There was death at every window;
          And hell at one dark window;
For Bess could see, through her casement, the road that
    he would ride.

They had tied her up to attention, with many a sniggering
    jest.[9]
50 They had bound a musket beside her, with the muzzle
    beneath her breast!
"Now, keep good watch!" and they kissed her. She heard
    the doomed man say—
Look for me by moonlight;
        Watch for me by moonlight;
I'll come to thee by moonlight, though hell should bar
    the way!

55 She twisted her hands behind her; but all the knots held
    good!
She writhed her hands till her fingers were wet with
    sweat or blood!
They stretched and strained in the darkness, and the
    hours crawled by like years,
Till, now, on the stroke of midnight,
        Cold, on the stroke of midnight,
60 The tip of one finger touched it! The trigger at least was
    hers!

The tip of one finger touched it. She **strove** no more for
    the rest.
Up, she stood up to attention, with the muzzle beneath
    her breast.
She would not risk their hearing; she would not strive
    again;

◀ **strove**
(strōv) *v.* struggled;
made great efforts

---

9. sniggering (snig´ ər iŋ) **jest** sly joke.

For the road lay bare in the moonlight;

65   Blank and bare in the moonlight;

And the blood of her veins, in the moonlight, throbbed to
her love's refrain.

Tlot-tlot; tlot-tlot! Had they heard it? The horsehoofs ringing
clear;

Tlot-tlot, tlot-tlot, in the distance? Were they deaf that
they did not hear?

Down the ribbon of moonlight, over the brow of the hill,

70   The highwayman came riding—

Riding—riding—

The redcoats looked to their priming![10] She stood up,
straight and still.

Tlot-tlot, in the frosty silence! *Tlot-tlot,* in the echoing
night!

Nearer he came and nearer. Her face was like a light.

75   Her eyes grew wide for a moment; she drew one last deep
breath,

Then her finger moved in the moonlight,

Her musket shattered the moonlight,

Shattered her breast in the moonlight and warned him—
with her death.

He turned. He spurred to the west; he did not know who
stood

80   Bowed, with her head o'er the musket, drenched with her
own blood!

Not till the dawn he heard it, and his face grew gray to
hear

How Bess, the landlord's daughter,

The landlord's black-eyed daughter,

Had watched for her love in the moonlight, and died in
the darkness there.

85   Back, he spurred like a madman, shouting a curse to the
sky,

With the white road smoking behind him and his rapier
brandished[11] high.

---

10. priming (prī´ miņ) *n.* explosive used to set off the charge in a gun.
11. brandished (bran´ dishd) *adj.* waved in a threatening way.

Blood-red were his spurs in the golden noon; wine-red
    was his velvet coat;
When they shot him down on the highway,
        Down like a dog on the highway,
90 And he lay in his blood on the highway, with a bunch of
    lace at his throat.

And still of a winter's night, they say, when the wind is in
    the trees,
When the moon is a ghostly galleon tossed upon cloudy
    seas,
When the road is a ribbon of moonlight over the purple
    moor,
A highwayman comes riding—
95   *Riding—riding—*
A highwayman comes riding, up to the old inn door.

Over the cobbles he clatters and clangs in the dark
    innyard.
He taps with his whip on the shutters, but all is locked
    and barred.
He whistles a tune to the window, and who should be
    waiting there
100 *But the landlord's black-eyed daughter,*
        Bess, the landlord's daughter,
Plaiting a dark red love knot into her long black hair.

ABOUT THE AUTHOR

Alfred Noyes (1880–1958)

Englishman Alfred Noyes's love for learning led
him to a career as a poet, an author, a professor,
and a critic. Noyes published his first volume of
poetry at the age of 21, and became quite popular
with the reading public. Despite his great love
for England's history and landscape, he moved to
the United States, where he taught at Harvard University and Princeton
University and lectured around the country. In 1913, Noyes received an
honorary Ph.D. from Yale University.

Close Reading Activities

READ

Comprehension

Reread all or part of the text to help you answer the following questions.

1. Where and when does the action of the poem take place?

2. Who overheard what the highwayman told Bess?

3. When does the highwayman plan to return?

4. What does the highwayman do when he hears Bess's warning?

Research: Clarify Details Choose a detail or reference in the poem that is unfamiliar to you and briefly research it. Then, explain how your research helped you understand an aspect of the poem.

Summarize Write an objective summary of the poem. Remember to omit your opinions and evaluations.

Language Study

Selection Vocabulary Identify synonyms for the boldfaced words from the poem, and then use the words in sentences of your own.

• The wind was a **torrent** of darkness among the gusty trees.

• But they gagged his daughter, and **bound** her, to the foot of her narrow bed.

• She **strove** no more for the rest.

Diction and Style Study the passage below. Then, answer the questions that follow.

> Yet, if they press me sharply, and harry me through the day, … I'll come to thee by moonlight, though hell should bar the way.

1. **(a)** What does "press me sharply" mean here? **(b)** What connotations, or feelings, associated with the word *sharply* affect the tone of the sentence?

2. **(a)** Use context to determine the meaning of *harry*. Use a dictionary to confirm your answer. **(b)** Why is *harry* a more effective word in this context than a synonym would be?

Conventions Reread the lines below and identify the dependent clause in the stanza. Tell which subordinating conjunction introduces the clause, and then explain what information the dependent clause provides.

> He rose upright in the stirrups. He scarce could reach her hand,/ But she loosened her hair in the casement. His face burnt like a brand/ As the black cascade of perfume came tumbling over his breast;/ And he kissed its waves in the moonlight, / (O, sweet black waves in the moonlight!)/ Then he tugged at his reign in the moonlight, and galloped away to the west.

Academic Vocabulary

The following words appear in blue in the instructions and questions on the facing page.

contrast   identify   opposing

Decide whether you know each word well, know it a little bit, or do not know it at all. Then, look up the definitions of the words you do not know well.

Literary Analysis

Reread the identified passages. Then, respond to the following questions.

> **Focus Passage 1** *(p. 401)*
>
> The wind was a torrent of darkness… His rapier hilt a-twinkle under the jeweled sky.

> **Focus Passage 2** *(p. 404)*
>
> *Tlot-tlot; tlot-tlot!* Had they heard it?… and warned him—with her death.

Key Ideas and Details

1. Summarize: In your own words, describe the character, setting, and action presented in these stanzas.

Craft and Structure

2. (a) Analyze: What examples of figurative language does the poet use to describe the night? **(b) Interpret:** What mood does this description establish?

3. Analyze: What do the poem's descriptive details suggest about the highwayman? Support your answer.

Integration of Knowledge and Ideas

4. Compare and Contrast: How does the description of the setting compare and **contrast** with the description of the highwayman?

Key Ideas and Details

1. (a) What does Bess do in this passage? **(b) Interpret:** Why does she do it?

Craft and Structure

2. (a) Distinguish: Identify the sound device that Noyes uses in lines 67, 68, and 73. **(b) Analyze:** How does the use of this sound device create a feeling of tension in the poem?

3. Analyze: What effect does Noyes achieve by repeating "riding" in lines 70–71?

Integration of Knowledge and Ideas

4. (a) Interpret: In the second stanza from this passage, what two words with **opposing** connotations are linked together with rhyme? **(b) Analyze:** What is the effect of this contrast?

Repetition

Poets use the **repetition** of words or phrases to link and emphasize ideas. A repeated phrase in a poem can make an image more powerful. Reread "The Highwayman," noting how the poet uses repetition.

1. (a) Identify the repetition in lines 28–30. **(b)** What effect does this repetition achieve?

2. Heroes and Outlaws (a) In lines 40–42, how does Noyes use repetition and rhythm to complement the visual image he creates? **(b)** Explain how the repetition in these lines creates a connection between the soldiers and the highwayman.

 **Common Core State Standards**

RL.7.1, RL.7.2, RL.7.3, RL.7.4, RL.7.5
[For full standards wording, see the chart in the front of this book.]

DISCUSS

From Text to Topic Group Discussion

Discuss lines 19–27 with a group of classmates. Contribute your own ideas, and support them with examples from the poem.

> And dark in the dark old innyard a stable wicket creaked ... before the morning light; (pp. 401–402)

WRITE

Writing to Sources Informative Text

Assignment

Write a **character analysis** of the highwayman. Review the poet's descriptions of the highwayman's character and actions to determine whether he is a hero, an outlaw, or a little bit of both.

Prewriting and Planning As you review the poem, record details about the highwayman, including his characteristics, motivations, and actions. Review your notes to develop your analysis of the highwayman's character.

Drafting Begin with a thesis statement—one sentence in which you present your main idea about the highwayman's character. In the body of your essay, support your thesis by presenting the reasons for your interpretation of the highwayman's character. Support each reason with details from the poem and, when appropriate, from real life. In your conclusion, explain why the poet characterized the highwayman as he did.

Revising Reread your essay to ensure that you have clearly supported your main points. If your main points require additional support, consider adding direct quotations from the poem. If you add quotations, be sure to use quotation marks to clearly distinguish them from your own writing.

Editing and Proofreading Make sure that the pronouns in your essay match their antecedents. Then, edit your essay to clarify relationships between facts, characters, and events. One way to clarify relationships in your writing is by adding transitions, such as *as a result, because of,* and *in other words.*

QUESTIONS FOR DISCUSSION:

1. Do you think Bess is aware of Tim's feelings for her? Why or why not?

2. What details in the poet's description of Tim characterize Tim as a villain or a hero?

CONVENTIONS

Pronouns must agree with their antecedents in number and gender. Use singular pronouns with singular antecedents and plural pronouns with plural antecedents.

THE
HIGHWAYMAN

Alfred Noyes

RESEARCH

Research **Investigate the Topic**

Heroes and Outlaws in Literature Heroes and outlaws have been subjects in literature for thousands of years. Sometimes, outlaws are portrayed as heroes. Robin Hood, a folk hero of British literature, is one such heroic outlaw.

Assignment

Conduct research to learn about an outlaw hero of folk literature. Investigate where and when the person or character lived, and why he or she was considered both an outlaw and a hero. Consult print and electronic resources. Take clear notes that carefully identify your sources. Compare and contrast the subject of your research with the highwayman in the poem. Share your findings in an **informal presentation** to the class.

PREPARATION FOR ESSAY

You may use the knowledge you gain during this research assignment to support your claims in an essay you will write at the end of this section.

Gather Sources Locate authoritative print and digital sources. Use library catalogs and databases to find books, stories, and articles about outlaw heroes. To find online sources, use Internet databases and search engines. Remember not all online sources are reliable, so you must verify the validity of the information you find.

Take Notes Take notes on each source using an organized note-taking strategy. You may write your notes on notecards or record them in one or more electronic files.

- For sources that provide historical information, such as articles and encyclopedias, make a separate note for each source. Label the top of each note with the type of information it contains.

- For sources that provide stories about outlaw heroes, identify the source, and write a brief summary of the story in your own words.

- For Internet sources, record the Web site and the date you accessed the information.

Synthesize Multiple Sources Assemble the information from your research into a cohesive presentation. Select and organize important historical facts and other information you want to share. Draw conclusions about why your subject is both an outlaw and a hero, and compare his or her story with that of the highwayman. Then, outline your presentation.

Organize and Present Ideas Review your outline and practice delivering your presentation. Be ready to answer questions from your audience.

 Common Core State Standards

W.7.2, W.7.4, W.7.7, W.7.8, W.7.9, W.7.10; SL.7.1, SL.7.4, SL.7.6; L.7.1, L.7.1.a, L.7.4.a, L.7.4.d, L.7.5.b
[For full standards wording, see the chart in the front of this book.]

CARNEGIE HERO
Fund Commission

History

"I do not expect to stimulate or create heroism by this fund, knowing well that heroic action is impulsive; but I do believe that, if the hero is injured in his bold attempt to serve or save his fellows, he and those dependent upon him should not suffer pecuniarily."[1]

—Andrew Carnegie

Heroes of Civilization

A massive coal mine disaster in 1904 prompted Andrew Carnegie to establish a commission to recognize acts of civilian[2] heroism.

Pittsburgh steelmaker Andrew Carnegie had long held the idea that ordinary citizens who perform extraordinary acts of heroism should be recognized for their deeds. A massive explosion on January 25, 1904, in a coal mine at Harwick, Pa., near Pittsburgh, claiming 181 lives, inspired him to act … two of the victims had entered the mine after the explosion in ill-fated rescue attempts.

Within three months of the disaster, Carnegie had set aside $5 million under the care of a commission to recognize "civilization's heroes" … and to provide financial assistance for those disabled and the dependents of those killed helping others.

The **Carnegie Hero Fund Commission** carries out the founder's wishes by awarding the **Carnegie Medal** throughout the United States and Canada.

Over the 108 years of its existence, the Fund has awarded more

---

1. **pecuniarily** (pi kyo͞o′nē er′ i lē) *adv.* monetarily; relating to money.
2. **civilian** (sə vil′yən) *n.* any person not an active member of the armed forces and not employed as a police officer or firefighter.

"We live in a heroic age."

The Carnegie Medal

than 9,500 medals and $34 million in accompanying grants, including scholarship aid and continuing assistance. Ten hero funds established in Europe carry out a similar mission. The Carnegie Hero Fund Trust for Great Britain was set up in 1908 and was followed a year later by the Foundation Carnegie in France. In quick succession came hero funds in Germany, Norway, Switzerland, the Netherlands, Sweden, Denmark, Belgium, and Italy.

commemorated ▶
(kə mem′ə rāt′ id)
v. honored the
memory of

The Hero Fund's heritage was **commemorated** in 1996 by the Pennsylvania Historical and Museum Commission through the issuance of a roadside marker, which was installed along Pittsburgh Street in Springdale, Pa., near the sites of both the mine and the cemetery in which many of the disaster's victims are buried. More than 2,000 such markers have been issued by the state since the program's inception in 1946. The blue and gold signs dotting the state's highways commemorate subjects having meaningful impact and statewide or national significance.

prompted ▶
(prämpt′id) *v.*
urged into action

The Harwick explosion, remaining one of the worst U.S. mining disasters of the century, claimed 179 lives. It was the deaths of the two rescuers which **prompted** Carnegie to act on his thoughts about civilian heroism. Within three months of the explosion, Carnegie established a $5 million trust and appointed a 21-member commission to carry out his wish that "heroes and those dependent upon them should be freed from pecuniary cares resulting from their heroism." Further, the heroic acts were to be recognized by the granting of a medal.

More than a century later, the Carnegie Hero Fund Commission continues to carry out those goals.

What Is a Hero?

The Commission's definition of a hero has been largely unchanged since 1904: A civilian who knowingly risks his or her own life to an extraordinary degree while saving or attempting to save the life of another person. The cases submitted for consideration—in excess of 85,000 to date—are scrutinized by a full-time staff before formal review by the Commission itself. Persons selected for recognition receive a bronze medal and a financial grant, and each becomes **eligible** for scholarship aid. Those disabled in their heroic acts or the dependents of those killed are eligible for additional benefits, including ongoing aid to meet living expenses.

Approximately 20 percent of the awards are made posthumously,[3] reflecting a verse from the New Testament embossed on each medal: "Greater love hath no man than this, that a man lay down his life for his friends" (John 15:13).

A Heroic Age

The marker in Dunfermline reads, "The false heroes of barbarous man are those who can only boast of the destruction of their fellows. The true heroes of civilisation are those alone who save or greatly serve them. Young Hunter was one of those and deserves an enduring monument."—Carnegie

"We live in a heroic age," Carnegie wrote in 1904 in the opening lines of the fund's deed of trust. "Not seldom are we thrilled by deeds of heroism where men or women are injured or lose their lives in attempting to preserve or rescue their fellows; such the heroes of civilization. The heroes of barbarism maimed or killed theirs."

Similar thinking first surfaced in 1886, when Carnegie donated toward the cost of a marker honoring a 17-year-old boy who drowned in a rescue attempt in Carnegie's native Scotland. The philanthropist's[4] thoughts on heroism are chiseled into the youth's stone marker in a cemetery in Dunfermline, Carnegie's boyhood home.

The deaths of the Harwick rescuers 18 years later provided impetus for Carnegie to act on his peace-loving convictions, and he took great satisfaction in the establishment of the Hero Fund. Carnegie biographer Joseph Frazier Wall (Andrew Carnegie, Oxford University Press, New York), writes, "Every other philanthropic fund that Carnegie had ever established had been proposed to him—often forced upon him—by others. The Hero Fund came out of his own head and heart, and it delighted him."

---

3. **posthumously** (päs´choo məs´ lē) *adv.* after one's death.
4. **philanthropist** (fə lan´thrə pist) *n.* wealthy person who helps others, especially through gifts or charity.

READ

Comprehension

Reread the text as needed to answer the following questions.

1. Who was Andrew Carnegie?
2. What event inspired Carnegie to create the Hero Fund?
3. What is the purpose of the fund?

Research: Clarify Details Choose an unfamiliar detail from the article and conduct research to learn more. Then, explain how your research helped you understand the article.

Summarize Write an objective summary of the article. Remember to leave out your opinions and evaluations.

Language Study

Selection Vocabulary Write two related words for each boldfaced word from the selection (example: *assist, assistance, assisted*).

- The Hero Fund's heritage was **commemorated** in 1996 …

- It was the deaths of the two rescuers which **prompted** Carnegie to act…
- … the dependents of those killed are **eligible** for additional benefits …

Literary Analysis

Reread the identified passage. Then, respond to the following questions.

> **Focus Passage** (*p. 413*)
>
> **A Heroic Age** The marker in Dunfermline reads … Carnegie's boyhood home.

Key Ideas and Details

1. **(a)** Who is "young Hunter"? **(b) Interpret:** How does he fit the **definition** of a hero that appears on the marker in Dunfermline?

Craft and Structure

2. **(a) Interpret: Explain** in your own words what "Not seldom are we thrilled by deeds of heroism" means. **(b) Evaluate:** Explain the effect of the negative construction "Not seldom."

Integration of Knowledge and Ideas

3. **(a)** What groups that are commonly considered heroes might Carnegie call "heroes of barbarous man"? **(b)** According to Carnegie, what is the key **characteristic** of a "true hero of civilization"?

Structure

The **structure** of a text helps determine the organization of key ideas. Features such as headings, type size and style, and placement on a page reveal a text's structure. Take notes on this Web article's structure.

1. What text features identify the key ideas of the article? Cite examples.
2. **Heroes and Outlaws (a)** Why is the first section set off from the rest of the text? **(b)** What key idea about heroes does this section present?

DISCUSS • RESEARCH • WRITE

From Text to Topic **Group Discussion**

Discuss the following passage with a group of classmates. Take notes during the discussion. Contribute your own ideas, and support them with examples from the text.

> The Commission's definition of a hero has been largely unchanged since 1904: A civilian who knowingly risks his or her own life to an extraordinary degree while saving or attempting to save the life of another person.

Research **Investigate the Topic**

Civilization's Heroes Carnegie's fund has been in place since 1904, and thousands of cases of heroism are still submitted every year for review.

Assignment

Conduct research to learn the story of a past winner of the Carnegie Hero Fund Commission award. Consult the Internet to find a winner and learn the basic details of his or her story. Then, consult news sources to learn additional details. Take clear notes and carefully identify your sources so that you can easily access the information later. Share your findings in a brief **hero profile**.

Writing to Sources **Argument**

The Carnegie Hero Fund Commission selects winners from nominations that are submitted by members of the public.

Assignment

Write a **persuasive letter** in which you nominate someone you have read or heard about for a Carnegie Medal. Follow these steps:

- State your intention of nominating the person for the medal.
- Describe in detail the nature of the person's heroic act and its outcome.
- Present strong evidence that your nominee knowingly risked his or her life to save someone.
- Conclude by reflecting on why you consider the person a hero.

QUESTIONS FOR DISCUSSION

1. What words in this passage define who is eligible for an award? Who might not be eligible?

2. Why do you think these restrictions are in place? Do you agree with them? Explain.

PREPARATION FOR ESSAY

You may use the results of your research to support your ideas in the essay you will write at the end of this section.

ACADEMIC VOCABULARY

Academic terms appear in blue on these pages. If these words are not familiar to you, use a dictionary to find their definitions. Then, use the words as you speak and write about the text.

 **Common Core State Standards**

RI.7.1, RI.7.2, RI.7.3, RI.7.4, RI.7.5; W.7.1, W.7.4, W.7.7, W.7.8; SL.7.1; L.7.5
[For full standards wording, see the chart in the front of this book.]

Jesse James, 1875

The MYTH of the OUTLAW

Ruth M. Hamel

Life in the United States was hard after the Civil War. In many places, farmland had been ruined, factories burned, and homes destroyed. Not much work was available for the returning soldiers. But not only was life hard, it also was dull. People needed heroes to liven things up.

Outlaws such as Billy the Kid, Jesse James, William Quantrill, Belle Starr, and Sam Bass led lives that sounded exciting to many Americans. Their crimes were written up in newspapers and told around campfires, and the stories changed each time they were told.

Eventually, it seemed, every outlaw was on the side of the poor.

Outlaws also were featured in the new "dime novels." These small paperbacks sold for ten cents—affordable for the common man—and were filled with exciting stories of heroes such as Deadeye Dick and Fearnot Fred. Often the stories were purely fictional.

In 1882, the year after Pat Garrett killed Billy the Kid, Garrett's book *Billy the Kid* was published. He said that so many lies had been told about Billy that someone had to tell the truth. Billy himself had invented some of the lies. For instance, he had bragged about killing twenty-one men by the time he was twenty-one years old, but records show that he had killed only four and helped in the killing of five others.

In stories and songs, Billy is handsome and generous, having been forced into a life of crime when someone insulted his mother. But instead of having a face "fine and fair," Billy was, according to one source, "**nondescript**, narrow-chested, stoop-shouldered and **repulsive** looking." He was a cattle thief and a killer, but after his death someone said, "The Kid had principle ... outside of some loose notions about rustling cattle.[1] This was stealing, but I don't believe it struck him that way."

Similarly, Jesse James was portrayed in a sympathetic light both while he was alive and after he was dead. Indeed, seventeen men claimed to be the "real" Jesse James after his death, and at last count four hundred fifty articles and movies tell of his life and crimes. *Jesse James at Bay* portrays James as a kind of Robin Hood who helped widows and orphans.

When artist Thomas Hart Benton was **commissioned** to paint a mural celebrating the state of Missouri at the state capitol in 1935 ... , he included a handsome picture of James. In addition, one of Benton's best-known lithographs[2] is of James killing two men during a train robbery.

Just in case the outlaws might be forgotten, a set of trading cards was issued in the 1930s. The cards were called "The Roundup Series," and all of the outlaws pictured look handsome, likable, kind, and generous. Just the way they were in real life—at least in people's minds.

◄ **commissioned**
(kə mish′ənd) *v.* appointed or hired to carry out a duty or task

◄ **nondescript**
(nän′di skript′) *adj.* hard to describe; not interesting

◄ **repulsive**
(ri pul′siv) *adj.* causing intense dislike; disgusting

---

1. **rustling cattle** stealing cattle.
2. **lithographs** (lith′ə grafs′) *n.* prints made from a flat stone or metal plate.

READ

Comprehension

Reread all or part of the text to help you answer the following questions.

1. What was life like after the Civil War? Why?

2. In the years following the Civil War, how were outlaws portrayed?

3. What is the author's attitude toward these stories?

Research: Clarify Details Choose an unfamiliar detail from the article and briefly research it. Then, explain how your research helps you understand the article.

Summarize Write an objective summary of the article. Remember to omit any opinions or evaluations.

Language Study

Selection Vocabulary List a synonym for each boldfaced word from the article. Then, use the boldfaced word in a sentence of your own.

• Billy was, according to one source, "**nondescript,** narrow-chested, stoop-shouldered and **repulsive** looking."

• When artist Thomas Hart Benton was **commissioned** to paint a mural…

Literary Analysis

Reread the passage indicated below.

> **Focus Passage** *(p. 417)*
> In stories and songs … helped widows and orphans.

Key Ideas and Details

1. Compare and Contrast: What are two contrasting ideas about Billy the Kid?

Craft and Structure

2. (a) Infer: What does the comment about Billy the Kid's "loose notions" suggest

about the **attitude** of the person who made this remark? **(b) Speculate:** Why does the author include this quotation?

3. (a) Analyze: Why does the author begin the paragraph about Jesse James with the word *similarly*? **(b) Draw Conclusions:** What does this suggest about James?

Integration of Knowledge and Ideas

4. Connect: How does the information in this passage **reflect** the title of the article? Cite details from the article to support your answer.

Diction

Through **diction**, or word choice, an author can create vivid images and reveal his or her **viewpoint** on a subject. Take notes on the author's diction in this article.

1. (a) In the opening paragraph, what vivid words does the author use to describe life

after the Civil War? **(b)** What image do these words create?

2. Heroes and Outlaws (a) What image of Billy the Kid does the word "repulsive" create? **(b)** Why does the author include a quotation with this word in the article?

DISCUSS • RESEARCH • WRITE

From Text to Topic **Partner Discussion**

Discuss the following passage with a partner. Take notes, contribute your own ideas, and support them with examples from the text.

> When artist Thomas Hart Benton was commissioned to paint a mural celebrating the state of Missouri at the state capitol in 1935 ..., he included a handsome picture of James. In addition, one of Benton's best-known lithographs is of James killing two men during a train robbery.

Research **Investigate the Topic**

Outlaws After the Civil War Many outlaws besides Billy the Kid and Jesse James became famous after the Civil War.

Assignment

Conduct research to learn about a famous outlaw of the post-Civil War era. Use Web sites to find the popular version of his or her story. Consult biography databases and authoritative print sources to find more objective accounts. Take clear notes and identify sources for different accounts of the same information. Share your findings in a brief **oral report** to the class.

Writing to Sources **Argument**

There was considerable controversy about several scenes, including the image of Jesse James, in Thomas Hart Benton's mural *A Social History of the State of Missouri.*

Assignment

Write an **argument** in which you recommend preserving the mural as it is, or removing the scene with Jesse James because it glorifies criminal activity. Follow these steps:

- Go online to view a reproduction of Benton's mural.
- State your position in your opening paragraph.
- Present your reasons and evidence in body paragraphs.
- Acknowledge opposing arguments and respond to them.
- Use a formal tone that is free from slang.
- Provide a concluding paragraph.

QUESTIONS FOR DISCUSSION

1. What does James's portrayal in the mural suggest about the state's attitude toward him?

2. Can art affect the ways in which people perceive a hero or an outlaw? Explain.

PREPARATION FOR ESSAY

You may use the results of your research to support your ideas in the essay you will write at the end of this section.

ACADEMIC VOCABULARY

Academic terms appear in blue on these pages. If these words are not familiar to you, use a dictionary to find their definitions. Then, use the words as you speak and write about the text.

Common Core State Standards

RI.7.1, RI.7.2, RI.7.4, RI.7.6; W.7.1, W.7.1.d, W.7.4, W.7.7, W.7.8; SL.7.1, SL.7.4; L.7.5.b
[For full standards wording, see the chart in the front of this book.]

The Real Story of a Cowboy's Life

Geoffrey C. Ward

discipline ▶
(dis′ ə plin′) *n.*
strict control

gauge ▶
(gāj) *v.* estimate
or judge

A drive's success depended on **discipline** and planning. According to Teddy Blue,[1] most Texas herds numbered about 2,000 head with a trail boss and about a dozen men in charge—though herds as large as 15,000 were also driven north with far larger escorts. The most experienced men rode "point" and "swing," at the head and sides of the long herd; the least experienced brought up the rear, riding "drag" and eating dust. At the end of the day, Teddy Blue remembered, they "would go to the water barrel . . . and rinse their mouths and cough and spit up . . . black stuff. But you couldn't get it up out of your lungs."

They had to learn to work as a team, keeping the herd moving during the day, resting peacefully at night. Twelve to fifteen miles a day was a good pace. But such steady progress could be interrupted at any time. A cowboy had to know how to **gauge** the temperament of his cattle, how to chase down

---

1. **Teddy Blue** Edward C. Abbot, a cowboy who rode in a successful trail drive in the 1880s.

a stray without alarming the rest of the herd, how to lasso a steer using the horn of his saddle as a tying post. His saddle was his most prized possession; it served as his chair, his workbench, his pillow at night. Being dragged to death was the most common death for a cowboy, and so the most feared occurrence on the trail was the nighttime stampede.

As Teddy Blue recalled, a sound, a smell, or simply the sudden movement of a jittery cow could set off a whole herd.

> If . . . the cattle started running—you'd hear that low rumbling noise along the ground and the men on herd wouldn't need to come in and tell you, you'd know—then you'd jump for your horse and get out there in the lead, trying to head them and get them into a mill[2] before they scattered. It was riding at a dead run in the dark, with cut banks and prairie dog holes all around you, not knowing if the next jump would land you in a shallow grave.

Most cowboys had guns, but rarely used them on the trail. Some outfits made them keep their weapons in the chuck wagon to eliminate any chance of gunplay. Charles Goodnight[3] was still more **emphatic**: "Before starting on a trail drive, I made it a rule to draw up an article of agreement, setting forth what each man was to do. The main clause stipulated[4] that if one shot another he was to be tried by the outfit and hanged on the spot, if found guilty. I never had a man shot on the trail."

◄ **emphatic**
(em fat′ ik) *adj.*
expressing strong feeling

Regardless of its ultimate destination, every herd had to ford[5] a series of rivers—the Nueces, the Guadalupe, the Brazos, the Wichita, the Red.

A big herd of longhorns swimming across a river, Goodnight remembered, "looked like a million floating rocking chairs," and crossing those rivers one after another, a cowboy recalled, was like climbing the rungs of a long ladder reaching north.

> "After you crossed the Red River and got out on the open plains," Teddy Blue remembered, "it was sure a pretty sight to see them strung out for almost a mile, the sun shining on their horns." Initially, the

2. **mill** (mil) *n.* slow movement in a circle.
3. **Charles Goodnight** cowboy who rode successful trail drives beginning in the 1860s.
4. **stipulated** (stip′ yə lāt′ əd) *v.* stated as a rule.
5. **ford** (fôrd) *v.* cross a river at a shallow point.

land immediately north of the Red River was Indian territory, and some tribes charged tolls for herds crossing their land— payable in money or beef. But Teddy Blue remembered that the homesteaders, now pouring onto the Plains by railroad, were far more nettlesome:

> There was no love lost between settlers and cowboys on the trail. Those jay-hawkers would take up a claim right where the herds watered and charge us for water. They would plant a crop alongside the trail and plow a furrow around it for a fence, and then when the cattle got into their wheat or their garden patch, they would come cussing and waving a shotgun and yelling for damages. And the cattle had been coming through there when they were still raising punkins in Illinois.

The settlers' hostility was entirely understandable. The big herds ruined their crops, and they carried with them a disease, spread by ticks and called "Texas fever," that devastated domestic livestock. Kansas and other territories along the route soon established quarantine lines,[6] called "deadlines," at the western fringe of settlement, and insisted that trail drives not cross them. Each year, as settlers continued to move in, those deadlines moved farther west.

Sometimes, farmers tried to enforce their own, as John Rumans, one of Charles Goodnight's hands, recalled:

> Some men met us at the trail near Canyon City, and said we couldn't come in. There were fifteen or twenty of them, and they were not going to let us cross the Arkansas River. We didn't even stop. . . . Old man [Goodnight] had a shotgun loaded with buckshot and led the way, saying: "John, get over on that point with your Winchester and point these cattle in behind me." He slid his shotgun across the saddle in front of him and we did the same with our Winchesters. He rode right across, and as he rode up to them, he said: "I've monkeyed as long as I want to with you," and they fell back to the sides, and went home after we had passed.

There were few diversions on the trail. Most trail bosses banned liquor. Goodnight prohibited gambling, too. Even the songs for which cowboys became famous grew directly out of doing a job, remembered Teddy Blue:

> The singing was supposed to soothe [the cattle] and it did; I don't know why, unless it was that a sound they was used to

---

6. **quarantine** (kwôr´ ən tēn) **lines** n. boundaries created to prevent the spread of disease.

would keep them from spooking at other noises. I know that if you wasn't singing, any little sound in the night—it might be just a horse shaking himself—could make them leave the country; but if you were singing, they wouldn't notice it.

The two men on guard would circle around with their horses on a walk, if it was a clear night and the cattle was bedded down and quiet, and one man would sing a verse of song, and his partner on the other side of the herd would sing another verse; and you'd go through a whole song that way. . . . "Bury Me Not on the Lone Prairie" was a great song for awhile, but . . . they sung it to death. It was a saying on the range that even the horses nickered it and the coyotes howled it; it got so they'd throw you in the creek if you sang it.

The number of cattle on the move was sometimes staggering: once, Teddy Blue rode to the top of a rise from which he could see seven herds strung out behind him; eight more up ahead; and the dust from an additional thirteen moving parallel to his. "All the cattle in the world," he remembered, "seemed to be coming up from Texas."

At last, the herds neared their destinations. After months in the saddle—often wearing the same clothes every day, eating nothing but biscuits and beef stew at the chuck wagon, drinking only water and coffee, his sole companions his fellow cowboys, his herd, and his horse—the cowboy was about to be paid for his work, and turned loose in town.

ABOUT THE AUTHOR

Geoffrey C. Ward (b. 1940)

Historian Geoffrey C. Ward strives to present an accurate portrayal of the past. He has written more than a dozen books about the United States and the people who played key roles in its growth. Ward's book *A First-Class Temperament,* about Franklin D. Roosevelt, won the 1989 National Book Critics Circle Award for biography. Ward has also written biographies of Mark Twain, Susan B. Anthony, Harry Truman, and Billy the Kid. In addition to his books, Ward has written or co-written more than twenty screenplays for films, many of which have appeared on public television. Ward teamed up with filmmaker Ken Burns to create the Emmy Award-winning PBS documentaries *The Civil War* and *Baseball.*

READ

Comprehension

Reread to answer these questions.

1. How did trail bosses reduce the likelihood of violence between cowboys?

2. Why did cowboy songs become commonplace?

3. What was the relationship between cowboys and settlers?

Research: Clarify Details Choose an unfamiliar reference from the essay and briefly research it. Then, explain how your research helps you understand the essay.

Summarize Write an objective summary of the essay. Remember that an objective summary is free from opinion and evaluation.

Language Study

Selection Vocabulary Define each boldfaced word from the essay, and then use each word in a sentence.

- **discipline**
- **gauge**
- **emphatic**

Literary Analysis

Reread the identified passage. Then, respond to the following questions.

> **Focus Passage** *(pp. 421–422)*
>
> "After you crossed the Red River and got out on the open plains," … when they were still raising punkins in Illinois."

Key Ideas and Details

1. (a) What **challenge** did some Indian tribes present for the cowboys? **(b)** How did the cowboys deal with this challenge?

Craft and Structure

2. Interpret: A nettle is a plant with painful, stinging fibers. How does the word *nettlesome* characterize the settlers?

3. Analyze: *Jay hawker* is a slang term for "thief." How does Teddy Blue's use of the term contribute to the meaning and mood of the passage?

Integration of Knowledge and Ideas

4. Connect: How does Blue's comment about "raising punkins in Illinois" sum up his **attitude** toward the settlers?

Primary Sources

Quotations from **primary sources**—original, first-hand accounts of an event—lend strong credibility and vivid details to an author's writing. **Evaluate** how Geoffrey Ward uses primary sources in this essay.

1. Why is Teddy Blue's description of a nighttime stampede more effective than a description by the author would be?

2. Heroes and Outlaws How do the primary sources strengthen or weaken the popular opinion that cowboys are ideal folk heroes?

DISCUSS • RESEARCH • WRITE

From Text to Topic **Debate**

Debate the following passage in small groups, with half the group taking the cowboys' side and half the group taking the settlers' side. Respond to the previous speaker's ideas, and contribute your own ideas, supporting them with examples from the text.

> The settlers' hostility was entirely understandable… and they fell back to the sides, and went home after we had passed. (p. 422)

Research **Investigate the Topic**

Cowboys and Settlers Cowboys were not the only ones who had a difficult time in the Great Plains of the 1880s. The settlers who moved west faced harsh conditions, disease, and separation from their families, as well as opposition from the cowboys.

> ### Assignment
> Conduct research about Great Plains settlers during the 1880s to learn about the challenges they faced. Take notes on the books, magazines, and Internet resources you consult, and record your sources. Share your findings in a brief **research report**. Explain whether you consider the settlers heroes, outlaws, or a combination of the two.

Writing to Sources **Argument**

The cowboys in the essay blamed the settlers for disputes between the groups. The settlers blamed the cowboys.

> ### Assignment
> Write an **argument** in which you agree or disagree that the cowboys had the right to drive their cattle along the same trails and lands they had always used, even after famers settled that land. Follow these steps:
> - Begin by introducing the issue and stating your position.
> - Present your arguments in the body of your essay. Cite facts and details from the essay to support your claims.
> - Anticipate and address opposing arguments.
> - Write a strong conclusion that reflects on the importance of your position.

QUESTIONS FOR DISCUSSION

1. Should decades of cattle drives have established the cowboys' rights to the land? Explain.

2. Does Goodnight's behavior in this passage characterize him as a hero or an outlaw? Explain.

PREPARATION FOR ESSAY

You may use the results of your research to support your ideas in the essay you will write at the end of this section.

ACADEMIC VOCABULARY

Academic terms appear in blue on these pages. If these words are not familiar to you, use a dictionary to find their definitions. Then, use the words as you speak and write about the text.

 **Common Core State Standards**

RI.7.1, RI.7.2, RI.7.3, RI.7.4; W.7.1, W.7.4; SL.7.1, SL.7.4, SL.7.6; L.7.4
[For full standards wording, see the chart in the front of this book.]

After Twenty Years O. Henry

The policeman on the beat moved up the avenue impressively. The impressiveness was habitual and not for show, for spectators were few. The time was barely 10 o'clock at night, but chilly gusts of wind with a taste of rain in them had well nigh[1] de-peopled the streets.

Trying doors as he went, twirling his club with many intricate and artful movements, turning now and then to cast his watchful eye down the pacific thoroughfare,[2] the officer, with his stalwart form and slight swagger, made a fine picture of a guardian of the peace. The vicinity was one that kept early hours. Now and then you might see the lights of a cigar store or of an all-night lunch counter; but the majority of the doors belonged to business places that had long since been closed.

When about midway of a certain block the policeman suddenly slowed his walk. In the doorway of a darkened hardware store a man leaned, with an unlighted cigar in his mouth. As the policeman walked up to him the man spoke up quickly.

"It's all right, officer," he said, reassuringly. "I'm just waiting for a friend. It's an appointment made twenty years ago.

---

1. **well nigh** *adv.* very nearly.
2. **pacific thoroughfare** calm street.

Sounds a little funny to you, doesn't it? Well, I'll explain if you'd like to make certain it's all straight. About that long ago there used to be a restaurant where this store stands—'Big Joe' Brady's restaurant."

"Until five years ago," said the policeman. "It was torn down then."

The man in the doorway struck a match and lit his cigar. The light showed a pale, square-jawed face with keen eyes, and a little white scar near his right eyebrow. His scarfpin was a large diamond, oddly set.

"Twenty years ago tonight," said the man, "I dined here at 'Big Joe' Brady's with Jimmy Wells, my best chum, and the finest chap in the world. He and I were raised here in New York, just like two brothers, together. I was eighteen and Jimmy was twenty. The next morning I was to start for the West to make my fortune. You couldn't have dragged Jimmy out of New York; he thought it was the only place on earth. Well, we agreed that night that we would meet here again exactly twenty years from that date and time, no matter what our conditions might be or from what distance we might have to come. We figured that in twenty years each of us ought to have our destiny worked out and our fortunes made, whatever they were going to be."

"It sounds pretty interesting," said the policeman. "Rather a long time between meets, though, it seems to me. Haven't you heard from your friend since you left?"

"Well, yes, for a time we corresponded," said the other. "But after a year or two we lost track of each other. You see, the West is a pretty big proposition, and I kept hustling around over it pretty lively. But I know Jimmy will meet me here if he's alive, for he always was the truest, stanchest old chap in the world. He'll never forget. I came a thousand miles to stand in this door tonight, and it's worth it if my old partner turns up."

The waiting man pulled out a handsome watch, the lids of it set with small diamonds.

"Three minutes to ten," he announced. "It was exactly ten o'clock when we parted here at the restaurant door."

simultaneously ▶
(sĭ mǝl tā′ nē ǝs lē)
adv. at the
same time

"Did pretty well out West, didn't you?" asked the policeman.

"You bet! I hope Jimmy has done half as well. He was a kind of plodder, though, good fellow as he was. I've had to compete with some of the sharpest wits going to get my pile. A man gets in a groove in New York. It takes the West to put a razor-edge on him."

The policeman twirled his club and took a step or two.

"I'll be on my way. Hope your friend comes around all right. Going to call time on him sharp?"

"I should say not!" said the other. "I'll give him half an hour at least. If Jimmy is alive on earth he'll be here by that time. So long, officer."

"Good-night, sir," said the policeman, passing on along his beat, trying doors as he went.

There was now a fine, cold drizzle falling, and the wind had risen from its uncertain puffs into a steady blow. The few foot passengers astir in that quarter hurried dismally and silently along with coat collars turned high and pocketed hands. And in the door of the hardware store the man who had come a thousand miles to fill an appointment, uncertain almost to absurdity,[3] with the friend of his youth, smoked his cigar and waited.

About twenty minutes he waited, and then a tall man in a long overcoat, with collar turned up to his ears, hurried across from the opposite side of the street. He went directly to the waiting man.

"Is that you, Bob?" he asked, doubtfully.

"Is that you, Jimmy Wells?" cried the man in the door.

"Bless my heart!" exclaimed the new arrival, grasping both the other's hands with his own. "It's Bob, sure as fate. I was certain I'd find you here if you were still in existence. Well, well, well!— twenty years is a long time. The old restaurant's gone, Bob; I wish it had lasted, so we could have had another dinner there. How has the West treated you, old man?"

"Bully;[4] it has given me everything I asked it for. You've changed lots, Jimmy. I never thought you were so tall by two or three inches."

"Oh, I grew a bit after I was twenty."

"Doing well in New York, Jimmy?"

"Moderately. I have a position in one of the city departments. Come on, Bob; we'll go around to a place I know of, and have a good long talk about old times."

The two men started up the street, arm in arm. The man from

---

3. **absurdity** (ab sur′dǝ tē) *n.* nonsense.
4. **bully** *interj.* very good.

the West, his egotism enlarged by success, was beginning to outline the history of his career. The other, submerged in his overcoat, listened with interest.

At the corner stood a drug store, brilliant with electric lights. When they came into this glare each of them turned **simultaneously** to gaze upon the other's face.

The man from the West stopped suddenly and released his arm.

"You're not Jimmy Wells," he snapped. "Twenty years is a long time, but not long enough to change a man's nose from a Roman to a pug."[5]

"It sometimes changes a good man into a bad one," said the tall man. "You've been under arrest for ten minutes, 'Silky' Bob. Chicago thinks you may have dropped over our way and wires us she wants to have a chat with you. Going quietly, are you? That's sensible. Now, before we go to the station here's a note I was asked to hand to you. You may read it here at the window. It's from Patrolman Wells."

The man from the West unfolded the little piece of paper handed him. His hand was steady when he began to read, but it trembled a little by the time he had finished. The note was rather short.

> Bob,
> I was at the appointed place on time. When you struck the match to light your cigar I saw it was the face of the man wanted in Chicago. Somehow I couldn't do it myself, so I went around and got a plain clothes man to do the job.
> Jimmy.

ABOUT THE AUTHOR

O. Henry (1862–1910)

O. Henry is the pen name of William Sydney Porter. He is known for his warm, witty short stories featuring ordinary people. Born and raised in Greensboro, North Carolina, Porter moved to Texas at the age of 20. While he was working at a bank, a discrepancy was found with the accounts and Porter was accused of stealing bank funds. He was tried, found guilty, and sentenced to prison. While in prison, Porter began to write short stories. Upon his release, he moved to New York City and started a career as a writer. He used the name O. Henry to hide the fact that he had been in prison. Many of his 300 stories are inspired by his time in prison, where he gained an understanding of people on both sides of the law.

---

5. **change a man's nose from a Roman to a pug** A Roman nose has a high, prominent bridge, but a pug nose is short, thick, and turned up at the end.

READ

Comprehension

Reread all or part of the text to help you answer the following questions.

1. For whom is the man in the doorway waiting?

2. Why has it been so long since the two men have seen each other?

3. Who finally comes to meet Bob?

Language Study

Selection Vocabulary Define each boldfaced word from the story, and then write a paragraph that includes all three words.

• … for **spectators** were few.

Literary Analysis

Reread the identified passage. Then, respond to the following questions.

> **Focus Passage** (p. 426)
>
> The policeman on the beat … that had long since been closed.

Key Ideas and Details

1. Why is the street deserted?

2. **(a) Infer:** Does this story more likely take place in the country or the city? **(b) Support:** What details support your answer?

Irony

Irony is a literary element that involves a **contradiction** or contrast. In *situational irony,* something takes place that is the opposite of what you expect to happen. Take notes on O. Henry's use of irony in this story.

1. **(a)** Is Bob's description of Jimmy as "the truest, stanchest old chap in the world"

Research: Clarify Details Choose an unfamiliar detail from the story and briefly research it. Explain how your research helps you understand the story.

Summarize Write an objective summary of the story. Remember to omit your opinions and evaluations.

• … twirling his club with many **intricate** and artful movements…

• … each of them turned **simultaneously** …

Craft and Structure

3. **(a) Evaluate:** Cite details that convey a clear picture of the policeman.
(b) Interpret: Based on the text, describe the policeman in your own words.

Integration of Knowledge and Ideas

4. **(a) Analyze:** How does the author use details about the setting to **communicate** a mood? **(b) Draw Conclusions:** What impact does this mood have on the reader's expectations for the rest of the story?

accurate? **(b)** What makes the description ironic?

2. **(a)** In what way is the story's ending ironic? **(b)** If Jimmy had let Bob go free, would the story's ending still create irony? Explain.

DISCUSS • RESEARCH • WRITE

From Text to Topic **Group Discussion**

Discuss Jimmy's note with a group of classmates. **Contribute** your own ideas, and support them with examples from the text.

> Bob,
> I was at the appointed place on time. When you struck the match to light your cigar I saw it was the face of the man wanted in Chicago. Somehow I couldn't do it myself, so I went around and got a plain clothes man to do the job.
> Jimmy

Research **Investigate the Topic**

Police Heroes Although Jimmy did not face obvious danger in this story, police officers often do encounter situations that require courage and, sometimes, heroism.

Assignment

Conduct research to learn about one or more police officers who have been heroes. Consult electronic news sources as well as books and magazines. Take clear notes and carefully identify your sources so that you can easily access the information later. Share your findings about one of the heroes in a **group discussion** with the class.

Writing to Sources: **Narrative**

O. Henry's story ends with a surprising and ironic twist. But until the very end, the story could have gone in another direction.

Assignment

Develop a **fictional narrative** by writing a different ending to "After Twenty Years." Keep the first part of O. Henry's story, but then cut away to your own narrative before Bob meets the plainclothes policeman. Follow these instructions:

- Refer to the text to make sure that your characters' new actions are consistent with what has already happened.
- Address the concept of "heroes and outlaws" in your narrative.
- Make sure your story has a conflict and a climax in the plot.
- Use realistic dialogue and detailed descriptions.

QUESTIONS FOR DISCUSSION

1. Was it right for Jimmy to send someone else to arrest Bob? Explain.
2. Should Jimmy have turned Bob in? Why or why not?

PREPARATION FOR ESSAY

You may use the results of your research to support your ideas in the essay you will write at the end of this section.

ACADEMIC VOCABULARY

Academic terms appear in blue on these pages. If these words are not familiar to you, use a dictionary to find their definitions. Then, use the words as you speak and write about the text.

Common Core State Standards

RL.7.1, RL.7.2, RL.7.3, RL.7.6, W.7.3, W.7.4; SL.7.1, SL.7.4
[For full standards wording, see the chart in the front of this book.]

Harriet Tubman

*Africans in America: America's Journey
Through Slavery* PBS

Harriet Tubman is perhaps the most well-known of all the Underground Railroad's "conductors." During a ten-year span she made 19 trips into the South and escorted over 300 slaves to freedom. And, as she once proudly pointed out to Frederick Douglass, in all of her journeys she "never lost a single passenger."

Tubman was born a slave in Maryland's Dorchester County around 1820. At age five or six, she began to work as a house servant. Seven years later she was sent to work in the fields. While she was still in her early teens, she suffered an injury that would follow her for the rest of her life. Always ready to stand up for someone else, Tubman blocked a doorway to protect another field hand from an angry overseer.[1] The overseer picked up and threw a two-pound weight at the field hand. It fell short, striking Tubman on the head. She never fully recovered from the blow, which **subjected** her to spells in which she would fall into a deep sleep.

Around 1844 she married a free black named John Tubman and took his last name. (She was born Araminta Ross; she later changed her first name to Harriet, after her mother.) In 1849, in fear that she, along with other slaves on the plantation, was to be sold, Tubman resolved to run away. She set out one night on foot. With some assistance from a friendly white woman, Tubman was on her way. She followed the North Star by night, making her way to Pennsylvania and soon after to Philadelphia, where she found work and saved her money. The following year she returned to Maryland and escorted her sister and her sister's

---

1. overseer (ōˊvər sēˊər) *n.* person hired by a landowner to run a plantation and supervise slaves.

two children to freedom. She made the dangerous trip back to the South soon after to rescue her brother and two other men. On her third return, she went after her husband, only to find he had taken another wife. Undeterred, she found other slaves seeking freedom and escorted them to the North.

Tubman returned to the South again and again. She devised clever techniques that helped make her "forays" successful, including using the master's horse and buggy for the first leg of the journey; leaving on a Saturday night, since runaway notices couldn't be placed in newspapers until Monday morning; turning about and heading south if she encountered possible slave hunters; and carrying a drug to use on a baby if its crying might put the fugitives in danger. Tubman even carried a gun which she used to threaten the fugitives if they became too tired or decided to turn back, telling them, "You'll be free or die."

By 1856, Tubman's capture would have brought a $40,000 reward from the South. On one occasion, she overheard some men reading her wanted poster, which stated that she was illiterate. She promptly pulled out a book and **feigned** reading it. The ploy was enough to fool the men.

Tubman had made the perilous trip to slave country 19 times by 1860, including one especially challenging journey in which she rescued her 70-year-old parents. Of the famed heroine, who became known as "Moses," Frederick Douglass said, "Excepting John Brown—of sacred memory—I know of no one who has willingly encountered more perils and hardships to serve our enslaved people than [Harriet Tubman]."

And John Brown, who **conferred** with "General Tubman" about his plans to raid Harpers Ferry, once said that she was "one of the bravest persons on this continent."

Becoming friends with the leading abolitionists of the day, Tubman took part in antislavery meetings. On the way to such a meeting in Boston in 1860, in an incident in Troy, New York, she helped a fugitive slave who had been captured.

During the Civil War Harriet Tubman worked for the Union as a cook, a nurse, and even a spy. After the war she settled in Auburn, New York, where she would spend the rest of her long life. She died in 1913.

◀ **feigned**
(fānd) *v.* pretended or imitated

◀ **subjected**
(səb jekt´ id) *v.* caused one to experience

◀ **conferred**
(kən furd´) *v.* met to discuss

READ

Comprehension

Reread all or part of the text to help you answer the following questions.

1. For what is Harriet Tubman famous?

2. How was Tubman injured as a teen?

3. What "techniques" did Tubman use to make successful journeys?

Research: Clarify Details Choose an unfamiliar detail from the article and research it. Explain how your research helps you understand the article.

Summarize Write an objective summary of the article. Do not include opinions.

Language Study

Selection Vocabulary Define each boldfaced word from the article, and use it in a sentence of your own. What part of speech do all the words share?

• She never fully recovered from the blow, which **subjected** her to spells …

• She promptly pulled out a book and **feigned** reading it.

• And John Brown, who **conferred** with "General Tubman" about his plans to raid Harper's Ferry …

Literary Analysis

Reread the identified passage. Then, answer the following questions.

> **Focus Passage** *(pp. 432–433)*
>
> Around 1844 … escorted them to the North.

Key Ideas and Details

1. Why did Tubman first decide to run away?

2. What did Tubman do before she attempted to help her sister escape to freedom?

Craft and Structure

3. **(a)** What organizational pattern does the author use in this paragraph? **(b)** What words and phrases establish this pattern? **(c) Evaluate:** Why is this organizational pattern appropriate for the subject?

Integration of Knowledge and Ideas

4. **(a) Interpret:** What point does the author make in describing Tubman as "undeterred"? **(b) Support:** What details in the passage support the idea that Tubman was often "undeterred"?

Author's Viewpoint

An **author's viewpoint** includes the author's attitudes, opinions, and feelings toward a subject. Viewpoint is revealed through word choice and tone. Take notes on how the author's viewpoint is expressed in this article.

1. Heroes and Outlaws (a) Does the author portray Harriet Tubman as an outlaw or a hero? **(b)** What details in the text support this viewpoint?

2. Why does the author include quotations from Frederick Douglass and John Brown?

DISCUSS • RESEARCH • WRITE

From Text to Topic **Group Discussion**

Discuss the following passage with a group of classmates. Take notes during the discussion. Contribute your own ideas, and support them with examples from the text.

> Tubman even carried a gun which she used to threaten the fugitives if they became too tired or decided to turn back, telling them, "You'll be free or die."

Research **Investigate the Topic**

The Underground Railroad Harriet Tubman was a "conductor" on the Underground Railroad, a network of safe houses and routes that slaves used to escape to free northern states and Canada.

Assignment

Conduct research to find out more about the heroes and outlaws who helped slaves escape to freedom on the Underground Railroad. Consult books and articles on the topic, and search the Internet to find information. Take clear notes and identify your sources. Create or find illustrative charts and graphics, and use them in an **informal media presentation** for the class.

Writing to Sources **Narrative**

This article describes some of the steps Tubman and her "passengers" had to take in order to escape to freedom.

Assignment

As one of Tubman's "passengers," write a **fictional narrative** in the form of several diary entries. Writing from the perspective of a runaway slave, describe the problems you encounter and explain how you **solve** them by using some of Tubman's techniques that are described in the article. Follow these steps:

- Use diary format and style. Write from the first-person perspective, using the pronouns *I, me,* and *mine.*
- Include two or three entries in your diary.
- In each entry, use vivid details to describe the events of the day, what Tubman said and did, and your **reactions** to your experiences.

QUESTIONS FOR DISCUSSION

1. What does Tubman's threat tell you about the way she viewed her mission?

2. Was Tubman an outlaw, a hero, or both? Explain.

PREPARATION FOR ESSAY

You may use the results of your research to support your ideas in the essay you will write at the end of this section.

ACADEMIC VOCABULARY

Academic terms appear in blue on these pages. If these words are not familiar to you, use a dictionary to find their definitions. Then, use the words as you speak and write about the text.

RI.7.1, RI.7.2, RI.7.3, RI.7.4, RI.7.5, RI.7.6; W.7.3, W.7.4, W.7.7, W.7.8; SL.7.1, SL.7.5; L.7.4
[For full standards wording, see the chart in the front of this book.]

WANTED

Harriet Tubman, Abolitionist

She is a "Conductor" of the underground RailRoad that leads slave up north and away from our plantations causing a shortage in laborers. She threatens to shoot her passangers who want to make the right discion and turn back. She had never allowed on of our slaves to escape her grasp. This illiterate woman attends the insolent antislave meetings. The sooner she is turned in, the better it is for all us Southerners.

Tubman was born a slave in Maryland's Dorchester County and worked as a house servent around age five. About seven years later, she was sent to work in the fields. In her early teen years, she quite problematic for the overseers, constantly getting in the was of their slaves disapline. Later, she ran away from the plantation, then procceeded to set other slaves free too.

$40,000 REWARD

READ • RESEARCH • WRITE

Comprehension

Review the poster to help you answer the following questions.

1. Who might have produced and displayed this poster? Cite details to support your answer.

2. According to the poster, what damage was Tubman causing?

Critical Analysis

Key Ideas and Details

1. **Analyze:** What was the author's purpose for creating this poster?

Craft and Structure

2. **Generalize:** Based on the grammar and language of the poster, is it surprising that Tubman is referred to as "illiterate"? Explain.

3. **Analyze:** How does the poster appeal to the viewer's desire to belong to a group? Cite an example from the poster.

Integration of Knowledge and Ideas

4. **(a) Evaluate:** How important was Tubman's capture to the people who would have displayed this poster? **(b) Support:** What details support your answer?

Research **Investigate the Topic**

Abolitionist Leader Conduct research to find out about another hero of the American abolitionist movement during the 1800s. Note the qualities that made the person both a hero and an outlaw. Share your findings in an **informal presentation** for the class.

Writing to Sources **Explanatory Text**

Review the Web article about Harriet Tubman on pages 432–433. Then, write a **comparison-and-contrast essay** in which you examine the similarities and differences in the ways in which Tubman is portrayed in the article and in the wanted poster. Analyze the use of visual images and word choice as well as the impact of the information each author chose to include. Follow these steps:

- Organize your essay to show comparisons and contrasts.

- Use details from the selections, such as examples of logical reasoning, **facts**, and moral claims, to support your ideas.

- **Conclude** by evaluating which medium's portrayal is more **convincing**.

Common Core State Standards

RI.7.1, RI.7.4, RI.7.6, RI.7.9; W.7.1, W.7.4, W.7.7; SL.7.4
[For full standards wording, see the chart in the front of this book.]

ACADEMIC VOCABULARY

Academic terms appear in blue on these pages. If these words are not familiar to you, use a dictionary to find their definitions. Then, use the words as you speak and write about the text.

Speaking and Listening: **Group Discussion**

Heroes and Outlaws The texts in this section vary in genre, length, style, and perspective. However, all of the texts address, in some way, our fascination with heroes and outlaws. The ways in which we define both heroes and outlaws are related to the Big Question addressed in this unit: **What is the best way to communicate?**

Assignment

Conduct discussions. With a small group of classmates, conduct a discussion on how we communicate our ideas about heroes and outlaws. Refer to the texts in this section, other texts you have read, and your personal experience and knowledge to support your ideas. Begin your discussion by addressing the following questions:

- What defines a "hero"? Is everyone's definition the same? Why or why not?
- Why are certain individuals seen as heroes to some people and outlaws to others?
- Do heroes and outlaws create themselves, or do we create them through the ideas we communicate about them?

Summarize and present your ideas. After you have fully explored the topic, summarize your discussion and present your findings to the class as a whole.

▲ Refer to the selections you read in Part 3 as you complete the activities on this assessment.

Criteria for Success

✓ **Organizes the group effectively**
Appoint a group leader and a timekeeper. The group leader should present the discussion questions. The timekeeper should make sure the discussion takes no longer than 20 minutes.

✓ **Maintains focus of discussion**
As a group, stay on topic and avoid straying into other subject areas.

✓ **Involves all participants equally and fully**
No one person should monopolize the conversation. Rather, everyone should take turns speaking and contributing ideas.

✓ **Follows the rules for collegial discussion**
As each group member speaks, others should listen carefully. Build on one another's ideas and support viewpoints and opinions with sound reasoning and evidence. Express disagreement respectfully.

USE NEW VOCABULARY

As you speak and share ideas, work to use the vocabulary words you have learned in this unit. The more you use new words, the more you will "own" them.

Writing: **Narrative**

Heroes and Outlaws Heroes and outlaws have been the subjects of popular stories for thousands of years. Sometimes, the same person may be a hero in some stories and an outlaw (or villain) in others. The difference may be simply a matter of communication: how the character is described and how the events are presented.

Common Core State Standards

W.7.3.a–b, W.7.3.d–e; SL.7.1.a–d

[For full standards wording, see the chart in the front of this book.]

> ### Assignment
>
> Write a **fictional narrative** about a hero, an outlaw, or a combination of the two in which communication plays a role in introducing or resolving a conflict. The "outlaw" in your story can be someone who actually breaks the law, or someone who simply breaks rules. Use the knowledge and insights you gained in this section to help you compose your story.

Criteria for Success

Purpose/Focus
✓ **Connects specific incidents with larger ideas**
   Make clear connections between your characters and plot and the texts you have read in this section.

✓ **Clearly conveys the significance of the story**
   Provide a conclusion in which the conflict is resolved, either positively or negatively, in a satisfying and logical manner.

Organization
✓ **Sequences events logically**
   Structure your narrative so that individual events build on one another to create a coherent whole.

Development of Ideas/Elaboration
✓ **Supports insights**
   Include examples and details that draw from the texts you have read in this section.

✓ **Uses narrative techniques effectively**
   Use narrative techniques, such as flashback and foreshadowing, to build interest and suspense.

Language
✓ **Uses description effectively**
   Use descriptive details to paint word pictures that help readers see settings and characters.

Conventions
✓ **Does not have errors**
   Check your narrative to eliminate errors in grammar, spelling, and punctuation.

WRITE TO EXPLORE

Writing is a way to explore what you feel and think: This means that you may change your mind or get new ideas as you work. As you write your fictional narrative, explore your ideas on the role communication plays in depicting heroes and outlaws.

Writing to Sources: Explanatory Text

Heroes and Outlaws The authors in this section communicate their ideas about what makes a hero and what makes an outlaw in many different ways. They raise questions, such as the following:

- Are people who follow a law always right? Are people who break a law always wrong?
- How does the way we communicate through literature and other media affect our own and others' perceptions of heroes and outlaws?
- Can a person be both a hero and an outlaw?

Focus on the question that intrigues you the most, and then complete the following assignment.

Assignment

Write an **explanatory essay** in which you compare and contrast the ways in which two or more of the selections portray heroes and outlaws. As you analyze each selection, pay particular attention to the ways in which the author's attitude toward the subject influences his or her portrayal of a hero or an outlaw. Clearly present, develop, and support your ideas with examples and details from the texts.

Prewriting and Planning

Choose texts. Review the texts in this section to determine the ones you will cite in your essay. Select at least two that will provide strong material to support your main idea.

Gather details and identify key ideas. Use a chart like the one shown to develop your key ideas.

Focus Question: How does the way we communicate in literature and other media affect our perception of heroes and outlaws?

Text	Passage	Notes
The Highwayman	They had tied her up to attention, with many a sniggering jest. They had bound a musket beside her, with the muzzle beneath her breast!	The author portrays the legal authorities (King George's soldiers) as cruel and evil—moral outlaws.
Harriet Tubman	She devised clever techniques that helped make her "forays" successful, including using the master's horse and buggy for the first leg of the journey;	The author implies that, though Tubman broke laws, she was a hero because she protected a basic human right.

Example Key Idea: An author may apply moral standards rather than legal standards in defining and portraying heroes and outlaws.

INCORPORATE RESEARCH

In your essay, use the information you gathered as you completed the brief research assignments related to the selections in this section.

Organize your details. Gather the descriptions, examples, and quotations you will use to make comparisons and contrasts. Organize your details in a Venn diagram or two-column chart. Make sure you have details that support all of your main points.

Drafting

Follow an appropriate organizational pattern. To show comparisons and contrasts among two or more selections, you may decide to use the block method of organization. In this organization, present all the details about one selection first, then all the details about the second selection, and so on.

Plan your introduction. Begin your essay with a strong introductory paragraph that does the following:

- presents the selections you are comparing and contrasting
- identifies the features of heroes and outlaws that you will discuss
- states a main idea about your subjects

Revising and Editing

Review supporting details. Underline the key ideas in your essay. Confirm that each one is supported with details from the texts in this section or from your research. Add additional support if necessary.

Check subject-verb agreement. Circle the verbs in your essay. Make sure that sentences with singular subjects have singular verbs, and sentences with plural subjects have plural verbs.

Common Core State Standards

W.7.2.a–b, W.7.4, W.7.9, W.7.10; L.7.1, L.7.3
[For full standards wording, see the chart in the front of this book.]

CITE RESEARCH CORRECTLY

Avoid plagiarism by properly crediting the ideas of others. Refer to the Citing Sources pages in the Introductory Unit for information on citing sources.

Self-Evaluation Rubric

Use the following criteria to evaluate the effectiveness of your essay.

Criteria	Rating Scale
Purpose/Focus Clearly analyzes the similarities and differences between two or more related subjects	not very ... very 1 2 3 4
Organization Provides a clear organization that highlights the major points of comparison; uses appropriate transitions to create cohesion and clarify relationships among ideas; provides a strong introduction	1 2 3 4
Development of Ideas/Elaboration Develops the topic with concrete details that illustrate both similarities and differences between the subjects; provides relevant facts, definitions, quotations, and examples	1 2 3 4
Language Uses precise language and domain-specific vocabulary to compare and contrast a topic or topics	1 2 3 4
Conventions Uses proper grammar, including correct subject-verb agreement	1 2 3 4

Independent Reading

Titles for Extended Reading

In this unit, you have read texts in a wide variety of genres. Continue to read on your own. Select works that you enjoy, but challenge yourself to explore new authors and works of increasing depth and complexity. The titles suggested below will help you get started.

INFORMATIONAL TEXT

Discoveries: Pushing the Boundaries

In this book, you can read about many different ways to communicate. The **nonfiction articles** in this collection include "The Samurai of Feudal Japan" and "Challenging Assumptions."

This Land Was Made for You and Me: The Life and Songs of Woody Guthrie

by Elizabeth Partridge   EXEMPLAR TEXT ©

During the Great Depression of the 1930s, folk singer Woody Guthrie wandered the nation, meeting everyday people and writing songs. This **biography** of Guthrie includes photographs, posters, letters, and drawings.

Vincent van Gogh: Portrait of an Artist

by Jan Greenberg and Sandra Jordan   EXEMPLAR TEXT ©

The painter Vincent van Gogh surprised the art world of the late nineteenth century with his broad brushstrokes, vivid colors, and dreamlike landscapes. Meet Van Gogh in this exciting **biography**.

LITERATURE

It Doesn't Always Have to Rhyme
by Eve Merriam

This **poetry** collection is full of playful poems about poetry, including "How to Eat a Poem," "Metaphor," and "Onomatopoeia."

The Poetry of Robert Frost: The Collected Poems
by Robert Frost   EXEMPLAR TEXT ©

In his poetry, Robert Frost can capture a single thought or moment in a way that is personal but also universal. This **poetry** collection includes many of Frost's most popular poems.

When I Dance
by James Berry

James Berry was born in Jamaica but moved to England as a young man. Many of the poems in this **poetry** collection pulse with the rhythms of life in the Caribbean.

The Music of Dolphins
by Karen Hesse

After a plane crash, the main character in this exciting **novel** is raised by dolphins until the Coast Guard finds her. Mila "the Dolphin Girl" learns to speak, but she longs to return to the sea.

ONLINE TEXT SET

AUTOBIOGRAPHY
from **Angela's Ashes** Frank McCourt

SHORT STORY
Seventh Grade Gary Soto

WEB SITE
Safe Routes to School

Preparing to Read Complex Texts

Attentive Reading As you read on your own, ask yourself questions like these to enrich your reading experience.

When reading poetry, ask yourself...

Comprehension: **Key Ideas and Details**

- Who is the speaker of the poem? What kind of person does the speaker seem to be? How do I know?
- What is the poem about?
- If the poem is telling a story, who are the characters and what happens to them?
- Does any one line or section state the poem's theme, or meaning, directly? If so, what is that line or section?
- If there is no direct statement of a theme, what details help me to see the poem's deeper meaning?

Text Analysis: **Craft and Structure**

- How does the poem look on the page? Is it long and rambling or short and concise? Does it have long or short lines?
- Does the poem have a formal structure or is it free verse?
- Do I notice repetition, rhyme, or meter? Do I notice other sound devices? How do these techniques affect how I read the poem?
- Even if I do not understand every word, do I like the way the poem sounds? Why or why not?
- Do any of the poet's word choices seem especially interesting or unusual? Why?
- What images do I notice? Do they create clear word-pictures in my mind? Why or why not?

Connections: **Integration of Knowledge and Ideas**

- Has the poem helped me understand its subject in a new way? If so, how?
- Does the poem remind me of others I have read? If so, how?
- In what ways is the poem different from others I have read?
- What information, ideas, or insights have I gained from reading this poem?
- Would I like to read more poems by this poet? Why or why not?

Common Core State Standards

Reading Literature/ Informational Text

10. By the end of the year, read and comprehend literature, including stories, dramas, and poems, and literary nonfiction in the grades 6–8 text complexity band proficiently, with scaffolding as needed at the high end of the range.

UNIT 4

Do others see us more clearly than we see ourselves?

UNIT PATHWAY

PART 1
SETTING EXPECTATIONS

- INTRODUCING THE BIG QUESTION
- CLOSE READING WORKSHOP

PART 2
TEXT ANALYSIS
GUIDED EXPLORATION

DRAMATIC TRANSFORMATIONS

PART 3
TEXT SET
DEVELOPING INSIGHT

LEADERS AND FOLLOWERS

PART 4
DEMONSTRATING INDEPENDENCE

- INDEPENDENT READING
- ONLINE TEXT SET

CLOSE READING TOOL

Use this tool to practice the close reading strategies you learn.

STUDENT eTEXT

Bring learning to life with audio, video, and interactive tools.

ONLINE WRITER'S NOTEBOOK

Easily capture notes and complete assignments online.

Find all Digital Resources at **pearsonrealize.com.**

Do others see us more clearly than we see ourselves?

We are constantly learning about ourselves through our experiences and our interactions with others. Sometimes we feel that another person truly knows and understands us. Other times, however, we might suspect that someone is making an assumption about us based on appearance or other factors. To see ourselves and others clearly, it helps to reflect on the unique characteristics of each person. Our individual qualities and beliefs about ourselves influence how others see us and how we react to the people around us.

Exploring the Big Question

Collaboration: Group Discussion Start thinking about the Big Question by making a list of the ways you form impressions about other people and the ways that other people form impressions about you. Describe one specific example of each of the following:

- An impression based on appearance
- An impression influenced by prejudice, or bias
- An insight about the way another person treats you or others
- A time another person seemed to understand your thoughts
- A perception based on another person's reaction to a difficult situation

Share your examples with a small group. Discuss whether or not each situation helped someone see another person more clearly. As you conduct your discussion, use the words related to self-perception listed on the next page.

Connecting to the Literature Each reading in this unit will give you additional insight into the Big Question.

Vocabulary

Acquire and Use Academic Vocabulary The term "academic vocabulary" refers to words you typically encounter in scholarly and literary texts and in technical and business writing. Review the definitions of these academic vocabulary words.

Common Core State Standards

Speaking and Listening
1. Engage effectively in a range of collaborative discussions with diverse partners on grade 7 topics, texts, and issues, building on others' ideas and expressing their own clearly.

Language
6. Acquire and use accurately grade-appropriate general academic and domain-specific words and phrases; gather vocabulary knowledge when considering a word or phrase important to comprehension or expression.

appreciate (ə prē′ shē āt′) *v.* be thankful for

assumption (ə sump′ shən) *n.* act of accepting something as true without proof

bias (bī′ əs) *n.* slanted or prejudiced viewpoint

characteristic (kar′ ək tər is′ tik) *n.* trait; feature

define (dē fīn′) *v.* describe; explain

focus (fō′ kəs) *n.* direction; point of concentration

identify (ī den′ tə fī′) *v.* recognize; point out

ignore (ig nôr′) *v.* pay no attention to

Gather Vocabulary Knowledge Additional words related to self-perception are listed below. Categorize the words by deciding whether you know each one well, know it a little bit, or do not know it at all.

appearance	perception	reflect
image	perspective	reveal
	reaction	

Then, do the following:

1. Work with a partner to determine and write each word's definition.
2. Verify definitions by looking them up in a print or online dictionary and revising as needed.
3. Then, for each word, write an original sentence about how we see ourselves and others. Provide enough information so the meaning of each word is clear.
4. Exchange sentences with your partner to see if he or she agrees with your main points and your use of the vocabulary words.

Close Reading Workshop

In this workshop, you will learn an approach to reading that will deepen your understanding of literature and will help you better appreciate the author's craft. The workshop includes models for close reading, discussion, research, and writing. After you have reviewed the strategies and models, practice your skills with the Independent Practice selection.

 **Common Core State Standards**

RL.7.1, RL.7.2, RL.7.3, RL.7.4, RL.7.5; W.7.2, W.7.7; SL.7.1, SL.7.4

[For full standards wording, see the chart in the front of this book.]

CLOSE READING: DRAMA

In Part 2 of this unit you will focus on reading excerpts from various dramas. Use these strategies as you read the texts.

Comprehension: Key Ideas and Details

- Read first to unlock basic meaning.
- Use context clues to help you determine the meanings of unfamiliar words.
- Identify unfamiliar details that you might need to clarify through research.

Ask yourself questions such as these:
- Who are the main characters?
- When and where does the action take place?
- What conflicts do the characters face?

Text Analysis: Craft and Structure

- Think about the genre of the work and how the author presents ideas.
- Consider how stage directions can convey information about characters, sound effects, lighting, and props.
- Analyze how dialogue is used to reveal characters' personalities and emotions.

Ask yourself questions such as these:
- How does the author reveal information about characters and their conflicts?
- How do characters' actions advance the plot?
- How do stage directions help bring the drama to life?

Connections: Integration of Knowledge and Ideas

- Look for relationships among key ideas.
- Analyze how the author develops characters. Then, synthesize details about the characters to determine theme.
- Compare and contrast this work with similar works you have read.

Ask yourself questions such as these:
- How has this work broadened my knowledge of drama?
- How do elements work together to help the reader "see" the drama?
- Would I recommend this work to others? Why or why not?

Read

As you read this excerpt from a drama, take note of the annotations that model ways to closely read the text.

Reading Model

from *Sorry, Wrong Number* by Lucille Fletcher

[SCENE: *As curtain rises, we see a divided stage, only the center part of which is lighted and furnished as* MRS. STEVENSON'S *bedroom. Expensive, rather fussy furnishings.*[1] *A large bed, on which* MRS. STEVENSON, *clad in bed-jacket, is lying. A night-table close by, with phone, lighted lamp, and pill bottles. A mantle, with clock, R. A closed door, R. A window, with curtains closed, rear. The set is lit by one lamp on night-table. It is enclosed by three flats. Beyond this central set, the stage, on either side, is in darkness.*[1]

MRS. STEVENSON *is dialing a number on the phone, as curtain rises. She listens to phone, slams down receiver in irritation.*[2]

As she does so, we hear sound of a train roaring by in the distance. She reaches for her pill bottle, pours herself a glass of water, shakes out pill, swallows it, then reaches for the phone again, dials number nervously.][2]

SOUND: *Number being dialed on phone: Busy signal.*

MRS. STEVENSON (*A querulous, self-centered neurotic.*)[2] : Oh—dear! (*Slams down receiver, dials* OPERATOR.)

[SCENE: *A spotlight, L. of side flat, picks up out of peripheral darkness, figure of* 1ST OPERATOR, *sitting with headphones at a small table. If spotlight not available, use flashlight, clicked on by* 1ST OPERATOR, *illuminating her face.*][3]

OPERATOR: Your call, please?

MRS. STEVENSON: Operator? I've been dialing Murray Hill 4-0098 now for the last three-quarters of an hour, and the line is always busy. But I don't see how it could be that busy that long. Will you try it for me, please?

OPERATOR: Murray Hill 4-0098? One moment, please. [SCENE: *She makes gesture of plugging in call through a switchboard.*]

MRS. STEVENSON: I don't see how it could be busy all this time. It's my husband's office. He's working late tonight, and I'm all alone here in the house. My health is very poor—and I've been feeling so nervous all day....[4]

OPERATOR: Ringing Murray Hill 4-0098. ... (SOUND: *Phone buzz. It rings three times. Receiver is picked up at other end.*)

Craft and Structure

1 Stage directions give details that help create the mood. The description of a "fussy" bedroom surrounded by darkness conveys an unsettling feeling.

Key Ideas and Details

2 You might consult a dictionary to learn that *querulous* means "complaining" and a *neurotic* is an anxious person. If you combine these details with the other character traits described, you may conclude that Mrs. Stevenson is easily upset.

Craft and Structure

3 In this stage direction, the playwright gives specific instructions for lighting the scene in order to create the desired atmosphere.

Integration of Knowledge and Ideas

4 Mrs. Stevenson's dialogue reveals an internal conflict. She is uneasy because she is sick, alone, and cannot reach her husband.

[SCENE: *Spotlight picks up figure of a heavyset man, seated at desk with phone on right side of dark periphery of stage. He is wearing a hat. Picks up phone, which rings three times.*][5]

MAN: Hello.

MRS. STEVENSON: Hello …? (*A little puzzled*) Hello. Is Mr. Stevenson there?

MAN: (*into phone, as though he had not heard.*) Hello. … (*Louder*) Hello.

[SCENE: *Spotlight on left now moves from* **OPERATOR** *to another man,* **GEORGE**. *A killer type*,[6] *also wearing a hat, but standing as in a phone booth. A three-sided screen may be used to suggest this.*]

2ND MAN: (*slow, heavy quality, faintly foreign accent*). Hello.

1ST MAN: Hello, George?

GEORGE: Yes, sir.

MRS. STEVENSON: (*louder and more imperious, to phone*). Hello. Who's this? What number am I calling, please?[7]

1ST MAN: We have heard from our client. He says the coast is clear for tonight.

GEORGE: Yes, sir.

1ST MAN: Where are you now?

GEORGE: In a phone booth.

1ST MAN: OK. You should know the address. At eleven o'clock the private patrolman goes around to the bar on Second Avenue for a beer. Be sure that all the lights downstairs are out. There should be only one light visible from the street. At eleven-fifteen a subway train crosses the bridge. It makes a noise in case her window is open and she should scream.

MRS. STEVENSON: (*shocked*). Oh—HELLO! What number is this, please?

GEORGE: OK. I understand.

1ST MAN: Make it quick. As little blood as possible. Our client does not wish to make her suffer long.

GEORGE: A knife OK, sir?

1ST MAN: Yes. A knife will be OK. And remember—remove the rings and bracelets and the jewelry in the bureau drawer. Our client wishes it to look like simple robbery.[8]

GEORGE: OK—I get—[SCENE: *Spotlight suddenly goes out on* **GEORGE**.]

(*SOUND: A bland buzzing signal*)

Craft and Structure

5 These stage directions indicate a scene change. They describe the new setting and introduce a new character.

Key Ideas and Details

6 The playwright includes this detail to communicate that George is a threatening character. Stage directions like this can help a director choose the right actor for the role.

Integration of Knowledge and Ideas

7 Mrs. Stevenson can hear the two men, but they cannot hear her. This situation emphasizes her isolation and develops the theme.

Craft and Structure

8 This dialogue builds tension and suspense, and moves the action forward.

Discuss

Sharing your own ideas and listening to the ideas of others can deepen your understanding of a text and help you look at a topic in a whole new way. As you participate in collaborative discussions, work to have a genuine exchange in which classmates build upon one another's ideas. Support your points with evidence and ask meaningful questions.

Discussion Model

Student 1: The playwright includes a lot of information about Mrs. Stevenson in stage directions. Stage directions describe her "expensive, rather fussy" bedroom. They also describe Mrs. Stevenson's slamming down the receiver and picking it up again, which shows she feels frustrated.

Student 2: We also learn about Mrs. Stevenson through dialogue. She tells the operator that she's been trying to reach her husband, and that she's alone, sick, and nervous. When she overhears the dialogue between the men, we see her confusion and anxiety build—she keeps asking what number she is calling.

Student 3: What I noticed is that the dialogue clearly shows that this scene takes place decades ago. Mrs. Stevenson is calling "Murray Hill 4-0098." What does *Murray Hill* mean in a phone number?

Research

Targeted research can clarify unfamiliar details and shed light on various aspects of a text. Consider questions that arise in your mind as you read, and use those questions as the basis for research.

Research Model

Questions: *What does* Murray Hill *mean in a phone number? Where would someone with this phone number be located?*

Key Words for Internet Search: "Murray Hill" + name + telephone

Result: New York City telephone exchanges after December 1930.

What I Learned: Numbers that include names such as *Murray Hill* came into usage during the 1930s and '40s. Each name was a separate telephone exchange, and Murray Hill covered part of Manhattan in New York City.

Write

The following model essay evaluates Lucille Fletcher's use of stage directions and dialogue to reveal important details.

Writing Model: Argument

Stage Directions and Dialogue in *Sorry, Wrong Number*

If a play does not have a narrator to provide important details about characters and story events, the playwright must rely on stage directions and dialogue to convey information to readers. In this scene from *Sorry, Wrong Number*, Lucille Fletcher skillfully uses detailed stage directions and dialogue to reveal the main character's personality and move the action forward.

In the first paragraph, the writer introduces the main argument by providing a strong thesis statement.

Fletcher's stage directions are a major source of crucial details. As the scene opens, a long stage direction describes the setting: Mrs. Stevenson's "expensive, rather fussy" bedroom. This description does three important things. First, it suggests that Mrs. Stevenson herself is wealthy and fussy. Second, it helps readers picture the room clearly. Finally, by mentioning the darkness surrounding the room, it conveys a feeling of isolation and unease.

The writer makes a claim and supports it with specific details.

As the scene unfolds, stage directions provide further details about Mrs. Stevenson's personality and her growing internal conflict. The first time Mrs. Stevenson fails to reach her husband by phone, she slams down the receiver. She then takes a pill and dials a second time, nervously. She is described as a "querulous, self-centered neurotic." These details portray a character who is impatient, selfish, and anxious.

The writer draws a conclusion based on specific details provided in the stage directions.

Dialogue is another source of important details in this scene. Mrs. Stevenson tells the operator that she has been trying to reach her husband for almost an hour, and that she is alone, in poor health, and nervous. The dialogue also reveals specific information about the setting. The Murray Hill telephone exchange Mrs. Stevenson asks the operator for once covered a part of Manhattan. This detail reveals that her husband works somewhere in New York City.

By incorporating evidence from research, the writer provides an interesting fact about the setting.

When Mrs. Stevenson overhears two men plotting a murder, she keeps asking what number she is calling. The confusion further develops her mounting anxiety. The men cannot hear her and continue discussing their murder plans. As the tension and suspense build, the action of the play moves forward.

Through her skillful use of stage directions and dialogue, Lucille Fletcher reveals important details enabling readers to picture the scene and experience the building tension and suspense.

The conclusion restates the main idea and provides a strong closing.

As you read the following text, apply the close reading strategies you have learned. You may need to read the drama excerpt multiple times.

from the novel *Dragonwings*
by Laurence Yep

I do not know when I fell asleep, but it was already way past sunrise when I woke up. The light crept through the cracks in the walls and under the shutters and seemed to delight especially in dancing on my eyes. Father lay huddled, rolled up in his blanket. He did not move when the knock came at our door. I was still in my clothes because it was cold. I crawled out of the blankets and opened the side door.

The fog lay low on the hill. Tendrils drifted in through the open doorway. At first I could not see anything but shadows, and then a sudden breeze whipped the fog away from the front of our barn. Hand Clap stood there as if he had appeared by magic. He bowed.

"There you are." He turned and called over his shoulder. "Hey, everybody, they're here."

I heard the clink of harness and the rattle of an old wagon trying to follow the ruts in the road. Toiling up the hill out of the fog was Red Rabbit, and behind him I saw Uncle on the wagon seat. The rest of the wagon was empty—I suppose to give Red Rabbit less of a load to pull. Behind the wagon came the Company, with coils of ropes over their shoulders and baskets of food. I ran down the hill, my feet pounding against the hard, damp earth. I got up on the seat and almost bowled Uncle over. For once Uncle did not worry about his dignity but caught me up and returned my hug.

Meet the Author

"Sometimes I think of myself as a professional daydreamer," **Laurence Yep** (b. 1948) once said. His vivid imagination— along with the influences of his Chinese-American background and his interest in mythology and fantasy—have led him to write more than sixty novels, stories, and plays.

CLOSE READING TOOL

Read and respond to this selection online using the **Close Reading Tool.**

"Ouch," he said, and pushed me away. He patted himself lightly on his chest. "I'm not as young as I used to be."

Then Hand Clap, Lefty, and White Deer crowded around.

"Am I ever glad you're here," I said. "Poor Father—"

Uncle held up his hands. "We know. That's why we came."

"But how? Why?" I was bursting with a dozen questions all at once.

"Why, to help you get that thing up to the top of the hill," Uncle said. "Why else would we close up our shop and take a boat and climb this abominable hill, all on the coldest, wettest day ever known since creation?"

"But you don't believe in flying machines."

"I still don't," Uncle said sternly. "But I still feel as if I owe you something for what was done to you by that man who once was my son.[1] I'll be there to haul your machine up the hill, and I'll be there to haul it back down when it doesn't fly."

"We were all getting fat anyway," White Deer said, "especially Uncle."

---

1. **man who once was my son** Black Dog, who robbed the narrator and his father.

from the dramatization of *Dragonwings*

by Laurence Yep

RED RABBIT a horse that pulls the company's laundry wagon	**MOON SHADOW** the narrator of the story
UNCLE BRIGHT STAR another laundry owner	**MISS WHITLAW** owner of a stable in San Francisco where the narrator and his father live
WHITE DEER the third laundry owner	**WINDRIDER** Moon Shadow's father

Scene 9 *Piedmont, later that day outside the stable.*

MOON SHADOW: September twenty-second, Nineteen-ought-nine. Dear Mother. I have bad news. We are going to lose Dragonwings before father can fly it. Black Dog stole all we have, and the landlord will not give us an extension on our rent. So we'll have to move and leave Dragonwings behind. We have asked Miss Whitlaw for help, but her new house has taken up all of her money. And even if Uncle would speak to us, he has probably spent all he has on rebuilding his laundry.

[*UNCLE BRIGHT STAR and MISS WHITLAW enter from L.*]

MISS WHITLAW: I could have gotten down from the wagon by myself.

UNCLE BRIGHT STAR: Watch gopher hole.

MISS WHITLAW: I'm younger than you.

MOON SHADOW: Uncle, Miss Whitlaw!

MISS WHITLAW: How are you?

[*Shaking MOON SHADOW's hand. WINDRIDER enters from U. He now wears a cap.*]

WINDRIDER: Come to laugh, Uncle?

UNCLE BRIGHT STAR: I came to help you fly your contraption.

MOON SHADOW: But you don't believe in flying machines.

UNCLE BRIGHT STAR: And I'll haul that thing back down when it doesn't fly. Red Rabbit and me were getting fat anyway. But look at how tall you've grown. And how thin. And ragged. [*Pause.*] But you haven't broken your neck which was more than I ever expected.

MISS WHITLAW: As soon as I told your uncle, we hatched the plot together. You ought to get a chance to fly your aeroplane.

UNCLE BRIGHT STAR: Flat purse, strong backs.

WINDRIDER: We need to pull Dragonwings to the very top.

UNCLE BRIGHT STAR: That hill is a very steep hill.

WINDRIDER: It has to be that one. The winds are right.

UNCLE BRIGHT STAR: Ah, well, it's the winds.

WINDRIDER: Take the ropes. *[Pantomimes taking a rope over his shoulder as he faces the audience.]* Got a good grip?

OTHERS: *[Pantomiming taking the ropes.]* Yes, right, etc.

WINDRIDER: Then pull.

*[They strain. **MOON SHADOW** stumbles but gets right up. Stamping his feet to get better footing, he keeps tugging.]*

MOON SHADOW: *[Giving up.]* It's no good.

UNCLE BRIGHT STAR: Pull in rhythm. As we did on the railroad.[1]
*[In demonstration, **UNCLE BRIGHT STAR** stamps his feet in a slow rhythm to set the beat and the others repeat. The rhythm picks up as they move.]*
Ngúng, ngúng.
Dew gùng

OTHERS: Ngúng, ngúng.
Dew gùng

UNCLE BRIGHT STAR: *[Imitating the intonation of the Cantonese.]*
Púsh, púsh.
Wòrk, wòrk.

OTHERS: Púsh, púsh.
Wòrk, wòrk.

UNCLE BRIGHT STAR: Seen gà,
Gee gá.

[High rising tone on the last syllable.]

OTHERS: Seen gà,
Gee gá.

[High rising tone on the last syllable.]

---

1. railroad Uncle Bright Star had helped dig tunnels through the mountains for the railroad.

UNCLE BRIGHT STAR: Get rich,
Go home.

OTHERS: Get rich,
Go home.

[MOON SHADOW, WINDRIDER, UNCLE BRIGHT STAR and MISS WHITLAW arrive D.]

MOON SHADOW: *[Panting.]* We made it. Tramp the grass down in front.

[WINDRIDER stands C as the others stamp the grass. They can't help smiling and laughing a little.]

WINDRIDER: That's enough.

MOON SHADOW: [To **MISS WHITLAW.**] Take that propeller.

[MISS WHITLAW takes her place before the right propeller with her hands resting on the blade. MOON SHADOW takes his place beside the left propeller. WINDRIDER faces U., his back to the audience.]

MISS WHITLAW: Listen to the wind on the wings.

UNCLE BRIGHT STAR: It's alive.

WINDRIDER: All right.

[MOON SHADOW and MISS WHITLAW pull down at the propellers and back away quickly. We hear a motor cough into life. Propellers begin to turn with a roar.]

UNCLE BRIGHT STAR: *[Slowly turning.]* What's wrong? Is it just going to roll down the hill?

[MISS WHITLAW crosses her fingers as they all turn to watch the aeroplane.]

MISS WHITLAW: He's up!

[WINDRIDER starts to do his flight ballet.]

MOON SHADOW: *[Pointing.]* He's turning.

UNCLE BRIGHT STAR: He's really flying.

MISS WHITLAW: I never thought I'd see the day. A human up in the sky. Off the ground.

[They turn and tilt their heads back.]

MISS WHITLAW: *[Cont'd.]* Free as an eagle.

Uncle Bright Star: *[Correcting her.]* Like dragon.

Moon Shadow: Father, you did it. *[Wonderingly.]* You did it.

*[The aeroplane roars loudly overhead. **Moon Shadow** as adult steps forward and addresses the audience.]*

Moon Shadow: I thought he'd fly forever and ever. Up, up to heaven and never come down. But then some of the guy wires[2] broke, and the right wings separated. Dragonwings came crashing to earth. Father had a few broken bones, but it was nothing serious. Only the aeroplane was wrecked. Uncle took him back to the laundry to recover. Father didn't say much, just thought a lot—I figured he was busy designing the next aeroplane. But when Father was nearly well, he made me sit down next to him.

Windrider: Uncle says he'll make me a partner if I stay. So the western officials would have to change my immigration class. I'd be a merchant, and merchants can bring their wives here. Would you like to send for Mother?

Moon Shadow: *[Going to **Windrider**.]* But Dragonwings?

Windrider: When I was up in the air, I tried to find you. You were so small. And getting smaller. Just disappearing from sight. *[Handing his cap to **Moon Shadow**.]* Like you were disappearing from my life. *[He begins his ballet again.]* I knew it wasn't the time. The Dragon King[3] said there would be all sorts of lessons.

*[**Moon Shadow** turns to audience as an adult.]*

Moon Shadow: We always talked about flying again. Only we never did. *[Putting on cap.]* But dreams stay with you, and we never forgot.

*[**Windrider** takes his final pose. A gong sounds.]*

---

2. **guy wires** wires that help to steady the plane's two sets of wings.
3. **Dragon King** In Chinese legends, most dragons are not evil creatures. Earlier in the story, Windrider relates a dream sequence in which he was given his name by the Dragon King and learned he had once been a flying dragon.

Close Reading Activities

Read

Comprehension: **Key Ideas and Details**

1. In the novel excerpt, what reason does Uncle Bright Star give for helping Windrider?

2. (a) In the novel excerpt, how does Uncle plan to get the flying machine up the hill? **(b) Compare:** In the scene from the drama, what helps the audience grasp how Dragonwings will be moved?

3. (a) What happens to Dragonwings? **(b) Infer:** How is Windrider changed by his flight? **(c) Interpret:** What does Moon Shadow mean when he says, "dreams stay with you, and we never forgot"?

4. Summarize: Write a brief, objective summary of Scene 9 from *Dragonwings*. Include important textual details.

Text Analysis: **Craft and Structure**

5. (a) Interpret: Why does the playwright have the characters chant? **(b) Draw Conclusions:** Why do they chant in both Chinese and English?

6. Analyze: If *Dragonwings* were a three-act play, in which act do you think you would find the excerpt you read? Explain.

7. (a) Compare and Contrast: How is the dialogue in the drama similar to and different from the dialogue in the novel excerpt? **(b) Analyze:** Which version—the novel or the drama—is more effective in helping you picture the action? Why?

Connections: **Integration of Knowledge and Ideas**

Discuss
Conduct a **small-group discussion** about the stage directions in this scene. Find and discuss examples of directions that show action, reveal thoughts and feelings, or describe the setting. Then, answer this question: Are stage directions as useful to readers as they are to actors? Explain your answer.

Research
In his final speech, Windrider mentions the Dragon King, a character from Chinese mythology. Briefly research the Dragon King to find out what he looks like and what powers he has. Take notes as you perform your research. Then, write a brief

explanation of why the Dragon King is important to Windrider.

Write
Conflicts can lead people to change their goals. In an **essay,** identify Windrider's original goal and explain how conflict changed it. Support your analysis with details from the scene.

 Do others see us more clearly than we see ourselves?

Based on his letter and his words and actions in the scene, what qualities do you see in Moon Shadow that he may not see in himself?

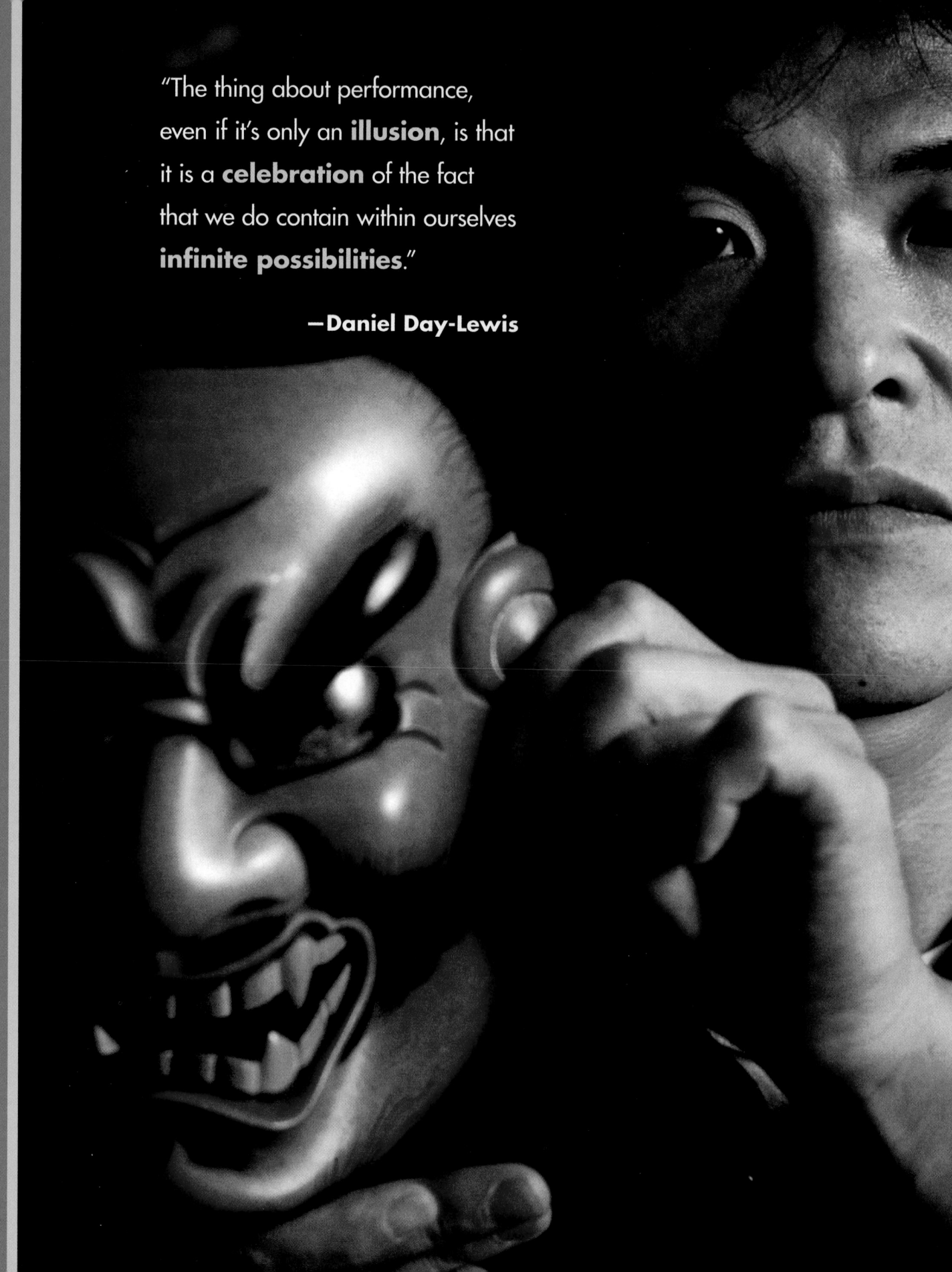

"The thing about performance, even if it's only an **illusion**, is that it is a **celebration** of the fact that we do contain within ourselves **infinite possibilities**."

—**Daniel Day-Lewis**

DRAMATIC TRANSFORMATIONS

As you read the drama in this section, pay careful attention to the ways in which characters change and grow in reaction to both internal and external conflicts. The quotation on the opposite page will help you explore the idea that everyone possesses the potential for change.

◀ **CRITICAL VIEWING** What dramatic transformation is about to take place in the photo on the opposite page?

READINGS IN PART 2

DRAMA
**A Christmas Carol:
Scrooge and Marley,
Act I**
Israel Horovitz (p. 468)

DRAMA
**A Christmas Carol:
Scrooge and Marley,
Act II**
Israel Horovitz (p. 502)

CLOSE READING TOOL

Use the **Close Reading Tool** to practice the strategies you learn in this unit.

Elements of Drama

A **drama** is a story that is meant to be performed.

A **drama,** or **play,** is a story that is performed for an audience. Some dramas are presented live on a stage, while others are recorded on film. No matter what the form, a drama brings to life the words of its author, the **playwright.**

Drama is similar to fiction in many ways. Like fiction, drama focuses on **characters,** made-up people who interact in a particular **setting,** or environment. The characters are caught up in a struggle, or **conflict.** This drives the **plot**—a series of actions that build to a **climax.** The climax is the highest point of tension. The action then winds down in a **resolution.**

Unlike fiction, drama is meant to be performed. Instead of *reading* a playwright's words, audiences see and hear actors speak the words.

The written text of a drama is called a **script.** A script consists of **dialogue,** the words spoken by the actors, and **stage directions,** the playwright's instructions about how the drama should be performed. **Acts** are the units of action in a drama. Acts are often divided into parts called **scenes.**

Elements of Drama	
Stage Directions	Stage directions are the playwright's instructions about how to perform the drama. They tell how actors should speak and move, and give details about lighting, sound effects, and costumes. These abbreviations are often used in stage directions: **C:** center stage **D:** downstage (nearest to audience) **U:** upstage (farthest from audience) **L:** stage left (audience's right) **R:** stage right (audience's left)
Dialogue	Dialogue is conversation between or among characters.
Set/Scenery	*Set* and *scenery* are terms used to describe the construction onstage that suggests the time and place of the action.
Props	Props are small movable items, such as a doctor's clipboard or a student's notebook, that actors use to make their actions look realistic.
Acts and Scenes	Acts and scenes are the basic units of action in a drama. A full-length drama may consist of several acts.

Changing Forms of Drama

Early Drama The earliest known written dramas came to us from the ancient Greeks. The Greeks divided drama into two basic categories that we still use today: **comedy** and **tragedy.**

Comedy	• features ordinary people in funny or ridiculous situations • usually has a happy ending • is meant to entertain, but also may point out human weaknesses and the faults of a society
Tragedy	• shows the downfall of the main character, known as the **tragic hero** • the tragic hero may be an admirable person with a fault that brings about his or her destruction • the hero might also be an ordinary person destroyed by an evil force in society

The biggest difference between a comedy and a tragedy is the way that the story ends. Comedies end in happy events, such as reunions or weddings. Tragedies end in sad events, such as deaths or partings. After the great plays of the ancient Greeks, drama went into a decline that lasted more than one thousand years. It bloomed again during the time of English playwright William Shakespeare (1564–1616). Shakespeare and his fellow dramatists wrote both comedies and tragedies.

Drama Today The modern period has seen a tremendous growth in dramatic writing, and this growth has brought change—even in the meaning of the term *drama*. Contemporary plays and films that treat serious subjects tend to be called *dramas* now, rather than *tragedies*. These serious works are different from contemporary comedies, which, as expected, are lighter and more entertaining.

An even more important change is the way different media have altered people's experience with drama. For several thousand years, people saw dramas in only one way: live. Today, the world of drama is not limited to the stage. Here are some other common types of dramas:

- **Screenplays** are the scripts for films. They include camera angles and can allow for more scene changes than a stage play.

- **Teleplays** are scripts written for television. They contains elements similar to those in a screenplay.

- **Radio plays** are written to be performed as radio broadcasts. They include sound effects and do not require a set.

Common Core State Standards

Reading Literature

3. Analyze how particular elements of a story or drama interact (e.g., how setting shapes the characters or plot).

5. Analyze how a drama's or poem's form or structure (e.g., soliloquy, sonnet) contributes to its meaning.

Analyzing Drama

Drama has its own unique way of telling stories about **characters**.

Structure in Drama The **structure,** or framework, of a drama affects the way the audience or reader finds meaning in the performance or script. The following is a typical structure for a three-act drama.

Act I	The characters, setting, and **conflict**, or problem, are introduced in the **exposition**.
Act II	In the **rising action**, the main character, or **protagonist**, tries to solve the conflict, but faces obstacles that prevent an easy solution.
Act III	The **climax**, or highest point of interest, represents a turning point in the drama. During the **falling action**, the plot moves toward the **resolution** of the conflict.

Of course, not all dramas follow a three-act structure. Many classic dramas, including most works by the Ancient Greeks and by Shakespeare, consist of five acts. One-act plays, on the other hand, contain a single act. Some one-act plays are divided into multiple scenes.

Conflict in Drama Dramatic action is driven by **conflict,** or struggle. There are two types of conflict in drama. **External conflict** occurs between a character and an outside force, such as another character. **Internal conflict** occurs within the mind of a character, as when a character is torn between opposing feelings or goals.

Example: External Conflict

- Two young people want to marry, but their parents will not allow it.
- A family must flee their war-torn country.

Example: Internal Conflict

- A girl must decide if she should turn in her friend, who has committed a crime.
- A man struggles to overcome a violent past.

Action: Showing, Not Telling

Drama is moved forward entirely by spoken dialogue and physical action. Audiences who watch a play or film are not *told* what is happening. Rather, they are *shown* what happens. For example, the audience may recognize conflict by hearing anger in an actor's voice or seeing tension in his body. As a drama unfolds, various elements work together to bring the story to life. A dimly lit stage may create an emotional effect; one character's tone of voice may make another character respond in a certain way.

Obviously, the experience of reading a drama differs from that of seeing it performed. Readers experience a script more fully if they imagine the setting described in the stage directions and the way the actors' voices and movements bring the dialogue to life.

Character Development In drama, two elements are key to the development of character: stage directions and dialogue. Playwrights use **stage directions** to tell how characters speak, move, and interact with other characters. Playwrights create **dialogue** to reveal character in several ways.

- A character may directly express private thoughts, feelings, and conflicts in a speech.
- Personality traits may be revealed as a character interacts with other characters.
- A character may comment on another character.

In addition, playwrights may have characters deliver different types of speeches.

- A **monologue** is a long, uninterrupted speech spoken by one character to another.
- A **soliloquy** is a speech in which a character is alone and reveals private thoughts. Sometimes a soliloquy is spoken to the audience. Other times, the character is speaking only to himself or herself.
- An **aside** is a comment made by a character to the audience. It is not meant to be heard by the other characters.

To engage the audience and reader, playwrights create **complex characters** who resemble real people. Complex characters are involved in complicated relationships. These characters change as a play progresses.

Theme in Drama As in most other literary genres, drama conveys **themes,** or insights about life and human nature.

Examples of Theme in Drama

Dramatic Subject	Theme
A basketball team with a losing record comes back to win the championship.	If you think positively, you can overcome past failures.
The special relationship between a brother and sister helps them adjust to their new school.	Friends may come and go, but family members will always be there for you.

The various elements of a drama work together to convey its theme. To determine and analyze the theme of a drama, notice how the characters respond to conflicts and decide whether they change or grow as a result of their experiences. Consider how the setting impacts characters or events. Finally, look for central ideas that are emphasized throughout the drama through the words and actions of the characters. Considering all of these elements will lead you to the central insight in a dramatic work.

Meet the Author

As a teenager, **Israel Horovitz** (b. 1939) did not like books by Charles Dickens. As he got older, however, he came to appreciate Dickens's style and stories. Today, Horovitz refers to Dickens as "a masterful storyteller." He imagines that if Dickens were alive today, he would be "our greatest television writer, or perhaps screenwriter." As Horovitz adapted Dickens's novel into a play, he thought about which character was his favorite. Surprisingly, it is Scrooge, who reminds Horowitz of his own father.

© **Common Core State Standards**

Reading Literature
3. Analyze how particular elements of a story or drama interact.
5. Analyze how a drama's or poem's form or structure contributes to its meaning.

Language
6. Acquire and use accurately grade-appropriate general academic and domain-specific words and phrases; gather vocabulary knowledge when considering a word or phrase important to comprehension or expression.

? Do others see us more clearly than we see ourselves?

Explore the Big Question as you read *A Christmas Carol: Scrooge and Marley*, Act I. Take notes on how the main character sees himself and how others see him.

CLOSE READING FOCUS

Key Ideas and Details: **Purpose for Reading**

Setting a purpose gives you a focus as you read. You may set one or more of these purposes:

- To learn about a subject
- To be entertained
- To gain understanding
- To take action or make a decision
- To be inspired
- To complete a task

To help you set a purpose, preview a text before reading. Look at the title, pictures, captions, and beginnings of passages to help you determine your reason for reading the text.

Craft and Structure: **Dialogue**

Dialogue is a conversation between characters. In a play, dialogue serves several key functions. When the play is viewed as a performance, the characters are developed entirely through dialogue. Characters' words and speech patterns give clues to their personalities. Dialogue also advances the plot and develops the conflict. In a dramatic script, a character's name appears before the lines he or she speaks, as in the following example.

 MRS. PEREZ. Come on, kids! We're leaving.
 JEN. Wait for me! *Please* wait for me!

Vocabulary

You will encounter the following words in *A Christmas Carol: Scrooge and Marley*, Act I. Copy the words into your notebook, and record their definitions.

implored	morose	destitute
void	conveyed	gratitude

CLOSE READING MODEL

The passage below is from Israel Horovitz's play *A Christmas Carol: Scrooge and Marley,* Act I. The annotations to the right of the passage show ways in which you can use close reading skills to set a purpose for reading and to analyze dialogue.

from *A Christmas Carol: Scrooge and Marley,* Act I

MARLEY. How is it that I appear before you in a shape that you can see, I may not tell. I have sat invisible beside you many and many a day. That is no light part of my penance. I am here tonight to warn you that you have yet a chance and hope of escaping my fate.[1] A chance and hope of my procuring, Ebenezer.

SCROOGE. You were always a good friend to me. Thank'ee!

MARLEY. You will be haunted by Three Spirits.[2]

SCROOGE. Would that be the chance and hope you mentioned, Jacob?

MARLEY. It is.

SCROOGE. I think I'd rather not.

MARLEY. Without their visits, you cannot hope to shun the path I tread. Expect the first one tomorrow, when the bell tolls one.

SCROOGE. Couldn't I take 'em all at once, and get it over, Jacob?[3]

MARLEY. Expect the second on the next night at the same hour. The third upon the next night when the last stroke of twelve has ceased to vibrate.[4] Look to see me no more. Others may, but you may not. And look that, for your own sake, you remember what has passed between us!

Purpose for Reading
1 At this point, your purpose for reading may be to learn more about Scrooge and to discover what hope there is for him to escape his fate.

Dialogue
2 You may sense from this dialogue that Marley's remarks will have a strong impact on the plot.

Dialogue
3 Based on his words, Scrooge seems nervous about what is to come. By revealing Scrooge's unease, this dialogue helps you gain new insight into Scrooge's personality.

Purpose for Reading
4 Marley has revealed that Scrooge's "chance and hope" lies in the visits from three spirits. At this point, your purpose for reading may broaden. You may read on to find out what role the Three Spirits play in Scrooge's fate.

A Christmas Carol:

SCROOGE AND MARLEY

Israel Horovitz
from A Christmas Carol
by Charles Dickens

JACOB MARLEY, a specter
EBENEZER SCROOGE, not yet dead, which is to say still alive
BOB CRATCHIT, Scrooge's clerk
FRED, Scrooge's nephew
THIN DO-GOODER
PORTLY DO-GOODER
SPECTERS (VARIOUS), carrying money-boxes
THE GHOST OF CHRISTMAS PAST
FOUR JOCUND TRAVELERS
A BAND OF SINGERS
A BAND OF DANCERS
LITTLE BOY SCROOGE
YOUNG MAN SCROOGE
FAN, Scrooge's little sister
THE SCHOOLMASTER
SCHOOLMATES
FEZZIWIG, a fine and fair employer
DICK, young Scrooge's co-worker
YOUNG SCROOGE
A FIDDLER
MORE DANCERS
SCROOGE'S LOST LOVE

SCROOGE'S LOST LOVE'S DAUGHTER
SCROOGE'S LOST LOVE'S HUSBAND
THE GHOST OF CHRISTMAS PRESENT
SOME BAKERS
MRS. CRATCHIT, Bob Cratchit's wife
BELINDA CRATCHIT, a daughter
MARTHA CRATCHIT, another daughter
PETER CRATCHIT, a son
TINY TIM CRATCHIT, another son
SCROOGE'S NIECE, Fred's wife
THE GHOST OF CHRISTMAS FUTURE, a mute Phantom
THREE MEN OF BUSINESS
DRUNKS, SCOUNDRELS, WOMEN OF THE STREETS
A CHARWOMAN
MRS. DILBER
JOE, an old second-hand goods dealer
A CORPSE, very like Scrooge
AN INDEBTED FAMILY
ADAM, a young boy
A POULTERER
A GENTLEWOMAN
SOME MORE MEN OF BUSINESS

ACT I

THE PLACE OF THE PLAY Various locations in and around the City of London, including Scrooge's Chambers and Offices; the Cratchit Home; Fred's Home; Scrooge's School; Fezziwig's Offices; Old Joe's Hide-a-Way.

THE TIME OF THE PLAY The entire action of the play takes place on Christmas Eve, Christmas Day, and the morning after Christmas, 1843.

SCENE 1

[*Ghostly music in auditorium. A single spotlight on* JACOB MARLEY, D.C. *He is ancient; awful, dead-eyed. He speaks straight out to auditorium.*]

MARLEY. [*Cackle-voiced*] My name is Jacob Marley and I am dead. [*He laughs.*] Oh, no, there's no doubt that I am dead. The register of my burial was signed by the clergyman, the clerk, the undertaker . . . and by my chief mourner . . . Ebenezer Scrooge . . . [*Pause; remembers*] I am dead as a doornail.

[*A spotlight fades up, Stage Right, on* SCROOGE, *in his counting-house,*[1] *counting. Lettering on the window behind* SCROOGE *reads:* "SCROOGE AND MARLEY, LTD." *The spotlight is tight on* SCROOGE's *head and shoulders. We shall not yet see into the offices and setting. Ghostly music continues, under.* MARLEY *looks across at* SCROOGE; *pitifully. After a moment's pause*] I present him to you: Ebenezer Scrooge . . . England's most tightfisted hand at the grindstone, Scrooge! a squeezing, wrenching, grasping, scraping, clutching, covetous, old sinner! secret, and self-contained, and solitary as an oyster. The cold within him freezes his old features, nips his pointed nose, shrivels his cheek, stiffens his gait; makes his eyes red, his thin lips blue; and speaks out shrewdly in his grating voice. Look at him. Look at him . . .

[SCROOGE *counts and mumbles.*]

SCROOGE. They owe me money and I will collect. I will have

---

1. **counting-house** office for keeping financial records and writing business letters.

Purpose for Reading
Based on the images, title, and other information you can quickly preview, what is your purpose for reading this play?

Comprehension
Where and when does this drama take place?

them jailed, if I have to. They owe me money and I will collect what is due me.

[MARLEY *moves towards* SCROOGE; *two steps. The spotlight stays with him.*]

MARLEY. [*Disgusted*] He and I were partners for I don't know how many years. Scrooge was my sole executor, my sole administrator, my sole assign, my sole residuary legatee,[2] my sole friend and my sole mourner. But Scrooge was not so cut up by the sad event of my death, but that he was an excellent man of business on the very day of my funeral, and solemnized[3] it with an undoubted bargain. [*Pauses again in disgust*] He never painted out my name from the window. There it stands, on the window and above the warehouse door: Scrooge and Marley. Sometimes people new to our business call him Scrooge and sometimes they call him Marley. He answers to both names. It's all the same to him. And it's cheaper than painting in a new sign, isn't it? [*Pauses; moves closer to* SCROOGE] Nobody has ever stopped him in the street to say, with gladsome looks, "My dear Scrooge, how are you? When will you come to see me?" No beggars implored him to bestow a trifle, no children ever ask him what it is o'clock, no man or woman now, or ever in his life, not once, inquire the way to such and such a place. [MARLEY *stands next to* SCROOGE *now. They share, so it seems, a spotlight.*] But what does Scrooge care of any of this? It is the very thing he likes! To edge his way along the crowded paths of life, warning all human sympathy to keep its distance.

[*A ghostly bell rings in the distance.* MARLEY *moves away from* SCROOGE, *now, heading D. again. As he does, he "takes" the light:* SCROOGE *has disappeared into the black void beyond.* MARLEY *walks D.C., talking directly to the audience. Pauses*]

The bell tolls and I must take my leave. You must stay a while with Scrooge and watch him play out his scroogey

---

2. **my sole executor** (eg zek′ yōō tər), **my sole administrator, my sole assign** (ə sīn′), **my sole residuary legatee** (ri zij′ ōō er′ ē leg′ ə tē′) legal terms giving one person responsibility to carry out the wishes of another who has died.
3. **solemnized** (säl′ əm nīzd′) *v.* honored or remembered. Marley is being sarcastic.

Dialogue
What do these lines reveal about Marley's character?

Vocabulary ▶
implored (im plôrd′) *v.* begged

life. It is now the story: the once-upon-a-time. Scrooge is busy in his counting-house. Where else? Christmas eve and Scrooge is busy in his counting-house. It is cold, bleak, biting weather outside: foggy withal: and, if you listen closely, you can hear the people in the court go wheezing up and down, beating their hands upon their breasts, and stamping their feet upon the pavement stones to warm them . . .

[*The clocks outside strike three.*]

Only three! and quite dark outside already: it has not been light all day this day.

[*This ghostly bell rings in the distance again.* MARLEY *looks about him. Music in.* MARLEY *flies away.*]

[*N.B.* MARLEY's *comings and goings should, from time to time, induce the explosion of the odd flash-pot. I.H.*]

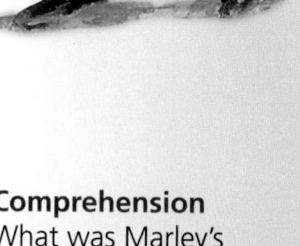

▼ **Critical Viewing**
How does this portrayal of Scrooge compare with the image you picture as you read?

SCENE 2

[*Christmas music in, sung by a live chorus, full. At conclusion of song, sound fades under and into the distance. Lights up in set: offices of Scrooge and Marley, Ltd.* SCROOGE *sits at his desk, at work. Near him is a tiny fire. His door is open and in his line of vision, we see* SCROOGE's *clerk,* BOB CRATCHIT, *who sits in a dismal tank of a cubicle, copying letters. Near* CRATCHIT *is a fire so tiny as to barely cast a light: perhaps it is one pitifully glowing coal?* CRATCHIT *rubs his hands together, puts on a white comforter*[4] *and tries to heat his hands around his candle.* SCROOGE's NEPHEW *enters, unseen.*]

SCROOGE. What are you doing, Cratchit? Acting cold, are you? Next, you'll be asking to replenish your coal from my coal-box, won't you? Well, save your breath, Cratchit! Unless you're prepared to find employ elsewhere!

NEPHEW. [*Cheerfully; surprising* SCROOGE] A merry Christmas to you, Uncle! God save you!

SCROOGE. Bah! Humbug![5]

Comprehension
What was Marley's relationship to Scrooge?

---

4. **comforter** (kum' fər tər) *n.* long, woolen scarf.
5. **Humbug** (hum' bug') *interj.* nonsense.

NEPHEW. Christmas a "humbug," Uncle? I'm sure you don't mean that.

SCROOGE. I do! Merry Christmas? What right do you have to be merry? What reason have you to be merry? You're poor enough!

NEPHEW. Come, then. What right have you to be dismal? What reason have you to be **morose**? You're rich enough.

SCROOGE. Bah! Humbug!

NEPHEW. Don't be cross, Uncle.

SCROOGE. What else can I be? Eh? When I live in a world of fools such as this? Merry Christmas? What's Christmas-time to you but a time of paying bills without any money; a time for finding yourself a year older, but not an hour richer. If I could work my will, every idiot who goes about with "Merry Christmas" on his lips, should be boiled with his own pudding, and buried with a stake of holly through his heart. He should!

NEPHEW. Uncle!

SCROOGE. Nephew! You keep Christmas in your own way and let me keep it in mine.

Vocabulary ▶
morose (mə rōs´) *adj.*
gloomy; ill-tempered

Do others see us more clearly than we see ourselves?

Nephew. Keep it! But you don't keep it, Uncle.

Scrooge. Let me leave it alone, then. Much good it has ever done you!

Nephew. There are many things from which I have derived good, by which I have not profited, I daresay. Christmas among the rest. But I am sure that I always thought of Christmas time, when it has come round—as a good time: the only time I know of, when men and women seem to open their shut-up hearts freely, and to think of people below them as if they really were fellow-passengers to the grave, and not another race of creatures bound on other journeys. And therefore, Uncle, though it has never put a scrap of gold or silver in my pocket, I believe that it *has* done me good, and that it *will* do me good; and I say, God bless it!

[*The* Clerk *in the tank applauds, looks at the furious* Scrooge *and pokes out his tiny fire, as if in exchange for the moment of impropriety.* Scrooge *yells at him.*]

Scrooge. [*To the clerk*] Let me hear another sound from *you* and you'll keep your Christmas by losing your situation. [*To the nephew*] You're quite a powerful speaker, sir. I wonder you don't go into Parliament.[6]

Nephew. Don't be angry, Uncle. Come! Dine with us tomorrow.

Scrooge. I'd rather see myself dead than see myself with your family!

Nephew. But, why? Why?

Scrooge. Why did you get married?

Nephew. Because I fell in love.

Scrooge. That, sir, is the only thing that you have said to me in your entire lifetime which is even more ridiculous than "Merry Christmas"! [*Turns from* Nephew] Good afternoon.

Nephew. Nay, Uncle, you never came to see me before I married either. Why give it as a reason for not coming now?

Scrooge. Good afternoon, Nephew!

Dialogue
How does this exchange between Scrooge and his nephew show the contrast between the two characters?

Comprehension
What invitation does Scrooge's nephew offer?

---

6. **Parliament** (pär′ lə mənt) national legislative body of Great Britain, in some ways like the United States Congress.

NEPHEW. I want nothing from you; I ask nothing of you; why cannot we be friends?

SCROOGE. Good afternoon!

NEPHEW. I am sorry with all my heart, to find you so resolute. But I have made the trial in homage to Christmas, and I'll keep my Christmas humor to the last. So A Merry Christmas, Uncle!

SCROOGE. Good afternoon!

NEPHEW. And A Happy New Year!

SCROOGE. Good afternoon!

NEPHEW. [*He stands facing* SCROOGE.] Uncle, you are the most . . . [*Pauses*] No, I shan't. My Christmas humor is intact . . . [*Pause*] God bless you, Uncle . . . [NEPHEW *turns and starts for the door; he stops at* CRATCHIT's *cage.*] Merry Christmas, Bob Cratchit . . .

CRATCHIT. Merry Christmas to you sir, and a very, very happy New Year . . .

SCROOGE. [*Calling across to them*] Oh, fine, a perfection, just fine . . . to see the perfect pair of you: husbands, with wives and children to support . . . my clerk there earning fifteen shillings a week . . . and the perfect pair of you, talking about a Merry Christmas! [*Pauses*] I'll retire to Bedlam![7]

NEPHEW. [*To* CRATCHIT] He's impossible!

CRATCHIT. Oh, mind him not, sir. He's getting on in years, and he's alone. He's noticed your visit. I'll wager your visit has warmed him.

NEPHEW. Him? Uncle Ebenezer Scrooge? *Warmed?* You are a better Christian than I am, sir.

CRATCHIT. [*Opening the door for* NEPHEW; *two* DO-GOODERS *will enter, as* NEPHEW *exits*] Good day to you, sir, and God bless.

NEPHEW. God bless . . . [*One man who enters is portly, the other is thin. Both are pleasant.*]

CRATCHIT. Can I help you, gentlemen?

Dialogue
What can you infer about the nephew's character from his words to Cratchit?

7. **Bedlam** (bed´ ləm) hospital in London for the mentally ill.

THIN MAN. [*Carrying papers and books; looks around* CRATCHIT *to* SCROOGE] Scrooge and Marley's, I believe. Have I the pleasure of addressing Mr. Scrooge, or Mr. Marley?

SCROOGE. Mr. Marley has been dead these seven years. He died seven years ago this very night.

PORTLY MAN. We have no doubt his liberality[8] is well represented by his surviving partner . . . [*Offers his calling card*]

SCROOGE. [*Handing back the card; unlooked at*] . . . Good afternoon.

THIN MAN. This will take but a moment, sir . . .

PORTLY MAN. At this festive season of the year, Mr. Scrooge, it is more than usually desirable that we should make some slight provision for the poor and destitute, who suffer greatly at the present time. Many thousands are in want of common necessities; hundreds of thousands are in want of common comforts, sir.

SCROOGE. Are there no prisons?

PORTLY MAN. Plenty of prisons.

SCROOGE. And aren't the Union workhouses still in operation?

THIN MAN. They are. Still. I wish that I could say that they are not.

SCROOGE. The Treadmill[9] and the Poor Law[10] are in full vigor, then?

THIN MAN. Both very busy, sir.

SCROOGE. Ohhh, I see. I was afraid, from what you said at

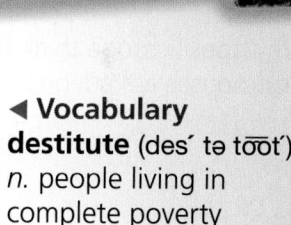

◄ **Vocabulary**
destitute (des´ tə t$\overline{oo}$t´) *n.* people living in complete poverty

Comprehension
Who do the thin man and the portly man want to help?

---

8. **liberality** (lib´ ər al´ i tē) generosity.
9. **the Treadmill** (tred´ mil´) kind of mill wheel turned by the weight of people treading steps arranged around it; this device was used to punish prisoners.
10. **the Poor Law** the original 16th-century Poor Laws called for overseers of the poor in each neighborhood to provide relief for the needy. The New Poor Law of 1834 made the workhouses in which the poor sometimes lived and worked extremely hard and unattractive.

Social Studies Connection

Union Workhouses

In Victorian England, many people who were poverty-stricken, orphaned, old, or sick lived in workhouses. On a typical day, workers woke at 5 A.M. and spent ten hours doing physical labor, such as crushing stones, sewing, cleaning, and milling corn. Bedtime was 8 P.M. There was not enough food to eat. Typically, breakfast was a piece of bread; dinner was a piece of bacon and a piece of bread or a potato; supper was a piece of bread and a piece of cheese.

Connect to the Literature

Why does Scrooge think the workhouses are adequate?

first, that something had occurred to stop them from their useful course. [*Pauses*] I'm glad to hear it.

PORTLY MAN. Under the impression that they scarcely furnish Christian cheer of mind or body to the multitude, a few of us are endeavoring to raise a fund to buy the Poor some meat and drink, and means of warmth. We choose this time, because it is a time, of all others, when Want is keenly felt, and Abundance rejoices. [*Pen in hand; as well as notepad*] What shall I put you down for, sir?

SCROOGE. Nothing!

PORTLY MAN. You wish to be left anonymous?

SCROOGE. I wish to be left alone! [*Pauses; turns away; turns back to them*] Since you ask me what I wish, gentlemen, that is my answer. I help to support the establishments that I have mentioned: they cost enough: and those who are badly off must go there.

THIN MAN. Many can't go there; and many would rather die.

SCROOGE. If they would rather die, they had better do it, and decrease the surplus population. Besides—excuse me—I don't know that.

THIN MAN. But you might know it!

SCROOGE. It's not my business. It's enough for a man to understand his own business, and not to interfere with other people's. Mine occupies me constantly. Good afternoon, gentlemen!
[SCROOGE *turns his back on the gentlemen and returns to his desk.*]

PORTLY MAN. But, sir, Mr. Scrooge . . . think of the poor.

SCROOGE. [*Turns suddenly to them. Pauses*] Take your leave of my offices, sirs, while I am still smiling.

[*The* THIN MAN *looks at the* PORTLY MAN. *They are undone. They shrug. They move to the door.* CRATCHIT *hops up to open it for them.*]

THIN MAN. Good day, sir . . . [*To* CRATCHIT] A merry Christmas to you, sir . . .

CRATCHIT. Yes. A Merry Christmas to both of you . . .

PORTLY MAN. Merry Christmas . . .

[CRATCHIT *silently squeezes something into the hand of the* THIN MAN.]

THIN MAN. What's this?

CRATCHIT. Shhhh . . .

[CRATCHIT *opens the door; wind and snow whistle into the room.*]

THIN MAN. Thank you, sir, thank you.

[CRATCHIT *closes the door and returns to his workplace.* SCROOGE *is at his own counting table. He talks to* CRATCHIT *without looking up.*]

SCROOGE. It's less of a time of year for being merry, and more a time of year for being loony . . . if you ask me.

CRATCHIT. Well, I don't know, sir . . . [*The clock's bell strikes six o'clock.*] Well, there it is, eh, six?

SCROOGE. Saved by six bells, are you?

CRATCHIT. I must be going home . . . [*He snuffs out his candle and puts on his hat.*] I hope you have a . . . very very lovely day tomorrow, sir . . .

SCROOGE. Hmmm. Oh, you'll be wanting the whole day tomorrow, I suppose?

CRATCHIT. If quite convenient, sir.

SCROOGE. It's not convenient, and it's not fair. If I was to stop half-a-crown for it, you'd think yourself ill-used, I'll be bound?

[CRATCHIT *smiles faintly.*]

CRATCHIT. I don't know, sir . . .

SCROOGE. And yet, you don't think me ill-used when I pay a day's wages for no work . . .

▼ **Critical Viewing**
How does this portrayal of Cratchit compare to your idea of how Cratchit would look?

Comprehension
How does Scrooge feel about Christmas?

CRATCHIT. It's only but once a year . . .

SCROOGE. A poor excuse for picking a man's pocket every 25th of December! But I suppose you must have the whole day. Be here all the earlier the next morning!

CRATCHIT. Oh, I will, sir. I will. I promise you. And, sir . . .

SCROOGE. Don't say it, Cratchit.

CRATCHIT. But let me wish you a . . .

SCROOGE. Don't say it, Cratchit. I warn you . . .

CRATCHIT. Sir!

SCROOGE. Cratchit!

[CRATCHIT *opens the door.*]

CRATCHIT. All right, then, sir . . . well . . . [*Suddenly*] Merry Christmas, Mr. Scrooge!

[*And he runs out the door, shutting same behind him.* SCROOGE *moves to his desk; gathering his coat, hat, etc. A* BOY *appears at his window. . . .*]

BOY. [*Singing*] "Away in a manger . . ."

[SCROOGE *seizes his ruler and whacks at the image of the* BOY *outside. The* BOY *leaves.*]

SCROOGE. Bah! Humbug! Christmas! Bah! Humbug! [*He shuts out the light.*]

A note on the crossover, following Scene 2:

[SCROOGE *will walk alone to his rooms from his offices. As he makes a long slow cross of the stage, the scenery should change. Christmas music will be heard, various people will cross by* SCROOGE, *often smiling happily.*

There will be occasional pleasant greetings tossed at him.

SCROOGE, *in contrast to all, will grump and mumble. He will snap at passing boys, as might a horrid old hound.*

In short, SCROOGE'S *sounds and movements will define him in contrast from all other people who cross the stage: he is the misanthrope,*[11] *the malcontent, the miser. He is* SCROOGE.

▶ **Critical Viewing**
How does the image on the facing page compare with the scene you pictured after reading the stage directions describing Scrooge's walk home?

---

11. misanthrope (mis′ ən thrōp′) *n.* person who hates or distrusts everyone.

Do others see us more clearly than we see ourselves?

This statement of SCROOGE's *character, by contrast to all other characters, should seem comical to the audience.*

During SCROOGE's crossover to his rooms, snow should begin to fall. All passers-by will hold their faces to the sky, smiling, allowing snow to shower them lightly. SCROOGE, by contrast, will bat at the flakes with his walking-stick, as might an insomniac swat at a sleep-stopping, middle-of-the-night swarm of mosquitoes. He will comment on the blackness of the night, and, finally, reach his rooms and his encounter with the magical specter:[12] MARLEY, his eternal mate.]

Dialogue
What do you learn about Scrooge through his words as he shuts out the light?

Comprehension
Why is Cratchit taking a day off?

---

12. **specter** (spek´ tər) *n.* ghost.

SCENE 3

Vocabulary ▶
void (void) *n.* emptiness

SCROOGE. No light at all . . . no moon . . . *that* is what is at the center of a Christmas Eve: dead black: **void** . . .

[SCROOGE *puts his key in the door's keyhole. He has reached his rooms now. The door knocker changes and is now* MARLEY'S *face. A musical sound; quickly: ghostly.* MARLEY'S *image is not at all angry, but looks at* SCROOGE *as did the old* MARLEY *look at* SCROOGE. *The hair is curiously stirred; eyes wide open, dead: absent of focus.* SCROOGE *stares wordlessly here. The face, before his very eyes, does deliquesce.*[13] *It is a knocker again.* SCROOGE *opens the door and checks the back of same, probably for* MARLEY'S *pigtail. Seeing nothing but screws and nuts,* SCROOGE *refuses the memory.*]

Pooh, pooh!

[*The sound of the door closing resounds throughout the house as thunder. Every room echoes the sound.* SCROOGE *fastens the door and walks across the hall to the stairs, trimming his candle as he goes; and then he goes slowly up the staircase. He checks each room: sitting room, bedrooms, lumber-room. He looks under the sofa, under the table: nobody there. He fixes his evening gruel on the hob,*[14] *changes his jacket.* SCROOGE *sits near the tiny low-flamed fire, sipping his gruel. There are various pictures on the walls: all of them now show likenesses of* MARLEY. SCROOGE *blinks his eyes.*]

Bah! Humbug!

[SCROOGE *walks in a circle about the room. The pictures change back into their natural images. He sits down at the table in front of the fire. A bell hangs overhead. It begins to ring, of its own accord. Slowly, surely, begins the ringing of every bell in the house. They continue ringing for nearly half a minute.* SCROOGE *is stunned by the phenomenon. The bells cease their ringing all at once. Deep below* SCROOGE, *in the basement of the house, there is the sound of clanking, of some enormous chain being dragged across the floors; and now up the stairs. We hear doors flying open.*]

Purpose for Reading
Preview Scene 3. If your purpose were to find out what happens to Scrooge next, what details would you look for in the scene?

13. **deliquesce** (del′ i kwes′) *v.* melt away.
14. **gruel** (grōō′ əl) **on the hob** (häb) thin broth warming on a ledge at the back or side of the fireplace.

Bah still! Humbug still! This is not happening! I won't
believe it!

[MARLEY'S GHOST *enters the room. He is horrible to look at:
pigtail, vest, suit as usual, but he drags an enormous
chain now, to which is fastened cash-boxes, keys,
padlocks, ledgers, deeds, and heavy purses fashioned
of steel. He is transparent.* MARLEY *stands opposite the
stricken* SCROOGE.]

How now! What do you want of me?

MARLEY. Much!

SCROOGE. Who are you?

MARLEY. Ask me who I was.

SCROOGE. Who were you then?

MARLEY. In life, I was your business partner: Jacob Marley.

SCROOGE. I see . . . can you sit down?

MARLEY. I can.

SCROOGE. Do it then.

MARLEY. I shall. [MARLEY *sits opposite* SCROOGE, *in the chair
across the table, at the front of the fireplace.*] You don't
believe in me.

SCROOGE. I don't.

MARLEY. Why do you doubt your senses?

SCROOGE. Because every little thing affects them. A slight
disorder of the stomach makes them cheat. You may be
an undigested bit of beef, a blot of mustard, a crumb of
cheese, a fragment of an underdone potato. There's more of
gravy than of grave about you, whatever you are!

[*There is a silence between them.* SCROOGE *is made nervous by
it. He picks up a toothpick.*]

Humbug! I tell you: humbug!

[MARLEY *opens his mouth and screams a ghosty, fearful
scream. The scream echoes about each room of the house.
Bats fly, cats screech, lightning flashes.* SCROOGE *stands
and walks backwards against the wall.* MARLEY *stands
and screams again. This time, he takes his head and lifts it*

Dialogue
Based on this dialogue,
what is Scrooge's at-
titude toward Marley's
Ghost?

Comprehension
What does Scrooge see
in the door knocker?

from his shoulders. His head continues to scream. MARLEY'S *face again appears on every picture in the room: all scream-ing.* SCROOGE, *on his knees before* MARLEY.]

Mercy! Dreadful apparition,[15] mercy! Why, O! why do you trouble me so?

MARLEY. Man of the worldly mind, do you believe in me, or not?

SCROOGE. I do. I must. But why do spirits such as you walk the earth? And why do they come to me?

MARLEY. It is required of every man that the spirit within him should walk abroad among his fellow-men, and travel far and wide; and if that spirit goes not forth in life, it is condemned to do so after death. [MARLEY *screams again; a tragic scream; from his ghosty bones.*] I wear the chain I forged in life. I made it link by link, and yard by yard. Is its pattern strange to *you?* Or would you know, you, Scrooge, the weight and length of the strong coil you bear yourself? It was full as heavy and long as this, seven Christmas Eves ago. You have labored on it, since. It is a ponderous chain.

[*Terrified that a chain will appear about his body,* SCROOGE *spins and waves the unwanted chain away. None, of course, appears. Sees* MARLEY *watching him dance about the room.* MARLEY *watches* SCROOGE; *silently.*]

SCROOGE. Jacob. Old Jacob Marley, tell me more. Speak comfort to me, Jacob . . .

MARLEY. I have none to give. Comfort comes from other regions, Ebenezer Scrooge, and is conveyed by other ministers, to other kinds of men. A very little more, is all that is permitted to me. I cannot rest, I cannot stay, I cannot linger any-where . . . [*He moans again.*] my spirit never walked beyond our counting-house—mark me!—in life my spirit never roved beyond the narrow limits of our money-changing hole; and weary journeys lie before me!

SCROOGE. But you were always a good man of business, Jacob.

MARLEY. [*Screams word "business"; a flash-pot explodes with him.*] BUSINESS!!! Mankind was my business. The

---

15. apparition (ap′ ə rish′ ən) *n.* ghost.

Purpose for Reading
What purpose for reading might Scrooge's question suggest to readers?

Vocabulary ▶
conveyed (kən vād′) *v.* made known; expressed

Do others see us more clearly than we see ourselves?

common welfare was my business; charity, mercy, forbearance, benevolence, were, all, my business. [SCROOGE *is quaking.*] Hear me, Ebenezer Scrooge! My time is nearly gone.

SCROOGE. I will, but don't be hard upon me. And don't be flowery, Jacob! Pray!

MARLEY. How is it that I appear before you in a shape that you can see, I may not tell. I have sat invisible beside you many and many a day. That is no light part of my penance. I am here tonight to warn you that you have yet a chance and hope of escaping my fate. A chance and hope of my procuring, Ebenezer.

SCROOGE. You were always a good friend to me. Thank'ee!

MARLEY. You will be haunted by Three Spirits.

SCROOGE. Would that be the chance and hope you mentioned, Jacob?

MARLEY. It is.

SCROOGE. I think I'd rather not.

MARLEY. Without their visits, you cannot hope to shun the path I tread. Expect the first one tomorrow, when the bell tolls one.

SCROOGE. Couldn't I take 'em all at once, and get it over, Jacob?

MARLEY. Expect the second on the next night at the same hour. The third upon the next night when the last stroke of twelve has ceased to vibrate. Look to see me no more. Others may, but you may not. And look that, for your own sake, you remember what has passed between us!

▲ **Critical Viewing**
How do the characters' gestures and positions reinforce the emotion of the scene?

Comprehension
Why does Marley visit Scrooge?

MARLEY *places his head back upon his shoulders. He approaches the window and beckons to* SCROOGE *to watch. Outside the window, specters fly by, carrying money-boxes and chains. They make a confused sound of lamentation.* MARLEY, *after listening a moment, joins into their mournful dirge. He leans to the window and floats out into the bleak, dark night. He is gone.]*

SCROOGE. [*Rushing to the window*] Jacob! No, Jacob! Don't leave me! I'm frightened! [*He sees that* MARLEY *has gone. He looks outside. He pulls the shutter closed, so that the scene is blocked from his view. All sound stops. After a pause, he re-opens the shutter and all is quiet, as it should be on Christmas Eve. Carolers carol out of doors, in the distance.* SCROOGE *closes the shutter and walks down the stairs. He examines the door by which* MARLEY *first entered.]* No one here at all! Did I imagine all that? Humbug! [*He looks about the room.*] I did imagine it. It only happened in my foulest dream-mind, didn't it? An undigested bit of . . . [*Thunder and lightning in the room; suddenly*] Sorry! Sorry!

[*There is silence again. The lights fade out.]*

SCENE 4

[*Christmas music, choral, "Hark the Herald Angels Sing," sung by an onstage choir of children, spotlighted, D.C. Above,* SCROOGE *in his bed, dead to the world, asleep, in his darkened room. It should appear that the choir is singing somewhere outside of the house, of course, and a use of scrim[16] is thus suggested. When the singing is ended, the choir should fade out of view and* MARLEY *should fade into view, in their place.]*

MARLEY. [*Directly to audience*] From this point forth . . . I shall be quite visible to you, but invisible to him. [*Smiles*] He will feel my presence, nevertheless, for, unless my senses fail me completely, we are—you and I—witness to the changing of a miser: that one, my partner in life, in business, and in eternity: that one: Scrooge. [*Moves to staircase, below* SCROOGE] See him now. He endeavors to pierce the

---

16. scrim (skrim) *n.* see-through fabric used to create special effects in the theater.

Do others see us more clearly than we see ourselves?

darkness with his ferret eyes.[17] [*To audience*] See him, now. He listens for the hour.

[*The bells toll.* SCROOGE *is awakened and quakes as the hour approaches one o'clock, but the bells stop their sound at the hour of twelve.*]

SCROOGE. [*Astonished*] Midnight! Why this isn't possible. It was past two when I went to bed. An icicle must have gotten into the clock's works! I couldn't have slept through the whole day and far into another night. It isn't possible that anything has happened to the sun, and this is twelve at noon! [*He runs to window; unshutters same; it is night.*] Night, still. Quiet, normal for the season, cold. It is certainly not noon. I cannot in any way afford to lose my days. Securities come due, promissory notes,[18] interest on investments: these are things that happen in the daylight! [*He returns to his bed.*] Was this a dream?

[MARLEY *appears in his room. He speaks to the audience.*]

MARLEY. You see? He does not, with faith, believe in me fully, even still! Whatever will it take to turn the faith of a miser from money to men?

SCROOGE. Another quarter and it'll be one and Marley's ghosty friends will come. [*Pauses; listens*] Where's the chime for one? [*Ding, dong*] A quarter past [*Repeats*] Half-past! [*Repeats*] A quarter to it! But where's the heavy bell of the hour one? This is a game in which I lose my senses! Perhaps, if I allowed myself another short doze . . .

MARLEY. . . . Doze, Ebenezer, doze.

[*A heavy bell thuds its one ring; dull and definitely one o'clock. There is a flash of light.* SCROOGE *sits up, in a sudden. A hand draws back the curtains by his bed. He sees it.*]

SCROOGE. A hand! Who owns it! Hello!
[*Ghosty music again, but of a new nature to the play. A strange figure stands before* SCROOGE—*like a child, yet at the same time like an old man: white hair, but unwrinkled skin, long, muscular arms, but delicate legs and feet. Wears*

Dialogue
What important information in Marley's opening speech will influence the rest of the play?

Spiral Review
CONFLICT How do details about the setting work together to increase the tension?

Comprehension
Why is Scrooge confused when he wakes up?

---

17. **ferret eyes** a ferret is a small, weasel-like animal used for hunting rabbits; this expression means to stare continuously, the way a ferret hunts.
18. **promissory** (pram′ i sôr′ ē) **notes** written promises to pay someone a certain sum of money.

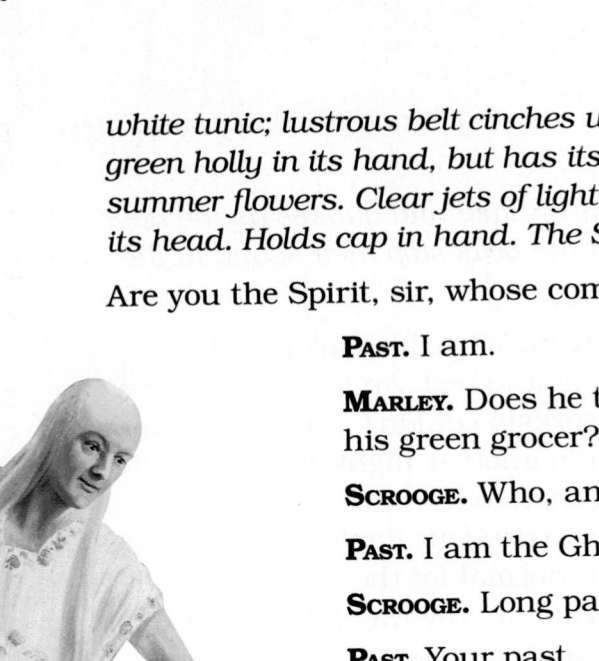

white tunic; lustrous belt cinches waist. Branch of fresh green holly in its hand, but has its dress trimmed with fresh summer flowers. Clear jets of light spring from the crown of its head. Holds cap in hand. The Spirit is called PAST.]

Are you the Spirit, sir, whose coming was foretold to me?

PAST. I am.

MARLEY. Does he take this to be a vision of his green grocer?

SCROOGE. Who, and what are you?

PAST. I am the Ghost of Christmas Past.

SCROOGE. Long past?

PAST. Your past.

SCROOGE. May I ask, please, sir, what business you have here with me?

PAST. Your welfare.

SCROOGE. Not to sound ungrateful, sir, and really, please do understand that I am plenty obliged for your concern, but, really, kind spirit, it would have done all the better for my welfare to have been left alone altogether, to have slept peacefully through this night.

PAST. Your reclamation, then. Take heed!

SCROOGE. My what?

PAST. [*Motioning to* SCROOGE *and taking his arm*] Rise! Fly with me! [*He leads* SCROOGE *to the window.*]

SCROOGE. [*Panicked*] Fly, but I am a mortal and cannot fly!

PAST. [*Pointing to his heart*] Bear but a touch of my hand here and you shall be upheld in more than this!

[SCROOGE *touches the spirit's heart and the lights dissolve into sparkly flickers. Lovely crystals of music are heard. The scene dissolves into another. Christmas music again*]

Dialogue
Based on this dialogue, how has Scrooge been affected by what has happened to him so far?

Do others see us more clearly than we see ourselves?

SCENE 5

[SCROOGE *and the* GHOST OF CHRISTMAS PAST *walk together across an open stage. In the background, we see a field that is open; covered by a soft, downy snow: a country road.*]

SCROOGE. Good Heaven! I was bred in this place. I was a boy here!

[SCROOGE *freezes, staring at the field beyond.* MARLEY's *ghost appears beside him; takes* SCROOGE's *face in his hands, and turns his face to the audience.*]

MARLEY. You see this Scrooge: stricken by feeling. Conscious of a thousand odors floating in the air, each one connected with a thousand thoughts, and hopes, and joys, and care long, long forgotten. [*Pause*] This one—this Scrooge—before your very eyes, returns to life, among the living. [*To audience, sternly*] You'd best pay your most careful attention. I would suggest rapt.[19]

[*There is a small flash and puff of smoke and* MARLEY *is gone again.*]

PAST. Your lip is trembling, Mr. Scrooge. And what is that upon your cheek?

SCROOGE. Upon my cheek? Nothing . . . a blemish on the skin from the eating of overmuch grease . . . nothing . . . [*Suddenly*] Kind Spirit of Christmas Past, lead me where you will, but quickly! To be stagnant in this place is, for me, unbearable!

PAST. You recollect the way?

SCROOGE. Remember it! I would know it blindfolded! My bridge, my church, my winding river! [*Staggers about, trying to see it all at once. He weeps again.*]

PAST. These are but shadows of things that have been. They have no consciousness of us.

[*Four jocund travelers enter, singing a Christmas song in four-part harmony—"God Rest Ye Merry Gentlemen."*]

SCROOGE. Listen! I know these men! I know them! I remember the beauty of their song!

Comprehension
Who appears to Scrooge during Scene 4?

---

19. **rapt** (rapt) *adj.* giving complete attention; totally carried away by something.

PAST. But, why do you remember it so happily? It is Merry Christmas that they say to one another! What is Merry Christmas to you, Mr. Scrooge? Out upon Merry Christmas, right? What good has Merry Christmas ever done you, Mr. Scrooge? . . .

SCROOGE. [*After a long pause*] None. No good. None . . . [*He bows his head.*]

PAST. Look, you, sir, a school ahead. The schoolroom is not quite deserted. A solitary child, neglected by his friends, is left there still.

[SCROOGE *falls to the ground; sobbing as he sees, and we see, a small boy, the young* SCROOGE, *sitting and weeping, bravely, alone at his desk: alone in a vast space, a void.*]

SCROOGE. I cannot look on him!

PAST. You must, Mr. Scrooge, you must.

SCROOGE. It's me. [*Pauses; weeps*] Poor boy. He lived inside his head . . . alone . . . [*Pauses; weeps*] poor boy. [*Pauses; stops his weeping*] I wish . . . [*Dries his eyes on his cuff*] ah! it's too late!

PAST. What is the matter?

SCROOGE. There was a boy singing a Christmas Carol outside my door last night. I should like to have given him something: that's all.

PAST. [*Smiles; waves his hand to* SCROOGE] Come. Let us see another Christmas.

[*Lights out on little boy. A flash of light. A puff of smoke. Lights up on older boy*]

SCROOGE. Look! Me, again! Older now! [*Realizes*] Oh, yes . . . still alone.

[*The boy—a slightly older* SCROOGE —*sits alone in a chair, reading. The door to the room opens and a young girl enters. She is much, much younger than this slightly older* SCROOGE. *She is, say, six, and he is, say, twelve. Elder* SCROOGE *and the* GHOST OF CHRISTMAS PAST *stand watching the scene, unseen.*]

FAN. Dear, dear brother, I have come to bring you home.

Dialogue
How do these lines reveal that a change is taking place in Scrooge?

Do others see us more clearly than we see ourselves?

Boy. Home, little Fan?

Fan. Yes! Home, for good and all! Father is so much kinder than he ever used to be, and home's like heaven! He spoke so gently to me one dear night when I was going to bed that I was not afraid to ask him once more if you might come home; and he said "yes" . . . you should; and sent me in a coach to bring you. And you're to be a man and are never to come back here, but first, we're to be together all the Christmas long, and have the merriest time in the world.

Boy. You are quite a woman, little Fan!

[*Laughing; she drags at boy, causing him to stumble to the door with her. Suddenly we hear a mean and terrible voice in the hallway, Off. It is the* SCHOOLMASTER.]

Schoolmaster. Bring down Master Scrooge's travel box at once! He is to travel!

Fan. Who is that, Ebenezer?

Boy. O! Quiet, Fan. It is the Schoolmaster, himself!

[*The door bursts open and into the room bursts with it the* SCHOOLMASTER.]

Schoolmaster. Master Scrooge?

Boy. Oh, Schoolmaster. I'd like you to meet my little sister, Fan, sir . . .

[*Two boys struggle on with* SCROOGE'S *trunk.*]

Fan. Pleased, sir . . . [*She curtsies.*]

Schoolmaster. You are to travel, Master Scrooge.

Scrooge. Yes, sir. I know sir . . .

[*All start to exit, but* FAN *grabs the coattail of the mean old* SCHOOLMASTER.]

Boy. Fan!

Schoolmaster. What's this?

Fan. Pardon, sir, but I believe that you've forgotten to say your goodbye to my brother, Ebenezer, who stands still now

Purpose for Reading
What questions do you have about Scrooge's family? Read on to see if they are answered.

Comprehension
Where is Scrooge when his sister arrives to take him home?

awaiting it . . . [*She smiles, curtsies, lowers her eyes.*] pardon, sir.

SCHOOLMASTER. [*Amazed*] I . . . uh . . . harumph . . . uhh . . . well, then . . . [*Outstretches hand*] Goodbye, Scrooge.

BOY. Uh, well, goodbye, Schoolmaster . . .

[*Lights fade out on all but* BOY *looking at* FAN; *and* SCROOGE *and* PAST *looking at them.*]

SCROOGE. Oh, my dear, dear little sister, Fan . . . how I loved her.

PAST. Always a delicate creature, whom a breath might have withered, but she had a large heart . . .

SCROOGE. So she had.

PAST. She died a woman, and had, as I think, children.

SCROOGE. One child.

PAST. True. Your nephew.

SCROOGE. Yes.

PAST. Fine, then. We move on, Mr. Scrooge. That warehouse, there? Do you know it?

SCROOGE. Know it? Wasn't I apprenticed[20] there?

PAST. We'll have a look.

[*They enter the warehouse. The lights crossfade with them, coming up on an old man in Welsh wig:* FEZZIWIG.]

SCROOGE. Why, it's old Fezziwig! Bless his heart; it's Fezziwig, alive again!

[FEZZIWIG *sits behind a large, high desk, counting. He lays down his pen; looks at the clock: seven bells sound.*]

Quittin' time . . .

FEZZIWIG. Quittin' time . . . [*He takes off his waistcoat and laughs; calls off*] Yo ho, Ebenezer! Dick!

[DICK WILKINS *and* EBENEZER SCROOGE—*a young man version—enter the room.* DICK *and* EBENEZER *are* FEZZIWIG'S *apprentices.*]

Dialogue
What surprising aspect of Scrooge's character does this scene reveal?

---

20. **apprenticed** (ə pren′ tist) *v.* receiving instruction in a trade as well as food and housing or wages in return for work.

▼ **Critical Viewing**
Based on this painting, what kind of a man is Fezziwig?

SCROOGE. Dick Wilkins, to be sure! My fellow-'prentice! Bless my soul, yes. There he is. He was very much attached to me, was Dick. Poor Dick! Dear, dear!

FEZZIWIG. Yo ho, my boys. No more work tonight. Christmas Eve, Dick. Christmas, Ebenezer!
[*They stand at attention in front of* FEZZIWIG; *laughing*]
Hilli-ho! Clear away, and let's have lots of room here! Hilli-ho, Dick! Chirrup, Ebenezer!
[*The young men clear the room, sweep the floor, straighten the pictures, trim the lamps, etc. The space is clear now. A fiddler enters, fiddling.*]
Hi-ho, Matthew! Fiddle away . . . where are my daughters?

[*The fiddler plays. Three young daughters of* FEZZIWIG *enter followed by six young male suitors. They are dancing to the music. All employees come in: workers, clerks, housemaids, cousins, the baker, etc. All dance. Full number wanted here. Throughout the dance, food is brought into the feast. It is "eaten" in dance, by the dancers.* EBENEZER *dances with all three of the daughters, as does* DICK. *They compete for the*

Comprehension
Who is Fezziwig?

daughters, happily, in the dance. FEZZIWIG *dances with his daughters.* FEZZIWIG *dances with* DICK *and* EBENEZER. *The music changes:* MRS. FEZZIWIG *enters. She lovingly scolds her husband. They dance. She dances with* EBENEZER, *lifting him and throwing him about. She is enormously fat. When the dance is ended, they all dance off, floating away, as does the music.* SCROOGE *and the* GHOST OF CHRISTMAS PAST *stand alone now. The music is gone.*]

PAST. It was a small matter, that Fezziwig made those silly folks so full of **gratitude**.

SCROOGE. Small!

PAST. Shhh!

[*Lights up on* DICK *and* EBENEZER]

DICK. We are blessed, Ebenezer, truly, to have such a master as Mr. Fezziwig!

YOUNG SCROOGE. He is the best, best, the very and absolute best! If ever I own a firm of my own, I shall treat my apprentices with the same dignity and the same grace. We have learned a wonderful lesson from the master, Dick!

DICK. Ah, that's a fact, Ebenezer. That's a fact!

PAST. Was it not a small matter, really? He spent but a few pounds[21] of his mortal money on your small party. Three or four pounds, perhaps. Is that so much that he deserves such praise as you and Dick so lavish now?

SCROOGE. It isn't that! It isn't that, Spirit. Fezziwig had the power to make us happy or unhappy; to make our service light or burdensome; a pleasure or a toil. The happiness he gave is quite as great as if it cost him a fortune.

PAST. What is the matter?

SCROOGE. Nothing particular.

PAST. Something, I think.

SCROOGE. No, no. I should like to be able to say a word or two to my clerk just now! That's all!

Vocabulary ▶
gratitude (grat′ i tood′) *n.* thankful appreciation

Dialogue
What does this dialogue reveal about Scrooge's feelings for Fezziwig?

---

21. pounds (poundz) *n.* common type of money used in Great Britain.

[EBENEZER *enters the room and shuts down all the lamps. He stretches and yawns. The* GHOST OF CHRISTMAS PAST *turns to* SCROOGE *all of a sudden.*]

PAST. My time grows short! Quick!

[*In a flash of light,* EBENEZER *is gone, and in his place stands an* OLDER SCROOGE, *this one a man in the prime of his life.*
Beside him stands a young woman in a mourning dress. She is crying. She speaks to the man, with hostility.]

WOMAN. It matters little . . . to you, very little. Another idol has displaced me.

MAN. What idol has displaced you?

WOMAN. A golden one.

MAN. This is an even-handed dealing of the world. There is nothing on which it is so hard as poverty; and there is nothing it professes to condemn with such severity as the pursuit of wealth!

WOMAN. You fear the world too much. Have I not seen your nobler aspirations fall off one by one, until the master-passion, Gain, engrosses you? Have I not?

SCROOGE. No!

MAN. What then? Even if I have grown so much wiser, what then? Have I changed towards you?

WOMAN. No . . .

MAN. Am I?

WOMAN. Our contract is an old one. It was made when we were both poor and content to be so. You are changed. When it was made, you were another man.

MAN. I was not another man: I was a boy.

WOMAN. Your own feeling tells you that you were not what you are. I am. That which promised happiness when we were one in heart is fraught with misery now that we are two . . .

Dialogue
What personal change in Scrooge does this dialogue show?

Comprehension
What does the woman tell Scrooge about himself?

SCROOGE. No!

WOMAN. How often and how keenly I have thought of this, I will not say. It is enough that I have thought of it, and can release you . . .

SCROOGE. [*Quietly*] Don't release me, madame . . .

MAN. Have I ever sought release?

WOMAN. In words. No. Never.

MAN. In what then?

WOMAN. In a changed nature; in an altered spirit. In everything that made my love of any worth or value in your sight. If this has never been between us, tell me, would you seek me out and try to win me now? Ah, no!

SCROOGE. Ah, yes!

MAN. You think not?

WOMAN. I would gladly think otherwise if I could, heaven knows! But if you were free today, tomorrow, yesterday, can even I believe that you would choose a dowerless girl[22]—you who in your very confidence with her weigh everything by Gain; or, choosing her, do I not know that your repentance and regret would surely follow? I do; and I release you. With a full heart, for the love of him you once were.

SCROOGE. Please, I . . . I . . .

MAN. Please, I . . . I . . .

WOMAN. Please. You may—the memory of what is past half makes me hope you will—have pain in this. A very, very brief time, and you will dismiss the memory of it, as an unprofitable dream, from which it happened well that you awoke. May you be happy in the life that you have chosen for yourself . . .

---

22. a dowerless (dou´ er les) **girl** a girl without a dowry, the property or wealth a woman brought to her husband in marriage.

Do others see us more clearly than we see ourselves?

SCROOGE. No!

WOMAN. Yourself . . . alone . . .

SCROOGE. No!

WOMAN. Goodbye, Ebenezer . . .

SCROOGE. Don't let her go!

MAN. Goodbye.

SCROOGE. No!

> [*She exits.* SCROOGE *goes to younger man: himself.*]
> You fool! Mindless loon! You fool!

MAN. [*To exited woman*] Fool. Mindless loon. Fool . . .

SCROOGE. Don't say that! Spirit, remove me from this place.

PAST. I have told you these were shadows of the things that have been. They are what they are. Do not blame me, Mr. Scrooge.

SCROOGE. Remove me! I cannot bear it!

[*The faces of all who appeared in this scene are now projected for a moment around the stage: enormous, flimsy, silent.*]
   Leave me! Take me back! Haunt me no longer!

[*There is a sudden flash of light: a flare. The* GHOST OF CHRISTMAS PAST *is gone.* SCROOGE *is, for the moment, alone onstage. His bed is turned down, across the stage. A small candle burns now in* SCROOGE's *hand. There is a child's cap in his other hand. He slowly crosses the stage to his bed, to sleep.* MARLEY *appears behind* SCROOGE, *who continues his long, elderly cross to bed.* MARLEY *speaks directly to the audience.*]

MARLEY. Scrooge must sleep now. He must surrender to the irresistible drowsiness caused by the recognition of what was. [*Pauses*] The cap he carries is from ten lives past: his boyhood cap . . . donned atop a hopeful hairy head . . . askew, perhaps, or at a rakish angle. Doffed now in honor of regret.[23] Perhaps even too heavy to carry in his present state of weak remorse . . .

Dialogue
What do you learn about Scrooge's past from the dialogue here?

Comprehension
Why does the woman leave Scrooge?

---

23. **donned . . . regret** To *don* and *doff* a hat means to put it on and take it off, *askew* means "crooked," and *at a rakish angle* means "having a dashing or jaunty look."

Purpose for Reading
How does this speech by Marley influence your purpose for reading Act 2?

[SCROOGE *DROPS THE CAP*. *He lies atop his bed. He sleeps.* *To audience*]

He sleeps. For him, there's even more trouble ahead. [*Smiles*] For you? The play house tells me there's hot cider, as should be your anticipation for the specter Christmas Present and Future, for I promise you both. [*Smiles again*] So, I pray you hurry back to your seats refreshed and ready for a miser—to turn his coat of gray into a blazen Christmas holly-red. [*A flash of lightning. A clap of thunder. Bats fly. Ghosty music.* MARLEY *is gone.*]

Language Study

Vocabulary Rewrite the numbered sentences so that each includes one of the vocabulary words listed below and also retains the same basic meaning.

implored   **morose**   **destitute**   **void**   **conveyed**

1. Jack's gloomy expression showed that he had lost the game.
2. Her sudden inheritance meant that she would no longer live among the poor.
3. The party helped to ease the emptiness I was feeling.
4. The grin on Dr. Jackson's face expressed his relief.
5. We begged the guard not to close the gate.

WORD STUDY

The **Latin root -grat-** means "thankful" or "pleasing." In this play, Bob Cratchit expresses his **gratitude**, or thankfulness, for a day off from work on Christmas.

Word Study

Part A Explain how the **Latin root -grat-** contributes to the meanings of the words *gratuity, ingrate,* and *gratification*. Consult a dictionary if necessary.

Part B Use the context of the sentences and what you know about the Latin root -grat- to explain your answer to each question.

1. If a friend helped you out of a difficult situation, would you feel *grateful*?
2. Would *congratulations* be in order if you failed an exam?

Literary Analysis

Key Ideas and Details

1. Purpose for Reading What clues in the title helped you preview the content of the play?

2. Purpose for Reading (a) What is your purpose for reading this play? **(b)** How might your purpose be different if you were reading a nonfiction play about life in the workhouses of Victorian England?

3. (a) What scenes from his past does Scrooge visit? **(b) Draw Conclusions:** How does each event contribute to his current attitude and personality?

4. (a) Deduce: What does Scrooge value in life? Support your answer with examples and quotations from the text. **(b) Draw Conclusions:** Do his values make Scrooge a happy man? Explain.

Craft and Structure

5. Dialogue Complete a chart like the one on the right by identifying important examples of dialogue. **(a)** For each line of dialogue in the first row, use the second row to tell what it means. **(b)** In the third row, tell why this dialogue is important for advancing the action of the play or developing characters.

What Does It Say?
What Does It Mean?
Why Is It Important?

Integration of Knowledge and Ideas

6. (a) Connect: What hints in the text suggest to you that Scrooge may change for the better? **(b) Speculate:** In the future, how might Scrooge's interactions with others differ from his interactions in the present? **(c) Predict:** Do you think you will see examples of Scrooge's changed behavior in the second act of the play? Why or why not?

7. (a) Deduce: What effects have Scrooge's past experiences had on the person he has become? **(b) Evaluate:** Based on Scrooge's past experiences, do you think he should be excused for his current attitudes and behavior? Explain.

8. Speculate: What do you think would have happened to Scrooge if he had not been visited by Marley's Ghost and the Ghost of Christmas Past? Support your ideas with details from the text.

9. **Do others see us more clearly than we see ourselves?** How do the people in Scrooge's past reveal his own behavior to him?

ACADEMIC VOCABULARY

As you write and speak about *A Christmas Carol: Scrooge and Marley*, Act I, use the words related to self-perception that you explored on p. 447 of this textbook.

Conventions: Prepositions and Prepositional Phrases

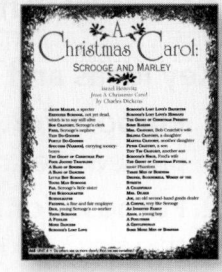

A **preposition** relates a noun or a pronoun that follows it to another word in the sentence. In the sentence *The book is on the table*, the preposition *on* relates the noun *table* to another word in the sentence, *book*.

A **prepositional phrase** begins with a preposition and ends with a noun or pronoun—called the **object of the preposition**. In the prepositional phrase *on the table*, the preposition is *on*, and the object of the preposition is *table*.

Commonly Used Prepositions			
above	below	in	over
across	beneath	into	through
after	between	near	to
against	by	of	toward
along	down	on	under
at	during	onto	until
before	for	out	up
behind	from	outside	with

Practice A

Identify the prepositional phrase in each sentence. Then, identify the preposition and the object of the preposition.

1. Scrooge is sitting in his countinghouse.
2. Marley points at Scrooge's window.
3. Marley describes visits from three spirits.
4. Scrooge is weak with fear.

Reading Application In *A Christmas Carol: Scrooge and Marley*, Act I, find three sentences with prepositional phrases and identify the prepositions.

Practice B

Identify the preposition and the object of the preposition in each prepositional phrase. Then, use each prepositional phrase to write a sentence about Scrooge's past.

1. by his friends
2. near a chair
3. in Fezziwig's warehouse
4. of gratitude

Writing Application Choose three prepositions from the drama and use them in a paragraph describing a time you were persuaded to change.

Writing to Sources

Argument Write a **letter** to Scrooge, telling him what he is missing in life by being cranky and negative toward the people around him. Begin your letter with a salutation, or greeting. Then, support the main points of your argument with clear reasons and evidence. Conclude with a closing and your signature.

- Present a balanced argument by carefully organizing the body of your letter. Fully support each claim with logical reasons and relevant evidence from the text. Use transitional phrases like "another issue is . . ." or "in addition" to help unify the main argument—that there are many things Scrooge is missing.

- If you handwrite your letter, write legibly.
  (For a model of a friendly-letter format, refer to the Writing Handbook at the back of this book.)

Grammar Application Check your writing to be sure you have used prepositions and prepositional phrases correctly.

Research and Technology

Build and Present Knowledge Prepare **costume plans** for this play. With a small group, research the clothing that was worn during the Victorian era in England.

- Use the Internet and library resources to gather information, photos, sketches, and descriptions.

- Review *A Christmas Carol* and note the social positions of the characters. Based on their social positions, determine what types of clothing different characters would have worn. Be sure the costumes reflect the season in which the play is set. Also, find out about the fabrics and materials that were available during the time period.

- Use the information you find to plan costumes for two different characters. In your plan, show or describe the types of clothing, including the colors and fabrics. Include pictures or sketches with your descriptions.

- Ask your classmates for feedback as to whether or not your costume plans reflect what they imagined as they read Act I. Feedback should be supported with specific textual details.

 **Common Core State Standards**

Writing
1. Write arguments to support claims with clear reasons and relevant evidence.
1.a. Introduce claim(s), acknowledge alternate or opposing claims, and organize the reasons and evidence logically.
1.b. Support claim(s) with logical reasoning and relevant evidence, using accurate, credible sources and demonstrating an understanding of the topic or text.
1.c. Use words, phrases, and clauses to create cohesion and clarify the relationships among claim(s), reasons, and evidence.
7. Conduct short research projects to answer a question, drawing on several sources and generating additional related, focused questions for further research and investigation.

Language
1.a. Explain the function of phrases and clauses in general and their function in specific sentences.

Do others see us more clearly than we see ourselves?

Think about the Big Question as you read *A Christmas Carol: Scrooge and Marley*, Act II. Take notes on the ways in which Scrooge gains insights about himself.

CLOSE READING FOCUS

Key Ideas and Details: **Purpose for Reading**

Your **purpose for reading** affects the way you read and the speed of your reading. Adjust your reading rate to suit your purpose.

- As you read drama, slow down to read stage directions carefully. They may reveal action that is not shown in the dialogue.
- Speed up to read short lines of dialogue quickly to create the feeling of conversation.
- Slow down to read longer speeches by a single character so that you can reflect on the character's words.
- If one of your purposes is to appreciate an *author's style*, or unique way of writing, slow your pace as you read.

Craft and Structure: **Stage Directions**

The **script** is the written text of a play. **Stage directions**, a part of the script, instruct actors on how to move and speak or describe what the stage should sound and look like. If you are reading a play instead of watching a performance, you get certain information only from the stage directions. Stage directions are usually written in italic type and set off by brackets or parentheses, as in this example:

[Jen bursts through the door, stage left. There is a crack of thunder. Then, the lights go dark.]

Vocabulary

Copy the words from the drama into your notebook. Write a synonym for each word you know.

astonish	compulsion	severe
meager	audible	intercedes

Common Core State Standards

Reading Literature
3. Analyze how particular elements of a story or drama interact.
5. Analyze how a drama's or poem's form or structure contributes to its meaning.

Language
4.b. Use common, grade-appropriate Greek or Latin affixes and roots as clues to the meaning of a word.
5.b. Use the relationship between particular words (e.g., synonym/antonym, analogy) to better understand each of the words.

CLOSE READING MODEL

The passage below is from Israel Horvitz's play *A Christmas Carol: Scrooge and Marley*, Act II. The annotations to the right of the passage show ways in which you can use close reading skills to set a purpose for reading and to analyze stage directions.

from *A Christmas Carol: Scrooge and Marley*, Act II

[Winter music. Choral group behind scrim, sings. When the song is done and the stage is re-set, the lights will fade up on a row of shops, behind the singers. The choral group will hum the song they have just completed now and mill about the streets, carrying their dinners to the bakers' shops and restaurants. They will, perhaps, sing about being poor at Christmastime, whatever.][1]

PRESENT. These revelers, Mr. Scrooge, carry their own dinners to their jobs, where they will work to bake the meals the rich men and women of this city will eat as their Christmas dinners. Generous people these . . . to care for the others, so . . .

[PRESENT walks among the choral group and a sparkling incense falls from his torch on to their baskets, as he pulls the covers off of the baskets. Some of the choral group become angry with each other.][2]

MAN #1. Hey, you, watch where you're going.

MAN #2. Watch it yourself, mate!

[PRESENT sprinkles them directly, they change.][3]

MAN #1. I pray go in ahead of me. It's Christmas. You be first!

MAN #2. No, no, I must insist that YOU be first!

MAN #1. All right, I shall be, and gratefully so.

MAN #2. The pleasure is equally mine, for being able to watch you pass, smiling.[4]

Stage Directions
1 These stage directions help you picture the scene by describing actions, sounds, and lighting effects.

Purpose for Reading
2 Stage directions may reveal details not shown in the dialogue. Read them slowly so you do not overlook important information or actions.

Stage Directions
3 These stage directions are brief but they convey an important detail. When Present sprinkles incense on the people, "they change." Without this information, you, as a reader, might not understand why the angry people suddenly become friendly.

Purpose for Reading
4 Speed up your reading rate to read short lines of dialogue like these. Doing so will help you "hear" the conversational nature of the characters' exchange.

A Christmas Carol:

SCROOGE AND MARLEY

Israel Horovitz
from A Christmas Carol
by Charles Dickens

ACT II

SCENE 1

[*Lights. Choral music is sung. Curtain.* SCROOGE, *in bed, sleeping, in spotlight. We cannot yet see the interior of his room.* MARLEY, *opposite, in spotlight equal to* SCROOGE'S. MARLEY *laughs. He tosses his hand in the air and a flame shoots from it, magically, into the air. There is a thunder clap, and then another; a lightning flash, and then another. Ghostly music plays under. Colors change.* MARLEY'S *spotlight has gone out and now reappears, with* MARLEY *in it, standing next to the bed and the sleeping* SCROOGE. MARLEY *addresses the audience directly.*]

MARLEY. Hear this snoring Scrooge! Sleeping to escape the nightmare that is his waking day. What shall I bring to him now? I'm afraid nothing would astonish old Scrooge now. Not after what he's seen. Not a baby boy, not a rhinoceros, nor anything in between would astonish Ebenezer Scrooge just now. I can think of nothing . . . [*Suddenly*] that's it! Nothing! [*He speaks confidentially.*] I'll have the

Stage Directions
What sounds establish this as a scary scene?

◄ **Vocabulary**
astonish (ə stän´ ish)
v. amaze

Comprehension
What is Marley trying to figure out?

clock strike one and, when he awakes expecting my second messenger, there will be no one . . . nothing. Then I'll have the bell strike twelve. And then one again . . . and then nothing. Nothing . . . [*Laughs*] nothing will . . . astonish him. I think it will work.

[*The bell tolls one.* SCROOGE *leaps awake.*]

SCROOGE. One! One! This is it: time! [*Looks about the room*] Nothing!

[*The bell tolls midnight.*]

Midnight! How can this be? I'm sleeping backwards.

[*One again*]

Good heavens! One again! I'm sleeping back and forth! [*A pause.* SCROOGE *looks about.*] Nothing! Absolutely nothing!

[*Suddenly, thunder and lightning.* MARLEY *laughs and disappears. The room shakes and glows. There is suddenly springlike music.* SCROOGE *makes a run for the door.*]

MARLEY. Scrooge!

SCROOGE. What?

MARLEY. Stay you put!

SCROOGE. Just checking to see if anyone is in here.

[*Lights and thunder again: more music.* MARLEY *is of a sudden gone. In his place sits the* GHOST OF CHRISTMAS PRESENT—*to be called in the stage directions of the play,* PRESENT—*center of room. Heaped up on the floor, to form a kind of throne, are turkeys, geese, game, poultry, brawn, great joints of meat, suckling pigs, long wreaths of sausages, mince-pies, plum puddings, barrels of oysters, red hot chestnuts, cherry-cheeked apples, juicy oranges, luscious pears, immense twelfth cakes, and seething bowls of punch, that make the chamber dim with their delicious steam. Upon this throne sits* PRESENT, *glorious to see. He bears a torch, shaped as a Horn of Plenty.*[1] SCROOGE *hops out of the door, and then peeks back again into his bedroom.* PRESENT *calls to* SCROOGE.]

---

1. **Horn of Plenty** a horn overflowing with fruits, flowers, and grain, representing wealth and abundance.

► **Critical Viewing**
Based on your knowledge of the play so far, whom do you expect the character in the green robe to be? Explain.

Purpose for Reading
At what rate would you read these stage directions? Why?

PRESENT. Ebenezer Scrooge. Come in, come in! Come in and know me better!

SCROOGE. Hello. How should I call you?

PRESENT. I am the Ghost of Christmas Present. Look upon me.

[PRESENT *is wearing a simple green robe. The walls around the room are now covered in greenery, as well. The room seems to be a perfect grove now: leaves of holly, mistletoe and ivy reflect the stage lights. Suddenly, there is a mighty roar of flame in the fireplace and now the hearth burns with a lavish, warming fire. There is an ancient scabbard girdling the* GHOST'S *middle, but without sword. The sheath is gone to rust.*]

You have never seen the like of me before?

SCROOGE. Never.

PRESENT. You have never walked forth with younger members of my family; my elder brothers born on Christmases past.

SCROOGE. I don't think I have. I'm afraid I've not. Have you had many brothers, Spirit?

PRESENT. More than eighteen hundred.

SCROOGE. A tremendous family to provide for! [PRESENT *stands*] Spirit, conduct me where you will. I went forth last night on **compulsion**, and learnt a lesson which is working now. Tonight, if you have aught to teach me, let me profit by it.

PRESENT. Touch my robe.

[SCROOGE *walks cautiously to* PRESENT *and touches his robe. When he does, lightning flashes, thunder claps, music plays. Blackout*]

◀ **Vocabulary**
compulsion (kəm pul′ shən) *n.* driving, irresistible force

Comprehension
Who visits Scrooge in Scene 1?

SCENE 2

[*PROLOGUE:* MARLEY *stands spotlit, L. He speaks directly to the audience.*]

MARLEY. My ghostly friend now leads my living partner through the city's streets.

[*Lights up on* SCROOGE *and* PRESENT]

See them there and hear the music people make when the weather is severe, as it is now.

Vocabulary ▶
severe (sə vir´) *adj.*
harsh

[*Winter music. Choral group behind scrim, sings. When the song is done and the stage is re-set, the lights will fade up on a row of shops, behind the singers. The choral group will hum the song they have just completed now and mill about the streets,*[2] *carrying their dinners to the bakers' shops and restaurants. They will, perhaps, sing about being poor at Christmastime, whatever.*]

PRESENT. These revelers, Mr. Scrooge, carry their own dinners to their jobs, where they will work to bake the meals the rich men and women of this city will eat as their Christmas dinners. Generous people these . . . to care for the others, so . . .

[PRESENT *walks among the choral group and a sparkling incense*[3] *falls from his torch on to their baskets, as he pulls the covers off of the baskets. Some of the choral group become angry with each other.*]

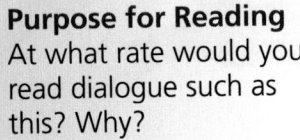

Purpose for Reading
At what rate would you read dialogue such as this? Why?

MAN #1. Hey, you, watch where you're going.

MAN #2. Watch it yourself, mate!

[PRESENT *sprinkles them directly, they change.*]

MAN #1. I pray go in ahead of me. It's Christmas. You be first!

MAN #2. No, no, I must insist that YOU be first!

MAN #1. All right, I shall be, and gratefully so.

MAN #2. The pleasure is equally mine, for being able to watch you pass, smiling.

MAN #1. I would find it a shame to quarrel on Christmas Day . . .

---

2. **mill about the streets** walk around aimlessly.
3. **incense** (in´ sens) *n.* any of various substances that produce a pleasant odor when burned.

MAN #2. As would I.

MAN #1. Merry Christmas then, friend!

MAN #2. And a Merry Christmas straight back to you!

[*Church bells toll. The choral group enter the buildings: the shops and restaurants; they exit the stage, shutting their doors closed behind them. All sound stops.* SCROOGE *and* PRESENT *are alone again.*]

SCROOGE. What is it you sprinkle from your torch?

PRESENT. Kindness.

SCROOGE. Do you sprinkle your kindness on any particular people or on all people?

PRESENT. To any person kindly given. And to the very poor most of all.

SCROOGE. Why to the very poor most?

PRESENT. Because the very poor need it most. Touch my heart . . . here, Mr. Scrooge. We have another journey.

[SCROOGE *touches the* GHOST'S *heart and music plays, lights change color, lightning flashes, thunder claps. A choral group appears on the street, singing Christmas carols.*]

SCENE 3

[MARLEY *stands spotlit in front of a scrim on which is painted the exterior of* CRATCHIT'S *four-roomed house. There is a flash and a clap and* MARLEY *is gone. The lights shift color again, the scrim flies away, and we are in the interior of the* CRATCHIT *family home.* SCROOGE *is there, with the* spirit (PRESENT), *watching* MRS. CRATCHIT *set the table, with the help of* BELINDA CRATCHIT *and* PETER CRATCHIT, *a baby, pokes a fork into the mashed potatoes on his highchair's tray. He also chews on his shirt collar.*]

SCROOGE. What is this place, Spirit?

PRESENT. This is the home of your employee, Mr. Scrooge. Don't you know it?

SCROOGE. Do you mean Cratchit, Spirit? Do you mean this is Cratchit's home?

Vocabulary ▶
meager (mē´ gər) *adj.*
small in amount;
of poor quality

PRESENT. None other.

SCROOGE. These children are his?

PRESENT. There are more to come presently.

SCROOGE. On his **meager** earnings! What foolishness!

PRESENT. Foolishness, is it?

SCROOGE. Wouldn't you say so? Fifteen shillings[4] a week's what
he gets!

PRESENT. I would say that he gets the pleasure of his family,
fifteen times a week times the number of hours a day!
Wait, Mr. Scrooge. Wait, listen and watch. You might
actually learn something . . .

MRS. CRATCHIT. What has ever got your precious father then?
And your brother, Tiny Tim? And Martha warn't as late
last Christmas by half an hour!

[MARTHA *opens the door, speaking to her mother as she does.*]

MARTHA. Here's Martha, now, Mother! [*She laughs. The*
CRATCHIT CHILDREN *squeal with delight.*]

BELINDA. It's Martha, Mother! Here's Martha!

PETER. Marthmama, Marthmama! Hullo!

BELINDA. Hurrah! Martha! Martha! There's such an enormous
goose for us, Martha!

MRS. CRATCHIT. Why, bless your heart alive, my dear, how late
you are!

MARTHA. We'd a great deal of work to finish up last night, and
had to clear away this morning, Mother.

Purpose for Reading
How does Mrs.
Cratchit's use of
language affect your
reading rate? Explain.

MRS. CRATCHIT. Well, never mind so long as you are come. Sit
ye down before the fire, my dear, and have a warm, Lord
bless ye!

BELINDA. No, no! There's Father coming. Hide, Martha, hide!

[MARTHA *giggles and hides herself.*]

MARTHA. Where? Here?

PETER. Hide, hide!

---

4. **Fifteen shillings** a small amount of money for a week's work.

BELINDA. Not there! *THERE!*

MARTHA *is hidden.* BOB CRATCHIT *enters, carrying* TINY TIM *atop his shoulder. He wears a threadbare and fringeless comforter hanging down in front of him.* TINY TIM *carries small crutches and his small legs are bound in an iron frame brace.*]

BOB AND TINY TIM. Merry Christmas.

BOB. Merry Christmas my love, Merry Christmas Peter, Merry Christmas Belinda. Why, where is Martha?

MRS. CRATCHIT. Not coming.

BOB. Not coming: Not coming upon Christmas Day?

MARTHA. [*Pokes head out*] Ohhh, poor Father. Don't be disappointed.

BOB. What's this?

MARTHA. 'Tis I!

BOB. Martha! [*They embrace.*]

TINY TIM. Martha! Martha!

MARTHA. Tiny Tim!

[TINY TIM *is placed in* MARTHA'S *arms.* BELINDA *and* PETER *rush him offstage.*]

BELINDA. Come, brother! You must come hear the pudding singing in the copper.

TINY TIM. The pudding? What flavor have we?

PETER. Plum! Plum!

TINY TIM. Oh, Mother! I love plum!

[*The children exit the stage, giggling.*]

MRS. CRATCHIT. And how did little Tim behave?

BOB. As good as gold, and even better. Somehow he gets thoughtful sitting by himself so much, and thinks the

▲ **Critical Viewing**
How do you think seeing the happy Cratchit family will affect Scrooge's attitude?

Comprehension
Why does Martha hide?

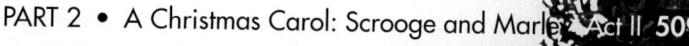

strangest things you ever heard. He told me, coming home, that he hoped people saw him in the church, because he was a cripple, and it might be pleasant to them to remember upon Christmas Day, who made lame beggars walk and blind men see. [*Pauses*] He has the oddest ideas sometimes, but he seems all the while to be growing stronger and more hearty . . . one would never know. [*Hears* TIM's *crutch on floor outside door*]

Stage Directions
Why is the pause in Bob's speech important here?

PETER. The goose has arrived to be eaten!

BELINDA. Oh, mama, mama, it's beautiful.

MARTHA. It's a perfect goose, Mother!

TINY TIM. To this Christmas goose, Mother and Father I say . . . [*Yells*] Hurrah! Hurrah!

OTHER CHILDREN. [*Copying* TIM] Hurrah! Hurrah!

[*The family sits round the table.* BOB *and* MRS. CRATCHIT *serve the trimmings, quickly. All sit; all bow heads; all pray.*]

BOB. Thank you, dear Lord, for your many gifts . . . our dear children; our wonderful meal; our love for one another; and the warmth of our small fire—[*Looks up at all*] A merry Christmas to us, my dear. God bless us!

ALL. [*Except* TIM] Merry Christmas! God bless us!

TINY TIM. [*In a short silence*] God bless us every one.

All freeze. Spotlight on PRESENT *and* SCROOGE]

SCROOGE. Spirit, tell me if Tiny Tim will live.

PRESENT. I see a vacant seat . . . in the poor chimney corner, and a crutch without an owner, carefully preserved. If these shadows remain unaltered by the future, the child will die.

SCROOGE. No, no, kind Spirit! Say he will be spared!

PRESENT. If these shadows remain unaltered by the future, none other of my race will find him here. What then? If he be like to die, he had better do it, and decrease the surplus population.

[SCROOGE *bows his head. We hear* BOB's *voice speak* SCROOGE's *name.*]

Bob. Mr. Scrooge . . .

Scrooge. Huh? What's that? Who calls?

Bob. [*His glass raised in a toast*] I'll give you Mr. Scrooge, the Founder of the Feast!

Scrooge. Me, Bob? You toast *me?*

Present. Save your breath, Mr. Scrooge. You can't be seen or heard.

Mrs. Cratchit. The Founder of the Feast, indeed! I wish I had him here, that miser Scrooge. I'd give him a piece of my mind to feast upon, and I hope he'd have a good appetite for it!

Bob. My dear! Christmas Day!

Mrs. Cratchit. It should be Christmas Day, I am sure, on which one drinks the health of such an odious, stingy, unfeeling man as Mr. Scrooge . . .

Comprehension
What is wrong with Tiny Tim?

Scrooge. Oh, Spirit, must I? . . .

Mrs. Cratchit. You know he is, Robert! Nobody knows it better than you do, poor fellow!

Bob. This is Christmas Day, and I should like to drink to the health of the man who employs me and allows me to earn my living and our support and that man is Ebenezer Scrooge . . .

Mrs. Cratchit. I'll drink to his health for your sake and the day's, but not for his sake . . . a Merry Christmas and a Happy New Year to you, Mr. Scrooge, wherever you may be this day!

Scrooge. Just here, kind madam . . . out of sight, out of sight . . .

Bob. Thank you, my dear. Thank you.

Scrooge. Thank you, Bob . . . and Mrs. Cratchit, too. No one else is toasting me, . . . not now . . . not ever. Of that I am sure . . .

Bob. Children . . .

All. Merry Christmas to Mr. Scrooge.

Bob. I'll pay you sixpence, Tim, for my favorite song.

Tiny Tim. Oh, Father, I'd so love to sing it, but not for pay. This Christmas goose—this feast—you and Mother, my brother and sisters close with me: that's my pay—

Bob. Martha, will you play the notes on the lute, for Tiny Tim's song.

Belinda. May I sing, too, Father?

Bob. We'll all sing.

[*They sing a song about a tiny child lost in the snow— probably from Wordsworth's poem.* Tim *sings the lead vocal; all chime in for the chorus. Their song fades under, as the* Ghost of Christmas Present *speaks.*]

▼ **Critical Viewing**
Martha plays a lute like this one while her family sings. If this play were set in modern times, what instrument would Martha probably play?

Stage Directions
What does the song— and its subject—add to the mood of the scene?

Present. Mark my words, Ebenezer Scrooge. I do not present the Cratchits to you because they are a handsome, or brilliant family. They are not handsome. They are not brilliant. They are not well-dressed, or tasteful to the times. Their shoes are not even waterproofed by virtue of money or cleverness spent. So when the pavement is wet, so are the insides of their shoes and the tops of their toes. These are the Cratchits, Mr. Scrooge. They are not highly special. They are happy, grateful, pleased with one another, contented with the time and how it passes. They don't sing very well, do they? But, nonetheless, they do sing . . . [*Pauses*] think of that, Scrooge. Fifteen shillings a week and they do sing . . . hear their song until its end.

Scrooge. I am listening. [*The chorus sings full volume now, until . . . the song ends here.*] Spirit, it must be time for us to take our leave. I feel in my heart that it is . . . that I must think on that which I have seen here . . .

Present. Touch my robe again . . .

[Scrooge *touches* Present's *robe. The lights fade out on the* Cratchits, *who sit, frozen, at the table.* Scrooge *and* Present *in a spotlight now. Thunder, lightning, smoke. They are gone.*]

Spiral Review
CHARACTER What point is the Ghost of Christmas Present trying to impress upon Scrooge as he describes the Cratchits?

SCENE 4

[Marley *appears D.L. in single spotlight. A storm brews. Thunder and lightning.* Scrooge *and* Present *"fly" past, U. The storm continues, furiously, and, now and again,* Scrooge *and* Present *will zip past in their travels.* Marley *will speak straight out to the audience.*]

Marley. The Ghost of Christmas Present, my co-worker in this attempt to turn a miser, flies about now with that very miser, Scrooge, from street to street, and he points out partygoers on their way to Christmas parties. If one were to judge from the numbers of people on their way to friendly gatherings, one might think that no one was left at home to give anyone welcome . . . but that's not the case, is it? Every home is expecting company and . . . [*He laughs.*] Scrooge is amazed.

Comprehension
What does Scrooge observe the Cratchits doing?

[SCROOGE *and* PRESENT *zip past again. The lights fade up around them. We are in the* NEPHEW'S *home, in the living room.* PRESENT *and* SCROOGE *stand watching the* NEPHEW: FRED *and his wife, fixing the fire.*]

SCROOGE. What is this place? We've moved from the mines!

PRESENT. You do not recognize them?

SCROOGE. It is my nephew! . . . and the one he married . . .

[MARLEY *waves his hand and there is a lightning flash. He disappears.*]

FRED. It strikes me as sooooo funny, to think of what he said . . . that Christmas was a humbug, as I live! He believed it!

WIFE. More shame for him, Fred!

FRED. Well, he's a comical old fellow, that's the truth.

WIFE. I have no patience with him.

FRED. Oh, I have! I am sorry for him; I couldn't be angry with him if I tried. Who suffers by his ill whims? Himself, always . . .

SCROOGE. It's me they talk of, isn't it, Spirit?

FRED. Here, wife, consider this. Uncle Scrooge takes it into his head to dislike us, and he won't come and dine with us. What's the consequence?

WIFE. Oh . . . you're sweet to say what I think you're about to say, too, Fred . . .

FRED. What's the consequence? He don't lose much of a dinner by it, I can tell you that!

WIFE. Ooooooo, Fred! Indeed, I think he loses a very good dinner . . . ask my sisters, or your bachelor friend, Topper . . . ask any of them. They'll tell you what old Scrooge, your uncle, missed: a dandy meal!

FRED. Well, that's something of a relief, wife. Glad to hear it! [*He hugs his wife. They laugh. They kiss.*] The truth is, he misses much yet. I mean to give him the same chance every year, whether he likes it or not, for I pity him. Nay, he is my only uncle and I feel for the old miser . . . but, I tell you, wife: I see my dear and perfect mother's face on his own wizened cheeks and brow: brother and sister they were, and I cannot erase that from each view of him I take . . .

WIFE. I understand what you say, Fred, and I am with you in your yearly asking. But he never will accept, you know. He never will.

FRED. Well, true, wife. Uncle may rail at Christmas till he dies. I think I shook him some with my visit yesterday . . . [*Laughing*] I refused to grow angry . . . no matter how nasty he became . . . [*Whoops*] It was HE who grew angry, wife! [*They both laugh now.*]

SCROOGE. What he says is true, Spirit . . .

FRED AND WIFE. Bah, humbug!

FRED. [*Embracing his wife*] There is much laughter in our marriage, wife. It pleases me. You please me . . .

WIFE. And you please me, Fred. You are a good man . . . [*They embrace.*] Come now. We must have a look at the meal . . . our guests will soon arrive . . . my sisters, Topper . . .

FRED. A toast first . . . [*He hands her a glass.*] A toast to Uncle Scrooge . . . [*Fills their glasses*]

WIFE. A toast to him?

FRED. Uncle Scrooge has given us plenty of merriment, I am sure, and it would be ungrateful not to drink to his health. And I say . . . *Uncle Scrooge!*

WIFE. [*Laughing*] You're a proper loon,[5] Fred . . . and I'm a

Comprehension
What scenes does the Ghost of Christmas Present show Scrooge?

---

5. **a proper loon** a silly person.

proper wife to you . . . [*She raises her glass.*] Uncle Scrooge!
[*They drink. They embrace. They kiss.*]

Vocabulary ▶
audible (ô′ də bəl) *adj.*
loud enough
to be heard

SCROOGE. Spirit, please, make me visible! Make me **audible**! I
want to talk with my nephew and my niece!

[*Calls out to them. The lights that light the room and* FRED *and
wife fade out.* SCROOGE *and* PRESENT *are alone, spotlit.*]

PRESENT. These shadows are gone to you now, Mr. Scrooge.
You may return to them later tonight in your dreams.
[*Pauses*] My time grows short, Ebenezer Scrooge. Look you
on me! Do you see how I've aged?

SCROOGE. Your hair has gone gray! Your skin, wrinkled! Are
spirits' lives so short?

PRESENT. My stay upon this globe is very brief. It ends tonight.

SCROOGE. Tonight?

PRESENT. At midnight. The time is drawing near!

[*Clock strikes 11:45.*]

Stage Directions
Why is the clock on
stage important to the
action?

Hear those chimes? In a quarter hour, my life will have
been spent! Look, Scrooge, man. Look you here.

[*Two gnarled baby dolls are taken from* PRESENT'S *skirts.*]

SCROOGE. Who are they?

PRESENT. They are Man's children, and they cling to me,
appealing from their fathers. The boy is Ignorance; the girl
is Want. Beware them both, and all of their degree, but
most of all beware this boy, for I see that written on his
brow which is doom, unless the writing be erased.
[*He stretches out his arm. His voice is now amplified: loudly
and oddly.*]

SCROOGE. Have they no refuge or resource?

PRESENT. Are there no prisons? Are there no workhouses?
[*Twelve chimes*] Are there no prisons? Are there no
workhouses?

[*A* PHANTOM, *hooded, appears in dim light,* D., *opposite.*]
Are there no prisons? Are there no workhouses?

[PRESENT *begins to deliquesce.* SCROOGE *calls after him.*]

SCROOGE. Spirit, I'm frightened! Don't leave me! Spirit!

PRESENT. Prisons? Workhouses? Prisons? Workhouses . . .

[*He is gone.* SCROOGE *is alone now with the* PHANTOM, *who is, of course, the* GHOST OF CHRISTMAS FUTURE. *The* PHANTOM *is shrouded in black. Only its outstretched hand is visible from under his ghostly garment.*]

SCROOGE. Who are you, Phantom? Oh, yes, I think I know you! You are, are you not, the Spirit of Christmas Yet to Come? [*No reply*] And you are about to show me the shadows of the things that have not yet happened, but will happen in time before us. Is that not so, Spirit? [*The* PHANTOM *allows* SCROOGE *a look at his face. No other reply wanted here. A nervous giggle here.*] Oh, Ghost of the Future, I fear you more than any Specter I have seen! But, as I know that your purpose is to do me good and as I hope to live to be another man from what I was, I am prepared to bear you company. [FUTURE *does not reply, but for a stiff arm, hand and finger set, pointing forward.*] Lead on, then, lead on. The night is waning fast, and it is precious time to me. Lead on, Spirit!

[FUTURE *moves away from* SCROOGE *in the same rhythm and motion employed at its arrival.* SCROOGE *falls into the same pattern, a considerable space apart from the* SPIRIT. *In the space between them,* MARLEY *appears. He looks to* FUTURE *and then to* SCROOGE. *He claps his hands. Thunder and lightning. Three* BUSINESSMEN *appear, spotlighted singularly: One is D.L.; one is D.R.; one is U.C. Thus, six points of the stage should now be spotted in light.* MARLEY *will watch this scene from his position,* C. SCROOGE *and* FUTURE *are R. and L. of* C.]

FIRST BUSINESSMAN. Oh, no, I don't know much about it either way, I only know he's dead.

SECOND BUSINESSMAN. When did he die?

FIRST BUSINESSMAN. Last night, I believe.

SECOND BUSINESSMAN. Why, what was the matter with him? I thought he'd never die, really . . .

FIRST BUSINESSMAN. [*Yawning*] Goodness knows, goodness knows . . .

Stage Directions
The stage direction calls for Future to stretch out his hand. How does this action add to the drama of the scene?

Spiral Review
CHARACTER What valuable information does Scrooge reveal about himself?

Comprehension
What warning does the Ghost of Christmas Present give Scrooge?

THIRD BUSINESSMAN. What has he done with his money?

SECOND BUSINESSMAN. I haven't heard. Have you?

FIRST BUSINESSMAN. Left it to his Company, perhaps. Money to money; you know the expression . . .

THIRD BUSINESSMAN. He hasn't left it to *me*. That's all I know . . .

FIRST BUSINESSMAN. [*Laughing*] Nor to me . . . [*Looks at* SECOND BUSINESSMAN] You, then? You got his money???

SECOND BUSINESSMAN. [*Laughing*] Me, me, his money? Nooooo!

[*They all laugh.*]

THIRD BUSINESSMAN. It's likely to be a cheap funeral, for upon my life, I don't know of a living soul who'd care to venture to it. Suppose we make up a party and volunteer?

SECOND BUSINESSMAN. I don't mind going if a lunch is provided, but I must be fed, if I make one.

FIRST BUSINESSMAN. Well, I am the most disinterested among you, for I never wear black gloves, and I never eat lunch. But I'll offer to go, if anybody else will. When I come to think of it, I'm not all sure that I wasn't his most particular friend; for we used to stop and speak whenever we met. Well, then . . . bye, bye!

SECOND BUSINESSMAN. Bye, bye . . .

THIRD BUSINESSMAN. Bye, bye . . .

[*They glide offstage in three separate directions. Their lights follow them.*]

SCROOGE. Spirit, why did you show me this? Why do you show me businessmen from my streets as they take the death of Jacob Marley? That is a thing past. You are *future!*

[JACOB MARLEY *laughs a long, deep laugh. There is a thunder clap and lightning flash, and he is gone.* SCROOGE *faces* FUTURE, *alone on stage now.* FUTURE *wordlessly stretches*

▲ **Critical Viewing**
How does the Ghost of Christmas Future differ from the other ghosts?

Do others see us more clearly than we see ourselves?

out his arm-hand-and-finger-set, pointing into the distance, U. There, above them, scoundrels "fly" by, half-dressed and slovenly. When this scene has passed, a woman enters the playing area. She is almost at once followed by a second woman; and then a man in faded black; and then, suddenly, an old man, who smokes a pipe. The old man scares the other three. They laugh, anxious.]

Stage Directions
If you were staging this play, how could you make people appear to "fly" by?

FIRST WOMAN. Look here, old Joe, here's a chance! If we haven't all three met here without meaning it!

OLD JOE. You couldn't have met in a better place. Come into the parlor. You were made free of it long ago, you know; and the other two ain't strangers [*He stands; shuts a door. Shrieking*] We're all suitable to our calling. We're well matched. Come into the parlor. Come into the parlor . . . [*They follow him* D. SCROOGE *and* FUTURE *are now in their midst, watching; silent. A truck comes in on which is set a small wall with fireplace and a screen of rags, etc. All props for the scene.*] Let me just rake this fire over a bit . . .

[*He does. He trims his lamp with the stem of his pipe. The* FIRST WOMAN *throws a large bundle on to the floor. She sits beside it, crosslegged, defiantly.*]

FIRST WOMAN. What odds then? What odds, Mrs. Dilber? Every person has a right to take care of themselves. HE always did!

MRS. DILBER. That's true indeed! No man more so!

FIRST WOMAN. Why, then, don't stand staring as if you was afraid, woman! Who's the wiser? We're not going to pick holes in each other's coats, I suppose?

MRS. DILBER. No, indeed! We should hope not!

FIRST WOMAN. Very well, then! That's enough. Who's the worse for the loss of a few things like these? Not a dead man, I suppose?

MRS. DILBER. [*Laughing*] No, indeed!

FIRST WOMAN. If he wanted to keep 'em after he was dead, the wicked old screw, why wasn't he natural in his lifetime? If he had been, he'd have had somebody to look after him

Comprehension
What does Scrooge think the spirit is showing him?

Purpose for Reading
What question about the characters directs your purpose for reading this dialogue?

when he was struck with Death, instead of lying gasping out his last there, alone by himself.

MRS. DILBER. It's the truest word that was ever spoke. It's a judgment on him.

FIRST WOMAN. I wish it were a heavier one, and it should have been, you may depend on it, if I could have laid my hands on anything else. Open that bundle, old Joe, and let me know the value of it. Speak out plain. I'm not afraid to be the first, nor afraid for them to see it. We knew pretty well that we were helping ourselves, before we met here, I believe. It's no sin. Open the bundle, Joe.

FIRST MAN. No, no, my dear! I won't think of letting you being the first to show what you've . . . earned . . . earned from this. I throw in mine.

[*He takes a bundle from his shoulder, turns it upside down, and empties its contents out on to the floor.*]

It's not very extensive, see . . . seals . . . a pencil case . . . sleeve buttons . . .

FIRST WOMAN. Nice sleeve buttons, though . . .

FIRST MAN. Not bad, not bad . . . a brooch there . . .

OLD JOE. Not really valuable, I'm afraid . . .

FIRST MAN. How much, old Joe?

OLD JOE. [*Writing on the wall with chalk*] A pitiful lot, really. Ten and six and not a sixpence more!

FIRST MAN. You're not serious!

OLD JOE. That's your account and I wouldn't give another sixpence if I was to be boiled for not doing it. Who's next?

MRS. DILBER. Me! [*Dumps out contents of her bundle*] Sheets, towels, silver spoons, silver sugar-tongs . . . some boots . . .

OLD JOE. [*Writing on wall*] I always give too much to the ladies. It's a weakness of mine and that's the way I ruin myself. Here's your total comin' up . . . two pounds-ten . . . if you asked me for another penny, and made it an open question, I'd repent of being so liberal and knock off half-a-crown.

FIRST WOMAN. And now do MY bundle, Joe.

OLD JOE. [*Kneeling to open knots on her bundle*] So many knots, madam . . . [*He drags out large curtains; dark*] What do you call this? Bed curtains!

FIRST WOMAN. [*Laughing*] Ah, yes, bed curtains!

OLD JOE. You don't mean to say you took 'em down, rings and all, with him lying there?

FIRST WOMAN. Yes, I did, why not?

OLD JOE. You were born to make your fortune and you'll certainly do it.

FIRST WOMAN. I certainly shan't hold my hand, when I can get anything in it by reaching it out, for the sake of such a man as he was, I promise you, Joe. Don't drop that lamp oil on those blankets, now!

OLD JOE. His blankets?

FIRST WOMAN. Whose else's do you think? He isn't likely to catch cold without 'em, I daresay.

OLD JOE. I hope that he didn't die of anything catching? Eh?

FIRST WOMAN. Don't you be afraid of that. I ain't so fond of his company that I'd loiter about him for such things if he did. Ah! You may look through that shirt till your eyes ache, but you won't find a hole in it, nor a threadbare place. It's the best he had, and a fine one, too. They'd have wasted it, if it hadn't been for me.

OLD JOE. What do you mean "They'd have wasted it?"

FIRST WOMAN. Putting it on him to be buried in, to be sure. Somebody was fool enough to do it, but I took it off again . . .

[*She laughs, as do they all, nervously.*]

If calico[6] ain't good enough for such a purpose, it isn't good enough then for anything. It's quite as becoming to the body. He can't look uglier than he did in that one!

SCROOGE. [*A low-pitched moan emits from his mouth; from the bones.*] OOOOOOOoooooOOOOOooooOOOOOOO oooooOOOOOOoooooOO!

Stage Directions
How do the stage directions help you picture the action in this scene?

Comprehension
Whose possessions are these people selling?

---

6. **calico** (kal´ i kō) *n.* coarse and cheap cloth.

OLD JOE. One pound six for the lot. [*He produces a small flannel bag filled with money. He divvies it out. He continues to pass around the money as he speaks. All are laughing.*] That's the end of it, you see! He frightened every one away from him while he was alive, to profit us when he was dead! Hah ha ha!

ALL. HAHAHAHAhahahahahahah!

SCROOGE. *OOOoooOOOoooOOOoooOOOooo OOoooOOoooOOOooo!* [*He screams at them.*] Obscene demons! Why not market the corpse itself, as sell its trimming??? [*Suddenly*] Oh, Spirit, I see it, I see it! This unhappy man—this stripped-bare corpse . . . could very well be my own. My life holds parallel! My life ends that way now!

[SCROOGE *backs into something in the dark behind his spotlight.* SCROOGE *looks at* FUTURE, *who points to the corpse.* SCROOGE *pulls back the blanket. The corpse is, of course,* SCROOGE, *who screams. He falls aside the bed; weeping.*]

Spirit, this is a fearful place. In leaving it, I shall not leave its lesson, trust me. Let us go!

[FUTURE *points to the corpse.*]

Spirit, let me see some tenderness connected with a death, or that dark chamber, which we just left now, Spirit, will be forever present to me.

[FUTURE *spreads his robes again. Thunder and lightning. Lights up, U., in the* CRATCHIT *home setting.* MRS. CRATCHIT *and her daughters, sewing*]

TINY TIM'S VOICE. [*Off*] And He took a child and set him in the midst of them.

SCROOGE. [*Looking about the room; to* FUTURE] Huh? Who spoke? Who said that?

MRS. CRATCHIT. [*Puts down her sewing*] The color hurts my eyes. [*Rubs her eyes*] That's better. My eyes grow weak sewing by candlelight. I shouldn't want to show your father weak eyes when he comes home . . . not for the world! It must be near his time . . .

Stage Directions
What is the effect of the spirit's silence?

▶ **Critical Viewing**
How does this portrayal of the Cratchit family compare with the picture on page 511?

PETER. [*In corner, reading. Looks up from book*] Past it, rather. But I think he's been walking a bit slower than usual these last few evenings, Mother.

MRS. CRATCHIT I have known him walk with . . . [*Pauses*] I have know him walk with Tiny Tim upon his shoulder and very fast indeed.

PETER. So have I, Mother! Often!

DAUGHTER. So have I.

MRS. CRATCHIT. But he was very light to carry and his father loved him so, that it was not trouble—no trouble. [BOB, *at door*]
And there is your father at the door.

[BOB CRATCHIT *enters. He wears a comforter. He is cold, forlorn.*]

PETER. Father!

BOB. Hello, wife, children . . .

[*The daughter weeps; turns away from* CRATCHIT.]

Children! How good to see you all! And you, wife. And look at this sewing! I've no doubt, with all your industry,

Comprehension
Whose corpse does Scrooge see?

we'll have a quilt to set down upon our knees in church on Sunday!

MRS. CRATCHIT. You made the arrangements today, then, Robert, for the . . . service . . . to be on Sunday.

BOB. The funeral. Oh, well, yes, yes, I did. I wish you could have gone. It would have done you good to see how green a place it is. But you'll see it often. I promised him that I would walk there on Sunday, after the service. [*Suddenly*] My little, little child! My little child!

ALL CHILDREN. [*Hugging him*] Oh, Father . . .

BOB. [*He stands*] Forgive me. I saw Mr. Scrooge's nephew, who you know I'd just met once before, and he was so wonderful to me, wife . . . he is the most pleasant-spoken gentleman I've ever met . . . he said "I am heartily sorry for it and heartily sorry for your good wife. If I can be of service to you in any way, here's where I live." And he gave me this card.

PETER. Let me see it!

BOB. And he looked me straight in the eye, wife, and said, meaningfully, "I pray you'll come to me, Mr. Cratchit, if you need some help. I pray you do." Now it wasn't for the sake of anything that he might be able to do for us, so much as for his kind way. It seemed as if he had known our Tiny Tim and felt with us.

MRS. CRATCHIT. I'm sure that he's a good soul.

BOB. You would be surer of it, my dear, if you saw and spoke to him. I shouldn't be at all surprised, if he got Peter a situation.

MRS. CRATCHIT. Only hear that, Peter!

MARTHA. And then, Peter will be keeping company with someone and setting up for himself!

PETER. Get along with you!

BOB. It's just as likely as not, one of these days, though there's plenty of time for that, my dear. But however and whenever we part from one another, I am sure we shall none of us forget poor Tiny Tim—shall we?—or this first parting that was among us?

Purpose for Reading
What plot information does this dialogue provide about a possible future for the Cratchits?

ALL CHILDREN. Never, Father, never!

BOB. And when we recollect how patient and mild he was, we shall not quarrel easily among ourselves, and forget poor Tiny Tim in doing it.

ALL CHILDREN. No, Father, never!

LITTLE BOB. I am very happy, I am, I am, I am very happy.

[BOB *kisses his little son, as does* MRS. CRATCHIT, *as do the other children. The family is set now in one sculptural embrace. The lighting fades to a gentle pool of light, tight on them.*]

SCROOGE. Specter, something informs me that our parting moment is at hand. I know it, but I know not how I know it.

[FUTURE *points to the other side of the stage. Lights out on* CRATCHITS. FUTURE *moves slowing, gliding.* SCROOGE *follows.* FUTURE *points opposite.* FUTURE *leads* SCROOGE *to a wall and a tombstone. He points to the stone.*]

Am I that man those ghoulish parasites[7] so gloated over? [*Pauses*] Before I draw nearer to that stone to which you point, answer me one question. Are these the shadows of things that will be, or the shadows of things that MAY be, only?

▼ **Critical Viewing**
What emotions do you think Scrooge might be feeling in this scene?

Comprehension
What has happened to Tiny Tim?

---

7. ghoulish parasites (gōōl′ ish par′ ə sīts) man and women who stole and divided Scrooge's goods after he died.

[FUTURE *points to the gravestone.* MARLEY *appears in light well U. He points to grave as well. Gravestone turns front and grows to ten feet high. Words upon it:* EBENEZER SCROOGE: *Much smoke billows now from the grave. Choral music here.* SCROOGE *stands looking up at gravestone.* FUTURE *does not at all reply in mortals' words, but points once more to the gravestone. The stone undulates and glows. Music plays, beckoning* SCROOGE. SCROOGE *reeling in terror*]

Oh, no. Spirit! Oh, no, no!

[FUTURE's *finger still pointing*]

Spirit! Hear me! I am not the man I was. I will not be the man I would have been but for this intercourse. Why show me this, if I am past all hope?

[FUTURE *considers* SCROOGE's *logic. His hand wavers.*]

Oh, Good Spirit, I see by your wavering hand that your good nature **intercedes** for me and pities me. Assure me that I yet may change these shadows that you have shown me by an altered life!

[FUTURE's *hand trembles; pointing has stopped.*]

I will honor Christmas in my heart and try to keep it all the year. I will live in the Past, the Present, and the Future. The Spirits of all Three shall strive within me. I will not shut out the lessons that they teach. Oh, tell me that I may sponge away the writing that is upon this stone!

[SCROOGE *makes a desperate stab at grabbing* FUTURE's *hand. He holds firm for a moment, but* FUTURE, *stronger than* SCROOGE, *pulls away.* SCROOGE *is on his knees, praying.*]

Spirit, dear Spirit, I am praying before you. Give me a sign that all is possible. Give me a sign that all hope for me is not lost. Oh, Spirit, kind Spirit, I beseech thee: give me a sign . . .

[FUTURE *deliquesces, slowly, gently. The* PHANTOM's *hood and robe drop gracefully to the ground in a small heap. Music in. There is nothing in them. They are mortal cloth. The* SPIRIT *is elsewhere.* SCROOGE *has his sign.* SCROOGE *is alone. Tableau. The lights fade to black.*]

Vocabulary ▶
intercedes (in'tər sēdz')
v. makes a request on behalf of another

Stage Directions
What action described in the stage directions gives Scrooge hope that he may change the future?

SCENE 5

[*The end of it.* MARLEY, *spotlighted, opposite* SCROOGE, *in his bed, spotlighted.* MARLEY *speaks to audience, directly.*]

MARLEY. [*He smiles at* SCROOGE.] The firm of Scrooge and Marley is doubly blessed; two misers turned; one, alas, in Death, too late; but the other miser turned in Time's penultimate nick.[8] Look you on my friend, Ebenezer Scrooge . . .

SCROOGE. [*Scrambling out of bed; reeling in delight*] I will live in the Past, in the Present, and in the Future! The Spirits of all Three shall strive within me!

MARLEY. [*He points and moves closer to* SCROOGE's *bed.*] Yes, Ebenezer, the bedpost is your own. Believe it! Yes, Ebenezer, the room is your own. Believe it!

SCROOGE. Oh, Jacob Marley! Wherever you are, Jacob, know ye that I praise you for this! I praise you . . . and heaven . . . and Christmastime! [*Kneels facing away from* MARLEY] I say it to ye on my knees, old Jacob, on my knees! [*He touches his bed curtains.*] Not torn down. My bed curtains are not at all torn down! Rings and all, here they are! They are here: I am here: the shadows of things that would have been, may now be dispelled. They will be, Jacob! I know they will be!

[*He chooses clothing for the day. He tries different pieces of clothing and settles, perhaps, on a dress suit, plus a cape of the bed clothing: something of color.*]

I am light as a feather, I am happy as an angel, I am as merry as a schoolboy. [*Yells out window and then out to audience*] Merry Christmas to everybody! Merry Christmas to everybody! A Happy New Year to all the world! Hallo here! Whoop! Whoop! Hallo! Hallo! I don't know what day of the month it is! I don't care! I don't know anything! I'm quite a baby! I don't care! I don't care a fig! I'd much rather be a baby than be an old wreck like me or Marley! (Sorry, Jacob, wherever ye be!) Hallo! Hallo there!

[*Church bells chime in Christmas Day. A small boy, named* ADAM, *is seen now D.R., as a light fades up on him.*]

---

8. **in Time's penultimate nick** just at the last moment.

Purpose for Reading
Why might you read this speech by Scrooge quickly?

Comprehension
What promises does Scrooge make?

Media Connection

The Many Faces of Scrooge
The part of Ebenezer Scrooge has been played by many different actors over the years.

1983 Scrooge McDuck

1938 Reginald Owen

1951 Alistair Sim

1962 Mister Magoo

1992 Michael Caine

Connect to the Literature
Which of these actors best portrays Scrooge as you imagine him from your reading? Explain.

Hey, you boy! What's today? What day of the year is it?

ADAM. Today, sir? Why, it's Christmas Day!

SCROOGE. It's Christmas Day, is it? Whoop! Well, I haven't missed it after all, have I? The Spirits did all they did in one night. They can do anything they like, right? Of course they can! Of course they can!

ADAM. Excuse me, sir?

SCROOGE. Huh? Oh, yes, of course, what's your name, lad?

[SCROOGE *and* ADAM *will play their scene from their own spotlights.*]

ADAM. Adam, sir.

SCROOGE. Adam! What a fine, strong name! Do you know the poulterer's[9] in the next street but one, at the corner?

ADAM. I certainly should hope I know him, sir!

SCROOGE. A remarkable boy! An intelligent boy! Do you know whether the poulterer's have sold the prize turkey that was hanging up there? I don't mean the little prize turkey, Adam. I mean the big one!

ADAM. What, do you mean the one they've got that's as big as me?

SCROOGE. I mean, the turkey the size of Adam: that's the bird!

ADAM. It's hanging there now, sir.

SCROOGE. It is? Go and buy it! No, no, I am absolutely in earnest. Go and buy it and tell 'em to bring it here, so that I may give them the directions to where I want it delivered, as a gift. Come back here with the man, Adam, and I'll give you a shilling. Come back here with him in less than five minutes, and I'll give you half-a-crown!

ADAM. Oh, my sir! Don't let my brother in on this.

[ADAM *runs offstage.* MARLEY *smiles.*]

MARLEY. An act of kindness is like the first green grape of summer: one leads to another and another and another. It would take a queer man indeed to not follow an act of kindness with an act of kindness. One simply whets the tongue for more . . . the taste of kindness is too too sweet. Gifts—goods—are lifeless. But the gift of goodness one feels in the giving is full of life. It . . . is . . . a . . . wonder.

[*Pauses; moves closer to* SCROOGE, *who is totally occupied with his dressing and arranging of his room and his day. He is making lists, etc.* MARLEY *reaches out to* SCROOGE.]

ADAM. [*Calling, off*] I'm here! I'm here!

[ADAM *runs on with a man, who carries an enormous turkey.*]

Here I am, sir. Three minutes flat! A world record! I've got the poultryman and he's got the poultry! [*He pants, out of breath.*] I have earned my prize, sir, if I live . . .

---

9. **poulterer's** (pōl′ tər ərz) *n.* British word for a store that sells poultry.

Comprehension
What does Scrooge instruct Adam to do?

[*He holds his heart, playacting.* SCROOGE *goes to him and embraces him.*]

SCROOGE. You are truly a champion, Adam . . .

MAN. Here's the bird you ordered, sir . . .

SCROOGE. *Oh, my, MY!!!* Look at the size of that turkey, will you! He never could have stood upon his legs, that bird! He would have snapped them off in a minute, like sticks of sealingwax! Why you'll never be able to carry that bird to Camden-Town. I'll give you money for a cab . . .

MAN. Camden-Town's where it's goin', sir?

SCROOGE. Oh, I didn't tell you? Yes, I've written the precise address down just here on this . . . [*Hands paper to him*] Bob Cratchit's house. Now he's not to know who sends him this. Do you understand me? Not a word . . . [*Handing out money and chuckling*]

MAN. I understand, sir, not a word.

SCROOGE. Good. There you go then . . . this is for the turkey . . . [*Chuckle*] and this is for the taxi. [*Chuckle*] . . . and this is for your world-record run, Adam . . .

ADAM. But I don't have change for that, sir.

SCROOGE. Then keep it, my lad. It's Christmas!

ADAM. [*He kisses* SCROOGE's *cheek, quickly.*] Thank you, sir. Merry, Merry Christmas! [*He runs off.*]

MAN. And you've given me a bit overmuch here, too, sir . . .

SCROOGE. Of course I have, sir. It's Christmas!

MAN. Oh, well, thanking you, sir. I'll have this bird to Mr. Cratchit and his family in no time, sir. Don't you worry none about that. Merry Christmas to you, sir, and a very happy New Year, too . . .

[*The man exits.* SCROOGE *walks in a large circle about the stage, which is now gently lit. A chorus sings Christmas music far in the distance. Bells chime as well, far in the distance. A gentlewoman enters and passes.* SCROOGE *is on the streets now.*]

SCROOGE. Merry Christmas, madam . . .

Purpose for Reading
The positive change in Scrooge is becoming more noticeable. Will your reading rate change from here until the end of the act? Why or why not?

WOMAN. Merry Christmas, sir . . .

[*The portly businessman from the first act enters.*]

SCROOGE. Merry Christmas, sir.

PORTLY MAN. Merry Christmas, sir.

SCROOGE. Oh, you! My dear sir! How do you do? I do hope that you succeeded yesterday! It was very kind of you. A Merry Christmas.

PORTLY MAN. Mr. Scrooge?

SCROOGE. Yes, Scrooge is my name though I'm afraid you may not find it very pleasant. Allow me to ask your pardon. And will you have the goodness to—[*He whispers into the man's ear.*]

PORTLY MAN. Lord bless me! My dear Mr. Scrooge, are you *serious!?!*

Comprehension
Where does Scrooge want the turkey delivered?

SCROOGE. If you please. Not a farthing[10] less. A great many back payments are included in it, I assure you. Will you do me that favor?

PORTLY MAN. My dear sir, I don't know what to say to such munifi—

SCROOGE. [*Cutting him off*] Don't say anything, please. Come and see me. Will you?

PORTLY MAN. I will! I will! Oh I will, Mr. Scrooge! It will be my pleasure!

SCROOGE. Thank'ee, I am much obliged to you. I thank you fifty times. Bless you!

[*Portly man passes offstage, perhaps by moving backwards.* SCROOGE *now comes to the room of his* NEPHEW *and* NIECE. *He stops at the door, begins to knock on it, loses his courage, tries again, loses his courage again, tries again, fails again, and then backs off and runs at the door, causing a tremendous bump against it. The* NEPHEW *and* NIECE *are startled.* SCROOGE, *poking head into room*]

    Fred!

NEPHEW. Why, bless my soul! Who's that?

NEPHEW AND NIECE. [*Together*] How now? Who goes?

SCROOGE. It's I. Your Uncle Scrooge.

NIECE. Dear heart alive!

SCROOGE. I have come to dinner. May I come in, Fred?

NEPHEW. *May you come in???!!!* With such pleasure for me you may, Uncle!!! What a treat!

NIECE. What a treat, Uncle Scrooge! Come in, come in!

[*They embrace a shocked and delighted* SCROOGE: FRED *calls into the other room.*]

NEPHEW. Come in here, everybody, and meet my Uncle Scrooge! He's come for our Christmas party!

[*Music in. Lighting here indicates that day has gone to night and gone to day again. It is early, early morning.* SCROOGE *walks alone from the party, exhausted, to his offices, opposite*

---

10. farthing (fär′ *thin*) *n.* small British coin.

Stage Directions
What do Scrooge's actions tell you about his feelings at this point?

Stage Directions
How could lighting be used to show the passage of time?

side of the stage. He opens his offices. The offices are as they were at the start of the play. Scrooge seats himself with his door wide open so that he can see into the tank, as he awaits CRATCHIT, *who enters, head down, full of guilt.* CRATCHIT, *starts writing almost before he sits.*]

SCROOGE. What do you mean by coming in here at this time of day, a full eighteen minutes late, Mr. Cratchit? Hallo, sir? Do you hear me?

BOB. I am very sorry, sir. I *am* behind my time.

SCROOGE. You are? Yes, I certainly think you are. Step this way, sir, if you please . . .

BOB. It's only but once a year, sir . . . it shall not be repeated. I was making rather merry yesterday and into the night . . .

SCROOGE. Now, I'll tell you what, Cratchit. I am not going to stand this sort of thing any longer. And therefore . . .

[*He stands and pokes his finger into* BOB'S *chest.*]

I am . . . about . . . to . . . raise . . . your salary.

BOB. Oh, no, sir, I . . . [*Realizes*] what did you say, sir?

SCROOGE. A Merry Christmas, Bob . . . [*He claps* BOB'S *back.*] A merrier Christmas, Bob, my good fellow! than I have given you for many a year. I'll raise your salary and endeavor to assist your struggling family and we will discuss your affairs this very afternoon over a bowl of smoking bishop.[11] Bob! Make up the fires and buy another coal scuttle before you dot another i, Bob. It's too cold in this place! We need warmth and cheer, Bob Cratchit! Do you hear me? DO . . . YOU . . . HEAR . . . ME?

[BOB CRATCHIT *stands, smiles at* SCROOGE: BOB CRATCHIT *faints. Blackout. As the main lights black out, a spotlight appears on* SCROOGE: *C. Another on* MARLEY: *He talks directly to the audience.*]

MARLEY. Scrooge was better than his word. He did it all and infinitely more; and to Tiny Tim, who did NOT die, he was a second father. He became as good a friend, as good a master, as good a man, as the good old city knew, or any other good old city, town, or borough in the good old world.

Stage Directions
What information in the stage directions might be funny to audiences? Why?

Comprehension
What has Scrooge promised to give Bob?

---

11. **smoking bishop** hot sweet orange-flavored drink.

And it was always said of him that he knew how to keep Christmas well, if any man alive possessed the knowledge. [*Pauses*] May that be truly said of us, and all of us. And so, as Tiny Tim observed . . .

TINY TIM. [*Atop* SCROOGE's *shoulder*] God Bless Us, Every One . . .

[*Lights up on chorus, singing final Christmas Song.* SCROOGE *and* MARLEY *and all spirits and other characters of the play join in. When the song is over, the lights fade to black.*]

Language Study

Vocabulary The words listed below appear in *A Christmas Carol: Scrooge and Marley,* Act II. Answer each question, then explain your answer.

astonish   compulsion   severe   meager   audible

1. When you speak, do you want your voice to be *audible*?
2. Would it *astonish* you if an elephant sang?
3. Would you take cover if a *severe* storm were approaching?
4. Can a family with a *meager* income build a large, fancy house?
5. Would a person with a *compulsion* to save money give away a million dollars?

WORD STUDY

The **Latin prefix** *inter-* means "between" or "among." In this act, the Ghost of Christmas Future **intercedes** on behalf of Scrooge by going between him and a terrible future to protect Scrooge from what might be.

Word Study

Part A Explain how the **Latin prefix** *inter-* contributes to the meanings of the words *interplanetary*, *interpersonal*, and *interject*. Consult a dictionary if necessary.

Part B Use the context of the sentences and what you know about the Latin prefix *inter-* to explain your answers.

1. Would you make an *international* phone call to the person next door?
2. Does an *intermission* usually occur at the start of a play?

Close Reading Activities

Literary Analysis

Key Ideas and Details

1. **Purpose for Reading** Which did you read more quickly: the dialogue or the stage directions? In your answer, explain how your purpose affected your reading rate.

2. **Purpose for Reading** When you read long speeches that contain difficult words, what happens to your reading rate? Explain, giving a specific example from the text.

3. **(a)** In Scene 3, what does Scrooge learn about the Cratchit family? **(b) Analyze:** Why does Scrooge care about the fate of Tiny Tim? **(c) Draw Conclusions:** In what way is Scrooge changing? Support your answer with a quotation from the play.

4. **(a)** In Scene 4, what happens to Scrooge's belongings in Christmas future? **(b) Draw Conclusions:** What does Scrooge learn from this experience?

Craft and Structure

5. **Stage Directions** Reread the stage directions at the beginning of Scene 1. Then, complete a chart like the one on the right to record the information the directions reveal.

6. **Stage Directions (a)** Which stage direction in Scene 4 is especially effective in making the scene mysterious? **(b)** What specific details contribute to the mysterious feeling?

Integration of Knowledge and Ideas

7. **(a) Analyze:** Why is Scrooge happy at the end of the play? **(b) Predict:** How well do you think Scrooge will live up to his promise to learn his "lessons"? **(c) Support:** What details in the play support your prediction?

8. **Take a Position:** Do you think Cratchit and Scrooge's nephew do the right thing by forgiving Scrooge immediately? Explain, using details from the play to support your answer.

9. **Do others see us more clearly than we see ourselves?** Discuss the following questions with a small group. **(a)** What does Scrooge learn from the experience of watching his own life? **(b)** How does he change his behavior to reflect his new insight?

Characters on Stage
Movement of Characters
Description of Lighting
Description of Sound
Other Special Effects

ACADEMIC VOCABULARY

As you write and speak about *A Christmas Carol: Scrooge and Marley*, Act II, use the words related to self-perception that you explored on p. 447 of this textbook.

Conventions: Appositives and Appositive Phrases

An **appositive** is a noun or pronoun placed after another noun or pronoun to identify, rename, or explain it.

An **appositive phrase** is a noun or pronoun with modifiers. It stands next to a noun or pronoun and adds information that identifies, renames, or explains it.

Appositive	Appositive Phrase
Our cat, Midnight, likes to sleep on my bed.	Karina—a talented violinist—played a solo.

- If the information in an appositive or appositive phrase is essential to understanding the sentence, *do not* set it off with commas or dashes.
  Example: Do you watch the TV show <u>Nature</u>?

- If the sentence is clear without the information, *do* use commas or dashes to set off the appositive or appositive phrase.
  Example: My boss, <u>Ms. Parks</u>, works late every night.

Practice A

Identify the appositive or appositive phrase in each sentence and indicate which noun or pronoun it identifies, renames, or explains.

1. The play *A Christmas Carol* is a story about how a man is changed by the spirit of Christmas.

2. Ebenezer Scrooge, one of the richest men in London, was a miserly man.

3. He collected high rents from his tenants—mostly poor people—without mercy.

Reading Application Find an appositive phrase in *A Christmas Carol: Scrooge and Marley,* Act II. Note whether or not it is set off by commas or dashes and explain why.

Practice B

Identify the appositive or appositive phrase in each sentence. Then, write a new sentence about the play, using the same appositive or appositive phrase.

1. Bob Cratchit's daughter Martha hid in the closet.

2. The second spirit, the Ghost of Christmas Present, visits Scrooge at midnight.

3. The crook Old Joe was eager to see the bed curtains.

Writing Application Use appositive phrases in three original sentences about *A Christmas Carol.* Set off nonessential appositives with commas or dashes.

Writing to Sources

Argument Respond to the play by writing a **tribute**, or expression of admiration, to the changed Scrooge. In your tribute, share examples from the drama that show how Scrooge has transformed his life, and reflect on the events or experiences that caused Scrooge to change. As you draft, identify the new traits that make Scrooge worthy of a tribute, and include evidence from the play to support your analysis. Conclude by stating your opinion of the play and providing your own insights about whether there is a lesson that everyone can learn from Scrooge's story. Support your opinion and insights with details from the play.

Grammar Application Check your writing to be sure that you have used and punctuated appositives and appositive phrases correctly.

Speaking and Listening

Presentation of Ideas Review the sections of Act II where Scrooge encounters the ghosts. Then, choose one section to be the focus of a **dramatic monologue** in which you share Scrooge's thoughts.

- As you draft your monologue, write as Scrooge from the first-person point of view, using the word *I*.
- Include stage directions to indicate gestures and emotions.
- Punctuate your monologue correctly. Use a period after the speaker's name and brackets to set off stage directions.

As you prepare to present your monologue, consider these tips:

- Project your voice so that everyone can hear you.
- Follow stage directions that tell how to move or speak.
- As you rehearse, refer to the play to determine how Scrooge might have read the monologue. Try pausing at appropriate moments, speaking at different speeds where a tempo change makes sense, and raising and lowering your voice for effect. After reading your monologue in several different ways, decide which techniques work best and use these in your final presentation.

Common Core State Standards

Writing

2. Write informative/explanatory texts to examine a topic and convey ideas, concepts, and information through the selection, organization, and analysis of relevant content.

9. Draw evidence from literary or informational texts to support analysis, reflection, and research.

Speaking and Listening

6. Adapt speech to a variety of contexts and tasks, demonstrating command of formal English when indicated or appropriate.

Language

1.a. Explain the function of phrases and clauses in general and their function in specific sentences.

2. Demonstrate command of the conventions of standard English capitalization, punctuation, and spelling when writing.

ANALYZING ARGUMENTATIVE TEXTS

EDITORIAL

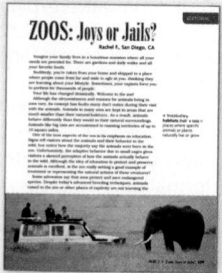

EDITORIAL

Common Core State Standards

Reading Informational Text

6. Determine an author's point of view or purpose in a text and analyze how the author distinguishes his or her position from that of others.

9. Analyze how two or more authors writing about the same topic shape their presentations of key information by emphasizing different evidence or advancing different interpretations of facts.

Writing

1.a. Introduce claims, and organize the reasons and evidence logically.

1.b. Support claim(s) with logical reasoning and relevant evidence, demonstrating an understanding of the topic or text.

Reading Skill: Analyze Point of View

Editorials reflect a writer's **point of view,** or opinion, on an issue. An editorial writer develops his or her point of view by clearly stating a claim and supporting it with specific evidence and persuasive language. When writers with differing points of view write about the same subject, each may focus only on evidence that supports his or her own argument. Use the chart to help you **analyze the authors' point of view** in the editorials that follow.

Techniques for Developing Point of View	Example
A clearly stated claim	"School dress codes promote a sense of unity."
Supporting statistics, facts, and examples	"Students are more focused when distractions such as fashion choices are eliminated."
Persuasive techniques and language	"The self-confident manner of uniformed students makes a positive impression on visitors."
Arguments that address opposing views	"Some people believe that dress codes discourage individuality, yet there are many other creative outlets."
A concluding statement that reinforces the author's point of view	"Schools with dress codes shift the focus from fashion to education, which is exactly where it should be."

Content-Area Vocabulary

These words appear in the selections that follow. You may also encounter them in other content-area texts.

- habitats
- vulnerable
- resources

ZOOS: Joys or Jails?

Rachel F., San Diego, CA

Imagine your family lives in a luxurious mansion where all your needs are provided for. There are gardens and daily walks and all your favorite foods.

Suddenly, you're taken from your home and shipped to a place where people come from far and wide to ogle at you, thinking they are learning about your lifestyle. Sometimes, your captors force you to perform for thousands of people.

Your life has changed drastically. Welcome to the zoo!

Although the circumstances and reasons for animals being in zoos vary, its concept has faults many don't notice during their visit with the animals. Animals in many zoos are kept in areas that are much smaller than their natural **habitats**. As a result, animals behave differently than they would in their natural surroundings. Animals like big cats are accustomed to roaming territories of up to 10 square miles.

One of the best aspects of the zoo is its emphasis on education. Signs tell visitors about the animals and their behavior in the wild, but notice how the majority say the animals were born in the zoo. Unfortunately, the adaptive behavior due to small cages gives visitors a skewed perception of how the animals actually behave in the wild. Although the idea of education to protect and preserve animals is excellent, is the zoo really setting a good example of treatment or representing the natural actions of these creatures?

Some advocates say that zoos protect and save endangered species. Despite today's advanced breeding techniques, animals raised in the zoo or other places of captivity are not learning the

◀ **Vocabulary**
habitats (hab´ ə tats) *n.* places where specific animals or plants naturally live or grow

Vocabulary ▶
vulnerable (vul′ nər ə
bəl) *adj.* open to attack

survival techniques they would in the wild. These animals would be very **vulnerable** if released and would encounter difficulties coping. Would it not be more beneficial to raise them in their natural habitat?

In this way scientists wouldn't face as many risks in reintroducing captive animals raised into the wild.

Helping endangered species in the wild gives them a better chance for survival and reproduction. Scientists should only revert to the zoo if the necessary funding or habitat for breeding is not available.

Animals are not just brought to the zoo to protect their species, but also to provide entertainment. Many animals' lives will include performing for visitors. Four shows are performed every day at the San Diego Zoo. The zoo should be reserved for education and protecting endangered species, not an amusement park where animals are trained to perform.

Although the zoo is trying to be helpful in providing shows about the animals, it is harming those it intends to protect. The zoo has good intentions in its educational purposes, and in breeding endangered species, but animals shouldn't perform or be treated in a manner that could change their behaviors from how they act in the wild.

Though zoos are meant to be a joy to viewers and teach lessons about our earth, the zoo jails its inhabitants and passes on faulty knowledge. The wild animals in our world are a wonder, and they must be preserved. At the zoo they are treated with care, but they should be treated with reverence.

Next time you visit a zoo, look at the enclosure of the tigers and watch the seals balance a ball on their noses, and then think about what you are really learning from your day at the zoo.

Kid Territory:
WHY DO WE NEED ZOOS?

San Diego Zoo Staff

It's an interesting question that many people wonder about. Why have people created zoos, and why are they important now?

The idea of a zoo actually started a long time ago, in the ancient cultures of China, the Middle East, and then the Roman Empire. As people started to travel more, for longer distances to explore the unknown, they began to discover animals and plants that they had never seen or heard of before. They were fascinated by these amazing creatures. Travelers reported back to their communities and their leaders what they had seen. Rulers like emperors, sultans, and kings often wanted to prove how wealthy and powerful they were, to each other and to their subjects. One way to do that was to "collect" some of these animals, and allow people to come and see them. These collections were called menageries, and usually only the rich and powerful had them.

But that changed as time went on, and eventually it was countries and then individual cities that had collections of exotic animals for people to come and see, and they were no longer reserved only for wealthy rulers. Zoology is the study of animals, so these became zoological collections. You guessed it—that was then shortened to the word we use now: zoos.

Zoos open to the public

At first most zoos only had a limited number of animals, usually the ones people had heard about but never seen in person, like lions, bears, giraffes, hippos, and other big and impressive species. Then as zoos became more popular, and traveling to get animals became more possible, zoos started to represent animals from particular countries and parts of the world. Zoologists studied these animals to find out more about them: what they ate, how they grew, how they had young, and how they behaved, among other things. But zoos were open to the general public, too, so everyone could find out about animals.

Connecting with critters

Zoos today still serve that important purpose: they allow us to study and find out more about animals that we would not understand otherwise.

People are curious and want to know about the world around them, and that especially includes the animals and plants with which we share the Earth. In addition to studying animals in zoos, scientists are also able to go out to the countries where animals live and study them in the field, or their habitat. But most people cannot do that, so zoos allow them to see and connect with what would otherwise be unavailable to them.

Helping wildlife

These days we also have cable TV, though, and there are lots of wild animal shows that we can watch. So why still have zoos? One of the most important reasons is conservation. Humans are destroying the Earth's habitats at a very fast pace, in order to make space, food, and products for ourselves. But that leaves less and less room for animals and plants. Zoos and wildlife parks are places where we can protect species that are in trouble, so they don't disappear from the Earth completely.

People do have different opinions about that, though. Some people think that animals should not be kept by humans for any reason, and that if they go extinct, then that's the way it should be. Other people think that animals are precious **resources**, an important part of the Earth, and that we should do everything we can to protect them, especially since we are the ones putting them in danger in the first place. Some people feel that there is lots of wild space and that animals should only live there. Other people feel that there is very little wild space left, that animals are contained by humans in some way no matter where they are, and it is up to us to take care of them the best we can. It's a discussion that will probably go on for a long time, especially as more and more species become endangered.

There is another thing that zoos accomplish, which could be one of the most important of all. Zoos give people the opportunity to see animals in person, often up close, to watch them, realize how alike we are in many ways, to understand them, and to appreciate them. It's amazing to come almost face to face with an elephant or tiger, for example, to see how big it is, to feel its power, to look in its eyes; or to see an orangutan or gorilla amble right by you, holding its baby or playing chase with its brother or sister. It is said that people only love what they understand, and they only protect what they love. Zoos may be the last stand for wild species, the place where humans can grow to love them, and then work to protect them.

**Vocabulary ▶
resources** (rē´ sôrs´ əz) *n.* natural features that enhance the quality of human life

Comparing Argumentative Texts

1. Identify the two strongest points each author makes to support the point of view presented in his or her article.

2. Compare the arguments to determine which author makes the strongest case. Explain your reasoning, citing details from the texts.

Content-Area Vocabulary

3. Use the words *habitats, vulnerable,* and *resources* in a paragraph in which you explain whether or not you think zoos are a good idea.

 Timed Writing

Argument: Editorial

Write a brief editorial for a school newspaper about an issue that affects your community or the nation—for example, building affordable housing or protecting animal habitats. Use supporting details to develop your argument. **(35 minutes)**

5-Minute Planner

Complete these steps to write your editorial:

1. Jot down two or three issues currently affecting your community or the nation. Review your list. Choose the issue you feel most strongly about as the topic for your editorial.

2. Write a sentence that clearly states your point of view and claim about your topic.

3. Make notes that give reasons, facts, descriptions, and examples that support your claims.
   TIP: You can sway your readers by including language that evokes positive or negative emotions.

4. Review the two editorials to see how the authors developed their arguments and structured their writing. Finalize your organizational plan.

5. Consult your notes as you write your editorial.

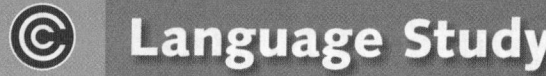

Connotation and Denotation

 **Common Core State Standards**

The **denotation** of a word is its dictionary meaning. A word's **connotations** are the ideas associated with that word. Those ideas and feelings might be positive or negative. Understanding connotations can help you to choose the right words in your writing. The following chart shows an example of three words with the same denotation and different connotations. Notice the various shades of meaning among the three words.

Language
4.c. Consult general and specialized reference materials, both print and digital, to find the pronunciation of a word or determine or clarify its precise meaning or its part of speech.
5.b. Use the relationship between particular words (e.g., synonym/antonym, analogy) to better understand each of the words.
5.c. Distinguish among the connotations (associations) of words with similar denotations (definitions).

Word	Denotation	Connotation	Example Sentence
postpone	to put off until a later time	to reschedule, usually due to something out of one's control	We had to *postpone* the party because the hostess became ill.
delay		to hold off on something for a short amount of time	The heavy morning traffic will *delay* the city's buses.
procrastinate		to put something off that is undesirable by doing another thing	I *procrastinate* every day by watching television before doing my homework.

Practice A

Each of the following words has a positive, neutral, or negative connotation. For each word pair, identify which word has a more positive connotation. If necessary, use a dictionary to check each word's denotation.

1. noise, sound
2. screech, holler
3. grab, obtain
4. discontinue, quit
5. brainy, intelligent
6. aware, alert

Practice B

Sometimes, the connotations of words can help you see degrees of meaning. For example, the words *large* and *enormous* have the same basic meaning, but *enormous* implies greater size than *large*. Rewrite each of the following sentences by replacing the italicized word. The new word should have the same denotation but a connotation that implies a greater degree of the original word. If necessary, use a dictionary or a thesaurus to help you.

1. The coach was *angry* after the team's poor performance.
2. My little sister loves to *bother* me when I have friends over.
3. We *eat* our lunch as soon as we sit down at the table.
4. The marching band from Southern California was *good*.
5. My mother was *happy* when I told her my grade on the test.
6. The weather in the desert is *hot*.
7. The rides at the amusement park were *fun*.
8. My cousin from Georgia is *nice*.
9. I drank a *large* glass of water after the race.
10. After playing a game of "fetch," my dog was *tired*.

Activity Each of the following words has neutral connotations. Use a thesaurus to find synonyms, or words with a similar meaning, for each word. Find at least one synonym with positive connotations and one synonym with negative connotations. Use a graphic organizer like the one shown to organize your synonyms. The first one has been completed as an example.

difficult   aged   calm   brave   humble

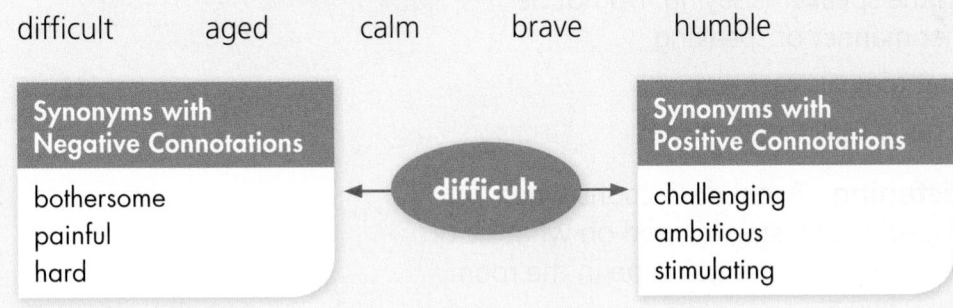

Synonyms with Negative Connotations

bothersome
painful
hard

difficult

Synonyms with Positive Connotations

challenging
ambitious
stimulating

Comprehension and Collaboration

Work with a partner to write two separate paragraphs about a fictional inventor. One partner's paragraph should describe the inventor as a visionary. The other's should describe the inventor as a dreamer. When you have finished writing, exchange paragraphs and discuss how the connotations of the words *visionary* and *dreamer* influenced your descriptions of the inventor.

Conducting an Interview

When you research a topic, you may sometimes find it necessary to interview someone in order to get the information you need. Follow these steps to conduct a successful interview.

Learn the Skills

An interview is a conversation that is powered by questions and answers. Before the interview, have a list of probing questions that will elicit the information you need.

Identify your purpose. It is important that you know what kind of information you would like to get from the interview. Conduct background research on your topic to focus your questions.

Create probing questions. Use your research notes to help you generate a list of questions. You will use this list at the interview, but you can also ask other questions that come to mind as you listen. You may need to ask follow-up questions to clarify points and get examples.

Listen carefully. Listening is more than just hearing. Sometimes you think you know what someone is going to say, so you do not really hear what they *are* saying. Break this habit by rephrasing what the speaker said, or by asking for clarification before moving on. If you are listening to acquire new information or to evaluate a point of view, pay close attention to both main points and details. Here are some tips for listening effectively:

- Do not look around. Focus your eyes and ears on the speaker.
- Concentrate on what the speaker is saying. Do not be distracted by his or her manner of speaking.
- Put away anything that may distract you.
- Keep a pencil and paper handy to take notes.

Eliminate barriers to listening. Avoid distractions when listening. Sit close to the speaker and stay focused on what he or she is saying, not on other things that are going on in the room.

Take notes. Taking notes will help you remember what a speaker says. Do not write down every word. Instead, try to capture the speaker's main points and a few supporting details. Later, review your notes to be sure you understand them.

 **Common Core State Standards**

Speaking and Listening

1.a. Come to discussions prepared, having read or researched material under study; explicitly draw on that preparation by referring to evidence on the topic, text, or issue to probe and reflect on ideas under discussion.

1.b. Follow rules for collegial discussions, track progress toward specific goals and deadlines, and define individual roles as needed.

1.c. Pose questions that elicit elaboration and respond to others' questions and comments with relevant observations and ideas that bring the discussion back on topic as needed.

2. Analyze the main ideas and supporting details presented in diverse media and formats (e.g., visually, quantitatively, orally) and explain how the ideas clarify a topic, text, or issue under study.

Practice the Skills

Presentation of Knowledge and Ideas Use what you have learned in this workshop to complete the following activity.

ACTIVITY: Conduct an Interview

Interview a community member, friend, or relative on a subject about which he or she is knowledgeable. If possible, ask a partner to videotape your interview. Follow the steps below.

- Before the interview, do background research on your topic.
- Make a list of focused questions that are based on your research.
- Listen carefully, analyze main ideas and details, rephrase what the speaker says, and ask for clarification as needed.
- Focus on what the speaker is saying, and block out distractions.
- Take notes to capture the main ideas and details.

Refer to the Interview Checklist as you prepare for your interview. If it is possible for you and your classmates to videotape your interviews, use the checklist to give each other feedback.

Interview Checklist

Preparing for the Interview
Does the preparation meet all of the requirements of the activity? Check all that apply.

- ❑ The purpose of the interview is clear.
- ❑ The interviewer has performed background research on the topic.
- ❑ The list of questions is designed to draw out interesting answers.
- ❑ The questions are focused and clear.

Conducting the Interview
Did the interviewer follow rules for listening? Check all that apply.

- ❑ The interviewer concentrated on what the speaker said.
- ❑ The interviewer rephrased main ideas and details and asked for clarifications.
- ❑ The interviewer sat close to the speaker and avoided distractions.
- ❑ The interviewer took notes.

Comprehension and Collaboration With your classmates, review the completed Interview Checklists. As a group, discuss which aspects of the interview process were most challenging and which were most rewarding.

Write an Argument

Response to Literature: Review of a Short Story

Defining the Form In a **response to literature,** the writer develops an argument that addresses one or more aspects of a literary work. You might use elements of a literary response in a letter to an author, or in a book or movie review.

Assignment Write a review of a short story you have read. A review is a kind of argument, so it should rely on reasons and evidence. Include these elements in your response:

✓ a *clearly stated claim* about the impact of the story

✓ a logical and consistent *organization*

✓ *relevant evidence from the text* to support your analysis

✓ use of words, phrases, and clauses that *clarify the relationships* between claims and the reasons that support them

✓ a *formal style* and tone

✓ a clear understanding of the distinctions between the *denotations and connotations* of words

✓ error-free writing, including *correct use of participles* to combine sentences smoothly

To preview the criteria on which your oral response may be judged, see the rubric on page 555.

Common Core State Standards

Writing

1. Write arguments to support claims with clear reasons and relevant evidence.

1.b. Support claim(s) with logical reasoning and relevant evidence, using credible sources and demonstrating an understanding of the topic or text.

1.c. Use words, phrases, and clauses to clarify the relationship among claim(s) and reasons.

1.d. Establish and maintain a formal style.

9. Draw evidence from literary or informational texts to support analysis, reflection, and research.

Language

5.c. Distinguish among the connotations of words with similar denotations.

FOCUS ON RESEARCH

When you write a response to literature, you must use strong evidence from the text to support your position.

• Reread the story closely to identify the key elements that shape your response.

• Take notes on important aspects of character, plot, setting, and theme.

• Find passages that support your claims about the author's use of language.

Prewriting/Planning Strategies

Choose a story to review. Make a list of stories you have read recently. Put a star next to the ones that elicited a strong response in you—either positive or negative. To evaluate the stories, ask yourself questions such as these:

- Do I identify strongly with a character or situation in the story?
- Does the story seem believable?
- Are there passages in the story that are especially moving or exciting?
- What is special or unusual about the author's use of language?
- Did the story's ending surprise me?

Find connections. After you have decided on a story, reread it carefully to find a topic for your review. To help you narrow your focus, complete a chart like the one shown. Fill in each column by answering the leading question. Look over what you have written and highlight details that connect in ways that interest you. To create a focused topic, sum up the highlighted details in a sentence.

Story Element	Leading Questions	Interesting Details
Characters	Who did the action?	
Settings	When or where was it done?	
Actions	What was done?	
Motivations	Why was it done?	

Find supporting evidence. To write an effective short story review, you must provide evidence to support your claims. Review the story to find details that support your response. Think of the incidents of the plot, the characters' actions and words, and the author's descriptions of the characters and setting. Record these details on notecards with a heading that indicates how each is connected to your topic. If you wish to quote directly from the story, be sure to copy the words accurately.

Drafting Strategies

Define and develop your focus. Review your prewriting notes to find a main idea or focus for your response. The focus statement, or thesis, sums up your reaction to one aspect of the story. Answer questions like the ones shown. Then, write one good sentence that states the focus and references a literary element. Include this sentence in your introduction, and elaborate on it in the body of your review.

1. My Response	2. What Causes It	3. My Focus
What is my main response to my topic? I thoroughly enjoyed the story.	What features of the story cause my reaction? • the suspense • the believability of the characters	What conclusion can I draw about the story's features? The author creates suspense and believable characters, producing a realistic story.

Organize your review. Your review should have three parts: an introduction, a body, and a conclusion.

- In the **introduction,** identify the author and title of the story and present a brief summary. Present your thesis, a single sentence that states the focus of your response.

- In the **body** of your review, present the evidence that supports your response. You might decide to organize each paragraph to focus on the analysis of a different story element, such as characters, plot, and word choice.

- In the **conclusion,** tie your review together by restating your thesis. Then, go a step further by making a final point or presenting a final insight.

Use examples to provide support. Rely on examples from the story to help you support your main arguments and claims. Refer to specific scenes, characters, images, and actions. Justify your interpretations with direct quotations from the text. However, avoid simply retelling the story. It is important that you share your responses to various aspects of the text.

 Common Core State Standards

Writing

1.a. Introduce claim(s) and organize the reasons and evidence clearly.

1.b. Support claim(s) with logical reasoning and relevant evidence, using credible sources and demonstrating an understanding of the topic or text.

1.d. Establish and maintain a formal style.

1.e. Provide a concluding statement or section that follows from the argument presented.

9. Draw evidence from literary or informational texts to support analysis, reflection, and research.

9.a. Apply grade 7 Reading standards to literature.

Language

5.c. Distinguish among the connotations of words with similar denotations.

Finding the Perfect Word

Word choice is the specific language a writer selects in order to create a strong impression. Critics choose memorable words and phrases to emphasize their arguments and to grab readers' attention. Follow these tips as you write your review.

Developing Tone The tone of your writing reveals your attitude toward your audience or subject. Ask yourself:

- How did the plot of this short story make me feel?
- Did I like the characters or dislike them? Why?
- How effective was the author's use of literary elements such as pacing and description?
- Would I recommend this story to others?

Write your answers to these questions in complete sentences. Then use your responses as you draft your review, using a formal style that is appropriate for a review.

Choosing Language As you write, use language that helps you develop your arguments and that accurately captures your feelings about an aspect of the story. Include colorful words, phrases, and comparisons. Consider the **connotations** of words, or the feelings and associations they convey, as well as their **denotations,** or meanings. For example, if you liked the climax of a story, you might describe it as *dramatic*. If you did not like it, you might describe it as *exaggerated*. Add examples and quotations to support your descriptions. The chart shows descriptive words that you might use.

Plot	Characters	Dialogue	Description
suspenseful	hideous	unrealistic	unique
predictable	flat	engaging	extensive
confusing	intriguing	humorous	uninteresting

Supporting Claims With Reasons Choose words that support your claims. For example, if you claim that a character is overly dramatic, you might use words that emphasize the character's hysterical reactions to an ordinary event.

Checking Language With a partner, review your word choices for fairness, accuracy, and consistency.

Revising Strategies

Revise to organize around your strongest idea. Review your draft with a partner to find places to support your main point. Follow these steps:

1. Circle your strongest point—your most profound insight or the quotation that pulls your review together. Consider moving this point to the end, just before your concluding statement.

2. If you move your strongest point to the end, revise your last paragraph to add a transition sentence that clearly explains the connection between this point and your other ideas.

3. Go back to other paragraphs to link each paragraph to your concluding point. For example, use connecting language like this: *Another example that shows the story's humor is . . .*

Show relationships clearly. Read the final sentence of each paragraph. Then, read the opening sentence of the next paragraph. If one or both sentences clearly show the relationship between paragraphs, underline them. If you do not find a relationship, add a transitional word, phrase, or sentence to link them together. Use these tips as you revise.

Using Effective Transitions	
To add to an idea or show sequence	also, next, equally important, furthermore, first, second, third, likewise, still, too, another, besides
To contrast ideas	alternatively, despite, although, yet, conversely, instead, on the other hand, however, otherwise, regardless
To give examples or clarify ideas	after all, in other words, certainly, for example, such as
To show cause and effect	after all, in other words, certainly, for example, such as

Peer Review

Review your draft with a partner to find places where you can add stronger support for your thesis. In addition, ask your partner to identify any grammatical or spelling errors in your review. If necessary, refer to a grammar handbook or dictionary for help with correcting the errors.

Common Core State Standards

Writing
1.c. Use words, phrases, and clauses to create cohesion and clarify the relationships among claim(s), reasons, and evidence.

1.e. Provide a concluding statement or section that follows from and supports the argument presented.

5. With some guidance and support from peers and adults, develop and strengthen writing as needed by planning, revising, editing, rewriting, or trying a new approach, focusing on how well purpose and audience have been addressed.

9. Draw evidence from literary or informational texts to support analysis, reflection, and research.

9.a. Apply *grade 7 Reading standards* to literature.

Language
1.c. Place phrases and clauses within a sentence, recognizing and correcting misplaced and dangling modifiers.

3. Use knowledge of language and its conventions when writing, speaking, reading, or listening.

Revising Sentences Using Participles

To make your writing flow smoothly, combine sentences using participles and participial phrases. A **participle** is a verb form that acts as an adjective, modifying a noun or pronoun. **Present participles** end in *-ing*. **Past participles** usually end in *-ed,* but may have an irregular ending, such as the *-en* in *spoken*.

> past participle   noun
>
> She banged her fist against the <u>closed</u> <u>windows</u>.

A **participial phrase** includes a participle and other words, such as modifiers. A **misplaced modifier** is placed far away from the word it describes.

> **Misplaced modifier:** I heard her voice listening to the song.
>
> **Solution:** Listening to the song, I heard her voice.

A **dangling modifier** is not logically connected to any word in the sentence.

> **Dangling modifier:** Raising the flag, the <u>wind</u> felt strong.
>
> **Solution:** Raising the flag, the <u>sailors</u> felt the strong wind.

Fixing Choppy Passages Using Participles To fix a choppy passage, identify sentences that can be combined. Then rewrite the passage using one or more of the following methods:

1. **Combine sentences using a present participle.**
   - ▶ **Example:** We arranged a tour. We would walk the grounds.
     We arranged a <u>walking</u> tour of the grounds.
2. **Combine sentences using a past participle.**
   - ▶ **Example:** The food is cooked. It will not spoil.
     The <u>cooked</u> food will not spoil.
3. **Combine sentences using a participial phrase.**
   - ▶ **Example:** Marissa ate her food quickly. She was running late.
     <u>Running late,</u> Marissa ate her food quickly.

Grammar in Your Writing

Choose three paragraphs in your draft. Read the paragraphs aloud, highlighting any passages that sound choppy. Using one of the methods above, fix the choppy passages by combining sentences.

Common Core State Standards

Language
2.b. Spell correctly.

The Lesson of "Rikki-tikki-tavi"

The short story "Rikki-tikki-tavi" is a well-known short story written by Rudyard Kipling, who also wrote many novels, such as *Kim* and *Captains Courageous*. "Rikki-tikki-tavi" is a story about two natural enemies: a mongoose and a cobra. The message of the story is that although you may be small, you can still overcome major enemies. This story is enjoyable because it can teach you helpful morals while keeping you entertained at the same time.

The beginning of this story is heavyhearted and dramatic. A small boy named Teddy thinks that the mongoose is dead following a bout with its first enemy—a flood that swept him away from his burrow. The mood of the story changes when the boy realizes that the mongoose is still alive, but weak. He decides to keep it, and takes care of it much like a pet, feeding it and naming it Rikki-tikki-tavi.

When Rikki-tikki goes outside into the little boy's garden to explore his surroundings, he comes upon a bird, which he confronts. The story switches back to a gloomy mood when the mongoose discovers that Nag, a cobra, ate one of the bird's eggs. When Rikki-tikki hears this, Nag comes out of the tall grass behind him.

This is when the story gets scary because Rikki faces another enemy. Nag quickly spreads his hood to intimidate the small mongoose. Then, Nagaina, Nag's wife, pulls a surprise attack on Rikki-tikki and nearly eats him. Because Rikki-tikki is young and dodges the cobra's blow from behind, he gains plenty of confidence. Readers wonder whether the mongoose will stay safe.

As the story progresses, Rikki meets Karait, another snake, and this builds excitement and tension. This snake isn't after the mongoose, although he is after the family. When Teddy runs out to pet Rikki-tikki, the snake strikes at the boy, but Rikki-tikki lunges at the snake and paralyzes it by biting it before it can bite Teddy.

Later, after Rikki-tikki discovers that the cobras are going to go after his owners, he is filled with rage and he takes on the challenge. The moment the reader is waiting for arrives. The mongoose and the cobra fight to kill. At one point Rikki-tikki has his teeth in Nag as Nag flings himself about. Readers may think that Rikki-tikki will surely die from the beating that he is taking, but he holds on and, thankfully, Teddy's dad hears the fighting and shoots Nag behind the hood with a shotgun, easily ending the brutal battle, which leaves Nag dead and Rikki-tikki dizzy, but alive.

This story is exciting and thought provoking. It ends, leaving me and other readers to think about its real meaning. Most people can relate to a time when they have faced a challenge in their life but have felt that they were unable to overcome it. However, when they kept trying and put their minds to it, they eventually ended with success, as Rikki-tikki did.

Tyler focuses on the message, or theme, of the story.

Tyler summarizes the most important plot events in the story in the order in which they occur.

Tyler supports his ideas about the story by giving examples of how Rikki-tikki fights several enemies even though he is small.

Tyler explains what message readers can take away from the story.

Editing and Proofreading

Spell tricky syllables correctly. The syllables in some words are barely heard. Because of this, letters are often left out in spelling. Double-check the spellings of words such as *different, average,* and *restaurant* in a dictionary. Notice how each word is broken into syllables. Say the word aloud while you look at it, and exaggerate your pronunciation of the sounds and syllables.

Focus on quotations. A response to a literary work should include a number of quotations from the work. Pay careful attention to the punctuation, indentation, and capitalization of quotations. Use quotation marks to set off short quotations. Longer quotations of four or more lines should begin on a new line, be indented, and appear without quotation marks.

Spiral Review
Earlier in the unit, you learned about **prepositional phrases** (p. 498) and **appositive phrases** (p. 536). Review your essay to be sure that you have used these types of phrases correctly.

Publishing and Presenting

Consider these ideas to share your writing with a larger audience:

Share your review. Discuss your response with a group of classmates. Invite classmates to respond with their opinions and reactions.

Build a collection. Work with your classmates to assemble a book of responses to literature for your school or local library.

Reflecting on Your Writing

Writer's Journal Jot down your answer to this question:

How did writing about the work help you to understand it?

Rubric for Self-Assessment

Find evidence in your writing to address each category. Then, use the rating scale to grade your work.

Criteria	Rating Scale			
	not very ....very			
Purpose/Focus Introduces the topic and make a clear claim	1	2	3	4
Organization Organizes reasons and evidence clearly and logically; provides a concluding section that follows from the argument presented	1	2	3	4
Development of Ideas/Elaboration Supports the claim with clear reasons and relevant evidence; draws evidence from the text to support analysis; establishes and maintains a formal style	1	2	3	4
Language Uses words, phrases, and clauses to clarify the relationships among claims and reasons; shows awareness of the denotations and connotations of words	1	2	3	4
Conventions Uses participles and participial phrases effectively to create smooth sentences	1	2	3	4

SELECTED RESPONSE

© Common Core
State Standards

RL.7.3, RL.7.5; L.7.4.a; W.7.2
[For full standards wording, see the chart in the front of this book.]

I. Reading Literature

Directions: *Read the excerpt from the dramatization of "Alice in Wonderland" by Alice Gerstenberg. Then, answer each question that follows.*

[*A soft radiance follows the characters mysteriously. As the curtain rises ALICE comes through the looking glass; steps down, looks about in wonderment and goes to see if there is a "fire." The RED QUEEN rises out of the grate and faces her <u>haughtily</u>.*]

ALICE: Why, you're the Red Queen!

RED QUEEN: Of course I am! Where do you come from? And where are you going? Look up, speak nicely, and don't twiddle your fingers!

ALICE: I only wanted to see what the looking glass was like. Perhaps I've lost my way.

RED QUEEN: I don't know what you mean by *your* way; all the ways about here belong to *me*. Curtsey while you're thinking what to say. It saves time.

ALICE: I'll try it when I go home; the next time I'm a little late for dinner.

RED QUEEN: It's time for you to answer now; open your mouth a *little* wider when you speak, and always say, "Your Majesty." I suppose you don't want to lose your name?

ALICE: No, indeed.

RED QUEEN: And yet I don't know, only think how convenient it would be if you could manage to go home without it! For instance, if the governess wanted to call you to your lessons, she would call out "come here," and there she would have to leave off, because there wouldn't be any name for her to call, and of course you wouldn't have to go, you know.

ALICE: That would never do, I'm sure; the governess would never think of excusing me from lessons for that. If she couldn't remember my name, she'd call me "Miss," as the servants do.

RED QUEEN: Well, if she said "Miss," and didn't say anything more, of course you'd miss your lessons. I dare say you can't even read this book.

ALICE: It's all in some language I don't know. Why, it's a looking-glass book, of course! And if I hold it up to a glass, the words will all go the right way again.

JABBERWOCKY

'Twas brillig, and the slithy toves
 Did gyre and gimble in the wabe;
All mimsy were the borogoves,
 And the mome raths outgrabe.

It seems very pretty, but it's *rather* hard to understand; somehow it seems to fill my head with ideas, only I don't exactly know what they are.

---

1. Which answer choice best describes this **drama** excerpt?
   A. dialogue
   B. monologue
   C. act
   D. set

2. What do the following lines reveal about the Red Queen's **character?**

   It's time for you to answer now; open your mouth a *little* wider when you speak, and always say, "Your Majesty."

   A. The Red Queen is hard of hearing.
   B. The Red Queen is silly and entertaining.
   C. The Red Queen is ill at ease.
   D. The Red Queen is bossy and self-important.

3. **Part A** Which answer choice best describes Alice in the drama excerpt?
   A. She is cold.
   B. She is confused.
   C. She is late for her lessons.
   D. She does not know the Red Queen.

   Part B Which lines from the drama best support the answer to Part A?
   A. "I only wanted to see what the looking glass was like."
   B. "I'll try it when I get home; the next time I'm a little late for dinner."
   C. ". . . the governess would never think of excusing me from lessons for that."
   D. ". . . somehow it seems to fill my head with ideas, only I don't exactly know what they are."

4. How do the **stage directions** contribute to the drama excerpt?
   A. They tell which character is speaking and present his or her exact words.
   B. They tell the audience where to look.
   C. They give readers information about the characters and action.
   D. They tell readers where the play has been performed.

5. Which answer choice best explains the appropriate **reading rate** for reading stage directions?
   A. You should read stage directions slowly and carefully because they may reveal action that is not shown in the dialogue.
   B. You should read stage directions slowly in order to appreciate the playwright's style of writing.
   C. You should read stage directions quickly, or you may forget what the characters are saying and doing.
   D. You should skim stage directions because the information they contain may not be important.

6. Which event in the drama's **plot** happens first?
   A. The Red Queen reads a book.
   B. The Red Queen sees Alice.
   C. Alice misses her lessons.
   D. Alice is asked to curtsey.

7. Which answer choice is the best definition of the underlined word *haughtily?*
   A. sadly
   B. directly
   C. proudly
   D. with caution

⏱ Timed Writing

8. In a short essay, explain how the playwright develops **characters** through the use of **dialogue.** Support your answer with details from the text.

GO ON

II. Reading Informational Text

Directions: *Read the passage. Then, answer each question that follows.*

© **Common Core State Standards**

RI.7.1, RI.7.5; L.7.1.a, L.7.1.c
[For full standards wording, see the chart in the front of this book.]

Would you like to sleep an extra hour each morning? If so, you are not alone. Most American teenagers get about seven hours of sleep each night. However, sleep researchers say adolescents and young teens actually need 9.2 hours of sleep. That is more than adults and young children need.

Stumbling through the day like a zombie can be dangerous. For example, the National Highway Traffic Safety Administration says young, sleepy drivers are involved in about 50,000 accidents each year. Lack of sleep can also result in poor grades for teenagers.

Some adults think teenagers who sleep late are lazy. However, Professor Mary Carskadon, a sleep researcher at Brown University, says sleeping late can be healthy. She thinks schools should start later. Most high schools in the United States start classes at 7 A.M. Carskadon says 8:00, or 8:30, would be a better time.

Not only do teenagers need more sleep, but they need it at different times than other people do. Melatonin is a hormone produced daily by the human brain. It tells you that you are sleepy. Research shows that teenagers produce melatonin later at night than other people do. The result is that teenagers are often wide awake when their parents want them to go to sleep. Teenagers' melatonin levels remain high in the early morning. That means they may still be sleepy, even after school has started.

1. **Part A** What is the author's main argument?
   A. Schools should start classes later.
   B. Mary Carskadon is the expert on sleep.
   C. Teenagers should sleep more at night.
   D. Teenagers need more sleep in the morning.

   Part B Which of the following claims supports the argument you identified in Part A?
   A. Teenagers produce melatonin later at night than other people.
   B. Schools should begin at 8 or 8:30.
   C. Most teenagers are lazy because they do not get enough sleep.
   D. Teenagers are forced to go to bed when they are wide awake.

2. Which piece of evidence supports Professor Carskadon's assertion that it is healthy for teenagers to sleep late?
   A. Teenagers produce more melatonin than older and younger people produce.
   B. Teenagers' melatonin levels remain high in the morning.
   C. Teenagers are often sleepy even after school has started.
   D. Sleepy drivers are involved in car accidents.

III. Writing and Language Conventions

Directions: *Read the passage. Then, answer each question that follows.*

(1) Many students, including me, depend on our cell phones to talk with our parents. (2) Every day I hear about my mother what time she will pick me up. (3) The problem is that Mr. Galindo wants to ban cell phones from school. (4) The solution is simple. (5) We should be allowed to bring our cell phones to school, but we will only use them when school is over. (6) Calls will be missed. (7) They can be returned after school. (8) This way everyone—teachers, parents, and students—wins.

1. Which of the following revisions *best* corrects the use of a **preposition** in sentence 2?
- **A.** Change *about* to *from*.
- **B.** Change *about* to *through*.
- **C.** Change *about* to *of*.
- **D.** Leave as is.

2. Which revision to sentence 4 would include a more informative **prepositional phrase?**
- **A.** The solution is simple and useful.
- **B.** The solution simply depends on our cell phones.
- **C.** The solution is simple and makes sense.
- **D.** The solution to the problem is simple.

3. Which revision combines sentence 6 and sentence 7 with a **past participle?**
- **A.** Missing calls will mean returning them after school.
- **B.** Students can return calls after school.
- **C.** Missed calls can be returned after school.
- **D.** After school, you can return your calls.

4. Which sentence includes an **appositive phrase?**
- **A.** sentence 1
- **B.** sentence 5
- **C.** sentence 6
- **D.** sentence 8

5. Which sentence adds more information to sentence 3 by using an **appositive?**
- **A.** The problem, declared today, is that Mr. Galindo wants to ban cell phones from school.
- **B.** The problem is that Principal Galindo wants to ban cell phones from school.
- **C.** The problem is that Mr. Galindo, our principal, wants to ban cell phones from school.
- **D.** The problem is that Mr. Galindo wants to ban cell phones from Arthur High School.

CONSTRUCTED RESPONSE

 **Common Core State Standards**

RL.7.2, RL.7.3, RL.7.5, RL.7.7;
W.7.2, W.7.2.c, W.7.7, W.7.8;
SL.7.4, SL.7.5

[For full standards wording, see the chart in the front of this book.]

Directions: *Follow the instructions to complete the tasks below as required by your teacher.*

As you work on each task, incorporate both general academic vocabulary and literary terms you learned in Parts 1 and 2.

Writing

TASK 1 ▶ Literature [RL.7.3; W.7.2]

Analyze Setting

Write an essay in which you analyze how the setting of A Christmas Carol: Scrooge and Marley *shapes the characters and plot.*

- Identify details from the play that reveal the time period as nineteenth-century England.
- Explain how the playwright uses dialogue to move the plot forward.
- Discuss how the playwright used the historical time to support the major points in the play. Point out the kinds of work people did and the ways in which they socialized. Discuss differences between the wealthy and the poor, and analyze why these class differences existed.
- Develop your analysis with relevant details, information, and specific examples from the play.
- Use appropriate transitions to show relationships between or among your ideas. Show comparisons with transitions such as *likewise, similarly,* and *in addition to.* Show contrasts with transitions such as *on the other hand* or *in contrast.*

TASK 2 ▶ Literature [RL.7.5; W.7.2]

Analyze Dramatic Structure

Write an essay in which you analyze how a drama's structure adds to its meaning.

- Analyze the parts of *A Christmas Carol: Scrooge and Marley,* including its division into acts and scenes and its dialogue and stage directions. Explain how each part of the drama contributes to characterization, setting, mood, and tone.

- Develop your analysis with examples from the drama. Use transitions to clarify the relationships between or among ideas.

TASK 3 ▶ Literature [RL.7.3; W.7.2, W.7.2.c]

Analyze Characters' Motives

Write an essay in which you analyze the motives of various characters in A Christmas Carol: Scrooge and Marley.

Part 1

- Select at least two characters from the play upon which to base your essay.
- Cite several examples of dialogue that reveal each character's reasons for taking an action. Remember that information contained in stage directions might provide clues to a character's motives.

Part 2

- Write an essay in which you explain the connections between each characters' actions and specific events in the plot. Cite evidence from the play to support your response.
- Use a strategy such as comparison-and-contrast organization to organize your ideas logically. Use transitions and transitional phrases to connect your sentences and paragraphs smoothly.
- Provide a concluding statement that follows logically from the information in your essay.

Speaking and Listening

TASK 4 Literature [RL.7.7; SL.7.5]

Analyze Techniques in Different Media

Give a multimedia presentation in which you compare and contrast the script for A Christmas Carol: Scrooge and Marley *to its film or stage version.*

- Reread *A Christmas Carol: Scrooge and Marley*, noting how you visualize the drama as you read. Then, view a film or stage version of the same play.

- Compare and contrast the written drama with its film or stage version. Analyze the effects of techniques that are unique to each medium. For example, consider the effects of lighting, sound, color, and camera angles in a film.

- In your presentation, include multimedia components, such as film clips, tape recordings, or visual displays to clarify your claims about the different techniques used in the formats and to emphasize your main points.

- Choose words and phrases for your intended effect and eliminate wordiness or repeated ideas in your presentation.

TASK 5 Literature [RL.7.3, RL.7.5; SL.7.4]

Analyze Dialogue

Give an oral presentation in which you analyze the dialogue in A Christmas Carol: Scrooge and Marley.

- Analyze examples of dialogue in the play that provide key information about a character. Discuss the character's word choice, syntax, and possibly dialect.

- Cite specific passages of dialogue to support your analysis of the character. In addition, explain how the dialogue advances the plot and develops the conflict in the play.

- As you give your oral presentation, use appropriate eye contact, adequate volume, and clear pronunciation.

- If necessary, consult a digital dictionary to find the pronunciations of unknown words from the text.

Research

TASK 6 Literature [RL.7.2; W.7.7, W.7.8]

Do others see us more clearly than we see ourselves?

In Part 2, you have read literature about ways people form impressions about each other. Now, you will conduct a short research project on a person who was judged for his or her appearance, beliefs, or treatment of others.

Use both the literature you have read and your research to reflect on this unit's Big Question. Review the following guidelines before you begin your research:

- Focus your research on one person.
- Gather relevant information from at least two reliable print or digital sources.
- Take notes as you research the person you chose to write about.
- Cite your sources.

When you have completed your research, write a response to the Big Question. Discuss how your initial ideas have been either changed or reinforced. Support your response with an example from literature and an example from your research.

"There go **my people**.
I must **follow** them,
for I am their **leader**."
—**Mahatma Gandhi**

LEADERS AND FOLLOWERS

The selections in this unit all deal with the Big Question: **Do others see us more clearly than we see ourselves?** As you read the texts in this section, think about the characteristics that make someone a leader. Also, consider the different reasons people have for following others. You may find that our ideas about leaders and followers are influenced by our own self-perception.

◄ CRITICAL VIEWING What does the quotation on the opposite page reveal about Gandhi's ideas regarding leadership? Does the photograph reinforce those ideas? Why or why not?

CLOSE READING TOOL

Use the **Close Reading Tool** to practice the strategies you learn in this unit.

READINGS IN PART 3

THE MONSTERS ARE DUE ON MAPLE STREET

ROD SERLING

CHARACTERS

| NARRATOR | FIGURE ONE | FIGURE TWO |

RESIDENTS OF MAPLE STREET

STEVE BRAND	DON MARTIN	PETE VAN HORN
CHARLIE'S WIFE	SALLY (TOMMY'S MOTHER)	CHARLIE
MRS. GOODMAN	LES GOODMAN	TOMMY
MRS. BRAND	MAN ONE	
WOMAN	MAN TWO	

ACT I

[*Fade in on a shot of the night sky. The various nebulae and planet bodies stand out in sharp, sparkling relief, and the camera begins a slow pan across the Heavens.*]

NARRATOR'S VOICE. There is a fifth dimension beyond that which is known to man. It is a dimension as vast as space, and as timeless as infinity. It is the middle ground between light and shadow—between science and superstition. And it lies between the pit of man's fears and the summit of his knowledge. This is the dimension of imagination. It is an area which we call The Twilight Zone.

[*The camera has begun to pan down until it passes the horizon and is on a sign which reads "Maple Street." Pan down until we are shooting down at an angle toward the street below. It's a tree-lined, quiet residential American street, very typical of the small town. The houses have front porches on which people sit and swing on gliders, conversing across from house to house.* STEVE BRAND *polishes his car parked in front of his house. His neighbor,* DON MARTIN, *leans against the fender watching him. A Good Humor man rides a bicycle and is just in the process of stopping to sell some ice cream to a couple of kids. Two women gossip on the front lawn. Another man waters his lawn.*]

NARRATOR'S VOICE. Maple Street, U.S.A., late summer. A tree-lined little world of front porch gliders, hop scotch, the laughter of children, and the bell of an ice cream vendor.

[*There is a pause and the camera moves over to a shot of the Good Humor man and two small boys who are standing alongside, just buying ice cream.*]

NARRATOR'S VOICE. At the sound of the roar and the flash of light it will be precisely 6:43 P.M. on Maple Street.

[*At this moment one of the little boys,* TOMMY, *looks up to listen to a sound of a tremendous screeching roar from overhead. A flash of light plays on both their faces and then it moves down the street past lawns and porches and rooftops and then disappears.*

    Various people leave their porches and stop what they're doing to stare up at the sky. STEVE BRAND, *the man who's been polishing his car, now stands there* transfixed, *staring upwards. He looks at DON MARTIN, his neighbor from across the street*]

STEVE. What was that? A meteor?

DON. [*Nods*] That's what it looked like. I didn't hear any crash though, did you?

STEVE. [*Shakes his head*] Nope. I didn't hear anything except a roar.

MRS. BRAND. [*From her porch*] Steve? What was that?

STEVE. [*Raising his voice and looking toward porch*] Guess it was a meteor, honey. Came awful close, didn't it?

MRS. BRAND. Too close for my money! Much too close.

[*The camera pans across the various porches to people who stand there watching and talking in low tones.*]

NARRATOR'S VOICE. Maple Street. Six-forty-four P.M. on a late September evening. [*A pause*] Maple Street in the last calm and reflective moment . . . before the monsters came!

[*The camera slowly pans across the porches again. We see a man screwing a light bulb on a front porch, then getting down off the stool to flick the switch and finding that nothing happens.*

    Another man is working on an electric power mower. He plugs in the plug, flicks on the switch of the power mower, off and on, with nothing happening.

Through the window of a front porch, we see a woman pushing her finger back and forth on the dial hook. Her voice is indistinct and distant, but intelligible and repetitive.]

WOMAN. Operator, operator, something's wrong on the phone, operator!

[MRS. BRAND *comes out on the porch and calls to* STEVE.]

MRS. BRAND. [*Calling*] Steve, the power's off. I had the soup on the stove and the stove just stopped working.

WOMAN. Same thing over here. I can't get anybody on the phone either. The phone seems to be dead.

[*We look down on the street as we hear the voices creep up from below, small, mildly disturbed voices highlighting these kinds of phrases:*]

VOICES.

Electricity's off.

Phone won't work.

Can't get a thing on the radio.

My power mower won't move, won't work at all.

Radio's gone dead!

[PETE VAN HORN, *a tall, thin man, is seen standing in front of his house.*]

VAN HORN. I'll cut through the back yard . . . See if the power's still on on Floral Street. I'll be right back!

[*He walks past the side of his house and disappears into the back yard.*
The camera pans down slowly until we're looking at ten or eleven people standing around the street and overflowing to the curb and sidewalk. In the background is STEVE BRAND'S *car.*]

STEVE. Doesn't make sense. Why should the power go off all of a sudden, and the phone line?

DON. Maybe some sort of an electrical storm or something.

CHARLIE. That don't seem likely. Sky's just as blue as anything. Not a cloud. No lightning. No thunder. No nothing. How could it be a storm?

WOMAN. I can't get a thing on the radio. Not even the portable.

[*The people again murmur softly in wonderment and question.*]

flustered ▶
(flus´ tərd) adj.
nervous; confused

CHARLIE. Well, why don't you go downtown and check with the police, though they'll probably think we're crazy or something. A little power failure and right away we get all **flustered** and everything.

STEVE. It isn't just the power failure, Charlie. If it was, we'd still be able to get a broadcast on the portable.

[*There's a murmur of reaction to this.* STEVE *looks from face to face and then over to his car.*]

STEVE. I'll run downtown. We'll get this all straightened out.

[*He walks over to the car, gets in it, turns the key. Looking through the open car door, we see the crowd watching him from the other side.* STEVE *starts the engine. It turns over* sluggishly *and then just stops dead. He tries it again and this time he can't get it to turn over. Then, very slowly and reflectively, he turns the key back to "off" and slowly gets out of the car.*

The people stare at STEVE. *He stands for a moment by the car, then walks toward the group.*]

STEVE. I don't understand it. It was working fine before . . .

DON. Out of gas?

STEVE. [*Shakes his head*] I just had it filled up.

WOMAN. What's it mean?

CHARLIE. It's just as if . . . as if everything had stopped. [*Then he turns toward* STEVE.] We'd better walk downtown.

[*Another murmur of assent at this.*]

STEVE. The two of us can go, Charlie. [*He turns to look back at the car.*] It couldn't be the meteor. A meteor couldn't do *this.*

[*He and* CHARLIE *exchange a look, then they start to walk away from the group.*

We see TOMMY, *a serious-faced fourteen-year-old in spectacles who stands a few feet away from the group. He is halfway between them and the two men, who start to walk down the sidewalk.*]

TOMMY. Mr. Brand . . . you better not!

STEVE. Why not?

TOMMY. They don't want you to.

[STEVE *and* CHARLIE *exchange a grin, and* STEVE *looks back toward the boy.*]

STEVE. Who doesn't want us to?

TOMMY. [*Jerks his head in the general direction of the distant horizon*] Them!

STEVE. Them?

CHARLIE. Who are them?

TOMMY. [*Very intently*] Whoever was in that thing that came by overhead.

[STEVE *knits his brows for a moment, cocking his head questioningly. His voice is intense.*]

STEVE. What?

TOMMY. Whoever was in that thing that came over. I don't think they want us to leave here.

[STEVE *leaves* CHARLIE *and walks over to the boy. He kneels down in front of him. He forces his voice to remain gentle. He reaches out and holds the boy.*]

STEVE. What do you mean? What are you talking about?

TOMMY. They don't want us to leave. That's why they shut everything off.

STEVE. What makes you say that? Whatever gave you that idea?

WOMAN. [*From the crowd*] Now isn't that the craziest thing you ever heard?

persistently ▶
(pər sist′ ənt lē) adv.
firmly and steadily

TOMMY. [*Persistently but a little intimidated by the crowd*] It's always that way, in every story I ever read about a ship landing from outer space.

WOMAN. [*To the boy's mother,* SALLY, *who stands on the fringe of the crowd*] From outer space, yet! Sally, you better get that boy of yours up to bed. He's been reading too many comic books or seeing too many movies or something.

SALLY. Tommy, come over here and stop that kind of talk.

STEVE. Go ahead, Tommy. We'll be right back. And you'll see. That wasn't any ship or anything like it. That was just a . . . a meteor or something. Likely as not—[*He turns to the group, now trying to weight his words with an optimism he obviously doesn't feel but is desperately trying to instill in himself as well as the others.*] No doubt it did have something to do with all this power failure and the rest of it. Meteors can do some crazy things. Like sunspots.

DON. [*Picking up the cue*] Sure. That's the kind of thing—like sunspots. They raise Cain[1] with radio reception all over the world. And this thing being so close—why, there's no telling the sort of stuff it can do. [*He wets his lips, smiles nervously.*] Go ahead, Charlie. You and Steve go into town and see if that isn't what's causing it all.

[STEVE *and* CHARLIE *again walk away from the group down the sidewalk. The people watch silently.*

TOMMY *stares at them, biting his lips, and finally calling out again.*]

TOMMY. *Mr. Brand!*

[*The two men stop again.* TOMMY *takes a step toward them.*]

TOMMY. Mr. Brand . . . please don't leave here.

[STEVE *and* CHARLIE *stop once again and turn toward the boy. There's a murmur in the crowd, a murmur of irritation and concern as if the boy were bringing up fears that shouldn't be brought up; words which carried with them a strange kind of validity that came without logic but nonetheless registered and had meaning and effect. Again we hear a murmur of reaction from the crowd.*

TOMMY *is partly frightened and partly* defiant *as well.*]

defiant ▶
(dē fī′ ənt) adj.
boldly resisting

TOMMY. You might not even be able to get to town. It was that way in the story. Nobody could leave. Nobody except—

---

1. raise Cain badly disturb.

STEVE. Except who?

TOMMY. Except the people they'd sent down ahead of them. They looked just like humans. And it wasn't until the ship landed that—

[*The boy suddenly stops again, conscious of the parents staring at them and of the sudden hush of the crowd.*]

SALLY. [*In a whisper, sensing the antagonism of the crowd*] Tommy, please son . . . honey, don't talk that way—

MAN ONE. That kid shouldn't talk that way . . . and we shouldn't stand here listening to him. Why this is the craziest thing I ever heard of. The kid tells us a comic book plot and here we stand listening—

[STEVE *walks toward the camera, stops by the boy.*]

STEVE. Go ahead, Tommy. What kind of story was this? What about the people that they sent out ahead?

TOMMY. That was the way they prepared things for the landing. They sent four people. A mother and a father and two kids who looked just like humans . . . but they weren't.

[*There's another silence as* STEVE *looks toward the crowd and then toward* TOMMY. *He wears a tight grin.*]

STEVE. Well, I guess what we'd better do then is to run a check on the neighborhood and see which ones of us are really human.

[*There's laughter at this, but it's a laughter that comes from a desperate attempt to lighten the atmosphere. It's a release kind of laugh. The people look at one another in the middle of their laughter.*]

CHARLIE. There must be somethin' better to do than stand around makin' bum jokes about it.

[*Rubs his jaw nervously*] I wonder if Floral Street's got the same deal we got. [*He looks past the houses.*] Where is Pete Van Horn anyway? Didn't he get back yet?

[*Suddenly there's the sound of a car's engine starting to turn over. We look across the street toward the driveway of* LES GOODMAN's *house. He's at the wheel trying to start the car.*]

SALLY. Can you get it started, Les? [*He gets out of the car, shaking his head.*]

GOODMAN. No dice.

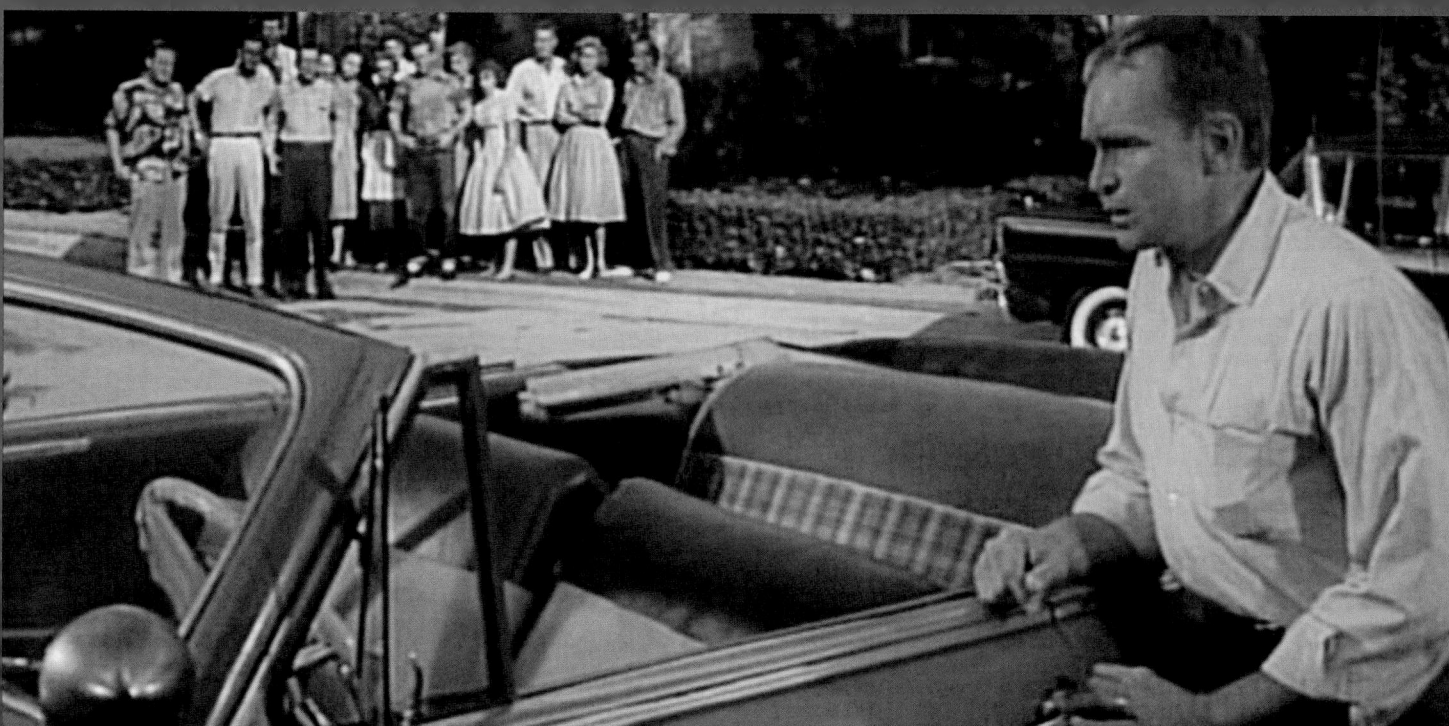

[*He walks toward the group. He stops suddenly as behind him, inexplicably and with a noise that inserts itself into the silence, the car engine starts up all by itself.* GOODMAN *whirls around to stare toward it.*

    The car idles roughly, smoke coming from the exhaust, the frame shaking gently.
    GOODMAN's *eyes go wide, and he runs over to his car.*
    The people stare toward the car.]

MAN ONE. He got the car started somehow. He got his car started!

[*The camera pans along the faces of the people as they stare, somehow caught up by this revelation and somehow, illogically, wildly, frightened.*]

WOMAN. How come his car just up and started like that?

SALLY. All by itself. He wasn't anywheres near it. It started all by itself.

[DON *approaches the group, stops a few feet away to look toward* GOODMAN's *car and then back toward the group.*]

DON. And he never did come out to look at that thing that flew overhead. He wasn't even interested. [*He turns to the faces in the group, his face taut and serious.*] Why? Why didn't he come out with the rest of us to look?

CHARLIE. He always was an oddball. Him and his whole family. Real oddball.

DON. What do you say we ask him?

[*The group suddenly starts toward the house. In this brief fraction of a moment they take the first step toward performing a metamorphosis that changes people from a group into a mob. They begin to head purposefully across the street toward the house at the end.* STEVE *stands in front of them. For a moment their fear almost turns their walk into a wild stampede, but* STEVE'S *voice, loud, incisive, and commanding, makes them stop.*]

STEVE. Wait a minute . . . wait a minute! Let's not be a mob!

[*The people stop as a group, seem to pause for a moment, and then much more quietly and slowly start to walk across the street.* GOODMAN *stands alone facing the people.*]

GOODMAN. I just don't understand it. I tried to start it and it wouldn't start. You saw me. All of you saw me.

[*And now, just as suddenly as the engine started, it stops and there's a long silence that is gradually intruded upon by the frightened murmuring of the people.*]

GOODMAN. I don't understand. I swear . . . I don't understand. What's happening?

DON. Maybe you better tell us. Nothing's working on this street. Nothing. No lights, no power, no radio. [*And then meaningfully*] Nothing except one car—yours!

[*The people pick this up and now their murmuring becomes a loud chant filling the air with accusations and demands for action. Two of the men pass* DON *and head toward* GOODMAN, *who backs away, backing into his car and now at bay.*]

GOODMAN. Wait a minute now. You keep your distance—all of you. So I've got a car that starts by itself—well, that's a freak thing, I admit it. But does that make me some kind of a criminal or something? I don't know why the car works—it just does!

[*This stops the crowd momentarily and now* GOODMAN, *still backing away, goes toward his front porch. He goes up the steps and then stops to stand facing the mob.*
  We see a long shot of STEVE *as he comes through the crowd.*]

STEVE. [*Quietly*] We're all on a monster kick, Les. Seems that the general impression holds that maybe one family isn't what we think they are. Monsters from outer space or something. Different than us. Fifth columnists[2] from the vast beyond. [*He chuckles.*] You know anybody that might fit that description around here on Maple Street?

GOODMAN. What is this, a gag or something? This a practical joke or something?

[*We see a close-up of the porch light as it suddenly goes out. There's a murmur from the group.*]

GOODMAN. Now I suppose that's supposed to incriminate me! The light goes on and off. That really does it, doesn't it? [*He looks around the faces of the people.*] I just don't understand this— [*He wets his lips, looking from face to face.*] Look, you all know me. We've lived here five years. Right in this house. We're no different from any of the rest of you! We're no different at all. Really . . . this whole thing is just . . . just weird—

WOMAN. Well, if that's the case, Les Goodman, explain why—

[*She stops suddenly, clamping her mouth shut.*]

GOODMAN. [*Softly*] Explain what?

STEVE. [*Interjecting*] Look, let's forget this—

CHARLIE. [*Overlapping him*] Go ahead, let her talk. What about it? Explain what?

WOMAN. [*A little reluctantly*] Well . . . sometimes I go to bed late at night. A couple of times . . . a couple of times I'd come out on the porch and I'd see Mr. Goodman here in the wee hours of the morning standing out in front of his house . . . looking up at the sky. [*She looks around the circle of faces.*] That's right, looking up at the sky as if . . . as if he were waiting for something. [*A pause*] As if he were looking for something.

[*There's a murmur of reaction from the crowd again.*

We cut suddenly to a group shot. As GOODMAN *starts toward them, they back away frightened.*]

GOODMAN. You know really . . . this is for laughs. You know what I'm guilty of? [*He laughs.*] I'm guilty of insomnia. Now what's the penalty for insomnia? [*At this point the laugh, the humor, leaves his voice.*] Did you hear what I said? I said it was insomnia. [*A pause as he looks around, then shouts.*]

---

2. **Fifth columnists** people who help an invading enemy from within their own country.

I said it was insomnia! You fools. You scared, frightened rabbits, you. You're sick people, do you know that? You're sick people—all of you! And you don't even know what you're starting because let me tell you . . . let me tell you—this thing you're starting—that should frighten you. As God is my witness . . . you're letting something begin here that's a nightmare!

ACT II

[*We see a medium shot of the* Goodman *entry hall at night. On the side table rests an unlit candle.* Mrs. Goodman *walks into the scene, a glass of milk in hand. She sets the milk down on the table, lights the candle with a match from a box on the table, picks up the glass of milk, and starts out of scene.*

Mrs. Goodman *comes through her porch door, glass of milk in hand. The entry hall, with table and lit candle, can be seen behind her.*

Outside, the camera slowly pans down the sidewalk, taking in little knots of people who stand around talking in low voices. At the end of each conversation they look toward Les Goodman's *house. From the various houses we can see candlelight but no electricity, and there's an all-pervading quiet that blankets the whole area, disturbed only by the almost whispered voices of the people as they stand around. The camera pans over to one group where* Charlie *stands. He stares across at* Goodman's *house.*

We see a long shot of the house. Two men stand across the street in almost sentry-like poses. Then we see a medium shot of a group of people.]

SALLY. [*A little timorously*] It just doesn't seem right, though, keeping watch on them. Why . . . he was right when he said he was one of our neighbors. Why, I've known Ethel Goodman ever since they moved in. We've been good friends—

CHARLIE. That don't prove a thing. Any guy who'd spend his time lookin' up at the sky early in the morning—well, there's something wrong with that kind of person. There's something that ain't legitimate. Maybe under normal circumstances we could let it go by, but these aren't normal circumstances. Why, look at this street! Nothin' but candles. Why, it's like goin' back into the dark ages or somethin'!

[STEVE *walks down the steps of his porch, walks down the street over to* LES GOODMAN's *house, and then stops at the foot of the steps.* GOODMAN *stands there, his wife behind him, very frightened.*]

GOODMAN. Just stay right where you are, Steve. We don't want any trouble, but this time if anybody sets foot on my porch, that's what they're going to get—trouble!

STEVE. Look, Les—

GOODMAN. I've already explained to you people. I don't sleep very well at night sometimes. I get up and I take a walk and I look up at the sky. I look at the stars!

MRS. GOODMAN That's exactly what he does. Why this whole thing, it's . . . it's some kind of madness or something.

STEVE. [*Nods grimly*] That's exactly what it is—some kind of madness.

CHARLIE'S VOICE. [*Shrill, from across the street*] You best watch who you're seen with, Steve! Until we get this all straightened out, you ain't exactly above suspicion yourself.

STEVE. [*Whirling around toward him*] Or you, Charlie. Or any of us, it seems. From age eight on up!

WOMAN. What I'd like to know is—what are we gonna do? Just stand around here all night?

CHARLIE. There's nothin' else we can do! [*He turns back looking toward* STEVE *and* GOODMAN *again.*] One of 'em'll tip their hand. They got to.

STEVE. [*Raising his voice*] There's something you can do, Charlie. You could go home and keep your mouth shut. You could quit strutting around like a self-appointed hanging judge and just climb into bed and forget it.

CHARLIE. You sound real anxious to have that happen, Steve. I think we better keep our eye on you too!

DON. [*As if he were taking the bit in his teeth, takes a hesitant step to the front*] I think everything might as well come out now. [*He turns toward* STEVE.] Your wife's done plenty of talking, Steve, about how odd you are!

CHARLIE. [*Picking this up, his eyes widening*] Go ahead, tell us what she's said.

[*We see a long shot of* STEVE *as he walks toward them from across the street.*]

STEVE. Go ahead, what's my wife said? Let's get it all out. Let's pick out every idiosyncrasy of every single man, woman, and child on the street. And then we might as well set up some kind of kangaroo court.[3] How about a firing squad at dawn, Charlie, so we can get rid of all the suspects? Narrow them down. Make it easier for you.

DON. There's no need gettin' so upset, Steve. It's just that . . . well . . . Myra's talked about how there's been plenty of nights you spent hours down in your basement workin' on some kind of radio or something. Well, none of us have ever seen that radio—

[*By this time* STEVE *has reached the group. He stands there defiantly close to them.*]

CHARLIE. Go ahead, Steve. What kind of "radio set" you workin' on? I never seen it. Neither has anyone else. Who you talk to on that radio set? And who talks to you?

STEVE. I'm surprised at you, Charlie. How come you're so dense all of a sudden? [*A pause*] Who do I talk to? I talk to monsters from outer space. I talk to three-headed green men who fly over here in what look like meteors.

[STEVE'S *wife steps down from the porch, bites her lip, calls out.*]

MRS. BRAND. Steve! Steve, please. [*Then looking around, frightened, she walks toward the group.*] It's just a ham radio set, that's all. I bought him a book on it myself. It's just a ham radio set. A lot of people have them. I can show it to you. It's right down in the basement.

STEVE. [*Whirls around toward her*] Show them nothing! If they want to look inside our house—let them get a search warrant.

CHARLIE. Look, buddy, you can't afford to—

STEVE. [*Interrupting*] Charlie, don't tell me what I can afford! And stop telling me who's dangerous and who isn't and who's safe and who's a menace. [*He turns to the group and shouts.*] And you're with him, too—all of you!

---

3. **kangaroo court** unofficial court that does not follow normal rules.

You're standing here all set to crucify—all set to find a scapegoat[4]—all desperate to point some kind of a finger at a neighbor! Well now look, friends, the only thing that's gonna happen is that we'll eat each other up alive—

[*He stops abruptly as* CHARLIE *suddenly grabs his arm.*]

CHARLIE. [*In a hushed voice*] That's not the only thing that can happen to us.

[*Cut to a long shot looking down the street. A figure has suddenly materialized in the gloom and in the silence we can hear the clickety-clack of slow, measured footsteps on concrete as the figure walks slowly toward them. One of the women lets out a stifled cry. The young mother grabs her boy as do a couple of others.*]

TOMMY. [*Shouting, frightened*] It's the monster! It's the monster!

[*Another woman lets out a wail and the people fall back in a group, staring toward the darkness and the approaching figure.*

We see a medium group shot of the people as they stand in the shadows watching. DON MARTIN *joins them, carrying a shotgun. He holds it up.*]

DON. We may need this.

STEVE. A shotgun? [*He pulls it out of Don's hand.*] Good Lord—will anybody think a thought around here? Will you people wise up? What good would a shotgun do against—

[*Now* CHARLIE *pulls the gun from* STEVE's *hand.*]

CHARLIE. No more talk, Steve. You're going to talk us into a grave! You'd let whatever's out there walk right over us, wouldn't yuh? Well, some of us won't!

[*He swings the gun around to point it toward the sidewalk. The dark figure continues to walk toward them.*

The group stands there, fearful, apprehensive, mothers clutching children, men standing in front of wives. CHARLIE *slowly raises the gun. As the figure gets closer and closer he suddenly pulls the trigger. The sound of it explodes in the stillness. There is a long angle shot looking down at the figure, who suddenly lets out a small cry, stumbles forward onto his knees and then falls forward on his face.* DON, CHARLIE, *and* STEVE *race forward*

---

4. **scapegoat** person or group blamed for the mistakes or crimes of others.

over to him. STEVE *is there first and turns the man over. Now the crowd gathers around them.*]

STEVE. [*Slowly looks up*] It's Pete Van Horn.

DON. [*In a hushed voice*] Pete Van Horn! He was just gonna go over to the next block to see if the power was on—

WOMAN. You killed him, Charlie. You shot him dead!

CHARLIE. [*Looks around at the circle of faces, his eyes frightened, his face contorted*] But . . . but I didn't know who he was. I certainly didn't know who he was. He comes walkin' out of the darkness—how am I supposed to know who he was? [*He grabs* STEVE.] Steve—you know why I shot! How was I supposed to know he wasn't a monster or something? [*He grabs* DON *now.*] We're all scared of the same thing. I was just tryin' to . . . tryin' to protect my home, that's all! Look, all of you, that's all I was tryin' to do. [*He looks down wildly at the body.*] I didn't know it was somebody we knew! I didn't know—

[*There's a sudden hush and then an intake of breath. We see a medium shot of the living room window of* CHARLIE's *house. The window is not lit, but suddenly the house lights come on behind it.*]

WOMAN. [*In a very hushed voice*] Charlie . . . Charlie . . . the lights just went on in your house. Why did the lights just go on?

DON. What about it, Charlie? How come you're the only one with lights now?

GOODMAN. That's what I'd like to know.

[*A pause as they all stare toward* CHARLIE.]

GOODMAN. You were so quick to kill, Charlie, and you were so quick to tell us who we had to be careful of. Well, maybe you had to kill. Maybe Peter there was trying to tell us something. Maybe he'd found out something and came back to tell us who there was amongst us we should watch out for—

[CHARLIE *backs away from the group, his eyes wide with fright.*]

CHARLIE. No . . . no . . . it's nothing of the sort! I don't know why the lights are on. I swear I don't. Somebody's pulling a gag or something.

[*He bumps against* STEVE, *who grabs him and whirls him around.*]

Steve. *A gag?* A gag? Charlie, there's a dead man on the sidewalk and you killed him! Does this thing look like a gag to you?

[CHARLIE *breaks away and screams as he runs toward his house.*]

Charlie. No! No! Please!

[*A man breaks away from the crowd to chase* CHARLIE.

We see a long angle shot looking down as the man tackles CHARLIE *and lands on top of him. The other people start to run toward them.* CHARLIE *is up on his feet, breaks away from the other man's grasp, lands a couple of desperate punches that push the man aside. Then he forces his way, fighting, through the crowd to once again break free, jumps up on his front porch. A rock thrown from the group smashes a window alongside of him, the broken glass flying past him. A couple of pieces cut him. He stands there perspiring, rumpled, blood running down from a cut on the cheek. His wife breaks away from the group to throw herself into his arms. He buries his face against her. We can see the crowd converging on the porch now.*]

Voices.

It must have been him.

He's the one.

We got to get Charlie.

[*Another rock lands on the porch. Now* CHARLIE *pushes his wife behind him, facing the group.*]

Charlie. Look, look I swear to you . . . it isn't me . . . but I do know who it is . . . I swear to you, I do know who it is.
I know who the monster is here. I know who it is that doesn't belong. I swear to you I know.

Goodman. [*Shouting*] What are you waiting for?

Woman. [*Shouting*] Come on, Charlie, come on.

Man One. [*Shouting*] Who is it, Charlie, tell us!

DON. [*Pushing his way to the front of the crowd*] All right, Charlie, let's hear it!

[CHARLIE's *eyes dart around wildly.*]

CHARLIE. It's . . . it's . . .

MAN TWO. [*Screaming*] Go ahead, Charlie, tell us.

CHARLIE. It's . . . it's the kid. It's Tommy. He's the one!

[*There's a gasp from the crowd as we cut to a shot of* SALLY *holding her son* TOMMY. *The boy at first doesn't understand and then, realizing the eyes are all on him, buries his face against his mother.*]

SALLY. [*Backs away*] That's crazy! That's crazy! He's a little boy.

WOMAN. But he knew! He was the only one who knew! He told us all about it. Well, how did he know? How could he have known?

[*The various people take this up and repeat the question aloud.*]

VOICES.

How could he know?

Who told him?

Make the kid answer.

DON. It was Charlie who killed old man Van Horn.

WOMAN. But it was the kid here who knew what was going to happen all the time. He was the one who knew!

[*We see a close-up of* STEVE.]

STEVE. Are you all gone crazy? [*Pause as he looks about*] Stop.

[*A fist crashes at* STEVE's *face, staggering him back out of the frame of the picture.*

There are several close camera shots suggesting the coming of violence. A hand fires a rifle. A fist clenches. A hand grabs the hammer from VAN HORN's *body, etc. Meanwhile, we hear the following lines.*]

DON. Charlie has to be the one—Where's my rifle—

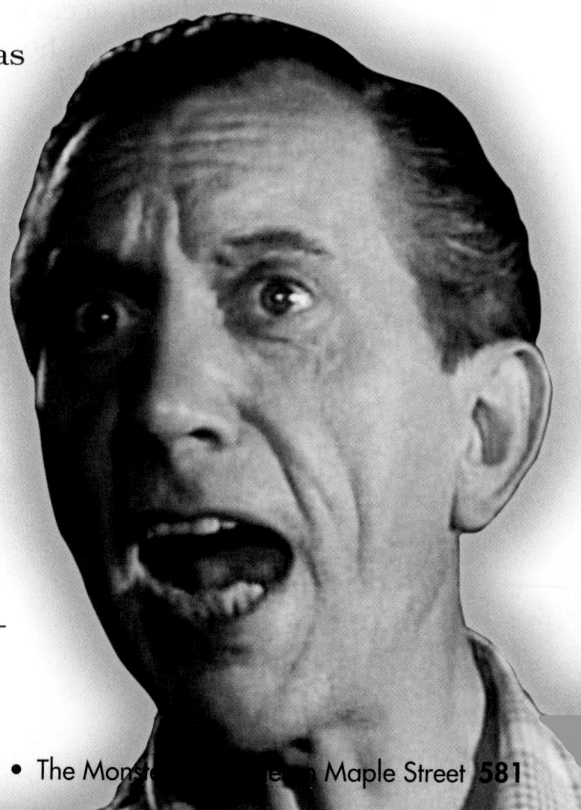

WOMAN. Les Goodman's the one. His car started! Let's wreck it.

MRS. GOODMAN. What about Steve's radio—He's the one that called them—

MR. GOODMAN. Smash the radio. Get me a hammer. Get me something.

STEVE. Stop—Stop—

CHARLIE. Where's that kid—Let's get him.

MAN ONE. Get Steve—Get Charlie—They're working together.

[*The crowd starts to converge around the mother, who grabs the child and starts to run with him. The crowd starts to follow, at first walking fast, and then running after him.*

We see a full shot of the street as suddenly CHARLIE'S *lights go off and the lights in another house go on. They stay on for a moment, then from across the street other lights go on and then off again.*]

MAN ONE. [*Shouting*] It isn't the kid . . . it's Bob Weaver's house.

WOMAN. It isn't Bob Weaver's house. It's Don Martin's place.

CHARLIE. I tell you it's the kid.

DON. It's Charlie. He's the one.

[*We move into a series of close-ups of various people as they shout, accuse, scream, interspersing these shots with shots of houses as the lights go on and off, and then slowly in the middle of this nightmarish morass of sight and sound the camera starts to pull away, until once again we've reached the opening shot looking at the Maple Street sign from high above.*

The camera continues to move away until we dissolve to a shot looking toward the metal side of a space craft, which sits shrouded in darkness. An open door throws out a beam of light from the illuminated interior. Two figures silhouetted against the bright lights appear. We get only a vague feeling of form, but nothing more explicit than that.]

FIGURE ONE. Understand the procedure now? Just stop a few of their machines and radios and telephones and lawn mowers . . . throw them into darkness for a few hours, and then you just sit back and watch the pattern.

FIGURE TWO. And this pattern is always the same?

FIGURE ONE. With few variations. They pick the most dangerous enemy they can find . . . and it's themselves. And all we need do is sit back . . . and watch.

FIGURE TWO. Then I take it this place . . . this Maple Street . . . is not unique.

FIGURE ONE. [*Shaking his head*] By no means. Their world is full of Maple Streets. And we'll go from one to the other and let them destroy themselves. One to the other . . . one to the other . . . one to the other—

[*Now the camera pans up for a shot of the starry sky and over this we hear the narrator's voice.*]

NARRATOR'S VOICE. The tools of conquest do not necessarily come with bombs and explosions and fallout. There are weapons that are simply thoughts, attitudes, prejudices—to be found only in the minds of men. For the record, prejudices can kill and suspicion can destroy and a thoughtless frightened search for a scapegoat has a fallout all its own for the children . . . and the children yet unborn. [*A pause*] And the pity of it is . . . that these things cannot be confined to . . . The Twilight Zone!

ABOUT THE AUTHOR

Rod Serling (1924–1975)

Rod Serling once said that he did not have much imagination. This is an odd statement from a man who wrote more than 200 television scripts.

Serling did not become serious about writing until he was in college. Driven by a love for radio drama, he earned second place in a national script contest. Soon after, he landed his first staff job as a radio writer. Serling branched out into writing for a new medium—television—and rocketed to fame with his weekly television series, *The Twilight Zone*.

READ

Comprehension

Reread all or part of the text to help you answer the following questions.

1. What strange event occurs just before Maple Street loses electricity?

2. Why does Tommy try to stop Steve Brand from leaving Maple Street?

3. Why does Steve try to stop people heading for Les Goodman's house?

4. What is the surprise at the end of the teleplay?

Research: Clarify Details This teleplay may include references that are unfamiliar to you. Choose at least one unfamiliar detail and briefly research it. Then, explain how the information you learned from research sheds light on an aspect of the drama.

Summarize Write an objective summary of *The Monsters Are Due on Maple Street*. Do not include opinions or evaluations.

Language Study

Selection Vocabulary Define each boldfaced word, and then use the word in a sentence of your own.

• A little power failure and right away we get all **flustered** and everything.

• [**Persistently** but a little intimidated by the crowd]

• [… TOMMY *is partly frightened and partly* **defiant** *as well.*]

Diction and Style Study the passage from the teleplay. Answer the questions that follow.

[*This stops the crowd momentarily and now* GOODMAN, *still backing away, goes toward his front porch. He goes up the steps and then stops to stand facing the mob …*]

1. **(a)** What is the meaning of *crowd* in the first sentence? **(b)** What does *mob* mean in the second sentence?

2. **(a)** How are meanings of *crowd* and *mob* similar? How are they different? **(b)** Which word—*crowd* or *mob*—has a stronger connotation? Explain.

Conventions Identify the prepositions and prepositional phrases in this passage. Then, explain how the prepositional phrases enhance the description.

[*We see a medium shot of the* GOODMAN *entry hall at night. On the side table rests an unlit candle.* MRS. GOODMAN *walks into the scene, a glass of milk in hand. She sets the milk down on the table, lights the candle with a match from a box on the table, picks up the glass of milk, and starts out of scene.*]

Academic Vocabulary

The following words appear in blue in the instructions and questions on the facing page.

affect   **identify**   **convince**

Categorize the words into words you know, know a little, or do not know at all. Then, use a dictionary to look up the definitions.

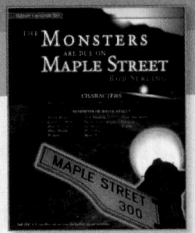

Literary Analysis

Reread the identified passages. Then, respond to the questions that follow.

> **Focus Passage 1** *(p. 566)*
>
> **NARRATOR'S VOICE.** Maple Street, U.S.A., late summer ... What was that? A meteor?

> **Focus Passage 2** *(pp. 580–581)*
>
> **CHARLIE.** Look, look I swear to you ... It's Tommy. He's the one!

Key Ideas and Details

1. **Draw Conclusions:** At the beginning of the teleplay, what type of place is Maple Street? Support your answer with details from the text.

2. **(a) Interpret:** What does the flash of light represent? **(b)** How do people react to the flash of light?

Craft and Structure

3. **(a)** What information does the narrator convey to the audience? **(b) Analyze:** Why might a writer use an outside narrator to describe events in a drama?

Integration of Knowledge and Ideas

4. **Compare and Contrast:** How do the events in this passage **affect** Maple Street's "little world"?

Key Ideas and Details

1. **(a) Deduce:** Why does Charlie claim he knows who the monster is? **(b) Support:** What details show that Charlie finds it hard to **identify** the person to blame?

2. **Infer:** Why does Goodman ask what Charlie is waiting for?

Craft and Structure

3. **Analyze:** How does dialogue create suspense in the passage?

4. **Interpret:** What information do the stage directions convey?

Integration of Knowledge and Ideas

5. **(a) Infer:** Does Charlie really know who the monster is? Explain. **(b) Analyze Cause and Effect:** Why does Charlie say Tommy is "the one"?

Characters' Motives

Motives are the reasons behind a character's actions. Reread the teleplay, taking notes on the ways that Rod Serling conveys the characters' motives.

1. **(a)** Why is Tommy determined that no one leave Maple Street? **(b)** Why is Tommy's mother concerned about the crowd's response to her son?

2. Why does Les Goodman first laugh and then shout as he tries to **convince** the crowd he has insomnia?

3. **Leaders and Followers (a)** Why does Charlie shoot Pete Van Horn? **(b)** Is he acting as the group's leader at this point? Explain. **(c)** What motivates most of the characters to be followers, and who are they following?

Common Core State Standards

RL.7.1, RL.7.2, RL.7.3, RL.7.4; L.7.1a, L.7.5c, L.7.6
[For full standards wording, see the chart in the front of this book.]

DISCUSS

From Text to Topic **Panel Discussion**

The Monsters Are Due on Maple Street is an episode of the television show *The Twilight Zone,* which ran from 1959 to 1964. Locate and watch the television episode with a small group of classmates. As you watch, take notes on the ways in which lighting, sound, and camera effects contribute to the television production. After viewing, hold a panel discussion in which you compare and contrast the written teleplay with the television episode. Analyze the techniques that are unique to each medium—film and print—and support your key points with evidence from both the television episode and the text.

QUESTIONS FOR DISCUSSION

1. Which medium is more effective in portraying the mob mentality?

2. What specific techniques made the portrayal more effective?

WRITE

Writing to Sources **Argument**

> ### Assignment
> Write an **argumentative essay** in which you make a claim about individuals who stand up to the crowd or individuals who follow others. Support your claim with details about characters in *The Monsters Are Due on Maple Street.*

Prewriting and Planning Reread the drama, looking for characters whose actions show them to be leaders or followers. Record your notes in web organizers that link characters and their actions.

Drafting Most argumentative writing includes the following:

- **Claim:** The writer's position on the issue
- **Evidence:** Relevant examples that support the claim and follow logical reasoning
- **Responses to Counterclaims:** Acknowledgement of opposing viewpoints
- **Conclusion:** A strong, concluding statement

In your draft, cite examples from the teleplay to support your points.

Revising Reread your essay, making sure you have clearly shown the relationships between claims and evidence.

Editing and Proofreading A sentence fragment is a group of words that is incorrectly punctuated as a sentence. A fragment is missing a subject, a predicate, or both. Proofread your essay to make sure all sentences are complete.

CONVENTIONS
When you write sentences, use the correct end punctuation. A period follows a statement, a question mark follows a question, and an exclamation point follows an exclamation.

RESEARCH

Research **Investigate the Topic**

Crowds and Their Actions Many individuals will follow a crowd's actions. For example, when spectators at a sports event start chanting, others join in. Mob behavior may occur when people are unsure of what "should" be done in a difficult situation. Because the members of a crowd are anonymous, it can be hard to tell who is responsible for the crowd's actions.

Assignment

Conduct research to learn about the factors that can influence people to act as a mob. Search online library databases using the keywords *crowd* and *mob*. Take clear notes and carefully identify your sources. Share your findings in an **oral presentation** for the class.

Gather Sources Locate authoritative sources. Primary sources, such as psychological research studies, provide firsthand information. You may also want to consult secondary sources, such as encyclopedias of the social sciences. Look for sources that feature expert authors and up-to-date information.

Take Notes Record notes on each of your sources, either electronically or on notecards. Use an organized note-taking strategy.

- Write a separate note for each source.

- Use quotation marks when you record exact wording.

- Do not try to note every detail from a source. Summarize the main points and most important details.

Synthesize Multiple Sources Assemble data from your sources and organize it into a cohesive presentation. Use what you learned to draw conclusions about the relationship between mobs and the actions of leaders and followers. Use your notes to construct an outline for your presentation. Follow accepted conventions to cite all sources you use in your presentation. See the Citing Sources pages in the Introductory Unit of this textbook for additional guidance.

Organize and Present Ideas Review your outline and practice delivering your presentation. Be prepared to answer questions from your audience.

PREPARATION FOR ESSAY

You may use the knowledge you gain during this research assignment to support your claims in an essay you will write at the end of this section.

Common Core State Standards

RL.7.7; W.7.1.a–c, W.7.1.e, W.7.4, W.7.7, W.7.8, W.7.10; SL.7.1, SL.7.4, SL.7.6

[For full standards wording, see the chart in the front of this book.]

Ray Bradbury
All Summer in a Day

"Ready?" "Ready." "Now?" "Soon."

"Do the scientists really know? Will it happen today, will it?"

"Look, look; see for yourself!"

The children pressed to each other like so many roses, so many weeds, intermixed, peering out for a look at the hidden sun.

It rained.

It had been raining for seven years; thousands upon thousands of days compounded and filled from one end to the other with rain, with the drum and gush of water, with the sweet crystal fall of showers and the concussion of storms so heavy they were tidal waves come over the islands. A thousand forests had been crushed under the rain and grown up a thousand times to be crushed again. And this was the way life was forever on the planet Venus and this was the schoolroom of the children of the rocket men and women who had come to a raining world to set up civilization and live out their lives.

"It's stopping, it's stopping!"

"Yes, yes!"

Margot stood apart from them, from these children who could never remember a time when there wasn't rain and rain and rain. They were all nine years old, and if there had been a day, seven years ago, when the sun came out for an hour and showed its face to the stunned world, they could not recall. Sometimes, at night, she heard them stir, in remembrance, and she knew they were dreaming and remembering gold or a yellow crayon or a coin large enough to buy the world with. She knew they thought they remembered a warmness, like a blushing in the face, in the body, in the arms and legs and trembling hands. But then they always awoke to the tatting drum, the endless shaking down of clear bead necklaces upon the roof, the walk, the gardens, the forests, and their dreams were gone.

All day yesterday they had read in class about the sun. About how like a lemon it was, and how hot. And they had written small stories or essays or poems about it:

I think the sun is a flower,
That blooms for just one hour.

That was Margot's poem, read in a quiet voice in the still classroom while the rain was falling outside.

"Aw, you didn't write that!" protested one of the boys.

"I did," said Margot. "I did."

"William!" said the teacher.

But that was yesterday. Now the rain was slackening, and the children were crushed in the great thick windows.

"Where's teacher?"

"She'll be back."

"She'd better hurry, we'll miss it!"

They turned on themselves, like a feverish wheel, all fumbling spokes.

Margot stood alone. She was a very frail girl who looked as if she had been lost in the rain for years and the rain had washed out the blue from her eyes and the red from her mouth and the yellow from her hair. She was an old photograph dusted from an album, whitened away, and if she spoke at all her voice would be a ghost. Now she stood, separate, staring at the rain and the loud wet world beyond the huge glass.

"What're you looking at?" said William.

Margot said nothing.

"Speak when you're spoken to." He gave her a shove. But she did not move; rather she let herself be moved only by him and nothing else.

They edged away from her, they would not look at her. She felt them go away. And this was because she would play no games with them in the echoing tunnels of the underground city. If they tagged her and ran, she stood blinking after them and did not follow. When the class sang songs about happiness and life and games her lips barely moved. Only when they sang about the sun and the summer did her lips move as she watched the drenched windows.

slackening ▶
(slak´ ən iŋ) *adj.*
easing; becoming
less active

And then, of course, the biggest crime of all was that she had come here only five years ago from Earth, and she remembered the sun and the way the sun was and the sky was when she was four in Ohio. And they, they had been on Venus all their lives, and they had been only two years old when last the sun came out and had long since forgotten the color and heat of it and the way it really was. But Margot remembered.

"It's like a penny," she said once, eyes closed.

"No, it's not!" the children cried.

"It's like a fire," she said, "in the stove."

"You're lying, you don't remember!" cried the children.

But she remembered and stood quietly apart from all of them and watched the patterning windows. And once, a month ago, she had refused to shower in the school shower rooms, had clutched her hands to her ears and over her head, screaming the water mustn't touch her head. So after that, dimly, dimly, she sensed it, she was different and they knew her difference and kept away.

There was talk that her father and mother were taking her back to Earth next year; it seemed vital to her that they do so, though it would mean the loss of thousands of dollars to her family. And so, the children hated her for all these reasons of big and little consequence. They hated her pale snow face, her waiting silence, her thinness, and her possible future.

"Get away!" The boy gave her another push. "What're you waiting for?"

Then, for the first time, she turned and looked at him. And what she was waiting for was in her eyes.

"Well, don't wait around here!" cried the boy savagely. "You won't see nothing!"

Her lips moved.

"Nothing!" he cried. "It was all a joke, wasn't it?" He turned to the other children. "Nothing's happening today. Is it?"

They all blinked at him and then, understanding, laughed and shook their heads. "Nothing, nothing!"

"Oh, but," Margot whispered, her eyes helpless. "But this is the day, the scientists predict, they say, they know, the sun . . ."

"All a joke!" said the boy, and seized her roughly. "Hey, everyone, let's put her in a closet before teacher comes!"

"No," said Margot, falling back.

◀ **vital**
(vīt′ ′l) *adj.*
extremely important or necessary

They surged[1] about her, caught her up and bore her, protesting, and then pleading, and then crying, back into a tunnel, a room, a closet, where they slammed and locked the door. They stood looking at the door and saw it tremble from her beating and throwing herself against it. They heard her muffled cries. Then, smiling, they turned and went out and back down the tunnel, just as the teacher arrived.

"Ready, children?" She glanced at her watch.

"Yes!" said everyone.

"Are we all here?"

"Yes!"

The rain slackened still more.

They crowded to the huge door.

The rain stopped.

It was as if, in the midst of a film concerning an avalanche, a tornado, a hurricane, a volcanic eruption, something had, first, gone wrong with the sound apparatus, thus muffling and finally cutting off all noise, all of the blasts and repercussions and thunders, and then, second, ripped the film from the projector and inserted in its place a peaceful tropical slide which did not move or tremor. The world ground to a standstill. The silence was so immense and unbelievable that you felt your ears had been stuffed or you had lost your hearing altogether. The children put their hands to their ears. They stood apart. The door slid back and the smell of the silent, waiting world came in to them.

The sun came out.

It was the color of flaming bronze and it was very large. And the sky around it was a blazing blue tile color. And the jungle burned with sunlight as the children, released from their spell, rushed out, yelling, into the springtime.

"Now, don't go too far," called the teacher after them. "You've only two hours, you know. You wouldn't want to get caught out!"

But they were running and turning their faces up to the sky and feeling the sun on their cheeks like a warm iron; they were taking off their jackets and letting the sun burn their arms.

"Oh, it's better than the sun lamps, isn't it?"

"Much, much better!"

They stopped running and stood in the great jungle that covered Venus, that grew and never stopped growing, tumultuously, even as you watched it. It was a nest of octopi, clustering up great arms of fleshlike weed, wavering, flowering

---

1. **surged** (sʉrjd) v. moved in a violent swelling motion.

in this brief spring. It was the color of rubber and ash, this jungle, from the many years without sun. It was the color of stones and white cheeses and ink, and it was the color of the moon.

The children lay out, laughing, on the jungle mattress, and heard it sigh and squeak under them, **resilient** and alive. They ran among the trees, they slipped and fell, they pushed each other, they played hide-and-seek and tag, but most of all they squinted at the sun until tears ran down their faces, they put their hands up to that yellowness and that amazing blueness and they breathed of the fresh, fresh air and listened and listened to the silence which suspended them in a blessed sea of no sound and no motion. They looked at everything and savored everything. Then, wildly, like animals escaped from their caves, they ran and ran in shouting circles. They ran for an hour and did not stop running.

And then—

◀ **resilient**
(ri zil′ yənt) *adj.*
able to spring
back into shape

In the midst of their running one of the girls wailed.

Everyone stopped.

The girl, standing in the open, held out her hand.

"Oh, look, look," she said, trembling.

They came slowly to look at her opened palm.

In the center of it, cupped and huge, was a single raindrop.

She began to cry, looking at it.

They glanced quietly at the sky.

"Oh, Oh."

A few cold drops fell on their noses and their cheeks and their mouths. The sun faded behind a stir of mist. A wind blew cool around them. They turned and started to walk back toward the underground house, their hands at their sides, their smiles vanishing away.

A boom of thunder startled them and like leaves before a new hurricane, they tumbled upon each other and ran. Lightning struck ten miles away, five miles away, a mile, a half mile. The sky darkened into midnight in a flash.

They stood in the doorway of the underground for a moment until it was raining hard. Then they closed the door and heard the gigantic sound of the rain falling in tons and avalanches, everywhere and forever.

"Will it be seven more years?"

"Yes. Seven."

Then one of them gave a little cry.

"Margot!"

"What?"

"She's still in the closet where we locked her."

"Margot."

They stood as if someone had driven them, like so many stakes, into the floor. They looked at each other and then looked away. They glanced out at the world that was raining now and raining and raining steadily. They could not meet each other's glances. Their faces were solemn and pale. They looked at their hands and feet, their faces down.

"Margot."

One of the girls said, "Well . . .?"

No one moved.

"Go on," whispered the girl.

They walked slowly down the hall in the sound of cold rain. They turned through the doorway to the room in the sound of the storm and thunder, lightning on their faces, blue and terrible. They walked over to the closet door slowly and stood by it.

Behind the closet door was only silence.

They unlocked the door, even more slowly, and let Margot out.

READ

Comprehension

Answer the following questions.

1. How do the other children feel about Margot?

2. How do the children react when they realize that Margot missed the sun because of their prank?

Research: Clarify Details Choose at least one unfamiliar detail from the story and briefly research it.

Summarize Write an objective summary of the story that is free from opinion and evaluation.

Language Study

Selection Vocabulary Create a word map with at least one synonym and one antonym for each boldfaced word. Then, use each word in a sentence of your own.

- Now the rain was **slackening**, and the children were crushed in the great thick windows.

- … it seemed **vital** to her that they do so, though it would mean the loss of thousands of dollars to her family.

- The children lay out, laughing, on the jungle mattress, and heard it sigh and squeak under them, **resilient** and alive.

Literary Analysis

Reread the identified passage.

> **Focus Passage** *(pp. 589–590)*
>
> Margot stood apart from them, … and their dreams were gone.

Key Ideas and Details

1. (a) Interpret: How has seven years of constant rain affected the children?
(b) Interpret: How much do the children know about the sun?

2. How well does Margot fit in with the class? Explain.

Craft and Structure

3. (a) To what does the author compare the sun in this passage? **(b) Analyze:** What are the effects of these metaphors?

Integration of Knowledge and Ideas

4. Generalize: What does the sun represent? Cite details in the story to support your answer.

Setting

The **setting** is the time and place of a story's action. Reread the story, and take notes on ways the author uses setting.

1. How was Margot's environment on Earth different from the **environment** of Venus?

2. How do the children act when the sun comes out?

3. How does the children's behavior change when the rain begins to fall again?

DISCUSS • RESEARCH • WRITE

From Text to Topic **Partner Discussion**

Discuss the following passage from page 592 with a partner. Contribute your own ideas, and support them with examples from the story.

> They surged about her, caught her up and bore her, protesting, and then pleading, and then crying, back into a tunnel, a room, a closet, where they slammed and locked the door …
>
> "Ready, children?" She glanced at her watch.
> "Yes!" said everyone.
> "Are we all here?"
> "Yes!"

Research **Investigate the Topic**

Bullying To *bully* means to frighten someone by using force. Margot's classmates bully her by locking her in a closet.

Assignment

Conduct research to find out why people may follow a bully and to learn what is being done to develop **awareness** of this problem. Take clear notes and carefully identify your sources. Share your findings in a **research report**.

Writing to Sources **Informative Text**

"All Summer in a Day" describes a major event in a fictional world.

Assignment

Write a **news report** based on "All Summer in a Day" in which you explain the events that occurred on the day the sun appeared on Venus. Mention the **incident** between Margot and her classmates, describing who acted as leaders and who acted as followers.

- First, list answers to the questions, *Who? What? Where? When? Why,* and *How?* Base your answers on details from the story.
- Write an engaging *lead,* or opening sentence, and present the most important information in your first paragraph.
- Include quotations from people who were on the scene.

QUESTIONS FOR DISCUSSION

1. Would you describe the children as leaders or followers? Why?

2. What lesson might Ray Bradbury have wanted to teach with this story?

PREPARATION FOR ESSAY

You may use the results of your research to support your ideas in the essay you will write at the end of this section.

ACADEMIC VOCABULARY

Academic terms appear in blue on these pages. If these words are not familiar to you, use a dictionary to find their definitions. Then, use the words as you speak and write about the text.

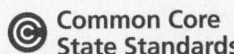

Common Core State Standards

RL.7.1, RL.7.2, RL.7.3, RL.7.4; W.7.2.a, W.7.2.b, W.7.7; SL.7.1; L.7.5.b, L.7.6
[For full standards wording, see the chart in the front of this book.]

Joseph R. McCarthy

from Prentice Hall United States History

The early Cold War[1] years saw one ominous event after another. The fall of China, Soviet nuclear bombs, and the exposure of Soviet agents in the United States all undermined American confidence. At that time, as Americans worried about the nation's security, a clever and **unscrupulous** man began to take advantage of this sense of fear and helplessness. He suggested that these setbacks were really caused by the work of traitors inside the United States.

unscrupulous ▶
(unskro͞o′pyə ləs) *adj.*
not held back by ideas of right and wrong; untrustworthy

Joseph McCarthy during the televised Army-McCarthy hearings

---

1. **Cold War** a period of conflict, without physical war, between the U.S. and the communist Soviet Union (1945–1991).

Primary Source "The reason why we find ourselves in a position of [weakness] is not because the enemy has sent men to invade our shores, but rather because of the traitorous actions of those who have had all the benefits that the wealthiest nation on earth has had to offer—the finest homes, the finest college educations, and the finest jobs in Government we can give. . . .I have here in my hand a list of 205 [individuals] that were known to the Secretary of State as being members of the Communist Party and who nevertheless are still working and shaping the policy of the State Department."

—Joseph McCarthy, February 9, 1950

McCarthy Makes Accusations

In February 1950, a little-known senator from Wisconsin made a speech in Wheeling, West Virginia. The senator, **Joseph R. McCarthy,** charged that the State Department was infested with communist agents. He waved a piece of paper, which, he said, contained the names of State Department employees who were secretly communists.

The charge provoked a **furor**. When challenged to give specific names, McCarthy said he had meant that there were "205 bad security risks" in the department. Then, he claimed that 57 employees were communists. Over the next months, the numbers on his list changed. McCarthy never did produce the list of communists. Still, with the outbreak of the Korean War in June 1950, McCarthy's accusations grabbed the attention of the American public.

At the time of the above speech, McCarthy was finishing his first term in the Senate. He had accomplished very little in that term and was looking for a popular issue on which to focus his 1952 reelection campaign. Anticommunism seemed to be just the issue. McCarthy was easily reelected to a second term.

◀ **furor**
(fyoor´ ôr´) *n.* outburst of public anger or excitement

McCarthy's Power Increases

In the following four years, McCarthy put forward his own brand of anticommunism—so much so that the term **McCarthyism** became a catchword for extreme, reckless charges. By making irresponsible allegations, McCarthy did more to discredit legitimate concerns about domestic communism than any other single American.

Between 1950 and 1954, McCarthy was perhaps the most powerful politician in the United States. Piling baseless accusations on top of charges that could not be proved, McCarthy became chairman of an investigations subcommittee. Merely being accused by McCarthy caused people to lose their jobs and destroyed their reputations. He attacked ruthlessly. When caught in a lie, he told another. When one case faded, he introduced a new one.

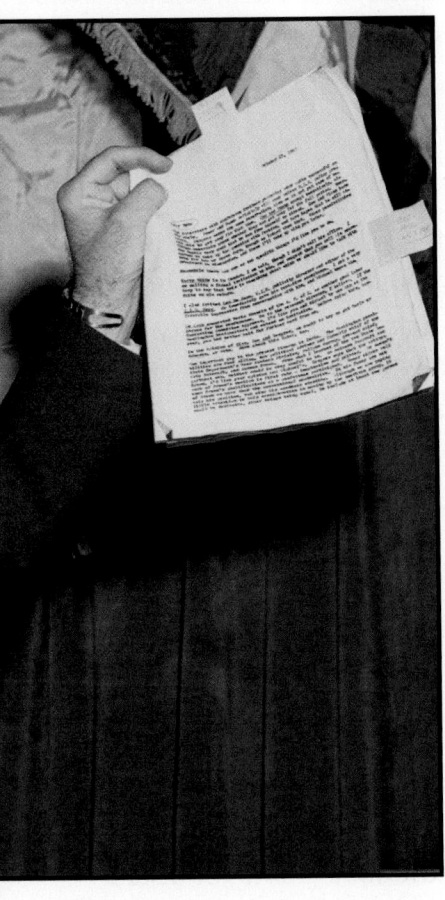

Joseph McCarthy delivers a "report" that accuses Democratic presidential candidate Adlai Stevenson of associating with alleged subversive groups.

Confident because of his increasing power, McCarthy took on larger targets. He attacked former Secretary of State George Marshall, a national hero and author of the Marshall Plan.[2] Even other senators came to fear McCarthy. They worried that he would brand them as communist sympathizers.

McCarthy Falls From Power

In 1954, McCarthy went after the United States Army, claiming that it, too, was full of communists. Army leaders responded that McCarthy's attacks were personally motivated. Finally, the Senate decided to hold televised hearings to sort out the allegations. For weeks, Americans were **riveted** to their television sets. Most were horrified by McCarthy's bullying tactics. For the first time, the public saw McCarthy badger witnesses, twist the truth, and snicker at the suffering of others. It was an upsetting sight for many Americans.

◄ **riveted**
(riv´ it id) *v.* anchored; completely absorbed by

By the time the hearings ended in mid-June, the senator had lost many of his strongest supporters. The Senate formally censured, or condemned, him for his reckless accusations. Although McCarthy continued to serve in the Senate, he had lost virtually all of his power and influence.

The end of the Korean War in 1953 and McCarthy's downfall in 1954 signaled the decline of the Red Scare.[3] The nation had been damaged by the suppression of free speech and by the lack of open, honest debate. However, Americans had come to realize how important their democratic institutions were and how critical it was to preserve them.

---

2. **Marshall Plan** (officially known as the European Recovery Program, ERP) a U.S. program that provided financial aid for rebuilding European economies after World War II in an effort to prevent the spread of Soviet communism.
3. **Red Scare** a term that refers to the promotion of widespread public fear of the possible rise of communism.

READ

Comprehension

Reread as needed to answer these questions.

1. Who was Joseph McCarthy?

2. Why did many Americans believe McCarthy at first?

3. What happened when the Army-McCarthy hearings were broadcast on television?

Research: Clarify Details Research an unfamiliar detail in the selection. Explain how your research helps you understand the text.

Summarize Write an objective summary of the textbook article. Omit your opinions and **evaluations**.

Language Study

Selection Vocabulary Define each boldfaced word below and use it in an original sentence.

• . . . a clever and **unscrupulous** man began to take advantage of this sense of fear . . .

• The charge provoked a **furor**.

• For weeks, Americans were **riveted** to their television sets.

Literary Analysis

Reread the passage and answer the following questions.

> **Focus Passage** *(pp. 600–601)*
>
> **McCarthy's Power Increases** . . . he would brand them communist sympathizers.

Key Ideas and Details

1. How did McCarthy become very powerful in the early 1950s?

Craft and Structure

2. Analyze: According to the textbook article, McCarthy made "irresponsible allegations"

and "baseless accusations", and "attacked ruthlessly." What picture do these descriptions paint of McCarthy?

3. (a) Identify two examples that show cause and effect in the passage. **(b) Evaluate:** Why is cause-and-effect organization useful in a textbook article?

Integration of Knowledge and Ideas

4. Connect: Review word choice in this passage, including the examples in question 2. How do vivid details and descriptions help you understand a particular period in U.S. history?

Main Idea

The **main idea** of a text or passage is the most important idea that it presents.

1. (a) What is the main idea of the first paragraph? **(b)** What sentence best supports the main idea?

2. Leaders and Followers (a) How did support for McCarthy change in 1954? **(b)** Identify three key details that support this main idea.

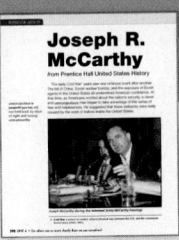

DISCUSS • RESEARCH • WRITE

From Text to Topic **Debate**

Use the following passage to prepare for a **debate**. With a team of classmates, choose a position based on one of the discussion questions, and then prepare your argument. Take notes and respond to the points raised by a team with an opposing viewpoint. Cite evidence from the text in your discussion.

> **McCarthy Falls From Power** . . . It was an upsetting sight for many Americans. (p. 601)

Research **Investigate the Topic**

McCarthyism *McCarthyism* is the term that describes the **investigations** of suspected Communist activities in the United States during the 1950s.

> ### Assignment
> Conduct research to find out about the U.S. Senate investigation of communism and its followers during the 1950s. Use multiple print and digital sources to gather relevant information. Take detailed notes and carefully identify your sources. Share your findings in an **outline**.

Writing to Sources **Argument**

"Joseph R. McCarthy" describes the fall of Senator McCarthy following televised hearings in the Senate.

> ### Assignment
> Write an **argument** in which you take a position on the value of the rapid communication of information to the public. Is it right to broadcast information before all the facts are known, or can this practice lead to miscommunication? Cite evidence from the selection in your argument. Follow these steps:
>
> - Choose your position on the issue and state your claim.
> - Support your claim with evidence from "Joseph R. McCarthy."
> - Anticipate and address counterarguments.
> - Maintain a formal style in your argument.
> - Provide a concluding statement that summarizes your position.

QUESTIONS FOR DISCUSSION

1. Is it ever right to pursue accusations based on a strong belief but no concrete proof? Explain.

2. Should cameras be allowed in Senate hearings and other court proceedings? Explain.

PREPARATION FOR ESSAY

You may use the results of your research to support your ideas in the essay you will write at the end of this section.

ACADEMIC VOCABULARY

Academic terms appear in blue on these pages. If these words are not familiar to you, use a dictionary to find their definitions. Then, use the words as you speak and write about the text.

 **Common Core State Standards**

RI.7.1, RI.7.2, RI.7.3, RI.7.4, RI.7.5; W.7.1, W.7.7, W.7.8; SL.7.1, SL.7.4; L.7.4.a, L.7.4.c, L.7.6
[For full standards wording, see the chart in the front of this book.]

The Salem Witch Trials of 1692

The Salem Witch Museum

I n January of 1692, the daughter and niece of Reverend Samuel Parris of Salem Village became ill. When they failed to improve, the village doctor, William Griggs, was called in. His diagnosis of bewitchment put into motion the forces that would ultimately result in the death by hanging of nineteen men and women. In addition, one man was crushed to death; seven others died in prison, and the lives of many were irrevocably[1] changed.

---

1. irrevocably (i rev´ə kə blē) *adv.* permanently; unable to be undone.

To understand the events of the Salem witch trials, it is necessary to examine the times in which **accusations** of witchcraft occurred. There were the ordinary stresses of 17th-century life in Massachusetts Bay Colony. A strong belief in the devil, factions among Salem Village fanatics and rivalry with nearby Salem Town, a recent small pox epidemic and the threat of attack by warring tribes created a fertile ground for fear and suspicion. Soon prisons were filled with more than 150 men and women from towns surrounding Salem. Their names had been "cried out" by tormented young girls as the cause of their pain. All would await trial for a crime punishable by death in 17th-century New England, the practice of witchcraft.

In June of 1692, the special Court of Oyer (to hear) and Terminer (to decide) sat in Salem to hear the cases of witchcraft. Presided over by Chief Justice William Stoughton, the court was made up of magistrates[2] and jurors. The first to be tried was Bridget Bishop of Salem who was found guilty and was hanged on June 10. Thirteen women and five men from all stations of life followed her to the gallows on three **successive** hanging days before the court was **disbanded** by Governor William Phipps in October of that year. The Superior Court of Judicature, formed to replace the "witchcraft" court, did not allow spectral evidence. This belief in the power of the accused to use their invisible shapes or specters to torture their victims had sealed the fates of those tried by the Court of Oyer and Terminer. The new court released those awaiting trial and pardoned those awaiting execution. In effect, the Salem witch trials were over.

As years passed, apologies were offered, and restitution[3] was made to the victims' families. Historians and sociologists have examined this most complex episode in our history so that we may understand the issues of that time and apply our understanding to our own society. The parallels between the Salem witch trials and more modern examples of "witch hunting" like the McCarthy hearings of the 1950's, are remarkable.

◄ **accusations**
(ak´yōō zā´shənz)
n. charges
made against a
person for doing
something wrong

◄ **successive**
(sək ses´iv) *adj.*
following, in order

◄ **disbanded**
(dis band´ əd) *v.*
broken up; dismissed

---

2. magistrates (maj´is trāt´s) *n.* civil officers in charge of enforcing the law.
3. restitution (res´tə tōō´shən) *n.* payment made for losses or damage.

READ

Comprehension

Reread as needed to answer these questions.

1. What made life stressful during the time of the Salem witch trials?

2. Who were the accusers?

3. What happened to end the trials?

Research: Clarify Details Research an unfamiliar reference from the Web article. Explain how your findings help you better understand the article.

Summarize Write an objective summary of the article. Remember to leave out your opinions and evaluations.

Language Study

Selection Vocabulary Define each boldfaced word. Then, identify related words for each one. Use a dictionary, if necessary.

• To understand the events of the Salem witch trials, it is necessary to examine the times in which **accusations** of witchcraft occurred.

• Thirteen women and five men from all stations of life followed her to the gallows on three **successive** hanging days before the court was **disbanded** by Governor William Phipps in October of that year.

Literary Analysis

Reread the passage and answer the questions.

> **Focus Passage** *(p. 604)*
> In January of 1692, … were irrevocably changed.

Key Ideas and Details

1. Where and when did the events that resulted in the Salem witch trials begin?

2. Analyze Causes and Effects: What was the outcome of these events?

Craft and Structure

3. Generalize: Describe the mood that is **established** through the use of the words *death, hanging,* and *prison*.

Integration of Knowledge and Ideas

4. Hypothesize: Why might the people of Salem have believed that William Griggs was correct in his **determination** of what was ailing Samuel Parris's daughter and niece?

Tone

Tone is the writer's attitude toward his or her audience and subject. For example, the tone might be **formal** or informal, serious or playful. Reread the article, noting the tone.

1. How does the writer's word choice establish tone? Cite examples from the text.

2. Leaders and Followers Why does the writer compare the Salem witch trials to the McCarthy hearings?

DISCUSS • RESEARCH • WRITE

From Text to Topic **Group Discussion**

Discuss the following passage with a group of classmates. Take notes during the discussion. Contribute your own ideas, and support them with examples from the text.

> As years passed, apologies were offered, and restitution was made to the victims' families. Historians and sociologists have examined this most complex episode in our history so that we may understand the issues of that time and apply our understanding to our own society.

Research **Investigate the Topic**

Mass Hysteria Mass hysteria is a situation in which a group of people **simultaneously** experience anxiety, irrational behavior, or symptoms of an illness that cannot be explained.

Assignment

Conduct research to learn more about mass hysteria and how it relates to the the concept of leaders and followers. Gather relevant information from a variety of print and digital sources, making sure that all sources are accurate and credible. Take detailed notes and carefully identify your sources. Share your findings in a **visual presentation**.

Writing to Sources **Explanatory Text**

"The Salem Witch Trials of 1692" describes the events that followed a diagnosis of bewitchment in two young girls.

Assignment

Write a **comparison-and-contrast essay** in which you analyze the similarities and differences between "The Salem Witch Trials of 1692" and a fictional portrayal of the Salem witch trials.

- Find and read a fictional account of the Salem witch trials.
- Organize your essay using the point-by-point or block method.
- Note the similarities and differences between each work's depiction of the time period, setting, characters, and events.
- Conclude your essay by assessing how the author of the fictional account uses or alters history.

QUESTIONS FOR DISCUSSION

1. Why is it important to study events that took place more than three hundred years ago?
2. What can we learn from the Salem Witch Trials?

PREPARATION FOR ESSAY

You may use the results of your research to support your ideas in the essay you will write at the end of this section.

ACADEMIC VOCABULARY

Academic terms appear in blue on these pages. If these words are not familiar to you, use a dictionary to find their definitions. Then, use the words as you speak and write about the text.

 **Common Core State Standards**

RL.7.9; RI.7.1, RI.7.2, RI.7.3, RI.7.4; W.7.2, W.7.7; SL.7.1.a, SL.7.1.c, SL.7.4; L.7.4.c, L.7.6
[For full standards wording, see the chart in the front of this book.]

Herd Mentality?
The Freakonomics[1] of Boarding a Bus

Stephen J. Dubner

A few days a week, I bring my daughter to nursery school on the East Side of Manhattan. (On the other days, I bring my son to kindergarten; next year, they will blessedly attend the same school.) We live on the West Side, and usually take the bus across town. It is a busy time of day. At the bus stop closest to our apartment (we'll call this Point A), there are often 40 or 50 people waiting for the bus. This is largely because there is a subway stop right there; a lot of people take the train from uptown or downtown, then go aboveground to catch the crosstown bus.

I don't like crowds much in general (I know: what am I doing living in New York?), and I especially don't like fighting a crowd when I'm trying to cram onto a bus with my five-year-old daughter. Because there are so many people waiting for a

---

1. **Freakonomics** Stephen J. Dubner co-wrote the bestsellers *Freakonomics* and *SuperFreakonomics* with economist Steven D. Levitt. The authors also have a popular blog called *Freakonomics*.

bus at Point A, we have perhaps a 30% chance of getting aboard the first bus that stops there, and probably an 80% chance of getting aboard one of the first *two* buses that stop at Point A. (The first bus to come along after a very crowded bus is usually less crowded, but not always.)

As for getting a seat on the bus, I'd say we have perhaps a 10% chance of sitting down on either of the first two buses at Point A. It's not such a long ride across town, maybe 15 minutes, but standing on a crowded bus in winter gear, my daughter's lunch getting smushed in her backpack, isn't the ideal way to start the day. Point A is so crowded that when eastbound passengers get *off* the bus at Point A, using the bus's back door, a surge of people rush *onto* the bus via the back door, which means that a) they don't pay, since the paybox is up front and b) they take room away from the people who are legitimately waiting at the head of the crowd to get on the bus.

So a while ago, we started walking a block west to catch the bus at what we'll call Point B. Point B is perhaps 250 yards west of—that is, further from our East Side destination—than Point A. But at Point B, the lines are considerably shorter, and the buses arrive less crowded. At Point B, we have a 90% chance of getting aboard the first bus that arrives, and perhaps a 40% chance of getting a seat. To me, this seems well worth the effort and time of walking 250 yards.

Once we hit upon this solution, we haven't boarded a single bus at Point A. We get to sit; we get to listen to the iPod together; … we don't arrive with a smushed lunch.

But what I can't figure out is why no other bus passengers at Point A do what we do. To anyone standing at Point A morning after morning, the conditions there are plainly bad. The conditions at Point B are clearly better since a) Point B is close enough to see with the naked eye and b) the buses that arrive at Point A from Point B often have room on them, although only for the first 10 or 20 passengers trying to board at Point A.

As for getting a seat on the bus, I'd say we have perhaps a 10% chance of sitting down on either of the first two buses at Point A.

At Point B, we have a 90% chance of getting aboard the first bus that arrives, and perhaps a 40% chance of getting a seat.

Personally, I am happy that more people at Point A *don't* go to Point B (which would make me have to consider boarding at Point C), but I don't understand why this is so. Here are a few possibilities:

1. Walking 250 yards doesn't seem like a worthwhile **investment** to improve a short, if miserable, experience.

2. Having just gotten off the subway, the Point A passengers are already broken in spirit and can't **muster** the energy to improve their commuting lot.

3. Perhaps some Point A passengers simply never think about the existence of a Point B, or at least the conditions thereof.

4. There is a herd at Point A; people may not *like* being part of a herd, but psychologically they are somehow comforted by it; they **succumb** to "herd mentality" and unthinkingly tag along—because if everyone else is doing it, it must be the thing to do.

Personally, I am persuaded that all four points may be valid in varying measures, and there are undoubtedly additional points to be made. But if I had to pick an outright winner, I'd say No. 4: the herd mentality.

What do you think? And what are some other examples of herd mentality that you have encountered?

◄ **succumb**
(sə kum´) *v.*
give way to;
submit to

◄ **investment**
(in vest´mənt) *n.*
act of devoting
time or effort
to a particular
undertaking with
the expectation of
a worthwhile result

◄ **muster**
(mus´tər) *v.*
gather together
or summon

MEET THE AUTHOR

Stephen J. Dubner (b. 1963)

Stephen J. Dubner is an award-winning writer. His first published work appeared in the magazine *Highlights for Children* when he was eleven years old. More recently, Dubner co-wrote the popular books *Freakonomics* and *SuperFreakonomics* with economist Steven D. Levitt. Both books explore the topic of human behavior. Dubner regularly contributes articles to periodicals such as *Time* and *The New Yorker.* He lives in New York City with his wife, who is a photographer, and their two children.

READ

Comprehension

Reread as needed to answer these questions.

1. For Dubner and his daughter, what makes the bus ride from Point A unpleasant?

2. What is the disadvantage of boarding the bus at Point B?

3. What is the meaning of "herd mentality"?

Research: Clarify Details Choose an unfamiliar detail from the blog post and research it. Then, explain how your findings clarify an aspect of the blog post.

Summarize Write an objective summary of the blog post. Remember to leave out your opinions and evaluations.

Language Study

Selection Vocabulary Define each boldfaced word below, and then use the word in a sentence of your own.

• Walking 250 yards doesn't seem like a worthwhile **investment** to improve a short, if miserable, experience.

• Having just gotten off the subway, the Point A passengers are already broken in spirit and can't **muster** the energy to improve their commuting lot.

• … they **succumb** to "herd mentality" and unthinkingly tag along …

Literary Analysis

Reread the indicated passage.

> **Focus Passage** *(p. 610)*
> So a while ago … board at point A.

Key Ideas and Details

1. (a) Analyze: Why is Point B a good place to board the bus? **(b) Connect:** Why does Dubner choose not to go back to boarding at Point A?

2. Interpret: What puzzles Dubner about the other bus riders' **behavior**?

Craft and Structure

3. (a) What types of numerical details does Dubner use in this passage? **(b) Analyze:** How does the use of these details **contribute** to Dubner's message?

Integration of Knowledge and Ideas

4. Synthesize: What details in the passage support the idea that Dubner is interested in human behavior?

Author's Argument

An **author's argument** is his or her position on a topic. Reread the blog post, and take notes on the author's argument.

1. What are Dubner's **assumptions** about boarding the bus at Point B?

2. Leaders and Followers (a) What format does Dubner use to present the possible reasons that other bus riders do not follow his example? **(b)** Which reason most clearly relates to leaders and followers?

DISCUSS • RESEARCH • WRITE

From Text to Topic **Partner Discussion**

Discuss the following passage with a partner. Take notes during the discussion. Contribute your own ideas, and support them with examples from the text.

> There is a herd at Point A; people may not *like* being part of a herd, but psychologically they are somehow comforted by it; they succumb to "herd mentality" and unthinkingly tag along—because if everyone else is doing it, it must be the thing to do.

Research **Investigate the Topic**

Herd Mentality The term "herd mentality" describes the behavior that results when people follow the crowd rather than thinking and acting for themselves.

Assignment

Conduct research to learn more about herd mentality. Consult the Internet to find sources, and make sure each source you find is accurate and credible. Take careful notes and identify your sources. Share your findings in an **informal speech** for the class.

Writing to Sources **Narrative**

"Herd Mentality? The Freakonomics of Boarding a Bus" focuses on the author's observations that people are likely to follow what the group does, even when there is a better solution to a problem.

Assignment

Write an **autobiographical narrative** in which you describe a time when you went along with the crowd or observed others doing so. Explain the situation, describe the group's behavior, and identify other options that might have been possible. Follow these steps:

- Establish the situation and the people involved.
- Use narrative techniques such as description, pacing, and dialogue. Consider using some of the techniques Dubner uses in his blog post.
- Compare your experience to Dubner's experience.
- Bring the narrative to a satisfying conclusion.

QUESTIONS FOR DISCUSSION

1. Why do people go along with the crowd?

2. What evidence in the blog post shows that not everyone will follow a crowd?

PREPARATION FOR ESSAY

You may use the results of your research to support your ideas in the essay you will write at the end of this section.

ACADEMIC VOCABULARY

Academic terms appear in blue on these pages. If these words are not familiar to you, use a dictionary to find their definitions. Then, use the words as you speak and write about the text.

 **Common Core State Standards**

RI.7.1, RI.7.2, RI.7.5, RI.7.6; W.7.3, W.7.7, W.7.8; SL.7.1.a, SL.7.6; L.7.4.a, L.7.6
[For full standards wording, see the chart in the front of this book.]

Follow the Leader: Democracy in Herd Mentality

Michael Schirber

Bees do it. Birds do it. So do fish and wildebeests. They are all able to gracefully flock or swarm in a particular direction even though not every member of the group knows where they are going.

Even human beings will tend to follow each other with a herd mentality—say, out of a crowded theater. New research provides some surprising insight into what's going on, including a group penchant for democratic decisions.

Even human beings will tend to follow each other with a herd mentality. . .

"Groups of animals move purposefully, yet often only relatively few individuals have **pertinent** information as to where to travel," said Iain Couzin of the University of Oxford.

Biologists have often wondered if there is some complex communication that goes on between the informed and the uninformed. But Couzin and his collaborators have shown in simulations that a simple set of behavioral rules can control a group.

"There's no **explicit** signaling in our model," Couzin told *LiveScience*. "No one is saying, 'I know something—come follow me.'"

The only requirement seems to be a balance between a need to stay in the group and a desire on the part of some to go off in their own preferred direction. These goal-oriented individuals look just like their naïve colleagues.

"No **inherent** differences, genetic or otherwise, such as dominance or body size, need to be invoked to explain leadership," Couzin said.

The fact that the followers in the simulation have no way to recognize who is leading them may explain how animals efficiently move in crowded environments, where they can only see their nearest neighbors.

"[This study] demonstrates the power of the little guy," said Daniel Rubenstein of Princeton University, who did not participate in the study. "You don't need avowed[1] leaders, you don't need complex signaling."

The results, published in the Feb. 3 issue of the journal *Nature*, might be useful in developing swarms of robots for exploring the oceans or other planets.

Follow the virtual leader

In computer simulations, Couzin and his colleagues programmed virtual animals with the instinct to stay near others—an important survival trait in many species. The researchers then endowed some members in the flock with a preferred direction—be it toward a food source or a new nesting site.

They then determined how close the group would come to arriving at this goal.

◄ **pertinent**
(purt´'n ənt) *adj.*
connected or related to the topic

◄ **explicit**
(eks plis´it) *adj.* clearly stated; readily seen

◄ **inherent**
(in hir´ ənt) *adj.*
natural, basic, or inborn

---

1. **avowed** (ə voud´) *adj.* openly declared.

Accuracy increased as more of the members knew where to go. But at a certain point, adding more informed individuals did not increase the accuracy by very much. To give an example, a group of 10 gets about the same advantage from having five leaders as having six.

The minimum percentage of informed individuals needed to achieve a certain level of accuracy depended on the size of the group. If 10 virtual buffaloes need 50 percent of the herd to know where the watering hole is, a group of 200 can get by with only 5 percent.

In nature, it is likely that the number of leaders is kept as low as possible. Couzin gave the example of bees, for which scouting out a new nest site is dangerous, as well as time-consuming. Studies have shown that only five percent of a hive's population gets involved with scouting.

Democratic principles

As is the case in human interactions, there will sometimes be a disagreement between those who are in the know.

For instance, there may be five individuals who know of a food supply to the east, but four others who have spotted food to the north. The researchers found that the entire group will tend to settle on the direction with the greater number of informed individuals.

"In the real world, you do have individuals with different information, needs and preferences," Couzin explained. "What we show is that—using very simple rules—the group will choose the majority. It's almost like a democratic decision."

To test whether these simple rules actually apply in real animals, Couzin's team has begun experiments in which certain fish are trained to associate one direction with a reward. These informed individuals will then be mixed with untrained fish to see if the group can be led.

Informed humans and robots

The scientists also plan to look at human crowds. Couzin thinks there may be a similar sort of mechanism to explain, say, how we walk along a busy street.

"We do it more or less on autopilot," he said.

Perhaps we are subconsciously reconciling two simple commands: get to work on time and avoid stepping on anyone's shoes.

Migrating wildebeest cross the Mara River in Africa

"The mechanism of coordination we propose is very simple and requires only limited cognitive ability," Couzin said. "This simplicity, generality and the effectiveness of the mechanism lend support to its being selected for in populations."

The simple network of commands may also be an efficient way to program teams of robots. Couzin has previously worked with researchers at Princeton University, who are designing underwater robots that can act autonomously.[2]

Robots that learn the location of a certain target could lead other robots to it without any human supervision.

---

2. autonomously (ô tän´ ə məs lē) *adv.* independently; without being controlled by others.

READ

Comprehension

Answer the following questions.

1. Why did Iain Couzin study groups of animals?

2. According to Couzin, what happens when two parts of the same group want to go in different directions to access a food supply?

3. How might the research described in this article be useful in the future?

Research: Clarify Details Conduct research on an unfamiliar detail in the article. Explain how your findings help clarify the article.

Summarize Write an objective summary of the article. Remember to leave out your opinions and evaluations.

Language Study

Selection Vocabulary Define each boldfaced term. Then, identify at least one synonym for each word.

- … relatively few individuals have **pertinent** information as to where to travel … .

- "There's no **explicit** signaling in our model … ."

- "No **inherent** differences, genetic or otherwise … need to be invoked to explain leadership … ."

Literary Analysis

Reread the passage and answer the questions.

> **Focus Passage** *(p. 615)*
>
> "Groups of animals move purposefully … just like their naïve colleagues.

Key Ideas and Details

1. **Distinguish:** What is the difference between "informed" and "uninformed" members of a group of animals?

2. What question about **transmitting** signals did biologists want to answer?

Craft and Structure

3. **(a)** Which animals are the "goal-oriented individuals"? Which animals are the "naïve colleagues"? **(b) Interpret:** What ideas about the animals do these terms convey?

Integration of Knowledge and Ideas

4. **Synthesize:** What distinguishes leaders from followers in a group of animals?

Expository Writing

In a piece of **expository writing,** the author provides explanations and information on a topic. Reread the article, and note how the author explains how groups of animals move.

1. **(a)** What behavior does the article explain? **(b)** Based on the research, is this behavior simple or **complex**?

2. **Leaders and Followers** In what ways is the behavior of humans similar to the behavior of animals?

DISCUSS • RESEARCH • WRITE

From Text to Topic **Group Discussion**

Discuss the following passage with a group of classmates. Take notes during the discussion. Contribute your own ideas, and support them with examples from the text.

> "In the real world, you do have individuals with different information, needs and preferences," Couzin explained. "What we show is that—using very simple rules—the group will choose the majority. It's almost like a democratic decision."

Research **Investigate the Topic**

Wisdom of the Crowd According to some studies, a group that acts as a whole can make smarter decisions than an individual who acts alone. This concept is referred to as "the wisdom of the crowd."

Assignment

Conduct research to learn more about the concept of "the wisdom of the crowd." Consult multiple print and Internet sources. Take detailed notes and carefully identify your sources so that you can easily access the information later. Share your findings with the class in an **informal presentation**.

Writing to Sources **Argument**

"Follow the Leader: Democracy in Herd Mentality" implies that leaders are motivated to change while followers are motivated to go along with the majority. Consider how this idea relates to the concept of "the wisdom of the crowd."

Assignment

Write an **argument** in which you agree or disagree that decisions made democratically, with each person having a say, are better than decisions made by one expert individual. Follow these steps:

- State your claim about democratic decisions versus expert decisions.
- Support your position. Provide logical reasons and relevant evidence from your own research and from the article.
- Address and **refute** counterarguments.
- Provide a concluding statement that supports your argument.

QUESTIONS FOR DISCUSSION

1. Are leaders always in the majority? Explain, using examples to support your answer.

2. For humans, is it usually a good decision to follow the majority? Explain.

PREPARATION FOR ESSAY

You may use the results of your research to support your ideas in the essay you will write at the end of this section.

ACADEMIC VOCABULARY

Academic terms appear in blue on these pages. If these words are not familiar to you, use a dictionary to find their definitions. Then, use the words as you speak and write about the text.

 **Common Core State Standards**

RI.7.1, RI.7.2, RI.7.3; W.7.1, W.7.7, W.7.8; SL.7.1.a; L.7.4.a, L.7.4.c, L.7.5.b, L.7.6
[For full standards wording, see the chart in the front of this book.]

Martin Luther King, Jr., Memorial

Washington, D.C.

Dedication ceremony, October 16, 2011

VIEW • RESEARCH • WRITE

© **Common Core State Standards**

RI.7.4; W.7.1, W.7.4, W.7.7; L.7.4.c, L.7.6
[For full standards wording, see the chart in the front of this book.]

Comprehension

View the photograph again to help you answer the following questions.

1. Examine the photograph closely and describe the memorial.

2. What is the general purpose of a memorial?

3. Why is Washington, D.C., an appropriate setting for this memorial?

Critical Analysis

Key Ideas and Details

1. **(a) Infer:** What can you tell about the setting from this photograph? **(b) Interpret:** What does the photograph show about the size of the memorial?

Craft and Structure

2. **Analyze:** Carved into the memorial are the words, "Out of the mountain of despair, a stone of hope." These lines come from King's "I Have a Dream" speech. How do these words help you **understand** the design of the memorial?

Integration of Knowledge and Ideas

3. How do you think the sculptor wanted to portray King? What features of the memorial led you to your answer?

Research **Investigate the Topic**

Memorial to a Leader Use credible Internet sources to learn how the creator of the memorial, Lei Yixin, was chosen and what inspired him. Learn more about the memorial itself, such as the **materials** used to build it, its location in Washington, D.C., and the significance of the rolled-up paper in King's hand. Share your findings in an **oral presentation** to the class.

Writing to Sources **Argument**

Write a brief **argument** in which you state your position on how effectively the photograph shows the memorial. Based on what you learned from your research, evaluate how well this photograph captures the memorial's **significance**. Remember to support your claim with reasons and evidence.

ACADEMIC VOCABULARY

Academic terms appear in blue on these pages. If these words are not familiar to you, use a dictionary to find their definitions. Then, use the words as you speak and write about the text.

Speaking and Listening: **Group Discussion**

Leaders and Followers The texts in this section vary in genre, length, style, and perspective. However, all of the texts bring up issues that relate to group behavior. The insights we can gain from literature, history, and research about people's tendency to follow the crowd relate to the Big Question this unit addresses: **Do others see us more clearly than we see ourselves?**

Assignment

Conduct discussions. With a small group of classmates, conduct a discussion about issues of leadership, following the crowd, and seeing ourselves as others do. Refer to the texts in this section, other texts you have read, and your personal experience and knowledge to support your ideas. Begin your discussion by addressing the following questions:

- What traits do leaders have?
- What motivates individuals to follow the crowd?
- How can others help us understand our own behavior?
- When is it good to follow what others are doing? When is it bad to be a follower?

Summarize and present your ideas. After you have fully explored the topic, summarize your discussion and present your findings to the class as a whole.

Criteria for Success

✓ **Organizes the group effectively**
Appoint a group leader and a timekeeper. The group leader should present the discussion questions. The timekeeper should make sure the discussion takes no longer than 20 minutes.

✓ **Maintains focus of discussion**
As a group, stay on topic and avoid straying into other subject areas.

✓ **Involves all participants equally and fully**
No one person should monopolize the conversation. Everyone should take turns speaking and contributing ideas.

✓ **Follows the rules for collegial discussion**
As each group member speaks, others should listen carefully. Build on one another's ideas and support viewpoints and opinions with sound reasoning and evidence. Express disagreement respectfully.

▲ Refer to the selections you read in Part 3 as you complete the activities on this assessment.

USE NEW VOCABULARY

As you speak and share ideas, work to use the vocabulary words you have learned in this unit. The more you use new words, the more you will "own" them.

Writing: **Narrative**

Leaders and Followers Many authors of both fiction and nonfiction want to help us see ourselves more clearly. We can better understand our own behavior—and how our behaviour relates to social forces at work in groups—by reading about leaders and followers.

Common Core State Standards

W.7.3.a–b, W.7.3.d–e; SL.7.1.a–d

[For full standards wording, see the chart in the front of this book.]

Assignment

Write an **autobiographical narrative**, a true story about your own life, in which you describe an experience you had as a member of a group. Did you follow the crowd, or did you go your own way? Explain the factors that influenced your actions. Remember that an effective autobiographical narrative explores the significance of an event in the writer's life.

Criteria for Success

Purpose/Focus

✓ **Connects specific incidents with larger ideas**
Make meaningful connections between your experiences and the texts you have read in this section.

✓ **Clearly conveys the significance of the story**
Provide a conclusion in which you reflect on what you experienced.

Organization

✓ **Sequences events logically**
Structure your narrative so that individual events build on one another to create a coherent whole.

Development of Ideas/Elaboration

✓ **Supports insights**
Include both personal examples and details from the texts you have read in this section.

✓ **Uses narrative techniques effectively**
Even though an autobiographical narrative is nonfiction, it may include storytelling elements like those found in fiction. Consider using dialogue to help readers "hear" how characters sound.

Language

✓ **Uses description effectively**
Use vivid details to help readers understand the significance of your experience.

Conventions

✓ **Does not have errors**
Check your narrative to eliminate errors in grammar, spelling, and punctuation.

WRITE TO EXPLORE

Writing is a way to clarify what you feel and think. This means that you may change your mind or get new ideas as you work. Allowing for this will improve your final draft.

Writing to Sources: **Argument**

Leaders and Followers The related readings in this section present a range of ideas about leaders and followers. They raise questions, such as the following, about individual and group behavior.

- What conflicts can arise between leaders and followers? How can these conflicts be resolved?
- What can a person learn by being a leader? What can a person learn by being a follower?
- Can someone be both a leader and a follower?
- Can historical events have meaning for human behavior today?
- How does research on animals help us understand human behavior? Is it ever wrong to make generalizations about humans based on research on animals?

INCORPORATE RESEARCH

In your essay, use information you gathered as you completed the brief research assignments related to the selections in this section.

Assignment

Write an **argumentative essay** in which you state and defend a claim about the issues surrounding leadership and the factors that motivate people to follow a group. Build evidence for your claim by analyzing the presentation of leaders and followers in two or more texts from this section. Clearly present, develop, and support your ideas with examples and details from the texts.

Prewriting and Planning

Choose texts. Review the texts in the section to determine which ones you will cite in your essay. Select at least two that will provide strong material to support your argument.

Gather details and craft a working thesis, or claim. Use a chart like the one shown to develop your claim.

Focus Question: How are group conflicts best resolved?

Text	Passage	Notes
The Monsters Are Due on Maple Street	STEVE. Wait a minute … wait a minute! Let's not be a mob!	Steve tries to stop the group before it gets out of control.
"Follow the Leader"	… they succumb to "herd mentality" and unthinkingly tag along— because if everyone else is doing it, it must be the thing to do.	"Herd mentality"; people follow group because others are going along

Example Claim: It takes more courage to be a leader in an attempt to stop a group from acting wrongly than it takes to be a follower.

Drafting

Structure your ideas and evidence. Create an informal outline or list of ideas you want to present. Decide where you will include evidence and which evidence you will use to support each point.

Address counterclaims. Strong argumentation takes differing ideas into account and addresses those ideas directly. As you organize your draft, build in sections in which you present opposing opinions or differing interpretations. Then, write a reasoned, well-supported response to those counterclaims.

Add interest to your writing. Write an introduction that will capture your readers' attention. Consider beginning with a compelling quotation or a startling fact. Use precise, vivid language to make your ideas clear and interesting.

Revising and Editing

Review content. Make sure that your claim is clearly stated and that you have supported it with convincing evidence from the texts. Underline main ideas in your paper and confirm that each one is supported. Add additional support as needed.

Review style. Revise to shorten passages that are unnecessarily wordy. Check that you have found the clearest, simplest way to communicate your ideas.

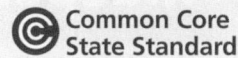

Common Core State Standards

W.7.1.a–b; L.7.3.a
[For full standards wording, see the chart in the front of this book.]

CITE RESEARCH CORRECTLY

When you quote from a source directly, use quotation marks to indicate that the words are not your own.

Self-Evaluation Rubric

Use the following criteria to evaluate the effectiveness of your essay.

Criteria	Rating Scale
	not very .... *very*
Purpose/Focus Introduces a precise claim and distinguishes the claim from (implied) alternate or opposing claims; provides a concluding section that follows from and supports the argument presented	1 2 3 4
Organization Establishes a logical organization; uses words, phrases, and clauses to link the major sections of the text, create cohesion, and clarify relationships among claims, reasons, and evidence, and between claims and counterclaims	1 2 3 4
Development of Ideas/Elaboration Develops the claim and counterclaims fairly, supplying evidence for each while pointing out the strengths and limitations of both	1 2 3 4
Language Establishes and maintains a formal style and objective tone	1 2 3 4
Conventions Uses correct conventions of grammar, spelling, and punctuation	1 2 3 4

Titles for Extended Reading

In this unit, you have read texts in a variety of genres. Continue to read on your own. Select works that you enjoy, but challenge yourself to explore new authors and works of increasing depth and complexity. The titles suggested below will help you get started.

INFORMATIONAL TEXT

Creating the X-Men: How Comic Books Come to Life
by James Buckley, Jr.

In this **nonfiction** text, comic book creators take readers behind the scenes to show how they use character, dialogue, plot, and design to bring their popular superheroes to life.

Gandhi: A Photographic Story of a Life
by Amy Pastan

Gandhi proved that nonviolent, peaceful movements can succeed in creating powerful changes. His **biography** shows the impact one person can have, even when confronting a mighty empire.

A Night to Remember   EXEMPLAR TEXT ©
by Walter Lord

This work of **historical nonfiction,** based on true accounts by survivors of the *Titanic,* details the sinking of the famous ship.

LITERATURE

Roald Dahl's Charlie and the Chocolate Factory: A Play
Adapted by Richard R. George

In this **play,** adapted from Dahl's novel, poor Charlie Bucket wins one of five golden tickets to tour Willy Wonka's chocolate factory. As his spoiled competitors start disappearing, the question remains: Can Charlie outlast the others in Wonka's fun-house world of chocolate rivers and everlasting chewing gum?

Eight Science Fiction Plays

In this wide-ranging science fiction collection, you will find **plays** such as *Only Slightly Different* by Bruce Goldstone and *A Clash of Wills* by Mary Canrobert.

Sorry, Wrong Number *and* The Hitchhiker
by Lucille Fletcher   EXEMPLAR TEXT ©
Dramatists Play Service, Inc., 1998

In the first of these two suspenseful **plays,** a woman overhears a murder plot. In the second, a man on a cross-country trip is followed by a ghostly hitchhiker.

Dragonwings   EXEMPLAR TEXT ©
by Laurence Yep
Dramatists Play Service, Inc., 1998

In this **play,** set in the early twentieth century, eight-year-old Moon Shadow sails from China to San Francisco to live with his father, whom he has never met. He quickly comes to admire his fascinating father, Windrider, who dreams of building a flying machine and is willing to endure scorn, hardship, and prejudice to make his dream come true.

ONLINE TEXT SET

POEM
Loo Wit Wendy Rose

QUESTION AND ANSWER ARTICLE
What Gives the Sunrise and Sunset its Orange Glow? GantDaily

AFRICAN AMERICAN FOLK TALE
How the Snake Got Poison Zora Neale Hurston

Preparing to Read Complex Texts

Attentive Reading As you read on your own, ask yourself questions like these to enrich your reading experience.

When reading drama, ask yourself...

Comprehension: **Key Ideas and Details**

- Who is the main character? What struggles does this character face?
- What other characters are important? How do these characters relate to the main character?
- Where and when does the play take place? Do the time and place of the setting affect the characters? If so, how?
- Do the characters, settings, and events seem real? Why or why not?
- How does the play end? How does the ending make me feel?

Text Analysis: **Craft and Structure**

- Does the play have a narrator? If so, what information does the narrator provide?
- How many acts are in this play? What happens in each act?
- Does the dialogue sound like real speech? Are there specific passages that seem especially real? Are there any that seem false?
- What do the stage directions tell me about the ways characters move, speak, and feel? In what other ways do I learn about the characters?
- At what point in the play do I feel the most suspense? Why?
- What speech or passage in the play do I like the most? Why?
- Does the playwright seem to have a positive or a negative point of view? How do I think the playwright's point of view affects the story?
- Do I agree with the playwright's point of view? Why or why not?

Connections: **Integration of Knowledge and Ideas**

- Does the play remind me of others I have read or seen? If so, how?
- In what ways is the play different from others I have read or seen?
- What new information or ideas have I gained from reading this play?
- What actors would I choose to play each role in this play?
- If I were to be in this play, what role would I want?
- Would I recommend this play to others? Why or why not?

**Common Core
State Standards**

**Reading Literature/
Informational Text**
10. By the end of the year, read and comprehend literature, including stories, dramas, and poems, and literary nonfiction in the grades 6–8 text complexity band proficiently, with scaffolding as needed at the high end of the range.

THE BIG
?

Community or individual—which is more important?

UNIT PATHWAY

PART 1
SETTING
EXPECTATIONS

- INTRODUCING
  THE BIG QUESTION
- CLOSE READING
  WORKSHOP

PART 2
TEXT ANALYSIS
GUIDED EXPLORATION

EXPLAINING THE WORLD

PART 3
TEXT SET
DEVELOPING INSIGHT

BECOMING AMERICAN

PART 4
DEMONSTRATING
INDEPENDENCE

- INDEPENDENT
  READING
- ONLINE TEXT SET

CLOSE READING TOOL

Use this tool to practice the close reading strategies you learn.

STUDENT eTEXT

Bring learning to life with audio, video, and interactive tools.

ONLINE WRITER'S NOTEBOOK

Easily capture notes and complete assignments online.

Find all Digital Resources at **pearsonrealize.com.**

Community or individual— which is more important?

In many parts of our lives, we celebrate the individual—encouraging people to reach their personal best and to pursue their own dreams. Each individual has unique qualities and beliefs. However, an individual may also be part of a family or group that shares common cultural beliefs, traditions, or customs. Even these families and groups are part of a larger community.

Communities help individuals by providing services, support, and opportunities. Yet, sometimes the rights or desires of an individual may conflict with those of his or her community. In these cases, it can be difficult to find a fair solution.

Exploring the Big Question

Collaboration: One-on-One Discussion Start thinking about the Big Question by making a list of conflicts between individuals and their communities. Describe one specific example of each of the following situations:

- A school rule that students do not believe is fair
- A situation in which one family member does not want to do what the rest of the family is doing
- A sacrifice that one person is asked to make in order to help many others
- A decision made by someone in power that affects a large group of people

Share your examples with a partner. For each example, discuss whether the interests of the community or the individual seem more important. Use the vocabulary words on the next page in your discussion.

Connecting to the Literature Each reading in this unit will give you additional insight into the Big Question.

Vocabulary

Acquire and Use Academic Vocabulary The term "academic vocabulary" refers to words you typically encounter in scholarly and literary texts and in technical and business writing. Review the definitions of these academic vocabulary words.

common (käm´ ən) *adj.* shared; public

community (kə myōō´ nə tē) *n.* group of people who share an interest or who live near each other

culture (kul´ chər) *n.* customs of a group or community

diversity (də vʉr´ sə tē) *n.* variety, as of groups or cultures

duty (dōōt´ ē) *n.* responsibility

environment (en vī´ rən mənt) *n.* surroundings; the natural world

individual (in´də vij´ ōō əl) *n.* single person or thing

team (tēm) *n.* group with a common goal

tradition (trə dish´ ən) *n.* customs, as of a social group or culture

unify (yōō´ nə fī´) *v.* bring together as one

unique (yōō nēk´) *adj.* one of a kind

Common Core State Standards

Speaking and Listening
1. Engage effectively in a range of collaborative discussions with diverse partners on *grade 7 topics, texts, and issues,* building on others' ideas and expressing their own clearly.

Language
6. Acquire and use accurately grade-appropriate general academic and domain-specific words and phrases; gather vocabulary knowledge when considering a word or phrase important to comprehension or expression.

Gather Vocabulary Knowledge Additional words related to community and the individual are listed below. Categorize the words by deciding whether you know each one well, know it a little bit, or do not know it at all.

custom	family	group
ethnicity		

Then, do the following:

1. Discuss the meaning of each word with a partner. Then, verify each meaning using a dictionary.
2. Next, use each word in an original paragraph that gives examples of what community and individuality mean to you. Provide context clues for every vocabulary word you use.
3. Remember that context clues might be definitions, synonyms, antonyms, examples, or explanations.
4. Finally, take turns reading your paragraph with a partner. If, during the readings, the meaning of any vocabulary word is still unclear, work with your partner to clarify it.

Close Reading Workshop

In this workshop you will learn an approach to reading that will deepen your understanding of literature and will help you better appreciate the author's craft. The workshop includes models for close reading, discussion, research, and writing. After you have reviewed the strategies and models, practice your skills with the Independent Practice selection.

 **Common Core State Standards**

RL.7.1, RL.7.2, RL.7.3; W.7.2.b, W.7.7, W.7.9.a; SL.7.1
[For full standards wording, see the chart in the front of this book.]

CLOSE READING: **THE ORAL TRADITION**

Use these strategies as you read the texts in Part 2.

Comprehension: **Key Ideas and Details**

- Use context clues to help you determine the meanings of unfamiliar words.
- Identify unfamiliar details that you might need to clarify through research.
- Distinguish between what is stated directly and what must be inferred.

Ask yourself questions such as these:
- What unique qualities do the characters exhibit?
- What motivates the characters to act as they do?
- What conflicts do the characters encounter?

Text Analysis: **Craft and Structure**

- Think about the genre of the work and how the author presents ideas.
- Analyze how the setting influences characters and story events.
- Identify elements of folk literature, including the use of fantasy, exaggeration, and repeated patterns.

Ask yourself questions such as these:
- How does the author's purpose determine the form of folk literature?
- What details in the story reflect the background, customs, and beliefs of the culture from which the story comes?
- What insight does the story present?

Connections: **Integration of Knowledge and Ideas**

- Look for relationships among key ideas.
- Look for repeated patterns or ideas and analyze their deeper meaning. Then, synthesize to determine the theme or central insight conveyed by the author.

Ask yourself questions such as these:
- How has this work increased my knowledge of a culture, an author, or the genre of folk literature?
- What is the moral of this story?
- What theme, or insight about life, does this work express?

Read

As you read this fable, take note of the annotations that model ways to closely read the text.

Reading Model

"The Travelers and the Bear" from *Aesop's Fables* retold by Jerry Pinkney

Two men were traveling through the forest together on a lonely trail. Soon they heard a sound up ahead as if heavy feet were trampling through the underbrush.[1]

"It could be a bear!" one whispered with alarm, and quickly as he could, he scrambled up a tall tree. He had barely reached the first branch when a huge brown bear thrust aside the bushes and stepped out onto the path.[2]

Hugging the trunk with both arms, the first traveler refused to lend a hand to his terrified companion,[3] who threw himself on the ground and prepared for death.

The bear lowered its great head and sniffed at the man, ruffling his hair with its nose. Then, to the amazement of both men, the fierce beast walked away.

The first traveler slid down from his tree. "Why, it almost looked as if the bear whispered something in your ear," he marveled.

"It did," said the second traveler.[4] "It told me to choose a better companion for my next journey."

Misfortune is the true test of friendship.[5]

Craft and Structure

1 The forest is a typical threatening setting in folk literature. The words *lonely* and *heavy* suggest that the travelers may encounter something dangerous.

Key Ideas and Details

2 You may sense that the threatening appearance of the bear will propel the story's action forward.

Craft and Structure

3 Folk literature often features *flat,* or one-sided, characters who display one main trait, such as the first traveler's selfish lack of concern for his companion.

Craft and Structure

4 The bear "whispered" to the second traveler. In folk literature, animal characters often behave like humans.

Integration of Knowledge and Ideas

5 As is often the case in fables, the author directly states the moral, or lesson, in the last line. This technique makes the theme of the story very clear to readers.

Discuss

Sharing your own ideas and listening to the ideas of others can deepen your understanding of a text and help you look at a topic in a whole new way. As you participate in collaborative discussions, work to have a genuine exchange in which classmates build upon one another's ideas. Support your points with evidence and ask meaningful questions.

Discussion Model

Student 1: I was really surprised when the bear walked away. I was sure it would attack the second traveler.

Student 2: I thought it was more surprising that the bear whispered to the man. I wonder why the author gave the bear the human ability to speak. Maybe this contributes to the fable's meaning and theme.

Student 3: I think the bear's ability to speak is crucial to the theme. The author ends with a moral: "Misfortune is the true test of friendship." If the bear couldn't speak, this lesson might be lost.

Student 4: I agree. Jerry Pinkney probably decided to retell this fable because its message still has meaning today.

Research

Targeted research can clarify unfamiliar details and shed light on various aspects of a text. Consider questions that arise in your mind as you read, and use those questions as the basis for research.

Research Model

Question: *Why does Jerry Pinkney's retelling of Aesop's fable have meaning today?*

Key Words for Internet Search: Pinkney AND fable

Result: *The New York Times,* "The Same Old Stories," a book review by Rosemary Wells

What I Learned: In a review of three books of fables, Rosemary Wells refers to the universal appeal of fables today. She attributes this appeal to the fact that fables provide valuable, timeless lessons in brief, action-packed stories. She praises Pinkney's retelling and attributes his understanding of the fables to the important role they played in his childhood view of the world.

Write

Writing about a text will deepen your understanding of it and will also allow you to share your ideas more formally with others. The following model essay evaluates the universal appeal of Aesop's fables and cites evidence to support the main ideas.

Writing Model: Informative Text

The Universal Appeal of Fables

According to *New York Times* book reviewer Rosemary Wells, fables have universal appeal. Jerry Pinkney's retelling of Aesop's "The Travelers and the Bear" is an example that shows how a fable can effectively convey a universal message with a brief story. Through the short, eventful story, Pinkney demonstrates the basic wisdom that characterizes a long tradition of fables.

> Introducing the focus of the essay in the first paragraph is an effective way to begin a short response assignment.

One appeal of Aesop's fables is that the stories are usually short and to the point. Wells writes, "The fables are compact, action-filled—the reader, or listener, must charge into the story's full-blown drama in the first sentence." In "The Travelers and the Bear," Pinkney retells Aesop's fable in under 200 words. In the first two sentences, he sets the scene. He introduces characters, describes the setting, and advances the action of the story all within the first paragraph. Despite the short length of the introduction, the author is able to create a sense of danger and mystery, "Soon they heard a sound up ahead as if heavy feet were trampling through the underbrush."

> The writer introduces the first claim with a clear topic sentence.

> The writer concludes this paragraph by supporting the claim with a quotation from the selection.

Another reason Aesop's fables have universal appeal is the clarity of the lesson or moral, which is traditionally summarized in one sentence at the end of the story. Wells is critical of renditions of Aesop's fables that neglect to include these summarizing sentences, which she calls "part and parcel of Aesop." In "The Travelers and the Bear," Pinkney maintains this tradition, by directly stating the moral: "Misfortune is the true test of friendship." The clarity of the moral in Aesop's fables makes the fables accessible to readers and listeners of all ages. Wells explains, "Without it, children must draw their own conclusions about the story's meaning."

> Evidence from research effectively supports the claim introduced in the third paragraph.

Aesop's fables have been an important part of the oral tradition for centuries. They have been retold by different cultures all over the world. Despite originating more than 2,000 years ago, Aesop's fables have endured and continue to have universal appeal for modern listeners and readers of all ages.

> The essay ends with a strong concluding statement that restates and clarifies the main idea.

As you read the following selections, apply the close reading strategies you have learned. You may need to read the stories multiple times.

Before he wrote books, **Jon Scieszka** (SHEH ska) (b. 1954) worked as a house painter, a lifeguard, and a teacher. One of his favorite books is also one of the first books he ever read—Dr. Seuss's *Green Eggs and Ham.* It showed Scieszka "that books could be goofy."

CLOSE READING TOOL

Read and respond to this selection online using the **Close Reading Tool.**

"Grasshopper Logic" from *Squids Will Be Squids*

by Jon Scieszka and Lane Smith

One bright and sunny day, Grasshopper came home from school, dropped his backpack, and was just about to run outside to meet his friends.

"Where are you going?" asked his mom.

"Out to meet some friends," said Grasshopper.

"Do you have any homework due tomorrow?" asked his mom.

"Just one small thing for History. I did the rest in class."

"Okay" said Mom Grasshopper. "Be back at six for dinner."

Grasshopper hung out with his friends, came home promptly at six, ate his dinner, then took out his History homework.

His mom read the assignment and freaked out.

"Rewrite twelve Greek myths as Broadway musicals. Write music for songs. Design and build all sets. Sew original costumes for each production."

"How long have you known about this assignment?" asked Mom Grasshopper, trying not to scream.

"I don't know," said Grasshopper.

Moral

There are plenty of things to say to calm a hopping mad Grasshopper mom. "I don't know" is not one.

"The Other Frog Prince" from *The Stinky Cheese Man and Other Fairly Stupid Tales*

by Jon Scieszka and Lane Smith

Once upon a time there was a frog. One day when he was sitting on his lily pad, he saw a beautiful princess sitting by the pond. He hopped in the water, swam over to her, and poked his head out of the weeds.

"Pardon me, O beautiful princess," he said in his most sad and pathetic voice. "I wonder if you could help me."

The princess was about to jump up and run, but she felt sorry for the frog with the sad and pathetic voice.

So she asked, "What can I do to help you, little frog?"

"Well," said the frog. "I'm not really a frog, but a handsome prince who was turned into a frog by a wicked witch's spell. And the spell can only be broken by the kiss of a beautiful princess."

The princess thought about this for a second, then lifted the frog from the pond and kissed him.

"I was just kidding," said the frog. He jumped back into the pond and the princess wiped the frog slime off her lips.

The End.

"Duckbilled Platypus vs. BeefSnakStik®" from *Squids Will Be Squids*

by Jon Scieszka and Lane Smith

"I have a bill like a duck and a tail like a beaver," bragged Duckbilled Platypus.

"So what?" said BeefSnakStik®. "I have beef, soy protein concentrate, and dextrose."

"I also have webbed feet and fur," said Duckbilled Platypus.

"Who cares?" said BeefSnakStik®. "I also have smoke flavoring, sodium erythorbate, and sodium nitrite."

"I am one of only two mammals in the world that lay eggs," said Duckbilled Platypus.

"Big deal," said BeefSnakStik®. "I have beef lips."

Moral
Just because you have a lot of stuff, don't think you're so special.

Close Reading Activities

Read

Comprehension: Key Ideas and Details

1. (a) Summarize: Summarize the plot of each story, making sure not to include your own opinions or judgments. **(b) Analyze:** Which of the stories has a surprise ending?

2. (a) Infer: Why does Grasshopper call his History assignment "small"? **(b) Generalize:** What makes the details

of the assignment funny? Cite an example from the text.

3. (a) Describe: What is the argument between Duckbilled Platypus and BeefSnakStik® about? **(b) Draw Conclusions:** Why is neither of these characters likely to win the argument?

Text Analysis: Craft and Structure

4. (a) Analyze: How does the author make the moral of each tale funny? **(b) Evaluate:** In your opinion, which story is the funniest, and why?

5. (a) Describe: What tone of voice does the frog use with the princess? **(b) Compare:** Does the frog have the same attitude

or tone of voice as BeefSnakStik®? **(c)** What makes these characters funny?

6. (a) Interpret: Explain the attitude toward life and literature that the fables reflect. **(b) Apply:** Is one type of reader more likely than other types to appreciate this attitude? Explain.

Connections: Integration of Knowledge and Ideas

Discuss
Conduct a **small group discussion** about the ways the three Scieszka stories reflect common elements of traditional folk literature. For example, consider surprise endings, animals that talk and act like people, and the way the author conveys themes. Use textual examples to support your points.

Research
Fables and fairy tales are two common types of folk literature. Briefly research the similarities and differences between these two types of stories. Consider these elements:
a. stylistic elements
b. common character types
c. types of themes or morals

Take notes as you research. Then, write a brief **comparison** of fables and fairy tales.

Write
Writers often use unexpected combinations of reality and fantasy to create humor. Write an **essay** in which you analyze the humorous elements in Scieszka's stories and explain the techniques the author uses to create humor. Use details from the texts to support your analysis.

 Community or individual— which is more important?
Are the morals in Scieszka's stories more useful to an individual or to a community as a whole? Explain.

"The **songs** of our **ancestors** are also the **songs** of our **children**."

—**Philip Carr-Gomm**

EXPLAINING THE WORLD

As you read the selections in this section, analyze the insights about life and human nature that the authors present through various forms of folk literature. The quotation on the opposite page will help you start to think about the ways in which the traditional tales of our ancestors can still guide us in explaining and celebrating the world around us.

◄ **CRITICAL VIEWING** People pass down traditions through stories, celebrations, and clothing, such as that worn by the woman in this photograph. What is the value of preserving cultural traditions?

READINGS IN PART 2

GREEK MYTH
Demeter and Persephone
Anne Terry White
(p. 648)

MEXICAN LEGEND
Popocatepetl and Ixtlaccihuatl
Juliet Piggott Wood
(p. 660)

ZUNI FOLK TALE
Sun and Moon in a Box
Alfonso Ortiz and Richard Erdoes (p. 674)

AFRICAN EXEMPLAR TEXT ⓒ
AMERICAN FOLK TALE
The People Could Fly
Virginia Hamilton
(p. 684)

CLOSE READING TOOL

Use the **Close Reading Tool** to practice the strategies you learn in this unit.

Elements of Folk Literature

Folk literature is a genre of writing that has its roots in the oral tradition.

The Oral Tradition Stories were told long before reading and writing began. These stories were handed down through the ages by word of mouth. The sharing of stories by word of mouth is called the **oral tradition.**

Folk literature is a genre of writing that originated in the oral tradition. Once writing and books were invented, the stories were collected and retold in print. Myths, legends, folk tales, and fables are all forms of folk literature.

The Importance of the Storyteller Stories in the oral tradition were created thousands of years ago. No one knows for sure who the first storytellers were. As stories were passed down, new storytellers added and changed details. These details reflected the storyteller's roots and **cultural perspective,** or view of the world. That viewpoint was shaped by the storyteller's background and experiences.

Theme is the central idea, message, or insight about life that a story conveys.

Some works of folk literature have **universal themes**—themes that are repeated across many cultures and over many time periods. They express insights into life and human nature that many people understand and find important. The struggle of good against evil is an example of a universal theme.

Other works of folk literature— especially fables—present their theme in the form of a **moral.** A moral is a lesson about life that is stated directly, usually at the very end of the work.

Purposes of Folk Literature The **purpose** of a piece of literature is the reason it was written. The purpose of some forms of folk literature may be to explain or teach. For example, a myth may explain a natural phenomenon, and a fable may teach a lesson about life. Other types of folk literature may have the simple purpose of entertaining readers.

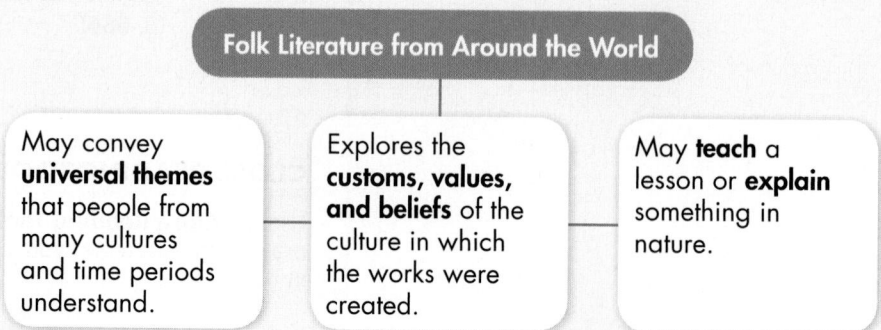

Folk Literature from Around the World

May convey **universal themes** that people from many cultures and time periods understand.

Explores the **customs, values, and beliefs** of the culture in which the works were created.

May **teach** a lesson or **explain** something in nature.

Forms of Folk Literature

Myths are tales that relate the actions of gods, goddesses, and the heroes who interact with them. Many cultures have their own collections of myths, or **mythology.**

Legends are traditional stories based on real-life events. As these stories are told and retold, fact often changes to fiction, and the characters often become larger than life.

Tall tales often focus on a central hero who performs impossible feats.

Folk tales may deal with real people or magical characters. They reflect the values and beliefs of the culture in which they were created.

Fables are brief stories or poems that often feature animal characters who act and speak like humans. They usually end with a moral that is directly stated.

Epics are long narrative poems important to the history of a nation or culture. They tell of a larger-than-life hero who goes on a dangerous journey, or **quest.**

Common Core State Standards

Reading Literature
2. Determine a theme or central idea of a text and analyze its development over the course of the text; provide an objective summary of the text.

Characteristics of Folk Literature

Here are some common characteristics you will see as you read folk literature.

Characteristic	Definition	Often Featured In...
Heroes and heroines	Larger-than-life figures who overcome obstacles or participate in exciting adventures	Myths Legends Epics
Trickster	A clever character who can fool others but often gets into trouble	Folk tales Fables
Personification	A type of figurative language in which nonhuman subjects are given human qualities	Myths Fables
Hyperbole	A type of figurative language that uses exaggeration, either for comic effect or to express strong emotion	Tall tales Myths Epics
Dialect	Language spoken by people in a particular region or group	Tall tales Folk tales

Analyzing Structure and Theme in Folk Literature

The **structural elements** of a work of folk literature contribute to its **theme**, or insight about life and human nature.

Folk literature is rich with humor, adventure, romance, suspense, and drama. At the same time, it is the themes of these stories that have made them meaningful to readers of many generations and cultures.

Stated Themes Themes in folk literature take different forms. Sometimes, the theme is directly stated at the end of the story as a moral, or lesson. For example, look at the retelling of Aesop's fable, "The Lion and the Mouse."

> ### Example: The Lion and the Mouse
>
> A tiny mouse accidentally crossed paths with a ferocious lion. The lion was about to eat the mouse, when the mouse pleaded with the lion to let him go. "If you do, I promise to help you one day," the mouse said. The mighty lion doubted he would ever need the help of a tiny mouse, but he let the mouse go. One day, the lion became trapped in a hunter's net. The little mouse heard the lion's roars and came to his aid. In a few minutes, the mouse had gnawed his way through the net, setting the lion free.
>
> **Moral:** *One act of kindness often leads to another.*

Implied Themes As in other literary genres, themes in folk literature are sometimes implied, or suggested, rather than stated. Clues to these themes lie in the details that describe setting, characters, and plot. Stories with implied themes require the reader to analyze the details to see what they reveal about the deeper meaning of the story.

Universal Themes A universal theme is an insight or lesson that appears in literature across cultures and throughout different periods in history. These themes are "universal" because they express ideas that are meaningful to most people. Here are a few universal themes that are commonly found in folk literature. They reflect ideas that have been understood for many generations.

- Goodness is eventually rewarded.
- Inner beauty is more important than outward appearance.
- Those who always want more are never satisfied.
- Cleverness and courage can overcome brute strength.

Folk literature of various types contains structural elements that contribute to the development of theme. As you read, look for these elements.

Repetition Folk literature often features the repetition of events, dialogue, descriptions, and sound patterns. Repetition adds rhythm to the text. It can also help build suspense and emphasize main ideas. For example, in the well-known tale of "The Three Little Pigs," the following lines of dialogue are repeated three times.

Example: Repetition
"Little pig, little pig, let me come in." "Not by the hair of my chinny chin chin." "Then I'll huff, and I'll puff, and I'll blow your house in."

Patterns Many works of folk literature share a common pattern, or repeated element. For example, many stories begin and end with such familiar phrases as "Once upon a time" and "They lived happily ever after." Another common structural element found in folk literature is the pattern of three. Many stories feature three important characters, three wishes, or three tasks.

Archetypes An archetype is an element that occurs regularly in literature from around the world and throughout history. Oral storytellers have used archetypes to convey such universal themes as the power of love or the importance of bravery. Here are some common archetypes found in folk literature:

Plot	• a dangerous journey • a struggle between a good character and an evil one • an explanation of how something came to be
Characters	• a brave hero • trickster, or wise fool • talking animals
Ideas	• magic in the normal world • hero or heroine helped by supernatural forces • evil disguised as good

Flat Characters Folk literature often features characters who seem to have only one main trait, such as kindness, cruelty, wisdom, or foolishness. Such characters are **flat,** or one-sided. They are not like real people, who usually have many different sides to their personalities. Flat characters can help storytellers express important themes. For example, in "Snow White," the evil queen remains evil throughout the tale, while Snow White herself remains kind and good. Together, these opposing characters help develop the theme that kindness is stronger than cruelty.

Building Knowledge

 Community or individual—which is more important?

Think about the Big Question as you read "Demeter and Persephone." Take notes on the ways in which the myth explores the concepts of community and the individual.

CLOSE READING FOCUS

Key Ideas and Details: **Cause and Effect**

A **cause** is an event, action, or feeling that produces a result. That result is called an **effect**. In some literary works, multiple causes result in a single effect. In other works, a single cause results in multiple effects. Effects can also become causes for events that follow. In a narrative, this linking of causes and effects propels the action forward. To analyze cause-and-effect relationships, ask yourself questions, such as *What happened? Why?* and *What will happen as a result of this?*

Craft and Structure: **Myth**

Since time began, people have tried to understand the world around them. Ancient peoples created **myths**—stories that explain natural occurrences and express beliefs about right and wrong. Most myths were composed orally and then passed from generation to generation by word of mouth. Every ancient culture has its own mythology, or collection of myths. Greek and Roman myths are known collectively as *classical mythology.*

In many myths, gods and goddesses have human traits, while human heroes possess superhuman traits. As you read, notice the ways that myths explain the world and explore universal themes.

Vocabulary

You will encounter the following words in this myth. Copy the words into your notebook. Circle the words that you think relate to ruling or governing a community of people.

defies	monarch	dominions
intervene	realm	abode

Meet the Author

Anne Terry White (1896–1980) was born in Ukraine, which was then part of Russia. She was one of the leading writers of nonfiction for children. White's first two books were *Heroes of the Five Books,* a look at figures of the Old Testament, and *Three Children and Shakespeare,* a family discussion of four of Shakespeare's plays. She wrote these books to introduce her own children to great works of literature. In addition to being a writer, White was an editor, a translator, and an authority on ancient Greece.

Common Core State Standards

Reading Literature
3. Analyze how particular elements of a story or drama interact (e.g., how setting shapes the characters or plot).

Language
4.b. Use common, grade-appropriate Greek or Latin affixes and roots as clues to the meaning of a word.

CLOSE READING MODEL

The passage below is from Anne Terry White's myth "Demeter and Persephone." The annotations to the right of the passage show ways in which you can use close reading skills to analyze cause-and-effect relationships and explore the elements of a myth.

from **"Demeter and Persephone"**

Now the goddess of love and beauty, fair Aphrodite, was sitting on a mountainside playing with her son, Eros.[1] She saw Pluto as he drove around with his coal-black horses and she said:

"My son, there is one who defies your power and mine. Quick! Take up your darts! Send an arrow into the breast of that dark monarch. Let him, too, feel the pangs of love. Why should he alone escape them?"[2]

At his mother's words, Eros leaped lightly to his feet. He chose from his quiver his sharpest and truest arrow, fitted it to his bow, drew the string, and shot straight into Pluto's heart.

The grim King had seen fair maids enough in the gloomy underworld over which he ruled. But never had his heart been touched. Now an unaccustomed warmth stole through his veins. His stern eyes softened.[3] Before him was a blossoming valley, and along its edge a charming girl was gathering flowers. She was Persephone, daughter of Demeter, goddess of the harvest.[4] She had strayed from her companions, and now that her basket overflowed with blossoms, she was filling her apron with lilies and violets. The god looked at Persephone and loved her at once.

Myth
1 The reference to Aphrodite as the "goddess of love and beauty" gives you a clue that this story is a myth. Like Aphrodite and Eros, mythical gods often possess human traits and exhibit human behavior.

Cause and Effect
2 Aphrodite resents Pluto because he "defies" her power—the power of love. As a result, she orders Eros to shoot Pluto with an arrow that will cause him to feel love. Note the effects of this action as you read on.

Cause and Effect
3 This sentence shows the immediate effect caused by Eros's arrow. You may guess that this event will cause other effects that will propel the action forward.

Myth
4 Mythical gods often rule over important aspects of human life. This detail about Demeter may help you infer that the harvest was important to the ancient Greeks, who first told this myth.

Demeter and Persephone

Anne Terry White

eep under Mt. Aetna, the gods had buried alive a number of fearful, fire-breathing giants. The monsters heaved and struggled to get free. And so mightily did they shake the earth that Pluto, the king of the underworld, was alarmed.

"They may tear the rocks asunder and leave the realm of the dead open to the light of day," he thought. And mounting his golden chariot, he went up to see what damage had been done.

Now the goddess of love and beauty, fair Aphrodite (af´ rə dīt´ ē), was sitting on a mountainside playing with her son, Eros.[1] She saw Pluto as he drove around with his coal-black horses and she said:

"My son, there is one who **defies** your power and mine. Quick! Take up your darts! Send an arrow into the breast of that dark **monarch**. Let him, too, feel the pangs of love. Why should he alone escape them?"

At his mother's words, Eros leaped lightly to his feet. He chose from his quiver[2] his sharpest and truest arrow, fitted it to his bow, drew the string, and shot straight into Pluto's heart.

The grim King had seen fair maids enough in the gloomy underworld over which he ruled. But never had his heart been touched. Now an unaccustomed warmth stole through his veins. His stern eyes softened. Before him was a blossoming valley, and along its edge a charming girl was gathering flowers. She was Persephone (pər sef´ ə nē), daughter of Demeter (di mēt´ ər), goddess of the harvest. She had strayed from her companions, and now that her basket overflowed with blossoms, she was filling her apron with lilies and violets. The god looked at Persephone and loved her at once. With one sweep of his arm he caught her up and drove swiftly away.

"Mother!" she screamed, while the flowers fell from her apron and strewed the ground. "Mother!"

And she called on her companions by name. But already they were out of sight, so fast did Pluto urge the horses on.

She saw Pluto as he drove around with his coal-black horses...

---

1. **Eros** (er´ äs) in Greek mythology, the god of love; identified by the Romans as Cupid.
2. **quiver** (kwiv´ ər) case for arrows.

In a few moments they were at the River Cyane.[3] Persephone struggled, her loosened girdle[4] fell to the ground, but the god held her tight. He struck the bank with his trident.[5] The earth opened, and darkness swallowed them all—horses, chariot, Pluto, and weeping Persephone.

From end to end of the earth Demeter sought her daughter. But none could tell her where Persephone was. At last, worn out and despairing, the goddess returned to Sicily. She stood by the River Cyane, where Pluto had cleft the earth and gone down into his own dominions.

Now a river nymph[6] had seen him carry off his prize. She wanted to tell Demeter where her daughter was, but fear of Pluto kept her dumb. Yet she had picked up the girdle Persephone had dropped, and this the nymph wafted[7] on the waves to the feet of Demeter.

The goddess knew then that her daughter was gone indeed, but she did not suspect Pluto of carrying her off. She laid the blame on the innocent land.

"Ungrateful soil!" she said. "I made you fertile. I clothed you in grass and nourishing grain, and this is how you reward me. No more shall you enjoy my favors!"

That year was the most cruel mankind had ever known. Nothing prospered, nothing grew. The cattle died, the seed would not come up, men and oxen toiled in vain. There was too much sun. There was too much rain. Thistles[8] and weeds were the only things that grew. It seemed that all mankind would die of hunger.

"This cannot go on," said mighty Zeus. "I see that I must intervene." And one by one he sent the gods and goddesses to plead with Demeter.

Myth
What details in this paragraph reveal that the story is a myth?

◀ **Vocabulary**
dominions (də min´ yəns) *n.* governed countries or territories
intervene (in tər vēn´) *v.* come between in an effort to influence or help settle an action or argument

Comprehension
Who is Pluto?

---

3. **River Cyane** (sī an) a river in Sicily, an island just south of Italy.
4. **girdle** (gurd´ əl) *n.* belt or sash for the waist.
5. **trident** (trīd´ ənt) *n.* spear with three points.
6. **river nymph** (nimf) *n.* goddess living in a river.
7. **wafted** (wäft´ əd) *n.* carried.
8. **thistles** (this´ əlz) *n.* stubborn, weedy plants with sharp leaves and usually purplish flowers.

But she had the same answer for all: "Not till I see my daughter shall the earth bear fruit again."

Zeus, of course, knew well where Persephone was. He did not like to take from his brother the one joyful thing in his life, but he saw that he must if the race of man was to be preserved. So he called Hermes[9] to him and said:

"Descend to the underworld, my son. Bid Pluto release his bride. Provided she has not tasted food in the **realm** of the dead, she may return to her mother forever."

Down sped Hermes on his winged feet, and there in the dim palace of the king, he found Persephone by Pluto's side. She was pale and joyless. Not all the glittering treasures of the underworld could bring a smile to her lips.

"You have no flowers here," she would say to her husband when he pressed gems upon her. "Jewels have no fragrance. I do not want them."

When she saw Hermes and heard his message, her heart leaped within her. Her cheeks grew rosy and her eyes

Vocabulary ▶
realm (relm)
n. kingdom

---

9. **Hermes** (hŭr´ mēz) a god who served as a messenger.

Mythology Connection

Gods and Goddesses

The ancient Greeks and Romans had different names for their gods and goddesses. In the diagram below, the Roman name for the god or goddess is given in parentheses. In their traditions, each god and goddess had control or power in a different area.

Poseidon (Neptune) god of the sea   **Zeus** (Jupiter) ruler of gods and men   **Hera** (Juno) goddess of marriage   **Demeter** (Ceres) goddess of agriculture   **Hades** (Pluto) god of the underworld

Hermes (Mercury) messenger of the gods   **Aphrodite** (Venus) goddess of beauty   **Ares** (Mars) god of war   **Athena** (Minerva) goddess of wisdom   **Persephone** (Proserpina) goddess of springtime

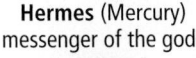 **Connect to the Literature**   **Why do you think that ancient peoples told stories about gods and goddesses such as Demeter and Persephone?**

---

sparkled, for she knew that Pluto would not dare to disobey his brother's command. She sprang up, ready to go at once. Only one thing troubled her—that she could not leave the underworld forever. For she had accepted a pomegranate[10] from Pluto and sucked the sweet pulp from four of the seeds.

With a heavy heart Pluto made ready his golden car.[11] He helped Persephone in while Hermes took up the reins.

"Dear wife," said the King, and his voice trembled as he spoke, "think kindly of me, I pray you. For indeed I love you truly. It will be lonely here these eight months you are away.

Comprehension
What does Zeus want Pluto to do?

---

10. **pomegranate** (päm´ ə gran´ it) *n.* round fruit with a red leathery rind and many seeds.
11. **car** (kär) *n.* chariot.

And if you think mine is a gloomy palace to return to, at least remember that your husband is great among the immortals. So fare you well—and get your fill of flowers!"

Straight to the temple of Demeter at Eleusis, Hermes drove the black horses. The goddess heard the chariot wheels and, as a deer bounds over the hills, she ran out swiftly to meet her daughter. Persephone flew to her mother's arms. And the sad tale of each turned into joy in the telling.

So it is to this day. One third of the year Persephone spends in the gloomy **abode** of Pluto—one month for each seed that she tasted. Then Nature dies, the leaves fall, the earth stops bringing forth. In spring Persephone returns, and with her come the flowers, followed by summer's fruitfulness and the rich harvest of fall.

Vocabulary ▶
abode (ə bōd) *n.* home; residence

Language Study

Vocabulary The words listed below appear in "Demeter and Persephone." For each numbered item, write a single sentence using the words indicated.

| defies | monarch | intervene | realm | abode |

1. realm; distant

2. intervene; argument

3. monarch; ancient

4. defies; stubborn

5. abode; family

WORD STUDY

The **Latin root -dom-** means "master" or "building." Pluto snatches Persephone and takes her to his underground **dominions**, the territories he rules.

Word Study

Part A Explain how the **Latin root -dom-** contributes to the meaning of the words *domain, dominant,* and *predominate.* Consult a dictionary if necessary.

Part B Use the context of the sentences and your knowledge of the Latin root -dom- to explain your answer to each question.

1. If you are behaving in a *domineering* manner, are you being humble?

2. If a building *dominates* a city skyline, is it hard to see?

Close Reading Activities

Literary Analysis

Key Ideas and Details

1. **Cause and Effect** Answer these questions to analyze cause-and-effect in the myth: **(a)** What happens to Persephone at the end of the myth? Why? **(b)** What happens to Demeter? Why?

2. **Cause and Effect** Describe the effect of the giants struggling to get free at the beginning of the myth.

3. **(a)** Why did Pluto take Persephone to his kingdom? **(b) Analyze:** What does Pluto's nickname, "the grim King," suggest about his emotional outlook on the world?

4. **Cause and Effect (a)** How does nature change as Persephone moves between Earth and the underworld? **(b)** How do the powerful emotions of the main characters account for the changing of the seasons?

Craft and Structure

5. **Myth** What human qualities does Pluto possess? Use specific details from the myth to support your answers.

6. **Myth** Complete a chart like the one on the right to describe the lessons the myth teaches through the characters of Demeter, Persephone, and Pluto.

Character: Demeter	
Lesson:	How Taught:
Character: Persephone	
Character: Pluto	

Integration of Knowledge and Ideas

7. **(a)** What does Demeter do when she discovers her daughter is lost? **(b) Make a Judgment:** Do you think her actions were justifiable? Why or why not? Find evidence in the text to support your opinion. **(c) Discuss:** Share your answer with a classmate. Then, evaluate how your response has changed.

8. **(a)** How is Persephone reunited with her mother? **(b) Speculate:** How might their experiences in this myth change each of the three main characters? Cite specific textual evidence to support your ideas.

9. **THE BIG ?** **Community or individual—which is more important?** **(a)** What was the consequence of Demeter's actions? **(b)** How did humankind suffer as a result of one individual's impulses? **(c)** What does this myth suggest about the effects of an individual's actions on the community as a whole?

ACADEMIC VOCABULARY

As you write and speak about "Demeter and Persephone," use the words related to community and the individual that you explored on page 631 of this textbook.

Conventions: Infinitive Phrases and Gerund Phrases

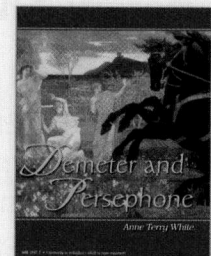

> An **infinitive** is a verb form that acts as a noun, an adjective, or an adverb. An infinitive usually begins with the word *to*. An **infinitive phrase** is an infinitive plus its own modifiers, objects, or complements.

Noun (functioning as subject): <u>*To speak*</u> *Spanish fluently* is my goal.

Adjective (modifying *one*): She is the one <u>*to see*</u> *immediately* if you need help.

Adverb (modifying *waited*): Everyone waited <u>*to hear*</u> *the news*.

> An **gerund** is a verb form that ends in *-ing* and acts as a noun. It can function as a subject, an object, a predicate noun, or the object of a preposition. A **gerund phrase** is a gerund plus its own modifiers, objects, or complements.

Subject: <u>*Remodeling*</u> *the building* was a good idea.

Direct Object: Mischa enjoys <u>*painting*</u> *with watercolors*.

Predicate Noun: Her favorite sport is *cross-country* <u>*skiing*</u>.

Object of the Preposition: Lucille never gets tired of <u>*singing*</u> *holiday songs*.

Practice A

Identify each infinitive and infinitive phrase or gerund and gerund phrase.

1. To get free, the monsters heaved and struggled beneath the mountain.

2. Persephone did not want to return to the underworld.

3. Spending time with Pluto is not enjoyable to Persephone.

4. Demeter wanted to see her daughter.

Reading Application In the myth, find a sentence that contains an infinitive phrase and a sentence that contains a gerund phrase. Explain how each functions.

Practice B

Identify each infinitive phrase or gerund phrase. Determine the function each phrase performs in the sentence. Then, use each infinitive or gerund to write a new sentence.

1. Pluto wants to keep Persephone with him.

2. To get her daughter back is Demeter's goal.

3. Neglecting the Earth was Demeter's revenge.

4. Demeter hates waiting for Persephone to return.

Writing Application Choose a sentence from the myth and rewrite it to include an infinitive phrase or a gerund phrase.

Writing to Sources

Narrative Text You may have wondered why leaves change colors in the fall or what causes an earthquake. Write a short **myth** that explains a natural phenomenon. Follow these steps:

- Think of a natural phenomenon and a creative explanation for its occurrence.
- Limit the number of characters in your myth to keep the story simple.
- Develop your characters by describing their personalities and actions and by showing how they relate to other characters.
- Plan the action by developing a well-structured sequence of events that unfolds naturally and logically.

Exchange your finished myth with a partner and compare your partner's myth to the myth of "Demeter and Persephone." Identify specific ways the two myths are similar and different using details from the selection.

Grammar Application Check your writing to be sure that you have properly used infinitive phrases and gerund phrases.

Speaking and Listening

Comprehension and Collaboration With a small group, conduct a **debate** on whether or not Demeter was justified in changing the weather on Earth. Each side should prepare an argument and material to support the argument, including specific details and examples from the text.

- Appoint a leader for your debate team and choose a person to act as a moderator, or discussion leader.
- Before the debate, consider what the opposing arguments might be and prepare text-based counterarguments to address them.
- Volunteer your own relevant opinions and make contributions to your team. Cite logical evidence to support your ideas.
- Respond directly to questions, and pose your own questions in response to others' comments.
- After the debate, meet with your group to provide constructive feedback about how well speakers conveyed their ideas.

Common Core State Standards

Writing

3. Write narratives to develop real or imagined experiences or events using effective technique, relevant descriptive details, and well-structured event sequences.

3.a. Engage and orient the reader by establishing a context and point of view and introducing a narrator and/or characters; organize an event sequence that unfolds naturally and logically.

3.b. Use narrative techniques, such as dialogue, pacing, and description, to develop experiences, events, and/or characters.

Speaking and Listening

1.a. Come to discussions prepared, having read or researched the material under study; explicitly draw on that preparation by referring to evidence on the topic, text, or issue to probe and reflect on ideas under discussion.

1.c. Pose questions that elicit elaboration and respond to others' questions and comments with relevant observations and ideas that bring the discussion back on topic as needed.

Language

1.a. Explain the function of phrases and clauses in general and their function in specific sentences.

Meet the Author

Juliet Piggott Wood
(1924–1996) discovered
her love for learning about
different cultures while
living in Japan, where her
grandfather was a legal
advisor to Prince Ito. Wood's
interest in Japan inspired
her to produce several
books on Japanese history
and folklore. Her fascination
with one culture led to
research about others.
She went on to co-author
a book retelling famous
fairy tales from around
the world.

© **Common Core**
State Standards

Reading Literature
3. Analyze how particular elements
of a story or drama interact (e.g.,
how setting shapes the characters
or plot).

Language
4.b. Use common, grade-
appropriate Greek or Latin affixes
and roots as clues to the meaning
of a word.

? **Community or individual—which is more important?**

Explore the Big Question as you read. Take notes on the ways in which the legend explores the concepts of community and the individual.

CLOSE READING FOCUS

Key Ideas and Details: **Cause and Effect**

A **cause** is an event or situation that produces a result. An **effect** is the result produced. In a literary work, each effect may eventually become a cause for the next event. This results in a cause-and-effect chain that propels the action forward.

If you do not clearly see the cause-and-effect relationships in a passage of text, reread to look for connections among the words and sentences. Some words that identify causes and effects are *because, due to, for this reason,* and *as a result.*

Craft and Structure: **Legend and Fact**

A **legend** is a traditional story about the past. A **fact** is something that can be proved to be true. Before legends were written down, they were passed on orally. Legends are based on facts that have grown into fiction through many retellings over generations.

Every culture has its own legends to immortalize famous people. Most legends include these elements:

- a human who is larger than life
- fantastic elements
- roots or basis in historical facts
- events that reflect the culture that created the story

Vocabulary

You will encounter the following words in this legend. Copy the words into your notebook. Circle the two words that share a suffix. How does this suffix contribute to the meaning of each word?

shortsightedness	routed	decreed
relished	unanimous	feebleness

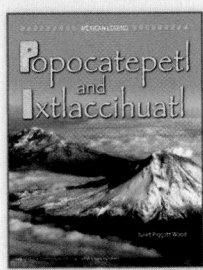

CLOSE READING MODEL

The passage below is from Juliet Piggott Wood's Aztec legend "Popocatepetl and Ixtlaccihuatl." The annotations to the right of the passage show ways in which you can use close reading skills to analyze cause-and-effect relationships and distinguish between legend and fact.

from "Popocatepetl and Ixtlaccihuatl"

There was once an Aztec Emperor in Tenochtitlan. He was very powerful. Some thought he was wise as well, whilst others doubted his wisdom. He was both a ruler and a warrior and he kept at bay those tribes living in and beyond the mountains surrounding the Valley of Mexico, with its huge lake called Texcoco in which Tenochtitlan was built.[1] His power was absolute and the splendor in which he lived was very great.

It is not known for how many years the Emperor ruled in Tenochtitlan, but it is known that he lived to a great age.[2] However, it was not until he was in his middle years that his wife gave him an heir, a girl. The Emperor and Empress loved the princess very much and she was their only child. She was a dutiful daughter and learned all she could from her father about the art of ruling, for she knew that when he died she would reign in his stead in Tenochtitlan.[3]

Her name was Ixtlaccihuatl. Her parents and her friends called her Ixtla. She had a pleasant disposition and, as a result, she had many friends.[4] The great palace where she lived with the Emperor and Empress rang with their laughter when they came to the parties her parents gave for her. As well as being a delightful companion, Ixtla was also very pretty, even beautiful.

Legend and Fact

1 The Aztecs were a real civilization and Tenochtitlan was an actual place. These true historical details are the basis for this legend.

Legend and Fact

2 The Emperor's absolute power, great splendor, and great age create the impression of a larger-than-life, legendary figure.

Cause and Effect

3 In this sentence, the word *for* means "because." It signals a cause-and-effect relationship between the daughter's knowledge of her future duties (cause) and her current desire to learn the art of ruling (effect).

Cause and Effect

4 The phrase *as a result* signals a cause-and-effect relationship: the princess had many friends because she had a pleasant disposition.

Popocatepetl and Ixtlaccihuatl

Juliet Piggott Wood

Before the Spaniards came to Mexico and marched on the Aztec capital of Tenochtitlan[1] there were two volcanoes to the southeast of that city. The Spaniards destroyed much of Tenochtitlan and built another city in its place and called it Mexico City. It is known by that name still, and the pass through which the Spaniards came to the ancient Tenochtitlan is still there, as are the volcanoes on each side of that pass. Their names have not been changed. The one to the north is Ixtlaccihuatl [ēs′ tlä sē′ wät′ əl] and the one on the south of the pass is Popocatepetl [pô pô kä te′ pet′ əl]. Both are snowcapped and beautiful, Popocatepetl being the taller of the two. That name means Smoking Mountain. In Aztec days it gushed forth smoke and, on occasion, it does so still. It erupted too in Aztec days and has done so again since the Spaniards came. Ixtlaccihuatl means The White Woman, for its peak was, and still is, white.

Perhaps Ixtlaccihuatl and Popocatepetl were there in the highest part of the Valley of Mexico in the days when the earth was very young, in the days when the new people were just learning to eat and grow corn. The Aztecs claimed the volcanoes as their own, for they possessed a legend about them and their creation, and they believed that legend to be true.

There was once an Aztec Emperor in Tenochtitlan. He was very powerful. Some thought he was wise as well, whilst others doubted his wisdom. He was both a ruler and a warrior and he kept at bay those tribes living in and beyond the mountains surrounding the Valley of Mexico, with its huge lake called Texcoco [tā skō′ kō] in which Tenochtitlan was built. His power was absolute and the splendor in which he lived was very great.

It is not known for how many years the Emperor ruled in Tenochtitlan, but it is known that he lived to a great age. However, it was not until he was in his middle years that his wife gave him an heir, a girl. The Emperor and Empress loved the princess very much and she was their only child. She was a dutiful daughter and learned all she could from her father about the art of ruling, for she knew that when he died she would reign in his stead in Tenochtitlan.

◀ **Critical Viewing**
Why do you think volcanoes like these inspired ancient peoples?

Comprehension
Explain the meaning of each mountain's name.

---

1. **Tenochtitlan** (tā noch′ tēt län′) the Aztec capital, conquered by the Spanish in 1521.

Vocabulary ▶
shortsightedness
(short´ sīt´ id ness)
n. condition of not
considering the future
effects of something

Cause and Effect
What causes Ixtla to
be serious?

Her name was Ixtlaccihuatl. Her parents and her friends called her Ixtla. She had a pleasant disposition and, as a result, she had many friends. The great palace where she lived with the Emperor and Empress rang with their laughter when they came to the parties her parents gave for her. As well as being a delightful companion Ixtla was also very pretty, even beautiful.

Her childhood was happy and she was content enough when she became a young woman. But by then she was fully aware of the great responsibilities which would be hers when her father died and she became serious and studious and did not enjoy parties as much as she had done when younger.

Another reason for her being so serious was that she was in love. This in itself was a joyous thing, but the Emperor forbade her to marry. He wanted her to reign and rule alone when he died, for he trusted no one, not even his wife, to rule as he did except his much loved only child, Ixtla. This was why there were some who doubted the wisdom of the Emperor for, by not allowing his heiress to marry, he showed a selfishness and shortsightedness towards his daughter and his empire which many considered was not truly wise. An emperor, they felt, who was not truly wise could not also be truly great. Or even truly powerful.

The man with whom Ixtla was in love was also in love with her. Had they been allowed to marry their state could have been doubly joyous. His name was Popocatepetl and Ixtla and his friends all called him Popo. He was a warrior in the service of the Emperor, tall and strong, with a capacity for gentleness, and very brave. He and Ixtla loved each other very much and while they were content and even happy when they were together, true joy was not theirs because the Emperor continued to insist that Ixtla should not be married when the time came for her to take on her father's responsibilities.

This unfortunate but moderately happy relationship between Ixtla and Popo continued for several years, the couple pleading with the Emperor at regular intervals and the Emperor remaining constantly adamant. Popo loved Ixtla no less for her father's stubbornness and she loved him no less while she studied, as her father demanded she should do, the art of ruling in preparation for her reign.

When the Emperor became very old he also became ill. In his **feebleness** he channeled all his failing energies towards instructing Ixtla in statecraft, for he was no longer able to exercise that craft himself. So it was that his enemies, the tribes who lived in the mountains and beyond, realized that the great Emperor in Tenochtitlan

was great no longer, for he was only teaching his daughter to rule and not ruling himself.

The tribesmen came nearer and nearer to Tenochtitlan until the city was besieged. At last the Emperor realized himself that he was great no longer, that his power was nearly gone and that his domain was in dire peril.

Warrior though he long had been, he was now too old and too ill to lead his fighting men into battle. At last he understood that, unless his enemies were frustrated in their efforts to enter and lay waste to Tenochtitlan, not only would he no longer be Emperor but his daughter would never be Empress.

Instead of appointing one of his warriors to lead the rest into battle on his behalf, he offered a bribe to all of them. Perhaps it was that his wisdom, if wisdom he had, had forsaken him, or perhaps he acted from fear. Or perhaps he simply changed his mind. But the bribe he offered to whichever warrior succeeded in lifting the siege of Tenochtitlan and defeating the enemies in and around the Valley of Mexico was both the hand of his daughter and the equal right to reign and rule, with her, in Tenochtitlan. Furthermore, he **decreed** that directly he learned that his enemies had been defeated he would instantly cease to be Emperor himself. Ixtla would not have to wait until her father died to become Empress and, if her father should die of his illness or old age before his enemies were vanquished,

Cause and Effect
What is one effect of the Emperor's becoming old and ill?

◀ **Vocabulary**
feebleness (fē´ bəl nəs) *n.* weakness

decreed (di krēd´) *v.* officially ordered

Comprehension
What does the Emperor forbid Ixtla to do?

Vocabulary ▶
relished (rel´isht)
v. enjoyed; liked

▼ Critical Viewing
How does this picture relate to the details of the battle in the story?

he further decreed that he who overcame the surrounding enemies should marry the princess whether he, the Emperor, lived or not.

Ixtla was fearful when she heard of her father's bribe to his warriors, for the only one whom she had any wish to marry was Popo and she wanted to marry him, and only him, very much indeed.

The warriors, however, were glad when they heard of the decree: there was not one of them who would not have been glad to have the princess as his wife and they all **relished** the chance of becoming Emperor.

And so the warriors went to war at their ruler's behest, and each fought trebly² hard for each was fighting not only for the safety of Tenochtitlan and the surrounding valley, but for the delightful bride and for the right to be the Emperor himself.

Even though the warriors fought with great skill and even though each one exhibited a courage he did not know he possessed, the war was a long one. The Emperor's enemies were firmly entrenched around Lake Texcoco and Tenochtitlan by the time the warriors were sent to war, and as battle followed battle the final outcome was uncertain.

The warriors took a variety of weapons with them; wooden clubs edged with sharp blades of obsidian,³ obsidian machetes,⁴ javelins which they hurled at their enemies from troughed throwing boards, bows and arrows, slings and spears set with obsidian fragments, and lances, too. Many of them carried shields woven from wicker and covered in tough hide and most wore armor made of thick quilted cotton soaked in brine.

The war was long and fierce. Most of the warriors fought together and in unison, but some fought alone. As time went on natural leaders emerged and, of these, undoubtedly Popo was the best. Finally it was he, brandishing his club and shield,

---

2. **trebly** (tre´ blē) *adv.* three times as much; triply.
3. **obsidian** (əb sid´ ē ən) *n.* hard, usually dark-colored or black, volcanic glass.
4. **machetes** (mə shet´ ēz) *n.* large, heavy-bladed knives.

who led the great charge of running warriors across the valley, with their enemies fleeing before them to the safety of the coastal plains and jungles beyond the mountains.

The warriors acclaimed Popo as the man most responsible for the victory and, weary though they all were, they set off for Tenochtitlan to report to the Emperor and for Popo to claim Ixtla as his wife at last.

But a few of those warriors were jealous of Popo. Since they knew none of them could rightly claim the victory for himself (the decision among the Emperor's fighting men that Popo was responsible for the victory had been **unanimous**), they wanted to spoil for him and for Ixtla the delights which the Emperor had promised.

These few men slipped away from the rest at night and made their way to Tenochtitlan ahead of all the others. They reached the capital two days later, having traveled without sleep all the way, and quickly let it be known that, although the Emperor's warriors had been successful against his enemies, the warrior Popo had been killed in battle.

It was a foolish and cruel lie which those warriors told their Emperor, and they told it for no reason other than that they were jealous of Popo.

When the Emperor heard this he demanded that Popo's body be brought to him so that he might arrange a fitting burial. He knew the man his daughter had loved would have died courageously. The jealous warriors looked at one another and said nothing. Then one of them told the Emperor that Popo had been killed on the edge of Lake Texcoco and that his body had fallen into the water and no man had been able to retrieve it. The Emperor was saddened to hear this.

After a little while he demanded to be told which of his warriors had been responsible for the victory but none of the fighting men before him dared claim the successful outcome of the war for himself, for each knew the others would refute him. So they were silent. This puzzled the Emperor and he decided to wait for the main body of his warriors to return and not to press the few who had brought the news of the victory and of Popo's death.

Legend and Fact
What does the account of the battle suggest about the Aztecs' attitudes toward war?

◀ **Vocabulary**
unanimous (yo͞o nan′ ə məs) *adj.* based on complete agreement

Comprehension
What is the outcome of the battle?

Social Studies Connection

Tenochtitlan Archaeologists believe that at one time, more than 200,000 people lived in Tenochtitlan, the Aztec capital city in the middle of the giant lake Texcoco. Approximately one half of the population were farmers. Much of the farming was done on small island gardens surrounding the city. People living in Tenochtitlan depended on food the farmers grew outside the city. They also depended on water from outside the city, which was carried to the city by a system of aqueducts.

Because of its location and dependence on outside food and water, the city would have been helpless in the face of a siege. With no way to get in or out to get food, a siege would soon lead to starvation.

Connect to the Literature

Based on the situation, do you think the rewards offered by the Emperor in this story were appropriate? Explain.

Then the Emperor sent for his wife and his daughter and told them their enemies had been overcome. The Empress was thoroughly excited and relieved at the news. Ixtla was only apprehensive. The Emperor, seeing her anxious face, told her quickly that Popo was dead. He went on to say that the warrior's body had been lost in the waters of Lake Texcoco, and again it was as though his wisdom had left him, for he spoke at some length of his not being able to tell Ixtla who her husband would be and who would become Emperor when the main body of warriors returned to Tenochtitlan.

But Ixtla heard nothing of what he told her, only that her beloved Popo was dead. She went to her room and lay down. Her mother followed her and saw at once she was very ill. Witch doctors were sent for, but they could not help the princess, and neither could her parents. Her illness had no name, unless it was the illness of a broken heart. Princess Ixtlaccihuatl did not wish to live if Popocatepetl was dead, and so she died herself.

The day after her death Popo returned to Tenochtitlan with all the other surviving warriors. They went straight to the palace and, with much cheering, told the Emperor that his enemies had been **routed** and that Popo was the undoubted victor of the conflict.

The Emperor praised his warriors and pronounced Popo to be the new Emperor in his place. When the young man asked first to see Ixtla, begging that they should be married at once before being jointly proclaimed Emperor and Empress, the Emperor had to tell Popo of Ixtla's death, and how it had happened.

Popo spoke not a word.

He gestured the assembled warriors to follow him and together they sought out the few jealous men who had given the false news of his death to the Emperor. With the army of warriors watching, Popo killed each one of them in single combat with his obsidian studded club. No one tried to stop him.

That task accomplished Popo returned to the palace and, still without speaking and still wearing his stiff cotton armor, went to Ixtla's room. He gently lifted her body and carried it out of the palace and out of the city, and no one tried to stop him doing that either. All the warriors followed him in silence.

When he had walked some miles he gestured to them again and they built a huge pile of stones in the shape of a pyramid. They all worked together and they worked fast while Popo stood and watched, holding the body of the princess in his arms. By sunset the mighty edifice was finished. Popo climbed it alone, carrying Ixtla's corpse with him. There, at the very top, under a heap of stones, he buried the young woman he had loved so well and for so long, and who had died for the love of him.

That night Popo slept alone at the top of the pyramid by Ixtla's grave. In the morning he came down and spoke for the first time since the Emperor had told him the princess was dead. He told the warriors to build another pyramid, a little to the southeast of the one which held Ixtla's body and to build it higher than the other.

He told them too to tell the Emperor on his behalf that he, Popocatepetl, would never reign and rule in Tenochtitlan. He would keep watch over the grave of the Princess Ixtlaccihuatl for the rest of his life.

The messages to the Emperor were the last words Popo ever spoke. Well before the evening the second mighty pile of stones was built. Popo climbed it and stood at the top, taking a torch of resinous pine wood with him.

◀ **Vocabulary**
routed (rout´ əd) *v.*
completely defeated

Comprehension
What does Popo ask the Emperor when he returns?

Legend and Fact
Are the volcanoes real?
How do you know?

And when he reached the top he lit the torch and the warriors below saw the white smoke rise against the blue sky, and they watched as the sun began to set and the smoke turned pink and then a deep red, the color of blood.

So Popocatepetl stood there, holding the torch in memory of Ixtlaccihuatl, for the rest of his days.

The snows came and, as the years went by, the pyramids of stone became high white-capped mountains. Even now the one called Popocatepetl emits smoke in memory of the princess whose body lies in the mountain which bears her name.

▶ **Critical Viewing**
What details in this photo are similar to the description of Popo's actions in the story?

Language Study

Vocabulary The words listed below appear in "Popocatepetl and Ixtlaccihuatl." Answer each question and then explain your answer.

decreed   routed   shortsightedness   feebleness   relished

1. If something is *decreed,* is it undecided?

2. If one's enemies have been *routed,* have the enemies won?

3. Is *shortsightedness* useful when making decisions for the future?

4. Would *feebleness* prevent a person from exercising?

5. If you *relished* the last book you read, did you enjoy it?

WORD STUDY

The **Latin prefix uni-** means "having or consisting of only one." In this legend, the Aztec warriors are **unanimous**, or sharing one opinion, about who is responsible for their victory.

Word Study

Part A Explain how the **Latin prefix uni-** contributes to the meanings of the words *unity, unilateral,* and *uniform.* Consult a dictionary if necessary.

Part B Use the context of the sentences and your knowledge of the Latin prefix *uni-* to explain your answer to each question.

1. How many wheels does a *unicycle* have?

2. If two people speak in *unison,* do they speak at the same time?

Close Reading Activities

Literary Analysis

Key Ideas and Details

1. **Cause and Effect** Reread the legend to find an effect for each of these causes.
   (a) The Emperor does not allow his daughter to marry.
   (b) The Emperor spends all his time teaching Ixtla statecraft.
   (c) The warriors lie to the Emperor about Popo's death.
   (d) Ixtla hears that Popo is dead.

2. **Cause and Effect** According to the legend, what causes the volcano to smoke? Cite textual evidence to support your answer.

3. **(a)** Why are Ixtla and Popo unable to marry? **(b) Analyze:** What qualities make the two well matched? Support your answer.

Craft and Structure

4. **Legend and Fact (a)** Identify two facts in this legend.
   (b) How do you know they are facts?

5. **Legend and Fact** Use a chart like the one on the right to help you identify which events in this legend might have been based on historical events.

6. **Legend and Fact (a)** What details in the legend convey the size and magnificence of Tenochtitlan and the Aztec empire?
   (b) What elements are present in the legend that you would not find in a factual account?

Events from Legend
Possible Historic Connections

Integration of Knowledge and Ideas

7. **(a)** Why does Popo refuse to become emperor and rule Tenochtitlan? **(b) Draw Conclusions:** Based on this legend, what traits do you think the Aztecs admired? **(c) Relate:** Do you think these traits are still valued today? Provide examples to support your response.

8. **(a) Interpret:** What lesson does the legend suggest?
   (b) Evaluate: Can this lesson be applied in modern times? Cite details from the text and your own experience to support your answer.

9. **Community or individual—which is more important?**
   (a) Was the Emperor's decision at the legend's beginning better for the individual or the community? **(b)** Is it ever important to consider the needs of a community over the needs of an individual? Explain.

ACADEMIC VOCABULARY

As you write and speak about "Popocatepetl and Ixtlaccihuatl," use the words related to community and the individual that you explored on page 631 of this textbook.

Conventions: **Punctuation Marks**

Punctuation marks are used to make the meaning of written text clearer. Each punctuation mark serves a specific function.

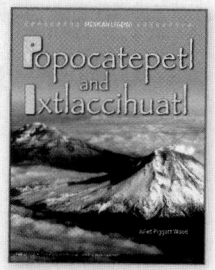

Punctuation/Usage	Example
colon (:) A *colon* introduces information that defines, explains, or provides a list of what is referred to before.	Lily brought many toys to the beach: buckets, shovels, balls, and floats.
semicolon (;) *Semicolons* join related clauses to form compound sentences.	We spent all morning riding our bikes; then we had a picnic.
hyphen (-) A *hyphen* is used to join two or more separate words into a single word.	Billy ordered a double-scoop, bubble-gum-flavored ice cream cone.
dash (—) *Dashes* are used to set off information that interrupts a thought.	On our way to the theater—it had just opened—we stopped for gas.
brackets ([ ]) *Brackets* are used to add clarifying information within a quotation.	Ames said, "In that year [2013] we won our first championship."
parentheses (( )) *Parentheses* are used to include extra information without changing the meaning of the sentence.	My brother Raf (the shyest person in our family) declined to make a speech at the party.

Practice A

Identify each punctuation mark in this paragraph and explain its function.

Ixtla had many admirable qualities: grace, beauty, loyalty, and devotion. Her only love was Popo—they had met when they were both young—and he returned her love. Her father (a powerful, wealthy man) would not let Ixtla marry Popo; he wanted her to be unmarried when she took his place as ruler of Tenochtitlan.

Reading Application In the legend, find one sentence that contains parentheses and one that contains a hyphen.

Practice B

Rewrite the paragraph below, using punctuation, so that each sentence makes sense.

Ixtlaccihuatl her beauty was legendary waited nervously for Popocatepetl to return from battle. She hoped they would be married the marriage was previously forbidden. Then she heard that he had died she lay down and died soon after.

Writing Application Write a brief paragraph about the legend using at least one hyphen, one dash, one colon, one semicolon, and one set of parentheses.

Writing to Sources

Informative Text Write a short **description** of the ancient city of Tenochtitlan based on two sources: the legend "Popocatepetl and Ixtlaccihuatl" and a nonfiction article about Tenochtitlan. You might consult library or Internet resources, or you may read "Tenochtitlan: Inside the Aztec Capital," a social studies article you will find in your eText.

- As you read both the fiction and the nonfiction selection, jot down details about the time, place, and overall environment of the city as well as details about the lives of its inhabitants.
- Refer to your notes as you draft your description.
- Draw on your description to write a brief **comparison** of the selections. Identify common historical elements to which the article and the legend refer.
- Finally, explain the ways in which the legend adapts or alters historical fact.

Grammar Application Check your writing to be sure that you have used punctuation marks properly.

Speaking and Listening

Presentation of Ideas Deliver a **persuasive speech** based on the legend. Your goal is to persuade the Emperor to allow Popo and Ixtla to marry.

- On a note card, write your position and a short statement explaining the reasons for your position.
- Use relevant evidence, including specific details and quotations from the legend, to demonstrate your understanding of the issues and to overcome opposing views.
- Jot down phrases that will remind you of your key points, rather than writing complete sentences.
- Refer to your note cards as you deliver your speech.
- While you are delivering your speech, establish eye contact, adjust the volume of your voice, when appropriate, and pronounce each word clearly.

Meet the Authors

Richard Erdoes
(1912–2008) was born
in Vienna, Austria. He
studied art and later
sketched humorous
portraits for daily
newspapers. He moved to
New York in 1940, where
he worked as an illustrator
for newspapers and
magazines. He has written
more than twenty books on
the American West.

Alfonso Ortiz (1939–1997)
was born in San Juan, a
Tewa pueblo in northern
New Mexico. He earned
degrees in both sociology
and anthropology, and
spent many years of his life
as a university professor.
He also served as president
of the Association on
American Indian Affairs for
fifteen years.

**Ⓒ Common Core
State Standards**

Reading Literature
2. Determine a theme or central idea
of a text and analyze its development
over the course of the text; provide
an objective summary of the text.

Language
5.b. Use the relationship between
particular words to better
understand each of the words.

⑦ Community or individual—which is more important?

Explore the Big Question as you read "Sun and Moon in a Box."
Take notes on the ways in which the selection explores the concepts
of community and the individual.

CLOSE READING FOCUS

Key Ideas and Details: **Compare and Contrast**

- A **comparison** tells how two or more things are alike.
- A **contrast** tells how two or more things are different.

Often, you can understand an unfamiliar concept by using your
prior knowledge to compare and contrast. For example, you may
understand an ancient culture better if you look for ways it is
similar to and different from your own culture. You might also find
similarities and differences between a story told long ago and one
that is popular today. To compare and contrast stories, ask yourself
questions about the characters, plots, settings, and themes.

Craft and Structure: **Cultural Context**

Stories such as fables, folk tales, and myths are influenced by
the **cultural context**, or the background, customs, and beliefs
of the people who originally told them. Recognizing the cultural
context can help you understand and appreciate a literary work.
As you read, consider the impact that cultural context might have
on the author's intended theme, or message about life.

Vocabulary

You will encounter the following words in this folk tale. Decide
whether you know each word well, know it a little bit, or do not
know it at all. After you read the selection, see how your knowledge
of each word has increased.

regretted	reliable	curiosity
pestering	relented	cunning

CLOSE READING MODEL

The passage below is from Richard Erdoes and Alfonso Ortiz's "Sun and Moon in a Box." The annotations to the right of the passage show ways in which you can use close reading skills to compare and contrast to increase your understanding and analyze cultural context.

from **"Sun and Moon in a Box"**

Coyote and Eagle were hunting. Eagle caught rabbits. Coyote caught nothing but grasshoppers. Coyote said: "Friend Eagle, my chief, we make a great hunting pair."

"Good, let us stay together," said Eagle.[1]

They went toward the west. They came to a deep canyon. "Let us fly over it," said Eagle.

"My chief, I cannot fly," said Coyote. "You must carry me across."

"Yes, I see that I have to," said Eagle.[2] He took Coyote on his back and flew across the canyon. They came to a river. "Well," said Eagle, "you cannot fly, but you certainly can swim. This time I do not have to carry you."

Eagle flew over the stream, and Coyote swam across. He was a bad swimmer. He almost drowned. He coughed up a lot of water. "My chief," he said, "when we come to another river, you must carry me." Eagle regretted to have Coyote for a companion.[3]

Cultural Context

1 Coyote addresses Eagle as "my chief," and the characters agree that they make "a great hunting pair." From these details, you may infer that in the Zuni culture, hunting is an important way of life, a chief is a respected member of the group, and cooperation is valued.

Cultural Context

2 The conversation between Coyote and Eagle sounds similar to a conversation between two human beings. This may lead you to believe that the folk tale originates from a culture in which people greatly respect animals and feel a kinship with them.

Compare and Contrast

3 A growing contrast has emerged between Eagle and Coyote. Eagle is skilled and able, while Coyote is not. Coyote has become a burden because he is needy and often requires Eagle's assistance.

SUN AND MOON IN A BOX

Richard Erdoes and Alfonso Ortiz

Coyote and Eagle were hunting. Eagle caught rabbits. Coyote caught nothing but grasshoppers. Coyote said: "Friend Eagle, my chief, we make a great hunting pair."

"Good, let us stay together," said Eagle.

They went toward the west. They came to a deep canyon. "Let us fly over it," said Eagle.

"My chief, I cannot fly," said Coyote. "You must carry me across."

"Yes, I see that I have to," said Eagle. He took Coyote on his back and flew across the canyon. They came to a river. "Well," said Eagle, "you cannot fly, but you certainly can swim. This time I do not have to carry you."

Eagle flew over the stream, and Coyote swam across. He was a bad swimmer. He almost drowned. He coughed up a lot of water. "My chief," he said, "when we come to another river, you must carry me." Eagle regretted to have Coyote for a companion.

Spiral Review
THEME In some cultures, coyotes are trickster characters. How might Eagle's willingness to listen to Coyote contribute to this folk tale's theme?

◀ **Vocabulary**
regretted (ri gret′ əd) *v.* felt sorry about

Comprehension
Why do Eagle and Coyote stay together?

They came to Kachina Pueblo.[1] The Kachinas were dancing. Now, at this time, the earth was still soft and new. There was as yet no sun and no moon. Eagle and Coyote sat down and watched the dance. They saw that the Kachinas had a square box. In it they kept the sun and the moon. Whenever they wanted light they opened the lid and let the sun peek out. Then it was day. When they wanted less light, they opened the box just a little for the moon to look out.

"This is something wonderful," Coyote whispered to Eagle.

"This must be the sun and the moon they are keeping in that box," said Eagle. "I have heard about these two wonderful beings."

"Let us steal the box," said Coyote.

"No, that would be wrong," said Eagle. "Let us just borrow it."

When the Kachinas were not looking, Eagle grabbed the box and flew off. Coyote ran after him on the ground. After a while Coyote called Eagle: "My chief, let me have the box. I am ashamed to let you do all the carrying."

"No," said Eagle, "you are not **reliable**. You might be curious and open the box and then we could lose the wonderful things we borrowed."

For some time they went on as before—Eagle flying above with the box, Coyote running below, trying to keep up. Then once again Coyote called Eagle: "My chief, I am ashamed to let you carry the box. I should do this for you. People will talk badly about me, letting you carry this burden."

"No, I don't trust you," Eagle repeated. "You won't be able to refrain from opening the box. **Curiosity** will get the better of you."

"No," cried Coyote, "do not fear, my chief, I won't even think of opening the box." Still, Eagle would not give it to

Cultural Context
What details show that this is a Native American story set in the Southwest?

Vocabulary ►
reliable (ri lī′ ə bəl) *adj.* dependable

curiosity (kyσor′ ē äs′ ə tē) *n.* desire to learn or know

1. **Kachina Pueblo** (kə chē′ nə pweb′ lō) Native American village.

him, continuing to fly above, holding the box in his talons. But Coyote went on pestering Eagle: "My chief, I am really embarrassed. People will say: 'That lazy, disrespectful Coyote lets his chief do all the carrying.'"

"No, I won't give this box to you," Eagle objected. "It is too precious to entrust to somebody like you."

They continued as before, Eagle flying, Coyote running. Then Coyote begged for the fourth time: "My chief, let me carry the box for a while. My wife will scold me, and my children will no longer respect me, when they find out that I did not help you carry this load."

Then Eagle relented, saying: "Will you promise not to drop the box and under no circumstances to open it?"

"I promise, my chief, I promise," cried Coyote. "You can rely upon me. I shall not betray your trust."

Then Eagle allowed Coyote to carry the box. They went on as before, Eagle flying, Coyote running, carrying the box in his mouth. They came to a wooded area, full of trees and bushes. Coyote pretended to lag behind, hiding himself behind some bushes where Eagle could not see him. He could not curb his curiosity. Quickly he sat down and opened the box. In a flash, Sun came out of the box and flew away, to

Compare and Contrast
How do Coyote's and Eagle's feelings about responsibility differ?

◀ **Vocabulary**
pestering (pes′ tər iŋ)
v. annoying; bothering
relented (ri lent′ əd)
v. gave in

the very edge of the sky, and at once the world grew cold, the leaves fell from the tree branches, the grass turned brown, and icy winds made all living things shiver.

Then, before Coyote could put the lid back on the box, Moon jumped out and flew away to the outer rim of the sky, and at once snow fell down from heaven and covered the plains and the mountains.

Eagle said: "I should have known better. I should not have let you persuade me. I knew what kind of low, cunning, stupid creature you are. I should have remembered that you never keep a promise. Now we have winter. If you had not opened the box, then we could have kept Sun and Moon always close to us. Then there would be no winter. Then we would have summer all the time."

Language Study

Vocabulary Use one of the words in blue to complete each *analogy*. An analogy shows the relationship between a pair of words or phrases. Your choice should make a word pair that matches the relationship between the first pair of words or phrases.

regretted   reliable   pestering   relented   cunning

1. came in : went out :: _____ : stood firm

2. insult : anger :: _____ : annoyance

3. famous : unknown :: _____ : undependable

4. felt pride : accomplishment :: _____ : mistake

5. amiable : friendly :: _____ : sly

WORD STUDY

The **Latin suffix -ity** means "state," "quality," or "condition of." This folk tale shows how too much **curiosity**, the state of feeling a strong desire to know, can lead one to make unwise choices.

Word Study

Part A Explain how the **Latin suffix -ity** contributes to the meanings of the words *density, integrity,* and *reliability.* Consult a dictionary if necessary.

Part B Use the context of the sentences and what you know about the Latin suffix *-ity* to explain your answer to each question.

1. Would a supervisor appreciate a worker's *productivity*?

2. If I show *sensitivity,* am I being thoughtful?

Close Reading Activities

Literary Analysis

Key Ideas and Details

1. Compare and Contrast Use a Venn diagram like the one on the right to compare and contrast Eagle and Coyote. Think about how they look, their abilities, and how they react to responsibility.

2. (a) Support: Make a two-column chart. In the first column, write sentences or comments from other characters or the narrator that give details about what Coyote is like. In the second column, explain what you think each detail reveals about Coyote.
(b) Discuss: In a small group, discuss your lists. Then, choose the best details from each list to share with the class.

3. (a) What does Coyote say to Eagle when Eagle is carrying the box? **(b) Speculate:** Why do you think he says this? **(c) Infer:** Why do you think Eagle finally agrees to give the box to Coyote?

Craft and Structure

4. Cultural Context (a) Describe where Coyote and Eagle are when they first see the box. **(b)** How do these details help you understand the cultural context of the story?

5. Cultural Context What Zuni beliefs and values are revealed in this folk tale? Identify details that support your answer.

Integration of Knowledge and Ideas

6. (a) Evaluate: Compare and contrast the environment enjoyed by the Kachina tribe before and after their box with the sun and the moon was stolen. What did the Kachina lose? **(b) Make a Judgement:** Do you think they gained anything? Why or why not? Cite textual evidence to support your answer.

7. Make a Judgment: In your opinion, does Eagle share any responsibility for the appearance of the first winter? Why or why not? Support your answer with evidence from the folk tale.

8. **Community or individual—which is more important?** **(a)** How do Coyote's ignorance and selfishness cause harm to others? **(b)** Which character bears more blame for losing the sun and moon? Why? **(c)** What does this folk tale imply about the individual's responsibility to the community?

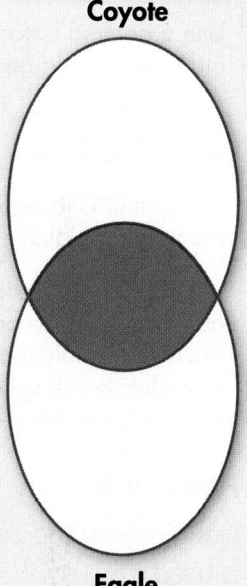

Coyote

Eagle

ACADEMIC VOCABULARY

As you write and speak about "Sun and Moon in a Box," use the words related to community and the individual that you explored on page 631 of this textbook.

Conventions: Commas

A **comma** signals a brief pause.

Review the chart to learn the functions of commas.

Using Commas	Example
Use a comma before a conjunction that joins independent clauses in a compound sentence.	John thought he was late, and he rushed through the parking lot.
Use a comma after an introductory word, phrase, or clause.	If you go to the play, how will you get your homework finished?
Use commas to separate three or more words, phrases, or clauses in a series.	The café offered fruit juice, iced tea, and sparkling water.
Use a comma to separate coordinate adjectives. These are adjectives in a row that each separately modify the noun that follows. Coordinate adjectives can be linked smoothly together with the word *and*.	We received a warm, joyful welcome. [We received a warm *and* joyful welcome.]

Practice A

Explain how the comma in each sentence is used.

1. Eagle caught rabbits, but Coyote caught only grasshoppers.
2. The winter weather grew cold, wet, and dreary.
3. Eagle thought that Coyote was a cunning, stupid creature.
4. When they got to the river, Eagle flew across it.

Reading Application In "Sun and Moon in a Box," find three sentences that contain commas and explain the function of each comma.

Practice B

Rewrite the following sentences, inserting commas as necessary.

1. Coyote was a very bad swimmer so he almost drowned.
2. Since Coyote could not control his curiosity he opened the box.
3. Coyote begged complained and moaned until Eagle gave him the box.
4. It was a cold dark world without the sun.

Writing Application Write five sentences about a folk tale with which you are familiar. At least one of the sentences should be a compound sentence, one should contain items in a series, one should use coordinate adjectives, and one should start with an introductory word, phrase, or clause.

Writing to Sources

Informative Text Write a **plot summary** of "Sun and Moon in a Box."

- Review the folk tale, taking notes to describe the setting, major characters, main events, and final outcome.
- Use your notes to write your summary. Include one major event from the beginning, one from the middle, and one from the end of the story.
- Conclude your summary by stating a possible theme that is logically supported by the ideas in your summary.

Remember to remain objective. Include the folk tale's main ideas and details, but do not include personal opinions or judgments.

Grammar Application Check your writing to be sure that you have used commas correctly.

Speaking and Listening

Comprehension and Collaboration Prepare and present a **retelling** of "Sun and Moon in a Box" from either Coyote's or Eagle's point of view. Review the folk tale, noting the traits and behaviors of the character you have chosen. Consider these details to determine how Coyote or Eagle would think and feel about the folk tale's events. Make your retelling entertaining and effective by using these strategies:

- Organize the plot of your retelling so that it unfolds naturally and is engaging and interesting.
- Include narrative techniques, such as dialogue and description to express the character's emotions and reactions to events.
- Create suspense by withholding certain details until the end of the story.
- As you present, use facial expressions and body movements to enhance and support your retelling.
- Adjust your speaking rate, volume, and tone to suit the action. Pronounce words clearly, and use appropriate expression.
- Make eye contact with your audience from time to time.
- After your presentation, have classmates critique the retelling based on their own interpretations of the folk tale.

Common Core State Standards

Reading Literature

2. Determine a theme or central idea of a text and analyze its development over the course of the text; provide an objective summary of the text.

Writing

2. Write informative/explanatory texts to examine a topic and convey ideas, concepts, and information through the selection, organization, and analysis of relevant content.

2.b. Develop the topic with relevant facts, definitions, concrete details, quotations, or other information and examples.

2.f. Provide a concluding statement or section that follows from and supports the information or explanation presented.

3. Write narratives to develop real or imagined experiences or events using effective technique, relevant descriptive details, and well-structured event sequences.

3.a. Organize an event sequence that unfolds naturally and logically.

3.b. Use narrative techniques, such as dialogue, pacing, and description, to develop experiences, events, and/or characters.

Language

2. Demonstrate command of the conventions of standard English capitalization, punctuation, and spelling when writing.

2.a. Use a comma to separate coordinate adjectives.

Speaking and Listening

4. Use appropriate eye contact, adequate volume, and clear pronunciation.

Virginia Hamilton
(1934–2002) is the author
of countless novels, stories,
and collections of African
American folk tales. She
was raised in a house of
gifted storytellers. Hamilton
described her childhood
as ideal, saying "I heard
'tells' every day of my life
from parents and relatives."
Some of those stories were
about slavery, and most
were about the past. As
a result, the past came to
play an important role in
Hamilton's writing. She
developed a unique style,
combining elements of
history, myth, legend, and
dream to bring her stories
to life.

© **Common Core
State Standards**

Reading Literature
3. Analyze how particular elements
of a story or drama interact.
Language
4.b. Use common, grade-
appropriate Greek or Latin affixes
and roots as clues to the meaning
of a word.

❓ Community or individual—which is more important?

Think about the Big Question as you read "The People Could Fly."
Take notes on the ways in which the folk tale explores the concepts
of community and the individual.

CLOSE READING FOCUS

Key Ideas and Details: **Compare and Contrast**

When you **compare and contrast,** you analyze similarities and
differences. You can compare and contrast elements in a literary
work by using a graphic organizer, such as a Venn diagram or
a two-column chart, to help you keep track of character traits,
situations, and ideas.

- First, reread the text to locate the details you will compare.
- Then, write the details in your graphic organizer.

Recording details in this way will help you understand the
similarities and differences in a literary work.

Craft and Structure: **Folk Tales**

A **folk tale** is a fictional story that is composed orally and then
passed from person to person by word of mouth. Although they
originate in this oral tradition, most folk tales are eventually
collected and written down. Similar folk tales are told by different
cultures throughout the world, using common character types,
plot elements, and themes. Folk tales often teach a lesson about
life and clearly differentiate between good and evil. As you read,
notice how the different elements of a folk tale work together to
give meaning to the story.

Vocabulary

You will encounter the following words in this folk tale. Copy
the words into your notebook, circling the words with multiple
meanings. Then, record the different meanings you know.

shed	scorned	hoed
croon	mystery	shuffle

CLOSE READING MODEL

The passage below is from Virginia Hamilton's folk tale "The People Could Fly." The annotations to the right of the passage show ways in which you can use close reading skills to compare and contrast the elements of a literary work and to understand folk tales.

from **"The People Could Fly"**

They say the people could fly. Say that long ago in Africa, some of the people knew magic. And they would walk up on the air like climbin up on a gate. And they flew like blackbirds over the fields. Black, shiny wings flappin against the blue up there.

Then, many of the people were captured for Slavery. The ones that could fly shed their wings. They couldn't take their wings across the water on the slave ships. Too crowded, don't you know.[1]

The folks were full of misery, then. Got sick with the up and down of the sea. So they forgot about flyin when they could no longer breathe the sweet scent of Africa.[2]

Say the people who could fly kept their power, although they shed their wings. They kept their secret magic in the land of slavery.[3] They looked the same as the other people from Africa who had been coming over, who had dark skin. Say you couldn't tell anymore one who could fly from one who couldn't.

One such who could was an old man, call him Toby. And standin tall, yet afraid, was a young woman who once had wings. Call her Sarah. Now Sarah carried a babe tied to her back. She trembled to be so hard worked and scorned.

Folk Tales

1 The informal language in this folk tale shows that the story was once told aloud. The author drops the final *g* in the words *climbin* and *flappin,* and uses casual expressions such as "don't you know." These details suggest spoken rather than written language.

Compare and Contrast

2 After they are "captured for Slavery," the people's situation changes dramatically. You can contrast the image of the people "flyin" and breathing "the sweet scent of Africa" with the image of them feeling "full of misery" and "sick" on the slave ship.

Folk Tales

3 Magic is a common element of folk tales. You may begin to wonder how the people will use their "power" and "secret magic" to overcome their terrible situation.

The People Could Fly

African American Folk Tale

Virginia Hamilton

Folk Tales
What informal language here suggests that this story has been passed on orally?

Vocabulary ▶
shed (shed) *v.* cast off or lost

scorned (skôrnd) *adj.* looked down upon

They say the people could fly. Say that long ago in Africa, some of the people knew magic. And they would walk up on the air like climbin up on a gate. And they flew like blackbirds over the fields. Black, shiny wings flappin against the blue up there.

Then, many of the people were captured for Slavery. The ones that could fly shed their wings. They couldn't take their wings across the water on the slave ships. Too crowded, don't you know.

The folks were full of misery, then. Got sick with the up and down of the sea. So they forgot about flyin when they could no longer breathe the sweet scent of Africa.

Say the people who could fly kept their power, although they **shed** their wings. They kept their secret magic in the land of slavery. They looked the same as the other people from Africa who had been coming over, who had dark skin. Say you couldn't tell anymore one who could fly from one who couldn't.

One such who could was an old man, call him Toby. And standin tall, yet afraid, was a young woman who once had wings. Call her Sarah. Now Sarah carried a babe tied to her back. She trembled to be so hard worked and **scorned**.

The slaves labored in the fields from sunup to sundown.
The owner of the slaves callin himself their Master. Say he
was a hard lump of clay. A hard, glinty[1] coal. A hard rock
pile, wouldn't be moved. His Overseer[2] on horseback pointed
out the slaves who were slowin down. So the one called
Driver[3] cracked his whip over the slow ones to make them
move faster. That whip was a slice-open cut of pain. So they
did move faster. Had to.

Sarah hoed and chopped the row as the babe on her back
slept.

Say the child grew hungry. That babe started up bawling
too loud. Sarah couldn't stop to feed it. Couldn't stop to
soothe and quiet it down. She let it cry. She didn't want to.
She had no heart to croon to it.

"Keep that thing quiet," called the Overseer. He pointed his
finger at the babe. The woman scrunched low. The Driver

◀ Vocabulary
hoed (hōd) *v.* weeded
or loosened soil with
a metal hand tool
croon (krōōn) *v.* sing
or hum quietly and
soothingly

Comprehension
What special gift do
some of the people in
this tale have?

---

1. **glinty** (glint′ ē) *adj.* shiny; reflecting light.
2. **Overseer** (ō′ vər sē′ ər) *n.* someone who watches over and directs the work of others.
3. **Driver** *n.* someone who forced (drove) the slaves to work harder.

cracked his whip across the babe anyhow. The babe hollered like any hurt child, and the woman fell to the earth.

The old man that was there, Toby, came and helped her to her feet.

"I must go soon," she told him.

"Soon," he said.

Sarah couldn't stand up straight any longer. She was too weak. The sun burned her face. The babe cried and cried, "Pity me, oh, pity me," say it sounded like. Sarah was so sad and starvin, she sat down in the row.

"Get up, you black cow," called the Overseer. He pointed his hand, and the Driver's whip snarled around Sarah's legs. Her sack dress tore into rags. Her legs bled onto the earth. She couldn't get up.

Toby was there where there was no one to help her and the babe.

"Now, before it's too late," panted Sarah. "Now, Father!"

"Yes, Daughter, the time is come," Toby answered. "Go, as you know how to go!"

He raised his arms, holding them out to her. *"Kum . . . yali, kum buba tambe,"* and more magic words, said so quickly, they sounded like whispers and sighs.

The young woman lifted one foot on the air. Then the other. She flew clumsily at first, with the child now held tightly in her arms. Then she felt the magic, the African mystery. Say she rose just as free as a bird. As light as a feather.

The Overseer rode after her, hollerin. Sarah flew over the fences. She flew over the woods. Tall trees could not snag her. Nor could the Overseer. She flew like an eagle now, until she was gone from sight. No one dared speak about it. Couldn't believe it. But it was, because they that was there saw that it was.

Say the next day was dead hot in the fields. A young man slave fell from the heat. The Driver come and whipped him. Toby come over and spoke words to the fallen one. The words of ancient Africa once heard are never remembered completely. The young man forgot them as soon as he heard them. They went way inside him. He got up and rolled over on the air. He rode it awhile. And he flew away.

Compare and Contrast
How does the Overseer's treatment of Sarah compare with Toby's treatment of her?

Vocabulary ▶
mystery (mis´ tə rē) *n.* something unexplained, unknown, or kept secret

Another and another fell from the heat. Toby was there. He cried out to the fallen and reached his arms out to them. "*Kum kunka yali, kum . . . tambe!*" Whispers and sighs. And they too rose on the air. They rode the hot breezes. The ones flyin were black and shinin sticks, wheelin above the head of the Overseer. They crossed the rows, the fields, the fences, the streams, and were away.

"Seize the old man!" cried the Overseer. "I heard him say the magic *words*. Seize him!"

The one callin himself Master come runnin. The Driver got his whip ready to curl around old Toby and tie him up. The slaveowner took his hip gun from its place. He meant to kill old, black Toby.

But Toby just laughed. Say he threw back his head and said, "Hee, hee! Don't you know who I am? Don't you know some of us in this field?" He said it to their faces. "We are ones who fly!"

And he sighed the ancient words that were a dark promise. He said them all around to the others in the field under the whip,

"*. . . buba yali . . . buba tambe. . . .*"

There was a great outcryin. The bent backs straightened up. Old and young who were called slaves and could fly joined hands. Say like they would ring-sing.[4] But they didn't **shuffle** in a circle. They didn't sing. They rose on the air. They flew in a flock that was black against the heavenly blue. Black crows or black shadows. It didn't matter, they went so high. Way above the plantation, way over the slavery land. Say they flew away to *Free-dom.*

And the old man, old Toby, flew behind them, takin care of them. He wasn't cryin. He wasn't laughin. He was the seer.[5] His gaze fell on the plantation where the slaves who could not fly waited.

___
4. **ring-sing** joining hands in a circle to sing and dance.
5. **seer** (sē´ ər) *n.* one who has supposed power to see the future; prophet.

▲ **Critical Viewing**
What are some reasons why a person might wish to fly?

◄ **Vocabulary**
shuffle (shuf´ əl) *v.* walk with dragging feet

Comprehension
What did Sarah do to escape the Overseer?

Compare and Contrast
How is Toby's position now different from his position at the beginning of the story?

"Take us with you!" Their looks spoke it but they were afraid to shout it. Toby couldn't take them with him. Hadn't the time to teach them to fly. They must wait for a chance to run.

"Goodie-bye!" The old man called Toby spoke to them, poor souls! And he was flyin gone.

So they say. The Overseer told it. The one called Master said it was a lie, a trick of the light. The Driver kept his mouth shut.

The slaves who could not fly told about the people who could fly to their children. When they were free. When they sat close before the fire in the free land, they told it. They did so love firelight and *Free-dom*, and tellin.

They say that the children of the ones who could not fly told their children. And now, me, I have told it to you.

Language Study

Vocabulary The words listed below appear in "The People Could Fly." For each numbered item, write a single sentence correctly using the words indicated.

shed	scorned	hoed	croon	shuffle

1. shuffle; dance
2. scorned; opinion
3. croon; lullaby
4. shed; leaves
5. hoed; planting

WORD STUDY

The **Greek root -myst-** means "secret." This folk tale tells a story about the African **mystery**, or secret, of people who could fly.

Word Study

Part A Explain how the **Greek root -myst-** contributes to the meanings of the words *mystique*, *mystical*, and *mysticism*. Consult a dictionary if necessary.

Part B Use the context of the sentences and what you know about the Greek root -myst- to explain your answer to each question.

1. Would a *mysterious* disappearance be easy to solve?
2. If I am *mystified* by your answer to my question, how might I respond?

Close Reading Activities

Literary Analysis

Key Ideas and Details

1. **Compare and Contrast (a)** How are the personalities of Toby and the Overseer similar? **(b)** How are they different? Use details from the text to support your answer to each question.

2. **(a)** What happens when Toby says the "magic words"?
   (b) Draw Conclusions: What do you think "flying" really means?
   (c) Support: Cite textual evidence to support your answer.

3. **Compare and Contrast** Use a Venn diagram or two-column chart to compare and contrast "The People Could Fly" with another story you have read in this book. In your diagram, include details about the setting, the plot, and the characters.

Craft and Structure

4. **Folk Tales** Use a chart like the one on the right to identify examples of the elements of folk tales that you find in this story and explain how they contribute to the story's meaning.

5. **Folk Tales (a)** What are the "magic words" Toby says?
   (b) Why do you think the author includes these words in the story?

Integration of Knowledge and Ideas

6. **(a) Describe:** What words would you use to describe the living conditions of many African Americans during the time this story originated? **(b) Support:** Describe three details from the story that help you understand these living conditions. **(c) Speculate:** How do you think these conditions impacted the community?

7. **(a)** Who is called Master? **(b) Contrast:** Who is the real "master" in the story? **(c) Evaluate:** Do you think this folk tale inspires hope? Explain.

Characters
Plot Events
Lesson
Theme

8. **Community or individual—which is more important?** Discuss the following questions with a small group of classmates. **(a) Speculate:** What effect might freedom tales, like this folk tale, have had on enslaved or otherwise oppressed people? **(b) Generalize:** How can folk tales and other stories from the oral tradition inspire and support a community?

ACADEMIC VOCABULARY

As you write and speak about "The People Could Fly," use the words related to community and the individual that you explored on page 631 of this textbook.

Conventions: **Capitalization**

> **Capital letters** signal the beginning of a sentence or quotation and identify proper nouns and proper adjectives.

Proper nouns include the names of people, geographical locations, specific events and time periods, organizations, languages, historical events and documents, and religions. **Proper adjectives** are derived from proper nouns, as in *French* (from *France*) and *Canadian* (from *Canada*).

Sentence beginning: **M**y dog ran away.

Quotation: I yelled, "**C**ome back!"

Proper nouns: **M**ichael, **Q**ueen **E**lizabeth, **U.S. C**onstitution, **F**riday

Proper adjectives: **M**exican, **J**effersonian, **I**rish

Practice A

Identify the proper nouns and proper adjectives in each sentence, and tell what each names (geographic location, historical event, etc.) or describes.

1. Virginia Hamilton wrote many collections of African American folk tales.

2. Hamilton was born on March 12, 1934.

3. She was born in Yellow Springs, Ohio, and went to college in Columbus, Ohio.

4. Virginia met poet Arnold Adoff in New York City, and they were married in 1960.

5. Hamilton's novel *The House of Dies Drear* won the Edgar Allan Poe Award.

Reading Application In "The People Could Fly," find two sentences that contain quotations and two additional sentences that each contain a different type of capitalized word.

Practice B

Rewrite the following sentences, correcting the capitalization.

1. hamilton's grandfather levi perry was brought to ohio as an infant via the underground railroad.

2. in 1974, virginia hamilton became the first african american to win the newbery award.

3. she received this award for her most successful novel, *m. c. higgins, the great.*

4. hamilton's daughter is named leigh, and her son is named jaime.

5. the library of congress houses a collection of hamilton's papers.

Writing Application Write three sentences about "The People Could Fly" or another folk tale you have read. In your sentences, use at least one quotation, one proper adjective, and two proper nouns.

Writing to Sources

Argument Write a **review** of "The People Could Fly" in which you state your position on whether or not other readers will enjoy this folk tale.

- Reread the folk tale, reviewing story elements, such as characters, description, dialogue, and plot, in order to choose your position.

- State your opinion clearly, acknowledging that some readers may not agree with you. Then, support your ideas with details from the story. Organize an effective argument by giving your strongest reasons or evidence at the beginning.

- Provide a concluding paragraph that summarizes your review and supports your arguments.

Revise your word choice to use words that are precise and descriptive. For example, replace "good" with "entertaining" or "comical," or change "boring" to "simplistic" or "predictable."

Grammar Application Check your writing to be sure that you have used correct conventions of capitalization.

Speaking and Listening

Presentation of Ideas Prepare a **television news report** that provides a clear interpretation of the events in "The People Could Fly."

- Begin by summarizing the main points of the story, starting with the most important point or event. Follow each main point with supporting ideas.

- Describe events in your own words. Tell when and where the incidents took place, using details from the folk tale.

- Include an interview with an eyewitness—someone who saw events and can provide an on-the-scene reaction. In your report, use quotations to add credibility and bring the action to life.

- Conclude your report with an insight about the meaning of the events and the characters' actions.

- Present your news report to a small group. Speak clearly and vary the tone of your voice to emphasize key points.

 **Common Core State Standards**

Writing

1. Write arguments to support claims with clear reasons and relevant evidence.

1.a. Introduce claim(s), acknowledge alternate or opposing claims, and organize the reasons and evidence logically.

1.b. Support claim(s) with logical reasoning and relevant evidence, using accurate, credible sources and demonstrating an understanding of the topic or text.

2.a. Introduce a topic clearly, previewing what is to follow; organize ideas, concepts, and information, using strategies such as definition, classification, comparison/contrast, and cause/effect.

2.b. Develop the topic with relevant facts, definitions, concrete details, quotations, or other information and examples.

2.f. Provide a concluding statement or section that follows from and supports the information or explanation presented.

Language

2. Demonstrate command of the conventions of standard English capitalization, punctuation, and spelling when writing.

3.a. Choose language that expresses ideas precisely and concisely, recognizing and eliminating wordiness and redundancy.

Speaking and Listening

4. Present claims and findings, emphasizing salient points in a focused, coherent manner with pertinent descriptions, facts, details, and examples; use appropriate eye contact, adequate volume, and clear pronunciation.

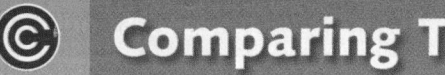

Community or individual—which is more important?

Explore the Big Question as you read the following selections. Both show that travel can enrich individuals and shape their views.

READING TO COMPARE UNIVERSAL THEMES

As you read, compare how these two authors explore universal themes, even though they are writing in different genres.

"The Voyage" *from* Tales from the Odyssey

Mary Pope Osborne (b. 1949)
Mary Pope Osborne has lived an adventurous life. Her father was in the military, and the family moved seven times before Mary was fifteen. As a young adult, she explored sixteen Asian countries with friends. Osborne began to write in her thirties. Today, she is best known for her series, *The Magic Tree House*. "There is no career better suited to my eccentricities, strengths, and passions than that of a children's book author," Osborne says.

"To the Top of Everest"

Samantha Larson (b. 1988)
In 2007, American Samantha Larson became the youngest person to climb the "Seven Summits"—the highest mountains on each of the seven continents. Larson climbed her first, Mount Kilimanjaro in Africa, at the age of 12. She finished her quest when she successfully reached the top of Mt. Everest at age 18. Larson calls Everest "much harder, longer, and higher" than the other peaks. "It was one big challenge," she recalls, but adds, "Deep down I thought I would make it."

Comparing Universal Themes

A **universal theme** is a message about life that is expressed repeatedly in many different cultures and time periods. Universal themes include concepts such as the value of courage and the danger of greed. You can identify the universal theme in a literary work by focusing on the main character, thinking about conflicts the character faces, and noticing the changes that the character undergoes as a result of those conflicts.

Universal themes are important ideas, so many cultures present these themes in **epics**—stories or long poems about larger-than-life heroes. In many ways, an epic can be seen as a portrait of the culture that produced it. Epics express a culture's values and its perspective on universal themes, such as bravery. Other **epic conventions**, or elements typical of epics, are listed in the chart below.

Epics and their themes are an important part of the literature of different cultures. Ancient epics were recited as entertainment and passed down from storyteller to storyteller. New generations often create works inspired by these epics. For example, it is not unusual to find an allusion, or reference, to the ancient Greek epic the *Odyssey* in a new adventure story. As you read these selections, use a chart like this to note the examples of epic conventions that help point toward a universal theme.

Common Core State Standards

Reading Literature
2. Determine a theme or central idea of a text and analyze its development over the course of the text; provide an objective summary of the text.

3. Analyze how particular elements of a story or drama interact.

Reading Informational Text
9. Analyze how two or more authors writing about the same topic shape their presentations of key information by emphasizing different evidence or advancing different interpretations of facts.

Writing
2. Write informative/explanatory texts to examine a topic and convey ideas, concepts, and information through the selection, organization, and analysis of relevant content.

Language
5.a. Interpret figures of speech (e.g., literary, biblical, and mythological allusions) in context.

Epic Conventions	"The Voyage" from *Tales from the Odyssey*	"To the Top of Everest"
dangerous journey		
characters who help	Goddesses Ino and Athena	
broad setting		
serious, formal style		

THE VOYAGE

FROM TALES FROM THE ODYSSEY

MARY POPE OSBORNE

In the early morning of time, there existed a mysterious world called Mount Olympus. Hidden behind a veil of clouds, this world was never swept by winds, nor washed by rains. Those who lived on Mount Olympus never grew old; they never died. They were not humans. They were the mighty gods and goddesses of ancient Greece.

The Olympian gods and goddesses had great power over the lives of the humans who lived on earth below. Their anger once caused a man named Odysseus to wander the seas for many long years, trying to find his way home.

Almost three thousand years ago, a Greek poet named Homer first told the story of Odysseus' journey. Since that time, storytellers have told the strange and wondrous tale again and again. We call that story the Odyssey.

With his hands gripping the rudder, Odysseus skillfully guided his raft over the waves. He never slept. All night, he kept his eyes fixed on the stars that Calypso had told him to watch—the Pleiades and the Bear.

Day after day and night after night, Odysseus sailed the seas. Finally, on the eighteenth day, he saw the dim outline of mountains on the horizon.

As Odysseus steered his raft toward the shore, dark clouds gathered overhead. The water began to rise. The wind began to blow, until it was roaring over the earth and sea.

Has Poseidon discovered my raft? Odysseus wondered anxiously. *Does he now seek his final revenge?*

For many years, Poseidon, mighty ruler of the sea, had been angry with Odysseus for blinding his son, the Cyclops. Now it seemed he was trying to destroy Odysseus once again. The wind roared from the north, south, east, and west. Daylight plunged into darkness. Odysseus feared he was about to come to a terrible, lonely end.

Suddenly an enormous wave crashed down on Odysseus' raft. Odysseus was swept overboard and pulled deep beneath the sea. He struggled wildly to raise his head above the water and breathe.

When his head finally broke the surface, Odysseus saw his raft swiftly moving away across the water. He swam as fast as he could toward the wooden craft. He grabbed the timbers and pulled himself aboard.

Then, as the wind swirled the raft across the water, Odysseus saw an astonishing sight. A sea goddess was floating like a gull on top of the waves.

Seemingly impervious to the great storm, she floated near his raft and climbed aboard.

"My friend," she said, "I am Ino, the White Goddess, who guides sailors in storms. I know not why Poseidon is angry with you. But I know this: for all the torture he has inflicted upon you, he will not kill you. But you must leave your raft at once and swim for the shore. Take my veil, for it is enchanted. You will come to no harm as long as you possess it. As soon as you reach land, you must throw it back into the sea."

◀ **Vocabulary**
impervious (im pur′ vē əs) *adj.* not affected by something

inflicted (in flikt′ əd) *v.* delivered something painful

Comprehension
Who climbs aboard Odysseus' raft?

With these words, the White Goddess removed her enchanted veil and gave it to Odysseus. Then she disappeared back into the wild seas.

At that moment, a huge wave crashed down on Odysseus' raft, ripping it to pieces. Clutching Ino's veil, Odysseus pulled himself onto a wooden plank and rode it as if it were a horse. Then he dove down into the sea.

Universal Themes
Which epic convention appears in this paragraph?

Suddenly, all the winds died down—except the north wind. Odysseus felt that Athena[1] was holding the other winds back, so he could swim safely and swiftly to some distant shore. For two days and two nights, with the north wind gently flattening the waves before him, he swam and floated on the calm sea.

On the third day, the north wind died away and the sea was completely calm. Odysseus saw land ahead. With a burst of joy, he swam toward the rocky shore.

In an instant, the wind and waves returned. With a thundering roar, sea spray rained down on him.

Odysseus struggled to keep his head above the churning water, seeking a place to go ashore.

Spiral Review
THEME What is Odysseus' relationship to the sea?

Angry waves were pounding the reefs with great force. *I'll be dashed against the rocks if I try to swim ashore now*, he thought desperately.

But once again, Odysseus felt the presence of Athena. A giant wave picked him up and carried him over the rocks toward the beach. But before Odysseus could crawl ashore to safety, another wave dragged him back into the sea and pulled him under the water.

Odysseus swam desperately, escaping the waves pounding the shore. Soon he came to a sheltered cove. He saw a riverbank free of rough stones. As he swam toward the bank, he prayed to the gods to save him from the angry attack of Poseidon.

Suddenly the waves were still. But when Odysseus tried to haul himself ashore, his body failed him. He had been defeated by the storm. It had ripped his flesh and robbed his muscles of their strength. He was passing in and out of consciousness.

---

1. Athena *n.* goddess of wisdom and protector of Odysseus.

Gasping for breath, he pulled off Ino's veil and threw it back into the sea. Then he used his last bit of strength to drag himself out of the water and throw himself into the river reeds.

If I lie here all night, I shall die from the cold and damp, he thought. *If I go farther ashore and pass out in a thicket, wild beasts will devour me.* No matter what evils lay ahead, he knew he had to push on. On bleeding hands and knees, he crawled to a sheltered spot under an olive tree, a tree sacred to the goddess Athena.

Odysseus lay down in a pile of dead leaves. With his bloody hands, he spread leaves over his torn body. Like a farmer spreading ashes over the embers of his fire, he tried to protect the last spark of life within him.

Mercifully, the gray-eyed goddess slipped down from the heavens and appeared at his side. She closed his weary eyes and pulled him down into a sweet sleep that took away his pain and sorrow.

Universal Themes
Based on this paragraph, what trait do you think the ancient Greeks valued in heroes?

Critical Thinking

1. **Key Ideas and Details (a)** How does Odysseus react to the storm at sea? **(b) Generalize:** Choose three adjectives that describe Odysseus. **(c) Speculate:** Why do you think the goddesses help Odysseus?

2. **Key Ideas and Details (a) Make a Judgment:** Do you think Odysseus will survive his injuries? **(b) Support:** Find several passages in the text that support your answer.

3. **Integration of Knowledge and Ideas** How would you describe ancient Greek culture after reading this passage based on an ancient Greek myth?

4. **Integration of Knowledge and Ideas** Odysseus struggles mightily against beings more powerful than he is. Do you think his story can teach lessons to individuals, communities, or both? Explain your answer, using details from the text. *[Connect to the Big Question: Community or individual—which is more important?]*

To the Top of Everest

Samantha Larson

Friday, March 30, 2007

Here we go ⟶ Kathmandu!

Today is the day! Our bags are (nearly) packed and we're (just about) ready to go. I've got eleven hours to run around doing last minute errands before our plane takes off.

I arrived back in Long Beach from New York last Saturday, where I've been since our return from Cho Oyu. When I wasn't training by running, swimming at the pool, taking dance classes, or rock climbing, I was taking oboe lessons, French, and photography classes. Hopefully I'll be able to take some great pictures on this expedition!

It has been a very exciting week in all our general trip preparation mayhem, filled with lots of gear sorting and fedex package arrivals. But now my dad and I are pretty much all set to go.

See you in Kathmandu!

◄ Critical Viewing
Which details in this photograph suggest Larson is about to go on a dangerous journey?

Comprehension
How did Larson train for her expedition?

Monday, April 2, 2007
Kathmandu
After nearly 24 hours of travel we finally arrived in Kathmandu yesterday afternoon. Doug, my dad, and I met up with the rest of the team (Victor, James, and Wim) at our hotel in Kathmandu. We had a group meeting where we went over the route we are going to take to base camp, and then we picked up some odds and ends at one of the dozens of local climbing stores.

The team is flying to Lukla to begin the trek to base camp early tomorrow morning.

Wednesday, April 4, 2007
Namche Bazar
Yesterday after a very scenic flight and a heart-stopping landing on a small airstrip perched on the side of a mountain, we arrived in Lukla to begin the trek to base camp. Lukla was filled with excitement as porters organized their loads and trekkers began their journeys. From Lukla, we hiked for about 4 hours through the beautiful Nepalese countryside, passing through several villages until we reached the village of Monjo, where we stayed the night in the Monjo Guesthouse. I think my dad and I got the big sleep that we needed to catch up on our jetlag; around 4 in the afternoon, we decided to take a "nap" that lasted until 7 the next morning!

Thursday, April 12, 2007
Base Camp
We made it to base camp yesterday afternoon. Today we are going to practice crossing the ladders over the Khumbu Icefall. We are well and safe.

En route here we visited Lama Gesa and he blessed our journey. It was an amazing experience!

I am going to try and connect my laptop and charge it with my solar charger—we will see if that works.

More to follow.....

Monday, April 16, 2007
Rest Day

Yesterday we got an early start for our first time through the icefall. We left around 6:30 in the morning, with the idea that we would turn around 11—we did not necessarily have a destination in mind, it was more for acclimatization[1] and to get an idea of what the icefall was like. However, at 11 we were about half an hour from the top of the icefall, so we decided to just continue to the top.

It was quite fun climbing up the icefall. The ladders that we had to cross over crevasses[2] were especially exciting. I was pretty tired by the time we got back to base camp, but today was a rest day (our first), so I've had plenty of time to recover.

Tomorrow we are going up to camp one to spend the night. Camp one is about an hour further than we went yesterday. The next day we will go up to tag camp two and then come back down to base camp.

Thursday, April 19, 2007
Puja

The day before yesterday we all made it up to camp one to spend the night. This time we were able to get through the Khumbu Icefall an hour quicker than the last. We had a pretty good night at camp one; my dad and I both had a bit of a headache at first, but we were both able to eat and sleep well.

Camp one is at the start of the Western Cwm.[3] Yesterday, from camp one we continued up the Cwm to camp two. The cwm

▲ **Critical Viewing**
Why might someone take a lot of risks to visit a place like this?

Universal Themes
How is Lama Gesa's role in this selection similar to Athena's role in "The Voyage"?

Comprehension
How long did it take to travel to Kathmandu?

---

1. **acclimatization** (ə klī′ mə tə zā′ shən) *n.* process of allowing the body to adjust to the climate, especially at high altitude.
2. **crevasses** (krə vas′ əz) *n.* deep cracks in ice or a glacier.
3. **Western Cwm** *n.* a broad valley at the base of Mount Everest.

is infamous for being very uncomfortably hot, but yesterday it was actually really nice. It was very beautiful, and we could see the summit of Everest, which we haven't been able to see since before we got to base camp. After we tagged camp two we came all the way back down to base camp. It was a long day, and we all returned pretty tired. However, it was nice to be back in base camp, and after dinner we watched Mission Impossible III on Ben's laptop (from the London Business School team). Unfortunately the power ran out about half way through, but I have been asked to charge up my laptop so we can finish tonight.

Spiral Review
CULTURAL
PERSPECTIVE Why do you think the Sherpas organize a blessing ceremony?

Today was the Puja, which is a ceremony that the Sherpas organize. A Lama comes up and performs many chants to ask the mountain gods for permission to climb the mountain, and to ask for protection. I had my ice ax and my crampons[4] blessed in the ceremony. As part of the ceremony, they also put out long lines of prayer flags coming out from the stupa where the ceremony was performed. Afterwards, they passed out lots of yummy treats.

While we were up at camp one, the shower tent was set up here at base camp. It's just a little bucket of water with a hose attached to it, but definitely 15 minutes of heaven.

Saturday, April 28, 2007
Base Camp

Universal Themes
Which details in this entry show that Larson and her team face great dangers as they continue to climb?

We are back at base camp! We came down from camp two yesterday, and arrived just in time for lunch. We were delayed a bit in the morning because we were radioed from base camp that there was a break in the icefall, and we didn't want to leave until we knew that the "ice doctors" had fixed up the route. As we came down, we found that the break was in a flat area known as the "football field" that we had previously designated as a "safe" area to take a little rest. And the whole shelf just collapsed!

Vocabulary ▶
designated (dez´ ig nāt´ əd) v. identified; pointed out

Now that we have spent a night at camp three, we are done with the acclimatization process. We are going to take a few days for rest and recovery, and then we just wait for good weather to make a summit bid. We plan to go back down to Pengboche tomorrow so we can really get a good rest at lower altitude before our summit attempt.

---

4. **crampons** (kram´ pənz) n. metal plates with spikes that are attached to boots to provide greater traction.

Here is what we have been up to these past few days:

4/23/07
Yesterday we all made it up to camp one for the night. We were joined by Tori from the London Business School team, because she wasn't feeling 100% when her team went up the day before.

Today we all came up to camp two. It was very hot coming up the Cwm this time, and we all had heavy packs because we had to bring up what we had left at camp one the last time we stayed there. It certainly made it a lot harder work!

4/24/07
Despite the fact that I caused us to get a later start than planned this morning (I had a particularly hard time getting out of my warm sleeping bag into the cold air) we accomplished our goal for the day. We went up the very first pitch of the Lhotse Face, and are now back at camp two for the evening.

4/26/07
Yesterday we went about halfway up the Lhotse Face to camp three to spend the night. This was a new record for my dad and me, as our highest night ever! Camp three is at about 23,500 feet, and our previous highest night was at camp two on Cho Oyu, at 23,000 feet. We arrived at camp three around noon, and then had a lot of time to kill in our tents, as it wasn't really safe to go more than five feet outside the tent without putting on crampons and clipping into the fixed ropes. Thankfully, I had not yet reached a hypoxic[5] level where I couldn't enjoy my book.

Coming up the Lhotse Face was a bit windy, and some parts were pretty icy. It gets fairly steep, so I was glad to have my ascender, which slides up the rope, but not back down, so you can use it as a handhold to pull yourself up.

Comprehension
What did the Lama ask for during the Puja?

---

5. **hypoxic** (hī päk´ sik) *adj.* having too little oxygen.

Sunday, May 6, 2007
Back from Holiday
We're back at base camp from our little holiday down the mountain.

Now that we are back in base camp, we are just waiting till we can go for our summit attempt. The ropes are not yet fixed to the summit. Once the ropes are fixed, we hope there will soon be a good weather window.

Friday, May 11, 2007
Base Camp
We're still at base camp. Hopefully we'll be able to go up soon though.

We've tried to hold on to our fitness these past few days by doing some sort of activity each day. We've been ice climbing in a really neat cave near base camp, and we've also been on hikes up Pumori to Pumori base camp, and then up to camp one. Pumori is a 7145-meter mountain near Everest.

Saturday, May 12, 2007
Still at Base Camp
It looks like we're going to be able to go up soon for our summit attempt. Fingers crossed!

We've gotten our oxygen masks and tested them out. I was able to get my oxygen saturation back up to 100% this morning! After I turned off the oxygen, I only had a few seconds of being at pseudo sea-level before it went back down, though.

We're all getting a little restless hanging around base camp.

Monday, May 14, 2007
Camp 2
We finally started our summit push yesterday, making our way from base camp to camp two. We don't have internet access up here, but we were able to relay this information to our correspondents in New York via satellite phone. We're taking a rest day today, and plan to press on tomorrow. If all goes well, we should summit on the 17th.

Universal Themes
How do you know that Larson is willing to face challenges to meet her goal?

Vocabulary ▶
saturation (sach′ ə rā′ shən) *n.* state of being completely filled

Thursday, May 17, 2007

Summit!

We made it to the top! Now all we have to do is get back down...

Wednesday, May 23, 2007

Back Home!

We've been in a big rush getting back home, and I haven't been able to update for awhile, as I have not had internet access. We woke up this morning at 16,000 feet in a village called Lobuche, and this evening my dad and I arrived back at sea-level in Long Beach! The rest of the team are celebrating in Kathmandu—my dad and I skipped out on the celebration to make it back in time for my brother Ted's college graduation in New York.

The day after we summited, we came down from the South Col (camp 4) to camp 2. I was very tired at that point, but glad that we had all made it back safely lower on the mountain. It was amazing how after being to almost 30,000 feet, 20,000-foot camp 2 felt like it was nearly at sea-level!

The day after that, we came back down to base camp, where we received lots of warm hugs and congratulations. We only had one night back at base camp, as the next day (the 20th), we packed up our bags and headed down the valley. Base camp had a strange, empty feeling—it was sad to leave my little tent that had been my home for the past 2 months! My dad, Doug, Wim, and I were hoping to get a helicopter out of Lobuche on the 21st to save a little time, but Victor and

Comprehension
How does Larson stay fit while waiting to go to the summit?

We made it to the top! Now all we have to do is get back down...

James decided to walk down to the Lukla airstrip to fly out to Kathmandu on the 23rd. However, even though we awoke on the 21st to a beautiful, clear day in Lobuche, apparently there were clouds lower down the valley, so the helicopter couldn't fly in until the 23rd either. It was kind of hard waiting those two days in Lobuche. We were just an hour away from a hot shower and a big meal, if only those clouds would clear!

Universal Themes
What details here suggest some people consider Larson and her team heroes?

Once the helicopter landed in Kathmandu, I was greeted by a mob of journalists and cameramen. I was so surprised! After nearly 20 hours of travel, my dad and I landed at LAX[6] and were greeted by my family, and some more news people. Now we only have a few hours before we jump back on a plane to go to New York! I am very excited to see my mom and brother though.

Thank you everyone for all of your wonderful comments and your support!!!

---

6. **LAX** *n.* Los Angeles International Airport.

Critical Thinking

1. **Key Ideas and Details** **(a)** What are some of the things Larson does to prepare for her journey before leaving home? **(b) Infer:** Why is it important for Larson to be in top physical shape? **(c) Deduce:** How might her other lessons and interests affect her trip?

2. **Key Ideas and Details** **(a)** How much time does Larson spend on the mountain before trying to reach the summit? **(b) Summarize:** List five things the team does with its time on the mountain before heading out for the summit. **(c) Deduce:** What prevents the team from trying to summit earlier?

3. **Integration of Knowledge and Ideas** Why might climbers of many faiths want to take part in the Puja ceremony?

4. **Integration of Knowledge and Ideas** Climbing Mt. Everest takes an incredible amount of time, effort, and money. **(a)** How might a journey like Larson's enrich her as an individual? **(b)** Do you think the community also gains from her success? Explain. *[Connect to the Big Question: Community or individual—which is more important?]*

Writing to Sources

Comparing Universal Themes

1. Key Ideas and Details Compare and contrast Larson's voyage with Odysseus's voyage.

	Odysseus	Samantha Larson
Journey undertaken		
Attitude of character		
Obstacles character must overcome		
Outcome		

2. Craft and Structure (a) Why might you include an allusion to the *Odyssey* if you were writing about Larson for your school paper? **(b)** Would you describe her as a "hero"? Explain.

3. Integration of Knowledge and Ideas One theme of the *Odyssey* is the triumph of bravery over power. Do you think "To the Top of Everest" expresses the same message? Why or why not? If not, how would you state its central idea?

⏱ Timed Writing

Explanatory Text: Essay

In an essay, compare and contrast the themes of the classic epic tale "The Voyage" with the modern account "To the Top of Everest." Explain how time and place influence the theme of each selection. **(40 minutes)**

5-Minute Planner

1. Read the prompt carefully and completely.

2. Jot down answers to these questions:

- What is the universal theme of each selection?

- How do the heroes overcome obstacles?

- How do the two authors affect your response by the way they emphasize different evidence?

3. Reread the prompt, and then draft your essay.

USE ACADEMIC VOCABULARY

As you write, use academic language, including the following words or their related forms:

attitude

challenge

environment

outcome

For more information about academic vocabulary, see pages xlvi–l.

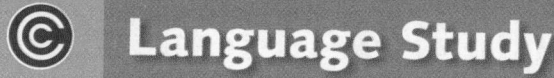

Figurative Language

 **Common Core State Standards**

Figurative language is language that is not meant to be taken literally. Most types of figurative language are based on imaginative comparisons, lending ordinary things extraordinary qualities. The use of figurative language makes writing vivid and expressive. The chart below contains examples of common types of figurative language.

Language

5. Demonstrate understanding of figurative language, word relationships, and nuances in word meanings.

5.a. Interpret figures of speech in context.

5.b. Use the relationship between particular words to better understand each of the words.

Type of Figurative Language	Example
Simile: a figure of speech that uses *like* or *as* to make a direct comparison between two unlike ideas	The sky is <u>like</u> a patchwork quilt.
Metaphor: a description of one thing as if it were another	The sky <u>is</u> a patchwork quilt.
Analogy: an extended comparison of relationships. An analogy shows how the relationship between one pair of things is like the relationship between another pair	Walter lives like a sheet of paper blown along a windy street. He is carried this way and that way with no control of his direction.
Personification: a figure of speech in which a nonhuman subject is given human characteristics	The <u>sea</u> was <u>angry</u> that day, my friends.
Paradox: a statement, an idea, or a situation that seems contradictory but actually expresses a truth	The more things change, the more they stay the same.
Idiom: an expression whose meaning differs from the meanings of its individual words	It was raining cats and dogs last night.

Practice A Identify each instance of figurative language in these sentences as a *simile* or *metaphor*.

1. Because I studied for several nights, the quiz was a breeze.

2. The winter night was so quiet that every sound was as clear as a bell.

3. My dog is the sunshine of my life.

4. After shoveling snow for several hours, I slept like a log last night.

5. A ghost of a moon shone over the fields.

Practice B Identify the *simile, metaphor, idiom,* or *analogy* in each sentence. Then, use context clues to explain the meaning of each.

1. Tyrone understands people very well; he reads them like a book.
2. I tried to get my friend to change his mind, but he was a mule.
3. Two peas in a pod, Simon and Jack liked exactly the same music.
4. Seeing the fascinating art in the museum sparked my interest in sculpture.
5. After she won the diving competition, Elana was as happy as a lark.
6. Learning the multiplication tables is like riding a bike; once you learn it, you never forget it.
7. After losing the concert tickets, Kevin was as mad as a hornet.
8. Her hair was a cloud of snowy white.

Activity With a partner, browse through some current magazines. Search through the articles to find examples of at least four types of figurative language. Use a notecard like the one shown to list the examples you have found. Then, explain the meaning of each example. Use the context clues in the article to aid your understanding.

Comprehension and Collaboration

With a partner, write a scene with dialogue between two characters, taking care to use no figurative language. Then, rewrite the dialogue, adding idioms, analogies, similes, and metaphors. Compare your scenes. Which one sounds more realistic? Why?

Similes:
Metaphors:
Analogies:
Personifications:
Paradoxes:
Idioms:

Research Presentation

These guidelines will help you through the processes of conducting research, writing a report, and presenting it to an audience.

Learn the Skills

Generate questions. Consider what you would like to discover about your topic. Pose relevant and concise questions to guide your research and help you to stay on topic.

Evaluate your sources. Prepare to use both print and electronic sources, such as databases, the Internet, and magazines. Evaluate the credibility, scope, and objectivity of each source.

- Is the source known for its correct facts?
- Does a Web site have *.edu, .gov,* or *.org* at the end of its Web address?
- Does the publication date fall within the last three years?

Organize your information. Take notes from each source to answer your research questions. Include only the information that is meaningful to your topic. Use your notes to develop an outline.

Write the report. Organize the report to include an introduction, several body paragraphs, and a conclusion. Avoid plagiarism by paraphrasing instead of copying information directly from each source. Credit your sources by citing them at the end of your report on a Bibliography or Works Cited page.

Present your report. Practice your presentation using the following techniques.

- Use graphics, such as charts, graphs, photographs, or a slideshow to enhance the main points in your report.
- Credit sources by using phrases like "According to . . ." and "In the book by . . . ."
- Vary your speaking rate and pitch to engage your listeners and retain their interest. Pronounce words clearly and speak loudly enough for everyone to hear.
- Use a natural but serious tone. Speak in formal English. For example, avoid using "filler" phrases, such as "as you know." Make eye contact and use hand gestures to emphasize certain points.

 **Common Core State Standards**

Speaking and Listening

1.c. Pose questions that elicit elaboration and respond to others' questions and comments with relevant observations and ideas that bring the discussion back on topic as needed.

2. Analyze the main ideas and supporting details presented in diverse media and formats (e.g., visually, quantitatively, orally) and explain how the ideas clarify a topic, text, or issue under study.

4. Present claims and findings, emphasizing salient points in a focused, coherent manner with pertinent descriptions, facts, details, and examples; use appropriate eye contact, adequate volume, and clear pronunciation.

5. Include multimedia components and visual displays in presentations to clarify claims and findings and emphasize salient points.

6. Adapt speech to a variety of contexts and tasks, demonstrating command of formal English when indicated or appropriate.

Practice the Skills

Presentation of Knowledge and Ideas Use the skills you learned in this workshop to complete the following activity.

ACTIVITY: **Delivering a Research Report**

Prepare a research presentation by following the steps below. Then, deliver the report to your class.

- Develop your major research question and additional questions that address your topic.
- Gather research and organize your report.
- Present your research report to your classmates.
- Use the Research Guide to plan your report.

Use a Research Guide like the one below to develop your presentation.

Research Guide

Major Research Question:

Brainstorm to list ideas that address the research topic:

Open-ended research questions:

1.   3.
2.   4.

Research plan: Jot down notes explaining your plan for researching each question.

Assessment of sources: Briefly demonstrate the reliability and credibility of each source. Then, explain why one source is more useful than another.

Synthesize the research: Draw conclusions about and summarize or paraphrase each source to synthesize the research.
Conclusions:
Summary:

Organize your research: Think about your purpose and audience when you organize your presentation.
Purpose of the research:
Audience:

Comprehension and Collaboration At the end of your presentation, invite your audience to discuss, respond to, or ask questions about your presentation. Then, listen as your classmates present their reports. Interpret the purpose of each report by explaining the content, evaluating the delivery of the presentation, and asking questions or making comments about the evidence that supports the presenter's claims.

Write an Explanatory Text

Cause-and-Effect Essay

Defining the Form A **cause-and-effect essay** explains why something happens or what happens as a result of something else. You may use this type of writing in lab reports, historical accounts, persuasive essays, magazine articles, and speeches.

Assignment Write a cause-and-effect essay about a question or issue that interests you. Include the following elements in your essay:

✓ a *well-defined* topic that can be covered in a few pages

✓ information drawn from *several credible sources*

✓ *detailed, factual explanations* of events or situations and the *relationships among them*

✓ a *clear and coherent organization* with *effective transitions that show causes and effects*

✓ a style *appropriate to the task, purpose, and audience*

✓ error-free writing, including the *correct use of commas with coordinate adjectives*

To preview the criteria on which your cause-and-effect essay may be judged, see the rubric on page 719.

FOCUS ON RESEARCH

When you conduct research to write a cause-and-effect essay, bear these points in mind:

- Some experts might emphasize one or two causes over others. Other experts might emphasize different causes. Evaluate the evidence each expert offers to determine which position makes the most sense to you.

- Experts might also differ on which effects are most serious. Again, study their evidence to see which side you support.

If a source seems extremely partial to one point of view, you might not want to rely on that source. Look for sources that are balanced. Examples include encyclopedias, news articles, and Web pages from organizations with a reputation for fairness.

ⓒ Common Core State Standards

Writing

2. Write informative/explanatory texts to examine a topic and convey ideas, concepts, and information through the selection, organization, and analysis of relevant content.

7. Conduct short research projects to answer a question, drawing on several sources and generating additional related, focused questions for further research and investigation.

READING-WRITING CONNECTION

To get the feel for cause-and-effect writing, read "Life Without Gravity" by Robert Zimmerman on page 194.

Prewriting/Planning Strategies

Choose a topic. Use one of these strategies:

- **Brainstorming** Sometimes the best way to find a topic is to just start writing. Write for five minutes about whatever questions come to mind. Use phrases such as "What causes . . ." or "Why does . . ." to begin each question. Circle any questions that you think would make an interesting topic.

- **Imagining a Walk** Close your eyes and imagine yourself walking through a house, apartment, or other place you know well. Observe the objects, people, or activities that you "see" along the way. To find items that suggest cause-and-effect relationships, ask, "What caused this?" or "What effects does this have?" Jot down several ideas, then choose your topic from these items.

Narrow your topic. A topic with many causes and effects, such as the causes and effects of storms, is far too broad. Narrow a broad topic to focus on a single cause or a single effect. For example, the effects of a tornado—a single cause—would be an appropriate topic. Use a web like the one shown to narrow your topic. Write your topic in the center and surround it with subtopics. Then, note causes or effects connected to each subtopic. Consider whether any of the subtopics would make a good focus for your essay.

Conduct research. Do research to fill in any gaps in your knowledge about your topic. First write down a series of questions about your topic to guide your research. Then, use library resources and online references, or interview an expert on the topic to find answers to the questions you posed. Continue to generate focused questions for further research. Use a two-column chart to help you gather details. In one column, list the causes involved in your event or situation. In the other column, list the effects.

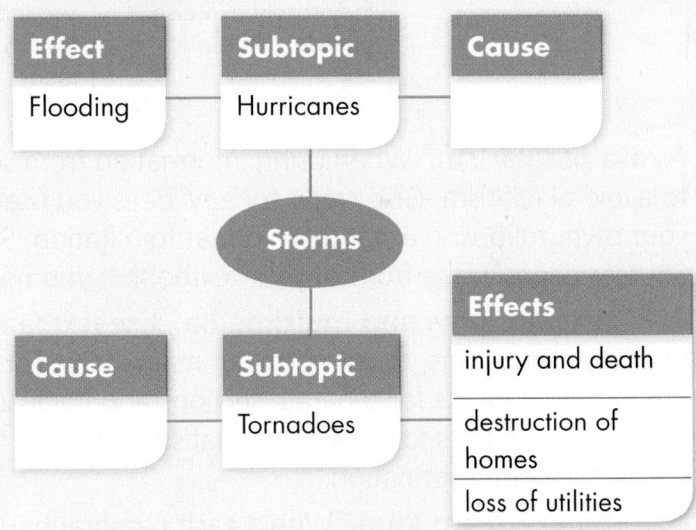

Drafting Strategies

**Common Core
State Standards**

Writing

2.a. Introduce a topic clearly, previewing what is to follow; organize ideas, concepts, and information, using strategies such as definition, classification, comparison/contrast, and cause/effect; include formatting, graphics, and multimedia when useful to aiding comprehension.

2.b. Develop the topic with relevant facts, definitions, concrete details, quotations, or other information and examples.

2.c. Use appropriate transitions to create cohesion and clarify the relationships among ideas and concepts.

4. Produce clear and coherent writing in which the development, organization, and style are appropriate to task, purpose, and audience.

Write a strong introduction. Your introduction is the first thing your audience will read. Include a sentence or two that explains the importance of your topic. Then, identify the main points you will address in your essay.

Explain causes and effects logically. Explain the logic of each cause-and-effect relationship you present. Support your statements with specific facts, statistics, names, and dates whenever possible. Opinions and trivial, or unimportant, details are not strong support for an argument.

Unsupported Statement	Supported Statement	Difference
Children watch too much TV nowadays.	Studies show that children watch an average of 15 hours of TV every week.	The first statement is an opinion. The second is a statement of fact.
I have a neighbor who never exercises.	In a survey of 100 teens, 32 percent said they rarely exercise outside school.	The first statement is a trivial example. The second cites evidence from a survey of many teens.

Avoid plagiarism. When using information from sources, be sure to avoid plagiarism. Give credit for any ideas you use that are not your own, following a standard format for citation. See the Citing Sources pages in the front of your textbook if you need guidance.

Add text features and multimedia. Use text features, such as headings and charts, to support your main ideas. For example, you might use headings for separate sections about causes and effects. You may use charts to present key statistics. Be sure to credit the sources of your information.

Use the SEE technique. Within each paragraph, use the **SEE** technique to add depth to your essay.

- In a paragraph, first write a **S**tatement of the main idea.
- Next, write a sentence that **E**xtends that idea.
- Finally, write a sentence that **E**laborates on the extension.

Organize Logically

Before you begin to write your essay, decide how you want to organize your details. You might try one of these suggestions:

- If you are writing about a single cause with many effects, devote a paragraph to each effect.
- If you are writing about one effect with many causes, devote one paragraph to each cause and one paragraph to the effect.
- If you are writing about a series of causes and effects, organize your paragraphs in chronological, or time, order.

The chart shows how the paragraphs of the body of the essay would be organized in these three arrangements.

Body Paragraph	Single Cause, Many Effects	Many Causes, Single Effect	Series of Causes and Effects
1	**Cause** Mount Saint Helens erupts	**Cause 1** Increased TV watching	**Cause** Growing power of computers
2	**Effect 1** People, animals, and plants die	**Cause 2** Increased junk-food eating	**Effect/Cause** Computers have more uses
3	**Effect 2** Forest fires, mudslides, floods	**Cause 3** Less exercise	**Effect/Cause** Computers become more popular
4	**Effect 3** Loss of buildings, roads, bridges	**Effect** A generation of children is gaining weight	**Effect** People rely on computers in many areas of life

Indicate Relative Importance Some causes or effects are more important than others. You might wish to build up from the least important to the most important point. Alternatively, you may decide to begin with your most important point. For instance, in the first example in the chart above, loss of life is listed as the first effect because the writer thinks that detail is the most important.

Whatever organization you choose, use transition words to clearly show the relationships among ideas. For example, beginning a paragraph with the words *Most important . . .* tells your readers that the effect you are about to describe is more serious than others you have mentioned.

Revising Strategies

State main ideas clearly. By starting a new paragraph, you signal readers that you are introducing a new idea. Effective writers clearly state the main idea in each paragraph. To analyze the connections among your other sentences, use color-coding.

Reread each paragraph. Use two highlighters—one color to mark phrases that present causes and another color to mark phrases that indicate effects. Evaluate the connections between the two. Go back and add transitions such as *because of* and *as a result* to help readers see cause-and-effect connections.

**Common Core
State Standards**

Writing
2.c. Use appropriate transitions to create cohesion and clarify the relationships among ideas and concepts.
5. With some guidance and support from peers and adults, develop and strengthen writing as needed by planning, revising, editing, rewriting, or trying a new approach, focusing on how well purpose and audience have been addressed.

Language
1. Demonstrate command of the conventions of standard English grammar and usage when writing or speaking.
2.a. Use a comma to separate coordinate adjectives.

> **Model: Color-Coding Causes and Effects**
> A generation of children is gaining weight. Instead of running and playing outside, many children sit in front of the TV, play video games or surf the Internet. While doing so, young children often eat junk food to pass the time. Because this time is so unstructured, they don't monitor how much food they are actually eating. In time, these young children are becoming very overweight.

Use the appropriate verb tense. Generally, you should use one verb tense consistently throughout your essay. However, to show the order of events, you may need to shift tenses. Review your draft to determine the tenses of most of your verbs. Circle any verbs that are in a different tense. If these verbs do not show events happening at different times or if they show a recurring event, consider changing them.

> **Events at different times:**
>   past
> Because I **missed** my math test
>   present
> yesterday, I **need** to take it today.
>
> ———————————————————————
>
> **Events that recur:**
>   past   present
> Last week, I **missed** French. Because I **leave** school early
>   present
> on Wednesdays, I **miss** one class every week.

Peer Review

Ask a classmate to review your draft to help you determine whether you have logically and clearly stated cause-and-effect links.

Revising Incorrect Use of Commas

A **comma** is a punctuation mark used to indicate a brief pause. The following examples illustrate some common misuses of commas. Misused commas are shown in red.

Rule: Commas separate **coordinate adjectives**—or two adjectives that modify the same noun—but not the adjective from the noun:

> **Misused:** My favorite drink is a cool, refreshing, lemonade.

> **Correct:** My favorite drink is a cool, refreshing lemonade.

Rule: Commas do not separate parts of a compound subject or object.

> **Misused:** After dinner, my friend Annie, and her sister Emma, left.

> **Correct:** After dinner, my friend Annie and her sister Emma left.

> **Misused:** He made a sundae with whipped cream, and sprinkles.

> **Correct:** He made a sundae with whipped cream and sprinkles.

Rule: Commas separate clauses that include both a subject and its verb, not parts of a compound verb.

> **Misused:** The candidate looked out at the audience, and laughed.

> **Correct:** The candidate looked out at the audience and laughed.

Fixing Incorrect Use of Commas Follow these rules:

1. Add a comma or commas:

- before a conjunction that separates two independent clauses in a compound sentence.
- to separate three or more words, phrases, or clauses in a series.
- to separate coordinate adjectives.
- to set off an introductory adverb clause.

2. Eliminate the comma:

- if it comes directly between the subject and the verb of a sentence.
- if it separates an adjective from the noun that follows it.
- if it separates a compound subject, verb, or object.

Grammar in Your Writing

Reread your cause-and-effect essay, noting coordinate adjectives and compound subjects, verbs, and objects. If necessary, fix the use of commas.

**Common Core
State Standards**

Language
2.b. Spell correctly.

The Invention of Cell Phones

Imagine our world today without cell phones. This portable way of communicating is a part of many people's everyday lives. If we did not have cell phones, moms would not be able to call from the store, more kids might have trouble staying in touch, and emergencies would be harder to report.

However people did, and still do, manage without them. Cell phones weren't invented that long ago. In 1973, Dr. Martin Cooper invented the first portable handset and soon after created the first pro-totype of a cellular phone. Four years later, cell phones became available to the public and cell phone testing began.

What effect has the invention of cell phones had on the world? With everything in life there are pros and cons. Today, most teenagers own cell phones. This means there is no excuse for not letting a parent or guardian know where you are or for not having your cell phone charged. And of course the most important thing is never to lose your phone.

Cell phones have caused a change in our economy. Although the cost of cell phones has gone down greatly over the years, they are still very expensive. As a result, for families that are not very wealthy, owning a cell phone might affect their income badly. However, loads of money is coming in to phone companies every month from cell phone bills.

Many people say that cell phones cause a disturbance. You cannot go on a train or shop in a mall without constantly hearing phones ring and listening to other people's conversations. The effect of this is that more people are stressed and being disturbed by cell phones. Others are disturbed by not having cell phones. A teacher in school left her cell phone at school over the weekend. She was in the office on Monday recalling her story angrily, reporting that it was an awful experience and that she could not function without her phone.

Although there are many negative aspects of cell phones, these items have also caused our world to be more secure. If you ask people why they first bought their cell phone, many will mention safety. Cell phones are very effective when people get into car accidents and can call "911" immediately. Parents can always know where their kids are.

The invention of cell phones has changed our lives immensely. There are positive and negative effects. However, despite the nuisance some cell phones present, I believe the safety issues cell phones solve can make us all feel a little more secure.

Sarah defines her topic in the first paragraph.

Sarah uses facts in her explanation.

Sarah restates her topic and begins to support it with examples.

Sarah gives examples to show how cell phones can be disturbing.

Sarah sums up the effects of cell phones in her conclusion.

Editing and Proofreading

Focus on spelling irregular plurals.

- Change *y* to *i* and add *-es* to nouns that end in a consonant and *y* (*memory* / *memories*).
- Do not change the *y,* but add *-s* to nouns that end in a vowel and *y* (*play* / *plays, key* / *keys*).
- For most nouns ending in *f* or *fe,* change the *f* or *fe* to *ve* and add *-s* (*elf* / *elves, wife* / *wives*).

Some nouns' base spelling changes in the plural form (*foot* / *feet*). Nouns that are not countable do not have plural forms (*cash*).

Spiral Review
Earlier in the unit, you learned about **punctuation marks** (p. 670) and **capitalization** (p. 690). Check your essay to be sure that you have used end marks correctly to punctuate your sentences.

Publishing and Presenting

Consider one of the following ways to share your writing:

Present a diagram. On a posterboard or an overhead slide, create a diagram of the cause-and-effect chain in your essay.

Produce a talk show. Work with a partner, taking turns being a talk-show host and a guest expert. Answer questions about your topic.

Reflecting on Your Writing

Writer's Journal Jot down your answer to this question:
Which prewriting strategy was most useful for generating a topic?

Rubric for Self-Assessment

Find evidence in your writing to address each category. Then, use the rating scale to grade your work.

Criteria	Rating Scale			
	not very ....*very*			
Purpose/Focus Creates informative and explanatory text that examines a topic using a cause-and-effect strategy	1	2	3	4
Organization Organizes information to show causes and effects; writes clearly and coherently; uses formatting, graphics, and multimedia	1	2	3	4
Development of Ideas/Elaboration Provides support through relevant facts, definitions, concrete details, quotations, and examples; uses information from and cites several sources; maintains a formal style	1	2	3	4
Language Writes in a style appropriate to the task, purpose, and audience; uses transitions to clarify relationships among ideas	1	2	3	4
Conventions Demonstrates command of the conventions of standard English; uses commas to separate coordinate adjectives	1	2	3	4

SELECTED RESPONSE

**Common Core
State Standards**

RL.7.2; W.7.1.b; L.7.4.a
[For the full wording of the standards, see the standards chart in the front of your textbook.]

I. Reading Literature

Directions: *Read the excerpt from "Icarus and Daedalus" by Josephine Preston Peabody. Then, answer each question that follows.*

Among all those mortals who grew so wise that they learned the secrets of the gods, none was more cunning than Daedalus.

He once built, for King Minos of Crete, a wonderful Labyrinth of winding ways so cunningly tangled up and twisted around that, once inside, you could never find your way out again without a magic clue. But the king's favor veered with the wind, and one day he had his master architect imprisoned in a tower. Daedalus managed to escape from his cell; but it seemed impossible to leave the island, since every ship that came or went was well guarded by order of the king.

At length, watching the sea-gulls in the air—the only creatures that were sure of liberty—he thought of a plan for himself and his young son Icarus, who was captive with him.

Little by little, he gathered a store of feathers great and small. He fastened these together with thread, molded them in with wax, and so fashioned two great wings like those of a bird. When they were done, Daedalus fitted them to his own shoulders, and after one or two efforts, he found that by waving his arms he could winnow the air and cleave it, as a swimmer does the sea. He held himself aloft, <u>wavered</u> this way and that with the wind, and at last, like a great fledgling, he learned to fly.

Without delay, he fell to work on a pair of wings for the boy Icarus, and taught him carefully how to use them, bidding him beware of rash adventures among the stars. "Remember," said the father, "never to fly very low or very high, for the fogs about the earth would weigh you down, but the blaze of the sun will surely melt your feathers apart if you go too near."

For Icarus, these cautions went in at one ear and out by the other. Who could remember to be careful when he was to fly for the first time? Are birds careful? Not they! And not an idea remained in the boy's head but the one joy of escape.

1. **Part A** What type of story is "Icarus and Daedalus"?

    A. a legend

    B. a myth

    C. a folk tale

    D. a poem

    Part B Which detail from the story best supports the answer to Part A?

    A. "they learned the secrets of the gods"

    B. "like a great fledgling, he learned to fly"

    C. "you could never find your way out again without a magic clue"

    D. "but the king's favor veered with the wind"

2. Which answer choice expresses a **universal theme?**

    A. Mortals do not have magic powers.

    B. Birds fly by flapping their wings.

    C. Too much pride can lead to a fall.

    D. Crete is the largest of the Greek islands.

3. Which passage from the story expresses a **cause-and-effect** relationship?

    A. "He once built, for King Minos of Crete, a wonderful Labyrinth of winding ways . . ."

    B. "Little by little, he gathered a store of feathers great and small."

    C. ". . . the blaze of the sun will surely melt your feathers apart if you go too near.'"

    D. "And not an idea remained in the boy's head but the one joy of escape."

4. Which passage from the story expresses **comparison and contrast?**

    A. "Among all those mortals who grew so wise that they learned the secrets of the gods, none was more cunning than Daedalus."

    B. "But the king's favor veered with the wind, and one day he had his master architect imprisoned in a tower."

    C. "When they were done, Daedalus fitted them to his own shoulders . . ."

    D. "Without delay, he fell to work on a pair of wings for the boy Icarus . . ."

5. Which answer choice describes **cultural context?**

    A. customs and beliefs

    B. plot and setting

    C. dialogue and description

    D. facts and examples

6. Which answer choice states a key feature of stories such as this one that come from the **oral tradition?**

    A. The stories tell the true story of a real person's life.

    B. The stories were passed down orally from generation to generation.

    C. The stories are all set in ancient Greece.

    D. The stories have happy endings.

7. **Part A** Which is the best definition of the underlined word *wavered?*

    A. flew

    B. swayed

    C. followed

    D. fell

    Part B Which phrase from the story helps you understand the meaning of *wavered?*

    A. "as a swimmer does the sea"

    B. "He held himself"

    C. "this way and that"

    D. "he learned to fly"

 Timed Writing

8. Write your own ending to the excerpt from "Icarus and Daedelus." Develop your ending to follow logically from the events described in the excerpt and to express a **universal theme.**

GO ON

II. Reading Informational Text

Directions: *Read the passage. Then, answer each question that follows.*

Common Core State Standards

RI.7.6, RI.7.8; L.7.1.a, L.7.2, L.7.2.a
[For full standards wording, see the chart in the front of this book.]

Pet ownership is a wonderful way for children to learn responsibility. I didn't always think so, but then my daughter changed my mind.

Anna was four when she began asking for a dog. I always said no. Anna was the kind of child who "forgot" her homework and never made her bed. Whenever Anna asked for a dog, I'd tell her that she needed to be more responsible before I would feel comfortable putting her in charge of a living creature.

Then, one day a little dog followed Anna home. We put up signs, but nobody claimed the dog. It seemed like she was meant to be ours.

Anna was twelve when the lost dog we named Coco joined the family. I didn't expect her to take care of the dog without help, but I was pleasantly surprised. Anna used to dawdle on her way home from school, always taking the long way. Suddenly, she was running home to feed Coco and take her for a walk. Anna used to tease me for picking up garbage at the park. Now she carries a bag and a glove with her so she can pick up broken glass. She doesn't want Coco to cut her paws. More surprisingly, Anna has become more responsible about things that have nothing to do with Coco—things like getting dressed in the morning and remembering her homework. Anna isn't the only one who is happy that Coco followed her home. I'm happy too!

1. Part A What is the author's argument at the beginning of the passage?

A. Children should demonstrate responsibility before getting a pet.

B. Owning a pet can teach responsibility.

C. Twelve is too young to own a dog.

D. Children should do chores at home.

Part B Which of the following is a claim that supports the argument you identified in Part A?

A. Anna runs home from school to take care of Coco.

B. No one claimed the dog that followed Anna home.

C. Anna was four when she began asking for a dog.

D. Anna used to tease her mother for picking up garbage at the park.

2. In what order does the author present events in the passage?

A. in spatial order

B. in chronological order

C. in backwards order

D. in order of importance

3. For what purpose did the author most likely write this selection?

A. To entertain readers with stories about her daughter.

B. To inform pet owners about how to care for a dog.

C. To convince cat owners that dogs make good pets.

D. To persuade parents that it is beneficial for children to care for pets.

III. Writing and Language Conventions

Directions: *Read the passage. Then, answer each question that follows.*

(1) October 3, 2015
(2) Dear Johnson Construction:
  (3) The Red aces baseball team has not replaced its uniforms in five years. (4) A $200 donation would allow for purchasing new shirts for each team member. (5) To show our thanks and gratitude we will put the name of your business on each shirt. (6) Spectators will see that you support an organization that gives kids a positive healthful afterschool activity. (7) Please help support this talented Pleasantville team.
  (8) Thank you,

  (9) Joe Green

1. Which revision to sentence 4 includes an **infinitive phrase?**
   A. A $200 donation would mean we could purchase new shirts for each team member.
   B. A $200 donation would allow us to purchase new shirts for each team member.
   C. A $200 donation would allow for our purchasing new shirts for each team member.
   D. A $200 donation would allow new shirts for each team member.

2. Which of the following revisions correctly uses a **comma** and a **hyphen?**
   A. positive, healthful, after-school
   B. positive, healthful after-school
   C. positive healthful afterschool
   D. positive, health-ful afterschool

3. Which of the following revisions uses **capitalization** correctly?
   A. The Red Aces baseball team
   B. The Red Aces Baseball team
   C. the Red Aces baseball team
   D. The red aces Baseball Team

4. Which of the following revisions correctly uses a **comma?**
   A. To show our thanks, and gratitude, we will put the name of your business on each shirt.
   B. To show our thanks and gratitude, we will put the name of your business on each shirt.
   C. To show, our thanks and gratitude, we will put the name of your business on each shirt.
   D. To show our thanks and gratitude we will put the name of your business, on each shirt.

CONSTRUCTED RESPONSE

 **Common Core State Standards**

RL.7.2, RL.7.3, RL.7.9;
W.7.7, W.7.8, W.7.9.a;
SL.7.1, SL.7.4
[For full standards wording, see the chart in the front of this book.]

Directions: *Follow the instructions to complete the tasks below as required by your teacher.*

As you work on each task, incorporate both general academic vocabulary and literary terms you learned in Parts 1 and 2.

Writing

TASK 1 Literature [RL.7.9; W.7.9.a]

Analyze the Use of Historical Fact in Fiction and Nonfiction

Write an essay in which you compare and contrast the use of facts in a work of fiction and a work of nonfiction.

- Explain that you will discuss similarities and differences in the use of facts in "Popocatepetl and Ixtlaccihuatl" and "Tenochtitlan: Inside the Aztec Capital," which you can find in your eText.

- Identify at least three facts in the article and three facts in the legend. Explain at least two similarities and differences in the ways each author uses these facts. Consider the purpose each fact serves.

- Explain whether the author of the legend has changed any facts. If so, identify how the fact was changed and state the likely purpose for the change.

- Write a thesis statement in which you present your key ideas.

- Support your thesis statement by citing specific details from the texts.

- Summarize your ideas in a conclusion.

TASK 2 Literature [RL.7.2; W.7.9.a]

Analyze the Development of a Theme

Analyze a theme in a literary work from Part 2, and write an objective summary of that story.

- Choose a story from Part 2 to analyze. Identify a theme that the story expresses.

- Explain how the theme is developed through characters' actions and story events.

- To make sure you understand the development of the theme, write an objective summary of the story. Use your own words to retell main ideas and details.

- Include events from each part of the story to ensure completeness.

- Leave out minor details and avoid including your personal opinions.

TASK 3 Literature [RL.7.2; W.7.9.a]

Analyze a Universal Theme

Write an essay in which you analyze a universal theme from a story in Part 2.

Part 1

- Identify a universal theme in a story in Part 2. Be sure that the theme contains a message about life that can be found in other cultures and eras.

- Take notes in which you connect the universal theme to specific details from the story, including character traits, settings, conflicts, and the changes or results of these conflicts.

Part 2

- Write an essay in which you explain how the same theme can be found in other works you have read.

- Cite examples from the story from Part 2 and from other stories that share its universal theme.

Speaking and Listening

TASK 4 · Literature [RL.7.3; SL.7.4]

Analyze the Characters in a Folk Tale

Plan a presentation in which you analyze character development in a folk tale in Part 2.

- Choose a folk tale from Part 2 that features interesting and memorable characters. Identify specific details about the characters, including their personality traits, the conflicts they face, how the setting influences their choices, and what they learn as a result of their conflicts.

- Jot down details and quotations from the folk tale that contribute to character development. Plan to use these in your presentation.

- Extend the ideas in your presentation by discussing the ways in which the characters' behavior reflects the beliefs of the culture that produced the folk tale.

- Practice delivering your presentation. Use your notes for reference as you speak, but strive to make eye contact periodically with your audience.

TASK 5 · Literature [RL.7.2; SL.7.1]

Analyze and Discuss Theme

Analyze a theme from a story in Part 2 and determine which customs and beliefs it reflects. Then, organize a discussion with a small group of classmates about the value of the story's message.

- Determine the theme of a story in Part 2. Analyze how the theme is developed over the course of the story through plot events and characters' actions.

- List questions about customs and beliefs that arise as you analyze the theme. Explore one question in your analysis. Conduct research as needed.

- Evaluate whether the story still contains a meaningful message for today's readers. Support your arguments with clear and relevant reasons.

- Discuss your findings with a small group, using vocabulary that accurately expresses your ideas.

Research

TASK 6 · Literature [RL.7.2; W.7.7, W.7.8]

Community or individual— Which is more important?

In Part 2, you have read literature about conflicts between individuals and their communities. Now you will conduct a short research project about a current conflict that is happening between individuals and a community, such as a school or city. Use the literature you have read as well as your research to reflect on this unit's Big Question. Review the following guidelines before you begin your research:

- Focus your research on one conflict between individuals and a community.

- Gather relevant information from at least two reliable print or digital sources.

- Take notes as you research the conflict.

- Cite your sources.

When you have completed your research, write a response to the Big Question. Discuss how your initial ideas have been changed or reinforced. Support your response with an example from literature and an example from your research.

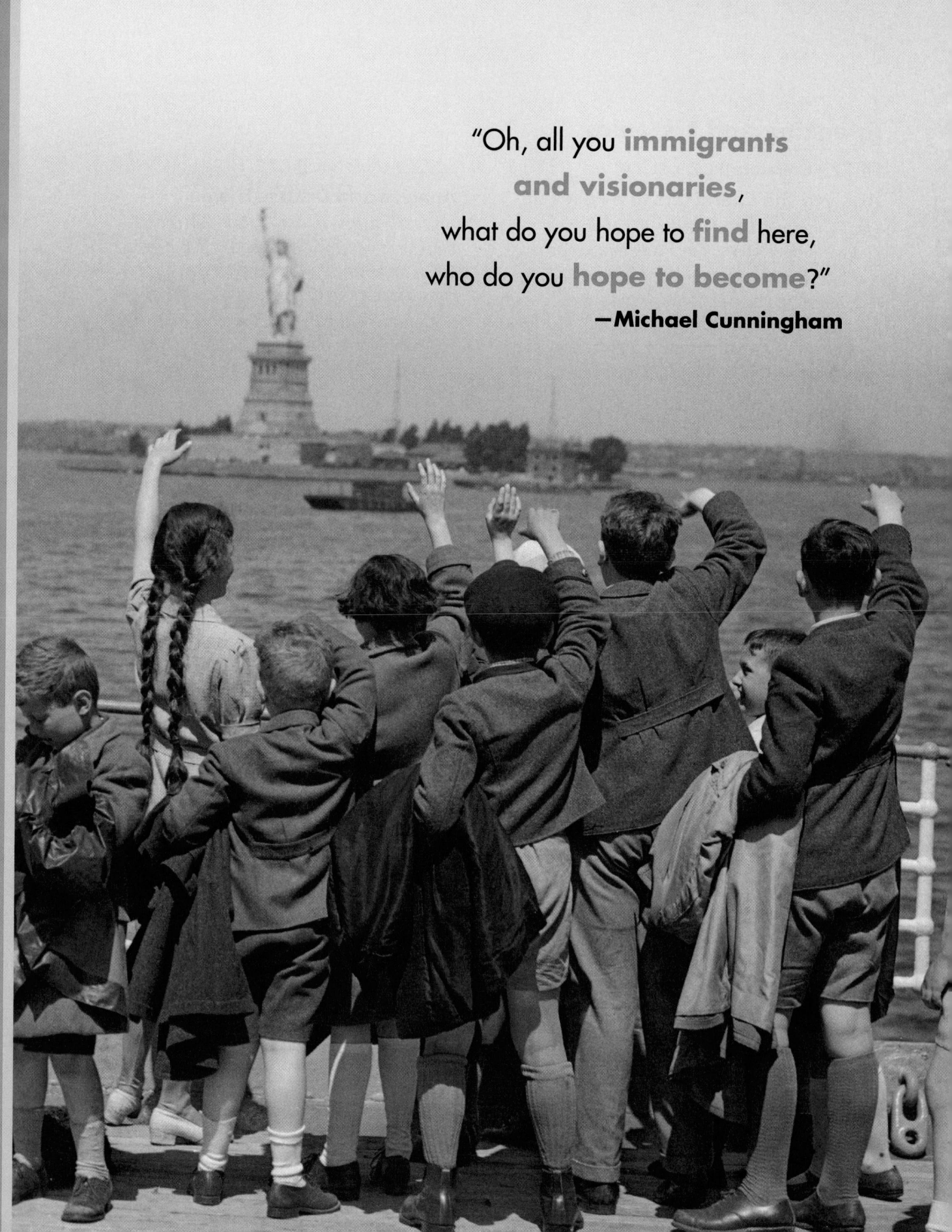

"Oh, all you **immigrants and visionaries**, what do you hope to **find** here, who do you **hope to become**?"

—**Michael Cunningham**

BECOMING AMERICAN

The selections in this unit all deal with the Big Question: **Community or individual—which is more important?** As you read the texts in this section, analyze the ways in which our varied backgrounds, cultures, and traditions shape our communities and help us explore what it means to become American.

◀ **CRITICAL VIEWING** What do you imagine are some of the hopes and dreams of the children in the photograph?

CLOSE READING TOOL

Use the **Close Reading Tool** to practice the strategies you learn in this unit.

My First Free Summer
Julia Alvarez

vowed ▶
(voud) *v.*
promised
solemnly

I never had summer—I had summer school. First grade, summer school. Second grade, summer school. Thirdgradesummerschoolfourthgradesummerschool. In fifth grade, I **vowed** I would get interested in fractions, the presidents of the United States, Mesopotamia; I would learn my English.

That was the problem. English. My mother had decided to send her children to the American school so we could learn the language of the nation that would soon be liberating us. For thirty years, the Dominican Republic had endured a bloody and repressive dictatorship. From my father, who was involved in an underground plot, my mother knew that *los américanos*[1] had promised to help bring democracy to the island.

"You have to learn your English!" Mami kept scolding me.

"But why?" I'd ask. I didn't know about my father's activities. I didn't know the dictator was bad. All I knew was that my friends who were attending Dominican schools were often on holiday to honor the dictator's birthday, the dictator's saint day, the day the dictator became the dictator, the day the dictator's oldest son was born, and so on. They marched in parades and visited the palace and had their picture in the paper.

Meanwhile, I had to learn about the pilgrims with their funny witch hats, about the 50 states and where they were on the map, about Dick and Jane[2] and their tame little pets, Puff

---

1. **los américanos** (lōs ä me′ rē kä′ nōs) *n.* Spanish for "the Americans."
2. **Dick and Jane** characters in a reading book commonly used by students in the 1950s.

and Spot, about freedom and liberty and justice for all—while being imprisoned in a hot classroom with a picture of a man wearing a silly wig hanging above the blackboard. And all of this learning I had to do in that impossibly difficult, rocks-in-your-mouth language of English!

Somehow, I managed to scrape by. Every June, when my prospects looked iffy, Mami and I met with the principal. I squirmed in my seat while they arranged for my special summer lessons.

"She is going to work extra hard. Aren't you, young lady?" the principal would quiz me at the end of our session.

My mother's eye on me, I'd murmur, "Yeah."

"Yes, what?" Mami coached.

"Yes." I sighed. "Sir."

It's a wonder that I just wasn't thrown out, which was what I secretly hoped for. But there were extenuating circumstances, the grounds on which the American school stood had been donated by my grandfather. In fact, it had been my grandmother who had encouraged Carol Morgan to start her school. The bulk of the student body was made up of the sons and daughters of American diplomats and business people, but a few Dominicans—most of them friends or members of my family—were allowed to attend.

"You should be grateful!" Mami scolded on the way home from our meeting. "Not every girl is lucky enough to go to the Carol Morgan School!"

In fifth grade, I straightened out. "Yes, ma'am!" I learned to say brightly. "Yes, sir!" To wave my hand in sword-wielding swoops so I could get called on with the right answer. What had changed me? Gratitude? A realization of my luckiness? No, sir! The thought of a fun summer? Yes, ma'am! I wanted to run with the pack of cousins and friends in the common yard that connected all our properties. To play on the trampoline and go off to la playa[3] and get brown as a berry. I wanted to be free. Maybe American principles had finally sunk in!

The summer of 1960 began in bliss: I did not have to go to summer school! *Attitude much improved. Her English progressing nicely. Attentive and cooperative in classroom.*

---

3. la playa (lä plä′ yä) *n.* Spanish for "the beach."

I grinned as Mami read off the note that accompanied my report card of Bs.

But the yard replete with cousins and friends that I had dreamed about all year was deserted. Family members were leaving for the United States, using whatever connections they could drum up. The plot had unraveled. Every day there were massive arrests. The United States had closed its embassy and was advising Americans to return home.

My own parents were terrified. Every night black Volkswagens blocked our driveway and stayed there until morning. "Secret police," my older sister whispered.

"Why are they secret if they're the police?" I asked.

"Shut up!" my sister hissed. "Do you want to get us all killed?"

Day after day, I kicked a deflated beach ball around the empty yard, feeling as if I'd been tricked into good behavior by whomever God put in charge of the lives of 10-year-olds. I was bored. Even summer school would have been better than this!

One day toward the end of the summer, my mother **summoned** my sisters and me. She wore that too-bright smile she sometimes pasted on her terrified face.

"Good news, girls! Our papers and tickets came! We're leaving for the United States!"

Our mouths dropped. We hadn't been told we were going on a trip anywhere, no less to some place so far away.

I was the first to speak up, "But why?"

My mother flashed me the same look she used to give me when I'd ask why I had to learn English.

I was about to tell her that I didn't want to go to the United States, where summer school had been invented and everyone spoke English. But my mother lifted a hand for silence. "We're leaving in a few hours. I want you all to go get ready! I'll be in to pack soon." The desperate look in her eyes did not allow for **contradiction**. We raced off, wondering how to fit the contents of our Dominican lives into four small suitcases.

Our flight was scheduled for that afternoon, but the airplane did not appear. The terminal lined with soldiers wielding machine guns, checking papers, escorting passengers into a small interrogation room. Not everyone returned.

"It's a trap," I heard my mother whisper to my father.

This had happened before, a cat-and-mouse game the dictator liked to play. Pretend that he was letting someone go, and then at the last minute, their family and friends

summoned ▶
(sum´ ənd) v.
called together

contradiction ▶
(kän´ trə dik´ shən) n.
difference between two conflicting things that means they both cannot be true

conveniently gathered together—wham! The secret police would haul the whole clan away.

Of course, I didn't know that this was what my parents were dreading. But as the hours ticked away, and afternoon turned into evening and evening into night and night into midnight with no plane in sight, a light came on in my head. If the light could be translated into words, instead, they would say: Freedom and liberty and justice for all . . . I knew that ours was not a trip, but an escape. We had to get to the United States.

The rest of that night is a blur. It is one, then two the next morning. A plane lands, lights flashing. We are walking on the runway, climbing up the stairs into the cabin. An American lady wearing a cap welcomes us. We sit down, ready to depart. But suddenly, soldiers come on board. They go seat by seat, looking at our faces. Finally, they leave, the door closes, and with a powerful roar we lift off and I fall asleep.

Next morning, we are standing inside a large, echoing hall as a stern American official reviews our documents. What if he doesn't let us in? What if we have to go back? I am holding my breath. My parents' terror has become mine.

He checks our faces against the passport pictures. When he is done, he asks, "You girls ready for school?" I swear he is looking at me.

"Yes, sir!" I speak up.

The man laughs. He stamps our papers and hands them to my father. Then wonderfully, a smile spreads across his face. "Welcome to the United States," he says, waving us in.

ABOUT THE AUTHOR

Julia Alvarez (b. 1950)

Shortly after her birth, Julia Alvarez moved from New York City to the Dominican Republic with her family. When Alvarez was ten years old, however, her family was forced to return to the United States because her father was involved in a failed rebellion against the country's dicta-tor, Rafael L. Trujillo. Alvarez had trouble adjusting to her new home. Turning inward, she began to read books and to write. Later, she said, "I fell in love with how words can make you feel complete in a way that I hadn't felt complete since leaving the island."

READ

Comprehension

Reread all or part of the text to help you answer the following questions.

1. What is the setting of the essay?

2. What historical conflict is described in the essay?

3. How did Alvarez usually spend her summers? Why?

4. What happened in the summer after Alvarez completed fifth grade?

Research: Clarify Details Choose at least one unfamiliar detail or reference and briefly research it. Then, explain how the information you learned from your research helped you understand an aspect of the essay.

Summarize Write an objective summary of the essay. Remember that an objective summary is free from opinion and evaluation.

Language Study

Selection Vocabulary The following sentences appear in "My First Free Summer." Define each boldfaced word, and then use the word in a sentence of your own.

- In fifth grade, I **vowed** I would get interested in fractions …

- One day toward the end of the summer, my mother **summoned** my sisters and me.

- The desperate look in her eyes did not allow for **contradiction**.

Diction and Style Study the following sentences from the essay. Then, answer the questions that follow.

> I wanted to run with the pack of cousins and friends. … To play on the trampoline and go off to la playa and get brown as a berry. I wanted to be free. Maybe American principles had finally sunk in!

1. What does the word *free* mean to Alvarez at age 10?

2. At this point in her life, what is Alvarez's understanding of "American principles"?

Conventions Read this passage from the essay. Identify and label the punctuation marks. Then, explain how the author's use of varied punctuation adds meaning to the passage.

> In fifth grade, I straightened out. "Yes, ma'am!" I learned to say brightly. "Yes, sir!" To wave my hand in sword-wielding swoops so I could get called on with the right answer. What had changed me? Gratitude? A realization of my luckiness? No, sir! The thought of a fun summer? Yes, ma'am!

Academic Vocabulary

The following words appear in blue in the instructions and questions on the facing page.

explain   **perspective**   **strategy**

Decide whether you know each word well, know it a little bit, or do not know it at all. Then, look up the definitions of the words you do not know well or do not know at all.

Literary Analysis

Reread the identified passages. Then, respond to the following questions.

Focus Passage 1 *(p. 728)*

That was the problem … had their picture in the paper.

Focus Passage 2 *(pp. 730–731)*

This had happened before … We had to get to the United States.

Key Ideas and Details

1. **(a)** Why does Alvarez's mother send her to the American school? **(b) Contrast:** How does this school differ from other schools on the island?

2. **Infer:** Why does Alvarez initially dismiss the importance of learning English?

Craft and Structure

3. **(a)** What information does Alvarez list in the sentence that begins, "All I knew was …" **(b) Analyze: Explain** the effect of the repeated use of the word *dictator* in this sentence.

4. **(a) Distinguish:** Does Alvarez write from the **perspective** of her young self or her adult self? **(b) Interpret:** How does this perspective add meaning to the passage?

Integration of Knowledge and Ideas

5. **Speculate:** Why do you think Alvarez's parents did not tell their children about their father's involvement in an underground plot?

Key Ideas and Details

1. **(a)** What do Alvarez's parents fear? **(b) Draw Conclusions:** Do they have a legitimate reason to be afraid? Use details from the text to support your answer.

Craft and Structure

2. **(a)** Explain the use of parallel structure in the sentence that begins, "But as the hours …" **(b) Interpret:** How does this structure add meaning to the passage?

3. **(a)** What term does Alvarez use to describe the dictator's **strategy**? **(b) Analyze:** How does this figurative language illustrate the nature of the family's situation?

Integration of Knowledge and Ideas

4. **(a) Hypothesize:** What might Alvarez want readers to learn from this story? **(b) Support:** What details in the essay support your answer?

Symbolism

A **symbol** is an object or idea that represents something other than itself. For example, spring can be a symbol of hope or rebirth. Reread the essay, and take notes on how the author uses symbolism.

1. What does summer symbolize for Alvarez?

2. Why do you think Alvarez titled her essay "My First Free Summer"?

3. **Becoming American** Identify symbols in the essay that relate to the idea of becoming American.

Common Core State Standards

RI.7.1, RI.7.2, RI.7.3, RI.7.4, RI.7.6; L.7.4, L.7.5
[For full standards wording, see the chart in the front of this book.]

DISCUSS

From Text to Topic **Group Discussion**

Discuss the following passage with a group of classmates. Take notes during the discussion. Contribute your own ideas, and support them with examples from the text.

> Meanwhile, I had to learn about the pilgrims with their funny witch hats, about the 50 states and where they were on the map, about Dick and Jane and their tame little pets, Puff and Spot, about freedom and liberty and justice for all—while being in a hot classroom with a picture of a man wearing a silly wig hanging above the blackboard. And all of this learning I had to do in that impossibly difficult, rocks-in-your-mouth language of English!

QUESTIONS FOR DISCUSSION

1. How do phrases such as "funny witch hats" and "silly wig" develop Alvarez's feelings about American history and culture?

2. Why is American school difficult for Alvarez?

WRITE

Writing to Sources **Informative Text**

Assignment

Write a **comparison-and-contrast essay** in which you analyze the changes Alvarez goes through during the time period she describes in "My First Free Summer." Examine similarities and differences between Alvarez's feelings, motivations, and actions at the beginning and at the end of her narrative.

Prewriting and Planning Reread the essay, looking for details that describe Alvarez's feelings, motivations, and actions. Record your notes in a two-column chart listing details from before her family moved to the U.S. on one side and details from after they moved on the other side.

Drafting Review your notes to find the main focus for your essay. Then, write a sentence that sums up your main idea. Include this sentence in your introduction, and elaborate on it in the body of your essay. As you draft, cite specific examples from the essay to support your key points.

Revising Reread your essay to make sure you have supported your key ideas with evidence from the text.

Editing and Proofreading Make sure that you have used adjectives correctly. Comparative adjectives, such as *older* and *more,* compare two things. Superlative adjectives, such as *oldest* and *most,* compare three or more things.

CONVENTIONS

Like adverbs, adverbial clauses modify verbs, adjectives, and adverbs. Adverbial clauses are introduced by subordinate conjunctions such as *before, since,* and *as.* An introductory adverbial phrase is usually followed by a comma.

RESEARCH

Research **Investigate the Topic**

Politics and Becoming American Alvarez's family had to flee the Dominican Republic because her father was part of a failed rebellion against the country's brutal dictator, Rafael L. Trujillo. Like Alvarez's family, many people come to the United States hoping to escape political oppression that threatens their physical safety.

Assignment

Conduct research to learn different reasons that people immigrate to the United States. Then, choose a past or current political situation (such as Trujillo's dictatorship) on which to focus. Consult primary, government, and historical sources. Take clear notes and carefully identify your sources so that you can easily access the information later. Share your findings in an **oral presentation** for the class.

Gather Sources Locate authoritative print and electronic sources. Primary sources, such as letters, journals, diaries, or memoirs, provide authentic firsthand information. You should also use secondary sources, such as government and historical Web sites, especially those that compile information about immigrants. Look for sources that feature expert authors and up-to-date information.

Take Notes Take notes on each source, either electronically or on notecards. Use an organized note-taking strategy:

- Review past and current political situations that have caused people to emigrate and choose one to use as the focus for your presentation.
- Find appropriate sources and use a separate set of notecards for each source. Record source information to use in citations.
- In your notes, use quotation marks around direct quotations from your sources to avoid accidental plagiarism.

Synthesize Multiple Sources Assemble data from your sources and organize it into a cohesive presentation. Use your notes to construct an outline for your presentation. Create a Works Cited list as described in the Citing Sources pages in the Introductory Unit of this textbook.

Organize and Present Ideas Review your outline and practice delivering your presentation. Be ready to respond to questions from your audience.

PREPARATION FOR ESSAY

You may use the knowledge you gain during this research assignment to support your claims in an essay you will write at the end of this section.

Common Core State Standards

W.7.2.a–b, W.7.2.d, W.7.4, W.7.5, W.7.7, W.7.8, W.7.9; SL.7.1, SL.7.4
[For full standards wording, see the chart in the front of this book.]

How I Learned English

Gregory Djanikian

It was in an empty lot
Ringed by elms and fir and honeysuckle.
Bill Corson was pitching in his buckskin[1] jacket,
Chuck Keller, fat even as a boy, was on first,
His t-shirt riding up over his gut,
Ron O'Neill, Jim, Dennis, were talking it up
In the field, a blue sky above them
Tipped with cirrus.[2]
                              And there I was,
Just off the plane and plopped in the middle
Of Williamsport, Pa., and a neighborhood game,
Unnatural and without any moves,
My **notions** of baseball and America
Growing fuzzier each time I whiffed.[3]

So it was not impossible that I,
Banished to the outfield and daydreaming
Of water, or a hotel in the mountains,
Would suddenly find myself in the path
Of a ball stung[4] by Joe Barone.
I watched it closing in
Clean and untouched, **transfixed**
By its easy arc before it hit
My forehead with a thud.
                              I fell back.

notions ▶
(nō′shənz) *n.*
general ideas

transfixed ▶
(trans fikst′) *adj.*
rooted to the spot

5

10

15

20

---

1. **buckskin** *adj.* yellowish-gray leather made from the hide of a deer.
2. **cirrus** (sir′ əs) *n.* high, thin clouds.
3. **whiffed** (hwift) *v.* struck out.
4. **stung** *v.* hit hard.

25 Dazed, clutching my brow,
Groaning, "Oh my shin, oh my shin,"
And everybody peeled away from me
And dropped from laughter, and there we were,
All of us **writing** on the ground for one reason
30 Or another.
                    Someone said "shin" again,
There was a wild stamping of hands on the ground,
A kicking of feet, and the fit
Of laughter overtook me too,
35 And that was important, as important
As Joe Barone asking me how I was
Through his tears, picking me up
And dusting me off with hands like swatters,
And though my head felt heavy,
40 I played on till dusk
Missing flies and pop-ups and grounders
And calling out in desperation things like
"Yours" and "take it," but doing all right,
Tugging at my cap in just the right way,
45 Crouching low, my feet set,
"Hum baby" sweetly on my lips.

◄ **writing**
(rīth′ iŋ) v. squirming,
often in response
to pain

ABOUT THE AUTHOR

Gregory Djanikian (b. 1949)

Born in Alexandria, Egypt, Gregory Djanikian moved to the United States with his family when he was eight years old. Since 1983, he has been a creative writing professor, as well as the head of the Creative Writing Department, at the University of Pennsylvania in Philadelphia. Djanikian's poetry has been published in many journals and magazines, and he is the author of five books of poetry. He has received many awards and honors, including a National Endowment for the Arts fellowship. "How I Learned English" is from his 1989 poetry collection *Falling Deeply into America*.

READ

Comprehension

Reread as needed to answer the questions.

1. Where is the poem set?
2. What happens to the speaker in the outfield?
3. What happens after the boys start laughing?

Research: Clarify Details Choose an unfamiliar detail from the poem and research it. Then, explain how your research helped you understand the poem.

Summarize Write an objective summary of the poem.

Language Study

Selection Vocabulary Write a synonym or an antonym for each boldfaced word.

- My **notions** of baseball and America/ Growing fuzzier each time I whiffed.

- Clean and untouched, **transfixed**/By its easy arc before it hit/My forehead with a thud.
- All of us **writhing** on the ground for one reason/Or another.

Literary Analysis

Reread the identified passage. Then, respond to the following questions.

Focus Passage *(pp. 736–737)*

So it was not impossible … one reason/ Or another.

Key Ideas and Details

1. **(a) Infer:** Why might the speaker be "daydreaming / Of water, or a hotel in the mountains"? **(b) Interpret:** What might make it difficult for the speaker to focus on the game?

2. What happens to the speaker in this stanza?

Craft and Structure

3. **(a) Determine:** How is line 24 different from the other lines in the stanza? **(b) Analyze:** Why might the poet have presented this line in a different way?

Integration of Knowledge and Ideas

4. **(a) Infer:** Why does the speaker groan, "Oh my shin, oh my shin"? **(b) Analyze:** What is the effect of these words? **(c) Interpret:** How does the incident that is described in this stanza change the speaker's **relationship** to the other players?

Narrative Poem

A **narrative poem** is a story told in verse. Narrative poetry includes elements of short stories.

1. **(a)** How does the poet describe the speaker? **(b)** What do these descriptions show the reader?

2. **Becoming American (a)** What is the main conflict in the poem? **(b)** How does the resolution help the speaker "become American"?

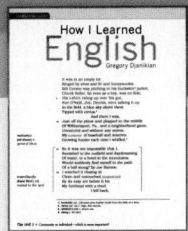

DISCUSS • RESEARCH • WRITE

From Text to Topic **Partner Discussion**

Discuss the following passage with a partner. Take notes during the discussion. Contribute your own ideas, and support them with examples from the text.

> Someone said "shin" again … And dusting me off with hands like swatters, (p. 737)

Research **Investigate the Topic**

Help in "Becoming American" The speaker of Djanikian's poem learns some English and absorbs American culture on the baseball field. Today, recent immigrants can find help in many places in their quest to "become American."

Assignment

Conduct research to find resources that help recent immigrants to the United States learn about their new home. Consult the websites of government agencies and cultural organizations. Share your findings in a brief **research report.**

Writing to Sources **Narrative**

In "How I Learned English," the speaker describes a situation in which he felt as if he did not fit in. Everyone has felt that way at one time or another.

Assignment

Write an **autobiographical narrative** in which you describe a time when you felt like you did not fit in. Follow these steps:

- Introduce the time, place, and situation.
- **Explain** why you felt that you did not fit in. Then, describe how the situation turned out.
- Use the elements of a short story—plot, conflict, characterization, and dialogue—to make your experience "come alive" for the reader.
- In your conclusion, explain what you learned from the experience. Make connections between your situation and that of the poem's speaker.

QUESTIONS FOR DISCUSSION

1. Why does the speaker think it is important that he joined in the laughter?

2. How might the **outcome** of the day have been different if the speaker had not been hit in the head or if he had been angered by the boys' laughter?

PREPARATION FOR ESSAY

You may use the results of your research to support your ideas in the essay you will write at the end of this section.

ACADEMIC VOCABULARY

Academic terms appear in blue on these pages. If these words are not familiar to you, use a dictionary to find their definitions.

 **Common Core State Standards**

RL.7.1, RL.7.2, RL.7.5; W.7.3, W.7.4, W.7.7; SL.7.1; L.7.4, L.7.5.b, L.7.6
[For full standards wording, see the chart in the front of this book.]

mk
Jean Fritz

I suspect for most of us MKs[1] China not only sharpened our sense of time but our sense of place. We always knew where we were in relation to the rest of the world. And we noticed. Perhaps because we knew we would be leaving China sometime (we wouldn't be MKs or even Ks forever), we developed the habit of observing our surroundings with care. We have strong memories, which explains why as an adult, walking along a beach in Maine, I suddenly found myself on the verge of tears. In front of me, pushing up from the crevice of a rock, was a wild bluebell[2] like the wild bluebells I had known in my summers at Kuling.[3] Suddenly I was a child again. I was back in China, welcoming bluebells back in my life.

For a long time it was hard for me to unscramble the strings that made up my quest. I have noticed, however, that those MKs who were born in China and stayed there through their high school years were more likely to commit their lives in some way to China. After finishing their higher education in the States, they would return to China as consuls, as teachers, as businessmen and women, as writers, as historians.

I wouldn't be staying through high school. My family planned to return to America when I had finished seventh grade, whether I was finished with China or not. Of course I knew I had to become an American, the sooner the better. So far away from America, I didn't feel like a real American. Nor would I, I thought, until I had put my feet down on American soil.

---

1. **MKs** (em′ kāz′) *n.* Missionary Kids; the children of missionaries.
2. **bluebell** (blo͞o′ bel′) *n.* plant with blue, bell-shaped flowers.
3. **Kuling** (ko͞ol′ iŋ) *n.* now called Lushan, a hill resort south of the Yangtze River in China.

I had just finished sixth grade at the British School in Wuhan,[4] so I would have one more year to go. Nothing would change that. I knew that there was fighting up and down the Yangtze River, but the Chinese were always fighting—warlord against warlord.[5] That had nothing to do with me. But as soon as I saw the servant from next door racing toward our house with a message for my mother, I knew something was happening. Since we had no phone, we depended on our German neighbors for emergency messages. My father had called, the servant explained. All American women and children had to catch the afternoon boat to Shanghai.[6] The army, which had done so much damage to Nanjing (just down the river), was on its way here.

As I helped my mother pack, my knees were shaking. I had only felt this once before. My mother and I had been in a ricksha on the way to the racecourse when farmers ran to the road, calling hateful words at us and throwing stones. The ricksha-pullers were fast runners, so we weren't hurt, but I told myself this was like Stephen in the Bible who was stoned to death. He just didn't have a ricksha handy. By the time we reached the boat that afternoon, my knees were normal. So was I. And I knew what our plans were. My father and other American men would work in the daytime, but for safety at night they would board one of the gunboats anchored in the river. The women and children going to Shanghai would be protected from bullets by steel barriers erected around the deck. And when we reached Shanghai, then what? I asked my mother.

---

4. **Wuhan** (wōō´ hän´) *n.* city in the central part of China, near the Yangtze River.
5. **warlord** (wôr´ lôrd´) *n.* military commander who exercises power by force.
6. **Shanghai** (shaŋ´ hī´) *n.* seaport in eastern China.

We would be staying with the Barretts, another missionary family, who had one son, Fletcher, who was two years younger than I and generally unlikable. Mr. Barrett met us in Shanghai and drove us to their home, where his wife was on the front porch. My mother greeted her warmly but I just held out my hand and said, "Hello, Mrs. Barrett," which I thought was adequate. She raised her eyebrows. "Have you become so grown up, Jean," she said, "that I'm no longer your 'Auntie Barrett'?"

I didn't say that I'd always been too grown up for the "auntie" business. I just smiled. In China all MKs called their parents' friends "auntie" or "uncle." Not me. Mrs. B. pushed Fletcher forward.

"Fletcher has been so excited about your visit, Jean," she said. "He has lots of games to show you. Now, run along, children."

Fletcher did have a lot of games. He decided what we'd play—rummy, then patience, while he talked a blue streak. I didn't pay much attention until, in the middle of an Uncle Wiggley game, he asked me a question.

"Have you ever been in love, Jean?" he asked.

What did he think I was? I was twelve years old, for heaven's sakes!

Ever since first grade I'd been in love with someone. The boys never knew it, of course.

Fletcher hadn't finished with love. "I'm in love now," he said. "I'll give you a hint. She's an MK."

"Naturally."

"And she's pretty." Then he suddenly shrieked out the answer as if he couldn't contain it a second longer. "It's you," he cried. "Y-O-U."

Well, Fletcher Barrett was even dumber than I'd thought. No one had ever called me "pretty" before. Not even my parents. Besides, this conversation was making me sick. "I'm tired," I said. "I think I'll get my book and lie down."

At the last minute I had slipped my favorite book in my suitcase. It was one my father and I had read last year—*The Courtship of Miles Standish*[7]—all about the first settlers in America. I knew them pretty well now and often visited with Priscilla Alden.

◄ adequate
(ad′ i kwət)
adj. enough

---

7. *The Courtship of Miles Standish* *n.* narrative poem by Henry Wadsworth Longfellow, written in 1858. One character in the poem is Priscilla Alden.

Settled on the bed in the room I'd been told was mine, I opened the book and let the Pilgrims step off the *Mayflower* into Shanghai. Priscilla was one of the first.

"You're still a long way from Plymouth," I told her, "but you'll get there. Think you'll like it?"

"I know I will," she answered promptly. "Everything will be better there."

"How do you know?"

"It's a new country. It will be whatever we make it."

"It may be hard," I warned her.

"Maybe," she admitted. "But I'll never give up. Neither will John," she added.

I was being called for supper. I waited for the Pilgrims to get back on the *Mayflower*. Then I closed the book and went downstairs.

The days that followed, I spent mostly with Fletcher, whether I liked it or not. Fletcher was fussing now that the summer was almost over and he'd have to go back to school soon.

"I thought you'd like it," I said. "After all, it's an American school and you're an American."

"So what?"

"Don't you feel like an American when you're in school?"

"What's there to feel?"

He was impossible. If he had gone to a British school, the way I had all my life, he might realize how lucky he was. The Shanghai American School was famous. Children from all over China were sent there to be boarders. Living in Shanghai, Fletcher was just a day student. But even so!

Then one day my mother got a letter from my father. The danger was mostly over, he thought, but some foreign businesses were not reopening. The British School had closed down. (Good news!)

The Yangtze River boats went back in service the next week, so my mother went downtown to buy our tickets back to Wuhan. Fletcher was back in school now, and as soon as he came home, he rushed to see me, his face full of news.

"Your mother is only buying one ticket," he informed me. "You're not going. You're going to the Shanghai American School as a boarder."

"My mother would never do that. You're crazy," I replied. "Where did you get such an idea?"

"I overheard our mothers talking. It's true, Jean."

"Yeah, like cows fly."

When my mother came back, I could see that she was upset. Fletcher did a disappearing act; I figured he didn't want to be caught in a lie.

"Oh, I'm sorry, Jean," my mother said, her eyes filling with tears. She put her arms around me. "Since the British School is closed," she said, "I've arranged for you to be a boarder at the American School. It won't be for long. We may even go back to America early. At least I'll know you're safe."

I knew my mother was worried that I'd be homesick, so I couldn't let on how I really felt. (Just think, I told myself, I'd have almost a year to practice being an American.) I buried my head on her shoulder. "I'll be okay," I said, sniffing back fake tears. Sometimes it's necessary to **deceive** your parents if you love them, and I did love mine.

After my mother left on the boat, Mr. Barrett took me to the Shanghai American School (SAS for short). I guess I expected some kind of immediate transformation. I always felt a

◀ **deceive**
(dē sēv′) *v.* make someone believe something that is not true

▲ Jean Fritz (center, in white) and her classmates.

tingling when I saw the American flag flying over the American consulate. Surely it would be more than a tingling now; surely it would overwhelm me. But when we went through the iron gates of the school grounds, I didn't feel a thing. On the football field a group of high school girls were practicing cheerleading. They were jumping, standing on their hands, yelling rah, rah, rah. It just seemed like a lot of fuss about football. What was the matter with me?

The dormitory where I'd be living was divided in half by a swinging door. The high school girls were on one side of the door; the junior high (which included me) were on the other. On my side there were two Russian girls and two American MKs, the Johnson sisters, who had long hair braided and wound around their heads like Sunday school teachers. And there was Paula, my American roommate, who looked as though she belonged on the other side of the door. Hanging in our shared closet I noticed a black velvet dress. And a pair of high heeled shoes. She wore them to tea dances, she explained, when one of her brother's friends came to town. She was squinting her eyes as she looked at me, sizing up my straight hair and bangs.

"I happen to know you're an MK," she said, "but you don't have to look like one." The latest style in the States, she told me, was a boyish bob.[8] She'd give me one, she decided.

So that night she put a towel around my shoulders and newspaper on the floor, and she began cutting. This might make all the difference, I thought, as I watched my hair travel to the floor.

---

8. bob (bäb) *n.* woman's or child's short haircut.

It didn't. My ears might have felt more American, but not me. After being in hiding all their lives, my ears were suddenly outdoors, looking like jug handles on each side of my face. I'd get used to them, I told myself. Meanwhile I had to admit that SAS was a big improvement over the British School. Even without an American flag feeling, I enjoyed the months I was there.

What I enjoyed most were the dances, except they weren't dances. There were too many MKs in the school, and the Ms didn't approve of dancing. Instead, we had "talk parties." The girls were given what looked like dance cards and the boys were supposed to sign up for the talk sessions they wanted. Of course a girl could feel like a wallflower[9] if her card wasn't filled up, but mine usually was. These parties gave me a chance to look over the boys in case I wanted to fall in love, and actually I was almost ready to make a choice when my parents suddenly appeared. It was early spring. Just as my mother had suspected, we were going to America early.

I knew that three weeks crossing the Pacific would be different from five days on the Yangtze but I didn't know how different. My father had given me a gray-and-green plaid steamer rug that I would put over me when I was lying on my long folding deck chair. At eleven o'clock every morning a waiter would come around with a cup of "beef tea." I loved the idea of drinking beef tea under my steamer rug but it didn't happen often. The captain said this was the roughest crossing he'd ever made, and passengers spent most of their time in their cabins. If they came out for a meal, they were lucky if they could get it down before it came back up again. I had my share of seasickness, so of course I was glad to reach San Francisco.

I couldn't wait to take my first steps on American soil, but I expected the American soil to hold still for me. Instead, it swayed as if we were all still at sea, and I lurched about as I had been doing for the last three weeks. I noticed my parents were having difficulty, too. "Our heads and our legs aren't ready for land," my father explained. "It takes a little while." We spent the night in a hotel and took a train the next day for Pittsburgh where our relatives were meeting us.

It was a three-day trip across most of the continent, but it didn't seem long. Every minute America was under us and rushing past our windows—the Rocky Mountains, the

---

9. **wallflower** (wôl′ flou′ ər) *n.* person who stands against the wall and watches at a dance due to shyness or lack of popularity.

Mississippi river, flat ranch land, small towns, forests, boys dragging school bags over dusty roads. It was all of America at once splashed across where we were, where we'd been, where we were going. How could you not feel American? How could you not feel that you belonged? By the time we were settled at my grandmother's house, I felt as if I'd always been a part of this family. And wasn't it wonderful to have real aunts and uncles, a real grandmother, and yes, even a real bathroom, for heaven's sakes?

I wanted to talk to Priscilla, so I took my book outside, and when I opened it, out tumbled the Pilgrims, Priscilla first. I smiled. Here we were, all of us in America together, and it didn't matter that we came from different times. We all knew that America was still an experiment and perhaps always would be. I was one of the ones who had to try to make the experiment work.

"You'll have disappointments," Priscilla said. "But it will help if you get to know Americans who have spent their lives working on the experiment."

I wasn't sure just what she meant, but I knew it was important. "I'll try," I said.

"Try!" Priscilla scoffed. "If you want to be a real American, you'll have to do more than that." Her voice was fading. Indeed, the Pilgrims themselves were growing faint. Soon they had all slipped away.

I learned about disappointment as soon as I went to school. Of course I was no longer an MK, but I was certainly a curiosity. I was the Kid from China. "Did you live in a mud hut?" one boy asked me. "Did you eat rats and dogs? Did you eat with sticks?"

ignorant ▶
(ig´ nə rənt) *adj.*
not knowing
facts or
information

I decided that American children were **ignorant**. Didn't their teachers teach them anything? After a while, as soon as anyone even mentioned China, I shut up. "What was the name of your hometown?" I was asked, but I never told. I couldn't bear to have my hometown laughed at.

"Not all American children are ignorant," my mother pointed out. "Just a few who ask dumb questions."

Even in high school, however, I often got the same questions. But now we were studying about the American Revolution and George Washington. Of course I'd always known who Washington was, but knowing history and understanding it are two different things. I had never realized how much he had done to make America into America. No matter how much he was asked to do for his country, he did it, even though he could hardly wait to go back home and be a farmer again. Of course there were disappointments on the way; of course he became discouraged. "If I'd known what I was getting into," he said at the beginning of the Revolution, "I would have chosen to live in an Indian teepee all my life." He never took the easiest way. When he thought his work was over at the end of the Revolution, he agreed to work on the Constitution. When the country needed a president, he took the oath of office. When his term was over, he was persuaded to run once again. Everyone had confidence that as long as he was there, the new government would work.

Although Washington was the first, there were many more like him who were, as Priscilla would say, "real" Americans. As I went through college and read about them, I knew I wanted to write about them someday. I might not talk to them in the same way I talked to Priscilla, but I would try to make them as real as they were when they were alive.

I had the feeling that I was coming to the end of my quest. But not quite. One day when someone asked me where I was born, I found myself smiling. I was for the moment standing beside the Yangtze River. "My hometown," I said, "was Wuhan, China." I discovered that I had to take China with me wherever I went.

ABOUT THE AUTHOR

Jean Fritz (b. 1915)

An only child of missionary parents, Jean Fritz spent the first thirteen years of her life in China. Although she had not yet been to the United States, she read and heard from her father about American heroes, such as George Washington and Teddy Roosevelt. Her fascination with these heroes inspired her career as a writer of American history. Fritz fills her biographies with unusual but true details about her subjects, which she researches thoroughly. "History is full of gossip; it's real people and emotion," she says. The details make her books about historical figures, such as Pocahontas or Sam Adams, spring to life. Fritz has received many awards and honors over her long career. In 1983, her autobiography *Homesick: My Own Story*—from which "mk" comes— won a National Book Award and was named a Newbery Honor Book.

READ

Comprehension

Reread as needed to answer the questions.

1. What is an "MK"?

2. Why does Fritz's family move in with the Barretts?

3. What happens to Fritz when the British School closes?

Research: Clarify Details Choose an unfamiliar detail from the autobiography, and conduct research to learn more about it.

Summarize Write an objective summary of the autobiography. Remember to leave out your opinions and evaluations.

Language Study

Selection Vocabulary For each boldfaced word, write its definition and list two other words in the same word family (example: *express, expressive, expression*).

- **adequate**
- **deceive**
- **ignorant**

Literary Analysis

Reread the identified passage.

> **Focus Passage** *(p. 744)*
>
> Settled on the bed in the room I'd been told was mine, ... "But I'll never give up. Neither will John," she added.

Key Ideas and Details

1. To whom is Fritz speaking in this passage?

2. **Connect:** What does Fritz have in common with this person?

Craft and Structure

3. **Analyze:** Fritz writes, *I opened the book and let the Pilgrims step off the Mayflower into Shanghai.* What idea do these words **communicate**?

Integration of Knowledge and Ideas

4. **(a) Draw Conclusions:** What does this conversation reveal about Fritz's concerns about moving to America? **(b) Predict:** Based on this conversation, would you **predict** that Fritz will adjust well to her new home in the U.S.? Why or why not?

Narration

Narration is the act or **process** of telling a story. Take notes on the narration in this autobiography.

1. **(a)** What is the point of view of the selection? **(b)** How does this point of view help readers learn about Fritz?

2. **Becoming American** The order of events is important in narration. **(a)** What is the first thing Fritz sees as she goes through the iron gates of the Shanghai American School? **(b)** Why is this information important to the story?

DISCUSS • RESEARCH • WRITE

From Text to Topic **Group Discussion**

Discuss the following passage with a group of classmates. Take notes during the discussion. Contribute your own ideas, and support them with examples from the text.

> I had the feeling that I was coming to the end of my quest. . . . I discovered that I had to take China with me wherever I went. (p. 749)

Research **Investigate the Topic**

American Literature "The Courtship of Miles Standish" is a long narrative poem by American poet Henry Wadsworth Longfellow.

Assignment

Conduct research to find out why "The Courtship of Miles Standish" is important to American literature. Consult literary and historical sources. Review a plot summary, and read at least part of the poem to get a feel for the language. Consider why Fritz was attracted to this poem as an American child living in China. Write a **short research paper** in which you share your findings.

Writing to Sources **Explanatory Text**

In "mk," Jean Fritz describes her experiences as a "missionary kid" who does not move to America until she is thirteen years old.

Assignment

Write a **comparison-and-contrast essay** in which you examine Fritz's feelings about America before and after she arrives in the United States. Follow these steps:

- Review "mk" and gather story details in a two-column chart. In the first column, list details that show Fritz's thoughts and feelings about America when she was living in China. In the second column, list her thoughts and feelings when she lived in the U.S.

- First, write an engaging introduction. Then, in the body of your essay, organize the information from your chart to show clear comparisons and contrasts.

- Sum up your main idea in a strong concluding paragraph.

QUESTIONS FOR DISCUSSION

1. Why did Fritz avoid naming her hometown in China at first?

2. Why was she finally able to name her hometown?

PREPARATION FOR ESSAY

You may use the results of your research to support your ideas in the essay you will write at the end of this section.

ACADEMIC VOCABULARY

Academic terms appear in blue on these pages. If these words are not familiar to you, use a dictionary to find their definitions. Then, use the words as you speak and write about the text.

Common Core State Standards

RI.7.1, RI.7.2, RI.7.3, RI.7.4, RI.7.6; W.7.2.a, W.7.2.f, W.7.4, W.7.7; SL.7.1
[For full standards wording, see the chart in the front of this book.]

The Statue of Liberty - Ellis Island Foundation, Inc.

Byron Yee: Discovering a Paper Son

Angel Island, San Francisco

For actor Byron Yee, family history provides the inspiration for his one-man show. "My name is Byron Yee. I am the second son of Bing Quai Yee. I am the son of a paper son.

"My father was an immigrant. He came to America to escape the Japanese invasion of China in 1938. He was 15 years old and he didn't know a word of English. He didn't have a penny in his pocket and he was living in a crowded apartment in New York City with relatives he had never met. I know nothing about my father's history, about his past."

With little to go on, Byron set out to **decipher** his father's story. He started at Angel Island, located in the middle of San Francisco Bay. "Angel Island has been called the Ellis Island of the West and for the most part, all the Chinese who came to the United States came through here, from a period of 1910 to 1940. But the rules were a little bit different. European settlers, Russian settlers were processed within an hour. The Japanese were kept for one day. But the Chinese were detained anywhere from three weeks to two years for their **interrogations**. So this was not so much the Ellis Island of the West for the Chinese; it was more like Alcatraz."

decipher ▶
(dē sī´fər) v. make out the meaning of

interrogations ▶
(in ter´ə gā´shənz) n. formal examinations that involve questioning the subject

In 1882, Congress passed a law prohibiting Chinese laborers from immigrating to the United States. The Chinese Exclusion Act was the only immigration law ever based on race alone. But people found ways around the act: U.S. law states that children of American citizens are automatically granted citizenship themselves, no matter where they were born. Taking advantage of that opening, some immigrants claimed to be legitimate offspring of U.S. citizens when in fact they were not. These individuals, mostly male, were called paper sons.

Byron's next step was to find his father's immigration file. The National Archives regional office in San Bruno, California contains thousands of files related to Angel Island. While Byron did not find his father's records there, he did find those of his grandfather, Yee Wee Thing. In one of the documents in his grandfather's file, Byron found a cross reference to his father, Yee Bing Quai. To avoid the **scrutiny** of Angel Island, Byron's father had sailed through Boston. Byron found his file at the National Archives in Massachusetts.

◀ **scrutiny**
(skro͞ot′ 'n ē) *n.* close, thorough inspection

"My father at 15. He is asked 197 questions: 'When did your alleged father first come to the United States?' 'Have you ever seen a photograph of your alleged father?' 'How many trips to China has your alleged father made since first coming to the United States?'" The lengthy interrogation made Byron suspect that his father was in fact a paper son. Maybe this was why he never knew his father's story.

Though Byron's mother knew very little about her husband's past, she did have an old photo, which she sent to Byron—a portrait of his father's family back in China. Byron learned that the baby on the left was his father. The boy in the middle was Yee Wee Thing, not Byron's grandfather at all, but his uncle.

"It kind of floored me because all of a sudden it made a lot of sense—why he was the way he was, why he never really talked about his past, why he was very secretive. It explained a lot about him and about his history.

"You see my story is no different from anyone else's. . . In all of our collective past, we've all had that one ancestor that had the strength to break from what was familiar to venture into the unknown. I can never thank my father and uncle enough for what they had to do so that I could be here today. One wrong answer between them and I would not be here."

READ

Comprehension

Reread the text as needed to answer the questions.

1. What was the Chinese Exclusion Act?

2. What were "paper sons"?

3. What did Byron Yee discover about Yee Wee Thing and his father?

Research: Clarify Details Conduct research on an unfamiliar detail from the selection. Then, explain how your research helped you understand the public document.

Summarize Write an objective summary of the article. Remember that an objective summary is free from opinion and evaluation.

Language Study

Selection Vocabulary Define each boldfaced word, and then use the word in a sentence of your own.

- With little to go on, Byron set out to **decipher** his father's story.

- But the Chinese were detained anywhere from three weeks to two years for their **interrogations.**

- To avoid the **scrutiny** of Angel Island, Byron's father had sailed through Boston.

Literary Analysis

Reread the identified passage. Then, respond to the following questions.

> **Focus Passage** (p. 753)
>
> "My father at 15 … about him and about his history.

Key Ideas and Details

1. (a) Infer: Why was Byron Yee's father asked so many questions? **(b) Interpret:** Why did the officials repeatedly use the word *alleged*?

2. (a) What does Byron Yee **discover** when he examines the photograph his mother sent?

(b) Draw Conclusions: Why did it make sense that Byron Yee's father "never really talked about his past"?

Craft and Structure

3. (a) Analyze: Why does the author combine Byron Yee's own words with passages of explanatory text? **(b) Evaluate:** Would the account be as effective if it had consisted only of questions and answers? Explain.

Integration of Knowledge and Ideas

4. Interpret: How does the discovery about Yee Wee Thing change Byron Yee's attitude toward his father?

Direct Quotation

Direct quotations are a person's exact words.

1. (a) Who is the source of all of the direct quotations? **(b)** How do the quotations **enhance** the article?

2. Becoming American How do the quotations help convey to readers the experience of "becoming American"?

DISCUSS • RESEARCH • WRITE

From Text to Topic **Partner Discussion**

Discuss the following passage with a partner. Take notes during the discussion. Contribute your own ideas, and support them with examples from the text.

> You see my story is no different from anyone else's … In all of our collective past, we've all had that one ancestor that had the strength to break from what was familiar to venture into the unknown.

Research **Investigate the Topic**

The Chinese Exclusion Act The article **cites** a law that restricted immigration to the United States: "The Chinese Exclusion Act was the only immigration law ever based on race alone." The law affected countless numbers of people, many of whom found ways around the law.

Assignment

Conduct research to learn why the Chinese Exclusion Act was passed, and when and why it was repealed. In addition, find out approximately how many people became "paper sons" in the U.S. as a result of the Act. Consult government and historical sources. Share your findings in an **informal speech** for the class.

Writing to Sources **Explanatory Text**

"Byron Yee: Discovering a Paper Son" focuses on one man's attempts to discover the truth about his father's immigration to the United States.

Assignment

Write an **expository essay** in which you explain how and why Byron Yee's father became a "paper son." Follow these steps:

- Write an introduction in which you provide a thesis statement.
- Introduce new paragraphs with clear transitions to explain the chain of events that preceded Bing Quai Yee's admittance into the United States.
- Provide a conclusion that summarizes the chain of events and the causes of Bing Quai Yee's actions.
- During your revision process, make sure there are no gaps in your essay's chain of events.

QUESTIONS FOR DISCUSSION

1. How did Bing Quai Yee display courage in his quest to become an American citizen?

2. How is Byron Yee's story "no different from anyone else's"?

PREPARATION FOR ESSAY

You may use the results of your research to support your ideas in the essay you will write at the end of this section.

ACADEMIC VOCABULARY

Academic terms appear in blue on these pages. If these words are not familiar to you, use a dictionary to find their definitions. Then, use them as you speak and write about the text.

 **Common Core State Standards**

RI.7.1, RI.7.2, RI.7.3, RI.7.4, RI.7.5; W.7.2, W.7.4, W.7.7; SL.7.1, SL.7.4; L.7.4
[For full standards wording, see the chart in the front of this book.]

FROM GRANDPA AND THE STATUE

ARTHUR MILLER

Sheean. [*Slight brogue*[1]] A good afternoon to you, Monaghan.

Monaghan. How're you, Sheean, how're ya?

Sheean. Fair, fair. And how's Mrs. Monaghan these days?

Monaghan. Warm. Same as everybody else in summer.

Sheean. I've come to talk to you about the fund, Monaghan.

Monaghan. What fund is that?

Sheean. The Statue of Liberty fund.

Monaghan. Oh, that.

Sheean. It's time we come to grips with the subject, Monaghan.

Monaghan. I'm not interested, Sheean.

Sheean. Now hold up on that a minute. Let me tell you the facts. This here Frenchman has gone and built a fine statue of Liberty. It costs who knows how many millions to build. All they're askin' us to do is contribute enough to put up a base for the statue to stand on.

Monaghan. I'm not . . . !

Sheean. Before you answer me. People all over the whole United States are puttin' in for it. Butler Street is doin' the same. We'd like to hang up a flag on the corner saying—"Butler Street, Brooklyn, is one hundred per cent behind the Statue of Liberty." And Butler Street is a hundred per cent subscribed except for you. Now will you give us a dime, Monaghan? One dime and we can put up the flag. Now what do you say to that?

◀ **subscribed**
(səb skrīb′ əd) *v.*
promised to give
money in support
of something

---

1. brogue (brōg) *n.* Irish accent.

Monaghan. I'm not throwin' me good money away for somethin' I don't even know exists.

Sheean. Now what do you mean by that?

Monaghan. Have you seen this statue?

Sheean. No, but it's in a warehouse. And as soon as we get the money to build the pedestal they'll take it and put it up on that island in the river, and all the boats comin' in from the old country will see it there and it'll raise the hearts of the poor immigrants to see such a fine sight on their first look at this country.

Monaghan. And how do I know it's in this here warehouse at all?

Sheean. You read your paper, don't you? It's been in all the papers for the past year.

Monaghan. Ha, the papers! Last year I read in the paper that they were about to pave Butler Street and take out all the holes. Turn around and look at Butler Street, Mr. Sheean.

Sheean. All right. I'll do this: I'll take you to the warehouse and show you the statue. Will you give me a dime then?

Monaghan. Well . . . I'm not sayin' I would, and I'm not sayin' I wouldn't. But I'd be more likely if I saw the thing large as life, I would.

peeved ▶
(pēvd) *adj.* irritated; annoyed

Sheean. [Peeved] All right, then. Come along.

[Music up and down and out]
[Footsteps, in a warehouse . . . echo . . . they come to a halt.]
Now then. Do you see the Statue of Liberty or don't you see it?

Monaghan. I see it all right, but it's all broke!

Sheean. *Broke!* They brought it from France on a boat. They had to take it apart, didn't they?

Monaghan. You got a secondhand statue, that's what you got, and I'm not payin' for new when they've shipped us something that's all smashed to pieces.

Sheean. Now just a minute, just a minute. Visualize what I'm about to tell you, Monaghan, get the picture of it. When

this statue is put together it's going to stand ten stories high. Could they get a thing ten stories high into a four-story building such as this is? Use your good sense, now Monaghan.

MONAGHAN. What's that over there?

SHEEAN. Where?

MONAGHAN. That tablet there in her hand. What's it say? July Eye Vee (IV) MDCCLXXVI . . . what . . . what's all that?

SHEEAN. That means July 4, 1776. It's in Roman numbers. Very high class.

MONAGHAN. What's the good of it? If they're going to put a sign on her they ought to put it: Welcome All. That's it. Welcome All.

SHEEAN. They decided July 4, 1776, and July 4, 1776, it's going to be!

MONAGHAN. All right, then let them get their dime from somebody else!

SHEEAN. Monaghan!

MONAGHAN. No, sir! I'll tell you something. I didn't think there was a statue but there is. She's all broke, it's true, but she's here and maybe they can get her together. But even if they do, will you tell me what sort of a welcome to immigrants it'll be, to have a gigantic thing like that in the middle of the river and in her hand is July Eye Vee MCDVC . . . whatever it is?

SHEEAN. That's the date the country was made!

MONAGHAN. The divil with the date! A man comin' in from the sea wants a place to stay, not a date. When I come from the old country I git off at the dock and there's a feller says to me, "Would you care for a room for the night?" "I would that," I sez, and he sez, "All right then, follow me." He takes me to a rooming house. I no sooner sign me name on the register—which I was able to do even at that time—when I look around and the feller is gone clear away and took my valise[2] in the bargain. A statue anyway can't move off so fast, but if she's going to welcome let her say welcome, not this MCDC. . . .

---

2. **valise** (və lēs′) *n.* small suitcase.

Sheean. All right, then, Monaghan. But all I can say is, you've laid a disgrace on the name of Butler Street. I'll put the dime in for ya.

Monaghan. Don't connect me with it! It's a **swindle**, is all it is. In the first place, it's broke; in the second place, if they do put it up it'll come down with the first high wind that strikes it.

Sheean. The engineers say it'll last forever!

Monaghan. And I say it'll topple into the river in a high wind! Look at the inside of her. She's all hollow!

Sheean. I've heard everything now, Monaghan. Just about everything. Good-bye.

Monaghan. What do you mean, good-bye? How am I to get back to Butler Street from here?

Sheean. You've got legs to walk.

Monaghan. I'll remind you that I come on the trolley.

Sheean. And I'll remind you that I paid your fare and I'm not repeating the kindness.

Monaghan. Sheean? You've stranded me!

[Music up and down]

ABOUT THE AUTHOR

Arthur Miller (1915–2005)

Arthur Miller was born in New York City in 1915. His father, who ran a small manufacturing business, went bankrupt during the Great Depression. After graduating from high school, Miller worked for two years to earn money so he could attend college. He had many jobs during this time, including one as a clerk in a warehouse. Miller began to write plays while attending college. Today, he is considered among the finest American playwrights. Most of his plays—which have won multiple Tony Awards and other honors—focus on the problems of ordinary people. One of his most famous plays, *Death of a Salesman* (1949), won a Pulitzer Prize and made him internationally famous.

Close Reading Activities

READ

Comprehension

Reread as needed to answer the questions.

1. What does Sheean want from Monaghan?

2. What are two reasons Monaghan gives for his lack of participation?

3. What happens at the end of the selection?

Research: Clarify Details Choose one unfamiliar detail from the play and research it.

Summarize Write an objective summary of the play excerpt. Remember that an objective summary is free from opinion and evaluation.

Language Study

Selection Vocabulary Use each boldfaced word from the play in a sentence that shows the word's meaning.

• And Butler Street is a hundred per cent **subscribed** except for you.

• SHEEAN. [Peeved] All right, then. Come along.

• It's a **swindle,** is all it is.

Literary Analysis

Reread the identified passage.

> **Focus Passage** *(p. 760)*
>
> **Monaghan.** The divil with the date! . . . not this MCDC. . . .

Key Ideas and Details

1. (a) Summarize: What happened when Monaghan arrived in the United States?
(b) Speculate: How did this experience affect his feelings toward the United States?

2. (a) What does Monaghan say new immigrants want? **(b) Analyze:** According to Monaghan, how does the statue fail to meet this need?

Craft and Structure

3. (a) Distinguish: How would you **characterize** Monaghan's way of speaking? Give examples from the text to support your answer. **(b) Draw Conclusions:** What does his style of speech tell you about Monaghan?

Integration of Knowledge and Ideas

4. (a) Compare and Contrast: How does Sheean's opinion of the Statue of Liberty differ from Monaghan's? **(b) Draw Conclusions:** What might be the author's purpose in having these two particular characters discuss the Statue of Liberty?

Dialogue

A **dialogue** is a conversation between characters. Reread the excerpt from the play, taking notes on the dialogue.

1. (a) What characteristics of Monaghan are revealed through his dialogue?

(b) What characteristics of Sheean are revealed through his lines?

2. Becoming American Based on the dialogue, which of the two men feels more comfortable in the United States? Explain.

DISCUSS • RESEARCH • WRITE

From Text to Topic **Debate**

Debate the following passage with your classmates. When it is your turn to speak, respond to the previous speaker and then add your own ideas. Support your ideas with examples from the text.

> **MONAGHAN**. That tablet there in her hand. What's it say? July Eye Vee [IV] MDCCLXXVI . . . what . . . what's all that?
>
> **SHEEAN**. That means July 4, 1776. It's in Roman numbers. Very high class.
>
> **MONAGHAN**. What's the good of it? If they're going to put a sign on her they ought to put it: Welcome All. That's it. Welcome All.

Research **Investigate the Topic**

"The New Colossus" A poem titled "The New Colossus," by Emma Lazarus, is inscribed on the base of the Statue of Liberty. The poem is a spirited explanation of the American ideals that the statue represents.

> ### Assignment
>
> Find and read "The New Colossus" and conduct research to **discover** more about the poem and its meaning for people "becoming American." Consult government and historical sources. Read the poem to the class and share your findings about it in a short **research paper**.

Writing to Sources **Argument**

The excerpt from "Grandpa and the Statue" focuses on two differing opinions about the Statue of Liberty.

> ### Assignment
>
> Write an **argument** in which you evaluate the characters' reasons for and against contributing to the Statue of Liberty Fund. In your essay, state a claim about whose reasons are strong and supported with evidence, and whose reasons are weak. Follow these steps:
>
> - Write a thesis statement that clearly states your claim about which character—Sheean or Monaghan—presents a better argument.
> - Use evidence and quotations from the play to support your argument.
> - Proofread your essay, and correct errors in grammar, spelling, and capitalization.

QUESTIONS FOR DISCUSSION

1. Why does Monaghan object to the Roman numbers on the tablet?
2. What does Sheean think of the tablet?
3. What different attitudes about coming to the United States do these opinions show?

PREPARATION FOR ESSAY

You may use the results of your research to support your ideas in the essay you will write at the end of this section.

ACADEMIC VOCABULARY

Academic terms appear in blue on these pages. If these words are not familiar to you, use a dictionary to find their definitions. Then, use them as you speak and write about the text.

Common Core State Standards

RL.7.1, RL.7.2, RL.7.3, RL.7.4, RL.7.6; W.7.1, W.7.4, W.7.7; SL.7.1
[For full standards wording, see the chart in the front of this book.]

Melting Pot

Anna Quindlen

fluent ▶
(flōō´ ənt) *adj.* able to write or speak easily and smoothly

My children are upstairs in the house next door, having dinner with the Ecuadorian family that lives on the top floor. The father speaks some English, the mother less than that. The two daughters are **fluent** in both their native and their adopted languages, but the youngest child, a son, a close friend of my two boys, speaks almost no Spanish. His parents thought it would be better that way. This doesn't surprise me; it was the way my mother was raised, American among Italians.

I always suspected, hearing my grandfather talk about the "No Irish Need Apply" signs outside factories, hearing my mother talk about the neighborhood kids, who called her greaseball, that the American fable of the melting pot was a myth. Here in our neighborhood it exists, but like so many other things, it exists only person-to-person.

The letters in the local weekly tabloid[1] suggest that everybody hates everybody else here, and on a macro level they do. The old-timers are angry because they think the new moneyed professionals are taking over their town. The professionals are tired of being blamed for the neighborhood's rising rents, particularly since they are the ones paying them. The old immigrants are suspicious of the new ones. The new ones think the old ones are **bigots**. Nevertheless, on a micro level most of us get along. We are friendly with the Ecuadorian family, with the Yugoslavs across the street, and with the Italians next door, mainly by virtue of our children's sidewalk friendships. It took awhile. Eight years ago we were the new people on the block, filling dumpsters with old plaster and lath, . . . (sitting) on the stoop with our demolition masks hanging around our necks like goiters.[2] We thought we could feel people staring at us from behind the sheer curtains on their windows. We were right.

My first apartment in New York was in a gritty warehouse district, the kind of place that makes your parents wince. A lot of old Italians lived around me, which suited me just fine because I was the granddaughter of old Italians. Their own children and grandchildren had moved to Long Island and New Jersey. All they had was me. All I had was them.

I remember sitting on a corner with a group of half a dozen elderly men, men who had known one another since they were boys sitting together on this same corner, watching a glazier install a great spread of tiny glass panes to make one wall of a restaurant in the ground floor of an old building across

◄ **bigots**
(big´ əts)
n. narrow-minded, prejudiced people

---

1. **tabloid** (tab´ loid´) *n.* small newspaper.
2. **goiters** (goit´ ərz) *n.* swellings in the lower front of the neck caused by an enlarged thyroid gland.

the street. The men laid bets on how long the panes, and the restaurant, would last. Two years later two of the men were dead, one had moved in with his married daughter in the suburbs, and the three remaining sat and watched **dolefully** as people waited each night for a table in the restaurant. "Twenty-two dollars for a piece of veal!" one of them would say, apropos of nothing.[3] But when I ate in the restaurant they never blamed me. "You're not one of them," one of the men explained. "You're one of me." It's an argument familiar to members of almost any embattled race or class: I like you, therefore you aren't like the rest of your kind, whom I hate.

Change comes hard in America, but it comes constantly. The butcher whose old shop is now an antiques store sits day after day outside the pizzeria here like a lost child. The old people across the street cluster together and discuss what kind of money they might be offered if the person who bought their building wants to turn it into condominiums. The greengrocer stocks yellow peppers and fresh rosemary for the gourmands, plum tomatoes and broad-leaf parsley for the older Italians, mangoes for the Indians. He doesn't carry plantains, he says, because you can buy them in the bodega.[4]

Sometimes the baby slips out with the bath water. I wanted to throw confetti the day that a family of rough types who propped their speakers on

3. **apropos** (ap´ rə pō´) **of nothing** without connection.
4. **bodega** (bō dā´ gə) *n.* small, Hispanic grocery store.

their station wagon and played heavy metal music at 3:00 a.m. moved out. I stood and smiled as the seedy bar at the corner was transformed into a slick Mexican restaurant. But I liked some of the people who moved out at the same time the rough types did. And I'm not sure I have that much in common with the singles who have made the restaurant their second home.

Yet somehow now we seem to have reached a nice mix. About a third of the people in the neighborhood think of squid as calamari, about a third think of it as sushi, and about a third think of it as bait. Lots of the single people who have moved in during the last year or two are easygoing and good-tempered about all the kids. The old Italians have become philosophical about the new Hispanics, although they still think more of them should know English. The firebrand community organizer with the storefront on the block, the one who is always talking about people like us as though we stole our houses out of the open purse of a ninety-year-old blind widow, is pleasant to my boys.

Drawn in broad strokes, we live in a pressure cooker: oil and water, us and them. But if you come around at exactly the right time, you'll find members of all these groups gathered around complaining about the condition of the streets, on which everyone can agree. We melt together, then draw apart. I am the granddaughter of immigrants, a young professional—either an interloper[5] or a longtime resident, depending on your concept of time. I am one of them, and one of us.

---

5. **interloper** (in′ tər lō′ pər) *n.* one who intrudes on another.

ABOUT THE AUTHOR

Anna Quindlen (b. 1953)

Anna Quindlen spent five years reporting for the *New York Times,* often covering issues related to her family and her neighborhood. "Melting Pot" originally appeared in "Life in the 30s," a popular column that Quindlen wrote in the 1980s. In 1992, Quindlen won a Pulitzer Prize for her columns. Later, she left journalism to write novels. She has published several bestsellers, including *One True Thing, Black and Blue,* and *Blessings.* She has also written children's books, nonfiction books, and a memoir.

READ

Comprehension

Reread as needed to answer the questions.

1. What is the setting of this article?

2. How long has Quindlen lived in her **community**?

3. Why did Quindlen get along with the people who lived near her first apartment?

Research: Clarify Details Choose one unfamiliar detail from the text and research it. Then, explain how your research helped you understand the newspaper column more fully.

Summarize Write an objective summary of the newspaper column.

Language Study

Selection Vocabulary Use each boldfaced word in a sentence that shows the word's meaning.

• The two daughters are **fluent** in both their native and their adopted languages …

• The new ones think the old ones are **bigots.**

• … the three remaining sat and watched **dolefully** as people waited each night for a table in the restaurant.

Literary Analysis

Reread the identified passage. Then, respond to the following questions.

Focus Passage *(pp. 765–766)*

I remember sitting on a corner… your kind, whom I hate.

Key Ideas and Details

1. On what do the elderly men lay bets?

2. **Analyze:** Why do the men comment on the restaurant's prices?

Craft and Structure

3. **(a)** What words indicate a time shift in the middle of in this passage? **(b)** Draw **Conclusions:** What has changed? What has stayed the same?

Integration of Knowledge and Ideas

4. **(a) Interpret:** What does the man mean when he says, "You're not one of them. You're one of me."? **(b) Hypothesize:** How does this **attitude** show that the man is resistant to change?

Idiom

An **idiom** is an expression with a meaning that is different from the meanings of its individual words. Review the text, and take notes on the idioms that Quindlen uses.

1. **(a)** What do you think the expression "the baby slips out with the bath water" (p. 766)

means? **(b)** What idea does Quindlen express through the use of this idiom?

2. **Becoming American (a)** What is the meaning of "the melting pot"? **(b)** Why does Quindlen say that the "fable of the melting pot was a myth" when people become American?

DISCUSS • RESEARCH • WRITE

From Text to Topic **Write and Discuss**

Write a short response to this passage, and then share and discuss it with a small group of classmates. Take notes during the discussion. Contribute your own ideas, and support them with examples from the text.

> Drawn in broad strokes, we live in a pressure cooker:… I am one of them, and one of us. (p. 767)

Research **Investigate the Topic**

Urban "Melting Pots" In this newspaper column, Quindlen describes a neighborhood that is made up of people from many different countries. Many urban neighborhoods in the U.S. have large populations of immigrants.

Assignment

Conduct research to learn about U.S. cities with large immigrant populations. Consult government websites and other print and online sources. Choose one area on which to focus your research. Share your findings in a **visual presentation**.

Writing to Sources **Argument**

In "Melting Pot," Anna Quindlen writes about some of the challenges that are faced by members of a multicultural community.

Assignment

Write a **problem-and-solution essay** in which you propose solutions for some of the conflicts Quindlen describes in her column. Follow these steps:

- Review "Melting Pot" to identify one or more problems to address in your essay. Brainstorm for possible solutions.
- **Compose** a thesis statement in which you present an argument for the best solutions to the problems you have identified.
- Support your thesis statement with evidence from the text, and explain why the solutions you propose are better than alternative solutions.
- Proofread to ensure correct spelling, punctuation, and grammar.

QUESTIONS FOR DISCUSSION

1. According to Quindlen, what can bring different groups of people together?

2. Why might a person feel as if he or she is part of more than just one group of people?

PREPARATION FOR ESSAY

You may use the results of your research to support your ideas in the essay you will write at the end of this section.

ACADEMIC VOCABULARY

Academic terms appear in blue on these pages. If these words are not familiar to you, use a dictionary to find their definitions. Then, use them as you speak and write about the text.

 Common Core State Standards

RI.7.1, RI.7.2, RI.7.3, RI.7.4; W.7.1, W.7.4, W.7.7; SL.7.1, SL.7.4; L.7.4, L.7.5
[For full standards wording, see the chart in the front of this book.]

United States Immigration Statistics

Legal Permanent Resident Flow by Region and Country of Birth:

Fiscal Years 2009 to 2011

Region and country of birth	2011		2010		2009	
	Number	Percent	Number	Percent	Number	Percent
REGION						
Total...............	1,062,040	100.0	1,042,625	100.0	1,130,818	100.0
Africa.............	100,374	9.5	101,355	9.7	127,046	11.2
Asia...............	451,593	42.5	422,063	40.5	413,312	36.5
Europe.............	83,850	7.9	88,801	8.5	105,476	9.3
North America.........	333,902	31.4	336,553	32.3	375,180	33.2
Caribbean...........	133,680	12.6	139,951	13.4	146,071	12.9
Central America......	43,707	4.1	43,951	4.2	47,868	4.2
Other North America...	156,515	14.7	152,651	14.6	181,241	16.0
Oceania.............	4,980	0.5	5,345	0.5	5,578	0.5
South America.........	86,096	8.1	87,178	8.4	102,860	9.1
Unknown.............	1,245	0.1	1,330	0.1	1,366	0.1
COUNTRY						
Total...............	1,062,040	100.0	1,042,625	100.0	1,130,818	100.0
Mexico.............	143,446	13.5	139,120	13.3	164,920	14.6
China, People's Republic..	87,016	8.2	70,863	6.8	64,238	5.7
India...............	69,013	6.5	69,162	6.6	57,304	5.1
Philippines...........	57,011	5.4	58,173	5.6	60,029	5.3
Dominican Republic.....	46,109	4.3	53,870	5.2	49,414	4.4
Cuba...............	36,452	3.4	33,573	3.2	38,954	3.4
Vietnam.............	34,157	3.2	30,632	2.9	29,234	2.6
Korea, South..........	22,824	2.1	22,227	2.1	25,859	2.3
Colombia............	22,635	2.1	22,406	2.1	27,849	2.5
Haiti...............	22,111	2.1	22,582	2.2	24,280	2.1
Iraq................	21,133	2.0	19,855	1.9	12,110	1.1
Jamaica.............	19,662	1.9	19,825	1.9	21,783	1.9
El Salvador...........	18,667	1.8	18,806	1.8	19,909	1.8
Bangladesh...........	16,707	1.6	14,819	1.4	16,651	1.5
Burma..............	16,518	1.6	12,925	1.2	13,621	1.2
Pakistan.............	15,546	1.5	18,258	1.8	21,555	1.9
Iran................	14,822	1.4	14,182	1.4	18,553	1.6
Peru...............	14,064	1.3	14,247	1.4	16,957	1.5
Ethiopia.............	13,793	1.3	14,266	1.4	15,462	1.4
Canada.............	12,800	1.2	13,328	1.3	16,140	1.4
All other countries......	357,554	33.7	359,506	34.5	415,996	36.8

Source: U.S. Department of Homeland Security, Computer Linked Application Information Management System (CLAIMS),
Legal Immigrant Data, Fiscal Years 2009 to 2011.

READ • RESEARCH • WRITE

**Common Core
State Standards**

W.7.3, W.7.7; SL.7.2
[For full standards wording, see the chart in the front of this book.]

Comprehension

Study the infographic to help you answer the questions.

1. What information appears in the table?

2. **(a)** What agency released the data table? **(b)** How are **legal** permanent residents (LPRs) classified in the table?

Critical Analysis

Key Ideas and Details

1. **(a) Interpret: Approximately** how many people, in total, became legal permanent residents in the United States from 2009 to 2011?
   (b) Identify: From which continent did the majority of the new LPRs come? **(c)** From which country did the most new LPRs come?

Craft and Structure

2. **Draw Conclusions:** Why does the table include an entry for "All other countries"?

Integration of Knowledge and Ideas

3. **Generalize:** Why might the information in this table be useful to immigration officials in the United States?

**ACADEMIC
VOCABULARY**

Academic terms appear in blue on this page. If these words are not familiar to you, use a dictionary to find their definitions. Then, use the words as you speak and write about the text.

Research **Investigate the Topic**

Immigration to the United States This table shows the number of people who became legal permanent residents of the United States from 2009 to 2011. The process of becoming a LPR is often long and difficult.

> **Assignment**
> Conduct research to learn about the current immigration process for people who want to move to the U.S. today. Investigate the reasons why people want to come here, and find out what they need to do in their home countries before they leave. Consult government sources for information. Share your findings in an **informal presentation.**

Writing to Sources **Narrative**

Write a brief **short story** in which you describe the experiences of an **individual** or a family who is immigrating to the United States.

Speaking and Listening: Group Discussion

Becoming American The texts in this section vary in genre, length, style, and perspective. However, all of the texts comment in some way on the experience of becoming American and on the Big Question addressed in this unit: **Community or individual—which is more important?**

Assignment

Conduct discussions. With a small group of classmates, conduct a discussion connecting issues related to becoming American with the relationship between the community and the individual. Refer to the texts in this section, other texts you have read, and your personal experience and knowledge to support your ideas. Begin your discussion by addressing the following questions:

- In what ways may an individual change if he or she moves to another country? In what ways may he or she stay the same?
- What are some different types of communities to which people belong in the United States?
- Can a person who moves to the U.S. from another country bring elements of his or her community along? If so, how?
- Are the needs of an individual ever more important than the needs of a community? Explain.

Summarize and present your ideas. After you have fully explored the topic, summarize your discussion and present your findings to the class.

▲ Refer to the selections you read in Part 3 as you complete the activities on this assessment.

Criteria for Success

✓ **Organizes the group effectively**
Appoint a group leader and a timekeeper. The group leader should present the discussion questions. The timekeeper should make sure the discussion takes no longer than 20 minutes.

✓ **Maintains focus of discussion**
As a group, stay on topic and avoid straying into other subject areas.

✓ **Involves all participants equally and fully**
No one person should monopolize the conversation. Rather, everyone should take turns speaking and contributing ideas.

✓ **Follows the rules for collegial discussion**
As each group member speaks, others should listen carefully. Build on one another's ideas and support viewpoints and opinions with sound reasoning and evidence. Express disagreement respectfully.

USE NEW VOCABULARY

As you speak and share ideas, work to use the vocabulary words you have learned in this unit. The more you use new words, the more you will "own" them.

Writing: **Narrative**

Becoming American As Americans, we may come from different ethnic, religious, and economic backgrounds. One thing we all share, however, is the experience of navigating our way through the various communities in our lives: our families, religious institutions, neighborhoods, schools, and workplaces.

Common Core State Standards

W.7.3.a–b, W.7.3.d–e, W.7.4; SL.7.1.a–d, SL.7.4, SL.7.6
[For full standards wording, see the chart in the front of this book.]

Assignment

Write an **autobiographical narrative**—a true story about your own life—in which you discuss an experience you have had as an individual functioning within a community. Frame your narrative around a problem or conflict that you had to address or are still addressing. For example, you might describe a conflict that resulted from the collision of one of your communities with another. In your narrative, compare your experience to the experience of someone you read about in one of the texts in this section. Explain how your experience relates to the idea of becoming, or being, American.

Criteria for Success

Purpose/Focus
✓ **Connects specific incidents with larger ideas**
Make meaningful connections between your experiences and the texts you have read in this section.

✓ **Clearly conveys the significance of the story**
Provide a conclusion in which you reflect on what you experienced.

Organization
✓ **Sequences events logically**
Structure your narrative so that individual events build on one another to create a coherent whole.

Development of Ideas/Elaboration
✓ **Supports insights**
Include both personal examples and details from the texts you have read.

✓ **Uses narrative techniques effectively**
Consider using storytelling elements such as figurative language, dialogue, and symbolism.

Language
✓ **Uses description effectively**
Use descriptive details to engage your readers.

Conventions
✓ **Does not have errors**
Eliminate errors in grammar, spelling, and punctuation.

WRITE TO EXPLORE

Writing is a way to explore what you feel and think: You may change your mind or get new ideas as you work. As you write your autobiographical narrative, explore your ideas on becoming American and on community and the individual.

Writing to Sources: **Explanatory Text**

Becoming American The related readings in this section present a range of ideas about becoming American. The selections raise questions, such as those below, about the differing experiences of individuals within communities, both in the U.S. and in other countries.

- What does it mean to be an individual?
- What happens when the needs of an individual conflict with the needs of the community?
- How does living in the United States make it easier or more difficult to belong to multiple communities?
- What actions do people take to "become American"? What is involved in the process?

Focus on the question that intrigues you the most, and then complete the following assignment.

> **Assignment**
>
> Write an **explanatory essay** in which you explore what it means to "become American" by comparing and contrasting characters in two or more texts from this section. Clearly present, develop, and support your ideas with examples and details from the texts.

Prewriting and Planning

Choose texts. Review the texts in the section to determine which ones you will cite in your essay. Select at least two texts that will provide strong material to support your thesis statement.

Gather details and craft a working thesis statement. Use a chart like the one shown to develop your thesis statement.

Focus Question: What actions does one have to take to "become American"? What is involved in the process?

Text	Passage	Notes
"My First Free Summer"	If the light could be translated into words, instead, they would say: Freedom and liberty and justice for all …	Alvarez begins to understand the American ideals she has learned at school.
"Melting Pot"	I am one of them, and one of us.	Quindlen recognizes that she belongs to multiple communities.

Example Thesis Statement: In these texts, becoming American involves embracing both the principles upon which the U.S. was founded, and the different groups of people gathered together under those principles.

INCORPORATE RESEARCH

In your essay, use the information you gathered as you completed the brief research assignments related to the selections in this section.

Drafting

Present a clear thesis. Review your notes to develop a single sentence, or thesis statement, in which you clearly present the main idea of your essay. Include this sentence in your opening paragraph.

Organize for clarity. For clarity and readability, address one key point in each paragraph. Make sure that all of your points connect to your thesis statement.

Use transition words and phrases. Use transitions that help you create a smooth flow between paragraphs and between ideas. Examples of transitions include: *next, although, as a result, therefore, however, furthermore,* and *finally.*

Revising and Editing

Check support for your thesis. Make sure that your thesis is clearly stated and that you have supported it with convincing textual evidence. Check your conclusion to make sure it reinforces your thesis while providing a sense of closure for your essay.

Maintain a formal style. Review your writing to ensure you have maintained a formal style. If necessary, revise to eliminate slang and contractions and to correct incomplete sentences and other grammatical errors.

Common Core State Standards

W.7.2.a–f, W.7.4, W.7.9; L.7.1, L.7.3
[For full standards wording, see the chart in the front of this book.]

CITE RESEARCH CORRECTLY

When you quote from a source directly, use quotation marks to indicate that the words are not your own.

Self-Evaluation Rubric

Use the following criteria to evaluate the effectiveness of your essay.

Criteria	Rating Scale
Purpose/Focus Introduces a clear thesis statement; provides a concluding section that follows from and supports the information or explanation presented	*not very* .... *very* 1 2 3 4
Organization Organizes complex ideas, concepts, and information to make important connections and distinctions; uses appropriate and varied transitions to link the major sections, create cohesion, and clarify relationships among ideas	1 2 3 4
Development of Ideas/Elaboration Develops the topic with well-chosen, relevant and sufficient facts, extended definitions, concrete details, quotations or other information and examples appropriate to the audience's knowledge of the topic	1 2 3 4
Language Uses precise language and domain-specific vocabulary to manage the complexity of the topic; establishes and maintains a formal style and objective tone	1 2 3 4
Conventions Uses correct conventions of grammar, spelling, and punctuation	1 2 3 4

Titles for Extended Reading

In this unit, you have read texts in a variety of genres. Continue to read on your own. Select works that you enjoy, but challenge yourself to explore new authors and works of increasing depth and complexity. The titles suggested below will help you get started.

INFORMATIONAL TEXT

Around the World in a Hundred Years
by Jean Fritz

 This entertaining **nonfiction** book describes what happened when explorers, such as Columbus and Magellan, met the inhabitants of the lands they called "the Unknown."

The Great Fire   EXEMPLAR TEXT ©
by Jim Murphy

In this **nonfiction** book, Jim Murphy uses a variety of personal accounts to tell the story of the tragic Great Chicago Fire of 1871. This fascinating history tells how the fire began, how people responded to it, and how it was finally contained.

Discoveries: Truth Is Stranger Than Fiction

 The **essays** in this book explore a variety of topics, including "The Wonders of the World," "Snakes in the Sky!," "Reel Time," and "Math Tricks."

LITERATURE

The People Could Fly: American Black Folktales   EXEMPLAR TEXT ©
by Virginia Hamilton

 These twenty-four **folk tales** celebrate the strength and resourcefulness of the people who survived slavery. The collection includes the selection "The People Could Fly," which is featured in this unit.

Trojan Horse
by David Clement-Davies

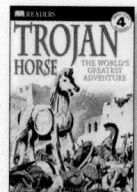 In this modern retelling of the classic **myth,** the Greeks cleverly use a huge wooden horse to enter and destroy the city of Troy.

The Time Warp Trio: It's All Greek to Me
by Jon Scieszka

 In this funny **novel,** Joe and his friends accidentally find themselves trapped in ancient Greece. With only a cardboard thunderbolt and a painted apple as weapons, they must outwit the gods to survive the dangers of Hades and Mount Olympus.

Thirteen Moons on Turtle's Back
by Joseph Bruchac

 The thirteen **poems** in this collection of myths and legends represent the thirteen moon cycles that make up the year in traditional Native American folklore.

ONLINE TEXT SET

POEM
Martin Luther King Raymond R. Patterson

SHORT STORY
The Bear Boy Joseph Bruchac

CONTRACT
Theater Show Contract Crystal Springs Upland School

Preparing to Read Complex Texts

Attentive Reading As you read on your own, ask yourself questions like these to enrich your reading experience.

When reading texts from the oral tradition, ask yourself...

Comprehension: **Key Ideas and Details**

- From what culture does this text come? What do I know about that culture?
- What type of text am I reading? For example, is it a myth, a legend, or a tall tale? What characters and events do I expect to find in this type of text?
- What elements of the culture do I see in the text? For example, do I notice beliefs, foods, or settings that have meaning for the people of this culture?
- Does the text teach a lesson or a moral? If so, is this a valuable lesson?

Text Analysis: **Craft and Structure**

- Who is retelling or presenting this text? Do I think the author has changed the text from the original? If so, how?
- Does the text include characters and tell a story? If so, are the characters and plot interesting?
- What do I notice about the language used in the text? Which aspects seem similar to or different from the language used in modern texts?
- Does the text include symbols? If so, do they have a special meaning in the original culture of the text? Do they also have meaning in modern life?

Connections: **Integration of Knowledge and Ideas**

- What does this text teach me about the culture from which it comes?
- What, if anything, does this text teach me about people in general?
- Does this text seem like others I have read or heard? Why or why not?
- Do I know of any modern versions of this text? How are they similar to or different from this one?
- If I were researching this culture for a report, would I include passages from this text? If so, what would those passages show?
- Do I enjoy reading this text and others like it? Why or why not?

Common Core State Standards

Reading Literature/ Informational Text
10. By the end of the year, read and comprehend literature, including stories, dramas, and poems, and literary nonfiction in the grades 6–8 text complexity band proficiently, with scaffolding as needed at the high end of the range.

Resources

Literary Terms

ALLITERATION *Alliteration* is the repetition of initial consonant sounds. Writers use alliteration to draw attention to certain words or ideas, to imitate sounds, and to create musical effects.

ALLUSION An *allusion* is a reference to a well-known person, event, place, literary work, or work of art. Allusions allow the writer to express complex ideas without spelling them out. Understanding what a literary work is saying often depends on recognizing its allusions and the meanings they suggest.

ANALOGY An *analogy* makes a comparison between two or more things that are similar in some ways but otherwise unalike.

ANECDOTE An *anecdote* is a brief story about an interesting, amusing, or strange event. Writers tell anecdotes to entertain or to make a point.

ANTAGONIST An *antagonist* is a character or a force in conflict with a main character, or protagonist.

See *Conflict* and *Protagonist.*

ARGUMENT See *Persuasion.*

ATMOSPHERE *Atmosphere,* or *mood,* is the feeling created in the reader by a literary work or passage.

AUTHOR'S ARGUMENT An *author's argument* is the position he or she puts forward, supported by reasons.

AUTHOR'S PURPOSE An *author's purpose* is his or her main reason for writing. For example, an author may want to entertain, inform, or persuade the reader. Sometimes an author is trying to teach a moral lesson or reflect on an experience. An author may have more than one purpose for writing.

AUTOBIOGRAPHY An *autobiography* is the story of the writer's own life, told by the writer. Autobiographical writing may tell about the person's whole life or only a part of it.

Because autobiographies are about real people and events, they are a form of nonfiction. Most autobiographies are written in the first person.

See *Biography, Nonfiction,* and *Point of View.*

BIOGRAPHY A *biography* is a form of nonfiction in which a writer tells the life story of another person. Most biographies are written about famous or admirable people. Although biographies are nonfiction, the most effective ones share the qualities of good narrative writing.

See *Autobiography* and *Nonfiction.*

CHARACTER A *character* is a person or an animal that takes part in the action of a literary work. The main, or *major,* character is the most important character in a story, poem, or play. A *minor* character is one who takes part in the action but is not the focus of attention.

Characters are sometimes classified as flat or round. A *flat character* is one-sided and often stereotypical. A *round character,* on the other hand, is fully developed and exhibits many traits—often both faults and virtues. Characters can also be classified as dynamic or static. A *dynamic character* is one who changes or grows during the course of the work. A *static character* is one who does not change.

See *Characterization, Hero/Heroine,* and *Motive.*

CHARACTERIZATION *Characterization* is the act of creating and developing a character. Authors use two major methods of characterization—*direct* and *indirect.* When using direct characterization, a writer states the *characters' traits,* or characteristics.

When describing a character indirectly, a writer depends on the reader to draw conclusions about the character's traits. Sometimes the writer tells what other participants in the story say and think about the character.

See *Character* and *Motive.*

CLIMAX The *climax,* also called the turning point, is the high point in the action of the plot. It is the moment of greatest tension, when the outcome of the plot hangs in the balance.

See *Plot.*

COMEDY A *comedy* is a literary work, especially a play, which is light, often humorous or satirical, and ends happily. Comedies frequently depict ordinary characters faced with temporary difficulties and conflicts. Types of comedy include *romantic comedy,* which involves problems between lovers, and the *comedy of manners,* which satirically challenges social customs of a society.

CONCRETE POEM A *concrete poem* is one with a shape that suggests its subject. The poet arranges the letters, punctuation, and lines to create an image, or picture, on the page.

CONFLICT A *conflict* is a struggle between opposing forces. Conflict is one of the most important elements of stories, novels, and plays because it causes the action. There are two kinds of conflict: external and internal.

An *external conflict* is one in which a character struggles against some outside force, such as another person. Another kind of external conflict may occur between a character and some force in nature.

An *internal conflict* takes place within the mind of a character. The character struggles to make a decision, take an action, or overcome a feeling.

See *Plot.*

CONNOTATIONS The *connotation* of a word is the set of ideas associated with it in addition to its explicit meaning. The connotation of a word can be personal, based on individual experiences. More often, cultural connotations—those recognizable by most people in a group—determine a writer's word choices.

See also *Denotation.*

COUPLET A *couplet* is two consecutive lines of verse with end rhymes. Often, a couplet functions as a stanza.

CULTURAL CONTEXT The *cultural context* of a literary work is the economic, social, and historical environment of the characters. This includes the attitudes and customs of that culture and historical period.

DENOTATION The *denotation* of a word is its dictionary meaning, independent of other associations that the word may have. The denotation of the word *lake,* for example, is "an inland body of water." "Vacation spot" and "place where the fishing is good" are connotations of the word *lake.*

See also *Connotation.*

DESCRIPTION A *description* is a portrait, in words, of a person, place, or object. Descriptive writing uses images that appeal to the five senses —sight, hearing, touch, taste, and smell.

See *Images.*

DEVELOPMENT See *Plot.*

DIALECT *Dialect* is the form of a language spoken by people in a particular region or group. Dialects differ in pronunciation, grammar, and word choice. The English language is divided into many dialects. British English differs from American English.

DIALOGUE A *dialogue* is a conversation between characters. In poems, novels, and short stories, dialogue is usually set off by quotation marks to indicate a speaker's exact words.

In a play, dialogue follows the names of the characters, and no quotation marks are used.

DICTION *Diction* is a writer's word choice and the way the writer puts those words together. Diction is part of a writer's style and may be described as formal or informal, plain or fancy, ordinary or technical, sophisticated or down-to-earth, old-fashioned or modern.

DRAMA A *drama* is a story written to be performed by actors. Although a drama is meant to be performed, one can also read the script, or written version, and imagine the action. The *script* of a drama is made up of dialogue and stage directions. The *dialogue* is the words spoken by the actors. The *stage directions,* usually printed in italics, tell how the actors should look, move, and speak. They also describe the setting, sound effects, and lighting.

Dramas are often divided into parts called *acts.* The acts are often divided into smaller parts called *scenes.*

DYNAMIC CHARACTER See *Character.*

ESSAY An *essay* is a short nonfiction work about a particular subject. Most essays have a single major focus and a clear introduction, body, and conclusion.

There are many types of essays. An *informal essay* uses casual, conversational language. A *historical essay* gives facts, explanations, and insights about historical events. An *expository essay* explains an idea by breaking it down. A *narrative essay* tells a story about a real-life experience. An *informational essay* explains a process. A *persuasive essay* offers an opinion and supports it. A *humorous essay* uses humor to achieve the author's purpose. A *reflective essay* addresses an event or experience and includes the writer's personal insights about the event's importance.

See *Exposition, Narration,* and *Persuasion.*

EXPOSITION In the plot of a story or a drama, the *exposition,* or introduction, is the part of the work that introduces the characters, setting, and basic situation.

See *Plot.*

EXPOSITORY WRITING *Expository writing* is writing that explains or informs.

EXTENDED METAPHOR In an *extended metaphor,* as in a regular metaphor, a subject is spoken or written of as though it were something else. However, extended metaphor differs from regular metaphor in that several connected comparisons are made.

See *Metaphor.*

EXTERNAL CONFLICT See *Conflict.*

FABLE A *fable* is a brief story or poem, usually with animal characters, that teaches a lesson, or moral. The moral is usually stated at the end of the fable.

See *Irony* and *Moral.*

FANTASY A *fantasy* is highly imaginative writing that contains elements not found in real life. Examples of fantasy include stories that involve supernatural elements, stories that resemble fairy tales, stories that deal with imaginary places and creatures, and science-fiction stories.

See *Science Fiction.*

FICTION *Fiction* is prose writing that tells about imaginary characters and events. Short stories and novels are works of fiction. Some writers base their fiction on actual events and people, adding invented characters, dialogue, settings, and plots. Other writers rely on imagination alone.

See *Narration, Nonfiction,* and *Prose.*

FIGURATIVE LANGUAGE *Figurative language* is writing or speech that is not meant to be taken literally. The many types of figurative language are known as *figures of speech.* Common figures of speech include metaphor, personification, and simile. Writers use figurative language to state ideas in vivid and imaginative ways.

See *Metaphor, Personification, Simile,* and *Symbol.*

FIGURE OF SPEECH See *Figurative Language.*

FLASHBACK A *flashback* is a scene within a story that interrupts the sequence of events to relate events that occurred in the past.

FLAT CHARACTER See *Character.*

FOIL A *foil* is a character whose behavior and attitude contrast with those of the main character.

FOLK TALE A *folk tale* is a story composed orally and then passed from person to person by word of mouth. Folk tales originated among people who could neither read nor write. These people entertained one another by telling stories aloud—often dealing with heroes, adventure, magic, or romance. Eventually, modern scholars collected these stories and wrote them down.

Folk tales reflect the cultural beliefs and environments from which they come.

See *Fable, Legend, Myth,* and *Oral Tradition.*

FOOT See *Meter.*

FORESHADOWING *Foreshadowing* is the author's use of clues to hint at what might happen later in the story. Writers use foreshadowing to build their readers' expectations and to create suspense.

FREE VERSE *Free verse* is poetry not written in a regular, rhythmical pattern, or meter. The poet is free to write lines of any length or with any number of stresses, or beats. Free verse is therefore less constraining than *metrical verse,* in which every line must have a certain length and a certain number of stresses.

See *Meter.*

GENRE A *genre* is a division or type of literature. Literature is commonly divided into three major genres: poetry, prose, and drama. Each major genre is, in turn, divided into lesser genres, as follows:

1. *Poetry:* lyric poetry, concrete poetry, dramatic poetry, narrative poetry, epic poetry

2. *Prose:* fiction (novels and short stories) and nonfiction (biography, autobiography, letters, essays, and reports)

3. *Drama:* serious drama and tragedy, comic drama, melodrama, and farce

See *Drama, Poetry,* and *Prose.*

HAIKU The *haiku* is a three-line Japanese verse form. The first and third lines of a haiku each have five syllables. The second line has seven syllables. A writer of haiku uses images to create a single, vivid picture, generally of a scene from nature.

HERO/HEROINE A *hero* or *heroine* is a character whose actions are inspiring or noble. Often heroes and heroines struggle to overcome the obstacles and problems that stand in their way. Note that the term *hero* was originally used only for male characters, while heroic female characters were always called *heroines.* However, it is now acceptable to use *hero* to refer to females as well as to males.

HISTORICAL CONTEXT The *historical context* of a literary work includes the actual political and social events and trends of the time. When a work takes place in the past, knowledge about that historical time period can help the reader understand its setting, background, culture, and message, as well as the attitudes and actions of its characters. A reader must also take into account the historical context in which the writer was creating the work, which may be different from the time period of the work's setting.

HUMOR *Humor* is writing intended to evoke laughter. While most humorists try to entertain, humor can also be used to convey a serious theme.

IDIOM An *idiom* is an expression that has a meaning particular to a language or region. For example, in "Seventh Grade," Gary Soto uses the idiom "making a face," which means to contort one's face in an unusual, usually unattractive way.

IMAGERY See *Images.*

IMAGES *Images* are words or phrases that appeal to one or more of the five senses. Writers use images to describe how their subjects look, sound, feel, taste, and smell. Poets often paint images, or word pictures, that appeal to the senses. These pictures help you to experience the poem fully.

INTERNAL CONFLICT See *Conflict.*

IRONY *Irony* is a contradiction between what happens and what is expected. There are three main types of irony. *Situational irony* occurs when something happens that directly contradicts the expectations of the characters or the audience. *Verbal irony* is something contradictory that is said. In *dramatic irony,* the audience is aware of something that the character or speaker is not.

JOURNAL A *journal* is a daily, or periodic, account of events and the writer's thoughts and feelings about those events. Personal journals are not normally written for publication, but sometimes they do get published later with permission from the author or the author's family.

LEGEND A *legend* is a widely told story about the past—one that may or may not have a foundation in fact. Every culture has its own legends—its familiar, traditional stories.

See *Folk Tale, Myth,* and *Oral Tradition.*

LETTERS A *letter* is a written communication from one person to another. In personal letters, the writer shares information and his or her thoughts and feelings with one other person or group. Although letters are not normally written for publication, they sometimes do get published later with the permission of the author or the author's family.

LIMERICK A *limerick* is a humorous, rhyming, five-line poem with a specific meter and rhyme scheme. Most limericks have three strong stresses in lines 1, 2, and 5 and two strong stresses in lines 3 and 4. Most follow the rhyme scheme *aabba.*

LYRIC POEM A *lyric poem* is a highly musical verse that expresses the observations and feelings of a single speaker. It creates a single, unified impression.

MAIN CHARACTER See *Character.*

MEDIA ACCOUNTS *Media accounts* are reports, explanations, opinions, or descriptions written for television, radio, newspapers, and magazines. While some media accounts report only facts, others include the writer's thoughts and reflections.

METAPHOR A *metaphor* is a figure of speech in which something is described as though it were something else. A metaphor, like a simile, works by pointing out a similarity between two unlike things.

See *Extended Metaphor* and *Simile.*

METER The *meter* of a poem is its rhythmical pattern. This pattern is determined by the number of *stresses,* or beats, in each line. To describe the meter of a poem, read it emphasizing the beats in each line. Then, mark the stressed and unstressed syllables, as follows:

My fáth | ĕr wás | thĕ fírst | tŏ héar |

As you can see, each strong stress is marked with a slanted line (´) and each unstressed syllable with a horseshoe symbol (˘). The weak and strong stresses are then divided by vertical lines (|) into groups called feet.

MINOR CHARACTER See *Character.*

MOOD See *Atmosphere.*

MORAL A *moral* is a lesson taught by a literary work. A fable usually ends with a moral that is directly stated. A poem, novel, short story, or essay often suggests a moral that is not directly stated. The moral must be drawn by the reader, based on other elements in the work.

See *Fable.*

MOTIVATION See *Motive.*

MOTIVE A *motive* is a reason that explains or partially explains a character's thoughts, feelings, actions, or speech. Writers try to make their characters' motives, or motivations, as clear as possible. If the motives of a main character are not clear, then the character will not be believable.

Characters are often motivated by needs, such as food and shelter. They are also motivated by feelings, such as fear, love, and pride. Motives may be obvious or hidden.

MYTH A *myth* is a fictional tale that explains the actions of gods or heroes or the origins of elements of nature. Myths are part of the oral tradition. They are composed orally and then passed from generation to generation by word of mouth. Every ancient culture has its own mythology, or collection of myths. Greek and Roman myths are known collectively as *classical mythology.*

See *Oral Tradition.*

NARRATION *Narration* is writing that tells a story. The act of telling a story is also called narration. Each piece is a *narrative.* A story told in fiction, nonfiction, poetry, or even drama is called a narrative.

See *Narrative, Narrative Poem,* and *Narrator.*

NARRATIVE A *narrative* is a story. A narrative can be either fiction or nonfiction. Novels and short stories are types of fictional narratives. Biographies and autobiographies are nonfiction narratives. Poems that tell stories are also narratives.

See *Narration* and *Narrative Poem.*

NARRATIVE POEM A *narrative poem* is a story told in verse. Narrative poems often have all the elements of short stories, including characters, conflict, and plot.

NARRATOR A *narrator* is a speaker or a character who tells a story. The narrator's perspective is the way he or she sees things. A *third-person narrator* is one who stands outside the action and speaks about it. A *first-person narrator* is one who tells a story and participates in its action.

See *Point of View.*

NONFICTION *Nonfiction* is prose writing that presents and explains ideas or that tells about real people, places, objects, or events. Autobiographies, biographies, essays, reports, letters, memos, and newspaper articles are all types of nonfiction.

See *Fiction.*

NOVEL A *novel* is a long work of fiction. Novels contain such elements as characters, plot, conflict, and setting. The writer of novels, or novelist, develops these elements. In addition to its main plot, a novel may contain one or more subplots, or independent, related stories. A novel may also have several themes.

See *Fiction* and *Short Story.*

NOVELLA A fiction work that is longer than a short story but shorter than a novel.

ONOMATOPOEIA *Onomatopoeia* is the use of words that imitate sounds. *Crash, buzz, screech, hiss, neigh, jingle,* and *cluck* are examples of onomatopoeia. *Chickadee, towhee,* and *whippoorwill* are onomatopoeic names of birds.

Onomatopoeia can help put the reader in the activity of a poem.

ORAL TRADITION *Oral tradition* is the passing of songs, stories, and poems from generation to generation by word of mouth. Folk songs, folk tales, legends, and myths all come from the oral tradition. No one knows who first created these stories and poems.

See *Folk Tale, Legend,* and *Myth.*

OXYMORON An *oxymoron* (pl. *oxymora*) is a figure of speech that links two opposite or contradictory words in order to point out an idea or situation that seems contradictory or inconsistent but on closer inspection turns out to be somehow true.

PERSONIFICATION *Personification* is a type of figurative language in which a nonhuman subject is given human characteristics.

PERSPECTIVE See *Narrator* and *Point of View.*

PERSUASION *Persuasion* is used in writing or speech that attempts to convince the reader or listener to adopt a particular opinion or course of action. Newspaper editorials and letters to the editor use persuasion. So do advertisements and campaign speeches given by political candidates. An *argument* is a logical way of presenting a belief, conclusion, or stance. A good argument is supported with reasoning and evidence.

See *Essay.*

PLAYWRIGHT A *playwright* is a person who writes plays. William Shakespeare is regarded as the greatest playwright in English literature.

PLOT *Plot* is the sequence of events in which each event results from a previous one and causes the next. In most novels, dramas, short stories, and narrative poems, the plot involves both characters and a central conflict. The plot usually begins with an *exposition* that introduces the setting, the characters, and the basic situation. This is followed by the *inciting incident,* which introduces the central conflict. The conflict then increases during the *development* until it reaches a high point of interest or suspense, the *climax.* The climax is followed by the *falling action,* or end, of the central conflict. Any events that occur during the *falling action* make up the *resolution* or *denouement.*

Some plots do not have all of these parts. Some stories begin with the inciting incident and end with the resolution.

See *Conflict.*

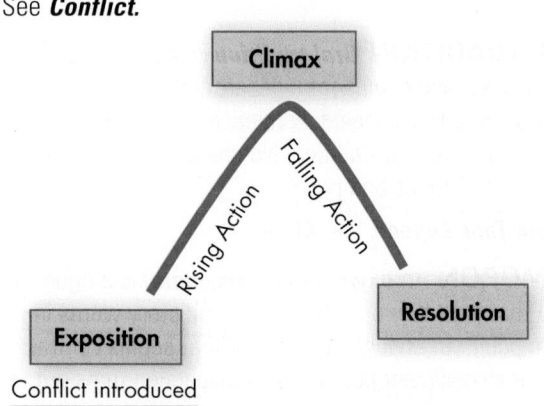

Conflict introduced

POETRY *Poetry* is one of the three major types of literature, the others being prose and drama. Most poems make use of highly concise, musical, and emotionally charged language. Many also make use of imagery, figurative language, and special devices of sound such as rhyme. Major types of poetry include *lyric poetry, narrative poetry,* and *concrete poetry.*

See *Concrete Poem, Genre, Lyric Poem,* and *Narrative Poem.*

POINT OF VIEW *Point of view* is the perspective, or vantage point, from which a story is told. It is either a narrator outside the story or a character in the story. *First-person point of view* is told by a character who uses the first-person pronoun "I."

The two kinds of *third-person point of view,* limited and omniscient, are called "third person" because the narrator uses third-person pronouns such as he and she to refer to the characters. There is no "I" telling the story.

In stories told from the *omniscient third-person point of view,* the narrator knows and tells about what each character feels and thinks.

In stories told from the *limited third-person point of view,* the narrator relates the inner thoughts and feelings of only one character, and everything is viewed from this character's perspective.

See *Narrator.*

PROBLEM See *Conflict.*

PROSE *Prose* is the ordinary form of written language. Most writing that is not poetry, drama, or song is considered prose. Prose is one of the major genres of literature and occurs in fiction and nonfiction.

See *Fiction, Genre,* and *Nonfiction.*

PROTAGONIST The *protagonist* is the main character in a literary work. Often, the protagonist is a person, but sometimes it can be an animal.

See *Antagonist* and *Character.*

REFRAIN A *refrain* is a regularly repeated line or group of lines in a poem or a song.

REPETITION *Repetition* is the use, more than once, of any element of language—a sound, word, phrase, clause, or sentence. Repetition is used in both prose and poetry.

See *Alliteration, Meter, Plot, Rhyme,* and *Rhyme Scheme.*

RESOLUTION The *resolution* is the outcome of the conflict in a plot.

See *Plot.*

RHYME *Rhyme* is the repetition of sounds at the ends of words. Poets use rhyme to lend a songlike quality to their verses and to emphasize certain words and ideas. Many traditional poems contain *end rhymes,* or rhyming words at the ends of lines.

Another common device is the use of *internal rhymes,* or rhyming words within lines. Internal rhyme also emphasizes the flowing nature of a poem.

See *Rhyme Scheme.*

RHYME SCHEME A *rhyme scheme* is a regular pattern of rhyming words in a poem. To indicate the rhyme scheme of a poem, one uses lowercase letters. Each rhyme is assigned a different letter, as follows in the first stanza of "Dust of Snow" by Robert Frost:

The way a crow	*a*
Shook down on me	*b*
The dust of snow	*a*
From a hemlock tree	*b*

Thus, the stanza has the rhyme scheme *abab.*

RHYTHM *Rhythm* is the pattern of stressed and unstressed syllables in spoken or written language.

See *Meter.*

ROUND CHARACTER See *Character.*

SCENE A *scene* is a section of uninterrupted action in the act of a drama.

See *Drama.*

SCIENCE FICTION *Science fiction* combines elements of fiction and fantasy with scientific fact. Many science-fiction stories are set in the future.

SENSORY LANGUAGE *Sensory language* is writing or speech that appeals to one or more of the five senses.

See *Images.*

SETTING The *setting* of a literary work is the time and place of the action. The setting includes all the details of a place and time—the year, the time of day, even the weather. The place may be a specific country, state, region, community, neighborhood, building, institution, or home. Details such as dialects, clothing, customs, and modes of transportation are often used to establish setting. In most stories, the setting serves as a backdrop—a context in which the characters interact. Setting can also help to create a feeling, or atmosphere.

See *Atmosphere.*

SHORT STORY A *short story* is a brief work of fiction. Like a novel, a short story presents a sequence of events, or plot. The plot usually deals with a central conflict faced by a main character, or protagonist. The events in a short story usually communicate a message about life or human nature. This message, or central idea, is the story's theme.

See *Conflict, Plot,* and *Theme.*

SIMILE A *simile* is a figure of speech that uses *like* or *as* to make a direct comparison between two unlike ideas. Everyday speech often contains similes, such as "pale as a ghost," "good as gold," "spread like wildfire," and "clever as a fox."

SOUND DEVICES *Sound devices* are techniques used by writers to give musical effects to their writing. Some of these include *onomatopoeia, alliteration, rhyme, meter,* and *repetition.*

SPEAKER The *speaker* is the imaginary voice a poet uses when writing a poem. The speaker is the character who tells the poem. This character, or voice, often is not identified by name. There can be important differences between the poet and the poem's speaker.

See *Narrator.*

SPEECH A *speech* is a work that is delivered orally to an audience. There are many kinds of speeches suiting almost every kind of public gathering. Types of speeches include *dramatic, persuasive,* and *informative.*

STAGE DIRECTIONS *Stage directions* are notes included in a drama to describe how the work is to be performed or staged. Stage directions are usually printed in italics and enclosed within parentheses or brackets. Some stage directions describe the movements, costumes, emotional states, and ways of speaking of the characters.

STAGING *Staging* includes the setting, lighting, costumes, special effects, and music that go into a stage performance of a drama.

See *Drama.*

STANZA A *stanza* is a group of lines of poetry that are usually similar in length and pattern and are separated by spaces. A stanza is like a paragraph of poetry—it states and develops a single main idea.

STATIC CHARACTER See *Character.*

SURPRISE ENDING A *surprise ending* is a conclusion that is unexpected. The reader has certain expectations about the ending based on details in the story. Often, a surprise ending is *foreshadowed,* or subtly hinted at, in the course of the work.

See *Foreshadowing* and *Plot.*

SUSPENSE *Suspense* is a feeling of anxious uncertainty about the outcome of events in a literary work. Writers create suspense by raising questions in the minds of their readers.

SYMBOL A *symbol* is anything that stands for or represents something else. Symbols are common in everyday life. A dove with an olive branch in its beak is a symbol of peace. A blindfolded woman holding a balanced scale is a symbol of justice. A crown is a symbol of a king's status and authority.

SYMBOLISM *Symbolism* is the use of symbols. Symbolism plays an important role in many different types of literature. It can highlight certain elements the author wishes to emphasize and also add levels of meaning.

THEME The *theme* is a central message in a literary work. A theme can usually be expressed as a generalization, or a general statement, about human beings or about life. The theme of a work is not a summary of its plot. The theme is the writer's central idea.

Although a theme may be stated directly in the text, it is more often presented indirectly. When the theme is stated indirectly, or implied, the reader must figure out what the theme is by looking at what the work reveals about people or life.

TONE The *tone* of a literary work is the writer's attitude toward his or her audience and subject. The tone can often be described by a single adjective, such as *formal* or *informal, serious* or *playful, bitter* or *ironic.* Factors that contribute to the tone are word choice, sentence structure, line length, rhyme, rhythm, and repetition.

TRAGEDY A *tragedy* is a work of literature, especially a play, that results in a catastrophe for the main character. In ancient Greek drama, the main character is always a significant person—a king or a hero—and the cause of the tragedy is a tragic flaw, or weakness, in his or her character. In modern drama, the main character can be an ordinary person, and the cause of the tragedy can be some evil in society itself. The purpose of tragedy is not only to arouse fear and pity in the audience, but also, in some cases, to convey a sense of the grandeur and nobility of the human spirit.

TURNING POINT See *Climax.*

UNIVERSAL THEME A *universal theme* is a message about life that is expressed regularly in many different cultures and time periods. Folk tales, epics, and romances often address universal themes like the importance of courage, the power of love, or the danger of greed.

WORD CHOICE See *Diction.*

Tips for Literature Circles

As you read and study literature, discussions with other readers can help you understand and enjoy what you have read. Use the following tips.

• Understand the purpose of your discussion

Your purpose when you discuss literature is to broaden your understanding of a work by testing your own ideas and hearing the ideas of others. Keep your comments focused on the literature you are discussing. Starting with one focus question will help to keep your discussion on track.

• Communicate effectively

Effective communication requires thinking before speaking. Plan the points that you want to make and decide how you will express them. Organize these points in logical order and use details from the work to support your ideas. Jot down informal notes to help keep your ideas focused.

Remember to speak clearly, pronouncing words slowly and carefully. Also, listen attentively when others are speaking, and avoid interrupting.

• Consider other ideas and interpretations

A work of literature can generate a wide variety of responses in different readers. Be open to the idea that many interpretations can be valid. To support your own ideas, point to the events, descriptions, characters, or other literary elements in the work that led to your interpretation. To consider someone else's ideas, decide whether details in the work support the interpretation he or she presents. Be sure to convey your criticism of the ideas of others in a respectful and supportive manner.

• Ask questions

Ask questions to clarify your understanding of another reader's ideas. You can also use questions to call attention to possible areas of confusion, to points that are open to debate, or to errors in the speaker's points. To move a discussion forward, summarize and evaluate conclusions reached by the group members.

When you meet with a group to discuss literature, use a chart like the one shown to analyze the discussion.

Work Being Discussed:	
Focus Question:	
Your Response:	Another Student's Response:
Supporting Evidence:	Supporting Evidence:

Tips for Improving Reading Fluency

When you were younger, you learned to read. Then, you read to expand your experiences or for pure enjoyment. Now, you are expected to read to learn. As you progress in school, you are given more and more material to read. The tips on these pages will help you improve your reading fluency, or your ability to read easily, smoothly, and expressively.

Keeping Your Concentration

One common problem that readers face is the loss of concentration. When you are reading an assignment, you might find yourself rereading the same sentence several times without really understanding it. The first step in changing this behavior is to notice that you do it. Becoming an active, aware reader will help you get the most from your assignments. Practice using these strategies:

- Cover what you have already read with a note card as you go along. Then, you will not be able to reread without noticing that you are doing it.

- Set a purpose for reading beyond just completing the assignment. Then, read actively by pausing to ask yourself questions about the material as you read.

- Use the Reading Strategy instruction and notes that appear with each selection in this textbook.

- Stop reading after a specified period of time (for example, 5 minutes) and summarize what you have read. To help you with this strategy, use the Reading Check questions that appear with each selection in this textbook. Reread to find any answers you do not know.

Reading Phrases

Fluent readers read phrases rather than individual words. Reading this way will speed up your reading and improve your comprehension. Here are some useful ideas:

- Experts recommend rereading as a strategy to increase fluency. Choose a passage of text that is neither too hard nor too easy. Read the same passage aloud several times until you can read it smoothly. When you can read the passage fluently, pick another passage and keep practicing.

- Read aloud into a tape recorder. Then, listen to the recording, noting your accuracy, pacing, and expression. You can also read aloud and share feedback with a partner.

- Use *Hear It!* Prentice Hall Literature Audio program CDs to hear the selections read aloud. Read along silently in your textbook, noticing how the reader uses his or her voice and emphasizes certain words and phrases.

Understanding Key Vocabulary

If you do not understand some of the words in an assignment, you may miss out on important concepts. Therefore, it is helpful to keep a dictionary nearby when you are reading. Follow these steps:

- Before you begin reading, scan the text for unfamiliar words or terms. Find out what those words mean before you begin reading.

- Use context—the surrounding words, phrases, and sentences—to help you determine the meanings of unfamiliar words.

- If you are unable to understand the meaning through context, refer to the dictionary.

Paying Attention to Punctuation

When you read, pay attention to punctuation. Commas, periods, exclamation points, semicolons, and colons tell you when to pause or stop. They also indicate relationships between groups of words. When you recognize these relationships you will read with greater understanding and expression. Look at the chart below.

Punctuation Mark	Meaning
comma	brief pause
period	pause at the end of a thought
exclamation point	pause that indicates emphasis
semicolon	pause between related but distinct thoughts
colon	pause before giving explanation or examples

Using the Reading Fluency Checklist

Use the checklist below each time you read a selection in this textbook. In your Language Arts journal or notebook, note which skills you need to work on and chart your progress each week.

Reading Fluency Checklist
☐ Preview the text to check for difficult or unfamiliar words.
☐ Practice reading aloud.
☐ Read according to punctuation.
☐ Break down long sentences into the subject and its meaning.
☐ Read groups of words for meaning rather than reading single words.
☐ Read with expression (change your tone of voice to add meaning to the word).

Reading is a skill that can be improved with practice. The key to improving your fluency is to read. The more you read, the better your reading will become.

Types of Writing

Good writing can be a powerful tool used for many purposes. Writing can allow you to defend something you believe in or to show how much you know about a subject. Writing can also help you share what you have experienced, imagined, thought, and felt. The three main types of writing are argument, informative/explanatory, and narrative.

Argument

When you think of the word *argument,* you might think of a disagreement between two people, but an argument is more than that. An argument is a logical way of presenting a belief, conclusion, or stance. A good argument is supported with reasoning and evidence.

Argument writing can be used for many purposes, such as to change a reader's point of view or opinion or to bring about an action or a response from a reader.

There are three main purposes for writing a formal argument:

- to change the reader's mind

- to convince the reader to accept what is written

- to motivate the reader to take action, based on what is written

The following are some types of argument writing:

Advertisements An advertisement is a planned message meant to be seen, heard, or read. It attempts to persuade an audience to buy a product or service, accept an idea, or support a cause. Advertisements may appear in print, online, or in broadcast form.

Several common types of advertisements are public-service announcements, billboards, merchandise ads, service ads, and political campaign literature.

Persuasive Essay A persuasive essay presents a position on an issue, urges readers to accept that position, and may encourage a specific action. An effective persuasive essay

- Explores an issue of importance to the writer

- Addresses an issue that is arguable

- Uses facts, examples, statistics, or personal experiences to support a position

- Tries to influence the audience through appeals to the readers' knowledge, experiences, or emotions

- Uses clear organization to present a logical argument

Forms of persuasion include editorials, position papers, persuasive speeches, grant proposals, advertisements, and debates.

Informative/Explanatory

Informative/explanatory writing should rely on facts to inform or explain. Informative/explanatory writing serves some closely related purposes: to increase readers' knowledge of a subject, to help readers better understand a procedure or process, or to provide readers with an enhanced comprehension of a concept. It should also feature a clear introduction, body, and conclusion. The following are some examples of informative/explanatory writing:

Cause-and-Effect Essay A cause-and-effect essay examines the relationship between events, explaining how one event or situation causes another. A successful cause-and-effect essay includes

- A discussion of a cause, event, or condition that produces a specific result

- An explanation of an effect, outcome, or result

- Evidence and examples to support the relationship between cause and effect

- A logical organization that makes the explanation clear

Comparison-and-Contrast Essay A comparison-and-contrast essay analyzes the similarities and differences between or among two or more things. An effective comparison-and-contrast essay

- Identifies a purpose for comparison and contrast

- Identifies similarities and differences between or among two or more things, people, places, or ideas

- Gives factual details about the subjects

- Uses an organizational plan suited to the topic and purpose

Descriptive Writing Descriptive writing creates a vivid picture of a person, place, thing, or event. Most descriptive writing includes

- Sensory details—sights, sounds, smells, tastes, and physical sensations

- Vivid, precise language

- Figurative language or comparisons

- Adjectives and adverbs that paint a word picture

- An organization suited to the subject

Types of descriptive writing include descriptions of ideas, observations, remembrances, travel brochures, physical descriptions, functional descriptions, and character sketches.

Problem-and-Solution Essay A problem-and-solution essay describes a problem and offers one or more solutions to it. It describes a clear set of steps to achieve a result. An effective problem-and-solution essay includes

- A clear statement of the problem, with its causes and effects summarized for the reader

- The most important aspects of the problem

- A proposal of at least one realistic solution

- Facts, statistics, data, or expert testimony to support the solution

- A clear organization that makes the relationship between problem and solution obvious

Research Writing Research writing is based on information gathered from outside sources. A research paper—a focused study of a topic—helps writers explore and connect ideas, make discoveries, and share their findings with an audience. An effective research paper

- Focuses on a specific, narrow topic, which is usually summarized in a thesis statement

- Presents relevant information from a wide variety of sources

- Uses a clear organization that includes an introduction, body, and conclusion

- Includes a bibliography or works-cited list that identifies the sources from which the information was drawn

Other types of writing that depend on accurate and insightful research include multimedia presentations, statistical reports, annotated bibliographies, and experiment journals.

Workplace Writing Workplace writing is probably the format you will use most after you finish school. In general, workplace writing is fact-based and meant to communicate specific information in a structured format. Effective workplace writing

- Communicates information concisely

- Includes details that provide necessary information and anticipate potential questions

- Is error-free and neatly presented

Common types of workplace writing include business letters, memorandums, résumés, forms, and applications.

Narrative

Narrative writing conveys experience, either real or imaginary, and uses time to provide structure. It can be used to inform, instruct, persuade, or entertain. Whenever writers tell a of story, they are using narrative writing. Most narrative-writing types share certain elements, such as characters, a setting, a sequence of events, and, often, a theme. The following are some types of narration:

Autobiographical Writing Autobiographical writing tells a true story about an important period, experience, or relationship in the writer's life. Effective autobiographical writing includes

- A series of events that involve the writer as the main character

- Details, thoughts, feelings, and insights from the writer's perspective

- A conflict or an event that affects the writer

- A logical organization that tells the story clearly

- Insights that the writer gained from the experience

Types of autobiographical writing include personal narratives, autobiographical sketches, reflective essays, eyewitness accounts, and memoirs.

Short Story A short story is a brief, creative narrative. Most short stories include

- Details that establish the setting in time and place

- A main character who undergoes a change or learns something during the course of the story

- A conflict or a problem to be introduced, developed, and resolved

- A plot, the series of events that make up the action of the story

- A theme or message about life

Types of short stories include realistic stories, fantasies, historical narratives, mysteries, thrillers, science-fiction stories, and adventure stories.

Writing Friendly Letters

Writing Friendly Letters

A friendly letter is much less formal than a business letter. It is a letter to a friend, a family member, or anyone with whom the writer wants to communicate in a personal, friendly way. Most friendly letters are made up of five parts:

- ✔ the heading
- ✔ the salutation, or greeting
- ✔ the body
- ✔ the closing
- ✔ the signature

The purpose of a friendly letter is often one of the following:

- ✔ to share personal news and feelings
- ✔ to send or to answer an invitation
- ✔ to express thanks

Model Friendly Letter

In this friendly letter, Betsy thanks her grandparents for a birthday present and gives them some news about her life.

11 Old Farm Road
Topsham, Maine 04011

April 14, 20—

> **The heading** includes the writer's address and the date on which he or she wrote the letter.

Dear Grandma and Grandpa,

Thank you for the sweater you sent me for my birthday. It fits perfectly, and I love the color. I wore my new sweater to the carnival at school last weekend and got lots of compliments.

The weather here has been cool but sunny. Mom thinks that "real" spring will never come. I can't wait until it's warm enough to go swimming.

School is going fairly well. I really like my Social Studies class. We are learning about the U.S. Constitution, and I think it's very interesting. Maybe I will be a lawyer when I grow up.

When are you coming out to visit us? We haven't seen you since Thanksgiving. You can stay in my room when you come. I'll be happy to sleep on the couch. (The TV is in that room!!)

Well, thanks again and hope all is well with you.

> **The body** is the main part of the letter and contains the basic message.

Love,

Betsy

> Some common **closings** for personal letters include "Best wishes," "Love "Sincerely," and "Yours truly."

Writing Business Letters

Formatting Business Letters

Business letters follow one of several acceptable formats. In **block format,** each part of the letter begins at the left margin. A double space is used between paragraphs. In **modified block format,** some parts of the letter are indented to the center of the page. No matter which format is used, all letters in business format have a heading, an inside address, a salutation or greeting, a body, a closing, and a signature. These parts are shown and annotated on the model business letter below, formatted in modified block style.

Model Business Letter

In this letter, Yolanda Dodson uses modified block format to request information.

Students for a Cleaner Planet
c/o Memorial High School
333 Veteran's Drive
Denver, CO 80211

January 25, 20—

Steven Wilson, Director
Resource Recovery Really Works
300 Oak Street
Denver, CO 80216

Dear Mr. Wilson:

Memorial High School would like to start a branch of your successful recycling program. We share your commitment to reclaiming as much reusable material as we can. Because your program has been successful in other neighborhoods, we're sure that it can work in our community. Our school includes grades 9–12 and has about 800 students.

Would you send us some information about your community recycling program? For example, we need to know what materials can be recycled and how we can implement the program.

At least fifty students have already expressed an interest in getting involved, so I know we'll have the people power to make the program work. Please help us get started.

Thank you in advance for your time and consideration.

Sincerely,

Yolanda Dodson

Yolanda Dodson

The **heading** shows the writer's address and organization (if any) and the date.

The **inside address** indicates where the letter will be sent.

A **salutation** is punctuated by a colon. When the specific addressee is not known, use a general greeting such as "To whom it may concern:"

The **body** of the letter states the writer's purpose. In this case, the writer requests information.

The **closing** "Sincerely" is common, but "Yours truly" or "Respectfully yours" are also acceptable. To end the letter, the writer types her name and provides a **signature.**

Grammar, Usage, and Mechanics Handbook

Parts of Speech

Nouns A **noun** is the name of a person, place, or thing. A **common noun** names any one of a class of people, places, or things. A **proper noun** names a specific person, place, or thing.

Common Nouns	*Proper Nouns*
writer	Francisco Jiménez

Use *apostrophes* with nouns to show ownership. Add an apostrophe and *s* to show the **possessive case** of most singular nouns. Add just an apostrophe to show the possessive case of plural nouns ending in *s* or *es*. Add an apostrophe and *s* to show the possessive case of plural nouns that do not end in *s* or *es*.

Pronouns A **pronoun** is a word that stands for a noun or for a word that takes the place of a noun. A **personal pronoun** refers to (1) the person speaking, (2) the person spoken to, or (3) the person, place, or thing spoken about.

	Singular	*Plural*
First Person	I, me, my, mine	we, us, our, ours
Second Person	you, your, yours	you, your, yours
Third Person	he, him, his, she, her, hers, it, its	they, them, their, theirs

A **demonstrative pronoun** directs attention to a specific person, place, or thing.

These are the juiciest pears I have ever tasted.

An **interrogative pronoun** is used to begin a question.

Who is the author of "Jeremiah's Song"?

An **indefinite pronoun** refers to a person, place, or thing, often without specifying which one.

Many of the players were tired.

Everyone bought something.

Verbs A **verb** is a word that expresses time while showing an action, a condition, or the fact that something exists. An **action verb** indicates the action of someone or something. A **linking verb** connects the subject of a sentence with a noun or a pronoun that renames or describes the subject. A **helping verb** can be added to another verb to make a single verb phrase.

Adjectives An **adjective** describes a noun or a pronoun or gives a noun or a pronoun a more specific meaning. Adjectives answer the questions *what kind, which one, how many,* or *how much.*

The articles *the, a,* and *an* are adjectives. *An* is used before a word beginning with a vowel sound.

A noun may sometimes be used as an adjective.

family home	*science* fiction

Adverbs An **adverb** modifies a verb, an adjective, or another adverb. Adverbs answer the questions *where, when, in what way,* or *to what extent.*

Prepositions A **preposition** relates a noun or a pronoun following it to another word in the sentence.

The ball rolled <u>under</u> the table.

Conjunctions A **conjunction** connects other words or groups of words. A **coordinating conjunction** connects similar kinds or groups of words. **Correlative conjunctions** are used in pairs to connect similar words or groups of words.

both Grandpa *and* Dad	*neither* they *nor* I

Interjections An **interjection** is a word that expresses feeling or emotion and functions independently of a sentence.

"Ah!" says he—

Phrases, Clauses, and Sentences

Sentences A **sentence** is a group of words with two main parts: a complete subject and a complete predicate. Together, these parts express a complete thought.

We read that story last year.

A **fragment** is a group of words that does not express a complete thought.

"Not right away."

Subject The **subject** of a sentence is the word or group of words that tells whom or what the sentence is about. The simple subject is the essential noun, pronoun, or group of words acting as a noun that cannot be left out of the complete subject. A **complete subject** is the **simple subject** plus any modifiers. In the following example, the complete subject is underlined. The simple subject is italicized.

<u>Pony express *riders*</u> carried packages for miles.

A **compound subject** is two or more subjects that have the same verb and are joined by a conjunction.

Neither the horse nor the driver looked tired.

Predicate The **predicate** of a sentence is the verb or verb phrase that tells what the complete subject of the sentence does or is. The **simple predicate** is the essential verb or verb phrase that cannot be left out of the complete predicate. A **complete predicate** is the simple predicate plus any modifiers or complements. In the following example, the complete predicate is underlined. The simple predicate is italicized.

Pony express riders <u>*carried* packages for miles.</u>

A **compound predicate** is two or more verbs that have the same subject and are joined by a conjunction.

She *sneezed and coughed* throughout the trip.

Complement A **complement** is a word or group of words that completes the meaning of the predicate of a sentence. Five different kinds of complements can be found in English sentences: *direct objects, indirect objects, objective complements, predicate nominatives,* and *predicate adjectives.*

A **direct object** is a noun, pronoun, or group of words acting as a noun that receives the action of a transitive verb.

We watched the *liftoff.*

An **indirect object** is a noun, pronoun, or group of words that appears with a direct object and names the person or thing that something is given to or done for.

He sold the *family* a mirror.

An **objective complement** is an adjective or noun that appears with a direct object and describes or renames it.

I called Meg my *friend.*

A **subject complement** is a noun, pronoun, or adjective that appears with a linking verb and tells something about the subject. A subject complement may be a *predicate nominative* or a *predicate adjective.*

A **predicate nominative** is a noun or pronoun that appears with a linking verb and renames, or explains the subject.

Kiglo was the *leader.*

A **predicate adjective** is an adjective that appears with a linking verb and describes the subject of a sentence.

Roko became *tired.*

Sentence Types There are four types of sentences:

1. A **simple sentence** consists of a single independent clause.
2. A **compound sentence** consists of two or more independent clauses joined by a comma and a coordinating conjunction or by a semicolon.
3. A **complex sentence** consists of one independent clause and one or more subordinate clauses.
4. A **compound-complex sentence** consists of two or more independent clauses and one or more subordinate clauses.

There are four functions of sentences:

1. A **declarative sentence** states an idea and ends with a period.
2. An **interrogative sentence** asks a question and ends with a question mark.
3. An **imperative sentence** gives an order or a direction and ends with either a period or an exclamation mark.
4. An **exclamatory sentence** conveys a strong emotion and ends with an exclamation mark.

Phrases A phrase is a group of words, without a subject and a verb, that functions in a sentence as one part of speech.

A **prepositional phrase** is a group of words that includes a preposition and a noun or a pronoun that is the object of the preposition.

near the town   with them

An **adjective phrase** is a prepositional phrase that modifies a noun or a pronoun by telling what kind or which one.

The house *on the corner* is new.

An **adverb phrase** is a prepositional phrase that modifies a verb, an adjective, or an adverb by pointing out where, when, in what manner, or to what extent.

Bring your saddle *to the barn.*

An **appositive phrase** is a noun or a pronoun with modifiers, placed next to a noun or a pronoun to add information and details.

The story, a *tale of adventure,* takes place in the Yukon.

A **participial phrase** is a participle modified by an adjective or an adverb phrase or accompanied by a complement. The entire phrase acts as an adjective.

Running at top speed, he soon caught up.

An **infinitive phrase** is an infinitive with modifiers, complements, or a subject, all acting together as a single part of speech. An infinitive is the verb form that starts with *to.*

I was happy *to sit down.*

Clauses A clause is a group of words with its own subject and verb. An **independent clause** can stand by itself as a complete sentence.

"I think it belongs to Rachel."

A **dependent clause** has a subject and a verb but cannot stand as a complete sentence; it can only be part of a sentence.

"Although it was late"

Using Verbs, Pronouns, and Modifiers

Principal Parts A **verb** has four principal parts: the present, the present participle, the past, and the past participle.

Regular verbs form the past and past participle by adding *-ed* to the present form.

Present: walk   *Past:* walked
Present Participle: (am) walking   *Past Participle:* (have) walked

Irregular verbs form the past and past participle by changing form rather than by adding *-ed.*

Present: go   *Past:* went
Present Participle: (am) going   *Past Participle:* (have) gone

Verb Tense A **verb tense** tells whether the time of an action or condition is in the past, the present, or the future. Every verb has six tenses: *present, past, future, present perfect, past perfect,* and *future perfect.* The **present tense** shows actions that happen in the present. The **past tense** shows actions that have already happened. The **future tense** shows actions that will happen. The **present perfect tense** shows actions that begin in the past and continue to the present. The **past perfect tense** shows a past action or condition that ended before another past action. The **future perfect tense** shows a future action or condition that will have ended before another begins.

Pronoun Case The **case** of a pronoun is the form it takes to show its use in a sentence. There are three pronoun cases: *nominative, objective,* and *possessive.* The **nominative case** is used to name or rename the subject of the sentence. The nominative case pronouns are *I, you, he, she, it, we, you, they.*

  As the subject: She is brave.
  Renaming the subject: The leader is *she.*

The **objective case** is used as the direct object, indirect object, or object of a preposition. The objective case pronouns are *me, you, him, her, it, us, you, them.*

  As a direct object: Tom called *me.*
  As an indirect object: My friend gave *me* advice.
  As an object of a preposition: She went without *me.*

The **possessive case** is used to show ownership. The possessive pronouns are *my, your, his, her, its, our, their, mine, yours, his, hers, its, ours, theirs.*

Subject-Verb Agreement To make a subject and a verb agree, make sure that both are singular or both are plural. Two or more singular subjects joined by *or* or *nor* must have a singular verb. When singular and plural subjects are joined by *or* or *nor,* the verb must agree with the closest subject.

  He is at the door.   They *drive* home.
  Either *Joe* or *you are* going.   Both *pets are* hungry.

Pronoun-Antecedent Agreement **Pronouns** must agree with their antecedents in number and gender. Use singular pronouns with singular antecedents and plural pronouns with plural antecedents. Many errors in pronoun-antecedent agreement occur when a plural pronoun is used to refer to a singular antecedent for which the gender is not specified.

  Incorrect: Everyone did their best.
  Correct: Everyone did his or her best.

The following indefinite pronouns are singular: *anybody, anyone, each, either, everybody, everyone, neither, nobody, no one, one, somebody, someone.* The following indefinite pronouns are plural: *both, few, many, several.* The following indefinite pronouns may be either singular or plural: *all, any, most, none, some.*

Modifiers The *comparative* and *superlative* degrees of most adjectives and adverbs of one or two syllables can be formed in either of two ways: Use *-er* or *more* to form a comparative degree and *-est* or *most* to form the superlative degree of most one- and two-syllable modifiers.

More and *most* can also be used to form the comparative and superlative degrees of most one- and two-syllable modifiers.

These words should not be used when the result sounds awkward, as in "A greyhound is *more* fast than a beagle."

Glossary of Common Usage

accept, except: *Accept* is a verb that means "to receive" or "to agree to." *Except* is a preposition that means "other than" or "leaving out." Do not confuse these two words.

  Aaron sadly *accepted* his father's decision to sell Zlata.
  Everyone *except* the fisherman had children.

affect, effect: *Affect* is normally a verb meaning "to influence" or "to bring about a change in." *Effect* is usually a noun, meaning "result."

among, between: *Among* is usually used with three or more items. *Between* is generally used with only two items.

bad, badly: Use the predicate adjective *bad* after linking verbs such as *feel, look,* and *seem.* Use *badly* whenever an adverb is required.

  Mouse does not feel *bad* about tricking Coyote.
  In the myth, Athene treats Arachne *badly.*

beside, besides: *Beside* means "at the side of" or "close to." *Besides* means "in addition to."

can, may: The verb *can* generally refers to the ability to act. The verb *may* generally refers to permission to act.

different from, different than: *Different from* is generally preferred over *different than.*

farther, further: Use *farther* when you refer to distance. Use *further* when you mean "to a greater degree or extent" or "additional."

fewer, less: Use *fewer* for things that can be counted. Use *less* for amounts or quantities that cannot be counted.

good, well: Use the predicate adjective *good* after linking verbs such as *feel, look, smell, taste,* and *seem.* Use *well* whenever you need an adverb.

its, it's: The word *its* with no apostrophe is a possessive pronoun. The word *it's* is a contraction for *it is.* Do not confuse the possessive pronoun *its* with the contraction *it's,* standing for "it is" or "it has."

lay, lie: Do not confuse these verbs. *Lay* is a transitive verb meaning "to set or put something down." Its principal parts are *lay, laying, laid, laid. Lie* is an intransitive verb meaning "to recline." Its principal parts are *lie, lying, lay, lain.*

like, as: *Like* is a preposition that usually means "similar to" or "in the same way as." *Like* should always be followed by an object. Do not use *like* before a subject and a verb. Use *as* or *that* instead.

of, have: Do not use *of* in place of *have* after auxiliary verbs like *would, could, should, may, might,* or *must.*

raise, rise: *Raise* is a transitive verb that usually takes a direct object. *Rise* is intransitive and never takes a direct object.

set, sit: *Set* is a transitive verb meaning "to put (something) in a certain place." Its principal parts are *set, setting, set, set. Sit* is an intransitive verb meaning "to be seated." Its principal parts are *sit, sitting, sat, sat.*

than, then: The conjunction *than* is used to connect the two parts of a comparison. Do not confuse *than* with the adverb *then,* which usually refers to time.

that, which, who: Use the relative pronoun *that* to refer to things or people. Use *which* only for things and *who* for people.

when, where, why: Do not use *when, where,* or *why* directly after a linking verb such as *is.* Reword the sentence.

> *Faulty:* Suspense is *when* an author increases tension.
>
> *Revised:* An author uses suspense to increase tension.

who, whom: Use *who* only as a subject in clauses and sentences and *whom* only as an object.

Mechanics

Capitalization

1. Capitalize the first word of a sentence.
   > Young Roko glances down the valley.
2. Capitalize all proper nouns and adjectives.
   > Mark Twain   Amazon River   Thanksgiving Day
3. Capitalize a person's title when it is followed by the person's name or when it is used in direct address.
   > Doctor   General Khokhotov   Mrs. Price
4. Capitalize titles showing family relationships when they refer to a specific person, unless they are preceded by a possessive noun or pronoun.
   > Granny-Liz   Margie's mother
5. Capitalize the first word and all other key words in the titles of books, periodicals, poems, stories, plays, paintings, and other works of art.
   > from *Tom Sawyer*   "Grandpa and the Statue"
6. Capitalize the first word and all nouns in letter salutations and the first word in letter closings.
   > Dear Willis,   Yours truly,

Punctuation

End Marks

1. Use a **period** to end a declarative sentence, an imperative sentence, and most abbreviations.
2. Use a **question mark** to end a direct question or an incomplete question in which the rest of the question is understood.
3. Use an **exclamation mark** after a statement showing strong emotion, an urgent imperative sentence, or an interjection expressing strong emotion.

Commas Use commas:

1. before the conjunction to separate two independent clauses in a compound sentence.
2. to separate three or more words, phrases, or clauses in a series.
3. to separate adjectives of equal rank. Do not use commas to separate adjectives that must stay in a specific order.
4. after an introductory word, phrase, or clause.
5. to set off parenthetical and nonessential expressions.
6. with places and dates made up of two or more parts.
7. after items in addresses, after the salutation in a personal letter, after the closing in all letters, and in numbers of more than three digits.

Semicolons Use semicolons:

1. to join independent clauses that are not already joined by a conjunction.
2. to join independent clauses or items in a series that already contain commas.

Colons Use colons:

1. before a list of items following an independent clause.
2. in numbers giving the time, in salutations in business letters, and in labels used to signal important ideas.

Quotation Marks

1. A **direct quotation** represents a person's exact speech or thoughts and is enclosed in quotation marks.
2. An **indirect quotation** reports only the general meaning of what a person said or thought and does not require quotation marks.
3. Always place a comma or a period inside the final quotation mark of a direct quotation.
4. Place a question mark or an exclamation mark inside the final quotation mark if the end mark is part of the quotation; if it is not part of the quotation, place it outside the final quotation mark.

Titles

1. Underline or italicize the titles of long written works, movies, television and radio shows, lengthy works of music, paintings, and sculptures.
2. Use quotation marks around the titles of short written works, episodes in a series, songs, and titles of works mentioned as parts of collections.

Hyphens Use a **hyphen** with certain numbers, after certain prefixes, with two or more words used as one word, and with a compound modifier that comes before a noun.

Apostrophes Use apostrophes:

1. to show the possessive case of most singular nouns.
2. to show the possessive case of plural nouns ending in *s* and *es.*
3. to show the possessive case of plural nouns that do not end in *s* or *es.*
4. in a contraction to indicate the position of the missing letter or letters.

Glossary

PRONUNCIATION KEY

Symbol	Sample Words	Symbol	Sample Words
a	at, tap, mat	oi	oil, toy, royal
ā	ate, rain, break	ou	out, now, sour
ä	car, father, heart	u	mud, ton, trouble
ch	chew, nature, such	ʉ	her, sir, word
e	end, feather, said	'l	cattle, paddle, cuddle
ē	sea, steam, piece	'n	sudden, hidden, sweeten
ə	ago, pencil, lemon	ŋ	ring, anger, pink
i	it, stick, gym	sh	shell, mission, fish
ī	nice, lie, sky	th	thin, nothing, both
ō	no, oat, low	*th*	then, mother, smooth
ô	all, law, taught	zh	vision, treasure, seizure
oo	look, would, pull	yoo	cure, furious
o͞o	boot, drew, tune	yo͞o	cute, few, use

Academic terms appear in blue type.

A

abode (ə bōd) *n.* home; residence

accusations (ak´yoo zā´shənz) *n.* charges made against a person for doing something wrong

acknowledge (ak näl´ ij) *v.* recognize and admit

adaptation (ad´əp tā´shən) *n.* gradual change in behavior to adjust to accepted norms in society

adequate (ad´ i kwət) *adj.* sufficient; enough

advocacy (ad´və kə sē) *n.* support for a particular idea or mission

affect (ə fekt´) *v.* do something that produces a change in someone or something; influence

aggressive (ə gres´iv) *adj.* forceful, especially in a destructive or mean way

ajar (ə jär´) *adj.* slightly open

analyze (an´ə līz´) *v.* break into parts in order to study closely

appearance (ə pir´əns) *n.* how a person or thing looks or seems

appreciate (ə prē´shē āt´) *v.* be thankful for

approximately (ə präk´sə mit lē) *adv.* in a close, but not exact, way

aptitude (ap´ tə tood) *n.* talent; ability

arid (ar´id) *adj.* getting little rain, and therefore very dry

assumption (ə sump´shən) *n.* act of accepting something as true without proof

assumptions (ə sump´shənz) *n.* acts of accepting something as true without proof

astonish (ə stän´ ish) *v.* amaze

attitude (at´ə tood´) *n.* person's opinions and feelings about someone or something

audible (ô´ də bəl) *adj.* loud enough to be heard

aversion (ə vʉr´zhən) *n.* intense dislike

awareness (ə wer´ nəs) *n.* knowledge or understanding of a particular subject or situation

B

behavior (bē hāv´yər) *n.* manner of conducting oneself

bias (bī´əs) *n.* slanted or prejudiced viewpoint

bigots (big´ əts) *n.* narrow-minded, prejudiced people

blander (bland´ ər) *adj.* more tasteless

blunt (blunt) *v.* lessen; make less forceful

bound (bound) *v.* tied

C

challenge (chal´ənj) *n.* something that tests your skills and abilities

characteristic (kar´ək tər is´tik) *n.* trait; feature

characterize (kar´ək tər īz´) *v.* 1. be typical of someone or something; 2. describe someone or something in a particular way

cite (sīt) *v.* 1. mention something as proof or an example of something else; 2. refer to

coax (kōks) *v.* use gentle persuasion

commemorated (kə mem´ə rāt´ id) *v.* honored the memory of

commissioned (kə mish´ənd) *v.* appointed or hired to carry out a duty or task

common (käm´ən) *adj.* 1. ordinary; expected; 2. shared; public

communal (kə myoon´ əl) *adj.* shared by all

communicate (kə myoo´ni kāt´) *v.* share ideas, thoughts or feelings; make known to others

communication (kə myoo´ni kā´shən) *n.* process of sharing information or expressing thoughts and feelings

community (kə myoo´nə tē) *n.* group of people who share an interest or who live near each other

competition (käm´pə tish´ən) *n.* event or game in which people or sides attempt to win

complex (käm pleks´) *adj.* 1. difficult to understand; 2. having many connected parts

compose (kəm pōz´) *v.* write or create a piece of music, art, or text

compromise (käm´prə mīz´) *n.* settling of differences in a way that allows both sides to feel satisfied

compulsion (kəm pul´ shən) *n.* driving, irresistible force

conclude (kən klood´) *v.* finish; bring to a logical end

conferred (kən furd´) *v.* met to discuss

conflict (kän flikt´) *n.* struggle between opposing forces

consolation (kän´ sə lā´ shən) *n.* something that comforts a disappointed person

conspired (kən spīrd´) *v.* planned together secretly

contradiction (kän´ trə dik´ shən) *n.* difference between two conflicting things that means they both cannot be true

contraption (kən trap´ shən) *n.* strange device or machine

contrast (kän´trast´) *v.* compare two things to show how they are different from each other

contribute (kən trib´yoot) *v.* 1. add to; enrich; 2. provide

conveyed (kən vād´) *v.* made known; expressed

convince (kən vins´) *v.* cause to accept a point of view

convincing (kən vins´ iŋ) *adj.* persuasive

coveted (kuv´ it əd) *v.* wanted; desired

cremated (krē´māt´ əd) *v.* burned a dead body to ashes

croon (kroon) *v.* sing or hum quietly and soothingly

crucial (kroo´ shəl) *adj.* important; critical

crystal (kris´ təl) *adj.* made of clear, brilliant glass

culminated (kul´ mə nāt´ əd) *v.* reached its highest point, or climax

culprit (kul´ prit) *n.* guilty person

culture (kul´chər) *n.* customs of a group or community

cunning (kun´ iŋ) *adj.* sly; crafty

cunningly (kun´ iŋ lē) *adv.* cleverly

curdled (kurd´ 'ld) *adj.* rotten

curiosity (kyoor´ ē äs´ ə tē) *n.* desire to learn or know

custom (kus´təm) *n.* accepted practice

D

dabbling (dab´ liŋ) *v.* wetting by dipping, splashing, or paddling in the water

danger (dān´jər) *n.* exposure to possible harm, injury, or loss

debate (dē bāt´) 1. *v.* discuss formally in front of others; 2. *n.* discussion or argument on a subject in which people express different opinions

deceive (dē sēv´) *v.* make someone believe something that is not true

decipher (dē sī´fər) *v.* make out the meaning of

decreed (di krēd´) *v.* officially ordered

defiant (dē fī´ ənt) *adj.* boldly resisting

defies (dē fīz´) *v.* boldly resists or opposes

define (dē fīn´) *v.* describe; explain

definition (def´ə nish´ən) *n.* sentence or phrase that states exactly what an idea, word, or phrase means

describe (di skrīb´) *v.* say what someone or something is like by giving details

designated (dez´ ig nāt´ əd) *v.* identified; pointed out

desire (di zīr´) *n.* wish or want

desolate (des´ ə lit) *adj.* lonely; solitary

destitute (des´ tə toot´) *n.* people living in complete poverty

deteriorates (dē tir´ē ə rāts) *v.* gets worse

determination (dē tur´mi nā´shən) *n.* decision or conclusion

devastated (dev´ ə stāt´ əd) *v.* destroyed; completely upset

devastating (dev´ ə stāt´ iŋ) *adj.* destructive; overwhelming

diagram (dī´ə gram´) *n.* chart, drawing, or plan that makes something clearer to read and understand

disagreement (dis´ə grē´mənt) *n.* difference or conflict between people or groups

disbanded (dis band´ əd) *v.* broken up; dismissed

discipline (dis´ ə plin´) *n.* strict control

discover (di skuv´ər) v. find something hidden or previously unknown; find out

dispute (di spyoot´) n. disagreement

distinct (di stiŋkt´) adj. separate and different

diversity (də vur´sə tē) n. variety, as of groups or cultures

dolefully (dōl´fəl lē) adv. with sadness and sorrow

dominions (də min´ yəns) n. governed countries or territories

downy (dou´ nē) adj. soft and fluffy

duty (doot´ē) n. responsibility

E

effective (e fek´tiv) adj. successful in producing the desired result

eligible (el´i jə bəl) adj. fit to be chosen; qualified

emerged (ē murjd´) v. came out

emphatic (em fat´ ik) adj. expressing strong feeling

endeavors (en dev´ərz) n. attempts; efforts

enhance (en hans´) v. improve; make something better

enrich (en rich´) v. make better; improve in quality

entertain (ent´ər tān´) v. 1. amuse; 2. put on a performance

environment (en vi´rən mənt) n. 1. surroundings; 2. the natural world

envying (en´ vē iŋ) v. wanting something that someone else has

epidemic (ep´ ə dem´ ik) n. outbreak of a contagious disease

equality (ē kwôl´ ə tē) n. social state in which all people are treated the same

ethnicity (eth nis´ə tē) n. racial or cultural background

evading (ē vād´ iŋ) v. avoiding

evaluate (ē val´yoo āt´) v. judge or rate

evaluations (ē val´yoo ā´shənz) n. 1. acts of judging or rating something or someone; 2. judgments or interpretations

evaporated (ē vap´ ə rāt əd) v. changed from a liquid to a gas

evidently (ev´ ə dent´ lē) adv. clearly; obviously

examine (eg zam´ən) v. study in depth in order to find or check something

exertion (eg zur´ shən) n. physical work

expectations (ek´ spekt tā´ shənz) n. things looked forward to

experiment (ek sper´ə mənt) n. test to determine a result

explain (ek splān´) v. 1. describe; 2. make understandable

explicit (eks plis´it) adj. clearly stated; readily seen

explore (ek splôr´) v. 1. travel through an unfamiliar area to find out what it is like; 2. thoroughly discuss a topic

express (ek spres´) v. say or communicate a feeling

exquisite (eks´ kwiz it) adj. beautiful in a delicate way

F

facts (fakts) n. true information about a topic

family (fam´ə lē) n. people related by blood or having a common ancestor

fascinated (fas´ ə nāt´ əd) adj. very interested

fathom (fath´ əm) n. unit of length used to measure the depth of water

feeble (fē´ bəl) adj. weak

feebleness (fē´ bəl nəs) n. weakness

feigned (fānd) v. pretended or imitated

fluent (floo´ ənt) adj. able to write or speak easily and smoothly

flushed (flusht) v. drove from hiding

flustered (flus´ tərd) adj. nervous; confused

focus (fō´kəs) n. direction; point of concentration

forage (fôr´ ij) n. food for domestic animals

formal (fôr´məl) adj. following established rules or customs

formidable (fôr´ mə də bəl) adj. impressive

fosters (fôs´tərz) v. promotes the growth or development of

fragrant (frā´ grənt) adj. sweet smelling

fundamental (fun´ də ment´ 'l) adj. basic; forming a foundation

furor (fyoor´ôr´) n. outburst of public anger or excitement

furrowed (fur´ōd) v. wrinkled

G

gauge (gāj) v. estimate or judge

globules (gläb´ yoolz) n. drops of liquid

granite (gran´ it) n. hard, gray rock

gratitude (grat´ i tood´) n. thankful appreciation

group (groop) n. collection or set, as of people

groves (grōvz) n. small groups of trees

gumption (gump´ shən) n. determination; initiative

H

habitats (hab´ ə tats) n. places where specific animals or plants naturally live or grow

haunches (hônch´ əz) n. upper legs and hips of an animal

hexagons (hek´ sə gänz´) n. six-sided figures

hoarding (hôr´ diŋ) n. accumulation and storage of supplies

hoed (hōd) v. weeded or loosened soil with a metal hand tool

I

identify (ī den´tə fī´) v. 1. recognize; 2. point out

ignorant (ig´ nə rənt) adj. not knowing facts or information

ignore (ig nôr´) v. pay no attention to

illustrate (il´ə strāt´) v. make something clear by providing examples

image (im´ij) n. picture; representation

immensely (i mens´ lē) *adv.* a great deal; very much

impervious (im pʉr´ vē əs) *adj.* not affected by something

implored (im plôrd´) *v.* begged

imposters (im päs´tərz) *n.* people or things pretending to be someone or something else

impromptu (im prämp´tŏŏ´) *adj.* unscheduled; unplanned

incessantly (in ses´ ənt lē) *adv.* without stopping

individual (in´də vij´ŏŏ əl) *n.* single person or thing

inflicted (in flikt´ əd) *v.* delivered something painful

inform (in fôrm´) *v.* tell; give information about

information (in´fər mā´shən) *n.* knowledge gained through study or experience

inherent (in hir´ ənt) *adj.* natural, basic, or inborn

inquire (in kwīr´) *v.* ask someone for information

inquiry (in´kwər ē) *n.* official process to find out why something happened

insight (in´sīt´) *n.* 1. ability to understand something clearly; 2. an understanding

integration (in´ tə grā´ shən) *n.* end of separation of cultural or racial groups

intercedes (in´tər sēdz´) *v.* makes a request on behalf of another

interrogations (in tər´ə gā´shənz) *n.* formal examinations that involve questioning the subject

intervene (in tər vēn´) *v.* come between in an effort to influence or help settle an action or argument

interview (in´tər vyŏŏ´) *v.* ask a series of questions of a person in order to gain information

intricate (in´ tri kit) *adj.* complex; detailed

investigate (in ves´tə gāt´) *v.* examine thoroughly

investigations (in ves´tə gā´shənz) *n.* official attempts to find out the reasons for something, such as a crime or a problem

investment (in vest´mənt) *n.* act of devoting time or effort to a particular undertaking with the expectation of a worthwhile result

J

justifies (jus´ tə fīz´) *v.* 1. excuses; 2. explains

K

knowledge (näl´ij) *n.* result of learning; awareness

L

laborious (lə bôr´ ē əs) *adj.* taking much work or effort

learn (lʉrn) *v.* gain knowledge or skills

legal (lē´gəl) *adj.* lawful

legislation (lej´ is lā´ shən) *n.* act of making laws; law-making

listen (lis´ən) *v.* pay attention to; heed

literally (lit´ər əl ē) *adv.* exactly

loathed (lōthd) *v.* hated

luminous (lŏŏ´ mə nəs) *adj.* giving off light

M

maestro (mīs´ trō) *n.* great musician

malicious (mə lish´ əs) *adj.* hateful; spiteful

manned (mand) *adj.* having human operators on board

materials (mə tir´ē əlz) *n.* things used for making or doing something

maximize (mak´ sə mīz´) *v.* make the most of

meager (mē´ gər) *adj.* 1. small in amount; 2. of poor quality

media (mē´dē ə) 1. *n. pl.* sources of information or expression, such as newspapers, television, and the Internet; 2. *adj.* relating to media

meek (mēk) *adj.* timid; not willing to argue

minnow (min ō) *n.* small fish

misunderstanding (mis´un dər stan´diŋ) *n.* state where words or a point of view fail to be communicated

monarch (man´ ərk) *n.* ruler, such as a king or queen

morose (mə rōs´) *adj.* gloomy; ill-tempered

mortality (môr tal´ ə tē) *n.* condition of being mortal, or having to die eventually

mourning (môr´niŋ) *v.* expressing grief, especially after someone dies

muster (mus´tər) *v.* gather together or summon

mystery (mis´ tə rē) *n.* something unexplained, unknown, or kept secret

N

negatives (neg´ ə tivz) *n.* photographic images in which the light and dark areas are reversed

nonchalantly (nän´ shə länt´ lē) *adv.* seemingly uninterested

nondescript (nän´di skript´) *adj.* 1. hard to describe; 2. not interesting

notions (nō´shənz) *n.* general ideas

O

observe (əb zʉrv´) *v.* watch someone or something carefully; notice

obstacle (äb´stə kəl) *n.* something in the way

ominous (äm´ ə nəs) *adj.* threatening

opinion (ə pin´ yən) *n.* belief based on what seems true or probable to one's own mind

opposing (ə pōz´ iŋ) *adj.* opposite; completely different

opposition (äp´ə zish´ən) *n.* person, group, or force that tries to prevent you from accomplishing something

optimal (äp´tə məl) *adj.* best or most favorable; optimum

optimist (äp´ tə mist) *n.* someone who takes the most hopeful view of matters

outcome (out´kum´) *n.* way a situation turns out; result or consequence

P

peeved (pēvd) *adj.* irritated; annoyed

perceive (pər sēv´) *v.* see or view

perception (pər sep´shən) *n.* act of becoming aware of through one or more of the senses

perceptions (pər sep´shənz) *n.* observations, sensations, or mental images

perilous (per´ ə ləs) *adj.* dangerous

perpetual (pər pech´ ōō əl) *adj.* constant; unending

persistently (pər sist´ ənt lē) *adv.* firmly and steadily

perspective (pər spek´tiv) *n.* point of view; viewpoint

pertinent (purt´´n ənt) *adj.* connected or related to the topic

pestering (pes´ tər iŋ) *v.* annoying; bothering

predict (prē dikt´) *v.* say that something will happen before it happens

presumptuous (prē zump´ chōō əs) *adj.* 1. overconfident; 2. lacking respect

process (prä´ses´) *n.* method; series of actions taken to achieve a particular result

produce (prə dōōs´) *v.* make; create

promote (prə mōt´) *v.* encourage; contribute to the growth of

prompted (prämpt´id) *v.* urged into action

psychologists (sī käl´ ə jists) *n.* experts who study the human mind and behavior

purpose (pur´pəs) *n.* reason for doing something

Q

question (kwes´chən) *v.* challenge the accuracy of; place in doubt

R

rash (rash) *adj.* too hasty

react (rē akt´) *v.* respond to

reaction (rē ak´shən) *n.* response to an influence, action, or statement

readapted (rē ə dapt´ əd) *v.* gradually adjusted again

realm (relm) *n.* kingdom

reassuring (rē ə shōōr´ iŋ) *adj.* having the effect of restoring confidence

reflect (ri flekt´) *v.* express or show

refute (ri fyōōt´) *v.* prove wrong

regretted (ri gret´ əd) *v.* felt sorry about

relationship (ri lā´shən ship´) *n.* connection

relented (ri lent´ əd) *v.* gave in

reliable (ri lī´ ə bəl) *adj.* dependable

relished (rel´isht) *v.* enjoyed; liked

remote (ri mōt´) *adj.* far away from anything else

reproach (ri prōach´) *n.* disapproval; criticism

repulsive (ri pul´siv) *adj.* causing intense dislike; disgusting

resilient (ri zil´ yənt) *adj.* able to spring back into shape

resolution (rez´ə lōō´shən) *n.* working out of a problem or conflict

resources (rē´ sôrs´ əz) *n.* natural features that enhance the quality of human life

reveal (ri vēl´) *v.* make known; show

revived (ri vīvd´) *v.* came back to life or consciousness

riveted (riv´ it id) *v.* anchored; completely absorbed by

routed (rout´ əd) *v.* completely defeated

S

saturation (sach´ ə rā´ shən) *n.* state of being completely filled

scorned (skôrnd) *adj.* looked down upon

scrutiny (skrōōt´´n ē) *n.* close, thorough inspection

sensitive (sen´ sə tiv) *adj.* easily hurt or affected

sentimental (sen tə ment´ əl) *adj.* emotional; showing tender feeling

severe (sə vir´) *adj.* harsh

shed (shed) *v.* cast off or lost

shortsightedness (shôrt´ sīt´ id nəs) *n.* condition of not considering the future effects of something

shuffle (shuf´ əl) *v.* walk with dragging feet

significance (sig nif´ə kəns) *n.* importance

simultaneously (sī´ məl tā´ nē əs lē) *adv.* at the same time

slackening (slak´ ən iŋ) *adj.* easing; becoming less active

smattering (smat´ ər iŋ) *n.* small number

snare (sner) *v.* catch; capture

solemn (säl´ əm) *adj.* serious; somber

solve (sälv) *v.* figure out an answer

speak (spēk) *v.* use oral language

spectators (spek´ tāt´ erz) *n.* people who watch

spines (spīnz) *n.* backbones

spur (spur) *v.* cause

sputters (sput´ erz) *v.* makes hissing or spitting noises

strategy (strat´ə jē) *n.* method or plan

strove (strōv) *v.* struggled; made great efforts

struggle (strug´əl) *n.* fight

subjected (səb jekt´ id) *v.* caused one to experience

subscribed (səb skrīb´ əd) *v.* promised to give money in support of something

successive (sək ses´iv) *adj.* following, in order

succumb (sə kum´) *v.* give way to; submit to

sufficient (sə fish´ənt) *adj.* enough

summoned (sum´ ənd) *v.* called together

supple (sup´ əl) *adj.* able to bend easily; flexible

swerve (swurv) *n.* curving motion

swindle (swin´dəl) *n.* act of cheating or fraud

T

teach (tēch) *v.* share information or knowledge

team (tēm) *n.* group with a common goal

technology (tek näl´ə jē) *n.* machines, equipment, and ways of doing things that are based on modern knowledge about science

tentatively (ten´ tə tiv lē) *adj.* hesitantly; with uncertainty

theory (thē´ə rē) *n.* explanatory idea not yet proved to be true

tolerant (täl´ ər ənt) *adj.* accepting; free from bigotry or prejudice

torrent (tôr´ ənt) *n.* flood

tout (tout) *v.* promote

tradition (trə dish´ən) *n.* customs, as of a social group or culture

transfixed (trans fikst´) *adj.* rooted to the spot

translates (trans´ lāts) *v.* expresses the same thing in another form

translucent (trans lo͞o´ sənt) *adj.* allowing some light through

transmit (trans mit´) *v.* send or give out

transmitting (trans mit´ tiŋ) *v.* sending or conveying from one thing to another

trivialness (triv´ē əl nes) *n.* state of having little importance

U

unanimous (yo͞o nan´ ə məs) *adj.* based on complete agreement

uncommonly (un käm´ ən lē) *adv.* remarkably

understand (un´dər stand´) *v.* grasp or reach knowledge with respect to something

understanding (un´dər stan´diŋ) *n.* agreement

unify (yo͞o´nə fī´) *v.* bring together as one

unique (yo͞o nēk´) *adj.* one of a kind

unscrupulous (un´skro͞o´pyə ləs) *adj.* 1. not held back by ideas of right and wrong; 2. untrustworthy

utter (ut´ ər) *v.* speak

V

veranda (və ran´ də) *n.* open porch, usually with a roof

verge (vʉrj) *n.* edge; brink

viewpoint (vyo͞o point´) *n.* particular way of thinking about a subject

vital (vīt´ 'l) *adj.* extremely important or necessary

void (void) *n.* emptiness

vowed (voud) *v.* promised solemnly

vulnerable (vul´ nər ə bəl) *adj.* open to attack

W

whimper (hwim´ pər) *v.* make low, crying sounds

withered (with´ ərd) *adj.* dried up

writhing (rīth´ iŋ) *v.* squirming, often in response to pain

Spanish Glossary

El vocabulario académico aparece en **azul**.

A

abode / domicilio *s.* hogar; residencia

accusations / acusaciones *s.* cargos en contra de una persona por hacer algo incorrecto o ilegal

acknowledge / reconocer *v.* aceptar; admitir

adaptation / adaptación *s.* cambio gradual en el comportamiento para ajustarse a las normas aceptadas por la sociedad

adequate / adecuado *adj.* bastante; suficiente

advocacy / defensa *s.* apoyo para una idea o misión en particular

affect / afectar *v.* hacer algo que produce un cambio en alguien o algo; influenciar

aggressive / agresivo *adj.* violento, propenso a actuar en forma destructiva o grosera

ajar / entreabierto *adj.* abierto a medias

analyze / analizar *v.* separar las partes de un todo para examinarlo detenidamente

appearance / apariencia *s.* aspecto o parecer de una persona o cosa

appreciate / apreciar *v.* estar agradecido

approximately / aproximadamente *adv.* de una forma cercana o casi correcta mas no exacta

aptitude / aptitud *s.* talento; habilidad

arid / árido *adj.* muy seco; baldío

assumption / suposición *s.* creencia o aceptación de la existencia de algo sin tener pruebas

assumptions / suposiciones *s.* actos de aceptación de algo como una realidad sin tener pruebas

astonish / asombrar *v.* causar sorpresa grande y a veces repentina; maravillar; pasmar

attitude / actitud *s.* opiniones y sentimientos de una persona acerca de alguien o algo

audible / audible *adj.* lo suficientemente alto para que se pueda oír

aversion / aversión *s.* fuerte disgusto o repugnancia frente a alguien o algo

awareness / conciencia *s.* conocimiento adquirido por medio de la percepción o de información

B

behavior / comportamiento *s.* la forma en la que uno se porta o actúa

bias / parcialidad *s.* tendencia a interpretar las cosas de manera sesgada o prejuiciosa

bigots / intolerantes *s.* personas de mentalidad cerrada, prejuiciosas

blander / más insípido *adj.* que tiene menos sabor

blunt / suavizar *v.* disminuir; hacer menos fuerte; reducir el filo

bound / sujeto *v.* atado

C

challenge / desafío *s.* algo que pone a prueba las habilidades de una persona; reto

characteristic / característica *s.* rasgo; facción

characterize / caracterizar *v.* 1. ser típico de alguien o algo; 2. describir a alguien o a algo en una forma particular

cite / citar *v.* 1. mencionar algo como prueba o ejemplo de alguna otra cosa; 2. referirse a

coax / convencer *v.* persuadir de manera sutil

commemorated / conmemoró *v.* honró la memoria de

commissioned / comisionó *v.* designó o empleó para llevar a cabo una labor o un trabajo

common / común *adj.* 1. ordinario; frecuente; 2. compartido; público

communal / comunal *adj.* compartido por todos

communicate / comunicar *v.* compartir ideas, pensamientos o sentimientos, usualmente con palabras

communication / comunicación *s.* acto de compartir información o de expresar pensamientos y sentimientos

community / comunidad *s.* grupo de personas que tienen un interés en común o que viven cerca el uno del otro

competition / competencia *s.* evento o juego en que las personas o bandos pretenden ganar

complex / complejo *adj.* 1. difícil de entender; 2. que tiene muchas partes conectadas

compose / componer *v.* escribir o crear una pieza musical, una obra de arte o un texto

compromise / solución *s.* convenio satisfactorio entre dos partes

compulsion / compulsión *s.* impulso irresistible

conclude / concluir *v.* terminar; finalizar

conferred / deliberó *v.* se discutió

conflict / conflicto *s.* choque o lucha entre grupos opuestos

consolation / consolación *s.* algo que alivia la pena de una persona decepcionada

conspired / conspiró *v.* planeó de manera secreta

contradiction / contradicción *s.* diferencia entre dos cosas conflictivas que demuestra que sólo una es cierta

contraption / artilugio s. aparato o mecanismo extraño

contrast / contrastar v. comparar dos cosas para mostrar sus diferencias

contribute / contribuir v. 1. agregar; enriquecer; 2. proveer

conveyed / comunicó v. hizo saber; expresó

convince / convencer v. persuadir; incitar a aceptar un punto de vista

convincing / convincente adj. persuasivo

coveted / codició v. quiso; deseó

cremated / cremado v. quemar un cadáver hasta convertirlo en cenizas

croon / canturrear v. cantar o tararear suave y dulcemente

crucial / crucial adj. importante; crítico

crystal / cristal adj. hecho de vidrio claro y brillante

culminated / culminó v. alcanzó su punto más alto o clímax

culprit / inculpado s. persona culpable

culture / cultura s. conjunto de modos de vida y costumbres de un grupo o una comunidad

cunning / astuto adj. hábil; ingenioso

cunningly / astutamente adv. ingeniosamente

curdled / cortado adj. podrido

curiosity / curiosidad s. deseo de aprender o saber más sobre un tema

custom / costumbre s. lo que se hace comúnmente; práctica aceptada

D

dabbling / chapuzar v. zambullirse, sumergirse o patalear en el agua

danger / peligro s. exposición a posible daño, lesión o pérdida

debate / debatir 1. v. discutir formalmente; 2. s. discusión o argumento sobre un tema en el que se expresan distintas opiniones

deceive / engañar v. hacer a alguien creer lo que no es cierto

decipher / descifrar v. encontrar el significado de

decreed / decretó v. creó un mandato oficial

defiant / desafiante adj. que resiste valientemente

defies / desafía v. se resiste o se opone valientemente o de manera abierta

define / definir v. determinar la naturaleza o establecer el significado de algo

definition / definición s. oración o frase que expresa el significado exacto de una palabra o frase

describe / describir v. decir cómo es algo o alguien al dar detalles acerca de éste

designated / designó v. señaló; marcó

desire / deseo s. acción de desear o querer

desolate / desolado adj. solo; solitario

destitute / indigentes adj. personas que viven en pobreza absoluta

deteriorates / se deteriora v. que se empeora

determination / determinación s. decisión o conclusión

devastated / devastado v. destruido; completamente disgustado

devastating / devastador adj. destructivo; arrollador

diagram / diagrama s. un cuadro, dibujo o plan que ayuda a que algo sea más fácil de entender

disagreement / desacuerdo s. diferencia o conflicto entre grupos o personas

disbanded / desbandado v. dividido; liquidado

discipline / disciplina s. entrenamiento; autocontrol o control estricto

discover / descubrir v. encontrar algo previamente desconocido; explorar

dispute / disputa s. desacuerdo

distinct / distinto adj. separado y diferente

diversity / diversidad s. variedad, como de grupos o culturas

dolefully / tristemente adv. de manera triste y penosa

dominions / dominios s. países o territorios gobernados

downy / suave adj. blando y esponjoso

duty / deber s. responsabilidad; obligación

E

effective / efectivo adj. exitoso en producir los resultados deseados

eligible / elegible adj. apto para ser escogido; calificado

emerged / emergió v. apareció a la vista; se volvió visible

emphatic / enfático adj. que se siente o se hace con fuerza

endeavors / esfuerzos s. intentos; empeños

enhance / mejorar v. pasar algo a un estado mejor

enrich / enriquecer v. mejorar

entertain / entretener v. 1. divertir; 2. hacer una presentación

environment / medio ambiente s. 1. lo que nos rodea; 2. el mundo natural

envying / envidiando v. queriendo lo que otro posee

epidemic / epidemia s. proliferación de una enfermedad contagiosa

equality / igualdad s. estado de la sociedad en el que todas las personas se tratan de la misma manera

ethnicity / etnicidad s. origen cultural o racial

evading / evadiendo v. evitando

evaluate / evaluar v. juzgar; determinar el significado o valor de algo

evaluations / evaluaciones s. 1. actos de juzgar o calificar algo o alguien; 2. juicios o interpretaciones

evaporated / evaporó v. cambió de líquido a gas

evidently / evidentemente adv. claramente; obviamente

examine / examinar v. estudiar a fondo para hallar o verificar algo; observar detenidamente

exertion / esfuerzo s. trabajo físico

expectations / expectativas s. esperanzas de lo que viene

experiment / experimento s. prueba que determina un resultado

explain / explicar v. 1. describir; 2. esclarecer o aclarar

explicit / explícito adj. expresado claramente; visto de inmediato

explore / explorar v. 1. viajar por un área desconocida para descubrir cómo es; 2. discutir un tema detalladamente

express / expresar v. hablar de o comunicar un sentimiento

exquisite / refinado adj. hermoso y delicado

F

facts / hechos s. la verdad o la realidad; información correcta acerca de un tema

family / familia s. personas de relación consanguínea o que tienen un antepasado en común

fascinated / fascinado adj. encantado; muy interesado

fathom / braza s. unidad de longitud para medir la profundidad del agua

feeble / débil adj. flojo; enclenque

feebleness / debilidad s. falta de fuerza

feigned / fingió v. pretendió; imitó

fluent / fluido adj. que escribe o habla con facilidad y soltura

flushed / expulsó v. obligó a salir de un lugar

flustered / agitado adj. nervioso; confuso

focus / enfoque n. punto central o tema de investigación

forage / forraje s. comida para animales domésticos

formal / formal adj. que sigue reglas o costumbres establecidas

formidable / formidable adj. imponente; impresionante

fosters / fomenta v. promueve el crecimiento o desarrollo de

fragrant / fragante adj. que emana un aroma dulce

fundamental / fundamental adj. básico; que forma una base

furor / furor s. explosión de ira o emoción pública

furrowed / arrugado v. hecho pliegues

G

gauge / medir v. estimar o juzgar

globules / glóbulos s. gotas de un líquido

granite / granito s. piedra dura de color gris

gratitude / gratitud s. agradecimiento

group / grupo s. conjunto o agrupación, como de personas

groves / arboledas s. grupos pequeños de árboles

gumption / arrojo s. osadía o coraje; empuje

H

habitats / hábitats s. lugares en los cuales ciertos animales o plantas viven o crecen de forma natural

haunches / ancas s. las patas posteriores de un animal

hexagons / hexágonos s. figuras de seis lados

hoarding / acaparando v. acumulando y almacenando provisiones como reservas

hoed / limpió con la azada v. cavó y removió tierra con una herramienta de metal

I

identify / identificar v. 1. reconocer como existente; 2. señalar

ignorant / ignorante adj. que no sabe los hechos o que no tiene la información apropiada

ignore / ignorar v. hacer caso omiso; desconocer

illustrate / ilustrar v. aclarar algo al proveer un ejemplo

image / imagen n. retrato; representación

immensely / inmensamente adv. en grado extremo; muchísimo

impervious / insensible adj. que no es afectado por algo

implored / implorado v. suplicado

imposters / impostores s. personas o cosas que aparentan ser algo o alguien que no son

impromptu / improvisado adj. no planeado

incessantly / incesantemente adv. sin parar

individual / individuo s. una sola persona o cosa

inflicted / inflijió v. causó sufrimiento o daño

inform / informar v. decir; dar información de algo

information / información s. conocimiento adquirido por medio del estudio o de la experiencia

inherent / inherente adj. natural, básico o innato

inquire / preguntar v. cuestionar con el fin de obtener información

inquiry / indagación s. proceso oficial con el fin de encontrar el porqué ocurrió algo

insight / perspicacia s. 1. habilidad de ver la verdad; 2. entendimiento claro

integration / integración s. fin de la separación de grupos culturales o raciales

intercedes / intercede v. actúa o pide por otra persona

interrogations / interrogatorios s. serie de preguntas formales dirigidas a un sujeto que tiene que contestarlas

intervene / interviene v. se interpone en una situación como influencia para ayudar a resolver una acción o argumento

interview / entrevistar *v.* hacer una serie de preguntas a una persona con el fin de obtener información

intricate / intricado *adj.* complejo; detallado

investigate / investigar *v.* examinar a fondo

investigations / investigaciones *s.* procesos oficiales para encontrar las razones por las cuales ocurrió algún suceso, como un crimen o problema

investment / inversión *s.* el acto de dedicar tiempo y esfuerzo a algo en particular con la expectativa de obtener un resultado que valga la pena

J

justifies / justifica *v.* 1. da escusas; 2. explica

K

knowledge / conocimiento *s.* el resultado del aprendizaje; acción de tener presente

L

laborious / laborioso *adj.* que cuesta bastante trabajo o esfuerzo

learn / aprender *v.* obtener conocimiento o destrezas

legal / legal *adj.* conforme a las leyes

legislation / legislación *s.* ley

listen / escuchar *v.* prestar atención a; atender

literally / literalmente *adv.* exactamente

loathed / abominado *v.* odiado

luminous / luminoso *adj.* que despide luz

M

maestro / maestro *s.* un gran músico

malicious / malicioso *adj.* que tiene mala intención; odioso

manned / tripulado *adj.* que tiene un operador humano abordo

materials / materiales *s.* cosas utilizadas para hacer algo

maximize / maximizar *v.* tomar el máximo provecho de algo

meager / escaso *adj.* precario; de poca cantidad

media / medios de comunicación *s.* conjunto de fuentes de información o expresión, tales como periódicos, televisión y la Internet

meek / manso *adj.* tímido; que no demuestra enfado

minnow / pececillo *s.* pez pequeño

misunderstanding / malentendido *s.* estado en el que palabras o un punto de vista no logra ser comunicado

monarch / monarca *s.* dominio por carácter hereditario, como el de un rey o una reina

morose / lúgubre *adj.* sombrío

mortality / mortalidad *s.* condición de ser mortal, o de tener que morir en algún momento

mourning / luto *s.* expresión de pena, especialmente después de que alguien muere

muster / reunir *v.* juntar las fuerzas; convocar

mystery / misterio *s.* algo inexplicable, desconocido o que se mantiene bajo secreto

N

negatives / negativos *s.* imágenes fotográficas en las cuales la luz y las áreas oscuras se encuentran invertidas

nonchalantly / con toda tranquilidad *adv.* de manera despreocupada; con indiferencia

nondescript / indefinido *adj.* 1. difícil de describir; 2. no interesante; soso

notions / nociones *s.* ideas generales

O

observe / observar *v.* ver algo o a alguien detalladamente; notar

obstacle / obstáculo *s.* algo que se interpone en el camino

ominous / siniestro *adj.* amenazante

opinion / opinión *s.* creencia basada en lo que parece ser cierto o probable según uno mismo

opposing / opuesto *adj.* contrario; completamente diferente

opposition / oposición *s.* persona, grupo o fuerza que trata de impedir el logro de algo

optimal / óptimo *adj.* mejor o más favorable

optimist / optimista *s.* alguien que tiende a ver las cosas de la manera más favorable

outcome / resultado *s.* la manera en que algo se resuelve; consecuencia

P

peeved / molesto *adj.* irritado; fastidiado

perceive / percibir *v.* aceptar desde cierto punto de vista; ver

perception / percepción *s.* acto de darse cuenta de algo por medio de uno o más sentidos

perceptions / percepciones *s.* observaciones, sensaciones o imágenes mentales

perilous / arriesgado *adj.* peligroso

perpetual / perpetuo *adj.* constante; sin fin

persistently / persistentemente *adv.* de manera firme y constante

perspective / perspectiva *s.* punto de vista

pertinent / pertinente *adj.* conectado o relacionado con el tema

pestering / molestando *v.* fastidiando; irritando

predict / predecir *v.* decir que algo va a pasar antes de que suceda

presumptuous / presumido *adj.* 1. con exceso de confianza en sí mismo; 2. arrogante

process / proceso *s.* método; serie de acciones realizadas para lograr un resultado particular

produce / producir *v.* hacer; crear

promote / promover v. impulsar; contribuir al crecimiento de algo

prompted / impulsó v. llevó a la acción

psychologists / psicólogos s. expertos que estudian la mente y el comportamiento humanos

purpose / propósito s. razón por la cual se hace algo

Q

question / cuestionar v. desafiar la verdad de algo; poner en duda

R

rash / imprudente adj. muy precipitado

react / reaccionar v. responder; hacer algo al respecto

reaction / reacción s. respuesta a una influencia, acción o afirmación

readapted / se adaptó de nuevo v. se ajustó gradualmente otra vez

realm / dominio s. reino

reassuring / tranquilizante adj. que alivia, asegura o da confianza

reflect / reflejar v. expresar o mostrar

refute / refutar v. probar que alguien o algo está equivocado

regretted / se arrepintió v. sintió pesar por algo

relationship / relación s. conexión

relented / cedió v. se dejó convencer

reliable / confiable adj. del que se puede depender

relished / se deleitó v. gozó; disfrutó de

remote / remoto adj. muy lejos de todo lo demás

reproach / reproche s. acto de culpar; crítica

repulsive / repulsivo adj. que causa disgusto; que da asco

resilient / resistente adj. fuerte; que puede recobrar su estado original

resolution / resolución s. fin satisfactorio de un problema o conflicto

resources / recursos s. elementos naturales que mejoran la calidad de vida humana

reveal / revelar v. hacer saber; dar a conocer; demostrar

revived / revivió v. volvió a la vida o recobró conciencia

riveted / cautivado v. absorbido completamente por algo o alguien

routed / derrotó v. venció de manera decisiva

S

saturation / saturación s. condición en la que se está completamente lleno

scorned / desdeñado adj. menospreciado

scrutiny / escrutinio s. inspección minuciosa

sensitive / sensible adj. que se hiere o afecta con facilidad

sentimental / sentimental adj. emotivo; que demuestra sentimientos tiernos

severe / severo adj. duro

shed / mudó v. perdió o cambió

shortsightedness / falta de visión s. carencia de proyección en el futuro; acto de no considerar los efectos futuros de una acción

shuffle / arrastrar v. caminar sin levantar los pies

significance / significado s. importancia

simultaneously / simultáneamente adv. al mismo tiempo

slackening / aminorando v. disminuyendo; volviéndose menos activo

smattering / poquito s. cantidad pequeña

snare / apresar v. atrapar; capturar

solemn / solemne adj. serio; sombrío

solve / resolver v. descifrar una respuesta

speak / hablar v. usar lenguaje oral; expresar con palabras

spectators / espectadores s. personas que miran con atención

spines / espinazos s. vértebras

spur / estimular v. causar

sputters / chisporrotea v. hace ruidos chispeantes o sibilantes

strategy / estrategia s. método o plan para alcanzar el éxito o lograr un objetivo

strove / se esforzó v. luchó; hizo un gran esfuerzo

struggle / lucha s. pelea

subjected / sometió v. forzó; causó

subscribed / suscribió v. prometió dar apoyo monetario a algo

successive / sucesivo adj. que sigue a otro; en orden

succumb / sucumbir v. ceder; someterse

sufficient / suficiente adj. cantidad satisfactoria

summoned / convocó v. citó o llamó a una reunión

supple / ágil adj. que usa su cuerpo con facilidad y soltura

swerve / viraje s. movimiento en curva

swindle / estafa s. acto de hacer trampa o fraude

T

teach / enseñar v. compartir información o conocimiento

team / equipo s. grupo unido por una meta en común

technology / tecnología s. aplicación práctica de las ciencias en la industria; máquinas, equipo y procesos basados en el conocimiento moderno de la ciencia

tentatively / tentativamente adv. dudosamente; sin certeza y con vacilación

theory / teoría s. una idea explicativa que aún no ha sido comprobada

tolerant / tolerante adj. que acepta; libre de resistencia o prejuicios

torrent / torrente s. inundación

tout / promover v. promocionar; fomentar

tradition / tradición s. costumbre, como de un grupo social o cultura

transfixed / embelesado *adj.* fascinado

translates / traduce *v.* expresa la misma cosa en otra forma

translucent / translúcido *adj.* que permite pasar cierta cantidad de luz

transmit / transmitir *v.* enviar o repartir

transmitting / transmitiendo *v.* enviando o transfiriendo de una cosa a otra

trivialness / trivialidad *s.* estado de tener poca importancia

U

unanimous / unánime *adj.* basado en un acuerdo total

uncommonly / extraordinariamente *adv.* fuera de lo común

understand / entender *v.* llegar a conocer y comprender algo

understanding / entendimiento *s.* acuerdo; fin de un conflicto

unify / unificar *v.* juntar para formar uno solo

unique / único *adj.* sin otro de su especie

unscrupulous / inescrupuloso *adj.* 1. que no actúa según lo que es o no es correcto; 2. que no genera confianza

utter / pronunciar *v.* articular; hablar

V

veranda / veranda *s.* porche abierto, usualmente con techo

verge / borde *s.* orilla; límite

viewpoint / punto de vista *s.* pensamientos particulares con respecto a un tema

vital / vital *adj.* de extrema importancia o necesario

void / vacío *s.* espacio desocupado

vowed / juró *v.* prometió solemnemente

vulnerable / vulnerable *adj.* que puede ser atacado

W

whimper / lloriquear *v.* emitir un llanto o lamento débil

withered / marchitado *adj.* que se ha secado

writhing / retorciéndose *v.* contorcionándo, usualmente a causa de dolor

Index of Skills

Literary Analysis

Comprehension Skills

Rubrics for Self-Assessment

Speaking and Listening
Activities

Strategies

Research

Activities

Language Conventions

Revising Sentences Using Participles, 553

Revising to Combine Sentences Using Conjunctions, 255

Vocabulary

Academic Vocabulary
domain-specific, 43, 65, 77, 95, 199, 209, 229, 337, 347, 371, 497, 535, 543, 655, 669, 679, 689
general, 3, 113, 175, 274, 313, 379, 445, 584, 631, 682, 707, 732

Language Study
antonyms/synonyms, 114, 144, 361, 406, 545
connotations/denotations, 191, 326, 375, 542, 544–545, 549, 551, 544, R2
context clues, use, 314, 315, 448, 632
descriptive/vivid words, use, 120, 251, 301, 691
dictionary/thesaurus, use, 114–115
etymology/word origins, 42, 64, 76, 94, 114, 198, 208, 216, 228, 246–247, 336, 346, 358, 370, 486, 496, 534, 654, 668, 678, 688. *See also* Word Study/

Etymology
idioms, 708, 768, R4
multiple-meaning words, 380–381
onomatopoeia, 315, 325, 350
precise words, use, 231, 252, 289, 691
sensory words, use, 231, 289, 375
spelling
   irregular plural nouns, 257
   tricky syllables, 555
technical language/specialized terms, 295
time-order words, use, 289
transitional words in nonfiction, 193
word choices, make, 121, 169, 252, 434, 551, 691

Word Study/Etymology
Prefixes
   inter-, 534
   mal-, 76
   un-, 370
   uni-, 668
Roots
   -dom-, 654
   -grat-, 486
   -just-, 208
   -leg-, 216

   -lum-, 336
   -myst-, 668
   -sol-, 228
   -spir-, 64
Suffixes
   -er, 346
   -ious, 94
   -ity, 678
   -less, 358
   -ness, 198
   -tion, 42

Assessment

Assessment: Synthesis, 166–169, 304–307, 438–441, 622–625, 772–775

Constructed Response, 130–131, 262–263, 396–397, 560–561, 724–725

Selected Response, 126–129, 258–261, 392–395, 556–559, 720–723

Timed Writing, 113, 127, 245, 259, 379, 543, 557, 707

Index of Authors and Titles

The following authors and titles appear in the print and online versions of Pearson Literature.

Additional Selections: Author and Title Index

The following authors and titles appear in the Online Literature Library.

Grateful acknowledgment is made to the following for copyrighted material: *English—Language Arts Content Standards for California Public Schools* reproduced by permission, California Department of Education, CD Press, 1430 N Street, Suite 3207, Sacramento, CA 95814.

All Children's Hospital c/o Florida Suncoast Safe Kids Coalition "2006 Safe Kids "Walk This Way" Program" from *http://www.allkids.org/body.cfm?xyzpdqabc=0&id=396&action=detail&ref=28*. Copyrgiht © 2007 All Children's Hospital. All rights reserved. Used by permission.

Miriam Altshuler Literary Agency "Treasure of Lemon Brown" by Walter Dean Myers from *Boy's Life Magazine, March 1983*. Copyright © 1983, by Walter Dean Myers. Used by permission of Miriam Altshuler Literary Agency, on behalf of Walter Dean Myers.

American Broadcasting Music, Inc. "Conjunction Junction" composed by Jack Sheldon and Bob Dorough. Copyright © 1973 American Broadcasting Music, Inc. Used by permission.

Americas Magazine "Mongoose on the Loose" reprinted from *Americas,* a bimonthly magazine published by the General Secretariat of the Organization of American States in English and Spanish. Content may not be copied without written permission. Used by permission.

Arte Publico Press, Inc. "Maestro" is used with permission from the publisher of *Borders* by Pat Mora. (Houston: Arte Publico Press - University of Houston © 1986). "Bailando" from *Chants* by Pat Mora. Used with permission from the publisher of *Chants* (Houston: Arte Publico Press - University of Houston copyright © 1985).

Atheneum Books for Young Readers, an imprint of Simon & Schuster "Papa's Parrot" from *Every Living Thing* by Cynthia Rylant. Text copyright © 1985 Cynthia Rylant. Used by permission of Atheneum Books for Young Readers, an imprint of Simon & Schuster Children's Publishing Division.

Bantam Books, a division of Random House, Inc. "The Eternal Frontier" from *Frontier* by Louis L'Amour, Photographs by David Muench, copyright © 1984 by Louis L'Amour Enterprises, Inc. Used by permission of Bantam Books, a division of Random House, Inc.

Susan Bergholz Literary Services "My First Free Summer" by Julia Alvarez, copyright © 2003 by Julia Alvarez. First published in *Better Homes and Gardens, August 2003*. Used by permission of Susan Bergholz Literary Services, New York, NY and Lamy, NM. All rights reserved.

Brandt & Hochman Literary Agents, Inc. "The Third Wish" from *Not What You Expected: A Collection of Short Stories* by Joan Aiken. Copyright © 1974 by Joan Aiken. Any electronic copying or redistribution of the text is expressly forbidden. Used by permission of Brandt & Hochman Literary Agents, Inc.

Brooks Permissions "Jim" Copyright © 1956 from *Bronzeville Boys and Girls* by Gwendolyn Brooks. Copyright © 1956 by Gwendolyn Brooks. Used by consent of Brooks Permissions.

Curtis Brown Ltd. "Two Haiku" ("O foolish ducklings..." and "After the moon sets...") first appeared in *Cricket Songs: Japanese Haiku,* published by Harcourt. Copyright © 1964 by Harry Behn. "Suzy and Leah" first published in *American Girl Magazine*. Copyright © 1993 by Jane Yolen. From *Dragonwings* by Laurence Yep from *Theatre For Young Audiences: Around The World In 21 Plays*. Copyright © 1992 by Laurence Yep. First appeared in *American Theatre Magazine*. Now appears in *Norton Anthology of Children's Literature*. Used by permission of Curtis Brown, Ltd. CAUTION: Professionals and amateurs are hereby warned that *Dragonwings*, being fully protected under the copyright Laws of the United States of America, the British Empire, including the Dominion of Canada, and all other countries of the Universal Copyright and Berne Conventions, are subject to royalty. All rights, including professional, amateur, motion picture, recitation, lecturing, public reading, radio and television broadcasting, and the rights of translation into foreign languages, are strictly reserved. All inquiries for *Dragonwings* should be addressed to Curtis Brown Ltd.

CA Walk to School Headquarters "Walk to School" from *www.cawalktoschool.com*. Copyright © 2006 California Center for Physical Activity.

Canadian Broadcasting Corporation "Charles Dickens's A Christmas Carol: A Radio Interview" from *http://www.victorianweb.org/authors/dickens/xmas/pva303.html*. Originally broadcast on the Canadian Broadcasting Corporation (The Great Northwest, Dec. 4, 2000). Copyright © Canadian Broadcasting Corporation. Used by courtesy of Canadian Broadcasting Corporation.

Carnegie Hero Fund Commission "The History of the Carnegie Hero Fund Commission." © The Carnegie Hero Commission. Reused with permission.

Carus Publishing Company "The Rhythms of Rap" by Kathiann M. Kowalski from *Odyssey's March 2002 issue: Music: Why Do We Love It?* Copyright © 2002, Cobblestone Publishing, 30 Grove Street, Suite C, Peterborough, NH 03458. All rights reserved. Used by permission of Carus Publishing Company.

CBS News "Win Some, Lose Some" by Charles Osgood. © 2001. Reprinted with permission of CBS News Archives.

Chronicle Books "The Travelers and the Bear" by Jerry Pinkney from *Aesop's Fables*. Copyright © 2000 by Jerry Pinkney.

City of Melbourne Stormwater Management Web Page from *http://www.melbourneflorida.org/stormwater/howyoucanhelp.htm*. Copyright City of Melbourne.

City of Oceanside City of Oceanside Clean Water Program from *www.oceansidecleanwaterprogram.org/kids.asp*. Copyright © City of Oceanside. Used by permission.

ClearyWorks "The Fox Outwits the Crow" by William Cleary from *www.clearyworks.com*. Used by permission of William Cleary, Burlington, Vermont.

Cobblestone Publishing "The Myth of the Outlaw" by Ruth M. Hamel. Copyright © 1996, *Cobblestone,* May96: Vol. 17, Issue 5. Carus Publishing. Used by permission.

Code Entertainment *The Monsters Are Due on Maple Street* by Rod Serling from *The Monsters Are Due on Maple Street.* Copyright © 1960 by Rod Serling; Copyright © 1988 by Carolyn Serling, Jodi Serling, and Anne Serling. Used by permission. CAUTION: Professionals and amateurs are hereby warned that *The Monsters Are Due on Maple Street,* being fully protected under the copyright laws of the United States of America, the British Commonwealth countries, including Canada, and the other countries of the Copyright Union, is subject to royalty. All rights, including professional, amateur, motion picture, recitation, lecturing, public reading, radio, television and cable broadcasting, and the rights of translation into foreign languages, are strictly reserved. All inquiries should be addressed to Code Entertainment.

Don Congdon Associates, Inc. "All Summer In A Day" by Ray Bradbury, published in *The Magazine of Fantasy and Science Fiction, March 1954.* Copyright © 1954, copyright © renewed 1982 by Ray Bradbury. From *No Gumption* by Russell Baker. Copyright © 1982 by Russell Baker. Used by permission of Don Congdon Associates, Inc.

The Emma Courlander Trust "All Stories Are Anansi's" from *The Hat-Shaking Dance And Other Ashanti Tales From Ghana* by Harold Courlander with Albert Kofi Prempeh Copyright © 1957, 1985 by Harold Courlander. Used by permission of The Emma Courlander Trust.

Crystal Springs Uplands School Crystal Springs Uplands School Theatre Contract from *http://www.csus.com/pageprint.cfm?p=1212.* Copyright © Crystal Springs Uplands School. Used by permission of the Crystal Springs Uplands School and John Hauer, Theater Manager and Production & Design Teacher.

Dell Publishing, a division of Random House, Inc. "The Luckiest Time of All" from *The Lucky Stone* by Lucille Clifton. Copyright © 1979 by Lucille Clifton. Used by permission of Dell Publishing, a division of Random House, Inc.

Dial Books for Young Readers, a division of Penguin Young Readers Group "The Three Century Woman" copyright © 1999 by Richard Peck, from *Past Present, Perfect Tense* by Richard Peck. Used by permission of Dial Books for Young Readers, a division of Penguin Young Readers Group, a member of Penguin Group (USA) Inc., 345 Hudson Street, New York, NY 10014. All rights reserved.

Gregory Djanikian "How I Learned English" by Gregory Djanikian from *Falling Deeply Into America,* Carnegie Mellon University, Copyright © 1989. Used by permission of the author.

Dramatists Play Service Inc. "Sorry, Wrong Number" by Lucille Fletcher. Copyright © renewed 1976, Lucille Fletcher. All rights reserved.

Dutton Children's Books From "The Tale of Mandarin Ducks" by Katherine Paterson, copyright © 1990 by Katherine Paterson, text. Used by permission of Dutton Children's Books, A Division of Penguin Young Readers Group, A Member of Penguin Group (USA) Inc. All rights reserved.

Gulf Publishing Look for the Differences (park sign) from *A Field Guide To Snakes Of California* by Philip R. Brown. Copyright © 1997.

Farrar, Straus & Giroux, LLC "Seal" from *Laughing Time: Collected Nonsense* by William Jay Smith. Copyright © 1990 by William Jay Smith. "Train Tune" from *The Blue Estuaries* by Louise Bogan. Copyright © 1968 by Louise Bogan. Copyright renewed © 1996 by Ruth Limmer. Used by permission of Farrar, Straus & Giroux, Inc.

Joanna Farrell for the Estate of Juliet Piggott Wood "Popocatepetl and Ixtlaccihuatl" by Juliet Piggott from *Mexican Folktales.* Used by permission of Mrs. J.S.E. Farrell.

Food Security Learning Center Food Security Learning Center from *www.worldhungeryear.org.* Copyright © 2007. All rights reserved. Used by permission.

Freakonomics LLC "Herd Mentality? The Freakonomics of Boarding a Bus" by Stephen J. Dubner. Copyright © 2007. Freakonomics LLC.

Estate of Mona Gardner "The Dinner Party" by Mona Gardner from *McDougal, Littell.* Copyright © 1942, 1970. Reprinted by permission.

Georgia Department of Transportation "Safe Routes to School: It's Happening in Metro Atlanta" from *http://www.atlantabike.org/srtsfrontpage.html.* Copyright © 2007. Used by permission of Georgia Department of Transportation, Atlanta Bicycle Campaign, and the Federal Highway Administration.

Golden Books, an imprint of Random House Children's Book "The Bride of Pluto"(retitled "Demeter and Persephone") from *The Golden Treasury of Myths and Legends* by Anne Terry White, illustrated by Alice and Martin Provensen, copyright © 1959, renewed copyright © 1987 by Random House, Inc. Used by permission of Golden Books, an imprint of Random House Children's Books, a division of Random House, Inc.

June Hall Literary Agency c/o PFD "One" from *When I Dance* by James Berry (Copyright © James Berry 1990) is reproduced by permission of PFD (www.pfd.co.uk) on behalf of James Berry.

Harcourt, Inc. Excerpt from "Seventh Grade" in *Baseball in April and Other Stories,* copyright © 1990 by Gary Soto. "Fog" from *Chicago Poems* by Carl Sandburg, copyright © 1916 by Holt, Rinehart and Winston and renewed copyright © 1944 by Carl Sandburg. This material may not be reproduced in any form or by any means without the prior written permission of the publisher. Used by permission of Harcourt, Inc.

Harcourt Education Limited "Tenochtitlan: Inside the Aztec Capital" from *The Aztecs: Worlds Of The Past* by Jacqueline Dineen. Used by permission of Harcourt Education.

HarperCollins Publishers, Inc. "Sarah Cynthia Sylvia Stout Would Not Take the Garbage Out" from *Where the Sidewalk Ends* by Shel Silverstein. Copyright © 2004 by Evil Eye Music, Inc. Used with permission from the Estate of Shel Silverstein and HarperCollins Children's Books. From *An American Childhood.* Copyright © 1987 by Annie Dillard. "How the Snake Got Poison" from *Mules and Men* by Zora Neale Hurston. Copyright © 1935 by Zora Neale Hurston. Copyright renewed © 1963 by John C. Hurston and Joel Hurston. Used by permission of HarperCollins Publishers.

HarperTrophy, an Imprint of HarperCollins Publishers Inc. From *Dragonwings* by Laurence Yep. Copyright © 1975 by Laurence Yep. Used by permission of HarperCollins Publishers.

Harvard University Press "I'm Nobody (#288)" by Emily Dickinson. Used by permission of the publishers and the Trustees of Amherst College from *The Poems Of Emily Dickinson,*

Thomas H. Johnson, ed., Cambridge, Mass.: The Belknap Press of Harvard University Press, Copyright © 1951, 1955, 1979, 1983 by the President and Fellows of Harvard College.

Helmut Hirnschall "I am a Native of North America" by Chief Dan George from *My Heart Soars*. Copyright © 1974 by Clarke Irwin. Used by permission.

Edward D. Hoch "Zoo" by Edward D. Hoch, copyright © 1958 by King Size Publications, Inc.; © renewed 1991 by Edward D. Hoch. Used by permission of the author.

The Barbara Hogenson Agency, Inc. "The Night the Bed Fell" from *My Life and Hard Times* by James Thurber. Copyright © 1933, 1961 by James Thurber. Used by arrangement with Rosemary Thurber and The Barbara Hogensen Agency, Inc. All rights reserved.

Holiday House, Inc. Copyright © 2006 by Russell Freedman From *Freedom Walkers: The Story of the Montgomery Bus Boycott*. All rights reserved. Used by permission of Holiday House, Inc.

Meghan Holohan "What Gives the Sunrise and Sunset Its Orange Glow" by Meghan Holohan from *www.gantdaily.com*. Used by permission of the author.

Henry Holt and Company, Inc. Excerpt from "My Dear Cousin Tovah" from *Letters From Rifka* by Karen Hesse. Copyright © 1992 by Karen Hesse. "Stopping by Woods on a Snowy Evening" from *The Poetry Of Robert Frost* edited by Edward Connery Lathem. Copyright © 1923, 1969 by Henry Holt and Company, copyright 1951 by Robert Frost. Used by permission of Henry Holt and Company, LLC. All rights reserved.

Houghton Mifflin Harcourt "Prayers of Steel" from *The Complete Poems of Carl Sandburg,* Revised and Expanded Edition, copyright © 1970, 1969 by Lilian Steichen Sandburg, Trustee, reprinted by permission of Houghton Mifflin Harcourt Publishing Company. The material may not be reproduced in any form or by any means without the prior written permission of the publisher.

Hyperion Books for Children "The Voyage" (including the Prologue) from *Tales From The Odyssey - Book Four: The Gray-Eyed Goddess* by Mary Pope Osborne. Copyright © 2003 by Mary Pope Osborne. Used by permission of Hyperion Books for Children. All rights reserved.

Information Please® "Fall of the Hindenburg" *www.infoplease.com*. Information Please® Database, Copyright © Pearson Education, Inc. All rights reserved. Used by permission.

Jacksonville Zoo and Gardens "Jacksonville Zoo & Gardens Leading the Charge in Northeast Florida to Save the Frogs!" from *http://www.jaxzoo.org/about/amphibianconservationpr.asp*. All content copyright © 2008 Jacksonville Zoo and Gardens. Special appreciation to Jacksonville Zoo & Gardens, Jacksonville, FL, for information on the frog crisis.

Japan Publications, Inc. "On sweet plum blossoms," "Has spring come indeed?" and "Temple bells die out" by Bashō from *One Hundred Famous Haiku* by Daniel C. Buchanan. Copyright © 1973. Used by permission of Japan Publications, Inc.

Stanleigh Jones "He-y, Come on O-ut!" by Shinichi Hoshi translated by Stanleigh Jones from *The Best Japanese Science Fiction Stories*. Reprinted with the permission of Stanleigh Jones.

The Estate of Barbara Jordan "All Together Now" by Barbara Jordan from *Sesame Street Parents*. Used by permission of Hilgers Bell & Richards Attorneys at Law for the Estate of Barbara Jordan.

The Kansas City Star "The Wrong Orbit: Senator Has No Legitimate Business Blasting Into Space" *Kansas City Star* Editorial from *The Kansas City Star, 1/20/98*. Used with permission of *The Kansas City Star* © Copyright 2007 *The Kansas City Star*. All rights reserved. Format differs from original publication. Not an endorsement.

Kinseido Publishing Co., Ltd. "Conversational Ballgames" by Nancy M. Sakamoto from *Polite Fictions: Why Japanese And Americans Seem Rude To Each Other*. Used by permission.

Alfred A. Knopf, Inc. "Mother to Son" from *The Collected Poems of Langston Hughes* by Langston Hughes, edited by Arnold Rampersad with David Roessel, Associate Editor. Copyright © 1994 by The Estate of Langston Hughes. Used by permission of Alfred A. Knopf, a division of Random House, Inc.

Alfred A. Knopf Children's Books "The People Could Fly" from *The People Could Fly: American Black Folktales* by Virginia Hamilton, copyright © 1985 by Virginia Hamilton, illustrations copyright © 1985 by Leo and Diane Dillon. Used by permission of Alfred A. Knopf, an imprint of Random House Children's Books, a division of Random House, Inc.

Barbara S. Kouts Literary Agency "The Bear Boy" by Joseph Bruchac from *Flying with the Eagle, Racing the Great Bear*. Copyright © 1993 by Joseph Bruchac. Used with permission.

Samantha Larson "Everest 2007" by Samantha Larson from *www.samanthalarson.blogspot.com*. Copyright © 2006 SamanthaLarson.com. Used by permission.

Little, Brown and Company, Inc. "The Real Story of a Cowboy's Life" (The Grandest Enterprise Under God 1865–1874) from *The West: An Illustrated History* by Geoffrey Ward. Little Brown and Company. Copyright © 1996 by The West Book Project, Inc. Used by permission.

Gina Maccoby Literary Agency "mk" from *Open Your Eyes* by Jean Fritz. Copyright © 2003 by Jean Fritz. Used by permission of The Gina Maccoby Literary Agency.

Naomi Long Madgett "Life" by Naomi Long Madgett from *One and the Many,* copyright © 1956; *Remembrances of Spring: Collected Early Poems,* copyright © 1993. Used by permission of the author.

Dennis Martin Chart: "Maslow's Theory of Motivation and Human Needs" by Abraham Maslow. Reprinted by permission of Dennis C. Martin, Retired Los Angeles County Public Reference Librarian and Idea Curator Webmaster and Creator of the Alphabetical Brain Vocabulary at: *www.self-lib.com*

Meriwether Publishing Ltd. "My Head is Full of Starshine" from *Acting Natural* by Peg Kehret, copyright © 1991 Meriwether Publishing Ltd. Used by permission.

Eve Merriam c/o Marian Reiner "Onomatopoeia" from *It Doesn't Always Have To Rhyme* by Eve Merriam. Copyright © 1964, 1992 Eve Merriam. Used by permission of Marian Reiner Literary Agency.

Edna St. Vincent Millay Society "The Courage That My Mother Had" by Edna St. Vincent Millay, from *Collected Poems,*

Credits

Staff Credits

Dori Amtmann, Tricia Battipede, Rachel Beckman, Nancy Bolsover, Laura Brancky, Odette Calderon, Pam Carey, Kelly Casanova, Geoff Cassar, Jessica Cohn, Kyle Cooper, Sarah Cunningham, Anthony DeSacia, Kim Doster, Irene Ehrmann, Andy Ekedahl, Sandy Engleman, Samantha Fahy, Janet Fauser, Amy Fleming, Pam Gallo, Mark Gangi, Nicole Gee, Susan Graef, Leslie Griffin, Elaine Goldman, Brian Hawkes, Steve Hernacki, Martha Heller, Amanda House, Rick Hickox, Patricia Isaza, Etta Jacobs, Blair Jones, Jim Kelly, Nathan Kinney, Sarah Kraus, Gregory Lynch, Nancy Mace, Jim McPherson, Charles Morris, Pa Moua, Elizabeth Nielsen, Kim Ortell, Kathleen Pagliaro, Jennie Rakos, Sheila Ramsay, Karen Randazzo, Julianne Regnier, Christopher Richardson, Melissa Schreiner, Hillary Schwei, Jeff Shagawat, Susan Sheehan, Charlene Smith, DeAnn Smith, Sheila Smith, Cynthia Summers, Morgan Taylor, Brian Thomas, Lucia Tirondola, Karen Tully, Merle Uuesoo, Kristen Varina, Jackie Westbrook, Jessica White

W9-BXG-581

CANADA

Lake Superior

Duluth

MINNESOTA

Minneapolis ★ St. Paul

WISCONSIN

Madison
★ Milwaukee

MICHIGAN

Lake Michigan

Lake Huron

Grand
Rapids

Flint
Detroit
Lansing

Sioux City

IOWA

Cedar
Rapids

Des Moines
Iowa City

Omaha

CENTRAL LOWLAND

Chicago

Peoria

ILLINOIS

★ Springfield

INDIANA

Muncie

Indianapolis

Wabash R.

Toledo

Cleveland

OHIO

Columbus

Wheeling

Cincinnati

Lake Erie

Lake Ontario

Buffalo

Rochester

NEW YORK

Albany

Hartford

VERMONT

Montpelier ★

Concord

Manchester

Springfield

MAINE

Augusta

Portland

NEW HAMPSHIRE

Boston

MASSACHUSETTS

★ Providence

RHODE ISLAND

CONNECTICUT

Newark

PENNSYLVANIA

Harrisburg ★

Pittsburgh

New York City

Trenton

NEW JERSEY

Philadelphia

St. Lawrence R.

Kansas
City

Jefferson City ★

MISSOURI

St. Louis

Louisville

Frankfort
Lexington

KENTUCKY

Bowling Green

Topeka

Missouri R.

OZARK

PLATEAU

Tulsa

ARKANSAS

Little Rock

Memphis

Ohio R.

WEST
VIRGINIA

Charleston

Baltimore

Annapolis

Washington, D.C. ⊛

MARYLAND

Dover

DELAWARE

Richmond ★

VIRGINIA

Norfolk

APPALACHIAN MTS.

Knoxville

★ Nashville

TENNESSEE

Chattanooga

Winston-
Salem

★ Raleigh

NORTH CAROLINA

Charlotte

Columbia

SOUTH CAROLINA

ATLANTIC
OCEAN

Shreveport

LOUISIANA

Lake
Charles

Baton Rouge ★

New Orleans

Houston

Birmingham

ALABAMA

★ Montgomery

MISSISSIPPI

★ Jackson

Mobile

Pensacola

Macon

GEORGIA

★ Atlanta

Charleston

Savannah

ATLANTIC COASTAL PLAIN

★ Tallahassee

Jacksonville

Orlando

Tampa

St. Petersburg

FLORIDA

Miami

Key West

GULF OF MEXICO

Elevation

Feet		Meters
10,000		3,050
5,000		1,525
2,000		610
1,000		305
500		153
Sea level		Sea level
Below sea level		Below sea level

⊛ National capital

★ State capital

• Other city

0   100   200   300   400   500 miles

0   200   400   600   800 kilometers

A PEOPLE AND A NATION

A People and a Nation

A History of the United States

SIXTH EDITION

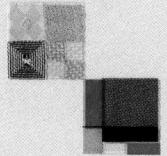

Mary Beth Norton
Cornell University

David M. Katzman
University of Kansas

David W. Blight
Amherst College

Howard P. Chudacoff
Brown University

Thomas G. Paterson
University of Connecticut

William M. Tuttle, Jr.
University of Kansas

Paul D. Escott
Wake Forest University

Houghton Mifflin Company   Boston   New York

The icons used throughout Chapters 1–16 are details from "Sampler Block Quilt" by Evelyn Derr. National Museum of American Art, Smithsonian Institution, Washington, D.C./Art Resource, N.Y.

Sponsoring Editor: Colleen S. Kyle
Development Editor: Ann Hofstra Grogg
Editorial Assistant: Michael Kerns
Senior Project Editor: Christina M. Horn
Senior Production/Design Coordinator: Carol Merrigan
Senior Designer: Henry Rachlin
Senior Manufacturing Coordinator: Sally Culler
Senior Marketing Manager: Sandra McGuire

Picture research by Pembroke Herbert and Sandi Rygiel, Picture Research Consultants & Archives.

Cover design: Diana Coe / ko Design Studio
Cover image: *Near Andersonville*, 1865–1866, by Winslow Homer. Oil on canvas. The Newark Museum, Newark, N.J./Art Resource, N.Y.

Text credits:

Pages 787–788: Adapted from *The Greatest Generation*, by Tom Brokaw. Copyright © 1998 by Tom Brokaw. Used by permission of Random House, Inc.

Page 798: Robert Thomas, "Self-Analysis," from *Senior Scholastic*, October 6, 1947. Copyright © 1947 by Scholastic, Inc. Reprinted by permission of Scholastic, Inc.

Printed in the U.S.A.

Library of Congress Catalog Card Number: 00-103884

ISBN: 0-618-00550-1

1 2 3 4 5 6 7 8 9-VH-04 03 02 01 00

Brief Contents

CONTENTS

MAPS

CHARTS

PREFACE

"What? Another edition?" asked one of our friends. "History hasn't changed that much in the last few years!" Wrong. "History" *has* changed, in several ways. More of "history's" story has been told in new books and articles and revealed in newly released documents. Our interpretation of "history" has changed because new perspectives on familiar topics have continued to emerge from the prolific writings of historians, anthropologists, and other scholars. And, last, our understanding of "history" has changed as our engagement with current events reshapes how we remember the past.

Like other teachers and students, we are always recreating our past, restructuring our memory, rediscovering the personalities and events that have influenced us, inspired us, and bedeviled us. This book represents our rediscovery of America's history—its diverse people and the nation they created and have nurtured. As this book demonstrates, there are many different Americans and many different memories. We have sought to present all of them, in both triumph and tragedy, in both division and unity.

Although much is new in this Sixth Edition in coverage, interpretation, and organization, we have sustained the qualities that have marked *A People and a Nation* from the beginning: our approach of telling the story of all the people; our study of the interaction of the private sphere of everyday life with the public sphere of politics and government; our integration of political and social history; our spirited narrative based on diaries, letters, oral histories, and other sources; and our effort to challenge readers to think about the meaning of American history, not just to memorize facts. Students and instructors have commented on how enjoyable the book is to read. Scholars have commended the book for its up-to-date scholarship.

About *A People and a Nation*

Readers have also told us that we have demonstrated, in section after section and in the "How Do Historians Know?" feature, how the historian's mind works asking questions and teasing conclusions out of vast and often conflicting evidence. Each chapter's highlighted "How Do Historians Know?" explains how historians go about using sources—such as artifacts, cartoons, census data, medical records, and popular art—to arrive at conclusions. This feature also helps students understand how scholars can claim knowledge about historical events and trends. Chapter-opening vignettes, dramatically recounting stories of people contending with their times, continue to define the key questions of each chapter. Succinct introductions and summaries still frame each chapter. As before, myriad illustrations, maps, tables, and graphs tied closely to the text encourage visual and statistical explorations. Readability, scholarship, critical thinking, clear structure, instructive illustrative material—these strengths have been sustained in this edition.

What's New in This Edition

Guided by Houghton Mifflin's excellent editorial and design staffs, by instructors' thorough reviews, by the authors' ongoing research, and by our frank and friendly planning sessions and critical reading of one another's chapters, we worked to improve every aspect of the book. We added a distinguished new author, David W. Blight, whose expertise on the antebellum period, slavery, the Civil War, and historical memory has strengthened these topics in the book. To reflect new scholarship and to satisfy instructors' needs for improved chronological flow, we substantially reorganized the chapters that cover the antebellum and post-1945 periods. We have expanded our treatment of slavery, women, religion in America's social and political life, race theory and the social construction of racial identity, the West, the South's relationship to the nation, cultural expansion as a dimension of foreign relations, and the globalization of the U.S. economy. Throughout the book, we reexamined every sentence, interpretation, map, chart, illustration, and caption, refining the narrative, presenting new examples, and rethinking and labeling the Summary section for each chapter. More than half of the chapter-opening vignettes are new to this edition, as are more than one-third of the "How Do Historians Know?" entries. The "Important Events" tables have been trimmed for easier reference. The "Suggestions for Further Reading" have been revised to include new literature and conveniently consolidated at the end of the book.

Eager to help students link the past to the present, to identify the origins of issues of current interest, we have introduced in each chapter a new feature: "Legacy for a People and a Nation." Appearing after each chapter's Summary, the Legacy feature spotlights a specific contemporary topic; examples include Columbus Day, women's education, Bible Belt, revolutionary violence, Fourteenth Amendment, ethnic food, intercollegiate athletics, Peace Corps, atomic waste, and the Internet. After exploring the subject's beginnings, a few tightly focused paragraphs trace its important history to the present, inviting students to think about the historical roots of their world today and to understand the complexity of issues that on the surface seem so simple. For students who ask what history has to do with the immediate events and trends that swirl around them—or who wonder why we study history at all—these timely legacies provide telling answers.

New "Legacy for a People and a Nation"

As in previous editions, several themes and questions stand out in our concerted effort to incorporate the most recent scholarship that integrates political, social, and cultural history. We study the many ways Americans have defined themselves—gender, race, class, region, ethnicity, religion, sexual orientation—and the many subjects that have reflected their multidimensional experiences: social, political, economic, diplomatic, military, environmental, intellectual, cultural, technological, and more. We highlight the remarkably diverse everyday life of the American people—in cities and on farms and ranches, in factories and in corporate headquarters, in neighborhood meetings and in powerful political chambers, in love relationships and in hate groups, in recreation and in work, in the classroom and in military uniform, in secret national security conferences and in public foreign relations debates, in church and in prison, in polluted environments and in conservation areas. We pay particular attention to lifestyles, diet and dress, family life and structure, labor conditions, gender roles, and childbearing and child rearing. We explore how Americans have entertained and informed themselves by discussing their music, sports, theater, print media, film, radio, television, graphic arts, and literature, in both "high" culture and "low" culture. We study how technology has influenced Americans' lives, such as through the internal combustion engine and the computer.

Themes in This Book

The private sphere of everyday life always interacts with the public sphere of politics and government. To understand how Americans have sought to protect their different ways of life and to work out solutions to thorny problems, we emphasize their expectations of governments at the local, state, and federal levels; governments' role in providing answers; the lobbying of interest groups; the campaigns and outcomes of elections; and the hierarchy of power in any period. Because the United States has long been a major participant in world affairs, we explore America's descent into wars, interventions in other nations, empire-building, immigration patterns, images of foreign peoples, cross-national cultural ties, and international economic trends.

Mary Beth Norton, who had primary responsibility for Chapters 1–8, expanded and revised her coverage of the peopling of the Americas and early settlements, the Salem witchcraft crisis, and masculinity and public rituals in the colonial period. She reorganized Chapter 3 to highlight new scholarship identifying the 1670s as a crucial turning point in the relationships of Europeans and Indians in several regions of North America, and to emphasize the key role of the slave trade in the economy of all the colonies. In Chapter 4, she added a discussion of regional differences in African American family life. Chapters 3, 4, and 8, moreover, all incorporate recent scholarship on the complex relationship between the development of the slave system and the creation of racial categories.

Section-by-Section Changes in This Edition

David M. Katzman, who had primary responsibility for Chapters 9–12, substantially reorganized the early-nineteenth-century chapters. Chapters 9–11 now have a more focused chronological narrative, integrating political events with related social, economic, and cultural developments. The antebellum chapters give added emphasis to regional interconnections in the emerging market economy, Indian–white relations and Native American adaptations to the market economy, demographic changes, internal migration, popular culture, and the formation of racial ideas. Katzman also gives new attention to the Barbary captives, the Lewis and Clark expedition, early Texas settlement, and population movements. He also explores anew immigration, ethnicity and race, frontier communities in the West, and the links between reform politics and religion.

David W. Blight, who had primary responsibility for Chapters 13–16, brought fresh perspectives to the antebellum South and its relation to the nation's cultural life and market revolution. He added new material on slave culture and resistance, slavery's intersection with westward expansion, the War with Mexico, and the Underground Railroad. In his discussion of the South, he increased coverage of free blacks and social reform movements. In the Civil War and Reconstruction chapters, Blight has revised the history of military battles, women and nursing, emancipation, wartime reconstruction, the meanings of freedom for former slaves, and the Fourteenth Amendment. He has introduced the problem of memory—especially Americans' difficulty in confronting the Reconstruction period of their history. Replacing Paul D. Escott, who brought distinction to *A People and a Nation* for five editions and whose fine writing and scholarship remain evident throughout, Blight has worked with co-author Katzman to reorganize all the antebellum period chapters.

Howard P. Chudacoff, who had primary responsibility for Chapters 17–21 and 24, reconfigured material throughout these chapters. Chapter 17 now focuses solely on the West, with additions on Indian economic and cultural life, women in frontier communities, mining, irrigation, and transportation. In his other chapters, he has increased the coverage of southern industrialization, immigrants and migrants in southern cities, and southern Progressivism. He also presents new discussion of the characteristics of the industrial revolution, race and ethnicity in urban borderlands, Mexican American farmers, religion and science, technology, the clash between modernism and fundamentalism, women's political activities, and the causes of the Great Depression.

Thomas G. Paterson, who had primary responsibility for Chapters 22–23, 26, 29, and 31, and shared responsibility for 33, and who served as the book's co-ordinating author, offers new material throughout on cultural expansion and on the influence of ideology and images of foreign peoples on foreign policy decisions. He has augmented coverage of religious missionaries, Anglo-American cooperation, and navalism. Labor issues, Indian soldiers, weapons technology, and gas warfare receive new treatment for World War I. As part of the restructuring of the post-1945 chapters, Chapters 29 and 31 are newly designed to parallel chapters on domestic history. Paterson reexamines the Korean War, U.S. Information Agency activities, and popular fears of nuclear war. For the Vietnam War, he has revisited presidential leadership, the war's impact on domestic reform, and military experiences. The last

chapter newly explores environmental diplomacy, the globalization of U.S. culture, intrastate wars, and humanitarian intervention.

William M. Tuttle, Jr., had primary responsibility for Chapters 25, 27–28, 30, and 32, and shared responsibility for 33. In Chapter 25, he expanded treatment of New Deal cultural programs, unionism, and the question of "whiteness." For World War II, he added new material on the cultural history of the home front, the wartime economy, technological research, and homosexuals in the armed forces. In his post-1945 chapters, Tuttle has revised his coverage of McCarthyism, race relations, the New Left and counterculture, Indian protest, immigration legislation, the Reagan presidency, AIDS, and the anti-abortion movement. In the last chapter, Tuttle has expanded his discussion of political violence and public dissatisfaction with government, and he has included new material on school shootings and the presidential impeachment crisis.

The multidimensional Appendix, prepared by Thomas G. Paterson, has been brought up to date. Once again, the Appendix includes a guide to reference works on key subjects in American history. Students may wish to use this updated and enlarged list of encyclopedias, atlases, chronologies, and other books, for example, when they start to explore topics for research papers, when they seek precise definitions or dates, when they need biographical profiles, or when they chart territorial or demographic changes. The tables of statistics on key features of the American people and nation also have been updated, as have the tables on the states (and the District of Columbia and Puerto Rico), presidential elections, presidents and vice presidents, party strength in Congress, and the justices of the Supreme Court. Other information, including the Articles of Confederation and a complete table of the cabinets by administration, is available on the *A People and a Nation* web site.

A People and a Nation continues to be supported by an extensive supplements package. For this edition, many more resources will be available to students and instructors online and on CD-ROM. We have also revised and updated all elements of our existing package.

Study and Teaching Aids

A new version of *@history*, Houghton Mifflin's CD-ROM featuring nearly one thousand primary source materials, including video, audio, visual, and textual resources, has been keyed to the organization of the Sixth Edition of *A People and a Nation*. Available in both instructor's and student's versions, *@history* is an interactive multimedia tool that can improve the analytical skills of students and introduce them to historical sources.

American History GeoQuest is a CD-ROM designed to improve students' geographical literacy. The program consists of thirty interactive historical maps, each of which provides background information and a series of self-correcting quizzes so that students can master the information on their own.

The *A People and a Nation* web site has been redesigned, updated, and augmented for users of the Sixth Edition. An *Instructor's Web Site* includes the *Online Instructor's Resource Manual* (see below), downloadable PowerPoint lecture outline slides, interactive Legacy activities, online primary sources with teaching instructions, and annotated links to other sites. The *Student's Web Site* includes ACE reading self-quizzes; online primary sources, including text, photo, and audio resources; an annotated guide of the top historical research Web sites; and interactive Legacy activities.

The *Study Guide*, prepared by George Warren of Central Piedmont Community College, includes an introductory chapter on studying history that focuses on interpreting historical facts, test-taking hints, and critical analysis. The guide also includes learning objectives, a thematic guide, lists of terms, multiple choice and essay questions with answer keys, and map exercises.

A new *Online Instructor's Resource Manual*, also created by George Warren, will now be downloadable from Houghton Mifflin's web site. For each chapter, the manual includes a content overview, a brief list of learning objectives, a comprehensive chapter outline, ideas for classroom activities, discussion questions, and ideas for paper topics.

A *Test Bank*, also prepared by George Warren, provides approximately 1,700 new multiple choice questions, more than 1,000 identification questions, and approximately 500 essay questions. This content is also available in a *Computerized Test Bank* for both Windows and Macintosh platforms.

A set of *American History Map Transparencies* is also available to instructors upon adoption.

At each stage of this revision, a sizable panel of historian reviewers read drafts of our chapters. Their suggestions, corrections, and pleas helped guide us through this momentous revision. We could not include all of their recommendations, but the book is better for our having heeded most of their advice. We heartily thank

Acknowledgments

Patrick Allitt, *Emory University*

Cara Anzilotti, *Loyola Marymount University*

Felix Armfield, *Western Illinois University*

Robert Becker, *Louisiana State University*

Jules Benjamin, *Ithaca College*

Roger Bromert, *Southwestern Oklahoma State University*

Jonathan Chu, *University of Massachusetts at Boston*

Nathaniel Comfort, *George Washington University*

Mary DeCredico, *U.S. Naval Academy*

Judy DeMark, *Northern Michigan University*

Jonathan Earle, *University of Kansas*

Alice Fahs, *University of California, Irvine*

Neil Foley, *University of Texas*

Colin Gordon, *University of Iowa*

Robert Gough, *University of Wisconsin at Eau Claire*

Brian Greenberg, *Monmouth University*

Harland Hagler, *University of North Texas*

Elizabeth Haiken, *University of British Columbia*

Benjamin Harrison, *University of Louisville*

Elizabeth Cobbs Hoffman, *San Diego State University*

Marianne Holdzkom, *Ohio State University*

John Inscoe, *University of Georgia*

Frank Lambert, *Purdue University*

David Rich Lewis, *Utah State University*

Nancy Mitchell, *North Carolina State University*

Patricia Moore, *University of Utah*

John Neff, *University of Mississippi*

James Reed, *Rutgers University*

Joseph Rowe, *Sam Houston State University*

Sharon Salinger, *University of California, Riverside*

Richard Stott, *George Washington University*

Daniel B. Thorp, *Virginia Polytechnic Institute and State University*

Marilyn Westerkamp, *University of California, Santa Cruz*

John Wigger, *University of Missouri, Columbia*

John Scott Wilson, *University of South Carolina*

The authors once again thank the extraordinary Houghton Mifflin people who designed, edited, produced, and nourished this book. Their high standards and acute attention to both general structure and fine detail are cherished in the publishing industry. Many thanks, then, to Colleen Shanley Kyle, sponsoring editor; Ann Hofstra Grogg, freelance development editor; Christina Horn, senior project editor; Jean Woy, editor-in-chief; Sandra McGuire, senior marketing manager; Pembroke Herbert, photo researcher; Charlotte Miller, art editor; and Michael Kerns, editorial assistant.

The authors also extend their thanks to the following for helping us: Sandra Greene, Karin Beckett, Nancy Board, Frank Couvares, Jan D. Emerson, Alice Fahs, Jeffrey Ferguson, Irwin Hyatt, Steven Jacobson, Andrea Katzman, Eric Katzman, Henry W. Katzman, Julie Stephens Katzman, Sharyn Katzman, Ariela Katzman-Jacobson, Elizabeth Mahan, Terri Rockhold, Martha Sandweiss, Martha Saxton, Barry Shank, John David Smith, Kathryn Nemeth Tuttle, and Samuel Watkins Tuttle.

We welcome comments from instructors and students about this new edition of *A People and a Nation*, which can be communicated through its accompanying web site, found at **http://college.hmco.com.**

For the authors, THOMAS G. PATERSON

THE AUTHORS

Mary Beth Norton

Born in Ann Arbor, Michigan, Mary Beth Norton received her B.A. from the University of Michigan (1964) and her Ph.D. from Harvard University (1969). She is now Mary Donlon Alger Professor of American History at Cornell University. Her dissertation won the Allan Nevins Prize. She has written *The British-Americans* (1972), *Liberty's Daughters* (1980), and *Founding Mothers and Fathers* (1996), which was one of three finalists for the Pulitzer Prize in 1997. She has coedited *To Toil the Livelong Day* (1987), *Women of America* (1979), and *Major Problems in American Women's History* (1995). Her articles have appeared in such journals as the *William and Mary Quarterly, Signs,* and the *American Historical Review.* Mary Beth has served on the National Council on the Humanities, as president of the Berkshire Conference of Women Historians, as vice president for research of the American Historical Association, and as general editor of the *AHA Guide to Historical Literature* (1995). In 1999 she was elected a fellow of the American Academy of Arts and Sciences. The National Endowment for the Humanities, Guggenheim Foundation, and Rockefeller Foundation have assisted her scholarship.

David M. Katzman

Born in New York City and a graduate of Queens College (B.A., 1963) and the University of Michigan (Ph.D., 1969), David M. Katzman is professor of American studies and courtesy professor of history and African American studies at the University of Kansas. He has written *Before the Ghetto* (1973) and *Seven Days a Week* (1978), which won the Philip Taft Labor History Prize. He has coedited *Plain Folk* (1982) and *Technical Knowledge in American Culture* (1996). He has also coauthored *Three Generations in Twentieth-Century America* (1982). David has been a visiting professor at University College, Dublin, Ireland, the University of Birmingham, England, Hong Kong University, and the University of Tokushima, Japan. He has also directed National Endowment for the Humanities Summer Seminars for College Teachers. He has sat on the Board of Directors of the National Commission on Social Studies and is coeditor of *American Studies*. At the University of Kansas, he is a former director of the College Honors Program. The Guggenheim Foundation, National Endowment for the Humanities, Ford Foundation, and Rockefeller Foundation have supported his research.

David W. Blight

Born in Flint, Michigan, David W. Blight received his B.A. from Michigan State University (1971) and his Ph.D. from the University of Wisconsin (1985). He is now Class of 1959 Professor of History and Black Studies at Amherst College. For the first seven years of his career, David was a public high school teacher in Flint. He has written *Frederick Douglass's Civil War* (1989) and *Race and Reunion: The Civil War in American Memory, 1863–1915* (2000). His edited works include *When This Cruel War Is Over: The Civil War Letters of Charles Harvey Brewster* (1992), *Narrative of the Life of Frederick Douglass* (1993), W. E. B. Du Bois, *The Souls of Black Folk* (with Robert Gooding Williams, 1997), *Union and Emancipation* (with Brooks Simpson, 1997), and *Caleb Bingham, The Columbian Orator* (1997). David's essays have appeared in the *Journal of American History, Civil War History,* and Gabor Boritt, ed., *Why the Civil War Came* (1996), among others. In 1992–1993 he was senior Fulbright Professor in American Studies at the University of Munich, Germany. A consultant to several documentary films, David appeared in the 1998 PBS series, *Africans in America.* In 1999 he was elected to the Council of the American Historical Association. David also teaches summer seminars for secondary school teachers, as well as for park rangers and historians of the National Park Service.

Howard P. Chudacoff

A University Professor and professor of history at Brown University, Howard P. Chudacoff was born in Omaha, Nebraska. He earned his A.B. (1965) and Ph.D. (1969) from the University of Chicago. He has written *Mobile Americans* (1972), *The Evolution of American Urban Society* (with Judith Smith, 1999), *How Old Are You?* (1989), and *The Age of the Bachelor* (1999). He has also edited *Major Problems in American Urban History* (1993). His articles have appeared in such journals as the *Journal of Family History*, *Reviews in American History*, and *Journal of American History*. At Brown University, Howard has cochaired the American Civilization Program, chaired the Department of History, and since 1990 has been faculty adviser to the women's basketball team. He has also served on the board of directors of the Urban History Association. The National Endowment for the Humanities, Ford Foundation, and Rockefeller Foundation have given him awards to advance his scholarship.

Thomas G. Paterson

Born in Oregon City, Oregon, and graduated from the University of New Hampshire (B.A., 1963) and the University of California, Berkeley (Ph.D., 1968), Thomas G. Paterson is professor emeritus of history at the University of Connecticut. He has written *Soviet-American Confrontation* (1973), *Meeting the Communist Threat* (1988), *On Every Front* (1992), *Contesting Castro* (1994), *American Foreign Relations* (with J. Garry Clifford and Kenneth J. Hagan, 2000), and *America Ascendant* (with Clifford, 1995). Tom has also edited *Kennedy's Quest for Victory* (1989), *Explaining the History of American Foreign Relations* (with Michael J. Hogan, 1991), and *Major Problems in American Foreign Relations* (with Dennis Merrill, 2000). With Bruce Jentleson he was senior editor for the four-volume *Encyclopedia of U.S. Foreign Relations* (1997). He has served on the ed-itorial boards of the *Journal of American History* and *Diplomatic History*. He has been president of the Society for Historians of American Foreign Relations and has directed National Endowment for the Humanities Summer Seminars for College Teachers. He has won fellowships from the Guggenheim Foundation, among others. In 2000 the New England History Teachers Association awarded him the Kidger Award for excellence in teaching and mentoring.

William M. Tuttle, Jr.

A native of Detroit, Michigan, William M. Tuttle, Jr., received his B.A. from Denison University (1959) and his Ph.D. from the University of Wisconsin (1967). A professor of history and American studies at the University of Kansas, Bill has written *Race Riot* (1996) and *"Daddy's Gone to War"* (1993). He has also edited *W. E. B. Du Bois* (1973) and coedited *Plain Folk* (1982). His articles have appeared in such journals as the *Journal of American History*, *American Studies*, and *Child Welfare*. He has been a research associate at the Institute of Human Development at the University of California, Berkeley. As a historical consultant, Bill has helped prepare several public television documentaries and docudramas, including *The Killing Floor*, which appeared on PBS's *American Playhouse*. Bill's scholarly work has been assisted by the American Council of Learned Societies, Institute of Southern History at Johns Hopkins University, Charles Warren Center, Guggenheim Foundation, Stanford Humanities Center, Radcliffe College, and National Endowment for the Humanities. In 1998 Bill was awarded the William T. Kemper Fellowship for Teaching Excellence.

A People and a Nation

Prom Lupi

Portus Regalis ſiue F. S. Helenæ.

5

As they neared the village called Cofitachequi on May 1, 1540, the band of Spanish explorers led by Hernán de Soto beheld a surprising scene. Villagers came to meet the Europeans, carrying their female chief, or *cacica*, "with much prestige on a litter covered in white (with thin linen)." The Lady of Cofitachequi, a Spanish chronicler recorded, was "young and of fine appearance." Speaking to Soto "with much grace and self-assurance," she welcomed the weary Spaniards to her domain in today's western South Carolina, giving Soto a string of pearls from her neck. Her people offered gifts of "well tanned hides and blankets, all very good, and a large amount of jerked venison and dry wafers, and much and very good salt." Later, she gave the hungry men huge quantities of corn and, seeing that they especially valued pearls, suggested they take the ones they would find in nearby burial chambers.

The Spanish explorers had landed at Tampa Bay, Florida, about a year earlier. They would wander through what is now the southeastern United States for three more years, encountering many different peoples, whom they often treated with great cruelty. Always they futilely sought the greatest riches of all— gold and silver. The people of Cofitachequi told the Spaniards they might find these treasures in another ruler's domain, about twelve days' travel away. When Soto left, he took the Lady with him as a captive. But the chronicler reported that she, "going one day with her slave women who were carrying her, stepped aside from the road and went into a wood saying that she had to attend to her necessities. Thus she deceived them and hid herself in the woods." Presumably, she then returned home.

Why had the Lady greeted Soto's force so kindly? Perhaps she did not have enough men to resist the Europeans. Her people had been devastated by an unknown "pestilence" two years earlier, the Spaniards observed, describing deserted settlements and reporting the residents' explanations. Or possibly messengers had informed the Lady about Soto's vicious

THREE OLD WORLDS CREATE A NEW 1492–1600

A 1591 print depicted what French adventurers saw in 1562 when they sailed into Port Royal River near today's Beaufort, South Carolina. From Theodor de Bry's *America,* the first book illustrating American scenes for a European audience. (John Carter Brown Library at Brown University)

treatment of villages he had previously encountered. Whatever her reasoning, the strategy worked: Soto and his men moved on, and although they destroyed other villages and peoples, Cofitachequi survived to be recorded by Spanish, French, and finally English visitors in the course of the next 130 years.

For thousands of years before 1492, human societies in the Americas had developed in isolation from the rest of the world. The era that began in the Christian fifteenth century brought that long-standing isolation to an end. As Europeans sought treasure and trade, peoples from different cultures came into regular contact for the first time. All were profoundly changed. The brief encounter of Soto and the Lady of Cofitachequi illustrated many of the elements of those contacts and changes: cruelty and kindness, greed and deception, trade and theft, surprise and sickness, captivity and enslavement. By the time Soto and his men landed in Florida in 1539, the age of European expansion and colonization was already well under way. Over the next 350 years, Europeans would spread their influence across the globe. The history of the tiny colonies that would become the United States must be seen in this broad context of European exploration and exploitation.

The continents that European sailors reached in the late fifteenth century had their own history, one the interlopers largely ignored. The residents of the Americas were the world's most skillful plant breeders; they had developed vegetable crops more nutritious and productive than those grown in Europe, Asia, or Africa. They had invented systems of writing and mathematics and created calendars as accurate as those used on the other side of the Atlantic. In the Americas, as in Europe, states rose and fell as leaders succeeded or failed in expanding their political and economic power. The arrival of Europeans immeasurably altered the Americans' struggles with one another.

After 1400, European nations not only warred on their own continent but also tried to acquire valuable colonies and trading posts elsewhere in the world. Initially interested primarily in Asia and Africa, many Europeans eventually focused their attention on the Americas. Their contests for trade and conquest changed the course of history on four continents. Even as Europeans slowly achieved dominance, their fates were shaped by the strategies of Americans and Africans, such as that of the Lady of Cofitachequi. In the Americas of the fifteenth and sixteenth centuries, three old worlds came together to produce a new. ■

American Societies

 Human beings originated on the continent of Africa, where humanlike remains about 3 million years old have been found in what is now Ethiopia. Over many millennia, the growing population slowly dispersed to the other continents. Because the climate was then far colder than it is now, much of the earth's water was concentrated in huge rivers of ice called glaciers. Sea levels were accordingly lower, and land masses covered a larger proportion of the earth's surface than they do today. Scholars have long believed that all the earliest inhabitants of the Americas crossed a land bridge known as Beringia (at the site of the Bering Strait) approximately 12,000 to 14,000 years ago. Yet striking new archaeological discoveries in both North and South America suggest that some parts of the Americas may have been settled much earlier, perhaps by seafarers crossing from northern Europe by island-hopping from Iceland to Greenland to Baffin Island, much as the Vikings did many millennia later (see Map 1.1 on page 8). When approximately 12,000 years ago the climate warmed and sea levels rose, Americans were separated from the peoples living on the connected continents of Asia, Africa, and Europe.

The first Americans are called Paleo-Indians. Nomadic hunters of game and gatherers of wild plants, they spread throughout North and **Paleo-Indians** South America, probably moving as bands composed of extended families. By about 11,500 years ago the Paleo-Indians were making fine stone projectile points, which they attached to wooden spears and used to kill and butcher bison (buffalo), woolly mammoths, and other large mammals then living in the Americas. But as the Ice Age ended and the human population increased, all the large American mammals except the bison disappeared. Scholars cannot agree whether overhunting or the change in climate caused their demise. In either case, deprived of their primary source of meat, the Paleo-Indians found new ways to survive.

By approximately 9,000 years ago, the residents of what is now central Mexico began to cultivate food crops, especially maize (corn), **Importance of** squash, beans, and peppers. In the **Agriculture** Andes Mountains of South America, people started to grow potatoes. As knowledge of agricultural techniques

IMPORTANT EVENTS

15,000–10,000 B.C.E. Paleo-Indians begin migrating from Asia to North America across the Beringia land bridge

7000 B.C.E. Cultivation of food crops begins in America

c. 1000 B.C.E. Olmec civilization appears

c. 300–600 C.E. Height of influence of Teotihuacán

c. 600–900 C.E. Classic Mayan civilization

1000 C.E. Anasazi settlements in modern states of Arizona and New Mexico flourish as trading centers

1001 Norse establish settlement in "Vinland"

1050–1250 Height of influence of Cahokia; prevalence of Mississippian culture in midwestern and southeastern United States

14th century Aztec rise to power

1450s–80s Portuguese explore and colonize islands in the Mediterranean Atlantic and São Tomé in Gulf of Guinea

1477 Publication of Marco Polo's *Travels*, describing China

1492 Columbus reaches Bahamas

1494 Treaty of Tordesillas divides land claims between Spain and Portugal in Africa, India, and South America

1496 Last Canary Island falls to Spain

1497 Cabot reaches North America

1513 León explores Florida

1518–30 Smallpox epidemic devastates Indian population of West Indies and Central and South America

1519 Cortés invades Mexico

1521 Tenochtitlán surrenders to Cortés; Aztec Empire falls to Spaniards

1524 Verrazzano sails along Atlantic coast of United States

1534–35 Cartier explores St. Lawrence River

1539–42 Soto explores southeastern United States

1540–42 Coronado explores southwestern United States

1587–90 Raleigh's Roanoke colony vanishes

1588 Harriot publishes *A Briefe and True Report of the New Found Land of Virginia*

improved and spread through the Americas, vegetables and maize proved a more reliable source of food than hunting and gathering. Except for those living in the harshest climates, most Americans started to adopt a more sedentary style of life so they could tend fields regularly. Some established permanent settlements; others moved several times a year among fixed sites. They became adept at clearing forests through the use of controlled burning. The fires not only created cultivable lands by killing trees and fertilizing the soil with ashes but also opened meadows that attracted deer and other wildlife. All the American cultures emphasized producing sufficient food to support themselves. Although they traded such items as shells, flint, salt, and copper, no society ever became dependent on another group for items vital to its survival.

Wherever agriculture dominated the economy, complex civilizations flourished. Such societies, assured of steady supplies of grains and vegetables, no longer had to devote all their energies to subsistence. Instead, they were able to accumulate wealth, produce ornamental objects, trade with other groups, and create elaborate rituals and ceremonies. In North America, the successful cultivation of nutritious crops such as maize, beans, and squash seems to have led to the growth and development of all the major civilizations: first the large city-states of Mesoamerica (modern Mexico and Guatemala), and then the urban clusters known collectively as the Mississippian culture and located in the present-day United States. Each of these societies, many historians and archaeologists now believe, reached its height of population and influence only after achieving success in agriculture. Each later declined and collapsed after reaching the limits of its food supply, with dire political and military consequences.

The earliest major Mesoamerican civilization was that of the Olmecs, who about 3,000 years ago lived near the Gulf of Mexico in large cities dominated by temple pyramids.

Mesoamerican Civilizations

More than 1,000 years later, the Mayan civilization developed on the Yucatán Peninsula, in today's eastern Mexico. The Mayas built large urban centers containing tall pyramids and temples with brightly painted stuccoed and carved façades. They studied astronomy, created the first writing system in the Americas, and developed a richly symbolic religious life in which rituals of bloodletting played a major role. By the fifth century C.E. (Common Era), or about 1,500 years ago, the kings of the Mayan city-states started to war with one another, attempting conquest on a grand scale. But no king or city could win total victory. Eventually, the constant fighting combined with an inadequate food supply to cause the collapse of the most powerful cities, ending the classic era of Mayan civilization by 900 C.E. By the time Spaniards arrived five hundred years later, only a few remnants of the once-mighty society remained intact.

Some of the more than 100,000 residents of Teotihuacán, the largest Mesoamerican metropolis, traded regularly with the Mayas. That city, founded in the Valley of Mexico about 300 B.C.E. (Before the Common Era)—some 2,300 years ago—was one of the most heavily populated urban areas in the world in the fifth century C.E. (By contrast, Paris had only about 10,000 residents at the time.) The rulers of Teotihuacán gained their position chiefly through commerce; their trading network extended hundreds of miles in all directions. Thousands of craftspeople lived in the city, many especially skilled in working the green glass called obsidian, which was valued throughout the region as a source of fine knives and mirrors. Teotihuacán also served as a religious center; pilgrims must have come long distances to visit the impressive Pyramid of the Sun, Pyramid of the Moon, and the great temple of Quetzalcoatl—the feathered serpent, the primary god of central Mexico.

Teotihuacán's influence was felt so widely in Mesoamerica before its decline in the eighth century C.E. that some scholars have argued that this Mexican city-state also influenced societies farther north, in what is now the United States. The Moundbuilders of the Ohio River region, who flourished about 2,000

Moundbuilders, Anasazi, and Mississippians

years ago, just as Teotihuacán rose to prominence, constructed earthen mounds. But the Ohioan mounds were used as burial sites, not as bases for temple pyramids. Also, the Moundbuilders' economy, which was based on hunting and gathering, bore little resemblance to that of Mesoamerica. Trade goods from as far away as the Great Lakes and the Gulf of Mexico have been found in the mounds, but direct evidence of contact with Teotihuacán is lacking.

Nor is there evidence of contact with Teotihuacán in sites inhabited by the Anasazi peoples in the modern states of Arizona and New Mexico. Pueblo Bonito, one of nine "Great Houses" in Chaco Canyon, by 1100 C.E. consisted of a series of large adobe buildings constructed along the sides of the canyon. Chaco Canyon, with a population of perhaps two thousand, sat at the juncture of over 400 miles of roads and served as a major regional trading center for turquoise, used then as now to create beautiful ornamental objects. The Anasazi constructed extensive irrigation systems in order to cultivate maize and other Mesoamerican crops in an arid environment, but they did not construct temple pyramids, nor did their towns resemble those built by their contemporaries in what is now Mexico.

More likely, Teotihuacán had an impact on the development of the Mississippian culture, which included the village of Cofitachequi and which flourished around 1000 C.E. in what is now the midwestern and southeastern United States. (Indeed, the historian Francis Jennings has argued that some of the Mississippians were "colonists" dispatched from Teotihuacán.) This civilization, like those to the south, depended on the cultivation of maize, beans, and squash. Not until after 800 C.E. were these nutritious crops grown successfully in the present-day United States. That introduction of agriculture made possible the growth of large cities, many of which included plazas and earthen pyramids. The largest of the urban centers was the City of the Sun (now called Cahokia), near modern St. Louis. At its peak (in the twelfth century), the City of the Sun covered more than 5 square miles and had a population of about twenty thousand—small by Mesoamerican standards but larger than any other northern community. Like Teotihuacán and Chaco Canyon, Cahokia was a religious and trading center. Its main pyramid, today called Monks Mound, was at the time of its construction the third largest structure of any description in the Western Hemisphere; it remains the largest earthwork ever built anywhere in the Americas.

Pueblo Bonito in Chaco Canyon in what is now the state of New Mexico. More than six hundred buildings were present on the well-defended site. The circular structures were kivas, used for food storage and for religious rituals. (David Muench photography)

The Aztecs' histories tell of the long migration of their people (who called themselves Mexica) into the Valley of Mexico during the twelfth century. The uninhabited ruins of Teotihuacán, which by then had been deserted for at least two hundred years, awed and mystified the migrants. The Aztecs' primary god, Huitzilopochtli, was a god of war represented by an eagle. The chronicles record that Huitzilopochtli directed the Aztecs to establish their capital at the spot on an island where they saw an eagle eating a serpent (thus symbolizing Huitzilopochtli's triumph over Quetzalcoatl). That island city became Tenochtitlán, the center of a rigidly stratified society composed of hereditary classes of warriors, merchants, priests, common folk, and slaves.

Aztecs

The Aztecs conquered their neighbors, forcing them to pay tribute in luxury items, raw materials, and human beings who could be sacrificed to Huitzilopochtli. They also engaged in ritual combat, known as "flowery wars," to obtain further sacrificial victims. The war god's taste for blood was not easily quenched. In the Aztec year Ten Rabbit (1502) at the coronation of Motecuhzoma II (the Spaniards could not pronounce his name correctly, so they called him Montezuma), five thousand people are thought to have

been sacrificed by having their still-beating hearts torn from their bodies.

The Aztecs believed that they lived in the age of the Fifth Sun. Four times previously, they wrote, the earth and all the people who lived on it had been destroyed. They predicted that their own world would end in earthquakes and hunger. In the Aztec year Thirteen Flint, volcanoes erupted, sickness and hunger spread, wild beasts attacked children, and an eclipse of the sun darkened the sky. Did some priest wonder whether the Fifth Sun was approaching its end? In time, the Aztecs learned that Thirteen Flint was called 1492 by the Europeans.

North America in 1492

Over the centuries, the Americans who lived north of Mexico adapted their once-similar ways of life to very different climates and terrains, thus creating the diverse cultures that the Europeans encountered when they first arrived (see Map 1.1). Scholars often refer to such cultures by language group (such as Algonquian or Iroquoian), since neighboring Indian nations commonly spoke related languages. Bands that lived in environments not well suited to agriculture—because of

Map 1.1 Native Cultures of North America The natives of the North American continent effectively used the resources of the regions in which they lived. As this map shows, coastal groups relied on fishing, residents of fertile areas engaged in agriculture, and other peoples employed hunting (often combined with gathering) as a primary mode of subsistence.

inadequate rainfall or poor soil, for example—followed a nomadic lifestyle similar to that of the Paleo-Indians. Within the area of the present-day United States, these groups included the Paiutes and Shoshones, who inhabited the Great Basin (now Nevada and Utah). Because of the difficulty of finding sufficient food for more than a few people, such hunter-gatherer bands were small, usually composed of one or more related families. The men hunted small animals and women gathered seeds and berries. Where large game was more plentiful and food supplies therefore more certain, as in present-day central and western Canada and the Great Plains, bands of hunters were somewhat larger.

In more favorable environments, larger groups combined agriculture with gathering, hunting, and fishing. Those who lived near the seacoasts, like the Chinooks of present-day Washington and Oregon, consumed fish and shellfish in addition to growing crops and gathering seeds and berries. Residents of the interior (for example, the Arikaras of the Missouri River valley) hunted large animals while also cultivating maize, squash, and beans. The peoples of what is now eastern Canada and the northeastern United States also combined hunting and agriculture. They regularly used controlled fires both to open land for cultivation and to assist in hunting.

Societies that relied primarily on hunting large animals like deer and buffalo assigned that task to men and allotted food preparation, clothing production, and child rearing to women. Before such nomadic bands acquired horses from the Spaniards, women—occasionally assisted by dogs—also carried the family's belongings whenever the band relocated. Such a sexual division of labor was universal among hunting peoples, regardless of their location. Agricultural societies, by contrast, differed in their assignments of work to the sexes. In what is now the southwestern United States, the Pueblo peoples, who lived in sixty or seventy autonomous villages and spoke five different languages, defined agricultural labor as men's work. In the east, large clusters of peoples speaking Algonquian, Iroquoian, and Muskogean languages allocated most agricultural chores to women, although men cleared the land. In all the farming societies, women gathered wild foods, prepared food for consumption or storage, and cared for children, while men were responsible for hunting.

Sexual Division of Labor in North America

The southwestern and eastern agricultural peoples had similar social organizations. They lived in villages, sometimes sizable ones with a thousand or more inhabitants. The Pueblos, descendants of the Anasazi, lived in large, multistory buildings constructed on terraces along the sides of cliffs or other easily defended sites. Northern Iroquois villages (in modern New York State) were composed of large, rectangular, bark-covered structures, or long houses; the name Haudenosaunee (which the Iroquois called themselves) means "People of the Long House." In the present-day southeastern United States, Muskogeans and southern Algonquians lived in large houses made of thatch. Most of the eastern villages were surrounded by wood palisades and ditches to aid in fending off attackers.

Social Organization

In all the agricultural societies, each dwelling housed an extended family defined matrilineally (through a female line of descent). Mothers, their married daughters, and their daughters' husbands and children all lived together. Matrilineal descent did not imply matriarchy, or the wielding of power by women, but rather served as a means of reckoning kinship. Extended families were linked into clans defined by matrilineal ties. The nomadic bands of the Great Plains, by contrast, were most often related patrilineally (through the male line). They lacked settled villages and defended themselves from attack primarily through their ability to move to safer locations when necessary.

The defensive design of eastern and western villages discloses the significance of warfare in pre-Columbian America. Long before Europeans arrived, residents of the continent fought one another for control of the best hunting and fishing territories, the most fertile agricultural lands, or the sources of essential items like salt (for preserving meat) and flint (for making knives and arrowheads). Bands of Americans protected by wooden armor battled while standing in ranks facing each other, the better to employ their clubs and throwing spears, which were effective only at close quarters. (They began to shoot arrows from behind trees only when they confronted the more accurate and longer-range European guns, which also rendered their armor useless.) People captured by the enemy in such wars were sometimes enslaved and dishonored by losing their previous names and identities, but slavery was never an important source of labor in pre-Columbian America.

War and Politics

Jacques Le Moyne, an artist accompanying the French settlement in Florida in the 1560s (see page 34), produced some of the first European images of North American peoples. His depiction of native agricultural practices shows the sexual division of labor: men breaking up the ground with fish-bone hoes before women drop seeds into the holes. But Le Moyne's version of the scene cannot be accepted uncritically: unable to abandon a European view of proper farming methods, he erroneously drew plowed furrows in the soil.   (John Carter Brown Library at Brown University)

American political structures varied considerably. Among Pueblo and Muskogean peoples, the village council, composed of ten to thirty men, was the highest political authority; no government structure connected the villages. Nomadic hunters also lacked formal links among separate bands. The Iroquois, by contrast, had an elaborate political hierarchy incorporating villages into nations and nations into a confederation; a council comprising representatives from each nation made crucial decisions of war and peace for the entire confederacy. In all the North American cultures, political power was divided between civil and war leaders, who wielded authority only so long as they retained the confidence of the people. Autocratic rule of the sort common in Europe (see page 15) was unusual in these political systems. Women more often assumed leadership roles among agricultural peoples, especially those in which females were the primary cultivators, than among nomadic hunters. Female sachems (rulers) led Algonquian villages in what is now Massachusetts, but women never became heads of Great Plains hunting bands. Iroquois women did not become chiefs, yet clan matrons nevertheless exercised political power. The older women of each village chose its chief and could both start wars (by calling for the capture of prisoners to replace dead relatives) and stop them (by refusing to supply warriors with necessary foodstuffs).

Americans' religious beliefs varied even more than did their political systems, but all the peoples were polytheistic, worshiping a multitude of gods. Each group's most important beliefs and rituals were closely tied to its means of subsistence. The major deities of agricultural peoples like the Pueblos and Muskogeans were associated with cultivation, and their chief festivals centered on planting and harvest. The most important gods of hunters (such as those liv-

Religion

ing on the Great Plains) were associated with animals, and their major festivals were related to hunting. A band's economy and women's role in it helped to determine women's potential as religious leaders. Women held the most prominent positions in those agricultural societies (like the Iroquois) in which they were also the chief food producers, whereas in hunting societies men took the lead in religious as well as political affairs.

A wide variety of cultures, comprising more than 5 million people, thus inhabited mainland North America when Europeans arrived. The hierarchical kingdoms of Mesoamerica bore little resemblance to the nomadic hunting societies of the Great Plains or to the agricultural societies that dominated a significant share of the continent. The diverse inhabitants of North America spoke well over one thousand different languages. For obvious reasons, they did not consider themselves one people, nor did they—for the most part—think of uniting to repel the European invaders.

African Societies

 Fifteenth-century Africa, like fifteenth-century America, housed a variety of cultures adapted to different terrains and climates (see Map 1.2). Many of these cultures were of great antiquity. In the north, along the Mediterranean Sea, lived the Berbers, a Muslim people. (Muslims are adherents of Islam, founded by the prophet Mohammed in the seventh century C.E.) On the east coast of Africa, Muslim city-states engaged in extensive trade with India, the Moluccas (part of modern Indonesia), and China. In these ports, sustained contact and intermarriage among Arabs and Africans created the Swahili language and culture. Through the East African city-states passed waterborne commerce between the eastern Mediterranean and East Asia; the rest followed the long land route across Central Asia known as the Silk Road.

South of the Mediterranean coast in the African interior lie the great Saharan and Libyan deserts, vast expanses of nearly waterless terrain crisscrossed by trade routes passing through oases. The introduction of the camel in the fifth century C.E. made such long-distance travel possible, and as Islam expanded after the ninth century, commerce controlled by Muslim merchants helped to spread similar religious and cultural ideas throughout the region. Below the deserts, much of the continent is divided between tropical rain forests (along the coasts) and grassy plains (in the interior). People speaking a variety of languages and pursuing different subsistence strategies lived in a wide belt south of the deserts. South of the Gulf of Guinea, the grassy landscape came to be dominated by Bantu-speaking peoples, who left their homeland in modern Nigeria about 2,000 years ago and slowly migrated south and east across the continent.

West Africa was a land of tropical forests and savanna grasslands where fishing, cattle herding, and agriculture had supported the inhabitants for at least 10,000 years before Europeans set foot there in the fifteenth century. The northern region of West Africa, or Upper Guinea, was heavily influenced by the Islamic culture of the Mediterranean. As early as the eleventh century C.E., many of the region's inhabitants had become Muslims. Trade via camel caravans between Upper Guinea and the Muslim Mediterranean was sub-Saharan Africa's major connection to Europe and West Asia. In return for salt, dates, silk, and cotton cloth, Africans exchanged ivory, gold, and slaves with northern merchants. Most of the enslaved people carried to North America came from this region, which Europeans called Guinea.

West Africa (Guinea)

Upper Guinea runs northeast-southwest from Cape Verde to Cape Palmas. The people of its northernmost region, the so-called Rice Coast (present-day Gambia, Senegal, and Guinea), fished and cultivated rice in coastal swamplands. The Grain Coast, the next region to the south, was thinly populated and not readily accessible from the sea because it had only one good harbor (modern Freetown, Sierra Leone). Its people concentrated on farming and raising livestock. Both the Rice and the Grain Coasts—especially the former—supplied slaves destined for sale in the Americas, but even more enslaved people came from Lower Guinea, known as the Gold and Slave Coasts, to the east of Cape Palmas, and from the Bight of Biafra (modern Nigeria) and Angola.

In the fifteenth century, most Africans in Lower Guinea were farmers who practiced traditional religions, not the precepts of Islam. Believing that spirits inhabited particular places, they invested those places with special significance. As did the agricultural peoples of the Americas, they developed rituals intended to ensure good harvests. Throughout the region, individual villages composed of kin groups were linked into hierarchical kingdoms. At the time of initial European contact, decentralized political and social authority characterized the region's polities.

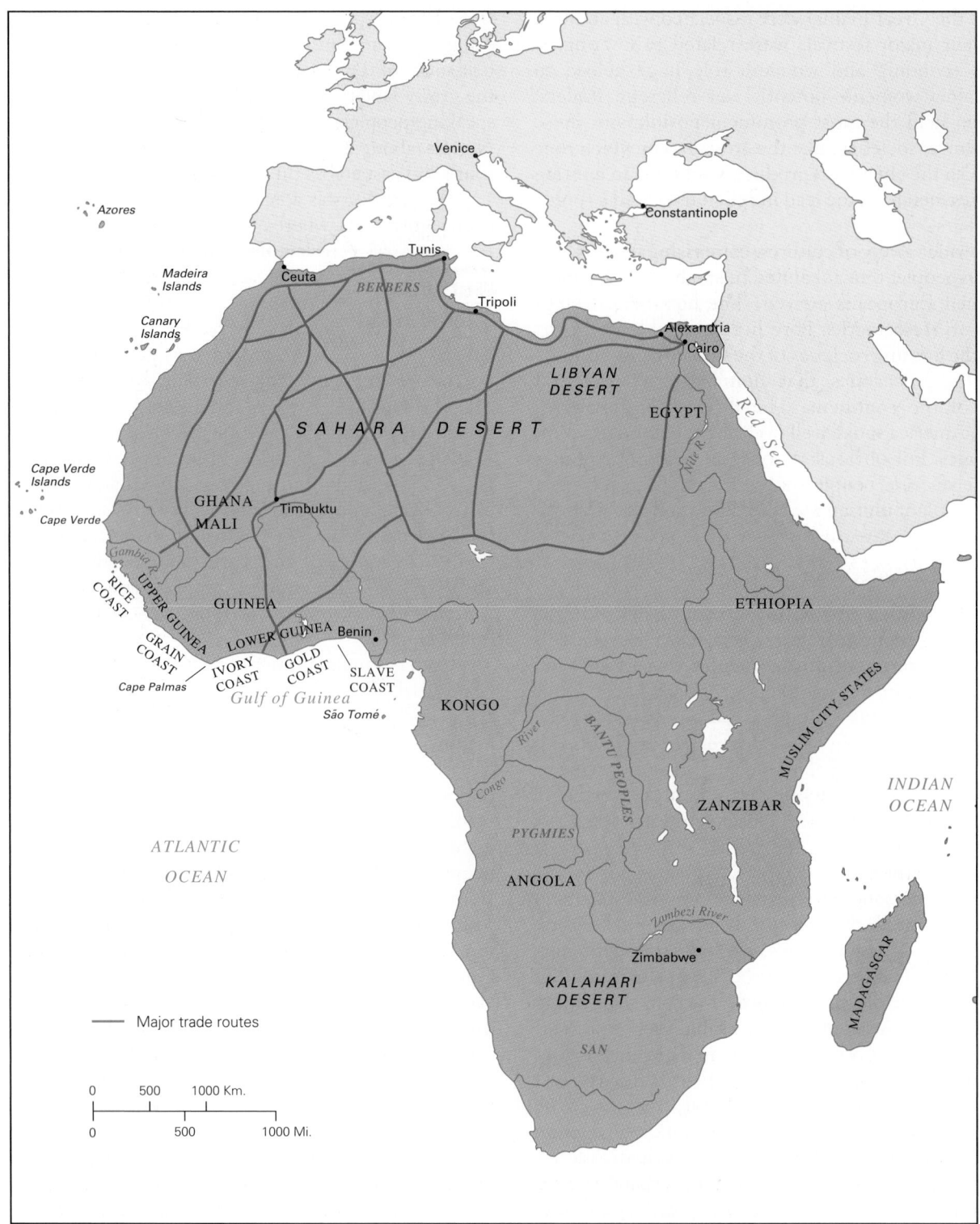

Map 1.2   Africa and Its Peoples, c. 1400   On the African continent resided many different peoples in a variety of ecological settings and political units. Even before Europeans began to explore Africa's coastlines, its northern regions were linked to the Mediterranean (and thus to Europe) by a network of trade routes.

West African law recognized both individual and communal land ownership, but men seeking to accumulate wealth needed access to

Slavery in West Africa

labor—wives, older children, or slaves—who could work the land. Africans held in slavery on their own continent (primarily criminals, debtors, or wartime captives, and their descendants) were therefore essential components of the economy. An African who possessed slaves had a right to the products of their labor, although the degree to which slaves were exploited varied greatly. Some slaves were held as chattel; others could engage in trade, retaining a portion of their profits; and still others achieved prominent political or military positions. All, however, found it difficult to overcome the social stigma of enslavement.

Many of the first slaves destined for sale across the Atlantic came from the Gold Coast, composed of thirty little kingdoms known as the Akan States. By the eighteenth century, though, the area farther east and south—the modern nations of Togo, Benin, Nigeria, and Angola—supplied most of the slaves sold in the English colonies. The Adja kings of the Slave Coast encouraged the founding of slave-trading posts and served as middlemen in the trade. Access to valuable European trade goods enhanced their positions in their own societies and improved their kingdoms' standing relative to their neighbors. When Europeans in America increasingly demanded slave labor, Africans responded by selling male prisoners of war, instead of killing them. Europeans then transported the purchased captives to the colonies.

The societies of West Africa, like those of the Americas, assigned different tasks to men and women. In general, the sexes shared agricul-

Sexual Division of Labor in West Africa

tural duties. Men also hunted, managed livestock, and did most of the fishing. Women were responsible for childcare, food preparation, and cloth manufacture. Everywhere in West Africa women were the primary local traders. They managed the extensive local and regional networks through which goods were exchanged among the various families, villages, and small kingdoms.

Despite their different economies and the rivalries among states, the peoples of Lower Guinea had similar social systems organized on the basis of what anthropologists have called the dual-sex principle. In Lower Guinea, each sex handled its own affairs: just as male political and religious leaders governed men, so

This decorative brass weight, created by the Asante peoples of Lower Guinea, was used for measuring gold dust. It depicts a family pounding fu-fu, a food made by mashing together plantains (a kind of banana), yams, and cassava. The paste was then shaped into balls to be eaten with soup. This weight, probably used in trading with Europeans, shows a scene combining foods of African origin (plantains and yams) with an import from the Americas (cassava), thus bringing the three continents together in ways both symbolic and real. (Trustees of the British Museum. Photo by Michael Holford)

females ruled women. In the Dahomean kingdom, for example, every male official had his female counterpart; in the Akan States, chiefs inherited their status through the female line, and each male chief had a female assistant who supervised other women. Many West African societies practiced polygyny (one man having several wives, each of whom lived separately with her children). Thus few adults lived permanently in marital households, but the dual-sex system ensured that their actions were subject to scrutiny by members of their own sex, if not by a spouse.

Throughout Upper Guinea religious beliefs stressed complementary male and female roles. Both

West African Religion

women and men served as heads of the cults and secret societies that directed the spiritual life of the villages. Young women were initiated into the Sandé cult, young men into Poro.

Neither cult was allowed to reveal its secrets to the opposite sex. Although West African women (unlike some of their Native American contemporaries) rarely held formal power over men, female religious leaders did govern other members of their sex within the Sandé cult, enforcing conformity to accepted norms of behavior and overseeing their spiritual well-being.

The West Africans carried to the Americas, then, were agricultural peoples, skilled at tending livestock, hunting, fishing, and manufacturing cloth from plant fibers and animal skins. Both men and women were accustomed to working communally, alongside other members of their own sex or in family groups. They were also accustomed to a relatively egalitarian relationship between the sexes, especially within the context of religion. In the Americas, they entered societies that used their labor but had little respect for their cultural traditions.

European Societies

 In the fifteenth century, Europeans, too, were agricultural peoples. The daily lives of Europe's rural people had changed little for several hundred years. Split into numerous small, warring countries, Europe was divided linguistically, politically, and economically, yet in social terms Europeans' lives were more similar than different. European societies were hierarchical: a few families wielded autocratic power over the majority of the people. English society in particular was organized as a series of interlocking hierarchies; that is, each person (except those at the very top or bottom) was superior to some, inferior to others. At the base of such hierarchies were people held in a variety of forms of bondage. Although Europeans were not subjected to perpetual slavery, Christian doctrine permitted the enslavement of "heathens" (all non-Christians), and some Europeans' freedom was restricted by such conditions as serfdom, which tied them to the land if not to specific owners. In short, Europe's kingdoms resembled those of Africa or Mesoamerica but differed greatly from the more egalitarian societies found in America north of Mexico.

Most Europeans, like most Africans and Americans, lived in small villages. Only a few cities dotted the landscape, most of them political capitals. European farmers, who were called peasants, owned or leased separate landholdings, but they worked the fields communally. Because fields had to lie fallow (unplanted) every second or third year to regain fertility, a family could not ensure itself a regular food supply unless the work and the crops were shared annually by all the villagers. Men did most of the fieldwork; women helped out chiefly at planting and harvest. In some areas men concentrated on herding livestock. Women's duties consisted primarily of childcare and household tasks, including preserving food, milking cows, and caring for poultry. If a woman's husband was a city artisan or storekeeper, she might assist him in business. Since Europeans kept domesticated animals (pigs, goats, sheep, and cattle) for meat, hunting had little economic importance in their cultures. Instead, hunting was primarily a sport for male aristocrats.

Sexual Division of Labor in Europe

Unlike in African and American societies, in which women often played prominent roles in politics and religion, men dominated all areas of life in Europe. A few women—notably Queen Elizabeth I of England—achieved status or power by right of birth, but the vast majority were excluded from positions of political authority. In the Roman Catholic Church and later in the new Protestant denominations, leadership roles were reserved for men. Husbands and fathers likewise expected to control their families. European women generally held inferior social, economic, and political positions, yet within their own families they wielded power over children and servants.

Black Death

When the fifteenth century began, European nations were slowly recovering from the devastating epidemic of plague known as the Black Death, which first struck them in 1346. Bubonic plague, spread by rats and fleas as well as by human contact, arrived in Europe from China, traveling with long-distance traders along the Silk Road to the eastern Mediterranean. The disease then recurred with particular severity in the 1360s and 1370s. Although no precise figures are available and the impact of the Black Death varied from region to region, the best estimate is that fully one-third of Europe's people died during those terrible years. That decimation led to a precipitous economic decline—in some regions more than half of the workers were lost—and to severe social, political, and religious disruption because of the deaths of clergymen and other leading figures.

As plague ravaged the population, England and France waged the Hundred Years War (1337–1453), initiated because the English monarchy claimed the French throne. The war interrupted overland trade routes through France connecting England and the

Netherlands to the Italian city-states and thence to Central Asia. Merchants in the eastern Mediterranean thus had to find new ways of reaching their northern markets. They solved that dilemma by forging a regular maritime link with the Netherlands to replace the overland route. The use of a triangular, or lateen, sail (rather than the then-standard square rigging) improved the maneuverability of ships, enabling them to sail out of the Mediterranean and north around the European coast. Also of key importance was the perfection of navigational instruments like the astrolabe and the quadrant, which allowed oceangoing sailors to estimate their position (latitude) by measuring the relationship of the sun, moon, or certain stars to the horizon.

In the aftermath of the Hundred Years War, European monarchs forcefully consolidated their previously diffuse political power and raised new revenues through increased taxation of an already hard-pressed peasantry. The long military struggle led to new pride in national identity, which eclipsed the prevailing regional and dynastic loyalties, and to heightened hostility toward foreigners. In England, Henry VII in 1485 founded the Tudor dynasty and began uniting a previously divided land. In France, the successors of Charles VII unified the kingdom and levied new taxes. Most successful of all were Ferdinand of Aragón and Isabella of Castile. In 1469 they married and combined their kingdoms, thereby creating the foundation of a strongly Catholic Spain. In 1492 they defeated the Muslims, who had lived in Spain and Portugal for centuries, thereafter expelling all Jews and Muslims from their domain.

The fifteenth century also brought technological change to Europe. Movable type and the printing press, invented in Germany in the 1450s, made information more accessible than ever before. Printing stimulated the Europeans' curiosity about fabled lands across the seas, lands they could now read about in books. The most important such work was Marco Polo's *Travels*, first published in 1477, which recounted a Venetian merchant's adventures in thirteenth-century China and, most intriguing, described that nation as bordered on the east by an ocean. Polo's account circulated widely among Europe's educated elites, first in manuscript and later in print. The book led many Europeans to believe that they could trade directly with China in oceangoing vessels instead of relying on the Silk Road or the route through East Africa. A transoceanic route, if it existed, would allow northern Europeans to circumvent the Muslim and Mediterranean merchants who hitherto had controlled their access to Asian goods.

Technological advances and the growing strength of newly powerful national rulers made possible the European explorations of the fifteenth and sixteenth centuries. Each country craved easy access to desirable African and Asian goods—spices like pepper, cloves, cinnamon, and nutmeg (to season the bland European diet), silk, dyes, perfumes, jewels, sugar, and gold. Avoiding Muslim and Venetian middlemen and acquiring such valuable products directly would improve a nation's income and its standing relative to other countries.

A secondary concern for spreading Christianity around the world supplemented the economic motive. The linking of materialist and spiritual goals might seem contradictory today, but fifteenth-century Europeans saw no necessary conflict between the two. Explorers and colonizers could honestly want to convert "heathen" peoples to Christianity. At the same time they could hope to increase their nation's wealth by establishing direct trade with Africa, China, India, and the Moluccas (also known as the Spice Islands).

Early European Explorations

 Before European mariners could discover new lands, they had to explore the oceans. To reach Asia, seafarers needed not just the maneuverable vessels and navigational aids increasingly used in the fourteenth century, but also knowledge of the sea, its currents, and especially its winds. Wind would power their ships. But how did the winds run? Where would Atlantic breezes carry their square-rigged ships, which, even with the addition of a triangular sail, needed to run before the wind (that is, to have the wind directly behind the vessel)?

Europeans learned the answers to these questions in the region that has been called the Mediterranean Atlantic, the expanse of the Atlantic Ocean that is south and west of Spain and is bounded by the island groups of the Azores (on the west) and the Canaries (on the south), with the Madeiras in their midst (see Map 1.3). Europeans reached all three sets of islands during the fourteenth century—first the Canaries in the 1330s, then the Madeiras and the Azores. The

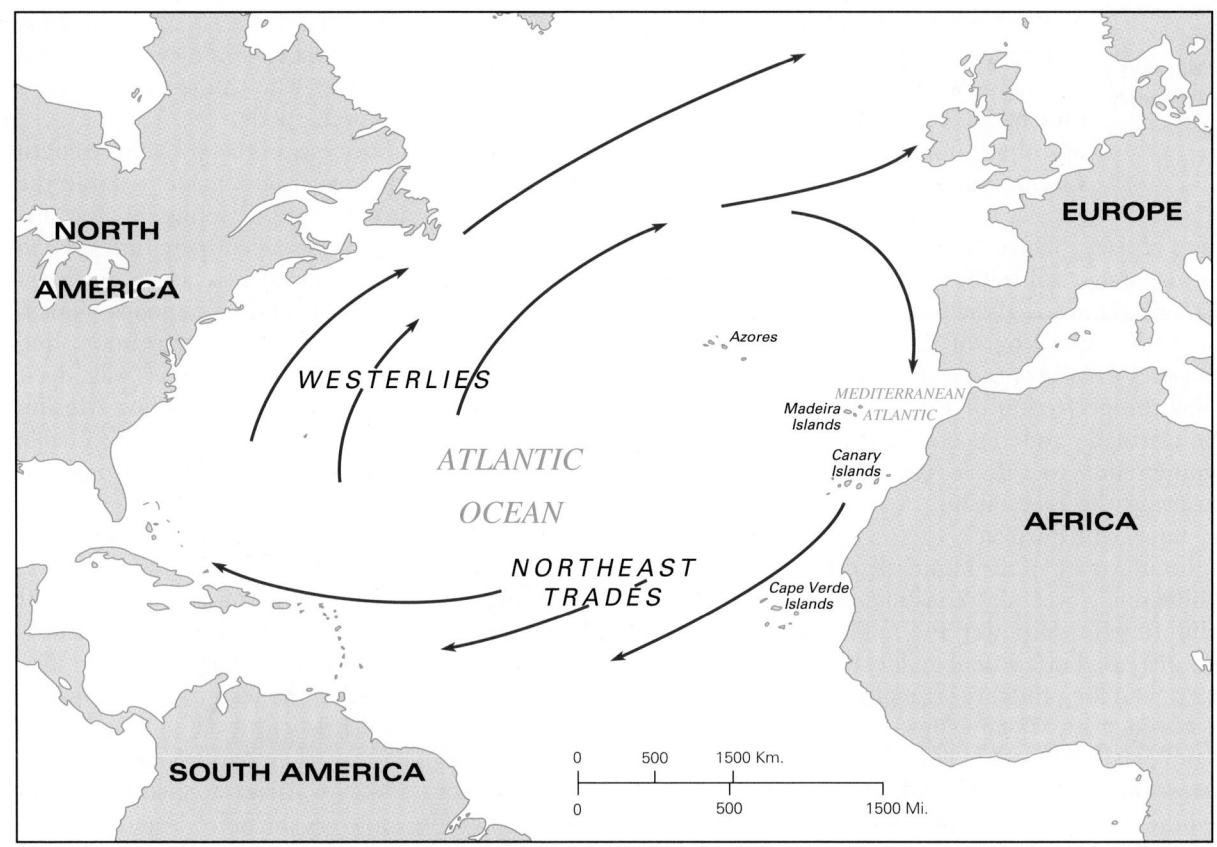

Map 1.3   Atlantic Winds and Islands   European mariners had to explore the oceans before they could find new lands. The first realm they discovered was that of Atlantic winds and islands.

Canaries proved a popular destination for mariners from Iberia, the peninsula that includes Spain and Portugal. Sailing to the Canaries from Europe was easy because strong winds known as the Northeast Trades blow southward along the Iberian and African coastlines. The voyage took about a week, and the volcanic peaks on the islands made them difficult to miss even with navigational instruments that were less than precise.

The problem was getting back. The Iberian sailor attempting to return home faced a major obstacle: the very winds that had brought him so quickly to the Canaries now blew directly at him. Early travelers to the islands sometimes used galleys powered by oarsmen as well as by sails, but even oarsmen had a difficult time fighting the contrary winds and currents. Another alternative was similarly tedious: tacking back and forth to the east and west, attempting each time to make more headway north. The problem seemed intractable, and in earlier eras European sailors had been

unable to solve it. When confronted with contrary winds, they simply waited for the wind to change. But for the most part, the Northeast Trades did not change. They blew steadily, shifting slightly with the seasons but never reversing course.

What could be done? Some unknown seafarer figured out the answer: sailing "around the wind." If a mariner could not sail against the trade winds, he had to sail as close as possible to the direction from which the wind was coming without being forced to tack. In the Mediterranean Atlantic, that meant pointing his vessel northwest into the open ocean, away from land, until—weeks later—he reached the winds that would carry him home, the so-called Westerlies. Those winds blow (we now know, though the mariners at first did not) northward along the coast of North America before heading east toward Europe.

This solution must at first have seemed to defy common sense, but it became the key to successful exploration of both the Atlantic and the Pacific Oceans.

In the fifteenth and sixteenth centuries, caravels ventured into the open oceans, thereby changing the contours of the known world. This illustration from a manuscript account of William Barents's 1594 expedition into the Arctic Ocean shows the combination of square rigging and lateen sails that gave ships greater maneuverability and allowed them to navigate along unfamiliar coastlines far from their home ports.   (Bridgeman Art Library)

Once a sailor understood the winds and their allied currents, he no longer feared leaving Europe without being able to return. Faced with a contrary wind, all he had to do was sail around it until he found a wind to carry him in the proper direction. This strategy might seem to take him hundreds of miles out of the way, but in the long run it was safer and surer than attempting the monumental task of tacking against the wind.

During the fifteenth century, armed with knowledge of the winds and currents of the Mediterranean Atlantic, Iberian seamen regularly visited the three island groups, all of which they could reach in two weeks or less. The uninhabited Azores were soon settled by Portuguese migrants who raised wheat for sale in Europe and sold livestock to passing sailors. The Madeiras also had no native peoples, and by the 1450s Portuguese colonists were employing slaves (probably Jews and Muslims brought from Iberia) to grow large quantities

Islands of the Mediterranean Atlantic

of sugar for export to the mainland. Madeira developed by the 1470s into the world's first colonial plantation economy.

The Canaries, by contrast, did have indigenous residents—the Guanche people, who began trading animal skins and dyes with their European visitors. In 1402 the French attacked one of the islands; thereafter, Portuguese and Spanish expeditions continued the sporadic assaults. The Guanches resisted vigorously, even though they were weakened by their susceptibility to alien European diseases. One by one the seven islands fell to Europeans, who then carried off Guanches as slaves to the Madeiras or the Iberian Peninsula. Spain conquered the last island in 1496 and subsequently devoted the land to sugar cultivation. Collectively, the Canaries and Madeira became known as the Wine Islands because much of their sugar production was directed to making sweet wines.

While some Europeans concentrated on exploiting the islands of the Mediterranean Atlantic, others used them as steppingstones to Africa. In 1415 Portugal seized control of Ceuta, a Muslim city in North Africa (see Map 1.2). Prince Henry the Navigator, son of King John I of Portugal, knew that vast wealth awaited the first European nation to tap the riches of Africa and Asia directly. Each year he dispatched ships southward along the African coast, attempting to discover an oceanic route to Asia. But not until after Prince Henry's death did Bartholomew Dias round the southern tip of Africa (1488) and Vasco da Gama finally reach India (1498).

Long before that, Portugal reaped the benefits of its seafarers' voyages. Although West African states successfully resisted European penetration of the interior, they allowed the Portuguese to establish trading posts along their coasts. Charging the traders rent and levying duties on goods they imported, the African kingdoms set the terms of exchange and benefited considerably from their new, easier access to European manufactures. The Portuguese gained too, for they no longer had to rely on trans-Saharan camel caravans. Their vessels earned immense profits by swiftly transporting African gold, ivory, and slaves to Europe. When they carried previously enslaved Africans back to Iberia, the Portuguese introduced black slavery into Europe.

Portuguese Trading Posts in Africa

An island off the African coast, previously uninhabited, proved critical to Portuguese success. São Tomé, located in the Gulf of Guinea (see Map 1.2), was colonized in the 1480s. By that time Madeira had already reached the limit of its capacity to produce sugar. The soil of São Tomé proved ideal for raising that valuable crop, and plantation agriculture there expanded rapidly. Planters imported large numbers of slaves from the mainland to work in the cane fields, thus creating the first economy based primarily on the bondage of black Africans.

By the 1490s, even before Christopher Columbus set sail to the west, Europeans had learned three key lessons of colonization in the Mediterranean Atlantic. First, they learned how to transplant their crops and livestock successfully to exotic locations. Second, they discovered that the native peoples of those lands could be either conquered (the Guanches) or exploited (the Africans). Third, they developed a viable model of plantation slavery—an exploitative economy based on the labor of large numbers of people held in perpetual bondage—

Lessons of Early Colonization

and a system for supplying nearly unlimited quantities of such workers. The stage was set for a pivotal moment in world history.

The Voyages of Columbus, Cabot, and Their Successors

 Christopher Columbus was well schooled in the lessons of the Mediterranean Atlantic. Born in 1451 in the Italian city-state of Genoa, Columbus, the largely self-educated son of a wool merchant, was by the 1490s an experienced sailor and mapmaker. Like many mariners of the day, he was drawn to Portugal and its islands, especially Madeira, where he commanded a merchant vessel. At least once he voyaged to the Portuguese outpost on the Gold Coast. There he acquired an obsession with gold, and there he came to understand the economic potential of the slave trade.

Like all accomplished seafarers, Columbus knew the world was round. (So, indeed, did most educated people: the idea that his contemporaries believed the world to be flat is a myth dating from the nineteenth century.) But he differed from other cartographers in his estimate of the earth's size: he thought that China lay only 3,000 miles from the southern European coast. Thus, he argued, it would be easier to reach Asia by sailing west than by making the difficult voyage around the southern tip of Africa. Experts scoffed at this crackpot notion, accurately predicting that the two continents lay 12,000 miles apart. When Columbus in 1484 asked the Portuguese authorities to back his plan to sail west to Asia, they rejected the proposal. After all, why should they adopt such a crazy scheme just as their efforts to round the Cape of Good Hope promised success?

Ferdinand and Isabella of Spain, ruling a newly united kingdom and jealous of Portugal's successes in Africa, were more receptive to Columbus's ideas. Urged on by some Spanish noblemen and a group of Italian merchants residing in Castile, the monarchs agreed to finance the risky voyage, in part because they hoped the profits would pay for an expedition to conquer Muslim-held Jerusalem. And so, on August 3, 1492, in command of three ships—the *Pinta*, the *Niña*, and the *Santa Maria*—Columbus set sail from the Spanish port of Palos.

Columbus's Voyage

The first part of the journey must have been very familiar, for the ships steered down the Northeast Trades to the Canary Islands. There Columbus refitted his square-rigged ships, adding triangular sails to make them more maneuverable. On September 6, the ships weighed anchor and headed out into the unknown ocean.

Just over a month later, pushed by favorable trade winds, the vessels found land approximately where Columbus had predicted (see Map 1.4). On October 12, he and his men landed on an island in the Bahamas, which its inhabitants called Guanahaní but which he renamed San Salvador. (Because Columbus's description of his landfall can be variously interpreted, three different places—Samana Cay, Plana Cays, and Mayaguana Cay—are today proposed as the most likely locations for his landing site.) Later he went on to explore the islands now known as Cuba and Hispaniola, which their residents, the Taíno people, called Colba and Bohío. Because he thought he had reached the Indies, Columbus referred to the inhabitants of the region as Indians.

Three themes predominate in Columbus's log, the major source of information on this first encounter.

Columbus's Observations

First, he insistently asked the Taínos where he could find gold, pearls, and valuable spices. Each time, his informants replied (largely via signs) that such products could be obtained on other islands, on the mainland, or in cities in the interior. Eventually he came to mistrust such answers, noting, "I am beginning to believe . . . they will tell me anything I want to hear."

Second, Columbus wrote repeatedly of the strange and beautiful plants and animals. "Here the fishes are

This map, produced in 1489 by Henricus Marcellus, represents the world as Christopher Columbus knew it, for it incorporates information obtained after Bartholomew Dias, a Portuguese sailor, rounded the Cape of Good Hope at the southern tip of Africa in 1488. Marcellus did not try to estimate the extent of the ocean separating the west coast of Europe from the east coast of Asia.   (Trustees of the British Library)

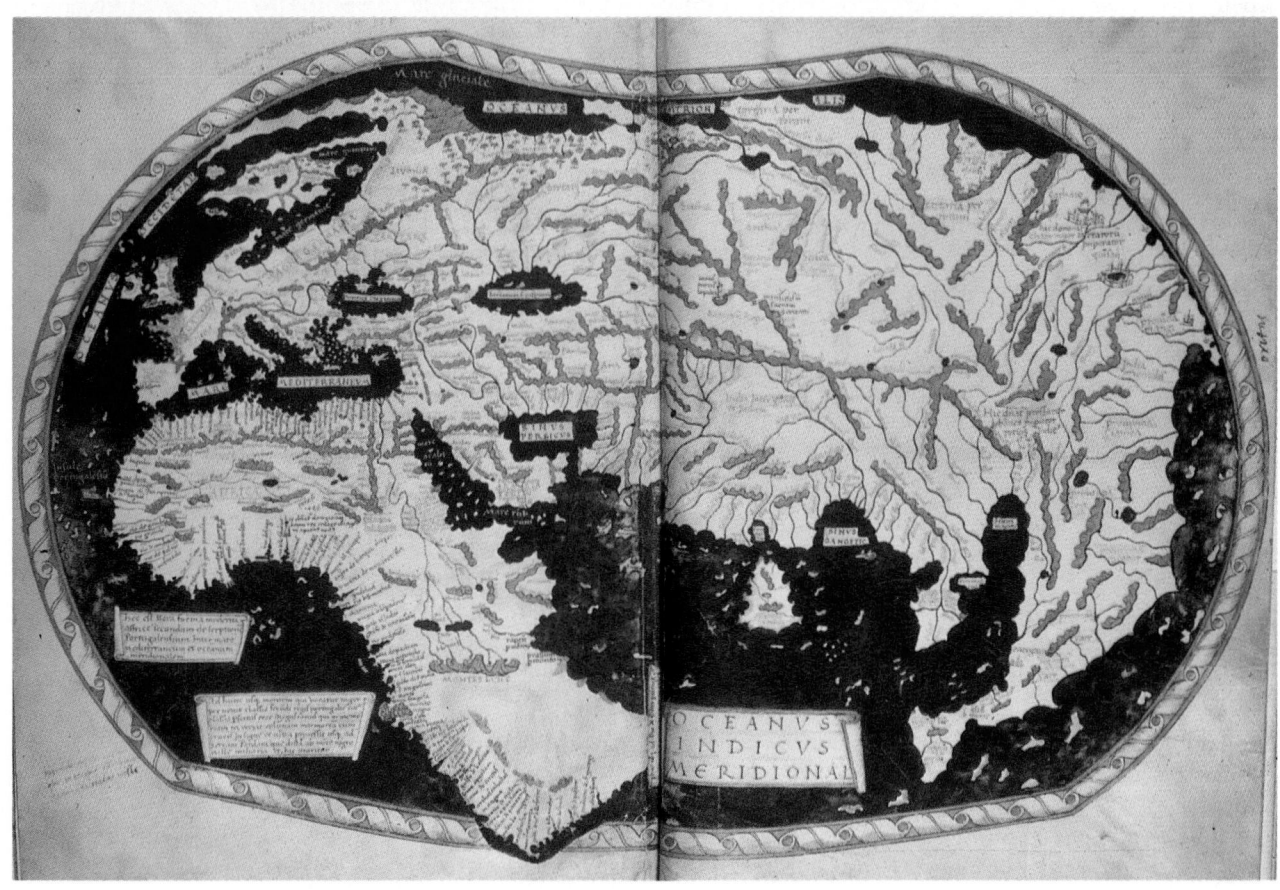

so unlike ours that it is amazing. . . . The colors are so bright that anyone would marvel," he noted, and again, "The song of the little birds might make a man wish never to leave here. I never tire from looking at such luxurious vegetation." Yet Columbus's interest was not only aesthetic. "I believe that there are many plants and trees here that could be worth a lot in Spain for use as dyes, spices, and medicines," he observed, adding that he was carrying home to Europe "a sample of everything I can," so that experts could examine them.

Third, Columbus also described the islands' human residents, and he seized some to take back to Spain. The Taínos were, he said, very handsome, gentle, and friendly, though they told him of fierce people who lived on other nearby islands and raided

The Taíno People

their villages. The Caniba (today called Caribs), from whose name the word *cannibal* is derived, were reported to eat their captives (today scholars disagree about whether the tales were true). Columbus believed the Taínos to be likely converts to Catholicism, remarking that "if devout religious persons knew the Indian language well, all these people would soon become Christians." But he had more in mind than conversion. The islanders "ought to make good and skilled servants," Columbus declared. It would be easy to "subject everyone and make them do what you wished."

Thus the records of the first encounter between Europeans and America and its residents revealed the themes that would be of enormous significance for

In 1507 Martin Waldseemüller, a German mapmaker, was the first person to designate the newly discovered southern continent as "America." He named the continent after Amerigo Vespucci, the Italian explorer who realized that he had reached a "new world" rather than islands off the coast of Asia.   (John Carter Brown Library at Brown University)

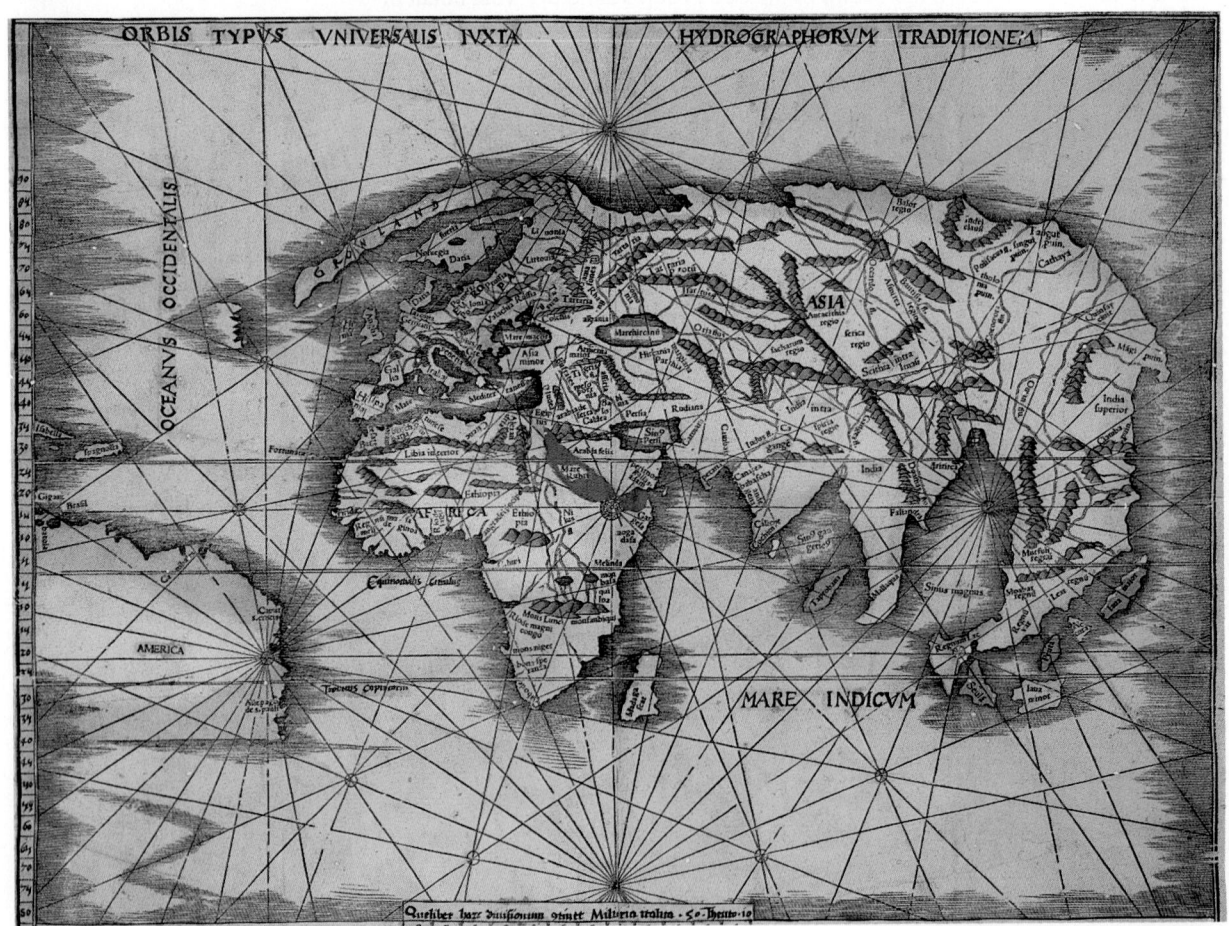

centuries to come, motivating such later explorers as Hernán de Soto as well. Above all, Europeans wanted to extract profits from North and South America by exploiting their natural resources, including plants, animals, and peoples alike.

Christopher Columbus made three more voyages to the west, exploring most of the major Caribbean is-

Naming of America

lands and sailing along the coasts of Central and South America. Until the day he died in 1506 at the age of fifty-five, Columbus believed that he had reached Asia. Even before his death, others knew better. Because the Florentine Amerigo Vespucci, who explored the South American coast in 1499, was the first to publish the idea that a new continent had been discovered, Martin Waldseemüller in 1507 labeled the land "America," as is evident in his map (reproduced on page 20). By then, Spain, Portugal, and Pope Alexander VI had signed the Treaty of Tordesillas (1494), confirming Portugal's dominance in Africa—and later Brazil—in exchange for Spanish preeminence in the rest of the Americas.

The mariners who explored the region of North America that was to become the United States and

Northern Voyages

Canada followed a very different route. Some historians argue that European sailors may have found the rich Newfoundland fishing grounds in the 1480s, even before Columbus's first voyage, but kept their discoveries a secret so that they alone could exploit the sea's bounty. Whether or not fishermen crossed the entire width of the Atlantic, they thoroughly explored its northern reaches. In the same way the Portuguese traveled regularly in the Mediterranean Atlantic, fifteenth-century seafarers voyaged among the European continent, England, Ireland, and Iceland.

The winds these sailors confronted posed problems on their outbound rather than homeward journeys. The same Westerlies that carried Columbus and other southern voyagers back to Europe blew in the faces of northerners looking west. But mariners soon learned that the strongest winds shifted southward during the winter and that, by departing from northern ports in the spring, they could make adequate headway if they steered northward to catch sporadic easterly breezes. Thus, whereas the first landfall of most sailors to the south was somewhere in the Caribbean, those taking the northern route usually reached America along the coast of what is now Maine or the Canadian maritime provinces.

Artifacts from L'Anse aux Meadows, Newfoundland, a site the Vikings called Straumond. These inconspicuous items reveal a great deal to archaeologists investigating the Norse settlements in North America. The small circular object, a spindle whorl for use in spinning yarn, discloses women's presence at Straumond; the nut comes from a tree that grows only south of the St. Lawrence River, thus indicating the extent of Viking travel along the coast.   (L'Anse aux Meadows, Canada)

Five hundred years before Columbus, about the year 1001, the Norseman Leif Ericsson and other Viking explorers sailed to North

Norse Seafarers

America across the Davis Strait, which separated their villages in Greenland from Baffin Island (located northeast of Hudson Bay; see Map 1.1) by just 200 nautical miles, settling at a site they named Vinland. Attacks by local residents forced them to depart hurriedly from Vinland after just a few years, the tale of their exploits subsequently being preserved in oral-history sagas. (In the 1960s, archaeologists determined that the Vikings had established an outpost at what is now L'Anse aux Meadows, Newfoundland, but Vinland itself was probably located farther south.) The European generally credited with "discovering" North America is John Cabot. More precisely, Cabot brought to Europe the first formal knowledge of the northern coastline of the continent.

Like Columbus, Cabot was a master mariner from the Italian city-state of Genoa. He is known to have

John Cabot's Explorations

been in Spain when Columbus returned from his first trip to America. Calculating that England—which traded with Asia only through a long series of middlemen stretching from Belgium to Venice to the Muslim world—would be eager to sponsor exploratory voyages, Cabot sought and

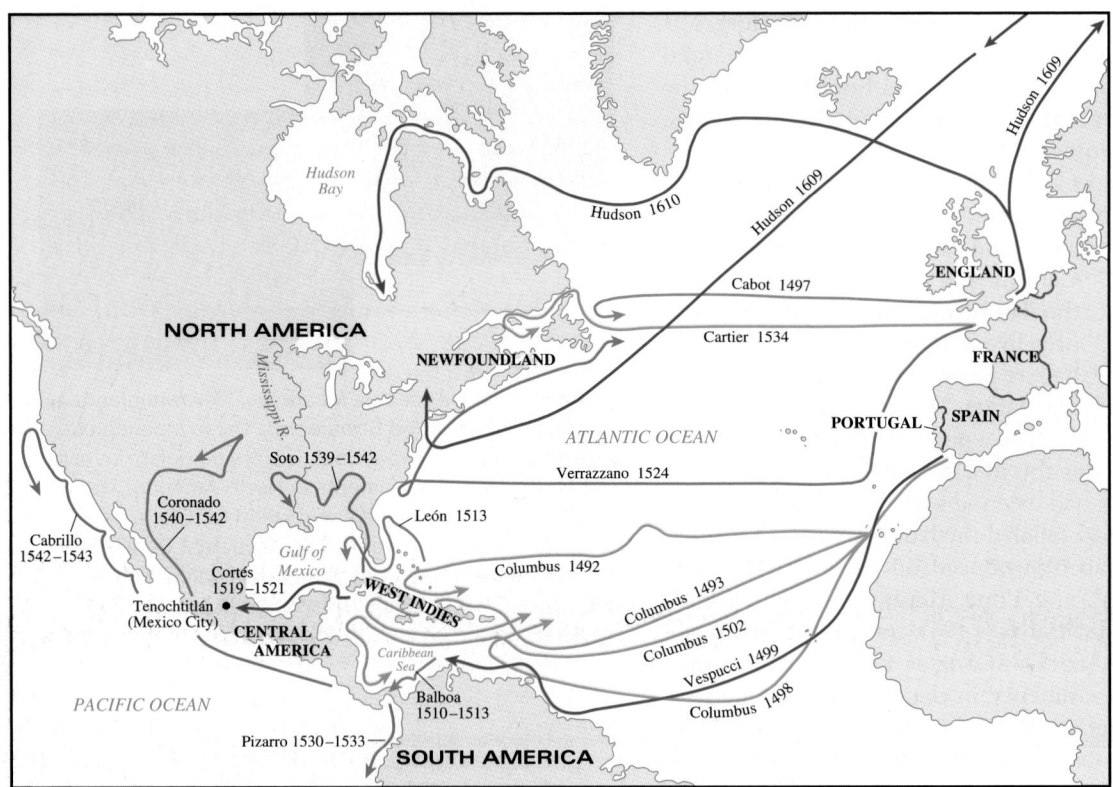

Map 1.4   European Explorations in America   In the century following Columbus's voyages, European adventurers explored the coasts and parts of the interior of North and South America.

won the support of King Henry VII. He set sail from Bristol in late May 1497 in the *Mathew*, reaching his destination on June 24. Scholars disagree about the location of his landfall (some say it was Cape Breton Island, others Newfoundland), but all recognize the importance of his month-long exploration of the coast. Having achieved his goal, Cabot rode the Westerlies back to England, arriving just fifteen days after he left North America.

The voyages of Columbus, Cabot, and their successors finally brought the Eastern and Western Hemispheres together. The Portuguese explorer Pedro Alvares Cabral reached Brazil in 1500; John Cabot's son Sebastian followed his father to North America in 1507; France financed Giovanni da Verrazzano in 1524 and Jacques Cartier in 1534; and in 1609 and 1610 Henry Hudson explored the North American coast for the Dutch West India Company (see Map 1.4). All these men were primarily searching for the legendary, nonexistent "Northwest Passage" through the Americas, hoping to find an easy route to the

riches of Asia. Although they did not attempt to plant colonies in the Western Hemisphere, their discoveries interested European nations in exploring North and South America.

Spanish Exploration and Conquest

 Only in the areas that Spain explored and claimed did colonization begin immediately. On his second voyage in 1493, Columbus brought to Hispaniola seventeen ships loaded with twelve hundred men, seeds, plants, livestock, chickens, and dogs—along with microbes, rats, and weeds. The settlement named Isabela (in the modern Dominican Republic) and its successors became the staging area for the Spanish invasion of America. On the islands of Cuba and Hispaniola the Europeans learned to adapt to the new environment, as did the horses, cattle, and hogs they imported. When the Spaniards moved on to explore the main-

land, they rode island-bred horses and ate island-bred cattle and hogs.

At first, Spanish explorers fanned out around the Caribbean basin. In 1513 Juan Ponce de León reached Florida and Vasco Núñez de Balboa crossed the Isthmus of Panama to the Pacific Ocean. In the 1530s and 1540s, conquistadors traveled farther, exploring many regions claimed by the Spanish monarchs: Francisco Vásquez de Coronado journeyed through the southwestern portion of what is now the United States at approximately the same time as Hernán de Soto explored the southeast and encountered the Lady of Cofitachequi. Juan Rodriguez Cabrillo sailed along the California coast; and Francisco Pizarro, who ventured into western South America, acquired the richest silver mines in the world by conquering and enslaving the Incas. But the most important conquistador was Hernán Cortés, who in 1521 seized control of the Aztec Empire.

Hernán Cortés and Malinche

Cortés, an adventurer who first arrived in the West Indies in 1504, embarked for the mainland in 1519 in search of wealthy cities rumored to exist there. As he moved his force inland from the Gulf of Mexico, local Mayas presented him with a gift of twenty young female slaves. One of them, Malinche (soon baptized as a Christian and renamed Doña Marina by the Spaniards), who had been sold into slavery by the Aztecs and raised by the Mayas, became Cortés's translator and mistress. Did she do so willingly? No one knows, but perhaps she felt little loyalty to those who had enslaved her. Malinche bore Cortés a son, Martín—one of the first *mestizos*, or mixed-blood children—and eventually married one of his officers. When the Aztec capital Tenochtitlán fell to the Spaniards in 1521, Cortés and his men seized a fabulous treasure of gold and silver. Thus not long after Columbus's first voyage, the Spanish monarchs—who treated the American territories as their personal possessions—controlled the richest, most extensive empire Europe had known since ancient Rome.

Spanish Colonization

Spain established the model of colonization that other countries later attempted to imitate, a model with three major elements. First, the Crown maintained tight control over the colonies, imposing a hierarchical government that allowed little autonomy to New World jurisdictions. That control included, for example, limiting the number of people permitted to emigrate to America and insisting that the colonies import all their manufactured goods from Spain. Roman Catholic priests ensured the colonists' conformity with orthodox religious views. Second, most of the colonists sent from Spain were male. They took Indian—and later African—women as their sexual partners, thereby creating the racially mixed population that characterizes much of Latin America to the present day.

Third, the colonies' wealth was based on the exploitation of both the native population and slaves imported from Africa. The Mesoamerican peoples, many of whom lived in urban areas, were accustomed to autocratic rule. Spaniards simply took over roles once assumed by native leaders, who had also exacted labor and tribute from their subjects. The *encomienda* system, which granted tribute from Indian villages to

A European artist recorded this scene of a Carib war dance. The leaders in the middle of the circle blow tobacco smoke on the dancers to give them courage in the coming battles.   (1996 MAPes MONDe Ltd.)

How do historians know...

that Indians and Europeans interacted in complex ways as early as the sixteenth century? The study of artifacts such as this plate fragment (shown here, with a clearer drawing underneath) can reveal much about the early years of intercultural contact. Called the Coosawattee plate, it was discovered in 1984 on a farm in northwestern Georgia. The site was once an Indian village (abandoned before 1600), and the plate was found in the grave of a ten-year-old child.

Archaeologists believe that an Aztec artisan made the plate in Mexico before 1560. It probably represents the Annunciation of the Virgin Mary, with a rendering of the Virgin dominating the middle (her modesty shown by her torn and mended skirt, a common Aztec symbol), the angel, who announced that she would bear God's son, carrying a torch of illumination on the left, and an ox (more often seen in Nativity scenes) on the right. Originally manufactured as a cover for a Bible, it almost certainly belonged to a Franciscan friar attached to a Spanish expedition that traveled to northwest Georgia twenty years after the initial visit of Hernán de Soto. An Indian punched holes in the

plate (the small black circles in the drawing) to turn it into a ceremonial necklace, and it was eventually buried with the child, perhaps its last owner. The object not only reveals the Aztecs' syncretic Christianity but also illustrates how Indians creatively used items they obtained from Europeans. (Photos: Courtesy James B. Langford, Jr.)

individual conquistadors as a reward for their services to the Crown, in effect legalized Indian slavery. Yet in 1542 a new code of laws reformed the system, forbidding Spaniards from enslaving Indians while still allowing them to collect money and goods from their tributary villages. In response, the conquerors, familiar with slavery in Spain, began to import Africans in order to increase the labor force under their direct control. They employed Indians and Africans primarily in gold and silver mines, on sugar plantations, and on huge horse, cattle, and sheep ranches. Yet African slavery was far more common in the Greater Antilles (the major Caribbean islands) than on the mainland.

The New World's gold and silver, initially a boon, ultimately brought about the decline of Spain as a ma-

Gold, Silver, and Spain's Decline

jor power. The influx of unprecedented wealth led to rapid inflation, which (among other adverse effects) caused Spanish products to be overpriced in international markets and imported goods to become cheaper in Spain. The once-profitable Spanish textile-manufacturing industry collapsed, as did scores of other businesses. The seemingly endless income from American colonies emboldened successive Spanish monarchs to spend lavishly on wars against the Dutch and the English. Several times in the late sixteenth and early seventeenth centuries the monarchs repudiated the state debt, wreaking havoc on the nation's finances. When the South American gold and silver mines started to give out in the mid-seventeenth century, Spain's economy crumbled and the nation lost its international importance.

Spanish wealth derived from American suffering. The Spaniards deliberately leveled American cities, building cathedrals and monasteries on sites once occupied by Aztec, Incan, and Mayan temples. Some conquistadors sought to erase all vestiges of the great Indian cultures by burning the written records they found. With traditional ways of life in disarray, devastated by disease, and compelled to labor for their conquerors, many demoralized residents of Mesoamerica accepted the Christian religion brought to New Spain by friars of the Franciscan and Dominican orders.

The friars devoted their energies to persuading Mesoamerican people to move into new towns and to build Roman Catholic churches. In

Christianity in New Spain

such towns, Indians were exposed to European customs and religious rituals designed to assimilate Catholic and pagan beliefs. Friars deliberately juxtaposed the cult of the Virgin Mary with that of the corn goddess, and the Indians adeptly melded aspects of their traditional world-view with Christianity, in a process called syncretism. Thousands of Indians residing in Spanish territory embraced Catholicism, at least partly because it was the religion of their new rulers and they were accustomed to obedience.

The Columbian Exchange

A broad mutual transfer of diseases, plants, and animals (called the Columbian Exchange by the historian Alfred Crosby) resulted directly from the European voyages of the fifteenth and sixteenth centuries and from Spanish colonization. The two hemispheres had evolved separately for thousands of years, developing widely different forms of life. Many large mammals like cattle and horses were native to the connected continents of Europe, Asia, and Africa, but the Americas contained no domesticated beasts larger than dogs and llamas. The vegetable crops of the Americas—particularly corn, beans, squash, cassava, and potatoes—were more nutritious and produced higher yields than those of Europe and Africa, such as wheat, millet, and rye. In time, native peoples learned to raise and consume European livestock, and Europeans and Africans became accustomed to planting and eating American crops. The diets of all three peoples were consequently vastly enriched. Partly as a result, the world's population doubled over the next three hundred years.

Diseases carried from Europe and Africa, though, had a devastating impact on the Americas. Indians fell

Smallpox and Other Diseases

victim to microbes that had long infested the other continents and had repeatedly killed hundreds of thousands but had also left survivors with some measure of immunity. The

A male effigy dating from 200–800 C.E., found in a burial site in Nayarit, Mexico. The lesions covering the figurine suggest that the person it represents is suffering from syphilis, which, untreated, produces these characteristic markings on the body in its later stages. Such evidence as this pre-Columbian effigy has now convinced most scholars that syphilis originated in the Americas—a hypothesis in dispute for many years.   (Private Collection)

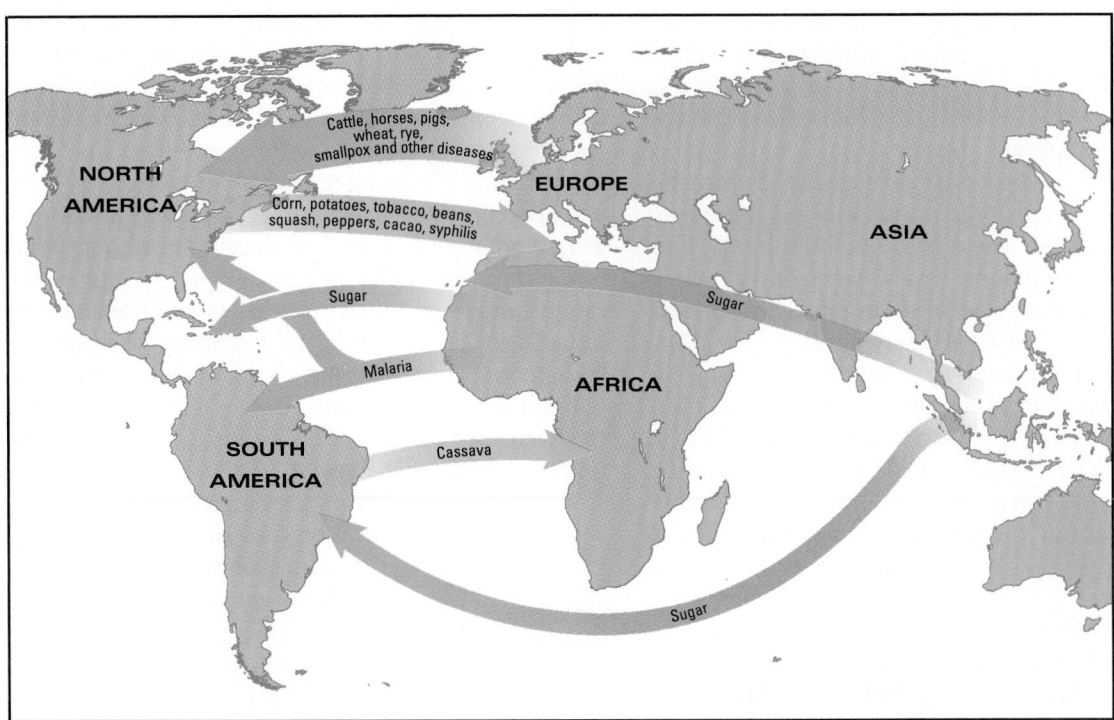

Figure 1.1   Major Items in the Columbian Exchange   As European adventurers traversed the world in the fifteenth and sixteenth centuries, they initiated the "Columbian Exchange" of plants, animals, and diseases. These events changed the lives of the peoples of the world forever, bringing new foods and new pestilence to both sides of the Atlantic.

statistics are staggering. When Columbus landed on Hispaniola in 1492, approximately half a million people resided there. Fifty years later, fewer than two thousand native inhabitants were still alive. Within thirty years of the first landfall at Guanahaní, not one Taíno survived in the Bahamas. Overall, historians estimate that the arrival of the alien microorganisms could have reduced the precontact American population by as much as 90 percent, especially because the epidemics continued to recur at twenty- to thirty-year intervals.

Although measles, typhus, influenza, malaria, and other illnesses severely afflicted the Native Americans, the greatest killer was smallpox, spread primarily by direct human contact. A Spanish priest recorded the vivid words of an old Aztec man who survived the first smallpox epidemic in Tenochtitlán. That epidemic, which began on Hispaniola in December 1518, was carried to the mainland by Spaniards in the spring of 1520. The epidemic peaked about six months later, fatally weakening Tenochtitlán's defenders. "It spread over the people as great destruction," the elderly Aztec remembered. "Some it quite covered [with pustules]

on all parts—their faces, their heads, their breasts. . . . There was great havoc. Very many died of it." Largely as a consequence, Tenochtitlán surrendered, and the Spaniards built Mexico City on its site.

Far to the north, where smaller American populations encountered only a few Europeans, disease also ravaged the countryside. A great epidemic, probably smallpox coupled with measles, swept through the villages along the coast north of Cape Cod from 1616 to 1618. Again the mortality rate may have been as high as 90 percent. An English traveler several years later commented that the people had "died on heapes, as they lay in their houses," and that bones and skulls covered the ruins of villages. Because of this dramatic depopulation of the area, just a few years later English colonists were able to establish settlements virtually unopposed.

The Americans, though, took a revenge of sorts. They gave the Europeans syphilis, a virulent venereal disease. The first recorded European case of the new ailment occurred in Barcelona, Spain, in 1493, shortly after Columbus's return from the

Syphilis

A Spanish map from 1519 showing the coast of Hispaniola, focusing on what is now the modern nation of Haiti. The decorative figures, shown with tools for hunting and cultivation, appear to be African slaves imported as laborers to replace the Indian population, already being rapidly depleted by disease and mistreatment.   (Bibliothèque Nationale)

Caribbean. Although less likely than smallpox to cause immediate death, syphilis was dangerous and debilitating. Carried by soldiers, sailors, and prostitutes, it spread quickly through Europe and Asia, reaching as far as China by 1505.

The exchange of three commodities had significant impacts on Europe and the Americas. Sugar, which was first domesticated in the East Indies, was being grown on the islands of the Mediterranean Atlantic by 1450 (see page 17). The insatiable European demand for sugar, which after initially being regarded as a medicine became a desirable luxury foodstuff, led Columbus to take Canary Island sugar canes to Hispaniola on his 1493 voyage. By the 1520s,

Sugar

plantations in the Greater Antilles worked by African slaves regularly shipped cargoes of sugar to Spain. Half a century later, the Portuguese colony in Brazil (founded 1532) was producing sugar on an even larger scale for the European market, and after 1640 (see pages 39–40), sugar cultivation became the crucial component of English and French colonization in the Caribbean.

Horses, which like sugar were brought to America by Columbus in 1493, fell into the hands of North American natives during the seventeenth century. Through trade and theft, horses spread among the peoples of the Great Plains, reaching most areas by 1750. Sioux, Comanches, and Crows,

Horses

among others, came to use horses for transportation and hunting, calculated their wealth in the number of horses owned, and waged wars primarily from horseback. Women no longer had to carry the bands' belongings on their backs. Some groups that previously had cultivated crops abandoned agriculture altogether. Because of the acquisition of horses, a mode of subsistence that had been based on hunting several different animals, in combination with gathering and agriculture, became one focused almost wholly on hunting buffalo.

In America, Europeans encountered tobacco, which at first they believed to have beneficial medicinal effects. Smoking and chewing the

Tobacco

"Indian weed" became a fad in Europe after it was planted in Turkey in the sixteenth century. Despite the efforts of such skeptics as King James I of England, who in 1604 pronounced smoking "loathsome to the eye, hatefull to the Nose, harmfull to the brain, [and] dangerous to the Lungs," tobacco's popularity climbed. Its contribution to lung cancer was discovered only in the twentieth century.

The European and African invasion of the Americas therefore had a significant biological component, for the invaders carried plants and animals with them. Some creatures, such as livestock, they brought deliberately. Others, including rats (which infested their ships), weeds, and diseases, arrived unexpectedly. And the same process occurred in reverse. When the Europeans returned home, they deliberately took back such crops as corn, potatoes, and tobacco, along with that unanticipated stowaway, syphilis.

Europeans in North America

Northern Europeans, denied access to the wealth of Mesoamerica by the Spanish and beaten to South America by the Portuguese, were initially more interested in exploiting North America's abundant natural resources than in the difficult task of establishing colonies on the mainland. John Cabot reported that fish were so plentiful along the North American coast that they could be caught merely by lowering baskets over the side of a vessel. Europeans rushed to take advantage of the abundance of fish, a product in great demand in their homelands as an inexpensive source of nourishment. By the 1570s, more than 350 ships, primarily from France and England, were capitalizing on the bounty of the Newfoundland Banks each year.

European fishermen soon learned that they could augment their profits by exchanging cloth and metal goods like pots and knives for the na-

Trade Among Indians and Europeans

tive trappers' beaver pelts, which Europeans used to make fashionable hats. At first the Europeans conducted their trading from ships sailing along the coast, but later they established permanent outposts on the mainland to centralize and control the traffic in furs (see page 36). All were inhabited chiefly by male adventurers, whose major aim was to send as many pelts as possible home to Europe.

The Europeans' demand for furs, especially beaver, was matched by the Indians' desire for European goods that could make their lives easier and establish their superiority over their neighbors. Some bands began to concentrate so completely on trapping for the European market that they abandoned their traditional economies. The Abenakis of Maine, for example, became partially dependent on food supplied by their neighbors to the south, the Massachusett tribe, because they devoted most of their energies to catching beaver to sell to French traders. The Massachusetts, in turn, intensified their production of foodstuffs, which they traded to the Abenakis in exchange for the European metal tools they preferred to their own handmade stone implements. The intensive trade in pelts also had serious ecological consequences. In some regions, beavers were completely wiped out. The disappearance of their dams led to soil erosion, especially when combined with the extensive clearing of forests by later European settlers.

Although their nation reaped handsome profits from fishing, English merchants and political leaders

Contest of Spain and England

watched enviously as Spain's American possessions enriched Spain immeasurably. In the mid-sixteenth century, English "sea dogs" like John Hawkins and Sir Francis Drake began to raid Spanish treasure fleets sailing home from the West Indies. Their actions caused friction between the two countries and helped to foment a war that in 1588 culminated in the defeat of a huge invasion force—the Spanish Armada—off the English coast. As a part of the contest with Spain, English leaders started to think about planting colonies in the Western Hemisphere, thereby gaining better access to valuable trade goods and simultaneously preventing their enemy from dominating the Americas.

The first English colonial planners saw Spain's possessions as both a model and a challenge. They hoped to reproduce Spanish successes by dispatching to America men who would similarly exploit the native peoples for their own and their nation's benefit. In the mid-1570s, a group that included Sir Humphrey Gilbert and his younger half-brother Sir Walter Raleigh began to promote a scheme to establish outposts that could trade with the Indians and provide bases for attacks on New Spain. Approving the idea, Queen Elizabeth I authorized first Gilbert, then Raleigh, to colonize North America.

Sir Walter Raleigh's Roanoke Colony

Gilbert failed to plant a colony in Newfoundland, dying in the attempt, and Raleigh was only briefly more successful. After two preliminary expeditions, in 1587 he sent 117 colonists to the territory he named Virginia, after Elizabeth, the "Virgin Queen." They established a settlement on Roanoke Island, in what is now North Carolina, but in 1590 a resupply ship—delayed in leaving England because of the Spanish Armada—could not find them. The colonists had vanished, leaving only the word Croatoan (the name of a nearby island) carved on a tree. Recent tree-ring studies have shown that the North Carolina coast experienced a severe drought between 1587 and 1589, which would have created a subsistence crisis for the settlers and which could well have led them to abandon the Roanoke site.

Thus England's first attempt to plant a permanent settlement on the North American coast failed, as had similar efforts by Portugal on Cape Breton Island (early 1520s) and France in northern Florida (mid-1560s). All three enterprises collapsed because of the hostility of their neighbors and their inability to be self-sustaining in foodstuffs. Spanish soldiers wiped out the French colony in 1565 (see page 34), and neither the Portuguese nor the English were able to maintain friendly relations with local Indians.

The explanation for such failings becomes clear in Thomas Harriot's *A Briefe and True Report of the New Found Land of Virginia*, published in 1588 to publicize Raleigh's colony. Harriot, a noted scientist who sailed with the second of the preliminary voyages to Roanoke, described the animals, plants, and people of the re-

Thomas Harriot's *Briefe and True Report*

John White, an artist with Raleigh's 1585 expedition (and later the governor of the ill-fated 1587 colony), illustrated three different fishing techniques used by Carolina Indians: to the left, the construction of weirs and traps; in the background, spearfishing in shallow water; in the foreground, fishing from dugout canoes. The fish are accurately drawn and can be identified today.   (Trustees of the British Museum)

gion for an English readership. His account revealed that although the explorers depended on nearby villagers for most of their food, they needlessly antagonized their neighbors by killing some of them for what Harriot himself admitted were unjustifiable reasons.

The scientist advised later colonizers to deal with the native peoples of America more humanely than his comrades had. But the content of his book suggested why that advice would rarely be followed. *A Briefe and True Report* examined the possibilities for economic development in America. Harriot stressed three points: the availability of commodities familiar to Europeans, like grapes, iron, copper, and fur-bearing animals; the potential profitability of exotic American products such as maize, cassava, and tobacco; and the relative ease of manipulating the native population to the Europeans' advantage. Should the Americans attempt to resist the English by force, Harriot asserted, the latter's advantages of disciplined soldiers and superior weaponry would quickly deliver victory.

Harriot's *Briefe and True Report* depicted for his English readers a bountiful land full of opportunities for quick profit. The people already residing there would, he thought, "in a short time be brought to civilitie" through conversion to Christianity, admiration for European superiority, or conquest—if they did not die from disease, the ravages of which he witnessed. Thomas Harriot understood the key elements of the story, but his prediction was far off the mark. European dominance of North America would be difficult to achieve. Indeed, some historians today argue that it never was fully achieved, in the sense Harriot and his compatriots intended, and that the societies that subsequently developed in North America owed as much to their native origins as to their immigrant ones.

Summary

 The process of initial contact between Europeans and Americans that ended with Thomas Harriot near the close of the sixteenth century began approximately 250 years earlier when Portuguese sailors first set out to explore the Mediterranean Atlantic and to settle on its islands. That region of the Atlantic so close to European and African shores nurtured the mariners who, like Christopher Columbus, ventured into previously unknown waters—those who sailed to India and Brazil as well as to the Caribbean and the North American coast. When Columbus first reached the Americas, he thought he had found Asia, his intended destination. Later explorers knew better but, except for the Spanish, regarded the Americas primarily as a barrier that prevented them from reaching their long-sought goal of an oceanic route to the riches of China and the Moluccas. Ordinary European fishermen were the first to realize that the northern coasts had valuable products to offer: fish and furs, both much in demand in their homelands.

The wealth of the north could not compare to that of Mesoamerica. The Aztec Empire, heir to the trad-

ing networks of Teotihuacán as well as to the intellectual sophistication of the Mayas, dazzled the conquistadors with the magnificence of its buildings and its seemingly unlimited wealth. As an old man, Cortés's aide Bernal Diaz del Castillo recalled his first sight of Tenochtitlán, situated in the midst of Lake Texcoco: "We were amazed and said that it was like the enchantments . . . on account of the great towers and cues [temples] and buildings rising from the water, and all built of masonry." Some soldiers asked, he remembered, "whether the things that we saw were not a dream."

The Aztecs had predicted that their Fifth Sun would end in earthquakes and hunger. Hunger they surely experienced after Cortés's invasion; and, if there were no earthquakes, the great temples tumbled to the ground nevertheless, as the Spaniards used their stones (and Indian laborers) to construct cathedrals honoring their God and his son Jesus rather than Huitzilopochtli. The conquerors employed first American and later enslaved African workers to till the fields, mine the precious metals, and herd the livestock that earned immense profits for themselves and their mother country.

The initial impact of Europeans on the Americas proved devastating. Flourishing civilizations were, if not entirely destroyed, markedly altered in just a few short decades. The Europeans' diseases and livestock, along with a wide range of other imported animals and plants, irrevocably changed the American environment, affecting the lives of the Western Hemisphere's inhabitants. By the end of the sixteenth century, fewer people resided in North America than had lived there before Columbus's arrival, even taking into account the arrival of many Europeans and Africans. And the people who did live there—Indian, African, and European—resided in a world that was indeed new—a world engaged in the unprecedented process of combining foods, religions, economies, styles of life, and political systems that had developed separately for millennia. Understandably, conflict and dissension permeated that process.

LEGACY FOR A PEOPLE AND A NATION
Columbus Day

Each year, the United States celebrates the second Monday in October as a tribute to Christopher Columbus's landing in the Bahamas in 1492. When viewed in the context of other holidays that mark the birthdays of great Americans or key events in the nation's past, Columbus Day is an anomaly. After all, the Genoese mariner never set foot on North American soil.

The first known U.S. celebration of Columbus's voyage occurred in New York City on October 12, 1792, when a men's social club gave a dinner to mark its three hundredth anniversary. In the late 1860s, Italian American communities in New York City and San Francisco began to celebrate October 12, but not until the four hundredth anniversary in 1892 did a congressional resolution order a one-time national commemoration. Columbus Day was first observed as a national holiday in 1971, although a majority of the states already celebrated it (Colorado was the first, in 1907).

More than thirty years ago Congress proclaimed Columbus Day as a national holiday with little opposition, except from Americans of Scandinavian descent who would have preferred to honor the Norse explorers of 1001. Today, though, the annual observances can arouse strong emotions. The American Indian Movement (AIM), founded in 1968, has declared that "from an indigenous vantage point, Columbus' arrival was a disaster." Terming Columbus a "murderer," the AIM contends that he "deserves no recognition or acco-

lades"—certainly not a holiday. At the same time, as immigration has increased the Latino presence in the United States, people of Hispanic descent have claimed Columbus as their own, insisting that his voyage was "a thoroughly Spanish event." In some cities—most notably New York—their celebrations rival those long organized by Italian Americans; in others, such as Miami, Hispanics control the official commemorations. Still other Latinos, especially those of Mexican descent living in Los Angeles, call October 12 Día de la Raza and use it as an occasion to protest current U.S. immigration policy.

As ethnic diversity has increased in the nation, and as peoples of different origins have sought to claim a share of the American heritage, holidays have unsurprisingly become the occasion for heated contests. Each fall, the American people and nation therefore continue to confront the controversial legacy of Columbus's 1492 voyage.

For Further Reading, see page A-1 of the Appendix. For Web resources, go to http://college.hmco.com.

La V.ᵃ Mᵉ. Maria de Iesus de Agreda. Predicando
à los Chichimecas del Nuebo-mexico. Antt.º de Costro fᵗ

In August 1630, Fray Alonso de Benavides brought thrilling news to Madrid. Franciscan priests in the remote territory called New Mexico had successfully converted at least eighty thousand heathens to Roman Catholicism. In village after village and even among the nomadic Apaches and Navajos, Indians had eagerly embraced baptism in the new faith, had built beautiful churches and schools with their own hands, and had demonstrated their willing adherence to the true religion of Jesus Christ. Moreover, the priests' missionary activities had repeatedly benefited from God's "wonders and miracles." For example, when an old woman from Taos tried to convince four others to renounce their Christian marriages, "a bolt of lightning flashed from a clear untroubled sky, killing that infernal agent of the demon."

Fray Alonso, who was born in the Azores in the 1570s, supervised the New Mexico missions from 1626 to 1629. His account of the Franciscans' miraculous successes created a sensation in Europe. Alonso's *Memorial* not only was immediately published in Spanish but also was quickly translated into Latin, French, Dutch, and German. Fray Alonso undertook the arduous journey to Spain to convince the king to increase his financial and administrative support of the Franciscan missions. He achieved that goal: King Philip IV agreed to send additional priests to New Mexico at his own personal expense, and he ordered the colonial governor to assist the missionaries' efforts actively.

Yet even Fray Alonso de Benavides's enthusiastic and optimistic report contained a troubling undercurrent. Only about 250 Spaniards (along with another 750 Pueblos and *mestizos*) inhabited the colonial capital at Santa Fe. The soldiers were "few and poorly equipped," and the church had been "a miserable hut" before Fray Alonso ordered the construction of a new one. Furthermore, not all the local Indians had been receptive to the priests' message. The residents of Picurís, for one, were "treacherous" and "on various occasions" had tried to murder the priests stationed there. Many of the miracles Fray Alonso described

When Fray Alonso de Benavides arrived in Spain (see text above), he visited a Franciscan nun, Maria de Jesús de Agreda, who claimed to have traveled in spirit to preach to the Indians of New Mexico. In this 1631 woodcut, an artist depicted the missionizing revealed in her visions. The Indians, she declared, could see her, but Spaniards in the colony could not. (University of Texas at Austin, Benson Latin Center for American History)

EUROPEANS COLONIZE NORTH AMERICA 1600–1640

(such as the one recounted above) had been occasioned by the Indians' rejection of Christianity. For example, some Hopis' skepticism about Christian teachings had led one priest to cause a boy blind from birth to see for the first time, and a Franciscan attempting to convert a group of Apaches had been saved from death only because at the last minute his attackers miraculously "did not dare shoot" the arrows they were aiming at him.

So, while praising the Spaniards' stunning successes in New Mexico, Fray Alonso revealed their equally striking weaknesses: many Native Americans resisted their proselytizing; both priests and soldiers lacked adequate financial resources; and the one tiny, impoverished European settlement was surrounded by tens of thousands of potentially troublesome Pueblos, Apaches, and Navajos. Fray Alonso furthermore failed to identify an additional problem: royal governors often clashed with the Franciscans in a struggle for control of the region. A half-century later, the Pueblo peoples capitalized on such Spanish weaknesses in a successful revolt.

By the time Fray Alonso arrived in Madrid in 1630, England, France, and the Netherlands had also founded permanent colonies in North America. No longer were the Spaniards the only Europeans on that vast continent. Just as Franciscans played a major role in the Spanish settlements, so too Jesuit priests were active in New France. The French and Dutch colonies, like the Spanish outposts, were settled largely by European men. Like the conquistadors, French and Dutch merchants (on the mainland) and planters (in the Caribbean islands) hoped to make a quick profit and then perhaps return to their homelands. The English, as Thomas Harriot made clear in the 1580s, were just as interested in profiting from North America. But they pursued those profits in a different way.

In contrast to other Europeans, most of the English settlers came to America intending to stay. Especially along the northeast Atlantic coast of the continent, in the area that came to be known as New England, they arrived in family groups, sometimes along with friends and relatives from neighboring villages back home. They recreated European society and family life to an extent not possible in the other colonies, where migrant men found their sexual partners within the Native American or African populations. Among the English colonies, those in the Chesapeake region and on the Caribbean islands most closely resembled colonies founded by other nations. Their economies, like those of Hispaniola or Brazil, soon came to be based on large-scale production for the international market by a labor force composed of bonded servants and slaves.

Wherever they settled, the English, like other Europeans, prospered only after they learned to adapt to the alien environment. The first permanent English colonies survived because nearby Indians assisted the newcomers. The settlers had to learn to grow unfamiliar American crops such as maize (corn) and tobacco. They also had to develop extensive trading relationships with Native Americans and with colonies established by other European countries. Needing laborers for their fields, they first used English indentured servants, then later began to import African slaves, copying the example of the Spanish in the Atlantic and Caribbean islands, and the Portuguese in São Tomé and Brazil. Thus the early history of the region that became the United States and the English Caribbean is best understood not as an isolated story of English colonization but rather as a series of complex interactions among a variety of European, African, and American peoples and environments. ■

New Spain, New France, and New Netherland

 Spaniards were the first Europeans to establish a permanent settlement within the boundaries of the modern United States, but they were not the first to attempt that feat. Twice in the 1560s groups of French Protestants (Huguenots) sought to escape from persecution in their homeland by planting colonies on the south Atlantic coast. The first colony, in present-day South Carolina, collapsed, and its starving inhabitants had to be rescued by a passing ship. The second, near modern Jacksonville, Florida, was destroyed in 1565 by a Spanish expedition under the command of Pedro Menéndez de Avilés. To ensure Spanish domination of the strategically important region (located near sea-lanes used by Spanish treasure ships bound for Europe), Menéndez set up a small fortified outpost, which he named St. Augustine—now the oldest continuously inhabited European settlement in the United States. Franciscan missionaries soon followed, but nearby Indians fiercely resisted the priests' efforts to Christianize them. Only after the native peoples were forcibly moved to mission towns did many assent to baptism. Even so, by the end of the sixteenth century a chain of Franciscan missions stretched across northern Florida.

IMPORTANT EVENTS

1533 Henry VIII divorces Catherine of Aragon; English Reformation begins

1558 Elizabeth I becomes queen

1565 Founding of St. Augustine (Florida), oldest permanent European settlement in present-day United States

1598 Oñate conquers Pueblos in New Mexico for Spain

1603 James I becomes king

1607 Jamestown founded, first permanent English settlement in North America

1608 Quebec founded by the French

1609 Hudson explores Hudson River for the Dutch

1610 Founding of Santa Fe, New Mexico

1611 First Virginia tobacco crop

1614 Fort Orange (Albany) founded by the Dutch

1619 Virginia House of Burgesses established, first representative assembly in the English colonies

1620 Plymouth colony founded, first permanent English settlement in New England

1622 Powhatan Confederacy attacks Virginia colony

1624 Dutch settle on Manhattan Island (New Amsterdam)
English colonize St. Kitts, first island in Lesser Antilles to be settled by Europeans
James I revokes Virginia Company's charter

1625 Charles I becomes king

1630 Massachusetts Bay colony founded

1634 Maryland founded

1636 Williams expelled from Massachusetts Bay; founds Providence, Rhode Island
Connecticut founded

1637 Pequot War in New England

1638 Hutchinson expelled from Massachusetts Bay colony; goes to Rhode Island

c. 1640 Sugar cultivation begins on Barbados

1642 Montreal founded by the French

1646 Treaty ends hostilities between Virginia and Powhatan Confederacy

---

More than thirty years passed after the founding of St. Augustine before conquistadors ventured anew into the present-day United States. In 1598, drawn northward by rumors of rich cities, Juan de Oñate, a Mexican-born adventurer, led a group of about five hundred soldiers and settlers to New Mexico. At first, the Pueblos greeted the newcomers cordially. When the Spaniards began to use torture, murder, and rape to extort food and clothing from the villagers, however, the residents of Acoma killed several soldiers. The invaders responded ferociously, killing more than eight hundred people and capturing the remainder. All the captives above the age of twelve were ordered enslaved for twenty years, and men older than twenty-five had one foot amputated. Not surprisingly, the other Pueblo villages surrendered.

Yet Oñate's bloody victory proved illusory, for New Mexico held little wealth. It also was too far from the Pacific coast to assist in protecting Spanish sea-lanes, which had been one of Oñate's aims (he, like others, initially believed the continent to be much nar-

New Mexico

The women of Acoma pueblo have long been accomplished potters. Before the arrival of Europeans with iron utensils, residents of the pueblo stored food and water in pots like this. The unusual shape derived from its function: the low center of gravity allowed a woman to balance the pot easily on her head as she carried water from a cistern to the top of the mesa.   (The Field Museum, #A109998c)

Table 2.1   The Founding of Permanent European Colonies in North America, 1565–1640

Colony	Founder(s)	Date	Basis of Economy
Florida	Pedro Menéndez de Avilés	1565	Farming
New Mexico	Juan de Oñate	1598	Livestock
Virginia	Virginia Company	1607	Tobacco
New France	France	1608	Fur trading
New Netherland	Dutch West India Company	1614	Fur trading
Plymouth	Pilgrims	1620	Farming, fishing
Maine	Sir Ferdinando Gorges	1622	Fishing
St. Kitts, Barbados, et al.	European immigrants	1624	Sugar
Massachusetts Bay	Massachusetts Bay Company	1630	Farming, fishing, fur trading
Maryland	Cecilius Calvert	1634	Tobacco
Rhode Island	Roger Williams	1636	Farming
Connecticut	Thomas Hooker	1636	Farming, fur trading
New Haven	Massachusetts migrants	1638	Farming
New Hampshire	Massachusetts migrants	1638	Farming, fishing

rower than it actually is). Many of the Spaniards returned to Mexico, and officials considered abandoning the isolated colony, which lay 800 miles north of the nearest Spanish settlement. Instead, in 1609, the authorities decided to maintain a small military outpost and a few Christian missions in the area, with the capital at Santa Fe (founded in 1610). This was the constricted world in which Fray Alonso de Benavides arrived in 1626 and on which he made his mark (see Map 3.3 on page 68).

After Spain's destruction of France's Florida settlement in 1565, the French turned their attention northward, to the area that Jacques Cartier had explored in the 1530s.

Quebec and Montreal

Several times they tried futilely to establish permanent bases along the Canadian coast, not succeeding until 1605, with the founding of Port Royal. Then in 1608 Samuel de Champlain set up a trading post at an interior site the local Iroquois had called Stadacona when Cartier spent the winter there seventy-five years earlier. Champlain renamed it Quebec. He had chosen well: Quebec was the most easily defended spot in the entire St. Lawrence River valley, a stronghold that controlled access to the heartland of the continent. In 1642 the French established a second post, Montreal, at the falls of the St. Lawrence (and thus at the end of navigation by oceangoing vessels), a place the Indians called Hochelaga.

Before the founding of these settlements, French fishermen served as the major transporters of North American beaver pelts to France, but the new posts quickly took over control of the lucrative trade in furs (see Table 2.1). Only a few Europeans resided in New France; most were men, some of whom married Indian women. The colony's leaders gave land grants along the river to wealthy seigneurs (nobles), who then imported tenants to work their farms. A small number of Frenchmen brought their wives and took up agriculture; even so, more than twenty-five years after Quebec's founding, it had just sixty-four resident families, along with traders and soldiers. With respect to territory occupied and farmed, northern New France never grew much beyond the confines of the river valley between Quebec and Montreal (see Map 2.1).

One other important group composed part of the population of New France: missionaries of the Society of Jesus (Jesuits), a Roman Catholic order dedicated to converting non-believers to Christianity. First arriving in Quebec in 1625, the Jesuits, whom the Indians called Black Robes, initially tried to persuade indigenous peoples to live near French settlements and to adopt European agricultural methods as well as the Europeans' religion. When that effort failed, the Jesuits concluded that they could introduce Roman Catholicism to their new charges without insisting that they fundamentally

Jesuit Missions in New France

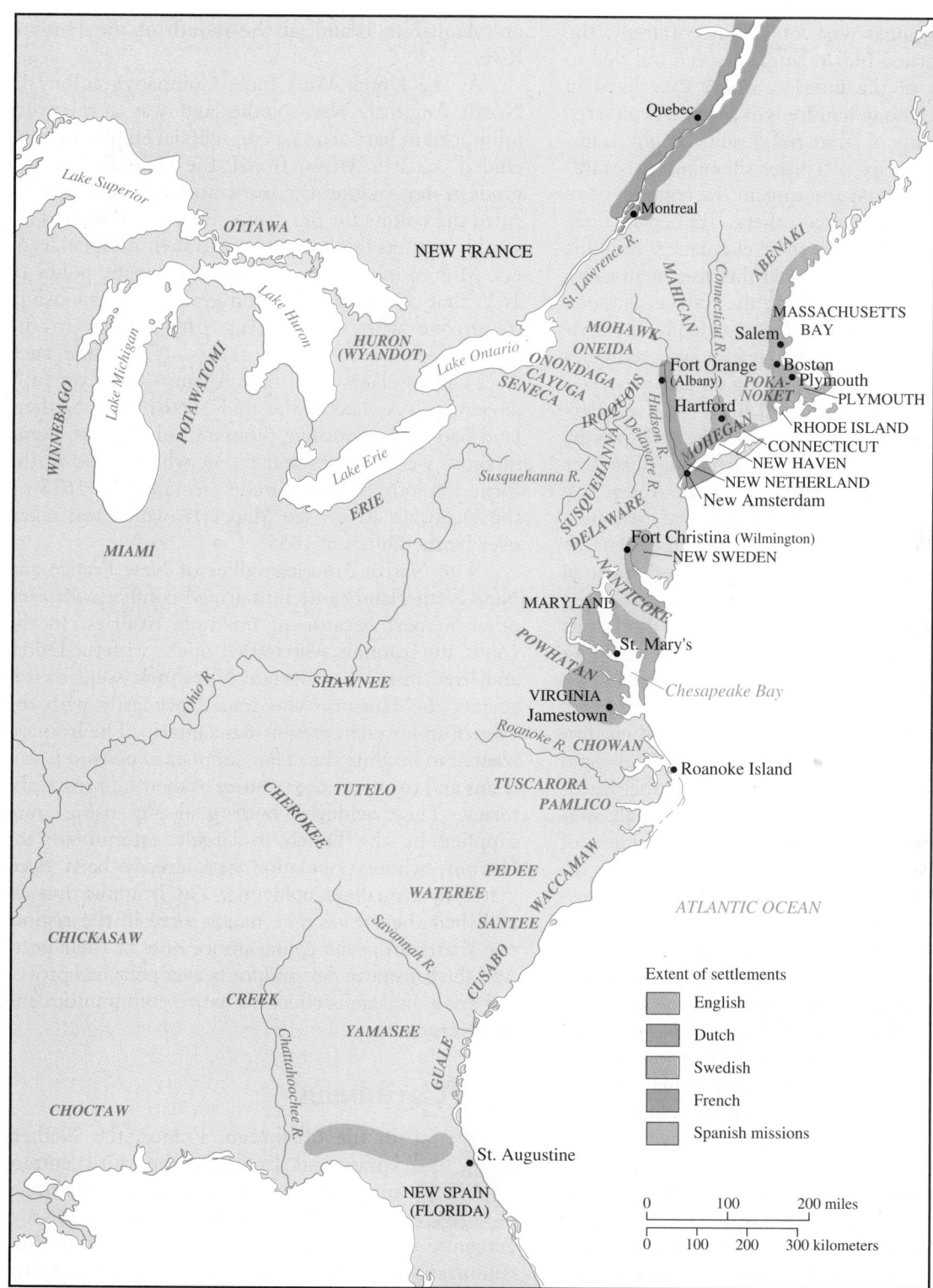

Map 2.1   European Settlements and Indian Tribes in Eastern North America, 1650
The few European settlements established in the east before 1650 were widely scattered, hugging the shores of the Atlantic Ocean and the banks of its major rivers. By contrast, America's native inhabitants controlled the vast interior expanse of the continent and Spaniards had begun to move into the West.

alter their traditional ways of life. Accordingly, the Black Robes learned Indian languages and traveled to remote regions of the interior, where they lived in twos and threes among hundreds of potential converts.

Using a variety of strategies, Jesuits sought to undermine the authority of village shamans (the traditional religious leaders) and to gain the confidence of leaders who could influence others. Trained in rhetoric, they won admirers by their eloquence. Immune to smallpox (for all had survived the disease already), they explained epidemics among the Indians as God's punishment for sin, their arguments aided by the ineffectiveness of the shamans' traditional remedies against the new pestilence. Drawing on European science, Jesuits predicted solar and lunar eclipses. Perhaps most important, they amazed the villagers by communicating with each other over long distances and periods of time by employing marks on paper. The Indians' desire to learn how to harness the extraordinary power of literacy was one of the critical factors making them receptive to the missionaries' spiritual message.

Although the process took many years, the Jesuits slowly gained thousands of converts, some of whom moved to reserves set aside for Christian Indians. In those communities they followed Catholic teachings with fervor and piety. The converts replaced their own culture's traditional equal treatment of men and women with notions more congenial to the Europeans' insistence on male dominance and female subordination. Further, they altered their practice of allowing premarital sexual relationships and easy divorce because Catholic doctrine prohibited both customs.

Jesuit missionaries faced little competition from other Europeans for Native Americans' souls, but French fur traders had to confront a direct challenge. In 1614, only five

New Netherland

years after Henry Hudson sailed up the river that now bears his name, his sponsor, the Dutch West India Company, established an outpost (Fort Orange) on that river at the site of present-day Albany, New York. Like the French, the Dutch sought beaver pelts, and their presence so close to Quebec posed a threat to French domination of the region. The Netherlands, at the time the world's dominant commercial power, was interested primarily in trade rather than colonization. Thus New Netherland, like New France, remained small, mostly confined to a river valley that offered easy access to its settlements. The colony's southern anchor was New Amsterdam, a town founded in 1624 on Manhattan Island, at the mouth of the Hudson River.

As the Dutch West India Company's colony in North America, New Netherland was a relatively unimportant part of a vast commercial empire that included posts in Africa, Brazil, the West Indies, and modern-day Indonesia. Autocratic directors-general ruled the colony for the company; with no elected assembly, settlers felt little loyalty to their nominal leaders. Migration was sparse. Even a company policy of 1629 that offered a large land grant, or patroonship, to anyone who would bring fifty settlers to the province failed to attract takers. (Only one such tract—Rensselaerswyck, near Albany—was ever fully developed.) As late as the mid-1660s, New Netherland had only about five thousand inhabitants. Some of those were Swedes and Finns, who resided in the former colony of New Sweden (founded in 1638 on the Delaware River; see Map 2.1), which was taken over by the Dutch in 1655.

The Native American allies of New France and New Netherland came into armed conflict with each other in part because of fur-trade rivalries. In the 1640s, the Iroquois, who traded chiefly with the Dutch and lived in modern upstate New York, went to war against the Hurons, who traded primarily with the French and lived in present-day Ontario. The Iroquois wanted to become the major supplier of pelts to Europeans and to ensure the security of their hunting territories. They achieved both goals by using guns supplied by the Dutch to largely exterminate the Hurons, whose population had already been decimated by a smallpox epidemic. The Iroquois thus established themselves as a major force in the region, one that Europeans could ignore only at their peril. And the European demand for beaver pelts had proved to have a disastrous effect on native communities and their interactions.

The Caribbean

In the Caribbean, France, the Netherlands, and England—the third entrant into the contest for North America—clashed openly in the first half of the seventeenth century. The Spanish concentrated their colonization efforts on the Greater Antilles—Cuba, Hispaniola, Jamaica, and Puerto Rico. They left many smaller islands alone, partly because of resistance by their Carib inhabitants, partly because the mainland offered greater wealth for less effort. But the tiny islands attracted other European powers: they could

provide bases from which to attack Spanish vessels loaded with American gold and silver, and they could serve as sources of valuable tropical products such as spices, dyes, and fruits.

England was the first northern European nation to establish a permanent foothold in the smaller West Indian islands (the Lesser Antilles). English people settled on St. Christopher (St. Kitts) in 1624, then later on other islands such as Barbados (1627). France was able to colonize Guadeloupe and Martinique only by defeating the Caribs, whereas the Dutch more easily gained control of St. Eustatius (strategically located near St. Kitts). In addition to indigenous inhabitants, Europeans had to worry about conflicts with Spaniards and with one another. Most of the islands were attacked at least once during the course of the century, and some changed hands. For example, the English drove the Spanish out of Jamaica in 1655, and the French soon thereafter took over half of Hispaniola, creating the colony of St. Domingue (modern Haiti).

Why did other Europeans devote so much energy to gaining control of these tiny bits of land neglected by Spain? The primary answer to that question is sugar. Early in the 1640s, English residents of Barbados discovered that the island's soil and climate were ideally suited for cultivating sugar cane, grown at the time primarily in the Wine Islands, São Tomé, and Brazil. Europeans loved sugar, which provided its users with both a sweet taste and a quick energy boost. Entering the European market in substantial quantities at approximately the same time as coffee and tea, the stimulating, addictive, and bitter Asian drinks improved by the addition of a sweetener, sugar quickly became a crucial element of Europeans' diet.

The Importance of Sugar

The Dutch helped to introduce sugar cane into the newly colonized Lesser Antilles. In 1630 they seized control of northeastern Brazil, holding the region until 1654. There the Dutch learned how to grow

In the 1660s, a French book illustrated the various phases of sugar processing for curious European readers. Teams of oxen (A) turned the mill, the rollers of which crushed the canes (C), producing the sap (D), which was collected in a vat (E), then boiled down into molasses (K). African slaves, with minimal supervision by a few Europeans (foreground), managed all phases of the process.   (Library Company of Philadelphia)

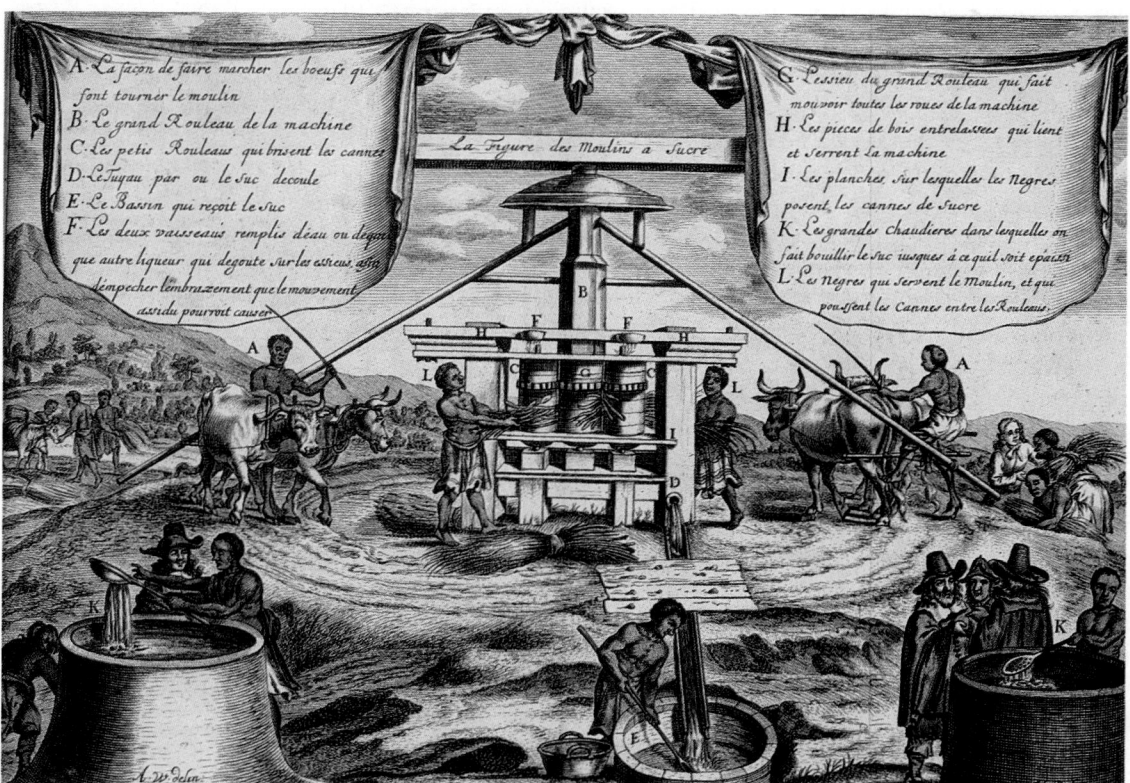

the canes and to process them into molasses and refined brown and white sugars. When they taught those skills to Barbadians, they were not being altruistic. The Dutch expected to sell African slaves to West Indian planters and to carry to Europe barrels of molasses and rum, which was distilled from sugar. The results must have exceeded their wildest dreams. The Barbados sugar boom in the 1640s was both explosive and lucrative. Planters, slave traders, and Dutch shipping interests alike earned immense profits.

As other Caribbean planters adopted sugar-cane cultivation, Barbadians' profits fell. Even so, sugar remained the most valuable American commodity for more than one hundred years. In the eighteenth century, sugar grown by slaves in British Jamaica and French St. Domingue dominated the world market. Yet, in the long run, the future economic importance of the Europeans' American colonies lay on the mainland rather than in the Caribbean.

English Interest in Colonization

The failure of Raleigh's Roanoke colony ended English efforts to settle in North America for nearly two decades. When the English decided in 1606 to try once more, they again planned colonies that imitated the Spanish model. Success came only when they abandoned that model and founded settlements very different from those of other European powers. Unlike Spain, France, or the Netherlands, England eventually sent large numbers of men and women to set up agriculturally based colonies on the mainland. Two major developments prompted approximately 200,000 ordinary English men and women to move to North America in the seventeenth century and led their government to encourage their emigration.

The first impetus that led English folk to move to North America was the onset of dramatic social and economic change caused by a population boom. In the 150-year period after 1530, largely as a result of the introduction of nutritious American crops into Europe, England's population doubled. All those additional people needed food, clothing, and other goods. The competition for goods led to high inflation, coupled with a fall in real wages as the number of workers increased. In these new economic and demographic circumstances, some English people—especially those with sizable landholdings that could produce food and clothing fibers for the

Social Change in England

growing population—substantially improved their lot. Others, particularly landless laborers and those with very small amounts of land, fell into unremitting poverty. When landowners raised rents, took over common lands previously open to use by peasants, or decided to combine small holdings into large units, they forced tenants off the land. As a result, geographical as well as social mobility increased, and the population of the cities swelled. London, for example, more than tripled in size between 1550 and 1650. By the latter year 375,000 residents were living on its crowded streets.

Well-to-do English people reacted with alarm to what they saw as the disappearance of traditional ways of life. Steady streams of the landless and homeless filled the streets and highways. Obsessed with the problem of maintaining order, officials came to believe that England was overcrowded. They concluded that colonies established in North America could siphon off England's "surplus population," thus easing social strains at home. For similar reasons, many English people decided that they could improve their circumstances by migrating from a small, land-scarce, apparently overpopulated island to a large, land-rich, apparently empty continent. Such economic considerations were rendered even more significant in light of the second development, a major change in English religious practice.

The sixteenth century witnessed a religious transformation that eventually led large numbers of English dissenters to leave their homeland. In 1533 Henry VIII, wanting a male heir and infatuated with Anne Boleyn, sought to annul his marriage to his Spanish-born queen, Catherine of Aragon, despite nearly twenty years of marriage and the birth of a daughter. When the pope refused to approve the annulment, Henry left the Roman Catholic Church. He founded the Church of England and—with Parliament's concurrence—proclaimed himself its head. In general, English people welcomed the schism. Many had little respect for the English Catholic Church, which at the time was filled with corrupt bishops and ignorant priests. At first the reformed Church of England differed little from Catholicism in its practices, but under Henry's daughter Elizabeth I (child of his marriage to Anne Boleyn), new currents of religious belief that had originated on the European continent early in the sixteenth century dramatically affected the English church.

The English Reformation

The leaders of the continental Protestant Reformation were Martin Luther, a German monk, and

John Calvin, a French cleric and lawyer. Combating the Catholic doctrine that priests must serve as intermediaries between laypeople and God, Luther and Calvin insisted that people could interpret the Bible for themselves. One result of that notion was the spread of literacy: to understand and interpret the Bible, people had to learn how to read. Both Luther and Calvin rejected Catholic rituals and denied the need for an elaborate church hierarchy. They also asserted that salvation rested on faith alone, rather than—as Catholic teaching had it—on a combination of faith and good works. Calvin, though, went further than Luther in stressing God's omnipotence and emphasizing the need for people to submit totally to God's will.

Elizabeth I tolerated religious diversity among her subjects as long as they generally acknowledged her authority as head of the Church of England. Accordingly, during her long reign (1558–1603) Calvin's ideas gained influence within the English church. By the late sixteenth century, many English

Puritans

Calvinists—those who came to be called Puritans because they wanted to purify the Church of England—believed that the English Reformation had not gone far enough. Henry had simplified the church hierarchy; they wanted to abolish it altogether. Henry had subordinated the church to the interests of the state; they wanted a church free from political interference. And the Church of England, like the Roman Catholic Church, continued to include all English people in its membership. The Puritans preferred a more restricted definition; they wanted to confine church membership to persons they believed to be "saved"—those God had selected for salvation before birth.

Paradoxically, though, a key article of the Puritans' faith insisted that people could not know for certain if they were "saved" because mere mortals could not comprehend or affect their predestination to heaven or hell. Thus pious Puritans daily confronted serious dilemmas: If the saved (or "elect") could not be identified with certainty, how could proper churches be constituted? If one was predestined for heaven or hell and could not alter one's fate, why should one

London in 1616, with London Bridge at center right. Overcrowding in the city led many observers to conclude that American colonization could remove "excess" population and provide new employment for poverty-stricken persons. The rapidly growing community of London merchants also sought to develop new sources of overseas profits. (Trustees of the British Library)

attend church or do good works? Puritans dealt with the first conundrum by admitting that their judgments as to eligibility for church membership only approximated God's unknowable decisions. And they resolved the second by reasoning that God gave the elect the ability to accept salvation and to lead a good life. Therefore, even though one could not earn a place in heaven by piety and good works, such practices could indicate one's place in the ranks of the saved.

Elizabeth I's Stuart successors, her cousin James I (1603–1625) and his son Charles I (1625–1649), were

The First Stuart Monarchs

less tolerant of Puritans than she. As Scots, they also had little respect for the traditions of representative government that had developed in England under the Tudors and their predecessors (see Table 2.2). The wealthy landowners who sat in Parliament had grown accustomed to having considerable influence on government policies, especially taxation. But James I, taking a position later endorsed by his son, publicly declared his adherence to the theory of the divine right of kings. The Stuarts insisted that a monarch's power came directly from God and that his subjects had a duty to obey him. A king's authority was absolute, they argued, just like the authority of a father over his children.

Both James I and Charles I believed that their authority included the power to enforce religious conformity among their subjects. Because Puritans were challenging many of the most important precepts of the English church, the monarchs authorized the removal of Puritan clergymen from their pulpits. In the 1620s and 1630s a number of English Puritans decided to move to America, where they hoped to put their religious beliefs into practice unmolested by the Stuarts or the church hierarchy. Some fled hurriedly to avoid arrest and imprisonment.

Table 2.2 Tudor and Stuart Monarchs of England, 1509–1649		
Monarch	**Reign**	**Relation to Predecessor**
Henry VIII	1509–1547	Son
Edward VI	1547–1553	Son
Mary I	1553–1558	Half-sister
Elizabeth I	1558–1603	Half-sister
James I	1603–1625	Cousin
Charles I	1625–1649	Son

The Founding of Virginia

 The initial impulse that would lead to England's first permanent colony in the Western Hemisphere came not from the Puritans but from a group of merchants and wealthy gentry. In 1606, envisioning the possibility of earning great profits by finding precious metals and opening new trade routes, the men established a joint-stock venture, the Virginia Company, to plant colonies in America.

Joint-stock companies had been developed in England during the sixteenth century as a mechanism for

Joint-Stock Companies

pooling the resources of many small investors. Stock sales funded these forerunners of modern corporations. Until the creation of the Virginia Company, they had been used primarily to finance trading voyages. For that purpose they worked well: no one risked too much money, and investors usually received quick returns. But joint-stock companies turned out to be a poor way to finance colonies because the early settlements required enormous amounts of capital and, with rare exceptions, failed to return much immediate profit. Colonies founded by joint-stock companies consequently suffered from a chronic lack of capital and from constant tension between stockholders and colonists, who claimed they were not being adequately supported by the investors.

The Virginia Company was no exception. Chartered by James I in 1606, the company tried but failed

Jamestown

to start a colony in Maine and barely succeeded in planting one in Virginia. In 1607 it dispatched to North America an expedition consisting exclusively of men and boys. In May, 104 Englishmen landed in a region the native inhabitants called Tsenacomoco. There they established the settlement called Jamestown on a swampy peninsula in a river they also named for their monarch. Ill-equipped for survival in the unfamiliar environment, the colonists were afflicted by dissension and disease. Moreover, through sheer bad luck they arrived in the midst of a severe drought (now known to be the worst in the region for nearly eight hundred years), which persisted until 1612. The lack of rainfall not only made it difficult to cultivate crops but also polluted their drinking water.

By January 1608, only thirty-eight of the original colonists remained alive. Many of the first immigrants were gentlemen unaccustomed to working with their hands and artisans with irrelevant skills like glassmaking. A few were soldiers who had fought against Spain in the Netherlands. Having come to Virginia expecting to make easy fortunes, many could not adjust to the conditions they encountered. They resisted hard labor, retaining elaborate English dress and casual work habits despite their desperate circumstances. Such attitudes, combined with the effects of chronic malnutrition and epidemic disease, took a terrible toll. Only when Captain John Smith, one of the colony's founders, imposed military discipline on the colonists in 1608 was Jamestown saved from collapse. But after Smith's departure the settlement experienced a severe "starving time" (the winter of 1609–1610), during which at least one colonist resorted to cannibalism. Although more settlers (including a few women and children) arrived in 1608 and 1609 and living conditions slowly improved, as late as 1624 only 1,300 of approximately 8,000 English immigrants to Virginia remained alive.

The survival of Jamestown may be attributed not to the English but rather to the Native Americans within whose territories they settled,

The Powhatan Confederacy

a group of six Algonquian tribes known as the Powhatan Confederacy (see Map 2.1). A shrewd and powerful leader, Powhatan was aggressively consolidating his authority over some twenty-five smaller bands when the Europeans arrived. Fortunately for the colonists, Powhatan at first viewed them as potential allies. He found the English colony a reliable source of useful items such as steel knives and guns, which gave him a technological advantage over his Indian neighbors. In return, Powhatan's people traded their excess corn and other foodstuffs to the starving settlers. The initially cordial relationship soon deteriorated, however. The English colonists kidnapped Powhatan's daughter, Pocahontas, holding her as a hostage in retaliation for Powhatan's seizure of several settlers. In captivity, she agreed in 1614 to marry a colonist, John Rolfe; she sailed with him to England, where she died in 1616.

The Jamestown colony and the coastal Indians had an uneasy relationship. English and Algonquian peoples had much in common: deep

Algonquian and English Cultural Differences

religious beliefs, a lifestyle oriented around agriculture, clear political and social hierarchies, and sharply defined gender roles. Yet the English and the Powhatans themselves focused on their cultural differences, not their similarities. English men regarded Indian men as lazy because they did not cultivate crops and spent much of their

time hunting (a sport, not work, in English eyes). Indian men thought English men effeminate because they did "women's work" of cultivation. In the same vein, the English believed that Algonquian women were oppressed because they did heavy field labor.

Other differences between the two cultures caused serious misunderstandings. Although both societies were hierarchical, the nature of the hierarchies differed considerably. Among the East Coast Algonquians, people were not born to positions of leadership, nor were political power and social status necessarily inherited through the male line. Members of the English gentry inherited their position from their fathers, and English political and military leaders tended to rule autocratically. By contrast, the authority of Algonquian leaders rested on consensus. Accustomed to the European concept of powerful kings, the English sought such figures in native villages. Often (for example, when negotiating treaties) they willfully overestimated the ability of chiefs to make independent decisions for their people.

Furthermore, the Algonquians and the English had very different notions of property ownership. In most Algonquian villages, land was held communally by the entire group. It could not be bought or sold absolutely, although certain rights to use the land (for example, for hunting or fishing) could be transferred. English people, in contrast, were accustomed to individual farms and to buying and selling land. The English also refused to accept the validity of Indians' claims to traditional hunting territories, insisting that only land intensively cultivated could be regarded as owned or occupied. As one colonist put it, "salvadge peoples" who "rambled" over a region without farming it could claim no "title or propertye" in the land. Ownership of such "unclaimed" property, the English believed, lay with the English monarchy, in whose name John Cabot had laid claim to North America in 1497.

Above all, the English settlers believed unwaveringly in the superiority of their civilization. Although in the early years of colonization they often anticipated living peacefully alongside Native Americans, they always assumed that they would dictate the terms of such coexistence. Like Thomas Harriot at Roanoke, they expected Native Americans to adopt English customs and to convert to Christianity. They showed little respect for traditional Indian ways of life, especially when they believed their own interests were at stake. The Virginia colony's treatment of the Powhatan Confederacy in subsequent years clearly revealed that attitude.

How do historians know...

that the Jamestown settlers traded extensively with the neighboring Powhatan Indians?

The few surviving written descriptions of life in early Jamestown omit many details that would interest historians today. But excavations conducted each year since 1994 have located the site of the first permanent English settlement in North America (previously thought to have eroded long ago into the James River) and have unearthed artifacts that speak volumes about the settlers' lives in the first years of Virginia. The small scraps of copper and the Irish copper coins illustrated here, for example, were found within the remains of the original James Fort, constructed in 1607 and abandoned by 1624. The fragments show that Englishmen quickly learned that the Powhatans placed a great value on copper ornaments, which, before the English arrived, they could obtain only by trade with Indians living far to the west. So settler craftsmen fashioned items for Indian trade from coins that the English regarded as nearly worthless and perhaps from copper brought from Europe for the purpose. Undoubtedly the Jamestown residents gave such objects to the Powhatans in exchange for the food they desperately needed. Copper ornaments of English manufacture have been found in Indian burials at Pasbehegh, the Powhatan village nearest to Jamestown. (Photos: The Association for the Preservation of Virginia Antiquities)

The Cultivation of Tobacco

The spread of tobacco cultivation upset the balance of power in early Virginia. In tobacco—the American crop previously introduced to Europe by the Spanish—the settlers and the Virginia Company found the salable commodity for which they had been searching. John Rolfe planted the first crop in 1611. Nine years later Virginians exported 40,000 pounds of cured leaves, and by the late 1620s shipments had jumped dramatically to 1.5 million pounds. The great tobacco boom had begun, fueled by high prices and substantial profits for planters. The price later fell almost as sharply as it had risen, fluctuating wildly from year to year in response to increasing supply and international competition. Nevertheless, tobacco made Virginia prosper, and the colony developed from a small outpost peopled exclusively by males into an agricultural settlement inhabited by both men and women.

Successful tobacco cultivation required abundant land, since the crop quickly drained soil of nutrients. Farmers soon learned that a field could produce only about three satisfactory crops before it had to lie fallow for several years to regain its fertility. Thus the once-small English settlements began to expand rapidly: eager applicants asked the Virginia Company for large land grants on both sides of the James River and its tributary streams. Lulled into a false sense of security by years of peace, Virginians established farms at some distance from one another along the river banks—a settlement pattern convenient for tobacco cultivation but dangerous for defense.

Virginia Company Policies

To attract more settlers to the colony, the Virginia Company in 1617 developed the "headright" system. Every new arrival paying his or her own way was promised a land grant of 50 acres; those who financed the passage of others received similar headrights for each person. To ordinary English farmers, many of whom owned little or no land, the headright system offered a powerful incentive to move to Virginia. To wealthy gentry, it promised even more: the possibility of establishing vast agricultural enterprises worked by large numbers of laborers. Two years later, the company introduced a second reform, authorizing the landowning men of the major Virginia settlements to elect representatives to an assembly called the House of Burgesses. Although England was a monarchy, English landholders had long been accustomed to electing members of Parliament and controlling their own local governments; therefore, they expected the same privilege in the nation's colonies.

Opechancanough, Powhatan's brother and successor, watched the English colonists steadily encroaching on the confederacy's lands and attempting to convert its members to Christianity. Recognizing the danger his brother had overlooked, the war leader launched coordinated attacks all along the James River on March 22, 1622. By the end of the day, 347 colonists (about one-quarter of the total) lay dead, and only a timely warning from two Christian converts saved Jamestown itself from destruction.

Indian Uprisings

Virginia reeled from the blow but did not collapse. Reinforced by new shipments of men and arms from England, the settlers attacked Opechancanough's villages. For some years an uneasy peace prevailed, but then in April 1644 Opechancanough tried one last time to repel the invaders. He failed, losing his life in the war that ensued. In 1646, survivors of the Powhatan Confederacy accepted a treaty formally subordinating them to English authority. Although they continued to live in the region, their alliance crumbled and their efforts to resist the spread of European settlement ended.

The 1622 Powhatan uprising that failed to destroy the colony succeeded in killing its parent. The Virginia Company never made any profits from the enterprise, for all its earnings were offset by the heavy cost of supporting the settlers and by internal corruption. In 1624 James I revoked the charter, transforming Virginia into a royal colony—a colony ruled by the king through appointed officials. James continued the headright policy the company had adopted. Because he distrusted legislative bodies, though, James at first abolished the assembly. But Virginians protested so vigorously that by 1629 the House of Burgesses was functioning once again. Only two decades after the first permanent English settlement was planted in North America, the colonists successfully insisted on governing themselves at the local level. Thus the political structure of England's American possessions came to differ from that of New Spain, New France, and New Netherland, all of which were ruled autocratically.

End of the Virginia Company

Life in the Chesapeake

By the 1630s, tobacco was firmly established as the staple crop and chief source of revenue in Virginia. It quickly became just as important in the second English colony planted on Chesapeake Bay: Maryland, given by Charles I to George Calvert, first Lord Baltimore, as a personal possession (proprietorship), which was settled in 1634. (Because Virginia and Maryland both border Chesapeake Bay—see Map 2.1—they are often referred to collectively as "the Chesapeake.") Members of the Calvert family intended the colony to serve as a haven for their fellow Roman Catholics, then being persecuted in England. Cecilius Calvert, second Lord Baltimore, became the first colonizer to offer freedom of religion to all Christian settlers; he understood that protecting the Protestant majority could also ensure Catholics' rights. (The policy was codified in Maryland's Act of Religious Toleration in 1649.)

In everything but religion the two Chesapeake colonies resembled each other. In Maryland as in Virginia, tobacco planters spread out along the river banks, establishing isolated farms instead of towns. The region's deep, wide rivers offered dependable water transportation in an age of few and inadequate roads. Each farm or group of farms had its own wharf, where oceangoing vessels could take on or discharge cargo. As a result, Virginia and Maryland had few towns, for their residents did not need commercial centers in order to buy and sell goods.

The planting, cultivation, and harvesting of tobacco had to be done by hand; such tasks were repetitious, time-consuming, and labor-intensive. Clearing land for new fields, necessary every few years, was also a laborious job. Above all else, then, successful Chesapeake tobacco farms required laborers. But where and how could they be obtained? Nearby Indians, their numbers reduced by war and disease, could not supply the needed workers. Nor were enslaved Africans readily available: merchants could more easily and profitably sell those slaves to Caribbean sugar planters. In the first half of the seventeenth century, therefore, only a few people of African descent, some of them free or indentured laborers rather than slaves, arrived in the Chesapeake. By 1650 about three hundred blacks lived in Virginia—a tiny fraction of the population.

Need for Laborers

Chesapeake tobacco farmers thus looked primarily to England to supply their labor needs. Because of the headright system (which Maryland also adopted in

1640), a tobacco farmer anywhere in the Chesapeake could simultaneously obtain both land and labor by importing workers from England. Good management would make the process self-perpetuating: a farmer could use his profits to pay for the passage of more workers and thereby gain title to more land. Success could even bring movement into the ranks of the planter gentry that began to develop in the region.

Because men did the agricultural work in European societies, colonists assumed that field laborers should be men. Such male laborers, along with a few

A surveyor's plat from Charles County, Maryland, late in the seventeenth century. The courthouse, the ordinary (inn), and the pillory and stocks are surrounded by old houses and a peach orchard, with roads and still un-cleared land nearby. Such a landscape would have been familiar to any resident of the early Chesapeake.
(Maryland State Archives, Charles County Court records, No. 1 MDHR 8132)

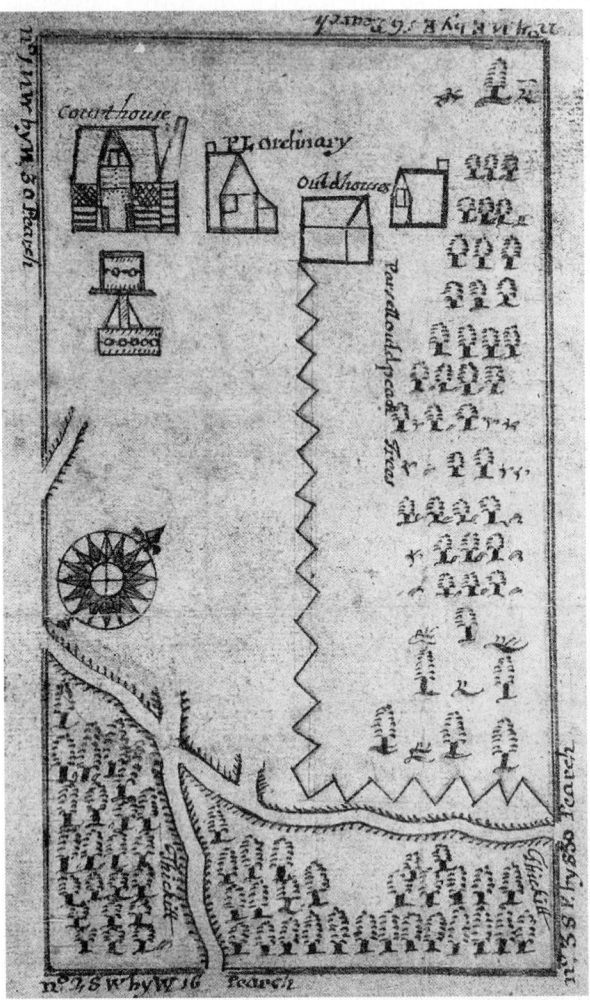

Indentured Servant Immigrants

women, immigrated to America as indentured servants—that is, in return for their passage they contracted to work for farmers for periods ranging from four to seven years. Indentured servants accounted for 75 to 85 percent of the approximately 130,000 English immigrants to Virginia and Maryland during the seventeenth century. The rest tended to be young couples with one or two children.

Males between the ages of fifteen and twenty-four composed roughly three-quarters of the servants; only one immigrant in five or six was female. Most of these young men came from farming or laboring families, and many originated in regions of England experiencing severe social disruption. Some had already moved several times within England before relocating to America. Often they came from the middling ranks of society—what their contemporaries called the "common sort." Their youth indicated that most probably had not yet established themselves in their homeland.

For such people the Chesapeake appeared to offer good prospects. Servants who fulfilled the terms of their indentures earned "freedom dues" consisting of clothes, tools, livestock, casks of corn and tobacco, and sometimes even land. From a distance at least, America seemed to hold out chances for advancement unavailable in England. Yet immigrants' lives were difficult. Servants typically worked six days a week, ten to fourteen hours a day, in a climate much warmer than England's. Their masters could discipline or sell them, and they faced severe penalties for running away. Even so, the laws did offer them some protection. For example, their masters were supposed to supply them with sufficient food, clothing, and shelter, and they were not to be beaten excessively. Cruelly treated servants could turn to the courts for assistance, sometimes winning verdicts directing that they be sold to more humane masters or released from their indentures.

Conditions of Servitude

Servants and their owners alike had to contend with epidemic disease. Immigrants first had to survive the process the colonists called "seasoning"—a bout with disease (probably malaria) that usually occurred during their first Chesapeake summer. They then had to endure recurrences of malaria, along with dysentery, typhoid fever, and other diseases. As a result, approximately 40 percent of male servants did not survive long enough to become freedmen. Even young men of twenty-two who successfully weathered their seasoning could expect to live only another twenty years at best.

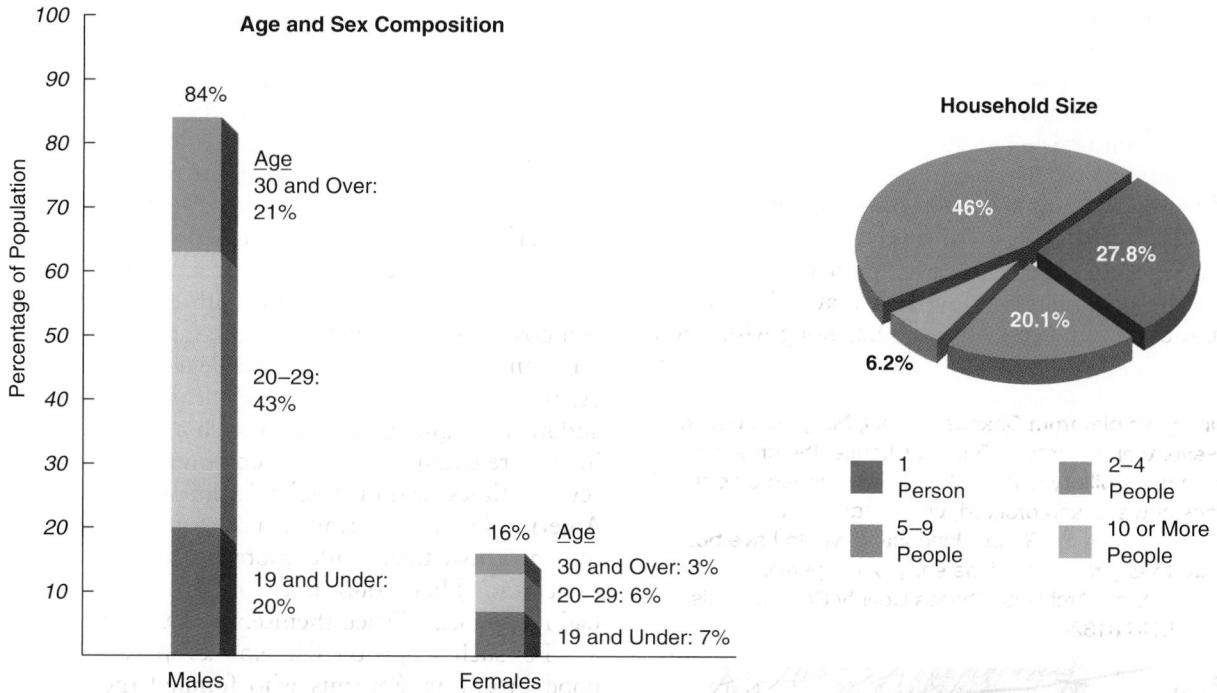

Figure 2.1 | Population of Virginia, 1625   The only detailed census taken in the English mainland North American colonies during the seventeenth century was prepared in Virginia in 1625. It listed a total of 1,218 people, constituting 309 "households" and living in 278 dwellings—so some houses contained more than one family. The chart shows, on the left, the proportionate age and gender distribution of the 765 individuals for whom full information was recorded, and, on the right, the percentage variation in the sizes of the 309 households. The approximately 42 percent of the residents of the colony who were servants were concentrated in 30 percent of the households. Nearly 70 percent of the households had no servants at all. (Source of data: Robert V. Wells, *The Population of the British Colonies in America Before 1776: A Survey of Census Data* [Princeton: Princeton University Press, 1975], tables V-5 and V-6 and pp. 165–166.)

For those who survived the term of their indentures, however, the opportunities for advancement were real. Until the last decades of the seventeenth century, former servants were usually able to become independent farmers ("freeholders") and to live a modest but comfortable existence. Some even assumed positions of political prominence such as justice of the peace or militia officer. But in the 1670s tobacco prices entered a fifty-year period of stagnation and decline. Simultaneously, good land grew increasingly scarce and expensive. In 1681 Maryland dropped its legal requirement that servants receive land as part of their freedom dues, forcing large numbers of freed servants to live for years as wage laborers or tenant farmers. By 1700 the Chesapeake was no longer the land of opportunity it once had been.

Life in the early Chesapeake was hard for everyone, regardless of sex or status. Farmers (and sometimes their wives) toiled in the fields alongside

Standard of Living

servants, laboriously clearing land, then planting and harvesting tobacco and corn. Because hogs could forage for themselves in the forests and needed little tending, Chesapeake households subsisted mainly on pork and corn, a filling diet but not sufficiently nutritious. Families supplemented this monotonous fare by eating fish, shellfish, and wildfowl, in addition to vegetables such as lettuce and peas, which they grew in small gardens. The near impossibility of preserving food for safe winter consumption magnified the health problems caused by epidemic disease. Salting, drying, and smoking, the only methods the colonists knew, did not always prevent spoilage.

Few households had many material possessions other than farm implements, bedding, and basic cooking and eating utensils. Chairs, tables, candles, and knives and forks were luxury items. Most people rose and went to bed with the sun, sat on crude benches or storage chests, and held plates or bowls in their hands while eating meat and vegetable stews with spoons. The ramshackle houses commonly had just one or two rooms. Colonists devoted their income to improving their farms, buying livestock, and purchasing more laborers rather than to improving their standard of living. Instead of making items such as clothing and tools, tobacco-growing families imported necessary manufactured goods from England.

The predominance of males, the incidence of servitude, and the high mortality rates combined to produce unusual patterns of family life. Female servants normally could not marry during their terms of indenture because masters did not want pregnancies to deprive them of workers. Many male ex-servants could not marry at all because of the scarcity of women; such men lived alone, in pairs, or as the third member of a household containing a married couple. In contrast, nearly every adult free woman in the Chesapeake married, and widows usually remarried within a few months of a husband's death. Yet because of high infant mortality and because almost all marriages were delayed by servitude or broken by death, Chesapeake women commonly reared only one to three healthy children, in contrast to English women, who normally had at least five.

Chesapeake Families

Thus Chesapeake families were few, small, and short-lived. Youthful immigrants came to America as individuals free of familial control and tended to die while their children were still young. In one Virginia county, for example, more than three-quarters of the children had lost at least one parent by the time they either married or reached age twenty-one. For the most part, then, Chesapeake men (unlike their English fathers; see page 14) could not establish long-term control over their spouses or offspring. And the large number of orphaned children prompted a legal innovation: the establishment of orphans' courts to oversee the management of orphans' property and to ensure that such young people received the appropriate inheritance when they reached adulthood.

Because of the low rate of natural increase, throughout the seventeenth century immigrants composed a majority of the Chesapeake population, with important implications for regional political patterns. Most of the members of Virginia's House of Burgesses and Maryland's House of Delegates (established in 1635) were immigrants; they also dominated the governor's council,

Chesapeake Politics

which was simultaneously each colony's highest court, part of the legislature, and executive adviser to the governor. A cohesive, native-born ruling elite did not emerge until the early eighteenth century. Before that, the Chesapeake colonies' immigrant leaders engaged in bitter and prolonged struggles for power and personal economic advantage.

Representative institutions based on the consent of the governed usually function as a major source of political stability. In the seventeenth-century Chesapeake, most property-owning white males could vote, and such freeholders chose as their legislators the local elites who seemed to be the natural leaders of their respective areas. But because most such men were immigrants without strong ties to one another or to the colonies, the assemblies' existence did not create political stability. Unusual demographic patterns thus contributed to the region's contentious politics.

The Founding of New England

The economic motives that prompted English people to move to the Chesapeake colonies also drew men and women to New England (see Map 2.2). But because Puritans organized the New England colonies, and also because of environmental differences between the two regions, the northern settlements turned out very differently from those in the South. The northern climate was too cold and the soil too infertile to raise tobacco on a large scale or to raise sugar cane at all. Accordingly, diversified small farms dominated the landscape.

Except for the few Catholics who moved to Maryland, immigrants to the Chesapeake seem to have been little affected by religious motives. Yet religion motivated many, although certainly not all, of the people who colonized New England. Puritan congregations quickly became key institutions in colonial New England, whereas neither the Church of England nor Roman Catholicism had much impact on the settlers or the early development of the Chesapeake colonies. Catholic and Anglican bishops in England paid little attention to their coreligionists in America, and Chesapeake congregations languished in the absence of sufficient numbers of properly ordained clergymen. (For example, in 1665 an observer noted that only ten of the fifty Virginia parishes had resident ministers.) Not until the 1690s did the Church of England begin to

Contrasting Regional Religious Patterns

take firmer root in Virginia; by then (see page 82) it had also replaced Catholicism as the established church in Maryland.

By contrast, religion was a constant presence in the lives of pious Puritans, who regularly reassessed the state of their souls. Many devoted themselves to self-examination and Bible study, and families prayed together each day under the guidance of the husband and father. Yet because even the most pious could never be certain that they were numbered among the elect, anxiety about their spiritual state troubled devout Puritans. That anxiety lent a special intensity to their religious beliefs and to their concern with proper behavior—their own and others'.

Some Puritans (called Congregationalists) wanted to reform the Church of England rather than abandon

Congregationalists and Separatists

it. Other groups, known as Separatists, thought the Church of England too corrupt to be salvaged. Only by starting anew could the church be purified, they argued, and so they established their own religious bodies, with membership restricted to the saved, as nearly as they could be identified.

Separatists were the first to move to New England. In 1609 a Separatist congregation relocated to Leiden, in the Netherlands, where they found the freedom of worship denied them in Stuart England. But the Netherlands' tolerant atmosphere worried them: the nation that tolerated them also tolerated religions and behaviors that they abhorred. Hoping to isolate themselves and their children from the corrupting influence of worldly temptations, these people, who were to become known as Pilgrims, received permission from the Virginia Company to colonize the northern part of its territory.

In September 1620, more than one hundred people, only thirty of them Separatists, set sail from England on the old and crowded

Plymouth

Mayflower. Two months later they landed in America, but farther north than they had intended. Still, given the lateness of the season, they decided to stay where they were. Establishing their settlement on a fine harbor—the site of an Indian village wiped out by the epidemic of 1616–1618—the English people named it Plymouth.

Even before they landed, the Pilgrims had to surmount their first challenge—from the "strangers," or non-Puritans, who sailed with them to America. Because they landed outside the jurisdiction of the Virginia Company, some of the strangers questioned the

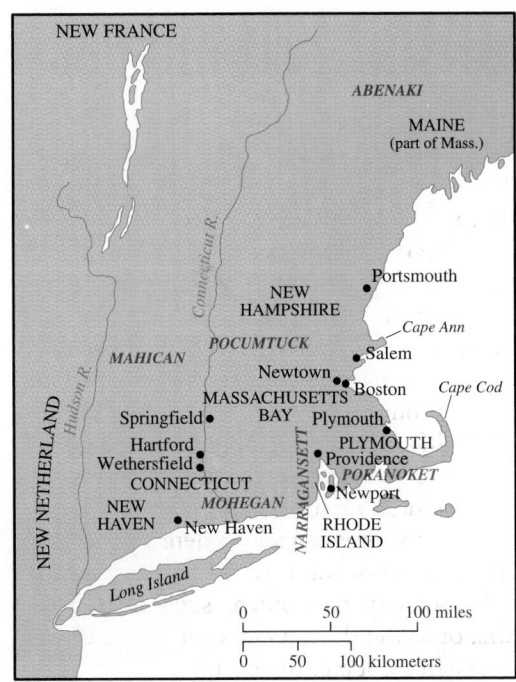

Map 2.2 New England Colonies, 1650 The most densely settled region of the mainland was New England, where English settlements and Indian villages existed side by side.

authority of the colony's leaders. In response, the Mayflower Compact, signed in November 1620 while everyone was still on board the ship, established a "Civil Body Politic" and a rudimentary legal authority for the colony. The settlers elected a governor and at first made all decisions for the colony at town meetings. Later, after more towns had been founded and the population increased, Plymouth, like Virginia and Maryland, created an assembly to which the landowning male settlers elected representatives.

A second challenge facing the Pilgrims was simple survival. Like the Jamestown settlers before them, they were poorly prepared to subsist in the new environment. Winter quickly descended, compounding their difficulties. Only half the *Mayflower*'s passengers were still alive by spring. But, again like the Virginians, the Pilgrims benefited from the political circumstances of nearby Indians.

The Pokanokets (a branch of the Wampanoags) controlled the area in which the Pilgrims settled.

Pokanokets

Their villages had suffered terrible losses in the recent epidemic, so to protect themselves from the powerful Narragansetts of the southern New England coast (who had been

Some scholars now believe that this 1638 painting by the Dutch artist Adam Willaerts depicts the Plymouth colony about fifteen years after its founding. The shape of the harbor, the wooden gate, and the houses straggling up the hill all coincide with contemporary accounts of the settlement. No one believes that Willaerts himself visited Plymouth, but people returning from the colony to Holland, where the Pilgrims had lived for years before emigrating, could well have described Plymouth to him.   (© J. D. Bangs, Courtesy of Leiden American Pilgrim Museum, The Netherlands)

spared the ravages of the disease), the Pokanokets decided to ally themselves with the newcomers. In the spring of 1621, their leader, Massasoit, signed a treaty with the Pilgrims, and during the colony's first difficult years the Pokanokets supplied the English with essential foodstuffs. The settlers were also assisted by Squanto, a Pokanoket, who, like Malinche (see page 23), served as a conduit between the Native Americans and the Europeans. Captured by fishermen in the early 1610s and taken to Europe, Squanto learned to speak English. Upon returning to North America, he discovered that his village had been wiped out by the epidemic. Squanto became the Pilgrims' interpreter and a major source of information about the unfamiliar environment.

Before the 1620s ended, another group of Puritans—this time Congregationalists, not Separatists—

Massachusetts Bay Company

launched the colonial enterprise that would come to dominate New England and would absorb Plymouth in 1691. Charles I, who became king in 1625, was more hostile to Puritans than his father had been. Under his leadership, the Church of England attempted to suppress Puritan practices, driving clergymen from their pulpits and forcing congregations to hold clandestine meetings for worship. A group of Congregationalist merchants, concerned about their long-term prospects in England, sent out a body of colonists to Cape Ann (north of Cape Cod) in 1628. The following year the merchants obtained a royal charter, constituting themselves as the Massachusetts Bay Company.

The new joint-stock company quickly attracted the attention of Puritans of the "middling sort" who were becoming increasingly convinced that they no longer would be able to practice their religion freely in their homeland. They remained committed to the goal of reforming the Church of England but concluded that they should pursue that aim in America. In a dramatic move, the Congregationalist merchants boldly decided to transfer the Massachusetts Bay Company's headquarters to New England. The settlers would then be answerable to no one in the mother country and would be able to handle their affairs, secular and religious, as they pleased.

The most important recruit to the new venture was John Winthrop, a member of the lesser English gentry. In October 1629, the Massachusetts Com-

Governor John Winthrop

pany elected Winthrop as its governor. (Until his death twenty years later, he served the colony continuously in one leadership post or another.) It fell to Winthrop to organize the initial segment of the great Puritan migration to America. In 1630 more than one thousand English men and women moved to Massachusetts—most of them to Boston, which soon became the largest town in English North America. By 1643 nearly twenty thousand compatriots had followed them.

On board the *Arbella*, en route to New England in 1630, John Winthrop preached a sermon, "A Model of Christian Charity," laying out his expectations for the new colony. Above all, he stressed the communal nature of the endeavor on which he and his fellow settlers had embarked. God, he explained, "hath so disposed of the condition of mankind as in all times some must be rich, some poor, some high and eminent in power and dignity, others mean and in subjection." But differences in status did not imply differences in worth. On the contrary: God had planned the world so that "every man might have need of other, and from hence they might be all knit more nearly together in the bond of brotherly affection." In America, Winthrop asserted, "we shall be as a city upon a hill, the eyes of all people are upon us." If the Puritans failed to carry out their "special commission" from God, "the Lord will surely break out in wrath against us."

Winthrop's was a transcendent vision. He foresaw in Puritan America a true commonwealth, a community in which each person put the good of the whole ahead of his or her private concerns. Although, as in seventeenth-century England, that society would be characterized by social inequality and clear hierarchies of status and power, Winthrop hoped that its members would live according to the precepts of Christian love. Of course, such an ideal was beyond human reach. Early New England had its share of bitter quarrels and unchristian behavior. What is remarkable is that the ideal persisted well into the third and fourth generations of the immigrants' descendants.

The Puritans expressed their communal ideal chiefly in the doctrine of the covenant. They believed

Ideal of the Covenant

God had made a covenant—that is, an agreement or contract—with them when they were chosen for the special mission to America. In turn they covenanted with one another, promising to work together toward their goals. The founders of churches and towns in the new land often drafted formal documents setting forth the principles

on which such institutions would be based. The same was true of the colonial governments of New England. The Pilgrims' Mayflower Compact was a covenant; so too was the Fundamental Orders of Connecticut (1639), which laid down the basic law for the settlements established along the Connecticut River valley in 1636 and thereafter.

The leaders of Massachusetts Bay likewise transformed their original joint-stock company charter into the basis for a covenanted community based on mutual consent. Under strong and persistent pressure from landowning male settlers, they gradually changed the General Court—officially the company's small governing body—into a colonial legislature. They also granted the status of freeman, or voting member of the company, to all property-owning adult male church members. Like Virginia men who won the reestablishment of the House of Burgesses after the king had abolished it, the male residents of Massachusetts insisted that their reluctant leaders allow them a greater voice in their government. Less than two decades after the first large group of Puritans arrived in Massachusetts Bay, the colony had a functioning system of self-government composed of a governor and a two-house legislature. The General Court also established a judicial system modeled on England's, although the laws they adopted differed from those of their homeland (see page 55).

The colony's method of distributing land helped to further the communal ideal. Unlike Virginia and Maryland, where individual applicants acquired headrights

An English beaver felt hat, made by combining American beaver fur with wool and other fibers. Men and women in England and on the European continent wore such fashionable items, thus creating the insatiable demand for pelts that fueled the fur trade for many years.   (The Pilgrim Society, Plymouth, Massachusetts)

New England Towns

and sited their farms separately, in Massachusetts groups of men—often from the same region of England—applied together to the General Court for grants of land on which to establish towns (novel governance units that did not exist in England). The men receiving such a grant determined how the land would be distributed. Understandably, the grantees copied the villages from which they had come. First they laid out lots for houses and a church. Then they gave each family parcels of land scattered around the town center: a pasture here, a woodlot there, an arable field elsewhere. They reserved the best and largest plots for the most distinguished among them (including the minister). People who had been low on the social scale in England received much smaller and less desirable allotments. Still, every man obtained land, thus sharply differentiating these villages from their English counterparts.

Thus New England settlements initially tended to be more compact than those of the Chesapeake. Town centers grew up quickly, developing in three distinctly different ways. Some, chiefly isolated agricultural settlements in the interior, tried to sustain Winthrop's vision of harmonious community life based on diversified family farms. A second group, the coastal towns like Boston and Salem, became bustling seaports, serving as focal points for trade and places of entry for thousands of new immigrants. The third category, commercialized agricultural towns, grew up in the Connecticut River valley, where easy water transportation made it possible for farmers to sell surplus goods readily. In Springfield, Massachusetts, for example, the merchant-entrepreneur William Pynchon and his son John began as fur traders and ended as large landowners with thousands of acres. Even in New England, then, the entrepreneurial spirit characteristic of the Chesapeake found some room for expression.

Internal Migration

When migrants began to move beyond the territorial limits of the Massachusetts Bay colony into Connecticut (1636), New Haven (1638), and New Hampshire (1638), the same pattern of land grants was maintained. (Only Maine, with coastal regions thinly populated by fishermen and their families, deviated from the standard practice.) The migration to the Connecticut valley ended the Puritans' relative freedom from clashes with nearby Indians. The first English people in the valley moved there from Massachusetts Bay under the direction of their minister, Thomas Hooker. Although their new settlements were remote from other English towns, the wide river promised ready access to the ocean. The site had just one problem: it fell within the territory controlled by the powerful Pequots.

Pequot War

The Pequots' dominance stemmed from their role as primary middlemen in the trade between New England Indians and the Dutch in New Netherland. The arrival of English settlers signaled the end of the Pequots' power over such regional trading networks, for previously subordinate bands could now trade directly with Europeans. Clashes between Pequots and English colonists began even before the establishment of settlements in the Connecticut valley, but their founding tipped the balance toward war. The Pequots tried without success to enlist other Indians in resisting English expansion. After two English traders were killed (not by Pequots), the English raided a Pequot village. In return, the Pequots attacked the new town of Wethersfield in April 1637, killing nine and capturing two of the colonists. To retaliate, a Massachusetts Bay expedition the following month attacked and burned the main Pequot town on the Mystic River. The Englishmen and their Narragansett allies slaughtered at least four hundred Pequots, mostly women and children, capturing and enslaving many of the survivors.

For the next thirty years, the New England Indians accommodated themselves to the spread of European

Among John Eliot's principal converts to Christianity was a young Native American named Daniel Takawampbartis. Ordained as a minister, he served at the head of the Indian congregation at Natick, Massachusetts, a "Praying Town," until his death in 1716. Members of his congregation made this desk for him in about 1677, incorporating elements of English design (brass pulls), Native American motifs (incised lines), and uniquely American hooved feet. The top, a hinged box, is intended to hold a Bible. (The Morse Institute, Natick, Massachusetts. Photo by Mark Sexton of the Peabody Essex Museum, Salem)

settlement. They traded with the newcomers and sometimes worked for them, but for the most part they resisted acculturation or incorporation into English society. Native Americans persisted in using traditional farming methods, which did not employ plows or fences, and women rather than men continued to be the chief cultivators. When Indian men learned "European" trades in order to survive, they chose those—like broom making, basket weaving, and shingle splitting—that most nearly accorded with their customary occupations and simultaneously ensured both independence and income. The one European practice they adopted was keeping livestock, for domesticated animals provided excellent sources of meat once earlier hunting territories had been turned into English farms and wild game had consequently disappeared.

John Eliot and the Praying Towns

Although the official seal of the Massachusetts Bay colony showed an Indian crying "Come over and help us," most colonists showed little interest in converting the Algonquians to Christianity. Only a few Massachusetts clerics, most notably John Eliot, seriously undertook missionary activities. Eliot insisted that converts reside in towns, farm the land in English fashion, assume English names, wear European-style clothing and shoes, cut their hair, and stop observing a wide range of their own customs. Since Eliot was demanding a total cultural transformation from his adherents—on the theory that Indians could not be properly Christianized unless they were also "civilized"—he understandably met with little success. At the peak of Eliot's efforts, only eleven hundred Native Americans (out of many thousands) lived in the fourteen "Praying Towns" he established, and just 10 percent of those town residents had been formally baptized.

Puritan, Franciscan, and Jesuit Missions Compared

The Jesuits' successful missions in New France contrasted sharply with the Puritans' failure to win many converts and the Franciscans' mixed results in New Mexico. Initially, Catholicism had several advantages over Puritanism (advantages more fully exploited by Jesuits than by Franciscans). The Catholic Church employed beautiful ceremonies, instructed converts that through good works they could help to earn their own salvation, and offered Indian women an inspiring role model—the Virgin Mary. In Montreal and Quebec but not in New Mexico, communities of nuns taught Indian women and children and ministered to their needs. Furthermore, the few French colonists on the St. Lawrence

Father Claude Chauchetière, a Jesuit in New France, sketched scenes of life in the colony's missions. His drawing of Indian women worshiping at a shrine of the Virgin Mary includes (at the rear) a view of one woman cutting her hair to conform more closely to European fashion. The other female converts show no evidence of having adopted European dress or hairstyles.   (Archives Départmentales de la Gironde, France)

did not alienate potential converts by encroaching steadily on their lands (as did New Englanders) or by demanding labor tribute (as did New Mexicans). Perhaps most important, the Jesuits understood that Christian beliefs could be compatible with Native American culture. Unlike Puritans and Franciscans, Jesuits accepted converts who did not wholly adopt European styles of life.

What attracted Indians to these religious ideas? Conversion often alienated the new Christians (both Catholic and Puritan) from their relatives and traditions—a likely outcome that must have caused many potential converts to think twice about making such a commitment. But surely many hoped to use the Europeans' religion as a means of coping with the dramatic changes the intruders had wrought. The combination of disease, alcohol, new trading patterns, and loss of territory disrupted customary ways of life to an unprecedented extent. Shamans had little success in restoring traditional ways. Many Indians must have concluded that the Europeans' own ideas could provide the key to survival in the new circumstances.

John Winthrop's description of the great smallpox epidemic that swept through southern New England in the early 1630s reveals the relationship among smallpox, conversion to Christianity, and English land claims. "A great mortality among the Indians," he noted in his diary in 1633. "Divers of them, in their sickness, confessed that the Englishmen's God was a good God; and that if they recovered, they would serve him." But most did not recover: in January 1634 an English scout reported that smallpox had spread "as far as any Indian plantation was known to the west."

In 1664 an eight-year-old girl, Elizabeth Eggington, became the subject of the earliest known dated New England painting. Her mother died shortly after her birth, perhaps because of childbirth complications; the girl's rich clothing, elaborate jewelry, and feather fan not only reveal her family's wealth but also suggest that she was much loved by her father, a merchant and ship captain. Unfortunately, Elizabeth died about the time this portrait was painted; perhaps it—like some other colonial portraits of young children—was actually painted after her death to memorialize her. (Wadsworth Atheneum, Hartford. Gift of Mrs. Walter H. Clark. Endowed by her daughter, Mrs. Thomas L. Archibald)

By July, Winthrop observed that most of the Indians within a 300-mile radius of Boston had died of the disease. Therefore, he declared with satisfaction, "the Lord hath cleared our title to what we possess."

Life in New England

 New England's colonizers adopted lifestyles that differed considerably from those of both their Indian neighbors and their European counterparts in the Chesapeake. Algonquian bands usually moved four or five times each year to take full advantage of their environment. In spring, women planted the fields, but once crops were established, they did not need regular attention for several months. Villages then divided into small groups, women gathering wild foods and men hunting and fishing. The villagers returned to their fields for harvest, then separated again for fall hunting. Finally, the people wintered together in a sheltered spot before returning to the fields to start the cycle anew the following spring.

Unlike the mobile Algonquians, English people lived year-round in the same location. And unlike residents of the Chesapeake, New Englanders constructed sturdy dwellings intended to last. (Many still survive to this day.) They used the same fields again and again, believing it was less arduous to employ manure as fertilizer than to clear new fields every few years. Furthermore, they fenced their croplands to prevent them from being overrun by the cattle, sheep, and hogs that were their chief sources of meat. When New Englanders began to spread out over the countryside, the reason was less human crowding than animal crowding. All that livestock constantly needed more pasturage.

Because Puritans commonly moved to America in family groups, the age range in early New England was wide; and because many more

New England Families

women went to New England than to the tobacco colonies, the population could immediately begin to reproduce itself. Lacking such tropical diseases as malaria, New England was much healthier than the Chesapeake. Once Puritan settlements had survived the difficult first few years and established self-sufficiency in foodstuffs, New England proved to be even healthier than the mother country. Adult male migrants to the Chesapeake lost about ten years from their English life expectancy of fifty to fifty-five years; their Massachusetts counterparts gained five or more years.

Consequently, while Chesapeake population patterns gave rise to families that were few in number, small in size, and transitory, the demographic characteristics of New England made families there numerous, large, and long-lived. In New England most men married; immigrant women married young (at age twenty, on the average); and marriages lasted longer and produced more children, who were more likely to live to maturity. If seventeenth-century Chesapeake women could expect to rear one to three healthy children, New England women could anticipate raising five to seven.

The nature of the population had other major implications for family life. New England in effect created grandparents, since in England people rarely lived long enough to know their children's children. And whereas early Chesapeake parents commonly died before their children married, New England parents exercised a good deal of control over their adult offspring. Young men could not marry without acreage to cultivate, and because of the communal land-grant system they had to depend on their fathers to give them that land. Daughters, too, needed a dowry of household goods supplied by their parents. Yet parents relied on their children's labor and often were reluctant to see them marry and start their own households. These needs at times led to considerable conflict between the generations. On the whole, though, children seem to have obeyed their parents' wishes, for they had few alternatives.

Impact of Religion

Another important difference lay in the influence of religion on New Englanders' lives. Puritans controlled the governments of Massachusetts Bay, Plymouth, Connecticut, and all the other early northern colonies. Congregationalism was the only officially recognized religion; except in Rhode Island, founded by dissenters from Massachusetts, members of other sects had no freedom of worship. Some non-Puritans voted in town meetings, but in Massachusetts Bay and New Haven, church membership was a prerequisite for voting in colony elections. All the early colonies taxed residents to build meetinghouses and pay ministers' salaries, but only in New England were provisions of criminal codes based on the Old Testament. Massachusetts's first bodies of law (1641 and 1648) incorporated regulations drawn from scriptures; New Haven, Plymouth, New Hampshire, and Connecticut later copied those codes. All colonists were required to attend religious services, whether or not they were church members, and people who expressed contempt for ministers or

their preaching could be punished with fines or whippings.

The Puritan colonies attempted to enforce strict codes of moral conduct. Colonists there were frequently tried for drunkenness, card playing, even idleness. Couples who had sex during their engagement—as revealed by the birth of a baby less than nine months after their wedding—were fined and publicly humiliated. (Maryland, by contrast, did not penalize premarital pregnancy, only bastardy.) More harshly treated were men—and a handful of women—who engaged in behaviors that today would be called homosexual. (The term did not then exist, nor were some people thought to be more likely than others to perform such acts.) Several men who had consenting same-sex relationships were hanged, as were other men suspected of bestiality (sex with animals). Executions for such offenses were far more common in New England than in the Chesapeake, even though men's behavior in the two regions was probably similar.

In New England, church and state were thus intertwined to a greater extent than they were in the Chesapeake. Puritans objected to secular interference in religious affairs but at the same time expected the church to influence the conduct of politics and the affairs of society. They also believed that the state was obliged to support and protect the one true church—theirs. As a result, although they came to America seeking freedom to worship as they pleased, they saw no contradiction in refusing to grant that freedom to others.

Roger Williams

Roger Williams, a Separatist who immigrated to Massachusetts Bay in 1631, quickly ran afoul of that Puritan orthodoxy. He told his fellow settlers that the king of England had no right to grant them land already occupied by Indians, that church and state should be kept entirely separate, and that Puritans should not impose their religious beliefs on others. Because Puritan leaders placed a heavy emphasis on achieving consensus in both religion and politics, they could not long tolerate significant dissent. In October 1635, the Massachusetts General Court tried Williams for challenging the validity of the colony's charter and for maintaining that New England Congregationalists had not separated themselves, their churches, or their polity sufficiently from England's corrupt institutions and practices.

Convicted and banished, Williams journeyed in early 1636 to the head of Narragansett Bay, where he founded the town of Providence on land he obtained from the Narragansetts and Wampanoags. Because

Williams believed that government should not interfere with religion in any way, Providence and other towns in what became Rhode Island adopted a policy of tolerating all religions, including Judaism. Along with Maryland (see page 45), the tiny colony founded by Williams thus presaged the religious freedom that eventually became one of the hallmarks of the United States.

A dissenter who presented a more sustained challenge to Bay colony leaders was Mistress Anne Marbury Hutchinson. (The title "Mistress" meant she had high status.) A skilled medical practitioner popular with the women of Boston, she greatly admired John Cotton, a minister who stressed the covenant of grace, or God's free gift of salvation to unworthy human beings. By contrast, most Massachusetts clerics emphasized the need for Puritans to engage in good works, study, and reflection in preparation for receiving God's grace. (In its most extreme form, such a doctrine could verge on the covenant of works, or the idea that people could earn their salvation.) After spreading her ideas for months in the context of childbed gatherings—when no men were present—Mistress Hutchinson began holding women's meetings in her home to discuss Cotton's sermons. She emphasized the covenant of grace more than did Cotton himself, and she even adopted the belief that the elect could be assured of salvation and communicate directly with God. Such ideas had an immense appeal for Puritans. Anne Hutchinson offered them certainty of salvation instead of a state of constant anxiety. Her approach also lessened the importance of the institutional church and its ministers.

Anne Hutchinson

Hutchinson's ideas posed a dangerous threat to Puritan orthodoxy. So in November 1637, officials charged her with having maligned the colony's ministers by accusing them of preaching the covenant of works. For two days she defended herself cleverly, matching scriptural references and wits with John Winthrop himself. But then Anne Hutchinson triumphantly and boldly declared that God had spoken to her directly, explaining that he would curse the Puritans' descendants for generations if they harmed her. That assertion assured her banishment, for what member of the court could acknowledge the legitimacy of such a revelation? After she had also been excommunicated from the church, she and her family, along with some faithful followers, were exiled to Rhode Island. Several years later, after she moved to New Netherland, she and most of her children were killed by Indians.

The authorities in Massachusetts Bay perceived Anne Hutchinson as doubly dangerous to the existing order: she threatened not only religious orthodoxy but also traditional gender roles. Puritans believed in the equality before God of all souls, including those of women, but they considered actual women (as distinct from their spiritual selves) inferior to men. Christians had long followed Saint Paul's dictum that women should keep silent in church and be submissive to their husbands. Mistress Hutchinson did neither. The magistrates' comments during her trial reveal that they were almost as outraged by her "masculine" behavior as by her religious beliefs. Winthrop charged her with having set wife against husband, since so many of her followers were women. A minister at her church trial told her bluntly: "You have stept out of your place, you have rather bine a Husband than a Wife and a preacher than a Hearer; and a Magistrate than a Subject."

The New England authorities' reaction to Anne Hutchinson reveals the depth of their adherence to European gender-role concepts. To them, an orderly society required the submission of wives to husbands as well as the obedience of subjects to rulers. English people intended to change many aspects of their lives by colonizing North America, but not the sexual division of labor or the assumption of male superiority.

Summary

By the middle of the seventeenth century, Europeans had unquestionably come to North America to stay, a fact that signaled major changes for the peoples of both hemispheres. Europeans had indelibly altered not only their own lives but also those of Native Americans. Europeans killed Indians with their weapons and diseases and had but limited success in converting them to European religions. Contacts with the Native Americans taught Europeans to eat new foods, speak new languages, and recognize—however reluctantly—the persistence of other cultural patterns. The prosperity and even survival of many of the European colonies depended heavily on the cultivation of American crops (maize and tobacco) and an Asian crop (sugar), thus attesting to the importance of post-Columbian ecological change.

European political rivalries, once confined to Europe, now spread around the globe, as England, Spain, Portugal, France, and the Netherlands vied for control of the peoples and resources of Asia, Africa, and the

Americas. In America, Spaniards reaped the benefits of their South and Central American gold and silver mines, while French people earned their primary profits from Indian trade (in Canada) and cultivating sugar cane (in the Caribbean). Sugar also enriched the Portuguese. The Dutch, by contrast, concentrated on commerce—trading in furs and sugar as well as carrying human cargoes of enslaved Africans to South America and the Caribbean.

Of these nations, only France and Spain went beyond the economic relationships they established with native peoples to attempt to Christianize them. In missions scattered in remote locations such as northern Florida, the St. Lawrence valley, and New Mexico, Catholic priests like Fray Alonso de Benavides worked with dedication to convert the Indians and to persuade them of the truth of Europeans' religious beliefs.

Although the English colonies, too, at first sought to rely on trade, they quickly took another form altogether when so many English people of the "middling sort" decided to migrate to North America. To a greater extent than their European counterparts, the English transferred the society and politics of their homeland to a new environment. Their sheer numbers, coupled with their need for vast quantities of land on which to grow their crops and raise their livestock, inevitably brought them into conflict with their Native American neighbors. New England and the Chesapeake differed in the sex ratio and age range of their immigrant populations, in the nature of their developing economies, in their settlement patterns, and in the impact of religious beliefs on their settlers' lives. Yet both were English in origin, and in the years to come both regions would be drawn into the increasingly fierce rivalries besetting the European powers. Those rivalries would continue to affect Americans of all races until after France and England in the mid-eighteenth century fought the greatest war yet known, and the Anglo-American colonies had won their independence.

LEGACY FOR A PEOPLE AND A NATION
The Foxwoods Casino and the Mashantucket Pequot Museum

In 1992 the Mashantucket Pequots opened the enormously successful Foxwoods Resort Casino on their small reservation in southeastern Connecticut. Just six years later, in August 1998, the Pequots proudly inaugurated a new museum (built with some of their

substantial profits) presenting their people's story, meticulously researched by historians and archaeologists. Both developments surprised many Americans, who associated Indians only with territories west of the Mississippi and did not realize that Native Americans still lived in New England. The existence of the Pequots was particularly startling, because histories had long recorded that the nation was destroyed in the Pequot War of 1637.

Survivors of the Mystic River massacre had regrouped in the Mashantucket swamps, building lives as farmers, laborers, and craftspeople. Some left the area, finding work on whaling vessels or eventually migrating to Wisconsin. But a few Pequots remained—the 1910 census, the source today for determining Pequot tribal membership, counted sixty-six residents of a reservation just 213 acres in size. By the 1970s, the residents had been reduced to two, and the state of Connecticut threatened to turn the reservation into a park. But an elder, Elizabeth George, persuaded several hundred people tracing descent from those listed in 1910 to return to live on the reservation. In 1983 the determined Pequots won formal federal recognition, and in turn that allowed them to build the profitable casino, a hotel, and several restaurants, and to begin purchasing more land.

Now the museum introduces the history of the Pequots and of eastern Algonquian peoples to hundreds of thousands of visitors each year. At its heart is a re-creation of a Pequot village as it would have looked shortly before Europeans first arrived on Connecticut's shores, complete with sounds and smells controlled by state-of-the-art computers. Exhibits detail the origins of the Pequot War, and a film narrates the tale of the massacre. Furthermore, excavations nearby continue to uncover new evidence about the overlooked history of these indomitable descendants of America's early residents.

The Pequots' success has helped to embolden other eastern Algonquian nations—for example, Wampanoags and Mashpees—to reassert publicly their long-suppressed Indian identities. The Pequot people's dedication to preserving their culture and reaffirming their history has created a remarkable legacy for the nation.

For Further Reading, see page A-2 of the Appendix. For Web resources, go to http://college.hmco.com.

The *Seaflower*, Captain Thomas Smith, master, lay at anchor in Boston harbor in early September 1676, awaiting official documents signed by Governor John Leverett of Massachusetts and his Plymouth counterpart, Josiah Winslow. Like other mariners of the period, Smith expected to sell the cargo in his hold in the West Indies. But that cargo differed from most: it comprised human beings, nearly two hundred "heathen Malefactors—men, women, and Children."

The certificates from the governors, dated September 12, explained "To all People" the origins of Captain Smith's human cargo: "Philip an heathen Sachem . . . with others his wicked complices and abettors have treacherously and perfidiously rebelled against" these colonies. "By due and legall procedure" the captives on board the *Seaflower* were "Sentenced & condemned to perpetuall Servitude" as punishment for their "inhumane and barbarous crueltys murder, outrages and vilainies." The Pokanoket leader King Philip (called Metacom at birth and later renamed "Philip" by New Englanders) had been killed a month earlier in the war that bore his name. His captured wife and young son subsequently languished for months in a Boston jail; her fate is unknown, but the boy seems to have been sold into slavery, along with many shiploads of Philip's followers.

Only one prominent New Englander objected on moral grounds to the policy of selling the vanquished Algonquians into West Indian slavery. The Reverend John Eliot (see page 53) reminded the authorities that the Bay colony's charter called for the conversion of Indians, "not theire exstirpation." The colonists had a solemn duty, he contended, to "inlarge the kingdom of Jesus Christ"; "to sell them away for slaves, is to hinder the inlargement of his kingdom." If the Indians deserved to die, then "godly governors" should ensure that they died "penitently," rather than depriving them

Captain Thomas Smith, a Boston mariner, painted this remarkable self-portrait in the late seventeenth century. It links his sailing career—illustrated in the background battle scene, which is thought to represent a combined Anglo-Dutch assault on a North African fort in 1670—with his pious Puritan faith. The skull under his hand serves to remind viewers of the brevity of life, which the poem underscores. "Why, why should I the World be minding?" the poet asks, looking forward to a future in which "The Eternall" would "Crowne me (after Grace) with Glory." (Worcester Art Museum, Worcester, Massachusetts, Museum purchase)

AMERICAN SOCIETIES TAKE SHAPE 1640–1720

of "all meanes of grace" by selling them as slaves. Not even Eliot, then, argued against enslavement itself, nor did he deny that the captured Algonquians deserved punishment. Rather, he believed that the chosen penalty would subvert God's plan for Massachusetts.

What the pious Captain Thomas Smith (whose self-portrait is reproduced on page 58) thought about his human cargo is unknown. The *Seaflower* arrived in Jamaica in November, and perhaps he disposed of some of the captives there. But the Reverend Eliot learned from a correspondent seven years later that at least a few New England Algonquians had ended up in Tangier (in the modern nation of Morocco) because so many countries had turned away the vessels carrying them.

The tale of Thomas Smith and the *Seaflower*'s human cargo illustrates not only the English colonists' willingness to enslave "heathen" peoples and their increasingly contentious relationship with Native Americans, but also the participation of the mainland colonies in a growing international network. North America, like England itself, was becoming embedded in a worldwide matrix of trade and warfare. The web woven by oceangoing vessels—once composed of only a few strands spun by Christopher Columbus, John Cabot, and their successors—now crisscrossed the globe, carrying European goods to America and Africa, West Indian sugar to New England and Europe, Africans to the Americas, and New England fish and wood products—and occasionally Indian slaves—to the Caribbean. Formerly tiny outposts, the North American colonies expanded their territorial claims and diversified their economies after the mid-seventeenth century.

Three developments shaped life in the mainland English colonies between 1640 and 1720: the introduction of a system of slavery, especially in the southern coastal regions; changes in the colonies' political and economic relationships with England; and escalating conflicts with Indians and other European colonies in North America.

The explosive growth of the slave trade significantly altered the Anglo-American economy. Carrying human cargoes paid off handsomely, as many mariners and ship owners learned; planters who could afford to buy slaves also reaped huge profits. At first primarily encompassing Indians and already enslaved Africans from the Caribbean, the trade soon came to focus almost exclusively on cargoes brought to the American mainland directly from Africa. The arrival of large numbers of West African peoples dramatically re-

shaped colonial society and fueled the international trading system.

The burgeoning North American economy, invigorated by the arrival of so many laborers, attracted new attention from colonial administrators. Especially after the Stuarts had been restored to the throne in 1660 (having lost it for a time as a result of the English Civil War), rulers and bureaucrats in London attempted to supervise the American settlements more effectively and to ensure that the mother country benefited from their economic growth. By the early eighteenth century, following a period of upheaval, a new stability characterized colonial political institutions.

Neither English colonists nor London administrators could ignore other peoples living on the North American continent. As the English settlements expanded, they came into violent conflict not only with powerful Indian nations but also with the Dutch, the Spanish, and especially the French. Moreover, all the European colonies confronted significant crises during the decade of the 1670s. By 1720, war—between Europeans and Indians, among Europeans, and among Indians allied with different colonial powers—had become an all-too-familiar feature of American life. No longer isolated from each other or from Europe, the people and products of the North American colonies had become integral to the world trading system and inextricably enmeshed in its conflicts. ■

The Restoration Colonies

 In 1642 England erupted into civil war. Disputes over taxation, religion, and other issues led to armed conflict between supporters of the Stuart King Charles I and the Puritan-dominated Parliament. After four years of warfare, Parliament triumphed. Following the execution of Charles I in 1649, the parliamentary army's leader, Oliver Cromwell, assumed control of the government. Yet after Cromwell's death in 1658 Parliament decided to restore the monarchy if Charles I's son and heir would agree to restrictions on his authority. In 1660, Charles II ascended the throne (see Table 3.1), having promised to support the Church of England and to seek Parliament's consent for any new taxes. Thus the Stuart Restoration ended the tumultuous chapter in English history known as the Interregnum (Latin for "between reigns") or Commonwealth period.

The English Civil War, the Interregnum, and the reign of Charles II (1660–1685) had far-reaching sig-

IMPORTANT EVENTS

1642–46	English Civil War
1649	Charles I executed
1651	First Navigation Act passed to regulate colonial trade
1660	Stuarts restored to throne; Charles II becomes king
1663	Carolina chartered
1664	English conquer New Netherland; New York founded
	New Jersey established
1670s	Marquette, Jolliet, and La Salle explore the Great Lakes and Mississippi valley for France
1675–76	King Philip's War devastates New England
1676	Bacon's Rebellion disrupts Virginia government; Jamestown destroyed
1680–92	Pueblo revolt temporarily drives Spaniards from New Mexico
1681	Pennsylvania chartered
1685	James II becomes king
1686–89	Dominion of New England established, superseding all charters of colonies from Maine to New Jersey
1688–89	James II deposed in Glorious Revolution; William and Mary ascend throne
1689–97	King William's War fought on northern New England frontier
1692	Witchcraft crisis in Salem; nineteen executions result
1696	Board of Trade and Plantations established to coordinate English colonial administration
1701	Iroquois adopt neutrality policy toward France and England
1702–13	Queen Anne's War fought by French and English
1711–13	Tuscarora War (North Carolina) leads to capture or migration of most Tuscaroras
1715	Yamasee War nearly destroys South Carolina
1718	New Orleans founded in French Louisiana

Proprietorships nificance for the Anglo-American colonies. During the Civil War and the Commonwealth period, Puritans controlled the English government. Thus their migration to New England largely ceased, and some colonists packed up to return home. The subsequent reign of Charles II saw the founding of six of the thirteen colonies that eventually would form the American nation: New York, New Jersey, Pennsylvania (including Delaware), and North and South Carolina (see Map 3.1). All were proprietorships; in each of them, as in Maryland, one man or several men held title to the soil and controlled the government. Charles II gave such vast American holdings as rewards to men who had supported his family during the Civil War. Several of his favorites even shared in more than one grant. Collectively, these became known as the Restoration colonies because they were created by the restored Stuart monarchy.

Charles's younger brother James, the duke of York, quickly benefited from his brother's generosity. In 1664, acting as though the Dutch colony of New Netherland did not exist, Charles II gave James the re-

New York gion between the Connecticut and Delaware Rivers, including the Hudson valley and Long Island. James immediately organized an invasion fleet. In August James's warships anchored off Manhattan Island and demanded New Netherland's surrender. The colony complied without resistance. Although the Netherlands briefly retook the colony in a later war in 1672, the Dutch permanently ceded the province in 1674.

Table 3.1 Stuart Monarchs of England, 1660–1714

Monarch	Reign	Relation to Predecessor
Charles II	1660–1685	Son
James II	1685–1688	Brother
Mary	1688–1694	Daughter
William	1688–1702	Son-in-law
Anne	1702–1714	Sister, sister-in-law

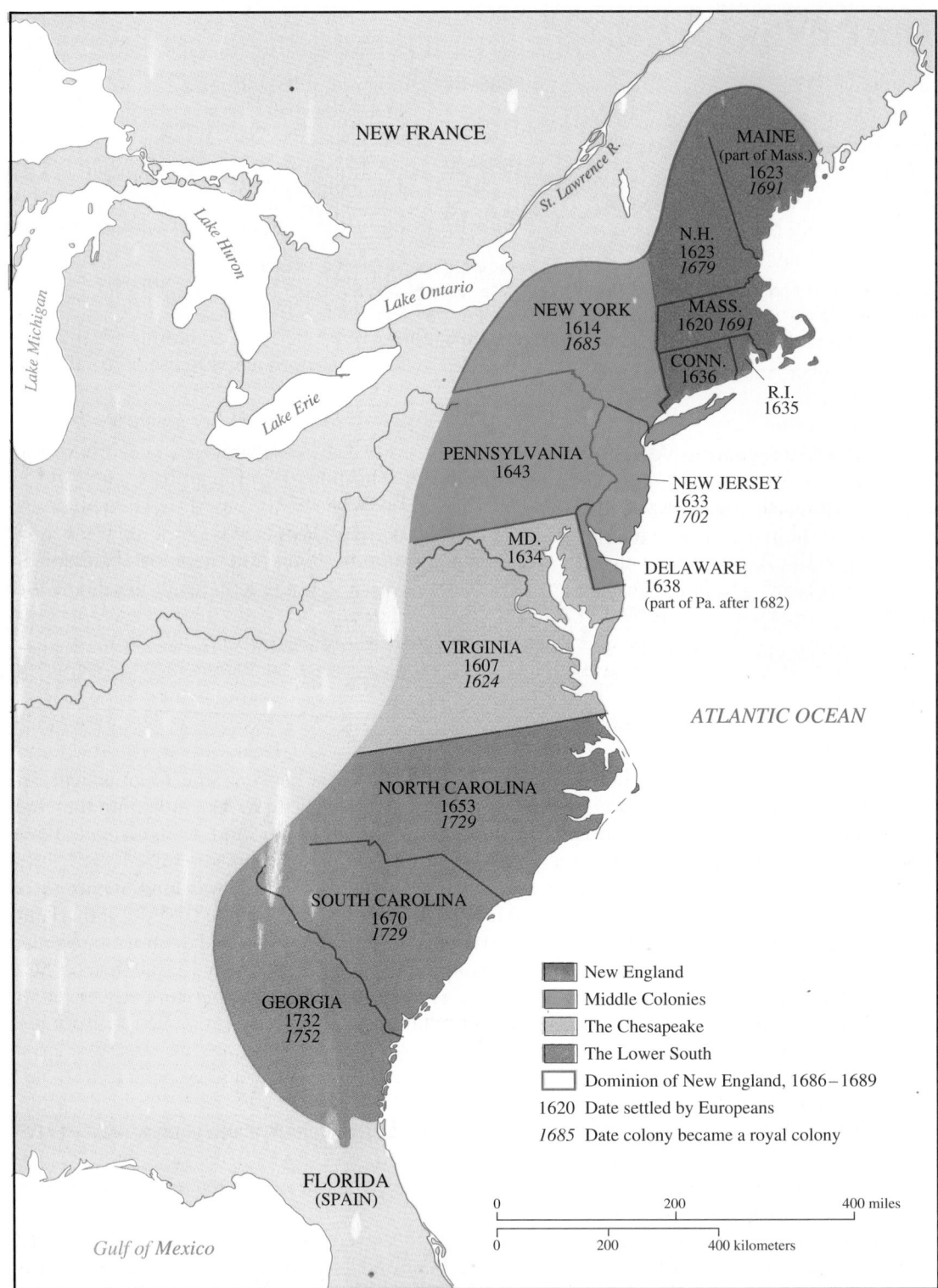

NEW FRANCE

Lake Huron

Lake Michigan

Lake Ontario

Lake Erie

St. Lawrence R.

MAINE
(part of Mass.)
1623
1691

N.H.
1623
1679

NEW YORK
1614
1685

MASS.
1620 *1691*

CONN.
1636

R.I.
1635

PENNSYLVANIA
1643

NEW JERSEY
1633
1702

MD.
1634

DELAWARE
1638
(part of Pa. after 1682)

VIRGINIA
1607
1624

ATLANTIC OCEAN

NORTH CAROLINA
1653
1729

SOUTH CAROLINA
1670
1729

GEORGIA
1732
1752

FLORIDA
(SPAIN)

Gulf of Mexico

New England
Middle Colonies
The Chesapeake
The Lower South
Dominion of New England, 1686–1689
1620 Date settled by Europeans
1685 Date colony became a royal colony

| 0 | | 200 | | 400 miles |
| 0 | 200 | | 400 kilometers | |

Map 3.1   The Anglo-American Colonies in the Early Eighteenth Century   By the early
eighteenth century, the English colonies nominally dominated the Atlantic coastline of North
America. But the colonies' formal boundary lines are deceiving because the western reaches
of each colony were still largely unfamiliar to Europeans and because much of the land was
still inhabited by Native Americans.

About 1650 a Dutch artist produced this copper engraving of New Amsterdam. Dominated by a prominent windmill, tall government buildings, and European-style row houses, the small community closely resembled towns in the Netherlands. Note the many contrasts to the view of Plymouth on page 50. (Museum of the City of New York. Gift of Dr. N. Sulzberber)

Thus James acquired a heterogeneous possession, which he renamed New York (see Table 3.2). In 1664 an appreciable minority of English people (mostly Puritan New Englanders who had moved to Long Island) already lived there, along with sizable numbers of Indians, Africans, Germans, French-speaking Walloons (from the southern part of modern Belgium), Scandinavians, and a smattering of other European peoples. The Dutch West India Company, the world's greatest slave-trading power at midcentury (see page 75), had actively imported slaves into the colony, intending some for resale in the Chesapeake. Many, though, remained in New Netherland as laborers; at the time of the English conquest, almost one-fifth of Manhattan's approximately fifteen hundred inhabitants were of African descent. Indeed, slaves then made up a higher proportion of New York's urban population than of the Chesapeake's rural people.

Recognizing the population's diversity, the duke of York's representatives moved cautiously in their efforts to establish English authority. The **The Duke's Laws** Duke's Laws, a legal code proclaimed in 1665, at first applied solely to the English settlements on Long Island, only later being extended to the rest of the colony. Dutch forms of local government were maintained, Dutch land titles confirmed, and Dutch residents allowed to maintain customary legal practices. Each town was permitted to decide which church (Dutch Reformed, Congregational, or Church of England) to support with its tax revenues. Much to the dismay of English residents of the colony, the Duke's Laws made no provision for a representative assembly. Like other Stuarts, James distrusted legislative bodies, and not until 1683 did he agree to the colonists' requests for an elected legislature. Before then, an auto-

cratic governor ruled New York, just as had been the practice under the Dutch.

The English takeover thus had little immediate effect on the colony. Its population grew slowly, barely reaching eighteen thousand by the time of the first English census in 1698. Until the second decade of the eighteenth century, New York City remained a commercial backwater within the orbit of Boston.

The English conquest brought so little change to New York primarily because the duke of York in 1664 **Founding of New Jersey** regranted the land between the Hudson and Delaware Rivers—East and West Jersey—to his friends Sir George Carteret and John Lord Berkeley. That grant left the duke's own colony hemmed in between Connecticut to the east and the Jerseys to the west and south, depriving it of much fertile land and hindering its economic growth. He also failed to promote migration. Meanwhile, the Jersey proprietors acted rapidly to attract settlers, promising generous land grants, limited freedom of religion, and—without authorization from the Crown—a representative assembly. In response, large numbers of Puritan New Englanders migrated southward to the Jerseys, along with some Barbadians and Dutch New Yorkers. New Jersey grew quickly; in 1726, at the time of its first census as a united colony, it had 32,500 inhabitants, only 8,000 fewer than New York.

Within twenty years, Berkeley and Carteret sold their interests in the Jerseys to separate groups of investors. The purchasers of all of Carteret's share (West Jersey) and portions of Berkeley's (East Jersey) were members of the Society of Friends, seeking a refuge from persecution in England. The Society of Friends, also called Quakers, rejected earthly and religious

Table 3.2   The Founding of English Colonies in North America, 1664–1681

Colony	Founder(s)	Date	Basis of Economy
New York (formerly New Netherland)	James, duke of York	1664	Farming, fur trading
New Jersey	Sir George Carteret, John Lord Berkeley	1664	Farming
North Carolina	Carolina proprietors	1665	Tobacco, forest products
South Carolina	Carolina proprietors	1670	Rice, indigo
Pennsylvania	William Penn	1681	Farming

hierarchies and denied the need for intermediaries between individuals and God. They believed that anyone could be saved by the "inner light" and that all people were equal in God's sight. With no formally trained clergy, Quakers allowed anyone, male or female, to speak in meetings or become a "public Friend" and travel to spread God's word. The Quaker message of radical egalitarianism was not welcome in the hierarchical society of seventeenth-century England or, for that matter, in Puritan New England. For example, Mary Dyer—who had followed Anne Hutchinson into exile—became a Quaker, returned to Boston as a missionary, and was hanged in 1660 (along with several men) for preaching Quaker doctrines.

The Quakers obtained their own colony in 1681, when Charles II granted the region between Maryland and New York to his close friend William Penn, a prominent member of the sect. Penn was then thirty-seven years old; he held the colony as a personal proprietorship, one that earned profits for his descendants until the American Revolution. Even so, Penn, like the Roman Catholic Calverts of Maryland before him, saw his province not merely as a source of revenue but also as a haven for persecuted coreligionists. Penn offered land to all comers on liberal terms, promised toleration of all religions (although only Christians were given the vote), guaranteed English liberties such as the right to bail and trial by jury, and pledged to establish a representative assembly. He also publicized the ready availability of land in Pennsylvania through promotional tracts printed in German, French, and Dutch and distributed widely throughout Europe.

Pennsylvania: A Quaker Haven

Penn's activities and the Quakers' attraction to his lands gave rise to a migration whose magnitude equaled the Puritan exodus to New England in the 1630s. By mid-1683, more than three thousand people—among them Welsh, Irish, Dutch, and Germans—had already moved to Pennsylvania, and within five years the population reached twelve thousand. (By contrast, it took Virginia more than thirty years to achieve a comparable population.) Philadelphia, carefully sited on the easily navigable Delaware River and planned to be the major city in the province, drew merchants and artisans from throughout the English-speaking world. From mainland and Caribbean colonies alike came Quakers seeking religious freedom; they brought with them years of experience on American soil and well-established trading connections. Pennsylvania's plentiful and fertile lands soon enabled its residents to begin exporting surplus flour and other foodstuffs to the West Indies. Practically overnight Philadelphia acquired more than two thousand citizens and started to challenge Boston's commercial dominance.

A pacifist with egalitarian principles, Penn attempted to treat Native Americans fairly. He learned to speak the language of the Delawares (or Lenapes), from whom he purchased tracts of land to sell to European settlers. Penn also established strict regulations for trade and forbade the sale of alcohol to Indians. His policies attracted native peoples who moved to Pennsylvania near the end of the seventeenth century to escape repeated clashes with English colonists in Maryland, Virginia, and North Carolina. Most important were the Tuscaroras, whose experiences are described later in this chapter. Likewise, Shawnees and Miamis chose to move eastward from the Ohio valley. By a supreme irony, however, the same toleration that attracted Native Americans also brought non-Quaker Europeans who showed little respect for Indian claims to the soil.

William Penn's Indian Policy

William Penn, later the proprietor of Pennsylvania, as he looked during his youth in Ireland. In such pamphlets as the one shown here, Penn spread the word about his new colony to thousands of readers in England and its other colonial possessions. (Historical Society of Pennsylvania)

In effect, Penn's policy was so successful that it caused its own downfall. The Scots-Irish, Germans, and Swiss who settled in Pennsylvania in the first half of the eighteenth century clashed repeatedly over land with Indians who had also recently migrated to the colony.

The southernmost proprietary colony, granted by Charles II in 1663, encompassed a huge tract of land stretching from the southern boundary of Virginia to Spanish Florida. The area had great strategic importance: a successful English settlement there would prevent Spaniards from pushing farther north. The fertile semitropical land also held forth the promise of producing exotic and valuable commodities such as figs, olives, wines, and silk. The proprietors named their new province Carolina in honor of Charles, whose Latin name was Carolus. The "Fundamental Constitutions of Carolina," which they asked the political philosopher John Locke to draft for them, set forth an elaborate plan for a colony governed by a hierarchy of landholding aristocrats and characterized by a carefully structured distribution of political and economic power.

Founding of Carolina

But Carolina failed to follow the course the proprietors laid out. Instead, it quickly developed two distinct population centers, which in 1729 split into separate colonies. Virginia planters settled the Albemarle region that became North Carolina. They established a society much like their own, with an economy based on cultivating tobacco and exporting such forest products as pitch, tar, and timber. Because North Carolina lacked a satisfactory harbor, its planters relied on Virginia's ports and merchants to conduct their trade, and the colonies remained tightly linked. The other population center, which eventually formed the core of South Carolina, developed at Charles Town, founded in 1670 near the juncture of the Ashley and Cooper Rivers. Many of its early residents migrated from Barbados, which was already overcrowded less than fifty years after English people first settled there.

South Carolina's first years were difficult. After learning that many tropical plants would not grow successfully on the mainland, Carolinians began to raise corn and herds of cattle, which they sold to Caribbean sugar planters hungry for foodstuffs. Like so many other colonists before them, they depended on trade with nearby Indians to supply the only commodity for which they found a ready market in Europe: deerskins, which were almost as valuable as beaver pelts. During the first decade of the eighteenth century, South Carolina exported an average of 54,000 skins annually, and exports later peaked at 160,000 a year.

1670–1680: A Decade of Crisis

As the Restoration colonies were extending the range of English settlement on the North American landscape, existing English colonies and French and Spanish settlements in North America faced new crises caused primarily by their changing relationships with America's indigenous peoples. Between 1670 and 1680, New England, Virginia, New France, and New Mexico experienced bitter conflicts as their interests col-

lided with those of America's original inhabitants. All the early colonies changed irrevocably as a result.

In the mid-1670s, Louis de Buade de Frontenac, the governor-general of Canada, decided to expand New France's reach into the south and west, hoping to establish a trade route to Mexico and to gain direct control of the valuable fur trade on which the prosperity of the colony rested. Accordingly, he encouraged the explorations of Father Jacques Marquette, Louis Jolliet, and Robert Cavelier de La Salle in the Great Lakes and Mississippi valley regions. His goal, however, brought him into conflict with the powerful Iroquois Confederacy, comprising not one Indian nation but five—the Mohawks, Oneidas, Onondagas, Cayugas, and Senecas. (In 1722 the Tuscaroras became the sixth.)

New France and the Iroquois

Under the terms of a unique defensive alliance forged early in the sixteenth century, a representative council made decisions of war and peace for the entire Iroquois Confederacy, although each nation still retained some autonomy and could not be forced to comply with a council directive against its will. Before the arrival of Europeans, the Iroquois waged wars pri-

Trade between Europeans and Indians provided both societies with essential items. The Europeans manufactured tomahawks specifically for the Native American market. Likewise, the Indians of Long Island increased their production of wampum (made from clam shells) when English and Dutch colonists adopted the purple and white beads as a medium of exchange. Wampum served as a substitute for European coins, which were scarce in the remote colonial outposts. (Peabody Essex Museum/Peabody Museum Collections. Photos by Mark Sexton)

marily to acquire captives to replenish their population. Contact with foreign traders brought ravaging disease as early as 1633, intensifying the need for captives. Simultaneously, the Europeans' presence created an economic motive for warfare: the desire to dominate the fur trade and to gain unimpeded access to European goods. The war with the Hurons in the 1640s (see page 38) was but the first of a series of conflicts with other Indians known as the Beaver Wars, in which the Iroquois fought to achieve control of the lucrative peltry trade. Iroquois warriors did not themselves trap beaver; instead, they raided other villages in search of caches of pelts or attacked Indians from the interior as they carried furs to European outposts. Then the Iroquois traded that booty for European-made blankets, knives, guns, alcohol, and other desirable items.

In the mid-1670s, as Iroquois dominance grew, the French stepped in, for an Iroquois triumph would have destroyed France's plans to trade directly with western Indians. Over the next twenty years the French launched repeated attacks on Iroquois villages. The English offered little assistance other than weapons to their trading partners, even though in 1677 New Yorkers and the Iroquois established a formal alliance known as the Covenant Chain. Its people and resources depleted by constant warfare, the Confederacy in 1701 finally negotiated a neutrality treaty with France and other Indians. For the next half-century the Iroquois nations maintained their power through trade and skillful diplomacy rather than warfare.

The wars against the Iroquois initiated in the 1670s were crucial components of French Canada's plan to penetrate the heartland of North America. Unlike Spaniards, French adventurers did not attempt to subjugate the Indians they encountered. Nor, at first, did they even formally claim large territories for France. Still, when France decided to strengthen its presence near the Gulf of Mexico by founding New Orleans in 1718—to counter both westward thrusts of the English colonies and eastward moves of the Spanish—the Mississippi posts became the glue of empire. *Coureurs de bois* (literally, "forest runners") used the rivers and lakes of the American interior to travel regularly between Quebec and Louisiana, carrying French goods to outposts such as Michilimackinac (at the junction of Lakes Michigan and Huron), Cahokia and Kaskaskia (in present-day

French Expansion into the Mississippi Valley

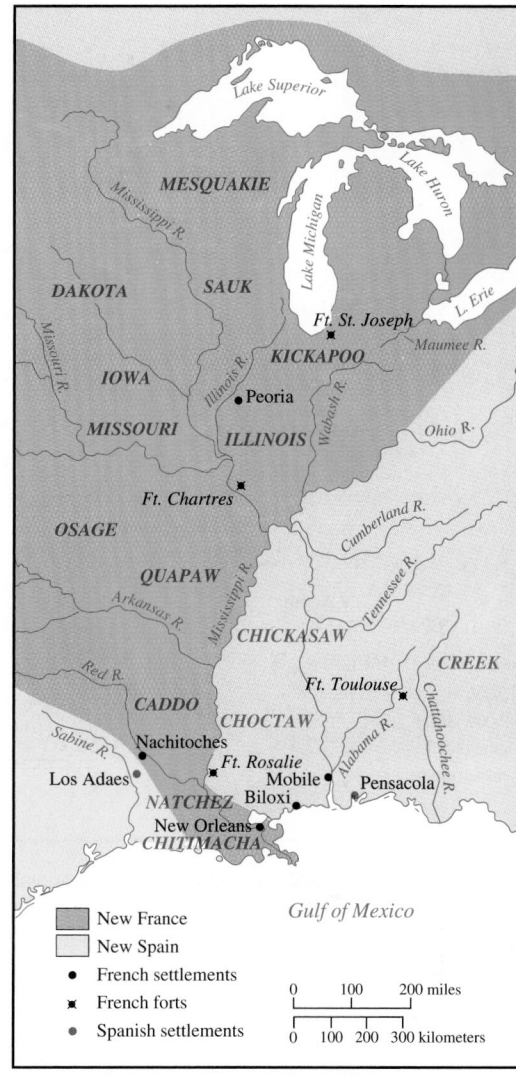

Map 3.2 Louisiana, c. 1720 By 1720 French forts and settlements dotted the Mississippi River and its tributaries in the interior of North America. Two isolated Spanish outposts were situated near the Gulf of Mexico. (Source: Adapted from *France in America,* by William J. Eccles. Copyright © 1972 by William J. Eccles. Reprinted by permission of HarperCollins Publishers, Inc.)

Illinois), and Fort Rosalie (Natchez), on the lower Mississippi River (see Map 3.2).

At most such sites lived a small military garrison and a priest, surrounded by powerful nations such as the Choctaws, Chickasaws, and Osages. Indians gained easy access to valuable European goods by tolerating the minimal European presence, and France's

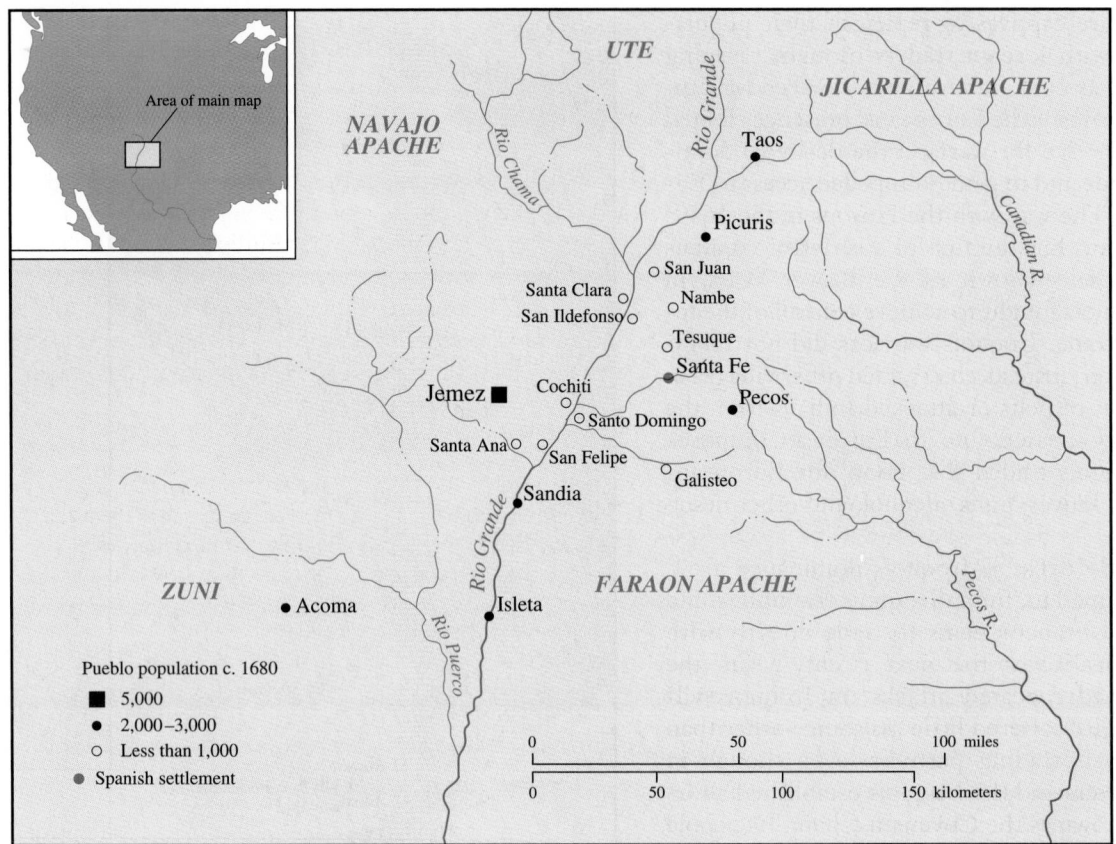

Map 3.3   New Mexico, c. 1680   In 1680, the lone Spanish settlement at Santa Fe was surrounded and vastly outnumbered by the many Pueblo villages nearby.   (Source: Adapted from *Apache, Navaho, and Spaniard,* by Jack D. Forbes. Copyright © 1960 by the University of Oklahoma Press. Used by permission.)

primarily political and economic aims did not include systematic missionary work. The largest French settlements in the region, known collectively as *le pays de Illinois* ("the Illinois country"), never totaled much above three thousand in population. Located along the Mississippi just south of modern St. Louis and north of Fort Chartres, the settlements produced wheat for export to New Orleans. In all the French outposts, the shortage of European women led to interracial unions between French men and Indian women and to the creation of mixed-race people known as *metís.*

In New Mexico, too, events of the 1670s led to a crisis with long-term consequences. Over the years under Spanish domination, the Pueblo peoples had added Christianity to their religious beliefs while still retaining traditional rituals, engaging in syncretic practices as had

Popé and the Pueblo Revolt

Mesoamericans (see pages 24–25). But decade by decade Franciscans adopted increasingly brutal and violent tactics in order to erase all traces of the native religion. Priests and secular colonists who held *encomiendas* also placed heavy labor demands on the population. In 1680 the Pueblos revolted under the leadership of Popé, a respected shaman, successfully driving the Spaniards out of New Mexico (see Map 3.3). Although Spain managed to restore its authority in 1692, imperial officials had learned their lesson. Afterward, Spanish governors stressed cooperation with the Pueblos, no longer attempting to reduce them to bondage or to violate their cultural integrity. The Pueblo revolt of 1680 instigated the most successful and longest-sustained Indian resistance movement in colonial North America.

When the Spanish expanded their territorial claims to the east and north, they followed the same

Spain's North American Possessions

strategy they had adopted in New Mexico, establishing their presence through military outposts and Franciscan missions. The army's role was to maintain order among the subject Indians—to protect them from attack and ensure the availability of their labor—and to guard the boundaries of the New Spain from possible incursions, especially by the French. The friars concentrated on conversions and allowed religious syncretism. By the late eighteenth century, Spain claimed a vast territory that stretched from California (first colonized in 1769 to prevent Russian sea-otter trappers from taking over the region) through Texas (settled after 1700) to the Gulf Coast. Throughout that region, the Spanish presence consisted of a mixture of missions and forts dotting the countryside, sometimes at considerable distances from one another.

In the more densely settled English colonies, hostilities developed in the decade of the 1670s not over religion (as in New Mexico) or trade (as in New France) but rather over land. Put simply, the rapidly expanding Anglo-American population wanted more of it. In both New England and Virginia—though for different reasons—settlers began to encroach on territories that until then had remained in the hands of Native Americans.

In the north, the expansion of the population resulted not from continued immigration (for that largely ceased after the outbreak of the English Civil War in 1642) but rather from natural increase. The

Population Pressures in New England

original settlers' many children also produced many children, and subsequent generations followed suit. By the 1670s, New England's population had more than tripled to reach approximately seventy thousand. Such a rapid increase placed great pressure on available land. Colonial settlement spread far into the interior of Massachusetts and Connecticut, and many members of the third and fourth generations had to migrate—north to New Hampshire or Maine, south to New York or New Jersey, west beyond the Connecticut River—to find sufficient farmland for themselves and their children. Others abandoned agriculture and learned such skills as blacksmithing or carpentry to support themselves in the growing towns.

Colonial settlements eventually surrounded the ancestral lands of the Pokanokets (Wampanoags) on Narragansett Bay. The Pokanoket chief, King Philip, was the son of Massasoit, who had welcomed

King Philip's War

the Pilgrims in 1621. Troubled by the loss of Pokanoket lands and concerned about the impact of European culture and Christianity on his people, King Philip led his warriors in attacks on nearby communities in June 1675. Other Algonquian peoples, among them Nipmucks and Narragansetts, soon joined King Philip's forces. In the fall, the Indian nations jointly attacked settlements in the northern Connecticut River valley. In early 1676, they devastated well-established villages and even attacked Plymouth and Providence. Altogether, the alliance

In September 1671 a large number of Wampanoags renewed their long-standing alliance with the Plymouth colony by signing this document. Yet less than four years later the peace collapsed as King Philip launched devastating attacks on settlements in southern New England. (Boston Athenaeum)

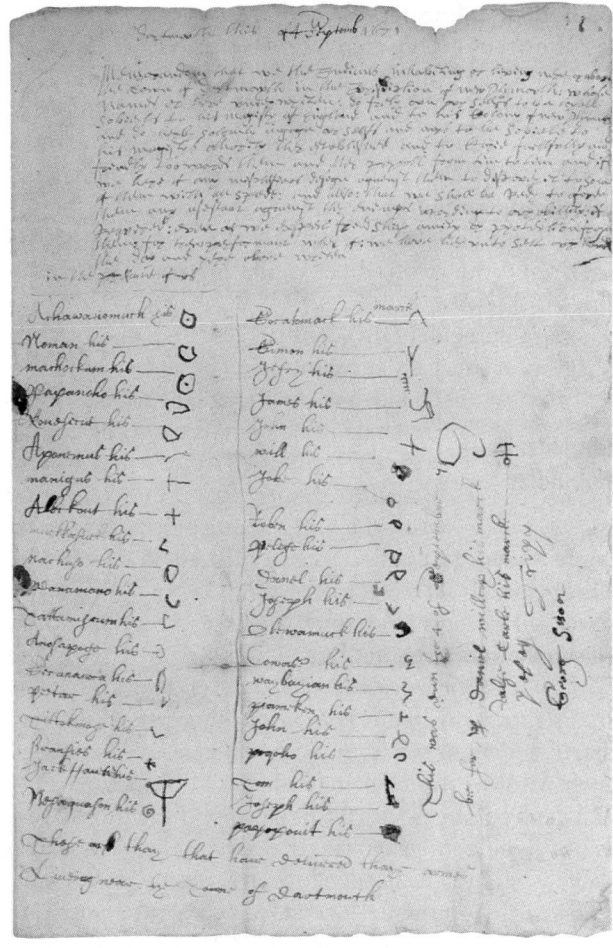

wholly or partially destroyed twenty-five of the ninety Puritan towns and attacked forty others, pushing the line of English settlement back toward the coast.

Still, the tide turned in the summer of 1676. The Indian coalition ran short of food and ammunition, and colonists began to use Christian Indians as guides and scouts. On June 12, the Mohawks—who as Iroquois were ancient enemies of the New England Algonquians—devastated a major Wampanoag encampment while most of the warriors were away attacking an English town on the Connecticut River. After King Philip's death that August, the alliance crumbled. As the chapter-opening vignette reveals, many surviving Pokanokets, Nipmucks, and Narragansetts were captured and sold into slavery, and still more died of starvation and disease. New Englanders had broken the power of the coastal tribes. Thereafter the Indians lived in small clusters, subordinated to the colonists and often working as servants or sailors. Only on the isolated island of Martha's Vineyard did some Wampanoags who had not participated in the war preserve their cultural identity intact.

But the settlers paid a terrible price for their victory in King Philip's War: an estimated one-tenth of the able-bodied adult male population was killed or wounded. Proportional to population, it was the most costly conflict in American history. New Englanders did not fully rebuild abandoned interior towns for another three decades, and not until the American Revolution did the region's per capita income again reach pre-1675 levels.

Not coincidentally, conflict with Indians wracked Virginia at precisely the same time. By the early 1670s, land-hungry Virginians eagerly eyed rich lands north of the York River reserved for Native Americans by early treaties. Using as a pretext the July 1675 killing of an English servant by some Doeg Indians, settlers attacked not only the Doegs but also the Susquehannocks, a powerful nation that had recently occupied the area. In retaliation, Susquehannock bands raided outlying farms in the winter of 1676. Governor William Berkeley, the leader of an entrenched coterie of large landowners, resisted starting a major war to further the aims of disgruntled men who overtly challenged his hold on power. Dissatisfied colonists, including former indentured servants unable to establish their own tobacco farms, rallied behind the leadership of a recent immigrant, the wealthy Nathaniel Bacon, who like other new ar-

Bacon's Rebellion

rivals had found that all the desirable land in settled areas was already claimed by earlier residents.

Berkeley and Bacon soon clashed. After Bacon held members of the House of Burgesses hostage until they authorized him to attack the Indians, Berkeley declared Bacon and his men to be in rebellion. As the chaotic summer of 1676 wore on, Bacon alternately pursued Indians and battled the governor's supporters. In September Bacon marched on Jamestown itself, burning the capital to the ground. But when Bacon died of dysentery the following month, the rebellion began to collapse. Even so, the rebels had made their point, and a new treaty signed in 1677 opened much of the disputed territory to English settlement.

The war, a turning point in Virginia's relationship with nearby Indians, also marked a turning point in the colony's internal race relations. After Bacon's Rebellion, Virginia landowners began to purchase large numbers of imported African slaves for the first time. Historians disagree as to whether they did so in part because they feared dealing with successive waves of the discontented ex-servants who had followed Bacon's lead. But regardless of their motives, in the last two decades of the seventeenth century Anglo-Americans in the Chesapeake irrevocably altered the racial composition of their labor force.

The Introduction of African Slavery

In the 1670s and 1680s, the prosperity of the Chesapeake rested on tobacco, and successful tobacco cultivation depended, as it always had, on an ample labor supply. But fewer and fewer English men and women proved willing to indenture themselves for long terms of service in Maryland and Virginia. Population pressures had eased in England, and the founding of the Restoration colonies meant that people could choose other American destinations. Furthermore, fluctuating tobacco prices and the growing scarcity of land made the Chesapeake less appealing to potential immigrants. That posed a problem for wealthy Chesapeake tobacco growers, whose farms had by then developed into plantations—large enterprises encompassing a number of fields worked by many laborers. Where could they obtain the workers they needed? They found the answer in the Caribbean sugar islands, where since the 1640s Dutch, French, English, and Spanish planters had eagerly purchased African slaves.

European traders hoped to avoid purchasing sick slaves who would carry diseases on board their vessels, thereby causing high mortality rates among other bondspeople and destroying the profitability of the voyages. Some mistakenly believed that by tasting the slaves' sweat they could determine their captives' health. An artist sketched just such a scene in 1725. (*Traite général du commerce de l'Amérique,* by Chambon. Bibliothèque Municipale, Nantes, France)

Slavery had been practiced in Europe (although not in England) for centuries. European Christians—both Catholics and Protestants—

Why African Slavery?

believed that enslaving heathen peoples, especially those of exotic origin, was justifiable in religious terms. Some argued, piously, that holding heathens in bondage would lead to their conversion. Others believed that any heathen taken prisoner in wartime could legitimately be enslaved. Consequently, when Portuguese mariners reached the sub-Saharan African coast and encountered non-Christian societies holding enslaved prisoners of war (see page 18), they did not hesitate to buy such slaves. After the 1440s, Portugal imported large numbers of these captives into the Iberian Peninsula and the Wine Islands; one historian has estimated that by 1500, enslaved Africans composed about one-tenth of the population of Lisbon and Seville, the chief cities of Portugal and Spain.

Iberians then exported African slavery to their American possessions, New Spain and Brazil. Because the Catholic Church prevented the formal enslavement of Indians in those domains (see pages 23–24) and free laborers saw no reason to work voluntarily in mines or on sugar plantations when they could earn better wages under easier conditions elsewhere, African bondspeople (who had no choice) became mainstays of the Caribbean and Brazilian economies. Sugar planters on English islands, who had the same problems of labor supply as did their French, Dutch, and Spanish counterparts, also purchased slaves.

Yet that slave system—well-established in the West Indies by the mid-1650s—did not immediately

Atlantic Creoles in Societies with Slaves

take root in the English mainland colonies, in large part because the colonies were then well-supplied with English laborers. Before the 1660s, the few residents of African descent on the mainland varied in status: some were free, some indentured, some en-slaved. All came from a population that the historian Ira Berlin has termed Atlantic creoles. Often of mixed race, many came to the English colonies from else-where in the Americas. Already familiar with Euro-peans, the Atlantic creoles fitted easily into established niches in the many-faceted hierarchical social struc-tures of the early colonies. Berlin has characterized all the early mainland colonies as "societies with slaves"—that is, societies in which some people were held in perpetual bondage but that did not rely wholly on slave labor. He usefully contrasts such communities with "slave societies," or societies in which slavery served as the fundamental basis of the economy.

The many ambiguities of status in societies with slaves are evident in early laws adopted by the Chesa-peake assemblies. In several Virginia statutes the term *Christian* was used to mean "free person"; when at least one slave therefore claimed freedom as a consequence of conversion to Christianity, the House of Burgesses provided (in 1667) that "the blessed sacrament of bap-tism" would not liberate bondspeople from perpetual servitude. The two colonies did not agree on how slave status would be transmitted to the next generation: Virginia in 1662 declared that slavery followed "the condition of the mother," whereas Maryland two years later provided that children would be slaves "as their fathers were." And when in 1670 the House of Burgesses sought to define for the first time who was enslaveable and who was not, it declared that "all ser-vants not being christians imported into this colony by shipping shalbe slaves for their lives," but similar ser-vants that "shall come by land" would serve only for a term of years. The awkward phrases attempted to dif-ferentiate Africans from Indians; Virginians clearly saw both groups as distinguishable from English people, but expressed those distinctions in terms of re-ligion and geography rather than race.

Yet just a few years later, Chesapeake legislators started to employ racial terminology. As increasing numbers of slaves arrived each year, first from the Caribbean and then di-rectly from Africa, the majority of the enslaved population changed from acculturated creole to newly imported African. Virginia in 1682 altered its definition of who could be enslaved, declar-ing bluntly that "Negroes, Moors, Mollatoes or Indi-ans" arriving "by sea or land" could all be held in bondage for life if their "parentage and native country

The Beginnings of Mainland Slave Societies

are not christian." Most of the English colonies, even those without many bondspeople, adopted detailed codes to govern slaves' behavior. By 1700 African sla-very was firmly established as the basis of the economy in the Chesapeake and South Carolina as well as in the Caribbean. Under Berlin's definition, those colonies had become "slave societies."

English enslavers evidently had few moral qualms about these actions. Few at the time questioned the decision to hold Africans and their descendants—or Indians captured in wars, such as the New England Al-gonquians—in perpetual bondage. The convoluted and contradictory early attempts to define slave status and how it would pass to the next generation suggest, however, that seventeenth-century English colonists nevertheless initially lacked clear conceptual cate-gories defining both "race" and "slave." They devel-oped such categories and their meanings over time, through their experience with the institution of African (and Indian) slavery, which they originally adopted for economic reasons.

Between 1492 and 1770 more Africans than Euro-peans came to the Americas, the overwhelming major-ity of them as slaves. Most went to Brazil or the Caribbean: of at least 10 million enslaved people brought to the Americas during the existence of sla-very, only about 120,000 by 1740, or 260,000 by 1775, were imported into the region that later became the United States. This massive trade in human beings is best understood within the context of the Atlantic trading system that developed during the middle years of the seventeenth century.

The Web of Empire and the Atlantic Slave Trade

The elaborate Atlantic economic system is commonly called the triangular trade. In that context, the traffic in slaves from Africa to the Americas has become known as the middle passage because it constituted the mid-dle leg of such a theoretical triangle. But both *trian-gular trade* and *middle passage* fail to convey the complexities of the commercial relationships that by the late seventeenth century linked the various ele-ments of the Atlantic trading system in Europe, Africa, North and South America, and the Caribbean. People and products did not move across the ocean in easily diagrammed patterns. Instead, their movements created a complicated web of exchange that inextrica-

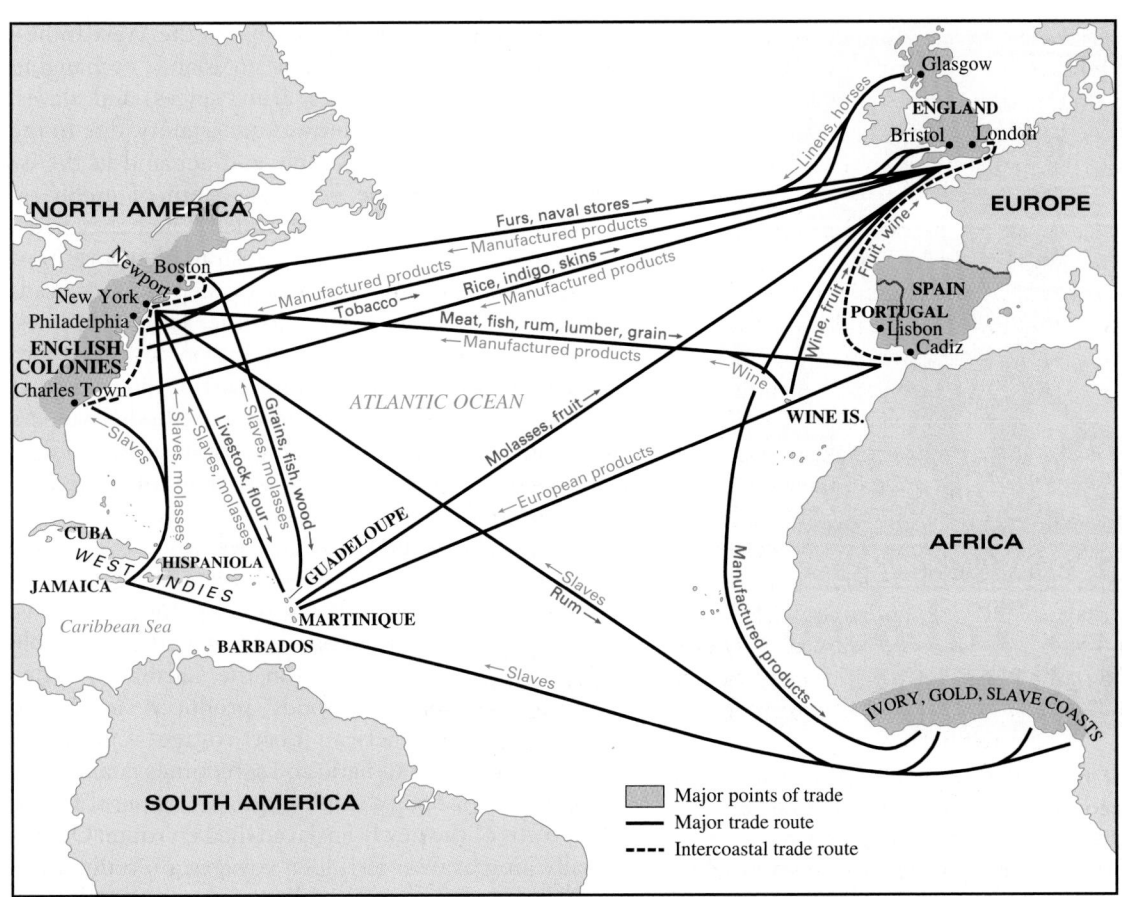

Map 3.4   Atlantic Trade Routes   By the late seventeenth century, an elaborate trade network linked the countries and colonies bordering the Atlantic Ocean. The most valuable commodities exchanged were enslaved people and the products of slave labor.

bly tied the peoples of the Atlantic world together (see Map 3.4).

The traffic in enslaved human beings served as the linchpin of the system. The expanding network of trade between Europe and its colonies was fueled by the sale and transport of slaves, the exchange of commodities produced by slave labor, and the need to feed and clothe so many bound laborers. Yet the various elements had different relationships within the system and with the wider web of exchange. Chesapeake tobacco and Caribbean and Brazilian sugar were in great demand in Europe, so planters shipped their products directly to their home countries. The profits paid for both the African laborers who grew their crops and European manufactured goods. The African coastal rulers who

Atlantic Trading System

ran the entrepots where European slavers acquired their human cargoes received their payment in European manufactures; they had little need for most American products. Europeans purchased slaves from Africa for resale in their colonies and acquired sugar and tobacco from America, in exchange dispatching their manufactures everywhere.

New England had the most complex relationship to the trading system. The region produced only one item England wanted: tall trees to serve as masts for sailing vessels. To buy English manufactures, New Englanders therefore needed profits earned elsewhere—the Wine Islands and such English islands as Barbados and St. Kitts. Those islands lacked precisely the items that New England could produce in abundance: cheap

New England and the Caribbean

York Tobacco LONDON

By the middle of the eighteenth century, American tobacco had become closely associated with African slavery. An English woodcut advertising tobacco from the York River in Virginia accordingly depicted not a Chesapeake planter but rather an African, shown with a hoe in one hand and a pipe in the other. Usually, of course, slaves would not have smoked the high-quality tobacco produced for export, although they were allowed to cultivate small crops for their own use.   (Colonial Williamsburg Foundation)

food (primarily corn and salt fish) to feed the burgeoning slave population and wood for barrels to hold wine and molasses (the liquid form in which sugar was shipped). By the late 1640s, decades before the Chesapeake economy became dependent on *production* by slaves, New England's already rested on *consumption* by slaves and their owners. The sale of foodstuffs and wood products to Caribbean sugar planters provided New England farmers and merchants with a major source of income. After the founding of Pennsylvania, New York, and New Jersey, those colonies too participated in the lucrative West Indian trade.

Shopkeepers in the interior of New England and the middle colonies bartered with local farmers for grains, livestock, and barrel staves, then traded those items to merchants located in port towns. Such merchants then dispatched their ships to the West Indies, where they sailed from island to island, exchanging their cargoes for molasses, fruit, spices, and slaves. The system's sole constant was uncertainty, due to the weather, rapid shifts in supply and demand in the island markets, and the delicate system of credit on which the entire structure depended. Once they had a full load, the ships returned to Boston, Newport, New York, or Philadelphia to dispose of their cargoes, trading the items they did not use to other nearby colonies. Americans then distilled West Indian molasses into rum, a crucial aspect of the only part of the trade that could accurately be termed triangular. Rhode Islanders took rum to Africa and traded it for slaves, whom they carried to the West Indies to exchange for more molasses to produce still more rum.

Tying the system together was the voyage that brought Africans (sold by coastal rulers, bought by European slavers) to the Americas, where they cultivated the profitable crops and—in the Caribbean—consumed foods produced in North America. That voyage was always traumatic and sometimes fatal for the people who made up a ship's cargo. An average of 10 to 20 percent of the newly enslaved died en route. On unusually long or disease-ridden voyages, mortality rates could be much higher. In addition, some slaves died either before the ships left Africa or shortly after their arrival in the Americas. Their European captors also died at high rates, chiefly through exposure to such diseases as yellow fever and malaria, which were endemic to Africa. Just 10 percent of the men sent to run the Royal African Company's forts in Lower Guinea lived to return home to England, and one in every four or five European sailors died on slaving voyages. Once again, the exchange of diseases caused unanticipated death and destruction.

The Human Tragedy of the Slave Trade

Olaudah Equiano, just eleven years old in 1756 when African raiders kidnapped him from his Ibo village in what is now Nigeria, has left one of the most vivid accounts of such a voyage—as applicable to a century earlier as to his own time. Terrified by the light complexions, long hair, and strange language of the sailors, he feared that he "had gotten into a world of bad spirits and that they were going to kill me." Placed below decks, Equiano found that "with the loathsomeness of the stench and crying together, I became so sick and low that I was not able to eat, nor had I the least desire to taste anything."

Equiano's Story

The slavers flogged him to make him eat. Equiano thought about killing himself by jumping overboard but was too closely watched. At last some other Ibos told him that they were being taken to their captors' country to work. "I then was a little revived," Equiano remembered, "and thought if it were no worse than working, my situation was not so desperate."

After a long voyage during which many of the Africans died of disease brought on by the cramped, unsanitary conditions and poor food, the ship arrived at Barbados. Equiano and his shipmates suspected that "these ugly men" were cannibals, but experienced slaves came on board to assure them that they would not be eaten and that many Africans like themselves lived on the island. Equiano recalled that "sure enough soon after we landed there came to us Africans of all languages." Along with other less desirable slaves in the cargo, the youthful Equiano was carried to Virginia, where he was sold and put to work on an isolated part of a tobacco plantation. Resold to a visiting ship captain, he became a sailor, learned English, purchased his own freedom, and eventually published his autobiography.

The slave trade had political and economic consequences for the nations of West Africa. Coastal rulers served as middlemen, allowing the establishment of permanent slave-trading posts in their territories and supplying resident Europeans with slaves to fill ships that stopped regularly at the coastal forts. Such rulers controlled European traders' access to slaves and at the same time controlled inland peoples' access to desirable European goods such as cloth, alcohol, tobacco, firearms, and iron bars that could be made into useful tools. The centralizing tendencies of the slave trade helped to create such powerful eighteenth-century kingdoms as Dahomey and Asante (formed from the Akan States; see page 13). Traffic in slaves thus destroyed smaller polities and disrupted traditional economic patterns, as trade once sent north toward the Mediterranean was redirected to the coast, and as local manufactures declined in the face of European competition.

West Africa and the Slave Trade

The trade in human beings did not uniformly depopulate Guinea, a fertile and densely inhabited region. Instead, the slave trade affected African societies unevenly. Because they primarily bartered prisoners of war with European slavers, coastal rulers' participation in the trade depended on their involvement in warfare. For example, the growing state of Benin actively sold wartime captives to the Portuguese in the late fifteenth century; did not do so at the height of its power in the sixteenth and seventeenth centuries; and renewed the sale of prisoners in the eighteenth century when its waning power led to conflict with neighboring states. Because American planters preferred to purchase male slaves, the trade did have an impact on the sex ratio of the remaining population. The relative shortage of men increased work demands on women, encouraged polygyny, and opened new avenues for advancement to women and their children.

This traffic in slaves chiefly benefited Europeans, despite its importance to some African kings. The European economy, previously oriented toward the Mediterranean and Asia, shifted its emphasis to the Atlantic Ocean. Whereas European merchants' profits had once come primarily from trade with North Africa, the eastern Mediterranean, and China, by the late seventeenth century commerce in slaves and the products of slave labor constituted the basis of the European economic system. The irony of Columbus's discoveries thus became complete: seeking the wealth of Asia, Columbus instead found the lands that—along with Africa—ultimately replaced Asia as the source of European prosperity.

European Rivalries and the Slave Trade

European nations fought bitterly to control the slave trade. The Portuguese, who at first dominated the trade, were supplanted by the Dutch in the 1630s. The Dutch in turn lost out to the English, who controlled the trade through the Royal African Company, a joint-stock company chartered by Charles II in 1672. Holding a monopoly on all English trade with sub-Saharan Africa, the company built and maintained seventeen forts and trading posts, dispatched to West Africa hundreds of ships carrying English manufactured goods, and transported about 100,000 slaves to England's Caribbean colonies. It paid regular dividends averaging 10 percent yearly, and some of its agents made fortunes. Yet even before the company's monopoly expired in 1712, many individual English traders had illegally entered the market for slaves. By the early eighteenth century, such independent traders carried most of the Africans imported into the colonies, earning huge profits from successful voyages.

English officials seeking a new source of revenue after the disruptions of the Civil War decided to tap into the profits produced by the expanding Atlantic trading system. Chesapeake tobacco and West Indian sugar had obvious value, but other colonial products also had considerable potential. Additional tax revenues could put

The harbor of Christiansted, St. Croix, in the Danish West Indies. Although this view was painted over one hundred years after the events discussed in this chapter, the town had not changed much in the interim. Scenes like this would have been very familiar to seventeenth- and eighteenth-century colonial mariners, for such ports existed all over the Caribbean. Anchored merchant vessels await the hogsheads of molasses being prepared for shipment at the wharf.   (1996 MAPes MONDe Ltd.)

England back on a sound financial footing, and English merchants wanted to ensure that they—not their Dutch rivals—reaped the benefits of trading with English colonies. Parliament and the restored Stuart monarchs accordingly began to draft laws designed to confine the proceeds of the English imperial web of trade primarily to the mother country.

Like other European nations, England based its commercial policy on a series of assumptions about the operations of the world's economic

Mercantilism

system. Collectively, these assumptions are usually called mercantilism, although neither the term itself nor a unified mercantilist theory would be formulated until a century later. The theory viewed the economic world as a collection of national states, whose governments actively competed for shares of a finite amount of

wealth. What one nation gained, another nation automatically lost. Each nation sought to become as economically self-sufficient as possible while maintaining a favorable balance of trade with other countries by exporting more than it imported. Colonies had an important role to play in such a scheme. They could supply the mother country with valuable raw materials to be consumed at home or sent abroad, and they could serve as a market for the mother country's manufactured goods.

Parliament applied mercantilist thinking to the American colonies in laws known as the Navigation

Navigation Acts

Acts. The major acts—passed between 1651 and 1673—established three main principles. First, only English or colonial merchants and ships could engage in trade in the colonies.

Second, certain valuable American products could be sold only in the mother country or in other English colonies. At first, these "enumerated" goods included wool, sugar, tobacco, indigo, ginger, and dyes; later acts added rice, naval stores (masts, spars, pitch, tar, and turpentine), copper, and furs to the list. Third, all foreign goods destined for sale in the colonies had to be shipped by way of England, paying English import duties. Some years later, a new series of laws established a fourth principle: the colonies could not export items (such as wool clothing, hats, or iron) that competed with English products.

The Navigation Acts aimed at forcing American trade to center on England. The mother country would benefit from colonial imports and exports both. England had first claim on the most valuable colonial exports, and all foreign imports into the colonies had to pass through England first, enriching its customs revenues in the process. The laws adversely affected some colonies, like those in the West Indies and the Chesapeake, because planters there could not seek new markets for their staple crops. In others, the impact was minimal or even positive. Builders and owners of ships benefited from the monopoly on American trade given to English and colonial merchants; the laws stimulated the creation of a lucrative colonial shipbuilding industry, especially in New England. And the northern and middle colonies produced many unenumerated goods—for example, fish, flour, meat and livestock, and barrel staves. Such products could be traded directly to the French and Dutch Caribbean islands as long as they were carried in English or American ships.

The English authorities soon learned that writing mercantilist legislation was far easier than enforcing it. The many harbors of the American coast provided ready havens for smugglers, and colonial officials often looked the other way when illegally imported goods were offered for sale. In ports such as St. Eustatius in the Dutch West Indies, American merchants could easily dispose of enumerated goods and purchase foreign items on which duty had not been paid. Consequently, Parliament in 1696 enacted another Navigation Act. This law established in America a number of vice-admiralty courts, which operated without juries. In England such courts dealt only with cases involving piracy, vessels taken as wartime prizes, and the like. But since American juries had already demonstrated a tendency to favor local smugglers over customs officers (a colonial customs service was instituted in 1671), Parliament decided to remove Navigation Act cases from the regular colonial courts.

England took another major step in colonial administration in 1696 by creating the fifteen-member Board of Trade and Plantations, which thereafter served as the chief organ of government concerned with the American colonies. (Previously, no single body in London had that responsibility.) It gathered information, reviewed Crown appointments in America, scrutinized legislation passed by colonial assemblies, supervised trade policies, and advised successive ministries on colonial issues. Still, the Board of Trade did not have any direct powers of enforcement. It also shared jurisdiction over American affairs not only with the customs service and the navy but also with the secretary of state for the southern department, the member of the ministry responsible for the colonies. In short, although the Stuart monarchs' reforms considerably improved the quality of colonial administration, supervision of the American provinces remained decentralized and haphazard.

Board of Trade and Plantations

Enslavement in North America

The voyage Olaudah Equiano described was typical, for most slave ships followed the Northeast Trades to the Caribbean before heading north to the Chesapeake. So many Africans were imported into Virginia and Maryland so rapidly that as early as 1690 those colonies contained more slaves than English indentured servants, and by 1710 people of African descent composed one-fifth of the region's population. Even so, and despite sizable continuing imports, a decade later American-born slaves already outnumbered their African-born counterparts in the Chesapeake, and the native-born continued to grow thereafter as a proportion of the slave population.

Slaves brought from Africa tended to be assigned to outlying parts of the plantations (called quarters), at least until they learned some English and the routines of tobacco cultivation. Those from Upper Guinea might have grown the crop in Africa; one historian has speculated that slaves from that region, whence tobacco was exported by the 1680s, could have offered expert advice to Chesapeake planters, who at the time were still experimenting with curing and processing techniques. Such Africans—the vast majority of them men—lived in quarters composed of ten to fifteen workers housed

Enslavement in the Chesapeake

together in one or two buildings and supervised by an Anglo-American overseer. Each man was expected to cultivate about two acres of tobacco a year. Their lives must have been filled with toil and loneliness, for few spoke the same language and all were expected to work for their owners six days a week. On Sundays, planters allowed them a day off. Many used that time to cultivate their own gardens or to hunt or fish to supplement their meager diets. Only rarely could they form families because of the scarcity of women among newly imported Africans.

Such slaves usually cost about two and a half times as much as indentured servants, but they repaid the greater investment with a lifetime of service, assuming they survived—which large numbers, weakened by the voyage and sickened by exposure to new diseases, did not. Many planters could not afford to purchase such expensive workers. Thus the transition from indentured to enslaved labor increased the social and economic distance between richer and poorer planters. Those with enough money could acquire slaves, accumulate greater wealth, and establish large plantations worked by tens, if not hundreds, of bondspeople, whereas the less affluent could not even buy indentured servants, whose price rose because of scarcity. As time passed, Anglo-American society in the Chesapeake became more and more stratified— that is, the gap between rich and poor steadily widened. The introduction of large numbers of Africans into the Chesapeake thus had a significant impact on the shape of Anglo-American society, in addition to reshaping the population as a whole.

Impact of Slavery on the Anglo-American Chesapeake

Africans who had lived in the Caribbean came with their masters to South Carolina from Barbados in 1670, composing one-quarter to one-third of the early population. The Barbadian slaveowners quickly discovered that African-born slaves had a variety of skills well suited to the semitropical environment of South Carolina. African-style dugout canoes became the chief means of transportation in the colony, which was crossed by rivers. Fishing nets copied from African models proved more efficient than those of English origin. Baskets that enslaved laborers wove and gourds that they hollowed out came into general use as containers for food and drink. Africans' skill at killing crocodiles equipped them to handle alligators. And, finally, Africans adapted their traditional techniques of cattle

Enslavement in South Carolina

herding for use in America. Since meat and hides numbered among the colony's chief exports in its earliest years, Africans contributed significantly to South Carolina's prosperity.

Not until after 1700 did South Carolinians begin to import slaves directly from Africa. Nevertheless, by 1710 African-born slaves already outnumbered those born in the Americas, and they constituted a majority of the slave population in South Carolina until about midcentury. The similarity of the South Carolinian and West African environments, coupled with the large proportion of Africans in the population, ensured that more aspects of West African culture survived in that colony than elsewhere on the North American mainland. Only in South Carolina did enslaved parents continue to give their children African names; only there did a dialect develop that combined English words with African terms. (Known as Gullah, it has survived to the present day in isolated areas.) African skills remained useful, so techniques lost in other regions when the migrant generation died were instead passed down to the migrants' children. And in South Carolina African women became the primary petty traders, dominating the markets of Charles Town as they did those of Guinea.

The importation of large numbers of Africans coincided with the successful introduction of rice as a staple crop in South Carolina. English people knew little about the techniques of growing and processing rice, and they failed at their first attempts to raise the crop. But people from Africa's Rice Coast (see page 11) had spent their lives working with rice. Although the evidence is circumstantial, it seems likely that the Africans' expertise assisted their English masters in cultivating the crop profitably. Slaves on rice plantations, which were far larger than Chesapeake tobacco quarters, were each expected to cultivate three to four acres of rice a year. To cut expenses, planters also expected slaves to grow part of their own food. A universally adopted task system of predefined work assignments provided that after bondspeople had finished their set "tasks" for the day, they could then relax or work in their own garden plots or on other projects. Experienced slaves could often complete their tasks by early afternoon; after that, as on Sundays, their masters had no legitimate claim on their time.

Rice and Indigo

When South Carolina developed a second staple crop, its planters too used the task system and drew on slaves' specialized skills. Indigo was much prized in

How do historians know...

that enslaved Africans preserved important aspects of their culture in America? The vast majority of slaves could not read or write, so they did not leave the documentary evidence on which historians customarily rely to develop interpretations of cultural continuity among other peoples. Yet European observers commented on the activities and skills of Africans in their homelands and in the Americas, and the conjunctions are sometimes highly revealing. In 1726, for example, William Smith, an employee of the Royal African Company, drew the sketch below, showing an African musician playing a traditional marimba-like instrument called the *balafo*. Anglo-Americans reported seeing and hearing similar instruments both in the Caribbean islands and on the mainland. John Harrower, a schoolmaster who was an indentured servant in Virginia, recorded in his journal in March 1775 a visit to a tutor on another plantation. After dinner, he wrote, "I spent the afternoon with him in conversation & hearing him play the Fiddle. He also made a Niger come & play on an Instrument call'd a Barrafou." Harrower's description makes it clear that the instrument he heard closely resembled the one Smith had seen half a century earlier in Guinea: "The body of it is an oblong box with the mouth up & stands on four sticks put in bottom, & cross the [top] is laid 11 lo[o]se sticks upon [which] he beats." It is impossible to know who made the *balafo* Harrower heard, or whether the musician was African- or American-born. But the sketch and the description, taken together, show that African music came to North America along with the enslaved multitudes. (Photo: Joseph Regenstein Library, University of Chicago)

Europe as a source of blue dye for cloth. In the early 1740s, Eliza Lucas, a young woman managing her father's plantations, began to experiment with indigo cultivation. Drawing on the knowledge of slaves and overseers from the West Indies, she developed the planting and processing techniques later adopted throughout the colony. Indigo grew on high ground, and rice was planted in low-lying swamps; rice and indigo also had different growing seasons. Thus the two crops complemented each other. South Carolina indigo never matched the quality of that from the Caribbean, but the indigo industry flourished because Parliament offered Carolinians a bounty on every pound they exported to Great Britain.

Indian Enslavement in North and South Carolina

Among the many people held in slavery in both the Carolinas were Indians, many of them Catholic converts from Spanish missions in northern Florida who had been captured by Englishmen or their Native American allies. A widespread traffic in Indian slaves developed in South Carolina, as some Indian nations (for example, the Creeks and the Tuscaroras) sold their captives to the colonists, who either retained them or exported them to other colonies. There are no reliable statistics on the extent of the trade in Indian slaves, but in 1708 they composed 14 percent of the South Carolina population.

Bitter conflicts between North Carolina settlers and indigenous peoples produced not only Indian slaves but also mass migrations. In 1711 the Tuscaroras, an Iroquoian people, attacked a Swiss-German settlement at New Bern that had expropriated their lands without payment. Because the Tuscaroras had been avid slavers, their Algonquian neighbors took the opportunity to settle old scores, joining with the English colonists to defeat their enemy in a bloody two-year war. In the end, more than a thousand Tuscaroras were themselves sold into slavery, and the remnants of the group drifted northward, where they joined the Iroquois Confederacy (see page 66).

The slave trade's abuses led as well to another Indian war in South Carolina. Colonial traders were well known for cheating Native Americans, physically abusing them, and selling friendly peoples into slavery when no enemy captives came readily to hand. In the spring and summer of 1715, the Yamasees, aided by Creeks and others, retaliated by attacking English settlements. Refugees by the hundreds streamed into Charles Town; the Creek-Yamasee offensive came close to driving the colonists from South Carolina. But reinforcements arrived from the north, the colonists hastily armed their slaves to help defend the territory, and Cherokees joined the English settlers to fight the Creeks, their ancient foes. In the end, the Creeks were forced to retreat to villages in the west and the Yamasees moved south into Florida, seeking refuge among the Spanish.

Yamasee War

Indian or African slavery was never of great importance in the economy of Spain's North American territories. (Required labor tribute from the Indian population supplied the Spaniards' needs.) But as slavery took deeper root in South Carolina, Florida officials in 1693 offered freedom to fugitives who would convert to Catholicism. Hundreds of South Carolina runaways took advantage of the offer; although not all won their liberty, others enlisted as free men in the Florida militia. Many settled in a town founded for them near St. Augustine, Gracia Real de Santa Teresa de Mose, which was led by a former slave and militia captain, Francisco Menéndez.

Slaves in Spanish North America

In early Louisiana, too, slaves—some Indians, some Atlantic creoles—at first composed only a tiny proportion of the residents. But a growing European population demanded that the French government

Slaves in French Louisiana

supply them with slaves, and in 1719 officials finally acquiesced, dispatching more than six thousand Africans (most from Senegal) over the next decade. The residents failed to develop a successful crop (although they experimented with both tobacco and indigo), but they did succeed in angering the Natchez Indians, whose lands they had usurped. In 1729 the Natchez, assisted by newly arrived slaves, attacked northern reaches of the colony, killing more than 10 percent of its European people. The French struck back, slaughtering the Natchez and their enslaved allies, but throughout much of the century Louisiana remained a society with slaves rather than a slave society.

Atlantic creoles from the West Indies composed almost all the bondspeople in the northern mainland colonies; few vessels arrived in Boston, Newport, or Philadelphia directly from Africa. Yet the intricate involvement of northerners in the web of commerce surrounding the slave trade ensured that many people of African descent lived in America north of Virginia. Some bondspeople resided in urban areas, especially New York, which in 1700 had a larger black population than any other mainland city. Women tended to work as domestic servants, men as unskilled laborers, and one or two slaves were commonly found in the households of well-to-do families (including three-quarters of wealthy Philadelphians at the end of the seventeenth century). Yet even in the north most enslaved people worked in the countryside, the majority at agricultural tasks. Some men toiled in new rural enterprises such as ironworks, working with hired laborers and indentured servants at forges and foundries. Indeed, ironmasters owned some of the largest numbers of slaves in the north.

Enslavement in the North

Colonial Political Development, Imperial Reorganization, and the Witchcraft Crisis

 The crises of the 1670s in Virginia and New England focused the attention of reform-minded English officials on the mainland colonies. In the early 1680s, London administrators confronted a bewildering array of colonial governments. Massachusetts Bay (includ-

ing Maine) functioned under its original charter. Neighboring Connecticut (having absorbed New Haven) and Rhode Island were granted charters by Charles II in 1662 and 1663, respectively, but Plymouth remained autonomous. Virginia, a royal colony, was joined in that status by New Hampshire in 1679 and New York in 1685 when its proprietor ascended the throne as James II. All the other mainland settlements were proprietorships.

Colonial Political Structures

Still, the colonies shared characteristic political structures. A governor and a legislature ruled most. In New England, property-holding men or the legislature elected the governors; in other regions, the king or the proprietor appointed such leaders. A council, either elected or appointed, advised the governor on matters of policy and sometimes served as the colony's highest court. The councils also served as upper houses of colonial legislatures. At first, councilors and elected representatives met jointly to debate and adopt laws affecting the colony. But as time passed, the fundamental differences between the two legislative groups' purposes and constituencies led them to separate (the first such division occurred in Massachusetts in 1644). Thus developed the two-house legislature still used in all but one of the states.

Meanwhile, local political institutions took shape. In New England, elected selectmen initially governed the towns, but by the end of the seventeenth century, town meetings—held at least annually and attended by most free adult male residents—handled matters of local concern. In the Chesapeake colonies and both of the Carolinas, appointed justices of the peace ran local governments. At first the same was true in Pennsylvania, but by the early eighteenth century elected county officials began to take over some government functions. And in New York, local elections were the rule even before the establishment of the colonial assembly in 1683.

A Tradition of Autonomy Challenged

By late in the seventeenth century, therefore, Anglo-American colonists everywhere had become accustomed to exercising a considerable degree of local political autonomy. The tradition of consent was especially firmly established in New England. Massachusetts, Plymouth, Connecticut, and Rhode Island operated essentially as independent entities, subject neither to the direct authority of the king nor

to a proprietor. Everywhere in the English colonies, free adult men who owned more than a minimum amount of property (which varied from place to place) expected to have an influential voice in their governments—and especially in decisions concerning taxation.

After James II became king in 1685, such expectations clashed with those of the monarch. The new king and his successors sought to bring order to the apparently chaotic state of colonial administration by tightening the reins of government and by reducing the colonies' political autonomy. (Simultaneously, officials used the Navigation Acts to reduce the colonies' economic autonomy.) Administrators began to chip away at the privileges granted in colonial charters and to reclaim proprietorships for the Crown. Massachusetts (1691), New Jersey (1702), and the Carolinas (1729) all became royal colonies. The charters of Rhode Island, Connecticut, Maryland, and Pennsylvania were temporarily suspended but ultimately were restored to their original status.

Dominion of New England

The most drastic reordering of colonial administration targeted Puritan New England. Reports from America convinced English officials that New England was a hotbed of smuggling. Moreover, Puritans refused to allow freedom of religion to non-Congregationalists and insisted on maintaining laws that ran counter to English practice. New England thus seemed an appropriate place to exert English authority with greater vigor. The charters of all the colonies from New Jersey to Maine were revoked, and a Dominion of New England established in 1686. (For the boundaries of the Dominion, see Map 3.1.) Sir Edmund Andros, the governor, had immense power: Parliament dissolved all the assemblies, and Andros needed only the consent of an appointed council to make laws and levy taxes.

Glorious Revolution in America

New Englanders endured Andros's autocratic rule for more than two years. Then came the dramatic news that James II had been overthrown in a bloodless coup known as the Glorious Revolution and had been replaced on the throne by his daughter Mary and her husband, the Dutch prince William of Orange. James II, like his father Charles I, had levied taxes without parliamentary approval. He also had announced his conversion to Roman Catholicism. When Parliament offered the throne to

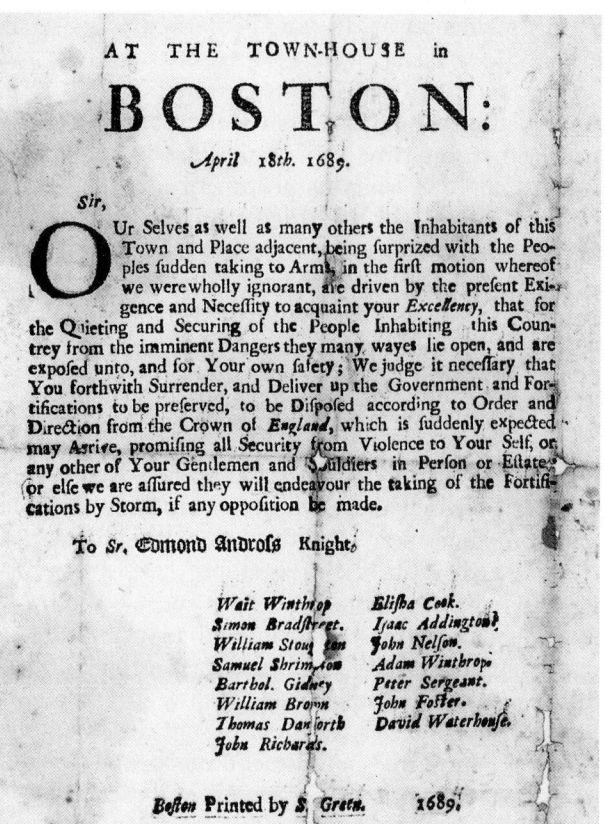

Sir Edmund Andros (1637–1714), the much-detested autocratic governor of the Dominion of New England, and a broadside issued at the height of the crisis caused by the Glorious Revolution, calling on Andros to surrender control of the government. The signers were the foremost leaders of the Massachusetts Bay colony, among them a son and grandson of John Winthrop. (Portrait: Massachusetts State Archives; Broadside: Massachusetts Historical Society)

the Protestants William and Mary, the Glorious Revolution affirmed the supremacy of both Parliament and Protestantism.

Seizing the opportunity to rid themselves of the hated Dominion, New Englanders jailed Andros and his associates, proclaimed their loyalty to William and Mary, and wrote to England for instructions about the form of government they should adopt. Most of Massachusetts Bay's political leaders hoped that the new monarchs would renew their original charter, revoked in 1684 prior to establishment of the Dominion. In other colonies, too, the Glorious Revolution emboldened people for revolt. In Maryland the Protestant Association overturned the government of the Catholic proprietor, and in New York a militia officer of German origin, Jacob Leisler, assumed control of the gov-

ernment. Like New Englanders, the Maryland and New York rebels allied themselves with the supporters of William and Mary. They saw themselves as carrying out the colonial phase of the English revolt against Stuart absolutism.

William and Mary, however, like James II, believed that England should exercise tighter control over its unruly American possessions. Consequently, only the Maryland rebellion received royal sanction, primarily because of its anti-Catholic thrust. In New York, Jacob Leisler was hanged for treason, and Massachusetts (including the formerly independent jurisdiction of Plymouth) became a royal colony with an appointed governor. The province retained its town meeting system of local government and continued to elect its council, but the new charter issued in 1691 (which arrived in Boston with the new governor in May 1692) eliminated the traditional religious test for voting and officeholding. A parish of the Church of England appeared in the heart of Boston. The "city upon a hill," as John Winthrop had envisioned it, was no more.

A war with the French and their Algonquian allies compounded New England's difficulties in a time of political upheaval and economic

King William's War

uncertainty. King Louis XIV of France allied himself with the deposed James II, and England declared war on France in 1689. In Europe, this conflict was known as the War of the League of Augsburg, but the colonists called it King William's War. Indian attacks wholly or partially destroyed a number of English settlements, including Schenectady (New York) and such Maine communities as Casco and Wells. Expeditions organized by the colonies against Montreal and Quebec in 1690 both failed miserably, and throughout the rest of the conflict New England found itself on the defensive. Even the Peace of Ryswick (1697), which formally ended the war in Europe, failed to bring much of a respite from warfare to the northern frontiers. For instance, Maine could not be fully resettled for several decades because of continuing unrest.

Early in the conflict, New Englanders understandably feared a repetition of the devastation of King

The 1692 Witchcraft Crisis

Philip's War. For eight months in 1692, witchcraft accusations spread like wildfire through the rural communities of northeastern Massachusetts—precisely the area most threatened by the Indian attacks in southern Maine and New Hampshire. Like their contemporaries elsewhere, seventeenth-century New Englanders believed in the existence of witches, whose evil powers came from the Devil. If people could not find other explanations for their troubles, they tended to suspect they were bewitched. Before 1689, about one hundred New Englanders, most of them middle-aged women, had been charged with practicing witchcraft, chiefly by neighbors who attributed misfortunes to the suspected witch. Only a few of the accused were convicted, and fewer still were executed. Such isolated incidents involving personal disputes bore little relationship to the witch fears that convulsed the region in 1692 while the war raged just to the north.

The crisis began in late February when several girls in Salem Village (an outlying precinct of the bustling port of Salem) accused some older female neighbors of having bewitched them. Soon other accusers chimed in, many of them female domestic servants who had been orphaned in the Indian attacks on Maine. (One, for example, lost her grandparents in King Philip's War and her parents in King William's War.) These traumatized young women, perhaps the most powerless people in a region apparently powerless to affect its fate, offered their fellow New Englanders a compelling explanation for the seemingly endless chain of troubles afflicting them: their province was under direct attack not only by the Indians but also by the Devil and his allied witches. Before the crisis ended, fourteen women and five men were hanged, one man was pressed to death with heavy stones, and more than one hundred fifty people were jailed, some for many months.

In October, the crisis ended rapidly, for three main reasons. First, the colony's ministers, led by the Reverend Increase Mather, formally expressed serious reservations about the validity of the evidence used to convict many of the accused. Second, the full implementation of the new royal charter ended the worst period of political uncertainty, eliminating one of the sources of stress and regularizing legal procedures. Third, opponents of the trials gained the ear of the new governor, publicly disparaging the "hysterical girls" who had begun the crisis and casting doubt on their credibility.

With the end of the witchcraft crisis and with colonial administration firmly in place, Massachusetts and the rest of the English colonies

Accommodation to Empire

in America accommodated themselves to the new imperial order. Most colonists resented alien officials who arrived in America determined to implement the policies of king and Parliament, but they adjusted to their demands and to the trade restrictions imposed by the Navigation Acts. They fought another imperial war—the War of the Spanish Succession, or Queen Anne's War—from 1702 to 1713, without enduring the stresses of the first, despite the heavy economic burdens the conflict imposed. Colonists who allied themselves with royal government received patronage in the form of offices and land grants and composed "court parties" that supported English officials. Others, who were either less fortunate in their friends or more principled in defense of colonial autonomy, made up the opposition, or "country" interest. By the end of the first quarter of the eighteenth century, most men in both groups had been born in America and were members of elite families whose wealth derived from staple-crop production in the South and commerce in the North.

The Reverend Cotton Mather of Boston, twenty-nine years old in 1692 at the time of the Salem witchcraft crisis, rushed this book—*The Wonders of the Invisible World*—into print shortly after the trials ended. He tried to explain to his fellow New Englanders the "Grievous Molestations by Daemons and Witchcrafts which have lately annoy'd the Countrey" by providing both brief trial narratives and examples of similar recent occurrences elsewhere, most notably in Mohra, Sweden. (Massachusetts Historical Society)

Summary

The eighty years from 1640 to 1720 established the basic economic and political patterns that were to structure subsequent changes in mainland colonial society. In 1640 just two isolated centers of English population, New England and the Chesapeake, existed along the seaboard, along with the tiny Dutch colony of New Netherland. In 1720 nearly the entire east coast of North America was in English hands, and Indian control east of the Appalachian Mountains had been broken by the outcomes of King Philip's War, Bacon's Rebellion, and Queen Anne's War. To the west of the mountains, though, Iroquois power still reigned supreme. What had been an immigrant population was now mostly American-born, except for the many African-born people in South Carolina; economies originally based on trade in fur and skins had become far more complex and more closely linked with the mother country; and a wide variety of political structures had been reshaped into a more uniform pattern. Yet at the same time the introduction of large-scale slavery into the Chesapeake and the Carolinas differentiated their societies from those of the colonies to the north. The production of tobacco, rice, and indigo for international markets distinguished the southern regional economies. They had become true slave societies, heavily reliant on a system of perpetual servitude, not societies with slaves, in which a few bondspeople mingled with larger numbers of indentured servants and laborers of other descriptions.

Even the economies of the northern colonies, though, rested on profits derived from the Atlantic trading system, the key element of which was traffic in enslaved humans, primarily Africans but also including Indians. New England sold corn, salt fish, and wood products to the West Indies, where slaves consumed the foodstuffs and planters shipped molasses in barrels made from staves crafted by northern farmers. Pennsylvania and New York too found in the Caribbean islands a ready market for their livestock, grains, and wheat flour. The rapid growth of enslavement drove all the English colonial economies in these years.

Meanwhile, from a small outpost in Santa Fe, New Mexico, and missions in Florida, the Spanish had expanded their influence throughout the Gulf Coast region and, by just after midcentury, as far north as California. The French had moved from a few settlements along the St. Lawrence to dominate the length of the Mississippi River and the entire Great Lakes region. Both groups of colonists lived near Indian nations and depended on the indigenous people's labor and goodwill. The French and Spanish could not fully control their Native American allies—and the French did not even try. The extensive Spanish and French presence to the south and west of the English settlements meant that future conflicts among the European powers in North America were nearly inevitable.

By 1720, the essential elements of the imperial administrative structure that would govern the English colonies until 1775 had been put firmly in place. The regional economic systems originating in the late seventeenth and early eighteenth centuries also continued to dominate North American life for another century—until after independence had been won. And Anglo-Americans had developed the commitment to autonomous local government that later would lead them into conflict with Parliament and the king.

LEGACY FOR A PEOPLE AND A NATION
"Witch Hunts"

Since the eighteenth century, the Salem witchcraft crisis has fascinated Americans, both scholars in many different fields and the general public. Movies, plays, television shows, and innumerable books and articles have examined the episode from a variety of perspectives. Some authors attribute the hysteria to food poisoning or disease (encephalitis); some accuse a "girl gang" of delinquents of making mischief because they were repressed by Puritan culture (or perhaps because they were simply bored with their lives); one historian even asserts that there really *were* practicing witches in Salem in 1692.

Yet everyone today agrees that what happened in northeastern Massachusetts in 1692 was a "witch hunt." Americans now regularly apply that term to a misguided search for scapegoats on whom to blame as-

sorted troubles. In the early 1690s, those troubles stemmed from concerns about the future of the Bay colony—fears caused both by the absence of a fully implemented charter and by the ongoing King William's War being fought immediately to the north. Because seventeenth-century people believed that those who allied themselves with the Devil could thereby gain the power to harm individuals and animals, they singled out some of their unpopular neighbors as witches and jailed or hanged them.

During the last half-century, some Americans have likewise used the term "witch hunt" as a code phrase to describe searches for scapegoats of various sorts. In the early 1950s it was employed with respect to Senator Joseph McCarthy's campaign against reputed Communists in the State Department and the Army, and the House Un-American Activities Committee's attack on prominent stage and film professionals for Communist Party membership. In the early 1980s, prosecutions of daycare workers accused of child sexual abuse and engaging in satanic rituals were likewise termed "witch hunts" by their critics. Democrats charged that the 1999 impeachment of President Bill Clinton by the House of Representatives was yet another "witch hunt." Always the term is used pejoratively by opponents of the actions in question, for because of the episode commonly known simply as "Salem," the phrase "witch hunt" has become an American byword for unjustified and unfair legal proceedings that appear to result from communal hysteria. The accusations that so shook the people who lived in the tiny settlements of northeastern Massachusetts more than three hundred years ago have thus left an indelible legacy for the nation.

For Further Reading, see page A-3 of the Appendix. For Web resources, go to http://college.hmco.com.

Maturina, a free black resident of New Orleans, awoke with a start at 3 A.M. on June 2 to the shouts of her neighbor, a slave woman named Louisa. "Maturina, someone has stolen your hens!" Louisa yelled. Leaping from her bed, Maturina ran to investigate, accompanied by her son and her brother Nicolas. They quickly located three of the hens, which had escaped from the robber's grasp, but could search no more until daylight.

Maturina knew where to look for missing chickens. At dawn, she and her relatives went to the city market on the levee (river bank), where they soon encountered a man carrying three fowls they recognized as hers. By threatening him with prosecution, they extracted the information that he had purchased the hens from a French grocer named La Rochelle. So the three confronted La Rochelle at his hut, where they found yet another of the birds. Under their questioning, the grocer reluctantly admitted that "it was a negro who had brought them to him to sell," informing Maturina and Nicolas that the culprit "must be on the levee, or in some of the huts."

Suspicious, Maturina searched La Rochelle's own hut, rousting out the thief, who was hiding within. He tried to escape, but Nicolas pursued and captured him. Brought before the authorities, the thief proved to be Juan, a runaway slave from the countryside. The official investigation revealed that several times in the previous month Juan had successfully sold other stolen poultry at the levee market, and he was convicted of theft.

That much of the action in the story of Maturina, Nicolas, and Juan took place on the Mississippi River levee is not surprising. In the mid-eighteenth century, the crude market centered there was as much a focal point of New Orleans as were its formal government buildings. (The theft occurred in 1782, when New Orleans was ruled by Spain [see page 120], but the same events could easily have happened under French governance, during the decades covered by this chapter.)

More than fifty years after Maturina found her missing chickens at the New Orleans market (see text above), Benjamin Henry Latrobe sketched these "Market Folks" buying and selling goods on the levee. Maturina would have recognized this scene, even though it occurred in 1819. African Americans, European Americans, and Native Americans all actively participated in market exchanges in both eras. (Maryland Historical Society, Baltimore)

4

A WORLD TRANSFORMED 1720–1770

To the levee came Indian traders, French and German farmers, free and enslaved Africans—all intent on buying and selling. One contemporary observed in 1761 that the Germans' Saturday morning market on the levee supplied the city with "cabbages, salads, fruits, greens . . . as well as vast quantities of wildfowl, salt pork, and many excellent sorts of fish." About two thousand people, or one-fourth of the population of Louisiana, lived in New Orleans in 1763, and they regularly mingled at the levee market.

The lively markets in New Orleans and Anglo-American cities such as Boston, Charles Town, and Philadelphia illuminate several key themes of colonial development in the mid-eighteenth century: population growth, ethnic diversity, the increasing importance of colonial urban centers, the creation of an urban elite that purchased food and clothing from other colonists, rising levels of consumption for all social ranks, and the new significance of internal markets. In the French and English mainland colonies, exports continued to dominate the economy. Settlers along the Atlantic and Gulf of Mexico coasts were tied to an international commercial system that fluctuated wildly for reasons having little to do with the colonies but inescapable in their effects. Yet expanding local populations demanded greater quantities and types of goods, and Europe could not supply all those needs. Therefore, in English and French America, as well as in the northern portions of New Spain known as the Borderlands (where exports were never an important element of the economy), colonists came increasingly to depend on exploiting and consuming their own resources.

Ethnic diversity was especially pronounced in the small colonial cities, but even the countryside attracted settlers from many European nations. For example, an Englishman traveling in the vicinity of New Orleans in 1770 encountered not merely the French, Indian, and African residents one might expect, but also Germans, Acadians (see page 120), Irish, Scots, a native of the Spanish island of Minorca, a Slav, and several Anglo-Americans. The Spanish Borderlands and rural New England were the only exceptions; they attracted few new immigrants of any description, their population growth stemming almost entirely from natural increase. The middle and southern Anglo-American colonies attracted by far the largest number of newcomers. Their arrival not only swelled the population but also altered political balances and affected the religious climate by introducing new sects. Unwilling immigrants too (slaves and transported con-

victs) clustered primarily in the middle and southern colonies.

Intermarried networks of wealthy families developed in each of Europe's American possessions by the 1760s. These well-off, educated colonists participated in transatlantic intellectual life, such as the movement known as the Enlightenment, whereas many colonists of the "lesser sort" could neither read nor write. The elites lived in comfortable houses and enjoyed leisure-time activities. Most colonists, whether free or enslaved, struggled just to survive, working daily from dawn to dark. Such divisions were most pronounced in British America, the largest and most prosperous settlements on the continent. By the last half of the century, the social and economic distance among different ranks of Anglo-Americans had widened noticeably. As such stratification increased, so did conflicts—political, economic, and even religious—among people of diverse origins and social ranks.

In 1720 much of the North American continent still fell under Indian control. By 1770, in sharp contrast, settlements of Europeans and Africans ruled by Great Britain filled almost all of the region between the Appalachian Mountains and the Atlantic Ocean; and the British, thanks to their victory over France in the Seven Years War (see pages 118–120), dominated the extensive system of rivers and lakes running through the heart of the continent. Spanish missions extended in a great arc from present-day northern California to the Gulf Coast. Such geographical, economic, and social changes transformed the character of Europe's North American possessions. ∎

Population Growth and Ethnic Diversity

 Dramatic population growth characterized the English mainland colonies in the eighteenth century. Only about 250,000 European and African Americans resided in the colonies in 1700. Thirty years later, that number had more than doubled, and by 1775 it had become 2.5 million. Such rapid expansion appears even more remarkable when it is compared with the modest changes that occurred in Louisiana, New Mexico, California, and Texas. By the last quarter of the eighteenth century, Texas contained only about 2,500 Spanish residents and California even fewer; the largest Spanish colony, New Mexico, included just 20,000 or so. The total European population of New France ex-

IMPORTANT EVENTS

1690	Locke's *Essay Concerning Human Understanding* published, a key example of Enlightenment thought
1720–40	Black population of Chesapeake begins to grow by natural increase, contributing to rise of large plantations
1732	Founding of Georgia
1739	Stono Rebellion (South Carolina) leads to increased white fears of slave revolts George Whitefield arrives in America; Great Awakening broadens
1739–48	King George's War disrupts American economy
1741	New York City "conspiracy" reflects whites' continuing fears of slave revolts
1760s	Baptist congregations take root in Virginia
1760–75	Peak of eighteenth-century European and African migration to English colonies
1765–66	Hudson River land riots pit tenants and squatters against large landlords
1767–69	Regulator movement (South Carolina) tries to establish order in backcountry
1771	North Carolina Regulators defeated by eastern militia at Battle of Alamance

panded from approximately 15,000 in 1700 to about 70,000 in the 1760s, but only along the St. Lawrence River between Quebec and Montreal and in New Orleans were there significant concentrations of French settlers.

Although migration accounted for a considerable share of the growth in English America, most of the gain resulted from natural increase. Once the difficult early decades of settlement had passed, the American population doubled approximately every twenty-five years. Such a rate of growth, unparalleled in human history until very recent times, had a variety of causes, chief among them women's youthful age at the onset of childbearing (early twenties for European Americans, late teens for African Americans). Since married women became pregnant every two or three years, women normally bore five to ten children. Because the colonies were relatively healthful places to live (especially north of Virginia), a large proportion of children who survived infancy reached maturity and began families of their own. As a result, about half of the American population was under sixteen years old in 1775. (By contrast, only about one-third of the American population was under sixteen in 1990.)

Newcomers from Africa and Europe

Africans (about 260,000) constituted the largest racial or ethnic group that came to the mainland English colonies during the eighteenth century. In the slaveholding societies of South America and the Caribbean, a surplus of males over females and appallingly high mortality rates meant that only a large, continuing flow of enslaved Africans could maintain the captive work force at constant levels. South Carolina, where rice cultivation was difficult and unhealthy (chiefly because malaria-carrying mosquitoes bred in the rice swamps), and where planters preferred to purchase men, bore some resemblance to such colonies because it too required an inflow of Africans to sustain as well as expand its labor force. But in the Chesapeake the number of black residents grew especially rapidly because the new imports were added to an African American population that began to sustain itself through natural increase after 1740. Even in South Carolina, where imports continued, African-born slaves had become a minority by 1750.

The offspring of slaves were also slaves, whereas the children of servants were free. The consequences of this important difference between enslaved and indentured labor first became clear when the enslaved population began to grow primarily through natural increase. A planter who owned adult female slaves could watch the size of his labor force increase steadily—through the births of their children, by then declared to be slaves in all the colonies—without making additional major investments in workers. Not coincidentally, the first truly large Chesapeake plantations appeared in the 1740s. Some years later, the slaveholder Thomas Jefferson indicated that he fully understood the connections when he declared, "I consider a woman who brings a child every two years more profitable than the best man of the farm. What she produces is an addition to the capital, while his labors disappear in mere consumption."

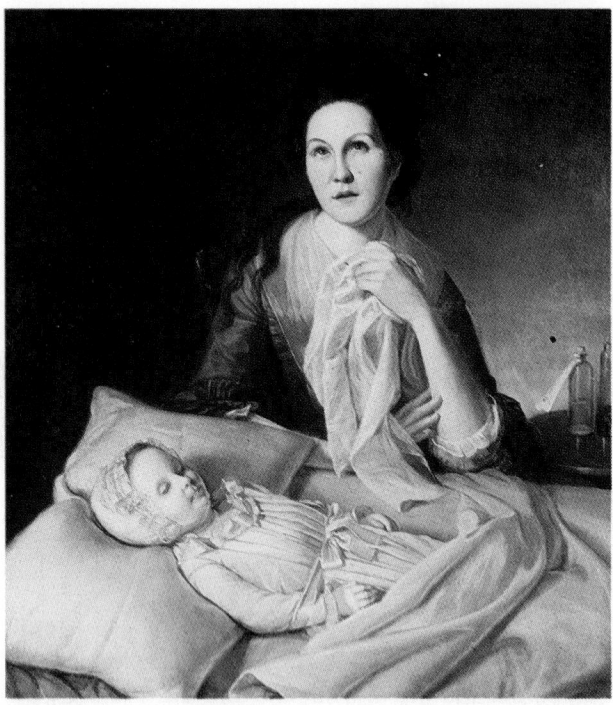

"Rachel Weeping," by Charles Willson Peale, conveys as few other colonial portraits can the affection of eighteenth-century parents for their children and the grief they felt when those children died (as was so often the case) at an early age. Peale movingly revealed his wife's sorrow at the death of their daughter; thus his painting helps to refute the interpretation—advanced by some historians—that high levels of infant mortality led colonists to avoid becoming too attached to their young children. (Philadelphia Museum of Art, the Barra Foundation)

In addition to the new group of Africans, about 585,000 Europeans moved to North America during the eighteenth century, most of them after 1730. Late in the seventeenth century, English officials decided to recruit foreign Protestant colonists in order to prevent further large-scale emigration from England itself, for, influenced by mercantilist thought, they had come to regard a large, industrious population at home as an asset rather than a liability. Thus they ordered the deportation to the colonies of "undesirables"—convicts and Jacobite rebels (supporters of the deposed Stuart monarchs)—but otherwise discouraged emigration. They offered foreign Protestants free lands and religious toleration, even financing the passage of some groups (for example, Germans sent to New York in the 1710s). After 1740 they relaxed citizenship (naturalization) requirements, insisting on only the payment of a small fee, seven years' colonial residence, evidence of adherence to Protestant beliefs, and an oath of allegiance to the king.

One of the largest groups of immigrants—nearly 150,000—came from Ireland or Scotland. About 66,000 Scots-Irish descendants of Presbyterian Scots who had settled in the north of Ireland during the seventeenth century joined some 35,000 people who came directly to America from Scotland (see Table 4.1). Another 43,000, both Protestants and Catholics, migrated from southern Ireland. Fleeing economic distress and (in Ireland) religious discrimination, they hoped to obtain their own land. Scots, Irish, and Scots-Irish immigrants usually landed in Philadelphia. They moved west and south, settling chiefly in Pennsylvania, Maryland, Virginia, and the Carolinas. Frequently unable to afford any acreage, they settled illegally on land belonging to Indians, land speculators, or colonial governments.

Scots-Irish, Germans, and Scots

Migrants from Germany numbered about 85,000. Most emigrated from the Rhineland between 1730 and 1755, also usually arriving in Philadelphia. They became known locally as Pennsylvania Dutch (a corruption of *Deutsch*, as the Germans called themselves); late in the century they and their descendants accounted for one-third of Pennsylvania's residents. But many other Germans moved west and then south along the eastern slopes of the Appalachian Mountains, eventually finding homes in western Maryland and Virginia. Others landed in Charles Town and settled in the southern interior. The Germans belonged to a wide variety of Protestant sects—primarily Lutheran, German Reformed, and Moravian—and therefore added to the already substantial religious diversity of Pennsylvania and New York.

The most concentrated period of immigration to the colonies fell between 1760 and 1775. Tough economic times in Germany and the British Isles led many to decide to seek a better life in America; simultaneously, the slave trade burgeoned. In those fifteen years alone more than 220,000 persons arrived—nearly 10 percent of the entire population of British North America in 1775. Late-arriving free immigrants had little choice but to remain in the cities or move to the edges of settlement; land elsewhere was fully occupied (see Map 4.1). In the peripheries they became the tenants of, or bought property from, land speculators who had purchased giant tracts in the (usually vain) hope of making a fortune.

Table 4.1   Who Moved to America from England and Scotland in the Early 1770s, and Why?

	English Emigrants	Scottish Emigrants	Free American Population
Destination			
13 British colonies	81.1%	92.7%	—
Canada	12.1	4.2	—
West Indies	6.8	3.1	—
Age Distribution			
Under 21	26.8	45.3	56.8%
21–25	37.1	19.9	9.7
26–44	33.3	29.5	20.4
45 and over	2.7	5.3	13.1
Sex Distribution			
Male	83.8	59.9	—
Female	16.2	40.1	—
Unknown	4.2	13.5	—
Traveling Alone or with Families			
In families	20.0	48.0	—
Alone	80.0	52.0	—
Known Occupation or Status			
Gentry	2.5	1.2	—
Merchandising	5.2	5.2	—
Agriculture	17.8	24.0	—
Artisanry	54.2	37.7	—
Laborer	20.3	31.9	—
Why They Left			
Positive reasons (e.g., desire to better one's position)	90.0	36.0	—
Negative reasons (e.g., poverty, unemployment)	10.0	64.0	—

Note: Between December 1773 and March 1776, the British government questioned individuals and families leaving ports in Scotland and England for the American colonies to learn who they were, where they were going, and why they were leaving. This table summarizes just a few of the findings of the official inquiries, which revealed a number of significant differences between the Scottish and English emigrants.

Source of data: Bernard Bailyn, *Voyagers to the West* (New York: Knopf, 1986), Tables 4.1, 5.2, 5.4, 5.7, 5.23, and 6.1.

Because of these migration patterns and the concentration of slaveholding in the South, half the colonial population south of New England had non-English origins by 1775. Whether the migrants assimilated readily into Anglo-American culture depended on patterns of set-

Maintaining Ethnic Identities

tlement, the size of the group, and the strength of the migrants' ties to their common culture. For example, the Huguenots—French Protestants who fled religious persecution in their homeland after 1685—settled in tiny enclaves in American cities like Charles Town and New York. Unable to sustain either their language or their religious practices, they had almost

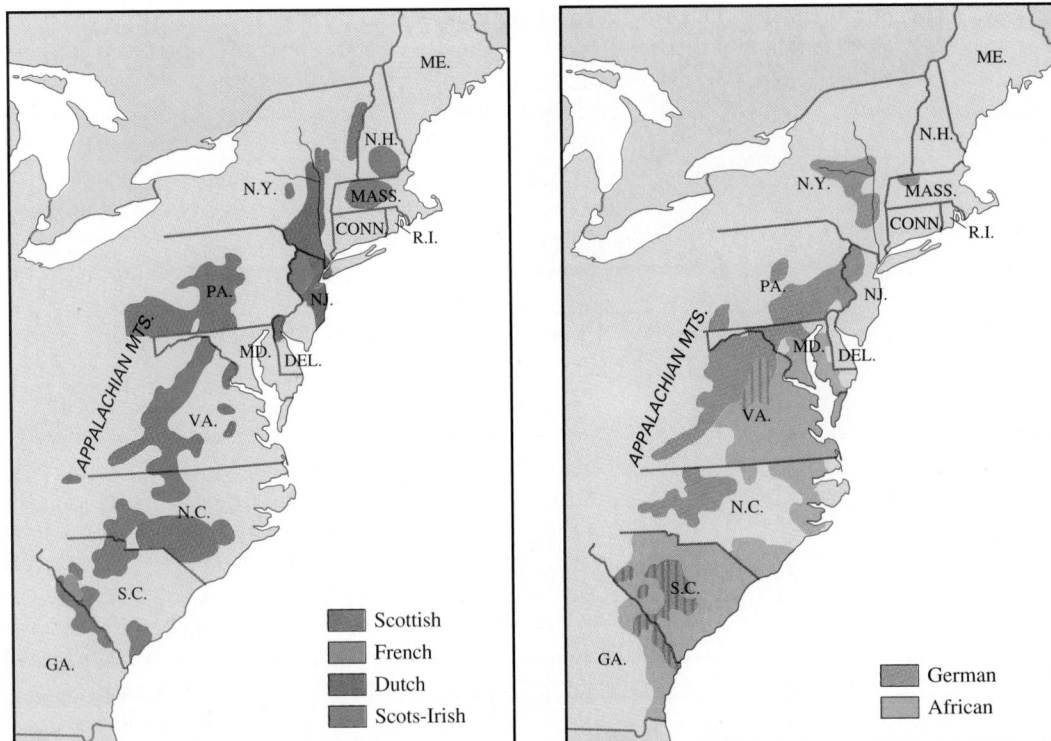

Map 4.1   Non-English Ethnic Groups in the British Colonies, c. 1775   Non-African immigrants arriving in the years after 1720 were pushed to the peripheries of settlement, as is shown by these maps. Scottish, Scots-Irish, French, and German newcomers had to move to the frontiers. The Dutch remained where they had originally settled in the seventeenth century. Africans were concentrated in coastal plantation regions.

wholly assimilated into the dominant culture within two generations. By contrast, the equally small group of colonial Jews maintained a distinct identity. Most were Sephardic, descended from Spanish and Portuguese Jews who had escaped persecution in those countries by migrating to the Netherlands and later to Dutch colonies in America. In a few cities—notably New York and Newport, Rhode Island—they established synagogues and worked actively to preserve their culture. For instance, when Phila Franks, the daughter of a prominent New York Jewish family, married a Christian in 1742, her devastated mother Abigail declared, "I am Determined I never will See nor Lett none of ye Family Goe near her." Few colonial children could defy such strong familial pressures.

Members of the larger groups of migrants (Germans, Irish, and Scots) found it easier to sustain Old World ways. Different ethnic groups each dominated certain localities. Near Frederick, Maryland, a visitor would have heard more German than English; in Anson and Cumberland Counties, North Carolina, the

same visitor might have thought she was in Scotland. Where migrants from different countries settled in the same region, ethnic antagonisms often surfaced. One German clergyman in Pennsylvania, for example, explained his efforts to prevent German youths from marrying people of different ethnic origins by asserting that the Scots-Irish were "lazy, dissipated and poor" and that "it is very seldom that German and English blood is happily united in wedlock."

Recognizing the benefits of keeping other racial and ethnic groups divided, the English elites on occasion deliberately fostered such antagonisms, and they frequently subverted the naturalization laws, thus depriving even long-resident immigrants of a voice in government. When the targets of their policies were European migrants, they hoped to maintain their political and economic power. When they targeted Indians and Africans, as in South Carolina, the stakes were considerably higher. In 1758 one official reported, "It has been allways the policy of this government to create an aversion in them [Indians] to Negroes."

South Carolinians of English origin, a minority of the population, wanted to prevent Indians and Africans from making common cause against them. To keep slaves from running away to join the Indians, Anglo-Americans hired Indians as slave catchers. To keep Indians from trusting Africans, slaves were employed as soldiers in Indian wars.

The elites probably would have preferred to ignore the English colonies' growing racial and ethnic diversity, but they could not do so for long and still maintain their power. When such men decided to lead a revolution in the 1770s, they recognized that they needed the support of non-English Americans. Quite deliberately, they began to speak of "the rights of man," rather than "English liberties," when they sought recruits for their cause.

Economic Growth and Development

 The dramatic increase in the population of Anglo America served as one of the few sources of stability for the colonial economy, which was primarily driven by the vagaries of international markets. A comparison to French and Spanish America reveals significant differences. The population and economy of New Spain's Borderlands both stagnated. The isolated settlements produced few items for export (notably, hides and skins, most obtained through trade with Indians); residents were more likely to exchange goods illegally with their French and English neighbors than with the distant centers of Spanish Mexico or the Caribbean. French Canada exported large quantities of furs and fish, but monopolistic trade practices ensured that most of the profits ended up in the home country. The Louisiana colony required substantial government subsidies to survive, despite its active internal trade and some agricultural exports. Of France's American possessions, only the Caribbean islands flourished economically.

In British North America, by contrast, each year the rising population generated ever-greater demands

Overview of the Anglo-American Economy

for goods and services, which led to the development of small-scale colonial manufacturing and a complex network of internal trade. As the area of settlement expanded, roads, bridges, roads, mills, and stores were built to serve the new communities. A lively coastal trade developed; by the late 1760s, 54 percent of the vessels leaving Boston harbor were sailing to other mainland colonies rather than to foreign ports. Such ships not only collected goods for export and distributed imports but also sold items made in America. The colonies thus began to move away from their earlier pattern of near total dependence on Europe for manufactured goods. For the first time, the American population generated sufficient demand to encourage manufacturing enterprises. The largest indigenous industry was iron making; by 1775, 82 American furnaces and 175 forges produced more iron than did England itself. Almost all of that iron was for domestic consumption.

The major energizing, yet destabilizing, influence on the colonial economy nevertheless remained foreign trade. Colonial prosperity still depended heavily on overseas demand for American products like tobacco, rice, indigo, fish, and barrel staves. The sale of such items earned the colonists the credit they needed to purchase English and European imports. If demand for American exports slowed, the colonists' income dropped and so did their ability to buy imported goods. Merchants were particularly vulnerable to economic downswings, and bankruptcies were common.

Despite fluctuations, the economy slowly grew during the eighteenth century. That growth, which

Growth of Consumption

resulted in part from Americans' higher earnings from their exports, in turn produced better standards of living for all property-owning Americans. In the first two decades of the century, as the price of British manufactures fell in relation to Americans' incomes, households began to acquire amenities such as chairs and earthenware dishes. Diet also improved as trading networks brought access to more varied foodstuffs. After 1750, luxury items like silver plate could be found in the homes of the wealthy, and the "middling sort" started to purchase imported English ceramics and teapots. Even the poorest property owners had more and better household possessions. Thus the colonists became consumers, in the sense that for the first time they could make choices among a wide variety of products and also could afford to buy items not absolutely essential for survival and subsistence.

Yet the benefits of economic growth were unevenly distributed: wealthy Americans improved their position relative to other colonists. The native-born elite families who dominated American political, economic, and social life by 1750 had begun the century with sufficient capital to take advantage of the changes caused by population growth. They were the urban merchants who exported raw materials and imported luxury goods, the large landowners who rented small farms to immigrant tenants, the slave traders who supplied equally wealthy planters with their bondspeople, and the owners of rum distilleries. The rise of this group of moneyed families helped to make the social and economic structure of mid-eighteenth-century America more stratified than before.

New arrivals did not have the opportunities for advancement that had greeted their predecessors.

Urban Poverty

Even so, there seems to have been relatively little severe poverty among free settlers in rural areas, where over 90 percent of the colonists lived. But in the cities, circumstances differed. Families of urban laborers lived on the edge of destitution. In Philadelphia, for instance, a male laborer's average annual earnings fell short of the amount needed to supply his family with the bare necessities. Even in a good year, his wife or children had to do wage work; in a bad year, the family could be reduced to beggary. By the 1760s

public urban poor-relief systems were overwhelmed with applicants for assistance, and some cities began to build workhouses or almshouses to shelter the growing number of poor people. Among them were recent immigrants, the elderly and infirm, and widows, especially those with small children.

Within this overall picture, it is important to distinguish among the various regions: New England, the middle colonies (Pennsylvania, New York, and New Jersey), the Chesapeake (including North Carolina), and the Lower South (South Carolina and Georgia). Each region of the colonies had its own economic rhythm derived from the nature of its export trade.

In New England, three elements combined to influence economic development: the nature of the landscape, New England's leadership in colonial shipping, and the impact of imperial wars. New England's poor soil did not produce surpluses other than livestock, so wood products constituted important salable commodities. Farms were worked primarily by family

Figure 4.1   Regional Trading Patterns: New England   New England's major exports—salt fish, livestock, and wood products—were sold primarily in the West Indies.   (Source: James F. Shepherd and Gary M. Walton, *Shipping, Maritime Trade, and the Economic Development of Colonial North America* [Cambridge: Cambridge University Press, 1972]. Copyright 1972. Used by permission of Cambridge University Press.)

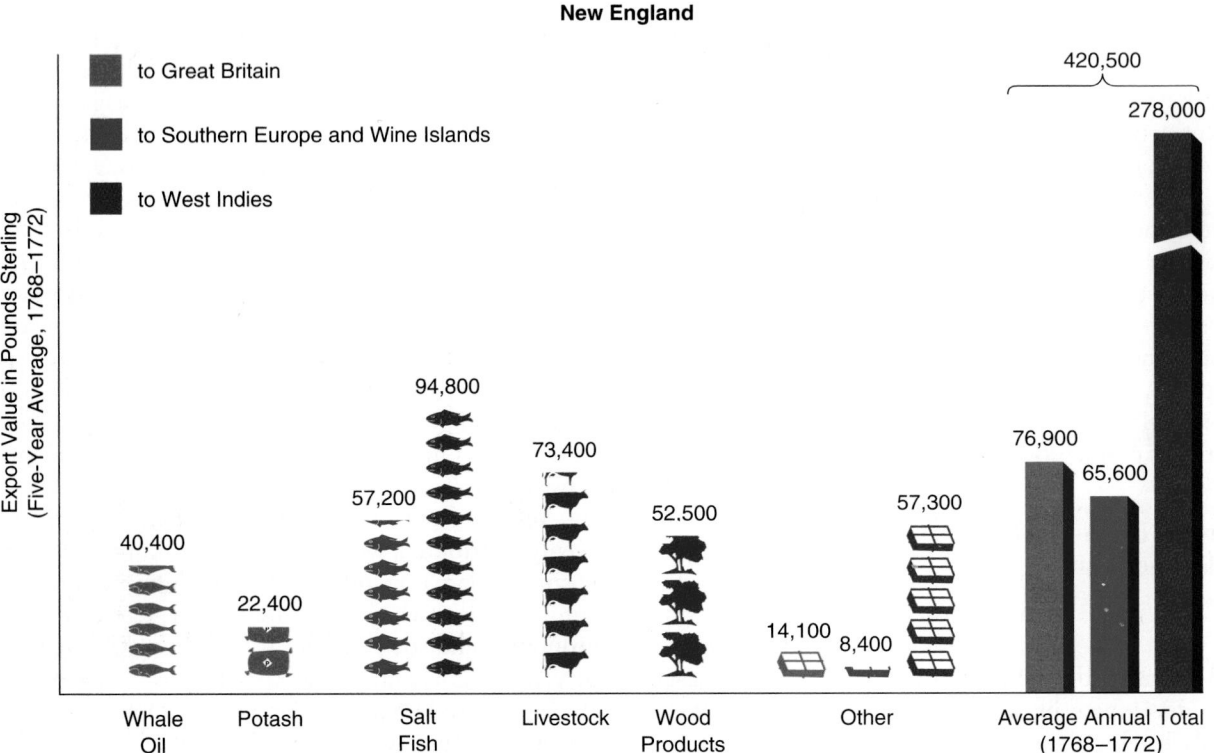

members; the region had relatively few hired laborers. It also had the lowest average wealth per freeholder in the colonies. But New England had many wealthy men: merchants and professionals whose income was drawn from trade with the West Indies in items such as salt fish, livestock, and molasses. (See Figure 4.1.)

Boston, by the 1730s a major shipbuilding center, soon felt the effects when warfare between European powers resumed in 1739. British vessels clashed with Spanish ships in the Caribbean, setting off a conflict that became known in America as King George's War. Nominally the war (called the War of the Austrian Succession in Europe) concerned who would sit on the Austrian throne, but European commercial rivalries in the Americas contributed greatly to its motivations. At first, the war had a positive impact on Boston's economy, for ships—and sailors—were in great demand to serve as privateers (privately owned vessels authorized

New England and King George's War

by the British to capture the enemy's commercial shipping). Wealthy merchants became even wealthier by profiting from contracts to supply military expeditions.

But New England suffered heavy losses of manpower in Caribbean battles and forays against Canada. In 1745 the most successful and expensive expedition captured the French fortress of Louisbourg (in modern Nova Scotia), which guarded the sea-lanes leading to New France. Afterward, though, Massachusetts had to levy heavy taxes on its residents to pay for the costly effort. For decades Boston's economy felt the continuing effects of King George's War. The city was left with unprecedented numbers of widows and children on its relief rolls. The boom in shipbuilding ended when the war did, and taxes remained high. As a final blow to the colony, Britain gave Louisbourg back to France in the Treaty of Aix-la-Chapelle (1748).

King George's War and its aftermath affected the middle colonies more positively because of the greater

Figure 4.2 Regional Trading Patterns: Middle Colonies The middle colonies' major trading partners were the West Indies, the Wine Islands, and southern Europe. Bread, flour, and grains were the region's most valuable exports. (Source: James F. Shepherd and Gary M. Walton, *Shipping, Maritime Trade, and the Economic Development of Colonial North America* [Cambridge: Cambridge University Press, 1972]. Copyright 1972. Used by permission of Cambridge University Press.)

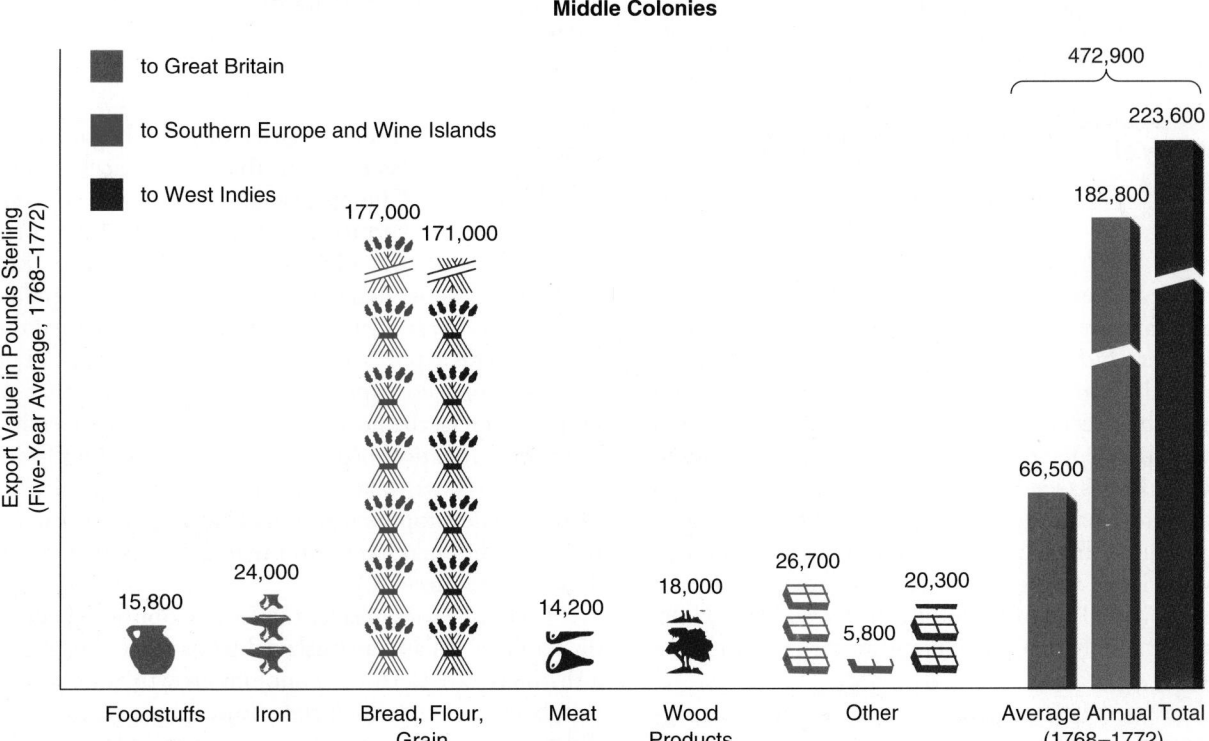

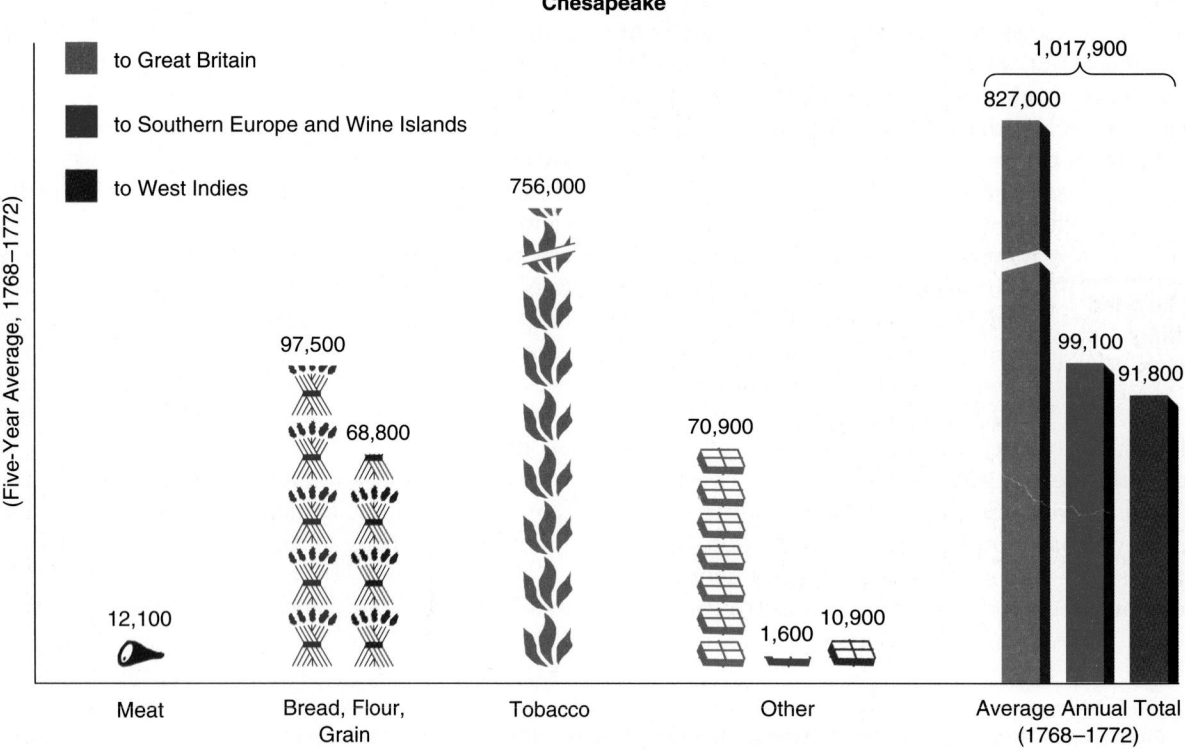

Chesapeake

to Great Britain

to Southern Europe and Wine Islands

to West Indies

Export Value in Pounds Sterling (Five-Year Average, 1768–1772)

1,017,900

827,000

756,000

97,500

68,800

70,900

99,100

91,800

12,100

1,600   10,900

Meat

Bread, Flour, Grain

Tobacco

Other

Average Annual Total (1768–1772)

Figure 4.3   Regional Trading Patterns: The Chesapeake   Tobacco—legally exported only to Great Britain under the terms of the Navigation Acts—was the Chesapeake's dominant product. Grain made up an increasing proportion of the crops this region sold to other destinations.   (Source: James F. Shepherd and Gary M. Walton, *Shipping, Maritime Trade, and the Economic Development of Colonial North America* [Cambridge: Cambridge University Press, 1972]. Copyright 1972. Used by permission of Cambridge University Press.)

Prosperity of the Middle Colonies

fertility of the soil in New York and Pennsylvania, where commercial farming prevailed. An average Pennsylvania farm family consumed only 40 percent of what it produced, selling the rest. New York and New Jersey both had many tenant farmers, who rented acreage from large landowners and often paid their rental fees by sharing crops with their landlords. Prosperous landlords and farmers thus occupied an ideal position to profit from the wartime demand for grain and meat, especially in the West Indies (see Figure 4.2). After the war a series of poor grain harvests in Europe caused flour prices to rise rapidly. Philadelphia and New York, which could draw on large fertile grain- and livestock-producing areas, took the lead in the foodstuffs trade. Meanwhile, Boston, which had no such fertile hinterland, found its economy stagnating.

Increased European demand for grain had a significant impact on the Chesapeake as well. After 1745,

Change in the Chesapeake

when the price of grain began rising faster than that of tobacco, some Chesapeake planters began to convert tobacco fields to wheat and corn.

By diversifying their crops, they could avoid dependency on one product for their income. Tobacco still ruled the region and remained the largest single export from the mainland colonies. (The value of tobacco exports was nearly double that of grain products, the next contender.) Yet the conversion to grain cultivation brought about the first significant change in Chesapeake settlement patterns by encouraging the development of port towns (like Baltimore) to house the merchants who marketed the new products. (See Figure 4.3.)

Like the Chesapeake, the Lower South depended on staple crops and an enslaved labor force, but it had a distinctive pattern of economic growth. In contrast to tobacco prices, which rose slowly through the middle decades of the century, rice prices climbed steeply,

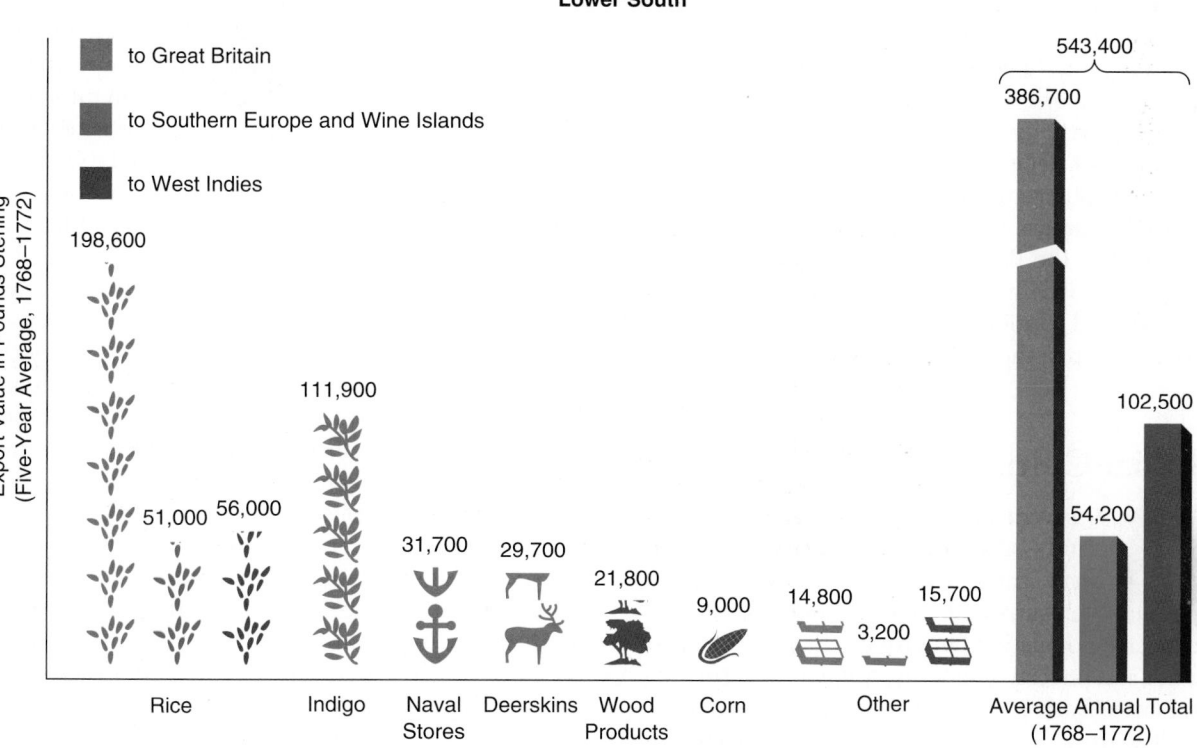

Figure 4.4   Regional Trading Patterns: The Lower South   Rice and indigo, sold primarily in the mother country, dominated the exports of the Lower South.   (Source: James F. Shepherd and Gary M. Walton, *Shipping, Maritime Trade, and the Economic Development of Colonial North America* [Cambridge: Cambridge University Press, 1972]. Copyright 1972. Used by permission of Cambridge University Press.)

Trade and the Lower South

doubling by the late 1730s, primarily because of heavy demand for rice in southern Europe (see Figure 4.4). After Parliament removed rice from the list of enumerated products (see page 77) in 1730, South Carolinians did what colonial tobacco planters could never do: trade directly with continental Europe. But dependence on European sales had its drawbacks, as rice growers discovered when the outbreak of King George's War in 1739 disrupted trade with the continent. Rice prices plummeted, and South Carolina entered a depression from which it did not emerge for a decade. Still, prosperity returned by the 1760s because of rapidly rising European demand for South Carolina's exports; indeed, the Lower South experienced more rapid economic growth in that period than did the other regions of the colonies. Partly as a result, it had the highest average wealth per freeholder in Anglo America by the time of the American Revolution.

Georgia

Closely linked to South Carolina geographically, demographically, and economically was the newest colony on the mainland, Georgia, chartered in 1732 as a haven for English debtors. Its founder James Oglethorpe envisioned Georgia as a garrison province peopled by sturdy farmers who would defend the southern flank of English settlement against Spanish Florida, and so its charter prohibited slavery. But Carolina rice planters successfully won the removal of the restriction in 1751. Thereafter, they essentially invaded Georgia, which—despite remaining politically independent and becoming a royal colony in 1752—developed into a rice-planting slave society resembling South Carolina.

King George's War at first helped New England and hurt the Lower South, but in the long run those effects were reversed. In the Chesapeake and the middle colonies, the war ushered in a long period of prosperity. These variations in economic experience point up a crucial fact about the English mainland colonies: they did not compose a unified whole. Although linked economically into regions, they had few political or social ties beyond or even within those regions. Despite the growing coastal trade, the individual colonies' economic fortunes depended not on their neighbors in America but rather on the shifting markets of Europe and the West Indies. Had it not been for an unprecedented crisis in the British imperial system (discussed in Chapter 5), it is hard to see how they could have been persuaded to join in a common endeavor. Even with that impetus, they found unity difficult to maintain.

Colonial Cultures

 A seventeenth-century resident of England's American possessions miraculously transported to 1750 would have been surprised not only by the denser and more diverse population but also by the new extremes of wealth and poverty, primarily visible in the growing cities. Native-born colonial elites sought to distinguish themselves from ordinary folk in a variety of ways as they consolidated their hold on the local economy and political power.

One historian has termed these processes "the refinement of America." Those colonists who acquired wealth through trade, agriculture, or

Genteel Culture

manufacturing spent their money ostentatiously, dressing at the height of fashion, traveling in horse-drawn carriages driven by uniformed servants, and entertaining one another at lavish parties. Most notably, they built large houses containing rooms specifically designed for such forms of socializing as dancing, cardplaying, or drinking tea. Sufficiently well-off to enjoy "leisure" time (a first for North America), they attended concerts and the theater, gambled at horse races, and played billiards and other games. They also cultivated polite manners, adopting stylized forms of address and paying attention to "proper" ways of behaving. Although the effects of accumulated wealth were most pronounced in Anglo America, elite families in New Mexico, Louisiana, and Quebec as well set themselves off from the "lesser sort." Together these wealthy families deliberately constructed a genteel culture quite different from that of the seventeenth-century colonies or of ordinary colonists in their own day.

Men from such families prided themselves not only on their possessions and on their positions in the

Education

colonial political, social, and economic hierarchy, but also on their level of education and their intellectual connections to Europe. Many had been tutored by private teachers hired by their families; some even attended college in Europe or America. (Harvard, the first colonial college, founded in 1636, was joined by William and Mary in 1693, Yale in 1701, and later by several others—for example, Princeton, established in 1747.) In the seventeenth century, only aspiring clergymen attended college, and their studies focused heavily on ancient languages and theology. But by the mid-eighteenth century, colleges broadened their curricula to include courses on mathematics, the natural sciences, law, and medicine. Accordingly, young men from elite or upwardly mobile families enrolled in college to study for careers other than the ministry. American women were mostly excluded from advanced education, with the exception of some who joined nunneries in Canada or Louisiana, and there could engage in sustained study within convent walls.

The intellectual current known as the Enlightenment deeply affected the learned clergymen who headed colonial colleges and their

The Enlightenment

students. Around the middle of the seventeenth century, some European thinkers began to analyze nature in an effort to determine the laws that govern the universe. They employed experimentation and abstract reasoning to discover general principles behind phenomena such as the motions of planets and stars, the behavior of falling objects, and the characteristics of light and sound. Above all, Enlightenment philosophers emphasized acquiring knowledge through reason, taking particular delight in challenging previously unquestioned assumptions. John Locke's *Essay Concerning Human Understanding* (1690), for example, disputed the notion that human beings are born already imprinted with innate ideas. All knowledge, Locke asserted, derives from one's observations of the external world.

The Enlightenment had an enormous impact on educated, well-to-do people in Europe and America. It supplied them with a common vocabulary and a unified view of the world, one that insisted that the enlightened eighteenth century was better, and wiser, than all previous ages. It joined them in a common endeavor, the effort to make sense of God's orderly creation. Thus American naturalists like John and William Bartram supplied European scientists with information about New World plants and animals so

The profits earned by tobacco planters with large holdings of land and slaves enabled them to buy luxurious items unimaginable to earlier colonists. This handpainted ivory fan and elaborate gold and enamel watch belonged to female members of the Byrd family of Virginia in the mid-eighteenth century.   (Virginia Historical Society)

that they could be included in newly formulated universal classification systems. So, too, Americans interested in astronomy took part in an international effort to learn about the solar system by studying a rare occurrence, the transit of Venus across the face of the sun in 1769. A prime example of America's participation in the Enlightenment was Benjamin Franklin, who retired from a successful printing business in 1748 when he was just forty-two, thereafter devoting himself to scientific experimentation and public service. His *Experiments and Observations on Electricity* (1751) established the terminology and basic theory of electricity still used today.

The Enlightenment had its greatest impact on the lives of ordinary Americans through advances in medicine—specifically, the treatment of smallpox. The Reverend Cotton Mather, a prominent Puritan cleric, read in a British publication about the benefits of inoculation (deliberately infecting a person with a mild case of a disease) as a protection against smallpox. When Boston in 1720–1721 suffered a major smallpox epidemic, Mather urged the adoption of inoculation despite fierce opposition from the city's leading physician. Mortality rates eventually supported Mather—of those inoculated, just 3 percent died; of others, 15 percent. Although inoculation was not widely accepted until midcentury, Enlightenment sci-

ence had provided colonial Americans with a means of preventing the greatest killer disease of all.

Enlightenment rationalism affected politics as well as science. Locke's *Two Treatises of Government*

Contract Theory of Government

(1691) and other works by French and Scottish philosophers challenged previous concepts of a divinely sanctioned, hierarchical political order originating in the power of fathers over families. Men created governments and so could alter them, Locke declared. A ruler who broke his contract with the people and failed to protect their rights could legitimately be ousted from power by peaceful—or even violent—means. Government should aim at the good of the people, Enlightenment theorists proclaimed. A proper political order could prevent the rise of tyrants; God's natural laws governed even the power of monarchs.

The world in which such ideas were discussed was that of the few, not the many. Most residents of North

Oral Cultures

America did not know how to read or write. Even those with basic literacy skills—a small proportion in French or Spanish America, about half of the people in British America—knew only the rudiments. Books were scarce and expensive, and ordinary folk rarely had occasion to write a letter. No colony required children to attend school; European American youngsters who learned to read usually did so in their own homes, taught by their parents or older siblings. A few months at a private "dame school" run by a literate local widow might complete their education by teaching them the basics of writing and simple arithmetic. Few Americans other than some Church of England missionaries in the South tried to teach enslaved children the rudiments. And only the most zealous Indian converts learned Europeans' literacy skills.

Thus the cultures of colonial North America were primarily oral, communal, and—at least through the first half of the eighteenth century—intensely local. In the absence of literacy, face-to-face conversation served as the major means of communication. Infor-

Religious Rituals

mation tended to travel slowly and within relatively confined regions. Different locales developed divergent cultural traditions, and racial and ethnic variations heightened those differences. Public rituals served as the chief means through which the colonists forged their cultural identities.

Attendance at church was perhaps the most important such ritual. In Congregational (Puritan) churches, church leaders assigned seating to reflect standing in the community. In early New England, men and women sat on opposite sides of a central aisle, arranged in ranks according to age, wealth, and church membership. By the mid-eighteenth century, wealthy

One of the very few institutions of higher learning open to females in eighteenth-century North America is clearly marked on this 1769 map from a Dutch atlas: the Ursuline convent in New Orleans. There young women studied religion and other subjects. As indicated in the label to the left, the convent is located at letter *k,* in the lower right corner of the map (which shows the area of the modern city known as the French Quarter).   (Private Collection)

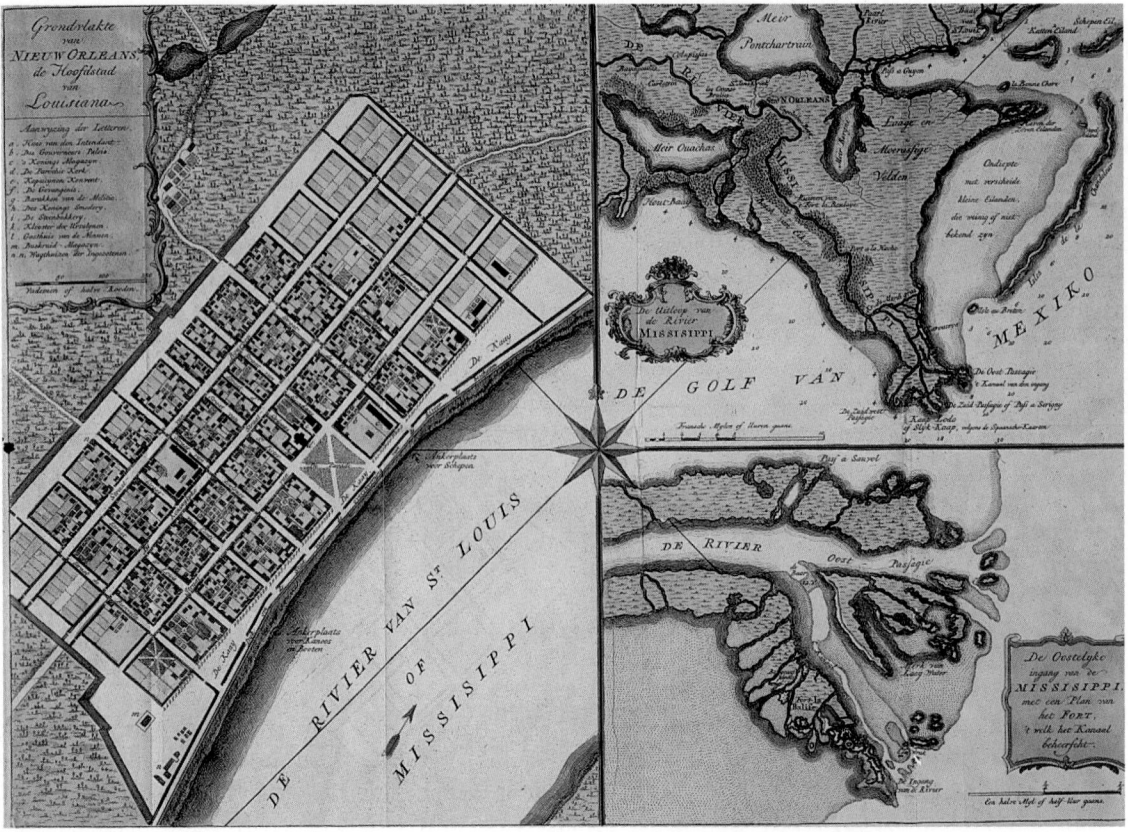

Convicted criminals were publicly punished and shamed in front of their friends, relatives, and neighbors. A man might be put in the stocks for offenses such as contempt of authority, drunken and disorderly conduct, or theft. The intent was not simply to deter him from future misbehavior but to let his fate serve as a warning to all who saw his humiliating posture. (Library of Congress)

men and their wives sat in privately owned pews; their children, servants, and the less fortunate still sat in sex-segregated fashion at the rear or sides of the church. In eighteenth-century Virginia, seating in Church of England parishes also conformed to the local status hierarchy. Planter families purchased their own pews, and in some parishes landed gentlemen customarily strode into church as a group just before the service, deliberately drawing attention to their exalted position. In Quebec city, formal processions of men into the parish church celebrated Catholic feast days; each participant's rank determined his placement in the procession. By contrast, Quaker meetinghouses in Pennsylvania and elsewhere used an egalitarian but sex-segregated seating system. The varying rituals surrounding people's entrance into and seating in colonial churches thus symbolized their place in society and the values of the local community.

Communal culture also centered on the civic sphere. In New England, colonial governments proclaimed official days of thanksgiving (for good harvests, victories in war, and so forth) and days of fasting and prayer (when the colony was experiencing difficulties such as droughts or epidemics). Everyone was expected to participate in the public rituals held in churches on such occasions. Monthly militia musters (known as training days) also brought the community together, since all able-bodied men between the ages of sixteen and sixty participated in the militia.

Civic Rituals

In the Chesapeake, important cultural rituals occurred on court and election days. When the county court met, men came from miles around to file suits, appear as witnesses, serve as jurors, or observe the goings-on. Attendance at court functioned as a method of civic education; from watching the proceedings men learned what behavior their neighbors expected of them. Elections served the same purpose, for property-holding men voted in public. An election official, often flanked by the candidates for the office in question, would call each man forward to declare his preference. The voter would then be thanked politely by the gentleman for whom he had cast his oral ballot. Traditionally, the candidates afterward treated their supporters to rum at nearby taverns.

Everywhere in colonial North America, the public punishment of criminals served not just to humiliate the offender but also to remind the community of proper standards of behavior. Public hangings and whippings expressed the community's outrage about crimes and restored harmony to its ranks. Judges often assigned penalties that shamed miscreants in especially appropriate ways. In San Antonio, Texas, for example, one cattle thief was sentenced to be led through the town's streets "with the entrails hanging from his neck"; and when a New Mexico man assaulted his father-in-law, he was directed not merely to pay medical expenses but also to kneel before him and to beg his forgiveness publicly, in front of the entire community. New Englanders convicted of capital offenses but not hanged did not thereby escape public humiliation:

How do historians know...

that the residents of colonial North America began to purchase luxury items in the eighteenth century from wide-ranging international trade networks?

Probate inventories—written records of what people possessed at the time of their deaths—are a useful documentary source for scholars. But perhaps even more revealing are the results of archaeological excavations at the sites of colonial settlements. The shards shown here were found at one of the first French outposts in Louisiana—Old Mobile, established in 1702 on Mobile Bay, in what is now Alabama. The pots, of which only these small pieces remain (see the complete example), represent the final stage in a long trade route originating in China. The Chinese sold ceramics to traders in the Philippines, which Spain controlled, in exchange for Mexican silver. Spanish ships then carried the porcelain across the Pacific to Mexico, where it was purchased at annual fairs in Acapulco, carried by mule train across Mexico to Vera Cruz, then shipped to Caribbean and Gulf of Mexico ports and to Spain itself. The three hundred or so residents of Old Mobile bought such items

from the Spanish settlement at Pensacola in nearby Florida. A brief description in an inventory could not convey so much information nearly as vividly as do these small bits of pottery. (Photos: Chinese porcelain fragments: The Magazine Antiques; Chinese porcelain pot: The Metropolitan Museum of Art, Purchased by subscription, 1879)

frequently they were ordered to wear nooses around their necks for years as a constant reminder to themselves, their families, and their neighbors of their heinous violation of community norms.

The wide availability of consumer goods after the early years of the eighteenth century fostered new rituals centered on consumption, establishing novel links among the various residents of North America and creating what historians have termed "an empire of goods." The rituals began with the acquisition of desirable items. In the seventeenth century, settlers acquired necessities by bartering with neighbors or by ordering products from a home-country merchant. By the middle of the eighteenth century, specialized shops selling nonessentials had proliferated in cities such as New York, Philadel-

Rituals of Consumption

phia, and New Orleans. In 1770 Boston alone had more than five hundred stores, which offered consumers a vast selection of millinery, sewing supplies, tobacco, gloves, tableware, and the like. Even small and medium-size towns had one or two retail establishments. A colonist with money to spend would set aside time to "go shopping," a novel and pleasurable activity. The purchase of a desired object—for example, a ceramic bowl, a mirror, or a length of beautiful fabric—marked only the beginning of consumption rituals.

Consumers would then deploy their purchases in an appropriate manner: hanging the mirror prominently on a wall of the house, displaying the bowl on a table or sideboard, turning the fabric into a special piece of clothing. Individual colonists took pleasure in owning lovely objects, but they also could take pride in

This trade card (advertisement) issued by a Philadelphia tobacco dealer in 1770 shows a convivial group of wealthy men at a tavern. Both the leisurely activity depicted here and the advertisement itself were signs of the new rituals of consumption. Merchants began to advertise only when their customers could choose among different ways of spending money. (Library Company of Philadelphia)

displaying their acquisitions (and thus their wealth and good taste) publicly to kin and neighbors. A particularly rich man might even hire a portraitist to paint his family using the objects and wearing the clothing, thereby creating a pictorial record that also would be displayed for admiration.

Tea drinking played an especially important role in Anglo-American consumption rituals. From early in the eighteenth century, households with aspirations to genteel status sought to acquire the items necessary for the proper consumption of tea: not just pots and cups but also strainers, sugar tongs, bowls, and even special tables. Tea provided a focal point for socializing and, because of its cost, served as a crucial marker of status. A hot and mildly stimulating drink, it was seen as healthful as well. Thus poor households also consumed tea, although they could not afford the fancy equipment used by their better-off neighbors. Even some Mohawk Indians adopted the custom, much to the surprise of a traveler from Sweden, who observed them drinking tea in the late 1740s.

Importance of Tea

Other sorts of rituals allowed the disparate cultures of colonial North America to interact with one another. Particularly important rituals developed on what the historian Richard White has termed the "middle ground"—that is, the psychological and geographical space in which Indians and Europeans encountered each other. Most of those cultural encounters occurred in the context of trade or warfare.

Rituals on the "Middle Ground"

When Europeans sought to trade with Indians, they came into contact with an indigenous system of exchange that stressed gift giving rather than formalized buying and selling. Although French and English traders complained constantly about the need to present Indians with gifts prior to negotiating with them for furs and skins, successful bargaining required such a step. Over time, an appropriate ritual developed. A European trader arriving at a village would give gifts (cloth, rum, gunpowder, and other items) to Indian hunters. Eventually, those gifts would be reciprocated, and further exchanges would then take place. To the detriment of Indian societies, rum became a crucial component of these intercultural trading rituals. Traders soon concluded that drunken Indians would sell their furs more cheaply; and some Indians refused to hunt or trade unless they first received rum. Alcohol abuse hastened the deterioration of villages already devastated by disease and dislocation.

Intercultural rituals also developed to deal with murders. Indians and Europeans both believed that murders required a compensatory act, but the two groups had different notions of what that act should be. Europeans sought primarily to identify the murderer and to punish, perhaps even kill, the malefactor. To Indians, such "eye for an eye" revenge was just one of many possible responses to murder. Compensation could also be accomplished by capturing someone who could take the dead person's place or—most important for maintaining peace on the frontiers—by "covering the dead," or providing the family of the deceased with goods that compensated for the loss. Eventually, the French and the Algonquians in particular evolved an elaborate ritual for handling frontier murders—a ritual that encompassed elements of both societies' traditions: murders were investigated and murderers identified, but by mutual agreement deaths were usually "covered" by trade goods rather than by blood revenge.

Colonial Families

Families (rather than individuals) constituted the basic units of colonial society. People living together as families, commonly under the direction of a marital pair, were everywhere the chief mechanisms for both production and consumption. Yet family forms and structures varied widely in the mainland colonies, and not all were headed by couples.

As Europeans consolidated their hold on the North American continent during the first three-quarters of the eighteenth century, **Indian Families** Native Americans had to adapt to novel circumstances. As Chapter 1 reveals, Spanish horses dramatically changed the lives of Plains Indians, and diseases ravaged even those groups that had little direct contact with Europeans. Bands reduced in numbers by disease and warfare recombined into new units; for example, the group later known as the Catawbas emerged in the 1730s in the western Carolinas from the fragmentary remains of several earlier Indian nations, including the

Yamasees. Likewise, Indian family forms were reshaped under pressure from European secular and religious authorities. Whereas many Indian societies had permitted easy divorce, English, French, and Spanish missionaries frowned on such practices; and those societies that had allowed polygynous marriages (including New England Algonquians) redefined such relationships, designating one wife as "legitimate" and others as "concubines."

Continued high mortality rates created Indian societies in which extended kin took on new importance, for when parents died, aunts, uncles, and other relatives—even occasionally nonkin—assumed child-rearing responsibilities. Furthermore, once Europeans established dominance in any region, Indians there could no longer pursue traditional modes of subsistence. That led to unusual family forms as well as to a variety of economic strategies. In New England, for instance, Algonquian husbands and wives often could not live together, for adults supported themselves by working separately for Anglo-Americans (perhaps wives as domestic servants, husbands as sailors). And in New Mexico, detribalized Navajos, Pueblos, and Apaches employed as servants by Spanish settlers clustered in the small towns of the Borderlands. Known collectively as *genizaros*, they lost contact with Indian cultures, instead living on the fringes of Hispanic society.

Wherever the population contained relatively few European women, sexual liaisons (both inside and outside marriage) occurred among European men and Indian women. The **Mixed-Race Families** resulting mixed-race population of *mestizos* and *métis* worked as a familial "middle ground" to ease other cultural interactions. In New France and the Anglo-American backcountry, such families frequently resided in Indian villages and were enmeshed in trading networks; often, children of these unions became prominent leaders of Native American societies. (For example, Peter Chartier, the son of a Shawnee mother and a French father, led a pro-French Shawnee band in western Pennsylvania in the 1740s.) By contrast, in the Spanish Borderlands the offspring of Europeans and *genizaros* were treated as degraded individuals. Largely denied the privilege of legal marriage, they bore generations of "illegitimate" children of various racial mixtures, giving rise in Hispanic society to a wide range of labels describing degrees of skin color with a precision unknown in English or French America.

Eighteenth-century Anglo-Americans used the word *family* to mean all the people who occupied one household (including any resident servants or slaves). Family life among the many European migrants to North America was far more stable than that among Indian and *mestizo* peoples. European men or their widows headed households considerably larger than American families today. In 1790 the average home in the United States housed 5.7 free people, and such sizable co-resident groups did not for the most part include extended kin like aunts, uncles, or grandparents. Family members—bound by ties of blood or servitude—worked together to produce goods for consumption or sale. The head of the household represented it to the outside world, managing the finances and holding legal authority over the rest of the family—his wife, his children, and his servants or slaves.

European American Families

In English, French, and Spanish America alike, the vast majority of European families supported themselves through agriculture by cultivating crops and raising livestock. The scale and nature of the work varied: the production of indigo in Louisiana or tobacco in the Chesapeake required different sorts of labor from subsistence farming in New England or cattle ranching in New Mexico and Texas. Still, just as in the European, African, and Native American societies discussed in Chapter 1, household tasks were allocated by sex. The master, his sons, and his male servants or slaves performed one set of chores; the mistress, her daughters, and her female servants or slaves, a different set.

The mistress took responsibility for what Anglo-Americans called "indoor affairs." She and her female helpers prepared food, cleaned the house, did laundry, and often made clothing. Preparing food alone involved planting and cultivating a garden, harvesting and preserving vegetables, salting and smoking meat, drying apples and pressing cider, milking cows and making butter and cheese, not to mention cooking and baking. The head of the household and his male helpers, responsible for "outdoor affairs," also had heavy workloads. They planted and cultivated the fields, built fences, chopped wood for the fireplace, harvested and marketed crops, cared for livestock, and butchered cattle and hogs to provide the household with meat. So extensive was the work involved in maintaining a farm household that a married couple

One of the few extant depictions of a mixed-race family in eighteenth-century North America, by the Mexican artist Miguel Cabrera, 1763. The Spanish father and Indian mother have produced a *mestiza* daughter. Families such as this would have been frequently seen in New Mexico as well.   (Private Collection)

could not do it alone. If they had no children to help them, they turned to servants or slaves.

Most African American families lived as components of European American households—often on plantations that masters perceived as one large family. More than 95 percent of colonial African Americans were held in perpetual bondage. Although many African Americans lived on farms with only one or two other slaves, others had the experience of living and working in a largely black setting. In South Carolina, a majority of the population was of African origin; in Georgia, about half; and in the Chesapeake, 40 percent. Portions of the Carolina low country were nearly 90 percent African American by 1790.

African American Families

The setting in which African Americans lived determined the shape of their family lives. In the North, the scarcity of other blacks often made it difficult for bondspeople to form stable family units. In the Chesapeake, men and women who regarded themselves as married (slaves could not legally wed) frequently lived on different quarters or even on different plantations. Children generally resided with their mothers, seeing their fathers only on Sundays. Simultaneously, the natural increase of the population created wide American-born kinship networks among Chesapeake slaves. On large Carolina and Georgia rice plantations, enslaved couples not only usually lived together with their children but also accumulated property through working for themselves after they had completed their daily "tasks" (see page 78). Some Georgia slaves sold their surplus produce at the market in Savannah, thereby earning money to buy nice clothing or such luxuries as tobacco or jewelry, but rarely enough to purchase themselves.

Running Away and Other Forms of Resistance

Because all the English colonies legally permitted slavery, bondspeople had few options other than Florida (see page 80) if they considered running away. Some recently arrived Africans stole boats to try to return home or ran off in groups to frontier regions to join the Indians or to establish independent communities. Among American-born slaves, family ties strongly affected such decisions. South Carolina planters soon learned, as one wrote, that slaves "love their families dearly and none runs away from the other," so many owners sought to keep families together for purely practical reasons. In the Chesapeake, where family members often lived separately, affectionate ties could by contrast cause slaves to run away, especially if a family member had been sold or moved to a distant quarter.

Although colonial slaves rarely rebelled collectively, they often resisted enslavement in other ways.

William L. Breton's watercolor of "The Old London Coffee House" in eighteenth-century Philadelphia shows a slave auction taking place on its porch. That such a scene could have occurred in front of such a prominent and popular meeting place serves as a reminder of the ubiquity of slavery in the colonies, north as well as south. (Historical Society of Pennsylvania)

Bondspeople uniformly rejected any attempts by their owners to commandeer their labor on Sundays without compensation. Slaves established strong family structures in which youngsters often carried relatives' names. Extended-kin groups protested excessive punishment of relatives and sought to live near each other. The links that developed among African American families who had lived on the same plantation for several generations served as insurance against the uncertainties of existence under slavery. If parents and children were separated by sale, other relatives could help with child rearing and similar tasks. Among African Americans, just as among Indians, the extended family thus served a more important function than it did among European Americans.

Most slave families managed to carve out a small measure of autonomy, especially in their working and spiritual lives and especially in the Lower South. Enslaved Muslims often clung to their Islamic faith, a pattern especially evident in Louisiana and South Carolina. Some African Americans preserved traditional beliefs and others converted to Christianity, finding comfort in the assurances of their new religion that all people would be free and equal in heaven. South Carolina and Georgia slaves jealously guarded their customary ability to control their own time after the completion of their "tasks." Even on Chesapeake tobacco plantations, slaves were allowed to plant their own gardens, hunt, or fish in order to supplement the minimal diet their masters supplied. Late in the century, some Chesapeake planters with a surplus of laborers began to hire out slaves to others, often allowing the workers to keep a small part of their earnings. Such accumulated property could buy desired goods or serve as a legacy for children.

Just as African and European Americans lived together on plantations, so too both groups were found side by side in cities. (Indeed, in **Life in the Cities** 1760s Philadelphia one-fifth of the work force was enslaved, and by 1775 blacks composed nearly 15 percent of the population of New York City.) Yet such cities were nothing but large towns by today's standards. In 1750 the largest, Boston and Philadelphia, had just seventeen thousand and thirteen thousand inhabitants, respectively. Life in the cities differed considerably from that on northern farms, southern plantations, or southwestern ranches. City dwellers everywhere, not just those in New Orleans who went to the levee, purchased foodstuffs and wood at markets and cloth in shops instead of laboriously producing such items themselves. Urban residents lived by the clock rather than the sun, and men's jobs frequently took them away from their households. City people also had much more contact with the world beyond their own homes than did their rural counterparts.

By the 1750s, most major cities had at least one weekly newspaper, and some had two or three. Anglo-American newspapers printed the latest "advices from London" (usually two to three months old) and news from other English colonies, as well as local reports. Newspapers were available at taverns, coffeehouses, and inns, so people who could not afford to buy them could catch up on the news. Even illiterates could do so, since literate customers often read the papers aloud. Contact with the outside world, however, had its drawbacks. Sailors sometimes brought exotic and deadly diseases into port. Boston, New York, Philadelphia, and New Orleans endured terrible epidemics of smallpox and yellow fever, which Europeans and Africans in the countryside largely escaped.

Politics: Stability and Crisis in British America

 In the first decades of the eighteenth century, Anglo-American political life exhibited a new stability. Despite substantial migration from overseas, most residents of the mainland had been born in America. Men from genteel families dominated the political structures in each province, for voters (free male property holders) tended to defer to their well-educated "betters" on election days.

Throughout the Anglo-American colonies, political leaders sought to increase the powers of elected assemblies relative to the powers of the **Rise of the Assemblies** governors and other appointed officials. Assemblies began to claim privileges associated with the British House of Commons, such as the rights to initiate all tax legislation and to control the militia. The assemblies also developed effective ways of influencing British appointees, especially by threatening to withhold their salaries. In some colonies (Virginia and South Carolina, for example), elite members of the assemblies usually presented a united front to royal officials, but in others (such as New York), they fought among themselves long and bitterly. To win hotly contested elections, New York's genteel leaders began to appeal to "the people," competing openly for

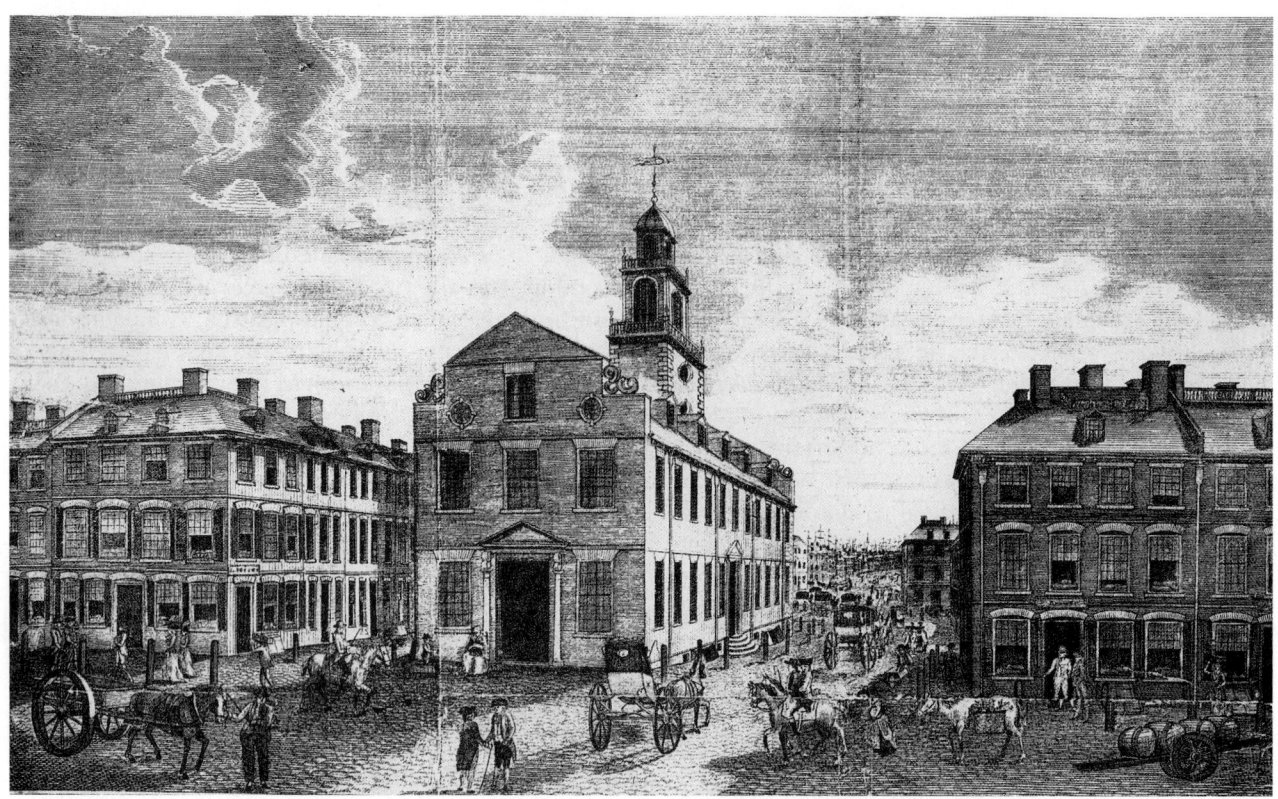

In 1713 the colony of Massachusetts constructed its impressive State House in Boston. Here met the assembly and the council. The solidity and imposing nature of the building must have symbolized for its users the increasing consolidation of power in the hands of the Massachusetts legislature.   (The Bostonian Society)

the votes of ordinary voters. Yet in 1733 that same New York government imprisoned a newspaper editor, John Peter Zenger, who had too vigorously criticized its actions. Defending Zenger against the charge of "seditious libel," his lawyer argued that the truth could not be defamatory, thus helping to establish a free-press principle now found in American law.

Eighteenth-century assemblies bore little resemblance to twentieth-century state legislatures. Much of their business would today be termed administrative; only on rare occasions did they formulate new policies or pass laws of real importance. Members of the assemblies also saw their roles differently than do modern legislators. Instead of believing that they should act positively to improve the lives of their constituents, eighteenth-century assemblymen saw themselves as acting defensively to prevent encroachments on the people's rights. In their minds, their primary function was, for example, stopping governors from imposing oppressive taxes, rather than passing laws that would actively benefit their constituents.

By midcentury, politically aware colonists commonly linked their own governmental structures to Great Britain's balance of king, lords, and commons—a combination that had been thought to produce a stable polity since the days of ancient Greece and Rome. Drawing rough analogies, political leaders equated their governors with the monarch, their councils with the aristocracy, and their assemblies with the House of Commons. All three were believed essential to good government, but Americans did not regard them with the same degree of approval. They viewed governors and appointed councils as potential threats to colonial freedoms and customary ways of life, since such people primarily represented Britain. Colonists saw the assemblies, however, as the people's protectors. And in

Interpretations of the Assemblies

turn the assemblies regarded themselves as representatives of the people.

Again, though, such beliefs should not be equated with modern practice. The assemblies, firmly controlled by dominant families whose members were reelected year after year, rarely responded to the concerns of their poorer constituents. Although settlements continually expanded, assemblies failed to reapportion themselves to provide adequate representation for newer communities—a lack of action that led to serious grievances among frontier dwellers, especially those from non-English ethnic groups. The colonial ideal of the assembly as the defender of the people's liberties must therefore be distinguished from the colonial reality: the most dearly defended were the wealthy colonists, particularly the assembly members themselves.

At midcentury, the political structures that had stabilized in a period of relative calm confronted a series of crises. None affected all the mainland provinces, but no colony escaped wholly untouched. The crises of various descriptions—ethnic, racial, economic—exposed the internal tensions building in the pluralistic American society, foreshadowing the greater disorder of the revolutionary era. Most important, they demonstrated that the political accommodations arrived at in the aftermath of the Glorious Revolution were no longer adequate to govern Britain's American empire. Once again, changes appeared necessary, and imminent.

One of the first and greatest crises occurred in South Carolina. Early one morning in September 1739, about twenty South Carolina slaves, most from Angola, gathered near the Stono River south of Charles Town. Seizing guns and ammunition from a store, they killed the storekeepers and some nearby planter families. Then, joined by other local slaves, they headed toward Florida in hopes of finding refuge at Gracia Real de Santa Teresa de Mose. By midday, however, the alarm had been sounded among slaveowners in the district. That afternoon a troop of militia attacked the fugitives, who then numbered about a hundred, killing some and dispersing the rest. More than a week later, most of the remaining conspirators were captured. The colony quickly executed those not killed on the spot, but for over two years rumors about escaped renegades haunted the colony.

Stono Rebellion

The Stono Rebellion shocked slaveholding South Carolinians as well as residents of other colonies.

New York Conspiracy

Throughout British America, laws governing the behavior of African Americans were stiffened. The most striking response came in New York City, which had suffered a slave revolt in 1712. There the news from the South, coupled with fears of Spain generated by the outbreak of King George's War, set off a reign of terror in the summer of 1741. Hysterical whites suspected a biracial gang of thieves and arsonists of conspiring to foment a slave uprising under the guidance of a supposed priest in the pay of Spain. By summer's end, thirty-one blacks and four whites had been executed for participating in the alleged plot. The Stono Rebellion and the New York conspiracy not only exposed and confirmed Anglo-Americans' deepest fears about the dangers of slaveholding but also revealed the assemblies' inability to prevent serious internal disorder. Events of the next two decades confirmed that pattern.

By midcentury most of the fertile land east of the Appalachians had been purchased or occupied. As a result, conflicts over land titles and conditions of landholding grew in number and frequency as colonists competed for control of land good for farming. In 1746, for example, some New Jersey farmers clashed violently with agents of the East Jersey proprietors. The proprietors claimed the farmers' land as theirs and demanded annual payments, called quit-rents, for the use of the property. Similar violence occurred in the 1760s in the region that later became Vermont. There, farmers holding land grants issued by New Hampshire battled with speculators claiming title to the area through grants from New York authorities.

Land Riots in New Jersey and New York

The most serious land riots of the period took place along the Hudson River in 1765–1766. Late in the seventeenth century, the governor of New York had granted huge tracts in the lower Hudson valley to prominent colonial families. The proprietors in turn divided these estates into small farms, which they rented chiefly to poor Dutch and German migrants who regarded tenancy as a step on the road to independent freeholder status. By the 1750s some proprietors earned large sums annually from quit-rents and other fees.

After 1740, though, increasing migration from New England brought conflict to the great New York estates. The New Englanders did not want to become tenants. Many squatted on vacant portions of the manors, resisting all attempts at eviction. In the mid-

1760s the Philipse family sued New Englanders who had lived on Philipse land for two decades or more. New York courts upheld the Philipse claim, ordering squatters to make way for tenants with valid leases. Instead of complying, the farmers rebelled, terrorizing proprietors and loyal tenants, freeing their friends from jail, and on one occasion battling a county sheriff and his posse. The rebellion lasted nearly a year, ending only when British troops finally captured its leaders.

Violent conflicts of a different sort erupted just a few years later in the Carolinas. The Regulator movements of the late 1760s (South Carolina) and early 1770s (North Carolina) pitted backcountry farmers against wealthy eastern planters who controlled the provincial governments. Frontier dwellers, most of Scots-Irish origin, protested their lack of an adequate voice in colonial political affairs. South Carolinians for months policed the countryside in vigilante bands, complaining of lax and biased law enforcement. North Carolinians, who primarily objected to heavy taxation, fought and lost a battle with eastern militiamen at Alamance in 1771. Regional, ethnic, and economic tensions thus combined to create these disturbances, which ultimately arose from frontier people's dissatisfaction with the Carolina governments.

Regulators in the Carolinas

A Crisis in Religion

The most widespread crisis was religious. From the mid-1730s through the 1760s, waves of religious revivalism—today known collectively as the First Great Awakening—swept over various parts of the colonies, primarily New England (1735–1745) and Virginia (1750s and 1760s). Orthodox Calvinists sought to combat Enlightenment rationalism, which denied innate human depravity. Simultaneously, the economic and political uncertainty accompanying King George's War made colonists receptive to the spiritual certainty offered by evangelical religion. In addition, many recent immigrants and residents of the backcountry had no prior religious affiliation, thus presenting evangelists with a potential source of converts.

The Great Awakening began in New England, where descendants of the Puritan founding generation still composed the membership of Congregational churches. Whether in full or "halfway" communion—

New England and the Great Awakening

the latter, a category established in 1662 to ensure that people who had not experienced saving faith would be subject to church discipline—such members were primarily female. From the beginnings of the Awakening, though, both men and women responded with equal fervor. During 1734 and 1735, Reverend Jonathan Edwards, a noted preacher and theologian, noticed a remarkable reaction among the youthful members of his church in Northampton, Massachusetts, to a message based squarely on Calvinist principles. Individuals could attain salvation, Edwards contended, only through recognition of their own depraved natures and the need to surrender completely to God's will. Such surrender brought to Congregationalists of both sexes an intensely emotional release from sin and came to be seen as a single identifiable moment of conversion.

The effects of such conversions remained isolated until 1739, when George Whitefield, a Church of England clergyman already celebrated for leading revivals in England, arrived in America. For fifteen months he toured the British colonies, preaching to large audiences from Georgia to New England and concentrating his efforts in the major cities: Boston, New York, Philadelphia, Charles Town, and Savannah. A gripping orator, Whitefield in effect generated the Great Awakening. The historian Harry Stout has termed him "the first modern celebrity" because of his skillful self-promotion and clever manipulation of both his listeners and the newspapers. Everywhere he traveled, his fame preceded him. Thousands of free and enslaved folk turned out to listen—and to experience conversion. Whitefield's journey, the first such ever undertaken, created new interconnections among the previously distinct colonies.

George Whitefield

Regular clerics initially welcomed Whitefield and the American-born itinerant evangelist preachers who sprang up to imitate him. Soon, however, many clergymen began to realize that although "revived" religion filled their churches, it ran counter to their own approach to doctrine and matters of faith. They disliked the emotional style of the revivalists, whose itinerancy also disrupted normal patterns of church attendance because it took churchgoers away from the services they usually attended. Particularly troublesome to the orthodox were the dozens of female exhorters who took to streets and pulpits, proclaiming their right (even duty) to expound God's word.

Opposition to the Awakening heightened rapidly, causing congregations to splinter. "Old Lights"—traditional clerics and their followers—engaged in bitter disputes with the "New Light" evangelicals. Already characterized by numerous sects, American Protestantism became further divided as the major denominations split into Old Light and New Light factions and as new evangelical sects—Methodists and Baptists—gained adherents. Paradoxically, the angry fights and the rapid rise in the number of distinct denominations eventually led to an American willingness to tolerate religious diversity. No single sect could make an unequivocal claim to orthodoxy, so they had to coexist if they were to exist at all.

Most significantly, the Awakening challenged traditional modes of thought, for the revivalists' message directly contested the colonial tradition of deference. Itinerant preachers, only a few of whom were ordained clergymen, claimed they understood the will of God better than did elite college-educated clerics. Moreover, they and their followers divided the world into two groups—the saved and the damned—without respect to gender, age, or status, the previously dominant social categories. The Awakening's emphasis on emotion rather than learning undermined the validity of received wisdom, and New Lights questioned not only religious but also social and political orthodoxy. For example, New Lights began to defend the rights of groups and individuals to dissent from a community consensus, thereby challenging one of the most fundamental tenets of colonial political life. Ordinary folk were especially attracted, and many elites repelled, by the egalitarian themes of the Awakening.

Impact of the Awakening

Nowhere was this trend more evident than in Virginia, where the Church of England, the established religion, was supported by tax moneys, and the plantation gentry and their ostentatious lifestyle dominated society. By the 1760s Baptists had gained a secure foothold in Virginia; inevitably, their beliefs and behavior clashed with the way most genteel families lived. They rejected as sinful the horseracing, gambling, and dancing that occupied much of the gentry's leisure time. They dressed plainly, in contrast to the gentry's fashionable opulence. They addressed one another as "brother" and

Virginia Baptists

Reverend George Whitefield, the charismatic evangelist who sparked the First Great Awakening in the mainland British colonies, attracted harsh critics as well as avid admirers. Here an English cartoonist satirizes him as a money-grubbing charlatan who hoodwinks his gullible followers into believing that he is a "Pious Churchman" motivated by "Holy Zeal." Whitefield's crossed eyes, obvious in this image as in others, played a prominent role in contemporary depictions of him.   (Trustees of the British Museum)

"sister" regardless of social status, and they elected the leaders of their congregations—more than ninety of them by 1776. Their monthly "great meetings," which attracted hundreds of people, introduced new public rituals that rivaled the weekly Anglican services.

Strikingly, almost all the Virginia Baptist congregations included both free and slave members. At the founding of the Dan River Baptist Church in 1760, for example, eleven of seventy-four members were African Americans; some congregations had African American majorities. Church rules applied equally to all members; interracial sexual relationships, divorce, and adultery were off limits to all. In addition, congregations forbade masters from breaking up slave couples through sale. Biracial committees investigated complaints about church members' misbehavior. Churches excommunicated slaves for stealing from their masters, but they also excommunicated masters for physically abusing their slaves. One such slaveowner so dismissed in 1772 experienced a true conversion. Penalized for "burning" one of his slaves, Charles Cook apologized to the congregation and became a preacher in a largely African American church. Other Baptists decided that owning slaves was "unrighteous" and freed their bondspeople; the immensely wealthy Robert Carter manumitted more than nine hundred slaves.

Summary

 The Great Awakening thus injected an egalitarian strain into Anglo-American life at midcentury. Although primarily a religious movement, the Awakening had important social and political consequences, calling into question habitual modes of behavior in the secular as well as the religious realm. In short, the Great Awakening helped to break Anglo-Americans' ties to their seventeenth-century origins. So, too, did the newcomers from Germany, Scotland, Ireland, and Africa, who brought their languages, customs, and religions to British North America. The European immigrants settled throughout the English colonies but were concentrated in the growing cities and in the backcountry. By contrast, enslaved migrants from Africa lived and worked primarily within 100 miles of the Atlantic coast. In many areas of the colonial South, 50 to 90 percent of the population was of African origin.

The economic life of all Europe's North American colonies proceeded simultaneously on two levels. On the farms, plantations, and ranches on which most colonists resided, the daily, weekly, monthly, and yearly rounds of chores for men, women, and children alike dominated people's lives while providing the goods consumed by households and sold in the markets. Simultaneously, the British, French, and Spanish colonies were enmeshed in an international network of trade that affected their local economic circumstances. The bitter wars fought by European nations during the eighteenth century inevitably involved the colonists by creating new opportunities for overseas sales or by disrupting their traditional markets. The volatile colonial economy fluctuated for reasons beyond Americans' control. Those fortunate few who—through skill, control of essential resources, or luck—reaped the profits of international trade made up the wealthy class of merchants and landowners who dominated colonial political and social life.

A century and a half after European peoples first settled in North America, the colonies mixed diverse European, American, and African traditions into a novel cultural blend that owed much to Europe but just as much, if not more, to North America itself. Europeans who interacted regularly with peoples of African and American origin—and with Europeans who came from nations other than their own—had to develop new methods of accommodating intercultural differences in addition to creating ties within their own potentially fragmenting communities. Yet at the same time the dominant colonists continued to identify themselves as French, Spanish, or British rather than as Americans. That did not change in Canada, Louisiana, or the Spanish Borderlands, but in the 1760s some Anglo-Americans began to realize that their interests did not necessarily coincide with those of Great Britain or its monarch. For the first time, they offered a direct challenge to British authority.

LEGACY FOR A PEOPLE AND A NATION
Anti-Immigrant Sentiments

In 1751 Benjamin Franklin tried to convince British authorities to halt immigration from Germany to the colonies. In *Observations Concerning the Increase of Mankind*, he contended that Britain's mainland possessions would be peopled by natural increase alone, so immigration was unnecessary. "Why should the Palatine [German] Boors be suffered to swarm into our Settlements, and by herding together establish their Language and Manners to the Exclusion of ours?" he asked. Pennsylvania would soon become "a Colony of *Aliens*," who would "Germanize us instead of our Anglifying them"; and, he predicted, they "will never adopt our Language or Customs."

Such sentiments have a familiar ring, because policymakers and others today make similar comments about recent arrivals, primarily those from South and Central America and Asia. As the twenty-first century opens, the United States is grappling once again with immigration policy. State legislators, members of Congress, the courts, and public interest groups vie over such questions as how many immigrants to admit each year, what services and rights immigrants are entitled to, and how to deal with illegal aliens. Nativist groups argue for new controls on immigration, opposed by immigrants' rights organizations urging more lenient policies.

These current controversies have deep roots in American soil. More than two decades before Franklin published his essay, for example, Pennsylvania already levied heavy duties on all incoming aliens in hopes of preventing the immigration of "lewd, idle and ill-affected persons." And ever since the nation's founding, immigration policy has periodically caused vitriolic debates, as Americans argued over the admission of French and Haitian immigrants in the 1790s,

Irish immigrants in the 1840s and 1850s, Chinese and Japanese in the 1870s and 1880s, and eastern and southern Europeans around the turn of the century. Often, these debates ended with the passage of restrictive legislation—for example, Asian exclusion acts in the 1880s and laws setting immigration quotas for foreign countries in 1921 and 1924 (not removed until 1965).

Franklin's fears have thus been voiced repeatedly during the intervening 250 years. The first substantial wave of foreign immigration to the colonies and reactions to it have thereby left an enduring legacy to the American people.

For Further Reading, see page A-5 of the Appendix. For Web resources, go to http://college.hmco.com.

SEVERING THE BONDS OF EMPIRE 1754–1774

The two men must have found the occasion remarkable. The artist customarily painted portraits of the wealthy and high born, not of artisans, even well-connected, affluent ones. The subject himself was an artist—a maker of beautiful silver and gold objects, an engraver of cartoons and townscapes. The political sympathies of the painter, John Singleton Copley, lay primarily with Boston's conservatives, whereas the sitter, Paul Revere, was a noted leader of resistance to British policies. Yet sometime in 1768 Revere commissioned Copley to paint his portrait, and the result (opposite page) is one of the greatest works of American art.

Copley was thirty, Revere thirty-four. Each man had learned his trade from a parent. Revere's father Apollos, who had arrived in Boston as a teenage Huguenot refugee early in the century, was an accomplished gold- and silversmith; Paul served as his father's apprentice and took over the family business when Apollos died in 1754. Copley, whose Irish parents had immigrated to Boston in the 1730s, was taught to paint by his stepfather, Peter Pelham, an English artist. The two young tradesmen had undoubtedly known each other for years. In 1763 and thereafter, Copley hired Revere to make silver and gold frames for the miniature portraits that were among his earliest works.

But their finest collaboration was the painting reproduced here. Copley portrayed Revere surrounded by the tools of his trade and contemplating a teapot he was crafting. The silversmith wears a loose-fitting linen shirt and an open vest rather than the formal dress usually worn by colonial artists' subjects. Even so, Revere is not actually at work: his clothes are too clean, and the table is too polished to be a work surface. The silversmith's pose and apparel convey an impression of thoughtfulness, virtuous labor, and solidity. The teapot too carries a message, especially in the year 1768. Simultaneously a reflection of a craftsman's skills and a prominent emblem of the new "empire of goods" in British America, it resonated with symbolism because, as shall be seen later in this chapter, tea

John Singleton Copley's portrait of Paul Revere is generally regarded as one of his masterpieces. Copley captured Revere's character as a hard-working, respectable artisan—a man unafraid of displaying his humble origins to the world. (Museum of Fine Arts, Boston. Gift of Joseph W., William B., and Edward H. R. Revere)

boycotts were an important component of colonial resistance to Great Britain. Both artist and subject, indeed, were to be active participants (though in very different ways) in the 1773 event known to history as the Boston Tea Party.

In retrospect, John Adams identified the years between 1760 and 1775 as the era of the true American Revolution. The Revolution, Adams declared, ended before the fighting started, for it was "in the Minds of the people," involving not the actual winning of independence but a fundamental shift of allegiance from Britain to America. Today, not all historians would concur with Adams that the shift he identified constituted the Revolution. But none would deny the importance of the events of those crucial years, which divided the American population along political lines and set the colonies on the road to independence.

The story of the 1760s and early 1770s describes an ever-widening split between Great Britain and Anglo America and among their respective supporters in the colonies. In the long history of British settlement in the Western Hemisphere, considerable tension had occasionally marred the relationship between individual provinces and the mother country. Still, that tension had rarely persisted for long, nor had it been widespread, except during the crisis following the Glorious Revolution in 1689. The primary divisions affecting the colonies had been internal rather than external. In the 1750s, however, a series of events began to draw the colonists' attention from domestic matters to their relations with Great Britain. It all started with the Seven Years War.

Britain's overwhelming victory in that war, confirmed by treaty in 1763, forever altered the balance of power in North America. France was ousted from the continent and Spain from Florida, events with major consequences for both the indigenous peoples of the interior and the residents of the British colonies. Indians could no longer play off European powers against one another and so lost one of their major diplomatic tools. Anglo-Americans, for their part, no longer had to fear the French threat on their northern and western borders or the Spanish in the Southeast. The British colonies along the coast would never have dared to break with their mother country, some historians contend, if France had still controlled the Mississippi River and the Great Lakes.

The British victory in 1763, then, dramatically affected all the residents of North America. That victory also had a significant impact on Great Britain, one that soon involved the colonies. Britain's massive war-related debt needed to be paid, and so Parliament for the first time imposed revenue-raising taxes on the colonies in addition to the customs duties that had long regulated trade. That decision exposed differences in the political thinking of Americans and Britons—differences that until then had been obscured by a shared political vocabulary.

During the 1760s and early 1770s a broad coalition of the residents of Anglo America, men and women alike, resisted new tax levies and attempts by British officials to tighten controls over provincial governments. The colonies' elected leaders became ever more suspicious of Britain's motives as the years

Table 5.1	The Colonial Wars, 1689–1763					
American Name	**European Name**	**Dates**	**Participants**	**American Sites**	**Dispute**
King William's War	War of the League of Augsburg	1689–97	England, Holland versus France, Spain	New England, New York, Canada	French power
Queen Anne's War	War of Spanish Succession	1702–13	England, Holland, Austria versus France, Spain	Florida, New England	Throne of Spain
King George's War	War of Austrian Succession	1739–48	England, Holland, Austria versus France, Spain, Prussia	West Indies, New England, Canada	Throne of Austria
French and Indian War	Seven Years War	1756–63	England versus France, Spain	Ohio country, Canada	Possession of Ohio country

IMPORTANT EVENTS

1754 Albany Congress meets to try to forge
colonial unity
Fighting breaks out with Washington's
defeat at Fort Necessity

1756 Britain declares war on France; Seven Years
War officially begins

1759 British forces take Quebec

1760 American phase of war ends with fall of
Montreal to British troops
George III becomes king

1763 Treaty of Paris ends Seven Years War
Pontiac's allies attack British forts in West
Proclamation of 1763 attempts to close land
west of Appalachians to English settlement

1764 Sugar Act lays new duties on molasses,
tightens customs regulations
Currency Act outlaws paper money issued
by the colonies

1765 Stamp Act requires stamps on all printed
materials in colonies
Sons of Liberty formed

1766 Stamp Act repealed
Declaratory Act insists that Parliament can
tax the colonies

1767 Townshend Acts lay duties on trade within
the empire, send new officials and judges
to America

1768–70 Resistance to Townshend duties takes
form of boycotts and public demonstrations but divides merchants and urban
artisans

1770 Lord North becomes prime minister
Townshend duties repealed, except for tea
tax
Boston Massacre kills five colonial rioters

1772 Boston Committee of Correspondence
formed

1773 Tea Act aids East India Company
Boston Tea Party protests the Tea Act

1774 Coercive Acts punish Boston and Massachusetts as a whole
Quebec Act reforms government of Quebec

---

passed. They laid aside old antagonisms to coordinate their responses to the new measures, and they slowly began to reorient their political thinking. As late as the summer of 1774, though, most were still seeking a solution within the framework of the empire; few harbored thoughts of independence. ■

Renewed Warfare Among Europeans and Indians

The English colonies along the Atlantic seaboard were surrounded by hostile, or potentially hostile, neighbors: Indians everywhere, the Spanish in Florida and along the coast of the Gulf of Mexico, the French along the great inland system of rivers and lakes that stretched from the St. Lawrence to the Mississippi. The Spanish outposts posed little direct threat, for Spain's days as a major power had passed. The French were another matter. Their long chain of forts and settlements dominated the North American interior, facilitating trading partnerships and alliances with the Indians. In none of the three wars fought between

1689 and 1748 was England able to shake France's hold on the American frontier. Under the Peace of Utrecht, which ended Queen Anne's War in 1713, the English won control of such peripheral northern areas as Newfoundland, Hudson's Bay, and Nova Scotia (Acadia). But Britain made no territorial gains in King George's War (see Table 5.1 and Map 5.2).

During both Queen Anne's War and King George's War, the Iroquois Confederacy maintained the policy of neutrality it first developed in 1701. While British and French forces fought for nominal control of the North American continent, the confederacy—which actually dominated a large portion of that continent—skillfully manipulated its favors with the Europeans, refusing to commit warriors fully to either side despite being showered with gifts by both. Instead, the Iroquois fought only their southern enemies, the Catawbas. Since France repeatedly urged them to attack the Catawbas, who were allied with Britain, the Iroquois achieved desirable goals. They appeased the French while simultaneously consolidating their control over the entire interior region north of Virginia. The cam-

Iroquois Neutrality

An eighteenth-century Iroquois warrior as depicted by a European artist. Such men of the Six Nations confederacy dominated the North American interior before the Seven Years War. Lines drawn on maps by colonizing powers and the incursions of traders made little impact on their power. (Library of Congress, Rare Book and Special Collections Division)

paign against a common enemy also enabled the confederacy to cement its alliance with its weaker tributaries, the Shawnees and Delawares, and to ensure the continued subordination of those groups.

But even careful Iroquois diplomats could not prevent the region inhabited by the Shawnees and Delawares (now western Pennsylvania and eastern Ohio) from providing the spark that set off a major war. That conflict spread from America to Europe (a significant reversal of previous patterns), proving decisive in the contest for North America. Trouble began in 1752 when Anglo-American fur traders ventured into the area known as the Ohio country (see Map 5.1). The French could not permit their rivals to gain a foothold in the region, for it contained the source of the Ohio River, which offered direct access by water to French posts on the Mississippi. A permanent British presence in the Ohio country could challenge France's control of the western fur trade and even threaten its prominence in the Mississippi valley. Accordingly, in 1753 the French pushed southward from Lake Erie, building fortified outposts at strategic points.

In response to the French threat to their western frontiers, delegates from seven northern and middle colonies gathered in Albany, New York, in June 1754. With the backing of administrators in London, they sought two goals: to persuade the Iroquois to abandon their traditional neutrality and to coordinate the defenses of the colonies. They succeeded in neither. The Iroquois listened politely to the colonists' arguments but saw no reason to change a policy that had served them well for half a century. And although the Albany Congress delegates adopted a Plan of Union (which would have established an elected intercolonial legislature with the power to tax), their provincial governments uniformly rejected the plan—primarily because those governments feared a loss of autonomy.

Albany Congress

While the Albany Congress delegates deliberated, the war they sought to prepare for was already beginning. Governor Robert Dinwiddie of Virginia sent a small militia force westward to counter the French moves. Virginia claimed ownership of the Ohio country, and Dinwiddie hoped to prevent the French from establishing a permanent post there. But the Virginia militiamen arrived too late, for the French were already engaged in constructing Fort Duquesne at the strategic point—now Pittsburgh—where the Allegheny and Monongahela Rivers meet to form the Ohio. The inexperienced young officer who commanded the Virginians attacked a French detachment and then allowed himself to be trapped in his crudely built Fort Necessity at Great Meadows, Pennsylvania. After a day-long battle (on July 3, 1754), during which more than one-third of his men were killed or wounded, twenty-two-year-old George Washington surrendered. He and his men were allowed to return to Virginia.

Washington had blundered grievously, setting off a war that eventually would encompass nearly the entire world. He also ensured that the Ohio Indians, many of whom had moved west to escape Iroquois domination and to trade with the French, would support France in that conflict. The Indians took Washington's mistakes as an indication of Britain's weakness, and nothing that occurred in the next four years made them alter that judgment. In July 1755, a few miles south of Fort

Seven Years War

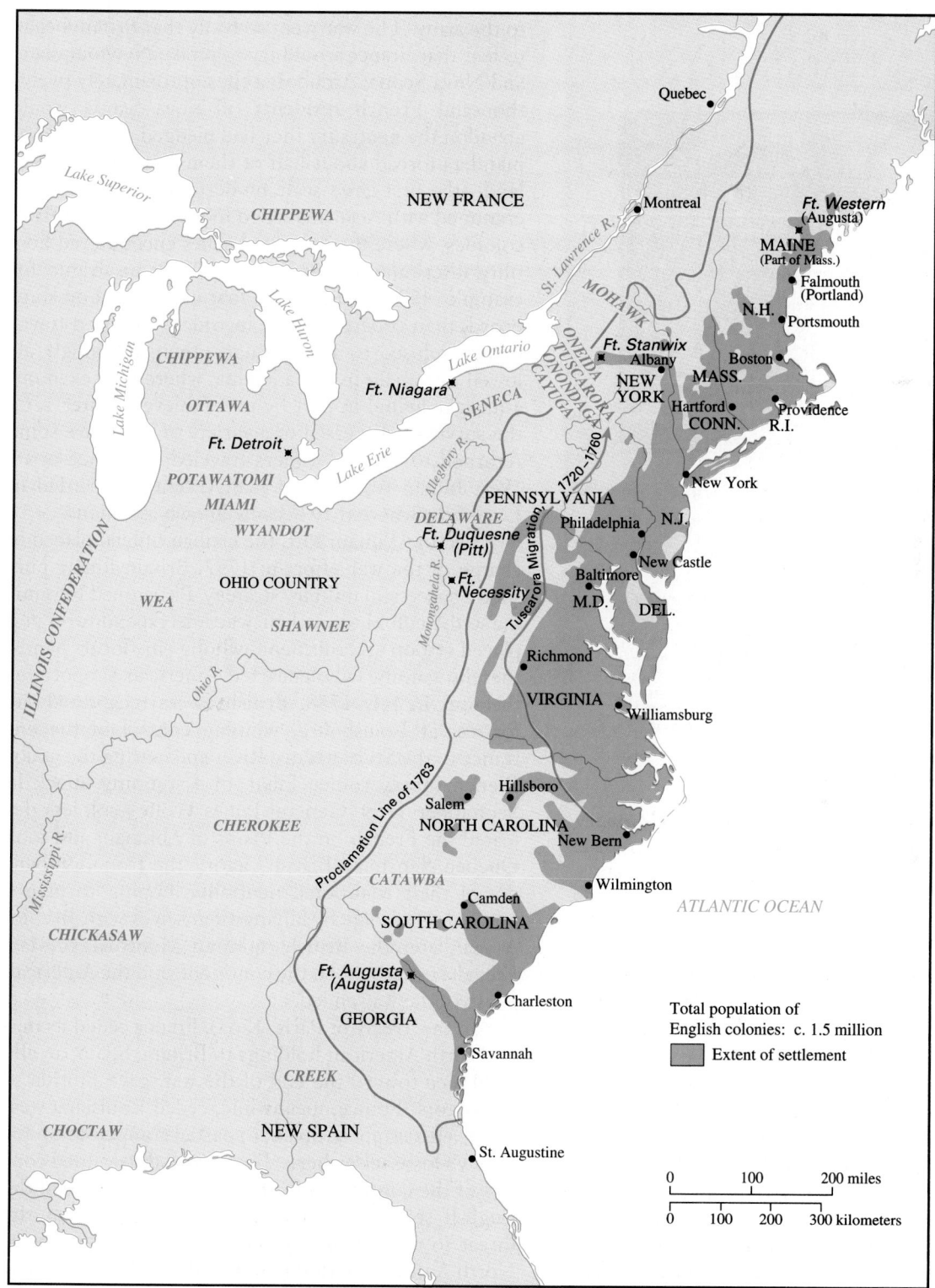

Map 5.1   European Settlements and Indians, 1754   By 1754, Europeans had expanded the limits of the English colonies to the eastern slopes of the Appalachian Mountains. Few independent Indian nations still existed in the East, but beyond the mountains they controlled the countryside. Only a few widely scattered English and French forts maintained the Europeans' presence there.

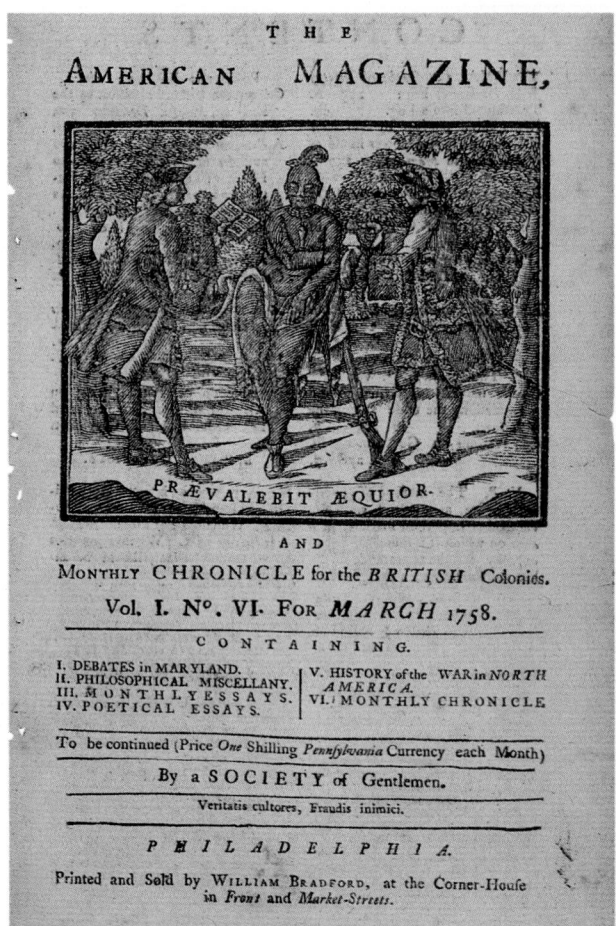

The frontispiece of *The American Magazine and Monthly Chronicle* for March 1758 reflected the struggle for the allegiance of Ohio valley Indians during the Seven Years War. The French representative on the left offers an undecided warrior a tomahawk and a flintlock, while the Englishman on the right presents him with bolts of cloth and a Bible. The Latin phrase at the base of the image translates as "grease takes precedence"; or, in other words, the better gift will win the contest for the Indians' assistance.   (Library of Congress)

Duquesne, a combined force of French and Indians ambushed British and colonial troops readying a renewed assault on the fort. In the devastating defeat, General Edward Braddock was killed and his surviving soldiers were demoralized. After news of the debacle reached London, Britain declared war on France in 1756, thus formally beginning the conflict known as the Seven Years War.

For three more years one disaster followed another. British officers tried without much success to coerce the colonies into supplying men and materiel to the army. The war went so badly that Britain began to fear that France would try to retake Newfoundland and Nova Scotia. Afraid that the approximately twelve thousand French residents of Nova Scotia would abandon the neutrality they had pledged, British commanders forced about half of them from their homeland—the first large-scale modern deportation. Ships crammed with Acadians sailed to each of the mainland colonies, where the dispirited exiles encountered hostility, discrimination, and disease. In Pennsylvania, for example, 450 Acadians were first imprisoned on shipboard, then ordered to live in widely scattered towns (which refused to accept them), then grudgingly allowed to remain in Philadelphia, where they eked out a meager living, in part by petty thievery. After 1763 the survivors dispersed to a variety of locations: some returned to Canada, others traveled to France or its West Indian islands, and many eventually settled in Louisiana, where they became known as Cajuns.

Led by William Pitt, the civilian official placed in charge of the war effort in 1757, Britain finally pursued a successful military strategy. Pitt agreed to reimburse the colonies for their wartime expenditures and placed troop recruitment wholly in local hands, thereby gaining wholehearted American support for the war. In July 1758, British forces recaptured the fortress at Louisbourg, winning control of the entrance to the St. Lawrence River and cutting the major French supply route. Then, in a stunning attack in September 1759, General James Wolfe's soldiers defeated the French on the Plains of Abraham and took Quebec. Sensing a British victory, the Iroquois abandoned their traditional neutrality, hoping to gain a postwar advantage by allying themselves with Britain. A year later the British captured Montreal, the last French stronghold on the continent, and the American phase of the war ended.

In the Treaty of Paris (1763), France ceded its major North American holdings to Britain. Spain, an ally of France toward the end of the war, gave Florida to the victors. France, meanwhile, ceded Louisiana west of the Mississippi to Spain, in partial compensation for its ally's losses elsewhere. The British thus gained control of the continent's fur trade. No longer would the English seacoast colonies have to worry about the threat to their existence posed by France's extensive North American territories (see Map 5.2).

Because most of the fighting occurred in the Northeast, the war had especially pronounced effects on New Englanders. As many as one-third of all Massachusetts men between the ages of sixteen and

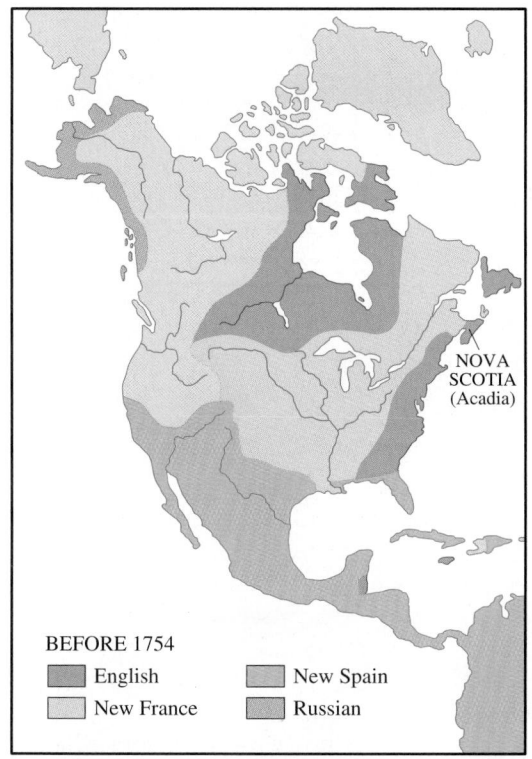

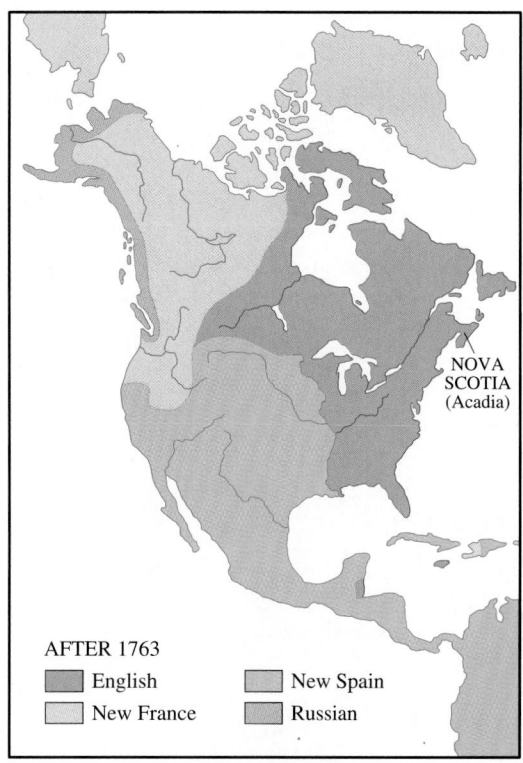

Map 5.2   European Claims in North America   The dramatic results of the British victory in the Seven Years (French and Indian) War are vividly demonstrated in these maps, which depict the abandonment of French claims to the mainland after the Treaty of Paris in 1763.

American Soldiers

twenty-nine served for a time in the provincial army. Wartime service left a lasting impression on these soldiers. For the first time, ordinary Americans came into extended contact with Britons—and they did not like what they saw. The provincials regarded the British troops (called "redcoats" because of the color of their uniforms) as haughty, profane Sabbath-breakers who arbitrarily imposed overly harsh punishments on anyone who broke the rules. Nearly sixty years later a veteran still vividly recalled an incident in 1762 when a British soldier inflicted hundreds of lashes on three men for "some trifling offense. . . . I felt at the time as though I could have taken summary vengeance on those who were the authors of it," he wrote in his memoirs.

The New England soldiers also learned that British troops did not share their adherence to principles of contract and consensus—the values that governed their lives at home. Colonial regiments mutinied or

rebelled en masse if they believed they were being treated unfairly, as happened, for instance, when they were not allowed to leave when their enlistments expired. One private in these circumstances grumbled in his journal in 1759, "Although we be Englishmen born, we are debarred Englishmen's liberty. . . . [The British soldiers] are but little better than slaves to their officers. And when I get out of their [power] I shall take care how I get in again." Such men would later recall their personal experience of British "tyranny" when they decided to support the Revolution.

The overwhelming British triumph stimulated some Americans to think expansively. People like the Philadelphia printer Benjamin Franklin, who had long touted the colonies' wealth and potential, predicted a glorious new future for British North America—a future that included not just geographical expansion but also economic development and population growth. Such men were to lead the resistance to British measures in the years after 1763. They uniformly opposed

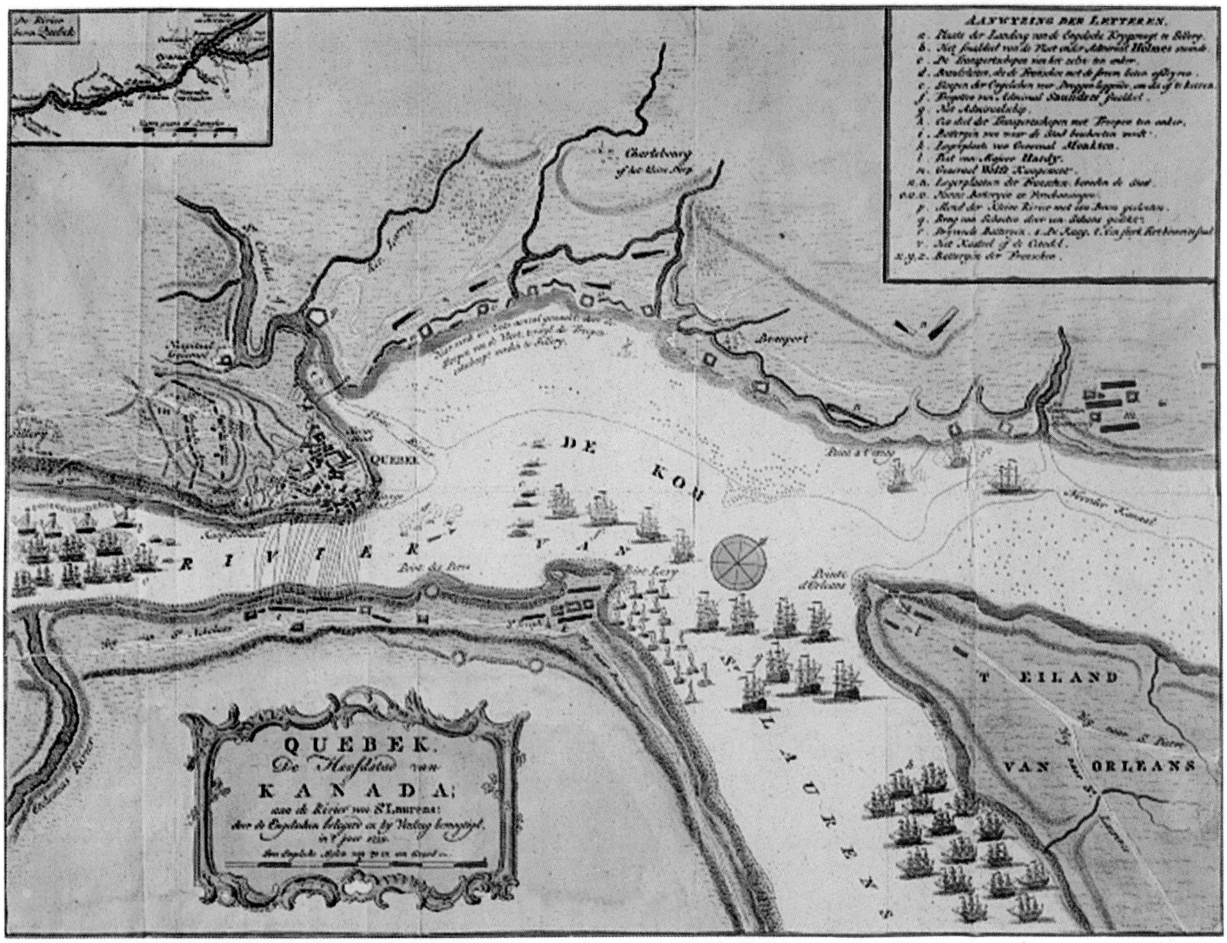

A 1769 Dutch atlas charted the successful British attack on Quebec ten years earlier. Ships of the British fleet fill the St. Lawrence River. Cannon on the southern shore bombard the fortified town (indicated by the lines across the river). And to the left of the city, on the Plains of Abraham, the string of small red blocks represents the British troops who had stealthily climbed the heights at night to confront Quebec's French defenders (the blue blocks). (Private Collection)

any laws that would retard America's growth and persistently supported steps to increase Americans' control over their own destiny.

1763: A Turning Point

The great victory over France had an irreversible impact on North America, felt first by the indigenous peoples of the interior. With France excluded from the continent altogether and Spanish territory now confined to west of the Mississippi, the diplomatic strategy that had served the Indians well for so long was now obsolete. The consequences were immediate and devastating.

Even before the Treaty of Paris, southern Indians had to adjust to the new circumstances. After Britain gained the upper hand in the American war in 1758, Creeks and Cherokees lost their ability to force concessions by threatening to turn instead to France or Spain. In desperation, and in retaliation for British atrocities, Cherokees attacked the Carolina and Virginia frontiers in 1760. Though initially victorious, the Indians were defeated the following year by a force of British regulars and colonial militia. Late in 1761 the two sides concluded a treaty under which the Cherokees allowed the construction of British forts in their territories and opened a large tract of land to European settlement.

The fate of the Cherokees in the South portended events in the Ohio country. There, the Ottawas, Chippewas, and Potawatomis reacted

Neolin and Pontiac

angrily when Great Britain, no longer facing French competition, raised the price of trade goods and ended traditional gift-giving practices. Britain also allowed settlers to move into the Monongahela and Susquehanna valleys, onto Delaware and Iroquois lands. A shaman named Neolin (also known as the Delaware Prophet) urged Indians to oppose British incursion on their lands and European influence on their culture. Contending that native peoples were destroying themselves by becoming dependent on European goods and especially alcohol, Neolin advocated resistance, both peaceful and armed. If all Indians west of the mountains united to reject the invaders, Neolin declared, the Great Spirit would replenish the depleted deer herds and once again look kindly upon his people.

Pontiac, the war chief of an Ottawa village near Detroit, became the leader of a movement based on Neolin's precepts. In the spring of 1763, Pontiac forged an unprecedented alliance among Hurons, Chippewas, Potawatomis, Delawares, Shawnees, and Mingoes (Pennsylvania Iroquois). Pontiac then laid siege to Fort Detroit while war parties attacked other British outposts in the Great Lakes region. Detroit withstood the siege, but by late June all the other forts west of Niagara and north of Fort Pitt (formerly the French Fort Duquesne) had fallen to the alliance. Indians then raided the Virginia and Pennsylvania frontiers at will throughout the summer, killing at least two thousand settlers. Still, they failed to take the strongholds of Niagara, Fort Pitt, or Detroit. In early August, colonial militiamen soundly defeated a combined force of Delawares, Shawnees, Hurons, and Mingoes at Bushy Run, Pennsylvania. Conflict ceased when Pontiac broke off the siege of Detroit in late October. A treaty ending the war was finally negotiated three years later.

The uprising showed Great Britain that the huge territory just acquired from France would not be easy

Proclamation of 1763

to govern. Officials in London had no prior experience managing such a vast area, particularly one inhabited by such restive peoples—the remaining French settlers along the St. Lawrence and the many different Indian communities. In October, the ministry issued the Proclamation of 1763, which declared the headwaters of rivers flowing

Benjamin West, the first well-known American artist, engraved this picture of a prisoner exchange at the end of Pontiac's Uprising, with Colonel Henry Bouquet supervising the return of settlers abducted during the war. In the foreground, a child resists leaving the Indian parents he had grown to love. Many colonists were fascinated by the phenomenon West depicted—the reluctance of captives to abandon their adoptive Indian families.   (Ohio Historical Society)

into the Atlantic from the Appalachian Mountains to be the temporary western boundary for colonial settlement (see Map 5.1). The proclamation was intended to prevent clashes by forbidding colonists to move onto Indian lands until tribes had given up their territory by treaty. But many Anglo-Americans had already established farms or purchased property west of the proclamation line; among them were wealthy speculators who hoped to control large tracts of fertile land. From the outset, then, the unenforceable policy was doomed to failure.

The hard-won victory in the Seven Years War had cost Britain millions of pounds and created an immense war debt. The problem of paying it bedeviled

George III

George III, who succeeded his grandfather, George II, on the British throne in 1760. The twenty-two-year-old king, a man of mediocre intellect and even more mediocre education, was unfortunately also an erratic judge of character. During the crucial years between 1763 and 1770, when the rift with the colonies grew ever wider and he faced a series of political crises in England, the king replaced ministries with bewildering rapidity. Although determined to assert the power of the monarchy, George III was immature and unsure of himself. He often substituted stubbornness for cleverness, and he regarded adherence to the status quo as the hallmark of patriotism.

The man he selected as prime minister in 1763, George Grenville, believed that the American colonies should be more tightly administered than in the past. Grenville confronted a financial crisis: England's burden of indebtedness had nearly doubled since 1754, from £73 million to £137 million. Annual expenditures before the war had amounted to no more than £8 million; now the yearly interest on the debt alone came to £5 million. Grenville's ministry had to find new sources of funds, and the British people themselves were already heavily taxed. Since the colonists had benefited greatly from the wartime expenditures, Grenville concluded that Anglo-Americans should be asked to pay a greater share of the cost of running the empire.

Grenville did not question Great Britain's right to levy taxes on the colonies. Like all his countrymen, he

Theories of Representation

believed that the government's legitimacy derived ultimately from the consent of the people, but he defined consent far more loosely than did the colonists. Americans had come to believe that they could be represented only by men who lived nearby and for whom they or their property-holding neighbors actually voted; otherwise, they could not count on legislators to represent their interests properly. Grenville and his English contemporaries, however, believed that Parliament—king, lords, and commons acting together—by definition represented all British subjects, wherever they resided (even overseas) and whether or not they could vote.

Parliament saw itself as collectively representing the entire nation; the particular constituency that chose a member of the House of Commons had no special claim on that member's vote, nor did he have to live near his constituents. According to this theory of government, called virtual representation, the colonists were seen as virtually, if not actually, represented in Parliament. Thus their consent to acts of Parliament could be presumed. In the colonies, by contrast, members of the lower houses of the assemblies were viewed as specifically representing the regions that had elected them. Before Grenville proposed to tax the colonists, the two notions coexisted because no major conflict arose to expose the central contradiction. But events of the 1760s revealed the incompatibility of the two definitions of representation.

The same events threw into sharp relief Americans' attitudes toward political power. The colonists had become accustomed to a central

Real Whigs

government that wielded only limited authority over them, affecting their daily lives very little. Consequently, they believed that a good government was one that largely left them alone, a view in keeping with the theories of a group of British writers known as the Real Whigs. Drawing on a tradition of dissenting thought that reached back to John Locke and even to the English Civil War, the Real Whigs stressed the dangers inherent in a powerful government, particularly one headed by a monarch. Some of them even favored republicanism, which proposed to eliminate monarchs altogether and rest political power more directly on the people. Real Whigs warned the people to guard constantly against government's attempts to encroach on their liberty and seize their property. Political power was always to be feared, wrote John Trenchard and Thomas Gordon in their essay series *Cato's Letters* (originally published in London in 1720–1723 and reprinted many times thereafter in the colonies). Rulers would try to corrupt and oppress the people. Only the perpetual vigilance of people and their elected representatives could preserve their precious yet fragile liberty, which was closely linked to their right to hold private property.

Britain's attempts to tighten the reins of government and to raise revenues from the colonies in the 1760s and early 1770s convinced many Americans that the Real Whigs' reasoning applied to their circumstances, especially because of the link between liberty and property rights. Excessive and unjust taxation, they believed, could destroy their freedoms. They began to interpret British measures in light of the Real Whigs' warnings and to see oppressive designs behind the actions of Grenville and his successors. Historians disagree over the extent to which those perceptions were correct, but by 1775 a large number of colonists believed they were. In the mid-1760s, however, colonial leaders did not immediately accuse Grenville of conspiring to oppress them. They at first merely questioned the wisdom of the laws he proposed.

Parliament passed the first such measures, the Sugar and Currency Acts, in 1764. The Sugar Act (also known as the Revenue Act) revised existing customs regulations, laid new duties on some foreign imports into the colonies, and aimed at stopping the widespread smuggling of molasses, one of the chief commodities in American trade. It also established a vice-admiralty court at Halifax, Nova Scotia. (Vice-admiralty courts considered cases arising under maritime law and operated without juries.) Although the Sugar Act appeared to resemble the Navigation Acts, which the colonies had long accepted as legitimate, it broke with tradition in being explicitly designed to raise revenue, not to channel American trade through Britain. The Currency Act effectively outlawed colonial issues of paper money. (British merchants had long complained that Americans were paying their debts in inflated local currencies.) Americans could accumulate little sterling, since they imported more than they exported; thus the act seemed to the colonists to deprive them of a useful medium of exchange.

Sugar and Currency Acts

The Sugar and Currency Acts were imposed on an economy already in the midst of depression. A business boom accompanied the Seven Years War, but the brief spell of prosperity ended abruptly in 1760 when the war shifted overseas. Urban merchants could not sell all their imported goods to colonial customers alone, and without the military's demand for foodstuffs, American farmers found fewer buyers for their products. The bottom dropped out of the European tobacco market, threatening the livelihood of Chesapeake planters. Sailors were thrown out of work, and artisans found few customers. In such circumstances, the prospect of increased import duties and inadequate supplies of currency aroused merchants' hostility.

Individual American essayists and incensed colonial governments protested the new policies. But, lacking any precedent for a united campaign against acts of Parliament, Americans in 1764 took only hesitant and uncoordinated steps. Eight colonial legislatures sent separate petitions to Parliament requesting the Sugar Act's repeal. They argued that its commercial restrictions would hurt Britain as well as the colonies and that they had not consented to its passage. The protests had no effect. The law remained in force, and Grenville proceeded with another revenue plan.

The Stamp Act Crisis

 The Stamp Act (1765), Grenville's most important proposal, was modeled on a law that had been in effect in Great Britain for almost a century. It touched nearly every colonist by requiring tax stamps on most printed materials, but it placed the heaviest burden on merchants and other members of the colonial elite, who used printed matter more frequently than did ordinary folk. Anyone who purchased a newspaper or pamphlet, made a will, transferred land, bought dice or playing cards, applied for a liquor license, accepted a government appointment, or borrowed money would have to pay the tax. Never before had a revenue measure of such scope been proposed for the colonies. The act also required that tax stamps be paid for with sterling, which was scarce, and that violators be tried in vice-admiralty courts. Americans feared the loss of their right to trial by a jury of their peers. Finally, such a law would break decisively with the colonial tradition of self-imposed taxation.

The most important colonial pamphlet protesting the Sugar Act and the proposed Stamp Act was *The Rights of the British Colonies Asserted and Proved*, by James Otis, Jr., a brilliant young Massachusetts attorney. Otis starkly exposed the ideological dilemma that confounded the colonists for the next decade. How could they justify their opposition to certain acts of Parliament without questioning Parliament's authority over them? On the one hand, Otis asserted, Americans were "entitled to all the natural, essential, inherent, and inseparable rights" of Britons, including the right not to be taxed without their consent. "No man or body of men, not excepting the parliament . . . can take [those rights] away," he declared. On the other hand, Otis was forced to admit, under the British system established after the Glorious Revolution, "the power of parliament is uncontrollable but by themselves, and we must obey. . . . Let the parliament lay what burthens they please on us, we must, it is our duty to submit and patiently bear them, till they will be pleased to relieve us."

James Otis's Rights of the British Colonies

Otis's first contention, drawing on colonial notions of representation, implied that Parliament could not constitutionally tax the colonies because Americans were not represented in its ranks. Yet his second point both acknowledged political reality and accepted the prevailing theory of British government: that Parliament was the sole, supreme authority in the empire. Even unconstitutional laws enacted by Parliament had to be obeyed until Parliament decided to repeal them.

According to orthodox British political theory, there could be no middle ground between absolute submission to Parliament and a frontal challenge to its authority. Otis tried to find such a middle ground by proposing colonial representation in Parliament, but his idea was never taken seriously on either side of the

In 1765 a clerk in the offices of British tax officials prepared this register to contain examples of the tax stamps intended for use in the American colonies. But because the law was never enforced and soon repealed, the register is largely empty, and the other volumes the clerk anticipated were never readied at all.   (The British Library Philatelic Section, Inland Revenue Archives)

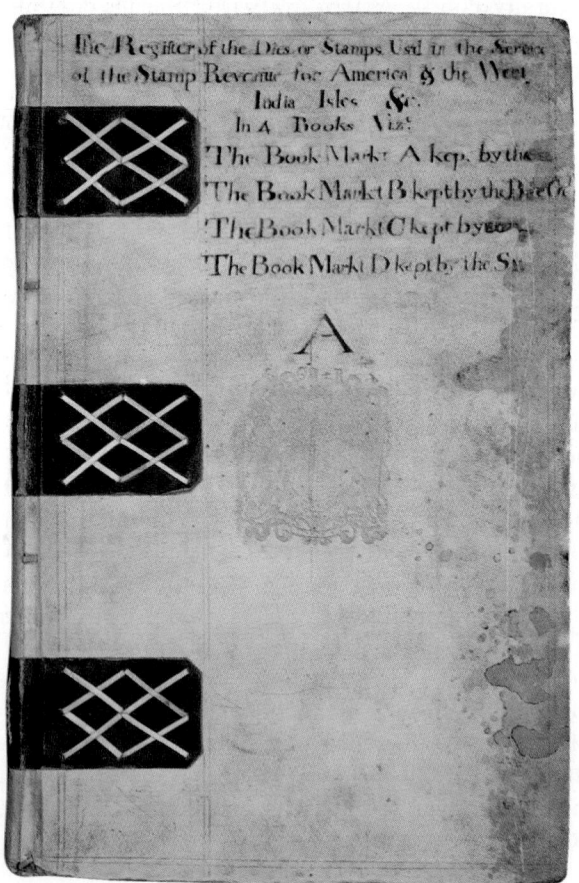

Atlantic. The British believed that colonists were already virtually represented in Parliament, and Anglo-Americans quickly realized that a handful of colonial delegates to London would simply be outvoted.

Otis published his pamphlet before the Stamp Act was passed. When Americans first learned of the act's adoption in the spring of 1765, they reacted indecisively. Few colonists—even appointed government officials—publicly favored the law. But colonial petitions had already failed to prevent its adoption, and further lobbying appeared futile. Perhaps Otis was correct: the only course open to Americans was to pay the stamp tax, reluctantly but loyally. Acting on that assumption, colonial agents in London sought the appointment of their American friends as stamp distributors so that the law would at least be enforced equitably.

Not all the colonists resigned themselves to paying the new tax. A twenty-nine-year-old lawyer serving his first term in the Virginia House of Burgesses was appalled by his fellow legislators' unwillingness to oppose the Stamp Act. Patrick Henry later recalled that he was "young, inexperienced, unacquainted with the forms of the house and the members that composed it"—but he decided to act. "Alone, unadvised, and unassisted, on a blank leaf of an old law book," he wrote the Virginia Stamp Act Resolves.

Patrick Henry and the Virginia Stamp Act Resolves

Little in Henry's earlier life foreshadowed his success in the political arena he entered so dramatically. The son of a prosperous Scottish immigrant to western Virginia, Henry had little formal education. After marrying at eighteen, he failed at both farming and storekeeping before turning to the law as a means of supporting his wife and their six children. Henry lacked legal training, but his oratorical skills made him an effective advocate, first for his clients and later for his political beliefs. A prominent Virginia lawyer observed, "He is by far the most powerful speaker I ever heard. Every word he says not only engages, but commands the attention; and your passions are no longer your own when he addresses them."

Patrick Henry introduced his seven proposals near the end of the legislative session, when many burgesses had already departed for home. Henry's fiery speech led the Speaker of the House to accuse him of treason. (Henry denied the charge, contrary to the nineteenth-century myth that he exclaimed, "If this be treason, make the most of it!") The few burgesses remaining in Williamsburg adopted five of Henry's resolutions by a bare majority. Although they repealed the most radical of the five the next day, their action had far-reaching effects. Some colonial newspapers printed Henry's seven original resolutions as if they had been uniformly passed by the House, even though one was rescinded and two others were never debated or voted on at all.

The four propositions adopted by the burgesses repeated Otis's arguments, asserting that the colonists had never forfeited the rights of British subjects, among which was consent to taxation. The other three resolutions went much further. The one that was repealed claimed for the burgesses "the only exclusive right" to tax Virginians, and the final two (those never considered) asserted that residents of Virginia need not obey tax laws passed by other legislative bodies (namely Parliament), terming any opponent of that opinion "an Enemy to this his Majesty's Colony."

The burgesses' decision to accept only the first four of Henry's resolutions anticipated the position

Continuing Loyalty to Britain

most Americans would adopt throughout the following decade. Though willing to contend for their rights, the colonists did not seek independence. They rather wanted some measure of self-government.

Accordingly, they backed away from the assertions that they owed Parliament no obedience and that only their own assemblies could tax them. Indeed, declared the Maryland lawyer Daniel Dulany, whose *Considerations on the Propriety of Imposing Taxes on the British Colonies* was the most widely read pamphlet of 1765, "The colonies are dependent upon Great Britain, and the supreme authority vested in the king, lords, and commons, may justly be exercised to secure, or preserve their dependence." But, warned Dulany, a superior did not have the right "to seize the property of his inferior when he pleases"; there was a crucial distinction between a condition of "dependence and inferiority" and one of "absolute vassalage and slavery."

Over the next ten years, America's political leaders searched for a formula that would enable them to control their internal affairs, especially taxation, but remain under British rule. The chief difficulty lay in British officials' inability to compromise on the issue of parliamentary power. The notion that Parliament could exercise absolute authority over all colonial possessions inhered in the British theory of government. Even the harshest British critics of the ministries of the 1760s and 1770s questioned only the wisdom of specific policies, not the principles on which they rested. In effect, the Americans wanted British leaders

In 1795 the artist Lawrence Sully painted the only known life portrait of Patrick Henry. The old man's fierce gaze reflects the same intensity that marked his actions thirty years earlier, when he introduced the Virginia Stamp Act Resolves in the House of Burgesses.   (Mead Art Museum, Amherst College. Bequest of Herbert L. Pratt, Class of 1985)

to revise their fundamental understanding of the workings of their government. But that was simply too much to expect.

The ultimate effectiveness of Americans' opposition to the Stamp Act rested on more than ideological arguments over parliamentary power. The decisive and inventive actions of some colonists during the late summer and fall of 1765 gave the resistance its primary force.

In August the Loyal Nine, a Boston social club of printers, distillers, and other artisans, organized a

Loyal Nine

demonstration against the Stamp Act. Hoping to show that people of all ranks opposed the act, they approached the leaders of the city's rival laborers' associations, based in Boston's North End and South End neighborhoods. The two gangs, composed of unskilled workers and poor tradesmen, often battled each other, but the Loyal Nine convinced them to lay aside their differences to participate in the demonstration. All colonists, not just affluent ones, would have to pay the stamp taxes.

Early on August 14, the demonstrators hung an effigy of Andrew Oliver, the province's stamp distributor, from a tree on Boston Common. That night a large crowd led by a group of about fifty well-dressed tradesmen paraded the effigy around the city. The crowd tore down a small building they thought was intended as the stamp office, making a bonfire near Oliver's house with wood from the structure. Beheading the effigy, they added it to the flames. Demonstrators broke most of Oliver's windows and threw stones at officials who tried to disperse them. In the midst of the melée, the North End and South End leaders drank a toast to their successful union. The Loyal Nine achieved success when Oliver publicly promised not to fulfill the duties of his office. One Bostonian jubilantly wrote to a relative, "I believe people never was more Universally pleased not so much one could I hear say he was sorry, but a smile sat on almost every ones countinance."

But another crowd action twelve days later, aimed this time at Oliver's brother-in-law, Lieutenant Governor Thomas Hutchinson, drew no praise from Boston's respectable citizens. On the night of August 26, a mob reportedly led by the South End leader Ebenezer MacIntosh attacked the homes of several customs officers. The crowd then completely destroyed Hutchinson's elaborately furnished townhouse in one of Boston's most fashionable districts. The lieutenant governor reported that by the next morning "one of the best finished houses in the Province had nothing remaining but the bare walls and floors." His trees and garden were ruined, his valuable library was lost, and the mob "emptied the house of every thing whatsoever except a part of the kitchen furniture." But Hutchinson took some comfort in the fact that "the encouragers of the first mob never intended matters should go this length and the people in general express the utmost detestation of this unparalleled outrage." (A portrait of Hutchinson is on page 137.)

The differences between the two Boston mobs of August 1765 exposed divisions that would continue to characterize subsequent colonial protests. Few residents of the colonies sided with Great Britain during the 1760s, but various colonial groups had divergent goals. The skilled craftsmen who composed the Loyal Nine, and merchants, lawyers, and other members of the educated elite preferred orderly demonstrations con-

Americans' Divergent Interests

fined to political issues. For the city's laborers, by contrast, economic grievances may have been paramount. Certainly, their "hellish Fury" as they wrecked Hutchinson's house suggests a resentment against his ostentatious display of wealth.

Colonists, like Britons, had a long tradition of crowd action in which disfranchised people took to the streets to redress deeply felt local grievances. But the Stamp Act controversy drew ordinary urban folk into the vortex of transatlantic politics for the first time. Matters that previously had been of concern only to the gentry or to members of colonial legislatures were now discussed on every street corner. Benjamin Franklin's daughter observed as much when she informed her father, then serving as a colonial agent in London, that "nothing else is talked of, the Dutch [Germans] talk of the stompt act the Negroes of the tamp, in short every body has something to say."

The entry of unskilled workers, slaves, and women into the realm of imperial politics both threatened and aided the elite men who wanted to mount effective opposition to British measures. On the one hand, crowd action could have a stunning impact. Anti–Stamp Act demonstrations occurred in cities and towns stretching from Halifax in the north to the Caribbean island of Antigua in the south (see Map 5.3). They were so successful that by November 1, when the law was scheduled to take effect, not one stamp distributor was willing to carry out his official duties. Thus the act could not be enforced. But on the other hand, wealthy men recognized that mobs composed of the formerly powerless—whose goals were not always identical to theirs (as the Boston experience showed)—could endanger their own dominance of the society. What would happen, they wondered, if the "hellish Fury" of the crowd turned against them?

They therefore attempted to channel resistance into acceptable forms by creating an intercolonial association, the Sons of Liberty. New Yorkers organized the first such group in early November, and branches spread rapidly through the coastal cities. Composed of merchants, lawyers, and prosperous tradesmen like Paul Revere, the Sons of Liberty by early 1766 linked protest leaders from Charleston, South Carolina, to Portsmouth, New Hampshire.

Sons of Liberty

The Sons of Liberty could influence events but not control them. In Charleston in October 1765, an informally organized crowd shouting "Liberty Liberty and stamp'd paper" forced the resignation of the South

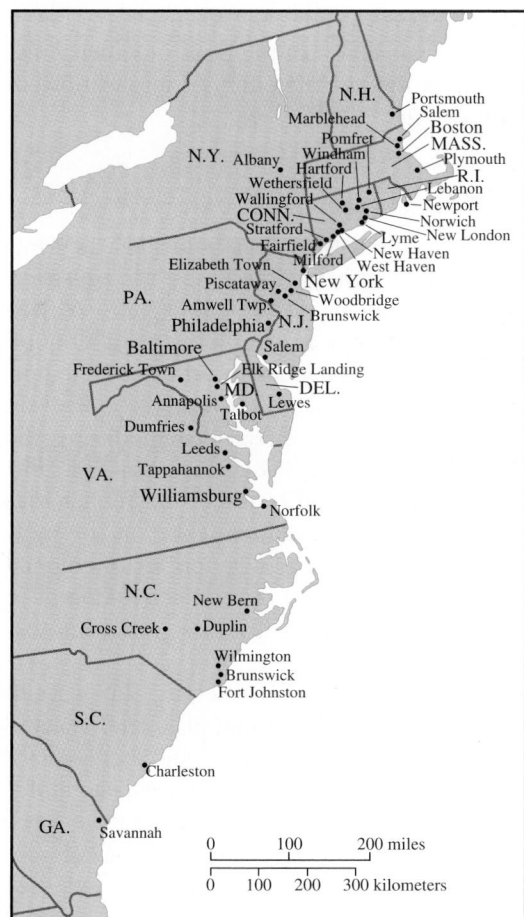

Map 5.3   Sites of Major Demonstrations Against the Stamp Act   Every place named on these maps was the site of a demonstration against the Stamp Act of 1765; British colonies outside the eventual United States joined in the nearly universal opposition to the hated measure. (Source: From Lester J. Cappon et al., eds., *Atlas of Early American History: The Revolutionary Era, 1760–1790.* Copyright © 1976 by Princeton University Press. Reprinted by permission of Princeton University Press.)

Carolina stamp distributor. The victory celebration a few days later—the largest demonstration the city had ever known—featured a British flag with the word "Liberty" emblazoned on it. But the new Charleston chapter of the Sons of Liberty was horrified when in January 1766 local slaves paraded through the streets similarly crying "Liberty!" Freedom from slavery was not the sort of liberty elite slaveowners had in mind.

In Philadelphia, too, resistance leaders were dismayed when an angry mob threatened to attack Benjamin Franklin's house. The city's laborers believed Franklin to be partly responsible for the Stamp Act, since he had obtained the post of stamp distributor for a close friend. But Philadelphia's artisans—the backbone of the opposition movement there and elsewhere—were fiercely loyal to Franklin, one of their own who had made good. They gathered to protect his home and family from the crowd. The house was

saved, but the resulting split between the better-off tradesmen and the common laborers prevented the establishment of a successful workingmen's alliance like that of Boston.

During the fall and winter of 1765–1766, opposition to the Stamp Act proceeded on three separate fronts. Colonial legislatures petitioned Parliament to repeal the hated law, and courts closed because they could not obtain the stamps now required for all legal documents. In October nine colonies sent delegates to a general congress, the first since the 1754 Albany Congress. The Stamp Act Congress met in New York to draft a unified but conservative statement of protest that stressed the law's adverse economic effects rather than its perceived violations of Americans' rights. At the same time, the Sons of Liberty held mass meetings, attempting to rally public support for the resistance movement. Finally, American merchants organized nonimportation associations to pressure British exporters. By the 1760s, one-quarter of all British exports went to the colonies, and American merchants reasoned that London merchants whose sales suffered severely would lobby for repeal. Since times were bad and American merchants were finding few customers for imported goods anyway, a general moratorium on future purchases would also help to reduce their bloated inventories.

In March 1766, Parliament repealed the Stamp Act. The nonimportation agreements had had the anticipated effect, creating allies for the colonies among wealthy London merchants. But boycotts, formal protests, and crowd actions were less important in winning repeal than was the appointment of a new prime minister, chosen by George III for reasons unrelated to colonial politics. Lord Rockingham, who replaced Grenville in the summer of 1765, had opposed the Stamp Act, not because he believed Parliament lacked power to tax the colonies but because he thought the law unwise and divisive. Thus although Rockingham proposed repeal, he linked it to passage of a Declaratory Act, which asserted Parliament's authority to tax and legislate for Britain's American possessions "in all cases whatsoever."

Repeal of the Stamp Act

News of the repeal arrived in Newport, Rhode Island, in May, and the Sons of Liberty quickly dispatched messengers to carry the welcome tidings throughout the colonies. They organized celebrations commemorating the glorious event, all of which stressed the Americans' unwavering loyalty to Great Britain. Their goal achieved, the Sons of Liberty dissolved. Few colonists saw the ominous implications of the Declaratory Act.

Resistance to the Townshend Acts

The colonists had accomplished their immediate aim, but the long-term prospects were unclear. In the summer of 1766, another change in the ministry in London revealed how fragile their victory had been. The new prime minister, William Pitt, had fostered cooperation between the colonies and Great Britain during the Seven Years War (see page 118). Now, however, Pitt was ill much of the time, and another minister, Charles Townshend, became the dominant force in the ministry. An ally of Grenville and a supporter of colonial taxation, Townshend decided to renew the attempt to obtain additional funds from Britain's American possessions (see Table 5.2.).

The duties Townshend proposed in 1767 were to be levied on trade goods like paper, glass, and tea, and thus seemed to be nothing more than extensions of the existing Navigation Acts. But the Townshend duties differed from previous customs levies in two ways. First, they applied to items imported into the colonies from Britain, not from foreign countries. Thus they violated mercantilist theory (see page 76). Second, they were designed to raise money to pay the salaries of some royal officials in the colonies. That posed a direct challenge to the colonial assemblies, which derived considerable power from threatening to withhold officials' salaries. In addition, Townshend's scheme provided for the creation of an American Board of Customs Commissioners and of vice-admiralty courts at Boston, Philadelphia, and Charleston. Both moves angered merchants, whose profits would be threatened by more vigorous enforcement of the Navigation Acts.

In 1765, months had passed before the colonists began to protest the Stamp Act. The passage of the Townshend Acts, however, drew a quick response. One series of essays in particular, *Letters from a Farmer in Pennsylvania* by the prominent lawyer John Dickinson, expressed a broad consensus. Eventually all but four colonial newspapers printed Dickinson's essays; in pamphlet form they went through seven American editions. Dickinson con-

John Dickinson's Farmer's Letters

Table 5.2	British Ministries and Their American Policies	
Head of Ministry	**Major Acts**
George Grenville	Sugar Act (1764)
	Currency Act (1764)
	Stamp Act (1765)
Lord Rockingham	Stamp Act repealed (1766)
	Declaratory Act (1766)
William Pitt/ Charles Townshend	Townshend Acts (1767)
Lord North	Townshend duties (except for the tea tax) repealed (1770)
	Coercive Acts (1774)
	Quebec Act (1774)

tended that Parliament could regulate colonial trade but could not exercise that power to raise revenue. By drawing a distinction between trade regulation and unacceptable commercial taxation, Dickinson avoided the sticky issue of consent and how it affected colonial subordination to Parliament. But his argument created a different, and equally knotty, problem. In effect it obligated the colonies to assess Parliament's motives in passing any law pertaining to trade before deciding whether to obey it. That was in the long run an unworkable position.

The Massachusetts assembly responded to the Townshend Acts by drafting a letter to circulate among the other colonial legislatures, calling

Massachusetts Assembly Dissolved

for unity and suggesting a joint petition of protest. Not the letter itself but the ministry's reaction to it united the colonies. When Lord Hillsborough, recently named to the new post of secretary of state for America, learned of the circular letter, he ordered Governor Francis Bernard of Massachusetts to insist that the assembly recall it. He also directed other governors to prevent their assemblies from discussing the letter. Hillsborough's order gave

colonial assemblies the incentive they needed to join forces to oppose this new threat to their prerogatives. In late 1768 the Massachusetts legislature met, debated, and resoundingly rejected recall by a vote of 92 to 17. Bernard immediately dissolved the assembly, and other governors followed suit when their legislatures debated the circular letter.

The number of votes cast against recalling the circular letter—92—assumed ritual significance for the supporters of resistance. The figure 45 already had symbolic meaning because John Wilkes, a radical Londoner sympathetic to the American cause, had been jailed for libel in Britain for publishing an essay entitled *The North Briton*, No. 45. In Boston, Paul Revere made a punchbowl weighing 45 ounces that held 45 gills (half-cups) and was engraved with the names of the 92 legislators; James Otis, John Adams, and others publicly drank 45 toasts from it (see the photo below). In Charleston the city's tradesmen decorated a tree with 45 lights and set off 45 rockets. Carrying 45 candles, they adjourned to a tavern, where 45 tables were set with 45 bowls of wine, 45 bowls of punch, and 92 glasses.

Rituals of Resistance

Paul Revere crafted a punchbowl to commemorate the 92 members of the Massachusetts Assembly who in 1768 voted against rescinding the circular letter. The bowl was also linked symbolically to John Wilkes by its size and weight, and through its use in rituals incorporating the number 45.   (Courtesy, Museum of Fine Arts, Boston. Gift by Subscription and Francis Bartlett Fund. Reproduced with permission. © 1999 Museum of Fine Arts, Boston. All rights reserved.)

Such public rituals served important educational functions. Just as the pamphlets by Otis, Dulany, Dickinson, and others acquainted literate colonists with the issues raised by British actions, so public rituals taught illiterate Americans about the reasons for resistance and familiarized them with the terms of the argument. When Boston's revived Sons of Liberty invited hundreds of city residents to dine with them each August 14 to commemorate the first Stamp Act uprising, and the Charleston Sons of Liberty held their meetings in public, crowds gathered to watch and listen. Likewise, the public singing of songs supporting the American cause helped to spread the word. The participants in such events openly expressed their commitment to the cause of resistance and encouraged others to join them.

During the campaign against the Townshend duties, the Sons of Liberty and other American leaders made a deliberate effort to involve ordinary folk in the resistance movement. Most important, they urged colonists of all ranks and both sexes to sign agreements not to purchase or consume British products. The new consumerism that previously had linked colonists economically now linked them politically as well, supplying them with a ready method of displaying their allegiance. As "A Tradesman" wrote in a Philadelphia paper in 1770, it was essential "for the Good of the Whole, to strengthen the Hands of the Patriotic Majority, by agreeing not to purchase British Goods."

As the primary purchasers of textiles and household goods, women played a central role in the nonconsumption movement. In Boston more than three hundred matrons publicly promised not to buy or drink tea, "Sickness excepted." The women of Wilmington, North Carolina, burned their tea after walking through town in a solemn procession. Women throughout the colonies exchanged recipes for tea substitutes or drank coffee instead. The best known of the protests, the so-called Edenton Ladies Tea Party, actually had little to do with tea. It was a meeting of prominent North Carolina women who pledged formally to work for the public good and to support resistance to British measures.

Daughters of Liberty

Women also encouraged home manufacturing. In many towns, young women calling themselves Daughters of Liberty met to spin in public in an effort to persuade other women to make homespun, thereby ending the colonies' dependence on British cloth. These symbolic displays of patriotism—publicized by newspapers and broadsides—served the same purpose as the male rituals involving the numbers 45 and 92. When young ladies from well-to-do families sat publicly at spinning wheels all day, eating only American food and drinking local herbal tea, and later listening to patriotic sermons, they were serving as political instructors. Many women took great satisfaction in their newfound role. When a New England satirist hinted that women discussed only "such triffling subjects as Dress, Scandal and Detraction" during their spinning bees, three Boston women replied angrily: "Inferior in abusive sarcasm, in personal invective, in low wit, we glory to be, but inferior in veracity, sincerity, love of virtue, of liberty and of our country, we would not willingly be to any."

But the colonists were by no means united in support of nonimportation and nonconsumption. If the Stamp Act protests had occasionally (as in Boston and Philadelphia) revealed a division between artisans and merchants on the one side and common laborers on the other, resistance to the Townshend Acts exposed new splits in American ranks. The most significant—which arose from a change in economic circumstances—divided urban artisans and merchants, allies in 1765 and 1766.

Divided Opinion over Boycotts

The Stamp Act boycotts had helped to revive a depressed economy by creating a demand for local products and reducing merchants' inventories. But in 1768 and 1769, merchants were enjoying boom times and had no financial incentive to support a boycott. As a result, merchants signed the agreements only reluctantly, sometimes violating them secretly. In contrast, artisans supported nonimportation enthusiastically, recognizing that the absence of British goods would create a ready market for their own manufactures. Thus tradesmen formed the core of the crowds that coerced both importers and their customers by picketing stores, publicizing offenders' names, and sometimes destroying property.

Such tactics were effective: colonial imports from England dropped dramatically in 1769, especially in New York, New England, and Pennsylvania. But they also aroused heated opposition, creating a second major division among the colonists. Some Americans who supported resistance to British measures began to question the use of violence to force others to join the boycott. In addition, wealthier and more conservative colonists were frightened by the threat to private property inherent in the campaign. Political activism by ordinary colonists challenged the ruling elite's domination, just as its members had feared in 1765.

Disclosures that leading merchants had violated the nonimportation agreement caused dissension in the ranks of the boycotters, so Americans were relieved when news arrived in April 1770 that the Townshend duties had been repealed, with the exception of the tea tax. A new prime minister, Lord North, persuaded Parliament that duties on trade within the empire were ill-advised. Although some colonial leaders argued that nonimportation should continue until the tea tax was repealed, merchants quickly resumed importing. The rest of the Townshend Acts remained in force, but repealing the duties made the other provisions (establishing vice-admiralty courts and the American Board of Customs Commissioners, and promising to pay officials' salaries from customs revenues at some time in the future) appear less objectionable.

Repeal of the Townshend Duties

Confrontations in Boston

At first the new ministry in London did nothing to antagonize the colonists. Yet on the very day Lord North proposed repeal of the Townshend duties, a confrontation between civilians and soldiers in Boston led to the death of five Americans. The origins of the event that patriots called the Boston Massacre lay in repeated clashes between customs officers and the people of Massachusetts. The decision to base the American Board of Customs Commissioners in Boston was the source of the problem.

Mobs targeted the customs commissioners from the day they arrived in November 1767. In June 1768 their seizure of the patriot leader John Hancock's sloop *Liberty* on suspicion of smuggling caused a riot in which prominent customs officers' property was destroyed. The riot in turn helped to convince the ministry in London that troops were needed to maintain order in the unruly port. The assignment of two regiments of regulars to their city confirmed Bostonians' worst fears; the redcoats constantly reminded city dwellers of the oppressive potential of British power. Guards on Boston Neck, the entrance to the city, checked all travelers and their goods. Redcoat patrols

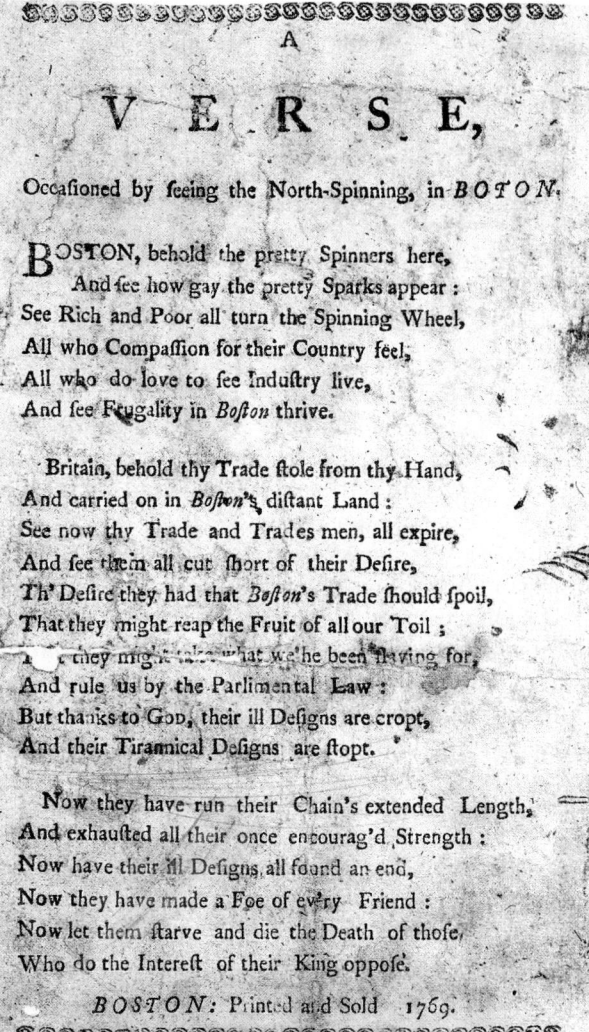

A 1769 Boston broadside commended the spinners, "Rich and Poor," who had "Compassion for their Country" and promoted "Frugality" during the Townshend Act crisis. The poet put into verse precisely the message the spinners intended to convey.   (Massachusetts Historical Society)

roamed the city day and night, questioning and sometimes harassing passersby. Military parades were held on Boston Common, accompanied by martial music and often the public whipping of deserters and other violators of army rules. Parents began to fear for the safety of their daughters, who were subjected to soldiers' coarse sexual insults. But the greatest potential for violence lay in the uneasy relationship between the soldiers and Boston laborers. Many redcoats sought employment in their off-duty hours, competing for unskilled jobs with the city's ordinary workingmen. Members of the two groups brawled repeatedly in taverns and on the streets.

Early on the evening of March 5, 1770, a crowd of laborers began throwing hard-packed snowballs at soldiers guarding the Customs House.

Boston Massacre

Goaded beyond endurance, the sentries acted against express orders to the contrary and fired on the crowd, killing four and wounding eight, one of whom died a few days later. Resistance leaders idealized the dead rioters as martyrs for the cause of liberty, holding a solemn funeral and later commemorating March 5 annually with patriotic orations. Paul Revere's engraving of the massacre (based on a drawing by John Singleton Copley's half-brother Henry Pelham and reproduced on page 135) was part of the propaganda campaign.

Leading patriots wanted to ensure that the soldiers did not become martyrs as well. Despite the political benefits the patriots derived from the massacre, they probably did not approve the crowd action that provoked it. Ever since the destruction of Hutchinson's house in August 1765, men allied with the Sons of Liberty had supported orderly demonstrations and expressed distaste for uncontrolled riots, of which the Boston Massacre was a prime example. Thus when the soldiers were tried for the killings in November, John Adams and Josiah Quincy, Jr., both unwavering patriots, acted as their defense attorneys. All but two of the accused men were acquitted, and those convicted were released after being branded on the thumb. Undoubtedly the favorable outcome of the trials prevented London officials from taking further steps against the city.

For more than two years after the Boston Massacre and the repeal of the Townshend duties, a superficial calm descended on the colonies.

A British Plot?

The most outspoken colonial newspapers, such as the *Boston Gazette*, the *Pennsylvania Journal*, and the *South Carolina Gazette*, published essays drawing on Real Whig ideology and accusing Great Britain of deliberately scheming to oppress the colonies. After the Stamp Act's repeal, the patriots had praised Parliament; following repeal of the Townshend duties, they warned of impending tyranny. What had seemed to be an isolated mistake, a single ill-chosen stamp tax, now appeared to be part of a plot against American liberties. Essayists pointed to Parliament's persecution of

the British radical John Wilkes, the stationing of troops in Boston, and the growing number of vice-admiralty courts as evidence of plans to enslave the colonists. Indeed, patriot writers played repeatedly on the word *enslavement*. Most white colonists had direct knowledge of slavery (either as slaveholders themselves or as neighbors of slaveowners), and the threat of enslavement by Britain must have hit them with peculiar force.

Still, no one yet advocated complete independence from the mother country. Although the patriots were becoming increasingly convinced that they should seek freedom from parliamentary authority, they continued to acknowledge their British identity and their allegiance to George III. They began, therefore, to envision a system that would enable them to be ruled by their own elected legislatures while remaining loyal to the king. But any such scheme violated Britons' conception of the nature of their government, which posited that Parliament wielded sole undivided sovereignty over the empire. Furthermore, in the British mind, Parliament encompassed the king as well as lords and commons, so separating the monarch from the legislature was impossible.

Then, in the fall of 1772, the North ministry began to implement the Townshend Act that provided for governors and judges to be paid from customs revenues. In early November, voters at a Boston town meeting established a Committee of Correspondence to publicize the decision by exchanging letters with other Massachusetts towns. Heading the committee was the man who had proposed its formation, Samuel Adams.

Fifty-one in 1772, Samuel Adams was thirteen years older than his distant cousin John and by a decade the senior of most other leaders of American resistance. He had

Samuel Adams

been a Boston tax collector, a member and clerk of the Massachusetts assembly, an ally of the Loyal Nine, and a member of the Sons of Liberty. His primary forum was the Boston town meeting. Unswerving in his devotion to the American cause, Adams drew a sharp contrast between a corrupt, vice-ridden Britain and the colonies, peopled by simple, liberty-loving folk. An experienced political organizer, Adams continually stressed the necessity of prudent collective action. His Committee of Correspondence thus undertook the task of creating an informed consensus among all the residents of Massachusetts.

How do historians know...

that ordinary people became familiar with the ideas propounded by the leaders of the American Revolution?

This is a difficult question to answer because most of the evidence about the patriots' ideology comes from pamphlets and newspapers aimed at the well-educated. People who could read at only a basic level might not have been able to understand the sophisticated criticisms of British policies advanced in such writings. But because an engraver made his point visually rather than verbally, anyone, even illiterate folk, could interpret an image such as Paul Re-

vere's masterful portrayal of the Boston Massacre. The label "Butcher's Hall" on the Customs House merely reinforces the patriot view of the incident on March 5, 1770. The British soldiers are shown firing on an unresisting crowd, not the aggressive, angry mob described at the soldiers' trial. Even worse, a gun with smoke drifting up from its barrel emerges from a window above the redcoats, suggesting the complicity of civilian officials in what the patriots interpreted as an outrageous act. (Photo: Courtesy of the John Carter Brown Library, Brown University)

Such committees, which were eventually established throughout the colonies, represented the next logical step in the organization of American resistance. Until 1772, the protest movement was largely confined to the seacoast and primarily to major cities and towns (see Map 5.3).

Boston Committee of Correspondence

Adams realized that the time had come to widen the movement's geographic scope, to attempt to involve the residents of the interior in the struggle. Accordingly, the Boston town meeting directed the Committee of Correspondence "to state the Rights of the Colonists and of this Province in particular," to list "the Infringements and Violations thereof that have been, or from time to time may be made," and to send copies to the other towns in the province. In return, Boston requested "a free communication of their Sentiments on this Subject."

The statement of colonial rights prepared by the Bostonians declared that Americans had absolute rights to life, liberty, and property. The idea that "a British house of commons, should have a right, at pleasure, to give and grant the property of the colonists" was "irreconcileable" with "the first principles of natural law and Justice . . . and of the British Constitution in particular." The list of grievances complained of taxation without representation, the presence of unnecessary troops and customs officers on American soil, the use of imperial revenues to pay colonial officials, the expanded jurisdiction of vice-admiralty courts, and even the nature of the instructions given to American governors by their superiors in London.

The entire document, which was printed as a pamphlet for distribution to the towns, exhibited none of the hesitation that had characterized colonial claims against Parliament in the 1760s. No longer were patriots—at least in Boston—preoccupied with defining the precise limits of parliamentary authority. No longer did they mention the necessity of obedience to Parliament. They were committed to a course that placed American rights first, loyalty to Great Britain a distant second.

The response of the Massachusetts towns to the committee's pamphlet must have caused Samuel Adams to rejoice. Some towns disagreed with Boston's assessment of the state of affairs, but most aligned themselves with the city. From Braintree came the assertion that "all civil officers are or ought to be Servants to the people and dependent upon them for their official Support, and every instance to the Contrary from the Governor downwards tends to crush and destroy civil liberty." The town of Holden declared that "the People of New England have never given the People of Britain any Right of Jurisdiction over us." The citizens of Petersham commented that resistance to tyranny was "the first and highest social Duty of this people." And Pownallborough warned, "Allegiance is a relative Term and like Kingdoms and commonwealths is local and has its bounds." Beliefs like these made the next crisis in Anglo-American affairs the final one.

Tea and Turmoil

The tea tax was the only Townshend duty still in effect by 1773. In the years after 1770, some Americans continued to boycott English tea, while others resumed drinking it either openly or in secret. As was explained in Chapter 4, tea figured prominently in both the colonists' diet and their social lives, so observing the boycott required them not only to forgo a favorite beverage but also to alter habitual forms of socializing. Tea thus retained an explosively symbolic character even though the boycott began to fall apart after 1770.

In May 1773, Parliament passed an act designed to save the East India Company from bankruptcy.

Tea Act

The company, which held a monopoly on British trade with the East Indies, was critically important to the British economy (and to the financial well-being of many prominent British politicians who had invested in its stock). According to the Tea Act, legal tea would henceforth be sold in America only by the East India Company's designated agents, which would enable the company to avoid middlemen in both England and the colonies and to price its tea competitively with that offered by smugglers. The net result would be cheaper tea for American consumers. Resistance leaders, however, interpreted the new measure as a pernicious device to make them admit Parliament's right to tax them, for the less-expensive tea would still be taxed under the Townshend law. Others saw the Tea Act as the first step in the establishment of an East India Company monopoly of all colonial trade. Residents of the four cities designated to receive the first shipments of tea accordingly prepared to respond to what they perceived as a new threat to their freedom.

In New York City, the tea ships failed to arrive on schedule. In Philadelphia, the governor of Pennsylvania persuaded the captain to turn around and sail back to Britain. In Charleston, the tea was unloaded and stored; some was destroyed, the rest sold in 1776 by the new state government. The only confrontation occurred in Boston, where both sides—the town meeting, joined by participants from nearby towns, and Governor Thomas Hutchinson, two of whose sons were tea agents—rejected compromise.

The Boston Tea Party

The first of three tea ships, the *Dartmouth*, entered Boston harbor on November 28. The customs laws required cargo to be landed and the appropriate duty paid by its owners within twenty days of a ship's arrival; otherwise, the cargo had to be seized by customs officers and sold at auction. After a series of mass meetings, Bostonians voted to post guards on the wharf to prevent the tea from being unloaded. Hutchinson refused to permit the vessels to leave the harbor. John Singleton Copley, whose father-in-law was a tea agent, tried to mediate the dispute.

On December 16, one day before the cargo would have been confiscated, more than five thousand people (nearly a third of the city's population) crowded into Old South Church. The meeting, chaired by Samuel Adams, made a final attempt to persuade Hutchinson to send the tea back to England. But the governor remained adamant. In the early evening Adams reportedly announced "that he could think of nothing further to be done—that they had now done all they could for the Salvation of their Country." Cries then rang out from the back of the crowd: "Boston harbor a tea-pot tonight! The Mohawks are come!" Small groups pushed their way out of the meeting. Within a few minutes, about sixty men crudely disguised as Indians assembled at the wharf, boarded the three ships, and dumped the cargo into the harbor. By 9 P.M. their work was done: 342 chests of tea worth approximately £10,000 floated in splinters on the water.

Among the "Indians" were many representatives of Boston's artisans, including the silversmith Paul Revere. Five masons, eleven carpenters and builders, three leatherworkers, a blacksmith, two barbers, a coachmaker, a shoemaker, and twelve apprentices have been identified as participants. That their ranks also included four farmers from outside Boston, ten merchants, two doctors, a teacher, and a bookseller illustrated the widespread support for the resistance

Thomas Hutchinson, the governor of Massachusetts, helped to incite the Boston Tea Party by refusing to allow the tea ships to leave the harbor. This portrait conveys the governor's haughty demeanor.   (Massachusetts Historical Society)

movement. The next day John Adams exulted in his diary that the Tea Party was "so bold, so daring, so firm, intrepid and inflexible" that "I cant but consider it as an Epocha in history."

The North administration reacted with considerably less enthusiasm when it learned of the Tea Party.

Coercive and Quebec Acts

In March 1774, Parliament adopted the first of four laws that became known as the Coercive, or Intolerable, Acts. It ordered the port of Boston closed until the tea was paid for, prohibiting all but coastal trade in food and firewood. Later in the spring, Parliament passed three other punitive measures. The Massachusetts Government Act altered the province's charter, substituting an appointed council for the elected one, increasing the governor's powers, and forbidding most town meetings. The Justice Act provided that a person accused of committing murder in the course of suppressing a riot or enforcing the laws could be tried outside the colony where the incident had occurred. Finally, the Quartering Act allowed military officers to commandeer privately owned buildings to house their troops. Thus the Coercive Acts punished not only Boston but also Massachusetts as a whole, alerting other colonies to the possibility that their residents, too, could be subject to retaliation if they opposed British authority.

After passing the last of the Coercive Acts, Parliament turned its attention to much-needed reforms in the government of Quebec. The Quebec Act thereby became linked with the Coercive Acts in the minds of the patriots. Intended to ease strains that had arisen since the British conquest of the formerly French colony, the Quebec Act granted greater religious freedom to Catholics—alarming Protestant colonists, who equated Roman Catholicism with religious and political despotism. It also reinstated French civil law, which had been replaced by British procedures in 1763, and it established an appointed council (rather than an elected legislature) as the governing body of the colony. Finally, in an attempt to provide northern Indians with some protection against Anglo-American settlement, the act annexed to Quebec the area east of the Mississippi River and north of the Ohio River. That region, parts of which were claimed by individual seacoast colonies, was thus removed from their jurisdiction.

Members of Parliament who voted for the punitive legislation believed that the acts would be obeyed and that at long last they had solved the problem posed by the troublesome Americans. But the patriots showed little inclination to bow to the wishes of Parliament. In their eyes, the Coercive Acts and the Quebec Act proved what they had feared since 1768: that Great Britain had embarked on a deliberate plan to oppress them. If the port of Boston could be closed, why not the ports of Philadelphia or New York? If the royal charter of Massachusetts could be changed, why not the charter of South Carolina? If certain people could be transferred to distant colonies for trial, why not any violator of any law? If troops could be forcibly quartered in private houses, did not that action pave the way for the occupation of all of America? If the Roman Catholic Church could receive favored status in Quebec, why not everywhere? It seemed as though the full dimensions of the plot against American rights and liberties had at last been revealed.

Implications of the Coercive Acts

The Boston Committee of Correspondence urged all the colonies to join in an immediate boycott of British goods. But the other provinces hesitated to take such a drastic step. Rhode Island, Virginia, and Pennsylvania each suggested that another intercolonial congress be convened to consider an appropriate response, and in mid-June 1774 Massachusetts acquiesced. Few people wanted to take hasty action; even the most ardent patriots remained loyal to Britain and hoped for reconciliation with its leaders. Despite their objections to British policy, they continued to see themselves as part of the empire. Americans were approaching the brink of confrontation, but they had not committed themselves to an irrevocable break. So the colonies agreed to send delegates to Philadelphia in September to attend a Continental Congress.

Summary

 Just twenty years earlier, at the outbreak of the Seven Years War in the wilderness of western Pennsylvania, no one could have predicted that the future would bring such swift and dramatic change to Britain's mainland colonies. Yet that conflict—which simultaneously removed France from North America and created a huge war debt Britain had to find ways to pay—set in motion the process leading to the convening of the First Continental Congress.

In the years after the war ended in 1763, momentous changes occurred in the ways colonists thought about themselves and their allegiances. The number of colonists who defined themselves as political actors increased substantially. Once linked unquestioningly to Great Britain, they began to develop a sense of their own identity as Americans, including a recognition of the cultural and social gulf that separated them from Britons. They started to realize that their concept of the political process differed from that held by people in the mother country. They also came to understand that their economic interests did not necessarily coincide with those of Great Britain. Colonial political leaders reached such conclusions only after a long train of events, some of them violent, altered their understanding of their relationship with the mother country. Parliamentary acts such as the Stamp Act and the Townshend Acts elicited colonial responses—both ideological and practical—that produced further responses from Britain. Tensions escalated until they climaxed in the Tea Party. From that point on, there was to be no turning back.

In the late summer of 1774, the Americans were committed to resistance but not to independence. Even so, they had started to sever the bonds of empire. During the next decade, they would forge the bonds of a new American nationality to replace those rejected Anglo-American ties.

LEGACY FOR A PEOPLE AND A NATION
The Census and Reapportionment

When in the prerevolutionary years American colonists argued that "they were not represented in" Parliament, they developed a definition of *representation* very different from the understanding traditionally accepted in Great Britain. There, numbers did not matter: the entire British population was seen as being "virtually" represented in Parliament, regardless of how many men had the vote or how many electors lived in each district. In eighteenth-century Britain, some districts had few or no voters, some had many, and some heavily populated areas could vote for no one, because Parliament had not been reapportioned for centuries.

Americans, by contrast, placed great emphasis on the importance of being represented in government by someone for whom they—or at least their better-off male neighbors—had actually voted. And that carried with it the related desire for election districts that were regularly reapportioned in accordance with the movements and increase of the population; otherwise the goal of actual representation could not be ensured. Article 1, Section 2, of the U.S. Constitution thus provides for an "actual enumeration" of the nation's residents every ten years so that "representatives and direct taxes shall be apportioned among the several States . . . according to their respective numbers." Only once, in the 1790s, did Congress levy direct taxes, so the chief effect of this clause has been its requirement for a decennial census. Each decade, from 1790 to 2000, the government has tried to count the nation's residents accurately—although, according to historians and demographers, it has often failed to achieve that goal. Even Thomas Jefferson, who as secretary of state oversaw the first census in 1790, recognized that it undercounted the population and should be adjusted upward.

The planning for the year 2000 census led to heated debates in Congress and to a Supreme Court decision outlining appropriate techniques for conducting the mandated "actual enumeration" of the American population. In other years as well (especially 1920, near the close of an era of dramatic demographic change), planning and conducting the census proved extremely contentious. The origin of such contests lies in Americans' prerevolutionary experience, for the clause the Founding Fathers incorporated into the Constitution stemmed from ideological battles of the 1760s.

Thus every ten years the nation must still wrestle with an enduring legacy of the colonial period: the need to enumerate the American people and to alter the boundaries of electoral districts according to the results.

For Further Reading, see page A-6 of the Appendix. For Web resources, go to http://college.hmco.com.

The Shawnee chief Blackfish named his new captive Sheltowee, or Big Turtle, and adopted him as his son. Blackfish's warriors had easily caught the lone hunter, who was returning with a slaughtered buffalo to an encampment of men making salt at the briny spring known as Blue Licks. The captive then persuaded his fellow frontiersmen to surrender to the Shawnees (who were allied to the British) without a fight. It was February 1778. The hunter was Daniel Boone, who less than three years earlier had moved his family from North Carolina to the western region of Virginia known as Kentucke. Both his contemporaries and some historians have wondered about Boone's allegiance during the American Revolution, for he moved to the frontier just as the war began. His encounter with the Shawnees in 1778, which can be interpreted in several ways, highlights many of the ambiguities of revolutionary-era loyalties.

The Shawnees were seeking captives to cover the death (see page 104) of their chief Cornstalk, who had been killed several months earlier while a prisoner of American militiamen in the Ohio country. Of the twenty-six men taken at the spring, about half were adopted into Shawnee families; the others—less willing to conform to Indian ways—were dispatched as prisoners to the British fort at Detroit. Boone, who assured Blackfish that in the spring he would negotiate the surrender of the women and children remaining at his home settlement of Boonesborough, watched and waited, outwardly content with his new life. In June 1778 he escaped, hurrying home to warn the Kentuckians of impending attack.

When Blackfish's Shawnees and their British allies appeared outside the Boonesborough stockade in mid-September, Boone proved amenable to negotiations. Although the settlers adamantly refused to move back across the mountains, fragmentary evidence suggests that they agreed to swear allegiance to the British in order to avert a bloody battle. But the discussions dissolved into a melee and the Indians then futilely

A statue of George III standing in the Bowling Green in New York City was one of the first casualties of the American Revolution, as colonists marked the adoption of the Declaration of Independence by pulling it down. Much of the metal was melted to make bullets, but in the twentieth century the head—largely intact—was unearthed in Connecticut. (Lafayette College Art Collection, Easton, Pennsylvania)

6

A Revolution, Indeed 1774–1783

besieged the fort for a week before withdrawing. With that threat gone, Boone was charged with treason and court-martialed by Kentucky militia. Although he was cleared, questions about the incident at Blue Licks and its aftermath haunted him for the rest of his life.

Where did Daniel Boone's loyalties lie? To the British? to the Americans? to other Kentuckians? His actions could be viewed in all three lights. Had he betrayed the settlers to Shawnees and sought to establish British authority in Kentucky? Had he—as he later claimed—twice deceived the Shawnees? Or had he rather made the survival of the fragile settlements his highest priority? Kentucky was a borderland—a region where British, Indians, and various groups of American settlers all vied for control. Boone and other residents of the Appalachian backcountry did not always face clear-cut choices as they struggled to establish themselves securely under such precarious circumstances.

Daniel Boone was not the only American of uncertain or shifting allegiance in the 1770s. As a civil war that affected much of North America east of the Mississippi River, the American Revolution uprooted thousands of families, disrupted the economy, reshaped society by forcing many colonists into permanent exile, led Americans to develop new conceptions of politics, and created a nation from thirteen separate colonies. Much more than a series of clashes between the British and patriot armies, it marked a significant turning point in Americans' collective history.

The struggle for independence required revolutionary leaders to accomplish three separate but closely related tasks. The first was political and ideological: transforming a consensus favoring loyal resistance into a coalition supporting independence. Pursuing a variety of measures (ranging from persuasion to coercion) to enlist all European Americans in the patriot cause, the colonies' elected leaders also tried to ensure the neutrality of Indians and slaves in the impending conflict.

The second task involved foreign relations. To win independence, patriot leaders knew they needed international recognition and aid, particularly from France. Thus they dispatched to Paris the most experienced American diplomat, Benjamin Franklin, who had served for years as a colonial agent in London. Franklin skillfully negotiated the Franco-American alliance of 1778, which was to prove crucial to winning independence.

Only the third task directly involved the British. George Washington, commander-in-chief of the American army, soon recognized that his primary goal should be not to win battles but to avoid losing them decisively. The outcome of any one battle was less important than ensuring that his army survived to fight another day. Consequently, the story of the Revolutionary War reveals British action and American reaction, British attacks and American defenses and withdrawals. The American war effort was aided by the failure of British military planners to analyze accurately the problem confronting them. Until it was too late, they treated the war against the colonists as they treated wars against other Europeans: they concentrated on winning battles and did not consider the difficulties of achieving their main goal, retaining the colonies' allegiance. In the end, the Americans' triumph owed more to their own endurance and to Britain's mistakes than to their military prowess. ■

Government by Congress and Committee

 When the fifty-five delegates to the First Continental Congress convened in Philadelphia in September 1774, they knew that any measures they adopted were likely to enjoy support among many of their fellow countrymen and countrywomen. That summer, open meetings held throughout the colonies had endorsed the idea of another nonimportation pact. Participants in such meetings promised (in the words of the freeholders of Johnston County, North Carolina) to "strictly adhere to, and abide by, such Regulations and Restrictions as the Members of the said General Congress shall agree to and judge most convenient." Committees of correspondence publicized these meetings so effectively that Americans everywhere knew about them. Most of the congressional delegates were selected by extralegal provincial conventions whose members were chosen at local gatherings, since governors had forbidden regular assemblies to conduct formal elections. Thus the very act of designating delegates to attend the Congress involved Americans in open defiance of British authority.

The colonies' leading political figures—most of them lawyers, merchants, and planters representing every colony but Georgia—attended the Philadelphia Congress. The Massachusetts delegation included both Samuel Adams, the experienced organizer of Boston resistance, and

First Continental Congress

IMPORTANT EVENTS

1774 First Continental Congress meets in
Philadelphia, adopts Declaration of
Rights and Grievances
Continental Association implements
economic boycott of Britain; committees of observation established to
oversee boycott

1774–75 Provincial conventions replace collapsing colonial governments

1775 Battles of Lexington and Concord; first
shots of war fired
Second Continental Congress begins
Dunmore's proclamation offers freedom
to patriots' slaves who join British
forces

1776 Paine publishes *Common Sense*, advocating
independence

British evacuate Boston
Declaration of Independence adopted
New York City falls to British

1777 British take Philadelphia Burgoyne
surrenders at Saratoga

1778 French alliance brings vital assistance to
the United States British evacuate
Philadelphia

1779 Sullivan expedition destroys Iroquois
villages

1780 British take Charleston

1781 Cornwallis surrenders at Yorktown

1782 Peace negotiations begin

1783 Treaty of Paris signed, granting
independence to the United States

---

his younger cousin John, an ambitious lawyer. Among others, New York sent John Jay, a talented young attorney. From Pennsylvania came the conservative Joseph Galloway and his long-time rival, John Dickinson. Virginia elected Richard Henry Lee and Patrick Henry, both noted for their patriotic zeal, as well as George Washington. Most of these men had never met, but in the weeks, months, and years that followed they became the chief architects of the new nation.

The congressmen faced three tasks when they convened at Carpenters Hall on September 5, 1774. The first two were explicit: defining American grievances and developing a plan for resistance. The third—articulating their constitutional relationship with Great Britain—was less clear-cut and proved troublesome. The most radical congressmen, like Lee of Virginia, argued that colonists owed allegiance only to George III and that Parliament was nothing more than a local legislature for Great Britain with no authority over the colonies. The conservatives—Joseph Galloway and his allies—proposed a formal plan of union that would have required Parliament and a new American legislature to consent jointly to all laws pertaining to the colonies. After heated debate, delegates narrowly rejected Galloway's proposal, but they were not prepared to embrace the radicals' position either.

Finally, they accepted a compromise position worked out by John Adams. The crucial clause that Adams drafted in the Congress's Declaration of Rights and Grievances read in part: "From the necessity of the case, and a regard to the mutual interest of both countries, we cheerfully consent to the operation of such acts of the British parliament, as are bona fide, restrained to the regulation of our external commerce." Notice the key phrases. "From the necessity of the case" declared that Americans would obey Parliament only because they thought that doing so was in the best interest of both countries. "Bona fide, restrained to the regulation of our external commerce" made it clear to Lord North that they would continue to resist taxes in disguise, like the Townshend duties. Most striking of all was that such language—which only a few years before would have been regarded as irredeemably extreme—could be presented and accepted as a compromise in the fall of 1774. The Americans had come a long way since their first hesitant protests against the Sugar Act ten years earlier.

Declaration of Rights and Grievances

With the constitutional issue resolved, the delegates readily agreed on the laws they wanted repealed (notably the Coercive Acts) and decided to implement an economic boycott while petitioning the king for

In 1775 a British cartoonist demonstrated his contempt for the pronouncements of the Continental Congress by setting his satire in a privy, or "necessary house," and showing a politician who has used a torn congressional resolution as toilet paper. The person at right is poring over a political pamphlet while portraits of John Wilkes and a man who has been tarred and feathered decorate the walls.   (Library of Congress)

relief. They adopted the Continental Association, which called for nonimportation of British goods (effective December 1, 1774), nonconsumption of British products (effective March 1, 1775), and nonexportation of American goods to Britain and the British West Indies (effective September 10, 1775, so that southern planters could market their 1774 tobacco crop, which had to be dried and cured before sale).

To enforce the Continental Association, Congress recommended the election of committees of observation and inspection in every Ameri-

Committees of Observation

can locality. By specifying that committee members be chosen by all persons qualified to vote for members of the lower house of the colonial legislatures, Congress guaranteed the committees a broad popular base. In some places the committeemen were former local officeholders; in other towns they were men who had never before held office. Everywhere, these committeemen—perhaps seven to eight thousand of them in the colonies as a whole—became the local leaders of American resistance.

Such committees were officially charged only with overseeing implementation of the boycott, but over the next six months they became de facto governments. They examined merchants' records and published the names of those who continued to import British goods. They also promoted home manufactures, encouraging Americans to adopt simple modes of dress and behavior to symbolize their commitment to liberty and virtuous conduct. Since expensive leisure-time activities were believed to reflect vice and corruption, Congress urged Americans to forgo dancing, gambling, horseracing, cockfighting, and other forms of "extravagance and dissipation." Some committees extracted apologies from people caught gambling, partying, or racing, prohibited the slaughter of lambs (so that sheep could grow up to produce wool), and offered prizes for the best locally made cloth.

Thus the committees gradually extended their authority over many aspects of American life. They attempted to identify opponents of American resistance, developing elaborate spy networks, circulating copies of the Continental Association for signatures, and investigating reports of dissident remarks and activities. Suspected dissenters were first urged to support the colonial cause; if they failed to do so, the committees had them watched, restricted their movements, or tried to force them to leave the area. People engaging in casual political exchanges with friends one day could find themselves charged with "treasonable conversation" the next. One Massachusetts man, for example, was called before his local committee for maligning the Congress as "a Pack or Parcell of Fools" that was "as tyrannical as Lord North and ought to be opposed & resisted." When he refused to recant, the committee put him under surveillance.

Those who dissented more openly received harsher treatment, as the experiences of the Reverend John Agnew of Virginia demonstrate. Agnew, an Anglican, insisted on warning his congregation of "the danger and sin of rebellion." He rejected the committee's summons and was thereafter ostracized by its order. Millers would not grind his corn, and doctors would not treat his sick wife and children. The committee tried to intimidate him by sending armed men to his church to beat drums and drill during services. When that failed, patriots nailed shut the church's doors and windows. Finally Agnew and his oldest son fled, but the persecution of his wife and younger children continued. She was, she later recalled, "daily insulted and robbed . . . [and] searched under various pretense."

While the committees of observation were expanding their power during the winter and early spring of 1775, the regular colonial governments were collapsing. Only a few legislatures continued to meet without encountering patriot challenges to their authority. In most colonies, popularly elected provincial conventions took over the task of running the government, sometimes entirely replacing the legislatures and at other times holding concurrent sessions. In late 1774 and early 1775, these conventions approved the Continental Association, elected delegates to the Second Continental Congress (scheduled for May), organized militia units, and gathered arms and ammunition. Unable to stem the tide of resistance, the British-appointed governors and councils watched helplessly as their authority crumbled.

Provincial Conventions

The frustrating experience of Governor Josiah Martin of North Carolina is a case in point. After a provincial convention was called to meet at New Bern on April 4, 1775—the same day the legislature was to convene—Martin asked all citizens to "renounce disclaim and discourage all such meetings cabals and illegal proceedings . . . which can only tend to introduce disorder and anarchy." When the convention met at New Bern, its membership proved to be virtually identical to that of the colonial legislature. The delegates proceeded to act alternately in both capacities and even passed some joint resolves. Continuing the farce, the exasperated Martin delivered a speech to the assembly denouncing the convention. Three days later, Martin wrote to officials in London, admitting that his government was "absolutely prostrate, impotent, and that nothing but the shadow of it is left."

Royal officials in other colonies suffered similar humiliations. Courts were prevented from holding sessions; taxes were paid to the conventions' agents rather than to provincial tax collectors; sheriffs' powers were challenged; and militiamen would muster only when committees ordered. In short, during the six months preceding the battles at Lexington and Concord, independence was being won at the local level, but without formal acknowledgment and for the most part without bloodshed. Not many Americans fully realized what was happening. The vast majority still proclaimed their loyalty to Great Britain, denying that they sought to leave the empire. Among the few

who clearly recognized the trend toward independence were those who opposed it.

Choosing Sides: Loyalists, African Americans, and Indians

 The first protests against British measures in the mid-1760s won the support of most colonists. Only in the late 1760s and early 1770s did a significant number of Americans begin to question both the aims and the tactics of the resistance movement. By 1774 and 1775 such people found themselves in a difficult position. Like their more radical counterparts, most of them objected to parliamentary policies, favoring some kind of constitutional reform. Joseph Galloway, for instance, was a conservative by American standards, but his plan for restructuring the empire was too novel for Britain to accept. Nevertheless, if forced to a choice, colonists like Galloway sympathized with Great Britain rather than with an independent America. The events of the crucial year between the passage of the Coercive Acts and the outbreak of fighting in Massachusetts crystallized their thinking. Their objections to violent protest, their desire to uphold legally constituted government, and their fears of anarchy combined to make them especially sensitive to the dangers of resistance.

Some conservatives thus began to publish essays and pamphlets critical of the Congress and its allied committees. In New York City a group of Anglican clergymen publicly supported maintaining a cordial connection between Britain and America. In Pennsylvania, Joseph Galloway published *A Candid Examination of the Mutual Claims of Great Britain and the Colonies*, attacking the Continental Congress for rejecting his plan of union. In Massachusetts the young attorney Daniel Leonard, writing under the pseudonym Massachusettensis, engaged in a prolonged newspaper debate with Novanglus (John Adams). Leonard and others realized that what had begun as a dispute over the nature of American subordination to Parliament was now raising the question of whether the colonies would remain linked to Great Britain at all. "Rouse up at last from your slumber!" the Reverend Thomas Bradbury Chandler of New Jersey penned passionately. "There is a set of people among us . . . who have formed a scheme for establishing an independent government or empire in America."

Loyalists

John Singleton Copley married into a loyalist family. His father-in-law, Richard Clarke, was one of the Boston tea agents in 1773. Copley was in Italy studying art when the war began but joined his exiled wife and father-in-law in London in 1776. His sentimental portrait of the family (with himself in the background) commemorated their reunion. The only person in the painting who ever returned to America was his daughter Elizabeth *(center),* who grew up to marry a Bostonian. (Andrew W. Mellon Fund, © 1996 Board of Trustees, National Gallery of Art, Washington, D.C.)

Some colonists did heed the conservative pamphleteers' warnings. About one-fifth of the European American population remained loyal to Great Britain, firmly rejecting independence. Most loyalists had one thing in common: they had long opposed the men who became patriot leaders, though for varying reasons. British-appointed government officials; Anglican clergy everywhere and lay Anglicans in the North, where their denomination was in the minority; tenant farmers, particularly those whose landlords sided with the patriots; members of persecuted religious sects; many of the backcountry southerners who had rebelled against eastern rule in the late 1760s and early 1770s; and non-English ethnic minorities, especially Scots: all these groups feared the power wielded by those who controlled the colonial assemblies and who had shown little concern for their welfare in the past. Joined by merchants whose trade depended on imperial connections and by former officers and enlisted men from the British army who had settled in America after 1763, they formed a loyalist core that remained true to a self-conception that revolutionaries proved willing to abandon.

During the war, loyalists congregated in cities held by the British army. When those posts were evacuated at war's end, loyalists scattered to different parts of the British Empire—Britain, the West Indies, and especially Canada. In the provinces of Nova Scotia, New Brunswick, and Ontario they re-created their lives as colonists, laying the foundations of British Canada. All told, perhaps as many as 100,000 Americans preferred to leave their homeland rather than live in a nation independent of British rule.

Active revolutionaries, who accounted for about two-fifths of the population, came chiefly from the groups that had dominated colonial society, either numerically or politically. Among them were yeoman farmers, members of dominant Protestant sects (both Old and New Lights), Chesapeake gentry, merchants dealing mainly in American commodities, city artisans, elected office-holders, and people of English descent. Wives usually but not always adopted their husbands' political beliefs. Although all these patriots supported the Revolution, they pursued divergent goals within the broader coalition, as they had in the 1760s. Some sought limited political reform, others extensive political change, and still others social and economic reforms. (The ways in which their concerns interacted are discussed in Chapter 7.)

Patriots and Neutrals

Between the patriots and the loyalists, there remained in the middle perhaps two-fifths of the European American population. Some of those who tried to avoid taking sides were sincere pacifists, such as Quakers. Others opportunistically shifted their allegiance to whatever side happened to be winning at the time. Still others simply wanted to be left alone; they cared little about politics and usually obeyed whoever was in power. Such colonists also resisted British and Americans alike when the demands on them seemed too heavy—when taxes became too high, for example, or when calls for militia service came too often. Their attitude might best be summed up in the phrase "a plague on both your houses." Such people made up an especially large proportion of the population in the southern backcountry (including Boone's Kentucky), where Scots-Irish settlers had little love for either the patriot gentry or the English authorities.

To patriots, apathy or neutrality was a crime as heinous as loyalism: those who were not for them were

Barzillai Lew, a free African American born in Groton, Massachusetts, in 1743, served in the Seven Years War before enlisting with patriot troops in the American Revolution. An accomplished fifer, Lew fought at the Battle of Bunker Hill. Like other freemen in the north, he cast his lot with the revolutionaries, in contrast to southern bondspeople, who tended to favor the British. (Courtesy of Mae Theresa Bonitto)

surely against them. By the winter of 1775–1776, the Second Continental Congress was recommending that all "disaffected" persons be disarmed and arrested. State legislatures passed laws prescribing severe penalties for suspected loyalists or neutrals. Many began to require all voters (or, in some cases, all free adult men) to take oaths of allegiance; the penalty for refusal was usually banishment or extra taxes. After 1777 many states confiscated the property of banished persons, using the proceeds for the war effort.

The patriots' policies helped to ensure that their scattered and persecuted opponents could not band together to threaten the revolutionary cause. But loyalists and neutrals were not the patriots' only worry, for they also feared that Indians and slaves might join the forces arrayed against them. Early in the war, free blacks from New England enthusiastically enlisted in local patriot militias, but the revolutionaries could not assume that *enslaved* African Americans would also support the struggle for independence.

Bondspeople faced a dilemma at the beginning of the Revolution: how could they best pursue their goal of escaping slavery? Should they fight with or against their masters? African Americans made different decisions, but to most slaves, supporting the British appeared more promising. Thus news of slave conspiracies surfaced in different parts of the colonies in late 1774 and early 1775. All shared a common element: a plan to assist the British army in return for freedom. One group of slaves futilely petitioned General Thomas Gage, the commander-in-chief of British forces in Boston, promising to fight for the redcoats if he would liberate them. The most serious incident occurred in 1775 in Charleston, where Thomas Jeremiah, a free black harbor pilot, was brutally executed after being convicted of attempting to foment a slave revolt.

The Slaves' Dilemma

Although the Caribbean islands too had protested British taxation in the 1760s (see Map 5.3 on page 129), sugar planters in the British West Indies were more cautious in opposing parliamentary policies than were residents of the mainland. On most of the Caribbean islands, slaves outnumbered their masters by six or seven to one. With the ever-present threat of slave revolt or foreign attack hanging over their heads, planters could not afford to risk opposing Britain, their chief protector. The Jamaica assembly agreed with the mainland colonial legislatures that citizens should not be bound by laws to which they had not consented. Nevertheless, its members assured the king in 1774 that "it cannot be supposed, that we now intend, or ever could have intended Resistance to Great Britain." They cited as reasons Jamaica's "weak and feeble" condition, "its very small number of white inhabitants, and . . . the incumbrance of more than Two hundred thousand Slaves."

Slavery affected politics on the mainland as well. In New England, with few resident slaves, revolutionary fervor reached a peak. In Virginia and Maryland, where free people constituted a safe majority, the potential for slave revolts raised occasional but not disabling fears. By contrast, South Carolina and Georgia, where slaves composed more than half of the population, were no-

Slavery and Revolutionary Fervor

ticeably less enthusiastic about resistance. Georgia sent no delegates to the First Continental Congress and reminded its representatives at the second one to consider its circumstances, "with our blacks and tories [loyalists] within us," when voting on the question of independence.

The slaveowners' worst fears were realized in November 1775, when Lord Dunmore, the governor of Virginia, offered to free any slaves and indentured servants who would leave their patriot masters to join the British forces. Dunmore hoped to use African Americans in his fight against the revolutionaries and to disrupt the economy by depriving planters of their labor force. But at most only two thousand African Americans rallied to the British standard, and many of them perished in a smallpox epidemic. Even so, Dunmore's proclamation led Congress in January 1776 to modify an earlier policy that had prohibited the enlistment of African Americans in the regular American army.

Although slaves did not pose a serious threat to the revolutionary cause in its early years, the patriots turned rumors of slave uprisings to their own advantage. In South Carolina resistance leaders argued that unity under the Continental Association would protect masters from their slaves at a time when royal government was unable to muster adequate defense forces. Undoubtedly many wavering Carolinians were drawn into the revolutionary camp by fear that an overt division among the colony's free people would encourage rebellion among the bondspeople.

Similarly, the threat of Indian attacks helped persuade some reluctant westerners to support the struggle against Great Britain. In the years since the Proclamation of 1763, British officials had won the Indians' trust by attempting to protect them from land-hungry European Americans. The British-appointed superintendents of Indian affairs, John Stuart in the South and Sir William Johnson in the North, lived among and understood the Indians. In 1768 Stuart and Johnson negotiated separate agreements modifying the proclamation line and trying to draw realistic, defensible boundaries between tribal holdings and European American settlements. The treaties supposedly established permanent western borders for the colonies. But just a few years later, in 1770 and 1773, the British pushed the southern boundary even farther west to accommodate the demands of settlers in western Georgia and Kentucky.

By 1775 many Indian groups were provoked beyond endurance by such aggressive pressure on their lands. Bitterness, misunderstanding, and occasional

Indians' Grievances

bloody encounters characterized relationships on the frontier. Such grievances and the tribes' confidence in Stuart and Johnson predisposed most Indians toward an alliance with Great Britain. Even so, the latter hesitated to make full and immediate use of these potential allies. The superintendents knew that neither the Indians' style of fighting nor their war aims would necessarily be compatible with those of the British. Accordingly, Stuart and Guy Johnson (who became northern superintendent following his uncle's death) at first sought from native peoples only a promise of neutrality. The superintendents even helped to avert a general Indian uprising in the summer of 1774 by preventing the Shawnees from recruiting allies for attacks on Kentucky villages. Lord Dunmore's War, between the Shawnees and the Virginia militia, ended with Kentucky being opened to European American settlers such as Daniel Boone and his associates, but with hunting and fishing rights still reserved to the Shawnees.

Recognizing that their standing with native peoples was poor, the patriots also sought the Indians' neutrality. In 1775 the Second Continental Congress sent a general message to Indian communities describing the war as "a family quarrel between us and Old England" and requesting that they "not join on either side" since "you Indians are not concerned in it." A group of Cherokees led by Chief Dragging Canoe nevertheless decided that the "family quarrel" would allow them to settle some old scores. They attacked settlements along the western borders of the Carolinas and Virginia in the summer of 1776. But a militia campaign destroyed many of their towns, along with crops and large quantities of supplies. Dragging Canoe and his diehard followers fled to the west, establishing new outposts; the rest of the Cherokees agreed to a treaty that ceded still more of their land.

Bands of Shawnees and Cherokees continued to attack frontier settlements in Kentucky and elsewhere throughout the war, but dissent in their own ranks crippled their efforts.

Indians During the Revolution

The British victory over France in 1763 had destroyed the Indian nations' most effective means of maintaining their independence: their ability to play European powers off against one another. Successful strategies were difficult to envision under these new circumstances, and Indian leaders could no longer concur on a unified course of action. Communities split asunder as older and younger men, or civil and

In 1776 the American artist Benjamin West—based in London after the mid-1760s—painted Colonel Guy Johnson, the superintendant of Indian affairs for the northern district, while he was in London for consultations with British officials. In the background is the Iroquois chief Karonghyontye, also known as Captain David Hill.
(Andrew W. Mellon Collection, © 1996 Board of Trustees, National Gallery of Art, Washington, D.C.)

war leaders, disagreed vehemently over what policy to adopt. Only a few communities (among them the Stockbridge Indians of New England and the Oneidas in New York) unwaveringly supported the American revolt; most other native villages either tried to remain neutral or at least partly aligned themselves with the British. Warfare between settlers and Indian bands allied with the British persisted on the frontier long after fighting between the main armies had ceased, and even after the signing of the peace treaty.

Although patriots could never completely ignore the threats posed by loyalists, neutrals, slaves, and Indians, only rarely did fear of these groups seriously hamper the revolutionary movement. Occasionally frontier militiamen refused to turn out for duty on the seacoast because they feared Indians would attack in their absence. Sometimes southern troops refused to serve in the North because they (and their political leaders) were unwilling to leave their regions unprotected against a slave insurrection. But the practical impossibility of a large-scale slave revolt, coupled with dissension in Indian communities and the patriots' successful campaign to disarm and neutralize loyalists, ensured that the revolutionaries would by and large remain firmly in control of the countryside as they fought for independence.

War and Independence

On January 27, 1775, Lord Dartmouth, secretary of state for America, addressed a fateful letter to General Thomas Gage in Boston. Expressing his belief that American resistance was nothing more than the response of a "rude rabble without plan," Dartmouth urged Gage to take a decisive step. Opposition could not be "very formidable," Dartmouth wrote, and even if it were, "it will surely be better that the Conflict should be brought on, upon such ground, than in a riper state of Rebellion."

Dartmouth's letter did not reach Gage until April 14. He responded by sending an expedition to confiscate provincial military supplies stockpiled at Concord. Bostonians dispatched two messengers, William Dawes and Paul Revere (later joined by Dr. Samuel Prescott), to rouse the countryside. So when the British vanguard of several hundred men approached Lexington at dawn on April 19, they found a ragtag group of seventy militiamen—about half of the adult male population of the town—drawn up before them on the common. The Americans' commander ordered his men to withdraw, realizing they could not halt the redcoats' advance. But as they began to disperse, a shot rang out; the British soldiers then fired several volleys. When they stopped, eight Americans lay dead and another ten had been wounded. The British moved on to Concord, 5 miles away.

Battles of Lexington and Concord

There the contingents of militia were larger, Concord residents having been joined by groups of men from nearby towns. An exchange of gunfire at the North Bridge spilled the first British blood of the Revolution: three men were killed and nine wounded.

Thousands of militiamen then fired from houses and from behind trees and bushes at the British forces as they retreated to Boston. By the end of the day, the redcoats had suffered 272 casualties, including 70 deaths. Only the arrival of reinforcements and the American militia's lack of coordination prevented much heavier British losses. The patriots suffered just 93 casualties.

By the evening of April 20, perhaps as many as twenty thousand American militiamen had gathered around Boston, summoned by local committees that spread the alarm across the countryside. Many did not stay long since they were needed at home for spring planting, but those who remained dug in along siege lines encircling the city. For nearly a year the two armies sat and stared at each other across those lines. The redcoats attacked their besiegers only once, on June 17, when they drove the Americans from trenches atop Breed's Hill in Charlestown. In that misnamed Battle of Bunker Hill, the British incurred their greatest losses of the entire war: over 800 wounded and 228 killed. The Americans, though forced to abandon their position, lost less than half that number.

First Year of War

During the same eleven-month period, patriots captured Fort Ticonderoga, a British fort on Lake Champlain, acquiring much-needed cannon. Trying to bring Canada into the war on the American side, they also mounted an uncoordinated northern campaign that ended in disaster at Quebec in early 1776. But the chief significance of the war's first year lay in the long lull in fighting between the main armies at Boston. The delay gave both sides a chance to regroup, organize, and plan their strategies.

Lord North and his new American secretary, Lord George Germain, made three central assumptions about the war they faced. First, they concluded that patriot forces could not withstand the assaults of trained British regulars. They and their generals were convinced that the 1776 campaign would be the first and last of the war. Accordingly, they dispatched to America the largest force Great Britain had ever assembled anywhere: 370 transport ships carrying 32,000 troops and tons of supplies, accompanied by 73 naval vessels and 13,000 sailors. Such an extraordinary effort, they thought, would ensure a quick victory. Among the troops were thousands of German mercenaries (many from the German state of Hesse); eighteenth-century armies were often composed of

British Strategy

In 1775 an unknown artist painted the redcoats entering Concord. The fighting at North Bridge, which occurred just a few hours after this triumphal entry, signaled the start of open warfare between Britain and the colonies.　(Photography Courtesy of Concord Museum, Concord, Mass.)

such professional soldiers who hired out to the highest bidder.

Second, British officials and army officers treated this war as comparable to wars they had fought successfully in Europe. They adopted a conventional strategy of capturing major American cities and defeating the rebel army decisively without suffering serious casualties themselves. Third, they assumed that a clear-cut military victory would automatically bring about their goal of retaining the colonies' allegiance.

All these assumptions proved false. North and Germain, like Lord Dartmouth before them, vastly underestimated Americans' commitment to armed resistance. Battlefield defeats did not lead patriots to abandon their political aims and sue for peace. The

ministers in London also failed to recognize the significance of the American population's dispersal over an area 1,500 miles long and more than 100 miles wide. Although Great Britain would control each of the most important American ports at one time or another during the war, less than 5 percent of the population lived in those cities. Furthermore, the coast offered so many excellent harbors that essential commerce was easily rerouted. In other words, the loss of cities did little to damage the American cause, while redcoat generals repeatedly squandered their resources to capture such ports.

Most of all, British officials did not at first understand that military triumph would not necessarily lead to political victory. Securing the colonies permanently

The plight of the redcoat soldiers besieged in Boston during the fall and winter of 1775–1776 attracted the sympathies of a British cartoonist. For "Six-Pence a Day," he noted, soldiers were exposed to "Yankees, Fire and Water, Sword and Famine," while their wives and children begged for assistance at home. The artist hoped to persuade men not to enlist in the British army.   (Courtesy of the British Museum, Department of Prints and Drawings, Satires)

would require hundreds of thousands of Americans to return to their original allegiance. The conquest of America was thus a far more complicated task than the defeat of France twelve years earlier. Great Britain needed not only to overpower the patriots but also to convert them. After 1778 the ministry adopted a strategy designed to achieve that goal through the expanded use of loyalist forces and the restoration of civilian authority in occupied areas. But the new policy came too late. Britain's leaders never fully realized that they were fighting not a conventional European war but rather an entirely new kind of conflict: the first modern war of national liberation.

Great Britain at least had a bureaucracy ready to supervise the war effort. The Americans had only the Second Continental Congress, originally planned as a brief gathering to consider the ministry's response to the Continental Association. Instead, the delegates who convened in Philadelphia on May 10, 1775, had to assume the man-

Second Continental Congress

tle of intercolonial government. "Such a vast Multitude of objects, civil, political, commercial and military, press and crowd upon us so fast, that we know not what to do first," John Adams wrote a close friend early in the session. Yet as the summer passed, Congress slowly organized the colonies for war. It authorized the printing of money with which to purchase necessary goods, established a committee to supervise relations with foreign countries, and took steps to strengthen the militia. Most important, it created the Continental Army and appointed its generals.

Until Congress met, the Massachusetts provincial congress had taken responsibility for organizing the militiamen encamped at Boston. But that army, composed of men from all over New England, constituted a heavy drain on limited local resources. Consequently, Massachusetts asked the Continental Congress to assume the task of directing the army. As a first step, Congress had to choose a commander-in-chief, and many delegates recognized the importance of naming someone who was not a New Englander. John

Adams later recalled that in mid-June he proposed the appointment of a Virginian "whose Skill and Experience as an Officer, whose independent fortune, great Talents and excellent universal Character, would command the Approbation of all America": George Washington. The Congress unanimously concurred.

Washington was no fiery radical, nor was he a reflective political thinker. He had not played a prominent role in the prerevolutionary agitation, but his devotion to the American cause was unquestioned. He was dignified, conservative, and respectable—a man of unimpeachable integrity. The younger son of a Virginia planter, Washington did not expect to inherit substantial property, planning to make his living as a surveyor. But the early death of his older brother and his marriage to the wealthy widow Martha Custis made George Washington one of the largest slaveholders in Virginia. Though unmistakably an aristocrat, he was unswervingly committed to representative government and—thanks to his service in the Seven Years War (see page 118)—he had considerable military experience. He had other desirable traits as well. His stamina was remarkable: in more than eight years of war, Washington never had a serious illness and took only one brief leave of absence. Moreover, he both looked and acted like a leader. More than six feet tall in an era when most men were five inches shorter, he displayed a stately and commanding presence. Other patriots praised his judgment, steadiness, and discretion, and even a loyalist admitted that Washington could "atone for many demerits by the extraordinary coolness and caution which distinguish his character."

George Washington: A Portrait of Leadership

Washington needed all the coolness and caution he could muster when he took command of the army outside Boston in July 1775. It took him months to impose hierarchy and discipline on the unruly troops and to bring order to the supply system. But by March 1776, when the arrival of cannon from Ticonderoga finally enabled him to put direct pressure on the redcoats in the city, the army was prepared to act. As it happened, an assault on Boston proved unnecessary. Sir William Howe, who had replaced Gage, had for some time been considering an evacuation; he wanted to transfer his troops to New York City. The patriots' new cannon decided the matter. On March 17, the British and more than a thousand of their loyalist allies abandoned Boston forever.

British Evacuation of Boston

That spring of 1776, as the British fleet left Boston for the temporary haven of Halifax, Nova Scotia, the colonies were moving inexorably toward the act the Massachusetts loyalists on board the British ships feared most: a declaration of independence. Even months after fighting began, American leaders still denied seeking a break with Great Britain. But in January 1776 there appeared a pamphlet by a man who advocated such a step.

Thomas Paine's *Common Sense* exploded on the American scene like a bombshell. Within three months of publication, it sold 120,000 copies. The author, a radical English printer who had lived in America only since 1774, called stridently for independence. Paine also challenged many

Thomas Paine's *Common Sense*

That America's patriot leaders read Thomas Paine's inflammatory *Common Sense* soon after it was published in early 1776 is indicated by this first edition, owned by George Washington himself. (Boston Athenaeum)

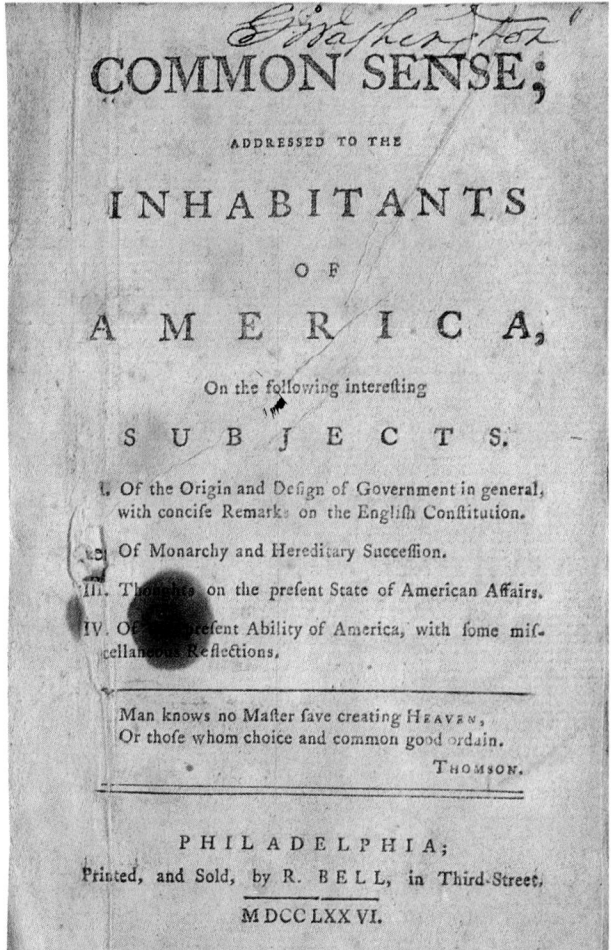

common American assumptions about government and the colonies' relationship to Britain. Rejecting the notion that a balance of monarchy, aristocracy, and democracy was necessary to preserve freedom, he advocated the establishment of a republic, a government by the people with no king or nobility. Instead of acknowledging the benefits of links to the mother country, Paine insisted that Britain had exploited the colonies unmercifully. And for the frequently heard assertion that an independent America would be weak and divided, he substituted an unlimited confidence in America's strength once freed from European control.

He expressed these striking sentiments in equally striking prose. Scorning the rational style of most other pamphleteers, Paine adopted an enraged tone, describing the king as a "royal brute," a "wretch" who only pretended concern for the colonists' welfare. His pamphlet reflected the oral culture of ordinary folk. Couched in everyday language, it relied heavily on the Bible—the only book familiar to most Americans—as a primary source of authority. No wonder the pamphlet had a wider distribution than any other political publication of its day.

There is no way of knowing how many people were converted to the cause of independence by reading *Common Sense*. But by late spring in 1776 independence had become inevitable. On May 10, the Second Continental Congress formally recommended that individual colonies "adopt such governments as shall, in the opinion of the representatives of the people, best conduce to the happiness and safety of their constituents in particular, and America in general." From that source stemmed the first state constitutions. Perceiving the trend of events, the few loyalists still connected with Congress severed their ties to that body.

Then on June 7 came confirmation of the movement toward independence. Richard Henry Lee of Virginia, seconded by John Adams of Massachusetts, introduced the crucial resolution: "that these United Colonies are, and of right ought to be, free and independent States, that they are absolved of all allegiance to the British Crown, and that all political connection between them and the State of Great Britain is, and ought to be, totally dissolved." Congress debated but did not immediately adopt Lee's resolution. Instead, it postponed a vote until early July, to allow time for consultation and public reaction. In the meantime, a five-man committee—including Thomas Jefferson, John Adams, and Benjamin Franklin—was directed to draft a declaration of independence.

The committee assigned primary responsibility for writing the declaration to Jefferson, who was well known for his apt and eloquent style. Years later John Adams recalled that Jefferson had modestly protested his selection, suggesting that Adams prepare the initial draft. The Massachusetts revolutionary recorded his frank response: "You can write ten times better than I can."

Thomas Jefferson and the Declaration of Independence

The thirty-four-year-old Thomas Jefferson, a Virginia lawyer, had been educated at the College of William and Mary and in the law offices of a prominent attorney. A member of the House of Burgesses, he had read widely in history and political theory. That broad knowledge was evident not only in the declaration but also in his draft of the Virginia state constitution, completed just a few days before his appointment to the committee. Jefferson, an intensely private man, loved his home and family deeply. This early stage of his political career was marked by his beloved wife Martha's repeated difficulties in childbearing. While he wrote and debated in Philadelphia, she suffered a miscarriage at their home, Monticello. Not until after her death in 1782, from complications following the birth of their sixth (but only third surviving) child in ten years of marriage, did Jefferson fully commit himself to public service.

The draft of the declaration was laid before Congress on June 28, 1776. The delegates officially voted for independence four days later, then debated the wording of the declaration for two more days, adopting it with some changes on July 4. Since Americans had long ago ceased to see themselves as legitimate subjects of Parliament, the Declaration of Independence concentrated on George III (see the appendix). That focus also provided an identifiable villain. The document accused the king of attempting to destroy representative government in the colonies and of oppressing Americans through the unjustified use of excessive force.

The declaration's chief long-term importance, however, did not lie in its lengthy catalogue of grievances against George III (including, in a section deleted by Congress, Jefferson's charge that the British monarchy had introduced slavery into America). It lay instead in the ringing statements of principle that have served ever since as the ideal to which Americans aspire: "We hold these truths to be self-evident: That all men are created equal; that they are endowed by their

Creator with certain unalienable rights; that among these are life, liberty and the pursuit of happiness; that, to secure these rights, governments are instituted among men, deriving their just powers from the consent of the governed; that whenever any form of government becomes destructive of these ends, it is the right of the people to alter or to abolish it, and to institute new government." These phrases have echoed down through American history like no others.

The delegates in Philadelphia who voted to accept the Declaration of Independence did not have the advantage of our two centuries of hindsight. When they adopted the declaration, they risked their necks: they were committing treason. Therefore, when they concluded the declaration with the assertion that they "mutually pledge[d] to each other our lives, our fortunes, and our sacred honor," they spoke no less than the truth. The real struggle still lay before them, and not many of them had Thomas Paine's boundless confidence in success.

The Long Struggle in the North

In late June 1776, the first ships carrying Sir William Howe's troops from Halifax appeared off the coast of New York (see Map 6.1). On July 2, the day Congress voted for independence, redcoats landed on Staten Island. Washington marched his army of seventeen thousand south from Boston to defend Manhattan. Because Howe waited until more troops arrived from England before attacking, the American army was able to prepare to defend the city.

But Washington and his men, still inexperienced in fighting and maneuvering, made major mistakes, losing battles at Brooklyn Heights and on Manhattan Island. The city fell to the British, who captured nearly three thousand American soldiers. Those men spent most of the rest of the war imprisoned on British vessels anchored in New York harbor, where many died of disease.

Loss of New York

During the autumn months, Washington retreated across New Jersey, with Howe in leisurely pursuit. The British took control of most of the state, and hundreds of New Jerseyites and Pennsylvanians (among them Joseph Galloway) accepted pardons for their "treasonous" activities. Occupying troops met little opposition, and the revolutionary cause appeared to be in disarray. "These are the times that try men's souls," wrote Thomas Paine in his pamphlet *The Cri-*

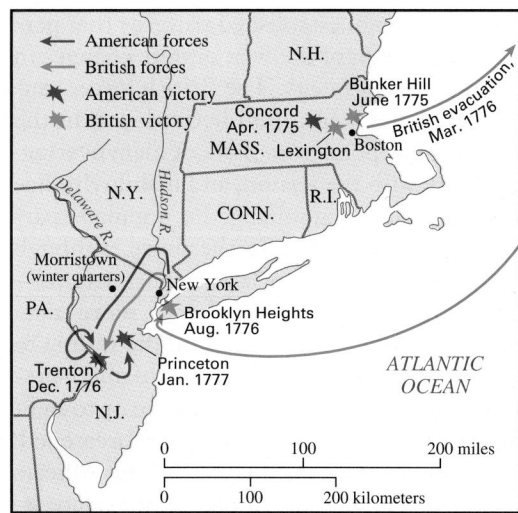

Map 6.1 The War in the North, 1775–1777
The early phase of the Revolutionary War was dominated by British troop movements in the Boston area, the redcoats' evacuation to Nova Scotia in the spring of 1776, and the subsequent British invasion of New York and New Jersey.

sis. "The summer soldier and the sunshine patriot will, in this crisis, shrink from the service of his country; . . . yet we have this consolation with us, that the harder the conflict, the more glorious the triumph."

The British let their advantage slip away as redcoats stationed in New Jersey went on a rampage of rape and plunder. Because the invading troops failed to distinguish between loyalists and patriots, families on both sides suffered losses of livestock, crops, and firewood. Redcoats looted and burned houses and desecrated churches and public buildings. The murder and rape of innocent civilians alienated potentially loyal New Jerseyites whose allegiance the British could ill afford to lose. It also spurred Washington's determination to strike back. Moving quickly, he attacked a Hessian encampment at Trenton early in the morning of December 26, while the redcoats were still reeling from their Christmas celebration. The patriots captured more than nine hundred Hessians and killed another thirty; only three Americans were wounded. A few days later, Washington attacked again at Princeton. Having gained command of the field and buoyed American spirits with the two swift victories, Washington set up winter quarters at Morristown, New Jersey.

Battles in New Jersey

The 1776 campaign established patterns that persisted throughout much of the war, despite changes in British leadership and strategy. The British forces usually outnumbered and were often better led than the Americans. But their ponderous style of maneuvering, lack of familiarity with the terrain, and inability to live off the land without antagonizing the populace partially offset those advantages. Furthermore, although Washington always seemed to lack regular troops—the Continental Army never numbered more than 18,500 men—he could usually count on the militia to join him at crucial times. American militiamen preferred not to enlist for long terms of service or to fight far from home; but when their homes were threatened, they rallied to the cause. Washington and his officers complained about the militiamen's habit of disappearing during planting or harvesting. But time and again their presence, however brief, enabled the Americans to launch an attack or counter a strategic British thrust.

As the war dragged on, the Continental Army and the militia took on decidedly different characters.

The American Army

State governments, responsible for filling military quotas, discovered that most men willing to enlist for long periods in the regular army were young, single, and footloose. Farmers with families tended to prefer short-term militia duty. As the supply of men willing to join the Continentals dwindled, recruiters in northern states turned increasingly to African Americans, both slave and free. Approximately five thousand blacks eventually served in the army, most of them winning their freedom as a result. They commonly served in racially integrated units but were assigned tasks that others shunned, such as cooking, foraging for food, and driving wagons. Also attached to the American forces were a number of women, the wives and widows of poor soldiers. Such camp followers worked as cooks, nurses, and launderers in return for rations and low wages.

At the Battle of Princeton in early 1777, American forces under George Washington cemented the victory they had won a few days earlier at Trenton. This view was painted in 1787 by James Peale, who fought in the battle. (Princeton University Library)

The presence of women, as well as militiamen who floated in and out of the American camp at irregular intervals, made for an unwieldy army that officers found difficult to manage. Yet the army's shapelessness also reflected its greatest strength: an almost unlimited reservoir of manpower and womanpower.

The officers of the Continental Army—those who enlisted for long periods or for the war's duration—developed an intense sense of pride and commitment to the revolutionary cause. The hardships they endured, the battles they fought, the difficulties they overcame all helped to forge an *esprit de corps* that outlasted the war. The realities of warfare were often dirty, messy, and corrupt, but the officers drew strength from a developing image of themselves as professionals who sacrificed personal gain for the good of the entire nation. When Benedict Arnold—an officer who fought heroically for the patriot cause early in the war—violated that virtuous self-image by defecting to the British, they made his name a metaphor for villainy. "How black, how despised, loved by none, and hated by all," wrote one patriot.

The flashy "Gentleman Johnny" Burgoyne, a playboy general as much at home at London's gaming tables as on the battlefield, planned

**Planning the
1777 Campaign**

the major British effort in 1777. A subordinate of Howe, Burgoyne spent the winter in London, where he gained the ear of Lord George Germain. Burgoyne convinced Germain that he could lead an invading force of redcoats and Indians down the Hudson River from Canada, cutting off New England from the rest of the states. He proposed to rendezvous near Albany with a similar force that would move east along the Mohawk River valley. The combined forces would then presumably link up with Sir William Howe's troops in New York City.

That Burgoyne's scheme would give "Gentleman Johnny" all the glory and relegate Howe to a supporting role did not escape Sir William's notice. While Burgoyne plotted in London, Howe prepared his own plans in New York. Joseph Galloway and other Pennsylvania loyalists persuaded Howe that Philadelphia could be taken easily and that many loyal residents would welcome his troops. Just as Burgoyne omitted Howe from his plans, so too Howe omitted Burgoyne, and officials in London failed to order them to coordinate their campaigns. The two major British armies in America would operate independently in 1777; the result would be a disaster (see Map 6.2).

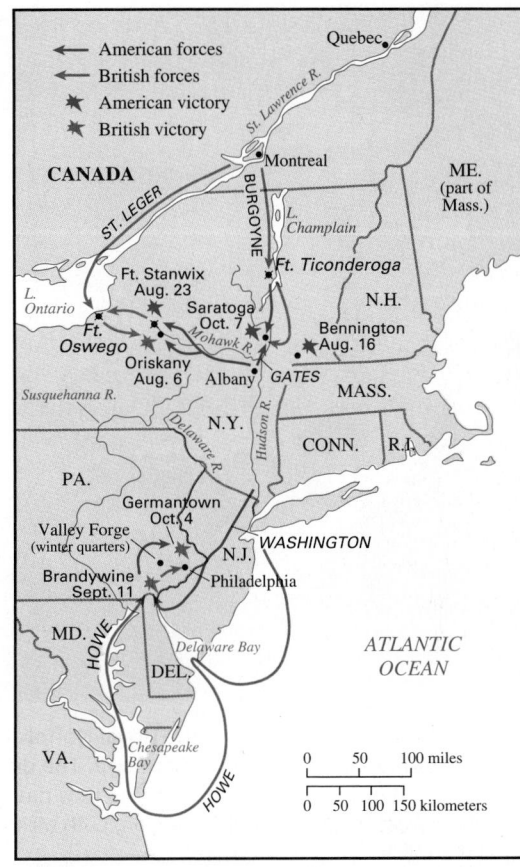

Map 6.2   Campaign of 1777   The crucial campaign of 1777 was fought on two fronts: along the upper Hudson and Mohawk River valleys, and in the vicinity of Philadelphia. The rebels won in the north; the British triumphed—at least nominally—in the south. The capture of Philadelphia, however, did the redcoats little good, and they abandoned the city the following year.

Howe captured Philadelphia, but he did so in inexplicable fashion, delaying for months before beginning the campaign, then taking six

**Howe Takes
Philadelphia**

weeks to transport his troops by sea instead of marching them overland. That maneuver cost him at least a month, debilitated his men, and depleted his supplies. Incredibly, at the end of the lengthy voyage, he ended up only 40 miles closer to Philadelphia than when he started. By the time Howe advanced on Philadelphia, Washington had had time to prepare its defenses. Twice, at Brandywine Creek and again at Germantown, the two armies clashed near the patriot capital. Although the British won both en-

This kettledrum belonged to the band of the Royal Norfolk Regiment, a British infantry unit that surrendered to the Americans at Saratoga. The drum was sent to West Point, where it has remained ever since, a symbol of the new nation's first great victory of the Revolution.   (The West Point Museum Collection, U.S. Military Academy, West Point, N.Y. Photo by Paul Warchal)

gagements, the Americans handled themselves well. The redcoats took Philadelphia in late September, but to little effect. The campaign season was nearly over; the revolutionary army had gained confidence in itself and its leaders; few welcoming loyalists had materialized; and, far to the north, Burgoyne was going down to defeat.

Burgoyne's Campaign in New York

Burgoyne and his men set out from Montreal in mid-June 1777, floating down Lake Champlain into New York in canoes and flat-bottom boats. They easily captured Fort Ticonderoga from its outnumbered and outgunned patriot defenders. Trouble began, however, when Burgoyne started an overland march. His clumsy artillery carriages and baggage wagons foundered in the heavy forests and ravines. Patriot militia felled giant trees across his path to slow his progress. Consequently, Burgoyne's troops took twenty-four days to travel 23 miles. In August the campaign suffered two sharp blows—first, when the redcoats and Indians marching east along the Mohawk River turned back after a battle at Oriskany, New York; second, when in a clash near Bennington, Vermont, American militiamen nearly wiped out eight hundred of Burgoyne's German mercenaries. Yet the general continued to dawdle, giving the Americans more than enough time to prepare for his coming. After several skirmishes with an American army commanded by General Horatio Gates, Burgoyne was surrounded near Saratoga, New York. On October 17, 1777, he surrendered his entire force of more than six thousand men.

Split of the Iroquois Confederacy

The August 1777 battle at Oriskany divided the Iroquois Confederacy (see pages 66–67). In 1776 the Six Nations formally pledged to remain neutral in the Anglo-American struggle. But two influential Mohawk leaders worked tirelessly to persuade their fellow Iroquois to join the British. Both Mary Brant, a powerful tribal matron and the widow of the Indian superintendent Sir William Johnson, and her younger brother Joseph, a renowned warrior, strongly believed that the

Six Nations should ally themselves with the British in order to prevent American encroachment on their lands. The Brants won over to the British the Senecas, Cayugas, and Mohawks, all of whom contributed warriors to the 1777 expedition. But the Oneidas—who had been converted to Christianity by Protestant missionaries—preferred the American side and brought the Tuscaroras with them. The Onondagas split into three factions, one on each side and one supporting neutrality. At Oriskany, some Oneidas and Tuscaroras joined patriot militiamen in fighting their Iroquois brethren, shattering a league of friendship that had survived for over three hundred years.

The collapse of Iroquois unity and the confederacy's abandonment of neutrality had significant consequences. In 1778 Iroquois warriors allied with the British raided frontier villages in Pennsylvania and New York. To retaliate, the Americans the following summer dispatched an expedition under General John Sullivan to burn Iroquois crops, orchards, and settlements. The resulting devastation forced many bands to leave their ancestral homeland to seek food and shelter north of the Great Lakes during the winter of 1779–1780. A large number of Iroquois people never returned to New York but settled permanently in British Canada.

Burgoyne's surrender at Saratoga brought joy to patriots, discouragement to loyalists and Britons. In exile in London, Thomas Hutchinson wrote of "universal dejection" among loyalists there. "Everybody in a gloom," he commented; "most of us expect to lay our bones here." The disaster prompted Lord North to authorize a peace commission to offer the Americans what they had requested in the Declaration of Rights and Grievances in 1774—in effect, a return to the imperial system of 1763. That proposal came far too late: the patriots rejected the overture, and the peace commission sailed back to England empty-handed in mid-1778.

Most important, the American victory at Saratoga drew France formally into the conflict. Ever since 1763, the French had sought to avenge their defeat in the Seven Years War, and the American Revolution gave them that opportunity. Even before Benjamin Franklin arrived in Paris in late 1776, France covertly supplied the revolutionaries with military necessities. Indeed, 90 percent of the gunpowder used by the Americans during the war's first two years came from France.

Benjamin Franklin worked tirelessly to strengthen ties between the two nations. He deliberately assumed

Joseph Brant, the Iroquois leader who helped to persuade the Mohawks, Senecas, and Cayugas to support the British in the latter stages of the Revolution, as painted by Charles Willson Peale in 1797.   (Independence National Historic Park Collection)

Franco-American Alliance of 1778

a plain style of dress that made him stand out amid the luxury of the court of King Louis XVI. Presenting himself as a representative of American simplicity, Franklin played on the French image of Americans as virtuous yeomen. His efforts culminated in 1778 when the countries signed two treaties. In the Treaty of Amity and Commerce, France recognized American independence, establishing trade ties with the new nation. In the Treaty of Alliance, France and the United States promised—assuming that France would go to war with Britain, which it soon did—that neither would negotiate peace with the enemy without consulting the other. France also formally abandoned any claim to Canada and to North American territory east of the Mississippi River. In the years that followed, the most visible symbol of Franco-American cooperation was the Marquis de Lafayette, a young nobleman who volunteered for service with George Washington in 1777 and fought with American forces until the conflict ended.

The French alliance had two major benefits for the patriot cause. First, France began to aid the Americans

A British cartoon published in 1780. Even after Spain and the Netherlands had joined
France in supporting the Americans' quest for independence, this artist had confidence in
Britain's ability to outweigh the alliance in "The Ballance of Power."   (Print Collection,
Miriam and Ira D. Wallach Division of Art, Prints and Photographs. The New York Public
Library, Astor, Lenox, and Tilden Foundations)

openly, sending troops and naval vessels in addition to arms, ammunition, clothing, and blankets. Second, Great Britain could no longer focus solely on the American mainland, for it had to fight France in the Caribbean and elsewhere. Spain's entry into the war in 1779 as an ally of France (but not of the United States) further magnified Britain's problems, for the Revolution then became a global war. The French aided the Americans throughout the conflict, but in its last years the assistance was particularly vital.

The Long Struggle in the South

In the aftermath of the Saratoga disaster, Lord George Germain and British military officials reassessed their strategy. Maneuvering in the North had done them little good; perhaps shifting the field of battle southward would bring success. Many loyalist exiles in London encouraged this line of thinking. They argued that loyal southerners would welcome the redcoat army as liberators and that the region could serve as a base for attacking the North, once it had been pacified and returned to friendly civilian control.

Sir Henry Clinton, who replaced Howe, therefore oversaw the regrouping of British forces in America.

British Victories in South Carolina

He ordered the evacuation of Philadelphia in June 1778 and then dispatched a small expedition to Georgia at the end of the year. When Savannah and then Augusta fell easily into British hands, Clinton became convinced that a southern strategy would succeed. In late 1779 he sailed down the coast from New York to besiege Charleston, the most important city in the South (see Map 6.3). The Americans held out for months, but on May 12, 1780, General Benjamin Lincoln surrendered the entire southern army—5,500 men—to the invaders. In the following weeks, the redcoats spread through South Carolina, establishing garrisons at key points in the interior. Hundreds of South Carolinians renounced allegiance to the United States, proclaiming their renewed loyalty to the Crown. Clinton organized loyalist regiments, and the process of pacification began.

Yet the triumph was less complete than it appeared. The success of the southern campaign depended on control of the seas, for the British armies were so widely dispersed and travel by land was so difficult that only through British naval vessels could the armies coordinate their efforts. For the moment, the Royal Navy safely dominated the American coastline, but French naval power posed a threat to the entire southern enterprise. Moreover, the redcoats never managed to establish full control of the areas they seized. Patriot bands operated freely throughout the state, and loyalists could not be guaranteed protection against their enemies. Last but not least, the fall of Charleston failed to dishearten the patriots; instead, it spurred them to greater exertions. As one Marylander declared confidently, "The Fate of America is not to be decided by the Loss of a Town or Two." Patriot women in four states formed the Ladies Association, which collected money to purchase shirts for needy soldiers. Recruiting efforts were stepped up.

Nevertheless, the war in South Carolina went badly for the patriots throughout most of 1780. At Camden in August, forces under Lord Cornwallis, the new British commander in the South, crushingly defeated a reorganized southern army led by Horatio Gates. Hundreds, even thousands, of enslaved African Americans joined the redcoats, seeking freedom on the basis of Lord Dunmore's 1775 proclamation. Running away from their patriot masters individually and as families, they seriously disrupted planting and harvesting in the Carolinas in 1780 and 1781. More than fifty-five thousand slaves were lost to their owners as a result of the war. Not all of them joined the British or won their freedom if they did, but their flight had exactly the effect Dunmore sought. Many served the British well as scouts, guides, and laborers.

After the Camden defeat, Washington (who had to remain in the North to contain the British army occupying New York) appointed General Nathanael Greene to command the southern campaign. Appalled by the conditions in South Carolina, Greene told a friend that "the word difficulty when applied to the

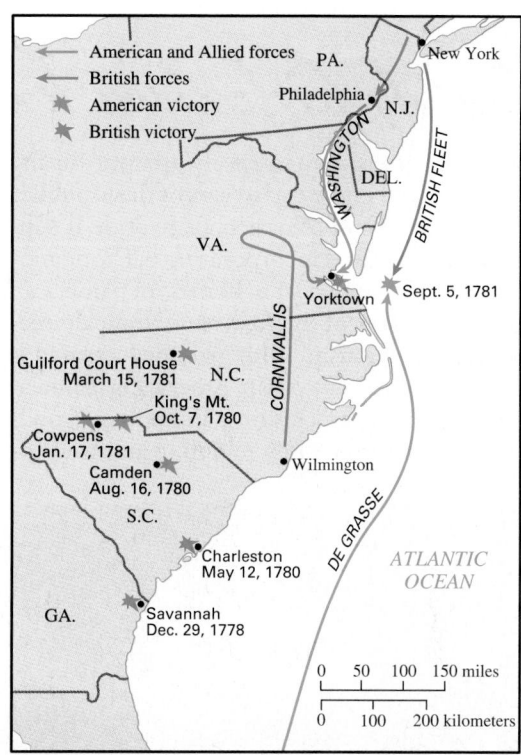

Map 6.3 The War in the South   The southern war—after the British invasion of Georgia in late 1778—was characterized by a series of British thrusts into the interior, leading to battles with American defenders in both North and South Carolina. Finally, after promising beginnings, Cornwallis's foray into Virginia ended with disaster at Yorktown in October 1781.

Greene and the Southern Campaign

state of things here . . . is almost without meaning, it falls so far short" of reality. His troops needed clothing, blankets, and food, but "a great part of this country is already laid waste and in the utmost danger of becoming a desert." Incessant guerrilla warfare had, he commented, "so corrupted the principles of the people that they think of nothing but plundering one another."

In such dire circumstances, Greene had to move cautiously. Adopting a conciliatory policy toward loyalists and neutrals, he persuaded the governor of South Carolina to pardon those who had fought for the British if they would now join the patriot militia. He also ordered his troops to treat captives fairly and not to loot loyalist property. Recognizing that the patriots needed to convince a war-weary populace that they could bring stability to the region, he helped the

How do historians know...

that many Americans were intensely patriotic during the Revolution and in the early years of the republic?

Evidence of a wave of nationalistic pride is supplied by the many items incorporating patriotic motifs that soon decorated the homes of American citizens. The artisans of the new nation quickly recognized that "patriotism sold," so they created a wide variety of objects to satisfy Americans' demand for furniture, wallpaper, curtains, and pottery goods displaying such themes. Only middling and well-to-do Americans could afford to buy such items, but a less-well-off American woman could produce some of these goods for herself. We do not know who made this eagle hooked rug, but a poor woman with just a few moments to spare each day could well have labored for months to display her allegiance to the newly independent United States in this fashion. (Photo: New York State Historical Association, Cooperstown)

shattered provincial congresses of Georgia and South Carolina to reestablish civilian authority in the interior—a goal the British were never able to accomplish. Since he had so few regulars (only sixteen hundred when he took command), Greene had to rely on western volunteers and could not afford to have frontier militia companies occupied in defending their homes from Indian attack. He accordingly pursued diplomacy aimed at keeping the Indians out of the war. Although royal officials cooperating with the redcoat invaders initially won some Indian allies, Greene's careful maneuvers eventually proved successful. By war's end, only the Creeks remained allied with Great Britain.

Even before Greene took command of the southern army in December 1780, the tide had begun to turn. In October, at King's Mountain, a force from the settlements west of the Appalachians defeated a large party of redcoats and loyalists. Then in January 1781 Greene's trusted aide Daniel Morgan brilliantly routed the crack British regiment Tarleton's Legion at Cowpens. Greene himself confronted the main body of British troops under Lord Cornwallis at Guilford Court House, North Carolina, in March. Although

Cornwallis controlled the field at the end of the day, most of his army had been destroyed. He had to retreat to Wilmington, on the coast, to receive supplies and fresh troops from New York by sea. Meanwhile, Greene returned to South Carolina, where, in a series of swift strikes, he forced the redcoats to abandon their interior posts and retire to Charleston.

Yorktown and the Treaty of Paris

 Lord Cornwallis headed north into Virginia, where he joined forces with a detachment of redcoats commanded by the American traitor Benedict Arnold. Instead of acting decisively with his new army of 7,200 men, Cornwallis withdrew to the peninsula between the York and James Rivers, where he fortified Yorktown and awaited more supplies and reinforcements. Seizing the opportunity, Washington quickly moved more than 7,000 troops south from New York City. When a French fleet under the Comte de Grasse arrived from the Caribbean in time to defeat the Royal Navy vessels sent to relieve Cornwallis, the British general was trapped (see Map 6.3). On October 19, 1781, Cornwallis surrendered to the combined American and French forces.

When news of the surrender reached London, Lord North's ministry fell. Parliament voted to cease offensive operations in America, authorizing peace negotiations. Washington returned with the main army to the environs of New York, where his underpaid—and, they thought, underappreciated—officers grew restive. In March 1783 they threatened to mutiny unless Congress guaranteed them adequate compensation for their services. Washington, warned in advance of the so-called Newburgh Conspiracy, met the challenge brilliantly. Summoning his officers, he defused the crisis with a well-reasoned but emotional speech drawing on their patriotism. How could they, he asked, "open the flood Gates of Civil discord, and deluge our rising Empire in Blood"? When at one point he fumbled for glasses, remarking in passing that "I have grown gray in your service and now find myself growing blind," eyewitnesses reported that many of the rebellious officers began to cry. At the end of the year, he stood before Congress and formally resigned his commission as commander-in-chief. Through such actions at the end of the conflict, Washington established an enduring precedent: civilian control of the American military.

The war had been won, but at terrible cost. More than twenty-five thousand American men died in the

The Cost of Victory

war, only about one-quarter of them from wounds suffered in battle. The rest were declared missing in action or died of disease or as prisoners of war. In the South, years of guerrilla warfare and the loss of thousands of runaway slaves shattered the economy. Indebtedness soared, and local governments were crippled for lack of funds, since few people could afford to pay their taxes. In the 1780s in Charles County, Maryland, for example, men commonly refused to serve in elective or appointive office because their personal estates would become liable for any taxes or fines they were unable to collect. Many of the county's formerly wealthy planters descended into insolvency, and in the 1790s a traveler observed that "the country . . . wears a most dreary aspect," remarking on the "old dilapidated mansions" that had once housed well-to-do slaveowners.

Yet Charles County residents and Americans in general "all rejoiced" when they learned of the signing

Treaty of Paris

of the preliminary peace treaty at Paris in November 1782. The American diplomats—Benjamin Franklin, John Jay, and John Adams—ignored their instructions from Congress to be guided by France and instead negotiated directly with Great Britain. Their instincts were sound: the French government was more an enemy to Britain than a friend to the United States. In fact, French ministers worked secretly behind the scenes to try to prevent the establishment of a strong and unified government in America. Spain's desire to lay claim to the region between the Appalachian Mountains and the Mississippi River further complicated the negotiations. But the American delegates proved adept at power politics, achieving their main goal: independence as a united nation. Weary of war, the new British ministry, headed by Lord Shelburne (formerly an outspoken critic of Lord North's American policies), made numerous concessions—so many, in fact, that Parliament ousted the ministry shortly after peace terms were approved.

The treaty, signed formally on September 3, 1783, granted the Americans unconditional independence. Generous boundaries delineated the new nation: to the north, approximately the present-day boundary with Canada; to the south, the 31st parallel (about the modern northern border of Florida); to the west, the Mississippi River. Florida, which Britain had acquired

Measles, typhus, diphtheria, dysentery, and other diseases ravaged military encampments, so medicine chests like the one shown here were essential equipment for the army. Doctors used crude remedies that often did more harm than good, for little was known about the causes of such afflictions. Smallpox was one of the few epidemics that eighteenth-century doctors could combat: inoculation was known to be an effective preventive measure as early as the 1720s.   (The West Point Museum Collection, U.S. Military Academy, West Point, N.Y. Photo by Josh Nefsky)

in 1763, reverted to Spain. The Americans also gained unlimited fishing rights off Newfoundland. In ceding so much land to the United States, Great Britain ignored the territorial rights of its Indian allies, sacrificing their interests to the demands of European politics. British diplomats also poorly served loyalists and British merchants. The treaty's ambiguously worded clauses pertaining to the payment of prewar debts and the postwar treatment of loyalists caused trouble for years to come, proving impossible to enforce.

Summary

The long war finally over, the victorious Americans could look back on their achievement with satisfaction and awe. Having unified the disparate mainland colonies, they had claimed their place in the family of nations and forged a successful alliance with France. With an inexperienced ragtag army, they had taken on the greatest military power in the world—and eight years later they had won. They accomplished their goal more through persistence and commitment than through brilliance on the battlefield. Actual victories were few, but their army always survived defeats and standoffs to fight again. Ultimately, the Americans simply wore their enemy down.

In winning the war, the Americans reshaped the physical and mental landscapes in which they lived. They abandoned the British identity once so important to them, excluding from their new nation all those unwilling to make a break with the mother country. In the Continental Army in particular they began the process of creating loyalty to an entity that had no prior existence—a nation they named "the United States of America." They also established a claim to most of the territory east of the Mississippi River and south of the Great Lakes, thereby greatly expanding the land potentially open to their settlements.

In achieving independence, Americans surmounted formidable challenges. But in the future they faced perhaps even greater ones: establishing stable republican governments at the state and national levels to replace the monarchy they had rejected, and ensuring their government's continued existence in a world of bitter rivalries among the major powers—Britain, France, and Spain. Those European rivalries worked to the Americans' advantage during the war, but in the decades to come they would pose significant threats to the survival of the new nation.

LEGACY FOR A PEOPLE AND A NATION
The Black Patriots' Memorial

The Black Patriots Foundation has been actively soliciting private funds to build a memorial to the approximately five thousand African Americans who fought in the revolutionary army. The National Capital Planning Commission has approved a site on the mall in Washington, D.C., and a commemorative silver dollar, authorized by Act of Congress, is being sold to raise money. A sculptor has been selected, a design chosen. The black soldiers of the Revolution "provided critical service to the founding of America," declared a foundation supporter at a Memorial Day, 1996, ceremony. Their "gallant efforts . . . have been tragically overlooked by history. It's time—past time—that we right this historical wrong by honoring their noble service with a fitting memorial."

Although historians of the American Revolution appreciate the impulse behind the campaign, many find the project ironic. A prime example of what scholars have termed "contribution history"—that is, the notion that a people's history is important primarily insofar as it has contributed to the history of the nation—the Black Patriots' Memorial would enshrine in bronze the story of only approximately 10 percent of the African Americans who fought in the Revolutionary War. The other 90 percent aligned themselves with the British.

And with good reason. Enslaved African Americans understandably sought their own personal freedom during the Revolution. The British held out that prospect to *any* slave of a rebel—man, woman, or child—who joined them during the conflict. Only a few African American men received similar promises from individual patriots or from the states. Black loy-

alists, who at the end of the war emigrated to the Bahamas, England, or Nova Scotia, and some of whom later founded Sierra Leone on the African continent, represented the vast majority of black participants in the Revolution.

The Black Patriots' Memorial thus ignores the experience of most revolutionary-era African Americans. Moreover, its exclusive focus on patriots obscures the fact that—judging by the number of slaves who seized freedom by joining the British forces—the Revolution was by far the most successful slave revolt in American history. Through their devotion to personal liberty and their open challenge to enslavement, the black people who chose loyalism have left at least as great a legacy to the nation today as did the much smaller number of black patriots who contributed more formally to the nation's founding.

For Further Reading, see page A-7 of the Appendix. For Web resources, go to http://college.hmco.com.

On December 26, 1787, a group of Federalists—supporters of the proposed Constitution—gathered in Carlisle, a town on the Pennsylvania frontier. The men planned to fire a cannon to celebrate their state convention's ratification vote two weeks earlier, but a large crowd of Antifederalists prevented them from doing so. First the Antis stood in front of the cannon, refusing to budge even though the Federalists threatened to fire the gun anyway. Then, moving from passive to active resistance, they attacked the Federalists, who eventually fled the scene as the angry Antis publicly burned a copy of the Constitution.

The next day, the Federalists returned in force to fire their cannon and to read the convention's ratification proclamation. Choosing not to create another violent confrontation, Antifederalists instead paraded around the town effigies of two supporters of the Constitution, then burned them. When Federalist officials later arrested several Antifederalists on riot charges, the Antifederalist-dominated militia mustered to break the men out of jail. Only a flaw in the warrant—which freed the arrestees legally—prevented another bloody brawl.

For several weeks thereafter, the participants in these events argued back and forth in the Carlisle newspaper about the meaning of the demonstrations and counterdemonstrations. Pro-Federalist authors proclaimed that the respectable initial celebrants acted with "good order and coolness"; their Antifederalist opponents, by contrast, were "obscure" men, nothing but "a few worthless ragamuffins." In response, "One of the People" pronounced the Federalists "an unhallowed riotous mob." Although the Constitution's supporters had declared themselves to be "friends of government," he wrote, in fact they were not: through their support of a form of government that aimed to suppress the people's liberties, they had revealed their true identity as secret aristocrats.

FORGING A NATIONAL REPUBLIC 1776–1789

William Smith, painted with his grandson in 1788 by Charles Willson Peale, presented the public image appropriate to a dignified citizen of the new republic. Peale and other artists of the time tried to promote republican values visually in their work. Here, the images of the well-tended farm, a mill, books, and a cherished child combine to symbolize virtuous labor, rational thought, and a concern for the "rising generation." (Virginia Museum of Fine Arts)

The Carlisle riots presaged violent disputes over the new Constitution in Albany (New York), Providence (Rhode Island), and other cities. In late 1787, Carlisle witnessed one incident in an ongoing struggle that began in 1775 and continued until the end of the century. In that contest, Americans argued continually—in print and in person—over how to implement republican principles and who represented the people's will. Easterners debated with westerners; in both regions, elites contended with ordinary folk. Public celebrations, like those in the small Pennsylvania town, played an important part in the struggle. After all, in a world in which only relatively few property-holding men had the right to vote, other people—and even voters themselves—expressed their political opinions in the streets rather than at the ballot box.

Republicanism—the idea that governments should be based wholly on the consent of the people—originated with political theorists in ancient Greece and Rome. Republics, theorists declared, were desirable yet fragile forms of government. Unless their citizens were especially virtuous—that is, sober, moral, and industrious—and largely in agreement on key issues, republics were doomed to failure. When Americans left the British Empire, they abandoned the idea that the best system of government balanced monarchy, aristocracy, and democracy—or, to put it another way, that a stable polity required participation by a king, the nobility, and the people. They substituted a belief in the superiority of republicanism, in which the people, not Parliament, were sovereign. During and after the war, Americans had to deal with the potentially unwelcome consequences of that decision, such as those evident in the Carlisle demonstrations. How could they best ensure political stability? How could they foster consensus among the populace? How could they create and sustain a virtuous republic?

America's political and intellectual leaders worked hard to inculcate virtue in their fellow countrymen and countrywomen. After 1776, American literature, theater, art, architecture, and education all pursued explicitly moral goals. The education of women was considered particularly important, for as the mothers of the republic's children, they were primarily responsible for ensuring the nation's future. On such matters Americans could agree, but they disagreed on many other critical issues. Almost all white men assumed that women, Indians, and African Americans should have no formal role in politics, but they found it diffi-cult to reach a consensus on how many of their own number should be included, how often elections should be held, or how their new governments should be structured.

Republican citizens had to make many other decisions as well. Should a republic's diplomacy differ from that of other nations? (For example, should the United States work to advance the cause of republicanism elsewhere?) And then there were Thomas Jefferson's words in the Declaration of Independence: "all men are created equal." Given that bold statement of principle, how could white republicans justify holding African Americans in perpetual bondage? Some answered that question by freeing their slaves or by voting for state laws that abolished slavery. Others responded by denying that blacks were "men" in the same sense as whites.

The most important task facing Americans in these years was the construction of a genuinely national government. Before 1765 the British mainland colonies had rarely cooperated on common endeavors. Many circumstances separated them: their diverse economies, varying religious traditions and ethnic compositions, competing land claims (especially in the West), and different political systems. But fighting the Revolutionary War brought them together and created a new nationalistic spirit, especially among those who served in the Continental Army or the diplomatic corps. Wartime experiences broke down at least some of the boundaries that previously had divided Americans, replacing loyalties to state and region with loyalties to the nation.

Still, forging a national republic (as opposed to a set of loosely connected state republics) was neither easy nor simple. America's first such government, under the Articles of Confederation, proved too weak and decentralized. But some of the nation's political leaders learned from their experiences and tried another approach when they drafted the Constitution in 1787. Some historians have argued that the Articles of Confederation and the Constitution reflect opposing political philosophies, the Constitution representing an "aristocratic" counterrevolution against the "democratic" Articles. The two documents are more accurately viewed as successive attempts to solve the same problems—for instance, the relationship of states and nation and the extent to which authority should be centralized. Both applied theories of republicanism to practical problems of governance; neither was entirely successful in resolving those difficulties. ◼

IMPORTANT EVENTS

1776 Second Continental Congress directs states to draft constitutions

1777 Articles of Confederation sent to states for ratification

Vermont becomes first state to abolish slavery

1781 Articles of Confederation ratified

1786 Annapolis Convention meets, discusses reforming government

1786–87 Shays's Rebellion in western Massachusetts raises questions about future of the republic

1787 Northwest Ordinance organizes territory north of Ohio River and east of Mississippi River

Constitutional Convention drafts new form of government

1788 Hamilton, Jay, and Madison write *The Federalist* to urge ratification of the Constitution by New York

Constitution ratified

1794 Wayne defeats Miami Confederacy at Fallen Timbers

1795 Treaty of Greenville opens Ohio to white settlement

1800 Weems publishes his *Life of Washington*

Creating a Virtuous Republic

 When the colonies declared their independence from Great Britain, John Dickinson recalled many years later, "there was no question concerning forms of Government, no enquiry whether a Republic or a limited Monarchy was best. . . . We knew that the people of this country must unite themselves under some form of Government and that this could be no other than the republican form"—in short, self-government by the people. But how should that goal be implemented?

Three different definitions of *republicanism* emerged in the new United States. Ancient history and political theory informed the first, held chiefly by members of the educated elite (such as the Adamses of Massachusetts). The histories of popular governments in Greece and Rome suggested that republics could succeed only if they were small in size and homogeneous in population. Unless a republic's citizens were willing to sacrifice their own private interests for the good of the whole, the government would collapse. A truly virtuous man, classical republican theory insisted, had to forgo personal profit and work solely for the best interests of the nation. In return for sacrifices, though, a republic offered its citizens equality of opportunity.

Varieties of Republicanism

Under such a government, rank would be based on merit rather than on inherited wealth and status. Society would be governed by members of a "natural aristocracy," men whose talent had elevated them from what might have been humble beginnings to positions of power and privilege. Rank would not be abolished but instead would be founded on merit.

A second definition, advanced by other members of the elite but also by some skilled craftsmen, drew more on economic theory than on political thought. Instead of perceiving the nation as an organic whole composed of people nobly sacrificing for the common good, this version of republicanism followed the Scottish theorist Adam Smith in emphasizing individuals' pursuit of rational self-interest. The huge profits some men reaped from patriotism by selling supplies to the army underscored such an approach. The nation could only benefit from aggressive economic expansion, argued men such as Alexander Hamilton. When republican men sought to improve their own economic and social circumstances, the entire nation would benefit. Republican virtue would be achieved through the pursuit of private interests, rather than through subordination to some communal ideal. Such thinking decisively abandoned the old notion of the Puritan covenant, which the first definition perpetuated in its emphasis on consensus though not in its stress on an aristocracy of talent rather than birth (see page 51).

When the great French sculptor Jean-Antoine Houdon prepared this bust of George Washington in 1785, he chose to show the revolutionary leader in classical garb rather than in contemporary clothing. Such images linked the aspirations of the new nation to the ancient republics American thinkers revered.   (Collection of Dr. Gary Milan)

The third notion of republicanism was less influential but more egalitarian than the other two, which both contained considerable potential for inequality. Many of its illiterate or barely literate proponents could write little to promote their beliefs. Men who advanced the third version of republicanism, the most prominent of whom was Thomas Paine, called for widening men's participation in the political process. They also wanted government to respond directly to the needs of ordinary folk, rejecting any notion that the "lesser sort" should automatically defer to their "betters." They were, indeed, democrats in more or less the modern sense. For them, republican virtue was embodied in the untutored wisdom of the people as a whole, rather than in the special insights of a natural aristocracy or the pronouncements of wealthy individuals.

Despite the differences, the three strands of republicanism shared many of the same assumptions.

For example, all three contrasted the industrious virtue of America to the corruption of Britain and Europe. In the first version, that virtue manifested itself in frugality and self-sacrifice; in the second, it would prevent self-interest from becoming vice; in the third, it was the justification for including even propertyless free men in the ranks of voters. "Virtue, Virtue alone . . . is the basis of a republic," asserted Dr. Benjamin Rush of Philadelphia, an ardent patriot, in 1778. His fellow Americans concurred, even if they defined virtue differently. Most agreed that a virtuous country would be composed of hard-working citizens who would dress simply and live plainly, elect wise leaders to public office, and forgo the conspicuous consumption of luxury goods.

As citizens of the United States set out to construct their republic, they believed they were embarking on an unprecedented enterprise.

Virtue and the Arts

With great pride in their new nation, they expected to replace the vices of monarchical Europe—immorality, selfishness, and lack of public spirit—with the sober virtues of republican America. They wanted to embody republican principles not only in their governments but also in their society and culture. They looked to painting, literature, drama, and architecture to convey messages of nationalism and virtue to the public, focusing on such themes until after the turn of the century.

Americans faced a crucial contradiction at the very outset of their efforts. To some republicans, the fine arts themselves were manifestations of vice. Their existence in a virtuous society, many contended, signaled the arrival of luxury and corruption. What need did a frugal yeoman have for a painting—or, worse yet, a novel? Why should anyone spend hard-earned wages to see a play in a lavishly decorated theater? The first American artists, playwrights, and authors thus confronted an impossible dilemma. They wanted to produce works embodying virtue, but those very works, regardless of their content, were viewed by many as corrupting.

Still, they tried. William Hill Brown's *The Power of Sympathy* (1789), the first novel written in the United States, was a lurid tale of seduction intended as a warning to young women, who made up a large proportion of America's fiction readers. In Royall Tyler's *The Contrast* (1787), the first successful American play, the virtuous conduct of Colonel Manly was contrasted (hence the title) with the reprehensible behavior of the fop Billy Dimple. The most popular book of the era,

Mason Locke Weems's *Life of Washington*, published in 1800 shortly after George Washington's death, was intended by its author to "hold up his great Virtues . . . to the imitation of Our Youth." Weems could hardly be accused of subtlety. The famous tale he invented—six-year-old George bravely admitting cutting down his father's favorite cherry tree—ended with George's father exclaiming, "Run to my arms, you dearest boy. . . . Such an act of heroism in my son, is worth more than a thousand trees, though blossomed with silver, and their fruit of purest gold."

Painting and architecture, too, were expected to embody high moral standards. Two of the most prominent artists of the period, Gilbert Stuart and Charles Willson Peale, painted innumerable portraits of upstanding republican citizens. John Trumbull's vast canvases depicted milestones of American history such as the Battle of Bunker Hill, Burgoyne's surrender at Saratoga, and Cornwallis's capitulation at Yorktown. Such portraits and historical scenes were intended to instill patriotic sentiments in their viewers. Architects likewise hoped to convey in their buildings a sense of the young republic's ideals. When the Virginia government asked Thomas Jefferson, then minister to France, for advice on the design of the state capitol in Richmond, Jefferson unhesitatingly recommended copying a Roman building, the Maison Carrée at Nîmes. "It is very simple," he explained, "but it is noble beyond expression." Jefferson set forth ideals that would guide American architecture for a generation to come: simplicity of line, harmonious proportions, a feeling of grandeur.

Despite the artists' efforts (or, some would have said, because of them), some Americans began to detect signs of luxury and corruption by the mid-1780s. The resumption of European trade after the war brought a return to fashionable clothing for both men and women and abandonment of the simpler homespun garments patriots had once worn with pride. Elite families again attended balls and concerts. Parties no longer seemed complete without gambling and cardplaying. Social clubs for young people multiplied; Samuel Adams worried in print about the opportunities for corruption lurking behind plans for tea drinking and genteel conversation among Boston youths. Especially alarming to fervent republicans was the establishment in 1783 of the Society of the Cincinnati, a hereditary association for Revolutionary War officers and their descendants. Although the organizers hoped to advance the notion of the citizen-soldier, opponents feared that the group would become the nucleus of a native-born aristocracy. All these developments directly challenged the United States's self-image as a virtuous republic.

Americans' deep-seated concern for the future of the infant republic focused their attention on their children, the "rising generation."

Educational Reform

Education had previously been seen as a private means to personal advancement, a concern only for individual families. Now, though, schooling would serve a public purpose. If young people were to resist the temptations of vice and become useful citizens prepared for self-government, they would need a better education. In fact, the very survival of the nation depended on it. The 1780s and 1790s thus witnessed two major changes in educational practice.

First, in contrast to the colonies, where nearly all education had been privately financed, some northern states began to use tax money to support public elementary schools. In 1789 Massachusetts became one of the first states to require towns to offer their citizens free public elementary education. Second, schooling for girls was improved. Americans' recognition of the importance of the rising generation led to the realization that mothers would have to be properly educated if they were to instruct their children adequately. Therefore, Massachusetts insisted in its 1789 law that town elementary schools be open to girls as well as boys. Throughout the United States, private academies were founded to give teenage girls from well-to-do families an opportunity for advanced schooling. No one yet proposed opening colleges to women, but a few fortunate girls could study history, geography, rhetoric, and mathematics. The academies also trained female students in fancy needlework—the only artistic endeavor considered appropriate for genteel women.

The chief theorist of women's education in the early republic was Judith Sargent Murray of Gloucester, Massachusetts.

Judith Sargent Murray and Women's Education

In a series of essays published in the 1780s and 1790s, Murray argued that women and men had equal intellectual capacities, although women's inadequate education might make them seem less intelligent. "We can only reason from what we know," she declared, "and if an opportunity of acquiring knowledge hath been denied us, the inferiority of our sex cannot fairly be deduced from thence." Therefore, concluded Murray, boys and girls should be offered equivalent scholastic training.

She further contended that girls should be taught to support themselves by their own efforts: "Independence should be placed within their grasp."

Murray's direct challenge to the traditional colonial belief that, as one man put it, girls "knew quite enough if they could make a shirt and a pudding" was part of a general rethinking of women's position that occurred as a result of the Revolution. Male patriots who enlisted in the army or served in Congress were away from home for long periods of time. In their absence their wives, who previously had handled only the "indoor affairs" of the household, shouldered the responsibility for "outdoor affairs" as well. As the wife of a Connecticut militiaman later recalled, her husband "was out more or less during the remainder of the war [after 1777], so much so as to be unable to do anything on our farm. What was done, was done by myself."

The American artist Benjamin Blythe painted this portrait of Abigail Smith Adams in 1766, shortly after her marriage. Less than a decade later she would join her husband John in eager support of the revolutionary cause. At the same time, however, she forthrightly challenged him to "remember the ladies" in the nation's "new code of laws." (Massachusetts Historical Society)

Similarly, John and Abigail Adams took great pride in Abigail's developing skills as a "farmeress." Like her female contemporaries, Abigail Adams stopped calling the farm "yours" in letters to her husband and began referring to it as "ours"—a revealing change of pronoun. Both men and women realized that female patriots had made vital and important contributions to winning the war through their work at home and that their notions of proper gender roles had to be rethought. Americans began to develop new ideas about the role women should play in a republican society.

The best-known expression of those new ideas appears in a letter Abigail Adams addressed to her husband in March 1776. "In the new Code of Laws which I suppose it will be necessary for you to make I desire you would Remember the Ladies," she wrote. "Remember all Men would be tyrants if they could. . . . If perticuliar care and attention is not paid to the Laidies [*sic*] we are determined to foment a Rebelion, and will not hold ourselves bound by any Laws in which we have no voice, or Representation." With these words, Abigail Adams took a step that was soon to be duplicated by other disfranchised Americans. She deliberately applied the ideology developed to combat parliamentary supremacy to purposes revolutionary leaders had never intended. Since men were "Naturally Tyrannical," she argued, the United States should reform colonial marriage laws, which made wives subordinate to their husbands.

Abigail Adams: "Remember the Ladies"

Abigail Adams did not ask that women be allowed to vote, but others claimed that right. The men who drafted the New Jersey state constitution in 1776 defined voters carelessly as "all free inhabitants" who met certain property qualifications. They thereby unintentionally gave the vote to property-holding white spinsters and widows, as well as to free black landowners. Qualified women and African Americans regularly voted in New Jersey's local and congressional elections until 1807, when they were disfranchised by the state legislature, which falsely alleged that they had engaged in widespread vote fraud. Yet the fact that women voted at all was evidence of their altered perception of their place in the political life of the country.

Such dramatic episodes were unusual. After the war, European Americans still viewed women in traditional terms, continuing to believe that women's primary function was to be good wives, mothers, and mistresses of households. They perceived significant

Women's Role in the Republic

differences between male and female characters. That distinction eventually enabled Americans to resolve the conflict between the two most influential strands of republican thought and led to new roles for some women. Because wives could not own property or participate directly in economic life, women in general came to be seen as the embodiment of self-sacrificing, disinterested republicanism. Through new female-run charitable associations founded after the war, better-off women assumed public responsibilities, in particular through caring for poor widows and orphaned children. Thus men were freed from the naggings of conscience as they pursued their economic self-interest (that other republican virtue), secure in the knowledge that their wives and daughters were fulfilling the family's obligation to the common good. The ideal republican man, therefore, was an individualist, seeking advancement for himself and his family. The ideal republican woman, by contrast, always put the well-being of others ahead of her own.

Together European American men and women established the context for the creation of a virtuous republic. But nearly 20 percent of the American population was of African descent. How did approximately 700,000 African Americans fit into the developing national plan?

The First Emancipation and the Growth of Racism

Revolutionary ideology exposed one of the primary contradictions in American society. Both European and African Americans saw the irony in slaveholders' claims that they sought to prevent Britain from "enslaving" them. Many revolutionary leaders voiced the theme. In 1773 Dr. Benjamin Rush called slavery "a vice which degrades human nature," warning ominously that "the plant of liberty is of so tender a nature that it cannot thrive long in the neighborhood of slavery." Common folk also saw the contradiction. When Josiah Atkins, a Connecticut soldier marching south, saw Washington's plantation, he observed in his journal: "Alas! That persons who pretend to stand for the rights of mankind for the liberties of society, can delight in oppression, & that even of the worst kind!"

African Americans did not need revolutionary ideology to tell them that slavery was wrong, but they quickly took advantage of that ideology. In 1779 a group of slaves from Portsmouth, New Hampshire, asked the state legislature "from what authority [our masters] assume to dispose of our lives, freedom and property," pleading "that the name of slave may not more be heard in a land gloriously contending for the sweets of freedom." The same year several bondspeople in Fairfield, Connecticut, petitioned the legislature for their freedom, characterizing slavery as a "dreadful Evil" and "flagrant Injustice." How could men who were "nobly contending in the Cause of Liberty," they asked, continue "this detestable Practice"?

Both legislatures responded negatively, but the postwar years witnessed the gradual abolition of slavery in the North, a process that has become known as "the first emancipation." Vermont abolished slavery in its 1777 constitution. Massachusetts courts decided in the 1780s that a clause in the state constitution prohibited slavery. Most of the other northern and middle states adopted gradual emancipation laws between 1780 (Pennsylvania) and 1804 (New Jersey). Although New Hampshire did not formally abolish slavery, only eight slaves were reported on the 1800 census, and none remained a decade later. No southern state adopted similar general emancipation laws, but the legislatures of Virginia (1782), Delaware (1787), and Maryland (1790 and 1796) altered laws that earlier had restricted slaveowners' ability to free their bondspeople. South Carolina and Georgia never considered adopting such acts, and North Carolina insisted that all manumissions (emancipations of individual slaves) be approved by county courts.

Emancipation and Manumission

Revolutionary ideology thus had limited impact on the well-entrenched economic interests of large slaveholders. Only in the North, where slaves were less common and where less money was invested in human capital, could state legislatures vote to abolish slavery. Even there, legislators' concern for property rights—the Revolution, after all, was fought for property as well as life and liberty—led them to favor gradual emancipation over immediate abolition. Most states provided only for the freeing of children born after passage of the law, not for the emancipation of adults. And even those children were to remain slaves until reaching adulthood. Still, by 1840 only one northern state—New Jersey—permitted holding African Americans in bondage.

Despite the slow progress of abolition, the number of free people of African descent in the United States grew dramatically in the first years after the

Robert Carter was one of the largest slaveholders in Virginia. After the state altered its manumission laws and he had become a Baptist, he decided to free all of his bondspeople. He worked out a plan of gradual emancipation, freeing some slaves each year for several years. Hannah, one of his weavers, wrote to him in April 1792, requesting that she be allowed to buy her loom when she was emancipated the following January. This is one of only a handful of documents known to be written by literate slave women during the eighteenth century. (Chicago Historical Society, Robert Carter Papers)

The Chesapeake, where manumissions were speeded by economic changes such as declining soil fertility and the shift from tobacco to grain production, felt the effects of the postwar trend most sharply. Since grain cultivation was less labor-intensive than tobacco growing, planters began to complain about "excess" slaves. They occasionally solved that problem by freeing some of their less productive or more favored bondspeople. The free black population of Virginia more than doubled between 1790 and 1810, and by the latter year nearly one-quarter of Maryland's African American population was no longer in legal bondage.

In the 1780s and thereafter, freed people from rural areas often made their way to northern port cities. Boston and Philadelphia, where slavery was abolished sooner than in New York City, were popular destinations. Women outnumbered men among the migrants by a margin of three to two, for they had better employment opportunities in the cities, especially in domestic service. Some freedmen also worked in domestic service, but larger numbers were employed as unskilled laborers and sailors. A few of the women and a sizable proportion of men (nearly one-third of those in Philadelphia in 1795) were skilled workers or retailers. These people chose new names for themselves, exchanging the surnames of former masters for names like Newman or Brown, and as soon as possible they established independent two-parent nuclear families instead of continuing to live in their employers' households. They also began to occupy distinct neighborhoods, probably as a result of discrimination.

Migration to Northern Cities

Emancipation did not bring equality. Even whites who recognized African Americans' right to freedom were unwilling to accept them as equals. Laws discriminated against freed people as they had against slaves. South Carolina, for example, did not permit free blacks to testify against whites in court. Public schools often refused to educate their children. Freedmen found it difficult to purchase property and find good jobs. And though in many areas African Americans were accepted as members—even ministers—of evangelical churches, they were rarely allowed an equal voice in church affairs.

Gradually, freed people developed their own institutions, often based in their own neighborhoods. In Charleston mulattos formed the Brown Fellowship Society, which provided insurance coverage for its members, financed a school, and helped to support or-

Growth of Free Black Population

Revolution. Before the war they had been few in number; in 1755, for example, only 4 percent of African Americans in Maryland were free. Most slaves emancipated before the war were mulattos, born of unions between bondswomen and their masters, who then manumitted the children. But wartime disruptions radically augmented the freed population. Slaves who had escaped from plantations during the war, others who had served in the American army, and still others who had been emancipated by their owners or by state laws were now free. By 1790 nearly 60,000 free people of color lived in the United States; ten years later they numbered more than 108,000, nearly 11 percent of the total African American population.

Freed People's Churches and Associations

phans. In 1794 former slaves in Philadelphia and Baltimore founded societies that eventually became the African Methodist Episcopal (AME) denomination. AME churches later sponsored schools in a number of cities and, along with African Baptist, African Episcopal, and African Presbyterian churches, became cultural centers of the free black community. Freed people quickly learned that, to survive and prosper, they had to rely on their own collective efforts rather than on the benevolence or goodwill of their white compatriots.

Their endeavors were all the more important because the postrevolutionary years witnessed the development of a formal racist theory in the United States. European Americans had long regarded their slaves as inferior, but the most influential writers attributed that inferiority to environmental factors. They argued that African slaves' seemingly debased character derived from their enslavement, rather than enslavement being the consequence of inherited inferiority. In the Revolution's aftermath, though, slaveowners needed to defend holding other human beings in bondage against the notion that "all men are created equal." Consequently, they began to argue that people of African descent were less than fully human and that the principles of republican equality applied only to European Americans. In other words, to avoid having to confront the contradiction between their practice and the egalitarian implications of revolutionary theory, they redefined the theory so that it would not apply to African Americans.

Development of Racist Theory

Simultaneously, the very notion of "race" appeared in coherent form, applied to groups defined by skin color as "whites" and "blacks." The rise of egalitarian thinking among European Americans both downplayed status distinctions within their own group and differentiated all "whites" from people of color—Indians and African Americans. (That differentiation soon manifested itself in new miscegenation laws adopted in both northern and southern states to forbid intermarriage among whites and blacks or Indians.) Meanwhile, a generation or two of experience as slaves on American soil forged the identity "African" or "black" from the various ethnic and national affiliations of people who had survived the transatlantic crossing. Strikingly, among the first to term themselves "Africans" were Olaudah Equiano (see pages 74–75) and his fellow oceanic sailors—men whose wide-ranging contacts with Europeans caused them to construct a unified (and separate) identity for themselves. Thus in the revolutionary era "whiteness" and "blackness"—along with the superiority of the former, the inferiority of the latter—developed as contrasting terms in tandem with each other.

Such racism had several intertwined elements. First came the assertion that, as Thomas Jefferson insisted in 1781, blacks were "inferior to the whites in the endowments both of body and mind." There followed the belief that blacks were congenitally lazy, dishonest, and uncivilized (or uncivilizable). Third, and of crucial importance, was the notion that all blacks were sexually promiscuous and that African American men lusted after European American women. The specter of interracial sexual intercourse involving black men and white women haunted early American racist thought. Significantly, the more common reverse circumstance—the sexual exploitation of enslaved women by their masters—aroused little comment or concern.

African Americans did not allow these developing racist notions to go unchallenged. Benjamin Banneker, a free black surveyor, astronomer, and mathematical genius, directly disputed Thomas Jefferson's belief in Africans' intellectual inferiority. In 1791 Banneker sent Jefferson a copy of his latest almanac (which included his astronomical calculations) as an example of blacks' mental powers. Jefferson's response admitted Banneker's capability but indicated that he regarded Banneker as exceptional; Jefferson insisted that he needed more evidence before he would change his mind.

At its birth, then, the republic was defined by its leaders as an exclusively white male enterprise. Indeed, some historians have argued that the subjugation of blacks and women was a necessary precondition for theoretical equality among white men. They have pointed out that identifying a common racial antagonist helped to create white solidarity and to lessen the threat to gentry power posed by the enfranchisement of poorer white men. Moreover, excluding women from the political realm preserved all power for men, specifically those of the "better sort." Some scholars have pointed out that it was less dangerous to allow white men with little property to participate formally in politics than to open the possibility that they might join with former slaves to question the rule of elites. That was perhaps one reason why after the Revolution the division of American

A Republic for White Men Only

How do historians know...

that the 1780s and 1790s marked a crucial turning point in the history of slavery and racism in the United States?

Emancipation, manumission, and miscegenation laws adopted by state legislatures, coupled with debates in pamphlets and newspapers, indicate a shift in Americans' thinking. A painting such as the one reproduced here, *Liberty Displaying the Arts and Sciences*, offers a unique visual perspective on the same developments. In 1792 the Library Company of Philadelphia, a private lending library founded in the mid-eighteenth century, commissioned the artist Samuel Jennings to produce a depiction of slavery and abolitionism showing the "figure of Liberty (with her Cap and proper Insignia) displaying the arts." The results reportedly pleased the library's directors. The painting, probably the first to celebrate emancipation, shows the blonde goddess presenting books (symbolizing knowledge and freedom) to several suppliant and grateful blacks, while in the background former slaves dance joyfully around a liberty pole. Although the theme is abolition and the African Americans in the foreground have realistic features, the portrayal of blacks in passive roles and diminutive sizes portended future stereotypes. Thus the picture linked emancipation and the growth of racism. (Photo: The Library Company of Philadelphia)

society between slave and free was transformed into a division between blacks—some of whom were free—and whites. The white male wielders of power ensured their continued dominance in part by substituting race for enslavement as the primary determinant of African Americans' status.

Designing Republican Governments

 In May 1776, even before adoption of the Declaration of Independence, the Second Continental Congress directed states to devise new republican governments to replace the provincial congresses and committees that had met since 1774. Thus American men initially concentrated on drafting state constitutions and devoted little attention to their national government—an oversight they later had to remedy.

At the state level, they immediately faced the problem of defining a "constitution." Americans wanted to create tangible documents specifying the fundamental structures of government, but at first legislators could not decide how best to accomplish that goal. States eventually concluded that their constitutions should not be drafted by regular legislative bodies. Following the lead established by Vermont in 1777 and Massachusetts in 1780, they began to elect conventions for the sole purpose of drafting constitutions. Thus states sought direct authorization from the people—the theoretical sovereigns in a republic—before establishing new governments. After preparing new constitutions, delegates submitted them to voters for ratification.

Drafting of State Constitutions

The framers of state constitutions concerned themselves primarily with outlining the distribution of and limitations on government power—both crucial to the survival of republics. If authority was improperly distributed among the branches of government, or not confined within reasonable limits, the states might become tyrannical, as Britain had. Americans' experience with British rule permeated every provision of their new constitutions. States experimented with different solutions to the problems the framers perceived, and the early constitutions varied considerably in specifics while remaining broadly comparable in outline.

Under their colonial charters, Americans had learned to fear the power of the governor—usually, the appointed agent of the king or proprietor—and to see the legislature as their defender. Accordingly, the first state constitutions typically provided for the governor to be elected annually (commonly by the legislature), limited the number of terms he could serve, and gave him little independent authority. Simultaneously, the constitutions expanded the legislature's powers. Every state except Pennsylvania and Vermont retained a two-house structure, with members of the upper house having longer terms and being required to meet higher property-holding standards than members of the lower house. But they also redrew electoral districts to reflect population patterns more accurately, and they increased the number of members in both houses. Finally, most states lowered property qualifications for voting. As a result the legislatures came to include some members who before the war would not have been eligible to vote. Thus the revolutionary era witnessed the first deliberate attempt to broaden the base of American government, a process that has continued into our own day.

But the state constitutions' authors knew that governments designed to be responsive to the people would not necessarily provide sufficient protection if tyrants were elected to office. They consequently included explicit limitations on government authority in the documents they composed, attempting to protect what they regarded as the inalienable rights of individual citizens. Seven of the constitutions contained formal bills of rights, and the others had similar clauses. Most guaranteed citizens freedom of the press and of religion, the right to a fair trial, the right of consent to taxation, and protection against general search warrants. An independent judiciary was charged with upholding such rights.

Limits on State Governments

In sum, the constitution makers put far greater emphasis on preventing state governments from becoming tyrannical than on making them effective wielders of political authority. Their approach to shaping governments was understandable, given the American experience with Great Britain. But establishing such weak political units, especially in wartime, practically ensured that the constitutions soon would need revision. Soon some states began to rewrite constitutions they had drafted in 1776 and 1777.

Invariably, the revised versions increased the powers of the governor and reduced the scope of the legislature's authority. In the mid-1780s, some American

Rewriting the State Constitutions

political leaders started to develop a theory of checks and balances as the primary means of controlling government power. (In the mid-1770s, constitutions prescribed powerful legislatures to ensure good government, but warime experiences led many to conclude that such arrangements often failed.) Americans sought to balance the powers of the legislative, executive, and judicial branches against one another. The national constitution they drafted in 1787 also embodied that principle.

Yet the constitutional theories that Americans applied at the state level did not at first influence their conception of national government. Since American officials initially focused on organizing the military struggle against Britain, the powers and structure of the Continental Congress evolved by default early in the war. Not until late 1777 did Congress send the Articles of Confederation to the states for ratification, and those Articles simply wrote into law the unplanned arrangements of the Continental Congress.

The chief organ of national government was a unicameral (one-house) legislature in which each state had one vote. Its powers included conducting foreign relations, mediating disputes between states, controlling maritime affairs, regulating Indian trade, and valuing state and national coinage. The Articles did not give the national government the ability to raise revenue effectively or to enforce a uniform commercial policy. The United States of America was described as "a firm league of friendship" in which each state "retains its sovereignty, freedom and independence, and every Power, Jurisdiction and right, which is not by this confederation expressly delegated to the United States, in Congress assembled." (See the appendix for the text of the Articles.)

Articles of Confederation

The Articles required unanimous consent of state legislatures for ratification or amendment, and a clause concerning western lands proved troublesome. The draft accepted by Congress allowed states to retain all land claims derived from their original charters. But states with definite western boundaries in their charters (such as Maryland and New Jersey) wanted other states to cede to the national government their landholdings west of the Appalachian Mountains. Otherwise, they feared, states with large claims could expand and overpower their smaller neighbors. Maryland refused to accept the Articles until 1781, when Virginia finally promised to surrender its western holdings to

national jurisdiction (see Map 7.1). Other states followed suit, establishing the principle that unorganized lands would be held by the nation as a whole.

The capacity of a single state to delay ratification for three years portended the fate of American government under the Articles of Confederation. The unicameral legislature, whether it was called the Second Continental Congress (until 1781) or the Confederation Congress (thereafter), was too inefficient and unwieldy to govern effectively. The Articles' authors had not given adequate thought to the distribution of power within the national government or to the relationship between the Confederation and the states. The Congress they created was simultaneously a legislative body and a collective executive (there was no judiciary), but it had no independent income and no authority to compel the states to accept its rulings. Under the Articles, national government lurched from crisis to crisis.

Trials of the Confederation

Finance posed the most persistent problem faced by both state and national governments. Because legislators at all levels levied taxes only reluctantly, both Congress and the states at first tried to finance the war simply by printing currency. Even though the money was backed by nothing but good faith, it circulated freely and without excessive depreciation during 1775 and most of 1776. Demand for military supplies and civilian goods was high, stimulating trade (especially with France) and local production. Indeed, the amount of money issued in those years was probably no more than what a healthy economy required as a medium of exchange.

But in late 1776, as the American army suffered reverses in New York and New Jersey, prices began to rise and inflation set in. The currency's value rested on Americans' faith in their government, a faith that was sorely tested in the years that followed, especially during the dark days of early British triumphs in the South (1779 and 1780). State governments fought inflation by controlling wages and prices and requiring acceptance of paper currency on an equal footing with hard money. States also borrowed funds, established lotteries, and even levied taxes. Their efforts were futile. So too was Congress's attempt to stop printing currency altogether and to rely solely on money contributed by the

Inflation and Taxation

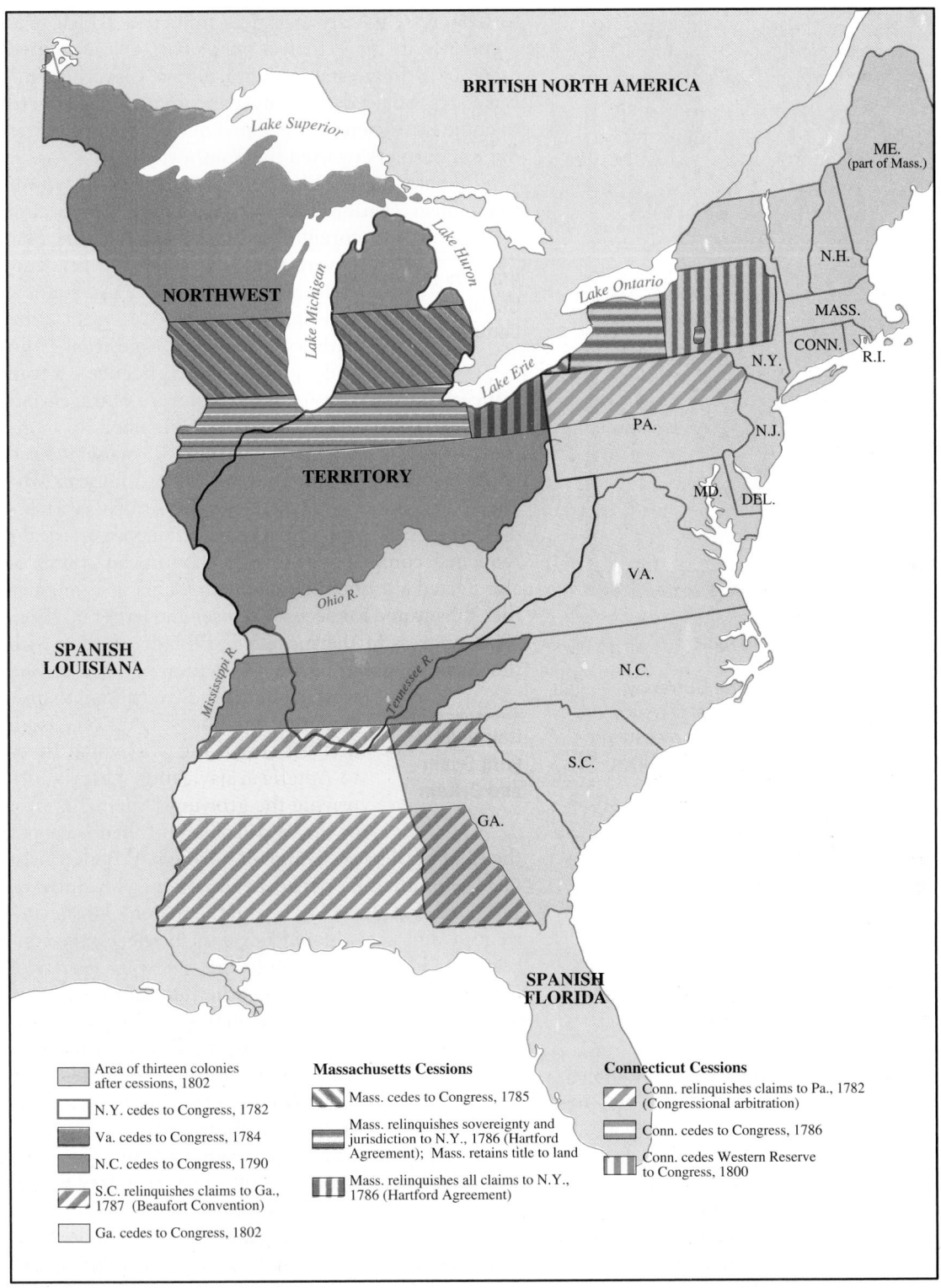

British North America

ME.
(part of Mass.)

N.H.

MASS.

CONN.

R.I.

N.Y.

PA.

N.J.

MD.

DEL.

VA.

N.C.

S.C.

GA.

NORTHWEST

TERRITORY

Lake Superior

Lake Michigan

Lake Huron

Lake Erie

Lake Ontario

Ohio R.

Mississippi R.

Tennessee R.

**SPANISH
LOUISIANA**

**SPANISH
FLORIDA**

Area of thirteen colonies
after cessions, 1802

N.Y. cedes to Congress, 1782

Va. cedes to Congress, 1784

N.C. cedes to Congress, 1790

S.C. relinquishes claims to Ga.,
1787 (Beaufort Convention)

Ga. cedes to Congress, 1802

Massachusetts Cessions

Mass. cedes to Congress, 1785

Mass. relinquishes sovereignty and
jurisdiction to N.Y., 1786 (Hartford
Agreement); Mass. retains title to land

Mass. relinquishes all claims to N.Y.,
1786 (Hartford Agreement)

Connecticut Cessions

Conn. relinquishes claims to Pa., 1782
(Congressional arbitration)

Conn. cedes to Congress, 1786

Conn. cedes Western Reserve
to Congress, 1800

Map 7.1   Western Land Claims and Cessions, 1782–1802   After the United States achieved
independence, states competed with each other for control of valuable lands to which they had
possible claims under their original charters. That competition led to a series of compromises
among the states or between individual states and the new nation, which are indicated on this map.

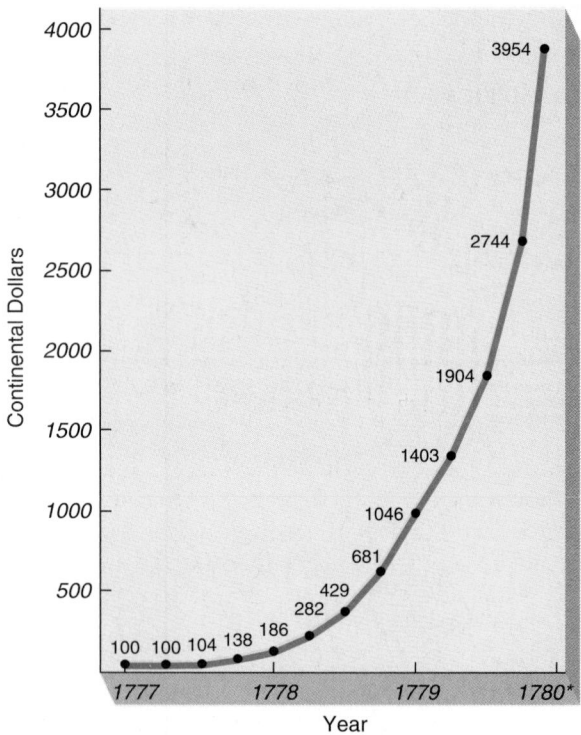

Year

* Currency abandoned in April 1780

Figure 7.1 Depreciation of Continental Currency, 1777–1780 The depreciation of Continental currency accelerated in 1778, as is shown in this graph measuring its value against one hundred silver dollars. Thereafter, its value dropped almost daily. (Source: Data from John J. McCusker, "How Much Is That in Real Money? A Historical Price Index for Use as a Deflator of Money Values in the Economy of the United States," *Proceedings of the American Antiquarian Society,* Vol. 101, Pt. 2 [1991], Table C-1.)

states. By early 1780 it took forty paper dollars to purchase one silver dollar. Soon, Continental currency was worthless (see Figure 7.1).

In 1781, faced with total collapse of the monetary system, the congressmen undertook ambitious reforms. After establishing a department of finance under the wealthy Philadelphia merchant Robert Morris, they asked the states to amend the Articles of Confederation to allow Congress to levy a duty of 5 percent on imported goods. Morris put national finances on a solid footing, but the customs duty was never adopted. First Rhode Island and then New York refused to agree to the tax. The states' resistance reflected fear of a too-powerful central government. As one worried citizen wrote in 1783, "If permanent Funds are given to Congress, the aristocratical Influence, which predominates in more than a major part of the United States, will fully establish an arbitrary Government." But states too needed revenue, and found it just as hard to come by. When they enacted new, heavy taxes after the war, farmers resisted their authority.

Because the Articles denied Congress the power to establish a national commercial policy, the realm of foreign trade also exposed the new government's weaknesses. Immediately after the war, Britain, France, and Spain restricted American trade with their colonies. Americans, who had hoped independence would bring about trade with all nations, were outraged but could do little to change matters. Members of Congress watched helplessly as British manufactured goods flooded the United States while American produce could no longer be sold in the British West Indies, once its prime market. Although Americans reopened commerce with other European countries and started a profitable trade with China in 1784, neither substituted for access to closer and larger markets.

Congress furthermore had difficulty dealing with the Spanish presence on the nation's southern and western borders. Determined to prevent the republic's expansion, Spain in 1784 closed the Mississippi River to American navigation, thereby depriving the growing settlements west of the Appalachians of their access to the Gulf of Mexico. Congress, through its department of foreign affairs, opened negotiations with Spain in 1785, but even John Jay, one of the nation's most experienced diplomats, could not win the necessary concessions. The talks collapsed the following year after Congress divided sharply: southerners and westerners insisted on navigation rights on the Mississippi; northerners were willing to abandon that claim in order to win commercial concessions in the West Indies. The impasse raised doubts about the possibility of any national consensus on foreign affairs.

Provisions of the 1783 Treaty of Paris too caused serious problems. Article Four, which promised the repayment of prewar debts (most of them owed by Americans to British merchants), and Article Five, which recommended that states allow loyalists to recover their confiscated property, aroused considerable opposition. States passed laws denying British subjects the right to sue for recovery of debts or property in American courts, and town meetings decried the loyal-

Inability to Regulate Commerce

Relations with Spain and Britain

Because of their citizens' resistance to taxation, the early state governments found it hard to raise sufficient revenues. Some, like Massachusetts, turned to state-run lotteries to make up the shortfall. Here a New Englander proudly poses with a lottery ticket, demonstrating his support for the state.   (Milwaukee Art Museum Purchase, Layton Art Collection)

ists' return. As residents of Norwalk, Connecticut, put it, few Americans wanted to permit the "Tory Villains" to return "while filial Tears are fresh upon our Cheeks and our Murdered Brethren scarcely cold in their Graves." State governments also had reason to oppose enforcement of the treaty. Sales of loyalists' land, houses, and other possessions had helped finance the war. Since most of the purchasers were prominent patriots, states had no desire to raise questions about the legitimacy of their property titles.

The refusal of state and local governments to comply with Articles Four and Five gave Britain an excuse to maintain military posts on the Great Lakes long after its troops were supposed to have withdrawn. Furthermore, Congress's inability to convince states to implement the treaty disclosed its lack of power, even in an area—foreign affairs—in which it had authority under the Articles of Confederation. Concerned nationalists argued publicly that enforcement of the

treaty, however unpopular, was a crucial test of the republic's credibility in foreign affairs. "Will foreign nations be willing to undertake anything with us or for us," asked Alexander Hamilton, "when they find that the nature of our governments will allow no dependence to be placed on our engagements?"

Order and Disorder in the West

 Congressmen also confronted knotty problems when they considered the status of land beyond the Appalachians. Although British and American diplomats did not discuss tribal claims, the United States assumed that the Treaty of Paris cleared its title to all land east of the Mississippi except the area still held by Spain. Still, recognizing that land cessions should be obtained from the most powerful tribes, Congress initiated negotiations with both northern and southern Indians (see Map 7.2).

At Fort Stanwix, New York, in 1784, American diplomats negotiated a treaty with chiefs who said they represented the Iroquois; and at Hopewell, South Carolina, in late 1785 and early 1786, they did the same with emissaries from the Choctaw, Chickasaw, and Cherokee nations. In 1786 the Iroquois formally repudiated the Fort Stanwix treaty, denying that the men who attended the negotiations had been authorized to speak for the Six Nations. The confederacy threatened new attacks on frontier settlements, but everyone knew the threat was empty; the flawed treaty stood by default. At intervals until the end of the decade New York State purchased large tracts of land from individual Iroquois nations. By 1790 the once-dominant confederacy was confined to a few scattered reservations. In the South as well the United States took the treaties as confirmation of its sovereignty, authorizing settlers to move onto the territories in question. European Americans poured over the southern Appalachians, provoking the Creeks—who had not agreed to the Hopewell treaties—to defend their territory by declaring war. Only in 1790 did they come to terms with the United States.

Western nations such as the Shawnees, Chippewas, Ottawas, and Potawatomis previously had allowed the Iroquois to speak for them. After the collapse of Iroquois power, they formed their own confederacy and demanded direct negotiations with the United States. They intended to present a united

Relations with the Indians

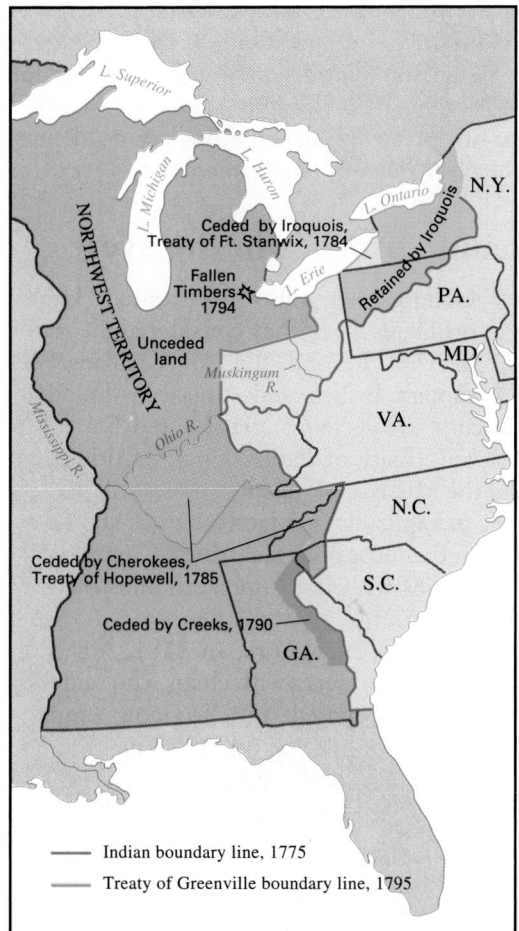

Map 7.2 Cession of Tribal Lands to the United States, 1775–1790 The land claims of the United States meant little as long as Indian nations still controlled vast territories within the new country's formal boundaries. A series of treaties in the 1780s and 1790s opened some lands to white settlement. (Source: From Lester J. Cappon et al., eds., *Atlas of Early American History: The Revolutionary Era, 1760–1790.* Copyright © 1976 by Princeton University Press. Reprinted by permission of Princeton University Press.)

front so as to avoid the piecemeal surrender of land by individual bands and villages. But they faced a difficult task. In the postwar world, Indian nations could no longer pursue the diplomatic strategy that had worked so well for so long: playing off European and American powers against one another. France was gone; Spanish territory lay far to the west and south; and British power was confined to Canada, north of the Great Lakes. Only the United States remained.

At first the national government ignored the western confederacy. Shortly after state land cessions were completed, Congress began to organize the Northwest Territory, bounded by the Mississippi River, the Great Lakes, and the Ohio River (see Map 7.1). Ordinances passed in 1784, 1785, and 1787 outlined the process through which the land could be sold to settlers and formal governments could be organized.

Ordinances of 1784 and 1785

To ensure orderly development, Congress in 1785 directed that the land be surveyed into townships 6 miles square, each divided into thirty-six sections of 640 acres (1 square mile). Revenue from the sale of the sixteenth section of each township was to be reserved for the support of public schools—the first instance of federal aid to education in American history. One dollar was the minimum price per acre; the minimum sale was one section. Thus Congress showed little concern for the small farmer: the resulting minimum outlay, $640, lay beyond the reach of ordinary Americans, except those veterans who received part of their army pay in land warrants. Proceeds from western land sales constituted the first independent revenues available to the national government.

The most important of the three land policies—the Northwest Ordinance of 1787—contained a bill of rights guaranteeing settlers freedom of religion and the right to a jury trial, forbidding cruel and unusual punishments, and nominally prohibiting slavery. Eventually, that prohibition became an important symbol for antislavery northerners, but at the time it had little effect. Some residents of the territory already held slaves, and Congress did not intend to deprive them of their property. Moreover, the ordinance also contained a provision allowing slaveowners to "lawfully reclaim" runaway bondspeople who took refuge in the territory—the first national fugitive slave law. The ordinance prevented slavery from taking deep root by discouraging slaveholders from moving into the territory with their human chattel, but not until 1848 was enslavement abolished throughout the region, now known as the Old Northwest.

Northwest Ordinance

The ordinance of 1787 also specified the process by which residents of the territory could organize state governments and seek admission to the Union "on an equal footing with the original States." Early in the nation's history, therefore, Congress laid down a policy of admitting new states on the same basis as the old

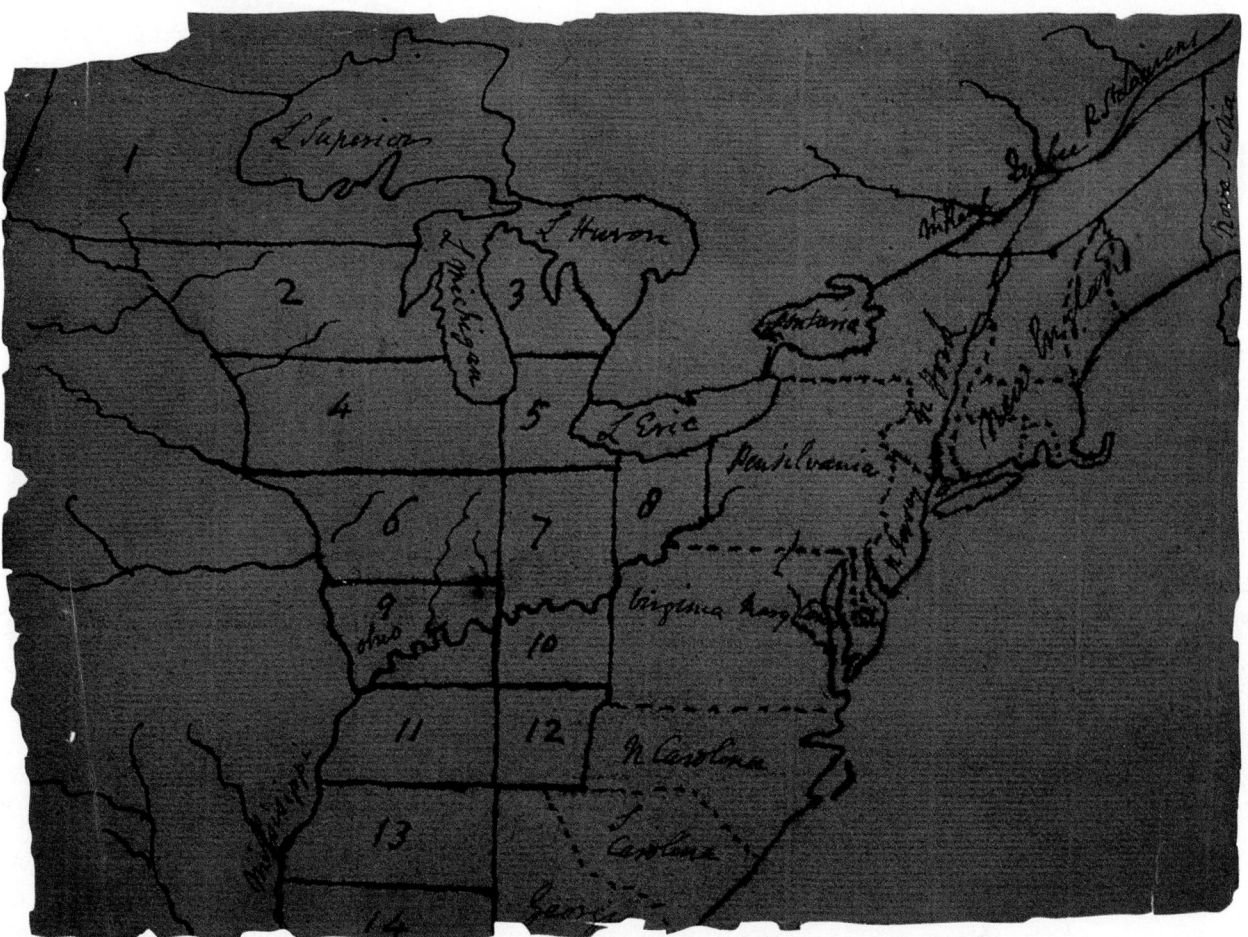

In 1784 Thomas Jefferson proposed a scheme for organizing the new nation's western lands. His plan would have divided the region on a grid pattern, yielding fourteen new states (with names such as "Metropotamia" and "Pelisipia") composed of 10-mile-square "hundreds." After a year of debate, Jefferson's plan was replaced by the one adopted in the Land Ordinance of 1785, which is described in the text.   (Clements Library, University of Michigan)

and assuring residents of the territories the same rights held by citizens of the original states. Having suffered under the rule of a colonial power, congressmen understood the importance of preparing the new nation's first "colony" for eventual self-government. Nineteenth- and twentieth-century Americans were to be less generous in their attitudes toward residents of later territories, many of whom were non-European or non-Protestant. But the nation never fully lost sight of the egalitarian principles of the Northwest Ordinance.

In a sense, though, in 1787 the ordinance was purely theoretical. The Miamis, Shawnees, and Delawares refused to acknowledge American sovereignty. They opposed settlement violently, attacking unwary pioneers who ventured too far north of the Ohio

River. In 1788 the Ohio Company, to which Congress had sold a large tract of land at reduced rates, established the town of Marietta at the juncture of the Ohio and Muskingum Rivers. But Indians prevented the company from extending settlement very far into the interior. After General Arthur St. Clair, the Northwest Territory's first governor, failed to negotiate a meaningful treaty with the Indians in early 1789, the United States could not avoid clashing with the western confederacy, composed of eight nations and led by the Miamis.

Little Turtle, the able war chief of the Miami Confederacy, defeated first General Josiah Harmar (1790) and then St. Clair himself (1791) in major battles near the present border between Indiana and

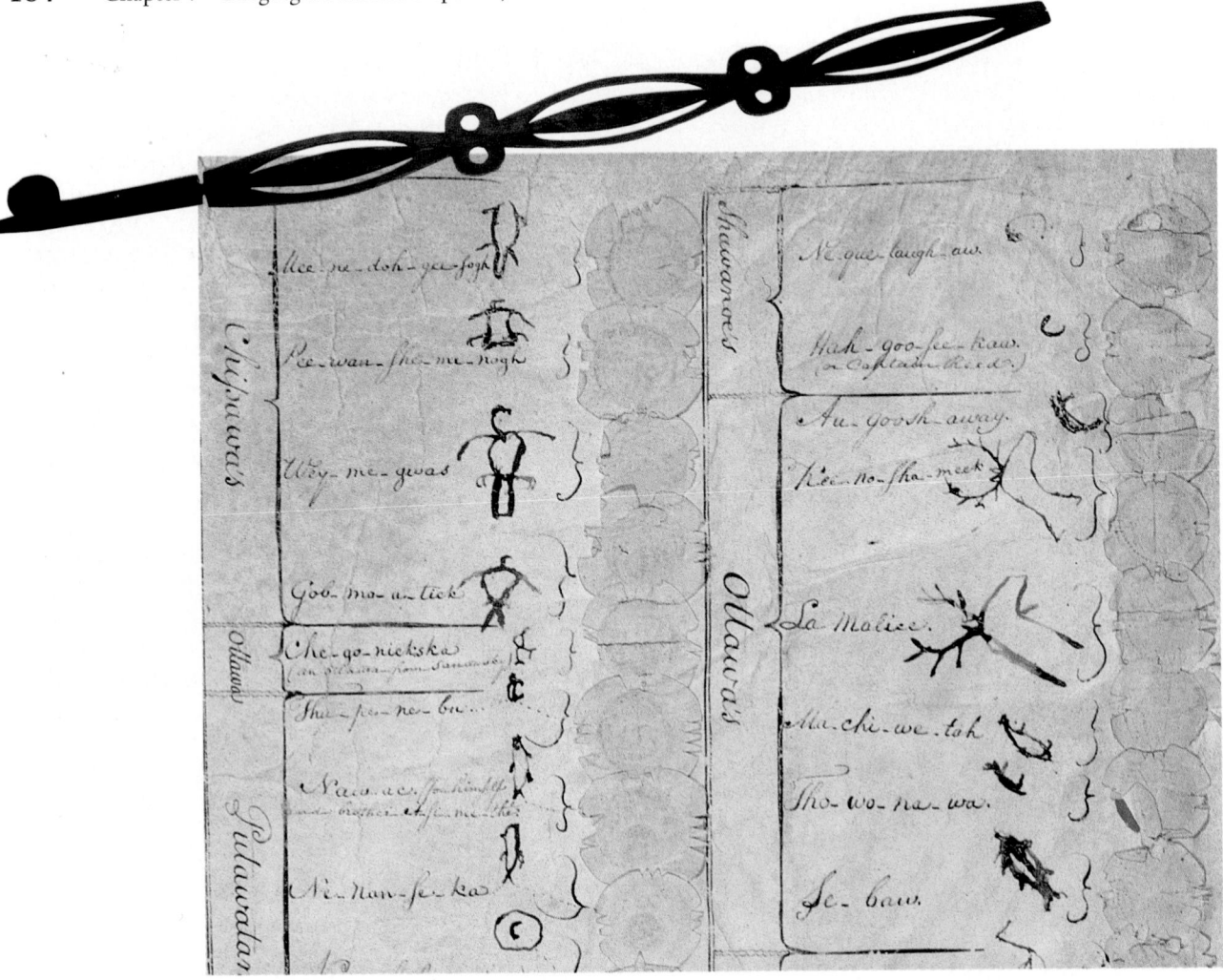

In the summer of 1795, the United States and the Miami Confederacy signed the Treaty of Greenville, bringing an end to open conflict after several years of warfare. All the participants smoked the calumet (peace pipe) pictured here, symbolizing their acceptance of the treaty. Because there were so many signatories, the ceremony took a long time. (Pipe: Ohio Historical Society; Treaty: National Archives)

War in the Old Northwest

Ohio. More than six hundred of St. Clair's men died, and scores more were wounded, in the United States' worst defeat in the entire history of the American frontier. In 1793 the Miami Confederacy declared that peace could be achieved only if the United States recognized the Ohio River as its northwestern boundary. But the national government refused to relinquish its claims in the region. A new army under the command of General Anthony Wayne, a Revolutionary War hero, attacked and defeated the confederacy in August 1794 at the Battle of Fallen Timbers (near present-day

Toledo, Ohio; see Map 7.2). Peace negotiations began after the victory.

By the summer of 1795, Wayne reached agreement with the Miami Confederacy. The Treaty of Greenville gave each side a portion of what it wanted. The United States gained the right to settle much of what was to become Ohio, the indigenous peoples retaining only the northwest corner of the region. Indians, though, received the acknowledgment they had long sought: American recognition of their rights to the soil. At Greenville, the United States formally accepted the principle of Indian sovereignty, by virtue of residence, over all lands the native peoples had not ceded. Never again would the United States government claim that it had acquired Indian territory solely through negotiation with a European or North American country.

The problems the United States encountered in ensuring safe settlement of the Northwest Territory revealed the basic weakness of the Confederation government. Not until after the Articles of Confederation were replaced with a new constitution could the United States muster sufficient force to implement the Northwest Ordinance. Thus, although the ordinance is often viewed as one of the few lasting accomplishments of the Confederation Congress, it must be seen within a context of political impotence.

From Crisis to the Constitution

Americans involved in finance, overseas trade, and foreign affairs became acutely aware of the inadequacies of the Articles of Confederation. In those areas the Articles had obvious deficiencies: Congress could not levy taxes, nor could it impose its will on the states to establish a uniform commercial policy or to ensure the enforcement of treaties. Partly as a result, the American economy slid into a depression less than a year after war's end. Exporters of staple crops (especially tobacco and rice) and importers of manufactured goods suffered from the postwar restrictions European powers imposed on American commerce. Although recovery began by 1786, the war's effects proved impossible to erase, particularly in the Lower South. Some estimates suggest that between 1775 and 1790 America's per capita gross national product declined by nearly 50 percent.

The war, indeed, wrought permanent change in the American economy. The near total cessation of foreign commerce in nonmilitary items during the war stimulated domestic manufacturing. Consequently, despite the influx of European goods after 1783, the postwar period witnessed the stirrings of American industrial development. For example, the first American textile mill began production in Pawtucket, Rhode Island, in 1793. Because of continuing population growth, the domestic market assumed greater relative importance in the overall economy. Moreover, foreign trade patterns shifted from Europe and toward the West Indies, continuing a trend that had begun before the war. Foodstuffs shipped to the French and Dutch

Economic Change

Caribbean islands became America's largest single export, replacing tobacco (and thus accelerating the Chesapeake's conversion from tobacco to grain production). South Carolina resumed importing slaves on a large scale, as planters sought to replace workers lost to wartime disruptions. Yet without British subsidies American indigo could not compete with that produced in the Caribbean, and even rice planters struggled to find new markets.

Recognizing the Confederation Congress's inability to deal with commercial matters, representatives of Virginia and Maryland met at Mt. Vernon (George Washington's plantation) in March 1785 to negotiate an agreement about trade on the Potomac River, which divided the two states for much of its length. The successful meeting led to an invitation to other states to discuss trade policy generally at a convention in Annapolis, Maryland. Although nine states named representatives to the meeting in September 1786, only five delegations attended. Those present realized that so few people could not have any significant impact on the political system. They issued a call for another convention, to be held in Philadelphia nine months later, "to devise such further provisions as shall . . . appear necessary to render the constitution of the federal government adequate to the exigencies of the Union."

Annapolis Convention

The other states did not respond immediately. But then an armed rebellion in Massachusetts did what a polite invitation to convene could not: convince doubters that reform was needed. Farmers from the western part of the state, many of them veterans, violently opposed high taxes (levied by the eastern-dominated legislature to pay off war debts) and an allied policy of foreclosing on the lands of tax defaulters. Daniel Shays, a former officer in the Continental Army, assumed the nominal leadership of the disgruntled western farmers. On January 25, 1787, he led about 1,500 men in an assault on the federal armory at Springfield, attempting to capture the military stores housed there. The militiamen mustered to defend the armory fired on their former comrades in arms, who then withdrew after suffering twenty-four casualties. The westerners did not confine to the battlefield their challenge to the legitimacy of a government controlled by eastern merchants. Terming Massachusetts "tyrannical," they insisted that "whenever any encroachments are made either upon the liberties or properties of the people, if redress

Shays's Rebellion

cannot be had without, it is virtue in them to disturb government." They thereby explicitly linked their rebellion to the earlier independence struggle.

Such explosive assertions convinced many political leaders that the nation's problems extended far beyond trade policy. To some, the rebellion confirmed the need for a much stronger federal government. After most of the states had already appointed delegates, the Confederation Congress belatedly endorsed the convention, "for the sole and express purpose of revising the Articles of Confederation." In mid-May 1787, fifty-five men, representing all the states but Rhode Island, assembled in Philadelphia to begin their deliberations.

The vast majority of delegates to the Constitutional Convention were men of property and substance. They all favored reform;

Constitutional Convention in Philadelphia

otherwise, they would not have come to Philadelphia. Most wanted to invigorate the national government and to give it new authority over taxation and foreign commerce. Many had been members of state legislatures, and some had helped to draft state constitutions. All were influenced in their Philadelphia deliberations by their under-

James Madison (1751–1836), the youthful scholar and skilled politician who earned the title "Father of the Constitution." (Library of Congress)

standing of the success or failure of those constitutions' provisions. Their ranks included merchants, planters, physicians, generals, governors, and especially lawyers—twenty-three had studied the law. Most had been born in America, and many came from families that had arrived in the seventeenth century. In an era when only a tiny proportion of the population had any advanced education, more than half of the delegates had attended college. A few had been educated in Britain, but most had graduated from American institutions: Princeton, with ten, counted the most alumni participants. The youngest delegate was twenty-six, the oldest—Benjamin Franklin—eighty-one. Like George Washington, whom they elected their presiding officer, most were in their vigorous middle years. A dozen men did the bulk of the convention's work. Of these, James Madison of Virginia was by far the most important; he deserves the title "Father of the Constitution."

The frail, shy James Madison was thirty-six years old in 1787. A Princeton graduate raised in western

James Madison: Father of the Constitution

Virginia, he served on the local Committee of Safety and was elected successively to the provincial convention, the state's lower and upper houses, and the Continental Congress (1780–1783). Although Madison returned to Virginia to serve in the state legislature in 1784, he remained in touch with national politics, partly through his continuing correspondence with his close friend Thomas Jefferson. A promoter of the Annapolis Convention, he strongly supported its call for further reform.

Madison stood out among the delegates for his systematic preparation for the Philadelphia meeting. Through Jefferson in Paris he bought more than two hundred books on history and government, carefully analyzing their accounts of past confederacies and republics. A month before the Constitutional Convention began, he summed up the results of his research in a lengthy paper entitled "Vices of the Political System of the United States." After listing the flaws he perceived in the current structure of the government (among them "encroachments by the states on the federal authority" and lack of unity "in matters where common interest requires it"), Madison revealed the conclusion that would guide his actions over the next few months. What the government most needed, he declared, was "such a modification of the sovereignty as will render it sufficiently neutral between the different interests and factions, to controul one part of the society from invading the rights of another, and at the

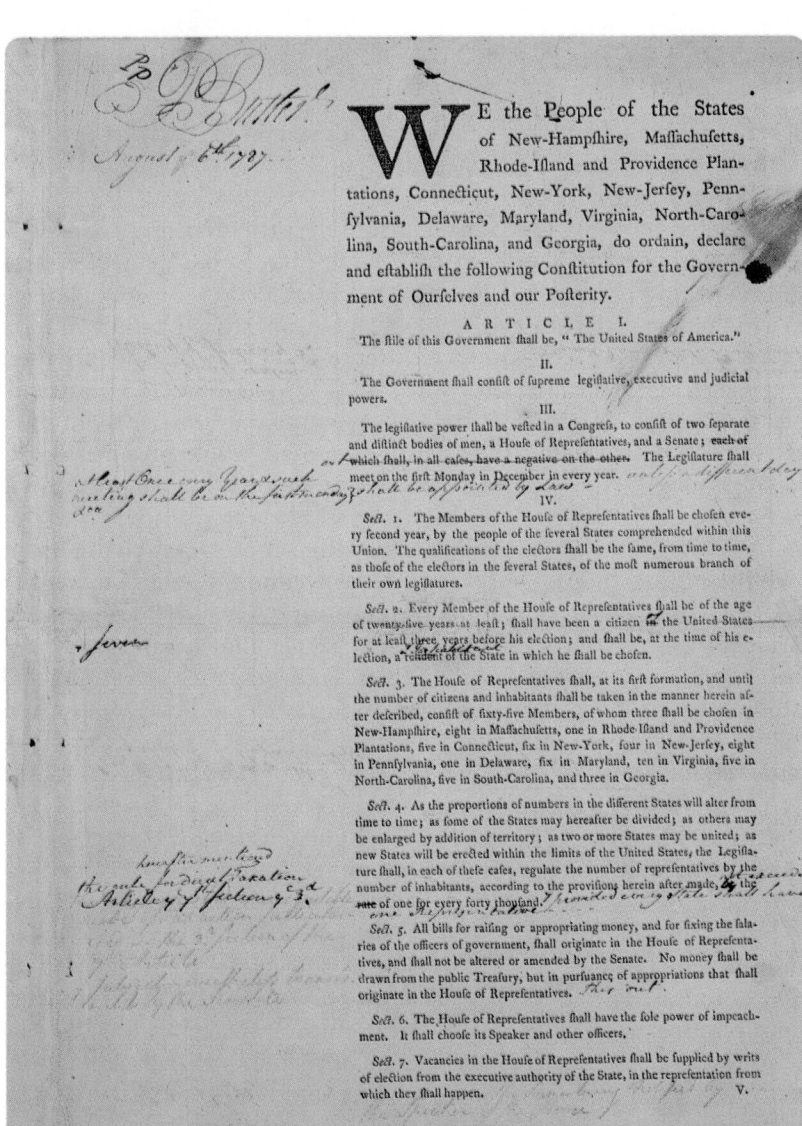

In August 1787 a first draft of the Constitution was secretly printed in Philadelphia for the use of convention members. Wide margins left room for additions and amendments, such as those made on this copy by the South Carolina delegate Pierce Butler. Note that in this early version the preamble does not yet read "We the people of the United States," but instead begins by listing the individual states.   (The Gilder Lehrman Collection, on deposit at the Pierpont Morgan Library/Art Resource, N.Y.)

same time sufficiently controuled itself, from setting up an interest adverse to that of the whole Society."

Thus Madison set forth the principle of checks and balances. The government, he believed, had to be constructed in such a way that it could not become tyrannical or fall wholly under the influence of a particular faction. He regarded the large size of a potential national republic as an advantage in that respect. Rejecting the common assertion that republics had to be small to survive, Madison argued that a large, diverse republic should be preferred. Because the nation would include many different factions, no one of them would be able to control the government. Political stability would result from compromises among the contending parties.

The so-called Virginia Plan, introduced on May 29 by Edmund Randolph, embodied Madison's con-

Virginia and New Jersey Plans

ception of national government. The plan provided for a two-house legislature, the lower house elected directly by the people and the upper house selected by the lower; representation in both houses proportional to property or population; an executive elected by Congress; a national judiciary; and congressional veto over state laws. The Virginia Plan gave Congress the broad power to legislate "in all cases to which the separate states are incompetent." Had it been adopted intact, it would have created a government in which national authority reigned unchallenged and state power was greatly diminished. Proportional representation in both houses (however reckoned) would also have given large states a dominant voice in the national government.

The convention included many delegates who recognized the need for change but believed the Virginia Plan went too far in the direction of national consolidation. After two weeks of debate on Randolph's proposal, disaffected delegates—particularly those from small states—united under the leadership of William Paterson of New Jersey. On June 15 Paterson presented an alternative scheme, the New Jersey Plan, calling for strengthening the Articles rather than completely overhauling the government. Paterson proposed retaining a unicameral congress in which each state had an equal vote, but giving Congress new powers of taxation and trade regulation. Paterson earlier had made his position clear in debate. Asserting that the Articles were "the proper basis of all the proceedings of the convention," he contended that the delegates' proper task was "to mark the orbits of the states with due precision and provide for the use of coercion" by the national government. Although the convention initially rejected Paterson's position, he and his allies won a number of victories in the months that followed.

The delegates began their work by discussing the structure and functions of Congress. They readily agreed that the new national government should have a two-house (bicameral) legislature. In addition, they concurred, in accordance with Americans' long-standing opposition to virtual representation (see page 124), that "the people" (however that term was defined) should be directly represented in at least one house of Congress. But they discovered that they differed widely in their answers to three key questions: Should representation in *both* houses of Congress be proportional to population? How was representation in either or both houses to be apportioned among the states? And, finally, how were the members of the two houses to be elected?

The Debates: Houses of Congress

The last issue proved the easiest to resolve. To quote John Dickinson, the delegates thought it "essential" that members of the lower branch of Congress be elected directly by the people and "expedient" that members of the upper house be chosen by state legislatures. Since legislatures had selected delegates to the Confederation Congress, they would expect a similar privilege in the new government. If the convention had not agreed to allow state legislatures to elect senators, the Constitution would have run into significant opposition among state political leaders. The plan also had the virtue of placing the election of one house of Congress one step removed from the "lesser sort," whose judgment the elites at the convention did not wholly trust.

The possibility of representation proportional to population in the Senate caused considerably greater disagreement. The delegates accepted without much debate the principle of proportional representation in the House of Representatives. But small states, through their spokesman Luther Martin of Maryland, argued for equal representation in the Senate. Such a scheme, they rightly supposed, would give them relatively more power at the national level. Large states, on the other hand, supported a proportional plan, for they would then be allotted more votes in the upper house. For weeks the convention deadlocked, neither side able to obtain a majority. A committee appointed to work out a compromise recommended equal representation in the Senate, coupled with a proviso that all appropriation bills originate in the lower house. But not until the convention accepted a suggestion that a state's two senators vote as individuals rather than as a unit was a breakdown averted.

The Debates: Slavery and Representation

The remaining critical question divided the nation along sectional lines rather than by size of state: how was representation in the lower house to be apportioned among states? Delegates from states with large numbers of slaves wanted African and European inhabitants to be counted equally; delegates from states with few slaves wanted only free people to be counted. Slavery thus became inextricably linked to the foundation of the new government. Delegates resolved the dispute by using a formula developed by the Confederation Congress in 1783 to allocate financial assessments among states: three-fifths of slaves would be included in population totals. (The formula reflected delegates' judgment that slaves were less efficient producers of wealth than free people, not that they were 60 percent human and 40 percent property.) The three-fifths compromise on representation won unanimous approval. Only two delegates, Gouverneur Morris of New York and George Mason of Virginia, later spoke out against the institution of slavery.

Constitutional Protections for Slavery

Although the words *slave* and *slavery* do not appear in the Constitution (the framers used euphemisms such as "other persons"), the document contained both direct and indirect protections for slavery. The three-fifths clause, for example, assured white southern male voters not only congressional representation out of proportion to their numbers but also a disproportionate influence on the selection of the president, since the number of each state's electoral votes was determined by the size of its congressional delegation. The Constitution prohibited Congress from outlawing the slave trade for at least twenty years, and the fugitive slave clause required all states to return runaways to their masters. By guaranteeing that the national government would aid any states threatened with "domestic violence," the Constitution promised aid in putting down future slave revolts, as well as incidents like Shays's Rebellion.

Once delegates agreed on the knotty, conjoined problems of slavery and representation, they readily achieved consensus on the other issues confronting them. All agreed that the national government needed the authority to tax and to regulate commerce. But instead of giving Congress the nearly unlimited scope proposed in the Virginia Plan, delegates enumerated congressional powers and then provided for flexibility by granting it all authority "necessary and proper" to carry out those powers. Discarding the congressional veto contained in the Virginia Plan, the convention implied but did not explicitly authorize a national judicial veto of state laws. The Constitution plus national laws and treaties would constitute "the supreme law of the land; and the judges in every state shall be bound thereby," Article VI declared ambiguously. As another means of circumscribing state powers, delegates drafted a long list of actions forbidden to states.

The convention placed primary responsibility for conducting foreign affairs in the hands of the president, who was also designated commander-in-chief of the armed forces.

The Presidency

That decision raised the question, left unspecified in the Constitution's text, of whether the president (or Congress, for that matter) acquired special powers in times of war. With the consent of the Senate, the president could appoint judges and other federal officers. To select the president, delegates established an elaborate mechanism, the electoral college, whose members would be chosen in each state by legislatures or qualified voters. This system, they hoped, would ensure that the executive would be independent of the national legislature—and of the people. They also agreed that the chief executive should serve a four-year term but be eligible for reelection.

The final document still showed signs of its origins in the Virginia Plan, but compromises created a system of government less powerful at the national

Separation of Powers

level than Madison and Randolph had envisioned. The key to the Constitution was the distribution of political authority—that is, separation of powers among executive, legislative, and judicial branches of the national government, and division of powers between states and nation. Two-thirds of Congress and three-fourths of the states, for example, had to concur on amendments. The branches balanced one another, their powers deliberately entwined to prevent each from acting independently. The president could veto congressional legislation, but that veto could be overriden by two-thirds majorities in both houses, and his treaties and major appointments required the Senate's consent. Congress could impeach the president and federal judges, but courts appeared to have the final say on interpreting the Constitution. These checks and balances would make it difficult for the government to become tyrannical. At the same time, though, the elaborate system would sometimes prevent the government from acting quickly and decisively. Furthermore, the Constitution drew such a vague line between state and national powers that the United States fought a civil war in the next century over that very issue.

The convention held its last session on September 17, 1787. Of the forty-two delegates present (others had returned home weeks earlier), only three refused to sign the Constitution, two of them in part because of the lack of a bill of rights. Benjamin Franklin had written a speech calling for unity; because his weak voice could not be heard, another delegate read it for him. "I confess that there are several parts of this constitution which I do not at present approve," Franklin admitted. Yet he urged its acceptance "because I expect no better, and because I am not sure, that it is not the best." Only then was the Constitution made public. The convention's proceedings had been entirely secret—and remained so until the delegates' private notes were published in the nineteenth century. (See the Appendix for the full text of the Constitution.)

Opposition and Ratification

Later the same month, the Confederation Congress submitted the Constitution to the states but did not formally recommend approval. The ratification clause provided for the new system to take effect once it was approved by special conventions in at least nine states, with delegates being elected by qualified voters. Thus the national Constitution, unlike the Articles of Confederation, would rest directly on popular authority (and the presumably hostile state legislatures would be circumvented).

As states began to elect delegates to the special conventions, discussion of the proposed government grew more heated. Newspaper essays and pamphlets vigorously defended or attacked the Philadelphia convention's decisions. The extent of the debate was unprecedented. Every newspaper in the country printed the full text of the Constitution, and most supported its adoption. It quickly became apparent, though, that disputes within the Constitutional Convention had been mild compared to divisions of opinion within the populace as a whole. Although most citizens concurred that the national government should have more power over taxation and foreign commerce, some believed that the proposed government held the potential for tyranny. As happened in Carlisle, Pennsylvania, the vigorous debate between the two sides frequently spilled out into the streets.

Those supporting the proposed Constitution called themselves Federalists. They built on the notions of classical republicanism, holding forth a vision of a virtuous, self-sacrificing republic vigorously led by a manly aristocracy of talent. Claiming that the nation did not need to fear centralized authority when good men drawn from the elite were in charge, they argued that the carefully structured government would preclude the possibility of tyranny. A republic could be large, they declared, if the government's design prevented any one group from controlling it. The separation of powers among legislative, executive, and judicial branches, and the division of powers between states and nation, would accomplish that goal. Thus people did not need to be protected from the powers of the new government in a formal way. Instead, their liberties would be guarded by "distinguished worthies"—men of the "better sort" whose only goal (said George Washington) was "to merit the approbation of good and virtuous men."

Federalists

The Federalists termed those who opposed the Constitution Antifederalists, thus tagging them with negative nomenclature. Antifederalists, while recognizing the need for a national source of revenue, feared a too-powerful central government. They saw the states as the chief protectors of individual rights; consequently, weakening the states could bring the onset of arbitrary power. Antifederalist argu-

Antifederalists

ments against the Constitution often consisted of lists of potential abuses of government authority.

Heirs of the Real Whig ideology of the late 1760s and early 1770s, Antifederalists stressed the need for constant popular vigilance to avert oppression. Indeed, some of the Antifederalists had originally promulgated those ideas—Samuel Adams, Patrick Henry, and Richard Henry Lee led the opposition to the Constitution. Such older Americans, whose political opinions had been shaped prior to the centralizing, nationalistic Revolution, peopled the Antifederalist ranks. Joining them were small farmers preoccupied with guarding their property against excessive taxation, and ambitious, upwardly mobile men who would benefit from an economic and political system less tightly controlled than that the Constitution envisioned. Federalists denigrated such men as disorderly, licentious, and even "unmanly" and "boyish" because they would not follow the elites' lead in supporting the Constitution.

As public debate continued, Antifederalists focused on the Constitution's lack of a bill of rights. Even if the new system weakened the states, Antis believed, people could still be protected from tyranny by specific guarantees of rights. The Constitution did contain some prohibitions on congressional power. For example, the writ of habeas corpus, which prevented arbitrary imprisonment, could not be suspended except in dire emergencies. But Antifederalists found such constitutional provisions to be few and inadequate. Nor were they reassured by Federalist assertions that the new government could not violate people's rights because it had only limited powers. Antis wanted the national governing document to incorporate a bill of rights, as had most state constitutions.

Importance of a Bill of Rights

Letters of a Federal Farmer, perhaps the most widely read Antifederalist pamphlet, listed the rights that should be protected: freedom of the press and religion, trial by jury, and guarantees against unreasonable searches. From Paris, Thomas Jefferson added his voice to the chorus. Replying to Madison's letter conveying a copy of the Constitution, Jefferson declared, "I like much the general idea" but not "the omission of a bill of rights. . . . A bill of rights is what the people are entitled to against every government on earth, general or particular, and what no just government should refuse, or rest on inference."

As state conventions considered ratification, the lack of a bill of rights loomed ever larger as a flaw in

Ratification of the Constitution

the proposed government. Four of the first five states to ratify did so unanimously, but serious disagreements then surfaced. Massachusetts, in which Antifederalist forces had been bolstered by a backlash against the state government's heavy-handed treatment of the Shays rebels, ratified by a majority of only 19 votes out of 355 cast. In June 1788, when New Hampshire ratified, the requirement of nine states was satisfied. But New York and Virginia had not yet voted, and everyone realized the new Constitution could not succeed unless those key states accepted it.

Despite a valiant effort by the Antifederalist Patrick Henry, pro-Constitution forces won by 10 votes in the Virginia convention. In New York, James Madison, John Jay, and Alexander Hamilton campaigned for ratification by publishing *The Federalist*, a political tract that explained the theory behind the Constitution and masterfully answered its critics. Their reasoned arguments, coupled with Federalists' promise to add a bill of rights to the Constitution, helped win the battle. On July 26, 1788, New York ratified the Constitution by the slim margin of 3 votes. Although the last states—North Carolina and Rhode Island—did not join the Union until November 1789 and May 1790, respectively, the new government was a reality.

Americans in many cities celebrated ratification (somewhat prematurely) with a series of parades on

Celebrating Ratification

July 4, 1788. The carefully planned processions dramatized the history and symbolized the unity of the new nation, seeking to counteract memories of the dissent that had so recently engulfed such cities as Carlisle, Pennsylvania (see page 167). Like pre-Revolution protest meetings, the parades served as political lessons for literate and illiterate Americans alike. The processions aimed to educate men and women about the significance of the new Constitution and to instruct them about political leaders' hopes for industry and frugality on the part of a virtuous American public.

Symbols expressing those goals filled the Philadelphia parade, planned by the artist Charles Willson Peale. About five thousand people participated in the procession, which featured floats portraying such themes as "The Grand Federal Edifice" and stretched for a mile and a half. Marchers representing the first pioneers and Revolutionary War troops paraded with groups of farmers and artisans dramatizing their work.

The Federal Almanack for 1789 trumpeted the virtues of the new Constitution. Not all Americans were so certain that the national government, here symbolized as an edifice supported by thirteen pillars, was as "solid, strong as time" as the printer proclaimed. (American Antiquarian Society)

More than forty groups of tradesmen, including barbers, hatters, printers, cloth manufacturers, and clockmakers, sponsored floats. Lawyers, doctors, clergymen of all denominations, and congressmen followed the artisans. A final group of marchers symbolized the nation's future: students from the University of Pennsylvania and other city schools bore a flag labeled "The Rising Generation."

The Philadelphia State House (the building now known as Independence Hall, but without its familiar tower), on the left; and, to its right, Congress Hall, where Congress met when Philadelphia served as the U.S. capital. Portrayed in front of the state house in this 1792 watercolor is the 33-foot-long vessel *Union,* an elaborately constructed ship carried through the city streets in the grand ratification parade of July 4, 1788. (Philadelphia Museum of Art, Lent by the Dietrich American Foundation)

Summary

 During the 1770s and 1780s the nation took shape as a political union. It began to develop an economy independent of the British Empire and attempted to chart its own course in the world in order to protect the national interest, defend the country's borders, and promote beneficial trade. Some Americans prescribed rules for the cultural and intellectual life they thought appropriate for a republic, outlining artistic and educational goals for a properly virtuous people. An integral part of the formation of the Union was the systematic formulation of American racist thought. Emphasizing race (rather than status as slave or free) as a determinant of African Americans' standing in the nation, and defining women as nonpolitical, allowed men who now termed themselves "white" to define *republicanism* to exclude all people but themselves and to ensure that they would dominate the country for the foreseeable future.

The experience of fighting a war and of struggling for survival as an independent nation altered the political context of American life in the 1780s. At the outset of the war, most Americans believed that "that government which governs best governs least," but by the late 1780s many had changed their minds. They were the drafters and supporters of the Constitution, who concluded from the republic's vicissitudes under the Articles of Confederation that the United States needed a more powerful central government. They contended during ratification debates that their proposed solution to the nation's problems was just as "republican" in conception (if not more so) as the Articles.

Both sides concurred in a general adherence to republican principles, but they emphasized different views of republicanism. Federalists advanced a position based on the principles of classical republicanism. Antifederalists, fearing that elected leaders would not subordinate personal gain to the good of the whole, wanted a weak central government, formal protection of individual rights, and a loosely regulated economy.

The Federalists won their point when the Constitution was adopted, however narrowly. The process of consolidating the states into a national whole was thereby formalized. The 1790s, the first decade of government under the Constitution, would witness hesitant steps toward the creation of a true nation, the United States of America.

LEGACY FOR A PEOPLE AND A NATION
Women's Education

In the early years of the twenty-first century, women comprise a slim majority of the students enrolled in U.S. colleges and universities. Because women were denied all access to collegiate education in this country until the middle of the nineteenth century, that is a remarkable development. Its roots lie deep, in the republican ideology of the 1770s and 1780s.

Once the United States had established republican forms of government at both state and national levels, its citizens began to worry about sustaining those governments—thought to be fragile and easily disrupted—for the decades and centuries to come. The future, everyone knew, lay in the hands of the nation's children, especially its sons. And theorists concluded that those sons could successfully perpetuate the republic only if they learned the lessons of patriotism from their mothers. Male and female reformers therefore began to argue that women in the United States should be better educated than those who lived under other forms of government. If American women were ignorant of the nation's history or principles of government, or if they did not know enough basic reading or arithmetic to assist their husbands in running farms or businesses, the republic was doomed to collapse in just a generation or two.

Some of those reformers accordingly founded private academies (roughly equivalent to modern high schools) to teach young women from leading families such subjects as history, geography, mathematics, and languages. Some of the women who attended those academies later started educational establishments of their own—including Mary Lyon, who in 1837 founded Mt. Holyoke College in western Massachusetts, the first institution of higher education for women in the United States. A few years later, some colleges for men (such as Oberlin, in Ohio) and state universities (for example, Michigan) admitted women as students, and a number of women's colleges were established. Not until the second half of the twentieth century, however, did American women gain truly equal access to higher education. In the 1970s such Ivy League universities as Yale and Princeton finally opened their doors to women students, and others (such as Cornell) that had sharply restricted women's enrollment through admissions quotas removed all constraints.

Along with the existence of the nation itself, increased educational opportunity for women is therefore one of the most important legacies of the revolutionary era for the American people.

For Further Reading, see page A-9 of the Appendix. For Web resources, go to http://college.hmco.com.

The twenty-eight-year-old guest on the Georgia plantation, a recent graduate of Yale College, had already proved himself to be good with his hands. His hostess, Catherine Greene (the widow of the Revolutionary War general Nathanael Greene), had complained that her embroidery frame was poorly designed—and so he quickly constructed a replacement. Thus when some neighboring planters discussed in Mrs. Greene's presence the seemingly insurmountable problem of extracting seeds from cotton fibers, she told them, "apply to my young friend, Mr. Whitney, he can make any thing."

Catherine Greene's "young friend," Eli Whitney, attacked the planters' challenge with the same ingenuity that had led him, while still a teenager, to develop methods for manufacturing nails on a large scale. Within ten days, he later recalled, he produced a small working model of the machine that would become known as the cotton gin. Whitney's device changed the lives of millions of people, for good and ill.

In the years after the Revolution, the United States sought another staple crop to augment such exports as tobacco and salt fish. When new spinning and weaving machines caused a boom in the British textile manufacturing industry in the 1780s, cotton seemed a possibility. But the only kind of cotton that could be grown widely in the United States had fibers that twisted tightly around its seeds. Removing the seeds by hand was costly, labor-intensive, and agonizingly slow. Before Whitney invented his cotton gin in 1793, few Americans planted much cotton because of such processing difficulties.

Whitney attached wire teeth to two adjacent rollers turned by a hand crank. The teeth tore the seeds from fibers fed between the rollers; the seeds then dropped through a screen into a receptacle. To prevent fibers from clogging the machine, Whitney also rigged a set of brushes that turned in the opposite direction, continually cleaning the rollers. This gin, its inventor proudly noted, processed cotton fifty times faster than hand workers could. The Georgia planters

Eli Whitney, the inventor of the cotton gin, in a portrait by his fellow Yale graduate Samuel F. B. Morse. Although the gin did not earn him the fortune Whitney had anticipated, it did eventually bring him great fame. (Yale University Art Gallery, Gift of George Hoadley, B.A., 1801)

THE EARLY REPUBLIC: CONFLICTS AT HOME AND ABROAD 1789–1800

Building a Workable Government
Domestic Policy Under Washington and Hamilton
The French Revolution and the Development of Partisan Politics
Partisan Politics and Relations with Great Britain
John Adams and Political Dissent
Race Relations at the End of the Century
LEGACY FOR A PEOPLE AND A NATION
Dissent During Wartime

who saw the machine quickly recognized its potential. Someone stole the model even before Whitney could request a patent on it, and thereafter he spent years in court defending his right to his invention. He did not fully establish his legal claims until shortly before the patent expired.

Whitney therefore did not profit greatly from the cotton gin, but many others did. Cotton exports became one of the mainstays of the American economy in the nineteenth century. The surge in cotton cultivation revived the institution of slavery, which in the immediate postrevolutionary period had appeared to be losing its reason for being, as Chesapeake tobacco planters switched to less labor-intensive grains, indigo cultivation collapsed, and new markets for rice had to be established. Southern planter families and New England capitalists gained a great deal by his invention, but enslaved people thus lost much more.

In the 1790s, before the full impact of Whitney's invention, the American economy still rested in large part on traditional exports. Americans found their vital commerce disrupted once more—with consequent fluctuations in their income and profits—when in 1793 England and France again went to war. The fight over ratifying the Constitution turned out to presage an even wider division over the major political, economic, and diplomatic questions confronting the young republic: the extent to which authority (especially fiscal authority) should be centralized in the national government; the relationship of national power and states' rights; the formulation of foreign policy in an era of continual warfare in Europe; and the limits of dissent. Americans did not anticipate the acrimonious disagreements that rocked the 1790s. Believing that the Constitution would resolve the problems that had arisen under the Confederation, they mistakenly expected the new government to rule largely by consensus. And no one predicted the difficulties that would develop as the United States attempted to deal with Indian nations now wholly encompassed within its borders.

Most important of all, perhaps, they could not understand or fully accept the division of America's political leaders into two factions—not yet political parties—known as Federalists and Democratic-Republicans, believing that only monarchies should experience such factional disputes. In republics, they believed, the rise of factions signified decay and corruption. As the decade closed with the first fully partisan presidential election, Americans still had not come to terms with the implications of partisan politics. ■

Building a Workable Government

 The nationalistic spirit expressed in the processions celebrating ratification of the Constitution carried over to the first session of Congress. Only a few Antifederalists ran for office in the congressional elections held late in 1788, and even fewer were elected. Thus the First Congress consisted chiefly of men who supported a strong national government. The drafters of the Constitution had deliberately left many key issues undecided, so the nationalists' domination of Congress meant that their views on those points quickly prevailed.

Congress faced four immediate tasks when it convened in April 1789: raising revenue to support the new government, responding to states' calls for a bill of rights, setting up executive departments, and organizing the federal judiciary. The last task was especially important. The Constitution established a Supreme Court but left it to Congress to decide whether to have other federal courts as well.

James Madison, who had been elected to the House of Representatives, soon became as influential in Congress as he had been at the

Madison and the First Congress

Constitutional Convention. A few months into the first session, he persuaded Congress to adopt the Revenue Act of 1789, imposing a 5 percent tariff on certain imports. Thus the First Congress quickly achieved what the Confederation Congress never had: an effective national tax law. The new government would have problems in its first years, but lack of revenue was not one of them.

Madison also took the lead with respect to constitutional amendments. At the convention and thereafter, he had consistently opposed additional limitations on the national government. He believed it unnecessary to guarantee people's rights explicitly when the government was one of limited powers. But Madison recognized that Congress should respond to public opinion as expressed in state ratifying conventions. Accordingly, he placed nineteen proposed amendments before the House. The states soon ratified ten, which officially became part of the Constitution on December 15, 1791 (see the appendix for the Constitution and all amendments, including the twenty-seventh, which was one of Madison's nineteen). Their adoption defused Antifederalist opposition and rallied support for the new government.

IMPORTANT EVENTS

1789	Washington inaugurated as first president
	Judiciary Act of 1789 organizes federal court system
	French Revolution begins
1790	Hamilton's *Report on Public Credit* proposes assumption of state debts
1791	First ten amendments (Bill of Rights) ratified
	First national bank chartered
1793	France declares war on Britain, Spain, and the Netherlands
	Washington's neutrality proclamation keeps the United States out of war
	Democratic-Republican societies founded, the first grassroots political organizations
1794	Whiskey Rebellion in western Pennsylvania protests taxation
1795	Jay Treaty with England
	Pinckney's Treaty with Spain
1796	First contested presidential election: Adams elected president, Jefferson vice president
1798	XYZ affair arouses American opinion against France
	Sedition Act penalizes dissent
	Virginia and Kentucky resolutions protest suppression of dissent
1798–99	Quasi-War with France
1800	Franco-American Convention ends Quasi-War
	Jefferson elected president, Burr vice president
	Gabriel's Rebellion threatens Virginia slaveowners

The First Amendment specifically prohibited Congress from passing any law restricting the right to freedom of religion, speech, press, peaceable assembly, or petition. The next two amendments arose directly from the former colonists' fear of standing armies as a threat to freedom. The Second Amendment guaranteed the right "to keep and bear arms" because of the need for a "well-regulated Militia." Thus the constitutional right to bear arms was based on the expectation that most able-bodied men would serve the nation as citizen-soldiers, and there would be little need for a standing army. The Third Amendment limited the conditions under which troops could be quartered in private homes. The next five pertained to judicial procedures. The Fourth Amendment prohibited "unreasonable searches and seizures"; the Fifth and Sixth established the rights of accused persons; the Seventh specified the conditions for jury trials in civil (as opposed to criminal) cases; and the Eighth forbade "cruel and unusual punishments." The Ninth and Tenth Amendments reserved to the people and the states other unspecified rights and powers. In short, the amendments' authors made clear that, in listing some rights, they did not mean to preclude the exercise of others.

While debating proposed amendments, Congress also considered the organization of the executive branch. It readily agreed to continue the three administrative departments established under the Articles of Confederation: War, Foreign Affairs (renamed State), and Treasury. Congress instituted two lesser posts: the attorney general—the nation's official lawyer—and the postmaster general. Controversy arose over whether the president alone could dismiss officials whom he originally had appointed with the Senate's consent. After some debate, the House and Senate agreed that he had such authority. Thus was established the important principle that the heads of executive departments are accountable solely to the president.

Aside from constitutional amendments, the most far-reaching piece of legislation enacted by the First Congress was the Judiciary Act of 1789, which defined the jurisdiction of the federal judiciary and established a six-member Supreme Court, thirteen district courts, and three circuit courts of appeal. Its most important provision, Section 25, allowed appeals from state courts to federal courts when cases raised certain types of constitutional issues. Section 25 thus implemented Article VI of the Constitution, which stated that federal laws and treaties were to be considered "the supreme Law of the Land." For Article VI to be enforced uniformly, the national judiciary had to be able to overturn state court decisions in cases involving the Constitution, federal laws, or treaties. Yet nowhere did the Constitution explicitly permit such action by federal courts.

The Judiciary Act of 1789 presumed that the wording of Article VI implied the right of appeal from state to federal courts. In the nineteenth century, however, judges and legislators committed to states' rights challenged that interpretation.

During its first decade, the Supreme Court handled few cases of any importance, and several members resigned. (John Jay, the first chief justice, served only six years.) But in a significant 1796 decision, *Ware v.*

Hylton, the Court for the first time declared a state law unconstitutional. That same year it also reviewed the constitutionality of an act of Congress, upholding its validity in the case of *Hylton v. U.S.* The most important case of the decade, *Chisholm v. Georgia* (1793), established that states could be sued in federal courts by citizens of other states. This decision, unpopular with state governments, was overruled five years later by the Eleventh Amendment to the Constitution.

Domestic Policy Under Washington and Hamilton

George Washington did not seek the presidency. In 1783 he returned to Mount Vernon eager for the peaceful life of a Virginia planter. But his fellow countrymen never regarded Washington as just another private citizen. Unanimously elected to preside at the Constitutional Convention, he did not participate in debates but consistently voted for a strong national government. After the adoption of the new governmental structure, Americans concurred that only George Washington had sufficient stature to serve as the republic's first president, an office designed largely with him in mind. The unanimous vote of the electoral college merely formalized that consensus.

Reluctant to return to public life, George Washington nevertheless knew he could not ignore his country's call. Awaiting the summons to New York City, the nation's capital, he wrote to an old friend, "My movements to the chair of Government will be accompanied by feelings not unlike those of a culprit who is going to the place of his execution. . . . I am sensible, that I am embarking the voice of my Countrymen and a good name of my own, on this voyage, but what returns will be made for them, Heaven alone can foretell."

Washington acted cautiously during his first months in office, knowing that whatever he did would set precedents for the future. When

Washington's First Steps

the title by which he should be addressed aroused controversy (Vice President John Adams favored "His Highness, the President of the United States of America, and Protector of their Liberties"), Washington said nothing. The accepted title soon became a plain "Mr. President." By using the heads of the executive departments collectively as his chief advisers, he created the cabinet. As the Constitution required, he sent Congress an annual State of the

When George Washington toured the nation during his first term in office, he was greeted by local leaders in elaborately orchestrated rituals. The organizers of the ceremony at Providence, Rhode Island, on August 17, 1790, issued this broadside to inform participants of their plans for a formal procession. While some Americans gloried in such displays of pomp, others feared they presaged the return of monarchy.   (The Huntington Library & Art Collections, San Marino, California)

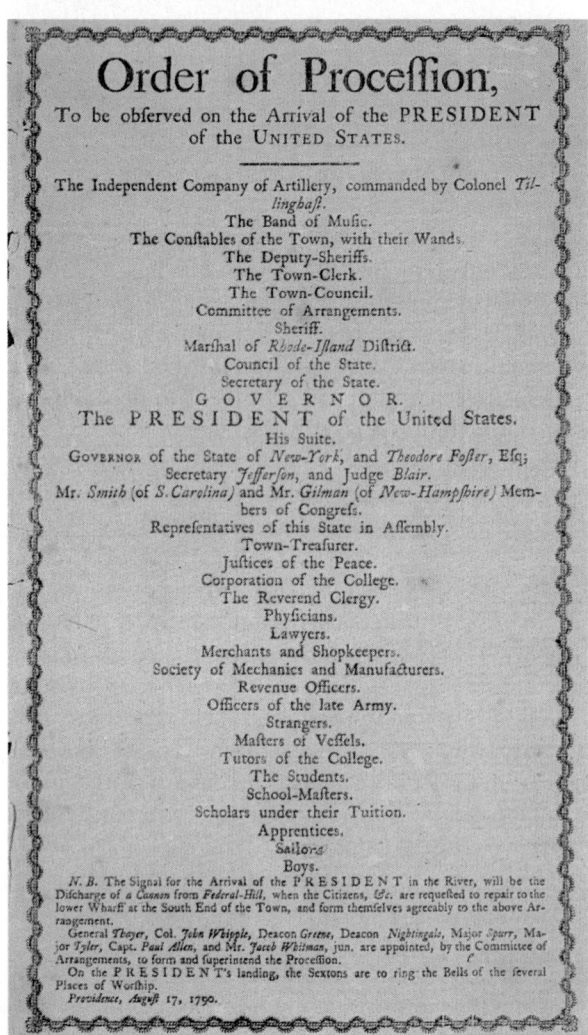

John Trumbull, known primarily for his larger-than-life portraits of patriot leaders, painted this miniature (c. 1792–1794) of George Washington, who posed for it during his presidency. (Division of Political History, Smithsonian Institution, Washington, D.C.)

Alexander Hamilton, by James Sharpless, about 1796. This profile of Hamilton, painted near the end of Washington's presidency, shows the secretary of the treasury as he looked during the years of his first heated partisan battles with Thomas Jefferson and James Madison (see page 203). (National Portrait Gallery, Smithsonian Institution/Art Resource, N.Y.)

Union message. Washington also concluded that he should exercise his veto power over congressional legislation very sparingly—only, indeed, if he became convinced a bill was unconstitutional.

Early in his term, Washington undertook elaborately organized journeys to all the states. At each stop, he was ritually welcomed by uniformed militia units, young women strewing flowers in his path, local leaders, groups of Revolutionary War veterans, and respectable citizens who presented him with formal addresses reaffirming their loyalty to the United States. The president thus personally came to embody national unity, simultaneously drawing ordinary folk into the sphere of national politics.

Washington's first major task as president was to choose the heads of the executive departments. For the War Department he selected an old comrade-in-arms, Henry Knox of Massachusetts, who had been his reliable general of artillery during much of the Revolution. His choice for the State Department was his fellow Virginian Thomas Jefferson, who had just re-

turned to the United States from his post as minister to France. And for the crucial position of secretary of the treasury, the president chose the brilliant, intensely ambitious Alexander Hamilton.

The illegitimate son of a Scottish aristocrat and a woman whose husband had divorced her for adultery and desertion, Hamilton was born in

Alexander Hamilton

the British West Indies in 1757. His early years were spent in poverty; after his mother's death when he was eleven, he worked as a clerk for a mercantile firm. In 1773 Hamilton enrolled in King's College (later Columbia University) in New York City. Only eighteen months later, in late 1774, the precocious seventeen-year-old contributed a pamphlet to the prerevolutionary publication wars. Devoted to the patriot cause, Hamilton volunteered for service in the American army, where he came to Washington's attention. In 1777 Washington appointed the young man as one of his aides, and the two developed great mutual affection.

The general's patronage helped the poor youth of dubious background to marry well. At twenty-three he took as his wife Elizabeth Schuyler, daughter of a wealthy New York family. After the war, Hamilton practiced law in New York City and served as a delegate first to the Annapolis Convention and then to the Constitutional Convention. Although he exerted little influence at either gathering, his contributions to *The Federalist* in 1788 revealed him as one of the chief political thinkers in the republic.

In his dual role as secretary of the treasury and one of Washington's major advisers, Hamilton exhibited two traits that distinguished him from most of his contemporaries. First, he displayed an undivided loyalty to the nation as a whole. As a West Indian who had lived on the mainland only briefly before the war, Hamilton had no ties to a particular state. He showed little sympathy for, or understanding of, demands for local autonomy. Thus the aim of his fiscal policies was always to consolidate power at the national level. Further, he never feared the exercise of centralized executive authority, as did older counterparts who had clashed repeatedly with colonial governors, nor was he afraid of maintaining close political and economic ties with Britain.

Second, Hamilton regarded his fellow human beings with unvarnished cynicism. Perhaps because of his difficult early life and his own overriding ambition, Hamilton believed people to be motivated primarily by self-interest—particularly economic self-interest. He placed no reliance on people's capacity for virtuous and self-sacrificing behavior. This outlook set him apart from those Americans who foresaw a rosy future in which public-spirited citizens would pursue the common good rather than their own private advantage. Although other Americans (for example, Madison) also stressed the role of private interests in a republic, Hamilton went beyond them in his emphasis on self-interest as the major motivator of human behavior. And his beliefs significantly influenced the way in which he tackled the monumental task before him: straightening out the new nation's tangled finances.

In 1789, Congress ordered the new secretary of the treasury to assess the public debt and to submit recommendations for supporting the government's credit. Hamilton found that the country's remaining war debts fell into three categories: those owed by the nation to foreign governments and investors, mostly to France (about $11 million); those owed by the national government to

National and State Debts

merchants, former soldiers, holders of revolutionary bonds, and the like (about $27 million); and, finally, similar debts owed by state governments (roughly $25 million). With respect to the national debt, few disagreed: Americans recognized that if their new government was to succeed, it would have to repay at full face value those financial obligations incurred by the nation while winning independence.

The state debts were another matter. Some states—notably Virginia, Maryland, North Carolina, and Georgia—already had paid off most of their war debts by levying taxes and handing out land grants in lieu of monetary payments. They would oppose the national government's assumption of responsibility for other states' debts because their citizens would be taxed to pay such obligations. Massachusetts, Connecticut, and South Carolina, by contrast, still had sizable unpaid debts and would welcome a system of national assumption. The possible assumption of state debts also had political implications. Consolidating the debt in the hands of the national government would help to concentrate economic and political power at the national level. A contrary policy would reserve greater independence of action for the states.

Hamilton's first *Report on Public Credit*, sent to Congress in January 1790, stimulated lively debate.

Hamilton's Financial Plan

The treasury secretary proposed that Congress assume outstanding state debts, combine them with national obligations, and issue new securities covering both principal and accumulated unpaid interest. Hamilton thereby hoped to ensure that holders of the public debt—many of them wealthy merchants and speculators—had a significant financial stake in the new government's survival. The opposition coalesced around James Madison, who was against the assumption of state debts for two reasons. Not only had his state already paid off most of its obligations, but he also wanted to avoid rewarding wealthy speculators who had purchased state and national debt certificates at a small fraction of their face value from needy veterans and farmers.

Prompted in part by Madison, the House initially rejected the assumption of state debts. The Senate, however, adopted Hamilton's plan largely intact. A series of compromises followed, in which the assumption bill became linked to the other major controversial issue of that congressional session: the location of the permanent national capital. The legend that Hamilton and Madison agreed over Jefferson's dinner table to exchange assumption of state debts for a southern site is not supported by the surviving evidence, but a political deal was undoubtedly struck. The Potomac River was designated as the site for the capital, and the first part of Hamilton's financial program became law in August 1790.

Four months later Hamilton submitted to Congress a second report on public credit, recommending the chartering of a national bank. This proposal too aroused much opposition, though primarily after Congress had already passed the bill to establish the bank.

Hamilton modeled his bank on the Bank of England. The Bank of the United States was to be capitalized at $10 million, of which only

First Bank of the United States

$2 million would come from public funds. Private investors would supply the rest. The bank's charter would run for twenty years, and the government would name one-fifth of the directors. The bank's notes would circulate as the nation's currency. The bank would also act as collecting and disbursing agent for the Treasury and would lend money to the government. Most political leaders recognized that such an institution would be beneficial, especially because it would solve the problem of America's perpetual shortage of an acceptable medium of exchange. But another issue loomed large: did the Constitution give Congress the power to establish such a bank?

James Madison answered that question with a resounding *no*. He pointed out that Constitutional Convention delegates had specifi-

Strict and Broad Constructions of the Constitution

cally rejected a clause authorizing Congress to issue corporate charters. Consequently, he argued, that power could not be inferred from other parts of the Constitution. Madison's contention disturbed President Washington, who decided to request other opinions before signing the bill into law. Edmund Randolph, the attorney general, and Thomas Jefferson, the secretary of state, agreed with Madison that the bank was unconstitutional. Jefferson referred to Article I, Section 8, of the Constitution, which gave Congress the power "to make all Laws which shall be necessary and

Although Congress did not react positively to the arguments in Hamilton's *Report on Manufactures,* the owners of America's burgeoning industries recognized the importance of the policy Hamilton advocated. Ebenezer Clough, a Boston maker of wallpaper, incorporated into his letterhead the exhortation "Americans, Encourage the Manufactories of your Country, if you wish for its prosperity."   (American Antiquarian Society)

proper for carrying into Execution the foregoing Powers." The key word, Jefferson argued, was *necessary*: Congress could do what was needed but without specific constitutional authorization could not do what was merely desirable. Thus Jefferson formulated the strict-constructionist interpretation of the Constitution.

Washington asked Hamilton to reply to the negative assessments of his proposal. Hamilton's *Defense of the Constitutionality of the Bank*, presented to the president in February 1791, brilliantly expounded a broad-constructionist view of the Constitution. Hamilton argued forcefully that Congress could choose any means not specifically prohibited by the Constitution to achieve a constitutional end. He reasoned thus: if the end was constitutional and the means was not *un*constitutional, then the means was constitutional.

Washington concurred, and the bill became law. The bank proved successful, as did the scheme for funding the national debt and assuming the states' debts. The new nation's securities became desirable investments for its own citizens and for wealthy foreigners, especially those in the Netherlands, who rushed to purchase American debt certificates. The influx of new capital, coupled with the high prices American produce now commanded in European markets, eased farmers' debt burdens and contributed to a new prosperity. But two other aspects of Alexander Hamilton's wide-ranging financial scheme did not fare so well.

In December 1791, Hamilton presented to Congress his *Report on Manufactures,* the third and last of his prescriptions for the American economy. In it he outlined an ambitious plan for encouraging and protecting the United States's infant industries, such as shoemaking and textile manufacturing. Hamilton argued that the nation could never be truly independent as long as it relied heavily on Europe for manufactured goods. He thus urged Congress to promote the immigration of technicians and laborers and to support industrial development through a limited use of protective tariffs. Many of Hamilton's ideas were implemented in later decades, especially after the United States greatly increased its cultivation of cotton and could therefore amply supply its textile mills, but few congressmen in 1791 could see much merit in his proposals. They firmly believed that America's future lay in agriculture and the carrying trade and that the mainstay of the republic was the virtuous small farmer. Therefore, Congress rejected the report.

Hamilton's Report on Manufactures

That same year Congress accepted another feature of Hamilton's financial program, levying a tax on whiskey produced within the United States. Although proceeds from the Revenue Act of 1789 covered the interest on the national debt, the decision to fund state debts meant that the national government required additional income. A tax on whiskey affected relatively few farmers—those west of the mountains who sold their grain in the form of distilled spirits as a means of avoiding the high cost of transportation—and might also reduce the consumption of whiskey. (Eighteenth-century Americans, notorious for their heavy drinking, consumed about twice as much alcohol per capita as today's rate.) Moreover, Hamilton knew that those western farmers were Jefferson's supporters, and he saw the benefits of taxing them rather than the merchants who supported his own policies.

News of the tax set off protests in frontier areas of Pennsylvania, where residents were already dissatisfied with the army's as yet unsuccessful attempts to defeat the Miami Confederacy (see pages 184–185). To their minds, the same government that protected them inadequately was now proposing to tax them disproportionately. Unrest continued for two years on the frontiers of Pennsylvania, Maryland, and Virginia. Large groups of men drafted petitions protesting the tax, deliberately imitated crowd actions of the 1760s, and occasionally harassed tax collectors.

Whiskey Rebellion

President Washington responded with restraint until violence erupted in July 1794, when western Pennsylvania farmers resisted a federal marshal and a tax collector trying to enforce the law. Three rioters were killed and several militiamen wounded. About seven thousand rebels convened on August 1 to plot the destruction of Pittsburgh but decided not to face the heavy guns of the fort guarding the town. Washington then took decisive action to prevent a crisis reminiscent of Shays's Rebellion. On August 7, he called on the insurgents to disperse and summoned nearly thirteen thousand militia from Pennsylvania and neighboring states. By the time federal forces marched westward in October and November (led at times by Washington himself), the disturbances had ceased. The troops met no resistance and arrested only twenty suspects. Two, neither of them prominent leaders of the rioters, were convicted of treason, but—continuing his policy of restraint—Washington pardoned both. The leaderless and unorganized rebellion ended with little bloodshed.

The chief importance of the Whiskey Rebellion lay not in military victory over the rebels—for there was none—but in the forceful message it conveyed to the American people. The national government, Washington had demonstrated, would not allow violent resistance to its laws. In the republic, change would be effected peacefully, by legal means. People dissatisfied with the law should try to amend or repeal it, not take extralegal action as they had during the colonial era.

The French Revolution and the Development of Partisan Politics

 By 1794, some Americans were already beginning to seek change systematically through electoral politics, even though traditional political theory regarded organized opposition—especially in a republic—as illegitimate. In a monarchy, formal opposition groups were to be expected. In a government of the people, by contrast, serious and sustained disagreement was taken as a sign of corruption and subversion. Such negative judgments, while widely held, still did not halt the growth of partisan sentiment.

Democratic-Republicans and Federalists

Thomas Jefferson and James Madison became convinced as early as 1792 that Hamilton's policies of favoring wealthy commercial interests at the expense of agriculture aimed at imposing a corrupt, aristocratic government on the United States. Characterizing themselves as the true heirs of the Revolution, they charged that Hamilton was plotting to subvert republican principles. To dramatize their point, Jefferson, Madison, and their followers in Congress began calling themselves Democratic-Republicans. Hamilton in turn accused Jefferson and Madison of the same crime: attempting to destroy the republic. Hamilton and his supporters began calling themselves Federalists, to legitimize their claims and link themselves with the Constitution. Each group accused the other of being an illicit faction working to sabotage the republican principles of the Revolution. (In the traditional sense of the term, a faction was by definition dangerous and opposed to the public good.)

At first, President Washington tried to remain aloof from the political dispute that divided Hamilton and Jefferson, his chief advisers. Yet the growing controversy helped persuade him to seek a second term of office in 1792 in hopes of promoting political unity.

MAD TOM in A RAGE

A Federalist political cartoon from the 1790s shows "Mad Tom" Paine "in a rage," trying to destroy the federal government as carefully constructed (in classical style) by President Washington and Vice President Adams. That Paine is being aided by the Devil underscores the hostility to partisanship common in the era. (The Huntington Library & Art Collections, San Marino, California)

But in 1793 and thereafter, developments in foreign affairs magnified the disagreements, for France—America's wartime ally—and Great Britain—America's most important trading partner—resumed the periodic hostilities that had originated a century earlier (see page 83).

The French Revolution

In 1789 Americans welcomed the news of the French Revolution. The French people's success in limiting, and then overthrowing, an oppressive monarchy seemed to vindicate the United States's own revolution. Americans saw themselves as the vanguard of an inevitable historical trend that would reshape the world in a republican mold. But by the early 1790s the reports from France were disquieting. Outbreaks of violence continued and ministries succeeded each other with bewildering rapidity. Executions mounted; the king himself was beheaded in early 1793. Although many Americans, including Jefferson and Madison, retained a sympathetic view of the revolution, others began to cite France as a prime example of the perversion of republicanism. As might be expected, Alexander Hamilton spoke for the latter group.

When France declared war on Britain, Spain, and Holland in 1793, the Americans faced a dilemma. The 1778 Treaty of Alliance with France bound them to that nation "forever," and a mutual commitment to republicanism created ideological bonds. Yet the United States was connected to Great Britain as well. In addition to their shared history and language, America and Britain had again become important economic partners. Americans still purchased most of their manufactured goods from Great Britain. Indeed, since the financial system of the United States depended heavily on import tariffs as a source of revenue, the nation's

economic health in effect required uninterrupted trade with the former mother country.

Citizen Genêt

The political and diplomatic climate grew even more complicated in April 1793, when Citizen Edmond Genêt, a representative of the French government, landed in Charleston, South Carolina. As Genêt made his way north to New York City, he recruited Americans for expeditions against British and Spanish colonies in the Western Hemisphere, freely distributing privateering commissions. Genêt's arrival raised troubling questions for President Washington. Should he receive Genêt, thus officially recognizing the French revolutionary government? Should he acknowledge an obligation to aid France under the terms of the 1778 Treaty of Alliance? Or should he proclaim American neutrality?

For once, Hamilton and Jefferson saw eye to eye. Both told Washington that the United States could not afford to ally itself with either side. Washington agreed. He received Genêt but also issued a proclamation informing the world that the United States would adopt "a conduct friendly and impartial toward the belligerent powers." In deference to Jefferson's continued support for France, though, the word *neutrality* did not appear in the declaration.

Genêt himself was removed from politics when his faction fell from power in Paris; he subsequently sought political asylum in the United States. But his disappearance from the diplomatic scene did not diminish the impact of the French Revolution in America. The domestic divisions Genêt helped to widen were perpetuated by clubs called Democratic-Republican societies, formed by Americans sympathetic to the French Revolution and worried about the policies of the Washington administration. Such societies reflected a growing grassroots concern about the same developments that troubled Jefferson and Madison.

Democratic-Republican Societies

More than forty Democratic-Republican societies organized between 1793 and 1800. Their members saw themselves as heirs of the Sons of Liberty, seeking the same goal as their predecessors: protection of people's liberties against encroachments by corrupt and self-serving rulers. To that end, they publicly protested government fiscal and foreign policy and repeatedly proclaimed their belief in "the equal rights of man," particularly the rights to free speech, free press, and assembly. Like the Sons of Liberty, the Demo-

Citizen Edmond Genêt's visit caused the first major diplomatic crisis in the new nation. His attempts to enlist Americans in support of the French Revolution raised troubling questions about the international role of the United States.   (Collection of the Albany Institute of History and Art. Bequest of George Genêt)

cratic-Republican societies chiefly comprised artisans and craftsmen, although professionals, farmers, and merchants also joined.

The rapid growth of such groups, outspoken in their criticism of the Washington administration for its failure to come to the aid of France and for its domestic economic policies, deeply disturbed Hamilton and eventually Washington himself. Some newspapers charged that the societies were subversive agents of a foreign power. Their "real design," one asserted, was "to involve the country in war, to assume the reins of government and tyrannize over the people." The counterattack climaxed in the fall of 1794, when Washington accused the societies of having fomented the Whiskey Rebellion.

In retrospect, Washington and Hamilton's reaction to the Democratic-Republican societies seems disproportionately hostile. But it must be recalled that factional disputes were believed to endanger the survival of republics. As the first organized political dissenters in the United States, the Democratic-Republican societies alarmed elected officials, who had not yet accepted the idea that one component of a free government was an organized loyal opposition.

Partisan Politics and Relations with Great Britain

In 1794 George Washington dispatched Chief Justice John Jay to London to negotiate four unresolved questions in Anglo-American relations. The first point at issue was recent British seizures of American merchant ships trading in the French West Indies. The United States wanted to establish the principle of freedom of the seas and to assert its right, as a neutral nation, to trade freely with both combatants. Second, in violation of the 1783 peace treaty, Great Britain had not yet evacuated its posts in the American Northwest. Settlers there believed that the British were responsible for the renewed warfare in the region (see pages 182–185), and they wanted that threat removed. The Americans also hoped for a commercial treaty and sought compensation for the slaves who left with the British army at the end of the war.

The negotiations in London proved difficult, since Jay had little to offer in exchange for the concessions he sought. Britain did agree to

Jay Treaty

evacuate the western forts and ease restrictions on American trade to England and the West Indies. (Some limitations were retained, however, violating the Americans' stated commitment to open commerce.) The treaty established two arbitration commissions—one to deal with prewar debts Americans owed to British creditors and the other to hear claims for captured American merchant ships—but Britain adamantly refused slaveowners compensation for their lost bondspeople. Under the circumstances, Jay did remarkably well: the treaty averted war with England at a time when the United States, which lacked an effective navy, could not have won such a conflict. Nevertheless, most Americans, including the president, expressed dissatisfaction with at least some parts of the treaty.

The Senate debated the Jay Treaty in secret, so members of the public did not learn its provisions until after Senate ratification (by a vote of 20 to 10) in June 1795. The Democratic-Republican societies led protests against the treaty. Especially vehement opposition arose in the South, as planters criticized the failure to obtain compensation for runaway slaves and objected to the commission on prewar debts, which might make them pay off sizable obligations to British merchants dating back to the 1760s. Once President Washington had signed the treaty, though, there seemed little the Democratic-Republicans could do to prevent it from taking effect. Just one opportunity remained: Congress had to appropriate funds to carry out the treaty provisions and, according to the Constitution, appropriation bills had to originate in the House of Representatives.

When the House debated the issue in March 1796, members opposing the treaty tried to prevent approval of the appropriations. To that end, they asked Washington to submit to the House all documents pertinent to the negotiations. In successfully resisting the House's request, Washington established the doctrine of executive privilege—the power of the president to withhold information from Congress if he believes circumstances warrant doing so.

The treaty's opponents initially appeared to be in the majority, but pressure for appropriating the necessary funds built as time passed. Frontier residents eagerly sought Britain's evacuation of its remaining outposts, for they feared a new outbreak of Indian war despite the signing of the Treaty of Greenville. Merchants wanted to reap benefits from expanded trade. Furthermore, Thomas Pinckney of South Carolina had negotiated a treaty with Spain giving the United States navigation privileges on the Mississippi River, which would be an economic boost to the West and

South. The popularity of Pinckney's Treaty (the Senate ratified it unanimously) helped to overcome opposition to the Jay Treaty. For all these reasons, the House appropriated the money by the narrow margin of 51 to 48.

Analysis of the vote reveals both the regional nature of the division and the growing cohesion of the Democratic-Republican and Federalist factions in Congress. Voting for the appropriations were 44 Federalists and 7 Democratic-Republicans; voting against were 45 Democratic-Republicans and 3 Federalists. The final tally also divided by region. Southerners (including three Virginia Federalists) cast the vast majority of votes against the bill. Its supporters hailed from New England and the middle states, with the exception of two South Carolina Federalists. The seven Democratic-Republicans who voted for the appropriations came from commercial areas in New York, Pennsylvania, and Maryland.

Partisan Divisions in Congress

The small number of defectors on both sides reveals a new force at work in American politics: partisanship. Voting statistics from the first four Congresses show the ever-increasing tendency of members of the House of Representatives to vote as cohesive groups, rather than as individuals. If factional loyalty is defined as voting together at least two-thirds of the time on national issues, the percentage of nonaligned congressmen dropped from 42 percent in 1790 to just 7 percent in 1796. Significantly, this trend toward party cohesion occurred even though Congress experienced heavy turnover. Most congressmen served only one or two terms in office, and fewer than 10 percent were reelected more than three times. During the 1790s the majority slowly shifted from Federalist to Democratic-Republican. Federalists controlled the first three Congresses, through the spring of 1795. Democratic-Republicans gained ascendancy in the Fourth Congress. Federalists returned to power with slight majorities in the Fifth and Sixth Congresses, but the Democratic-Republicans took over—more or less for good—in the Seventh Congress in 1801.

To describe these shifts is easier than to explain them. The terms used by Jefferson and Madison (aristocrats versus the people) or by Hamilton and Washington (true patriots versus subversive rabble) do not adequately explain the growing divisions. Simple economic differences between agrarian and commercial interests do not provide the answer either, since more than 90

Bases of Partisanship

percent of Americans still lived in rural areas. Moreover, Jefferson's vision of a prosperous agrarian America rested on commercial farming, not rural self-sufficiency. Nor did the divisions in the 1790s simply repeat the Federalist-Antifederalist debate of 1787–1788. Even though most Antifederalists became Democratic-Republicans, the party's leaders, Madison and Jefferson, had supported the Constitution.

Yet certain distinctions can be made. Democratic-Republicans, especially prominent in the southern and middle states, tended to be self-assured, confident, and optimistic about both politics and the economy. Southern planters, firmly in control of their region and of a class of enslaved laborers, did not fear instability, at least among the European American population. They foresaw a prosperous future based partly on continued westward expansion, a movement they expected to dominate. Democratic-Republicans employed democratic rhetoric to win the allegiance of small farmers south of New England. Members of non-English ethnic groups—especially Irish, Scots, and Germans—found Democratic-Republicans' words attractive. Artisans also joined the coalition; they saw themselves as the urban equivalent of small farmers and valued their independence from domineering bosses. Democratic-Republicans of all descriptions emphasized developing America's own resources, worrying less than Federalists did about the nation's place in the world. Democratic-Republicans also remained sympathetic to France in international affairs.

By contrast, Federalists, concentrated in New England, came mostly from English stock. Insecure and uncertain of the future, they drew considerable support from commercial interests. They stressed the need for order, authority, and regularity in the political world. Federalists had no grassroots political organization and put little emphasis on involving ordinary people in government. Wealthy New England merchants aligned themselves with the Federalists, but so too did the region's farmers who, prevented from expanding agricultural production because of New England's poor soil, gravitated toward the more conservative party. Federalists, like Democratic-Republicans, assumed that southern and middle-state interests would dominate the land west of the mountains, so they had little incentive to work actively to develop that potentially rich territory. In Federalist eyes, potential enemies—both internal and external—perpetually threatened the nation, which required a continuing alliance with Great Britain for its own protection. Their vision of international affairs may have been more accurate than that of the Democratic-

Republicans, given the warfare in Europe, but it was also narrow and unattractive. Since the Federalist view held out little hope of a better future to the voters of any region, the Democratic-Republicans unsurprisingly prevailed in the end.

The presence of the two organized groups—not yet parties in the modern sense but active contenders for office nonetheless—made the presidential election of 1796 the first serious contest for the position. Wearied by the criticism to which he had been subjected,

Washington's Farewell Address

George Washington decided to retire from office. (Presidents had not yet been limited to two terms, as they have been since the adoption of the Twenty-second Amendment in 1951.) In September Washington published his Farewell Address, most of which had been written by Hamilton. In it Washington outlined two principles that guided American foreign policy at least until the late 1940s: to maintain commercial but not political

How do historians know...

that in all probability starting in the 1790s Thomas Jefferson fathered the children born to his slave Sally Hemings?

Tales that Jefferson fathered Hemings's children surfaced early in his presidency. For many years historians rejected those stories as scurrilous rumors spread by Jefferson's enemies, accepting the Jefferson family's explanation that Sally Hemings's children (who resembled the third president) had been fathered by one of his sister's sons, Peter or Samuel Carr. Most scholars and Jefferson family members argued that the acknowledged special treatment accorded the entire Hemings clan at Monticello stemmed from the fact that Sally and her siblings were the acknowledged offspring of Jefferson's father-in-law by his mulatto slave mistress, Betty Hemings (and thus that Sally was Jefferson's dead wife's half-sister). In 1974, however, the historian Fawn Brodie's assertion in her *Thomas Jefferson: An Intimate History* that Jefferson had fathered the younger Hemingses reignited the controversy. Recent advances in DNA testing permitted a scientific analysis of the alternative theories, at least with respect to the parentage of Sally's youngest son, Eston Hemings. It is now

known that men pass Y chromosomes on to their male children largely intact. Because no sons were born to the marriage of Martha Randolph and Thomas Jefferson, male-line descendants of Jefferson's paternal uncle were tested, along with similar descendants of the Carr brothers and Eston Hemings. British scientists, working blindly—that is, without knowing the origins of the blood samples they were studying—demonstrated to their own satisfaction that Jefferson had indeed fathered Eston Hemings, and by implication Sally Hemings's earlier children as well. The DNA samples of the Hemings and Jefferson descendants match almost perfectly (as illustrated here), whereas those of the Carrs differ significantly from both of the others. (Photo: *Nature*, vol. 396)

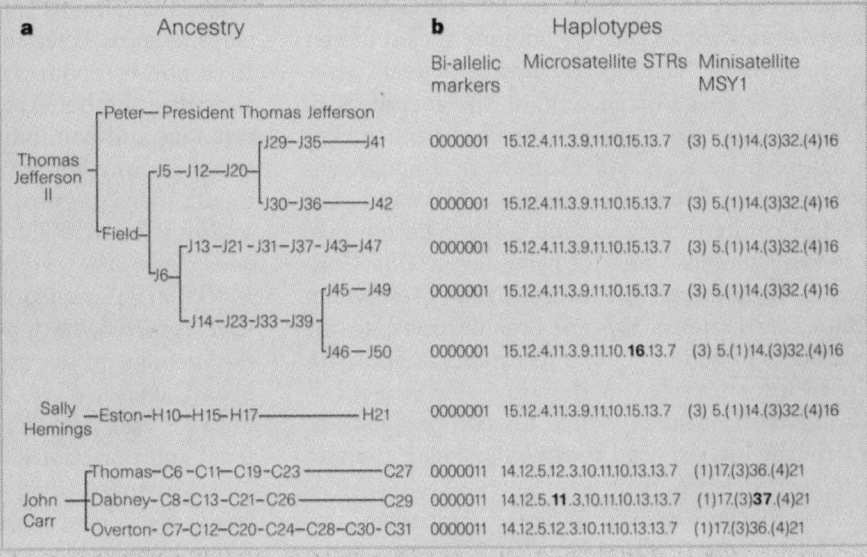

ties to other nations and to enter no permanent alliances. He also drew sharp distinctions between the United States and Europe, stressing America's uniqueness—its exceptionalism—and the need for unilateralism (independent action in foreign affairs).

Washington also lamented the existence of factional divisions among his countrymen. Historians have often interpreted his call for an end to partisan strife as the statement of a man who could see beyond political affiliations to the good of the whole. But in the context of the impending presidential election, the Farewell Address appears rather as an attack on the legitimacy of the Democratic-Republican opposition. Washington advocated unity behind the Federalist banner, which he viewed as the only proper political stance. The Federalists (like the Democratic-Republicans) continued to see themselves as the sole guardians of the truth and the only true heirs of the Revolution. Both sides perceived their opponents as misguided, unpatriotic troublemakers who sought to undermine revolutionary ideals.

To succeed Washington, the Federalists in Congress put forward Vice President John Adams, with the diplomat Thomas Pinckney as his running mate. Congressional Democratic-Republicans met and chose Thomas Jefferson as their presidential candidate; the lawyer, Revolutionary War veteran, and active Democratic-Republican politician Aaron Burr of New York agreed to run for vice president.

Election of 1796

That the election was contested does not mean that the people decided its outcome. Voters could cast their ballots only for electors, not for the candidates themselves, and not all electors publicly declared their preferences. State legislatures, not a popular vote, selected more than 40 percent of the members of the electoral college; some electors had been picked even before Federalists and Democratic-Republicans named their presidential candidates. Moreover, the method of voting in the electoral college did not take into account the possibility of party slates. The Constitution's drafters had not foreseen the development of competing national political organizations, so the Constitution provided no way to express support for one person for president and another for vice president. The electors simply voted for two people. The man with the highest total became president; the second highest, vice president.

This procedure proved to be the Federalists' undoing. Adams won the presidency with 71 votes, but a number of Federalist electors (especially those from New England) failed to cast ballots for Pinckney. Thomas Jefferson won 68 votes, 9 more than Pinckney, to become vice president. The incoming administration was thus politically divided. During the next four years the new president and vice president, once allies and close friends, became bitter enemies.

John Adams and Political Dissent

 John Adams took over the presidency peculiarly blind to the partisan developments of the previous four years. As president he never abandoned an outdated notion discarded by George Washington as early as 1794: that the president should be above politics, an independent and dignified figure who did not seek petty factional advantage. Thus Adams kept Washington's cabinet intact, despite its key members' allegiance to his chief rival, Alexander Hamilton. Adams often adopted a passive posture, letting others (usually Hamilton) take the lead when the president should have acted decisively. As a result, his administration gained a reputation for inconsistency. When Adams's term ended, the Federalists were severely divided, and the Democratic-Republicans had won the presidency. But Adams's detachment from Hamilton's maneuverings did enable him to weather the greatest international crisis the republic had yet faced: the Quasi-War with France.

The Jay Treaty improved America's relationship with Great Britain, but it provoked French retaliation. Angry that the United States had reached agreement with its enemy, the French government ordered its ships to seize American vessels carrying British goods. In response, Congress increased military spending, authorizing the building of ships and the stockpiling of weapons and ammunition. President Adams also sent three commissioners to Paris to negotiate a settlement. For months, the American commissioners sought talks with Talleyrand, the French foreign minister, but Talleyrand's agents demanded a bribe of $250,000 before negotiations could begin. The Americans retorted, "No, no; not a sixpence," and reported the incident in dispatches that the president received in early March 1798. Adams informed Congress of the impasse and recommended further increases in defense appropriations.

Convinced that Adams had deliberately sabotaged the negotiations, congressional Democratic-Republicans insisted that the dispatches be turned over

This cartoon drawn during the XYZ affair depicts the United States as a maiden being victimized by the five leaders of the French government's directorate. In the background, John Bull (England) watches from on high, while other European nations discuss the situation.   (The Lilly Library, Indiana University, Bloomington, Indiana)

XYZ Affair

to Congress. Adams complied, aware that releasing the reports would work to his advantage. He withheld only the names of the French agents, referring to them as X, Y, and Z. The revelation that the Americans had been treated with contempt stimulated a wave of anti-French sentiment in the United States. A journalist's version of the commissioners' reply, "Millions for defense, but not a cent for tribute," became the national slogan. Cries for war filled the air. Congress formally abrogated the Treaty of Alliance and authorized American ships to seize French vessels.

Thus began an undeclared war with France. Warships of the U.S. Navy and French privateers seeking to capture American merchant vessels fought the Quasi-War in Caribbean waters. Although Americans initially suffered heavy losses of merchant shipping, by early 1799 the U.S. Navy had established its superiority in the West

Quasi-War with France

Indies. Its ships captured eight French privateers and naval vessels, easing the threat to America's vital Caribbean trade.

The Democratic-Republicans, who opposed war and continued to sympathize with France, could do little to stem the tide of anti-French feelings. Since Agent Y had boasted of the existence of a "French party in America," Federalists flatly accused Democratic-Republicans of traitorous designs. A New York newspaper declared that anyone who remained "lukewarm" after reading the XYZ dispatches was a "criminal—and the man who does not warmly reprobate the conduct of the French must have a soul black enough to be fit for treason Strategems and spoils." John Adams wavered between calling the Democratic-Republicans traitors and acknowledging their right to oppose administration measures. His wife was less tolerant. "Those whom the French boast of as their Partizans," Abigail Adams declared, should be "adjudged traitors to their country." If Jefferson had been president, she added, "we should all have been sold to the French."

Federalists saw this climate of opinion as an opportunity to deal a death blow to their Democratic-Republican opponents. Now that the country seemed to see the truth of what they had been saying ever since the Whiskey Rebellion in 1794—that Democratic-Republicans were subversive foreign agents—Federalists sought to codify that belief into law. In 1798 the Federalist-controlled Congress adopted a set of four laws known as the Alien and Sedition Acts, intended to suppress dissent and to prevent further growth of the Democratic-Republican faction.

Alien and Sedition Acts

Three of the acts targeted recently arrived immigrants, whom Federalists accurately suspected of being Democratic-Republican in their sympathies. The Naturalization Act lengthened the residency period required for citizenship and ordered all resident aliens to register with the federal government. The two Alien Acts provided for the detention of enemy aliens in time of war and gave the president authority to deport any alien he deemed dangerous to the nation's security. Neither act was implemented during the Adams administration, however.

The fourth statute, the Sedition Act, sought to control both citizens and aliens. It outlawed conspiracies to prevent the enforcement of federal laws, setting the maximum punishment for such offenses at five years in prison and a $5,000 fine. The act also tried to control speech. Writing, printing, or uttering "false, scandalous and malicious" statements against the government or the president "with intent to defame . . . or to bring them or either of them, into contempt or disrepute" became a crime punishable by as much as two years' imprisonment and a fine of $2,000. Today any such law punishing speech alone would be considered unconstitutional. But in the eighteenth century, when organized political opposition was by definition suspect, many Americans supported the Sedition Act's restrictions on free speech.

The Sedition Act led to fifteen indictments and ten convictions. Outspoken Democratic-Republican newspaper editors who failed to mute their criticism of the administration composed most of the accused. But the first victim—whose story may serve as an example of the rest—was a hot-tempered Democratic-Republican congressman from Vermont, Matthew Lyon. The Irish-born Lyon, a former indentured servant who had purchased his freedom and fought in the Revolution, was indicted for declaring in print that John Adams had displayed "a continual grasp for

power" and "an unbounded thirst for ridiculous pomp, foolish adulation, and selfish avarice." Though convicted, fined $1,000, and sent to prison for four months, Lyon did not lapse into silence. He conducted his reelection campaign from jail, winning an overwhelming majority. Leading Democratic-Republicans from around the country contributed to pay his fine.

Faced with prosecutions of their supporters, Jefferson and Madison sought an effective means of combating the acts. Petitioning the Federalist-controlled Congress to repeal the laws would clearly fail. Furthermore, Federalist judges refused to allow accused individuals to question the Sedition Act's constitutionality. Accordingly, the Democratic-Republican leaders turned to the only other forum available for protest: state legislatures. Carefully concealing their own role—it would not have been desirable for the vice president to be indicted for sedition—Jefferson and Madison each drafted a set of resolutions. Introduced into the Kentucky and Virginia legislatures, respectively, in the fall of 1798, the resolutions differed somewhat but had the same import. Since a compact among the states created the Constitution, they contended, people speaking through their states had a legitimate right to judge the constitutionality of actions taken by the federal government. Both sets of resolutions pronounced the Alien and Sedition Acts unconstitutional, asking other states to join in a concerted protest against them.

Virginia and Kentucky Resolutions

Although no other state endorsed them, the Virginia and Kentucky resolutions nevertheless had considerable influence. First, they constituted superb political propaganda, rallying Democratic-Republican opinion throughout the country. They placed the opposition party squarely in the revolutionary tradition of resistance to tyrannical authority. Second, the theory of union they proposed inspired southern states' rights advocates in the 1830s and thereafter. Jefferson and Madison had identified a key constitutional issue: how far could states go in opposing the national government? How could a conflict between the two be resolved? These questions would not be definitively answered until the Civil War.

Just as the Sedition Act was being implemented and northern state legislatures were rejecting the Virginia and Kentucky resolutions, Federalists split over the course of action the United States should take toward France. Hamilton and his supporters

Convention of 1800

called for a declaration legitimizing the undeclared naval war. But Adams received a number of private signals that the French government regretted its treatment of the American commissioners. Acting on such assurances, he dispatched the envoy William Vans Murray to Paris. The United States sought two goals: compensation for ships the French had seized since 1793 and abrogation of the treaty of 1778. The Convention of 1800, which ended the Quasi-War, provided for the latter but not the former. Still, it freed the United States from its only permanent alliance, thus allowing it to follow the independent diplomatic course George Washington had urged in his Farewell Address.

The results of the negotiations did not become known in the United States until after the presidential election of 1800. Even so, since Hamilton and many of his followers wanted to widen the Quasi-War, Adams's decision to seek a peaceful settlement probably cost him reelection because of the divisions it caused in Federalist ranks.

The Democratic-Republicans entered the 1800 presidential race firmly united behind Thomas Jefferson and Aaron Burr, their candidates

Election of 1800

from four years earlier. Although they won the election, their lack of foresight almost cost them dearly. The system of voting in the electoral college, which Federalists understood better than Democratic-Republicans, nearly derailed the Democratic-Republicans' plans. The Federalists arranged in advance for one of their electors to fail to vote for Charles Cotesworth Pinckney, their vice-presidential candidate. John Adams thus received the higher number of Federalist votes (65 to Pinckney's 64). Democratic-Republicans failed to make the same distinction between their candidates, and all 73 of their electors cast ballots for both Jefferson and Burr (see Map 8.1). Because neither man had a plurality, the Constitution required that the contest be decided in the House of Representatives, with each state's congressmen voting as a unit. Since the new House, dominated by Democratic-Republicans, would not take office for some months, Federalist congressmen decided the election. It took them thirty-five ballots to decide that Jefferson would be a lesser evil than Burr, who revealed his ambition (and alienated Jefferson) by promoting his own candidacy for president. In response to the tangle, the Twelfth Amendment to the Constitution (1804) changed the method of voting in the electoral college to allow for a party ticket.

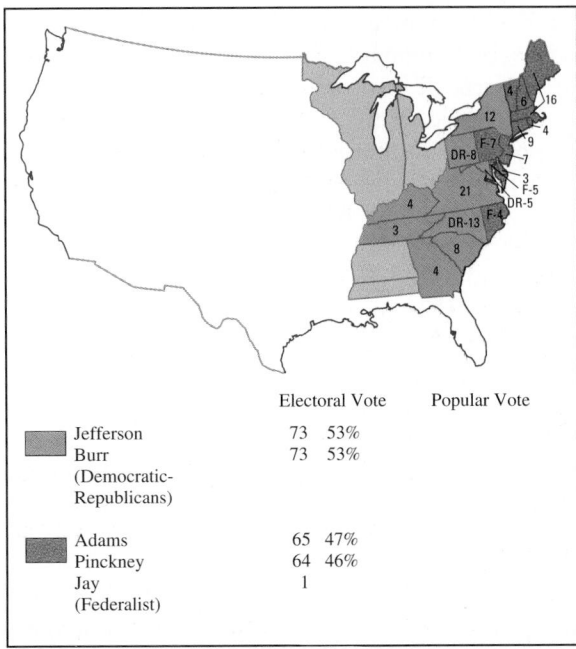

	Electoral Vote	Popular Vote
Jefferson	73	53%
Burr	73	53%
(Democratic-Republicans)		
Adams	65	47%
Pinckney	64	46%
Jay	1	
(Federalist)		

Map 8.1   Presidential Election, 1800   The Democratic-Republicans, with their candidates Thomas Jefferson and Aaron Burr, won the electoral votes of the southern states, while the Federalists, the party of John Adams and Charles Cotesworth Pinckney, received votes primarily in New England. The parties split the votes of the middle states, but the Democratic-Republicans dominated the electoral-vote count there and won the election.

Race Relations at the End of the Century

 As the nation anticipated the inauguration of a new president, it had added three states (Vermont, Kentucky, and Tennessee) to the original thirteen and more than 1 million people to the nearly 4 million counted by the 1790 census. Nine-tenths of the approximately 1 million resident African Americans—most still enslaved—lived in the Chesapeake or the Lower South. After the signing of the Treaty of Greenville in 1795 (see pages 184–185), all the Indian nations residing in U.S. territory east of the Mississippi River had made peace with the republic. Even though many Indian peoples still lived independently of federal authority, they came increasingly within the orbit of U.S. influence.

The new nation's policymakers, all of European American descent, could not ignore such large proportions of the population. How should the republic deal with eastern Indians, who no longer posed a military threat to the country? Did the growing population of bondspeople (augmented by more than ninety thousand imports directly from Africa before Congress ended the slave trade in 1808) present new hazards? The second question took on added significance after 1793, when in the French colony of Saint Domingue (Haiti), mulattos and blacks under the leadership of Toussaint L'Ouverture overthrew European rule in a bloody revolt characterized by numerous atrocities on both sides.

In 1789 Henry Knox, Washington's secretary of war, proposed that the new national government assume the task of "civilizing" America's indigenous population. "Instead of exterminating a part of the human race," he contended, the government

"Civilizing" the Indians

should "impart our knowledge of cultivation and the arts to the aboriginals of the country." The first step in such a project, Knox suggested, should be to introduce to Indian peoples "a love for exclusive property"; to that end, he proposed that the government give livestock to individual Indians. Four years later, the Indian Trade and Intercourse Act of 1793 codified Knox's plan, promising that the federal government would supply Indians with animals and agricultural implements and would also provide appropriate instructors.

The well-intentioned plan reflected federal officials' blindness to the realities of native peoples' lives. Not only did it incorrectly posit that the Indians' traditional commitment to communal notions of landowning (see page 43) could easily be overcome, it also ignored the centuries-long agricultural experience

In 1805, an unidentified artist painted Benjamin Hawkins, a trader and U.S. agent to the Indians of the Southeast, at the Creek agency near Macon, Georgia. Hawkins introduced European-style agriculture to the Creeks, who are shown here with vegetables from their fields. Throughout the eastern United States, Indian nations had to make similar adaptations of their traditional lifestyles in order to maintain their group identity.   (Collection of the Greenville County Art Museum, South Carolina)

of eastern Indian peoples. The policymakers focused only on Indian *men:* since they hunted, male Indians were "savages" who had to be "civilized" by being taught to farm. That in these societies *women* traditionally did the farming was irrelevant because in the eyes of the officials, Indian women—like those of European descent—should properly confine themselves to child rearing, household chores, and home manufacturing.

Indian nations at first responded cautiously to the "civilizing" plan. The Iroquois Confederacy had been devastated by the war; its people in the 1790s lived in what one historian has called "slums in the wilderness."

Iroquois and Cherokees

Restricted to small reservations increasingly surrounded by Anglo-American farmlands, men could no longer hunt and often spent their days in idle carousing. Quaker missionaries started a demonstration farm among the Senecas, intending to teach men to plow, but they quickly learned that women showed greater interest in their message. The same was true among the Cherokees of Georgia, where Indian agents found that women eagerly sought to learn both new farming methods and textile manufacturing skills. As their southern hunting territories were reduced, Cherokee men did begin to raise cattle and hogs, but they startled the reformers by treating livestock like wild game, allowing the animals to run free in the woods and simply shooting them when needed, in the same way they had once killed deer. Men also started to plow the fields, although Cherokee women continued to bear primary responsibility for cultivation and harvest.

Iroquois men became more receptive to the Quakers' lessons after the spring of 1799, when a Seneca named Handsome Lake experienced a remarkable series of visions. Like other prophets stretching back to Neolin (see page 123), Handsome Lake preached that Indian peoples should renounce alcohol, gambling, and other destructive European customs. Even though he directed his followers to reorient men's and women's work assignments as the Quakers advocated, Handsome Lake aimed above all to preserve Iroquois culture by doing so. He recognized that, since men could no longer obtain meat through hunting, only by adopting a sexual division of labor that had originated in Europe could the Iroquois retain an autonomous existence.

African Americans had long been forced to conform to European American notions of proper gender roles and, unlike Indians, they had embraced Christianity as well during the Great Awakening (see page

African Americans and Ideas of Freedom

110). Yet, just as Cherokees and Iroquois adapted the reformers' plans to their own purposes, so too enslaved blacks found new meanings in the dominant society's ideas. Like their white compatriots, African Americans (both slave and free) became familiar with concepts of liberty and equality during the Revolution. They also witnessed the benefits of fighting collectively for freedom, rather than resisting individually or running away—a message reinforced by the dramatic news of the successful slave revolt in St. Domingue in 1793. And, as white evangelicals by the end of the century began to back away from the earlier racial egalitarianism of their movement, African Americans increasingly formed their own separate Baptist and Methodist congregations in the Chesapeake, as they did in Philadelphia and other urban centers (see pages 174–175).

Such congregations near Richmond became the seedbeds of revolt. Gabriel, an enslaved blacksmith who argued that African Americans should fight for their freedom, carefully planned a large-scale revolt. Often accompanied by his brother Martin, a preacher, he visited Sunday church services, where blacks gathered outside of the watchful eyes of their owners. Gabriel first recruited to his cause other skilled African Americans who like himself lived in semifreedom under minimal supervision. Next he enlisted rural slaves (see Map 8.2). The conspirators planned to attack Richmond on the night of August 30, 1800, set fire to the city, seize the state capitol, and capture the governor, James Monroe. At that point, Gabriel believed, other slaves and sympathetic poor whites would join in.

Gabriel's Rebellion

The plan showed considerable political sophistication, but heavy rain forced a postponement. Several planters then learned of the plan from slave informers and spread the alarm. Gabriel avoided arrest for some weeks, but militia troops quickly apprehended and interrogated most of the other leaders of the rebellion. Twenty-six conspirators, including Gabriel himself, were hanged. Ironically, only those slaves who betrayed their fellows won their freedom as a consequence of the conspiracy.

That disastrous outcome did not end the unrest among Virginia's slaves. In 1802 a waterman named Sancho—a peripheral participant in Gabriel's plot—revived the plans for a revolt. This time word spread along Virginia and North Carolina rivers, carried by slaves who, like Sancho, worked on the boats that plied

Richmond, Virginia, at the time of Gabriel's Rebellion. This was the city as Gabriel knew it. The state capitol, the rebels' intended target, dominates the city's skyline as it dominated Gabriel's thinking. (Virginia Historical Society)

the two states' interconnected waterways. The incomplete plans disintegrated when the plots were revealed prematurely. Again, trials and executions followed, and twenty-five more African Americans lost their lives on the gallows.

At his trial two years earlier, one of Gabriel's followers had made explicit the links that so frightened Chesapeake slaveholders. He told his judges that, like George Washington, "I have adventured my life in endeavouring to obtain the liberty of my countrymen, and am a willing sacrifice in their cause." Southern state legislatures responded to such claims by increasing the severity of the laws regulating slavery. Before long, all talk of emancipation (gradual or otherwise) ceased, and slavery became even more firmly entrenched as an economic institution and way of life, especially as cotton cultivation spread rapidly in the wake of Whitney's invention of the cotton gin.

Summary

 As the nineteenth century began, inhabitants of the United States faced changed lives in the new republic. Indian peoples east of the Mississippi River found that they had to give up some parts of their traditional culture to preserve others. Some African Americans struggled unsuccessfully to free themselves from the inhuman bonds of slavery, then subsequently con-

fronted more constraints than ever because of increasingly restrictive laws.

European Americans too adjusted to changed circumstances. The first eleven years of government under the Constitution established many enduring precedents for congressional, presidential, and judicial action—among them the establishment of the cabinet, the interpretations of key clauses of the Constitution, and the stirrings of judicial review of state and federal legislation. Building on successful negotiations with Spain (Pinckney's Treaty), Britain (the Jay Treaty), and France (the Convention of 1800), the United States developed its diplomatic independence, striving to avoid entanglement with European powers. Yet especially after 1793 internal political consensus proved elusive. The 1790s spawned vigorous debates over foreign and domestic policy and saw the beginnings of a system of organized political factionalism, if not yet formal parties. The Whiskey Rebellion, instigated by westerners outraged at tax policies formulated by eastern elites, showed that regional conflicts continued even under the new government. And the waging of an undeclared war proved extremely contentious, splitting one faction and energizing another.

At the end of the 1790s, after more than a decade of struggle, the Jeffersonian view of the future of republicanism prevailed over Alexander Hamilton's vision of a powerful centralized economy and a strong national government. As a result, in the years to come

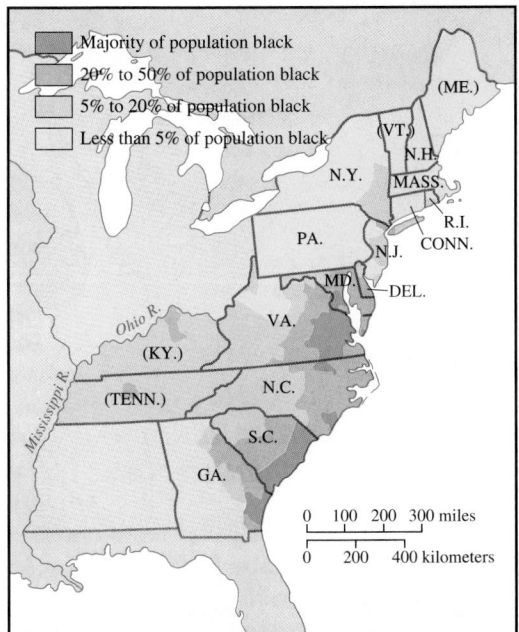

Map 8.2   African American Population, 1790: Proportion of Total Population   The first census clearly indicated that the African American population was heavily concentrated in just a few areas of the United States, most notably in coastal regions of South Carolina, Georgia, and Virginia. Although there were growing numbers of blacks in the backcountry—presumably taken there by migrating slaveowners—most parts of the North and East, with the exception of the immediate vicinity of New York City, had few African American residents.   (Source: From Lester J. Cappon et al., eds., *Atlas of Early American History: The Revolutionary Era, 1760–1790.* Copyright © 1976 by Princeton University Press. Reprinted by permission of Princeton University Press.)

the country would be characterized by a decentralized economy, minimal government (especially at the national level), and maximum freedom of action and mobility for individual white men. Jeffersonian Democratic-Republicans, like other white men before them, failed to extend to white women, Indian peoples, and African Americans the freedom and individuality they recognized as essential for themselves.

LEGACY FOR A PEOPLE AND A NATION

Dissent During Wartime

The Quasi-War with France in 1798 and 1799, the nation's first overseas conflict, brought the first attempt to suppress dissent. By criminalizing dissenting speech, the Sedition Act of 1798 tried to quiet the Democratic-Republicans' criticism of the war in general and President John Adams in particular. Fifteen men (including a member of Congress) were fined and jailed after being convicted under the statute's provisions.

Although Americans might assume that their right to free speech under the First Amendment, more fully accepted now than it was two hundred years ago, would today protect dissenters in the event of another war, the history of the nation suggests otherwise. Each major conflict fought under the Constitution—the Civil War, World War I, World War II, and Vietnam—has stimulated efforts by both government and individual citizens to suppress dissenting voices. For example, during the Civil War, the Union jailed civilian Confederate sympathizers, holding them under martial law for long periods. During the First World War, a later Sedition Act allowed the government to deport immigrant aliens who too vocally criticized the war effort, among them several outspoken Socialists and anarchists. Moreover, citizens who objected to government policies were subjected to a variety of formal and informal sanctions by their neighbors. World War II brought the silencing of isolationists' voices, as those who had opposed American entry into the war were denied public outlets for their ideas. The consequences of antiwar protests in the Vietnam era still affect the nation today, as the American people remain divided over whether the proper course of action in the 1960s was dissent from, or acquiescence in, government policy. And during the Gulf War in the early 1990s, military officials restricted reporters' access to the battlefront to forestall potential criticism.

Freedom of speech is never easy to maintain, and wartime conditions make it much more difficult. When the nation comes under attack from a foreign power, many patriotic Americans argue that the time for dissent has ceased and that all citizens should support the government. Others contend that, if freedom in the nation is to mean anything, people must have the right to speak their minds freely at all times. Tracing the history of wartime dissent in the United States suggests that this legacy will remain extremely contentious.

For Further Reading, see page A-10 of the Appendix. For Web resources, go to http://www.college.hmco.com.

HISTOIRE
DE
BARBARIE, ET DE SES
CORSAIRES.

Le R.P.F. PIERRE DAN, Bachelier en Theologie de la
Faculté de Paris, M.r et Superieur du Couuent de l'ordre de la S.
Trinité et Redemption des Captifs fondé au Chasteau de Fontaine-bleau.

SECONDE EDITION.
Reueuë et augmentée.

J ohn Foss, captured by "pirates" off the Barbary Coast of North Africa in the 1790s, wrote of the "hellish tortures and punishments" inflicted "on the unfortunate Christians." Marched through Algiers, the party of nine ragged sailors heard shouts from the Islamic crowds praising the victories over "Christian dogs," and in prison they learned of ten other American vessels recently captured. In Algiers they became white slaves under African masters. Eventually the United States ransomed the captives, and four of the nine made it back to America; the others died of plague.

In the early nineteenth century, the Barbary captivity stories had the drama of modern gothic novels. "Pirates" took American men and women hostage from ships, held them in confinement, stripped and beat them as Christians, and humiliated them as Americans. In telling of white slaves with black masters, the tales turned American assumptions of the natural order on their heads. Firsthand descriptions of Africa projected negative images of a despotic, depraved people, so very different from Americans. In the end, the Americans—at least those who survived to tell their stories—prevailed, and so the stories became epic affirmations of Western culture over "barbarians."

Americans loved to read these harrowing stories. John Foss's account of his captivity was reprinted twice in 1798. The fictional account of a woman held a slave in Algiers from 1800 to 1806, *History of the Captivity and Sufferings of Mrs. Maria Martin*, titillated Americans and went through twelve editions in eleven years following its 1807 printing. Chained in prison, Martin described how "the enormous iron round my neck pained me," and how "her mind sunk under this accumulation of miserable sufferings." Finally, she wrote, "my liberty had been purchased by my country," and she heard the door of the dungeon slam shut for the last time. As a Christian, in chains and afterward, she felt morally superior to her captors.

In reality the "pirates"—from what Europeans called the Barbary states and Africans the Maghreb— had challenged the United States in a most fundamental way: was this new nation an independent, sovereign

Christian monks purchase the freedom of Barbary Coast captives, held in chains, from their Muslim captors. (James Ford Bell Library, University of Minnesota)

"A WISE AND FRUGAL GOVERNMENT": THE DEMOCRATIC-REPUBLICANS IN POWER 1801–1815

state that could protect its citizens and commerce abroad?

The issue was money. In 1801 the *bashaw* of Tripoli, angry over the United States's refusal to pay tribute for safe passage of its ships, sailors, and passengers through the Mediterranean, declared war on the United States. President Thomas Jefferson responded by sending a naval squadron to protect American ships in the area. The only other alternative was to abandon the Mediterranean Sea, which would have severely damaged American trade. After two years of stalemate, Jefferson ordered a blockade of Tripoli, but the American frigate *Philadelphia* ran aground in its harbor and three hundred American officers and sailors were taken captive. Jefferson refused to ransom them. With the blockade still in place, seven marines and four hundred soldiers of fortune marched overland from Egypt to seize the port of Derne, on the shores of Tripoli. Finally, by treaty with Tripoli in 1805, the United States paid $60,000 to free the *Philadelphia* prisoners, and the war was over. But the United States continued to pay tribute to the other three Barbary states until 1815. Was the United States an independent sovereign nation? The question rankled, especially as Great Britain seemed to think not, and continued to treat the new nation as a colony.

American independence and stability passed a political test at home as well when presidential succession took place in 1801 by ballot rather than by arms, which some feared. Despite the bitterness of the campaign and the ensuing political intrigue, Thomas Jefferson replaced John Adams as president. The Constitution withstood the test, but the transfer of power to the Democratic-Republicans from the Federalists intensified political conflict. In the tradition of the Revolution, Democratic-Republican presidents soon sought to restrain the national government, believing that limited government would foster republican virtue. The Federalists, in contrast, advocated a strong national government with centralized authority to promote economic development. As both factions competed for popular support, they laid the basis for the evolution of party politics. Factionalism did not spring only from politics, however. Americans also divided along other lines: by class, race, ethnicity, gender, religion, and region.

Events abroad and in the West both encouraged and threatened Americans. Seizing one opportunity, the United States purchased the Louisiana Territory, adding a vast territory from which new states would soon be carved. But even as American interests turned westward, events in Europe and on the high seas of the Atlantic wrenched an about-face. Caught between the warring British and French, the United States found its ships seized, its foreign commerce interrupted, and its sailors impressed (forcibly drafted), all in violation of its rights as a neutral and independent nation. In what some have called the second war for independence, the United States fought Great Britain to a standoff, while on another front routing Indian resistance and shattering Native American unity. A peace treaty restored the prewar status quo, but the war and the treaty reaffirmed U.S. sovereignty and strengthened American's determination to steer clear of further European conflicts. The war also stimulated industry and nationalism. In 1815 a secure, independent, and self-confident nation looked to the future with optimism. ∎

The Jefferson Presidency and Marshall Court

 In later years Thomas Jefferson would always refer to his taking office as the "Revolution of 1800." He viewed his victory that year as a revolution that restored government to its limited role, restrained and frugal. He stressed the republican virtues of independence, self-reliance, and equality, and in contrast to the formality of the Federalist presidents, he and his fellow Democratic-Republicans preferred simplicity. They wore ordinary clothes instead of the aristocratic wigs and breeches (knee-length trousers) that George Washington and John Adams had favored. Jefferson believed that the austerity of the revolutionary period should be the model for personal conduct.

The election campaign of 1800 had been bitter, and writing to English scientist Joseph Priestly in 1801, Jefferson described his victory as defeating "the Barbarians." The Federalists, Jefferson wrote, had looked "backwards not forwards." But now, a new age had dawned: "The great extent of our republic is new. Its sparse habitation is new. The mighty wave of public opinion which has rolled over is new."

Yet in public, Jefferson sought unity by reaching out to his opponents, to heal the wounds of the campaign and to bridge policy differences. Unity and nation building were the order of the day and the theme of his inaugural address. Standing in the Senate chamber, the only part of the Capitol that had been completed, he

Jefferson's Inaugural

IMPORTANT EVENTS

1801 Marshall becomes chief justice of the United States

Jefferson inaugurated as first Republican president

1801–05 United States defeats Barbary pirates in Tripoli War

1803 *Marbury v. Madison* establishes judicial review

United States purchases Louisiana Territory from France

1804 Burr kills Hamilton in a duel

Jefferson reelected

1804–06 Lewis and Clark explore Louisiana Territory

1805 Prophet emerges as Shawnee leader

1807 *Chesapeake* affair almost leads to war with Great Britain

Embargo Act halts foreign trade

1808 Congress bans importation of slaves to the United States

Madison elected president

1808–13 Prophet and Tecumseh organize Native American tribal resistance

1808–15 Embargoes and war stimulate domestic manufacturing

1812–15 United States and Great Britain fight the War of 1812

1813 Death of Tecumseh ends effective pan-Indian resistance

New England capitalists form Boston Manufacturing Company

1814 Jackson's defeat of Creeks at Battle of Horseshoe Bend begins Indian removal from the South

Treaty of Ghent ends the War of 1812

1814–15 Hartford Convention undermines Federalists

1815 Battle of New Orleans makes Jackson a national hero

1816 James Monroe elected president

---

declared: "We are all republicans, we are all federalists." He thus appealed to the electorate not as party members but as citizens who shared common beliefs in republicanism and federalism. Nearly a thousand people strained to hear him lay out his vision of a restored republicanism: "A wise and frugal government, which shall restrain men from injuring one another, which shall leave them free to regulate their pursuits of industry and improvement, and shall not take from the mouth of labor the bread it has earned. This is the sum of good government," he concluded.

Still, Federalists and Democratic-Republicans continued to distrust each other. John Adams did not attend the inaugural; he had left Washington before dawn to avoid the Democratic-Republican takeover. He and Jefferson had once been close friends but now disliked each other intensely. Both were thin-skinned, quick to take offense and quick to give it.

To implement the restoration of republican values, Jefferson aggressively extended the Democratic-Republicans' grasp on the national government. Virtually all of the six hundred or so officials appointed during the administrations of Washington and Adams

Democratic-Republican Ascendancy

had been loyal Federalists; only six were known Democratic-Republicans. To bring into his administration men who shared his vision of an agrarian republic and individual liberty, Jefferson refused to recognize appointments that Adams had made in the last days of his presidency and dismissed Federalist customs collectors from New England ports. He awarded vacant treasury and judicial offices to Democratic-Republicans. By July 1803, Federalists held only 130 of 316 presidentially controlled offices. They accused Jefferson of "hunting the Federalists like wild beasts" and abandoning the olive leaf extended in his inaugural address.

The Democratic-Republican Congress, swept into office in the election of 1800, proceeded to affirm its belief in limited government. Albert Gallatin, secretary of the treasury, and John Randolph of Virginia, Jefferson's ally in the House of Representatives, translated ideology into policy, putting the federal government on a diet. Congress repealed all internal taxes, including the whiskey tax. Gallatin cut the army budget in half and reduced the 1802 navy budget by two-

This portrait of President Thomas Jefferson was painted by Rembrandt Peale in 1805. Charles Willson Peale (Rembrandt's father) and his five sons helped establish the reputation of American art in the new nation. Rembrandt Peale achieved fame for his presidential portraits; here he has captured Jefferson in a noble pose without the usual symbols of office or power, befitting the Republican age. (© Collection of The New-York Historical Society)

thirds. He then moved to reduce the national debt from $83 million to $57 million, as part of a plan to retire it altogether by 1817. If Alexander Hamilton had viewed the national debt as the engine of economic growth, Jefferson saw it as the source of government corruption. Jefferson even closed two of the nation's five diplomatic missions abroad—at The Hague and Berlin—to save money.

More than frugality, however, distinguished Democratic-Republicans from Federalists. Before Jefferson's election, opposition to the Alien and Sedition Acts of 1798 had helped unite Democratic-Republicans (see page 210). Jefferson now declined to use the acts against his opponents (as President Adams had done in suppressing Democratic-Republican editors) and pardoned those who had been convicted under their provisions. Congress let expire the Sedition Act in 1801 and the Alien Act in 1802. Congress also repealed the Naturalization Act of 1798, which had required fourteen years of residency for citizenship. The 1802 act that replaced it, while stipulating the registration of aliens, required of would-be citizens only five years of residency, loyalty to the Constitution, and the forsaking of foreign allegiance and titles. The new act would remain the basis of naturalized American citizenship into the twentieth century.

The Democratic-Republicans turned next to the judiciary, the last stronghold of Federalist power. To many Democratic-Republicans, the judiciary represented a centralizing force, one undemocratic by virtue of rule by unelected judges appointed for life. Especially galling to Jefferson, John Marshall had become chief justice of the United States, appointed after Adams's defeat. During the 1790s not a single Democratic-Republican had occupied the federal bench; thus the judiciary became a battlefield following the revolution of 1800.

War on the Judiciary

The first skirmish erupted over repeal of the Judiciary Act of 1801, which had been passed in the final days of the Adams administration. The act, designed to maintain Federalist control over the courts, created fifteen new judgeships, which Adams filled by signing "midnight" appointments until his term was just hours away from expiring. The act also reduced by attrition the number of justices on the Supreme Court from six to five. Since that reduction would have denied Jefferson a Supreme Court appointment until two vacancies occurred, the new Democratic-Republican–dominated Congress repealed the 1801 act.

Partisan Democratic-Republicans created another front in the war for control of the judiciary by targeting opposition judges for removal. Republicans were especially infuriated with the Federalist judges who had refused to review the Sedition Act under which Federalists had prosecuted critics of the Adams administration. At Jefferson's prompting, the House impeached (indicted) Federal District Judge John Pickering of New Hampshire, an elderly, emotionally disturbed alcoholic. He was an easy target, and in 1805 the Senate convicted him, removing him from office.

The day Pickering was ousted, the House impeached Supreme Court Justice Samuel Chase for judicial misconduct. A staunch Federalist, Chase had pushed for prosecutions under the Sedition Act, had actively campaigned for Adams in 1800, and repeatedly had denounced Jefferson's administration from the bench. The Democratic-Republicans, however, failed to muster the two-thirds majority of senators necessary to convict him. Chase's acquittal preserved the Court's independence at a critical time before the role of the judiciary as an equal branch of government had been established. In failing to remove Chase, the Senate established the precedent that criminal actions, not political disagreements, were the only proper grounds for impeachment. In his tenure as president, Jefferson appointed three new Supreme Court justices. Nonetheless, the Court remained a Federalist stronghold under Chief Justice John Marshall.

Jefferson and Marshall shared much in common. They were fellow Virginians, even distant cousins, and Marshall was of the generation of Madison and Monroe, the bright young men who formed Jefferson's intellectual entourage. Jefferson, however, viewed Marshall as a traitor to republicanism after Marshall became a Federalist in the 1790s. President Adams had appointed him secretary of state and then, in his last weeks as a lame-duck president, named Marshall as chief justice. Though an autocrat by nature, Marshall possessed a grace and openness of manner that complemented the new Republican political style. As a justice he adopted republican dress, wearing a plain black gown rather than the British robes of scarlet and ermine or the colorful academic garb worn by other justices. Charles de Saint-Memin's portrait of Marshall in 1801 captures both his autocratic bearing and his direct manner. Under Marshall's domination, however, the Supreme Court retained a Federalist outlook even after Democratic-Republican justices achieved a majority in 1811. Throughout his tenure (1801–1835), the Court consistently upheld federal supremacy over the states and protected the interests of commerce and capital.

John Marshall

Marshall made the Court an equal branch of government in practice as well as theory. Judicial service became a coveted honor for ambitious and talented men. Previously people regarded it lightly, and justices had served only short terms. No judicial building was constructed in Washington; Congress considered it unessential, and the Court continued to meet in a chamber of the Capitol. Marshall unified the Court, influencing the justices to issue joint majority opinions rather than a host of individual concurring judgments. Marshall himself became the voice of the majority: from 1801 through 1805 he wrote twenty-four of the

John Marshall (1755–1835) was chief justice of the United States from 1801 to 1835. He posed for this portrait by the French artist Charles Balthazar Julien Fevret de Saint-Memin in 1801, the year he joined the Court. The artist captured the power and strength with which Marshall would dominate the Court.   (Duke University Archives)

Court's twenty-six decisions; through 1810 he wrote 85 percent of the opinions, including every important one.

Marshall significantly increased the Supreme Court's power in the landmark case of *Marbury v. Madison* (1803), another skirmish in war over the judiciary. William Marbury, one of Adams's midnight appointees, had been named a justice of the peace in the District of Columbia. James Madison, Jefferson's new secretary of state, declined to certify Marbury's appointment so that the president could instead appoint a Democratic-Republican. Marbury sued, requesting a writ of mandamus (a court order forcing the president to appoint him). The case presented a political dilemma. If the Supreme Court ruled in favor of Marbury and issued a writ of mandamus, the president probably would not

Marbury v. Madison

comply with it, and the Court had no way to force him to do so. But if the Federalist-dominated bench refused to issue the writ, it would be handing the Democratic-Republicans a victory.

Marshall brilliantly recast the issue to avoid both pitfalls. Speaking for the Court, he ruled that Marbury had a right to his appointment but that the Supreme Court could not compel Madison to honor the appointment because the Constitution did not grant the Court power to issue a writ of mandamus. In the absence of any specific mention in the Constitution, Marshall ruled, the section of the Judiciary Act of 1789 that authorized the Court to issue such writs was unconstitutional. In *Marbury v. Madison*, the Supreme Court denied itself the power to issue writs of mandamus but established its far greater power to judge the constitutionality of laws passed by Congress.

In succeeding years Marshall fashioned the theory of judicial review, the power of the Supreme Court to decide the constitutionality of legislation and presidential acts. Since the Constitution was the supreme law, he reasoned, any federal or state act contrary to the Constitution must be null and void. The Supreme Court, whose duty it was to uphold the law, would decide whether or not a legislative act contradicted the Constitution. "It is emphatically the province and duty of the judicial department," Marshall ruled, "to say what the law is." The power of judicial review established in *Marbury v. Madison* permanently enhanced the independence of the judiciary and breathed life into the Constitution. "Marshall found the Constitution paper and made it power," President James A. Garfield later observed.

Louisiana and Lewis and Clark

 Democratic-Republicans and Federalists divided sharply over more than just the Court; Jefferson's acquisition of the Louisiana Territory in 1803 was another point of contention. Jefferson shared with many other Americans the belief that the United States was destined to expand its "empire of liberty," and his presidency made western expansion a national goal.

Since American independence, Louisiana had held a special place in the young nation's expansionist

Louisiana dreams. Louisiana defined the western border of the United States, which stretched along the Mississippi River from the Gulf of Mexico to present-day Minnesota. Spain had acquired the Louisiana Territory from France in 1763, at the end of

the Seven Years War (see page 118). By 1800 hundreds of thousands of Americans in search of land had settled in the rich Mississippi and Ohio River valleys, intruding on Indian lands. These settlers floated their farm goods down the Mississippi and Ohio Rivers to New Orleans for export. Whoever controlled the port of New Orleans thus had a hand on the throat of the American economy. Americans preferred Spanish control of Louisiana to control by France, a much stronger power.

In secret pacts with Spain in 1800 and 1801, however, France had acquired the territory once again. The United States learned of the transfer only in 1802, when Napoleon seemed poised to rebuild a French empire in the New World. "Every eye in the United States is now focused on the affairs of Louisiana," Jefferson wrote to Robert R. Livingston, the American minister in Paris. American concerns intensified in October of that year when Spanish officials, on the eve of ceding control to the French, violated Pinckney's Treaty (see pages 205–206) by denying Americans the privilege of storing their products at New Orleans prior to transshipment to foreign markets. "The Mississippi," Secretary of State James Madison wrote, "is to them [western settlers] everything. It is the Hudson, the Delaware, the Potomac and all navigable rivers of the Atlantic States formed into one stream." Western farmers and eastern merchants thought a devious Napoleon had closed the port; they grumbled and talked war.

Jefferson personally took charge. To relieve the pressure for war and to win western farm support, Jefferson prepared for war while sending

Louisiana Purchase Virginia governor James Monroe as his personal envoy to join Robert Livingston in France. Their mission: to buy the port of New Orleans and as much of the Mississippi valley as possible. Meanwhile, Congress authorized the call-up of eighty thousand militiamen in case war became necessary. Arriving in Paris in April 1803, Monroe was astonished to learn that France already had offered to sell all 827,000 square miles of Louisiana to the United States for a mere $15 million. Napoleon had lost interest in the New World. Once he failed to recapture independent Haiti, the idea of a New World empire dissolved and Louisiana became superfluous. At the same time he needed money for renewed warfare against Britain. On April 30 Monroe and Livingston signed a treaty buying the vast territory whose exact borders were not yet mapped and whose land was uncharted (see Map 9.1).

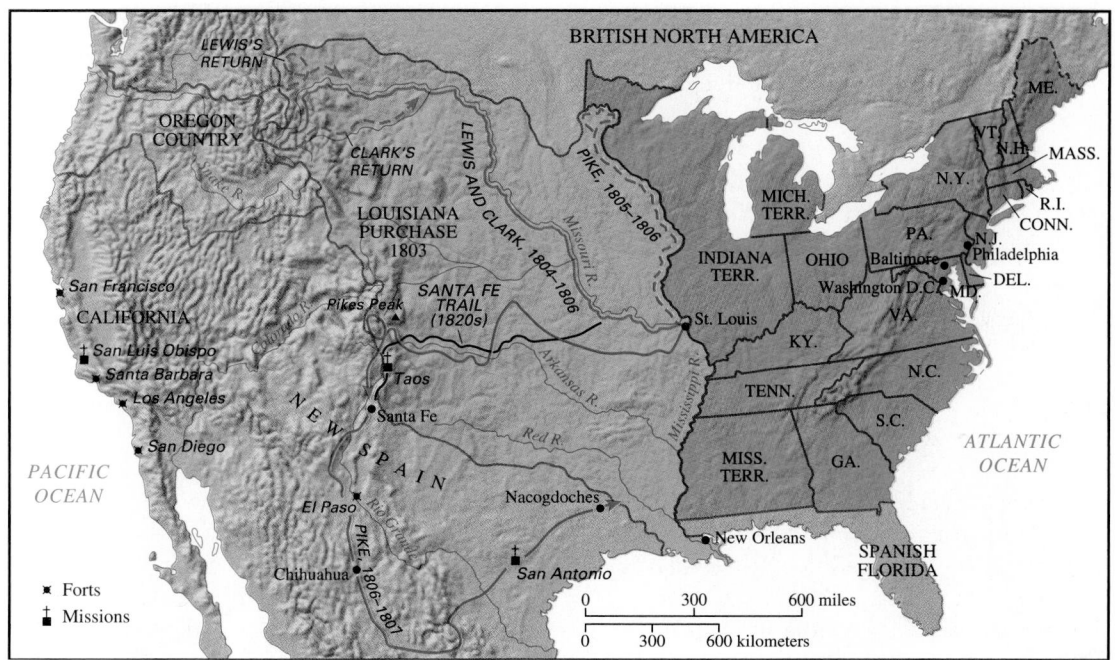

Map 9.1   Louisiana Purchase   The Louisiana Purchase (1803) doubled the area of the United States and opened the trans-Mississippi West for American settlement.

At one stroke of a pen, the Louisiana Purchase doubled the size of the nation and opened the way for continental expansion. It stood as the most popular achievement of Jefferson's presidency. But for Jefferson, the purchase presented a dilemma. For one thing, in purchasing Louisiana, Jefferson forgot his commitment to debt reduction. And some questioned Jefferson's power to make such a move. To be sure, the purchase promised fulfillment of his dream of a nation "with room enough for our descendants to the hundredth and thousandth generation." It provided a means to resolve Indian-settler conflict in the West by making available land to which eastern tribes could be forcibly removed. But was it constitutional? The Constitution nowhere authorized the president to acquire new territory and incorporate it into the nation.

Jefferson considered proposing a constitutional amendment to allow the purchase but decided against it. He believed that the president's implied powers to protect the nation justified the purchase. His long-standing interest in Louisiana and the West also allayed his constitutional concerns. As early as 1782, as an American envoy in France, Jefferson had suggested sending an exploratory mission across the continent to California. A naturalist and scientist, Jefferson seemed fascinated with every aspect of the West—its geography, people, plants, and animals; he had long wanted

to acquire, subdue, and exploit it. As secretary of state in the 1790s, he had been active in promoting a search for "the shortest & most convenient route of communications between the U.S. & the Pacific Ocean."

In 1803 Jefferson sent an expedition headed by Meriwether Lewis and William Clark to the Pacific coast via the Missouri and Columbia Rivers. The twenty-nine-year-old Lewis, a regular army officer in the 1790s, had exchanged rugged military life to be Jefferson's private secretary in 1801. As friend, teacher, leader, role model, and father figure, Jefferson gave Lewis a "crash course" on the botany and the environment of the West, and he proved an exceptional student. The thirty-year-old Clark was an explorer and former soldier who had fought against and negotiated with Native Americans. Aware of the risks as well as the scientific importance of their mission, both were eager for the commission. The expedition also had political import, for the publication of Alexander MacKenzie's *Voyages from Montreal* in 1801 described the first crossing of the continent in Canada in 1793. The publication raised fears that the British would dominate the Far West.

Lewis and Clark

Lewis and Clark officially started their journey in May 1804. They traveled up the Missouri River and wintered at Fort Mandan in present-day North

Western artist Charles Russell depicts a Hidatsa leader trying to rub the black pigment off York, William Clark's slave who was part of the "Corps of Discovery." Many Indians were astonished at York because they had not seen a black man before.   (Courtesy of the Montana Historical Society. Gift of the Artist)

Dakota. Here they selected their twenty-nine-member corps and were joined by Indian guides. In April 1805 they resumed their journey, traveling through present-day Montana. In August, having reached the navigable limits of the Missouri, the party continued the journey with horses. With the help of a local Shoshone guide, they crossed the Bitterroot Mountains. Traversing the Rockies, "the most terrible mountains I ever beheld," according to Sergeant Patrick Gass's diary, proved their most dangerous and treacherous venture. At times they lost their way; tumbled down steep mountain trails; and slept in the snow, bone cold. Short of food, they had to kill a horse for meat. In November 1805 they reached the Pacific Ocean in present-day Oregon, where they wintered, and the following March began the return trek. Lewis and Clark split up to explore alternate routes and reunited in August 1806. They arrived home in St. Louis on September 23, 1806.

The original Corps of Discovery was a diverse group. It included army regulars and young adventurers from Kentucky who became soldiers when they joined the corps.

Corps of Discovery

Clark's slave York, whom he inherited in 1799 from his father, came along as did two men who were half-French and half-Omaha and another who was son of a French Canadian father and a Shawnee mother. Immigrants included an Irishman and a German. Later at the Mandan villages the French Canadian trader Toussaint Charbonneau and his pregnant fifteen-year-old Shoshone wife, Sacagawea, joined the expedition. Lewis and Clark took Charbonneau because they wanted Sacagawea, who knew the languages of the mountain Indians, and she proved invaluable as a guide and translator; she knew the land and the people better than anyone else. The youngest member of the group was the newborn Jean Baptiste Charbonneau, son of Sacagawea, born on February 11, 1805.

Headed by army officers, the expedition followed military rules. But it also was, at times, much more informal and democratic than army regulations or even civilian society allowed. When trouble arose, Lewis and Clark held courts-martial to discipline corps members for such infractions as drunkenness. Contrary to army rules, enlisted men sat on the court. In more serious cases when an accused corps member faced the death penalty, such as a sentry falling asleep or an enlisted man deserting, Lewis and Clark presided. When Sergeant Charles Floyd died of a ruptured appendix at the beginning of the journey, Lewis and Clark allowed the soldiers to elect Private Patrick Gass as his successor, a most unusual move. Later, in November 1805, when the expedition voted where to locate their winter quarters on the Pacific coast, all voted, including the slave York and the Indian woman Sacagawea. Yet issues of race and gender were present. Along the way Indians were astonished at York; many had not seen a black man before. They were curious of his skin color, his "short, curling hair," and his strength. At the end of the journey the names of York and Sacagawea did not appear on the roster Lewis submitted to the War Department. Neither received pay for their work though their assistance had been indispensable.

Although some Americans still believed that the lands in the West were uninhabited, Lewis and Clark knew better. They anticipated a crowded wilderness and hoped to cement U.S. relations with Indians. The explorers carried with them twenty-one bags of gifts for Native American leaders, both to establish goodwill and to stimulate interest in trading for American manufactured goods. They brought back stories not only of various peoples, but also of fauna and flora unknown to the western scientific community; they encountered the grizzly bear, bighorn sheep, and mountain goats. Lewis sent boxes of natural-history specimens to Jefferson, including plant and tree cuttings.

In time, the expedition became legendary and Lewis and Clark fabled American explorers. Many of the artifacts they brought back became relics. They mapped the West and, with their reports and specimens, furthered dreams of a continental empire. The corps members were well rewarded and basked in their renown. But one among them reaped few rewards from the expedition: the slave York. In 1808 York demanded his freedom from Clark as a reward for his service to the expedition. York's wife, a slave, lived in Louisville, Kentucky, and he wished to join her. Clark let him visit her, and York proposed that he stay there, hiring himself out and sending money to Clark. Clark refused and in May 1809 York returned to Clark in St. Louis. Clark found York "insolent and sulky. I gave him a severe trouncing the other Day, and he has much mended" his ways.

Other explorations followed Lewis and Clark's and further publicized the land west of the Mississippi.

Exploration of the West

In 1805 and 1806 Lieutenant Zebulon Pike sought the source of the continent-cutting river and a navigable water route to the Far West. When Pike and his men wandered into Spanish territory to the south, the Spanish held them captive for several months in Mexico. After his release, Pike wrote an account of his experiences that set commercial minds spinning. He described a potential commercial market in southwestern Spanish cities as well as bountiful furs and precious minerals. Over the next few decades, Americans avidly read accounts of western exploration. The vision of a road to the Southwest became a reality with the opening of the Santa Fe Trail in the 1820s, and settlement followed the trail.

New Spain's *Tejas* (Texas) province bordered the Louisiana Territory. Provincial officials welcomed Americans interested in the land south of Louisiana, and American immigrants began to drift in. Some fought as volunteers with Indians and Mexican rebels in a twelve-year war with Spain that ended with Mexican independence in 1821. The establishment of an independent Mexico inspired these Americans to dream of an independent Texas nation—a place for Americans, not for Mexicans. It seems there was no place for people of color, including Mexicans—a mix of European, Indian, and African peoples—in the "empire of liberty."

Political Factionalism and Jefferson's Reelection

Prior to the Republican victory in 1800, most Federalists had disdained popular campaigning. They believed in government by the "best" people—those whose education, wealth, and experience qualified them to be leaders. For candidates to debate their own merits in front of their inferiors—the voters—was utterly demeaning, they thought. No wonder the direct appeals of the Democratic-Republicans struck the Federalists as a subversion of the natural political order.

After the resounding Federalist defeat in 1800, however, a younger generation of Federalists began to imitate the Democratic-Republicans.

A New Style of Campaigning

Led by such men as Josiah Quincy, a Massachusetts congressman, the Younger Federalists campaigned for popular support. Quincy cleverly presented the Federalists as the people's party, attacking Democratic-Republicans as autocratic planters. "Jeffersonian Democracy," Quincy gibed in 1804, was "an Indian word, signifying 'a great tobacco planter who had herds of black slaves.'" In attacking frugal government, the Federalists played on fears of a weakened army and navy. Eastern merchants depended on a strong navy to protect ocean trade; westerners looked to the army to defend them as they encroached on the territory of Native Americans.

In states where both factions organized and ran candidates, people became more active in politics. In some states about 90 percent of the eligible voters cast ballots between 1804 and 1816. But the base of eligible voters—nearly all of whom were white males—remained restricted: property qualifications for voting and holding office persisted, and in 1804 six state legislatures still selected presidential electors. Fearing the divisiveness of partisanship, some Democratic-Republicans restrained their organizational efforts, and most leaders shied away from formal, cohesive political organizations.

Yet political competition and a vigorous partisan press prompted grassroots electioneering. Political barbecues symbolized the new style of campaign. In New York the factions roasted oxen; on the New England coast they baked clams; in Maryland they served oysters. Guests washed down their meals with beer and punch and sometimes competed in corn-shucking or horse-pulling contests. Voters demonstrated their allegiance by attending these events and displaying images of their party leaders. Oratory became a popular form of entertainment, and candidates delivered lengthy and uninhibited speeches wherever crowds gathered. They often made wild accusations, which—given the slow speed of communications—might go unanswered until after the election.

Grassroots Electioneering

The Federalists never mastered the art of campaigning. Older Federalists remained opposed to blatant campaigning. And though strong in Connecticut, Delaware, and a few other states, the Federalists were weak at the national level and never offered the Democratic-Republicans sustained competition. Divisions among Federalists often undermined their success, and the extremism of some Older Federalists discredited most of the rest. A case in point was Timothy Pickering, a Massachusetts congressman and former secretary of state. Pickering opposed the Louisiana Purchase, feared Jefferson's reelection, and urged the secession of New England in 1803 and 1804. He won some support, but most Federalists balked at his plan for secession. Ever the opportunist, Vice President Aaron Burr, intrigued with Pickering's idea of northeastern independence, fantasized about leading New York into secession, with other states following. But when Burr lost his bid to become governor of New York in 1804, dreams of a northern confederacy evaporated.

Where Federalists were too weak to pose a threat, Democratic-Republicans fought among themselves. Politics suffered from divisiveness and personal animosities that were as strong a force as ideology, and the controversies surrounding Burr illustrate the convergence of the political and the personal. The United States was just beginning to build a tradition of nonviolent politics, and it would be a long time before it took root. Indeed some historians have speculated that political parties helped contain violence by establishing alternate rituals for nonviolent expression. But in the nation's early years political disagreements did erupt into violence. The most famous was the Burr-Hamilton duel, involving a former vice president and a former secretary of the treasury.

The charismatic and ambitious Aaron Burr and Alexander Hamilton had long despised each other. Hamilton relentlessly blocked Burr's path. He thwarted Burr's attempt to steal the election of 1800 from Jefferson, and in the 1804 mudslinging New York gubernatorial race, Burr lost to a rival Democratic-Republican faction backed by the Federalist Hamilton. Both Burr and Hamilton held grudges, and when Hamilton made derogatory remarks about him, Burr challenged his nemesis to a duel. Hamilton accepted even though he found dueling repugnant; his son Philip had died in 1801 from dueling wounds. Because New York had outlawed dueling, the two men met across the Hudson River at Weehawken, New Jersey. Hamilton did not fire, and he paid for that decision with his life. But in killing Hamilton, Burr only added to his dishonor in the

Hamilton-Burr Duel

How do historians know...

that popular interest in elections was increasing early in the nineteenth century? Election data are not available, but paintings like John Lewis Krimmel's *Election Day in Philadelphia* (1815) convey that interest. Only white males could vote at the time, and the crowd is composed mostly of white men, although at least one African American and some women and children are present. The artist depicts a festive occasion. Citizens riding on a float in the background carry their own flag; they have created a parade. A holiday spirit seems to prevail as men cluster in groups talking, arguing, sharing jokes, and generally appearing to be enjoying themselves. Perhaps there is a hint of overindulgence as well. The man sitting in front of an overturned chair *(left foreground)*, with his hat on the ground behind him, seems to have fallen,

perhaps from too much drink—a common affliction in the party atmosphere of election day. Among the spectators are two women *(right foreground)*, one of whom is holding the hand of a little girl. They suggest a restraining force on the raucous scene. The woman dressed in white and her friend offer a common female image of the time: the woman as an emblem of republican virtue. The space between the female and male figures suggests that the women stand apart not only as nonvoters but also as symbols of virtue and seriousness absent in the male world. Overall, the painting depicts a popular event, mixing a party atmosphere with civic duty. From a sober exercise of democratic responsibility, voting had become a popular event.   (Photo: Courtesy of Winterthur Museum)

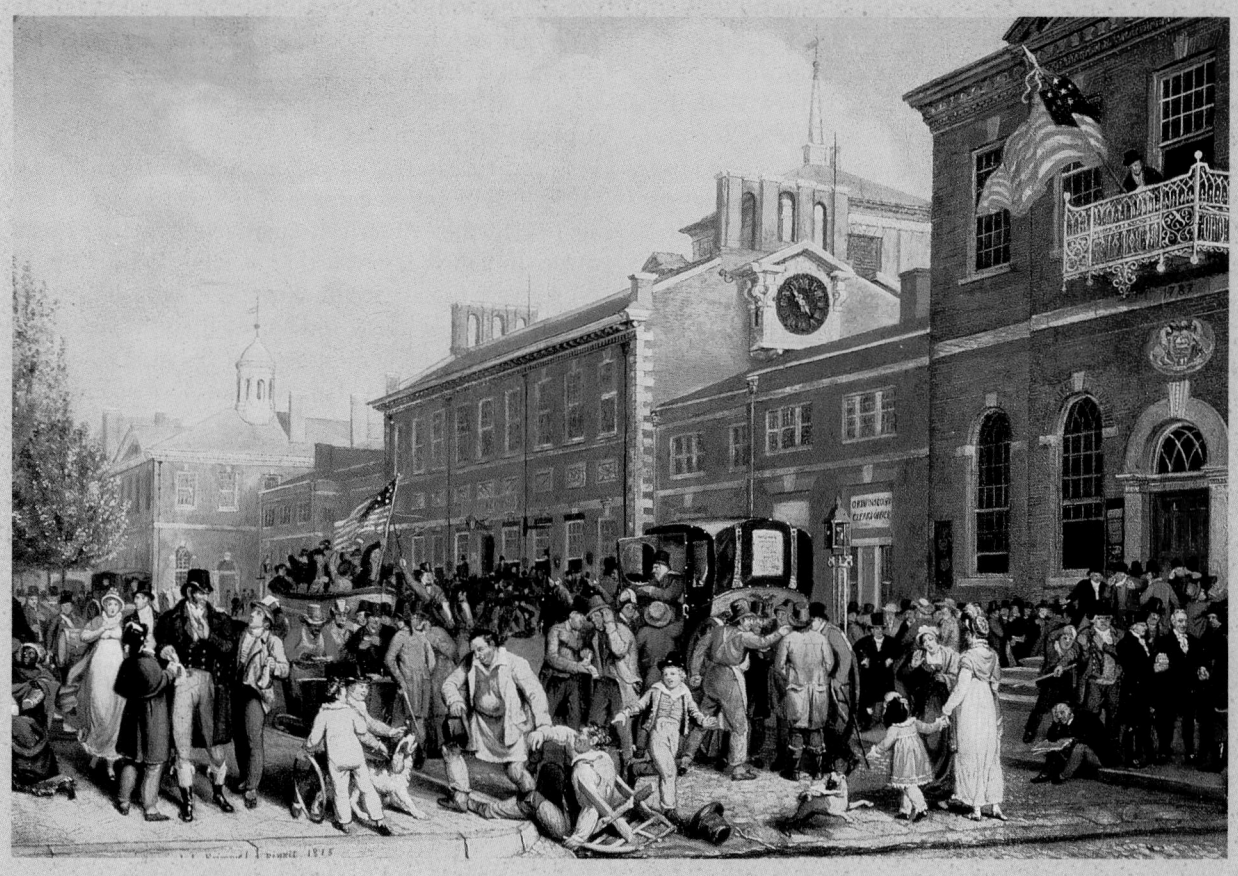

public's eyes. He was indicted for murder in New York and New Jersey and faced immediate arrest if he returned to either state.

Jefferson was appalled that politics could lead to personal violence. In 1808 he advised his grandson, Thomas Jefferson Randolph, to avoid political arguments. The president had witnessed too many politicians "getting warm, becoming rude, and shooting one another." It was not just the deaths of Philip and Alexander Hamilton that Jefferson had in mind. In 1806 the president's son-in-law, Congressman Thomas Mann Randolph, and his distant cousin, former Jefferson ally and now fierce opponent, John Randolph, chairman of the House Ways and Means Committee, tangled. Nasty floor speeches led the two Randolphs to arrange a duel, but Thomas Mann Randolph's apology averted gunfire. The embers of mistrust smoldered, and the possibility of a duel remained. After the War of 1812 dueling became rarer in politics and was confined mostly to the South as a traditional means of defending one's personal or family honor.

Rather than preserving his honor, Burr's killing of Hamilton made him an outcast. His political career in ruins, Burr plotted to create in the Southwest a new empire carved out of the Louisiana Territory. With the collusion of General James Wilkinson, the U.S. commander in the Mississippi valley, Burr planned to raise a private army to grab land from the United States or from Spain (his exact plans remain unknown). Wilkinson switched sides and informed President Jefferson of Burr's devious intention. Jefferson personally assisted the prosecution in Burr's 1807 trial for treason, over which Chief Justice Marshall presided. The jury acquitted Burr, who fled to Europe.

Campaigning for reelection in 1804, Jefferson took credit for the restoration of republican values and the acquisition of the Louisiana Territory. Jefferson and the Democratic-Republicans claimed they ended the Federalist threat to liberty by repealing the Alien and Sedition and Judiciary Acts. They also boasted that they had reduced the size of government by cutting spending. Despite his opponents' charges, Jefferson had demonstrated that Democratic-Republicans supported commerce and promoted free trade. American trade with Europe was flourishing. Federalists who earlier had criticized Jefferson for not seizing Louisiana now unwisely attacked the president for paying too much for it and for exceeding his powers in buying the territory.

Jefferson's Reelection

Jefferson's opponent in 1804 was Charles Cotesworth Pinckney, a wealthy South Carolina lawyer and former Revolutionary War aide to George Washington. As Adams's vice-presidential running mate in 1800, Pinckney had inherited the Federalist leadership. Jefferson dumped the disloyal and unreliable Aaron Burr from the 1804 ticket, and he and his running mate, George Clinton of New York, swamped Pinckney and New Yorker Rufus King in the electoral college by 162 votes to 14, carrying fifteen of the seventeen states.

Indian Resistance

Lewis and Clark's account testified to the Indian presence in the West, and most Americans viewed Native Americans, no matter where they lived, as obstacles to American settlement. Violations of treaties and coerced new ones, forcing Indians to cede ever more land to the United States, continually shrunk Indian territory. With less land, Indians found hunting and agriculture more difficult. Not only their traditional ways but also their independence and existence were threatened. Encroachment by whites and the periodic ravages of disease—smallpox, measles, and influenza—brought further misery.

In the early 1800s two Shawnee brothers, Prophet (1775–1837) and Tecumseh (1768–1813), led a revolt against further American encroachment by fostering a pan-Indian federation that stretched from the Old Northwest to the South. Prophet's early life typified the experiences of the Indians of the Old Northwest. Born in 1775 a few months after his father's death in battle, Prophet, called Lalawethika ("Noisemaker"), as a young man was expelled to Ohio along with other Shawnees under the 1795 Treaty of Greenville (see page 184), and he later moved to Indiana. Within Prophet and Tecumseh's own lifetimes the Shawnees had lost most of their Ohio land; by the 1800s they occupied scattered sites in Ohio and in the Michigan and Louisiana territories. Displacement left Lalawethika forlorn, and like many other Native Americans he turned to whiskey for escape. He also turned to traditional folk knowledge and remedies and in 1804 became a tribal medicine man. His medicine, however, could not stop the white man's diseases from ravaging his village.

Lalawethika emerged from his own battle with illness in 1805 as a new man, called Tenskwatawa ("the Open Door"), or "the Prophet." Claiming to have died

The Shawnee chiefs Tecumseh *(left)* and Prophet *(right)*. The two brothers led a revival of traditional Shawnee culture and preached Native American federation against white encroachment. In the War of 1812 they allied themselves with the British, but Tecumseh's death at the Battle of the Thames (1813) and British indifference thereafter caused Native Americans' resistance and unity to collapse.   (Tecumseh: Field Museum of Natural History, Chicago, FMNH Neg. #A93851; Prophet: National Museum of American Art, Smithsonian Institution, Washington, D.C.)

The Prophet

and been resurrected, he traveled widely in the Ohio River valley as a religious leader, attacking the decline of moral values among Native Americans, warning of damnation for those who drank whiskey, condemning intertribal battles, and stressing harmony and respect for elders. He urged Indians to return to the old ways and abandon white customs: to hunt with bows and arrows, not guns; to stop wearing hats; and to refrain from eating bread and instead to cultivate corn and beans. Whiskey, he preached, was made for whites; the forest had been created for Indians.

Prophet was building a religious movement that offered reassurance to the Shawnees, Potawatomis, and other displaced western Indians. As a leader his power came from his eloquence, deep conviction, and performance of miracles. By timing his invocations to coincide with a solar eclipse, he even seemed to darken the sun. His outspoken opposition to federal Indian policy drew others into his camp, and as his message spread to southern tribes, the federal government and white settlers became alarmed.

By 1808 Prophet and his older brother Tecumseh talked less about spiritual renewal and more about resisting American aggression. Tecumseh was turning Prophet's religious movement into a political one. The British, who looked for alliances with Native Americans after renewed Anglo-American hostilities (see page 236), encouraged Indians to defy eviction from lands claimed by the U.S. government. In repudiating land cessions to the government under the Treaty of Fort Wayne (1809), Tecumseh told Indiana's governor William Henry Harrison at Vincennes in 1810 that "the only way to check and stop this evil is, for all the red men to unite in claiming a common and equal right in the land, as it was at first, and should be

Tecumseh

yet; for it . . . belongs to all, for the use of each. . . . No part has a right to sell, even to each other, much less to strangers."

Tecumseh, a towering six-foot warrior and charismatic orator, soon overshadowed his brother as Shawnee leader. He dressed as a chief from a century before, exchanging his European shirts and cloth trousers for soft deerskin suits with fringes. He replaced the bright beads and ribbons sold by whites with dyed porcupine quills. He returned to traditional diet as well, refusing foreign food. Younger Indians flocked to him. Warriors found his political visions more relevant than Prophet's spirituality in protecting themselves against the United States. Convinced that only an Indian federation could stop the advance of white settlement, Tecumseh sought to unify northern and southern Indians by traveling widely, preaching Indian resistance. And he warned Harrison that Indians would resist white occupation of the 2.5 million acres on the Wabash River that they had ceded in the Treaty of Fort Wayne.

American Neutrality Imperiled by a World at War

 "Peace, commerce, and honest friendship with all nations, entangling alliance with none," President Jefferson had proclaimed in his first inaugural address. Jefferson's efforts to stand aloof from European conflict were successful until 1805. Thereafter the United States could not escape the web of European hostilities, and protection of American commerce and foreign relations occupied nearly all of Jefferson's second administration. The easy victory over the Barbary states would not be repeated against the British.

After the Senate ratified the Jay Treaty in 1795 (see page 205), the United States and Great Britain appeared to reconcile their differences. Britain withdrew from its western forts and interfered less in American trade with France. Since the United States was Britain's best customer, and the British Empire in turn bought the bulk of American exports, both sides worked hard for good relations.

But in May 1803, two weeks after Napoleon sold Louisiana to the United States, renewal of the Napoleonic wars between France and Britain (and later Britain's continental allies, Prussia, Austria, and Russia) again trapped the United States between Britain and France on the high seas. For two years American commerce benefited from the conflict. As the world's

largest neutral carrier, the United States became the chief supplier of food to Europe. American merchants also gained control of most of the West Indian trade.

But after defeating the French and Spanish fleets at the Battle of Trafalgar in October 1805, Britain's Royal Navy tightened its control of the oceans. Two months later Napoleon crushed the Russian and Austrian armies at Austerlitz. Stalemated, France and Britain launched a commercial war, blockading each other's trade. As a trading partner of both countries, the United States paid a high price.

All tension focused on the high seas, where Britain, commanding the world's largest navy, suffered a severe shortage of sailors. Too few men enlisted, and those in service frequently deserted, demoralized by harsh treatment. Some British sailors joined U.S. merchant ships, where conditions were better. The Royal Navy resorted to stopping American vessels and seizing British deserters, British-born naturalized American seamen, and other unlucky sailors suspected of being British. Perhaps six to eight thousand Americans were impressed in this way between 1803 and 1812. Moreover, alleged deserters—many of them American citizens—faced British courts-martial. Americans saw impressment as a direct assault on the independence of their new republic. The principle of "once a British subject, always a British subject" mocked U.S. citizenship and sovereignty.

Impressment of American Sailors

The British violated other American rights as well. They interfered with U.S. trade with the West Indies by blocking goods the United States believed were part of neutral trade. They also searched and seized U.S. vessels within American territory offshore.

In February 1806 Americans denounced British impressment as aggression and a violation of America's neutral rights. In protest, Congress passed the Non-Importation Act, barring British manufactured goods from entering American ports. Since the act exempted most cloth or metal articles, it had little impact on British trade; instead, it was a warning to the British of what to expect if they continued to violate American rights. In November Jefferson suspended the act temporarily while William Pinckney, a Baltimore lawyer, joined James Monroe in London to negotiate a settlement. But the treaty Monroe and Pinckney carried home violated their instructions—it did not so much as mention impressment—and Jefferson never submitted it to the Senate for ratification.

Anglo-American relations steadily deteriorated. Then in June 1807, the forty-gun frigate U.S.S. *Chesapeake* left Norfolk, Virginia, headed

Chesapeake Affair

to protect American ships in the Mediterranean. About 10 miles from shore, still inside American territorial waters, it met the fifty-gun British frigate *Leopard*. When the *Chesapeake* refused to be searched for deserters, the *Leopard* repeatedly fired its cannon broadside into the American ship. Three Americans were killed and eighteen wounded, including the ship's captain. The British seized four deserters from the Royal Navy—three of them American citizens; one of the deserters, British subject Jenkin Ratford, was hanged. Damaged and humiliated, the *Chesapeake* returned to port. Americans were outraged and united. "But one feeling pervades the nation," said a leading Democratic-Republican, former Congressman Joseph Nicholson. "All distinctions of Federalism and Democracy are banished." The *Chesapeake* affair

not only intensified the emotional impact of impressment but also exposed American military weakness.

Had the United States been better prepared militarily, the ensuing howl of public indignation might have brought about a declaration of war. But the still-fledgling country was ill equipped to defend its neutral rights with force; it was certainly no match for the British navy. With Congress in recess, Jefferson was able to avoid hostilities, choosing instead what he called "peaceable coercion." In July the president closed American waters to British warships to prevent similar incidents, and soon thereafter he increased military and naval expenditures. In December 1807 Jefferson again put economic pressure on Great Britain by invoking the Non-Importation Act, followed eight days later by a new restriction, the Embargo Act.

The Embargo Act was intended to avoid war. Jefferson thought of it as a short-term measure to prevent confrontation between American merchant vessels and British and French warships and to put pressure on

A painting of the British frigate *Leopard* firing its guns into the U.S.S. *Chesapeake* when the U.S. ship refused to be searched for British deserters. The British boarded the subdued *Chesapeake* and seized four deserters, three of them American citizens. Americans were humiliated and angered by the British violation of American rights. (Courtesy of William Gilkerson)

Embargo Act

France and England by denying them American products. The embargo forbade all exports from the United States to any country. Foreign ships delivering goods left American ports with empty holds. U.S. exports dropped some 80 percent in 1808, but smuggling blossomed overnight.

Few American policies were as well intentioned and as unpopular and unsuccessful as Jefferson's embargo. Although "peaceable coercion" had been an enlightened concept in international affairs, some Democratic-Republicans felt uneasy about interfering with trade. Federalists opposed the embargo vociferously. Some feared its impact abroad. "If England [were to] sink," Federalist vice-presidential candidate Rufus King said in 1808, expressing Federalist pro-British sympathies, "her fall will prove the grave of our liberties." Mercantile New England, the heart of Federalist opposition to Jefferson, took the brunt of the resulting economic depression. In the winter of 1808–1809, talk of secession spread through New England port cities.

Although general unemployment soared, some individuals benefited from the embargo. Merchants with ships abroad (those not idled by the embargo) and merchants willing to risk the lax enforcement to trade illegally could garner enormous profits. U.S. manufacturers—the early textile mills, for instance—received a boost, since the domestic market became theirs exclusively.

The embargo actually had little impact on Britain. The British most severely hurt—West Indians and factory workers in England—had no voice in policy. English merchants actually gained because they took over the Atlantic carrying trade from the stalled American ships. And because of a successful British blockade of Europe, the embargo had little practical effect on the French. Indeed, it gave France an excuse to set privateers against American ships that had evaded the embargo and were, possibly, heading to British ports. The French cynically claimed that such ships were British ships in disguise because the embargo prevented American vessels from sailing.

In the election of 1808, the Democratic-Republicans faced not only the Federalists but also factional dissent and dissatisfaction in seaboard states hobbled by the embargo.

Election of 1808

Although nine state legislatures passed resolutions urging Jefferson to run again, the president followed Washington's lead in renouncing a third term. He supported James Madison, his secretary of state, as the Democratic-

Republican standard-bearer. For the first time, however, the Democratic-Republican nomination was contested. Madison won the endorsement of the party's congressional caucus, but Virginia Democratic-Republicans put forth James Monroe, who later withdrew, and some easterners supported Vice President George Clinton.

Charles Cotesworth Pinckney and Rufus King again headed the Federalist ticket, but with new vigor. The Younger Federalists, led by Harrison Gray Otis and other Bostonians, made the most of the widespread disaffection with Republican policy, especially the embargo. Although Pinckney received only 47 electoral votes to Madison's 122, the Federalists offered genuine competition. Pinckney carried all of New England except Vermont, and he won Delaware and some electoral votes in two other states. Federalists also gained seats in Congress and captured the New York State legislature. The Federalist future looked promising.

Under the pressure of domestic opposition, the embargo eventually collapsed. In its place, the Non-

Non-Intercourse Act

Intercourse Act of 1809 reopened trade with all nations except Britain and France, and it authorized the president to resume trade with Britain or France if either of them ceased to violate neutral rights. On leaving office in March, Jefferson expressed the weight of his failure: "Never did a prisoner, released from his chains," he wrote, "feel such relief as I in shaking off the shackles of power."

The new act solved only the problems created by the embargo; it did not prevent further British and French interference with American commerce. For one brief moment it appeared to work. In June 1809 President Madison reopened trade with England after the British minister to the United States assured him that Britain would repeal restrictions on American trade. His Majesty's government in London, however, repudiated the minister's assurances, and Madison reverted to nonintercourse.

When the Non-Intercourse Act expired in 1810, Congress substituted a variant, Macon's Bill Number 2, that exchanged the proverbial stick for a carrot. The bill reopened trade with both Great Britain and France but provided that when either nation stopped violating American commercial rights, the president could suspend American commerce with the other. Madison, eager to avoid war, fell victim to French duplicity. When Napoleon accepted the offer, Madison declared nonintercourse with Great Britain in 1811. Napoleon, however, tricked him. The French continued to seize

American ships, and nonintercourse failed a second time. But because the Royal Navy dominated the seas, Britain, not France, became the main focus of American hostility.

Commerce and Industry

 The economy of the early republic relied heavily on shipping, and the commercial fleet played a significant role in extending American trade around the world. American fishermen explored the Atlantic, while whalers hunted for prey in the Atlantic and Pacific Oceans. The United States became a major supplier to Europe, taking advantage of the disruption in food production caused by European conflicts. Americans also exported cotton, lumber, sugar, and other commodities to Europe, and brought back manufactured goods. The slave trade lured American sailing ships to Africa. Boston, Salem, and Philadelphia merchants opened trade with China, sending cloth and metal to swap for furs with Chinook Indians on the Oregon coast, then sailing to China to trade for porcelain, tea, and silk. Greater profits could be made by importing manufactured goods than by producing them at home.

After 1807 embargoes and war, however, boosted domestic manufacturing. The disruptions in commerce made domestic manufactures profitable, and merchants began to shift their capital from shipping to manufacturing. In 1807 there were twenty cotton and woolen mills in New England; by 1813 there were more than two hundred.

Factories were still new in America. Samuel Slater set up the first American textile mill in Rhode Island in the 1790s. It used water-powered spinning machines that English immigrant Slater had built from memorized British models. Though Federalists like Alexander Hamilton, through his *Report on Manufactures* (see page 202), had pushed the United States to promote manufacturing, Jefferson envisioned an "empire of liberty" that was agricultural and commercial, not industrial. Holding fast to frugal, limited government, the Democratic-Republican policy did not promote industry.

This contemporary painting shows the Boston Manufacturing Company's 1814 textile factory at Waltham, Massachusetts. All manufacturing processes were brought together under one roof, and the company built its first factories in rural New England to tap roaring rivers as a power source.   (Courtesy of Gore Place Society, Waltham, Mass.)

Construction of the first American power loom and the chartering of the Boston Manufacturing Company in 1813 radically transformed textile manufacturing. Francis Cabot Lowell and other Boston merchants capitalized the corporation at $400,000—ten times the amount behind the first Rhode Island mills. The owners erected their factories in Waltham, Massachusetts, bringing all the manufacturing processes to a single location. They employed a resident manager to run the mill, thus separating ownership from management. Workers received wages, and the cloth they produced was sold throughout the United States.

Waltham or Lowell System

The cloth was so inexpensive that many women began to purchase it rather than make their own. While spinning and especially weaving remained women's work in many rural homes, women who formerly had spun their own yarn now received yarn from the mills and returned finished cloth. The change was subtle but significant: although the work itself was familiar, women were operating their looms for wages and producing cloth for the market, not primarily for their families.

The managers could not find enough hands in rural Waltham to staff the mill, so they recruited New England farm daughters, accepting responsibility for their living conditions. As inducements they offered cash wages, company-run boarding houses, and cultural events such as evening lectures—none of which were available on the farm. This paternalistic approach, called the Waltham or Lowell system, spread to other mills erected alongside New England rivers.

The early mills, dependent on waterpower, sprung up in rural areas. By erecting dams and watercourses, mill owners diverted water from farmers and destroyed fishing, an important source of income and protein in rural and village America. To protect their customary rights, fishermen and farmers fought the manufacturers in New England state legislatures, but petitions from job seekers in the mill environs supported the manufacturers. The ensuing compromises promoted mill development.

The War of 1812

Though unprepared for war in 1812, the United States seemed unable to avoid it. Economic pressure had failed to protect American ships and sailors. Having exhausted all efforts to alter British policy, and fearing for the survival of American independence, the United States drifted toward war. The Democratic-Republican "War Hawks," elected to Congress in 1810, cried loudest for war. Britain's response was too little and too late. In spring 1812, the admiralty ordered British ships to avoid clashes with the American navy and to avoid searches and seizures of American ships. Then in June 1812, Britain reopened the seas to American shipping. Hard times had hit the British Isles: the Anglo-French conflict had blocked much British commerce to the European continent, and exports to the United States had fallen 80 percent. But two days after the change in British policy, before word of it had crossed the Atlantic, Congress declared war.

In his message to Congress on June 1, 1812, President Madison enumerated familiar grievances: impressment, interference with neutral commerce, and British alliances with western Indians. More generally, the Democratic-Republicans resolved to defend American independence and honor, and some Americans hoped to conquer and annex British Canada.

The war Congress was a partisan one. Most militant were the War Hawks, land-hungry southerners and westerners, all Democratic-Republicans, led by John C. Calhoun of South Carolina and first-term congressman and House Speaker Henry Clay of Kentucky. John Randolph of Roanoke, an opponent of war, charged angrily, "Agrarian cupidity, not maritime rights, urges war." He heard "but one word" in Congress: "Canada! Canada! Canada!" Most representatives from the coastal states opposed war because armed conflict with the Royal Navy would interrupt American shipping. On June 4, the House voted 79 to 49 for war; two weeks later the Senate followed suit 19 to 13. Republicans favored war by a vote of 98 to 23; Federalists opposed it 39 to 0. On June 19, President Madison signed the bill. The United States went to war with Britain.

The Vote for War

The war unfolded as a series of scuffles and skirmishes, for which the U.S. Army and Navy and the state militias were unprepared. Officers executed campaigns poorly, and full-scale battles happened rarely (see Map 9.2). But the Americans had the advantage of fighting close to home.

Jefferson's warning that "our constitution is a peace establishment—it is not calculated for war" proved true. Though the U.S. Navy had a corps of experienced officers who had proved their mettle in the Barbary War, it was no match for the Royal Navy. The

Map 9.2   Major Campaigns of the War of 1812   The land war centered on the U.S.-Canadian border, the Chesapeake Bay, and the Louisiana and Mississippi Territories.

Recruiting an Army

U.S. Army had neither an able staff nor an adequate force of enlisted men. By 1812 the U.S. Military Academy at West Point, founded in 1802, had produced only eighty-nine regular officers. The American army depended on political leaders and state militias to recruit volunteers, but not all states cooperated. The government offered enlistees a sign-up bonus of $16, monthly pay of $5, a full set of clothes, and a promise of three months' pay and rights to purchase 160 acres of western land upon discharge. Forty-two percent of the enlistees were illiterate.

At first, recruitment in the West went well. Civic spirit, desire for land, and strong anti-Indian sentiment stimulated thousands of enlistments from the Old Northwest, Kentucky, Tennessee, and the southern frontier. The army made itself more acceptable to new recruits by abolishing flogging as punishment in 1812. Within a year, however, frontier enlistments declined. Word spread that the War Department failed to meet its payroll on time. By fall 1814, the army lagged six to twelve months behind in paying soldiers. Nor were supplies adequate; troops often went without shoes, uniforms, or blankets and the rations they received were sometimes spoiled.

Raising an army proved even more difficult in New England, where many viewed the conflict as a Democratic-Republican affair—"Mr. Madison's War"—and Federalists discouraged enlistments. Even some New England Democratic-Republicans declined to raise volunteer companies. Those who accepted promised their men that they would serve only in a defensive role, as in Maine where they guarded the coastline. Indeed, the inability of the United States to mount a successful invasion of Canada was due in part to the army's failure to assemble an effective force. Militias in New England and New York often refused to fight outside their state borders.

Nonetheless, Canada was tempting, and seemed takeable. The mighty Royal Navy could not reach the Great Lakes separating the United States and Canada because there was no river access to them from the Atlantic. Canada's population of just one-half million was a fraction of the United States's 7.5 million. Canada had seven thousand regulars in uniform; the United States, 12,000. And Americans hoped that the French in Canada might welcome U.S. forces.

Invasion of Canada

Begun with high hopes, the invasion of Canada ended in disaster. The American strategy concentrated on the West, aiming to split Canadian forces and isolate the pro-British Indians. At the outset of the war, Tecumseh joined the British, who promised him in return an Indian nation in the Great Lakes region. U.S. General William Hull, territorial governor of Michigan, marched his troops into Upper Canada, near Detroit. More experienced as a politician than as a soldier, Hull had surrounded himself with newly minted colonels as politically astute and militarily ignorant as he was. Although his forces in the area outnumbered the British and their Indian allies, Hull waged a timid campaign, retreating more than he attacked. His abandonment of Mackinac Island and Fort Dearborn in Chicago and his surrender of Fort Detroit left the entire Midwest exposed to the enemy. The only bright spot was the September 1812 defense of Fort Harrison in Indiana Territory by Captain Zachary Taylor, who

provided the Americans with their first land victory. By the winter of 1812–1813, the British controlled about half of the Old Northwest.

The United States had no greater success on the Niagara front, where New York borders Canada. At the Battle of Queenstown, Canada, north of Niagara, the U.S. Army met defeat because the New York militia refused to leave New York. This frustrating scenario was repeated near Lake Champlain, when the New York militia's refusal to cross the border into Canada foiled American plans to attack Montreal. And neither the French nor the American loyalists who had fled to Canada at the time of the American Revolution rose to welcome the Americans.

The navy provided the only good news in the first year of the war. The U.S.S. *Constitution*, the U.S.S. *Wasp*, and the U.S.S. *United States* all bested British warships on the Atlantic Ocean. The *Constitution*'s 1812 rout of H.M.S. *Guerrière* in the Atlantic emboldened the U.S. Navy and earned the American ship the nickname "Old Ironsides." In the first year of war the Americans lost 20 percent of their ships while in defeat the British lost just 1 percent of their vessels. The United States, however, could ill afford to lose *any* ships. Democratic-Republican frugality had left the navy with only seventeen ships in 1812. It could not fight the British in a general naval war and thus Britannia ruled the waves.

Naval Battles

The Royal Navy blockaded the Chesapeake and Delaware Bays in December 1812, and by 1814 the blockade covered nearly all American ports along the Atlantic and Gulf coasts. After 1811, American trade overseas had declined nearly 90 percent, and the decline in revenues from customs duties threatened to bankrupt the federal government and prostrate New England.

The contest for control of the Great Lakes, the key to the war in the Northwest, evolved as a shipbuilding race. Under Master Commandant Oliver Hazard Perry and shipbuilder Noah Brown, the United States outbuilt the British on Lake Erie and defeated them at the bloody Battle of Put-in-Bay on September 10, 1813. With this costly victory, the Americans gained control of Lake Erie.

Great Lakes Campaign

General William Henry Harrison then began the offensive that proved to be among the United States's most successful land campaigns in the war. A ragged group of Kentucky militia volunteers who had been drafted into the regular army marched 20 to 30 miles a day to join Harrison's forces in Ohio. They had received no training and were armed only with swords and knives. Now with forty-five hundred men, Harrison's force attacked and took Detroit. Then they crossed to Canada, pursuing and defeating the British, Shawnee, and Chippewa forces on October 5 at the Battle of the Thames. In victory the United States captured six hundred British troops and great amounts of war materiel; the United States regained control of the Old Northwest. Tecumseh died in the battle, and with his death expired Native American unity. Following the loss of their leader, some Indians joined the United States against Britain. After the Battle of the Thames, the Americans razed the Canadian capital of York (now Toronto). Though they did not have enough troops to hold the city, they looted and burned the Parliament building before withdrawing. The stunning land

victory had the added effect of stopping the British on Lake Ontario and occupying British operations on Lake Erie.

After defeating Napoleon in Europe in April 1814, the British launched a land counteroffensive against the United States, concentrating on the Chesapeake Bay region. In retaliation for the burning of York—and to divert American troops from Lake Champlain, where the British planned a new offensive—royal troops occupied Washington, D.C., in August and set it ablaze, leaving the presidential mansion and parts of the city burning all night. Chaos ruled. The president and cabinet had planned to rendezvous in Frederick, Maryland, but Madison and his advisers fled to Virginia. First Lady Dolley Madison oversaw removing cabinet documents to safety.

The British intended the attack on the capital only as a diversion. The major battle occurred in Septem-

Andrew Jackson imposed the Treaty of Fort Jackson on the Creek nation, ending the campaign against the Red Sticks. The treaty required the Creeks to pay the costs of the war, which Jackson estimated as the equivalent of 20 million acres. In moving the Creeks out of what is now central Alabama, Jackson initiated the Indians' forced removal from the South. Ironically, of the thirty-five chiefs who made their mark on the treaty, part of which is shown here, only one was a member of the Creek nation.   (National Archives)

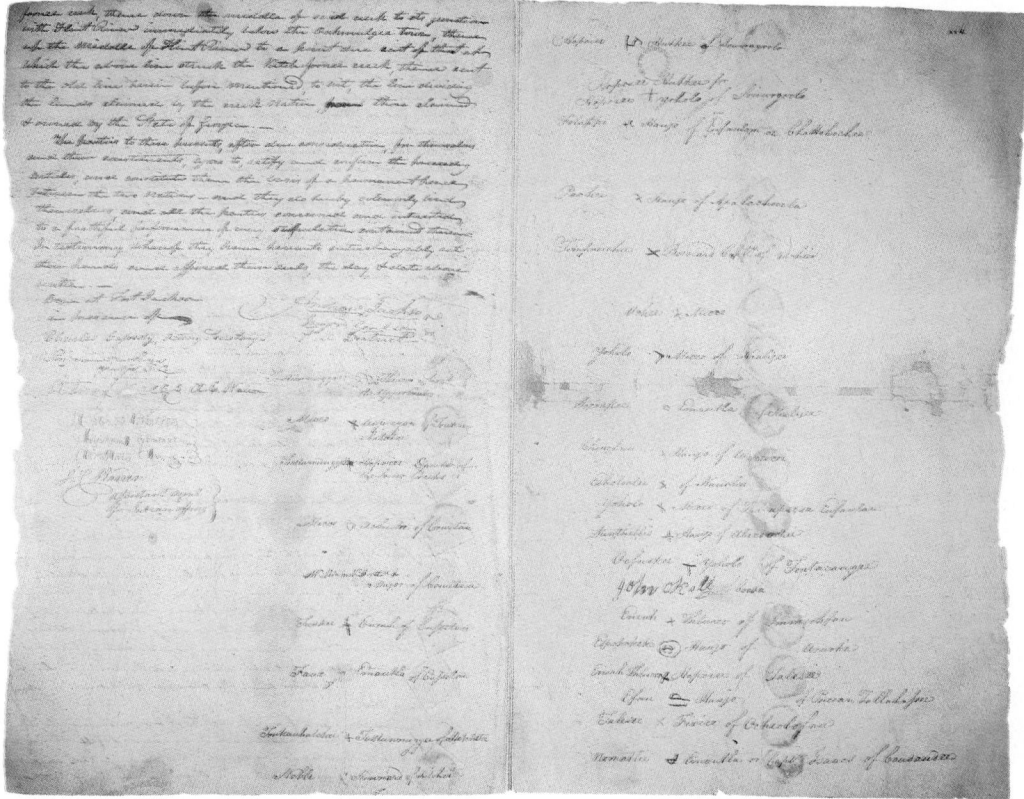

ber 1814 at Baltimore, where the Americans held firm. Francis Scott Key, detained on a British ship, watched the bombardment of Fort McHenry from Baltimore harbor and the next morning wrote the verses of "The Star-Spangled Banner" (which became the national anthem in 1931). Although the British inflicted heavy damage both materially and psychologically, they achieved little militarily. Their offensive at Lake Champlain proved equally unsuccessful when American ships turned back a British flotilla at Plattsburgh. The British halted their offense, and the war was stalemated.

The last campaigns of the war took place in the South, against the Creeks along the Gulf of Mexico and against the British around New Orleans (see Map 9.2). The Creeks had responded to the call of Tecumseh, whose mother was a Creek, to resist U.S. expan-

Campaign Against the Creeks

sion. Some had died in Indiana Territory, at Prophetstown on Tippecanoe Creek, when General Harrison's troops routed Shawnee forces there in 1811. In December 1812 General Andrew Jackson raised his Tennessee militia to fight the Creeks. By late 1813 his anti-Creek campaign stalled for lack of supplies. His men, who had signed up for a year, muttered about going home. Jackson refused to discharge them; they could not, he said, abandon their posts on enemy ground. Officers repeatedly threatened to shoot any man who left. Indeed, in March 1814 Jackson executed John Woods, a militiaman, for disobedience and mutiny. This act broke the opposition within the ranks, and Jackson's men defeated the Creek nation at the Battle of Horseshoe Bend in Mississippi Territory in March 1814.

Ballou's Pictorial Drawing-Room Companion depicts the Battle of New Orleans, the last campaign of the War of 1812. Andrew Jackson's troops—army regulars, Tennessee and Kentucky volunteers, and two companies of African American volunteers from New Orleans—held off the better-trained British troops in January 1815. The battle made Andrew Jackson a national hero.   (Historic New Orleans Collection)

The victory began Jackson's rise to political prominence. In the 1814 Treaty of Fort Jackson, the Creeks ceded two-thirds of their land

Battle of New Orleans

and withdrew to the southern and western part of Mississippi Territory (what is now Alabama); the removal of Indians from the South had begun. Jackson became a major general in the regular army and continued south toward the Gulf of Mexico. To forestall a British invasion at Pensacola Bay, which guarded an overland route to New Orleans, Jackson seized Pensacola—in Spanish Florida—in November 1814. Then, after securing Mobile, he marched on to New Orleans to defend it against the British.

The Battle of New Orleans was the last campaign of the war. Early in December the British fleet landed fifteen hundred men east of the city, hoping to seize the mouth of the Mississippi River and thus strangle the lifeline of the American West. They faced American regulars, Tennessee and Kentucky volunteers, and two companies of free African American volunteers from New Orleans. For three weeks the British under Sir Edward Pakenham and the Americans led by Jackson played cat-and-mouse. Finally, on January 8, 1815, the two forces met head-on. In fortified positions, Jackson's poorly trained army held its ground against two frontal assaults from a British contingent of six thousand. At day's end, more than two thousand British soldiers lay dead or wounded; the Americans suffered only twenty-one casualties. Andrew Jackson emerged a national hero, and Americans memorialized the battle in song and paintings. The Battle of New Orleans actually took place two weeks after the end of the war. Unknown to the participants, a treaty had been signed in Ghent, Belgium, on December 24, 1814.

Peace and Consequences

The U.S. government had gone to war reluctantly and throughout the conflict probed for a diplomatic end to hostilities. In 1813 President Madison eagerly accepted a Russian offer to mediate, but Great Britain balked. Three months later, British foreign minister Lord Castlereagh suggested opening peace talks. It took more than ten months to arrange meetings, but in August 1814 a team of American negotiators, including John Quincy Adams and Henry Clay, began talks with the British in Ghent.

The Ghent treaty made no mention of the issues that had led to war. The United States received no satisfaction on impressment, blockades, or other maritime rights for neutrals. British demands for an independent Indian nation in the Northwest and territorial cessions from Maine to Minnesota likewise went unsatisfied. The Treaty of Ghent essentially restored the prewar status quo. It provided for an end to hostilities with the British and with Native Americans, release of prisoners, restoration of conquered territory, and arbitration of boundary disputes.

Why did the negotiators settle for so little? Events in Europe had made peace and the status quo acceptable at the end of 1814, as they had not been in 1812. Napoleon's defeat allowed the United States to abandon its demands, since peace in Europe made impressment and interference with American commerce moot issues. Similarly, war-weary Britain—its treasury nearly depleted—stopped pressing for a military victory.

The War of 1812 affirmed the independence of the American republic. Nearly three hundred thousand troops had taken up arms to

Consequences of the War of 1812

maintain independence; almost two thousand died for the cause, and four thousand were wounded. Although conflict with Great Britain over trade and territory continued, it never again led to war. The experience strengthened America's resolve to steer clear of European politics because the Anglo-French conflagration had drawn the United States into war. At the same time, with Indian resistance broken, U.S. expansion would spread south and west, not north to Canada.

The war carried disastrous results for most Native Americans. Although they were not a party to the Treaty of Ghent, the ninth article of the pact pledged the United States to end hostilities and to restore "all the possessions, rights, and privileges" that Indians had enjoyed before the war. Midwestern Indians signed more than a dozen treaties with the United States in 1815, but they had little meaning. With the death of Tecumseh, the Indians had lost their most powerful political and military leader; with the withdrawal of the British, they had lost their strongest ally. The Shawnees, Potawatomis, Chippewas, and others had lost the means to resist American expansion.

The war exposed weaknesses in defense and transportation at home. American generals had found U.S. roads inadequate to move troops and supplies. In the Northwest, General Harrison's troops had depended on homemade cartridges and gifts of clothing from Ohio residents; in Maine, troops had melted down spoons to make bullets. Improved transportation and a well-equipped army became national priorities; both were vital for westward expansion. In 1815 President Madison responded by centralizing control of the military and building a line of forts for coastal defense, and Congress voted a standing army of ten thousand men—one-third of the army's wartime strength but three times the size of the army during Jefferson's administration. In 1818 the National Road reached Wheeling, Virginia (now West Virginia), from its Cumberland, Maryland, beginning and carried settlers westward (see page 253).

Perhaps most important of all, the war stimulated economic growth. The embargo, the Non-Importation and Non-Intercourse Acts, and the war itself spurred the production of manufactured goods because New England capitalists began to invest in home manufactures. The effects of these changes were far-reaching (see Chapter 10).

Finally, the war sealed the fate of the Federalists. Realizing that they could not win a presidential election in wartime, the Federalists joined renegade Democratic-Republicans in supporting New York City mayor DeWitt Clinton in September 1812. Federalist organization peaked at the state level as the Younger Federalists campaigned hard. Clinton nevertheless lost to President Madison by 128 to 89 electoral votes; areas that favored the war (the South and West) remained solidly Democratic-Republican. The Federalists gained some congressional seats and carried many local elections, but extremism, in the form of the Hartford Convention, undermined them.

During the war Federalists had revived talk of secession. With the war stalemated, delegates from New England met in Hartford, Connecticut, for three weeks in the winter of 1814–1815 to discuss revising the national compact or pulling out of the republic. Moderates prevented a resolution of secession, but convention members condemned the war and the embargo and endorsed radical changes in the Constitution. They wanted to restrict the presidency to one term and require a two-thirds congressional vote to admit new states to the Union. A barometer of their dissatisfaction was a proposal forbidding naturalized citizens from holding office. The delegates fruitlessly attempted to preserve New England Federalist political power as electoral strength

Hartford Convention

shifted to the South and West and immigrants became politically active.

The timing of the Hartford Convention proved lethal. The victory at New Orleans and news of the peace treaty made the convention, with its talk of secession and constitutional amendments, look ridiculous if not treasonous. Rather than harassing a beleaguered wartime administration, the Federalists found themselves in retreat before a rising tide of nationalism. Though the Federalists survived in a handful of states until the 1820s, the faction dissolved. The War of 1812, at first a source of revival as opponents of war flocked to the Federalist banner, helped speed its demise.

Summary

The 1800 election marked the peaceful transition in power from the Federalists to the opposition Democratic-Republicans. Thomas Jefferson replaced John Adams as president and sought both to unify the nation and to solidify Democratic-Republican control of the government. Jeffersonians favored frugal government, and they cut the budget, military forces, and diplomatic missions.

The Supreme Court under Chief Justice John Marshall remained a Federalist bastion. Both parties fought over the judiciary, and Marshall would ensure, until 1835, the dominance of Federalist principle: federal supremacy over the states and the protection of commerce and capital. In *Marbury v. Madison* (1803), the Supreme Court established its great power of judicial review.

Jefferson considered the acquisition of Louisiana Territory and the commissioning of Lewis and Clark's expedition among his significant presidential accomplishments. In a single act the United States doubled its size. Increasingly Americans looked westward, and Lewis and Clark's Corps of Discovery practiced "buckskin diplomacy" while exploring the land, flora, fauna, and people west of the Mississippi. Americans quickly moved to absorb Louisiana.

With Jefferson and his successor James Madison, the Democratic-Republicans won every presidential election in this period. Though the electorate was limited only to males and mostly to whites, both the Federalists and the Democratic-Republicans competed at the grassroots level for popular support. Political conflict was bitter, divisions real. Sometimes they could prove fatal as in the Burr-Hamilton duel.

Despite internal divisions, the greatest threats came from abroad. In the war with the Barbary states, the United States sought to guard its commerce and ships on the high seas. The second war with Britain—the War of 1812—was fought for similar reasons but against a much more formidable power. The peace treaty reaffirmed American independence; thereafter the nation was able to settle disputes with Great Britain at the bargaining table. The war also dealt a serious blow to Indian resistance in the West and South. At the same time, embargoes and war forced Americans to look toward building domestic markets and jump-started American manufacturing. Military and diplomatic assertiveness brought Americans a sense of national identity and self-confidence.

LEGACY FOR A PEOPLE AND A NATION
The Peaceful Transfer of Power

Among those in attendance at Jefferson's inauguration on March 4, 1801, was novelist Margaret Bayard Smith. Afterward she wrote: "The changes of administration, which in every government and in every age have most generally been epochs of confusion, villainy and bloodshed, in this happy country take place without any species of distraction, or disorder." It need not have been so. Washington, D.C., still under construction, was full of revolutionaries. Alexander Hamilton, Thomas Jefferson, Aaron Burr, and Charles Pinckney had once risked their lives and fortunes for political ends.

John Adams, another revolutionary, was so bitter over his loss that he exited the city before sunrise that morning. Adams had lost by a narrow margin in the electoral college, but Aaron Burr, Jefferson's running mate, threw the election into turmoil when he unsuccessfully tried to grab the presidency for himself. The campaign of 1800 had been particularly nasty and personal, and candidates hinted that were their opponents elected, chaos would ensue.

Why didn't it? After all, what would plague most new states in the nineteenth and twentieth centuries was the unwillingness of regimes to hand over power peacefully to legitimate successors. Coups, bloodshed, and military rule seemed to be most common.

In later years Jefferson called his election to the presidency the "Revolution of 1800." He meant that the Federalists, in control of the government since its inception in 1789, were turned out and the republican principles of the Revolution were about to be restored.

The real revolution, however, was that the Federalists had relinquished power to the Democratic-Republicans, without confusion or villainy or bloodshed, as Margaret Bayard Smith observed. It established the precedent that political battles, with the exception of the Civil War, would be waged not in the streets but at the polls, in Congress, and before the courts. The developing party system itself would channel political disagreements within acceptable, peaceful means. The "revolution" of 1800 established a unique legacy for a people and a nation that would define governance in the United States: the transfer of governmental power based on the ballot, not on arms.

For Further Reading, see page A-11 of the Appendix. For Web resources, go to http://www.college.hmco.com.

THE OLD GRANITE STATE,

Judson. Abby. John. Asa

A SONG,

Price 50 Cts Nett.

COMPOSED, ARRANGED AND SUNG, BY

THE HUTCHINSON FAMILY.

The Hutchinson Family, also known as the Tribe of Jesse, was the most popular singing group in nineteenth-century America. Abby, Asa, Jesse, John, and Judson Hutchinson—five of a family of sixteen children from rural New Hampshire—performed the patriotic, religious, and sentimental songs that had dominated popular music since the Revolution. They initiated new musical styles, wrote lyrics full of social commentary, and made entertainment a commodity, promoted and performed in the market economy.

Unlike most musical groups, the Tribe of Jesse not only sang but also presented well-rehearsed and elaborately produced performances. They used folk tunes that the audiences found familiar and enjoyed, but their lyrics explored controversial topics such as abolition and temperance. Their 1844 "Get Off the Track!" used imagery from railroads, the newest form of transportation, to hail the unstoppable power of the antislavery movement.

The Hutchinson Family traveled by rail, too, performing across the expanding United States, but drawing their largest audiences in the growing cities of the North. The family's fee for a single night in the 1840s reached $1,000, about 400 times a worker's daily wage. They had an entourage of managers, agents, and publishers. Hawkers sold sheet music, portraits, and songbooks at the Hutchinsons' concerts. The Hutchinson Family made a business of music and entertainment, selling nostalgia and reform.

The Hutchinsons' off-stage lives, too, bridged the old and the new. They had come from the farms of New Hampshire, they sang in "The 'Old Granite State.'" They left home, they explained in song, with the blessing of their "aged parents," to sing of liberty, traveling "round the World." Besides their musical talent, the Hutchinson Family offered their audiences reassurance in a time of rapid change. By setting their lyrics to familiar hymns (we are "good old fashioned singers"), they connected their advocacy of reform with the comfortable past. And by describing a bucolic future, they reassured their audiences that the present, with all its turmoil, would turn out well.

The Hutchinson Family celebrated their native rural New Hampshire in "The 'Old Granite State,'" their most popular song. They made a business of performing, and hawkers sold their sheet music at concerts. (Courtesy of Lynn Historical Society, hand-colored by Sandi Rygiel, Picture Research Consultants, Inc.)

10

NATIONALISM, EXPANSION, AND THE MARKET ECONOMY 1816–1845

The Hutchinsons' concert tours exemplified the market economy, in which goods and services sold in cash or credit transactions created a network of exchange that bound distant enterprises together. The family performed in western areas in the 1840s that had had no American settlements twenty years before. The canals and railroads that carried them also increasingly linked the nation's regions after the War of 1812. People moved inland from the seaboard, farmed the rich lands across the Appalachians, and sold their crops at home and abroad. Grain went east to coastal cities, cotton went to Europe, and ready-made men's garments from New York and Cincinnati sold across the nation. Increasingly, farmers turned to staple-crop agriculture and city people worked not for themselves but for others, for wages. These large-scale enterprises needed capital, and new financial institutions amassed and loaned it. Mechanization took hold; factories and precision-made machinery put home workshops and handcrafters out of business; on farms, horse-drawn reapers replaced farmhands. In turn, the increased specialization in plantation and commercial agriculture, manufacturing, transportation, and finance further fired the engines of the new nationwide, capitalist, market-oriented economy.

The end of the War of 1812 unleashed this growth. A new nationalist spirit encouraged the economy and promoted western expansion at home, trade abroad, and assertiveness throughout the Western Hemisphere. Economic growth and territorial expansion, however, generated new problems. Sectional conflicts over slavery and economic development created divisions. Migration, shifts in occupations, and changes in the ways people worked created new tensions. Not everyone profited in wealth and opportunity as the Hutchinson Family did. Journeyman tailors, displaced by retailers and cheaper labor, found their trades disappearing. New England farm daughters who became wage workers found their world changing no less radically. Moreover, boom-and-bust cycles, now on a national scale, wrenched livelihoods and lives. Mills, factories, roads, canals, and railroads altered or destroyed the landscape.

Everywhere Americans were on the move. Settlement, North and South, moved to the interior, and farms and cities, linked by rivers, then roads, canals, and railroads, stretched to the Ohio and Mississippi River valleys and beyond. The Indian inhabitants attempted to hold their ground but were in the end removed to the West, pushed off their lands by the same drive for profit, the same nationalist spirit, that was re-

shaping American national politics and the dynamic American economy. ■

Postwar Nationalism

 Nationalism surged after the War of 1812. Self-confident, the nation asserted itself at home and abroad as Democratic-Republicans borrowed a page from the Federalists' agenda and encouraged economic growth. Though James Monroe would follow James Madison as the last of the presidents who had attended the Constitutional Convention, political power began to shift away from the founders of the republic. Congressional leaders Henry Clay and John C. Calhoun, and those who vied for the presidency in the 1820s—John Quincy Adams and Andrew Jackson—formed a new generation of political leaders who were nationalistic in outlook.

James Madison inspired the postwar wave of nationalism. In his December 1815 message to Congress, he recommended economic development and military expansion. His agenda included a national bank (the charter of the first bank had expired in 1811) and improved transportation. To raise government revenues and foster manufacturing, Madison called for a protective tariff—a tax on imported goods designed to protect American manufactures. Yet his program acknowledged Jeffersonian republicanism; only a constitutional amendment, Madison argued, could authorize the federal government to build local roads and canals.

Congressional leaders saw Madison's program as a way of unifying the country. Democratic-Republican John C. Calhoun of South Carolina and House Speaker Henry Clay of Kentucky believed that the tariff would stimulate industry. The agricultural South and West would sell cotton to the churning mills of New England and food to its millworkers. New roads and canals would transport the goods, and tariff revenues would provide money to build them. A national bank would handle the transactions.

Nationalist Program

In the last year of Madison's administration, the Democratic-Republican Congress enacted much of the nationalist program. In 1816 it chartered the Second Bank of the United States to assist the government and to issue currency. Like its predecessor, the bank mixed public and private ownership; the government provided one-fifth of the bank's capital and appointed one-fifth of its directors.

IMPORTANT EVENTS

1815	Madison proposes internal improvements
1816	Second Bank of the United States chartered
	Tariff of 1816 imposes first substantial duties
	Monroe elected president
1817	Rush-Bagot Treaty limits British and American naval forces on Lake Champlain and Great Lakes
1819	*McCulloch v. Maryland* establishes supremacy of federal over state law
	Adams-Onís Treaty with Spain gives Florida to U.S. and defines Louisiana territorial border
1819–1823	Hard times bring unemployment
1820	Missouri Compromise creates formula for admitting slave and free states
	Monroe reelected
1820s	New England textile mills expand
1823	Monroe Doctrine closes Western Hemisphere to European intervention
1824	*Gibbons v. Ogden* affirms federal over state authority in interstate commerce
	Monroe proposes Indian removal

1825	Erie Canal completed
1830	Railroad era begins
	Congress passes Indian Removal Act
1830s	McCormick reaper and Deere steel plow patented
1830s–1840s	Cotton production shifts to Mississippi valley
1831	Cherokees turn to courts to defend treaty rights in *Cherokee Nation v. Georgia*
1832	Marshall declares Cherokee nation a distinct political community in *Worcester v. Georgia*
1834	Women workers strike at Lowell textile mills
1835–1842	Seminoles successfully resist removal in Second Seminole War
1836	Second Bank of the United States closes
1837	*Charles River Bridge v. Warren Bridge* encourages new enterprises
1839–1843	Hard times strike again
1842	*Commonwealth v. Hunt* declares strikes lawful
1844	Government grant sponsors first telegraph line

Congress also passed a protective tariff to aid industries that had flourished during the War of 1812 but were now threatened by the resumption of overseas trade. The Tariff of 1816 levied taxes on imported woolens and cottons, and on iron, leather, hats, paper, and sugar, in effect raising their prices in the United States. Foreshadowing a growing trend, support for the tariff divided along sectional lines: New England and the western and Middle Atlantic states stood to benefit and applauded it, but the South did not.

The South did press for better transportation. It was Congressman Calhoun of South Carolina, not the president, who promoted roads and canals to "bind the republic together." However, on March 3, 1817, the day before he left office, Madison vetoed Calhoun's internal improvements bill as unconstitutional. The president *did* approve funds for extending the National Road to Ohio, deeming it a military necessity.

James Monroe, Madison's successor, continued Madison's domestic program, supporting tariffs and vetoing internal improvements.

James Monroe   Monroe was the third Virginian elected president since 1801. A former senator and twice governor of Virginia, he had served under Madison as secretary of state and of war and used his close association with Jefferson and Madison to attain the presidency.

Among the nation's founders, Monroe was a most ordinary and colorless man who rarely had an original idea. But in 1816 he easily defeated the last Federalist presidential nominee, Rufus King, and swept all the electoral votes except for the Federalist strongholds of Massachusetts, Connecticut, and Delaware. The American people were "one great family." A Boston newspaper dubbed this one-party period the "Era of Good Feelings."

Led by Federalist chief justice John Marshall, the Supreme Court became the bulwark of a nationalist point of view. In *McCulloch v. Maryland* (1819), the Court struck down a Maryland law taxing a branch of the federally chartered Second Bank of the United States. Maryland had imposed the tax in an effort to destroy the bank's Baltimore branch. The issue was thus one of state versus federal jurisdiction. Speaking for a unanimous Court, Marshall asserted the supremacy of the federal government over the states. "The Constitution and the laws thereof are supreme," he declared. "They control the constitution and laws of the respective states and cannot be controlled by them."

McCulloch v. Maryland

The Court went on to consider whether Congress could issue a bank charter. The Constitution did not spell out such power, but Marshall noted that Congress had the authority to pass "all laws which shall be necessary and proper for carrying into execution" the enumerated powers of the government. Marshall ruled that Congress could legally exercise "those great powers on which the welfare of the nation essentially depends." If the ends were legitimate and the means were not prohibited, Marshall ruled, a law was constitutional. The Constitution was, in Marshall's words, "intended to endure for ages to come, and consequently, to be adapted to the various causes of human affairs." The bank charter was declared legal.

McCulloch v. Maryland thus joined nationalism and economics. By asserting federal supremacy, Marshall protected the commercial and industrial interests that favored a national bank; this was federalism in the tradition of Alexander Hamilton (see page 200). The decision was only one in a series of rulings that cemented the federalist view. In *Fletcher v. Peck* (1810), the Court had voided a Georgia law that violated individuals' rights to make contracts. In *Dartmouth College v. Woodward* (1819), the Court nullified a New Hampshire act altering the charter of Dartmouth College. Marshall ruled that the charter was a contract, and in protecting such contracts he thwarted state interference in commerce and business. *Gibbons v. Ogden* (1824) confirmed federal supremacy in interstate commerce.

Monroe's secretary of state, John Quincy Adams, matched the self-confident Marshall Court in assertiveness and nationalism. A small, austere man once described by a British official as a "bulldog among spaniels," Adams, the son of John and Abigail Adams, was a superb diplomat who spoke six languages. From 1817 to 1825 he brilliantly managed the nation's foreign policy, stubbornly pushing for expansion, fishing rights for Americans in Atlantic waters, political distance from the Old World, and peace. An ardent expansionist, he nonetheless believed that it must come about through negotiations, not war, and that newly acquired territories must bar slavery. The United States, Adams said in an 1821 Fourth of July speech, "goes not abroad, in search of monsters to destroy. She is the well-wisher to the freedom and independence of all."

John Quincy Adams as Secretary of State

An Anglophobe, Adams nonetheless worked to strengthen the peace with Great Britain negotiated at Ghent (1814). In 1817 the two nations agreed in the Rush-Bagot Treaty to limit their naval forces to one ship each on Lake Champlain and Lake Ontario and to two ships each on the four other Great Lakes. This first disarmament treaty of modern times led to the demilitarization of the border between the United States

John Quincy Adams (1767–1848), architect of the Monroe Doctrine, was secretary of state from 1817 to 1825. Thomas Sully's portrait, painted in 1825, captured Adams's determination and stubbornness. (New York State Office of Parks, Recreation, and Historic Preservation, Philipse Manor Hall State Historic Site)

and Canada. Adams then pushed for the Convention of 1818, which fixed the United States–Canadian border from Lake of the Woods in Minnesota westward to the Rockies along the 49th parallel (see Map 10.1). When agreement could not be reached on the territory west of the Rockies, Britain and the United States settled on joint occupation of Oregon for ten years (renewed indefinitely in 1827).

Adams's next moved to settle long-term disputes with Spain. Although the 1803 Louisiana Purchase had omitted reference to Spanish-ruled West Florida, the United States claimed the territory as far east as the Perdido River (the present-day Florida-Alabama border) but occupied only a small finger of the area. During the War of 1812 the United States had seized Mobile and the remainder of West Florida. After the war Adams took advantage of Spain's preoccupation with domestic and colonial troubles to negotiate for the purchase of East Florida. During the 1818 talks, General Andrew Jackson took it on himself to occupy much of present-day Florida on the pretext of suppressing Seminole raids against American settlements across the border. Adams was furious with Jackson but defended his brazen act.

The following year, Don Luís de Onís, the Spanish minister to the United States, agreed to cede Florida to the United States without payment. The Adams-Onís, or Transcontinental, Treaty also defined the southwestern boundary of the Louisiana Purchase and set the southern border of Oregon at the 42nd parallel (see Map 10.1). (Spain retained present-day Texas, New Mexico, and California.) The U.S. government assumed $5 million of claims by American citizens against Spain and gave up its dubious claim to northern Mexico (Texas). Expansion was achieved at little cost and without war.

Adams-Onís Treaty

When the Spanish flag was last lowered over St. Augustine on July 10, 1821, and at Pensacola on July 17, Florida residents differed in how they greeted the United States and the American colonial governor, General Andrew Jackson. Some planter-slaveholders and traders welcomed the American flag, but Creeks and Seminoles, free blacks, runaway slaves, and Spanish-speaking town dwellers did not. Many feared Jackson, who had led raids against the Seminoles in Florida in 1814 and 1818. The Spanish encouraged residents to resettle in Mexico, Cuba, or Texas, but most stayed put though wary of the United States.

Conflict between the United States and European nations was temporarily resolved by the Rush-Bagot Treaty, the Convention of 1818, and the Adams-Onís Treaty, but events to the south still threatened American interests. John Quincy Adams's desire to insulate the United States and the Western Hemisphere from European conflict brought about his greatest achievement: the Monroe Doctrine.

The immediate issue was the recognition of new governments in Latin America. Between 1808 and 1822, the United Provinces of the Río de la Plata (present-day northern Argentina, Paraguay, and Uruguay), Chile, Peru, Colombia, and Mexico all broke free from Spain. Monroe and Adams moved cautiously, seeking to avoid conflict with Spain and to be assured of the stability of the new regimes. Then in 1822, shortly after the Adams-Onís Treaty was signed and ratified, the United States became the first nation outside Latin America to recognize the new states, including Mexico.

Independent States in Latin America

Soon events in Europe again threatened the stability of the New World. Spain suffered a domestic revolt, and France, to bolster the weak Spanish monarchy against the rebels, occupied Spain. The United States feared that France would return the new Latin American states to colonial rule. Great Britain, similarly distrustful of France, proposed a joint United States–British declaration against European intervention in the Western Hemisphere and a joint disavowal of territorial ambitions in the region. Adams rejected the British overture. Following George Washington's admonition to avoid foreign entanglements, he insisted that the United States act independently.

Despite clamors to take joint action with Great Britain, Adams refused to budge. Those who favored a multilateral move believed the United States needed British naval power to prevent French or Russian expansion in the New World. But Adams won. "It would be more candid, as well as more dignified," he argued, "to avow our principles explicitly to Russia and France, than to come in as a cockboat in the wake of the British man-of-war." Adams interpreted the British disavowal of territorial ambitions as an attempt to thwart American expansion.

President Monroe presented the American position—the Monroe Doctrine—to Congress in December 1823. His message called for noncolonization of the Western Hemisphere by European nations, a principle that addressed American anxiety not only about Latin America but also about Russian expansion beyond Alaska and its settlements in California. He also demanded nonin-

Monroe Doctrine

tervention by Europe in the affairs of independent New World nations, and he pledged noninterference by the United States in European affairs, including those of Europe's existing New World colonies.

The Monroe Doctrine proved popular at home. It tapped American nationalism and anti-British and anti-European feelings, and it eventually became the foundation of American policy in the Western Hemisphere. Monroe's words, however, carried no force. Indeed, the policy could not have succeeded without the support of the British, who were committed to keeping other European nations out of the hemisphere to protect their dominance in the Atlantic trade. Europeans ignored the Monroe Doctrine; it was the Royal Navy they respected, not American policy.

While nationalism brought Americans together, the question of slavery divided them. Since the drafting of the Constitution, political leaders had tried to avoid the issue. The one exception was an act ending the foreign slave trade after January

"Fire Bell in the Night"

1, 1808, which passed without much opposition. The act followed the expiration of the constitutional ban (Article I, Section 9) on ending the slave trade before 1808. In 1819, however, slavery crept onto the political agenda when Missouri residents petitioned Congress for admission to the Union as a slave state. For two and a half years the issue dominated Congress. "This momentous question," wrote Thomas Jefferson, fearful for the life of the Union, "like a fire bell in the night, awakened and filled me with terror."

The debate transcended slavery in Missouri. The compromises that had kept the issue under wraps since the Constitutional Convention could collapse. Five new states had joined the Union since 1812: Louisiana (1812), Indiana (1816), Mississippi (1817), Illinois (1818), and Alabama (1819). Of these, Louisiana, Mississippi, and Alabama permitted slavery. Because Missouri was on the same latitude as free Illinois, Indiana, and Ohio (a state since 1803), its admission as a slave state would thrust slavery farther northward. It would also tilt the uneasy political balance in the Senate

Map 10.1 Missouri Compromise and the State of the Union, 1820 The compromise worked out by House Speaker Henry Clay established a formula that avoided debate over whether new states would allow or prohibit slavery. In the process, it divided the United States into northern and southern regions.

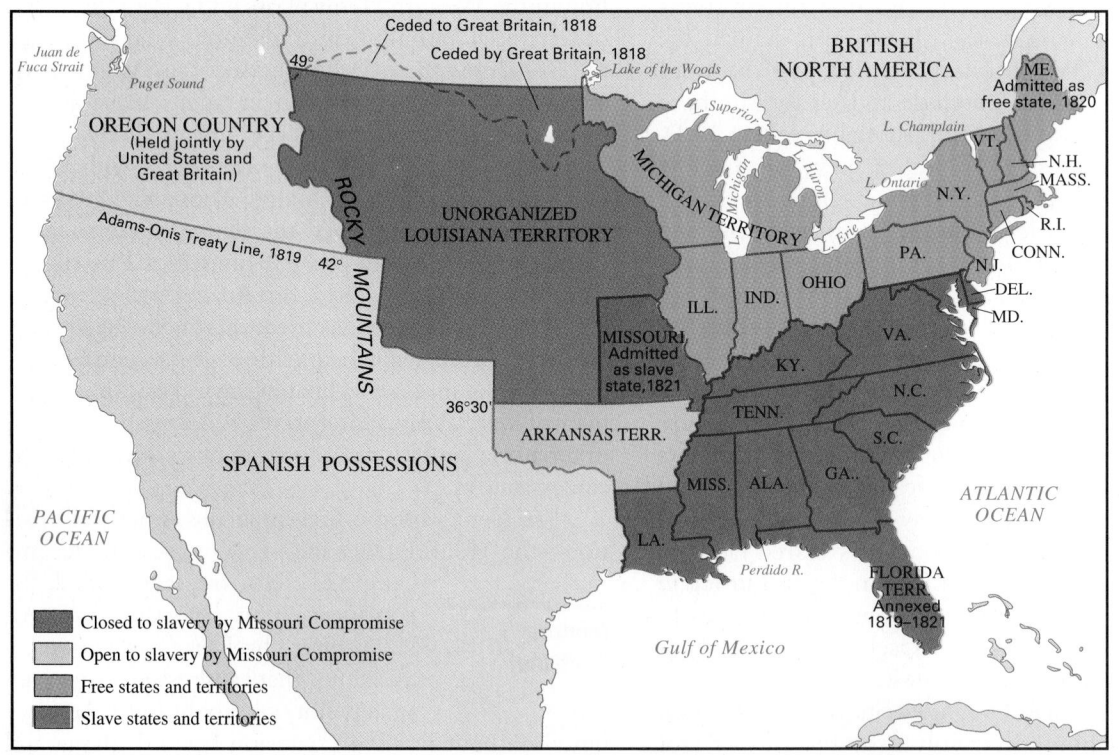

toward the slave states. In 1819 the Union consisted of eleven slave and eleven free states. If Missouri joined, slave states would have a one-vote edge in the Senate.

The moral issues made slavery an explosive question. Settlers from slave states—Kentuckians and Tennesseans—made up most of the new Missourians. But in the North slavery was slowly dying out, and many northerners had concluded that it was evil. When Representative James Tallmadge, Jr., of New York proposed gradual emancipation in Missouri, a passionate and sometimes violent debate ensued. Southerners accused the North of threatening to destroy the Union. "If you persist, the Union will be dissolved," Thomas W. Cobb of Georgia shouted at Tallmadge. "Seas of blood can only extinguish" the fire Tallmadge was igniting, Cobb warned. "Let it come," retorted Tallmadge. The House, which had a northern majority, passed the Tallmadge amendment, but the Senate rejected it. The two sides were deadlocked.

A compromise emerged in 1820 under pressure from House Speaker Henry Clay. Maine would enter as a free state, carved out of Massachusetts, while Missouri entered as a slave state. In the rest of the Louisiana Territory north of latitude 36°30' (Missouri's southern boundary), slavery was prohibited forever (see Map 10.1). The compromise carried, but the agreement almost unraveled in November when Missouri submitted a constitution that barred free blacks from entering the state. Opponents contended that the proposed state constitution violated the federal Constitution's provision that "the citizens of each State shall be entitled to all privileges and immunities of citizens in the several States." Proponents argued that many states, North and South, restricted black migrants from entering. In 1821 Clay produced a second compromise: Missouri guaranteed that none of its laws would discriminate against citizens of other states. (Once admitted to the Union, however, Missouri twice adopted laws banning free blacks.)

Missouri Compromise

The Market Economy and Government's Economic Role

Increasingly in the years after the War of 1812, Americans became involved in the market economy—growing crops and producing goods specifically for cash sale and using the cash to purchase items produced by other people. Farms and slave plantations produced crops for market sales. Plantations raised rice, tobacco, sugar, or cotton; farmers grew only one or two crops or raised animals for market. Farm women gave up spinning and weaving and purchased fabric made by wage-earning farm girls in Massachusetts textile mills. Nonfarm men and women sold not goods but their labor for cash, working for wages. Most free farmers and workers bought in stores, increasing the amount of goods produced in workshops and factories. Such a system encouraged specialization. It also energized transportation, as both goods and entertainment, like the Hutchinsons, circulated nationally.

Before canals and railroads, farmers had geared production to their own needs and to local and foreign, not national, markets. They lived in interdependent communities and exchanged labor and goods with their neighbors. Farm families produced much of what they needed—food, clothing, candles, soap, and the like—and traded for or purchased items they could not produce, such as cooking pots, horseshoes, coffee, tea, and sugar.

Mechanization, the division of labor, new methods of financing, and improvements in transportation all fueled the expansion of the economy. Goods and services multiplied. This growth, in turn, prompted new improvements and greater opportunities for wage labor. The effect was cumulative; by the 1840s the economy was growing faster than in the previous four decades. While per capita income increased 50 percent between 1800 and 1840, the price of manufactured goods and food fell.

The pace of economic growth, however, was uneven. Prosperity reigned during two long periods, from 1823 to 1835 and from 1843 to 1857. But there were long stretches of economic contraction as well. Contraction and deflation (decline in the general price level) occurred again during the hard times of 1819–1823 and 1839–1843. During these periods banks collapsed, businesses went under, wages and prices declined, and jobs were hard to find or to keep. Yet even during boom periods major industries like construction offered only cyclical employment. The boom-and-bust cycle was also seasonal and personal. Free laborers in Baltimore, for example, typically found steady work only from March through October, then unemployment and hunger from November through February.

Boom-and-Bust Cycles

In 1819 the postwar boom collapsed. Expansion had been built on easy credit; state banks had printed notes freely, fueling speculative buying of western land. Speculators had bought acreage to sell at a profit rather than to farm. When manufacturing fell in 1818, prices spiraled downward. The Second Bank of the United States cut back on loans, thus further shrinking the economy. With urban workers, farmers, and southern planters having less money to spend, the economy declined.

The contraction devastated workers and their families. As a Baltimore physician noted in 1819, working people felt hard times "a thousand fold more than the merchants." In the 1839 contraction in Baltimore, when hundreds of small manufacturers closed their doors, tailors, shoemakers, milliners, and shipyard and construction workers lost their jobs. Ninety miles to the north, Philadelphia took on an eerie aura. "The streets seemed deserted," Sidney George Fisher observed in 1842. "The largest [merchant] houses are shut up and to rent, there is no business . . . no money, no confidence." Only auctions boomed, as sheriffs sold off seized property at a quarter of pre-depression prices, a dismal scene as portrayed by artist E. Didier in *Auction in Chatham Street* in nearby New York (see the painting below). In Philadelphia and other cities, soup societies fed the hungry. In New York, bread lines and beggars crowded the sidewalks. In smaller cities like Lynn, Massachusetts, the poor became scavengers, digging for clams and harvesting dandelions.

What caused the boom-and-bust cycles that brought about such suffering? Generally speaking, they were a direct result of the market economy. As with the expansion following the War of 1812, prosperity stimulated demand for finished goods such as clothing and furniture. Increased demand in turn led not only to higher prices and still higher production but also, because of business optimism and expectation of higher prices, to speculation in land. Then, as with the hard times of 1819, production surpassed demand, causing prices and wages to fall; in response, land and stock values collapsed.

Cause of the Boom-and-Bust Cycles

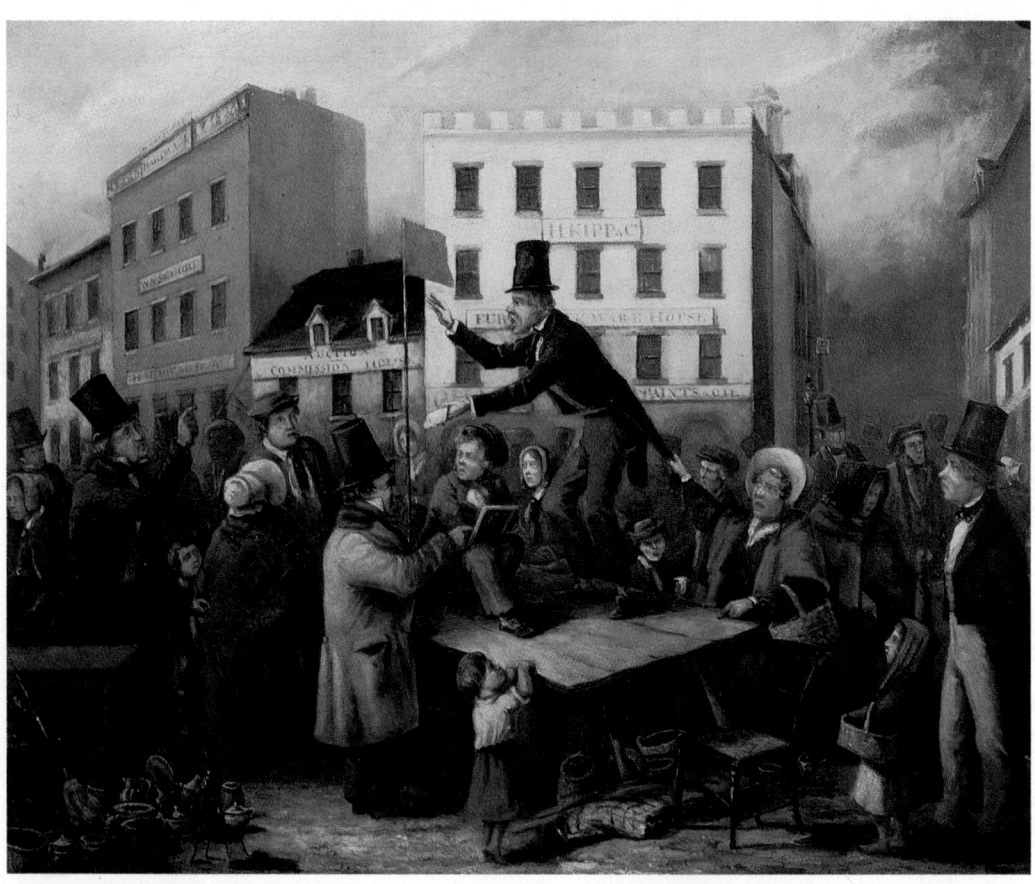

E. Didier painted *Auction in Chatham Street* in 1834. Auction houses in New York and other cities boomed during hard times. (Museum of the City of New York)

In the economic thinking of the time, some considered this process beneficial—a self-adjusting cycle that eliminated unprofitable economic ventures. In theory, people concentrated on the activities they did best, and the economy as a whole became more efficient. Advocates of the system also argued that it enhanced individual freedom, since theoretically each seller, whether of goods or labor, determined the price. But in fact the system tied workers to a perpetual roller coaster; they became dependent on wages—and on the availability of jobs—for their very existence. The cycles that governed the market economy influenced every corner of the country as even small localities became tied, or handcuffed, to regional and national markets.

The market economy also ushered in another type of boom-and-bust cycle: harvest and destruction. Canals and railroads spurred demand for distant resources, then accelerated the destruction of forests, natural waterways, and any landscape features that represented obstacles. Railroads made possible large-scale lumbering of pinewood forests in Michigan and Wisconsin. During the 1840s, lumber companies deforested millions of acres, leaving most of that land unfit even for agriculture. The process of harvest and destruction would eventually change the ecology of the United States.

The idea of a market economy drew on eighteenth-century republicanism. Advanced by members of the elite as well as by craftsmen, it

Government Economic Role

emphasized economic liberty and individualism (see page 168). Limited, not activist, government, adherents argued, fostered economic expansion because individuals pursuing their own private interests benefited the nation as a whole.

Nonetheless, the federal government played an active role in technological and industrial growth. Federal arsenals pioneered new manufacturing techniques and helped to develop the machine-tool industry. The United States Post Office fostered the circulation of information, a critical element in a market economy. The number of post offices grew from three thousand in 1815 to fourteen thousand in 1845. The post office also played a brief but crucial role in the development of the telegraph, financing the first telegraph line, from Washington to Baltimore, in 1844. Invented by artist Samuel F. B. Morse, the telegraph allowed information to travel faster, almost instantaneously, over long distances. To create an atmosphere conducive to economic growth and individual creativity, the government protected inventions and domestic industries. Patent laws gave inventors a seventeen-year monopoly on their inventions, and tariffs protected American industry from foreign competition.

Government policy also fostered farm life. Republicanism associated farming with virtue, independence, and productivity, essential values in the new republic, and the federal government surveyed public land and opened it to settlement. Internal improvements such as harbors, roads, and canals—some underwritten by government—linked new farms in the West to markets in the East. When Indians got in the way of expansion, the federal government moved them across the Mississippi River (see pages 269–274).

The federal judiciary validated government promotion of the economy and encouraged business enterprise and risk taking. In *Gibbons v.*

Legal Foundations of Commerce

Ogden (1824), the Supreme Court overturned the New York State law that gave Robert Fulton and Robert Livingston a monopoly on the New York–New Jersey steamboat trade. Aaron Ogden, their successor, lost the monopoly when Chief Justice John Marshall ruled that the congressional prerogative of licensing new enterprises took precedence over New York's grant of monopoly rights to Fulton and Livingston. Marshall declared that Congress's power under the commerce clause of the Constitution extended to "every species of commercial intercourse," including transportation systems. Within a year, forty-three steamboats were plying Ogden's route.

In defining interstate commerce broadly, the Marshall Court expanded federal powers over the economy while restricting the ability of states to control economic activity within their borders. Its action was consistent with the earlier decision in *Dartmouth College v. Woodward* (1819), which protected the sanctity of contracts against interference by the states (see page 246). "If business is to prosper," Marshall wrote, "men must have assurance that contracts will be enforced."

Federal and state courts, in conjunction with state legislatures, also encouraged the proliferation of corporations—organizations entitled to

Corporations

hold property and transact business as if they were individuals. Corporation owners, called shareholders, were granted *limited liability*, or freedom from responsibility for the company's debts beyond their original investments. An attractive feature to potential investors, limited liability encouraged people to back

The Marshall Court encouraged business competition by ending state-licensed monopolies on inland waterways. *Gibbons v. Ogden* (1824) opened up the New York–New Jersey trade to new lines, and within a short time dozens of steamboats were ferrying passengers and freight across the Hudson River.   (© Collection of The New-York Historical Society)

new business ventures. Shareholders elected managers who ran the corporation, though often managers controlled a majority of the voting stock. By 1817 the number of corporations in the United States had grown to two thousand, from three hundred in 1800. By 1830 the New England states alone had issued nineteen hundred charters, one-third to manufacturing and mining firms. At first each firm needed a special legislative act to incorporate, but after the 1830s applications became so numerous that states established routine procedures allowing firms to incorporate easily.

Though legislative action created corporations, the courts played a crucial role in extending their powers and protecting them. The Supreme Court in particular encouraged corporate development and free enterprise by ruling, in *Charles River Bridge v. Warren Bridge* (1837), that new enterprises could not be restrained by implied privileges under old charters. The case involved issues of great importance: should a new interest be allowed to compete against existing enterprises, and should the state protect existing privilege or encourage innovation and the growth of commerce through competition?

Charles River Bridge Case

The Massachusetts legislature had chartered the Charles River Bridge Company in 1785 and six years later extended its charter for seventy years. In return for assuming the risk of building a bridge between Charlestown and Boston, the owners received the right to collect tolls. In 1828 the legislature chartered another company to build the Warren Bridge across the Charles nearby; the owner would have the right to collect tolls for six years, after which the bridge would be turned over to the state and be free of tolls. The Charles River Bridge Company sued in 1829, claiming that the new bridge breached the earlier charter and contradicted the principles in *Dartmouth College v. Woodward*.

Speaking for the Court majority, Marshall's successor Roger Taney declared that the original charter did not confer the privilege of monopoly and that exclusivity could not therefore be implied. Focusing on the question of corporate privilege rather than the law of contracts, Taney ruled that charter grants should be interpreted narrowly and that ambiguities would be decided in favor of the public interest. New enterprises should not be restricted by old charters, and economic growth would best be served by narrowing the application of the *Dartmouth College* decision. In this way the judiciary promoted individual enterprise and competition.

In promoting the economy, state governments far surpassed the federal government. From 1815 through the 1840s, for example, government money, mostly from the states, financed three-fourths of the nearly $200 million invested in canals. In the 1830s the states started to invest in rail construction. Though the federal government played a larger role in constructing railroads than in building canals, state and local governments provided more than half of the capital for southern rail lines. State governments also invested in corporate and bank stocks, providing corporations and banks with much-needed capital. In fact, states actually equaled or exceeded private enterprise in their investments.

Pennsylvania, encompassing a vast area from the Delaware River to beyond the Appalachians, developed the nation's most extensive program of internal improvements to stimulate settlement and economic growth. The state invested a total of $100 million in canals, railroads, banks, and manufacturing firms; its appointees sat on more than 150 corporate boards of directors. But Pennsylvania and other states did more than invest resources in industry. Through special acts and incorporation laws, they regulated the nature and activities of corporations and banks and used their licensing capacities to control industrial operations. Georgia, for example, regulated the grading and marketing of tobacco.

Largely as a result of these government efforts, the United States experienced uneven but sustained economic growth from the end of the War of 1812 until midcentury. Political controversy raged over questions of state versus federal activity—especially with regard to internal improvements and banking—but all parties agreed on the general goal of economic expansion. Indeed, during these years the major restraint on government action was not philosophical but financial: the public purse was small. As the private sector grew more vigorous, entrepreneurs looked less to government for financial support, and the states played less of a role in investment.

Transportation Links

 Improved transportation was another factor facilitating economic growth. Northern, Middle Atlantic, and western states invested heavily in roads, canals, and railroads, with much of the financing borrowed from Europe. With regional and national financial institutions increasingly concentrated in New York, Boston, and Philadelphia, northeastern seaboard cities became the center of American commerce. New York financial and commercial houses dominated the American export trade, not only of New England textiles but also, through affiliates in southern port cities, of southern cotton. The South's staple crop was marketed to, and through, the North. The Deep South, with most of its capital invested in slave labor and land, built fewer canals, railroads, and factories and remained mostly rural.

Water routes provided the cheapest and most available transportation. Before the War of 1812 nearly all commerce moved on navigable rivers, and bulk shipments—cotton in the South and grain in the West—continued to move to ocean port cities by water. Increasingly, however, settlement extended beyond the river links, and the federal and state governments, followed by private corporations, invested heavily in alternative transportation modes.

East-West Links In the 1820s new arteries opened up east-west travel. The National Road—a stone-based, gravel-topped highway originating in Cumberland, Maryland—reached Columbus, Ohio, in 1833. More important, the Erie Canal, completed in 1825, linked the Great Lakes with New York City and the Atlantic Ocean. The canal carried easterners and then immigrants to settle the Old Northwest and the frontier beyond; in the opposite direction, it transported western grain to the large and growing eastern markets. Railroads and later the telegraph would solidify these east-west links. Other than for carrying cotton, links between the Deep South and the North were rarer.

Canals The 363-mile-long Erie Canal was a visionary enterprise. When the state of New York authorized its construction in 1817, the longest American canal was only 28 miles long. Vigorously promoted by Governor DeWitt Clinton, the Erie cost $7 million, much of it borrowed from British investors. The canal shortened the journey between Buffalo and New York City from twenty to six days and reduced freight charges from $100 to $5 a ton. By 1835 traffic was so heavy that the canal had to be widened from 40 to 70 feet and deepened from 4 to 7 feet. Skeptics who had called the canal "Clinton's big ditch" had long since fallen silent.

The success of the Erie Canal triggered an explosion of canal building. By 1840 canals crisscrossed the Northeast and Midwest, and total canal mileage reached 3,300—an increase of more than 2,000 miles in a single decade (see Map 10.2). Unfortunately for investors, none of these canals enjoyed the financial

The town of Lockport, New York, owed its existence to the Erie Canal, and serving boats, freight, and passengers was its major industry. This view of the town was rendered in 1836, eleven years after the canal was opened.   (Library of Congress, hand-colored by Sandi Rygiel, Picture Research Consultants, Inc.)

success achieved by the Erie. As the high cost of construction combined with an economic contraction, investment in canals began to slump in the 1830s. By midcentury more miles were being abandoned than built, and the canal era had unmistakably ended.

Meanwhile, railroad construction boomed. The railroad era in the United States began in 1830 when

Railroads

Peter Cooper's locomotive, "Tom Thumb," first steamed along 13 miles of Baltimore and Ohio Railroad track. In 1833 the nation's second railroad ran 136 miles from Charleston to Hamburg in South Carolina. By 1850 the United States had nearly 9,000 miles of railroad track.

The earliest railroads connected nearby cities, such as Philadelphia and Baltimore; not until the 1850s did railroads offer long-distance service at reasonable rates. The early lines had to overcome technical problems. Locomotives heavy enough to climb steep grades and pull long trains required strong rails and resilient track beds. Engineers met those needs by

replacing wooden tracks with iron rails and by supporting the rails with ties embedded in gravel. A new wheel alignment—the swivel truck—permitted heavy engines to hold the track on sharp curves. Other problems persisted: the lack of a standard gauge for the width of track thwarted development of a national system. Pennsylvania and Ohio railroads, for instance, had no fewer than seven different track widths. A journey from Philadelphia to Charleston, South Carolina, involved eight different gauges, which meant that passengers and freight had to change trains seven times. Only at Bowling Green, Kentucky, did northern and southern railroads connect directly with one another.

Technology and investments in transportation dramatically reduced travel time and shipping. Before

Reduction in Travel Time and Cost

1815 river transportation was the only feasible route for long-distance journeys. In 1815 a traveler took four days to go by stagecoach from New York City to Baltimore and nearly

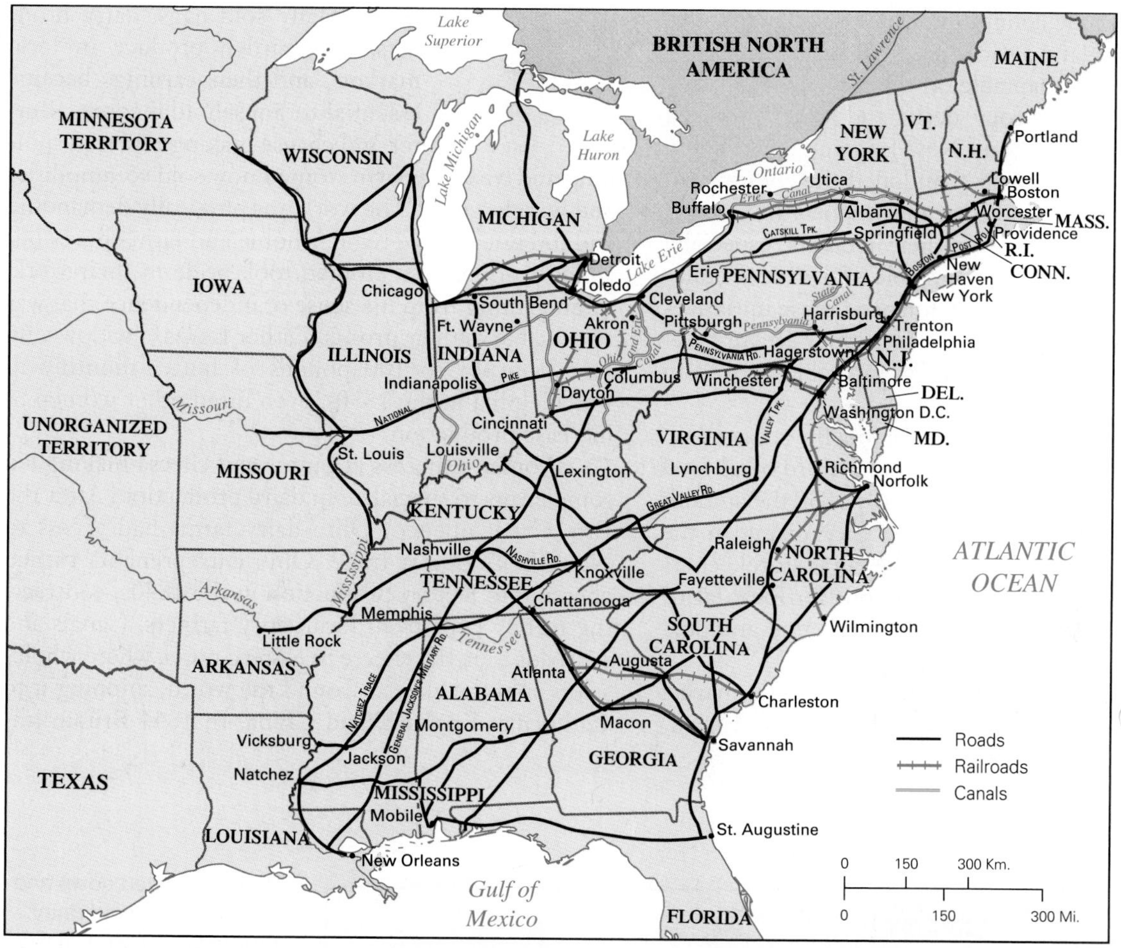

Map 10.2   Major Roads, Canals, and Railroads, 1850   A transportation network linked the seaboard to the interior. Settlers followed those routes westward, and they sent back grain, grain products, and cotton to the port cities.

four weeks to reach Detroit. By 1830 the New York–Baltimore journey took a day and a half, while the Erie Canal reduced the New York–Detroit journey to two weeks. Before the War of 1812 wagon transportation cost 30 to 70 cents per ton per mile. By midcentury railroads brought the cost of land transportation down 95 percent and reduced the journey to one-fifth the time.

Commercial Farming

Although manufacturing increased steadily, agriculture remained the backbone of the economy and American exports. But increasingly the market economy altered farming. Self-sufficient household and plantation economies gave way to market-oriented farming. Equally important, the center of commercial farming moved westward. In the 1830s and after, the plantation South shifted to the Mississippi River valley, while commercial farming came to dominate the Old Northwest and the Ohio River valley, then moved even farther westward to the prairies.

After the 1820s, northeastern agriculture began to decline. Eastern farmers had already cultivated all the

Northeastern Agriculture

land available to them; expansion was impossible. Moreover, small New England farms with their uneven terrains did not lend themselves to the new labor-saving farm implements introduced in the 1830s—mechanical sowers, reapers, threshers, and balers. As a result, many northern farmers either moved west or gave up farming for jobs in the merchant houses and factories.

But neither the countinghouse nor the factory depleted New England agriculture. The farmers who remained proved as adaptable on the farm as were their children working at copy desks and water-powered looms. By the 1850s many New England and Middle Atlantic farm families had abandoned the commercial production of wheat and corn and stopped tilling poor land. Instead, they improved their livestock, especially cattle, and specialized in vegetable and fruit production and dairy farming. They financed these initiatives through land sales and debt. In fact, their greatest potential profit was from increasing land values, not from farming itself.

Farm families everywhere gradually adjusted to market conditions. In 1820 about one-third of all food produced was intended for market. By 1850 the amount surpassed 50 percent. Middlemen specializing in the grain and food trades replaced the rural storekeepers who had once handled all transactions for local farmers, acting both as retailers and as marketing and purchasing agents.

Farm women had a distinctive role in the market economy aside from their work in fields and barn-

Women's Paid Labor

yards. Many sold eggs, dairy products, and garden produce in local markets, and their earnings became essential to household incomes. Butter and cheese making replaced spinning and weaving; farm women now sold commodities and bought cloth. The work was physically demanding and did not replace regular home and farm chores but added to them. Yet women took pride in their work, often gaining from it a sense of independence that was as valuable as their profits. Esther Lewis, a widow who sent from 75 to 100 pounds of butter monthly to Philadelphia in the 1830s, even hired other women to increase production.

Women's success at butter and cheese making led some farms to specialize in dairy production. After the Erie Canal opened, Ohio dairy farms had access to New York's export trade. Ohio entrepreneurs turned cheese into factory production in the 1840s, contracting to buy curd from local dairy farmers. Canals and railroads took the cheese to eastern ports, where wholesalers sold the cheese around the world, shipping it to California, England, and China. In 1844 Britain im-

Women tended cows and chickens and sold dairy products and eggs in the growing market economy. (Princeton University Library, Sinclair Hamilton Collection. Visual Materials Division, Department of Rare Books and Special Collections)

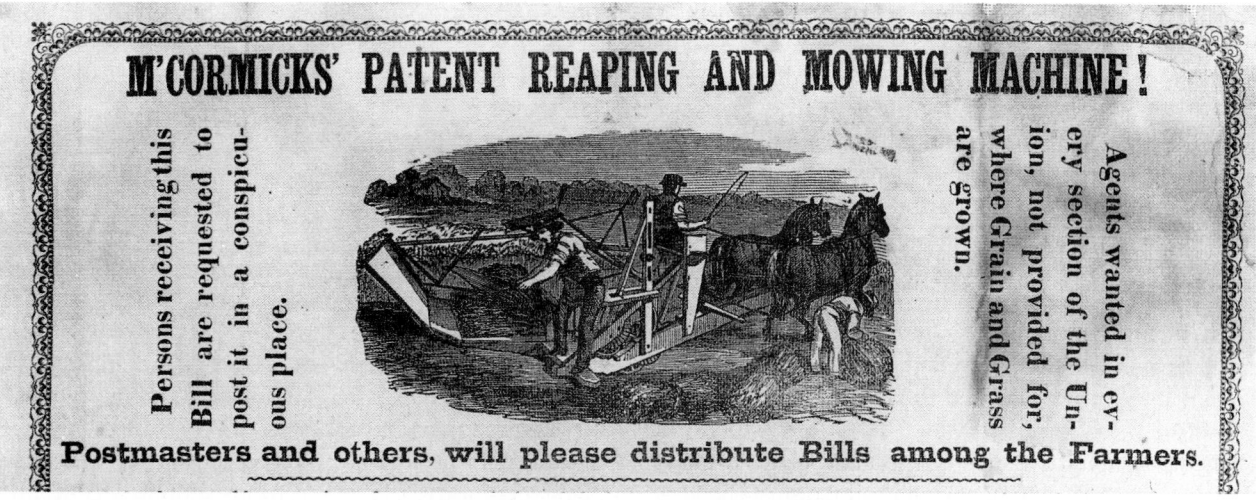

Cyrus McCormick invented the reaper in 1831, and midwestern farmers bought reapers as they mechanized their farms in the 1840s. Increased farm production fed the growing eastern cities and led to grain export.   (Chicago Historical Society)

ported more than 5 million pounds of cheese from the United States.

Most farm families welcomed the opportunities offered by the market economy. While continuing to take pride in self-sufficiency, they shifted toward specialization and market-oriented production. The rewards for such flexibility were great. Produce sold at market financed land and equipment purchases and made credit arrangements possible. Farm families who owned their land flourished.

Meanwhile, the economic distance widened between farm owners on the one hand and tenants and hired hands on the other. The rising cost of land and of farming made it harder to start up. By the 1840s it took more than ten years for a rural laborer to save enough money to farm for himself. Thus the number of tenant farmers increased. Previously farmers had relied mostly on the labor of unpaid family members or enslaved workers; now they had to secure waged farm labor.

Individually and collectively, Americans still valued agrarian life. State governments energetically promoted commercial agriculture to spur economic growth and sustain the values of an agrarian-based republic. Massachusetts in 1817 and New York in 1819 began to subsidize agricultural prizes and county fairs. New York required contestants to submit written descriptions of how they grew their prize crops; the state then published the essays to encourage new methods and specialization. The post office circulated farm journals that helped familiarize farmers with developments in agriculture.

Gradually the Old Northwest replaced the Northeast as the center of American family agriculture.

Mechanization of Agriculture

Farms in the Old Northwest were much larger, flatter, and better suited to the new mechanized farming implements than were their northeastern counterparts. Cyrus McCormick, a Virginia farmer, had invented the reaper in 1831. In one continuous motion, a revolving drum on the horse-drawn reaper positioned grain stalks in front of a blade and the cut grain fell onto a platform. Though ridiculed by the *London Times* as "a cross between a flying machine, a wheelbarrow, and an Astly chariot," the reaper was a great success. McCormick patented his machine in 1834 and built a factory in Chicago that by 1847 sold a thousand reapers a year. Midwestern farmers bought reapers on credit and paid for them with the profits from their high yields. Similarly, John Deere's steel plow, invented in 1837, replaced the traditional iron plow; steel blades kept the soil from sticking and were tough enough to break the roots of prairie grass.

And just in time. The Midwest was becoming one of the leading agricultural regions of the world. Midwestern farms fed the growing cities in the East, bursting with growing immigrant populations, and still produced enough to export to Europe.

At the end of the eighteenth century, southern agriculture was diverse. The South grew sufficient grain to feed itself. Although debt plagued Virginia's tobacco growers, farther south, along the coast, slaves grew rice and some indigo for the market. Cotton was profitable only for the Sea Island planters in South Carolina and Georgia, who grew the luxurious long and silky variety. Short-staple cotton, which grew readily in the interior and in all kinds of soil, was unmarketable because its sticky seeds lay tangled in the fibers. Then, in 1793, Eli Whitney invented the cotton gin (see pages 195–196). This machine, which separated the cotton from the seeds fifty times faster than by hand, made possible the expansion of cotton production at the very time that new textile mills in England and New England were increasing demand for cotton cloth. The result was a boom.

The Cotton South

After 1800 the cultivation of short-staple cotton spread rapidly. By the 1820s there were cotton plantations in the fertile lands of Louisiana, Mississippi, Alabama, Arkansas, and Tennessee. From 1820 to 1840, South Carolina sank from first to fifth in cotton production, and Mississippi rose to first. Each decade after 1820, the total crop doubled. By 1825 the South was the world's dominant supplier of cotton, and the white fibers were America's largest export. Southerners with capital bought more land and more slaves and planted ever more cotton.

No region was more tied to international markets than the South, yet the region seemed immune to its transforming power. It produced cotton exclusively as a market crop. Though some cotton production became mechanized, with steam engines used in place of horses to power gins and presses, most southern capital remained concentrated in land and slaves. It could not shift easily to support manufacturing and commerce. In many ways the cotton economy resembled a colonial economy. Planters depended on distant agents, some in southern cities, many in the North, and even some in Europe, to represent them and handle finances, which often included loans. Thus critical market decisions were made by bankers, financiers, and brokers, all outside the South. The South was engaged in the new market economy, but at a distance.

The cotton boom, dependent on slave labor, fixed the slave system to the land as it spread westward. Slaveholders sought profits, just as did commercial farmers, merchants, and entrepreneurs in the North. But they did not pay wages for labor; they bought laborers. Ultimately this "peculiar" system (see pages 332–338) would separate the South from the national economy and the nation.

The Rise of Manufacturing and Commerce

 Though at first Americans imported machines or copied British designs, they soon built their own. Matthew Baldwin made steam engines in Philadelphia in the 1820s, but in 1834, with railroads expanding, Baldwin turned to making steam locomotives. By 1839 he had produced 140 of them, or 45 percent of all American-made locomotives. A visitor to his shop in 1838 found twelve engines in various states of construction. "Those parts of the engine, such as the cylinder, piston, valves . . . in which good fitting and fine workmanship are indispensable to the efficient action of the machine, were very highly finished," the British visitor reported. By 1840 the United States exported railroad engines to Russia, some German states, and even Britain.

British visitors to the 1851 London Crystal Palace Exhibition, the first modern world's fair, were equally impressed by American design and fine tooling of working parts. American companies displayed hundreds of American machines and wares—from farm tools to exotic devices such as the reaper and an ice-cream freezer—that astonished observers. American manufacturers returned home with dozens of medals. Most impressive to the Europeans were three simple machines: Alfred C. Hobb's unpickable padlocks, Samuel Colt's revolvers, and Robbins and Lawrence's rifles fashioned with completely interchangeable parts. Like Baldwin's locomotives, all were machine-tooled rather than handmade, products of what the British called the American system of manufacturing.

The American system of manufacturing used precision machinery to produce interchangeable parts that did not require individual adjustment to fit. Eli Whitney, a Yale graduate and inventor of the cotton gin, had promoted the idea of interchangeable parts in 1798 when he contracted with the federal government to make ten thousand rifles in twenty-eight months. By the 1820s the United States Ordnance Department had contracted with private firms to in-

American System of Manufacturing

In the 1830s an unknown artist painted *Middlesex Company Woolen Mills,* portraying the hulking mass of the mill buildings. The company organized all the manufacturing processes at a single location, in Lowell, Massachusetts, on the Merrimack River. (Museum of American Textile History)

troduce machine-made interchangeable parts for firearms. The American system quickly spread beyond the arsenals, giving birth to the machine-tool industry—the manufacture of machines for the purposes of mass production. One outcome was an explosion in consumer goods. Because the time and skill involved in manufacturing were greatly reduced, the new system permitted mass production at low cost: Waltham watches, Yale locks, and other goods became household items, inexpensive yet of uniformly high quality.

Even larger than the machine-tool industry was the textile industry. New England mills began processing and weaving southern cotton in the same decade that Whitney patented his gin. Boosted by embargo and war, then protected by the tariff, the textile industry boomed with the expansion of cotton cultivation after the war (see Map 10.3). By the 1840s a cotton mill resembled a modern factory and textiles were the most important industry in the

Textile Mills

nation. Cotton cloth production rose from 4 million yards in 1817 to 323 million in 1840. The industry employed around eighty thousand workers in the mid-1840s, more than half of them women.

The industry's great innovation was that the machines, not the women, spun the yarn and wove the cloth. Workers watched the machines and intervened to maintain the operation. When a thread broke, the machine stopped automatically; a worker then found the break, pieced the ends together, and restarted the machine. The mills increasingly used specialized machines. Their application of the American system of manufacturing enabled American firms to compete successfully with British cotton mills.

Textile manufacturing changed New England and had its greatest impact on Lowell, Massachusetts. The population of Lowell, the "city of spindles" and the prototype of early American industrialization, grew from twenty-five hundred to thirty-three thousand between 1826 and midcentury. The largest of the cotton-

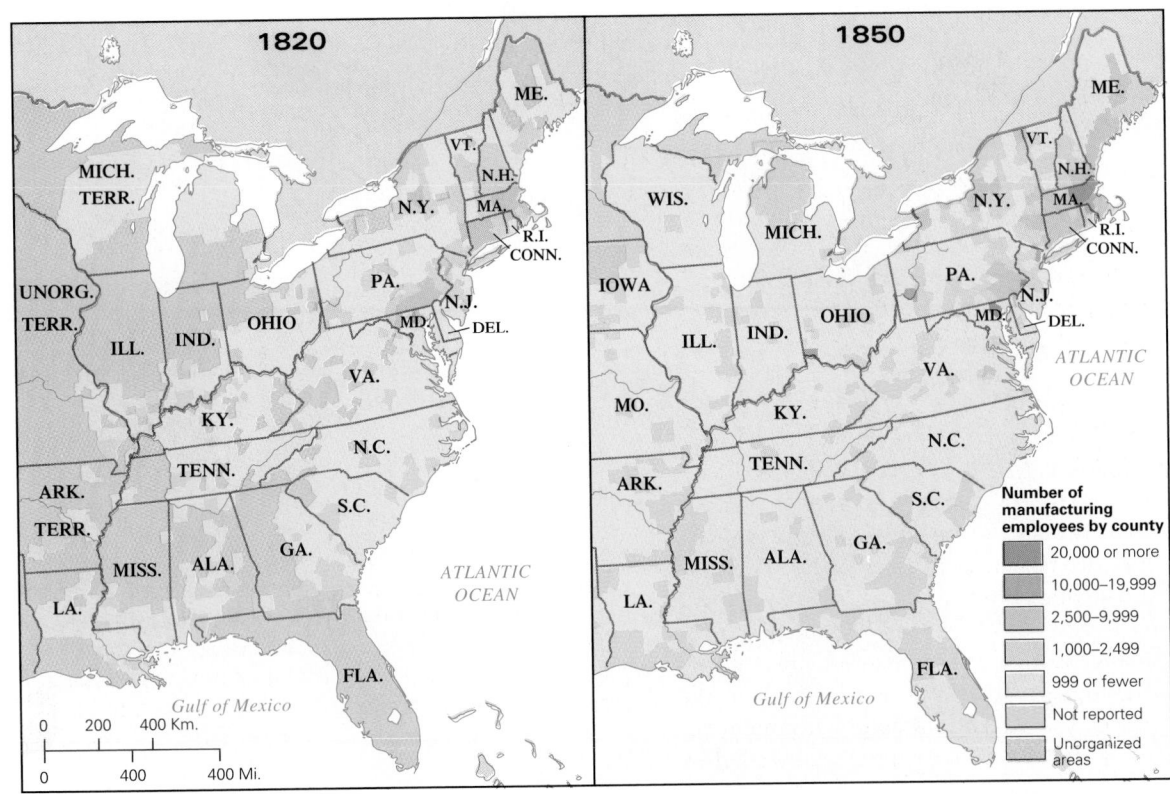

Map 10.3   U.S. Manufacturing Employment, 1820 and 1850   In 1820 manufacturing employment was concentrated mostly in the Northeast, where the first textile mills appeared. By 1850 the density of manufacturing in the Northeast had increased, but new manufacturing centers arose in Baltimore, Pittsburgh, and Cincinnati. (Source: *Historical Atlas of the United States,* 2d ed. [Washington, D.C.: National Geographic Society, 1993], p. 148. Reprinted by permission of National Geographic Maps/National Geographic Society Image Collection.)

mill towns and the front runner in technological change, Lowell boasted the biggest work force, the greatest output, and the most capital invested.

The success of the textile factories spawned the ready-made clothing industry. Before the 1820s, women sewed most clothing at home, and some people purchased used clothing. Tailors and seamstresses made wealthy men's and women's clothing to order. By the 1820s and 1830s, much clothing was mass-produced. Manufacturers used two methods, either separately or in combination. In one, the clothing was made in a factory; in the other, at home, through the putting-out system. In this arrangement, a journeyman tailor—a trained craftsman employed by a master tailor who owned the workshop—cut the fabric panels in the factory, and the masters "put out" the sewing at piece rates to women working in their own homes.

In 1832 Boston manufacturers employed three hundred journeyman tailors at $2 per day and thirteen

Ready-made Clothing

hundred women and one hundred boys at 50 cents a day. Apprentices, if used at all, were no longer learning a trade; they were a permanent source of cheap labor. Women learned their sewing skills at home, passed down from mother to daughter. In the 1840s as many as a dozen different pairs of hands contributed to making a single pair of pants under the putting-out system.

Most of the early mass-produced clothes, crudely made and limited to a few loose-fitting sizes, were produced for and purchased by men who lived in city boarding houses and rooming houses, far from the female kin who previously would have made their garments. Most women made their own clothes, but those who could afford to do so employed seamstresses. Improvements in fit and changes in men's fashion eventually made ready-to-wear apparel more acceptable to clerks and professional men. In the 1840s the short sack coat, which did not taper at the waist, began to replace the embroidered waistcoat. This forerunner of the modern suit jacket fit loosely and needed little custom tailoring. Now even upper-class men were willing to consider ready-made apparel.

Retail Merchants

Retail clothing stores well stocked with ready-made clothes appeared in the 1820s. T. S. Whitmarsh of Boston advertised in 1827 that "he keeps constantly for Sale, from 5 to 10,000 Fashionable ready-made Garments." Such merchants often bought goods wholesale, though many manufactured shirts and trousers in their own factories. Lewis and Hanford of New York City boasted of cutting more than one hundred thousand garments in the winter of 1848–1849. The New York firm sold most of its clothing in the South and owned its own retail outlet in New Orleans. Paul Tulane, a New Orleans competitor, owned a New York factory that made goods for his Louisiana store. In the West, Cincinnati became the center of the new men's clothing industry. By midcentury, Cincinnati's ready-to-wear apparel industry employed fifteen hundred men and ten thousand women. As in Boston, most of the women did outwork.

Specialization of Commerce

Commerce expanded hand in hand with manufacturing. Cotton, for instance, had once been traded by plantation agents, who sold the raw cotton and bought manufactured goods that they then sold to plantation owners, extending them credit when necessary. Cotton exports rose from 83 million pounds in 1815 to 298 million in 1830 to more than a billion pounds for the first time in 1849. Gradually, some agents came to specialize in finance alone: they were cotton brokers, who for a commission brought together buyers and sellers. Similarly, wheat and hog brokers sprang up in the West—in Cincinnati, Louisville, and St. Louis. The distribution of finished goods also became more specialized as wholesalers bought large quantities of particular items from manufacturers, and jobbers broke down the wholesale lots for retail stores and country merchants.

General Merchants

General merchants persisted longer in small towns than in cities. They continued to exchange some goods with local farm women—trading flour or pots and pans for eggs or other produce. And local craftsmen continued to sell their own finished goods, such as shoes and clothing. In some rural areas and on the frontier, peddlers acted as general merchants. But as transportation improved and towns grew, even small-town merchants began to specialize.

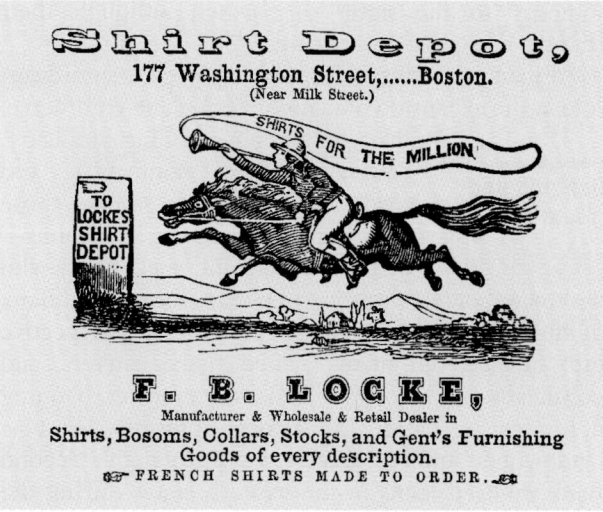

F. B. Locke adapted to the new market for ready-made clothing by becoming a manufacturer, wholesaler, and retailer of men's shirts. Although he continued to make shirts to order, the staple of his Shirt Depot was mass-produced shirts, as this advertisement from the *Boston Directory* for 1848–1849 indicates. (Warshaw Collection of Business Americana, Smithsonian Institution, Washington, D.C.)

Commercial specialization transformed some traders in big cities, especially New York, into virtual merchant princes. After the Erie Canal opened, New York City became a stop on every major trade route from Europe, the southern ports, and the West. New York traders were the middlemen for southern cotton and western grain. Merchants in other cities played a similar role within their own regions. Some traders in turn invested their profits in factories, further stimulating urban manufacturing. Some cities specialized: Rochester became a milling center, and Cincinnati— "Porkopolis"—became the first meatpacking center.

Merchants who engaged in complex commercial transactions required large office staffs. Most of the all-male office staff worked on high stools, laboriously copying business forms and correspondence. At the bottom of the office hierarchy were messenger boys, often preteens, who delivered documents. Above them were the ordinary copyists, who hand-copied as many documents as needed. Clerks processed documents and shipping papers and did translations. Above them were the bookkeeper and the confidential chief clerk. Those seeking employment in such an office, called a countinghouse, often took a course from a writing master to acquire a "good hand." All hoped to rise someday to the status of partner, although their chances of doing so were slim.

Financial institutions, which played a significant role in the expansion of manufacturing and commerce, also became a leading industry.

Banking and Credit Systems

Banks, insurance companies, and corporations linked savers—those who deposited money in banks—with producers and speculators who wished to borrow money. After 1816, the Second Bank of the United States injected a national perspective into finance, but many farmers, local bankers, and politicians denounced the bank as a monster, blaming it for serving national, not local, interests. Western landowners suffered severe losses when the Second Bank reduced loans in the western states during the Panic of 1819. In 1836 critics finally succeeded in killing the bank (see page 292).

The closing of the Second Bank in 1836 caused a nationwide credit shortage, which, in conjunction with the Panic of 1837, led to fundamental reforms in banking. Michigan and New York introduced charter laws promoting what was called *free banking*. Many other states soon followed suit. Previously, every new bank needed a special legislative charter before it could open for business; thus each bank incorporation was in effect a political decision. Under the new laws, any proposed bank that met certain minimum conditions—amount of capital invested, number of notes issued, and types of loans to be offered—would receive a state charter automatically. Banks in Michigan, New York, and, soon, other states were thus freer to incorporate, although the legislatures placed some restrictions on their operations to reduce the risk of bank failure.

Free banking proved to be a significant stimulus to the economy in the late 1840s and 1850s. New banks sprang up everywhere, providing merchants and manufacturers with the credit they needed. The free-banking laws also served as a precedent for general incorporation statutes that allowed manufacturing firms to receive state charters without special acts of the state legislature.

Workers and the Workplace

Loud the morning bell is ringing,
    Up, up sleepers, haste away;
Yonder sits the redbreast singing,
    But to list we must not stay.
        . . .

Sisters, haste, the bell is tolling,
    Soon will close the dreadful gate;
Then, alas! We must go strolling,
    Through the counting-room too late.
. . .

Now the sun is upward climbing,
    And the breakfast hour has come;
Ding, dong, ding, the bell is chiming,
    Hasten, sisters, hasten home.

The poet, writing in 1844 in the *Factory Girl's Garland*, uses the sound of the factory bell as a refrain to emphasize its incessant control, announcing when the workers are to wake, eat, begin work, stop work, and go to sleep. Night and day the millworkers felt the stress of factory schedules.

But the first generation of young single women who left New England villages and farms to work in the mills had come with great optimism. The mills offered steady work and good pay, plus airy boarding houses, prepared meals, and cultural activities. Though housekeepers enforced strict curfews, banned alcohol, and reported on workers' behavior and church attendance, mill work brought financial independence and friendship.

Sisters and cousins often worked in the same mill and lived in the same boarding house. They helped each other adjust, and their letters home drew kin to the mills. The benefits were not sufficient, however, to change their ambitions to be wives and mothers. Most arrivals were sixteen and stayed only about five years. When they left the mills to marry, other younger women interested in earning a wage took their places.

In the hard times from 1837 to 1842, demand for cloth declined, and most mills ran only part-time. Sub-

Boom and Bust in the Textile Mills

sequently managers pressured workers by means of the speed-up, the stretch-out, and the premium system. The speed-up increased the speed of the machines; the stretch-out increased the number of machines each worker had to operate; and premiums paid to the overseers whose departments produced the most cloth encouraged them to pressure workers for greater output. The result: between 1836 and 1850 the number of spindles and looms in Lowell increased 150 and 140 percent, respectively, while the number of workers increased by only 50 percent. The corporation's goal of building an industrial empire and maximizing profits took precedence over its paternalistic concern for workers' living conditions. In the race for profits, owners lengthened hours, cut wages, tightened discipline,

How do historians know...

that work in New England mills was regimented? This timetable from the Lowell Mills is among the rich sources historians consult to reconstruct workers' experiences in the mills. Textile factories were the first corporations to impose rigid work rules, necessitated by the size of the labor force, the management structure, and the organization of the work. Managers established exact times for beginning and ending work and for meals. Few workers carried a timepiece, so a system of bells regulated the lives of the factory community. For young mill women from the New England countryside, and later for Irish women, such regimentation must have seemed a world apart from the natural rhythms of rural life. (Photo: American Textile Museum)

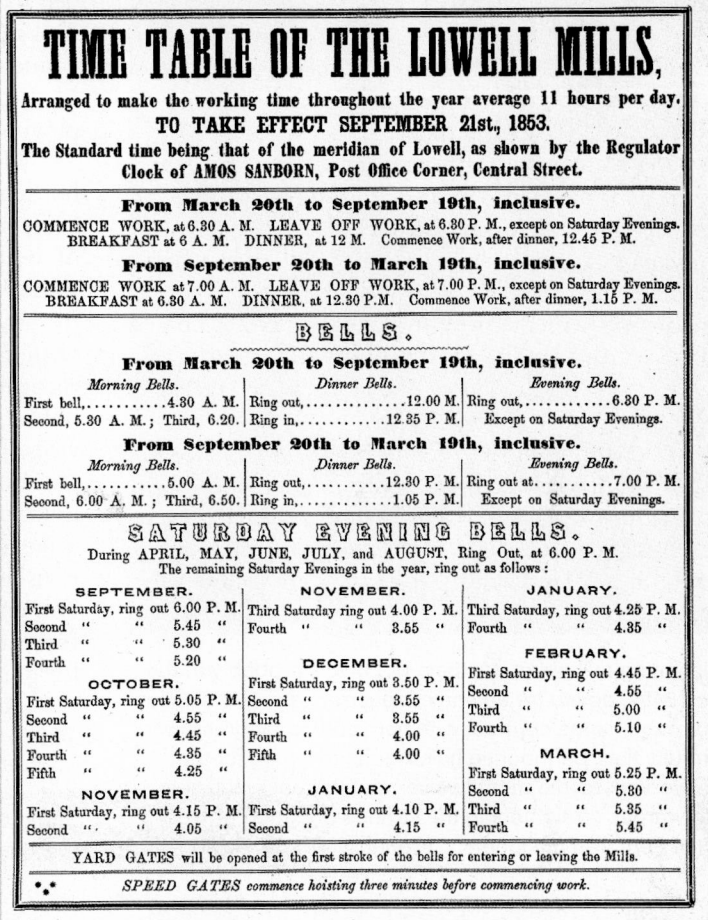

and packed the boarding houses. Some millworkers began to think of themselves as slaves.

New England millworkers responded to their deteriorating working conditions by organizing and striking. In 1834, in reaction to a 25 percent wage cut, they unsuccessfully "turned out" (struck) against the Lowell mills. Two years later, when boarding house fees increased, they turned out again. As conditions continued to worsen, workers adopted new methods of resistance. In the 1840s, strikes gave way to a concerted effort to shorten the workday. Massachusetts mill women and other workers joined forces to press for state legislation mandating a ten-hour day. Eliza R. Hemingway, a three-year veteran of two different Lowell mills, told a Massachusetts House of

Protests

Representatives committee in 1845 that workers' hours were too long. In the summer, work ran from 5:00 A.M. to 7:00 P.M., with time off for meals.

Women aired their complaints in worker-run newspapers: in 1842, the *Factory Girl* appeared in New Hampshire, the *Wampanoag and Operatives' Journal* in Massachusetts. Two years later they founded the *Factory Girl's Garland* and the *Voice of Industry*, nicknamed "the factory girl's voice." Even the *Lowell Offering*, the owner-sponsored paper that was the pride of millworkers and managers alike, became embroiled in controversy when workers charged its editors had suppressed articles criticizing working conditions.

The women's labor organizations were weakened by the short tenure of most workers. Few of the militant native-born millworkers stayed on to fight the managers

This young mill girl at Waltham or Lowell, probably in the late 1840s, posed for an early daguerreotype. Her swollen and rough hands contrast with her youth, neat dress, and carefully tied, beribboned hair. Her hands suggest that she worked, as did most twelve- and thirteen-year-olds, as a warper, straightening the strands of cotton or wool as they entered the looms.   (Courtesy of Jack Naylor)

and lived in a mostly female world. In the clothing and shoemaking industries, whose male artisans had once worked at home assisted by unpaid family labor, men began working outside the home while women continued to work at home through the putting-out system. Tasks and wages, too, became rigidly differentiated: women sewed, whereas men shaped materials and finished products, receiving higher wages in shops employing men only.

The market economy had an impact on unpaid household labor as well. As home and workplace became separate and labor came to be defined in terms of wages (what could be sold in the marketplace) rather than production (what could be made by hand), the unpaid labor of women was devalued. Cash exchanged was the measure, and as families increasingly recorded their incomes and expenditures in account books, there was no category for women's unpaid services. Yet those labors were extensive; indeed, the family depended on women's work within the household, ever more so as sons and even daughters sought wage work outside the home and had less time for household tasks. Thus gender defined household labor, and in the market economy it went unrecorded. Inevitably, it seemed to be worth little and was taken for granted.

The new textile mills, shoe factories, iron mills, and railroads were the antithesis of traditional workshop and household production. In factory workplaces authority was hierarchically organized. Factory workers lost their sense of autonomy as impersonal market forces seemed to dominate their lives. Their jobs were insecure, as competition frequently led to layoffs and replacement by cheaper, less-skilled workers or children. Moreover, the formal rules of the factory contrasted sharply with the more relaxed atmosphere of artisan shops and farm households. Journeymen recognized that the new system of manufacturing threatened them. When master craftsmen in shoemaking and textiles turned their workshops into small factories with themselves as managers, master and journeymen were distanced. In large factories, the distance was greater, as supervisors represented owners whom workers never saw. The division of labor and the use of machines narrowed the skills required. And the bell, the steam whistle, or the clock governed the flow of work, as the *Factory Girl's Garland* poem anxiously described.

Changes in the Workplace

One problem, of course, was the quickening pace of the work between the bells. Workers who at first

and owners, and gradually there were fewer New England daughters to enter the mills. They were replaced, in the 1850s, by Irish immigrant women who lived at home. Technological improvements in the looms and other machinery had made the work less skilled and more routine. The mills could thus pay lower wages and draw from a reservoir of unskilled labor.

A growing gender division in the workplace, especially in the textile, clothing, and shoemaking industries, was one important outcome of large-scale manufacturing. Although women and men in traditional agricultural and artisan households tended to perform different tasks, they worked as a family unit. As wage work spread, however, men's and women's work cultures became increasingly separate. The women and girls who left home for jobs in textile mills worked

Gender Divisions in Work

sought factory jobs for higher wages changed their minds in the face of wage reductions, speed-ups, and stretch-outs. Other conditions were trying, too. Mill-workers had to tolerate the roar of the looms, and all workers on power machines risked accidents that could maim or even kill. Perhaps most demoralizing, opportunities for advancement in the new system were virtually nil.

As a sense of distance from their employers took hold, so did deep-seated differences among workers. Initially, mill women drew on kinship, village, and gender ties to build supportive networks in factories. But in the 1840s, as recently arrived Irish immigrant women entered the mills, many workers found themselves working with total strangers. Once employed, their only bases for friendship and mutual support were their work experiences. Wage workers felt distanced from traditional culture as well. As wage work became common, the republican virtues associated with independent craft traditions eroded. The rigid rules of factory work and the swings in employment brought on by boom-and-bust cycles restricted individual freedom. At every turn, workers were hemmed in by formidable forces.

In response, some workers organized to resist changes wrought by the market economy and factories and to regain control of their work and their lives. Women textile work-

Labor Parties

ers organized into unions and demonstrated for better wages and conditions or lobbied legislatures for relief. Male workers, like shoemakers, also organized and protested, but because they were eligible to vote, they also organized political parties. Labor parties formed in Pennsylvania, New York, and Massachusetts in the 1820s, and later spread to other states, advocated free public education and an end to imprisonment for debt and opposed banks and monopolies. The interests of workers' parties often coincided with those of middle-class reformers: temperance, observance of the Sabbath, and suppression of vice (see Chapter 11). Ironically, however, reform politics also tended to divide workers. Many reforms—moral education, temperance, Sabbath closings—served the interests of merchants and industrialists seeking a more disciplined work force. Temperance and Sabbath closings pitted Protestants against Catholics who celebrated Sunday at public beer gardens. Anti-immigrant and anti-Catholic movements further divided workers.

Organized labor's greatest achievement during this period was to gain relief from the threat of conspiracy laws. When journeyman shoemakers

Emergence of a Labor Movement

organized during the first decade of the century, their employers accused them of criminal conspiracy. The cordwainers' (shoemakers') cases between 1806 and 1815 left labor organizations in a tenuous position. Although the courts acknowledged the journeymen's right to organize, judges ruled unlawful any coercive action by workers that would harm other businesses or the public. In other words, strikes were ruled illegal. Eventually a Massachusetts case, *Commonwealth v. Hunt* (1842), effectively reversed this status when Chief Justice Lemuel Shaw ruled that Boston journeyman bootmakers could strike "in such manner as best to subserve their own interests." Conspiracy laws no longer thwarted unionization.

Yet workers found permanent labor organizations difficult to sustain. Most workers outside the crafts were unskilled or semiskilled at best. Moreover, religion, race, ethnicity, and gender divided workers. The first unions arose among urban journeymen in printing, woodworking, shoemaking, and tailoring. These early unions tended to be local; the strongest resembled medieval guilds in that members sought to protect themselves against the competition of inferior workmen by regulating apprenticeship and establishing minimum wages. They also excluded women and African Americans. (Massachusetts mill women organized their own unions.) Umbrella organizations composed of individual craft unions, like the National Trades Union (1834), arose in several cities in the 1820s and 1830s. But the movement fell apart amid wage reductions and unemployment in the hard times of 1839–1843.

Labor organizations remained weak; individual producers—craftsmen, factory workers, and farmers—lost economic power; and workers increasingly forfeited control over their own work. While mill owners, corporate investors, large-scale landowners, and slave-holding planters reaped benefits from economic growth, workers' share of the national wealth declined after 1830.

Americans on the Move

 Growth in the years following the War of 1812 was not economic only. The Louisiana Purchase (1803) doubled the land area of the United States and acquisitions in the 1840s nearly doubled it again. Population soared, increasing by a third in each decade. The U.S.

Map 10.4   Settled Areas of the United States, 1820 and 1840   Removal of Indians and a growing transportation network opened up land to white and black settlers in the West and in the Southeast, as the U.S. population grew from 9.6 million in 1820 to 17.1 million in 1840.

population grew by 10.6 million people between 1820 and 1845, and immigration accounted for only a small amount; 89 percent of the population growth was from natural increase. In 1845, 20.2 million people lived in the United States.

In land and population the United States expanded outward, mostly westward, from its original seaboard base (see Map 10.4). The admission of new states tells the story: Indiana (1816), Mississippi (1817), Illinois (1818), Alabama (1819), Maine (1820), and Missouri

Westward Movement

(1821) brought the union to twenty-four states in the 1820s. Arkansas (1836) and Michigan (1837) soon followed, as did Florida and Texas (1845), Iowa (1846), and Wisconsin (1848) in the following decade.

Southerner and easterner, cotton raiser and grain farmer, black and white, slave and free person, owner and renter, investor and speculator, and settler and transient marched across the Appalachians. In the first two decades of the century Americans poured into the Ohio River valley; then, starting in the 1820s they moved into the Mississippi River valley and beyond, doubling the population living beyond the Appalachi-

Women who traveled west with their husbands found their domestic skills in great demand. In this watercolor entitled *Laying Out of Karns' City, Minnesota* (1856), E. Whitefield shows a woman preparing a meal out of her lean-to kitchen for her husband and their guests.   (Chicago Historical Society)

ans. By midcentury two-thirds of Americans lived west of the Appalachians. Mostly young and hard-working, they had visions of establishing family farms and achieving economic security.

Some 5 to 10 percent of Americans moved each year, their travel made ever faster and easier by the expanding transportation networks. Restless, they settled only temporarily and then moved on. "There is more travelling in the United States than in any part of the world," observed a commentator in 1828. "Here the whole population is in motion, whereas, in old countries, there are millions who have never been beyond the sound of the parish bell." People tended to move short distances; thus long moves were made in stages. Though most people lived on farms, there was also a steady rural to urban migration.

After the 1820s the heart of cotton cultivation and the plantation system shifted from the coastal

The South

states to Alabama and the newly settled Mississippi valley—Tennessee, Louisiana, Arkansas, and Mississippi. Southerners brought their institu-

tions with them; slaves moved with planters to the newer areas of the South, and yeoman farmers followed.

The shift was dramatic. The population of Mississippi soared from 73,000 in 1820 to 607,000 in 1850, with African American slaves in the majority. Across the Mississippi River, the population of Arkansas went from 14,000 in 1820 to 210,000 in 1850. Indian removal made expansion possible.

The South and cotton continued westward into Texas. In 1830 the 7,000 American immigrants living in northwest Mexico outnumbered Mexicans there two to one. By 1835 the American population reached 35,000, including 3,000 slaves. The American settlers were restless for independence or U.S. annexation and chafed at Mexico's resistance toward Anglo domination in Texas. Independence in 1836 spurred further American immigration into Texas. By 1845 "Texas fever" had boosted the Anglo population to 125,000. Statehood that year opened the floodgates.

Not all moves were westward. A steady stream drifted from the Upper South to the Ohio valley, from

Moves North and South

slave to free states. Abraham Lincoln's family, for example, took this path in moving from Kentucky to Indiana Territory and, later, to Illinois. Though northern black people moved westward as well, thousands of free people of color moved to northern states and Canada in the 1830s following the adoption of black codes and mob violence in the South (see pages 325–326). Fugitives from slavery too went north. Hispanics in the Southwest continued to move north into areas of Texas and present-day New Mexico and Utah. Hispanics and Indians competed for control of the land, but when the U.S. Army suppressed the Comanches, Apaches, Navajos, and Utes, Hispanic migration spread. After the United States acquired Florida and attempted to colonize and suppress the Indian peoples there, southerners poured into the new territory.

Settlers needed land and credit. Reflecting the nationalist outlook, the federal government served as real estate agent, transferring land to private hands, filling the West with non-Indian peoples, and promoting republican virtue. Some public lands were granted as rewards for military service; veterans of the War of 1812 received 160

Land Grants and Sales

acres. Until 1820 civilians could buy government land at $2 an acre (a relatively high price) on a liberal four-year payment plan, but the minimum purchase had been reduced in 1817 to 80 acres. After 1819 the government discontinued credit sales but reduced the price to an affordable $1.25 an acre.

Some eager pioneers settled land before it had been surveyed and offered for sale. Such illegal settlers, or squatters, then had to buy the land at auction and faced the risk of being unable to purchase it. In 1841, to facilitate settlement and end property disputes, Congress passed the Pre-emption Act, which legalized settlement prior to surveying.

Since most settlers needed to borrow money, private credit systems arose: banks, private investors, country storekeepers, and speculators all loaned money to farmers. Nearly all economic activity in the West involved credit, from land sales to produce shipments to railroad construction. In 1816 and 1836 easy credit boosted land prices. When tight credit, high interest, low prices, or destructive weather squeezed farmers' income, land values collapsed, ending the speculative bubble. Mortgage bankers and speculators then purchased land cheaply. As a consequence, many farmers became renters instead of own-

Credit

Henry Lewis's *St. Louis in 1846* depicts a pioneer family stopping to view the great Missouri city across the river. The contrast between the towering city, surrounded by modern steamboats and dominating the Mississippi and Missouri Rivers, and the pioneer family, with their wagons and horses, highlights the role cities played in western settlement and growth. (St. Louis Art Museum, Eliza McMillan Fund)

ers of land; tenancy became more common in the West than it had been in New England.

From the start, newly settled western areas depended on their links with towns and cities. Ohio

Frontier Cities

River cities—Louisville and Cincinnati—and the old French settlements—Detroit on the Great Lakes, St. Louis on the Mississippi River—predated and promoted the earliest western settlements. So too in the South, from New Orleans to Natchez to Memphis, towns spearheaded settlement and economic growth. Steamboats connected the river cities with eastern markets and ports, carrying grain east and returning with finished goods. Like cities in the Northeast, these western cities eventually developed into manufacturing centers as merchants shifted their investments from commerce to industry. Louisville, for instance, became a textile center. Smaller cities specialized in flour mills, and all produced consumer goods for the hinterlands. As commerce, urban growth, and industrialization overtook the farmers' frontier, the West was wed to the Northeast.

Native American Resistance and Removal

Indians were also on the move, but their migrations were more forced than voluntary. Indian removal made white expansion possible, but it uprooted the indigenous cultures of the eastern and southern woodlands. Perhaps 100,000 eastern and southern Indian people were removed between 1820 and 1850; about 30,000 died in the process. Those who remained became virtually invisible.

The U.S. Constitution acknowledged Indian distinctiveness by recognizing Indian sovereignty and by

Treaty Making

giving the federal government responsibility for dealing with Native Americans. In its relations with Indian leaders, the government followed international protocol. The federal government received Indian delegations with pomp and ceremony. They exchanged presents as tokens of friendships. Agreements between an Indian national and the United States were signed, sealed, and ratified like any other international treaty.

In practice, however, treaty making and Indian sovereignty were fictions. Protocol appeared to signify mutual respect and independence, but treaty negotiations exposed the sham. The American government used treaty making as a tactic to acquire Indian land, as

in the Lower Mississippi. Instead of bargains struck by two equal nations, treaties often were imposed by the victor on the vanquished. Old treaties gave way to new ones requiring Native Americans to cede their traditional holdings in exchange for other land in the West. Whether through arms or economic pressure, the federal government forced Native Americans to sign and relinquish treaties.

Indians could delay but not prevent removal. Though Indian resistance persisted after the War of 1812, it only slowed the inevitable. In the 1820s native peoples in Ohio, southern Indiana and Illinois, southwestern Michigan, most of Missouri, central Alabama, and southern Mississippi ceded lands under federal pressure. They gave up nearly 200 million acres for pennies an acre.

To maintain independence and preserve their ways of life, many Indian nations tried to accommodate to the expanding market econ-

Indians in the Market Economy

omy. In the first three decades of the century, the Choctaw, Chickasaw, and Creek peoples in the lower Mississippi responded to the growing cotton economy by becoming suppliers and traders. Under treaty provisions, Indian commerce took place through trading posts and stores that provided Indians with supplies and purchased or bartered Indian-produced goods. Indians exchanged hides, skins, and beeswax for cloth, ammunition, manufactured goods, and illegal liquor. The trading posts extended credit to chiefs, and increasingly they fell into debt. With pelt prices falling, the debts grew enormously and often could be paid off only by selling land to the federal government. The Choctaws, Creeks, and Chickasaws found themselves in a cycle of trade debt and land cessions. By 1822 the Choctaw nation had sold 13 million acres but still carried a debt of $13,000. The Indians struggled to adjust, increasing agriculture and hunting, working as farm hands and craftsman, and selling produce at market stalls in Natchez and New Orleans. Over time, however, they could not prevent the spread of the cotton economy that arose on their lands. With loss of land came dependency. The Choctaws came to rely on Europeans not only for manufactured goods but also for food.

Dependency facilitated removal of Native American peoples to western lands. While the population of other groups increased by leaps and bounds, the Indian population fell. Alexis de Tocqueville noticed the contrast. "Not only have these wild tribes receded, but they are destroyed," Tocqueville concluded, after personally observing the tragedy of forced removal, "and as they give way or perish, an immense and increasing people fill their place. There is no instance upon record of so prodigious a growth or so rapid a destruction." War, forced removal, disease, especially smallpox, and malnutrition reduced many Indian nations by 50 percent. More than half of the Pawnees, Omahas, Otoes, Missouris, and Kansas died in the 1830s alone.

The wanderings of the Shawnees, the people of Prophet and Tecumseh (see pages 228–230), illustrate the uprooting of Indian people. After giving up 17 million acres in Ohio in the 1795 Treaty of Greenville (see page 184), the Shawnees scattered to Indiana and eastern Missouri. After the War of 1812, Prophet's Indiana group withdrew to Canada under British protection. In 1822 other Shawnees sought Mexican protection and moved from Missouri to present-day eastern Texas. As the U.S. government promoted removal to Kansas, Prophet returned from Canada to lead a group to the new Shawnee lands in eastern Kansas in 1825. When Missouri achieved statehood in 1821, Shawnees living there were also forced to move to Kansas, where in the 1830s other Shawnees removed from Ohio or, expelled from Texas, joined them. By 1854 Kansas was open to white settlement, and the Shawnees had to cede seven-eighths of their land, or 1.4 million acres.

Shawnees

Removal had a profound impact on all Shawnees. The men lost their traditional role as providers; their methods of hunting and their knowledge of woodland animals were useless on the prairies of Kansas. As grain became the tribe's dietary staple, Shawnee women played a greater role as providers, supplemented by government aid under treaty provisions. (Typically, treaties required annual government distributions of grain, blankets, and cash payments.) Remarkably, the Shawnees preserved their language and culture in the face of these drastic changes. Although resistance proved incapable of protecting their lands, it did help maintain their culture.

Ever since the early days of European colonization, whites had sought the assimilation of Native Americans through education and Christianity (see page 53). This goal took on renewed urgency as the United States expanded westward. "Put into the hand of [Indian] children the primer and the hoe," the House Committee on Indian Affairs recommended in 1818, "and they will naturally, in time, take hold of the plough; and, as

Assimilation and Education

their minds become enlightened and expand, the Bible will be their book, and they will grow up in habits of morality and industry . . . and become useful members of society." In 1819, in response to missionary lobbying, Congress appropriated $10,000 annually for "civilization of the tribes adjoining the frontier settlements." Protestant missionaries administered the "civilizing fund" and established mission schools.

Within five years thirty-two boarding schools enrolled Indian students. They substituted English for Native American languages and taught agriculture alongside the Christian Gospel. The emphasis on agriculture taught the value of private property, hard work, and adaptation to the market economy, and laid the basis for Christian communities. But to settlers eyeing Indian land, assimilation through education seemed too slow a process. At the program's peak, schools across the United States enrolled fewer than fifteen hundred students; at that rate it would take centuries to assimilate all the Indians. Thus wherever Native Americans lived, illegal settlers disrupted their lives. Though obligated to protect the integrity of treaty lands, the federal government did so only half-heartedly. With government supporting westward expansion, legitimate Indian claims had to give way to the advance of white civilization.

In the 1820s it became apparent that neither economic dependency, education, nor Christianity could persuade Native Americans to cede enough land to satisfy the expansionists. Attention focused on southeastern tribes—Cherokees, Creeks, Choctaws, Chickasaws, and Seminoles—because much of their land remained intact after the War of 1812 and because they aggressively resisted white encroachment. Possessing some formal political institutions, they were better organized than the northern tribes to resist.

In his last annual message to Congress in late 1824, President James Monroe suggested that all Indians be moved beyond the Mississippi River. Three days later he sent a special message to Congress proposing removal. Monroe described his proposal as an "honorable" one that would protect Indians from invasion and provide them with independence for "improvement and civilization." Force would be unnecessary, he believed; Indians would willingly accept western land free from white encroachment.

Indian Removal as Federal Policy

Monroe's proposition targeted the Cherokees, Creeks, Choctaws, and Chickasaws, and they unanimously rejected it. Between 1789 and 1825 they had

Southern Indians attempted to remain in their ancestral lands in the South. Karl Bodmer's watercolor portrayed a Choctaw camp on the Mississippi River near Natchez, before the Indians were forced out of Mississippi and Alabama in 1830. (Joslyn Art Museum, Omaha, Nebraska)

negotiated thirty treaties with the United States, and they had reached their limits. Most wished to remain on what little was left of their ancestral land.

Pressure from Georgia had prompted Monroe's policy. Cherokees and Creeks lived in northwestern Georgia, and in the 1820s the state accused the federal government of not fulfilling its 1802 promise to remove the Indians in return for the state's renunciation of its claim to western lands. Georgia was satisfied neither by Monroe's removal messages nor by further cessions by the Creeks. In 1826, under federal pressure, the Creek nation ceded all but a small strip of its Georgia acreage. But Georgia still was not satisfied. Only the removal of the Georgia Creeks to the West could resolve the conflict between the state and the federal government.

For the Creeks the outcome was a devastating blow. In an ultimately unsuccessful attempt to hold fast to the remainder of their traditional lands, which were in Alabama, they radically altered their political structure. In 1829, at the expense of traditional village autonomy, they centralized tribal authority and forbade any chief from ceding land. In the end, they lost not only their land but also their traditional forms of social and political organization.

Adapting to American ways seemed no more successful than resistance in forestalling removal. No

Cherokees

people met the challenge of civilizing themselves by American standards more thoroughly than the Cherokees, whose traditional home centered on eastern Tennessee and northern Alabama and Georgia. Between 1819 and 1829 the tribe became economically self-sufficient and politically self-governing; during this Cherokee renaissance the twelve to fifteen thousand adult Cherokees came to think of themselves as a nation, not a collection of villages. In 1821 and 1822 Sequoyah, a self-educated Cherokee, devised an eighty-six-character phonetic alphabet that made possible a Cherokee-language Bible and a bilingual tribal newspaper, *Cherokee Phoenix* (1828). Between 1820 and 1823 the Cherokees created a formal government with a bicameral legislature, a court system, and a salaried bureaucracy. In 1827 they adopted a written constitution, modeled after that of the United States. Cherokee land laws, however, differed from U.S. law. The tribe collectively owned all Cherokee land and forbade land sales to outsiders. Nonetheless, the Cherokees assimilated American cultural patterns. By 1833 they held fifteen hundred black slaves whose legal status was the same as that of slaves held by southern whites. Moreover, missionaries had been so successful that the Cherokees could be considered a Christian community.

Although the Cherokees developed a political system similar to that of an American state, they failed to win respect or acceptance from southerners. In the 1820s, Georgia pressed them to sell the 7,200 square miles of land they held in the state. Congress appropriated $30,000 in 1822 to buy the Cherokee land in Georgia, but the Cherokees preferred to stay where they were. Impatient with their refusals to negotiate cession, Georgia annulled the Cherokees' constitution, extended the state's sovereignty over them, prohibited the Cherokee National Council from meeting except to cede land, and ordered their lands seized. The discovery of gold on Cherokee land in 1829 whetted Georgia's appetite for Cherokee territory.

Backed by sympathetic whites but not by the new president, Andrew Jackson, the Cherokees under Chief John Ross turned to the federal courts to defend their treaty with the United States and to disarm new

Cherokee Nation v. Georgia

threats by Georgia to seize their land. Their legal strategy reflected their growing political sophistication. In *Cherokee Nation v. Georgia* (1831), Chief Justice John Marshall ruled that under the federal Constitution an Indian tribe was neither a foreign nation nor a state and therefore had no standing in federal courts. Nonetheless, said Marshall, the Indians had an unquestionable right to their lands; they could lose title only by voluntarily giving it up. A year later, in *Worcester v. Georgia*, Marshall defined the Cherokee position more clearly. The Indian nation was, he declared, a distinct political community in which "the laws of Georgia can have no force" and into which Georgians could not enter without permission or treaty privilege. The Cherokees cheered. *Phoenix* editor Elias Boudinot called the decision "glorious news." But Georgia refused to comply.

Map 10.5 Removal of Native Americans from the South, 1820–1840   Over a twenty-year period, the federal government and southern states forced Native Americans to exchange their traditional homes for western land. Some tribal groups remained in the South, but most settled in the alien western environment.   (Acknowledgment is due to Martin Gilbert and George Weidenfeld and Nicholson Limited for permission to reproduce this map taken from *American History Atlas*)

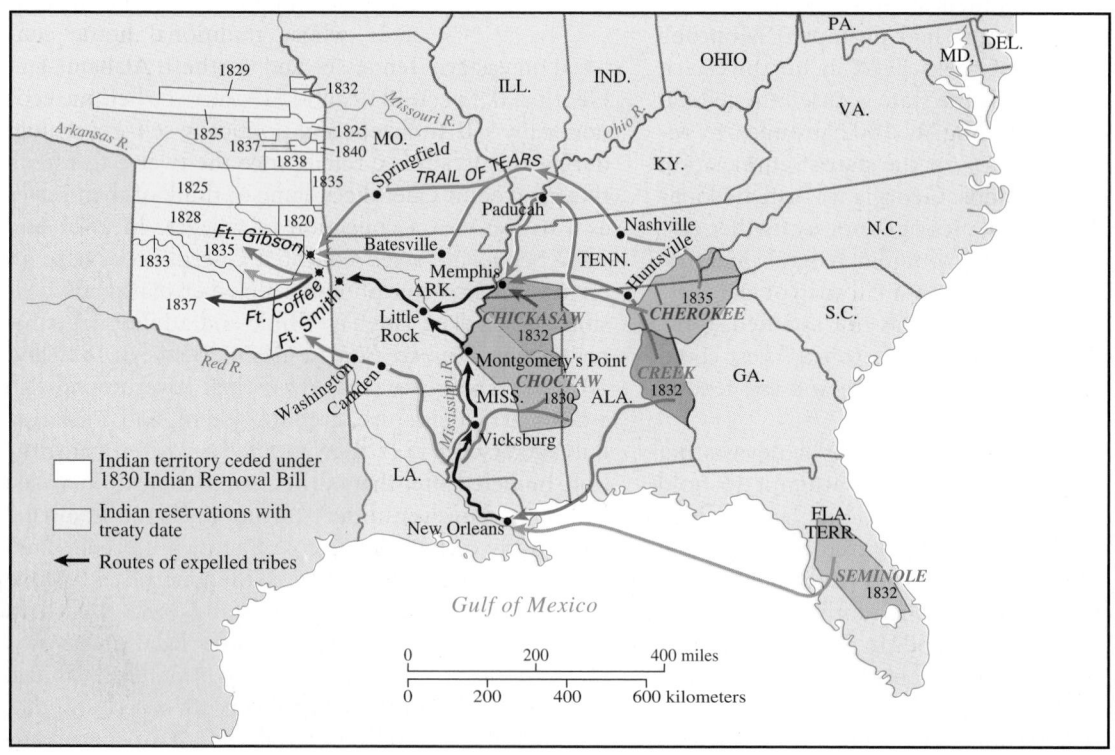

President Andrew Jackson, whose reputation had been built as an Indian fighter, refused to interfere because the case involved a state action. Newspapers widely reported that Jackson had said, "John Marshall has made his decision: now let him enforce it." Keen to open up new lands for settlement, Jackson favored expelling the Cherokees. In the Removal Act of 1830 Congress had provided Jackson with the funds he needed to negotiate new treaties and resettle the resistant tribes west of the Mississippi (see Map 10.5).

The Choctaws went first; they made the forced journey from Mississippi and Alabama to the West in the winter of 1831 and 1832. Alexis

Trail of Tears

de Tocqueville was visiting Memphis when they passed through: "The wounded, the sick, newborn babies, and the old men on the point of death. . . . I saw them embark to cross the great river," he wrote, "and the sight will never fade from my memory. Neither sob nor complaint rose from that silent assembly. Their afflictions were of long standing, and they felt them to be irremediable." Other tribes soon joined the forced march. The Creeks in Alabama resisted removal until

1836, when the army pushed them westward. A year later the Chickasaws followed.

Having fought removal in the courts, the Cherokees were divided. Some believed that further resistance was hopeless and accepted removal as the only chance to preserve their civilization. The leaders of this minority agreed in 1835 to exchange their southern home for western land in the Treaty of New Echota. Most, though, wanted to stand firm. John Ross, with petitions signed by fifteen thousand Cherokees, lobbied the Senate against ratification of the treaty. They lost. But when the time for evacuation came in 1838, most Cherokees refused to move. President Martin Van Buren sent federal troops to round them up. About twenty thousand Cherokees were evicted, held in detention camps, and marched to Indian Territory in present-day Oklahoma under military escort. Nearly one-quarter of them died of disease and exhaustion on what came to be known as the Trail of Tears.

When the forced march to the West ended, the Indians had traded about 100 million acres east of the Mississippi for 32 million acres west of the river plus

The Trail of Tears, by twentieth-century Pawnee artist Brummet Echohawk. About twenty thousand Cherokees were evicted in 1838–1839, and about one-quarter of them died on the forced march to present-day Oklahoma.   (Thomas Gilcrease Institute of American History and Art)

$68 million. Only a few scattered remnants, among them the Seminoles in Florida and the Cherokees in the southern Appalachian Mountains, remained in the East and South.

Forced removal had a disastrous impact on the Cherokees and the other displaced tribes. In the West they encountered an alien environment; lacking traditional ties, few felt at peace with the land. The animals and plants they found were unfamiliar. Unable to live off the land, many became dependent on government payments for survival. Removal also brought new internal conflicts. The Cherokees in particular struggled over their tribal government. In 1839 followers of John Ross assassinated the leaders of the protreaty faction. Violence continued sporadically until a new treaty in 1846 imposed a temporary truce.

Conflicts also arose among migrating Native American groups from the South and East and Indians already living in the West, as they were forced to share land and scarce resources. Nearly one hundred thousand newcomers settled west of the Mississippi, and the existing game could not support them all. The Osages and Pawnees grittily fought the newcomers who, under U.S. Army escort, were invading their land and homes.

In Florida a small band of Seminoles continued to resist. Some Seminole leaders agreed in the 1832

Second Seminole War

Treaty of Payne's Landing to relocate to the West within three years, but others opposed the treaty, and some probably did not know it existed. A minority under Osceola, a charismatic leader, refused to vacate their homes and fought the protreaty group. When federal troops were sent to impose removal in 1835, Osceola waged a fierce guerrilla war against them.

The Florida Indians were a varied group that included many Creeks and mixed Indian–African Americans (ex-slaves or descendants of runaway slaves). The U.S. Army, however, considered them all Seminoles, subject to removal. General Thomas Jesup believed that the runaway slave population was the key to the war. "This, you may be assured, is a Negro, not an Indian war," he wrote a friend in 1836, "and if it be not speedily put down, the South will feel the effects of it on their slave population before the end of the next season."

Osceola was captured under a white flag of truce and died in an army prison in 1838, but the Seminoles fought on under Chief Coacoochee (Wild Cat) and other leaders. In 1842 the United States abandoned

the removal effort. Most of Osceola's followers agreed to move west to Indian Territory in 1858, but many Seminoles remained in the Florida Everglades, proud of having resisted conquest.

Summary

Nationalism and self-confidence accompanied the end of the War of 1812. Under the Democratic-Republicans the federal government fostered expansion and economic growth through internal improvements, tariffs, the Second Bank of the United States, land sales, and Indian removal. The Supreme Court and American diplomats, too, asserted nationalism. The Monroe Doctrine was among John Quincy Adams's finest achievements.

But sectionalism accompanied nationalism and geographical expansion. Conflicts over tariffs, economic hard times, and slavery brought discord. The Missouri Compromise was a stopgap measure to avoid the explosive issue of slavery.

From 1816 through 1845 the United States experienced explosive growth. Population increased sixfold, mostly from natural increase, and moved westward. New farms grew cotton and grain for the market, and cities followed. In the process, Indians and Hispanics were pushed aside.

Agriculture remained the dominant industry, though by midcentury a booming manufacturing sector challenged farming. And agriculture itself was becoming market-oriented and mechanized. The market economy brought sustained growth; it also ushered in cycles of boom and bust. Hard times and unemployment became frequent occurrences. The growing economy also meant larger-scale destruction of the environment: mills exploited New England waterways as a source of power.

Large-scale manufacturing also altered traditional patterns of production and consumption. Farm families began to purchase goods formerly made by wives and daughters, and geared production to faraway markets. Farm women increasingly contributed income from market sales to the household purse. In New England many young women left the family farm to become the first factory workers in the new textile industry. As workshops and factories replaced home-based production, and the master-journeyman-apprentice system faded away, workplace relations became more impersonal, working conditions grew harsher, and men's and women's work became increasingly dissimilar. Industrial jobs began to attract large numbers of immigrants, and some workers organized labor unions.

Americans turned to controlling, resisting, or advocating change in the home and public spheres, through reform and politics.

LEGACY FOR A PEOPLE AND A NATION
A Mixed Economy

How active should the U.S. government be? Should it run, regulate, or leave to the market system healthcare, Social Security and private pensions, corporate concentration, and stock trading and investments? In other words, to what degree should the government be responsible for the well-being of the economy and individuals?

The Articles of Confederation limited government, the Constitution empowered it, and the Bill of Rights restricted it in specific areas. While Americans have continuously debated the appropriate role of government, the United States has generally occupied a middle ground: a mixed economy.

In the early nineteenth century, government played an active role in economic and social expansion. Federal and state governments built roads and canals, developed harbors, and operated post offices and the early telegraph. More commonly the government intervened to stimulate and regulate the private sector. In chartering corporations and banks and in land sales and grants, the United States created an infrastructure that laid the way for the market economy and industrialization.

In the late nineteenth century advocates of laissez-faire or hands-off government challenged the pre–Civil War traditions of an active government. Laissez faire dominated briefly until the 1880s and 1890s when large corporations and trusts accumulated so much power that governments stepped in to regulate railroads and business concentration. After the turn of the century the federal government extended regulation to food, drugs, the environment, working conditions, and fair business practices. Probably the most innovative example of the mixed economy was the creation in 1913 of the Federal Reserve System—a public system for overseeing currency and banking that left control in private hands. After a revival of laissez faire in the 1920s, the crisis of the Great Depression of the 1930s and World War II would lead the federal government to establish the modern welfare state, which operates through a mixed public/private structure.

As the United States begins the twenty-first century, its people again debate the appropriate role of government. Conservatives view government as the problem rather than the solution, arguing that government regulation hampers individual freedom and distorts the law of supply and demand. Advocates of an activist government argue that only the government has the power and resources to check economic concentration and to protect health, safety, and the environment. The framework of this debate is a legacy from before the Civil War.

For Further Reading, see page A-12 of the Appendix. For Web resources, go to http://college.hmco.com.

"I proceed, Gentlemen, briefly to call your attention to the present state of Insane persons confined within this Commonwealth," Dorothea Dix petitioned the Massachusetts legislature in 1843, "in cages, closets, stalls, pens! Chained, naked, beaten with rods and lashed into obedience."

Dix revealed the netherworld she had uncovered in investigating the treatment of the insane during the previous two years. She found appalling conditions in Massachusetts: men and women in cages, chained to walls, in dark dungeons, brutalized and held in solitary confinement. In a visit to a Newburyport almshouse in the summer of 1842, Dix expressed her surprise at the comfortable conditions for the "one idiotic" and seven insane inhabitants. On the grounds she discovered, however, one man residing in a shed whose door opened to the local "dead room" or morgue; his only companions were corpses. Shocked, she heard from an attendant about another insane inmate of whom no one spoke openly: "a woman in a cellar."

Dix asked to see the woman. The superintendent warned Dix that the woman "was dangerous to be approached; that 'she had lately attacked his wife,' and was often naked." Dix pressed on. "If you will not go with me," she said, "give me the keys and I will go alone." They unlocked the doors and entered an underground cell. Beneath the staircase was a tiny door. In the shadows Dix saw "a female apparently wasted to a skeleton, partially wrapped in blankets." She was withered, wrote Dix, "not by age, but by suffering." When the inmate saw the visitors, she wailed with despair: "Why am I consigned to hell? dark—dark—I used to pray, I used to read the Bible—I have done no crime in my heart. I had friends; why have all forsaken me!—my God! my God! why hast thou forsaken me?"

Dix described in the most personal and vivid terms her visits to jails, almshouses, and private homes, and the cruel treatment of the insane. Her petition to the General Court of Massachusetts was so graphic and shocking that the legislature voted to reprint it as a government pamphlet: "Memorial to the Massachusetts Legislature" (1843). Part petition, part sermon, and part autobiography, it made riveting reading.

Dorothea Dix's powerful personal descriptions of the brutal treatment of the mentally ill propelled her from reform to politics. This early photograph of Dix portrays both her austere demeanor and her crusading spirit. (Boston Athenaeum)

11

REFORM AND POLITICS IN THE AGE OF JACKSON 1824–1845

From Revival to Reform

Antimasonry

Abolitionism and the Women's Movement

Jacksonianism and Party Politics

Federalism at Issue: The Nullification and Bank Controversies

The Whig Challenge and the Second Party System

Manifest Destiny and Expansionism

LEGACY FOR A PEOPLE AND A NATION
The Bible Belt

The first-person narrative—"I tell what I have seen"—gave Dix's message power. She seemed, however, an unlikely herald. Reared in Massachusetts, she began teaching in Worcester at age fourteen in 1816. She wrote an elementary science text and published children's devotional verse and poetry. Her appearance was somber: she wore dark dresses with starched white collars and pulled her hair back tightly, making her face look more angular and austere. She never married and seemed aloof to other Bostonians, but she became an impassioned crusader for asylum reform, advocating hospitals for the mentally ill. In the 1840s she traveled more than 40,000 miles, exposing the inhumane treatment of the insane and petitioning state legislatures. From 1848 through 1856 she lobbied Congress annually to set aside 5 million acres to fund insane asylums. During the Civil War Dix recruited and supervised nurses for the federal government; afterward she resumed her efforts on behalf of the mentally ill. She died in 1887 in a hospital she had founded.

Dix epitomized much of early-nineteenth-century reform. She started with a religious belief in individual self-improvement and human perfectibility that led her to advocate collective responsibility, especially on behalf of those dependent on the kindness of others. She made reform her career, fearlessly entering the public arena at a time when women of her class were circumscribed to private life. In investigating asylums, in petitioning the Massachusetts legislature, and in lobbying other states and Congress, Dix moved from reform to politics, and she helped create a new public role for women, in the process broadening the base of political participation.

The religious and reform fervor of the period arose both as part of the spiritual renewal known as the Second Great Awakening and as a response to the enormous transformation that the United States experienced after the War of 1812. Immigration, the spread of a market economy, growing inequality, the westward advance of settlement, and territorial expansion all contributed to remaking the United States. Many Americans had difficulty keeping up with the rapid pace of change and felt they were no longer masters of their own fates.

Anxieties wrought by rapid change drove the impulse to reform society. Men and women organized to end the abuses of alcohol and prostitution, to improve conditions in prisons and asylums, to oppose secret and antidemocratic societies, to end slavery, and to achieve equal rights for women. Inevitably reform movements pushed men and women into politics,

though only men voted. Opponents of reform, however, were equally concerned about social problems. What distinguished them from reformers was their skepticism about human perfectibility and their distrust of institutions and the exercise of power, both public and private. To them, government coercion was the greater evil. They sought to reverse, not shape, change.

Two issues in particular bridged reform and politics: the short-lived Antimasonry frenzy against secret societies; and the intense, uncompromising crusade for immediate emancipation. Though Antimasons organized the first third-party movement, abolition eventually overrode all other concerns. No single issue evoked the passion that slavery did. It pitted neighbor against neighbor and region against region.

The Jacksonians, too, saw themselves as reformers. They opposed special privileges and the Second Bank of the United States with the same vigor with which reformers opposed sin. President Jackson believed that a strong federal government restricted individual freedom by favoring one group over another. Social and religious reformers disagreed. Wanting a more active federal role, they rallied around the new Whig Party, which became the vehicle of humanitarian reform. Democrats and Whigs constituted a new party system, characterized by strong organizations, intensely loyal followings, and energetic religious and ethnic competition.

Both parties eagerly promoted expansionism during the prosperous 1840s. Democrats saw the agrarian West as an antidote to urbanization and industrialization; Whigs focused on the new commercial opportunities it offered. Expanding the nation all the way to the Pacific seemed to be the manifest destiny of the United States. Texas, California, and Oregon, unknown to most Americans in 1800, had become familiar places by the 1830s and 1840s, and to lay hold of them, the United States would challenge its neighbors to the north and south. ■

From Revival to Reform

 Religion was probably the prime motivating force behind organized benevolence and reform. Beginning in the late 1790s religious revivals galvanized Protestants, especially women, into social action. The most famous was at Cane Ridge, Kentucky, in 1801, and it became legendary. One report estimated twenty-five thousand people attended the August meetings, at a time when

IMPORTANT EVENTS

1790s–1840s Second Great Awakening spreads religious fervor

1820s Reformers in New York and Pennsylvania establish model penitentiaries

1824 No presidential candidate wins a majority in the electoral college

1825 House of Representatives elects Adams president

1826 American Society for the Promotion of Temperance founded
Morgan affair is catalyst for Antimasonry movement

1828 Tariff of Abominations passed
Jackson elected president

1830 Webster-Hayne debate explores the nature of the Union

1830s–40s Democratic-Whig competition gels in second party system

1831 Garrison begins abolitionist newspaper *The Liberator*
First national Antimason convention

1832 Jackson vetoes rechartering of the Second Bank of the United States
Jackson reelected president

1832–33 South Carolina nullifies tariffs of 1828 and 1832, prompting nullification crisis

1836 Republic of Texas established after breaking from Mexico
Specie Circular ends credit purchase of public lands
Van Buren elected president

1837 *Caroline* affair sparks Anglo-U.S.-Canadian hostility
Financial panic ends boom of the 1830s

1838–39 United States and Canada mobilize their militias over Maine–New Brunswick border dispute

1839–43 Hard times spread unemployment and deflation

1840 Whigs win presidency under Harrison

1841 Tyler assumes the presidency after Harrison's death
"Oregon fever" attracts settlers to the Northwest and intensifies expansionism

1843 Dix petitions Massachusetts legislature regarding deplorable condition of insane asylums

1844 Polk elected president

1845 Texas admitted to the Union

1848 Woman's Rights Convention at Seneca Falls, New York, calls for women's suffrage

---

Kentucky's largest city, Lexington, had fewer than two thousand inhabitants. Revivals spread in waves, finding ready audiences in the frontier folk of the countryside. At camp meetings, sometimes lasting a week and attended by thousands of people, preachers exhorted sinners to repent and become genuine Christians. They offered salvation to all through personal conversion. At a time when only a minority could read and write, these itinerant evangelists were democratizing American religion, making it available to all.

Resembling the Great Awakening of the eighteenth century (see pages 110–111), the movement

Second Great Awakening

came to be called the Second Great Awakening. Under its influence, the role of churches and ministers in community life diminished as lay participation increased, and Chris-

tians in all parts of the country tried to right the wrongs of the world. Visiting the United States in the 1830s, Alexis de Tocqueville noted that "there is no country in the world where the Christian religion retains greater influence" than in America.

In the South, huge numbers of people regularly attended revivals, but they especially drew women and African Americans, free and slave. The call to personal repentance and conversion invigorated Protestantism, giving southern churches an evangelical base and giving evangelicalism a southern accent. In essence, the Second Great Awakening turned the South into the Bible belt. In the North, New York lawyer Charles G. Finney led the revival movement. After his 1821 soul-shaking conversion, which he interpreted as "a retainer from the Lord Jesus Christ to plead his cause," Finney abandoned the law to convert souls, staging three- to four-day camp meetings in western New York towns.

Salvation could be achieved, Finney preached, through spontaneous conversion like his own. He mesmerized his audiences, evoking emotional responses. In everyday language, Finney preached that "God has made man a moral free agent." In other words, evil was avoidable: Christians were not doomed by original sin, and anyone could achieve salvation. Finney's brand of revivalism transcended sects, class, and race but had a particularly strong base among Baptists and Methodists. These denominations grew the most because their structure maximized democratic participation and they drew their ministers from ordinary folk.

The Second Great Awakening raised people's hopes for the Second Coming of the Christian messiah and the establishment of the Kingdom of God on earth. Revivalists resolved to speed the Second Coming by combating the forces of evil and darkness. Some revivalists even believed that the United States had a special mission in God's design and therefore a special role in eliminating evil. As the pace of social change quickened in the 1830s and 1840s, western New York experienced such continuous and heated waves of revivalism that it became known as "the burned-over district." Migration patterns spread not only religion but also the impulse for moral reform.

Regardless of theology, all revivalists shared a belief in individual self-improvement. The doctrine of perfectibility demanded that Christians actively organize and convert others. Thus the Second Great Awakening bred reform, and evangelical Protestants became missionaries for both religious and secular salvation. Wherever they preached, evangelists generated new religious groups and voluntary reform societies. New sects like the Mormons arose out of this ferment. So did associations to address the pressing issues of the day: temperance, education, Sabbath observance, dueling, and later slavery. Religious zeal led believers to support missionaries abroad, particularly in Asia and Africa. Collectively these groups constituted a national web of benevolent and moral-reform societies, and strengthened by numbers, the privately persuaded inevitably moved toward public action.

More women than men answered the call of Christianity, sustaining the Second Great Awakening and invigorating local churches. Pious middle-class women in Rochester, New York, for instance, responded to Finney by spreading

Role of Women

the word to other women during the day while their husbands were at work. Gradually women brought their families and sometimes their husbands into church and reform. Although many businessmen recruited their employees to benevolent work, women more than men tended to feel personally responsible for counteracting the increasingly secular orientation of the expanding market economy. The emotionally charged conversion experience could return women to what they believed was the right path. It also offered them communal ties with other women.

Everywhere prayer groups and female missionary societies motivated organized religious and benevolent activity on an unprecedented scale. For women and some men, reform represented their first political involvement at a time when women did not cast votes. In reform organizations women represented themselves; by participating directly in service activities, they pioneered new, visible, public roles for women. Within churches and society, they dissented and opposed traditional political leaders.

An exposé of prostitution in New York City illustrates how reform led to political action and dissent.

The Plight of Prostitutes

John R. McDowall, a divinity student, published a report in 1830 documenting the prevalence of prostitution in New York City. Philip Hone, a prominent civic leader (see pages 316–317), denounced McDowall's report as "a disgraceful document," and he and other New York businessmen and politicians defended the city's good name against "those base slanders." Women, moved by the plight of "fallen women," revived the fight against prostitution in 1834. But whereas male reformers made the prostitutes the target of their zeal, the newly organized Female Moral Reform Society focused on the men who victimized young women, publicizing the names of clients who entered brothels in New York City. They organized a shelter for refuge and an employment agency to find jobs for prostitutes.

During the 1830s, the New York society expanded its activities and geographical scope, calling itself the American Female Moral Reform Society. By 1840 it had 555 affiliated chapters across the nation. The society also entered the political sphere. In New York State in the 1840s, the movement successfully crusaded for criminal sanctions against the men who seduced women into prostitution, as well as against the prostitutes themselves.

One of the most successful reform efforts was the campaign against alcohol. Drinking was more wide-

Temperance spread in the early nineteenth century than it is today. American men gathered in public houses and rural inns to gossip, talk politics, play cards, escape work and home, and to drink whiskey, rum, and hard cider. Contracts were sealed, celebrations commemorated, and harvests toasted with liquor. Respectable women did not drink in public, but many regularly tippled alcohol-based patent medicines promoted as cure-alls. Why then did temperance become such a vital issue? And why were women especially active in the movement? Like all nineteenth-century reform, temperance had a strong religious foundation.

Evangelicals considered drinking a sin; it created poverty, dependency, and crime. Moreover, in many denominations, forsaking alcohol was part of conversion. The sale of whiskey often violated the Sabbath, for workers commonly labored six days and spent Sunday at the public house drinking and socializing. Equally important, alcoholism destroyed families. In the early 1840s thousands of ordinary women formed Martha Washington societies to protect families by reforming alcoholics, raising children as teetotalers, and spreading the temperance message. Popular culture of the time was laced with domestic images of the damage alcohol left in its wake: abandoned wives, prodigal sons, drunken fathers. Timothy Shay Arthur dramatized all these evils in *Ten Nights in a Barroom* (1853), a classic American melodrama, as did Deacon Robert Peckham in his temperance paintings. Employers complained that drinkers took "St. Monday" as a holiday to recover from Sunday. In the new world of the factory, drinking was unacceptable.

Demon rum became a prime target of reformers. As the temperance movement gained momentum, its goal shifted from moderate use of alcohol to voluntary abstinence and finally to prohibition. The American Society for the Promotion of Temperance, organized in 1826 to sign drinkers to a pledge of abstinence, became a pressure group for state prohibition legislation. By the mid-1830s five thousand state and local temperance societies touted teetotalism, and more than a million people had taken the pledge. Several hundred thousand children, for instance, enlisted in the Cold Water Army.

Temperance Societies

The temperance movement's success was reflected in a sharp decline in alcohol use. Per capita consumption fell from 5 gallons in 1800 to below 2 gallons in the 1840s. Success bred more victories. Maine prohibited the manufacture and sale of alcohol except for medicinal purposes in 1851, and by 1855 similar laws

The evils of drinking and the bliss of temperance were a major theme in popular culture. Deacon Robert Peckham illustrated the contrast in two paintings from the 1840s: *The Woes of Liquor (Intemperance)* and *The Happy Abstemious Family (Temperance)*. (Worcester Historical Museum)

had been enacted throughout New England and in New York, Pennsylvania, and the Midwest.

Even as consumption was declining, opposition to alcohol was growing. From the 1820s on, many reformers expressed their prejudices by regarding alcohol as an evil introduced by Catholic immigrants. The Irish and Germans, the *American Protestant Magazine* complained in 1849, "bring the grog shops like the frogs of Egypt upon us." Rum and immigrants defiled the Sabbath; rum and immigrants brought poverty; rum and immigrants supported the feared papacy. Some Catholics took the pledge of abstinence and formed their own organizations, such as the St. Mary's Mutual Benevolent Total Abstinence Society in Boston. Even nondrinking Catholics tended to oppose state regulation of drinking, however; temperance seemed to them a question of individual choice. They favored self-control, not state coercion.

As the career of Dorothea Dix demonstrated, moral reform also stimulated the construction of asylums and other institutions to house prisoners, the mentally ill, orphans, delinquent children, and the poor. Such institutions were needed, reformers argued, to shelter victims of society's turbulence and impose on them a familial discipline. It was widely believed that criminals came from unstable families whose lack of restraint led to vice and drink. Idleness was both a symptom and a cause of crime; thus the clock governed a prisoner's day, and idleness was banished. Through discipline, inmates might become self-reliant and responsible. Even the most sinful could be redeemed.

Penitentiaries and Asylums

In the 1820s New York and Pennsylvania developed competing models for reforming criminals. Both rejected incarceration simply to punish criminals or to remove them from society, advocating instead that disciplined regimens would rehabilitate them. New York's Auburn (1819–1823) and Ossining (1825) prisons isolated prisoners in individual cells but brought them together in common workshops. Pennsylvania's Pittsburgh (1826) and Philadelphia (1829) prisons isolated prisoners completely, forcing them to eat, sleep, and work in their individual cells, allowing them contact only with guards and visitors. Both systems sought to separate criminals from evil influences and to expose them to a regimen of order and discipline.

Similar approaches were employed in insane asylums, hospitals, and orphanages. Formerly the prescribed treatment removed disturbed individuals from society and isolated them among strangers; many were incarcerated with criminals. Dorothea Dix argued that this treatment was inhumane. The new asylums were clean and orderly. In response to Dix's crusade and reform societies, twenty-eight of the thirty-three states had public institutions for the mentally ill by 1860.

Antimasonry

 More intense than the asylum movement but of shorter duration was the crusade against Freemasonry, a secret fraternity that had come to the United States from England in the eighteenth century. Sons of the Enlightenment such as Benjamin Franklin and George Washington were attracted to Masonry, with its emphasis on individual belief in a deity (as opposed to organized religion) and on brotherhood (as opposed to one church). In the early nineteenth century Freemasonry spread, attracting middle- and upper-class men prominent in commerce and civic affairs. For the ambitious, the Masons offered access to powerful community leaders. Monumental lodges called attention to the Mason's affluence and prominence.

Opponents of Masonry charged that the order's secrecy and appeal to elites were antidemocratic and antirepublican. Publications such as the *Anti Masonic Almanac* attacked Masonic initiation rites. Evangelicals labeled the order satanic. Antimasons argued that Masonry threatened the family because it excluded women and encouraged men to neglect their families for alcohol and ribald entertainments at Masonic lodges. As the temperance movement sought to liberate individuals from drink, Antimasons sought to liberate society from the grip of what they considered a powerful, antirepublican secret fraternity. Just as penitentiaries and asylums would rehabilitate the criminal and insane, so the Antimasons believed that the abolition of Masonry would reestablish communal moral discipline and harmony. The political arena quickly absorbed Antimasonry, and its short life illustrates the close association of politics and reform in the 1820s and after.

Morgan Affair

The catalyst for Antimasonry as an organized movement was the suspected murder of William Morgan, a disillusioned Mason who published an exposé in 1826, *The Illustration of Masonry, By One of the Fraternity Who Has Devoted Thirty Years to the Subject*. Even before the book appeared, a group of Masons abducted Morgan in Canandaigua, New York. It was widely believed that his kidnappers murdered him, though his body was never found.

Events seemed to confirm Masonry's antidemocratic character. Prosecutors who were Masons appeared to obstruct the investigation of Morgan's abduction. The public pressed for justice, and the series of notorious trials that ensued from 1827 through 1831 led many to suspect a conspiracy. The cover-up became as much of an issue as Masonry itself, and the movement spread to other states. Antimasonry coalesced overnight in the burned-over district of western New York, and it quickly became a political movement.

With a growing popular following and a call for public morality and republican principles, the Antimasons held conventions in 1827 to se-

Convention System

lect candidates to oppose Masons running for office. The next year the conventions supported the National Republican candidate, John Quincy Adams, and opposed Andrew Jackson because he was a Mason. The Antimasons held the first national political convention in Baltimore in 1831, and a year later they nominated William Wirt as their presidential candidate. Thus the Antimasons became a rallying point for those opposed to President Andrew Jackson. Their electoral strength lay in New England and New York: in Vermont the Antimasons became the dominant party for a brief time in 1833; in Massachusetts they replaced the Democrats as the second major party. Antimasonry found little support, however, in the slave South.

By the mid-1830s, Antimasonry had lost momentum as a moral and political phenomenon. A single-issue party, the Antimasons declined along with Freemasonry. Yet the movement left its mark on the politics of the era. As a moral crusade focused on public officeholders, it inspired broad participation in the political process. It drew new white voters into politics at a time when male suffrage was being extended, and it attracted the lower and middle classes by pitting them against the Masonic elite, exploiting their distrust of local political leaders. The Antimasons also changed party organization by pioneering the convention, rather than the caucus, for nominating candidates for office and by introducing the party platform.

Abolitionism and the Women's Movement

Antimasonry foreshadowed and had much in common with abolitionism. Indeed, as Antimasonry waned, the antislavery movement gathered momentum. Abolitionist William Lloyd Garrison at first ignored the frenzy over the Morgan affair but in 1832 he joined

Antimasonic publications, such as this 1831 almanac, made much of the allegedly sinister initiation rites that bound a new member "to keep all Masonic secrets, under the penalty of having his throat cut, his tongue torn out, and his body buried in the ocean." (Print collection, Miriam and Ira D. Wallach Division of Art, Prints, and Photographs, New York Public Library, Astor, Lenox and Tilden Foundations)

the ranks of Antimasons. Echoing his stand on emancipation, Garrison wrote: "I go for the immediate, unconditional and total abolition of Freemasonry." In his eyes, both slavery and Masonry undermined republican values. Eventually the issue of slavery became so compelling that it consumed all other reforms and threatened the nation itself. Those who advocated immediate emancipation saw slavery as, above all, a moral issue—a flaw in the character of the American nation.

Before the 1830s few whites advocated the abolition of slavery. In the Northeast and Old Northwest, where by 1820 slavery had been virtually abolished (five states had gradual emancipation plans), whites took little interest in the issue. Antislavery sentiment appeared strongest in the Upper South, though north-

Women played an activist role in reform, especially in abolitionism. A rare daguerreotype from August 1850 shows women and men, including Frederick Douglass, on the podium at an abolitionist rally in Cazenovia, New York. (Collection of J. Paul Getty Museum, Los Angeles, California)

ern involvement grew after the War of 1812. The American Colonization Society, founded in 1816 in Washington, D.C., advocated gradual, voluntary emancipation and resettlement of former slaves in Africa, establishing the colony of Liberia for that purpose in the 1820s. Society members did not believe that free blacks had a place in the United States, and its members included Jefferson and other slaveholders, some evangelicals and Quakers, and (briefly) a few blacks. In the 1830s the immediatists—those who demanded immediate, complete, and uncompensated emancipation—surpassed the gradualists as the dominant strand of abolitionism.

At first only African Americans demanded an immediate end to slavery. David Walker's *Appeal . . . to the Colored Citizens* (1829) was a clarion call read by northern black people. Walker, a southern-born free black, was Boston's leading abolitionist until his death in 1830. When Walker died, there were fifty black abolitionist soci-

Black Abolitionists

eties in the United States assisting fugitive slaves, lobbying for emancipation, exposing the evils of slavery, and reminding the nation that its mission as defined in the Declaration of Independence remained unfulfilled. A free black press spread the word by fighting in print for suffrage and civil rights for free blacks. So did former slaves like Frederick Douglass and Sojourner Truth, whose writings and speeches of their personal experiences as slaves mobilized northerners. Douglass and Underground Railroad champion Harriet Tubman joined forces in the 1840s with white reformers in the American Anti-Slavery Society. Their militant and unrelenting campaign also won European support. "Brethren, arise, arise, arise!" Henry Highland Garnet commanded the 1843 National Colored Convention. "Strike for your lives and liberties. Now is the day and hour. Let every slave in the land do this and the days of slavery are numbered. Rather die freemen than live to be slaves."

In the 1830s a small number of white reformers, driven by moral urgency, also crusaded for immediate emancipation. The most prominent and uncompromising immediatist, though not the most representative, was the incendiary William Lloyd Garrison, a talented journalist who broke with moderate abolitionists in 1831. That year he began publishing *The Liberator*, which for thirty-five years would be his major weapon against slavery. He declared in its first issue, "I am in earnest—I will not equivocate—I will not excuse—I will not retreat a single inch—and *I will be heard*."

William Lloyd Garrison

Garrison's staunch refusal to work with anyone who tolerated the delay of emancipation isolated him from other opponents of slavery. He even forswore political action on the grounds that it was government that permitted slavery. Garrison burned a copy of the Constitution on July 4, 1854, proclaiming, "So perish all compromises with tyranny." By his actions and rhetorical power, Garrison helped to push antislavery onto the agenda, though he had no specific plan for abolishing it. In essence, what Garrison called for was conversion of those who held slaves or cooperated with institutions that supported slavery; they must repent.

It is difficult to differentiate between those who became immediatists and those who did not. But immediatists like Garrison, Elizabeth Chandler, Amos Phelps, and Theodore Weld had much in common. They were young evangelicals active

Immediatists

How do historians know...

that African Americans and women played prominent roles in the abolitionist movement?

Abolitionists lived open lives. They used newspapers, pamphlets, speeches, and sermons to expose the evils of slavery, to mount a crusade for emancipation, and to build a movement. Weekly abolitionist newspapers, such as *The Liberator*, published by William Lloyd Garrison, printed their correspondence, their speeches, and minutes of their meetings.

The Liberator appeared from 1831 to 1866, and it recorded the activities of the immediatist aboli-

tionists. Under the banners "No Union with Slaveholders" and "The United States Constitution is a 'covenant with death, and an agreement with hell,'" it preached to the choir, printing passionate attacks on slavery and reports of local antislavery societies. *The Liberator*'s pages recorded the activities of black and women abolitionists, frequently in their own words. The subscription lists that have survived indicate that a majority of its subscribers probably were African Americans. (Photo: Trustees of the Boston Public Library)

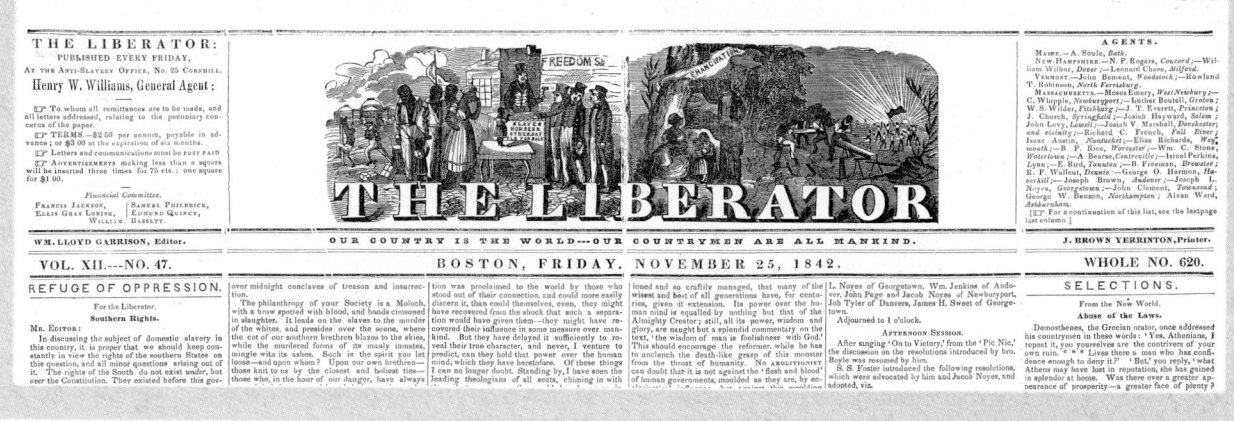

in benevolent societies in the 1820s; many became ordained ministers or started out intending ministry as a career; and many had personal contact with free blacks and were sympathetic to African American rights. They were convinced that slaveholding was a sin. Their common concern, in turn, made them more political: to abolish sin, they sought to change the institutions that harbored or fostered it. Finally, they shared great moral intensity. Because they were unwilling to compromise, their zeal made them forceful political activists. Their main organizational vehicle was the American Anti-Slavery Society, founded in 1833.

Most benevolent workers and reformers kept their distance from the immediatists. They shared with immediatists the view that slavery was a sin but believed in gradual emancipation. They feared that if they moved too fast, attacked sinners too harshly, or interfered too aggressively in time-honored customs and

beliefs, they would destroy the harmony and order they sought to bring about through peaceful reform. But peace was at a premium: unlike temperance, the antislavery movement faced fierce opposition, even mob violence.

Immediatists' greatest recruitment successes resulted from defending their own constitutional rights,

Opposition to Abolitionists

not the rights of slaves. Wherever they went, immediatists found their civil rights, especially free speech, at risk, threatened by hostile crowds. At Utica, New York, in 1835, merchants and professionals broke up the state Anti-Slavery Convention that had welcomed blacks and women. Mob violence peaked that year with more than fifty riots aimed at abolitionists or African Americans. In 1837 in Alton, Illinois, a mob murdered abolitionist editor Elijah P. Lovejoy, who had been driven out of slaveholding Missouri, and rioters sacked his printing office. But public outrage at Lovejoy's murder only broadened the base of antislavery support in the North.

In the South, mobs blocked the distribution of antislavery tracts. They destroyed pamphlets that the American Anti-Slavery Society sent out by the millions using new rotary printing presses. The state of South Carolina intercepted and burned abolitionist literature, and President Andrew Jackson proposed a law prohibiting the mailing of antislavery tracts. In 1835 proslavery assailants killed four abolitionists in South Carolina and Louisiana and forty supposed insurrectionists in Mississippi and Louisiana that summer. Riots in the South, unchecked by authorities, were violent and deadly.

At a rally in Boston's Faneuil Hall in 1835, former Federalist Harrison Gray Otis portrayed abolitionists as subversives. Attacking Garrison's American Anti-Slavery Society as "revolutionary," he accused it of having women "turn their sewing parties into abolition clubs." Soon, Otis charged, school primers would teach "that A stands for abolition." Abolitionists, he predicted, would turn to politics, causing unforeseeable calamity. "What will become of the nation?" Otis asked. "What will become of the union?"

But the furor between the abolitionists and their opponents was already being played out in the House of Representatives. Abolitionists were bombarding Congress with petitions to abolish slavery and the slave trade in the District of Columbia, which Congress governed. The House in 1836 adopted what abolitionists immediately labeled the "gag rule," which automatically tabled abolitionist petitions, effectively preventing debate on them. When the immediatists, in response, flooded Congress with nearly seven hundred thousand petitions, the gag rule gave new energy to the antislavery movement. In a dramatic defense of the right of petition, former president John Quincy Adams, now a representative from Massachusetts, took to the floor again and again to speak against the gag rule. (Its repeal in 1844 was anticlimactic.)

Gag Rule

The Missouri Compromise, censorship of the mails, and the gag rule represented attempts to keep the issue of slavery out of the political arena. Yet the more national leaders, especially Democrats, worked to avoid the matter, the more they hardened the resolve of the antislavery forces. The unlawful and violent tactics used by opponents of abolition actually unified the movement by forcing factions to work together for mutual defense.

At the outset abolition was highly factionalized, and its adherents fought one another as often as they fought the defenders of slavery. They were divided over Garrison's emphasis on "moral suasion"—winning over the hearts of slaveowners rather than coercing them—versus the practical politics of James G. Birney, the Liberty Party's candidate for president in 1840 and 1844, who sought to end slavery by electing abolitionists. Abolitionists also disagreed about the place of free people of color in American society. And the movement split over support for other reforms, especially the rights of women.

Women had been prominent in the antislavery movement from the first. They joined local female antislavery societies through their churches as part of the network of moral reform. In 1833 women in Boston founded the Female Anti-Slavery Society, which disbanded seven years later over the issue of politics, but in many antislavery organizations women were as active and politically involved as men. Lydia Maria Child, Maria Chapman, and Lucretia Mott served on the American Anti-Slavery Society's executive committee; Child edited its official paper, the *National Anti-Slavery Standard*, from 1841 to 1843, and Chapman coedited it from 1844 until 1848. Garrison's moral suasion attracted many women because it gave them a platform from which to oppose slavery. Yet some politically active societies excluded women because they could not vote.

Women Abolitionists

Opposition to women's prominent roles in reform movements led some women to reexamine their position in society at large. In the 1830s Angelina and Sarah Grimké challenged slavery and women's right to speak out. Born into a slaveholding family in Charleston, South Carolina, both sisters experienced conversion and independently became Quakers. When in 1834 they became activists, especially in abolitionism, they found in Garrison's immediatism a home. Yet they were soon attacked for speaking before mixed groups of men and women. Some New England Congregationalists, and even some abolitionists, joined in the criticism; one pastoral letter stated that women should obey, not lecture, men. This reaction turned the Grimkés' attention from slavery to women's condition. They attacked the concept of "subordination to man," insisting that men and women had the "same rights and same duties." Sarah Grimké's *Letters on the Equality of the Sexes and the Condition of Women* (1838) and her sister's *Letters to Catharine E. Beecher*, published the same year, were the opening volleys in the long war over the legal and social inequality of women.

It was only a matter of time before women involved with abolitionism crossed the path from pious and moral opposition against slavery

Women's Rights to political engagement on behalf of women's rights. Eight years after their humiliation in London, Elizabeth Cady Stanton and Lucretia Mott, with Lucy Stone, organized the convention they had resolved to hold. In July 1848 three hundred women and men reformers gathered at the Woman's Rights Convention at Seneca Falls, New York, to demand political, social, and economic equality for women. They protested women's legal disabilities—inability to vote, limited property rights—and their social restrictions—exclusion from advanced schooling and from most occupations. Their Declaration of Sentiments, modeled after the Declaration of Independence, indicted the injustices suffered by women and launched the women's rights movement. "All men and women are created equal," the declaration proclaimed. If women had the vote, participants argued, they could protect themselves and realize their full potential as moral and spiritual leaders. What is important is that the women lobbying for suffrage created new public, political roles for women.

Advocates of women's rights were slow to garner support, especially from men, who held most of the political and legal power. In the 1840s the question of women's rights split the antislavery movement. Some men joined the ranks, notably Garrison and Frederick Douglass, but most men actively opposed the movement. Not everyone at Seneca Falls signed the resolution on women's suffrage. Of the one hundred who did, only two would live to see the passage of the Nineteenth Amendment to the Constitution seventy-two years later.

Jacksonianism and Party Politics

In the 1820s, reform pushed its way into politics. No less than reformers, politicians sought to control the direction of change in the expanding nation. The 1824 presidential election ignited a political barn fire that reformers, abolitionists, and expansionists would continuously stoke. By the 1830s, politics had become the great nineteenth-century American pastime.

The election of 1824, in which John Quincy Adams and Andrew Jackson faced off for the first time,

Elizabeth Cady Stanton posed in 1848 with two of her sons, Henry Jr., left, and Neil. Stanton, one of the organizers of the Seneca Falls Woman's Rights Convention, traveled widely and agitated for women's equality while raising five children. (Collection of Rhoda Jenkins)

End of the Caucus System heralded a more open political system. From 1800 through 1820 the system in which a congressional caucus (House and Senate members of the political party) chose Jefferson, Madison, and Monroe as the Democratic-Republican nominees had worked well. That it limited voters' involvement in choosing candidates was not an anomaly because in 1800 only five of the sixteen states selected presidential electors by popular vote. In most of the others, state legislatures selected the electors who voted for president. By 1824, however, eighteen out of twenty-four states chose electors by popular vote.

The Democratic-Republican caucus in 1824 chose William H. Crawford of Georgia, secretary of the treasury, as its presidential candidate. But other Democratic-Republicans, emboldened by the chance to appeal directly to voters, put themselves forward as sectional candidates. John Quincy Adams drew support from New England, while westerners backed

Presidential candidate Andrew Jackson is portrayed on a trinket or sewing box in 1824. This is an example of how campaigns entered popular culture and also illustrates the active role of women, excluded from voting, in politics. (Collection of David J. and Janice L. Frent)

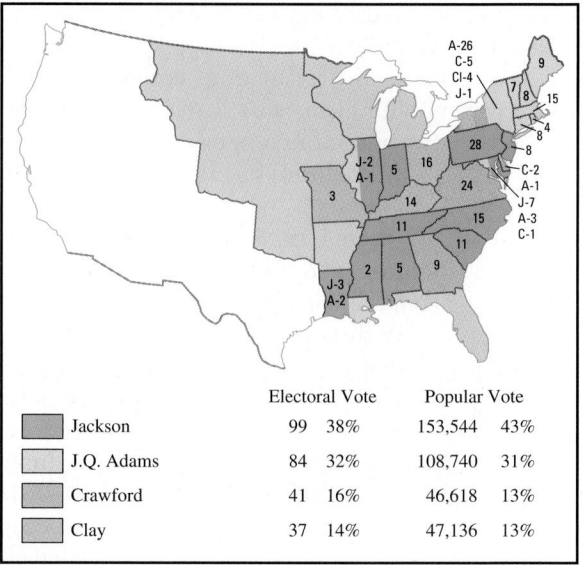

		Electoral Vote		Popular Vote	
	Jackson	99	38%	153,544	43%
	J.Q. Adams	84	32%	108,740	31%
	Crawford	41	16%	46,618	13%
	Clay	37	14%	47,136	13%

Map 11.1 Presidential Election, 1824 Andrew Jackson led in both electoral and popular votes but failed to win a majority of electoral college votes. The House elected John Quincy Adams president.

House Speaker Henry Clay of Kentucky. Secretary of War John C. Calhoun looked to the South for support and hoped to win Pennsylvania as well. The Tennessee legislature nominated Andrew Jackson, a popular military hero whose political views were unknown. Jackson had the most widespread support, but Crawford led in the party caucus. By boycotting the caucus and by attacking it as undemocratic, the four other candidates and their supporters ended the role of Congress in nominating presidential candidates.

Election of 1824 In the four-way presidential election of 1824, Andrew Jackson led in both electoral and popular votes, but no candidate received a majority in the electoral college (see Map 11.1). Adams finished second, and Crawford and Clay trailed far behind (Calhoun had dropped out of the race before the election). As required by the Constitution, the House of Representatives, voting by state delegation, one vote to a state, selected the next president from among the leaders in electoral votes. Clay, who had received the fewest votes, was dropped. Crawford, who had a stroke after the election, never received serious consideration. The influential Clay—Speaker of the House and leader of the Ohio valley states—backed Adams, who received the votes of thirteen of the twenty-four state delegations to win. Clay then became Adams's secretary of state, the traditional steppingstone to the presidency.

Angry Jacksonians denounced the outcome of the election as a "corrupt bargain" that had stolen the office. Jackson's bitterness reinforced his opposition to elitism and fueled his later emphasis on the people's will. The Democratic-Republican Party split. The Adams wing emerged as the National Republicans, and the Jacksonians became the Democrats; they immediately began planning a reversal for 1828.

After taking the oath of office, Adams proposed a strong nationalist policy incorporating Henry Clay's "American System," a program of protective tariffs, a national bank, and internal improvements. Adams believed the federal government should take an activist role not only in the economy but also in education, science, and the arts. He proposed establishing a national university in Washington, D.C. Brilliant as a diplomat and secretary of state, Adams was an inept president. The political skills he had demonstrated in winning the office eluded him as chief executive. He underestimated the lingering effects of the Panic of 1819 and the resulting staunch opposition to a national bank and protective tariffs. Meanwhile, supporters of Andrew Jackson sabotaged Adams's administration at every opportunity.

The 1828 election pitted Adams against Jackson in a rowdy campaign. Voters displayed their enthusiasm

Election of 1828

for Jackson with badges, medals, and other campaign paraphernalia, which were mass-produced for the first time. The contest was also intensely personal. Mudslinging was the order of the day. Jackson's supporters accused Adams of stealing the 1824 election and, when he was envoy to Russia, of having secured prostitutes for the czar. Anti-Jacksonians published reports that Rachel Jackson had had an affair with Jackson and married the young officer before her first husband divorced her in 1793; she was, they sneered, an adulterer and a bigamist. In 1806 Jackson had killed John Dickinson in a Kentucky duel defending Rachel's integrity, and the cry of murderer was revived in the election. After the election Rachel Jackson discovered a pamphlet defending her, and she was mortified by the extent of the charges. In December 1828 she died of a heart attack. Jackson never forgave her "murderers."

Although Adams kept the states he won in 1824, the opposition was unified, and Jackson swamped him (see Map 11.2). Jackson polled 56 percent of the popular vote and won in the electoral college by 178 to 83 votes. He and his supporters believed that the will of the people had finally been served. Through a lavishly financed coalition of state parties, political leaders, and newspaper editors, a popular movement had elected the president, and an era had ended. The Democratic Party became the first well-organized national political party in the United States, and tight party organization became the hallmark of nineteenth-century American politics.

Nicknamed "Old Hickory" after the toughest of American hardwoods, Andrew Jackson was a rough-and-tumble, ambitious man. Born in

Andrew Jackson

South Carolina in 1767, he rose from humble beginnings to become a wealthy Tennessee planter and slave-holder. Jackson was the first American president from the West and the first born in a log cabin; he was at ease among both frontiersmen and southern planters. Though vindictive and given to violent displays of temper, he could charm opposition into assent. A natural leader, Jackson inspired immense loyalty. He had an instinct for politics and picked both issues and supporters shrewdly.

Few Americans have been as celebrated as Jackson. Having served in the Revolution as a boy, he claimed a connection to the founding generation. In the Tennessee militia General Jackson led the campaign to remove Creeks from the Alabama and Geor-

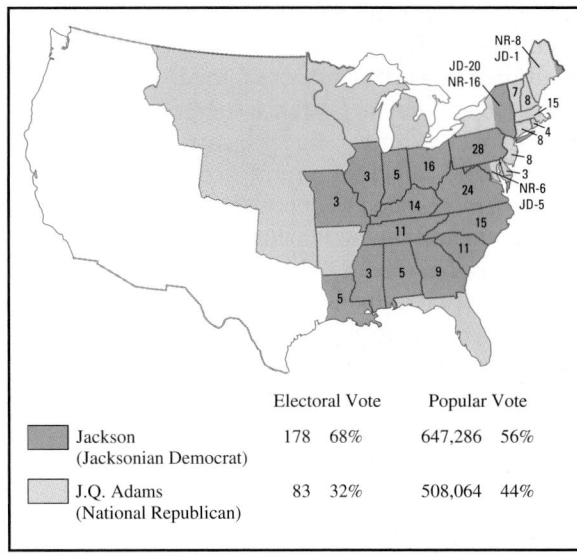

		Electoral Vote		Popular Vote	
■	Jackson (Jacksonian Democrat)	178	68%	647,286	56%
☐	J.Q. Adams (National Republican)	83	32%	508,064	44%

Map 11.2   Presidential Election, 1828   Andrew Jackson avenged his 1824 loss of the presidency, sweeping the election in 1828.

gia frontier (see page 238). He burst onto the national scene in 1815 as the great hero of the Battle of New Orleans, and in 1818 enhanced his glory in an expedition against Seminoles in Spanish Florida. Jackson also served as a congressman and senator from Tennessee, and as the first territorial governor of Florida (1821), before running for president in 1824.

Jackson and his supporters offered an alternative to the strong federal government advocated by John Quincy Adams. The Democrats represented a wide range of views but shared a fundamental commitment to the Jeffersonian concept of an agrarian society. They distrusted a powerful central government as the enemy of individual liberty. The 1824 "corrupt bargain" had strengthened their suspicion of Washington politics. Jackson himself, a backwoodsman and farmer, symbolized simpler times.

Democrats

Jacksonians feared the concentration of economic and political power. They believed that government intervention in the economy benefited special-interest groups and created corporate monopolies, which favored the rich. They sought to restore the independence of the individual—the artisan and the yeoman farmer—by ending federal support of banks and corporations and restricting the use of paper currency, which they distrusted. Their definition of the proper role of government tended to be negative, and Jackson's political power was largely expressed in negative acts. He exercised the veto more than all previous presidents combined.

Jackson and his supporters also opposed reform as a movement. Reformers eager to turn their programs into legislation called for a more activist government. But Democrats tended to oppose programs like educational reform and the establishment of a public education system. They believed, for instance, that public schools restricted individual liberty by interfering with parental responsibility and undermined freedom of religion by replacing church schools. Nor did Jackson share reformers' humanitarian concerns. He showed little sympathy for Native Americans, initiating the removal of the Cherokees along the Trail of Tears (see page 273).

Jacksonians considered themselves reformers in a different way. By restraining government and emphasizing individualism, they sought to restore traditional republican virtues, such as prudence and economy. No less zealous than reformers, Jackson sought to encourage self-discipline and self-reliance and to restore the harmony that he saw disrupted by economic and social change. In doing so, Jackson looked to Jefferson and the generation of the founders as models of traditional values. "My political creed," Jackson wrote to Tennessee congressman James K. Polk in 1826, "was formed in the old republican school."

Jacksonians as Reformers

Like Jefferson, Jackson strengthened the executive branch of government even as he weakened the federal role. Given his popularity and the strength of his personality, this concentration of power in the presidency was perhaps inevitable, but in combining the roles of party leader and chief of state, he centralized power in the White House. Jackson relied on political friends, his "Kitchen Cabinet," for advice; he rarely consulted his official cabinet. Enamored of power, Jackson never hesitated to confront his opponents with all the weapons at his disposal. He commanded enormous loyalty, and he rewarded his followers handsomely. Rotating officeholders, Jackson claimed, made government more responsive to the public will, but it allowed him to introduce a spoils system to appoint loyal Democrats to office. He removed fewer than one-quarter of the federal officeholders he inherited, but he used patronage to strengthen party organization and loyalty.

Jackson stressed rejection of elitism and special favors, rotation of officeholders, and belief in popular government. Time and again he declared that sovereignty resided with the people, not with the states or the courts. In this respect Jackson was a reformer; he returned government to majority rule. Yet it is hard to distinguish between Jackson's belief in himself as the instrument of the people and simple egotism and demagogic arrogance. After all, his opponents, too, claimed to represent the people.

Animosity grew year by year among President Jackson's supporters and opponents. Massachusetts senator Daniel Webster feared the men around the president; Henry Clay most feared Jackson himself. Rotation in office, they contended, corrupted government. Opponents mocked Jackson as "King Andrew I," charging him with abuse of power by ignoring the Supreme Court's ruling on Cherokee rights (see page 272), by using the spoils system, and by consulting his Kitchen Cabinet. Critics rejected his claim of restoring republican virtue and accused him of recklessly destroying the economy.

Amid all the agitation, Jackson pursued his agenda. He invigorated the philosophy of limited government. In 1830 he vetoed the Maysville Road bill—which would have funded construction of a 60-mile turnpike from Maysville to Lexington, Kentucky. A federally subsidized internal improvement confined to one state was unconstitutional, he charged; such projects were properly a state responsibility. The veto undermined Henry Clay's nationalist program and personally embarrassed Clay because the project was in his home district. Such federal-state issues were to loom even larger in the nullification crisis.

Federalism at Issue: The Nullification and Bank Controversies

Soon Jackson had to face directly the question of the proper division of sovereignty between state and central governments. The slave South feared federal power, no state more so than South Carolina, where the planter class was strongest and slavery most concentrated. Southerners also resented protectionist tariffs.

To protect manufactures, Congress in 1828 imposed high import duties on manufactured cloth and iron. But in protecting northern factories, the tariff raised the costs of these goods to southerners, who quickly labeled it the Tariff of Abominations.

Tariff of Abominations

To articulate their interests, South Carolina's political leaders turned to the doctrine of nullification, according to which a state had the right to overrule, or nullify, federal legislation. Nullification was based on the idea expressed in the Virginia and Kentucky resolutions of 1798 (see page 210)—that the states, representing the people, have a right to judge the constitutionality of federal actions. Jackson's vice president, John C. Calhoun of South Carolina, argued in his unsigned *Exposition and Protest* that, in any disagreement between the federal government and a state, a special state convention—like the conventions called to ratify the Constitution—should decide the conflict by either nullifying or affirming the federal law. Only the power of nullification, Calhoun asserted, could protect the minority against the tyranny of the majority.

In public, Calhoun let others take the lead in advancing nullification. As Jackson's running mate in 1828, he had avoided endorsing nullification and thus embarrassing the Democratic ticket; he also hoped to win Jackson's support as the Democratic presidential heir apparent. Thus in early 1830 Calhoun presided silently over the Senate and its packed galleries when Senator Daniel Webster of Massachusetts and Senator Robert Y. Hayne of South Carolina debated states' rights. The debate started over a resolution to restrict western land sales and engaged the tariff issue by exploring sectional differences. It quickly turned to the nature of the Union, with nullification a subtext. With Vice President Calhoun nodding in agreement, Hayne charged that the North was threatening to bring disunity, as it had done fifteen years earlier at the Hartford Convention (see page 240). Hayne accused reformers of wanting in "the spirit of false philanthropy" to destroy the South.

For two days Webster eloquently defended New England and the republic, as he kept nullification on the defense. Though debating Hayne, he aimed his remarks at Calhoun. At the climax of the debate, Webster invoked two powerful images. One was the outcome of nullification: "states dissevered, discordant, belligerent; on a land rent with civil feuds, or drenched . . . in fraternal blood!" The other was a patriotic vision of a great nation flourishing under the motto "Liberty and Union, now and forever, one and inseparable."

Though sympathetic to states' rights and distrustful of the federal government, Jackson rejected the idea of state sovereignty. He strongly believed that sovereignty rested with the people. Deeply loyal to the Union, he shared Webster's dread of nullification. Soon after the Webster-Hayne debate, the president made his position clear at a Jefferson Day dinner with the toast "Our Federal Union, it must and shall be preserved." Vice President Calhoun, when his turn came, toasted "The Federal Union—next to our liberty the most dear." Thus Calhoun revealed his adherence to states' rights. Calhoun and Jackson grew apart, and Jackson looked to Secretary of State Martin Van Buren, not Calhoun, as his successor.

Webster-Hayne Debate

Nullification Crisis

Tensions did not subside when Congress passed a new tariff in 1832 reducing some duties but retaining high taxes on imported iron, cottons, and woolens. Though a majority of southern representatives supported the new tariff, South Carolinians refused to go along. In their eyes, the constitutional right to control their own destiny had been sacrificed to the demands of northern industrialists. More than the duties, they feared that the act could set a precedent for congressional legislation on slavery. In November 1832 a South Carolina state convention nullified both tariffs, making it unlawful for federal officials to collect duties in the state.

Old Hickory was quick to respond. Privately he threatened to invade South Carolina and hang Vice President Calhoun; publicly he took measured steps. In December Jackson issued a proclamation opposing nullification. He moved troops to federal forts in South Carolina and prepared U.S. marshals to collect the required duties. At Jackson's request, Congress passed the Force Act, which gave the president authority to call up troops but also offered a way to avoid using force by collecting duties before foreign ships reached Charleston's harbor. At the same time, Jackson extended an olive branch by recommending tariff reductions.

Calhoun, disturbed by South Carolina's drift toward separatism, resigned as vice president and soon won election to represent South Carolina in the U.S. Senate. There he worked with Henry Clay to draw up the compromise Tariff of 1833. Quickly passed by Congress and signed by the president, the new tariff lengthened the list of duty-free items and reduced duties over nine years. Satisfied, South Carolina's convention repealed its nullification law. In a final salvo, it also nullified Jackson's Force Act. Jackson ignored the gesture.

Nullification offered a genuine debate on the nature and principles of the republic. Each side believed it was upholding the Constitution. Both sides felt they were opposing special privilege and subversion of republican values. South Carolina opposed the tyranny of the federal government and manufacturers who sought tariff protection. Jackson fought the tyranny of South Carolina, whose refusal to bow to federal authority threatened to split the republic. Neither side won a clear victory, though both claimed to have done so. It took another crisis, over a central bank, to define the powers of the federal government more clearly.

At stake was survival of the Second Bank of the United States, whose twenty-year charter was scheduled to expire in 1836. Like its predecessor, the bank served as a depository for federal funds and was an important source of credit for businesses. Its bank notes circulated as currency throughout the country; they could be readily exchanged for gold, and the federal government accepted them as payment in all transactions. Through its twenty-five branch offices, the Second Bank acted as a clearing-house for state banks, keeping them honest by refusing to accept bank notes of any state bank without sufficient gold in reserve. Most state banks resented the central bank's police role: by presenting a state bank's notes for redemption all at once, the Second Bank could easily ruin a state bank. Moreover, with less money in reserve, state banks found themselves unable to compete on an equal footing with the Second Bank.

Second Bank of the United States

Many state governments also regarded the national bank as unresponsive to local needs. Westerners and urban workers remembered with bitterness the bank's conservative credit policies during the Panic of 1819 (see page 249). As a private, profit-making institution, its policies reflected the interest of its owners, especially its president, Nicholas Biddle, who controlled the bank completely. An eastern patrician, Biddle symbolized all that westerners found wrong with the bank.

Rechartering was a volatile issue in the 1832 presidential campaign. The bank's charter was valid until 1836, but Henry Clay, the National Republican presidential candidate, persuaded Biddle to ask Congress to approve an early rechartering. This strategy was designed to pressure Jackson to sign the rechartering bill or to override his veto of it. The plan backfired, however. The president vetoed the bill, and the Senate failed to override. Jackson's veto message was an emotional attack on the undemocratic nature of the bank. "It is to be regretted," he wrote, "that the rich and powerful too often bend the acts of government to their selfish purposes."

The bank thus became the prime issue in the presidential campaign of 1832, with Jackson denouncing special privilege and economic power. With every state but South Carolina now choosing electors by popular vote, the Jacksonians used their party organization to mobilize voters by advertising the presidential election as the focal point of the political system. When the Antimasons adopted a party platform, the first in the nation's history, the Democrats and the National Republicans quickly followed suit. The Democratic convention nominated Jackson and Martin Van Buren, Jackson's first secretary of state and then American minister to Great Britain; the National Republican convention selected Clay and John Sergeant. South Carolina nominated its own candidate, John Floyd. Jackson was reelected easily in a Democratic Party triumph.

After his sweeping victory and second inauguration, Jackson moved in 1833 to dismantle the Second Bank of the United States. He deposited federal funds in state-chartered banks (critics called them his "pet banks"). Without federal money, the Second Bank shriveled. When its federal charter expired in 1836, it became just another Pennsylvania-chartered private bank. Five years later it closed its doors.

Jackson's Second Term

In conjunction with the demise of the Bank of the United States, Congress passed the Deposit Act of 1836 with Jackson's support. The act authorized the secretary of the treasury to designate one bank in each state and territory to provide the services formerly performed by the Bank of the United States. The act provided that the federal surplus in excess of $5 million be distributed to the states as interest-free loans beginning in 1837. These loans were never repaid—a fitting Jacksonian restraint on the federal purse.

The surplus had derived from wholesale speculation in public lands: speculators borrowed money to purchase public land, used the land as collateral for credit to buy additional acreage, and repeated the cycle. Between 1834 and 1836 federal receipts from land sales rose from $5 million to $25 million. The state banks providing the loans issued bank notes. Jackson, an opponent of paper money, feared that the speculative craze threatened the stability of state banks and undermined the interests of settlers, who could not compete with speculators in bidding for the best land.

Specie Circular

In keeping with his hard-money instincts and opposition to paper currency, the president ordered Treasury Secretary Levi Woodbury to issue the Specie Circular. It provided that after August 1836 only

An 1832 anti-Jackson cartoon depicts Andrew Jackson and three rivals playing a game of brag, a bluffing card game. The stakes: the 1832 election. Henry Clay, on the left, reveals what the cartoonist presents as the winning hand: the cards for "U.S. Bank," "Internal Improvements," and "Domestic Manufactures." In the foreground, John C. Calhoun folds his hand of "Nullification" and "Anti-Tariff," which cannot match Clay's. Former Attorney General William Wirt "bolts" with his "Anti-Masonic" card, a loser. A decrepit Jackson has the weakest cards: "Intrigue," "Corruption," and "Imbecility," which have no value once his bluff is called. In the election, however, Jackson followed through in bragging of strength; he easily won reelection.   (Library Company of Philadelphia)

specie—gold or silver—or Virginia scrip (paper money) would be accepted as payment for land. By ending credit sales, it significantly reduced purchases of public land and the federal budget surplus. As a result the government suspended payments to the states soon after they began.

The policy was a disaster. Although federal land sales were sharply reduced, speculation continued as available land for sale became scarce. The increased demand for specie squeezed banks, and many suspended the redemption of bank notes for specie. Credit contracted further as banks issued fewer notes and made fewer loans. Jackson aggravated the situation by instinctively pursuing a tight money policy. More important, the Specie Circular was similar to a bill defeated in the Senate just three months earlier. Jackson's opponents thus saw King Andrew at work. In the waning days of Jackson's administration, Congress voted to repeal the circular, but the president pocket-vetoed the bill by holding it unsigned until Congress adjourned. Finally in mid-1838, a joint resolution of Congress overturned the circular. Restrictions on land sales ended, but the speculative fervor was over.

From George Washington to John Quincy Adams, the first six presidents had vetoed nine bills; Jackson alone vetoed twelve. Previous presidents believed that vetoes were justified only on constitutional grounds, but Jackson considered policy disagreement legitimate grounds as well. He made the veto an effective weapon for controlling Congress, since representatives and senators had to consider the possibility of a presidential veto in their deliberations on any bill. In effect, Jackson made the executive for the first time a rival branch of government, equal in power to Congress.

Use of the Veto

The Whig Challenge and the Second Party System

 Most historians view the 1830s and 1840s as an age of reform and popularly based political parties. Only when the passions of reformers and abolitionists spilled over into politics did party differences become paramount and party loyalties solidify. For the first time in American history, grassroots political groups, organized from the bottom up, set the tone of political life. And both parties were national, drawing voters and winning counties in every region.

Opponents of the Democrats, including remnants of the National Republican Party, found shelter under a common umbrella, the Whig Party, in the 1830s. Resentful of Jackson's domination of Congress, the Whigs borrowed the name of the British party that had opposed the tyranny of Hanoverian monarchs in the eighteenth century. From 1834 through the 1840s, the Whigs and the Democrats competed on a nearly equal footing. They fought at the city, county, state, and national levels and achieved a stability previously unknown in American politics. The political competition of this period—known as the second party system—was more intense and well organized than that of the first party system of Democratic-Republicans versus Federalists.

Reform and the party system changed politics. As political participation broadened, the electoral process opened up. By the 1830s only a handful of states significantly restricted adult white male suffrage. Some even allowed immigrants who had taken out citizenship papers to vote. Hotly contested elections further stimulated public interest in politics. The net effect was a sharp increase in the number of votes cast in presidential elections. Between 1824 and 1828 that number increased threefold, from 360,000 to over 1.1 million. In 1840, 2.4 million men cast votes. The proportion of eligible voters who cast ballots also increased, from about 27 percent in 1824 to more than 80 percent in 1840.

Increasingly the parties diverged. Whigs favored economic expansion through an activist government, Democrats through limited central government. Whigs supported corporate charters, a national bank, and paper currency; Democrats were opposed to all three. Whigs also favored more humanitarian reforms than did Democrats, including public schools, abolition of capital

Whigs and Reformers

punishment, prison and asylum reform, and temperance. Whigs were more optimistic than Democrats, generally speaking, and more enterprising. They did not object to helping a specific group if doing so would promote the general welfare. The chartering of corporations, they argued, expanded economic opportunity for everyone, laborers and farmers alike. Democrats, distrustful of concentrated economic power and of moral and economic coercion, held fast to the Jeffersonian principle of limited government.

Religion and ethnicity, not economics and class, most influenced party affiliation. The Whigs' support for energetic government and humanitarian and moral reform won the favor of evangelical Protestants, especially those involved in religious revival. Methodists and Baptists were overwhelmingly Whigs, as were the small number of free black voters. Democrats, by contrast, tended to be foreign-born Catholics and nonevangelical Protestants, both of whom preferred to keep religion and politics separate.

The Whig Party was the vehicle of revivalist Protestantism. In many locales the membership rolls of reform societies overlapped those of the party. Indeed, Whigs practiced a kind of political revivalism. Their rallies resembled camp meetings; in their speeches they employed pulpit rhetoric; their programs embodied the perfectionist beliefs of reformers. This potent blend of religion and politics—"intimately united" in America, according to Tocqueville—greatly intensified political loyalties.

In their appeal to evangelicals, Whigs alienated members of other faiths. The evangelicals' ideal Christian state had no room for Catholics, Mormons, Unitarians, Universalists, or religious freethinkers. Those groups opposed Sabbath laws and temperance legislation in particular and state interference in moral and religious questions in general. As a result, more than 95 percent of Irish Catholics, 90 percent of Reformed Dutch, and 80 percent of German Catholics voted Democratic.

Vice President Martin Van Buren, handpicked by Jackson, headed the Democratic ticket in the 1836 presidential election. Van Buren was a shrewd politician who had built a political machine—the Albany Regency—in New York and then left to join Jackson's cabinet in 1829. Having helped found the Democratic Party, Van Buren was a professional politician; he made his career in party politics.

Election of 1836

Because the Whigs in 1836 had not yet coalesced into a national party, they entered three sectional candidates: Daniel Webster of New England, Hugh White of the South, and William Henry Harrison of the West. By splintering the vote, they hoped to throw the election into the House of Representatives. Van Buren, however, comfortably captured the electoral college even though he had only a 25,000-vote edge out of a total of 1.5 million votes cast. No vice-presidential candidate received a majority of electoral votes, and for the only time in American history the Senate decided a vice-presidential race, selecting Democratic candidate Richard M. Johnson of Kentucky.

Van Buren took office just weeks before the American credit system collapsed. In response to the impact of the Specie Circular, New York banks stopped redeeming paper currency with gold in mid-1837. Soon all banks suspended payments in hard coin. Thus began a downward economic spiral that curtailed bank loans and strangled business confidence. Credit contraction made things worse; after a brief recovery, hard times persisted from 1839 until 1843.

Van Buren and Hard Times

Ill advisedly, Van Buren followed Jackson's hard-money policies. He cut federal spending, which caused prices to drop further, and he opposed a national bank, which would have expanded credit. Even worse, the president proposed a new regional treasury system for government deposits. The proposed treasury branches would accept and pay out only gold and silver coin; they would not accept paper currency or checks drawn on state banks. Van Buren's independent treasury bill became law in 1840. By increasing the demand for hard coin, it deprived banks of gold and further accelerated price deflation. Whigs and Democrats faced off at the state level over these issues. Whigs favored new banks, more paper currency, and readily available corporate and bank charters. As the party of hard money, Democrats favored eliminating paper currency altogether. Increasingly the Democrats became distrustful even of state banks, and by the mid-1840s a majority favored eliminating all bank corporations.

With the nation in the grip of hard times, the Whigs prepared confidently for the election of 1840. Their strategy was simple: hold on to loyal supporters and win over independents by blaming hard times on the Democrats. The Whigs rallied behind a military hero, General William Henry Harrison, conqueror of the Shawnees at Tippecanoe

William Henry Harrison and the Election of 1840

Creek in 1811 (see page 238). The Democrats renominated President Van Buren at a somber convention.

Harrison, or "Old Tippecanoe," and his running mate, John Tyler of Virginia, ran a "log cabin and hard cider" campaign—a people's crusade—against the aristocratic president in "the Palace." Though descended from a Virginia plantation family, Harrison presented himself as an ordinary farmer. The Whigs wooed supporters and independents alike with huge rallies, parades, songs, posters, campaign mementos, and a party newspaper, *The Log Cabin*. Harrison took a position above the issues, earning himself the nickname "General Mum," but party hacks bluntly blamed the hard times on the Democrats. In a huge turnout, 80 percent of eligible voters cast ballots. Harrison won the popular vote by a narrow margin but swept the electoral college by 234 to 60.

Immediately after taking office in 1841, President Harrison convened a special session of Congress to pass the Whig program: repeal of the independent treasury system, a new national bank, and a higher protective tariff. But the sixty-eight-year-old Harrison caught pneumonia and died within a month of his inauguration. His successor, John Tyler, was a former Democrat who had left the party to protest Jackson's nullification proclamation.

In office, Tyler turned out to be more of a Democrat than a Whig. As critical of the Whigs' economic nationalism as he had been of Jackson's use of executive power, Tyler consistently opposed his own party's congressional agenda. He repeatedly vetoed Henry Clay's protective tariffs, internal improvements, and bills aimed at reviving the Bank of the United States. The only important measures that became law during his term were repeal of the independent treasury system and passage of a higher tariff. Two days after Tyler's second veto of a bank bill, the entire cabinet except Secretary of State Daniel Webster resigned; Webster, busy negotiating a new treaty with Great Britain, left shortly thereafter. Tyler became a president without a party, and the Whigs lost the presidency without losing an election. Disgusted Whigs referred to Tyler as "His Accidency."

Hard times in the late 1830s and early 1840s deflected attention from a renewal of Anglo-American tensions that had multiple sources: northern commercial rivalry with Britain, the default of state governments and corporations on British-held debts during the Panic of 1837, rebellion in Canada, boundary disputes, southern

Anglo-American Tensions

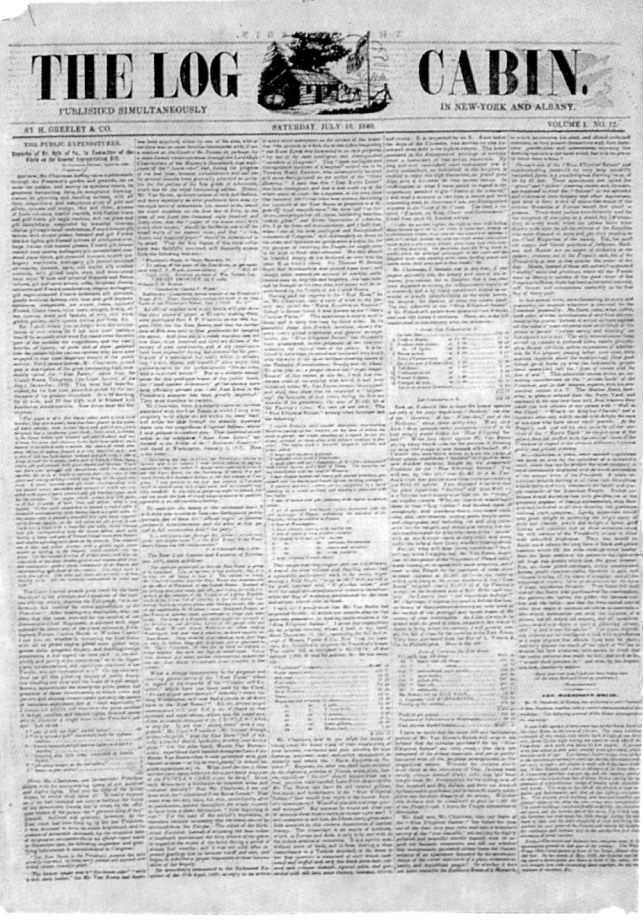

Using techniques that look familiar to politicians today, General William Henry Harrison in 1840 ran a "log cabin and hard cider" campaign against Jackson's heir, President Martin Van Buren. The campaign handkerchief shows Harrison welcoming two of his comrades to his log cabin, with a barrel of cider outside. *The Log Cabin,* a newspaper edited by Horace Greeley, was the voice of the Harrison campaign, and it reached eighty thousand partisans. (Handkerchief: © Collection of The New-York Historical Society; Newspaper: Division of Political History, Smithsonian Institution, Washington, D.C.)

alarm over West Indian emancipation, and American expansionism.

One of the most troublesome disputes arose from the *Caroline* affair. A U.S. citizen, Amos Durfee, had been killed when Canadian militia set afire the privately owned steamer *Caroline* in the Niagara River. (The *Caroline* had supported an unsuccessful uprising against Great Britain in 1837.) Britain refused to apologize, and American newspapers called for revenge. Fearing that popular support for the Canadian rebels would ignite war, President Van Buren posted troops at the border to discourage raids. Tensions subsided in late 1840 when Alexander McLeod, a Canadian deputy sheriff, was arrested in New York for the murder of Durfee. McLeod eventually was acquitted. Had he been found guilty and executed, Lord Palmerston, the British foreign minister, might have sought war.

At almost the same time an old border dispute between Maine and New Brunswick disrupted Anglo-American relations. Great Britain had accepted an 1831 arbitration decision fixing a new boundary, but the U.S. Senate rejected it. Thus when Canadian lumbermen cut trees in the disputed region in the winter of 1838–1839, the citizens of Maine attempted to expel them. The lumbermen captured the Maine land agent and posse, both sides mobilized their militias, and Congress authorized a call-up of fifty thousand men. Ultimately, no blood was spilled. General Winfield Scott, who had patrolled the border during the *Caroline* affair, was dispatched to Aroostook, Maine, where he arranged a truce. The two sides compromised on their conflicting land claims in the Webster-Ashburton Treaty (1842).

These border disputes with Great Britain prefigured the conflicts that were to erupt in the 1840s over the expansion of the United States. With Tyler's succession to power in 1841 and James K. Polk's Democratic victory in the presidential election of 1844, federal activism in the domestic sphere ended for the rest of the decade, as attention turned to territorial expansion. Reform, however, was not dead. Its passions would resurface before the decade was over in the debate about slavery in the territories.

Manifest Destiny and Expansionism

 The belief that American expansion westward and southward was inevitable, just, and divinely ordained was first labeled manifest destiny by John L. O'Sullivan, editor of the *United States Magazine and Domestic Review*. The annexation of Texas, O'Sullivan wrote in 1845, was "the fulfillment of our manifest destiny to overspread the continent allotted by Providence for the free development of our yearly multiplying millions." Armed with such sentiments, expansionism reached a new fervor in the 1840s.

Since colonial days Americans had hungered for more land. Acquisition of the Louisiana Territory (1803) and Florida (1819) had set the process in motion (see Map 9.1 on page 223). As the proportion of Americans living west of the Appalachians grew from one-quarter to one-half between 1830 and 1860, both national parties joined the popular clamor for expansion. Agrarian Democrats sought western land to balance urbanization. Enterprising Whigs looked to the new commercial opportunities the West offered. Southerners envisioned the extension of slavery and more slave states.

Fierce national pride spurred the quest for land. Subdued during hard times, it reasserted itself after 1843 when the economy recovered. Americans were convinced that theirs was the greatest country on earth, with a special role to play in the world. As reform sought to perfect American society, so too expansionism promised to extend the benefits of America's republican system of government to the unfortunate and the inferior.

In part, racism contributed to manifest destiny as well. The impulse to colonize and develop the West was based on the belief that Euro-Americans could use the land more productively than Native Americans or Hispanics. Euro-Americans viewed Native Americans and Hispanics as inferior peoples, best controlled or conquered. Thus the same racial attitudes that justified discrimination against black people and slavery supported expansion in the West.

The desire to secure the nation from perceived external threats also fed expansionist fever. The internal enemies of the 1830s—banks, corporations, paper cur-

rency, alcohol—seemed pale in comparison to the opportunities Americans saw along their borders in the 1840s. Expansion, some believed, was necessary to preserve American independence.

Among the long-standing objectives of expansionists was Texas, which in addition to present-day Texas included parts of Oklahoma, Kansas, Colorado, Wyoming, and New Mexico (see Map 11.3). After winning its independence from Spain in 1821, Mexico encouraged the development of its remote northern province, offering large tracts of land virtually free to U.S. settlers called *empresarios*. The settlers in turn agreed to become Mexican citizens, adopt the Catholic religion, and bring hundreds of American families into the area. Moses and Stephen Austin, who had helped to formulate the policy, responded eagerly.

Republic of Texas

By 1835 thirty-five thousand Americans, including many slaveholders, lived in Texas. As the new settlers' numbers and power grew, they tended to ignore their commitments to the Mexican government. In response, the dictatorship of General Antonio López de Santa Anna tightened control over the region. In turn,

Texans believed that their war for independence paralleled the Revolutionary War. The lady of liberty on this banner, carried by Texans in 1836, brings to mind similar images that stirred patriots during the American Revolution. (Archives Division, Texas State Library)

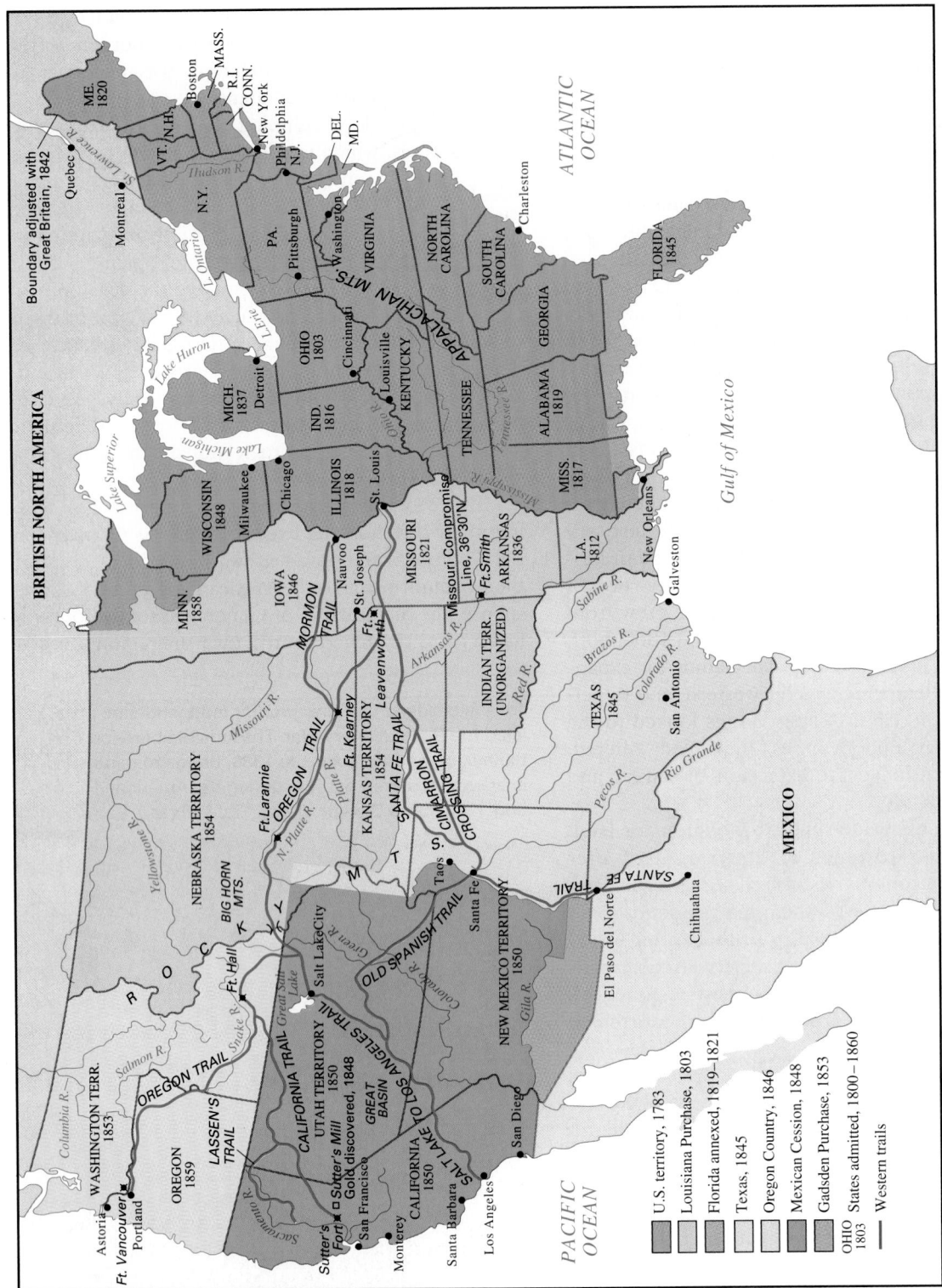

Map 11.3 Westward Expansion, 1800–1860 Through exploration, purchase, war, and treaty, the United States became a continental nation, stretching from the Atlantic to the Pacific.

the Anglo immigrants and *Tejanos*—Mexicans living in Texas—rebelled. At the Alamo mission in San Antonio in 1836, fewer than two hundred Texans made a heroic but unsuccessful stand against three thousand Mexicans under General Santa Anna. "Remember the Alamo" became the Texans' rallying cry. By the end of the year the Texans had won independence, delighting most Americans. Some saw the victory as a triumph of Protestants over Catholic Mexico; others cheered that proslavery Texans had defeated antislavery Mexicans.

Texas established the independent Lone Star Republic but soon sought annexation to the United States. Sam Houston, president of the Texas republic, opened negotiations with Washington, but the issue quickly became politically explosive. Southerners favored annexing proslavery Texas; abolitionists, many northerners, and most Whigs opposed annexation. In recognition of the political dangers, President Jackson reneged on his promise to recognize Texas, and President Van Buren ignored annexation. Rebuffed by the United States, Texans talked about closer ties with the British and extending their republic to the Pacific coast. With Britain controlling Canada, the prospect of a rival republic to the south caused some Americans to fear encirclement. If Texas reached the ocean and became an English ally, would not American independence be threatened?

President Tyler, committed to expansion, pushed for annexation. Eager to gain the 1844 Democratic nomination, Tyler hoped his position would build a political base in the South. Southerners also pressed for annexation; they lobbied former president Jackson, who responded that the United States must have Texas, "peacefully if we can, forcibly if we must." But the Senate rejected annexation in 1844. A letter from Secretary of State Calhoun to the British minister, justifying annexation to protect slavery, so outraged senators that the treaty was defeated 16 to 35.

Just as southerners sought expansion to the Southwest, so northerners looked to the Northwest. "Oregon fever" struck thousands in 1841. Lured by the glowing reports of missionaries who seemed as enthusiastic about the Northwest's riches and beauty as about conversion of Indians, migrants in wagon trains took to the Oregon Trail. Their enthusiasm was tempered by apprehension. Lavinia Porter feared that her husband did not have "the training to make a living on the plains of the West or the crossing of the continent in an ox team a successful venture." The 2,000-mile journey took six months or more, but

Oregon Fever

within a few years five thousand settlers had arrived in the fertile Willamette valley south of the Columbia River.

Britain and the United States had jointly occupied the disputed Oregon Territory since the Convention of 1818 (see pages 246–247). Beginning with the administration of President John Quincy Adams, the United States had tried to fix the boundary at the 49th parallel, but Britain was determined to maintain access to Puget Sound and the Columbia River. Time only increased the American appetite. In 1843 a Cincinnati convention of expansionists demanded the entire Oregon Country for the United States, up to its northernmost border at latitude 54°40'. Soon "Fifty-four Forty or Fight" became the rallying cry of American expansionists.

Expansion into Oregon and rejection of the annexation of Texas, both favored by antislavery forces, worried southern leaders. Anxious about their diminishing ability to control the debate over slavery, they persuaded the 1844 Democratic convention to adopt a rule requiring the presidential nominee to receive two-thirds of the convention votes. In effect, the southern states acquired a veto, and they wielded it to block Van Buren as the nominee; most southerners objected to his opposition to slavery and Texas annexation. Instead, the party chose "Young Hickory," House Speaker James K. Polk, a hard-money Jacksonian, avid expansionist, and slaveholding cotton planter from Tennessee. The Whig leader Henry Clay, who opposed annexation, won his party's nomination handily. The Democratic platform called for occupation of the entire Oregon Territory and annexation of Texas. The Whigs, while favoring annexation, argued that the Democrats' belligerent nationalism would lead the nation into war with Great Britain or Mexico or both. Clay favored expansion through negotiation.

With a well-organized campaign, Polk and the Democrats won the election by 170 electoral votes to 105. (They won the popular vote by just 38,000 out of 2.7 million votes cast.) Polk won New York's 36 electoral votes by just 6,000 popular votes. Abolitionist James G. Birney, the Liberty Party candidate, had drawn almost 16,000 votes away from Clay, handing New York and the election to Polk. Abolitionist forces thus unwittingly brought about the choice of a slaveholder as president, but they viewed Polk as more moderate than Clay on slavery and thus the lesser of two evils.

James K. Polk and the Election of 1844

An unknown artist depicted, in rich detail, the election campaign of 1844. A team of Polk supporters offers a campaign handbill to the seated voter. Passions were so high and party organization was so extensive that door-to-door politicking became the norm. (Courtesy, Nathan Liverant & Son)

Interpreting Polk's victory as a mandate for annexation, President Tyler proposed in his final days in office that Texas be admitted by joint resolution of Congress. The usual method of annexation, by treaty negotiation, required a two-thirds vote in the Senate—which expansionists clearly did not have, since there were sufficient opponents to slavery who would vote against annexation. Joint resolution required only a simple majority in each house. The resolution passed the House by 120 to 98 and the Senate by 27 to 25. Three days before leaving office, Tyler signed the measure. Mexico, which had never recognized Texas independence, immediately broke relations with the United States. In October the citizens of Texas ratified annexation, and Texas joined the Union in December 1845.

Summary

Religion, reform, and expansionism shaped politics from 1824 through the 1840s. As the Second Great Awakening spread through villages and towns, the converts, especially women, organized to reform a rapidly changing society. Religion imbued men and women with zeal to right the wrongs of American society and the world. Reformers pursued perfectionism and republican virtue by battling with the evils of slavery, prostitution, and alcohol. As reformers, they sought to improve insane asylums and penitentiaries. In the process, women entered public arenas as advocates of reform. Two issues elicited particular intensity: the comet of Antimasonry and the smoldering fire of abolitionism. The passions that both aroused were so potent, and success so elusive, that Antimasons and abolitionists transformed their moral crusades into political movements. Women's rights and nationalism contributed to the brew, and the new mixture made politics far more important and critical than just voting at elections.

Reform remade politics and politics remade public discourse. So too did American nationalism and economic cycles. As did reformers, President Adams raised expectations about an expanded governmental role. The organized parties of the 1820s and the struggles between the National Republicans and the Democrats, then between the Democrats and the Whigs, stimulated even greater interest in campaigns and political issues. The Democrats, who rallied around Andrew Jackson, and Jackson's opponents, who found shelter under the Whig tent, competed almost equally for the loyalty of voters. Both parties built strong organizations that faced off in national and local elections. And both parties favored economic expansion. Their world-views, however, were fundamentally different. Whigs were more optimistic and favored greater centralized government initiative. Democrats harbored a deep-seated belief in limited government. The controversies over the Second Bank of the United States and nullification allowed Americans to debate the principles of the republic. Jackson, however, did not hesitate to use presidential authority, and his opponents called him King Andrew.

No less than reform and politics, American people and communities experienced dramatic change in this period. As the nation became larger and its inhabitants more diverse, its manifest destiny divided rather than united, for along with expanding territories went the issue of slavery.

LEGACY FOR A PEOPLE AND A NATION
The Bible Belt

Had an eighteenth-century visitor to North America asked for the Bible belt, she would have been directed to New England, whose colonies were all founded for religious purposes. Early southerners tended to be more secular than religious. By the 1830s, however, the South was the most churched region, and southerners were the most devout. The Second Great Awakening, beginning with the Cane Ridge revival in 1801, spread like wildfire through the South. By the 1830s more than half of whites and one-quarter of

black southerners had undergone a conversion experience, and religion and the South formed a common identity. Embracing the Bible as the revealed word of God, it became known as the Bible belt.

Religion helped define southern distinctiveness. Southern Protestant liturgy and cadences were as much African as European; thus southern and northern denominations grew apart. They formally separated in the 1840s when Southern Baptists and Methodists withdrew from the national organizations that had barred slaveowners from church offices. Presbyterians withdrew later. After the Civil War evangelical denominations remained divided in northern and southern organizations.

Southern religion maintained tradition and resisted modern ways. Protestantism dominated, making the South more religiously homogeneous than other regions. Mostly evangelical, southern religion emphasized conversion and a personal battle against sin. By the twentieth century, fundamentalism, which stressed a literal reading of the Bible, reinforced resistance to modernism. Yet southern Protestantism lost ground as a political force in opposing evolution and in alliances with nativist groups.

But evangelicalism rose again in the 1960s, especially after a Catholic—John F. Kennedy—won the Democratic nomination for president. Many evangelicals began to vote their religion, moving to the Republican Party, and in 1964 Republican Barry Goldwater won the Bible belt states, breaking up the solid Democratic block. His conservative rhetoric resonated with southerners concerned about desegregation and erosion of religious values. *Time* called 1976 the "Year of the Evangelical" when born-again Southern Baptist Jimmy Carter was elected president.

In the 1980s and 1990s the Bible belt became the base of mobilized evangelical political action led by the Moral Majority. Religious and cultural issues rallied southern evangelicals: defending the traditional family and advocating prayer in schools, and opposing abortion, the Equal Rights Amendment, and gay rights legislation. In their own eyes, fundamentalist evangelical Protestants were defending biblical principles.

Thus the revivals that began in Kentucky in 1801 have rippled in ever wider circles across the South for two centuries, shaping the distinctive southern blend of culture and politics.

For Further Reading, see page A-13 of the Appendix. For Web resources, go to http://college.hmco.com.

"I hope that things will get better," Anna Maria Klinger wrote from New York to her family in Württemberg, Germany, in March 1849. She felt "lonely and forlorn in a foreign land." Twenty-eight-year-old Anna Maria had crossed the Atlantic among strangers, but her religious faith kept her going. "The dear Lord is my shield and refuge," she wrote home.

Anna's passage to America had taken fifteen weeks, including seven docked in Plymouth, England, while the ship was fitted. Three other young women migrants to America proved unsuitable as traveling companions. They "started behaving so badly" with young men, Anna Maria wrote her parents, that "I got annoyed because I couldn't stand such loose behavior."

Her luck improved in New York. She quickly found work as a domestic servant with a German family at $4 a day. New York was so large, she reported in letters home, that she could not walk around it in one day. She was the first in her immediate family to come to America, though two cousins had preceded her years before. Soon after arriving in New York, she met her future husband, Franz Schano, a deserter from the Bavarian army. Over the next decade she and Schano brought five of her siblings to New York: Babett, Gottlieb, Katharina, Daniel, and finally in 1858 the youngest, Rosina.

Finding work could be difficult—Franz, a stone-cutter, was unemployed for a time—but teenagers like Babett and Katharina found jobs as servants. Babett, who came in 1852, adjusted quickly. She now called herself Barbara and adopted the New York custom of wearing a hat. "If I were to run into you," she wrote her parents, "none of you would recognize me with my hat on." With her earnings as a servant, first for an English family then for a French family, Barbara repaid her sister for her fare to America.

Within a year of Barbara's arrival, Franz wrote home that she had taken up with a young man whom "we could see from the start would not be to her advantage." They "tried everything to dissuade her, but to no use." She soon gave birth to a baby son, "for whom she has a father all right but no husband, and when we noticed that she was expecting, we urged him to marry her but then he said he had never promised to

In 1851 the *Cornelius Grinnell* brought Irish immigrants from Liverpool to New York. John A. Rolph's 1851 ink wash caught the families taking fresh air, a relief from the miserable conditions below deck. (© J. Welles Henderson Collection)

PEOPLE AND COMMUNITIES IN THE NORTH AND WEST 1830–1860

marry her and he wouldn't ever marry her." He provided a cash settlement of $80 to Barbara.

Anna Maria, assisted by Franz, guided the family, keeping them together by sheer force of will. But the siblings' lives diverged. In 1855 Anna Maria and Franz moved to Albany, where Franz opened his own business and they bought a house for $1,000. Barbara went west, leaving her son with Anna Maria and Franz. Settled in Indiana, married, and living in a log cabin on a 40-acre homestead, Barbara complained that rural Indiana was boring. In 1861 her son joined her. Widowed and remarried again, she raised seven "Christian children" on her Indiana farm.

In 1860 Franz Schano died of consumption. Thirteen months later Anna Maria married Adam Plantz, a Prussian-born blacksmith; he, too, died of consumption only five weeks after. Then brother Gottlieb assumed the role of head of the family. Gottlieb and Daniel settled in Albany near Anna Maria and rode the roller coaster of the economy, prospering in good times, unemployed in hard times. Gottlieb ran a saloon, lost it, then worked in a piano factory and later as a wood carver. Daniel worked as a teamster. Eventually, they lost touch with two of their sisters. After Katharina, a widow, married a prosperous New York grocer, they no longer heard from her. They also lost contact with Rosina, who had moved to Canada. Years later they heard she was living again in New York and had "a whole brood of children" with her tinsmith husband.

The Klingers represented both the old values of traditional culture and the new values of the market system. Anna Maria worked hard, saved money, and found success in Albany even though widowhood twice threatened her security. Barbara, an unwed mother, lived a hardscrabble life. She reestablished herself 700 miles from New York, eventually finding peace in a German American rural community. Ambitious Katharina spent most of her income on herself, saving very little; her siblings complained of her selfishness. Even after years in the United States, the Klinger siblings were only partially Americanized. They always lived in German neighborhoods, and they socialized almost exclusively with family and fellow immigrants from Württemberg. Despite jealousies and conflicts, they helped one another and regularly sent money to their parents.

The Klinger family's experiences were similar to those of many immigrants. From the 1830s through the 1850s, millions of Europeans arrived on America's shores. Immigration added to the rapidly growing population and transformed the nation's character.

Within large cities and in the countryside, whole districts became enclaves of ethnic and religious groups.

What it meant to be an American was obviously changing. The Revolution and early nation building diminished as sources of American identity. European immigrants, slaves, free people of color, Hispanics, and Native Americans had cultural traditions different from those of the American colonial past. Increasingly some white Americans came to see the differences as racial rather than cultural. Free people of color in the North established the institutions and communities that would be the basis of modern African American life, but they found themselves as the black "other," racial outsiders like Hispanics in the Southwest. Immigrants, too, experienced antipathy. White native-born Americans rioted against them. In a society growing ever more diverse and complex, conflict became common.

The market economy both energized and accentuated the differences among Americans. In the nation's cities, opulent mansions rose within sight of notorious slums, and both wealth and poverty reached extremes unknown in agrarian communities. As in the past, Americans sought community in their neighborhoods, not in the nation, but ethnic background, race, religion, and class divided Americans. Farm families attempted to maintain cohesive, rural villages, while utopians and groups like the Mormons sought to create self-governing communal havens.

The market economy altered family life too. With the growth of commerce and industry, the home began to lose its function as a workplace. Goods formerly made at home were now mass-manufactured in factories and bought in stores. Public schools took over much of the family's traditional role as prime educator. Leisure, too, became a commodity to be purchased by those who could afford it. Families shrank in size, and more people lived outside family units. In the North and West the market economy, urban growth, and immigration challenged economic and social conventions. ■

Country Life

Rural life changed significantly in the first half of the nineteenth century. Established rural communities lost population as families went west in search of more fertile and cheaper land. New communities in the West arose almost overnight, linked by the new transportation networks to the markets of the East. European immigrants and free people of color from the East and

IMPORTANT EVENTS

1827 *Freedom's Journal*, first African American newspaper, appears

1830 Smith founds Mormon Church
First National Negro Convention

1830s–50s Urban riots commonplace

1832 Rice debuts in New York minstrel show

1835 Arkansas passes first women's property law

1837 Emerson delivers "The American Scholar" address
Boston employs paid policemen

1837–48 Mann heads the Massachusetts Board of Education

1838 Mormons driven out of Missouri

1841–47 Brook Farm combines spirituality, work, and play in a utopian rural community

1842 Knickerbocker baseball club formed

1844 Nativist riots peak in Philadelphia
Smith brothers murdered in Illinois

1845 Irish potato blight begins
Narrative of the Life of Frederick Douglass appears

1846–47 Mormon trek to the Great Salt Lake

1847–57 Immigration at peak pre–Civil War levels

1848 Abortive revolution in German states
U.S. acquires Alta California in Treaty of Guadalupe Hidalgo
Gold discovered in California

1849 California gold rush transforms the West Coast

1852 Stowe's *Uncle Tom's Cabin* published

1854 Railroad reaches the Mississippi River
Large-scale Chinese immigration begins

1855 New York establishes Castle Garden as immigrant center

Upper South joined the population stream seeking farmland in the prairies. Religious fervor following from the Second Great Awakening inspired some to seek spiritual regeneration, rather than cash-crop profits, through the establishment of utopian communities.

In the 1850s, western settlement, technological improvements, competition, economic recovery, and a desire for national unity prompted development of regional and, eventually, national rail networks. By 1853 rail lines linked Chicago to eastern cities, and a year later track reached the Mississippi River. By 1860 rails stretched as far west as St. Joseph, Missouri, as railroad track tripled during the 1850s, reaching 30,600 miles in 1860.

Railroads

The farm village, with its churches, post office, general store, railroad or wagon depot, and tavern, remained the center of rural life and linked farmers with the world. Communal values still ruled. Families gathered on one another's farms to accomplish as a community what they could not manage individually. Barn-raisings regularly brought people together. A farm family with the help of an itinerant carpenter would prepare the walls.

Farm Communities

The neighbors would come by buggy to help the family raise walls into position and build a roof. Afterward everyone celebrated with a hearty communal feast and sang, danced, and played games. They might compete in foot races, wrestling, or marksmanship, and on occasion they raced horses. Similar gatherings took place at harvest time and on special occasions.

Farm men and women had active social lives. Men met frequently at general stores, weekly markets, and taverns, and hunted and fished together. Some women also attended market, especially those engaged in dairy farming. More typically they met at after-church dinners, prayer groups, sewing and corn-husking bees, and quilting parties. These were cherished opportunities to exchange experiences, thoughts, and spiritual support, and to swap letters, books, and news.

Irene Hardy, who grew up in rural Ohio in the 1840s, left a memoir of the gatherings she had attended as a girl. Fifty years later she recalled apple bees at which neighbors gathered to make apple butter or preserves. After the day's work, Hardy recalled, the elders gossiped while the youngsters joked and teased each other and flirted. "Then came supper, apple and pumpkin pies, cider, doughnuts, cakes, cold chicken and turkey," Hardy wrote,

Bees

The Lackawanna Valley (1855) by George Inness. Hired by the Lackawanna Railroad to paint a picture showing the company's new roundhouse at Scranton, in northeastern Pennsylvania, Inness combined landscape and locomotive technology into an organic whole. Industrialism, Inness seems to say, belonged to the American landscape; it would neither overpower nor obliterate the land. (Gift of Mrs. Huttleston Rogers, © Board of Trustees, National Gallery of Art, Washington, D.C.)

"after which games, 'Forfeits,' 'Building a Bridge,' 'Snatchability,' even 'Blind Man's Bluff' and 'Pussy Wants a Corner.'" Traditional country bees had their town counterparts. Fredrika Bremer, a Swedish visitor, described a sewing bee in Cambridge, Massachusetts, in 1849, at which neighborhood women made clothes for "a family who had lost all their clothing by fire." Yet town bees were not the all-day family affairs of the countryside, and when the Hardy family moved to the town of Eaton, Ohio, Irene missed the country gatherings. The families of Eaton seldom held bees; instead, they purchased the goods country people made. They were wage earners and consumers, and the market economy shaped and controlled their daily lives.

Americans were increasingly conscious of such changes, and a few resisted, seeking to avoid the untamed growth of cities and, in utopian rural communities, to restore traditional work tasks and social cohesion. The religious ferment of the Second Great Awakening (see pages 279–280) promoted new religious communities as well. Virtually all these communities broke with tradition by experimenting with communal living, innovative (sometimes shocking) family arrangements, and more egalitarian gender roles in a cooperative rather than competitive environment.

The Shakers, the largest of the communal utopian experiments, reached their peak between 1820 and 1860. In those years six thousand members lived in twenty settlements in eight states. Shaker communities emphasized agriculture and handcrafts; most managed to become self-sufficient and profitable enterprises. Shaker furniture became famous for its simplicity, excellent construction, and beauty of design.

Shakers

The Shakers had been established in England a half-century earlier. Founder Ann Lee brought the phenomenon to America in 1774. Named for the way they danced at worship services, the Shakers believed that the end of the world was near and that sin entered the world through sexual intercourse. They considered existing churches too worldly and viewed the Shaker community as the instrument of salvation.

Though economically conservative, the Shakers were social radicals. They abolished individual families; each colony was one large family. They also elected women to lead. During its period of greatest growth, a woman, Lucy Wright, headed the Shaker ministry. The sect's practice of celibacy, however, led it to depend on enlisting new recruits, and its strict rules proved unattractive to many Americans, especially as interest in utopian communities faded.

The most successful communitarian group was the Church of Jesus Christ of Latter-day Saints, known as the Mormons. During the religious ferment of the 1820s, Joseph Smith, a young farmer in western New York, reported that an angel called Moroni had visited him and given him engraved divine gold plates. Smith published his revelations as the *Book of Mormon* and

Mormon Community of Saints

organized a church in western New York in 1830. The next year they moved west to Ohio to build a "New Jerusalem" to await the second coming of Jesus.

Violence stalked the Mormons; angry mobs drove them from Ohio, and they settled in Missouri. Still, their rapid growth created antagonism, as did their claim that only Mormons would be saved upon Jesus' return. Anti-Mormons charged that Mormonism was fraudulent, a scam by Joseph Smith. Opponents also feared Mormon political power. In 1838 the governor of Missouri charged Smith with fomenting insurrections and gathered evidence to indict Smith and other leaders for treason.

Joseph Smith and his followers resettled in Nauvoo, Illinois. The state legislature gave them a city charter, which made them self-governing, and authorized a local militia. After 1841, when Smith introduced the practice of polygamy, allowing men to have several wives at once, opponents, who now included some ex-Mormons, became furious. In 1842 Smith became mayor, and this consolidation of religious and political power antagonized opponents further. They faced their worst fears when in 1843 Nauvoo petitioned the federal government to be a self-governing territory. Schisms within Mormonism added to the controversies. In 1844 the authorities indicted Smith and

Violence stalked the Mormons until they found safety in the Great Salt Lake valley. Here a Mormon family—a father, three wives, and five children—poses for a photographer in the 1850s in Salt Lake City. (Church of Jesus Christ of Latter-Day Saints)

others with plotting to murder their opponents, but the Nauvoo courts released them. Then Joseph and his brother Hyrum were arrested for treason and jailed in Carthage, Illinois. The militia from Warsaw, Nauvoo's neighbor, stormed the jail and killed the two brothers. The next year the Mormons began a trek westward to find security in the wilderness. They found a home in the Great Salt Lake valley, in unorganized territory. There, under Brigham Young, head of the Twelve Apostles (the Mormons' governing body), they established a patriarchal, cooperative "community of saints." They found in the distant desert West both religious freedom and political autonomy.

In Utah the Mormons distributed agricultural land according to family size. An extensive irrigation system, constructed by men who contributed their labor in proportion to the quantity of land they received and the amount of water they expected to use, transformed the arid valley into a rich oasis. As the colony developed, the church elders gained control of water, trade, industry, and eventually the territorial government of Utah.

Religious conviction fortified the Latter-day Saints to withstand persecution. The Mormons offered success and community in this world and salvation in the next to anyone who would join. Indeed, many recruits were poor and uneducated. To those who rejected existing churches, the Mormons also offered fellowship and religious certainty within a tight-knit society and cooperative economic system.

Not all utopian communities gravitated to the wilderness. The Brook Farm cooperative in West Roxbury, Massachusetts, near

Brook Farm

Boston, had a lasting impact although its achievements were more artistic than economic. Inspired by transcendentalism—the belief that the physical world is secondary to the spiritual realm, which human beings can know by ignoring custom and experience and relying instead on intuition—Brook Farm's members rejected materialism in favor of rural communalism, combining spirituality, manual labor, intellectual life, and play. Founded in 1841 by the Unitarian minister George Ripley, a literary critic and friend of transcendentalist lecturer and essayist Ralph Waldo Emerson, Brook Farm attracted farmers, craftsmen, and writers, among them the novelist Nathaniel Hawthorne. Indeed, the fame of Brook Farm rested on the intellectual achievements of its members. Its school drew students from outside the community, and its residents contributed regularly to the *Dial*, the leading

transcendentalist journal. In 1845 Brook Farm's hundred members organized themselves into model phalanxes (working-living units) suggested by French utopian Charles Fourier. Rigid regimentation replaced individualism, and membership dropped. After a disastrous fire in 1846, the experiment collapsed in 1847.

Though short-lived, Brook Farm played a significant role in the flowering of a national literature. During these years Hawthorne, Emerson, and *Dial* editor Margaret Fuller joined Henry David Thoreau, Herman Melville, and others in a literary outpouring known today as the American Renaissance. In philosophical intensity and moral idealism, their work was both distinctively American and an outgrowth of the European romantic movement. Their themes were universal, their settings and characters American. Hawthorne, for instance, used Puritan New England as a backdrop, and Melville wrote of great spiritual quests as seafaring adventures.

The essayist Ralph Waldo Emerson was the prime mover of the American Renaissance and a pillar of the transcendental movement. Emerson

Ralph Waldo Emerson

had followed his father and grandfather into the ministry but quit his Boston Unitarian pulpit in 1831. After a two-year sojourn in Europe, he returned to lecture and write, preaching individualism and self-reliance. "We live in succession, in division, in parts, in particles," Emerson wrote. "We see the world piece by piece, as the sun, the moon, the animal, the tree; but the whole, of which these are the shining parts, is the soul." Intuitive experience of God is attainable, insisted Emerson, because "the Highest dwells" within every individual in the form of the "Over-soul." What gave Emerson's writings force was, for his times, a simple, direct prose. In his first book, *Nature* (1836), and in "The American Scholar" (1837), a Phi Beta Kappa address at Harvard, Emerson explored human nature and American culture. Widely admired, he influenced Thoreau, Fuller, Hawthorne, and other members of Brook Farm.

Whether intellectual, spiritual, or economic in their origins, utopian communities can be seen as attempts to recapture the cohesiveness of traditional agricultural and artisan life in reaction to the competitive pressures of the market economy and urbanization. Utopians resembled Puritan perfectionists; like the Separatists of seventeenth-century New England (see page 49), they sought to begin anew in their own colonies.

The West

In the 1840s a trickling stream of migrants followed the Oregon Trail to the West Coast. Then, in 1848, gold was discovered in California. The next year a pioneer observed that the Oregon Trail "bore no evidence of having been much traveled." Traffic flowed south instead, and California became the new population center on the Pacific slope. One measure of this shift was the overland mail routes. In the 1840s the Oregon Trail had been the main communications link between the Midwest and the Pacific. Ten years later the post office routes terminated in California, not Oregon; in fact, in the 1850s there was no mail route north of Sacramento.

When the United States acquired Alta California from Mexico in the 1848 Treaty of Guadalupe Hidalgo

Discovery of Gold

(see page 364), the province was inhabited mostly by Indians, with some Mexicans living on large estates. A chain of small settlements surrounded military forts (*presidios*) and missions. That changed almost overnight after James Marshall, a carpenter, spotted gold particles in the mill-race at Sutter's Mill (now Coloma, California, northwest of Sacramento) in January 1848. Word of the discovery spread and Californians rushed to scrabble for instant fortunes. When the military explorer John C. Frémont reached San Francisco five months later, he found that "all, or nearly all, its male inhabitants had gone to the mines." The town, "which a few months before was so busy and thriving, was then almost deserted."

By 1849 the news had sped around the world, and hundreds of thousands of fortune seekers, mostly

The discovery of gold in California brought tens of thousands to participate in "Nature's Great Lottery scheme." This daguerreotype captured a group of black and white miners sifting for gold traces at Spanish Flats in 1852 California. (California State Library)

young men, streamed in from Mexico, England, Germany, France, Ireland, and from all over the United States, including some African Americans. They mined the lodes and washed away the surface soil with hydraulic works, leaving the land unsuitable for anything after they abandoned it.

Gold mining seemed to offer instant riches, and indeed, some made fortunes. In 1848 a California male servant earned $2,000 mining for gold and returned to Monterey a rich man. Peter Brown, a black man from Ste. Genevieve, Missouri, went to California alone, as did most "forty-niners." He wrote his wife in 1851 that "California is the best country in the world to make money. It is also the best place for black folks on the globe." He had earned $300 in two months.

Most "forty-niners," however, never found enough gold to pay their expenses. "The stories you hear frequently in the States," one gold seeker wrote home, "are the most extravagant lies imaginable—the mines are a humbug." Another gold seeker called gold mining "Nature's Great Lottery scheme." Many found work in California's cities and agricultural districts more profitable. Meanwhile, enterprising merchants rushed to supply, feed, and clothe the new settlers. One such merchant was Levi Strauss, a German Jewish immigrant, whose tough mining pants found a ready market among the prospectors.

San Francisco, the former *presidio* and mission of Yerba Buena, had in 1848 been a small settlement of about a thousand Mexicans, Anglos, soldiers, friars, and Indians. As the West Coast gateway to the interior, it now became an instant city, ballooning to thirty-five thousand people in 1850. Ships bringing people and supplies continuously jammed the harbor. A French visitor in that year wrote, "At San Francisco, where fifteen months ago one found only a half dozen large cabins, one finds today a stock exchange, a theater, churches of all Christian cults, and a large number of quite beautiful homes."

The forty-niners had their eyes on gold nuggets, but they had to be fed. Thus began the great California agricultural boom. Farmers preferred wheat; it required minimal investment, was easily planted, and offered a quick return at the end of a relatively short growing season. California farmers eagerly imported horse-drawn machines, since labor was scarce (and expensive). By the mid-1850s, California exported wheat and had become firmly linked, through commerce, to the rest of the United States. Farmers on the West Coast cleared the land and constructed log

Farming

cabins. Success often depended on their access to water, and they sought to divert the streams and rivers of the West to irrigate their land.

In contrast to the Midwest, where family farms were the basic unit of production, in California men dominated mining, grazing, and large-scale wheat farming. Most men came alone, drawn by a sense of adventure and personal opportunity. Women who accompanied their husbands—only one-seventh of the travelers on the overland trails were women—experienced the migration differently. Their lives drastically changed as they left behind networks of friends and kin to journey, often with children, along an unknown and hazardous path to a strange environment. Yet in the West their domestic skills were in great demand. They received high fees for cooking, laundering, and sewing, and they ran boarding houses and hotels (men shunned domestic work).

Women Settlers

City Life

 When Anna Maria Klinger arrived in America in 1849, she first settled in New York City. She and other immigrants as well as migrants from New England and the Middle Atlantic states poured into New York and other cities in the 1830s, 1840s, and 1850s. Cities, especially northern ones, expanded geometrically. The nation's population increased during this period from 12.9 million to 31.4 million. Europeans spread westward, and small rural settlements quickly became towns. In 1830 the nation had only 23 cities with 10,000 or more people and only 7 with more than 25,000. By 1860, 93 towns exceeded 10,000, 35 towns had more than 25,000, and 9 exceeded 100,000 (see Map 12.1). The Northeast was most heavily urban, and the percentage of people living in urban areas there grew from 14 to 35 percent between 1830 and 1860.

Some cities became great metropolitan centers. By 1830 New York City had been the nation's most populous city and major commercial center for twenty years. At midcentury Baltimore and New Orleans dominated the South, and San Francisco was the leading West Coast city. In the Midwest, the new lake cities (Chicago, Detroit, and Cleveland) began to pass the frontier river cities (Cincinnati, Louisville, and Pittsburgh) founded a generation earlier. The largest cities of the North anchored a nationwide network linked by canals, roads, railroads, and the telegraph (see Chapter 10).

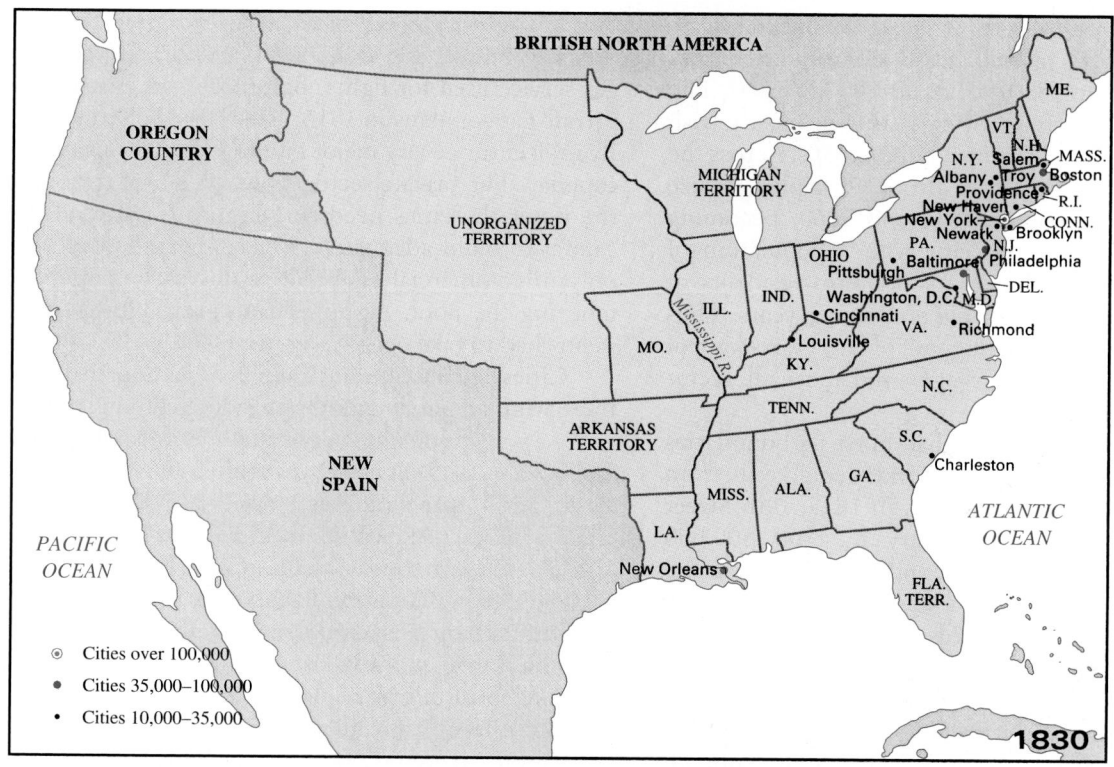

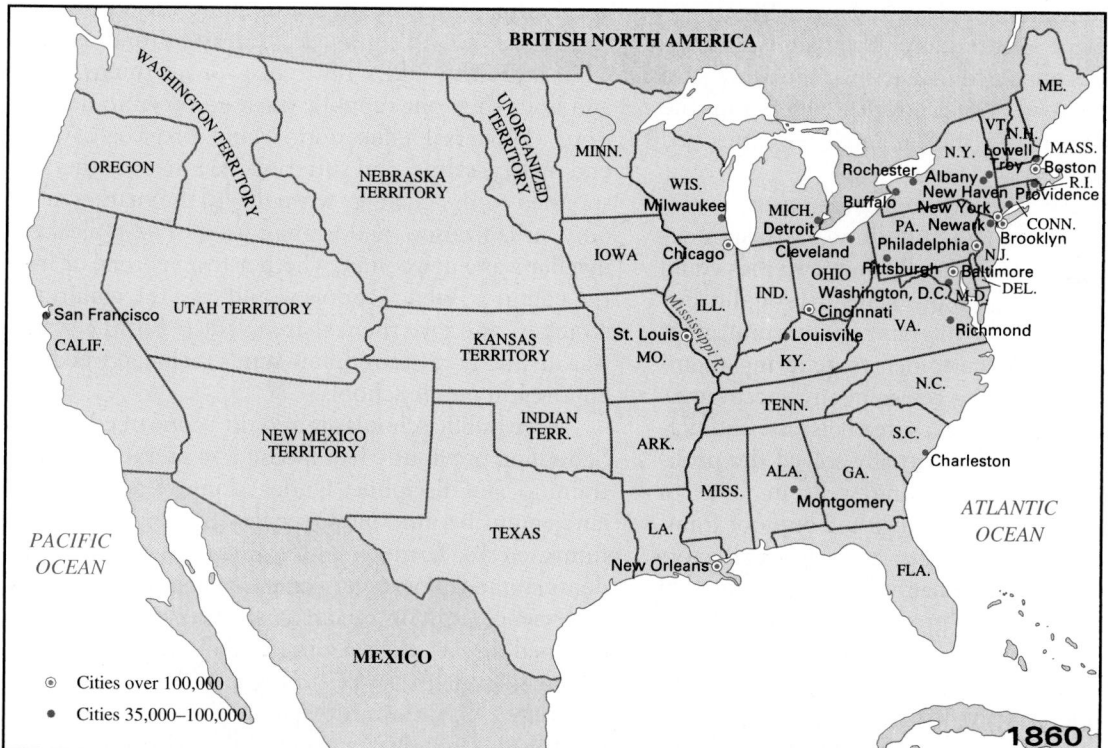

Map 12.1   Major American Cities in 1830 and 1860   The number of Americans who lived in cities increased rapidly between 1830 and 1860, and the number of large cities grew as well. In 1830 only New York City had a population exceeding one hundred thousand; thirty years later, eight more cities had surpassed that level.

As the nation's premier city, New York grew from 202,000 people in 1830 to over 814,000 in 1860. The immigrant port city was mostly Irish and German by the 1850s. Across the East River, Brooklyn tripled in size between 1850 and 1860, becoming the nation's third-largest city, with a population of 279,000. Many people were short-term residents of the two cities; the majority did not stay ten years. Thus New York was ever changing, full of energy, reeking of sweat, horse dung, and garbage—and above all, teeming with people.

New York City

New York City literally had burst its boundaries around 1830. Until then New Yorkers could walk from one end to the other in an hour. In 1825, 14th Street was the city's northern boundary. By 1860, 400,000 people lived above that divide, and 42nd Street was the city's northern limit. Gone were the cow pastures, kitchen gardens, and orchards of the eighteenth century. George Templeton Strong, a New York lawyer, recorded in his diary in 1856 that he had attended a party on 37th Street: "It seems but the other day that thirty-seventh Street was an imaginary line running through a rural district and grazed over by cows." Mass transit made city expansion possible. Horse-drawn omnibuses appeared in New York in 1827, and the Harlem Railroad, completed in 1832, ran the length of Manhattan. By the 1850s all big cities had horse-drawn streetcars.

Urban Problems

By modern standards nineteenth-century cities were disorderly, unsafe, and unhealthy. Expansion occurred so rapidly that few cities could handle the problems it brought. For example, migrants from rural areas were accustomed to relieving themselves outside and throwing refuse in any vacant area. In the city, such waste smelled, spread disease, and polluted water. New York City partially solved the problem in the 1840s by abandoning wells in favor of reservoir water piped into buildings and outdoor fountains. In some districts, scavengers and refuse collectors carted away garbage and human waste, but in much of the city it just rotted on the ground. Only one-quarter of New York City's streets had sewers by 1857.

New York and other cities lacked adequate taxing power to provide services for all. The best the city could do was to tax property adjoining new sewers, paved streets, and water mains. Thus new services and basic sanitation depended on residents' ability to pay. As a result, those most in need of services got them last. Another solution was to charter private compa-

nies to sell basic services. This plan worked well with gas service used for lights. Baltimore first chartered a private gas company in 1816; New York did so in 1842. By midcentury every major city was lit by a private gas supplier. The private sector, however, failed to supply the water the cities needed. Private firms lacked the capital to build adequate systems, and they laid pipe only in commercial and well-to-do residential areas, ignoring the poor. As population grew, city governments had to take over.

Cities led in offering public education. In 1800 there were no public schools outside New England; by 1860 every state offered some public education to whites. Under Horace Mann, secretary of the state board of education from 1837 to 1848, Massachusetts led the way. It established a minimum school year of six months and formalized the training of teachers.

Horace Mann and Public Schools

Mann was an evangelist for public education and school reform; his preaching on behalf of free, state-sponsored education changed schooling throughout the nation. "If we do not prepare children to become good citizens," Mann argued, "if we do not develop their capacities, . . . imbue their hearts with the love of truth and duty, and a reverence for all things sacred and holy, then our republic must go down to destruction." Universal education, Mann proposed, would end misery, crime, and suffering. Mann and others responded to the changes wrought by the market economy, urbanization, and immigration. The typical city dweller was a newcomer, whether from abroad or from the country. Public schools would take the children of strangers and give them shared values. But the system was distinctly racialized; few states included free black children in public schools.

Free public schools altered the scope of education. Schooling previously had focused on literacy, religious training, and discipline. Under Mann's leadership, the curriculum became more secular and appropriate for future clerks, farmers, and workers of America. Students studied geography, American history, arithmetic, and science. Schools retained moral education, but they dropped direct religious indoctrination. Nonetheless, primers like *McGuffey's Eclectic Readers* still used Protestant Scripture to teach children to accept their positions in society. A good child, *McGuffey* taught, does not envy the rich: "It is God who makes some poor and others rich." *McGuffey* further preached that "the rich have troubles which we know nothing of; and . . . the poor, if they are good, may be very happy."

Catholics, immigrants, blacks, and working-class people sought to control their own schools, but the state legislatures established secular statewide standards under Protestant educators. Catholics in New York responded by building their own educational system over the next half-century. When Los Angeles became a city in 1850, it attempted to establish bilingual Spanish-English instruction. Trained bilingual teachers could not be found, however, and when the schools opened, they offered only English instruction.

Towns and cities created new patterns of leisure as well as work. In rural society, as Irene Hardy recalled, both social activities and work often

Leisure

took place at home. But in cities, dedicated spaces—streets, theaters, sports fields—constituted a social sphere where people could come together away from home. Through the sale of admission tickets or membership in associations, leisure became a commodity to be purchased. As the population became more diverse, leisure associations reflected ethnic, racial, and class divisions.

Traditional rural pursuits continued in the city. Men frequented taverns and spent spare time drinking and playing games of skill and strength—arm wrestling, ninepins, and pitching coins. Though city dwellers had less opportunity than their rural counterparts to ride and hunt, fishing remained popular among both men and women. Churches continued to serve as social centers and the Second Great Awakening increased women's involvement. Church clubs combined socializing with good works.

Americans not only played more but read more. Thanks to the expansion of public education, the vast majority of native-born white Americans were literate by the 1850s. In

Reading

cities, urban newspapers and magazines proliferated and bookstores spread. Power printing presses and better transportation made possible wide distribution of books and periodicals. The religious press—of both traditional sects and dissenters—produced pamphlets, hymnals, Bibles, and religious newspapers. Americans also read secular publications. Newspapers and magazines—political organs, literary journals, and the voices of specialized groups like millworkers—abounded in the 1830s and after. In Brookfield, Massachusetts, in 1798, the mails brought one weekly newspaper; fifty years later, in 1848, fifty different newspapers and another fifty-five monthly magazines regularly arrived on subscribers' doorsteps.

Fiction and autobiographies competed with religious tracts as popular literature. Newspapers and magazines printed fiction, and bookstores and stationers in large cities sold novels and autobiographies. Frederick Douglass's powerful attack on slavery in the *Narrative of the Life of Frederick Douglass, an American Slave, Written by Himself* (1845) sold widely. Many popular novels, some written by women, often for women, were set in the home and upheld Christian values. They reflected growing gender differences in American society in their exploration of the divisions between home and work, between emotion and authority, and between sentimentality and power. Yet in their support of traditional female moral roles, they also can be read as a challenge to prevailing values. Although Susan Warner's *The Wide, Wide, Wide World* (1850), Nathaniel Hawthorne's *The House of the Seven Gables* (1851), and Fanny Fern's *Ruth Hall* (1855) did not challenge women's traditional domestic roles, they gave women a special moral bearing. In giving a positive cast to notions of community and republican virtue, they implicitly criticized the growing market economy. By the 1850s popular fiction circulated widely. Harriet Beecher Stowe's antislavery novel, *Uncle Tom's Cabin, or Life Among the Lowly* (1852), which appeared serially in 1851–1852, sold 300,000 copies in book form in its first year.

A major attraction, theater provided a social sphere in which both men and women gathered. A

Theater

theater was often the second public building constructed in a town—after a church. Large cities boasted two or more theaters catering to different classes. In New York City the Park Theater enjoyed the patronage of the carriage trade, the Bowery drew the middle class, and the Chatham attracted workers. Some plays cut across class lines. Shakespeare was performed so often and appreciated so widely that even illiterate theatergoers knew his plays well. In the 1840s musical and dramatic presentations took on a more professional tone; like the Hutchinson Family (see pages 243–244), newly popular minstrel shows and traveling circuses offered carefully rehearsed routines. Dancing and music remained popular and took new forms, as in blackfaced minstrelsy.

By the 1840s hundreds of traveling minstrel troupes performed a complete evening's entertainment in American theaters. Minstrel acts

Minstrel Show

had first appeared twenty or thirty years earlier, when white men, in burnt cork makeup, imitated African Americans in song, dance, and patter. In the early 1830s Thomas D. Rice of New York became famous for his role as Jim Crow, an old southern slave. In ill-fitting patched clothing and torn shoes, the blackface Rice shuffled, danced, and sang on stage. Another stereotyped image soon joined him: Zip Coon, a black Bowery Boy. What minstrels presented was a European version of African American culture.

Minstrelsy combined contradictory elements. At one level, performers masked as people of color told jokes mocking economic and political elites. At the same time the actors stereotyped black people by exaggerating physical features. They also presented blacks as sensual and lazy, thus stoking the fires of racism with ridicule. In blending black culture with white humor, African dance with English folktunes, and the African banjo with the Irish fiddle, minstrelsy seemed to represent the new urban potpourri. In portraying foils to sexual purity and work discipline, minstrelsy also constituted a resistance to the moral demands and factory regimens of the era. Ultimately, minstrelsy furthered growing racial divisions in the United States. The fictional representation of blacks on stage not only defined "blackness" but also defined "whiteness." Whiteness as a racial category took on meaning as laughing white audiences distinguished themselves from the black characters.

Increasingly, urban recreation and sports became more formal commodities to be purchased. One had to

Sports

buy a ticket to go to the theater, the circus, P. T. Barnum's American Museum in New York City, the racetrack, or the ballpark.

Spectator sports became increasingly popular. From 1831 enthusiasts could read the all-sports newspaper, *Spirit of the Times.* By 1849 news of boxing was so much in demand that a round-by-round account of a Maryland boxing match was telegraphed throughout the East. Horseracing, walking races, and, in the 1850s, baseball began to attract large urban male crowds.

Organized leagues replaced spontaneity. A group of Wall Street office workers formed the Knickerbocker Club in 1842 and in 1845 drew up rules for the game of baseball. Their rules were widely adopted and continue to serve as the basis for the game.

Ironically, public leisure soon developed a private dimension. Exclusive private clubs and associations

City Culture

arose to provide space and occasions for leisure set apart from the crowds and rowdiness of public events. As cities grew, their populations seemed

increasingly fragmented. Finding people similar to oneself required more of a conscious effort. The new associations that evolved served as a bulwark against the cultures of other groups—immigrants, migrants, blacks, and artisans. Middle- and upper-class New Yorkers who felt alienated in the city of their birth founded exclusive clubs. Some joined the Masonic order, which offered everything the bustling, chaotic city did not: an elaborate hierarchy, an orderly code of deference between ranks, harmony, and shared values. Members knew one another. Masons played a political role as well: they recruited officeholders and marched in the parades that were a regular feature of the city's political life.

Ethnic, racial, and religious groups seeking to socialize and preserve similar shared traditions formed their own clubs and societies. The Irish formed the Hibernian Society and the Sons of Erin; Germans brought Turnvereine physical-cultural clubs from across the Atlantic; Jews founded B'nai B'rith as a men's club; and African Americans had chapters of the Prince Hall Masons in their communities. Women, too, organized their own associations, ranging from social organizations to benevolent societies. Americans of all sorts—native- and foreign-born, black and white—also formed churches and church-associated clubs. Associations brought together like people, but they also formalized divisions among groups.

Divisions seemed to occur naturally on city streets. In the 1840s, a youth culture developed on the Bowery, one of New York's entertainment strips. In the evenings the lamp-lit promenade, lined with theaters, dance halls, and cafés, became an urban midway. Older New Yorkers feared the "Bowery boys and gals," whose ostentatious dress and behavior seemed threatening to them. Around 1847 artist Nicholino Calyo depicted three Bowery boys in a watercolor painting (see page 315). A Bowery boy had long hair, often greased into a roll. He wore a broad-brimmed black hat, an open shirt collar, a black frock coat that reached below the knee, and as much jewelry as he could afford. His swaggering gait, especially when he had a girlfriend on his arm, frightened many in the middle class. Equally disturbing to old New Yorkers were the young working women who strolled the Bowery. They came in groups to enjoy each other's company and to meet Bowery boys. Unlike more genteel ladies who wore modest veils or bonnets, Bowery "gals" drew attention to themselves with outlandish costumes and ornate hats.

Nicholino Calyo's watercolor *Soap-Locks, or Bowery Boys* (c. 1847) captured the bold body language and showy dress of the youths who controlled the sidewalks of the Bowery. (© Collection of The New-York Historical Society)

Much more than on the stage, racial, ethnic, and class divisions were played out on city streets. Most working people spent much of their lives outdoors; they worked in the streets as laborers, shopped in open markets, paraded on special occasions, and socialized in all these places. Young people courted, neighbors argued, and ethnic and racial groups defended their turf on the streets. Increasingly, urban streets served as a political arena as crowds formed to listen to speakers, to respond and to demonstrate, and sometimes to take mob action.

Economic, political, social, racial, and ethnic conflict erupted on city streets. In the 1830s riots became commonplace as professionals, merchants, craftsmen, and laborers vented their rage against political and economic rivals. "Gentlemen of property and standing," unnerved by antislavery proponents, sacked abolitionist and antislavery organizations, even murdering newspaper editor Elijah Lovejoy in Alton, Illinois, in 1837. In the 1840s "respectable" citizens drove the Mormons out of Missouri and Illinois. In Philadelphia native-born workers attacked Irish weavers in 1828, and whites and blacks fought on the docks in 1834 and 1835. Residents of

Urban Riots

North Philadelphia took to the streets continuously from 1840 to 1842 until the construction of a railroad through their neighborhood was abandoned. These disturbances came to a head in the Philadelphia riots of 1844, in which mostly Protestant skilled workers attacked Irish Catholics. Smaller cities, too, became battlegrounds as nativist riots peaked in the 1850s; Louisville, for instance, witnessed an anti-German riot in 1855. By 1840 more than 125 people had died in urban riots, and by 1860 fatalities exceeded 1,000.

As public disorder spread, Boston hired uniformed policemen in 1837 to supplement its part-time watchmen and constables, and New York in 1845 established a uniformed force. Nonetheless, middle-class city dwellers did not venture out alone at night. The police tried to control and suppress street activity, as did local ordinances that regulated street vendors. Local laws against vagrancy and disturbing the peace often were used against free blacks and immigrants. The continuing inflow of immigrants to the cities worsened social tensions by pitting groups against one other in the contest for jobs, housing, and street space. In the midst of so much noise, crime, and conflict, the lavish uptown residences of the very rich rose like an affront to those struggling to survive.

Extremes of Wealth

The French nobleman Alexis de Tocqueville and other observers characterized the United States before the Civil War as primarily a place of equality and opportunity for white males. Tocqueville and his companion Gustave de Beaumont traveled 4,000 miles and visited all twenty-four states over a nine-month period in 1831 and 1832. Tocqueville opened *Democracy in America*, his classic analysis of the American people and nation, with this observation: "No novelty in the United States struck me more vividly during my stay there than the equality of conditions."

Tocqueville attributed American equality—the relative fluidity of the social order—to Americans' mobility and restlessness. Geographic mobility, he felt, offered people a chance to start anew regardless of where they came from or who they were. Wealth and family mattered little; a person could be known by deeds alone. Indeed, Americans seemed driven by an itch to move and ambition. "An American will build a house in which to pass his old age," Tocqueville wrote, "and sell it before the roof is on; he will plant a garden and rent it just as the trees are coming into bearing; he will clear a field and leave others to reap the harvest; he will take up a profession and leave it, settle in one place and soon go off elsewhere with his changing desires."

Others disagreed with the egalitarian view of American life. *New York Sun* publisher Moses Yale

"If Not an Aristocracy" Beach believed a new aristocracy based on wealth and power was forming. Author of twelve editions of *Wealth* and *Biography of the Wealthy Citizens of New York City*, Beach listed 750 New Yorkers with assets of $100,000 or more in 1845. John Jacob Astor, with a fortune of $25 million, led the list of nineteen millionaires. Ten years later, Beach reported more than a thousand New Yorkers worth $100,000, among them twenty-eight millionaires. Combining gossip-column items with wild guesses at people's wealth, Beach's publications suggest the enormous wealth of New York's upper class. Tocqueville himself, sensitive to conflicting trends in American life, had described the new industrial wealth. The rich and well educated "come forward to exploit industries," Tocqueville wrote, and become "more and more like the administrators of a huge empire. . . . What is this if not an aristocracy?"

Wealth throughout the United States was becoming concentrated in the hands of a relatively small number of people. In New York City between 1828 and 1845, the richest 4 percent of the city's population increased their holdings from an estimated 63 percent to 80 percent of all individual wealth. Meanwhile, the holdings of many ordinary people virtually disappeared. In Brooklyn between 1810 and 1841, the share of wealth held by the bottom two-thirds of families decreased from 10 percent to almost nothing. By 1860 the top 5 percent of American families owned more than half of the nation's wealth, and the top 10 percent owned nearly three-quarters.

A cloud of uncertainty hovered over working men and women. Anxious that hard times were always imminent, many resented the compe-

Urban Poverty tition of immigrants and goods produced by slave labor. They dreaded poverty, chronic illness, disability, old age, widowhood, and desertion. Women feared raising a family without a spouse. And they had good reason: few women could find a job that paid enough to support a family. Fear of poverty prompted the Klinger sisters, for instance, to marry again and again.

Poverty dogged the urban working class. Newly arrived immigrants, free blacks, the working poor, and thieves, beggars, and prostitutes eked out a living in urban slums. New York City's Five Points, a few blocks from City Hall, lacked running water and sewers and was notorious for its squalor. Dominated by the Old Brewery, which had been converted to housing in 1837, the neighborhood was predominantly immigrant Irish and recently freed black people. Contemporaries estimated that more than a thousand people lived in the Old Brewery's rooms, cellars, and subcellars. Throughout the city, workers' housing was at a premium. Houses built for two families often held four; tenements built for six families held twelve. Families took in lodgers to help pay the rent.

A world apart from Five Points and the people of the streets, though only a short walk away, lived the upper-class elite society of Philip

The Urban Elite Hone, one-time mayor of New York. Hone's diary, meticulously kept from 1826 until his death in 1851, records the life of an American aristocrat. On February 28, 1840, for instance, Hone attended a masked ball at the Fifth Avenue mansion of Henry Breevoort, Jr., and Laura Carson Breevoort. The ball began at the fashionable hour of 10 P.M., and the five hundred invited ladies and gentlemen wore costumes adorned with ermine and gold. For more than a week, Hone believed, the affair "occupied the minds of people of all stations,

A visible sign of urban poverty in the 1850s was the homeless and orphaned children, most of them immigrants, who wandered the streets of New York City. The Home for the Friendless Orphanage, at Twenty-ninth Street and Madison Avenue, provided shelter for some of the orphan girls. (© Collection of The New-York Historical Society)

ranks, and employments." Similar parties were held in Boston, Philadelphia, Baltimore, and Charleston.

Hone regularly attended elegant dinner parties graced by fine cuisine and imported wines. The New York elite who filled the pages of Hone's diary—the 1 percent of the population who owned half of the city's wealth—lived in mansions attended by servants. Country estates, ocean resorts, mineral spas, and grand tours of Europe offered relief from the winter and spring social seasons and escape from the heat and smells of the summer.

Much of this wealth was inherited. For every John Jacob Astor who made millions in the western fur trade or George Law who left a farm to become a millionaire contractor and investor, ten others had inherited or married money. Andrew H. Mickle, a poor Irish immigrant who became a millionaire and mayor of New York City, derived his fortune from marrying the daughter of his employer. Many of the wealthiest New Yorkers bore the names of the colonial commercial elite: Breevoort, Roosevelt, Van Rensselaer, and Whitney. These rich New Yorkers were not idle; they worked at increasing their fortunes and power. Urban capitalists like Philip Hone and the fashionable society, like their Boston counterparts who founded the Boston Manufacturing Company, invested in and profited enormously from commerce and manufacturing. Wealth begat wealth, and marriage cemented upper-crust family ties.

Meanwhile, a distinct middle class appeared on the urban scene. Small in number, they were the city

The Middle Class

businessmen, traders, and professionals in the market economy. The growth and specialization of trade rapidly increased their numbers.

Middle-class families enjoyed the new consumer items: wool carpeting, fine wallpaper, and rooms full of furniture replaced the bare floors, whitewashed walls, and relative sparseness of eighteenth-century homes. Houses were large, often having from four to six rooms. Middle-class children slept one to a bed, and by the 1840s and 1850s middle-class families used indoor toilets. When Philadelphia publishing agent Joseph Engles died in 1861, an inventory of his estate indicated that his parlor contained two sofas, thirteen chairs, three card tables, a fancy table, a piano,

John Lewis Krimmel painted this portrait of himself and his sister-in-law and her children around 1812. It shows a prosperous middle-class Philadelphia German family that had been in the United States around five years. The dress and home of the Krimmel children stand in sharp contrast to the homeless and orphaned children of New York City. (The Warner Collection of Gulf States Paper Corporation, Tuscaloosa, Alabama. Photo courtesy of The Schwarz Gallery, Philadelphia)

a mirror, and a fine carpet. Other rooms were similarly furnished.

Middle-class families formed the backbone of the clubs and societies that Tocqueville had observed in America. They filled the family pews in church on Sundays; their children pursued whatever educational opportunities were available. They were as distant from Philip Hone's world as they were from the milieu of the working class and the poor. Increasingly they looked to the family and home as the core of middle-class life.

Women, Families, and the Domestic Ideal

 Once primarily an economic unit, urban families in the nineteenth century lost their role as producers (see Chapter 10). As manufacturing left the home, so did wage workers. One result was specialization of roles by gender and by life stage.

Men dominated American families. English common law gave husbands absolute control over the family. The men owned their wives' personal property; they were legal guardians of the children; and they owned whatever family members produced or earned. A father still had the legal authority to oppose his daughter's choice of husband. Nonetheless, most American women, with their parents' blessing, chose their own marriage partners.

Marriage and family life were the central adult experiences of most women. Although married women still had limited legal rights and standing, they made modest gains in property and spousal rights from the 1830s on. Arkansas in 1835 passed the first married women's property law, and by 1860 sixteen more states had followed suit. In those states, women—single, married, or widowed—could own and convey property. When a wife inherited, earned, or acquired property, it was hers, not her husband's; and she could write a will. In the 1830s states began to liberalize divorce, adding cruelty and desertion as grounds for divorce. Nonetheless divorce was rare.

As the urban workplace and home became separate entities, men worked for wages outside the home, and so did their offspring. In New England daughters left farms to work in textile mills, sons to work in urban commerce. In the 1840s the new urban department stores hired young women as clerks and cash runners. Many women worked for a time as teachers, usually for two to five years. Paid employment typically represented a brief stage in women's lives before they left their parental households and entered their marital households.

Supporting Families

Working-class women—the poor, widows, and free blacks—worked to support themselves and their families. Leaving their parental homes as early as age twelve, they earned wages most of their lives, with only short respites for bearing and rearing children. But unlike men and New England farm daughters, most of these women did not work in the new shops and factories. Instead, they sold their domestic skills for wages outside their own households. Unmarried girls and women worked as domestic servants in other women's homes; married and widowed women worked as laundresses, seamstresses, and cooks. Some hawked food and wares on city streets; others did piecework sewing at home, earning wages in the putting-out system; and some became prostitutes. Few of these occupations enabled them to support themselves or a family at a respectable level.

Most women continued to perform unpaid labor in the home. As the urban family lost its role in the production of goods, household upkeep and child rearing claimed women's full-time attention. Religion, morality, domestic arts, and music and literature filled the void left by the decline in the economic functions of the family; these realms came to be known as woman's sphere. A woman who achieved mastery in these areas lived up to the middle-class ideal of the cult of domesticity.

Idealizing the Family

Middle-class Americans idealized the family as a moral institution characterized by selflessness and cooperation. The world of work—the market economy—was seen as an arena of conflict increasingly identified with men and dominated by base self-interest. In a rapidly changing world, the family represented stability and traditional values. The domestic ideal restricted the range of paying jobs available to middle-class women. One occupation was considered consonant with the genteel female role: teaching. In 1823 the Beecher sisters, Catharine and Mary, established the Hartford Female Seminary

Rebecca Lukens pioneered in an unusual role for a woman in early-nineteenth-century America: she ran the Lukens Steel Company in eastern Pennsylvania from 1825 until she died in 1854. The deaths of her father in 1823 and of her husband in 1825 left her with the mill and large debts. She revived the steel company and soon was shipping iron plates as far away as Europe.   (Courtesy of Lukens, Inc., Coatesville, Pa.)

and offered history and science in addition to the traditional women's curriculum of domestic arts and religion. A decade later Catharine Beecher successfully campaigned for teacher-training schools for women. By 1850 school teaching had become a woman's profession. "Females govern with less resort to physical force," Horace Mann asserted, "and exert a more kindly, humanizing and refining influence upon the dispositions and manners of their pupils." Most urban teachers were unmarried women, who earned about half the salary of male teachers.

Meanwhile, family size was shrinking. In 1830 American women bore an average of five or six children; by 1860 the figure had dropped to five. This decline occurred even though many immigrants with

Decline in Family Size

large-family traditions were settling in the United States; thus the birth rate among native-born women declined even more steeply. Although rural families remained larger than their urban counterparts, birth rates among both groups declined comparably.

A number of factors reduced family size. Small families were viewed as increasingly desirable in an economy in which the family was a unit of consumption rather than production. Children in smaller families would have greater opportunities: parents could give them more attention, better education, and more financial help. Evidence suggests many wives and husbands made deliberate decisions to limit the size of families. Where farmland was relatively expensive in eastern states, for instance, family size was smaller than in cheaper agricultural districts to the west. In urban areas, children tended to become an economic burden rather than an asset as the family lost its role as a producer of goods.

How did men and women limit their families in the early nineteenth century? Average age at marriage rose, thus shortening the period of potential childbearing. Women also bore their last child at a younger age, dropping from around forty in the mid-eighteenth century to around thirty-five in the mid-nineteenth. This change suggests family planning. Many couples used traditional forms of birth control, such as coitus interruptus (withdrawal of the male before completion of the sexual act) and breast-feeding, which makes some women temporarily infertile. Medical devices, however, were beginning to compete with these ancient and imperfect practices. Although animal-skin condoms imported from France were too expensive for popular use, cheap rubber condoms became available in the 1850s. Some couples used the rhythm method—attempting to confine intercourse to a woman's infertile periods. Awareness of the "safe period," however, was uncertain, even among physicians.

Limiting Families

If all else failed, women resorted to abortions, especially after 1830. Ineffective folk methods of self-induced abortion had been around for centuries, but in the 1830s abortionists, mostly women, advertised surgical services in large cities. To protect women from unqualified abortionists, and in response to reformers opposed to abortion, states began to regulate the procedure. Between 1821 and

Abortion

1841, ten states and one territory either restricted late-term abortions or prohibited abortion altogether; by 1860 twenty states had adopted such restrictions.

Significantly, the birth-control methods that women themselves controlled—the rhythm method, abstinence, and abortion—became increasingly common. The new emphasis on domesticity encouraged women's autonomy in the home and by extension gave them greater control over their own bodies. Women ruled the household, including the bedroom, with refinement and purity. As one woman put it, "Woman's duty was to subdue male passions, not to kindle them."

Smaller families and fewer births changed women's lives. At one time birth and infant care had occupied nearly the entire span of women's adult lives, and few mothers lived to see their youngest child reach maturity. Smaller families also allowed women to devote more time to their older children, and childhood gradually came to be perceived as a distinct period in the life span. The expansion of public education in the 1830s and the policy of grouping schoolchildren by age reinforced this trend.

Urban life always offered a place for men outside families. Rooming and boarding houses provided them with places to live. The expansion of cities and the market economy offered independence for women outside families as well. Single women departed from the centuries-old pattern in which a woman moved from her father's to her husband's household. Louisa May Alcott (1832–1888), the author of *Little Women* (1868) who lived most of her life in Massachusetts, sought independence and financial security for herself. Her father, the philosopher Bronson Alcott, never adequately supported his family. Not even the family's participation in a utopian cooperative put enough food on the table. Alcott worked as a seamstress, governess, teacher, and housemaid before her writing brought her success. "I think I shall come out right, and prove that though an Alcott, I can support myself," she wrote her father in 1856. "I like the independent feeling; and though not an easy life, it is a free one, and I enjoy it. I can't do much with my hands; so I will make a battering-ram of my head and make a way through this rough-and-tumble world."

Single Men and Women

Louisa May Alcott forswore marriage. She and other unmarried women pursued careers and lives defined by female relationships. Given the difficulty women had finding ways to support themselves, they undertook independence at great risk. Nonetheless, the proportion of single women in the population increased significantly in the nineteenth century. In Massachusetts in 1850, 17 percent of native-born women never married—a far larger percentage than in colonial days. Independent white women, in sum, were taking advantage of new opportunities offered by the market economy and urban expansion.

Immigrant Lives in America

 The United States continued to be a nation of newcomers. The 5 million immigrants who came to the United States between 1830 and 1860 outnumbered the entire population of the country recorded in the first

census in 1790. The vast majority were European (see Figure 12.1). During the peak period of pre–Civil War immigration, from 1847 through 1857, 3.3 million immigrants entered the United States; 1.3 million were from Ireland and 1.1 million, like the Klingers, came from the German states. By 1860, 15 percent of the white population was foreign-born.

This massive migration had been set in motion decades earlier. At the turn of the nineteenth century, the Napoleonic wars gave rise to one of the greatest population shifts in history; ultimately it lasted more than a century. War, revolution, famine, religious persecution, and the lure of industrialization led many Europeans to leave home. From the other side of the

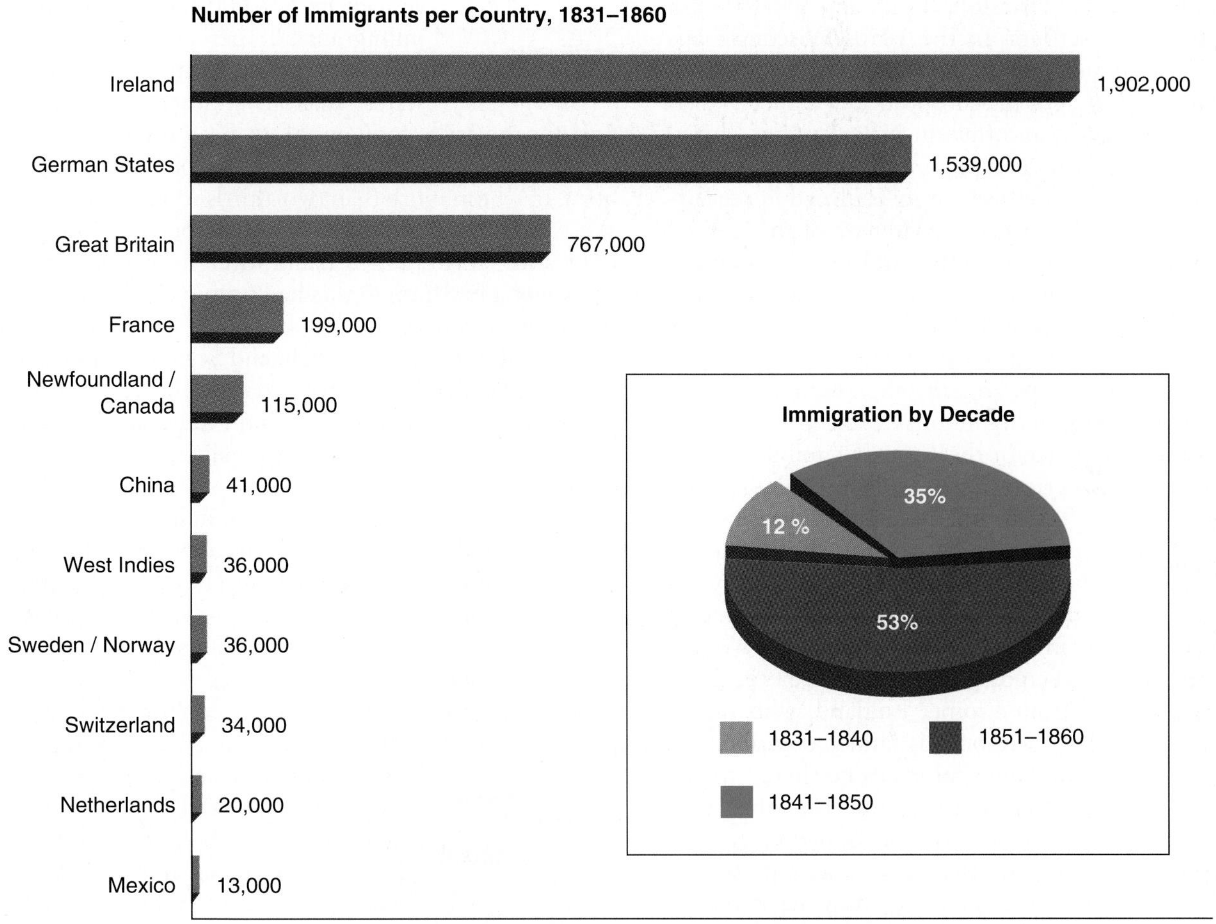

Number of Immigrants per Country, 1831–1860

- Ireland 1,902,000
- German States 1,539,000
- Great Britain 767,000
- France 199,000
- Newfoundland / Canada 115,000
- China 41,000
- West Indies 36,000
- Sweden / Norway 36,000
- Switzerland 34,000
- Netherlands 20,000
- Mexico 13,000

Immigration by Decade

35% — 1831–1840 (12%), 1841–1850 (35%), 1851–1860 (53%)

Figure 12.1 Major Sources of Immigration to the United States, 1831–1860 Most immigrants came from two areas: Great Britain, of which Ireland was a part, and the German states. These two areas sent more immigrants between 1830 and 1860 than the inhabitants of the United States enumerated at the first census in 1790. By 1860, 15 percent of the white population was of foreign birth. (Source: Data from Stephan Thernstrom, ed., *Harvard Encyclopedia of American Ethnic Groups* [Cambridge, Mass., and London: Harvard University Press, 1980], 1047.)

world, Chinese immigration to the United States was just beginning; 41,000 Chinese, nearly all men, entered the United States from 1854 through 1860 to work mostly in heavy construction. The United States attracted immigrants as its economy offered jobs and its Constitution protected religious freedom.

Promotion of Immigration

The market economy needed workers. Large construction projects and massive mining operations sought strong young men, and textile mills sought young women. To fill these jobs both private firms and governments recruited European immigrants. Midwestern and western states lured potential settlers to promote economic growth. Two transplanted New Yorkers, Augustus and Joe Kirby Allen, for instance, in 1836 set themselves up in what became Houston, Texas, and advertised in newspapers for settlers. In the 1850s Wisconsin appointed a commissioner of emigration, who advertised the state's advantages in European newspapers. Wisconsin also opened an office in New York and hired European agents to compete with other states and with firms like the Illinois Central Railroad in recruiting immigrants. Europeans' awareness of the United States grew as employers, states, and shipping companies promoted opportunities across the Atlantic. Often the message was stark: work and prosper in America or starve in Europe. The price of a ticket on the regularly scheduled sailing ships crossing the ocean after 1848 was within easy reach of millions of Europeans.

Letters Home

As the experience of the Klinger family exemplifies, success in America stimulated further emigration. "I wish, and do often say that we wish you were all in this happy land," wrote shoemaker John West of Germantown, Pennsylvania, to his kin in Corsley, England, in 1831, adding: "A man nor woman need not stay out of employment one hour here." John Down, a weaver from Frome, England, who immigrated to New York without his family, described for his wife in 1830 the bountiful meals he shared with a farmer's family. The farm hands sat at the same table with their masters and ate a banquet of puddings, pies, fruits and vegetables of the season, and preserves. Though Down sorely missed his family, he wrote, "I do not repent of coming, for you know that there was nothing but poverty before me." Such testimonials to the success of pauper immigrants in America circulated widely in Europe.

They endured the hardships of travel and of living in a strange land. The average transatlantic crossing took six weeks; in bad weather it could take three months. Disease spread unchecked among people packed together like cattle in steerage. More than seventeen thousand immigrants, mostly Irish, died from "ship fever" in 1847. On arrival, con artists and swindlers preyed on the newcomers. Boarding house and employment agents tried to lure them from their chosen destinations. In response, New York State established Castle Garden as an immigrant center in 1855. There, at the tip of Manhattan Island, the major port for European entry, immigrants were somewhat sheltered from fraud. Authorized transportation companies maintained offices in the large rotunda and assisted new arrivals with their travel plans.

Settling In

Most immigrants gravitated toward cities, and many stayed in New York City itself. By 1855, 52 percent of its 623,000 inhabitants were immigrants, 28 percent from Ireland and 16 percent from the German states. Boston, another major entry port for the Irish, took on a European tone; throughout the 1850s the city was about 35 percent foreign-born, of whom more than two-thirds were Irish. In the West, St. Louis's population was 61 percent foreign-born and San Francisco had a foreign-born majority.

Only a few immigrants had farming experience or the means to purchase land, but those who did settled in rural areas. German, Dutch, and Scandinavian farmers, in particular, headed toward the Midwest. Greater percentages of Scandinavians and Netherlanders took up farming than did other nationalities; both groups came mostly as religious dissenters and migrated in family units. The Dutch who founded colonies in Michigan and Wisconsin, for instance, had seceded from the official Reformed Church of the Netherlands, fleeing persecution in their native land to establish new and more pious communities such as Holland and Zeeland in Michigan.

Immigrant Disenchantment

Not all immigrants found success in the United States; hundreds of thousands returned to their homelands disappointed. Before the famines of the late 1840s hit Ireland, American recruiters had lured many Irish to swing picks and shovels on American canals and railroads and to work in construction. The promise that "he should soon become a wealthy man" lured Michael Gaugin, who had worked for thirteen years as an assistant engineer in the construction of a Dublin canal. The Irish agent for a New York firm convinced him to quit his job, which included a house and an acre of ground, to come to America. But Gaugin landed in New York City during the financial panic of 1837. He could not find work, and within two months he was broke, struggling to find the means to return to Ireland.

Before the great famine, caused by a blight that turned the potato crop—Ireland's food staple—rotten and inedible, there had been a small

Irish Immigrants

but steady stream of migration from Ireland to the United States. From 1845 to 1849, death from starvation, malnutrition, and typhus spread in Ireland. In all, 1 million died and about 1.5 million fled, two-thirds of them to the United States. Ireland's major export became its people. At the peak of Irish immigration, from 1847 to 1854, 1.2 million Irish men and women entered the United States. In every year but one between 1830 and 1854, the Irish constituted the largest group of immigrants. By the end of the nineteenth century there would be more Irish in the United States than in Ireland.

Most of the new immigrants from Ireland were young, female, poor, from rural counties, and Roman Catholic. In America, the women found work in textile mills and households. Young Irishmen worked in transportation and construction. The Irish supported their families back home and in Irish enclaves in cities, built Catholic churches and schools, and established networks of charitable and social organizations.

This wave of Irish immigrants, descended from the ancient Celts who spoke Gaelic, differed greatly

Racial Ideas

from the Irish who had migrated earlier to the American colonies. In the eighteenth century (see page 90), the Protestant Scots-Irish predominated; they were considered British. But the Celts were considered inferior. The British had thought them barbaric, and colonists carried those views to America. Dr. Robert Knox of the Edinburgh College of Surgeons believed the British stood for liberty, whereas "the source of all evil lies in the race, the Celtic race of Ireland." "Race is everything," he declared in an 1850 study published in Philadelphia; "literature, science, art, in a word, civilization, depends upon it." Many Americans agreed, describing Irish immigrants in negative, racial terms. They talked about Celtic racial characteristics: a small upturned nose, high forehead, and black tint of skin. As scientists like Knox began to classify peoples into biological types, scientific theory buttressed the developing notion of race.

With the immigration of new groups to the United States—Celts, Jews, and Catholics, for instance—with

Though the popular slogan "No Irish Need Apply" excluded Irish immigrants from jobs and housing, it was used by Kathleen O'Neil to attack such exclusion in her lyrics and spirited melody. In the song the Irishman meets discrimination head on, and "No Irish Need Apply" is banished.   (Special Collections, Milton S. Eisenhower Library, The Johns Hopkins University)

the black population expanding, and with territorial expansion bringing Hispanics and more Indians into the United States as well, native-born white Americans were increasingly confronted with people who did not look like them. Many considered these non-British, non-European, non-Protestant people separate races, distinct from their own. Ralph Waldo Emerson, while rejecting the extremes of Dr. Knox's argument, asserted the importance of race in *English Traits* (1856). To Emerson, as a son inherits his ancestors' "every mental and moral property," so too does a race pass on to its members its physical, intellectual, and moral characteristics. "Race avails . . . that all Celts are Catholics," Emerson wrote. "Race is a controlling influence in the Jew. . . . Race in the negro (sic) is of appalling importance. The French in Canada, cut off from all intercourse with the parent people, have held their national traits."

Were the Irish part of the white majority? In the 1840s and 1850s native-born white Americans and British and German immigrants often treated Irish men and women as if they were nonwhites. Posting placards warning "No Irish Need Apply," they excluded the Irish from many occupations. The Irish immigrants who lived with blacks in Five Points seemed to many observers to be much closer to black than white.

Closely related to racial stereotyping in its causes and nasty effects was anti-Catholicism, which became strident in the 1830s and was most overt and cruel in Boston, where a great many Irish had settled. Anti-Catholic riots were almost commonplace. In Charlestown, Massachusetts, a mob burned a convent in 1834; in Philadelphia a crowd attacked priests and nuns and vandalized churches in 1844; and in Lawrence, Massachusetts, a mob leveled the Irish neighborhood in 1854.

Anti-Catholicism

The native-born whites who rejected the Irish and hated Catholics were motivated in part by economic competition and anxiety. Competition was stiffest among the lowest paid and least desirable jobs, from women's textile millwork and domestic service to men's day-laboring jobs. To apprehensive workers, racializing the Irish as Celts was a way of keeping them out of the running. Irish-Catholics were also blamed for nearly every social problem, from immorality and alcoholism to poverty and economic upheaval. Impoverished native-born workers complained to the Massachusetts legislature in 1845 that the Irish displaced "the honest and respectable laborers of the State . . . and from their manner of living . . . work for much less per day . . . being satisfied with food to support the animal existence alone." American workers, they claimed, "not only labor for the body but for the mind, the soul, and the State."

In emphasizing "the soul, and the State," native-born workers added a political dimension to their racial expression. Republicanism depended on broad participation and the consent of the governed, and it seemed to American nativists that the Irish, a non-white, non-British "race," were not fit to participate.

The experience of German immigrants differed from that of the Irish. By and large Americans viewed most Germans, especially the majority Protestant group, as white. They shared a racial stock with the English, who according to Emerson, "come mainly from the Germans."

German Immigrants

Americans stereotyped Germans as hard working, self-reliant, and intelligent, attributes also applied to white people. Many believed that Germans fit more easily into American culture.

In the ten years from 1846 to 1855, 977,000 immigrants from the German states entered the United States, including the Klinger family. In 1854 Germans replaced the Irish as the largest group of new arrivals. Potato blight also prompted emigration from the German states in the 1840s; other hardships added to the steady stream. Many people came from regions where small landholdings made it hard to eke out a living. Craftsmen displaced by the industrial revolution sought jobs in the American expanding market economy. Political refugees—liberals, freethinkers, socialists, communists, and anarchists—fled to the United States after the abortive revolutions of 1848.

Germans shared a German language, though neither a single German state nor a common culture united them. While New York's sizable German population made it the world's third largest German-speaking city—after Vienna and Berlin—Germans settled elsewhere in the United States as well. In the South they were peddlers and merchants; in the North and West they worked as farmers, urban laborers, and businessmen. Their tendency to migrate as families and groups helped them maintain German customs and institutions. Many settled in small towns and rural areas where they could preserve their language and regional German cultures. In larger cities immigrants from the same German states tended to cluster together. Their presence transformed the tone of cities like Cincinnati and Milwaukee, as they became major producers of German beer and sausage and built shops and factories based on German crafts skills, from cigar making to tool works.

Non-Protestant Germans did not fare so well, frequently encountering hostility fed by religious and racial prejudice. A significant number of German immigrants were Jewish, and Jews were considered a separate race. Anti-Catholics attacked the German immigrants who were Catholic. The Sunday tradition of urban German families gathering at beer gardens to eat and drink, to dance and sing, and sometimes to play cards outraged Protestants, who viewed this behavior as violating the sanctity of the Lord's day.

From Florida to Texas and the Southwest to California, Hispanic inhabitants of the borderlands became "immigrants" without actually moving; treaties placed them in the United States. Some Mexicans were unhappy to find themselves in a new

Hispanics

country, while others welcomed the political self-government that the United States seemed to promise.

But reality did not live up to promise. In Nueces County, Texas, at the time of the Texas Revolution (1836), Mexicans held all the land; twenty years later, they had lost it. The new Anglo owners produced crops for the market economy; *rancheros* and *vaqueros*—cowboys—became obsolete. Although many Mexicans, called *Tejanos*, had fought for Texas's independence, new Anglo settlers tended to treat them as inferiors and foreigners. They became second-class citizens on land where they had lived for generations. Still they retained their culture. They held fast to their language, Roman Catholic religion, and cultural traditions. San Antonio, Mexican from 1821 to 1836 and thereafter a Texas city, illustrates *Tejano* persistence. The church, free public schools (established in 1827), newspapers, mutual aid societies, public holidays, and celebrations of life-cycle events from baptism to marriage to funerals all perpetuated *Tejano* culture.

In California—unlike in Texas, New Mexico, and Arizona—Hispanic society and political power quickly gave way to American and European culture. *Californios*, the Mexican population, numbered 10,000 in 1848, or two-thirds of the non-Indian population. By the end of the century the Hispanic population was 15,000 out of 1.5 million, and Hispanic culture was only a remnant, though Mexican immigrants would reestablish it in the twentieth century.

White Americans considered Hispanics, a group descended from Indians and Spaniards, as a separate, nonwhite race. Anglo-Americans also inherited the British view of Spaniards as sneaky, cowardly, lazy, and decadent, stereotypes they applied to Hispanics. Racializing Hispanics helped to justify the attitudes and actions of aggressive whites, who pushed aside any who stood in the way of expansion and settlement.

This painting (c. 1840) of Saint Isadore of Madrid, patron saint of farmers, is attributed to Rafael Aragon. Hispanic farmers in the Southwest sought the aid of Saint Isadore as they struggled to raise crops and preserve their culture.   (Courtesy of Dr. and Mrs. Ward Alan Minge)

Free People of Color

 African Americans were the most visible nonwhite group in the early nineteenth century. As their numbers grew, from 2.3 million in 1830 to 4.4 million in 1860, they were increasingly viewed solely as a racial group, a people racially apart from English and other European groups. In law and society most black people found themselves as outsiders in the land of their birth.

The free African American population rose from 320,000 in 1820 to almost 500,000 in 1860. Nearly half lived in the North, some in rural settlements but far more in cities such as Philadelphia, New York, and Cincinnati. Baltimore, in the border state of Maryland, had the largest community. An estimated 60,000 free blacks lived in Canada as exiles from the United States. Despite differences in occupation, wealth, education, religion, and social status, the necessity of self-defense promoted solidarity among free blacks.

Ex-slaves constantly increased the ranks of free people of color. Some, like Frederick Douglass and Harriet Tubman, were fugitives. Douglass, a Baltimore ship caulker, escaped in 1838 by bluffing his way to Philadelphia and freedom. Tubman, a slave in Maryland, escaped to Philadelphia in 1849 when it was rumored that she would be sold out of the state. Over the next two years she returned twice to free her two children, her sister, her mother, and her brother and his family. Some slaves received freedom in owners' wills when masters sought, at death, to rid themselves of the stain of owning slaves. Some owners released elderly slaves rather than support them in old age. Others freed their children, offspring of liaisons and forced relations with slaves.

Free people of color forged cohesive communities and created autonomous institutions within them.

African American Communities

Swept up by the Second Great Awakening, blacks turned to religion and reform. The African Methodist Episcopal Church, founded in Philadelphia in 1816, run by and for free people of color, led the way, and other churches soon followed, many of them evangelical. Black churches were the center of community life, and pastors became political leaders. Pastors taught religious and secular classes, and their chapels and social halls functioned as town halls, housing schools, political forums and conventions, protest meetings, and benevolent and self-help associations.

Black churches—especially the African Methodist Episcopal Church, run by and for free people of color—were central in the communal and religious life of free people of color. Mrs. Juliann Jane Tillman, an AME minister in Philadelphia, was a popular preacher. Peter S. Duval printed this 1844 life drawing of Tillman by Alfred Hoffy. (Library of Congress)

A network of voluntary associations became the hallmark of black communities. Besides the churches, men and women organized fraternal and benevolent associations, literary societies, and schools. In Philadelphia in the 1840s, more than half of the black population belonged to mutual beneficiary societies, and female benevolent societies and schools flourished. The Prince Hall Masons had more than fifty lodges in seventeen states by 1860. Many black leaders believed that these mutual aid societies would encourage thrift, industry, and morality, thus assisting their members to improve their lot. But no amount of effort could counteract the burden of white racism, which impinged on every aspect of their lives. For example, blacks in effect paid double for education: their taxes supported white public schools, which excluded black children; then they raised additional funds to educate their own children.

In the majority of states where free blacks were excluded from the ballot, they formed protest organizations to fight for equal rights. Among the early efforts to organize for self-defense was the Negro Convention movement. From 1830 to 1835, and irregularly thereafter, free blacks held national conventions with delegates drawn from city and state organizations. Under the leadership of the small black middle class, which included the Philadelphia sail manufacturer James Forten and the orator Reverend Henry Highland Garnet, the convention movement served as a forum to attack slavery and agitate for equal rights. Militant new black newspapers joined the struggle. *Freedom's Journal*, the first black weekly, appeared in 1827; in 1837 the *Weekly Advocate* began publication in New York City. Both papers circulated throughout the North, disseminating African American political analysis and promoting activism.

Activists fought the relegation of blacks to second-class status. The Constitution acknowledged slavery but the Bill of Rights seemed to apply to free African Americans. The Fifth Amendment specified that "no person shall . . . be deprived of life, liberty, or property, without due process of law." But eighteenth-century political theory had defined the republic as being for whites only (see page 173), and early federal legislation excluded blacks from common rights. The first naturalization law in 1790 limited citizenship to "free white persons." It implied that black people were not fit for self-government. Thus from the start legislation excluded free people of color from citizenship rights. When Congress created militias in 1792, they included only whites. After the admission of Missouri

How do historians know...

that African Americans were intensively engaged in political thought and activism in the early nineteenth century? One important source is publications of black institutions like the National Negro Conventions, first held in 1830. Free people of color held at least eleven national conventions and almost forty state conventions between 1830 and 1860. Bishop Richard Allen of the African Methodist Episcopal Church presided over the first national convention, in Philadelphia. The delegates called for pursuing "all legal means for the speedy elevation of ourselves and brethren to the scale and standing of men" and discussed emigration to Canada. The reports of the conventions document the involvement of African Americans in the reforms of the times and the importance they placed on education and equal rights. In the 1850s the conventions turned more nationalistic.

The convention movement was democratic. Most communities elected their delegates to the national conventions at public meetings or at local and state conventions. Although the minutes reveal a wide range of opinion within black communities, delegates universally agreed on abolishing slavery, immediate emancipation, and equal rights for free people of color.   (Photo: Title page for the Minutes of the Proceedings of the National Negro Convention, 1831)

> **CONSTITUTION**
>
> OF THE
>
> **AMERICAN SOCIETY**
>
> OF
>
> **FREE PERSONS OF COLOUR,**
>
> FOR IMPROVING THEIR CONDITION IN THE UNITED STATES; FOR PURCHASING LANDS; AND FOR THE ESTABLISHMENT OF A SETTLEMENT IN UPPER CANADA.
>
> ALSO
>
> **THE PROCEEDINGS OF THE CONVENTION,**
>
> WITH THEIR
>
> **ADDRESS**
>
> TO
>
> **THE FREE PERSONS OF COLOUR**
>
> IN THE
>
> **UNITED STATES.**
>
> ————————
>
> PHILADELPHIA:
> PRINTED BY J. W. ALLEN, NO 26, STRAWBERRY-ST.
> **1831.**

in 1821, every new state admitted until the Civil War, free and slave, banned blacks from voting. When Congress organized the Oregon and New Mexico Territories, it reserved public land grants for whites. Clearly free people of color were defined as an alien race; they could not participate in the republican ideal that government rested on the consent of the governed.

Even in the North, states attempted to exclude African Americans. While southern states, which found the existence of free people of color incompatible with slavery, restricted black rights as a way of encouraging free blacks to leave their states, these people were not welcome in most northern and western states

either. Many states barred free blacks or required them to post bonds ranging from $500 to $1,000 to guarantee their good conduct, as did Illinois (1819), Michigan (1837), and Oregon (1857). Only in Massachusetts, New Hampshire, Vermont, and Maine could blacks vote on an equal basis with whites throughout the early nineteenth century. In 1842 African Americans gained the right to vote in Rhode Island (where all voters faced restrictive property qualifications), but they had lost it earlier in Pennsylvania and Connecticut. Only Massachusetts permitted blacks to serve on juries. Four midwestern states and California did not allow African Americans to testify against whites. In

Oregon blacks could not own real estate, make contracts, or sue in court. The laws were meant to render African Americans powerless.

Throughout the United States white social custom became more rigid in excluding or segregating free people of color. Hotels and restaurants barred them, as did most theaters and white churches. Abolitionist Frederick Douglass was repeatedly turned away from public facilities during a speaking tour of the North in 1844.

Racial Exclusion and Segregation

Economic discrimination solidified social segregation. Black people were banned from the jobs opening up in the expanding market economy. The jobs available were consistent with white views of blacks as an inferior race, fit only for hard physical labor or servile work. Countinghouses, retail stores, and factories refused to hire black men except as janitors and handymen. New England mills hired only whites. Except for a small professional and skilled elite, free black men in the North found steady work elusive; most toiled as unskilled daily laborers.

African American women found jobs more easily than men did. Their domestic skills were in great demand in the cities; they worked as servants, cooks, laundresses, and seamstresses, and kept boarding houses. Unlike their white counterparts, these women did not view paid employment as a temporary phase in their lives; around 40 percent of black women worked for wages during their child-rearing years.

African American Women

But gender roles also restricted black women. In religious organizations they participated regularly but rarely held leadership positions. Besides holding paid work outside the home, they were expected to perform domestic duties, which included responsibility for education. A number of black women participated in abolitionist as well as literary societies, but they, like their white sisters, were discouraged from speaking in public. Black women also had to deal with black men's needs to be strong and protect women, roles men found impossible in slavery and difficult in freedom. Both men and women carried the burden of refuting racial stereotypes, but black women bore the additional burden of gender stereotypes.

The mood of free blacks turned pessimistic in the late 1840s and 1850s. Many felt frustrated by the failure of the abolitionist movement and angered by the passage of the stringent Fugitive Slave Act of 1850 (see

Black Nationalism

page 368). Some fled to Canada, others became more militant, and a few joined John Brown in his plans for a slave uprising (see page 380). Many more were swept up in a wave of black nationalism that stressed racial solidarity, self-help, and a growing interest in Africa. Before this time, efforts to send African Americans "back to Africa" had originated with whites seeking to rid the United States of blacks. But in the 1850s blacks held emigrationist conventions of their own under the leadership of abolitionists Henry Bibb and Martin Delany. Delany led an exploration party to the Niger valley as the emissary of a black convention, there signing a treaty with Yoruba rulers allowing him to settle American blacks in their African kingdom.

Nothing illustrates the poignant position of free blacks in the United States better than the flight of black Americans to Canada and Africa in search of freedom while millions of European migrants were flooding to the United States for liberty and opportunity. With the coming of the Civil War, the status of blacks would move onto the national political agenda, and African Americans would focus on their position at home.

Summary

The American people and communities in the North and West were far more diverse and turbulent in the 1850s than they had been in the 1820s. The market economy and westward movement altered farm life, city life, and class structure; heavy immigration, growing racial ideas, and the anguished position of free people of color added to the tensions. Inequality increased as did the gap between the haves and the have-nots. As the nation grew more populous and the market economy upset work and social relations, many felt a loss of tradition and community. Some longed to return to old values. Utopians like the Shakers, Mormons, and Brook Farmers sought to counter isolation and individualism.

Increasingly cities became the center of American life, with New York the predominant metropolis. Growing populations brought new problems, however, and cities struggled to provide adequate public health and safety and education for their residents. Large cities offered rich leisure activities, from entertainment to sporting events. Increasingly, however, people divided along class, ethnic, and racial lines.

Whether formal, as in the Masonic order, or informal as in the youth culture of the Bowery, divisions became more rigid. The gap between rich and poor widened.

In the midst of these changes, middle-class families sought to insulate their homes from the competition of the market economy. Many wives and mothers found fulfillment in the domestic ideal; others found "woman's sphere" confining. Middle-class urban women became associated with nurturing roles, first in homes and schools, then in churches and reform societies. Working-class women had more modest goals: escaping poverty and winning respect. Most Americans found some comfort in religion.

Famine and oppression in Europe propelled millions of people across the Atlantic, most from Ireland and the German states. American expansion added Hispanics to the nation. Diversity, competition, and religious and scientific thought fueled racial ideas. Many European descendants began to view the Irish, Hispanics, and African Americans as inferior races rather than as cultural groups. Racism justified second-class citizenship for Hispanics and black people.

LEGACY FOR A PEOPLE AND A NATION

White Fascination with and Appropriation of Black Culture

White Americans' fascination with and appropriation of black culture blossomed in the early nineteenth century. Whites performed songs and dances from blackface minstrel reviews, while urban young people imitated black language, dress, and hairstyles. In the 1850s white songwriter Stephen Foster's "Old Folks at Home," "Susanna," and "Camptown Races" were enormously popular. Whites believed they were traditional black folk songs, though they romanticized the slave South.

American popular culture combined African, European, and African American traditions. Its emphasis on performance, improvisation, strong rhythms, vernacular language, multiple meanings, and integration into everyday life is evident of strong African ties. These elements appealed to whites because of their ex-

pressive powers. Whites also believed that black cultural forms were "exotic" and offered "natural" forms of expression.

Black traditions continue to influence twentieth-century popular culture. Minstrelsy turned into vaudeville and Broadway theater, which gave birth to American popular music. Popular dance and music, performed mostly by whites, drew heavily on black gospel, slave spirituals, the blues, and jazz, and spread through live performance, recorded music, and later radio and television. Black traditions influenced the swing bands of the 1930s, and after World War II, they shaped rhythm and blues, rock 'n' roll, and, later, rap, hip-hop, and ska.

Until recently, most whites experienced black culture as appropriated by whites. Minstrels in blackface and Stephen Foster's songs modified black culture for white audiences. But in the late twentieth century, a synthesis of black and white traditions became notable. In the early 1950s Bill Haley and the Comets, a white country-western group, combined black rhythm and blues with white country and western music. Their 1954 sensation, "Shake, Rattle & Roll," for instance, was a sanitized version of Big Joe Turner's rhythm and blues hit. White audiences responded enthusiastically, and when Haley and the Comets played "Rock Around the Clock" in the 1955 movie *Blackboard Jungle*, rock 'n' roll took off. Elvis Presley too synthesized rhythm and blues and gospel with country music and middle-of-the-road popular music. Rap and hip-hop built on the talking blues, call and response, and urban black and Chicano/a dance styles of the 1970s. White suburban youth made them dominant popular forms.

Popular music and dance, with its African American roots, is uniquely American. Young people fostered this popular culture and used its expressive elements to define themselves. Thus African American culture has given the people and nation a unique cultural legacy.

For Further Reading, see page A-15 of the Appendix. **For Web resources**, go to http://www.college.hmco.com

A slaveholder in debt was a dangerous man. Pierce Butler was broke. It was late winter of 1859, fear of disunion dominated national life, and Butler's slave auction had all of coastal Georgia and South Carolina talking. Butler was the grandson of Major Pierce Butler, a framer of the Constitution, a senator from South Carolina, and a wealthy planter. Butler the younger divided his time between the family's ostentatious home in Philadelphia and 1,500 acres of cotton plantations on Butler Island and St. Simons Island in Georgia, worked by eight hundred slaves. His marriage to the famous British actress Fanny Kemble had ended in divorce; she could not bear the realities of slavery on her husband's cotton plantations, and he could not bear her protests. By 1859 Butler had squandered a fortune of $700,000 through speculation and gambling. Allegedly, he blew $25,000 on one hand of cards.

Most of Butler's properties and possessions in Philadelphia were sold to satisfy his creditors. Then came the largest slave auction in American history. In the last week of February, 436 Butler slaves were taken to Savannah by railroad and steamboat. They were housed for several days in horse-and-carriage sheds at the Ten Broeck racetrack. People of all ages—infants, husbands, wives, children, grandparents—huddled in fearful expectation. Joseph Bryan, a slave broker and auctioneer, managed the sale. Among the planters and speculators who were there to buy was an undercover *New York Tribune* reporter. The auction, held in the racecourse's grandstand, lasted an agonizing two days in a driving rainstorm.

If possible, families were sold intact for group prices; thus the old and infirm could still be liquidated, while the closest kin stayed together. A seventeen-year-old "Prime woman" named Dorcas and her three-month-old son, Joe, went for $2,200. A nineteen-year-old "prime young man," Abel, netted $1,295. Some families of four, such as Goin and Cassander and their two daughters, Emiline and Judy, brought only $1,600 together. At the end of the second day of what blacks

Thomas S. Noble's painting *The Last Sale of Slaves* depicts the public drama and family horror of slave auctions. Noble's work stimulated a heated newspaper debate in St. Louis over its abolitionist message. The sight of people treated as property, and bills of sale signed on the table, leave slavery's most haunting images.   (Missouri Historical Society)

People and Communities in a Slave Society: The South 1830–1860

in the region called the "weeping time," Butler had amassed $303,850 by selling 436 human beings. It would have been impossible to convince the numbed and despairing African Americans who traveled away from Savannah in wagons or railcars that slavery did not cause the war that would soon follow. Their sorrow was soon the nation's as well.

Many northerners remained undisturbed during the antebellum era by the growth of human bondage, even its worst elements such as the Butler auction. But a growing number came to see it as threatening and immoral. By the 1830s the North was an emerging market economy embarking on an industrial revolution.

Meanwhile, the South, with a different kind of growth and prosperity, also participated in the market revolution. New lands were settled and new states peopled, and steadily the South emerged as the world's most extensive and vigorous slave economy, linked to an international cotton trade and textile industry. Slavery had a far-reaching influence on the whole society. The Old South's wealth came from export crops, land, and slaves; and its population was almost wholly rural. In the land where cotton became king, racial slavery affected not only economics but values, customs, laws, and the region's relationship to the nation. ■

The "Peculiar" South?

 The South, the section composed of the slaveholding states from the Chesapeake region to Missouri and from Florida to Texas, has often been considered America's most distinctive region. Historians have long asked the "old perennial" question: how was the Old South like or unlike the rest of the nation? Was the South behind national economic growth and development? Or, put most directly, was the South "backward" in comparison to the industrializing North?

There has long been a tendency to equate certain American values such as materialism, individualism, and faith in progress with the North in the nineteenth century, and to equate values such as tradition, conservatism, and family loyalty to the South. The South, so the stereotype has it, was static, and the North dynamic in the decades leading up to the Civil War. Indeed, the great fact of secession and the Confederacy will always give the South a distinct place in American history. But there are many measures of just how different South was from North in the antebellum era. It depends on which measures one chooses.

The South was peculiar because of its commitment to slavery, but it was also much like the rest of the

New Orleans, the South's largest city and a major port, was a wealthy hub of a thriving market economy, rooted in cotton and woven together by river trade. This view from 1860 shows hundreds of cotton bales and dozens of steamboats waiting to receive them.   (Chicago Historical Society)

IMPORTANT EVENTS

1810–20	137,000 slaves are forced to move from North Carolina and the Chesapeake to Alabama, Mississippi, and other western regions
1822	Vesey's plot is discovered in South Carolina
1831	Turner leads a violent slave rebellion in Virginia
1832	Virginia holds last serious debate in South about the future of slavery
	Publication of Dew's proslavery tract, "Abolition of Negro Slavery"
1832 and after	Legislators in several states increase restrictions on slaves
1830s	Class tensions lead to electoral reforms in much of the South
	The cotton trade provides much of the export capital to finance northeastern economic growth

1836	Arkansas gains admission to the Union
1839	Mississippi's Married Women's Property Act gives married women some property rights
1840s	Southern slave economy prospers, but northern, urban economic growth is less dependent on it
1845	Florida and Texas gain admission to the Union
	Publication of Douglass's *Narrative of the Life of Frederick Douglass, An American Slave*
1850–60	Of some 300,000 slaves who migrate from Upper to Lower South, 60–70% go by outright sale
1857	Helper denounces the slave system in *The Impending Crisis*
	Publication of Fitzhugh's "Southern Thought," an aggressive defense of slavery

South-North Similarity

nation. The geographic sizes of the South and the North were roughly the same. By the 1830s southerners shared a heritage from the era of the American Revolution, the same heroes and political ideology, with their fellow free citizens in the North. With varying accents, southerners spoke the same language and worshiped the same Protestant God as northerners. White Americans in the South lived under the same cherished Constitution as northerners, and they shared a common mixture of nationalism and localism in their attitudes toward government. Down to the 1840s, northerners and southerners invoked the doctrine of states' rights against federal authority with nearly equal frequency. A faith in the future fueled by a sense of American mission and the dreams inspired by the westward movement were as much a part of southern as of northern experience.

Indeed, some of the most eloquent visions of America as a land of independent, self-sufficient farmers expanding westward had come from a southerner, Thomas Jefferson. Jefferson believed that "virtue" rested in those who tilled the soil, that farmers made the best citizens. In 1804 Jefferson declared his "moral and physical preference of the agricultural over the manufacturing man." But as slavery and the plantation economy expanded (see Map 13.1), the South did not become a land of individual opportunity in quite the same manner as the North.

During the thirty years before the Civil War, the South shared in the nation's economic booms and busts. Research has shown that despite its enormous cruelties, slavery was a profitable labor system for planters. In purely economic measures, slavery was not a drag on the South's prosperity. Southerners and northerners shared an expanding capitalist economy. As it grew, the slave-based economy of money-crop agriculture reflected the rational choices of planters. More land and more slaves generally converted into more wealth. By the eve of the Civil War in 1860, the distribution of wealth and property in the two sections was almost identical: 50 percent of free adult males owned only 1 percent of real and personal property, while the richest 1 percent owned 27 percent of the wealth. One study comparing Texas and Wisconsin in 1850 shows that the richest 2 percent of families in each state owned 31 to 32 percent of the wealth. So, both North and South had ruling classes, even if their wealth was invested in different kinds of property. Entrepreneurs in both sections, whether forging plantations out

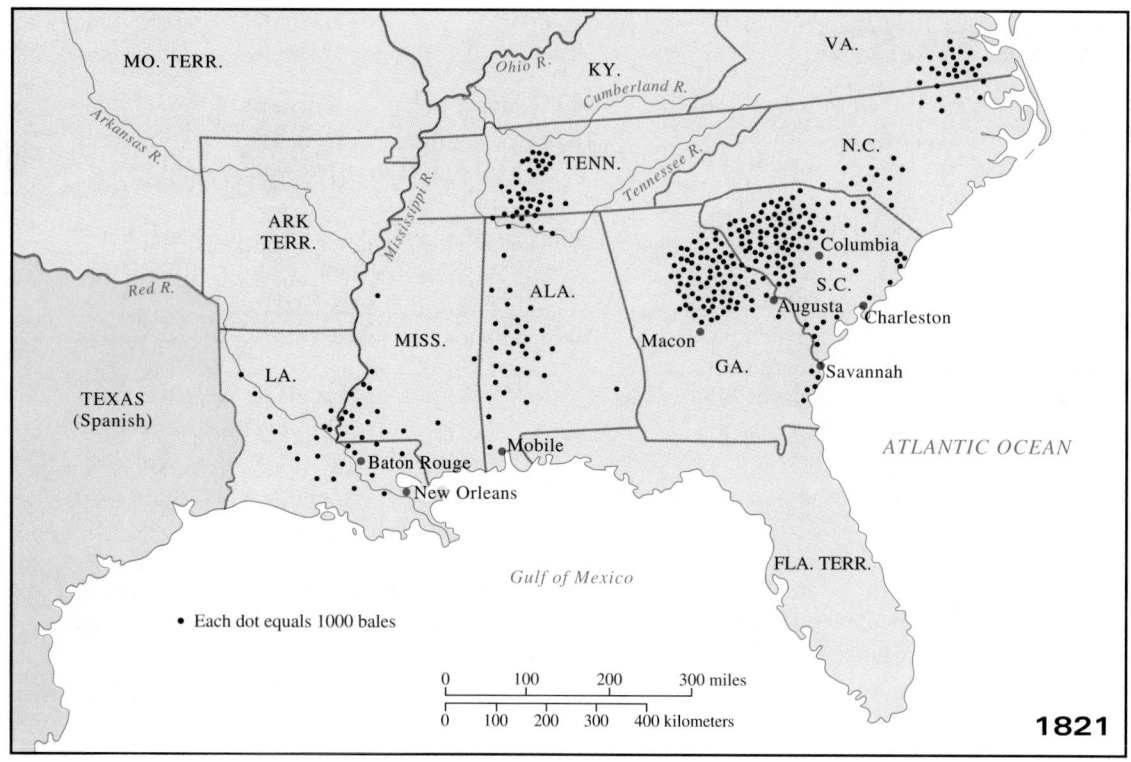

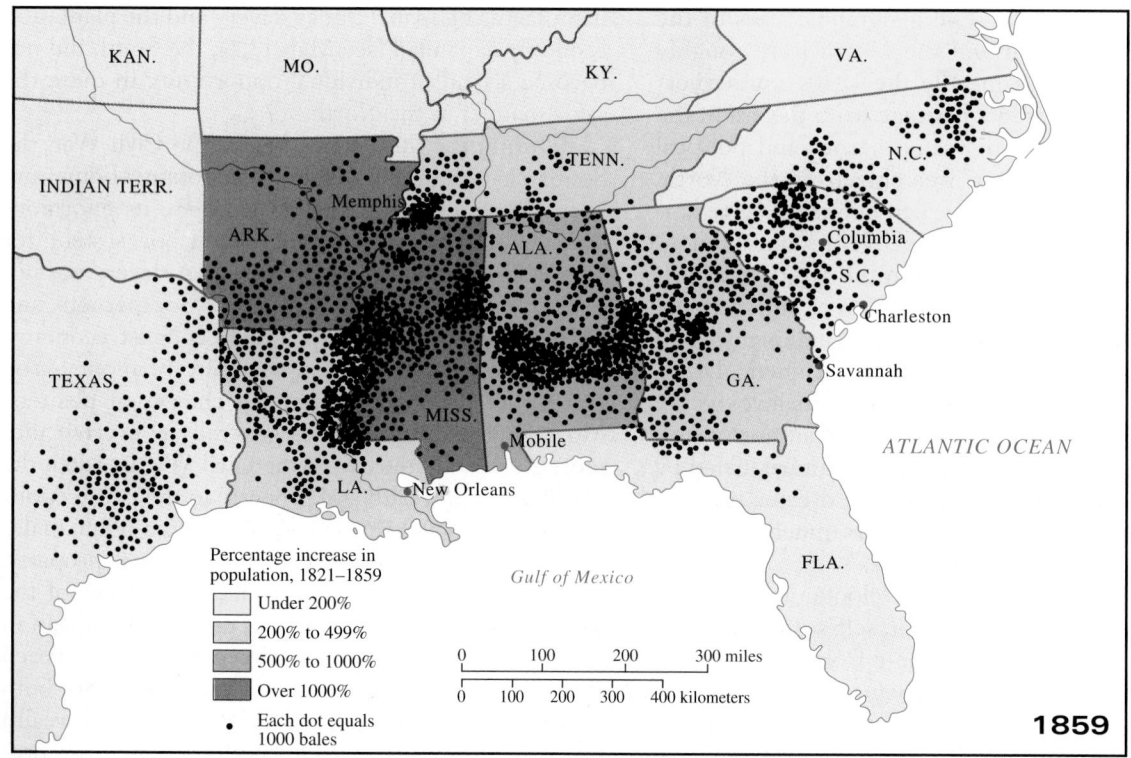

Map 13.1 Cotton Production in the South These two maps reveal the rapid westward expansion of cotton production and its importance to the antebellum South.

of Mississippi Delta land or shoe factories and textile mills in New England river towns, sought their fortunes in an expanding market economy.

But there were also important differences between the North and the South. The South's climate and longer growing season gave it an unmistakable rural and agricultural destiny. Its people, white and black, developed an intense attachment to place, to the ways people were related to the land and to one another. It developed as a biracial society of brutal inequality, where the liberty of one race directly depended on the enslavement of another.

South-North Dissimilarity

In this agrarian society, cotton growers spread out over as large an area as possible to maximize production and income. Population density was low in the older plantation states and extremely low in the frontier areas. By 1860 there were only 2.3 people per square mile in vast and largely unsettled Texas, 15.6 in Louisiana, and 18.0 in Georgia. By contrast, population density in the nonslaveholding states east of the Mississippi River was almost three times higher. The Northeast had an average of 65.4 people per square mile. Massachusetts had 153.1 people per square mile, and New York City compressed 86,400 people into each square mile. When in the 1850s young Frederick Law Olmsted of Connecticut, later renowned as a landscape architect, toured the South as a journalist, he traveled mostly on horseback along primitive trails. Between Columbus, Georgia, and Montgomery, Alabama, Olmsted found "a hilly wilderness, with a few dreary villages, and many isolated cotton farms." For the designer of Central Park in New York City, this was just too much ruralness.

Where people were scarce, it was difficult to finance and operate schools, churches, libraries, or even inns and restaurants. Southerners were strongly committed to their churches, and some believed in the importance of universities, but all such institutions were far less developed than those in the North. Factories

Eastman Johnson's *Fiddling His Way* (1866) depicts rural life by representing the visit of an itinerant black musician to a farm family. Expressions and gestures suggest remarkable ease between the races at the yeoman level of southern society.   (The Chrysler Museum of Art, Norfolk, Virginia. Bequest of Walter P. Chrysler, Jr.)

were rare because planters invested most of their capital in slaves. A few southerners did invest in iron or textiles on a small scale. But the largest southern "industry" was lumbering, and the largest factories used slave labor to make cigars. More decisively, the South was slower than the North to develop a unified market economy and a regional transportation network. Despite concerted efforts, the South had only 35 percent of the nation's railroad mileage in 1860.

The South lagged way behind the North in nearly any measure of industrial growth. It always had its reformist voices, however, who advocated commercial development. The South did have urban centers, especially ports like New Orleans and Charleston, which became bustling crossroads of commerce and small-scale manufacturing. But slavery slowed urban growth. As a system of labor and racial control, slavery did not work well in cities. As one historian has said, southern urban centers were small market towns, dependent on agricultural trade—"urbanization without cities." Likewise, the South did not attract immigrants as readily as the North. By 1860 only 13 percent of the nation's foreign-born population lived in the slave states.

Like northerners, antebellum southerners were adherents to evangelical Christianity. Americans from all regions held in common a faith in a personal God and in conversion and piety as the means to salvation. But southern evangelicalism was distinct from its northern practice. In the South, Baptists and Methodists concentrated on personal rather than social improvement. By the 1830s in the North, evangelicalism was a major wellspring of reform movements (see Chapter 11); but in the states where blacks were so numerous and unfree, and where the very social structure was under increasingly aggressive attacks from abolitionists, religion, as one scholar has written, preached "a hands-off policy concerning slavery." Although blacks themselves began to convert to Christianity in the early-nineteenth-century South, many southern whites feared a reform impulse that would foster what one historian has called an "interracial communion" in their churches and in their communities. The only reform movements that did take hold in the emerging Bible belt of the South, such as temperance, focused on personal behavior, not social reform.

When antebellum southerners built prisons or hospitals, these institutions tended to fit into a conservative social structure. Southern law restricted the authority of the courts, reinforcing a tradition of planter control. Penitentiaries tended to house only white prisoners, as most blacks were under the authority of personal masters. Law-breaking in the South tended to be crimes of violence rather than crimes against property. Similarly, the rural character of the South and the significance of the plantation as a self-sufficient social unit meant that the section put few resources into improving disease control and public health. So, in a host of ways, the South was distinct.

Perhaps in no way was the South more peculiar than in its embrace of a particular world-view, a system of thought and meaning held especially by the planter class, but also influencing all groups of whites. Like those of all people, southerners' values, beliefs, and habits and their rationalizations for slavery were not so different from those of any civilization trying to defend the institutions it inherits. But at the heart of the proslavery argument was a deep and abiding racism. The persistence of modern racism in all sections of the United States is all the more reason to comprehend antebellum southerners' justifications for human slavery, from whence so many modern racial assumptions are derived.

A Southern World-View and the Proslavery Argument

By 1830 white southerners defended slavery as a "positive good," and not merely a "necessary evil." They used the Bible and its many references to slaveholding, as well as the ancient roots of slavery, to foster a historical argument for bondage. They arrayed a variety of assumptions about the superiority and inferiority of races in support of slavery as the natural status of blacks. Whites were the more intellectual race and blacks the race more inherently physical, and therefore destined for labor. Proslavery writers did not mince words. In a proslavery tract written in 1851, John Campbell confidently declared that "there is as much difference between the lowest tribe of negroes and the white Frenchman, Englishman, or American, as there is between the monkey and the negro."

Some southerners defended slavery in practical terms; they simply saw their bondsmen as economic necessity and as symbols of their quest of prosperity. Others, such as James Henry Hammond of South Carolina, in 1845, argued that slaveholding was essentially a matter of property rights. He spoke for many southerners in his unwillingness to "deal in abstractions" about the "right and wrong" of slavery: property was sacred and slaves were legal property—end of argument.

The deepest root of the proslavery argument was a conservative, hierarchical view of human relations, a concern for social order as slavery's defenders believed God or nature had prescribed it. Southerners cherished stability, duty, and honor, believing social change

Most slaveowners lived in comfortable country homes rather than in stately mansions. This rare daguerreotype, dating from about 1853, shows a family in front of their home. Notice the presence of a male slave in the left background. (The J. Paul Getty Museum, Los Angeles, California)

should come only in slow increments, if at all. As the Virginia legislature debated the gradual abolition of slavery in 1832, in the wake of a major slave rebellion, Thomas R. Dew contended, "There is a time for all things, and nothing in this world should be done before its time."

Southern defenders of slavery held views decidedly different from those of northern reformers on the concept of freedom, progress, and equality. They turned natural law doctrine to their favor, arguing that the natural state of mankind was inequality of ability and condition, not equality. A former U.S. senator in South Carolina, William Harper, charged in 1837 that Jefferson's famous dictum about equality in the Declaration of Independence was no more than a "sentimental phrase." "Is it not palpably nearer the truth to say that no man was ever born free," Harper argued, "and that no two men were ever born equal?" Proslavery writers believed that people were born to certain stations or purposes in life; they stressed dependence over autonomy, and duty over rights, as the human condition. As the Virginia writer George Fitzhugh put it in 1854, "men are not born entitled to equal rights. It would be far nearer the truth to say, that some were born with saddles on their backs, and others booted and spurred to ride them."

Hence, however differently their slaves may have interpreted the relationship, many slaveholders believed that their ownership of people bound them, by honor, to a set of paternal obligations. They saw themselves as guardians of a familial relationship between masters and slaves given to them by fate and heritage. Although contradicted by countless examples of slave resistance and escape, planters needed to believe in, and exerted great energy in constructing, the idea of the faithful, contented slave. Slaveholders had come to understand, and needed to endlessly justify, how much the freedom of whites depended on the slavery of blacks. All these ideas about honor and mutual dependency were, of course, weighed against profits.

What the South had become by the 1830s, and grew even more fully into by 1860, was not merely a society with slaves, but a slave society (see page 72). In this way, the region was most distinct within the larger American nation. Slavery and race affected everything in the Old South. Whites and blacks alike grew up, were socialized, married, reared children, worked, invested their incomes or conceived of property, and honed their most basic habits of behavior under the influence of slavery. This was true of slaveholding and nonslaveholding whites, as well as of blacks who were slave and free. Slavery shaped the social structure of the South, fueled almost anything meaningful in its economy, and came to dominate its politics.

A Slave Society

This does not mean that the Old South did not share a common culture, political system, and economy with the North, and with Europe. The South was interdependent with the North and the West in a growing capitalist market system. Southerners relied on northern banks, northern steamship companies working the great western rivers, and northern merchants to keep the cotton trade flowing. But there were elements of that system that southerners increasingly rejected during the antebellum era, especially urbanism, the wage labor system, a broadening right to vote, and any threats to the racial and class order on which they so depended. Although enmeshed in a national economy, the Old South became anti-modern, disdainful of some of the very changes that increasingly made it different and eventually overwhelmed it.

In the antebellum era, as later, there were many Souths, depending on whether one considered the South Carolina low country or the Appalachian highlands of east Tennessee, the Mississippi Delta or the piney woods regions of the same state. But Americans have always been determined to define what one historian called the "Dixie difference." "The South is both American and something different," writes another historian, "at times a mirror or magnifier of national traits and at other times a counterculture." This was most acutely true in the decades before the Civil War.

Just how peculiar the South was will always be debated. Culturally, the South developed a proclivity to tell its own story. Its ruralness and its sense of tradition may have given southerners a special habit of telling tales. "Southerners . . . love a good tale," says Mississippi writer Eudora Welty. "They are born reciters, great memory retainers, diary keepers, letter exchangers, and letter savers, history tracers, and debaters, and—outstaying all the rest—great talkers." The South's tragic and distinct story begins in the Old South. The story was peculiar and national all at once.

Free Southerners: Farmers, Planters, and Free Blacks

 A large majority of white southern families (three-quarters in 1860) owned no slaves. Some lived in towns and ran stores or businesses, but most were yeoman farmers who owned their own land and grew their own food. The social distance between different groups of whites was great. Still greater was the distance between whites and blacks.

These farmers were individualistic and hard working. Unlike their northern counterparts, their lives were not being transformed by improvements in transportation. They could be independent thinkers as well, but their status as a numerical majority did not mean that they set the political or economic direction of the slave society. Often isolated, always absorbed in the work of their farms, they operated both apart from and within the slave-based staple-crop economy. They valued their self-reliance and freedom from others' control.

Yeoman Farmers

Yeomen pioneered the southern wilderness, moving into undeveloped regions and building log cabins. After the War of 1812 they moved in successive waves down the southern Appalachians into new Gulf lands, first as herders of livestock and then as farmers. In large sections of the South, especially inland from the coast and away from large rivers, small, self-sufficient farms that grew staple crops were the norm. Lured by stories of good land, many men uprooted their wives and children repeatedly. So many shared the excitement over new lands that one North Carolinian wrote in alarm, "The Alabama Fever rages here with great violence. . . . I am apprehensive if it continues to spread as it has done, it will almost depopulate the country."

On the southern frontier men worked hard to clear fields and establish farms, while their wives labored in the household economy and patiently re-created the social ties—to relatives, neighbors, fellow churchgoers—that enriched everyone's experience. Women seldom shared the men's excitement about moving. They dreaded the isolation and loneliness of the frontier. "We have been [moving] all our lives," lamented one woman. "As soon as ever we git comfortably settled, it is time to be off to something new."

Some yeomen acquired large tracts of level land, purchased slaves, and became planters. These people made up part of the new wealth of the boom states of Mississippi and Louisiana, the region to which the southern political power base shifted by the 1840s and 1850s. Others clung to familiar mountainous areas or kept moving as independent farmers because, as one frontiersman put it, he disliked "seeing the nose of my neighbor sticking out between the trees."

The yeomen enjoyed a folk culture based on family, church, and local region. Their speech patterns and inflections recalled their Scots-Irish and Irish backgrounds. They flocked to religious revivals called camp meetings, and in between they got together for

Yeoman Folk Culture

house-raisings, logrollings, quilting bees, corn-shuckings, and hunting for both food and sport. Such occasions combined work with fun, offering food in abundance, and usually liquor as well. They also provided welcome fellowship to isolated rural dwellers.

A demanding round of work and family responsibilities shaped women's lives in the home. At harvest they helped in the fields, and throughout the year the care and preparation of food consumed much of their time. Household tasks continued during frequent pregnancies and childcare. Primary nursing and medical care also fell to the mother, who might have a book of remedies to aid her but often relied on folk wisdom.

Among the men there were many who aspired to wealth, eager to join the race for slaves and cotton profits.

Yeoman Livelihoods

North Carolinian John F. Flintoff kept a diary of his struggle for success. At age eighteen in 1841, Flintoff went to Mississippi to seek his fortune. Like other aspiring yeomen, he worked as an overseer of slaves but often found it impossible to please his employers. At one point he gave up and returned to North Carolina, where he married and lived for a while in his parents' house. But Flintoff was "impatient to get along in the world," so he tried Louisiana next and then Mississippi again.

Flintoff's health suffered in the Gulf region and, routinely, "first rate employment" alternated with "very low wages." Moreover, as a young man working on isolated plantations, Flintoff often felt lonely. Even a revival meeting in 1844 proved "an extremely cold time" with "little warm feeling." His uncle and other employers found fault with his work, and in 1846 Flintoff concluded in despair that "managing negroes and large farms is soul destroying."

But a desire to succeed at this very economic proposition kept him going. At twenty-six, even before he owned any land, Flintoff bought his first slave, "a negro boy 7 years old." Soon he had purchased two more children, the cheapest slaves available. Conscious of his status as a slaveowner, Flintoff resented the low wages he was paid. In 1853, with nine young slaves and a growing family, Flintoff faced "the most unhappy time of my life." Fired by his uncle, he returned to North Carolina, sold some of his slaves, and purchased 124 acres with help from his in-laws. Flintoff grew corn, wheat, and tobacco and earned extra cash hauling wood. By 1860 he owned three horses, twenty-six hogs, ten head of cattle, and several slaves

and was paying off his debts. As the Civil War approached, he looked forward to freeing his wife from labor, and possibly sending his sons to college. Although Flintoff demonstrated that a farmer could move in and out of the slaveholding class, his path had been wrenching, and he never achieved the cotton planter status he desired.

Probably more typical of the southern yeoman was Ferdinand L. Steel, who as a young man moved from North Carolina to Tennessee to work as a river boatman but eventually took up farming in Mississippi. Steel rose every day at five and worked until sundown. With the help of his family he raised corn, wheat, pork, and vegetables. Cotton was his cash crop: he sold five or six bales (about 2,000 pounds) a year to obtain money for sugar, coffee, salt, calico, gunpowder, and a few other store-bought goods.

Thus Steel entered the market economy as a small farmer, but with mixed results. He picked his own cotton and complained that cotton cultivation was brutal work. He felt like a serf in cotton's kingdom. When cotton prices fell, a small grower like Steel could be driven into debt and lose his farm. In fact, he wanted to grow less cotton. "We are too weak handed" to manage it, he noted in his diary. "We had better . . . raise corn and keep out of debt and we will have no necessity of raising cotton."

Steel's life in Mississippi in the 1840s retained much of the flavor of the frontier. He made all the family's shoes; his wife and sister sewed dresses, shirts, and "pantiloons." The Steel women also rendered their own soap and spun and wove cotton into cloth; the men hunted game. Steel doctored his illnesses with boneset tea and other herbs. As the nation fell deeper into crisis over the future of free or slave labor, this independent southern farmer never came close to owning a slave.

The focus of Steel's life was family and religion. Family members prayed together daily, and he studied Scripture for an hour after lunch. "My Faith increases, & I enjoy much of that peace which the world cannot give," he wrote in 1841. Seeking to prepare himself for Judgment Day, Steel borrowed histories, Latin and Greek grammars, and religious books from his church. Eventually he became a traveling Methodist minister. "My life is one of toil," he reflected, "but blessed be God that it is as well with me as it is."

Toil with even less security was the lot of two other groups of free southerners: landless whites and free blacks. A sizable minority of white southern workers—from 25 to 40 percent, depending on the state—

Landless Whites were unskilled laborers who owned no land and worked for others in the countryside and towns. Their property consisted of a few household items and some animals—usually pigs—that could feed themselves on the open range. The landless included some immigrants, especially Irish, who did heavy and dangerous work such as building railroads and digging ditches.

In the countryside, white farm laborers struggled to purchase land in the face of low wages or, if they rented, unpredictable market prices for their crops. By scrimping and saving and finding odd jobs, some managed to climb into the ranks of yeomen. When James and Nancy Bennitt of North Carolina succeeded in their ten-year struggle to buy land, they decided to avoid the unstable market in cotton; thereafter they raised extra corn and wheat as sources of cash. People like the Bennitts were both participants in and victims of an economy dominated by cotton producers who relied on slave labor.

Herdsmen who viewed pigs and livestock as a major economic asset always had a desperate struggle to succeed. By 1860, as the South anticipated war to preserve its society, between 300,000 and 400,000 white people in the four states of Virginia, North and South Carolina, and Georgia lived in genuine poverty, approximately one-fifth of the total white population. Their lives were harsh to say the least. An early antebellum traveler in central South Carolina described the white folk he encountered in the countryside: "The people looked yellow, poor, and sickly. Some of them lived the most miserably I ever saw any poor people live." In many ways the cotton boom only made the poor poorer.

Free Blacks For the nearly quarter-million free blacks in the South in 1860, conditions were generally worse than the yeoman's and often little better than the slave's. The free blacks of the Upper South were usually descendants of men and women manumitted by their owners in the 1780s and 1790s. A remarkable number of slaveholders in Virginia and the Chesapeake region had freed their slaves because of religious principles and revolutionary ideals in the wake of American independence (see Chapter 7). Many also became free as runaways, especially by the 1830s, disappearing into the southern population or making their way northward.

White southerners were increasingly desperate to restrict this growing free black presence in their midst in the antebellum years. "It seems the number of free Negroes," complained a Virginia slaveholder, "always exceeds the number of Negroes freed." Some free blacks made substantial progress in towns or cities, but most lived in rural areas and struggled to survive. They usually did not own land and had to labor in someone else's fields, often beside slaves. By law free blacks could not own a gun, buy liquor, violate curfew, assemble except in church, testify in court, or (throughout the South after 1835) vote. Despite these obstacles, a minority bought land, and others found jobs as skilled craftsmen.

A few free blacks prospered and bought slaves, most of them purchasing their own wives and children (whom they could not free, since laws required newly emancipated blacks to leave their states). In 1830 there were 3,775 free black slaveholders in the South; 80 percent lived in the four states of Louisiana, South Carolina, Virginia, and Maryland, and approximately one-half of the total lived in the two cities of New Orleans and Charleston. Hundreds of petitions survive in which black slaveholders asked to be exempted from antimanumission laws passed in most southern states. At the same time, a few mulattos in New Orleans were active slave traders in its booming market.

Free Black Communities In the cotton and Gulf regions, a large proportion of free blacks were mulattos, the privileged offspring of wealthy white planters. Not all planters freed their mixed-race offspring, but those who did often recognized a moral obligation and gave their children a good education and financial backing. In a few cities like New Orleans, Charleston, and Mobile, extensive interracial sex, as well as migrations from the Caribbean, had produced a mulatto population that was recognized as a distinct class.

In many southern cities by the 1840s, free black communities formed, especially around an expanding number of churches. By the late 1850s, Baltimore had fifteen churches, Louisville nine, and Nashville and St. Louis four each, and most of them were African Methodist Episcopal. Class and race distinctions were important to southern free blacks, but outside a few cities, which developed fraternal orders of skilled craftsmen and fellowships of light-skinned people, most mulattos experienced more disadvantages than benefits. In the United States, "one drop" of black "blood" made them black, and potentially enslaveable.

At the top of the southern social pyramid were slaveholding planters. As a group they lived well and enjoyed luxuries. But most lived in comfortable farmhouses, not on the opulent scale that legend suggests.

Planters

The grand plantation mansions, with fabulous gardens and long rows of outlying slave quarters, are an enduring symbol of the Old South. But a few statistics tell the fuller story: in 1850, 50 percent of southern slaveholders had fewer than five slaves; 72 percent had fewer than ten; 88 percent had fewer than twenty. Thus the average slaveholder was not a wealthy aristocrat but an aspiring farmer, usually a person of humble origins, with little formal education.

Consider the Louisiana cotton planter Bennet Barrow, a newly rich planter of the 1840s who was preoccupied with moneymaking. He worried constantly over his cotton crop, filling his diary with weather reports and gloomy predictions of his yields. Yet Barrow also strove to appear above such worries. Barrow hunted frequently and had a passion for racing horses and raising hounds. He could report the loss of a slave without feeling, but emotion broke through his laconic manner when illness afflicted his sporting animals. "Never was a person more unlucky than I am," he mourned. "My favorite pup never lives." His strongest feelings surfaced when his horse Jos Bell—equal to "the best Horse in the South"—"broke down running a mile . . . ruined for Ever." The same day the

This grand portrait (1851) by William Frye of Minor Winn Gracey and his wife, Mourning Smith Gracey, of Alabama, celebrates the planter class's wealth and status in the artifacts surrounding the couple.
(Loaned by William M. Spencer III, Birmingham Museum of Art)

distraught Barrow gave his field hands a "general Whipping." In 1841 diary entries he worried about a rumored slave insurrection. He gave a "severe whipping" to several of his slaves when they disobediently killed a hog. And when a slave named Ginney Jerry "sherked" his cotton-picking duties and was rumored "about to run off," Barrow whipped him one day, and the next, recorded matter-of-factly: "took my gun found him in the Bayou behind the Quarter, shot him in his thigh—etc. raining all around."

The richest planters used their wealth to model genteel sophistication. Extended visits, parties, and balls to which women wore the latest fashions provided opportunities for friendship, courtship, and display. Such parties were held during the Christmas holidays, but also on such occasions as a molasses stewing, a Bachelor's Ball, a horse race, or the crowning of the May Queen. These entertainments were especially important as diversions for plantation women. Young women relished social events to break the monotony of their domestic lives. In 1826 a Virginia girl was ecstatic about the "week . . . I was in Town." "There were five beaux and as many belles in the house constantly," she declared, and all she and her companions did was "eat, visit, romp, and sleep. . . ."

Some old Virginia and South Carolina families were represented among the proud new "cotton snobs" of Alabama and Mississippi, but most of the planters in these cotton boom states were newly rich by the 1840s. As one historian put it, "a number of men mounted from log cabin to plantation mansion on a stairway of cotton bales, accumulating slaves as they climbed." And many did not live like rich men. Some lived for decades in their original log cabins, improved only by clapboards or a frame addition. They put their new wealth into cotton acreage and slaves even as they sought refinement and high social status.

William Faulkner immortalized the new wealthy planter in a fictional character, Thomas Sutpen, in his novel *Absalom, Absalom!* (1936). Sutpen arrives in a Mississippi county in the 1830s, buys a huge plantation he calls Sutpen's Hundred, and with his troop of slaves converts it into a wealthy enterprise. Sutpen marries a local girl, and although he is always viewed as a mysterious outsider by many earlier residents of the county, he becomes a pillar of the slaveholding class. Sutpen eventually serves as an officer in the Confederate Army, but he achieves his status largely because he was a self-made man of indomitable will and slave-based wealth. Although his ambition is ultimately his undoing, one of the earliest lessons Sutpen had learned

about success in the South he migrated into was, as he says, that "you got to have land and niggers and a fine house. . . ."

The cotton boom in the Mississippi valley created one-generation aristocrats. A nonfictional case in point is Greenwood Leflore, a Chocktaw chieftain who owned a plantation in Mississippi with four hundred slaves. After selling his cotton on the world market, he spent $10,000 in France to furnish one room of his mansion. The floor was covered with a handwoven Aubusson carpet, and the furniture was all Louis XIV period pieces, upholstered in crimson and gold leaf. A table and cabinet were ornamented with tortoise-shell inlay and brasswork, and the room also featured a variety of mirrors and paintings, and a clock and candelabra in brass and ebony completed Leflore's conspicuous display of wealth.

Slaveholding men dominated society and, especially among the wealthiest and oldest families, justified their dominance through a paternalistic ideology. Instead of stressing the profitable aspects of commercial agriculture, they focused on their *obligations*, viewing themselves as custodians of the welfare of society in general and of the black families they owned in particular. The paternalistic planter saw himself not as an oppressor but as the benevolent guardian of an inferior race. He developed affectionate feelings toward his slaves (as long as they knew their place) and was genuinely shocked at criticism of his behavior. Even yeomen who moved in and out of the slaveowning class shared this attitude of racial paternalism.

Southern Paternalism

Paul Carrington Cameron, who was North Carolina's largest slaveholder, exemplifies this mentality. After a period of sickness among his one thousand North Carolina slaves (he had hundreds more in Alabama and Mississippi), Cameron wrote, "I fear the Negroes have suffered much from the want of proper attention and kindness under this late distemper . . . no love of lucre shall ever induce me to be cruel. . . ." On another occasion he described to his sister the sense of responsibility he felt: "Do you remember a cold & frosty morning, during [our mother's] illness, when she said to me 'Paul my son the people ought to be shod' this is ever in my ears, whenever I see any ones shoes in bad order; and in my ears it will be, so long as I am master."

It was comforting to rich planters to see themselves in this way, and slaves—accommodating to the realities of power—encouraged their masters to think their benevolence was appreciated. Paternalism also served as a defense against abolitionist criticism. Still, paternalism was often a matter of style, covering harsher assumptions. As talk of paternalistic duties increased, theories about the complete and permanent inferiority of blacks multiplied. In reality, paternalism grew as a give-and-take relationship between masters and slaves, each extracting from the other as much as they could of what they desired—labor from the bondsmen, a measure of autonomy and living space from the slaveowners. But it also evolved as a theory of black slavery and white dominance. As one historian has argued, paternalism "grew out of the necessity to discipline and morally justify a system of exploitation, . . . a fragile bridge across the intolerable contradictions inherent" in a slave society dependent on "the willing reproduction and productivity of its victims."

Even Paul Cameron's benevolence vanished with changed circumstances. After the Civil War, he bristled at African Americans' efforts to be free and made sweeping economic decisions without regard to their welfare. Writing on Christmas Day 1865, Cameron showed little Christian charity (but a healthy profit motive) when he declared, "I am convinced that the people who gets rid of the free negro first will be the first to advance in improved agriculture. Have made no effort to retain any of mine [and] will not attempt a crop beyond the capacity of 30 hands." With that he turned off his land nearly a thousand black people, rented his fields to several white farmers, and invested in industry.

Relations between men and women in the planter class were similarly paternalistic. The upper-class

Plantation Mistresses

southern woman was raised and educated to be a wife, mother, and subordinate companion to men. South Carolina's Mary Boykin Chesnut wrote of her husband, "He is master of the house. To hear is to obey. . . . All the comfort of my life depends upon his being in a good humor." In a social system based on the coercion of an entire race, women were not allowed to challenge society's rules on sexual or racial relations.

Planters' daughters usually attended one of the South's rapidly multiplying boarding schools. There they formed friendships with other girls and received an education that emphasized grammar, composition, penmanship, geography, literature, and languages. Typically the young woman could entertain suitors whom her parents approved. But very soon she had to choose

a husband and commit herself for life to a man whom she generally had known for only a brief time. Young women were often alienated and emotionally unfulfilled. They had to follow the wishes of their families, especially fathers. "It was for me best that I yielded to the wishes of papa," wrote a young North Carolinian in 1823. "I wonder when my best will cease to be painful and when I shall begin to enjoy life instead of enduring it."

Upon marriage, a planter class woman ceded to her husband most of her legal rights, becoming part of his family. Most of the year she was isolated on a large plantation, where she had to oversee the cooking and preserving of food, manage the house, supervise care of the children, and attend sick slaves. All these realities were more rigid and confining on the frontier, where isolation was even greater. Women sought refuge in their extended families and associations with other women. In 1821 a Georgia woman wrote to her brother of the distress of a cousin's wife: "They are living . . . in the frontiers of the state and [a] perfectly uncivilized place. Cousin W. gets a good practice [the husband]—but she is almost crazy to get to Alabama where one of her sisters is living." Men on plantations could occasionally escape into the public realm—to town, business, or politics. Women could retreat from rural plantation culture only into kinship.

It is not surprising that a perceptive young woman sometimes approached marriage with anxiety. Women

Marriage and Family

could hardly help viewing their wedding days, as one put it in 1832, as "the day to fix my fate." Lucy Breckinridge, a wealthy Virginia girl of twenty, lamented the autonomy she surrendered at the altar. In her diary she recorded this unvarnished observation on marriage: "If [husbands] care for their wives at all it is only as a sort of servant, a being made to attend to their comforts and to keep the children out of the way. . . . A woman's life after she is married, unless there is an immense amount of love, is nothing but suffering and hard work."

Lucy loved young children but knew that childbearing often involved grief, poor health, and death. In 1840 the birth rate for white southern women in their childbearing years was almost 30 percent higher than the national average. The average southern white woman could expect to bear eight children in 1800; by 1860 the figure had decreased to only six, with one or more miscarriages likely. For those women who wanted to plan their families, methods of contraception and medical care were uncertain. Complications of childbirth were a major cause of death, occurring twice as often in the hot, humid South as in the Northeast.

Slavery was another source of problems that white women had to endure but were not supposed to notice. "Violations of the moral law . . . made mulattoes as common as blackberries," protested a woman in Georgia, but wives had to play "the ostrich game." "A magnate who runs a hideous black harem," wrote Mrs. Chesnut, ". . . poses as the model of all human virtues to these poor women whom God and the laws have given him. From the height of his awful majesty, he scolds and thunders at them, as if he never did wrong in his life."

Southern men tolerated little discussion by women of the slavery issue. In the 1840s and 1850s, as abolitionist attacks on slavery increased, southern men published a barrage of articles stressing that women should restrict their concerns to the home. The *Southern Quarterly Review* declared, "The proper place for a woman is at home. One of her highest privileges, to be politically merged in the existence of her husband."

But some southern women were beginning to seek a larger role. A study of women in Petersburg, Virginia, a large tobacco-manufacturing town, revealed behavior that valued financial autonomy. Over several decades before 1860, the proportion of women who never married, or did not remarry after the death of a spouse, grew to exceed 33 percent. Likewise the number of women who worked for wages, controlled their own property, and ran millinery or dressmaking businesses increased. In managing property, these and other women benefited from legal changes; to protect families from the husband's indebtedness during business panics and recessions, reforms gave married women some property rights.

Slave Life and Labor

 For African Americans, slavery was a burden that destroyed some people and forced others to develop modes of survival. Slaves knew a life of poverty, coercion, toil, and resentment. They provided the physical strength, and much of the know-how, to build a burgeoning agricultural empire. But their daily lives embodied the nation's most basic contradiction: in the world's model republic, they were on the wrong side of a brutally unequal power relationship between masters and slaves.

Southern slaves enjoyed few material comforts beyond the bare necessities. Although they generally had enough to eat, their diet was plain and monotonous. Clothing too was plain, coarse, and inexpensive. Few slaves received more than one or two changes of clothing for hot and cold seasons and one blanket each winter. Children of both sexes ran naked in hot weather and wore long cotton shirts in winter. Many slaves had to go without shoes until December, even as far north as Virginia. The shoes they received were frequent objects of complaint—uncomfortable brass-toed brogans or stiff wraparounds made from tanned leather. The bare feet of slaves were often symbolic of their status, and one reason why, after freedom, many black parents were so concerned to provide their children with shoes.

Slaves' Everyday Conditions

Summer and winter, slaves typically lived in small one-room cabins, possibly with a window opening but no glass. Some of the richer plantations provided more substantial houses, but the average slave lived in crude accommodations, where dirt was the only floor. The gravest drawback of slave cabins was not lack of comfort but their unhealthfulness. Each small cabin housed one or two entire families. Crowding and lack of sanitation fostered the spread of infection and contagious diseases such as typhoid fever, malaria, and dysentery.

Hard work was the central fact of slaves' existence. The long hours and large work gangs that characterized Gulf Coast cotton districts operated almost like factories in the field. Overseers rang the morning bell before dawn—so early that some slaves remembered being "afraid to start work for fear that they would cover the cotton plants with dirt because they couldn't see clearly." Slaves who cultivated tobacco in the Upper South worked long hours picking the sticky, sometimes noxious, tobacco leaves under harsh discipline. And, as one woman recalled when interviewed in the 1930s, "it was way after sundown 'fore they could stop that field work. Then they had to hustle to finish their night work [such as watering livestock or cleaning cotton] in time for supper, or go to bed without it."

Slaves' Work Routines

Working "from sun to sun" became a norm in much of the South. Long hours and hard work were among the advantages that slave labor gave southern planters. As one planter put it, slaves were the best la-

George Fuller, an itinerant painter from Massachusetts, worked from 1856 to 1858 in Alabama, where he made this sketch in ink and pencil of a mistress joining her slave at work on washday.   (Pocumtuck Valley Memorial Association)

bor because "you could command them and make them do what was right." Profit took precedence over paternalism. Slave women did heavy fieldwork, often as much as the men and even during pregnancy. Old people—of whom there were few—were kept busy caring for young children, doing light chores, or carding, ginning, and spinning cotton. Children had to gather kindling, carry water to the fields, or sweep the yard. The black abolitionist orator Frances Ellen Watkins captured this grinding economic reality of slavery in an 1857 speech, charging that slaveholders had "found out a fearful alchemy by which . . . blood can be transformed into gold. Instead of listening to the cry of agony, they listen to the ring of dollars and stoop down to pick up the coin."

Different jobs, talents, and circumstances created variations in status and rivalries among slaves. But only one-quarter of all slaves lived on plantations of fifty or more blacks, so few experienced a wide chasm separating house servants and lowly field hands. Many slaves did both housework and fieldwork, depending on their age and the season, and this arrangement helped create a sense of group unity.

But incentives had to be part of the labor regime and the master-slave relationship as well. Planters in the South Carolina and Georgia low country used a task system whereby slaves were assigned measured amounts of work to be performed in a given amount of time. So much cotton on a daily basis was to be picked from a designated field; so many rows hoed or plowed in a particular slave's specified section. When the task system worked best, slaves and masters alike embraced it, fostering a degree of reciprocal trust.

By the 1830s slaveowners found that labor could be regulated and motivated by the clock. When their task and "clock time" was up, slaves' time was their own, for working in garden plots, tending to hogs, or even hiring out their own extra labor. The system's incentives afforded many slave families life-sustaining material and psychological benefits. From this experience and personal space, many slaves developed their own sense of property ownership.

Slaves could not demand autonomy too much, of course, because the owner enjoyed a monopoly on force and violence. Whites throughout the South believed that slaves "can't be governed except with the whip." One South Carolinian frankly explained to a northern journalist that he whipped his slaves regularly, "say once a fort-

Violence Against Slaves

night; . . . the fear of the lash kept them in good order." Evidence suggests that whippings were less frequent on small farms than on large plantations. But beatings symbolized authority to the master and tyranny to the slaves, who made them a benchmark for evaluating a master. In the words of former slaves, a good owner was one who did not "whip too much," whereas a bad owner "whipped till he's bloodied you and blistered you."

As these reports suggest, terrible abuses could and did occur. The master wielded virtually absolute authority on his plantation, and courts did not recognize the word of chattel. Slaveholders rarely had to answer to the law or to the state. Pregnant women were whipped, and there were burnings, mutilations, tortures, and murders. Yet physical cruelty may have been less prevalent in the United States than in other slaveholding parts of the New World. In sugar-growing operations in Brazil and mining regions in Peru in the 1800s, slaves were regarded as an expendable resource to be replaced after several years. Especially in some of the sugar islands of the Caribbean, treatment was so poor and death rates were so high that the heavily male slave population shrank in size. In the United States, by contrast, the slave population experienced a steady natural increase as births exceeded deaths and each generation grew larger. Indeed, the North American slave population was the only one in the New World to naturally reproduce itself.

The worst evil of American slavery was not its physical cruelty but the nature of slavery itself: coercion, lack of freedom, belonging to another person, virtually no hope for mobility or change. Recalling their time in bondage, some former slaves emphasized the physical abuse, or the "bullwhip days," as one woman described her past. But memories of physical punishment focused on the tyranny of whipping as much as the pain. Delia Garlic made the essential point: "It's bad to belong to folks that own you soul an' body. I could tell you 'bout it all day, but even then you couldn't guess the awfulness of it." Thomas Lewis put it this way: "There was no such thing as being good to slaves. Many people were better than others, but a slave belonged to his master and there was no way to get out of it." To be a slave was to be the object of another person's will and material gain, to be owned, as the saying went, "from the cradle to the grave."

As these comments reveal, the great majority of American slaves retained their mental independence and self-respect despite their bondage. Contrary to popular belief at the time, they were not loyal partners in their own oppression. They had to be subservient and speak honeyed words to their masters, but they talked and behaved quite differently among themselves. The evidence of their resistant attitudes comes from their actions and their own life stories. In his *Narrative* (1845), Frederick Douglass wrote that most slaves, when asked about "their condition and the character of their masters, almost universally say they are contented, and that their masters are kind." Slaves did this, said Douglass, because they were governed by the maxim that "a still tongue makes a wise head," especially in the presence of unfamiliar people. Because they were "part of the human family," slaves often quarreled over who had the best master. But at the end of the day, Douglass remarked, when one had a bad master, he sought a better master; and when he had a better one, he wanted to "be his own master."

Some former slaves remembered warm feelings between masters and slaves, but the prevailing attitudes were distrust and antagonism. Slaves saw through acts of kindness. One woman said her mistress was "a mighty good somebody to belong to" but only "'cause she was raisin' us to work for her." A man recalled that his owners took good care of their slaves, "and Grandma Maria say, 'Why shouldn't they—it was their money.'" Slaves also resented being used as beasts of burden. One man observed that his master "fed us reg'lar on good, 'stantial food, just like you'd tend to your horse, if you had a real good one." Another recalled his master eyeing the slave children and saying, "'That one will be worth a thousand dollars.' . . . You see, it was just like raisin' young mules."

Slave-Master Relationships

Slaves were alert to the thousand daily signs of their degraded status. One man recalled the general rule that slaves ate cornbread and owners ate biscuits. If blacks did get biscuits, "the flour that we made the biscuits out of was the third-grade sorts." A former slave recalled, "Us catch lots of 'possums," but "the white folks ate 'em. Our mouths would water for some of that 'possum, but it wasn't often they let us have none." If the owner took his slaves' garden produce to town and sold it for them, the slaves often suspected him of pocketing part of the profits.

Suspicion often grew into hatred. When a yellow fever epidemic struck in 1852, many slaves saw it as God's retribution. An elderly ex-slave named Minnie Fulkes cherished the conviction that God was going to punish white people for their cruelty to blacks. She described the whippings that her mother had to endure, and then she exclaimed, "Lord, Lord, I hate white people and the flood waters goin' to drown some more."

On the plantation, of course, slaves had to keep such thoughts to themselves. Often they expressed one feeling to whites, another within their own households. In their daily lives slaves created many ways to survive and to sustain their humanity in this world of repression.

Slave Culture

 A people is always "more than the sum of its brutalization," wrote the African American novelist Ralph Ellison in 1967. What people create in the face of hard luck and oppression is what provides hope. The resource that enabled slaves to maintain such defiance was their culture: a body of beliefs, values, and practices born of their past and maintained in the present. As best they could, they built a community knitted together by sto-

ries, music, a religious world-view, leadership, the smells of their cooking, the sounds of their own voices, and the tapping of their feet. "The values expressed in folklore," wrote the African American poet Sterling Brown, provided a "wellspring to which slaves . . . could return in times of doubt to be refreshed."

Slaves had few of the basic hopes one generation wishes to transmit to the next that were not denied. That they endured and found loyalty and strength among themselves is a tribute to their courage and triumph of the human spirit.

Slave culture changed significantly after 1800, as fewer and fewer slaves were African-born. For a few years South Carolina reopened the

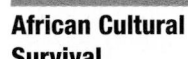
African Cultural Survival

international slave trade, but after 1808 Congress banned further importations. By the 1830s, the vast majority of slaves in the South were native-born Americans. Many blacks, therefore, can trace their American ancestry back farther than many white Americans.

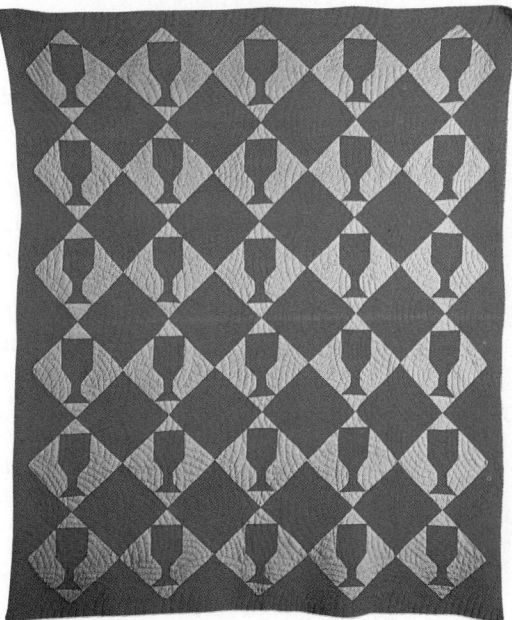

In addition to the heavy labor required on southern plantations, slaves also performed work of fine craftsmanship in furniture making, needlework, and other areas. This dining room corner cupboard is walnut veneer on pine and cedar and was built around 1840. The quilt, emblazoned with chalice cups to celebrate the annual visit of an Anglican bishop, was made around 1860. Both are from Texas. (Cupboard: Courtesy of the Witte Museum and the San Antonio Museum Association, San Antonio, Texas; Quilt: The American Museum in Britain, photo courtesy of The Museum of the Confederacy)

that the slaves' daily feelings, yearnings, crises, or hardships were reflected in their songs? In the slave narratives, autobiographies written by ex-slaves after their escapes, former bondsmen and bondswomen left many clues to the meanings of slave culture. In *Narrative of the Life of Frederick Douglass, An American Slave* (1845), the most famous black abolitionist gave many answers to the riddles of the slaves' psychological world. Slaves interpreted their experience from a sacred world-view in which God and the spirit could enter daily life at any time. It was also a world of paradoxes and ironic reversals. Douglass's discussion of slave life constantly moves between the slaves' endurance of dehumanization and their ability to fashion creative resistance. He argues that the slaves' humanity manifests itself in a cunning accommodation to, and subversion of, evil authority.

Douglass, seen here when he was in his early thirties, anticipates modern historians' treatment of slave culture most directly in his discussion of slave music (see excerpt below). Through imagination, he invites the future scholar into the piney woods around the Wye River plantation (the "Great House Farm") on the slaves' "allowance day" (when food and clothing were distributed), and there, in silence, to "analyze the sounds that shall pass through the chambers of

his soul." *Analyze the sounds:* Since the 1960s, in the study of folklore, especially the lyrics of the spirituals, this is precisely what historians of slave culture have done. By coming to understand the form and substance of slave music, folktales, and religious practices, scholars have been able to better comprehend the psychological and spiritual survival of American bondspeople. They have come to see that cultural behavior is how all people find self-definition and resist those elements of life that threaten to control their souls. In many studies of slave communities, scholars have taken Douglass up on his invitation. (Photo: Metropolitan Museum of Art, The Rubel Collection, Promised Gift of William Rubel [L.1997.84.8])

The slaves selected to go to the Great House Farm, for the monthly allowance for themselves and their fellow-slaves, were peculiarly enthusiastic. While on their way, they would make the dense old woods, for miles around, reverberate with their wild songs, revealing at once the highest joy and the deepest sadness. They would compose and sing as they went along, consulting neither time nor tune. . . . They would . . . sing most exultingly the following words:—

> I am going away to the Great House Farm!
> O, yea! O, yea! O!

This they would sing, as a chorus, to words to which to many would seem unmeaning jargon, but which, nevertheless, were full of meaning to themselves. I have sometimes thought that the mere hearing of those songs would do more to impress some minds with the horrible character of slavery, than the reading of whole volumes of philosophy on the subject could do.

I did not, when a slave, understand the deep meaning of those rude and apparently incoherent songs. I was myself within the circle; so that I neither saw nor heard as those without might see and hear. They told a tale of woe which was then altogether beyond my feeble comprehension; they were tones loud, long, and deep; they breathed the prayer and complaint of souls boiling over with the bitterest anguish. Every tone was a testimony against slavery, and a prayer to God for deliverance from chains. The hearing of those wild notes always depressed my spirit, and filled me with ineffable sadness, I have frequently found myself in tears while hearing them. . . . Those songs still follow me, to deepen my hatred of slavery, and quicken my sympathies for my brethren in bonds. If any one wishes to be impressed with the soul-killing effects of slavery, let him go to Colonel Lloyd's plantation, and, on allowance-day, place himself in the deep pine woods, and there let him, in silence, analyze the sounds that shall pass through the chambers of his soul. . . .

The songs of the slave represent the sorrows of his heart; and he is relieved by them, only as an aching heart is relieved by its tears. . . .

Despite lack of firsthand memory, African influences remained strong, especially in appearance and forms of expression. Some slave men plaited their hair into rows and fancy designs; slave women often wore their hair "in string"—tied in small bunches secured by a string or piece of cloth. A few men and many women wrapped their heads in kerchiefs of the styles and colors of West Africa. Some could remember the names of African ancestors passed on to them by family lore. In burial practices, slaves used jars and other glass objects to decorate graves, following similar African traditions.

Music, religion, and folktales were parts of daily life for most slaves. Borrowing partly from their African background, as well as forging new American folkways, they developed what scholars have called a "sacred world-view," which affected all aspects of work, leisure, and self-understanding. Slaves made musical instruments with carved motifs that resembled African stringed instruments. Their drumming and dancing followed African patterns that made whites marvel. One visitor to Georgia in the 1860s described a ritual dance of African origin: "A ring of singers is formed. . . . They then utter a kind of melodious chant, which gradually increases in strength, and in noise, until it fairly shakes the house, and it can be heard for a long distance." This observer of the "ring shout" also noted the agility of the dancers and the African call-and-response pattern in their chanting.

Many slaves continued to believe in spirit possession. Whites, too, believed in ghosts and charms, but the slaves' belief resembled the African concept of the living dead—the idea that deceased relatives visit the earth for many years until the process of dying is complete. Slaves also practiced conjuration, voodoo, and quasi-magical root medicine. By the 1850s the most notable conjurers and root doctors were reputed to live in South Carolina, Georgia, Louisiana, and other isolated coastal areas with high slave populations. But even in Maryland, a young Frederick Douglass carried a special root that had to be positioned "always on the right side," given him by an "old advisor" who lived alone in the woods.

These cultural survivals provided slaves with a sense of their separate past and their own special ways. Such practices and beliefs were not static "African-isms" or mere "retentions." They were cultural adaptations, living traditions reformed in the Americas in response to new experience.

As they became African Americans, slaves also developed a sense of racial identity. In the colonial period, Africans had arrived in America from many different states and kingdoms, represented in distinctive languages, body markings, and traditions. Planters had used ethnic differences to create occupational hierarchies. By the early antebellum period, however, old ethnic identities gave way as American slaves increasingly saw themselves as a single group unified by race. Africans had arrived in the New World with virtually no concept of "race"; by the antebellum era, their descendants had learned through bitter experience that race was now the defining feature of their lives. They were a transplanted and transformed people.

As African culture gave way to a maturing African American culture, more and more slaves adopted Christianity. But they fashioned Christianity into an instrument of support and resistance. Theirs was a religion of justice and deliverance, quite unlike their masters' religious propaganda directed at them as a means of control. "You ought to have heard that preachin'," said one man. "'Obey your master and mistress, don't steal chickens and eggs and meat,' but nary a word about havin' a soul to save." Slaves believed that Jesus cared about their souls and their plight. In their interpretations of biblical stories, as one historian has said, they were "literally willing themselves reborn." They rejected the idea that in heaven whites would have "the colored folks . . . there to wait on 'em." Instead, slaveholders would be "broilin' in hell for their sin" when God's justice came.

Slaves' Religion and Music

For slaves, Christianity was a religion of personal and group salvation. Devout men and women worshiped every day, "in the field or by the side of the road," or in special "prayer grounds" that afforded privacy. Some slaves held fervent secret prayer meetings that lasted far into the night. Many slaves nurtured an unshakable belief that God would enter history and end their bondage. This faith—and the joy and emotional release that accompanied worship—sustained them.

Slaves also adapted Christianity to African practices. In West African belief, devotees are possessed by a god so thoroughly that the god's own personality replaces the human personality. In the late antebellum era, Christian slaves experienced possession by the Protestant "Holy Spirit." The combination of shouting, singing, and dancing that seemed to overtake black worshipers formed the heart of their religious faith. "The old meeting house caught fire," recalled an ex-slave preacher. "The spirit was there. . . . God saw our need and came to us. I used to wonder what made people shout but now I don't. There is a joy on the inside and it wells up so strong that we can't keep still. It is fire in the bones. Any time that fire touches a man, he will jump." Out in brush arbors or in meetinghouses, slaves took in the presence of God and sang away their woes. Some travelers observed "bands" of "Fist and Heel Worshippers." "He who could sing loudest and longest led the 'Band,'" said a suspicious black bishop from the North who opposed emotional religion, "a handkerchief in hand with which he kept time, while his feet resounded on the floor like the drumsticks of a bass drum." Many post-slavery black choirs could not perform properly without a good wooden floor to use as their "drum."

Rhythm and physical movement were crucial to slaves' religious experience. In their own preachers' chanted sermons, which reached out to gather the sinner into a narrative of meanings and cadences along the way to conversion, an American tradition was born. The chanted sermon was both a message from Scripture and a patterned form that required audience response punctuated by "yes sirs!" and "amens!" But it was in song that the slaves left their most sublime gift to American culture.

Through the spirituals, slaves tried to impose order on the chaos of their lives. Many themes run through the lyrics of slave songs. Often referred to later as the "sorrow songs," they also anticipate imminent rebirth. Sadness could give way immediately to joy: "Did you ever stan' on a mountain, wash yo hands in a cloud?" Rebirth was at the heart as well of the famous hymn "Oh, Freedom": "Oh, Oh, Freedom / Oh, Oh, Freedom over me— / But before I'll be a slave, / I'll be buried in my grave, / And go home to my Lord, / And Be Free!"

This tension and sudden change between sorrow and joy animates many songs: "Sometimes I feel like a motherless chile . . . / Sometimes I feel like an eagle in the air, / Spread my wings and fly, fly, fly!" Many songs also express a sense of intimacy and closeness with God. Some songs display an unmistakable rebelliousness, such as the enduring "He said, and if I had my way / If I had my way, if I had my way, / I'd tear this building down!" And some spirituals reached for a collective sense of hope in the black community as a whole:

O, gracious Lord! When shall it be,
That we poor souls shall all be free;
Lord, break them slavery powers—

Will you go along with me?
Lord break them slavery powers,
Go sound the jubilee!

In many ways, American slaves converted the Christian God to themselves. They sought an alternative world to live in—a home other than the one fate had given them on earth. In a thousand variations on the 'Brer Rabbit folktales, in which power and success could be reversed, and in the countless refrains of their songs, they fashioned survival and resistance out of their own cultural imagination.

The main source of support for individuals was the family, which faced severe pressures. Many families were separated by the forced migration and sale of an estimated 2 million slaves between 1820 and 1860 into the region extending from western Georgia to eastern Texas. When the Union Army registered thousands of black marriages in Mississippi and Louisiana in 1864 and 1865, fully 25 percent of the men over forty reported that they had been forcibly separated from a previous wife. Thousands of black families were disrupted every year to serve the needs of the expanding cotton economy.

The Slave Trade and Separation

Many antebellum white southerners made their livings from the slave trade. In South Carolina alone by the 1850s, there were over one hundred slave-trading firms selling an annual average of approximately 6,500 slaves to southwestern states. Although southerners often denied it, vast numbers of slaves moved west by outright sale and not by migrating with their owners. A typical trader's advertisement read: "NEGROES WANTED. I am paying the highest cash prices for young and likely NEGROES, those having good front teeth and being otherwise sound."

Slave traders were practical, roving businessmen. They were sometimes considered degraded by white planters, but many became prominent citizens, and whatever their status, many slaveowners did business with them. Market forces, as the Butler auction indicates, drove this commerce in humanity. At slave "pens" in cities such as New Orleans, traders promoted a "large and commodious showroom . . . prepared to accommodate over 200 Negroes for sale." Traders did their utmost to make their slaves appear young, healthy, and happy, cutting gray whiskers off men, using "paddles" as discipline so as not to scar their merchandise, and forcing people to dance and sing as buyers arrived for an auction. When trans-

...ograph of five generations of a slave family, taken in Beaufort, South Carolina, in ...lent but powerful testimony to the importance that enslaved African Americans ...their ever-threatened family ties.   (Library of Congress)

...was often the name not of their current mas-
...f the owner under whom their family had be-
...r bondage in America.
...al abuse and rape by white masters of slave
...vere ever-present threats. Harriet Jacobs, who
...ıch of her youth and early adult years dodging
...ıer's relentless sexual pursuit, described this
...ance as "the war of my life." In recollecting
...erate effort to protect her children and help
...ıd a way north to freedom, Jacobs asked a
...g question that many slave women carried with
...their graves: "Why does the slave ever love?
...ow the tendrils of the heart to twine around
...which may at any moment be wrenched away
...and of violence?"
...es hated interference in their family lives. In-
...me individuals refused separations and strug-
...years to keep their children together and
...ısh contact with lost loved ones. Kinship net-
...indeed, were often what held family life to-
...ı many slave communities.

Slave Resistance and Rebellion

Slaves brought to their efforts at resistance the same common sense and determination that characterized their family lives. The scales weighed heavily against overt revolution, and the slaves knew it. But they seized opportunities to alter their work conditions. They sometimes slacked off when they were not being watched. Thus owners complained that slaves "never would lay out their strength freely." One exasperated Virginia planter voiced his irritation (and the racism nurtured by slavery) when he said, "You can make a nigger work, *but you cannot make him think.*" These attitudes made many whites disbelievers in the prospect of black free labor after the Civil War.

Daily discontent and desperation were also manifest in sabotage of equipment, in wanton carelessness about work, in theft of food, livestock, or crops, or in getting drunk on stolen liquor. Some slaves who were

A slave coffle [...]
newly settled s[...]
(Collection of W[...]

This p[...]
1862, [...]
placed[...]

ported to the southwestern markets, slaves were often chained together in "coffles," which made journeys of 500 miles or more on foot.

The complacent mixture of racism and business among traders is evident in their own language. "I refused a girl 20 year[s] old at 700 yesterday," one trader wrote to another in 1853. "If you think best to take her at 700 I can still get her. She is very badly whipped but good teeth." Some sales were transacted at owners' requests. "Bought a cook yesterday that was to go out of state," wrote a trader; "she just made the people mad that was all." Some traders demonstrated how deeply slavery and racism were intertwined. "I have bought the boy Isaac for 1100," wrote a trader in 1854 to his partner. "I think him very prime. . . . He is a . . . house servant . . . first rate cook . . . and splendid carriage driver. He is also a fine painter and varnisher and . . . says he can make a fine panel door. . . . Also he performs well on the violin. . . . He is a genius and its strange to say I think he is smarter than I am."

But separation did not mean that slave families could not endure. American slaves clung tenaciously

The Black Family in Slavery

to the pers[...]
gave meanin[...]
ican law did [...]
ilies, masters [...]
slaveowners [...]
families and have children. As [...]
rapidly expanding edge of the [...]
was a normal ratio of men t[...]
Studies have shown that on s[...]
plantations of South Carolina [...]
their slaves increased autono[...]
system, the property accumula[...]
more stable and healthier fam[...]

Following African kinship [...]
icans avoided marriage betw[...]
place among aristocratic slave[...]
African customs, they did not [...]
ers but did expect a young wo[...]
mous relationship after one p[...]
By naming their children afte[...]
ations, African Americans e[...]
histories. If they chose to bea[...]

owner[...]
ter bu[...]
gun th[...]

S[...]
wome[...]
spent [...]
her o[...]
circun[...]
her de[...]
them [...]
haunti[...]
them [...]
Why [...]
object[...]
by the[...]

Sl[...]
deed, [...]
gled f[...]
reesta[...]
works[...]
gether[...]

Strategies of Resistance

hired out for as much as a year away from their families might show their anger by hoarding their earnings. Or, they might just fall into recalcitrance. "I have a boy in my employ called Jim Archer," complained a Vicksburg, Mississippi, slaveholder in 1843. "Jim does not want to be under anyones control and says . . . he wants to go home this summer." A woman named Ellen, hired as a cook in Tennessee in 1856, quietly put mercury poison into a roasted apple for her unsuspecting mistress.

Many male, and some female, slaves acted out their defiance by violently attacking overseers or even their owners. Southern court records and newspapers are full of accounts of these resistant slaves who gave the lie to the syrupy image of the docile bondsmen. The price they paid was high. Such lonely rebels were customarily secured and flogged, sold away, or hanged. One Louisiana planter reported strapping two especially uncooperative slaves to a stake and delivering 150 lashes to one and 175 to the other.

Many individual slaves attempted to run away to the North, and some received assistance from the loose network known as the Underground Railroad (see page 369). But it was more common for slaves to run off temporarily to hide in the woods. Fear, disgruntlement over treatment, family separation, and a hundred other complaints might motivate slaves to try to stay at large in the Upper South states for weeks or months at a time. Only a minority of those who tried such escapes ever made it to freedom in the North, but these fugitives made slavery a very insecure institution by the 1850s.

American slavery produced some fearless revolutionaries. Gabriel's Rebellion involved as many as a thousand slaves when it was discovered in 1800, just before it exploded in Richmond, Virginia (see pages 213–214). A similar conspiracy in Charleston in 1822, led by a free black named Denmark Vesey, involved many of the prominent whites' most trusted slaves. Born a slave, Vesey won a lottery of $1,500 in 1800 and bought his own freedom. As a literate religious leader, he struck terror into South Carolina as he combined biblical teachings with revolutionary, natural rights ideology to justify his conspiracy to overthrow the slaveholding regime. The Vesey plot began in 1821 when white authorities closed a black church founded three years earlier in a split between white and black Methodists. Betrayed by whites and blacks alike, the Vesey rebellion and its potential horrors deeply unnerved official white South Carolina. When the arrests and trials were over, thirty-seven conspirators were executed and more than three dozen others were banished from the state.

The most famous rebel of all, Nat Turner, struck for freedom in Southampton County, Virginia, in 1831. The son of an African woman who passionately hated her enslavement, Nat Turner was a precocious child who learned to read when he was very young. Encouraged by his first owner to study the Bible, he enjoyed certain privileges but also endured hard work and changes of masters. His father successfully escaped to freedom.

Nat Turner's Insurrection

Eventually young Nat became a preacher with a reputation for eloquence and a tendency toward mysticism. After nurturing his plan for several years, Turner led a band of rebels from farm to farm in the predawn darkness of August 22, 1831. The group severed limbs and crushed skulls with axes or killed their victims with guns. Before alarmed planters stopped them, Nat Turner and his followers had slaughtered sixty whites of both sexes and all ages in forty-eight hours. The rebellion was soon put down, and in retaliation, whites killed slaves at random all over the region, including in adjoining states. Turner was eventually caught and then hanged. As many as two hundred African Americans, including innocent victims of marauding whites, lost their lives as a result of the rebellion.

Nat Turner remains one of the most haunting symbols in America's unresolved history with racial slavery and discrimination. While in jail awaiting execution, Turner was interviewed by a Virginia lawyer and slaveholder, Thomas R. Gray. Their intriguing, collaborative creation, *The Confessions of Nat Turner*, became a bestseller within a month of Turner's hanging. Turner told of his early childhood, his religious visions, his zeal to be free; Gray called the rebel a "gloomy fanatic," but in a manner that made him fascinating and produced one of the most remarkable documents in the annals of American slavery. In the wake of Turner's insurrection, many states passed stiffened legal codes against black education and religious practice.

Most importantly, in 1832 the state of Virginia, shocked to its core, held a full-scale legislative and public debate over gradual emancipation as a means of ridding itself of slavery and of blacks. The plan debated would not have freed any slaves until 1858, and it provided that eventually all blacks would be colonized outside Virginia. Fear and anti-black sentiments drove this debate. In the end, Virginia opted out of this pivotal moment by doing nothing except reinforcing its own moral and economic defenses of slavery. When the House of Delegates finally voted, the motion favoring gradual abolition lost by 73 to 58. Ironically, if the Virginia debate had gone the other way, Nat Turner's Rebellion would have succeeded in destroying slavery because racism had triumphed. At the very least, Turner got the nation's attention.

Harmony and Tension in a Slave Society

From 1830 to 1860, slavery impinged on laws and customs, individual values, and, increasingly, every aspect of southern politics. In all things, from their workaday movements to Sunday worship, slaves fell under the supervision of whites. State courts held that a slave "has no civil right" and could not hold property "except at the will and pleasure of his master." Revolts like Nat Turner's tightened the legal straitjacket even more. As political conflicts between North and South deepened, fears of slave revolt grew, and restrictions on slaves increased accordingly.

State and federal laws aided the capture of fugitive slaves and required nonslaveholders to support the slave system. All white male citizens had a legal duty to participate in slave patrols. Ship captains, harbor masters, and other whites in strategic positions in both North and South were required to scrutinize the papers of African Americans who might be attempting to escape bondage.

Slavery deeply affected southern values precisely because it was the main determinant of wealth. Ownership of slaves guaranteed the labor

Slavery, Wealth, and Social Standing

to produce cotton and other crops on a large scale. Slaves were therefore vital to the acquisition of a fortune. Beyond that, they were a commodity and an investment, much like gold; people bought them on speculation, hoping for a steady rise in their market values. Across the South, variations in wealth from county to county corresponded very closely to variations in slaveholding.

Wealth in slaves also translated into political power: a solid majority of political officeholders were slaveholders, and the most powerful were usually large-scale planters. Lawyers and newspaper editors were sometimes influential, but they were dependent on planters for business and support.

Slavery's influence spread throughout the social system until even the values and mores of nonslaveholders bore its imprint. The availability of slave labor tended to devalue free labor: where strenuous work under supervision was reserved for an enslaved race, few free people relished it. When Alexis de Tocqueville crossed from Ohio into Kentucky in his celebrated travels of 1831, he observed "the effect that slavery produces on society. On the right bank of the Ohio [River] everything is activity, industry; labor is honoured; there are no slaves. Pass to the left bank and the scene changes so suddenly that you think yourself on the other side of the world; the enterprising spirit is gone. There, work is not only painful; it is shameful. . . ." Tocqueville's own class impulses found a home in the South, however. There he found a "veritable aristocracy which . . . combines many prejudices with high sentiments and instincts."

The values of the aristocrat—lineage, privilege, pride, and refinement of person and manner—commanded respect throughout the South. Many of those qualities were in short supply, however, in the recently settled portions of the cotton kingdom, where frontier values of courage and self-reliance ruled. Thus independence and defense of one's honor became highly valued traits for planter and frontier farmer alike.

Aristocratic Values and Frontier Individualism

Instead of gradually disappearing as it did in the North, dueling, which required men to defend their honor through violence, lasted much longer in the South. In North Carolina in 1851 a wealthy planter named Samuel Fleming responded to a series of disputes with the lawyer William Waightstill Avery by "cowhiding" (whipping) him on a public street. According to the code, Avery had two choices: to redeem his honor violently or to brand himself a coward through inaction. Three weeks later Avery shot Fleming dead at point-blank range during a session of Burke County Superior Court, with Judge William Battle and numerous spectators looking on. A jury later took only ten minutes to find Avery not guilty, and the spectators gave him a standing ovation. Though Judge Battle was troubled by this outcome, most white males seemed satisfied.

Other aristocratic values of the planter class were less acceptable to the average voter. Planters believed they were better than other people. In their pride, they expected not only to wield power but to receive deference from poorer whites. Independent and proud, the yeoman class resented infringements of their rights, and many belonged to evangelical faiths that exalted values of simplicity that were alien to the planters' love of wealth. Also conscious of national democratic ideals, yeomen sometimes challenged or rejected the aristocratic pretensions of planters.

Class tensions emerged in the western, nonslaveholding parts of the seaboard states by the 1830s.

Yeoman Demands for Political Reform

There yeoman farmers resented their underrepresentation in state legislatures and the corruption in local government. After vigorous debate, the reformers won many battles. Voters in more recently settled areas—Alabama, Mississippi, Tennessee, Arkansas, and Texas—adopted white manhood suffrage and other electoral reforms, including popular election of governors, legislative apportionment based on white population only, and locally chosen county government. Kentucky, Georgia, Florida, Louisiana, Maryland, and North Carolina adopted most or some of these measures. Only South Carolina and Virginia effectively defended property qualifications for office, legislative malapportionment, and selection of the governor by state legislatures. The structure of southern government thus became more democratic than planters wished.

Slaveowners knew that a more open government structure could permit troubling issues to arise. In Virginia, it was nonslaveholding westerners who petitioned and initiated the debate over abolition in the wake of Nat Turner's Rebellion in 1832, the last public debate on slavery in the antebellum South.

Given such tensions, it was perhaps remarkable that slaveholders and nonslaveholders did not experience more overt conflict. Why were

Antebellum White Class Relations

class confrontations among whites so infrequent? Historians have given several answers. One of the most important factors was race. The South's racial ideology stressed the superiority of all whites to blacks. Thus slavery became the basis of equality among whites, and racism inflated the status of poor whites and gave them a common interest with the rich. Moreover, family ties linked some nonslaveholders to wealthy planters, especially on the expanding frontier.

The "Old South" was a new and mobile society in which many people rose in status by acquiring land or

A bill of sale documents that this slave woman, Louisa, was owned by the young child whom she holds on her lap. In the future Louisa's life would be subject to the child's wishes and decisions.   (Missouri Historical Society, St. Louis)

slaves, and those who did not wished they could. Even in cotton-rich Alabama in the 1850s, fewer than half of the richest families in a typical county belonged to its elite ten years later. Most did not die or lose their wealth; they merely moved on to some new state. This constant mobility in an expanding plantation economy meant that southern society did not settle into an utterly rigid social pattern.

Most importantly, in their daily lives yeomen and slaveholders were seldom in conflict. Before the Civil War most yeomen were able to pursue unhindered their independent lifestyle. They worked their farms, avoided debt, and marked progress for their families that in their rural habitats was unrelated to slaveholding. Likewise, slaveholders pursued their goals quite independently of yeomen. Planters farmed for the market but also for themselves. Thus the planter did not depend on the nonslaveholder as a producer of food crops.

Suppression of dissent also played an increasing role. After 1830 white southerners who criticized the slave system out of moral conviction or class resentment were intimidated, attacked, or legally prosecuted. (Some, like James Birney, went north and joined the antislavery movement. Two sisters from Charleston, Angelina and Sarah Grimké, became leading advocates of both abolition and women's rights—see page 286.) By the 1850s the defense of slavery's interests exerted an ever more powerful influence on southern politics and society.

Hardening of Class Lines

Still, there were signs that the relative lack of conflict between slaveholders and nonslaveholders was coming to an end in the late antebellum period. As cotton lands filled up, nonslaveholders saw their opportunities beginning to narrow; meanwhile, wealthy planters enjoyed expanding profits. The risks of entering cotton production were becoming too great and the cost of slaves too high for many yeomen to rise in society. From 1830 to 1860 the percentage of white southern families holding slaves declined steadily from 36 to 25 percent. At the same time, the monetary gap between the classes was widening. Although slaveowners accounted for this smaller portion of the population, planters' share of the South's agricultural wealth remained at between 90 and 95 percent.

Urban artisans and mechanics felt the pinch acutely. Their numbers were few and in bad times they were often the first to lose work as markets collapsed. Moreover, they faced stiff competition from urban slaves, whose masters wanted to hire them out to practice trades. White workers in the port cities of Charleston and Wilmington and elsewhere staged protests demanding that economic competition from slaves be forbidden, but they were ignored. The angry protests of white workers resulted in harsh restrictions on free African American laborers and craftsmen, who had no powerful allies to defend their interests. On the eve of the Civil War, many successful free blacks actually felt compelled to leave Charleston for fear of being reenslaved.

Pre–Civil War politics reflected these tensions as well. Anticipating possible secession and the prospect of a war to defend slavery, slaveowners expressed growing fear about the loyalty of nonslaveholders. Schemes to widen the ownership of slaves were discussed, including reopening the African slave trade. In North Carolina, a prolonged and increasingly bitter controversy erupted over the combination of high taxes on land and low taxes on slaves. When nonslaveholder Hinton R. Helper denounced the slave system in *The Impending Crisis*, published in 1857, discerning planters feared the eruption of such controversies in every southern state.

But for the moment slaveowners stood secure. In the 1850s they occupied from 50 to 85 percent of the seats in state legislatures and a similarly high percentage of the South's congressional seats. Planters had established their point of view in all the other major social institutions. Professors who criticized slavery had been dismissed from colleges and universities; schoolbooks that contained "unsound" ideas had been replaced. And almost all the Methodist and Baptist clergy had become slavery's most vocal defenders.

Summary

During the thirty years before the Civil War the South grew as part of America's westward expansion. Ideologically and economically, the southern states developed in many distinctive ways; at the same time, they were also deeply enmeshed in the nation's heritage and political economy. Far more than the North, the antebellum South was a biracial society; whites grew up directly influenced by black folkways and culture, and blacks, the vast majority of whom were slaves, became predominantly native-born Americans and the cobuilders with whites of a rural, agricultural society.

With the sustained thirty- to forty-year cotton boom, the South grew fatefully into a much larger slave society than it had been early in the century. The coercive influence of slavery affected virtually every element of southern life and politics, and increasingly produced a leadership determined to preserve a conservative, hierarchical social and racial order. Despite the white supremacy that united them, the democratic values of yeomen often clashed with the profit motives of aristocratic planters. The benevolent self-image and paternalistic ideology of slaveholders had to ultimately stand the test of the slaves' own judgments. African American slaves responded by fashioning over time a rich expressive folk culture and a religion of personal and group deliverance. Their experiences could be profoundly different from one region and kind of labor to another. Some blacks were crushed by bondage;

many others transcended it in an epic of survival and resistance.

From the Old South on to modern times, white and black southerners have always shared a tragic, mutual history. By 1850, through their own wits and on the backs of African labor, white southerners had aggressively built one of the last profitable, expanding slave societies on earth. North of them, deeply intertwined with them in the same nation, market economy, constitutional system, and history, a different kind of society had grown even faster—one driven by industrialism and individualistic free labor. The clash of these two deeply connected, yet mutually fearful and divided societies was about to explode in political storms over how the nation would define its future.

LEGACY FOR A PEOPLE AND A NATION
The Black Family

In the late 1830s Virginia slaveholder Robert Bruce prepared a list of the slaves on his plantation. He noted that three maternal grandmothers performed the primary care of small children whose mothers either were dead or had been sold away. Bruce made no mention of slave fathers.

Bruce's list illustrates one of slavery's deepest legacies—its impact on family life. The questions are still with us. Can poverty and broken families since emancipation be attributed to the slave experience? Does slavery's heritage require persistent redistributive justice in our current society? And who or what is responsible for continuing disparities in the family stability of blacks and whites: history (the nation's policies) or individuals (personal behavior)?

Slavery put unbearable pressures on black family life, and ever since emancipation, popular lore supported the idea that a nuclear family could not survive the masters' economic and sexual power. In 1939 the black sociologist E. Franklin Frazier argued that "no social organization" survived from African heritage among American slaves, and that the family "went to pieces." In the 1960s Daniel Patrick Moynihan conducted a study that concluded that blacks had plunged into urban poverty because of a set of behaviors drawn from the past that eroded stable families. The values alleged to cause this "culture of poverty" are self-indulgence, low educational aspiration, and lack of thrift. This analysis thrives on the image of the black male adult's absence from familial responsibilities.

Historians challenged the "damage" thesis in the 1970s, revealing evidence of strong families during and after slavery. Moreover, sociologists argued that the fact of poverty, not a "culture" developed from it, severs marriages and families. But even these new theses are challenged by studies of widespread family separation during slavery, the women-centered character of slave life, and the ravages of sharecropping and segregation.

Much damage was done by slavery to black family life. Exactly what the long-term effects are may never produce a consensus. But this question drives nearly every policy debate Americans face over the relationships among race, history, and social welfare. Many single black women raise well-adjusted children; and kin networks are still crucial in African American family life. But troubling facts remain: a majority of black children still live in families that include their mothers but not their fathers, whereas about four of five white children under eighteen live with both parents.

For Further Reading, see page A-16 of the Appendix. For Web resources, go to http://college.hmco.com.

JOHN C. FREMONT.
THE REPUBLICANS CHOICE FOR PRISIDENT AND VICE PRESIDENT FROM 1857 TO 1861.
WM L. DAYTON.

GRAND NATIONAL REPUBLICAN BANNER.
FREE LABOR, FREE SPEECH, FREE TERITORY.

As the delegates filed into the Musical Fund Hall in Philadelphia on June 17, 1856, they knew they had created something special in American politics. The first national nominating convention of the Republican Party met to approve a platform and select their presidential ticket. Formed just two years earlier, the party drew together a broad coalition of northern politicians who opposed the expansion of slavery, as well as the growing power of the South in the federal government. Most American political conventions in those years were raucous affairs; but at this gathering, according to a journalist, there was only "a slight quantity of liquor consumed, very little profane swearing . . . and . . . intense propriety." Republicans had come to Philadelphia for the solemn business of offering the American electorate a genuinely antislavery national future.

Their coalition combined men who had been former Democrats; men who had been founding members of the American Party, a group that wanted to prohibit foreigners, especially Catholics, from settling in the United States; and many former Whigs, whose party had been shattered by the crisis over slavery and its expansion. They consisted of conservatives, moderates, and radicals; some believed slavery and all its influences a moral evil, while others saw it as a political problem.

At this convention, a radical temper prevailed. The convention was only minutes old when the temporary chairman, Robert Emmet of New York, brought the delegates to their feet by using the Declaration of Independence to label slavery a great political danger to the nation's future. Permanent chairman Henry S. Lane of Indiana followed by declaring the "vital principle of the Republican party" to be "no more slave states," an aim he rooted in the "natural rights of man." Speaker after speaker declared that their party would render "freedom national" and "slavery sectional" by using the power of Congress to outlaw human bondage in all western territories.

Born as an antislavery coalition out of the controversy over the spread of slavery into the West, the Republican Party nominated John C. Frémont for president and William L. Dayton for vice president at its first national convention in Philadelphia in June 1856. The Republicans altered America's political landscape nearly overnight; southern slaveholders feared them, and a broad base of northerners flocked to their free-soil vision of the nation's future. (Collection of Janice L. and David J. Frent)

SLAVERY AND AMERICA'S FUTURE: THE ROAD TO WAR 1845–1861

The convention's platform committee was fittingly chaired by David Wilmot, a former Democrat who was no friend of black civil and political rights. But Wilmot, like others, was firmly opposed to slavery's expansion and just as firmly endorsed the protection of free white men's labor and land ownership across the continent. The platform denounced the South's interest in the acquisition of Cuba, supported the building of a transcontinental railroad, and nodded gently against nativism. But these were all "like a tail to the antislavery kite," as one historian put it. At the heart of the platform was the short, direct credo calling upon Congress to "prohibit in the territories those twin relics of barbarism—polygamy and slavery."

The Republicans nominated the famous western explorer and former California senator, John C. Frémont, for president. In the election that followed, Americans began to vote by section and not by party as never before. The Republican coalition began to unify the North around keeping the West free and alarmed the South, which now saw the future of its slave society endangered by a political movement determined to limit if not destroy slavery. Frémont would lose the 1856 election, but Republicans made the best showing ever in American history of a newly born party in its first presidential bid.

As the Republicans engaged in their near miss at winning the presidency in 1856, a larger drama of conflict and violence had begun to envelop the nation. In Kansas territory, open warfare had exploded between proslavery and antislavery settlers. On the floor of the U.S. Senate a southern representative beat a northern senator senseless. A new fugitive slave law sent thousands of blacks fleeing into Canada in fear for their liberty and their lives. The tradition of compromise on political problems related to slavery teetered on the brink of complete collapse. Within a year the Supreme Court had issued a dramatic decision about slavery, its constitutionality in westward expansion, and the status of African American citizenship—to the delight of most southerners and the dread of most northerners. And abolitionist John Brown was planning a raid into Virginia to start a slave rebellion.

The political culture of the American republic, now under the leadership of Americans born after the passing of the Revolutionary War generation, was disintegrating. As the 1850s advanced, slavery pulled Americans, North and South, into a maelstrom of dispute that its best statesmen, ultimately, could not subdue. The prosperous, model republic, riven by stark contradictions, was on the road to a terrible war.

Divergent economic and political aims, which had long been held in check, now flew apart over the issue of slavery. The old nationwide political parties fractured, and a realignment that reinforced sectional interests took their place. The means for compromise steadily slipped from the nation's grasp.

Slavery had aroused passions that could be neither contained nor resolved. What began as a dark cloud over the territories became a storm engulfing the nation. Between 1845 and 1853 the United States added Texas, California, Oregon Country, and the Southwest to its domain and launched the settlement of the Great Plains. During the administration of President James K. Polk alone (1845–1849), the nation increased its land mass by two-thirds. Each time the nation expanded, it confronted a thorny issue: should new territories and states be slave or free?

The ensuing political storms gave rise to a feeling in both North and South that America's future was at stake—the character of its economy, its labor system, its definition of liberty under the Constitution, and its racial self-definition. The new Republican Party believed that America's future depended on the unbounded labor of free men, whose rights were protected by a government devoted to liberty. They charged southerners with using the power of the federal government to make slavery legal throughout the Union. Southern leaders defended slavery and charged the North with unconstitutional efforts to destroy it. To these southerners enslavement of blacks was the foundation of civilization and equality among whites; a government that failed to protect slavery was unworthy of their loyalty.

For blacks, the growing dispute brought hope and despair. They could take heart that the country's political strife over slavery might somehow lead to their liberation. But in a nation now trying to define its future, blacks had to wonder whether they had a future at all in America. In 1855 Frederick Douglass spoke for slaves and former slaves when he wrote that "the thought of only being a creature of the present and the past, troubled me, and I longed to have a future—a future with hope in it." In those words, Douglass spoke as well to the nation's central dilemma. ■

The War with Mexico and Its Consequences

 In the 1840s, territorial expansion surged forward under the leadership of President James K. Polk of North Carolina. The annexation of Texas (see page 300) just be-

IMPORTANT EVENTS

1846 War with Mexico begins
Oregon Treaty negotiated
Wilmot Proviso inflames sectional divisions

1847 Cass proposes idea of popular sovereignty

1848 Treaty of Guadalupe Hidalgo gives United
States new territory in the Southwest
Free-Soil Party formed
Taylor elected president

1849 Gold discovered in California, which applies
for admission to Union as free state

1850 Compromise of 1850 passed in separate bills

1852 Stowe publishes *Uncle Tom's Cabin*
Pierce elected president

1854 Publication of "Appeal of the Independent
Democrats"
Kansas-Nebraska Act wins approval and
ignites controversy
Republican Party formed
Return of fugitive Burns from Boston to
slavery in Virginia

1856 Bleeding Kansas troubles nation
Brooks attacks Sumner in Senate chamber
Buchanan elected president but Republican
Frémont wins most northern states

1857 *Dred Scott v. Sandford* endorses southern
views on black citizenship and slavery in
territories
Economic panic and widespread unemployment begins

1858 Kansas voters reject Lecompton Constitu-
tion
Lincoln-Douglas debates attract attention
Douglas proposes Freeport Doctrine

1859 Brown raids Harpers Ferry

1860 Democratic Party splits in two; southern
Democrats demand "Slave Code for the
Territories"
Lincoln elected president
Crittenden Compromise fails
South Carolina secedes from Union

1861 Six more Deep South states secede
Confederacy established at Montgomery,
Alabama
Attack on Fort Sumter begins Civil War
Four states in the Upper South join the
Confederacy

fore his inauguration did not necessarily make war with Mexico inevitable, but by design and through a series of calculated decisions, Polk made the conflict all but unavoidable. Mexico broke off relations with the United States, and as the annexation process took hold in 1845, Polk urged Texans to seize all land to the Rio Grande and claim the river as their southern and western border. Mexico held that the Nueces River was the border; hence the stage was set for conflict. Nothing could weaken Polk's determination to fulfill the nation's "manifest destiny" to rule the continent. He wanted Mexico's territory all the way to the Pacific, and all of Oregon Country, since 1818 jointly occupied with Britain, as well. He and his expansionist cabinet achieved their goals but were largely unaware of the price in domestic harmony that expansion would exact.

During the 1844 campaign, Polk's supporters had threatened war with Great Britain to gain all of Oregon. As president, however, Polk turned first to diplomacy. Not wanting to fight Mexico and Great Britain at the same time, he tried to avoid

Oregon

bloodshed in the Northwest, where America and Britain had for decades jointly occupied disputed territory. Dropping the demand for a boundary at latitude 54°40', he pressured the British to accept the 49th parallel. In 1846 Great Britain agreed. The Oregon Treaty gave the United States all of present-day Oregon, Washington, and Idaho and parts of Wyoming and Montana (see Map 14.1).

Toward Mexico, Polk was more aggressive. In early 1846, he ordered American troops under "Old Rough and Ready," General Zachary Taylor, to march south and defend the contested border of the Rio Grande across from the town of Matamoros (see Map 14.2 on page 363). Polk especially desired California as the prize in his expansionist strategy, and to that end he attempted to buy from the angry Mexicans a huge tract of land extending to the Pacific. When that effort failed, Polk waited for war. Negotiations between troops on the Rio Grande were awkwardly conducted in French because no American officer spoke Spanish and no Mexican

"Mr. Polk's War"

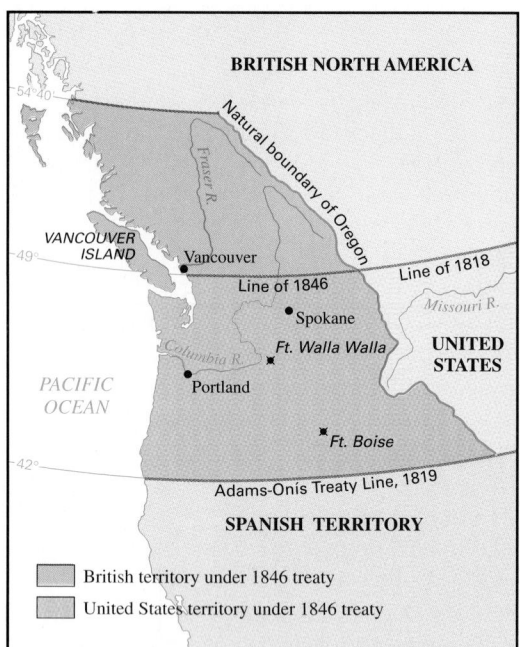

Map 14.1 American Expansion in Oregon
The slogan of Polk's supporters had been "Fifty-four forty or fight," but negotiation of a boundary at the 49th parallel avoided the danger of war with Great Britain.

spoke English. After a three-week standoff, the tense situation came to a head. On April 24, 1846, Mexican cavalry ambushed a U.S. cavalry unit on the north side of the river; eleven Americans were killed and sixty-three taken captive. On April 26 Taylor sent a dispatch overland to Washington, D.C., which took two weeks to arrive, announcing: "Hostilities may now be considered as commenced."

Polk now drafted a message to Congress: Mexico had "passed the boundary of the United States, had invaded our territory and shed American blood on American soil." In the bill accompanying the war message, Polk deceptively declared that "war exists by the act of Mexico itself" and summoned the nation to arms. Two days later on May 13, the House recognized a state of war with Mexico by a vote of 174 to 14, and the Senate by 40 to 2, with numerous abstentions. Some antislavery Whigs had tried to oppose the war but were barely allowed to gain the floor of Congress to speak. Since Polk withheld key facts, the full reality of what had happened on the distant Rio Grande was not known. But the theory and practice of manifest destiny had launched the United States into its first war on foreign territory.

The idea of war unleashed great public celebrations. Huge crowds gathered in southern cities such as Richmond and Louisville to voice support for the war effort. Twenty thousand Philadelphians and even more New Yorkers rallied in the same spirit. After news came of General Taylor's first two battlefield victories at Palo Alto and Resaca de la Palma, volunteers swarmed recruiting stations. From his home in Lansingburgh, New York, the writer Herman Melville remarked that "the people here are all in a state of delirium. . . . A military ardor pervades all ranks. . . . Nothing is talked of but the 'Halls of the Montezumas.'" Publishers rushed books into print about Mexican geography; "Palo Alto" hats and root beer went on sale. And the advent of daily newspapers, printed on new rotary presses, boosted sales by giving the war a romantic appeal.

Foreign War and the Popular Imagination

Here was an adventurous war of conquest in a far-off, exotic land. Here was the fulfillment of Anglo-Saxon–Christian destiny to expand and possess the North American continent and to take "civilization" to the "semi-Indian" Mexicans. For many, racism fueled the expansionist spirit. In 1846 an Illinois newspaper justified the war on the basis that Mexicans were "reptiles in the path of progressive democracy." For those who read newspapers, the War with Mexico became the first national event experienced with immediacy. The battles south of the border were reported by war correspondents. From Vera Cruz on the Gulf Coast of Mexico, ships carried news dispatches to New Orleans, whose nine daily newspapers ran a faster steamer out to meet them. With stories set in type before even reaching shore, the news was then sent by riders toward the North. With the extension of the telegraph by the end of the war, news traveled in only three days from New Orleans to Washington.

The war spawned an outpouring of poetry, song, drama, travel literature, and lithographs that captured the popular imagination and glorified the war. New lyrics to the tune "Yankee Doodle" proclaimed: "They attacked our men upon our land / and crossed our river too sir / now show them all with sword in hand / what yankee boys can do sir." Most of the war-inspired flowering in the popular arts was patriotic. But not everyone cheered. The abolitionist James Russell Lowell considered the war a "national crime committed in behoof of slavery, our common sin." Ralph Waldo Emerson confided to his journals in 1847: "The United States will conquer Mexico, but it will be as the

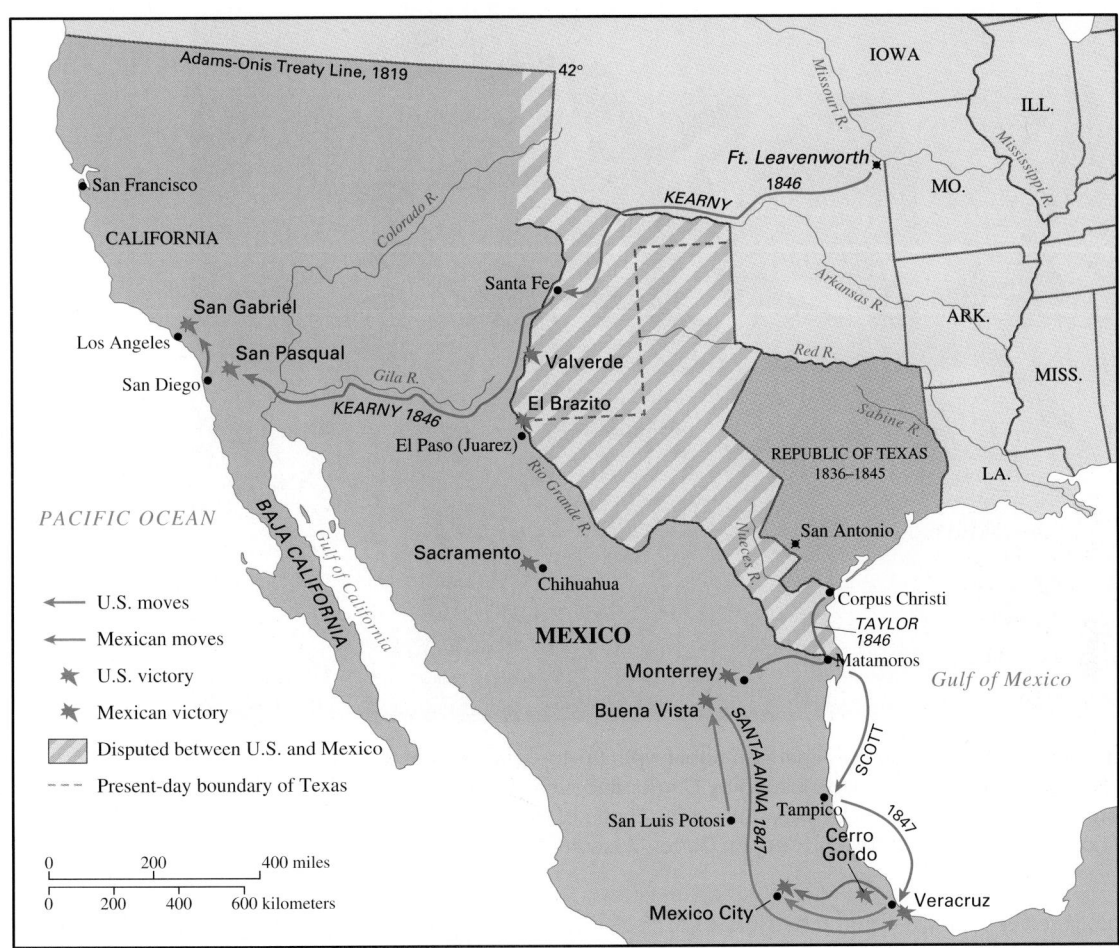

Map 14.2   The War with Mexico   This map shows the territory disputed between the United States and Mexico. After U.S. gains in northeastern Mexico and in New Mexico and California, General Winfield Scott captured Mexico City in the decisive campaign of the war.

man swallows arsenic, which brings him down in turn. Mexico will poison us." Even proslavery spokesman John C. Calhoun saw the perils of expansionism. Mexico, he said, was "the forbidden fruit; the penalty of eating it would be to subject our institutions to political death."

Early in the war U.S. forces made significant gains. The troops proved unruly and undisciplined, and their politically ambitious commanders often quarreled among themselves. Nevertheless, progress was steady. In May 1846 Polk ordered Colonel Stephen Kearny and a small detachment to invade the remote and thinly populated provinces of New Mexico and California. Taking Santa Fe without opposition, Kearny pushed into Cal-

Conquest

ifornia, where he joined forces with rebellious American settlers led by Captain John C. Frémont and with a couple of U.S. naval units. General Zachary Taylor's forces attacked and occupied Monterrey, which surrendered in September, securing northeastern Mexico (see Map 14.2). American soldiers soon established dominion over distant California before the end of 1846.

Because losses on the periphery of their large country had not broken Mexican resistance, General Winfield Scott carried the war to the enemy's heartland. Landing at Veracruz, he led fourteen thousand men toward Mexico City. This daring invasion proved the decisive campaign of the war. Scott's men, outnumbered and threatened by yellow fever, encountered a series of formidable Mexican defenses, but engineers repeatedly discovered flanking routes around

Enthusiastic publishers vied to furnish the American public with up-to-date news of the War with Mexico. This is one of three lithographs issued by Currier and Ives in 1846 to celebrate U.S. forces' capture of Mexico's General La Vega during the Battle of Resaca de la Palma, fought near the border of Texas and Mexico. (Amon Carter Museum, Fort Worth, Texas)

their foes. After a series of hard-fought battles, U.S. troops captured the Mexican capital.

Representatives of both countries signed the Treaty of Guadalupe Hidalgo in February 1848. The United States gained California and New Mexico (including present-day Nevada, Utah, and Arizona, and parts of Colorado and Wyoming) and recognition of the Rio Grande as the southern boundary of Texas. In return, the American government agreed to settle the claims of its citizens against Mexico ($3.2 million) and to pay Mexico a mere $15 million (before the war Polk had been prepared to pay up to $40 million).

Treaty of Guadalupe Hidalgo

The costs of the war included the deaths of thirteen thousand Americans (mostly from disease) and fifty thousand Mexicans, plus Mexican American enmity that endured into the twentieth century. The domestic cost to the United States was even higher. Public opinion was sharply divided, despite widespread hostility toward Mexicans. Southwesterners were enthusiastic about the war, as were most southern planters; New Englanders strenuously opposed it.

Whigs in Congress charged that Polk, a Democrat, had "provoked" an unnecessary war and "usurped the power of Congress." The aged John Quincy Adams denounced the war; and a tall, young, Illinois Whig named Abraham Lincoln called Polk's justifications the "half insane mumbling of a fever-dream." Abolitionists and a small minority of antislavery Whigs charged that the war was no less than a plot to extend slavery. Congressman Joshua Giddings of Ohio charged that Polk's purpose was "to render slavery secure in Texas" and to extend slavery's dominion over vast expanses of new territory.

These charges fed northern fear of the so-called Slave Power. Abolitionists had long warned of a slaveholding oligarchy that intended to dominate the nation through its hold on federal power. These dangerous aristocrats had gained control of the South by persecuting critics of slavery and suppressing dissent. They had forced the gag rule on Congress in 1836 (see page 286) and threatened northern liberties. To many white northerners, even those who saw nothing wrong with slavery, it was

"Slave Power Conspiracy"

the battle over free speech and the right of petition that first made the idea of a Slave Power credible. The War with Mexico deepened such fears. Why, asked antislavery northerners, had claims to part of Oregon been abandoned and a questionable war begun for vast, new slave territory?

Northern opinion on slavery expansion began to shift, but the impact of events on southern opinion was even more dramatic. At first some southern leaders criticized the War with Mexico. Southern Whigs attacked the Democratic president for causing the war, and few southern congressmen saw defense of slavery as the paramount issue. Even John C. Calhoun—despite his earlier schemes to annex Texas for slavery—strongly opposed the seizure of large amounts of land from Mexico. Many whites in both North and South feared that large land seizures would bring thousands of nonwhite Mexicans into the United States and upset the racial order. An Indiana politician did not want "any mixed races in our Union, nor men of any color except white, unless they be slaves." And the *Charleston Mercury* of South Carolina asked if the nation expected "to melt into our population eight millions of men, at war with us by race, by language, by religion, manners and laws." Despite their racism, many statesmen soon saw other prospects in the outcomes of a war of conquest in the Southwest.

The War with Mexico proved generally popular with southern voters, and no southern Whig could oppose it once slavery became the central issue. That happened in August 1846, when David Wilmot, a Pennsylvania Democrat, proposed an amendment, or proviso, to a military appropriations bill: that "neither slavery nor involuntary servitude shall ever exist" in any territory gained from Mexico. Although the proviso never passed both houses of Congress, its repeated introduction by northerners transformed the debate.

Wilmot Proviso

Southerners suddenly circled their wagons to protect the future of a slave society. Alexander H. Stephens, only recently "no defender of slavery," now declared that slavery was based on the Bible and above moral criticism, and John C. Calhoun asserted a radical new southern position. The territories, Calhoun insisted, belonged to all the states, and the federal government could do nothing to limit the spread of slavery there. Southern slaveholders had a constitutional right rooted in the Fifth Amendment, Calhoun claimed, to take their slaves (as property) anywhere in the territories.

This position, often called "state sovereignty," which quickly became a test of orthodoxy among southern politicians, was a radical reversal of history. In 1787 the Confederation Congress had excluded slavery from the Northwest Territory (see pages 182–183); Article IV of the federal Constitution had authorized Congress to make "all needful rules and regulations" for the territories; and the Missouri Compromise had barred slavery from most of the Louisiana Purchase. Now, however, southern leaders demanded protection and future guarantees for slavery.

In the North, the Wilmot Proviso became a rallying cry for abolitionists. Eventually the legislatures of fourteen northern states endorsed it—and not because all its supporters were abolitionists. David Wilmot, significantly, was neither an abolitionist nor an antislavery Whig. He denied having any "squeamish sensitiveness upon the subject of slavery" or "morbid sympathy for the slave." Instead, his goal was to defend "the rights of white freemen" and to obtain California "for free white labor." Wilmot sought opportunity for "the sons of toil, of my own race and own color." His involvement in antislavery controversy is a measure of the remarkable ability of the territorial issue to alarm northerners of many viewpoints.

As Wilmot demonstrated, it was possible, however, to be both a racist and an opponent of slavery. The vast majority of white northerners were not active abolitionists, and their desire to keep the West free from slavery was often matched by their desire to keep blacks from settling there. Fear of the Slave Power was thus building a potent antislavery movement that united abolitionists and antiblack voters. The latter's concern was to protect from the Slave Power an abiding version of the American Dream: the free, individual, immigrant farmer's access to social mobility through acquisition of land and jobs in the West. This sacred ideal of free labor, and its dread of concentrated power, fueled a new political persuasion in America. Opposition to slavery's extension and fear of a conspiratorial Slave Power were growing. And as northerners became increasingly antislavery, southern slaveholders felt deep alarm.

The slavery question divided northerners and southerners in both parties and could not be kept out of national politics. After Polk renounced a second term as president, the Democrats nominated Senator Lewis Cass of Michigan for president and General William Butler of Kentucky for vice president. Cass, a party loyalist who had served in Jackson's cabinet, had

The Election of 1848 and Popular Sovereignty

devised in 1847 the idea of "popular sovereignty" for the territories—letting residents in the territories decide the question of slavery for themselves. His party's platform declared that Congress lacked the power to interfere with slavery and criticized those who pressed the question. The Whigs nominated General Zachary Taylor, a southern slaveholder and war hero; Congressman Millard Fillmore of New York was his running mate. The Whig convention similarly refused to assert that Congress had power over slavery in the territories.

But the issue would not stay in the background. Many southern Democrats distrusted Cass and eventually voted for Taylor because he was a slaveholder. Among northerners, concern over slavery led to the formation of a new party. New York Democrats committed to the Wilmot Proviso rebelled against Cass and nominated former president Martin Van Buren. Antislavery Whigs and former supporters of the Liberty Party then joined them to organize the Free-Soil Party, with Van Buren as its candidate (see Table 14.1). This party, whose slogan was "Free Soil, Free Speech, Free Labor, and Free Men," won almost 300,000 northern votes. For a new third party to win 10 percent of the national vote was a signal achievement. Taylor polled 1.4 million votes to Cass's 1.2 million and won the White House, but the results were more ominous than decisive. The War with Mexico made the political issue of slavery expansion into a moral issue. Politics split along sectional lines as never before. Religious denominations, too, were splitting into northern and southern wings. Judgments about slavery in America rarely lacked a religious dimension in these years; many Protestants, North and South, began to fear that God had an appointment with America, either to destroy the national sin of slavery or to help the South defend it as part of his divine order.

The conflicts of 1848 would dominate politics throughout the 1850s, as slavery in the territories colored every other national issue. The nation's uncertain attempts to deal with economic and social change gave way to more pressing questions about the nature of the Union itself.

1850: Compromise or Armistice?

The first sectional battle of the new decade involved California. More than eighty thousand Americans flooded into California during the gold rush of 1849 (see page 309). With Congress unable to agree on a formula to govern the territories, President Taylor urged these settlers to apply directly for admission to the Union. They promptly did so, proposing a state constitution that did not allow for slavery. Because California's admission as a free state would upset the sectional balance of power in the Senate (the ratio of slave to free states was 15 to 15), southern politicians wanted to postpone admission and make California a slave territory, or at least to extend the Missouri Compromise line west to the Pacific. Representatives from nine southern states, meeting in Nashville, asserted the South's right to part of the territory.

Henry Clay, the venerable Whig leader, sensed that the Union was in peril. Twice before—in 1820 and 1833—Clay, the "Great Pacificator," had taken the lead in shaping sectional compromise; now he struggled one last time to preserve the nation. To hushed Senate galleries Clay presented a series of compromise measures in the winter of 1850. At one point Clay held up what he claimed was a piece of George Washington's coffin as a means of inspiring unity. Over the weeks that followed, he and Senator Stephen A. Douglas of Illinois, the "Little Giant," steered their omnibus bill, or compromise package, through debate and amendment.

Table 14.1	**New Political Parties**		
Party	**Period of Influence**	**Area of Influence**	**Outcome**
Liberty Party	1839–1848	North	Merged with other antislavery groups to form Free-Soil Party
Free-Soil Party	1848–1854	North	Merged with Republican Party
Know-Nothings (American Party)	1853–1856	Nationwide	Disappeared, freeing most to join Republican Party
Republican Party	1854–present	North (later nationwide)	Became rival of Democratic Party and won presidency in 1860

The problems to be solved were numerous and difficult. Would California, or part of it, become a free state? How should the territory acquired from Mexico be organized? Texas, which allowed slavery, claimed large portions of the new land as far west as Santa Fe, so that claim, too, had to be settled. Southerners complained that fugitive slaves were not being returned as the Constitution required, and northerners objected to the sale of human beings in the nation's capital. Eight years earlier, in *Prigg v. Pennsylvania* (1842), the Supreme Court had ruled that enforcement of the fugitive slave clause in the Constitution was a federal obligation, thus fueling southern desires to bring this issue to a head. But most troublesome of all was the status of slavery in the territories.

Clay and Douglas hoped to avoid a specific formula, for Lewis Cass's idea of popular sovereignty possessed what one historian called the "charm of ambiguity" that appealed to practical politicians. Ultimately Congress would have to approve statehood for a territory, but "in the meantime," said Cass, it should allow the people living there "to regulate their own concerns in their own way."

Those simple words proved all but unenforceable. When could settlers prohibit slavery? To avoid dissension within their party, northern and southern Democrats explained Cass's statement to their constituents in two incompatible ways. Southerners claimed that neither Congress nor a territorial legislature could bar slavery. Only late in the territorial process, when settlers were ready to draft a state constitution, could they take that step, thus allowing time for slavery to take root. Northerners, however, insisted that Americans living in a territory were entitled to local self-government and thus could outlaw slavery at any time, especially early in the process.

The cause of compromise gained a powerful supporter when Senator Daniel Webster committed his prestige and eloquence to Clay's bill. "I wish to speak today," Webster declaimed on March 7 in a scene of high drama, "not as a Massachusetts man, nor as a Northern man, but as an American. I speak today for the preservation of the Union. Hear me for my cause." Abandoning his earlier support for the Wilmot Proviso, Webster urged northerners not to "taunt or reproach" the South with antislavery measures. To southern firebrands he issued a warning that disunion inevitably would cause violence and destruction. For his efforts at compromise, Webster was condemned by many former abolitionist friends in New England who accused him of going over to the "devil."

Only three days earlier, with equal drama, Calhoun was carried from his sickbed to deliver a speech opposing the compromise. Unable to stand and speak, his address was read for him by Senator James Mason of Virginia. Grizzled and dying, the South's intellectual defender warned that the "cords which bind these states" were "already greatly weakened." Calhoun did not address the specific measures in the bill; he predicted disunion if southern demands were not met, thereby frightening some into support of compromise.

Yet Webster's influence and rising fear were not enough. After months of labor, Clay and Douglas finally brought their legislative package to a vote, and lost. But the determined Douglas would not give up. With Clay sick and absent from Washington, Douglas reintroduced the compromise measures one at a time. Though there was no majority for compromise, Douglas shrewdly realized that different majorities might be created for the separate measures. Because southerners favored some bills and northerners the rest, the small bloc for compromise could vote first with one section and then with the other. The strategy worked, and Douglas's resourcefulness salvaged a positive result from more than eight months of congressional crisis. The Compromise of 1850 became law.

The compromise had five essential measures: California became a free state; the Texas boundary was set at its present limits (see Map 14.3 on page 372) and the United States paid Texas $10 million in compensation for the loss of New Mexico territory; the territories of New Mexico and Utah were organized on a basis of popular sovereignty; the fugitive slave law was strengthened; and the slave trade was abolished in the District of Columbia. Jubilation greeted passage of the compromise; crowds in Washington and other cities celebrated the happy news. "On one glorious night," records a modern historian, "the word went abroad that it was the duty of every patriot to get drunk. Before the next morning many a citizen had proved his patriotism."

Compromise of 1850

In reality, there was less cause for celebration than people hoped. At best, the Compromise of 1850 was an artful evasion. As one historian has argued, the legislation was more an "armistice," delaying greater conflict, than a compromise. Douglas had found a way to pass the five proposals without convincing northerners and southerners to agree on fundamentals. The compromise bought time for the nation, but it did not provide a real settlement of the territorial questions.

Furthermore, the compromise had two basic flaws. The first concerned the ambiguity of territorial legislation: how exactly was popular sovereignty to be enforced? During debate, southerners insisted there would be no prohibition of slavery during the territorial stage, and northerners declared that settlers could bar slavery whenever they wished. The compromise even allowed for the appeal of a territorial legislature's action to the Supreme Court. One witty politician remarked that the legislators had enacted a lawsuit instead of a law.

The second flaw lay in the Fugitive Slave Act, which gave new—and controversial—protection to slavery. The law empowered slave-

Fugitive Slave Act

owners to go into court in their own states to present evidence that a slave who owed them service had escaped. The resulting transcript and a description of the fugitive would then serve as legal proof of a person's slave status, even in free states and territories. Specially appointed court officials adjudicated the identity of the person described, not whether he or she was indeed a slave. Penalties made it a felony to harbor fugitives, and the law stated that northern citizens could be summoned to hunt fugitives. The fees paid to U.S. marshals favored slaveholders: $10 if the alleged fugitive was returned to the slaveowner, $5 if not returned.

Abolitionist newspapers quickly attacked the Fugitive Slave Act as a violation of fundamental American rights. Why, in a land of freedom, were alleged fugitives denied a trial by jury? Why were they given no chance to present evidence or cross-examine witnesses? Why did the law give authorities a financial incentive to send suspected fugitives into bondage? These arguments convinced some northerners that free blacks could be sent into slavery with no means to defend themselves. Protest meetings were held all over the North, especially in staunchly abolitionist communities.

Between 1850 and 1854, violent resistance to slave catchers occurred in dozens of northern towns. Sometimes a captured fugitive was broken out of jail or from the clutches of slave agents by abolitionists, as in the case of Shadrach Minkins in 1851 in Boston, who was spirited by a series of wagons and trains across Massachusetts, up through Vermont, to Montreal, Canada. Also in 1851, a fugitive named Jerry McHenry was freed by an abolitionist mob in Syracuse, New York, and hurried into Canadian freedom. That same year as well, the small black community in Lancaster County, Pennsylvania, rose up in arms to defend four escaped slaves from a federal posse charged with reenslaving them. At this "Christiana riot," the fugitives shot and killed Edward Gorsuch, the Maryland slaveowner who sought the return of his "property." Amid increasing border warfare over fugitive slaves, a headline reporting the Christiana affair screamed "Civil War, The First Blow Struck!"

Many abolitionists became convinced by their experience of resisting the Fugitive Slave Act that violence was a legitimate means of opposing slavery. In an 1854 column entitled "Is It Right and Wise to Kill a Kidnapper?" Frederick Douglass said that the only way to make the fugitive slave law "dead letter" was to make a "few dead slave catchers."

At this point a novel portrayed the humanity and suffering of slaves in a way that touched millions of northerners. Harriet Beecher Stowe,

Uncle Tom's Cabin

whose New England family had produced many prominent ministers, wrote *Uncle Tom's Cabin* out of deep moral conviction. Her story, serialized in 1851 and published as a book in 1852, conveyed the agonies faced by slave families and described a mother's dash to freedom with her child across the frozen Ohio River. Stowe also portrayed slavery's evil effects on slaveholders, indicting the institution itself more harshly than she indicted the southerners caught in its web. Moreover, Stowe exposed northern racism and complicity with slavery by making the worst slaveholder a man of New England birth, and a visiting relative on a plantation a squeamish Vermont woman who could hardly cope with the near presence of blacks.

In nine months the book sold over three hundred thousand copies, by mid-1853 over a million. Countless people saw *Uncle Tom's Cabin* performed as a stage play or heard the story in dramatic readings or read similar novels inspired by it. Stowe brought home the evil of slavery to many who had never given it much thought. Indeed, for generations, the characters in *Uncle Tom's Cabin*—Eliza, George, Little Eva, Simon Legree, Miss Ophelia, Augustine St. Clair, and Uncle Tom himself—became touchstones of the American imagination about the entire era of slavery and the Civil War.

The popularity of *Uncle Tom's Cabin* alarmed anxious southern whites. In politics and now in popular literature they saw threats to their way of life. Behind the South's aggressive claims about territorial rights lay the fear that if nearby areas became free soil, they would be used as bases from which to spread abolitionism into the slave states. To most white southerners, a moral condemnation of slaveholding anywhere meant the same thing everywhere.

To protect slavery in the arena of ideas, southerners needed to counter indictments of the institution as a moral wrong. Accordingly, some fifteen to twenty proslavery novels were published in the 1850s as responses to *Uncle Tom's Cabin*. Most of these anti–Uncle Tom books paled in comparison to Mrs. Stowe's masterpiece, but southern writers continued to defend their system as more humane than wage labor, and they blamed the slave trade on the "outside interference" of Yankee speculators. In awkward stories such as J. W. Page's *Uncle Robin in His Cabin and Tom Without One in Boston*, slaves were induced to run away by visiting abolitionists, and then all but starved in northern cities.

In reality, slaveholders were especially disturbed by the 1850s over what was widely called the Underground Railroad. This loose, illegal network of abolitionist stations all over the border state region (the area all along the Ohio River and the boundaries between Pennsylvania and Maryland and Virginia), spiriting runaways to freedom in safe houses, secret hideouts, and wagons, had never been very organized. Thousands of slaves did escape by these routes but largely through their own wits and courage, and through the assistance of black vigilance committees in some northern cities. Lewis Hayden in Boston, David Ruggles in New York, William Still in Philadelphia, John Parker in Ripley, Ohio, and Jacob Gibbs in Washington, D.C., were only some of the many black abolitionists who managed fugitive slave escapes through their regions.

The Underground Railroad

Moreover, Harriet Tubman, herself an escapee in 1848, returned to her native Maryland and to Virginia nearly twenty times, and through clandestine measures helped as many as three hundred slaves to freedom, some of them her own family members. Maryland planters were so outraged at her heroic success that they offered a $40,000 reward for her capture.

In Ohio numerous white abolitionists, often Quakers, joined with blacks as agents of slave liberation at various points along the river border between slavery and freedom. In the wake of the Fugitive Slave Act, an estimated twenty thousand blacks, most of them fugitive slaves, moved from the northern states into Canada seeking security. The Underground Railroad also had numerous maritime routes, as coastal slaves escaped aboard ship out of Virginia or the Carolinas, or from a major port like New Orleans. This constant, dangerous flow of humanity was a testament to human courage, good luck, and the will for free

The Webb Family toured the North, presenting dramatic readings of *Uncle Tom's Cabin*. Performances by the Webbs and others deepened the already powerful impact of Harriet Beecher Stowe's novel.   (Harriet Beecher Stowe Center, Hartford, Conn.)

dom. It never reached the scale that some angry slaveholders believed, but in reality and in legend it applied pressure to the slavery crisis and served as a symbol and a national conscience against oppression.

The 1852 election gave southern leaders hope that slavery would be secure under the administration of a new president. Franklin Pierce, a Democrat from New Hampshire, won an easy victory over the Whig presidential nominee, General Winfield Scott. Pierce defended each section's rights as essential to the nation's unity, and southerners hoped that his firm support for the Compromise of 1850 might end the season of crisis. Because Scott's views on the compromise had been unknown and the Free-Soil candidate, John P. Hale of New Hampshire, had openly rejected it, Pierce's victory suggested widespread support for the compromise.

Election of 1852 and the Collapse of Compromise

Pierce's victory, however, derived less from his strengths than from the Whig Party's weakness. The

In *Still Life of Harriet Tubman with Bible and Candle,* we see the youthful, calm, determined leader of the Underground Railroad. Appearing gentle, Tubman was in her own way a revolutionary who liberated nearly three hundred of her people. (© 2000 Louis Psihoyos/Matrix)

Whigs were a congressional and state-based party that never had achieved much success in presidential politics. Sectional discord was splitting the party in two, further undermining its national competitiveness, and the deaths of President Taylor, Daniel Webster, and Henry Clay had deprived Whigs of decisive leadership. In 1852 the Whig Party was all but dead.

President Pierce's embrace of the compromise appalled many northerners. His vigorous enforcement of the Fugitive Slave Act provoked outrage and fear of the Slave Power, especially in the case of the fugitive slave Anthony Burns. Burns had fled Virginia by stowing away on a ship. In Boston, thinking he was safe in a city known for abolitionism, Burns began a new life. But in 1854 federal marshals found and placed him under guard in Boston's courthouse. An interracial crowd of abolitionists attacked the courthouse, killing a jailor, in an unsuccessful attempt to free Burns, whose case attracted nationwide attention.

Pierce moved decisively to enforce the Fugitive Slave Act. He telegraphed local officials to "incur any expense to insure the execution of the law" and sent marines, cavalry, and artillery to Boston. When Burns's owner seemed willing to sell his property, the U.S. attorney blocked the sale and won a decision that Anthony Burns must return to slavery. U.S. troops marched Burns to Boston harbor through streets draped in black and hung with American flags at half-mast. At a cost of $100,000, a single black man was returned to slavery through the power of federal law.

The national will to sustain the future of slavery was now tested at every turn. This demonstration of federal support for slavery radicalized opinion, even among many conservatives. Textile manufacturer Amos A. Lawrence observed that "we went to bed one night old fashioned, conservative, Compromise Union Whigs & waked up stark mad Abolitionists." Juries refused to convict the abolitionists who had stormed the courthouse, and New England states began to pass personal-liberty laws designed to impede or block federal enforcement. Before the end of the 1850s, nine northern states passed such laws. Where northerners now saw evidence of a dominating Slave Power, outraged slaveholders saw the legal defense of their rights.

Pierce seemed unable to avoid sectional conflict in other arenas as well. His proposal for a transcontinental railroad derailed when congressmen fought over its location, North or South. His attempts to acquire foreign territory stirred more trouble. An annexation treaty with Hawai'i failed because southern senators would not vote for another free state, and efforts to acquire slaveholding Cuba angered northerners. Events in the Pacific also caused division at home. With two orchestrated landings in the Bay of Tokyo, in 1853 and 1854, Commodore Matthew Perry established U.S. intentions to trade with Japan, whether that country sought such contact or not. Offended and intrigued, the Japanese were impressed with Perry's steam-powered warships, the first such black smoke-belching floating machines they had seen. Perry's Treaty of Kanagawa in March 1854 negotiated two ports as coaling stations for American ships. The much sought-after trading arrangements were slow in coming, although this did not stop merchants and bankers from lavishing on Perry a hero's honors when he returned to the United States. In his meetings with the Japanese, the pompous Perry had given his hosts, whom he considered an inferior people, a telegraph system, a quarter-scale railroad train, a bound history of the War with Mexico, and 100 gallons of Kentucky whiskey.

Soon back home another territorial bill threw Congress and the nation into even greater turmoil and the Compromise of 1850 fell into complete collapse.

Slavery Expansion and Collapse of the Party System

The new controversy began in a surprising way. Stephen A. Douglas, one of the architects of the Compromise of 1850, introduced a bill to establish the Kansas and Nebraska Territories. Talented and ambitious, Douglas was known for compromise, not sectional quarreling. But he did not view slavery as a fundamental problem, and he was willing to risk some controversy to win economic benefits for Illinois, his home state. A transcontinental railroad would encourage settlement of the Great Plains and stimulate the economy of Illinois; but no company would build such a railroad before Congress organized the territories it would cross. Thus interest in promoting the construction of such a railroad drove Douglas to introduce a bill that inflamed sectional passions.

The Kansas-Nebraska bill exposed the first flaw of the Compromise of 1850—the conflicting interpretations of popular sovereignty. Douglas's bill left "all questions pertaining to slavery in the Territories . . . to the people residing therein." Northerners and southerners, however, still disagreed violently over what territorial settlers could constitutionally do. Moreover, the Kansas and Nebraska Territories lay within the Louisiana Purchase, and the Missouri Compromise prohibited slavery in all that land from latitude 36°30' north to the Canadian border. If popular sovereignty were to mean anything in Kansas and Nebraska, it had to mean that the Missouri Compromise was no longer in effect and that settlers could establish slavery there.

The Kansas-Nebraska Bill

Southern congressmen, anxious to establish slaveholders' right to take slaves into any territory, pressed Douglas to concede this point. They demanded an explicit repeal of the 36°30' limitation as the price of their support. During a carriage ride with Senator Archibald Dixon of Kentucky, Douglas debated the point at length. Finally he made an impulsive decision: "By God, Sir, you are right. I will incorporate it in my bill, though I know it will raise a hell of a storm."

Perhaps Douglas underestimated the storm because he believed that conditions of climate and soil would keep slavery out of Kansas and Nebraska. Nev-

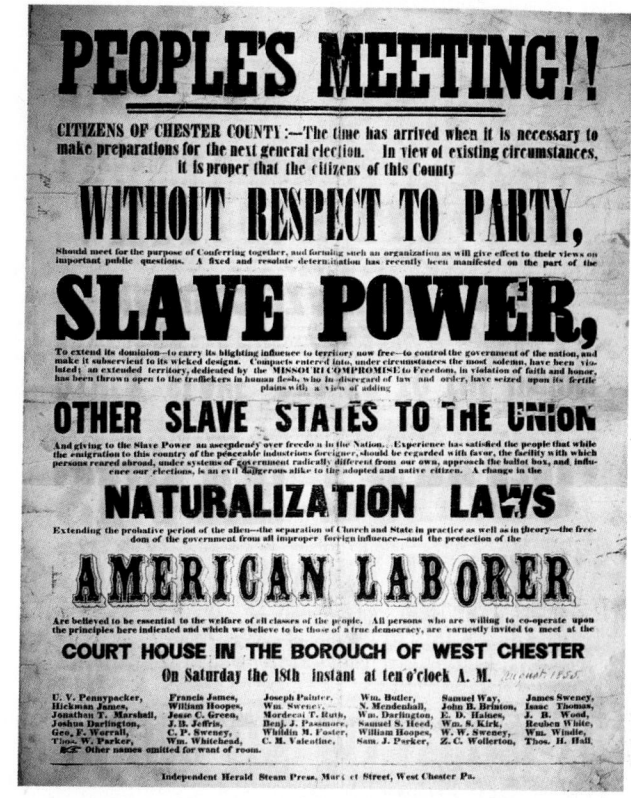

Throughout the North the Kansas-Nebraska Act kindled fires of alarm over the Slave Power's "determination to extend its dominion" and "control the government of the nation." Public meetings like the one announced here, held in West Chester, Pennsylvania, aided the new Republican Party.   (American Antiquarian Society)

ertheless, his bill threw open to slavery land from which it had been prohibited for thirty-four years. Opposition from Free-Soilers and antislavery forces was immediate and enduring; many considered this turn of events a betrayal of a sacred trust. The titanic struggle in Congress lasted three and a half months. Douglas won the support of President Pierce and eventually prevailed: the bill became law in May 1854 by a vote that demonstrated the dangerous sectionalization of American politics (see Map 14.3 and Table 14.2).

But the storm was just beginning. Abolitionists charged sinister aggression by the Slave Power, and northern fears of slavery's influence deepened. Opposition to the Fugitive Slave Act grew dramatically; between 1855 and 1859 Connecticut, Rhode Island, Massachusetts, Michigan, Maine, Ohio, and Wisconsin passed personal-liberty laws. These laws enraged southern leaders by providing counsel for alleged fugitives and requiring trial by jury. More important was

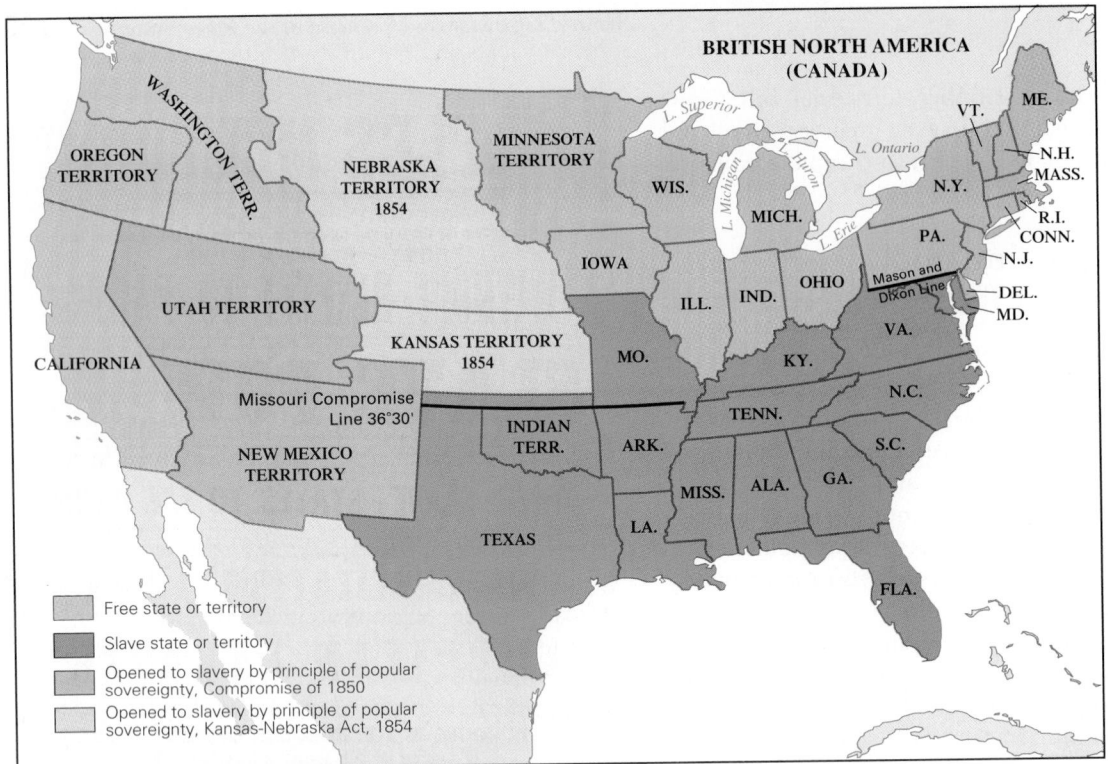

Map 14.3 The Kansas-Nebraska Act and Slavery Expansion, 1854 The vote on the Kansas-Nebraska Act (see also Table 14.2) in the House of Representatives demonstrates the sectionalization of American politics due to the slavery question.

the devastating impact of the Kansas-Nebraska Act on political parties. The weakened Whig Party broke apart into northern and southern wings that could no longer cooperate nationally. One of the two foundations of the second party system (see pages 294–295) was now gone. The Democrats survived, but their support in the North fell drastically in the 1854 elections. Northern Democrats lost sixty-six of their ninety-one congressional seats and lost control of all but two free-state legislatures.

The beneficiary of northern voters' wrath was a new political party. During debate on the Kansas-Nebraska bill, six congressmen had published an "Appeal of the Independent Democrats." Joshua Giddings, Salmon Chase, and Charles Sumner—the principal authors of this protest—attacked Douglas's legislation as a "gross violation of a sacred pledge" (the Missouri Compromise) and a "criminal betrayal of precious rights" that would make free territory a "dreary region of despotism." Their appeal tapped a reservoir of deep concerns in the North, cogently expressed by Illinois's Abraham Lincoln.

Birth of the Republican Party

Although Lincoln did not personally condemn southerners—"They are just what we would be in their situation"—he exposed the meaning of the Kansas-Nebraska Act. Denying "that there can be moral right in the enslaving of one man by another," Lincoln argued that the founders, from love of liberty, had banned slavery from the Northwest Territory, kept the word *slavery* out of the Constitution, and treated it overall as a "cancer" on the republic. Rather than encouraging liberty, the Kansas-Nebraska Act put slavery "on the high road to extension and perpetuity," and that constituted a "moral wrong and injustice." America's future, Lincoln warned, was being mortgaged to slavery and all its influences.

Thousands of ordinary northerners agreed. During the summer and fall of 1854, antislavery Whigs and Democrats, Free-Soilers, and other reformers throughout the Old Northwest met to form the new Republican Party, dedicated to keeping slavery out of the territories. The influence of the Republicans rapidly spread to the East, and they won a stunning victory in the 1854 elections. In their first appearance on the ballot, Republicans captured a majority of northern House seats. Antislavery sentiment had created a new party and caused roughly a quarter of northern Democrats to desert their party.

For the first time, too, a sectional party had gained significant power in the political system. Now the

Table 14.2   The Vote on the Kansas-Nebraska Act

The vote was 113–100 in favor.

	Aye	Nay
Northern Democrats	44	42
Southern Democrats	57	2
Northern Whigs	0	45
Southern Whigs	12	7
Northern Free-Soilers		4

Whigs were gone, and only the Democrats struggled to maintain national membership. The Republicans absorbed the Free-Soil Party and grew rapidly in the North. Indeed, the emergence of the Republican coalition of antislavery interests is the most rapid transformation in party allegiance and voter behavior in American history. This fact alone attests to the centrality of slavery expansion in the causation of the Civil War.

And Republicans were not the only new party. For a brief period, an anti-immigrant organization, the American Party, blossomed. This

Know-Nothings party, popularly known as the Know-Nothings (because its first members kept their purposes secret, answering "I know nothing" to all questions), exploited nativist fear of foreigners and Catholics. Between 1848 and 1860, nearly 3.5 million immigrants entered the United States—proportionally the heaviest inflow of foreigners ever in American history (see pages 321–323). Democrats courted the votes of these new citizens, but many native-born, Anglo-Saxon Protestants believed that Irish and German Catholics would owe primary allegiance to the Pope in Rome and not to the American nation.

In 1854 anti-immigrant fears gave the Know-Nothings spectacular success in some northern states. They triumphed especially in Massachusetts, electing 11 congressmen, a governor, all state officers, all state senators, and all but 2 of 378 state representatives. The temperance movement also gained new strength early in the 1850s with its promises to stamp out the evils associated with liquor and immigrants (a particularly anti-Irish campaign). In this context the Know-Nothings strove to reinforce Protestant morality and restrict voting and officeholding to the native-born. As the Whig Party faded from the scene, the Know-Nothings temporarily filled the void. But their terror tactics against immigrant voters drove many potential supporters away. And, like the Whigs, the Know-Nothings could not keep their northern and southern wings together, and they dissolved after 1856. The growing Republican coalition wooed the nativists with temperance ordinances and laws postponing suffrage for naturalized citizens (see Table 14.1 on page 366).

With nearly half of the old electorate up for grabs, the demise of the Whig Party ensured a major realignment of the political system. To win over these homeless Whigs, the remaining parties made appeals to various segments of the electorate. Immigration, temperance, homestead bills, the tariff, internal improvements—all played important roles in attracting voters during the 1850s. The Republicans appealed strongly to those interested in the economic development of the West. Commercial agriculture was booming in the Ohio–Mississippi–Great Lakes area, but residents of that region desired more canals, roads, and river and harbor improvements to reap the full benefit of their labors. Because credit was scarce, a homestead program attracted voters: its proponents argued that western land should be made available free to individual farmers. Seizing their opportunity, the Republicans added internal improvements and land-grant planks to their platform. They also backed higher tariffs as an enticement to industrialists and businessmen, whose interest in tariff protection grew after a financial panic in 1857.

Partisan ideological appeals became the currency of the realigned political system. As Republicans preached "Free Soil, Free Labor, Free Men," they captured a self-image of many northerners. These phrases resonated with traditional ideals of equality, liberty, and opportunity under self-government—the heritage of republicanism. Invoking that heritage also undercut charges that the Republican Party was radical and unreliable.

"Free Soil, Free Labor, Free Men" seemed an appropriate motto for a northern economy that was energetic, expanding, and prosperous. Thousands of farmers had moved west to establish productive farms and growing communities. Midwesterners multiplied their yields by using new machines such as disk harrows and mechanical reapers. Railroads were carrying their crops to urban markets. And industry was beginning to perform wonders of production, making available goods that only recently had been beyond the reach of the average person. As northerners surveyed the general growth and prosperity, they thought they saw a reason for it.

Party Realignment and the Republicans' Appeal

The key to progress appeared, to many people, to be free labor—the dignity of work and the incentive of opportunity. Any hard-working and virtuous man, it was thought, could improve his condition and achieve economic independence by seizing opportunities that the country had to offer. Republicans argued that the South, with little industry and its slave labor system, was backward and retrograde by comparison, and their arguments captured much of the spirit of the age in the North.

Republican Ideology

Traditional republicanism hailed the virtuous common man as the backbone of the country. In Abraham Lincoln, a man of humble origins who had become a successful lawyer and political leader, Republicans had a symbol of that tradition. They portrayed their party as the guardian of economic opportunity, giving individuals a chance to work, acquire land, and attain success. In the words of an Iowa Republican, the United States was thriving because its "door is thrown open to all, and even the poorest and humblest in the land, may, by industry and application, gain a position which will entitle him to the respect and confidence of his fellow-men."

At stake in the enveloping crises of the 1850s were thus two competing definitions of "liberty": southern planters' claims to protection of their liberty in the possession and transport of their slaves anywhere in the land, and northern workers' and farmers' claims to protection of their liberty to seek a new start on free land, unimpeded by a system that defined labor as slave and black. Thus, a growing number of northerners expressed the fear that the rising political storm was an "irrepressible conflict."

Opposition to the extension of slavery had brought the Republicans into being, but party members carefully broadened their appeal by adopting the causes of other groups. Their coalition ideology consisted of many elements: resentment of southern political power, devotion to unionism, antislavery based on free labor arguments, moral revulsion to slavery, and racial prejudice. As the *New York Tribune* editor Horace Greeley wrote in 1856, "It is beaten into my bones that the American people are not yet anti-slavery." Four years later, Greeley again observed that "an Anti-Slavery man per se cannot be elected." But, he added, "a Tariff, River-and-Harbor, Pacific Railroad, Free Homestead man, may succeed although he is Anti-Slavery." As these elements joined the Republican Party, they also grew to fear slavery even more.

In the South, the disintegration of the Whig Party had left many southerners at loose ends politically; they

Southern Democrats

included a good number of wealthy planters, smaller slaveholders, and urban businessmen. Some gravitated to the American Party, but not for long. In the increasingly tense atmosphere of sectional crisis, these people were highly susceptible to strong states' rights positions and defense of slavery. The security of their own communities seemed to be at stake. In the 1850s, Democratic leaders managed to convert most of the formerly Whig slaveholders, who responded to their class interests.

Most southern Democrats, however, were not slaveholders. Since Andrew Jackson's day, small farmers had been the heart of the Democratic Party. Democratic politicians, though often slaveowners themselves, lauded the common man and argued that their policies advanced his interests. According to the southern version of republicanism, white citizens in a slave society enjoyed liberty and social equality because black people were enslaved. As Jefferson Davis put it in 1851, in other societies distinctions were drawn "by property, between the rich and the poor." But in the South, slavery elevated every white person's status and allowed the nonslaveholder to "stand upon the broad level of equality with the rich man." To retain the support of ordinary whites, southern Democrats emphasized this appeal to racism. The issue in the sectional crisis, they warned, was "shall negroes govern white men, or white men govern negroes?"

Southern leaders also portrayed sectional controversies as matters of injustice and insult to the South. The rights of all southern whites were in jeopardy, they argued, because antislavery and Free-Soil forces threatened an institution protected in the Constitution. The stable, well-ordered South was the true defender of constitutional principles, the rapidly changing North their destroyer.

Racial fears and traditional political loyalties helped keep the political alliance between yeoman farmers and planters largely intact through the 1850s. Across class lines, white southerners joined together in the interest of community security against what they perceived as the Republican Party's capacity to cause slave unrest in their midst. Potential conflicts between slaveholders and nonslaveholders were not discussed, and no viable party emerged to replace the Whigs. The result was a one-party system that emphasized sectional issues and loyalty. In the South as in the North, political realignment sharpened sectional identities.

Political leaders of both sections used race in their arguments about opportunity, but northerners and southerners saw different futures. The *Montgomery* (Alabama) *Mail* warned southern whites in 1860 that the Republicans intended "to free the negroes and force amalgamation between them and the children of the poor men of the South. The rich will be able to keep out of the way of the contamination." Republicans warned northern workers that if slavery entered the territories, the great reservoir of opportunity for ordinary citizens would be poisoned.

In the territory of Kansas a succession of events, like hammer blows, deepened the conflict. The Kansas-Nebraska Act spawned hatred and violence as land-hungry claim jumpers and partisans in the sectional struggle clashed repeatedly in Kansas Territory. Abolitionists and religious groups sent in armed Free-Soil settlers; southerners sent in their reinforcements to establish slavery and prevent "northern hordes" from stealing Kansas away. Conflicts led to bloodshed, and soon the whole nation was talking about "Bleeding Kansas."

Politics in the territory resembled war more than democracy. During elections for a territorial legislature in 1855, thousands of proslavery Missourians—known as Border Ruffians—invaded the polls and ran up a large but fraudulent majority for slavery candidates. The resulting legislature legalized slavery, and in response Free-Soilers held an unauthorized convention at which they cre-

Bleeding Kansas

ated their own government and constitution. In the spring of 1856, a proslavery posse sent to arrest the Free-Soil leaders sacked the Kansas town of Lawrence, killing several people. In revenge John Brown, a radical abolitionist who saw himself as God's instrument to destroy slavery, murdered five proslavery settlers living along Pottawatomie Creek. Soon, armed bands of guerrillas roamed the territory, battling over land claims as well as slavery.

These passions brought violence to the U.S. Senate in May 1856, when Charles Sumner of Massachusetts denounced "the Crime against Kansas." Radical in his antislavery views, Sumner bitterly assailed the president, the South, and Senator Andrew P. Butler of South Carolina. Soon thereafter Butler's cousin, Representative Preston Brooks, approached Sumner at the latter's Senate desk, raised his cane, and began to beat Sumner on the head. Trapped behind his desk, which was bolted in place, Sumner tried to rise, eventually wrenching the desk free before he collapsed, bleeding, on the floor.

Shocked northerners recoiled from what they saw as another southern assault on free speech and the South's readiness to use violence to have its way. William Cullen Bryant, editor of the *New York Evening Post*, asked, "Has it come to this, that we must speak with bated breath in the presence of our southern masters?" As if in reply, the *Richmond Enquirer* denounced "vulgar Abolitionists in the Senate" who "have been

The Border Ruffians, depicted in this pen-and-ink drawing, were proslavery Missourians who periodically invaded Kansas to vote and help establish slavery there. Conflicts over land claims further complicated the violence in Bleeding Kansas.   (Yale University Art Gallery, Mabel Brady Garvan Collection)

suffered to run too long without collars. They must be lashed into submission." Popular opinion in Massachusetts strongly supported Sumner; South Carolina voters reelected Brooks and sent him dozens of commemorative canes. The country was becoming polarized.

The election of 1856 showed how extreme that polarization had become. When Democrats met to select a nominee, they shied away from prominent leaders whose views on the territories were well known. Instead, they chose James Buchanan of Pennsylvania, whose chief virtue was that for the past four years he had been ambassador to Britain, uninvolved in territorial controversies. This anonymity and superior party organization helped Buchanan win 1.8 million votes and the election, but he owed his victory to southern support. Hence, he was tagged with the label "a northern man with southern principles." Eleven of sixteen free states voted against him, and Democrats did not regain ascendancy in those states for decades. The Republican candidate, John C. Frémont, won those eleven free states and 1.3 million votes; Republicans had become the dominant party in the North after only two years of existence. The Know-Nothing candidate, Millard Fillmore, won almost 1 million votes, but this election was to be his party's last hurrah. The coming battle would pit a sectional Republican Party against an increasingly divided Democratic Party.

Slavery and the Nation's Future

 For years the issue of slavery in the territories had convulsed Congress, and for years Congress had tried to settle the issue with vague formulas. In 1857 a different branch of government stepped into the fray. The Supreme Court took up this emotionally charged subject and attempted to silence controversy with a definitive verdict.

A Missouri slave named Dred Scott had sued his owner for his freedom. Scott based his claim on the fact that his former owner, an army surgeon, had taken him for several years into Illinois, a free state, and into the Wisconsin Territory, from which slavery had been barred by the Missouri Compromise. Scott first won and then lost his case as it moved on appeal through the state courts, into the federal system, and finally after eleven years to the Supreme Court.

Dred Scott Case

Normally Supreme Court justices were reluctant to inject themselves into political issues, and it seemed likely that the Court would stay out of this one. An 1851 decision had declared that state courts determined the status of Negroes who lived within their jurisdictions. The Supreme Court had only to follow this precedent to avoid ruling on substantive, and very controversial, issues: Was a black person like Dred Scott a citizen of the United States and thus eligible to sue in federal court? Had residence in a free state or territory made him free? Did Congress have the power to prohibit slavery in a territory or to delegate that power to a territorial legislature?

Initially the Supreme Court seemed ready to dispose of *Dred Scott v. Sanford* by following the 1851 precedent. The chief justice even assigned one justice the task of writing such an opinion. Then, for a number of reasons, the Court decided to rule on the Missouri Compromise after all. Two northern justices indicated that they would dissent from the assigned opinion and argue for Scott's freedom and the constitutionality of the Missouri Compromise. Their decision emboldened southerners on the Court, who were growing eager to declare the 1820 geographical restriction on slavery unconstitutional. Southern sympathizers in Washington were pressing for a proslavery verdict, and several justices simply felt they should try to resolve sectional strife once and for all.

In March 1857, Chief Justice Roger B. Taney of Maryland delivered the majority opinion of a divided Court. Taney declared that Scott was not a citizen of either the United States or Missouri; that residence in free territory did not make Scott free; and that Congress had no power to bar slavery from any territory. The decision not only overturned a sectional compromise that had been honored for years; it also invalidated the basic ideas of the Wilmot Proviso and probably popular sovereignty as well.

The Slave Power seemed to have won a major constitutional victory. African Americans were especially dismayed, for Taney's decision asserted that the founders had never intended for black people to be citizens. At the nation's founding, the chief justice wrote, blacks had been regarded "as beings of an inferior order" with "no rights which the white man was bound to respect." Taney was mistaken, however. African Americans had been citizens in several of the original states. Nevertheless, the ruling seemed to shut the door permanently on their hopes for justice and equal rights. Blacks, after 1857, lived in the land of the *Dred Scott* decision.

Northern whites who rejected the decision's content were suspicious of the circumstances that produced it. Five of the nine justices were southerners;

Dred Scott, a slave who brought suit in Missouri for his freedom, and Chief Justice Roger Taney, a descendant of Maryland's slaveholding elite, were principal figures in the most controversial Supreme Court decision of the nineteenth century. (Scott: Missouri Historical Society; Taney: Maryland Historical Society, Baltimore)

three of the northern justices actively dissented or refused to concur in crucial parts of the decision. The only northerner who supported Taney's opinion, Justice Robert Grier of Pennsylvania, was known to be close to President Buchanan. In fact, Buchanan had secretly brought to bear improper but effective influence.

A storm of angry reaction broke in the North. The decision seemed to confirm every charge against the aggressive Slave Power. "There is such a thing as the slave power," warned the *Cincinnati Daily Commercial.* "It has marched over and annihilated the boundaries of the states. We are now one great homogenous slaveholding community." The *Cincinnati Freeman* asked, "What security have the Germans and the Irish that their children will not, within a hundred years, be reduced to slavery in this land of their adoption?" "Where will it end?" asked the *Atlantic Monthly.* "Is the success of this conspiracy to be final and eternal?" The poet James Russell Lowell expressed the anxieties of poor northern whites when he had his Yankee character Ezekiel Biglow say:

> Wy, it's just ez clear ez figgers,
> Clear ez one an' one make two,
> Chaps thet make black slaves o' niggers,
> Want to make wite slaves o' you.

Republican politicians used these fears to strengthen their antislavery coalition. Abraham Lincoln stressed that the territorial question affected every citizen. "The whole nation," he had declared as

Abraham Lincoln on the Slave Power

early as 1854, "is interested that the best use shall be made of these Territories. We want them for homes of free white people. This they cannot be, to any considerable extent, if slavery shall be planted within them." The territories must be reserved, he insisted, "as an outlet for free white people everywhere" so that immigrants could come to America and "find new homes and better their condition in life."

More importantly, Lincoln warned of slavery's increasing control over the nation. The founders had created a government dedicated to freedom, Lincoln insisted. Admittedly they had recognized slavery's existence, but the public mind, he argued in 1858, had always rested in the belief that slavery would die either naturally or by legislation. The next step in the unfolding Slave Power conspiracy, Lincoln alleged, would be a Supreme Court decision "declaring that the Constitution does not permit a State to exclude slavery from its limits. . . . We shall lie down pleasantly, dreaming that the people of Missouri are on the verge of making their State free; and we shall awake to the reality instead, that the Supreme Court has made Illinois a slave State." This charge was not pure hyperbole, for lawsuits soon challenged state laws that freed slaves brought within their borders.

Lincoln's most eloquent statement against the Slave Power was his famous "House Divided" speech, delivered as he announced his campaign for the U.S.

How do historians know...

that Abraham Lincoln despised slavery? Lincoln, of course, was a politician who made many public addresses and statements. Later, as president, he mastered the form of the public letter sent to leading newspapers. Lincoln paid close attention to his understanding of public opinion on the issues of slavery and emancipation, and when the war came, he put saving the Union ahead of freeing slaves as a matter of policy, until the two causes became interdependent. But before he received the Republican nomination for president in 1860, he was long on record as a leading voice of his party's intention to put slavery on a "course of ultimate extinction." This photograph was taken in Chicago in 1859, the year before the Illinois lawyer was elected president.

Lincoln also produced many private writings. The page reproduced here comes from a notebook in which he recorded his reactions to a proslavery book, *Slavery Ordained of God*, by Reverend Fred A. Ross. Criticizing Ross, Lincoln revealed his dislike of privilege and exposed the self-interest of those who would exploit others: "Dr. Ross sits in the shade, with gloves on his hands, and subsists on the bread that Sambo is earning in the burning sun" rather than "delv[ing] for his own bread." Lincoln was no radical abolitionist, and his various stands on slavery represented both his pragmatic politics and his personal views. But there can be no doubt that, when it came to his own convictions, he hated slavery as an idea and as an institution. (Photos: Notebook: Courtesy of the Illinois State Historical Library; Lincoln: Chicago Historical Society)

Senate in 1858. Using biblical metaphor and extraordinary grace, he declared:

> 'A house divided against itself cannot stand.' I believe this government cannot endure, permanently half slave and half free. I do not expect the Union to be dissolved—I do not expect the House to fall—but I do expect it to cease to be divided. It will become all one thing or all the other. Either the opponents of slavery will arrest the further spread of it, and place it where the public mind shall rest in the belief that it is in the course of ultimate extinction; or its advocates will push it forward, till it shall become alike lawful in all the States, old as well as new, North as well as South.

Lincoln warned repeatedly that the latter possibility was real, and events convinced countless northerners that slaveholders were nearing their goal of making slavery a national institution. And southerners never forgot Lincoln's use of the direct words "ultimate extinction."

Politically, these forceful Republican arguments offset the difficulties that the *Dred Scott* decision posed. By endorsing the South's doctrine of state sovereignty, the Court had in effect declared that the central position of the Republican Party—no extension of slavery—was unconstitutional. Republicans could only repudiate the decision, appealing to a "higher law," or hope to change the personnel of the Court. They did both and gained politically as fear of the Slave Power grew. But fear also grew among free blacks, as they wondered if they had any future in America. Frederick Douglass continued to try to fashion hope among his people, but concluded a speech in the wake of the *Dred Scott* decision bleakly: "I walk by faith, not by sight."

For northern Democrats like Stephen Douglas, the Court's decision posed an awful dilemma. North-

The Lecompton Constitution

ern voters were alarmed by the prospect that the territories would be opened to slavery. To retain their support, Douglas had to find some way to reassure them. Yet, given his ambitions to lead the national Democratic Party and become president, Douglas could not afford to alienate southern Democrats.

Douglas chose to stand by his principle of popular sovereignty, even if the result angered southerners. In 1857 Kansans voted on a proslavery constitution that had been drafted at Lecompton. It was defeated by more than ten thousand votes. The evidence was overwhelming that Kansans did not want slavery, yet President Buchanan tried to force the Lecompton Constitution through Congress in an effort to hastily organize the territory.

Never had the Slave Power's influence over the government seemed more blatant; the Buchanan administration and southerners demanded a proslavery outcome, contrary to the popular will of the majority in Kansas. Breaking with the administration, Douglas threw his weight against the Lecompton Constitution. He gauged opinion in Kansas correctly, for in 1858 voters there rejected the constitution again. But his action infuriated southern Democrats. After the *Dred Scott* decision, southerners like Senator Albert G. Brown of Mississippi believed that slavery was protected in the territories: "The Constitution as expounded by the Supreme Court awards it. We demand it; we mean to have it."

Douglas further alienated the southern wing of his party in his well-publicized debates with Abraham

Stephen Douglas and the Freeport Doctrine

Lincoln, who challenged him for the Illinois Senate seat in 1858. Speaking at Freeport, Illinois, Douglas attempted to revive the concept of popular sovereignty with some tortured arguments. Asserting that the Supreme Court had ruled only on the powers of Congress, not on the powers of a territorial legislature, Douglas claimed that citizens in a territory could still bar slavery either by passing a law against it or by doing nothing. Without the patrol laws and police regulations that supported slavery, he reasoned, the institution could not exist. This argument, called the Freeport Doctrine, temporarily shored up Douglas's crumbling position in the North. But it gave southern Democrats further evidence that Douglas was unreliable, and many turned viciously against him. Many southerners studied the trend in northern opinion and concluded that southern rights and slavery would be safe only in a separate nation.

Such feelings were not new. As early as 1838, the Louisiana planter Bennet Barrow had written in his diary: "Northern States meddling with slavery . . . openly speaking of the sin of Slavery in the southern states . . . must eventually cause a separation of the Union." In 1856 a calmer, more polished Georgian named Charles Colcock Jones, Jr., rejoiced at James Buchanan's defeat of Republican John C. Frémont for the presidency. The result guaranteed four more years of peace and prosperity, wrote Jones, but "beyond that period . . . we scarce dare expect a continuance of our present relations." Increasingly, slaveowners lived with a sense of crisis about the fate of the Union.

The immediate consequence for politics, however, was the likelihood of a split in the Democratic Party. Northern Democrats could not support the territorial protection for slavery that southern Democrats insisted was theirs as a constitutional right. Thus, in the North and in the South the issue of slavery in the territories continued to destroy moderation and promote militancy.

Disunion

 It is worth remembering that in the late 1850s most Americans were not caught up daily in the slavery crisis. They were preoccupied with personal affairs, especially coping with the effects of the economic panic that had begun in the spring of 1857. They were worried about widespread unemployment, a sick cow, the plummeting price of wheat, the declining wages at a textile mill,

or a son who wanted to marry and needed land. In the Midwest, clerks, mechanics, domestics, railroad hands, and lumber camp workers lost jobs by the thousands. Bankers were at a loss for what to do about a weak credit system caused by frenzied western land speculation that began early in the decade. In parts of the South, such as Georgia, the panic intensified class divisions between upcountry yeomen and coastal slaveholding planters. Farmers blamed the tight money policies of Georgia's budding commercial banking system on wealthy planters who controlled the state's Democratic Party.

By 1858 Philadelphia had 40,000 unemployed workers, and New York City nearly 100,000. Fear of bread riots and class warfare gripped many cities in the North. True to form, blame for such economic woe became sectionalized, as southerners saw their system justified by the temporary collapse of industrial prosperity, and northerners feared even more the incursions of the Slave Power on an insecure future.

The earliest known photograph of John Brown, probably taken in 1846 in Massachusetts, shows him pledging his devotion to an unidentified flag, possibly an abolitionist banner. Already Brown was aiding runaway slaves and pondering ways to strike at slavery. (Ohio Historical Society)

Soon, however, the entire nation's focus would be thrown again on a new dimension of the slavery question—armed rebellion. Born in Connecticut in 1800, John Brown had been raised by staunchly religious and antislavery parents. Between 1820 and 1855, he engaged in some twenty business ventures, including farming, nearly all of them failures. But Brown had a distinctive vision of abolitionism, though he never joined any antislavery organizations. He relied on an Old Testament conception of justice—"an eye for an eye"—and he had a puritanical obsession with the wickedness of others, especially southern slaveowners. Brown believed that slavery was an "unjustifiable" state of war conducted by one group of people against another. He also believed that violence in a righteous cause was a holy act, even a rite of purification for those who engaged in it. To Brown, the destruction of slavery in America required revolutionary ideology and revolutionary acts.

John Brown's Raid on Harpers Ferry

On October 16, 1859, Brown led a small band of whites and blacks (eighteen men in all) in an attack on the federal arsenal at Harpers Ferry, Virginia. Hoping to trigger a slave rebellion, Brown failed miserably and was quickly captured. In a celebrated trial in November, and a highly guarded but widely publicized execution in December, in Charles Town, Virginia, Brown became one of the most enduring martyrs, as well as villains, of American history. His attempted insurrection struck fear into the South.

Then it became known that Brown had received financial backing from several prominent abolitionists. When northern intellectuals such as Emerson and Henry David Thoreau praised Brown as a holy warrior who "would make the gallows as glorious as the cross," and as "an angel of light," white southerners' outrage multiplied. The South almost universally interpreted Brown's attack at Harpers Ferry as the act of midnight terrorism, as the fulfillment of their long-stated dread of "abolition emissaries" who would infiltrate the region to incite slave rebellion.

Perhaps most telling of all was the fact that the pivotal election of 1860 was less than a year away when Brown went so eagerly to the gallows, handing a note to his jailer with the famous prediction: "I John Brown am now quite certain that the crimes of this guilty land will never be *purged away, but with blood.*" Most troubling to southerners, perhaps, was their awareness that while Republican politicians condemned Brown's crimes, they did so in a way that deflected attention onto the still greater crime of slavery.

Many Americans believed that the election of 1860 would decide the fate of the Union. Only the Democratic Party remained as an organization that was truly national in scope. "One after another," wrote a Mississippi editor, "the links which have bound the North and South together, have been severed . . . [but] the Democratic party looms gradually up . . . and waves the olive branch over the troubled waters of politics." But at its 1860 convention in Charleston, South Carolina, the Democratic Party split.

Election of 1860

Stephen A. Douglas wanted his party's presidential nomination, but he could not afford to alienate northern voters by accepting the southern position on the territories. Southern Democrats, however, insisted on recognition of their rights—as the *Dred Scott* decision had defined them—and they moved to block Douglas's nomination. When Douglas obtained a majority for his version of the platform, delegates from the five Gulf states plus South Carolina, Georgia, and Arkansas walked out of the convention. After efforts at compromise failed, the Democrats presented two nominees: Douglas for the northern wing, and Vice President John C. Breckinridge of Kentucky for the southern.

The Republicans nominated Abraham Lincoln at a rousing convention in Chicago. Lincoln's choice reflected the growing power of the Midwest, and he was perceived as more moderate on slavery than the early front runner, Senator William H. Seward of New York. A Constitutional Union Party, formed to preserve the nation but strong only in the Upper South, nominated John Bell of Tennessee.

Bell's only issue in the ensuing campaign was the urgency of preserving the Union, and Douglas desperately wanted to hold his northern and southern supporters together. Even Breckinridge quickly backed away from the appearance of extremism, and his sup-porters in several states stressed his unionism. Although Lincoln and the Republicans denied any intent to interfere with slavery in the states where it existed, they stood firm against the extension of slavery into the territories.

The election of 1860 was sectional in character, and the only one in American history in which the losers refused to accept the result. Lincoln won, but Douglas, Breckinridge, and Bell together received most of the votes. Douglas had broad-based support but won few states. Breckinridge carried nine southern states, all in the Deep South. Bell won pluralities in Virginia, Kentucky, and Tennessee. Lincoln prevailed in the North, but in the four border states that ultimately remained loyal to the Union (Missouri, Kentucky, Maryland, and Delaware) he gained only a plurality, not a majority (see Table 14.3). Lincoln's victory was won in the electoral college. He polled only 40 percent of the total vote and was not even on the ballot in ten slave states.

Opposition to slavery's extension was the core issue of the Republican Party, and Lincoln's alarm over slavery's growing political power was genuine. Moreover, abolitionists and supporters of free soil in the North worked to keep the Republicans from compromising on their territorial stand. Meanwhile in the South, proslavery advocates and secessionists whipped up public opinion and demanded that state conventions assemble to consider secession.

Lincoln made the crucial decision not to soften his party's position on the territories. He wrote of the necessity of maintaining the bond of faith between voter and candidate and of declining to set "the minority over the majority." But Lincoln's refusal to compromise derived both from conviction and from concern for the unity of the Republican Party. Although many conservative Republicans—eastern businessmen and former Whigs who did not feel strongly about slavery—hoped for a compromise, the original and most

Table 14.3 **Presidential Vote in 1860 (by State)**	
Lincoln (Republican)	Carried all northern states and all electoral votes except 3 in New Jersey
Breckinridge (Southern Democrat)	Carried all slave states except Virginia, Kentucky, Tennessee, and Missouri
Bell (Constitutional Union)	Carried Virginia, Kentucky, Tennessee
Douglas (Northern Democrat)	Carried only Missouri

Lincoln received only 26,000 votes in the entire South and was not even on the ballot in ten slave states. Breckinridge was not on the ballot in three northern states.

committed Republicans—antislavery voters and "conscience Whigs"—were adamant for free soil. Lincoln chose to stand firm against slavery's extension.

In the winter of 1860–1861, southern leaders in the Senate were willing, conditionally, to accept a compromise drawn up by Senator John J. Crittenden of Kentucky. Hoping to don the mantle of Henry Clay and avert disunion, Crittenden proposed that the two sections divide the territories between them at latitude 36°30'. But the southerners would agree to this only if the Republicans did, too, for they wanted no less and knew that extremists in the South would demand much more. When Lincoln ruled out concessions on the territorial issue, Crittenden's peacemaking effort, based on old and discredited measures, collapsed.

Meanwhile, the Union was being destroyed. On December 20, 1860, South Carolina passed an ordinance of secession amid jubilation and cheering. This

Secession

step marked the inaugural success of a strategy favored by secessionists: separate-state secession. Recognizing the difficulty of persuading all the southern states to challenge the federal government simultaneously, secessionists concentrated their efforts on the most extreme proslavery state. They hoped South Carolina's secession would induce other states to follow, with each decision building momentum for disunion.

The strategy proved effective. By reclaiming its independence, South Carolina raised the stakes in the sectional confrontation. No longer was secession an unthinkable step; the Union was broken. Secessionists now argued that other states should follow South Carolina and that those who favored compromise could make a better deal outside the Union than in it. Moderates found it difficult to dismiss such arguments, since most of them—even those who felt deep affection for the Union—were committed to defending southern rights and the southern way of life.

Southern extremists soon got their way in the Deep South. Overwhelming their opposition, they

The Confederate States of America

called separate state conventions and passed secession ordinances in Mississippi, Florida, Alabama, Georgia, Louisiana, and Texas. By February 1861 these states had joined South Carolina to form a new government in Montgomery, Alabama: the Confederate States of America. The delegates at Montgomery chose Jefferson Davis as their president, and the Confederacy began to function independently of the United States.

This apparent unanimity of action was deceiving. Confused and dissatisfied with the alternatives, many southerners who in 1860 had voted in the U.S. presidential election stayed home a few months later rather than vote for delegates who would decide on secession. Even so, in some state conventions the vote to secede was close, with secession decided by overrepresentation of plantation districts. Furthermore, the conventions were noticeably unwilling to let voters ratify their acts. Four states in the Upper South—Virginia, North Carolina, Tennessee, and Arkansas—flatly rejected secession and did not join the Confederacy until after fighting had begun. In the border states, popular sentiment was deeply divided; minorities in Kentucky and Missouri tried to secede, but these slave states ultimately came under Union control, along with Maryland and Delaware (see Map 14.4).

Such misgivings were not surprising. Secession posed new and troubling issues for southerners, espe-

On February 18, 1861, in Montgomery, Alabama, Jefferson Davis took an oath as president of the Confederate States of America. Davis later recalled that he foresaw "troubles innumerable" but was committed to seek independence as his paramount goal.   (Boston Athenaeum)

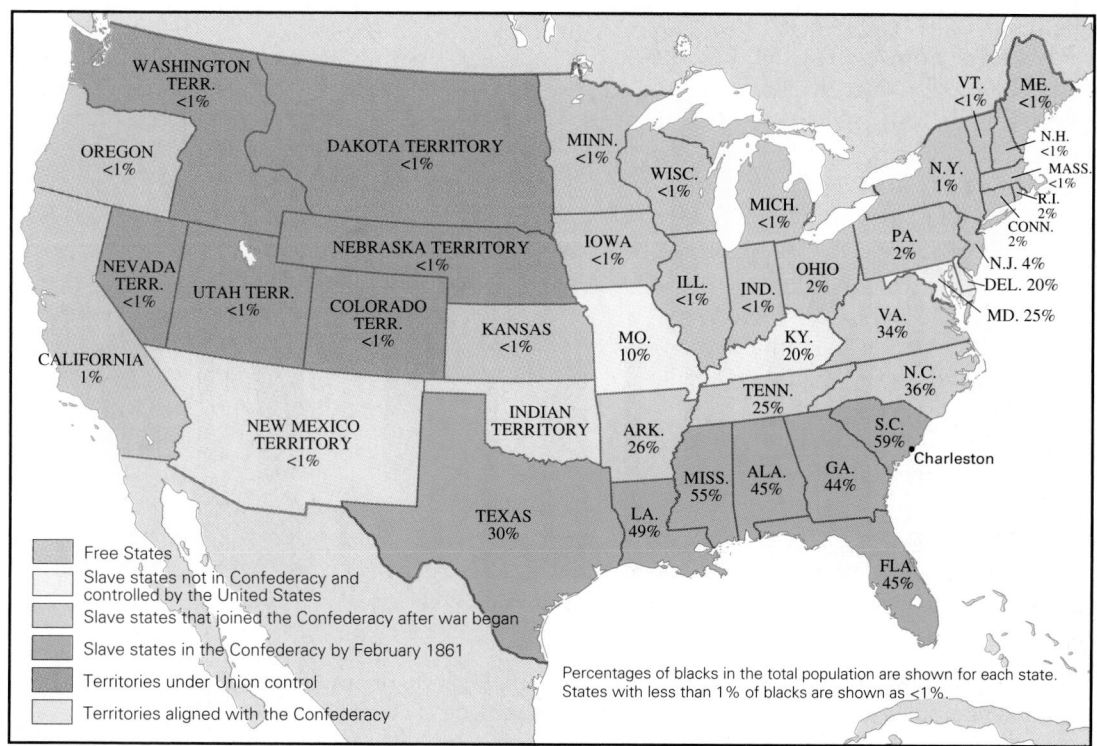

Map 14.4   The Divided Nation—Slave and Free Areas, 1861   After fighting began, the Upper South joined the Deep South in the Confederacy. How does the nation's pattern of division correspond to the distribution of slavery and the percentage of blacks in the population?

cially the possibility of war, where it would be fought, and who would die. Analysis of election returns from 1860 and 1861 indicates that slaveholders and nonslaveholders were beginning to part company politically. Heavily slaveholding counties strongly supported secession. But nonslaveholding areas that had favored Breckinridge in the presidential election proved far less willing to support secession: most counties with few slaves took an antisecession position or were staunchly Unionist (see Figure 14.1). Large numbers of yeomen also sat out the election. With war on the horizon, nonslaveholders were beginning to consider their class interests and to ask themselves how far they would go to support slavery and slaveowners.

After Alabama's convention approved secession, one delegate wrote: "Here I set & from my window see the nasty little thing [flag] flaunting in the breeze which has taken the place of that glorious banner which has been the pride of millions of Americans and the boast of freemen the wide world over." Although such sentiments presented problems for the Confederacy, they were not sufficiently developed to prevent secession.

The dilemma facing President Lincoln on inauguration day in March 1861 was how to maintain the authority of the federal government without provoking war. Proceeding cautiously, he sought only to hold on to forts in the states that had left the Union, reasoning that in this way he could assert federal sovereignty while waiting for a restoration of relations. But Jefferson Davis, who could not claim to lead a sovereign nation if the Confederate ports were under foreign (that is, United States) control, was unwilling to be so patient. A collision was inevitable.

Fort Sumter and Outbreak of War

It arrived in the early morning hours of April 12, 1861, at Fort Sumter in Charleston harbor. A federal garrison there ran low on food, and Lincoln notified the South Carolinians that he was sending a ship to resupply the fort. For the Montgomery government, the alternatives were to attack the fort or to acquiesce to Lincoln's authority. After the Confederate cabinet met, the secretary of war ordered local commanders to obtain a surrender or attack the fort. After two days of

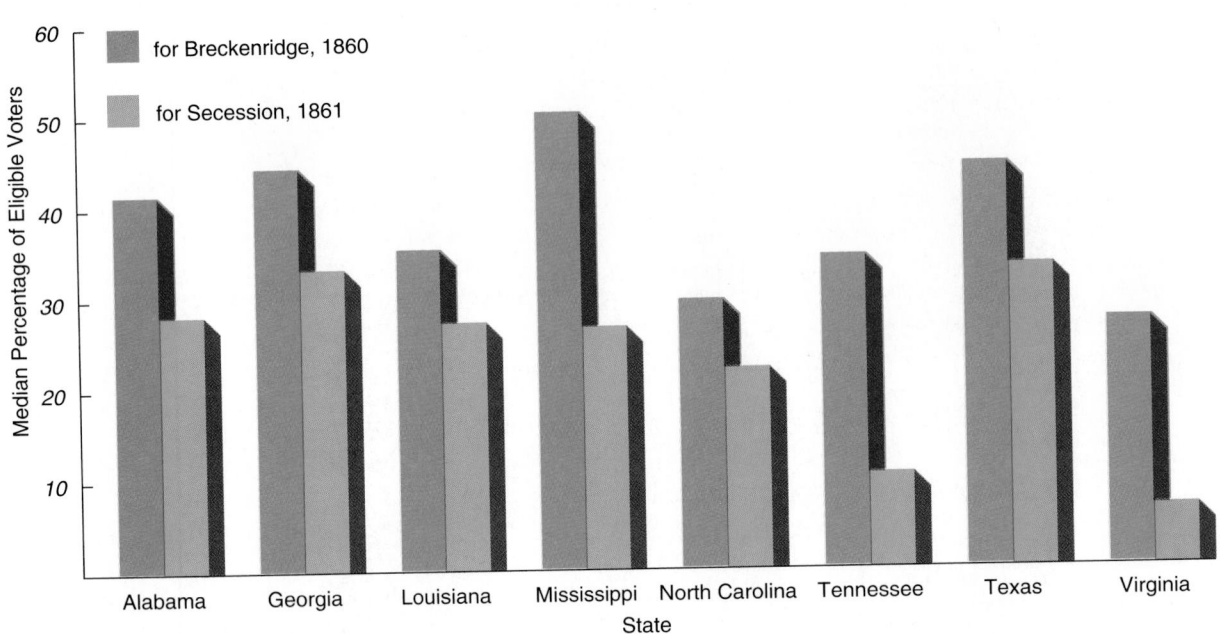

Figure 14.1 Voting Returns of Counties with Few Slaveholders, Eight Southern States, 1860 and 1861   This graph depicts voting in counties whose percentage of slaveholders ranked them among the lower half of the counties in their state. How does voters' support for secession in 1861 compare with support for John Breckinridge, the southern Democratic candidate in 1860? Why was their support for secession so weak? At this time counties with many slaveholders were giving increased support to secession.

heavy bombardment, the federal garrison finally surrendered. No one died in battle, though an accident during postbattle ceremonies killed two Union soldiers. Confederates permitted the U.S. troops to sail away on unarmed vessels while Charlestonians celebrated wildly. The Civil War—the bloodiest war in America's history—had begun.

Summary

 Throughout the 1840s and 1850s many able leaders had worked diligently to avert this outcome. Most people, North and South, had hoped to keep the nation together. As late as 1858 even Jefferson Davis had declared, "This great country will continue united," saying that "to the innermost fibers of my heart I love it all, and every part." Secession dismayed northern editors and voters, and it also plunged some planters into depression. Paul Cameron, the largest slaveowner in North Carolina, confessed that he was "very unhappy. I love the Union." Many blacks, however, shared Frederick Douglass's outlook. "The contest

must now be decided," he wrote in March 1861, "and decided forever, which of the two, Freedom or Slavery, shall give law to this Republic. Let the conflict come."

Why had war broken out? Why had all efforts to prevent it failed? The conflict slavery generated was fundamental and beyond adjustment. The emotions bound up in attacking and defending it were too powerful, and the interests it affected too vital, for compromise. Because it was deeply entwined with major policy questions of the present and the foreseeable future, each section ultimately regarded slavery as too important to be put aside.

Even if one excludes extreme views, North and South had fundamentally different attitudes toward the institution. The logic of Republican ideology tended in the direction of abolishing slavery, even though Republicans denied any such intention. The logic of southern arguments led toward establishing slavery everywhere, though southern leaders too denied such a motive. Lincoln put these facts succinctly. In a postelection letter to his old friend Alexander Stephens of Georgia, soon to be vice president of the Confederacy, Lincoln offered assurance that Republicans would not attack slavery in the states where it existed. But Lincoln continued, "You think slavery is right and ought to be expanded; while we think it is wrong and ought to be restricted. That I suppose is the rub."

A nation may face unresolvable issues yet manage to get past them. New events can capture people's attention; time can alter interests and attitudes—this is why historians always remind us of the importance of "contingency" in human affairs. That is precisely what the advocates of compromise hoped for. They tried to contain conflict and buy time for the nation, to avoid issues that could not be settled, and to preserve areas of consensus among Americans. But their efforts were doomed to failure.

Territorial expansion generated disputes so frequently that the nation never enjoyed a breathing space. Every southern victory increased fear of the Slave Power, and each new expression of Free-Soil sentiment made alarmed slaveholders more insistent in their demands. Eventually even those opposed to war could see no way to avoid it. In the profoundest sense, slavery was the root of the war. But as the fighting began, this, the war's central issue, was shrouded in confusion. How would the Civil War affect slavery, its place in the law, and African Americans' place in society? Would the institution survive a short war, but not a long war? As a people and a nation, Americans had reached the most fateful turning point in their history. Answers would now come from the battlefield and from the mobilization of two societies to wage war on a scale they had not imagined.

LEGACY FOR A PEOPLE AND A NATION

Revolutionary Violence

The greatest significance of John Brown's raid on Harpers Ferry in 1859 rests in its long aftermath in American memory. "Men consented to his death," wrote Frederick Douglass of Brown, "and then went home and taught their children to honor his memory." Brown is as important as a symbol as he is for his deeds. He has been at once one of the most beloved and most loathed figures in American history. In the song that bears his name, "John Brown's Body," a popular marching tune during the Civil War, his "soul goes marching on." As the poet Stephen Vincent Benet wrote: "You can weigh John Brown's body well enough, / But how and in what balance weigh John Brown?"

In the wake of his execution, in painting, song, and poetry, people constructed a John Brown mythology. Was he the Christ-like figure who died for the nation's sins, who had to commit crimes in order to expose the nation's larger crime? Or was he the terrorist thief, who murdered in the name of his own peculiar vision of God's will? Brown can be disturbing and inspiring, majestic and foolish, a monster or a warrior saint. He represented the highest ideals and ruthless deeds. He killed for justice. Perhaps Brown was one of the avengers of history who does the work the rest of us won't, couldn't, or shouldn't.

Brown forces us to ask when and how revolutionary violence—violence in the name of a political or spiritual end—is justified. The 1850s and the turn of the twenty-first century are two different contexts. But in today's world, terrorist, revolutionary violence is commonplace in our weekly news: an airliner is blown up over Lockerbie, Scotland; buses are strafed in Jerusalem; a federal building explodes in Oklahoma City; the Irish Republican Army plants bombs in London subways; American embassies are attacked in Africa and Europe—a truck bomb here, a car bomb there. Many organizations over the years have adopted John Brown as their justifying symbol, from left-wing students opposing American foreign policy to current anti-abortion groups who target clinics and doctors. The story of John Brown's raid in 1859 forces us to confront the question of when revolutionary violence is right or wrong.

For Further Reading, see page A-17 of the Appendix. For Web resources, go to http://college.hmco.com.

15

TRANSFORMING FIRE: THE CIVIL WAR 1861–1865

He was an ordinary twenty-seven-year-old store clerk from a New England town. But he went off, as though directed by a manly compass, to seek the extraordinary experiences of comradeship and war. In the spring of 1861, Charles Brewster, a member of a militia unit in Northampton, Massachusetts, left his mother and two sisters behind and joined Company C of the Tenth Massachusetts Volunteers. At that moment, Brewster had no idea of his capacity for leadership or his ability to uphold such values as courage and manliness. But the war released him from the boredom and failure of his life.

On April 18, only three days after the surrender of Fort Sumter, a mustering of Company C turned into a large public rally where forty new men enlisted. By April 24 seventy-five Northampton women committed their labor to sew uniforms for the company. Some women worked at home, while others sewed in the town hall. Local poets came to the armory to recite patriotic verses to the would-be soldiers. Yesterday farmers, clerks, and mechanics, today they were the heroes who would "whip secesh." By June 10, after weeks of drilling, Brewster's company attended a farewell ball, and four days later they strode down Main Street amid a cheering throng of spectators. Flags waved everywhere, several brass bands competed, and Brewster and his company boarded a train going south. En route the soldiers continued the joyous fervor of the day by singing "patriotic airs" to the accompaniment of a lone accordion.

Before their three-year enlistment ended, the Tenth Massachusetts participated in nearly every major battle fought by the Army of the Potomac from early 1862 to the summer of 1864. When the survivors of the Tenth were mustered out, only 220 of the nearly 1,000 in the original regiment were still on active duty. Their summer outing had transformed into the bloodiest war in history. They had seen thousands die of disease, practiced war upon civilians and the southern landscape, and loyally served the cause as variously defined, trying their best to fulfill their communities' expectations. In more than two hundred sometimes

War drastically altered the lives of millions of Americans. Many young men found in soldiering a combination of comradeship, devotion, boredom, and horror. Winslow Homer gave the ironic title *Home, Sweet, Home* to this painting of Union soldiers in camp about 1863. (Private Collection, photograph courtesy of Hirschl and Adler Galleries, New York)

lyrical letters to his mother and sisters, Brewster, who rose to lieutenant and adjutant of his regiment, left a trove of commentary on the meaning of war, the character of slavery and why it had to be destroyed, and especially the values of common, mid-nineteenth-century American men.

Brewster was as racist as many southerners in his perceptions of blacks. He was no "desperate hero" about battlefield courage, and he nearly died of dysentery more than once. He was personally eager for rank and recognition, and he eventually held only contempt for civilians who stayed at home. He was often miserably lonely and homesick, and he described battlefield carnage with an honest realism. The early romantic was transformed into a mature veteran by what he called the "terrible, terrible business" of war.

Most tellingly, Brewster grew in his attitudes about race. In 1862 he defied orders and took in a seventeen-year-old ex-slave as his personal servant, patronizingly clothing him with his own old pants sent from home. In 1864, after surviving some of the worst battles of the war in Virginia, which destroyed his regiment, and frightened of civilian life, Brewster reenlisted to be a recruiter of black troops. In this new role, Brewster worked from an office in Norfolk, Virginia, where his principal job was writing "love letters" for illiterate black women to their soldier husbands at the front. In imagining Brewster sitting at a table with a lonely freedwoman, swallowing his prejudices toward blacks and women, and repeatedly writing or reciting the phrases "give my love to . . ." and "your Husband untall Death," we can glimpse the enormous potential for human transformation at work in this war.

The Civil War brought astonishing, unexpected changes not only to Charles Brewster but everywhere in both North and South. Countless southern soldiers experienced similar transformations. But they, and their families, also experienced what few other groups of Americans have—utter defeat. For some Americans, wealth changed to poverty and hope to despair; for others, the suffering of war spelled opportunity. Contrasts abounded, between noble and crass motives and between individuals seeking different goals. Even the South's slaves, who hoped that they were witnessing God's "Holy War"—the "coming of the jubilee"—encountered unsympathetic liberators. When a Yankee soldier ransacked a slave woman's cabin, stealing her best quilts, she denounced him as a "nasty, stinkin' rascal" who had betrayed his cause of freedom. Angrily the soldier contradicted her, saying, "I'm fightin' for $14 a month and the Union."

Northern troops were not the only ones to feel anger over their sacrifices. Impoverished by the war, one southern farmer had endured inflation, taxes, and shortages to support the Confederacy. Then an impressment agent arrived to take still more from him—grain and meat, horses and mules, and wagons. In return, the agent offered only a certificate promising repayment sometime in the future. Bitter and disgusted, the farmer spoke for many by declaring, "The sooner this damned Government falls to pieces, the better it will be for us."

Many northern businessmen, however, viewed the economic effects of the war with optimistic anticipation. The conflict ensured vast government expenditures, a heavy demand for goods, and lucrative federal contracts. *Harper's Monthly* reported that an eminent financier expected a long war—the kind of war that would mean huge purchases, paper money, active speculation, and rising prices. "The battle of Bull Run," predicted the financier, "makes the fortune of every man in Wall Street who is not a natural idiot."

For millions, the Civil War was a life-changing event. It obliterated the normal patterns and circumstances of life. Millions of men were swept away into training camps and battle units. Armies numbering in the hundreds of thousands marched over the South, devastating once-peaceful countrysides. Families struggled to survive without their men; businesses tried to cope with the loss of workers. Women in both North and South took on extra responsibilities in the home and moved into new jobs in the work force. Many women joined the ranks of nurses and hospital workers. No sphere of life was untouched.

Change was most drastic in the South, where the leaders of the secession movement had launched a conservative revolution for their section's national independence. Born of states' rights doctrine, their break with the Union now had to be transformed into a centralized nation to fight a vast war. Never were men more mistaken: their revolutionary means were fundamentally incompatible with their conservative purpose. Southern whites had feared that a peacetime government of Republicans would interfere with slavery and upset the routine of plantation life. Instead their own actions led to a war that turned southern life upside down and imperiled the very existence of slavery. Jefferson Davis, president of the Confederate States of America, devised policies more objectionable to the elite than any proposed by President-elect Lincoln. Life in the Confederacy proved to be a shockingly unsouthern experience.

IMPORTANT EVENTS

1861 Battle of Bull Run
McClellan organizes Union Army
Union blockade begins
U.S. Congress passes first confiscation act
Trent affair
Some slaves admitted to Union lines as "contraband" of war

1862 Union captures Fort Henry and Fort Donelson
U.S. Navy captures New Orleans
Battle of Shiloh shows the war's destructiveness
Confederacy enacts conscription
McClellan's Peninsula Campaign fails to take Richmond
U.S. Congress passes second confiscation act, initiating emancipation
Confederacy mounts offensive in Maryland and Kentucky
Battle of Antietam ends Lee's drive into Maryland in September
British intervention in the war on Confederate side is averted by events and northern diplomacy

1863 Emancipation Proclamation takes effect
U.S. Congress passes National Banking Act
Union enacts conscription
African American soldiers join Union Army
Food riots occur in southern cities

Battle of Chancellorsville ends in Confederate victory but Jackson's death
Union wins key victories at Gettysburg and Vicksburg
Draft riots take place in New York City
Battle of Chattanooga leaves South vulnerable to Sherman's march into Georgia

1864 Battles of the Wilderness and Spotsylvania produce heavy casualties on both sides in the effort to capture and defend Richmond
Battle of Cold Harbor continues carnage in Virginia
Lincoln requests Republican Party plank abolishing slavery
Sherman captures Atlanta
Confederacy begins to collapse on the home front, as southern hardship destroys morale
Lincoln wins reelection, eliminating any Confederate hopes for a negotiated end to war
Jefferson Davis proposes emancipation within the Confederacy
Sherman marches through Georgia to the sea

1865 Sherman marches through Carolinas
U.S. Congress approves Thirteenth Amendment
Lee abandons Richmond and Petersburg
Lee surrenders at Appomattox Court House
Lincoln assassinated
Death toll in war reaches 620,000

War altered the North as well, but less sharply. Because most of the fighting took place on southern soil, northern farms and factories remained virtually unscathed. The drafting of workers and the changing need for products slowed the pace of industrialization somewhat, but factories and businesses remained busy. Workers lost ground to inflation, but the economy hummed. A new pro-business atmosphere dominated Congress, where the seats of southern representatives were empty. To the alarm of many, the powers of the federal government and of the president increased during the war.

The war created social strains in both North and South. Disaffection was strongest in the Confederacy, where poverty and class resentment fed a lower-class antagonism to the war that threatened the Confederacy from within as federal armies assailed it from without. In the North, dissent also flourished, and antiwar sentiment occasionally erupted into violence.

Ultimately, the Civil War forced on the nation a social and political revolution regarding race. Its greatest effect was to compel leaders and citizens to deal directly with the issue they had struggled over but had been unable to resolve: slavery. This issue, in complex and indirect ways, had caused the war. Now the scope and demands of the war forced reluctant Americans to confront it. And blacks themselves embraced what was for them the most fundamental turning point in their experience as Americans. ■

America Goes to War, 1861–1862

 Few Americans understood what they were getting into when the war began. The onset of hostilities sparked patriotic sentiments, optimistic speeches, and joyous ceremonies in both North and South. Northern communities, large and small, raised companies of

In *Departure of the Seventh Regiment* (1861), flags and the spectacle of thousands of young men from New York marching off to battle give a deceptively gay appearance to the beginning of the Civil War. (Museum of Fine Arts, Boston; M. and M. Karolik Collection)

volunteers eager to save the Union and sent them off with fanfare (a scene captured in the painting *Departure of the Seventh Regiment*). In the South, confident recruits boasted of whipping the Yankees and returning home at least before Christmas. Southern women sewed dashing uniforms for men who soon would be lucky to wear drab gray or butternut homespun. Americans went to war in 1861 with decidedly romantic notions of what they would experience.

Through the spring of 1861 both sides scrambled to organize and train their undisciplined armies. On July 21, 1861, the first battle took place outside Manassas Junction, Virginia, near a stream called Bull Run. General Irvin McDowell and 30,000 Union troops attacked General P. G. T. Beauregard's 22,000 southerners (see Map 15.1 on page 394). As raw recruits struggled amid the confusion of their first battle, federal forces began to gain ground. Then they ran into a line of Virginia troops under General Thomas Jackson. "There is Jackson standing like a stone wall," shouted one Confederate. "Stonewall" Jackson's line held, and the arrival of 9,000 Confederate reinforcements won the day for the South. Union troops fled back to Washington and shocked northern congressmen and spectators,

First Battle of Bull Run

who had watched the battle from a point 2 miles away; a few of them were actually captured for their folly.

The unexpected rout at Bull Run gave northerners their first hint of the nature of the war to come. While the United States enjoyed an enormous advantage in resources, victory would not be easy. Pro-Union feeling was growing in western Virginia, and loyalties were divided in the four border slave states—Missouri, Kentucky, Maryland, and Delaware. But the rest of the Upper South, the states of North Carolina, Virginia, Tennessee, and Arkansas, had joined the Confederacy in the wake of the attack on Fort Sumter. Moved by an outpouring of regional loyalty, half a million southerners volunteered to fight, so many that the Confederate government could hardly arm them all. The United States therefore undertook a massive mobilization of troops around Washington, D.C.

Lincoln gave command of the army to General George B. McClellan, an officer who proved to be better at organization and training than at fighting. McClellan put his growing army into camp and devoted the fall and winter of 1861 to readying a formidable force of a quarter-million men whose mission would be to take Richmond, established as the Confederate capital by July 1861. "The vast preparation of the enemy," wrote one southern soldier, produced a "feeling of despondency" in the South for the first time. But southern morale remained high early in the war.

While McClellan prepared, the Union began to implement other parts of its overall strategy, which called for a blockade of southern **Grand Strategy** ports and eventual capture of the Mississippi River. Like a constricting snake, this "Anaconda plan" would strangle the Confederacy (see Map 15.2 on page 412). At first the Union Navy had too few ships to patrol 3,550 miles of coastline and block the Confederacy's avenues of commerce and supply. Gradually, however, the navy increased the blockade's effectiveness, though it never stopped southern commerce completely.

Confederate strategy was essentially defensive. A defensive posture was not only consistent with the South's claim of independence, but acknowledged the North's advantage in resources (see Figure 15.1). Furthermore, communities all across the South demanded their defense. Jefferson Davis, however, wisely rejected a static or wholly defensive strategy. The South would pursue an "offensive defensive," taking advantage of opportunities to attack and using its interior lines of transportation to concentrate troops at crucial points. In its war aims, the Confederacy did not need to conquer the North; the Union effort, however, as time would tell, required conquest of the South.

Strategic thinking on both sides slighted the importance of "the West," that vast expanse of territory between Virginia and the Mississippi River. When the war began, both sides were unprepared for large-scale operations in the West, but before the end of the war they would prove to be decisive. Guerrilla warfare broke out in 1861 in the politically divided state of Missouri, and key locations along the Mississippi and other major rivers in the West would prove to be crucial prizes in the North's eventual victory. In the Far West, beyond the Mississippi River, the Confederacy hoped to gain an advantage by negotiating treaties with the Creeks, Choctaws, Chickasaws, Cherokees, Seminoles, and smaller tribes of Plains Indians. Although early strategy evolved haphazardly, both sides would soon know they were in a war the scale of which few people had ever imagined.

The last half of 1861 brought no major land battles, but the North made gains by sea. Late in the summer Union naval forces captured **Union Naval Campaign** Cape Hatteras and then seized Hilton Head, one of the Sea Islands off Port Royal, South Carolina. A few months later, similar operations secured vital coastal points in North Carolina, as well as Fort Pulaski, which defended Savannah. Federal naval operations established significant beachheads along the Confederate coastline (see Map 15.2).

The coastal victories off South Carolina foreshadowed a revolution in slave society. At the federal gunboats' approach, frightened planters abandoned their lands and fled. For a while, Confederate cavalry tried to round up slaves and move them to the interior as well. But thousands of slaves greeted what they hoped to be freedom with rejoicing and broke the hated cotton gins. Some entered their masters' homes and absconded with clothing and furniture, which they conspicuously displayed. Their jubilation and the growing stream of runaways who poured into the Union lines eliminated any doubt about which side slaves would support, given the opportunity. Unwilling at first to

Figure 15.1 Comparative Resources, Union and Confederate States, 1861   The North had vastly superior resources. Although the North's advantages in manpower and industrial capacity proved very important, the South still had to be conquered, its society and its will crushed. (Source: *The Times Atlas of World History.* Time Books, London, 1978. Used with permission.)

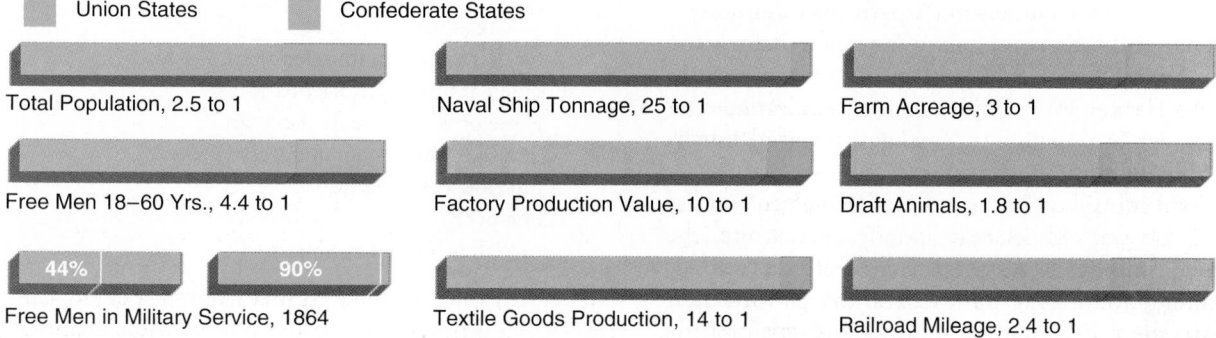

| Union States | | Confederate States |

Total Population, 2.5 to 1

Naval Ship Tonnage, 25 to 1

Farm Acreage, 3 to 1

Free Men 18–60 Yrs., 4.4 to 1

Factory Production Value, 10 to 1

Draft Animals, 1.8 to 1

44%   90%
Free Men in Military Service, 1864

Textile Goods Production, 14 to 1

Railroad Mileage, 2.4 to 1

wage a war against slavery, the federal government did not acknowledge the slaves' freedom—though it began to use their labor in the Union cause. This swelling tide of emancipated slaves, defined by many Union officers as "contraband" of war (confiscated enemy property), forced first a bitter and confused debate within the Union Army and government over how to treat the freedmen, and then a forthright attempt to harness their power.

The coastal incursions worried southerners, but the spring of 1862 brought even stronger evidence of the war's gravity. In March two ironclad ships—the *Monitor* (a Union warship) and the *Merrimack* (a Union ship recycled by the Confederacy)—fought each other for the first time; their battle, though indecisive, ushered in a new era in naval design. In April Union ships commanded by Admiral David Farragut smashed through log booms blocking the Mississippi River and fought their way upstream to capture New Orleans. Farther west three full Confederate regiments were organized, mostly of Cherokees, from Indian Territory, but a Union victory at Elkhorn Tavern, Arkansas, shattered southern control of Indian Territory. Thereafter, dissension within Native American groups and a Union victory the following year at Honey Springs, Arkansas, reduced Confederate operations in Indian Territory to guerrilla raids.

In February 1862 land and river forces in northern Tennessee won significant victories for the Union.

Grant's Tennessee Campaign and the Battle of Shiloh

A hard-drinking Union commander named Ulysses S. Grant saw the strategic importance of Fort Henry and Fort Donelson, the Confederate outposts guarding the Tennessee and Cumberland Rivers. If federal troops could capture these forts, Grant realized, they would open two prime routes into the heartland of the Confederacy. In just ten days he seized the forts, cutting off the Confederates so completely that he demanded unconditional surrender of Fort Donelson. A path into Tennessee, Alabama, and Mississippi now lay open before the Union Army. Grant's achievement of such a surrender from his former West Point roommate, Confederate commander Simon Bolivar Buckner, inspired northern public opinion that spring.

Grant moved on into southern Tennessee and the first of the war's shockingly bloody encounters, the Battle of Shiloh. On April 6 Confederate general Albert Sidney Johnston caught federal troops with their backs to the water awaiting reinforcements along the Tennessee River. The Confederates attacked early in the morning and inflicted heavy damage all day. Close to victory, General Johnston was shot from his horse and killed. Southern forces almost achieved a breakthrough, but Union reinforcements arrived that night. The next day the tide of battle turned, and after ten hours of terrible combat, Grant's men forced the Confederates to withdraw.

Neither side won a victory at Shiloh, yet the losses were staggering. Northern troops lost 13,000 men (killed, wounded, or captured) out of 63,000; southerners sacrificed 11,000 out of 40,000. Total casualties in this single battle exceeded those in all three of America's previous wars combined. Now both sides were beginning to sense the true nature of the war. "I saw an open field," Grant recalled, "over which Confederates had made repeated charges . . . , so covered with dead that it would have been possible to walk across the clearing, in any direction, stepping on dead bodies, without a foot touching the ground." Shiloh utterly changed Grant's thinking about the war. He had hoped that southerners soon would be "heartily tired" of the conflict. After Shiloh, "I gave up all idea of saving the Union except by complete conquest." Memories of Shiloh battlefield, and many others to come, would haunt the soldiers who survived for the rest of their lives. Herman Melville's "Shiloh, A Requiem" captures the pathos of that spring day when armies learned the truth about war.

> Skimming lightly, wheeling still,
>   The swallows fly low
> Over the field in clouded days,
>   The forest-field of Shiloh—
> Over the field where April rain
> Solaced the parched ones stretched in pain
> Through the pause of night
> That followed the Sunday fight
>   Around the church of Shiloh—
> The church so lone, the log-built one,
> That echoed to many a parting groan
>   And natural prayer
>   Of dying foemen mingled there—
> Foemen at morn, but friends at eve—
>   Fame or country least their care:
> (What like a bullet can undeceive!)
>   But now they lie low,
> While over them the swallows skim,
>   And all is hushed at Shiloh.

Meanwhile, on the Virginia front, President Lincoln had a different problem. General McClellan was

Both armies experienced religious revivals during the war. This photograph shows members of a largely Irish regiment from New York celebrating Mass at the beginning of the war. Notice the presence of some female visitors in the left foreground. (Library of Congress)

McClellan and the Peninsula Campaign

slow to move. Only thirty-six, Mc-Clellan had already achieved notable success as an army officer and railroad president. Keenly aware of his historic role, he did not want to fail and insisted on having everything in order before he attacked. Habitually overestimating the size of enemy forces, McClellan called repeatedly for reinforcements and ignored Lincoln's directions to advance. McClellan advocated war of limited aims that would lead to a quick reunion. He intended no disruption of slavery, nor any war on noncombatants. McClellan's conservative vision of the war was practically outdated before he ever moved his army into Virginia. Finally he chose to move by a water route, sailing his troops down the Chesapeake, landing them on the peninsula between the York and James Rivers, and advancing on Richmond from the east (see Map 15.1).

After a bloody but indecisive battle at Fair Oaks on May 31–June 1, the federal armies moved to within 7 miles of the Confederate capital. They could see the spires on Richmond churches. The Confederate commanding general, Joseph E. Johnston, was badly wounded at Fair Oaks, and President Jefferson Davis placed his chief military adviser, Robert E. Lee, in command. The fifty-five-year-old Lee was an aristocratic Virginian, a life-long military officer, and a veteran of distinction from the War with Mexico. Although he opposed secession and found slavery distasteful, Lee loyally gave his allegiance to his state. He soon foiled McClellan's legions.

First, he sent Stonewall Jackson's corps of 17,000 northwest into the Shenandoah valley behind Union forces, where they threatened Washington, D.C., and with rapid-strike mobility drew some federal troops away from Richmond to protect their own capital. Further, in mid-June, in an extraordinary four-day ride around the entire Union Army, Confederate cavalry under J. E. B. Stuart, a self-styled Virginia cavalier, with red cape and plumed hat, confirmed the exposed position of a major portion of McClellan's army north of the rain-swollen Chickahominy River. Then, in a series of engagements known as the Seven Days Battles, June 26–July 1, Lee struck at McClellan's army. Lee never managed to close his pincers around the retreating Union forces, but the daring move of taking the majority of his army northeast and attacking the Union right flank, while leaving only a small force to

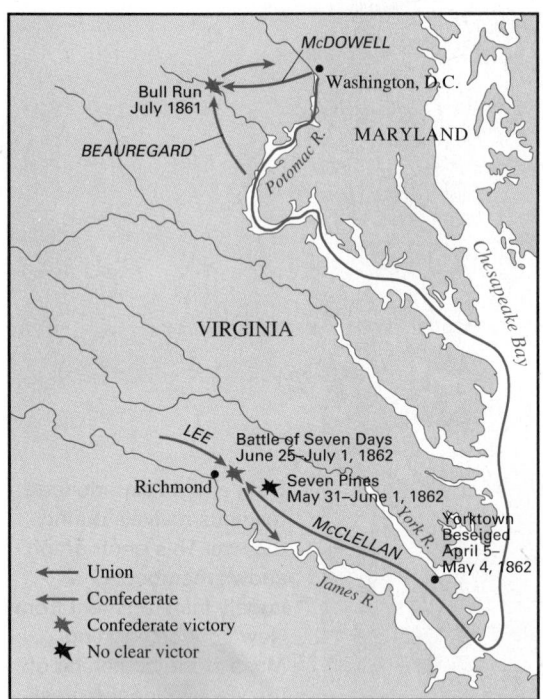

Map 15.1 McClellan's Campaign The water route chosen by McClellan to threaten Richmond during the peninsular campaign.

Union. This was a coordinated effort to take the war to the North, to contest the allegiance of the border states, and to try to force a decisive turning point.

The plan was promising, but every part of the offensive failed. In the bloodiest day of the entire war, September 17, 1862, McClellan turned Lee back from Sharpsburg, Maryland. In the Battle of Antietam 5,000 men died (3,500 had died at Shiloh), and another 18,000 were wounded. Lee was lucky to escape destruction, for McClellan had intercepted a lost battle order, wrapped around cigars for each Confederate corps commander and inadvertently dropped by a courier. But McClellan moved slowly, failed to use his larger forces in simultaneous attacks all along the line, and allowed Lee's stricken army to retreat to safety across the Potomac. In the wake of Antietam, Lincoln removed McClellan from command.

In Kentucky Generals Smith and Bragg secured Lexington and Frankfurt, but their effort to force the Yankees back to the Ohio River was stopped at the Battle of Perryville on October 8. Bragg's army retreated back into Tennessee where, on December 31, 1862, to January 2, 1863, they fought an indecisive but much bloodier battle at Murfreesboro. Casualties exceeded even those of Shiloh and many lives were sacrificed on a bitter winter landscape.

Confederate leaders had marshaled all their strength for a breakthrough but had failed. Outnumbered and disadvantaged in resources, the South could not continue the offensive. Profoundly disappointed, Davis admitted to a committee of Confederate representatives that southerners were entering "the darkest and most dangerous period we have yet had." Tenacious defense and stoic endurance now seemed the South's only long-range hope.

But 1862 also brought painful lessons to the North. Confederate general J. E. B. Stuart executed a daring cavalry raid into Pennsylvania in October. Then on December 13 Union general Ambrose Burnside, now in command of the Army of the Potomac, unwisely ordered his soldiers to attack Lee's army, which held fortified positions on high ground at Fredericksburg, Virginia. Lee's men performed so coolly and controlled the engagement so thoroughly that Lee was moved to say, "It is well that war is so terrible. We should grow too fond of it." Burnside's repeated assaults up Marye's Heights shocked even the opponents. "The Federals had fallen like the steady dripping of rain from the eaves of a house," remarked Confederate general James Longstreet. And a Union officer observed the carnage of 1,300 dead and 9,600

defend Richmond, forced McClellan (always believing he was outnumbered) to retreat toward the James River.

During the sustained fighting of the Seven Days, the Union forces suffered 20,614 casualties, and the Confederates 15,849. After repeated rebel assaults against entrenched positions on high ground at Malvern Hill, an officer concluded: "It was not war, it was murder." By August 3 McClellan withdrew his army back to the Potomac and the environs of Washington. Richmond remained safe for almost two more years.

Buoyed by these results, Jefferson Davis conceived an ambitious plan to turn the tide of the war and gain recognition of the Confederacy by European nations. He ordered a general offensive, sending Lee north into Maryland and Generals Kirby Smith and Braxton Bragg into Kentucky. Calling on residents of Maryland and Kentucky to make a separate peace with his government, Davis also invited northwestern states like Indiana, which sent much of their trade down the Mississippi to New Orleans, to leave the

Confederate Offensive in Maryland and Kentucky

In October 1862 in New York City, photographer Mathew Brady opened an exhibition of photographs from the Battle of Antietam. Although few knew it, Brady's vision was very poor, and this photograph of Confederate dead was actually made by his assistants, Alexander Gardner and James F. Gibson. (Library of Congress)

wounded Union soldiers: "The whole plain was covered with men, prostrate and dropping. . . . I had never before seen fighting like that—nothing approaching it in terrible uproar and destruction . . . the next brigade coming up in succession would do its duty, and melt like snow coming down on warm ground."

The rebellion was far from being suppressed. Both sides were learning that they would have to pay a terrible price. And people on both home fronts had now to decide just what they would endure to win a war of one society against the other.

War Transforms the South

The war caused tremendous disruptions in civilian life and altered southern society beyond all expectations. One of the first traditions to fall was the southern preference for local and limited government. States' rights had been a formative ideology for the Confederacy, but state governments were weak and sketchy operations. The average citizen, on whom the hand of gov-ernment had rested lightly, probably knew county authorities best. To withstand the massive power of the North, however, the South needed to centralize; like the colonial revolutionaries, southerners faced a choice of join together or die separately. No one saw the necessity of centralization more clearly than Jefferson Davis. If the states of the Confederacy insisted on fighting separately, said Davis, "we had better make terms as soon as we can."

Promptly Davis moved to bring all arms, supplies, and troops under his control. But by early 1862 the

The Confederacy and Centralization of Power

scope and duration of the conflict required something more. Tens of thousands of Confederate soldiers had volunteered for just one year's service, planning to return home in the spring to plant their crops. To keep southern armies in the field, the War Department encouraged reenlistments and called for new volunteers. However, as one official admitted, "the spirit of volunteering had died out." Three states threatened or instituted a draft. Finally, faced with a critical shortage of troops, in April

This Confederate soldier, like thousands of his comrades, took advantage of an opportunity to pose with his wife and brother. As the death toll mounted and suffering increased, southern women grew less willing to urge their men into battle.   (Collection of Larry Williford)

1862 the Confederate government enacted the first national conscription (draft) law in American history. Thus the war forced unprecedented change on states that had seceded out of fear of change.

Jefferson Davis was a strong chief executive. He adopted a firm leadership role toward the Confederate Congress, which raised taxes and later passed a tax-in-kind—paid in farm products. Almost three thousand agents dispersed to collect the tax, assisted by almost fifteen hundred appraisers. Where opposition arose, the government suspended the writ of habeas corpus (which prevented individuals from being held without trial) and imposed martial law. In the face of political opposition that cherished states' rights, Davis proved unyielding. This tax system, however, proved inadequate to the South's war effort.

To replace the food that men in uniform would have grown, Davis exhorted farmers to switch from cash crops to food crops; he encouraged the states to require them to do so. But the army remained short of food and labor. In emergencies the War Department resorted to impressing slaves to work on fortifications, and after 1861 the government relied heavily on con-

fiscation of food to feed the troops. Officers swooped down on farms in the line of march and carted away grain, meat, wagons, and draft animals.

Soon the Confederate administration in Richmond gained virtually complete control over the southern economy. Because it controlled the supply of labor through conscription, the administration could compel industry to work on government contracts and supply the military's needs. The Confederate Congress also gave the central government almost complete control of the railroads. New statutes even limited corporate profits and dividends. A large bureaucracy sprang up to administer these operations: over seventy thousand civilians staffed the Confederate administration. By the war's end, the southern bureaucracy was larger in proportion to population than its northern counterpart. Early in the war, Davis hoped that such centralization would inspire a new national loyalty across the South.

Clerks and subordinate officials crowded the towns and cities where Confederate departments set up their offices. The sudden population booms that resulted overwhelmed the housing supply and stimulated new construction. The pressure was especially great in Richmond, whose population increased 250 percent. Mobile's population jumped from 29,000 to 41,000; Atlanta began to grow; and 10,000 people poured into war-related industries in little Selma, Alabama.

Wartime Southern Cities and Industry

As the Union blockade disrupted imports of manufactured products, the traditionally agricultural South forged industries. Many planters shared Davis's hope that industrialization would bring "deliverance, full and unrestricted, from all commercial dependence" on the North or the world. Indeed, beginning almost from scratch, the Confederacy achieved tremendous feats of industrial development. Chief of Ordnance Josiah Gorgas increased the capacity of Richmond's Tredegar Iron Works and other factories to the point that by 1865 his Ordnance Bureau was supplying all Confederate small arms and ammunition. Meanwhile, the government constructed new railroad lines to improve the efficiency of the South's transportation system. Much of the labor on railroads and ironworks consisted of slaves relocated from farms and plantations.

White women, restricted to narrow roles in antebellum society, gained substantial new responsibilities in wartime. The wives and mothers of soldiers now headed households and performed men's work, including raising crops and tending animals. Women in non-

Changing Roles of Women

slaveowning families cultivated fields themselves, while wealthier women suddenly had to manage field hands unaccustomed to female overseers.

In the cities, white women—who had been virtually excluded from the labor force—found a limited number of respectable new paying jobs. Clerks had always been males, but the war changed that, too. "Government girls" staffed the Confederate bureaucracy, and female schoolteachers appeared in the South for the first time.

Some women gained confidence from their new responsibilities. Among these was Janie Smith, a young North Carolinian. Raised in a rural area by prosperous parents, she now faced grim realities as the war reached her farm and troops turned her home into a hospital. "It makes me shudder when I think of the awful sights I witnessed that morning," she wrote to a friend. "Ambulance after ambulance drove up with our wounded. . . . Under every shed and tree, the tables were carried for amputating the limbs. . . . The blood lay in puddles in the grove; the groans of the dying and complaints of those undergoing amputation were horrible." But Janie Smith learned to cope with crisis. She ended her account with the proud words, "I can dress amputated limbs now and do most anything in the way of nursing wounded soldiers."

Patriotic sacrifice appealed to some women, but others resented their new burdens. Many among the wealthy found their war-imposed tasks difficult and their changed situation distasteful. A Texas woman who had struggled to discipline slaves pronounced herself "sick of trying to do a man's business." Others grew angry over shortages and resented cooking and unfamiliar contact with lower-class women. Some women grew scornful of the war and demanded that their men return to help provide for families.

For millions of ordinary southerners change brought privation and suffering. Mass poverty descended for the first time on a large minority of the white population.

Human Suffering, Hoarding, and Inflation

Many yeoman families had lost their breadwinners to the army. As a South Carolina newspaper put it, "The duties of war have called away from home the sole supports of many, many families. . . . Help must be given, or the poor will suffer." The poor sought help from relatives, neighbors, friends, anyone. Sometimes they pleaded their cases to the Confederate government. "In the name of humanity," begged one woman, "discharge my husband he is not able to do your government much good and he might do his children some good . . . my poor children have no home nor no Father." To the extent that the South eventually lost the will to fight in the face of defeat, women played a key role in bringing the war to an end.

Other factors aggravated the effect of the labor shortage. The South was in many places so sparsely populated that the conscription of one skilled craftsman could work a hardship on the people of an entire county. Often they begged in unison for the exemption or discharge of the local miller or the neighborhood tanner, wheelwright, or potter. Physicians also were in short supply. Most serious, however, was the loss of a blacksmith. As a petition from Alabama explained, "Our Section of County [is] left entirely Destitute of any man that is able to keep in order any kind of Farming Tules."

The blockade of Confederate shipping created shortages of common but important items—salt, sugar, coffee, nails—and speculation and hoarding made the shortages worse. Greedy businessmen cornered the supply of some commodities; prosperous citizens stocked up on food. The *Richmond Enquirer* criticized a planter who purchased so many wagonloads of supplies that his "lawn and paths looked like a wharf covered with a ship's loads." "This disposition to speculate upon the yeomanry of the country," lamented the *Richmond Examiner*, "is the most mortifying feature of the war." North Carolina's Governor Zebulon Vance worried about "the cry of distress . . . from the poor wives and children of our soldiers. . . . What will become of them?"

Inflation raged out of control, fueled by the Confederate government's heavy borrowing and inadequate taxes, until prices had increased almost 7,000 percent. Inflation particularly imperiled urban dwellers without their own sources of food. As early as 1861 and 1862, newspapers reported that "want and starvation are staring thousands in the face," and troubled officials predicted that "women and children are bound to come to suffering if not starvation." Some families came to the aid of their neighbors, and "free markets," which disbursed goods as charity, sprang up in various cities. But other people would not cooperate: "It is folly for a poor mother to call on the rich people about here," raged one woman. "Their hearts are of steel they would sooner throw what they have to spare to the dogs than give it to a starving child." Private charity, as well as a rudimentary relief program organized by the Confederacy, failed to meet the need.

As their fortunes declined, people of once-modest means looked around and found abundant evidence that all classes were not sacrificing equally. And they noted that the Confederate government enacted policies that favored the upper class. Until the last year of the war, for example, prosperous southerners could avoid military service by hiring substitutes. Prices for substitutes skyrocketed until it cost a man $5,000 or $6,000 to send someone to the front in his place. Well over 50,000 upper-class southerners purchased such substitutes. Mary Boykin Chesnut knew of one young aristocrat who "spent a fortune in substitutes. . . . He is at the end of his row now, for all able-bodied men are ordered to the front. I hear he is going as some general's courier." The rich traded on their social connections to avoid danger. "It is a notorious fact," complained an angry Georgian, that "if a man has influential friends—or a little money to spare—he will never be enrolled." A Confederate senator from Mississippi, James Phelan, informed Jefferson Davis that apparently "nine tenths of the youngsters of the land whose relatives are conspicuous in society, wealthy, or influential obtain some safe perch where they can doze with their heads under their wings."

Inequities of the Confederate Draft

Anger at such discrimination exploded in October 1862 when the Confederate Congress exempted from military duty anyone who was supervising at least twenty slaves. "Never did a law meet with more universal odium," observed one representative. "Its influence upon the poor is most calamitous." Protests poured in from every corner of the Confederacy, and North Carolina's legislators formally condemned the law. Its defenders argued, however, that the exemption preserved order and aided food production, and the statute remained on the books. The twenty-slave law is indicative of the racial fears many Confederates felt as the war threatened to overturn southern society.

Dissension spread and alert politicians and newspaper editors warned of class warfare. The bitterness of letters to Confederate officials suggests the depth of the people's anger. "If I and my little children suffer [and] die while there Father is in service," threatened one woman, "I invoke God Almighty that our blood rest upon the South." Another woman swore to the secretary of war that unless help was provided to poverty-stricken wives and mothers "an allwise god . . . will send down his fury and judgment in a very grate manar . . . [on] those that are in power." War magnified existing social tensions in the Confederacy, and created a few new ones.

Wartime Northern Economy and Society

 With the onset of war, a tidal wave of change rolled over the North as well. Factories and citizens' associations geared up to support the war, and the federal government and its executive branch gained new powers. The energies of an industrializing, capitalist society were harnessed to serve the cause of the Union. Idealism and greed flourished together, and the northern economy proved its awesome productivity. Northern factories ran overtime, and unemployment was low. Northern farms and factories came through the war unharmed, whereas most of the South suffered extensive damage. To Union soldiers on the battlefield, sacrifice was a grim reality, but northern civilians experienced the bustle and energy of wartime production.

At first the war was a shock to business. Northern firms lost their southern markets, and many companies had to change their products and find new customers in order to remain open. Southern debts became uncollectible, jeopardizing not only northern merchants but also many western banks. In farming regions, families struggled with an aggravated shortage of labor. A few enterprises never pulled out of the tailspin caused by the war. Cotton mills lacked cotton; construction declined; shoe manufacturers sold few of the cheap shoes that planters had bought for their slaves.

Northern Business, Industry, and Agriculture

But certain entrepreneurs, such as wool producers, benefited from shortages of competing products, and soaring demand for war-related goods swept some businesses to new success. To feed the hungry war machine, the federal government pumped unprecedented sums into the economy. The Treasury issued $3.2 billion in bonds and paper money called greenbacks, and the War Department spent over $360 million in revenues from new taxes, including a broad excise tax and the nation's first income tax. Government contracts soon totaled more than $1 billion.

Secretary of War Edwin M. Stanton's list of the supplies needed by the Ordnance Department indicates the scope of government demand: "7,892 cannon, 11,787 artillery carriages, 4,022,130 small-arms, . . . 1,022,176,474 cartridges for small-arms, 1,220,555,435 percussion caps, . . . 26,440,054 pounds of gunpowder, 6,395,152 pounds of niter, and 90,416,295 pounds of lead." Stanton's list covered only weapons; the government also purchased huge quantities of uniforms, boots, food, camp equipment, saddles, ships, and other necessities. War-related spending revived business in many northern states. In 1863 a merchants' magazine examined the effects of the war in Massachusetts: "Seldom, if ever, has the business of Massachusetts been more active or profitable than during the past year. . . . In every department of labor the government has been, directly or indirectly, the chief employer and paymaster." Government contracts saved Massachusetts shoe manufacturers from ruin.

Nothing illustrated the wartime partnership between business and government better than the work of Jay Cooke, a wealthy New York financier. Cooke threw himself into the marketing of government bonds to finance the war effort. With imagination and energy, he convinced both large investors and ordinary citizens to invest enormous sums, in the process earning hefty commissions for himself. But the financier's profit served the Union cause, as the interests of capitalism and government, finance and patriotism, merged. The booming economy, the Republican alliance with business, and the frantic wartime activity combined to create a new pro-business atmosphere in Washington.

War aided some heavy industries in the North, especially iron and steel production. Although new railroad construction slowed, repairs helped the manufacture of rails to increase. Of considerable significance for the future was the railroad industry's adoption of a standard gauge (width) for track, which eliminated the unloading and reloading of boxcars and created a unified transportation system.

The northern economy also grew because of a complementary relationship between agriculture and industry. Mechanization of agriculture had begun before the war. Wartime recruitment and conscription, however, gave western farmers an added incentive to purchase labor-saving machinery. The shift from human labor to machines created new markets for industry and expanded the food supply for the urban industrial work force. The boom in the sale of agricultural tools was tremendous. Cyrus and William McCormick built an industrial empire in Chicago from the sale of their reapers. Between 1862 and 1864 the manufacture of mowers and reapers doubled to 70,000 yearly; even so, manufacturers could not satisfy the demand. By the end of the war, 375,000 reapers were in use, triple the number in 1861. Large-scale commercial agriculture had become a reality. As a result, northern farm families whose breadwinners went to

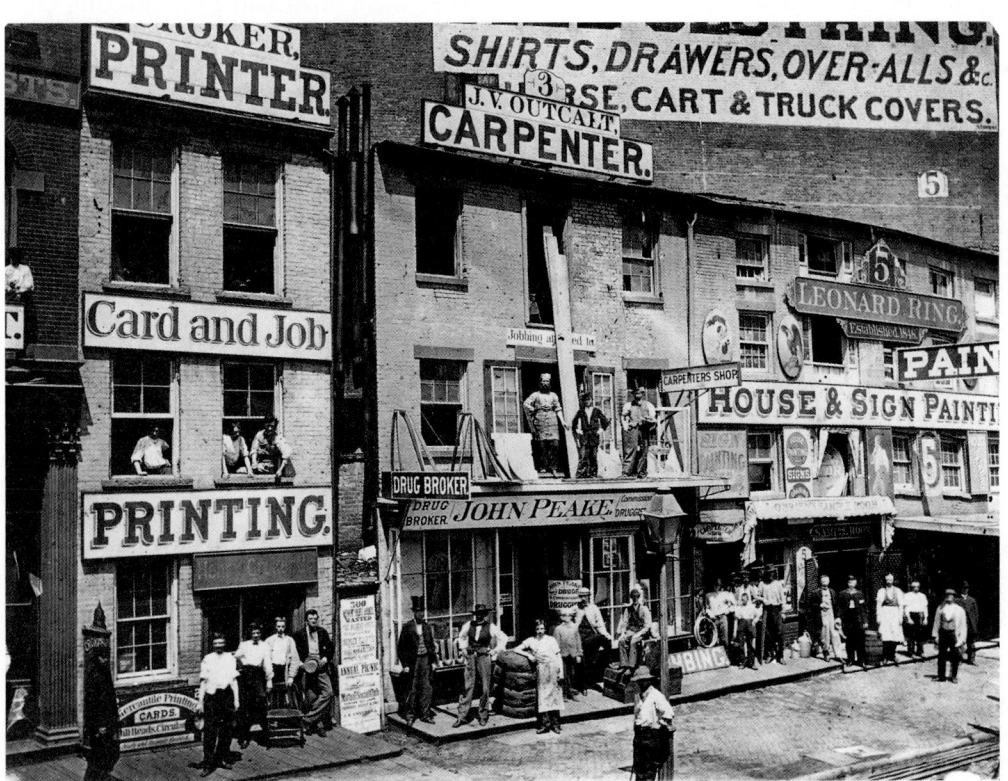

Despite initial problems, the task of supplying a vast war machine kept the northern economy humming. This photograph shows businesses on the west side of Hudson Street in New York City in 1865. (© Collection of The New-York Historical Society)

war did not suffer as much as their counterparts did in the South. "We have seen," one magazine observed, "a stout matron whose sons are in the army, cutting hay with her team . . . and she cut seven acres with ease in a day, riding leisurely upon her cutter."

Northern industrial and urban workers did not fare as well. After the initial slump, jobs became plentiful, but inflation ate up much of a worker's paycheck. The price of coffee had tripled; rice and sugar had doubled; and clothing, fuel, and rent had all climbed. Between 1860 and 1864 consumer prices rose at least 76 percent, while daily wages rose only 42 percent. Workers' families consequently suffered a substantial decline in their standards of living.

New Militancy Among Northern Workers

As their real wages shrank, industrial workers lost job security. To increase production, some employers were replacing workers with labor-saving machines. Other employers urged the government to promote immigration to secure cheap labor. Workers responded by forming unions and sometimes by striking. Skilled craftsmen organized to combat the loss of their jobs and status to machines; women and unskilled workers, who were excluded by the craftsmen, formed their own unions. In recognition of the increasingly national scope of business activity, thirteen occupational groups—including tailors, coal miners, and railway engineers—formed national unions during the Civil War, and the number of strikes climbed steadily.

Employers reacted with hostility to this new labor independence. Manufacturers viewed labor activism as a threat to their freedom of action and accordingly formed statewide or craft-based associations to cooperate and pool information. These employers shared blacklists of union members and required new workers to sign "yellow dog" contracts (promises not to join a union). To put down strikes, they hired strikebreakers from among blacks, immigrants, and women, and sometimes used federal troops to break the will of unions.

Despite the unions' emerging presence, they did not prevent employers from making profits, nor from profiteering on government contracts. Unscrupulous businessmen took advantage of the suddenly immense demand for army supplies by selling clothing and blankets made of "shoddy"—wool fibers reclaimed from rags or worn cloth. Shoddy goods often came apart in the rain; most of the shoes purchased in the early months of the war were worthless. Contractors sold inferior guns for double the usual price and passed off tainted meat as good. Corruption was so widespread that it led to a year-long investigation by the House of Representatives. A group of contractors who had demanded $50 million for their products dropped their claims to $17 million as a result of the findings of the investigation. Those who romanticize the Civil War era rarely learn of these historical realities.

Legitimate enterprises also made healthy profits. The output of woolen mills increased so dramatically that dividends in the industry nearly tripled. Some cotton mills made record profits on what they sold, even though they reduced their output. Brokerage houses worked until midnight and earned unheard-of commissions. Railroads carried immense quantities of freight and passengers, increasing their business to the point that railroad stocks doubled and tripled in value. The price of Erie Railroad stock rose from $17 to $126 a share during the war.

Government and Business Partnership

Railroads also were a leading beneficiary of government largesse. With the South absent from Congress, the northern, rather than southern, route of the transcontinental railroad quickly prevailed. In 1862 and 1864 Congress chartered two corporations, the Union Pacific Railroad and the Central Pacific Railroad, and assisted them financially in connecting Omaha, Nebraska, with Sacramento, California. For each mile of track laid, the railroads received a loan of from $16,000 to $48,000 in government bonds plus 20 square miles of land along a free 400-foot-wide right of way. Overall, the two corporations gained approximately 20 million acres of land and nearly $60 million in loans.

Economic Nationalism

Other businessmen benefited handsomely from the Morrill Land Grant Act (1862). To promote public education in agriculture, engineering, and military science, Congress granted each state 30,000 acres of federal land for each of its congressional districts. The states could sell the land, as long as they used the income for the purposes Congress had intended. The law eventually fostered sixty-nine colleges and universities, but one of its immediate effects was to enrich a few prominent speculators. Hard-pressed to meet wartime expenses, some states sold their land cheaply to wealthy entrepreneurs. At the same time, the Homestead Act of 1862 offered cheap, and sometimes free, land to people who would settle the West and improve their property.

Before the war, there was no national banking, taxation, or currency. Banks operating under state charters issued no fewer than seven thousand different kinds of notes, which were difficult to distinguish from forgeries. During the war, Congress and the Treasury Department established a national banking system empowered to issue national bank notes. At the close of the war in 1865, Congress forced most state banks to join the national system by means of a prohibitive tax. This process created sounder currency, but also inflexibility in the money supply and an eastern-oriented financial structure that, later in the century, pushed farmers in need of credit and cash to revolt.

In response to the war, the Republicans created an activist federal government. They converted the sale of war bonds into a crusade, affirming that the country could absorb any level of debt or expense for the cause of union. Indeed, with agricultural legislation, the land grant colleges, higher tariffs, and railroad subsidies, the federal government entered the economy forever. Moreover, Republican economic policies bonded people to the nation as never before. As freeing the slaves became a fundamental war aim, this economic nationalism would loom important as a buttress for a controversial cause.

The powers of the federal government and the president grew steadily during the crisis. Abraham Lincoln, like Jefferson Davis, found that war required active presidential leadership. At the beginning of the conflict, Lincoln launched a major shipbuilding program without waiting for Congress to assemble. The lawmakers later approved his decision, and Lincoln continued to act in advance of Congress when he deemed such action necessary. In one striking exercise of executive power, Lincoln suspended the writ of habeas corpus for everyone living between Washington, D.C., and Philadelphia. There was scant legal justification for this act, but the president's motive was practical: to ensure the loyalty of Maryland, which surrounded the capital on three sides. Later in the war, with congressional approval, Lincoln repeatedly suspended habeas corpus and invoked martial law, mainly in the border states but elsewhere as well. Between fifteen and twenty thousand U.S. citizens were arrested on suspicion of disloyal acts. These measures have led some to claim that Lincoln achieved "dictatorial" powers as a wartime president.

On occasion Lincoln used his wartime authority to bolster his own political fortunes. He and his gener-

Expansion of Presidential Power

als proved adept at furloughing soldiers so they could vote in close elections; those whom Lincoln furloughed, of course, usually voted Republican. He also came to the aid of other officeholders in his party. When the Republican governor of Indiana, who was battling Democrats in his legislature who sought a negotiated end to the war, ran short of funds, Lincoln had the War Department supply $250,000. This procedure lacked constitutional sanction, but it advanced the Union cause.

In thousands of self-governing towns and communities, northern citizens felt a personal connection to representative government. Secession threatened to destroy their system, and northerners rallied to its defense. Secular and church leaders supported the cause, and even ministers who preferred to separate politics and pulpit denounced "the iniquity of causeless rebellion." In the first two years of the war, northern morale remained remarkably high for a cause that today may seem abstract—the Union—but at the time meant the preservation of a social and political order that people cherished.

The Union Cause

But social attitudes on the northern home front evolved in directions that would have shocked the soldiers in the field. In the excitement of moneymaking, an eagerness to display one's wealth flourished in the largest cities. *Harper's Monthly* reported that "the suddenly enriched contractors, speculators, and stock-jobbers . . . are spending money with a profusion never before witnessed in our country, at no time remarkable for its frugality. . . . The men button their waistcoats with diamonds . . . and the women powder their hair with gold and silver dust." The *New York Herald* summarized that city's atmosphere: "Not to keep a carriage, not to wear diamonds, . . . is now equivalent to being a nobody. This war has entirely changed the American character. . . . The individual who makes the most money—no matter how—and spends the most—no matter for what—is considered the greatest man."

Yet idealism coexisted with ostentation. Many churches endorsed the Union cause as God's cause. One Methodist newspaper described the war as a contest between "equalizing, humanizing Christianity" and "disunion, war, selfishness, [and] slavery." Abolitionists campaigned to turn the war into a crusade against slavery. Free black communities and churches both black and white responded to the needs of slaves who flocked to the Union lines, sending clothing, ministers, and teachers to aid the freedpeople. Indeed, northern blacks gave wholehearted support to the war, volunteering by the thousands at first and drilling their own militia units in spite of the initial rejection they received from the Lincoln administration.

Northern women, like their southern counterparts, took on new roles. Those who stayed home or-

Northern Women

ganized over ten thousand soldiers' aid societies, rolled bandages, and raised $3 million to aid injured troops. Women were instrumental in pressing for the first trained ambulance corps in the Union armies, and they formed the backbone of the U.S. Sanitary Commission, a civilian agency officially recognized by the War Department in 1861. The Sanitary Commission provided crucial nutritional and medical aid to soldiers. Although most of its officers were men, the bulk of its volunteers who ran its seven thousand auxiliaries were women. Women organized elaborate "Sanitary Fairs" all across the North to raise money and awareness for soldiers' health and hygiene.

Approximately 3,200 women also served as nurses in frontline hospitals, where they pressed for better care of the wounded. Yet women were only about one-quarter of all nurses, and they had to fight for a chance to serve at all. The professionalization of medicine

Walt Whitman, now America's most celebrated wartime poet. His *Drum Taps* series, part of his evolving masterpiece *Leaves of Grass,* left some of the most haunting and moving poetic images of both the death and new life wrought by the war.   (National Portrait Gallery, Smithsonian Institution, Washington, D.C.)

since the Revolution had created a medical system dominated by men, and many male physicians did not want women's aid. Even Clara Barton, famous for her persistence in working in the worst hospitals at the front, was ousted from her post in 1863. But with Barton, women such as the stern Dorothea Dix (see page 277), well-known for her efforts to reform asylums for the insane, and an Illinois widow, Mary Ann Bickerdyke, who served tirelessly in Sherman's army in the West, established a heroic tradition for Civil War nurses. They also advanced the professionalization of nursing as several schools of nursing were established in northern cities during or after the war.

The poet Walt Whitman left a record of his experiences as a volunteer nurse in Washington, D.C. As

Walt Whitman's War

he dressed wounds and tried to comfort suffering and lonely men, Whitman found "the marrow of the tragedy concentrated in those Army Hospitals." But despite "indescribably horrid wounds," he also found inspiration in such suffering and a deepening faith in American democracy. Whitman celebrated the "incredible dauntlessness" and sacrifice of the common soldier who fought for the Union. As he had written in the preface to his great work *Leaves of Grass* (1855), "The genius of the United States is not best or most in its executives or legislatures, but always most in the common people." Whitman worked this idealization of the common man into his poetry, which also explored homoerotic themes and rejected the lofty meter and rhyme of European verse to strive for a "genuineness" that would appeal to the masses.

In "The Wound Dresser," Whitman meditated unforgettably on the deaths he witnessed on both sides:

> On, on I go, (open doors of time! open hospital doors!)
> The crush'd head I dress, (poor crazed hand tear not
>   the bandage away,)
> The neck of the cavalry-man with the bullet through
>   and through I examine,
> Hard the breathing rattles, quite glazed already the eye,
>   yet life struggled hard,
> (Come sweet death! be persuaded O beautiful death!
>   In mercy come quickly.)

Whitman mused for millions in the war who suffered the death of a husband, brother, father, or friend. Indeed, the scale of death in this war shocked many Americans into believing that this conflict had to be for purposes larger than themselves.

Thus northern society embraced strangely contradictory tendencies. Materialism and greed flourished alongside idealism, religious conviction, and self-sacrifice. While some soldiers risked their lives willingly out of a desire to preserve the Union or extend freedom, many others openly sought to avoid service. Under the law, a draftee could stay at home by providing a substitute or paying a $300 commutation fee. Many wealthy men chose these options, and in response to popular demand, clubs, cities, and states provided the money for others to escape conscription. In all, 118,000 substitutes were provided and 87,000 commutations paid before Congress ended the commutation system in 1864. Naturally, in decades to come Americans would commemorate and build monuments to soldiers' sacrifice and idealism, not to opportunism.

The Advent of Emancipation

Despite the sense of loyalty to cause that animated soldiers and civilians on both sides, the governments of the United States and the Confederacy lacked clarity about the purpose of the war. Throughout the first several months of the struggle, both Davis and Lincoln studiously avoided references to slavery. Davis realized that emphasis on the issue could increase class conflict in the South. To avoid identifying the Confederacy only with the interests of slaveholders, he articulated a broader, traditional ideology. Davis told southerners that they were fighting for constitutional liberty: northerners had betrayed the founders' legacy, and southerners had seceded to preserve it. As long as Lincoln also avoided making slavery an issue, Davis's line seemed to work.

Lincoln had his own reasons for not mentioning slavery. It was crucial at first not to antagonize the Union's border slave states, whose loyalty was tenuous. Also for many months Lincoln hoped that a pro-Union majority would assert itself in the South. It might be possible, he thought, to coax the South back into the Union and stop the fighting, short of what he later called "the result so fundamental and astounding"—emancipation. Raising the slavery issue would severely undermine both goals. Powerful political considerations also dictated Lincoln's reticence. The Republican Party was a young and unwieldy coalition. Some Republicans burned with moral outrage over slavery; others were frankly racist, dedicated to protecting free whites from the Slave Power and the competition of cheap slave labor. A forthright stand by Lincoln on the subject of slavery could split the party, gratifying some groups and alienating others. No

northern consensus on what to do about slavery existed early in the war.

The president's hesitancy ran counter to some of his personal feelings. Lincoln was a compassionate man whose humility and moral anguish during the war were evident in his speeches and writings. But as a politician, Lincoln distinguished between his own moral convictions and his official acts. His political positions were studied and complex, calculated for maximum advantage.

Lincoln, the Gradual Emancipator

Many blacks furiously attacked Lincoln during the first year of the war for his refusal to convert the struggle into an "abolition war." When Lincoln countermanded General John C. Frémont's order of liberation for slaves owned by disloyal masters in Missouri in September 1861, the *Anglo-African* declared that the president, by his actions, "hurls back into the hell of slavery thousands . . . rightfully set free." As late as July 1862, Frederick Douglass condemned Lincoln as a "miserable tool of traitors and rebels," and characterized administration policy as reconstruction of "the old union on the old and corrupting basis of compromise, by which slavery shall retain all the power that it ever had." Douglass wanted the old union destroyed and a new one created in the crucible of a war that would destroy slavery and rewrite the Constitution in the name of human equality. To his own amazement, within a year, just such a profound result began to take place.

Lincoln first broached the subject of slavery in a substantive way in March 1862, when he proposed that the states consider emancipation on their own. He asked Congress to promise aid to any state that decided to emancipate, appealing especially to border state representatives. What Lincoln proposed was gradual emancipation, with compensation for slaveholders and colonization of the freed slaves outside the United States. To a delegation of free blacks he explained that "it is better for us both . . . to be separated."

Until well into 1864 Lincoln's administration promoted a wholly impractical scheme to colonize blacks in Central America or the Caribbean. Lincoln saw colonization as one option among others in dealing with the impending freedom of America's 4.2 million slaves. As yet, he was unconvinced that America had any prospect as a truly biracial society, and he desperately feared that white northerners might not support a war for black freedom. Led by Frederick Douglass, black abolitionists vehemently opposed these machinations by the Lincoln administration.

Other politicians had much greater plans for a struggle against slavery. A group of Republicans in Congress, known as the Radicals and led by men such as George Julian, Charles Sumner, and Thaddeus Stevens, dedicated themselves to a war for emancipation. They were instrumental in creating a special House-Senate committee on the conduct of the war, which investigated Union reverses, sought to make the war effort more efficient, and prodded the president to take stronger measures. Early in the war these Radicals, with widening support, turned their attention to slavery.

In August 1861, at the Radicals' instigation, Congress passed its first confiscation act. Designed to punish the Confederates, the law

Confiscation Acts

confiscated all property used for "insurrectionary purposes." Thus if the South used slaves in a hostile action, those slaves were declared seized and liberated as contraband of war. A second confiscation act (July 1862) went much further: it confiscated the property of anyone who supported the rebellion, even those who merely resided in the South and paid Confederate taxes. Their slaves were declared "forever free of their servitude." The logic behind these acts was that the insurrection—as Lincoln termed it— required strong measures to stop it. Let the government use its full powers, free the slaves, and crush the insurrection, urged the Radicals.

Lincoln refused to adopt that view in the summer of 1862. He stood by his proposal of voluntary gradual emancipation by the states and made no effort to enforce the second confiscation act. His stance provoked a public protest from Horace Greeley, editor of the powerful *New York Tribune*. In an open letter to the president entitled "The Prayer of Twenty Millions," Greeley pleaded with Lincoln to "execute the laws" and declared, "On the face of this wide earth, Mr. President, there is not one disinterested, determined, intelligent champion of the Union cause who does not feel that all attempts to put down the Rebellion and at the same time uphold its inciting cause are preposterous and futile." Lincoln's reply was an explicit statement of his calculated approach to the question. He disagreed, he said, with all those who would make the maintenance or destruction of slavery the paramount issue of the war. "I would save the Union," announced Lincoln. "If I could save the Union without freeing any slave I would do it, and if I could save it by freeing all the slaves I would do it; and if I could save it by freeing some and leaving others alone I would also do that.

What I do about slavery, and the colored race, I do because I believe it helps to save the Union." Lincoln closed with a personal disclaimer: "I have here stated my purpose according to my view of official duty; and I intend no modification of my oft-expressed personal wish that all men everywhere could be free."

When he wrote those words, Lincoln had already decided to boldly issue a presidential Emancipation Proclamation. He was waiting, however, for a Union victory so that it would not appear to be an act of desperation. Yet the letter to Greeley was not simply an effort to stall; it was an integral part of Lincoln's approach to the future of slavery, as the text of the Emancipation Proclamation would show. Lincoln was concerned to condition public opinion as best he could for the coming social revolution.

On September 22, 1862, shortly after Union success at the Battle of Antietam, Lincoln issued the first part of his two-part proclamation.

Emancipation Proclamations

Invoking his powers as commander-in-chief of the armed forces, he announced that on January 1, 1863, he would emancipate the slaves in the states "in rebellion against the United States." Lincoln made plain that he would judge a state to be in rebellion in January if it lacked bona fide representatives in the U.S. Congress. Thus his September proclamation was less a declaration of the right of slaves to be free than a threat to southerners: unless they put down their arms and returned to Congress, they would lose their slaves. "Knowing the value that was set on the slaves by the rebels," said Garrison Frazier, a black Georgia minister, "the President thought that his proclamation would stimulate them to lay down their arms . . . and their not doing so has now made the freedom of the slaves a part of the war." Lincoln had little expectation that southerners would give up their effort, but he was careful to offer them the option, thus trying to put the onus of emancipation on them.

In the fateful January 1 proclamation, Lincoln excepted (as areas in rebellion) every Confederate county or city that had fallen under Union control. Those areas, he declared, "are, for the present, left precisely as if this proclamation were not issued." Nor did Lincoln liberate slaves in the border slave states that remained in the Union. "The President has purposely made the proclamation inoperative in all places where . . . the slaves [are] accessible," charged the anti-administration *New York World*. "He has proclaimed emancipation only where he has notoriously no power to execute it." Partisanship aside, even Secretary of

State Seward, a moderate Republican, said sarcastically, "We show our sympathy with slavery by emancipating slaves where we cannot reach them and holding them in bondage where we can set them free." A British official, Lord Russell, commented on the "very strange nature" of the document, noting that it did not declare "a principle adverse to slavery." Russell may have missed the point.

Lincoln was worried about the constitutionality of his acts. Making the liberation of the slaves "a fit and necessary war measure" raised a variety of legal questions. How long did a war measure remain in force? Did it expire with the suppression of a rebellion? The proclamation did little to clarify the status or citizenship of the freed slaves, although it did open the possibility of military service for blacks. How indeed would this change the character and purpose of the war?

Thus the Emancipation Proclamation was an ambiguous document that said less than it seemed to say. But if as a legal document it was wanting, as a moral and political document it had great meaning. Because the proclamation defined the war as a war against slavery, radicals could applaud it, even if the president had not gone as far as Congress. Yet at the same time it protected Lincoln's position with conservatives, leaving him room to retreat if he chose and forcing no immediate changes on the border slave states. It was a delicate balancing act, but one from which there was no real turning back.

Most important, though, thousands of slaves had already reached Union lines in various sections of the South. They had "voted with their feet" for emancipation, as many said, well before the proclamation. And now, every advance of federal forces into slave society was a liberating step. This Lincoln knew in taking his own initially tentative, and then forthright, steps toward emancipation.

Across the North and in Union-occupied sections of the South, blacks and their white allies celebrated the Emancipation Proclamation with unprecedented fervor. Full of praise songs, these celebrations demonstrated that whatever the fine print of the proclamation, black folks knew that they had lived to see a new day. At a large "contraband camp" in Washington,

A group of "contrabands" (liberated slaves), photographed at Cumberland Landing, Virginia, May 14, 1862, at a sensitive point in the war when their legal status was still not fully determined. The faces and generations of the women, men, and children represent the human drama of emancipation.   (Library of Congress)

D.C., some six hundred black men, women, and children gathered at the superintendent's headquarters on New Year's Eve and sang through the night. In chorus after chorus of "Go Down, Moses," they announced the magnitude of their painful but beautiful exodus. One newly supplied verse concluded with "Go down, Abraham, away down in Dixie's land, tell Jeff Davis to let my people go!"

The need for men soon convinced the administration to recruit northern and southern blacks for the Union Army. By the spring of 1863, African American troops were answering the call of a dozen or more black recruiters barnstorming the cities and towns of the North. Lincoln came to see black soldiers as "the great available and yet unavailed of force for restoring the Union." African American leaders hoped that military service would secure equal rights for their people. Once the black soldier had fought for the Union, wrote Frederick Douglass, "there is no power on earth which can deny that he has earned the right of citizenship in the United States." If black soldiers turned the tide, asked another man, "would the nation refuse us our rights?"

In June 1864 Lincoln gave his support to a constitutional ban on slavery. Reformers such as Elizabeth Cady Stanton and Susan B. Anthony were pressing for an amendment that would write emancipation into the Constitution. On the eve of the Republican national convention, Lincoln called the party's chairman to the White House and instructed him to have the party "put into the platform as the keystone, the amendment of the Constitution abolishing and prohibiting slavery forever." The party promptly called for the Thirteenth Amendment. Republican delegates probably would have adopted such a plank without his urging, but Lincoln demonstrated his commitment by lobbying Congress for quick approval of the measure. The proposed amendment passed in early 1865 and was sent to the states for ratification. The war to save the Union had also become the war to free the slaves.

It has long been debated whether Abraham Lincoln deserved the label (one he never claimed for himself) of "Great Emancipator." Was

Who Freed the Slaves?

Lincoln ultimately a reluctant emancipator, following rather than leading Congress and public opinion? Or did Lincoln give essential presidential leadership to the most transformative and sensitive aspect of the war by going slow on emancipation, but once moving, never backpedaling on the main issue—black freedom. Once he had realized the total character of the war and decided to prosecute it to the unconditional surrender of the Confederates, Lincoln made the destruction of slavery central to the war's purpose.

Others have argued, however, that the slaves themselves are the central story in the achievement of their own freedom. When they were in proximity to the war zones, or had opportunities as traveling laborers, slaves fled for their freedom by the thousands. Some worked as camp laborers for the Union armies, and eventually more than 180,000 black men served in the Union Army and Navy. Sometimes freedom came as a combination of confusion, fear, and joy in the rural hinterlands of the South. Some found freedom as individuals in 1861, and some not until 1865 as members of trains of refugees. Some slaves remained supportive of their masters' welfare until the war was over. Some freedmen traversed great distances to reach contraband camps.

However freedom came to individuals, emancipation was a historical confluence of two essential forces: one, a policy directed by and dependent on the military authority of the president in his effort to win the war; and two, the will and courage necessary for acts of self-emancipation. In his annual message in December 1862, Lincoln asserted that "in *giving* freedom to the slave, we *assure* freedom to the free." Likewise, most blacks understood the long-term meaning in those words—in the midst of total war they comprehended their freedom as both given and taken.

Before the war was over, the Confederacy, too, addressed the issue of emancipation. Jefferson Davis himself offered a proposal for black freedom of a kind. He was dedicated to independence, but late in the war he was willing to sacrifice slavery to achieve that goal. Davis concluded late in 1864 that the military situation of the Confederacy was so desperate that independence with emancipation was preferable to defeat with emancipation. He proposed that the Confederate government purchase forty thousand slaves to work for the army as laborers, with a promise of freedom at the end of their service. Soon Davis upgraded the idea, calling for the recruitment and arming of slaves as soldiers, who likewise would gain their freedom at war's end. The wives and children of these soldiers, he made plain, must also receive freedom from the states. Davis and his advisers envisioned an "intermediate" status for ex-slaves of "serfage or peonage." Thus at the bitter end, a few southerners were willing to sacrifice some of the racial, if not class, destiny for which they had launched their revolution.

A Confederate Plan of Emancipation

How do historians know...

that ex-slaves fully embraced their new freedom? Jourdon Anderson was a former slave from Tennessee. Residing in Dayton, Ohio, with his family in August 1865, four months after the war ended, Anderson received a letter from his former owner, Colonel P. H. Anderson, asking him to return to the old place. "I have often felt uneasy about you," Anderson told his old master. As for the "good chance . . . you propose," Anderson said to the former slaveholder, "we have concluded to test your sincerity by asking you to send us our wages for the time we served you." With remarkable wit and irony, Anderson described the dignity with which he and his family lived in freedom (his children were in school and his wife was called "Mrs. Anderson"). Published in the *Cincinnati Commercial* and the *New York Tribune*, this astonishing letter, dictated by Anderson, demonstrates that freedom meant everything to the freedpeople: a free public identity, choice, education, and, not least, the "justice" represented by wages. (Photo: *New York Daily Tribune*, August 22, 1865)

Dayton, Ohio, August 7, 1865

To My Old Master, Colonel P. H. Anderson,
Big Spring, Tennessee

Sir: I got your letter and was glad to find you had not forgotten Jourdon, and that you wanted me to come back and live with you again, promising to do better for me than anybody else can. I have often felt uneasy about you. I thought the Yankees would have hung you long before this for harboring Rebs they found at your house. . . . Although you shot at me twice before I left you, I did not want to hear of your being hurt, and am glad you are still living. It would do me good to go back to the dear old home again and see Miss Mary and Miss Martha and Allen, Esther, Green, and Lee. Give my love to them all, and tell them I hope we will meet in the better world, if not in this. . . .

I want to know particularly what the good chance is you propose to give me. I am doing tolerably well here; I get $25 a month, with victuals and clothing; have a comfortable home for Mandy (the folks here call her Mrs. Anderson), and the children, Milly, Jane and Grundy, go to school and are learning well; the teacher says Grundy has a head for a preacher. . . . Now, if you will write and say what wages you will give me, I will be better able to decide whether it would be to my advantage to move back again.

As to my freedom, which you say I can have, there is nothing to be gained on that score, as I got my free-papers in 1864. . . . Mandy says she would be afraid to go back without some proof that you are sincerely disposed to treat us justly and kindly—and we have concluded to test your sincerity by asking you to send us our wages for the time we served you. This will make us forget and forgive old scores, and rely on your justice and friendship in the future. I served you faithfully for thirty-two years and Mandy twenty years. At $25 a month for me, and $2 a week for Mandy, our earnings would amount to $11,680. Add to this the interest for the time our wages has been kept back and deduct what you paid for our clothing and three doctor's visits to me, and pulling a tooth for Mandy, and the balance will show what we are in justice entitled to. Please send the money by Adams Express, in care of V. Winters, esq, Dayton, Ohio. If you fail to pay us for faithful labors in the past we can have little faith in your promises in the future. We trust the good Maker has opened your eyes to the wrongs which you and your fathers have done to me and my fathers, in making us toil for you for generations without recompense. Here I draw my wages every Saturday night, but in Tennessee there was never any pay day for the negroes any more than for the horses and cows. . . .

In answering this letter please state if there would be any safety for my Milly and Jane, who are now grown up and both good-looking girls. You know how it was with poor Matilda and Catherine. I would rather stay here and starve and die if it comes to that than have my girls brought to shame by the violence and wickedness of their young masters. You will also please state if there has been any schools opened for the colored children in your neighborhood, the great desire of my life now is to give my children an education, and have them form virtuous habits.

P.S.—Say howdy to George Carter, and thank him for taking the pistol from you when you were shooting at me.

From your old servant,
Jourdon Anderson

Bitter debate over Davis's plan resounded through the Confederacy. When the Confederate Congress approved slave enlistments without the promise of freedom in March 1865, Davis insisted on more. He issued an executive order to guarantee that owners would emancipate slave soldiers, and his allies in the states started to work for emancipation of the soldiers' families.

The war ended before much could come of these desperate policy initiatives on the part of the Confederacy. By contrast, Lincoln's Emancipation Proclamation stimulated a vital infusion of forces into the Union armies. Before the war was over, 134,000 slaves (and 52,000 free African Americans) had fought for freedom and the Union. Their participation aided northern victory while it discouraged recognition of the Confederacy by foreign governments, especially Great Britain, which had freed the slaves in its empire thirty years earlier. As both policy and process, emancipation had profound practical and moral implications for the new nation to be born out of the war.

The Soldiers' War

 The intricacies of policymaking and social revolutions were far from the minds of most ordinary soldiers. Military service completely altered their lives. Enlistment took young men from their homes and submerged them in large organizations whose military discipline ignored their individuality. Army life meant tedium, physical hardship, and separation from loved ones. Yet the military experience had powerful attractions as well. It molded men on both sides so thoroughly that they came to resemble one another far more than they resembled civilians back home. Many soldiers forged amid war a bond with their fellows and a connection to a noble purpose that they cherished for years afterward.

Union soldiers may have sensed most clearly the massive scale of modern war. Most were young; the average soldier was between eighteen and twenty-one. Many went straight from small towns and farms into large armies supplied by extensive bureaucracies. By late 1861 there were 640,000 volunteers in arms, a stupendous increase over the regular army of 20,000 men. Many soldiers found adapting to camp life and military discipline daunting.

Soldiers benefited from certain new products, such as canned condensed milk, but blankets, clothing, and arms were often of poor quality. Vermin abounded. Hospitals were badly managed at first.

Hospitals and Camp Life

Rules of hygiene in large camps were scarcely enforced; latrines were poorly made or carelessly used. One investigation turned up "an area of over three acres, encircling the camp as a broad belt, on which is deposited an almost perfect layer of human excrement." Water supplies were unsafe and typhoid epidemics common. About 57,000 men died from dysentery and diarrhea; in fact, 224,000 Union troops died from disease or accidents, far more than the 140,000 who died as a result of battle. Confederate troops were less well supplied, especially in the latter part of the war, and they had no sanitary commission. Still, an extensive network of hospitals, aided by many white female volunteers and black women slaves, sprang up to aid the sick and wounded.

On both sides troops quickly learned that soldiering was far from glorious. "The dirt of a camp life knocks all its poetry into a cocked hat," wrote a North Carolina volunteer in 1862. One year later he marveled at his earlier innocence. Fighting had taught him "the realities of a soldier's life. We had no tents after the 6th of August, but slept on the ground, in the woods or open fields, without regard to the weather. . . . I learned to eat fat bacon raw, and to like it. . . . Without time to wash our clothes or our persons, and sleeping on the ground all huddled together, the whole army became lousy more or less with body lice." Union troops "skirmished" against lice by boiling their clothes or holding them over a hot fire, but, reported one soldier, "I find some on me in spite of all I can do."

Few had seen violent death before, but war soon exposed them to the blasted bodies of their friends and comrades. "Any one who goes over a battlefield after a battle," wrote one Confederate, "never cares to go over another. . . . It is a sad sight to see the dead and if possible more sad to see the wounded—shot in every possible way you can imagine." Many men died gallantly; there were innumerable striking displays of courage. But far more often soldiers gave up their lives in mass sacrifice, in tactics that made little sense.

Advances in technology made the Civil War particularly deadly. By far the most important were the rifle and the "minie ball." Bullets fired from a smoothbore musket tumbled and wobbled as they flew through the air and thus were not accurate at distances over 80 yards. Cutting spiraled grooves inside the barrel gave the projectile a spin and much greater accuracy, but rifles remained

The Rifled Musket

Union soldiers in camp, posing for a photograph, with black servants. The drudgery of camp life never prohibited soldiers from displaying their individuality. (National Archives)

difficult to load and use until the Frenchman Claude Minie and the American James Burton developed a new kind of bullet. Civil War bullets were sizable lead slugs with a cavity at the bottom that expanded upon firing so that the bullet "took" the rifling and flew accurately. With these bullets, rifles were accurate at 400 yards and useful up to 1,000 yards.

This meant, of course, that soldiers assaulting a position defended by riflemen were in greater peril than ever before. Even though Civil War rifles were cumbersome to load (relatively few of the new, untried, breechloading and repeating rifles were ordered), the defense gained a significant advantage. While artillery now fired from a safe distance, there was no substitute for the infantry assault or the popular turning movements aimed at an enemy's flank. Thus advancing soldiers had to expose themselves repeatedly to accurate rifle fire. Because medical knowledge was rudimentary, even minor wounds often led to amputation, and to death through infection. Never before in Europe or America had such massive forces pummeled each other with weapons of such destructive power. As losses mounted, many citizens wondered at what Union soldier (and future Supreme Court justice) Oliver Wendell Holmes, Jr., called "the butcher's bill."

Still, Civil War soldiers developed deep commitments to each other and to their task. As campaigns dragged on, fighting and dying with their comrades became their reality, and most soldiers who did not desert grew determined to see the struggle through. "We now, like true Soldiers go determined not to yield one inch," wrote a New York corporal. When at last the war was over, "it seemed like breaking up a family to separate," one man observed. Another admitted, "We shook hands all around, and laughed and seemed to make merry, while our hearts were heavy and our eyes ready to shed tears."

The bonding may have been most dramatic among officers and men in the northern black regiments, for there white and black troops took their first steps toward bridging a deep racial divide. Racism in the Union Army was strong. Most white soldiers wanted nothing to do with black people and regarded them as inferior. "I never came out here for to free the black devils," wrote one soldier, and another objected to fighting beside African Americans because, "We are a too superior race for that." For many, acceptance of black troops grew only because they could do heavy labor and "stop Bullets as well as white people." A

The Black Soldier's Fight for Manhood

popular song celebrated "Sambo's Right to Be Kilt" as the only justification for black enlistments.

But among some a change occurred. While recruiting black troops in Virginia in late 1864, Charles Brewster sometimes denigrated the very men he sought to enlist. But he was delighted at the sight of a black cavalry unit because it made the local "secesh" furious, and he praised black soldiers who "fought nobly" and filled hospitals with "their wounded and mangled bodies." White officers who volunteered to lead black units only to gain promotion found that experience altered their opinions. After just one month with black troops, a white captain informed his wife, "I have a more elevated opinion of their abilities than I ever had before. I know that many of them are vastly the superiors of those . . . who would condemn them all to a life of brutal degradation." One general reported that his "colored regiments" possessed "remarkable aptitude for military training," and another observer said, "They fight like fiends."

Black troops created this change through their own dedication. They had a mission to destroy slavery and demonstrate their equality. "When Rebellion is crushed," wrote a black volunteer from Connecticut, "who will be more proud than I to say, 'I was one of the first of the despised race to leave the free North with a rifle on my shoulder, and give the lie to the old story that the black man will not fight.'" Corporal James Henry Gooding of Massachusetts's black Fifty-fourth Regiment explained that his unit intended "to live down all prejudice against its color, by a determination to do well in any position it is put." After an engagement he was proud that "a regiment of white men gave us three cheers as we were passing them," because "it shows that we did our duty as men should."

Through such experience under fire the blacks and whites of the Fifty-fourth Massachusetts forged deep bonds. Just before the regiment launched its costly assault on Fort Wagner in Charleston harbor, in July 1863, a black soldier called out to abolitionist Colonel Robert Gould Shaw, who would perish that day, "Colonel, I will stay by you till I die." "And he kept his word," noted a survivor of the attack. "He has never been seen since." Indeed, the heroic assault on Fort Wagner was celebrated for demonstrating the valor of black men. This bloody chapter in the history of American racism proved many things, not least of which was that black men had to die in battle to be acknowledged as men.

Such valor emerged despite persistent discrimination. Off-duty black soldiers were sometimes attacked by northern mobs; on duty, they did most of the "fa-

Company E, 4th U.S. Colored Infantry, photographed at Fort Lincoln, Virginia, in 1864. Nothing so symbolized the new manhood and citizenship among African Americans in the midst of the war as such young black men in blue.   (Chicago Historical Society)

tigue duty," or heavy labor. The Union government, moreover, paid white privates $13 per month plus a clothing allowance of $3.50, whereas black privates earned only $10 per month less $3 for clothing. Outraged by this injustice, several regiments refused to accept any pay whatsoever, and Congress eventually remedied the inequity. In this instance, at least, the majority of legislators agreed with a white private that black troops had "proved their title to manhood on many a bloody field fighting freedom's battles."

1863: The Tide of Battle Turns

 The fighting in the spring and summer of 1863 did not settle the war, but it began to suggest the outcome. The campaigns began in a deceptively positive way for Confederates, as their Army of Northern Virginia performed brilliantly in the Battle of Chancellorsville.

For once, a large Civil War army was not slow and cumbersome but executed tactics with speed and precision.

Battle of Chancellorsville

On May 2 and 3, west of Fredericksburg, Virginia, some 130,000 members of the Union Army of the Potomac bore down on fewer than 60,000 Confederates. Boldly, as if they enjoyed being outnumbered, Lee and Stonewall Jackson divided their forces, ordering 30,000 men under Jackson on a day-long march westward to gain position for a flank attack. This classic turning movement was boldly carried out in the face of great numerical disadvantage. Arriving at their position late in the afternoon, Jackson's seasoned "foot cavalry" found unprepared Union troops laughing, smoking, and playing cards. The Union soldiers had no idea they were under attack until frightened deer and rabbits bounded out of the forest, followed by gray-clad troops. The Confederate attack drove the entire right side of the Union Army back in confusion. Eager to press his advantage, Jackson rode forward with a few officers to study the ground. As they returned at twilight, southern troops mistook them for federals and fired, fatally wounding their commander. The next day Union forces left in defeat. Chancellorsville was a remarkable southern victory but costly because of the loss of Stonewall Jackson.

July brought crushing defeats for the Confederacy in two critical battles—Vicksburg and Gettysburg—that severely damaged Confederate hopes for independence. Vicksburg was a vital western citadel, the last major fortification on the Mississippi River in

Siege of Vicksburg

southern hands (see Map 15.2). After months of searching through swamps and bayous, General Ulysses S. Grant found an advantageous approach to the city. He laid siege to Vicksburg in May, bottling up the defending army of General John Pemberton. If Vicksburg fell, Union forces would control the river, cutting the Confederacy in two and gaining an open path into its interior. To stave off such a result, Jefferson Davis gave command of all other forces in the area to General Joseph E. Johnston and beseeched him to go to Pemberton's aid. Meanwhile, at a council of war in Richmond, General Robert E. Lee proposed a Confederate invasion of the North. Although such an offensive would not relieve Vicksburg directly, it could stun and dismay the North and, if successful, possibly even lead to peace. By invading the North a second time, Lee hoped to take the war out of war-weary Virginia, garner civilian support in Maryland, win a major victory on northern soil, threaten major cities, and thereby force a Union capitulation on his terms.

Lee's troops streamed through western Maryland and into Pennsylvania, threatening both Washington and Baltimore. As his emboldened army advanced, the possibility of a major battle near the Union capital became more and more likely. Confederate prospects along the Mississippi, however, darkened. Davis repeatedly wired General Johnston, urging him to concentrate his forces and attack Grant's army. Johnston, however, did little, telegraphing back, "I consider saving Vicksburg hopeless." Grant's men, meanwhile, were supplying themselves from the abundant crops of the Mississippi River valley and could continue their siege indefinitely. Their rich meat-and-vegetables diet became so tiresome, in fact, that one day, as Grant rode by, a private looked up and muttered, "Hardtack," referring to the dry biscuits that were the usual staple of soldiers' diets. Soon a line of soldiers was shouting "Hardtack! Hardtack!" demanding respite from turkey and sweet potatoes.

In such circumstances the fall of Vicksburg was inevitable, and on July 4, 1863, its commander surrendered.

Battle of Gettysburg

The same day a battle that had been raging for three days concluded at Gettysburg, Pennsylvania (see Map 15.3). On July 1 Confederate forces hunting for a supply of shoes had collided with part of the Union Army. Heavy fighting on the second day over two steep hills left federal forces in possession of high ground along

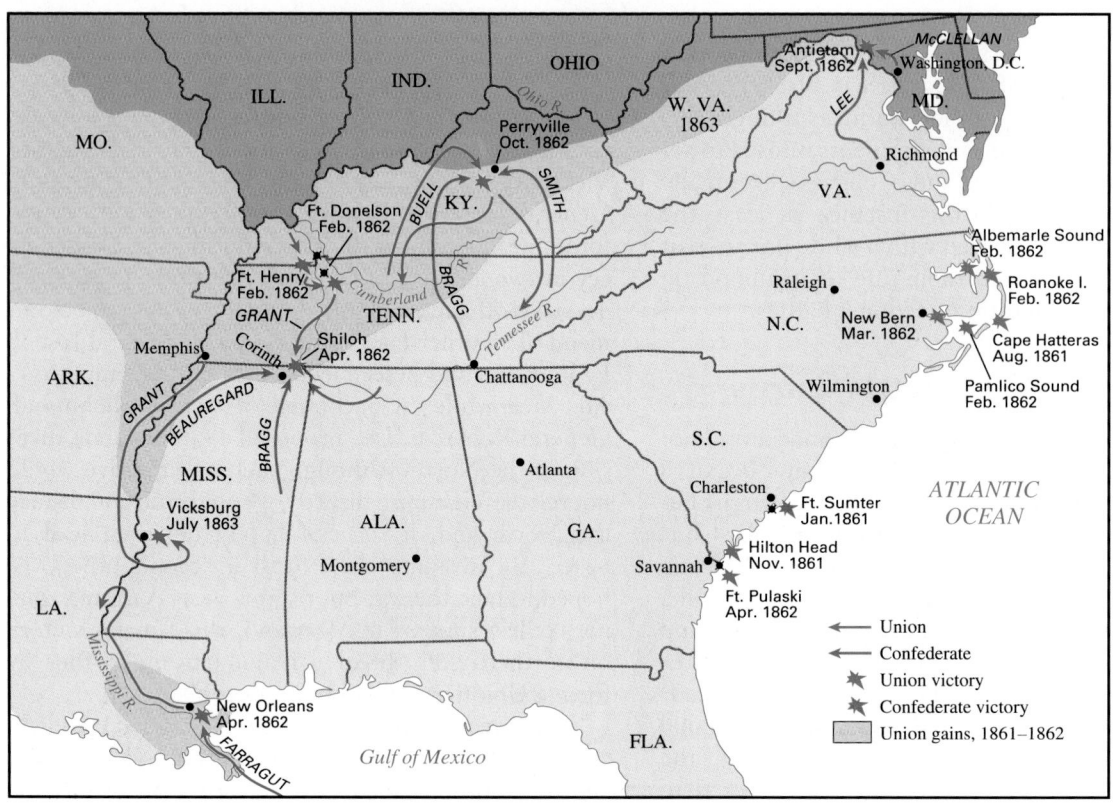

Map 15.2 War in the West, 1861–1863 Here is an overview of the Union's successful campaigns in the west and its seizure of key points on the Mississippi River, as well as along the Atlantic coast in 1862 and 1863. These actions were decisive in paving the way for ultimate northern victory.

Cemetery Ridge, running more than a mile south of the town. There they enjoyed the protection of a stone wall and a clear view of their foe across almost a mile of open field.

Undaunted, Lee believed his reinforced troops could break the Union line, and on July 3 he ordered a direct assault. Full of foreboding, General James Longstreet warned Lee that "no 15,000 men ever arrayed for battle can take that position." But Lee stuck to his plan. Virginians under General George E. Pickett and North Carolinians under General James Pettigrew methodically marched up the slope in a doomed assault known as Pickett's Charge. For a moment a few hundred Confederates breached the enemy's line, but most fell in heavy slaughter. On July 4 Lee had to withdraw, having suffered almost 4,000 dead and about 24,000 missing and wounded. The Confederate general reported to President Davis that "I am alone to blame" and offered to resign. Davis replied that to find a more capable commander was "an impossibility."

The Confederacy had reached what many consider its "high water mark" on that ridge at Gettysburg.

Southern troops displayed unforgettable courage and dedication at Gettysburg, and the Union Army, which suffered 23,000 casualties (nearly one-quarter of the force), under General George G. Meade exhibited the same bravery in stopping the Confederate invasion. But the results there and at Vicksburg were disastrous for the South. The Confederacy was split in two; west of the Mississippi General E. Kirby Smith had to operate on his own, virtually independent of Richmond. Moreover, the heartland of Louisiana, Tennessee, and Mississippi lay exposed to invasion, and Lee's defeat spelled the end of major southern offensive actions. Too weak to prevail in attack, the Confederacy henceforth would have to conserve its limited resources and rely on a prolonged defense. By refusing to be beaten, and wearing down northern morale, the South might yet win, but its prospects were darker than ever before.

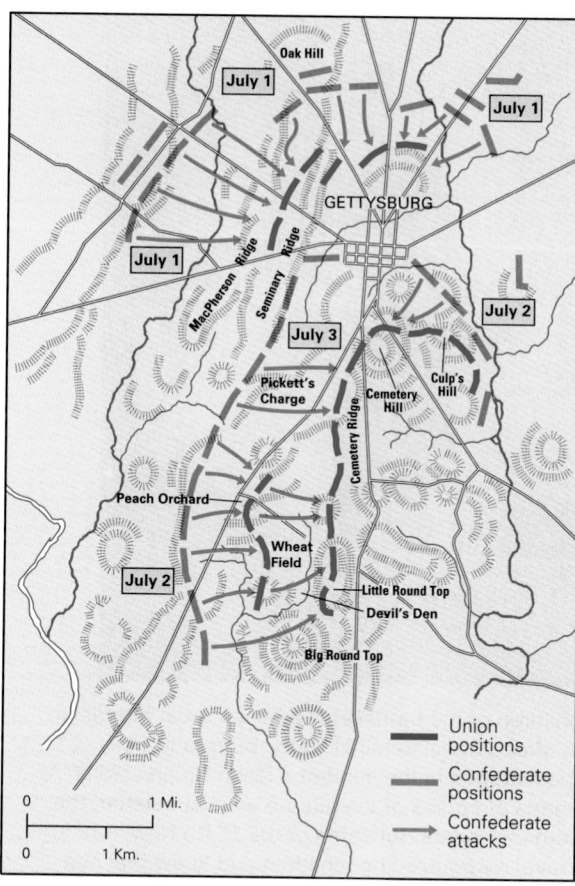

Map 15.3   Battle of Gettysburg   In the war's greatest battle, fought around a small market town in southern Pennsylvania, Lee's invasion of the North was repulsed. Union forces had the advantage of high ground, shorter lines, and superior numbers. The casualties for the two armies—dead, wounded, and missing—exceeded 50,000 men.

Disunity, South and North

 Both northern and southern governments waged the final two years of the war in the face of increasing opposition at home. Dissatisfactions that had surfaced earlier grew more intense and sometimes violent. The gigantic costs of a *civil* war that neither side seemed able to win fed the unrest. But protest also arose from fundamental stresses in the social structures of North and South.

The Confederacy's problems were both more serious and more deeply rooted than the North's. Vastly disadvantaged in industrial capacity, natural resources,

Disintegration of Confederate Unity

and labor, southerners felt the cost of the war more quickly, more directly, and more painfully than northerners. But even more fundamental were the Confederacy's internal problems; crises that were integrally connected with the southern class system threatened the Confederate cause.

One ominous development was the planters' increasing opposition to their own government. Not only did the Richmond government impose new taxes and the tax-in-kind, but Confederate military authorities also impressed slaves to build fortifications. And when Union forces advanced on plantation areas, Confederate commanders burned stores of cotton that lay in the enemy's path. Such interference with plantation routines and financial interests was not what planters had expected of their government, and they complained bitterly.

Nor were the centralizing policies of the Davis administration popular. The increasing size and power of the Richmond government startled and alarmed planters who had condemned federal usurpations. In fact, the Confederate constitution had granted substantial powers to the central government, especially in time of war. But many planters assumed with R. B. Rhett, editor of the *Charleston Mercury*, that the Confederate constitution "leaves the States untouched in their Sovereignty, and commits to the Confederate Government only a few simple objects, and a few simple powers to enforce them." Governor Joseph E. Brown of Georgia took a similarly inflated view of the importance of the states. During the brief interval between Georgia's secession from the Union and its admission to the Confederacy, Brown sent an ambassador to Europe to seek recognition for the sovereign republic of Georgia from Queen Victoria, Napoleon III, and the king of Belgium.

Years of opposition to the federal government within the Union had frozen southerners in a defensive posture. Now they erected the barrier of states' rights as a defense against change, hiding behind it while their capacity for creative statesmanship atrophied. Planters sought, above all, a guarantee that their plantations and their lives would remain untouched; many were not deeply committed either to building a southern nation or to winning independence. If the Confederacy had been allowed to depart from the Union in peace and continue as a semideveloped cotton-growing region, they would have been content. When secession revolutionized their world, they could not or would not adjust.

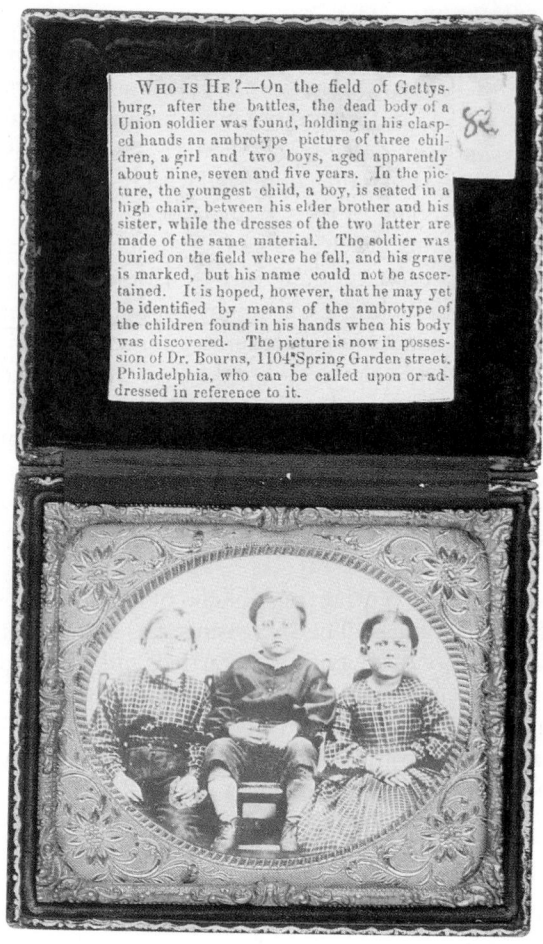

WHO IS HE?—On the field of Gettysburg, after the battles, the dead body of a Union soldier was found, holding in his clasped hands an ambrotype picture of three children, a girl and two boys, aged apparently about nine, seven and five years. In the picture, the youngest child, a boy, is seated in a high chair, between his elder brother and his sister, while the dresses of the two latter are made of the same material. The soldier was buried on the field where he fell, and his grave is marked, but his name could not be ascertained. It is hoped, however, that he may yet be identified by means of the ambrotype of the children found in his hands when his body was discovered. The picture is now in possession of Dr. Bourns, 1104 Spring Garden street, Philadelphia, who can be called upon or addressed in reference to it.

These "children of the battlefield" aroused great interest in the North after a burial detail at Gettysburg found this ambrotype clutched in the hand of a fallen Union soldier. After thousands of copies of the picture were circulated, the wife of Sergeant Amos Humiston of the 154th New York Infantry *(above)* recognized her children and knew that she was a widow.   (The C. Craig Caba Gettysburg Collection, from *Gettysburg.* Larry Sherer © 1991 Time-Life Books, Inc.)

Confused and embittered planters struck out at Jefferson Davis. Conscription, thundered Governor Brown, was "subversive of [Georgia's] sovereignty, and at war with all the principles for the support of which Georgia entered into this revolution." Searching for ways to frustrate the law, Brown bickered over draft exemptions and ordered local enrollment officials not to cooperate with the Confederacy. The *Charleston Mercury* told readers that "conscription . . . is . . . the very embodiment of Lincolnism, which our gallant armies are today fighting." In a gesture of stubborn selfishness, Robert Toombs of Georgia, a former U.S. senator, refused to switch from cotton to food crops, defying the wishes of the government, the newspapers, and his neighbors' petitions. His action bespoke the inflexibility of the southern elite at a crucial point in the Confederacy's struggle to survive.

The southern courts ultimately upheld Davis's power to conscript. Despite his cold formality and inability to disarm critics, Davis possessed two important virtues: iron determination and total dedication to

independence. These qualities kept the Confederacy afloat. But his actions earned him the hatred of most influential and elite citizens.

Meanwhile, for ordinary southerners, the dire predictions of hunger and suffering were becoming a reality. Food riots occurred in the spring of 1863 in Atlanta, Macon, Columbus, and Augusta, Georgia, and in Salisbury and High Point, North Carolina. On April 2 a crowd assembled in Richmond to demand relief. A passerby, noticing the excitement, asked a young girl, "Is there some celebration?" "We celebrate our right to live," replied the girl. "We are starving. As soon as enough of us get together we are going to the bakeries and each of us will take a loaf of bread." Soon they did just that, sparking a riot that Davis himself had to quell at gunpoint.

Food Riots in Southern Cities

Throughout the rural South, ordinary people resisted more quietly—by refusing to cooperate with conscription, tax collection, and impressments of food. "In all the States impressments are evaded by every means which ingenuity can suggest, and in some openly resisted," wrote a high-ranking commissary officer. Farmers who did provide food for the army refused to accept payment in certificates of credit or government bonds, as required by law. Conscription officers increasingly found no one to draft—men of draft age were hiding out in the forests. "The disposition to avoid military service is general," observed one of Georgia's senators in 1864. In some areas tax agents were killed in the line of duty.

Jefferson Davis was ill equipped to deal with such discontent. Austere and private by nature, he failed to communicate with the masses. Often he buried himself in military affairs or administrative details. His class perspective also distanced him from the sufferings of the common people. While his social circle in Richmond dined on duck and oysters, ordinary southerners recovered salt from the drippings on their smokehouse floors and went hungry. State governors who responded to people's needs won the public's loyalty, but Davis failed to reach out to the plain folk and thus lost their support.

Such discontent was certain to affect the Confederate armies. "What man is there that would stay in the army and no that his family is

Desertions from the Confederate Army

suffering at home?" an angry citizen wrote anonymously to the secretary of war. Worried about their loved ones and resentful of what they saw as a rich man's war, large numbers of men did indeed leave the armies. Their friends and neighbors gave them support. Mary Boykin Chesnut observed a man being dragged back to the army as his wife looked on. "Desert agin, Jake!" she cried openly. "You desert agin, quick as you kin. Come back to your wife and children."

Desertion did not become a serious problem for the Confederacy until mid-1862, and stiffer policing solved the problem that year. But from 1863 on, the number of men on duty fell rapidly as desertions soared. By mid-1863, John A. Campbell, the South's assistant secretary of war, wondered whether "so general a habit" as desertion could be considered a crime. Campbell estimated that 40,000 to 50,000 troops were absent without leave and that 100,000 were evading duty in some way. Furloughs, amnesty proclamations, and appeals to return had little effect; by November 1863 Secretary of War James Seddon admitted that one-third of the army could not be accounted for. The situation would worsen.

The defeats at Gettysburg and Vicksburg dealt a heavy blow to Confederate morale. When the news

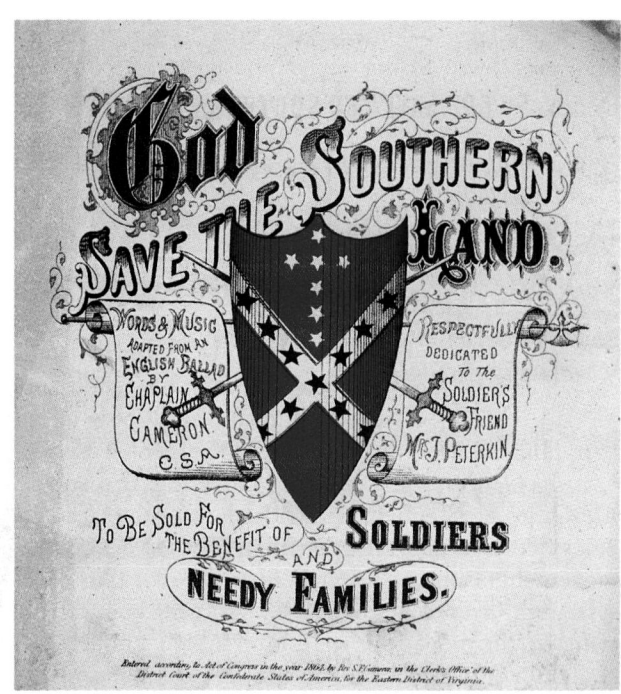

The impoverishment of nonslaveholding white families was a critical problem for the Confederacy. The sale of this sheet music was intended not only to boost morale but also to raise money that could be used to aid the hungry and needy. This effort and larger government initiatives, however, failed to solve the problem.   (Chicago Historical Society)

reached Josiah Gorgas, the genius of Confederate ordnance operations, he confided to his diary, "Today absolute ruin seems our portion. The Confederacy totters to its destruction." In desperation President Davis and several state governors resorted to threats and racial scare tactics to drive southern whites to further sacrifice. Defeat, Davis warned, would mean "extermination of yourselves, your wives, and children." Governor Charles Clark of Mississippi predicted "elevation of the black race to a position of equality—aye, of superiority, that will make them your masters and rulers."

From this point on, the internal disintegration of the Confederacy quickened. A few newspapers began to call openly for peace. "We are for peace," admitted the *Raleigh* (North Carolina) *Daily Progress*, "because there has been enough of blood and carnage, enough of widows and orphans." A neighboring journal, the *North Carolina Standard*, tacitly admitted that defeat was inevitable and called for negotiations. Similar proposals were made in several state legislatures, though they were presented as plans for independence on honorable terms. Confederate leaders began to realize that they were losing the support of the common people. Governor Zebulon Vance of North Carolina wrote privately that victory would require more "blood and misery . . . and our people will not pay this price I am satisfied for their independence."

In North Carolina a peace movement grew under the leadership of William W. Holden, a popular Dem-

Southern Peace Movements

ocratic politician and editor. Over one hundred public meetings took place in the summer of 1863 in support of peace negotiations, and many seasoned political observers believed that Holden had the majority of the people behind him. In Georgia early in 1864, Governor Brown and Alexander H. Stephens, vice president of the Confederacy, led a similar effort. Ultimately, however, these movements came to naught. The lack of a two-party system threw into question the legitimacy of any criticism of the government; even Holden and Brown could not entirely escape the taint of dishonor and disloyalty. That the movement existed at all demonstrates deep disaffection.

The results of the 1863 congressional elections strengthened dissent in the Confederacy. Everywhere secessionists and supporters of the administration lost seats to men not identified with the government. Many of the new representatives were former Whigs who opposed the Davis administration or publicly favored peace. In the last years of the war, Davis's support in the Confederate Congress dwindled. Davis used the government bureaucracy and the army to enforce his unpopular policies. A few editors and a core of courageous, determined soldiers kept the Confederacy alive in spite of disintegrating popular support.

By 1864 much of the opposition to the war had moved entirely outside the political sphere. Southerners were simply giving up the struggle and withdrawing their cooperation from the government. Deserters dominated whole towns and counties. Secret societies favoring reunion, such as the Heroes of America and the Red Strings, sprang up. Active dissent was particularly common in upland and mountain regions. "The condition of things in the mountain districts of North Carolina, South Carolina, Georgia, and Alabama," admitted Assistant Secretary of War Campbell, "menaces the existence of the Confederacy as fatally as either of the armies of the United States." The government was losing the support of its citizens.

In the North opposition to the war was similar but less severe. Alarm intensified over the growing cen-

Antiwar Sentiment in the North

tralization of government, and by 1863 war-weariness was widespread. Resentment of the draft sparked protest, especially among poor citizens, and the Union Army struggled with a desertion rate as high as the Confederates'. But the Union was so much richer than the South in human resources that none of these problems ever threatened the effectiveness of the government. Fresh recruits were always available, especially after black enlistments began, and there were no shortages of food and other necessities.

Also, Lincoln possessed a talent that Davis lacked: he knew how to stay in touch with the ordinary citizen. Through letters to newspapers and to soldiers' families, he reached the common people and demonstrated that he had not forgotten them. The daily carnage, the tortuous political problems, and the ceaseless criticism weighed heavily on him. But this president—a self-educated man of humble origins—was able to communicate his suffering. His moving words helped to contain northern discontent, though they could not remove it.

Much of the wartime protest in the North was political in origin. The Democratic Party fought to

Peace Democrats

regain power by blaming Lincoln for the war's death toll, the expansion of federal powers, inflation and the high tariff, and the emancipation of blacks. Appealing to tradition, its leaders called for an end to the war and reunion on the basis of "the Constitution as it is and the Union as it was." The Democrats denounced conscription and martial law and defended states' rights and the interests of agriculture. They charged repeatedly that Republican policies were designed to flood the North with blacks, depriving white males of their status, their jobs, and their women. These claims appealed to southerners who had settled north of the Ohio River, to conservatives, to many poor people, and to some eastern merchants who had lost profitable southern trade. In the 1862 congressional elections, the Democrats made a strong comeback, and peace Democrats—who would go much further than others in their party to end the war—had influence in New York State and majorities in the legislatures of Illinois and Indiana.

Led by outspoken men like Representative Clement L. Vallandigham of Ohio, the peace Democrats made themselves highly visible. Vallandigham criticized Lincoln as a dictator who had suspended the writ of habeas corpus without congressional authority and had arrested thousands of innocent citizens. Like other Democrats, he condemned both conscription and emancipation and urged voters to use their power at the polls to depose "King Abraham." Vallandigham stayed carefully within legal bounds, but his attacks seemed so damaging to the war effort that military authorities arrested him for treason after Lincoln suspended habeas corpus. Lincoln wisely decided against punishment—and martyr's status—for the Ohioan and exiled him to the Confederacy. (Eventually Vallandigham returned to the North through Canada.)

Lincoln believed that antiwar Democrats were linked to secret organizations that harbored traitorous ideas. These societies, he feared, encouraged draft resistance, discouraged enlistment, sabotaged communications, and plotted to aid the Confederacy. Likening such groups to a poisonous snake, Republicans sometimes branded them—and by extension the peace Democrats—as "Copperheads." Though Democrats were connected with these organizations, most engaged in politics rather than treason. And though some saboteurs and Confederate agents were active in the North and Canada, they never genuinely threatened the Union war effort.

More violent opposition to the government arose from ordinary citizens facing the draft, which became law in 1863. The urban poor and immigrants in strongly Democratic areas were especially hostile to conscription. Federal enrolling officers made up the lists of eligibles, a procedure open to personal favoritism and prejudice. Many men, including some of modest means, managed to avoid the army by hiring a substitute or paying commutation, but the poor viewed the commutation fee as discriminatory, and many immigrants suspected (wrongly, on the whole) that they were called in disproportionate numbers. (Approximately 200,000 men born in Germany and 150,000 born in Ireland served in the Union Army.)

New York City Draft Riots

As a result, there were scores of disturbances and melees. Enrolling officers received rough treatment in many parts of the North, and riots occurred in New Jersey, Ohio, Indiana, Pennsylvania, Illinois, and Wisconsin. By far the most serious outbreak of violence occurred in New York City in July 1863. The war was unpopular in that Democratic stronghold, and racial, ethnic, and class tensions ran high. Shippers had recently broken a longshoremen's strike by hiring black strikebreakers to work under police protection.

Mobs in the New York City draft riots directed much of their anger at African Americans. Rioters burned an orphanage for black children and killed scores of blacks. This wood engraving, which appeared in the *Illustrated London News* on August 8, 1863, depicts a lynching in Clarkson Street.   (Chicago Historical Society)

Working-class New Yorkers feared an inflow of black labor from the South and regarded blacks as the cause of the war. Poor Irish workers resented being forced to serve in the place of others who could afford to avoid the draft.

Military police officers came under attack first, and then mobs crying "Down with the rich" looted wealthy homes and stores. But blacks became the special target. Those who happened to be in the rioters' path were beaten; soon the mob rampaged through African American neighborhoods, destroying an orphan asylum. At least seventy-four people died in the violence, which raged out of control for three days. Only the dispatch of army units fresh from Gettysburg ended the episode.

Discouragement and war-weariness reached a peak in the summer of 1864, when the Democratic Party nominated the popular General George B. McClellan for president and inserted a peace plank into its platform. The plank, written by Vallandigham, condemned "four years of failure to restore the Union by the experiment of war," called for an armistice, and spoke vaguely about preserving the Union. Lincoln, running with Tennessee's Andrew Johnson on a "National Union" ticket, concluded that it was "exceedingly probable that this Administration will not be reelected." During a publicized interchange with Confederate officials sent to Canada, Lincoln insisted that the terms for peace include reunion and "the abandonment of slavery." A wave of protest arose in the North from voters who were weary of war and dedicated only to reunion. Lincoln quickly backtracked, denying that his offer meant "that nothing *else* or *less* would be considered, if offered." He would insist on freedom only for those slaves (about 134,000) who had joined the Union Army under his promise of emancipation. Lincoln's action showed his political weakness, but the fortunes of war soon changed the electoral situation.

1864–1865: The Final Test of Wills

 During the final year of the war, the Confederates could still have won their version of victory if military stalemate and northern antiwar sentiment had forced a negotiated settlement to end the war. But events, northern determination, and Lincoln's insistence on the unconditional surrender of Confederate forces prevailed as Americans endured the bloodiest nightmare in their history.

The North's long-term diplomatic strategy succeeded in 1864. From the outset, the North had pur-

Northern Diplomatic Strategy

sued one paramount goal: to prevent recognition of the Confederacy by European nations. Foreign recognition would belie Lincoln's claim that the United States was fighting an illegal rebellion and would open the way to the financial and military aid that could ensure Confederate independence. The British elite, however, felt considerable sympathy for southern planters, whose aristocratic values were similar to their own. And both England and France stood to benefit from a divided and weakened America. Thus to achieve their goal, Lincoln and Secretary of State Seward needed to avoid both serious military defeats and controversies with the European powers.

Aware that the textile industry employed one-fifth of the British population directly or indirectly, southerners banked on British recognition of the Confederacy. But at the beginning of the war, British mills had a 50 percent surplus of cotton on hand; later on, new sources of supply in India, Egypt, and Brazil helped to meet Britain's needs. And throughout the war, some southern cotton continued to reach Europe, despite the Confederacy's embargo on cotton production, an ill-fated policy initiative aimed at securing British sup-

port. Refusing to be stampeded into recognition of the Confederacy, the British government kept its eye on the battlefield. France, though sympathetic to the South, was unwilling to act independently of Britain. Confederate agents managed to purchase valuable arms and supplies in Europe and obtained loans from European financiers, but they never achieved a diplomatic breakthrough.

More than once the Union strategy nearly broke down. An acute crisis occurred in 1861 when the overzealous commander of an American frigate stopped the British steamer *Trent* and removed two Confederate ambassadors, James Mason and John Slidell, sailing to Britain. They were imprisoned in Boston after being brought ashore. This action was cheered in the North, but the British interpreted it as a violation of freedom of the seas and demanded the prisoners' release. Lincoln and Seward waited until northern public opinion cooled and then released the two southerners. Soon forgotten, the incident nevertheless strained U.S.-British relations at a sensitive early stage in the war.

Then the sale to the Confederacy of warships constructed in England sparked vigorous protest from U.S. ambassador Charles Francis Adams. A few English-built ships, notably the *Alabama*, reached open water to serve the South. Over a period of twenty-two months, without entering a southern port (because of the Union blockade), the *Alabama* destroyed or captured more than sixty U.S. ships. But the British government, as a neutral power, soon barred delivery of warships such as the Laird rams (built by a private company), formidable vessels whose pointed prows were designed to end the blockade by battering the Union ships.

On the battlefield, the northern victory was far from won in 1864. General Nathaniel Banks's Red

Battlefield Stalemate and a Union Strategy for Victory

River campaign, designed to capture more of Louisiana and Texas, quickly fell apart, and the capture of Mobile Bay in August did not cause the fall of Mobile. Union general William Tecumseh Sherman commented that the North had to "keep the war South until they are not only ruined, exhausted, but humbled in pride and spirit." Sherman soon brought total war to the southern heartland. On the eastern front during the winter of 1863–1864, the two armies in Virginia settled into a stalemate awaiting yet another spring offensive by the North.

Military authorities throughout history have agreed that deep invasion is very risky: the farther an

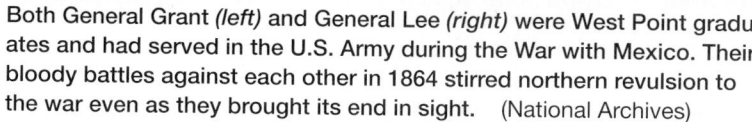

Both General Grant *(left)* and General Lee *(right)* were West Point graduates and had served in the U.S. Army during the War with Mexico. Their
bloody battles against each other in 1864 stirred northern revulsion to
the war even as they brought its end in sight.   (National Archives)

army penetrates enemy territory, the more vulnerable
its own communications and supply lines. Moreover,
observed the Prussian expert Karl von Clausewitz, if
the invader encountered a "truly national" resistance,
his troops would be "everywhere exposed to attacks
by an insurgent population." Thus if southerners
mounted such a "truly national" resistance, their defiance and the South's vast size could make a northern
victory improbable.

General Grant, by now in command of all the federal armies, decided to test these conditions—and
southern will—with a strategic innovation of his own:
raids on a massive scale. Grant, less tied to tradition
and maneuver by the book than most other Union
commanders, proposed to use whole armies, not just
cavalry, to destroy Confederate railroads, thus ruining
the enemy's transportation and damaging the South's
economy. Abandoning their lines of support, Union
troops would live off the land while laying to waste all
resources useful to the military and to the civilian population of the Confederacy. After General George H.
Thomas's troops won the Battle of Chattanooga in
November 1863 by ignoring orders and charging up
Missionary Ridge, the heartland of Georgia lay open.
Moving to Virginia, Grant entrusted General Sherman with 100,000 men for an invasion deep into the
South, toward the rail center of Atlanta.

Jefferson Davis countered by positioning the army
of General Joseph E. Johnston in Sherman's path.
Davis's entire political strategy for
1864 was based on demonstrating
Confederate military strength and
successfully defending Atlanta. The
U.S. presidential election of 1864 was approaching,
and Davis hoped that southern resolve would lead to
the defeat of Lincoln and the election of a president
who would sue for peace. When General Johnston
slowly but steadily fell back toward Atlanta, Davis
grew anxious and sought assurances that Atlanta would
be held. From a purely military point of view, Johnston
maneuvered skillfully, but the president of the Confederacy could not take a purely military point of view.
When Johnston provided no information and continued to retreat, Davis replaced him with the one-legged

Atlanta

General John Hood, who knew his job was to fight. "Our all depends on that army at Atlanta," wrote Mary Boykin Chesnut. "If that fails us, the game is up."

For southern morale, the game was up. Hood attacked but was beaten, and Sherman's army occupied Atlanta on September 2, 1864. The victory buoyed northern spirits and ensured Lincoln's reelection. "There is no hope," Mary Chesnut acknowledged; and a government clerk in Richmond wrote, "Our fondly-cherished visions of peace have vanished like a mirage of the desert." Davis exhorted southerners to fight on and win new victories before the federal elections, but he had to admit that "two-thirds of our men are absent . . . most of them absent without leave." In a desperate diversion, Hood's army marched north to cut Sherman's supply lines and force him to withdraw, but Sherman began to march sixty thousand of his men straight to the sea, planning to live off the land and destroying Confederate resources as he went (see Map 15.4).

Sherman's army was an unusually formidable force, composed almost entirely of battle-tested veterans and officers who had risen through the ranks from

Sherman's March to the Sea

the midwestern states. Before the march began, army doctors weeded out any men who were weak or sick. Tanned, bearded, tough, and unkempt, the remaining veterans were determined, as one put it, "to Conquer this Rebelien or Die." They believed "the South are to blame for this war" and were ready to make the South pay. Although many harbored racist attitudes, most had come to support emancipation because, as one said, "Slavery stands in the way of putting down the rebellion." Confederate General Johnston later commented, "There has been no such army since the days of Julius Caesar."

As Sherman's men moved across Georgia, they cut a path 50 to 60 miles wide and more than 200 miles long. The totality of the destruction they caused was awesome. A Georgia woman described the "Burnt Country" this way: "The fields were trampled down and the road was lined with carcasses of horses, hogs, and cattle that the invaders, unable either to consume or to carry with them, had wantonly shot down to starve our people and prevent them from making their crops. The stench in some places was unbearable."

Map 15.4 Sherman's March to the Sea   The West proved a decisive theater at the end of the war. From Chattanooga, Union forces drove into Georgia, capturing Atlanta. Then General Sherman embarked on his march of destruction through Georgia to the coast and then northward through the Carolinas.

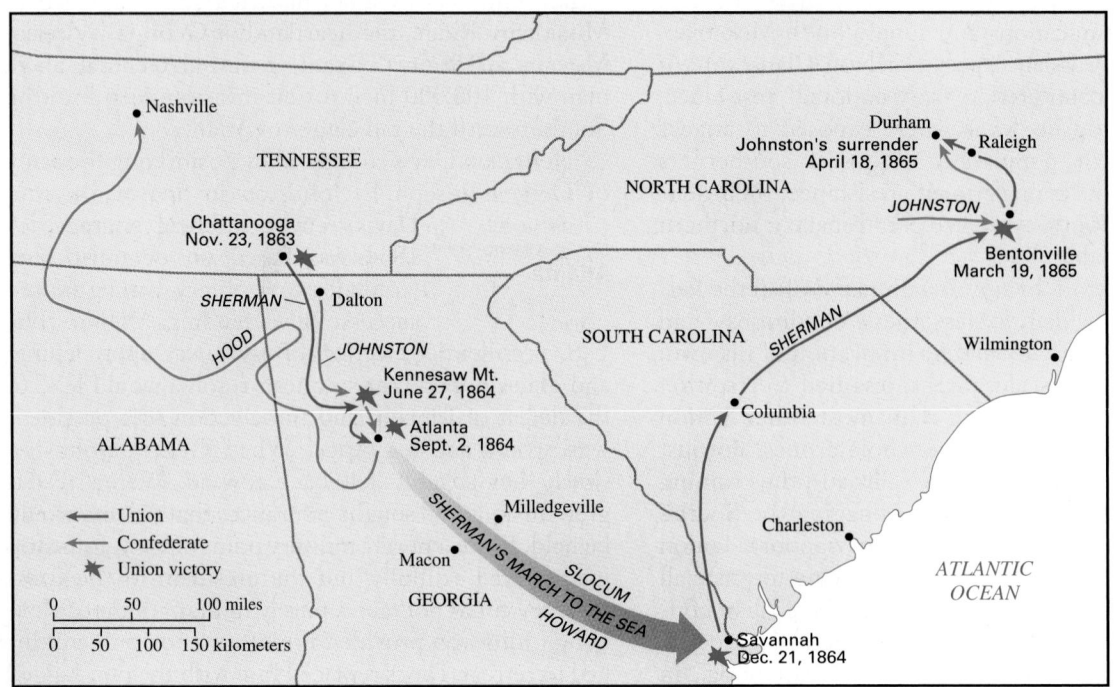

Such devastation diminished the South's material resources and sapped its will to resist.

After reaching Savannah in December, Sherman marched his armies north into the Carolinas. To his soldiers, South Carolina was "the root of secession." They burned and destroyed as they moved through, encountering little resistance. The opposing army of General Johnston was small, but Sherman's men should have been prime targets for guerrilla raids and harassing attacks by local defense units. The absence of both led South Carolina's James Chesnut, Jr. (a politician and the husband of Mary Chesnut), to write that his state "was shamefully and unnecessarily lost. . . . We had time, opportunity and means to destroy him. But there was wholly wanting the energy and ability required by the occasion." The South put up no "truly national" resistance; its people had lost the will to continue the struggle.

Sherman's march drew additional human resources to the Union cause. In Georgia alone as many as nineteen thousand slaves gladly took the opportunity to escape bondage and join the Union troops as they passed through the countryside. Others remained on the plantations to await the end of the war, either from an ingrained wariness of whites or negative experiences with federal soldiers. The destruction of food harmed slaves as well as white rebels, and many blacks lost livestock, clothing, crops, and other valuables to their liberators. In fact, the brutality of Sherman's troops shocked these veterans of the whip. "I've seen them cut the hams off of a live pig or ox and go off leavin' the animal groanin'," recalled one man. "The master had 'em kilt then, but it was awful."

It was awful, too, in Virginia, where the path to victory proved protracted and ghastly. Throughout

Virginia's Bloody Soil

the spring and summer of 1864, intent on capturing Richmond, Grant hurled his troops at Lee's army in Virginia and suffered appalling losses: almost 18,000 casualties in the Battle of the Wilderness, where skeletons poked out of the shallow graves dug one year before; more than 8,000 at Spotsylvania; and 12,000 in the space of a few hours at Cold Harbor (see Map 15.5).

Before the assault at Cold Harbor (which Grant later admitted was a grave mistake), Union troops pinned scraps of paper bearing their names and addresses to their backs, certain they would be mowed down as they rushed Lee's trenches. In four weeks in May and June, Grant lost as many men as were enrolled in Lee's entire army. From early May until July,

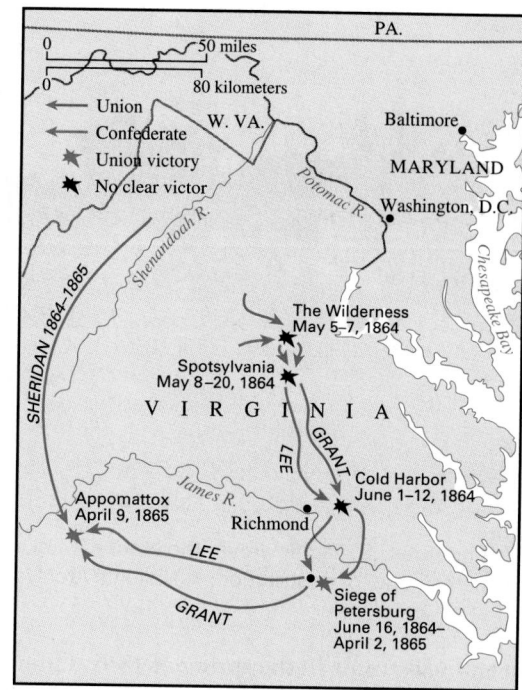

Map 15.5   The War in Virginia, 1864–1865   At great cost, Grant hammered away at Lee's army until the weakened southern forces finally surrendered at Appomattox Court House.

when Union forces had marched and fought all the way from forests west of Fredericksburg to Petersburg, south of Richmond, which they besieged, the two armies engaged each other nearly every day, often in full-scale battles. The war had reached a horrible modern scale. Wagon trains carrying thousands of Union wounded crawled back toward Washington. "It was as if war," wrote historian Bruce Catton, "the great clumsy machine for maiming people, had at last been perfected. Instead of turning out its grist spasmodically, with long waits between each delivery, it was at last able to produce every day, without any gaps at all."

Undaunted, Grant kept up the pressure, saying, "I propose to fight it out along this line if it takes all summer." Though costly, and testing northern morale to its limits, these battles prepared the way for eventual victory: Lee's army shrank until offensive action was no longer possible, while Grant's army kept replenishing its forces with new recruits. The siege of Petersburg, with the armies facing each other in miles of trenches, lasted throughout the winter of 1864–1865.

At the war's end, the U.S. flag flew over the state capitol in Richmond, Virginia, which bore many marks of destruction.   (National Archives)

The end finally came in the spring of 1865. Grant kept battering Lee, who tried but failed to break through the Union line. With the numerical superiority of Grant's army now greater than two to one, Confederate defeat was inevitable. On April 2 Lee abandoned Richmond and Petersburg. On April 9, hemmed in by Union troops, short of rations, and with fewer than thirty thousand men left, Lee surrendered at Appomattox Court House. Grant treated his rival with respect and paroled the defeated troops, allowing cavalrymen to keep their horses and take them home. The war was over at last. Within weeks, Confederate forces under Johnston surrendered and Davis, who had fled Richmond but wanted the war to continue, was captured in Georgia. The North rejoiced, and most southerners fell into despair, expecting waves of punishment. In the profound relief and stillness of the surrender field at Appomattox, no one could know the tasks of healing and justice that lay ahead.

Surrender at Appomattox

With Lee's surrender, Lincoln knew that the Union had been preserved, yet he lived to see but a few days of war's aftermath. On the evening of Good Friday, April 14, he accompanied his wife to Ford's Theatre in Washington to enjoy a popular comedy. There John Wilkes Booth, an embittered southern sympathizer, shot the president in the head at point-blank range. Lincoln died the next day. Twelve days later, troops tracked down and killed Booth. The Union had lost its wartime leader, and millions publicly mourned the martyred chief executive along the route of the funeral train that took his body home to Illinois. Relief at the war's end mingled hauntingly with a renewed sense of loss and anxiety about the future. Millions never forgot where they were and how they felt at the news of Lincoln's assassination.

Property damage and financial costs were enormous, though difficult to tally. U.S. loans and taxes during the conflict totaled almost $3 billion, and interest on the war debt was $2.8 billion. The Confederacy borrowed over $2 billion but lost far more in the destruction of homes, crops, livestock, and other property. As an example of the wreckage that attended four years of conflict on southern soil, the number of hogs in South Carolina plummeted from 965,000 in 1860 to approximately 150,000 in 1865, leaving many families without their primary source of meat.

Financial Tally

In southern war zones the landscape was desolated. Over wide regions fences and crops were destroyed; houses, barns, and bridges burned; and fields abandoned and left to erode. Union troops had looted factories and put two-thirds of the South's railroad system out of service. Visitors to the countryside were struck by how empty and impoverished it looked.

Estimates of the total cost of the war exceed $20 billion—five times the total expenditures of the federal government from its creation to 1861. The northern government increased its spending by 700 percent in the first full year of the war; by the last year its spending had soared to twenty times the prewar level. By 1865 the federal government accounted for over 26 percent of the gross national product.

Many of these changes were more or less permanent. In the 1880s, interest on the war debt still accounted for approximately 40 percent of the federal budget and Union soldiers' pensions for as much as 20 percent. The federal government had used its power to support manufacturing and business interests by means of tariffs, loans, and subsidies, and wartime measures left the government more deeply involved in the banking and transportation systems. If southerners had hoped to remove government from the economy, the war had now irrepressibly bound them together.

The human costs of the Civil War were especially staggering. The total number of military casualties on both sides exceeded 1 million—a frightful toll for a nation of 31 million people. Approximately 360,000 Union soldiers died, 110,000 of them from wounds suffered in battle. Another 275,175 Union soldiers were wounded but survived. On the Confederate side, an estimated 260,000 lost their lives, and almost as many suffered wounds. More men died in the Civil War than in all other American wars combined until Vietnam. Of an estimated 194,743 northerners in southern prisons, 30,218 died, compared with 25,976 of 214,865 southerners who died in northern prisons. The prison story from the war is one in

Death Toll

which neither side could claim pride, although it caused embittered debate in war memory for decades.

These unprecedented losses flowed from fundamental strife over the nature of the Union and the liberty of black people. Both sides saw vital interests in the struggle. As Julia Ward Howe wrote in her famous "Battle Hymn," they had heard "the trumpet that shall never call retreat." And so the war took its horrifying course. The first great legacy of the war in the lives of its survivors was, therefore, death itself. Although precise figures on enlistments are impossible to obtain, it appears that 700,000 to 800,000 men served in the Confederate armies. Far more, possibly 2.3 million, served in the Union armies. All these men were taken from home, family, and personal goals; their lives, if they survived at all, were disrupted in ways that were never repaired.

Summary

The Civil War altered American society forever. During the war, in both North and South, women had taken on new roles. Industrialization and large economic enterprises grew in power. Ordinary citizens found that their futures were increasingly tied to huge organizations. The character and extent of government power changed markedly. Under Republican leadership, the federal government had expanded its

The death of President Lincoln caused a vast outpouring of grief in the North. As this Currier and Ives print shows, on its way to Illinois, his funeral train stopped at several cities to allow local services to be held. (Anne S. K. Brown Military Collection, John Hay Library, Brown University)

power not only to preserve the Union but also to extend freedom. A social revolution and government authority emancipated the slaves, and Lincoln had called for "a new birth of freedom" in America. A republic desperately divided against itself had survived, yet in new constitutional forms yet to take shape under tremendous political strife during Reconstruction.

It was unclear, however, how or whether the nation would use its power to protect the rights of the former slaves. Secession was dead, but whether Americans would continue to embrace a centralized nationalism remained to be seen. How would white southerners, embittered and impoverished, respond to efforts to reconstruct the nation? How long would military occupation last in the South, and who would rule its civil society? How would the country care for the maimed, the orphans, the farming women without men to work their land, and all the dead who had to be properly found and buried? And of central importance: what would be the place of black men and women in American life? Black veterans and former slaves eagerly sought an answer. They would find it during Reconstruction.

In the Civil War Americans had undergone an epic of destruction and survival. White southerners had experienced defeat as few other Americans have ever faced. Blacks were walking proudly but anxiously from slavery to freedom. White northerners were, by and large, self-conscious victors in a massive war for the nation's existence and for new definitions of what freedom meant in America. The war, including all its drama, sacrifice, and social and political changes, left a compelling memory in American hearts and minds for generations.

LEGACY FOR A PEOPLE AND A NATION
The Confederate Battle Flag

The most widespread and controversial symbol to emerge from the Civil War era is the Confederate flag. Rather than the official flag of the Confederacy, it was a battle flag that soldiers carried to mark the center of a unit's position in the confusion of combat. Over time, this flag has taken on powerful emotional meanings.

At Confederate veterans' reunions and parades from the 1870s well into the twentieth century, the flag was an emblem of the South's Lost Cause. After extended controversy, many captured Confederate flags were returned by the federal government to southern states in 1905 as a gesture of reconciliation. Increasingly, Confederate remembrance merged with white supremacy at the turn of the twentieth century and African Americans resented the flag's appearance.

In the late 1940s the flag became a fixture of popular culture with heightened racial meanings. In 1948 it was a symbol of the States' Rights ("Dixiecrat") Party. By the 1950s waving the Confederate flag became a demonstration of defiance among southern whites against the civil rights revolution. With the spread of American popular culture abroad, the Confederate flag can now be found all over the world.

What does this flag mean as a symbol? Some southern whites argue that it is merely a marker of regional pride and identity. Some stress the flag's countercultural value as a symbol of rebellion against the establishment, or "political correctness." But to most blacks and to many whites, it expresses racism. The flag is loaded with coded meanings that can be interpreted in opposite ways. Some claim it represents the "nobility" of southern military tradition; others conclude that it stands for the hatred embodied in the history of the Ku Klux Klan.

In recent times, the Confederate flag has been the center of legal and political controversy. Disputes have emanated from city councils, high schools, and universities over public and private uses of the flag. Most visible of all have been the debates in the states of Georgia, South Carolina, and Alabama over whether to cease flying the Confederate flag at official sites. The debate over the meaning and legacy of the Confederate flag may never end. At issue are important questions and traditions: free speech, equal protection under law, perception versus reality, official government endorsement of collective symbols, the significance of race and racism in our national memory, and the meaning of the Civil War itself.

For Further Reading, see page A-18 of the Appendix. For Web resources, go to http://college.hmco.com.

In 1861 Robert Smalls was a slave in South Carolina, while Wade Hampton was a South Carolina legislator and one of the richest planters in the South. The events of the next fifteen years turned each man's world upside down more than once.

Robert Smalls became a Union hero in 1862 when he escaped from slavery by stealing a Confederate ship from Charleston harbor and piloting it to the blockading federal fleet. Thereafter, Smalls guided Union gunboats and toured the North recruiting black troops. Though he enjoyed celebrity status, Smalls encountered racial discrimination in the North and found in 1865 that neither his heroism nor his freedom entitled him to vote. But by 1868 that, too, had changed, and he began a career in politics. Smalls helped write his state's constitution, served in the legislature, and won election to Congress. There he denounced white violence and worked for educational and economic opportunity for his people. But Smalls was helpless to prevent the return of white control in South Carolina in 1877.

Wade Hampton joined the Confederate Army in 1861 and soon became a general. The South's defeat profoundly shocked him; and as Union forces closed in, he spoke wildly of "forc[ing] my way across the Mississippi" with "a devoted band of Cavalry" and continuing to fight. The postwar years brought further painful changes, including forced bankruptcy. In 1867 Hampton surprised other privileged whites by supporting suffrage for a few educated and propertied former slaves. By 1876, though, Hampton's fortunes were again on the rise: Democrats nominated him for governor, promising that he would "redeem" South Carolina from Republican misrule. Among Hampton's white supporters were the paramilitary Red Shirts who pledged to "control the vote of at least one Negro, by intimidation, purchase," or other means. Hampton won the governor's chair, then a seat in the U.S. Senate, and eventually an honored place as a distinguished Confederate veteran.

As the careers of Smalls and Hampton suggest, Reconstruction was revolutionary, but revolutions can

On January 6, 1874, Congressman Robert B. Elliott of South Carolina made an eloquent defense of the proposed civil rights bill. After a review of legal issues, he called on Congress to ignore the opposition of southerners, who he said had tried to destroy the nation, and deal justly with the Negro race, which had faithfully defended the Union. (Chicago Historical Society)

RECONSTRUCTION: AN UNFINISHED REVOLUTION 1865–1877

go backward. Robert Smalls rose from bondage to experience glory, emancipation, political power, and, ultimately, disappointment. Wade Hampton fell from privilege to endure defeat, failure, bankruptcy, and, eventually, a return to leadership in his state. Unprecedented changes took place in American society, but the underlying realities of economic power, racial prejudice, and judicial conservatism limited Reconstruction's revolutionary potential.

Nowhere was the turmoil of Reconstruction more evident than in national politics. Lincoln's successor, Andrew Johnson, fought bitterly with Congress over the shaping of a plan for Reconstruction. Though a southerner, Johnson had always been a foe of the South's wealthy planters, and his first acts as president suggested that he would be tough on "traitors." Before the end of 1865, however, Johnson's policies changed direction, and he became the friend and protector of southern interests. Jefferson Davis stayed in prison for two years, but Johnson quickly pardoned other rebel leaders and allowed them to occupy high offices. He also ordered the return of plantations to their original owners, including abandoned coastal lands on which forty thousand freed men and women had settled by order of General William Tecumseh Sherman early in 1865. Burdened by a train of thousands of black refugees following his army on the march to the sea, Sherman issued special Field Order Number 15 in February 1865. The order set aside 400,000 acres of land in the Georgia and South Carolina Sea Islands region for the exclusive settlement of the freedpeople. Hope swelled among ex-slaves as 40-acre plots, mules, and "possessary titles" were promised to them. But President Johnson ordered them removed in October and returned the land to its original owners under army protection.

Johnson imagined a lenient and rapid "restoration" of the South to the Union rather than the fundamental "reconstruction" that Republican congressmen favored. Between 1866 and 1868, the president and the Republican leadership in Congress engaged in a bitterly antagonistic power struggle over how to put the United States back together again.

Before these struggles were over, Congress had impeached the president, enfranchised the freed men, and given them a role in reconstructing the South. The nation also adopted the Fourteenth and Fifteenth Amendments, ushering equal protection of the law, a definition of citizenship, and universal manhood suffrage into the Constitution. Yet some underlying realities never changed. Little was done to open the doors of economic opportunity to black southerners, and throughout this period of upheaval, the cause of equal rights for African Americans as the central aim of Reconstruction rose and fell.

By 1869 the Ku Klux Klan employed extensive violence and terror to thwart Reconstruction and undermine black freedom. As white Democrats in the South recaptured state governments, undoing the political revolution, they encountered little opposition from the North. Voters had grown weary and suspicious of the use of federal power to prop up failing Republican governments. Moreover, as the 1870s advanced, industrial growth accelerated, creating new opportunities and raising new priorities. A new economic depression after 1873 refocused northerners' attention. Political corruption became a nationwide scandal, bribery a way of doing business. "Money has become the God of this country," wrote one disgusted observer, "and men, otherwise good men, are almost compelled to worship at her shrine."

Thus Reconstruction became a revolution eclipsed. The white South's desire to take back control of their states and of race relations overwhelmed the national interest in stopping them. But Reconstruction left enduring legacies the nation has struggled with ever since. ■

Wartime Reconstruction

 Civil wars leave immense challenges of healing, justice, and physical rebuilding. Anticipating that process, Reconstruction of the Union was an issue as early as 1863, well before the war ended. Many key questions loomed on the horizon when and if the North succeeded on the battlefield. How would the nation be restored? How would southern states and leaders be treated? As errant brothers, or as traitors? What was the constitutional basis for readmission of states to the Union and where, if anywhere, could American statesmen look for precedence or guidance? More specifically, four vexing problems compelled early thinking and would haunt the Reconstruction era throughout. One, *who* would rule in the South once it was defeated? Two, *who* would rule in the federal government, Congress or the president? Three, what were the dimensions of *black freedom*, and what rights under law would the freedmen enjoy? And four, would Reconstruction be a preservation of the *old* republic, or a second revolution, a re-invention of a *new* republic?

IMPORTANT EVENTS

1865 Johnson begins rapid and lenient
Reconstruction
Confederate leaders regain power
White southern governments pass
restrictive black codes
Congress refuses to seat southern
representatives
Thirteenth Amendment ratified

1866 Congress passes Civil Rights Act and
renewal of Freedmen's Bureau over
Johnson's veto
Congress approves Fourteenth Amendment
Most southern states reject Fourteenth
Amendment
In *Ex parte Milligan* the Supreme Court
reasserts its influence
In congressional elections, Republicans
win more than two-thirds majority, a
renunciation of Johnson's plan of
Reconstruction

1867 Congress passes Reconstruction Act and
Tenure of Office Act
Secretary of State William Seward arranges
purchase of Alaska
Constitutional conventions called in
southern states

1868 House impeaches Johnson; Senate
acquits him
Most southern states gain readmission to
the Union under Radical plan
Fourteenth Amendment ratified
Grant elected president

1869 Congress approves Fifteenth Amendment
(ratified in 1870)

1870 Congress passes first Enforcement Act

1871 Congress passes second Enforcement Act
and Ku Klux Klan Act
Treaty with England settles *Alabama* claims

1872 Amnesty Act frees almost all remaining
Confederates from restrictions on holding
office
Liberal Republicans organize and oppose
Grant
Debtors urge government to keep greenbacks
in circulation
Grant reelected

1873 *Slaughter-House* cases limit power of
Fourteenth Amendment
Panic of 1873 sends economy into extended
depression, leading to widespread
unemployment and labor strife

1874 Grant vetoes increase in supply of paper
money
Democrats win majority in House of
Representatives

1875 Several Grant appointees indicted for
corruption
Congress passes weak Civil Rights Act
Congress requires that after 1878 greenbacks
be convertible into gold
Democratic Party continues to "redeem"
control of southern states with white
supremacy campaigns

1876 *U.S. v. Cruikshank* and *U.S. v. Reese* further
weaken Fourteenth Amendment
Presidential election disputed

1877 Congress elects Hayes president
Exodusters migrate to Kansas
"Home rule" returns to three remaining
southern states not yet controlled by
Democrats; Reconstruction considered
over

Abraham Lincoln had never been antisouthern,
though he had grown to become the leader of an
antislavery war. He lost three broth-

**Lincoln's
10 Percent Plan**

ers-in-law killed in the war on the
Confederate side. His worst fear was
that the war would collapse at the
end into guerrilla warfare across the
South, with surviving bands of Confederates carrying
on resistance. Lincoln insisted that his generals give
lenient terms to southern soldiers once they surrendered. He planned early for a swift and moderate
Reconstruction process. In his Second Inaugural Address, delivered only a month before his assassination,
Lincoln promised "malice toward none; with charity
for all," as Americans strove to "bind up the nation's
wounds."

In his "Proclamation of Amnesty and Reconstruction," issued in December 1863, Lincoln proposed to replace majority rule with "loyal rule" as a means of reconstructing southern state governments before hostilities ended. He envisioned Reconstruction as a process of experimentation. He proposed pardons to all ex-Confederates except the highest ranking military and civilian officers. Then, as soon as 10 percent of the voting population in the 1860 election had taken an oath and established a government, it would be recognized. Lincoln did not consult Congress in these plans, and "loyal" assemblies (known as "Lincoln governments") were created in Louisiana, Tennessee, and Arkansas in 1864, states largely occupied by Union troops. These governments were weak and dependent on northern armies for survival.

Congress responded with great hostility to Lincoln's moves to readmit southern states in what seemed such a premature manner. Many Radical Republicans, strong proponents of emancipation and aggressive prosecution of the war against the South, considered the 10 percent plan a "mere mockery" of democracy. Led by Thaddeus Stevens of Pennsylvania in the House and Charles Sumner of Massachusetts in the Senate, congressional Republicans locked horns with Lincoln and proposed a longer and harsher approach to Reconstruction. Stevens advocated a "conquered provinces" theory, and Sumner, recovered from his beating at the hands of Preston Brooks (see page 375), employed an argument of "state suicide." Both contended that southerners had organized as a foreign nation to make war on the United States and, by secession, had destroyed their status as states. They therefore must be treated as "conquered foreign lands" and reverted to the status of "unorganized territories" before any process of readmission could be entertained (by Congress).

Congress and the Wade-Davis Bill

In July 1864, the Wade-Davis bill, named for its sponsors, Senator Benjamin Wade of Ohio and Congressman Henry W. Davis of Maryland, emerged from Congress with three specific conditions for southern readmission: one, it demanded a "majority" of white male citizens participating in the creation of a new government; two, to vote or be a delegate to constitutional conventions, men had to take an "iron-clad" oath (declaring they had never aided the Confederate war effort); and three, all officers above the rank of lieutenant, and all civil officials in the Confederacy,

would be disfranchised and deemed "not a citizen of the United States." The Confederate states were to be defined as "conquered enemies," said Davis, and the process of readmission was to be harsh and slow. Lincoln, ever the adroit politician, pocket-vetoed the bill and issued a conciliatory proclamation of his own announcing that he would not be inflexibly committed to any "one plan" of Reconstruction.

The timing of this exchange came during Grant's bloody campaign in Virginia against Lee. The outcome of the war and Lincoln's reelection were still in doubt. Radical members of his own party, indeed, were organizing a dump-Lincoln campaign for the 1864 election. On August 5, Radical Republicans issued the "Wade-Davis Manifesto" to newspapers, which contained an unprecedented attack on a sitting president by members of his own party. They accused Lincoln of usurpation of presidential powers and disgraceful leniency toward an eventually conquered South. What emerged in 1864–1865 was a clear-cut debate and a potential constitutional crisis. Lincoln saw Reconstruction as a means of weakening the Confederacy and winning the war; the Radicals saw it as a longer-term transformation of the political and racial order of the country.

In early 1865, Congress and Lincoln joined in passing two important measures that recognized slavery's centrality to the war. On January 31, with strong administration backing, Congress passed the Thirteenth Amendment, which had two provisions. It abolished involuntary servitude everywhere in the United States and declared that Congress shall have power to enforce this outcome by "appropriate legislation." When the measure passed by 119 to 56, a mere two votes more than the necessary two-thirds, unprecedented rejoicing broke out in Congress. A Republican recorded in his diary: "Members joined in the shouting and kept it up for some minutes. Some embraced one another, others wept like children. I have felt ever since the vote, as if I were in a new country."

Thirteenth Amendment and the Freedmen's Bureau

Potentially as significant, on March 3, 1865, Congress created the Bureau of Refugees, Freedmen, and Abandoned Lands—the Freedmen's Bureau, an unprecedented agency of social uplift, necessitated by the ravages of the war. Americans had never engaged in federal aid to citizens on such a scale. With thousands of refugees, white and black, displaced in the South, the government continued what private freedmen's aid societies had started as early as 1862. In the mere four years of its existence, the Freedmen's Bureau supplied food and medical services, built several thousand schools and some colleges, negotiated several hundred thousand employment contracts between freedmen and their former masters, and tried to manage confiscated land.

The Bureau would be a controversial aspect of Reconstruction, within the South where whites generally hated it, and within the federal government where politicians divided over its constitutionality. Some Bureau agents were devoted to freedmen's rights, while others were opportunists who exploited the chaos of the postwar South. The war had forced into the open an eternal question of republics: What are the social welfare obligations of the state toward its people, and what do people owe their governments in return? Apart from their conquest and displacement of the eastern Indians, Americans were relatively inexperienced at the Freedmen's Bureau's task—social reform through military occupation.

The Meanings of Freedom

Black southerners entered into life after slavery with hope and circumspection. A Texas man recalled his father telling him, even before the war was over, "Our forever was going to be spent living among the Southerners, after they got licked." Expecting hostility, freed men and women tried to gain as much as they could from their new circumstances. Often the changes they valued the most were personal—alterations in location, employer, or living arrangements.

For America's former slaves, Reconstruction had one paramount meaning: a chance to explore freedom.

The Feel of Freedom

A southern white woman admitted in her diary that the black people "showed a natural and exultant joy at being free." Former slaves remembered singing far into the night after federal troops, who confirmed rumors of their emancipation, reached their plantations. The slaves on a Texas plantation shouted for joy, their leader proclaiming,

Post-emancipation society in the South brought about the renegotiation of old relationships, as in the scene depicted in Winslow Homer's *A Visit From the Old Mistress* (1876). (National Gallery of American Art/Art Resource)

"We is free—no more whippings and beatings." A few people gave in to the natural desire to do what had been impossible before. One angry grandmother dropped her hoe and ran to confront her mistress. "I'm free!" she yelled. "Yes, I'm free! Ain't got to work for you no more! You can't put me in your pocket [sell me] now!" Another man recalled that he and others "started on the move," either to search for family members or just to exercise the human right of mobility.

Many freed men and women reacted more cautiously and shrewdly, taking care to test the boundaries of their new condition. "After the war was over," explained one man, "we was afraid to move. Just like terrapins or turtles after emancipation. Just stick our heads out to see how the land lay." As slaves they had learned to expect hostility from white people, and they did not presume it would instantly disappear. Life in freedom might still be a matter of what was allowed, not what was right. "You got to say master?" asked a freedman in Georgia. "Naw," answered his fellows, but "they said it all the same." One sign of this shrewd caution was the way freed people evaluated potential employers. "Most all the Negroes that had good owners stayed with 'em, but the others left. Some of 'em come back and some didn't," explained one man. After considerable wandering in search of better circumstances, a majority of blacks eventually settled as agricultural workers back on their former farms or plantations. But they relocated their houses and did their utmost to control the conditions of their labor.

Former slaves concentrated on improving their daily lives. Throughout the South they devoted themselves to reuniting their families, separated during slavery by sale or hardship, and during the war by dislocation and the emancipation process. The search for family members who had been sold away during slavery was awe inspiring. With only shreds of information to guide them, thousands of freed people embarked on odysseys in search of a husband, wife, child, or parent. By relying on the black community for help and information, and placing ads in black newspapers that continued to appear well into the 1880s, some succeeded in their quest, sometimes almost miraculously. Others trudged through several states and never found loved ones.

Reunion of African American Families

Husbands and wives who had belonged to different masters established homes together for the first time, and parents asserted the right to raise their own children. A mother bristled when her old master claimed a right to whip her children. She informed him that "he warn't goin' to brush none of her chilluns no more." The freed men and women were too much at risk to act recklessly, but, as one man put it, they were tired of punishment and "sure didn't take no more foolishment off of white folks."

Many black people wanted to minimize contact with whites because, as Reverend Garrison Frazier told General Sherman in January 1865, "There is a prejudice against us . . . that will take years to get over." To avoid contact with overbearing whites who were used to supervising them, blacks abandoned the slave quarters and fanned out to distant corners of the land they worked. "After the war my stepfather come," recalled Annie Young, "and got my mother and we moved out in the piney woods." Others described moving "across the creek to [themselves]" or building a "saplin house . . . back in the woods." Some rural dwellers established small all-black settlements that still exist today along the back roads of the South.

Blacks' Search for Independence

Even once-privileged slaves desired such independence and social separation. One man turned down the master's offer of the overseer's house and moved instead to a shack in "Freetown." He also declined to let the former owner grind his grain for free because it "make him feel like a free man to pay for things just like anyone else." One couple, a carriage driver and trusted house servant during slavery, passed up the fine cooking of the "big house" to move "in the colored settlement."

In addition to a fair employer, what freed men and women most wanted was the ownership of land. Land represented their chance to farm for themselves, to enjoy the independence that self-sufficient farmers value. It represented compensation for generations of travail in bondage.

African Americans' Desire for Land

A northern observer noted that slaves freed in the Sea Islands of South Carolina and Georgia made "plain, straight-forward" inquiries as they settled the land set aside for them by Sherman. They wanted to be sure the land "would be theirs after they had improved it." Everywhere, blacks young and old thirsted for homes of their own.

But how much of a chance would whites give to blacks? Most members of both political parties opposed genuine land redistribution to the freedmen. Even northern reformers who with Lincoln's encouragement had administered the Sea Islands during the war showed little sympathy for black aspirations. The former Sea Island slaves wanted to establish small, self-sufficient farms. Northern soldiers, officials, and missionaries of both races brought education and aid to the freedmen but also insisted that they grow cotton. They emphasized profit, cash crops, and the values of competitive capitalism.

"The Yankees preach nothing but cotton, cotton!" complained one Sea Island black. "We wants land," wrote another, but tax officials "make the lots too big, and cut we out." Indeed, the U.S. government sold thousands of acres in the Sea Islands for nonpayment of taxes, but 90 percent of the land went to wealthy investors from the North. At a protest against evictions from a contraband camp in Virginia in 1866, freedman Bayley Wyatt made black desires and claims clear: "We has a right to the land where we are located. For why? I tell you. Our wives, our children, our husbands, has been sold over and over again to purchase the lands we now locates upon; for that reason we have a divine right to the land."

Ex-slaves reached out for valuable things in life that had been denied them. One of these was education. Blacks of all ages hungered for the knowledge in books that had been permitted only to whites. With freedom, they started schools and filled classrooms both day and night. On log seats and dirt floors, freed men and women studied their letters in old almanacs and discarded dictionaries. Young children brought infants to school with them, and adults attended at night or after "the crops were laid by." Many a teacher had "to make herself heard over three other classes reciting in concert" in a small room. The desire to escape slavery's ignorance was so great that, despite their poverty, many blacks paid tuition, typically $1 or $1.50 a month. These small amounts constituted major portions of a person's agricultural wages and added up to more than $1 million by 1870.

The federal government and northern reformers of both races assisted this pursuit of education. In its brief life the Freedmen's Bureau founded over four thousand schools, and idealistic men and women from the North established and staffed others founded by private northern philanthropy. The Yankee schoolmarm—dedicated, selfless, and religious—became an agent of progress in many southern communities. Thus did African Americans seek a break from their pasts through learning. The results included the beginnings of a public school system in each southern

The Black Embrace of Education

African Americans of all ages eagerly pursued the opportunity in freedom to gain an education. This young woman in Mt. Meigs, Alabama, is helping her mother learn to read.   (Smithsonian Institute, photo by Rudolf Eickemeyer)

state and the enrollment of over six hundred thousand African Americans in elementary school by 1877.

Blacks and their white allies also saw the need for colleges and universities to train teachers, ministers, and professionals for leadership. The American Missionary Association founded seven colleges, including Fisk and Atlanta Universities, between 1866 and 1869. The Freedmen's Bureau helped to establish Howard University in Washington, D.C., and northern religious groups such as the Methodists, Baptists, and Congregationalists supported dozens of seminaries and teachers' colleges. By the late 1870s black churches had joined in the effort, founding numerous colleges despite limited resources.

During Reconstruction, African American leaders often were highly educated individuals; many of them came from the prewar elite of free people of color. This group had benefited from its association with wealthy whites, many of whom were blood relatives; some planters had given their mulatto children an outstanding education. Francis Cardozo, who held various offices in South Carolina, had attended universities in Scotland and England. P. B. S. Pinchback, who became lieutenant governor of Louisiana, was the son of a planter who had sent him to school in Cincinnati. Both of the two black senators from Mississippi, Blanche K. Bruce and Hiram Revels, possessed privileged educations. Bruce was the son of a planter who had provided tutoring at home; Revels was the son of free North Carolina mulattos who had sent him to Knox College in Illinois. These men and many self-educated former slaves brought to political office their experience as artisans, businessmen, lawyers, teachers, and preachers.

Freed from the restrictions and regulations of slavery, blacks could build their own institutions as they saw fit. The secret churches of slavery came into the open; in countless communities throughout the South, ex-slaves "started a brush arbor." A brush arbor was merely "a sort of . . . shelter with leaves for a roof," but the freed men and women worshiped in it enthusiastically. "Preachin' and

Growth of Black Churches

shouting sometimes lasted all day," they recalled, for the opportunity to worship together freely meant "glorious times."

Within a few years independent branches of the Methodist and Baptist denominations had attracted the great majority of black Christians in the South. By 1877, in South Carolina alone, the African Methodist Episcopal Church had 1,000 ministers, 44,000 members, and its own school of theology, while the A.M.E. Zion Church had 45,000 members. In the rapid growth of churches, some of which became the wealthiest and the most autonomous institutions in black life, the freedpeople demonstrated their most secure claim on freedom as they created enduring communities.

The desire to gain as much independence as possible also shaped the former slaves' economic arrangements. Since most of them lacked money to buy land, they preferred the next best thing: renting the land they worked. But the South had a cash-poor economy with few sources of credit, and few whites would consider renting land to blacks. Most blacks had no means to get cash before the harvest, and thus other alternatives had to be tried.

Rise of the Sharecropping System

Churches became a center of African American life, for social and political purposes as well as for worship. This engraving, which appeared in *Harper's Weekly* in 1874, shows the minister of the First African Baptist Church of Richmond, Virginia, preaching to the congregation from an elevated pulpit.   (The Valentine Museum, Richmond, Virginia)

Sharecropping became an oppressive system in the postwar South. At plantation stores like this one, photographed in Mississippi in 1868, merchants recorded in their ledger books debts that few sharecroppers were able to repay. (Recordbook: Smithsonian Institute, Division of Community Life; Plantation store: Amistad Foundation Collection at the Wadsworth Athenaeum, Hartford, Connecticut)

Black farmers and white landowners therefore turned to sharecropping, a system in which farmers kept part of their crop and gave the rest to the landowner while living on his property. The landlord or a merchant "furnished" food and supplies needed before the harvest, and he received payment from the crop. Republican laws gave laborers the first lien, or legal claim, on the crop, enhancing their sense of ownership. Although landowners tried to set the laborers' share at a low level, black farmers had some bargaining power, at least at first. Sharecroppers would hold out, or move and try to switch employers from one year to another.

The sharecropping system, which materialized as early as 1868 in parts of the South, originated as a desirable compromise. It eased landowners' problems with cash and credit, and provided them a permanent, dependent labor force; blacks accepted it because it gave them more freedom from daily supervision. Instead of working under a white overseer, as in slavery, they farmed a plot of land on their own in family groups. But sharecropping later proved to be a disaster. Owners and merchants developed a monopoly of control over the agricultural economy, as sharecroppers found themselves riveted into ever-increasing debt (see pages 563–564).

The fundamental problem, however, was that southern farmers as a whole still concentrated on cotton, a crop with a bright past and a dim future. During the Civil War, India, Brazil, and Egypt had begun to supply cotton to Britain, and the South lost markets as well as income. In freedom, black women, like their white counterparts, often stayed away from the fields. Black families placed greater value on human dignity than on reaching higher levels of production. By 1878 the South had recovered its prewar share of British cotton purchases. But even as southerners grew more cotton, their reward diminished. Cotton prices began a long decline, as world demand fell off.

Overdependence on Cotton

In these circumstances overspecialization in cotton was a mistake, but for most southern farmers there was no alternative. Landowners required sharecroppers to grow the salable cash crop. Thus southern agriculture slipped deeper and deeper into depression. Black sharecroppers struggled under a growing burden of debt that reduced their independence and bound them to landowners and to furnishing merchants almost as oppressively as slavery had bound them to their masters. Many white farmers became debtors, too, and gradually lost their land. This economic transformation took place as the nation struggled to put its political house back in order.

Johnson's Reconstruction Plan

 When Reconstruction began under President Andrew Johnson, many expected his policies to be harsh. Throughout his career in Tennessee he had criticized the wealthy planters and championed the small farmers. When an assassin's bullet thrust Johnson into the presidency, many former slaveowners shared the dismay of a North Carolina woman who wrote, "Think of Andy Johnson [as] the president! What will become of us— 'the aristocrats of the South' as we are termed?" Northern Radicals also had reason to believe that Johnson would deal sternly with the South. When one of them suggested the exile or execution of ten or twelve leading rebels to set an example, Johnson replied, "How are you going to pick out so small a number? . . . Treason is a crime; and crime must be punished."

Like his martyred predecessor, Johnson followed a path in antebellum politics from obscurity to power. With no formal education, he became a tailor's apprentice. But from 1829, while in his early twenties, he held nearly every office in Tennessee politics: alderman, state representative, congressman, two terms as governor, and U.S. senator by 1857. Although elected as a southern Democrat, Johnson was the only senator from a seceded state who refused to follow his state out of the Union. Lincoln appointed him war governor of Tennessee in 1862, and hence, his symbolic place on the ticket in the president's bid for reelection in 1864.

Who Was Andrew Johnson?

Johnson's political beliefs made him look a little like a Republican, but at heart he was an old Jacksonian Democrat. And as they said in the mountainous region of east Tennessee, where Johnson established a reputation as a stump speaker, "Old Andy never went back on his 'raisin." Although a staunch Unionist, he was also an ardent states' rightist. Before the war, Johnson had supported tax-funded public schools and homestead legislation, fashioning himself as a champion of the common man. Although he vehemently opposed secession, Johnson advocated limited government. Above all, when it came to race, Johnson was a thoroughgoing white supremacist. He shared none of the Radicals' expansive conception of federal power. Johnson accepted emancipation as a result of the war, but he did not favor black civil and political rights. His philosophy toward Reconstruction may be summed up in the slogan he adopted: "The Constitution as it is, and the Union as it was."

Through 1865 Johnson alone controlled Reconstruction policy, for Congress recessed shortly before he became president and did not reconvene until December. In the following eight months, Johnson put into operation his own plan, forming new state governments in the South by using his power to grant pardons. Johnson followed Lincoln's leniency by extending even easier terms to southerners. But which southerners would be allowed to vote?

Johnson's Leniency and Racial Views

Johnson held that black suffrage could never be imposed on a southern state by the federal government. His racism put him on a collision course with the Radicals. Johnson held what one politician called "unconquerable prejudices against the African race." In perhaps the most blatantly racist official statement ever delivered by an American president, Johnson declared in his annual message of 1867 that blacks possessed less "capacity for government than any other race of people. No independent government of any form has ever been successful in their hands; . . . wherever they have been left to their own devices they have shown a constant tendency to relapse into barbarism."

This racial conservatism had an enduring effect on Johnson's policies. Where whites were concerned, however, Johnson seemed to be pursuing changes in class relations. He proposed rules that would keep the wealthy planter class at least temporarily out of power. White southerners were required to swear an oath of loyalty as a condition of gaining amnesty or pardon, but Johnson barred several categories of people from taking the oath: former federal officials, high-ranking Confederate officers, and political leaders or graduates of West Point or Annapolis who had violated their oaths to support the United States by aiding the Confederacy. To this list Johnson added another important group: all southerners who aided the rebellion and whose taxable property was worth more than $20,000. These individuals had to apply personally to the president for pardon and restoration of their political rights.

Thus it appeared that the leadership class of the Old South would be removed from power, for virtually all the rich and powerful whites of prewar days needed Johnson's special pardon. The president, it seemed, meant to take revenge on the haughty

Johnson's Pardon Policy

aristocrats and thereby promote a new leadership of deserving yeomen.

Johnson appointed provisional governors who began the Reconstruction process by calling constitutional conventions. The delegates chosen for these conventions had to draft new constitutions that eliminated slavery and invalidated secession. After ratification of these constitutions, new governments could be elected, and the states would be restored to the Union with full congressional representation. But only those southerners who had taken the oath of amnesty and been eligible to vote on the day the state seceded could participate in this process. Thus unpardoned whites and former slaves were not eligible.

If Johnson intended to strip the old elite of its power, he did not hold to his plan. The old white leadership proved resilient and influential; prominent Confederates (a few with pardons but many without) won elections and turned up in various appointive offices. Then, surprisingly, Johnson helped to subvert his own plan: he started pardoning aristocrats and leading rebels who should not have been in office. He hired additional clerks to write out the necessary documents and then began to issue pardons to large categories of people. By September 1865 hundreds were being issued in a single day. These pardons, plus the rapid return of planters' abandoned lands, restored the old elite to power and quickly gave Johnson the image as the South's champion. He further gained southern loyalty with his hostility to the Freedmen's Bureau.

Why did Johnson allow the planters to regain power? Perhaps vanity betrayed his judgment. Too long an isolated outsider, Johnson may have succumbed to the attention and flattery of the pardon seekers. He was also determined upon a rapid Reconstruction in order to deny the Radicals the opportunity for the more thorough racial and political changes they desired in the South. And, given Johnson's need for southern support in the 1866 elections, he decided to endorse the new governments and declare Reconstruction complete only eight months after Appomattox. Thus in December 1865 many Confederate congressmen traveled to Washington to claim seats in the U.S. Congress. Even Alexander Stephens, vice president of the Confederacy, returned to Capitol Hill as a senator-elect.

The election of such prominent rebels troubled many northerners. So did other results of Johnson's program. Some of the state conventions were slow to repudiate secession; others admitted only grudgingly that slavery was dead. Two refused to take any action

Combative and inflexible, President Andrew Johnson contributed greatly to the failure of his own Reconstruction program.   (Library of Congress)

to repudiate the large Confederate debt, which northerners felt should not be paid. Even Johnson admitted that these acts showed "something like defiance, which is all out of place at this time."

Furthermore, to define the status of freed men and women and control their labor, some legislatures merely revised large sections of the slave codes by substituting the word *freedmen* for *slaves*. The new black codes compelled the former slaves, now supposedly free, to carry passes, observe a curfew, live in housing provided by a landowner, and give up hope of entering many desirable occupations. Stiff vagrancy laws and restrictive labor contracts bound supposedly free laborers to plantations, and "anti-enticement" laws punished anyone who tried to lure these workers to other employment. State-supported schools and orphanages excluded blacks entirely.

Black Codes

It seemed to northerners that the South was intent on returning African Americans to servility and that

Johnson's Reconstruction policy held no one responsible for the terrible war. But memories of the war—not yet a year over—were still raw, and would dominate political behavior for several elections to come. Thus the Republican majority in Congress decided to call a halt to the results of Johnson's plan. On reconvening, the House and Senate considered the credentials of the newly elected southern representatives and decided not to admit them. Instead, they bluntly challenged the president's authority and established a joint committee to study and investigate a new direction for Reconstruction.

The Congressional Reconstruction Plan

Northern congressmen were hardly unified, but they did not doubt their right to shape Reconstruction policy. The Constitution mentioned neither secession nor reunion, but it gave Congress the primary role in the admission of states. Moreover, the Constitution declared that the United States shall guarantee to each state a republican form of government. This provision, legislators believed, gave them the authority to devise policies for Reconstruction.

They soon found that other constitutional questions affected their policies. What, for example, had rebellion done to the relationship between southern states and the Union? Lincoln had always insisted that states could not secede—they had engaged in an "insurrection"—and that the Union remained intact. Not even Andrew Johnson, however, accepted the southern position that state governments of the Confederacy could simply reenter the nation. Johnson argued that the Union had endured, though individuals had erred—thus the use of his power to grant or withhold pardons. Congressmen who favored vigorous Reconstruction measures argued that the war had broken the Union, and that the South was subject to the victor's will. Moderate congressmen held that the states had forfeited their rights through rebellion and thus had come under congressional supervision.

These theories mirrored the diversity of Congress itself. Northern Democrats, weakened by the war most of them had opposed in its final year, denounced any idea of racial equality and supported Johnson's policies. Conservative Republicans, despite their party loyalty, favored a limited federal role in Reconstruction. The Radical Republicans, led by

The Radicals

Thaddeus Stevens, Charles Sumner, and George Julian, wanted to transform the South. Although they were a minority within their party, they had the advantage of a clearly defined goal. They believed it was essential to democratize the South, establish public education, and ensure the rights of freed people. They favored black suffrage, often supported land confiscation and redistribution, and were willing to exclude the South from the Union for several years if necessary to achieve their goals. Born of the war and its outcome, the Radicals brought a new civic vision to American life; they wanted to create an activist federal government and the beginnings of racial equality. A large group of moderate Republicans did not want to go as far as the Radicals but believed some reworking of Johnson's policies was necessary.

One overwhelming political reality faced all four groups: the 1866 elections were approaching in the fall. Having questioned Johnson's program, Congress needed to develop an alternative plan and avoid going before the voters empty-handed. Ironically, Johnson and the Democrats sabotaged the possibility of a conservative coalition. They refused to cooperate with conservative or moderate Republicans and insisted that Reconstruction was over, that the new state governments were legitimate, and that southern representatives should be admitted to Congress. To devise a Republican program, conservative and moderate elements in the party had to work with the Radicals, whose influence grew in proportion to Johnson's intransigence.

Trying to work with Johnson, Republicans believed a compromise had been reached in the spring of 1866. Under its terms Johnson would agree to two modifications of his program: extension of the life of the Freedmen's Bureau for another year and passage of a civil rights bill to counteract the black codes. This bill would force southern courts to practice equality before the law by allowing federal judges to remove from state courts cases in which blacks were treated unfairly. Its provisions applied to public, not private, acts of discrimination. The civil rights bill of 1866 was the first statutory definition of the rights of American citizens.

Congress Wrests Control from Johnson

Johnson destroyed the compromise, however, by vetoing both bills (they later became law when Congress overrode the president's veto). Denouncing any change in his program, the president condemned Congress's action and revealed his own racism. Because the civil rights bill defined U.S. citizens as native-born

How do historians know...

that the Radical Republican vision of Reconstruction had a popular base and was not solely the creation of a few ambitious politicians? How do we understand and evaluate the contending wills and bitterness that existed in North and South as Reconstruction policies developed? Moreover, why did the Republicans take back control of the Reconstruction process from President Andrew Johnson in late 1865 and throughout 1866? This excerpt from a letter by Brigadier General James S. Brisbin on December 29, 1865, to Congressman Thaddeus Stevens (the principal architect of Radical Reconstruction) indicates both practical and philosophical reasons why many northerners supported a harsher plan for bringing the South back into the Union than Johnson had put in place. Brisbin had just read Stevens's speech on Reconstruction in Congress, in which the congressman had called for a halt to the seating of any representatives elected by the "Johnson governments" and proposed a lengthy investigation of southern conditions. Brisbin speaks as soldier and citizen, fearing that "the fruits of our toils and battles and sieges were to be bartered away and treason made as honorable as loyalty." Brisbin, who was commanding occupation troops in Arkansas, encouraged Stevens in his effort to slow down Reconstruction. "These people are not loyal," he writes; "they are only conquered." The letter anticipates much of what soon occurred in the bitter struggle to bind up sectional hatreds and respond to the profound challenges of emancipation and reunion. If Stevens needed any encouragement or justification in leading Congress in taking control of Reconstruction, he received it in this letter. This photograph of Congressman Thaddeus Stevens was taken during the early years of Reconstruction. (Photo: National Archives)

After four years of war during which we suffered all that men could suffer and after finally beating the rebles in battle we began to fear that the fruits of our toils our battles and seiges were to be bartered away and treason made as honorable as loyalty. For the assurance that rebles whose hands red with the blood of our brothers, are not just yet to be allowed to set themselves up to rule over us, thousands of loyal soldiers will thank you. . . .

These people are not loyal; they are only conquered, I tell you there is not as much loyalty in the South to day as there was the day Lee surrendered to Grant. The moment they lost their cause in the field they set about to gain by politics what they had failed to obtain by force of arms. . . .

My God can any sane man look at the men who fill their so called state Legislatures and then say the states are loyal. . . .

The bones of our dead brothers, falling in the great struggle lie buried in the soil of every Southern state and at least until they have returned to dust and their graves grown green we should not shake the bloody hands of the men who robbed them of life. The immodest haste (and it should be called brazen impudence) of the Southern people in attempting to get their delegations into Congress should be sufficient to arouse the suspicions of every Northern man that they were not sincere. . . .

These people are most anxious to renew their practical relations with the Federal Govt because . . . then they can go to work in earnest in their state Legislatures to pass vagrant laws and reduce the blacks to a slavery worse than that from which they have just escaped. Loyal men will not be elected to office in the South until the blacks are allowed to vote and I hope you will not allow any Southern member of his seat until he comes there elected by a majority _of all the people of his District_. I am no politician but what I see I know and I tell you you are right in what you said on re-construction. . . .

In 1866, as Congress reviewed the progress of Reconstruction, news from the South had a considerable impact. Violence against black people, like the riot in Memphis depicted here, helped convince northern legislators that they had to modify President Johnson's policies. (Library of Congress)

persons who were taxed, Johnson claimed it discriminated against "large numbers of intelligent, worthy, and patriotic foreigners . . . in favor of the negro." The bill, he said, operated "in favor of the colored and against the white race."

All hope of presidential-congressional cooperation was now dead. In 1866 newspapers reported daily violations of blacks' rights in the South and carried alarming accounts of antiblack violence—notably in Memphis and New Orleans, where police aided brutal mobs in their attacks. In Memphis forty blacks were killed and twelve schools burned by white mobs, and in New Orleans the toll was thirty-four African Americans dead and two hundred wounded. Such violence convinced Republicans, and the northern public, that more needed to be done. A new Republican plan took the form of a proposed amendment to the Constitution, forged out of a compromise between radical and conservative elements of the party. The Fourteenth Amendment, passed and sent to the states in June 1866, was Congress's alternative to Johnson's program of Reconstruction.

Of the four parts of the Fourteenth Amendment, the first would have the greatest legal significance in later years. It conferred citizenship on the freedmen

The Fourteenth Amendment

and prohibited states from abridging their constitutional "privileges and immunities" (see the Constitution in this book's Appendix). It also barred any state from taking a person's life, liberty, or property "without due process of law" and from denying "equal protection of the laws." These resounding phrases became powerful guarantees of African Americans' civil rights—indeed, of the rights of all citizens—in the twentieth century.

Nearly universal agreement emerged among Republicans on the amendment's second and third provisions. The second declared the Confederate debt null and void and guaranteed the war debt of the United States. Northerners rejected the notion of paying taxes to reimburse those who had financed a rebellion, and business groups agreed on the necessity of upholding the credit of the U.S. government. The third provision barred Confederate leaders from holding state and federal office. Only Congress, by a two-thirds vote of each house, could remove the penalty. The amendment thus guaranteed a degree of punishment for the leaders of the Confederacy.

The fourth part of the amendment dealt with representation and embodied the compromises that produced the document. Northerners disagreed about whether black citizens should have the right to vote. As a citizen of Indiana wrote to a southern relative, there was strong feeling in favor of "humane and liberal laws for the government and protection of the colored population." But there was prejudice, too. "Although there is a great deal [of] profession among us for the relief of the darkey yet I think much of it is far from being sincere. I guess we want to compell you to do right by them while we are not willing ourselves to do so." Those arched words are indicative of not only how revolutionary Reconstruction had become, but also how far the public will lagged behind the enactments that became new constitutional cornerstones.

Republican congressmen shied away from confronting this ambivalence, but political reality required them to do something. Emancipation made every former slave a full rather than three-fifths of a person, which would increase southern representation. Thus the postwar South stood to gain power in Congress, and if white southerners did not allow blacks to vote, former secessionists would derive the political benefit from emancipation. That was more irony than most northerners could bear. So Republicans determined that if a southern state did not grant black men the vote, their representation would be reduced proportionally. If they did enfranchise black men, their representation would be increased proportionally. This compromise avoided a direct enactment of black suffrage, but would deliver future black voters to the Republican Party.

The Fourteenth Amendment paved the way for black male suffrage but ignored female citizens, black and white. For this reason it provoked a strong reaction from the women's rights movement. Advocates of women's equality had worked with abolitionists for decades, often subordinating their cause to that of the slaves. During the drafting of the Fourteenth Amendment, however, female activists demanded to be heard. When legislators defined women as nonvoting citizens, prominent leaders such as Elizabeth Cady Stanton and Susan B. Anthony decided that it was time to end their alliance with abolitionists and fight more determinedly for themselves. Thus the amendment infused new life into the women's rights movement and caused considerable strife among old allies. Many male former abolitionists, white and black, were willing to delay the day of woman suffrage in favor of securing freed men the right to vote in the South.

In 1866, however, the major question in Reconstruction politics was how the public would respond to the congressional initiative. Johnson did his best to

The South's and Johnson's Defiance, 1866

block the Fourteenth Amendment in both North and South. Condemning Congress for its refusal to seat southern representatives, the president urged state legislatures in the South to vote against ratification. Every southern legislature except Tennessee's rejected the amendment by a wide margin. In three other states the amendment received no support at all.

To present his case to northerners, Johnson organized a National Union Convention and took to the stump himself. In an age when active personal campaigning was rare for a president, Johnson boarded a special train for a "swing around the circle" that carried his message deep into the Northeast, the Midwest, and then back to Washington. In city after city, he criticized the Republicans in a ranting, undignified style. Increasingly, audiences rejected his views and hooted and jeered at him. In this whistle-stop tour, Johnson began to hand out American flags with thirty-six rather than twenty-five stars, declaring that the Union was already restored. At many towns he likened himself to a "persecuted" Jesus who might now be martyred "upon the cross" for his magnanimity toward the South. And, repeatedly, he labeled the Radicals "traitors" for their efforts to take over Reconstruction. Johnson was shouted down and forced from the stage in Pittsburgh.

The elections of 1866 were a resounding victory for Republicans in Congress. Radicals and moderates whom Johnson had denounced won reelection by large margins, and the Republican majority grew to two-thirds of both houses of Congress. The North had spoken clearly: Johnson's policies were prematurely giving the advantage to rebels and traitors. Although the Radicals may have been out ahead of public opinion, most northerners feared for "the future peace and safety of the Union" if Johnson's approach to Reconstruction prevailed. Thus Republican congressional leaders won a mandate to pursue their Reconstruction plan.

But, thanks to Johnson and southern intransigence, that plan had reached an impasse. Nothing could be accomplished as long as the "Johnson governments" existed and the southern electorate remained exclusively white. Republicans resolved to form new state governments in the South and enfranchise the freedmen. The unavoidable logic of the situation forced the majority to accept the Radical plan. (See Table 16.1.)

After some embittered debate in which Republicans and the remaining Democrats in Congress argued

Table 16.1   Plans for Reconstruction Compared

	Johnson's Plan	Radicals' Plan	Fourteenth Amendment	Reconstruction Act of 1867
Voting	Whites only; high-ranking Confederate leaders must seek pardons	Give vote to black males	Southern whites may decide but can lose representation if they deny black suffrage	Black men gain vote; whites barred from office by Fourteenth Amendment cannot vote while new state governments are being formed
Officeholding	Many prominent Confederates regain power	Only loyal white and black males eligible	Confederate leaders barred until Congress votes amnesty	Fourteenth Amendment in effect
Time out of Union	Brief	Several years; until South is thoroughly democratized	Brief	3–5 years after war
Other change in southern society	Little; gain of power by yeomen not realized; emancipation grudgingly accepted, but no black civil or political rights	Expand public education; confiscate land and provide farms for freedmen; expansion of activist federal government	Probably slight, depending on enforcement	Considerable, depending on action of new state governments

The Reconstruction Acts of 1867–1868

over the meaning and memory of the Civil War itself, the First Reconstruction Act passed in March 1867. This plan, under which the southern states were actually readmitted to the Union, incorporated only a part of the Radical program. Union generals, commanding small garrisons of troops and charged with supervising all elections, assumed control in five military districts in the South (see Map 16.1). Confederate leaders designated in the Fourteenth Amendment were barred from voting until new state constitutions were ratified. The act guaranteed freedmen the right to vote in elections for state constitutional conventions and in subsequent elections. In addition, each southern state was required to ratify the Fourteenth Amendment, to ratify its new constitution by majority vote, and to submit it to Congress for approval.

Thus African Americans gained an opportunity to fight for a better life through the political process, and ex-Confederates were given what they interpreted as a bitter pill to swallow in order to return to the Union. The Second, Third, and Fourth Reconstruction Acts, passed between March 1867 and March 1868, provided for the details of operation for voter registration boards, the adoption of constitutions, and the administration of "good faith" oaths on the part of white southerners.

In the words of one historian, the Radicals succeeded in "clipping Johnson's wings." But they had hoped Congress could do much more. Thaddeus Stevens, for example, argued that economic opportunity was essential to the freedmen. "If we do not furnish them with homesteads from forfeited and rebel property," Stevens declared, "and hedge them around with protective laws . . . we had better left them in bondage." Stevens therefore drew up a plan for extensive confiscation and redistribution of land. Only one-tenth of the land affected by his plan was earmarked for freedmen, in 40-acre plots. The rest was to be sold to generate money for Union veterans' pensions, compensation to loyal southerners for damaged property, and payment of the federal debt.

The Failure of Land Redistribution

By these means Stevens hoped to win support for a basically unpopular measure. But he failed, and in general the Radicals were not able to generate public support. Northerners were accustomed to a limited role for government, and the business community staunchly opposed any interference with private property rights, even for former Confederates. Thus black

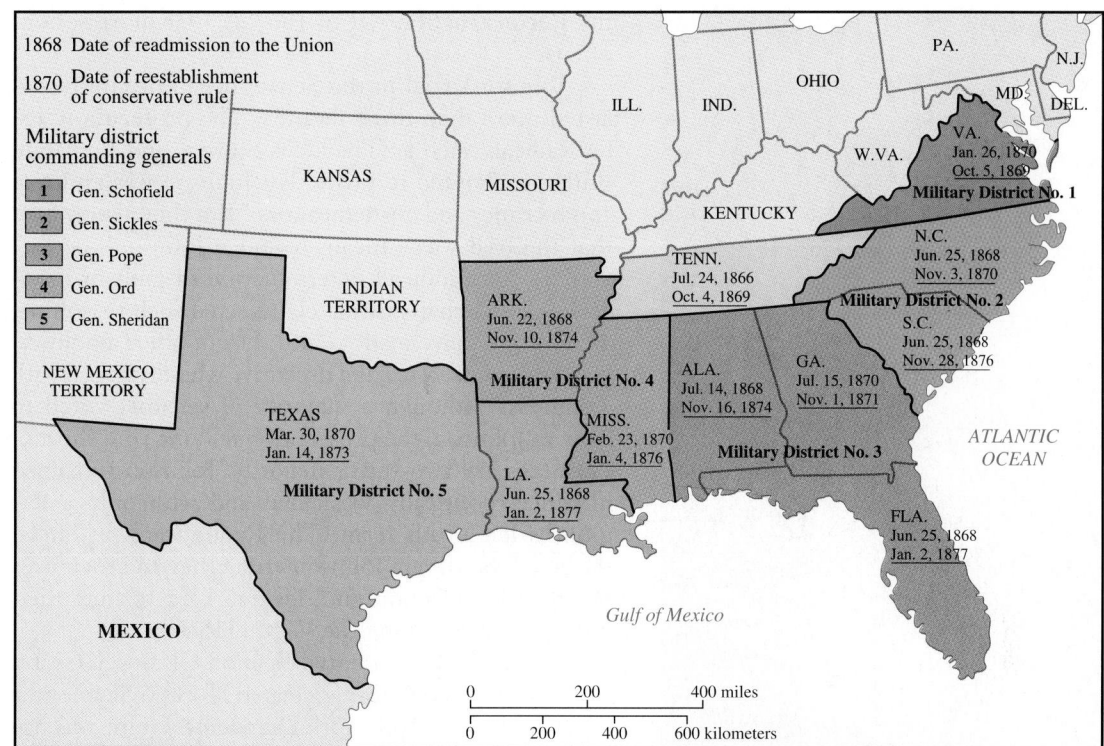

1868 Date of readmission to the Union

1870 Date of reestablishment of conservative rule

Military district commanding generals

1 Gen. Schofield

2 Gen. Sickles

3 Gen. Pope

4 Gen. Ord

5 Gen. Sheridan

Map 16.1   The Reconstruction   This map shows the five military districts established when Congress passed the Reconstruction Act of 1867. As the dates within each state indicate, conservative Democratic forces quickly regained control of government in four southern states. So-called Radical Reconstruction was curtailed in most of the others as factions within the weakened Republican Party began to cooperate with conservative Democrats.

farmers were forced to seek work in a hostile environment in which landowners opposed their acquisition of land, even as renters.

Congress's role as the architect of Reconstruction was not quite over, for its quarrels with Andrew Johnson were growing more bitter. To

Constitutional Crisis

restrict Johnson's influence and safeguard its plan, Congress passed a number of controversial laws. First, it set the date for its own reconvening—an unprecedented act, for the president traditionally summoned legislators to Washington. Then it limited Johnson's power over the army by requiring the president to issue military orders through the General of the Army, Ulysses S. Grant, who could not be dismissed without the Senate's consent. Finally, Congress passed the Tenure of Office Act, which gave the Senate power to approve changes in the president's cabinet. Designed to protect Secretary of War Stanton, who sympathized with the Radicals, this law violated the tradition that a president controlled appointments to his own cabinet.

All of these measures, as well as each of the Reconstruction Acts, were passed by a two-thirds override of presidential vetoes. The situation led some to believe that the federal government had reached a stage of "congressional tyranny," and others to conclude that Johnson had become an obstacle to the legitimate will of the people in reconstructing the nation on a just and permanent basis.

Johnson took several belligerent steps of his own. He issued orders to military commanders in the South limiting their powers and increasing the powers of the civil governments he had created in 1865. Then he removed military officers who were conscientiously enforcing Congress's new law, preferring commanders who allowed disqualified Confederates to vote. Finally, he tried to remove Secretary of War Stanton. With that attempt the confrontation reached its climax.

Impeachment is a political procedure provided for in the Constitution. It is a remedy for crimes or serious abuses of power by presidents, federal judges, and other high officials in the government. Those who are impeached (judged or politically indicted) in the

Thomas Waterman Wood, who had painted portraits of society figures in Nashville before the war, sensed the importance of Congress's decision in 1867 to enfranchise the freedmen. This oil painting, one of a series on suffrage, emphasizes the significance of the ballot for the black voter. (Cheekwood Museum of Art, Nashville, Tennessee)

Impeachment of President Johnson

House are then tried in the Senate. Historically, this power has generally not been used as a means to investigate and judge the private lives of presidents, although in recent times it was used in this manner in the case of President Bill Clinton.

Twice in 1867, the House Judiciary Committee had considered impeachment of Johnson, rejecting the idea once and then recommending it by only a 5-to-4 vote. That recommendation was decisively defeated by the House. After Johnson tried to remove Stanton, however, a third attempt to impeach the president carried easily. The indictment concentrated on his violation of the Tenure of Office Act, though modern scholars regard his efforts to impede enforcement of

the Reconstruction Act of 1867 as a far more serious offense.

Johnson's trial in the Senate began promptly and lasted more than three months. The prosecution, led by Radicals such as Thaddeus Stevens and Benjamin Butler, attempted to prove that Johnson was guilty of "high crimes and misdemeanors." But they also argued that the trial was a means to judge Johnson's performance, not a judicial determination of guilt or innocence. The Senate ultimately rejected such reasoning, which could have made removal from office a political weapon against any chief executive who disagreed with Congress. Although a majority of senators voted to convict Johnson, the prosecution fell one vote short of the necessary two-thirds majority. Johnson remained in office, politically weakened and with only a few months left in his term. The Republicans, in effect, managed the vote in Johnson's trial; they had their eyes on the 1868 election and did not want to hurt their prospects of regaining the White House.

In the 1868 presidential election Ulysses S. Grant, running as a Republican, defeated Horatio Seymour, a New York Democrat. Grant was not a Radical, but his platform supported congressional Reconstruction and endorsed black suffrage in the South. (Significantly, Republicans stopped short of endorsing it in the North.) The Democrats, meanwhile, vigorously denounced Reconstruction and thus renewed the sectional conflict. Indeed, in the 1868 election, the Democrats conducted the most openly white supremacist campaign to that time in American history. Both sides waved the "bloody shirt," accusing each other as the villains of the war's sacrifices. By associating themselves with rebellion and with Johnson's repudiated program, the Democrats went down to defeat in all but eight states, though the popular vote was fairly close. Participating in their first presidential election ever on a wide scale, blacks decisively voted en masse for General Grant.

Election of 1868

In office Grant acted as an administrator of Reconstruction but not as its enthusiastic advocate. He vacillated in his dealings with the southern states, sometimes defending Republican regimes and sometimes currying favor with Democrats. On occasion Grant called out federal troops to stop violence or enforce acts of Congress. But he never imposed a true military occupation on the South. Rapid demobilization had reduced a federal army of more than 1 million to 57,000 within a year of the surrender at Appomattox. Thereafter the number of troops in the South continued to fall, until in 1874 there were only 4,000

A Republican Party brass band in action during the 1868 election campaign in Baton Rouge, Louisiana. The Union regimental colors and soldier caps demonstrate the strong federal presence in the South at this pivotal moment in radical Reconstruction. (Andrew D. Lytle Collection, Louisiana and Lower Mississippi Valley Collections, LSU Libraries, Louisiana State University, Baton Rouge, La.)

in the southern states outside Texas. Throughout Reconstruction, the strongest federal units were in Texas and the West, fighting Indians, not white southerners. The later legend of "military rule," so important to southern claims of victimization during Reconstruction, was steeped in myth.

In 1869, in an effort to write democratic principles into the Constitution, the Radicals passed the Fifteenth Amendment. This measure forbade states to deny the right to vote "on account of race, color, or previous condition of servitude." Such wording did not guarantee the right to vote. It deliberately left states free to restrict suffrage on other grounds so that northern states could continue to deny suffrage to women and certain groups of men—Chinese immigrants, illiterates, and those too poor to pay poll taxes.

Fifteenth Amendment

Ironically, the votes of four uncooperative southern states—compelled by Congress to approve the amendment as an added condition to rejoining the Union—proved necessary to impose even this language on parts of the North. Although several states outside the South refused to ratify, three-fourths of the states approved the measure, and the Fifteenth Amendment became law in 1870. It too had been a political compromise, and though African Americans rejoiced all across the land at its enactment, it left open the possi-

bility for states to create countless qualification tests to obstruct voting in the future.

With passage of the Fifteenth Amendment, many Americans, especially supportive northerners, considered Reconstruction essentially completed. "Let us have done with Reconstruction," pleaded the *New York Tribune* in April 1870. "The country is tired and sick of it. . . . Let us have Peace!" But some northerners, like radical abolitionist Wendell Phillips, worried. "Our day," he warned, "is fast slipping away. Once let public thought float off from the great issue of the war, and it will take . . . more than a generation to bring it back again."

Reconstruction Politics in the South

 From the start, Reconstruction encountered the resistance of white southerners. In the black codes and in private attitudes, many whites stubbornly opposed emancipation, and the former planter class proved especially unbending. In 1866 a Georgia newspaper frankly observed that "most of the white citizens believe that the institution of slavery was right, and . . . they will believe that the condition, which comes nearest to slavery, that can now be established will be the best."

Thomas Nast, in this 1868 cartoon, pictured the combination of forces that threatened the success of Reconstruction: southern opposition and the greed, partisanship, and racism of northern interests.   (Library of Congress)

Fearing loss of control over their slaves, some planters attempted to postpone freedom by denying or misrepresenting events. Former slaves reported that their owners "didn't tell them it was freedom" or "wouldn't let [them] go." Agents of the Freedmen's Bureau reported that "the old system of slavery [is] working with even more rigor than formerly at a few miles distant from any point where U.S. troops are stationed." To hold onto their workers, some landowners claimed control over black children and used guardianship and apprentice laws to bind black families to the plantation.

White Resistance

Whites also blocked blacks from acquiring land. A few planters divided up plots among their slaves, but most condemned the idea of making blacks landowners. A Georgia woman whose family was known for its support of religious education for slaves was outraged that two property owners planned to "rent their lands

to the Negroes!" Such action was, she declared, "injurious to the best interest of the community."

Adamant resistance by propertied whites soon manifested itself in other ways, including violence. In one North Carolina town a local magistrate clubbed a black man on a public street, and bands of "Regulators" terrorized blacks in parts of that state and in Kentucky. Such incidents were predictable in a defeated society in which many planters believed, as a South Carolinian put it, that blacks "can't be governed except with the whip."

After President Johnson encouraged the South to resist congressional Reconstruction, white conservatives worked hard to capture the new state governments. Many whites also boycotted the polls in an attempt to defeat Congress's plans; by sitting out the elections, whites might block the new constitutions, which had to be approved by a majority of registered voters. This tactic was tried in North Carolina and succeeded in Alabama, forcing Congress to base ratification of the Fourteenth Amendment and of new state constitutions on a majority of "votes cast" (the provision of the Fourth Reconstruction Act).

Very few black men stayed away from the polls. Enthusiastically and hopefully, they voted Republican.

Black Voters and Emergence of a Southern Republican Party

Most agreed with one man who felt he should "stick to the end with the party that freed me." Illiteracy did not prohibit blacks (or uneducated whites) from making intelligent choices. Although Mississippi's William Henry could read only "a little," he testified that he and his friends had no difficulty selecting the Republican ballot. "We stood around and watched," he explained. "We saw D. Sledge vote; he owned half the county. We knowed he voted Democratic so we voted the other ticket so it would be Republican." Women, who could not vote, encouraged their husbands and sons, and preachers exhorted their congregations to use the franchise. With such group spirit, zeal for voting spread through the entire black community.

Thanks to a large black turnout and the restrictions on prominent Confederates, a new southern Republican Party came to power in the constitutional conventions of 1868–1870. Republican delegates consisted of a sizable contingent of blacks (265 out of the total of just over 1,000 delegates throughout the South), some northerners who had moved to the South, and native southern whites who favored change. Together these Republicans brought the South into line with progressive reforms adopted earlier in the rest of the nation. The new constitutions were more democratic. They eliminated property qualifications for voting and holding office, and they turned many appointed offices into elective posts. They provided for public schools and institutions to care for the mentally ill, the blind, the deaf, the destitute, and the orphaned.

The conventions broadened women's rights in property holding and divorce. Usually, the goal was not to make women equal with men but to provide relief to thousands of suffering debtors. In families left poverty-stricken by the war and weighed down by debt, it was usually the husband who had contracted the debts. Thus giving women legal control over their own property provided some protection to their families. The goal of some delegates, however, was to elevate women. Blacks in particular called for laws to provide for woman suffrage, but they were ignored by their white colleagues.

Under these new constitutions the southern states elected Republican-controlled governments. For the

Triumph of Republican Governments

first time, the ranks of state legislators in 1868 included some black southerners. It remained to be seen now how much social change these new governments would bring about. Contrary to what white southerners would later claim, the Republican state governments did not disfranchise ex-Confederates as a group. The vexing questions of land reform and the assurance of racial equality all but overwhelmed the "radical" governments.

These new biracial regimes appreciated the realities of power and the depth of racial enmity. In most states, whites were in the majority and former slaveowners controlled the best land and other sources of economic power. James Lynch, a leading black politician from Mississippi, explained why African Americans shunned the "folly" of disfranchisement. Unlike northerners who "can leave when it becomes too uncomfortable," landless former slaves "must be in friendly relations with the great body of the whites in the state. Otherwise . . . peace can be maintained only by a standing army." Despised and lacking economic or social power, southern Republicans strove for acceptance and legitimacy.

Blacks also believed in the principle of universal suffrage and the Christian goal of reconciliation. Far from being vindictive toward the race that had enslaved them, they treated leading rebels with generosity and appealed to white southerners to adopt a spirit of fairness and cooperation. In this way the South's Republican Party condemned itself to defeat if white

voters would not cooperate. Within a few years Republicans were reduced to the embarrassment of making futile appeals to whites while ignoring the claims of their strongest supporters, blacks. But for a time both Republicans and their opponents, who called themselves Conservatives or Democrats, moved to the center and appealed for support from a broad range of groups. Some propertied whites accepted congressional Reconstruction as a reality and declared themselves willing to compete under the new rules. All sides found an area of agreement in economic policies.

Reflecting northern ideals and southern necessity, the Reconstruction governments enthusiastically promoted industry. Confederates had

Industrialization

seen how industry aided the North during the war. Accordingly, Reconstruction legislatures encouraged investment with loans, subsidies, and exemptions from taxation for periods up to ten years. The southern railroad system was rebuilt and expanded, and coal and iron mining made possible Birmingham's steel plants. Between 1860 and 1880, the number of manufacturing establishments in the South nearly doubled.

This emphasis on big business, however, produced higher state debts and taxes, drew money away from schools and other programs, and multiplied possibilities for corruption. It also locked Republicans into a conservative strategy. In courting elite whites who never joined the Republican Party, Republicans lost the opportunity of building support among poorer whites.

Policies appealing to African American voters never went beyond equality before the law. In fact, the

Republican Policies on Racial Equality

whites who controlled the southern Republican Party were reluctant to allow blacks a share of offices proportionate to their electoral strength. Aware of their weakness, black leaders did not push very far for revolutionary economic or social change. In every southern state, they led efforts to establish public schools, although they did not press for integrated facilities. In 1870 South Carolina passed the first comprehensive school law in the South. By 1875, 50 percent of black school-age children in that state were enrolled in school, and approximately one-third of the three thousand teachers were black.

Some African American politicians did fight for civil rights and integration. Most were mulattos from cities such as New Orleans or Mobile, where large populations of light-skinned free blacks had existed before the war. Their experience in such communities

One notable success in Reconstruction efforts to stimulate industry was Birmingham, Alabama. Here workers cast molten iron into blocks called pigs.   (Birmingham Public Library)

had made them sensitive to issues of status, and they spoke out for open and equal public accommodations. Laws requiring equal accommodations won passage throughout the Deep South, but they often went unenforced or required an injured party to bring expensive legal action for enforcement.

Economic progress was uppermost in the minds of most freed people and black representatives from rural districts. Black southerners needed land, but only a few promoted confiscation. In fact, much land did fall into state hands for nonpayment of taxes and was offered for sale in small lots. But most freedmen had too little cash to bid against investors or speculators, and few acquired land in this way. South Carolina established a land commission, but it could help only those with money to buy. Any widespread redistribution of land had to arise from Congress, which never supported such action. The lack of genuine land redistribution remained the significant lost opportunity of Reconstruction.

Within a few years, as centrists in both parties met with failure, white hostility to congressional Reconstruction began to dominate. Some conservatives had always desired to fight Reconstruction through pressure and racist propaganda. They put

The Myth of "Negro Rule"

economic and social pressure on blacks: one black Republican reported that "my neighbors will not employ me, nor sell me a farthing's worth of anything." Charging that the South had been turned over to ignorant blacks, conservatives deplored "black domination," which became a rallying cry for a return to white supremacy.

Such attacks were inflammatory propaganda, and part of the growing myth of "Negro rule," which would serve as a central theme in battles over the memory of Reconstruction. African Americans participated in politics but hardly dominated or controlled events. They were a majority in only two out of ten state constitutional writing conventions (transplanted northerners were a majority in one). In the state legislatures, only in the lower house in South Carolina did blacks ever constitute a majority; among officeholders, their numbers generally were far fewer than their proportion in the population. Sixteen blacks won seats in Congress before Reconstruction was over, but none was ever elected governor. Only eighteen served in a high state office such as lieutenant governor, treasurer, superintendent of education, or secretary of state. In all, some four hundred blacks served in political office during the Reconstruction era. Although they never dominated the process, they established a rich tradition of government service and civic activism. Elected officials, such as Robert Smalls in South Carolina, labored tirelessly for cheaper land prices, better healthcare, access to schools, and the enforcement of civil rights for their people. The black politicians of Reconstruction are lost in the mists, the forgotten heroes of this seedtime of America's long civil rights movement.

Conservatives also assailed the allies of black Republicans. Their propaganda denounced whites from the North as "carpetbaggers," greedy crooks planning to pour stolen tax revenues into their sturdy luggage made of carpet material. Immigrants from the North, who held the largest share of Republican offices, were all tarred with this brush.

Carpetbaggers and Scalawags

In fact, most northerners who settled in the South had come seeking business opportunities or a warmer climate and never entered politics. Those who did enter politics generally wanted to democratize the South and to introduce northern ways, such as industry, public education, and the spirit of enterprise. Carpetbaggers' ideals were tested by hard times and ostracism by white southerners.

In addition to tagging northern interlopers as carpetbaggers, Conservatives invented the term *scalawag* to discredit any native white southerner who cooperated with the Republicans. A substantial number of southerners did so, including some wealthy and prominent men. Most scalawags, however, were yeoman farmers, men from mountain areas and nonslaveholding districts who had been restive under the Confederacy. They saw that they could benefit from the education and opportunities promoted by Republicans. Banding together with freedmen, they pursued common class interests and hoped to make headway against the power of long-dominant planters. Cooperation even convinced a few scalawags that "there is but little if any difference in the talents of the two races," as one observed, and that all should have "an equal start." Yet this black-white coalition was vulnerable to the race issue, and most scalawags did not support racial equality. Republican tax policies also cut into upcountry yeoman support because reliance on the property tax hit many small landholders hard.

Taxation was a major problem for the Reconstruction governments. Republicans wanted to maintain prewar services, repair the war's destruction, stimulate industry, and support important new ventures such as public schools. But the Civil War had destroyed much of the South's tax base. One category of valuable property—slaves—had disappeared entirely. And hundreds

Albion Winegar Tourgee, a former Union soldier severely wounded at the Battle of Bull Run in 1861, became a carpetbagger and was elected a district judge in North Carolina during Reconstruction. In 1879 he published a best-selling novel, *A Fool's Errand,* which told his own story of travail as a Yankee immigrant in the South confronting the Ku Klux Klan and implementing freedmen's rights. (Chautauqua County Historical Society, Westfield, N.Y.)

Tax Policy and Corruption as Political Wedges

of thousands of citizens had lost much of the rest of their property—money, livestock, fences, and buildings—to the war. Thus an increase in taxes was necessary even to maintain traditional services, and new ventures required still higher taxes. Inevitably, Republican tax policies aroused strong opposition, especially among the yeomen.

Corruption was another serious charge levied against the Republicans. Unfortunately, it often was true. Many carpetbaggers and black politicians engaged in fraudulent schemes, sold their votes, or padded expenses, taking part in what scholars recognize was a nationwide surge of corruption in an age ruled by "spoilsmen" (see pages 554–556). Corruption carried no party label, but the Democrats successfully pinned the blame on unqualified blacks and greedy carpetbaggers among southern Republicans.

All these problems hurt the Republicans, whose leaders also allowed factionalism along racial and class lines to undermine party unity. But in many southern states the deathblow came through violence. The Ku Klux Klan, a secret veterans' club that began in

Ku Klux Klan

Tennessee in 1866, spread through the South and rapidly evolved into a terrorist organization. Violence against African Americans occurred from the first days of Reconstruction but became far more organized and purposeful after 1867. Klansmen rode to frustrate Reconstruction and keep the freedmen in subjection. Nighttime harassment, whippings, beatings, and murder became common, and terrorism dominated some counties and regions.

Although the Klan persecuted blacks who stood up for their rights as laborers or individuals, its main purpose was political. Lawless nightriders made active Republicans the target of their attacks. Leading white and black Republicans were killed in several states. After freedmen who worked for a South Carolina scalawag started voting, terrorists visited the planta-

Members of the Ku Klux Klan devised ghoulish costumes to heighten the terror inspired by their acts. This photograph shows the costume of a Mississippi Klansman from 1871. (Courtesy of Mr. Herbert Peck, Jr.)

tion and, in the words of one victim, "whipped every nigger man they could lay their hands on." Klansmen also attacked Union League clubs—Republican organizations that mobilized the black vote—and schoolteachers who were aiding the freedmen.

Klan violence was not a spontaneous outburst of racism; very specific social forces shaped and directed it. In North Carolina, for example, Alamance and Caswell Counties were the sites of the worst Klan violence. Slim Republican majorities there rested on cooperation between black voters and white yeomen, particularly those whose Unionism or discontent with the Confederacy had turned them against local Democratic officials. Together, these black and white Republicans had ousted officials long entrenched in power. The wealthy and powerful men in Alamance and Caswell who had lost their accustomed political control were the Klan's county officers and local chieftains. They organized a deliberate campaign of terror, recruiting members and planning atrocities. By whipping up racism or intimidating enough Republicans, the Ku Klux Klan weakened the Republican coalition and restored a Democratic majority.

Klan violence injured Republicans across the South. No fewer than one-tenth of the black leaders who had been delegates to the 1867–1868 state constitutional conventions were attacked, seven fatally. In one judicial district of North Carolina the Ku Klux Klan was responsible for twelve murders, over seven hundred beatings, and other acts of violence, including rape and arson. A single attack on Alabama Republicans in the town of Eutaw left four blacks dead and fifty-four wounded. In South Carolina five hundred masked Klansmen lynched eight black prisoners at the Union County jail, and in nearby York County the Klan committed at least eleven murders and hundreds of whippings. According to historian Eric Foner, the Klan "made it virtually impossible for Republicans to campaign or vote in large parts of Georgia."

Thus a combination of difficult fiscal problems, Republican mistakes, racial hostility, and terror brought down the Republican regimes. In most southern states, "Radical Reconstruction" lasted only a few years (see Map 16.1). The most enduring failure of Reconstruction, however, was not political; it was social and economic. Reconstruction failed to alter the South's social structure or its distribution of wealth and power. Without land of their own, freed men and women were dependent on white landowners who could and did use their economic power to compromise blacks' political freedom.

Failure of Reconstruction

Armed only with the ballot, freed men in the South had little chance to effect major changes.

To reform the southern social order, Congress would have had to redistribute land, but most lawmakers opposed an attack on private property. Radical Republicans like Albion Tourgée, a former Union soldier who moved to North Carolina and was elected a judge, condemned Congress's timidity. Turning the freedman out on his own without protection, said Tourgée, constituted "cheap philanthropy." Indeed, African Americans who had to live with the consequences of Reconstruction considered it a failure, for the North "threw all the Negroes on the world without any way of getting along." Moreover, without careful supervision by Congress, the situation of the freed men and women deteriorated. Whenever the North lost interest, Reconstruction would collapse.

Reconstruction Reversed

 Northerners had always been more interested in suppressing rebellion than in aiding southern blacks, and by the early 1870s the North's commitment to bringing about change in the South was weakening. Criticism of the southern governments grew, new issues captured public attention, and sentiment for national reconciliation gained popularity in politics. In one southern state after another, Democrats regained control, and they threatened to defeat Republicans in the North as well. Whites in the old Confederacy referred to this decline of Reconstruction as "southern redemption," and by the 1870s, "redeemer" Democrats claimed to be the saviors of the South from alleged "black domination" and "carpetbag rule." And for one of only a few times in American history, violence and terror emerged as a tactic in normal politics.

In 1870 and 1871 the violent campaigns of the Ku Klux Klan forced Congress to pass two Enforcement Acts and an anti-Klan law. These laws made actions by individuals against the civil and political rights of others a federal criminal offense for the first time. They also provided for election supervisors and permitted martial law and suspension of the writ of habeas corpus to combat murders, beatings, and threats by the Klan. Federal prosecutors used the laws rather selectively. In 1872 and 1873 Mississippi and the Carolinas saw many prosecutions; but in other states where violence flourished, the laws were virtually ignored. Southern juries sometimes refused to convict Klansmen; out of a total

Political Implications of Klan Terrorism

of 3,310 cases, only 1,143 ended in convictions. Though many Klansmen (roughly two thousand in South Carolina alone) fled their states to avoid prosecution, and the Klan officially disbanded, the threat of violence did not end. Paramilitary organizations known as Rifle clubs and Red Shirts often took the Klan's place.

Klan terrorism openly defied Congress, yet even on this issue there were ominous signs that the North's commitment to racial justice was fading. Some conservative but influential Republicans opposed the anti-Klan laws. Rejecting other Republicans' arguments that the Thirteenth, Fourteenth, and Fifteenth Amendments had made the federal government the protector of the rights of citizens, these dissenters echoed an old Democratic charge that Congress was infringing on states' rights. Senator Lyman Trumbull of Illinois declared that the states remained "the depositories of the rights of the individual." If Congress could punish crimes like assault or murder, he asked, "what is the need of the State governments?" For years Democrats had complained of "centralization and consolidation"; now some Republicans seemed to agree with them. This opposition foreshadowed a more general revolt within Republican ranks in 1872.

Disenchanted with Reconstruction, a group calling itself the Liberal Republicans bolted the party in 1872 and nominated Horace Greeley, the well-known editor of the *New York Tribune*, for president. The Liberal Republicans were a varied group, including civil service reformers, foes of corruption, and advocates of a lower tariff. Normally such disparate elements would not cooperate with one another, but two popular and widespread attitudes united them: distaste for federal intervention in the South and an elitist desire to let market forces and the "best men" determine events, both in the South and in Washington.

The Liberal Republican Revolt

The Democrats also gave their nomination to Greeley in 1872. The combination was not enough to defeat Grant, who won reelection, but it reinforced Grant's desire to avoid confrontation with white southerners. Greeley's campaign for North-South reunion, for "clasping hands across the bloody chasm," was a bit premature to win at the polls, but a harbinger of the future of American politics. Organized Blue-Gray fraternalism (gatherings of Union and Confederate veterans) began as early as 1874 in some states. Grant continued to use military force sparingly and in 1875 refused a desperate request for troops from the governor of Mississippi to quell racial and political terrorism in that state.

Dissatisfaction with Grant's administration grew during his second term. Strong-willed but politically naive, Grant made a series of poor appointments. His secretary of war, his private secretary, and officials in the Treasury and Navy Departments were involved in bribery or tax-cheating scandals. Instead of exposing the corruption, Grant defended some of the culprits. In 1874, as Grant's popularity and his party's prestige declined, the Democrats recaptured the House of Representatives. This stunning turnabout signaled the beginning of the end of the old Radical Republican vision of Reconstruction. The Republican Party faced more unfavorable publicity in 1875, when several of Grant's appointees were indicted for corruption.

The effect of Democratic gains in Congress was to weaken legislative resolve on southern issues. Congress had already lifted the political disabilities of the Fourteenth Amendment from many former Confederates. In 1872 it had adopted a sweeping Amnesty Act, which pardoned most of the remaining rebels and left only five hundred barred from political officeholding. In 1875 Congress passed a Civil Rights Act, partly as a tribute to the recently deceased Charles Sumner, purporting to guarantee black people equal accommodations in public places, such as inns and theaters, but the bill was watered down and contained no effective provisions for enforcement. (The Supreme Court later struck down this law; see page 562.)

A General Amnesty

Democrats regained power in the South rather quickly, redeeming control of state governments in four states before 1872 and in a total of eight by January 1876 (see Map 16.1). In the North Democrats successfully stressed the failure and scandals of Reconstruction governments. As opinion shifted, historian Brooks Adams, the grandson and great-grandson of presidents, published an article condemning the enfranchisement of blacks as "a wholesale creation of the most ignorant mass of voters to be found in the civilized world." Many Republicans sensed that their constituents were tiring of southern issues and the legacies of the war. Despite the consequences for the freedpeople, sectional reconciliation now seemed crucial for commerce. The nation was expanding westward rapidly, and the South was a new frontier for investment.

Both industrialization and immigration were surging, hastening the pace of change in national life. Within only eight years, postwar industrial production increased by an impressive 75 percent. For the first time, nonagricultural workers outnumbered farmers, and only Britain's industrial output was greater than that of the United States. Government financial policies did much to bring about this rapid growth. Soon after the war Congress used a portion of tax revenues to pay off the interest-bearing war debt: the debt fell from $2.33 billion in 1866 to only $587 million in 1893, and every dollar repaid was a dollar injected into the economy for potential reinvestment. Low taxes on investment and high tariffs on manufactured goods also aided industrialists. With such help, the northern economy quickly recovered its prewar rate of growth.

Reconciliation and Industrial Expansion

Between 1865 and 1873, 3 million new immigrants entered the country, most of them joining the labor force of industrial cities in the North and West. As the number of immigrants rose, a corresponding revival of suspicion and hostility among native-born Americans took place. Also prominent was the question of how Utah's growing Mormon community, which practiced polygamy, could be reconciled to American law.

Then the Panic of 1873 ushered in over five years of economic contraction. Three million people lost their jobs, and the clash between labor and capital became the major issue of the day (see Chapter 18). Class attitudes diverged, especially in the large cities. Debtors and the unemployed sought easy money policies to spur economic expansion (workers and farmers desperately needed cash). Businessmen, disturbed by the widespread strikes and industrial violence that accompanied the panic, became increasingly concerned about the defense of property.

Class conflict fueled a monetary issue: whether paper money—the Civil War greenbacks—should be kept in circulation. In 1872 Democratic farmers and debtors urged this policy to expand the money supply and raise prices, but businessmen, bankers, and creditors overruled them. Now hard times swelled the ranks of the "greenbackers"—voters who favored easy money.

Greenbacks Versus Sound Money

Congress voted in 1874 to increase the number of greenbacks in circulation, but Grant vetoed the bill in deference to the opinions of financial leaders. The next year, "sound money" interests prevailed in Congress, winning passage of a law requiring that greenbacks be convertible into gold after 1878. The chasm between farmers and workers and wealthy industrialists grew even wider.

In international affairs, there was renewed pressure for, and controversy about, expansion (see Chapter 22).

Foreign Expansion

In 1867 Secretary of State William H. Seward arranged a vast addition of territory to the national domain through the purchase of Alaska from the Russian government for $7.2 million. Opponents ridiculed Seward's venture, calling Alaska Frigidia, the Polar Bear Garden, and Walrussia. But Seward convinced important congressmen of Alaska's economic potential, and other lawmakers favored the dawning of friendship with Russia.

Also in 1867 the United States took control of the Midway Islands, a thousand miles from Hawai'i. And in 1870 President Grant tried unsuccessfully to annex the Dominican Republic. Seward and his successor, Hamilton Fish, also resolved troubling Civil War grievances against Great Britain. Through diplomacy they arranged a financial settlement of claims on Britain for damage done by the *Alabama* and other cruisers built in England and sold to the Confederacy (see page 616).

Meanwhile, the Supreme Court played its part in the northern retreat from Reconstruction. During the Civil War the Court had been cautious and inactive. Reaction to the *Dred Scott* decision (1857) had been so violent, and the Union's wartime emergency so great, that the Court avoided interference with government actions. The justices breathed a collective sigh of relief, for example, when legal technicalities prevented them from reviewing the case of Clement Vallandigham, a Democratic opponent of Lincoln's war effort, who had been convicted by a military tribunal of aiding the enemy. But in 1866 a similar case, *Ex parte Milligan*, reached the Court through proper channels.

Judicial Retreat from Reconstruction

Lambdin P. Milligan of Indiana had plotted to free Confederate prisoners of war and overthrow state governments. For these acts a military court sentenced Milligan, a civilian, to death. Milligan challenged the authority of the military tribunal, claiming that he had a right to a civil trial. The Supreme Court declared that military trials were illegal when civil courts were open and functioning, and its language indicated that the Court intended to reassert its authority.

In the 1870s the Court successfully renewed its challenge to Congress's actions when it narrowed the meaning and effectiveness of the Fourteenth Amendment. The *Slaughter-House* cases (1873) began in 1869, when the Louisiana legislature granted one company a monopoly on the slaughtering of livestock in New Orleans. Rival butchers in the city promptly sued. Their attorney, former Supreme Court justice John A. Campbell, argued that Louisiana had violated the rights of some of its citizens in favor of others. The Fourteenth Amendment, Campbell contended, had revolutionized the constitutional system by bringing individual rights under federal protection. Campbell thus articulated an original goal of the Republican Party: to nationalize civil rights and guard them from state interference.

But in the *Slaughter-House* decision, the Supreme Court dealt a stunning blow to the scope and vitality of the Fourteenth Amendment. Refusing to accept Campbell's argument, it interpreted the "privileges and immunities" of citizens so narrowly that it reduced them almost to trivialities. State citizenship and national citizenship were separate, the Court declared. National citizenship involved only matters such as the right to travel freely from state to state and to use the navigable waters of the nation, and only these narrow rights were protected by the Fourteenth Amendment.

The Supreme Court also concluded that the butchers who sued had not been deprived of their rights or property in violation of the due-process clause of the amendment. Shrinking from a role as "perpetual censor upon all legislation of the States, on the civil rights of their own citizens," the Court's majority declared that the framers of the recent amendments had not intended to "destroy" the federal system, in which the states exercised "powers for domestic and local government, including the regulation of civil rights." Thus the justices severely limited the amendment's potential for securing and protecting the rights of black citizens—its original intent.

The next day the Court decided *Bradwell v. Illinois*, a case in which Myra Bradwell, a female attorney, had been denied the right to practice law in Illinois on account of her gender. Pointing to the Fourteenth Amendment, Bradwell's attorneys contended that the state had unconstitutionally abridged her "privileges and immunities" as a citizen. The Supreme Court rejected her claim, alluding to women's traditional role in the home.

In 1876 the Court weakened the Reconstruction era amendments even further by emasculating the enforcement clause of the Fourteenth Amendment and revealing deficiencies inherent in the Fifteenth Amendment. In *U.S. v. Cruikshank* the Court overruled the conviction under the 1870 Enforcement Act of Louisiana whites who had attacked a meeting of blacks and conspired to deprive them of their rights. The justices ruled that the Fourteenth Amendment did not give the federal government power to act against these whites. The duty of protecting citizens' equal rights, the Court said, "rests alone with the States." Such judicial conservatism had profound impact down through the next century, as the revolutionary potential in the Civil War amendments was blunted, if not destroyed.

As the 1876 elections approached, most political observers saw that the North was no longer willing to pursue the goals of Reconstruction.

Disputed Election of 1876 and the Compromise of 1877

The results of a disputed presidential election confirmed this fact. Samuel J. Tilden, the Democratic governor of New York, ran strongly in the South and needed only one more electoral vote to triumph over Rutherford B. Hayes, the Republican nominee. Nineteen electoral votes from Louisiana, South Carolina, and Florida (the only southern states yet "unredeemed" by Democratic rule) were disputed; both Democrats and Republicans claimed to have won in those states despite fraud committed by their opponents. One vote from Oregon was undecided because of a technicality (see Map 16.2).

To resolve this unprecedented situation, on which the Constitution gave little guidance, Congress established a fifteen-member electoral commission. In the interest of impartiality, membership on the commission was to be balanced between Democrats and Republicans. But one independent Republican, Supreme Court Justice David Davis, refused appointment in order to accept his election as a senator. A regular Republican took his place, and the Republican Party prevailed 8 to 7 on every attempt to count the returns, along strict party lines. Hayes would become president if Congress accepted the commission's findings.

Congressional acceptance was not certain. Democrats controlled the House and could filibuster to block action on the vote. Many citizens worried that the nation had entered a major constitutional crisis and would slip once again into civil war, as some southerners vowed "Tilden or Fight." The crisis was resolved when Democrats acquiesced in the election of Hayes based on a "deal" cut in a Washington hotel. Negotiations took place between Hayes's supporters and southerners who wanted federal aid to railroads, internal improvements, federal patronage, and removal of troops from southern states. Neither party was well enough organized to implement and enforce the various parts of this bargain between the sections. Northern and southern Democrats simply decided they could not win and did not contest the election of a Republican who was not going to continue Reconstruction. Thus Hayes became president, inaugurated privately inside the White House to avoid any threat of violence, southerners relished their promises of economic aid, and Reconstruction was unmistakably over.

Southern Democrats rejoiced, but African Americans grieved over the betrayal of their hopes for equality. Tens of thousands considered leaving the South, where real freedom was no longer a possibility. "[We asked] whether it was possible we could stay under a people who had held us in bondage," said Henry Adams, who led a migration to Kansas. In South Carolina, Louisiana, Mississippi, and other southern states, thousands gathered up their possessions and migrated to Kansas. They were known as Exodusters, disappointed people still searching for their share in the American dream. Even in Kansas they met disillusionment, as the welcome extended by

Betrayal of Black Rights and the Exodusters

Map 16.2   Presidential Election of 1876 and the Compromise of 1877   In 1876 a combination of solid southern support and Democratic gains in the North gave Samuel Tilden the majority of popular votes, but Rutherford B. Hayes won the disputed election in the electoral college, after a deal satisfied Democratic wishes for an end to Reconstruction.

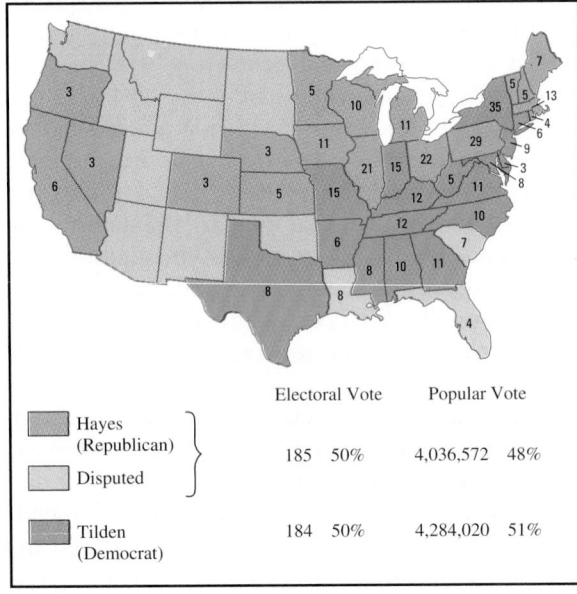

	Electoral Vote		Popular Vote	
Hayes (Republican)	185	50%	4,036,572	48%
Disputed				
Tilden (Democrat)	184	50%	4,284,020	51%

These cartoons reveal the North's readiness to give up on a strong Reconstruction policy. According to the images on the left, only federal bayonets could support the "rule or ruin" carpetbag regimes that oppressed the South. What do the background and foreground of the cartoon on the right suggest will be the results of President Hayes's "Let 'Em Alone Policy"?   (Library of Congress)

the state's governor soon gave way to hostile public reactions.

Blacks now had to weigh their options, which were not much wider than they had ever been. The Civil War had brought emancipation, and Reconstruction had guaranteed their rights under law. But events and attitudes in larger white America were foreboding. In a Fourth of July speech in Washington, D.C., in 1875, Frederick Douglass anticipated this predicament. He reflected anxiously on the American centennial to be celebrated the following year. The nation, Douglass feared, would "lift to the sky its million voices in one grand Centennial hosanna of peace and good will to all the white race . . . from gulf to lakes and from sea to sea." Douglass looked back on fifteen years of unparalleled change for his people and worried about the hold of white supremacy on America's historical memory: "If war among the whites brought peace and liberty to the blacks, what will peace among the whites bring?" Douglass's question would echo down through American political culture for decades.

Summary

Reconstruction left a contradictory record. It was an era of tragic aspirations and failures, but also of unprecedented legal, political, and social change. The Union victory brought about an increase in federal power, stronger nationalism, sweeping federal intervention in the southern states, and landmark amendments to the Constitution. But northern commitment to make these changes endure had eroded, and the revolution remained unfinished.

By 1876 in South Carolina, Wade Hampton ran successfully for governor, relying on a campaign of terror and intimidation carried out by his "Red Shirt" followers, crushing the black vote in many counties and ending Republican rule. Robert Smalls, however, managed to stay in office despite Democratic Party efforts to oust him. He won his final congressional election in 1884 against the viciously racist "Pitchfork" Ben Tillman. After leaving Congress, Smalls served from 1890 until 1913 as customs collector in his native Beaufort.

The North embraced emancipation, black suffrage, and constitutional alterations strengthening the central government. But it did so to defeat the rebellion and secure the peace. As the pressure of these crises declined, strong underlying continuities emerged and placed their mark on Reconstruction. The American people and the courts maintained a preference for state authority and a distrust of federal power. The ideology of free labor dictated that property should be respected and that individuals should be self-reliant. Racism endured and transformed into the even more virulent forms of Klan terror and theories that freedom would send blacks as a race back toward "barbarism." Concern for the human rights of African Americans was strongest when their plight threatened to undermine the interests of whites, and reform frequently had less appeal than moneymaking in an individualistic, enterprising society.

A host of other issues had arisen from industrialization. How would the country develop its immense resources in an increasingly interconnected national economy? How would farmers, industrial workers, immigrants, and capitalists fit into the new social system? Industrialization not only promised a higher standard of living but wrought increased exploitation of labor. Moreover, industry increased the nation's power and laid the foundation for an enlarged American role in international affairs. The American imagination again turned to the conquest of new frontiers.

In the wake of the Civil War Americans faced two profound tasks—the achievement of healing and the dispensing of justice. Both had to occur, but they never developed in historical balance. Making sectional reunion compatible with black freedom and equality overwhelmed the imagination in American political culture, and the nation still faced much of this dilemma more than a century later.

LEGACY FOR A PEOPLE AND A NATION
The Fourteenth Amendment

Before the Civil War, no definition of civil rights existed in America. Reconstruction legislation, especially the Fourteenth Amendment, changed that forever. Approved by Congress in 1866, the Fourteenth Amendment enshrined in the Constitution the ideas of birthright citizenship and equal rights. The Fourteenth Amendment was designed to secure and protect the rights of the freedpeople. But over time, the "equal protection of the law" clause became one of the most important and malleable provisions in the Constitution. It has been used at times to support the rights of states, cities, corporations, immigrants, women, religious organizations, gays and lesbians, students, and labor unions. It has advanced both tolerance and intolerance, affirmative action and anti-affirmative action programs. It provides the legal wellspring for the generations-old civil rights movement in the United States.

The amendment as originally written required individuals to pursue grievances through private litigation, alleging state denial of a claimed federal right. At first the Supreme Court interpreted it conservatively, especially on racial matters, and by 1900 the idea of color-blind liberty in America was devastated by Jim Crow laws, disfranchisement, and unpunished mob violence.

But Progressive reformers used the equal protection clause to advocate government support of health, union organizing, municipal housing, a progressive income tax, and the protection of woman and child laborers. In the 1920s and 1930s, a judicial defense of civil liberties and free speech took hold, especially from Justice Louis Brandeis. The Supreme Court expanded the amendment's guarantee of equality by a series of decisions upholding the rights of immigrant groups to resist "forced Americanization," especially Catholics in their creation of parochial schools. And, from its inception in 1910, the NAACP waged a long campaign to reveal the inequality of racial segregation in schooling and every other kind of public facility. Led by Charles Houston and Thurgood Marshall, this epic legal battle culminated in the *Brown v. Board of Education* desegregation decision of 1954. In the multilayered Civil Rights Act of 1964, the equal protection tradition was reenshrined into American law. Since 1964 Americans have lived in a society where the Fourteenth Amendment's legacy is the engine of expanded liberty for women and all minorities, as well as a political battleground for defining the nature and limits of human equality, and for redistributing justice long denied.

For Further Reading, see page A-20 of the Appendix. For Web resources, go to http://college.hmco.com.

In 1893 a young historian named Frederick Jackson Turner delivered a stunning scholarly paper at the Columbian Exposition in Chicago. In it, Turner expounded a theory that would occupy the textbooks of high school and college students for several generations. Titled "The Significance of the Frontier in American History," the paper argued the "frontier thesis" that the existence of "free land, its continuous recession, and the advancement of American settlement westward" had created a distinctively American spirit of democracy and egalitarianism. The conquest of a succession of frontier Wests, in other words, explained American progress and character.

At a covered arena just across the street from this same world's fair, the folk character Buffalo Bill Cody staged two performances daily of an extravaganza he called the "Wild West." Though Cody also dramatized the conquest of frontiers, his perspective differed markedly from Turner's. While Turner described the relatively peaceful settlement of largely empty western land, Cody portrayed violent conquest of territory formerly occupied by savage Indians. Turner's heroes were persevering farmers who tamed the wilderness with axes and plows. Buffalo Bill's heroes were rugged scouts who braved danger and defeated Indians with rifles and bullets. Turner used images of log cabins, wagon trains, and wheat fields to argue that the western frontier fashioned a new, progressive race. Cody, who used a cast of actual Indians and soldiers (plus himself) to stage scenes of Indian attacks and clashes between native warriors and white cavalry, depicted the West as a place of brutal aggression and heroic victory.

In spite of their contradictions, exaggerations, and inaccuracies, both Turner and Cody were to some degree correct. The American West inspired material and cultural progress, and it also witnessed the forceful domination of one group of humans over another and over the environment. Both Turner and Cody believed that by the 1890s the era of the frontier had come to an end. In fact, Turner's essay had been sparked by an announcement from the superintendent of the 1890 cen-

17

THE DEVELOPMENT OF THE WEST 1877–1900

The Economic Activities of Native Peoples

The Transformation of Native Cultures

The Extraction of Natural Resources

Irrigation and Transportation

Farming the Plains

The Ranching Frontier

LEGACY FOR A PEOPLE AND A NATION

The West and Rugged Individualism

This painting (1874) by Thomas Moran shows an American Indian dwarfed but not threatened by nature. The interaction of humans with the environment provided the major themes of western history in the nineteenth century. (Detail of *Cliffs of Green River*, Thomas Moran, oil on canvas, 1874, 1975.28. Copyright Amon Carter Museum, Fort Worth, Texas)

sus that "at present the unsettled area [of the West] has been so broken into by isolated bodies of settlement that there can be hardly said to be a frontier line." Over time, Turner's theory was abandoned (even by Turner himself) as too simplistic, and Buffalo Bill was relegated to the gallery of rogues and showmen (though he subsequently became an advocate of irrigated farming). Even so, both of the Wests that they depicted persist in the romance of American history, while the real story of western development in the late nineteenth century is much more complex than either myth.

One fact is certain. Much of the West was never empty, and those who inhabited it utilized its resources in quite different ways. Indians had managed the environment and sustained their needs for centuries before white settlers arrived on the scene. The Pawnees of the Plains, for example, planted crops in the spring, left their fields to hunt buffalo, then returned for harvesting. They sometimes battled with Cheyennes and Arapahos, who wanted hunting grounds and crops for their own purposes. Pawnee technology was simple. Though they sometimes splurged when feasting on buffalo, they survived by developing and using natural resources in limited ways. Concepts of private property and profit had little meaning for them.

For white Americans, however, expanses of land and water were assets to be utilized for economic gain. As whites settled the West in the late nineteenth century, they exploited the environment for profit far more extensively than did the Indians. They excavated deep into the earth to remove valuable minerals, cut down forests for lumber to construct homes and other buildings, built railroads to carry goods and link markets, and dammed the rivers and plowed the soil with machines to grow crops. Their goal was not survival; rather, it was buying and selling and opening markets nationally and internationally. As they transformed the landscape, the triumph of their market economies transformed the entire nation.

The West, which by 1870 referred to the vast area between the Mississippi River and the Pacific Ocean, actually consisted of several regions and a variety of economic potential. Abundant rainfall along the Pacific Coast fed huge forests. Farther south into California woodlands and grasslands existed, with fertile valleys capable of supporting vegetable fields and orange groves. Eastward, between the Cascade and Sierra Mountains and the Rocky Mountains where gold, silver, and other minerals lay buried, was an arid, desolate plateau that descended into the hot desert of

southeastern California and western Arizona. On the eastern side of the Rockies were the Great Plains, divided into a semiarid western side of few trees and tough buffalo grass and an eastern area of ample rainfall and tall grasses. The Plains could support grain crops and livestock.

Much of this territory had long been the scene of great migrations. Before contact with whites, thousands of Indian peoples had moved around and through the region. As they searched for food and shelter, they warred, traded, and sometimes negotiated with one another. In parts of the Southwest, Hispanics had built towns, farms, and ranches. But after the Civil War, white people flooded into the West overwhelming the native peoples. Between 1870 and 1890, the population living in the region swelled from 7 million to nearly 17 million.

The abundance of exploitable land, food, and raw materials in the West filled white Americans with faith that anyone eager and persistent enough could succeed. But this self-confidence rested on a belief that white people were somehow special, and individual advantage often asserted itself at the expense of people of color and the poor, as well as the environment. Americans rarely thought about conserving resources because there always seemed to be more territory to exploit and bring into the market economy.

By 1890 farms, ranches, mines, towns, and cities could be found in almost every corner of the present-day continental United States. Though of great symbolic importance, the fading of the frontier had little direct impact on people's behavior, for vast stretches of land remained unsettled. Pioneers who failed in one locale rarely starved to death; they moved on and tried again somewhere else. Although life in the West was less than comfortable, expanses of seemingly uninhabited land gave Americans the feeling that they would always have a second chance. It was this belief in an infinity of second chances, more than Turner's theory of frontier democracy or Cody's reenactments of western battles, that left a deep imprint on the American character. ■

The Economic Activities of Native Peoples

Historians once defined the American frontier as "the edge of the unused," implying, as Frederick Jackson Turner had, that the frontier disappeared once white men and women arrived to occupy supposedly open

IMPORTANT EVENTS

1862 Homestead Act grants free land to citizens who live on and improve the land

Morrill Land Grant Act gives states public lands to finance agricultural and industrial colleges

1864 Chivington's militia massacres Black Kettle's Cheyennes at Sand Creek

1872 Yellowstone becomes first national park

1873 Barbed wire invented, enabling western farmers to enclose and protect fields cheaply

1876 Sioux annihilate Custer's federal troops at Little Big Horn

1877 Nez Percé Indians under Young Joseph surrender to U.S. troops

1878 Timber and Stone Act allows citizens to buy timber land cheaply but also enables large companies to acquire huge tracts of forestland

1879 Utes surrender after resisting territorial concessions in western Colorado

Carlisle School for Indians established in Pennsylvania

Colorado creates water divisions to regulate water rights

1880–81 Manypenny's *Our Indian Wards* and Jackson's *A Century of Dishonor* influence public conscience about poor government treatment of Indians

1881 Shootout at OK Corral between Clantons and Earps

1881–82 Chinese Exclusion Acts prohibit Chinese immigration to the U.S.

1883 National time zones standardized

1884 U.S. Supreme Court first defines Indians as wards under government protection

1887 Dawes Severalty Act ends communal ownership of Indian lands and grants land allotments to individual Native American families.

Hatch Act provides for agricultural experiment stations in every state

California passes law permitting farmers to organize into districts that would sponsor the construction and operation of irrigation projects

1887–88 Devastating winter on Plains destroys countless livestock and forces farmers into economic hardship

1889 Statehood granted to North Dakota, South Dakota, Washington, and Montana

1890 Final suppression of Plains Indians by U.S. Army at Wounded Knee

Census Bureau announces closing of the frontier

Statehood granted to Wyoming and Idaho

Yosemite National Park established

Wyoming makes its rivers public property subject to state supervision

1892 Muir helps found Sierra Club

1893 Turner presents "frontier thesis" at Columbian Exposition

1896 Rural Free Delivery made available

Statehood granted to Utah

1902 Newlands Reclamation Act passed

land for farming or the building of cities. Scholars now acknowledge that Native Americans had settled and developed the West long before other Americans migrated there. Neither passive nor powerless in the face of nature, Indians had been shaping their environment—for better and for worse—for centuries. Nevertheless, almost all native economic systems weakened in the late nineteenth century. Why and how did these declines happen?

Western Indian cultures varied. Some Indians lived in permanent settlements; others moved their camps and villages. Seldom completely isolated, most Indians were participants and recipients in a large-scale flow of goods, culture, language, and disease carried by migrating bands who moved from one region to another. But regardless of their type of settlement, all Indians based their

Subsistence Cultures

The horses, sometimes numbering more than one hundred, and the women and children, usually twenty or thirty, were a liability as well as a help to a Plains Indian camp. The horses competed with buffalo for valuable pasturage, and the women and children made camps vulnerable when white soldiers attacked. (Denver Public Library, Western History Division)

economies to differing degrees on four activities: crop raising; livestock raising; hunting, fishing, and gathering; and trading and raiding. Corn was the most common crop; sheep and horses, acquired from Spanish colonizers, were the livestock; and buffalo (American bison) were the primary prey of hunts. Indians raided one another for food, tools, hides, and horses, which in turn they used in trading with other Indians and with whites. They also attacked one another to avenge wrongs and to displace competitors from hunting grounds. To achieve their standards of living, Indians tried to balance their economic systems. When a buffalo hunt failed, they could subsist on crops. When their crops failed, they could still hunt buffalo and steal food and horses in a raid or trade livestock and furs for necessities.

For Indians on the Great Plains, whether they were nomads such as the Lakotas or village dwellers such as the Pawnees, everyday life focused on the buffalo. They cooked and preserved buffalo meat; fashioned hides into clothing, shoes, and blankets; used sinew for thread and bowstrings; and carved tools from bones and horns. Buffalo were so valuable to them that the Pawnees and Lakotas often came into conflict over access to herds. The Plains Indians also depended on horses, which they used for transportation and hunt-

ing, and as symbols of wealth. To provide food for their herds, Pawnees and other Plains Indians altered the environment by periodically setting fire to tallgrass prairies. The fires burned away dead plants, facilitating the growth of new grass in the spring so horses could feed all summer.

In the Southwest, Indians were herders and placed great value on sheep, goats, and horses. Old Man Hat, a Navajo, explained, "The herd is money. . . . You know that you have some good clothing; the sheep gave you that. And you've just eaten different kinds of food; the sheep gave that food to you. Everything comes from the sheep." He was not speaking of money in a business sense, though. To the Navajos, the herds provided status and security. Like many Indians, the Navajos emphasized generosity and distrusted private property and wealth. Within the family, sharing was expected; outside the family, gifts and reciprocity governed personal relations. Southwestern Indians, too, altered the environment, building elaborate irrigation systems to maximize use of scarce water supplies.

What buffalo were to the Plains Indians and sheep were to Southwestern Indians, salmon were to Indians of the Northwest. Before the mid-nineteenth century, the Columbia River and its tributaries supported the densest population of native peoples in North America, all of whom fished the river for salmon in the summer and stored dried fish for the winter. The Clatsops, Klamathets, and S'Klallam applied their own technology of stream diversion, platform construction over the water, and special baskets to better harvest fish. Like natives of other regions, many of these Indians also traded for horses, buffalo robes, beads, cloth, and knives.

On the Plains and in parts of the Southwest, this native world began to dissolve after 1850 when whites entered the West and competed with Indians for access to and control over natural resources. Perceiving the buffalo and the Indians as hindrances to their ambitions, whites endeavored to eliminate both. Railroads sponsored hunts in which eastern sportsmen shot at the bulky targets from slow-moving trains. The army distributed ammunition to hunters and refused to enforce treaties that reserved hunting grounds for exclusive Indian use. Some hunters collected from $1 to $3 from tanneries for hides that were sent east to be used mainly as belts to drive industrial machinery; others did not even stop to pick up their kill.

Slaughter of Buffalo

Unbeknownst to both Indians and whites, however, a complex combination of circumstances had already doomed the buffalo before the slaughter of the late 1800s. Indians themselves were contributing to the depletion of the herds by increasing their kills, especially to obtain hides for trade with whites and other Indians. Also, a period of generally dry years in the 1840s and 1850s had forced Indians to set up camps in more fertile river basins, where they competed with buffalo for space and water. As a result, the bison were pushed out of important grazing territory and faced threats of starvation. When whites arrived on the Plains, they too sought to settle in the same river basin areas, thereby further forcing buffalo away from nutritious grasslands. At the same time, lethal animal diseases such as anthrax and brucellosis, brought in by white-owned livestock, were decimating buffalo, many of whom had been weakened by malnutrition and drought. The increased numbers of horses, oxen, and sheep owned by white newcomers, as well as by some Indians, also upset the grazing patterns of the bison by devouring grasses that buffalo depended on at certain times of the year. In sum, a convergence of human and environmental shocks created vulnerability among the buffalo to which the mass killing only struck the final blow. By the 1880s only a few hundred remained of the estimated 25 million bison that had existed in 1820.

In the Northwest, the basic wild source of Indian food supply, salmon, suffered a similar fate as the buffalo, but for different reasons. In the Lower Columbia and Willamette River valleys, diseases such as smallpox and malaria, caught from white explorers and fur traders, by the 1870s had decimated some two-thirds of northwestern Indian populations. As a result, fewer Indians were fishing for salmon. But as white commercial fishermen and canneries moved into the region, they greatly diminished the salmon runs on the Columbia by the 1880s. Increasing numbers of salmon running up the river to spawn were being caught before they laid their eggs so that the fish supply was not being replenished. By the twentieth century, the construction of dams on the river and its tributaries further impeded the salmon's ability to reproduce. The government protected Indian fishing rights on the river and hatcheries helped restore some of the fish supply, but the need for electrical power from dams, combined with depletion of the salmon from overfishing and pollution, ended the abundance of this resource in the Northwest.

Decline of Salmon

The Transformation of Native Cultures

Buffalo slaughter and salmon reduction undermined Indian subsistence, but a unique mix of human circumstances contributed as well. For most of the nineteenth century, the white population that migrated into western lands inhabited by Indians was overwhelmingly young and male. In 1870 white men outnumbered white women by three to two in California, two to one in Colorado, and two to one in Dakota Territory. By 1900, preponderances of men remained throughout these places. Most of these males were in their twenties and thirties, unmarried, and at the stage of life when they were most prone to violent behavior. In other words, the whites that Indians were most likely to come into contact with first were explorers, traders, trappers, soldiers, prospectors, and cowboys—almost all of whom possessed guns and had few qualms about using their weapons against animals and humans who got in their way.

Violence

Moreover, these men subscribed to prevailing attitudes that Indians were primitive, lazy, devious, and cruel. Such contempt made exploiting and killing natives all the easier, and violence was often "justified" by

Using buffalo hides to fashion garments, Indians often exhibited artistic skills in decorating their apparel. This Ute Indian hide dress shows symbolic as well as aesthetic representations. (Denver Art Museum)

claims of preempting threats to life and property. When Indians raided white settlements, they sometimes did mutilate bodies, burn buildings, and kidnap women, acts that were embellished in campfire stories, pamphlets, and popular fiction—all with the result of reinforcing images of Indians as savages. Among the bachelor society of saloons and cabins, men boasted of their exploits in Indian fighting and showed off trophies of scalps and other body parts taken from victims.

Indian warriors also were young, armed, and prone to violence. Sensitive to values of bravery and vengeance, they boasted of fighting white interlopers. But Indian communities contrasted with those of whites in that they contained excesses of women and children, making native bands less mobile and therefore vulnerable to attack. They also were vulnerable to the bad habits of the bachelor white society. Indians copied white behavior of bingeing on cheap whiskey and indulging in prostitution. The syphilis and gonorrhea they contracted from Indian women infected by whites killed many and reduced the ability of natives to reproduce, a consequence that their already declining population could not afford. Thus the age and gender structure of the white frontier population combined with attitudes of racial contempt created a serious threat to Indian existence in the West.

Government policy reinforced individual efforts to remove Indians from the path of white ambitions.

Lack of Native Unity

North American natives were organized not so much into tribes, as whites believed, but rather into hundreds of bands and confederacies in the Plains and towns and villages in the Southwest and Northwest. Some two hundred distinct languages and dialects separated these groups and made it difficult for Indians to unite against white invaders. Although a language group could be defined as a tribe, separate bands and clans within each language group had their own leaders, and seldom did a tribal chief hold significant power. Moreover, bands usually spent more time quarreling among themselves than with white settlers, and sometimes bands from completely different peoples, such as Kiowas and Comanches in the southern Plains, lived together.

Nevertheless, the U.S. government needed some way of categorizing the natives so as to fashion a policy toward them. It did so by imputing more meaning to tribal organization than was warranted. After the Treaty of Greenville in 1795, American officials considered Indian tribes to be separate nations with which they could make treaties that ensured peace and defined boundaries between Indian and white lands. But a chief or chiefs who agreed to a treaty could not guarantee that all bands within the group would abide by it. Moreover, whites seldom accepted treaties as guarantees of the Indians' future land rights. In the Northwest, whites considered treaties protecting Indians' fishing rights at certain sites on the Columbia River to be nuisances and pushed Indians aside from the best locations so they could use their mechanical devices that harvested thousands of fish a day. On the Plains, whites assumed that they could settle wherever they wished, and they rarely hesitated to commandeer choice farmland along river basins. As white settlers pressed into Indian territories, treaties made one week were violated the next.

Territorial Treaties

From the 1860s to the 1880s, the federal government tried to force Indians onto reservations, where, it

Reservation Policy

was thought, they could be "civilized." Reservations usually consisted of those areas of a group's previous territory that were least desirable to whites. When assigning Indians to such parcels, the government promised protection from white encroachment and agreed to provide food, clothing, and other necessities.

The new post–Civil War reservation policy helped make way for the market economy. In the early years of contact in the West, trade had benefited both Indians and whites and had taken place on a nearly equal footing, much as it had between eastern Indians and whites in the years before the American Revolution. Indians had acquired clothing, guns, and horses in return for furs, jewelry, and, sometimes, military service. In the West, however, whites' needs and economic power grew disproportionate to the needs and power of Indians. Indians became more dependent, and whites increasingly dictated what was to be traded and on what terms. For example, white traders persuaded Navajo weavers in the Southwest to produce heavy rugs suitable for eastern customers and to adopt new designs and colors to boost sales. Meanwhile, Navajos raised fewer crops and were forced to buy food because the market economy lured them away from subsistence agriculture. Soon they were selling their land and labor to whites as well, which made it easier to force them onto reservations.

Reservation policy had degrading consequences. First, Indians had no say over their own affairs on reservations. Supreme Court decisions in 1884 and 1886 defined them as wards (falling, like helpless children, under government protection) and denied them the right to become U.S. citizens. Thus they were unprotected by the Fourteenth and Fifteenth Amendments,

Reformers established boarding schools to take Indian children off the reservations and teach them a new and allegedly better culture. As one white leader remarked, "They should be educated, not as Indians, but as Americans." At the Carlisle School in Pennsylvania, one of twenty-four such schools, Sioux youths *(left)* received new attire to make them look *(right)* as their teachers wanted them to look. (Smithsonian Institute, Washington, D.C.)

which had extended to African Americans the privileges and legal protections of citizenship. Second, pressure from white farmers, miners, and herders who continually sought Indian lands for their own purposes made it difficult for the government to preserve reservations intact. Third, the government ignored native history, even combining on the same reservation Indian bands that habitually had waged war against each other. Rather than serving as civilizing communities, reservations weakened every aspect of Indian life, except the resolve of some to survive.

Not all Indians succumbed to market forces and reservation restrictions. Pawnees in the Midwest, for example, resisted extensive trading and the disadvantageous deals that whites tried to impose on them. And some natives tried to preserve their cultures even as they became dependent on whites. Pawnees, for example, agreed to leave their Nebraska homelands for a reservation in the hope that they could hunt buffalo and grow corn as they once had done.

Native Resistance

As they had done earlier in the East, whites responded to western Indian recalcitrance and revolt with organized military aggression. In 1864, for example, in order to eliminate Indians who blocked white ambitions in the Sand Creek region of Colorado, a militia force led by Methodist minister John Chivington attacked a Cheyenne band under Black Kettle, killing almost everyone. In 1877 four detachments of troops, aided by Crow and Cheyenne scouts, chased eight hundred Nez Percé Indians over rugged terrain in the Northwest, finally surrounding and killing many before one of their leaders, Young Joseph, surrendered. In 1879 four thousand U.S. soldiers mobilized and forced a surrender from Utes, who already had given up most of their ancestral territory in western Colorado but were resisting further concessions.

Indian Wars

The most infamous of Indian battles occurred in June 1876 when 2,500 Lakotas led by Chiefs Rain-in-the-Face, Sitting Bull, and Crazy Horse surrounded and annihilated 256 government troops led by the rash Colonel George A. Custer near the Little Big Horn River in southern Montana. Though Indians consistently demonstrated military skill in such battles, shortages of supplies and relentless pursuit by U.S. soldiers, who often utilized Indian scouts from an enemy tribe, eventually overwhelmed armed Indian resistance. Native Americans were not so much conquered in battle as they were starved into submission.

By the 1870s and 1880s, government officials and reformers sought more peaceful means of dealing with western natives. Instead of being considered foreign nations, Indians would be "civilized" and "uplifted" through landholding and education.

Reform of Indian Policy

This meant changing their identities, community structures, and relationships to the federal government. With government encouragement, white missionaries and teachers would attempt to persuade Native Americans to adopt values of the new American work ethic: ambition, thrift, and materialism. To achieve this transformation, however, Indians would have to abandon their traditional cultures. Also, reform treatises—George Manypenny's *Our Indian Wards* (1880) and Helen Hunt Jackson's *A Century of Dishonor* (1881), for example—and unfavorable comparison with Canada's management of Indian affairs aroused the American conscience. Canada had granted native peoples the rights of British subjects, and the Royal Mounted Police defended them against whites. Canadian officials were more tolerant and proceeded more slowly than Americans in efforts to acculturate Indians. A high rate of intermarriage between Indians and Canadian whites also promoted smoother relations.

In the United States, the two most active Indian reform organizations were the Women's National Indian Association (WNIA) and the Indian Rights Association (IRA). The WNIA, composed mainly of white women who sought to use women's domestic skills to help people in need, urged gradual assimilation of Indians. The IRA, which was more influential but numbered few Native Americans among its members, supported citizenship and landholding by individual Indians. Most reformers believed Indians were culturally inferior to whites and assumed Indians could succeed economically only if they adopted middle-class values of diligence, monogamy, and education.

Reformers particularly deplored Indians' sexual division of labor. Women seemed to do all the work—tending crops, raising children, cooking, curing hides, making tools and clothes—and to be servile to men, who hunted but were otherwise idle. Ignoring the fact that white men were not always considerate of white women, groups such as the WNIA and IRA wanted Indian men to bear more responsibilities, to treat Indian women more respectfully, and to resemble male heads of white middle-class households. But because these groups often tried to coax Indian men and

How do historians know...

that Indians expressed values and messages in non-verbal ways? The Plains Indians did not write books or letters as whites did, but they did tell stories and spread news through art. Plains Indians painted scenes on buffalo hides and, later, in notebooks that they acquired from whites, a form of artwork called ledger drawings. These illustrations not only depict scenes but, together, also tell a story with motion, drama, and message almost as a motion picture might today. The drawings also conveyed important information such as directions to new campsites, the location of enemy bands, and messages of love. Look at the drawing reproduced here. It was painted in the 1870s by a Cheyenne named Howling Wolf, who signed his work not in letters but with a symbol of a wolf with its mouth open in a howl. Howling Wolf made himself the hero of the scene, identified by the line drawn from the wolf to the warrior on the left. The discharging pistol hanging in midair and the blood pouring from the enemy's chest and mouth show that Howling Wolf has earlier wounded his adversary, and the path of hoof prints shows the movement of the battle. With his gun back in his belt, Howling Wolf holds a long spear that has dislodged his opponent from his horse, and victory clearly is imminent. Within the limits of a small page, Howling Wolf has described his own heroic exploits with an active narrative. But he has also left an indication of how highly Cheyenne culture esteemed bravery and individual male conquest, how important guns and horses were to Indian combat, and how Indians dressed and prepared for battle.

Ledger drawings represent one of several ways that historians can discover cultural aspects of people who did not produce written records. Other forms of evidence include artwork such as the totems of Pacific Northwest Indians and oral testimonies from southwestern and Plains Indians. (Photo: Allen Memorial Art Museum, Oberlin College, Oberlin, Ohio)

women into adopting a model of white society, in which women were supposed to be submissive and private, Indian women lost much of the power over daily life as well as the economic independence that they once had.

In 1887 Congress reversed its reservation policy and passed the Dawes Severalty Act. The act, which

Dawes Severalty Act

achieved a goal long recommended by reformers, authorized dissolution of community-owned Indian property and granted land allotments to individual Native American families. The land was held in trust by the government for twenty-five years so the families could not sell their allotments. The act also awarded citizenship to all who accepted allotments (though an act of Congress in 1906 delayed citizenship for those Indians who had not yet taken their allotment). It also entitled the government to sell unallocated land to whites.

Indian policy, as carried out by the Interior Department, now took on two main features, both of which aimed at assimilating Indians into European and white American forms of culture. First and foremost, as required by the Dawes Act, the federal government

Attempts at Assimilation

distributed reservation land to individual families in the belief that the American institution of private property would fashion good citizens and integrate Indians into the larger society. Second, officials believed that Indians would abandon their "barbaric" habits more quickly if their children were educated in boarding schools away from the reservations.

The Dawes Act reflected the Euro-American and Christian world-view, an earnest but narrow belief that a society of families headed by men was the most desired model. The reformers were deeply religious people who had long believed, as one expressed in 1887, that "civilization and the Gospel go hand in hand." They were joined by professional educators who viewed schools as tools to create a well-integrated, patriotic, industrial nation. Using the model of Hampton Institute, founded in Virginia in 1869 for the education of newly freed slaves, educators helped establish the Carlisle School in Pennsylvania in 1879, which served as the flagship of the government's Indian school system. In keeping with Euro-American custom, the boarding schools sought to impose white-defined sex roles: boys were taught farming and carpentry while girls learned sewing, cleaning, and cooking.

In 1890 the government made one last show of force—though such a demonstration was hardly necessary. With active resistance having

Ghost Dance

been suppressed, some Lakotas and other groups turned to the new religion of the Ghost Dance as a spiritual means of preserving native culture. Inspired by a Paiute prophet named Wovoka, the Ghost Dance involved movement in a circle until the dancers reached a trancelike state and envisioned dead ancestors. Some dancers believed these ancestral visitors heralded a day when buffalo would return to the plains and all elements of white civilization, including guns and whiskey, would be buried. The Ghost Dance expressed this messianic vision in a ritual involving several days of dancing and meditation.

Ghost Dancers forswore violence but appeared aggressive when they donned sacred shirts that they believed would repel the white man's bullets. As the religion spread, government agents became alarmed about the possibility of renewed Indian uprisings. Charging that the cult was anti-Christian, they began arresting Ghost Dancers. Late in 1890, the government sent the Seventh Cavalry, Custer's old regiment, to round up some Lakotas moving from the north toward Pine Ridge, South Dakota. Though the Indians were starving and seeking shelter, the army chose to assume they were armed for revolt. Overtaking the band at a creek called Wounded Knee, the troops massacred an estimated three hundred men, women, and children in the snow.

The Dawes Act effectively accomplished what whites wanted and Indians feared: it reduced native control over land. Eager speculators induced Indians to sell their newly acquired property, in spite of federal safeguards against such practices. Between 1887 and the 1930s, Indian landholdings dwindled from 138 million acres to 52 million. Land-grabbing whites were particularly cruel to the Ojibwas of the northern plains. In 1906 Senator Moses E. Clapp of Minnesota attached to an Indian appropriations bill a rider declaring that mixed-blood adults on the White Earth reservation were "competent" (meaning educated in white ways) enough to sell their land without having to observe the twenty-five-year waiting period stipulated in the Dawes Act. When the bill became law, speculators duped many Ojibwas, whom white experts had declared mixed-bloods on the basis of fraudulent evidence, into signing away their land in return for counterfeit money and worthless merchandise. The Ojibwas lost more than half of their original holdings, and economic ruin overtook them.

The Losing of the West

The government's policy had other harmful effects on Indians' ways of life. The boarding-school program enrolled thousands of children and tried to teach them that their inherited customs were inferior, but most returned to their families demoralized and confused rather than ready to assimilate into white society. Polingaysi Qoyawayma, a Hopi woman forced to take the Christian name Elizabeth Q. White, recalled after four years spent at the Sherman Institute in Riverside, California, "As a Hopi, I was misunderstood by the white man; as a convert of the missionaries, I was looked upon with suspicion by the Hopi people."

Ultimately, political and ecological crises overwhelmed most western Indian groups. White violence and military superiority alone did not defeat them. Their economic systems had started to break down before the military campaigns occurred. Buffalo extinction, enemy raids, and disease, in addition to force, combined to hobble subsistence culture to the point that Native Americans had no alternative but to yield their lands to market-oriented whites. Believing their culture to be superior, whites determined to transform the Indians into virtuous farmers by teaching them the value of private property, educating them in American ideals, and forcefully eradicating their "backward" languages, lifestyles, and religions. Although Indians tried to retain their culture by both adapting and yielding to the various demands they faced, by the end of the century they had lost control of the land and were under increasing pressure to shed their group identity. The West was won at their expense, and to this day they remain casualties of an aggressive age.

The Extraction of Natural Resources

 In sharp contrast to the Indians, who used land and water mostly to meet subsistence needs, most whites who migrated to the West and the Great Plains, first in the 1850s and increasingly after the Civil War, were driven by the desire to get rich quick. To their eyes, the vast stretches of territory lay as untapped reservoirs of resources and wealth (see Map 17.1). Extraction of these resources advanced settlement and created new markets at home and abroad; it also fueled the revolutions

Map 17.1   The Development and Natural Resources of the West   By 1890 mining, lumbering, and cattle ranching had penetrated many areas west of the Mississippi River, and railroads had linked together the western economy. These characteristics, along with the spread of agriculture, contributed to the Census Bureau's observation that the frontier had disappeared; yet, as the map shows, large areas remained undeveloped.

Legend:
- Forest
- Grassland
- Desert
- Copper mining
- Gold mining
- Silver mining
- Cattle trails
- Railroad routes
- 28-inch rainfall line

in transportation, agriculture, and industry that swept the United States in the late nineteenth century. At the same time, extraction of nature's wealth gave rise to wasteful interaction with the environment and fed habits of racial and sexual oppression.

In the mid-1800s, eager prospectors began to comb western forests and mountains for gold, silver, timber, and copper. The mining frontier advanced rapidly, drawing thousands of people to Nevada, Idaho, Montana, Utah, and Colorado. California, already a thriving state with more than three hundred thousand people by 1860, furnished many of the miners, who traveled from west to east in search of riches. Others followed traditional routes, moving from the East and Midwest to western mining regions.

Mining and Lumbering

By the 1880s, large-scale operations had replaced solitary prospectors in the extraction of minerals from western territories. Here, powerful sprays of water are being used to wash silver from a deposit in Alma, Colorado. (Colorado Historical Society)

Prospectors tended to be restless optimists, willing to climb mountains and trek across deserts in search of a telltale glint of precious metal. They shot game for food and financed their explorations by convincing merchants to advance credit for equipment in return for a share of the as-yet-undiscovered lode. Unlucky prospectors whose credit ran out took jobs and saved up for another search.

Digging for and transporting minerals was extremely expensive, so prospectors who did discover veins of metal seldom mined them. Instead, they sold their claims to large mining syndicates such as the Anaconda Copper Company. Financed by eastern capital, these companies could bring in engineers, heavy machinery, railroad lines, and work crews. Although discoveries of gold and silver first drew attention to the West and its resources, mining companies usually exploited less romantic but equally lucrative bonanzas of lead, zinc, tin, quartz, and copper.

Cutting fir and spruce trees for lumber to be used in construction, another large-scale extractive industry, needed vast tracks of forest land to be profitable. Lumber companies moving into the Northwest grabbed millions of acres under the Timber and Stone Act, passed by Congress in 1878 to stimulate settlement in California, Nevada, Oregon, and Washington. It allowed private citizens to buy, at a low price, 160-acre plots "unfit for cultivation" and "valuable chiefly for timber." Lumber companies hired seamen from waterfront boarding houses to register private claims to timberland and then transfer those claims to the companies. By 1900 private citizens had bought over 3.5 million acres, but most of that land belonged to corporations.

While lumber companies were acquiring timberlands in the Northwest, oil companies were beginning to drill for wells in the Southwest. In 1900 most of the nation's petroleum still came from the Appalachians and the Midwest, but rich oil reserves had been discovered in southern California and eastern Texas. Although oil and kerosene were still used mostly for lubrication and lighting, oil discovered in the Southwest later became a vital new source of fuel.

Though single white men numerically dominated the western natural-resource frontier, many communities did have substantial populations of white women who had come for the same reason as men: to find a fortune. But on the mining frontier as elsewhere, women's independence was limited; they usually accompanied a husband or fa-

Women in Mining Regions

ther and seldom prospected themselves. Even so, many women used their labor as a resource and realized opportunities to earn money by cooking and laundering and in some cases providing sexual services for the miners in houses of prostitution. In the Northwest, they worked in the canneries, cleaning and salting the fish that their husbands caught.

Women also helped to bolster family and community life as members of the home mission movement. Protestant missions had long carried out benevolent activities in foreign areas, such as China, and had been crucial in the settlement of Oregon in the 1840s. But in the mid-nineteenth century a number of women broke away from male-dominated missionary organizations. Their efforts focused on aiding women in countries that supported "barbaric" practices such as polygamy and female infanticide. Soon, these women—middle-class and white—were establishing missionary societies in the United States to fulfill their slogan, "Woman's work for woman." In the West, they exercised moral authority by building homes to rescue women—unmarried mothers, Mormons, Indians, and Chinese immigrants—who they believed had fallen prey to men or who had not yet accepted the conventions of Christian virtue.

The West became a rich multiracial society, including not only Native Americans and native-

A Complex Population

born white migrants but also Hispanics, African Americans, and Asians. A crescent of territory, a borderland stretching from western Texas through New Mexico and Arizona to northern California, supported Hispanic ranchers and sheepherders, descendants of the Spanish who originally had claimed the land. In New Mexico, Hispanics had mixed with Indians to form a *mestizo* population of small farmers and ranchers. All along the southwest border, Mexican immigrants moved into American territory to find work. Some returned to Mexico seasonally; others stayed. And, before federal law excluded them in 1881 and 1882, some two hundred thousand Chinese immigrants—most of them young, male, and single—came to the United States and constituted a sizable proportion of the work force in California, Oregon, and Washington. Japanese and eastern European immigrants also inhabited mining and agricultural communities. The region consequently developed its own migrant economy, with workers moving back and forth within a large geographical area as they took short-term jobs in mining, farming, and railroad construction. They periodically

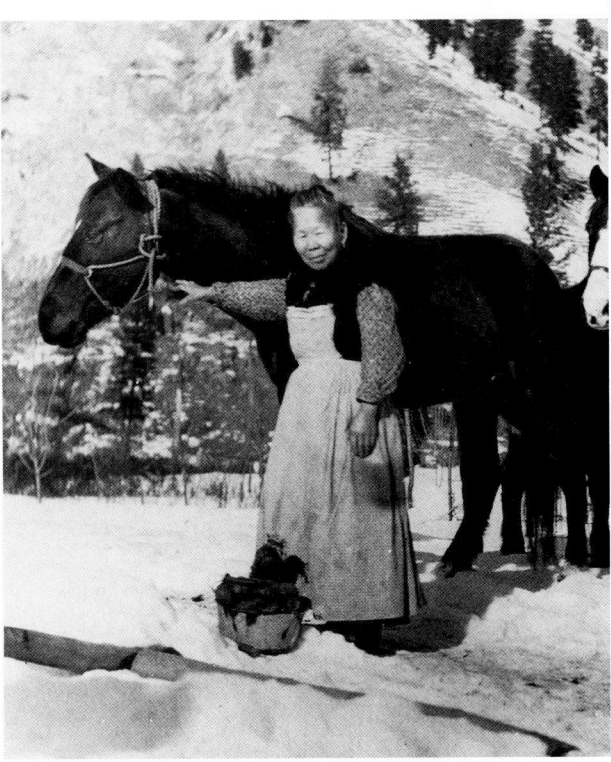

Born in China, Polly Bemis, pictured here, came to America when her parents sold her as a slave. An Idaho saloon-keeper bought her, and she later married a man named Charlie Bemis, who won her in a card game. Her life story was common among the few Chinese women who immigrated to the United States in the 1860s and 1870s (most Chinese immigrants were men). Unlike many Chinese, however, she lived peacefully after her marriage until her death in 1933.   (Idaho Historical Society Library and Archives)

returned to their home villages where women preserved a domestic base.

To control labor and social relations within this complex population, white settlers made race an important distinguishing social charac-

Significance of Race

teristic in the West. They usually identified four nonwhite races: Indians, Mexicans (both Mexican Americans, who had originally inhabited western lands, and Mexican immigrants), "Mongolians" (a term applied to Chinese), and African Americans. In creating these categories, whites imposed racial distinctions on people who, with the possible exception of blacks, had never before considered themselves to be a "race." Whites using these categories ascribed demeaning characteristics to all non-

Dressed formally for the opening ceremony of the Mullan Tunnel in Montana in 1884, these Chinese railroad workers, who helped build the tunnel, have temporarily cast aside their traditional work clothes and are showing their embrace of a new culture.   (Montana Historical Society)

whites, judging them to be not only inferior but permanently so.

Racial minorities in western communities occupied the bottom half of a two-tiered labor system. Whites dominated the top tier of managerial and skilled labor positions. Unskilled laborers, often Irish, Chinese, and Mexicans, worked in the mines, on railroad construction, and as agricultural laborers. Blacks also worked in railroad and mining camps, doing cooking and cleaning, while Indians barely participated in the white-controlled labor system at all. All nonwhite groups plus the Irish encountered prejudice, especially as whites tried to reserve for themselves whatever riches the West might yield. The few Chinese who went into commercial fishing or agriculture found their activities limited by federal laws and local persecution that resulted in loss of their property. Many became low-paid workers in California's laundry, tobacco, and domestic service establishments. Mexicans, many of whom had been the original owners of the land, saw their property claims ignored or stolen by white miners and farmers. In California, they

too became an urban population, working at unskilled, low-paying jobs.

The multiracial quality of western society, however, also included a cross-racial quality. Because so many male migrants to these states, as well as to Texas and New Mexico, were single, intermarriage with Mexican and Indian women was common. Such intermarriage was acceptable for white men, but not for white women, especially where Asian immigrants were involved. Most miscegenation laws passed by western legislatures were intended to prevent Chinese and Japanese men from marrying white women.

As whites were wresting control of the land from the Indians and Spanish inhabitants of the Southwest and California, questions arose over control of the nation's oil, mineral, and timber resources. Much of the remaining undeveloped land west of the Mississippi was in the public domain, and some people believed that the federal government, as its owner, should limit its exploitation. Others, however, believed that their own and the na-

Conservation Movement

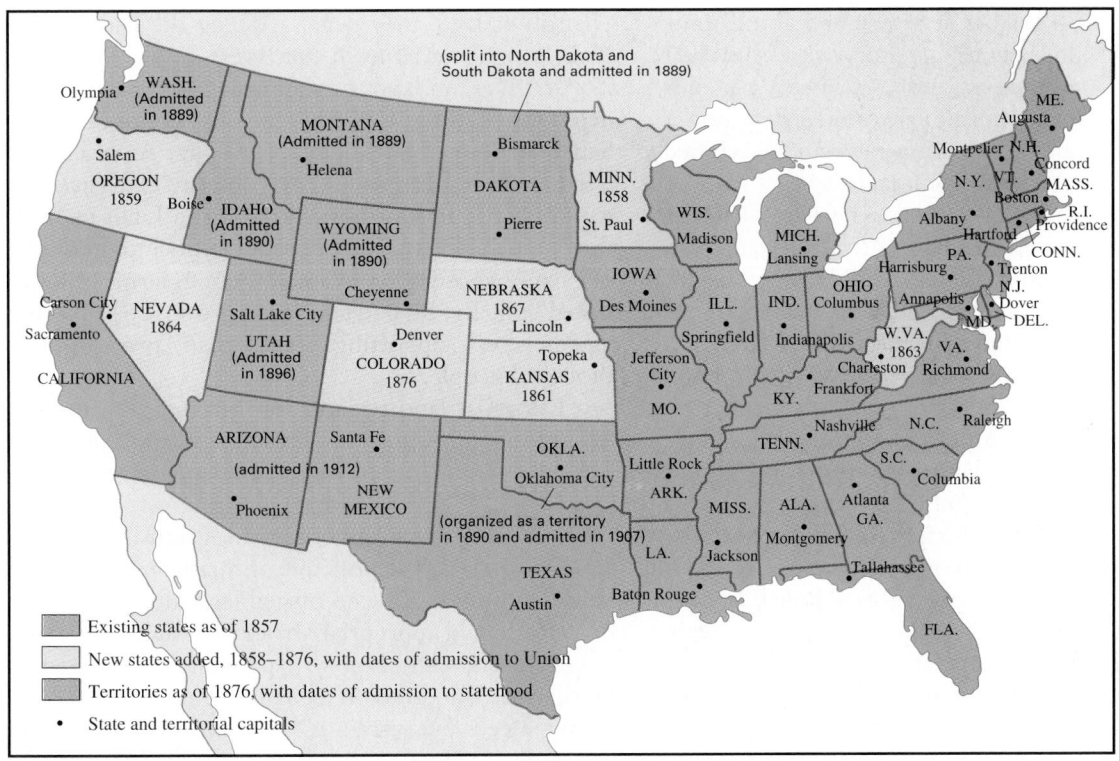

Map 17.2 The United States, 1876–1912 A wave of admissions between 1889 and 1912 brought remaining territories to statehood and marked the final creation of new states until Alaska and Hawai'i were admitted in the 1950s.

tion's prosperity depended on unlimited use of the land.

Questions about natural resources caught Americans between a desire for progress and a fear of spoiling the land. By the late 1870s, people eager to protect the natural landscape began to organize a conservation movement. They made Yellowstone Park in Wyoming the first national park in 1872. A prominent conservationist, naturalist John Muir, helped to establish Yosemite National Park in 1890. The next year, pressured by Muir and others, Congress authorized President Benjamin Harrison to create forest reserves—public lands protected from private-interest cutting. Such policies met with strong objections. Opposition came from lumber companies, lumber dealers, railroads, and householders accustomed to cutting timber freely for fuel and building material. Public opinion also split along sectional lines. Most supporters of conservation came from eastern states, where resources already had become less plentiful. Despite Muir's activism and efforts by the Sierra Club (which

Muir helped found in 1892), opposition was loudest in the West, where people remained eager to take advantage of nature's bounty.

Development of the mining and forest regions, and of the farms and cities that followed, brought western territories to the threshold of statehood (see Map 17.2). In 1889 Republicans seeking to solidify their control of Congress passed an omnibus bill granting statehood to North Dakota, South Dakota, Washington, and Montana. Wyoming and Idaho were admitted the following year. Congress denied statehood to Utah until 1896, wanting assurances from the Mormons, who constituted a majority of the territory's population and controlled its government, that they would give up polygamy.

Admission of New States

Those states' mining towns and lumber camps spiced American folk culture and fostered a go-getter optimism that distinguished the American spirit. The lawlessness and hedonism of places such as Deadwood,

Legends of the West

in Dakota Territory, and Tombstone, in Arizona Territory, gave the West notoriety and romance. Legends grew up almost immediately about characters whose lives both typified and magnified western experience.

Arizona's mining towns, with their free-flowing cash and loose law enforcement, attracted gamblers, thieves, and opportunists whose names came to stand for the Wild West. Near Tombstone, the infamous Clanton family and their partner John Ringgold (known as Johnny Ringo) engaged in smuggling and cattle rustling. Inside the town, the Earp brothers— Wyatt, Jim, Morgan, Virgil, and Warren—and their friends William ("Bat") Masterson and John Henry ("Doc") Holliday operated on both sides of the law as gunmen, gamblers, and politicians. A feud between the Clanton and Earp clans climaxed on October 26, 1881, in a shootout at the OK Corral, where three Clantons were killed and Holliday and Morgan Earp were wounded. These characters and their exploits provided material for many movies and television programs in future years.

Mark Twain, Bret Harte, and other writers captured for posterity the flavor of mining life, and characters like Buffalo Bill, Annie Oakley, Wild Bill Hickok, Poker Alice, and Bedrock Tom became western folk heroes. But violence and eccentricity were far from common. Most miners and lumbermen worked long hours and had little time, energy, or money for gambling, carousing, or gunfights. Women worked as long or longer as teachers, cooks, laundresses, storekeepers, and housewives. Only a few were sharpshooters or dance-hall queens. For most, western life was a matter of adapting and surviving.

Irrigation and Transportation

Glittering gold, tall trees, and gushing oil shaped the popular image of the West, but water gave it life. If western territories and states promised wealth from mining, cutting, and drilling, their agricultural potential promised more—but only if settlers could find a way to bring water to the arid land. The economic development of the West is the story of how public and private interests used technology and organization to develop the region's river basins and make the land agriculturally productive. Just as control of land was central to western development, so too was control of water.

For centuries, Indians had irrigated southwestern lands to sustain their subsistence farming. When the Spanish arrived, they began tapping the Rio Grande River to irrigate farms in southwest Texas, New Mexico, and mission lands in California. Later they channeled water to the California mission communities of San Diego and Los Angeles. The first Americans of northern European ancestry to practice extensive irrigation were the Mormons. Arriving in Utah in 1847, they quickly diverted streams and rivers into networks of canals, whose water enabled them to farm the hardbaked soil. By 1890 Utah boasted over 263,000 irrigated acres supporting more than two hundred thousand people.

Efforts at land reclamation through irrigation in Colorado and California raised controversies over rights to the precious streams that flowed through the West. Americans had inherited the English commonlaw principle of riparian rights, which held that only those who owned land along the banks of a river could appropriate from the water's flow. The stream itself, according to riparianism, belonged to God; those who lived on its banks could take water for normal needs but were not to diminish the river. This principle, intended to protect nature, discouraged economic development because it prohibited each property owner from damming or diverting water at the expense of others who lived along the banks.

Rights to Water

Americans who settled the West rejected riparianism in favor of the doctrine of prior appropriation, which awarded a river's water to the first person who claimed it. Westerners, taking cues in part from eastern Americans who had diverted waterways to power mills and factories, asserted that water, like timber, minerals, and other natural resources, existed to serve human needs and advance profits. They argued that anyone intending a beneficial or "reasonable" (economically productive) use of river water should have the right to appropriation, and the courts ultimately agreed.

Under appropriation, those who dammed and diverted water often reduced the flow of water downstream. People disadvantaged by such action could protect their interests either by suing those who deprived them of water or by establishing a public authority to regulate water usage. Thus in 1879 Colorado created a number of water divisions, each with a commissioner to determine and regulate water rights. In 1890 Wyoming enlarged the concept of control with a constitutional provision declaring that the state's rivers were public property subject to state supervision of their use.

Destined to become the most productive agricultural state, California developed a dramatic solution to

Water, aided by human resolve, coaxed crops from the dry soil and helped make the West habitable for whites. On this Colorado farm, a windmill pumps water for irrigation. (Longmont Museum, Longmont, Colorado)

California's Solution

the problem of water rights, sometimes called the "California Solution." In the 1860s a few individuals controlled huge tracts of land in the fertile Sacramento and San Joaquin River valleys, which they used for speculating in real estate, raising cattle, and growing wheat. But around the edges of the wheat fields lay unoccupied lands that could profitably support vegetable and fruit farming if irrigated properly.

Unlike western states that had opted for appropriation rights over riparian rights, California maintained a mixed legal system that upheld riparianism while allowing for some appropriation. This system put irrigators at a disadvantage and prompted them to seek a change in state law. In 1887 the state legislature passed a bill permitting farmers to organize into districts that would sponsor the construction and operation of irrigation projects. An irrigation district could use its public authority to purchase water rights, seize private property to build irrigation canals, and finance its projects through taxation or by issuing bonds. As a result of this legislation, California became the nation's leader in irrigated acreage, with more than 1 million irrigated acres by 1890, and the state's fruit and vegetable crops made its agriculture the most profitable in the country.

Though state irrigation provisions stimulated development, the federal government still owned most of western lands in the 1890s, ranging from 64 percent of California to 96 percent of Nevada. Prodded by land-hungry developers, the states wanted the federal government to transfer to them at least part of the public domain lands. States claimed that they could make these lands profitable through reclamation—providing them with irrigated water. For the most part, Congress refused such transfers because of the controversies they raised. If federal lands were transferred to state control for the purpose of water development, who would regulate waterways that flowed through more than one state or that potentially could provide water to a nearby state? If, for example, California received control of the Truckee River, which flowed westward out of Lake Tahoe on the California-Nevada border, how would Nevadans be assured that California would give them any water? Only the federal government, it seemed, had the power to regulate regional water development.

Newlands Reclamation Act

In 1902, after years of proposals and debates, Congress passed the Newlands Reclamation Act. Named for Nevada congressman Francis Newlands, the act allowed the federal government to sell western public lands to individuals in parcels not to exceed 160 acres, and to use the proceeds from such sales to finance irrigation projects. The Newlands Act provided for control but not conservation of water, because three-fourths of the water used in open-ditch irrigation, the most common form, was lost to evaporation. Thus the legislation fell squarely within the tradition of exploitation of nature for human profit. Often identified as an example of sensitivity to natural-resource conservation, the Newlands Reclamation Act in fact represented a decision by the federal government to aid the agricultural and general economic development of the West, just as state and federal subsidies to railroads during the 1850s and 1860s aided settlement of the West.

Railroad construction boomed after the Civil War. Between 1865 and 1890, total track in the United

Post–Civil War Railroad Construction

States grew from 35,000 to 200,000 miles (see Map 17.1). By the turn of the century, the United States contained one-third of all the railroad track in the world. A diverse mix of workers made up construction crews. The Central Pacific, built eastward from San Francisco, imported seven thousand Chinese to build its tracks; the Union Pacific, extending westward from Omaha, Nebraska, used mainly Irish construction gangs. Workers lived in shacks and tents that could be dismantled, loaded on flatcars, and relocated at intervals of about 60 or 70 miles. After 1880, when steel rails began to replace iron rails, railroads helped to boost the nation's steel industry to international leadership. Railroad expansion also spawned a number of related industries, including coal production, passenger- and freight-car manufacture, and depot construction.

Influential and essential, railroads performed a uniquely American function. Europeans usually built

Rails and Markets

railroads to link established market centers and to improve or replace existing routes for carrying raw materials, food, and manufactured goods. In the United States, railroads carried the same products, but they often created many of the very communities they were meant to serve and they carried traffic that had never before existed. With their ability to transport large loads of people and freight, lines such as the Union Pacific and Southern Pacific accelerated the growth of western regional centers such as Omaha, Kansas City, Cheyenne, Los Angeles, Portland, and Seattle.

Railroads accomplished these feats with the help of some of the largest government subsidies in Ameri-

can history. Executives argued that because railroads benefited the public, the government should aid them by giving them land from the public domain. Congress, dominated by Republicans during and after the Civil War, was sympathetic, as it had been when it aided steamboat companies navigating on the Great Lakes and the Mississippi River earlier in the nineteenth century. To encourage rail construction, the federal government granted railroad companies over 180 million acres, mostly for interstate routes. These grants usually consisted of a right of way, plus alternate sections of land in a strip 20 to 80 miles wide along the right of way. Railroads funded construction by using the land as security for bonds or by selling it for cash. States and localities heaped on further subsidies. State legislators, many of whom had financial interests in a railroad's success, granted some 50 million acres. Counties, cities, and towns also assisted, usually by offering loans or by purchasing railroad bonds or stocks.

Government subsidies had mixed effects. Though capitalists often argued against government interference in economic affairs of private companies, privately owned railroads nevertheless accepted government aid and pressured governments into meeting their needs. The Southern Pacific, for example, threatened to bypass Los Angeles unless the city came up with a bonus and built a depot. Localities that could not or would not pay withered. Without public help, few railroads could have prospered sufficiently to attract private investment, yet public aid was not always salutary. During the 1880s, the policy of assistance haunted communities whose zeal had prompted them to commit too much to railroads that were never built or that defaulted on loans. Some laborers and farmers fought subsidies, arguing that companies like the Southern Pacific would become too powerful. Many communities boomed, however, because they had linked their fortunes to the iron horse. Moreover, railroads drew farmers into the market economy.

Railroad construction brought about important technological and organizational reforms. By the late

Standard Gauge; Standard Time

1880s, almost all lines had adopted standard-gauge rails so their tracks could connect with one another. Air brakes, automatic car couplers, standardized handholds on freight cars, and other devices made rail transportation safer and more efficient. The need for gradings, tunnels, and bridges spurred the growth of the American engineering profession. Organizational advances included systems for coordinating complex passenger and freight schedules and the adoption of uniform freight-classification systems.

Railroads also altered conceptions of time and space. First, by surmounting physical barriers to travel, railroads transformed space into time. Instead of expressing the distance between places in miles, people began to refer to the amount of time it took to travel from one place to another. Second, railroad scheduling required nationwide standardization of time. Before railroads, local church bells and clocks struck noon when the sun was directly overhead, and people set their clocks and watches accordingly. But because the sun was not overhead at exactly the same moment everywhere, time varied from place to place. Clocks in Boston, for instance, differed from those in New York by almost twelve minutes. To impose regularity, railroads created their own time zones. By 1880 there were nearly fifty different standards, but in 1883 the railroads finally agreed—without consulting anyone in government—to establish four standard time zones for the whole country. Most communities adjusted their clocks accordingly, and railroad time became national time.

Farming the Plains

"You are in a sea of wheat," rhapsodized the author of an 1880 magazine article about Oliver Dalrymple's farm in Dakota Territory's Red River valley. "The railroad train rolls through an ocean of grain. . . . We encounter a squadron of war chariots . . . doing the work of human hands. . . . There are 25 [machines] in this one brigade of the grand army of 115, under the marksmanship of this Dakota farmer." Dalrymple's farm exemplified two important achievements of the late nineteenth century: the transforming of arid, windswept prairies into arable land that would yield crops to benefit humankind, and the transformation of agriculture into big business by means of mechanization, long-distance transportation, and scientific cultivation.

These achievements did not come easily. The climate and terrain of the Great Plains presented formidable challenges, and overcoming them did not guarantee success. Technological innovation and the mechanization of agriculture enabled farmers to feed the nation's burgeoning population and turned the United States into the world's breadbasket, but it also scarred the lives of hundreds of thousands of men and women who made that development possible.

Settlement of the Plains

During the 1870s and 1880s, hundreds of thousands of hopeful farmers streamed into the Great Plains region. More acres were put under cultivation in states such as Kansas, Nebraska, and Texas during these two decades than in the entire country during the previous 250 years. The number of farms tripled from 2 million to over 6 million between 1860 and 1910. Several states opened offices in the East and in European ports to lure migrants westward. Land-rich railroads were especially aggressive, advertising cheap land, arranging credit terms, offering reduced fares, and promising instant success. Railroad agents—often former immigrants—traveled to Denmark, Sweden, Germany, and other European nations to recruit settlers and greeted newcomers at eastern ports. In California after the turn of the century, fruit and vegetable growers imported laborers from Japan and Mexico to work in the fields and canneries.

Most migrants went west because opportunities there seemed to promise a better life. Railroad expansion gave farmers in remote regions a way to ship produce to market, and the construction of grain elevators

Train schedules not only changed the American economy but also altered how Americans timed their daily lives. As people and businesses ordered their day according to the arrival and departure of trains, distances became less important than hours and minutes.   (Library of Congress)

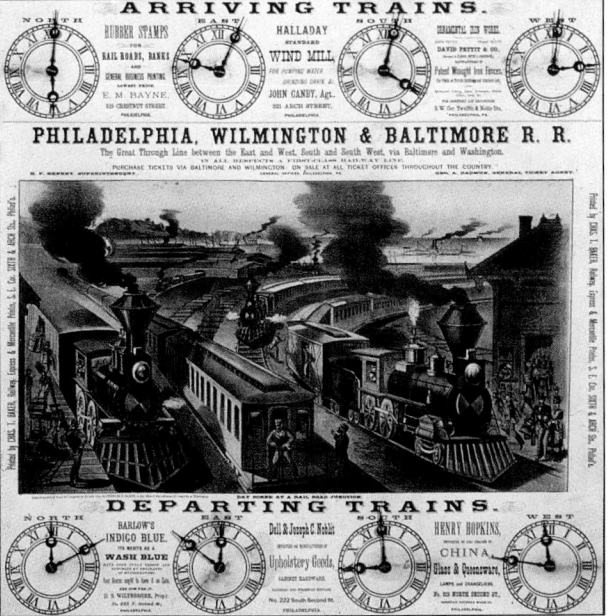

eased problems of shipping and storage. As a result of worldwide as well as national population growth, the demand for farm products grew rapidly, and the prospects for commercial agriculture—growing crops for profit and for shipment to distant, including international, markets—became more favorable than ever.

Life on the farm, however, was much harder than the advertisements and railroad agents suggested. Migrants often encountered scarcities of essentials they had once taken for granted. The open prairies contained little lumber for housing and fuel. Pioneer families were forced to build houses of sod and to burn manure for heat. Water for cooking and cleaning was sometimes as scarce as timber. Few families were lucky or wealthy enough to buy land near a stream that did not dry up in summer and freeze in winter. Machinery for drilling wells was expensive, as were windmills for drawing the water to the surface.

Even more formidable than the terrain was the climate. The climate between the Missouri River and the Rocky Mountains divides along a line running from Minnesota southwest through Oklahoma, then south, bisecting Texas. West of this line, annual rainfall averages less than 28 inches, not enough for most crops or trees (see Map 17.3), and even that scant life-giving rain was never certain. Heartened by adequate water one year, farmers gagged on dust and broke plows on hardened limestone soil the next.

Weather seldom followed predictable cycles. In summer, weeks of torrid heat and parching winds suddenly gave way to violent storms that washed away crops and property. The wind and cold of winter blizzards piled up mountainous snowdrifts that halted all outdoor movement. During the Great Blizzard that struck Nebraska and the Dakota Territory in January 1888, the temperature plunged to 36 degrees below zero, and the wind blew at 56 miles per hour. The storm not only caused livestock to perish but also stranded schoolchildren and killed several parents who ventured out to rescue them. In springtime, melting

Hardship of Life on the Plains

Map 17.3 Agricultural Regions of the United States, 1890 In the Pacific Northwest and east of the 28-inch-rainfall line, farmers could grow a greater variety of crops. Territory west of the line was either too mountainous or too arid to support agriculture without irrigation. The grasslands that once fed buffalo herds now could feed beef cattle.

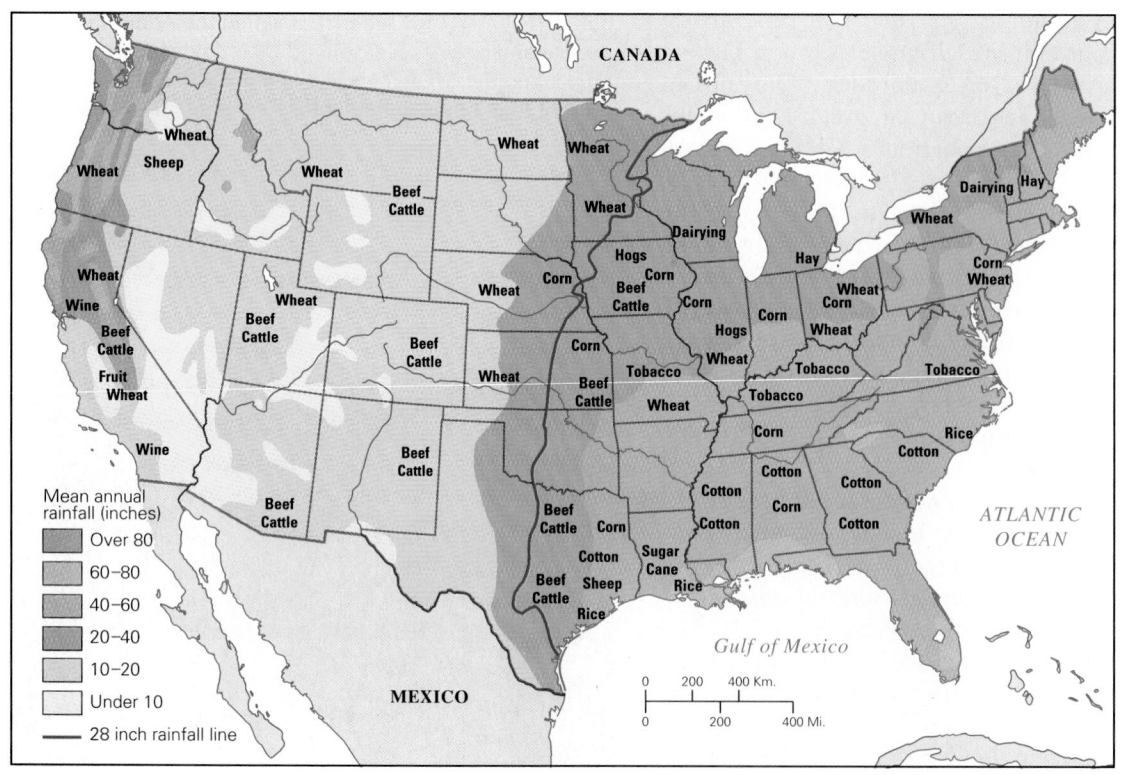

snow swelled streams, and floods threatened millions of acres. In the fall, a week without rain could turn dry grasslands into tinder, and the slightest spark could ignite a raging prairie fire.

Nature could be cruel even under good conditions. Weather that was favorable for crops was also good for breeding insects. Worms and flying pests ravaged corn and wheat. In the 1870s and 1880s swarms of grasshoppers virtually ate up entire farms. Heralded only by the din of buzzing wings, a mile-long cloud of insects would smother the land and devour everything: plants, tree bark, and clothes. As one farmer lamented, the "hoppers left behind nothing but the mortgage."

Settlers also had to contend with social isolation. Farmers in New England and in Europe lived in villages and traveled each day to nearby fields. This pattern was rare in the vast expanses of the Plains—and in the Far West and South as well—where peculiarities of land division compelled American rural dwellers to live apart from each other. The Homestead Act of 1862 and other measures to encourage western settlement offered cheap or free plots to people who would live on and improve their property. Because most plots acquired by small farmers were rectangular—usually encompassing 160 acres—at most

Social Isolation

four families could live near each other, but only if they congregated around the shared four-corner intersection. In practice, farm families usually lived back from their boundary lines, and at least a half-mile separated farmhouses.

Letters that Ed Donnell, a young Nebraska homesteader, wrote to his family in Missouri reveal how time and circumstances could dull optimism. In the fall of 1885, Donnell wrote to his mother: "I like Nebr first rate. . . . I have saw a pretty tuff time a part of the time since I have been out here, but I started out to get a home and I was determined to win or die in the attempt. . . . Have got a good crop of corn, a floor in my house and got it ceiled overhead." Already, though, Donnell was lonely. He went on: "There is lots of other bachelors here but I am the only one I know who doesn't have kinfolks living handy. . . . You wanted to know when I was going to get married. Just as quick as I can get money ahead to get a cow."

A year and a half later, Donnell's dreams were dissolving and, still a bachelor, he was beginning to look for a second chance elsewhere. As he explained to his brother, "The rats eat my sod stable down. . . . I may sell out this summer, land is going up so fast. . . . If I sell I am going west and grow up with the country." By fall things had worsened, and Donnell wrote, "We

Posing in front of their sod house, this proud Nebraska family displays the seriousness that derived from their hard lives on the Great Plains. Though bushes and other growth appear in the background, the absence of trees is notable. (Nebraska State Historical Society, Solomon D. Butcher Collection)

have been having wet weather for 3 weeks. . . . My health has been so poor this summer and the wind and the sun hurts my head so. I think if I can sell I will . . . move to town for I can get $40 a month working in a grist mill and I would not be exposed to the weather." Donnell's doubts and hardships, shared by thousands of other people, fed the cityward migration of farm folk that fueled late-nineteenth-century urban growth (see Chapter 19).

Farm families survived by sheer resolve and by organizing churches and clubs where they could socialize a few times a month. By 1900 two developments had brought rural settlers into closer contact with modern consumer society (though people in sparsely settled regions west of the 28-inch rainfall line remained isolated for several more decades). First, mail-order companies—Montgomery Ward and Sears, Roebuck—made new products available to almost everyone by the 1870s and 1880s. Emphasizing personal attention to customers, Ward's and Sears were outlets for sociability as well as material goods. Letters

Mail-Order Companies and Rural Free Delivery

from customers to Mr. Ward often reported family news and sought advice on everything from gifts to childcare. A Washington State man wrote, "As you advertise everything for sale that a person wants, I thought I would write you, as I am in need of a wife, and see what you could do for me." Another wrote: "I suppose you wonder why we haven't ordered anything from you since the fall. The cow kicked my arm and broke it and besides my wife was sick, and there was the doctor bill. But now, thank God, that is paid, and we are all well again, and we have a fine new baby boy, and please send plush bonnet number 29d8077."

Second, rural communities petitioned Congress for extension of the postal service during the 1890s, and in 1896 the government made Rural Free Delivery (RFD), which had begun earlier in West Virginia, widely available. Farmers previously had to go to town to pick up their mail. Now, they could receive letters, newspapers, and catalogues in a mailbox on a road near their home nearly every day. In 1913 the postal service inaugurated parcel post, which enabled people to receive packages, such as orders from Ward's and Sears, more cheaply.

By the late nineteenth century, the industrial revolution was making a significant impact on farming. This scene from a Colorado wheat farm shows a harvest aided by a steam tractor and belt-driven thresher, equipment that made large-scale commercial crop production possible.   (Colorado Historical Society)

The agricultural revolution that followed the Civil War would not have been possible without the expanded use of machinery. When the

Mechanization of Agriculture

Civil War drew men away from farms in the upper Mississippi River valley, the women and older men who remained behind began using reapers and other mechanical implements to satisfy demand for food and take advantage of high grain prices. After the war, continued demand and high prices encouraged farmers to depend more on machines, and inventors developed new implements for farm use. Seeders, combines, binders, mowers, and rotary plows, carried westward by railroads, were introduced on the Great Plains and in California in the 1870s and 1880s.

For centuries, the acreage of grain a farmer could plant had been limited by the amount that could be harvested by hand. Machines—driven first by animals, then by steam—increased productivity beyond farmers' imaginations. Before mechanization, a farmer working alone could harvest about 7.5 acres of wheat. Using an automatic binder that cut and bundled the grain, the same farmer could harvest 135 acres. Machines dramatically reduced the time and cost of farming other crops as well (see Table 17.1).

Meanwhile, Congress and scientists worked to improve existing crops and develop new ones. The 1862 Morrill Land Grant Act gave each

Legislative and Scientific Aids to Farming

state federal lands to sell in order to finance educational institutions that aided agricultural development. The act prompted establishment of state universities in Wisconsin, Illinois, Minnesota, California, and other states. (A second Morrill Act in 1890 aided more schools, including a number of black colleges.) The Hatch Act of 1887 provided for agricultural experiment stations in every state, further encouraging the advancement of farming science and technology.

Scientific advances enabled farmers to use the soil more efficiently. Researchers developed dry farming, a technique of plowing and harrowing that minimized evaporation of precious moisture. Botanists perfected varieties of "hard" wheat whose seeds could withstand northern winters, and millers invented a process for grinding the tougher wheat kernels into flour. Agriculturists also adapted new varieties of alfalfa from Mongolia, corn from North Africa, and rice from Asia. Californian Luther Burbank developed a multitude of new plants by crossbreeding. Chemist George Washington Carver of the Tuskegee Institute created hundreds of new products from peanuts, soybeans, sweet potatoes, and cotton wastes, and he introduced methods of soil improvement. Other scientists developed means of combating plant and animal diseases. These and other scientific and technological developments helped feed a burgeoning population and make America what one journalist called "the garden of the world."

The Ranching Frontier

 While commercial farming was overspreading the West, it ran headlong into one of the region's most romantic industries—cattle ranching. Early in the nineteenth century herds of cattle, introduced by the Spanish and expanded by Mexican ranchers, roamed southern Texas and bred with cattle brought by Anglo settlers. The re-

Longhorns and the Long Drive

sulting longhorn breed multiplied and became valuable by the 1860s, when population growth boosted the

Table 17.1	Time and Cost of Farming an Acre of Land by Hand and by Machine, 1890			
	Hours Required		**Labor Cost**	
Crop	**Hand**	**Machine**	**Hand**	**Machine**
Wheat	61	3	$3.65	$.66
Corn	39	15	$3.62	$1.51
Oats	66	7	$3.73	$1.07
Loose hay	21	4	$1.75	$.42

Source: Ray Allan Billington, *Westward Expansion: A History of the American Frontier,* 2d ed. (New York: Macmillan, 1960), p. 697.

A group of cowboys prepare for a roundup. Note the presence of African Americans, who, along with Mexicans, made up one-fourth of all cowboys. Though they rarely became trail bosses or ranch owners, black cowboys enjoyed an independence on the trails that was unavailable to them on tenant farms and city streets.   (Nebraska State Historical Society)

demand for beef and railroads simplified the transportation of food. By 1870 drovers were herding thousands of Texas cattle northward to Kansas, Missouri, and Wyoming (see Map 17.1). On these long drives, mounted cowboys (as many as 25 percent of whom were African American) tended the herds, which fed on open grassland along the way. At the northern terminus—usually Abilene, Dodge City, or Cheyenne—the cattle were sold to northern ranches or loaded onto trains bound for Chicago and St. Louis for slaughter and distribution to national and international markets.

The long drive gave rise to romantic lore but was not very efficient. Trekking 1,000 miles or more for two to three months made cattle sinewy and tough. Herds traveling through Indian lands and farmers' fields were sometimes shot at and later prohibited from such trespass by state laws. Ranchers adjusted by raising herds nearer to railroad routes. When ranchers discovered that crossing Texas longhorns with heavier Hereford and Angus breeds produced animals better able to survive northern winters, cattle raising spread across the Great Plains. Between 1860 and 1880 the cattle population of Kansas, Nebraska, Colorado,

Wyoming, Montana, and the Dakotas increased from 130,000 to 4.5 million, crowding out already declining buffalo herds.

Cattle raisers needed vast pastures to graze their herds, and they wanted to incur as little expense as possible in using such land. Thus

The Open Range

they often bought a few acres bordering a stream and turned their herds loose on adjacent public domain that no one wanted because it lacked water access. By this method, called open-range ranching, a cattle raiser could control thousands of acres by owning only a hundred or so. Neighboring ranchers often formed associations and allowed their herds to graze together. Owners identified their cattle by burning a brand into each animal's hide. Every ranch had its own brand—a shorthand method for labeling movable property. Cowboy crews rounded up the cattle twice each year, in the spring to brand new calves and in the fall to drive mature animals to market.

Roundups delighted easterners with colorful images of western life: bellowing cattle, rope-swinging cowboys, and smoky campfires. Opportunities for profit at first enriched ranchers in Texas and other

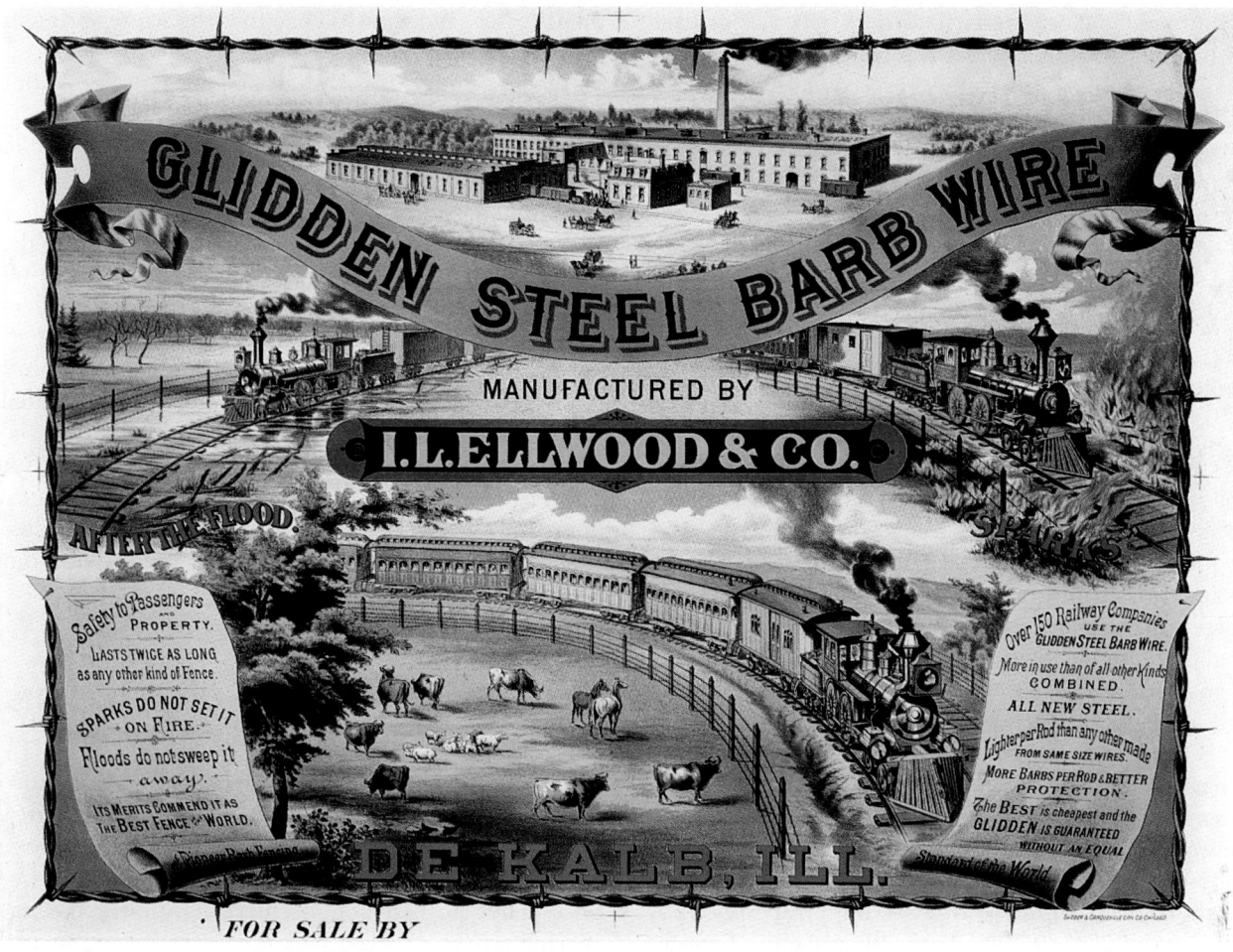

Bordered by the product it was promoting, this advertisement conveyed the message that railroads and farmers could protect their property from each other by utilizing a new type of fencing.   (Elwood House Museum, DeKalb, Illinois)

states. As one publication explained:

> A good sized steer when it is fit for the butcher market will bring from $45.00 to $60.00. The same animal at its birth was worth but $5.00. He has run on the plains and cropped the grass from the public domain for four or five years, and now, with scarcely any expense to its owner, is worth $40.00 more than when he started on his pilgrimage.

But as demand for beef kept rising and as ranchers and capital flowed into the Great Plains, cattle began to overrun the range.

Meanwhile, sheepherders from California and New Mexico also were using the public domain, spark-

Grazing Wars

ing conflict over land. Ranchers complained that sheep ruined grassland by eating down to the roots and that cattle refused to graze where sheep had been because the "woolly critters" left a repulsive odor. Armed conflict occasionally erupted when cowboys and sheepherders resorted to violence rather than settle disputes in court, where a judge might discover that both were using public land illegally.

More important, however, the farming frontier was advancing and generating new demands for land. Devising a way to organize the land resulted in an unheralded but highly significant invention. The problem was fencing. Lacking sufficient timber and stone for traditional fencing, western settlers faced a critical problem in defining and protecting their property. Tensions flared when farmers accused cattle raisers of allowing their herds to trespass on cropland and when herders in turn charged that farmers should fence their property against grazing animals. Ranchers and farmers alike may have wished to enclose their herds and fields, but they had no economical means of doing so.

Barbed Wire

The solution was barbed wire. Invented in 1873 by Joseph F. Glidden, a farmer in DeKalb, Illinois, these fences consist of two wires held in place by sharp spurs twisted around them. Mass-produced by the Washburn and Moen Manufacturing Company of Worcester, Massachusetts—80.5 million pounds worth in 1880 alone—barbed wire provided a cheap and durable means of enclosure. It opened the Plains to homesteaders by enabling them to protect their farms from grazing cattle. It also ended open-range ranching not only because it removed grazing land that often had been used illegally but also because it enabled large-scale ranchers to isolate their herds within massive stretches of private property.

Open-range ranching made beef a staple of the American diet and created a few fortunes, but its features could not survive the spurs of barbed wire and the rush of history. Moreover, a devastating winter in 1887–1888 destroyed countless herds and drove small ranchers out of business. By 1890 big businesses were taking over the cattle industry and applying scientific methods of breeding and feeding. Most ranchers now owned or leased the land they used, though some illegal fencing persisted. The myth of the cowboy's freedom and individualism lived on, but most cowboys became ordinary wage earners.

Summary

Americans of all races developed the West with courage and creativity. Indians, the region's original inhabitants, had used, and sometimes abused, the land to support subsistence cultures that included trade and war as well as hunting and farming. Living mostly in small groups, they depended heavily on fragile resources such as buffalo herds and salmon runs. When they came into contact with aggressive, migratory Euro-Americans, their resistance to the market economy,

the diseases, and the violence that the whites brought into the West failed.

White miners, timber cutters, farmers, and builders accomplished extraordinary feats. The extraction of raw minerals to supply eastern factories, the use of irrigation and mechanization to bring forth agricultural abundance from the land, the filling of pastures with cattle and sheep to expand food sources, and the construction of railroads to tie the nation together transformed half of the continent within a few decades. The new settlers, however, employed power, violence, and greed that sustained discrimination within a multiracial society, left many farmers feeling cheated and betrayed, kindled contests over use of water, and sacrificed environmental balance for market profits. The region's raw materials and agricultural products improved living standards and contributed to industrial progress, but not without human and environmental costs.

LEGACY FOR A PEOPLE AND A NATION
The West and Rugged Individualism

Though born in New York State, Theodore Roosevelt, twenty-sixth president of the United States, thought of himself as a westerner. In 1884, at the age of twenty-five, he moved to Dakota Territory to live on ranches he had bought there. He loved the uncharted world of what he called "vast silent spaces, a place of grim beauty," where he could mingle with cowboys, gamblers, and gunmen. In such a place, Roosevelt believed, he developed a character of "rugged individualism," an ability to conquer challenges through independent strength and fortitude. He once wrote of his experience that he "knew toil and hardship and hunger and thirst . . . but we felt the beat of hardy life in our veins, and ours was the glory of work and the joy of living."

Americans have long shared Roosevelt's fascination with the West and its reputation for rugged individualism. They have popularized western settings and characters in movies and on television. The film *Cimarron* (1930) was one of the first to win an Academy Award, and *Gunsmoke* held the record as one of the longest-running television series (1955–1975). Movie star John Wayne epitomized the rugged westerner in dozens of films. From *The Virginian*, first published in 1902, to the recent novels of Larry Mc-

Murtry, Americans have made stories about the West bestsellers. In each instance, a lone individual, usually male, overcomes danger and hardship with solitary effort. In their appreciation of this quality, Americans have not only infused political and moral rhetoric with references to rugged individualism; they also have tried to exhibit the quality in their attire. Over the years they have bought millions of dollars worth of Stetson cowboy hats, denim jeans, and buckskin jackets.

At the same time, however, the myth of rugged individualism that Roosevelt thought he could cultivate in the West had a different, ironic reality. In the late nineteenth century, migrants to the West traveled on railroads built with government subsidies, acquired land cheaply from the federal government under the Homestead and Timber and Stone Acts, depended on the army to remove Indians, and destroyed forests and diverted rivers with federal support. More recently, western politicians who oppose big government have received votes from constituents who depend on federal farm subsidies and price supports, free or subsidized water, and government-financed disaster relief from droughts, floods, and tornadoes.

Perhaps more important, the West could not have been settled and developed without both individualism *and* government assistance—what might be called "rugged cooperation." Here was the West's true legacy

Cliffs of Green River by Thomas Moran in 1874. A detail of this painting appears at the beginning of the chapter on page 458. (Amon Carter Museum, Fort Worth, Texas)

to a people and a nation. The federal government, with state assistance, created opportunities that tenacious miners, ranchers, and farmers took advantage of. Those who populated the West had to be rugged. Like Roosevelt they had to have the vision and determination to endure "toil and hardship and hunger and thirst." They survived, but they had—and continue to need—help.

For Further Reading, see page A-21 of the Appendix. For Web resources, go to http://college.hmco.com.

The shoemaker known only as "S" appeared a beaten and bitter man. Interviewed by the Massachusetts Bureau of the Statistics of Labor in 1871, "S" reported that he was fifty years old and had been plying his trade for forty years. He and his three children each worked in a shoe factory ten hours a day, five days a week, and nine hours on Saturdays. His wife toiled in another factory, stitching the covering on baseballs from 5:30 A.M. to 10 A.M. every day.

"S" told the interviewer that ever since his factory had introduced machinery, he had lost control of his craft. He could no longer teach his sons the skill of shoemaking because they had been moved to another room to carry out just one task instead of assembling the whole shoe or boot. "S" hoped his sons would not be factory workers all their lives, but he also realized they had little other choice. The cost of living had risen, making it impossible for his family to sustain itself in any other way, especially when the shoe factory laid off its work force for four months every year because of slow business.

When asked his opinion about the economic system, "S" responded with frustration and anger. "It is hard to see why it is not better to make the consumer pay two or three cents more a pair for his shoes, than to cut down a man who cannot, by hard toil at the wages given, make a comfortable living."

"S" felt embittered by the homage being paid to supply and demand: "We have it constantly dinned in our ears that supply and demand govern prices, but we have found out to a certainty that this is not so. . . . [W]ithout the aid of machinery, six men will make a case of 60 pairs [of shoes] in a day, . . . which would give each man about $1.70 a day; on the other hand, with the machinery, three men will do the same amount of work in the same time, and get about the same pay [$1.70] each, as the men on hand work. . . . Who gets the difference in money saved by machinery? and how far does supply and demand govern in these things?"

The pessimistic testimony of "S" reflected one worker's reaction to the industrialization that was re-

Steel became a vital component of American industrialization in the late nineteenth century, both as a product itself and as a material necessary for countless new machines. Steel mills—such as this one in Meadville, Pennsylvania—employed large work forces in ever more expansive, and dangerous, settings. (Library of Congress)

THE MACHINE AGE 1877–1920

lentlessly overtaking the nation's economy in the late 1800s. The new order was both exciting and daunting. Factories and machines divided production into minute, repetitive tasks and organized work according to the dictates of the clock. Workers like "S" who had long thought of themselves as valued producers found themselves struggling to avoid becoming slaves to machines. Meanwhile, in their quest for productivity, profits, and growth, corporations merged and amassed great power. Defenders of the new system devised theories to justify it, while critics tried to combat what they thought were abuses of power.

Industrialization is a complex process whose chief feature is production of goods by machine rather than by hand. In the early and mid-nineteenth century, an industrial revolution swept through parts of the United States, and the mechanization that characterized it set the stage for a second round in the latter half of the century. Three technological developments propelled this new stage: the rise of electric-powered machines; new applications in the use of chemicals; and expansion of engines powered by internal combustion. Earlier industrialization influenced the new technologies. Steam engines had reached their peak of utility, generating a need for a new power source—electricity. Chemical researchers experimented with dyes, bleaches, and cleaning agents in the textile industry. And the potential of railroad transportation spurred progress in automobile manufacture.

In 1860 only about one-fourth of the American labor force worked in manufacturing and transportation; by 1900 over half did so. As the twentieth century dawned, the United States was not only the world's largest producer of raw materials and food but also the most productive industrial nation (see Map 18.1). Between 1880 and 1920 migrants from farms and from abroad swelled the industrial work force (see Chapter 19); but machines, more than people, boosted American productivity. Innovations in business organization and marketing also fueled the drive for profits.

These developments had momentous effects on standards of living and everyday life. Between the end of Reconstruction and the end of the First World War, a new consumer society took shape. Farms and factories produced so much that growing numbers of Americans could afford to satisfy their material wants. What had once been accessible to a few was becoming available to many; what had formerly been luxuries were becoming necessities. Products such as canned foods and machine-made clothing that had hardly existed before the Civil War became common by the turn of the century. Yet the accomplishments of industrialism, like the natural resource extraction and agricultural expansion (see Chapter 17) that provided the raw materials on which the new industrialization was based, involved waste and greed. The vigor and creativity that marked the era gave rise to both constructive and destructive forces. ■

Technology and the Triumph of Industrialism

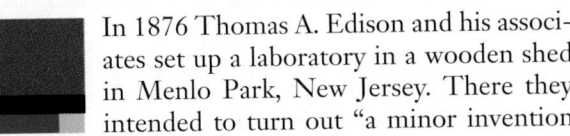

In 1876 Thomas A. Edison and his associates set up a laboratory in a wooden shed in Menlo Park, New Jersey. There they intended to turn out "a minor invention every ten days and a big thing every six months or so." Edison envisioned this structure as an invention factory, where creative people would pool ideas and skills to fashion marketable products. Here he would blend brash enthusiasm with a systematic work ethic. If Americans wanted new products, Edison believed, they had to organize and work purposefully to bring about progress. Such efforts reflected the forward-looking spirit that enlivened American industrialization at the end of the nineteenth century.

In the closing years of the nineteenth century, mechanization fired American optimism. Like the image of second chances represented by the West, the machine symbolized opportunity. The patent system, created by the Constitution to "promote the Progress of science and useful Arts," testifies to an outburst of American mechanical inventiveness. Between 1790 and 1860 the U.S. Patent Office granted a total of 36,000 patents. In 1897 alone, however, it granted 22,000, and between 1860 and 1930 it registered 1.5 million. The inventions often sprang from a marriage between technology and business organization. The harnessing of electricity, internal combustion, and industrial chemistry illustrates how this marriage worked.

Most of Edison's more than one thousand inventions used electricity to transmit light, sound, and images. Perhaps his biggest "big thing" project began in 1878 when he formed the Edison Electric Light Company and embarked on a search for a cheap, efficient means of indoor lighting. After tedious trial-and-error

Birth of the Electrical Industry

IMPORTANT EVENTS

1859	Great Atlantic Tea Company (A&P), the nation's first grocery chain, founded
1860	Knights of Labor founded
1873–78	Economic decline results from overly rapid expansion
1876	Bonsack invents machine for rolling cigarettes
1877	Widespread railroad strikes protest wage cuts
1878	Edison Electric Light Company founded
1879	George's *Progress and Poverty* argues against economic inequality
1880s	Chain-pull toilets spread across the United States
	Doctors begin to accept germ theory of disease
	Mass production of tin cans begins
1881	First federal trademark law begins spread of brand names
1882	Standard Oil Trust formed
1884–85	Economic decline results from numerous causes
1886	Haymarket riot in Chicago protests police brutality against labor demonstrators
	American Federation of Labor (AFL) founded
1888	Bellamy's *Looking Backward* depicts utopian world free of monopoly, politicians, and class divisions
1890	Sherman Anti-Trust Act outlaws "combinations in restraint of trade"
1892	Homestead (Pennsylvania) steelworkers strike against Carnegie Steel Company

1893–97	Economic depression causes high unemployment and business failures
1894	Workers at Pullman Palace Car Company strike against exploitative policies
1895	*U.S. v. E. C. Knight Co.* limits Congress's power to regulate manufacturing
1896	*Holden v. Hardy* upholds law regulating miners' work hours
1898	Taylor promotes scientific management as efficiency measure in industry
1901–03	U.S. Steel Corporation founded E. I. du Pont de Nemours and Company reorganized Ford Motor Company founded
1903	Women's Trade Union League founded
1905	*Lochner v. New York* overturns law limiting bakery workers' work hours and limits labor protection laws
	Industrial Workers of the World (IWW) founded
1908	*Muller v. Oregon* upholds law limiting women to ten-hour workday
	First Ford Model T built
1911	Triangle Shirtwaist Company fire in New York City leaves 146 workers dead
1913	First moving assembly line begins operation at Ford Motor Company
1914	Ford offers Five-Dollar-Day plan to workers
1919	Telephone operator unions strike in New England

experiments, Edison perfected an incandescent bulb that used a vacuum to reduce oxidation of the filament, thereby extending the useful life of the bulb. At the same time, he devised a system of power generation and distribution—an improved dynamo and a parallel circuit of wires—to provide convenient power to a large number of customers.

To market his ideas, Edison acted as his own publicist. During the 1880 Christmas season he illuminated Menlo Park with forty incandescent bulbs, and in 1882 he built a power plant that could light eighty-five buildings in New York's Wall Street financial district. When this plant began service, a *New York Times* reporter marveled that working in his office at night "seemed almost like writing in daylight."

Edison's system of direct current could transmit electric power only a mile or two. George Westinghouse, a young inventor from Schenectady, New York,

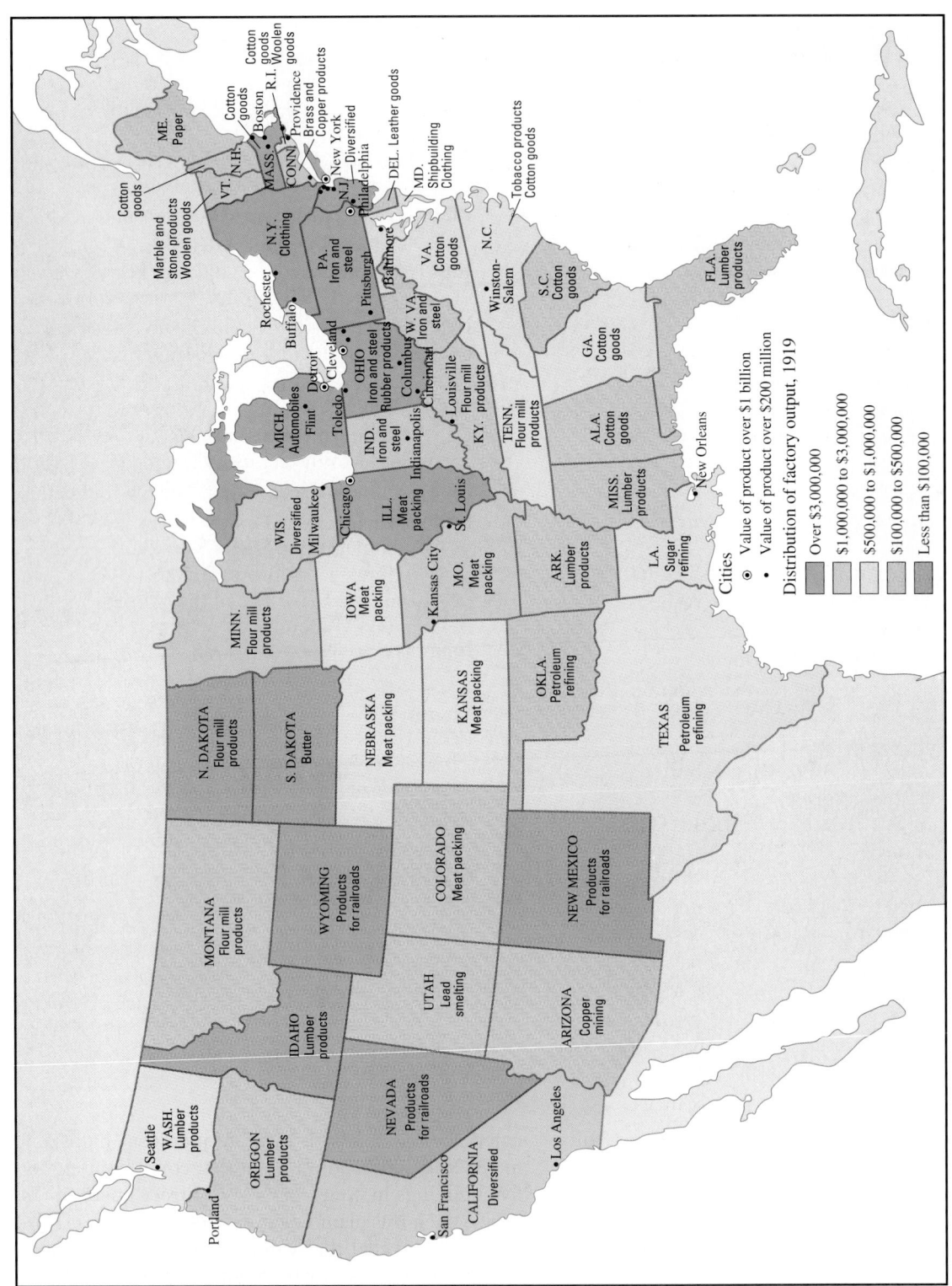

Map 18.1 Industrial Production, 1919 By the early twentieth century, each state could boast of at least one kind of industrial production. Although the value of goods produced was still highest in the Northeast, states like Minnesota and California had impressive dollar values of outputs. (Source: Data from U.S. Bureau of the Census, *Fourteenth Census of the United States, 1920,* Vol. IX, *Manufacturing* [Washington, D.C.: U.S. Government Printing Office, 1921].)

George Westinghouse

who had become famous for devising an air brake for railroad cars, solved the problem. Westinghouse purchased patent rights to generators that used alternating current and transformers that reduced high-voltage power to lower voltage levels, thus making transmission over long distances cheaper.

Other entrepreneurs utilized new business practices to market Edison's and Westinghouse's technological breakthroughs. Samuel Insull, Edison's private secretary, attracted investors and organized Edison power plants across the country, amassing an electric-utility empire. In the late 1880s and early 1890s financiers Henry Villard and J. P. Morgan bought up patents in electric lighting and merged small equipment-manufacturing companies into the General Electric Company. Equally important, General Electric and Westinghouse Electric encouraged the practical application of electricity, formerly an experimental field for scientists, by establishing research laboratories that paid scientists to create electrical products for everyday use.

As corporations organized the process of invention in company labs, individual inventors continued to work independently and tried, sometimes successfully and sometimes not, to sell their handiwork and patents to manufacturing companies. One such inventor, Granville T. Woods, an engineer called by some the "black Edison," patented thirty-five devices vital to electronics and communications. Among his inventions, most of which he sold to companies such as General Electric, were an automatic circuit breaker, an electromagnetic brake, and various instruments to aid communications between railroad trains.

Development of the internal-combustion engine in France and Germany inspired the era's most visionary manufacturer, Henry Ford. In the

Henry Ford and the Automobile Industry

1890s Ford, an electrical engineer in Detroit's Edison Company, experimented in his spare time with a gasoline-burning engine to power a vehicle. George Selden, a lawyer from Rochester, New York, had already been tinkering with internal-combustion engines, but Ford applied organizational genius to this invention and spawned a massive industry.

Like Edison, Ford had a scheme as well as a product. In 1909 he declared, "I am going to democratize the automobile. When I'm through, everybody will be

able to afford one, and about everyone will have one." Ford proposed to reach this goal by mass-producing thousands of identical cars in exactly the same way. Adapting methods of the meatpacking and metalworking industries, Ford engineers set up assembly lines that drastically reduced the time and cost of producing cars. Instead of performing numerous tasks, each worker was assigned only one task, performed repeatedly, using the same specialized machine. A conveyor belt moved past stationary workers who fashioned each component part, and progressively the entire car was assembled.

The Ford Motor Company began operation in 1903. In 1908, the first year it built the Model T, Ford sold 10,000 cars. In 1913 the company's first full assembly line began producing cars in Highland Park, outside Detroit, and the next year, 248,000 Fords were sold. Rising automobile production created more jobs, higher earnings, and greater profits in related industries such as oil, paint, rubber, and glass. As well, the internal-combustion engine helped give birth to the manufacture of trucks, buses, and, ultimately, airplanes.

By 1914 many Ford cars cost $490, only about one-fourth of their price a decade earlier. Yet even $490 was too much for many workers, who earned at best $2 a day. That year, however, Ford tried to spur productivity, prevent high labor turnover, head off unionization, and better enable his workers to buy the cars they produced by offering them the Five-Dollar-Day plan—combined wages and profit sharing equal to $5 a day.

During the same period, the du Pont family did for the chemical industry what Edison and Ford did for the electrical and automobile in-

Du Ponts and the Chemical Industry

dustries. Du Ponts had been manufacturing gunpowder since the early 1800s. In 1902 three cousins, Alfred, Coleman, and Pierre, took over E. I. du Pont de Nemours and Company and broadened production. In 1911 du Pont scientists and engineers working in the nation's first research laboratory adapted cellulose to the production of new materials such as photographic film, rubber, lacquer, textile fibers, and plastics; the innovation wrought a significant transformation in consumer products. The company also pioneered methods of efficient management, accounting, and reinvestment of earnings, all of which contributed to controlled production, better recordkeeping, and higher profits.

The assembly line broke the production process down into simple tasks that individual workers could efficiently repeat hour after hour. Here, assembly-line workers at the Ford plant in Highland Park, Michigan, outside Detroit, are installing pistons in engines of the Model T around 1914.   (Henry Ford Museum and Greenfield Village)

The South's two major staple crops, tobacco and cotton, propelled that region into the machine age.

Technology and Southern Industry

Before the 1870s, Americans used tobacco mainly for snuff, cigars, and chewing. But in 1876 a Virginian named James Bonsack, just eighteen years old, invented a machine for rolling cigarettes. Sales soared when James B. Duke of North Carolina, who popularized cigarettes just as Edison and Ford popularized their products, began marketing cigarettes in the North by enticing consumers with free samples, trading cards, and billboards. By 1900 his American Tobacco Company was a huge nationwide business, employing Jewish immigrant cigar makers who trained laborers in the mass production of cigarettes. Cigarette factories, located in southern cities, employed both black and white workers (including women), though in separate locations of the plant.

New technology also aided southern textile mills, which by 1900 numbered over four hundred and contained 4 million spindles. As the machinery of north-

Southern Textile Mills

ern mills became obsolete, the South, especially its small towns, had space for factory construction as well as a cheap labor force to tend new machines. Aided by electric motors, which could power individual machines rather than depend on a water-powered drive shaft with belts attached to numerous machines, southern mills could utilize automatic looms, which required fewer and less skilled workers. Moreover, southern mills could install electric lighting, which expanded the hours of production. The textile mills, financed mostly by local investors, paid women and children 50 cents a day for twelve or more hours of work—about half the wages northern workers received. Many companies built villages around their mills, where they controlled housing, stores, schools, and churches. Inside these towns, owners banned criticism of the company and squelched attempts at union organization.

Northern and European capitalists financed other southern industries. Between 1890 and 1900, northern lumber syndicates moved into pine forests

Tobacco production was one southern industry that traditionally hired African American laborers. This scene from a Richmond tobacco factory around 1880 shows women and children preparing leaves for curing by tearing off the stems.   (Valentine Museum)

of the Gulf states, boosting production 500 percent. During the 1880s, northern investors developed southern iron and steel manufacturing, much of it in the boom city of Birmingham. Except for some modernized plants, however, the South lacked the technological innovations, such as those in the machine-tool industry, that had enabled northern industries to compete with those of other industrializing nations.

Nevertheless, southern boosters heralded the emergence of a New South. Henry Grady, editor of the *Atlanta Constitution* and the most articulate voice of southern progress, proclaimed, "We have sowed towns and cities in the place of theories, and put business in place of politics. We have challenged your spinners in Massachusetts and your iron-makers in Pennsylvania. . . . We have fallen in love with work." Grady's optimism was premature. A New South would eventually emerge, but not until after the First World War.

In all regions of the country, the timing of technological innovation varied from one industry to another, but machines broadly altered the economy and everyday life. Telephones and typewriters revolutionized communications, making face-to-face con-

Influence of New Machines

versations less important and facilitating correspondence and record-keeping in the growing insurance, banking, and advertising firms. Sewing machines made mass-produced clothing available to almost everyone. Refrigeration changed dietary habits by enabling the preservation and shipment of meat, fruit, vegetables, and dairy products. Cash registers and adding machines revamped accounting and created new clerical jobs.

Profits resulted from higher production at lower costs. As technological innovations made large-scale production more economical, some owners replaced small factories with larger ones. Between 1850 and 1900 the average capital investment in a manufacturing firm increased from $700,000 to $1.9 million. Only large companies could afford to buy complex machines and operate them at full capacity. And large companies could best take advantage of discounts for shipping products in bulk and for buying raw materials in quantity. Economists call such advantages economies of scale.

Taken at the historic moment of liftoff, this photograph shows the first airplane flight at Kitty Hawk, North Carolina, December 17, 1903. With Orville Wright lying at the controls and brother Wilbur standing nearby, the plane was airborne only twelve seconds and traveled 120 feet. Even so, the flight marked the beginning of one of the twentieth century's most influential industries.   (Library of Congress)

Profitability depended as much on how production was arranged as on the machines in use. Where once shop-floor workers such as "S" had exercised control over how a product was made, by the 1890s engineers and managers with specialized knowledge acquired in specialized schools had assumed this responsibility and planned every task to increase output. Their efforts standardized production, which then required less skill and virtually no independent judgment from workers.

The most influential advocate of efficient production was Frederick W. Taylor. As foreman and engineer for the Midvale Steel Company in the 1880s, Taylor concluded that the best way a company could lessen fixed costs and increase profits was to apply scientific studies of "how quickly the various kinds of work . . . ought to be done." The "ought" in Taylor's formulation signified producing more for lower cost per unit, usually by eliminating unnecessary workers. Similarly, "how quickly" signified that time and money were equivalent. Above all, efficiency was a science.

Frederick W. Taylor and Efficiency

In 1898 Taylor took his stopwatch to the Bethlehem Steel Company to illustrate how his principles of scientific management worked. His experiments, he explained, required studying workers and devising "a series of motions which can be made quickest and best." Applying this technique to the shoveling of ore, Taylor designed fifteen kinds of shovels and prescribed the proper motions for using each one. He succeeded in reducing a crew of 600 men to 140.

As a result of Taylor's writings and experiments, time, as much as quality, became the measure of acceptable work, and science rather than experience determined the ways of doing things. As integral features of the assembly line, where work was divided into specific time-determined tasks, employees like "S" became another kind of interchangeable part.

Mechanization and the Changing Status of Labor

By 1880 the status of labor had undergone a dramatic shift in just a single generation. Technological innovation and assembly-line production created new jobs, but because most machines were labor-saving, fewer workers could produce more in less time. Moreover, as "S" knew firsthand, workers could no longer accurately be termed producers, as farmers and craftsmen had traditionally thought of themselves. The working class now consisted mainly of employees—men, women, and children who worked only when someone hired them. Producers had been paid by consumers in accordance with the quality of what they produced; now, employees received wages for time spent on the job.

As mass production subdivided manufacturing into small tasks, workers continually repeated the same specialized operation. One investigator found that the worker became "a mere machine. . . . Take the proposition of a man operating a machine to nail on 40 to 60 cases of heels in a day. That is 2,400 pairs, 4,800 shoes in a day. One not accustomed to it would wonder how a man could pick up and lay down 4,800 shoes in a day, to say nothing of putting them . . . into a machine. . . . That is the driving method of the manufacture of shoes under these minute subdivisions."

By reducing the manufacturing process to simplified tasks constantly repeated, and by coordinating production to the running of machinery, assembly lines also deprived employees of their independence. Workers could no longer decide when to begin and end the workday, when to rest, and what tools and techniques to use. As a Massachusetts factory operative testified in 1879, "During working hours the men are not allowed to speak to each other, though working close together, on pain of instant discharge. Men are hired to watch and patrol the shop." And workers were now surrounded by others who labored at the same rate for the same pay, regardless of the quality of their work.

Workers affected by these changes did not accept them passively. Employees struggled to retain independence and self-respect in the face of employers' ever-increasing power. As new groups encountered the industrial system, they resisted in various ways. Artisans such as cigar makers, glass workers, and coopers (barrel makers), caught in the transition from hand labor to machine production, fought to preserve their work pace and to retain shop customs such as appointing a fellow worker to read a newspaper aloud while they worked. When immigrants went to work in factories, they often persuaded foremen to hire their relatives and friends, thus preserving on-the-job family and village ties. Off the job, workers continued to gather for leisure-time activities such as social drinking and holiday celebrations, ignoring employers' attempts to control their social lives.

Employers established standards of behavior and work incentives that they thought would enhance effi-

ciency and productivity. To make workers docile (like the machines they operated), employers supported temperance and moral-reform societies, dedicated to combating immoderate drinking and debauchery. Ford Motor Company required workers to meet the company's behavior code before they became eligible for the profit-sharing segment of the Five-Dollar-Day plan. Other employers established piecework rates, paying workers an amount per item produced, rather than an hourly wage, to increase productivity and maximize use of machines.

As machines and assembly lines reduced the need for skilled workers, employers cut labor costs by hiring women and children. Between 1880 and 1900, the numbers of employed women soared from 2.6 million to 8.6 million. At the same time their occupational patterns underwent striking changes (see Figure 18.1). The proportion of women in domestic-service jobs (maids, cooks, laundresses)—the most common and lowest-paid form of female employment—dropped dramatically as jobs opened in other sectors. In manufacturing, women usually held menial positions in textile mills and food-processing plants that paid as little as $1.56 a week for seventy hours of labor. (Unskilled men received $7 to $10 for a similar workweek.) Though the number of female factory hands tripled between 1880 and 1900, the proportion of women workers in these jobs remained about the same.

Employment of Women

General expansion of the industrial and retail sectors, however, caused the numbers and percentages of women in clerical jobs—typists, bookkeepers, sales clerks—to skyrocket. By 1920 nearly half of all clerical workers were women; in 1880 only 4 percent had been women. Previously, when sales and office positions had required accounting and letter-writing skills, men had dominated such jobs. Then, new inventions such as the typewriter, cash register, and adding machine simplified these tasks. Companies eagerly hired women who had taken trade-school courses in typing and shorthand and were looking for the better pay and conditions that clerical jobs offered compared to factory and domestic work. An official of a sugar company observed in 1919 that "all the bookkeeping of this company . . . is done by three girls and three bookkeeping machines . . . one operator takes the place of three men." Though paid low wages, women also were attracted to sales jobs because of the respectability, pleasant surroundings, and contact

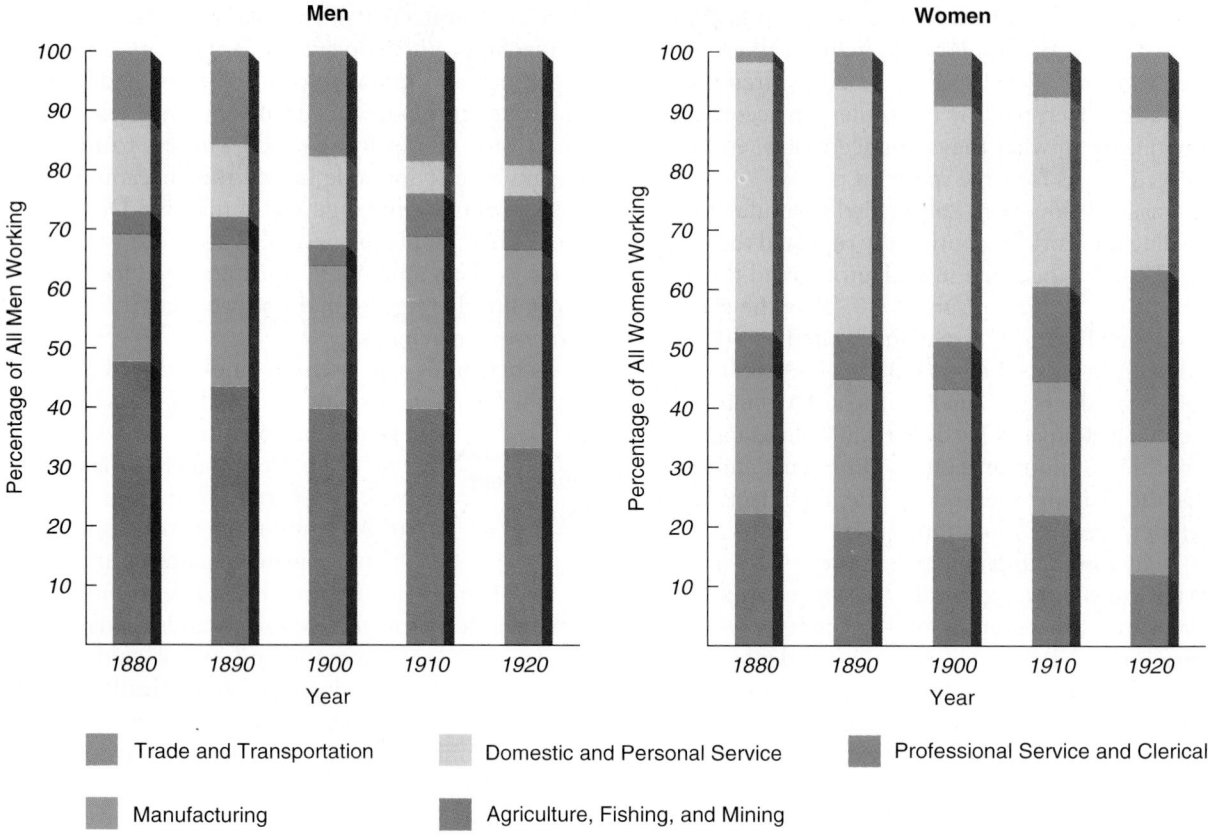

Figure 18.1 Distribution of Occupational Categories Among Employed Men and Women, 1880–1920 The changing lengths of the bar segments of each part of this graph represent trends in male and female employment. Over the forty years covered by this graph, the agriculture, fishing, and mining segment for men and the domestic service segment for women declined the most, while notable increases occurred in manufacturing for men and services (especially store clerks and teachers) for women. (Source: U.S. Bureau of the Census, *Census of the United States, 1880, 1890, 1900, 1910, 1920* [Washington: U.S. Government Printing Office].)

with affluent customers that such positions offered. Nevertheless, sex discrimination pervaded the clerical sector. In department stores, male cashiers took in cash and made change; women were seldom given responsibility for billing or counting money. The new jobs offered women some opportunities for advancement to supervisory positions, but males dominated the managerial ranks.

Although most children who worked toiled on their parents' farms, the number in nonagricultural occupations tripled between 1870 and 1900. In 1890 over 18 percent of all children between ages ten and fifteen were gainfully employed (see Figure 18.2). Textile and shoe factories in particular employed many workers below age sixteen. Mecha-

Child Labor

nization created numerous light tasks, such as running errands and helping machine operators, that children could handle at a fraction of adult wages. Conditions were especially hard for child laborers in the South, where burgeoning textile mills needed unskilled hands. Mill owners induced white sharecroppers and tenant farm families, who otherwise might not have had any jobs or income, to bind their children over to factories at miserably low wages.

Several states, especially in the Northeast, passed laws specifying minimum ages and maximum workday hours for child labor. But most large companies could evade regulations because state statutes could regulate only firms operating within state borders, not those engaged in interstate commerce. Enforcing age requirements proved difficult because many parents,

Factories employed children from the early nineteenth century well into the twentieth. In textile mills like the one pictured here, girls operated machines, and boys ran messages and carried materials back and forth. Mill girls had to tie up their hair to keep it from getting caught in the machines. The girl posing here with a shawl over her head would not have worn that garment while she was working. (National Archives)

needing income from child labor, lied about their children's ages and employers rarely asked. One woman who had worked in the huge Amoskeag Mills of Manchester, New Hampshire, recalled how easy it was to get a job without proof of age. "I was twelve years old when I arrived here and started work," she recalled. "All we had to do was show them that we were fourteen years old. Tall or short, it didn't matter; they'd just ask, 'Are you fourteen years old?' OK. That's all. So that's how I went in to work." By 1900 state laws and automation had reduced the number of children employed in manufacturing, but many more worked at street trades—shining shoes and peddling newspapers and other merchandise—and as helpers in stores. Not until the Progressive era did reformers seek federal legislation to control child labor (see Chapter 21).

Although working conditions were often dangerous and unhealthy, low wages most often acted as the catalyst of worker unrest. Many employers believed in the "iron law of wages," which dictated that employees

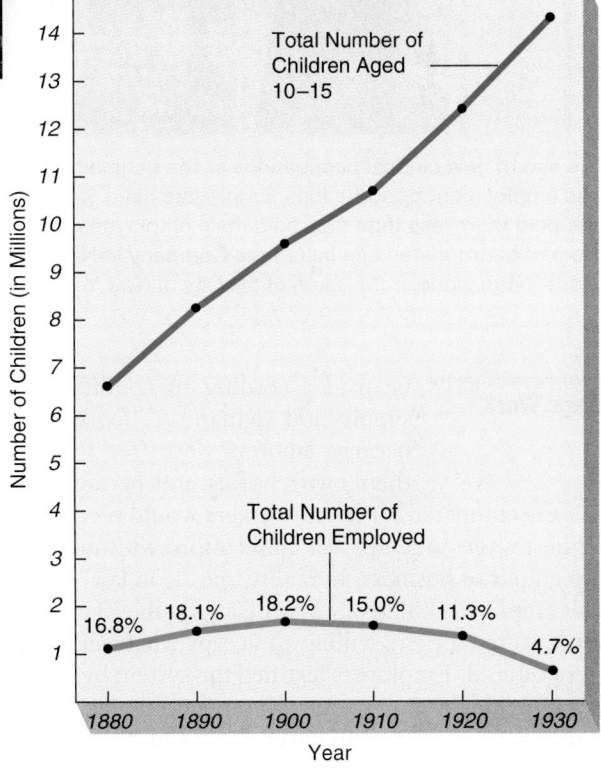

Figure 18.2   Children in the Labor Force, 1880–1930
The percentage of children in the labor force peaked around the turn of the century. Thereafter, the passage of state laws requiring children to attend school until age fourteen and limiting the ages at which children could be employed caused child labor to decline. (Source: Data from *The Statistical History of the United States from Colonial Times to the Present* [Stamford, Conn.: Fairfield Publishers, 1965].)

The rise of new clerical occupations at the beginning of the twentieth century gave women count-less employment opportunities. Employers hired women to file company records and type letters and paid them less than they paid male employees. The floor-to-ceiling file cases in the records room of Metropolitan Life Insurance Company in New York was the largest outfit of steel file cases in the world.   (Museum of the City of New York, Gift of Donald Beggs)

Wage Work

be paid according to conditions of supply and demand. Theoretically, because laborers were free to make their own choices and because employers competed for labor, workers would receive the highest wages an employer could afford without being driven out of business. In reality, the "iron law" meant that employers could pay as little as possible, as long as there were workers willing to accept whatever wages were offered. Employers justified the system by invoking individual freedom: a worker who did not like the wages being paid was free to quit and find a job elsewhere.

Courts regularly denied workers the right to organize and bargain collectively on the grounds that wages should be individually negotiated between employee and employer. In contrast, wage earners believed the system trapped them. A factory worker told Congress in 1879, "The market is glutted, and we have seasons of dullness; advantage is taken of men's wants, and the pay is cut down; our tasks are increased, and if we remon-

strate, we are told our places can be filled. I work harder now than when my pay was twice as high."

Even steady employment proved insecure. Repetitive tasks using high-speed machinery dulled concentration, and the slightest mistake could cause serious injury. Industrial accidents rose steadily before 1920, killing or maiming hundreds of thousands of people each year. As late as 1913, after factory owners had installed safety devices, some 25,000 people died in industrial mishaps, and close to 1 million were injured. Each year sensational disasters, such as explosions and mine cave-ins, aroused public clamor for better safety regulations. The most notorious tragedy was a fire at New York City's Triangle Shirtwaist Company in 1911, which killed 146 workers, most of them teenage Jewish immigrant women who had been trapped in locked workrooms. Equally tragic, however, were the countless accidents that left workers with mangled limbs, infected cuts, chronic illness, and death. Because

Industrial Accidents

disability insurance and pensions were almost nonexistent, families stricken by such accidents suffered acutely.

Prevailing free-market views hampered the passage of legislation that would regulate hours and working conditions, and employers denied responsibility for employees' well-being. As one railroad manager declared, "The regular compensation of employees covers all risk or liability to accident. If an employee is disabled by sickness or any other cause, the right to claim compensation is not recognized." The only recourse for a stricken family was to sue and prove in court that the killed or injured worker had not realized the risks involved and had not caused the accident, an expensive route that very few ever took.

Reformers and union leaders lobbied Congress for laws to improve working conditions, but the Supreme Court limited the scope of such legislation by narrowly defining what jobs were dangerous and which workers needed protection. In *Holden v. Hardy* (1896), the Court upheld a law regulating working hours of miners because overly long hours would increase the threat of injury. In *Lochner v. New York* (1905), however, the Court struck down a law limiting bakery workers to a sixty-hour week and a ten-hour day. Responding to the argument that states had the authority to protect workers' health and safety, the Court ruled that baking was not a dangerous enough occupation to justify restricting the right of workers to sell their labor freely. According to the Court, interference with the right of individuals to make contracts for their labor would violate the Fourteenth Amendment's guarantee that no state could "deprive any person of life, liberty, or property without due process of law."

Courts Restrict Labor Reform

In *Muller v. Oregon* (1908), the Court used a different rationale to uphold a law limiting women to a ten-hour workday in laundries. In this case, setting aside its *Lochner* argument, the Court asserted that women's health and reproductive functions required protection. According to the Court, a woman's well-being "becomes an object of public interest and care in order to preserve the strength and vigor of the race." Though the case represented a victory for those seeking government's right to regulate hours and working conditions, as a result of *Muller*'s success, later laws barred women from occupations such as printing and transportation, which required long hours or night work, and thus further confined women to menial, dead-end jobs.

Industrialization left numerous casualties from accidents involving machines and workers. Permanent disability and sometimes even death created dire hardship for working-class families living on the edge of subsistence.   (George Eastman House)

Throughout the nineteenth century, tensions rose and fell as workers confronted mechanization. Adjustments were made as different groups—rural migrants, foreign immigrants, women, and children—entered the industrial labor force. Some people submitted to the demands of the factory, machine, and time clock. Some tried to blend old ways of working into the new system. Some never adjusted and wandered from place to place, job to job. Others, however, turned to organized resistance.

The year 1877 marked a crisis for labor. In July a series of strikes broke out among unionized railroad workers who were protesting wage cuts. Violence spread from Pennsylvania and West Virginia to the Midwest, Texas, and California. Venting pent-up anger, rioters attacked railroad property, derailing trains and burning railroad yards. State militia companies, organized and commanded by employers, broke up picket lines and fired

Railroad Strikes of 1877

into threatening crowds. In several communities, factory workers, wives, and even merchants aided the strikers, while railroads enlisted strikebreakers to replace union men.

The worst violence occurred in Pittsburgh, where on July 21 militiamen bayoneted and fired on rock-throwing demonstrators, killing ten and wounding many more. Infuriated, the mob drove the soldiers into a railroad roundhouse and set fires that destroyed 39 buildings, 104 engines, and 1,245 freight and passenger cars. The next day, the troops shot their way out of the roundhouse and killed twenty more citizens before fleeing the city. After more than a month of unprecedented carnage, President Rutherford B. Hayes sent federal troops to end the strikes—the first significant use of soldiers to quell labor unrest.

The immediate cause of these strikes was the squeeze of hard times. In the economic slump that followed the Panic of 1873, railroad managers cut wages, increased workloads, and laid off workers, especially those who had joined unions. Such actions drove workers to strike and riot. Laborers in other industries sympathized with the strikers, as did residents of their communities. A Pittsburgh state militiaman, ordered out to break the 1877 strike, recalled, "I talked to all the strikers I could get my hands on, and I could find but one spirit and one purpose among them—that they were justified in resorting to any means to break down the power of the corporations."

The Union Movement

Knights of Labor

After 1877 anxiety over the loss of independence and a desire for better wages, hours, and working conditions pushed more workers into unions. Trade unions, which excluded everyone except skilled workers in particular crafts such as printing and iron molding, dated from the early nineteenth century, but the narrowness of their membership left them without broad power. The National Labor Union, founded in 1866, claimed 640,000 members in a variety of industries in 1868 but collapsed during the hard times of the 1870s. The only broad-based labor organization to survive that depression was the Knights of Labor.

Founded in 1869 by Philadelphia garment cutters, the Knights began recruiting other workers in the 1870s. In 1879 Terence V. Powderly, a machinist and mayor of Scranton, Pennsylvania, was elected grand master. Under his forceful guidance and, in contrast to most craft unions, willingness to welcome women, African Americans, immigrants, and all unskilled and semiskilled workers, Knights membership mushroomed, peaking at 730,000 in 1886.

The Knights tried to avert the bleak future that they believed industrialism portended by building a workers' alliance that would offer an alternative to profit-oriented industrial capitalism. They believed they could eliminate conflict by establishing a cooperative society in which laborers worked for themselves, not for those who possessed capital. The goal, argued Powderly, was to "eventually make every man his own master—every man his own employer. . . . There is no good reason why labor cannot, through cooperation, own and operate mines, factories, and railroads." Like many farmers, the Knights saw producer and consumer cooperatives as preferable to capitalist control. This view simultaneously strengthened and weakened the organization. The cooperative idea, attractive in the abstract, gave laborers little bargaining power because employers held all the economic leverage. Strikes offered one means of achieving immediate goals, but Powderly and other Knights leaders opposed strikes, arguing that they tended to divert attention from the long-term goal of a cooperative society and that workers tended to lose more strikes than they won.

Some Knights, however, did support militant action. In 1886 the Knights demanded higher wages and union recognition from railroads in the Southwest. Railroad magnate Jay Gould refused to negotiate, and a strike began March 1 in Texas and spread to Kansas, Missouri, and Arkansas. As violence increased, Powderly met with Gould and called off the strike, hoping to settle the conflict. But Gould again rejected concessions, and the Knights had to give in. Militant craft unions began to desert the Knights, upset by Powderly's compromising position and confident that they could attain more on their own. Membership in the Knights dwindled, although the union survived in a few small towns, where it made a brief attempt to unite with Populists in the 1890s (see Chapter 20). The special interests of craft unions replaced the Knights' broad-based but often vague appeal, and dreams of labor unity faded.

Haymarket Riot

Nevertheless, workers continued to strive to regain control of their work, and several groups rallied around the issue of an eight-hour workday. In Chicago on May 1, 1886, the campaign for the eight-hour day generated mass strikes and the largest spontaneous labor demonstration in the country's history. Some one hundred thousand workers

The Haymarket Riot of 1886 was one of the most violent incidents of labor unrest in the late nineteenth century. This drawing, from *Frank Leslie's Illustrated Newspaper,* shows workers fleeing while police beat demonstrators with nightsticks. As this clash was occurring, a bomb, allegedly set off by anarchists, exploded, killing both police and workers.   (Library of Congress)

turned out, including not only craft unions but also radical anarchists who believed in using violence to replace all government with voluntary cooperation. In Europe, labor radicals had made May 1 a day of special demonstration, and Chicago police, fearing that European radicals were transplanting their tradition of violence to the United States, mobilized to prevent disorder, especially among striking workers at the huge McCormick reaper plant. The day passed calmly, but two days later police stormed an area near the factory and broke up a battle between striking unionists and nonunion strikebreakers. Police shot and killed two unionists and wounded several others.

The next evening, labor groups rallied at Haymarket Square, near downtown Chicago, to protest police brutality. As a police company approached, a bomb exploded, killing seven and injuring sixty-seven. In reaction against immigrant radicals, mass arrests of anarchists and unionists followed. Eventually a court convicted eight anarchists of the bombing, though the evidence of their guilt was questionable. Four were executed and one committed suicide in prison. The remaining three were pardoned in 1893 by Illinois governor John P. Altgeld, who believed they had been victims of the "malicious ferocity" of the courts. Altgeld's act of conscience ruined his political career when supporters of capitalism denounced him as a friend of anarchy.

The Haymarket bombing, like the 1877 railroad strikes, drew attention to the growing discontent of labor and revived fear of radicalism. The participation of anarchists and socialists, many of them foreign-born, created a feeling that forces of law and order had to act swiftly to prevent social turmoil. To protect their city, private Chicago donors helped to establish a military base at Fort Sheridan and the Great Lakes Naval Training Station. Elsewhere, governments strengthened police forces and armories. Employer associations, coalitions of manufacturers in the same industry, countered labor militancy by drawing up blacklists of union activists whom they would not employ, and by agreeing to resist strikes.

The American Federation of Labor (AFL) emerged from the 1886 upheavals as the major workers' organization. An alliance of national craft unions, the AFL had about 140,000 members, most of them skilled workers. Led by Samuel Gompers, a pragmatic and opportunistic immigrant who headed the Cigar Makers' Union, the AFL avoided the Knights' and anarchists' idealistic rhetoric of worker solidarity to press for concrete goals: higher wages, shorter hours, and the right to bargain collectively. As Gompers's associate Adolph Strasser explained, "We are fighting only for immediate objects . . . that can be realized in a few years." In contrast to the Knights of Labor, the AFL accepted the industrial system and worked to improve conditions within the wage-and-hours system. Member unions retained autonomy in their own areas of interest but tried to develop a general policy that would suit all members. Since these unions tried to protect skilled workers by organizing by craft rather than by workplace, they had little interest in recruiting unskilled workers.

American Federation of Labor

The AFL grew to 1 million members by 1901 and 2.5 million by 1917, when it represented 111 national unions and 27,000 local unions. The national organization required constituent unions to hire organizers to expand membership, and it collected dues for a fund to aid members on strike. The AFL avoided party politics, adhering instead to Gompers's dictum to support labor's friends and oppose its enemies, regardless of party.

The AFL and the labor movement suffered a series of setbacks in the early 1890s, when once again labor violence stirred public fears. In July 1892 the AFL-affiliated Amalgamated Association of Iron and Steelworkers refused to accept pay cuts and went on strike in Homestead, Pennsylvania. Henry C. Frick, president of Carnegie Steel Company, then closed the plant. Shortly thereafter, Frick tried to protect the plant by hiring three hundred guards from the Pinkerton Detective Agency and floating them in by barge under cover of darkness. Lying in wait on the shore of the Monongahela River, angry workers attacked and routed the guards. State militiamen intervened, and after five months the strikers gave in. By then public opinion had turned against the union because of an attempt on Frick's life by a young anarchist who was not a striker.

In 1894 workers at the Pullman Palace Car Company walked out in protest over exploitative policies at the company town near Chicago.

Pullman Strike The paternalistic George Pullman provided everything for the twelve thousand residents of his so-called model town named after him. His company owned and controlled all land and buildings, the school, the bank, and the water and gas systems. It paid wages, fixed rents, and spied on disgruntled employees. As one laborer grumbled, "We are born in a Pullman house, fed from the Pullman shop, taught in the Pullman school, catechized in the Pullman church, and when we die we shall be buried in the Pullman cemetery and go to the Pullman hell."

One thing Pullman would not do was negotiate with workers. When the hard times that began in 1893 threatened his prosperity, Pullman protected profits and stock dividends by cutting wages 25 to 40 percent while holding firm on rents and prices in the town. Hard-pressed workers sent a committee to Pullman to protest his policies. He reacted by firing three members of the committee. Enraged workers, most of them from the American Railway Union, called a strike; Pullman retaliated by closing the factory. The union, led by the charismatic Eugene V. Debs, voted to aid the strikers by refusing to handle any Pullman cars attached to any trains. Pullman still rejected arbitration.

The railroad owners' association then enlisted aid from U.S. Attorney General Richard Olney, who obtained a court injunction to prevent the union from "obstructing the railways and holding up the mails." President Grover Cleveland ordered federal troops to Chicago, ostensibly to protect the rail-carried mails but in reality to crush the strike. Within a month strikers gave in, and Debs went to prison for defying the court injunction. The Supreme Court upheld Debs's six-month sentence on grounds that the federal government had the power to remove obstacles to interstate commerce.

In the West, radical labor activity arose among Colorado miners, who engaged in several bitter struggles and violent strikes. In 1905 these

IWW workers helped form a new labor organization, the Industrial Workers of the World (IWW). Unlike the AFL, the IWW strove like the Knights of Labor to unify all laborers, including the unskilled who were excluded from craft unions. Its motto was "An injury to one is an injury to all," and its goal was "One Big Union." But the "Wobblies," as IWW members were known, exceeded the goals of the Knights and espoused socialism and tactics of violence and sabotage.

Embracing the rhetoric of class conflict—"The final aim is revolution," according to IWW creed—and an ideology of socialism, Wobblies believed workers should seize and run the nation's industries. "Mother" Jones, an Illinois coalfield union organizer; Elizabeth Gurley Flynn, a fiery orator known as the "Joan of Arc of the labor movement"; and William D. (Big Bill) Haywood, the brawny, one-eyed founder of the Western Federation of Miners, led a series of strife-torn strikes. Demonstrations erupted in western lumber and mining camps, in the steel town of McKees Rocks, Pennsylvania (1907), and in the textile mills of Lawrence, Massachusetts (1912). Though the Wobblies' anticapitalist goals and aggressive tactics attracted considerable publicity, IWW membership probably never exceeded 150,000. The organization collapsed during the First World War when federal prosecution sent many of its leaders to jail and local police forces and mobs violently harassed IWW members.

Many unions, notably those of the AFL, openly rejected female members. Of 6.3 million employed women in 1910, fewer than 2 percent

Women and the Labor Movement belonged to unions. Male unionists often rationalized the exclusion of women by insisting that women should not be employed. According

In 1919, telephone operators, mostly female, went out on strike and shut down phone service throughout New England. These workers, who interrupted their picketing to pose for the photograph, showed that women could take forceful action in support of their labor interests. (Corbis-Bettmann)

to one labor leader, "Woman is not qualified for the conditions of wage labor. . . . The mental and physical makeup of woman is in revolt against wage service. She is competing with the man who is her father or husband or is to become her husband." Mostly, unionists feared competition. Because women were paid less than men, males worried that their own wages would be lowered or that they would lose their jobs if women invaded the workplace. Moreover, male workers, accustomed to sex segregation in employment, could not imagine working side by side with women.

Yet female employees could organize and fight employers as strenuously as men could. Since the early years of industrialization, women had formed their own unions. Some, such as the Collar Laundry Union of Troy, New York, organized in the 1860s, had successfully struck for higher wages. The "Uprising of the 20,000" in New York City, a 1909 strike by immigrant members—most of them women—of the International Ladies Garment Workers Union (ILGWU), was one of the country's largest strikes to that time. Women were also prominent in the 1912 Lawrence, Massachusetts, textile workers' "Bread and Roses" strike. Female trade-union membership swelled during the 1910s, but men monopolized national trade

union leadership, even in industries with large female work forces, such as garment manufacturing, textiles, and boots and shoes.

Women, however, did dominate one union: the Telephone Operators' Department of the International Brotherhood of Electrical Workers. Organized in Montana and San Francisco early in the twentieth century, the union spread throughout the Bell system, the nation's monopolistic telephone company and single largest employer of women. To promote solidarity among their mostly young members, union leaders organized dances, excursions, and bazaars. They also sponsored educational programs to enhance members' leadership skills. The union focused mainly on workplace issues. Intent on developing pride and independence among telephone operators, the union opposed scientific management techniques and tightening of supervision. In 1919 several militant union branches paralyzed the phone service of five New England states. The union collapsed after a failed strike, again in New England, in 1923, but not before women had proved to contemporaries that they could battle a powerful employer.

The first women's organization seeking to promote the interests of laboring women was the

Women's Trade Union League (WTUL), founded in 1903 and patterned after a similar organization in England. The WTUL sought protective legislation for female workers, sponsored educational activities, and campaigned for women's suffrage. It helped telephone operators organize their union, and in 1909 it supported the ILGWU's massive strike against New York City sweatshops. Initially the union's highest offices were held by middle-class women who sympathized with female wage laborers, but control shifted in the 1910s to forceful working-class leaders, notably Agnes Nestor, a glove maker; Rose Schneiderman, a cap maker; and Mary Anderson, a shoe worker. The WTUL advocated changes such as opening apprenticeship programs to women so they could enter skilled trades and training female workers to assume leadership roles. It served as a vital link between the labor and women's movements into the 1920s.

Immigrants, African Americans, and Labor Unions

Organized labor excluded most immigrant and African American workers, often fearing that such groups would depress wages. Some trade unions welcomed skilled immigrants—foreign-born craftsmen were prominent leaders of several unions—but only the Knights of Labor and the IWW had explicit policies of accepting immigrants and blacks. Blacks were prominent in the coal miners' union, and they were partially unionized in trades such as construction, barbering, and dock work, which had large numbers of African American workers. But they could belong only to segregated local unions in the South, and the majority of northern AFL unions had exclusion policies. Long-held prejudices were reinforced when blacks and immigrants, eager for any work they could get, worked as strikebreakers, hired to replace striking whites.

The dramatic labor struggles in the half-century following the Civil War make it easy to forget that only a small fraction of American wage workers belonged to unions. In 1900 about 1 million out of a total of 27.6 million workers were unionized. By 1920 total union membership had grown to 5 million, still only 13 percent of the work force. Unionization was strong in construction trades, transportation, communications, and, to a lesser extent, manufacturing. For many workers, getting and holding a job held priority over wages and hours. Job instability and the seasonal nature of work seriously hindered union-organizing efforts. Few companies employed a full work force all year round; most employers hired workers during peak seasons and laid them off during slack periods. Thus employment rates fluctuated wildly. The 1880 census showed that in some communities 30 percent of adult males had been jobless at some time during the previous year. Moreover, union organizers took no interest in large segments of the industrial labor force and intentionally barred others.

The millions of men, women, and children who were not unionized tried in their own ways to cope with pressures of the machine age. Increasing numbers, both native-born and immigrant, turned to fraternal societies such as the Polish Roman Catholic Union and the Jewish B'nai B'rith. For small monthly or yearly contributions these organizations provided members with life insurance, sickness benefits, and funeral expenses and became widespread by the early twentieth century.

Fraternal Societies

For most American workers, then, the machine age had mixed results. Industrial wages rose between 1877 and 1914, boosting purchasing power and creating a mass market for standardized goods. Yet in 1900 most employees worked sixty hours a week at wages that averaged 20 cents an hour for skilled work and 10 cents an hour for unskilled. Moreover, as wages rose, living costs increased even faster.

Standards of Living

Some Americans, like "S," distrusted machines, but few could resist the changes that mechanization brought to everyday life. The expansion of railroad, postal, telephone, and electrical service drew even isolated communities into the orbit of a consumer-oriented society. American ingenuity combined with mass production and mass marketing to make available myriad goods that previously had not existed or had been the exclusive property of the wealthy. The new material well-being, heralded by products such as ready-made clothes, canned foods, and home appliances, had a dual effect. It blended Americans of differing status into consumer communities defined not by place or class but by possessions, and it accentuated differences between those who could afford goods and services and those who could not.

If a society's affluence can be measured by how it converts luxuries into commonplace articles, the United States was indeed becoming affluent in the years between 1880 and 1920. In 1880 smokers rolled their own cigarettes; only wealthy women could afford

New Availability of Products

silk stockings; only residents of Florida, Texas, and California could enjoy fresh oranges; and people made candy and soap at home. By 1899 manufactured goods and perishable foodstuffs had become increasingly available. That year Americans bought 2 billion machine-produced cigarettes and 151,000 pairs of silk stockings, consumed oranges at the rate of 100 crates for every 1,000 people, and spent an average of $1.08 per person on store-bought candy and 63 cents per person on soap. By 1921 the transformation had advanced even further. Americans smoked 43 billion cigarettes that year (403 per person), bought 217 million pairs of silk stockings, ate 248 crates of oranges per 1,000 people, and spent $1.66 per person on confectionery goods and $1.40 per person on soap.

What people can afford obviously depends on their resources and incomes. Data for the period show that incomes rose broadly. The expanding economy spawned massive fortunes and created a new industrial elite. An 1891 magazine article estimated that 120 Americans were worth at least $10 million. By 1920 the richest 5 percent of the population received almost one-fourth of all earned income. (The proportion received by the richest 5 percent declined over the next fifty years but has risen again to match the 1920 level.)

Incomes also rose among the middle class. For example, average pay for clerical workers rose 36 percent between 1890 and 1910 (see Table 18.1). At the turn of the century, employees of the federal executive branch averaged $1,072 a year, and college professors $1,100—not handsome sums, but much more than manual workers received. With such incomes, the middle class, whose numbers were increasing as a result of new job opportunities, could afford relatively comfortable housing. A six- or seven-room house cost around $3,000 to buy or build and from $15 to $20 per month to rent.

Though wages for industrial workers increased, their income figures were deceptive because jobs were not always stable and workers had to expend a disproportionate amount of income on necessities. On average, annual wages of factory workers rose from $486 in 1890 to $630 in 1910, about 30 percent. In industries with large female work forces, such as shoe and paper manufacturing, hourly rates remained lower than in male-dominated industries such as coal mining and iron production. Regional variations were also wide. Nevertheless, as Table 18.1 shows, most wages moved upward. Income for farm laborers followed the same

Table 18.1   American Living Standards, 1890–1910

	1890	1910
Income and earnings		
Annual income		
Clerical worker	$848	$1,156
Public school teacher	256	492
Industrial worker	486	630
Farm laborer	233	336
Hourly wage		
Soft-coal miner	0.18[a]	0.21
Iron worker	0.17[a]	0.23
Shoe worker	0.14[a]	0.19
Paper worker	0.12[a]	0.17
Labor statistics		
Number of people in labor force	28.5 million	41.7 million[b]
Average workweek in manufacturing	60 hours	51 hours

a. 1892
b. 1920

trend, though wages remained relatively low because farm workers generally received free room and board.

Wage increases mean little, however, if living costs rise as fast or faster. That is what happened. The weekly cost of living for a typical wage earner's family of four rose over 47 percent between 1889 and 1913.

Cost of Living

In other words, a combination of food and other goods that cost $6.78 in 1889 increased, after a slight dip in the mid-1890s, to $10 by 1913. In few working-class occupations did income rise as fast as the cost of living.

How then could working-class Americans afford machine-age new goods and services? Many could not. The daughter of a textile worker, recalling her school days, described how "some of the kids would bring bars of chocolate, others an orange. . . . I suppose they were richer than a family like ours. My father used to buy a bag of candy and a bag of peanuts every payday. . . . And that's all we'd have until the next payday." Another woman explained how her family coped with high prices and low wages: "My mother made our clothes. People then wore old clothes. My mother would rip them out and make them over."

Still, a family could raise its income and partake modestly in consumer society by sending children and women into the labor market (see pages 495–497). In a household where the father made $600 a year, wages of other family members might lift total income, or the family wage, to $800 or $900. Many families also rented rooms to boarders and lodgers, a practice that could yield up to $200 a year. These means of increasing family income enabled people to spend more and save more. Between 1889 and 1901, working-class families markedly increased expenditures for life insurance, alcoholic beverages, and union dues as well as for new leisure activities (see Chapter 19). Workers were thus able to improve their living standards, but not without sacrifices.

Supplements to Family Income

More than ever, American working people engaged in a highly developed wage and money economy. Between 1890 and 1920, the labor force increased by 50 percent, from 28 million workers to 42 million. These figures, however, are somewhat misleading: in general, they represent a change in the nature of work as much as an increase in the number of available jobs. In the rural society that predominated in the nineteenth century, women and children performed jobs crucial to the family's daily existence—cooking, cleaning, planting, and harvesting—but they seldom appeared in employment figures because they earned no wages. But as the nation industrialized, and the agricultural sector's share of national income and population declined, paid employment became more common. Jobs in industry and commerce were easier to define and easier to count. The proportion of Americans who worked—whether in fields, households, factories, or offices—probably did not increase markedly. Most Americans, male and female, had always worked. What was new was the increase in paid employment, making purchases of consumer goods and services more affordable.

Science and technology eased some of life's struggles, and their impact on living standards grew after 1900. Advances in medical care, better diets, and improved housing sharply reduced death rates and extended the life span. Between 1900 and 1920, life expectancy rose by fully six years and the death rate dropped by 24 percent. During this period notable declines occurred in deaths from typhoid, diphtheria, influenza (except for a harsh pandemic in 1918 and 1919), tuberculosis, and intestinal ailments—diseases that had been scourges of earlier generations. There were, however, significantly more deaths from cancer, diabetes, and heart disease, afflictions of an aging population and of new environmental factors such as smoke and chemical pollution. Americans also found more ways to kill one another: although the suicide rate remained stable, homicides and automobile-related deaths—effects of a fast-paced urban society—increased dramatically.

Higher Life Expectancy

Not only were amenities and luxuries more available than in the previous half-century, but the means to upward mobility seemed more accessible as well. Education increasingly became the key to success. Public education, aided by construction of new schools and passage of laws that required children to stay in school to age fourteen, equipped young people to achieve a standard of living higher than their parents'. Between 1890 and 1922, the number of students enrolled in public high schools rose dramatically. The creation of managerial and sales jobs in service industries helped to counter the downward mobility that resulted when mechanization pushed skilled workers out of their crafts. Yet inequities that had pervaded earlier eras remained in place. Race, gender, religion, and ethnicity still determined access to opportunity.

The Quest for Convenience

The toilet stood at the vanguard of a revolution in American lifestyles. The chain-pull washdown water closet, invented in England around 1870, reached the United States in the 1880s. Shortly after 1900 the flush toilet appeared; thanks to mass production of enamel-coated fixtures, it became standard in American homes and buildings. The toilet, cheap and easy to install, brought about a shift in habits and attitudes.

Flush Toilets

Before 1880 only luxury hotels and estates had private indoor bathrooms. By the 1890s the germ theory of disease had raised fears about carelessly disposed human waste as a source of infection and water contamination. Much more rapidly than Europeans did, Americans combined a desire for cleanliness with an urge for convenience, and water closets became common, especially in middle-class urban houses. (Flush toilets were not prevalent in working-class homes until the 1920s.) Bodily functions took on an unpleasant image, and the home bathroom became a place of utmost privacy. Edward and Clarence Scott, who produced white tissue in perforated rolls, provided Americans a more convenient form of toilet paper than the rough paper they had previously used. At the same time, the toilet and the private bathtub gave Americans new ways to use—and waste—water. Plumbing advances belonged to a broader democratization of convenience that accompanied mass production and consumerism.

The tin can also altered lifestyles. Before the mid-nineteenth century, Americans typically ate only foods that were in season. Drying, smoking, and salting could preserve meat for a short time, but the availability of fresh meat and fresh milk was limited; there was no way to prevent spoilage. A French inventor developed the cooking-and-sealing process of canning around 1810, and in the 1850s an American man named Gail Borden devised a means of condensing and preserving milk. Canned goods and condensed milk became more common during the 1860s, but supplies remained low because cans had to be made by hand. By 1880, however, inventors had fashioned stamping and soldering machines to mass-produce cans from tin plate. Now, even people remote from markets, like sailors and cowboys, could readily con-

Processed and Preserved Foods

Industrialization enhanced the incomes of the middle classes, enabling them to purchase goods previously unavailable and to provide amenities to their families more conveniently. This advertisement for a portable stove shows a father heating up milk for a baby that the mother is coddling. Note the bottle, tube, and nipple that the father is holding as well as the rug, furniture, clothing, vases, clock, and other items of moderate affluence. (Private Collection)

sume tomatoes, milk, oysters, and other alternatives to previously monotonous diets. Housewives also preserved their own fruits and vegetables, "putting up" foods in sealed glass jars.

Other trends and inventions broadened Americans' diets. Growing urban populations created demands that encouraged fruit and vegetable farmers to raise more produce. Railroad refrigerator cars enabled growers and meatpackers to ship perishables greater distances and to preserve them for longer periods. By the 1890s northern city dwellers could enjoy southern and western strawberries, grapes, and tomatoes for up to six months of the year. Home iceboxes enabled middle-class families to store perishables. An easy means of producing ice commercially was invented in the 1870s, and by 1900 the nation had over two thousand commercial ice plants, most of which made home deliveries.

The availability of new foods also inspired health reformers to correct the American diet. In the 1870s John H. Kellogg, a nutritionist and manager of the Western Health Reform Institute in Battle Creek, Michigan, began serving patients healthy new foods, including peanut butter and wheat flakes. Several years later his brother, William K. Kellogg, invented corn flakes, and Charles W. Post introduced Grape-Nuts, revolutionizing breakfast by replacing eggs, potatoes, and meat with ready-to-eat cereal, which supposedly was healthier. Just before the First World War, scientists discovered the dietetic value of vitamins A and B (C and D were discovered after the war). Growing numbers of published cookbooks and the opening of cooking schools reflected heightened interest in food and its possibilities for health and enjoyment.

Dietary Reform

Even the working class enjoyed a more diversified diet. As in the past, the poorest people still ate cheap foods, heavy in starches and carbohydrates. Southern textile workers, for example, ate corn mush and fatback (the strip of meat from a hog's back) almost every day. Poor urban families seldom could afford meat. Now, though, many of them could purchase previously unavailable fruits, vegetables, and dairy products. Workers had to spend a high percentage of their income on food—almost half of the breadwinner's wages—but they never suffered the severe malnutrition that plagued other developing nations.

Just as tin cans and iceboxes made many foods widely available, the sewing machine brought about a revolution in clothing. Before 1850 nearly all the clothes Americans wore were made at home or by seamstresses and tailors, and a person's social status was apparent in what he or she wore. Then in the 1850s the sewing machine, invented in Europe but refined by Americans Elias Howe, Jr., and Isaac M. Singer, came into use in clothing and shoe manufacture. Demand for uniforms during the Civil War boosted the ready-made clothing industry, and by 1890 annual retail sales of mass-

Ready-made Clothing

produced garments reached $1.5 billion. Mass production enabled manufacturers to turn out good-quality apparel at relatively low cost and to standardize sizes to fit different body shapes. By 1900 only the poorest families could not afford "ready-to-wear" clothes. Tailors and seamstresses, once the originators of fashion, had been relegated to repair work. Some women continued to make clothing at home, to save money or as a hobby, but dress patterns intended for use with a sewing machine simplified the remaining home production of clothing and injected another form of standardization into everyday life.

Mass-produced clothing and dress patterns reinforced a concern for style. Restrictive Victorian fashions still dominated women's clothing, but women were abandoning the most burdensome features. As women's participation in work and leisure activities became more active, dress designers placed greater emphasis on comfort. In the 1890s long sleeves and skirt hemlines receded, and high-boned collars disappeared. Women began wearing tailored blouses called shirtwaists, mass-manufactured in factories such as the Triangle Shirtwaist Factory. Designers used less fabric; by the 1920s a dress required three yards of material instead of ten. Petite was still the ideal, however: the most desirable waist measurement was 18 to 20 inches, and corsets were big sellers. In the early 1900s, long hair tied behind the neck was the most popular style. By the First World War, when many women worked in hospitals and factories, shorter and less hindering hairstyles had become fashionable.

Men's clothes, too, became more lightweight and stylish. Before 1900 men in the middle and affluent working classes would have owned no more than two suits, one for Sundays and special occasions and one for everyday wear. After 1900, however, manufacturers began to produce garments from fabrics of different weights and for different seasons. Men replaced derbies with felt hats, and stiff collars and cuffs with soft ones; dark-blue serge gave way to lighter shades and more intricate weaves. Workingmen still needed the most durable, least expensive overalls, shirts, and shoes. But even for males of modest means, clothing was becoming something to be bought instead of made and remade at home.

Department stores and chain stores helped to create and serve this new consumerism. Between 1865 and 1900, Macy's in New York, Wanamaker's in Philadelphia, Marshall Field in Chicago, and Rich's in Atlanta became urban landmarks.

Department and Chain Stores

This photograph of the food counter at R. H. Macy's Department Store in 1902 indicates the large number of processed and preserved foods that became available to Americans at the end of the nineteenth century. The use of tin cans and glass bottles permitted food producers to sell products previously available only at limited times of the year.   (Museum of the City of New York, The Byron Collection)

Previously, working classes had bought their goods in stores with limited inventories, and wealthier people had patronized fancy shops; each was discouraged by price, quality of goods, and social custom from shopping at the other's establishments. Now department stores, with their open displays of clothing, housewares, and furniture—all available in large quantities to anyone with the purchase price—caused a merchandising revolution. They offered not only a wide variety but also home deliveries, exchange policies, and charge accounts.

Meanwhile, the Great Atlantic Tea Company, founded in 1859, became the first grocery chain. Renamed the Great Atlantic and Pacific Tea Company in 1869 (and known as A&P), the firm's stores bought in volume and sold to the public at low prices. By 1915 there were almost eighteen hundred A&P stores, and twelve thousand more were built in the next ten years. Other chains, such as Woolworth's, dime stores that sold inexpensive personal items and novelties, grew rapidly during the same period.

A society of scarcity does not need advertising: when demand exceeds supply, producers have no trouble selling what they market. But in a society of abundance such as industrial America, supply frequently outstrips demand, necessitating a means to increase and create demand. Thus advertising assumed a new scale and function. In 1865 retailers spent about $9.5 million on advertising; that sum reached $95 million by 1900 and nearly $500 million by 1919.

Advertising

A salesperson tries to convince an individual customer to buy a certain product—whether an insurance policy, an article of clothing, or a home appliance. Advertisers, by contrast, aim to invent needs and persuade large groups of people to buy a specific product—a brand of cigarettes, a particular cosmetic, a company's canned foods. In the late nineteenth century, large companies that mass-produced consumer goods charged advertisers to create "consumption communities," bodies of consumers loyal to a particular brand name.

How do historians know...

that traditional gender roles pervaded American consumer society in the late nineteenth century? Advertising, which developed into a powerful medium in the late nineteenth century, offers useful insights into prevailing social and cultural values, and advertisers, eager to sell new consumer products, helped shape those values with strong visual images. This 1882 advertisement for the W. J. Morgan Sewing Machine Company uses both explicit and implicit domestic images to reinforce a wife's role as homemaker. From the very onset of her family career, the ad implies, a woman assumes domestic tasks and obligations such as sewing and mending clothing, and her husband guides her into this role. The ad conveys other symbols and values as well, such as the devoted look on the woman's face and the strong and superior pose of the man. The clothing also implies a middle-class standard. Newspapers and magazine advertisements of the late nineteenth century are rich with clues about this period of flourishing consumerism.   (Photo: Library of Congress)

In 1881 Congress passed a trademark law enabling producers to register and protect brand names. Thousands of companies registered products as varied as Hires Root Beer, Uneeda Biscuits, and Carter's Little Liver Pills. Advertising agencies—a service industry pioneered by N. W. Ayer & Son of Philadelphia—in turn offered expert advice to companies that wished to cultivate brand loyalty. By the early 1900s, advertising techniques had been so perfected that French composer Jacques Offenbach observed, "Decidedly the American advertising men play upon the human mind as a musician plays on his piano."

Newspapers served as the prime vehicle for advertising. In the mid-nineteenth century, publishers began to pursue higher revenues by selling more ad space. Wanamaker's placed the first full-page ad in 1879, and advertisers began to print pictures of products. Such attention-getting techniques transformed advertising into news. More than ever before, people read newspapers to find out what was for sale as well as what was happening.

The Corporate Consolidation Movement

 Neither new products nor new marketing techniques could mask certain unsettling factors in the American economy. The huge capital investment in new technology meant that factories had to operate at near capacity to recover costs. But the more manufacturers produced, the more they had to sell. To sell more, they had to reduce prices. To increase profits and compensate for reduced prices, they further expanded production and often reduced wages. To expand, they borrowed money. And to repay loans, they had to produce and sell even more. This spiraling process strangled small firms that could not keep pace and thrust workers into constant uncertainty. The same cycle affected commerce, banking, and transportation as well as manufacturing.

In this environment, optimism could dissolve at the hint that debtors could not meet their obligations.

Indeed, financial panics afflicted the economy during every decade at the end of the nineteenth century, ruining businesses and destroying workers' security. Economic declines that began in 1873, 1884, and 1893 lingered for several years. Business leaders disagreed on what caused them. Some blamed overproduction; others pointed to underconsumption; still others blamed lax credit and investment practices. Whatever the explanation, businesspeople began seeking ways to combat the uncertainty of boom-and-bust business cycles. Many adopted centralized forms of business organization, notably corporations, pools, trusts, and holding companies.

Unlike laborers, industrialists never questioned the capitalist system. They sought new ways to build on the base that had supported economic growth since the early 1800s, when states adopted incorporation laws to encourage commerce and industry. Under such laws, almost anyone could start a company and raise money by selling stock to investors. Stockholders could share in profits without personal risk because laws limited their liability for company debts to the amount of their own investment; the rest of their wealth was protected should the company fail. Nor did investors need to concern themselves with a firm's day-to-day operation; responsibility for company administration rested with its managers.

Rise of Corporations

Corporations proved to be the best instruments to raise capital for industrial expansion, and by 1900 two-thirds of all goods manufactured in the United States were produced by corporate firms. Moreover, corporations won judicial protection in the 1880s and 1890s when the Supreme Court ruled that they, like individuals, are protected by the Fourteenth Amendment. That is, states could not deny corporations equal protection under the law and could not deprive them of rights or property without due process of law. Such rulings insulated corporations against government interference in their operations.

As downward swings of the business cycle threatened profits, corporation managers sought greater stability in new and larger forms of economic concentration. Between the late 1880s and early 1900s, an epidemic of business consolidation swept the United States, resulting in massive conglomerates that have since dominated the nation's economy. At first such alliances were tentative and informal, consisting mainly of cooperative agreements

Pools

among firms that manufactured the same product or offered the same service. Through these arrangements, called pools, competing companies tried to control the market by agreeing how much each should produce and sharing profits. Employed by railroads (to divide up traffic), steel producers, and whiskey distillers, pools depended on their members' honesty. Such "gentlemen's agreements" worked during good times when there was enough business for all; but during slow periods, the desire for profits often tempted pool members to evade their commitments by secretly reducing prices or by selling more than the agreed quota. The Interstate Commerce Act of 1887 outlawed pools among railroads (see page 556), but by then the usefulness of the pooling strategy was already fading.

John D. Rockefeller, boss of Standard Oil, disliked pools, calling them weak and undependable. In 1879 one of his lawyers, Samuel Dodd, devised a more stable means of dominating the market. Since state laws prohibited one corporation from holding stock in another corporation, Dodd adapted an old device called a trust, a legal arrangement whereby responsible individuals would manage the financial affairs of a person unwilling or unable to handle them alone. Dodd reasoned that one company could control an industry by luring or forcing stockholders of smaller companies in that industry to yield control of their stock "in trust" to the larger company's board of trustees. This device allowed Rockefeller to achieve horizontal integration of the profitable petroleum industry in 1882 by combining his Standard Oil Company of Ohio with other refineries he bought up.

Trusts

In 1888 New Jersey adopted new laws allowing corporations chartered there to own property in other states and to own stock in other corporations. (Trusts provided for trusteeship, not ownership.) This liberalization facilitated creation of the holding company, which owned a partial or complete interest in other companies. Holding companies could in turn merge their companies' assets (buildings, equipment, inventory, and cash) as well as their management. Under this arrangement, Rockefeller's holding company, Standard Oil of New Jersey, merged forty refining companies. By 1898 Standard Oil refined 84 percent of all oil produced in the nation, controlled most pipelines, and had moved into natural-gas production and ownership of oil-producing properties.

Holding Companies

Believing that Rockefeller's Standard Oil monopoly was exercising dangerous power, this political cartoonist depicts the trust as a greedy octopus whose sprawling tentacles already ensnare Congress, state legislatures, and the taxpayer, and are reaching for the White House.   (Library of Congress)

Standard Oil's expansion into operations besides refining exemplified a new form of economic integration. To dominate their markets, many holding companies sought control over all aspects of their operations, including raw materials, production, and distribution. A model of such vertical integration, which fused related business activities into one entity under unified management, was Gustavus Swift's meat-processing operation. During the 1880s, Swift invested in livestock, slaughterhouses, refrigerator cars, and marketing to ensure profits from the sale of his beef at prices he could control.

Mergers provided an answer to industry's search for order and profits. Between 1889 and 1903, some three hundred combinations were formed, most of them trusts and holding companies. The most spectacular was U.S. Steel Corporation, financed by J. P. Morgan in 1901. This enterprise, made up of iron-ore properties, freight carriers, wire mills, plate and tubing companies, and other firms, was capitalized at over $1.4 billion. Other mammoth combinations included the Amalgamated Copper Company, American Sugar Refining Company, and U.S. Rubber Company. In 1896 fewer than a dozen corporations were worth over $10 million; by 1903 three hundred were worth that much and seventeen had assets exceeding $100 million. At the same time, these huge companies ruth-

lessly put thousands of smaller competitors out of business.

The merger movement created a new species of businessman, one whose vocation was financial organizing rather than producing a particular good or service. Shrewd operators sought opportunities for combination, formed a holding company, then persuaded producers to sell their firms to the new company. These financiers raised money by selling stock and borrowing from banks. Their attention ranged widely. W. H. Moore organized the American Tin Plate Company, Diamond Match Company, and National Biscuit Company, and he acquired control of the Rock Island Railroad. Elbert H. Gary similarly participated in consolidation of the barbed-wire industry and then of U.S. Steel. Investment bankers like J. P. Morgan and Jacob Schiff piloted the merger movement, inspiring awe with their financial power and organizational skills.

The growth of corporations in the late nineteenth century turned financial stock and bond exchanges into hubs of activity. In 1886 trading on the New York Stock Exchange reached 1 million shares a day. By 1914 the number of industrial stocks traded reached 511, compared with 145 in 1869. Between 1870 and 1900, foreign investment in American companies rose

Financiers

from $1.5 billion to $3.5 billion. Personal savings and institutional investment also mushroomed: assets of savings banks, concentrated in the Northeast and West Coast, rose by 700 percent between 1875 and 1897 to a total of $2.2 billion. States loosened regulations to enable banks to invest in railroads and industrial enterprises. Commercial banks, insurance companies, and corporations also invested heavily. As one journal proclaimed, "Nearly the whole country (including the typical widow and orphan) is interested in the stock market." This exaggeration reflected what optimistic capitalists wanted to believe.

The Gospel of Wealth and Its Critics

Business leaders used corporate consolidation not to promote competition but to minimize it. To justify their tactics to a public committed to the free market, they called on the doctrine of Social Darwinism. Developed by British philosopher Herbert Spencer and preached in the United States by Yale professor William Graham Sumner, Social Darwinism loosely grafted Charles Darwin's theory of the survival of the fittest onto laissez faire, the doctrine that government should not interfere in private economic affairs. Social Darwinists reasoned that, in an unconstrained economy, power and wealth would flow naturally to the most capable people. Acquisition and possession of property were thus sacred and well-deserved rights. Civilization depended on this system, explained Sumner. "If we do not like the survival of the fittest," he wrote, "we have only one possible alternative, and that is survival of the unfittest." In this view, monopolies represented the natural accumulation of economic power by those best suited for wielding it.

Social Darwinism

Social Darwinists reasoned, too, that wealth carried moral responsibilities to provide for those less fortunate or less capable. Steel baron Andrew Carnegie asserted what he called "the Gospel of Wealth"—that he and other industrialists were guardians of society's wealth and that they had a duty to fulfill their obligation in humane ways. Over his lifetime, Carnegie donated more than $350 million to libraries, schools, peace initiatives, and the arts. Such philanthropy, however, also implied a right for benefactors like Rockefeller and Carnegie to define what was good and necessary for society; it did not translate into paying workers decent wages.

In contradiction, business leaders who extolled individual initiative and independence also pressed for government assistance. While denouncing efforts to legislate maximum working hours or regulate factory conditions as interference with natural economic laws, they lobbied forcefully and successfully for subsidies, loans, and tax relief to encourage business growth. Grants to railroads were one form of such assistance. Tariffs, which raised the prices of foreign products by placing an import tax on them, were another. When Congress imposed high tariffs on foreign goods such as kerosene, steel rails, woolen goods, and tin plate, American producers could raise prices on their own kerosene, rails, woolens, and tin to just under what comparable foreign goods would sell for with the tariff included. Since the inception of tariffs in the early nineteenth century, industrialists argued that tariff protection encouraged the development of new products and the founding of new enterprises. But tariffs also forced consumers to pay artificially high prices for many goods.

Government Assistance to Business

While defenders insisted that trusts and other forms of big business were a natural and efficient outcome of economic development, critics charged that these forms were unnatural because they stifled opportunity and originated from greed. Such charges emanating from farmers, workers, and intellectuals voiced an ardent fear of monopoly, the domination of an economic activity (such as oil refining) by one powerful company (such as Standard Oil). Those who feared monopoly believed—with considerable justification—that large corporations fixed prices, exploited workers by cutting wages, destroyed opportunity by crushing small businesses, and threatened democracy by corrupting politicians—all of which was not only unnatural but immoral. To critics, ethics eclipsed economics.

Dissenting Voices

Many believed in a better path to progress. By the mid-1880s, a number of intellectuals began to challenge Social Darwinism and laissez-faire economics. Sociologist Lester Ward attacked the application of evolutionary theory to social and economic relations. In *Dynamic Sociology* (1883), Ward argued that human control of nature, not natural law, accounted for the advance of civilization. A system that guaranteed survival only to the fittest was wasteful and brutal; instead, Ward reasoned, cooperative activity fostered by government intervention was more moral. Economists Richard Ely, John R. Commons, and Edward Bemis agreed that natural forces should be harnessed for the public good. They denounced the laissez-faire system for its "unsound morals" and praised the positive assistance that government could offer.

While academics endorsed intervention in the natural economic order, others more directly questioned why the United States had to have so many poor people while a few became fabulously wealthy.

Utopian Economic Schemes

Henry George was a San Francisco printer and writer who had fallen into desperate poverty during the depression of the 1870s. Alarmed at the exploitative power of large enterprises, he came to believe that inequality stemmed from the ability of a few to profit from rising land values. George argued that such profits made speculators rich simply because of increased demand for living and working space, especially in cities. To prevent profiteering, George proposed to replace all taxes with a "single tax" on the "unearned increment"—the rise in property values caused by increased market demand rather than by owners' improvements. George's scheme, argued forcefully in *Progress and Poverty* (1879), had great popular appeal and almost won him the mayoralty of New York City in 1886.

Unlike George, who accepted private ownership, novelist Edward Bellamy believed competitive capitalism promoted waste. Instead, he proposed establishment of a state in which government owned the means of production. Bellamy outlined his dream in *Looking Backward* (1888). The novel, which sold over a million copies, depicted Boston in the year 2000 as a peaceful community where everyone had a job and a technological elite managed the economy according to scientific principles. Though a council of elders ruled and ordinary people could not vote in this utopia, Bellamy tried to convince readers that a "principle of fraternal cooperation" could replace vicious competition and wasteful monopoly. His vision, which he called "Nationalism," sparked formation of Nationalist clubs from Boston to Los Angeles and kindled popular appeals for civil service reform, social welfare measures, and government ownership of railroads and utilities.

Few people supported the universal government ownership envisioned by Bellamy, but several states took steps to prohibit monopolies and regulate business. By the end of the nineteenth century, fifteen states had constitutional provisions outlawing trusts, and twenty-seven had laws

Antitrust Legislation

forbidding pools. Most were agricultural states in the South and West that were responding to antimonopolistic pressure from farm organizations. But state authorities lacked the staff and judicial support for an effective attack on big business, and corporations always found ways to evade restrictions. Only national legislation, it seemed, could work.

Congress moved hesitantly toward such legislation and in 1890 finally passed the Sherman Anti-Trust Act. Introduced by Senator John Sherman of Ohio and rewritten by pro-business eastern senators, the law made illegal "every contract, combination in the form of trust or otherwise, or conspiracy in the restraint of trade." Those found guilty of violating the law faced fines and jail terms, and those wronged by illegal combinations could sue for triple damages. However, the law was left purposely vague so as to attract broad support. It did not clearly define "restraint of trade" and consigned interpretation of its provisions to the courts, which at the time were strong allies of business.

Judges used the law's vagueness to blur distinctions between reasonable and unreasonable restraints of trade. When in 1895 the federal government prosecuted the so-called Sugar Trust for owning 98 percent of the nation's sugar-refining capacity, eight of the nine Supreme Court justices ruled that control of manufacturing did not necessarily mean control of trade (*U.S. v. E. C. Knight Co.*). According to the Court, the Constitution empowered Congress to regulate interstate commerce, but manufacturing (which in the Knight case took place entirely within the state of Pennsylvania) did not fall under congressional control.

Between 1890 and 1900 the federal government prosecuted only eighteen cases under the Sherman Anti-Trust Act. The most successful involved railroads directly involved in interstate commerce. Ironically, the act equipped the government with a tool for breaking up labor unions: courts that did not consider monopolistic production a restraint on trade willingly applied antitrust provisions to boycotts encouraged by striking unions.

Summary

Mechanization and new inventions thrust the United States into the vanguard of industrial nations and immeasurably altered daily life between 1877 and 1920. But in industry, as in farming and mining, massive size and aggressive consolidation engulfed the individual, changing the nature of work from individual activity undertaken by producers to mass production undertaken by wage earners. Laborers fought to regain control of their work but struggled to develop well-organized unions that could meet their needs. The outpouring of products created a new mass society based on consumerism, but even the democratization of consumption did not benefit all social groups.

The problems of enforcing the Sherman Anti-Trust Act reflected the uneven distribution of power. Corporations consolidated to control resources, production, and politics. Farmers, laborers, and reformers had numbers and ideas but lacked influence. They benefited from the material gains that technology and mass production provided, but they charged that business was acquiring too much influence and profiting at their expense. In factories and farms, some people were celebrating the industrial transformation while others were struggling with the dilemma of industrialism: whether a system based on ever-greater profits was the best way for Americans to fulfill the nation's democratic destiny.

The march of industrial expansion proved almost impossible to stop, however, because so many powerful and ordinary people were benefiting from it. Moreover, the waves of people pouring into the nation's cities were increasingly providing both workers and consumers for America's expanding productive capacity. The dynamo of American vitality now rested in the cities.

LEGACY FOR A PEOPLE AND A NATION
Rockefeller and Standard Oil

For a generation after he founded his oil trust in 1882, John D. Rockefeller and Standard Oil evoked awe and fear of their power and wealth. Then, in 1911, the U.S. Supreme Court enforced anti-trust law and dissolved the company into thirty-four pieces. After the breakup, the Rockefeller family and the oil business drifted apart, but both left legacies to American society, though in different ways.

John D. Rockefeller personified the big-business "Robber Baron" for decades, even after he retired from managing his empire of oil, steel, and railroads. His wealth inspired dreams, with sayings and song lyrics expressing a person's hope of becoming "rich as Rockefeller." For years he regularly gave away millions of dollars for educational and humanitarian purposes, and in 1913 he permanently endowed a philanthropic foundation "to promote the well-being of mankind throughout the world." Since then, the Rockefeller Foundation has disbursed some $100 million for education, the eradication of disease, food production, population research, and the arts and humanities. Rockefeller's only son, John, Jr., oversaw the foundation while he withdrew the family from the oil business in the 1920s and 1930s, and he sold oil stock to finance construction of the huge Rockefeller Center office complex in New York City. A grandson, John III, continued to give away money made by his grandfather.

Meanwhile, the business of oil refining became a critical element to everyday life, not just in the production of gasoline for cars, trucks, planes, and other machines driven by internal combustion, but also for the plastics industry that provides so many modern products that to list them would require volumes. In 1998, at the height of another era of corporate consolidation, the two largest segments of the former Standard Oil Trust—Exxon Corporation and Mobil Corporation (formerly Standard Oil of New Jersey and Standard Oil of New York)—negotiated an $83 billion merger that reunited them into the world's largest oil company with 123,000 employees and $200 billion in annual revenues. But the newly created Exxon Mobil did not presage the revival of a monopolistic trust. While in his day the senior Rockefeller controlled 90 percent of American refining capacity, the Exxon-Mobil combination would control 21 percent. Worldwide oil production has dispersed control of the industry, and competitive production has minimized the power of any one company.

The closest modern replica of Rockefeller might be William H. Gates, founder and chairman of Microsoft, the giant computer software firm. Also the target of anti-trust prosecution, Gates, like Rockefeller, drove rivals out of business through aggressive pricing and continually innovated to maintain a competitive edge. Gates also amassed a vast fortune, reputed to be the largest of any American, and gave away huge sums for humanitarian and educational purposes.

For Further Reading, see page A-21 of the Appendix. For Web resources, go to http://college.hmco.com.

It sounds like a movie story line. Rahel Gollop grew up in a village in western Russia. Her father, driven to desperation by persecution and poverty, left his family in 1890 to find a better life. Arrested by Russian soldiers, he escaped into Germany and found passage on a steamship bound for New York City. After two and a half years in the United States, he had saved enough to purchase tickets so Rahel and her aunt could join him in America. A year later, her mother, brothers, and sisters arrived.

Rahel's first impression of the American city was one of awe. "I was dazed by all there was to see," she recalled. "I looked with wonder at the tall houses, the paved streets, the street lamps. As I had never seen a large city and had had only a glimpse of a small one, I thought these things true only of America." But soon the Gollop's landlady, an immigrant who had been in the United States for several years, gave Rahel a dose of reality. Rahel wrote,

> When she asked us how we liked America, and we spoke of it with praise, she smiled a queer smile. "Life here is not all that it appears to the 'green horn' (new immigrant)," she said. She told us that her husband was a presser of coats and earned twelve dollars when he worked a full week. Aunt Masha thought twelve dollars a good deal. Again Mrs. Felesberg smiled. "No doubt it would be," she said, "where you used to live. You had your own house, and most of the food came from the garden. Here you will have to pay for everything; the rent!" she sighed, "for the light, for every potato, every grain of barley."

Like other immigrant families, the Gollops struggled and coped with this urban world where a family could not afford their own house and where they had to pay for everything. To help her parents and enable her brothers to attend school, Rahel, only twelve years old, went to work in a garment sweatshop. Before she was twenty, she held a variety of jobs, mostly doing

With hope and apprehension, millions of foreign immigrants poured into America's pulsing cities between 1880 and 1920. Bringing with them values, habits, and attire from the Old World, they faced a multitude of new experiences, expectations, and products in the New World and tried to negotiate their existence by combining the new with the old. (Albanian Woman, Ellis Island, 1905. © Collection for Creative Photography, The University of Arizona)

19

THE VITALITY AND TURMOIL OF URBAN LIFE 1877–1920

tailoring work. She witnessed—and went through—many of the travails suffered by other immigrants, including the beating of eastern European Jews on election night and the harassment of street vendors by drunken nativists. Like other immigrants, Rahel sought security by associating with her own kind, rarely mingling with strangers.

But gradually Rahel broke away. Health problems brought her into a Protestant hospital where she was exposed to another culture. She learned to read English and acquired an education. Rejecting the man whom her parents had selected for her husband, she married a grocer and became a writer. She published her autobiography in 1918 and died in 1925 at the age of forty-five, possibly of suicide.

The experiences of Rahel Gollop illustrate many themes characterizing urban life in America in the late nineteenth century and early twentieth. Where to live, where to work, how to support the family, the cash-based economy, ethnic consciousness and bigotry, the quest for individual independence and respectability—all these things and more made cities places of hope, frustration, satisfaction, and conflict. Their clanging trolleys, smoky air, crowded streets, and jumble of languages contrasted with the quiet pace of village and farm life.

Cities had exerted significant influence on the nation's history since its inception, but not until the 1880s did the United States begin to become a truly urban nation. The new industrialization and technological innovation of the late nineteenth century (see Chapter 18) fueled a tremendous social and geographical expansion that funneled millions of people into cities. By 1920 a milestone of urbanization was passed: that year's census showed that, for the first time, a majority of Americans (51.2 percent) lived in cities (settlements with more than 2,500 people). This new fact of national life was as symbolically significant as the disappearance of the frontier in 1890.

Cities served as marketplaces and forums, bringing together the people, resources, and ideas responsible for many of the changes in neighborhoods, politics, commerce, and leisure that American society was experiencing. By 1900 a network of small, medium, and large cities spanned every section of the country. Some people relished the opportunities and excitement cities offered; others found American cities disquieting and threatening. But whatever people's personal impressions, the city had become central to American life. The ways people built their cities and adjusted to the urban environment have shaped American society. ■

Electric trolley cars and other forms of mass transit enabled middle-class people like these women and men to reside on the urban outskirts and ride into the city center for work, shopping, and entertainment.   (Museum of the City of New York, The Byron Collection)

IMPORTANT EVENTS

1867 First law regulating tenements passes, in New York State

1870 One-fourth of Americans live in cities

1876 National League of Professional Baseball Clubs founded

1880s "New" immigrants from eastern and southern Europe begin to arrive in large numbers

1883 Brooklyn Bridge completed
Pulitzer buys *New York World* and creates a major vehicle for yellow journalism

1885 Safety bicycle invented

1886 First settlement house opens, in New York City

1889 Edison invents the motion picture and viewing device

1890s Electric trolleys replace horse-drawn mass transit

1893 Columbian Exposition opens in Chicago

1895 Hearst buys the *New York Journal*, another major popular yellow-journalism newspaper

1898 Race riot erupts in Wilmington, North Carolina

1900–10 Immigration reaches peak
Vaudeville rises in popularity

1903 Boston beats Pittsburgh in first baseball World Series

1905 Intercollegiate Athletic Association, forerunner of National College Athletic Association (NCAA), is formed and restructures rules of football

1906 Race riot erupts in Atlanta, Georgia

1915 Griffith directs *Birth of a Nation*, one of the first major technically sophisticated movies

1920 Majority (51.4 percent) of Americans live in cities

Industrial Growth and Transportation in the Modern City

 Though their initial functions had been commercial, cities became the main arenas for industrial growth in the late nineteenth century. As centers of labor, transportation, and communication, cities provided everything factories needed. Capital accumulated by the cities' mercantile enterprises fed industrial invest-

Urban Industrial Development ment. Urban populations also furnished consumers for myriad new products. Thus urban growth and industrialization wound together in a mutually advantageous spiral. The further industrialization advanced, the more opportunities it created for work and investment. Increased opportunity in turn drew more people to cities; as workers and as consumers, they fueled yet more industrialization.

Most cities housed a variety of industrial enterprises, but product specialization gradually became common. Mass production of clothing concentrated in New York; the shoe industry in Philadelphia; textiles in New England cities. Other cities processed products from surrounding agricultural regions: flour in

Minneapolis; cottonseed oil in Memphis; beef and pork in Chicago and Omaha. Still others processed natural resources: gold and copper in Denver; fish and lumber in Seattle; coal and iron in Pittsburgh and Birmingham; oil in Houston and Los Angeles. Such activities increased cities' magnetic attraction for people in search of steady employment.

Urban and industrial growth transformed the national economy and freed the United States from dependence on European capital and manufactured goods. Imports and foreign investments still flowed into the United States. But by the early 1900s, cities and their factories, stores, and banks were converting America from a debtor agricultural nation into an industrial, financial, and exporting power.

Late in the nineteenth century, the compact city of the early nineteenth century, where residences

Birth of the Modern City mingled among shops, factories, and warehouses, burst open. From Boston to Los Angeles, the built environment sprawled several miles beyond the original central core. No longer did walking distance determine a city's size. No longer did different social groups live close together, poor near rich, immigrant near native-born, black near white. Instead, cities subdivided into distinct districts:

working-class and ethnic neighborhoods, downtown, a ring of suburbs. Two forces were responsible for this new arrangement. One, mass transportation, was centrifugal, propelling people and enterprises outward. The other, economic change, was centripetal, drawing human and economic resources inward.

Mass transportation moved people faster and farther. By the 1870s, horse-drawn vehicles were disappearing from city streets, replaced by motor-driven conveyances. Cable cars (carriages that moved by clamping onto a moving underground wire) came first. By the 1880s, cable-car lines operated in Chicago, San Francisco, and many other cities. Then in the 1890s, electric-powered streetcars began replacing horse cars and cable cars. Designed in Montgomery, Alabama, and Richmond, Virginia, electric trolleys spread to nearly every large American city. Between 1890 and 1902, total extent of electrified track grew from 1,300 to 22,000 miles. In a few cities, companies raised track onto trestles, enabling vehicles to travel without interference above jammed downtown streets. In Boston,

Mechanization of Mass Transportation

New York, and Philadelphia, transit firms dug underground passages for their cars, also to avoid traffic congestion. Because elevated railroads and subways were extremely expensive to construct, they appeared only in the few cities where companies could amass enough capital to lay track and buy equipment and where there were enough riders to ensure profits.

Another form of mass transit, the electric interurban railway, helped link nearby cities. Usually built over shorter distances than steam railroads, the interurbans operated between cities in areas with growing suburban populations and furthered urban development by making outer regions attractive for home buyers and businesses. The extensive network of the Pacific Electric Railway in southern California, for example, facilitated both travel and economic development in that region.

Mass-transit lines launched millions of urban dwellers into outlying neighborhoods and created a commuting public. Those who could afford the fare—usually a nickel a ride—could live beyond the crowded central city and commute there for

Beginnings of Urban Sprawl

Along with mass-produced consumer goods such as clothing and appliances, Sears, Roebuck and Company marketed architectural plans for middle-class suburban housing. This drawing, taken from the Sears catalogue for 1911, illustrates the kind of housing developed on the urban outskirts in the early twentieth century.   (Sears, Roebuck and Company)

work, shopping, and entertainment. Working-class families, whose incomes rarely topped a dollar a day, found streetcar fares unaffordable. But the growing middle class could escape to quiet neighborhoods on the urban outskirts and live in bungalows with their own yards on tree-lined streets. Real-estate development boomed around the borders of cities. Between 1890 and 1920, for example, developers in the Chicago area opened 800,000 new lots—enough to house at least three times the city's 1890 population. A home several miles from downtown was inconvenient, but the benefits outweighed the costs. As one suburbanite wrote in 1902, "It may be a little more difficult for us to attend the opera, but the robin in my elm tree struck a higher note and a sweeter one yesterday than any prima donna ever reached."

Urban sprawl was essentially unplanned, but certain patterns did emerge. Eager to capitalize on commuting possibilities, thousands of small investors who bought land in anticipation of settlement paid little attention to the need for parks, traffic control, and public services. Construction of mass transit was guided by the profit motive and thus benefited the urban public unevenly. Streetcar lines serviced mainly those districts that promised the most riders—those whose fares would increase company profits.

Streetcars, elevateds, and subways altered commercial as well as residential patterns. When consumers moved outward, businesses followed. New commercial centers sprouted at trolley-line intersections and at elevated-railway stations. Branches of department stores and banks joined groceries, theaters, taverns, and shops to create neighborhood shopping centers, the forerunners of today's suburban malls. Meanwhile, the urban core became the work zone, where offices and stores loomed over streets clogged with people, horses, wagons, and trolleys. Districts such as Chicago's Loop and New Orleans's Canal Street employed thousands in commerce and finance.

Peopling the Cities: Migrants and Immigrants

Between 1870 and 1920, the number of Americans living in cities increased almost 550 percent, from 10 million to 54 million. During this period, the number of cities with more than 100,000 people grew from fifteen to sixty-eight; the number with more than 500,000 swelled from two to twelve (see Map 19.1).

These figures, dramatic in themselves, represent millions of stories of dreams and frustration, coping and confusion, success and failure.

How Cities Grew

A city can increase its population in three ways: by natural increase (an excess of births over deaths); by extending its borders to annex land and people; and by net migration (an excess of in-migrants over out-migrants). Between the 1870s and early 1900s, the number of people born in American cities was roughly equal to the number who died, so natural increase did not account for urban population growth in this period. Many cities, however, annexed nearby territory, thereby instantly increasing their populations. The most notable consolidation occurred in 1898 when New York City, which previously consisted of only Manhattan and the Bronx, merged with Brooklyn, Staten Island, and part of Queens and doubled overnight from 1.5 million to 3 million people. Suburbs often desired annexation for the schools, water, fire protection, and sewer systems that cities could provide. Sometimes annexation preceded settlement, adding vacant land where new city dwellers could live. In the 1880s, Chicago, Minneapolis, and Los Angeles incorporated hundreds of undeveloped square miles into their borders.

By far the greatest contribution to urban population growth was in-migration from the countryside and immigration from abroad. In fact, migration to cities nearly matched the massive migration to the West that was occurring at the same time. Urban newcomers arrived from two major sources: the American countryside and Europe. Asia, Canada, and Latin America also supplied immigrants, though in smaller numbers.

Migration from the Countryside

Despite land rushes in the West, rural populations declined as urban populations burgeoned. Low crop prices and high debts dashed white farmers' hopes and drove them off the land toward opportunities that cities seemed to offer. Such migration affected not only major cities such as Detroit, Chicago, and San Francisco but also secondary cities such as Indianapolis, Salt Lake City, Birmingham, Nashville, and San Diego. The thrill of city life beckoned especially to young people. A character in the play *The City* (1920) spoke for many youths when she exclaimed, "Who wants to smell new-mown hay, if he can breathe in gasoline on Fifth Avenue instead! Think of the theaters! The crowds! Think of being able to go out on the street and see someone you didn't know by sight!"

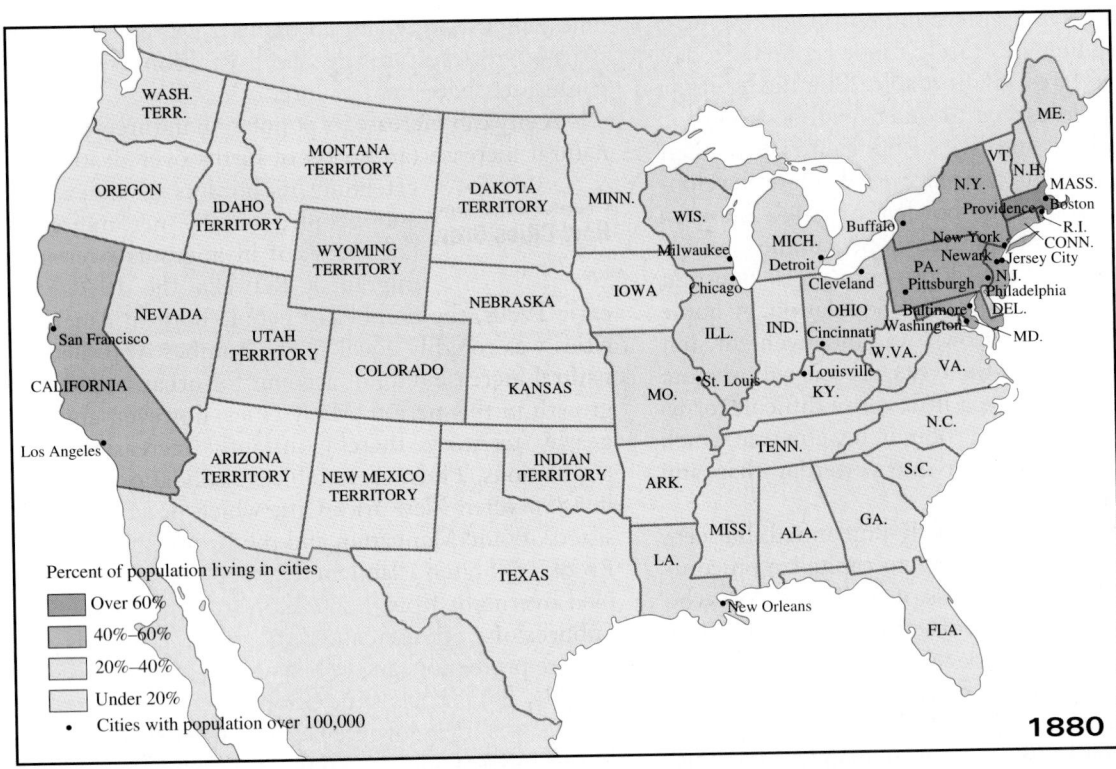

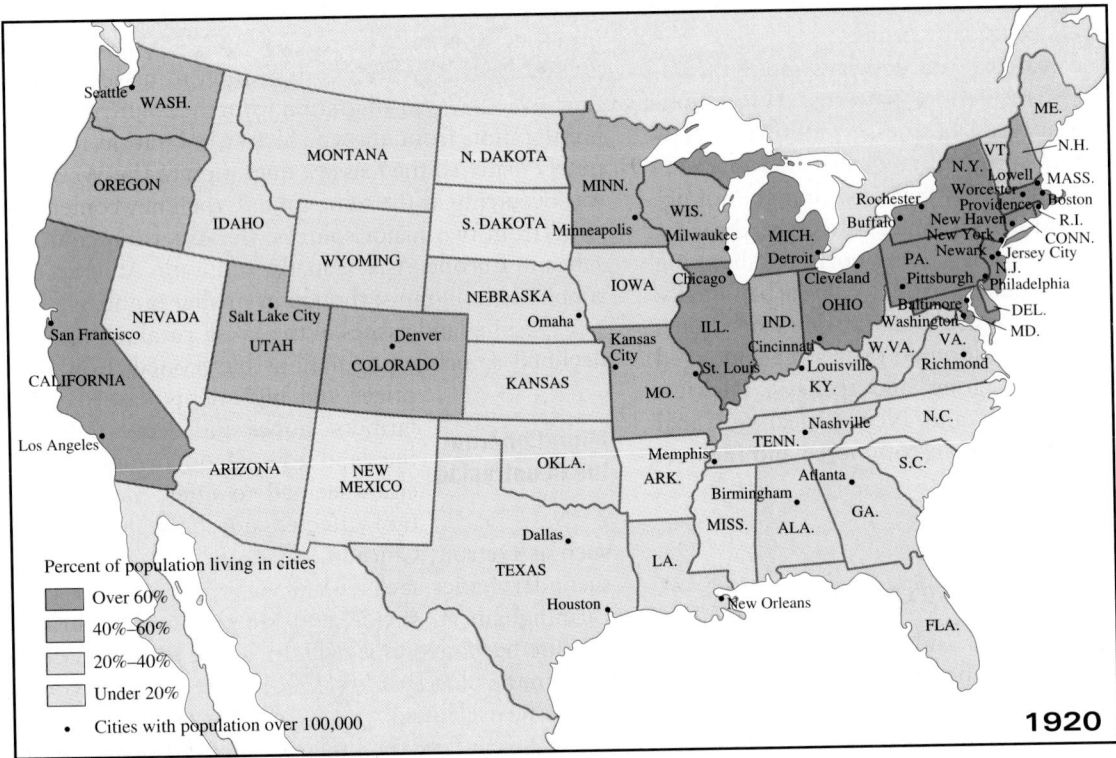

Map 19.1   Urbanization, 1880 and 1920   In 1880 the vast majority of states still were heavily rural. By 1920 only a few had less than 20 percent of their population living in cities.

The Caribbean as well as Europe sent immigrants to the United States. Proud and confident on arrival from their homeland of Guadeloupe, these women perhaps were unprepared for the double disadvantage they faced as both blacks and foreigners. (William Williams Papers, Manuscripts & Archives Division, The New York Public Library)

In the 1880s and 1890s, thousands of rural African Americans also moved cityward, seeking better employment and fleeing crop liens, ravages of the boll weevil on cotton crops, racial violence, and political oppression. Though black urban dwellers grew more numerous after 1915, thirty-two cities already had more than ten thousand black residents by 1900. Southern cities such as Baltimore, Atlanta, and Birmingham increased their black populations, but also northern and western places such as New York, Cleveland, and Chicago received thousands of African American migrants. These urban newcomers resembled other migrants in their rural backgrounds and economic motivations, but they differed in several important ways. Because few factories would employ African Americans, most found jobs in the service sector—cleaning, cooking, and driving—rather than in industrial trades. Also, because most service openings were traditionally female jobs, black women outnumbered black men in cities such as New York, Baltimore, and New Orleans. In the South, an enlarged population of African Americans migrating from the countryside served as an important source of unskilled labor in the region's growing cities. By 1900 almost 40 percent of the total population of both Atlanta, Georgia, and Charlotte, North Carolina, were blacks.

In the West, many Hispanics, who once had been a predominantly rural population, moved into cities. They took over unskilled construction and grading

African American and Hispanic Migration to Cities

jobs once held by Chinese laborers who were driven from southern California cities, and in some Texas cities native Mexicans (called *Tejanos*) held the majority of all unskilled jobs. In places such as Los Angeles, males often left for long periods of time to take temporary agricultural jobs, leaving behind many female heads of household.

Even more newcomers were immigrants from Europe who had fled foreign villages and cities for American shores. Smaller numbers from Asia, Canada, and

Those who wished to Americanize the immigrants believed the public schools could provide the best setting for assimilation. This 1917 poster from the Cleveland Board of Education and the Cleveland Americanization Committee used the languages most common to the new immigrants—Slovene, Italian, Polish, Hungarian, and Yiddish—as well as English to invite newcomers to free classes where they could learn "the language of America" and "citizenship."   (National Park Service Collection, Ellis Island Immigration Museum. Photo: Chermayeff & Geismar/MetaForm)

Immigration from Other Lands

Latin American came for the same reasons. The dream of many was not to stay but to make enough money to return home and live in greater comfort and security. For every hundred foreigners who entered the country, around thirty later left. Still, most of the 26 million immigrants who arrived between 1870 and 1920 and whose numbers peaked between 1900 and 1910 remained, and the great majority settled in cities, where they helped reshape American culture. Rahel Gollop, the Russian garment worker, fit this pattern of settlement and adaptation.

Immigrants to the United States were part of a worldwide movement pushing people away from traditional means of support and pulling them toward better opportunities. Population pressures, land redistribution, and industrialization induced millions of peasants, small farmers, and craftsmen to leave Europe and Asia for Canada, Australia, Brazil, and Argentina, as well as the United States. Religious persecution, too, particularly the violent pogroms and merciless military conscription that Jews suffered in eastern Europe, forced people to flee across the Atlantic. Migration always has been present in human history, but in the late nineteenth century technological developments in communications and transportation spread news of opportunities and made travel cheaper, quicker, and safer.

Immigrants from northern and western Europe had long made the United States their main destination, but after 1880 economic and demographic changes propelled a second wave of immigrants from other regions. Northern and western Europeans continued to arrive, but the new wave brought more people from eastern and southern Europe, plus smaller contingents from Canada, Mexico, and Japan (see Map 19.2 and Figure 19.1). Two-thirds of the newcomers who arrived in the 1880s came from Germany, England, Ireland, and Scandinavia; between 1900 and 1909, two-thirds came from Italy, Austria-Hungary, and Russia. By 1910 arrivals from Mexico were beginning to outnumber arrivals from Ireland, and large numbers of Japanese had moved to the West Coast and Hawai'i. Foreign-born blacks, chiefly from the West Indies, also increased in number. (See the Appendix for the nationalities of immigrants.)

The New Immigrants

Many Americans feared the customs, Catholic and Jewish faiths, and poverty of "new" immigrants, con-

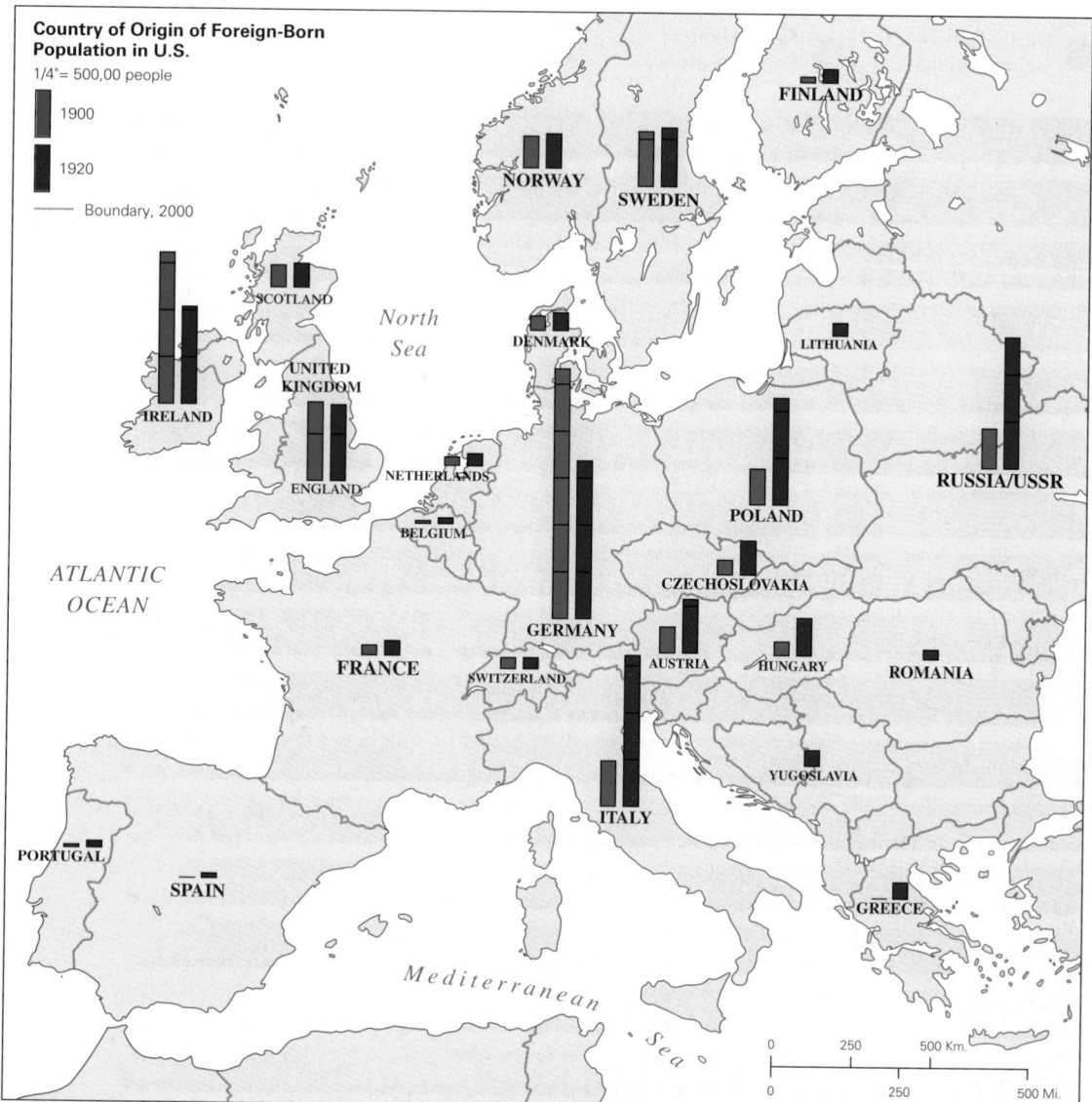

Map 19.2 Sources of European-born Population, 1900 and 1920 In just a few decades, the proportion of European immigrants to the United States who came from northern and western Europe decreased (Ireland and Germany) or remained relatively stable (England and Scandinavia), while the proportion from eastern and southern Europe dramatically increased. (Data from U.S. Census Bureau, "Historical Census Statistics on the Foreign-born Population of the United States: 1850–1990," Feb. 1999. Retrieved Feb. 12, 2000, from the World Wide Web: http://www.census.gov/population.)

sidering them less desirable than "old" immigrants, whose languages and beliefs seemed less alien. Unlike earlier arrivals from Great Britain and Ireland, new immigrants did not speak English and more than half worked in the lowest skilled occupations. In reality, however, old and new immigrants closely resembled each other in their strategies for coping. The majority of both groups came from societies that made the family the focus of all undertakings. As Rahel Gollop's case

illustrates, whether and when to emigrate was decided in light of the family's needs, and family bonds continued to prevail after immigrants reached the New World. New arrivals usually knew where they wanted to go and how to get there because they received aid from relatives who had already immigrated. In many instances, workers helped kin obtain jobs, and family members pooled resources to maintain, if not improve, their standard of living.

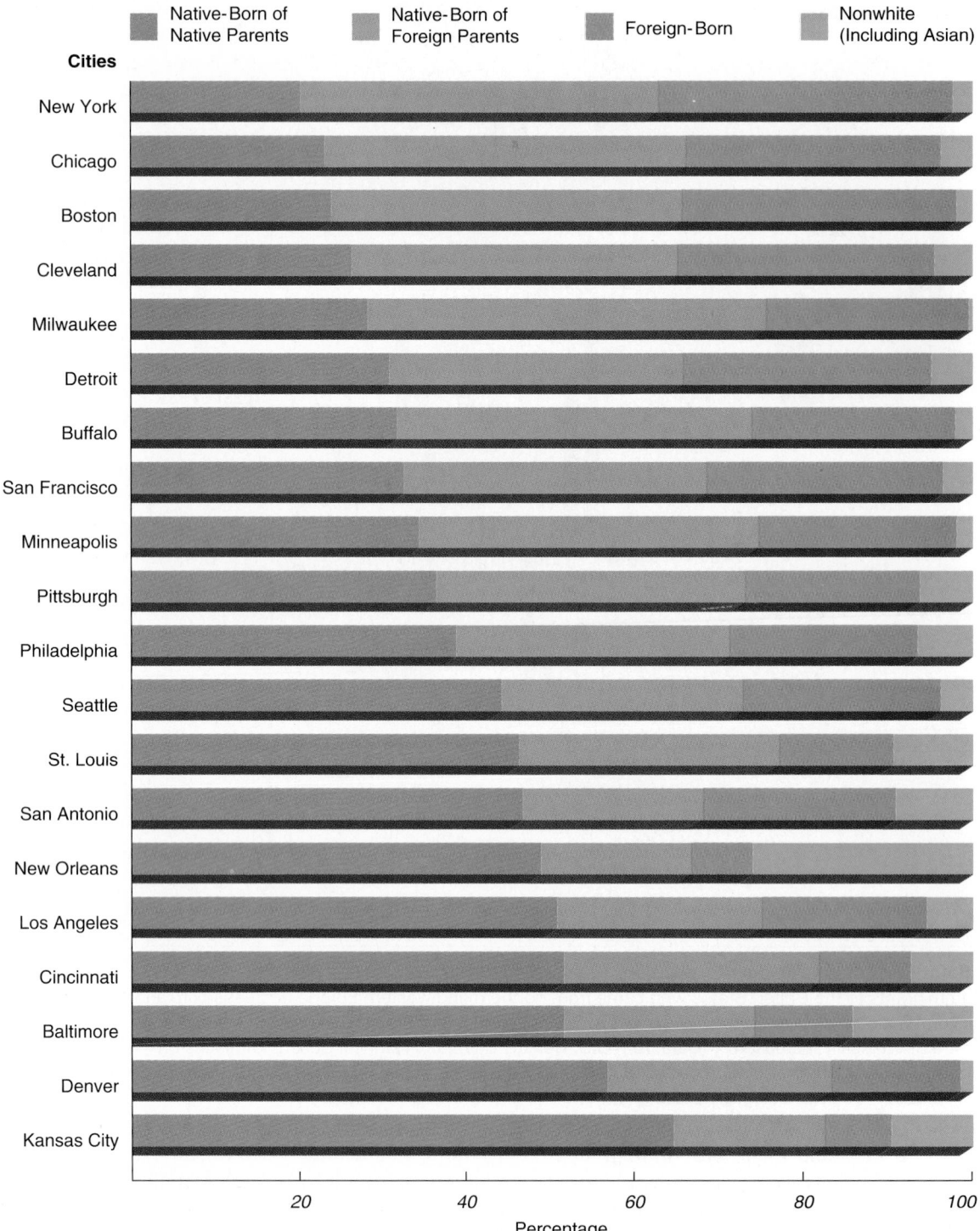

Figure 19.1 Composition of Population, Selected Cities, 1920 Immigration and migration made native-born whites of native-born parents minorities in almost every major city by the early twentieth century. Moreover, foreign-born residents and native-born whites of foreign parents (combining the green and purple segments of a line) constituted absolute majorities in numerous places.

The migration streams moving into American cities were only part of an extraordinary amount of movement because, once settled, in-migrants and immigrants rarely stayed put. Each year millions of families packed up and moved elsewhere. As early as 1847, a foreign visitor, amazed by American transiency, wrote, "If God were suddenly to call the world to judgment He would surprise two-thirds of the American population on the road like ants." The urge to move affected every region, every city. From Boston to San Francisco, from Minneapolis to San Antonio, no more than half of the families residing in a city at any one time were still there ten years later.

Residential Mobility

Many who migrated, particularly unskilled workers, did not improve their status; they simply floated from one low-paying job to another. Others did find greener pastures. Studies of Boston, Omaha, Atlanta, and other cities show that most men who rose occupationally or acquired property had migrated from somewhere else. Thus while cities frustrated the hopes of some, they offered opportunities to others.

In addition to movement between cities, countless numbers of people moved within the same city. In American communities today, one in every five families changes residence in a given year. A hundred years ago, the proportion was closer to one in four or one in three. It was not uncommon for a family to live at three or more different addresses over a ten- or fifteen-year period. Population turnover affected almost every neighborhood, every ethnic and occupational group.

Thus the peopling of American cities was a very dynamic process. Americans of all groups, native and foreign, were always seeking a better life, and hope for improved conditions elsewhere acted as a safety valve, relieving some of the tensions and frustrations that simmered inside the city. Sometimes families moved a short distance to another home or another neighborhood; sometimes they simply picked up and left town. A railroad ticket to another city cost only a few dollars; there was little to lose by moving.

Urban Neighborhoods

Looking back from the 1920s, literary critic Randolph Bourne dubbed the United States "a cosmopolitan federation of national colonies." Such an observation, based on an image of the social organization of the inner city of New York and other metropolises, implies that immigrants huddled together in their own neighborhood enclaves, where they steadily preserved national cultures and customs. But the reality was more complicated. With so many people moving about and interacting on city streets and in workplaces and shops, cultural change was hard to avoid.

It is true that in their new surroundings—where the language was a struggle, the workday followed the clock rather than the sun, and housing and employment often were uncertain—immigrants first anchored their lives to the rock they knew best: their cultures. Old World customs persisted in immigrant enclaves of Italians from the same province, Japanese from the same island district, or Russian Jews from the same *shtetl* (village). Fraternal societies were re-created along village and provincial lines. For example, Japanese transferred their *ken* societies, which organized social celebrations and relief services, and Chinese from Canton brought *hui* institutions, which raised money to help members acquire businesses. People practiced religion as they always had, held traditional feasts and pageants, married within their group, and pursued old feuds with people from rival villages. Among Orthodox Jews from eastern Europe, men grew sidelocks, women wore wigs, and children attended afternoon religious training.

Immigrant Cultures

Southern Italians transplanted the system whereby a *padrone* (boss) found jobs for unskilled workers by negotiating with—and receiving a payoff from—an employer. Italians also re-created mutual benefit associations to provide families emergency aid as well as sickness and death benefits. Pasquale Cruci, an immigrant from Salerno, explained that he helped to found such an association in Bridgeport, Connecticut, because "I felt that the Italian people of this city should have some security from death and accidents. The Italian people of this time didn't trust the big insurance companies because they thought they would get cheated. They felt that if some organization was Italian that it was all right."

Yet, as Rahel Gollop discovered, the diversity of American cities forced immigrants to modify their attitudes and habits. Few newcomers could avoid contact with people different from themselves, and few could prevent such contacts from altering their traditional ways of life. Although many foreigners identified themselves by their village or region of birth, native-born Americans categorized them by nationality. People from County Cork and County Limerick were lumped together as Irish; those from Schleswig and Württemberg were Germans; those from Calabria and Campobasso became Italians. Immigrant institutions, such as newspapers and churches, found they had to appeal to the entire nationality in order to survive.

In most large cities, immigrants inhabited multiethnic neighborhoods, places one historian has called "urban borderlands" where a diversity of people, identities, and lifestyles coexisted. Even within districts identified with a certain group, such as Little Italy, Jewtown, Polonia, or Greektown, rapid mobility constantly undermined residential stability as over a period as short as a few years former inhabitants dispersed to other neighborhoods and new inhabitants

Ethnic and Racial Borderlands

moved in. But seldom did a single ethnic group predominate. Rather, an area's businesses and institutions, such as its bakeries, butcher shops, churches, and club headquarters, gave the neighborhood its identity.

Nevertheless, though different groups jointly inhabited these urban borderlands, various ethnic and racial groups insulated themselves culturally, or were isolated by outside forces, from other immigrants and from the majority population. Some groups, such as Italians, Jews, and Poles, deliberately tried to maintain their separate religious, linguistic, and cultural lifestyles. For such European immigrants, their neighborhoods acted as havens until individuals were ready to cross from the borderland into the majority society. For people of color, however—African Americans, Asians, and Mexicans—the borderlands had a more persistent character that, because of discrimination, became less multiethnic over time.

Though Chinese immigrants struggled, like other immigrants, to succeed in American society, they often faced severe discrimination because of their different lifestyles. As this photo of a San Francisco grocery shows, Chinese looked, dressed, and ate differently than did white Americans. Occasionally, they suffered from racist violence that caused them to fear not only for their personal safety but also for the safety of establishments like this one that might suffer damage from resentful mobs.   (The Bancroft Library, University of California)

In industrial cities such as Chicago, Philadelphia, and Detroit, the availability of jobs and cheap housing prompted European immigrants initially to cluster together in inner-city neighborhoods. Though members of different ethnic groups lived nearby, members of the same group often tried to exclude outsiders from their neighborhoods and institutions. But these borderland experiences proved to be transitory. The expansion of mass transportation and outward movement of factories enabled many people to move to other neighborhoods, where they interspersed with families of their own socioeconomic class but not necessarily of their own ethnicity. European immigrants did encounter prejudice, such as the exclusion of Jews from certain professions and clubs or the inability of Italians to break into urban politics, but discrimination against them rarely was as systematic or complete as it was against blacks, Asians, and Mexicans.

Though African Americans originally may have lived in multiethnic, multiracial communities, by the early twentieth century institutional-

Ghettos

ized racial discrimination was forcing them into relatively permanent, highly segregated ghettos. By 1920 in Chicago, Detroit, Cleveland, and other cities outside the South, two-thirds or more of the total African American population lived in only 10 percent of the residential area. Circumscribed within color-line boundaries, blacks found it increasingly difficult to find jobs as well as housing outside the ghettos. The only way blacks could relieve the pressure resulting from increasing migration was to expand the ghetto borders into surrounding, previously white neighborhoods, a process often resulting in harassment and attacks on black families by white residents whose racist attitudes were intensified by fears that black neighbors would cause property values to decline.

Within the ghettos, African Americans, like other urban people, nurtured cultural institutions that helped them cope with urban life: shops, schools, clubs, theaters, dance halls, newspapers, and saloons. Churches, particularly those of the Baptist and African Methodist Episcopal (AME) branches of Protestantism, were especially influential. Pittsburgh blacks boasted twenty-eight such churches in the early 1900s. Membership in Cincinnati's black Baptist churches doubled between 1870 and 1900, from 1,027 to 2,011. In Louisville, blacks pooled their resources and built their own theological institute. In virtually all cities, black religious activity not only dominated ghetto life but also represented cooperation of blacks across class, cultural, and regional lines.

Asians encountered similar kinds of discrimination and ghetto experience. Although these immigrants often preferred to live in Chinatowns and Japanese sections, Anglos made every effort to keep them separated. In the 1880s, San Francisco's government, for example, prohibited Chinese laundries from locating in white neighborhoods, and its school board tried to isolate Japanese and Chinese children in Chinatown schools.

Mexicans in southwestern cities experienced somewhat more complex patterns. In some places, such as Los Angeles, Santa Barbara,

Barrios

and Tucson, Mexicans had been the original inhabitants and Anglos were migrants who overtook the city, pushing Mexicans into adjoining areas. Here, Mexicans became increasingly isolated in residential and commercial districts call *barrios*. Frequently, real-estate covenants, by which property owners pledge not to sell homes to Mexicans (or to African Americans, or to Jews), kept Mexican families confined in *barrios* of Los Angeles, Albuquerque, and San Antonio, though these areas tended to be located away from central city multiethnic borderlands housing European immigrants. To a considerable extent, then, race, more than any other factor, made the urban experiences of nonwhites unique compared to those of whites.

Everywhere, Old World culture mingled with New World realities. Immigrants struggled to maintain their native languages and to

Americanization

pass them down to younger generations. But English, taught in the schools and needed on the job, soon penetrated nearly every community. Foreigners fashioned homeland garments from American fabrics. Italians went to American doctors but still carried traditional amulets to ward off evil spirits. Chinese expanded their traditional gambling games to include poker. Music especially revealed adaptations. Polka bands entertained at Polish social gatherings, but their repertoires soon blended American and Polish folk music; once dominated by violins, the bands added accordions, clarinets, and trumpets so they could play louder. Mexican ballads acquired new themes that described the adventures of border crossing and the hardship of labor in the United States.

The influx of so many immigrants between 1870 and 1920 transformed the United States from a basically Protestant nation into one composed of Protestants, Catholics, Orthodox Christians, and Jews. Newcomers from Italy, Hungary, Polish lands, and Slovakia joined Irish and Germans to boost the proportion

Accommodation of Religion

of Catholics in many cities. In Buffalo, Cleveland, Chicago, and Milwaukee, Catholic immigrants and their offspring approached a majority of the population. Catholic Mexicans constituted over half of the population of El Paso. German and Russian immigrants gave New York one of the largest Jewish populations in the world.

Partly in response to Protestant charges that they could not retain Old World religious beliefs and still assimilate into American society, many Catholics and Jews tried to accommodate their faiths to the new environment. Catholic and Jewish leaders from more established immigrant groups supported liberalizing trends—the use of English in sermons, the phasing-out of Old World rituals such as saints' feasts, and a preference for public over religious schools. As long as new immigrants continued to arrive, however, these trends met stiff opposition.

Newcomers usually held on to familiar practices, whether the folk Catholicism of southern Italy or the Orthodox Judaism of eastern Europe. Because Catholic parishes served distinct geographical areas, immigrants who clustered in a particular area wanted clergy of their own kind in spite of church attempts to make American Catholicism more uniform. Bishops acceded to pressures from predominantly Polish congregations for Polish- rather than German-born priests. Eastern European Jews, convinced that Reform Judaism sacrificed too much to American ways, established the Conservative branch, which retained traditional ritual, though it abolished the segregation of women in synagogues and allowed English prayers.

Each of the three major migrant groups that peopled American cities—native-born whites, foreigners of various races, and native-born blacks—helped to mold modern American culture. The cities nurtured rich cultural variety: American folk music and literature, Italian and Mexican cuisine, Irish comedy, Yiddish theater, African American jazz and dance, and much more. Newcomers in the late nineteenth century changed their environment as much as they were changed by it.

Living Conditions in the Inner City

Urban population growth created intense pressures on the public and private sectors. The masses of people who jammed inner-city districts were recognized more for their problems than for their cultural contributions. American cities seemed to harbor all the afflictions that plague modern society: poverty, disease, crime, and other unpleasant conditions that occur when large numbers of people live close together. City dwellers coped as best they could. Although technology, private enterprise, and public authority could not solve every problem, city officials and engineers achieved some remarkable successes. In the late nineteenth and early twentieth centuries, construction of buildings, homes, streets, sewers, and schools proceeded at a furious pace. American cities set world standards for fire protection and water purification. But even a century later, many problems still await solution.

One of the most persistent shortcomings—the failure to provide adequate housing for all who need

Housing

it—has its origins in nineteenth-century urban development. In spite of massive construction in the 1880s and early 1900s, population growth outpaced housing supplies. Scarcity of inexpensive housing especially afflicted working-class families who, because of low wages, had to rent their living quarters. As cities grew, landlords took advantage of shortages in low-cost rental housing by splitting up existing buildings to house more people, constructing multiple-unit tenements, and hiking rents. Low-income families adapted to high costs and short supply by sharing space and expenses. Thus it became common in many big cities for a one-family apartment to be occupied by two or three families or by a single family plus several boarders.

The result was unprecedented crowding. In 1890 New York City's immigrant-packed Lower East Side averaged 702 people per acre, one of the highest population densities in the world. Low-rent districts had distinctive physical appearances in different cities: six- to eight-story barracks-like buildings in New York; dilapidated row houses in Baltimore and Philadelphia; converted slave quarters in Charleston and New Orleans; and crumbling two- and three-story frame houses in Seattle and San Francisco.

Inside these buildings, conditions were harsh. The largest rooms were barely ten feet wide, and interior rooms either lacked windows or opened onto narrow shafts that bred vermin and rotten odors. Describing such a shaft, one immigrant housekeeper said, "It's damp down there, and the families, they throw out garbage and dirty papers and the insides of chickens, and other unmentionable filth. . . . I just vomited when I first cleaned up the air shaft." Few buildings had indoor plumbing; the only source of heat was dangerous, polluting coal-burning stoves.

Housing problems aroused reform campaigns in several places. New York State took the lead by legislating light, ventilation, and safety codes for new tenement buildings in 1867, 1879, and 1901. These and similar laws in other states could not remedy the ills of existing buildings, but they did impose minimal obligations on landlords. A few reformers, such as journalist Jacob Riis and humanitarian Lawrence Veiller, advocated housing low-income families in "model tenements," with more spacious rooms and better facilities. Model tenements, however, required landlords to accept lower profits—a sacrifice few were willing to make. Both reformers and public officials opposed government financing of better hous-

Housing Reform

ing, fearing that such a step would undermine private enterprise. Still, the new housing codes and regulatory commissions strengthened the power of local government to oversee construction.

Eventually, new technology brought about unheralded but momentous changes in home life. As historian Thomas Schlereth has pointed out, new systems of central heating (furnaces), artificial lighting, and modern indoor plumbing created a new kind of consumption, first for middle-class households and later for most others. Whereas formerly families chopped wood for cooking and heating, made candles for light, and hauled water for bathing, they increasingly were connected to outside utilities for gas, electricity, and water. Moreover, these utilities helped foment new attitudes about privacy. Bedrooms and bathrooms enabled

Changes in Household Technology

Inner-city dwellers used not only indoor space as efficiently as possible but also what little outdoor space was available to them. Scores of families living in this cramped block of six-story tenements in New York strung clotheslines behind the buildings. Notice that there is virtually no space between buildings, so only rooms at the front and back received daylight and fresh air.   (Library of Congress)

How do historians know...

that urban reformers tried to manipulate public opinion? Journalist Jacob Riis wrote a landmark investigation of slum life in New York City, *How the Other Half Lives* (1890). Riis was one of the first to use the camera as a reform tool, supplementing his accounts of poverty and crowding with moving photographs of poor people (mostly immigrants) and their surroundings. For many readers, these photographs provided what one reformer called "added realism" and "an inherent attraction not found in other forms of illustration." But is a photograph always completely "real"? This Riis photo shows three "street arabs," homeless boys living and sleeping outdoors away from adult care. They are dressed in rags, and their look of innocence evokes the viewer's pathos. Because the shutter speed of his camera was slow (high-speed shutters of today did not exist in early

cameras) and because he wanted to maximize the emotional effect of his images, Riis staged his photographs. Here, he has carefully selected his subjects and focused on them in his own way to stir up sympathy and, he hoped, action. Though the picture contains a large portion of reality, it also serves notice that the historian must be aware that a photographer—any photographer—does more than record a scene. Even if not posed, every photograph in its selection of subjects, framing of the scene, and focus (long shot or close-up, for example) reveals as much about the photographer as it does about the subject. Thus, though photographs like this one may be valuable historical documents, historians must look beyond the image to consider what biases it might represent.   (Photo: Museum of the City of New York, the Jacob Riis Collection)

middle-class family members to withdraw into private spaces where they still could have the comfort of light, heat, and water. Instead of doubling or tripling up in one room or even one bed, children could have their own bedrooms, complete with individualized decoration. Finally, these utilities erased the inconveniences of nature. Though not affordable for the poor, central heat and artificial light made it possible for the middle class to enjoy a steady, comfortable temperature and turn night into day, while indoor plumbing removed the unpleasant experiences of the outhouse.

Housing reforms for the poor had only limited success, but scientific and technological advances eventually enabled city dwellers and the entire nation to live in greater comfort and safety. By the 1880s, some doctors had begun to accept the theory that microorganisms (germs) cause disease. In response, cities established more efficient systems of water purification and sewage disposal. Although disease and death rates remained higher in cities than in the countryside, and tuberculosis and other respiratory ills continued to plague inner-city districts, public health regulations as applied to water purity, sewage disposal, and food quality helped to control dread diseases such as cholera, typhoid fever, and diphtheria.

Sanitation and Construction Technology

Meanwhile, street paving, modernized firefighting equipment, and electric street lighting spread rapidly across urban America. Steel-frame construction, which supports a building with a metal skeleton rather than with masonry walls, made possible the erection of skyscrapers—and thus more efficient use of scarce and costly urban land. Electric elevators and steam-heating systems serviced these buildings. Steel-cable suspension bridges, developed by John A. Roebling and epitomized by his great Brooklyn Bridge (completed in 1883), linked metropolitan sections more closely.

None of these improvements, however, lightened the burden of poverty. The urban economy, though generally expanding, advanced erratically. Employment, especially for unskilled workers in manufacturing and construction, rose and fell with business cycles and changing seasons. An ever-increasing number of families lived on the margins of survival.

Urban Poverty

Since colonial days, Americans have disagreed about how much responsibility the public should assume for poor relief. According to traditional beliefs, still widespread at the turn of the century, anyone could escape poverty through hard work and clean living; indigence existed only because some people were morally weaker than others. Such reasoning bred fear that aid to poor people would encourage paupers to rely on public support rather than their own efforts. As the business cycle fluctuated and poverty increased, this attitude hardened, and city governments discontinued direct grants of food, fuel, and clothing to needy families. Instead, cities provided relief in return for work on public projects and sent special cases to state-run almshouses, orphanages, and homes for the blind, deaf, and mentally ill.

Efforts to rationalize relief fostered some change in attitude. Between 1877 and 1892, philanthropists in ninety-two cities formed Charity Organization Societies, an attempt to put social welfare on a systematic basis by merging disparate charity groups into coordinated units. Believing poverty to be caused by personal defects such as alcoholism and laziness, members of these organizations spent most of their time visiting poor families and encouraging them to be thriftier and more virtuous.

Close observation of the poor, however, prompted some humanitarians to conclude that people's environments, not their personal shortcomings, caused poverty. In turn, they had faith that poverty could be prevented and eliminated by improving housing, education, sanitation, and job opportunities rather than admonishing the poor to be more moral. This attitude, which had been gaining ground since the mid-nineteenth century, fueled drives for building codes, factory regulations, and public health measures in the Progressive era of the early twentieth century (see Chapter 20). Still, most middle- and upper-class Americans continued to endorse the creed that in a society of abundance only the unfit were poor and that poverty relief should be tolerated but never encouraged. As one charity worker put it, relief "should be surrounded by circumstances that shall . . . repel every one . . . from accepting it."

More than crowding and pauperism, crime and disorder nurtured fears that urban growth, especially the slums, threatened the nation. The more cities grew, it seemed, the more they shook with violence. While homicide rates declined in industrialized nations such as England and Germany, those in America rose alarmingly: 25 murders per million people in 1881; 107 per million in 1898. Pickpockets, swindlers, and burglars roamed

Crime and Violence

every city. Some acquired as much notoriety as western desperadoes. One infamous urban outlaw was Rufus Minor, alias Rufus Pine. Short, stocky, and bald, Minor resembled a shy clerk, but one police chief labeled him "one of the smartest bank sneaks in America." A sometime associate of Billy "The Kid" Burke, Minor often grew a heavy beard before holding up a bank, then shaved afterward to avoid identification by eyewitnesses. Minor was implicated in bank heists in New York City, Cleveland, Detroit, Providence, Philadelphia, Albany, Boston, and Baltimore—all between 1878 and 1882.

Despite fears of robberies and violence, urban crime may simply have become more conspicuous and sensational, rather than more prevalent. To be sure, concentrations of wealth and the mingling of different peoples provided opportunities for larceny, vice, and assault. But urban lawlessness and brutality probably did not exceed that of backwoods mining camps and southern plantations. Nativists were quick to blame immigrants for urban crime and disorder, but there is little evidence that more foreigners than native-born Americans populated the rogues' gallery. One investigation of jails in 1900 concluded that "we have ourselves evolved as cruel and cunning criminals as any that Europe may have foisted upon us."

The cityward movement of African Americans especially roused white fears, and as the twentieth century dawned, a series of race riots spread across the nation. In 1898 white citizens of Wilmington, North Carolina, resenting the success of African Americans in local politics, rioted and killed dozens of blacks. In the wake of the fury, whites expelled all black office-holders and instituted restrictions to prevent blacks from voting. In Atlanta in 1906, a series of newspaper accounts alleging attacks by black men on white women provoked a wave of shooting and killing that left twelve blacks dead and over seventy injured. An influx of African American unskilled laborers and strikebreakers into the industrial city of East St. Louis, Illinois, heightened racial tensions that erupted in 1917 when blacks fired back at a car whose occupants they believed had shot into their homes. When whites discovered that the black shooters had mistakenly killed two policemen riding in the car, a full-scale riot erupted that ended only after nine whites and thirty-nine blacks had been killed and over three hundred buildings had been destroyed. In addition to such mass violence, innumerable disruptions ranging from domestic violence to muggings to gang fights made cities scenes of constant turbulence.

Promises of Mobility

 The persistence of poverty, crime, and violence undercut the image of cities as places of opportunity, yet as locales of economic progress, cities could provide avenues by which people might achieve some modicum of success. The story of urban social mobility is not one of rags to riches but rather of countless small triumphs mixed with dashed hopes, discrimination, and failure. Basically, there were two ways a person could get ahead: occupational advancement (and the higher income that accompanied it) through experience, education, and the expansion of new occupations; and acquisition of property (and the wealth it represented). These options were open chiefly to white men.

Many women held paying jobs, owned property, and migrated, but their economic standing was usually defined by the men in their lives—usually their husbands or fathers. Women could improve their status by marrying men with wealth or potential, but other avenues were mostly closed. Laws limited what women could inherit; educational institutions blocked their training in professions such as medicine and law; and prevailing assumptions attributed higher aptitude for manual skills and business to men than to women. For African Americans, American Indians, Mexican Americans, or Asian Americans opportunities were even fewer. Assigned to the lowest-paying occupations by prejudice, they could make few gains.

For white men, however, occupational mobility was a reality, thanks to urban and industrial expansion. Thousands of businesses were needed to supply goods and services to burgeoning urban populations. As corporations grew and centralized their operations, they required new managerial personnel. Capital for a large business was hard to amass, but aspiring merchants could open a saloon or small shop for a few hundred dollars. Knowledge of accounting could qualify one for white-collar jobs that sometimes paid better than manual labor. Thus nonmanual work and the higher social status and income that tended to accompany it were attainable.

Occupational Mobility

Such advancement occurred often. To be sure, only a very few traveled the rags-to-riches path that Andrew Carnegie and Henry Ford discovered. The vast majority of the era's wealthiest businessmen began their careers with distinct advantages: American birth, Protestant religion, superior education, and relatively affluent parents. Yet considerable movement occurred along the road from poverty to moderate success, as men climbed from manual to nonmanual jobs. Personal successes like that of Meyer Grossman, a Russian immigrant to Omaha, Nebraska, who worked as a teamster before saving enough to open a successful furniture store, were common.

Rates of occupational mobility were slow but steady between 1870 and 1920. In fast-growing cities such as Atlanta, Los Angeles, and Omaha, approximately one in five white manual workers rose to white-collar or owner's positions within ten years—provided they stayed in the city that long. In older cities such as Boston and Philadelphia, upward mobility averaged closer to one in six workers in ten years. Some men slipped from a higher to a lower rung on the occupational ladder, but rates of upward movement usually doubled those of downward movement. Though patterns were not consistent, immigrants generally experienced less upward and more downward mobility than the native-born did. Still, regardless of birthplace, the chances for a white male to rise occupationally over the course of his career or to hold a higher-status job than his father had were relatively good.

What constitutes a better job, however, depends on one's definition of improvement. Many an immigrant artisan, such as a German carpenter or Italian shoemaker, would have considered an accountant's job demeaning. People with traditions of pride in manual skills neither desired nonmanual jobs nor encouraged their children to seek them. As one Italian tailor explained, "I learned the tailoring business in the old country. Over here, in America, I never have trouble finding a job because I know my business from the other side [Italy]. . . . I want that my oldest boy learn my trade because I tell him that you could always make at least enough for the family."

Business ownership, moreover, entailed risks. Failure rates were high among shopkeepers, saloon owners, and other small proprietors in working-class neighborhoods because the low incomes of their customers made business uncertain. Many manual workers sought security rather than mobility, preferring a steady wage to the risks of ownership. A Sicilian who lived in Bridgeport, Connecticut, observed that "the people that come here they afraid to get in business because they don't know how that business goes. In Italy these people don't know much about these things because most of them work on farms or in [their] trade."

In addition to advancing occupationally, a person might achieve social mobility by acquiring property

Acquisition of Property

such as a building or a house. But property was not easy to acquire. Banks and savings-and-loan institutions had far stricter lending practices than they did after the 1930s, when the federal government began to insure real-estate financing. Before then, mortgage loans carried high interest rates and short repayment periods. Thus renting, even of single-family houses, was common, especially in big cities. A general rise in wage rates nevertheless enabled many families to amass savings, which they could use as down payments on property. Ownership rates varied regionally—higher in western cities, lower in eastern cities—but 36 percent of all urban American families owned their homes in 1900, the highest homeownership rate of any Western nation except for Denmark, Norway, and Sweden.

The possibilities of upward mobility seemed to temper people's dissatisfaction. Although the gap between the very rich and the very poor widened, the expanding economies of American cities created room in the middle of the socioeconomic scale. Few could become another Rockefeller, but many did become respectable shopkeepers, foremen, clerks, and agents. Some also used politics and management of the city as routes to status and success.

Managing the City

 Those concerned with managing cities faced daunting challenges in the late nineteenth century. Burgeoning populations, business expansion, and technological change created urgent needs for sewers, police and fire protection, schools, parks, and other services. Such needs strained municipal resources beyond their capacities. Furthermore, city governments approached these needs in a disorganized fashion. Legislative and administrative functions were typically scattered among a mayor, city council, and independent boards that administered health regulations, public works, and poverty relief. Philadelphia at one time had thirty different boards, plus a mayor and council. Also, state governments often interfered in local matters, appointing board members and limiting cities' abilities to levy taxes and borrow money.

Since the mid-nineteenth century, city dwellers had gradually overcome their resistance to professional law enforcement and increasingly depended on the police to protect life and property. By the early 1900s, however, law enforcement had become compli-

Role of the Police

cated and controversial because various groups differed in their views of the law and how it should be enforced. Disadvantaged groups—notably ethnic and racial minorities—could not escape arrest as easily as those with economic or political influence. And police officers applied the law less harshly to members of their own ethnic groups and to people who bought exemptions with bribes.

As chief urban law enforcers, police forces, who often were poorly trained and prone to corruption, were caught between pressures for swift and severe action on one hand and leniency on the other. Some people clamored for crackdowns on drunkenness, gambling, and prostitution at the same time that others favored loose law enforcement so they could indulge in these customer-oriented crimes. As urban society diversified, different groups tried to protect their particular interests—such as keeping saloons open late at night, indulging in social gambling, or even applying their own notions of law and order. Achieving a balance between the idealistic intentions of criminal law and people's desire for individual freedom grew increasingly difficult, and it has remained so to this day.

Out of the apparent confusion surrounding urban management arose political machines, organizations whose main goals were the rewards—money, influence, and prestige—of getting and keeping political power. Machine politicians routinely used bribery and graft to further their ends. But machines needed popular support, and they could not have succeeded if they had not provided relief, security, and services to large numbers of people, especially to the hordes of newcomers who crowded into cities. By meeting those needs, machine politicians accomplished things that other agencies had been unable or unwilling to attempt.

The Machine

Machines bred leaders—bosses—who were adept at satisfying special-interest groups while simultaneously catering to the urban working classes. Bosses and machines established power bases among new immigrant voters and used politics to solve important urban problems. Most bosses had immigrant backgrounds and had grown up in the inner city, so they knew their constituents' needs firsthand. Machines made politics a full-time profession. According to George Washington Plunkitt, a small-time boss in New York City who published his memoirs in 1905, "As a rule [the boss] has no business or occupation other than politics. He plays politics every day and night in the year and his headquarters bears the inscription, 'Never closed.'"

Machines were rarely as dictatorial or corrupt as critics charged. To be sure, fraud, bribery, and thievery tainted the system. Bosses such as Philadelphia's "Duke" Vare, Kansas City's Tom Pendergast, and New York's Richard Croker lived like kings, though their official incomes were slim. A few bosses had no permanent organization; they were freelance opportunists who bargained for power, sometimes winning and sometimes losing. But from the 1880s onward, most machines evolved into highly organized political structures, such as New York's Tammany Hall, that wedded public accomplishments with personal gain.

The system rested on a popular base and was held together by loyalty and service. Machines usually were coalitions of smaller organizations that derived power directly from inner-city working-class neighborhoods. In return for votes, bosses provided jobs, built parks and bathhouses, distributed food and clothing to the needy, and helped when someone ran afoul of the law. Such personalized service cultivated mass attachment to the boss; never before had public leaders assumed such responsibility for people in need. Bosses, moreover, were genuinely public people. They attended weddings and wakes, joined clubs, and held open houses in saloons where neighborhood folk could talk to them personally.

The Boss

To finance their activities and campaigns, bosses exchanged favors for votes or money. Power over local government enabled machines to control the awarding of public contracts, the granting of utility or streetcar franchises, and the distribution of city jobs. Recipients of city business and jobs were expected to repay the machine with a portion of their profits or salaries and to cast supporting votes on election day. Critics called this process graft; bosses called it gratitude.

Machine-led city governments constructed public buildings, sewer systems, and mass-transit lines that otherwise might not have been built; but bribes and kickbacks made such projects costly to taxpayers. In the late nineteenth century, cities financed their expansion projects with loans from the public in the form of municipal bonds. Critics of bosses charged that these loans were inflated or unnecessary. Whether necessary or not, municipal bonds caused public debts to soar, and taxes had to be raised to repay their interest and principal. In addition, machines dispensed favors to legal and illegal businesses. Payoffs from

"Big Tim" Sullivan, a New York City ward boss, rewarded "repeat voters" with a new pair of shoes. Sullivan once explained, "When you've voted 'em with their whiskers on, you take 'em to a barber and scrape off the chin fringe. Then you vote 'em again. . . . Then to a barber again, off comes the sides and you vote 'em a third time with the mustache. . . . [Then] clean off the mustache and vote 'em plain face. That makes every one of 'em for four votes."   (Library of Congress)

gambling, prostitution, and illicit liquor traffic became important sources of machine revenue.

Bosses held power because they tended to problems of everyday life. Martin Lomasney, boss of Boston's South End, explained, "There's got to be in every ward somebody that any bloke can come to—no matter what he's done—and get help. Help, you understand, none of your law and justice, but help." The boss system, however, was neither neutral nor fair. Racial minorities and new immigrant groups such as Italians and Poles received only token jobs and nominal favors, if any. But in an age of economic individualism, bosses were no more guilty of self-interest and discrimination than were business leaders who exploited workers, spoiled the landscape, and manipulated government in pursuit of profits. Sometimes humane and sometimes criminal, bosses acted as brokers between various sectors of urban society and an uncertain world.

While bosses were consolidating their power, others were attempting to destroy them. Many middle- and upper-class Americans feared that immigrant-

Urban Reform

based political machines menaced the republic and that unsavory alliances between bosses and businesses wastefully depleted municipal finances. Anxious over the poverty, crowding, and disorder that accompanied population expansion, and convinced that urban services were making taxes too high, civic reformers organized to install more responsible leaders at the helm of urban administrations.

Urban reform arose in part from the industrial system's emphasis on eliminating inefficiency. Business-minded reformers believed government should be run like a company. The way to achieve this goal, they believed, was to elect officials who would hold down expenses and prevent corruption. Thus they advocated reducing city budgets, making public employees work more efficiently, and cutting taxes.

To implement business principles in government, civic reformers supported structural changes such as the city-manager and commission forms of government, which would place administration in the hands

Structural Reform in Government

of experts rather than politicians, and nonpartisan, citywide election of officials. Armed with such strategies, reformers believed they could cleanse party politics and weaken bosses' power bases in the neighborhoods. They rarely realized, however, that bosses succeeded because they used government to meet people's needs. Reformers noticed only the waste and corruption that machines bred.

A few reform mayors moved beyond structural changes to address social problems. Hazen S. Pingree of Detroit, Samuel "Golden Rule" Jones of Toledo, and Tom Johnson of Cleveland worked to provide jobs for poor people, reduce charges by transit and utility companies, and promote governmental responsibility for the welfare of all citizens. They also supported public ownership of gas, electric, and telephone companies, a quasi-socialist reform that alienated their business allies. But Pingree, Jones, and Johnson were exceptions. Civic reformers achieved temporary successes but could not match the bosses' political savvy; they soon found themselves out of power.

A different type of reform arose outside politics. Driven by an urge to improve as well as manage society, social reformers—mostly young and middle class—embarked on campaigns to identify and solve urban problems. Housing reformers pressed local governments for building codes to ensure safety in tenements. Educational reformers sought to use public schools as a means of preparing immigrant children for citizenship by teaching them American values.

Social Reform

Perhaps the most ambitious and inspiring feature of urban reform movements was the settlement house. Located in slum neighborhoods and run mostly by women, settlements were buildings where middle-class young people went to live and work in order to bridge the gulf between social classes. The first American settlement, patterned after London's Toynbee Hall, opened in New York City in 1886, and others quickly appeared in cities across the country. Early settlement leaders such as Jane Addams, founder of Hull House in Chicago and one of the country's most influential women, and Florence Kelley, a brilliant political strategist who pioneered laws to protect consumers and working women, wanted to improve the lives of slum dwellers by helping them obtain education, appreciation of the arts, better jobs, and decent housing. Although working-class and immigrant neighborhood residents sometimes mistrusted them as outsiders, settlement workers achieved important successes with activities such as vocational classes, childcare, and ethnic pageants.

As they broadened their scope to fight for school nurses, building and factory safety codes, and public playgrounds, settlement workers became reform leaders in cities and in the nation. Their efforts to involve national and local governments in the solution of social problems later made them the vanguard of the Progressive era, when a reform spirit swept the nation (see Chapter 21). Moreover, activities of settlement houses created new professional opportunities for women in social work, public health, and child welfare. These professions enabled female reformers to build a dominion of influence over social policy independent of male-dominated professions and to make valuable contributions to national as well as inner-city life.

A contrast developed, however, between white female reformers and black female reformers. Middle-class white women lobbied for government programs to aid needy people, mostly white immigrant and native-born working classes. Black women, barred by their race from political institutions, raised funds from private donors and focused on helping members of their own race. African American women were especially active in founding schools, old-age homes, and hospitals, but they also worked for advancement of the race and protection of black women from sexual exploitation. Their ranks included women such as Jane Hunter, who founded a home for unmarried black working women in Cleveland in 1911 and influenced the establishment of similar homes in other cities, and Modjeska Simkins, who organized a program to address health problems among blacks in South Carolina.

While female reformers tried to revive neighborhoods, a group of male reformers organized the City Beautiful movement to improve cities' attractiveness. Inspired by the Columbian Exposition of 1893, a dazzling world's fair held in a "White City" built on Chicago's South Side, architects and planners worked to redesign the urban landscape. Led by architect Daniel Burnham, City Beautiful advocates built civic centers, parks, and boulevards that would make cities more economically efficient as well as beautiful. "Make no little plans," Burnham urged. "Make big plans; aim high in hope and work." This attitude spawned beautifying projects in Chicago, San Francisco, and Washington, D.C., in the early 1900s.

Architects

Yet most big plans turned out to be only big dreams. Neither government nor private businesses could finance large-scale projects, and planners disagreed among themselves and with social reformers over whether beautification would do anything to solve urban problems.

Regardless of their focus, urban reformers wanted to save cities, not abandon them. They believed they could improve urban life by restoring cooperation among all citizens. They often failed to realize, however, that cities were places of great diversity and that different people held very different views about what reform actually meant. To civic reformers, distributing city jobs on the basis of civil service exams rather than party loyalty meant progress, but to working-class men civil service signified reduced employment opportunities. Moral reformers believed that prohibiting the sale of alcoholic beverages would prevent working-class breadwinners from squandering their wages and ruining their health, but immigrants saw such crusades as interference in their private lives. Planners saw new streets and civic buildings as modern necessities, but such structures often displaced the poor. Well-meaning humanitarians criticized immigrant mothers for the way they shopped, dressed, did housework, and raised children, without regard for the inability of these mothers to afford the products that the consumer economy created. Thus urban reform merged idealism with naiveté and insensitivity.

At the same time, efforts of still a different sort were making cities more livable. Providing sanitation, street lighting, bridge and street

Engineers

construction, and other such needs required technological creativity, not political or humanitarian action. In addressing these critical urban issues, the American engineering profession developed new systems and standards of worldwide significance.

Take, for example, the problem of refuse. Experts in 1900 estimated that every New Yorker generated annually some 160 pounds of garbage (food and bones), 1,200 pounds of ashes (from stoves and furnaces), and 100 pounds of rubbish (shoes, furniture, and other discarded items). Europeans of that era produced only about half as much trash. At the same time, there were as many as 3.5 million horses in American cities, each of which left behind about 20 pounds of manure and a gallon of urine daily. Overworked city horses died after only a few years, and each city had to dispose of thousands of carcasses every year. In past eras, trash, excrement, and dead animals could be dis-

missed as nuisances; by the twentieth century they became health and safety hazards, and citizens' groups protested against inadequate refuse collection and disposal.

The problem raised difficult questions. Who should be responsible for waste removal, city workers or a private contractor hired by the city? Previously, cities had dumped refuse on vacant land and in nearby rivers and lakes. What alternatives were there to these unsafe practices? How frequently should streets be cleaned, and by whom?

To solve such problems, cities increasingly depended on the technical expertise of engineers. By 1900 engineers were devising systems for incinerating refuse, dumping trash while safeguarding water supplies, constructing efficient sewers, and providing for regular street cleaning and snow removal. Engineers had similar influence in matters of street lighting, parks, and fire protection, and they also advised officials on budget and contracts. City officials, whether bosses or reformers, came to depend on the expertise of engineers, who seemed best qualified to supervise a city's expansion. Insulated within bureaucratic agencies from tumultuous party strife, engineers generally carried out their responsibilities efficiently and with little fanfare and made some of the most lasting contributions to urban management.

Family Life

Although the overwhelming majority of Americans continued to live within families, this basic social institution suffered strain during the era of urbanization and industrialization. New institutions—schools, social clubs, political organizations, and others—increasingly competed with the family to provide nurture, education, and security. Clergy and journalists warned that rising divorce rates, the growing separation between home and work, the entrance of numerous women into the work force, and loss of parental control over children spelled peril for home and family. Yet the family retained its fundamental role as a cushion in a hard, uncertain world.

Throughout modern Western history, most people have lived in two overlapping social units: household and family. A household is a

Family and Household Structures

group of people, related or unrelated, who share the same residence. A family is a group related by kinship, some members of which typically live

The Hedlund family of St. Paul, Minnesota, celebrates the Fourth of July together in 1911 with flags and fireworks. Consisting of two parents and three children, the family represents the modern household of two generations and limited family size.   (Minnesota Historical Society)

together. In the late nineteenth and early twentieth centuries, different patterns characterized the two institutions.

Since colonial times, the vast majority of American households (75 to 80 percent) have consisted of nuclear families—usually a married couple, with or without children. About 15 to 20 percent of households consisted of extended families—usually a married couple, with or without children, plus one or more relatives such as parents, adult siblings, grandchildren, aunts, and uncles. About 5 percent of households consisted of people living alone or in boarding houses and hotels. Despite slight variations, this pattern held relatively constant among ethnic, racial, and socioeconomic groups.

Several factors explain this pattern. Because immigrants tended to be young, the U.S. population as a whole was young. In 1880 the median age was under twenty-one, and by 1920 it was still only twenty-five. (Median age at present is about thirty-six.) Moreover, in 1900 the death rate among people aged forty-five to

sixty-four was double what it is today. As a result, there were relatively few older people: only 4 percent of the population was sixty-five or older, compared with about 15 percent today. Thus few families could form extended three-generation households, and fewer children than today had living grandparents. Migration separated many families, and the ideal of a home of one's own encouraged nuclear household organization.

The average size of nuclear families did change over time, though. Most of Europe and North America experienced falling birth rates in the nineteenth century. The decline in the United States began early in the 1800s and accelerated toward the end of the century. In 1880 the birth rate was 40 live births per 1,000 people; by 1900 it had dropped to 32; by 1920 to 28. Several factors explain this decline.

Declining Birth Rates

First, the United States was becoming an urban nation, and birth rates are historically lower in cities than in rural areas. On farms, where young children worked at home or in the fields, each child born represented a new set of hands for the family work force. In the wage-based urban economy, children could not contribute significantly to the family income for many years, and a new child represented another mouth to feed. Second, infant mortality fell as diet and medical care improved, and families did not have to bear many children just to ensure that some would survive. Third, awareness that smaller families meant improved quality of life seems to have stimulated decisions to limit family size—either by abstaining from sex during the wife's fertile period or by using contraception and abortion. Although fertility was higher among blacks, immigrants, and rural people than among white native-born city dwellers, birth rates of all groups fell. Families with six or eight children became rare; three or four became more usual. As a result, the nuclear family tended to reach its maximum size and then shrink faster than in earlier eras.

The household tended to expand and contract over the lifetime of a given family. Its size increased as children were born. Later, especially

Boarding

in working-class families, it shrank as children left home before they were twenty years old, usually to work. The process of leaving home altered household composition; huge numbers of young people—and some older people—lived as boarders and lodgers, especially in cities. Middle- and working-class families commonly took in boarders to occupy rooms vacated by grown children and to get additional income. Immigrants such as Rahel Gollop often lodged with relatives and fellow villagers until they could establish themselves. By the end of the nineteenth century, as many as 50 percent of city residents had lived either as, or with, boarders at some point during their lifetime. Housing reformers charged that boarding caused overcrowding and loss of privacy. Yet for those who boarded or took in boarders, the practice was highly useful. One immigrant woman recalled:

> We had four boarders and I had to cook for them. When I first came here I didn't want to do this because everybody want to have their own house. Well, I change my mind because everybody was doing this thing. That time some of the people that came from the other side didn't have no place to stay and we took some of the people in the house that we knew. . . .
> This is the way that everybody used to do it that time.

For people on the move, boarding was a transitional stage, providing them with a quasi-family environment until they set up their own households.

Some households took in extended-family members who lived as quasi-boarders. Especially in communities where economic hardship

Importance of Kinship

or rapid growth made housing expensive or scarce, newlyweds sometimes lived temporarily with one spouse's parents. Families also took in widowed parents or unmarried siblings who otherwise would have lived alone, and many young unmarried men and women continued to live at home although they had jobs and independent social lives.

At a time when welfare agencies were rare, the family was the institution to which people could turn in times of need. Even when relatives did not live together, they often lived nearby and aided one another with childcare, meals, shopping, advice, and consolation. They also obtained jobs for each other. Factory foremen who had responsibility for hiring often recruited new workers recommended by their employees. According to one new arrival, "After two days my brother took me to the shop he was working in and his boss saw me and he gave me the job."

But obligations of kinship were not always welcome. Immigrant families often pressured last-born children to stay at home to care for aging parents, a practice that stifled opportunities for education, marriage, and economic independence. As an aging Italian-American father confessed, "One of our daughters is an old maid [and] causes plenty of troubles. . . . It may be my fault because I always wished her to remain at home and not to marry for she was of great financial help." Tensions also developed between generations, such as when immigrant parents and American-born children clashed over the abandonment of Old World ways or the amount of money employed children should contribute to the household. Nevertheless, for better or worse, kinship provided people a means of coping with the stresses caused by an urban-industrial society. Social and economic change did not sever family ties.

Large numbers of city dwellers lived beyond the haven of traditional family relationships, however. In 1890 almost 42 percent of adult

Unmarried People

American men and 37 percent of women were single, almost twice as high as the figures for 1960. (The proportions today have risen back to beyond the 1890 levels.) About half of them still lived in their parents' household, but many others inhabited boarding houses or rooms in the homes of strangers. Mostly young, these men and women constituted a separate subculture that helped support institutions like dance halls, saloons, cafés, and the YMCA and YWCA.

Some of these unmarried people numbered among the homosexual population that thrived especially in large cities like New York and Boston. Though their numbers are difficult to estimate, gay men had their own subculture complete with clubs, restaurants, coffeehouses, theaters, and support networks. A number of gay couples, especially women, formed lasting marriage-type relationships, sometimes called "Boston marriages." Some men cruised in the sexual underground of the streets and bars. People in the gay subculture were categorized more by how they acted—men acting like women, women acting like men—than by who their sexual partners were. Thus the term *homosexual* was not used. For example, men who dressed and acted like women were called "fairies," and men who displayed masculine traits could be termed "normal" even though they might have sexual relations with fairies. Gay women remained even more hidden, and a lesbian subculture of clubs and commercial establishments seldom existed until the 1920s. The gay world, then, was a complex one that included a variety of relationships and institutions.

Although the family remained resilient and adaptable, subtle but momentous changes began to occur in individual life patterns. Before the twentieth century, stages of life were less distinct than they are today, and generations blended together with relatively little differentiation. Childhood, for instance, had been regarded as a period during which young people prepared for adulthood by gradually assuming more adult roles and responsibilities. The subdivisions of youth—toddlers, schoolchildren, adolescents, and the like—were not recognized or defined. Because married couples had more children over a longer time span than is common today, active parenthood occupied most of their adult lives. Older children, who cared for younger sisters and brothers, might begin parenting even before reaching adulthood. And because relatively few people lived to advanced ages or left work voluntarily, and because old-age homes were rare, older people were not isolated from other age groups.

By the late nineteenth century, demographic and social changes had altered these patterns. Decreasing birth rates shortened the period of parental responsibility, so more middle-aged couples experienced an empty nest when all their children grew up and left

Stages of Life

home. Longer life expectancy and a tendency by employers to force aged workers to retire separated the old from the young. At the same time, work became more specialized and education in grade schools more formalized, especially after states passed compulsory school-attendance laws in the 1870s and 1880s. Childhood and adolescence became more distinct from adulthood. As a result of these and other trends (including the lower birth rate, which gave people fewer sisters and brothers to relate to), Americans became more conscious of age and peer influence. People's roles in school, in the family, on the job, and in the community came to be determined by age more than by any other characteristic.

Thus by the early 1900s, family life and functions were both changing and holding firm. New institutions were assuming tasks formerly performed by the family. Schools were making education a community responsibility. Employment agencies, personnel offices, and labor unions were taking responsibility for employee recruitment and job security. Age-based peer groups were exerting greater influence over people's values and activities. In addition, migration and a soaring divorce rate seemed to be splitting families apart. Yet in the face of these pressures, the family adjusted by expanding and contracting to meet temporary needs, and kinship remained a dependable though not always appreciated institution. For the majority of people, family life was vital. "As I grew up, living conditions were a bit crowded," one woman reminisced, "but no one minded because we were a family . . . thankful we all lived together."

The New Leisure and Mass Culture

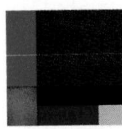

On December 2, 1889, as hundreds of workers paraded through Worcester, Massachusetts, in support of shorter working hours, a group of carpenters hoisted a banner proclaiming "Eight Hours for Work, Eight Hours for Rest, Eight Hours for What We Will." That last phrase was significant, for it laid claim to a special segment of daily life that belonged to the individual. Increasingly, among all urban social classes, leisure activities filled this time segment.

American inventors had long tried to create labor-saving devices, but not until the late 1800s did technology become truly time-saving. Mechanization and assembly-line production helped to cut the average

Increase in Leisure Time

workweek in manufacturing from sixty-six hours in 1860 to sixty in 1890 and forty-seven in 1920. These reductions meant shorter workdays and freer weekends. White-collar workers spent from eight to ten hours a day on the job and often worked only half a day or not at all on weekends. To be sure, thousands of laborers still endured twelve- or fourteen-hour shifts in steel mills and sweatshops and had no time or energy for leisure. But as the nation's economy shifted from one of scarcity and production to one of surplus and consumption, more Americans began to engage in a variety of diversions, and a substantial segment of the economy began providing for—and profiting from—leisure. By the early 1900s, many Americans were enmeshed in the business of play.

After the Civil War, amusement became an organized, commercial activity. The production of games, toys, and musical instruments for indoor family entertainment expanded. Games such as checkers and backgammon had existed for decades, but improvements in printing and paper production and the rise of new manufacturers such as Milton Bradley and Parker Brothers increased the popularity of board games markedly. Significantly, the content of board games shifted from moral lessons to topics involving transportation, finance, and sports. Also, by the 1890s, middle-class families were buying mass-produced pianos and sheet music that made the singing of popular songs a favored form of home entertainment.

The vanguard of new leisure pursuits, however, was sports. Formerly a fashionable indulgence of elites, organized sports quickly became the most popular pastime of all classes, attracting huge numbers of participants and spectators. Even those who could not play or watch became involved by reading about sports in the newspapers.

The most popular organized sport was baseball. An outgrowth of older bat, ball, and base-circling games, baseball was formalized in 1845 by a group of wealthy New Yorkers—the Knickerbocker Club—who codified the rules of play. By 1860 at least fifty baseball clubs existed, and informal games were being played on city lots and rural fields across the nation. In 1869 a professional club, the Cincinnati Red Stockings, went on a national tour, and other clubs quickly followed suit. The National League of Professional Baseball Clubs, founded in 1876, gave the sport a stable, businesslike structure. Not all athletes could benefit; as

Baseball

While baseball, football, boxing, and racing became popular sports for men, basketball became the most appealing sport for women, especially those in college. Special rules established in 1897 lessened the supposed dangers of rough, vigorous play by limiting the number of dribbles, confining players to particular zones on the court, and encouraging passing.   (Collection of Sally Fox)

early as 1867, a "color line" excluded black players from professional teams. Nevertheless, by the 1880s, professional baseball was a big business. In 1903 the National League and competing American League (formed in 1901) began a World Series between their championship teams, entrenching baseball as the national pastime. The Boston Red Socks beat the Pittsburgh Pirates in that first series.

Baseball appealed mostly to men. But croquet, which also swept the nation, attracted both sexes. Middle- and upper-class people held croquet parties and outfitted wickets with candles for night contests. In an era when the departure of paid work

Croquet and Cycling

from the home had separated men's from women's spheres, croquet increased opportunities for social contact between the sexes.

Meanwhile, cycling achieved a popularity rivaling that of baseball, especially after 1885, when the cumbersome velocipede, with huge front wheel and tall seat, gave way to the safety bicycle with pneumatic tires and wheels of identical size. By 1900 Americans owned over 10 million bicycles, and clubs like the League of American Wheelmen were pressing state governments to build more paved roads. One journal boasted that cycling cured dyspepsia, headaches, insomnia, and sciatica and gave "a vigorous tone to the whole system." Professional bicycle races brought success to riders such as Major Taylor, an African American who won fame in Europe and the United States. Like croquet, cycling brought men and women together, combining opportunities for courtship and exercise. Moreover, the bicycle played an influential role in freeing women from the constraints of Victorian fashions. In order to ride the dropped-frame female models, women had to wear divided skirts and simple undergarments. Gradually, cycling costumes influenced everyday fashions. As the 1900 census declared, "Few articles . . . have created so great a revolution in social conditions as the bicycle."

Other sports had their own patrons. Tennis and golf attracted both sexes but remained pastimes of the wealthy. Played mostly at private clubs, these sports lacked baseball's team competition and cycling's informality. American football also began as a sport for people of high social rank. As an intercollegiate competition, football attracted players and spectators wealthy enough to have access to higher education. By the end of the century, however, the game was appealing to a broader audience. The 1893 Princeton-Yale game drew fifty thousand spectators, and informal games were being played in yards and playgrounds throughout the country.

Football

At the same time, college football became a national scandal because of its violence and use of "tramp athletes," nonstudents whom colleges hired to help their teams win. Critics charged that football mirrored the worst features of American society. An editor of *The Nation* charged in 1890 that "the spirit of the American Youth, as of the American man, is to win, to 'get there,' by fair means or foul; and the lack of moral scruple which pervades the struggles of the business world meets with temptations equally irresistible in the miniature contests of the football field."

The scandals climaxed in 1905, when 18 players died from game-related injuries and over 150 were seriously injured. President Theodore Roosevelt, a strong advocate of athletics, convened a White House conference to discuss ways to eliminate brutality and foul play. The conference founded the Intercollegiate Athletic Association (renamed the National College Athletic Association in 1910) to police college sports. In 1906 the association altered the games to make football less violent and more open. New rules outlawed "flying wedge" rushes, extended from five to ten yards the distance needed to earn a first down, legalized the forward pass, and tightened player eligibility requirements.

As more women enrolled in college, they began to pursue physical activities besides croquet and cycling. Believing that intellectual success required active and healthy bodies, college women participated in sports such as rowing, track, and swimming. Eventually women made basketball their most popular intercollegiate sport. Invented in 1891 as a winter sport for men, basketball was given women's rules (which limited dribbling and running and encouraged passing) by Senda Berenson of Smith College in the 1890s.

Paralleling the rise of sports, American show business also became a mode of leisure created by and for common people. Circuses—traveling shows of acrobats and animals—had existed since the 1820s. But after the Civil War, railroads enabled them to reach cities and towns across the country. Circuses offered two main attractions: so-called freaks of nature, both human and animal, and the temptation and conquest of death. At the heart of their appeal was the astonishment that trapeze artists, lion tamers, acrobats, and clowns aroused. Writer Hamlin Garland captured the circus's effect on a community:

Circuses

> From the time the "advance man" flung his highly colored posters over the fence till the coming of the glorious day, we thought of little else. . . . It was our brief season of imaginative life. In one day—in a part of one day—we gained a thousand new conceptions of the world and of human nature. It was the embodiment of all that was skillful and beautiful in human action. . . . It gave us something to talk about.

Three branches of American show business— popular drama, musical comedy, and vaudeville—matured with the growth of cities. Theatrical performances offered audiences an escape from the harshness of urban-industrial life into melodrama, ad-

Popular Drama and Musical Comedy

venture, and comedy. Plots were simple, the heroes and villains recognizable. For urbanized people unfamiliar with the frontier, popular plays brought to life the mythical Wild West and Old South through stories of Davy Crockett, Buffalo Bill, and Civil War romances. Virtue, honor, and justice always triumphed in melodramas such as "Uncle Tom's Cabin" and "The Old Homestead," reinforcing faith that in an uncertain and disillusioning world, goodness would prevail.

Musical comedies entertained audiences with song, humor, and dance. American musical comedy grew out of lavishly costumed operettas common in Europe. By introducing American themes (often involving ethnic groups), folksy humor, and catchy tunes, these shows featured the nation's most popular songs and entertainers. George M. Cohan, a spirited singer, dancer, and songwriter born into an Irish family of entertainers, became the master of American musical comedy after the turn of the century. Drawing on urbanism, patriotism, and traditional values in songs like "Yankee Doodle Boy" and "You're a Grand Old Flag," Cohan helped bolster morale during the First World War. Comic opera, too, became popular. The first American comic operas imitated European musicals, but by the early 1900s composers like Victor Herbert were writing for American audiences. Shortly thereafter Jerome Kern began to compose more sophisticated musicals, and American musical comedy came into its own.

Because of its variety, vaudeville was probably the most popular entertainment in early-twentieth-century America. Shows included, in rapid succession, acts of jugglers, dancing bears, pantomimists, storytellers, magicians, puppeteers, acrobats, comedians, singers, and dancers. Around 1900, the number of vaudeville theaters and troupes skyrocketed. Sharp entrepreneurs, who did for entertain-

Vaudeville

Joe Weber and Lew Fields were one of the most popular comic teams in vaudeville. They and similar comedians used fast-paced dialogue to entertain audiences with routines such as this one: Doctor: Do you have insurance? Patient: I ain't got one nickel insurance. Doctor: If you die, what will your wife bury you with? Patient: With pleasure. (Corbis-Bettmann)

ment what Edison and Ford did for technology, made vaudeville big business. The famous promoter Florenz Ziegfeld brilliantly packaged shows in a stylish format—the Ziegfeld Follies—and gave the nation a new model of femininity, the Ziegfeld Girl, whose graceful dancing and alluring costumes suggested a haunting sensuality.

Show business provided new opportunities for female, African American, and immigrant performers, but it also encouraged stereotyping and exploitation. Comic opera diva Lillian Russell, vaudeville singer-comedienne Fanny Brice, and burlesque queen Eva Tanguay attracted intensely loyal fans, commanded handsome fees, and won respect for their talents. In contrast to the demure Victorian female, they conveyed pluck and creativity. There was something both shocking and refreshingly confident about Eva Tanguay when she sang earthy songs like "I Want Someone to Go Wild with Me," "It's All Been Done Before but Not the Way I Do It," and her theme song, "I Don't Care." But lesser female performers were often exploited by male promoters and theater owners, many of whom wanted only to titillate the public, for a price, with the sight of scantily clad women.

Before the 1890s, the chief form of commercial entertainment open to African American performers was the minstrel show, but vaudeville opened new opportunities to them. As stage settings shifted from the plantation to the city, music shifted from folk tunes to ragtime. Pandering to the prejudices of white audiences, composers and performers of both races ridiculed blacks. As songs like "He's Just a Little Nigger, but He's Mine All Mine" and "You May Be a Hawaiian on Old Broadway, but You're Just Another Nigger to Me" confirm, blacks on the stage suffered much as they did in society at large. Even Burt Williams, a talented and highly paid black comedian and dancer who achieved success by playing stereotypical roles of darky and dandy, was tormented by the humiliation he had to suffer.

An ethnic flavor gave much of American mass entertainment its uniqueness. Indeed, immigrants occupied the core of American show business. Vaudeville in particular utilized ethnic humor, exaggerating dialects and other national traits. Skits and songs reinforced ethnic stereotypes and made fun of ethnic groups, but such distortions were more self-conscious and sympathetic than those directed at blacks. Ethnic humor often focused on everyday difficulties that immigrants faced. A typical scene involving Italians, for example, revolved around a character's uncertain grasp of En-

glish, which caused him to confuse *mayor* with *mare*, *diploma* with the *plumber*, and *pallbearer* with *polar bear*. Such scenes allowed audiences to laugh with rather than at the foibles of the human condition. The conditions of African Americans, however, were subject to more vicious humor.

Shortly after 1900, live entertainment began to yield to a more accessible form of amusement: moving pictures. Perfected by Thomas Edison in the 1880s, movies began as slot-machine peepshows in penny arcades and billiard parlors. Eventually images were projected onto a screen so that large audiences could view them, and a new medium was born. At first, the subjects of films hardly mattered; scenes of speeding trains, acrobats, and writhing belly dancers were thrilling enough.

Movies

Producers soon discovered that a film could tell a story in exciting ways. Thanks to creative directors like D. W. Griffith, motion pictures became a distinct art form. Griffith's *Birth of a Nation* (1915), an epic film about the Civil War and Reconstruction, fanned racial prejudice by depicting African Americans as threats to white moral values. The National Association for the Advancement of Colored People (NAACP), formed in 1909, led an organized protest against it. But the film's innovative techniques—close-ups, fade-outs, and battle scenes—heightened the drama. By 1920, movies were popular among all classes (admission usually cost a nickel), and audiences idolized film stars such as Mary Pickford, Lillian Gish, and Charlie Chaplin.

The still camera, modernized by inventor George Eastman, enabled ordinary people to record their own visual images, especially useful for preserving family memories. The phonograph, another Edison invention, brought musical performances into the home. The spread of movies, photography, and phonograph records meant that access to live performances no longer limited people's exposure to art and entertainment. By making it possible to mass-produce sound and images, technology made entertainment a highly desirable consumer good.

News also became a consumer product. Using high-speed printing presses, cheap paper, and profits from growing advertisement revenues, a group of canny publishers created a medium that made people crave news just as they craved amusements. City life and increased leisure time seemed to nurture a fascination with the sensational, and from the 1880s onward popular urban newspapers increasingly whetted that appetite.

Joseph Pulitzer, a Hungarian immigrant who bought the *New York World* in 1883, pioneered journalism as a branch of mass culture.

Yellow Journalism

Believing that newspapers should be "dedicated to the cause of the people rather than to that of the purse potentates," Pulitzer filled the *World* with stories of disasters, crimes, and scandals. Sensational headlines, set in large bold type like that used for advertisements, screamed from every page. Pulitzer's journalists not only reported news but sought it out and even created it. *World* reporter Nellie Bly (real name, Elizabeth Cochrane) faked her way into an insane asylum and wrote a brazen exposé of the sordid conditions she found. Other reporters staged stunts and sought out heart-rending human-interest stories. Pulitzer also popularized comics, and the yellow ink they were printed in gave rise to the term *yellow journalism* as a synonym for sensationalism.

Pulitzer's strategy was immensely successful. In one year he increased the *World*'s daily circulation from 20,000 to 100,000, and by the late 1890s it reached 1 million. Soon other publishers, such as William Randolph Hearst, who bought the *New York Journal* in 1895 and started an empire of mass-circulation newspapers, adopted Pulitzer's techniques. Yellow journalism became a nationwide phenomenon, feeding interest in bizarre aspects of the human condition.

Pulitzer and his rivals boosted circulation further by emphasizing sports and women's news. Newspapers had previously reported sporting events, but yellow-journalism papers gave such stories far greater prominence by printing separate, expanded sports pages. Such sections promoted sports as a leisure-time attraction, as sports news re-created a game's drama through narrative and statistics. While increasing sports reporting, mostly for male readers, newspapers also added special sections devoted to household tips, fashion, decorum, and club news to capture female readers. Like crime and disaster stories, sports and women's sections helped to make news a mass commodity.

By the early twentieth century, mass-circulation magazines were overshadowing the expensive elitist journals of earlier eras. Publications

Magazines

such as *McClure's*, *Saturday Evening Post*, and *Ladies' Home Journal* offered human-interest stories, muckraking exposés (see page 581), titillating fiction, photographs, colorful covers, and eye-catching ads to a growing mass market. Meanwhile, the total number of books

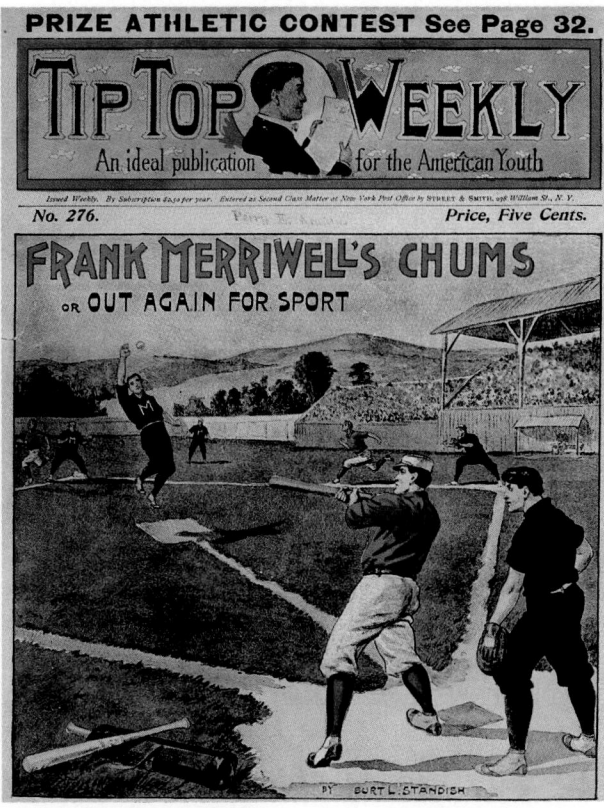

Frank Merriwell, the fictional hero of hundreds of stories written by Burt Standish (the pen name used by Gilbert Patten), was a popular character in the early 1900s. In a series of adventures, most involving sports, Frank used his physical skills, valor, and moral virtue to lead by example, accomplish the impossible, and influence others to behave in an upstanding way.   (Collection of Picture Research Consultants)

published more than quadrupled between 1880 and 1917. This rising popular consumption of news and books reflected growing literacy. Between 1870 and 1920, the proportion of Americans aged ten and over who could not read or write fell from 20 percent to 6 percent.

Other forms of communication also expanded. In 1891 there was fewer than one telephone for every 100 people in the United States; by 1901 the number had grown to 2.1, and by 1921 it had swelled to 12.6. In 1900 Americans used 4 billion postage stamps; in 1922 they used 14.3 billion. The term *community* took on new dimensions, as people used the media, mail, and telephone to extend their horizons far beyond their immediate localities. More than ever before, people in different parts of the country knew about and discussed the same news event, whether it was a sensational murder, a sex scandal, or the fortunes of a particular entertainer or athlete. America was becoming a mass society.

To some extent, the cities' new amusements and pastimes had a homogenizing influence, bringing together ethnic and social groups to share a common experience. Parks, ball fields, vaudeville shows, movies, and feature sections of newspapers and magazines were nonsectarian and apolitical, designed to appeal to everyone. Yet even though entrepreneurs were responsible for the spread of amusements, different groups of consumers often used them to reinforce their own cultural habits. In some cities, for example, working-class immigrants occupied parks and amusement areas as sites for family and ethnic gatherings. To the dismay of reformers who hoped that recreation would assimilate newcomers and teach them habits of restraint, immigrants used picnics and Fourth of July celebrations as occasions for boisterous drinking and sometimes violent behavior. Young working-class men and women resisted parents' and moralists' warnings and frequented urban dance halls, where they explored their own forms of courtship and sexual behavior. And children often used streets and rooftops to create their own entertainment rather than participate in adult-supervised games in parks and playgrounds. Thus as Americans learned to play, their leisure—like their work and their politics—expressed and was shaped by the pluralistic forces that thrived in the cities.

Mass Culture and Americanization

Summary

Much of what American society is today originated in the urbanization of the late nineteenth and early twentieth centuries. Though their governments and neighborhoods may have seemed chaotic, American cities experienced an "unheralded triumph" by the early 1900s. Amid corruption and political conflict, urban engineers modernized local infrastructures with new sewer, water, and lighting services, and urban governments made the environment safer by expanding professional police and fire departments. When native inventiveness met the traditions of European, African, and Asian cultures, a new kind of society emerged. This society seldom functioned smoothly; there really was no coherent urban community, only a collection of subcommunities. Yet the jumble of social classes, ethnic and racial groups, political organizations, and professional experts created a relatively stable though fragile harmony.

American cities exhibited bewildering diversity. Fearful and puzzled, native-born whites tried to Americanize and uplift immigrants, but newcomers stubbornly strained to protect their cultures. Optimists had envisioned the American nation as a melting pot, where various nationalities would blend to become a unified people. Instead, many ethnic groups proved unmeltable, and racial minorities got burned on the bottom of the pot. As a result of immigration and urbanization, the United States became a culturally pluralistic society—not so much a melting pot as a salad bowl, where ingredients retained their original flavor and occasionally blended. Often the results were hyphenated identifications: Irish-American, Italian-American, Polish-American, and the like.

Pluralism and interest-group loyalties enhanced the importance of politics. If America was not a melting pot, then different groups were competing for power, wealth, and status. Some people carried polarization to extremes and tried to suppress everything allegedly un-American. Efforts to enforce homogeneity generally failed, however, because the country's cultural diversity prevented domination by a single ethnic majority. By 1920, immigrants and their offspring outnumbered the native-born in many cities, and the national economy depended on these new workers and consumers. Migrants and immigrants transformed the United States into an urban nation. They gave American culture its rich and varied texture, and they laid the foundations for the liberalism that characterized American politics in the twentieth century.

LEGACY FOR A PEOPLE AND A NATION
Ethnic Food

Today, an ordinary American might eat a bagel for breakfast, a gyro sandwich for lunch, and wonton soup, shrimp creole, and rice pilaf for dinner, followed by chocolate mousse and espresso. An evening snack might consist of nachos and lager beer. These items, all identified with a different ethnic group, serve as tasty reminders that immigrants made important and lasting contributions to the nation's culinary culture. Yet also, the American diet represents one of the few genuine ways that the multicultural nation has served as a melting pot.

The American taste for ethnic food has a complicated history. Since the nineteenth century, the food business has offered immigrant entrepreneurs lucrative opportunities, many of which involved products unrelated to their own ethnic background. The industry is replete with success stories linked to names such as Hector Boiardi (Chef Boyardee), William Gebhardt (Eagle Brand chili and tamales), Jeno Paulucci (Chun-King), and Alphonse Biardot (Franco-American), all of whom immigrated to the United States in the late nineteenth or early twentieth century. But Americans have also supported unheralded immigrant merchants and restaurateurs who have offered special and regional fare—German, Chinese, Italian, Tex-Mex, "soul food," or Thai—in every era.

Unlike the strife that occurred over housing, jobs, schools, and politics when different nationalities collided, the evolution of American eating habits has been extremely peaceful. Occasionally, criticisms developed, such as when dietitians and reformers in the early twentieth century charged that Mexican immigrants were harming their digestion by overusing tomatoes and peppers and that the rich foods of eastern European Jews made them overly emotional and less capable of assimilating. But as historian Donna Gabaccia has observed, relatively conflict-free sharing and borrowing have characterized American foodways far more than "food fights" and intolerance. The sensory pleasure of eating has always overriden cultural loyalty, and mass marketers have been quick to capitalize.

As each wave of immigrants has entered the nation—and especially as these newcomers have occupied the cities, where cross-cultural contact has been inevitable—food has given them certain ways of becoming American, of finding some form of group acceptance, while also giving them a means of confirming their identity. At the same time, those who already thought of themselves as Americans have willingly made the cuisine of the newcomers a part of the existing culture and a part of themselves.

For Further Reading, see page A-22 of the Appendix. For Web resources, go to http://college.hmco.com.

GILDED AGE POLITICS 1877–1900

He had one eye and a bad temper. Born in back-country South Carolina, Benjamin Tillman was only two when his father died. Of his five brothers, two were murdered, another killed a man in a gambling dispute, and another died in the Civil War. Benjamin enlisted in the Confederate Army but had to quit almost immediately because an abscess caused blindness in one eye. He began farming a small plot that he received from his mother, but drought, crop failures, and debt forced him to sell much of his land. Driven by a belief that the southern power structure was causing the "decay of that sturdy independence of character, which was once marked in our people," he entered politics.

Associates called him "Pitchfork Ben" because when he ran for the U.S. Senate in 1894, he promised to "stick a pitchfork" into Grover Cleveland to make the president more receptive to his ideas. A former slaveholder, he epitomized southern extremism. He never wavered in his belief that African Americans were inferior to whites, and he worked to exclude them from voting and advocated lynching in cases of rape. Yet Benjamin Tillman, two-term governor and four-term senator from South Carolina, also helped his state open new colleges, supported laws to regulate railroads, accused steelmakers of profiting at public expense, equalized state taxes, increased the education budget, helped secure direct primaries for nomination of state officers, and fought tirelessly on behalf of embattled farmers.

Tillman's turbulent career paralleled an eventful era, one that can be characterized by three themes: special interests, legislative accomplishment, and political exclusion. When he attacked railroads, the steel industry, and the merchants and lawyers whom he accused of exploiting farmers, Tillman expressed the growing dissatisfaction with the ways in which powerful private interests—manufacturers, railroad managers, bankers, and wealthy men in general—were exercising monumental greed in large corporations across the continent. The era's venality seemed so widespread that when, in 1874, Mark Twain and Charles Dudley Warner satirized America as a land of shallow money

Politics in the late nineteenth century was a major community activity. In an age before movies, television, shopping malls, and widespread professional sports, forceful orators such as Socialist Party leader Eugene V. Debs, shown speaking in a railroad yard, attracted large audiences for speeches that sometimes lasted for hours.   (Brown Brothers)

grubbers in their novel, *The Gilded Age*, the name stuck. Historians have used the expression "Gilded Age" to characterize the late nineteenth century.

At the same time, Tillman's economic and political reforms reflected the era's accomplishments not just at the state level but also at the national level. Between 1877 and 1900, industrialization, urbanization, and the commercialization of agriculture altered national politics and government as much as they shaped everyday life. Congress achieved legislative landmarks in railroad regulation, tariffs, currency, civil service, and other important issues in spite of partisan and regional rivalries. Meanwhile, the judiciary actively supported big business by defending property rights against state and federal regulation. The presidency was occupied by honest, respectable men who, though not as exceptional as Washington, Jefferson, or Lincoln, prepared the office for its more activist character after the turn of the century.

Even so, exclusion—the third phenomenon—prevented the majority of Americans—including women, southern blacks, Indians, uneducated whites, and unnaturalized immigrants—from voting and from access to the tools of democracy. "Pitchfork Ben" Tillman represented an extreme example of individuals and groups who exacerbated a condition that plagued the nation in the years following Reconstruction.

Until the 1890s, those three phenomena of special interests, accomplishment, and exclusion existed within a delicate political equilibrium characterized by a stable party system and a balance of power among the country's geographical sections. Then in the 1890s rural discontent erupted in the West and South, and a deep economic depression bared flaws in the industrial system. Though he stood on the fringes of the mass agrarian reform movement, Tillman helped awaken the rural masses with his fiery rhetoric. Amid the economic and political disruption, a presidential campaign in 1896 stirred Americans as they had not been stirred for a generation. A new party arose, old parties split, sectional unity dissolved, and fundamental disputes about the nation's future climaxed. The nation emerged from the turbulent 1890s with new economic configurations and new political alignments. ■

The Nature of Party Politics

At no other time in the nation's history was public interest in elections more avid than between 1870 and 1896. Consistently, 80 to 90 percent of eligible voters (white and black males in the North, mostly white males in the South) cast ballots in local and national elections. (Under 50 percent typically do so today.) Politics served as a form of recreation, more popular than baseball or circuses. Actual voting provided only the final stage in a process that included parades, picnics, and speeches. As one observer remarked, "What the theatre is to the French, or the bull fight . . . to the Spanish . . . [election campaigns] and the ballot box are to our people."

Party loyalty in part reflected American pluralism. As different groups competed for power, wealth, and status, they formed coalitions to achieve their goals. But such coalitions were fragile, and their memberships shifted according to the issue in question. With some exceptions, groups who opposed interference by government in matters of personal liberty identified with the Democratic Party, and those who believed government could be an agent of moral reform identified with the Republican Party. Democrats included immigrant Catholics and Jews, who believed that ritual and sacraments should guide personal behavior and prove one's faith in God. Republicans consisted mostly of native-born Protestants, who believed that religious salvation could best be achieved by purging the world of evil and that legislation could protect people from sin. Democrats would restrict government power. Republicans believed in direct government action.

Cultural-Political Alignments

At state and local levels, adherents of these two cultural traditions battled over how much control government should exercise over people's lives. The most contentious issues were use of leisure time and celebration of Sunday, the Lord's day. Protestant Republicans tried to keep the Sabbath holy through legislation that prohibited bars, stores, and commercial amusements from being open on Sundays. Immigrant Democrats, accustomed to feasting and playing after church, fought saloon closings and other restrictions on the only day they had free from work. Similar splits developed over public versus parochial schools and prohibition versus the free availability of liquor.

These issues made politics a personal as well as a community activity. In an era before movie stars and media heroes, people formed strong loyalties to individual politicians, loyalties that often overlooked crassness and corruption. James G. Blaine—Maine's flamboyant and powerful congressman, senator, presidential aspirant, and two-time secretary of state—typified this appeal. Followers called him the "Plumed Knight," composed songs and organized parades in his

IMPORTANT EVENTS

1873 Congress ends coinage of silver dollars

1874 Twain and Warner's *The Gilded Age* appears and gives a name to its era

1873–78 Economic hard times hit

1876 Hayes elected president

1877 Georgia passes poll tax and begins legislative movement to disfranchise African Americans in the South
Munn v. Illinois upholds principle of state regulation

1878 Bland-Allison Act requires Treasury to buy between $2 and $4 million in silver each month
Anthony-backed woman suffrage amendment defeated in Congress

1880 Garfield elected president

1881 Garfield assassinated; Arthur assumes the presidency

1883 Pendleton Civil Service Act creates Civil Service Commission to oversee competitive examinations for some government positions
Supreme Court strikes down 1875 Civil Rights Act

1884 Cleveland elected president

1886 *Wabash* case declares that only Congress can limit interstate commerce rates

1887 Farm prices collapse
Farmers' Alliances form
Interstate Commerce Act creates commission to regulate rates and practices of interstate shippers

1888 B. Harrison elected president

1890 McKinley Tariff raises tariff rates
Sherman Silver Purchase Act commits Treasury to buying 4.5 million ounces of silver each month
"Mississippi Plan" uses poll taxes and literacy tests to prevent African Americans from voting
National American Woman Suffrage Association formed

1892 Populist convention in Omaha draws up reform platform
Cleveland elected president

1893–97 Major economic depression hits U.S.

1893 Sherman Silver Purchase Act repealed

1894 Wilson-Gorman Tariff attempts to reduce rates; Senate Republicans restore House cuts
Eugene V. Debs arrested and turns to socialism
Coxey's army marches on Washington, D.C.

1895 Cleveland cuts deal with bankers to save gold reserves

1896 McKinley elected president
Plessy v. Ferguson establishes "separate-but-equal" doctrine, allowing segregation of African Americans in public accommodations

1897 Dingley Tariff raises duties

1898 Louisiana implements "grandfather clause" that keeps blacks from voting

1899 *Cummins v. County Board of Education* applies separate-but-equal doctrine to schools

1900 Gold Standard Act requires all paper money to be backed by gold
McKinley reelected president

---

honor, and sat mesmerized by his long speeches, while disregarding his corrupt alliances with businessmen and his animosity toward laborers and farmers.

Allegiances to national parties and candidates were so evenly divided that no faction gained control for any sustained period of time. Between 1877 and 1897, Republicans held the presidency for three terms, Democrats for two. Rarely did the same party control both the presidency and Congress simultaneously. From 1876 through 1892, presidential elections were extremely close. The outcome often hinged on the popular vote in a few populous states—Connecticut, New York, New Jersey, Ohio, Indiana, and Illinois. Both parties tried to gain advantages by nominating presidential and vice-presidential candidates from these states (and also by committing vote fraud there on their candidates' behalf).

Moreover, internal quarrels split both the Republican and Democratic Parties. Among Republicans, a faction known as "Stalwarts" was led by New York's pompous Senator Roscoe Conkling. A physical-fitness devotee once labeled "the finest torso in public life," Conkling worked the spoils system to

Party Factions

President Rutherford B. Hayes (1822–1893) entered office amid numerous claims on him by special interests. This cartoon shows Hayes making the precarious journey from the Ohio State House, where he had served as governor, across a field of bayonets to his presidential chair, which is outfitted with a seat of spikes and propped up by the Republican Party. (Library of Congress)

win government jobs for his supporters. The Stalwarts' rivals were the "Half Breeds," led by James G. Blaine, who pursued influence as blatantly as Conkling did. On the sidelines stood more idealistic Republicans, or "Mugwumps" (supposedly an Indian term meaning "mug on one side of the fence, wump on the other"). Mugwumps such as Senator Carl Schurz of Missouri disliked the political roguishness that tainted the Republican Party and believed that only righteous, educated men like themselves should govern. Meanwhile, Democrats tended to subdivide into white-supremacy southerners, immigrant-stock and working-class urban political machines, and business-oriented advocates of low tariffs. Like Republicans, Democrats eagerly pursued the spoils of office.

At the state level, one party usually dominated, and within that party a few men typically held dictatorial power. Often the state "boss" was a senator. Until the Seventeenth Amendment to the Constitution was ratified in 1913, state legislatures elected U.S. senators, and a senator could wield enormous influence

with his command of federal jobs. Many senators parlayed their state power into national influence. Besides Conkling and Blaine, their ranks included Thomas C. Platt of New York, Nelson W. Aldrich of Rhode Island, Mark A. Hanna of Ohio, Matthew S. Quay of Pennsylvania, and William Mahone of Virginia.

Politics in the Industrial Age

 In Congress, issues of sectional controversies, patronage abuses, railroad regulation, tariffs, and currency provoked heated debates but also important legislation. Well into the 1880s, bitter hostilities left from the Civil War continued to divide Americans. Republicans capitalized on war memories by "waving the bloody shirt" at Democrats. As one Republican orator harangued in 1876, "Every man that tried to destroy this nation was a Democrat. . . . Soldiers, every scar you have on your heroic bodies was given you by a Democrat." In the South, Democratic candidates also waved the bloody shirt, calling Republicans traitors to white supremacy and states' rights.

Other Americans also sought advantages by invoking war memories. The Grand Army of the Republic, an organization of 400,000 Union Army veterans, allied with the Republican Party and cajoled Congress into providing generous pensions for former Union soldiers and their widows. Many pensions were deserved: Union troops had been poorly paid, and thousands of wives had been widowed. But for some veterans, the war's emotional memories furnished an opportunity to profit at public expense. Though the Union Army spent $2 billion to fight the Civil War, pensions to veterans ultimately cost taxpayers $8 billion, one of the largest welfare commitments the federal government has ever made. By 1900 soldiers' pensions accounted for roughly 40 percent of the federal budget. Confederate veterans received none of this money, though some southern states funded small pensions and built old-age homes for ex-soldiers.

Few politicians dared oppose Civil War pensions, but some attempted to dismantle the spoils system.

Civil Service Reform

The practice of awarding government jobs to party workers, regardless of their qualifications, had taken root before the Civil War and flourished after it. As the postal service, diplomatic corps, and other government agencies expanded, so did the public payroll. Between 1865 and 1891, the number of federal jobs tripled, from 53,000

How do historians know...

that Gilded Age politics evoked bitter criticism? Social commentary sometimes is expressed more effectively through art than with words. An artist can employ the tools of wit, caricature, and symbolism to make powerful statements from which historians can glean important insights into the past. Thomas Nast, whose political cartoons appeared in *Harper's Weekly* magazine between 1862 and 1885, expressed optimism after the Civil War and then disillusionment during the Gilded Age better than almost anyone else. A talented artist as well as a keen analyst, Nast used his skills to potent effect, influencing domestic policies as well as public attitudes. Thus his drawings, and the caricatures and cartoons of other artists, serve as important historical documents of American society and politics of the late nineteenth century.

This cartoon appeared in May 1881, at a time when Nast believed the federal government had little incentive to pass laws for national welfare and cared only about the spoils of office. Thus a sloth, a symbol of laziness, represents the lawmakers who occupy the Capitol and White House, in the background, and a beaver, the symbol of industriousness, represents the people busily toiling on behalf of workshops, banks, trade, and other economic institutions. While Citizen Beaver labors to achieve prosperity

and good government, Statesman Sloth lies on its back contemplating laws to exploit the people and line its own pockets (spoils). Such images could exert powerful influence on public opinion, but because they exaggerate reality, they also reflect personal bias. (*Harper's Weekly*, May 21, 1881)

May 21, 1881

Our Stumbling-Block.
While the Citizen Beaver labors for prosperity and good government, the "Statesman" Sloth lies on his back and obstructs and destroys.

to 166,000. Elected officials scrambled to control these jobs as a means of cementing support for themselves and their parties. In return for comparatively short hours and high pay, appointees to federal positions pledged their votes and a portion of their earnings to their patrons.

Shocked by such corruption, especially after the revelation of scandals in the Grant administration, some reformers began advocating appointments and promotions based on merit rather than political connections. Civil service reform accelerated in 1881 with the formation of the National Civil Service Reform

Before the Pendleton Act of 1883, many government positions were filled by patronage; hat in hand, job seekers beseeched political leaders to find a place for them. Here a member of Congress presents office-seeking friends to President Hayes.   (Library of Congress)

League, led by editors E. L. Godkin and George W. Curtis. The same year, the assassination of President James Garfield by a demented job seeker hastened the drive for change. The Pendleton Civil Service Act, passed by Congress in 1882 and signed by President Chester Arthur in 1883, created the Civil Service Commission to oversee competitive examinations for government positions. The act gave the commission jurisdiction over only 10 percent of federal jobs, though the president could expand the list. Because the Constitution barred Congress from interfering in state affairs, civil service at the state and local levels developed in a more haphazard manner. Nevertheless, the Pendleton Act marked a beginning and provided impetus for wider changes.

Veterans' pensions and civil service reform were not representative issues of the Gilded Age, however. Rather, economic policymaking occupied congressional business more than ever before. Railroad expansion had become a particularly controversial issue. As the rail network spread, so did competition. In their quest for customers, railroad lines reduced rates to outmaneuver rivals, but rate wars cut into profits and

wildly fluctuating rates angered shippers and farmers. Ironically, as freight rates generally fell, complaints about high rates rose. On noncompetitive routes, railroads often boosted charges as high as possible to compensate for unprofitably low rates on competitive routes, making pricing disproportionate to distance. Charges on short-distance shipments served by only one line could exceed those on long-distance shipments served by competing lines. Railroads also played favorites, reducing rates to large shippers and offering free passenger passes to preferred customers and politicians.

Such favoritism stirred farmers, small merchants, and reform politicians to demand public regulation of

Railroad Regulation

railroad rates. Their efforts occurred first at the state level. By 1880 fourteen states had established commissions to limit freight and storage charges of state-chartered lines. Railroads fought these measures, arguing that the Constitution guaranteed them freedom to acquire and use property without government restraint. But in 1877, in *Munn v. Illinois*, the Supreme Court upheld the principle of state regulation, declaring that the grain warehouses owned by the railroads were acting in the public interest and therefore must submit to regulation for "the common good."

State legislatures, however, could not regulate interstate lines, a limitation affirmed by the Supreme Court in the *Wabash* case of 1886, in which the Court declared that only Congress could limit rates involving interstate commerce. Reformers thereupon demanded federal action. Congress responded in 1887 by passing the Interstate Commerce Act. The law prohibited pools, rebates, and long-haul/short-haul rate discrimination, and it created the Interstate Commerce Commission (ICC) to investigate railroad rate-making methods, issue cease-and-desist orders against illegal practices, and seek court aid to enforce compliance. The legislation's lack of provisions for enforcement, however, left railroads room for evasion, and federal judges chipped away at ICC powers. In the *Maximum Freight Rate* case (1897), the Supreme Court ruled that the ICC did not have power to set rates; and in the *Alabama Midlands* case (1897), the Court overturned prohibitions against long-haul/short-haul discrimination. Even so, the principle of government regulation, though weakened, remained in force.

The economic issue of tariffs carried strong political implications. Congress initially had created tariffs

Tariff Policy

to protect American manufactured goods and agricultural products from European competition. But tariffs quickly became a tool by which special interests could protect and enhance their profits. By the 1880s these interests had succeeded in obtaining tariffs applied to more than four thousand items. A few economists and farmers argued for free trade, but most politicians still insisted that tariffs were a necessary form of government assistance to support industry and preserve jobs.

The Republican Party, claiming credit for economic growth, put protective tariffs at the core of its political agenda. Democrats complained that tariffs made prices artificially high by keeping out less expensive foreign goods, thereby benefiting manufacturers while hurting farmers whose crops were not protected and consumers who had to buy manufactured goods. For example, a yard of flannel produced abroad might cost 10 cents, but the imposition of an 8-cent tariff raised the price paid by American consumers to 18 cents. An American manufacturer of a similar yard of flannel, also costing 10 cents, could charge consumers 17 cents, underselling the foreign competition by 1 cent yet still pocketing a large profit because he did not have to pay the tariff.

During most of the Gilded Age, taxes, tariffs, and other levies created a surplus rather than a deficit in the federal budget. Most Republicans, being businessmen, liked the idea that the government was earning more than it spent and hoped to keep the extra money as a Treasury reserve or to spend it on projects like harbor improvement and federal buildings that would aid commerce. Democrats, however, pointed out that the federal government should not be a profit-making business. They insisted that the surplus should be reduced not by spending more but by reducing revenues—by cutting taxes and cutting tariffs. Democrats acknowledged a need for tariff protection of some manufactured goods and raw materials, but they favored lower rates to encourage foreign trade and to reduce the Treasury surplus.

Manufacturers and their congressional allies maintained control over tariff policy. The McKinley Tariff of 1890 boosted already-high rates by another 4 percent. When House Democrats supported by President Grover Cleveland passed a bill to reduce tariff rates in 1894, Senate Republicans, aided by southern Democrats eager to protect their region's infant industries, added six hundred amendments restoring most of the cuts (Wilson-Gorman Tariff). In 1897 the Dingley Tariff raised rates further. Attacks on the tariff, though unsuccessful, made tariffs the symbol of privileged business in the public mind and a target of reformers after 1900.

Monetary policy aroused even stronger emotions than tariffs did. When increased industrial and agricultural production caused prices to fall after the Civil War, debtors and creditors had opposing reactions.

Monetary Policy

Farmers suffered because the prices they received for their crops were dropping, but they had to pay high interest rates on money they borrowed to pay off their mortgages and other debts. They favored schemes like the coinage of silver to increase the amount of currency in circulation. An expanded money supply, they reasoned, would reduce interest rates, making their debts less burdensome, and their costs would be lower relative to the prices they received for their crops. Creditors believed that overproduction had caused prices to decline. They favored a more stable, limited money supply backed only by gold. They feared that the value of currency not backed by gold would fluctuate; the resulting uncertainty would threaten their wealth and undermine investors' confidence in the U.S. economy.

Arguments over the quantity and quality of money, however, transcended economics. Creditor-debtor tension translated into class divisions between haves and have-nots. The debate also represented sectional cleavages: western silver-mining areas and agricultural regions of the South and West against the more conservative industrial Northeast. And the issue carried moral, almost religious, overtones. Some Americans believed the beauty, rarity, and durability of gold gave it a magical potency. Others believed the gold standard for currency was too limiting; sustained prosperity, they insisted, demanded new attitudes.

By the 1870s, the currency controversy had boiled down to gold versus silver. Previously, the government had bought both gold and silver to back the national currency, setting a ratio that made a gold dollar worth sixteen times more than a silver dollar. Mining discoveries after 1848, however, increased the supply of gold and lowered its market price relative to that of silver. As a result, silver dollars disappeared from circulation—because of their inflated value relative to gold, owners hoarded them—and in 1873 Congress officially stopped coining silver dollars, an act that silver partisans later called the "Crime of '73." Europeans also stopped buying silver, and the United States and many of its trading partners unofficially adopted the gold standard, meaning that their currency was backed chiefly by gold.

Within a few years, new mines in the American West began to flood the market with silver, and its price dropped. Gold then became worth more than sixteen times the value of silver (the ratio reached twenty to one by 1890), and it became profitable to spend rather than hoard silver dollars. Silver producers wanted the government to resume buying silver at the old sixteen-to-one ratio, which amounted to a subsidy because they could sell silver to the government above market price. Debtors, hurt by falling prices and the economic hard times of 1873–1878, saw silver as a means of expanding the currency supply. They joined with silver producers to denounce the "Crime of '73" and to press for resumption of silver coinage at the old sixteen-to-one ratio.

With both parties split into silver and gold factions, Congress at first tried to compromise. The Bland-Allison Act of 1878 authorized the Treasury to buy between $2 million and $4 million worth of silver each month, and the Sherman Silver Purchase Act of 1890 increased the government's monthly purchase of silver by specifying weight (4.5 million ounces) rather than dollars. Neither act satisfied the different interest groups. The government paid for the silver with Treasury notes, not with gold dollars that silver interests wanted. Moreover, the acts failed to expand the money supply as substantially as debtors had hoped and failed to erase the impression that the government favored creditors' interests.

National politics was not a glamorous field of endeavor in the Gilded Age. For each constituent who received a patronage job, many more were disappointed. Senators and representatives received small salaries and usually had the financial burden of maintaining two homes: one in their home districts and one in Washington. Life in the nation's capital was oppressively hot in summer, muddy and icy in winter. Most members of Congress had no private office space, only a desk. They worked long hours responding to constituents' requests, wrote their own speeches, and had to pay for staff out of their own pockets. Yet, cynics to the contrary, most politicians were principled and dedicated. They managed to deal with important issues and pass significant legislation under difficult conditions.

Legislative Accomplishments

The Presidency Restrengthened

Operating under the cloud of Andrew Johnson's impeachment, Grant's scandals, and doubts about the legitimacy of the election of 1876 (see Chapter 16), American presidents between 1877 and 1900 moved gingerly to restore the authority of their office. Proper and honest, Presidents Rutherford Hayes (1877–1881), James Garfield (1881), Chester Arthur (1881–1885), Grover Cleveland (1885–1889 and 1893–1897), Benjamin Harrison (1889–1893), and William McKinley (1897–1901) tried to act as legislative as well as administrative leaders. Like other politicians, they used symbols. Hayes served lemonade at the White House to emphasize that he, unlike his predecessor Ulysses Grant, was no hard drinker. McKinley put aside his cigar in public so photographers would not catch him setting a bad example for youth. More important, each president initiated legislation and used the veto to guide national policy.

Hayes, Garfield, and Arthur

Rutherford B. Hayes had been a Union general and an Ohio congressman and governor before his disputed election to the presidency, an event that prompted opponents to label him "Rutherfraud." Though his party expected him to favor business interests, Hayes played a quiet role as reformer and conciliator. He emphasized national harmony over sectional rivalry and opposed violence of all kinds. He tried to overhaul the spoils system by appointing civil service reformer Carl Schurz to his cabinet and by battling New York's patronage king, Senator Conkling. (He fired Conkling's protégé, Chester Arthur, from the post of New York customs house collector.) Though he was too cautious to use government power to do so, Hayes believed society was obligated to help the oppressed, including American Chinese and Indians, and after retiring from the presidency he worked diligently to aid former slaves.

When Hayes declined to run for reelection in 1880, Republicans nominated another Ohio congressman and Civil War hero, James A. Garfield. A solemn and cautious man, Garfield defeated Democrat Winfield Scott Hancock, also a Civil War hero, by just forty thousand votes out of 9 million cast. By winning the pivotal states of New York and Indiana, however, Garfield carried the electoral college by a comfortable margin of 214 to 155.

Garfield spent most of his brief presidency trying to secure an independent position among party poten-

field lingered for seventy-nine days while doctors tried vainly to remove a bullet lodged in his back, but he succumbed to infection and died September 19.

Garfield's successor was Vice President Chester A. Arthur, the New York spoilsman whom Hayes had fired in 1878. Republicans had nominated Arthur for vice president only to help Garfield carry New York State. Though his elevation to the presidency made reformers shudder, Arthur became a dignified and temperate executive. He signed the Pendleton Civil Service Act, urged Congress to modify outdated tariff rates, and supported federal regulation of railroads. He wielded the veto aggressively, killing several bills that excessively benefited railroads and corporations. But congressional partisans frustrated his plans for reducing the tariff and strengthening the navy. Arthur wanted to run for reelection in 1884 but lost the nomination to James G. Blaine at the Republican national convention.

To oppose Blaine, Democrats named New York's governor Grover Cleveland, a bachelor who had tainted his reputation when he fathered an illegitimate son—a fact he admitted during the campaign. Both parties focused on the sordid. (Alluding to Cleveland's bastard son, Republicans chided him with catcalls of "Ma! Ma! Where's my pa?" To which Democrats replied, "Gone to the White House, Ha! Ha! Ha!") Distaste for Blaine prompted some Mugwump Republicans to desert their party for Cleveland. On election day Cleveland beat Blaine by only 29,000 popular votes; his tiny margin of 1,149 votes in New York gave him that state's 36 electoral votes, enough for a 219-to-182 victory in the electoral college. Cleveland may have won New York thanks to last-minute remarks of a local Protestant minister, who equated Democrats with "rum, Romanism, and rebellion." Democrats eagerly publicized the slur among New York's large Irish-Catholic population, urging voters to protest by supporting Cleveland.

Cleveland, the first Democratic president since James Buchanan (1857–1861), echoed his Republican

Cleveland and Harrison

predecessors' complaints about the "cursed constant grind" of his office. He tried, however, to exert vigorous leadership. He expanded civil service, vetoed hundreds of private pension bills, and urged Congress to cut tariffs on raw materials and manufactured goods. When advisers warned that his stand might weaken his chances for reelection, the president retorted, "What is the use of being elected or reelected, unless you stand for something?" But the Mills tariff bill of 1888, passed by the House in

By the late nineteenth century, political parties merchandised their candidates in the same way manufacturers advertised consumer goods. Coins and ribbons, such as these showing the Republican and Democratic candidates for president and vice president in 1888, were designed to sell dignified images to the voting republic—similar to the way that some retailers tried to give their consumer products public appeal.   (Collection of David J. and Janice L. Frent)

tates. He hoped to reduce the tariff and develop economic relations with Latin America but had to spend most days dealing with hordes of men seeking government jobs. "Once or twice," Garfield admitted, "I felt like crying out against the greed for office and its consumption of my time." He pleased civil service reformers by rebuffing Conkling's patronage demands, but his chance to make lasting contributions ended in July 1881 when Charles Guiteau, a disappointed patronage seeker, shot him in a Washington railroad station. Gar-

response to Cleveland's wishes, died in the Senate. When Democrats renominated Cleveland for the presidency in 1888, protectionists in the party convinced him to temper his attacks on high tariffs.

Republicans in 1888 nominated Benjamin Harrison, former senator from Indiana and grandson of President William Henry Harrison (1841). During the campaign, some Republicans manipulated the British minister into stating that Cleveland's reelection would be good for England. Irish Democrats, who hated England's colonial rule over Ireland, took offense, as intended, and Cleveland's campaign was weakened. Perhaps more helpful to Harrison were the bribery and multiple voting that helped him win Indiana by 2,300 votes and New York by 14,000. (Democrats also indulged in bribery and vote fraud, but this time Republicans proved more successful at such deceits.) Those states ensured Harrison's victory. Though Cleveland outpolled Harrison by 90,000 popular votes, Harrison carried the electoral vote by 233 to 168.

Harrison was the first president since 1875 whose party had majorities in both houses of Congress. Using a variety of methods, ranging from threats of vetoes to informal dinners and consultations, Harrison influenced the course of legislation. The Congress of 1889–1891 passed 517 bills, two hundred more than the average passed by Congresses between 1875 and 1889. Harrison also showed support for civil service by appointing the reformer Theodore Roosevelt a civil service commissioner. But neither the president nor Congress could resist pressures from special interests, especially those waving the bloody shirt. Harrison signed the Dependents' Pension Act, which provided pensions for Union veterans who had suffered war-related disabilities and granted aid to their widows and minor children. The bill doubled the number of welfare recipients from 490,000 to 966,000.

The Pension Act and other appropriations pushed the federal budget past $1 billion in 1890 for the first time in the nation's history. Democrats blamed the "Billion-Dollar Congress" on spendthrift Republicans. Voters reacted by unseating seventy-eight Republicans in the congressional elections of 1890. Seeking to capitalize on voter unrest, Democrats nominated Cleveland to run against Harrison again in 1892. This time Cleveland attracted large contributions from business and beat Harrison by 370,000 popular votes (3 percent of the total) and by 277 to 145 electoral votes.

In office again, Cleveland moved boldly to address problems of currency, tariffs, and labor unrest. But his actions reflected a narrow orientation toward interests of business and bespoke political weakness. During his campaign Cleveland had promised sweeping tariff reform, but he made little effort to line up support in the Senate, where protectionists undercut all efforts to reduce rates. And when 120,000 boycotting railroad workers paralyzed commerce in the Pullman strike of 1894, Cleveland bowed to requests from railroad managers and Attorney General Richard Olney to send in troops (see page 502). Though he pursued an expansionist foreign policy (see Chapter 22), throughout Cleveland's second term, events at home—particularly economic downturn and agrarian ferment—seemed to overwhelm the president.

Limits of Gilded Age Politics

 Though the scope and size of government activity expanded during the Gilded Age, policies of discrimination and exclusion continued to haunt more than half of the nation's population. Just as before the Civil War, issues of race gave a peculiar quality to politics in the South. There, poor whites, facing economic losses, feared that newly enfranchised African Americans would challenge whatever political and social superiority (real and imagined) they enjoyed. Wealthy white landowners and merchants fanned these fears, using racism to divide whites and blacks and to distract poor whites from protesting their own economic subjugation.

The majority of the nation's African Americans lived in the South and worked in agriculture. Although the abolition of slavery had altered their legal status, it had not markedly improved their economic opportunities. In 1880, 90 percent of all southern blacks depended for a living on farming or personal and domestic service—the same occupations they had held as slaves. The New South, moreover, proved to be as violent for blacks as the Old South had been. Weapons, including a gun commonly known as a "nigger killer," were plentiful, and whites seldom hesitated to use them. More dramatically, between 1889 and 1909, more than seventeen hundred African Americans were lynched in the South. Most lynchings occurred in sparsely populated districts where whites felt threatened by an influx of migrant blacks who had no friends, black or white, to vouch for them. Most lynching victims were usually accused of an assault—rarely proved—on a white woman.

Violence Against African Americans

With slavery dead, white supremacists fashioned further ways to keep blacks in a position of inferiority. Southern leaders, embittered by northern interference in race relations during Reconstruction and eager to reassert authority over people whom they believed to be inferior, instituted measures to prevent blacks from voting and to segregate them legally from whites.

The end of Reconstruction had not stopped blacks from voting. Despite threats and intimidation, blacks still formed the backbone of the southern Republican Party and won elective offices. In North Carolina, for example, eleven African American men served in the state senate and forty-three in the house between 1877 and 1890. White politicians sought to discourage the "Negro vote" by imposing restrictions that appeared neutral but actually barred blacks from the polls. Beginning with Georgia in 1877, southern states levied taxes of $1 to $2 on all citizens wishing to vote. These poll taxes proved prohibitive to most black voters, who were so poor and deeply in debt that they rarely had cash for any purpose. Other schemes disfranchised blacks who could not read.

Disfranchisement Begins

Disfranchisement was accomplished in other devious ways. The Supreme Court affirmed in *U.S. v. Reese* (1876) that the Fifteenth Amendment prohibited states from denying the vote "on account of race, color, or previous condition of servitude." But, said the Court, Congress had no control over local and state elections other than the explicit provisions of the Fifteenth Amendment. State legislatures found ways to exclude black voters without mentioning race, color, or servitude. For instance, an 1890 state constitutional convention established the "Mississippi Plan," requiring all voters to pay a poll tax eight months before each election, to present the tax receipt at election time, and to prove that they could read and interpret the state constitution. Registration officials applied stiffer standards to blacks than to whites, even declaring college graduates ineligible on grounds of illiteracy. In 1898 Louisiana enacted the first "grandfather clause," which established literacy and property qualifications for voting but exempted sons and grandsons of those eligible to vote before 1867, the year the Fifteenth Amendment had gone into effect. Other southern states initiated similar measures.

Such restrictions proved highly effective. In South Carolina, for example, 70 percent of eligible blacks voted in the presidential election of 1880; by 1896 the rate had dropped to 11 percent. By the 1900s African

In the years after Reconstruction, lynchings of African American men occurred with increasing frequency, chiefly in sparsely populated areas where whites looked on strangers, especially black strangers, with fear and suspicion. (© R. P. Kingston/Index Stock Imagery, Picture Cube Division)

Americans had effectively lost political rights in every southern state except Tennessee. Disfranchisement also affected poor whites, few of whom could meet poll tax, property, and literacy requirements. Thus the total number of eligible voters in Mississippi shrank from 257,000 in 1876 to 77,000 in 1892.

Racial discrimination also stiffened in social affairs. After the Civil War, the existing customs of racial separation were expanded in law. In a series of cases during the 1870s, the Supreme Court opened the door to discrimination by ruling that the Fourteenth Amendment protected citizens' rights only against infringement by state governments. The federal government, according to the

Legal Segregation

Court, lacked authority over what individuals or organizations might do. If blacks wanted legal protection, the Court said, they must seek it from the states, which under the Tenth Amendment retained all powers not specifically assigned to Congress.

These rulings climaxed in 1883 when in the *Civil Rights* cases the Court struck down the 1875 Civil Rights Act, which had prohibited segregation in public facilities such as streetcars, hotels, theaters, and parks. Again the Court declared that the federal government could not regulate the behavior of private individuals in matters of race relations. Subsequent lower court rulings established the principle that blacks could be restricted to "separate but equal" facilities. The Supreme Court upheld the separate-but-equal doctrine in *Plessy v. Ferguson* (1896) and applied it to schools in *Cummins v. County Board of Education* (1899).

Thereafter, segregation laws—known as Jim Crow laws—multiplied throughout the South, confronting African Americans with daily reminders of their inferior status. State and local laws restricted them to the rear of streetcars, to separate public drinking fountains and toilets, and to separate sections of hospitals and cemeteries. A Birmingham, Alabama, ordinance required that the races be "distinctly separated . . . by well defined physical barriers" in "any room, hall, theatre, picture house, auditorium, yard, court, ballpark, or other indoor or outdoor place." Local laws defined neighborhoods as all-black or all-white. Mobile, Alabama, passed a curfew requiring blacks to be off the streets by 10 P.M., and Atlanta mandated separate Bibles for the swearing-in of black witnesses in court.

African American women and men coped with the political climate in the South in several ways. In the optimistic days following Reconstruction, a number of blacks used higher education as a means of elevating their status. In all-black teachers' colleges, most of which were coeducational, blacks sought opportunities for themselves and their race. Education also seemed to present a way to foster interracial cooperation. But the white supremacy campaigns that soon developed taught southern blacks that they would have to negotiate in a biracial, rather than interracial, society.

Political disfranchisement pushed African American men, who in contrast to women had previously been able to vote, out of public life. In their place,

Livingston College in North Carolina was one of several institutions of higher learning established by and for African Americans in the late nineteenth century. With a curriculum that emphasized training for educational and religious work in the South and in Africa, these colleges were coeducational, operating on the belief that both men and women could have public roles. (Courtesy of Heritage Hall, Livingstone College, Salisbury, North Carolina)

African American women began using their traditional roles as mothers, educators, and moral guardians to seek services and reforms that reflected subtle yet important political activity. They participated in successful lobbying of local and state governments in the South for reforms such as cleaner city streets, better public health, expanded charity services, and vocational education. In less threatening means than casting ballots, black women found ways to join with white women for campaigns to improve the general community and to negotiate with the white male power structure to achieve their goals.

Women also contended head-on with male power structures. Their major goal was the vote; their successes in reaching this goal were

Woman Suffrage

limited. Prior to 1869, each state determined who was qualified to vote. The Fifteenth Amendment, adopted that year, forbade states to deny the vote "on account of race, color or previous condition" but omitted any reference to sex. For the next twenty years, two organizations—the National Woman Suffrage Association (NWSA) and the American Woman Suffrage Association (AWSA)—battled for female suffrage. The NWSA, led by militants Elizabeth Cady Stanton and Susan B. Anthony, advocated comprehensive women's rights in courts and workplaces as well as at the ballot box. The AWSA, led by former abolitionists Lucy Stone and Thomas Wentworth Higginson, focused more narrowly on suffrage.

In 1878 Susan B. Anthony, who had lost in the courts when she tried to vote in 1872, persuaded Senator A. A. Sargent of California to introduce a constitutional amendment stating that "the right of citizens of the United States to vote shall not be denied or abridged by the United States or by any state on account of sex." A Senate committee killed the bill, but the NWSA had it reintroduced repeatedly over the next eighteen years. On the few occasions when the bill reached the Senate floor, it was voted down by senators who claimed that suffrage would interfere with women's family obligations.

While the NWSA fought for suffrage on the national level, the AWSA worked to amend state constitutions. (The groups merged in 1890 to form the National American Woman Suffrage Association.) Though these campaigns succeeded only slightly, they helped train a corps of female leaders in political organizing and public speaking. Women did win partial victories. Between 1870 and 1910, eleven states (mostly in the West) legalized woman suffrage. By 1890 nineteen states allowed women to vote on school issues, and three granted suffrage on tax and bond issues. But the right to vote in national elections awaited a later generation.

Agrarian Unrest and Populism

While voting concerned those suffering from political exclusion, inequities in the economic order sparked a mass movement that would shake American society. The agrarian revolt—a mixture of strident rhetoric, nostalgic dreams, and hard-headed egalitarianism—began in Grange organizations in the early 1870s. The revolt accelerated when Farmers' Alliances formed in Texas in the late 1870s and spread across the Cotton Belt and Great Plains in the 1880s. The Alliance movement had appeal chiefly in areas where tenancy, debt, railroads, weather, and insects threatened the well-being of hopeful farmers. Once under way, the agrarian rebellion inspired visions of a truly cooperative and democratic society.

Agricultural expansion in the West and Great Plains exposed millions of people to the hardships of rural life (see Chapter 17). Farmers who had moved into these areas knew life would be hard, but they had hoped that the rewards would be more promising than they turned out to be.

Whereas before the Civil War laborlords (slave-owners) dominated southern agriculture, now land-

Sharecropping and Tenant Farming in the South

lords who employed sharecroppers and tenants characterized the system. Sharecropping and tenant farming entangled millions of black and white southerners in a web of debt and humiliation, at whose center stood the crop lien. Most farmers, too poor to have cash on hand, borrowed in order to buy necessities. They could offer as collateral only what they could grow. A farmer in need of supplies dealt with a nearby "furnishing merchant," who would exchange supplies for a lien, or legal claim, on the farmer's forthcoming crop. After the crop was harvested and brought to market, the merchant collected his debt by claiming the portion of the crop that would satisfy the loan. All too often, however, the debt exceeded the crop's value. The farmer could pay off only part of the debt to the merchant but still needed food and supplies for the coming year. The only way he could get these supplies was to sink deeper into debt by reborrowing and giving the merchant a new lien on his next crop.

Merchants frequently took advantage of indebted farmers' powerlessness by inflating prices and charging them interest ranging from 33 to 200 percent on the advances they received. Suppose, for example, that a cash-poor farmer needed a 20-cent bag of seed or 20-cent piece of cloth. The furnishing merchant would sell him the goods on credit but would boost the price to 28 cents. At year's end that 28-cent loan would have accumulated interest, raising the farmer's debt to 42 cents—more than double the item's original cost. The farmer, having pledged more than his crop's worth against scores of such debts, fell behind in payments and never recovered. If he fell too far behind, he could be evicted.

The crop-lien system caused hardship in former plantation areas where tenants and sharecroppers grew cotton for the same markets that had existed before the Civil War. In the southern backcountry, which in the antebellum era had been characterized by small farms, few slaves, and diversified agriculture, the crop-lien problem was compounded by other economic changes. New spending habits of backcountry farmers illustrate these changes. In 1884 Jephta Dickson of the northern Georgia hills bought $55.90 worth of flour, potatoes, peas, meat, corn, and syrup from merchants. Such expenditures would have been rare in the upcountry before the Civil War, when farmers grew almost all the food they needed. But after the war, yeomen like Dickson shifted to commercial farming; in the South that meant raising cotton. This change came about for two reasons: debts incurred during the war and Reconstruction forced farmers to grow a crop that would bring in cash, and railroad expansion enabled them to transport cotton to markets more easily than before. As backcountry yeomen devoted more acres to cotton, they raised less of what they needed on a daily basis and found themselves more frequently at the mercy of merchants.

In the Midwest, as growers cultivated more land, as mechanization boosted productivity, and as foreign competition increased, supplies exceeded national and worldwide demand for agricultural products. Consequently, prices for staple crops dropped steadily. A bushel of wheat that sold for $1.45 in 1866 brought only 80 cents in the mid-1880s and 49 cents by the mid-1890s. Meanwhile, transportation and storage fees remained high relative to other prices. Expenses for seed, fertilizer, manufactured goods, taxes, and mortgage interest trapped many farm families in troubling

Hardship in the Midwest and West

and sometimes desperate circumstances. In order to buy necessities and pay bills, farmers had to produce more. But the spiral wound ever more tightly: the more farmers produced, the lower prices for their crops dropped (see Figure 20.1).

The West suffered from special hardships. In Colorado absentee capitalists seized control of access to transportation and water, and concentration of technology in the hands of large mining companies pushed out small firms. Charges of monopolistic control by railroads echoed among farmers, miners, and stockmen in Wyoming and Montana. In California, Washington, and Oregon, wheat and fruit growers found their opportunities reduced by railroads' control of transportation and storage rates.

Even before they felt the full impact of these developments, farmers began to organize. With aid from Oliver H. Kelley, a clerk in the Department of Agriculture, farmers in almost every state during the 1860s and 1870s founded a network of local organizations called Granges. By 1875 the Grange had twenty thousand branches and a million members. Like other voluntary organizations throughout the country, Granges had constitutions, elected officers, and membership oaths. Strongest in the Midwest and South, Granges at first served a chiefly social function, sponsoring meetings and educational events to relieve the loneliness of farm life. Family-oriented and open to all, local Granges welcomed women's participation.

Grange Movement

As membership flourished, Granges turned to economic and political action. Local branches formed cooperative associations to buy supplies and to market crops and livestock. In a few instances, Grangers operated farm-implement factories and insurance companies. Most of these enterprises failed, however, because farmers lacked capital for cooperative buying and because competition from large manufacturers and dealers undercut them. For example, the mail-order firm Montgomery Ward could furnish rural customers with cheaper products more conveniently than could Granges. Also, a requirement that Grange cooperatives run on a cash-only basis excluded large numbers of farmers who rarely had cash.

Despite their efforts, Granges declined in the late 1870s. Their promotion of thrift and hard work hardly helped families already practicing both virtues. Grangers had some political successes, convincing states to establish agricultural colleges, electing sympathetic legislators, and pressing for so-called Granger

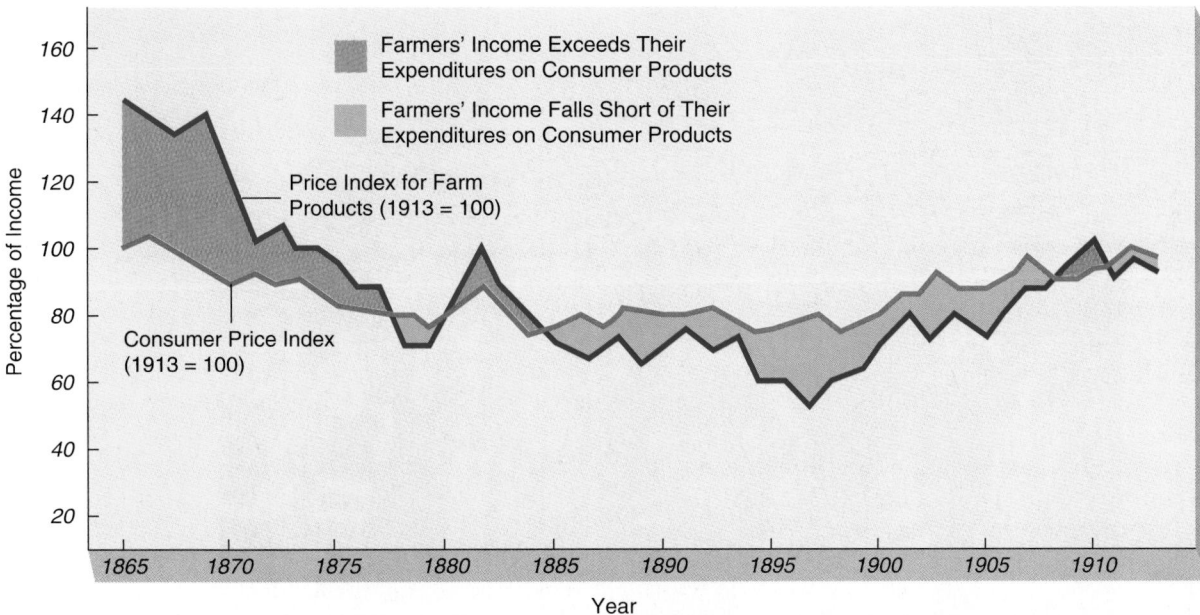

Figure 20.1   Consumer Prices and Farm Product Prices, 1865–1913   Until the late 1870s, in spite of falling farm prices, farmers were able to receive from their crops more income than they spent on consumer goods. But beginning in the mid-1880s, consumer prices leveled off and then rose while prices for farm products continued to drop. As a result, farmers found it increasingly difficult to afford consumer goods, a problem that plagued them well into the twentieth century.

laws to regulate transportation and storage rates. But these efforts faltered when corporations won court support to overturn Granger laws. Granges disavowed party politics but could not withstand the power of business interests within the two major parties. Thus after a brief assertion of economic and political influence, Granges again became farmers' social clubs.

In the Southwest, the movement of English-speaking ranchers into communal pastureland used by Mexican farmers and villagers sparked another kind of agrarian protest. In the late 1880s, a group calling itself *Las Gorras Blancas,* or White Hats, believed that they should have control of lands that their Mexican ancestors had once held. They harassed Anglo ranchers and destroyed the fences that they had erected on public land. Sounding like Grangers and Knights of Labor before them and Populists after them, the White Hats proclaimed in 1889, "Our purpose is to protect the rights and interest of the people in general and especially those of the helpless classes." Their cause, however, could not halt Anglos from legally buying and using public land, and by 1900 many Hispanics had given up farming on their

The White Hats

own to work as agricultural laborers or to migrate into the cities.

By 1890 rural activism shifted to the Farmers' Alliances, two networks of organizations—one in the Great Plains and one in the South—that constituted a new mass movement. (The West also had Alliance groups, but in that region they tended to be smaller and more closely linked to labor radicals, socialist clubs, and antimonopoly organizations.) The first Farmers' Alliances arose in Texas, where hard-pressed small farmers rallied against crop liens, merchants, and railroads in particular, and against money power in general. Using traveling lecturers to recruit members, Alliance leaders extended the movement into other southern states. By 1889 the southern Alliance boasted 2 million members, and a separate Colored Farmers' National Alliance claimed over 1 million black members. A similar movement flourished in the Plains, which by the late 1880s organized 2 million members in Kansas, Nebraska, and the Dakotas.

Farmers' Alliances

Like Granges, Farmers' Alliances fostered community loyalty through rallies, educational meetings,

Exhibited at the Chicago World's Fair of 1893, this cabin was the site of the first Farmers' Alliance meeting in Lampasas County, Texas. Using recruiters, rallies, and meetings replete with slogans such as "We Are All Mortgaged but Our Votes," the organization voiced the grievances of rural America and laid the groundwork for formation of the Populist party in the 1890s.   (Private Collection)

Subtreasury Plan

and cooperative buying and selling agreements. Also, women participated in all Alliance activities. Alliances also opened new paths. Beyond urging democratic cooperation, the Alliance movement proposed the subtreasury plan to relieve shortages of cash and credit, the most serious rural problems. The plan, originating in 1890, had two parts. One called for the federal government to construct warehouses where farmers could store nonperishable crops while awaiting higher prices; the government would then loan farmers Treasury notes amounting to 80 percent of the market price that the stored crops would bring. Farmers could use these notes as legal tender to pay debts and make purchases. Once the stored crops were sold, farmers would repay the loans plus small interest and storage fees. This provision would enable farmers to avoid the exploitative crop-lien system.

The second part of the subtreasury plan would have the government provide low-interest loans to farmers who wanted to buy land. These loans, along with the Treasury notes loaned to farmers who had temporarily stored crops in government warehouses, would inject cash into the economy and encourage the kind of inflation that advocates hoped would raise crop prices without raising other prices. If the government subsidized business through tariffs and land grants, reasoned Alliance members, why should it not help farmers earn a decent living, too?

If all Farmers' Alliances had been able to unite, they would have made a formidable political force; but sectional and racial differences and personality clashes thwarted early attempts at merging. At an 1889 meeting in St. Louis, white southerners, fearing reprisals from landowners and objecting to participation by blacks, rejected proposals that would have ended secret Alliance activities and whites-only membership rules. Northerners, too, renounced amalgamation, fearing domination by more experienced southern leaders. Differences on issues also prevented unity. Northern farmers, mostly Republicans, wanted protective tariffs to keep out foreign grain. White southerners, mostly Democrats, wanted low tariffs to hold down costs of foreign manufactured goods. Northern and southern Alliances both favored government regulation of transportation and communications, equitable taxation, currency reform, and prohibition of landownership by foreign investors.

Growing membership and rising confidence drew Alliances more deeply into politics. By 1890 farmers had elected several officeholders sympathetic to their programs, especially in the South, where Alliances controlled four governorships, eight state legislatures, and forty-seven seats in Congress (forty-four in the House, three in the Senate). In the Midwest, Alliance candidates often ran on third-party tickets and achieved some success in Kansas, Nebraska, and the Dakotas. Leaders crisscrossed the country organizing meetings to solidify support for a third party. During the summer of 1890, the Kansas Alliance held a "convention of the people" and nominated candidates who swept the state's fall elections. Formation of this People's Party, whose members were called Populists (from *populus*, the Latin word for "people"), gave a title to Alliance political activism.

Rise of Populism

Election results in 1890 energized efforts to unite Alliance groups into a single Populist party. A meeting in 1891 of northern and southern Alliances in Cincinnati failed when southerners chose to remain Democrats rather than risk joining a third party. But by 1892 southern Alliance members were ready for independent action. Meeting with northern counterparts in St. Louis, they summoned a People's Party convention in Omaha on July 4 to draft a platform and nominate a presidential candidate.

The new party's platform was an extraordinary reform document. Its preamble charged that the nation had been "brought to the verge of moral, political, and material ruin. Corruption dominates the ballot box, the legislatures, the Congress, and touches . . . even the [courts]." More important, inequality threatened to splinter American society. "The fruits of the toil of millions," the platform declared, "are boldly stolen to build up colossal fortunes for a few." Claiming that "wealth belongs to him that creates it," the Omaha platform addressed three central sources of rural unrest: transportation, land, and money. Frustrated with weak state and federal regulation, Populists demanded government ownership of railroad and telegraph lines. They urged the federal government to reclaim all land owned for speculative purposes by railroads and foreigners. The monetary plank called on the govern-

Mary E. Lease (1850–1933) was one of the founders of the Populist party in Kansas. Tall and intense, she had a deep, almost hypnotic voice that made her an effective publicist for the farmers' cause. She gave a seconding speech to the presidential nomination of James B. Weaver in 1892. (The Kansas State Historical Society, Topeka, Kansas)

ment to expand the currency by printing money to be made available for farm loans and by basing the money on free and unlimited coinage of silver. Other planks advocated a graduated income tax, postal savings banks, direct election of U.S. senators, and a shorter workday. As its presidential candidate, the People's Party nominated James B. Weaver of Iowa, a former Union general and supporter of an increased money supply.

The Populist campaign featured dynamic personalities and vivid rhetoric. The Kansas plains rumbled with speeches by "Sockless Jerry" Simpson, an unschooled but canny rural reformer, and by Mary Elizabeth Lease, a fiery orator who charged that "Wall Street owns the country. The great common people of the country are slaves, and monopoly is the master." The South produced equally forceful leaders, such as Texas's Charles

Election Rhetoric

W. Macune, Georgia's Tom Watson, and North Carolina's Leonidas Polk. Colorado's governor Davis "Bloody Bridles" Waite attacked mine owners with his prolabor and antimonopolist stance. Minnesota's Ignatius Donnelly, pseudoscientist and writer of apocalyptic novels, became chief ideologue of the northern plains and wrote the thunderous language in the Omaha platform. The campaign also attracted characters such as James Hogg, the 300-pound governor of Texas, and one-eyed Senator "Pitchfork Ben" Tillman of South Carolina, who were not genuine Populists but used the agrarian fervor for their own political ends.

Weaver garnered 8 percent of the popular vote in 1892, majorities in four states, and twenty-two electoral votes. Not since 1856 had a third party done so well in its first national effort. Nevertheless, disturbing factors had emerged. The party faced a dilemma of whether to uphold its principles at all costs or compromise in order to gain power. The election had been successful for Populists only in the West. The vote-rich Northeast had ignored Weaver, and Alabama was the only southern state that gave Populists as much as one-third of its votes. More ominously, by the end of 1892 Populist politics had diverted Alliance attention from social and economic reform, and defeat in all three areas caused the movement to wither.

Still, Populism gave rural dwellers in the South and West an emotional faith in the future. Although Populists were flawed egalitarians—they mistrusted blacks and foreigners—they sought change in order to fulfill their version of American ideals. Amid hardship and desperation, millions of people began to believe that a cooperative democracy in which government would ensure equal opportunity could overcome corporate power. A banner draped above the stage at the Omaha convention captured the movement's spirit: "We do not ask for sympathy or pity. We ask for justice."

The Depression of the 1890s

In 1893, shortly before Grover Cleveland's second presidency, the Philadelphia and Reading Railroad, once a thriving and profitable line, went bankrupt. Like other railroads, the Philadelphia and Reading had borrowed heavily to lay track and build stations and bridges. But overexpansion cut into profits, and ultimately the company was unable to pay its debts.

The same problem beset manufacturers. For example, output at McCormick farm machinery factories was nine times greater in 1893 than in 1879, but revenues had only tripled. To compensate, the company bought more factory equipment and squeezed more work out of fewer laborers. This strategy, however, only enlarged debt and unemployment. Jobless workers found themselves in the same plight as employers: they could not pay their creditors. Banks suffered, too, when their customers defaulted. The failure of the National Cordage Company in May 1893 accelerated a chain reaction of business and bank closings. By year's end, five hundred banks and sixteen hundred businesses had failed. A year later, an adviser warned President Cleveland, "We are on the eve of a very dark night." He was right. Between 1893 and 1897, the nation suffered a devastating economic depression.

Personal hardship followed business failures; nearly 20 percent of the labor force were jobless for a significant time during the depression. Falling demand caused prices to drop between 1892 and 1895, but layoffs and wage cuts more than offset declining living costs. Many people could not afford basic necessities. The New York police estimated that twenty thousand homeless and jobless people roamed the city's streets. Surveying the depression's impact on Boston, Henry Adams wrote, "Men died like flies under the strain, and Boston grew suddenly old, haggard, and thin."

As the depression deepened, the currency problem reached a crisis. The Sherman Silver Purchase Act of 1890 had committed the government to issue Treasury notes (silver certificates) to buy 4.5 million ounces of silver each month. These certificates could be redeemed in gold, at the ratio of one ounce of gold for every sixteen ounces of silver. But a western mining boom made silver more plentiful, causing its market value relative to gold to fall and prompting holders of Sherman silver notes and greenback currency issued during the Civil War to cash in their notes in exchange for gold whose worth remained fairly constant. As a result, the nation's gold reserve soon dwindled, falling below $100 million in early 1893.

Continuing Currency Problems

The $100 million level had psychological importance. If investors believed that the country's gold reserve was disappearing, they would lose confidence in America's economic stability and refrain from investing. British capitalists, for example, owned some $4 billion in American stocks and bonds. If the dollar were to depreciate too much, they would sell their holdings and stop investing in American economic growth. In fact, the lower the gold reserve dropped, the more people rushed to redeem their money and securities—to get gold before it disappeared. Panic spread, causing more bankruptcies and unemployment.

Vowing to protect the gold reserve from redeemers of silver certificates, President Cleveland called a special session of Congress to repeal the Sherman Silver Purchase Act. Repeal passed in late 1893, but the run on the Treasury continued through 1894. In early 1895 gold reserves fell to $41 million. In desperation, Cleveland accepted an offer of 3.5 million ounces of gold in return for $65 million worth of federal bonds from a banking syndicate led by financier J. P. Morgan. When the bankers resold the bonds to the public, they made about $2 million in profits. Cleveland claimed that he had saved the gold reserves, but discontented farmers, workers, silver miners, and even some of Cleveland's Democratic allies saw only humiliation in the president's deal with big businessmen. "When Judas betrayed Christ," charged Senator Tillman, "his heart was not blacker than this scoundrel, Cleveland, in betraying the [Democratic Party]."

Few people knew what the president was really enduring. At about the time Cleveland called Congress into special session, doctors discovered a malignant tumor on his palate that required immediate removal. Fearful that publicity of his illness would hasten the run on gold, and intent on preventing Vice President Adlai E. Stevenson, a silver supporter, from gaining influence, Cleveland kept his condition a secret. He announced that he was going sailing, and doctors removed his cancerous upper left jaw while the yacht floated outside New York City. Outfitted with a rubber jaw, Cleveland resumed a full schedule five days later, hiding terrible pain to dispel rumors that he was seriously ill. He eventually recovered, but those who knew of his surgery believed it had sapped his vitality.

The deal between Cleveland and Morgan did not end the depression. After improving slightly in 1895, the economy plunged again. Farm income, declining since 1887, continued to slide; factories closed; banks that remained open restricted withdrawals. The tight money supply depressed housing construction, drying up important jobs and reducing immigration. Cities such as Detroit allowed citizens to cultivate "potato patches" on vacant land to help alleviate food shortages. Each night urban police stations filled up with vagrants who had no place to stay.

Like previous hard times, the depression ultimately ran its course. In the final years of the century, gold discoveries in Alaska, good harvests, and industrial growth brought relief. But the downturn of the 1890s hastened the crumbling of the old economic

Effects of a New Economic System

system and the emergence of a new one. Since the 1850s, railroads had steered American economic development, opening new markets, boosting steel production, and invigorating banking. The central features of a new business system—consolidation and a trend toward bigness—were beginning to solidify just when the depression hit.

The American economy had become national rather than sectional; the fate of a large business in one part of the country had repercussions elsewhere. Before the depression many companies had expanded too rapidly. When contraction occurred, their reckless debts dragged them down, and they pulled other industries with them. In early 1893, for example, thirty-two steel companies, five hundred banks, and sixteen thousand other businesses filed for bankruptcy. European economies also slumped, and more than ever before the fortunes of one country affected the fortunes of other countries.

American farmers had to contend not only with discriminatory transportation rates and falling crop prices at home, but also with Canadian and Russian wheat growers, Argentine cattle ranchers, Indian and Egyptian cotton producers, and Australian wool producers. When farmers fell into debt and lost purchasing power, their depressed condition in turn affected the economic health of railroads, farm-implement manufacturers, banks, and other businesses. As well, the glutted domestic market persuaded businessmen to seek new markets abroad (see Chapter 22). The downward spiral ended late in 1897, but the depression exposed problems that demanded reform and set an agenda for future years.

Depression-Era Protests

The depression exposed fundamental tensions in the industrial system. Technological and organizational changes had been widening the gap between employees and employers for half a century. By the 1890s workers' protests against exploitation were threatening to spark an economic and political explosion. In 1894, the year the economy plunged into depression, there were over thirteen hundred strikes and countless riots. Contrary to accusations of business leaders, few protesters were anarchists or communists come from Europe to sabotage American democracy. Rather, the disaffected included thousands of men and women who believed that in a democracy their voices should be heard.

The era of protest began with the railroad strikes of 1877 (see page 499). The vehemence of those strikes, and the support they drew from working-class people, raised fears that the United States would experience a popular uprising like one in Paris six years earlier, which had briefly overturned the government and introduced communist principles. The Haymarket riot of 1886, a general strike in New Orleans in 1891, and a prolonged strike at the Carnegie Homestead Steel plant in 1892 (see page 502) heightened anxieties. In the West, embittered workers also took action. In 1892 violence erupted at a silver mine in Coeur d'Alene, Idaho. Angered by wage cuts and a lockout, striking miners seized the mine and battled federal troops sent to subdue them. Such defiance convinced some businessmen that only force could counter the radicalism allegedly promoted by socialists and anarchists.

Socialists

Small numbers of socialists did participate in these and other confrontations. Furthermore, personal experience convinced many workers who never became socialists to agree with Karl Marx (1818–1883), the German philosopher and father of communism, that whoever controls the means of production holds the power to determine how well people live. Marx wrote that industrial capitalism generates profits by paying workers less than the value of their labor and that mechanization and mass production alienate workers from their labor. Thus, Marx contended, capitalists and laborers engage in an inescapable conflict over how much workers will benefit from their efforts. According to Marx, only by abolishing the return on capital—profits—could labor receive its true value, an outcome possible only if workers owned the means of production. Marx predicted that workers throughout the world would become so discontented that they would revolt and seize factories, farms, banks, and transportation lines. This revolution would establish a socialist order of justice and equality. Marx's vision appealed to some workers because it promised independence and abundance. It appealed to some intellectuals because it promised to end class conflict and crude materialism.

In America, socialism suffered from lack of strong leadership and disagreement over how to achieve Marx's vision. It splintered into small groups, such as the Socialist Labor Party, led by Daniel DeLeon, a fiery West Indian–born lawyer. DeLeon and other socialist leaders failed to attract the mass of unskilled laborers, even though many immigrant workers had been exposed to socialism in Europe. American social-

ists often focused on fine points of doctrine while ignoring workers' everyday needs; they could not rebut the clergy and business leaders who celebrated opportunity, self-improvement, and consumerism. Social mobility and the philosophy of individualism also undermined socialist aims. Workers hoped that they or their children would benefit through education and acquisition of property or by becoming their own bosses; thus most workers sought individual advancement rather than the betterment of all.

Eugene V. Debs

Events in 1894 triggered changes within the socialist movement. That year an inspiring new leader arose in response to the government's quashing of the Pullman strike and of the newly formed American Railway Union. Eugene V. Debs, the union's intense and animated president, converted to socialism while serving a six-month prison term for defying an injunction against the strike (see page 502). Once released, Debs became the leading spokesman for American socialism, combining visionary Marxism with Jeffersonian and Populist antimonopolism. Though never good at organizing, Debs captivated audiences with passionate eloquence and indignant attacks on the free-enterprise system. "Many of you think you are competing," he would lecture. "Against whom? Against Rockefeller? About as I would if I had a wheelbarrow and competed with the Santa Fe [railroad] from here to Kansas City." By 1900 the group soon to be called the Socialist Party of America was uniting around Debs. It would make its presence felt more forcefully in the new century.

Coxey's Army

In 1894 Debs shared public attention with Jacob S. Coxey, a quiet businessman from Massillon, Ohio. Like Debs, Coxey had a vision. He was convinced that, to aid debtors, the government should issue $500 million of "legal tender" paper money, make low-interest loans to local governments, and use the loans and money to pay the unemployed to build roads and other public works. He planned to publicize his scheme by leading a march from Massillon to Washington, D.C., gathering a "petition in boots" of unemployed workers along the way. Coxey even christened his newborn son Legal Tender and proposed that his teenage daughter lead the procession on a white horse.

Coxey's army, about two hundred strong, left in March 1894. Moving across Ohio into Pennsylvania, they received food and housing in depressed industrial towns and rural villages, and they won new recruits. Elsewhere, a dozen similar processions from places such as Seattle, San Francisco, and Los Angeles also began the trek eastward. Sore feet prompted some marchers to commandeer trains, but most processions were peaceful and law-abiding. One official called the marchers the "idle, useless dregs of humanity," but the troops kept themselves and their camps clean and well organized.

While other marchers were still on the road, Coxey's citizen army of five hundred, including women and children, entered Washington on April 30. The next day (May Day, a date traditionally associated with socialist demonstrations), the group, armed with "war clubs of peace," marched to the Capitol. When Coxey and a few others vaulted the wall surrounding the Capitol grounds, mounted police moved in and routed the crowd. Coxey tried to speak from the Capitol steps, but police dragged him away. As arrests and clubbings continued, Coxey's dream of a demonstration of 400,000 jobless workers dissolved. Like the strikes, the first people's march on Washington yielded to police muscle.

Unlike socialists, who wished to replace the capitalist system, Coxey's troops merely wanted more jobs and better living standards. Today, in an age of union contracts, regulation of business, and government-sponsored unemployment relief, their goals do not appear radical. The brutal reactions of officials, however, reveal how threatening dissenters such as Coxey and Debs seemed to defenders of the existing social order.

Populists, the Silver Crusade, and the Election of 1896

Populists did not suffer the suppression that unions and Coxey's army experienced, but they encountered roadblocks just when their political goals seemed attainable. As late as 1894, Populist candidates made good showings in elections in the West and South. Like earlier third parties, though, Populists were underfinanced and underorganized. They had strong and colorful candidates but not enough of them to effectively challenge the major parties. Voters remained reluctant to abandon old loyalties to the Republicans or Democrats.

Issues of race also permeated politics. The possibility of biracial political action posed by Farmers' Alliances in the early 1890s failed for two reasons. First, as noted above, southern white Democrats had succeeded in creating restrictions on voting rights that prevented African Americans from becoming a political force. Second, raw racism impeded the acceptance

Stifling of Biracial Dissent

of blacks by white Populists. Some Populists did seek to unite distressed black and white farmers. Tom Watson, Georgia's prominent Populist, noted that "the crushing burdens which now oppress both races in the South will cause each to . . . see a similarity of cause and a similarity of remedy." But poor white farmers could not forgo their racism. Many came from families that had supported the Ku Klux Klan during Reconstruction. Some had owned slaves, considered African Americans a permanently inferior people, and took comfort in the belief that there always would be people worse off than they were. Thus few Populists addressed the needs of black farmers, and many used white-supremacist rhetoric to guard against accusations that they encouraged race-mixing.

In the national arena, the Populist crusade against "money power" settled on the issue of silver. Many people saw silver as a simple solution to the nation's complex ills. To them, free coinage of silver meant the end

Free Silver

Published in 1894, *Coin's Financial School* by William H. Harvey expressed the position of free silver in simple language and illustrations. Written in the form of lectures on the money question given by "Professor Coin," Harvey's book had enormous appeal to distressed farmers. (Trustees of the Boston Public Library)

mercilessly scourges the money changers in the Temple of the Republic.
—*New York Recorder.*

This book tells its readers more about gold, silver and currency generally than any other publication we know of, and in a way that every man can fully comprehend.
—*Chicago Inter Ocean.*

Coin's Financial School

PUBLISHERS
COIN PUBLISHING COMPANY

During the 1896 presidential campaign, Republicans depicted their candidate, William McKinley, as holding the key to prosperity for both the working man and the white-collar laborer, shown here raising their hats to the candidate. Republicans successfully made this economic theme, rather than the silver crusade of McKinley's unsuccessful opponent, William Jennings Bryan, the difference in the election's outcome.   (Collection of David J. and Janice L. Frent)

of special privileges for the rich and the return of government to the people. Populists agreed and made free coinage of silver their political battle cry.

As the election of 1896 approached, Populists had to decide how to translate their few previous electoral victories into larger success. Should they join with sympathetic factions of the major parties, thus risking a loss of identity, or should they remain an independent third party and settle for minor wins at best? Except in Rocky Mountain states, where free coinage of silver had strong support, Republicans were unlikely allies because their support for the gold standard and big-business orientation represented what Populists opposed.

In the North and West, alliance with Democrats was more plausible. There, the Democratic Party retained vestiges of antimonopoly ideology and some sympathy for a looser currency system, although "gold Democrats" such as President Cleveland and Senator David Hill of New York held powerful influence. Populists assumed they shared common interests with Democratic urban workers, who they believed suffered the same oppression that beset farmers. In the

South, fusion with Democrats seemed less likely, since there the party constituted the very power structure against which farmers had revolted in the late 1880s. Whichever option they chose, fusion or independence, Populists ensured that the political campaign of 1896 would be the most issue-oriented election since 1860.

The 1896 presidential election climaxed a generation of political turbulence. Each party was divided.

Republican Nomination of McKinley

Republicans, directed by Marcus A. Hanna, a prosperous Ohio industrialist, had only minor problems. For a year, Hanna had been maneuvering to win the nomination for Ohio's governor, William McKinley. By the time the party convened in St. Louis, Hanna had corralled enough delegates to succeed. "He had advertised McKinley," quipped Theodore Roosevelt, "as if he were a patent medicine." The Republicans' only distress occurred when they adopted a moderate platform supporting gold, rejecting a prosilver stance proposed by Colorado's Senator Henry M. Teller. Teller, who had been among the party's founders forty years earlier, walked out of the convention in tears, taking a small group of silver Republicans with him.

At the Democratic convention, prosilver delegates wearing silver badges and waving silver banners paraded through the Chicago Amphitheatre. Observing their tumultuous demonstrations, one delegate wrote, "For the first time I can understand the scenes of the French Revolution!" A *New York World* reporter remarked that "All the silverites need is a Moses." They soon found one in William Jennings Bryan.

Bryan, age thirty-six, arrived at the Democratic convention as a member of a contested Nebraska delegation. A former congressman whose support for coinage of silver had annoyed President Cleveland, he was highly distressed by the depression's impact on midwestern farmers. The convention seated Bryan and his colleagues instead of a competing faction that supported the gold standard. Shortly afterward, as a member of the party's resolutions committee, Bryan helped write a platform calling for free coinage of silver. When the committee presented the platform to the full convention, Bryan rose to speak on its behalf. Bryan's now-famous closing words ignited the delegates:

William Jennings Bryan

> Having behind us the producing masses of this nation and the world, supported by the commercial interests, the laboring interests, and the toilers everywhere, we will answer [the wealthy classes'] demand for a gold standard by saying to them: You shall not press down upon the brow of labor this crown of thorns, you shall not crucify mankind upon a cross of gold.

The speech could not have been better timed. Delegates who backed Bryan for president now had no trouble enlisting support. It took five ballots to win the nomination, but the magnetic "Boy Orator" proved irresistible. In accepting the silverite goals of southerners and westerners and repudiating Cleveland's policies in its platform, the Democratic Party became more attractive to discontented farmers. But like the Republicans, it, too, alienated a dissenting minority wing. Some gold Democrats withdrew and nominated their own candidate.

Bryan's nomination presented the Populist party (as it was now called) with a dilemma. Should Populists join Democrats in support of Bryan, or should they nominate their own candidate? Tom Watson, expressing opposition to fusion with Democrats, warned that "the Democratic idea of fusion [is] that we play Jonah while they play whale." Others reasoned that supporting a different candidate would split the anti-

William Jennings Bryan (1860–1925) posed for this photograph in 1896, when he first ran for president at the age of thirty-six. Bryan's emotional speeches turned agrarian unrest and the issue of free silver into a moral crusade.
(Library of Congress)

McKinley vote and guarantee a Republican victory. In the end the convention compromised, first naming Watson as its vice-presidential nominee to preserve party identity (Democrats had nominated Maine shipping magnate Arthur Sewall for vice president) and then nominating Bryan for president.

The campaign, as Kansas journalist William Allen White observed, "took the form of religious frenzy . . . as the crusaders of the revolution rode home, praising the people's will as though it were God's will and cursing wealth for its iniquity." The campaign rhetoric rang with emotionalism. Bryan preached that "every great economic question is in reality a great moral question." Republicans countered Bryan's evangelism and attacks on privilege by predicting chaos if he won. While Bryan raced around the country giving twenty speeches a day, Hanna invited thousands of people to

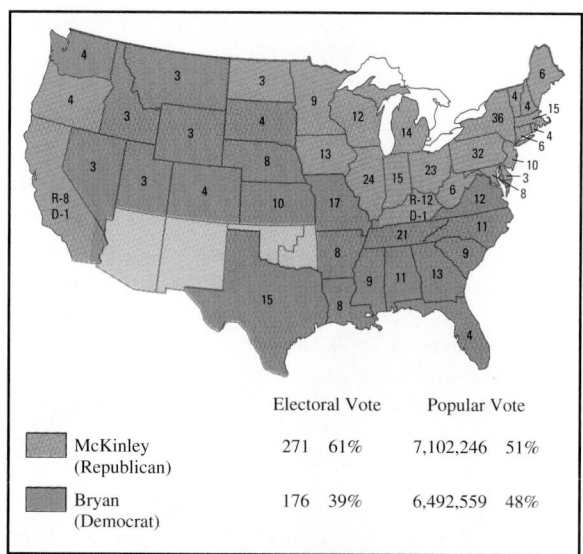

	Electoral Vote		Popular Vote	
McKinley (Republican)	271	61%	7,102,246	51%
Bryan (Democrat)	176	39%	6,492,559	48%

Map 20.1   Presidential Election, 1896   William Jennings Bryan had strong voter support in the South and West, but the numerically superior industrial states, plus California, created majorities for William McKinley.

McKinley's home in Canton, Ohio, where the candidate plied them with homilies on moderation and prosperity, promising something for everyone. In an appeal to working-class voters, Republicans stressed the new jobs that a protective tariff would create.

The election results revealed that the political standoff had finally ended. McKinley, symbol of Republican pragmatism and corporate ascendancy, beat Bryan by over 600,000 popular votes and won in the electoral college by 271 to 176 (see Map 20.1). It was the most lopsided presidential election since 1872.

Election Results

Bryan worked hard to rally the nation, but obsession with silver undermined his effort and prevented Populists from building the urban-rural coalition that would have expanded their political appeal. The silver issue diverted voters from focusing on broader reforms deriving from the Alliance movement and the Omaha platform of 1892. Reformer Henry Demarest Lloyd summarized the matter succinctly: "Free silver," he wrote, "is the cowbird of the reform movement. It waited till the nest had been built by the sacrifices and labor of others, and then it laid its eggs in it, pushing out the others which it smashed to the ground." Urban workers, who might have benefited from Populist goals, shied away from the silver issue out of fear that free coinage would reduce the value of their wages. Labor leaders such as the AFL's Samuel Gompers, though partly sympathetic, would not commit themselves fully because they viewed farmers as businessmen, not workers. And socialists such as Daniel DeLeon denounced Populists as "retrograde" because they, unlike socialists, believed in free enterprise. Thus the Populist crusade collapsed. Although Populists and fusion candidates won a few state and congressional elections in 1896, the Bryan-Watson ticket of the Populist party polled only 222,600 votes nationwide.

As president, McKinley signed the Gold Standard Act (1900), requiring that all paper money be backed by gold. A seasoned and personable politician, McKinley was best known for crafting protective tariffs; as a congressman from Ohio, he had guided passage of record-high tariff rates in 1890. He accordingly supported the Dingley Tariff of 1897, which raised duties even higher. Domestic tensions subsided during McKinley's presidency; an upward swing of the business cycle and a money supply enlarged by gold discoveries in Alaska, Australia, and South Africa helped restore prosperity. A believer in opening new markets abroad to sustain prosperity at home, McKinley encouraged imperialistic ventures in Latin America and the Pacific (see Chapter 22). Good times and victory in the Spanish-American-Cuban-Filipino War enabled him to beat Bryan again in 1900, using the slogan "The Full Dinner Pail."

The McKinley Presidency

Summary

 Government during the Gilded Age succeeded in making many modest, and some major, accomplishments. Guided by well-meaning, generally competent people, much of what occurred in statehouses, the halls of Congress, and the White House prepared the nation for the twentieth century. Laws encouraging economic growth with some principles of regulation, measures expanding government agencies while reducing crass patronage, federal intervention in trade and currency issues, and a more active presidency all evolved during the 1870s and 1880s. Extremists such as "Pitchfork Ben" Tillman and those who supported disfranchisement of African Americans and continued discrimination against both blacks and women still polluted politics. Nor could the system tolerate radical views such as those expressed by socialists, Coxey, or Populists. But many politicians concerned themselves with

more than patronage and influence; most genuinely wanted to create what they believed was a good society.

The 1896 election realigned national politics. The Republican Party, founded in the 1850s amid a crusade against slavery, became the majority party by emphasizing active government aid to business expansion, expanding its social base to include urban workers, and playing down its moralism. The Democratic Party miscalculated on the silver issue and held its traditional support only in the South. After 1896, however, party loyalties lacked the potency they once had. Suspicion of party politics increased, and voter participation rates declined. A new kind of politics was brewing, one in which technical experts and scientific organization would attempt to supplant the backroom deals and favoritism that had characterized the previous age.

In retrospect, it is easy to see that the Populists never had a chance. The political system lacked the ability to accept third parties. The structure of Congress was such that the two-party system had enormous power, making it difficult for the few Populist representatives even to speak, let alone serve on important committees and promote reform legislation.

Nevertheless, by 1920 many Populist goals were achieved, including regulation of railroads, banks, and utilities; shorter workdays; a variant of the subtreasury plan; a graduated income tax; direct election of senators; and the secret ballot. These reforms succeeded because a variety of groups united behind them. Immigration, urbanization, and industrialization had transformed the United States into a pluralistic society in which compromise among interest groups had become a political fact of life. As the Gilded Age ended, business was still in the ascendancy, and large segments of the population were still excluded from political and economic opportunity. But the winds of dissent and reform had begun to blow more strongly.

LEGACY FOR A PEOPLE AND A NATION
Politics and Popular Culture

The Wizard of Oz, one of the most popular movies of all time, began as a Populist fable penned by journalist L. Frank Baum in 1900. Originally titled "The Wonderful Wizard of Oz," the story used memorable characters to represent the conditions of overburdened farmers and laborers. Dorothy symbolized the well-intentioned common person; the Scarecrow, the struggling farmer; the Tin Man, the industrial worker.

Hoping for a better life, these new friends, along with the Cowardly Lion (William Jennings Bryan with a loud roar but little power), followed a yellow brick road (the gold standard) that led nowhere. Along their journey, they encountered the Wicked Witch of the East, who, Baum wrote, kept the little people (Munchkins) "in bondage, . . . making them slaves for her night and day." They also met the Wicked Witch of the West, who symbolized industrial corporations. The Emerald City they find is presided over by the Wizard of Oz (oz. is the abbreviation for ounces, the chief measurement of gold), who rules from behind a screen. A typical politician, the Wizard tries to be all things to all people, but Dorothy and her friends reveal him as a fraud, just "a little man, with a bald head and a wrinkled face." Dorothy is able to leave this muddled society and return to her simple Kansas farm family of Aunt Em and Uncle Henry by using her magical silver slippers (coinage of silver).

Baum used his tale to argue that powerful leaders were deceiving and manipulating ordinary people. He believed that if *Oz* exposed what really was going on, the people—no longer ignorant—would be outraged by the greed and deceit of politicians and industrialists, and would act. But this message disappeared when Metro Goldwyn Mayer (MGM) bought Baum's story and made it into a full-length motion picture to showcase their new child star, Judy Garland. The movie came out in 1939 and was an instant success. Broadcast on television since 1956, it is seen by millions each year.

The saga of *The Wizard of Oz* shows how modern popular culture can subsume politics. The adventures of four endearing characters came to have more appeal than their political symbolism. The rise of movies, television, and sports also altered the nature of fame. Whereas in the Gilded Age politicians held the spotlight as the nation's chief celebrities, by the twentieth century they had been bumped into the background. And instead of popular culture, such as Baum's fable, influencing politics, the legacy to a people and a nation has been the opportunity of some celebrities to use popular culture to become politicians. Thus the nation has seen movie stars and sports personalities become governors, senators, representatives, and even president.

For Further Reading, see page A-23 of the Appendix. For Web resources, go to http://college.hmco.com.

A coworker once described Florence Kelley as a "guerrilla warrior" in the "wilderness of industrial wrongs." A woman of sharp wit and commanding presence, Kelley accomplished as much as anyone in guiding the United States out of the tangled swamp of unregulated industrial capitalism into the uncharted seas of the twentieth-century welfare state.

Kelley's career traced a remarkable odyssey. Raised in middle-class comfort in Philadelphia, the daughter of a Republican congressman, Kelley graduated from Cornell in 1883. She prepared to study law, but the University of Pennsylvania denied her admission to its graduate school because of her gender. Instead, she traveled to Europe. In Zurich, Kelley joined a group of socialists who alerted her to the plight of the underprivileged. She married a socialist Russian medical student and returned to New York City in 1886. When the marriage collapsed from debts and physical abuse, Kelley took her three children to Chicago in 1891 to obtain a divorce. Later that year she moved into Hull House, a residence in the slums where middle-class reformers went to live in order to help and learn from working-class immigrants. There her transforming work truly began.

Until the 1890s, Kelley's life had been male-oriented, influenced first by her father, then by her husband. She had tried to enter public life by attending law school and participating in political organizations, but men had blocked her path at every turn. At Hull House, however, Kelley entered a female-dominated environment, where women sought to apply helping skills to the betterment of society. This environment encouraged Kelley to assert her powerful abilities.

Over the next decade, Kelley became the nation's most ardent advocate of improved conditions for working-class women and children. She investigated and publicized the exploitative sweatshop system in Chicago's garment industry, lobbied for laws to prohibit child labor and regulate women's working hours, and served as Illinois's first factory inspector. Her work

During the Progressive era, reformers advocated new ways of thinking and new techniques to achieve progress in a variety of fields. Progressive educators, for example, cast aside rigid methods of memorization and discipline in favor of encouraging children to use their minds and hands in ways that were relevant to their lives. (Library of Congress)

THE PROGRESSIVE ERA 1895–1920

helped create new professions for women in social service, and her strategy of investigating, publicizing, and crusading for action became a model for reform. Perhaps most significant, she and fellow reformers like Jane Addams and Lillian Wald enlisted government to aid in the solution of social problems.

During the 1890s economic depression, labor violence, political upheaval, and foreign entanglements shook the nation. Technology had fulfilled many promises, but great numbers of Americans continued to suffer from poverty and disease. Some critics regarded industrialists as monsters who controlled markets, wages, and prices for the sole purpose of maximizing profits. Others believed government was corroded by bosses who enriched themselves through politics. Tensions created by urbanization and industrialization seemed to be fragmenting society into conflicting interest groups.

By 1900, however, the political tumult of the previous decade had died down, and the economic depression seemed to be over. The nation emerged victorious from a war (see Chapter 22), and a new era of dynamic political leaders such as Theodore Roosevelt and Woodrow Wilson was dawning. A sense of renewal served both to intensify anxiety over continuing social and political problems and to raise hopes that somehow such problems could be fixed and democracy could be reconciled with capitalism.

From these circumstances there emerged a complex, and many-sided, reform campaign. By the 1910s many reformers were calling themselves "Progressives"; in 1912 they formed a political party by that name to embody their principles. Historians have uniformly used the term *Progressivism* to refer to the era's reformist spirit while disagreeing over its meaning and over which groups and individuals actually were Progressive. Nonetheless, the era between 1895 and 1920 included a series of movements, each aiming in one way or another to renovate or restore American society, values, and institutions.

This painting (1904) by Everett Shinn depicts the disastrous consequences of poverty and the unkept promise of American life. Unable to pay the rent, thousands of families, along with their meager belongings, were forced into the streets. A painter of the so-called Ashcan School, Shinn captured the distress of poverty-stricken families forced to experience this humiliation.   (National Museum of American Art, Washington, D.C./Art Resource, N.Y.)

IMPORTANT EVENTS

1893 Anti-Saloon League founded

1895 Washington gives Atlanta Compromise
speech
National Association of Colored Women
founded

1896 *Holden v. Hardy* upholds limits on miners'
working hours

1900 McKinley reelected

1901 McKinley assassinated; T. Roosevelt
assumes the presidency

1904 T. Roosevelt elected president
Northern Securities case dissolves railroad trust

1905 Niagara Conference promotes African
American rights
Lochner v. New York removes limits on
bakers' working hours

1906 Hepburn Act tightens control over railroads
Sinclair's *The Jungle* exposes poor condi-
tions in meatpacking plants
Meat Inspection Act passed
Pure Food and Drug Act passed

1907 Reckless speculation causes economic panic

1908 Taft elected president
Muller v. Oregon upholds limits on women's
working hours

1909 NAACP founded
Payne-Aldrich Tariff passed

1910 Mann-Elkins Act reinforces ICC powers
White Slave Traffic Act prohibits transportation of women for "immoral purposes"
Ballinger-Pinchot controversy angers conservationists

1911 Society of American Indians founded

1912 T. Roosevelt runs for president on the
Progressive (Bull Moose) ticket
Wilson elected president

1913 Sixteenth Amendment ratified, legalizing
federal income tax
Seventeenth Amendment ratified, providing
for direct election of U.S. senators
Underwood Tariff institutes income tax
Federal Reserve Act establishes central banking system

1914 Federal Trade Commission created to
investigate unfair trade practices
Clayton Anti-Trust Act outlaws monopolistic
business practices
Sanger indicted for sending articles on contraception through the mail

1916 Wilson reelected
Federal Farm Loan Act provides credit to
farmers
Adamson Act mandates eight-hour workday
for railroad workers

1919 Eighteenth Amendment ratified, establishing
prohibition of alcoholic beverages

1920 Nineteenth Amendment ratified, giving
women the vote in federal elections

1921 Sanger founds American Birth Control
League

The reform impulse had many sources. Industrial capitalism had created awesome technology, unprecedented productivity, and a cornucopia of consumer goods. But it also brought harmful overproduction, domineering monopolies, labor strife, and the spoiling of natural resources. Burgeoning cities facilitated the amassing and distribution of goods, services, and cultural amenities; they also bred poverty, disease, and crime. Inflows of immigrants and the rise of a new class of managers and professionals reconfigured the social order. And the depression of the 1890s forced many leading citizens to realize what working people had known for some time: the central promise of American life was not being kept; equality of opportunity was a myth.

In addressing these problems, Progressives organized their ideas and actions around three goals. First, they sought to end abuses of power. Attacks on unfair privilege, monopoly, and corruption were not new; Jacksonian reformers of the 1830s and 1840s and Populists of the 1890s belonged to the same tradition. Progressives, however, intensified the attacks. Trust-busting, consumers' rights, and good government became compelling political issues.

Second, Progressives aimed to supplant corrupt power with humane institutions such as schools,

Judge Ben Lindsey (1869–1943) of Denver was a Progressive reformer who worked for children's legal protection. Like many reformers of his era, Lindsey had an earnest faith in the ability of humankind to build a better world.   (Library of Congress)

charities, and medical clinics. Though eager to protect individual rights, they abandoned individualistic notions that hard work and good character automatically ensured success and that the poor had only themselves to blame for their plight. Instead, Progressives acknowledged that society had responsibility and power to improve individual lives, and they believed that government, acting for society at large, must intervene in social and economic affairs to protect the common good and elevate public interest above self-interest. Their revolt against fixed categories of thought challenged entrenched views on women's roles, race relations, education, legal and scientific thought, and morality.

Third, Progressives wanted to apply scientific principles and efficient management to economic, social, and political institutions. Their aim was to establish bureaus of experts that would end wasteful competition and promote social and economic order. Science and the scientific method—planning, control, and predictability—were their central values. Just as corporations applied scientific management techniques to achieve economic efficiency, Progressives advocated expertise and planning to achieve social and political efficiency.

Befitting their name, Progressives had deep faith in the ability of humankind to create a better world. They used phrases such as "humanity's universal growth" and "the upward spiral of human development." Optimism arising from rising incomes, new educational opportunities, and increased availability of goods and services created an aura of confidence that social improvement would follow. Judge Ben Lindsey of Denver, who spearheaded reform in the treatment of juvenile delinquents, expressed the Progressive creed when he wrote, "In the end the people are bound to do the right thing, no matter how much they fail at times." ◼

The Varied Progressive Impulse

 Progressive reformers addressed vexing issues that had surfaced in the previous half-century, but they did so in a new political climate. As the twentieth century dawned, party loyalty eroded and voter turnout declined. In northern states, voter participation in presidential elections dropped from Gilded Age levels of over 80 percent of the eligible electorate to less than 60 percent. In southern states, where taxes and literacy

tests excluded most African Americans and many poor whites from the polls, it fell below 30 percent. Parties and elections, it seemed, were losing influence over government policies. At the same time, the political system was opening to new interest groups, each of which championed its own cause.

Local voluntary associations had existed since the 1790s, but many organizations became nationwide in scope after the 1890s and tried to shape public policy to meet their needs and goals. These organizations included professional associations such as the American Bar Association; women's organizations such as the National American Woman Suffrage Association; issue-oriented groups such as the National Consumers League; civic clubs such as the National Municipal League; and minority-group associations, such as the National Negro Business League and the Society of American Indians. Because they usually acted independently of either of the established political parties, such groups made politics more fragmented and issue-focused than in earlier eras.

Also, American politics became receptive to foreign models and ideas for reorganizing society. A

Foreign Influences

variety of programs and proposals traveled across the Atlantic; some were introduced by Americans such as Florence Kelley who had observed reforms in England, France, and Germany, others by foreigners traveling in the United States. (Europeans also learned of American reforms, but the balance of the idea flow tilted toward the United States.) Such reforms as old-age insurance, subsidized workers' housing, city planning, and rural reconstruction originated abroad and were adopted or modified in America.

Although goals of the rural-based Populist movement lingered—moral regeneration, political democracy, and antimonopolism—the Progressive quest for social justice, educational and legal reform, and government streamlining had a largely urban bent. Between 1890 and 1920 the proportion of the nation's population living in cities swelled from 35 percent to 51 percent; the number of cities with fifty thousand or more people rose from 58 to 144. By utilizing advances in mail, telephone, and telegraph communications, urban reformers exchanged information and coordinated efforts to alleviate the consequences of this change.

Organizations and individuals intent on achieving Progressive goals—ending the abuse of power, reforming social institutions, and promoting bureaucratic and scientific efficiency—existed in almost all

Urban Middle-Class Reformers and Muckrakers

levels of society. But the new middle class—men and women in professions of law, medicine, engineering, social work, religion, teaching, and business—formed the vanguard of reform. Offended by inefficiency and immorality in business, government, and human relations, these people set out to apply rational techniques they had learned in their professions to problems of the larger society.

Their indignation motivated many middle-class Progressive reformers to seek an end to abuses of power. Their views were voiced by journalists whom Theodore Roosevelt dubbed muckrakers (after a character in the Puritan allegory *Pilgrim's Progress* who, rather than looking heavenward at beauty, looked downward and raked the muck to find what was wrong with life). Muckrakers fed public taste for scandal and sensation by exposing social, economic, and political wrongs. Their investigative articles in *McClure's*, *Cosmopolitan*, and other popular magazines attacked adulterated foods, fraudulent insurance, prostitution, and other offenses. Lincoln Steffens's articles in *McClure's*, later published as *The Shame of the Cities* (1904), epitomized the muckraking style. Steffens hoped his exposés of bosses' misrule would inspire mass outrage and, ultimately, reform. Other well-known muckraking efforts included Upton Sinclair's *The Jungle* (1906), a novel that disclosed crimes of the meatpacking industry; Ida M. Tarbell's critical history of Standard Oil (1904); Burton J. Hendrick's *Story of Life Insurance* (1907); and David Graham Phillips's *Treason of the Senate* (1906).

To improve politics, Progressives advocated nominating candidates through direct primaries instead of party caucuses and holding nonpartisan elections to prevent the fraud and bribery bred by party loyalties. To make officeholders more responsible, Progressives pressed for three reforms: the initiative, which permitted voters to propose new laws; the referendum, which enabled voters to accept or reject a law; and the recall, which allowed voters to remove offending officials and judges from office before their terms expired. Their goal, like that of the business-consolidation movement, was efficiency: they would reclaim government by replacing the boss system with accountable managers chosen by a responsible electorate.

The Progressive spirit also stirred some elite business leaders. Executives like Alexander Cassatt of the Pennsylvania Railroad supported some government regulation and political reforms to protect their interests from more radical reformers. Others, like

Upper-Class Reformers

E. A. Filene, founder of a Boston department store, and Tom Johnson, a Cleveland streetcar magnate, were humanitarians who worked unselfishly for social justice. Business-dominated organizations like the Municipal Voters League and U.S. Chamber of Commerce thought that running schools, hospitals, and local government like efficient businesses would help stabilize society. Elite women often led organizations like the Young Women's Christian Association (YWCA), which aided growing numbers of unmarried working women, and the Women's Christian Temperance Union (WCTU), the largest women's organization of its time, which supported numerous causes besides abstinence from drinking.

Not all Progressives were middle- or upper-class. Vital elements of what became modern American liberalism derived from working-class urban experiences. By 1900 many urban workers were pressing for government intervention to ensure safety and security. They advocated "bread-and-butter reforms" such as safe factories, shorter workdays, workers' compensation, better housing, and health safeguards. Often these were the same people who supported political bosses, supposedly the enemies of reform. In fact, bossism was not necessarily at odds with humanitarianism. When "Big Tim" Sullivan, an influential boss in New York City's Tammany Hall political machine, was asked why he supported a shorter workday for women, he explained, "I had seen me sister go out to work when she was only fourteen and I know we ought to help these gals by giving 'em a law which will prevent 'em from being broken down while they're still young."

Working-Class Reformers

After 1900, voters from urban working-class districts elected several Progressive legislators who had trained in the trenches of machine politics. New York's Alfred E. Smith and Robert F. Wagner, Massachusetts's David I. Walsh, and Illinois's Edward F. Dunne—all from immigrant backgrounds—earnestly supported reform at the state and national levels. They wanted government to take responsibility for alleviating hardships that resulted from urban-industrial growth. They opposed reforms such as prohibition, Sunday closing laws, civil service, and nonpartisan elections, which conflicted with their constituents' interests. They were most successful when they joined with other reformers to pass laws aiding labor and promoting social welfare.

Some disillusioned people moved beyond Progressive reform; they wanted a different society altogether.

Socialists

A blend of immigrant intellectuals, industrial workers, disaffected Populists, miners, and women's rights activists—they turned to the socialist movement. The majority of socialists united behind Eugene V. Debs (see page 570), the American Railway Union organizer who drew nearly 100,000 votes in the 1900 presidential election. Although Debs failed to develop a consistent program beyond opposition to war and bourgeois materialism, he was a spellbinding spokesman for radical causes. As the Socialist Party's presidential candidate Debs won 400,000 votes in 1904, and in 1912, at the pinnacle of his and his party's career, he polled over 900,000.

With stinging rebukes of exploitation and unfair privilege, Debs and socialists like Milwaukee's Victor Berger and New York's Morris Hilquit made compelling overtures to reform-minded people. Some, such as Florence Kelley, joined the Socialist Party. But most Progressives had too much at stake in the capitalist system to want to overthrow it. Municipal ownership of public utilities represented their limit of drastic change. In Wisconsin, where Progressivism was most advanced, reformers refused to ally with Berger's more radical group. California Progressives temporarily allied with reactionaries to prevent socialists from gaining power in Los Angeles. And few Progressives objected when Debs was jailed in 1918 for giving an antiwar speech.

Opponents of Progressivism

It would be a mistake to assume that a Progressive spirit captured all of American society between 1895 and 1920. Large numbers of people, heavily represented in Congress, disliked government interference in economic affairs and found no fault with existing power structures. Defenders of free enterprise opposed many regulatory measures out of self-interest and fear that government programs would undermine the individual initiative and competition that they believed was basic to the free-market system. Government interference, they contended, contradicted the natural law of survival of the fittest. "Old-guard" Republicans like Senator Nelson W. Aldrich of Rhode Island and House Speaker Joseph Cannon of Illinois championed this ideology. Outside Washington, D.C., tycoons like J. P. Morgan and John D. Rockefeller insisted that progress would result only from maintaining the profit incentive and an economy unfettered by government regulation.

Though their objectives sometimes differed from those of middle-class Progressive reformers, socialists also became a more active force in the early twentieth century. Socialist parades on May Day, such as this one in 1910, were meant to express the solidarity of all working people.   (Library of Congress)

Progressive reformers occupied the center of the ideological spectrum. Moderate, socially aware, sometimes contradictory, they believed on one hand that the laissez-faire system was obsolete and on the other that a radical shift away from free enterprise was dangerous. Like Thomas Jefferson, they expressed faith in the conscience and will of the people; like Alexander Hamilton, they desired strong central government to act in the interests of conscience. Their goals were both idealistic and realistic. As minister-reformer Walter Rauschenbusch wrote, "We shall demand perfection and never expect to get it."

Governmental and Legislative Reform

A mistrust of tyranny had traditionally prompted American theorists and ordinary citizens to believe that democratic government should be small and unobtrusive, should interfere in private affairs only in unique circumstances, and should withdraw when balance had been restored. But in the late 1800s this point of view

weakened when problems resulting from economic change seemed to overwhelm individual effort. Corporations pursued government aid and protection for their enterprises. Discontented farmers sought government regulation of railroads and other monopolistic businesses. And city dwellers, accustomed to favors performed by political machines, came to expect government to act on their behalf.

Progressive reformers supported the assumption that government should ensure justice and well-being.

Restructuring Government

Increasingly aware that a simple, inflexible government was inadequate in a complex industrial age, they reasoned that public authority needed to counteract inefficiency and exploitation. But before activists could effectively use such power, they would have to reclaim government from politicians whose greed had soiled the democratic system. Thus eliminating corruption from government was a central thrust of Progressive activity.

Prior to the Progressive era, reformers had attacked corruption in cities (see Chapter 19). Between 1870 and 1900, opponents of boss politics tried to restructure government through reforms such as civil service, nonpartisan elections, and tighter scrutiny of public expenditures. A few reformers advocated poverty relief, housing improvement, and prolabor laws, but most worked for efficient—meaning economical—government. After 1900 reform campaigns installed city manager and commission forms of government (in which urban officials were chosen for professional expertise, rather than political connections) and public ownership of utilities (to prevent monopolistic gas, electric, and transit companies from profiting at public expense).

Reformers, however, found the city too small an arena for the changes they sought. Frustrated by lim-

Robert M. La Follette (1855–1925) was one of the most dynamic of Progressive politicians. As governor of Wisconsin, he sponsored a program of political reform and business regulation known as the Wisconsin Plan. In 1906 he entered the U.S. Senate and continued to champion Progressive reform. The National Progressive Republican League, which La Follette founded in 1911, became the core of the Progressive Party. (State Historical Society of Wisconsin)

ited victories, they theorized that state and federal governments offered better opportunities for enacting needed legislation. Their goals tended to vary regionally. In the Great Plains and Far West, they rallied behind railroad regulation and government control of natural resources. In the South reformers continued the Populist crusade against big business and autocratic politicians. In the Northeast and Midwest, they attacked corrupt politics and unsafe labor conditions.

Faith in a strong, fair-minded executive prompted Progressives to support a number of skillful and charismatic governors. The most forceful Progressive governor was Wisconsin's Robert M. La Follette. A self-made small-town lawyer, La Follette rose through the state Republican Party and won the governorship in 1900. As governor he initiated a multipronged reform program including direct primaries, more equitable taxes, and regulation of railroad rates. He also appointed commissions staffed by experts, who supplied him with the facts and figures he used in fiery speeches to arouse public support for his policies. After three terms as governor, La Follette was elected to the U.S. Senate and carried his ideals into national politics. "Battling Bob" displayed a rare ability to approach reform scientifically while still exciting people with moving rhetoric. His goal, he asserted, "was not to 'smash' corporations, but to drive them out of politics, and then to treat them exactly the same as other people are treated."

Robert M. La Follette

The South experienced a brand of Progressive reform that in many ways resembled that of other regions. Essentially urban and middle class in nature, it included the same strategies of railroad and utility regulation, factory safety, pure food and drug legislation, and moral reform that existed in Wisconsin, California, and New York. The South led the way in political reform; the direct primary originated in North Carolina, the city commission plan arose in Galveston, Texas, and the city manager plan began in Staunton, Virginia. Progressive governors, such as Braxton Bragg Comer of Alabama and Hoke Smith of Georgia, introduced business regulation and other reforms that rivaled actions inspired by Robert La Follette.

Southern Progressivism

But racial bitterness tainted southern Progressive politics, largely excluding former slaves from many benefits of reform. The exclusion of black men from voting through poll taxes, literacy requirements, and other means (see Chapter 20) meant that electoral reforms affected only whites—and then only white men with enough cash and education to satisfy voting prerequisites. Smith, Comer, and other Progressive governors such as Charles B. Aycock of North Carolina and James K. Vardamann of Mississippi rested their power on appeals to white supremacy. Racism was not unique to the South; Governor Hiram Johnson of California, a leading western Progressive, promoted discrimination against Japanese Americans, and New Jersey's Woodrow Wilson had no sympathy for African Americans. Yet discrimination did not lessen in the South just because reformers held office.

At the same time, however, southern women, white and black, made notable contributions to Progressive causes, just as they did in the North. Southern white women crusaded against child labor, ran social service organizations, and challenged unfair wage rates. African American women, using a nonpolitical guise as homemakers and religious leaders—roles that whites found more acceptable than political activism—attempted to serve their communities by acting as spokespersons for street cleaning, better education, and health reforms. Thus, though much of southern Progressivism was racist, it would have been even more so without the reformist efforts of women, especially black women.

In all regions, crusades against corrupt politics produced notable changes. By 1916 all but three states had direct primaries, and many had adopted the initiative, referendum, and recall. Political reformers achieved a major goal in 1913 with adoption of the Seventeenth Amendment, which provided for direct election of U.S. senators (they previously had been elected by state legislatures, many of which Progressives thought were corrupt). Such measures did not always help. Party bosses, better organized and more experienced than reformers, were still able to control elections. Efforts to use the initiative, referendum, and recall often failed because special-interest groups spent large sums to influence the voting. Moreover, courts usually aided rather than reined in entrenched power.

State laws to improve labor conditions had greater impact than did political reforms because both reformers and bosses could sometimes agree on issues affecting working people. Many states used their constitutional powers to protect public health and

Labor Reform

safety (police power) and to enact factory inspection laws, and by 1916 nearly two-thirds of the states required compensation for victims of industrial accidents. A coalition of labor and humanitarian groups even induced some legislatures to grant aid to mothers with dependent children. Under pressure from the National Child Labor Committee, nearly every state set a minimum age for employment (varying from twelve to sixteen) and prohibited employers from working children more than eight or ten hours a day. Such laws had limited effect, though, because they seldom provided for the close inspection of factories that full enforcement required. And families that needed extra income evaded the laws by encouraging their children to work and to lie about their ages.

Several groups united to achieve restricted working hours for women. After the Supreme Court, in *Muller v. Oregon*, upheld Oregon's ten-hour limit in 1908 (see page 499), more states passed laws protecting female workers. Meanwhile, in 1914 efforts of the American Association for Old Age Security showed signs of success when Arizona established old-age pensions. The courts struck down the law, but demand for pensions continued, and in the 1920s many states enacted laws to provide for needy elderly people.

Reformers themselves did not always agree about what was Progressive, especially in human behavior. The main question was whether state intervention was necessary to enforce purity, especially in drinking habits and sexual behavior. For example, the Anti-Saloon League, formed in 1893, intensified the long-standing campaign against drunkenness and its costs to society. This organization allied with the Women's Christian Temperance Union (founded in 1873) to publicize the role of alcoholism in liver disease and other health problems. The League was especially successful in shifting attention from the individual's responsibility for temperance to the alleged link between the drinking that saloons encouraged and the accidents, poverty, and poor productivity that were consequences of drinking.

Moral Reform

The war on saloons prompted many states and localities to restrict consumption of liquor. By 1900 almost one-fourth of the nation's population lived in "dry" communities (which prohibited the sale of liquor). But consumption of alcohol, especially beer, increased after 1900, convincing prohibitionists that a nationwide ban was

The War on Alcohol

the best solution. By 1917 they had enlisted support from notables such as Supreme Court Justice Louis D. Brandeis and former president William Howard Taft. In 1918 Congress passed the Eighteenth Amendment (ratified in 1919 and implemented in 1920) outlawing the manufacture, sale, and transportation of intoxicating liquors. Not all prohibitionists were Progressive reformers, and not all Progressives were prohibitionists. Nevertheless, the Eighteenth Amendment can be seen as an expression of the Progressive goal to protect family and workplace through reform legislation.

Moral outrage erupted also when muckraking journalists charged that international gangs were kidnapping young women and forcing them into prostitution, a practice called white slavery. The charges were

In addition to crusading against drunkenness, moral reformers stirred up emotions over accusations that evil men were seducing innocent young women into prostitution—or white slavery, as it was called. In this posed photograph printed in a 1910 antivice publication, *The White Slave Hell: or, With Christ at Midnight in the Slums of Chicago*, the man supposedly has gotten the woman drunk and is about to lure her into a life of sin. (Collection of Perry R. Duis, from *The Saloon*)

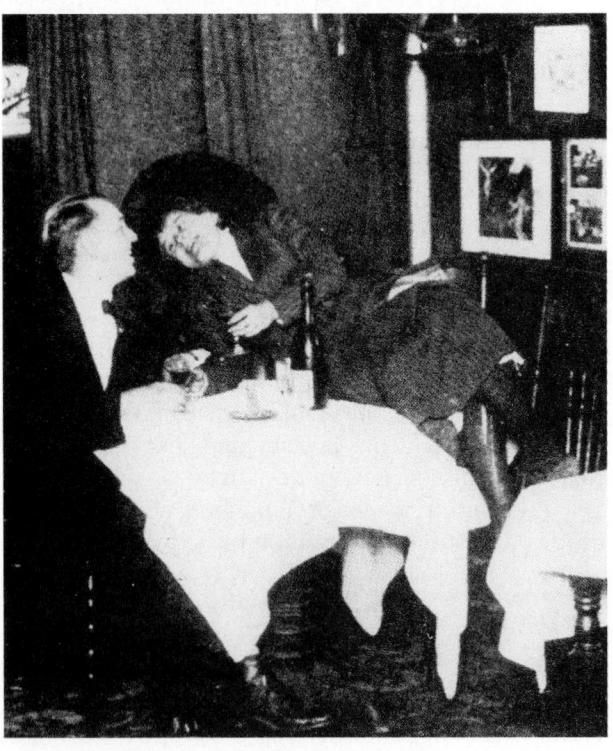

Prostitution and White Slavery

more imagined than real, but they alarmed some moralists who falsely perceived a link between immigration and prostitution and feared that prostitutes were producing genetically inferior children. Nevertheless, those fearful about the social consequences of prostitution prodded governments to investigate the problem and pass corrective legislation. The Chicago Vice Commission, for example, undertook a "scientific" survey and published its findings, titled *The Social Evil in Chicago*, in 1911. The report underscored the poverty, ignorance, and desperation that drove women into prostitution.

Such investigations found rising numbers of prostitutes but failed to prove that criminal organizations deliberately lured women onto the streets. Reformers nonetheless believed they could attack prostitution by punishing those who promoted it. In 1910 Congress passed the White Slave Traffic Act, known as the Mann Act, prohibiting interstate and international transportation of a woman for immoral purposes. By 1915 nearly every state had outlawed brothels and solicitation of sex. Such laws ostensibly protected young women from exploitation, but in reality they failed to address the more serious problem of sexual violence that women suffered at the hands of family members and presumed friends and at the workplace.

Like prohibition, the Mann Act reflected growing sentiment that government could improve behavior by restricting it. Reformers believed that the source of evil was not original sin or human nature but the social environment. And if evil was created by human will, it followed that it could be eradicated by human effort. Intervention in the form of laws could help create a heaven on earth.

New Ideas in Education, Law, Religion, and the Sciences

 In addition to legislative paths, reform impulses opened new vistas in ideas. Preoccupation with efficiency and scientific management infiltrated the realms of education, law, religion, and science. Darwin's theory of evolution had challenged traditional beliefs in a God-created world; immigration had created confusing social diversity; and technology had made old habits of production and consumption obsolete. Thoughtful people in a number of professions grappled with how

to respond to the new era yet preserve what was best from the past.

In education, changing patterns of school attendance required new ways of thinking. As late as 1870, when families needed children at home to do farm work, Americans attended school for an average of only four years. By 1900, however, cities contained multitudes of children who had more time for school. Compulsory-attendance laws required children to be in school to age fourteen, and swelling populations of immigrant and migrant children jammed schoolrooms. Meanwhile, the number of public high schools grew from five hundred in 1870 to ten thousand in 1910. Before the Civil War, curricula had consisted chiefly of moralistic pieties from *McGuffey's Reader*. But in the late nineteenth century, psychologist G. Stanley Hall and philosopher John Dewey asserted that modern education ought to prepare children differently. They insisted that personal development, not subject matter, should be the focus of the curriculum. Education, argued Dewey, must relate directly to experience; children should be encouraged to discover knowledge for themselves. Learning relevant to students' lives should replace rote memorization and outdated subjects.

John Dewey and Progressive Education

Progressive education, based on Dewey's *The School and Society* (1899) and *Democracy and Education* (1916), was a uniquely American phenomenon. Dewey believed that learning should focus on real-life problems and that children should be taught to use their intelligence and ingenuity as instruments for controlling their environments. From kindergarten through high school, Dewey asserted, children should learn through direct experience. Dewey and his wife, Alice, put these ideas into practice in their own Laboratory School located at the University of Chicago.

A more practical curriculum became the driving principle behind reform in higher education as well. Previously, the purpose of American colleges and universities had resembled that of European counterparts: to train a select few for careers in law, medicine, teaching, and religion. But in the late 1800s, institutions of higher learning multiplied, aided by land grants and an increase in the number of people who could afford tuition. Between 1870 and 1910 the number of colleges and universities in the United States grew from 563 to nearly 1,000. Curricula expanded as educators sought

Growth of Colleges and Universities

to make learning more appealing and to keep up with technological and social changes. Harvard University, under President Charles W. Eliot, pioneered in substituting electives for required courses and experimenting with new teaching methods. The University of Wisconsin and other public universities achieved distinction in new areas of study such as political science and sociology. Many schools, private and public, considered athletics vital to a student's growth, and intercollegiate sports became a permanent feature of student life as well as a source of school pride.

Southern states, in keeping with separate-but-equal policies, set up segregated land-grant colleges for blacks in addition to the public institutions for whites. Separate was a more accurate description of these institutions than equal. African Americans continued to suffer from inferior educational opportunities in both state institutions and private all-black colleges. Nevertheless, African American men and women found intellectual stimulation in all-black colleges and hoped to use their educations to promote better race relations.

As higher education expanded, so did female enrollments. Between 1890 and 1910 the number of women in colleges and universities swelled from 56,000 to 140,000. Of these, 106,000 attended coeducational institutions (mostly state universities); the rest attended women's colleges. By 1920, 283,000 women were attending college, accounting for 47 percent of total enrollment. But discrimination lingered in admissions and curriculum policies. Women were encouraged (indeed, they usually sought) to take home economics and education courses rather than science and mathematics, and most medical schools, including Harvard and Yale, refused to admit women. Barred from such institutions, women continued to attend their own schools, most of which were founded in the late nineteenth century, places such as Women's Medical College of Philadelphia and women's colleges such as Smith, Mount Holyoke, and Wellesley.

American educators adopted the prevailing attitude of business: more is better. They justifiably congratulated themselves for increasing enrollments and making instruction more meaningful. By 1920, 78 percent of children between ages five and seventeen were enrolled in public elementary and high schools; another 8 percent attended private and parochial schools. These figures represented a huge increase over 1870 attendance rates. And there were 600,000 college and graduate students in 1920, compared with only 52,000

Poised and proud, these members of the University of Michigan's Class of 1892 represent the student body of a publicly funded land-grant college in the late nineteenth century. With their varied curricula, inclusion of women, and increasing enrollments, such schools transformed American higher education in the Progressive era.   (University of Michigan)

in 1870. Yet few people looked beyond the numbers to assess how well schools were doing their jobs. Critical analysis seldom tested the faith that schools could promote equality and justice as well as personal growth and responsible citizenship.

The legal profession also embraced new emphases on experience and scientific principles. Harvard law professor Roscoe Pound, an influential proponent of the new outlook, urged that social reality should influence legal thinking. Oliver Wendell Holmes, Jr., associate justice of the Supreme Court between 1902 and 1932, led the attack on the traditional view of law as universal and unchanging. "The life of the law," said Holmes, sounding like Dewey, "has not been logic; it has been experience." The opinion that law should reflect society's needs challenged the practice of invoking inflexible legal precedents that often obstructed social legislation. Louis D. Brandeis, a lawyer who later joined Holmes on the Supreme Court, insisted that judges' opinions

Progressive Legal Thought

be based on factual, scientifically gathered information about social realities. Using the Progressive approach to problems, Brandeis collected extensive data on the harmful effects of long hours to convince the Supreme Court, in *Muller v. Oregon* (1908), to uphold Oregon's law limiting women's working hours.

The new legal thinking met with some resistance. Judges raised on laissez-faire economics and strict construction of the Constitution continued to overturn laws Progressives thought necessary for effective reform. Thus despite Holmes's forceful dissent, in 1905 the Supreme Court, in *Lochner v. New York*, revoked a New York law limiting bakers' working hours. As in similar cases, the Court's majority argued that the Fourteenth Amendment protected an individual's right to make contracts without government interference and that this protection superseded police power. Judges weakened other federal regulations by invoking the Tenth Amendment, which prohibited the federal government from interfering in matters reserved to the states.

Courts did uphold some regulatory measures, particularly those protecting public safety. A string of decisions beginning with *Holden v. Hardy* (1898), in which the Supreme Court sustained Utah's mining regulations, confirmed the use of state police power to protect health, safety, and morals. Judges also affirmed federal police power and Congress's authority over interstate commerce by supporting federal legislation such as the Pure Food and Drug Act, the Meat Inspection Law (see page 598), and the Mann Act. In these instances citizens' welfare took precedence over the Tenth Amendment.

But the concept of general welfare often conflicted with the concept of equal rights when the will of local majorities was imposed on minorities. Even if one agreed that laws should address society's needs, whose needs should prevail? The United States was a mixed nation; gender, race, religion, and ethnicity deeply influenced law. In many localities a native-born Protestant majority imposed Bible reading in public schools (offending Catholics and Jews), required businesses to close on Sundays, limited women's rights, restricted religious practices of Mormons and other groups, prohibited interracial marriage, and enforced racial segregation. Justice Holmes asserted that laws should be made for "people of fundamentally differing views," but were such laws possible in a nation of so many different interest groups? The debate continues to this day.

At the same time, social science—the study of society and its institutions—experienced changes similar to those engulfing law and education.

Social Science In economics a group of young scholars used statistics to argue that laws governing economic relationships were not timeless. Instead, they claimed, theory should reflect prevailing social conditions. Richard T. Ely of Johns Hopkins University and the University of Wisconsin, reflecting this point of view, argued that poverty and impersonality resulting from industrialization required intervention by "the united efforts of Church, state, and science." A new breed of sociologists led by Lester Ward, Albion Small, and Edward A. Ross agreed, adding that citizens should actively plan to cure social ills rather than passively waiting for problems to solve themselves. In the field of psychology, female researchers challenged age-old beliefs that women's minds were different from, and inferior to, men's.

Meanwhile, Progressive historians Frederick Jackson Turner, Charles A. Beard, and Vernon L. Parrington examined the past to explain present American society. Beard, like other Progressives, believed that the Constitution was a flexible document amenable to growth and change, not an inviolable code imposed by wise forefathers. His influential *Economic Interpretation of the Constitution* (1913) argued that a group of merchants and business-oriented lawyers created the Constitution to defend private property. If the Constitution had served special interests in one age, it could be changed to serve broader interests in another age. Meanwhile, political scientists like Woodrow Wilson emphasized the practical over the theoretical, advocating expansion of government power to ensure justice and progress.

In public health, organizations like the National Consumers League (NCL) joined physicians and social scientists to bring about some of the most far-reaching Progressive reforms. Founded by Florence Kelley in 1899, NCL activities included women's suffrage, protection of female and child laborers, and elimination of potential health hazards. After aiding in the success of *Muller v. Oregon* in 1908, the organization became active in sponsoring court cases on behalf of women workers and worked with reform lawyers Louis Brandeis and Felix Frankfurter in support of these cases. Local branches united with women's clubs to advance consumer protection measures such as the licensing of food vendors and inspection of dairies. They also urged city governments to fund neighborhood clinics that provided health education and medical care to the poor.

Much of Progressive reform rested on religious underpinnings. The distresses of modern society especially sparked new thoughts about fortifying social relations with moral principles. Particularly, a movement known as the Social Gospel, led by Protestant ministers Walter Rauschenbusch, Washington Gladden, and Charles Sheldon, would counter the brutality of competitive capitalism by interjecting Christian churches into practical, worldly matters such as arbitrating industrial harmony and improving the environment of the poor. Believing that service to fellow humans provided the way both to securing individual salvation and to creating God's kingdom on earth, Social Gospelers actively participated in social reform and governed their lives by asking, "What would Jesus do?"

The Social Gospel served as a reform response to Social Darwinism, the application of biological natural selection and survival of the fittest to human interac-

The Social Gospel

Eugenics

tions (see page 513). But another movement that flourished during the Progressive era, eugenics, sought to apply Darwinian principles to society in a more scientific way. The brainchild of Francis Galton, an English statistician and cousin of Charles Darwin, eugenics rested on the belief that human character and habits could be inherited. If good traits could be inherited so could bad traits, such as criminality, insanity, and feeblemindedness. Just as some Progressives believed that in order to create a better world, society had an obligation to intervene and erase poverty and injustice, eugenicists believed society had an obligation to prevent the reproduction of the mentally defective, the criminally inclined, and people generally deemed to be inferior. Inevitably such focus landed on immigrants and people of color.

There were two basic means by which followers of eugenics would eliminate people whose offspring might threaten American progress. One was to sterilize those identified as unfit to reproduce. Beginning around the turn of the century, several state legislatures began considering laws to legalize the sterilization (mostly involving vasectomies) of certain criminal and insane men. In 1907 Indiana enacted the country's first law permitting the involuntary sterilization of "confirmed criminals, idiots, imbeciles, and rapists" when a committee of experts considered such action advisable. By 1915 thirteen states had such laws, and by 1930 the number had reached thirty. The other method of protecting American society from reproduction by inferior people involved restricting immigration. Though not strictly a work of eugenics, the book *The Passing of the Great Race* (1916) by Madison Grant strongly bolstered theories that immigrants from southern and eastern Europe were threatening to weaken American society because they were inferior mentally and morally to earlier Nordic immigrants. Thus, many people, including some Progressives, concluded, new immigration laws should curtail the influx of Poles, Italians, Jews, and other eastern and southern Europeans. Such efforts reached fruition in the 1920s when restrictive legislation, often backed by eugenics theories, drastically closed the door to "new" immigrants (see page 682). Not all support for sterilization and immigration restriction came from eugenicists, but in the Progressive era, eugenics arose as an invidious way of applying science to social organization.

Thus a new breed of men and women pressed for institutional change as well as political reform in the two decades before the First World War. Largely middle class, trained in new professional standards, confident that new ways of thinking could bring about progress, these people helped broaden government's role to meet the needs of a mature industrial society. But their questioning of prevailing assumptions also unsettled conventional attitudes toward race and gender.

Challenges to Racial and Sexual Discrimination

The Progressive era, dominated as it was by white reformers, often ignored issues directly affecting former slaves, nonwhite immigrants, Indians, and women. Yet activists among these groups caught the Progressive spirit and strove for change in this time of challenge to entrenched ideas and customs. Their efforts, however, posed a dilemma. Should women and nonwhites aim to become just like white men, with white men's values as well as their rights? Or was there something unique about racial and sexual cultures that they should preserve at the risk of sacrificing some gains? Both groups fluctuated between attraction to and rejection of the culture that excluded them.

In 1900 nine-tenths of African Americans lived in the South, where repressive Jim Crow laws had multiplied in the 1880s and 1890s (see page 562). Denied legal and voting rights and officially segregated in almost all walks of life, southern blacks faced constant exclusion. In 1910 only 8,000 out of 970,000 high school–age blacks in the entire South were enrolled in high schools. And blacks met with constant violence. Between 1900 and 1914 white mobs, usually incensed over rumored sexual assaults or insults by black men on white women, lynched over a thousand blacks.

Disadvantages of African Americans

African Americans began to move northward in the 1880s, accelerating their migration after 1900. The conditions they found represented a relative improvement over the rural sharecropping existence, but job discrimination, inferior schools, and segregated housing existed in northern as well as southern cities. White authorities perpetuated segregation by maintaining separate and inferior institutions, such as hospitals and schools, for blacks. A half-century after slavery's abolition, most whites still agreed with historian James Ford Rhodes, who wrote that blacks were "innately inferior and incapable of citizenship."

African American leaders differed sharply over how—and whether—to pursue assimilation. In the wake of emancipation, ex-slave Frederick Douglass urged "ultimate assimilation through self-assertion, and on no other terms." Others favored separation from white society and supported migration to Africa or the establishment of all-black communities in Oklahoma Territory and Kansas. Others, as bitter as white racists, advocated militancy, believing, as one writer stated, "Our people must die to be saved and in dying must take as many along with them as it is possible to do with the aid of firearms and all other weapons."

Most blacks, however, could neither escape nor conquer white society. They sought other routes to economic and social improvement.

Booker T. Washington and Self-Help

Self-help, a strategy articulated by educator Booker T. Washington, offered one popular alternative. Born to slave parents in 1856, Washington obtained an education and in 1881 founded Tuskegee Institute in Alabama, a vocational school for blacks. There he developed a philosophy that blacks' best hopes for assimilation lay in at least temporarily accommodating to whites. Rather than fighting for political rights, Washington said, blacks should work hard, acquire property, and prove they were worthy of respect. Washington voiced his views in a speech at the Atlanta Exposition in 1895. "Dignify and glorify common labor," he urged in what became known as the Atlanta Compromise. "Agitation of questions of racial equality is the extremest folly." Envisioning a society where blacks and whites would remain apart but share similar goals, Washington observed that "in all things that are purely social we can be as separate as the fingers, yet one as the hand in all matters essential to mutual progress."

Whites welcomed Washington's accommodation policy because it urged patience and reminded black people to stay in their place. Because he said what they wanted to hear, white businesspeople, reformers, and politicians chose to regard Washington as representative of all African Americans. Yet though Washington endorsed a separate-but-equal policy, he projected a subtle racial pride that would find more direct expression in black nationalism later in the twentieth century, when some African Americans advocated control

Booker T. Washington's Tuskegee Institute helped train young African Americans in useful crafts such as shoemaking and shoe repair, as illustrated here. At the same time, however, Washington's intentions and the Tuskegee curriculum reinforced what many whites wanted to believe: that blacks were unfit for anything except manual labor.
(Tuskegee University Library)

of their own businesses and schools. Washington never argued that blacks were inferior to whites; he asserted that they could enhance their dignity through self-improvement.

Some blacks thought that Washington favored a degrading second-class citizenship. His southern-based philosophy did not appeal to educated northern African Americans, such as William Monroe Trotter, the fiery editor of the *Boston Guardian*, or social scientist T. Thomas Fortune. In 1905 a group of "anti-Bookerites" convened near Niagara Falls and pledged militant pursuit of rights such as unrestricted voting, economic opportunity, integration, and equality before the law. Spokesperson for the Niagara movement was W. E. B. Du Bois, an outspoken critic of the Atlanta Compromise.

A New Englander and the first black to receive a Ph.D. from Harvard, Du Bois was both a Progressive and a member of the black elite. He

W. E. B. Du Bois and the Niagara Movement

held an undergraduate degree from all-black Fisk University and had studied in Germany, where he learned about scientific investigation. While a faculty member at Atlanta University, Du Bois compiled fact-filled sociological studies of black ghetto dwellers and wrote poetically in support of civil rights. He treated Washington politely but could not accept white domination. "The way for a people to gain their reasonable rights," Du Bois asserted, "is not by voluntarily throwing them away." Instead, blacks must agitate for what was rightfully theirs.

Dissatisfied with Washington's strategy, Du Bois in 1905 organized a conference of blacks who favored more active opposition to racism. Meeting at Niagara Falls, the group took the name Niagara Conference and began meeting annually. Then, in 1909, Du Bois joined with a group of white liberals who also were discontented with Washington's accommodationism to form the National Association for the Advancement of Colored People (NAACP), which aimed to end racial discrimination and obtain voting rights by pursuing legal redress in the courts. By 1914 the NAACP had fifty branch offices and six thousand members.

Whatever their views, African Americans faced continued oppression. Those who managed to acquire property and education encountered white resentment, especially when they fought for equality. Black editor and reformer Ida B. Wells, who wrote *On Lynching* (1892) in support of antilynching legislation, suffered destruction of her property and threats against her life. The federal government only aggravated biases. During Woodrow Wilson's presidency, southern cabinet members supported racial separation in restrooms, restaurants, and government office buildings and balked at hiring black workers. Commenting on Wilson's racism in 1913, Booker T. Washington wrote, "I have never seen the colored people so discouraged and so bitter as they are at the present time."

African Americans still sought to fulfill the dream of success, but many wondered whether their goals should include membership in a corrupt white society. Du Bois voiced these doubts poignantly, observing that "one ever feels his twoness—an American, a Negro, two souls, two thoughts, two unreconciled strivings, two warring ideals in one dark body." Somehow blacks had to reconcile that "twoness" by combining racial pride with national identity. As Du Bois wrote in 1903, a black "would not Africanize America, for America has too much to teach the world and Africa. He would not bleach his Negro soul in a flood of white Americanism, for he knows that Negro blood has a message for the world. He simply wishes to make it possible for a man to be both a Negro and an American." That simple wish would haunt the nation for decades to come.

The dilemma of identity bedeviled Native Americans as well, but it had an added tribal dimension.

Society of American Indians

Since the 1880s, Native American reformers had belonged to white-led Indian organizations. In 1911 educated, middle-class Indians formed their own association, the Society of American Indians (SAI), to work for better education, civil rights, and healthcare. It also sponsored "American Indian Days" to cultivate pride and offset images of savage peoples promulgated in Wild West shows.

The SAI's emphasis on racial pride, however, was squeezed between pressures for assimilation from one side and tribal allegiance on the other. Its small membership did not genuinely represent the diverse and unconnected Indian nations, and its attempt to establish a governing body fizzled. Some tribal governments no longer existed to select representatives, and most SAI members simply promoted their own self-interest. At the same time, the goal of achieving acceptance in white society proved elusive. Individual hard work was not enough to overcome white prejudice and condescension, and attempts to redress grievances through legal action faltered for lack of funds. Ultimately, SAI had to rely on rhetoric and moral exhortation, which had little effect on poor and powerless Indians who seldom knew that SAI even existed. Torn by internal disputes, the association folded in the early 1920s.

The challenges to established social assumptions also raised questions of identity among women. The

"The Woman Movement"

ensuing quandaries resembled those faced by racial minorities: What tactics should women use to achieve equality? What should be their role in society? Novelist Henry James expressed the dilemma from a male point of view when he complained that women who wanted to become just like men were disregarding their own uniqueness. Or, as some women put it, could women achieve equality with men and at the same time change male-dominated society?

The answers that women found involved a subtle but important shift in women's politics. Before about 1910, crusaders for women's rights referred to themselves as "the woman movement." This label applied to middle-class women striving to move beyond the household into social welfare activities, higher education, and paid labor. Like some African American and Indian leaders, women argued that legal and voting rights were indispensable to such moves. These women's rights advocates based their claims on the theory that women's special, even superior, traits as guardians of family and morality would humanize all of society. Settlement-house founder Jane Addams, for example, endorsed women's suffrage by asking, "If women have in any sense been responsible for the gentler side of life which softens and blurs some of its harsher conditions, may not they have a duty to perform in our American cities?"

Women's clubs represented a unique dimension of the woman movement. Originating as middle-class literary and educational organizations,

Women's Clubs

women's clubs began taking stands on public affairs in the late nineteenth century. Because female activists were excluded from holding office, they were drawn less to government reform than to social betterment, an enterprise called social housekeeping. Rather than pressing for reforms such as trustbusting and direct primaries, these women worked for factory inspection, regulation of children's and women's labor, housing improvement, upgrading of education, and consumer protection.

Such efforts were not confined to white women. African American women had their own club move-

The rise of the settlement house movement and of the Visiting Nurse Association provided young middle-class women with opportunities to aid inner-city working-class neighborhoods and formed the basis of the social work profession. Here a group of visiting nurses prepare to apply their medical training to the disadvantaged.   (Corbis-Bettmann)

ment, including the Colored Women's Federation, which sought to establish a training school for "colored girls." Founded in 1895, the National Association of Colored Women was the nation's first African American social service organization; it concentrated on establishing nurseries, kindergartens, and retirement homes. Black women also developed their own reform organizations within Black Baptist and African Methodist Episcopal churches.

Around 1910 some of those concerned with women's place in society began using a new term, *feminism*, to refer to their ideas. Whereas

Feminism

the woman movement spoke generally of duty and moral purity, feminists—more explicitly conscious of

How do historians know...

that settlement houses structured their activities to satisfy middle-class objectives? Settlement houses were among the most influential agents of social reform during the Progressive era, attracting scores of young workers eager to help reform inner-city neighborhoods and residents. This document presents an actual listing of one week's activities at the Chicago Commons Settlement House in 1896. There are at least three ways to interpret these activities. First is the nature of the activities themselves: a blend of practical (savings bank, cooking, manual training) with intellectual (Shakespeare, French, elocution). Settlement workers were highly educated and believed that the people they served needed exposure to culture as well as life skills. Second is the age factor: note that the majority of entries are for children. As realists, settlement workers believed they had a greater chance of reaching the minds and hearts of the younger generation than the more suspicious parents. Third is the gender factor: though the settlement staff has scheduled a few activities for males, the selections are exclusively for boys, not adult men.

Moreover, the numerous activities for females reinforce prevailing stereotypes of women's role as housekeeper—though the daily kindergarten existed as a form of childcare for working mothers of young children. Even though many of the settlement workers were women, they still believed in maintaining women's traditional roles. (Photo: Library of Congress)

SCHEDULE OF OCCASIONS

LIST OF MEETINGS, CLASSES, CLUBS AND OTHER APPOINTMENTS OF THE WEEK AT CHICAGO COMMONS AND THE TABERNACLE DURING THE PAST WINTER.

AT THE COMMONS,
140 NORTH UNION STREET.

DAILY
All Day—House open for neighbors and friends.
9:00–12:00 a. m.—Free Kindergarten (except Saturday and Sunday). Mrs. Bertha Hofer Hegner, head kindergartner; Miss Alice B. Coggswell, assistant.
2:00–5:00 p. m.—Kindergarten Training Classes.
7:00 p. m.—Family Vespers (except Saturday).

SUNDAY
3:30 p. m.—Pleasant Sunday Afternoon.

MONDAY
4:00 p. m.—Manual Training (Girls.) Mr. N. H. Weeks.
7:30 p. m.—Penny Provident Bank.
8:00 p. m.—Girls' Clubs. Misses Coggswell, Taylor and Purnell.
　Cooking Class (Girls). Miss Manning.
　Girls' Progressive Club (Young Women). Classes in Art, Miss Cushman; Embroidery, Mrs. Gavit; Greek Mythology, Mrs. Follett; English History and Constitution, Miss Allen.
　Shakespere Class. Mr. Gavit.

TUESDAY
2:00 p. m.—Woman's Club.
4:00 p. m.—Cooking Class (Girls). Miss Cookinham.
　Manual Training. Mr. Weeks.
7:30 p. m.—Boys' Club. Mr. Weeks, Misses Alexander and Holdridge.
　French. Miss Sayer.
　Rhetoric. Mr. Wyatt.
　Stenography. Mr. Fisher.
　Cooking Class (Girls). Miss Thayer.
8:00 p. m.—Choral Club. Miss Hofer and Mr. C. E. Weeks.
8:15 p. m.—"The Tuesday Meeting," for Economic Discussion.

WEDNESDAY
4:00 p. m.—Kindergarten Clubs (children). Miss Purnell and Abbott.
　Dressmaking Class (Girls). Miss Temple.
　Piano. Miss Gavit.
7:00 p. m.—Piano. Miss Bemiss.
7:30 p. m.—Penny Provident Bank.
　Girls' Clubs. Misses Coggswell, Gavit, Bosworth, Bemiss, Etheridge.
　Boys' Club. Mr. Grant.
　Cooking Class (Young Women). Miss Temple.

THURSDAY
4:00 p. m—Cooking Class (for Women). Miss Temple.
　Elocution. Miss Ellis.
　Manual Training (Girls). Mr. Weeks.
7:30 p. m.—Girls' Club. Miss Chandler.
　Good Will ("Blue Ticket") Club. Mr. Weeks.
　Elocution. Miss Ellis.
　Grammar. Mr. Carr.
　Cooking (for Girls). Miss Manning.
　Mothers' Club (Fortnightly).
　Seventeenth Ward Municipal Club (Monthly).

FRIDAY
4:00 p. m.—Manual Training (Boys'). Mr. Weeks.
7:30 p. m.—Penny Provident Bank.
　Cooking Class (Girls). Miss Manning.
　Boys' Clubs. Messrs. Burt, Carr, Crocker, Young, C. E. Weeks, N. H. Weeks.
　Dressmaking. Mrs. Strawbridge.

SATURDAY
10:00 a. m.—Manual Training (Boys). Mr. Weeks.
2:00 p. m.—Manual Training (Boys). Mr. Weeks.
3:00 p. m.—Piano Lessons. Miss Bemiss.
6:30 p. m.—Residents' Meeting (for residents only).

Other Appointments, for Clubs, Study Classes, Social Gatherings, etc., are made from time to time and for special occasions.

their identity as women—emphasized rights and self-development. Feminism, however, contained an inherent contradiction. On one hand feminists argued that all women should unite in the struggle for rights because of their shared disadvantages as women. On the other, feminists insisted that sex-typing—treating women differently than men—must end because it re-

sulted in discrimination. Thus feminists advocated the contradictory position that women should unite as a gender group for the purpose of abolishing all gender-based distinctions.

Feminism focused primarily on economic and sexual independence. Charlotte Perkins Gilman articulated feminist goals in *Women and Economics* (1898),

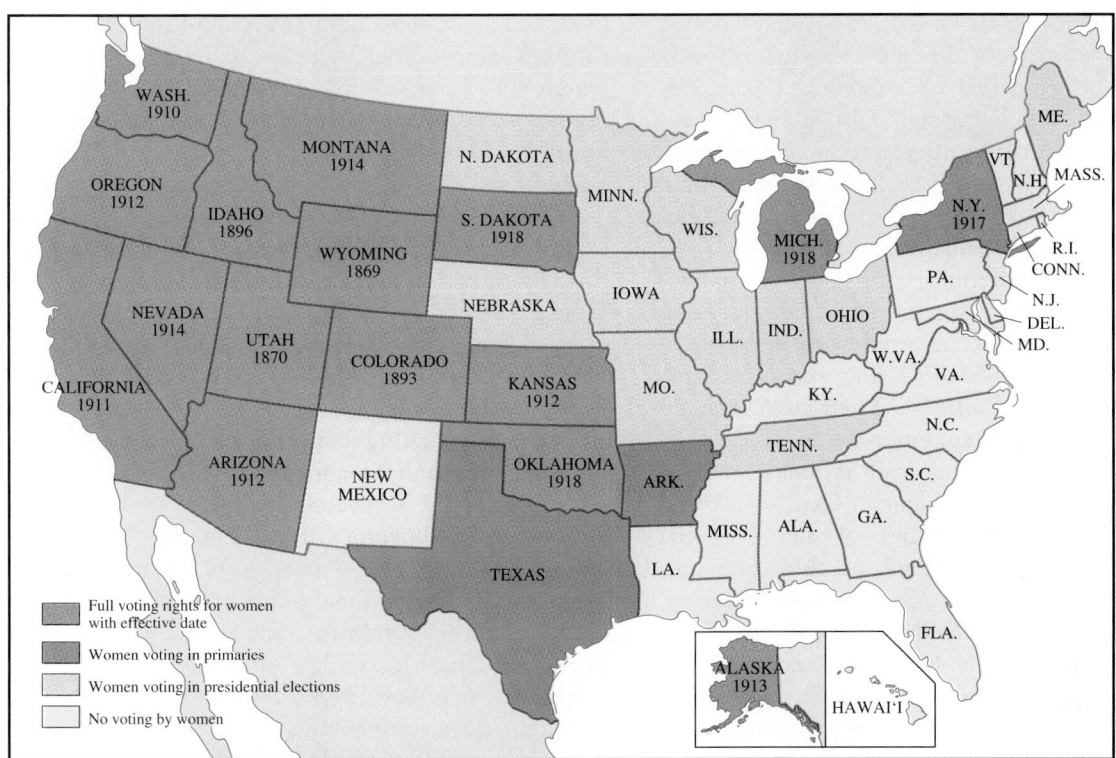

Map 21.1   Woman Suffrage Before 1920   Before Congress passed and the states ratified the Nineteenth Amendment, woman suffrage already existed, but mainly in the West. Several mid-western states allowed women to vote only in presidential elections, but legislatures in the South and Northeast generally refused such rights until forced to do so by constitutional amendment.

declaring that domesticity and female innocence were obsolete and attacking the male monopoly on economic opportunity. Gilman argued that modern women must take jobs in industry and the professions and that paid employees should handle domestic chores such as cooking, cleaning, and childcare.

Feminists also supported "sex rights"—a single standard of behavior for men and women—and several feminists joined the birth-control movement led by Margaret Sanger. As a visiting nurse in New York City's immigrant neighborhoods, Sanger attracted support from the Socialist Party in distributing information about contraception to help poor women prevent unwanted pregnancies. Though Sanger later gained acceptance among middle-class women, her actions initially aroused opposition from those who saw birth control as a threat to family and morality. In 1914 Sanger's opponents caused her to be indicted for defying an

Margaret Sanger's Crusade

1873 law that prohibited the sending of obscene literature (articles on contraception) through the mails, and she fled the country for a year. Sanger persevered and in 1921 formed the American Birth Control League, enlisting physicians and social workers to convince judges to allow distribution of birth-control information. Most states still prohibited the sale of contraceptives, but Sanger succeeded in introducing the issue into public debate and the American Birth Control League became Planned Parenthood, an organization currently at the forefront of birth-control issues.

During the Progressive era, a generation of feminists, represented by Harriot Stanton Blatch, who was the daughter of nineteenth-century suffragist Elizabeth Cady Stanton, carried on women's battle for the vote (see Map 21.1). Blatch made the improvement of working conditions for women a primary goal and agreed with those who saw the vote as the means by which women could effect

Woman Suffrage

such improvement. Declaring that all women worked, whether they performed paid labor or unpaid housework, Blatch believed that all women's efforts contributed to society's betterment. In Blatch's view, achievement rather than wealth and refinement was the best criterion for public influence. Thus women should exercise the vote not to enhance the power of elites but to promote and protect women's economic roles.

Despite internal differences, suffragists united behind their single goal and achieved some successes. Nine states, all in the West, allowed women to vote in state and local elections by 1912, and women continued to press for national suffrage. Their tactics ranged from moderate but persistent letter-writing and publications of the National American Woman Suffrage Association, led by Carrie Chapman Catt, to spirited meetings and militant marches of the National Woman's Party, led by Alice Paul. All these activities heightened public awareness. More decisive, however, were women's performances during the First World War as factory laborers, medical volunteers, and municipal workers (see pages 649–650). By convincing legislators that women could shoulder public responsibilities, women's wartime contributions gave final impetus to passage of the national suffrage amendment in 1920 (see Map 21.1).

The activities of women's clubs, feminists, and suffragists failed to create an interest group united or powerful enough to overcome men's political, economic, and social control. Like blacks, women knew that voting rights would mean little until society's attitudes changed. The Progressive era helped women to clarify issues that concerned them, but major reforms were not achieved until a later era. As feminist Crystal Eastman, echoing W. E. B. Du Bois, observed in the aftermath of the suffrage crusade: "Men are saying perhaps, 'Thank God, this everlasting women's fight is over!' But women, if I know them, are saying, 'Now at last we can begin.' . . . Now they can say what they are really after, in common with all the rest of the struggling world, is freedom."

Theodore Roosevelt and the Revival of the Presidency

The Progressive era's theme of reform—in politics, institutions, and social relations—drew attention to government, especially the federal government, as the foremost agent of change. Though the federal government had made some notable accomplishments during the preceding Gilded Age (see Chapter 20), its role mainly had been to support rather than control economic expansion, as when it transferred western public lands and resources to private ownership. Then, in September 1901, the political climate suddenly shifted. The assassination of President William McKinley by anarchist Leon Czolgosz vaulted Theodore Roosevelt, the vigorous young vice president, into the White House.

Political manager Mark Hanna had warned fellow Republicans against running Roosevelt for vice president in 1900. "Don't any of you realize," Hanna asked after the nominating convention, "that there's only one life between that madman and the presidency?" As governor of New York, Roosevelt had angered Republican bosses by showing sympathy for regulatory legislation, so they rid themselves of their pariah by pushing him into national politics. Little did they anticipate that they were providing the steppingstone for the nation's most forceful president since Lincoln and a president who bestowed the office with much of its twentieth-century character.

As a youth Roosevelt had suffered from asthma and near-sightedness. He was driven throughout his life by an obsession to overcome his physical limitations and exert what he and his contemporaries called "manliness," meaning a zest for physical exertion and display of courage. In his teens he became an expert marksman and horseman and later competed on Harvard's boxing and wrestling teams. In the 1880s he went to live on a Dakota ranch, where he roped cattle and brawled with cowboys. Descended from a Dutch aristocratic family, Roosevelt had wealth to indulge in such pursuits. But he also inherited a sense of civic responsibility that guided him into a career in public service. He served three terms in the New York State Assembly, ran for mayor of New York City in 1886 (finishing third), sat on the federal Civil Service Commission, served as New York City's police commissioner, and was assistant secretary of the navy. In these offices Roosevelt earned a reputation as a combative, politically crafty leader. He also distinguished himself as a historian, writing *The Naval War of 1812* (1882) and *The Winning of the West* (1889). In 1898 Roosevelt thrust himself into the Spanish-American-Cuban-Filipino War by organizing a volunteer cavalry brigade, called the Rough Riders, to fight in Cuba (see page 622). Though his dramatic act had little impact on the war's outcome, it

Theodore Roosevelt

Theodore Roosevelt (1858–1919) liked to think of himself as a great outdoorsman. He loved most the rugged countryside and believed that he and his country should serve as examples of "manliness." (California Museum of Photography, University of California)

excited the public's imagination. A publicity hound who craved the center of attention, Roosevelt returned a media hero.

As president, Roosevelt concurred with Progressives that a small, uninvolved government would not suffice in the industrial era. Instead, economic development necessitated a government powerful enough to guide national affairs broadly. "A simple and poor society," he observed, "can exist as a democracy on the basis of sheer individualism. But a rich and complex society cannot so exist." Especially in economic matters, he wanted the government to act as an umpire, deciding when big business was good and when it was bad. But his brash patriotism and dislike of weakness and indecisiveness, qualities he considered effeminate, also recalled earlier eras of unbridled expansion when raw power prevailed in social and economic affairs.

The federal regulation of the economy that characterized twentieth-century American history began with Roosevelt's presidency. Roosevelt turned his attention first to big business, where consolidation had

Regulation of Trusts

created massive, monopolistic trusts. Although Roosevelt was labeled a "trustbuster," he actually considered consolidation the most efficient means to achieve material progress. He believed in distinguishing between good and bad trusts and preventing bad ones from manipulating markets. Thus he instructed the Justice Department to use antitrust laws to prosecute railroad, meatpacking, and oil trusts, which he believed were unscrupulously exploiting the public. Roosevelt's policy triumphed in 1904 when the Supreme Court, convinced by the government's arguments, ordered the breakup of Northern Securities Company, the huge railroad combination created by J. P. Morgan and his business allies (*Northern Securities* case). Roosevelt chose, however, not to attack other gigantic trusts, such as U.S. Steel, another of Morgan's creations.

When prosecution of Northern Securities began, Morgan reportedly collared Roosevelt and offered, "If we have done anything wrong, send your man to my man and they can fix it up." The president refused but was more sympathetic to cooperation between business and government than his rebuff might suggest. Rather than prosecute at every turn, he urged the Bureau of Corporations (part of the newly created Department of Labor and Commerce) to assist companies on mergers and other forms of expansion. Through investigation and cooperation, the administration cajoled businesses to regulate themselves; corporations often accepted regulation because it helped them operate more efficiently and reduced overproduction.

Roosevelt also supported regulatory legislation, especially after his resounding electoral victory in 1904, in which he won votes from Progressives and businesspeople alike. After a year of wrangling, Roosevelt persuaded Congress to pass the Hepburn Act (1906), which gave the Interstate Commerce Commission (ICC) more authority to set railroad freight and storage rates, though it did allow the courts to overturn rate decisions. Progressive senator Robert La Follette complained that Roosevelt had compromised with congressional business allies to ensure the bill's passage. But Roosevelt chose to reaffirm the principle of regulation rather than risk defeat over unreachable, idealistic objectives.

Roosevelt showed similar willingness to compromise on legislation to ensure the purity of food and drugs. For decades reformers had been urging government regulation of processed meat and patent medicines. Public outrage at fraud and adulteration was heightened in 1906 when Upton Sinclair published *The Jungle*, a fictionalized exposé of Chicago meatpacking plants. Sinclair, a socialist whose prime objective was to improve working conditions, shocked public sensibilities with his vivid descriptions:

Pure Food and Drug Laws

> There would be meat stored in great piles in rooms; and the water from the leaky roofs would drip over it, and thousands of rats would race about on it. It was too dark in these storage places to see well, but a man could run his hand over these piles of meat and sweep off handfuls of dried dung of rats. These rats were a nuisance, and the packers would put poisoned bread out for them; they would die, and then rats, bread, and meat would go into the hoppers together.

After reading the novel, Roosevelt ordered an investigation. Finding Sinclair's descriptions accurate,

he supported the Meat Inspection Act, which passed in 1906. Like the Hepburn Act, this law reinforced the principle of government regulation, requiring that government agents monitor the quality of processed meat. But as part of a compromise to pass the bill, the government, rather than the meatpackers, had to finance inspections, and meatpackers could appeal adverse decisions in court. Nor were companies required to provide date-of-processing information on canned meats. Most large meatpackers welcomed the legislation anyway, because it helped them force out smaller competitors and restored falling confidence in American meat products in foreign markets.

The Pure Food and Drug Act (1906) not only prohibited dangerously adulterated foods but also addressed abuses in the patent medicine industry. Makers of tonics and pills had long been making undue claims about their products' effects and liberally using alcohol and narcotics as ingredients. Ads in popular publications, such as one for a "Brain Stimulator and Nerve Tonic" in the Sears, Roebuck catalogue, had wildly exaggerated claims. Although the law did not ban such products, it did require that labels list the ingredients—a goal consistent with Progressive confidence that if people knew the truth they would make wiser purchases.

Roosevelt's approach to labor resembled his stance toward business. When the United Mine Workers struck against Pennsylvania coal mine owners in 1902 over an eight-hour workday and higher pay, the president employed Progressive tactics of investigation and arbitration. Owners, however, stubbornly refused to recognize the union or arbitrate grievances. As winter approached and fuel shortages threatened, Roosevelt roused public opinion. He threatened to use federal troops to reopen the mines, thus forcing management to accept arbitration of the dispute by a special commission. The commission decided in favor of higher wages and reduced hours and required management to deal with grievance committees elected by the miners, but it did not mandate recognition of the union. The decision, according to Roosevelt, provided a "square deal" for all. The settlement also embodied Roosevelt's belief that the president or his representatives should have a say in which labor demands were legitimate and which were not. In Roosevelt's mind there were good and bad labor organizations (socialists, for example, were bad), just as there were good and bad business combinations.

Makers of unregulated patent medicines advertised exorbitant results from using their products. This ad, while warning against "fraudulent claims," asserts that a wide belt can cure a variety of ailments. The Pure Food and Drug Act of 1906 did not ban such products but tried to prevent manufacturers from making such unsubstantiated statements. (Picture Research Consultants & Archives)

Roosevelt did not originate government involvement in modern resource conservation; important developments in this area, especially the establishment of national parks, had begun in the late nineteenth century (see pages 472–473). But he did combine the Progressive impulse for efficiency with his love for the great outdoors to advance conservation policy. Roosevelt warned Congress in 1907, "We are prone to think of the resources of this country as inexhaustible; this is not so." In this regard, he drastically revised federal policy toward the nation's resources, particularly in the West. Previously, the government had habitually transferred ownership and control of natural resources on federal land to the states and to private interests. Roosevelt, however, believed the most efficient way to use and conserve these resources would be for the government to retain public management over those lands that remained in the public domain.

Conservation

Roosevelt took steps to exert federal power over resources in several ways. He tried, though unsuccessfully, to revise an 1873 law under which the government sold western coal and oil lands at very cheap prices to private concerns. Roosevelt wanted to retain government ownership and charge producers lease fees (such a policy was instituted in 1920). He did succeed in protecting waterpower sites from sale and instead charged permit fees for users who wanted to produce hydroelectricity. He also supported the Newlands Reclamation Act of 1902, which controlled sale of irrigated federal land in the West (see page 475). He tripled the number and acreage of national forests and supported conservationist Gifford Pinchot in creating the U.S. Forest Service.

As chief forester, Pinchot advocated scientific management of the nation's woodlands to protect the land and water from overuse by timber cutters, farmers, and herders. Pinchot had management of the national forests transferred from the Interior Department to his bureau in the Agriculture Department by arguing that forests were crops grown on "tree farms." Under his guidance, the Forest Service charged fees for grazing livestock within the national forests, supervised bidding for the cutting of timber, and hired university-trained foresters as federal employees.

Gifford Pinchot

As historian Richard White has pointed out, Pinchot and Roosevelt did not seek to lock up resources permanently; rather they wanted to guarantee their efficient use. Although antifederal, anticonservation attitudes remained in the West, many of those involved in natural-resource exploitation welcomed such a policy because, like regulation of food and drugs, it enabled them to minimize overproduction and to restrict competition. They simply had to try to influence federal bureaucracies and Congress to act in their behalf while at the same time denouncing federal interference. As a result of new federal policies, the West and its resources fell under the Progressive spell of management.

In 1907 Roosevelt had to compromise his principles in the face of economic crisis. That year a financial panic caused by reckless speculation forced some New York banks to close to prevent frightened depositors from withdrawing money. J. P. Morgan helped stem the panic by persuading financiers to stop dumping their stocks. In return for Morgan's aid, Roosevelt approved a deal allowing U.S. Steel to absorb the Tennessee Iron and Coal Company—a deal at odds with Roosevelt's trustbusting aims.

Panic of 1907

During his last year in office, Roosevelt retreated from the Republican Party's traditional friendliness to big business. He lashed out at the irresponsibility of "malefactors of great wealth" and supported stronger business regulation and heavier taxation of the rich. Having promised that he would not seek reelection, Roosevelt backed his friend Secretary of War William Howard Taft for the Republican nomination in 1908, hoping that Taft would continue his initiatives. Democrats nominated William Jennings Bryan for the third time, but the "Great Commoner" lost again. Aided by Roosevelt, who still enjoyed great popularity, Taft won by 1.25 million popular votes and a 2-to-1 margin in the electoral college.

Early in 1909 Roosevelt traveled to Africa to shoot game (his passion for the manly activity of hunting outweighed his support for conservation), leaving Taft to face political problems that his predecessor had managed to postpone. Foremost among them was the tariff; rates had risen to excessive levels. Honoring Taft's pledge to cut rates, the House passed a bill sponsored by Representative Sereno E. Payne that provided for numerous reductions. Protectionists in the Senate prepared, as in the past, to amend the House bill and revise rates upward. But Senate Progressives, led by La Follette, or-

Taft Administration

ganized a stinging attack on the tariff for benefiting special interests, trapping Taft between reformers who claimed to be preserving Roosevelt's antitrust campaign and protectionists who still dominated the Republican Party. In the end, Senator Aldrich and other protectionists restored many of the cuts the Payne bill had made, and Taft—who believed the bill had some positive provisions and understood that more extreme cuts were not politically possible—signed what became known as the Payne-Aldrich Tariff (1909). In the eyes of Progressives, Taft had failed the test of filling Roosevelt's shoes.

Progressive and conservative wings of the Republican Party were rapidly drifting apart. Soon after the tariff controversy, a group of insurgents in the House led by Nebraska's George Norris challenged Speaker "Uncle Joe" Cannon of Illinois, whose power over committee assignments and the scheduling of debates could make or break a piece of legislation. Taft first supported then abandoned the insurgents, who nevertheless managed to liberalize procedures by enlarging the influential Rules Committee and removing selection of its members from Cannon's control. In 1910 Taft also angered conservationists by firing Gifford Pinchot, who had protested Secretary of the Interior Richard A. Ballinger's plan to reduce federal supervision of western waterpower sites and his sale of coal lands in Alaska.

In reality Taft was as sympathetic to reform as Roosevelt was. He prosecuted more trusts than Roosevelt, expanded national forest reserves, signed the Mann-Elkins Act (1910), which bolstered the regulatory powers of the ICC, and supported labor reforms such as the eight-hour workday and mine safety legislation. The Sixteenth Amendment, which legalized the federal income tax, and the Seventeenth Amendment, which provided for direct election of U.S. senators, were initiated during Taft's presidency (and ratified in 1913). Like Roosevelt, Taft compromised with big business, but unlike Roosevelt he lacked the ability to manipulate the public with spirited rhetoric. Roosevelt had expanded presidential power and had infused the presidency with vitality. "I believe in a strong executive," he once asserted. "I believe in power." Taft, by contrast, believed in the strict restraint of law. He had been a successful lawyer and judge (and returned to the bench as chief justice of the United States between 1921 and 1930). His caution and unwillingness to offend disappointed those accustomed to Roosevelt's impetuosity.

In 1910, when Roosevelt returned from Africa boasting three thousand animal trophies, he found his party torn and tormented. Reformers, angered by Taft's apparent insensitivity to their causes, formed the National Progressive Republican League and rallied behind Robert La Follette for president in 1912, though many hoped Roosevelt would run. Another wing of the party remained loyal to Taft. Disappointed by Taft's performance (particularly his firing of Pinchot), Roosevelt began to speak out. He filled his speeches with references to "the welfare of the people" and stronger regulation of business. When La Follette became ill early in 1912, Roosevelt, proclaiming himself fit as a "bull moose," threw his hat into the ring for the Republican presidential nomination.

The Bull Moose Party

Taft's supporters controlled the Republican convention and nominated him for a second term. In protest, Roosevelt's supporters bolted the convention to form a third party—the Progressive, or Bull Moose, Party—and nominated the fifty-three-year-old former president. Meanwhile, Democrats took forty-six ballots to select their candidate, New Jersey's Progressive governor Woodrow Wilson. Socialists, by now an organized and growing party, again nominated Eugene V. Debs. The ensuing campaign exposed voters to the most thorough evaluation of the American system since 1896.

Woodrow Wilson and the Extension of Reform

In his acceptance speech before the Progressive Party, Theodore Roosevelt proclaimed, "We stand at Armageddon and we battle for the Lord." But on inauguration day in 1913, it was Woodrow Wilson who assumed command of the forces of good. "The Nation," he exhorted, "has been deeply stirred by a solemn passion. . . . The feelings with which we face this new age of right and opportunity sweep across our heartstrings like some air out of God's own presence, where justice and mercy are reconciled and the judge and the brother are one."

Election results illustrated the extent to which such moral pronouncements had swayed voter passions. Wilson won 42 percent of the popular vote. He was a minority president, though he did capture 435 out of 531 electoral votes (see Map 21.2). Roosevelt received

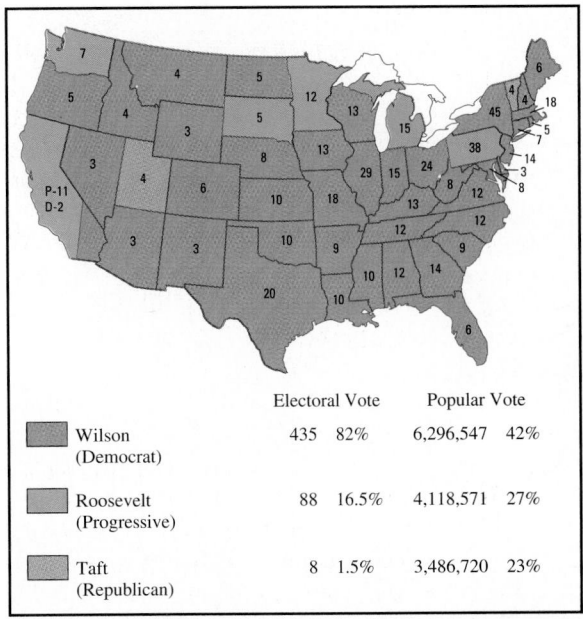

	Electoral Vote		Popular Vote	
Wilson (Democrat)	435	82%	6,296,547	42%
Roosevelt (Progressive)	88	16.5%	4,118,571	27%
Taft (Republican)	8	1.5%	3,486,720	23%

Map 21.2 Presidential Election, 1912 Though he won a minority of the popular votes, Woodrow Wilson captured so many states that he achieved an easy victory in the electoral college.

27 percent of the popular vote. Taft finished third, polling 23 percent of the popular vote and only 8 electoral votes. Debs won 901,000 votes, 6 percent of the total, but no electoral votes. Fully three-quarters of the electorate thus supported some alternative to the view of restrained government that Taft represented.

Sharp debate over Progressive fundamentals had characterized the campaign. Roosevelt offered voters the "New Nationalism," a term coined by reform editor Herbert Croly. Roosevelt foresaw an era of national unity in which government would coordinate and regulate economic activity. He would not destroy big business, which he viewed as an efficient organizer of production. Instead, he would establish regulatory commissions of experts who would protect citizens' interests and ensure wise use of economic power. "The effort at prohibiting all combinations has substantially failed," he claimed. "The way out lies . . . in completely controlling them."

New Nationalism and New Freedom

Wilson offered a more idealistic scheme, the "New Freedom," based on ideas of Progressive lawyer

Looking sober and stubborn, Woodrow Wilson (1856–1924) used a preacher's moralism and a professor's reasoning to raise expectations for the fulfillment of his idealistic promises. (National Portrait Gallery, Smithsonian Institution/Art Resource, N.Y.)

Both men strongly supported equality of opportunity (chiefly for white males), conservation of natural resources, fair wages, and social betterment for all. Neither would hesitate to expand government activity through strong personal leadership and bureaucratic reform. Thus even though Wilson received a minority of the total vote in 1912, he could interpret the election results as a mandate to subdue trusts and broaden the federal government's role in social reform.

The public fondly called Roosevelt "Teddy" and "TR," but Thomas Woodrow Wilson was too aloof ever to be nicknamed "Woody" or "WW." Born in Virginia in 1856 and raised in the South, Wilson was the son of a Presbyterian minister. He earned a B.A. at Princeton University, studied law at the University of Virginia, received a Ph.D. from Johns Hopkins University, and became a professor of history, jurisprudence, and political economy. Between 1885 and 1908, he published several respected books on American history and government.

Woodrow Wilson

Wilson's manner and bearing reflected his background. He exuded none of Roosevelt's flamboyance, yet he was a charismatic leader. A superb orator, he could inspire intense loyalty with religious imagery and eloquent expressions of American ideals. Wilson's convictions led him early into reform. In 1902 he became president of Princeton, where he upset tradition with curricular reforms and battles against the university's aristocratic elements. In 1910 New Jersey's Democrats, eager for respectability, nominated Wilson for governor. After winning the election, Wilson repudiated the party bosses and promoted Progressive legislation. A poor administrator, he often lost his temper and stubbornly refused to compromise. His accomplishments nevertheless attracted national attention and won him the Democratic nomination for president in 1912.

As president, Wilson found it necessary to blend New Freedom competition with New Nationalism regulation; in so doing he set the direction of future federal economic policy. The corporate merger movement had proceeded so far that restoration of open competition proved impossible. Wilson could only try to prevent corporate abuses by expanding government's regulatory powers. His administration moved toward that end with passage in 1914 of the Clayton Anti-Trust Act and a bill creating the Federal Trade

Wilson's Policy on Business Regulation

Louis Brandeis. Wilson argued that concentrated economic power threatened individual liberty and that monopolies had to be broken up so the marketplace could become genuinely open. But he would not restore laissez faire. Like Roosevelt, Wilson would enhance government authority to protect and regulate. "Freedom today," he declared, "is something more than being let alone. Without the watchful . . . resolute interference of the government, there can be no fair play between individuals and such powerful institutions as the trust." Wilson stopped short, however, of advocating the cooperation between business and government inherent in Roosevelt's New Nationalism.

Roosevelt and Wilson stood closer together than their rhetoric implied. In spite of his faith in experts as regulators, Roosevelt harbored a belief in individual freedom as strong as Wilson's. And Wilson was not completely hostile to concentrated economic power.

Commission (FTC). The Clayton Act corrected deficiencies of the Sherman Anti-Trust Act of 1890 (see page 514) by outlawing monopolistic practices such as price discrimination (efforts to destroy competition by lowering prices in some regions but not in others) and interlocking directorates (management of two or more competing companies by the same executives). The FTC would investigate companies and issue cease-and-desist orders against unfair trade practices. Accused companies could appeal FTC orders in court; nevertheless, the FTC represented another step toward consumer protection.

Wilson expanded regulation of banking with the Federal Reserve Act (1913), which established the nation's first central banking system since 1836 when the Second Bank of the United States expired. The act was intended to break the power that powerful banking syndicates such as that of J. P. Morgan held over the money supply and credit. It created twelve district banks to hold reserves of member banks throughout the nation. The district banks, supervised by the Federal Reserve Board, would lend money to member banks at a low interest rate called the discount rate. By adjusting this rate (and thus the amount a bank could afford to borrow), district banks could increase or decrease the amount of money in circulation. In other words, in response to the nation's needs, the Federal Reserve Board could loosen or tighten credit. Monetary affairs no longer would depend on the gold supply, and interest rates would be fairer, especially for small borrowers.

Like his predecessors, Wilson attempted to restore competition in commerce with the Underwood Tariff, passed in 1913. By the 1910s, prices for some consumer goods had become unnaturally high because tariffs had discouraged the importation of cheaper foreign materials and manufactured goods. By reducing or eliminating certain tariff rates, the Underwood Tariff encouraged imports. To replace revenues lost because of tariff reductions, the act levied a graduated income tax on U.S. residents—an option made possible when the Sixteenth Amendment was ratified earlier that year. The income tax was tame by today's standards. Incomes under $4,000 were exempt; thus almost all factory workers and farmers escaped taxation. Individuals and corporations earning between $4,000 and $20,000 had to pay a 1 percent tax; thereafter rates rose gradually to a maximum of 6 percent on earnings over $500,000.

Tariff and Tax Reform

The outbreak of the First World War (see Chapter 23) and approaching presidential election campaign prompted Wilson to support stronger reforms in 1916. Concerned that farmers needed a better system of long-term mortgage credit, the president backed the Federal Farm Loan Act. This measure created twelve federally supported banks (not to be confused with the Federal Reserve banks) that would lend money at moderate interest to farmers who belonged to credit institutions—a watered-down version of the subtreasury plan that Populists had promoted a generation earlier (see page 566).

To forestall railroad strikes that might disrupt transportation at a time of national emergency, Wilson pushed passage of the Adamson Act, which mandated an eight-hour workday and time-and-a-half overtime pay for railroad laborers. He pleased Progressives by appointing Brandeis, the "people's advocate," to the Supreme Court, though an anti-Semitic backlash almost blocked Senate approval of the Court's first Jewish justice. Also, Wilson courted support from social reformers by backing laws that regulated child labor and provided workers' compensation for federal employees who suffered work-related injuries or illness.

In selecting a candidate to oppose Wilson in 1916, Republicans snubbed Theodore Roosevelt in favor of Charles Evans Hughes, a Supreme Court justice and former reform governor of New York. Acutely aware of the First World War's impact on national affairs (Europe had been ablaze since 1914), Wilson ran for reelection on a platform of peace, Progressivism, and preparedness; his supporters used the campaign slogan "He Kept Us Out of War." Hughes and his fractured party could not muzzle Roosevelt, whose bellicose speeches suggested that Republicans would drag Americans into war. Wilson received 9.1 million votes to Hughes's 8.5 million, and the president barely won in the electoral college, 277 to 254. The Socialist candidate drew only 600,000 votes, down from 901,000 in 1912, largely because Wilson's reforms had won over some socialists and because the ailing Eugene Debs was no longer the party's standard-bearer.

Election of 1916

During Wilson's second term, involvement in the First World War increased government regulation of the economy. In his first term Wilson had become convinced that regulatory commissions, which could easily fall under the influence of the very interests they were meant to regulate, should not govern social and economic behavior. Mobilization for the war effort, he came to believe, required coordination of production and cooperation between the public and private sectors. The War Industries Board (see pages 646–647) exemplified this cooperation: private businesses regulated by the board submitted to its control on condition that their own profit motives would continue to be satisfied. After the war the Wilson administration dropped most cooperative and regulatory measures, including farm price supports, guarantees of collective bargaining, and high taxes. This retreat from regulation, prompted in part by the election of a Republican Congress in 1918, stimulated a new era of business ascendancy in the 1920s.

Summary

By 1920 a quarter-century of reform had wrought momentous changes. Government, economy, and society as they had existed in the nineteenth century were gone forever. In their efforts to achieve their goals of ending abuses of power, reforming institutions, and applying scientific principles and efficient management, Progressives established the principle of public intervention to ensure fairness, health, and safety. Concern over poverty and injustice reached new heights. For every American who suffered some form of deprivation, three or four enjoyed unprecedented material comforts; and amid growing affluence, reformers could not sustain their efforts indefinitely. Although Progressive values lingered after the First World War, a mass consumer society began to refocus people's attention from reform to materialism.

The Progressive era was characterized by multiple and sometimes contradictory goals. By no means was there a single Progressive movement. Reform programs on the national level ranged from Roosevelt's faith in big government as a coordinator of big business to Wilson's promise to dissolve economic concentrations and legislate open competition. At state and local levels, reformers pursued causes as varied as neighborhood improvement, government reorganization, public ownership of utilities, betterment of working conditions, and control of morality. Local organizations and national associations coordinated efforts on specific issues, but reformers with different goals often worked at cross-purposes.

In spite of their remarkable successes, the outright failure of many Progressive initiatives indicates the strength of the opposition, as well as weaknesses within the reform movements themselves. Courts asserted constitutional and liberty-of-contract doctrines in striking down key Progressive legislation, notably the federal law prohibiting child labor. In states and cities, adoption of the initiative, referendum, and recall did not encourage greater participation in government as had been hoped; those mechanisms either were seldom used or became tools of special interests. On the federal level, regulatory agencies rarely had enough resources for thorough investigations; they had to depend on information from the very companies they policed. Progressives thus failed in many respects to redistribute power. In 1920 as in 1900, government remained under the influence of business and industry, a state of affairs that many people considered quite satisfactory.

Yet the reform movements that characterized the Progressive era reshaped the nation's future. Trust-busting, however faulty, forced industrialists to become more sensitive to public opinion, and insurgents in Congress partially diluted the power of dictatorial politicians. Progressive legislation equipped government with tools to protect consumers against price fixing and dangerous products. The income tax, created to redistribute wealth, also became a source of government revenue. Social reformers relieved some ills of urban life. And perhaps most important, Progressives challenged old ways of thinking. Although the questions they raised about the quality of American life remained unresolved, Progressives made the nation acutely aware of its principles and promises.

LEGACY FOR A PEOPLE AND A NATION
Women and Social Work

By the year 2000, human services—occupations catering to people's personal needs in the areas of health, education, housing, income, and justice and public safety—constituted the sixth-fastest-growing career field in the United States. Social workers dominated this profession, and over three-fourths of social workers were female, a legacy from the actions of concerned women during the Progressive era.

Jane Addams, the indomitable founder and leader of the Hull House settlement, laid the groundwork for the social work profession with her activities to understand and improve the lives of disadvantaged people. Almost all early social work pioneers who aided her were women, including Florence Kelley, Alice Hamilton, and Edith and Grace Abbott. These and other women used the field of social welfare to create occupations for other educated, ambitious, and service-minded women not only in social work but also in areas of child welfare, juvenile justice, and healthcare. Their early efforts focused on reforming existing institutions and lobbying for government aid and intervention, but by the end of the Progressive era social workers had made casework an important part of their professional activity. This shift reflected the particular interest and experience women had in attending to needs of individuals and families.

In 1898 formal organization of the profession began with the establishment of The New York School of Philanthropy, later named the Columbia University School of Social Work. Thereafter, programs for educating social workers appeared in other cities. Women continued to dominate the profession. Of 111 individuals listed as "social work pioneers" by the National Association of Social Workers over the past one hundred years, 77 are female. These leaders and the profession in general served critical functions in bringing public resources to people in need, especially during major periods of social action such as the New Deal of the 1930s, the Great Society of the 1960s, and today—especially in the area of assisting new immigrants.

Women's activities in social service have had drawbacks as well as successes. Throughout the twentieth century, men have held most of the top administrative positions in social work organizations and schools. Women in the profession still tend toward casework while men more frequently are involved in social welfare policymaking. And women social workers receive lower salaries than men and are less likely to be promoted. Moreover, psychological principles, which have become central to social work theory, carry a sexist tone in that they are likely to define "normal" social behavior in male-oriented terms, making it more likely for social workers to view female clients with social problems as having "abnormal" traits. Thus the pioneer efforts by women in social service dating from the Progressive era have still not erased gender-based biases in American culture.

For Further Reading, see page A-24 of the Appendix. For Web resources, go to http://college.hmco.com.

THE QUEST
FOR EMPIRE
1865–1914

Devil!" they angrily shouted at Lottie Moon. "Foreign devil!" The Southern Baptist missionary braced herself against the antiforeign Chinese "rabble" she vowed to convert to Christianity. On a day in the 1880s, she walked "steadily and persistently" through the village hecklers, vowing to win their acceptance and then their souls. A daunting task.

Born in 1840 in Virginia and educated at what is now Hollins College, Charlotte Diggs Moon volunteered in 1873 for "woman's work" in northern China. There she taught and proselytized, largely among women and children because women seldom preached to men and men were forbidden to preach to women. This compassionate, pious, and courageous single woman, "putting love into action," worked in China until her death in 1912.

Lottie Moon (Mu Ladi or 幕拉第) made bold and sometimes dangerous evangelizing trips in the 1870s and 1880s to isolated Chinese hamlets. "O! The torture of human eyes upon you; scanning every feature, every look, every gesture!" Curious peasant women pinched her, pulling on her skirt, purring, "How white her hand is!" They peppered her with questions: "How old are you?" and "Where do you get money to live on?" Speaking in Chinese, she held high a picture book on Jesus Christ's birth and crucifixion, drawing the chattering crowd's attention to the "foreign doctrine" that she hoped would displace Confucianism, Buddhism, and Taoism.

In the 1890s a "storm of persecution" against foreigners swept China. Missionaries, because they were upending traditional ways and authority, became hated targets. One missionary conceded that in "believing Jesus," girls and women alarmed men who clamored that "disobedient wives and daughters" would no longer "worship the idols when told." In the village of Shaling in early 1890, Lottie Moon's Christian converts were beaten and the "foreign devils" ordered to move out. Fearing for her life, she had to flee. For several months in 1900, during the violent Boxer Rebellion, she had to leave China altogether as a multinational force (that included U.S. troops) intervened to save foreign missionaries, diplomats, and merchants.

The missionary Lottie Moon (1840–1912) is surrounded in 1901 by English-language students in Japan during her refuge from the Boxer Rebellion in China. (Virginia Baptist Historical Society & University Archives)

Lottie Moon and thousands of other missionaries managed to convert to Christianity only a very small minority of the Chinese people. Although she, like other missionaries, probably never shed the Western view that she represented a superior religion and culture, she seldom wavered from her affection for the Chinese people and from her devotion to the foreign missionary project—from her "rejoicing to suffer." In frequent letters and articles directed to a U.S. audience, she lobbied to recruit "a band of ardent, enthusiastic, and experienced Christian women," to stir up "a mighty wave of enthusiasm for Woman's Work for Woman." To this day, the Lottie Moon Christmas Offering in Southern Baptist churches raises millions of dollars for missions abroad.

Like so many other Americans who went overseas in the late nineteenth and early twentieth centuries, Lottie Moon helped spread American culture and implant U.S. influence abroad. In this complex process, other peoples sometimes adopted and sometimes rejected American ways. At the same time, American participants in this cultural expansion, and the cultural collisions it generated, became transformed. Lottie Moon, for example, strove to understand the Chinese people and learn their language. She abandoned the derogatory phrases "heathen Chinese" and "great unwashed" and even assumed their dress. She reminded other less sensitive missionaries that the Chinese rightfully took pride in their own ancient history and thus had no reason to "gape in astonishment at Western civilization."

Lottie Moon also changed—again, in her own words—from "a timid self-distrustful girl into a brave self-reliant woman." As she questioned the Chinese confinement of women, most conspicuous in arranged marriages, footbinding, and sexual segregation, she advanced women's rights. She understood that she could not convert Chinese women unless they had the freedom to listen to her appeals. Bucking the gender ideology of the times, she also uneasily rose to challenge the male domination of America's religious missions. When the Southern Baptist Foreign Mission Board, for example, denied women missionaries the right to vote in meetings, she resigned in protest. The board soon reversed itself.

Critics over the decades have labeled as "cultural imperialism" the activities of Lottie Moon and other missionaries, accusing the missionaries of seeking to subvert indigenous traditions and sparking destructive cultural clashes. Defenders of missionary work, on the other hand, have celebrated their efforts to break down cultural barriers and to bring the world's peoples closer together. Either way, Lottie Moon's story illustrates how Americans interacted with the world in diverse ways, how through their experiences the categories "domestic" and "foreign" intersected, and how they expanded abroad not only to seek land, trade, investments, and strategic bases but also to promote American culture, including the Christian faith.

Between the Civil War and the First World War, Americans ranked as unabashed expansionists and imperialists. Before the Civil War, Americans had repeatedly extended the frontier: they bought Louisiana; annexed Florida, Oregon, and Texas; pushed Indians out of the path of white migration westward; seized California and other western areas from Mexico; and acquired southern parts of present-day Arizona and New Mexico from Mexico (the Gadsden Purchase). Americans had also developed a lucrative foreign trade with most of the world and spread their culture wherever they traveled. They rekindled their expansionist course after the Civil War, building, managing, and protecting an overseas empire. In that imperialistic age of "living" and "dying" nations, as British prime minister Lord Salisbury observed, the international system witnessed an assertive Germany challenge an overextended Great Britain, an economic and military giant becoming, said one diplomat, the "weary titan" of the world. Japan expanded in Asia at the expense of both China and Russia. As for the "living" United States, it emerged as a great power with particular clout in Latin America, especially as the "dying" Spain declined and Britain disengaged from the hemisphere. "The old nations of the earth creep on at a snail's pace," the industrialist Andrew Carnegie bragged, but the United States "thunders past with the rush of the express [train]."

The United States's imperialist surge, however, sparked considerable opposition. Abroad, native nationalists, commercial competitors, and other imperial nations tried to block the spread of U.S. influence, while anti-imperialists at home stimulated a momentous debate over the fundamental course of American foreign policy. Most Americans applauded expansionism—the outward movement of goods, ships, dollars, people, and ideas—as a traditional feature of their nation's history. But many became uneasy whenever expansionism gave way to imperialism—the imposition of control over other peoples, undermining their sovereignty and usurping their freedom to make their own decisions. Imperial control could be imposed either formally (by military occupation, annexation, or

IMPORTANT EVENTS

1861–69 Seward sets expansionist course

1866 Transatlantic cable completed

1867 Alaska and Midway acquired

1868 Burlingame Treaty with China regulates immigration

1871 Anglo-American treaty sends *Alabama* claims issue to tribunal

1874 U.S. foreign trade shifts to favorable balance

1876 Pro-U.S. Díaz begins long rule in Mexico

1878 U.S. gains naval rights in Samoa

1880 Treaty limits Chinese immigration to the United States

1883 Congress votes funds for New Navy

1885 Strong's *Our Country* celebrates Anglo-Saxons

1887 U.S. gains naval rights to Pearl Harbor, Hawai'i

1889 First Pan-American Conference

1890 Mahan's *The Influence of Sea Power upon History* published

McKinley Tariff hurts Hawaiian sugar exports

1893 Severe economic depression begins

Turner sets forth frontier thesis

Hawaiian Queen Lili'uokalani overthrown

1894 Wilson-Gorham Tariff imposes duty on Cuban sugar

1895 Olney blasts Britain in Venezuelan crisis

Cuban revolution against Spain begins

Japan defeats China in war

1898 Publication of de Lôme letter

Sinking of the *Maine*

Spanish-American-Cuban-Filipino War

Hawai'i annexed by the United States

1899 Treaty of Paris enlarges U.S. empire

United Fruit Company forms and becomes influential in Central America

First Open Door note calls for equal trade opportunity in China

Philippine insurrection breaks out

Samoa partitioned

1900 Second Open Door note issued during Boxer Rebellion in China

U.S. exports total $1.5 billion

1901 Hay-Pauncefote Treaty allows U.S. canal

1903 Panama grants canal rights to U.S.

Platt Amendment subjugates Cuba

1904 Roosevelt Corollary declares U.S. a hemispheric "police power"

1905 Taft-Katsura Agreement gains Japanese pledge to respect Philippines

Portsmouth Conference ends Russo-Japanese War

U.S. financial supervision of Dominican Republic begins

1906 San Francisco school board segregates Asian schoolchildren

U.S. invades Cuba to quell revolt

1907 "Great White Fleet" makes world tour

"Gentleman's agreement" with Japan restricts immigration

1908 Root-Takahira Agreement with Japan reaffirms Open Door in China

1910 Mexican revolution threatens U.S. interests

1911 Treaty bans pelagic sealing in Bering Sea

1912 U.S. troops invade Cuba again

U.S. troops occupy Nicaragua

1914 U.S. troops invade Mexico

First World War begins

Panama Canal opens

colonialism) or informally (by economic domination, political manipulation, or the threat of intervention). As the informal methods indicate, imperialism meant far more than the taking of territory.

Critics in the late nineteenth century disparaged territorial imperialism as unbefitting the United States, and they opposed joining other great powers in the scramble for colonies in Asia and Africa. Would not an overseas territorial empire, incorporating people of color living far from the United States, weaken institutions at home, threaten American culture, invite perpetual war, and violate honored principles? Although the United States preferred the "annexation of trade" to the annexation of territory, as Secretary of State James G. Blaine once declared, it became clear that economic expansionism sometimes led to the grabbing of colonies. Most Americans endorsed economic expansion as essential to the nation's prosperity and security, but anti-imperialists drew the line between expansionism and imperialism: profitable and fair trade relationships, yes; exploitation, no. And, some advised, American business activity abroad should not drag the United States into unwanted diplomatic crises and wars. But it did.

In the late nineteenth century the federal government sometimes failed to fund adequately the vehicles of expansion (such as the navy until the 1880s) and most businessmen ignored foreign commerce in favor of the domestic marketplace. Still, the direction of U.S. foreign policy after the Civil War became unmistakable: Americans intended to exert their influence beyond the continental United States, to reach for more space, more land, more markets, more cultural penetration, and more power. Republican Senator Henry Cabot Lodge of Massachusetts, claiming that the "great nations" were seizing "the waste areas of the world," advised that "the United States must not fall out of the line of march," because "civilization and the advancement of the [Anglo-Saxon] race" were at stake.

U.S. activity abroad heightened in the tumultuous decade of the 1890s, when doubters' voices were drowned out by calls for war and foreign territory, and when American power was sufficient to deliver both. U.S. entry into the Spanish-American-Cuban-Filipino War in 1898 and the subsequent subjugation of other peoples ignited a major political debate while lifting the United States to great-power status. ■

Imperial Promoters: The Foreign Policy Elite and Economic Expansion

Foreign policy has always sprung from the domestic setting of a nation—its needs, wants, moods, ideology, and culture. The leaders who guided America's expansionist foreign relations were the same people who guided the economic development of the machine age, forged the transcontinental railroad, built America's bustling cities and giant corporations, and shaped a mass culture. They unabashedly espoused the idea that the United States was an exceptional nation, so different from and superior to others because of Americans' Anglo-Saxon heritage and their God-favored and prosperous history. The domestic and foreign spheres, as always, were inseparable.

"The people" may influence domestic policy, but they seldom shape foreign policy. Most Americans simply do not follow international relations or express themselves on **Foreign Policy Elite** foreign issues. The making of foreign policy, then, is usually dominated by what scholars have labeled the "foreign policy elite"—opinion leaders in politics, business, labor, agriculture, religion, journalism, education, and the military. In the post–Civil War era, this small group, whom Secretary of State Walter Q. Gresham called "the thoughtful men of the country," expressed the opinion that counted. Better read and better traveled than most Americans, more cosmopolitan in outlook, and politically active, they believed that U.S. prosperity and security depended on the exertion of U.S. influence abroad. Increasingly in the late nineteenth century, and especially in the 1890s, the expansionist-minded elite urged both formal and informal imperialism. These leaders created what the historian Emily Rosenberg has called "the promotional state"—a federal government committed to assisting American entrepreneurs who wished to trade and invest abroad and dedicated to making the United States a world power.

Ambitious and clannish, the imperialists often met in Washington, D.C., at the homes of the historian Henry Adams and the writer and diplomat John Hay (who became secretary of state in 1898) or at the Metropolitan Club. They talked about building a bigger navy and digging a canal across Panama, Central America, or Mexico, establishing colonies, and selling surpluses abroad. Theodore Roosevelt, appointed assistant secretary of the navy in 1897, was among them; so were Senator Henry Cabot Lodge, who joined the Foreign Relations Committee in 1896, and the corporate lawyer Elihu Root, who later would serve as both secretary of war and secretary of state. Such well-positioned luminaries kept up the drumbeat for empire.

These American leaders believed that selling, buying, and investing in foreign marketplaces were important to the United States. Why? One reason was profits from foreign sales. "It is my dream," declared the governor of Georgia in 1878, to see "in every valley . . . a cotton factory to convert the raw material of the neighborhood into fabrics which shall warm the limbs of Japanese and Chinese." Fear helped make the case for foreign trade as well because the nation's farms and factories produced more than Americans could consume, all the more so during the 1890s depression. Foreign commerce might serve as a safety valve to re-

As one expression of the theme of economic expansion, this poster, advertising the Uncle Sam stove manufactured in New York by the Abendroth Bros. company, announces that food links the United States with the rest of the world. Although the foods on the long list are international—potatoes from Ireland and macaroni from Italy, for example—the message here is that the United States itself is "feeding the world." The turkey being removed from the oven seems to be the only unique American offering, but many of the items on the list were also produced in the United States. The poster was issued in 1876, which explains the image of the Centennial building in Philadelphia and the patriotic red, white, and blue colors. (© Collection of The New-York Historical Society)

lieve overproduction, unemployment, economic depression, and the social tension that arose from them. Surpluses had to be exported, the economist David A. Wells warned, or "we are certain to be smothered in our own grease." Economic ties also permitted political influence to be exerted abroad and helped spread the American way of life, creating a world more hospitable to Americans. In an era when the most powerful nations in the world were also the greatest traders, vigorous foreign economic expansion symbolized national stature.

Foreign trade figured prominently in the tremendous economic growth of the United States after the

Foreign Trade Expansion

Civil War. Foreign commerce, in turn, stimulated the building of a larger protective navy, the professionalization of the foreign service, calls for more colonies, and a more interventionist foreign policy. In 1865 U.S. exports totaled $234 million; by 1900 they had climbed to $1.5 billion (see Figure 22.1). By 1914, at the outbreak of the First World War, exports had reached $2.5 billion, prompting some Europeans to protest an American "invasion" of goods. In 1874 the United States reversed its historically unfavorable balance of trade (importing more than it exported) and began to enjoy a long-term favorable balance (exporting more than it imported). Most of America's products went to Britain, continental Europe, and Canada, but increasing amounts flowed to new markets in Latin America and Asia. Meanwhile, direct American investments abroad reached $3.5 billion by 1914, placing the United States among the top four investor countries.

Agricultural goods accounted for about three-fourths of total exports in 1870 and about two-thirds in 1900, with grain, cotton, meat, and dairy products topping the export list that year. More than half of the annual cotton crop was exported each year. Midwestern

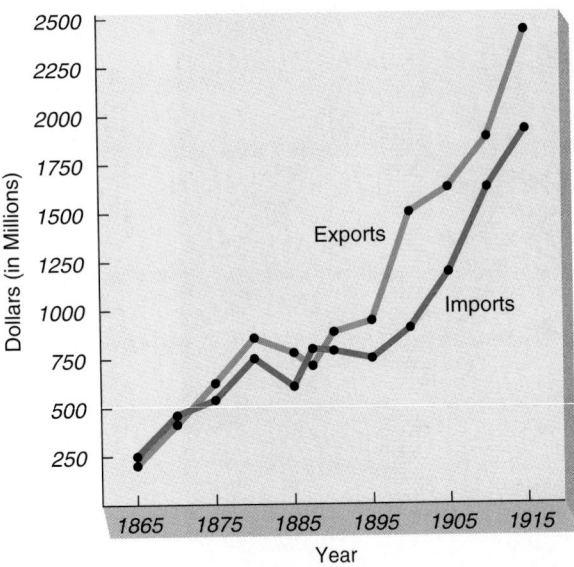

Figure 22.1 U.S. Trade Expansion, 1865–1914 This figure illustrates two key characteristics of U.S. foreign trade: first, that the United States began in the 1870s to enjoy a favorable balance of trade (exporting more than it imported); second, that U.S. exports expanded tremendously, making the United States one of the world's economic giants. (Source: Thomas G. Paterson, J. Garry Clifford, and Kenneth J. Hagan, *American Foreign Relations: A History,* 5th ed. Copyright © 2000 by Houghton Mifflin Company.)

farmers transported their crops by railroad to seaboard cities and then on to foreign markets. Farmers' livelihoods thus became tied to world-market conditions and the outcomes of foreign wars. Wisconsin cheesemakers shipped to Britain; the Swift and Armour meat companies exported refrigerated beef to Europe. To sell American grain abroad, James J. Hill of the Great Northern Railroad distributed wheat cookbooks translated into several Asian languages.

In 1913, when the United States outranked both Great Britain and Germany in manufacturing production (see Figure 22.2), manufactured goods led U.S. exports for the first time. Substantial proportions of America's steel, copper, and petroleum were sold abroad, making many workers in those industries dependent on American exports. George Westinghouse marketed his air brakes in Europe; almost as many Singer sewing machines were exported as were sold at home; and Cyrus McCormick's "reaper kings" harvested the wheat of Russian fields.

Ideology, Culture, and Empire

 In the American march toward empire, ideology and culture figured prominently. An intertwined set of ideas conditioned U.S. foreign relations. Nationalism, exceptionalism, capitalism, Social Darwinism, paternalism, and the categorization of foreigners in derogatory race-, age-, and gender-based terms—all influenced American leaders. Fear and prejudice infused many American ideas about the world and foreign peoples— fear of the social disorder stirred by revolution, fear of economic depression, fear of racial and ethnic mixing, fear of women's rights, fear of a closed frontier, fear of losing international stature. To calm their fears and promote their values, leaders exported American culture and sought to remake other societies in the image of the United States. "They are children and we are men in these deep matters of government," the future president Woodrow Wilson announced in 1898. The intersection of American and foreign cultures, however, bred not only adoption but rejection, not only imitation but clash, as Lottie Moon learned.

After the Civil War, leaders again put the United States on an expansionist course and championed a nationalism based on notions of American supremacy. The inflated **Race Thinking** rhetoric of American exceptionalism and manifest destiny revived, giving intensified voice to explanations for expansion based on race. Some Americans placed people with darker skin, such as blacks and Indians, at the bottom of a racial hierarchy, calling them "uncivilized." At the top sat "civilized" white Anglo-Saxon Americans. Near the top, but beneath Anglo-Saxons, came European peoples—"aggressive" Germans followed by "peasant" Slavs, "sentimental" French and Italians, and "Shylock" Jews. In the middle rank came Latinos, the Spanish-speaking people of Latin America. Theodore Roosevelt disparaged Latinos as "dagoes" and "darkeys" who lacked any ability to govern themselves. Americans debased Latin Americans as half-breeds needing close supervision, distressed damsels begging for manly rescue, or children requiring tutelage. Also midway in the hierarchy were East Asian peoples, the "Orientals" or "Mongolians" whom Americans thought inscrutable, crafty, and immoral, although, as in the case of the Japanese, sometimes capable of success.

Reverend Josiah Strong's popular and influential *Our Country* (1885) celebrated an Anglo-Saxon race

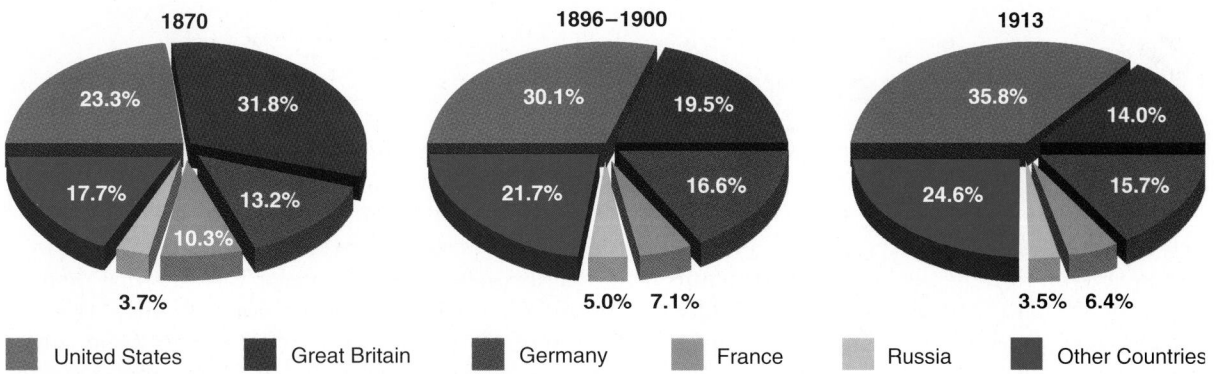

1870

23.3%   31.8%

17.7%   13.2%

10.3%

3.7%

1896–1900

30.1%   19.5%

21.7%   16.6%

5.0%   7.1%

1913

35.8%   14.0%

24.6%   15.7%

3.5%   6.4%

■ United States   ■ Great Britain   ■ Germany   ■ France   ■ Russia   ■ Other Countries

Figure 22.2   The Rise of U.S. Economic Power in the World   These pie charts showing percentage shares of world manufacturing production for the major nations of the world demonstrate that the United States came to surpass Great Britain in this significant economic measurement of power.   (Source: League of Nations data presented in Aaron L. Friedberg, *The Weary Titan: Britain and the Experience of Relative Decline, 1895–1905* [Princeton, N.J.: Princeton University Press, 1988], p. 26.)

destined to lead others. "As America goes, so goes the world," he declared. A few years later he wrote that "to be a Christian and an Anglo-Saxon and an American . . . is to stand at the very mountaintop of privilege." Social Darwinists saw Americans as a superior people certain to overcome all competition. Secretary of State Thomas F. Bayard (1885–1889) applauded the "overflow of our population and capital" into Mexico to "saturate those regions with Americanism," but, he added, "we do not want them" until "they are fit."

The magazine *National Geographic*, which published its first issue in 1888, chronicled with photographs America's new overseas possessions. The editors chose pictures that reflected prevailing American ethnocentric attitudes toward foreigners. Even when smiling faces predominated, the image portrayed was that of strange, exotic, premodern people who had not become "Western." Emphasizing this point, *National Geographic* regularly pictured women with naked breasts. Fairs, too, stereotyped other peoples as falling short of civilization. Fair managers not only celebrated the impressive technology of "Western civilization"; they also put people of color on display in the "freaks" or "midway" section. Alongside bearded women and the fattest man in the world were exhibits—as at the 1895 Atlanta and 1897 Nashville fairs—of Cubans and Mexicans in primitive village settings. Dog-eating Filipinos aroused particular comment at the 1904 St. Louis World's Fair.

Race thinking—popularized in world's fairs, magazine cartoons, postcards, school textbooks, and

political orations—reinforced notions of American greatness, influenced the way U.S. leaders dealt with other peoples, and obviated the need to think about the subtle textures of other societies. Such racism downgraded diplomacy and justified domination and war because self-proclaimed superiors do not negotiate with people ranked as inferiors.

A masculine ethos also characterized American views of foreigners. The language of U.S. leaders was weighted with words such as *manliness* and *weakling*. Member of Congress, son-in-law of Senator Lodge, and 1898 war veteran Augustus P. Gardner extolled the "arena of lust and blood, where true men are to be found." The warrior and president Theodore Roosevelt prized the White House as the "bully pulpit" and celebrated the "strenuous life" against the "flapdoodle pacifists and mollycoddlers." But, more, he and his imperialist cohorts often described other nations (and the American peace movement) as effeminate—unable, in contrast to a masculine Uncle Sam, to cope with the demands of world politics. The gendered imagery prevalent in U.S.-foreign relations joined race thinking to place women, people of color, and nations weaker than the United States in the low ranks of the hierarchy of power and, hence, in a necessarily dependent status justifying U.S. hegemony. During and after the war of 1898, some activists in women's organizations bemoaned the "intoxication with the hashish of conquest" and "martial spirit" prevalent among male

Male Ethos

How do historians know...

that Americans in the imperial age disparaged people of other societies as "uncivilized," needing "civilization" from a superior United States? Historians interpret speeches, diaries, letters, tourist industry advertisements, fair exhibits, and cartoons to identify racist, age-biased, and gender-biased American ideas about foreigners. Especially revealing are the images on picture postcards of the era because they capture expressions of supremacy in their depictions of the "civilized" (modern) and the "wild" (premodern). As photographs, postcards provide historians with a detailed documentary record, a testimony of feelings, and a visual representation of the values and attitudes of the time.

Government-made postcards were first issued in Austria in 1869 as a way to reduce the expense of corresponding by mail (they cost just a penny to post). Privately or commercially printed picture postcards appeared elsewhere in Europe in the 1880s and in the United States in the 1890s. Collecting postcards immediately became popular as a hobby; the collection and study of postcards today is called deltiology. At the turn of the century, card

subjects included humor, anniversaries, patriotic events, advertisements, street scenes, historic sites, romantic messages, famous leaders, art, and costumes. The images of foreign peoples on American postcards often communicated a message that denigrated indigenous life through contrast with "Western" ways. The Singer Manufacturing Company handed out the promotional postcard reproduced here as a souvenir from the firm's exhibit at the 1893 Columbian Exposition in Chicago. About three-quarters of all sewing machines sold in the world were Singers. The machine shown in this postcard was marketed in South Africa, where, the company advised, the "Zulus are a fine warlike people" who were moving toward "civilization," with Singer's help. (Photo: State Historical Society of Wisconsin)

ZULULAND.

COPYRIGHT 1892, BY THE SINGER MANUFACTURING CO.

---

imperialists who denied voting rights to both Filipinos and American women.

Issues of race and gender also marked the experiences of religious missionaries, many of whom were

Missionaries

single women (like Lottie Moon) or wives of clergymen. Missionaries dispatched to Asia and Africa helped spur the transfer of American culture

and power abroad—"the peaceful conquest of the world," as Reverend Frederick Gates put it. One organization, the Student Volunteers for Foreign Missions, began in the 1880s on college campuses and by 1914 had placed some six thousand missionaries abroad. In 1915 a total of 10,000 American missionaries worked overseas. In China by 1915 more than 2,500 American Protestant missionaries—most of them female—

labored to preach the gospel, to teach school, and to administer medical care. What motivated these women to endure such demanding work far from home and family? Many convictions led them to the mission field—deep piety, a theology of sacrificial service, the American tradition of volunteerism, a belief that a woman's mothering role made women especially suited to educate children, and a recognition that foreign missionary work empowered them as women at a time when men largely denied them a public life at home.

As they struggled to win converts, women missionaries also critiqued the Chinese gender system. When they judged non-Christian foreign societies as more exploitative of women than the United States was, in essence they perpetuated cultural stereotypes of Anglo-Saxon superiority that undergirded imperialism. *The Mother Goose Missionary Rhymes* betrayed traces of cultural imperialism: "Ten little heathen standing in a line; / One went to mission school, then there were but nine. . . . / Three little heathen didn't know what to do; / One learned our language, then there were two. . . . / One little heathen standing all alone; / He learned to love our flag, then there were none." At the same time, missionaries and Singer executives joined hands in promoting the "civilizing medium" of the sewing machine.

With a mixture of self-interest and idealism typical of American thinking on foreign policy, expansionists believed that empire benefited both Americans and those who came under their control. When the United States intervened in other lands or lectured weaker states, Americans claimed that in remaking foreign societies they were extending liberty and prosperity to less fortunate people. William Howard Taft, as civil governor of the Philippines (1901–1904), described the United States's mission in its new colony as lifting up Filipinos "to a point of civilization" that will make them "call the name of the United States blessed." Later, after becoming secretary of war (1904–1908), Taft said about the Chinese that "the more civilized they become . . . the wealthier they become, and the better market they become for us." "The world is to be Christianized and civilized," declared Reverend Josiah Strong. "And what is the process of civilizing but the creating of more and higher wants."

To critics at home and abroad, however, American paternalism appeared hypocritical—a violation of cherished principles. To impose on Filipinos an American-

The "Civilizing" Impulse

The missionaries Charles and Anna Hartwell, brother and sister, travel in 1901 on their "gospel boat," working out of the Fuzhou mission in China.   (ABCFM Pictures, courtesy of Houghton Library, Harvard University)

style political system, for example, U.S. officials censored the press, jailed critics, and picked candidates for public office. From this coercive experience, Filipinos may have learned more about how to fix elections than about how to make democracy work.

Ambitions Abroad, 1860s–1880s

The U.S. empire grew gradually, sometimes haltingly, as American leaders defined guiding principles and built institutions to support overseas ambitions. William H. Seward, one of its chief architects, argued relentlessly for extension of the American frontier as senator from New York (1849–1861) and secretary of state (1861–1869). "There is not in the history of the Roman Empire an ambition for aggrandizement so marked as that which characterizes the American people," he once said. Seward envisioned a large, coordinated U.S. empire encompassing Canada, the

Caribbean, Cuba, Central America, Mexico, Hawai'i, Iceland, Greenland, and Pacific islands. This empire would be built not by war but by a natural process of gravitation toward the United States. Commerce would hurry the process, as would a canal across Central America, a transcontinental American railroad to link up with Asian markets, and a telegraph system to speed communications.

Most of Seward's grandiose plans did not reach fruition in his own day. In 1867, for example, he signed a treaty with Denmark to buy the Danish West Indies (Virgin Islands), but his domestic political foes in the Senate and a hurricane that wrecked St. Thomas scuttled his effort. The Virgin Islanders, who had voted for annexation, had to wait until 1917 for official U.S. status. Also failing was Seward's scheme with unscrupulous Dominican Republic leaders to gain a Caribbean naval base at Samaná Bay. The stench of corruption rising over this unsavory deal-making wafted into the Ulysses S. Grant administration and foiled Grant's initiative in 1870 to buy the entire island nation. The Senate rejected annexation. Anti-imperialism, not just politics, blocked Seward. Anti-imperialists such as Senator Carl Schurz and E. L. Godkin, editor of the magazine *The Nation*, argued that the country already had enough unsettled land and that creating a showcase of democracy and prosperity at home would best persuade other peoples to adopt American institutions and principles. Some anti-imperialists, sharing the racism of the times, opposed the annexation of territory populated by dark-skinned people.

William H. Seward's Quest for Empire

Seward did enjoy some successes. In 1866, citing the Monroe Doctrine, he sent troops to the border with Mexico and demanded that France abandon its puppet regime there. Also facing angry Mexican nationalists, Napoleon III abandoned the Maximilian monarchy that he had installed by force three years earlier. In 1867 Seward paid Russia $7.2 million for the 591,000 square miles of Alaska—land twice the size of Texas. Some critics lampooned "Seward's Icebox," but the secretary of state extolled the Russian territory's rich natural resources, and the Senate voted overwhelmingly for the treaty. That same year, Seward laid claim to the Midway Islands in the Pacific Ocean.

Seward realized his dream of a world knit together into a giant communications system. In 1866, through the persevering efforts of the financier Cyrus Field, an underwater transatlantic cable linked European and American telegraph networks.

International Communications

Backed by J. P. Morgan's capital, the communications pioneer James A. Scrymser strung telegraph lines to Latin America, entering Chile in 1890. In 1903 a submarine cable reached across the Pacific to the Philippines; three years later it extended to Japan and China. Information about markets, crises, and war flowed steadily and quickly. Wire telegraphy—like radio (wireless telegraphy) later—shrank the globe. Nellie Bly, a reporter for the *New York World*, accented the impact of new technology in 1890 when she completed a well-publicized trip around the world in seventy-two days. Drawn closer to one another through improved communications and transportation, nations found that faraway events had more and more impact on their prosperity and security. Because of the communications revolution, "every nation elbows other nations to-day," observed Amherst College professor Edwin Grosvenor in 1898.

Gradually through the late nineteenth century, despite frequent squabbles over such issues as fishing rights along the North Atlantic coast, Britain and the United States worked to negotiate rather than fight over their differing interests. Seward's successor, Hamilton Fish (1869–1877), inherited the knotty problem of the *Alabama* claims. The *Alabama* and other vessels built in Great Britain for the Confederacy during the Civil War had preyed on Union shipping. Senator Charles Sumner demanded that Britain pay $2 billion in damages or cede Canada to the United States, but Fish favored negotiations. In 1871 Britain and America signed the Washington Treaty, whereby the British apologized and agreed to the creation of a tribunal, which later awarded the United States $15.5 million. Bitter controversy over sealing also ended in a peaceful settlement. Beginning in the late 1860s the United States sought to curb pelagic (open sea) sealing—especially the harvesting of fur seals as they swam in the Bering Sea. Pelagic poachers ignored the law as they slaughtered great numbers of breeding females. Despite U.S. seizures of ships, many of them Canadian, the seals faced extermination by the end of the century. Finally, in 1911, Great Britain, the United States, Russia, and Japan banned pelagic sealing altogether and limited land kills. The seal population gradually rejuvenated.

Anglo-Canadian-American Relations

The emerging Anglo-American rapprochement also figured in the outcome of a contest over Samoa, a group of South Pacific islands 4,000 miles from San Francisco on the trade route to Australia. In 1878 the United States gained exclusive right to a coaling station at Samoa's coveted port of Pago Pago. Also seek-

Contest over Samoa

ing imperial advantage, Britain and Germany began to cultivate ties with Samoan leaders. In the 1880s, responding to U.S. warnings to stay out, Berlin protested that Washington was treating the Pacific Ocean "as an American lake." Year by year tensions grew as the powers dispatched warships to Samoa and aggravated factionalism among Samoa's chiefs. Rather than go to war, Britain, Germany, and the United States met in Berlin in 1889 and, without consulting the Samoans, devised a three-part protectorate that limited Samoa's independence. Ten years later the three powers partitioned Samoa: the United States received Pago Pago through annexation of part of the islands (now called American Samoa and administered by the U.S. Department of the Interior); Germany took what is today independent Western Samoa; and Britain, for renouncing its claims to Samoa, obtained the Gilbert Islands and Solomon Islands. One result of the long-simmering Samoan crisis was an intensified U.S. Germanophobia, which also fed on testy German-American trade and naval rivalries and a growing perception that German autocracy and militarism threatened American democracy.

Americans realized far less gain in their relations with China. Missionaries became targets of Chinese nationalist anger, while American oil and textile companies sent their wares into a China market they dreamed was boundless but actually was limited. American religious leaders and business executives throughout the late nineteenth century appealed for official U.S. protection. At

Sino-American Troubles

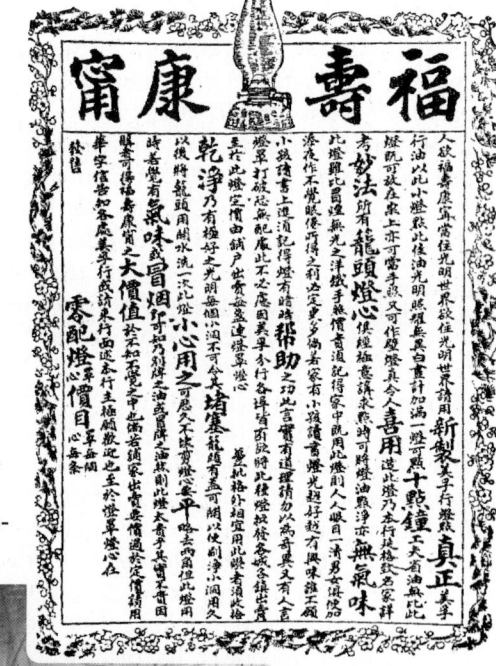

Beginning in the late nineteenth century, Standard Oil (the forerunner of Exxon Corporation) sent agents to China to persuade the Chinese to use American-made kerosene in their lamps and cooking stoves. To promote sales, the American entrepreneurs gave away small lamps, which the Chinese called *Mei Foo* (Beautiful Companion). One agent who popularized the lamp was William P. Coltman, shown here with Chinese business associates. At right is one of the advertisements.   (EXXON Corporation)

home, although the Burlingame Treaty (1868) provided for free immigration between the United States and China and pledged Sino-American friendship, Sinophobia in the American West erupted again and again in riots against Chinese immigrants—in Los Angeles (1871), San Francisco (1877), Denver (1880), and Seattle (1886). A new treaty in 1880 permitted Congress to suspend Chinese immigration to the United States, and it did so two years later. A violent incident occurred in Rock Springs, Wyoming, in 1885, when white coal miners and railway workers rioted and massacred at least twenty-five Chinese. Weakened by internal strife and the imperial powers' encroachments, leaders in Beijing could do little but protest and remember, although a short-lived Chinese boycott of American products in 1905 revealed China's lingering anger over racist American practices.

In Latin America, meanwhile, the convening in 1889 of the first Pan-American Conference in Washington, D.C., demonstrated growing U.S. influence in the Western Hemisphere. Conferees from Latin America toured U.S. factories and then pledged support for reciprocity treaties to improve hemispheric trade. To encourage inter-American cooperation, they founded the Pan-American Union. In 1891 Latin Americans wondered what Pan-Americanism really stood for after the United States flexed its naval muscle and coerced Chile into a humiliating apology and indemnity after drunken sailors from the *Baltimore* battled Chileans outside a Valparaiso bar; two Americans lost their lives. "The American Republic will stand no more nonsense from any power, big or little," boomed Senator George Shoup of Iowa.

Pan-American Conference

With eyes on all parts of the world, even on Africa, where U.S. interests were minimal, ardent expansionists embraced navalism—the campaign to build an imperial navy. They argued for a bigger, modernized navy, adding the "blue water" command of the seas to its traditional role of "brown water" coastline defense and riverine operations. Captain Alfred T. Mahan became a major popularizer for this "New Navy." Because foreign trade was vital to the United States, he argued, the nation required an efficient navy to protect its shipping; in turn, a navy required colonies for bases. "Whether they will or no," Mahan wrote, "Americans must now begin to look outward. The growing production of the country demands it." Mahan's lectures

Alfred T. Mahan, Navalism, and the New Navy

at the Naval War College in Newport, Rhode Island, where he served as president, were published as *The Influence of Sea Power upon History* (1890). This widely read book sat on every serious expansionist's shelf, and foreign leaders turned its pages. Theodore Roosevelt and Henry Cabot Lodge eagerly consulted Mahan, sharing his belief in the links between trade, navy, and colonies, and his growing alarm over "the aggressive military spirit" of Germany.

Moving toward naval modernization, Congress in 1883 authorized construction of the first steel-hulled warships. American factories went to work to produce steam engines, high-velocity shells, powerful guns, and precision instruments. The navy shifted from sail power to steam and from wood construction to steel. Often named for states and cities to kindle patriotism and local support for naval expansion, New Navy ships such as the *Maine*, *Oregon*, and *Boston* thrust the United States into naval prominence, especially during crises in the 1890s.

Crises in the 1890s: Hawai'i, Venezuela, and Cuba

 In the depression-plagued 1890s, crises in Hawai'i, Venezuela, and Cuba gave expansionist Americans opportunities to act on their zealous arguments for what Senator Lodge called a "large policy." Belief that the frontier at home had closed accentuated the expansionist case. In 1893 the historian Frederick Jackson Turner postulated that an ever-expanding continental frontier had shaped the American character. That "frontier has gone," Turner pronounced, "and with its going has closed the first period of American history." He did not explicitly say that a new frontier had to be found overseas in order to sustain the American way of life, but he did claim that "American energy will continually demand a wider field for its exercise."

Hawai'i, the Pacific Ocean archipelago of eight major islands located 2,000 miles from the West Coast of the United States, emerged as a new frontier for Americans. The Hawaiian Islands had long commanded American attention—commercial, religious missionary, naval, and diplomatic. Wide-eyed U.S. expansionists envisioned ships sailing from the eastern seaboard through a Central American canal to Hawai'i and then on to the fabled China market. Already by 1881 Secretary of

Annexation of Hawai'i

State James Blaine had declared the Hawaiian Islands "essentially a part of the American system." By 1890 Americans owned about three-quarters of Hawai'i's wealth and subordinated its economy to that of the United States through sugar exports that entered the U.S. marketplace duty-free. In Hawai'i's multiracial society Chinese and Japanese nationals far outnumbered Americans, who represented a mere 2.1 percent of the population. Prominent Americans on the islands—lawyers, businessmen, and sugar planters, many of them the sons of missionaries—organized secret clubs and military units to contest the royal government. In 1887 they forced the king to accept a constitution that granted foreigners the right to vote and shifted decision-making authority from the monarchy to the legislature. The same year, Hawai'i granted the United States naval rights to Pearl Harbor. Many native Hawaiians (53 percent of the population in 1890) believed that the *haole* (foreigners)—especially Americans—were taking their country from them.

The McKinley Tariff of 1890 created an economic crisis for Hawai'i that further undermined the native government. The tariff eliminated the duty-free status of Hawaiian sugar exports in the United States. Suffering declining sugar prices and profits, the American island elite pressed for annexation of the islands by the United States so that their sugar would be classified as domestic rather than foreign. When Princess Lili'uokalani assumed the throne in 1891, she sought to roll back the political power of the *haole*. The next year, the white oligarchy—questioning her moral rectitude, fearing Hawaiian nationalism, and reeling from the McKinley Tariff—formed the subversive Annexation Club.

The annexationists struck in January 1893 in collusion with John L. Stevens, the chief American diplomat in Hawai'i, who dispatched troops from the U.S.S. *Boston* to occupy Honolulu. The queen, arrested and confined, surrendered. However, rather than yield to the new provisional regime, headed by Sanford B. Dole, son of missionaries and a prominent attorney, she relinquished authority to the U.S. government. Up went the American flag. "The Hawaiian pear is now fully ripe and this is the golden hour to pluck it," a triumphant Stevens informed Washington. Against the queen's protests and those of Japan, President Benjamin Harrison hurriedly sent an annexation treaty to the Senate.

Sensing foul play, incoming President Grover Cleveland ordered an investigation, which confirmed a

Queen Lili'uokalani (1838–1917), ousted from her throne in 1893 by wealthy revolutionaries, vigorously protested in her autobiography and diary, as well as in interviews, the U.S. annexation of Hawai'i in 1898. For years she defended Hawaiian nationalism and emphasized that American officials in 1893 had conspired with Sanford B. Dole and others to overthrow the native monarchy.   (Courtesy of the Lili'uokalani Trust)

conspiracy by the economic elite in league with Stevens and noted that most Hawaiians opposed annexation. Down came the American flag. But when Hawai'i gained renewed attention as a strategic and commercial way station to Asia and the Philippines during the Spanish-American-Cuban-Filipino War, President William McKinley maneuvered annexation through Congress on July 7, 1898, by means of a majority vote (the Newlands Resolution) rather than by a treaty, which would have required a two-thirds count. Under the organic act of June 1900, the people of Hawai'i became U.S. citizens with the right to vote in local elections and to send a nonvoting delegate to Congress. Statehood for Hawai'i came in 1959.

The Venezuelan crisis of 1895 also saw the United States in an expansive mood. For decades Venezuela and Great Britain had quarreled over the border between Venezuela and British Guiana. The disputed

Venezuelan Boundary Dispute

territory contained rich gold deposits and the mouth of the Orinoco River, a commercial gateway to northern South America. Venezuela asked for U.S. help. President Cleveland decided that the "mean and hoggish" British had to be warned away. In July 1895, Secretary of State Richard Olney brashly lectured the British that the Monroe Doctrine prohibited European powers from denying self-government to nations in the Western Hemisphere. He aimed his spread-eagle words at an international audience, proclaiming the United States "a civilized state" whose "fiat is law" in the Americas. The United States, he declared, is "master of the situation and practically invulnerable as against any or all other powers." The British, seeking international friends to counter intensifying competition from Germany, quietly retreated from the crisis. In 1896 an Anglo-American arbitration board divided the disputed territory between Britain and Venezuela. The Venezuelans were barely consulted. Thus the United States displayed a trait common to imperialists: disregard for the rights and sensibilities of small nations.

In 1895 came yet another crisis, this one in Cuba. From 1868 to 1878 the Cubans had battled Spain for their independence. Slavery was abolished but independence denied. While the Cuban economy suffered depression, repressive Spanish rule continued. Insurgents committed to *Cuba Libre* waited for another chance. José Martí, one of the heroes of Cuban history, collected money, arms, and men in the United States. This was but one of the many ways the lives of Americans and Cubans intersected. Their cultures, for example, melded. Cubans of all classes settled in Baltimore, New York, Boston, and Philadelphia. Prominent Cubans on the island sent their children to schools in the United States. When Cuban expatriates returned home, many came in American clothes, spoke English, had American names, played baseball, and jettisoned Catholicism for Protestant denominations. Struggling with competing identities, Cubans admired American culture but resented U.S. economic hegemony.

U.S. Interests and Revolution in Cuba

The Cuban and U.S. economies became integrated. American investments of $50 million, most in sugar plantations, dominated the Caribbean island. More than 90 percent of Cuba's sugar was exported to the United States, and most island imports came from the United States. The Florida and Cuban economies also fused. Havana's famed cigar factories relocated to Key West and Tampa to evade protectionist U.S. tariff laws. Martí feared that this "economic union means political union," for "the nation that buys, commands" and "the nation that sells, serves." Watch out, he warned, for a U.S. "conquering policy" that reduced Latin American countries to "dependencies." A change in American tariff policy hastened the Cuban revolution against Spain and the island's further incorporation into "the American system." The Wilson-Gorman Tariff (1894) imposed a duty on Cuban sugar, which had been entering the United States duty-free under the McKinley Tariff. The Cuban economy, highly dependent on exports, plunged into deep crisis.

From American soil, Martí launched a revolution in 1895 that mounted in human and material costs. Rebels burned sugar-cane fields and razed mills, conducting an economic war and using guerrilla tactics to avoid head-on clashes with Spanish soldiers. "It is necessary to burn the hive to disperse the swarm," explained the insurgent leader Máximo Gomez. U.S. investments went up in smoke and Cuban-American trade dwindled. To separate the insurgents from their supporters among the Cuban people, Spanish general Valeriano Weyler instituted a policy of "reconcentration." Some three hundred thousand Cubans were herded into fortified towns and camps, where hunger, starvation, and disease led to tens of thousands of deaths. As reports of atrocity and destruction became headline news in the American yellow press (see page 547), Americans sympathized increasingly with the insurrectionists. In late 1897 a new government in Madrid modified reconcentration and promised some autonomy for Cuba, but the insurgents continued to gain ground.

President William McKinley had come to office as an imperialist who advocated foreign bases for the New Navy, the export of surplus production, and U.S. supremacy in the Western Hemisphere. Vexed by the turmoil in Cuba, he came to believe that Spain should give up its colony. At one point he explored the purchase of Cuba by the United States for $300 million. Events in early 1898 caused McKinley to lose faith in Madrid's ability to bring peace to Cuba. In January, when antireform pro-Spanish loyalists and army personnel rioted in Havana, Washington ordered the battleship *Maine* to Havana harbor to demonstrate U.S. concern and to protect American citizens. On February 15 an explosion ripped the *Maine*, killing 266 of 354 American officers and crew. Just a week earlier, William Randolph Hearst's inflammatory *New York Journal* had published a stolen private letter written by the Spanish minister

Sinking of the *Maine*

in Washington, Enrique Dupuy de Lôme, who belittled McKinley as a "cheap politician" and suggested that Spain would fight on. Congress soon complied unanimously with McKinley's request for $50 million in defense funds. The naval board investigating the *Maine* disaster then reported that a mine had caused the explosion. Vengeful Americans blamed Spain. (Later, official and unofficial studies attributed the sinking to an accidental internal explosion.)

The impact of these events narrowed McKinley's diplomatic options. He decided to send Spain an ulti-

McKinley's Ultimatum and War Decision

matum. In late March the United States insisted that Spain accept an armistice, end reconcentration altogether, and designate McKinley as arbiter. Madrid made concessions. It abolished reconcentration and rejected, then accepted, an armistice. The weary president hesitated, but he would no longer tolerate chronic disorder just 90 miles off the U.S. coast. On April 11 McKinley asked Congress for authorization to use force "to secure a full and final termination of hostilities between . . . Spain and . . . Cuba, and to secure in the island the establishment of a stable government, capable of maintaining order." American intervention, he said, meant "hostile constraint upon both the parties to the contest." McKinley listed the reasons for war: the "cause of humanity"; the protection of American life and property; the "very serious injury to the commerce, trade, and business of our people"; and, referring to the destruction of the *Maine*, the "constant menace to our peace." At the end of his message, McKinley mentioned Spain's recent concessions but made little of them. On April 19 Congress declared Cuba free and independent and directed the president to use force to remove Spanish authority from the island. The legislators also passed the Teller Amendment, which disclaimed any U.S. intention to annex Cuba or "control" the island "except for the pacification thereof." McKinley beat back a congressional amendment to recognize the rebel government. Believing that the Cubans were not ready for self-government, he argued that they needed a period of American tutoring.

On July 1, 1898, U.S. troops stormed Spanish positions on San Juan Hill near Santiago, Cuba. Both sides suffered heavy casualties. A *Harper's* magazine correspondent reported a "ghastly" scene of hundreds killed and thousands wounded. The American painter William Glackens (1870–1938) put to canvas what he saw. Because Santiago surrendered on July 17, propelling the United States to victory in the war, and because Rough Rider Theodore Roosevelt fought at San Juan Hill and later gave a self-congratulatory account of the experience, the human toll has often gone unnoticed.   (Wadsworth Atheneum, Hartford, Gift of Henry Schnakenberg)

The Spanish-American-Cuban-Filipino War and the Debate over Empire

Diplomacy had failed. By the time the Spanish concessions were on the table, events had already pushed the antagonists to the brink. Washington might have been more patient, and Madrid might have faced the fact that its once-grand empire had disintegrated. Still, prospects for compromise appeared dim because the advancing Cuban insurgents would settle for nothing less than full independence, and no Spanish government could have given up and remained in office. Nor did the United States welcome a truly independent Cuban government that might attempt to reduce U.S. interests. As the historian Louis A. Pérez, Jr., has argued, McKinley's decision for war may have been "directed as much against Cuban independence as it was against Spanish sovereignty." Thus came a war best titled the "Spanish-American-Cuban-Filipino War" so as to represent all the major participants and to identify where the war was fought and whose interests were most at stake.

The motives of Americans who favored war were mixed and complex. McKinley's April message ex-

Motives for War pressed a humanitarian impulse to stop the bloodletting, a concern for commerce and property, and the psychological need to end the nightmarish anxiety once and for all. Republican politicians advised McKinley that their party would lose the upcoming congressional elections unless he solved the Cuban question. Many businesspeople, who had been hesitant before the crisis of early 1898, joined many farmers in the belief that ejecting Spain from Cuba would open new markets for surplus production.

Inveterate imperialists saw war as an opportunity to fulfill expansionist dreams. Naval enthusiasts could prove the worth of the New Navy. Some religious leaders also saw merit in war. The Social Gospel advocate Washington Gladden remarked that "in saving others we may save ourselves." Conservatives, alarmed by Populism and violent labor strikes, welcomed war as a national unifier. One senator commented that "internal discord" was disappearing in the "fervent heat of patriotism." Sensationalism also figured in the march to war, with the yellow press exaggerating stories of Spanish misdeeds. Assistant Secretary of the Navy Theodore Roosevelt and others too young to remember the bloody Civil War looked on war as adventure and used masculine rhetoric to trumpet the call to arms. Anglo-Saxon supremacists such as the politician Albert Beveridge shouted, "God's hour has struck." Overarching all explanations for the 1898 war were expansionism and imperialism, whose momentum had been moving the nation ever outward in the last half of the nineteenth century.

More than 263,000 regulars and volunteers served in the army and another 25,000 in the navy during

The U.S. Military at War the war. Most of them never left the United States. The typical volunteer was young (early twenties), white, unmarried, native-born, and working-class. Deaths numbered 5,462—but only 379 in combat. The rest fell to yellow fever and typhoid, and most died in the United States, especially in camps in Tennessee, Virginia, and Florida, where in July and August a typhoid epidemic devastated the ranks. About 10,000 African American troops, assigned to segregated regiments, found no relief from racism and Jim Crow, even though black troops played a key role in the victorious battle for Santiago. For all, food, sanitary conditions, and medical care were bad. Still, Roosevelt could hardly contain himself. Although his Rough Riders, a motley unit of Ivy Leaguers and cowboys, proved undisciplined and often ineffective, they nonetheless received a good press largely because of Roosevelt's self-serving publicity efforts.

To the surprise of most Americans, the first war news actually came from faraway Asia, from the

Dewey in the Philippines Spanish colony of the Philippine Islands. On May 1, 1898, Commodore George Dewey's New Navy ship *Olympia* led an American squadron into Manila Bay and wrecked the outgunned Spanish fleet. Dewey and his sailors had been on alert in Hong Kong since February, when he received orders from imperial-minded Washington to attack the islands if war broke out. Manila ranked with Pearl Harbor and Pago Pago as a choice harbor, and the Philippines sat significantly on the way to China and its potentially huge market.

Facing rebels and Americans in both Cuba and the Philippines, Spanish resistance collapsed rapidly. U.S. ships blockaded Cuban ports to prevent Spain from resupplying its army, which suffered hunger and disease because Cuban insurgents had cut off supplies from the countryside. American troops saw their first ground-war action on June 22, the day several thousand of them landed near Santiago de Cuba and laid siege to the city. On July 3 U.S. warships sank the Spanish Caribbean squadron in Santiago harbor. American forces then assaulted the Spanish colony of Puerto Rico to obtain another Caribbean base for the navy and a strategic site to help protect a Central American canal. Losing on all fronts, Madrid sued for peace.

On August 12 Spain and the United States signed an armistice to end the war. In Paris, in December 1898, American and Spanish negotiators agreed on the peace terms: independence for Cuba from Spain; cession of the Philippines, Puerto Rico, and Guam (an island in the Pacific) to the United States; and American payment of $20 million to Spain for the territories. The U.S. empire now stretched deep into Asia; and the annexation of Wake Island (1898), Hawai'i (1898), and Samoa (1899) gave American traders, missionaries, and naval promoters other steppingstones to China.

Treaty of Paris

During the war with Spain, the *Washington Post* detected "a new appetite, a yearning to show our strength. . . . The taste of empire is in the mouth of the people." But as the nation debated the Treaty of Paris, anti-imperialists such as the author Mark Twain, the Nebraska politician William Jennings Bryan, the intellectual William Graham Sumner, the reformer Jane Addams, the industrialist Andrew Carnegie, and Senator George Hoar of Massachusetts argued vigorously against annexation of the Philippines. They were disturbed that a war to free Cuba had led to empire.

Some critics appealed to principle, citing the Declaration of Independence and the Constitution: the conquest of people against their wills violated the right of self-determination. The philosopher William James charged that the United States was throwing away its special place among nations; it was, he warned, about to "puke up its heritage." Other anti-imperialists argued that the United States could acquire markets without having to subjugate foreign peoples. To those who argued that the Filipinos were not yet fit for self-government, former senator Carl Schurz retorted that Manila's city council was probably less corrupt than Chicago's. Others claimed that to maintain empire, the president would repeatedly have to dispatch troops overseas. Because he could do so as commander-in-chief, he would not have to seek congressional approval, thus subverting the constitutional checks-and-balances system.

Anti-imperialist Arguments

Some anti-imperialists predicted that the very character of the American people was being corrupted by the imperialist zeal. Jane Addams, seeing children play war games in the streets of Chicago, pointed out that they were not freeing Cubans but were slaying Spaniards. Hoping to build a distinct foreign policy constituency out of networks of women's clubs and organizations, prominent women such as Addams endorsed peace and an end to imperial conquest. Some Americans protested that the United States was practicing a double standard—"offering liberty to the Cubans with one hand, cramming liberty down the throats of the Filipinos with the other, but with both feet planted upon the neck of the negro," as an African American politician from Massachusetts put it. Some white anti-imperialists, believing in a racial hierarchy, warned that annexing people of color would undermine Anglo-Saxon purity and supremacy at home.

Samuel Gompers and other anti-imperialist labor leaders worried about the possible undercutting of American labor by what Gompers called the "half-breeds and semi-barbaric people" of the new colonies. Might not the new colonials be imported as cheap contract labor to drive down the wages of American workers? Would not exploitation of the weak abroad become contagious and lead to further exploitation of the weak at home? Would not an overseas empire drain interest and resources from pressing domestic problems, delaying reform?

The anti-imperialists entered the debate with many handicaps and never launched an effective campaign. Although they organized the Anti-Imperialist League in November 1898, they differed so profoundly on domestic issues that they found it difficult to speak with one voice on a foreign question. They also appeared inconsistent: Gompers favored the war but not the postwar annexations; Carnegie would accept colonies if they were not acquired by force; Hoar voted for annexation of Hawai'i but not of the Philippines; Bryan backed the Treaty of Paris but only, he said, to hurry the process toward Philippine independence. Finally, possession of the Philippines was an established fact, very hard to undo.

The imperialists answered their critics with appeals to patriotism, destiny, and commerce. They sketched a scenario of American greatness: merchant ships plying the waters to boundless Asian markets; naval vessels cruising the Pacific to protect American interests; missionaries uplifting inferior peoples. It was America's duty,

Imperialist Arguments

they insisted, quoting a then-popular Rudyard Kipling poem, to "take up the white man's burden." Furthermore, insurgents were beginning to resist U.S. rule, and it seemed cowardly to pull out under fire. Germany and Japan, two powerful international competitors, were snooping around the Philippines, apparently ready to seize them if the United States's grip loosened. National honor dictated that Americans keep what they had shed blood to take. Senator Beveridge asked: "Shall [history] say that, called by events to captain and command the proudest, ablest, purest race of history in history's noblest work, we declined that great commission?"

In February 1899, by a 57-to-27 vote, the Senate passed the Treaty of Paris ending the war with Spain. Most Republicans voted "yes" and most Democrats "no." An amendment promising independence as soon as the Filipinos formed a stable government lost only by the tie-breaking ballot of the vice president. The Democratic presidential candidate Bryan carried the anti-imperialist case into the election of 1900, warning that repudiation of self-government in the Philippines would weaken the principle at home. But the victorious McKinley refused to apologize for American imperialism. "It is no longer a question of expansion with us," he asserted. "If there is any question at all it is a question of contraction; and who is going to contract?"

Asian Encounters: Open Door in China, Philippine Insurrection, and Japan

 In 1895, the same year as the Venezuelan crisis and the outbreak of the Cuban revolution, Japan claimed victory over China in a short war. Outsiders had been pecking away at China since the 1840s, but the Japanese onslaught intensified the international scramble. Taking advantage of the Qing (Manchu) dynasty's weakness, the major powers carved out spheres of influence (regions over which the outside powers claimed political control and exclusive commercial privileges): Germany in Shandong; Russia in Manchuria; France in Yunnan and Hainan; Britain in Kowloon and Hong Kong. Japan controlled Formosa and Korea as well as parts of China proper (see Map 22.1). American religious and business leaders petitioned Washington to halt the dismemberment of China before they were closed out.

Secretary Hay knew that the United States could not force the imperial powers out of China, but he was determined to protect American commerce and missionaries such as Lottie Moon. In September 1899 Hay sent the imperial nations active in China a note asking them to respect the principle of equal trade opportunity—an Open Door. The recipients sent evasive replies, privately complaining that the United States was seeking for free in China the trade rights that they had gained at considerable military and administrative cost. The next year, a Chinese secret society called the Boxers incited riots that killed foreigners, including missionaries. The Boxers laid siege to the foreign legations in Beijing. The United States, applauded by American merchants and missionaries alike, joined the imperial powers in sending troops to lift the siege. Hay also sent a second Open Door note in July that instructed other nations to preserve China's territorial integrity and to honor "equal and impartial trade." Hay's protests notwithstanding, China continued for years to be fertile soil for foreign exploitation, especially by the Japanese.

Open Door Policy

Though Hay's foray into Asian politics settled little, the Open Door policy became a cornerstone of U.S. diplomacy. The "open door" had actually been a long-standing American principle, for as a trading nation the United States opposed barriers to international commerce and demanded equal access to foreign markets. After 1900, however, when the United States began to emerge as the premier world trader, the Open Door policy became an instrument first to pry open markets and then to dominate them, not just in China but throughout the world. The Open Door also developed as an ideology with several tenets: first, that America's domestic well-being required exports; second, that foreign trade would suffer interruption unless the United States intervened abroad to implant American principles and keep markets open; and third, that the closing of any area to American products, citizens, or ideas threatened the survival of the United States itself.

In the Philippines, meanwhile, U.S. occupation authorities soon antagonized their new "wards," as McKinley labeled them. The president intended to "uplift and civilize" the Filipinos, but they denied that they needed U.S. paternalism. Emilio Aguinaldo, the Philippine nationalist leader who had been battling the

Philippine Insurrection and Pacification

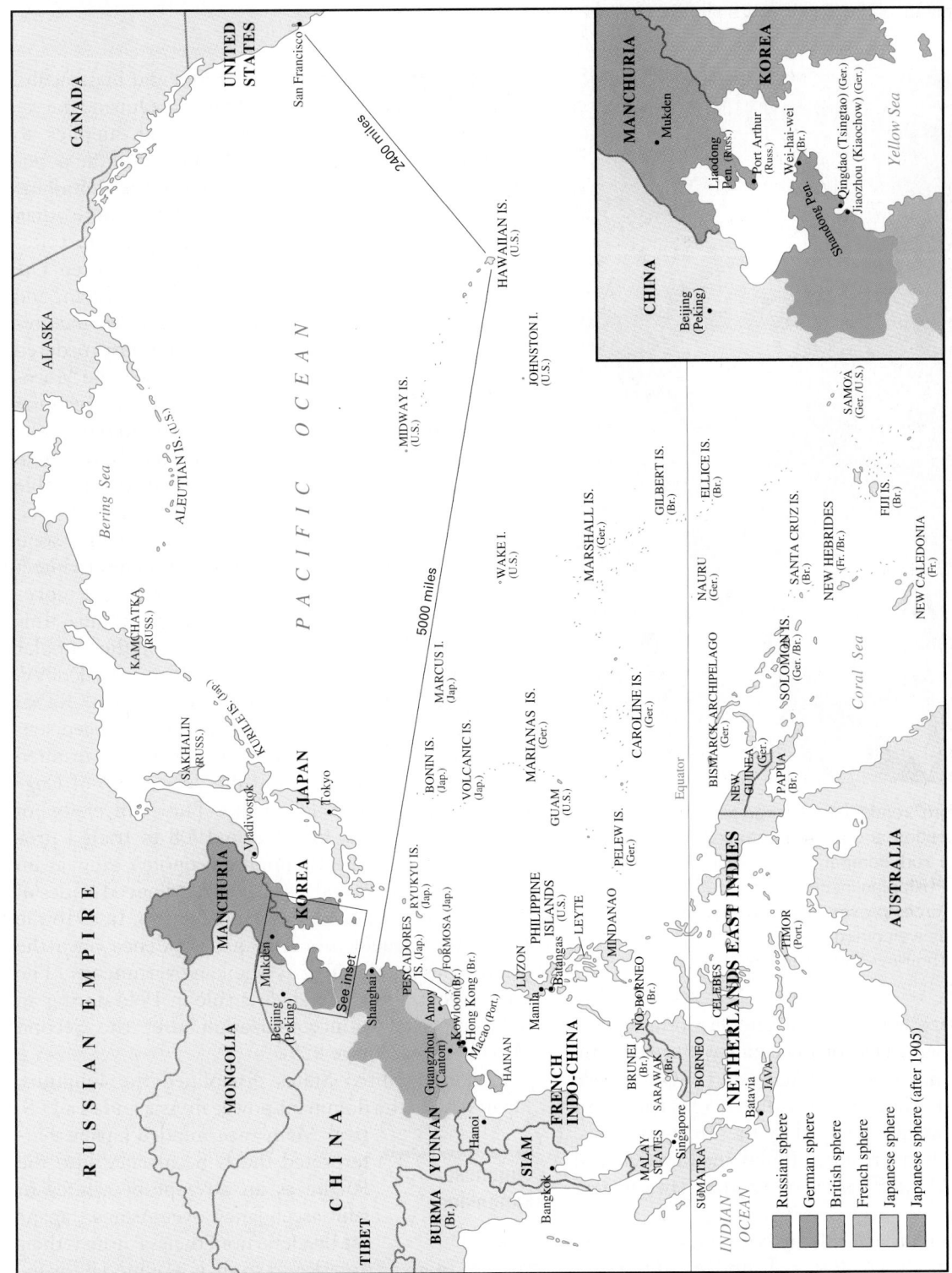

Map 22.1   Imperialism in Asia: Turn of the Century   China and the Pacific region had become imperialist hunting grounds by the turn of the century. The European powers and Japan controlled more areas than the United States, which nonetheless participated in the imperial race by annexing the Philippines, Wake, Guam, Hawai'i, and Samoa, announcing the Open Door policy, and expanding trade. As the spheres of influence in China demonstrate, that besieged nation succumbed to outsiders despite the Open Door policy.

"Know Our Empire" reads the message on the box cover of a patriotic question-and-answer card game produced in 1899 by the New York company McLoughlin Bros. The outbreak of the Philippine insurrection and its suppression by U.S. military forces proved false the suggestion on one card that Filipinos welcomed their new imperial masters. (© Collection of The New-York Historical Society)

Spanish for years, believed that American officials had promised independence for his country. But after the victory, U.S. officers ordered Aguinaldo out of Manila and isolated him from decisions affecting his nation. In January 1899, feeling betrayed by the Treaty of Paris, he proclaimed an independent Philippine Republic and took up arms. U.S. officials soon set their jaws against the rebellion.

In a war fought viciously by both sides, American soldiers burned villages, tortured captives, and introduced a variant of the reconcentration policy. Americans spoke of the "savage" Filipino; one soldier declared that the Philippines "won't be pacified until the niggers [Filipinos] are killed off like the Indians." In the province of Batangas, U.S. troops forced residents to live in designated zones in an effort to separate the insurgents from local supporters. Disaster

followed. Poor sanitation, starvation, and malaria and cholera killed several thousand people. Outside the secure areas, Americans destroyed food supplies to starve out the rebels. At least one-quarter of the population of Batangas died or fled. Before the Philippine insurrection was suppressed in 1902, more than 200,000 Filipinos and 5,000 Americans lay dead. Resistance to U.S. rule, however, did not abate. The fiercely independent, vehemently anti-Christian, and often violent Muslim Filipinos of Moro Province refused to knuckle under. The U.S. military ordered them to submit or be exterminated. In 1906 the Moros finally met defeat; six hundred of them, including many women and children, were slaughtered at the Battle of Bud Dajo. "Work of this kind," General Leonard Wood wrote Roosevelt, "has its disagreeable side."

U.S. officials, with a stern military hand, soon tried to Americanize the Philippines. The architect Daniel Burnham, leader of the City Beautiful movement (see page 538), planned modern Manila. Imported American teachers taught from the popular American primer *Baldwin Reader* (which included "A" for "apple," a fruit unknown to most Filipinos). Racial slurs—one teacher wrote home that he had been sent to Leyte "to teach these monkeys to talk"—insulted nationalistic Filipinos, as did the declaration of English as the official language. The University of the Philippines was founded in 1908 to train a pro-American elite. The Philippine economy grew as an American satellite, and a sedition act silenced critics of U.S. authority by sending them to prison. In 1916 the Jones Act vaguely promised independence once the Philippines established a "stable government." The United States finally ended its rule in 1946 during an intense period of decolonization after the Second World War (see page 829).

As the United States disciplined the Filipinos, Japan rose as the dominant power in Asia and as a U.S. rival. Many race-minded Japanese interpreted the U.S. advance into the Pacific as an attempt by whites to gain ascendancy over Asians. Japanese leaders nonetheless urged their citizens to go to America to study it as a model for industrializing and achieving world power. As the historian Walter LaFeber has put it: "The Japanese were determined to copy—not become subject to—the West." Although some Americans proudly proclaimed the Japanese the "Yankees of the East," gradually the United States had to make concessions to Japan to protect the vulnerable Philippines and to sustain the

Japanese Expansion

Open Door policy. Japan continued to plant interests in China and then smashed the Russians in the Russo-Japanese War (1904–1905). President Roosevelt mediated the crisis at the Portsmouth Conference in New Hampshire and won the Nobel Peace Prize for this ultimately vain effort to preserve a balance of power in Asia and shrink Japan's "big head."

In 1905, in the Taft-Katsura Agreement, the United States conceded Japanese hegemony over Korea in return for Japan's pledge not to undermine the U.S. position in the Philippines. Three years later, in the Root-Takahira Agreement, the United States recognized Japan's interests in Manchuria, whereas Japan again pledged the security of the United States's Pacific possessions and endorsed the Open Door in China. Roosevelt also built up American naval power to deter the Japanese; in late 1907 he sent on a world tour the navy's "Great White Fleet" (so named because the ships were painted white for the voyage). Duly impressed, the Japanese began to build a bigger navy of their own.

President William Howard Taft thought he might counter Japanese advances in Asia through dollar diplomacy—the use of private funds to serve American diplomatic goals and at the same time to garner profits for American financiers. In this case, Taft induced American bankers to join an international consortium to build a railway in China. Taft's venture seemed only to embolden Japan to solidify and extend its holdings in China, where internal discord continued after the nationalistic revolution of 1911 overthrew the Qing dynasty.

Japanese-American relations also became tense over the treatment of Japanese citizens living in the United States. In 1906 the San Francisco School Board, reflecting the anti-Asian bias of many West Coast Americans, ordered the segregation of all Chinese, Koreans, and Japanese in special schools. Tokyo protested the discrimination against its citizens. The following year, President Roosevelt quieted the crisis by striking a "gentleman's agreement" with Tokyo restricting the inflow of Japanese immigrants; San Francisco then rescinded its segregation order. Relations with Tokyo were jolted again in 1913 when the California legislature denied Japanese residents the right to own property in the state.

Anti-Japanese Bias in California

In 1914, when the First World War broke out in Europe, Japan seized Shandong and some Pacific islands from the Germans. In 1915 Japan issued its Twenty-One Demands, virtually insisting on hege-

mony over all of China. The Chinese door was being slammed shut, but the United States lacked adequate countervailing power in Asia to block Japan's imperial thrusts. President Woodrow Wilson worried about how the "white race" could blunt the rise of "the yellow race."

Latin America, Europe, and International Rivalry

 Intense international rivalry also characterized U.S. relations with Latin America, where U.S. economic and strategic interests and power towered (see Map 22.2), and with Europe, where repeated political and military disputes persuaded Americans to develop friendlier relations with Great Britain while avoiding entrapment in the continent's troubles, many of which Americans blamed on Germany.

As U.S. economic interests expanded in Latin America, so did U.S. political influence. Exports to Latin America, which exceeded $50 million in the 1870s, rose to more than $120 million in 1900 and then reached $300 million in 1914. Investments by U.S. citizens in Latin America climbed to a commanding $1.26 billion in 1914. In 1899 two large banana importers merged to form United Fruit Company. In Central America, United Fruit owned much of the land (more than a million acres in 1913) and the railroad and steamship lines, and the firm became an influential economic and political force in the region. The company also worked to eradicate yellow fever and malaria while it manipulated Central American politics.

Economic Hegemony in Latin America

After the destructive war in Cuba, U.S. citizens and corporations continued to dominate the island's economy, controlling the sugar, mining, tobacco, and utilities industries and most of the rural lands. Private U.S. investments in Cuba grew from $50 million before the revolution to $220 million by 1913, and U.S. exports to the island rose from $26 million in 1900 to $196 million in 1917. The Teller Amendment outlawed the annexation of Cuba, but officials in Washington soon used the document's call for "pacification" to justify U.S. control. American troops remained there until 1902. Favoring the "better classes," U.S. authorities restricted voting rights largely to propertied Cuban males, excluding two-thirds of adult men and all women. American officials also forced the

Cuba and the Platt Amendment

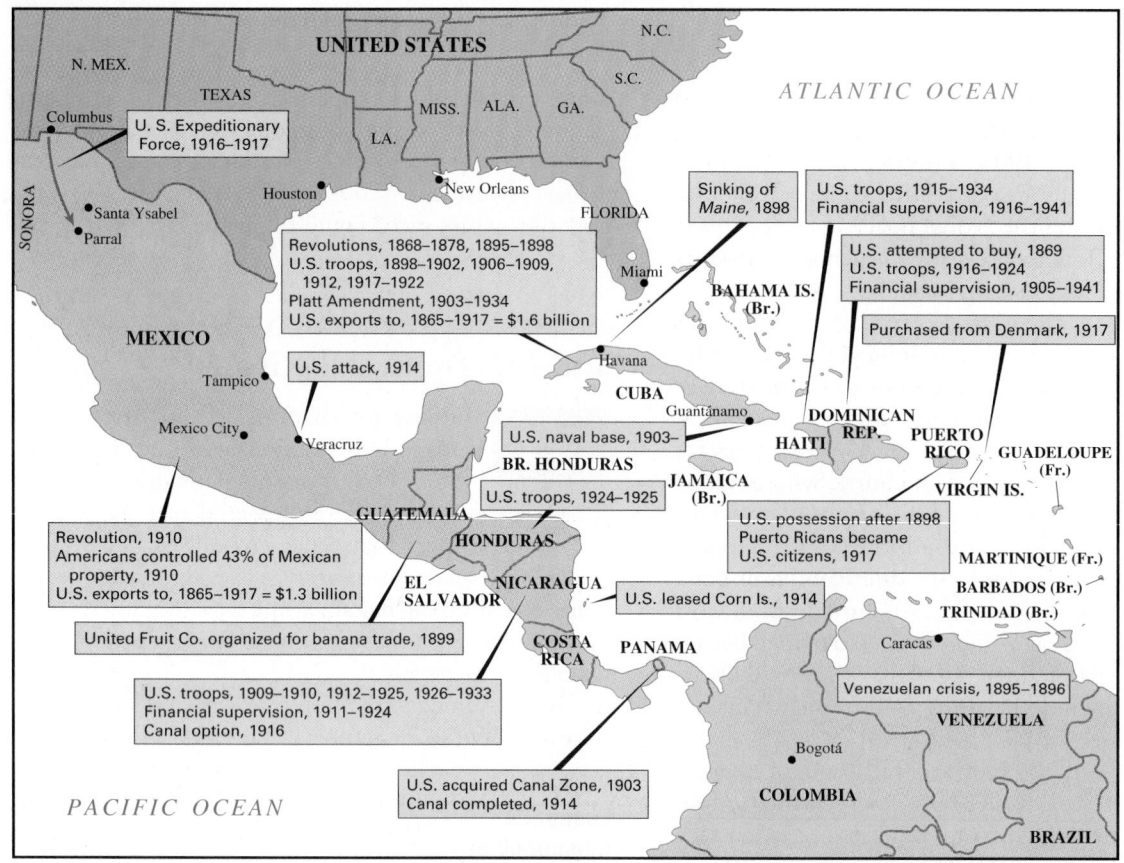

Map 22.2 **U.S. Hegemony in the Caribbean and Latin America** Through many interventions, territorial acquisitions, and robust economic expansion, the United States became the predominant power in Latin America in the early twentieth century. The United States often backed up the Roosevelt Corollary's declaration of a "police power" by dispatching troops to Caribbean nations, where they met nationalist opposition.

Cubans to append to their constitution a frank avowal of U.S. hegemony known as the Platt Amendment. This statement prohibited Cuba from making a treaty with another nation that might impair its independence; in practice, this meant that all treaties had to have U.S. approval. Most important, another Platt Amendment provision granted the United States "the right to intervene" to preserve the island's independence and to maintain domestic order. Cuba also had to lease a naval base (at Guantánamo Bay, and still under U.S. jurisdiction today). Formalized in a 1903 treaty, the amendment governed Cuban-American relations until 1934. "There is, of course, little or no independence left Cuba under the Platt Amendment," General Wood noted.

The Cubans, like the Filipinos, chafed under U.S. mastery. Widespread demonstrations protested the Platt Amendment, and a rebellion against the Cuban government in 1906 prompted Roosevelt to order another invasion of Cuba. The marines stayed until 1909, returned briefly in 1912, and occupied the island again from 1917 to 1922. All the while, U.S. officials helped to develop a transportation system, expand the

public school system, found a national army, and increase sugar production. When Dr. Walter Reed's experiments, based on the theory of the Cuban physician Carlos Finlay, proved that mosquitoes transmitted yellow fever, sanitary engineers controlled the insect and eradicated the disease.

Puerto Rico, the Caribbean island taken as a spoil of war in the Treaty of Paris, also developed under

U.S. Governance of Puerto Rico

U.S. tutelage. Although no Puerto Rican sat at the negotiating table for that treaty, the Puerto Rican elite at first welcomed the United States as an improvement over Spain. But disillusionment soon set in. The condescending U.S. military governor, General Guy V. Henry, regarded Puerto Ricans as naughty, ill-educated children who needed "kindergarten instruction in controlling themselves without allowing them too much liberty." Some residents warned against the "Yankee peril"; others applauded the "Yankee model" and futilely anticipated statehood (see page 631).

Panama, meanwhile, became the site of a bold U.S. expansionist venture. In 1869 the world had mar-

Panama Canal veled at the completion of the Suez Canal, a waterway that greatly facilitated travel between the Indian Ocean and Mediterranean Sea and enhanced the power of the British Empire. Surely that feat could be duplicated in the Western Hemisphere, possibly in Panama, a province of Colombia. One expansionist, U.S. navy captain Robert W. Shufeldt, predicted that a new canal would convert "the Gulf of Mexico into an American lake." Business interests joined politicians, diplomats, and navy officers in insisting that the United States control such an interoceanic canal. Daunting obstacles had to be overcome. The Clayton-Bulwer Treaty with Britain (1850) provided for joint control of a canal. The British, recognizing their diminishing influence in the region and cultivating friendship with the United States as a counterweight to Germany, stepped aside in the Hay-Pauncefote Treaty (1901) to permit a solely U.S.-run canal. When Colombia hesitated to meet Washington's terms, Roosevelt encouraged Panamanian rebels to declare independence and ordered American warships to the isthmus to back them. In 1903 the new Panama awarded the United States a canal zone and long-term rights to its control. The treaty also guaranteed Panama its independence. (In 1922 the United States paid Colombia $25 million in "conscience money" but did not apologize.) The completion of the Panama Canal in 1914 marked a major technological achievement. During the canal's first year of operation, more than one thousand merchant ships squeezed through its locks.

As for the rest of the Caribbean, Roosevelt resisted challenges to U.S. hegemony. Worried that Latin American nations' defaults on debts owed to European banks were provoking European intervention (England, Germany, and Italy sent warships to Venezuela in 1902), the president in 1904 issued the Roosevelt Corollary to the Monroe Doctrine. He warned Latin Americans to stabilize their politics and finances. "Chronic wrongdoing," the corollary lectured, might require "intervention by some civilized nation," and "in flagrant cases of such wrongdoing or impotence," the United States would have to assume the role of "an international police power." Laced with presumptions of superiority, Roosevelt's declaration provided the rationale for frequent U.S. interventions in Latin America.

From 1900 to 1917, the presidents ordered U.S. troops to Cuba, Panama, Nicaragua, the Dominican Republic, Mexico, and Haiti to quell civil wars, thwart

Roosevelt Corollary

The Panama-Pacific Exposition in San Francisco in 1915 celebrated the opening of the Panama Canal with this official poster by Perham Nahl, "The Thirteenth Labor of Hercules." The artist commemorates the ten-year construction feat by using symbols that reflect the imperialism and male hegemony of that time: a gigantic, muscular Hercules (the powerful United States) forcibly opens the land (a yielding Panama) to make space for the canal. When President Theodore Roosevelt asked Secretary of War Elihu Root whether he had adequately defended himself against charges that the United States had acted imperialistically in helping to sever Panama from Colombia in 1903, Root replied: "You have shown that you were accused of seduction and you have conclusively proved that you were guilty of rape." (Courtesy of the Oakland Museum of California)

challenges to U.S. influence, gain ports and bases, and forestall European meddling (see Map 22.2). U.S. authorities ran elections, trained national guards that became politically powerful, and renegotiated foreign debts, shifting them to U.S. banks. They also took over customs houses to control tariff revenues and government budgets (as in the Dominican Republic, from 1905 to 1941).

A TRUE AMERICAN ROUGH RIDER.

This chauvinistic *Judge* magazine cartoon of 1904 appeared after President Theodore Roosevelt proclaimed the United States a "police power" in the Western Hemisphere (the Roosevelt Corollary to the Monroe Doctrine). "A True American Rough Rider," Roosevelt gallops across Central America and Panama into South America, all the while knocking down or chasing away European nations from the United States's sphere of influence. (Collection of Janice L. and David J. Frent)

In neighboring Mexico, the long-time (1876–1910) dictator Porfirio Díaz aggressively recruited foreign investors through tax incentives

U.S.-Mexico Relations Under Díaz

and land grants. American capitalists came to own Mexico's railroads and mines and invested heavily in petroleum and banking. By the early 1890s, the United States dominated Mexico's foreign trade. By 1910 Americans controlled 43 percent of Mexican property and produced more than half of the country's oil; in the state of Sonora 186 of 208 mining companies were American-owned. The Mexican revolutionaries who ousted Díaz in 1910, like

nationalists elsewhere in Latin America, set out to reclaim their nation's sovereignty by ending their economic dependency on the United States (see page 640).

As the United States reaffirmed the Monroe Doctrine against European expansion in the hemisphere and demonstrated the power to enforce it, European nations reluctantly honored U.S. hegemony in Latin America. In turn, the United States held to its tradition of standing outside European embroilments. The balance of power in Europe was precarious, and seldom did an American president involve the United States directly. Roosevelt did help settle a Franco-German clash over Morocco by mediating a settlement at Algeciras, Spain (1906). But the president drew American criticism for entangling the United States in a European problem. Americans endorsed the ultimately futile Hague peace conferences (1899 and 1907) and negotiated various arbitration treaties, but on the whole stayed outside the European arena, except to profit from extensive trade with it.

A special feature of American-European relations was the flowering of the Anglo-American cooperation that had been growing throughout the late nineteenth century. One outcome of the intense German-British rivalry and the rise of the United States to world power was London's quest for friendship with Washington. Already prepared by racial ideas of Anglo-Saxon kinship, a common language, and respect for representative government and private-property rights, Americans appreciated British support in the 1898 war and the Hay-Pauncefote Treaty, and London's virtual endorsement of the Roosevelt Corollary and withdrawal of British warships from the Caribbean. As Mark Twain said of the two imperialist powers: "We are kin in sin."

Anglo-American Rapprochement

British-American trade and U.S. investment in Britain also secured ties. By 1914 more than 140 American companies operated in Britain, including H. J. Heinz's processed foods and F. W. Woolworth's "penny markets." Many Britons decried an Americanization of British culture. One journalist complained that a Briton "wakes in the morning at the sound of an American alarm clock; rises from his New England sheets, and shaves with . . . a Yankee safety razor. He . . . slips his Waterbury watch into his pocket [and] catches an electric train made in New York. . . . At his office . . . he sits on a Nebraskan swivel chair, before a Michigan roll-top desk." Such exaggerated fears and the always prickly character of the Anglo-American relationship, however, gave way to cooperation in world affairs, most evident in 1917 when the United States threw its weapons and soldiers into the First World War on the British side against Germany.

Summary

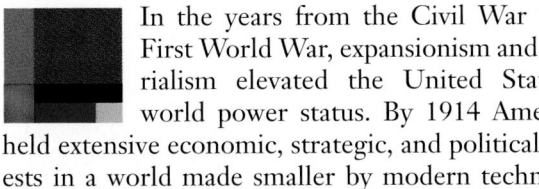 In the years from the Civil War to the First World War, expansionism and imperialism elevated the United States to world power status. By 1914 Americans held extensive economic, strategic, and political interests in a world made smaller by modern technology. The victory over Spain in 1898 was but the most dramatic moment in the long process. The outward reach of U.S. foreign policy from Seward to Wilson sparked opposition from domestic critics, other imperial nations, and foreign nationalists, but expansionists prevailed and the trend toward empire endured.

From Asia to Latin America, economic and strategic needs and ideology motivated and justified expansion and empire. The belief that the United States needed foreign markets to absorb surplus production to save the domestic economy joined missionary zeal to reform other societies through the promotion of American products and culture. Notions of racial and male supremacy and appeals to national greatness also fed the appetite for foreign adventure and commitments. The greatly augmented navy became a primary means for satisfying American ideas and wants.

Revealing the great diversity of America's intersection with the world, missionaries such as Moon in China, generals such as Wood in Cuba, companies such as Singer in Africa and Heinz in Britain, and politicians such as Taft in the Philippines carried American ways, ideas, guns, and goods abroad to a mixed reception. The conspicuous declarations of Olney, Hay, Roosevelt, and other leaders became the guiding texts for U.S. principles and behavior in world affairs. A world power with far-flung interests to protect, the United States had to face a tough test of its self-proclaimed greatness and reconsider its political isolation from Europe when a world war broke out in August 1914.

LEGACY FOR A PEOPLE AND A NATION
The Status of Puerto Rico

Ever since the U.S. invasion of their island in July 1898 and their transfer under the Treaty of Paris from Spain to the United States, Puerto Ricans have de-

bated their status, their very identity. Colony? territory? nation? state? or the "Commonwealth of Puerto Rico" that the U.S. Congress designated in 1952? A small Caribbean island with 3.8 million people (another 2.5 million Puerto Ricans live in the United States), Puerto Rico has held nonbinding plebiscites in 1967, 1993, and 1998, each time rejecting both statehood and independence in favor of commonwealth. In the 1998 referendum, 46.5 percent voted for statehood and 2.5 percent for independence. The U.S. Congress, which holds the constitutional authority to set the rules by which Puerto Ricans live, stands as sharply divided as the islanders, rejecting independent nationhood, unwilling to force statehood if Puerto Ricans do not want it, yet uneasy with the ambivalence that commonwealth status promotes.

Although a plurality of Puerto Ricans have narrowly endorsed commonwealth status, they remain troubled by their incomplete self-government. They are U.S. citizens (made so by the Jones Act of 1916) who can and do move freely between the island and the mainland and who are subject to the military draft, but they cannot vote in U.S. presidential elections. Although they send a delegate to the U.S. Congress, this representative cannot vote. Yet they have the attributes of a state, with a government modeled after the fifty states. Puerto Ricans pay Medicare and Social Security taxes, but not federal income taxes, and they receive benefits under federal programs. They also take pride in the symbols of nationalism, such as their own Olympic team, but the symbols do not signify independence.

The issue of cultural nationalism dominates the debate over Puerto Rico's political status. A majority of Puerto Ricans have rejected statehood because they fear it would mean giving up their Latin American culture and Spanish language. Most Puerto Ricans today, although bilingual, prefer Spanish over English, and many oppose the mandatory school courses in English. Commonwealthers warn that if Puerto Rico became a state, mainland conservatives might make English the official U.S. language. Puerto Rico's uncertain status persists as a legacy of turn-of-the-century empire building; then, as now, the issue centered on the rights of self-determination—in this case, the right to sustain a people's own culture.

For Further Reading, see page A-25 of the Appendix. For Web resources, go to http://college.hmco.com.

The medical case files listed him as "A.P.," an eighteen-year-old Marine Corps private who had volunteered to fight in the Great War. He thrived on the military life, and, like other young American soldiers, A.P. was ordered to the western front in France. During early 1918 the Germans relentlessly bombarded his position at Château-Thierry, where screeching shells and deafening explosions pounded the fresh American troops.

In June, A.P.'s company trudged forward to the battle lines, past the bodies of French soldiers dismembered by the big guns. His commanding officer detailed A.P. to bury the mangled corpses. For several nights thereafter the young man could not sleep. Artillery fire frightened him. During a bombardment on June 14, he began to tremble uncontrollably. Evacuated to a hospital, A.P. suffered horrifying dreams, and the slightest noise easily startled him.

Doctors who treated military casualties saw many such patients, whom they diagnosed as having a mental illness known as war neurosis or war psychosis—shell shock, for short. The symptoms: a fixed empty stare, violent tremors, paralyzed limbs, listlessness, jabbering, screaming, and haunting dreams. The illness could strike anyone; even those soldiers who appeared most manly and courageous cracked after days of incessant shelling and inescapable human carnage. "There was a limit to human endurance," one lieutenant explained.

Their nervous systems shattered, some one hundred thousand victims went to special military hospitals staffed by psychiatrists. A regimen of rest, military discipline, recreation, exercise, counseling, and reminders about patriotic duty restored many shell-shock victims to health. Some returned to the front lines, but others remained riven by anxiety and had to be assigned to noncombat duties. The very ill went home to the United States. Even cured shell-shocked soldiers had lingering mental problems—flashbacks, nightmares, and a persistent disorientation that made it difficult for them to make decisions or organize their lives. Thousands of the most severely afflicted remained in veterans' hospitals.

Harvey Dunn's 1918 painting (detail) of weary soldiers in the First World War captures the misery of frontline battle. (Smithsonian Institute, Division of Political History, Washington, D.C.)

23

AMERICANS IN THE GREAT WAR 1914–1920

Many Progressive era professionals and reformers found rewards and opportunities in the wrenching national emergency of World War I. The psychiatrists who treated the shell-shock victims, for example, wanted to apply their mental health expertise to help win the war. They also hoped to use their wartime medical experience later, at home, to improve care for the mentally ill. For them, the cataclysm of foreign crisis and the opportunity for domestic social betterment went hand in hand. That is what the philosopher and educator John Dewey meant when he said that the war presented "social possibilities." But the antiwar intellectual Randolph Bourne was not so sure that positive change could emerge from the war. "If the war is too strong for you to prevent," he lectured progressives, "how is it going to be weak enough for you to control and mold to your liberal purposes?"

The outbreak of the Great War in Europe in 1914 at first stunned Americans. For years their nation had participated in the international competition for colonies, markets, and weapons supremacy. But full-scale war seemed unthinkable. The new machine guns, howitzers, submarines, and dreadnoughts were such awesome death engines that leaders surely would not use them. When they did, moaned one social reformer, "civilization is all gone, and barbarism come." Progressives who had applauded Germany as a model of state welfare now wondered how it became so reactionary. Articulated by well-organized groups, peace sentiment in the United States strengthened with each grisly report from the European battlefield.

For almost three years President Woodrow Wilson kept America out of the war. During this time, he sought to protect U.S. trade interests and to improve the nation's military posture. He lectured the belligerents to rediscover their humanity and to respect international law. But American property, lives, and neutrality fell victim to British and German naval warfare. In April 1917, when the president finally asked Congress for a declaration of war, he did so with his characteristic crusading zeal. America entered the battle not just to win the war but to reform the postwar world—to "make the world safe for democracy," declared Wilson.

Even after more than a decade of Progressive reform, Americans remained a heterogeneous and fractious people at the start of the Great War. Headlines still trumpeted labor-capital confrontations such as the Ludlow Massacre in Colorado, in which two women and eleven children were killed when state militia fired on striking miners. Racial antagonisms were evident in

Wilson's decision to segregate federal buildings in Washington and in continued lynchings of African Americans (fifty-one in 1914). Nativists protested the pace of immigration; 1.2 million immigrants entered the United States in 1914 alone. Ethnic groups eyed one another suspiciously. Activist women argued for equality between the sexes and at the ballot box, but many men preferred restrictive traditions.

The war experience accentuated and intensified the nation's social divisiveness. Whites who did not like the northward migration of southern blacks to work in defense plants incited race riots. War hawks harassed pacifists and German Americans. The federal government itself, eager to stimulate patriotism, trampled on civil liberties to silence critics. And as communism implanted itself in Russia, a postwar Red Scare repressed radicals and tarnished America's reputation as a democratic society. After the war, groups that sought to consolidate wartime gains vied with those who sought to restore the prewar status quo.

America's participation in the war wrought massive changes and accelerated ongoing trends. Wars are emergencies, and during such times normal ways of doing things surrender to the extraordinary and exaggerated. The U.S. government, more than ever before, became a manager—of people, prices, production, and minds. A compulsory draft pulled men into the armed services. The presidency assumed greater powers. Unprecedented centralization and integration of the economy, increased standardization of products, and unusual cooperation between government and business also characterized the times. Although reformers continued to devote themselves to issues such as prohibition and woman suffrage, the war experience helped splinter the Progressive movement. Jane Addams sadly remarked that "the spirit of fighting burns away all those impulses . . . which foster the will to justice."

The United States emerged from the war a major power in an economically hobbled world. Yet Americans who had marched to battle as if on a crusade grew disillusioned with the peace process. They recoiled from the spectacle of the victors squabbling over the spoils, and they chided Wilson for failing to deliver the "peace without victory" he promised. As in the 1790s, the 1840s, and the 1890s, Americans once again engaged in a searching national debate about the fundamentals of their foreign policy. After negotiating the Treaty of Versailles at Paris, the president urged U.S. membership in the new League of Nations, which he touted as a vehicle for reforming world politics. The

IMPORTANT EVENTS

1914 U.S. troops invade revolutionary Mexico
First World War begins in Europe

1915 *Lusitania* sinks
Secretary of State Bryan resigns

1916 Congress rejects Gore-McLemore resolution limiting travel on belligerent ships
U.S. troops invade Mexico again
After torpedoing *Sussex*, Germany pledges not to attack merchant ships without warning
National Defense Act expands military
Wilson reelected on platform of peace, progressivism, and preparedness

1917 Germany declares unrestricted submarine warfare
Zimmermann telegram aggravates U.S.-Mexico troubles
Russian Revolution ousts the czar
United States enters First World War
Selective Service Act creates the draft
Espionage Act limits First Amendment rights
Race riot in East St. Louis, Illinois
War Industries Board created to manage the economy
War Revenue Act raises taxes to control war profiteering
Fuel crisis during severe winter

1918 Wilson announces Fourteen Points for new world order
Sedition Act further limits free speech
Debs imprisoned for antiwar speech
U.S. troops at Château-Thierry help blunt German offensive
U.S. troops intervene in Russia against Bolsheviks
Flu pandemic
Republicans hand Wilson a setback by winning congressional elections
Armistice ends the First World War

1919 Paris Peace Conference punishes Germany and launches League of Nations
May Day bombings help instigate Red Scare
American Legion organizes for veterans' benefits and antiradicalism
Chicago race riot
Steelworkers strike
Communist Party of the United States of America founded
Wilson suffers stroke after speaking tour
Senate rejects Treaty of Versailles and U.S. membership in League
Schenck v. U.S. upholds Espionage Act

1920 Palmer Raids round up suspected radicals

Senate rejected his appeal (the League nonetheless organized without U.S. membership) because many Americans feared that the League might entangle Americans in Europe's problems, threaten the U.S. empire, and compromise the country's traditional unilateralism, or nonaligned course in foreign relations. On many fronts, then, Americans during the era of the First World War were at war with themselves. ■

Precarious Neutrality

The war that erupted in August 1914 grew from years of European competition over trade, colonies, allies, and armaments. Two powerful alliance systems had formed: the Triple Alliance of Germany, Austria-Hungary, and Italy, and the Triple Entente of Britain, France, and Russia. All had imperial holdings and ambitions for more, but Germany seemed particularly bold as it rivaled Great Britain for world leadership. Many Americans saw Germany as a threat to U.S. interests in the Western Hemisphere and viewed Germans as an excessively militaristic people who embraced autocracy and spurned democracy.

Strategists said that Europe enjoyed a balance of power, but crises in the Balkan countries of southeastern Europe triggered a chain of events that shattered the "balance." Slavic nationalists sought to enlarge Serbia, an independent Slavic nation, by annexing regions such as Bosnia, then a province of the Austro-Hungarian Empire (see Map 23.1). On June 28, 1914, at Sarajevo, Bosnia, a member of the Black Hand, a Serbian terrorist group in collusion with Serbian officials, assassinated the heir to the Austro-Hungarian throne. Alarmed by the

Outbreak of the First World War

Map legend:
- Central Powers (Triple Alliance – except Italy – and allies)
- The Allies (Triple Entente and allies)
- Neutral nations

1. **June 28**
Assassination at Sarajevo

2. **July 28**
Austria-Hungary declares war on Serbia

3. **July 30**
Russia begins mobilization

4. **August 1**
Germany declares war on Russia

5. **August 3**
Germany declares war on France and invades Belgium

6. **August 4**
Great Britain declares war on Germany

7. **August 6**
Russia and Austria-Hungary at war

8. **August 12**
Great Britain declares war on Austria-Hungary

Map 23.1   Europe Goes to War, Summer 1914   Bound by alliances and stirred by turmoil in the Balkans, where Serbs repeatedly upended peace, the nations of Europe descended into war in the summer of 1914. Step by step a Balkan crisis escalated into the "Great War."

prospect of an engorged Serbia on its border, Austria-Hungary consulted its Triple Alliance partner Germany, which urged toughness. When Serbia called on its Slavic friend Russia for help, Russia in turn looked for backing from its ally France. In late July, Austria-Hungary declared war against Serbia. Russia then began to mobilize its armies.

Germany—having goaded Austria-Hungary toward war and believing war inevitable—struck first, declaring war against Russia on August 1 and against France two days later. Britain hesitated, but when German forces slashed into neutral Belgium to get at France, London declared war against Germany on August 4. Eventually Turkey (the Ottoman Empire) joined Germany and Austria-Hungary as the Central Powers, and Italy (switching sides) and Japan teamed up with Britain, France, and Russia as the Allies. Japan took advantage of the European war to seize Germany's sphere of influence in China, Shandong.

President Wilson at first sought to distance America from the conflagration by issuing a proclamation of neutrality—the traditional U.S. policy toward European wars. He also asked Americans to refrain from taking sides, to exhibit "the dignity of self-control." In private, the president said that "we definitely have to be neutral, since otherwise our mixed populations would wage war on each other." The United States, he fervently hoped, would stand apart as a sane, civilized nation in a deranged international system.

Wilson's lofty appeal for American neutrality and unity at home collided with several realities between August 1914 and April 1917. First, ethnic groups in the United States did take sides. Many German Americans and anti-British Irish Americans (Ireland was then trying to break free from British rule) cheered for the Central Powers. Americans of British and French ancestry and others with roots in Allied nations championed the Allied cause. Germany's attack on Belgium confirmed in many people's minds that Germany had become the archetype of unbridled militarism.

Taking Sides

The pro-Allied sympathies of Wilson's administration also weakened the U.S. neutrality proclamation. Honoring Anglo-American rapprochement (see page 630), Wilson shared the conviction with British leaders that a German victory would destroy free enterprise and government by law. If Germany won the war, he prophesied, "it would change the course of our civilization and make the United States a military nation." Wilson's chief advisers and diplomats—his assistant Edward House, Secretary of State Robert Lansing, and Ambassador to London Walter Hines Page—held similar anti-German views that often translated into pro-Allied policies.

U.S. economic links with the Allies also rendered neutrality difficult, if not impossible. England had long been one of the nation's best customers. Now the British flooded America with new orders, especially for arms. Sales to the Allies helped pull the American economy out of its recession. Between 1914 and 1916, American exports to England and France grew 365 percent, from $753 million to $2.75 billion. In the same period, however, largely because of Britain's naval blockade, exports to Germany dropped by more than 90 percent, from $345 million to only $29 million. Loans from private American banks—totaling $2.3 billion during the neutrality period—financed much of U.S. trade with the Allies. Germany received only $27 million in the same period. The Wilson administration, which at first frowned on these transactions, came to see them

Trade and Loans

as necessary to the economic health of the United States.

From Germany's perspective, the linkage between the American economy and the Allies meant that the United States had become the Allied arsenal and bank. Americans, however, faced a dilemma: cutting their economic ties with Britain would constitute an unneutral act in favor of Germany. Under international law, Britain—which controlled the seas—could buy both contraband (war-related goods) and noncontraband from neutrals. It was Germany's responsibility, not America's, to stop such trade in ways that international law prescribed—that is, by an effective blockade of the enemy's territory, by the seizure of contraband from neutral (American) ships, or by the confiscation of goods from belligerent (British) ships. Germans, of course, judged the huge U.S. trade with the Allies an act of unneutrality that had to be stopped.

The president and his aides believed, finally, that Wilsonian principles stood a better chance of international acceptance if Britain, rather than the Central Powers, sat astride the postwar world. "Wilsonianism," the cluster of ideas Wilson espoused, consisted of traditional American principles (such as democracy and the Open Door) and an ideology of internationalism and exceptionalism. The central tenet was that only the United States could lead the convulsed world into a new, peaceful era of unobstructed commerce, free-market capitalism, democratic politics, and open diplomacy. American Progressivism, it seemed, was to be projected onto the world. "America had the infinite privilege of fulfilling her destiny and saving the world," Wilson claimed. Empires had to be dismantled to honor the principle of self-determination. Armaments had to be reduced. Critics charged that Wilson often violated his own credos in his eagerness to force them on others—as his military interventions in Mexico in 1914, Haiti in 1915, and the Dominican Republic in 1916 testified. All agreed, though, that such ideals served the American national interest; in this way idealism and realism were married.

Wilsonianism

To say that American neutrality was never a real possibility given ethnic loyalties, economic ties, and Wilsonian preferences is not to say that Wilson sought to enter the war. He emphatically wanted to keep the United States out. Time and again, he tried to mediate the crisis to prevent one power from crushing another. In early 1917, the president remarked that "we are the only one of the great white nations that is free from war today, and it would be a crime against civilization for us to go in." But go in the United States finally did. Why?

Americans got caught in the Allied–Central Power crossfire. British naval policy aimed to sever neutral trade with Germany in order to cripple the German economy. The British, "ruling the waves and waiving the rules," declared a blockade of water entrances to Germany and mined the North Sea. They also harassed neutral shipping by seizing cargoes and defined a broad list of contraband (including foodstuffs) that they prohibited neutrals from shipping to Germany. American vessels bearing goods for Germany seldom reached their destination. Furthermore, to counter German submarines, the British flouted international law by arming their merchant ships and flying neutral (sometimes American) flags. Wilson frequently protested British violations of neutral rights, pointing out that neutrals had the right to sell and ship noncontraband goods to belligerents without interference. But London often deftly defused Washington's criticism by paying for confiscated cargoes, and German provocations made British behavior appear less offensive by comparison.

British Violations of Neutral Rights

Unable to win the war on land and determined to lift the blockade and halt American-Allied commerce, Germany looked for victory at sea by using submarines. In February 1915 Berlin created a war zone around the British Isles, warned neutral vessels to stay out so as not to be attacked by mistake, and advised passengers from neutral nations to stay off Allied ships. President Wilson informed Germany that the United States was holding it to "strict accountability" for any losses of American life and property.

The German Submarine and International Law

Wilson was interpreting international law in the strictest possible sense. The law that an attacker had to warn a passenger or merchant ship before attacking, so that passengers and crew could disembark safely into lifeboats, predated the emergence of the submarine as a major weapon. When Wilson refused to make adjustments, the Germans thought him unfair. As they saw the issue, the slender, frail, and sluggish *unterseebooten* (U-boats) should not be expected to surface to warn ships. Surfacing would nullify the U-boats' advantage of surprise and leave them vulnerable to British attack. Berlin protested that Wilson was denying it the one weapon that could break the British economic stranglehold, disrupt the Allies' substantial connection

with U.S. producers and bankers, and win the war. To all concerned—British, Germans, and Americans—this naval warfare became a matter of life and death.

Submarine Warfare and Wilson's Decision for War

Over the next few months the U-boats sank ship after ship. In May 1915 the swift, luxurious British passenger liner *Lusitania* left New York City carrying more than twelve hundred passengers and a cargo of food and contraband, including 4.2 million rounds of ammunition for Remington rifles. Before "Lucy's" departure, the German embassy warned in a newspaper announcement that travelers on British vessels should know that Allied ships in war-zone waters "are liable to destruction." Few passengers paid attention or shifted to an American vessel for the transatlantic trip. On May 7, off the Irish coast, submarine U-20 torpedoed the four-stacked vessel. The *Lusitania* sank quickly, taking to their deaths 1,198 people, 128 of them Americans. Even if the ship was carrying armaments, argued Wilson, the sinking was a brutal assault on innocent people. But he ruled out a military response. Secretary of State William Jennings Bryan advised that Americans be prohibited from travel on belligerent ships and that passenger vessels be prohibited from carrying war goods. "Germany has a right to prevent contraband going to the Allies," wrote Bryan, "and a ship carrying contraband should not rely on passengers to protect her from attack—it would be like putting women and children in front of an army."

The president rejected Bryan's counsel, insisting on the right of Americans to sail on belligerent ships and demanding that Germany cease its inhumane submarine warfare. When the Germans urged Wilson to rethink the relationship between international law and the submarine, the president fumed. After a stormy White House meeting marked by Bryan's charge that the cabinet was pro-Allied, Wilson reiterated his demand that submarines be kept in port. When the president refused to ban American travelers from belligerent ships, Bryan resigned in protest—an uncommon act for unhappy secretaries of state, who usually leave quietly. The pro-Allied Robert Lansing took Bryan's place. When criticized for pursuing a double standard in favor of the Allies, Wilson responded that the British were taking cargoes and vio-

Secretary Bryan's Resignation

lating property rights but the Germans were taking lives and violating human rights. Wilson's attitude toward Germany had noticeably hardened.

Seeking to avoid war with America, Germany ordered U-boat commanders to halt attacks on passenger liners. But in mid-August another British vessel, the *Arabic*, was sunk off Ireland and three Americans died. The Germans hastened to pledge that an unarmed passenger ship would never again be attacked without warning. But the sinking of the *Arabic* fueled debate over American passengers on belligerent vessels. Why not require Americans to sail on American craft? asked critics. From August 1914 to March 1917 only three Americans died on an American ship (the tanker *Gulflight* in May 1915), whereas about 190 were killed on belligerent ships.

In early 1916 Congress began to debate the Gore-McLemore resolution to prohibit Americans from traveling on armed merchant vessels or on ships carrying contraband. The resolution, its sponsors hoped, would prevent incidents such as the *Lusitania* sinking from hurtling the United States into war. But Wilson would tolerate no interference in the presidential making of foreign policy (he had just sent Edward House to Europe to mediate an end to the war) and no restrictions on American travel. The resolution, he argued, would destroy the "whole fine fabric of international law." After heavy politicking, Congress tabled the resolution, effectively killing it. Wilson's critics have pointed out that the Gore-McLemore resolution would have avoided or at least delayed a German-American confrontation over the submarine without undercutting U.S. interests or besmirching national honor.

Gore-McLemore Resolution

In March 1916 a U-boat attack on the *Sussex*, a French vessel crossing the English Channel, took the United States a step closer to war. Four Americans were injured on that ship, which the U-boat commander mistook for a minelayer. Stop the marauding submarines, Wilson lectured Berlin, or the United States will sever diplomatic relations. Again the Germans retreated, pledging not to attack merchant vessels without warning. At about the same time, relations with Britain soured. The British crushing of the Easter Rebellion in Ireland and further restriction of U.S. trade with the Central Powers aroused American anger.

As the United States became more entangled in the Great War, many Americans urged Wilson to keep the nation out. In early 1915, Jane Addams, Carrie Chapman Catt, and other suffragists helped found the

"Here's money for your Americans. I may drown some more," says Kaiser Wilhelm to President Wilson in this anti-German cartoon. It appeared in early 1916 after Germany finally expressed regret for having taken American lives almost a year earlier when a U-boat sank the *Lusitania*. The Germans offered an indemnity, but not until 1925 did a claims commission determine that Germany should pay $2.5 million to American claimants who had suffered losses because of the *Lusitania* tragedy. (*Life* magazine, April 13, 1916. The Boston Athenaeum)

Peace Advocates

Woman's Peace Party, the U.S. section of the Women's International League for Peace and Freedom. "The mother half of humanity," claimed women peace advocates, had a special role as "the guardians of life." Later that same year, some pacifist Progressives—including Oswald Garrison Villard, Paul Kellogg, and Lillian Wald—organized an antiwar coalition, the American Union Against Militarism. The businessman Andrew Carnegie, who in 1910 had established the Carnegie Endowment for International Peace, helped finance peace groups. So did Henry Ford, who in late 1915 sent a "peace ship" to Europe to propagandize for a negotiated settlement. Socialists such as Eugene Debs added their voices to the peace movement.

Antiwar advocates emphasized several points: that war drained a nation of its youth, resources, and reform impulse; that it fostered repression at home; that it violated Christian morality; and that wartime business barons reaped huge profits at the expense of the people. Militarism and conscription, Addams pointed out, were what millions of immigrants had left behind in Europe. Were they now—in the United States—to be forced into the decadent system they had escaped? Although the peace movement was splintered—some of its followers endorsing peace but not pacifism—it carried political and intellectual weight that Wilson could not ignore, and it articulated several ideas that he shared. In fact, he campaigned on a peace platform in the 1916 presidential election. After his triumph, Wilson futilely labored once again to bring the belligerents to the conference table. In early 1917 he advised them to temper their acquisitive war aims, appealing for "peace without victory."

Germany rejected Wilson's overture in early February 1917, when it launched unrestricted submarine warfare. All vessels—belligerent or

Unrestricted Submarine Warfare

neutral, warship or merchant—would be attacked if sighted in the declared war zone. This bold decision represented a calculated risk that submarines could impede American munitions shipments to England and permit Germany to defeat the Allies before U.S. troops could be ferried across the Atlantic. Wilson quickly broke diplomatic relations with Berlin.

This German challenge to American neutral rights and economic interests was soon followed by a German threat to U.S. security. In late February, British intelligence intercepted and passed to U.S. officials a telegram addressed to the German minister in Mexico from German Foreign Secretary Arthur Zimmermann. Its message: If Mexico joined a military alliance against the United States, Germany would help Mexico recover the territories it had lost in 1848, including several western states. Zimmermann hoped to "set new enemies on America's neck—enemies which give them plenty to take care of over there."

U.S. officials took the message seriously because Mexican-American relations had deteriorated recently. The Mexican revolution, which began in 1910, had descended into a

Zimmermann Telegram and Mexican Revolution

bloody civil war with strong anti-Yankee overtones, and the Mexican government intended to nationalize extensive American-owned proper-

ties (see Chapters 22 and 26). Wilson had twice ordered troops onto Mexican soil: in 1914, at Veracruz, to avenge a slight to the U.S. uniform and flag and to overthrow the nationalistic government of President Victoriano Huerta, who was also trying to import German weapons; and again in 1916, in northern Mexico, where General John J. "Black Jack" Pershing spent months pursuing Pancho Villa after the Mexican rebel had raided an American border town. Having failed to capture Villa and facing another nationalistic government led by Venustiano Carranza, U.S. forces departed in January 1917. Even though Mexico City rejected Germany's offer, the Wilson administration judged Zimmermann's telegram "a conspiracy against this country." Mexico still might let German agents use Mexican soil to propagandize against the United States if not sabotage American properties.

Soon after learning of Zimmermann's ploy, Wilson asked Congress for "armed neutrality" to defend American lives and commerce. He requested authority to arm American merchant ships and to "employ any other instrumentalities or methods that may be necessary." In the midst of the debate, Wilson released Zimmermann's telegram to the press. Americans expressed outrage. Still, antiwar senators Robert M. La Follette and George Norris, among others, saw the armed-ship bill as a blank check for the president to move the country to war, and they filibustered it to death. Wilson proceeded to arm America's commercial vessels anyway. The action came too late to prevent the sinking of several American ships. War cries echoed across the nation. In late March, an agonized Wilson called Congress into special session.

On April 2, 1917, the president stepped before a hushed Congress. Solemnly he accused the Germans of "warfare against mankind."

War Message and War Declaration

Passionately and eloquently, Wilson enumerated U.S. grievances: Germany's violation of freedom of the seas, disruption of commerce, fomenting trouble with Mexico, and breach of human rights by killing innocent Americans. The "Prussian autocracy" had to be punished by "the democracies." Russia was now among the latter, he was pleased to report, because the Russian Revolution had ousted the czar just weeks before. Congress declared war against Germany on April 6 by a vote of 373 to 50 in the House and 82 to 6 in the Senate. The first woman ever to sit in Congress, Montana's Jeannette Rankin, cast a ringing "no" vote. "Peace is a woman's job," she declared, "because men have a natural fear of being classed as cowards if they oppose war" and because mothers should protect their children from death-dealing weapons.

For principle, for morality, for honor, for commerce, for security, for reform—for all of these reasons, Wilson took the United States into World War I. The submarine was certainly the culprit that drew a reluctant president and nation into the maelstrom. Yet critics such as Bryan, Gore, McLemore, and La Follette did not attribute the U.S. descent into war to the U-boat alone. They emphasized Wilson's rigid definition of international law, which did not take account of the submarine's tactics. They faulted his contention that Americans should be entitled to travel anywhere, even on a belligerent ship loaded with contraband. They criticized his policies as unneutral. But they lost the debate. Most Americans came to accept Wilson's view that the Germans had to be checked to ensure an open, orderly world in which U.S. principles and interests would be safe.

America went to war to reform world politics, not to destroy Germany. Wilson once claimed that the United States was "pure air blowing in world politics, destroying illusions and cleaning places of morbid miasmic gasses." By early 1917 the president concluded that America would not be able to claim a seat at the postwar peace conference unless it became a combatant. At the peace conference, Wilson intended to promote the principles he thought essential to a stable world order, to advance democracy and the Open Door, and to outlaw revolution and aggression. A heady mission.

Jeannette Rankin (1880–1973) of Montana was the first woman to sit in the House of Representatives (elected in 1916) and the only member of Congress to vote against U.S. entry into both world wars (in 1917 and 1941). A lifelong pacifist, she led a march in Washington, D.C.—at age eighty-seven—against U.S. participation in the Vietnam War.   (Brown Brothers)

Taking Up Arms and Winning the War

Even before the U.S. declaration of war, the Wilson administration—encouraged by groups such as the National Security League and the Navy League and by mounting public outrage against Germany's submarine warfare—had been beefing up the military under the banner of "preparedness." When the pacifist song "I Didn't Raise My Boy to Be a Soldier" became popular, preparedness proponents retorted: "I Didn't Raise My Boy to Be a Coward." Nonetheless, Senator La Follette and House Majority Leader Claude Kitchin, among others, worked to prevent passage of the National Defense Act of 1916. They failed. This legislation provided for increases in the army and National

Guard and for summer training camps modeled on the one in Plattsburgh, New York, where a slice of America's social and economic elite had trained in 1915 as "citizen soldiers." The Navy Act of 1916 started the largest naval expansion in American history.

To raise an army after the declaration of war, Congress in May 1917 passed the Selective Service Act, requiring all males between the ages of twenty-one and thirty (later changed to eighteen and forty-five) to register. National service, proponents believed, would not only prepare the nation for battle but instill patriotism and respect for order, democracy, and personal sacrifice. One general claimed that compulsory national service would "heat up the melting pot." Critics feared that "Prussianism," not democratization, would be the likely outcome. On June 5, 1917, more than 9.5 million men signed up for

The Draft and the Soldier

the "great national lottery." By war's end, 24 million men had been registered by local draft boards. Of this number, 4.8 million had served in the armed forces, 2 million of that number in France. Among them were hundreds of thousands who had volunteered before December 1917, when the government prohibited enlistment because the military judged voluntarism too inefficient (many volunteers were more useful in civilian factories than in the army) and too competitive (enlistees got to choose the service they wanted, thus setting off recruiting wars). Millions of laborers received deferments from military duty because they worked in war industries or had dependents.

The typical soldier was a draftee in his early twenties, white, single, American-born, and poorly educated (most had not attended high school and perhaps 30 percent could not read or write). Tens of thousands of women enlisted in the Army Nurse Corps, served as "hello girls" in the Army Signal Corps, and became clerks in the Navy and Marine Corps. On college cam-

puses, 150,000 students joined the Student Army Training Corps or similar navy and marine units. At officer training camps, the army turned out "ninety-day wonders."

Some 400,000 African Americans also served in the military. Although some southern politicians feared arming African Americans, the army drafted them into segregated units and assigned them to menial labor. Draft boards frequently denied African Americans' legitimate requests for occupational or dependency deferments. Racist slang became common in the training camps. W. E. B. Du Bois, in July 1918, endorsed the NAACP's support for the war. He urged blacks to join the fight for "world liberty," in the hope that a war to make the world safe for democracy might also blur the color line at home. Sparking protest from some other black leaders who thought that wartime accommodationism would damage, not improve, race relations, Du Bois also accepted an army captaincy. A year earlier he had backed creation of a segregated, all-

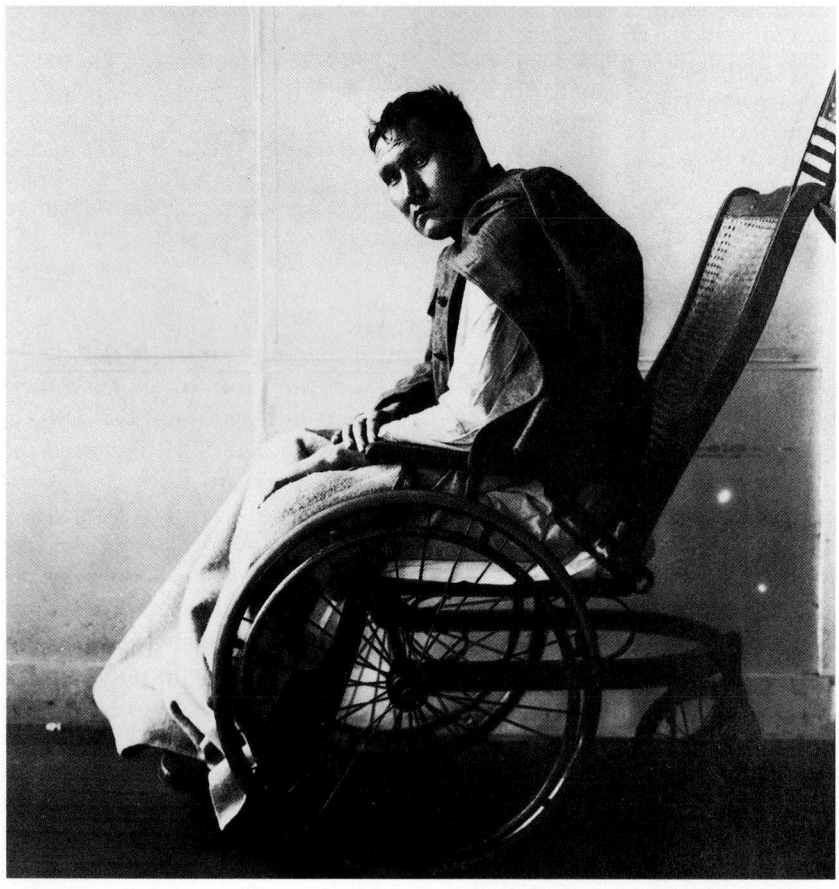

Fast Fred Horse, a Rosebud Sioux, recuperates in a New York hospital after suffering injury and paralysis during the Meuse-Argonne campaign of fall 1918. Unlike African Americans, Native Americans were not assigned to segregated units during the war. Native Americans participated in all major battles against German forces and suffered a high casualty rate in large part because they served as scouts, messengers, and snipers. (William Hammond Mathers Museum, Indiana University)

black officers' training camp: "We must choose then between the insult of a separate camp and the irreparable injury of strengthening the present custom of putting no black men in positions of authority." Blacks, he insisted, had to "take advantage of the disadvantage." Black colleges such as Hampton Institute and Fisk University encouraged students to join the camp. Eventually fourteen hundred black officers served in the war.

Some 15,000 Native Americans served, too. Most of them were enlistees who sought escape from restrictive Indian schools and lives of poverty, opportunities to develop new skills, and chances to prove their patriotism, which might later earn white respect. James McCarthy, a Papago from an Arizona reservation, volunteered because he wanted adventure; he got it: gas that blistered his body, a grenade wound, and German capture and imprisonment.

Indian Enlistees

Approximately 3 million men evaded draft registration. Some were arrested and others fled to Mexico or Canada, but most stayed at home and were never discovered. Another 338,000 men who had registered and been summoned by their draft boards failed to show up for induction. According to arrest records, most of these "deserters" and the more numerous "evaders" were lower-income agricultural and industrial laborers. Some simply felt overwhelmed by the government bureaucracy and stayed away; others were members of minority or ethnic groups who felt alienated. Although nearly 65,000 draftees initially applied for conscientious-objector status (refusing to bear arms for religious or pacifistic reasons), some changed their minds or, like so many others, failed preinduction examinations. Quakers and Mennonites were numerous among the 4,000 inductees actually classified as conscientious objectors (COs). General Leonard Wood called COs "enemies of the Republic," and the military harassed them. COs who refused noncombat service, such as in the Medical Corps, faced imprisonment.

American leaders worried that the young soldiers, once away from home, would be tempted by vice—especially by the saloons and houses of prostitution that quickly surrounded training camps. In the spirit of the Progressive era, to protect the supposed novices with "invisible armor," the government created the Commission on Training Camp Activities to coordinate

Commission on Training Camp Activities

the work of the Young Men's Christian Association (YMCA) and other groups that dispensed food, showed movies, held athletic contests, and distributed books. Men in uniform were not permitted to drink. Alarmed by the spread of venereal disease, commission officials declared "sin-free" zones around military bases and exhorted soldiers to abstain from sex. American Federation of Labor President Samuel Gompers thought the moralizing ridiculous and the prohibitions unenforceable because "real men will be men." Navy Secretary Josephus Daniels replied that "men must live straight if they would shoot straight."

General John J. Pershing, head of the American Expeditionary Forces (AEF), insisted that his "sturdy rookies" remain a separate, independent army. He was not about to turn over his "doughboys" to Allied commanders, who had become wedded to unimaginative and deadly trench warfare, producing a military stalemate and ghastly casualties on the western front. Zigzag trenches fronted by barbed wire and mines stretched across France. Between the muddy, stinking trenches lay "no man's land," denuded by artillery fire. When ordered out, soldiers would charge the enemy's trenches. Machine guns mowed them down; gas poisoned them. Little was gained. At the Battle of the Somme in 1916 the British and French suffered 600,000 dead or wounded to earn only 125 square miles; the Germans lost 500,000 men. Ambassador Page grew sickened by what Europe had become—"a bankrupt slaughter-house inhabited by unmated women."

Trench Warfare

The first American units landed in France on June 26, 1917, marched in a Fourth of July parade in Paris, and then moved by train toward the front. They soon learned about the horrors caused by advanced weaponry. An Army nurse probed one soldier's chest, finding his name tag deep in the "nasty" wound. "It probably saved his life." Poison gases (chlorine, phosgene, and mustard), first used by the Germans in spring 1915, blistered, incapacitated, and killed. Many men, like A.P., suffered shell shock. Providing some relief were Red Cross canteens, staffed by women volunteers, which gave soldiers way stations in a strange land and offered haircuts, food, and recreation. Some ten thousand Red Cross nurses also cared for the young warriors, while the American Library Association distributed 10 million books and magazines.

In Paris, where forty large houses of prostitution thrived, it became commonplace to hear that the

A U.S. soldier of Company K, 110th Infantry Regiment, receives aid during fighting at Verennes, France.   (National Archives)

Problem of Venereal Disease

British were drunkards, the French were whoremongers, and the Americans were both. Venereal disease became a serious problem. French Prime Minister Georges Clemenceau offered licensed, inspected prostitutes in "special houses" to the American army. When the generous Gallic offer reached Washington, Secretary of War Newton Baker gasped, "For god's sake . . . don't show this to the President or he'll stop the war." By war's end, about 15 percent of America's soldiers had contracted venereal disease, costing the army $50 million and 7 million days of active duty. Periodic inspections, chemical prophylactic treatments, and the threat of court-martial for infected soldiers kept the problem from being even more disastrous.

The influx of American men and materiel—and the morale boost they gave to the Allies—decided the outcome of the First World War. With both sides vir-

tually exhausted, the Americans tipped the balance toward the Allies. On the high seas, the U.S. Navy battled submarines and escorted troop carriers. Flying primarily French and British aircraft, pilots in the U.S. Air Service saw limited action, mostly against German ground troops and transport. But the aerial "dogfights" of such "aces" as Edward V. Rickenbacker helped advance the cause for military aviation. U.S. ground troops actually did not engage in much combat until after the lull in the fighting during the harsh winter of 1917–1918.

The Germans launched a major offensive in March 1918, after Russia left the war, permitting the shift of German troops from the eastern front to France. By May, Kaiser Wilhelm's forces had stormed to within 50 miles of Paris. Late that month, troops of the U.S. First Division helped blunt the German advance at Cantigny

AEF Battles in France

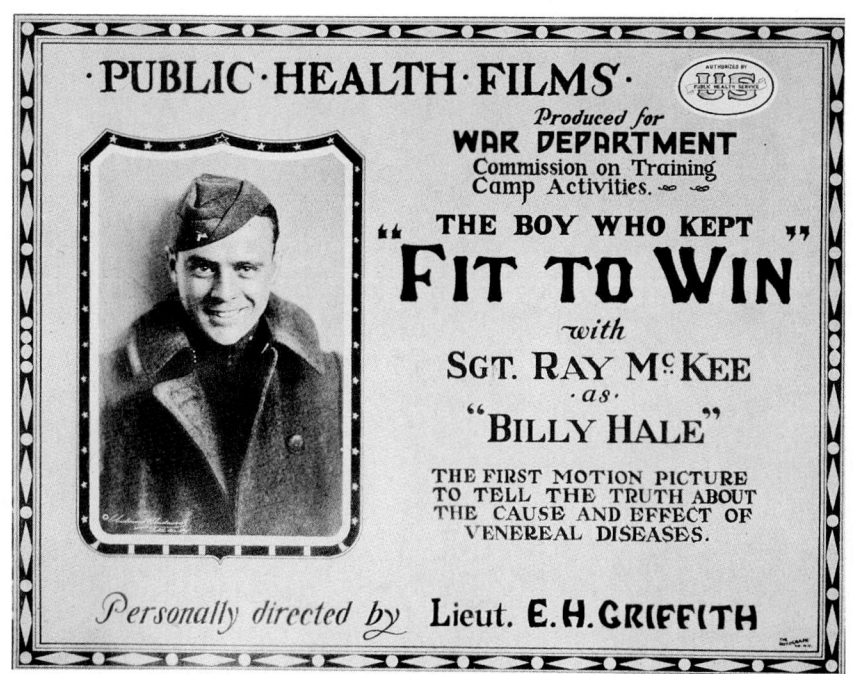

· PUBLIC · HEALTH · FILMS ·

AUTHORIZED BY U.S. PUBLIC HEALTH SERVICE

Produced for
WAR DEPARTMENT
Commission on Training
Camp Activities.

"THE BOY WHO KEPT"
FIT TO WIN
with
SGT. RAY MᶜKEE
· *as* ·
"BILLY HALE"

THE FIRST MOTION PICTURE
TO TELL THE TRUTH ABOUT
THE CAUSE AND EFFECT OF
VENEREAL DISEASES.

Personally directed by Lieut. E.H. GRIFFITH

During the First World War, the War Department promoted a film to combat sexually transmitted diseases. After the war, the New York State Board of Censors declared the film obscene. (Social Welfare History Archives Center, University of Minnesota)

(see Map 23.2). In June the Third Division and French forces held positions along the Marne River at Château-Thierry, and the Second Division soon attacked the Germans in the Belleau Wood. American soldiers won the battle after three weeks of fighting, but thousands died or were wounded after they made almost sacrificial frontal assaults against German machine guns.

Allied victory in the Second Battle of the Marne in July 1918 seemed to turn the tide against the Germans. In September French and American forces took St. Mihiel, a ferocious battle in which American gunners fired 100,000 rounds of phosgene gas shells. Then the Allies began their massive Meuse-Argonne offensive. More than 1 million Americans joined British and French troops in weeks of fierce combat; some 26,000 Americans died before the Allies claimed the Argonne Forest on October 10. For Germany—its ground war stymied, its submarine warfare failed, its troops and cities mutinous, its allies Turkey and Austria dropping out, and its kaiser abdicated—peace became imperative. The Germans accepted an armistice on November 11, 1918.

The belligerents counted 10 million soldiers and 6.6 million civilians dead and 21.3 million people wounded. Fifty thousand American soldiers died in

Casualties

battle, and another 62,000 died from disease—many from the influenza pandemic (see page 652). More than 200,000 Americans were wounded. Parents and widows pressed the War Department to return the remains of 70 percent of the American dead, but the others were buried in cemeteries in France, Belgium, and England.

Mobilizing and Managing the Home Front

"It is not an army that we must shape and train for war," declared President Wilson, "it is a nation." The United States was a belligerent for only nineteen months, but the war had a tremendous impact at home. The federal government quickly created a command economy to meet war needs and intervened in American life as never before. The vastly enlarged Washington bureaucracy managed the economy, labor force, military, public opinion, and more. Federal expenditures increased tremendously as the government spent more than $760 million a month from April 1917 to August 1919. War expenses ballooned to $33.5 billion (see

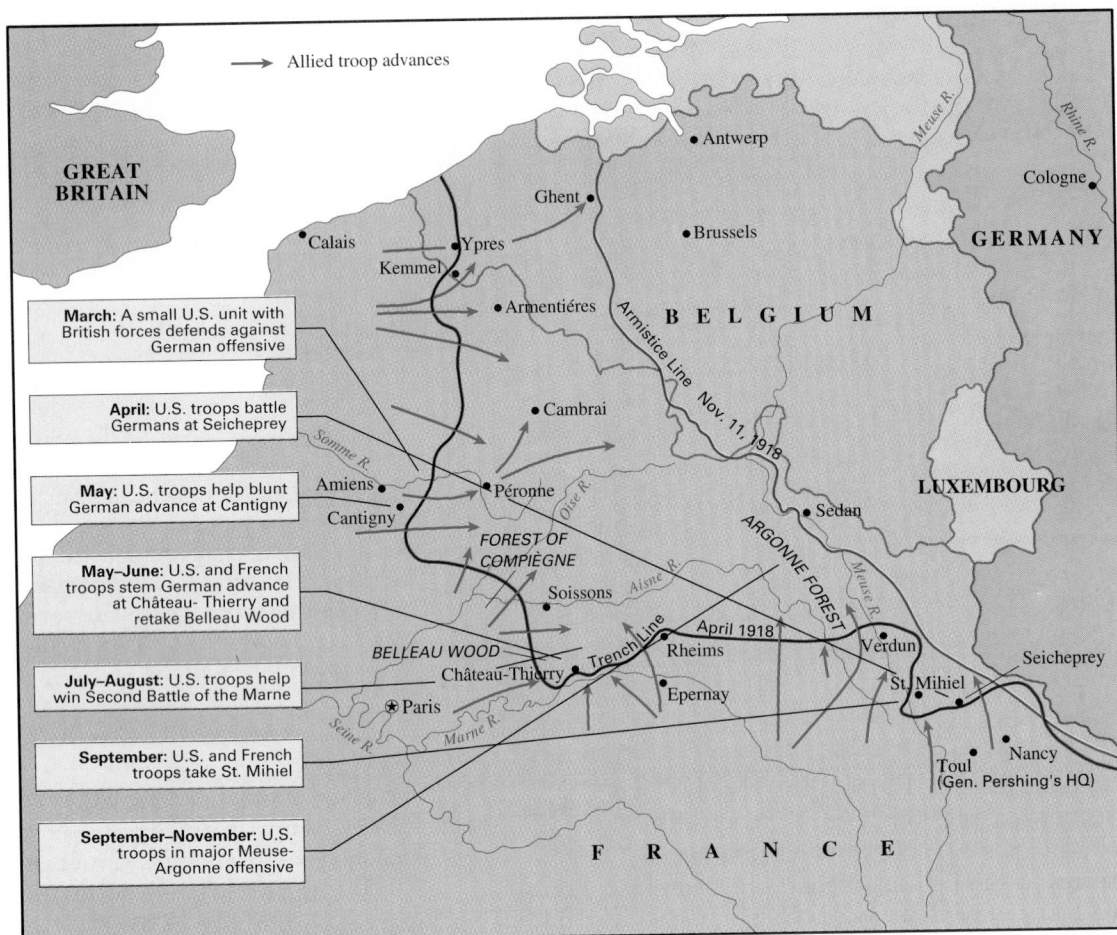

Map 23.2 American Troops at the Western Front, 1918 America's 2 million troops in France met German forces head-on, ensuring the defeat of the Central Powers in 1918.

Figure 23.1). The total cost of the war was probably triple that figure, since future generations would have to pay veterans' benefits and interest on loans. To Progressives of the New Nationalist persuasion, the wartime expansion and centralization of government power were welcome. To others, these changes seemed excessive, leading to concentrated, hence dangerous, federal power. "War is the health of the state," Randolph Bourne had warned.

The federal government and private business became partners during the war. Dollar-a-year executives flocked to the nation's capital from major companies; they retained their corporate salaries while serving in official administrative and consulting capacities. Early in the war, the government relied on several industrial committees for advice on purchases and prices. But evidence of self-interested businesspeople cashing in on the national interest aroused public protest. The head of the aluminum advisory committee, for example, was also president of the largest aluminum company. The assorted committees were disbanded in July 1917 in favor of a single manager, the War Industries Board. But the government continued to work closely with business through trade associations, which grew significantly to two thousand by 1920. The federal government suspended antitrust laws and signed cost-plus contracts, which guaranteed companies a healthy profit and a means to pay higher wages to head off labor strikes. Competitive bidding was virtually abandoned. Under these wartime practices, big business grew bigger.

Hundreds of new government agencies, staffed primarily by businesspeople, placed controls on the economy in order to shift the nation's resources to the

Business-Government Cooperation

New Agencies for Economic Management

Allies, the AEF, and war-related production. The Food Administration, led by the engineer and investor Herbert Hoover, launched voluntary programs to increase production and conserve food—Americans were urged to grow "victory gardens" and to eat meatless and wheatless meals—but it also set prices and regulated distribution. The Railroad Administration took over the snarled railway industry. The Fuel Administration controlled coal supplies and rationed gasoline. When strikes threatened the telephone and telegraph companies, the federal government seized and ran them.

The largest of the superagencies was the War Industries Board (WIB), headed by the financier Bernard Baruch. At one point, this Wall Streeter frankly told Henry Ford that he would dispatch the military to seize his plants if the automaker did not accept WIB limits on car production. Ford relented. Although the WIB seemed all-powerful, in reality it had to conciliate competing interest groups and compromise with the business executives whose advice it so valued. Designed as a clearing-house to coordinate the national economy, the WIB made purchases, allocated supplies, and fixed prices at levels that business requested. The WIB also ordered the standardization of goods to save materials and streamline production. The varieties of automobile tires, for example, were reduced from 287 to 3.

The performance of the mobilized economy was mixed, but it delivered enough men and materiel to France to ensure the defeat of the Central Powers. About a quarter of all American production was diverted to war needs. As farmers enjoyed boom years of higher prices, they put more acreage into production and mechanized as never before. From 1915 to 1920 the number of tractors in American fields jumped tenfold. Gross farm income for the period from 1914 to 1919 increased more than 230 percent. Although manufacturing output leveled off in 1918, some industries realized substantial growth because of wartime demand. Steel reached a peak production of 45 million tons in 1917, twice the prewar figure. As U.S. soldiers popularized American brands in Europe, tobacconists profited from a huge increase in cigarette sales: from 26 billion cigarettes in 1916 to 48 billion in 1918. Overall, the gross national product in 1920 stood 237 percent higher than in 1914.

Because massive assignments had to be completed in a hurry, mistakes mounted. Weapons deliveries fell

Economic Performance

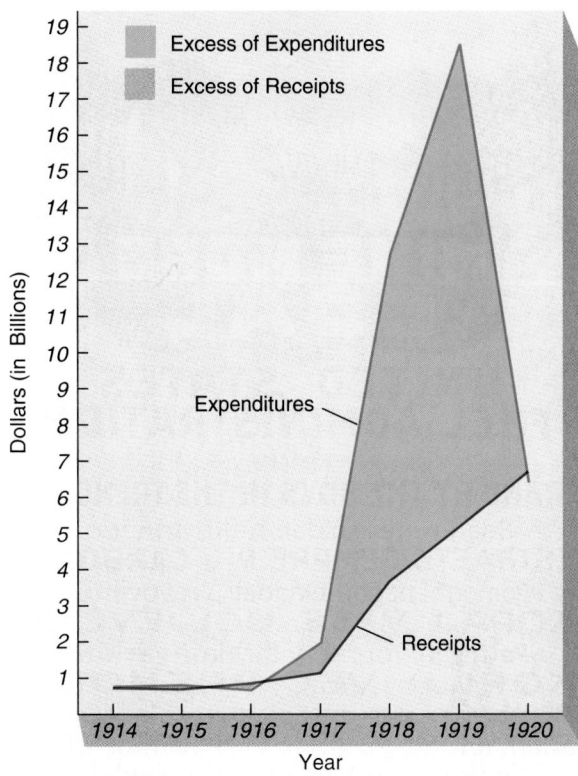

Figure 23.1 The Federal Budget, 1914–1920 During the First World War, the federal government spent more money than it received from increased taxes. It borrowed from banks or sold bonds through Liberty Loan drives. To meet the mounting costs of the war, in other words, the federal government had to resort to deficit spending. Expenditures topped receipts by more than $13 billion in 1919. Given this wartime fiscal pattern, moreover, the U.S. federal debt rose from $1 billion in 1914 to $25 billion in 1919. (Source: U.S. Department of Commerce, *Historical Statistics of the United States: Colonial Times to 1957* [Washington, D.C., Bureau of the Census, 1960], p. 711.)

short of demand; the bloated bureaucracy of the War Shipping Board failed to build enough ships. In the severe winter of 1917–1918, millions of Americans could not get coal. Coal companies held back on production to raise prices; railroads did not have enough coal cars; and harbors froze, closing out coal barges. In January, blizzards shut down midwestern railroads and factories, impeding the war effort. People died from pneumonia and freezing. A Brooklyn man went out in the morning to forage for coal and returned to find his two-month-old daughter frozen to death in her crib.

During the First World War, the United States Fuel Administration promoted economic mobilization at home in this poster printed in several languages. (National Park Service Collection, Ellis Island Immigration Museum. Photo Chermayeff and Geismar MetaForm)

Government officials failed to stem inflation. The wholesale price index was 98 percent higher in 1918 than it had been in 1913. Though partly stimulated by demand exceeding supply because of increases in Allied buying, inflation also sprang from the government's liberal credit policies and high price levels. By fixing prices on raw materials rather than on finished products, moreover, the government lost control of inflation. By bowing to southern politicians who wanted cotton left unregulated, the government permitted runaway cotton prices. Clothing tripled in cost, and food prices more than doubled. A quart of milk that cost 9 cents in 1914 climbed to 17 cents in 1920. Fuel prices also skyrocketed: the price for a 100-pound sack of coal rose 100 percent. Inflation pinched household budgets.

Inflation

Tax policies during the war sought to pull some of the profits reaped from high prices and defense contracts into the Treasury, reflecting the belief that wealth as well as labor should be conscripted. The Revenue Act in 1916 started the process by raising the surtax on high incomes and corporate profits, imposing a federal tax on large estates, and significantly increasing the tax on munitions manufacturers. Still, the government financed only one-third of the war through taxes. The other two-thirds came from loans, including Liberty bonds sold to the American people through aggressive campaigns. The War Revenue Act of 1917 provided for a more steeply graduated personal income tax, a corporate income tax, an excess-profits tax, and increased excise taxes on alcoholic beverages, tobacco, and luxury items. Although these taxes did curb excessive corporate profiteering, several loopholes tempted the unscrupulous. Sometimes companies inflated costs to conceal profits or paid high salaries and bonuses to their executives. Four officers of Bethlehem Steel, for example, divided bonuses of $2.3 million in 1917 and $2.1 million the next year. Corporate net earnings for 1913 totaled $4 billion; in 1917 they reached $7 billion; and in 1918, after the tax bite and the war's end, they still stood at $4.5 billion. Profits and patriotism went hand in hand in America's war experience. The abrupt cancellation of billions of dollars' worth of contracts at the end of the war, however, caused a brief economic downturn, a short boom, and then an intense depression (see Chapter 24).

Paying for the War

American workers benefited from the full-employment wartime economy, which increased their total earnings and gave many of them time-and-a-half pay for overtime work. Given the higher cost of living, however, workers saw minimal improvement in their economic standing. Turnover rates were high as workers switched jobs for higher pay and better conditions. Sometimes employers practiced "scamping": the pirating of laborers from other companies. Some employers sought to overcome labor shortages by expanding welfare and social programs and by establishing personnel departments—"specialized human nature engineers to keep its human machinery frictionless," as General Electric explained. To meet the labor crisis, the Department of Labor's U.S. Employment Service matched laborers with job vacancies, especially attracting workers from the South and Midwest to war industries in the East. The department also temporarily relaxed the literacy-test and head-tax

Labor Shortage

provisions of immigration law to attract farm labor, miners, and railroad workers from Mexico. Because the labor crisis also generated a housing crisis as workers crammed into cities, the U.S. Housing Corporation and Emergency Fleet Corporation, following British example, built row houses in Newport News, Virginia, and Eddystone, Pennsylvania.

In early 1918 Wilson instituted the National War Labor Board (NWLB), which discouraged strikes and lockouts and urged management to negotiate with existing unions. In July, after the Western Union Company fired eight hundred union members for trying to organize the firm's workers and then defied an NWLB request to reinstate the employees, the president nationalized the telegraph lines and put the laborers back to work. That month, too, the NWLB directed General Electric to raise wages and stop discriminating against metal trades union members in Schenectady, New York. On the other hand, in September the NWLB ordered striking Bridgeport, Connecticut, machinists back to munitions factories, threatening to revoke their draft exemptions (granted earlier because they worked in an "essential" industry).

National War Labor Board

For unions, the war seemed to offer opportunities for recognition and better pay through partnership with government. Samuel Gompers threw the AFL's loyalty to the Wilson administration, promising to deter strikes. Gompers and other moderate labor leaders accepted appointments to federal agencies. The antiwar Socialist Party blasted the AFL for becoming a "fifth wheel on [the] capitalist war chariot." But union membership climbed from roughly 2.5 million in 1916 to more than 4 million in 1919. The AFL, however, could not curb strikes by the radical Industrial Workers of the World (IWW) or rebellious AFL locals, especially those controlled by labor activists and socialists. In the nineteen war months, more than six thousand strikes expressed workers' demands for a "living wage" and improved working conditions (many called for an eight-hour workday). Exploiting Wilsonian wartime rhetoric, workers and their unions also sought to "de-Kaiser" American industry—that is, to create "industrial democracy," a more representative workplace with a role for labor in determining job categories and content and with workplace representation through shop committees. By 1920, in defiance of the national AFL, labor parties had sprung up in twenty-three states.

When immigration dropped off and some foreign nationals returned to Europe to fight for their home-

Women in the Work Force

lands, and when 16 percent of the male work force entered the military, business especially targeted women to fill vacancies. In Connecticut, a special motion picture, *Mr. and Mrs. Hines of Stamford Do Their Bit*, appealed to housewives' patriotism, urging them to take factory jobs. Although the total number of women in the work force increased slightly, the real story was that many changed jobs, sometimes moving into formerly male domains. Some white women left domestic service for factories, shifted from clerking in department stores to stenography and typing, or departed textile mills for employment in firearms plants. At least 20 percent of all workers in the wartime electrical-machinery, airplane, and food industries were women. Some one hundred

Using posters, many government agencies appealed to the American people to help win the war. This one, from the U.S. Employment Service, encouraged women to enter the work force.   (National Archives)

Stella Young (1896–1989), a Canadian-born woman from Chelsea, Massachusetts, became widely known as the "Doughnut Girl" because of her service during the First World War with the American branch of the Salvation Army, an international organization devoted to social work. She arrived in France in March 1918 and worked in emergency canteens near the battle front, providing U.S. troops with coffee, cocoa, sandwiches, doughnuts, pie, and fruit. Stella Young became famous when this picture of her wearing a khaki uniform and a "doughboy" steel helmet was widely circulated as a postcard. She served again in World War II. Chelsea named a city square in her honor in 1968. (Collection of Colonel Stuart S. Corning, Jr.)

segregated occupations, serving as typists, nurses, teachers, and domestic servants.

Some male workers, unaccustomed to working beside women, complained that women destabilized the work environment with their higher productivity and acceptance of lower pay. Women pointed out that male-dominated companies discriminated against them and that unions largely denied them membership. Male employees also resented the spirit of independence evident among women. Other critics charged that working mothers neglected their children and their housework. Day nurseries were scarce and beyond the means of most working-class families, and few employers provided childcare facilities. The war experience barely changed the attitude that women's proper sphere was the home, and most women workers lost their jobs to the returning veterans.

Women participated in the war effort in other ways. As volunteers, they made clothing for refugees and soldiers, served at Red Cross facilities, and taught French to nurses assigned to the war zone. Many worked for the Women's Committee of the Council of National Defense, whose leaders included Ida Tarbell and Carrie Chapman Catt. A vast network of state, county, and town volunteer organizations, the council publicized government mobilization programs, encouraged home gardens, sponsored drives to sell Liberty bonds, and continued the push for social welfare reforms. This patriotic work won praise from men and improved the prospects for passage of the Nineteenth Amendment (see page 595–596). "We have made partners of women in this war," Wilson said as he endorsed woman suffrage in 1918. "Shall we admit them only to a partnership of suffering and sacrifice . . . and not to a partnership of privilege and right?"

War mobilization wrought significant change for the African American community as southern blacks undertook a great migration to northern cities to work in railroad yards, packing houses, steel mills, shipyards, and coal mines. Between 1910 and 1920, Cleveland's black population swelled by more than 300 percent, Detroit's by more than 600 percent, and Chicago's by 150 percent. Much of the increase occurred between 1916 and 1919. All told, about a half-million African Americans uprooted themselves to move to the North. Families sometimes pooled savings to send one member; others sold their household goods to pay for the journey. Most of the migrants were males—young (in their early twenties), unmarried, and skilled or semi-skilled. Wartime jobs in the North provided an escape

African American Migration North

thousand women worked in the railroad industry. As white women took advantage of these new opportunities, black women took some of their places in domestic service and in textile factories. For the first time, department stores employed black women as elevator operators and cafeteria waitresses. Most working women were single and remained concentrated in sex-

A New York City street cleaner, wearing a gauze mask, takes no chances during the influenza pandemic of 1918. Many of the people who wore the masks said it was better to look ridiculous than to be dead. (Corbis-Bettmann)

from low wages, sharecropping, tenancy, crop liens, debt peonage, lynchings, and political disfranchisement. To a friend back in Mississippi, one African American wrote: "I just begin to feel like a man. . . . I don't have to humble to no one. I have registered. Will vote the next election."

But African Americans continued to experience discrimination in both North and South. When the United States entered the First World War, there was not one black judge in the entire country. Segregation remained social custom. The Ku Klux Klan was reviving, and racist films such as D. W. Griffith's *The Birth of a Nation* (1915) fed prejudice. Lynching statistics exposed the wide gap between wartime declarations of humanity and the American practice of inhumanity at home: between 1914 and 1920, 382 blacks were lynched, some of them in military uniform.

Northern whites who resented "the Negro invasion" vented their anger in riots, as in East St. Louis, Illinois, in July 1917 (see page 534).

Race Riots

The next month, in Houston, where African American soldiers faced white harassment and refused to obey seg-

regation laws, whites and blacks exchanged gunfire. Seventeen whites and two African Americans died, and the army sentenced thirteen black soldiers to death and forty-one to life imprisonment for mutiny. During the bloody "Red Summer" of 1919, race riots rocked two dozen cities and towns. The worst violence occurred in Chicago, a favorite destination for migrating blacks. In the very hot days of July 1919, a black youth swimming at a segregated white beach was hit by a thrown rock and drowned. Rumors spread, tempers flared, and soon blacks and whites were battling one another. Stabbings, burnings, and shootings went on for days until state police restored some calm. Thirty-eight people died, twenty-three African Americans and fifteen whites. By the time of this tragedy, a disillusioned W. E. B. Du Bois had already concluded that black support for the war had not diminished whites' adherence to inequality and segregation. That spring he vowed a struggle: "We return. We return from fighting. We return fighting."

Added to the nation's unsettling war experience was another home-front crisis that cut across race, gender, and class lines: the influenza pandemic that

Influenza Pandemic

engulfed the world in 1918–1919. Before it abated, as many as 40 million people died worldwide, killing the young more than the elderly. The first case of the extremely contagious flu virus was reported at Camp Funston, in Kansas, on March 4, 1918. It quickly spread to most American cities and then to Europe, carried there by U.S. troops. High fevers, aching muscles, and headaches staggered people. To fend off the virus, people received flu vaccines of questionable value or wore gauze masks. But mostly they had to wait until the virus tailed off. In many cases, severe pneumonia set in, and victims' lungs filled with fluid. Seven hundred thousand people died from the killer disease in the United States.

Through its concerted propaganda effort, the Committee on Public Information helped sell to the American people U.S. participation in the First World War. In this 1917 poster, the committee also warned against German spies, perhaps even German American spies, who might pick up secrets from unsuspecting citizens. (Private Collection)

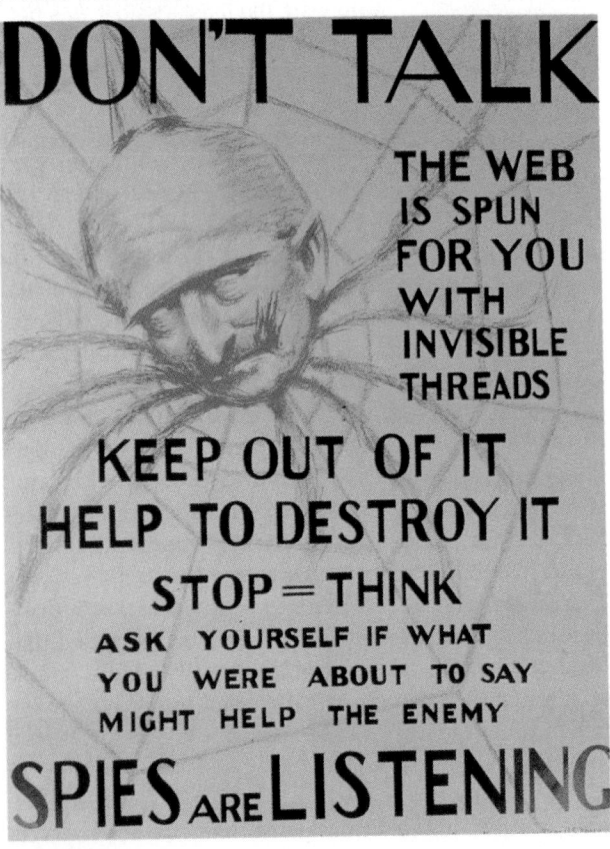

Emergence of the Civil Liberties Issue

"Woe be to the man that seeks to stand in our way in this day of high resolution," warned President Wilson. An official and unofficial campaign soon began to silence dissenters who questioned Wilson's decision for war or who protested the draft. In the end, the Wilson administration compiled one of the worst civil liberties records in American history. The targets of governmental and quasi-vigilante repression were the hundreds of thousands of Americans and aliens who refused to support the war: pacifists from all walks of life, conscientious objectors, socialists, radical labor groups, the debt-ridden tenant farmers of Oklahoma who staged the Green Corn Rebellion against the draft, the Non-Partisan League, reformers such as Robert La Follette and Jane Addams, and countless others. In the wartime process of debating the question of the right to speak freely in a democracy, the concept of "civil liberties" for the first time in American history emerged as a major public policy issue.

Shortly after the declaration of war in 1917, the president appointed George Creel, a Progressive journalist, to head the Committee on Public Information (CPI). Employing some of the nation's most talented writers and scholars, the CPI used propaganda to shape and mobilize public opinion. Pamphlets and films demonized the Germans, and CPI "Four-Minute Men" spoke at movie theaters, schools, and churches to pump up a patriotic mood. Encouraged by the CPI to promote American participation in the war, film companies and their trade association, the National Association of the Motion Picture Industry, produced documentaries, newsreels, and anti-German movies such as *The Kaiser, the Beast of Berlin* (1918) and *To Hell with the Kaiser* (1918). The committee also urged the press to practice "self-censorship" and encouraged people to spy on their neighbors. "Not a pin dropped in the home of any one with a foreign name," Creel claimed with satisfaction, "but that it rang like thunder on the inner ear of some listening sleuth." Exaggeration, fear-mongering, distortion, half-truths—such were the stuff of the CPI's "mind mobilization."

The Wilson administration also guided through an obliging Congress the Espionage Act (1917) and the Sedition Act (1918). The first statute forbade "false statements" designed to impede the draft or promote

Committee on Public Information

Espionage and Sedition Acts

military insubordination, and it banned from the mails materials considered treasonous. The Sedition Act made it unlawful to obstruct the sale of war bonds and to use "disloyal, profane, scurrilous, or abusive" language to describe the government, the Constitution, the flag, or the military uniform. These loosely worded laws gave the government wide latitude to crack down on critics. Fair-minded people could disagree over what constituted false or abusive language, but in the feverish home-front atmosphere of the First World War, the Justice Department's definition prevailed. More than two thousand people were prosecuted under the acts, and many others were intimidated into silence.

Stories of repression built up. The Woman's Peace Party's periodical *Four Lights* was denied use of the mails. When federal agents threatened to shut down the large-circulation black newspaper *Chicago Defender*, its editor reluctantly promised to refrain from criticizing the government. Put under surveillance by the Justice Department, Jane Addams also chose self-censorship, moderating her appeals for peace. Robert Goldstein, the producer of *The Spirit of '76* (1917), a film about the American Revolution complete with redcoats shooting minutemen, received a ten-year prison sentence for, said the judge, questioning the "good faith of our ally, Great Britain."

The war emergency gave Progressives and conservatives alike an opportunity to throttle the Industrial Workers of the World and the Socialist Party. Government agents raided IWW meetings, and the army marched into western mining and lumber regions to put down IWW strikes. By the end of the war most of the union's leaders were in jail. The Socialist Party fared little better. In summer 1918, with a government stenographer present, Socialist Party leader Eugene V. Debs delivered a spirited oration extolling socialism and freedom of speech—including the freedom to criticize the Wilson administration for taking America into the war. Federal agents arrested him. Debs told the court what many dissenters—and, later, many jurists and scholars—thought of the Espionage Act: it was "a despotic enactment in flagrant conflict with democratic principles and with the spirit of free institutions." Handed a ten-year sentence, Debs remained in prison until late 1921, when he received a pardon.

Imprisonment of Eugene V. Debs

Intolerance knew few boundaries. Local school boards dismissed teachers who questioned the war. At Wellesley College, economics professor Emily Greene Balch was fired because of her pacifist views (she won the Nobel Peace Prize in 1946). Three Columbia University students were picked up in mid-1917 for circulating an antiwar petition. Columbia also fired Professor J. M. Cattell, a distinguished psychologist, for his antiwar stand. His colleague Charles Beard, a historian with a prowar perspective, resigned in protest: "If we have to suppress everything we don't like to hear, this country is resting on a pretty wobbly basis."

Encouraged by official behavior, ultrapatriotic groups such as the Sedition Slammers and the American Defense Society sought to cleanse the nation through vigilantism. A German American miner in Illinois was wrapped in a flag and lynched. In Hilger, Montana, citizens burned history texts that mentioned Germany. By the end of the war, sixteen states had banned the teaching of the German language. To avoid trouble, the Kaiser-Kuhn grocery in St. Louis changed its name to Pioneer Grocery. Because towns had Liberty Loan quotas to fill, they sometimes bullied "slackers" into purchasing bonds. Nativist advocates of "100% Americanism" exploited the emotional atmosphere to exhort immigrants to throw off their Old World cultures. Companies offered English-language and naturalization classes in their factories and refused jobs and promotions to those who did not make adequate strides toward learning English. Even labor's drive for compulsory health insurance, which before the war had gained advocates in several states, including New York and California, became victimized by the poisoned war atmosphere. Many physicians and insurance companies had for years denounced health insurance as "socialistic"; after the United States entered the war, they discredited it as "Made in Germany."

Prior to World War I, American citizens of good standing could freely express mainstream political views, whereas people more marginal to a community (such as recent immigrants) or local leaders with radical opinions sometimes met with harsh treatment for exercising what today would be termed their freedom of speech. Before the war, few formally questioned these informal restrictions on political dissent. Yet the Wilson administration's vigorous suppression of dissidents led some Americans, most notably a conscientious objector named Roger Baldwin, to reformulate the traditional definition of allowable speech. Baldwin

Roger Baldwin and Free Speech

founded the Civil Liberties Bureau (forerunner of the American Civil Liberties Union) to defend the rights of those people accused under the Espionage and Sedition Acts. He was the first to advance the ideas that the content of political speech could be separated from the identity of the speaker and that a patriotic American could—indeed should—defend the right of someone to express political beliefs abhorrent to his or her own.

In unanimously upholding the Espionage Act in *Schenck v. U.S.* (1919), the Supreme Court adhered to the traditional view rather than that developed by Baldwin. In time of war, Justice Oliver Wendell Holmes wrote, the First Amendment could be restricted: "Free speech would not protect a man falsely shouting fire in a theater and causing panic." If, according to Holmes, words "are of such a nature as to create a clear and present danger that they will bring about the substantial evils that Congress has a right to prevent," free speech could be limited. A few months later, however, Holmes and Louis Brandeis dissented when the Court similarly upheld the Sedition Act, in *Abrams v. U.S.* (1919). In the interim, pressed by friends to adopt Baldwin's approach to freedom of speech and of the press, Holmes had changed his mind and accepted the notion that active political dissent was essential to a democratic government.

The Bolshevik Revolution, Labor Strikes, and the Red Scare

The line between wartime suppression of dissent and the postwar Red Scare is not easily drawn. In the name of patriotism, both harassed suspected internal enemies and deprived them of their constitutional rights; both had government sanction. Together they stabbed at the Bill of Rights and wounded radicalism in America. In the last few months of the war, guardians of Americanism began to label dissenters not only pro-German but pro-Bolshevik. After the Bolshevik Revolution in fall 1917, American hatred for the Kaiser's Germany was readily transferred to communist Russia. When the new Russian government under V. I. Lenin made a separate peace with Germany in early 1918, Americans grew angry because the closing of the eastern front would permit the Germans to move troops west. Many lashed out at American radicals, casually applying the term "Red" (derived from the red flag used by communists) to discredit them.

The ordeal of Victor Berger illustrates the blending of the wartime and postwar suppression of civil lib-

Case of Victor Berger

erties. A socialist living in a heavily German district in Milwaukee, Wisconsin, and a former member of Congress, Berger was indicted under the Espionage Act for denouncing U.S. entry into the war. Voters nonetheless elected him once again to Congress in 1918. Early the next year Berger was convicted and sentenced to twenty years in federal prison. The House of Representatives thereupon refused to admit him, calling him a pro-German Bolshevik. While out on bail pending an appeal, Berger won the special election held to replace him. The House again blocked his admission. Berger's nightmare did not end until 1921, when the Supreme Court reversed his conviction. He was elected to Congress again in 1924. This time he took his seat.

The Wilson administration's ardent anti-Bolshevism became clear in mid-1918 when the president ordered five thousand American troops to northern Russia and ten thousand more soldiers to Siberia, where they joined other Allied contingents. Wilson did not consult Congress. He said the military expeditions would guard Allied supplies and Russian railroads from German seizure and would also rescue a group of Czechs who wished to return home to fight the Germans. Worried that the Japanese were building influence in Siberia and closing the Open Door, Wilson also hoped to deter Japan from further advances in Asia. Mostly he wanted to smash the infant Bolshevik government, a challenge to his new world order. So he waged an undeclared war against the new Russian regime, already engaged in a civil war with its opponents.

Intervention in Russia Against Bolsheviks

Despite his famed devotion to the principle of self-determination, Wilson backed an economic blockade of Russia, sent arms to anti-Bolshevik forces, and refused to recognize the Bolshevik government. The United States also clandestinely passed military information to anti-Bolshevik forces and used food relief to shore up anti-Bolsheviks in the Baltic region. Later, at the Paris Peace Conference, Russia was denied a seat. U.S. troops did not leave Siberia until spring 1920, after the Bolsheviks had demonstrated their staying power. These interventions in Russia embittered Washington-Moscow relations for many decades.

At home, too, the Wilson administration moved against radicals and others imprecisely defined as Bolsheviks or communists. By the war's close, Americans had become edgy. The war had exacerbated racial tensions. It had disrupted the workplace and the family.

Americans had suffered an increase in the cost of living, and postwar unemployment loomed. To add to their worries, Russians in 1919 created the Communist (Third) International (or Comintern) to promote world revolution. Already hardened by wartime violations of civil liberties, Americans found it easy to blame their postwar troubles on new scapegoats.

In 1919 a rash of labor strikes seeking to raise wages to meet rising prices and to retain wartime bargaining rights sparked the Red Scare.

Labor Strikes and the Red Scare

All told, more than thirty-three hundred strikes involving 4 million laborers jolted the nation that year, including the Seattle general strike in January. On May 1, a day of celebration for workers around the world, bombs were sent through the mails to prominent Americans. Most of the devices were intercepted and dismantled, but police never captured the conspirators. Most people assumed, not unreasonably, that anarchists and others bent on the destruction of the American way of life were responsible. Next came the Boston police strike in September. Some sniffed a Bolshevik conspiracy, but others thought it ridiculous to label Boston's Irish-American Catholic cops "radicals." The conservative governor of Massachusetts, Calvin Coolidge, gained national attention by proclaiming that nobody had the right to strike against the public safety. State guardsmen soon replaced the striking policemen.

Unrest in the steel industry in September stirred more ominous fears. Many steelworkers worked twelve hours a day, seven days a week, and lived in squalid housing. They looked to local steel unions, organized by the National Committee for Organizing Iron and Steel Workers, to help them improve their lives. When postwar unemployment in the industry climbed and the U.S. Steel Corporation refused to meet with committee representatives, some 350,000 workers walked off the job demanding the right to collective bargaining, a shorter workday, and a living wage. The steel barons hired strikebreakers and sent agents to club strikers. Worried about both the 1919 strikes and Bolshevism, President Wilson warned against "the poison of disorder" and the "poison of revolt." But in the case of steel, the companies won; the strike collapsed in early 1920.

One of the leaders of the steel strike was William Z. Foster, an IWW member and militant labor organizer who later joined the Communist Party. His presence in a labor movement seeking bread-and-butter goals permitted political and business leaders to

❖ THE BULL IN THE CHINA SHOP ❖

This anti-Bolshevik cartoon, titled "The Bull in the China Shop," represented the view of U.S. leaders during the Red Scare that Russia's radical Bolshevik revolution was threatening American principles and values. (*San Francisco Chronicle,* February 27, 1919)

dismiss the steel strike as a foreign threat orchestrated by American radicals. There was in fact no conspiracy, and the American left was badly splintered. Two defectors from the Socialist Party, John Reed and Benjamin Gitlow, founded the Communist Labor Party in 1919. The rival Communist Party of the United States of America, composed largely of aliens, was launched the same year. Neither party commanded many followers—their combined membership probably did not exceed seventy thousand—and in 1919 the harassed Socialist Party could muster no more than thirty thousand members.

Although divisiveness among radicals actually signified weakness, both Progressives and conservatives

American Legion

interpreted the advent of the new parties as strengthening the radical menace. That is certainly how the American Legion saw the question. Organized in May 1919 to lobby for veterans' benefits, the Legion soon preached an anti-radicalism that fueled the Red Scare. By 1920, 843,000 Legion members, mostly middle and upper class, had become stalwarts of an impassioned Americanism that demanded conformity.

Wilson's attorney general, A. Mitchell Palmer, also insisted that Americans think alike. A Progressive reformer, Quaker, and ambitious politician, Palmer declared that "revolution" was "eating its way into the homes of the American workmen, licking the altars of the churches, leaping into the belfry of the school bell." Palmer appointed J. Edgar Hoover to head the Radical Division of the Department of Justice. The zealous Hoover compiled index cards bearing the names of allegedly radical individuals and organizations. During 1919 agents jailed IWW members; Palmer also saw to it that 249 alien radicals, including the anarchist Emma Goldman, were deported to Russia.

Again, state and local governments took their cue from the Wilson administration. States passed peacetime sedition acts under which hundreds of people were arrested. Vigilante groups and mobs flourished once again, their numbers swelled by returning veterans. In November 1919, in Centralia, Washington, American Legionnaires broke from a parade to storm the IWW hall. Several were wounded. A number of Wobblies were soon arrested, and one of them, an ex-soldier, was taken from jail by a mob, then beaten, castrated, and shot. The New York State legislature expelled five duly elected Socialist Party members in early 1920.

The Red Scare reached a climax in January 1920 in the Palmer Raids. Hoover planned and directed the operation; government agents in thirty-three cities broke into meeting halls and homes without search warrants. More than four thousand people were jailed and denied counsel. In Boston some four hundred people were kept in detainment on bitterly cold Deer Island; two died of pneumonia, one leaped to his death, and another went insane. Because of court rulings and the courageous efforts of Assistant Secretary of Labor Louis Post, who deliberately held up paperwork, most of the arrestees were released, although in 1920–1921 nearly six hundred were deported.

Palmer Raids

Palmer's disregard for elementary civil liberties drew criticism. Civil libertarians and lawyers charged that his tactics violated the Constitution. Many of the arrested "Communists" had committed no crimes.

When Palmer called for a peacetime sedition act, he alarmed both liberal and conservative leaders. His dire prediction that serious violence would mar May Day 1920 proved mistaken. With the steel strike over, the threat of Bolshevism in Europe receding, and the nation returning to postwar "normalcy," Palmer could no longer count on stampeding the public.

The campaigns against free speech from 1917 through 1920 left casualties. Debate, so essential to democracy, was wounded. Reform suffered as reformers either joined in the antiradicalism or became victims of it. Radical groups were badly weakened: the IWW became virtually extinct, and the Socialist Party became paralyzed. Throughout, the president made it appear that his critics were attacking the nation itself when they were actually questioning the policies of his administration. Wilson's intolerance of those who disagreed with him seemed to bespeak a fundamental distrust of democracy. At the very least, it illustrated that some Progressives were willing to use coercion to achieve their goal of a reformed society.

The Peace Conference, League Fight, and Postwar World

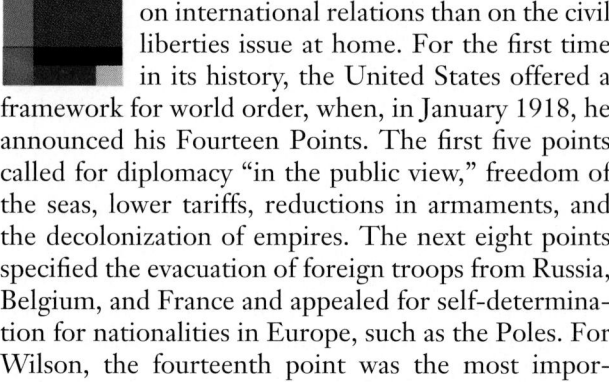

President Wilson seemed more focused on international relations than on the civil liberties issue at home. For the first time in its history, the United States offered a framework for world order, when, in January 1918, he announced his Fourteen Points. The first five points called for diplomacy "in the public view," freedom of the seas, lower tariffs, reductions in armaments, and the decolonization of empires. The next eight points specified the evacuation of foreign troops from Russia, Belgium, and France and appealed for self-determination for nationalities in Europe, such as the Poles. For Wilson, the fourteenth point was the most important—the mechanism for achieving all the others: "a general association of nations" or League of Nations. At the time of the armistice, the combatants reluctantly agreed that Wilson's principles should guide the peace negotiations.

When the president departed for the Paris Peace Conference in December 1918, he faced obstacles erected by his political enemies, by the Allies, and by himself. Some observers suggested that a cocky Wilson underestimated his task. During the 1918 congressional elections, Wil-

Obstacles to a Wilsonian Peace

son had urged a vote for Democrats as a sign of support for his peace goals. But the American people did just the opposite. The Republicans gained control of both houses, signaling trouble for Wilson in two ways. First, a peace treaty would have to be submitted for approval to a potentially hostile Senate. Second, the election results at home diminished Wilson's stature in the eyes of foreign leaders. Wilson aggravated his political problems by not naming a senator to his advisory American Peace Commission. He also refused to take any prominent Republicans with him to Paris or to consult with the Senate Foreign Relations Committee before the conference. It did not help that the president denounced his critics as "blind and little provincial people."

Another obstacle in Wilson's way was the Allies' determination to impose a harsh, vengeful peace on the Germans. Georges Clemenceau of France, David Lloyd George of Britain, and Vittorio Orlando of Italy—with Wilson, the Big Four—became formidable adversaries. They had signed secret treaties in 1915 to grab German- and Turkish-controlled territories. When the Russian Bolsheviks published the treaties in early 1918, Wilson snarled that his European allies seemed to be waging a war "for some imperial or capitalist purpose." Allied leaders scoffed at the pious, headstrong, self-impressed president who wanted to deny them the spoils of war while he sought to expand U.S. power. "How can I talk to a fellow who thinks himself the first man for two thousand years who has known anything about peace on earth," Clemenceau growled. "Wilson imagines that he is a second Messiah."

At the conference, held at the ornate palace of Versailles, the Big Four met behind closed doors. Critics quickly pointed out that Wilson had quickly abandoned the first of his Fourteen Points, diplomacy "in the public view." The victors demanded that Germany pay a huge reparations bill. Wilson instead called for a small indemnity, fearing that a resentful and economically hobbled Germany might turn to Bolshevism or disrupt the postwar community in some other way. Unable to moderate the Allied position, the president reluctantly gave way, agreeing to a clause blaming the war on the Germans and to the creation of a commission to determine the amount of reparations (later set at $33 billion). Wilson acknowledged that the peace terms were "hard," but he also came to believe that "the German people must be made to hate war."

Paris Peace Conference

As for the breaking up of empires and the principle of self-determination, Wilson could deliver on only some of his goals. Creating a League-administered "mandate" system, the conferees placed former German and Turkish colonies under the control of other imperial nations. France and Britain, for example, obtained parts of the Middle East, and Japan gained authority over Germany's colonies in the Pacific. In other arrangements, Japan replaced Germany as the imperial overlord of China's Shandong Peninsula, and France was permitted occupation rights in Germany's Rhineland. Elsewhere in Europe, Wilson's prescriptions fared better. Out of Austria-Hungary and Russia came the newly independent states of Austria, Hungary, Yugoslavia, Czechoslovakia, and Poland. Wilson and his colleagues also built a *cordon sanitaire* (buffer zone) of new westward-looking nations (Finland, Estonia, Latvia, and Lithuania) around Russia to quarantine the Bolshevik contagion (see Map 23.3).

Wilson worked hardest on the charter for the League of Nations. In the long run, he believed, such an organization would moderate the harshness of the Allied peace terms and temper imperial ambitions. The League reflected the power of large nations such as the United States: it consisted of an influential council of five permanent members and elected delegates from smaller states, an assembly of all members, and a World Court. Wilson identified Article 10 as the "kingpin" of the League covenant: "The Members of the League undertake to respect and preserve as against external aggression the territorial integrity and existing political independence of all Members of the League. In case of any such aggression or in case of any threat or danger of such aggression the Council shall advise upon the means by which this obligation shall be fulfilled." This collective-security provision, along with the entire League charter, became part of the peace treaty because Wilson insisted that there could be no future peace with Germany without a league to oversee it.

League of Nations and Article 10

German representatives at first refused to sign the punitive treaty but submitted in June 1919. They gave up 13 percent of Germany's territory, 10 percent of its population, all of its colonies, and a huge portion of its national wealth. Many people wondered how the League could function in the poisoned postwar atmosphere of revenge and humiliation. But Wilson waxed euphoric: "The stage is set, the destiny disclosed. It has come about by no plan of our conceiving, but by the hand of God."

Map 23.3 Europe Transformed by War and Peace After President Wilson and the other conferees at the Paris Peace Conference negotiated the Treaty of Versailles, empires were broken up. In eastern Europe, in particular, new nations emerged.

In March 1919, thirty-nine senators (enough to deny the treaty the necessary two-thirds vote) had signed a petition stating that the League's structure did not adequately protect U.S. interests. Wilson denounced his critics as "pygmy" minds, but he persuaded the peace conference to exempt the Monroe Doctrine and domestic matters from League jurisdiction. Having made these concessions to senatorial advice, Wilson would budge no more. Compromises with other nations had been necessary to keep the conference going, he insisted, and the League would rectify wrongs. Could his critics not see that membership in the League would give the United States "leadership in the world"?

The president was not the only one posing questions. The journalist Walter Lippmann asked: "How in our consciences are we to square the results with the promises?" Criticism of the peace process and the treaty mounted: Wilson had bastardized his own principles. He had conceded Shandong to Japan. He personally had killed a provision affirming the racial equality of all peoples. The treaty did not mention freedom of the seas, and tariffs were not reduced. Reparations promised to be punishing. Senator La Follette protested that the League would perpetuate empire. Conservative critics feared that the League would limit American freedom of action in world affairs, stymie U.S. expansion, and intrude on domestic questions. And Article 10 raised serious questions: Would the United States be *obligated* to use armed force to ensure collective security? And what about colonial rebellions, such as in Ireland or India? Would the League feel compelled to crush them? "Were a League of Nations in existence in the days when George Washington fought and won," an Irish American editor wrote, "we would still be an English colony."

Critics of the Treaty

Senator Henry Cabot Lodge of Massachusetts boldly disputed Wilson. A Harvard-educated Ph.D. and partisan Republican, Lodge packed the Foreign Relations Committee with critics and prolonged public hearings. He introduced several reservations to the treaty: one stated that the nation's immigration acts could not be subject to League decision; another held that Congress had to approve any obligation under Article 10.

In September 1919 Wilson embarked on a speaking tour of the United States. Growing more exhausted every day, he dismissed his antagonists as "contemptible quitters." Provoked by Irish American and German American hecklers, he lashed out in Red-Scare terms: "Any man who carries a hyphen about him carries a dagger which he is ready to plunge into the vitals of the Republic." While doubts about Article 10 multiplied, Wilson tried to highlight neglected features of the League charter—such as the arbitration of disputes and an international conference to abolish child labor. In Colorado, a day after delivering another passionate speech, the president awoke to nausea and

In October 1919 President Woodrow Wilson (1856–1924) receives assistance after his massive stroke, which made it difficult for him to maintain his train of thought and manage government affairs. Historians continue to debate the influence of Wilson's poor health on the president's losing battle for U.S. membership in the League of Nations. (Library of Congress)

How do historians know...

that President Wilson suffered a disabling illness that seriously impaired his leadership during the League debate and that his severe incapacity was deliberately hidden from the public? Historians had long suspected the worst, but not until the private memoranda and medical records kept by Wilson's private physician, Dr. Cary T. Grayson, were published in 1990 and 1991 (as part of editor Arthur S. Link's *The Papers of Woodrow Wilson*) did they have a detailed account of the bedridden president's condition.

After a massive stroke had incapacitated the president on October 2, 1919, Edith Bolling Wilson insisted that Grayson issue only "general statements" about her husband's status. Although at first Grayson publicly described Woodrow Wilson as "a very sick man," thereafter he delivered upbeat statements about the clarity of the president's mind and his "comfortable" days. No mention was ever made publicly that Wilson had suffered a debilitating stroke that made it difficult for him to focus on the nation's business.

Instead, as the newspaper reports printed here indicate, Grayson's bulletins simply stated that the president was down with "nervous exhaustion." White House Head Usher Irwin Hood Hoover remembered the conspiratorial "deception" to hide Wilson's actual condition. When Grayson published a memoir in 1960, he still did not reveal the truth.

Long before the major stroke, Wilson had been ill. His medical history included hypertension, arteriosclerosis (hardening of the arteries), and several small strokes (the first in 1896) that caused impaired reasoning and memory loss. Wilson and his doctors had conspired to keep this information from the American people. During the Paris Peace Conference and the League fight, Wilson's health had deteriorated further. He suffered severe headaches and insomnia. After a speech in Colorado on September 25, 1919, he collapsed.

The devastating stroke of October 2 left Wilson partially paralyzed. The prostrate president could not lead because he could not concentrate on any subject for very long and he secluded himself from cabinet members. Wilson grew very angry when Secretary of State Robert Lansing quietly suggested that the president was so incapacitated that the vice president should take over. (The Constitution reads that in case of the president's "inability to discharge the powers and duties" of his office, the "same shall devolve on the Vice President.") Always stubborn, Wilson became more intransigent and more irascible, refusing to compromise with senators who said that they would vote for U.S. membership in the League of Nations if he would accept changes in the charter. Given the serious issues raised by the collective-security provision of the covenant, some historians wonder whether even a healthy Wilson could have reversed the negative Senate vote. But other scholars argue that Wilson's illness so impaired his rationality and that the cover-up so distorted the truth that the Senate's defeat of the treaty can be understood only in the context of the stricken president's medical history as documented in Dr. Grayson's private accounts. (Photos: Copyright © 1919 by The New York Times Company. Reprinted by permission.)

Text of Admiral Grayson's Official Bulletins Reporting President Wilson's Condition

Special to The New York Times.

WASHINGTON, Oct. 11.—The bulletin on the President's condition, issued at the White House tonight, was as follows:

WHITE HOUSE, Saturday, Oct. 11, 9:45 P. M.
The President has had a comfortable day.
GRAYSON.

The morning bulletin read:

WHITE HOUSE, Saturday, Oct. 11, 12:40 P. M.
The President shows signs of continued improvement, but his condition is such as to necessitate his remaining in bed for an extended period.
GRAYSON,
DERCUM,
RUFFIN,
STITT.

This d[...]
nounced aft[...]
come to W[...]
condition f[...]
week, and [...]
Cary T. Gr[...]
Ruffin and [...]

Physicians' Bulletins Say President Had a Good Night and Restful Day

Special to The New York Times.

WASHINGTON, Oct. 12.—The following bulletin on the President's condition was issued by his physician tonight:

WHITE HOUSE, Oct. 12, 10 P. M.
The President is in good spirits and has had a restful day.
GRAYSON.

The morning bulletin read:

WHITE HOUSE, Oct. 12, 11:30 A. M.
There is no notable change in the President's condition. He had a good night.
GRAYSON.
RUFFIN
STITT.

uncontrollable facial twitching. "I just feel as if I am going to pieces," he said. A few days later, back in Washington, he suffered a massive stroke that paralyzed his left side. He became peevish and even more stubborn, increasingly unable to conduct presidential business. Advised to placate senatorial critics so the treaty would have a chance of passing, Wilson rejected "dishonorable compromise." From Senate Democrats he demanded utter loyalty—a vote against all reservations.

Twice in November the Senate rejected the Treaty of Versailles and thus U.S. membership in the League.

Senate Rejection of the Treaty and League

In the first vote, Democrats joined sixteen "Irreconcilables," mostly Republicans who opposed any treaty whatsoever, to defeat the treaty with reservations (39 for and 55 against). In the second vote, Republicans and Irreconcilables turned down the treaty without reservations (38 for and 53 against). In March 1920 the Senate again voted; this time a majority (49 for and 35 against) favored the treaty with reservations, but the tally fell short of the two-thirds needed. Had Wilson permitted Democrats to compromise—to accept reservations—he could have achieved his fervent goal of membership in the League, which, despite the U.S. absence, came into being. "I would rather fail in a cause that will ultimately triumph than triumph in a cause that will ultimately fail," he once said.

Who or what was responsible for the defeat of the treaty? The stroke incapacitated the president, sapping his energy and his ability to lead effectively. The bitter personal feud between Wilson and Lodge accounts for some conflict but does not explain the determination of the Irreconcilables. Certainly Wilson's concessions to a harsh peace at Paris undercut his case in the United States, but even so, two-thirds of the senators seemed willing to forgive his errors at Versailles if he would only accept some reservations.

At the core of the debate lay a basic issue in American foreign policy: whether the United States would

Collective Security versus Unilateralism

endorse collective security or continue to travel the path of unilateralism articulated in George Washington's Farewell Address and in the Monroe Doctrine. In a world dominated by imperialist states unwilling to subordinate their selfish ambitions to an international organization, Americans preferred their traditional nonalignment and freedom of choice over binding commitments to collective action. That is why

so many of Wilson's critics targeted Article 10 and why the president was so adamant in defending it.

In the end, Woodrow Wilson failed to create a new world order through reform. He promised more than he could deliver. Still, the United States emerged from the First World War an even greater world power. By 1920 the United States had become the world's leading economic power, producing 40 percent of its coal, 70 percent of its petroleum, and half of its pig iron. It also rose to first rank in world trade. American companies took advantage of the war to nudge the Germans and British out of foreign markets, especially in Latin America. Goodyear went into the Dutch East Indies for rubber. Meanwhile, the United States shifted from being a debtor to a creditor nation, becoming the world's leading banker.

After the disappointment of Versailles, appeals for arms control accelerated and the peace movement revitalized. At the same time, the military became better armed and more professional. The Reserve Officers' Training Corps (ROTC) became permanent; military "colleges" provided upper-echelon training; and the Army Industrial College, founded in 1924, pursued business-military cooperation in the area of logistics and planning. The National Research Council, created in 1916 with government money and Carnegie and Rockefeller funds, continued after the war as an alliance of scientists and businesspeople engaged in research relating to national defense. Tanks, quick-firing guns, armor-piercing explosives, and oxygen masks for high-altitude flying pilots were just some of the technological advances that emerged from the First World War.

The international system born in these years was unstable and fragmented. Espousing decolonization and taking to heart the Wilsonian

Unstable International System

principle of self-determination, nationalist leaders active during the First World War, such as Ho Chi Minh of Indochina and Mohandas K. Gandhi of India, vowed to achieve independence for their peoples. Communism became a disruptive force in world politics, and the Soviets bore a grudge against those invaders who had tried to thwart their revolution. The new states in central and eastern Europe proved weak, dependent on outsiders for security. Germans bitterly resented the harsh peace settlement, and the war debts and reparations problems dogged international order for years. As it entered the 1920s, the international system that Woodrow Wilson had vowed to reform wobbled.

Summary

 At the close of the First World War, the historian Albert Bushnell Hart observed that "it is easy to see that the United States is a new country." Actually, America came out of the war an unsettled mix of the old and the new. The war exposed deep divisions among Americans: white versus black, nativist versus immigrant, capital versus labor, men versus women, radical versus Progressive and conservative, pacifist versus interventionist, nationalist versus internationalist. It is little wonder that Americans—having experienced race riots, labor strikes, disputes over civil liberties, and the League fight—wanted to escape from what John Dewey called the "cult of irrationality" to what President Warren G. Harding called "normalcy."

During the war the federal government intervened in the economy and influenced people's everyday lives as never before. Centralization of control in Washington, D.C., and mobilization of the home front served as a model for the future. Although the Wilson administration shunned reconstruction or reconversion plans and quickly dismantled the many governmental agencies (war housing projects, for example, were sold to private investors), the World War I experience of the activist state served as guidance for 1930s reformers battling the Great Depression (see Chapter 25). The partnership of government and business in managing the wartime economy advanced the development of a mass society through the standardization of products and the promotion of efficiency. Wilsonian wartime policies also nourished the continued growth of oligopoly through the suspension of antitrust laws. Business power dominated the next decade. American labor, by contrast, entered lean years, although new labor management practices, including corporate welfare programs, survived.

Although the disillusionment evident after Versailles did not cause the United States to adopt a policy of isolationist withdrawal (see Chapter 26), skepticism about America's ability to right wrongs abroad marked the postwar American mood. The war was grimy and ugly, far less glorious than Wilson's lofty rhetoric suggested. People recoiled from photographs of shell-shocked faces and of bodies dangling from barbed wire. American soldiers, tired of idealism, craved the latest baseball scores and their regular jobs. Those Progressives who had believed that entry into the war would deliver the millennium, later marveled at their

naiveté. Many lost their enthusiasm for crusades, and many others turned away in disgust from the bickering of the victors. Some felt betrayed. The journalist William Allen White angrily wrote to a friend that the Allies "have—those damned vultures—taken the heart out of the peace, taken the joy out of the great enterprise of the war, and have made it a sordid malicious miserable thing like all the other wars in the world."

Woodrow Wilson himself had remarked, soon after taking office in 1913 and before the Great War, that "there's no chance of progress and reform in an administration in which war plays the principal part." From the perspective of 1920, looking back on distempers at home and abroad, Wilson knew that progress and reform had taken a beating.

LEGACY FOR A PEOPLE AND A NATION
Remembering War at the Tomb of the Unknown Soldier

The much visited Tomb of the Unknown Soldier, or Tomb of the Unknowns, is a solemn place to remember the First World War and others in which Americans have died. At the marble plaza in Virginia's Arlington National Cemetery, overlooking Washington, D.C., stern-faced military guards stiffly march back and forth, twenty-four hours a day. Buried there are the remains of three (until mid-1998, four) unidentified American soldiers "known but to God."

After World War I, U.S. leaders declared that the ceremonial burial of an anonymous hero would remind Americans of the war and symbolize national unity while saluting diversity, for it could not be determined whether the "Unknown Soldier" was white or nonwhite, immigrant or native, rich or poor, young or old, Protestant, Catholic, or Jewish. Few in those days, however, could imagine the unknown as anyone other than a native-born, white Protestant. In fall 1921, four unknowns were exhumed from graves in France; one was selected. On Armistice Day, November 11, American dignitaries reburied the unidentified combatant. On Memorial Day, May 26, 1958, an unknown from World War II and an unknown from the Korean War were interred in crypts beside the World War I soldier.

On May 28, 1984, U.S. leaders buried a fourth unknown, this one from the Vietnam War. Controversy ensued. Military authorities had initially classified the remains as those of twenty-four-year-old Lieutenant Michael J. Blassie, a pilot shot down in South Vietnam.

But officials then changed their designation to unidentified. The Blassie family pressed for reconsideration. In 1998, five years after a CBS television program publicized the issue, a reluctant Department of Defense finally agreed to disinter the Vietnam War unknown. A DNA sample (deoxyribonucleic acid, the cellular material that determines individual heredity characteristics) was removed from the pelvis and successfully matched to blood from Blassie's mother, Jean. Blassie's remains were shipped to Missouri for reburial.

One crypt at Arlington now sits empty, and will remain so given the use of DNA testing by forensic scientists. Since 1994, moreover, the Pentagon has compiled DNA "prints" of all military personnel, making certain the identification of killed, badly mangled U.S. soldiers separated from their ID tags. Watching the changing of the guards at Arlington and musing about the role of science in changing how Americans remember war, a history teacher from Kentucky recently remarked that "we are losing our sense of meaning. I guess this memorial will have to stand for more than soldiers that are unknown. We are going to have to look deeper now." And perhaps look to new labels, such as "disappeared soldier" or "missing-in-action soldier," to sustain a legacy for a people and a nation.

For Further Reading, see page A-26 of the Appendix. For Web resources, go to http://college.hmco.com.

Eager to win the $25,000 offered by a hotel owner to the first person to fly an airplane non-stop between New York and Paris, three different aircraft crews stood ready to go at Roosevelt Airfield in the spring of 1927. One man, Charles A. Lindbergh, the only one piloting his plane solo, decided to risk drizzly weather and start the trip May 20. For thirty-three hours, his craft, *The Spirit of St. Louis*, bounced across the Atlantic skies. The flight seized the attention of practically every American, as newspaper and telegraph reports followed Lindbergh's progress. He reached the Irish coast! He crossed over England! He entered France! And when he landed at Le Bourget Airfield, the nation rejoiced. The *New York Evening World* sold 114,000 extra newspapers on May 21; the *St. Louis Post-Dispatch* sold 40,000 extras. President Calvin Coolidge dispatched a warship to bring "Lucky Lindy" back home. Celebrants sent Lindbergh 55,000 telegrams and dropped 1,800 tons of shredded paper on him during a triumphant parade upon his return.

Charles Lindbergh was one of the most revered heroes in American history. Though he was not the first to fly across the ocean (in 1919 two men piloted a plane from Newfoundland to Ireland, and a crew of five reached Europe by way of the Azores) his feat temporarily united Americans and made a stunt pilot into an idol. During his flight, forty thousand spectators at New York's Yankee Stadium watching a boxing match stood in utter silence and prayed for Lindbergh's safety. One newspaper exclaimed that Lindbergh had accomplished "the greatest feat of a solitary man in the history of the human race." Among countless medals, Lindbergh received the Distinguished Flying Cross and the Congressional Medal of Honor. Promoters offered him millions of dollars to tour the world by air and $700,000 for a movie contract. Texas named a town after him.

Through it all, Lindbergh, nicknamed "The Lone Eagle," remained dignified, even aloof. His flight and its aftermath, however, open insights into his era. The burst of publicity and the thrill of celebration point to

Landing in France on May 21, 1927, Charles Lindbergh completed a flight across the Atlantic Ocean and instantly became one of the nation's most revered heroes. His accomplishment and the publicity surrounding it represented much of what made the 1920s a New Era. (Picture Research Consultants & Archives)

THE NEW ERA OF THE 1920S

the impact of commercialism, new technology, and mass entertainment. But Lindbergh himself epitomized individual achievement, high moral character, and patriotism—old-fashioned values that also vied for public allegiance in an era contemporaries themselves identified as "new."

During the 1920s, consumerism flourished. Although poverty beset small farmers, workers in declining industries, and nonwhites in inner cities, most other people enjoyed a high standard of living relative to previous generations. Spurred by advertising and installment buying, Americans eagerly acquired radios, automobiles, real estate, and stocks. As in the Gilded Age, government, as embodied in Congress, the presidency, and the Supreme Court, maintained a favorable climate for business. And in contrast to the Progressive era, few people worried about the abuse of private power. Yet state and local governments, extending the reach of public authority, undertook important reforms.

It was an era of contrast and complexity. Fads and frivolities coincided with new creativity in the arts and notable advances in science and technology. Changes in work habits, family responsibilities, and healthcare fostered new uses of time and new attitudes about behavior. While material bounty and leisure enticed Americans into new amusements, winds of change also stirred up waves of reaction. Liberal ideas repelled those who held tight to traditional beliefs.

An unseen storm lurked on the horizon, however. The glitter of consumer culture that dominated everyday life blinded Americans to rising debts and uneven prosperity. Just before the decade closed, a devastating depression brought the era to a brutal close. ∎

Big Business Triumphant

 The 1920s began with a jolting economic decline. Shortly after the First World War ended, industrial output dropped and unemployment rose as wartime orders dried up, consumer spending dwindled, and demobilized soldiers poured into the work force. As European agriculture recovered from the war, American exports contracted and farm income plunged. Unemployment, around 2 percent in 1919, passed 12 percent in 1921. Railroads and mining industries suffered in the West. Layoffs spread through New England as textile companies abandoned outdated factories for the convenient raw materials and cheap labor of the South.

Aided by electric energy, a recovery began in 1922 and continued unevenly until 1929. By decade's end, factories using electric motors dominated American industry, increasing productivity and sending thousands of steam engines to the scrap heap. Electric power helped manufacturers produce new metal alloys such as aluminum and synthetic materials such as rayon. As well, most urban households now had electric lighting and could utilize new appliances such as refrigerators, toasters, and vacuum cleaners.

As Americans acquired spending money and leisure time, service industries such as restaurants, beauty salons and barbershops, and movie theaters boomed. Installment or time-payment plans ("A dollar down and a dollar forever," one critic quipped) drove the new consumerism. Of 3.5 million automobiles sold in 1923, some 80 percent were bought on credit.

The economic expansion brought a continuation of the corporate consolidation movement that had created trusts and holding companies in the late nineteenth century. Although Progressive era trustbusting had reined in big business, it had not eliminated control of an entire industry by a few large firms. By the 1920s such oligopolies dominated not only production but also marketing, distribution, and even finance. In basic industries such as steel production and electrical equipment, a few sprawling companies such as U.S. Steel and General Electric predominated.

Business Consolidation and Lobbying

Business and professional organizations that had come into being around 1900 also expanded in the 1920s. Retailers and manufacturers formed trade associations to swap information and coordinate planning. Farm bureaus promoted scientific agriculture and tried to stabilize markets. Lawyers, engineers, and social scientists expanded their professional societies. These special-interest groups participated in what has been called the "new lobbying." In a complex society in which government was playing an increasingly influential role, hundreds of organizations sought to convince federal and state legislators to support their interests. One Washington, D.C., observer contended that "lobbyists were so thick they were constantly falling over one another."

Government assistance helped business thrive, and legislators came to depend on the expertise of lobbyists in making decisions. Prodded by lobbyists, Congress reduced taxes on corporations and wealthy individuals in 1921 and the next year raised tariff rates in the Fordney-McCumber Tariff Act. Presidents

IMPORTANT EVENTS

1920 Nineteenth Amendment ratified, legalizing the vote for women in federal elections

Harding elected president

KDKA transmits first commercial radio broadcast

1920–21 Postwar deflation and depression occurs

1921 Federal Highway Act funds national highway system

Johnson Act establishes immigration quotas

Sacco and Vanzetti convicted

Sheppard-Towner Act allots funds to states to set up maternity and pediatric clinics

Fordney-McCumber Tariff raises rates on imports

1922 Economic recovery raises standard of living

Coronado Coal Company v. United Mine Workers rules that strikes may be illegal actions in restraint of trade

Bailey v. Drexel Furniture Company voids restrictions on child labor

Federal government ends strikes by railroad shop workers and miners

1923 Harding dies; Coolidge assumes the presidency

Adkins v. Children's Hospital overturns a minimum-wage law affecting women

Ku Klux Klan activity peaks

Aimee Semple McPherson opens Angelus Temple in Los Angeles

1923–24 Government scandals (Teapot Dome) exposed

1924 Johnson-Reid Act revises immigration quotas

Coolidge elected president

1925 Scopes trial highlights battle between religious fundamentalists and modernists

1927 Sacco and Vanzetti executed

Lindbergh pilots solo transatlantic flight

Ruth hits sixty home runs

The Jazz Singer, the first movie with sound, is released

1928 Stock market soars

Hoover elected president

1929 Stock market crashes; Great Depression begins

Warren G. Harding, Calvin Coolidge, and Herbert Hoover appointed cabinet officers who pursued policies favorable to business. Regulatory agencies such as the Federal Trade Commission and Interstate Commerce Commission monitored company activities but, under the influence of lobbyists, cooperated with corporations more than they regulated them.

The Supreme Court, led by Chief Justice William Howard Taft, the former president, protected business and private property as aggressively as in the Gilded Age and abandoned its antitrust action of the Progressive era. Its key decisions sheltered business from government regulation and hindered organized labor's ability to achieve its ends through strikes and legislation. In *Coronado Coal Company v. United Mine Workers* (1922), Taft ruled that a striking union, like a trust, could be prosecuted for illegal restraint of trade. Yet in *Maple Floor Association v. U.S.* (1929), the Court decided that trade associations that distributed antiunion information were not acting in restraint of trade. The Court also voided restrictions on child labor (*Bailey v. Drexel Furniture Company*, 1922) and overturned a minimum-wage law affecting women because it infringed on liberty of contract (*Adkins v. Children's Hospital*, 1923).

Organized labor suffered other setbacks during the 1920s. Fearful of communism allegedly brought into the country by radical immigrants, public opinion turned against workers who disrupted everyday life with strikes. Perpetuating tactics used during the Red Scare (see pages 654–655), the Harding administration in 1922 obtained a sweeping court injunction to quash a strike by 400,000 railroad shop workers. The same year, the Justice Department helped put down a nationwide strike by 650,000 miners.

Fate of Organized Labor

Meanwhile, some large corporations countered the appeal of unions by offering pensions, profit sharing (which amounted to withholding wages for later distribution), and company-sponsored picnics and sporting events—a policy known as welfare capitalism.

State legislators aided employers by prohibiting closed shops (workplaces where union membership was mandatory) and permitting open shops (which could discriminate against nonunion workers). Concerned about job security, workers in turn shied away from unions; union membership fell from 5.1 million in 1920 to 3.6 million in 1929.

Agriculture was one sector of the national economy that languished during the 1920s. Pressed into competition with growers in other countries and trying hard to increase productivity by investing in new machines such as plows, harvesters, and tractors, American farmers found themselves further beset by debt. As in the 1880s and 1890s, overproduction and foreign competition depressed crop and livestock prices, in turn reducing incomes. Early in the decade, for example, the price that farmers could get for cotton dropped by two-thirds and that of hogs and cattle fell by half. As a result, farm income never recovered after the First World War, and the gap between a farmer's income and an urban worker's income widened. Many farmers became tenants because they lost their land; more quit farming altogether.

Farmers' Problems

Politics and Government

A series of Republican presidents in the 1920s extended Theodore Roosevelt's notion of government-business cooperation, but they made government a compliant coordinator rather than the active director Roosevelt had advocated. A symbol of government's goodwill toward business was President Warren G. Harding, elected in 1920 when the populace no longer desired national or international crusades. Democrats had nominated Ohio's Governor James M. Cox, who supported Woodrow Wilson's fading hopes for U.S. membership in the League of Nations. But Cox and his running mate, Franklin D. Roosevelt of New York, failed to excite voters. Harding, who kept his position on the League vague, captured 16 million popular votes to only 9 million for Cox. (The total vote in the 1920 presidential election was 36 percent higher than in 1916, reflecting the participation of women voters for the first time.)

A small-town newspaperman and senator from Ohio, Harding appointed some capable assistants, notably Secretary of State Charles Evans Hughes, Secre-

Harding Administration

tary of Commerce Herbert Hoover, Secretary of the Treasury Andrew Mellon, and Secretary of Agriculture Henry C. Wallace. Harding also backed some reforms. His administration helped streamline federal spending with the Budget and Accounting Act of 1921, supported antilynching legislation (rejected by Congress), and approved bills assisting farm cooperatives and liberalizing farm credit.

Harding's problem was that he had some predatory friends. "Warren, it's a good thing you wasn't born a gal," his father reputedly remarked. "You'd be in the family way all the time—you can't say no." Harding said "yes" often, appointing cronies who saw officeholding as an invitation to personal gain. Charles Forbes of the Veterans Bureau went to federal prison, convicted of fraud and bribery in connection with government contracts. Attorney General Harry Daugherty was implicated in bribery and other fraudulent schemes; he escaped prosecution by refusing to testify against himself. Most notoriously, a congressional inquiry in 1923 and 1924 revealed that Secretary of the Interior Albert Fall had accepted bribes to lease oil-rich government property to private oil companies. For his role in the affair—called the Teapot Dome scandal after a Wyoming oil reserve that had been turned over to Mammoth Oil Company—Fall was fined $100,000 and spent a year in jail, the first cabinet officer ever to be so disgraced.

Teapot Dome

By mid-1923, Harding had become disillusioned. Amid rumors of mismanagement and crime, he told a journalist, "My God, this is a hell of a job. I have no trouble with my enemies. . . . But my friends, my God-damned friends . . . they're the ones that keep me walking the floor nights." On a speaking tour that summer, Harding became ill and died in San Francisco August 2. Though his death preceded revelation of the Teapot Dome scandal, some people speculated that to avoid the embarrassment of impeachment Harding had committed suicide or was poisoned by his wife. Most evidence, however, points to death from natural causes, probably a heart attack. At any rate, Harding was truly mourned. A warm, dignified-looking man who relished a good joke and an evening of poker, he seemed suited to a nation recovering from world war and domestic hard times.

Vice President Calvin Coolidge, Harding's successor, was far more dour. (Alice Roosevelt Longworth, Teddy's daughter, quipped that Coolidge looked as if he had been weaned on a pickle.) As governor of Massachusetts, Coolidge had attracted national attention in 1919 with his active stand against striking Boston policemen, a policy that won him business support and the vice-presidential nomination in 1920. Ordinarily, however, he was content to let events take their course, prompting columnist Walter Lippmann to remark on the "grim, determined, alert inactivity, which keeps Mr. Coolidge occupied constantly."

Coolidge Prosperity

Coolidge's presidency coincided with business prosperity. Respectful of private enterprise and aided by Andrew Mellon, whom he retained as secretary of the treasury, Coolidge's administration reduced government debt, lowered income-tax rates (especially for the rich), and began construction of a national highway system. Congress took little initiative during these years, with the exception of farm policy. Responding to farmers' complaints of falling prices, Congress twice passed bills to establish government-backed price supports for staple crops (the McNary-Haugen Bills of 1927 and 1928). Resembling the subtreasury scheme that farm alliances had advocated in the 1890s (see page 566), these bills would establish a complex system whereby the government would buy surplus farm products and either hold them until prices rose or sell them abroad. Farmers argued that they deserved as much government protection as manufacturers got. Coolidge, however, vetoed the measure both times as improper government interference in the market economy.

"Coolidge prosperity" was the decisive issue in the presidential election of 1924. Both major parties ran candidates who favored private initiative. Republicans nominated Coolidge with little dissent. At their national convention, Democrats first debated whether to condemn the newly aroused Ku Klux Klan (see page 681), voting 542 to 541 against condemnation. They then endured 103 ballots deadlocked between southern prohibitionists, who supported former secretary of the treasury William G. McAdoo, and antiprohibition easterners, who backed New York's governor Alfred E. Smith. They finally compromised on John W. Davis, a New York corporation lawyer. Remnants of the Progressive movement, along with various farm, labor, and socialist groups, formed a new Progressive Party and nominated Robert M. La Follette, the aging Wisconsin reformer. The new party revived issues of the previous decades: public ownership of utilities, aid to farmers, rights for organized labor, and regulation of business.

Basically shy and introverted, Calvin Coolidge was content to let business have free rein in the pursuit of profits. This ironic cartoon shows the president accompanying the lively performance of big business with a saxophone and a song of praise. (*Life,* December 10, 1925)

The election results ratified Coolidge prosperity. Coolidge beat Davis by 15.7 million to 8.4 million popular votes, 382 to 136 electoral votes. La Follette finished third, receiving a respectable but ineffective 4.8 million popular votes and only 13 electoral votes. The electorate showed no desire for change and voiced its expectation of extended prosperity in the new era.

Impressed by the triumph of business influence, political analysts claimed that Progressivism had died.

State and Local Reform

They were partly right. The urgency for political and economic reform that had moved the previous generation faded in the 1920s. Much reform, however, occurred at state and local levels. Following initiatives begun before the First World War, thirty-four states instituted or expanded workers' compensation laws in the 1920s. Many states established employee-funded old-age pensions and welfare programs for the indigent. In cities, social workers strived for better housing and poverty relief. By 1926 every major city and many smaller ones had planning and zoning commissions that aimed to harness physical growth to the common good. The nation's statehouses, city halls, and universities trained a new generation of reformers who later influenced national affairs.

The federal government's generally apathetic Indian policy disturbed some reformers. Organizations such as the Indian Rights Associ-

Indian Affairs ation, the Indian Defense Association, and the General Federation of Women's Clubs worked to obtain justice and social services, including better education and return of tribal lands. But Native Americans, no longer a threat to whites' ambitions, were treated by the general population like other minorities: as objects of discrimination who were expected to assimilate. Severalty, the policy created by the Dawes Act of 1887 (see page 467) of allotting land to individuals rather than to tribes, had failed to make Indians self-supporting. Indian farmers had to endure poor soil, lack of irrigation, scarce medical care, and cattle thieves. Deeply attached to their land, they showed little inclination to move to cities. Whites still hoped to convert native peoples into "productive" citizens, but in a way that ignored indigenous cultures. Reformers were especially critical of Indian women, who refused to adopt middle-class homemaking habits and balked at sending their children to boarding schools.

Meanwhile, the federal government struggled to clarify Indians' citizenship status. The Dawes Act had conferred citizenship on all Indians who accepted allotments of land but not on those who remained on reservations. Also, the government retained a measure of control over Indian citizens that it did not exercise over other citizens. For example, because of allegations of drunkenness on reservations, federal law prevented the sale of liquor to Indians even before ratification of prohibition. After several court challenges, Congress finally passed a law in 1924 granting full citizenship to all Indians who previously had not received it. Also, the administration of President Herbert Hoover reorganized the Bureau of Indian Affairs and increased expenditures for health, education, and welfare. Much of the money, however, went to enlarge the bureaucracy rather than into Indian hands.

Even after achieving suffrage in 1920 with final ratification of the Nineteenth Amendment, politically active women remained excluded from local and national power structures, but their voluntary organiza-

Women and Politics tions used tactics that contributed to modern pressure-group politics. Whether the issue was birth control, peace, education, Indian affairs, or opposition to lynching, women in these associations publicized their causes and lobbied legislators rather than trying to elect their own candidates. For example, the League of Women Voters, reorganized out of the National American Woman Suffrage Association, did encourage women to run for office but more extensively worked for laws that would improve conditions for working women, the mentally ill, and the urban poor.

Action by women's groups persuaded Congress to pass the Sheppard-Towner Act (1921), which allotted funds to states to set up maternity and pediatric clinics. (The measure ended in 1929 when Congress, under pressure from private physicians, canceled funding.) The Cable Act of 1922 reversed the law under which an American woman who married a foreigner assumed her husband's citizenship; under the new law such a woman could retain U.S. citizenship. At the state level, women achieved other rights, such as the ability to serve on juries.

As new voters, however, women accomplished relatively little. The National Woman's Party remained the champion of feminism, but women pursued a variety of interests. African American women, for example, fought for the rights of minority women and men without support from either the National Woman's Party or the newly organized League of Women Voters. Some groups, such as the National Woman's Party, pressed for an equal rights amendment, to ensure women's equality with men under the law. But such activity alienated the National Consumers League, the Women's Trade Union League, the League of Women Voters, and other groups that supported protective legislation to limit the hours and improve conditions for employed women. And like men, women of all types seemed preoccupied by the new era's materialism.

Materialism Unbound

Between 1919 and 1929, the gross national product—the total value of all goods and services produced in the United States—swelled by 40

Expansion of Consumer Society percent. Wages and salaries also grew (though not as drastically), while the cost of living remained relatively stable. People had more purchasing power, and they spent as Americans had never spent. An article in *Survey* magazine contrasted one family's expenditures in 1900 with those of 1928:

1900

2 bicycles	$ 70*
wringer and washboard	5
brushes and brooms	5
sewing machine (mechanical)	25
Total	$ 105

1928

automobile	$ 700
radio	75
phonograph	50
washing machine	150
vacuum cleaner	50
sewing machine (electric)	60
other electrical equipment	25
telephone (per year)	35
Total	$1,145

The article's author cautioned that education and medical care had become costlier. Nevertheless, she regarded the change as worthwhile.

Technology's benefits were reaching more people than ever before. By 1929 two-thirds of all Americans lived in dwellings that had electricity, compared with one-sixth in 1912. In 1929 one-fourth of all families owned vacuum cleaners, and one-fifth had toasters. Many could afford goods such as radios, washing machines, and movie tickets only because more than one family member earned wages or because the breadwinner took a second job. Nevertheless, new products and services were available to more than just the rich.

The automobile stood as vanguard of all the era's material wonders. During the 1920s automobile registrations soared from 8 million to 23 million. Mass production and competition brought down prices, making cars affordable even to some working-class families. A Ford Model T cost less than $300 and a Chevrolet sold for $700 by 1926—when factory workers earned about $1,300 a year and clerical workers about $2,300. Used cars cost less. At those prices, people could consider the car a necessity rather than a luxury. "There is no such thing

Effects of the Automobile

---

* From *Another Part of the Twenties*, by Paul Carter. Copyright 1977 by Columbia University Press. Reprinted with permission of Paul A. Carter.

Electric appliances became commonplace in the 1920s and advanced the consumer economy. Note here the obvious link between a daughter and her mother, whose domestic tasks appear to be made easier and more appealing by an electric range, a vacuum cleaner, and an iron.   (Picture Research Consultants & Archives)

as a 'pleasure automobile,'" proclaimed one newspaper ad in 1925. "You might as well talk of 'pleasure fresh air,' or of 'pleasure beef steak.' . . . The automobile increases length of life, increases happiness, represents above all other achievements the progress and the civilization of our age."

The car altered American life as much as the railroad had seventy-five years earlier. City streets became much cleaner as autos replaced the numerous horses that had dumped tons of manure every day. Women who learned to drive achieved newfound independence, taking touring trips by themselves or with female friends, conquering muddy roads, and making

During the 1920s, the desire to own an automobile spread to members of all classes, races, and ethnic groups. Low prices and available credit enabled this family from Beaumont, Texas, to own a "touring car." (Tyrrell Historical Library)

repairs when their vehicles broke down. Families created "homes on wheels," packing up food and camping equipment to "get away from it all." By 1927 most autos were enclosed (they had previously been open), creating a new private space for courtship and sex. A vast choice of models (there were 108 automobile manufacturers in 1923) and colors allowed owners to express personal tastes. Some owners customized their cars, installing beds and mechanical gadgets such as special horns and starters. Most importantly, the car was the ultimate symbol of social equality. As one writer observed in 1924, "It is hard to convince Steve Popovich, or Antonio Branca, or plain John Smith that he is being ground into the dust by Capital when at will he may drive the same highways, view the same scenery, and get as much enjoyment from his trip as the modern Midas."

Americans' passion for driving necessitated extensive construction of roads and abundant supplies of fuel. Since the late 1800s farmers and bicyclists had been lobbying for improved roads. After the First World War motorists joined the campaign, and in the 1920s government aid made "automobility" truly feasible. In 1921 Congress passed the Federal Highway Act, providing money for state roads, and in 1923 the Bureau of Public Roads planned a national highway system. The oil industry, already vast and powerful, shifted emphasis from illumination and lubrication to propulsion. In 1920 the United States produced about 65 percent of the world's oil. The automobile also forced public officials to pay more attention to safety regulations and traffic control. General Electric Company produced the first timed stop-and-go traffic light in 1924.

Advertising whetted demand for automobiles and other goods and services. By 1929 more money was spent on advertising than on all types of formal education. Advertising became a new gospel for business-minded Americans. In his best-selling *The Man Nobody Knows* (1925), advertising executive Bruce Barton called Jesus "the founder of modern business" because he "picked up twelve men from the bottom ranks of business and forged them into an organization that conquered the world." About the same time, a pamphlet entitled *Moses, Persuader of*

Advertising

Men declared, "Moses was one of the greatest sales-men and real-estate promoters that ever lived." Cosmetics manufacturers such as Max Factor, Helena Rubenstein, and the African American entrepreneur Madame C. J. Walker used movie stars and beauty advice in magazine ads to induce women to buy their products. Blending psychological theory with practical cynicism, advertising theorists asserted confidently that any person's tastes could be manipulated.

As newspaper circulation declined, other media assumed vital advertising functions. Radio became one of the era's most influential agents.

Radio

By 1929 over 10 million families owned radios, which bombarded them with advertisements, and Americans were spending $850 million a year on radio equipment. In the early 1920s, Congress decided that radio should be a private enterprise, not a tax-supported public service as it was in Great Britain. As a result, American programming focused on entertainment rather than on educational content because entertainment attracted more audiences and therefore more profits from advertisers. Station KDKA in Pittsburgh, at first noncommercial, pioneered broadcasting in 1920. Soon stations began airing advertisements, and by 1922 there were 508 such stations. In 1929 the National Broadcasting Company began to assemble a network of stations and soon was charging advertisers $10,000 to sponsor an hour-long show. Highway billboards and commercials projected during intermissions at movie houses also reminded viewers to buy. Packaging and product display became sciences, all intended to entice consumers.

Although low-income people could not afford all modern products and services, some new trends benefited the working classes, especially those living in cities. Indoor plumbing and electricity became more common in private residences, and canned foods and ready-made clothes became more affordable. A little cash and a lot of credit enabled many wage earners to purchase an automobile. Spending became a national pastime. No wonder many Americans wanted Henry Ford to run for president in 1924.

Cities, Migrants, and Suburbs

Consumerism signified not merely an economically mature nation but an urbanized one. The 1920 federal census revealed that for the first time a majority of Americans lived in urban areas (defined as places with

America Acclaims *the* SUPERETTE
– the smallest *big* radio ever built

RCA Victor Radio

Between 1922 and 1930, the number of families owning radios swelled from 60,000 to almost 14 million. Manufacturers such as RCA produced a variety of sizes and shapes and took out full-page advertisements in popular publications to inform the public about the latest developments in design and technology. (Library of American Broadcasting, University of Maryland at College Park)

2,500 or more people); the city had become the focus of national experience. Growth in manufacturing and services helped propel urbanization. Industries such as steel, oil, and auto production energized cities like Birmingham, Houston, and Detroit; services and retail trades boosted expansion in Seattle, Atlanta, and Minneapolis. Explosive growth also occurred in warm-climate cities—notably Miami and San Diego—where promises of comfort and profit attracted thousands of speculators.

During the 1920s, 6 million Americans left their farms for the city. Midwestern migrants, particularly

Farm-to-City Migration

young single people, moved to regional centers like Kansas City and Indianapolis or to the West. Between 1920 and 1930, California's population increased 67 percent, and California became one of the nation's most urbanized states while retaining its status as a leading agricultural state. Meanwhile, streams of rural southerners moved to that region's burgeoning industrial cities or rode railroads northward to Chicago and Cleveland.

African Americans, involved in what has been called the Great Migration, made up a sizable portion of people on the move. Pushed from cotton farming by a boll weevil plague and lured by industrial jobs, 1.5 million blacks moved cityward during the 1920s, doubling the African American populations of New York, Chicago, Detroit, and Houston. Forced by low wages and discrimination to seek the cheapest housing, newcomers squeezed into low-rent ghettos. Unlike white migrants, who were free to move out from the inner-city when they could afford to, blacks found better housing closed to them. The only way they could expand their housing opportunities was to spill into nearby white neighborhoods, a process that sparked resistance and violence. Fears of such expansion prompted white neighborhood associations to adopt restrictive covenants, whereby homeowners pledged not to sell or rent property to blacks.

The Great Migration

In response to discrimination, threats, and violence, thousands of urban blacks joined movements that glorified racial independence. The most influential of these nationalist groups was the Universal Negro Improvement Association (UNIA), headed by Marcus Garvey, a Jamaican immigrant who believed blacks should separate themselves from corrupt white society. Proclaiming "I am the equal of any white man," Garvey cultivated racial pride with mass meetings and parades. He also promoted black-owned businesses. *Negro World*, Garvey's newspaper, refused to publish ads for hair straightening and skin-lightening cosmetics, and he set up the Black Star shipping line to help blacks emigrate to Africa.

Marcus Garvey

The UNIA declined in the mid-1920s after ten UNIA leaders were arrested on charges of anarchism, and Garvey was deported for mail fraud involving the bankrupt Black Star line—though the company's main problem was that unscrupulous dealers had sold it dilapidated ships. Middle-class black leaders like W. E. B. Du Bois and several ministers of black churches opposed the UNIA, fearing that its extremism would undermine their efforts and influence. Nevertheless, in New York, Chicago, Detroit, and other cities, the organization attracted a large following (contemporaries

estimated it at 500,000; Garvey claimed 6 million), and Garvey's speeches instilled many African Americans with a heightened sense of race pride.

The newest immigrants to American cities came from Mexico and Puerto Rico where, as in rural North America, declining fortunes pushed people off the land. Most Mexicans migrated to work as agricultural laborers in the Southwest, but many also were drawn to growing cities like Denver, San Antonio, Los Angeles, and Tucson. Like other immigrant groups, they generally lacked resources and skills, and men outnumbered women. Mexicans crowded into low-rent districts plagued by poor sanitation, poor police protection, and poor schools.

Mexican and Puerto Rican Immigrants

The 1920s also witnessed an influx of Puerto Ricans to the mainland. Puerto Rico had been a U.S. possession since 1898, and its natives were granted U.S. citizenship in 1917. A shift in the island's economy from sugar to coffee production created a surplus of workers. Attracted by contracts from employers seeking cheap labor, most Puerto Rican migrants moved to New York City, where they created *barrios* (communities) in Brooklyn and Manhattan and found jobs in manufacturing and in hotels, restaurants, and domestic service.

Within their communities, both Puerto Ricans and Mexicans maintained traditional customs and values and developed businesses—*bodegas* (grocery stores), cafés, boarding houses—and social organizations to help themselves adapt to American society. Educated elites—doctors, lawyers, business owners—tended to become community leaders.

As urban growth peaked, suburban growth accelerated. Although towns had clustered around cities since the nation's earliest years, prosperity and automobile transportation made the suburbs more accessible to those wishing to flee crowded urban neighborhoods in the 1920s. Between 1920 and 1930, suburbs of Chicago (such as Oak Park and Evanston), Cleveland (Shaker Heights), and Los Angeles (Burbank and Inglewood) grew five to ten times faster than did the central cities. Most suburbs were middle- and upper-class bedroom communities; some, like Highland Park (near Detroit) and East Chicago, were industrial satellites.

Growth of Suburbs

Increasingly, suburbs resisted annexation to core cities. Suburbanites wanted to escape big-city crime,

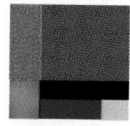

Mexican immigrants, like other immigrants, brought their homeland customs with them to the United States. Every year on May 5, Cinco de Mayo, with events such as this parade, held in 1914 in Mogollon, New Mexico, they commemorated the Mexican victory over French troops in the Battle of Puebla on May 5, 1862.   (Library of Congress)

dirt, and taxes, and they fought to preserve control over their own police, schools, and water and gas services. Particularly in the Northeast and Midwest, the suburbs' fierce independence choked off expansion by the central city and divided metropolitan areas in ways that would plague future generations. Moreover, automobiles and the dispersal of population spread the environmental problems of city life—trash, pollution, noise—across the entire metropolitan area.

Cities and suburbs fostered the mass culture that gave the decade its character. Most of the consumers who jammed shops, movie houses, and sporting arenas and who embraced fads like crossword puzzles, miniature golf, and marathon dancing lived in or around cities. These were the places where people defied law and morality by patronizing speakeasies (illegal saloons), wearing outlandish clothes, and listening to jazz. They were also the places where devout moralists strained to resist modernism. Yet the ideal of small-

town society survived. While millions thronged cityward, Americans reminisced about the innocence and simplicity of a world gone by. This was the dilemma the modern nation faced: how does one anchor oneself in a world of rampant materialism and rapid social change?

New Rhythms of Everyday Life

Amid changes to modern society, Americans developed new ways of using time. People increasingly split their daily lives into distinct compartments: work, family, and leisure. Each type of time was altered in the 1920s. For many people, time on the job shrank. Though strikes following the First World War had failed to reduce working hours, increased mechanization and higher productivity enabled employers to shorten the workweek for many industrial laborers from six days to

Wide highways, cheap land, and affordable housing allowed automobile commuters to move to the urban periphery. In this photo, young women wearing 1920s flapper-style outfits celebrate the phenomenal growth of Culver City, outside Los Angeles. Notice the strong presence of the motor car.   (Security Pacific National Bank Collection, Los Angeles Public Library)

five and a half. White-collar employees often worked a forty-hour week and enjoyed a full weekend off. Annual vacations became a standard job benefit for white-collar workers.

Family time is harder to measure, but certain trends are clear. Family size decreased between 1920 and 1930 as birth control became more widely practiced. Among American women who married in the 1870s and 1880s, well over half who survived to age fifty had five or more children; of their counterparts who married in the 1920s, however, just 20 percent had five or more children. Meanwhile, the divorce rate rose. In 1920 there was 1 divorce for every 7.5 marriages; by 1929 the national ratio was 1 in 6, and in many cities it was 2 in 7. In conjunction with longer life expectancy, lower birth rates and more divorce meant that adults were devoting a smaller portion of their lives to raising children.

Family Time

Housewives still worked long hours cleaning, cooking, and raising children, but machines now lightened some of their tasks and enabled them to use their time differently than their forebears had. Especially in middle-class households, electric irons and washing machines simplified some chores. Gas- and oil-powered central heating and hot-water heaters eliminated the hauling of wood, coal, and water, the upkeep of a kitchen fire, and the removal of ashes.

Household Management

Even as technology and economic change made life better and easier, they also created new demands on a woman's time. As daughters of working-class families stayed in school longer and as alternative forms of employment caused a shortage of servants in wealthier households, those who formerly had helped mothers and wives with cleaning, cooking, and childcare were less available. These factors, coupled with the spread of appliances such as washing machines, irons, and vacuum cleaners, shifted the entire task of household management to the wife. No longer a producer of food and clothing as her predecessors had been, a wife now became the chief shopper, responsible for making sure the family spent its money wisely. And the automobile made the wife a family's chief chauffeur. One survey found that urban housewives spent on average 13 percent of their work time, seven and a half hours per week, driving to shop and transport children.

A new emphasis on nutrition added a scientific dimension to housewives' responsibilities. With the discovery of vitamins between 1915 and 1930, nutritionists began advocating the consumption of certain foods to prevent illness. Giant food companies scrambled to advertise their products as filled with vitamins and minerals beneficial to growth and health. Not only did producers of milk and canned fruits and vegetables exploit the vitamin craze, but other companies made lofty claims that were hard to dispute because little was known about these invisible, tasteless ingredients. C. W. Post, for example, claimed that his Grape-Nuts contained "iron, calcium, phosphorus, and other mineral elements that are taken right up as vital food by the millions of cells in the body."

Nutrition

Better diets and improved sanitation made Americans generally healthier. Life expectancy at birth increased from fifty-four to sixty years between 1920 and 1930, and infant mortality decreased by two-thirds. Sanitation and research in bacteriology and immunology combined with better nutrition to reduce the risks of life-threatening diseases such as tuberculosis and diphtheria. But medical progress did not benefit all groups equally. Rates of infant mortality were 50 to 100 percent higher among nonwhites than among whites, and tuberculosis in inner-city slums remained alarmingly common. Moreover, fatalities from car accidents rose 150 percent, and deaths from heart disease and cancer—diseases of old age—increased 15 percent. Nevertheless, Americans in general were living longer: the total population over age sixty-five grew 35 percent between 1920 and 1930, while the rest of the population increased only 15 percent.

Longer life spans and the worsening economic status of the elderly stirred interest in government pensions and other forms of old-age assistance. Industrialism put a premium on youth and agility, pushing older people into poverty from forced retirement and

Older Americans and Retirement

reduced income. Recognizing the needs of aging citizens, most European countries established state-supported pension systems in the early 1900s. Many Americans, however, believed that individuals should prepare for old age by saving in their youth; pensions, they felt, smacked of socialism. As late as 1923 the Pennsylvania Chamber of Commerce labeled old-age assistance "un-American and socialistic . . . an entering wedge of communistic propaganda."

Yet conditions were alarming. Most inmates in state poorhouses were older people, and almost one-third of Americans age sixty-five and older depended financially on someone else. Few employers offered pension plans; most, including the federal government, did not provide for retired employees. Noting that the government fed retired horses until they died, one postal worker complained, "For the purpose of drawing a pension, it would have been better had I been a horse than a human being." Resistance to pension plans finally broke at the state level in the 1920s. Led by Isaac Max Rubinow and Abraham Epstein, reformers persuaded voluntary associations, labor unions, and legislators to endorse the principle of old-age assistance through pensions, insurance, and retirement homes. By 1933 almost every state provided at least minimal assistance to needy elderly people, and a path had been opened for a national program of old-age insurance.

As people were exposed to new influences in their time away from work and family, new habits and values were inevitable. Aided by new fabrics and chemical dyes, clothes became a means of self-expression and personal freedom. Both men and women wore more casual and gaily colored styles than their parents would have considered. The line between acceptable and inappropriate behavior blurred as smoking, drinking, swearing, and frankness about sex became fashionable. Birth-control advocate Margaret Sanger, who a decade earlier had been accused of promoting race suicide, gained a large following in respectable circles. Newspapers, magazines, motion pictures, and popular songs (such as "Hot Lips" and "Burning Kisses") made certain that Americans did not suffer from "sex starvation." A typical movie ad promised "brilliant men, beautiful jazz babies, champagne baths, midnight revels, petting parties in the purple dawn, all ending in one terrific smashing climax that makes you gasp."

Social Values

How do historians know...

that individual and family life in the 1920s was hardly homogeneous but reflected many variations? The manuscript census schedules (the pages on which census takers actually recorded information) from the 1920 federal census contain extraordinarily rich information. By sampling, tabulating, and analyzing large numbers of census entries—after trying to decipher often illegible handwriting—historians raise and attempt to answer questions about everyday life and the environments in which ordinary people lived. The excerpt on this page reproduces the records from a few families living on Stamford Street in Boston and yields numerous insights into how these households were organized.

The Bradley household at 16 Stamford consisted of a middle-aged husband, who was born in Massachusetts and worked as a railroad baggage master; his wife, born in New Brunswick (Nova Scotia) and of British descent; and a middle-aged boarder, who worked as a painter. Given the ages of the household's residents, it is possible to assume that the Bradleys had extra space for a boarder because their children had grown up and moved away.

The Milkowski household at 10 Stamford was larger and more complex. It contained ten people, including three young children and five lodgers. Mr. and Mrs. Milkowski were from Russia, but their lodgers came from a variety of places, leaving the impression that the Milkowskis intentionally used their residence to earn extra income. A lone Chinese man lived at 8 Stamford. He worked in a laundry, and the schedule notes that he was married. He presumably had immigrated alone and hoped either to return to China or to earn enough to send for his wife.

Census data often must be combined with other sources in order to validate such speculations. Nevertheless, manuscript censuses provide important information, especially about people previously excluded from the historical record because they did not leave diaries or letters and were not famous enough to be the subjects of newspaper stories. (Photo: National Archives Records and Census Bureau)

DEPARTMENT OF COMMERCE-BUREAU OF THE CENSUS

FOURTEENTH CENSUS OF THE UNITED STATES: 1920-POPULATION

STATE _Massachusetts_   ENUMERATOR _Harry Hoffman_
COUNTY _Suffolk_   ENUMERATED BY ME AN THE _7_ DAY OF _Jan_ 1920

TOWNSHIP OR OTHER DIVISION OF COUNTY _Tract 33 1413_   NAME OF INCORPORATED PLACE _Boston_

STREET	HOUSE NUMBER	NAME	RELATION	SEX	COLOR OR RACE	AGE	SINGLE, MARRIED, WIDOWED OR DIVORCED	CITIZENSHIP	YEAR OF IMMIGRATION	PERSON PLACE OF BIRTH	FATHER PLACE OF BIRTH	MOTHER PLACE OF BIRTH	ENGLISH SPEAKING	OCCUPATION
Stamford Street	22	Garrigan, James, step-son	M	W	20	S			Mass.	New York	Ireland	yes	chauffeur
		— Ellen, step-dghtr.	F	W	16	S			Mass.	New York	Ireland	yes	Laundry
	16	Bradley, George, Head	M	W	53	M			Mass.	Mass.	Mass.	yes	Railroad
		— Chas A. wife	F	W	52	M		1880	New Brunswick	New Brunswick	New Brunswick	yes	none
		Hart, Dennis, Lodger	M	W	49	wd.			Mass.	Ireland	Ireland	yes	Painter
	12	Sidlinger, Albert, Head	M	W	65	M			Maine	Maine	Maine	yes	none
		— Catherine, wife	F	W	49	M		1886	Nova Scotia	Ireland	Nova Scotia	yes	none Insurance
		— Albert K. son	M	W	29	S			Mass.	Maine	Nova Scotia		broker
	10	Milkowski, Tham, Head	M	W	34	M		1906	Russia	Russia	Russia	yes	cook
		— Mary, wife	F	W	27	M		1908	Russia	Russia	Russia	yes	none
		— Helen, dghtr	F	W	6 5/12	S			Mass.	Russia	Russia		none
		— Jennie, dghtr	F	W	5 5/12	S			Mass.	Russia	Russia		none
		— Peter, son	M	W	1 4/12	S			Mass.	Russia	Russia		none
		McQuaid, Francis, Lodger	M	W	33	M			Mass.	Ireland	Ireland	yes	Reporter
		— Frieda, wife	F	W	22	M		1899	Switzerland	Italy	Germany		none
		White, Irvin, Lodger	M	W	37	M		1897	England	England	England	yes	Hospital Handyman
		Blake, John, Lodger	M	W	38	M		1894	Ireland	Ireland	Ireland	yes	Labourer
		Miller, Harry, Lodger	M	W	44	S		1910	Norway	Norway	Norway	yes	waiters ship
	8	Ling, Chintung, Head	M	Ch	60	M		1890	China	China	China	no	Laundry
	6	Ross, Frank, Head	M	W	45	M		1889	Italy	Italy	Italy	yes	Marble Polisher
		— Effie, wife	F	W	43	M			New Hampshire	New Hampshire	Maine	yes	none

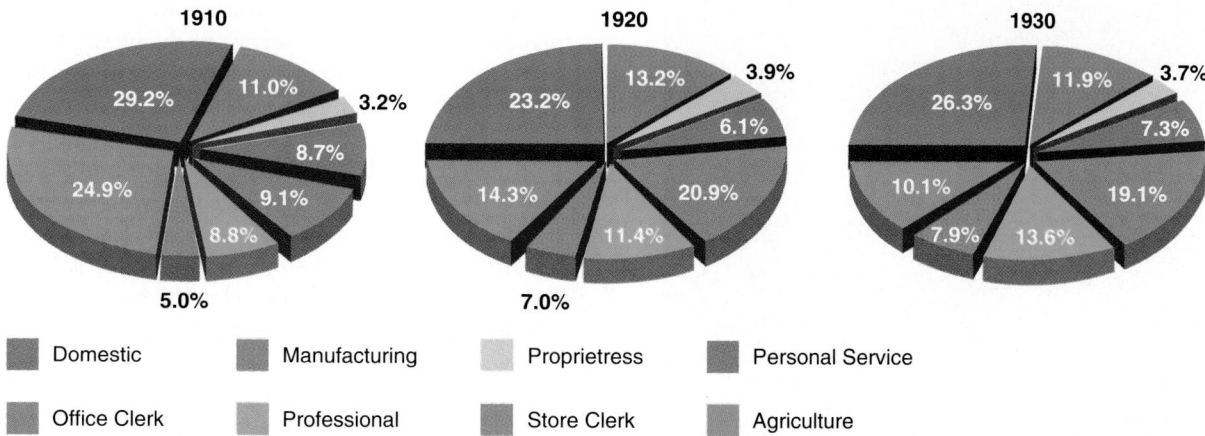

Figure 24.1   **Changing Dimensions of Paid Female Labor, 1910–1930**   These charts reveal the extraordinary growth in clerical and professional occupations among employed women and the accompanying decline in agricultural labor in the early twentieth century. Notice that manufacturing employment peaked in 1920 and that domestic service fluctuated as white immigrant women began to move out of these jobs and were replaced by women of color.

Other modern trends helped to weaken inherited customs. Because child-labor laws and compulsory-attendance rules kept children in school longer than ever before, peer groups played a more influential role in socializing children. In earlier eras, different age groups had shared the same activities: children had worked with older people in fields and kitchens, and young apprentices had toiled in workshops beside older journeymen and craftsmen. Now, graded school classes, sports, and clubs constantly brought together children of the same age, separating them from the company and influence of adults. Meanwhile, parents tended to rely less on family traditions of childcare and more on experts who wrote manuals on how best to raise children.

Employment for Women

After the First World War, women continued to stream into the labor force. By 1930, 10.8 million women held paying jobs, an increase of over 2 million since the war's end (see Figure 24.1). The sex segregation that had long characterized workplaces persisted; most women took jobs that men seldom sought and vice versa. Over 1 million women were teachers and nurses. Some 2.2 million were typists, bookkeepers, and office clerks, a tenfold increase since 1920. Another 736,000 were store clerks, and growing numbers became waitresses and hairdressers. Though almost 2 million women worked in factories, their numbers grew very little over the decade. Wherever women were employed, their wages seldom exceeded half of those paid to men.

For many women, employment outside the home represented an extension of family roles. Although women worked for a variety of reasons, their families' economic needs were paramount. The consumerism of the 1920s tempted working-class and middle-class families to satisfy their wants by living beyond their means or by sending women into the labor force. In previous eras, most extra-wage earners had been young and single. Even though the vast majority of married women remained outside the work force (only 12 percent were employed in 1930), married women as a proportion of the work force rose by 30 percent, and the number of employed married women swelled from 1.9 million to 3.1 million. These figures omit countless widowed, divorced, and abandoned women who held jobs and who, like married women, often had children to support.

Jobs for Minority Women

Women of racial minorities were the exception; the proportions of these women who worked for pay doubled that of white women. Often they entered the labor force because their husbands were unemployed or underemployed. The vast majority of African American women held domestic jobs doing cooking, cleaning, and laundry. The few who held factory jobs, such as in cigarette factories and meatpacking plants, performed the least desirable, lowest paying tasks. Some opportunities opened for

The expansion of service-sector jobs and new technology opened new opportunities for women in the 1920s. This telephone operator handled scores of phone calls at the same time and monitored a huge switchboard. Her dress and jewelry contrasted with the simpler styles worn by factory women, who had to be more careful in working with dangerous machines.   (George Eastman House)

educated black women in social work, teaching, and nursing, but even these women faced harsh discrimination and pressures on their families. Grandmothers and aunts helped with childcare when mothers took outside employment, but such arrangements did not lessen the economic burdens on African American households beset by lack of skills, poverty and prejudice.

Economic necessity also drew thousands of Mexican women into wage labor, although their tradition resisted the employment of women. Exact figures are difficult to uncover, but it is certain that many Mexican women in the Southwest worked as field laborers, operatives in garment factories, and domestic servants. Next to black women, Japanese American women were the most likely to hold paying jobs. They too worked as field hands and domestics. And, like Mexican American and African American women, Japanese American women encountered racial bias and low pay.

Employed or not, some women were remaking the image of femininity. In contrast to the heavy, floor-length dresses and long hair of previous generations, the short skirts and bobbed hair of the 1920s "flapper" symbolized independence and sexual freedom. Though few women lived the flapper life, the new look became fashionable among office workers and store clerks as well as college coeds. As models of female behavior, chaste, modest heroines were eclipsed by movie temptresses like Clara Bow, known as the "It Girl," and Gloria Swanson, notorious for her torrid love affairs on and off the screen. Many women were asserting a new social equality with men. One observer described "the new woman" as intriguingly independent:

The New Woman

> She takes a man's point of view as her mother never could. . . . She will never make you a hatband or knit you a necktie, but she'll drive you from the station . . . in her own little sports car. She'll don knickers and go skiing with you, . . . she'll dive as well as you, perhaps better, she'll dance as long as you care to, and she'll take everything you say the way you mean it.

The era's openness regarding sexuality also enabled the underground homosexual culture to emerge a little more than in previous eras. In nontraditional city neighborhoods, such as New York's Greenwich Village and Harlem, cheap rents and an apparent tolerance of alternate lifestyles attracted gay men and lesbians who patronized dance halls, speakeasies, cafés, and other gathering places. Such establishments that catered to a gay clientele remained targets for police raids, however, demonstrating that homosexual men and women could not expect tolerance from the rest of society.

Gay and Lesbian Culture

These trends represented a break with the more restrained culture of the nineteenth century. But social change rarely proceeds smoothly. As the decade wore on, various groups mobilized to defend older values.

Lines of Defense

 Early in 1920 the leader of a newly formed organization hired two public relations experts to recruit members. The experts, Edward Clarke and Elizabeth Tyler, canvassed communities in the South, Southwest, and Midwest, where they found thousands of men eager to pay a $10 membership fee and another $6 for a

white uniform. Clarke and Tyler pocketed $2.50 from each membership they sold. Their success helped build the organization to 5 million members by 1923.

No ordinary civic club like the Lions or Kiwanis, this was the Ku Klux Klan, a revived version of the hooded order that had terrorized southern communities after the Civil War. Its appeal was based on fear, and it vowed to protect female purity as well as racial purity. As one pamphlet distributed by Clarke and Tyler declared, "Every criminal, every gambler, every thug, every libertine, every girl ruiner, every home wrecker, every wife beater, every dope peddler, every moonshiner, every white slaver, every Rome-controlled newspaper, every black spider—is fighting the Klan. Think it over, which side are you on?"

Ku Klux Klan

Reconstituted in 1915 by William J. Simmons, an Atlanta evangelist and insurance salesman, the Klan was the most sinister reactionary movement of the 1920s. It revived the hoods, intimidating tactics, and mystical terminology of its forerunner (its leader was the Imperial Wizard, its book of rituals the Kloran). But the new Klan had broader membership, including a female auxiliary group, and objectives than the old. It fanned outward from the Deep South and for a time wielded frightening power in places as diverse as Oregon, Oklahoma, and Indiana. Unlike the original Klan, which directed terrorist tactics at emancipated blacks (see pages 449–450), the new Klan targeted a variety of racial and religious groups.

One phrase summed up Klan goals: "Native, white, Protestant supremacy." Native meant no immigration, no "mongrelization" of American culture. According to Imperial Wizard Hiram Wesley Evans, white supremacy was a matter of survival. "The world," he warned, "has been so made so that each race must fight for its life, must conquer, accept slavery, or die. The Klansman believes the whites will not become slaves, and he does not intend to die before his time." Evans praised Protestantism for promoting "unhampered individual development," and he accused the Catholic Church of discouraging assimilation and enslaving people to priests and a foreign pope.

Using threatening assemblies, violence, and political pressure, the Klan menaced many communities in the early 1920s. Klansmen meted out vigilante justice to suspected bootleggers, wife beaters, and adulterers; forced schools to adopt Bible reading and to stop teaching the theory of evolution; campaigned against Catholic and Jewish political candidates; and fueled racial tensions against Mexicans in Texas border cities. By 1925, however, the Invisible Empire was on the wane, as scandal undermined its moral base. In 1925 Indiana Grand Dragon David Stephenson kidnapped and raped a woman who later died either from taking poison or from infection caused by bites on her body; Stephenson was convicted of second-degree murder on grounds that he caused her suicide. More generally, the Klan's negative, exclusive brand of patriotism and purity could not compete in a pluralistic society.

The Ku Klux Klan had no monopoly on bigotry in the 1920s; intolerance pervaded American society. Nativists had been urging an end to free immigration since the 1880s. They charged that Catholic and Jewish immigrants clogged city slums, flouted community norms, and stubbornly held to alien religious and political beliefs. As naturalist Madison Grant, whose study of zoology prompted him to believe that certain human races, mainly Nordics, were superior to others, wrote in *The Passing of the Great Race* (1916): "These immigrants adopt the language of the native American, they wear his clothes, they steal his name and they are beginning to take his women, but they seldom adopt his religion or understand his ideals."

Guided by such sentiments, the movement to restrict immigration gathered support. Labor leaders warned that floods of aliens would depress wages and raise unemployment. Business executives, who formerly had opposed restrictions because they desired cheap immigrant laborers, changed their minds, having realized that they could keep wages low by mechanizing and by hiring black workers. Drawing support from such groups, Congress drastically reversed previous policy and set yearly immigration quotas for each nationality. The limits favored northern and western Europeans, reflecting nativist prejudices against immigrants from southern and eastern Europe. By stipulating that annual immigration of a given nationality could not exceed 3 percent of the number of immigrants from that nation residing in the United States in 1910, the Quota (Johnson) Act of 1921 discriminated against immigrants from southern and eastern Europe, whose numbers were small in 1910 relative to those from northern Europe.

Immigration Quotas

The Johnson Act did not satisfy restrictionists, so Congress replaced it with the Immigration Act (Johnson-Reid Act) of 1924. This law set quotas at 2 percent of each nationality residing in the United States in 1890. It limited total immigration to 165,000

O! CLOSE THE GATES.

Words by
A. W. NEEL

Music by
L. A. CLARK

Price fifty Cents

Frank Harding
Music Publisher and Printer
228 E. 22nd Street,   New York City.

Anti-immigrationists used songs, as well as speeches and posters, to promote their cause. This 1923 tune urges the government to "Close the Gates" lest foreigners betray the hard-won rights of Americans and "drag our Colors down." (National Park Service Collection, Ellis Island Immigration Museum)

people and further restricted southern and eastern Europeans, since fewer of those groups lived in the United States in 1890 than in 1910, though the law did allow wives and children of U.S. citizens to enter as nonquota immigrants. In 1929 the National Origins Act apportioned new quotas, totaling 150,000 possible immigrants, among European countries in proportion to the "national-origins" (country of birth or descent) of American people in 1920. People from Canada, Mexico, and Puerto Rico did not fall under the quotas (except for those whom the Labor Department might define as potential paupers), and soon they became the largest immigrant groups (see Figure 24.2).

Fear of immigrant radicalism, persisting from the Red Scare of 1919, fueled antiforeign flames. Heated debate occurred in 1921, when a court convicted Nicola Sacco and Bartolomeo Vanzetti, two immi-

Sacco and Vanzetti Case

grant anarchists, of murdering a guard and paymaster during a robbery in South Braintree, Massachusetts. Sacco and Vanzetti's main offenses seem to have been their political beliefs and Italian origins. Though the evidence failed to prove their guilt, Judge Webster Thayer openly sided with the prosecution and privately called the defendants "anarchist bastards." Appeals and protests failed to win a new trial, and the prisoners, who remained calm and dignified throughout their ordeal, were executed in 1927. Their deaths touched off rallies and riots in Europe, Asia, and South America, leaving doubts about the United States as the land that nurtured freedom of belief.

While nativists lobbied for racial purity, the pursuit of spiritual purity stirred religious fundamentalists. Millions of Americans sought

Fundamentalism

certainty and salvation against what they perceived as the skepticism and irreverence of a materialistic, hedonistic society by following evangelical denominations of Protestantism that accepted a literal interpretation of the Bible. Resolutely believing that God's miracles created life and the world, they were convinced that Darwin's theory of evolution was just that, a theory, and that if fundamentalists constituted a majority of a community, as they did throughout the South, they should be able to determine what would be taught in schools. Their enemies were "modernists," those who interpreted "truths" critically, using reasoning from psychology and anthropology. To modernists, the accuracy of the Bible did not matter; what was important was the historical relevance of God in culture and the role of science in advancing knowledge.

In 1925 Christian fundamentalism clashed with modernism in a celebrated case in Dayton, Tennessee.

Scopes Trial

Early that year the state legislature passed a law forbidding public school instructors to teach the theory that humans had evolved from lower forms of life rather than descended from Adam and Eve. Shortly thereafter, high school teacher John Thomas Scopes volunteered to serve in a test case and was arrested for violating the law. Scopes's trial that summer became a headline event. William Jennings Bryan, former secretary of state and three-time presidential candidate, argued for the prosecution, and a team of civil liberties lawyers headed by Clarence Darrow represented the defense. News correspondents

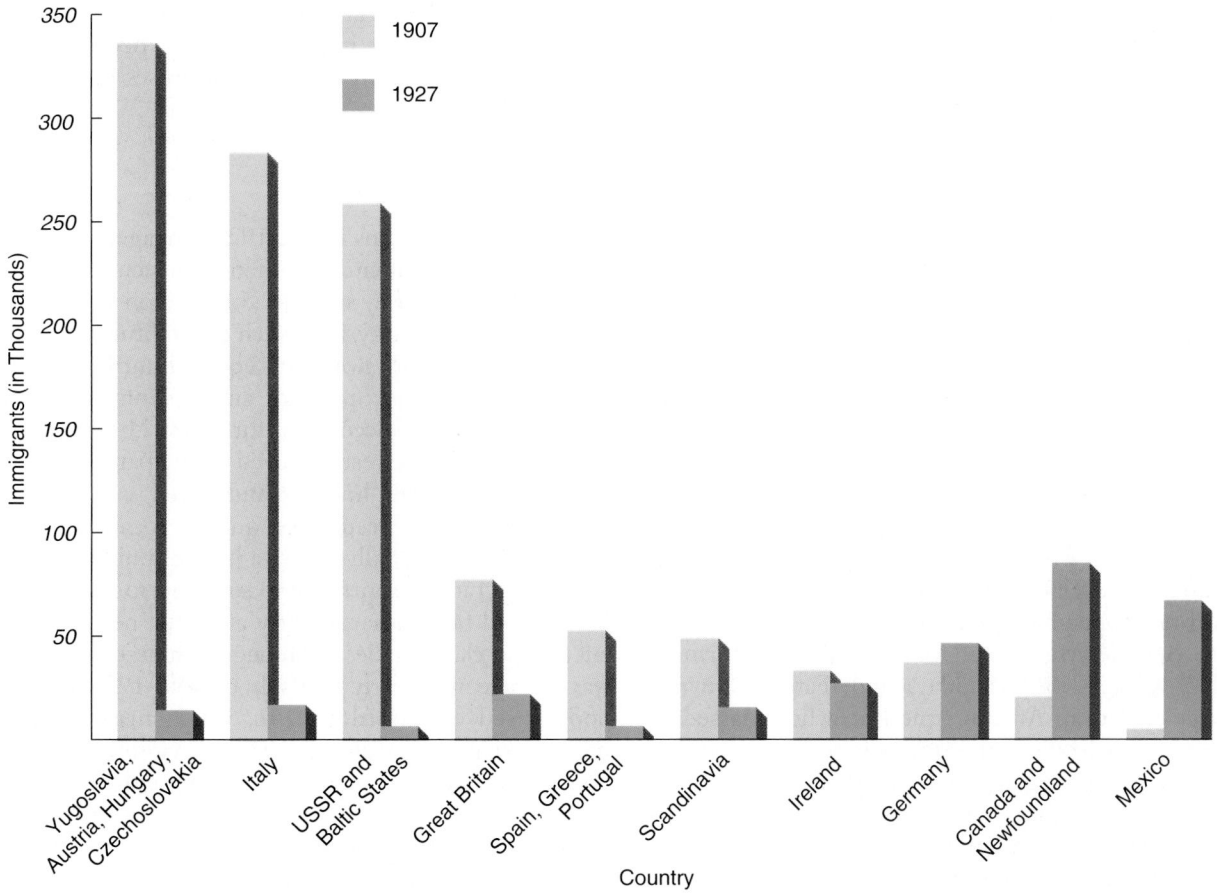

Figure 24.2 Sources of Immigration, 1907 and 1927 Immigration peaked in 1907 and 1908, when newcomers from southern and eastern Europe poured into the United States. After immigration restriction laws were passed in the 1920s, the greatest number of immigrants came from the Western Hemisphere (Canada and Mexico), which was exempted from the quotas, and the number coming from eastern and southern Europe shrank.

crowded into town, and radio stations broadcast the trial from coast to coast.

Although Scopes was convicted—clearly he had broken the law—modernists claimed victory. The testimony, they believed, showed fundamentalism to be illogical. The trial's climax occurred when Bryan himself took the witness stand as an expert on religion and science. Responding to Darrow's probing, Bryan asserted that Eve really had been created from Adam's rib, that the Tower of Babel was responsible for the diversity of languages, and that a big fish had swallowed Jonah. "One miracle is just as easy to believe as another," Bryan testified to cheering spectators. "I believe in creation [as told in the Bible], and if I am not able to explain it I will accept it."

After the contest between Bryan's blind faith and Darrow's bitter attack, one newspaper wrote, "Darrow succeeded in showing that Bryan knows little about the science of the world. Bryan succeeded in bearing witness bravely to the faith which he believes transcends all the learning of men." Most of the liberal press, however, mocked Bryan and his fundamentalist allies. Humorist Will Rogers quipped, "I see you can't say that man descended from the ape. At least that's the law in Tennessee. But do they have a law to keep a man from making a jackass of himself?" Nevertheless, fundamentalists were undeterred. They succeeded in getting many school boards to limit the teaching of evolution and influenced the content of high school biology books. As well, they created an independent subculture, with their own schools, camps, radio ministries, and missionary societies.

Klan rallies, immigration restriction, and fundamentalist literalism might appear as last gasps of a rural society yielding to modern urban-industrial values. Yet city dwellers swelled the ranks of all these movements. Nearly half the Klan's members lived in cities, especially in working-class neighborhoods where fear of invasion by racial minorities and foreigners was strong. Even urban reformers backed immigration restriction as a means of controlling poverty and quickening the assimilation of immigrants.

Cities also housed hundreds of Pentecostal churches, which attracted both blacks and whites struggling with economic insecurity and swayed by the pageantry and closeness to God that such churches offered. Using modern advertising techniques and elaborately staged services broadcast live on radio, magnetic preachers such as flamboyant Aimee Semple McPherson of Los Angeles, former baseball player Billy Sunday, and Father Divine (George Baker, an African American who amassed a huge interracial following especially in eastern cities) stirred revivalist fervor. And many urban dwellers supported prohibition, believing that eliminating the temptation of drink would help win the battle against poverty, vice, and corruption.

Revivalism

These emotional responses represented an attempt to sustain old-fashioned values in a fast-moving and materialistic world. Some Americans lashed out at "different" cultures and hedonistic trends in behavior. Millions of Americans firmly believed that nonwhites and immigrants were inferior people who imperiled national welfare. Clergy and teachers of all faiths condemned drinking, dancing, new dress styles, and sex on the movie screen and in parked cars. Yet even while mourning a lost past, most Americans tried to adjust to the modern order in one way or another. Few refrained from listening to the radio and attending movies, activities that proved less corrupting than critics feared. Radio featured music, news, and drama, most of which did not threaten traditional values. Movie producers, bowing to pressure from legislators, instituted self-censorship in 1927, forbidding nudity, rough language, and plots that did not end with justice and morality triumphant. More than ever, Americans sought fellowship in civic organizations. Membership swelled in Rotary, Elks, and women's clubs, and the number of Community Chests—associations that coordinated lo-

cal welfare projects—grew from 12 in 1919 to 361 in 1930. Perhaps most important, more people were finding release in recreation and new uses of leisure.

The Age of Play

Americans in the 1920s engaged in commercial entertainment as never before. In 1919 they spent $2.5 billion on leisure activities; by 1929 such expenditures topped $4.3 billion, a figure not again equaled until after the Second World War. Spectator amusements—movies, music, and sports—accounted for about 21 percent of the 1929 total; the rest involved participatory recreation, such as games, hobbies, and travel.

Entrepreneurs responded quickly to an appetite for fads, fun, and "ballyhoo"—a blitz of publicity that lent exaggerated importance to some person or event. Games and fancies particularly attracted newly affluent middle-class families. Mahjong, a Chinese tile game, was the rage in the early 1920s. In the mid-1920s people popularized crossword puzzles, which mass-circulation newspapers and magazines had begun printing a decade earlier. Next, fun seekers adopted miniature golf as their new fad. By 1930 the nation boasted thirty thousand miniature golf courses featuring tiny castles, windmills, and waterfalls. Dance crazes like the Charleston riveted public attention throughout the country, aided by live and recorded music on radio and the growing popularity of jazz.

In addition to indulging actively, Americans were avid spectators, particularly of movies and sports. In total capital investment, motion pictures became one of the nation's leading industries. Nearly every community had at least one theater, whether it was a hundred-seat Bijou on Main Street or a big-city "picture palace" with ornate lobbies and thousands of cushioned seats. In 1922 movies attracted 40 million viewers weekly; by 1930 the number reached 100 million—at a time when the nation's population was 120 million and total weekly church attendance was 60 million. The introduction of sound in *The Jazz Singer* in 1927, and of color a few years later, made movies even more exciting and realistic.

Movies

Responding to the tastes of mass audiences, the movie industry produced more escapist entertainment than art. The most popular films were spectacles such as Cecil B. DeMille's *The Ten Commandments* (1923)

BASE BALL STAR

BABE RUTH
Right Field

Babe Ruth had widespread appeal as one of the country's first sports superstars. Here a photograph of his mighty home run swing appears on a school notebook, showing the new link between sports and consumerism. (Private collection)

and *The King of Kings* (1927); lurid dramas such as *Souls for Sale* (1923) and *A Woman Who Sinned* (1924); and slapstick comedies starring Fatty Arbuckle, Harold Lloyd, and Charlie Chaplin. Ironically, comedies, with their poignant satires of the human condition, carried the most thought-provoking messages.

Spectator sports also boomed. Each year millions packed stadiums and parks to watch athletic events. Gate receipts from college football surpassed $21 million by the late 1920s. In an age when technology and mass production had robbed experiences and objects of their uniqueness, sports provided an unpredictability and drama that people craved. Newspapers and radio magnified this drama, feeding news to an eager public and glorifying events with such unrestrained narrative that sports promoters did not need to buy advertising.

Baseball's drawn-out suspense, variety of plays, and potential for keeping statistics attracted a huge following. After the "Black Sox scandal" of 1919, when eight members of the Chicago White Sox were banned from the game for allegedly throwing the World Se-

ries to the Cincinnati Reds (even though a jury acquitted them), baseball regained its respectability by transforming itself. Discovering that home runs excited fans, the leagues redesigned the ball to make it livelier. Attendance at games skyrocketed. A record three hundred thousand people attended the six-game 1921 World Series between the New York Giants and New York Yankees. Millions more gathered regularly to watch local teams, and even more listened to professional games on the radio.

Sports, movies, and the news created a galaxy of heroes. As technology and mass society made the individual less significant, people clung to heroic personalities as a means of identifying with the unique. Names such as Bill Tilden in tennis, Gertrude Ederle in swimming (in 1926 she became the first woman to swim across the English Channel), and Bobby Jones in golf became household words. But the power and action of boxing, football, and baseball produced the most popular sports heroes. Heavyweight

Sports Heroes

Rudolph Valentino became the idol of men and women alike in *The Sheik,* his most famous movie. With flashing eyes and wanton smile, Valentino carries a swooning woman to his tent. This immensely popular movie earned $1 million for Paramount Pictures.   (Museum of Modern Art Film Still Archive)

champion Jack Dempsey, a brawler from Manassa, Colorado, attracted the first of several million-dollar gates in his fight with Georges Carpentier in 1921. Harold "Red" Grange, running back for the University of Illinois football team, thrilled thousands with his speed and power and became the idol of sportswriters.

Baseball's foremost hero was George Herman "Babe" Ruth, who began his career as a pitcher but found he could use his prodigious strength to better advantage hitting home runs. Ruth hit 29 in 1919, 54 in 1920 (the year the Boston Red Sox traded him to the New York Yankees), 59 in 1924, and 60 in 1927—each year a record. His prowess on the field, defiant lifestyle, and boyish grin endeared him to millions. Known for overindulgence in food, drink, and women, he charmed fans into forgiving his excesses by appearing at public events and visiting hospitalized children.

While admiring the physical exploits of sports stars, Americans fulfilled a yearning for romance and adventure through movie stars. The films and personal lives of Douglas Fairbanks, Gloria Swanson, and Charlie Chaplin were discussed in parlors and pool

Movie Stars

halls across the country. One of the decade's most ballyhooed personalities was Rudolph Valentino, whose smooth seductiveness made women swoon and men imitate his pomaded hairdo and slick sideburns. Valentino's image exploited the era's sexual liberalism and flirtation with wickedness. In his most famous film, Valentino played a passionate sheik who carried away beautiful women to his boudoir tent, combining the roles of seducer and abductor. When he died at thirty-one of complications from ulcers and appendicitis, the press turned his funeral into a public extravaganza. Mourners lined up for over a mile to file past his coffin.

In their quest for fun and self-expression, some Americans became lawbreakers by refusing to give up drinking. The Eighteenth Amendment (1919) and the federal law (1920) that prohibited the manufacture, sale, and transportation of alcoholic beverages worked well at first. Per capita consumption of liquor dropped, as did arrests for drunkenness, and the price of illegal booze rose higher

Prohibition

than average workers could afford. But aside from passing supportive laws, legislators refrained from enforcing prohibition. In 1922 Congress gave the Prohibition Bureau only three thousand employees and less than $7 million for nationwide enforcement.

If the Eighteenth Amendment had applied only to hard liquor and not to beer and wine, it might have succeeded. But after 1925 the so-called noble experiment broke down as thousands of people made their own wine and bathtub gin, and bootleg importers along the country's borders and shorelines easily evaded the few patrols that attempted to curb them. Moreover, drinking, like gambling and prostitution, was a business with willing customers, and criminal organizations quickly capitalized on public demand. The most notorious of such mobs belonged to Al Capone, a burly tough who seized control of illegal liquor and vice in Chicago and maintained his grip on both politicians and the vice business through intimidation, bribery, and violence. But Capone contended, in a statement revealing of the era, "Prohibition is a business. All I do is supply a public demand." Americans wanted their liquor, and until 1931 when a federal court convicted and imprisoned him for income-tax evasion (the only charge for which authorities could obtain hard evidence), Capone supplied it. Reflecting on the contradictions inherent in Prohibition, columnist Walter Lippmann wrote in 1931, "The high level of lawlessness is maintained by the fact that Americans desire to do so many things which they also desire to prohibit."

Al Capone

Cultural Currents

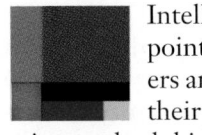

Intellectuals like Lippmann were quick to point to the era's hypocrisy. Serious writers and artists felt at odds with society, and their rejection of materialism and conformity was both biting and bitter.

Several writers of the so-called Lost Generation, including novelist Ernest Hemingway and poets Ezra Pound and T. S. Eliot, left the United States for Europe. Others, such as novelists William Faulkner and Sinclair Lewis, remained in America but, like the expatriates, expressed disillusionment with the materialism and hypocrisy that they witnessed. F. Scott Fitzgerald's *This Side of Paradise* (1920) and *The Great Gatsby* (1925); Lewis's *Babbitt*

Literature of Alienation

Florence Mills was a talented performer whose singing career received a major boost from her appearance in the musical comedy *Shuffle Along,* a show that heralded the beginning of the Harlem Renaissance.   (Howard Greenburg Galleries, © 1997 Donna VanDer Zee)

(1922), *Arrowsmith* (1925), and *Elmer Gantry* (1927); and Eugene O'Neill's plays exposed and derided Americans' preoccupation with money. Edith Wharton explored the clash of old and new moralities in novels such as *The Age of Innocence* (1921). Ellen Glasgow, one of the South's leading literary figures, lamented the trend toward impersonality in *Barren Ground* (1925). John Dos Passos's *Three Soldiers* (1921) and Hemingway's *A Farewell to Arms* (1929) interwove antiwar sentiment with critiques of the emptiness in modern relationships.

Spiritual discontent quite different from that of white writers inspired a new generation of African American artists. Middle class, well educated, and proud of their African heritage, these writers rejected white culture and exalted the militantly assertive "New Negro." Most of them lived in New York's Harlem; in this "Negro Mecca" black intellectuals and artists, aided by a few white patrons, celebrated black culture during what became known as the Harlem Renaissance.

Harlem Renaissance

This painting by the African American artist Archibald Motley represented the "Ash-Can" style, which considered no subject too undignified to paint, as well as the sensual relationship between jazz music and dancing within African American culture.   (Collection of Archie Motley and Valerie Gerrard Browne. Photo courtesy of The Art Institute of Chicago)

The popular 1921 musical comedy *Shuffle Along* is often credited with launching the Harlem Renaissance. The musical showcased talented African American artists such as lyricist Noble Sissle, composer Eubie Blake, and singers Florence Mills, Josephine Baker, and Mabel Mercer. Harlem in the 1920s also fostered a number of gifted writers, among them poets Langston Hughes, Countee Cullen, and Claude McKay; novelist Jean Toomer; and essayist Alain Locke. As well, the movement included visual artists such as Aaron Douglas, James A. Porter, and Augusta Savage.

Issues of identity troubled the Harlem Renaissance. Although intellectuals and artists cherished their African heritage, they realized that blacks had to come to terms with themselves as Americans. Thus Alain Locke urged that the New Negro should become "a collaborator and participant in American civilization." And Langston Hughes wrote, "We younger Negro artists who create now intend to express our individual dark-skinned selves without fear or shame. If white people are pleased, we are glad. If they are not, it doesn't matter. We know we are beautiful."

The Jazz Age, as the 1920s is sometimes called, owes its name to music that derived from black culture. Evolving from African and black American folk music, early jazz communicated an exuberance, humor, and authority that African Americans

Jazz

seldom expressed in their public and political lives. With emotional rhythms and emphasis on improvisation, jazz blurred the distinction between composer and performer and created intimacy between performer and audience. As African Americans moved northward, jazz traveled with them. Urban dance halls and bars often featured jazz, and gifted black performers like trumpeter Louis Armstrong, trombonist Kid Ory, and blues singer Bessie Smith enjoyed wide fame. Phonograph records and radio, better suited than sheet music to the spontaneity of jazz, helped to popularize it. Jazz greatly boosted the recording industry; music recorded by black artists and aimed at black consumers (sometimes called "race records") gave African Americans a place in the consumer culture. More important, jazz endowed America with its most distinctive art form.

In many ways the 1920s were the most creative years the nation had yet experienced. Painters such as

Experiments in Art and Music

Georgia O'Keeffe and John Marin tried to forge a uniquely American style of painting. European composers and performers still dominated classical music, but American composers such as Henry Cowell pioneered electronic music, and Aaron Copland built orchestral works around native folk motifs. George Gershwin blended jazz rhythms, classical forms, and folk melodies in his serious compositions (*Rhapsody in Blue*, 1924, and *Concerto in F*, 1925), musical dramas (*Funny Face*, 1927), and hit tunes such as "Summertime" and "Someone to Watch Over Me." In architecture the skyscraper boom drew worldwide attention, and Frank Lloyd Wright's "prairie-style" houses, churches, and schools celebrated the American landscape. At the beginning of the decade, essayist Harold Stearns had complained that "the most . . . pathetic fact in the social life of America today is emotional and aesthetic starvation." By 1929 that contention was hard to support.

The Election of 1928 and the End of the New Era

Intellectuals' uneasiness about materialism seldom affected the confident rhetoric of politics. Herbert Hoover voiced that confidence in his speech accepting the Republican nomination for president in 1928. "We in America today," Hoover boasted, "are nearer to the fi-

nal triumph over poverty than ever before in the history of any land. . . . We have not yet reached the goal, but, given a chance to go forward with the policies of the last eight years, we shall soon, with the help of God, be in sight of the day when poverty will be banished from this nation."

Hoover was an apt Republican candidate in 1928 (Coolidge had chosen not to seek reelection) because

Herbert Hoover

he fused the traditional value of individual hard work with modern emphasis on collective action. A Quaker from Iowa, orphaned at age ten, Hoover worked his way through Stanford University and became a wealthy mining engineer. During and after the First World War, he distinguished himself as U.S. food administrator and head of food relief for Europe.

As secretary of commerce under Harding and Coolidge, Hoover had what has been called an "associational vision." Recognizing the extent to which nationwide associations had come to dominate commerce and industry, Hoover tried to stimulate cooperation between business and government. He took every opportunity to make the Department of Commerce a center for the promotion of business, encouraging the formation of trade associations, holding conferences, and issuing reports, all aimed at improving production, marketing, and profits. His active leadership prompted one observer to quip that Hoover was "Secretary of Commerce and assistant secretary of everything else."

As Hoover's opponent, Democrats chose New York's governor Alfred E. Smith, whose background contrasted sharply with Hoover's.

Al Smith

Hoover had rural, native-born, Protestant, business roots and had never run for public office. Smith was an urbane, gregarious politician of immigrant stock with a career rooted in New York City's Tammany Hall. His relish for the give-and-take of city streets is apparent in his response during the campaign to a heckler who taunted him by shouting, "Tell them all you know, Al. It won't take long!" Smith unflinchingly retorted, "I'll tell them all we both know, and it won't take any longer!"

Smith was the first Roman Catholic to run for president on a major party ticket. His religion enhanced his appeal among urban ethnics, who were voting in increasing numbers, but intense anti-Catholic sentiments lost him southern and rural votes. Smith had compiled a strong record of promoting Progressive reforms and civil rights during his governorship, but his campaign failed to build a coalition of farmers and city dwellers because he stressed issues unlikely to unite these groups, particularly his opposition to prohibition.

Smith waged a spirited campaign, directly confronting anti-Catholic critics, but Hoover, who stressed national prosperity under Republican administrations, won the popular vote by 21 million to 15 million, the electoral vote by 444 to 87. Smith's candidacy nevertheless had beneficial effects on the Democratic Party. He carried the nation's twelve largest cities, which formerly had given majorities to Republican candidates, and he lured millions of foreign-stock voters to the polls for the first time. From 1928 onward, the Democratic Party solidified this urban base, which in conjunction with its traditional strength in the South would make the party a formidable force in national elections.

At his inaugural, Hoover proclaimed a New Day, "bright with hope." His cabinet, composed mostly of businessmen committed to the existing order, included six millionaires. To the lower ranks of government Hoover appointed young professionals who agreed with him that scientific methods could solve national problems. If Hoover was optimistic, so were most Americans. The belief was widespread that individuals were responsible for their own success and that unemployment or poverty suggested personal failing. Prevailing opinion also held that the ups and downs of the business cycle were natural and therefore not to be tampered with by government.

Hoover's Administration

This confidence dissolved in the fall of 1929 when stock prices suddenly plunged after soaring in 1928. Analysts explained the drop as temporary, caused by a "lunatic fringe." But on October 24, "Black Thursday," panic selling set in. Prices of many stocks hit record lows; some sellers could find no buyers. Stunned crowds gathered outside the frantic New York Stock Exchange. At noon, leading bankers met at the headquarters of J. P. Morgan and Company. To restore faith, they put up $20 million and ceremoniously began buying stocks. The mood changed and some stocks rallied. The bankers, it seemed, had saved the day.

Stock Market Crash

But as news of Black Thursday spread, panicked investors decided to sell their stocks rather than risk further losses. On "Black Tuesday," October 29, stock prices plummeted again. Hoover, who never had approved of what he called "the fever of speculation," assured Americans that the economy was sound. He shared the popular assumptions that the stock market's ills could be quarantined and that the economy was strong enough to endure until the market righted itself. Instead, the crash ultimately helped to unleash a devastating depression.

The economic weakness that underlay the Great Depression had several interrelated causes. One was declining demand. Since mid-1928, demand for new housing construction had faltered, leading to declining demand for building materials and unemployment among construction workers. Growth industries such as automobiles and electric appliances had been able to expand as long as consumers bought their products. Frenzied expansion, however, could not continue unabated. When demand leveled off, factory owners could not accumulate funds to build new plants and hire more workers. Instead, unsold inventories stacked up in warehouses, and laborers were laid off. Retailers also had amassed large inventories that crammed warehouses and store shelves, and in turn they were ordering less from manufacturers. Farm prices continued to sag, leaving farmers with less income to use in purchasing new machinery and goods. As wages and purchasing power stagnated, the workers who produced consumer products could not afford to buy them. Thus by 1929 a sizable population of underconsumers was causing serious repercussions.

Declining Demand

Underconsumption also resulted from the widening divisions in income distribution. As the rich grew richer, middle- and lower-income Americans made modest gains at best. Though average per capita disposable income (income after taxes) rose about 9 percent between 1920 and 1929, the income of the wealthiest 1 percent rose 75 percent, accounting for most of the increase. Much of this increase was put into stock market investments instead of being spent on consumer goods.

Furthermore, in their eagerness to expand and increase profits, many businesses overloaded themselves with debt. To obtain loans, they manipulated or misrepresented their assets in ways that weakened their ability to repay if forced to do so. Such practices, overlooked by lending agencies, put

Corporate Debt

As the stock market tumbled on October 24, 1929, a crowd of concerned investors gathered outside the New York Stock Exchange on Wall Street, unprepared for an unprecedented economic decline that would send the country into a tailspin for the next decade. (Corbis-Bettmann)

the nation's banking system also on precarious footing. When one part of the edifice collapsed, the entire structure crumbled.

The depression also derived from risky speculation on the stock market. Not only had corporations invested huge sums in stocks, but individuals also bought heavily on margin, meaning that they purchased stock by placing a down payment of only a fraction of the stock's actual price and then used stocks they had bought but not fully paid for as collateral for more stock purchases. When stock prices stopped rising, people tried to sell the holdings they had bought on margin to minimize their losses. But numerous investors selling at the same time caused prices to drop. As stock values collapsed, brokers demanded full payment for stocks bought on margin. Investors attempted to comply by withdrawing savings from banks

Speculation on the Stock Market

or selling stocks at a loss for whatever they could get. Bankers in turn needed cash and put pressure on brokers to pay back their loans, tightening the vise further. The more obligations went unmet, the more the system tottered. Inevitably, banks and investment companies collapsed.

International economic troubles also contributed to the crash and depression. During the First World War and postwar reconstruction, Americans had loaned billions of dollars to European nations. By the late 1920s, however, American investors were keeping their money at home, investing instead in the more lucrative U.S. stock market. Europeans, unable to borrow more funds and unable to sell their goods in the American market because of high tariffs, began to buy less from the United States. Moreover, the Allied nations depended on German war reparations to pay war debts

International Economic Troubles

to the United States. The German government depended on American bank loans to pay war reparations. When the depression choked off American loans, the Germans were unable to pay reparations debts, and in turn the Allies were unable to pay war debts. The world economy ground to a halt (see pages 735–736).

Government policies also contributed to the crash and depression. The federal government refrained from regulating wild speculation, contenting itself with occasionally scolding bankers and businesspeople. In keeping with government support of business expansion, the Federal Reserve Board pursued easy credit policies before the crash, charging low discount rates (interest rates on its loans to member banks) even though easy money was financing the speculative mania.

Drawbacks of Federal Policies

Partly because of optimism and partly because of the relatively undeveloped state of economic analysis, neither the experts nor people on the street realized what really had happened in 1929. Conventional wisdom, based on experiences from previous depressions, held that little could be done to correct economic problems; they simply had to run their course. So in 1929 people waited for the tailspin to ease, never realizing that the era of expansion and frivolity had come to an end and that society and politics, as well as the economy, would have to be rebuilt.

Summary

Two disturbing events, the First World War and the Great Depression, marked the boundaries of the 1920s. In the war's aftermath, traditional customs weakened as women and men sought ways to balance new liberation with old-fashioned mores. A host of new effects from science and technology, the automobile revolution, new conveniences such as electric appliances, and broadened exposure from mass media, movies, and travel influenced the lives of rich and poor alike. Moreover, the decade's general prosperity and freewheeling attitudes enabled countless Americans to emulate wealthier people not only by consuming more but also by trying to get rich through stock market speculation. The depression stifled some of these habits, but others were hard to break.

Beneath the "era of excess" lurked two important phenomena rooted in previous eras. One was the continued resurfacing of prejudice and intolerance that had long tainted the American dream. As prohibitionists, Klansmen, and immigration restrictionists made their voices heard, they encouraged discrimination against racial minorities and slurs against supposedly "inferior" ethnic groups. Meanwhile, the distinguishing forces of twentieth-century life—technological change, bureaucratization, and the growth of the middle class—accelerated, making the decade truly a "new era." Both phenomena would recur as major themes in the nation's history for the rest of the twentieth century.

LEGACY FOR A PEOPLE AND A NATION
Intercollegiate Athletics

In 1924 scandals of brutality, academic fraud, and illegal payments to recruits prompted the Carnegie Foundation for the Advancement of Higher Education to undertake a five-year investigation of college sports. Its 1929 report condemned coaches and alumni supporters for violating the amateur code. The report had minimal effect, however. As the career of Red Grange illustrated, football had become big-time during the 1920s, and other sports followed suit as scores of colleges and universities built stadiums and arenas to attract spectators, bolster alumni allegiance, and promote school spirit.

For most of the twentieth century, intercollegiate athletics ranked as one of the nation's major commercial entertainments. Highly paid coaches and highly recruited student-athletes have been common ever since the 1920s. At the same time, American colleges and universities have struggled to reconcile conflicts between the commercialism of athletic competition on one hand and the restraints of educational objectives and athletic amateurism on the other. Supposedly, cultivation of the mind is the main objective of higher education. But the economic potential of college sports coupled with rise in the 1920s of athletic departments, complete with athletic directors, staffs, and tutors as well as coaches and trainers, has created programs that compete with and sometimes overshadow the academic operations of the institutions that sponsor intercollegiate athletics.

Since the 1920s, recruiting scandals, cheating incidents, and accusations of academic fraud in college sports have sparked continual controversy and criticism. In 1952, after revelations of point-shaving (fixing the outcome) of college basketball games, the American Council on Education undertook a study of all college sports similar to that of the Carnegie Foundation a generation earlier. Its recommendations, including the abolition of bowl games, went largely unheeded. Then, in 1991, further abuses, especially in academics, prompted the Knight Foundation Commission on Intercollegiate Athletics to conduct a study that ultimately urged college presidents to take the lead in reforming intercollegiate athletics. Again, few significant changes resulted.

The most sweeping reforms followed court rulings in the 1990s that mandated expenditures for women's sports in proportion to women's share of a school's total enrollment (mandated under Title IX of the Educational Amendments Act of 1972). But as long as millions of dollars were involved and sports remained such a vital component of college as well as national culture, the system established in the 1920s has withstood most pressures for change.

For Further Reading, see page A-28 of the Appendix. For Web resources, go to http://college.hmco.com.

In late 1937 on a farm near Stigler, Oklahoma, Marvin Montgomery counted up his assets: $53 and a car—a 1929 Hudson that he had just bought to take himself, his wife, and their four children to California. Times in Oklahoma had been tough for Montgomery's family. Like other farm families on the Plains, Marvin explained, they had suffered from "the drought and such as that, it just got so hard, . . . I decided it would help me to change countries." The combined disasters of soil exhaustion, drought, and dust storms were driving farm families from their homes. In addition, machines, such as mechanical cotton pickers, were replacing the labor of men, women, and children in the cotton fields. Finally, farm policies under the New Deal of President Franklin D. Roosevelt often benefited landowners at the expense of tenant farmers and sharecroppers, tens of thousands of whom were evicted during the 1930s.

Marvin Montgomery believed that he could have held out. "I might have drug by like some of the rest of them," he said, "and sort of lived." But he wanted more than that. Above all, he wanted work. At the same time, circulars and newspaper advertisements held out the promise of jobs aplenty in the fields of California; and as many as four hundred thousand people decided to make the westward trek. Some of the migrants were from Arkansas, Texas, Missouri, and Kansas, but more came from Oklahoma than from any other state. Among them were Montgomery and his wife and children, who, on December 29, squeezed into the Hudson, along with their furniture, bedding, and pots and pans. "I had that old car loaded to the full capacity," Marvin acknowledged, "on top, the sides, and everywhere else." Traveling west on Route 66, the Montgomerys left Oklahoma for California.

There was never any doubt that the Montgomery family's destination would be California, where their married daughter and oldest son had already moved. "Yes, sir. I knew right where I was coming to," Marvin Montgomery told a congressional committee that in 1940 held hearings in a migratory labor camp in California's San Joaquin valley. But the trip had not been

Sharecropper, an oil painting by Jerry Bywaters, shows one of the major problems facing farmers on the southern plains in the 1930s: grasshoppers, which along with drought and dust storms ravaged crops in Oklahoma, Kansas, and other states.   (Dallas Museum of Art, Allied Arts Civic Prize, Eighth Annual Dallas Arts Exhibition)

THE GREAT DEPRESSION AND THE NEW DEAL 1929–1941

easy, largely because the Hudson proved to be an expensive gas-guzzler. "On the way, you know my car," he explained. "I got to where I had to blindfold it to get it past a filling station. It was taking on lots of gas and oil." The car also broke down twice. While they were crossing Arizona, their money ran out, and the family had to stop to work in the cotton fields for five weeks before they could afford to resume the trip. And once in California, Marvin said, there was little work: "Well, I hoed beets some; hoed some cotton, and I picked some spuds."

Their dream was one day to have a home and some land of their own in California, but they knew that low-paid farm work would never make the dream come true. In the meantime, though, the Montgomerys were relieved to be able to live in the housing provided for farm workers by the federal government through the Farm Security Administration (FSA). The FSA camp at Shafter in Kern County had 240 tents and forty small houses. For nine months the Montgomery family of six lived in a tent 14 by 16 feet, which rented for 10 cents a day plus four hours of volunteer labor a month. Then they proudly moved into an FSA house, "with water, lights, and everything, yes sir; and a little garden spot furnished."

What did the future hold for the Montgomerys? Marvin conceded that he became homesick for Oklahoma and "would rather be back on the farm, if you want to know." But his seventeen-year-old son Harvey saw a future for himself in California. When asked whether he wanted to return to Oklahoma, he replied: "I like California. . . . No. I would rather stay out here." And soon there were bountiful employment opportunities in California not only for the Montgomery family but for many other newcomers, in aircraft factories and shipyards mobilizing for the Second World War.

Statistics suggest the magnitude of the Great Depression's human tragedy. Between 1929 and 1933, a hundred thousand businesses failed, corporate profits fell from $10 billion to $1 billion, and the gross national product was cut in half. Banks failed by the thousands. Americans who believed that saving was a virtue discovered that their deposits had disappeared with the banks. Americans lost jobs as well. Thousands of men and women received severance slips every day. At the beginning of 1930 the number of jobless reached at least 4 million; by November it had jumped to 6 million. When President Herbert Hoover left office in 1933, about one-fourth of the labor force was idle—13 million workers—and millions more were underemployed, working only part-time. Unemployment strained relations within families. African Americans and other minorities sank deeper into destitution. Overall, the economic catastrophe aggravated old tensions: labor versus capital, white versus black, male versus female.

Elected amid prosperity and optimism, Herbert Hoover spent the years from late 1929 to his departure from office in March 1933 presiding over a gloomy and sometimes angry nation. Although he activated more of the federal government's resources than had any of his predecessors in an economic crisis, he opposed direct relief payments for the unemployed, and voters turned him out of office in 1932. His successor was Franklin D. Roosevelt, who promised vigorous action and projected hope in a time of despair.

From the first days of his presidency, Roosevelt displayed a buoyancy and willingness to experiment that helped to restore public confidence in the government and the economy. He acted not only to reform the banks and stock markets but also to provide central planning for industry and agriculture and direct government relief for the jobless. This sweeping emergency legislation was based on the concept of "pump priming," or pouring billions of federal dollars into the economy to generate business and industrial activity, thereby stimulating employment and consumer spending. Although Roosevelt's New Deal was opposed from both the left and the right, ultimately he prevailed, vastly expanding the scope of the federal government and the popularity of the Democratic Party, and in the process establishing America's welfare system.

During these years several million workers seized the chance to organize for better wages and working conditions. New Deal legislation made union organizing and collective bargaining legal. The new Congress of Industrial Organizations (CIO) established unions in the automobile, steel, meatpacking, and other major industries. Blacks registered political and economic gains, too, though they benefited less from the New Deal than did whites. Two and a half million additional women workers joined the labor force during the 1930s, but mostly in low-paying jobs that were not covered by New Deal legislation. Thus many women lacked Social Security coverage and minimum-wage protection.

The New Deal was not a revolution, but it transformed the United States. The elderly and disabled still collect Social Security payments. The Federal Deposit Insurance Corporation still insures bank deposits. The Securities and Exchange Commission still

IMPORTANT EVENTS

1929 Stock market crash (Oct.); Great Depression begins

Agricultural Marketing Act establishes Federal Farm Board to support crop prices

1930 Hawley-Smoot Tariff raises rates on imports

1931 Nine African American men arrested in Scottsboro affair

Hoover declares moratorium on First World War debts and reparations

1932 Reconstruction Finance Corporation established to make loans to banks, insurance companies, and railroads

Bonus Expeditionary Force marches on Washington

Roosevelt elected president

Revenue Act raises corporate, excise, and personal income taxes

1933 13 million Americans unemployed

National bank holiday suspends banking activities

Agricultural Adjustment Act (AAA) encourages decreased farm production

Civilian Conservation Corps provides jobs to young men

Tennessee Valley Authority established

Banking Act creates Federal Deposit Insurance Corporation

National Industrial Recovery Act (NIRA) attempts to spur industrial growth

Twentieth (Lame Duck) Amendment sets presidential inaugurations at January 20

Twenty-first Amendment repeals Eighteenth (Prohibition) Amendment

1934 Townsend devises Old Age Revolving Pensions plan

Long starts Share Our Wealth Society

Indian Reorganization (Wheeler-Howard) Act restores lands to tribal ownership

Taylor Grazing Act closes grasslands to further settlement

Democrats win victories in congressional elections

1935 Emergency Relief Appropriation Act authorizes establishment of public works programs

Works Progress Administration creates jobs in public works projects

Schechter v. U.S. invalidates NIRA

National Labor Relations (Wagner) Act grants workers the right to unionize

Social Security Act establishes insurance for the aged, the unemployed, and needy children

Committee for Industrial Organization established

Congress passes Public Utility Holding Company Act

Revenue (Wealth Tax) Act raises taxes on business and the wealthy

1936 9 million Americans unemployed

U.S. v. Butler invalidates AAA

Roosevelt defeats Landon

United Auto Workers hold sit-down strike against General Motors

1937 Roosevelt's court-packing plan fails

NLRB v. Jones & Laughlin upholds Wagner Act

Memorial Day Massacre of striking steel-workers

Farm Security Administration established to aid farm workers

National Housing Act establishes United States Housing Authority

1937–39 Business recession

1938 10.4 million Americans unemployed

AFL expels CIO unions

Fair Labor Standards Act establishes minimum wage

Missouri ex rel. Gaines v. Canada orders law school established for African Americans

1939 Marian Anderson performs at Lincoln Memorial

Social Security amendments add benefits for spouses and widows

1940 Roosevelt defeats Willkie

1941 African Americans threaten to march on Washington to protest unequal access to defense jobs

Fair Employment Practices Committee prohibits discrimination in war industries and government

monitors the stock exchanges. But the New Deal did not accomplish one of its goals—putting back to work all the people who wanted jobs. That would await the nation's entry into the Second World War in 1941. ■

Hoover and Hard Times: 1929–1933

 As the Great Depression deepened in the early 1930s, its underlying causes—principally overproduction and underconsumption—grew in severity (see Chapter 24). So too did instability in the banking industry. What happened to America's banks illustrates the cascading nature of the depression. Banks that had invested depositors' money in the stock market or foreign investments were badly weakened. When nervous Americans made runs on banks to salvage their threatened savings, a powerful momentum—panic—set in. In 1929, 659 banks folded; in 1930 the number of failures more than doubled to 1,350. The Federal Reserve Board blundered after the crash, drastically raising interest rates and thus tightening the money supply when just the opposite was needed: lowering interest rates to spur borrowing and spending. In 1931, 2,293 banks shut their doors, and another 1,453 ceased to do business in 1932. When banks failed, depositors lost everything.

Without jobs and without money, even necessities became luxuries. In the cities, some people quietly

No Food, No Home

lined up at soup kitchens or in bread lines. Others ate only potatoes, crackers, or dandelions or scratched through garbage cans for bits of food. As diets deteriorated, malnutrition became common, and the undernourished frequently fell victim to disease. Millions of Americans were not only hungry and ill; they were cold. Unable to afford fuel, they huddled in unheated tenements and shacks. Families doubled up in crowded apartments, and those unable to pay the rent were evicted. The homeless created shantytowns, called "Hoovervilles," where they lived in shacks made of everything from egg crates to discarded boards and bricks.

In the countryside, economic hardship deepened. Between 1929 and 1933 farm prices dropped 60 percent. At the same time, production decreased only 6 percent as individual farmers tried to make up for lower prices by producing more, thus adding to the surplus and depressing prices even further. The surplus could not be exported because foreign demand

had shrunk. Drought, foreclosure, clouds of hungry grasshoppers, and bank failures also plagued American farmers. Entire families, like the Montgomerys, left their homes in search of jobs or food; some men and women, including thousands of teenagers, jumped aboard freight trains as hoboes to seek salvation elsewhere.

Hard times also affected marriage patterns and family life. People postponed marriage, and married couples postponed having children. Out-of-work fathers felt frustrated and ashamed. "A child who was playing irritated him," recalled the son of an unemployed tool-and-die maker. "It wasn't just my own father. They all got shook up." Divorces declined, but desertions rose as husbands unable to provide for their families simply took off.

Most Americans met the crisis not with protest or violence but with bewilderment. Who was responsible? Hard-pressed citizens

Farmers' Holiday Association

blamed businesspeople and bankers, of course, but often faulted themselves as well. Some people were angry, though, and scattered protests raised the specter of popular revolt. Farmers in the Midwest prevented evictions and slowed foreclosures on farm properties by harassing sheriffs, judges, and lawyers. They also tried to stop farm produce from reaching the market. In Nebraska, Iowa, and Minnesota, farmers protesting low prices put up barricades of spiked logs and telegraph poles. They stopped trucks, smashed headlights, and dumped milk and vegetables in roadside ditches. Some of these demonstrations were organized by the Farmers' Holiday Association, which encouraged farmers to take a "holiday"—a strike that would keep farm products off the market until they commanded better prices.

Isolated protests also broke out in cities and in mining regions. In Chicago, Los Angeles, and Philadelphia, the unemployed marched on city halls. In Harlan County, Kentucky, when miners struck against wage reductions, mine owners responded with strikebreakers, bombs, the National Guard, the closing of relief kitchens, and evictions from company-owned housing.

The most spectacular confrontation shook Washington, D.C., in the summer of 1932. Congress was

Bonus Expeditionary Force

considering a bill to authorize immediate issuance of $2.4 billion in bonuses promised to First World War veterans by Congress in 1924, but not due for payment for twenty

In June 1932 unemployed veterans of the First World War board a truck in Girard, Alabama, and Columbus, Georgia, and travel to Washington, D.C., to join the "Bonus Army" and demand payment of their soldiers' bonuses. (Wide World Photos, Inc.)

years, or until 1945. To lobby for the bill, fifteen thousand unemployed veterans and their families converged on the tense nation's capital, calling themselves the Bonus Expeditionary Force (BEF), or "Bonus Army," and camping on vacant lots and in empty government buildings. President Hoover threw his weight against the bonus bill, and after much debate the Senate voted it down. One bonus marcher shouted: "We were heroes in 1917, but we're bums today."

Much of the BEF left Washington, but several thousand stayed on during the summer. Hoover carelessly labeled them "insurrectionists" and refused to meet with them. Then, in July, General Douglas MacArthur, assisted by Major Dwight D. Eisenhower and Major George S. Patton, confronted the veterans and their families with cavalry, tanks, and bayonet-wielding soldiers. The BEF hurled back stones and bricks. What followed shocked the nation. Men and women were chased down by horsemen; children were tear-gassed; shacks were set afire. When presidential hopeful Franklin D. Roosevelt heard about the attack on the Bonus Army, he turned to his friend Felix

Frankfurter and remarked, "Well, Felix, this will elect me."

With capitalism on its knees, American Communists in various parts of the nation encouraged the jobless to join "unemployment councils," which led urban demonstrations, agitated for jobs and food, and sought to raise class consciousness. On March 6, 1930, which the Communists labeled International Unemployment Day, hundreds of thousands of jobless Americans marched in the streets of New York, Chicago, and other cities. And in 1931 the Communists led a hunger march on Washington, D.C. In resisting efforts to evict jobless people, the unemployment councils often clashed with local police. The Communists' tangles with authority publicized the human tragedy of the depression. Still, total party membership in 1932 remained small at twelve thousand. The Socialist Party, which took issue with both capitalists and Communists, fared better. In 1932 the Socialist presidential candidate attracted 880,000 votes. More reformist than radical, the Social-

Communists and Socialists

ists also ran well in municipal elections after the stock market crash but scored few victories. Indeed, few Americans looked to left-wing doctrines, protest marches, or violence for relief from their misery. Americans were frightened, and they were angry, but they were not revolutionaries. They turned instead to their local, state, and federal governments.

But when urgent daily appeals for government relief for the jobless reached the White House, Hoover

Hoover's Response

at first became defensive, if not hostile, rejecting direct relief in the belief that it would undermine character and individualism. To a growing number of Americans, Hoover seemed heartless and inflexible. True to his beliefs, the president urged people to help themselves and their neighbors. He applauded the work of private voluntary relief through charities, but as the need increased, donations declined. State and urban officials found their treasuries drying up, too. Meanwhile, those calling for federal aid got no sympathy from Secretary of the Treasury Andrew Mellon, who believed that business cycles of boom and bust were not only inevitable but desirable. He advised Hoover to "let the slump liquidate itself. Liquidate labor, liquidate stocks, liquidate the farmers, liquidate real estate. . . . It will purge the rottenness out of the system."

As the depression intensified, Hoover's opposition to federal action gradually diminished. He rejected Mellon's insensitive counsel, hesitantly energizing the White House and federal agencies to take action—more action than the government had taken before. He won pledges from business and labor leaders to maintain wages and production and to avoid strikes. He urged state governors to increase their expenditures on public works. And he created the President's Organization on Unemployment Relief (POUR) to generate private contributions for relief of the destitute.

Though POUR proved ineffective, Hoover's spurring of federal public works projects (including Hoover and Grand Coulee Dams) did provide some jobs. Help also came from the Federal Farm Board, created under the Agricultural Marketing Act of 1929, which supported crop prices by lending money to cooperatives to buy crops and keep them off the market. But the board soon found itself short of money, and unsold surpluses jammed warehouses. To retard the collapse of the international monetary system, Hoover in 1931 announced a moratorium on the payment of First World War debts and reparations.

The president also asked Congress to charter the Reconstruction Finance Corporation (RFC). Created

Reconstruction Finance Corporation

in 1932 and eventually empowered with $2 billion, the RFC was designed to make loans to banks, insurance companies, and railroads and later to state and local governments. In theory, the RFC would lend money to large entities at the top of the economic system, and benefits would filter down to people at the bottom. It did not work; banks continued to collapse and small companies went into bankruptcy.

Despite warnings from prominent economists, Hoover also signed into law the Hawley-Smoot Tariff

Hawley-Smoot Tariff

(1930). The tariff raised duties by about one-third and further weakened the economy by making it even more difficult for foreign nations to sell their products and thus to earn dollars to pay back their debts to the United States and to buy American products.

Like most of his contemporaries, Hoover believed that a balanced budget was sacred and deficit spending sinful. In 1931 he therefore appealed for a decrease in federal expenditures and an increase in taxes. The following year he supported a sales tax on manufactured goods. The sales tax was defeated, but the Revenue Act of 1932 raised corporate, excise, and personal income taxes. Hoover seemed tangled in a contradiction: he urged people to spend to spur recovery, but his tax policies deprived them of spending money. Nor did he ever balance the budget.

Although Hoover expanded public works projects and approved loans to some institutions, he vetoed a

Hoover's Traditionalism

variety of relief bills presented to him by Congress. In rejecting a public power project for the Tennessee River, he argued that its inexpensive electricity would compete with power from private companies. Hoover's traditionalism also was well demonstrated by his handling of prohibition. Despite the Eighteenth Amendment, Americans were producing and drinking liquor with grand illegality and hypocrisy. Although the law was not and could not be enforced, Hoover resisted mounting public pressure for repeal. Opponents of prohibition argued not only that it encouraged crime but also that its repeal would stimulate economic recovery by reviving the nation's breweries and distilleries. But the president refused to tamper with the Constitution; he declared that the liquor industry, having no socially redemptive value, was best left depressed. After Hoover left office in 1933, prohibition was repealed through ratification of the Twenty-first Amendment.

Still, President Hoover stretched governmental activism as far as he thought he could without violating his cherished principles. On the eve of Hoover's departure from the presidency in 1933, the journalist William Allen White pondered "whether Herbert Hoover . . . by pointing the way to social recovery . . . is the first of the new Presidents . . . or whether . . . he is the last of the old." Perhaps he was both. Because Hoover mobilized the resources of the federal government as never before, some historians have depicted him as a bridge to the New Deal of the 1930s. If nothing else, he prepared the way for massive federal activity by giving private enterprise the opportunity to solve the depression—and to fail in the attempt.

Franklin D. Roosevelt and the Election of 1932

Herbert Hoover and the Republican Party faced dreary prospects in 1932. The president kept blaming international events for the economic crisis, but Americans were less concerned with abstract explanations than with tomorrow's meal. He grumbled and grew impatient with his critics. But what soured public opinion most was that Hoover did not offer leadership when the times required it. So unpopular had he become by 1932 that Republicans who did not want to be associated with a loser ran independent campaigns.

Franklin D. Roosevelt enjoyed quite a different reputation. Though born into the upper class of old money and privilege, the smiling, ingratiating governor of New York appealed to people of all classes, races, and regions, and he shared the American penchant for optimism. After serving as assistant secretary of the navy under Woodrow Wilson and running as the Democratic Party's vice-presidential candidate in 1920, Roosevelt was stricken with polio and left totally paralyzed in both legs. What should Roosevelt do next? Should he retire from public life, a rich invalid? His answer and his wife Eleanor's was "no." Throughout the 1920s the Roosevelts contended with his handicap. Rejecting self-pity, Franklin Roosevelt worked to rebuild his body. Friends commented that his fight against polio

Franklin D. Roosevelt

In November 1930 Franklin D. Roosevelt (1882–1945) read the good news. Reelected governor of New York by 735,000 votes, he immediately became a leading contender for the Democratic presidential nomination. Notice Roosevelt's leg braces, rarely shown in photographs because of an unwritten agreement by photographers to shoot him from the waist up.   (Corbis-Bettmann)

had given him new moral and physical strength. As Roosevelt explained it, "If you had spent two years in bed trying to wiggle your big toe, after that anything would seem easy."

For her part, Eleanor Roosevelt—who had grown up shy and sheltered—launched her own career in public life. In her memoirs, she described having changed in the 1920s from a depressed, isolated person into an independent woman with significant political commitments and personal relationships. Eleanor Roosevelt worked hard to become an effective public speaker and participated in the activities of the League of Women Voters, the Women's Trade Union League, and the Democratic Party. In a short time, she became a leading figure in a network of women activists. She became deeply committed to equal opportunity for women and for African Americans and wanted to alleviate the suffering of the poor. On these issues, she served as her husband's conscience.

Eleanor Roosevelt

Roosevelt was elected governor of New York in 1928 and reelected in 1930; his terms coincided with Hoover's presidency. But whereas Hoover appeared hardhearted and unwilling to help the jobless, Roosevelt seemed quite the opposite. He supported direct relief payments for the unemployed, declaring that

Roosevelt as Governor of New York

such aid "must be extended by Government, not as a matter of charity, but as a matter of social duty." As governor of New York, Roosevelt created jobs in publicly funded reforestation, land reclamation, and hydroelectric power projects, and he endorsed old-age pensions and protective legislation for labor unions. With his record, Roosevelt became an obvious prospect for the 1932 Democratic presidential nomination.

To prepare a national political platform, Roosevelt surrounded himself with a "Brain Trust" of lawyers and university professors. These experts reasoned that bigness was unavoidable in the modern American economy. It thus followed that the cure for the nation's ills was not to go on a rampage of trustbusting but to place large corporations, monopolies, and oligopolies under effective government regulation.

Roosevelt's "Brain Trust"

Roosevelt and his Brain Trust also agreed that it was essential to restore purchasing power to farmers, blue-collar workers, and the middle classes, and that the way to do so was to cut production. If demand for a product remained constant and the supply were cut, they reasoned, the price would rise. Producers would make higher profits, and workers would earn more. This method of combating a depression has been called "the economics of scarcity," which the Brain Trust at the time saw as the preferred alternative to pump priming through deficit spending, in which the government borrowed money to prime the economic pump and thereby revive purchasing power.

Roosevelt and Hoover both campaigned as fiscal conservatives committed to a balanced budget. But Roosevelt, unlike Hoover, also advocated immediate and direct relief to the unemployed. And Roosevelt demanded that the federal government engage in centralized economic planning and experimentation to bring about recovery.

Upon accepting the Democratic nomination, Roosevelt called for a "new deal for the American people." To that end, the Democrats were willing to abandon prohibition and to launch federal relief. More people went to the polls in 1932 than in any election since the First World War. In a crisis-ridden moment, Americans followed their traditional pattern and exchanged one government for another. The presidential election of 1932

1932 Election Results

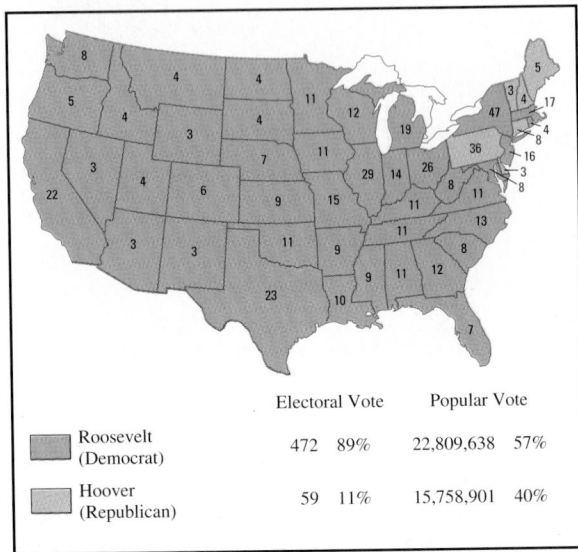

Map 25.1   Presidential Election, 1932   One factor above all decided the 1932 presidential election: the Great Depression. Roosevelt won forty-two states, Hoover six.

	Electoral Vote		Popular Vote	
Roosevelt (Democrat)	472	89%	22,809,638	57%
Hoover (Republican)	59	11%	15,758,901	40%

was never much of a contest: Roosevelt's 22.8 million popular votes far outdistanced Hoover's 15.8 million; Roosevelt won forty-two states to Hoover's six (see Map 25.1). Cities continued the trend, begun in 1928, of voting Democratic. Democrats also won overwhelming control of the Senate and the House.

Once elected, Roosevelt had to wait until his inauguration on March 4, 1933, to act. (To eliminate similar losses of time, the Twentieth Amendment to the Constitution—the so-called Lame Duck Amendment, ratified in 1933—shifted all future inaugurations to January 20.) It was a troubled four months. Millions of jobless Americans walked the streets; prices for agricultural and manufactured goods continued to plummet; industrial production sank to new depths. And throughout the United States, depositors lined up in front of banks to withdraw their savings. Banks with insufficient funds on hand to pay depositors had to close their doors and declare themselves insolvent. In February, Michigan and Maryland suspended banking operations, and by early March thirty-six other states, including New York, had declared bank holidays.

On March 2, 1933, President-elect Roosevelt and his family and friends boarded a train for Washington, D.C., and the inauguration ceremony. Roosevelt was carrying with him rough drafts of two presidential proclamations, one summoning a special session of Congress, the other declaring a national bank holiday, suspending banking transactions throughout the nation.

Launching the New Deal and Restoring Confidence

"First of all," declared the newly inaugurated president, "let me assert my firm belief that the only thing we have to fear is fear itself—nameless, unreasoning, unjustified terror." In his inaugural address Roosevelt scored his first triumph as president, instilling hope and courage in the American people. He invoked "the analogue of war," asserting that, if need be, "I shall ask the Congress for the one remaining instrument to meet the crisis—broad Executive power to wage a war against the emergency, as great as the power that would be given to me if we were in fact invaded by a foreign foe."

The next day, Roosevelt declared a four-day national bank holiday and summoned Congress to an emergency session, beginning March 9, that would

A gloomy Hoover and a buoyant Roosevelt ride to the inauguration in 1933. This magazine cover was never published, apparently because the editors of *The New Yorker* thought it inappropriate after an assassination attempt on the president-elect just three weeks before.   (Franklin D. Roosevelt Library)

Launching the New Deal

launch the New Deal. Roosevelt's first measure, the Emergency Banking Relief Bill, was introduced that very day, passed sight unseen by unanimous House vote, approved 73 to 7 in the Senate, and signed into law by the president that evening. The new law provided for the reopening, under Treasury Department license, of banks that were solvent and for the reorganization and management of those that were not. It also prohibited the hoarding and export of gold. It was, however, a fundamentally conservative law that upheld the status quo and left the same bankers in charge.

On the next day, March 10, the second bill of the New Deal was introduced in Congress. It too was conservative, and ten days later it became law. Called the Economy Act, its purpose was to balance the budget by reducing veterans' pensions and federal employees' pay. Under Roosevelt, the budget balancers had won a battle that could not have been won under Hoover.

On March 12, a Sunday evening, the president broadcast the first of his "fireside chats," and 60 million people heard his reassuring words on their radios.

Under the Agricultural Adjustment Act, farmers received government payments for not planting crops or for destroying crops they already had planted. Some farmers, however, needed help of a different kind. The Resettlement Administration, established by executive order in 1935, was authorized to resettle destitute farm families from areas of soil erosion, flooding, and stream pollution to homestead communities. This poster was done by Ben Shahn. (Library of Congress)

First Fireside Chat

His message: banks were once again safe places for depositors' savings. On Monday morning the banks opened their doors, but instead of queuing up to withdraw their savings, people were waiting outside to deposit their money. The bank runs were over; Roosevelt had reestablished people's confidence in their political leadership, their banks, even their economic system.

Roosevelt next pursued a measure, the Beer-Wine Revenue Act, that was deflationary because it actually took money out of people's pockets by imposing new taxes. The act, which legalized the sale of low-alcohol wines and beers, levied taxes on these products. (Congress had proposed repeal of prohibition in February 1933 in the Twenty-first Amendment, and the states ratified it by December 1933.) To many, levying new taxes seemed a strange way to restore purchasing power to people who could not afford to buy what they needed. Roosevelt knew that, but he predicted the situation would change. "It is simply inevitable," he wrote a friend, "that we must inflate." He added that his "banker friends may be horrified" by the large-scale federal spending that was to come.

Beer-Wine Revenue Act

In mid-March Roosevelt sent to Congress the Agricultural Adjustment Bill to restore farmers' purchasing power. If overproduction was the cause of farmers' problems, then the government had to encourage farmers to grow less. Under the domestic allotment plan, the government would pay farmers to reduce their acreage or plow under crops already in the fields. Farmers would receive payments based on *parity*, a system of regulated prices for corn, cotton, wheat, rice, hogs, and dairy products that would provide them the same purchasing power they had had during the prosperous period of 1909 to 1914. In paying price supports, the government was making up the difference between the current prices for farm products and the income that farmers needed to survive. The subsidies would be funded by taxes levied on the processors of agricultural commodities.

Agricultural Adjustment Act

Roosevelt's farm plan immediately encountered vehement opposition. How could there be crop surpluses when some Americans were hungry and even starving? Underconsumption, critics argued, was the result of a maldistribution of incomes and wealth.

Some politicians wanted to put more money into circulation by coining silver or printing greenbacks. Cheap money, they contended, not price supports, would make it easier for farmers to repay their debts. On May 12, Congress finally overcame opposition to the domestic allotment plan and passed the Agricultural Adjustment Act (AAA). A month later the Farm Credit Act was passed, providing short- and medium-term loans that enabled many farmers to refinance their mortgages and hang onto their homes and land. Another New Deal measure assisted homeowners in the towns and cities; the Home Owners Refinancing Act provided $2 billion in bonds to refinance nonfarm home mortgages.

Meanwhile, other relief measures became law. On March 21 the president requested direct cash grants to the states for relief payments to needy citizens and two federal programs that would create jobs. Ten days later Congress approved the Civilian Conservation Corps (CCC), a job agency that ultimately put 2.5 million young men aged eighteen to twenty-five to work planting trees, clearing camping areas and beaches, and building bridges, dams, reservoirs, fish ponds, and fire towers. Then on May 12 Congress passed the Federal Emergency Relief Act, which authorized $500 million in aid to state and local governments. Finally, on June 16 Title II of the National Industrial Recovery Act established the Public Works Administration (PWA) and appropriated $3.3 billion for hiring the unemployed to build roads, sewage and water systems, public buildings, and a host of other projects. These were worthwhile in themselves, but the key purpose of the PWA was to pump federal money into the economy.

Other Relief Measures

If the AAA was the agricultural cornerstone of the New Deal, the National Industrial Recovery Act was the industrial cornerstone. The act, which established the National Recovery Administration (NRA), was a testimony to the New Deal belief in national economic planning as opposed to an intensely competitive, laissez-faire economy. It was essential, planners argued, for businesses to cooperate in ending cutthroat competition and to raise prices by limiting production. Under NRA auspices, competing businesses met with each other, as well as with representatives of workers and consumers, to draft codes of fair competition, which limited production and established prices. With

National Recovery Administration

businesses enjoying new benefits from cooperation, workers wanted a share of the pie, too. Congress responded with Section 7(a) of the National Industrial Recovery Act, which guaranteed their right to unionize and to bargain collectively.

The New Deal also strengthened public confidence in the stock exchanges and banks. Roosevelt signed the Federal Securities Act, which compelled brokers to tell the truth about new securities issues, and the Banking Act of 1933, which set up the Federal Deposit Insurance Corporation (FDIC) for insuring bank deposits. In June Roosevelt also took the United States off the gold standard, no longer guaranteeing the gold value of the dollar abroad. Freed from the requirement that all paper money be backed by gold, the Federal Reserve Board could expand the supply of currency in circulation, thus enabling monetary policy to become another weapon for economic recovery.

One of the boldest programs enacted by Congress addressed the badly depressed Tennessee River valley, which runs through Virginia, North Carolina, Tennessee, Georgia, Alabama, Mississippi, and Kentucky (see Map 25.2). For years Progressives had advocated government operation of the Muscle Shoals electric power and nitrogen facilities on the Tennessee River. Roosevelt's Tennessee Valley Authority (TVA), established in May, was a much broader program. Its dams would not only control floods but generate hydroelectric power as well. In constructing public power facilities, the TVA would provide a yardstick for determining fair rates for privately produced electric power. Most important, the goal of the TVA was nothing less than enhancement of the economic well-being of the entire Tennessee River valley.

TVA

The TVA achieved its goals but, in the process, it became a major polluter. TVA strip mining caused soil erosion. Its coal-burning generators released sulfur oxides, which combined with water vapor to produce acid rain. Above all, the TVA degraded the water by dumping untreated sewage, toxic chemicals, and metal pollutants from strip mining into streams and rivers. Though an economic miracle, the TVA proved to be a monumental disaster in America's environmental history.

TVA's Environmental Legacy

The special session of Congress adjourned on June 16, 1933. In just over three months, Roosevelt had delivered fifteen messages to Congress proposing

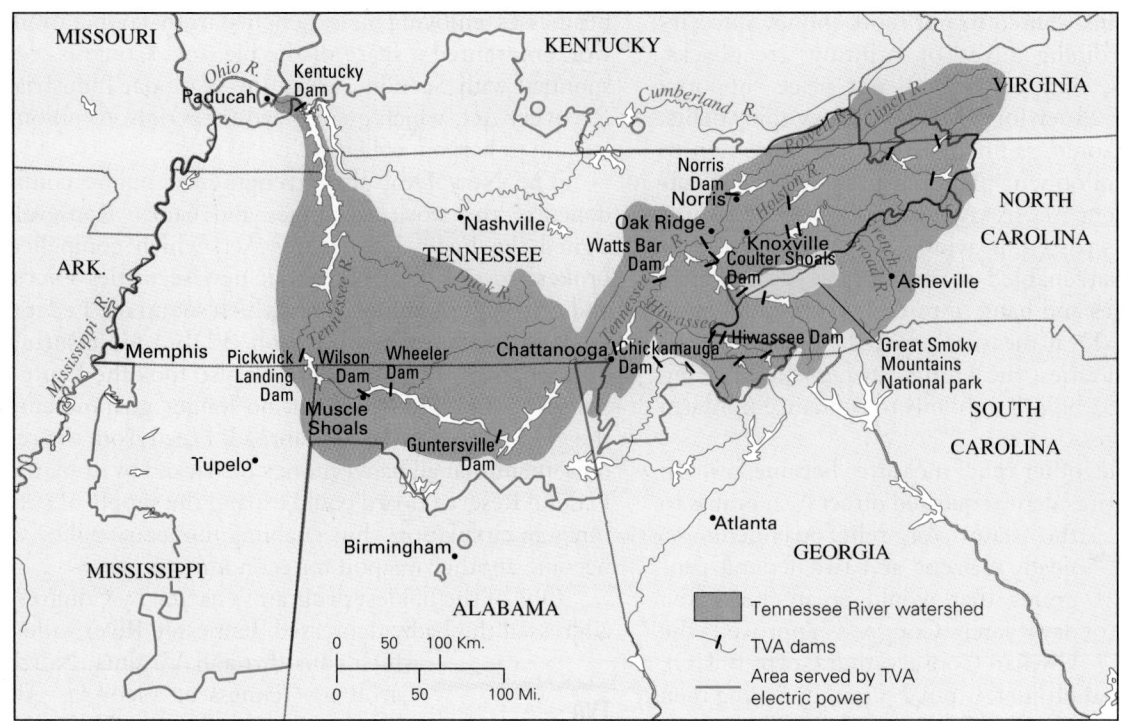

Map 25.2 The Tennessee Valley Authority To control flooding and to generate electricity, the Tennessee Valley Authority constructed dams along the Tennessee River and its tributaries from Paducah, Kentucky, to Knoxville, Tennessee.

End of the First Hundred Days

major legislation, and Congress had passed fifteen significant laws (see Table 25.1). The United States had rebounded from hysteria and near collapse. As columnist Walter Lippmann wrote, at the time of Roosevelt's inauguration the country was a collection of "disorderly panic-stricken mobs and factions. In the hundred days from March to June we became again an organized nation confident of our power to provide for our own security and to control our own destiny." Journalists called this period of remarkable achievement the Hundred Days.

Throughout the remainder of 1933 and the spring and summer of 1934, more New Deal bills became law, benefiting farmers, the unemployed, investors, homeowners, workers, and the environment. The Commodity Credit Corporation, organized in 1933, bolstered crop prices by lending farmers money secured by their underpriced crops, thereby allowing them to withhold

Other Legislation

their crops from the market until prices rose. In 1934 additional hundreds of millions of federal dollars were appropriated for unemployment relief and public works. Legislation that year also established the Securities and Exchange Commission, the National Labor Relations Board, and the Federal Housing Administration. In 1934, too, the Taylor Grazing Act was passed. For years, use of the public lands had been largely unregulated, and overgrazing of cattle had caused severe soil erosion. The Taylor Act, which created the Grazing Service (later to become the Bureau of Land Management), established federal supervision of most of the remaining public domain, and it closed 80 million acres of grasslands to further settlement and use.

New Deal legislation seemed to promise something for every group: industrial workers, urban dwellers, landowning farmers, and the jobless, not to mention industrialists, bankers, stockbrokers, educators, and social workers. This was interest-group democracy at work. In

Interest-Group Democracy

Table 25.1   New Deal Achievements

Year	Labor	Agriculture and Environment	Business and Industrial Recovery	Relief	Reform
1933	Section 7(a) of NIRA	Agricultural Adjustment Act Farm Credit Act	Emergency Banking Relief Act Economy Act Beer-Wine Revenue Act Banking Act of 1933 (guaranteed deposits) National Industrial Recovery Act	Civilian Conservation Corps Federal Emergency Relief Act Home Owners Refinancing Act Public Works Administration Civil Works Administration	TVA Federal Securities Act
1934	National Labor Relations Board	Taylor Grazing Act			Securities Exchange Act
1935	National Labor Relations (Wagner) Act	Resettlement Administration Rural Electrification Administration		Works Progress Administration National Youth Administration	Social Security Act Public Utility Holding Company Act Revenue Act (wealth tax)
1937		Farm Security Administration		National Housing Act	
1938	Fair Labor Standards Act	Agricultural Adjustment Act of 1938			

Source: Adapted from Charles Sellers, Henry May, and Neil R. McMillen, *A Synopsis of American History*, 6th ed. Copyright © 1985 by Houghton Mifflin Company. Reprinted by permission.

the midst of this coalition of special interests was President Roosevelt, the artful broker, who pointed to the economy as proof that this approach was working (see Figure 25.1). As the New Deal became law, unemployment fell steadily from 13 million in 1933 to 9 million in 1936. Net farm income rose from just over $3 billion in 1933 to $5.85 billion in 1935. Manufacturing salaries and wages also increased, from $6.25 billion in 1933 to almost $13 billion in 1937.

During the early years of Roosevelt's presidency, there was no question about the popularity of either the New Deal or the president. In the 1934 congressional elections, the Democrats gained nine seats in the House and nine in the Senate. The New Deal, ac-

cording to Arthur Krock of the *New York Times*, had won "the most overwhelming victory in the history of American politics."

Opposition to the New Deal

 There was, however, more than one way to read employment and income statistics and election returns. Although unemployment had dropped from a high of 25 percent in 1933 to 16.9 percent in 1936, it was still much higher than in 1929, when unemployment had been only 3.2 percent. And although manufacturing wages and salaries had reached almost $13 billion in

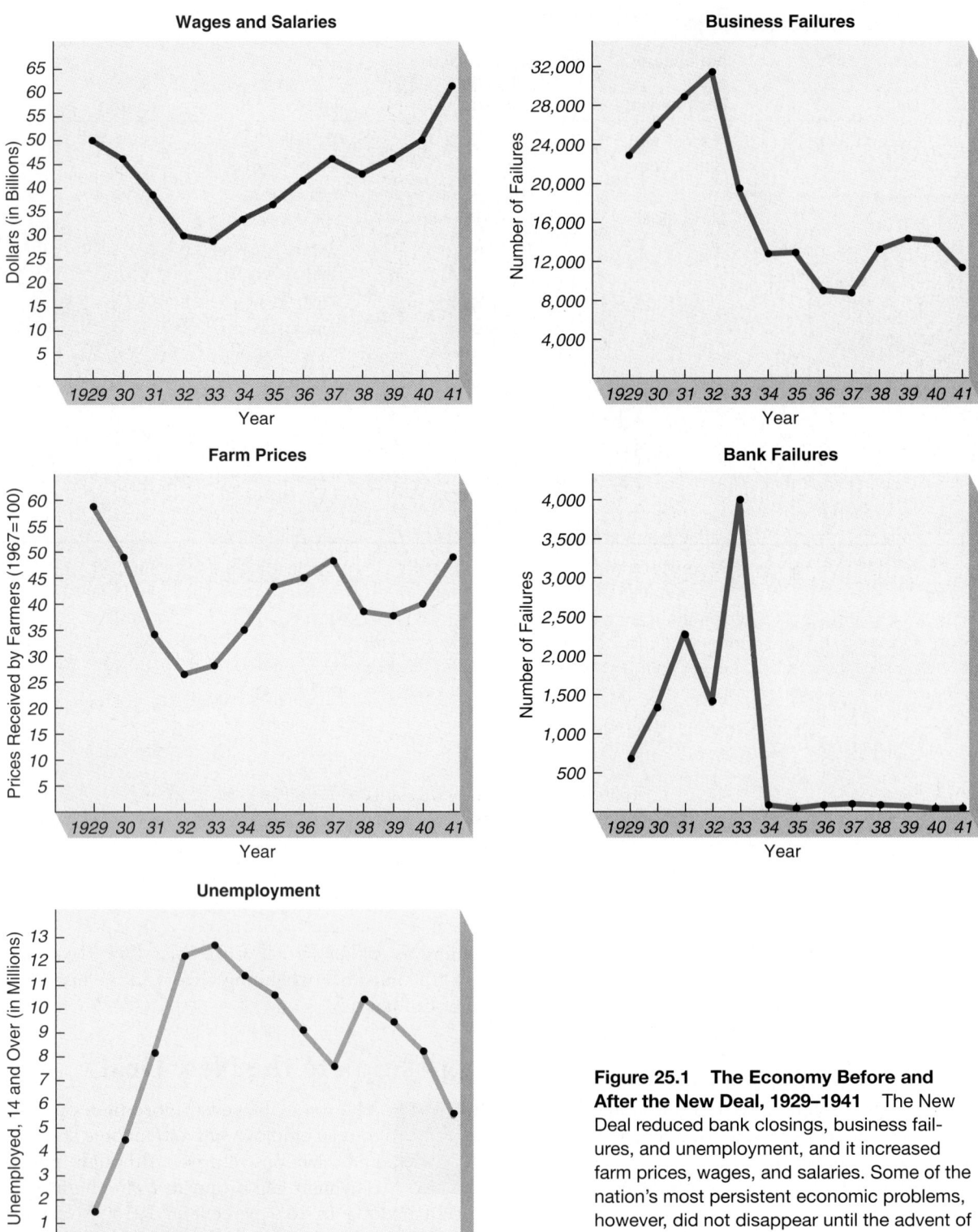

Figure 25.1 The Economy Before and After the New Deal, 1929–1941 The New Deal reduced bank closings, business failures, and unemployment, and it increased farm prices, wages, and salaries. Some of the nation's most persistent economic problems, however, did not disappear until the advent of the Second World War.

Plagued by dust storms and evictions, thousands of tenant farmers and sharecroppers were forced to leave their land during the Great Depression. Known as "Okies" and "Arkies," they took off for California with their few belongings. These refugees from drought-stricken Oklahoma experienced car trouble and were stalled on a New Mexico highway.   (Library of Congress)

1937, that figure was less than the total for 1929. In other words, the New Deal had a long way to go before reaching predepression standards.

With the arrival of partial economic recovery, many businesspeople and conservatives became vocal critics of the New Deal. Some charged that there was too much taxation and government regulation. Others condemned the deficit financing of relief and public works. In 1934 the leaders of several major corporations joined with Al Smith, John W. Davis, and disaffected conservative Democrats to establish the American Liberty League. Members of the Liberty League contended that the New Deal welfare payments were subverting individual initiative and self-reliance.

Conservative Critics of the New Deal

While businesspeople considered the government their enemy, others thought the government favored business too much. Critics argued that NRA codes favored industry's needs over those of workers and consumers. Farmers, labor unions, and individual entrepreneurs complained that the NRA set prices too high and favored large producers over small businesses. The federal courts also began to scrutinize the constitutionality of the legislation in cases brought by New Deal foes.

Farmers and Laborers

The AAA also came under attack for its encouragement of cutbacks in production. Farmers had plowed under 10.4 million acres of cotton and slaughtered 6 million pigs in 1933—a time when people were ill clothed and ill fed. Although for landowning farmers the program was successful, many others found such waste shocking. Tenant farmers and sharecroppers also were supposed to receive government payments for taking crops out of cultivation, but very few received what they were entitled to, especially if they were African American. Furthermore, the AAA's hopes that landlords would keep their tenants on the land even while cutting production were not fulfilled. In the South the number of sharecropper farms dropped by 30 percent between 1930 and 1940. The result was a homeless population, dispossessed Americans heading to cities and towns in all parts of the country.

Joining the migration to the West Coast were "Okies," such as Oklahoman Marvin Montgomery and his family traveling in their 1929 Hudson, and "Arkies" from Arkansas; many of them had been evicted from their tenant farms during the depression. Not all were driven by foreclosure; thousands took to the road to escape the drought that plagued the southern plains states of Kansas, Colorado, New Mexico, Oklahoma, Arkansas, and Texas—a region known in the mid-1930s as the Dust Bowl. The Dust Bowl was an ecological disaster. In the 1920s farmers on the southern plains had bought tens of thousands of tractors and plowed millions of acres. Then, in the 1930s, the rain stopped. Soil that had been plowed was particularly vulnerable to the

The Dust Bowl

drought that gripped the plains. Strong winds caused enormous dust storms; from 1935 through 1938, 241 dust storms suffocated the southern plains. Farmers shuttered their homes against the dust as tightly as possible, but, as a woman in western Kansas recounted in 1935, "those tiny particles seemed to seep through the very walls. It got into cupboards and clothes closets; our faces were as dirty as if we had rolled in the dirt; our hair was gray and stiff and we ground dirt between our teeth." Farm animals lacked protection. The photographer Margaret Bourke-White observed that "cattle quickly become blinded. They run around in circles until they fall and breathe so much dust that they die."

Some farmers blamed the government for their woes; others blamed themselves. As dissatisfaction mounted, so too did the appeal of various demagogues who presented an analysis of American society that people understood: the wealthy and powerful were ruling people's lives

Demagogic Attacks

In the 1930s, Senator Huey Long *(center)* had a mass following and presidential ambitions. But he was assassinated in 1935, the evening this photograph was taken. When Long was shot, he fell into the arms of James O'Connor *(left),* a political crony. Louisiana Governor O. K. Allen *(right)* seized a pistol and dashed into the corridor in pursuit of the murderer shouting, "If there's shooting, I want to be in on it."   (Wide World Photos, Inc.)

from distant cities, eroding community morale and ruining family farms and small businesses. One of the best-known demagogues was Father Charles Coughlin, a Roman Catholic priest whose weekly radio sermons offered a curious combination of anticommunism and anticapitalism. In addition to criticizing the New Deal, Coughlin became increasingly anti-Semitic, telling his listeners that the cause of their woes was an international conspiracy of Jewish bankers.

Another challenge to the New Deal came from Dr. Francis E. Townsend, a public health officer in Long Beach, California, who was thrown out of work at age sixty-seven with only $100 in savings. Disturbed by the plight of old people, Townsend devised the Old Age Revolving Pensions plan, under which the government would pay monthly pensions of $200 to all citizens older than sixty on condition that they spent the money in the same month they received it. Townsend claimed his plan not only would aid the aged but would cure the depression by pumping enormous purchasing power into the economy. The plan was fiscally impossible but recognized the real needs of elderly Americans.

Then there was Huey Long, perhaps the most successful demagogue in American history. Long was elected governor of Louisiana in 1928 with the slogan "Every Man a King, but No One Wears a Crown." As a U.S. senator, Long at first supported the New Deal, but he began to believe that Roosevelt had fallen captive to big business. Long countered in 1934 with the Share Our Wealth Society, which advocated the seizure by taxation of all incomes greater than $1 million and all inheritances of more than $5 million. With the resulting funds, the government would furnish each family a homestead allowance of $5,000 and an annual income of $2,000. By mid-1935 Long's movement claimed 7 million members, and few doubted that Long aspired to the presidency. An assassin's bullet extinguished his ambition in September 1935.

Some politicians, like Governor Floyd Olson of Minnesota, declared themselves socialists in the 1930s.

Left-wing Critics

In Wisconsin the left-wing Progressive Party reelected Robert La Follette, Jr. (son of "Battling Bob"), to the Senate in 1934, sent seven of the state's ten representatives to Washington, D.C., and placed La Follette's brother Philip in the governorship. And the old muckraker and socialist Upton Sinclair won the Democratic gubernatorial nomination in California in 1934 with the slogan "End Poverty in California."

Perhaps the most controversial alternative to the New Deal was the Communist Party of the United States of America. In 1935 the party leadership changed its strategy. Proclaiming "Communism Is Twentieth Century Americanism," the Communists disclaimed any intention of overthrowing the U.S. government and began to cooperate with left-wing labor unions, student groups, and writers' organizations in a "Popular Front" against fascism abroad and racism at home. In 1938, at its high point for the decade, the party had fifty-five thousand members.

In addition to challenges from the right and the left, the New Deal was also subject to challenge by the

Supreme Court Decisions Against the New Deal

Supreme Court. Many New Deal laws had been hastily drafted, and the majority of the justices feared that the legislation had vested too much power in the presidency. In 1935 the Court unanimously struck down the NIRA (*Schechter v. U.S.*), asserting that it granted the White House excessive legislative power and that the commerce clause of the Constitution did not give the federal government authority to regulate intrastate businesses. Roosevelt's industrial recovery program was dead. In early 1936 his farm program met a similar fate when the Court invalidated the AAA (*U.S. v. Butler*), deciding that agriculture was a local problem and thus, under the Tenth Amendment, subject to state, not federal, action.

The Second New Deal and Roosevelt's Second Term

As Roosevelt looked ahead to the presidential election of 1936, he foresaw the danger of losing his capacity to lead and to govern. His broad coalition of special interests was breaking up, radicals and demagogues were offering Americans alternative programs, and the Supreme Court was dismantling the New Deal. In early 1935 Roosevelt took the initiative once more. So impressive was the spate of new legislation that historians call it the Second New Deal.

The Second New Deal differed in important ways from the first. When the chief legislative goal had been economic recovery, Roosevelt had cooperated with business. Beginning in 1935, however, he denounced business leaders for placing their own selfish interests above the national welfare. The first triumph

Emergency Relief Appropriation Act

of the Second New Deal was an innocuous-sounding but momentous law called the Emergency Relief Appropriation Act, which authorized the president to establish massive public works programs for the jobless. Among the programs funded by the Emergency Relief Appropriation Act were the Resettlement Administration, which resettled destitute families and organized rural homestead communities and suburban greenbelt towns for low-income workers; the Rural Electrification Administration, which brought electricity to isolated rural areas; and the National Youth Administration, which sponsored work-relief programs for young adults and part-time jobs for students.

Perhaps the best-known program funded by the Emergency Relief Appropriation Act was the Works Progress Administration (WPA), later renamed the Work Projects Administration. The WPA ultimately employed more than 8.5 million people and built 650,000 miles of highways and roads, 125,000 public buildings, and 8,000 parks, as well as numerous bridges, reservoirs, irrigation systems, sewage treatment plants, and playgrounds and swimming pools. Among its construction projects, the WPA built or renovated 5,900 schools, 2,500 hospitals, and 1,000 airfields. The WPA also operated nurseries for preschool children, and it established schools in which 1.5 million adults were taught to read and write.

The WPA also sponsored a multitude of cultural programs, which not only provided employment for artists, musicians, writers, and actors,

The New Deal's Cultural Programs

but brought art in myriad forms to the people. The WPA's Federal Theater Project brought vaudeville, circuses, and theater, including African American and Yiddish plays, to cities and towns across the country; its Arts Project hired painters and sculptors to teach their crafts in rural schools, and it commissioned artists to decorate post office walls with murals depicting ordinary life in America past and present; and its Federal Music Project sponsored 225,000 concerts by symphony orchestras, jazz groups, and folk musicians. Perhaps the most ambitious of the New Deal's cultural programs was the WPA's Federal Writers Project, which hired talented authors such as John Steinbeck and Richard Wright to write local guidebooks and regional and folk histories. Many of these writers, like many of the artists, musicians, and actors, were politically sympathetic with the struggles of workers and farmers, and the WPA's arts projects were as a result often controversial. Critics assailed them as left-wing propaganda, and in fact some of these artists were Marxists and a few were communists. However, as the historian Michael Denning has observed, the goal of this "Popular Front" culture was not to overthrow the government, but to recover a tradition of American radicalism through remembering, and celebrating artistically, the lives and labor of America's plain folk. Among the best-known writers' projects, for example, are the poignant "slave narratives," which were collected from formerly enslaved women and men, and the interviews with sharecroppers and textile workers published in *These Are Our Lives* (1939).

In 1935 Roosevelt also wanted new legislation aimed at controlling the activities of big business.

Control of Business

The Supreme Court had dissolved the government-business cooperation that had been the foundation of the First New Deal. In addition, businesspeople had become increasingly critical of Roosevelt and the New Deal, complaining that they were overtaxed and overregulated. If big business would not cooperate with government, Roosevelt decided, government should "cut the giants down to size" through antitrust suits and heavy corporate taxes. In 1935 he asked Congress to enact several major bills, including a labor bill sponsored by Senator Robert Wagner of New York, a Social Security bill, a measure to regulate public-utility holding companies, and a "soak-the-rich" tax bill.

When the summer of 1935, which constituted the Second Hundred Days, was over, the president had everything he had requested. First,

National Labor Relations Act

the National Labor Relations (Wagner) Act granted workers the right to unionize and bargain collectively with management. The act also created a new National Labor Relations Board empowered to guarantee democratic union elections and to penalize unfair labor practices by employers, such as firing workers for union membership.

The Social Security Act was a milestone that established old-age insurance under which workers who paid Social Security taxes out of their wages, matched by their employers, would receive retirement benefits beginning at age sixty-five. The act also created several welfare programs, including a cooperative federal-state system of unem-

Social Security Act

ployment compensation and Aid to Dependent Children (later renamed Aid to Families with Dependent Children, AFDC) for needy children in single-parent families.

Although a milestone, Social Security was in some ways a conservative measure. First, the government did not pay for old-age benefits; workers and their bosses did. Second, the tax was regressive in that the more workers earned, the less they were taxed proportionally. Third, it was deflationary because it took out of people's pockets money that it did not repay for years. Finally, the law had a disparate impact on Americans, as it excluded agricultural labor, domestic service, and "casual labor not in the course of the employer's trade or business." Thus a disproportionally high number of women and people of color, who worked as farm laborers, as domestic servants, and in service jobs in hospitals and restaurants, received no benefits. Nevertheless, the Social Security Act was a highly significant development. With its passage, the federal government took responsibility not only for the aged but also for the temporarily jobless, dependent children, and disabled people.

In the next two weeks Roosevelt gained the remainder of what he had asked for, including the Public Utility Holding Company (Wheeler-Rayburn) Act and the Wealth Tax Act, which some critics saw as the president's attempt to "steal Huey Long's thunder." The tax act helped achieve a slight redistribution of income by raising the income taxes of the wealthy. It also imposed a new tax on excess business profits and increased taxes on inheritances, large gifts, and profits from the sale of property.

The Second Hundred Days made it unmistakably clear that the president was once again in charge and preparing to run for reelection.

Election of 1936

Roosevelt won by a landslide, easily defeating the Republican nominee, Governor Alf Landon of Kansas, by a margin of 27.8 million votes to 16.7 million. The Democrats also won huge majorities in the House and Senate. Some observers even worried that the two-party system was about to collapse.

By 1936 Roosevelt and the Democrats had forged what observers have called the "New Deal coalition."

New Deal Coalition

This new alliance consisted of the urban masses—especially immigrants from southern and eastern Europe and their sons and daughters—organized labor, the eleven states of the Confederacy (the "Solid South"), and northern blacks (before the 1930s, most African Americans had voted Republican). With the New Deal coalition, the Democratic Party came to dominate the two-party system and would occupy the White House for most of the next thirty years.

But even Roosevelt's buoyant optimism and landslide victory could not sustain forward momentum in his second term. Some of Roosevelt's own actions, in fact, helped bring about the end of the New Deal.

Concerned that the Supreme Court would invalidate much of the Second Hundred Days legislation, as it had done to the First Hundred Days, Roosevelt concluded that what the federal judiciary needed was a more progressive world-view. His Judiciary Reorganization Bill of 1937 requested the authority to add a federal judge whenever an incumbent failed to retire within six months of reaching age seventy; the president also wanted the power to name up to fifty additional federal judges, including six to the Supreme Court. Roosevelt frankly envisioned using the reorganization as a mandate to create a Supreme Court sympathetic to the New Deal. Liberals joined Republicans and conservative Democrats in resisting the bill, and the president had to concede defeat. The bill he signed into law provided pensions to retiring judges but denied him the power to increase the number of federal judges.

Roosevelt's Court-packing Plan

The episode had a final, ironic twist. During the public debate over court packing, swing-vote justices on the Supreme Court began to vote in favor of liberal, pro–New Deal rulings. In short order the Court upheld both the Wagner Act (*NLRB v. Jones & Laughlin Steel Corp.*), ruling that Congress's power to regulate interstate commerce also involved the power to regulate the production of goods for interstate commerce, and the Social Security Act. Moreover, the new pensions encouraged judges older than seventy to retire, and the president was able to appoint seven new associate justices in the next four years, including notables such as Hugo Black, Felix Frankfurter, and William O. Douglas.

Another New Deal setback was the renewed economic recession of 1937–1939. Roosevelt had never abandoned his commitment to a balanced budget. In 1937, confident that the depression had largely been cured, he began to order drastic cut-

Recession of 1937–1939

backs in government spending. At the same time the Federal Reserve Board, concerned about a 3.6 percent inflation rate, tightened credit. The two actions sent the economy into a tailspin: unemployment climbed from 7.7 million in 1937 to 10.4 million in 1938. Soon Roosevelt resumed deficit financing.

The New Deal was in trouble in 1937 and 1938, and there ensued a wide-ranging ideological struggle to chart the future of liberal reform. Some New Dealers urged vigorous trustbusting; others advocated the resurrection of national economic planning as it had existed under the National Recovery Administration. But in the end Roosevelt rejected these alternatives and instead chose deficit financing as a quick fix to stimulate consumer demand and create jobs. And in 1939, with conflict over events in Europe commanding more and more of the nation's attention, the New Deal came to an end. Roosevelt sacrificed further domestic reforms in return for conservative support for his programs of military rearmament and preparedness. The last significant New Deal laws enacted were the National Housing Act (1937), which established the United States Housing Authority and built housing projects for low-income families; a new Agricultural Adjustment Act (1938); and the Fair Labor Standards Act (1938), which forbade labor by children younger than sixteen and established a minimum wage and forty-hour workweek for many, but by no means all, workers.

Industrial Workers and the Rise of the CIO

 New Deal legislation that gave workers the right to organize unions and bargain collectively invigorated the labor movement. Organizers in the coal fields told miners that "President Roosevelt wants you to join the union"; and join they did. In Woonsocket, Rhode Island, textile workers embraced the union as a right of American citizenship, and they compared it to the independence for which the American revolutionaries had fought. And in Flint, Michigan, a striking auto worker proudly compared his actions to those of Davy Crockett: "Yes sir, Chevy [Plant] No. 4 was my Alamo." Unions and "Americanism" went hand in hand, and workers in need responded. In 1929 union membership stood at 3.6 million; in mid-1938 it surpassed 7 million.

The gains, however, did not always come easily. Management resisted vigorously in the 1930s, relying on the police or hiring armed thugs to intimidate workers and break up strikes. Violence erupted in the steel, automobile, and textile industries and among lumber workers in the Pacific Northwest and teamsters in the Midwest. In 1934 a strike of longshoremen was met with violence by police on the docks of San Francisco; two union members were killed, and workers' anger spread to other industries. Eventually 130,000 workers joined the general strike.

Rivalry Between Craft and Industrial Unions

Labor confronted yet another obstacle in the American Federation of Labor (AFL) craft unions' traditional hostility toward industrial unions. Craft unions typically consisted of skilled workers in a particular trade, such as carpentry or plumbing. Industrial unions represented all the workers, skilled and unskilled, in a given industry. The organizational gains of the 1930s were impressive in industrial unions, as hundreds of thousands of workers organized in industries such as autos, garments, rubber, and steel.

Craft and industrial unions competed bitterly for control of the growing labor movement. Attempts to reconcile the craft and industrial union movements failed; and in 1935 John L. Lewis, a leading industrial unionist and head of the United Mine Workers, resigned as vice president of the AFL. He and other industrial unionists then formed the Committee for Industrial Organization (CIO). The AFL responded by suspending the CIO unions, and in 1938 the CIO held its first national convention, calling itself the Congress of Industrial Organizations. By that time CIO membership had reached 3.7 million, slightly more than the AFL's 3.4 million.

Sit-down Strikes

The CIO evolved during the 1930s into a pragmatic, bread-and-butter labor organization that brought together millions of workers, including numerous women and African Americans who never before had had an opportunity to join a union. One union, the United Auto Workers (UAW), scored a major victory in late 1936. The UAW demanded recognition from General Motors (GM), Chrysler, and Ford. When GM refused, workers at the Fisher Body plant in Flint, Michigan, launched a sit-down strike and refused to leave the building. To discourage the strikers, GM turned off

During the 1937 sit-down strike by automobile workers in Flint, Michigan, a women's "emergency brigade" of wives, mothers, daughters, sisters, and sweethearts conducted daily demonstrations at the plants. When the police sought to force the men out of Chevrolet Plant No. 9 by filling it with tear gas, the women armed themselves with clubs and smashed out the plant's windows to let in fresh air.   (Wide World Photos, Inc.)

the heat. When that tactic failed, GM called in the police, who were met by a barrage of steel bolts, coffee mugs, and bottles. The police then resorted to tear gas, and the strikers turned the plant's water hoses on them.

The strike lasted for weeks. General Motors obtained a court order to evacuate the plant, but the strikers stood firm, risking imprisonment and fines. With the support of their families and neighborhoods, and a women's "emergency brigade" that picketed and delivered food and supplies to the strikers, the UAW prevailed. GM agreed to recognize the union. Chrysler signed a similar agreement, but Ford held out for four more years. With these victories, the tactic of the sit-down strike spread dramatically; it was used by workers in the textile, glass, and rubber industries, as well as by dime-store clerks, janitors, dressmakers, and bakers. Most important, participation in the sit-downs gave the strikers self-respect.

In 1937 the Steel Workers Organizing Committee (SWOC) signed a contract with the nation's largest steelmaker, U.S. Steel, that guaranteed an eight-hour workday and a forty-hour workweek. Other steel companies, however, refused to go along. Confrontations between the so-called little steel companies and the SWOC soon led to violence. On Memorial Day, strikers and their families joined sympathizers on the picket line in front of the Republic Steel plant in Chicago. Violence erupted, the police opened fire, ten strikers were killed, and forty suffered gunshot wounds. The police explained that the marchers had attacked them with clubs and bricks and that they had responded with reasonable force to defend themselves and disperse the mob. Some newspapers agreed, among them the anti-labor *Chicago Tribune*, which described the attack as an invasion by "a trained military unit of a revolutionary

Memorial Day Massacre

body." The strikers saw it differently; the police, they argued, without provocation had brutally attacked citizens who were peacefully asserting their constitutional rights.

Though senseless, the Memorial Day Massacre was not surprising. During the 1930s industries had hired private police agents and accumulated large stores of arms and ammunition for use in deterring workers from organizing and joining unions. Meanwhile, the CIO continued to enroll new members. By 1938 industrial unions had enlisted 600,000 miners, 375,000 steelworkers, 400,000 auto workers, and

How do historians know...

that police officers were largely responsible for the 1937 Memorial Day Massacre in Chicago? There is both photographic and medical evidence of the police's culpability. Covering the story at the Republic Steel plant were a cameraman from Paramount News and photographers from *Life* magazine and the Wide World Photos syndicate. Paramount News suppressed its film footage, claiming that releasing it "might very well incite local riots," but an enterprising reporter alerted a congressional committee to its existence, and a private viewing was arranged. Spectators at this showing, the reporter noted, "were shocked and amazed by scenes showing scores of uniformed policemen firing their revolvers pointblank into a dense crowd of men, women, and children, and then pursuing the survivors unmercifully as they made frantic efforts to escape." Medical evidence also substantiated the picketers' version: none of the ten people killed by police had been shot from the front. Clearly, the demonstrators had been trying to flee the police when they were shot or clubbed to the ground.   (Photo: World Wide Photos, Inc.)

300,000 textile workers. By the end of the decade the CIO had succeeded in organizing most of the nation's mass-production industries.

Mixed Progress for People of Color

 In 1930 about three-fourths of all African Americans lived in the South. Almost all southern blacks were prohibited from voting or serving on juries. They were routinely denied access to hospitals, universities, public parks, and swimming pools. And they were hired only for the least desirable, most menial jobs. Blacks living in rural areas in the South were propertyless sharecroppers, tenants, or wage hands. Caught in a cycle of poverty and disease, their life expectancy was ten years less than that of whites. The Great Depression plunged the vast majority of African Americans deeper into fear, political disfranchisement, Jim Crow segregation, and privation. And the specter of the lynch mob was a continuing threat in the South: in 1929, seven black men were lynched; in 1930, twenty; in 1933, twenty-four.

Racism also plagued African Americans living in the North. Southern blacks who migrated to northern cities found that employers discriminated against them. Black unemployment rates ran high; in Pittsburgh 48 percent of black workers were jobless in 1933, compared with 31 percent of white laborers. In northern industries in the 1930s, African Americans were the last hired and the first fired.

As African Americans were aware, President Herbert Hoover shared prevailing white racial attitudes.

Hoover and African Americans

Hoover sought a lily-white Republican Party and attempted to push blacks out of the party in order to attract white southern Democrats. He appointed few blacks to federal of-

Numerous African American families were evicted from their farms during the Great Depression. White planters who received government payments for taking land out of cultivation were supposed to share these payments with their tenants and sharecroppers. Instead, many kicked these families off the land and kept the money for themselves. This family in Putnam County, Georgia, loaded all its possessions into a rickety truck for the trip north.   (National Archives)

fice, rejected appeals for a federal antilynching law, and perpetuated the segregation of the army and of facilities in federal buildings in the nation's capital. In 1930 the president demonstrated his racial insensitivity by nominating Judge John J. Parker of North Carolina to the Supreme Court. Ten years earlier Parker had endorsed the disfranchisement of blacks. The NAACP remembered and protested his nomination. The AFL joined the protest, and the joint opposition plus liberal votes in the Senate defeated Parker's nomination, 41 to 39.

Shortly thereafter, a celebrated trial revealed the ugliness of race relations in the depression era. In

Scottsboro Trials

March 1931 nine African American teenagers who were riding a freight train near Scottsboro, Alabama, were arrested and charged with roughing up some white hoboes and throwing them off the train. Two white women removed from the same train claimed the nine men had raped them. Medical evidence later showed that the women were lying. But within two weeks, eight of the so-called Scottsboro boys were convicted of rape by all-white juries and sentenced to death. After the failure of several appeals, the first defendant, Haywood Patterson, was condemned to die. A Supreme Court ruling intervened, however, on the ground that African Americans were systematically excluded from juries in Alabama. Patterson was found guilty again in 1936 and was given a seventy-five-year jail sentence. Four of the other youths were sentenced to life imprisonment. Not until 1950 were all five out of jail—four by parole and Patterson by escaping from a work gang.

The Brotherhood of Sleeping Car Porters, under the astute leadership of A. Philip Randolph, fought for the rights of black workers. In

Organized Opposition

Harlem the militant Harlem Tenants League fought rent increases and evictions, and African American consumers began to boycott white merchants who refused to hire blacks as clerks. Their slogan was "Don't Buy Where You Can't Work." But America's white leaders made few concessions. Only the Supreme Court provided a measure of protection for African Americans at this time. It declared unconstitutional the Texas law that barred blacks from voting in the Democratic primaries, and it attempted to correct the abuse in the Scottsboro trials.

African Americans coped with their white-circumscribed environment and fought racism in a va-

riety of ways. Lawyers for the NAACP, notably Charles Hamilton Houston and Thurgood Marshall, sued southern and border state universities for providing facilities for African American students that were separate, but decidedly unequal. The NAACP was victorious in 1938, when the Supreme Court ruled (*Missouri ex rel. Gaines v. Canada*) that Missouri, by offering a legal education only to qualified white law students, gave whites a "privilege" that was "denied to Negroes by reason of their race." Thus the Supreme Court ordered Missouri to establish a separate law school for its qualified African Americans.

With the election of Franklin D. Roosevelt, blacks' attitudes toward government changed, as did their political affiliation. For African Americans—an important component of the New Deal coalition—Franklin D. Roosevelt would become the most appealing president since Abraham Lincoln. For one thing, Roosevelt was a decided improvement over Hoover, and the personal magnetism and buoyancy he exhibited in his fireside chats seemed to speak directly to them. Blacks also were heartened by photographs of African American visitors at the White House, many of whom came to see Eleanor Roosevelt, and by news stories about Roosevelt's black advisers. Most important, through the WPA and other relief programs, the New Deal aided black people in their struggle for economic survival.

The "Black Cabinet," or black brain trust assembled by Roosevelt, was unique in U.S. history. Never before had there been so many

Black Cabinet

African American advisers at the White House. Among the consultants were black lawyers, journalists, and Ph.D.'s and black experts on housing, labor, and social welfare. William H. Hastie and Robert C. Weaver, holders of advanced degrees from Harvard, served in the Department of the Interior. Mary McLeod Bethune, educator and president of the National Council of Negro Women, was director of the Division of Negro Affairs of the National Youth Administration. Also among the New Dealers were some whites who had committed themselves to first-class citizenship for African Americans. Foremost among these people was Eleanor Roosevelt. In 1939, when the acclaimed black contralto Marian Anderson was barred from performing in Washington's Constitution Hall by its owners, the Daughters of the American Revolution, Eleanor Roosevelt arranged for Anderson to sing at the Lincoln Memorial on Easter Sunday.

Mary McLeod Bethune, pictured here with her friend and supporter Eleanor Roosevelt, became the first African American woman to head a federal agency as director of the Division of Negro Affairs of the National Youth Administration.   (Corbis-Bettmann)

The president himself, however, remained uncommitted to African American civil rights. Fearful of alienating southern white Democrats, who controlled Congress and important committees such as the House Ways and Means Committee, he never endorsed two key goals of the civil rights struggle: a federal law against lynching and abolition of the poll tax. Moreover, many New Deal programs functioned in ways that were definitely damaging to African Americans. Rather than benefiting black tenant farmers and sharecroppers, the AAA had the effect of forcing many of them off the land. The Federal Housing Administration (FHA) refused to guarantee mortgages on houses purchased by blacks in white neighborhoods, the CCC was racially segregated, and the TVA followed local custom in handing out skilled jobs to whites first. Also, Social Security coverage and the minimum-wage provisions of the Fair Labor Standards Act of 1938 excluded menial occupations. This meant that janitors, farm workers, and domestics, many of whom were African Americans, received no benefits or protection.

Racism in the New Deal

Since its inception in the 1930s, America's welfare system has privileged white people over people of color, especially African Americans. With the New Deal's racial inequities in mind, the historian George Lipzitz has written that "the racialized nature of social democratic policies has . . . actually increased the possessive investment in whiteness among European Americans over the past half-century." Thus, while New Deal programs were generally inclusive of whites, they persistently excluded large numbers of blacks and other people of color from access to the things that American society defined as essential to first-class citizenship and human dignity, including decent housing and rewarding work.

"The Possessive Investment in Whiteness"

In short, although African Americans benefited from the New Deal, they did not get anything approaching their fair share. Even so, the large majorities they gave Roosevelt at election time demonstrated their appreciation for the aid they did receive. Not all African Americans, however, trusted the mixed message of the New Deal. Some concluded that they could depend only on themselves and organized self-help and direct-action movements. In 1934 black tenant farmers and sharecroppers joined with poor whites to form the Southern Tenant Farmers' Union. In the North, blacks organized tenants' unions, boycotted stores, and launched "Jobs for Negroes" campaigns. In 1935 when police in Harlem beat to death a black youth, a race riot erupted as mobs of poor and angry people smashed store windows and raided shelves. Working-class blacks criticized the NAACP for ignoring the economics of second-class citizenship and for being too middle class and legalistic in its war on racism. The NAACP was scoring notable victories in opening up graduate and professional schools to black students, but critics charged that these gains benefited only the middle class, not the masses who above all needed jobs.

Nowhere was the trend toward direct action more evident than in the March on Washington Movement in 1941. That year, billions of federal dollars flowed

March on Washington Movement

into American war industries as the nation rearmed for the possibility of another world war. Thousands of new jobs were created, but discrimination deprived blacks of a reasonable proportion of them. One executive notified black job applicants that "the Negro will be considered only as janitors and other similar capacities." Randolph, leader of the porters' union, proposed that blacks march on the nation's capital to demand equal access to jobs in defense industries.

By early summer thousands were ready to march. Fearing that the march might provoke riots and that communists might infiltrate the movement, Roosevelt announced that he would issue an executive order prohibiting discrimination in war industries and in the government if the march was canceled. The result was Executive Order No. 8802, which established the Fair Employment Practices Committee (FEPC). The March on Washington Movement anticipated future

In 1940 American Indians in Florida asked John Collier, U.S. commissioner of Indian affairs, to save their deer from slaughter in a government drive to eradicate cattle ticks. Collier (seated and wearing a white shirt) came to Miami to meet with Indians and hear their grievances.   (Wide World Photos, Inc.)

trends in the civil rights movement: it was all-black; its tactic was direct action, a threat by the masses to take to the streets; and its beneficiaries were the urban working class.

Another group, American Indians, sank further into malnutrition and disease during the Hoover ad-

A New Deal for Native Americans

ministration. In the early 1930s in Oklahoma, where the Choctaws, Cherokees, Seminoles, and other tribes lived on infertile soil, three-fourths of all Native American children were undernourished. Tu-

berculosis swept through the reservations. At the heart of the problem was a 1929 ruling by the U.S. comptroller general that landless tribes were ineligible for federal aid. Not until 1931 did the Bureau of Indian Affairs take steps to relieve the suffering. A federal relief program was launched to provide aid, and Congress substantially increased the bureau's budget that year; yet much of the money went to hire more bureaucrats.

Beginning in 1933, the New Deal approach to Native Americans differed greatly from that of earlier administrations; as a result, Indians benefited more directly than blacks from the New Deal. As commissioner of Indian affairs, Roosevelt appointed John Collier, founder of the American Indian Defense Association, who sought an end to the allotment policy established by the Dawes Severalty Act of 1887 (see page 467). The Indian Reorganization (Wheeler-Howard) Act (1934) aimed to reverse the increasing landlessness of Native Americans by restoring lands to tribal ownership and forbidding future division of Indian lands into individual parcels. Other provisions of the act enabled tribes to obtain loans for economic development and to establish self-government. Under Collier, the Bureau of Indian Affairs also encouraged the perpetuation of Indian religions and cultures. In a remarkable about-face, one order stated, "The cultural history of Indians is in all respects to be considered equal to that of any non-Indian group."

Mexican Americans also suffered extreme hardship during the Great Depression, but no government programs benefited them. During

Depression Hardships of Mexican Americans

these years many Mexicans and Mexican Americans packed up their belongings and moved south of the border; some did so willingly, but others were either deported by immigration officials or given one-way tickets to Mexico by California officials eager to purge

Many Mexican farm workers *(braceros)* were deported in the early 1930s, but by the end of the decade growers eager for the return of this source of cheap labor began to recruit trainloads of Mexicans as farm laborers in southwestern states. This photo, taken by Dorothea Lange in 1938, shows one of these workers.   (Dorothea Lange Collection, Oakland Museum of California, City of Oakland. Gift of Paul S. Taylor)

them from the relief rolls. According to the federal census, the Mexican-born population in the United States dropped from 617,000 in 1930 to 377,000 in 1940.

In addition, many employers changed their minds about the desirability of hiring Mexican American farm workers. Before the 1930s farmers had boasted that Mexican Americans were an inexpensive, docile labor supply and that they would not join unions. But in the 1930s Mexican Americans overturned the stereotype by engaging in prolonged and sometimes bloody strikes. In the San Joaquin valley, eighteen thousand cotton pickers walked off the fields in 1933 and set up a "strike city" after being evicted from the growers' camps. Shortly thereafter, their union hall was riddled with bullets, and two strikers died.

The New Deal offered Mexican Americans little help. The AAA was created to assist property-owning farmers, not migratory farm workers. The Wagner Act did not cover farm workers' unions, nor did the Social Security Act or the Fair Labor Standards Act cover farm laborers. One New Deal agency, the Farm Security Administration (FSA), was established in 1937 to help farm workers, in part by setting up migratory labor camps. But the FSA came too late to help Mexican Americans, most of whom by then had been replaced in the fields by dispossessed white farmers from the Dust Bowl states.

Women, Work, and the Great Depression

During the depression women had to work overtime to maintain themselves and their families. In *It's Up to the Women* (1933), Eleanor Roosevelt wrote that "women know that life must go on and that the needs of life must be met." Wives and mothers followed the maxim "Use it up, wear it out, make it do, or do without." Women bought day-old bread and cheap cuts of meat; they relined old coats with blankets, and they saved string, rags, and broken crockery for future use. Many families were able to maintain their standard of living only because of astute spending and because women substituted their own labor for goods and services they once purchased. Husbands shared these financial concerns, but it was usually women's responsibility to do the family budgeting; it was estimated that wives and mothers in the 1930s allocated over 80 percent of all family income.

While they were cutting corners to make ends meet, women were also seeking paid work outside the home. In 1930 approximately 10.5 million women were paid workers; ten years later, the female labor force exceeded 13 million. Many women were their families' sole providers and had to do it all, at home and on the job. Despite these social realities, most Americans believed that women should not take jobs outside the home, that they should strive instead to be good wives and mothers, and that women who worked were doing so for "pin money" to buy frivolous extras. When a 1936 Gallup poll asked whether wives should work if their husbands had jobs, 82 percent of the respondents (including 75 percent of the women) answered "no."

Women at Work Outside the Home

These attitudes resulted in severe job discrimination. For example, of the fifteen hundred urban school systems surveyed by the National Education Association in 1930 and 1931, 77 percent said that they refused to hire married women as teachers, and 63 percent said that they fired female teachers who married while employed. Most insurance companies, banks, railroads, and public utilities had similar policies against hiring married women. And from 1932 to 1937, federal law prohibited more than one family member from working for the civil service. Because wives usually earned less than their husbands, they were the ones who quit their government jobs.

Job Discrimination Against Married Women

In part, such thinking stemmed from the widely held belief that a woman who worked caused a man to be unemployed. That view missed the point, for three reasons. First, women were heavily concentrated in "women's jobs," including clerical positions, teaching, and nursing. Men rarely sought these jobs and probably would not have been hired to fill them had they applied. Second, most women workers (71 percent in 1930) were single and thus self-supporting. Third, the wages for "women's jobs" trailed far behind those for "men's jobs." Lagging further behind were women of color, some of whom lost their low-paying menial jobs to white women during the depression.

Although the preponderance of working women were single, married women too went to work during the depression. By 1940 married women constituted 35 percent of the female work force, up from 29 percent in 1930 and 15 percent in 1900. They worked to keep their families from slipping into poverty, but their assistance with family expenses did not improve their status. As the sociologists Robert and Helen Lynd observed at the time: "The men, cut adrift from their usual routine, lost most of their sense of time and dawdled helplessly and dully about the streets; while in the homes the women's world remained largely intact and the round of cooking, housecleaning, and mending became if anything more absorbing." And even though women were making greater contributions to the family, their husbands, including those without jobs, still expected to rule the roost and to remain exempt from childcare and housework.

Wives and Husbands Face Hard Times

The New Deal did take women's needs into account, but only when forcefully reminded to do so

Women in the New Deal

by the activist women who advised the administration. These women, mainly government and Democratic Party officials, formed a network united by their commitment to social reform, to protective laws for women's health and safety on the job, and to the participation of women in politics and government. The network's most prominent member was Eleanor Roosevelt, who was her husband's valued adviser. Secretary of Labor Frances Perkins was the nation's first woman cabinet officer. Other historic New Deal appointments included the first woman federal appeals judge and the first women ambassadors. Molly Dewson, head of the Democratic Party's Women's Division, noted with pride: "The change from women's status in government before Roosevelt is unbelievable."

Even with increased participation by women, however, New Deal provisions for women were mixed. The maximum-hour and minimum-wage provisions mandated by the NRA won women's support. Women workers in the lowest-paying jobs, many of whom labored under sweatshop conditions, had the most to gain from these standards. Some NRA codes mandated pay differentials based on gender, however, making women's minimum wages lower than men's. Federal relief agencies, such as the Civil Works Administration (1933) and the Federal Emergency Relief Administration, hired only one woman for every eight to ten men placed in relief jobs. A popular New Deal

Enacted in 1935, Social Security has been one of the most enduring of all New Deal programs. This poster urges eligible Americans to apply promptly for their Social Security cards. (Library of Congress)

program, the Civilian Conservation Corps, was limited to young men. And women in agriculture and domestic service were not protected by the 1938 Fair Labor Standards Act.

Most important, the 1935 Social Security Act excluded not only agricultural labor and domestic service, as already noted, but also occupations in the public sector. That meant that many teachers, nurses, librarians, and social workers, the majority of whom were women, went uncovered. Although Social Security originally contained no retirement provisions for spouses or widows, in 1939 Congress added such benefits. But the Social Security amendments of 1939 were also far from inclusive. They were based on the government's unstated social policy of preserving the traditional family in which the husband was the breadwinner and the wife was the stay-at-home caregiver. Accordingly, the Social Security amendments of 1939 provided retirement benefits for women who had been supported by their husbands, including widows, but not for single women who were separated or divorced.

Nevertheless, significant changes in women's lives were imminent. The reason for the changes, however, was not that the government would suddenly decide to address women's equality with men, but that beginning in 1941 the country would be at war—a war it could not win without employing womanpower in the nation's aircraft factories, shipyards, and munitions works.

The Election of 1940 and the Legacy of the New Deal

 No president had ever served more than two terms, and as the presidential election of 1940 approached, many Americans speculated about whether Franklin Roosevelt would run for a third term. Roosevelt seemed undecided until the spring of 1940, when Adolf Hitler's military advances in Europe apparently convinced him to stay on.

The Republican candidate was Wendell Willkie, an Indiana lawyer and utilities executive. A former Democrat, Willkie had become **Wendell Willkie** a prominent business opponent of Roosevelt's agenda and campaigned vigorously against the New Deal, contending that its meddling in business had failed to return the nation to prosperity. He also criticized the government's lack of military preparedness. But Roosevelt preempted the defense issue by expanding military and naval contracts. As workers streamed into the factories to fill new orders, unemployment figures dropped as well. When Willkie reversed his approach and accused Roosevelt of warmongering, the president promised Americans, "Your boys are not going to be sent into any foreign wars."

Willkie never did come up with an effective campaign issue, and on election day Roosevelt received 27 million popular votes to Willkie's 22 million. In the electoral college Roosevelt buried Willkie 449 to 82 (see Map 25.3). Willkie did manage to win the farm and small-town vote in the Midwest, but the New Deal coalition was triumphant. As in 1936, Roosevelt won in the cities, primarily among blue-collar workers, ethnic Americans, and African Americans. He also carried every state in the South. Although the New Deal was over at home, Roosevelt was still riding a wave of public approval.

Any analysis of the New Deal must begin with Franklin Delano Roosevelt himself. Assessments of his career varied widely during his presidency. Most historians consider him a truly great president, citing his

Map 25.3   Presidential Election, 1940   Roosevelt won an unprecedented third term in the 1940 presidential election. He did not repeat his landslide 1936 victory, in which he won all but two states. But he did capture thirty-eight states in 1940 to Republican Wendell Willkie's ten.

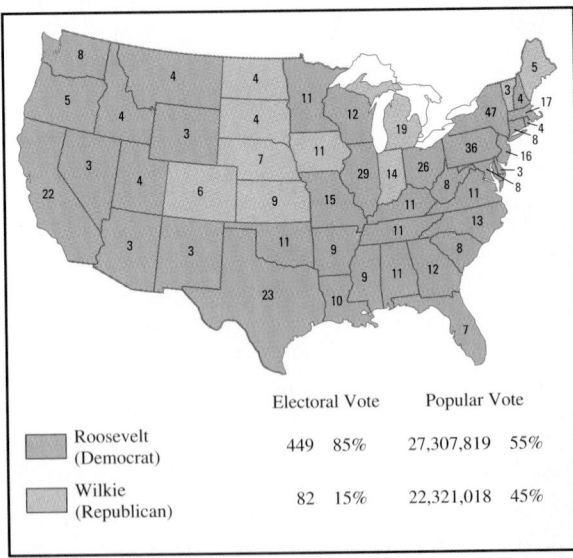

	Electoral Vote		Popular Vote	
Roosevelt (Democrat)	449	85%	27,307,819	55%
Wilkie (Republican)	82	15%	22,321,018	45%

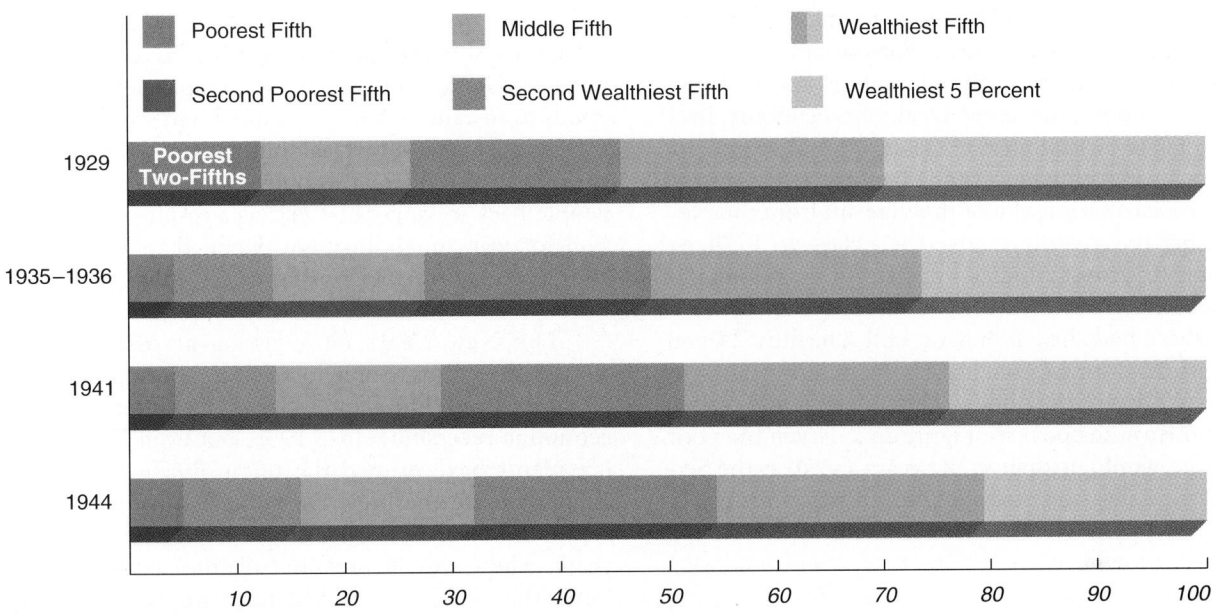

Figure 25.2   Distribution of Total Family Income Among the American People, 1929–1944 (Percentage)   Although the New Deal provided economic relief to the American people, it did not, as its critics so often charged, significantly redistribute income downward from the rich to the poor.   (Source: Adapted from U.S. Bureau of the Census, *Historical Statistics of the United States, Colonial Times to 1970,* 2 parts [Washington, D.C.: U.S. Government Printing Office, 1975], Part 1, p. 301.)

Roosevelt and the New Deal Assessed

courage and buoyant self-confidence, his willingness to experiment, and his capacity to inspire the nation during the most somber days of the depression. Those who criticize him charge that he lacked vision and failed to formulate a bold and coherent strategy of economic recovery and political and economic reform. He was not a socialist but a capitalist: he wanted to alleviate suffering but not at the expense of private property and the profit motive. Essentially he was a pragmatist whose goal was to preserve the system.

Even scholars who criticize Roosevelt's performance agree that he transformed the presidency. "Only Washington, who made the office, and Jackson, who remade it, did more than Roosevelt to raise it to its present condition of strength, dignity, and independence," according to political scientist Clinton Rossiter. Roosevelt personified the presidency, and with his fireside chats he became the first president to use the radio to appeal directly for the people's sup-

port. Other scholars, however, have charged that it was Roosevelt who initiated "the imperial presidency." Whether for good or ill, Roosevelt strengthened not only the presidency but the whole federal government. "For the first time for many Americans," the historian William Leuchtenburg has written, "the federal government became an institution that was directly experienced. More than state and local governments, it came to be the government."

In the past, the federal government had served primarily as an economic regulator and facilitator. During the New Deal the government not only added to its regulatory responsibilities, including overseeing the nation's stock markets, but it became an economic guarantor and stimulator as well. For the first time the federal government assumed a responsibility to offer relief to the jobless and the needy, and for the first time it resorted to deficit spending to stimulate the economy. Millions of Americans benefited from government

Origins of America's Welfare System

programs that are still operating today. The New Deal laid the foundation of the welfare system on which subsequent presidential administrations would build.

Although the government's role in the economy expanded under the New Deal, the economy itself continued to be capitalistic. The profit motive and private property remained fundamental to the system. Some redistribution of wealth did result from the New Deal, but the wealthy survived as a class. In 1929, for example, the most affluent 5 percent of the population received 30 percent of total family income. By 1941 their share had shrunk but was still a healthy 24 percent. Most of the income lost by the wealthy ended up in the pockets of the middle and upper-middle classes, not those of the poor (see Figure 25.2). Even the poor, however, would prosper in the years ahead, as the Second World War created jobs for all working Americans.

Summary

The New Deal brought about limited change in the nation's power structure. Beginning in the 1930s, business interests had to share their political clout with others. Labor gained influence in Washington, and farmers got more of what they wanted from Congress and the White House. If people wanted their voices to be heard, they had to organize into labor unions, trade associations, or other special-interest lobbies. Not everybody's voice was heard, however. Because of the persistence of racism, there was no real increase in the power of African Americans and other minorities.

The New Deal was a liberal, evolutionary reform program, not a revolutionary break with the past. Although the New Deal coalition emerged as a political force in the 1930s, New Deal ideas such as the TVA and Social Security had been around for decades. Moreover, prominent New Dealers had been active in reform movements since the Progressive era. Historians generally view the New Deal as a movement that benefited middle-class Americans. According to William Leuchtenburg, the New Deal "swelled the ranks of the bourgeoisie but left many Americans—sharecroppers, slum dwellers, most Negroes—outside of the new equilibrium."

The New Deal failed in one fundamental purpose: to put people back to work. As late as 1939, more than 10 million men and women were still jobless. That year, unemployment was 19 percent; over the next two years it fell no lower than 14 percent. What plagued the nation throughout the 1930s was underconsumption: people and businesses did not purchase enough goods to sustain high levels of employment. In the end it was not the New Deal but massive government spending during the Second World War that put people back to work. In 1941, as a result of mobilization for war, unemployment declined to 10 percent, and in 1944, at the height of the war, only 1 percent of the labor force was jobless.

The New Deal's most lasting accomplishments were its programs to ameliorate the suffering of unemployed people. The United States has suffered several economic recessions since 1945, but even Republican presidents have primed the pump during periods of slump. Before the New Deal, the United States had experienced a major depression every fifteen to twenty years. The Great Depression was the last of its kind. Since the New Deal, thanks to unemployment compensation, Social Security, and other measures, the United States has not experienced another such national nightmare.

LEGACY FOR A PEOPLE AND A NATION
Social Security for Retired Americans

In breaking with historical precedent by authorizing old-age insurance, as well as unemployment compensation and aid to dependent children, the Social Security Act of 1935 became the single most important piece of social welfare legislation in American history. Under Social Security, working Americans today still make monthly payments for old-age, survivors, and disability insurance (OASDI). Although Social Security initially excluded some of America's neediest citizens from participation in OASDI, such as people working in low-paying menial jobs, amendments to the law eased eligibility requirements. Twenty-four million Americans made monthly payments to the OASDI fund in 1939; ten years later, the figure had risen to 34 million. Legislation in the 1950s extended OASDI to self-employed workers, including farmers. By 1970, 69 million Americans were covered under OASDI; by 1980 that number had doubled; and by 1997 the figure had ballooned to 172 million. Prior to the enactment of Social Security, millions of elderly Americans had lived in poverty. But a 1999 study showed that Social Security benefits kept a third of the nation's elderly from slipping into poverty and helped significantly to narrow the income disparities between women and men in old age.

Today, Americans worry about the future of Social Security. They fear that the tens of millions of baby boomers born in the 1940s, 1950s, and early 1960s will bankrupt the system when they retire in the twenty-first century. Many also know that in the 1980s and 1990s the federal government raided the Social Security trust fund, diverting billions of dollars to pay for the skyrocketing national debt. Some reduction of the system's responsibilities has also occurred; in 1996, reflecting Americans' hostility to welfare, Congress passed and President Bill Clinton signed a law elimi-nating aid to families with dependent children and greatly tightening eligibility requirements for public assistance. The future of Social Security is hotly debated today, both in and out of government. Two of the most important proposals are, first, to allow Americans to invest their retirement contributions in the stock market and, second, to impose a federal "lock box" law that would safeguard Social Security's trust funds from future federal tampering.

For Further Reading, see page A-29 of the Appendix. For Web resources, go to http://college.hmco.com.

In 1921 the Rockefeller Foundation declared war on the mosquito in Latin America. As the carrier of yellow fever, the biting insect *Aedes aegypti* transmitted a deadly virus that caused severe headaches, vomiting, jaundice (yellow skin), and, for many, death. With clearance from the U.S. Department of State, the foundation dedicated several million dollars for projects to control yellow fever in Latin America, beginning with Mexico. Learning from the pioneering work of Carlos Juan Finlay of Cuba, Oswaldo Cruz of Brazil, and U.S. Army surgeon Walter Reed, scientists sought to destroy the mosquito in its larval stage, before it became an egg-laying adult.

Nothing less than U.S. hegemony in the hemisphere seemed at stake. U.S. diplomats, military officers, and business executives agreed with foundation officials that the disease threatened public health, which in turn disturbed political and economic order. When outbreaks occurred, ports were closed and quarantined, disrupting trade and immigration. The infection struck down American officials, merchants, investors, and soldiers stationed abroad. Workers became incapacitated, reducing productivity. Throughout Latin America, insufficient official attention to yellow-fever epidemics stirred public discontent against regimes the United States supported. When the Panama Canal opened its gates to ships from around the world in 1914, some leaders feared that the death-dealing disease would spread, even reinfecting the United States, which had suffered its last epidemic in 1905.

In Veracruz, a Mexican province of significant U.S. economic activity where American troops had invaded in 1914, a yellow-fever outbreak in 1920 killed 235 people. The next year, gradually overcoming strong local anti-U.S. feelings, Rockefeller personnel painstakingly inspected breeding places in houses and deposited larvae-eating fish in public waterworks. In 1924 La Fundación Rockefeller declared yellow fever eradicated in Mexico. In Latin America, the founda-

Officials of the Brazilian Federal Health Service, in cooperation with the Rockefeller Foundation, spray houses in Bahía to control mosquitoes during a campaign in the 1920s to battle yellow fever. (Courtesy of the Rockefeller Archive Center)

PEACESEEKERS AND WARMAKERS: AMERICANS IN THE WORLD 1920–1941

tion's antimosquito campaign proved successful in maritime and urban areas but less so in rural and jungle regions. Rockefeller Foundation efforts in the 1920s and 1930s also carried political effects: strengthening central governments by providing a national public health infrastructure and helping diminish anti-U.S. sentiment in a region known for virulent anti-Yankeeism.

The Rockefeller Foundation's drive to eradicate the mosquito exemplifies Americans' fervent but futile effort to build a stable international order between the First and Second World Wars. After World War I, Americans did not cut themselves off from international affairs, despite the tag "isolationist" that is sometimes still applied to U.S. foreign relations during the interwar decades. They remained very active in world affairs in the 1920s and 1930s—from gunboats on Chinese rivers, to negotiations in European financial centers, to marine occupations in Haiti and Nicaragua, to Hollywood films in Great Britain, to oil wells in the Middle East, to campaigns against diseases in Africa and Latin America. President Wilson had it right when he said after the First World War that the United States had "become a determining factor in the history of mankind, and after you have become a determining factor you cannot remain isolated, whether you want to or not."

"Internationalism has come," declared Senator Gilbert Hitchcock, "and we must choose what form the internationalism is to take." The most apt description of interwar U.S. foreign policy is "independent internationalism." That is, the United States was active on a global scale but retained its independence of action, its traditional unilateralism. American interests abroad were far-flung and vast—colonies, client states, naval bases, investments, trade, missionaries, humanitarian projects. Nevertheless, many Americans did think of themselves as isolationists, by which they meant that they wanted no part of Europe's political squabbles, military alliances and interventions, or the League of Nations, which might drag them unwillingly into war. Americans, then, were isolationists in their desire to avoid war but independent internationalists in their activities to shape the world to their liking.

In the aftermath of the First World War, Americans had grown disenchanted with military methods of achieving order and protecting American prosperity and security. "We can never herd the world into the paths of righteousness with the dogs of war," said Herbert Hoover. American diplomats thus increasingly sought to exercise the power of the United States through conferences, humanitarian programs, cultural penetration ("Americanization"), moral lectures and calls for peace, nonrecognition of disapproved regimes, arms control, and economic and financial ties under the Open Door principle. In Latin America, for example, U.S. leaders downgraded military interventions to fashion a Good Neighbor policy.

But a stable world order proved elusive. Some nations schemed to disrupt it, and severe economic problems undercut it. Public health projects saved countless lives but could not address the low living standards and staggering poverty of dependent peoples across the globe. The debts and reparations bills left over from the First World War bedeviled the 1920s, and the Great Depression of the 1930s shattered world trade and finance. The depression threatened America's prominence in international markets; it also spawned revolutions in Latin America and political extremism, militarism, and war in Europe and Asia. As Nazi Germany marched toward world war, the United States tried to protect itself from the conflict by adopting a policy of neutrality. At the same time, the United States sought to defend its interests in Asia against Japanese aggression by invoking the Open Door policy.

In the late 1930s, and especially after the outbreak of European war in September 1939, many Americans came to agree with President Franklin D. Roosevelt that Germany and Japan imperiled the national interest because they were building exclusive, self-sufficient spheres of influence based on military power and economic domination. Roosevelt first pushed for American military preparedness and then for the abandonment of neutrality in favor of aiding Britain and France. A German victory in Europe, he reasoned, would undermine Western political principles, destroy traditional economic ties, threaten U.S. influence in the Western Hemisphere, and place at the pinnacle of European power a fanatical man—Adolf Hitler—whose ambitions and barbarities seemed limitless.

At the same time, Japan seemed determined to dismember America's Asian friend China, to emasculate the Open Door principle by creating a closed economic sphere in Asia, and to endanger a U.S. colony—the Philippines. To deter Japanese expansion in the Pacific, the United States ultimately cut off supplies of vital American products such as oil. But economic warfare only intensified antagonisms. Japan's surprise attack on Pearl Harbor, Hawai'i, in December 1941 finally brought the United States into the Second World War. ■

IMPORTANT EVENTS

1921–22 Washington Conference limits naval arms
Rockefeller Foundation begins battle against yellow fever in Latin America

1922 Mussolini comes to power in Italy
Fordney-McCumber Tariff raises duties

1924 Dawes Plan eases German reparations
U.S. troops leave Dominican Republic

1926 U.S. troops occupy Nicaragua

1927 Jiang breaks with Communists in China

1928 Kellogg-Briand Pact outlaws war

1929 Great Depression begins
Young Plan reduces German reparations

1930 Hawley-Smoot Tariff raises duties

1931 Japan seizes Manchuria

1932 Stimson Doctrine protests Japanese control of Manchuria
Roosevelt elected president

1933 Hitler establishes Nazi regime in Germany
U.S. recognizes Soviet Union
Good Neighbor policy for Latin America

1934 Batista comes to power in Cuba
Export-Import Bank founded to expand trade
Johnson Act forbids loans to debt-defaulting countries
Reciprocal Trade Agreements Act lowers tariffs
U.S. troops withdraw from Haiti

1935 Italy invades Ethiopia
Neutrality Act stops U.S. arms shipments

1936 U.S. votes for nonintervention at Pan-American Conference
Germany reoccupies the Rhineland
Spanish Civil War breaks out between Loyalists and Franco's fascists

Neutrality Act forbids U.S. loans to belligerents
Rome-Berlin Axis created
Germany and Japan unite against Soviet Union in the Anti-Cominterm Pact

1937 Neutrality Act creates cash-and-carry trade with warring nations
Sino-Japanese War breaks out
Quarantine speech against aggressors
Ponce Massacre in Puerto Rico

1938 Mexico nationalizes American-owned oil companies
Munich Conference grants part of Czechoslovakia to Germany

1939 Nazi-Soviet Pact carves up eastern Europe
Germany invades Poland
Second World War begins
U.S. repeals arms embargo to help Allies

1940 Soviet Union invades Finland
Germany invades Denmark, Belgium, the Netherlands, and France
Committee to Defend America by Aiding the Allies formed
Germany, Italy, and Japan join in Tripartite Pact
U.S. and Great Britain swap destroyers for military bases
Isolationists form America First Committee
Selective Training and Service Act starts first peacetime draft

1941 Lend-Lease Act gives aid to Allies
Germany attacks Soviet Union
U.S. freezes Japanese assets
Atlantic Charter produced at Roosevelt-Churchill meeting
Roosevelt exploits *Greer* incident
Japanese flotilla attacks Pearl Harbor, Hawai'i
U.S. enters Second World War

Searching for Peace and Order in the 1920s

 In the early 1920s Secretary of State Charles Evans Hughes predicted that "there will be no permanent peace unless economic satisfactions are enjoyed." Like the nation's business leaders, Hughes expected Ameri-

can economic expansion to promote international stability—that is, out of economic prosperity would spring a world free from political extremes, revolution, arms races, aggression, and war.

The First World War left Europe in shambles. Between 1914 and 1921, Europe suffered 60 million casualties from world war, civil war, massacre, epidemic, and famine. Germany and France both lost 10 percent of their workers. Crops, livestock, factories, trains, forests, bridges—little was spared. The American Relief Administration and private charities delivered food to needy Europeans, including Russians wracked by famine in 1921 and 1922. Americans hoped not only to feed desperate Europeans but also to dampen any appeal political radicalism might have for them.

The Women's Peace Union (WPU) distributed this flier in the 1920s to remind Americans of the human costs of the First World War. One of many peace societies active in the interwar years, the WPU lobbied for a constitutional amendment requiring a national referendum on a declaration of war. In the 1930s Representative Louis Ludlow (Democrat of Indiana) worked to pass such a measure in Congress, but he failed. (Schwimmer-Lloyd Collection, Freida Langer Lazarus Papers. The New York Public Library, Astor, Lenox, and Tilden Foundations)

War Is a Crime Against Humanity

Gassed; Near Dun-sur-Meuse, in the Woods, France

To you who are filled with **horror** at the sufferings of war-ridden mankind;

To you who remember that **ten million men** were slaughtered in the last war;

To you who have the courage to face the reality of **war, stripped of its sentimental "glory"**;

We make this appeal:—

Eight years since the signing of the Armistice! And peace is still hard beset by preparations for war. In another war men, women and children would be more wantonly, more cruelly massacred, by death rays, gas, disease germs, and machines more fiendish than those used in the last war. Those whom you love must share in its universal destruction.

Can You Afford Not To Give Your Utmost To Cleanse The World Of This Black Plague Of Needless Death and Suffering?

Send your contribution to an uncompromising Peace organization

THE WOMEN'S PEACE UNION
39 Pearl Street, New York

We Believe that Violence and Bloodshed Are Always Wrong in Principle and Disastrous in Practice. We Are working to Make War Illegal and to Ensure World Peace.

Senator Henry Cabot Lodge gloated in 1920 that "we have destroyed Mr. Wilson's League of Nations and . . . we have torn up Wilsonism by the roots." Not quite. The Geneva-headquartered League of Nations, envisioned as a peacemaker, did prove feeble, not just because the United States did not join but because members failed to utilize the new organization to settle important disputes. And, starting in the mid-1920s, American officials participated discreetly in League meetings on public health, prostitution, drug and arms trafficking, counterfeiting of currency, and other questions. American jurists served on the Permanent Court of International Justice (World Court), though the United States also refused to join that League body. The Rockefeller Foundation donated $100,000 a year to the League to support its work in public health.

American peace societies worked for international stability, many of them keeping alive the Wilsonian preference for a world body. During the interwar years, peace groups such as the Fellowship of Reconciliation and the National Council for Prevention of War drew widespread public support. Women peace advocates gravitated to several of their own organizations because they lacked influence in the male-dominated groups and because of the popular assumption that women—as life givers and nurturing mothers—had a unique aversion to violence and war. Carrie Chapman Catt's moderate National Conference on the Cure and Cause of War, formed in 1924, and the more radical U.S. Section of the Women's International League for Peace and Freedom (WILPF), organized in 1915 under the leadership of Jane Addams and Emily Greene Balch, became the largest women's peace groups (see page 639). When Addams won the Nobel Peace Prize in 1931, she transferred her award money to the League of Nations.

Peace Groups

Most peace groups pointed to the carnage of the First World War and the futility of war as a solution to international problems, but they differed over strategies to ensure world order. Some urged cooperation with the League and World Court. Others championed the arbitration of disputes, disarmament and arms reduction, the outlawing of war, and strict neutrality during wars. The WILPF called for an end to U.S. economic imperialism, which, the organization claimed, compelled the United States to intervene militarily in Latin America to protect U.S. business interests. The Women's Peace Union (organized in 1921) lobbied for a constitutional amendment to require a national referendum on a declaration of war. The Carnegie Endowment for International Peace (founded in 1910) promoted peace education through publications. Quakers, YMCA officials, and Social Gospel clergy in 1917 created the American Friends Service Committee to identify pacifist alternatives to warmaking. All in all, peaceseekers believed that their various reform activities could and must deliver a world without war.

The Washington Conference of November 1921–February 1922 seemed to mark a substantial step toward peace through arms control.

Washington Conference on the Limitation of Armaments

At the invitation of the United States, delegates from Britain, Japan, France, Italy, China, Portugal, Belgium, and the Netherlands joined U.S. diplomats to discuss limits on naval armaments. Britain, the United States, and Japan were facing a naval arms race whose huge military spending endangered economic rehabilitation. American leaders also worried that an expansionist Japan, with the world's third largest navy, would overtake the United States, ranked second behind Britain.

The conference produced three treaties. The Five-Power Treaty set a ten-year moratorium on the construction of capital ships (battleships and aircraft carriers) and established total tonnage limits of 500,000 for Britain and the United States, 300,000 for Japan, and 175,000 for France and Italy. The first three nations actually agreed to dismantle some existing vessels to satisfy the 5:3:1.75 ratio. They also pledged not to build new fortifications in their Pacific possessions (such as the Philippines). In the Nine-Power Treaty, the conferees reaffirmed the Open Door in China, recognizing Chinese sovereignty. In the Four-Power Treaty, the United States, Britain, Japan, and France agreed to respect one another's Pacific possessions. The three treaties did not limit submarines, destroyers, or cruisers; nor did they provide enforcement powers for the Open Door declaration.

Peace advocates also welcomed the Locarno Pact of 1925, several agreements among European nations

Kellogg-Briand Pact

that sought to reduce tensions between Germany and France, and the Kellogg-Briand Pact of 1928. In the latter document, sixty-two nations agreed to "condemn recourse to war for the solution of international controversies, and renounce it as an instrument of national policy." The accord passed the Senate 85 to 1, but many senators

French Foreign Minister Aristide Briand (1862–1932) *(left)* and U.S. Secretary of State Charles Evans Hughes (1862–1948) join other diplomats at the Washington Conference of 1921–1922, where they negotiated a naval arms control agreement. Years later Briand helped craft the Kellogg-Briand Pact outlawing war. A graduate of Brown University and Columbia Law School, Hughes also served on the Supreme Court at two different times: 1910–1916 (associate justice) and 1930–1941 (chief justice). Conservative and reserved (Theodore Roosevelt called him "the bearded iceberg"), Hughes argued that the United States must be internationalist, leading the world to respect law and order.   (National Archives)

considered it little more than a statement of moral preference because it lacked enforcement provisions. Although weak, the Kellogg-Briand Pact reflected popular opinion that war was barbaric and wasteful, and the agreement stimulated serious public discussion of peace and war. But arms limitations, peace pacts, and efforts by peace groups and international institutions all failed to muzzle the dogs of war, which fed on the economic troubles that upended world order.

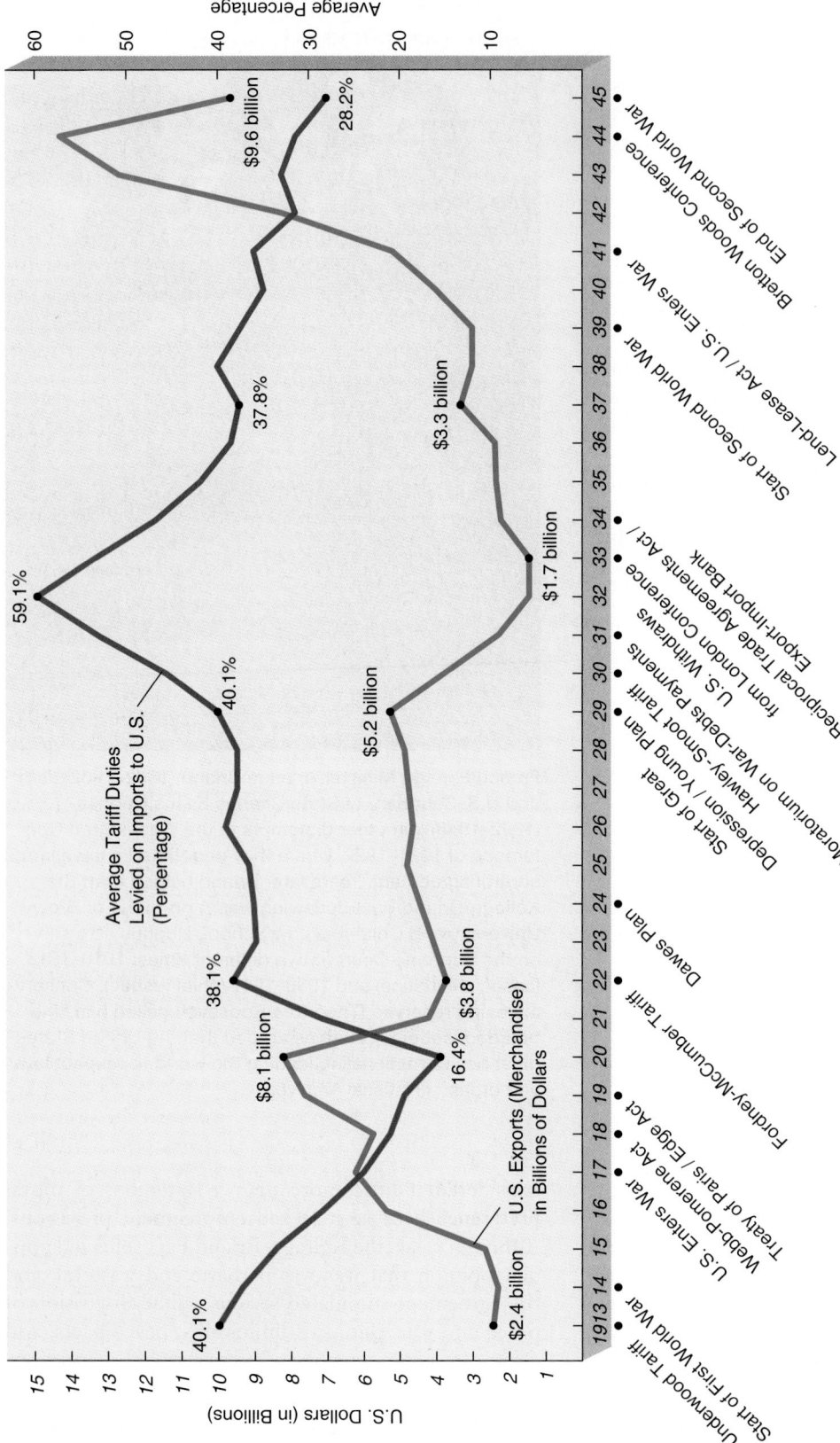

Figure 26.1 **The United States in the World Economy** In the 1920s and 1930s, global depression and war scuttled the United States's hope for a stable economic order. This graph suggests, moreover, that high American tariffs meant lower exports, further impeding world trade. The Reciprocal Trade Agreements program initiated in the early 1930s was designed to ease tariff wars with other nations. (Source: U.S. Bureau of the Census, *Historical Statistics of the United States, Colonial Times to 1970* [Washington, D.C., 1975].)

The World Economy, Cultural Expansion, and Great Depression

 While Europe struggled to recover from the ravages of the First World War, the international economy wobbled and then, in the early 1930s, collapsed. The Great Depression set off a political chain reaction that carried the world to war. Cordell Hull, secretary of state under President Franklin D. Roosevelt from 1933 to 1944, often pointed out that political extremism and militarism sprang from maimed economies. "We cannot have a peaceful world," he warned, "until we rebuild the international economic structure." Hull proved right.

For leaders such as Hughes and Hull, who believed that economic expansion by the United States would

U.S. Trade and Investment

stabilize world politics, America's prominent position in the international economy seemed opportune. Because of World War I, the United States became a creditor nation and the financial capital of the world (see Figure 26.1). From 1914 to 1930, private investments abroad grew fivefold to more than $17 billion. By the late 1920s the United States produced nearly half of the world's industrial goods and ranked first among exporters ($5.2 billion worth of shipments in 1929). For example, General Electric invested heavily in Germany, American companies began to exploit Venezuela's rich petroleum resources, and U.S. firms began to challenge British control of oil resources in the Middle East. Britain and Germany lost ground to American businesses in Latin America, where Standard Oil operated in eight nations and the United Fruit Company became a huge landowner.

America's economic prominence facilitated the export of American culture. Hollywood movies saturated the global market and stimu-

Cultural Expansion

lated interest in American ways and products. In Britain, where American silent and talkie films dominated, one woman from a mining town recalled seeing on the screen "all these marvelous [American] film stars. Everything was bright. I just wanted to go there and be like them." Although some foreigners warned against "Americanization," others aped American mass-production methods and emphasis on efficiency and modernization. Coca-Cola opened a bottling plant in Essen, Germany, and Ford built an automobile assembly plant in Cologne. The German writer Hans Joachim claimed that this cultural adop-

tion might help deliver a peaceful, democratic world because "our interest in elevators, radio towers, and jazz was . . . an attitude that wanted to convert the flame thrower into a vacuum cleaner." Germans marveled at Henry Ford's economic success and industrial techniques ("Fordismus"), buying out copies of his translated autobiography, *My Life and Work* (1922). In the 1930s, the Nazi leader Adolf Hitler sent German car designers to Detroit before he launched the Volkswagen. Further advertising the American capitalist model were the Phelps-Stokes Fund, exporting to black Africa Booker T. Washington's Tuskegee philosophy of education, and the Rockefeller Foundation, battling diseases in Latin America and Africa, supporting colleges to train doctors in Lebanon and China, and funding medical research and nurses' training in Europe.

The U.S. government assisted this cultural and economic expansion. The Webb-Pomerene Act (1918) excluded from antitrust prosecution those combinations set up for export trade; the Edge Act (1919) permitted American banks to open foreign branch banks; and the overseas offices of the Department of Commerce gathered and disseminated valuable market information. The federal government also stimulated foreign loans by American investors, discouraging those that might be used for military purposes. "In these days of competition," an American diplomat explained, "capital, trade, agriculture, labor, and statecraft all go hand in hand if a country is to profit." U.S. government support for the expansion of the telecommunications industry helped International Telephone and Telegraph (ITT), Radio Corporation of America (RCA), and the Associated Press (AP) become international giants by 1930. The U.S. Navy's cooperation with Juan T. Trippe's Pan American airline company helped its "flying boats" reach Asia.

Europeans watched American economic expansion with wariness and branded the United States

War Debts and German Reparations

stingy for its handling of World War I debts and reparations. Twenty-eight nations became entangled in the web of inter-Allied government debts, which totaled $26.5 billion ($9.6 billion of it owed to the U.S. government). Europeans owed private American creditors another $3 billion. Europeans urged Americans to erase the government debts as a magnanimous contribution to the war effort. During the war, they angrily charged, Europe had bled while America profited. "There is only one way we could be worse with the Europeans," remarked the humorist Will

John D. Rockefeller, Jr. (1874–1960), second from right, traveled to China in 1921 for the dedication of the Peking Union Medical College, a project of the Rockefeller Foundation, the philanthropic organization founded in 1913 by the oil industrialist John D. Rockefeller, Sr. At the center of this photograph is Xu Shi Chang (1855–1939), China's president. (Courtesy of the Rockefeller Archive Center)

Rogers, "and that is to have helped them out in two wars instead of one." American leaders insisted on repayment, some pointing out that the victorious European nations had gained vast territory and resources as war spoils. Senator George Norris of Nebraska, emphasizing domestic priorities, declared that the United States could build highways in "every county seat" if only the Europeans would pay their debts.

The debts question became linked to Germany's $33 billion reparations bill—an amount some believed Germany had the capacity but not the willingness to pay. In any case, hobbled by inflation and economic disorder, Germany began to default on its payments. To keep the nation afloat and to forestall the radicalism that might thrive on economic troubles, American bankers loaned millions of dollars. A triangular relationship developed: American investors' money flowed to Germany, Germany paid reparations to the Allies, and the Allies then paid some of their debts to the United States. The American-crafted Dawes Plan of 1924 greased the financial tracks by reducing Germany's annual payments, extending the repayment period, and providing still more loans. The United States also gradually scaled down Allied obligations, cutting the debt by half during the 1920s.

But the triangular arrangement depended on continued German borrowing in the United States, and in 1928 and 1929 American lending abroad dropped sharply in the face of more lucrative opportunities in the stock market at home (see Chapters 24 and 25). The U.S.-negotiated Young Plan of 1929, which reduced Germany's reparations, salvaged little as the world economy sputtered and collapsed. That year Britain rejected an offer from President Herbert Hoover to trade its total debt for British Honduras (Belize), Bermuda, and Trinidad. By 1931, when Hoover declared a moratorium on payments, the Allies had paid back only $2.6 billion. Staggered by the Great Depression—an international catastrophe—they defaulted on the rest. Annoyed with Europe, Congress in 1934 passed the Johnson Act, which forbade U.S. government loans to foreign governments in default on debts owed to the United States.

As the depression accelerated, tariff wars revealed a reinvigorated economic nationalism. By 1932 some twenty-five nations had retaliated against rising American tariffs (created in the Fordney-McCumber Act of 1922 and the Hawley-Smoot Act of 1930) by imposing higher rates on foreign imports. From 1929 to 1933, world trade declined in value by some 40 percent. Exports of American merchandise slumped from $5.2 billion to $1.7 billion.

Tariffs and Economic Nationalism

Many nations contributed to the worldwide economic cataclysm. The United States might have lowered its tariffs so that Europeans could sell their goods in the American market and thus earn dollars to pay off their debts. Americans also might have worked for a comprehensive, multinational settlement. Instead, at the London Conference in 1933, President Roosevelt barred U.S. cooperation in international currency stabilization. Vengeful Europeans might have trimmed Germany's huge indemnity. The Germans might have borrowed less from abroad and taxed themselves more. The Soviets might have agreed to pay rather than repudiate Soviet Russia's $4 billion debt.

A revival of world trade, Secretary Hull insisted, not only would help the United States pull itself out of the economic doldrums but also

Reciprocal Trade Agreements Act

would boost the chances for global peace. Calling the protective tariff the "king of evils," he successfully pressed Congress to pass the Reciprocal Trade Agreements Act in 1934. This important legislation empowered the president to reduce U.S. tariffs by as much as 50 percent through special agreements with foreign countries. The central feature of the act was the most-favored-nation principle, whereby the United States was entitled to the lowest tariff rate set by any nation with which it had an agreement. If, for example, Belgium and the United States granted each other most-favored-nation status, and Belgium then negotiated an agreement with Germany that reduced the Belgian tariff on German typewriters, American typewriters would receive the same low rate.

In 1934 Hull also helped create the Export-Import Bank, a government agency that provided loans to foreigners for the purchase of American goods. The bank stimulated trade and became a diplomatic weapon, allowing the United States to exact concessions through the approval or denial of loans. But in the short term, Hull's ambitious programs—examples of America's independent internationalism—brought only mixed results.

U.S. Hegemony in Latin America

Through the Platt Amendment, Roosevelt Corollary, Panama Canal, military intervention, and economic preeminence the United States had thrown an imperial net over Latin America in the early twentieth century (see Chapter 22). U.S. hegemony in the hemisphere

Cordell Hull (1871–1955) served as secretary of state from 1933 to 1944, concentrating on trade expansion, relations with Latin America, and negotiations with Japan. A Tennessean, Hull became known for his methodical style, hill-country drawl and lisp, and deep commitment to the premise that wars grow out of international economic competition. President Franklin Roosevelt, who relied on friends for advice and sent personal envoys on overseas diplomatic missions, often ignored Hull.   (Brown Brothers)

grew apace after the First World War. A prominent State Department officer patronizingly remarked that Latins were incapable of political progress because of their "low racial quality." They were, however, "very easy people to deal with if properly managed." And managed they were. American-made schools, roads, telephones, and irrigation systems dotted Caribbean and Central American nations. American "money doctors" in Colombia and Peru helped reform tariff and tax laws and invited U.S. companies to build public works. Washington forced private high-interest loans on the Dominican Republic and Haiti as ways to wield influence there. In El Salvador, Honduras, and Costa Rica, the State Department pressed governments to silence anti-imperialist intellectuals. U.S. soldiers occupied Cuba, the Dominican Republic, Haiti, Panama,

CANADA

Ottawa

ATLANTIC

OCEAN

UNITED
STATES

San Francisco

Washington, D.C.

Roosevelt's Good Neighbor Policy, 1933

U.S. troops, 1917–1922
U.S. investors dominate sugar industry
Revolution of 1933
U.S. abrogates Platt Amendment, 1934
Batista era, 1934–1959

U.S. upholds right of intervention at
Pan-American Conference, 1928

U.S. troops, 1915–1934
Financial supervision, 1916–1941

MEXICO

Gulf
of
Mexico

Miami

THE BAHAMAS
Nassau

U.S. financial supervision, 1905–1941
U.S. troops withdrawn, 1924
Trujillo era, 1930–1961

Constitution of 1917 challenges U.S. interests
Nationalization of foreign oil companies, 1938
U.S.-Mexico agreement settles oil dispute, 1942

Guantánamo
Havana CUBA
JAMAICA

DOMINICAN
REP.

San
Juan

VIRGIN IS. (US,UK)

Mexico
City

HAITI

PUERTO
RICO (US)

U.S. colony since 1917

Belmopan
BELIZE
HONDURAS
Tegucigalpa
NICARAGUA
Managua

Kingston
Port-au- Santo
Prince Domingo

U.S. colony
Jones Act grants U.S. citizenship, 1917

GUATEMALA
Guatemala City
EL SALVADOR San
Salvador

Caribbean Sea

U.S. invasion, 1924
United Fruit Company active

San José
COSTA
RICA
PANAMA

Caracas
Panama
VENEZUELA

Georgetown
Paramaribo
GUYANA Cayenne
SURINAM
FRENCH
GUIANA
(FR.)

U.S. financial supervision, 1911–1924
U.S. military occupation, 1912–1925
U.S. war against Sandino, 1926–1933
Somoza era, 1936–1979

Bogotá
COLOMBIA

U.S. control of Canal Zone
Declaration of Panama, 1939

ECUADOR
Quito

U.S. oil investments

PERU
Lima

BRAZIL

La Paz
BOLIVIA

Brasília

U.S. copper interests

PACIFIC

OCEAN

CHILE

PARAGUAY

Asunción

0   500   1000 Km.
0   500   1000 Mi.

Santiago

Buenos Aires URUGUAY
Montevideo
ARGENTINA

U.S. votes for nonintervention pledge
at Pan-American Conference, 1936

Map 26.1 The United States and Latin America Between the Wars The United States often
intervened in other nations to maintain its hegemonic power in Latin America, where nationalists resented outside meddling in their sovereign affairs. The Good Neighbor policy decreased U.S. military interventions, but U.S. economic interests remained strong in the hemisphere.

and Nicaragua. U.S. authorities maintained Puerto Rico as a colony (see Map 26.1).

By 1929 direct American investments in Latin America (excluding bonds and securities) totaled $3.5 billion, while U.S. exports dominated the trade of the area. Country after country experienced the repercussions of U.S. economic and political decisions. For example, the price that Americans set for Chilean copper determined the health of Chile's economy. North American oil executives bribed Venezuelan politicians for tax breaks. Latin American nationalists protested that their resources were being drained away as profits for U.S. companies, leaving too many nations in a status of dependency. A distinguished Argentine writer, Manuel Ugarte, asserted that the United States had become a new Rome that annexed wealth rather than territory, but unapologetic Americans believed that they were bringing not only material improvements to Latin American neighbors but also the blessings of liberty.

Criticism of U.S. imperialism in the region mounted in the interwar years. The president of Panama, a country dominated by the

Criticisms of U.S. Interventionism

Canal Zone and, in 1925, occupied by U.S. military forces seeking to put down a popular revolt, told a diplomat that he was tired of being "treated" by Washington "like a child." Senator William Borah of Idaho urged that Latin Americans be granted the right of self-determination, letting them decide their own futures. Others charged that U.S. presidents were usurping constitutional power by ordering troops abroad without a congressional declaration of war. Businesspeople feared that Latin American nationalists would direct their anti-Yankee feelings against American-owned property. Some Americans also became troubled by the double standard that prevailed. Hoover's secretary of state, Henry L. Stimson, acknowledged the problem in 1932 when he was protesting Japanese incursions in China: "If we landed a single soldier among those South Americans now . . . it would put me absolutely in the wrong in China, where Japan has done all this monstrous work under the guise of protecting her nationals with a landing force."

Renouncing unpopular military intervention, the United States shifted to other methods to maintain its influence in Latin America: Pan-Americanism, support for strong local leaders, the training of national guards, economic and cultural penetration, Export-Import Bank loans, financial supervision, and political

Good Neighbor Policy

subversion. Although this general approach predated his presidency, Franklin D. Roosevelt gave it a name in 1933: the Good Neighbor policy. It meant that the United States would be less blatant in its domination—less willing to defend exploitative business practices, less eager to launch military expeditions, and less reluctant to consult with Latin Americans. "Give them a share," Roosevelt recommended. In 1936, for example, the United States restored some sovereignty to Panama and increased that nation's income from the canal. Such acts greatly enhanced Roosevelt's popularity in Latin America.

To avoid military interventions and occupations, the United States trained Latin American national guards and supported dictators. For

National Guards and Dictators

example, before the United States withdrew its troops from the Dominican Republic in 1924, U.S. per-

This U.S. government recruiting poster captured the postwar American mood of independent internationalism by offering overseas duty to prospective marines.   (Library of Congress)

sonnel created a guard. One of its first officers was Rafael Leonidas Trujillo, who became head of the national army in 1928 and, through fraud and intimidation, became president two years later. Trujillo ruled the Dominican Republic with an iron fist until his assassination in 1961. "He may be an S.O.B.," Roosevelt supposedly remarked, "but he is our S.O.B."

Nicaraguans endured a similar experience. U.S. troops occupied Nicaragua from 1912 to 1925 and returned in late 1926 during a civil war. Nationalistic, anti-imperialist Nicaraguan opposition, led by César Augusto Sandino, who denounced the Monroe Doctrine as meaning "America for the Yankees," prompted Washington to end the occupation and move toward the Good Neighbor policy. In 1933 the marines departed, but they left behind a powerful national guard headed by General Anastasio Somoza, who "always played the game fairly with us," recalled a top U.S. officer. With backing from the United States, the Somoza family ruled Nicaragua from 1936 to 1979 through corruption, political suppression, and torture. The revolutionaries who overthrew the Somoza dictatorship in 1979 called themselves Sandinistas in honor of the patriot Sandino, who, more than three decades earlier, had battled the marines before he was assassinated by Somoza henchmen.

The marine occupation of black, French-speaking Haiti from 1915 to 1934 also left a negative legacy.

Marine Occupation of Haiti

U.S. officials censored the Haitian press, manipulated elections, wrote the constitution, jailed or killed protesters, managed government finances, and created a national guard. The National City Bank of New York became the owner of the Haitian Banque Nationale, and the United States became Haiti's largest trading partner. The American high commissioner, General John H. Russell of Georgia, boasted that the Haitian president "has never taken a step without first consulting me." In 1929 Haitians protested violently against foreign rule. U.S. soldiers withdrew, and Haiti continued to suffer Latin America's highest illiteracy rate, lowest per capita income, and poorest health, as well as dictatorship and police-state repression.

The Cubans, too, grew restless under North American domination. By 1929 North American investments in the Caribbean nation totaled $1.5 billion, including two-thirds ownership of the sugar industry. The U.S. military uniform remained conspicuous at the Guantá-

Backing Batista in Cuba

namo naval base. Especially among elites, American influences continued to permeate Cuban culture. In 1933 Cubans rebelled against the dictator and U.S. ally Gerardo Machado. In open defiance of U.S. warships cruising offshore, Professor Ramón Grau San Martín became president and declared the Platt Amendment null and void. His government also seized some North American–owned mills, refused to repay American bank loans, and debated land reform. Unsettled by this nationalistic "social revolution," U.S. officials plotted with army sergeant Fulgencio Batista to overthrow Grau in 1934.

During the Batista era, which lasted until Fidel Castro dethroned Batista in 1959 (see page 847), Cuba attracted and protected U.S. investments while it aligned itself with U.S. foreign policy goals. In return, the United States provided military aid and Export-Import Bank loans, abrogated the unpopular Platt Amendment, and gave Cuban sugar a favored position in the U.S. market. Cuba became further incorporated into the North American consumer culture, and American tourists flocked to Havana's night life of rum, rhumba, prostitution, and gambling. Nationalistic Cubans protested that their nation had become a mere extension—a dependency—of the United States.

In Puerto Rico throughout the 1920s and 1930s, incompetent and often tactless U.S. officials on the Caribbean island disparaged Puerto Ricans as people of color unfit to govern themselves. The Jones Act of 1916 had granted Puerto Ricans U.S. citizenship, but the United States rejected calls for the colony's independence or statehood. A few absentee American landowners and corporate barons made sugar the island's major economic activity. Under U.S. paternalism, schools and roads were improved, but 80 percent of the island's rural folk remained landless, and others crowded into urban slums. New Deal relief programs fell far short of need. Students, professors, and graduates of the Universidad de Puerto Rico formed the nucleus of islanders critical of U.S. tutelage. Some founded the Nationalist Party under the leadership of the Harvard-trained lawyer Pedro Albizo Campos, who eventually advocated the violent overthrow of U.S. rule. Police fired on a Nationalist Party march in 1937; nineteen people, including two policemen, died in the Ponce Massacre. Other Puerto Ricans followed the socialist Luis Muñoz Marín, whose Popular Democratic Party ultimately settled for the compromise of commonwealth status (officially conferred in 1952). To this day,

Control over Puerto Rico

Puerto Ricans remain divided into statehood, commonwealth, and independence factions (see page 631).

Mexico stood as a unique case in inter-American relations. Woodrow Wilson had sent troops there in 1914 and 1916 to tame the Mexican Revolution's anti-Americanism. But the opposite occurred. In 1917 the Mexicans openly threatened American-owned landholdings and oil interests by adopting a new constitution specifying that all "land and waters" and all subsoil raw materials (such as petroleum) belonged to the Mexican nation. U.S. officials worried that if Mexico succeeded in restricting the ownership of private property, other Latin Americans might also defy U.S. hegemony. For years, with some Americans claiming that Mexico had succumbed to Bolshevism, and Hollywood films disparagingly portraying Mexicans as villainous "greasers" and *bandidos*, Washington and Mexico City wrangled over the rights of U.S. economic interests. Still, the United States stood as Mexico's chief trading partner, accounting for 61 percent of Mexico's imports and taking 52 percent of its exports in 1934.

Clash with Mexican Nationalism

In 1938, during a petroleum workers' strike for higher wages and recognition, foreign oil companies, including Standard Oil, arrogantly rejected union appeals, hoping to send a message across the hemisphere that economic nationalism could never succeed. In a statement of economic independence, the Mexican government led by President Lázaro Cárdenas boldly expropriated the property of all foreign-owned petroleum companies, calculating that the approaching war in Europe would restrain the United States from attacking his country. The United States countered by reducing purchases of Mexican silver and promoting a multinational business boycott against the nation. But President Roosevelt decided to compromise because he feared that the Mexicans would increase oil sales to Germany and Japan. In a 1942 agreement the United States conceded that Mexico owned its raw materials and could treat them as it saw fit, and Mexico compensated the companies for their lost property. Although American investments in and trade with Mexico remained large, U.S. power there had been diminished. Nationalists across Latin America drew inspiration from Mexico's defiance of its giant neighbor.

Roosevelt's movement toward nonmilitary methods—the Good Neighbor policy—was also expressed in Pan-Americanism. Throughout the 1920s the United States had refused to renounce its self-declared

Ambassador Josephus Daniels (1862–1948) *(second from left)* and Mexican President Lázaro Cárdenas (1895–1970) *(second from right)* enjoy a cordial moment during the often stormy relations between the United States and Mexico in the 1930s. When Cárdenas attempted to regain control of his nation's oil resources from multinational corporations through expropriation, Daniels defended him as a "New Dealer" seeking to improve his country's living standards. Accepting Daniels's description and calling Cárdenas "one of the few Latin leaders who was actually preaching and trying to practice democracy," President Roosevelt compromised with Mexico in 1941. (Library of Congress)

Pan-Americanism

right of intervention in the hemisphere. In 1936, however, at the Pan-American Conference in Buenos Aires, U.S. officials endorsed nonintervention. The new policy marked a distinct change from the Roosevelt Corollary and marine expeditions. One payoff was the Declaration of Panama (1939), in which Latin American governments drew a security line around the hemisphere and warned aggressors away. In exchange for more U.S. trade and foreign aid, Latin Americans also reduced their sales of raw materials to Germany, Japan, and Italy and increased shipments to the United States. On the eve of the Second World War, then, the U.S. sphere of influence in the hemisphere seemed intact, and most Latin American regimes backed U.S. diplomatic objectives. For a long time, however, memories of American strong-arm methods fueled nationalism throughout the region.

Nazi Germany, the Soviet Union, and War in Europe

In depression-wracked Germany, Adolf Hitler came to power in 1933. Like Benito Mussolini, who had gained control of Italy in 1922, Hitler was a fascist. Fascism (called Nazism, or National Socialism, in Germany) was a collection of ideas and prejudices that celebrated supremacy of the state over the individual; of dictatorship over democracy; of authoritarianism over freedom of speech; of a regulated, state-oriented economy over a free-market economy; and of militarism and war over peace. The Nazis vowed not only to revive German economic and military strength but also to cripple communism and "purify" the German "race" by destroying Jews and other people, such as homosexuals and Gypsies, whom Hitler disparaged as inferiors.

The German leader Adolf Hitler (1889–1945) is surrounded in this propagandistic painting by images that came to symbolize hate, genocide, and war: Nazi flags with emblems of the swastika, the iron cross on the dictator's pocket, Nazi troops in loyal salute. The anti-Semitic Hitler denounced the United States as a "Jewish rubbish heap" of "inferiority and decadence" that was "incapable of conducting war." (U.S. Army Center of Military History)

Resentful of the punitive terms of the 1919 Treaty of Versailles, Hitler immediately withdrew Germany from the League of Nations, ended reparations payments, and began to rearm. While secretly laying plans for the conquest of neighboring states, he watched admiringly as Mussolini's troops invaded the African nation of Ethiopia in 1935. The next year Hitler ordered his own goose-stepping troopers into the Rhineland, an area that the Versailles treaty had demilitarized. When Germany's timid neighbor France did not resist this act, Hitler crowed: "The world belongs to the man with guts!"

German Aggression Under Hitler

Soon the aggressors joined hands. In 1936 Italy and Germany formed an alliance called the Rome-Berlin Axis. Shortly thereafter Germany and Japan united against the Soviet Union in the Anti-Comintern Pact. To these events Britain and France responded with a policy of appeasement, hoping to curb Hitler's expansionist appetite by permitting him a few territorial nibbles. The policy of appeasing Hitler proved disastrous, for the hate-filled German leader continually raised his demands.

In those hair-trigger times, a civil war in Spain soon turned into an international struggle. Beginning in 1936, the Loyalists defended Spain's elected republican government against Francisco Franco's fascist movement. About three thousand American volunteers, known as the Abraham Lincoln Battalion of the "International Brigades," joined the fight on the side of the Loyalist republicans, which also had the backing of the Soviet Union. Hitler and Mussolini sent military aid to Franco, who won in 1939, tightening the grip of fascism on the European continent.

Early in 1938 Hitler once again tested the limits of European tolerance when he sent soldiers into Austria to annex the nation of his birth. Then in September he seized the Sudeten region of Czechoslovakia. Appeasement reached its apex that month when France and Britain, without consulting the Czechs, agreed at Munich to allow Hitler this territorial bite. British Prime Minister Neville Chamberlain returned home to proclaim "peace in our time," confident that Hitler was satiated. In March 1939 Hitler swallowed the rest of Czechoslovakia (see Map 26.3 on page 749).

The Munich Conference

The Nazi leader next eyed another neighbor, Poland. Scuttling appeasement, London and Paris an-

Poland and the Outbreak of World War II

nounced that they would stand by their ally Poland. Undaunted, Berlin signed the Nazi-Soviet Pact with Moscow in August. Soviet leader Joseph Stalin believed that the West's appeasement of Hitler had left him no choice but to cut a deal with the Nazi ruler. But Stalin also coveted territory: a top-secret protocol attached to the pact carved eastern Europe into German and Soviet zones and permitted the Soviets to grab half of Poland and the three Baltic states of Lithuania, Estonia, and Latvia, formerly part of the Russian empire. On September 1 Hitler launched *blitzkrieg* (lightning war) attacks—highly mobile land forces and armor combined with tactical aircraft—against Poland. Britain and France declared war on Germany two days later. So started the Second World War.

As the world hurtled toward war, Soviet-American relations remained embittered. During the 1920s the United States refused to open diplomatic relations with the Soviet government, which had failed to pay $600 million for confiscated American-owned property and had repudiated preexisting Russian debts. To many Americans, the Communists ranked as godless, radical malcontents bent on destroying the American way of life through world revolution. American businesses such as General Electric and International Harvester nonetheless entered the Soviet marketplace. Henry Ford signed a contract in 1929 to build an automobile plant there. By 1930 the Soviet Union had become the largest buyer of American farm and industrial equipment.

In the early 1930s, when trade began to slump, some American business leaders lobbied for diplomatic recognition of the Soviet Union. "We would recognize the Devil with a false face if he would contract for some pitchforks," quipped the humorist Will Rogers. President Roosevelt himself concluded that nonrecognition had failed to alter the Soviet system, and he speculated that closer Soviet-American relations might deter Japanese expansion. In 1933 Roosevelt granted U.S. diplomatic recognition to the Soviet Union in return for Soviet agreement to discuss the debts question, to forgo subversive activities in the United States, and to grant Americans in the Soviet Union religious freedom and legal rights. The first U.S. embassy in Moscow opened in 1934, but relations soon deteriorated. Stalin's brutalities against his people and the

U.S. Recognition of the Soviet Union

Nazi-Soviet Pact of August 1939 outraged many Americans—further evidence for them that Europe had gone mad once again.

Isolationism, Neutrality Acts, and Roosevelt's Cautious Foreign Policy

As authoritarianism, race hatred, and military expansion swept over Europe in the 1930s, Americans sought to distance themselves from the tumult by embracing isolationism, whose key elements were abhorrence of war, limited military intervention abroad, and freedom of action in international relations. Americans had learned powerful negative lessons from the First World War: war damages reform movements, undermines civil liberties, dangerously expands federal and presidential power, disrupts the economy, and accentuates racial and class tensions (see Chapter 23). A 1937 Gallup poll found that nearly two-thirds of the respondents thought U.S. participation in World War I had been a mistake.

Conservative isolationists feared higher taxes and increased executive power if the nation went to war again. Liberal isolationists worried that domestic problems might go unresolved as the nation spent more on the military. Many isolationists predicted that in attempting to spread democracy abroad or to police the world, Americans would lose their freedoms at home. The vast majority of isolationists opposed fascism and condemned aggression, but they did not think the United States should have to do what Europeans themselves refused to do: block Hitler.

Variety of Isolationist Views

Isolationist sentiment was strongest in the Midwest and among anti-British ethnic groups, especially Americans of German or Irish descent, but it was a nationwide phenomenon that cut across socioeconomic, ethnic, party, and sectional lines and attracted a majority of the American people. Prominent isolationists in the 1930s included Republicans such as Representative Hamilton Fish of New York, Senator William Borah of Idaho, and former president Herbert Hoover; Democrats such as Representative Maury Maverick of Texas; Socialists such as Norman Thomas; Communists and Nazi sympathizers; and pacifists such as Representative Jeannette Rankin of Montana. They also included the publisher Robert R. McCormick of the *Chicago Tribune*, the historian Charles Beard, the physicist Albert Einstein, and the anti-Semitic radio priest Charles E. Coughlin. University students in 1936 organized the Veterans of Future Wars and asked for a bonus of $1,000 before going into battle because, they mockingly proclaimed, few would live through the next war. These dissimilar people united in the opinion that alternatives to American participation in another European war existed.

Some isolationists charged that corporate "merchants of death" had promoted war and were assisting the aggressors. After Dorothy Detzer

Nye Committee Hearings

of the WILPF diligently lobbied Senator Gerald P. Nye to take up the issue, a congressional committee held hearings from 1934 to 1936 on the role of business and financiers in the U.S. decision to enter the First World War. The Nye committee did not prove that American munitions makers had dragged the nation into that war, but it did uncover evidence that corporations practicing "rotten commercialism" had bribed foreign politicians to bolster arms sales in the 1920s and 1930s and had lobbied against arms control.

Isolationists grew suspicious of American business ties with Nazi Germany and fascist Italy that might endanger U.S. neutrality. Twenty-six of the top one hundred American corporations, including Du Pont, Standard Oil, and General Motors, had contractual agreements in 1937 with German firms. And after Italy attacked Ethiopia in 1935, American petroleum, copper, and scrap iron and steel exports to Italy increased substantially, despite Roosevelt's call for a moral embargo on such commerce. A Dow Chemical official stated: "We do not inquire into the uses of the products. We are interested in selling them." Not all American executives thought this way. The Wall Street law firm of Sullivan and Cromwell, for example, severed lucrative ties with Germany to protest the Nazi persecution of Jews.

Reflecting the popular desire for distance from Europe's disputes, President Roosevelt signed a series of neutrality acts. Congress sought to

Neutrality Acts

protect the nation by outlawing the kinds of contacts that had compromised U.S. neutrality during World War I. The Neutrality Act of 1935 prohibited arms shipments to either side in a war once the president had declared the existence of belligerency. Roosevelt had wanted the authority to name the aggressor and apply an arms embargo against it alone, but Congress would not grant the president such discretionary power. The Neutrality Act of 1936 forbade loans to belligerents. After a joint resolution in 1937 declared the United States neutral in the Spanish Civil War, Roosevelt embargoed arms shipments to both sides. The Neutrality Act of 1937 introduced the cash-and-carry principle: warring nations wishing to trade with the United States would have to pay cash for their nonmilitary purchases and carry the goods from U.S. ports in their own ships. The act also forbade Americans from traveling on the ships of belligerent nations.

President Roosevelt shared isolationist views in the early 1930s. Although prior to World War I he was

Roosevelt's Evolving Views

an expansionist and interventionist like his older cousin Theodore, during the interwar period Roosevelt talked less about preparedness and more about disarmament and the horrors of war, less about policing the world and more about handling problems at home. In a passionate speech delivered in August 1936 at Chautauqua, New York, Roosevelt expressed prevailing isolationist opinion and made a pitch for the pacifist vote in the upcoming election: "I have seen war. . . . I have seen blood running from the wounded. I have seen men coughing out their gassed lungs. . . . I have seen the agony of mothers and wives. I hate war." The United States, he promised, would remain unentangled in the European conflict. During the crisis over Czechoslovakia in 1938 Roosevelt endorsed appeasement and greeted the Munich accord with a "universal sense of relief."

All the while, Roosevelt grew troubled by the arrogant behavior of Germany, Italy, and Japan—aggressors he tagged the "three bandit nations." He condemned the Nazi persecution of the Jews and the Japanese slaughter of Chinese civilians. Privately he chastised the British and French for failing to collar Hitler. Because he worried that the United States was ill prepared to confront the aggressors, his New Deal public works programs included millions for the construction of new warships. In 1935 the president requested the largest peacetime defense budget in American history. Three years later, in the wake of Munich, he asked Congress for funds to build up the air force, which he believed essential to deter aggression. Pressed hard by Roosevelt in early 1938, the House of Representatives defeated a constitutional amendment proposed by Indiana Democrat Louis Ludlow to require a majority vote in a national refer-

President Franklin D. Roosevelt relaxes with his favorite hobby, stamp collecting, from which he said he learned history and geography. During World War II he once showed British Prime Minister Winston Churchill a stamp from "one of your colonies." Churchill asked: "Which one?" Roosevelt replied: "One of your last. . . . You won't have them much longer, you know."   (Franklin D. Roosevelt Library)

endum before a congressional declaration of war could go into effect (unless the United States were attacked). In January 1939 the president secretly decided to sell bombers to France, saying privately that "our frontier is on the Rhine." Although the more than five hundred combat planes delivered to France did not deter war, French orders spurred growth of the U.S. aircraft industry.

In early 1939 the president lashed out at the international lawbreakers and urged Congress to repeal the arms embargo and permit the sale of munitions to belligerents on a cash-and-carry basis. Roosevelt knew that repeal would aid Britain, which dominated the seas. When the Senate Foreign Relations Committee voted down repeal, Roosevelt raged: "I think we ought to introduce a bill for statues of [Senators] Austin, Vandenberg, Lodge and Taft . . . to be erected in Berlin and put the swastika on them." Feeling hampered by the isolationists, the president moved gradually toward a more interventionist posture, step by step, measuring public opinion while trying to change it. As a consummate politician, he developed a leadership style of caution, not wanting to get too far out front of popular isolationist sentiment. Roosevelt also liked to keep his options open. One scholar has likened him to a college professor who prefers to teach without a syllabus.

When Europe descended into the abyss of war in September 1939, Roosevelt declared neutrality and pressed again for repeal of the arms embargo. Isolationist senator Arthur Vandenberg of Michigan roared back that the United States could not be "an arsenal for one belligerent without becoming a target for the other." After much debate, however, Congress in November lifted the embargo on contraband and approved cash-and-carry exports of arms. Using "methods short of war," Roosevelt thus began to aid the Allies. Hitler sneered that a "half Judaized, half negrified" United States was "incapable of conducting war."

Repeal of the Arms Embargo

Japan, China, and a New Order in Asia

While Europe succumbed to political turmoil and war, Asia suffered the aggressive march of Japan. The United States had interests at stake in Asia: the Philippines and Pacific islands, religious missions, trade and investments, and the Open Door in China. In traditional missionary fashion, Americans also believed that they were China's special friend and protector. "With God's help," Senator Kenneth Wherry of Nebraska once proclaimed, "we will lift Shanghai up and up, ever up, until it is just like Kansas City." Pearl Buck's best-selling novel *The Good Earth* (1931), made into a widely distributed film six years later, countered prevailing images of the very different—and thus deviant—"heathen Chinee" by representing the Chinese as noble, persevering peasants. The daughter of Presbyterian missionaries, Buck helped shift negative American images of China to positive ones. By contrast, the aggressive Japan loomed as a threat to American attitudes and interests. The Tokyo government seemed bent on subjugating China and unhinging the Open Door doctrine of equal trade and investment opportunity.

The Chinese themselves were uneasy about the U.S. presence in Asia. Like the Japanese, they wished to reduce the influence of westerners. The Chinese Revolution of 1911 still rumbled in the 1920s as antiforeign riots damaged American property and imperiled American missionaries. Chinese nationalists criticized Americans for the imperialist practice of extraterritoriality (the exemption of foreigners accused of crimes from Chinese legal jurisdiction), and they demanded an end to this affront to Chinese sovereignty.

In the late 1920s, civil war broke out in China when Jiang Jieshi (Chiang Kai-shek) ousted Mao Zedong and his Communist followers from the ruling Guomindang Party.

Jiang Jieshi

Americans applauded this display of anti-Bolshevism and Jiang's conversion to Christianity in 1930. Jiang's new wife, Soong Meiling, also won their hearts. American-educated, Madame Jiang spoke flawless English, dressed in Western fashion, and cultivated ties with prominent Americans. Warming to Jiang, U.S. officials abandoned one imperial vestige by signing a treaty in 1928 restoring control of tariffs to the Chinese. U.S. gunboats and marines still remained in China to protect American citizens and property.

The Japanese grew increasingly suspicious of U.S. ties with China. In the early twentieth century, Japanese-American relations steadily deteriorated as Japan gained influence in Manchuria, Shandong, and Korea. The Japanese sought not only to oust Western imperialists from Asia but also to dominate Asian territories that produced the raw materials that their import-dependent island nation required. The Japanese also resented the discriminatory immigration law of 1924, which excluded them from emigrating to the United States. Secretary Hughes urged Congress not to pass the act; when it rejected his counsel, he sadly called the law "a lasting injury" to Japanese-American relations. Despite the Washington Conference treaties, naval competition continued. Also, although the volume of Japanese-American trade was twice that of Chinese-American trade, commercial rivalry strained relations between Japan and the United States. The importation of inexpensive Japanese goods, especially textiles, spawned "Buy America" campaigns and boycotts.

Relations further soured in 1931 after the Japanese military seized Manchuria in China (see Map 26.2). Larger than Texas, Manchuria

Manchurian Crisis

served Japan both as a buffer against the Soviets and as a vital source of coal, iron, timber, and food. More than half of Japan's foreign investments rested in Manchuria. "We are seeking room that will let us breathe," said a Japanese politician, ar-

William E. Borah (1865–1940), chair of the Senate Foreign Relations Committee (*left*), and Henry L. Stimson (1867–1950), secretary of state (*right*), often clashed over foreign policy even though both were Republicans. The Idaho senator became a passionate anti-imperialist and isolationist who protested U.S. interventions abroad. Because of critics such as Borah, Stimson grew eager to find nonmilitary means to maintain U.S. hegemony in the Western Hemisphere. (Corbis-Bettmann)

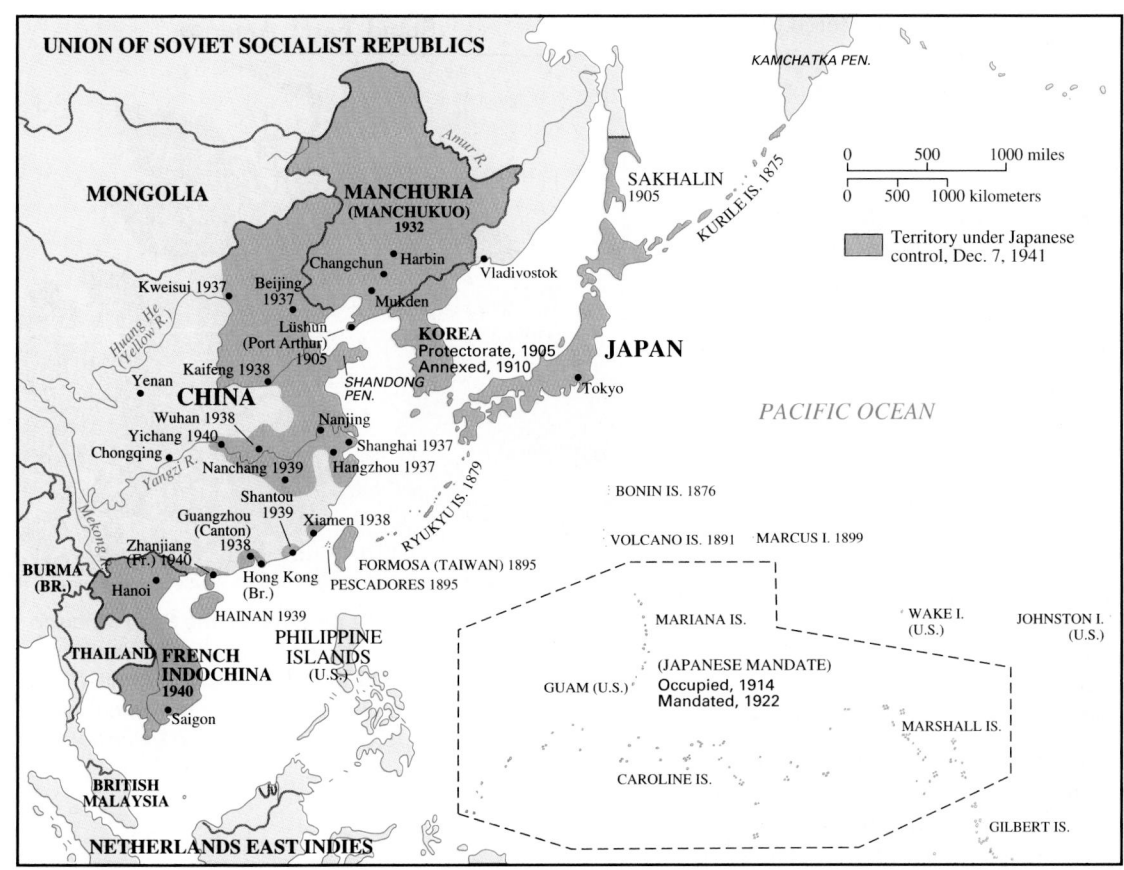

Map 26.2   Japanese Expansion Before Pearl Harbor   The Japanese quest for predominance began at the turn of the century and intensified in the 1930s. China suffered the most at the hands of Tokyo's military. Vulnerable U.S. possessions in Asia and the Pacific proved no obstacle to Japan's ambitions for a Greater East Asia Co-Prosperity Sphere.

guing that his heavily populated island nation (65 million people in an area slightly smaller than California) needed to expand in order to survive. Although the seizure of Manchuria violated the Nine-Power Treaty and the Kellogg-Briand Pact, the United States did not have the power to compel Japanese withdrawal, and the League of Nations did little but debate. The American response came as a moral lecture known as the Stimson Doctrine: the United States would not recognize any impairment of China's sovereignty or of the Open Door policy, Secretary Stimson declared in 1932. He himself later described his policy as largely "bluff."

Japan continued to harry China. In mid-1937 the Sino-Japanese War erupted. Japanese forces seized cities and bombed civilians. The gruesome bombing of Shanghai intensified anti-Japanese sentiment in the United States. Senator Norris, an isolationist who

moved further away from isolationism with each Japanese thrust, condemned the Japanese as "disgraceful, ignoble, barbarous, and cruel, even beyond the power of language to describe." In an effort to help China by permitting it to buy American arms, Roosevelt refused to declare the existence of war, thus avoiding activation of the Neutrality Acts.

In a speech denouncing the aggressors on October 5, 1937, the president called for a "quarantine" to curb the "epidemic of world lawlessness." People who thought Washington had been too gentle with Japan cheered. Isolationists warned that the president was edging toward war. On December 12 Japanese aircraft sank the American gunboat *Panay*, an escort for Standard Oil Company tankers on the Yangtze River. Two American sailors died during the attack. Roosevelt was much

Roosevelt's Quarantine Speech

relieved when Tokyo apologized and offered to pay for damages.

Japan's declaration of a "New Order" in Asia, in the words of one American official, "banged, barred, and bolted" the Open Door. Alarmed, the Roosevelt administration during the late 1930s gave loans and sold military equipment to the Chinese. Secretary Hull declared a moral embargo on the shipment of airplanes to Japan. Meanwhile, the U.S. Navy continued to grow, aided by a billion-dollar congressional appropriation in 1938. In mid-1939 the United States abrogated its trade treaty with Tokyo, yet Americans continued to ship oil, cotton, and machinery to Japan. The administration hesitated to initiate economic sanctions because such pressure might spark a Japanese-American war at a time when Germany posed a more serious threat and the United States was unprepared for war. When war broke out in Europe in fall 1939, Japanese-American relations were stalemated.

On a Collision Course with Japan and Germany, 1939–1941

 President Roosevelt remarked in 1939 that the United States could not "draw a line of defense around this country and live completely and solely to ourselves." Thomas Jefferson had tried that with his 1807 embargo—"the damned thing didn't work" and "we got into the War of 1812." America, the president insisted, could not insulate itself from world war. Polls showed that Americans strongly favored the Allies and that most supported aid to Britain and France, but the great majority emphatically wanted the United States to remain at peace. Troubled by this conflicting advice—oppose Hitler, aid the Allies, but stay out of the war—the president gradually moved the nation from neutrality to undeclared war against Germany and then, after the Japanese attack on Pearl Harbor, to full-scale war itself.

Because the stakes were so high, Americans vigorously debated the direction of their foreign policy from 1939 through 1941. Unprecedented numbers of Americans spoke out on foreign affairs and joined organizations that addressed the issues. Spine-chilling events and the widespread use of radio, the nation's chief source of news, helped stimulate this high level of public interest. So did ethnic affiliations with the various belligerents and victims of aggression. The American Legion, the

Foreign Policy Debate

Stand Fast! America

William Randolph Hearst's newspaper, the *San Francisco Examiner,* reflected the publisher's isolationist views in 1939 at the outbreak of World War II. Here the United States is depicted as an island of peace and democracy in a mad, menacing world. (*San Francisco Examiner,* Oct. 8, 1939)

League of Women Voters, labor unions, and local chapters of the Committee to Defend America by Aiding the Allies and the isolationist America First Committee (both organized in 1940) provided outlets for citizen participation in the national debate. African American churches organized anti-Italian boycotts to protest Mussolini's pummeling of Ethiopia.

In March 1940 the Soviet Union invaded Finland. In April Germany invaded Denmark and Norway (see Map 26.3). "The small countries are smashed up, one by one, like matchwood," sighed Winston Churchill, who became Britain's prime minister on May 10, 1940, the day Germany attacked Belgium, the Netherlands, and France. German divisions ultimately pushed French and British forces back to the English Channel. At Dunkirk, France, between May 26 and June 6, more than three hundred thousand Allied soldiers frantically escaped to Britain on a flotilla of small boats. The Germans occupied Paris a week later. A new French government located in the town of Vichy decided to collaborate with the conquering Nazis and, on June 22, surrendered France to Berlin. With France knocked out of the war,

The Fall of France

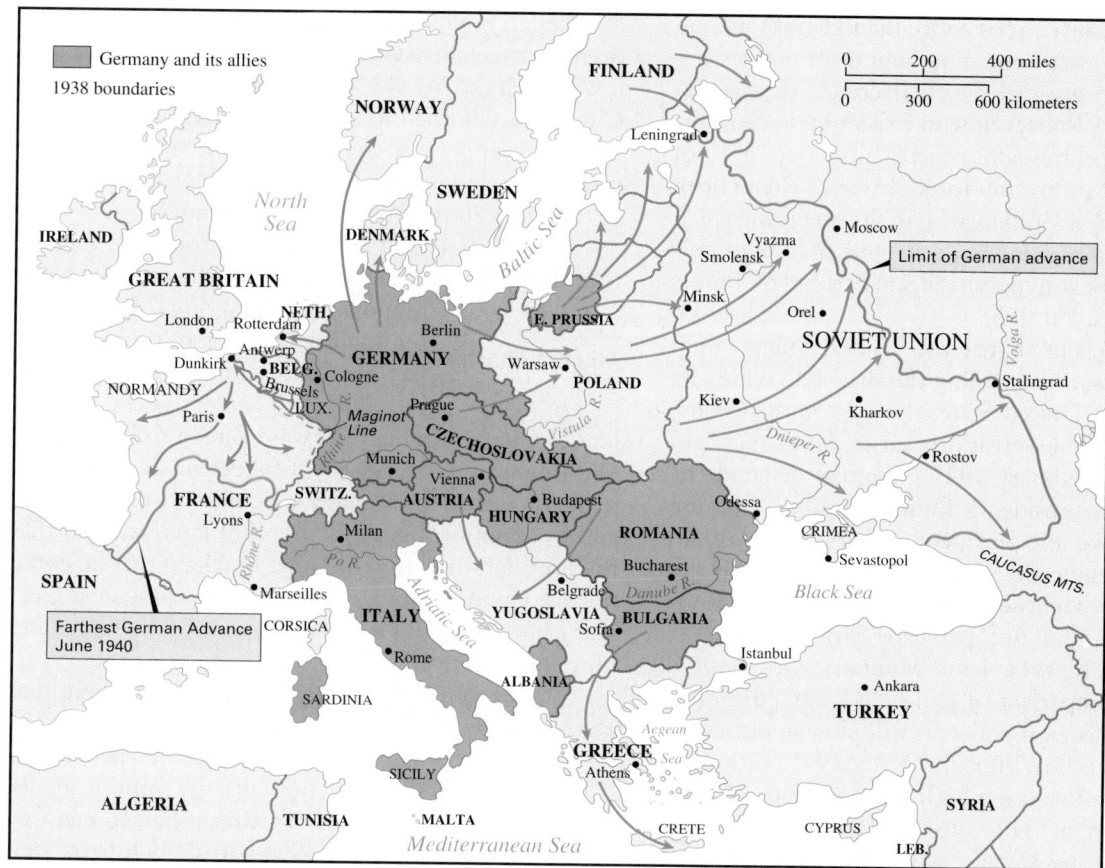

Map 26.3   The German Advance, 1939–1942   Hitler's drive to dominate Europe pushed German troops deep into France and the Soviet Union. Great Britain took a beating but held on with the help of American economic and military aid before the United States itself entered the Second World War in late 1941.

the German Luftwaffe (air force) launched massive bombing raids against Great Britain in preparation for a full-scale invasion. Stunned Americans asked, Could Washington or New York be the Luftwaffe's next target?

Alarmed by the swift defeat of one European nation after another, Americans gradually shed their isolationist sentiment. Some liberals left the isolationist fold; it became more and more the province of conservatives. Emotions ran high. Roosevelt called the isolationists "ostriches" and charged that some were pro-Nazi subversives. The White House began to turn over to the Federal Bureau of Investigation letters criticizing Roosevelt's foreign policy.

After Roosevelt tried futilely to draw the belligerents to the peace table, he told his advisers that he was "not willing to fire the first shot" but was waiting for some incident to bring the United States into the war.

In the meantime, assuring Americans that New Deal reforms would not have to be sacrificed to achieve military preparedness, Roosevelt began to aid the beleaguered Allies to prevent the fall of Britain. In May 1940 he ordered the sale of old surplus military equipment to Britain and France. In July he cultivated bipartisan support by naming Republicans Henry L. Stimson and Frank Knox, ardent backers of aid to the Allies, secretaries of war and the navy respectively. In September, by executive agreement, the president traded fifty over-age American destroyers for leases to eight British military bases, including Newfoundland, Bermuda, and Jamaica.

Two weeks later Roosevelt signed into law the hotly debated and narrowly passed Selective Training and Service Act, the first peacetime military draft in American history. The act called for the registration of all men between the ages of twenty-one and thirty-

First Peacetime Military Draft

five. Soon more than 16 million men had signed up, and draft notices began to be delivered. Meanwhile, Roosevelt won reelection in November 1940 with promises of peace: "Your boys are not going to be sent into any foreign wars." Republican candidate Wendell Willkie, who in the emerging spirit of bipartisanship had not made an issue of foreign policy, snapped, "That hypocritical son of a bitch! This is going to beat me!" It did.

Roosevelt claimed that the United States could stay out of the war by enabling the British to win. The United States, he said, must become the "great arsenal of democracy." In January 1941 Congress debated the president's Lend-Lease bill. Because Britain was broke, the president explained, the United States should lend rather than sell weapons, much as a neighbor lends a garden hose to fight a fire. Roosevelt's analogy did not persuade strict isolationist Senator Burton K. Wheeler of Montana, who shouted out another comparison: Lend-Lease was "the New Deal's triple A foreign policy; it will plow under every fourth American boy." But in March 1941, with pro-British sentiment running high, the House passed the Lend-Lease Act by 317 votes to 71; the Senate followed with a 60-to-31 tally. The initial appropriation was $7 billion, but by the end of the war the amount had reached $50 billion, more than $31 billion of it for Britain.

Lend-Lease Act

To ensure the safe delivery of Lend-Lease goods, Roosevelt ordered the U.S. Navy to patrol halfway across the Atlantic, and he sent American troops to Greenland. In July, arguing that Iceland was also essential to the defense of the Western Hemisphere, the president dispatched marines there. He also sent Lend-Lease aid to the Soviet Union, which Hitler had attacked in June. If the Soviets could hold off two hundred German divisions in the east, Roosevelt calculated, Britain would gain some breathing time. Churchill, who had long thundered against Communists, now applauded aid to the Soviets: "If Hitler invaded Hell, I would make at least a favorable reference to the Devil in the House of Commons."

In August 1941 Churchill and Roosevelt met for four days on a British battleship off the coast of Newfoundland. They got along well, trading naval stories and enjoying the fact that Churchill was half American. The two leaders issued the Atlantic Charter, a set of war aims reminiscent of Wilsonianism (see page 637): collective security, disarmament, self-determination, economic cooperation, and freedom of the seas. Churchill later recalled that the president told him in Newfoundland that he could not ask Congress for a declaration of war against Germany but "he would wage war" and "become more and more provocative."

Atlantic Charter

On September 4, 1941, came an incident that Roosevelt could exploit. In the Atlantic, a German submarine launched torpedoes at (but did not hit) the American destroyer *Greer*, after it had cooperated with British patrol bombers that dropped depth charges on the submarine (see page 755). Roosevelt declared that the German vessel, without warning, had fired first. Henceforth, he said, the U.S. Navy would shoot on sight. He also announced a policy he already had promised Churchill in private: American warships would convoy British merchant ships across the ocean.

***Greer* Incident**

Thus the United States entered into an undeclared naval war with Germany. When in early October a German submarine torpedoed the U.S. destroyer

The isolationist America First Committee published this bumper sticker in 1941 in a vain attempt to halt the United States's descent into war. America Firsters organized in September 1940 and attracted many prominent members, including the famed aviator Charles Lindbergh. (Herbert Hoover Presidential Library)

President Franklin D. Roosevelt *(left)* and British Prime Minister Winston Churchill (1874–1965) confer on board a ship near Newfoundland during their summit meeting of August 1941. During the conference, they signed the Atlantic Charter. Upon his return to Great Britain, Churchill told his advisers that Roosevelt had promised to "wage war" against Germany and do "everything" to "force an incident."   (Franklin D. Roosevelt Library)

Kearny off the coast of Iceland, the president announced that "the shooting has started. And history has recorded who fired the first shot." Later that month, when the destroyer *Reuben James* went down with the loss of more than one hundred American lives, Congress scrapped the cash-and-carry policy and further revised the Neutrality Acts to permit transport of munitions to Britain on armed American merchant ships. The United States was edging very close to full-scale war in Europe.

Why War Came: Pearl Harbor and U.S. Entry into World War II

In retrospect, it seems ironic that the Second World War came to the United States by way of Asia. Roosevelt had wanted to avoid war with Japan in order to concentrate American resources on the defeat of Germany. In September 1940, after Germany, Italy, and Japan had signed the Tripartite Pact, Roosevelt slapped an embargo on shipments of aviation fuel and scrap metal to Japan. Because the president believed the Japanese would consider a cutoff of oil a life-or-death matter, he did not embargo that vital commodity. But after Japanese troops occupied French Indochina in July 1941, Washington froze Japanese assets in the United States, virtually ending trade (including oil) with Japan. "The oil gauge and the clock stood side by side" for Japan, wrote one observer.

Tokyo recommended a summit meeting between President Roosevelt and Prime Minister Prince Konoye, but the United States rejected the idea. American officials insisted that the Japanese first agree to respect China's sovereignty and territorial integrity and to honor the Open Door policy—in short, to get out of China. According to polls taken in fall 1941, the American people seemed willing to risk war with Japan to thwart further aggression. For Roosevelt, Europe still claimed first priority, but he supported Secretary Hull's hard-line policy against Japan's pursuit of the Greater East Asia Co-Prosperity Sphere—the name

U.S. Demands on Japan

Tokyo gave to the vast Asian region it intended to dominate.

Roosevelt told his advisers to string out ongoing Japanese-American talks to gain time—time to fortify the Philippines and check the fascists in Europe. By breaking the Japanese diplomatic code and deciphering intercepted messages through Operation MAGIC, American officials learned that Tokyo's patience with diplomacy was fast dissipating (see page 763). In late November the Japanese rejected American demands that they withdraw from Indochina. An intercepted message that American experts decoded on December 3 instructed the Japanese embassy in Washington to burn codes and destroy cipher machines—a step suggesting that war was coming. Secretary Stimson explained later that the United States let Japan fire the first shot so as "to have the full support of the Ameri-can people" and "so that there should remain no doubt in anyone's mind as to who were the aggressors."

The Japanese plotted a daring raid on Pearl Harbor in Hawai'i. An armada of sixty Japanese ships, with a core of six carriers bearing 360 airplanes, crossed 3,000 miles of the Pacific Ocean. To avoid detection, every ship maintained radio silence.

Surprise Attack on Pearl Harbor

In the early morning of December 7, some 230 miles northwest of Honolulu, the carriers unleashed their planes, each stamped with a red sun representing the Japanese flag. They swept down on the unsuspecting American naval base and nearby airfields, dropping torpedoes and bombs and strafing buildings.

The battleship U.S.S. *Arizona* fell victim to a Japanese bomb that ignited explosives below deck,

The stricken U.S.S. *West Virginia* was one of eight battleships caught in the surprise Japanese attack at Pearl Harbor, Hawai'i, on December 7, 1941. In this photograph, sailors on a launch attempt to rescue a crew member from the water as oil burns around the sinking ship. (U.S. Army)

killing more than one thousand sailors. The U.S.S. *Nevada* tried to escape the inferno by heading out to sea, but a second wave of aerial attackers struck the ship. Altogether the invaders sank or damaged eight battleships and many smaller vessels and smashed more than 160 aircraft on the ground. Huddled in an air-raid shelter, sixteen-year-old Mary Ann Ramsey watched the injured come in "with filthy black oil covering shredded flesh. With the first sailor, so horribly burned, personal fear left me; he brought me the full tragedy of the day." A total of 2,403 died; 1,178 were wounded. By chance, three aircraft carriers at sea escaped the disaster. The Pearl Harbor tragedy, from the perspective of the war's outcome, amounted to a military inconvenience more than a disaster.

How could the stunning attack on Pearl Harbor have happened? After all, American cryptanalysts had broken the Japanese diplomatic code.

Explaining Pearl Harbor

Although the intercepted Japanese messages told policymakers that war lay ahead, the intercepts never revealed naval or military plans and never specifically mentioned Pearl Harbor. Roosevelt did not, as some critics charged, conspire to leave the fleet vulnerable to attack so that the United States could enter the Second World War through the "back door" of Asia. The base at Pearl Harbor was not on red alert because a message sent from Washington warning of the imminence of war had been too casually transmitted by a slow method and had arrived too late. Base commanders were too relaxed, believing Hawai'i too far from Japan to be a target for all-out attack. Like Roosevelt's advisers, they expected an assault against British Malaya, Thailand, or the Philippines (see Map 26.2). The Pearl Harbor calamity stemmed from mistakes and insufficient information, not from conspiracy.

On December 8, referring to the previous day as "a date which will live in infamy," Roosevelt asked Congress for a declaration of war against Japan. He noted that the Japanese had also attacked Malaya, Hong Kong, Guam, the Philippines, Wake, and Midway, and he expressed the prevailing sense of revenge when he vowed that Americans would never forget "the character of the onslaught against us." A unanimous vote in the Senate and a 388-to-1 vote in the House thrust America into war. Representative Jeannette Rankin of Montana voted "no," repeating her vote against entry into the First World War.

Three days later, Germany and Italy, honoring the Tripartite Pact they had signed with Japan in September 1940, declared war against the United States. "Hitler's fate was sealed," Churchill later wrote. "Mussolini's fate was sealed. As for the Japanese, they would be ground to powder. . . . I went to bed and slept the sleep of the saved and thankful." On January 1, 1942, the United States was among the twenty-six nations that signed the Declaration of the United Nations, pledging allegiance to the Atlantic Charter.

A fundamental clash of systems explains why war came. Germany and Japan preferred a world divided into closed spheres of influence. The

Clash of Systems

United States sought a liberal capitalist world order in which all nations enjoyed freedom of trade and investment. American principles manifested respect for human rights; fascists in Europe and militarists in Asia defiantly trampled such rights. The United States prided itself on its democratic system; Germany and Japan embraced authoritarian regimes backed by the military.

When the United States protested against German and Japanese expansion, Berlin and Tokyo reminded Washington of the United States's sphere in Latin America. German, Italian, and Japanese leaders also charged that Americans were applying a double standard, conveniently ignoring their own empire built through conquest, military occupation, and economic privilege. Americans rejected such comparisons and claimed that their expansionism had benefited not just themselves but the rest of the world. So many incompatible objectives and outlooks obstructed diplomacy and made war likely.

Summary

In the 1920s and 1930s, Americans proved unable to create a peaceful and prosperous world order. The Washington Conference treaties failed to curb a naval arms race or to protect China; the Dawes Plan collapsed; the Kellogg-Briand Pact proved ineffective; philanthropic activities fell short of need; the process of cultural "Americanization" provided no panacea; the aggressors Germany and Japan ignored repeated U.S. protests, from the Stimson Doctrine onward; recognition of the Soviet Union barely improved relations; U.S. trade policies, shifting from protectionist tariffs to reciprocal trade agreements, only minimally improved U.S. or international commerce in the era of the Great Depression; and the Neutrality Acts did not prevent U.S. entanglements in Europe. Even where

How do historians know...

that American leaders knew in December 1941, before the attack on Pearl Harbor, that Japan intended to go to war with the United States? In September 1940, U.S. cryptanalysts—code breakers—of the Signal Intelligence Service cracked the most secret diplomatic cipher used by the Japanese government, a machine they called PURPLE. The code breakers discovered patterns in the incoherent letters of telegraphed messages, produced texts, and even duplicated the complicated PURPLE machine (shown here). Thereafter, under Operation MAGIC, they decoded thousands of intercepted messages sent by Japanese officials around the world. Important intercepts such as the one shown below were delivered to a handful of top American leaders, including the president. These dispatches made increasingly clear through 1941 that Tokyo expected all-out war with the United States. An intercept on December 3, just a few days before the attack on Pearl Harbor, revealed that Tokyo had ordered the Japanese embassy in Washington to destroy all codes and cipher machines, a sure sign that war was imminent.

After the attack against Pearl Harbor, and after it became public knowledge that the United States had broken the Japanese diplomatic code, the cry sounded—especially from die-hard isolationists and Roosevelt-haters—that the president must have known what was coming yet failed to prepare the naval base for the assault. The many messages intercepted in the fall and winter of 1941, however, never revealed Japan's military plans. Not one intercepted message mentioned an attack on Pearl Harbor; indeed, even Japanese diplomats in Washington were never told that Pearl Harbor would be hit. (Photos: National Archives)

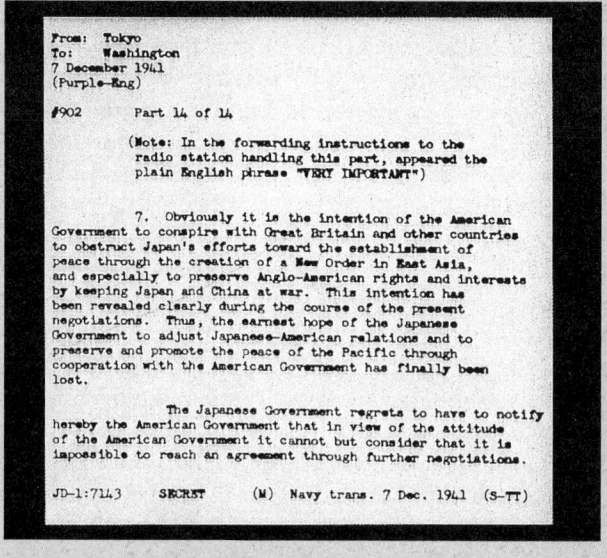

From: Tokyo
To: Washington
7 December 1941
(Purple-Eng)

#902   Part 14 of 14

(Note: In the forwarding instructions to the radio station handling this part, appeared the plain English phrase "VERY IMPORTANT")

7. Obviously it is the intention of the American Government to conspire with Great Britain and other countries to obstruct Japan's efforts toward the establishment of peace through the creation of a New Order in East Asia, and especially to preserve Anglo-American rights and interests by keeping Japan and China at war. This intention has been revealed clearly during the course of the present negotiations. Thus, the earnest hope of the Japanese Government to adjust Japanese-American relations and to preserve and promote the peace of the Pacific through cooperation with the American Government has finally been lost.

The Japanese Government regrets to have to notify hereby the American Government that in view of the attitude of the American Government it cannot but consider that it is impossible to reach an agreement through further negotiations.

JD-1:7143   SECRET   (M) Navy trans. 7 Dec. 1941 (S-TT)

American power and policies seemed to work to satisfy Good Neighbor goals—in Latin America—nationalist resentments simmered and Mexico challenged U.S. hegemony.

During the late 1930s and early 1940s, President Roosevelt hesitantly but steadily moved the United States from neutrality to aid for the Allies, to belligerency, and finally to a declaration of war after the attack on Pearl Harbor. Congress gradually revised and retired the Neutrality Acts in the face of growing danger and receding isolationism. Independent internationalism and economic and nonmilitary means to peace gave way to alliance-building and war.

The Second World War offered yet another opportunity for Americans to set things right in the world. As the publisher Henry Luce wrote in *American*

Century (1941), the United States must "exert upon the world the full impact of our influence, for such purposes as we see fit and by such means as we see fit." As they had so many times before, Americans flocked to the colors. Isolationists joined the president in spirited calls for victory. "We are going to win the war, and we are going to win the peace that follows," Roosevelt predicted.

LEGACY FOR A PEOPLE AND A NATION
Presidential Deception of the Public

Before U-652 launched two torpedoes at the *Greer*, heading for Iceland on September 4, 1941, the U.S. destroyer had stalked the German submarine for hours. Twice the *Greer* signaled the U-boat's location to British patrol bombers, one of which dropped depth charges on the submarine. After the torpedo attack, the *Greer* also released depth charges. In a dramatic radio "fireside chat" on September 11, President Roosevelt protested German "piracy" as a violation of the principle of freedom of the seas.

Throughout the twentieth century, presidents have exaggerated, distorted, withheld, or even lied about the facts of foreign relations in order to shape a public opinion favorable to their policies. One result: the growth of the "imperial presidency"—the president's grabbing of power from and supremacy over Congress, and the president's use of questionable means to reach his objectives. Franklin D. Roosevelt provided a telling example in the *Greer* incident. The president deliberately misrepresented the encounter in order to whip up anti-German passions, to discredit isolationist critics who opposed his pro-British interventionism in World War II, to announce his policy to convoy commercial ships across the Atlantic, and to issue an order to the navy to shoot German ships on sight.

In the *Greer* case, Roosevelt did not tell everything about the events of September 4, and what he did tell was misleading. In his radio message a week later, he described the clash as an unprovoked German attack.

He never mentioned that the U.S. ship had been cooperating with British warplanes, and he failed to note that the *Greer* had been tracking the submarine for hours. Despite his pleading, the incident had little to do with freedom of the seas, which related to neutral merchant ships not to U.S. warships operating in a war zone. Roosevelt's words amounted to a call to arms, yet he never asked Congress for a declaration of war against Germany. The president believed that he had to deceive the public in order to move hesitant Americans toward noble positions that they would ultimately see as necessary. Public opinion polls soon demonstrated that the practice worked, as most Americans approved the shoot-on-sight policy.

Several years later, in his book *The Man in the Street* (1948), Thomas A. Bailey defended Roosevelt. The historian argued that "because the masses are notoriously shortsighted, and generally cannot see danger until it is at their throats, our statesmen are forced to deceive them into an awareness of their own long-term interests." Roosevelt's critics, on the other hand, even those who agreed with him that Nazi Germany had to be stopped, have seen in his methods a danger to the democratic process, which cannot work in an environment of dishonesty and usurped powers. In the 1960s, during America's descent into the Vietnam War, Senator J. William Fulbright of Arkansas recalled the *Greer* incident: "FDR's deviousness in a good cause made it easier for LBJ to practice the same kind of deviousness in a bad cause." Indeed, during the Tonkin Gulf crisis of 1964, President Lyndon B. Johnson shaded the truth in order to gain from Congress wide latitude in waging war. In the 1980s Reagan administration officials, in the Iran-contra affair, consciously and publicly lied about U.S. arms sales to Iran and about covert aid to Nicaraguan terrorists. Practicing deception of the public and Congress—advancing the imperial presidency—was one of Roosevelt's legacies for a people and a nation.

For Further Reading, see page A-30 of the Appendix. For Web resources, go to http://college.hmco.com.

In 1942, when recruiters from the U.S. Marine Corps came to the Navajo reservation in Shiprock, New Mexico, William Dean Wilson was only sixteen years old and a student at the Shiprock Boarding School. The marines came seeking young men who spoke both English and Navajo, which is an exceedingly complex language; fewer than thirty non-Navajos, none of them Japanese, could understand the language at the outbreak of the war. The Navajo recruits of 1942 would become not only U.S. Marines but also "code talkers" in the war against the Japanese.

Wilson volunteered. "I said I was eighteen," he recalled, too young to be drafted but eager to join up. His parents had opposed his decision, but he removed a note from his file that read "Parents will not consent" and was inducted. Wilson, eager to see the world, was among an initial group of thirty Navajos chosen for a project with an important goal: to prevent the Japanese from deciphering radio messages sent by American troops landing on the shores of Pacific islands.

Organized as the 382nd Platoon, Wilson and his fellow recruits went first to marine boot camp, then to Camp Pendleton in California, where they trained as radio operators. At Camp Pendleton, they also helped to devise a code based on the Navajo language; the code had the beauty of being unbreakable. In preparation for battle, the code talkers memorized a special Navajo-coded dictionary of 413 military terms. While in the marines and even under battle conditions, the code talkers maintained traditional beliefs and practices. To prepare the young men to fight the enemy, Navajo families had special "Blessing Way" ceremonies performed for them; and many of the men went to battle carrying bags of sacred corn pollen.

By the time Wilson's seventeenth birthday arrived, he was fighting in the Pacific. Beginning with the Battle of Guadalcanal, he and others from the corps of 420 Navajo code talkers took part in every assault the marines conducted in the Pacific from 1942

THE SECOND WORLD WAR AT HOME AND ABROAD 1941–1945

Navajo "code talkers," who were U.S. Marines, were among the first assault forces to land on Pacific beaches. Dodging enemy fire, they set up radio equipment and transmitted vital information to headquarters, including enemy sightings and targets for American shelling. The Japanese never broke the special Navajo code. The artist is Colonel C. H. Waterhouse, U.S. Marine Corps (retired). (U.S. Marine Corps Art Collection/Colonel C. H. Waterhouse)

Winning the Second World War
Mobilizing the American Home Front
The Military Life
Enemy Aliens, Conscientious Objectors, and Japanese American Internees
Jobs and Racism on the Home Front
Women and Children in the War Effort
The Decline of Liberalism and the Election of 1944
Planning for Peace
LEGACY FOR A PEOPLE AND A NATION
Atomic Waste

to 1945. Usually, two code talkers were assigned to a battalion, one going ashore and the other remaining aboard ship. Those who went ashore led the assault forces landing on the beachheads. Often under hostile fire, they quickly set up their radio equipment and, using the special code, began transmitting, reporting sightings of enemy forces and directing shelling by American detachments.

Since the code talkers were responsible for the flow of vital battlefield information back to the ship and between advance units, they proved indispensable. Their work required great courage, and it paid off. "Were it not for the Navajos," declared Major Howard Conner, Fifth Marine Division signal officer, "the

"MEN MAKE THE NAVY . . . ," proclaims this U.S. Navy recruiting booklet, which encourages men to enlist by highlighting the good pay, food, and shipmates, as well as the possibility of "fighting action." One hundred thousand women also responded to the navy's recruiting efforts by joining the WAVES. (Private Collection)

Marines would never have taken Iwo Jima. The entire operation was directed by Navajo code. . . . I had six Navajo radio sets operating around the clock. In that period alone they sent and received over 800 messages without an error."

As it did for millions of other American fighting men and women, wartime service changed the Navajo code talkers' lives, broadening their horizons and often deepening their ambitions. Many became community leaders. William Dean Wilson, for example, became a tribal judge. From "the service," recalled Raymond Nakai, a navy veteran who became chairman of the Navajo nation, "the Navajo got a glimpse of what the rest of the world is doing." But in 1945 most Navajo war veterans were happy to return to their homes and traditional culture. And in accordance with Navajo ritual, the returning veterans participated in purification ceremonies to dispel the ghosts of the battlefield and invoke blessings for the future.

The Second World War marked a turning point in the lives of millions of Americans, as well as in the history of the United States. Most deeply affected were those who fought the war, on the beaches and battlefields, in the skies and at sea. For forty-five months Americans fought abroad to subdue the German, Italian, and Japanese aggressors. After military engagements against fascists in North Africa and Italy, American troops, together with Canadian, British, and Free French units, crossed the English Channel on D-Day in June 1944. The massive invasion forced the Germans to retreat through France to Germany. Battered by merciless bombing raids, leaderless after Adolf Hitler's suicide, and pressed by a Soviet advance from the east, the Nazis capitulated in May 1945. In the Pacific, Americans drove the Japanese back from one island to another before turning to the just-tested atomic bombs, which demolished Hiroshima and Nagasaki in August and helped spur a Japanese surrender.

Throughout the war the Allies—Britain, the Soviet Union, and the United States—stuck together to defeat Germany. But they squabbled over many issues: when to open a second front; how to structure a new international organization; how eastern Europe, liberated from the Germans, would be reconstructed; how Germany and Japan would be governed after defeat. At the end of the war, Allied leaders seemed more intent on retaining and expanding their own nations' spheres of influence than on building a community of mutual interest. Although the victors created the United Nations Organization, the prospects for postwar international cooperation seemed bleak, and the advent of the atomic age frightened everyone.

IMPORTANT EVENTS

1941 Germany invades Russia

Roosevelt issues Executive Order No. 8802, forbidding racial discrimination by defense industry employers

Japan attacks Pearl Harbor

U.S. enters Second World War

1942 National War Labor Board created to deal with labor-management conflict

War Production Board begins to oversee conversion to military production

West Coast Japanese Americans interned in prison camps

Congress of Racial Equality established

War Manpower Commission created to manage labor supply

Office of Price Administration created to control inflation

U.S. defeats Japanese forces at Battles of the Coral Sea and Midway

Office of War Information created to maintain support for the war at home

Manhattan Project set up to produce atomic bomb

Synthetic-rubber program begins

Allies invade North Africa

Republicans gain in Congress

1943 Red Army defeats German troops at Stalingrad

Soft-coal and anthracite miners strike

Congress passes War Labor Disputes (Smith Connally) Act

Race riots break out in Detroit, Harlem, and forty-five other cities

Allies invade Italy

Hirabayashi v. U.S. upholds restrictions on personal liberties of Japanese Americans because of their race

Roosevelt, Churchill, and Stalin meet at Teheran Conference

1944 Roosevelt requests Economic Bill of Rights

War Refugee Board established to set up refugee camps in Europe

GI Bill of Rights provides educational benefits for veterans

Allied troops land at Normandy on D-Day

Dumbarton Oaks Conference approves charter for United Nations

Roosevelt reelected

U.S. retakes the Philippines

Korematsu v. U.S. upholds removal of Japanese Americans from the West Coast

1945 Roosevelt, Stalin, and Churchill meet at Yalta Conference

Battles of Iwo Jima and Okinawa result in heavy American and Japanese losses

Roosevelt dies; Truman becomes president

United Nations founded

Germany surrenders

First atomic bomb explodes in test at Alamogordo, New Mexico

Potsdam Conference calls for Japan's "unconditional surrender"

Atomic bombs devastate Hiroshima and Nagasaki

Japan surrenders

The war transformed America's soldiers and sailors. Horizons expanded for the more than 16 million men and women who ultimately served in the armed forces, seeing new parts of the world and acquiring new skills. But at war's end they were older than their years, both physically and emotionally; some were physically injured and psychologically scarred, and many felt they had sacrificed the best years of their lives.

During the war nearly one of every ten Americans moved permanently to another state (see Map 27.1). Most headed for war-production centers, especially cities in the North and on the West Coast. Japanese Americans moved, too, but involuntarily, as they were rounded up by the army and placed in internment camps. And while the war offered new economic and political opportunities for numerous African Americans, encouraging them to demand their full rights as citizens, competition for jobs and housing created the conditions for an epidemic of race riots. For women, the war offered new job opportunities in the armed forces and in war industries. For some, work was an economic necessity; for others, it was a patriotic obligation; for all, it brought financial independence and enhanced self-esteem.

The United States underwent profound changes during the war. The American people united behind the war effort, collecting scrap iron, rubber, and newspapers for recycling and planting "victory gardens." But more than national unity and enthusiasm were re-

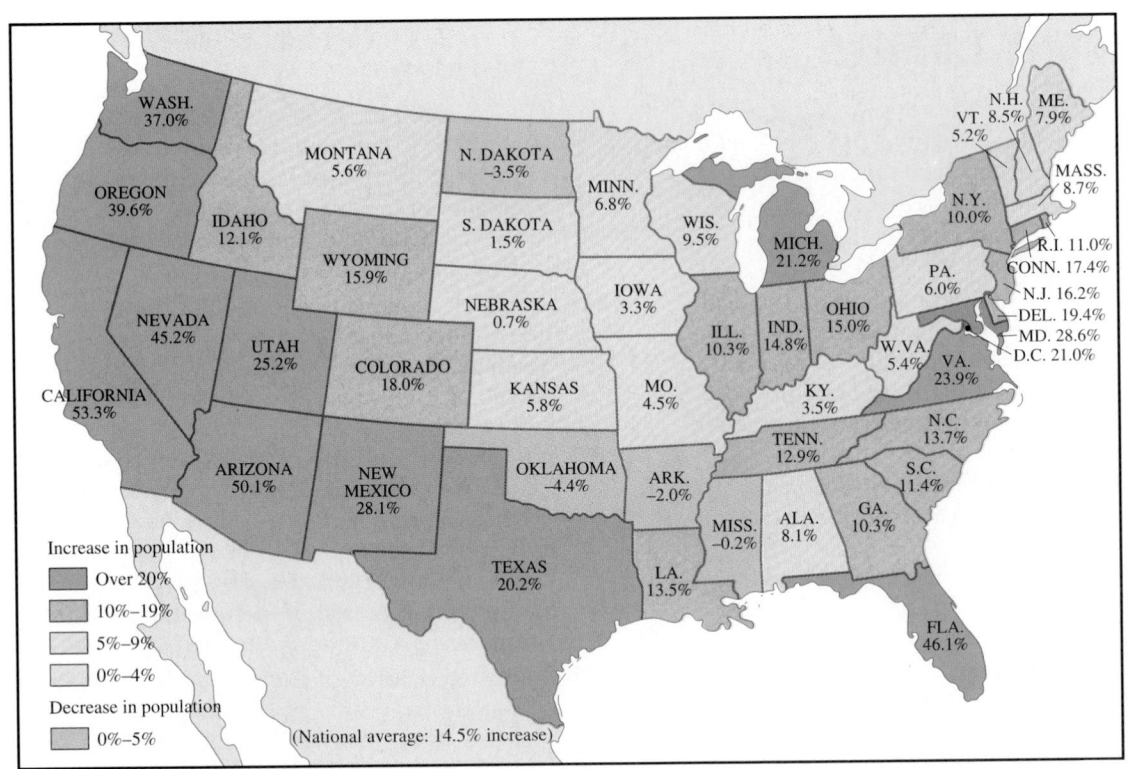

Map 27.1   A Nation on the Move, 1940–1950   American migration during the 1940s was the largest on record to that time. The farm population dropped dramatically as men, women, and children moved to war-production areas and to army and navy bases, particularly on the West Coast. Well over 30 million Americans migrated during the war. Many returned to their rural homes after the war, but 12 million migrants stayed in their new locations. Notice the population increases on the West Coast, as well as in the Southwest and Florida.

quired to win. Essential to victory was the mobilization of all sectors of the economy—industry, finance, agriculture, labor. America's big businesses got even bigger, as did its central government, labor unions, and farms. The federal government had the monumental task of coordinating activity in these spheres, as well as in two new ones: higher education and science. For this war was a scientific and technological war, supported by the development of new weapons such as radar and the atomic bomb. For all these reasons the Second World War transformed America. ■

Winning the Second World War

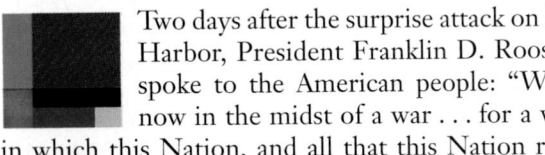 Two days after the surprise attack on Pearl Harbor, President Franklin D. Roosevelt spoke to the American people: "We are now in the midst of a war . . . for a world in which this Nation, and all that this Nation represents, will be safe for our children." Americans agreed with Roosevelt that they were defending their homes, families, and way of life against aggressive, even satanic, Japanese and Nazis.

Immediately, the United States became an "Ally" in the war against Germany, Japan, and Italy. But wartime relations among the United States, Great Britain, and the Soviet Union ran hot and cold. Allied leaders knew that military decisions had political consequences. If one Ally became desperate, for instance, it might destroy the alliance by pursuing a separate peace. The positions of troops at the end of the war, moreover, might determine the politics of the regions they occupied. Thus an undercurrent of mutual suspicion ran just beneath the surface of Allied cooperation. The Allies, however, did reach one important agreement: recognizing that if Germany gained control over Europe's resources, the Nazis might directly threaten the Americas, and worrying that the Germans would develop an atomic bomb before the Japanese did, Allied strategists devised a "Europe first" formula—knock out Germany and then concentrate on an isolated Japan.

Roosevelt, British prime minister Winston Churchill, and Soviet premier Joseph Stalin differed vehemently over the opening of a second, or western, front in Europe. After Germany conquered France in 1940 and invaded the Soviet Union in 1941, the Soviets bore the brunt of the war until mid-1944, suffering millions of casualties. By late 1941, before the fierce Russian winter stalled their onslaught, German troops had nearly reached Moscow and Leningrad (present-day St. Petersburg) and had slashed deeply into the Ukraine, taking Kiev. Stalin pressed for a British-American landing on the western coast to draw German troops away from the eastern front, but Churchill would not agree. The Red Army therefore did most of the fighting and dying on land, while the British and Americans concentrated on getting Lend-Lease supplies across the

Second-front Controversy

Atlantic and harassing the Germans from the air with attacks on factories and civilians alike.

Roosevelt was both sensitive to the Soviets' burden and fearful that the Soviet Union might be knocked out of the war, leaving Hitler free to invade England. In 1942 he told the Soviets that they could expect the Allies to cross the English Channel and invade France later that year. This was exactly what Stalin sought to take pressure off his wracked country. But Churchill balked. His preference was a series of small jabs at the enemy's Mediterranean forces. Churchill feared heavy losses in a premature cross-Channel invasion, but some American officials suspected that Churchill's strategy derived from his desire to reassert British imperial power in the Mediterranean.

Churchill won the debate. Instead of attacking France, the British and Americans invaded North Africa in November 1942 (see Map 27.2). "We are

The first wave of U.S. troops hits Omaha Beach during the D-Day invasion on June 6, 1944. Steven Spielberg's film *Saving Private Ryan* (1998) reconstructed the horrors that greeted the landing forces, including land mines and enemy machine-gun fire. This photo—one of the first D-Day photos released—was taken by daring war photographer Robert Capa, who landed in Normandy with the first troops.   (Robert Capa/Magnum Photos, Inc.)

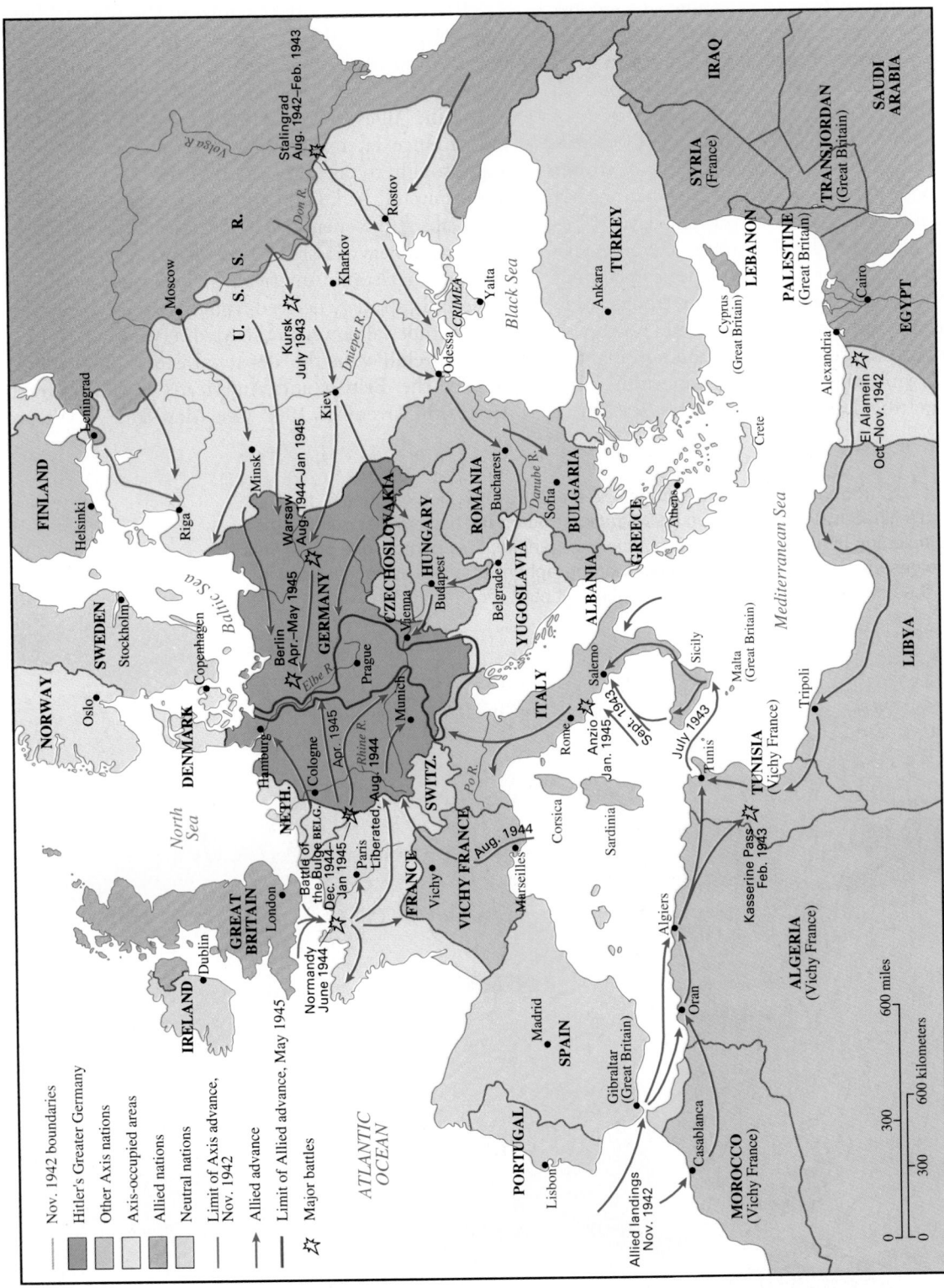

Map 27.2   The Allies on the Offensive in Europe, 1942–1945   The United States pursued a "Europe first" policy: first defeat Germany, then focus on Japan. American military efforts began in North Africa in late 1942 and ended in Germany in 1945 on May 8 (V-E Day).

striking back," Roosevelt declared. The news from the Soviet Union also buoyed Roosevelt. In the battle for Stalingrad (September 1942–January 1943)—probably the turning point of the European war—the Red Army defeated the Germans in bloody block-by-block fighting, forcing Hitler's divisions to retreat. But shortly thereafter, the president once again angered the Soviets by declaring another delay in launching the second front. Stalin was not mollified by the Allied invasion of Italy in the summer of 1943. Italy surrendered in September to American and British officers; Soviet officials were not invited to participate. Stalin grumbled that the arrangement smacked of a separate peace.

With the alliance badly strained, Roosevelt sought reconciliation through personal diplomacy. The three

Teheran Conference

Allied leaders met in Teheran, Iran, in December 1943. Stalin dismissed Churchill's repetitious justifications for further delaying the second front. Roosevelt had had enough, too; he also rejected Churchill's proposal for another peripheral attack, this time through the Balkans to Vienna. The three finally agreed to launch Operation Overlord—the cross-Channel invasion of France—in early 1944. And the Soviet Union promised to aid the Allies against Japan once Germany was defeated.

The second front opened in the dark morning hours of June 6, 1944—D-Day. In the largest

D-Day

amphibious landing in history, two hundred thousand Allied troops under the command of American general Dwight D. Eisenhower scrambled ashore at Normandy, France. Thousands of ships ferried the men within a hundred yards of the sandy beaches. Landing craft and soldiers immediately encountered the enemy; they triggered mines and were pinned down by fire from cliffside pillboxes. Meanwhile, Allied airborne troops dropped behind German lines. Although heavy aerial and naval bombardment and the clandestine work of saboteurs had softened the German defenses, the fighting was ferocious.

Allied troops soon spread across the countryside, liberating France and Belgium and entering Germany itself in September. In December, German armored divisions counterattacked in Belgium's Ardennes Forest, hoping to push on to Antwerp to halt the flow of Allied supplies through that Belgian port. After weeks of heavy fighting in what has come to be called the Battle of the Bulge—because of a noticeable bulge in the Allied line—the Allies pushed the enemy back

once again. Meanwhile, battle-hardened Soviet troops marched through Poland and cut a path to Berlin. American forces crossed the Rhine River in March 1945 and captured the heavily industrial Ruhr valley. Several units peeled off to enter Austria and Czechoslovakia, where they met up with Soviet soldiers. As the Americans marched east, a new president took office in Washington: Franklin D. Roosevelt died on April 12, and Harry S Truman became president and commander-in-chief. Eighteen days later, in bomb-ravaged Berlin, Adolf Hitler killed himself. On May 8 Germany surrendered.

The war in the Pacific was largely America's to fight, and at first, it did not go well. By mid-1942 Japan

The War in the Pacific

had seized the Philippines, Guam, Wake, Hong Kong, Singapore, Malaya, and the Dutch East Indies (Indonesia). In the Philippines in 1942, Japanese soldiers forced American and Filipino prisoners weakened by insufficient rations to walk 65 miles, clubbing, shooting, or starving to death about ten thousand of them. This so-called Bataan Death March intensified American hatred of the Japanese.

In April 1942 Americans began to hit back, initially by bombing Tokyo. In May, in the momentous

Battle of Midway

Battle of the Coral Sea, carrier-based American planes halted a Japanese advance toward Australia (see Map 27.3). The next month American forces defeated the Japanese at Midway, sinking four of the enemy's aircraft carriers. Thanks to the success of Operation MAGIC—the work of American experts who deciphered the secret code used by the Japanese to transmit messages—American naval officers knew ahead of time the approximate date and direction of the Japanese assault. The Battle of Midway was a turning point in the Pacific war, breaking the Japanese momentum and relieving the threat to Hawai'i. Thereafter, Japan was never able to match American fighting power or economic power.

American strategy was to "island-hop" toward Japan, skipping the most strongly fortified islands whenever possible and taking the weaker ones. In an effort to strand the Japanese armies on their island outposts and to cut off the supply of raw materials being shipped from Japan's home islands, Americans also set out to sink the Japanese merchant marine. The first U.S. offensive—at Guadalcanal in the Solomon Islands

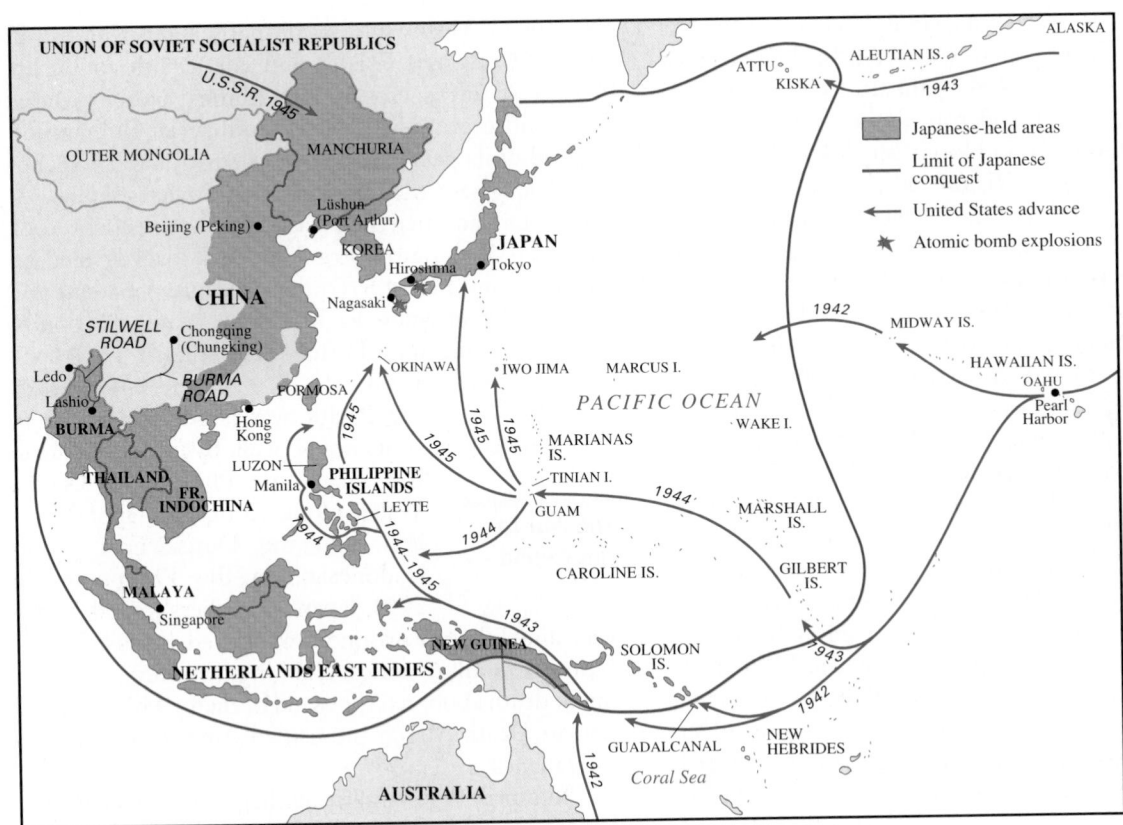

Map 27.3 The Pacific War The strategy of the United States was to "island-hop"—from Hawai'i in 1942 to Iwo Jima and Okinawa in 1945. Naval battles were also decisive, notably the Battles of the Coral Sea and Midway in 1942. The war in the Pacific ended with Japan's surrender on August 15, 1945 (V-J Day). (Source: Thomas G. Paterson, J. Garry Clifford, Kenneth J. Hagan, *American Foreign Policy: A History,* vol. 2, 3d ed. Copyright © 1991 by D. C. Heath Company. Used by permission of Houghton Mifflin Company.)

in mid-1942—gave American troops their first taste of jungle warfare: tropical heat, thick vegetation, savage mosquitoes. In 1943 and 1944 American troops attacked the enemy in the Gilbert, Marshall, and Mariana islands. And in October 1944, General Douglas MacArthur landed at Leyte to retake the Philippines for the United States.

Despite those victories, more tough fighting lay ahead in the Pacific. In February 1945 both sides took heavy losses at Iwo Jima, an island less than 5 miles long located 700 miles south of Tokyo. Stationed on the island were 21,000 Japanese troops living in pillboxes and miles of caves, trenches, and connecting tunnels. The American objective was Mount Suribachi, the highest point and most heavily fortified spot on Iwo Jima. From the outset, American casualties were heavy; the mountain had to be taken yard by yard.

Battles of Iwo Jima and Okinawa

After twenty days of fighting, victory finally came and marines planted the American flag atop Mount Suribachi. In this bitter battle, 6,821 Americans were killed along with all but 200 of the Japanese troops.

A month later, American troops landed on Okinawa, an island 350 miles from Japan. Fighting raged for two months; death was everywhere. Almost the entire Japanese garrison of 100,000 was killed, and there were 80,000 Okinawan civilian casualties. The American military lost 7,374 men. At sea, the supporting fleet reported almost 5,000 seamen killed or missing; most were the victims of *kamikaze* (suicide) attacks, in which Japanese pilots crashed their bomb-laden planes directly into American ships.

Still, Japanese leaders refused to admit defeat. Hoping to avoid a humiliating unconditional surrender (and to preserve the emperor's sovereignty), they hung on even while American bombers leveled their cities. In one staggering attack on Tokyo on May 23,

This scorched watch, found in the rubble at Hiroshima, stopped at the time of the blast—8:16. The shock waves and fires caused by the atomic bomb leveled great expanses of the city. Radiation released by the bomb caused lingering deaths for thousands who survived the explosion. The photo of Hiroshima shown above was taken eight months after the attack.   (Watch: John Launois/Black Star; Hiroshima: U.S. Air Force)

1945, American planes dropped bombs that engulfed the city in a firestorm, killing 83,000 people. Observers described the ghastly scene as a mass burning.

With victory in sight, American leaders began to plan a fall invasion of Japan's home islands, an expedition that was sure to incur high casualties. But the successful development of an atomic bomb by American scientists provided another route to victory. The secret atomic program, known as the Manhattan Project, had begun in August 1942, and the first bomb was exploded in the desert near Alamogordo, New Mexico, on July 16, 1945. Just three weeks later, on August 6, the Japanese city of Hiroshima was destroyed by a bomb dropped from an American B-29 plane called the *Enola Gay*, A

The Atomic Bomb

flash of dazzling light shot across the sky; then a huge purplish mushroom cloud boiled 40,000 feet into the atmosphere. Dense smoke, swirling fires, and suffocating dust soon engulfed the ground for miles. Much of the city was leveled almost instantly. Approximately 130,000 people were killed; tens of thousands more suffered severe burns and nuclear radiation poisoning.

American planes continued their devastating conventional bombing and also scattered leaflets over other Japanese cities, warning that they, too, would

How do historians know...

what motivated President Harry Truman to order the dropping of the atomic bomb? Truman explained that he did it for only one reason: to end the war as soon as possible and thus prevent the loss of 1 million American casulaties in an invasion of Japan. An earlier generation of historians, writing in the aftermath of the war, echoed President Truman's explanation. But more recently historians have revised this interpretation: they argue that Japan might have surrendered even if the atomic bombs had not been dropped, and they dispute Truman's high estimate of casualties as being pure fiction and several times the likely figure. These revisionists have studied the Potsdam Conference of July 1945 attended by Truman, Joseph Stalin, and Winston Churchill. In their research, they have demonstrated the value of diaries as historical evidence by consulting those kept by certain participants, notably Secretary of War Henry Stimson and Truman himself.

Scholars cite Stimson's diary (excerpted here) as evidence that Truman's chief motivations included not only ending the war but also impressing the Soviet Union with America's military might and minimizing the USSR's military participation in the final defeat and postwar occupation of Japan. On July 21 Stimson reported to Truman that the army had successfully tested an atomic device in New Mexico. Clearly emboldened by the news, Truman said that possession of the bomb "gave him an entirely new feeling of confidence. . . ." The next day, Stimson discussed the news with British prime minister Churchill. "Now I know what happened to Truman," Churchill responded. "When he got to the meeting after having read this report he was a changed man. He told the Russians just where they got off and generally bossed the whole meeting." A few historians contend that the decision to drop the atomic bomb was partly racist. As evidence, they point to Truman's handwritten diary entry in which he discussed using the bomb against "the Japs," whom he denounced as "savages, ruthless, merciless and fanatic." Others cite these words to claim that Truman desired to avenge the Japanese attack at Pearl Harbor. It is clear that while personal diaries can help to settle some historical disagreements, they can also generate new interpretive disputes.

The deeply emotional question about the necessity for dropping the atomic bomb has stirred debates among the public as well as among historians. In 1995, for example, the Smithsonian Institution provoked a furor with its plans for an exhibit prompted by the fiftieth anniversary of the decision to drop the bomb. Rather than incur the wrath of politicians, veterans' groups, and other Americans outraged by what they perceived to be an anti-American interpretation of events, the Smithsonian shelved most of the exhibit. (Photo: Henry L. Stimson Papers, Yale University Library)

TOP SECRET

I also discussed with him Harrison's two messages. He was intensely pleased by the accelerated timetable. As to the matter of the special target which I had refused to permit, he strongly confirmed my view, and said he felt the same way.

At ten forty Bundy and I again went to the British headquarters and talked to the Prime Minister and Lord Cherwell for over an hour. Churchill read Groves' report in full. He told me that he had noticed at the meeting of the three yesterday, Truman was evidently much fortified by something that had happened, and that he stood up to the Russians in a most emphatic and decisive manner, telling them as to certain demands that they absolutely could not have, and that the United States was entirely against them. Churchill said he now understood how this popping up had taken place and that he felt the same way. His own attitude confirmed this admission. He now not only was not worried about giving the Russians information of the matter, but was rather inclined to use it as an argument in our favor in the negotiations. The sentiment of the four of us was unanimous in thinking that it was advisable to tell the Russians at least that we were working on that subject, and intended to use it if and when it was successfully finished.

At twelve fifteen I called General Arnold over, showed him Harrison's two cables, showed him my answer to them and showed him Groves' report, which he read in its entirety. He told me that he agreed with me about the target which I had struck off the program. He said that it would take considerable hard work to organize the operations now that it was to move forward.

TOP SECRET

face atomic terror unless the Japanese Empire surrendered. On August 9 another atomic attack flattened Nagasaki, killing at least 60,000 people. Five days later the Japanese, who had been sending out peace feelers since June, surrendered. The victors promised that the Japanese emperor could remain as the nation's titular head. Formal surrender ceremonies were held September 2 aboard the battleship *Missouri*. The Second World War was over.

Use of the bomb to achieve victory had been the primary goal of the Manhattan Project. Most Americans agreed with President Truman

The Decision to Use the Atomic Bomb

that the atomic bombing of Hiroshima and Nagasaki was necessary to end the war as quickly as possible and to save American lives. At the highest government levels and among atomic scientists, alternatives had been discussed: detonating the bomb on an unpopulated Pacific island, with international observers as witnesses; blockading and bombing Japan conventionally; following up on Tokyo's peace feelers; encouraging a Soviet declaration of war on Japan. Truman, however, had rejected these options because he believed they would take too long and would not convince the tenacious Japanese that they had been beaten. Then, too, memories of Pearl Harbor played a part. "When you have to deal with a beast, you have to treat him as a beast," Truman said.

Diplomatic considerations also influenced the decision to use the bomb. American leaders wanted to take advantage of the real and psychological power the bomb would bestow on the United States. It might serve as a deterrent against aggression; it might intimidate the Soviet Union into making concessions in eastern Europe; it might end the war in the Pacific before the Soviet Union could claim a role in the postwar management of Asia. "If it explodes, as I think it will," Truman remarked, "I'll certainly have a hammer on those boys [the Soviets]."

Mobilizing the American Home Front

In the aftermath of Pearl Harbor, the American people rushed to the defense not only of their country but also of what President Roosevelt had called the "four essential human freedoms"—freedom of speech, freedom of worship, freedom from want, and freedom from fear. Women in war-production work, as well as men on the battlefields, believed they were fighting for

both democracy and the American family. Private advertisers as well as government agencies called on people to defend the "American Way of Life." For example, an advertisement for vacuum cleaners in the *Saturday Evening Post* urged women war workers to fight "for freedom and all that means to women everywhere. You're fighting for a little house of your own, and a husband to meet every night at the door. You're fighting for the right to bring up your children without the shadow of fear."

Despite nearly unanimous support for the war effort, government leaders worried that, in a long war, public willingness to sacrifice might

Why We Fight

lag. To elicit the people's support, in 1942 President Roosevelt established the Office of War Information (OWI), which took charge of domestic propaganda and hired Hollywood filmmakers and New York copywriters to sell the war at home. The army responded by hiring movie director Frank Capra to produce a series of propaganda films called *Why We Fight*, which portrayed the Allies as heroic partners united in a common effort against evil.

No wartime agency better exemplified Americans' willingness to sacrifice to win the war than the Office of Price Administration (OPA). Established by Congress in 1942 with

Office of Price Administration

the power to control inflation by fixing price ceilings on commodities, and by controlling rents in defense areas, the OPA instituted nationwide rationing for automobile tires and issued rationing books with coupons for sugar, coffee, and gasoline. Point rationing programs were introduced in 1943 with stamps for purchasing meats, butter and cheese, shoes, and other controlled commodities. Consumers became skilled at handling ration stamps, each worth ten points—red for meats and cheese, blue for canned goods. Most Americans abided by the rules, but some hoarded sugar and coffee or bought beef on the "black market"—under the counter or from the trunk of a car.

Women consumers were central to OPA's success. They enlisted in the "food fight for freedom" by signing "The Home Front Pledge" and promising to pay "no more than Ceiling Prices." The OPA was active in every community through its 5,525 local War Price and Rationing Boards, operated largely by women volunteers, which allocated coupons for each family. Some of the volunteers were veterans of labor unions and consumer groups, while others were ordinary shoppers determined to sacrifice for the war effort. But the

OPA's successes in enforcing price ceilings provoked opposition from businesses, large and small, which even in wartime wanted to charge whatever the market would bear. Ranging from local grocery stores to large trade associations, such as the National Association of Manufacturers, businesses blamed the OPA for the "scarcity" of consumer goods. The American Meat Institute attacked the OPA not only for the alleged shortages of meat, but also for alleged contamination of the meat supply. In fact, the packers' profits soared as war-working Americans with good jobs increased their annual consumption of meat from 127 to 150 pounds per capita.

While the guns boomed in Europe and Asia, the war was changing American lives and institutions.

War Production Board and War Manpower Commission

One month after Pearl Harbor, President Roosevelt established the War Production Board (WPB) and assigned to it the task of converting the economy from civilian to military production. Factories that had manufactured silk ribbons began to turn out silk parachutes; automobile companies switched to the production of tanks and airplanes; adding-machine companies started manufacturing automatic pistols. Factories had to be expanded and new ones built. Also established in 1942, the War Manpower Commission (WMC) recruited new workers for the nation's factories.

The war demanded sacrifices from Americans, but it also rewarded them with new highs in personal income (see Figure 27.1). Savings deposits jumped from $32.4 billion in 1942 to $51.4 billion in 1945. Corporations doubled their net profits between 1939 and 1943, and employees' wages and salaries rose more than 135 percent from 1940 to 1945. The government did not tax this extra income as heavily as it might have. Instead, it resorted to deficit financing and borrowed much of the cost of waging the war, about half of it in the form of war bonds sold to patriotic citizens. The national debt skyrocketed from $49 billion in 1941 to $259 billion in 1945.

The industrial mobilization was so successful that the production of durable goods more than tripled. Since this was the world's first massive air war, fighter planes and bombers were crucial, and America's factories responded to the need: the manufacture of military aircraft, which had totaled 6,000 in 1940, jumped to over 47,000 in 1942 and to 85,000 in 1943. Women workers made a major contribution to the rapidly expanding aircraft industry, whose female work force increased from 4,000 in December 1941 to 310,000 two years later.

The wartime emergency also spurred the establishment of totally new industries, most notably synthetic rubber. The Japanese, in their conquest of the South Pacific following Pearl Harbor, had captured 90 percent of the world's supply of crude rubber. The American government resorted to a national speed limit and gasoline rationing to save wear on tires, but the country still could not meet its wartime needs. So in 1942, with an investment of $700 million, the government underwrote the creation of a synthetic-rubber industry. By war's end the nation that had been the world's largest importer of rubber had become the world's largest exporter of rubber—all of it synthetic.

Government Incentives in Business

To gain the cooperation of business, the War Production Board and other government agencies met business more than halfway. The government guaranteed profits in the form of cost-plus-fixed-fee contracts, generous tax write-offs, and exemptions from antitrust prosecution. Such concessions made sense for a nation that wanted vast quantities of war goods manufactured in the shortest possible time. From mid-1940 through September 1944 the government awarded contracts totaling $175 billion, no less than two-thirds of which went to the top one hundred corporations. General Motors alone received 8 percent of the total; big awards also went to other automobile companies and to aircraft, steel, electrical, and chemical companies. Although the expression "military-industrial complex" had not yet been coined—President Dwight Eisenhower would do so in 1961 (see page 796)—the web of military-business interdependence had begun to be woven.

University Research and Weapons Development

In science and higher education, too, the big got bigger as federal contracts mobilized science and technology for the war effort. Massachusetts Institute of Technology was a major recipient for its development of radar. MIT received $117 million, followed by the California Institute of Technology, Harvard, and Columbia. Most federal research contracts with universities were for the development of devices for warfare, such as radar and the proximity fuse. The most spectacular result of such government contracts was the atomic bomb. The Manhattan Project, run by the army, financed research at the University of Chicago, which in 1942 was the site of the world's first

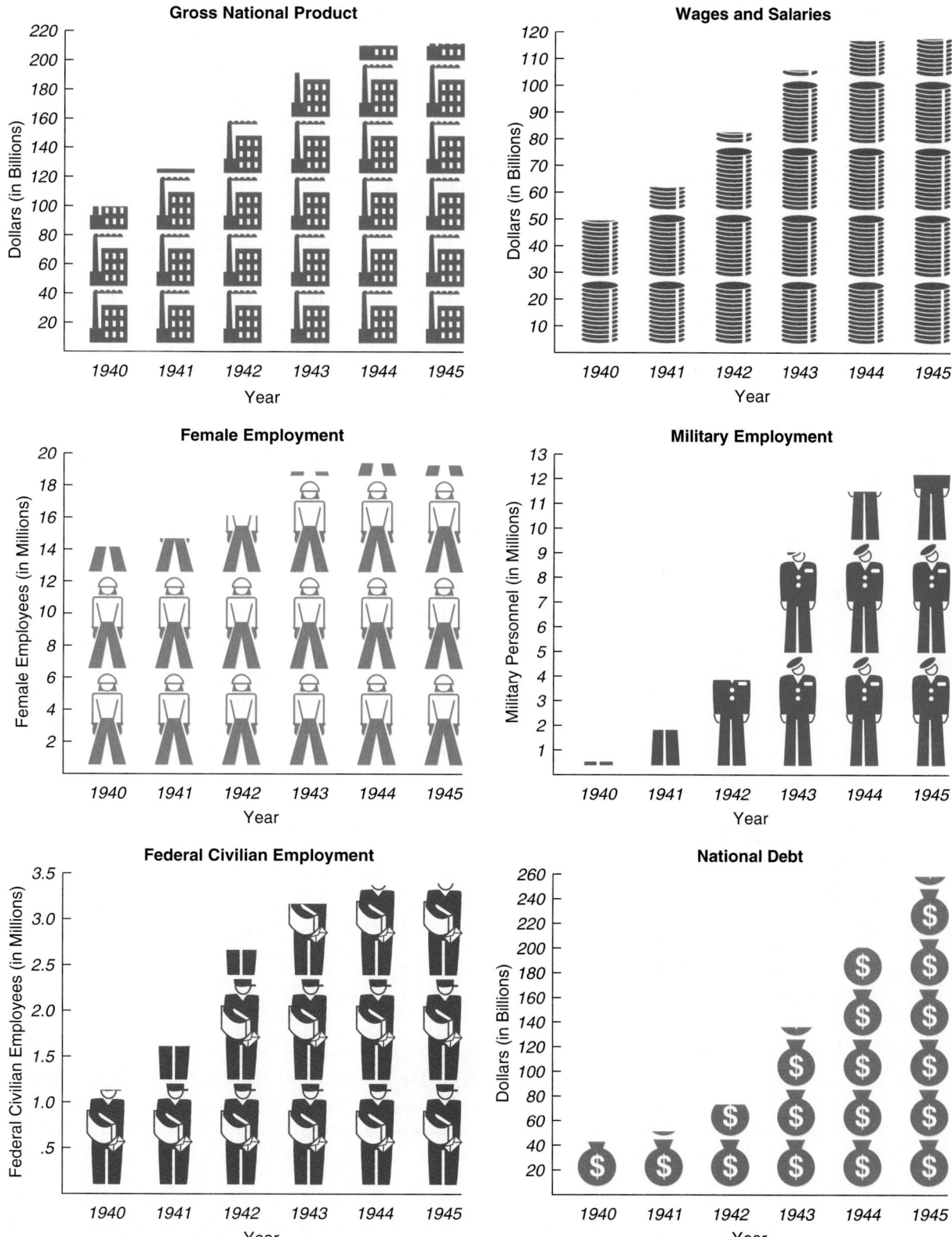

Figure 27.1   The Wartime Economic Boom, 1940–1945   War production finally ended the Great Depression. These graphs show the wartime increases in key economic indicators: gross national product; wages and salaries; female, military, and federal civilian employment; and national debt for financing the war.

sustained nuclear chain reaction. The University of California at Berkeley had a contract to operate the Los Alamos Scientific Laboratory in New Mexico, where the atomic bomb was tested. American universities became valued participants in the military-industrial complex.

Wartime contracts with universities also accelerated medical progress. Indeed, because of the development of antibiotics and sulfa drugs, which greatly reduced deaths from infected war wounds, the survival rate among injured soldiers was 90 percent, compared with 10 percent in the First World War. Penicillin made its debut in America in 1942, saving the life of a woman suffering from a once-fatal bacterial infection. The most dreaded home-front disease, especially by children, was polio. Although research for a polio vaccine advanced during the war, not until 1955 did the government approve a vaccine for public use (see Chapter 28).

Organized labor also grew during the war. Membership in unions ballooned from 8.5 million in 1940 to 14.75 million in 1945. Less than

Unions and Wartime Labor Strikes

a week after Pearl Harbor, a White House labor-management conference agreed to a no-strike/no-lockout pledge to guarantee uninterrupted war production. To minimize labor-management conflict, in 1942 President Roosevelt created the National War Labor Board (NWLB), sometimes referred to as the Supreme Court for labor disputes. Unions were permitted to enroll as many new members as possible, but workers could not be required to join a union. Thus the NWLB forged a temporary compromise between the unions' demand for a closed shop, in which only union members could be hired, and management's interest in open shops.

But when the NWLB attempted in 1943 to limit wage increases to cost-of-living pay hikes, workers responded with strikes that tripled the amount of lost production time over that of the previous year. The worst labor disruptions of 1943 occurred in the coal fields. To discourage further work stoppages, Congress passed the War Labor Disputes (Smith-Connally) Act in June 1943. The act gave the president authority to seize and operate any strike-bound plant deemed necessary to the national security, and it established a mandatory thirty-day cooling-off period before any new strike could be called. The Smith-Connally Act also gave the NWLB the legal authority to settle labor disputes for the duration of the war.

Agriculture also made an impressive contribution to the war effort, through hard work and the introduction of labor-saving machinery to re-

Wartime Changes in Agriculture

place men and women who had gone to the front or migrated to war-production centers. Before the war, farming had been in the midst of a transition from the family-owned and -operated farm to the large-scale, mechanized agribusiness dominated by banks, insurance companies, and farm co-ops. The Second World War accelerated the trend, for wealthy financial institutions were better able than family farmers to pay for expensive new machinery. From 1940 to 1945, while the value of farm machinery more than doubled, from $3.1 billion to $6.5 billion, the farm population fell from 30.5 million to 24.4 million people.

At the apex of the burgeoning national economy stood the federal government, the size and importance of which was mushrooming: from

Growth in the Federal Government

1940 to 1945 the federal bureaucracy expanded from 1.1 million workers to 3.4 million. The executive branch grew most dramatically. Besides raising the armed forces, mobilizing industrial production, and pacifying labor and management, the executive branch also had to manage the labor supply and control inflation. Although government-business-labor relations were sometimes bitter, and production was sometimes slowed as a result, Americans were generally ready to make personal sacrifices. They knew the war would be costly and long. In previous conflicts Americans had flocked to the colors with flags, wild rallies, and militaristic songs, but they fought the Second World War with a grim, realistic determination. They were in it "for the duration."

The Military Life

America's men and women responded eagerly to their nation's call to arms. In 1941, only 1.8 million people were serving on active duty, although Selective Service had been functioning for a full year. By the end of the war, more than 16.3 million women and men had served in the army, navy, and marines. Fighting a world war on two fronts required a massive force. To American servicepeople in Asia and in Europe, the Second World War was a dirty job. Like cartoonist Bill Mauldin's popular GI characters Willy and Joe, who were more interested in tasty food and dry socks than

Lining the rails of their ship, African American army nurses arrive at the European theater of operations in August 1944. These nurses, like their white counterparts in America's segregated army, served in field and base hospitals, often right behind the fighting front. (Library of Congress)

in abstractions, millions of GIs were simply eager to get it over with. American troops served overseas for an average of sixteen months. Some never returned: total deaths exceeded 405,000. In terms of lost American lives, the cost of the war was second only to that lost on both sides during the Civil War.

Military service demanded enormous personal adjustments. Soldiers and sailors who never had been more than a few miles from home became homesick; GIs joked, somewhat bitterly, about having found a new home in the army. But loneliness was inconsequential compared with the intense fear that soldiers admitted to feeling in battle. Combat veterans told a group of psychologists that a man who burst out weeping was "not regarded as a coward unless he made no apparent effort to stick to his job." Although the American Psychiatric Association did not identify the illness known as post-traumatic stress disorder until 1980, it is clear in retrospect that American veterans suffered from it after the war. The symptoms included nightmares and flashbacks to the battlefield, depression and anger, and widespread alcoholism.

Among the millions of Americans who left home to join the armed forces were men and women who

The Ordeal of Combat

Homosexuals on Active Duty

had experienced homosexual attraction in peacetime. Freed of their familial environments and serving in sex-segregated units, many acted on their feelings. "When I first got into the navy—in the recreation hall, for instance," recalled a chief petty officer, "there'd be eye contact. . . . All of a sudden you had a vast network of friends." The military court-martialed homosexuals, and nine thousand servicemen and -women were discharged because of their sexual orientation. Usually, however, gay relationships went unnoticed by the heterosexual world. For lesbians in the armed forces, the military environment offered friendships and a positive identity. "For many gay Americans," the historian John D'Emilio has written, "World War II created something of a nationwide coming out situation."

Wartime service not only broadened horizons but also fostered soldiers' ambitions. A soldier from the Midwest, who found himself "living among fellows from all over the country," observed that he had "picked up a lot of ideas from them . . . about how to live my own life and to get more out of it. I came out a lot more ambitious than I was before I went in." Many GIs returned to civilian

Postwar Ambitions

life with new skills they had learned in the military's technical schools. Still others took advantage of the educational benefits provided by the GI Bill of Rights (1944) to study for a college degree (see Chapter 28).

Still, after two or three years abroad, men and women in the service returned to the United States not knowing what to expect from civilian life. Some male war veterans expected that America's women, deeply appreciative of having been protected against a fearsome enemy, would repay their obligation with sexual favors. "We are not only fighting for the Four Freedoms," exclaimed one soldier, "we are also fighting for the priceless privilege of making love to American women." Many GIs, however, returned fearing that life at home had passed them by. They were much older in experience and exposure to brutality; many came back to the United States convinced that they had sacrificed their youth. And they found that home had changed as well. "Our friends are gone," one GI lamented. "The family and the town naturally had to go on even if we weren't there, and somehow it seems things have sort of closed in and filled that space we used to occupy."

Enemy Aliens, Conscientious Objectors, and Japanese American Internees

After the United States entered the war, American leaders had to consider whether enemy agents were operating within the nation's borders and threatening the war effort. It was clear that not all Americans were enthusiastic supporters of the nation's participation in the war. The Alien Registration (Smith) Act, passed in 1940, made it unlawful to advocate the overthrow of the U.S. government by force or violence or to join any organization that did so. After Pearl Harbor, the government drew upon this authority to take into custody thousands of Germans, Italians, and other Europeans as suspected spies and potential traitors. During the war, the government interned 14,426 Europeans in Enemy Alien Camps. Fearing subversion from aliens born in enemy countries, the government also prohibited ten thousand Italian Americans from living or working in restricted zones along the California coast, including San Francisco and Monterey Bay.

Some Americans had conscientious objections to war, particularly Quakers, Mennonites, and members of the Church of the Brethren. During the Second World War conscientious objectors (COs) had to have a religious (as opposed to a moral or an ethical) reason for refusing military service. About 12,000 COs were sent to civilian public service camps, where they worked on conservation projects or as orderlies in hospitals. Approximately 5,500, three-fourths of whom were Jehovah's Witnesses, refused to participate in any way; they were imprisoned.

Compared with the First World War, the nation's wartime civil liberties record was generally creditable.

"An Enemy Race"

But there was one enormous exception: the internment in "relocation centers" of, ultimately, 120,000 Japanese Americans. Of these people, 77,000 were Nisei—native-born citizens of the United States. Their imprisonment was based not on suspicion or evidence of treason; their crime was solely that they were of Japanese descent. General John L. DeWitt, chief of the Western Defense Command, warned, "The Japanese race is an enemy race and while many second and third generation Japanese born on United States soil, possessed of United States citizenship, have become 'Americanized,' the racial strains are undiluted. . . . It, therefore, follows that along the vital Pacific Coast over 112,000 potential enemies, of Japanese extraction, are at large today." With strained logic DeWitt rationalized the internment: "The very fact that no sabotage [by Japanese Americans] has taken place to date is a disturbing and confirming indication that such action will be taken."

General DeWitt was not alone in his racist paranoia and hatred. Popular racial stereotypes held that Japanese people abroad and at home were sneaky and evil, and the American people, feeling that the Japanese had to be repaid for Pearl Harbor, generally regarded Japan as the United States's chief enemy. Several factors, however, should have disproved the accusation that Japanese Americans were members of "an enemy race." In Hawai'i, for example, where 160,000 people—one-third of the population—were of Japanese descent, fewer than a thousand people were taken into custody and sent to the mainland for internment. More to the point, Japanese American soldiers fought valiantly for the United States. The all–Japanese American 442nd Regimental Combat Team, drawn heavily from young men in internment camps, was the most decorated unit of its size in the armed forces. Suffering heavy casualties in Italy and France, members of the 442nd were awarded a Congressional Medal of Honor, 47 Distinguished Service

Crosses, 350 Silver Stars, and more than 3,600 Purple Hearts.

During the war, charges of criminal behavior were never brought against any Japanese Americans; none was ever indicted or tried for espionage, treason, or sedition. Nevertheless in 1942 all the 112,000 Japanese Americans living in California, Oregon, and the state of Washington were rounded up and imprisoned. "It was really cruel and harsh," recalled Joseph Y. Kurihara, a citizen and a veteran of the First World War. "To pack and evacuate in forty-eight hours was an impossibility. Seeing mothers completely bewildered with children crying from want and peddlers taking advantage and offering prices next to robbery made me feel like murdering those responsible."

The internees were sent to flood-damaged lands at Relocation, Arkansas; to the intermountain terrain

Life in the Internment Camps

of Wyoming and the desert of western Arizona; and to other arid and desolate spots in the West. The camps were bleak and demoralizing. Behind barbed wire stood tarpapered wooden barracks where entire families lived in a single room furnished only with cots, blankets, and a bare light bulb. Toilets and dining and bathing facilities were communal; privacy was almost nonexistent. Japanese Americans were forced to sell property valued at $500 million, and they lost their positions in the truck-garden, floral, and fishing industries. Indeed, their economic competitors were among the most vocal proponents of their relocation.

The Supreme Court upheld the government's policy of internment. In wartime, the Court ruled in *Hirabayashi v. U.S.* (1943), "residents having ethnic af-

In February 1942 President Franklin D. Roosevelt ordered that all Japanese Americans living on the West Coast be rounded up and placed in prison camps. These families were awaiting a train to take them to an assembly center in Merced, California; from there, they would be sent to relocation camps in remote inland areas. (National Archives)

filiations with an invading enemy may be a greater source of danger than those of different ancestry." In *Korematsu v. U.S.* (1944), the Court, with three justices dissenting, approved the removal of the Nisei from the West Coast. One dissenter, Justice Frank Murphy, denounced the decision as the "legalization of racism."

In 1983, forty-one years after he had been sent to a government camp, Fred Korematsu had the satisfaction of hearing a federal judge rule that he—and by implication all detainees—had been the victim of "unsubstantiated facts, distortions and misrepresentations of at least one military commander whose views were affected by racism." A year earlier, the government's special Commission on Wartime Relocation and Internment of Civilians had recommended compensating the victims of this policy. Finally, in 1988, Congress voted to award $20,000 and a public apology to each of the surviving sixty thousand Japanese American internees.

Jobs and Racism on the Home Front

African Americans in Combat

Even before Pearl Harbor, African Americans asserted their determination to participate in the war effort. In response to the March on Washington Movement of 1941 (see pages 720–721), the Selective Service System and the War Department agreed to increase the number of African Americans in uniform by drafting blacks in proportion to their presence in the population: about 10 percent. At the height of the war, the army had more than 700,000 African American troops. An additional 187,000 black men and women enlisted in the navy, the Coast Guard, and the once all-white Marine Corps.

Although they served in segregated units, African Americans fought on the front lines. For the first time the War Department sanctioned the training of blacks as pilots. After instruction at Tuskegee Institute in Alabama, pilots saw heroic service in all-black units such as the Ninety-ninth Pursuit Squadron, winner of eighty Distinguished Flying Crosses. In 1940 Colonel Benjamin O. Davis was the first African American to be promoted to brigadier general. More important, black people distinguished themselves on the battlefield. The performance of black marines in the Pacific theater was such that the corps commandant pro-

claimed: "Negro Marines are no longer on trial. They are Marines, period."

Serious failures in race relations, however, undercut these accomplishments. Race riots instigated by whites broke out on military bases, and white civilians assaulted black soldiers and sailors throughout the South. In North Carolina a white bus driver who murdered an African American soldier in full view of the passengers was found not guilty. The worst racist outrage occurred at a munitions depot named Port Chicago in California. With a lack of training and a shocking disregard for safety by the navy, all-black squads of sailors were ordered to load explosives onto ships bound for the Pacific theater. On July 17, 1944, a tremendous ammunition explosion obliterated two vessels, shattered windows in San Francisco 35 miles away, and killed 320 people, including 202 African Americans. When the surviving black sailors were ordered to resume loading ammunition, fifty refused; the men were arrested, found guilty of mutiny by an all-white panel, dishonorably discharged, and sentenced to fifteen years at hard labor.

Experiences such as these caused African Americans to wonder what, in fact, they were fighting for.

Civil Rights Movement

They rankled at the remark of the governor of Tennessee when blacks urged him to appoint African Americans to local draft boards: "This is a white man's country. . . . The Negro had nothing to do with the settling of America." They noted that the Red Cross separated blood according to the race of the donor, as if there were some difference. Although some African Americans even argued that the Second World War was a white man's war and that American racism was little different from German racism, there were persuasive reasons for blacks to participate in the war effort. Perhaps, as the NAACP believed, this was an opportunity "to persuade, embarrass, compel and shame our government and our nation . . . into a more enlightened attitude toward a tenth of its people." Proclaiming that in the Second World War they were waging a "Double V" campaign (for victory at home and abroad), blacks were more militant than before and readier than ever to protest. Membership in civil rights organizations soared. The NAACP, 50,000 strong in 1940, had 450,000 members by 1946. And in 1942 civil rights activists founded the Congress of Racial Equality (CORE), which stressed "nonviolent direct action" and staged sit-ins to desegregate restaurants and movie theaters in northern cities.

A leader of the Tuskegee airmen, Benjamin O. Davis, Jr., was the fourth African American to graduate from West Point. During the war, Colonel Davis commanded the 332d Fighter Group, which destroyed over two hundred enemy planes in southern Europe. (National Archives)

The war also created opportunities in industry. Roosevelt's Executive Order No. 8802, issued in 1941,

African American War Workers

required employers in defense industries to make jobs available "without discrimination because of race, creed, color or national origin." To secure defense jobs, 1.5 million black Americans migrated from the South to the industrial cities of the North and West in the 1940s. Almost three-fourths settled in the urban-industrial states of California, Illinois, Michigan, New York, Ohio, and Pennsylvania. More than half a million became active members of CIO unions like the United Auto Workers and United Steel Workers. African American voters in northern cities were beginning to constitute a vital swing vote, not only in local and state elections but also in presidential contests.

For African Americans, however, the benefits of urban life came with a high price tag. Migrants from the rural South had to adjust to life in big cities, and white hostility made the adjustment more difficult. Southern whites who had migrated north brought

Race Riots of 1943

with them the racial prejudices of the Deep South. Also hostile were the northern whites. In 1942 more than half of them believed that African Americans should be segregated in separate schools and neighborhoods. Such attitudes, and the competition between blacks and whites for jobs and housing, caused many people to fear that the summer of 1943 would be like 1919—another "Red Summer" (see page 651). Indeed, in 1943 almost 250 racial conflicts exploded in forty-seven cities. Outright racial warfare bloodied the streets of Detroit in June. At the end of thirty hours of rioting, twenty-five blacks and nine whites lay dead. White mobs, undeterred by police, had roamed the city attacking blacks and overturning cars. Blacks had hurled rocks at police and hauled white passengers off streetcars. Surveying the damage, an elderly black woman said, "There ain't no North any more. Everything now is South."

The federal government did practically nothing to prevent further racial violence. From President Roosevelt on down, most federal officials put the war first,

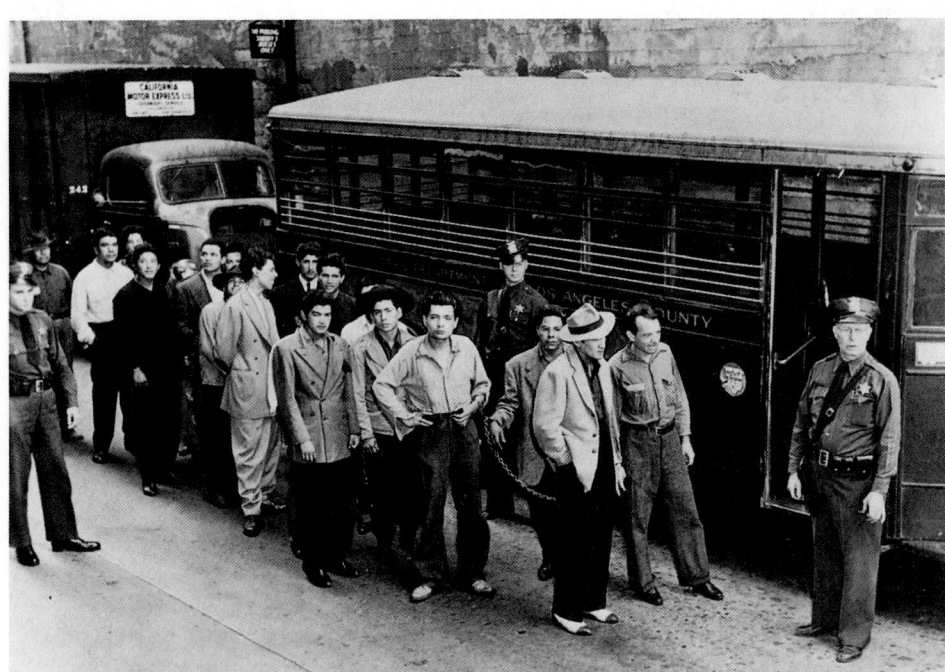

One hundred people were injured during the 1943 "zoot-suit riot" in Los Angeles, when white mobs attacked Mexican American men and tore off their zoot suits. During the riot, Los Angeles police arrested Mexican Americans for wearing such attire in violation of a city ordinance. These men in chains were headed to jail.   (Library of Congress)

domestic reform second. Unquestionably many government leaders held racist beliefs. Secretary of War Henry L. Stimson, for example, blamed the riots on "radical leaders of the colored race" who wanted to use the war to obtain "interracial marriages." But this time government neglect could not discourage African Americans and the century-old civil rights movement. By war's end they were ready—politically, economically, and emotionally—to wage a struggle for voting rights and for equal access to public accommodations and institutions.

Racial violence was not directed exclusively against blacks. Some whites judged people of Mexican origin as undesirable as those whose roots were African. In 1942 American farms and war industries needed workers, and the United States and Mexico had agreed to the *bracero* program, whereby Mexicans were admitted to the United States on short-term work contracts. Although the newcomers suffered racial discrimination and segregation, they seized the economic opportunities that had become available. In Los Angeles, seventeen thousand people of Mexican descent found shipyard jobs where before the war none had been available to them.

Ethnic and racial animosities intensified during the war. In 1943 Los Angeles witnessed the "zoot-suit riot," in which whites, most of them sailors and sol-

Bracero Program

diers, wantonly attacked Mexican Americans. Mexican American street gangs (*pachucos*) had adopted ducktail haircuts and zoot suits: long coats with wide padded shoulders, pegged pants, wide-brimmed hats, and dangling watch chains. White racist anger at the presumed arrogance of the zoot-suiters boiled over in June, and for four days mobs invaded Mexican American neighborhoods. According to one report, "Procedure was standard: grab a zooter. Take off his pants and frock coat and tear them up or burn them." Not only did white police officers look the other way during these assaults, but the city of Los Angeles passed an ordinance that made wearing a zoot suit within city limits a crime. Although the Second World War briefly provided economic opportunities for Mexican Americans, these years were not the transforming experience that they were for African Americans.

Women and Children in the War Effort

During the war large numbers of American women patriotically responded to their nation's call for help. The WACs (Women's Army Corps) enlisted 140,000 women, while 100,000 served in the navy's WAVES (Women Accepted for Volunteer Emergency Service)

and 39,000 in the Marine Corps and Coast Guard. Another 75,000 women served in the army and navy's Nursing Corps, where they saw duty during the invasions of North Africa, Italy, and France. Women also served as pilots in the WASP (Women Air Service Pilots), teaching basic flying, towing aerial targets for gunnery practice, ferrying planes across the country, and serving as test pilots. WASP flying duty was often hazardous; thirty-eight women lost their lives.

For economic as well as patriotic reasons, more than 6 million women entered the labor force during the war. During the Great Depression, when millions of men were unemployed, public opinion had been hostile to the hiring of women, but the war brought about a rapid increase in employment. Just when men were going off to war, industry had to recruit millions of new workers to supply the rapidly expanding need for military equipment. Filling these new jobs were African Americans, southern whites, Mexican Americans, and, above all, women.

No matter how impressive women's contributions were to the war effort, statistics tell only part of the story. Changes in people's attitudes were also important. Until early in the war, employers had insisted that women were not suited for industrial jobs. As labor shortages began to threaten the war effort, however, employers did an about-face. "Almost overnight," said Mary Anderson, head of the Women's Bureau of the Department of Labor, "women were reclassified by industrialists from a marginal to a basic labor supply for munitions making." Women became riveters, welders, crane operators, tool makers, shell loaders, lumberjacks ("lumberjills"), cowgirls, and police officers.

During the war years, the number of working women increased by 57 percent. Two million women took clerical jobs; another 2.5 million worked in manufacturing. The significance of these figures lay not

Women in War Production

Women workers mastered numerous job skills during the war. In 1942 crews of women cared for Long Island commuter trains like this one.   (Corbis-Bettmann)

just in the numbers themselves but also in the kinds of women who were entering the work force. The economist Claudia Goldin has observed that labor-force participation rates increased most for women over age forty-five, and that "married, rather than single women, were the primary means of bolstering the nation's labor force." Before the war the average female wage earner had been young, single, and largely self-supporting; by 1945 more working women were married than single, and more were over age thirty-five than under.

New employment opportunities also increased women's occupational mobility. Especially noteworthy were the gains made by African American women; over 400,000 quit work as domestic servants to enjoy the better working conditions, higher pay, and union benefits of industrial employment. To take advantage of the new employment opportunities, both black and white women willingly uprooted themselves. Over 7 million women moved to war-production areas, such as Willow Run, Michigan, site of a massive bomber plant, and southern California, home of both shipyards and aircraft factories.

As public opinion shifted to support women's war work, posters and billboards appeared urging women to "Do the Job HE Left Behind." Newspapers and magazines, radio, and movies proclaimed Rosie the Riveter a war hero. But few people asserted that women's war work should bring about a permanent shift in sex roles: it was merely a response to a national emergency. Once the victory was won, women should go back to nurturing their husbands and children, relinquishing their jobs to returning GIs. Wartime surveys, however, showed that many of the women wanted to remain in their jobs—80 percent of New York's women workers felt that way, as did 75 percent in Detroit. "War jobs have uncovered unsuspected abilities in American women," explained one woman. "Why lose all these abilities because of a belief that 'a woman's place is in the home'? For some it is," she added, "for others not."

Although women's wages rose when they acquired better jobs, they still received lower pay than men. In 1945 women in manufacturing earned only 65 percent of what men were paid. An important reason for this inequality was the sex-segregated labor market. Although the wartime emergency caused some traditionally male jobs to be reclassified for women, most jobs were defined as

Discrimination Against Women

either "women's work" or "men's work." Even in factories, most women worked in all-female shops. Working women, particularly working mothers, suffered in other ways as well. Early in the war, childcare centers were in short supply in war-boom areas. And even as mothers were being encouraged to work in the national defense, there was still opposition to their doing so. One form this campaign took was a series of exaggerated articles in mass-circulation magazines about the suffering of "eight-hour orphans" or "latchkey children," left alone or deposited in all-night movie theaters while their mothers worked eight-hour shifts in war plants.

By and large, however, the home-front children of working women were not neglected or abused during the war. Families made their own childcare arrangements, which often involved leaving children in the care of their grandmothers. Some families benefited from the Lanham Act of 1940, which provided federal aid to communities that had to absorb large war-related populations. Benefits included funds for childcare centers, hospitals, sewer systems, and additional police officers and firefighters. In late 1943, fewer than 60,000 children were enrolled in Lanham Act childcare centers; six months later, the number had more than doubled to 130,000. Another government program, Extended School Services, offered care for children before and after school; at the program's peak in 1943, it cared for 320,000 children. Although working mothers and their children received less of such help than they needed, the Second World War was a brief time of progress in the provision of childcare. Government support for these programs expired after the war.

Childcare in Wartime

America's children and youth made important contributions to the war effort. Children saved their nickels and dimes to buy war bonds, and they pulled wagons from house to house collecting old newspapers, rubber tires, and tin cans. "I became fiercely patriotic," recalled a Nebraska farm girl, "and participated in every war effort that I could." Thousands of young people also went to work during the war. In 1940, for example, 900,000 Americans between the ages of fourteen and eighteen were employed. By the spring of 1944 their number had climbed to 3 million—one-third of their age group. Teenagers were dropping out of high school in record numbers, and some observers believed that the most pressing social problem afflicting young people was not juvenile delinquency but failure to finish school. High-school enrollments hit new lows during the war, which prompted a back-to-school drive in 1944.

While millions of women were entering the work force, hundreds of thousands of women were also getting married. The number of

Increase in Marriage, Divorce, and Birth Rates

marriages rose from 73 per 1,000 unmarried women in 1939 to 93 in 1942. Some couples scrambled to get married so they could live together before the man was sent overseas; others doubtless married and had children to qualify for military deferments. Many of these hasty marriages did not survive long military separations, and divorces soared, too—from 25,000 in 1939 to 359,000 in 1943 and 485,000 in 1945. As might be expected, the birth rate also climbed: total births rose from about 2.4 million in 1939 to 3.1 million in 1943. Many births were "goodbye babies," conceived as a guarantee that the family would be perpetuated if the father died in battle overseas.

Ironically, women's efforts to hold their families together during the war posed problems for returning fathers. Women war workers had brought home the wages; they had taken over the budgeting of expenses and the writing of checks. In countless ways they had proved they could hold the reins in their husbands' absence. Many husbands returned home to find that the lives of their wives and children seemed complete without them. And what of the women who wanted to remain in the labor market? In 1945 many such women were pushed out of the factories and shipyards to make way for returning veterans. Others chose to leave their jobs for a year or two before returning to work. But those who tried later to return to high-paying industrial work were discouraged, and many were forced into low-paying jobs in restaurants and laundries.

The Decline of Liberalism and the Election of 1944

Even before Pearl Harbor, political liberals had suffered major defeats. Some Democrats hoped to revive the reform movement during the war, but Republicans and conservative Democrats were on guard against such a move. In the 1942 elections, the Republicans, aided by a small voter turnout, scored impressive gains, winning forty-six new seats in the House

and nine in the Senate and defeating Democratic governors in New York, California, and Michigan. Part of the Democrats' problem was that the war years, unlike the 1930s, were a time of full employment. Once people had acquired jobs and gained some economic security, they began to be more critical of New Deal policies. The New Deal coalition had always been a fragile alliance: southern white farmers had little in common with northern blacks or white factory workers. In northern cities, blacks and whites who had voted for Roosevelt in 1940 were competing for jobs and housing and soon would collide in race riots.

But though New Deal liberalism was enfeebled, it was far from dead. At its head still stood Franklin D. Roosevelt, and it had a program to

Wartime Liberalism

present to the American people. The liberal agenda began with a pledge to secure full employment. Roosevelt emphasized the concept in his Economic Bill of Rights, delivered as part of his 1944 State of the Union address. Every American, the president declared, had a right to a decent job, to sufficient food, shelter, and clothing, and to financial security in unemployment, illness, and old age. If to accomplish those goals the government had to operate at a deficit, Roosevelt was willing to do so. But first he had to be reelected.

In 1944 Franklin D. Roosevelt looked like an exhausted old man. His eyes were tired and puffy, and the loose flesh that hung on his

Roosevelt and Truman

large frame made him appear emaciated. The president's personal physician pronounced "nothing organically wrong with him at all—he's perfectly O.K.," but rumors of his ill health persisted. Whether or not Roosevelt expected to survive his fourth term, he selected a running mate who was inexperienced in international affairs: Senator Harry S Truman of Missouri. Truman, who represented a border state and a big-city machine (the Pendergast machine in Kansas City), was acceptable both to southerners and to the party bosses. An ardent and loyal New Dealer, the senator also enjoyed the approval of liberals. There was little evidence, however, that he possessed the capacities for national and world leadership that he would need as president. Nor did Roosevelt take Truman into his confidence, failing even to inform his running mate about the atomic bomb project.

Republicans were optimistic about their prospects for regaining the presidency. New York's Governor

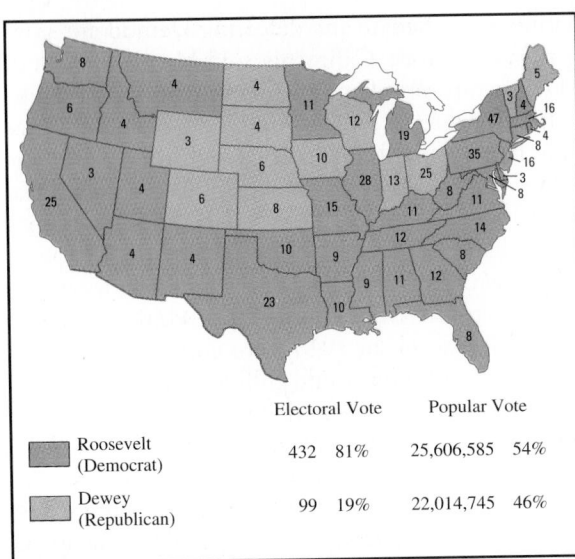

Map 27.4   Presidential Election, 1944   Franklin D. Roosevelt's fourth—and last—presidential election was his closest yet, but he still carried thirty-six of the country's forty-eight states.

Thomas E. Dewey, who won the nomination on the first ballot, was moderate in his criticism of Roosevelt's foreign policy and did not advocate repeal of the essentials of the New Deal—Social Security, unemployment relief, collective bargaining, and parity payments for farmers. Dewey had one great liability—his public image. He was stiff in manner and bland in personality.

Roosevelt won a fourth term, but with his narrowest-ever margin of victory. Nevertheless, he won 53.5 percent of the popular vote and 432 electoral votes to Dewey's 99 (see Map 27.4). It was the urban vote that returned Roosevelt to the White House. Wartime population shifts had enhanced the Democrats' political clout: southern whites who had been lifelong Democrats, along with southern blacks who had never voted before, had migrated to the urban industrial centers and cast Democratic ballots.

Roosevelt's Fourth-term Victory

Added to the Democrats' urban vote was a less obvious factor. Many voters seemed to be exhibiting what has been called "depression psychosis." Fearful that hard times would return once war contracts were terminated, they remembered New Deal relief programs and voted for Roosevelt. With victory within grasp, many Americans wanted Roosevelt's experienced hand

to guide both the nation and the world to a lasting international peace. Roosevelt's death in April 1945, however, meant that Harry Truman would deal with the postwar world.

Planning for Peace

The aftermath of the First World War weighed heavily on the minds of American diplomats throughout the war. Americans vowed to make a peace that would ensure a postwar world free from economic depression, totalitarianism, and war. American goals included the Open Door policy and lower tariffs; self-determination for liberated peoples; avoidance of the debts-reparations fiasco that had plagued Europe after the First World War; expansion of the United States's sphere of influence; gradual and orderly decolonization; and management of world affairs by what Roosevelt once called the Four Policemen: the Soviet Union, China, Great Britain, and the United States.

Although the Allies concentrated on defeating the aggressors, their suspicions of one another undermined cooperation. Questions about eastern Europe proved the most difficult. The Soviet Union sought to fix its boundaries where they had stood before Hitler attacked in 1941. This meant that the part of Poland that the Soviets had invaded and captured in 1939 would become Soviet territory. The British and Americans hesitated, preferring to deal with eastern Europe at the end of the war. Yet in an October 1944 agreement, Churchill and Stalin struck a bargain: the Soviet Union would gain Romania and Bulgaria as a sphere of influence; Britain would have the upper hand in Greece; and the two countries would share authority in Yugoslavia and Hungary.

Allied Disagreement over Eastern Europe

Poland stood as a special case. In 1943 Moscow had broken off diplomatic relations with the conservative Polish government-in-exile in London. The Poles had angered Moscow by asking the International Red Cross to investigate German charges, later substantiated, that the Soviets had massacred thousands of Polish army officers in the Katyn Forest in 1940. Then an uprising in Warsaw in 1944 complicated matters still further. Encouraged by approaching Soviet troops to expect assistance, the Warsaw underground rose against the occupying Germans. To the dismay of the world community, Soviet armies stood by as German troops slaughtered 166,000 people and devastated the city.

The Soviets then set up a pro-Communist government in Lublin. Thus near the end of the war Poland had two competing governments: one in London, recognized by America and Britain, and another in Lublin.

Early in the war the Allies had begun talking about a new international peacekeeping organization. At

Creation of the United Nations

Teheran in 1943 Roosevelt called for an institution controlled by the Four Policemen. The next year, at a Washington, D.C., mansion called Dumbarton Oaks, American, British, Soviet, and Chinese representatives conferred on the details. The conferees approved a preliminary charter for a United Nations Organization, providing for a supreme Security Council dominated by the great powers and a weak General Assembly. The Security Council would have five permanent members, each with veto power (Britain had insisted that France be one of the permanent members). Meanwhile, the Soviet Union, hoping to counter pro-American and pro-British blocs in the General Assembly, asked for separate membership in the General Assembly for each of the sixteen Soviet republics. This issue was not resolved at Dumbarton Oaks, but the meeting proved a success nevertheless.

Diplomatic action on behalf of the European Jews, however, proved to be a tragic failure. By war's

Jewish Refugees

end, about 6 million Jews had been forced into concentration camps and systematically murdered, most by firing squads and in gas chambers. The Nazis also exterminated as many as 250,000 Gypsies and about 60,000 gay men. During the depression, the United States and other nations had refused to relax their immigration restrictions to save Jews fleeing persecution. Because of anti-Semitism and concern over competition for scarce jobs, American immigration officials applied the rules so strictly—requiring legal documents that fleeing Jews could not possibly provide—that otherwise-

When the British liberated the Bergen-Belsen concentration camp near Hanover, Germany, in April 1945, they found this mass grave. It held the remains of thousands of Holocaust victims who had been starved, gassed, and machine-gunned by their Nazi jailers. This photograph and many others provide irrefutable proof of the Holocaust's savagery. (Imperial War Museum)

qualified refugees were kept out of the country. From 1933 to 1945, less than 40 percent of the German-Austrian immigration quota was filled.

Even the tragic voyage of the *St. Louis* did not change government policy. The vessel left Hamburg in mid-1939 carrying 930 desperate Jewish refugees who lacked proper immigration documents. Denied entry to Havana, the *St. Louis* headed for Miami, where Coast Guard cutters prevented it from docking. The ship was forced to return to Europe. Some of those refugees took shelter in countries that later were overrun by Hitler's legions. "The cruise of the *St. Louis*," wrote the *New York Times*, "cries to high heaven of man's inhumanity to man."

The Holocaust

As evidence mounted that Hitler intended to exterminate the Jews, British and American representatives met in Bermuda in 1943 but came up with no plans. Secretary of State Hull submitted a report to the president that emphasized "the unknown cost of moving an undetermined number of persons from an undisclosed place to an unknown destination." Appalled, Secretary of the Treasury Henry Morgenthau, Jr., charged that the State Department's foot-dragging made the United States an accessory to murder. "It takes months and months to grant the visa and then it usually applies to a corpse," he wrote bitterly. Early in 1944, stirred by Morgenthau's well-documented plea, Roosevelt created the War Refugee Board, which set up refugee camps in Europe and played a crucial role in saving 200,000 Jews from death. But, lamented one American official, "by that time it was too damned late to do too much."

The Yalta Conference

With the war in Europe nearing an end, and a host of political questions—including what to do with Germany—yet to be settled, President Roosevelt called for another summit meeting. The three Allied leaders met at Yalta, in the Russian Crimea, in early February 1945. Controversy has surrounded the conference ever since. Roosevelt was obviously ill, and critics of the Yalta agreements later charged that he was too weak to resist Stalin's cunning and that he struck a poor bargain. The evidence suggests, however, that Roosevelt was mentally alert and managed to sustain his strength during negotiations.

Each of the Allies arrived at Yalta with definite goals. Britain sought to make France a partner in the postwar occupation of Germany, to curb Soviet influence in Poland, and to ensure protection for the vulnerable British Empire. The Soviet Union wanted reparations from Germany to assist in the massive task of rebuilding at home, possessions in Asia, continued influence in Poland, and a permanently weakened Germany so that the Soviet Union would never again suffer a German attack. The United States lobbied for the United Nations Organization, in which it believed it could exercise influence; for a Soviet declaration of war against Japan to aid in ending the war in the Pacific; for recognition of China as a major power; and for compromise between rival factions in Poland.

Military positions at the time of the conference helped to shape the final agreements. Soviet troops occupied those countries in eastern Europe that they had liberated, including Poland, and Stalin repeatedly pointed out that twice in the century German armies had marched through Poland into Russian territory, killing millions. He insisted on a government friendly to Moscow—the Lublin regime—in order to prevent another German onslaught. He also demanded boundaries that would give Poland part of Germany in the west and the Soviet Union part of Poland in the east. Churchill boiled over in protest; he wanted the London government-in-exile to return to Poland.

With Roosevelt's help, a compromise was reached: a boundary favorable to the Soviet Union in the east; postponement of the western boundary issue; the creation of a "more broadly based" coalition government that would include members of the London regime; and free elections to be held sometime in the future. The agreement was vague but, given Soviet occupation of Poland, Roosevelt considered it "the best I can do."

As for Germany, the Big Three agreed that it would be divided into four zones, the fourth zone to be administered by France. Berlin, within the Soviet zone, also would be divided among the four victors. On the question of reparations, Stalin wanted a precise figure, but Churchill and Roosevelt insisted on determining Germany's ability to pay. With Britain abstaining, the Americans and Russians agreed that an Allied committee would consider the sum of $20 billion as a basis for discussion in the future, with half of the amount to go to the Soviet Union.

Other issues led to tradeoffs. Stalin promised to declare war on Japan two or three months after Hitler's defeat. Since the Japanese were still resisting the American advance in Asia and since the atomic bomb was still on the drawing boards, American military leaders applauded the commitment. The Soviet premier also agreed to sign a treaty of friendship and

The three Allied leaders—Winston Churchill, Franklin D. Roosevelt, and Joseph Stalin—met at Yalta in February 1945. Having been president for twelve years, Roosevelt showed signs of age and fatigue. Two months later, he died of a massive cerebral hemorrhage.   (Franklin D. Roosevelt Library)

alliance with Jiang Jieshi (Chiang Kai-shek), America's ally in China, rather than with the Communist Mao Zedong (Mao Tse-tung). In return, the United States agreed to the Soviet Union's recovery of holdings Russia had lost to Japan after the Russo-Japanese War in 1905: the southern part of Sakhalin Island and the Kurile Islands. Regarding the new world organization, Roosevelt and Churchill granted the Soviets three votes in the General Assembly (fifty nations officially launched the United Nations Organization three months later). Finally, the conferees issued the Declaration of Liberated Europe, a pledge to establish order and to rebuild economies by democratic methods.

Yalta marked the high point of the Grand Alliance; in the tradition of diplomatic give-and-take,

Potsdam Conference

each of the Allies came away with something it wanted. But as the great powers jockeyed for influence at the close of the war, neither the spirit nor the letter of Yalta held firm. The crumbling of the alliance became evident almost immediately, at the Potsdam Conference, which began in mid-July. Roosevelt had died in April, and Truman—a novice at international diplomacy—was less patient with the Soviets. Truman also was emboldened by learning during the conference that the atomic test in New Mexico had been successful.

Despite major differences at Potsdam, the Big Three did agree on general policies toward Germany: complete disarmament, dismantling of industry used for military production, dissolution of Nazi institutions and laws, and war crimes trials. In a compromise over reparations, they decided that each occupying nation should extract reparations from its own zone; but they could not agree on a total figure. The Potsdam Conference also called for the "unconditional surrender" of Japan.

Potsdam left much undone. As the war drew to a close, there was little that bound the Allies together. Roosevelt's cooperative style was gone; the spirit of Yalta was evaporating; the common enemy, Hitler, was defeated. And the United States, with the awesome atomic bomb in the offing to force defeat on Japan, no longer needed or even wanted the Soviet Union in the Pacific war. Moreover, each of the victors was seeking to preserve and enlarge its sphere of influence. Britain claimed authority in Greece and parts of the Middle East; the Soviet Union already dominated much of eastern Europe; and the United States retained its hegemony in Latin America. The United States also seized several Pacific islands as strategic outposts and laid plans to dominate a defeated Japan. Let the Americans have their Pacific bases, responded Churchill, "but 'Hands off the British Empire' is our maxim."

Summary

Hitler once prophesied, "We may be destroyed, but if we are, we shall drag a world with us—a world in flames." Indeed, *rubble* was the word most often invoked to describe the European landscape at the end of the war. Hamburg, Stuttgart, and Dresden had been laid to waste; three-quarters of Berlin was in ruins; and in England, Coventry and London were bombed out. In Asia as well as in Europe, ghostlike people wandered about, searching desperately for food and mourning those who would never come home. The Soviet Union had suffered by far the greatest losses: more than 21 million military and civilian war dead— one-ninth of the total Soviet population. The Chinese calculated their war losses at 10 million, the Germans and Austrians at 6 million, and the Japanese at 2.5 million. And 6 million Jews had been killed during the Holocaust. In all, the Second World War caused the deaths of 55 million people.

Only one major combatant escaped such grisly statistics: the United States. Protected by ocean barriers, its cities were not burned and its fields were not trampled. American deaths from the war—405,399—

were few compared with the losses of other nations. In fact, the United States emerged from the Second World War more powerful than it had ever been. It alone had the atomic bomb. The U.S. Air Force and Navy were the largest anywhere. What is more, only the United States had the capital and economic resources to spur international recovery. In the coming struggle to fashion a new world out of the ashes of the old, soon to be called the Cold War (see Chapter 29), the United States held a commanding position.

On the home front, life for many Americans was fundamentally different in 1945 from what it had been before Pearl Harbor. For one thing, the war finally ended the Great Depression, reducing unemployment practically to zero. War jobs demanded workers, and women, people of color, and other Americans responded by moving to war-production centers. Among the migrants were African Americans, Mexican Americans, whites, and women of all races. Employers' negative attitudes toward women workers eased during the war, and millions of married middle-class women, many of them over forty-five, took jobs in shipyards and aircraft factories.

But life differed in other ways, too, especially for the American men and women who fought the war. The Academy Award for 1946 went to *The Best Years of Our Lives*, a painful film about the postwar readjustments of three veterans and their families and friends. Many men returned home suffering flashbacks, nightmares, and deep emotional distress. "Dad came home a different man," recalled one girl; "he didn't laugh as much and he drank a lot."

On another front, the Second World War stimulated the trend toward bigness, not only in business and labor but also in government, agriculture, higher education, and science. Over the next few years, government agencies that had been conceived as temporary became permanent and grew in size and influence, resulting in the Department of Defense (consolidating the War and Navy Departments), the Central Intelligence Agency (succeeding the Office of Strategic Services), and the Atomic Energy Commission. The seeds of the military-industrial complex were sown during these years. Moreover, with the advent of the Cold War, millions of young men would be inducted into the armed forces during the next thirty years. War and the expectation of war would become part of American life.

At the same time, the Second World War was a powerful engine of social change in the United States.

The gains made during the war by African Americans and women were overdue. And by blending New Deal ideology and wartime urgency, the government assumed the responsibility of ensuring prosperity and stepping in when capitalism faltered. Americans emerged from the war fully confident that theirs was the greatest country in the world. The United States, they boasted, had preserved democracy and freedom around the globe. For better or worse—and clearly there were elements of each—the Second World War was a turning point in the nation's history.

LEGACY FOR A PEOPLE AND A NATION
Atomic Waste

Although victory in the Second World War tasted sweet to the American people, the war's environmental legacy proved noxious, not to mention toxic and deadly. New industries brought with them hazardous pollutants. The production of synthetic rubber spewed forth sulfur dioxide, carbon monoxide, and other dangerous gases. War industries fouled the water and the soil with both solid and petrochemical wastes. Air pollution—smog—was first detected in Los Angeles in 1943, the result of that city's rapid wartime industrialization combined with widespread dependence on the automobile. Although these were ominous signs, few people at the time worried about human-made threats to America's seemingly endless supplies of fresh air, water, and soil.

No wartime, or postwar, weapons program became more threatening to the natural environment than the project to develop the atomic bomb. Many of the bomb's ingredients, notably plutonium, beryllium, and mercury, are highly toxic and contaminate the environment. The storing of radioactive waste began during the war at Oak Ridge, Tennessee, and Hanford, Washington, where plutonium was produced. During the postwar nuclear arms race with the Soviet Union, the United States opened other production facilities, for example, at Rocky Flats in Colorado and on the Savannah River in South Carolina. At these sites, radioactive waste seeped from leaky barrels into the soil and water, threatening human life and killing fish, birds, and other wildlife. Moreover, during 1945–1963, nuclear testing, which was done above ground, killed an estimated 800,000 Americans from cancer attributable to radioactive fallout.

As the United States enters the twenty-first century, the environmental legacy of the atomic bomb continues to threaten the American people. The biggest problem of the new millennium remains the oldest problem: how to dispose of radioactive materials. In 1999, when the federal government opened the nation's first nuclear dump in New Mexico, the initial shipment came from the Los Alamos National Laboratory, New Mexico, birthplace of the atomic bomb. Scientists, however, are skeptical that current technology is up to the task of cleaning soil and water at the nuclear weapons sites. "The technology . . . used to remediate contaminated sites," said the chairman of a National Research Council task force that studied the problem, "is simply ineffective and unable to accomplish the massive job that needs to be done."

For Further Reading, see page A-31 of the Appendix. For Web resources, go to http://www.college.hmco.com.

POSTWAR AMERICA: COLD WAR POLITICS, CIVIL RIGHTS, AND THE BABY BOOM 1945–1961

In 1945 Bob Bush was only eighteen years old, but he was already a veteran of the Second World War. And he was one of 440 Americans in the war to be awarded the Congressional Medal of Honor for valor on the battlefield. On May 2, 1945, Bush, a Navy medical corpsman, was attached to a marine rifle company fighting on the Japanese island of Okinawa. Firing from heavily fortified positions, the Japanese were inflicting heavy casualties on the Americans. Bush was constantly on the run, patching up one wounded marine after another. Lying in the open was a critically wounded officer; Bush rushed to the man's side and began giving him blood plasma just as the enemy opened fire again. Holding the bottle of plasma high in one hand, he drew his pistol with the other. According to the citation accompanying Bush's medal, he "fired into the enemy ranks until his ammunition was expended. Quickly seizing a discarded carbine, he trained his fire on the Japanese charging point blank over the hill," killing six men, "despite his own serious wounds and the loss of one eye. . . ."

Recovering from his wounds in a hospital in Hawai'i, Bob Bush thought about his future in postwar America. And in the navy plane carrying him back to the United States, he made a promise to himself: he was going to put the war behind him. "I was eighteen. I had to get back to school in the fall. I had the girl-friend back home in [the state of] Washington." Her name was Wonda Spooner, and she too was eighteen. Bob wanted to ask her to marry him, and he was pleased when she said yes; that summer they were married. For their honeymoon, the couple boarded a train for Washington, D.C., where President Harry S Truman awarded Bush the Medal of Honor.

Back home, Bush completed his high-school requirements and, under the GI Bill, enrolled in business courses at the University of Washington. Anticipating a postwar housing boom, Bush and another veteran

In postwar America, millions of families shopped for new houses in the country's burgeoning suburbs. In the first decade after the Second World War, 4.3 million veterans used GI Bill loan provisions to purchase single-family residences. Many of these men and women were members of what Tom Brokaw, NBC's news anchor, has called "the greatest generation." They survived the Great Depression, served in the war, and became parents of America's baby boomers. (H. Armstrong Roberts)

then decided to buy a small lumberyard. As Tom Brokaw describes in his 1998 book *The Greatest Generation*, Bush was ambitious and hard working, putting in seven-day weeks and occasionally twenty-four-hour days. Like other veterans in postwar America, he felt he had to make up for lost time. "Everyone," Bush said, "should learn the meaning of that famous little four-letter word—*work*." In the 1940s and 1950s, his business boomed, and he acquired more lumberyards, eventually owning seven along with building supply stores, a ready-mix concrete business, and a mobile-home dealership.

Like so many veterans in postwar America, Bush had one overriding goal: to build a happy life for his family. While he was busy succeeding in business, Wonda was busy at home raising their baby-boom children, three boys and a girl. As in many families in the 1950s, Bob was often an absentee father. Wonda, on the other hand, was an indulgent mother who rose early to cook breakfast for the family, pack the school lunches, do laundry, and keep their comfortable house spotless. This division of gender roles and authority was the rule, not the exception, in postwar American homes.

The Bushes were not alone in having babies after the war. From 1946 until 1964, births hit record highs. During this period 76 million babies were born in the United States, compared with only 44 million during the period of depression and war from 1929 through 1945. The postwar baby boom was larger and in other ways different from increases in the birth rate that earlier generations had experienced. Parents who had grown up during the Great Depression were determined that their children's lives would be better than theirs had been. And many succeeded in making it so.

Material comfort was the hallmark for millions of middle-class families. In terms of both income level and lifestyle, more Americans were better off than ever before—and most expected their good fortune to continue. Often, however, both parents worked to pay for a new home and a second car. This meant that women had at least two jobs, for they still were expected to do the housework and cooking. In postwar America, "family togetherness" took on almost religious significance, including evenings watching television in the "family room" and family vacations to Disneyland.

Postwar America was not only prosperous, but also proud and boastful. From 1945 to the 1960s, the American people were in the grip of "victory culture"—that is, the belief that unending triumph was the nation's birthright and destiny. From the classroom, the pulpit, and the town hall, as well as from

popular-culture avenues, came self-congratulatory rhetoric about America's invincibility. And the country had an enemy in a new conflict known as the Cold War: communism in both the Soviet Union and China (see Chapter 29). Americans believed that their nation was the greatest in the world, not only the most powerful but the most righteous. And, Americans agreed, it was getting better all the time.

As evidence of the nation's perfectibility, Americans pointed to the postwar economic boom. The cornerstones of the boom, which began in 1945 and lasted twenty-five years, were the automobile, construction, and defense industries. As the gross national product (GNP) grew, income levels rose and property ownership spread. Automobiles rolled off the assembly lines; new houses and schools sprang up throughout the country. More and more people bought homes in the suburbs.

Although the postwar years constituted an age of consensus, Cold War politics were often volatile. When Harry Truman became president in 1945, his initial response to the challenge was a deep feeling of inadequacy. As vice president, Truman had been kept ignorant by Franklin D. Roosevelt about crucial foreign and military initiatives; nevertheless, he would have to deal with the closing months of the war and with the onset of the Cold War. In domestic matters, too, the ill-prepared president would need a crash course in the intricacies of governing the United States. The nation's reconversion from war back to peace was not smooth, and Truman angered liberals, conservatives, farmers, consumers, and union members.

In 1948, Truman seemed politically vulnerable, but he confounded experts by winning the presidency in his own right. His victory demonstrated the volatility of politics. The key domestic issues of the postwar period—civil rights for African Americans and the anti-Communist crusade to be called McCarthyism—were both highly charged. Later, the outbreak of the Korean War in 1950 intensified discontent. The war, inflation, and corruption in the White House caused Truman's popularity to plummet. After twenty years of Democratic presidents, Americans in 1952 elected the Republican nominee, General Dwight D. Eisenhower.

Eisenhower was a decisive and decorated war hero, but as president he moved cautiously and hesitantly, particularly in dealing with civil rights and McCarthyism. His major goal was to promote economic growth, and he pursued staunchly Republican goals: a balanced budget, reduced taxes and government spending, low inflation, and a return of power to the

IMPORTANT EVENTS

1945 Roosevelt dies; Truman becomes president
12 million GIs demobilized
Truman's economic message to Congress

1946 Baby boom begins
Spock's *Baby and Child Care* changes child-rearing practices
More than 1 million GIs enroll in colleges
Coal miners strike
Inflation reaches 18.2 percent
Republicans win both houses of Congress

1947 Truman institutes employee loyalty program
Taft-Hartley Act limits power of unions
To Secure These Rights issued by the President's Committee on Civil Rights
Planned community begun in Levittown, N.Y.

1948 Truman appoints committee to oversee racial desegregation of the armed forces
Truman elected president
Kinsey's *Sexual Behavior in the Human Male* published

1949 Soviet Union explodes an atomic bomb
Communists win revolution in China
National Housing Act promises decent housing for all Americans

1950 Fuchs arrested as an atomic spy
Hiss convicted of perjury
McCarthy alleges Communists in government
Korean War begins
Rosenbergs charged with conspiracy to commit treason
Internal Security (McCarran) Act requires members of "Communist front" organizations to register with the government

1951 Supreme Court upholds the Alien Registration (Smith) Act in *Dennis et al. v. U.S.*

1952 Ellison's *Invisible Man* shows African Americans' exclusion from the American Dream
Eisenhower elected president
Republicans win both houses of Congress

1953 Korean War ends
Rosenbergs executed

Congress adopts termination policy for Native Americans
Kinsey causes further public uproar with *Sexual Behavior in the Human Female*

1954 *Brown* decision reverses "separate-but-equal" doctrine
Communist Control Act makes Communist Party membership illegal
Senate condemns McCarthy

1955 AFL and CIO merge
Rebel Without a Cause idealizes youth subculture
Disneyland opens in Anaheim, California
Montgomery bus boycott begins

1956 Highway Act launches interstate highway system
Eisenhower reelected
Ginsberg's poem *Howl*, anthem of the Beat generation, published
Presley releases his first single

1957 King elected first president of the Southern Christian Leadership Conference
Little Rock, Arkansas, desegregation crisis
Congress passes Civil Rights Act
Soviet Union launches *Sputnik*
Kerouac criticizes white middle-class conformity in *On the Road*

1958 Congress passes National Defense Education Act to improve education in mathematics, foreign languages, and science
Adams resigns over scandal
St. Lawrence Seaway opens

1960 Sit-in in Greensboro, North Carolina
Student Nonviolent Coordinating Committee formed
Kennedy elected president

1961 Eisenhower warns against "military-industrial complex"

1962 Harrington's *The Other America* creates awareness of America's poor
Carson's *Silent Spring* warns of dangers of DDT

states. During Eisenhower's eight-year presidency, the nation was generally quiescent politically. Americans celebrated the American Dream and their economic system for providing a high standard of living, and they liked the president's traditionalism, caution, and moderation.

It was the infant civil rights movement that challenged the national consensus. Most African Americans, still farm workers in the South, were at the bottom of the economic ladder and were being denied constitutional rights such as the right to vote. How would blacks be incorporated into the consensus? The president, Congress, southern whites, and black civil rights activists all gave different answers as they debated *Brown v. Board of Education of Topeka*, the Supreme Court's momentous decision of 1954 invalidating racial segregation in public schools.

Still, however fragile, the age of consensus remained basically intact. President Eisenhower was succeeded in 1961 by a much younger man, Democratic senator John F. Kennedy of Massachusetts. The 1960s would be a far different decade. For one thing, the exceptions to the American Dream, ignored by affluent Americans in the 1950s, got attention. By the early 1960s, it was clear that the American poor were much more numerous than many people had imagined. Meanwhile, throughout the country from 1945 to 1961, race relations and urban conditions continued to deteriorate. In the 1960s the nation would have to deal with problems it had postponed addressing for too long. ■

Cold War Politics: The Truman Presidency

After the initial joyous reaction to the end of the Second World War, Americans faced a number of important questions. What would be the effect of reconversion—the cancellation of war contracts, termination of wage and price controls, and expiration of wartime labor agreements? Would depression recur as the artificial stimulus of the war was withdrawn, throwing people out of work and sending prices downward? Or would Americans spend the money they had saved during the war years and go on a buying spree?

Even before the war's end, cutbacks in production had caused layoffs. At Ford Motor Company's massive

Postwar Job Layoffs

Willow Run plant outside Detroit, where nine thousand Liberator bombers had been produced, most workers were let go in the spring of 1945. Ten days after the victory over Japan, 1.8 million people nationwide received pink slips, and 640,000 filed for unemployment compensation. The employment picture was made more complex by the return of millions of discharged GIs in 1945 and 1946; 12 million GIs were demobilized in 1945 alone. At the peak of postwar unemployment in March 1946, 2.7 million people searched for work.

Fearing that an economic depression might result from the cancellation of war contracts, President Tru-

man declared his determination not only to combat unemployment but also to expand on New Deal programs begun in the 1930s. In September 1945 he delivered to Congress a twenty-one-point message urging extension of unemployment compensation, an increase in the minimum wage, adoption of permanent farm price supports, and new public works projects. Truman also revived Roosevelt's Economic Bill of Rights—its linchpin, the right of every able-bodied American to hold a job. If the economy failed to provide one, the government should create it.

Despite high unemployment immediately after the war, the United States was hardly on the brink of depression. In fact, after a brief period of readjustment, the economy embarked on a quarter-century of unprecedented boom. People had plenty of savings to spend in 1945 and 1946, and, in time, there were new houses and cars for them to buy. Easy credit also promoted the buying binge. As a result, despite the winding down of war production, the GNP continued to rise in 1945. The nation's most immediate postwar economic problem was not depression but inflation, fueled by maddening shortages of consumer goods like meat and housing. Throughout 1945 and 1946 prices skyrocketed; inflation exceeded 18 percent in 1946.

Beginnings of the Postwar Economic Boom

As prices spiraled upward, many people were earning less in real income (actual purchasing power) than they had earned during the war. Industrial workers had complained during the war that the National War Labor Board limited their pay increases to barely perceptible cost-of-living increments. In the immediate postwar period they protested that the end of war production had eliminated much of their overtime work. A primary reason for workers' discontent was that as their wages and salaries declined slightly in 1946, net profits reached all-time highs. Indignant that they were not sharing in the prosperity, unions forced nationwide shutdowns in the coal, automobile, steel, and electric industries and halted railroad and maritime transportation.

Upsurges in Labor Strikes

By 1946 there was no doubt about the growing unpopularity of labor unions and their leadership. Many Americans blamed the unions for strikes, which restricted the output of consumer goods and inflated prices. In May, when a nationwide railroad strike was threatened, Truman made a dramatic appearance before a joint session of Congress. If strikers in an industry deemed vital to the national security refused to honor a presidential order to return to work, he would "request the Congress immediately to authorize the President to draft into the Armed Forces of the United States all workers who are on strike against their government." Truman's speech alienated not just the railroad workers but union members in general. Many vowed to defeat him in the upcoming 1948 presidential election.

Truman fared little better in his direction of the Office of Price Administration (OPA). Now that the war was over, powerful interests wanted price controls lifted. Consumers grew impatient with shortages and black-market prices, and manufacturers and farmers wanted to raise prices legally. Yet when most controls expired in mid-1946 and inflation rose further, consumers grumbled. Truman's approval rating plunged from 87 percent in late 1945 to 32 percent in 1946. Republicans made the most of public discontent. "Got enough meat?" asked Republican congressman John M. Vorys of Ohio. "Got enough houses? Got enough OPA? . . . Got enough inflation? . . . Got enough debt? . . . Got enough strikes?" In 1946 the Republicans won a majority in both houses of the Eightieth Congress, and the White House in 1948 seemed within their grasp.

Consumer Discontent

But the politicians who dominated the Eightieth Congress, whether Republicans or southern Democrats, were committed conservatives, and if Truman had alienated labor and consumers, the Eightieth Congress made them livid. Particularly unpopular with workers was the Taft-Hartley Act, which Congress approved over Truman's veto in 1947. A revision of the Wagner Act of 1935, the bill prohibited the closed shop, a workplace where membership in a particular union was a prerequisite for being hired. It also permitted the states to enact right-to-work laws banning union-shop agreements, which required all workers to join if a majority voted in favor of a union shop. In addition, the law forbade union contributions to political candidates in federal elections, required union leaders to swear in affidavits that they were not Communists, and mandated an eighty-day cooling-off period before carrying out strikes that imperiled the national security. Truman's veto of the Taft-Hartley Act vindicated him in the eyes of labor.

Throughout 1947 and 1948, the conservative Eightieth Congress offended not only unions but numerous other interest groups, such as farm organizations, which in turn swung back to Truman. Indeed,

After the war, American Indians lost sacred land to both big corporations and the federal government. In 1948 George Gillette *(left)*, chairman of the Fort Berthold, North Dakota, Indian Tribal Council, covers his face and weeps as Secretary of the Interior J. A. Krug signs a contract buying 155,000 acres of tribal land for a reservoir. (Wide World Photos, Inc.)

Republicans seemed oblivious to public opinion. Not since 1928 had they been so confident of capturing the presidency, and most political experts agreed. "Only a political miracle or extraordinary stupidity on the part of the Republicans," according to *Time*, "can save the Democratic party." At their national convention, Republicans strengthened their position by nominating the governors of two of the nation's most populous states: Thomas E. Dewey of New York for president and Earl Warren of California for vice president.

Democrats were up against more than Republicans in 1948. Two years before, Henry A. Wallace, the only remaining New Dealer in the cabinet, had been fired by Truman for publicly criticizing U.S. foreign policy. In 1948 Wallace ran for president on the Progressive Party ticket, which advocated friendly relations with the Soviet Union, racial desegregation, and nationalization of basic industries. A fourth party, the

Dixiecrats (States' Rights Democratic Party), was organized by southerners who walked out of the 1948 Democratic convention when it adopted a pro–civil rights plank; they nominated Governor Strom Thurmond of South Carolina. If Wallace's candidacy did not destroy Truman's chances, experts said, the Dixiecrats certainly would.

But Truman had a few ideas of his own. He called the Eightieth Congress into special session and challenged it to enact all the planks in the Republican platform. If Republicans really wanted to transform their convictions into law, said Truman, this was the time to do it. After Congress had debated for two weeks and accomplished nothing of significance, Truman took to the road, delivering scores of speeches denouncing the "do-nothing" Eightieth Congress. Still, no amount of furious campaigning by Truman seemed likely to change the predicted outcome.

Truman's Upset Victory

As the votes were counted, however, it was clear that Truman had confounded the experts. The final tally was 24 million popular votes and 303 electoral votes for Truman; 22 million popular votes and 189 electoral votes for Dewey (see Map 28.1). How and why did the upset occur? First, the United States was prosperous, at peace, and essentially united on foreign policy. Second, Roosevelt's legacy—the New Deal coalition—had endured: African Americans, union members, and voters in northern cities, along with most southern whites, had rallied to Truman's support. Many farmers also voted for Truman, fearful that the Republicans would drastically reduce price supports for agricultural goods. Finally, the extremist image of the Progressive and Dixiecrat Parties helped Truman by making the Democratic Party look moderate. Rather than receiving the predicted 5 million votes each, Wallace and Thurmond polled just over 1 million each.

Truman began his new term brimming with confidence. It was time, he believed, for government to fulfill its responsibility to provide economic security for the poor and the elderly. As he worked on his 1949 State of the Union message, he penciled in an expression of his intentions: "I expect to give every segment of our population a fair deal." Little of Truman's Fair Deal came to fruition, however, and he would leave office a highly unpopular president. One reason for the president's unpopularity was the Korean War, which broke out in 1950.

In June 1950, following the invasion of South Korea by North Korea, President Truman ordered American troops to fight in Korea (see Chapter 29). There was much grumbling among Americans as the nation again mobilized for war. People remembered the shortages of the last war and flocked to their grocery stores for sugar, coffee, and canned goods. Fueled by panic buying, inflation began to rise again. Moreover, people disliked the draft, and many reservists and national guardsmen resented being among those called to active duty. Thanks to an unpopular war and charges of influence peddling by some of Truman's cronies, the president's public approval rating slumped to an all-time low of 23 percent in 1951 and stayed at that level for a year. Once again the Democratic Party appeared doomed along with its leader—and this time appearances proved correct.

Korean War Discontent on the Home Front

Although Truman was highly unpopular when he left office in 1953, historians now rate him among the nation's ten best presidents. Truman was president at

Map 28.1   Presidential Election, 1948   In 1948 Harry S Truman won perhaps the biggest upset in a presidential election, defeating not only the Republican candidate but also challengers from the States' Rights Democratic (Dixiecrat) and Progressive Parties.

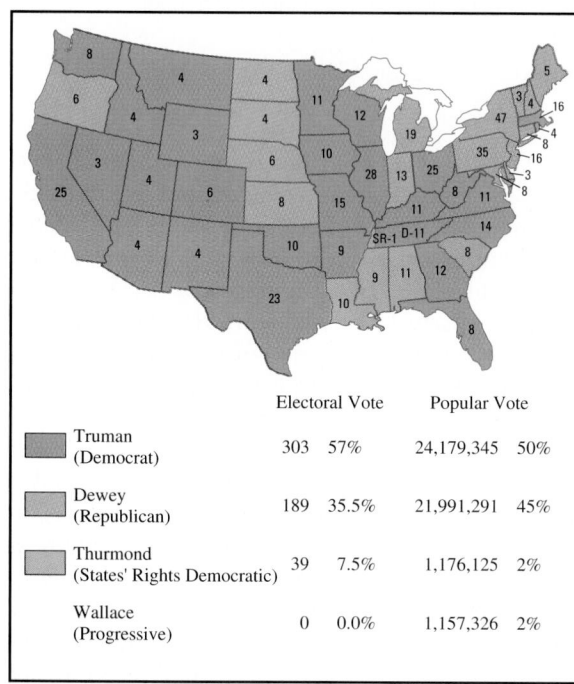

	Electoral Vote		Popular Vote	
Truman (Democrat)	303	57%	24,179,345	50%
Dewey (Republican)	189	35.5%	21,991,291	45%
Thurmond (States' Rights Democratic)	39	7.5%	1,176,125	2%
Wallace (Progressive)	0	0.0%	1,157,326	2%

So few pollsters predicted that President Harry S Truman (1884–1972) would win in 1948 that the *Chicago Tribune* announced his defeat before all the returns were in. Here a victorious Truman pokes fun at the newspaper for its premature headline.   (Corbis-Bettmann)

Truman's Historical Standing

the beginning of the Cold War, and in eight years he strengthened the powers of the presidency. Agencies that had been set up for temporary duty during the Second World War were made permanent, among them the Atomic Energy Commission. And legislation in 1947 created a unified Department of Defense and a permanent intelligence service, the Central Intelligence Agency (CIA). On the domestic front, Truman was a New Dealer who fought for programs to benefit workers, African Americans, farmers, homeowners, retired persons, and people in need of healthcare. He showed his spunk and courage in 1948 when he pulled off the biggest upset in American political history. Although little of Truman's Fair Deal was enacted during his presidency, much of it became law as part of the Great Society in the 1960s, in such legislation as Medicare and the Civil Rights Acts of 1964 and 1965 (see Chapter 30).

Consensus and Conflict: The Eisenhower Presidency

In the 1952 presidential election, voters agreed with the Republican campaign slogan "It's Time for a Change." What sealed the fate of the Democratic Party was the Republican candidacy of General Dwight D. Eisenhower. A bona fide war hero who had come from humble origins in Kansas, "Ike" had a warm, friendly smile, and he seemed to embody the virtues Americans most admired: integrity, decency, and lack of pretense. Eisenhower's unlucky Democratic opponent was Adlai Stevenson, the thoughtful and witty governor of Illinois. It was never much of a contest, especially after Eisenhower promised to "go to Korea," implying he would end the war. The result was a landslide: Eisenhower and his running mate, Senator Richard M. Nixon of California, won almost 34 million popular votes and 442 electoral votes, to the Democrats' 27

During the 1952 presidential campaign, Dwight D. Eisenhower (1890–1969) receives a delegation of Republican national committee women at his New York City headquarters. As the women chant "I Like Ike," the Republican candidate opens his arms to welcome them.   (Corbis-Bettmann)

million popular and 89 electoral votes. The Republicans even lured to their fold four states in the once-solid Democratic South. Moreover, Eisenhower's coattails were long enough to carry other Republicans to victory; the party gained control of both houses of Congress, though with only a one-seat margin in the Senate.

Smiling Ike, with his folksy style, garbled syntax, and frequent escapes to the golf course, provoked Democrats to charge that he failed to lead. But Dwight D. Eisenhower was not that simple. He was no stranger to hard work. His low-key, "hidden-hand" style was a way of playing down his role as politician and highlighting his role as chief of state. Eisenhower relied heavily on staff work, delegating authority to cabinet members. Sometimes he was not well informed on details and gave the impression that he was out of touch with his own government. In fact, he was not, and he remained a very popular president.

During Eisenhower's presidency most Americans clung to the status quo. It was an era of both self-congratulation and constant anxiety.

The "Consensus Mood"

British journalist Godfrey Hodgson has described the "consensus mood," writing that Americans were "confident to the verge of complacency

about the perfectibility of American society, anxious to the point of paranoia about the threat of communism." Demand for reform at such a time seemed to most Americans unnecessary, if not unpatriotic. Historian Henry Steele Commager saw conformity everywhere in the 1950s, as evidenced by "the uncritical and unquestioning acceptance of America as it is." College students shunned passionate political convictions. A weak minority on the American left advocated checks on the political power of corporations, and a noisy minority on the right accused the government of a wishy-washy campaign against communism. But both liberal Democrats and moderate Republicans avoided extremism, satisfied to be occupying what the historian Arthur M. Schlesinger, Jr., called "the vital center."

In this age of consensus, President Eisenhower approached his duties with a philosophy he called "dynamic conservatism." He meant being "conservative when it comes to money and liberal when it comes to human beings." Eisenhower's was unabashedly "an Administration representing business and industry," as Interior Secretary Douglas McKay acknowledged. The president and his appointees gave priority to reducing the federal budget, but they did not always succeed; and they rec-

"Dynamic Conservatism"

ognized that dismantling New Deal and Fair Deal programs was politically impossible. The administration did try to remove the federal government from agriculture, but the effort failed because of the political power of the farm lobby. Despite several changes in federal farm price support policy, the government found itself spending more money and stockpiling increased amounts of surplus farm commodities.

Eisenhower made headway in other spheres. In 1954 Congress passed legislation to construct a canal, the St. Lawrence Seaway, between Montreal and Lake Erie. This inland waterway, which opened in 1958, was intended to spur the economic development of the Midwest by linking the Great Lakes to the Atlantic Ocean. Also in 1954 Eisenhower signed into law amendments to the Social Security Act that raised benefits and added 7.5 million workers, mostly self-employed farmers, to the program's coverage. Congress also obliged the president with tax reform that raised business depreciation allowances and with the Atomic Energy Act of 1954, which granted private companies the right to own reactors and nuclear materials for the production of electricity.

Eisenhower also presided over a dramatic change in the lives of Native Americans. After little consultation with Native Americans, the

Termination Policy for Native Americans

government embarked on a radical departure from policies established under the New Deal's Indian Reorganization Act of 1934 (see page 721). In 1953 Congress adopted a policy known as *termination*: the forced assimilation of Native Americans into the dominant culture by terminating the Indian reservations, as well as by ending tribal sovereignty and federal services to Indians. Another act of the same year made Indians subject to state laws. Eisenhower administration officials applauded the changes because they would reduce federal costs and serve states' rights. Critics—including most Indians—denounced termination as one more attempt to grab Indian lands and exploit Native Americans.

Between 1954 and 1960, the federal government withdrew its benefits from sixty-one tribes. About one in eight Indians abandoned the reservations; many joined the ranks of the urban poor in low-paying jobs. The policy of termination and relocation was motivated largely by land greed. The Klamaths of Oregon, for example, lived on a reservation rich in ponderosa pine, which lumber interests coveted. Enticed by cash payments, almost four-fifths of the Klamaths accepted termination and voted to sell their shares of the forest-

land. With termination, their way of life collapsed. By the time termination was halted in the 1960s, so much human tragedy had struck Native Americans that observers compared the situation to the devastation their forebears had endured in the nineteenth century.

In the 1954 congressional elections, most Americans revealed that, though they still liked Eisenhower,

Election of 1956

they remained loyal to the Democratic Party. With a recession just winding down, the voters gave the Democrats control of both houses of Congress. Lyndon B. Johnson of Texas became the Senate's new majority leader. An energetic, pragmatic politician, Johnson worked with the Republican White House to pass legislation, including the Highway Act of 1956, which launched the largest public works program in American history, authorizing the construction over the next thirteen years of an interstate highway system. In 1955 Eisenhower suffered a heart attack but regained his strength and declared his intention to run again. The Democrats nominated Adlai E. Stevenson once more. Eisenhower, running again with Nixon, won a landslide victory in 1956: 36 million votes and 457 electoral votes to Stevenson's 26 million and 73. Americans decided to stick with an experienced military man and statesman at a time of world unrest. Still, the Democrats continued to dominate Congress.

Eisenhower faced rising federal expenditures in his second term, in part because of the tremendous expense of America's global activities (see Chapter 29). In the first three years of his presidency he had managed to trim the budget, largely by controlling defense spending. But the president discovered that he had to tolerate deficit spending to achieve his goals. In 1959 federal expenditures climbed to $92 billion, about half of which went to the military. In fact, Eisenhower balanced only three of his eight budgets. The administration's resort to deficit spending also was fueled by the need to cushion the impact of three recessions—in 1953–1954, 1957–1958, and 1960–1961. A sluggish economy and unemployment also reduced the tax dollars collected by the federal government.

Setbacks in 1958 made that year a low point for the Eisenhower administration. Scandal unsettled the White House when the president's chief aide, Sherman Adams, resigned under suspicion of influencing government regulatory decisions in exchange for luxury gifts such as a fur coat. Then came large Republican losses in the 1958 congressional elections. The Democrats took the Senate by 64 seats to 34 and the

House by 283 seats to 153. In 1960 the economy was in a recession, and the Soviets downed a Central Intelligence Agency U-2 spy plane (see page 842). First, Eisenhower denied that it was a spy plane; and his credibility suffered when he later conceded that it was.

Eisenhower Presidency Assessed

Assessments of the Eisenhower administration used to emphasize its conservatism, passive style, limited achievements, and reluctance to confront difficult issues. In recent years, interpretations have been changing as scholars have begun examining the now-declassified documents of the consensus era. Current evaluations often stress Eisenhower's command of policymaking, sensibly moderate approach to most problems, political savvy, and great popularity. Eisenhower no longer appears to be just an aging bystander but a competent, pragmatic leader who gave most Americans what they wanted at the time—a grandfatherly figure in the White House, economic comfort, and unrelenting anticommunism.

The record of Eisenhower's presidency is nonetheless mixed. At home he failed to deal with poverty, urban decay, and blatant denials of civil rights—problems that would wrack the country in the next decade. But in comparison with his successors in the 1960s, Eisenhower was measured and cautious. He kept military budgets under control and managed crises adroitly so that the United States avoided major military ventures abroad. But he authorized CIA covert actions to overthrow elected governments in Iran and Guatemala. At home the Eisenhower administration curbed inflation, strengthened the infrastructure by building an interstate highway system, and expanded Social Security coverage. Eisenhower brought dignity to the presidency, and the American people respected him.

The "Military-Industrial Complex"

Just before leaving office in early 1961, Eisenhower went on national radio and television to deliver his farewell address to the nation. Because of the Cold War, he observed, the United States had been "compelled to create a permanent industry of vast proportions," as well as a standing army of 3.5 million. "This conjunction of an immense military establishment and a large arms industry is new in the American experience," Eisenhower noted. "The total influence—economic, political, even spiritual—is felt in every city,

every statehouse, every office of the federal government." So powerful was this influence, the president declared, that it threatened the nation's democratic processes. Then Eisenhower issued a direct warning, urging Americans to "guard against . . . the military-industrial complex." They did not.

McCarthyism

One of the most volatile political issues in postwar America was the anti-Communist crusade known as McCarthyism. Both Truman and Eisenhower overreacted to the alleged threat of Communist subversion in government. Their alarmist rhetoric heightened public anxiety, and their loyalty programs ruined innocent people's lives and careers.

It is a misconception that anticommunism began in 1950 with the furious speeches of Senator Joseph R. McCarthy of Wisconsin. Actually, anticommunism had been a prominent strand in the American political fabric ever since the First World War and the Red Scare of 1919 and 1920. The Communist Party had never been strong in the United States, even during the hard times of the depression. But anticommunism persisted, and the Cold War heightened anti-Communist fears. In manipulating these fears to his own advantage, Joe McCarthy became the most successful and frightening redbaiter the country had ever seen.

Was there reason to fear Communist influence in the United States in the 1940s and 1950s? During the Second World War when the United States and the Soviet Union fought as allies, membership in the Communist Party of the United States of America (CPUSA) reached 80,000, up from 55,000 in 1938. In fact, as part of the war effort the United States voluntarily supplied valuable military intelligence to the Soviets, and 15,000 CPUSA members served in the American armed forces. In addition, however, documents selectively released in the 1990s from Russian archives suggest not only that Soviet spies had penetrated America's top-secret Manhattan Project to build the atomic bomb, but also that a handful of Americans working in sensitive government departments had provided classified documents to Soviet espionage agents. Was the CPUSA a tool of the Soviet Union? Its leaders were, but much of its membership was not. As the historian Ellen Schrecker has observed, the party "was both subservient to the Kremlin and genuinely dedicated to a wide range of social reforms," such as the elimination of racism in America.

In the postwar years, there was little hard evidence about Soviet espionage in the United States. Nevertheless, politicians of many stripes played on anti-Communist paranoia, and President Truman shared responsibility for initiating the postwar anti-Communist crusade. He was bothered by the revelation in 1945 that classified government documents had been found in a raid on the offices of *Amerasia*, a little-known magazine whose editors sympathized with the Communist revolution in China. Who had supplied the documents to the magazine, and why? Similar concerns greeted the release of a Canadian royal commission report in 1946, which asserted that Soviet spies were operating in Canada; among them, the report said, was a scientist who had transmitted atomic secrets to a Soviet agent.

Spurred by these revelations, Truman in 1947 ordered investigations into the loyalty of the more than 3 million employees of the U.S. government. In 1950 the government began discharging people deemed "security risks," among them alcoholics, homosexuals, and debtors thought to be susceptible to blackmail. In most cases there was no evidence of disloyalty. Others became victims of guilt by association. Their loyalty was considered questionable because they either knew or were related to people thought to be subversive or disloyal.

Truman's Loyalty Probe

The wellspring of this fear of communism was the Cold War: fear of internal subversion was intertwined with fear of external attack. Truman was not alone in peddling fear; conservatives and liberal Democrats joined him in accusing their political enemies of being "soft on communism." Republicans used the same methods to attack the Democratic candidates for president in 1948 and 1952; liberal Democrats used them to discredit the far-left, pro-Wallace wing of their party. The anti-Communist crusade of the late 1940s, created by professional politicians, was embraced and promoted by labor union officials, religious leaders, media moguls, and other influential figures.

Americans began to point accusing fingers at one another. "Reds, phonies, and 'parlor pinks,'" in Truman's words, seemed to lurk everywhere. Hollywood film personalities who had been ardent left-wingers such as Will Geer and Zero Mostel were blacklisted and could not find

Victims of Anti-Communist Hysteria

work in the movies; and ten screenwriters and directors (the "Hollywood Ten") were sent to prison for contempt of Congress when they refused to provide names of alleged Communists. Schoolteachers and college professors were fired for expressing dissenting viewpoints. Anti-Communists also exploited the hysteria to drive homosexuals from their jobs. "Sexual perverts have infiltrated our government in recent years," warned the Republican national chairman in 1950, adding that homosexuals were "perhaps as dangerous as the actual Communists."

In labor union elections and even in local parent-teacher associations, redbaiting became a convenient tactic for discrediting the opposition. The hysteria was particularly damaging to the labor movement, which forsook its class-conscious militancy of the 1930s in favor of anticommunism. In 1949 the CIO expelled eleven unions, with a combined membership of over 900,000, for alleged Communist domination. All this occurred at a time when membership in the Communist Party of the United States of America was declining, from a high of about 83,000 in 1947 to 55,000 in 1950 and 25,000 in 1954.

Despite the rampant false accusations, there was cause for anxiety—especially in 1949. In that year the Soviets detonated their first atomic bomb, and the Chinese Communists, finally victorious in their civil war, proclaimed the People's Republic of China. Furthermore, a former State Department official, Alger Hiss, was on trial for perjury for swearing to a grand jury that he had never passed classified documents to his accuser, former American Communist spy Whittaker Chambers, and that he in fact had not seen Chambers since 1936. When Truman and Secretary of State Dean Acheson came to Hiss's defense, some people began to suspect that the Democrats had something to hide. In 1948 Congressman Richard M. Nixon of California, a Republican member of the House Committee on Un-American Activities (HUAC), appeared before a federal grand jury to urge that Hiss be indicted for espionage. Two days later, he was, and in early 1950 he was convicted of perjury.

Hiss Case

At the same time, a British court sentenced and sent to prison Klaus Fuchs, a nuclear scientist and Nazi refugee, for turning over to Soviet agents secrets from the atomic bomb project at Los Alamos, New Mexico. "Fuchs and Acheson and Hiss and hydrogen bombs threatening outside and New Dealism eating away at the vitals of the nation," exclaimed a Republican

How do historians know...

that the advent of atomic weapons shaped popular culture in postwar United States? Historians have examined the era's popular culture, including feature films, comic books, newsreels, and television shows, as well as photographs in popular magazines such as *Life*. Especially influenced by the popular culture of the atomic age were America's children, some of whom saw a newsreel in 1946 with footage of Hiroshima shot after the August 1945 bombing. The victims' skin was seared; a man missing an ear appeared, then staggered on, as did a woman whose body was imprinted with the design of the dress she had been wearing. Children reported being shocked by this newsreel.

After the Soviets exploded their first atomic bomb in 1949, the United States initiated air raid drills in its schools and issued metal identification tags to girls and boys. But nothing drove home the point about the atomic threat as well as popular culture, in this case, an animated cartoon featuring Bert the Turtle, who warned schoolchildren to "Duck and Cover" during an atomic attack.

In the 1950s public concern mounted over the medical consequences of radioactive fallout from atomic bomb tests, especially when traces of strontium 90, a radioactive isotope, began showing up in milk. Feature films heightened Americans' anxiety. Monsters—atomic mutants—began to rampage through America's movies. In the movie *Them!* (1954), ants on a nuclear test range mutated into giants and swarmed toward Los Angeles. Watching *Them!* in theaters, people squirmed as soldiers used flamethrowers to blast the gigantic ants choking the city's sewer system. Sometimes, atomic contamination made people smaller, even microscopic, as in *The Incredible Shrinking Man* (1957). The historian Paul Boyer has written that "nuclear fear," generated by newsreels and films, "was a shaping cultural force in these years."

Because research on children's nuclear fears did not begin until the 1960s, historians may never know exactly what impact the pop-

ular culture of the atomic age had on America's boys and girls in the 1940s and 1950s. Still, there is anecdotal and even literary evidence of the intensity of children's fears. Early in the atomic age, in 1947, *Senior Scholastic* published this poem, written by a schoolboy:

I am a child of the Atom
And I must make my roots in this age.
But I am afraid
And I would go back into my mother's
    womb where it is dark and quiet. . . .

(Photo: Collection of Hershenson-Allen Archives)

Congressman Richard M. Nixon (1913–1994) appears to take little satisfaction in the newspaper headline proclaiming Alger Hiss's perjury conviction in early 1950. As a member of the House Un-American Activities Committee, Nixon led the investigation into charges that Hiss had been a Communist Party member and a spy in the 1950s. (Corbis-Bettmann)

senator. "In the name of heaven, is this the best America can do?"

The circumstances were ripe for a demagogue. It was in this bedeviled atmosphere that Senator Joseph McCarthy mounted a rostrum in Wheeling, West Virginia, in February 1950 and gave a name to the hysteria: McCarthyism. "The State Department," he asserted, was "thoroughly infested with Communists," and the most dangerous person in the department was Dean Acheson. The senator claimed to have a list of 205 Communists working in the department; McCarthy later lowered the figure to "57 card-carrying members," then raised it to 81. But the number did not matter. What McCarthy needed was a winning campaign issue, and he had found it. Republicans, distraught over losing what had appeared to be a sure victory in the 1948 presidential election, were eager to support his attack in hopes of capturing the White House in 1952.

McCarthy and McCarthyism gained momentum throughout 1950. McCarthy continued to display his unparalleled talent for demagoguery, implying guilt by association, interpreting writings out of context, and telling outright lies. Nothing seemed to slow the sena-

McCarthy's Attack on the State Department

tor down, not even attacks by other Republicans. Seven Republican senators, led by Maine's Margaret Chase Smith, broke with their colleagues in 1950 and publicly condemned McCarthy for his "selfish political exploitation of fear, bigotry, ignorance, and intolerance"; a Senate committee reported that his charges against the State Department were "a fraud and a hoax." But McCarthy had much to sustain him, including Julius and Ethel Rosenberg's 1950 arrest for conspiracy to commit espionage. During the war, they allegedly had recruited and supervised a spy who worked at the Los Alamos atomic laboratory. Perhaps even more helpful to McCarthy than the Rosenberg case was the outbreak of the Korean War in June 1950, also believed to be Moscow driven.

Widespread support for anti-Communist measures was also apparent in the adoption, over Truman's veto, of the Internal Security (McCarran) Act of 1950, which required members of "Communist-front" organizations to register with the government and prohibited them from holding defense jobs or traveling abroad. In a telling decision in 1951 (*Dennis et al. v. U.S.*), the Supreme Court upheld the Smith Act of 1940, under which eleven Communist Party leaders had been convicted and imprisoned. These government attacks on the CPUSA decimated its ranks.

The conduct of Senator Joseph R. McCarthy was one of the most vexing problems facing Eisenhower's first administration. The Wisconsin senator's no-holds-barred search for subversives in government turned up none and was an affront to political fair play, decency, and civil liberties. Eisenhower avoided confronting McCarthy, saying privately that he would not "get into the gutter with that guy"; the president also feared that a showdown would splinter the Republican Party. Instead, he hoped the media and Congress would bring McCarthy down.

Eisenhower's Reluctance to Confront McCarthy

While Eisenhower pursued this indirect strategy to undermine the senator, his administration practiced its own brand of anticommunism. A new executive order in 1953 expanded the criteria under which federal workers could be dismissed as "security risks." In its first three years in office, the Eisenhower administration dismissed fifteen hundred people, more than Truman had fired in twice the time. One of Eisenhower's most controversial decisions was his denial of clemency to Julius and Ethel Rosenberg, who had two young sons. The Rosenbergs, having been sentenced to death, were executed in 1953.

In 1954 the Communist Control Act demonstrated that both liberals and conservatives shared in the consensus on anticommunism. The measure, which in effect made membership in the Communist Party illegal, passed in the Senate unanimously and in the House by 265 votes to 2. Its chief sponsor, liberal Democratic senator Hubert H. Humphrey of Minnesota, told his colleagues just before he cast his vote: "We have closed all of the doors. These rats will not get out of the trap."

As for Senator McCarthy, he finally transgressed the limits of what the Senate and the public would tolerate. His crucial mistake was taking on the U.S. Army in front of millions of television viewers. At issue was the senator's wild accusation that the army was shielding and promoting Communists; he cited the case of one army dentist. The so-called Army-McCarthy hearings, held by a Senate subcommittee in 1954, became a showcase for the senator's abusive treatment of witnesses. McCarthy, apparently drunk, alternately ranted and slurred his words. Finally, after he maligned a young lawyer who was not even involved in the hearings, army counsel Joseph Welch protested, "Have you no sense of decency, sir?" The gallery erupted in applause, and McCarthy's career as a witch-hunter was over. The Senate finally condemned McCarthy, in a 67-to-22 vote in December 1954, not for defiling the Bill of Rights, but for sullying the dignity of the Senate. He remained a senator, but exhaustion and alcohol took their toll. McCarthy died in 1957 at the age of forty-eight.

Army-McCarthy Hearings

President Eisenhower's reluctance to discredit McCarthy publicly had given the senator, other right-wing members of Congress, and some private and public institutions enough rein to divide the nation and destroy the careers of many innocent people. McCarthyism demoralized and frightened federal workers, some of whom were driven from public service. The anti-Communist campaigns of the 1950s also discouraged people from freely expressing themselves and hence from debating critical issues. Fear, in short, helped sustain the Cold War consensus.

In 1954 Senator Joseph R. McCarthy, surrounded by his own newspaper headlines, adorns the cover of *Time* magazine. His downfall came later that year, during the televised Army-McCarthy hearings. McCarthy's wild accusations and abusive treatment of witnesses disgusted millions of viewers.   (© 1954 Time Inc.)

The Civil Rights Movement in the 1940s and 1950s

 Ironically, Cold War pressures benefited the civil rights movement. As the Soviet Union was quick to point out, the United States could hardly pose as the leader of the free world or condemn the denial of human rights in eastern Europe and the Soviet Union if it practiced segregation at home. Nor could the United States convince new African and Asian nations of its dedication to human rights if African Americans were subjected to segregation, discrimination, disfranchisement, and racial violence. To win the support of nonaligned nations, the United States would have to live up to its own ideals. That the nation was not doing so was evident.

Americans had seen the Second World War as a struggle for democracy and against hatred. African

African Americans' Political "Balance of Power"

Americans who had helped win the war were determined that their lives in postwar America would be better because of their sacrifices. Moreover, politicians were beginning to pay attention to black aspirations. Drawn by opportunities in war industries, in the 1940s more than a million African Americans migrated from the South to the North and West (see Chapter 27). In some urban-industrial states, black voters began to control the political "balance of power." Harry Truman and other politicians knew they would have to compete for the growing African American vote in California, New York, Illinois, Michigan, Pennsylvania, and other large states. Many Republicans cultivated the black vote. Dewey, who as governor of New York had pushed successfully for a fair employment practices commission, was particularly popular with African Americans.

President Truman, in short, had compelling political reasons for supporting African American civil rights. But he also felt a moral obligation to do something, for he genuinely believed it was only fair that every American, regardless of race, should enjoy the full rights of citizenship. Truman also was disturbed by the resurgence of racial terrorism. To suppress black aspirations for civil rights unleashed by the war, a revived Ku Klux Klan was again burning crosses and murdering blacks who had had the audacity to vote. But what really horrified Truman was the report that police in Aiken, South Carolina, had gouged out the

eyes of a black sergeant just three hours after he had been discharged from the army. Several weeks later, in December 1946, Truman signed an executive order establishing the President's Committee on Civil Rights.

The committee's report, *To Secure These Rights* (1947), would become the agenda for the civil rights movement for the next twenty years.

President Truman's Committee on Civil Rights

Among its recommendations were the enactment of federal antilynching and antisegregation legislation. *To Secure These Rights* also called for laws guaranteeing voting rights and equal employment opportunity and for the establishment of a permanent commission on civil rights. Although Congress failed to act and some evidence suggests that Truman's real goal was the African American vote in 1948, his action was significant. For the first time since Reconstruction, a president had acknowledged the federal government's responsibility to protect blacks and strive for racial equality.

Truman took this responsibility seriously, and in 1948 he issued two executive orders declaring an end to racial discrimination in the federal government. One proclaimed a policy of "fair employment throughout the federal establishment" and created the Employment Board of the Civil Service Commission to hear charges of discrimination. The other ordered the racial desegregation of the armed forces and appointed the Committee on Equality of Treatment and Opportunity in the Armed Services to oversee this process. Despite strong, even fierce, opposition to desegregation within the military, segregated units were being phased out by the time the Korean War broke out.

African Americans also benefited from a series of Supreme Court decisions. The trend toward judicial support of civil rights had begun in

Supreme Court Decisions on Civil Rights

the late 1930s, when the NAACP established its Legal Defense Fund under Charles Hamilton Houston and Thurgood Marshall. In the 1940s and 1950s, Marshall (who in 1967 would become the first African American Supreme Court justice) and his colleagues set out to destroy the separate-but-equal doctrine established in *Plessy v. Ferguson* (1896) by insisting on its literal interpretation. In higher education, the NAACP calculated, the cost of true equality in racially separate schools would be prohibitive. "You can't build a cyclotron for one student," as the president of the University of Oklahoma acknowledged. As a result of NAACP lawsuits, African

Jackie Robinson cracked the color line in major league baseball when he joined the Brooklyn Dodgers for the 1947 season. Sliding safely into third base, Robinson displays the aggressive style that won him rookie-of-the-year honors. He was later elected to the Baseball Hall of Fame.   (Hy Peskin, *Life* magazine © Time Inc.)

American students won admission to professional and graduate schools at a number of state universities. In *Smith v. Allwright* (1944), the Supreme Court also outlawed the whites-only primaries held by the Democratic Party in some southern states, branding them a violation of the Fifteenth Amendment's guarantee of the right to vote. Two years later the Court struck down segregation in interstate bus transportation (*Morgan v. Virginia*). And in *Shelley v. Kraemer* (1948), the Court held that racially restrictive covenants (private agreements among white homeowners not to sell to blacks) violated the equal protection clause of the Fourteenth Amendment.

A change in social attitudes accompanied these gains in black political and legal power. Books like Gunnar Myrdal's social science study *An American Dilemma* (1944) and Richard Wright's novels *Native Son* (1940) and *Black Boy* (1945) were increasing white awareness of the social injustices that plagued African Americans. A new black middle class was emerging, composed of college-educated activists, war veterans, and union workers. Blacks and whites also worked together in CIO unions and service organizations such as the National Council of Churches. In 1947 a black baseball player, Jackie Robinson, broke the major league color barrier and electrified Brooklyn Dodgers fans with his spectacular hitting and base running.

Even so, segregation was still standard practice in the 1950s, and blacks continued to suffer disfranchisement, job discrimination, and violence, including the bombing murder in 1951 of the Florida state director of the NAACP and his wife. But in 1954 the NAACP won a historic victory that stunned the white South and energized African Americans to challenge segregation on several fronts. *Brown v. Board of Education of Topeka* incorporated cases from several states, all involving segregated schools. Written by Earl Warren, whom President Eisenhower had named chief justice in 1953, the Court's unanimous decision concluded that "in the field of public education the doctrine of 'separate but equal' has no place. Separate educational facilities are inherently unequal." Such facilities, Warren wrote, produced in black children "a feeling of inferiority" and deprived them of "the equal protection of the laws guaranteed by the Fourteenth Amendment." But the ruling did not demand immediate compliance. A year later the Court finally ordered school desegregation, but only "with all deliberate speed."

Brown v. Board of Education of Topeka

The lack of a timetable encouraged the southern states to resist.

Some communities in border states like Kansas and Maryland quietly implemented the order, and many southern moderates advocated a gradual rollback of segregation. But the forces of white resistance soon came to dominate, urging southern communities to defy the Court. The Klan experienced another resurgence, and business and professional people created White Citizens' Councils for the express purpose of resisting the order. Known familiarly as "uptown Ku Klux Klans," the councils brought their economic power to bear against black civil rights activists. One of the most effective resistance tactics was enactment of state laws that paid the private-school tuition of white children who had left public schools to avoid integration. In some cases, desegregated public schools were ordered closed.

White Resistance to Civil Rights

White resistance to civil rights also gained strength in large northern cities, such as Chicago and Detroit. Because of migration to Chicago in the 1940s and 1950s, for example, the city's African American population jumped from 275,000 in 1940 to 800,000 in 1960. The newcomers gained not only good jobs in industry, but also political power due to their increased numbers. At the same time, blacks continued to be segregated in housing and education. White mobs in Chicago and Detroit resorted to violence to frighten African Americans out of white neighborhoods. In 1951 in Cicero, Illinois, adjoining Chicago, several thousand whites eager to keep blacks out provoked a race riot. So racially divided was Chicago that the U.S. Commission on Civil Rights in 1959 described it as "the most residentially segregated city in the nation." Detroit and other northern cities were not far behind.

Unlike Truman, President Eisenhower wanted to avoid dealing with civil rights, preferring instead gradual and voluntary change in race relations. He came to regret his appointment of Earl Warren as "the biggest damn fool mistake I ever made." Although the president disapproved of racial segregation, he objected to "compulsory federal law" in the belief that race relations would improve "only if it starts locally." He also feared that the ugly public confrontations likely to follow rapid desegregation would jeopardize Republican inroads in the South. Thus Eisenhower did not state forthrightly that the federal government would en-force the Court's decision as the nation's law. In short, instead of leading, he spoke ambiguously and thereby tacitly encouraged white noncompliance.

Events in Little Rock, Arkansas, forced the president to stop sidestepping the issue. In September 1957 Governor Orval E. Faubus intervened to defy a court-ordered desegregation plan for Little Rock's Central High School. Faubus ordered the Arkansas National Guard to block the entry of black students. Eisenhower made no effort to impede Faubus's actions. Later that month, bowing to a federal judge's order, Faubus withdrew the guardsmen. As hundreds of jeering whites threatened to storm the school, eight black children entered Central High. The next day, fearing violence, Eisenhower dispatched army paratroopers to Little Rock to ensure the black students' safety. Troops patrolled the school for the rest of the year; in response, Little Rock officials closed all public high schools in 1958 and 1959 rather than desegregate them.

Crisis in Little Rock, Arkansas

Elsewhere, African Americans did not wait for Supreme Court or White House decisions to claim equal rights. In 1955 Rosa Parks, a department store seamstress and active member of the NAACP, was arrested for refusing to give up her seat to a white man on a public bus in Montgomery, Alabama. Local black women's organizations and civil rights groups decided to boycott the city's bus system, and they elected Martin Luther King, Jr., a recently ordained minister who had just arrived in Montgomery, as their leader. King launched the boycott with a moving speech in which he declared: "If we are wrong, the Constitution is wrong. If we are wrong, God Almighty is wrong. If we are wrong, Jesus of Nazareth was merely a utopian dreamer. . . . If we are wrong, justice is a lie."

Montgomery Bus Boycott

Martin Luther King, Jr., was a twenty-six-year-old Baptist minister who recently had earned a Ph.D. at Boston University. Disciplined and analytical, he was committed to nonviolent protest in the spirit of India's leader Mohandas K. Gandhi. Although he was jailed for refusing to comply with an unjust law and a bomb blew out the front of his house, King persisted. "Absence of fear," according to civil rights leader Bayard Rustin, was what King gave to black Americans. In 1957 King became the first president of the Southern Christian

Martin Luther King, Jr.

In 1957 white teenagers in Little Rock, Arkansas, angrily confront African American students who, under federal court order, are attempting to enter, and thus desegregate, Central High School. The Supreme Court's *Brown* decision of 1954 was resisted by whites throughout the South. (Wide World Photos, Inc.)

Leadership Conference, organized to coordinate civil rights activities.

During the year-long Montgomery bus boycott, blacks young and old walked or carpooled. With the bus company near bankruptcy and downtown merchants hurt by declining sales, city officials adopted harassment tactics to frighten blacks into abandoning the boycott. King urged perseverance, and bolstered by a Supreme Court decision that declared Alabama's bus segregation laws unconstitutional, Montgomery blacks triumphed in 1956. They and others across the nation were further heartened when Congress passed the Civil Rights Act of 1957, which created the United States Commission on Civil Rights to investigate systematic discrimination, such as voting discrimination. But this measure, like a voting rights act passed three years later, proved ineffective. Critics charged that the Eisenhower administration was interested more in quelling the civil rights question than in addressing it.

African Americans responded by launching a campaign of sit-ins in the South. In February 1960 four black students from North Carolina Agricultural and

Sit-ins

Technical College in Greensboro ordered coffee at a dime-store lunch counter. Told they would not be served, the students refused to budge. "I felt as though I had gained my manhood," recalled one of the young men. Thus began the sit-in movement, which quickly spread throughout the South. And when whites brutally attacked the women and men sitting in at the lunch counters, the nightly news often featured the violence, provoking public sympathy for the civil rights movement. Inspired by the sit-ins, southern black college and high-school students met on Easter weekend in 1960 and organized the Student Nonviolent Coordinating Committee (SNCC). In the face of angry white mobs, SNCC members challenged the status quo, all the while singing the anthem of the civil rights movement, "We Shall Overcome," which includes the words "We are not afraid."

King personally joined the sit-in movement, and in October 1960 he was arrested at a sit-in to desegregate an Atlanta snack bar. Sent to a cold, cockroach-infested

For leading the movement to gain equality for blacks riding city buses in Montgomery, Alabama, Martin Luther King, Jr. (1929–1968), and other African Americans, including twenty-three other ministers, were indicted by an all-white jury for violating an old law banning boycotts. In late March 1956 King was convicted and fined $500. A crowd of well-wishers cheered a smiling King (here with his wife, Coretta) outside the courthouse, where King proudly declared, "The protest goes on!" King's arrest and conviction made the bus boycott front-page news across America.   (Corbis-Bettmann)

Civil Rights and the 1960 Election

state penitentiary where he faced four months at hard labor, he became ill. As an apathetic Eisenhower White House looked on, Senator John F. Kennedy, the Democratic presidential candidate, called King's wife, Coretta Scott King, to express support; and his brother, Robert F. Kennedy, persuaded the sentencing judge to release King on bond. In November grateful African Americans cast their ballots for Kennedy in the expectation that, as president, he would provide federal protection of their civil rights movement. Those committed to racial equality looked forward to great gains under Kennedy in the 1960s.

The Postwar Booms: Babies, Business, and Bigness

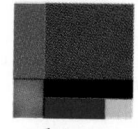

The postwar economic boom proved to be one of the longest periods of growth and prosperity the United States ever experienced. Its keys were increasing output and increasing demand. Despite occasional recessions

the gross national product more than doubled from $212 billion in 1945 to $520 billion in 1961 (see Figure 28.1).

The Harvard economist John Kenneth Galbraith gave a name to the United States during the postwar economic boom: the "affluent society." As U.S. productivity increased in the postwar years, so did Americans' appetite for goods and services.

The Affluent Society

During the depression and the Second World War, many Americans had dreamed of buying a home or a car. In the flush postwar years they finally could satisfy those deferred desires. Some families bought two cars and equipped their new homes with the latest appliances and amusements, such as television. Easy credit was the economic basis of the consumer culture; when people lacked cash to buy what they wanted, they borrowed money. Consumer credit to support the nation's shopping spree grew from $5.7 billion in 1945 to $58 billion in 1961.

When the economy produced more, Americans generally brought home bigger paychecks and had more money to spend. Between the end of the war and

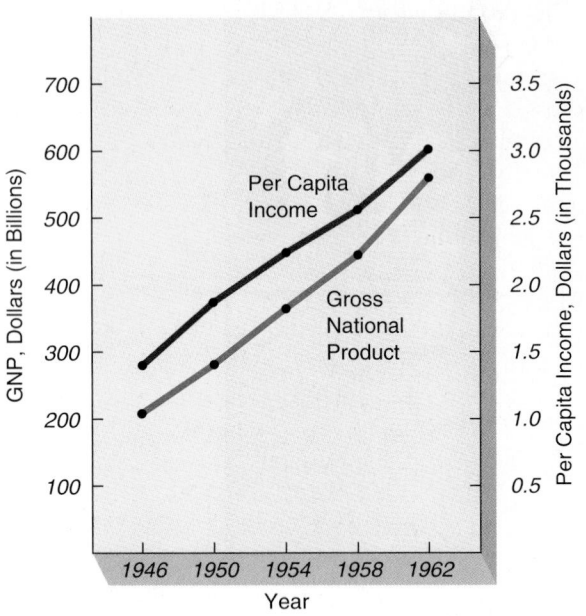

Figure 28.1 Gross National Product and Per Capita Income, 1946–1962 Both gross national product and per capita income soared during the economic boom from 1946 to 1962. (Source: Adapted from U.S. Bureau of the Census, *Historical Statistics of the United States, Colonial Times to 1970*, Bicentennial Edition [Washington, D.C., U.S. Government Printing Office, 1975], p. 224.)

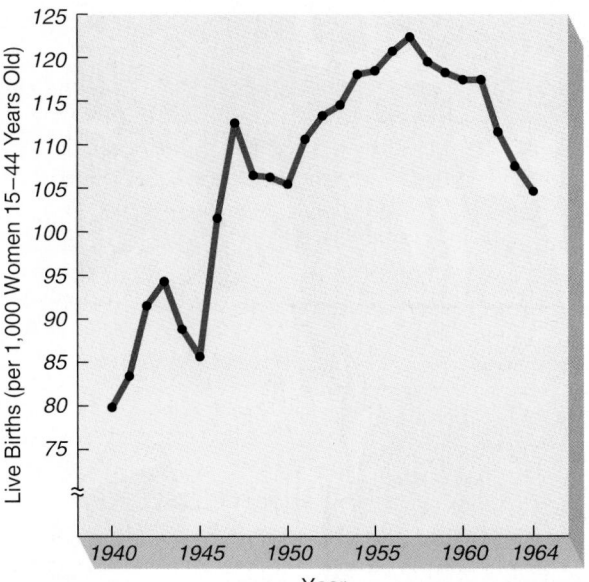

Figure 28.2 Birth Rate, 1945–1964 The birth rate began to rise in 1942 and 1943, but it skyrocketed during the postwar years beginning in 1946, reaching its peak in 1957. From 1954 to 1964, the United States recorded more than 4 million births every year. (Source: Adapted from U.S. Bureau of the Census, *Historical Statistics of the United States, Colonial Times to 1970*, Bicentennial Edition [Washington, D.C., U.S. Government Printing Office, 1975], p. 49.)

Increased Purchasing Power

1950, per capita real income (based on actual purchasing power) rose 6 percent—and that was only the beginning. In the 1950s it jumped another 15 percent; in the 1960s the increase was even greater—32 percent (see Figure 28.1). The result was a noticeable increase in the standard of living. To the vast majority of Americans, such prosperity was a vindication of the American system of free enterprise.

The baby boom was both a cause and an effect of prosperity. The birth rate, which had been very low during the 1930s, started to rise during the war. But the birth rate soared immediately after the war, and it continued to do so throughout the 1950s (see Figure 28.2). During the 1950s, the number of births exceeded 4 million per year, reversing the downward trend in birth rates that had prevailed for 150 years. Births began to decline after 1961 but con-

Baby Boom

tinued to exceed 4 million per year through 1964. The baby-boom generation was the largest by far in the nation's history. And as this vast age group grew older, it had successive impacts on housing, nursery schools, grade schools, and high schools, fads and popular music, colleges and universities, the job market, and retirement funds, including Social Security.

The baby boom meant business for builders, manufacturers, and school systems. "Take the 3,548,000 babies born in 1950," wrote Sylvia F. Porter in her syndicated newspaper column. "Bundle them into a batch, bounce them all over the bountiful land that is America. What do you get?" Porter's answer: "Boom. The biggest, boomiest boom ever known in history. Just imagine how much these extra people, these new markets, will absorb—in food, clothing, in gadgets, in housing, in services. Our factories must expand just to keep pace."

Of the three cornerstones of the postwar economic boom—construction, automobiles, and defense—two were directly related to the upsurge in births. Demand for housing and schools for all these children generated a building boom, furthered by construction of shopping centers, office buildings, and airports. Much of this construction took place in the suburbs. The postwar suburbanization of America in turn would have been impossible without automobile manufacturing, for the car provided access to the sprawling new communities. The number of registered automobiles climbed from 26 million in 1945 to 63 million in 1961.

Government funding helped new families to settle in the suburbs. Low-interest GI mortgages and Federal Housing Administration (FHA)

Housing Boom mortgage insurance made the difference for people who otherwise would have been unable to afford a home. This easy credit, combined with postwar prosperity, produced a construction boom. From 1945 to 1946, housing starts climbed from 326,000 to more than 1 million; they approached 2 million in 1950 and remained above 1.3 million in 1961. Never before had new starts exceeded 1 million.

To produce so much new, relatively inexpensive housing so fast, contractors had to operate on a massive scale. Arthur Levitt and Sons developed a system, adopted by other companies, of using interchangeable materials and designs to build nearly identical houses on uniform, treeless lots. In 1947 the construction of Levittown, New York, began; Levittowns also arose in New Jersey and Pennsylvania. To supply the new communities, shopping malls soon dotted the countryside.

As suburbia spread, pastures became neighborhoods with astounding rapidity. Highway construction was a central element in the transformation of rural land into suburbia.

Highway Construction In 1947 Congress authorized construction of a 37,000-mile chain of highways, and in 1956 President Eisenhower signed the Highway Act, which approved funds for a 42,500-mile interstate highway system, intended to facilitate commerce and enable the military to move around the nation more easily. The interstate highways invigorated the tourist industry, further weakened the railroads to the advantage of the truck-

Even during the Second World War, Americans dreamed about marriage, children, and a new house in the suburbs equipped with the latest kitchen appliances. This advertisement for Kelvinator appliances was published in *Life* magazine in December 1944.   (Ellen Kaiper Collection, Oakland, Calif.)

ing industry, and spurred the growth of suburbs farther and farther from the central cities.

Federal expenditures on highways swelled from $79 million in 1946 to $2.6 billion in 1961. State and local spending on highways also mushroomed. Highways both hastened suburbanization and homogenized the landscape. The high-speed trucking that highways made possible also accelerated the integration of the South into the national economy.

In the twenty-five years after the war, a mass movement was under way from the cities to the suburbs. In 1940, 19.5 percent of Americans lived in the suburbs. By 1970 that number had doubled, and for the first time in American history, more people lived in suburbs than in cities or in rural areas (see Table 28.1). A combination of motives drew people to the suburbs. Some wanted to leave behind the noise and smells of the city. Some white families moved out of urban neighborhoods because African American families were moving in. People living in row houses and apartments wanted to move into houses that had yards, family rooms, extra closets, and utility rooms. Many were also looking for a place where they could have a measure of political influence, particularly on the education their children received.

Growth of the Suburbs

Highway construction in combination with the growth of suburbia produced a new phenomenon, the *megalopolis*, a term coined by urban experts in the early 1960s to refer to the almost uninterrupted metropolitan complex stretching along the northeastern seaboard from Boston 600 miles south through New York, Philadelphia, and Baltimore all the way to Washington, D.C. "Boswash" encompassed parts of eleven states and a population of 49 million people, all linked by interstate highways. Another megalopolis that took shape was "Milipitts," a band of heavy industry and dense population stretching from Milwaukee to Pittsburgh.

Millions of Americans began their search for affluence by migrating to the Sunbelt—roughly, the southern third of the United States, running from southern California across the Southwest and South all the way to the Atlantic coast. Among the Sunbelt's booming cities were Houston, Phoenix, Los Angeles, San Diego, Dallas, and Miami. The population of Houston, which became a center not only of the aerospace industry but also of oil and petrochemical production, jumped from 385,000 in 1940 to 1,243,000 in 1960. California absorbed no less than one-fifth of the nation's entire population increase in the 1950s—enough by 1963 to make it the most populous state in the Union (see Map 28.2).

Growth of the Sunbelt

The mass migration to the Sunbelt had started during the war, when GIs and their families were ordered to new duty stations and war workers moved to defense plants in the West and South. The economic bases of the Sunbelt's spectacular growth were defense contractors, such as the aerospace industry, agribusiness, the oil industry, real-estate development, and recreation. Industry was drawn to the southern rim by right-to-work laws, which outlawed closed shops, and by low taxes and low heating bills. Government policies—generous tax breaks for oil companies, siting of military bases, and awarding of defense and aerospace contracts—were crucial to the Sunbelt's development. Crucial, too, was the air conditioning of houses, office buildings, and automobiles, which made bearable even the hottest Sunbelt days.

The third cornerstone of the postwar economic boom was military spending. When the Defense Department was established in 1947, its budget was just over $10 billion a year. In 1961 the total had risen to $98 billion. Many defense contracts went to industries and universities to develop weapons, and the government supported space research; funds spent on space research alone zoomed from $76 million in 1957 to almost $6 billion in 1966. Defense spending also helped stimulate rapid advances in the electronics industry. The ENIAC

Military Spending

Table 28.1	Geographic Distribution of the U.S. Population, 1930–1970 (in Percentages)		
Year	Central Cities	Suburbs	Rural Areas and Small Towns
1930	31.8%	18.0%	50.2%
1940	31.6	19.5	48.9
1950	32.3	23.8	43.9
1960	32.6	30.7	36.7
1970	31.4	37.6	31.0

Source: Adapted from U.S. Bureau of the Census, *Decennial Censuses, 1930–1970* (Washington, D.C., U.S. Government Printing Office).

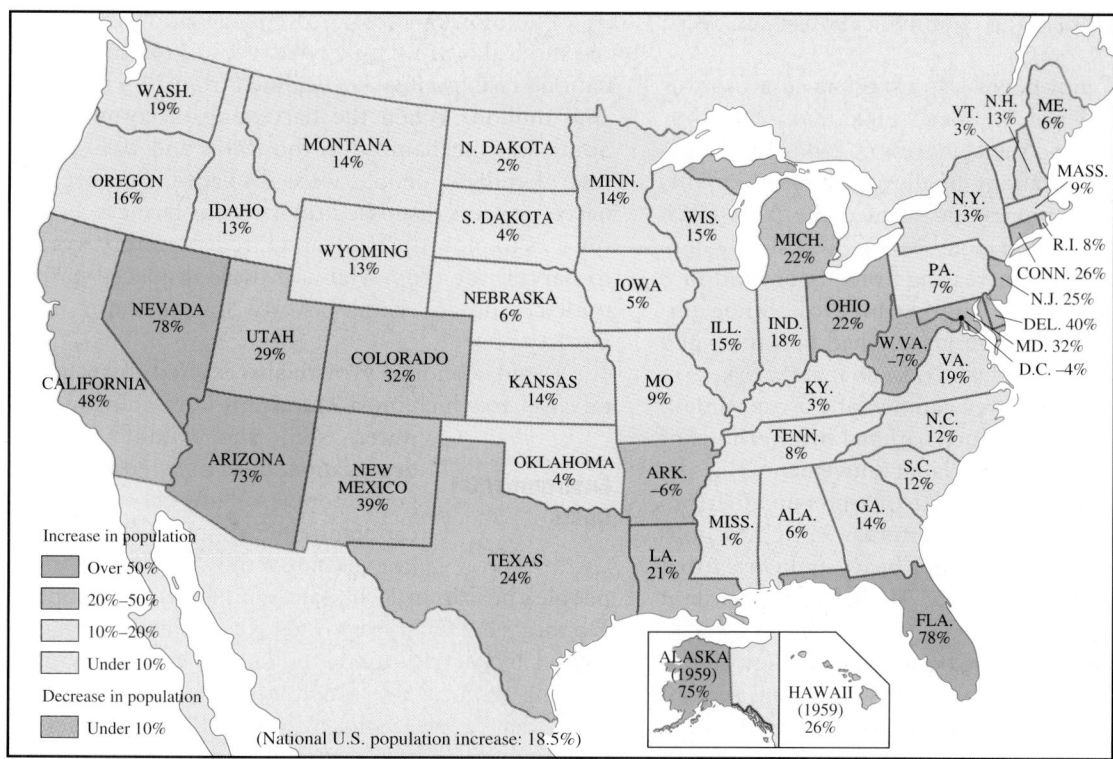

Map 28.2   Rise of the Sunbelt, 1950–1960   The years after the Second World War saw a continuation of the migration of Americans to the Sunbelt states of the Southwest and the West Coast.

computer, completed at the University of Pennsylvania in 1946, weighed fifty tons and required 18,000 vacuum tubes. Then, in the 1950s, introduction of the transistor accelerated the computer revolution; the silicon microchip in the 1960s inaugurated even more stunning advances in electronics. The microchip facilitated the shift from heavy manufacturing to high-technology industries in fiber optics, lasers, video equipment, robotics, and genetic engineering. Sales of office and business equipment reflected the growth in technology-based production.

The evolution of electronics meant a large-scale tradeoff for the American people. As industries automated, computerized processes replaced slower mechanical ones, increasing productivity but pushing people out of jobs. Electronic technology also promoted concentration of ownership in industry. Sophisticated technology was expensive, and small corporations were shut out of the market. Indeed, large corporations with capital and experience in high-tech fields expanded into related industries. General

Electric, which during the Second World War had manufactured electrical products, began producing computers, jet engines, and nuclear-powered generators.

Another kind of corporate expansion also marked the early 1950s. The third great wave of mergers swept across American business. The first two such movements, in the 1890s and 1920s, had tended toward vertical and horizontal integration, respectively (see pages 511 and 666). The postwar era was distinguished by conglomerate mergers. A *conglomerate* brings together companies in unrelated industries as a hedge against instability in a particular market. International Telephone and Telegraph (IT&T), for instance, bought up companies in several fields, including suburban development, insurance, and hotels. In keeping with the thrust of America's postwar boom, the country's ten largest corporations operated in core growth industries: automobiles (GM, Ford, Chrysler), oil (Exxon, Mobil, Tex-

Conglomerate Mergers

aco), and electronics and communications (GE, IBM, IT&T, AT&T).

The labor movement also experienced a postwar merger. In 1955 the American Federation of Labor

Labor Merger

and the Congress of Industrial Organizations finally put aside their differences and formed the AFL-CIO. Union membership grew slowly during the postwar years, increasing from just around 14.8 million in 1945 to 17.3 million in 1961. Some observers charged that union leaders had become smug and lost the zeal that had won over so many workers in the 1930s and 1940s; revelations of corrupt union practices, notably by the International Brotherhood of Teamsters, also tainted the labor movement. But the main reason for the slow growth of union membership was a shift in employment patterns. Most new jobs were being created not in the heavy industries that hired blue-collar workers but in the union-resistant white-collar service trades.

The postwar economic boom was good for unionized blue-collar workers, many of whom won real increases in wages sufficient to enjoy a middle-class lifestyle that previously had been the exclusive province of white-collar workers and professionals. Union workers could qualify for mortgages for suburban homes, especially if their spouses also worked. Many enjoyed job security, paid vacations, and retirement plans. They also could aspire to college educations for their children. And they were more protected against inflation: in 1948 General Motors and the United Auto Workers agreed on automatic cost-of-living adjustments (COLAs) in workers' wages, a practice that spread to other industries.

The trend toward economic consolidation also changed agriculture. New machines, such as mechanical cotton-, tobacco-, and grape-

Agribusiness

pickers and crop-dusting planes revolutionized farming methods, and the increased use of fertilizers and pesticides raised the total value of farm output from $24.6 billion in 1945 to $38.4 billion in 1961. At the same time, farm labor productivity tripled. The resulting improvement in profitability drew large investors into agriculture, and average acreage per farm increased from 195 in 1945 to 306 in 1961. By the 1960s it took money—sometimes big money—to become a farmer. In many regions only banks, insurance companies, and large businesses could afford the necessary land, machinery, and fertilizer.

The movement toward consolidation threatened the survival of the family farm. From 1945 to 1961 the nation's farm population declined from 24.4 million to 14.8 million. When the harvesting of cotton in the South was mechanized in the 1940s and 1950s, more than 4 million people were displaced. Southern tobacco growers dismissed their tenant farmers, bought tractors to plow the land, and hired migratory workers to harvest the crop. Many of these displaced farmers traded southern rural poverty for northern urban poverty.

Rapid economic growth also exacted environmental costs, to which most Americans were oblivious. Air, water, soil, and wildlife suffered

Environmental Costs

degradation. Steel mills, coal-powered generators, and internal-combustion car engines burning lead-based gasoline polluted the air and imperiled people's health. In 1948, for example, twenty people in Donora, Pennsylvania, died of respiratory failure caused by air pollution; the smoke and sulfur gases pouring from a zinc smelter in Donora became so thick that people could not see or breathe. America's water supplies suffered as well. Human and industrial waste befouled many rivers and lakes, making them unfit for consumption or recreation. Vast quantities of water were diverted from lakes and rivers to meet the needs of America's burgeoning Sunbelt cities, including the swimming pools that dotted parched Arizona and southern California. The extraction of natural resources—strip mining of coal, for example—also scarred the landscape, and toxic waste from chemical plants seeped deep into the soil. America was becoming a dumping ground as never before.

Defense contractors and farmers were among the country's worst polluters. Refuse from nuclear weapons facilities at Hanford, Washington, and at Colorado's Rocky Flats arsenal polluted soil and water resources for years. Agriculture began employing massive amounts of pesticides and other chemicals. A chemical called DDT, for example, which had been used on Pacific islands during the war to kill mosquitoes and lice, was released for public use in 1945. During the next fifteen years, farmers eliminated chronic pests with DDT. In 1962, however, *Silent Spring* by Rachel Carson, a wildlife biologist, specifically indicted DDT for the deaths of mammals, birds, and fish. DDT accumulates in the fatty tissues of eagles, trout, and other wildlife, causing cancer in the animals. Because of Carson's book, many Americans finally re-

During the Second World War, DDT was used to protect American troops against bug-borne diseases and was hailed as a miracle insecticide. The use of DDT spread in postwar America, but little attention was paid to its often fatal consequences for birds, mammals, and fish. In 1945, even as children ran alongside, this truck sprayed DDT as part of a mosquito-control program at New York's Jones Beach State Park.   (Corbis-Bettmann)

alized that there were costs to human conquest of the environment. The federal government finally banned the sale of DDT in 1972.

Much of America's continued economic growth encouraged habits that would make the country a "throwaway" society. The auto industry intentionally made cars less durable ("planned obsolescence") and through advertising and revamping designs urged consumers to buy a new model every year or two. Increasing numbers of disposable products such as plastic cups and paper diapers were marketed as conveniences. Moreover, as Americans consumed goods and services, they were using up the world's resources. By the 1960s the United States, with only 5 percent of the world's population, produced and consumed more than one-third of the world's goods and services.

A "Throwaway" Society

Conformity and Consumerism

For the generation of adults in postwar America—the women and men who had suffered economic deprivation during the depression and separation from loved ones during the war—the suburban home became a refuge, and family togetherness fulfilled a psychological need. But sociologists and other critics denounced the suburbs for breeding conformity and status seeking, and they scolded suburbanites for trying to keep up with the Joneses by buying new cars and appliances. William H. Whyte's *The Organization Man* (1956), a study of Park Forest, Illinois, pronounced these suburbanites mindless conservatives and extreme conformists. And the sociologist C. Wright Mills castigated white-collar suburbanites who "sell not only their time and energy but their personalities as well." Nonetheless, most residents of suburbia preferred their lifestyle to any other of which they were aware, and the vast majority of college students in the 1950s looked forward to settling in the suburbs.

Education at all levels, from preschool to graduate school, was a pressing concern for families in postwar America. Immediately after the Second World War, for example, many former GIs enrolled in college and set up housekeeping with their wives and babies in abandoned military barracks on college campuses. The legislation that made this possible was the Servicemen's Readjustment Act of 1944, popularly known as the GI Bill of Rights, which provided living allowances and tuition pay-

Pressures in Education

ments to college-bound veterans. Over 1 million veterans enrolled in 1946—accounting for one out of every two students. Despite pessimistic predictions, the veterans, who saw higher education as the key to upward mobility, succeeded as students. The downside of this success story was that colleges made places for male veterans by turning away qualified women.

As the baby boom became a grade-school boom in the 1950s, American families became preoccupied with the education of their children. Convinced that success in school was a prerequisite for success in adult life, parents joined parent-teacher associations so they would have a voice in the educational process. They worried that schools were overcrowded and that teachers were using obsolete methods. Then in 1957 education became a matter of national security. In that year the Soviet Union launched *Sputnik*, the first earth-orbiting satellite. The Soviet triumph threw into question American military and technological superiority, based ultimately on the nation's school system. Congress responded in 1958 with the National Defense Education Act (NDEA), which funded enrichment of elementary and high-school programs in mathematics, foreign languages, and the sciences, and offered fellowships and loans to college students.

As education became intertwined with national security, so religion became a matter of patriotism.

Growth of Religion

As President Eisenhower put it, "Recognition of the Supreme Being is the first, the most basic expression of Americanism." And in 1954 Eisenhower signed a law inserting the words "under God" after "one nation" in the Pledge of Allegiance to the flag. In America's Cold War with an atheistic enemy, religious leaders emphasized traditional values like family togetherness. The Bible topped the bestseller list, and a familiar refrain of the time was "The family that prays together stays together." Most impressive was the growth in membership in religious congregations; in the fifteen years after the Second World War, the total jumped 62 percent, from 71.7 million in 1945 to 116 million in 1961.

The postwar religious revival was also spurred by the introduction of a revolutionary influence in American life: television. The evangelist Billy Graham, who preached in stadiums throughout the country, and Catholic Bishop Fulton J. Sheen could reach mass audiences on televi-

Television Togetherness

By the mid-1950s, the proliferation of television sets had transformed American family life. The number of households with television sets increased eightfold between 1950 and 1955. Rather than talking, listening to the radio, reading, or going to the movies, families stayed home to watch their favorite shows. (Superstock)

sion. The growth of television was phenomenal. In 1946 only 8,000 households had TVs; that number skyrocketed to 3.9 million in 1950 and to more than 47 million in 1961. Most important, the introduction of television transformed family life in America. "And so the monumental change began in our lives and those of millions of other Americans," recalled a man whose parents bought their first television set in 1950. "More than a year passed before we again visited a movie theater. . . . Social evenings with friends became fewer and fewer still because we discovered we did not share the same television program interests." By 1950 television had loosened the grip of both radio and the movies on the American public.

Television was a crucial force in the evolution of both the consumer culture and family togetherness. "More appliances make mom's work easier," read a typical 1950s advertisement. TV told people what to buy; and as families strove to acquire the latest luxuries and conveniences, shopping became a form of recreation. TV's number-one product was entertainment, and situation comedies and action series were among the most popular shows. *Father Knows Best* and *Leave It to Beaver* celebrated family life. But as average TV-viewing time reached five hours a day in 1956 and continued to rise, critics worried that TV's distorted presentation of the world would significantly define people's sense of reality.

In 1946 the anthropologist Margaret Mead reflected on society's contradictory expectations of American women: "Choose any set of criteria you like, and the answer is the same: women—and men—are confused, uncertain, and discontented with the present definition of women's place in America." On the one hand, the home was premised on a full-time housewife who, with little regard for her own needs, provided her husband and children with a cozy haven from the outside world. On the other hand, women continued to enter the labor force for a variety of reasons. Many worked because they were their families' sole sources of income; they had to work. Others took jobs to supplement the family income. Indeed, the female labor force rose from 19.3 million in 1945 to 23.8 million in 1961 and to 31.6 million in 1970. Despite the cult of motherhood, most new entrants to the job market were married—a trend that had begun during the Second World War—and most were mothers (see Figure 28.3).

Women's Conflicting Roles and Dilemmas

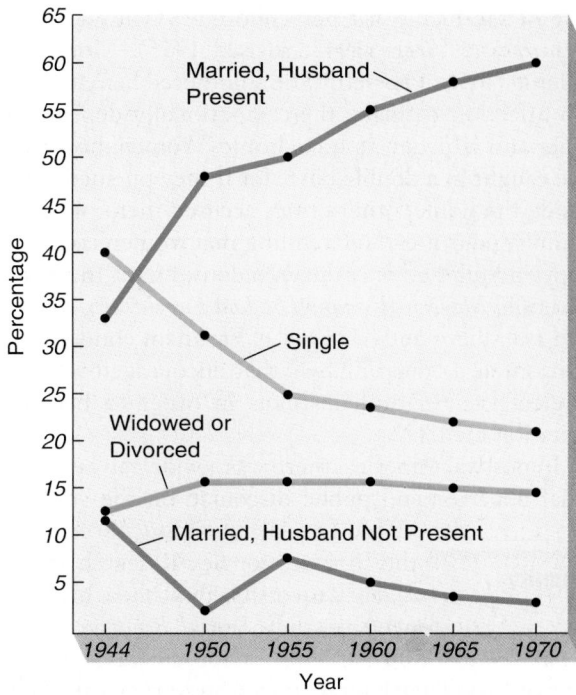

Figure 28.3 Marital Distribution of the Female Labor Force, 1944–1970 The composition of the female labor force changed dramatically from 1944 to 1970. In 1944, 41 percent of women in the labor force were single; in 1970, only 22 percent were single. During the same years, the percentage of the female labor force that had a husband in the home jumped from 34 to 59. The percentage who were widowed or divorced remained about the same from 1944 to 1970. (Source: Adapted from U.S. Bureau of the Census, *Historical Statistics of the United States, Colonial Times to 1970,* Bicentennial Edition [Washington, D.C., U.S. Government Printing Office, 1975], p. 133.)

Women's responsibilities also increased at home after the war. Some of the change was due to the publication of Dr. Benjamin Spock's *Baby and Child Care* (1946). Unlike earlier manuals, *Baby and Child Care* urged mothers always to think of their children first (Spock assigned fathers little formal role in child rearing). Dr. Spock based his advice on new findings about the importance of responding to a baby's needs; and the millions of women who embraced his teachings tried to be mother, teacher, psychologist, and playmate to their children. If they "failed" in any of these roles, guilt frequently was the outcome.

On the other hand, the social critic Philip Wylie denounced such selfless behavior as "Momism." In the guise of sacrificing for her children, Wylie wrote in *Generation of Vipers* (1942, revised 1955), Mom was pursuing "love of herself." She smothered her children with affection to make them emotionally dependent on her and reluctant to leave home. Women, however, were caught in a double bind, for if they pursued a life outside the home, other critics accused them of being "feminist neurotics," contending that women could be happy and fulfilled only through domesticity. In a popular book, *Modern Woman: The Lost Sex* (1947), Ferdinand Lundberg and Marynia F. Farnham condemned feminism as a "deep illness" that encouraged women to reject their natural instincts in order to become "imitation men."

In postwar America, there was a wide gap between sexual behavior and public discourse on the subject.

Sexuality

When Dr. Alfred Kinsey, director of the Institute for Sex Research at Indiana University, published his pioneering study *Sexual Behavior in the Human Male* (1948), the American public was shocked. But five years later Kinsey caused an uproar with *Sexual Behavior in the Human Female*, which claimed that 62 percent of his subjects masturbated and 50 percent had had intercourse before marriage. Some angry Americans condemned the report as a slanderous attack on motherhood and the family, and a congressman charged Kinsey with "hurling the insult of the century against our mothers, wives, daughters and sisters."

Family, church, state, and media alike warned Americans that sex outside marriage was wrong and that premarital, extramarital, and homosexual behavior would bring "familial chaos and weaken the country's moral fiber." Women often were blamed for the impending disaster; despite any evidence of significant increases in women's sexual activity from the 1920s to the 1960s, female lust was perceived to pose a threat to the future of the family. In fact, increased interest in sex was coming from a different direction: in 1953 men began reading about the sexual joys of bachelorhood in a new magazine, *Playboy*. Nevertheless, from Momism to promiscuity, American women were the victims of male-inspired stereotypes.

There was confusion for girls, too, in postwar America. Motherhood was venerated in American society, but many daughters sensed that their own mothers were deeply disappointed with their lives. In fact, a 1962 Gallup poll revealed that only 10 percent of mothers wanted their daughters to emulate them.

Some urged their daughters to avoid the trap of early marriage and domesticity and to develop personally fulfilling and economically independent lives. It is clear that the seeds of feminist protest in the later 1960s and 1970s were planted during the postwar years. As the historian Ruth Rosen has observed, the "invisible ghost haunting" young women "wore an apron and lived vicariously through the lives of her husband and children. Against her, the women's liberation movement was forged."

During the postwar years, a distinctive youth subculture emerged. "Teenagers all have the same basic problems," wrote a young columnist in 1958; "it's only natural we create our own special brand of music." In the 1950s the music industry catered to teens with inexpensive 45-rpm records. Bored with the era's syrupy music, young Americans were electrified by the driving energy and hard beat of Bill Haley and the Comets, Chuck Berry, Little Richard, and Buddy Holly. Although few white musicians acknowledged the debt, the roots of rock 'n' roll lay in African American rhythm and blues. The release of Elvis Presley's first single, "Heartbreak Hotel," in 1956, and his appearance on Ed Sullivan's Sunday night TV show touched off a frenzy of adoration and hero worship. The fact that parents were scandalized by Presley's suggestive gyrations did not lessen his appeal to their children.

The Youth Subculture

The motion picture industry also catered to teenagers. From 1946 to 1948, Americans had attended movies at the rate of nearly 90 million a week, but by 1960 the number had dropped to 40 million. The postwar years saw the steady closing of movie theaters—with the notable exception of drive-ins, which appealed to teenagers as well as to car-oriented suburban families. In fact, teenagers were the one exception to the downturn in moviegoing. By the late 1950s the first wave of the postwar baby boom had reached adolescence, and teens and young adults were flocking to the theaters. No less than 72 percent of moviegoers during the 1950s were under age thirty. Hollywood catered to this new audience with films portraying young people as sensitive and insightful, adults as boorish and hostile. *Rebel Without a Cause* (1955), starring James Dean, was one such movie. The cult of youth had been born.

Consumerism, which was crucial to the cult of youth, was also strikingly evident in Americans' postwar play and in the era's fads. Slinky, selling for a dollar, began loping down people's stairs in 1947; Silly Putty was introduced in 1950; and 3-D movies and Hula-Hoops were all the rage. Although most crazes were short-lived, they created multi-million-dollar industries and promoted dozens of movies and TV shows. Another postwar activity was the family vacation. With more money and leisure time and a much-improved highway system, middle-class families took vacations that formerly had been restricted to the rich. The destination of many family vacations was Disneyland, which opened in Anaheim, California, in 1955.

The consumer society was unreceptive to social criticism. The filmgoing public preferred noncontroversial doses of Doris Day and Rock

Beat Generation

Hudson and Dean Martin and Jerry Lewis. Even serious artists tended to ignore the country's social problems. But there were exceptions. Ralph Ellison's *Invisible Man* (1952) gave white Americans a glimpse of the psychic costs to black Americans of exclusion from the American Dream. And one group of writers noisily repudiated the materialistic and self-congratulatory world of the middle class and the suburbs. Beat (for "beatific") writers rejected both social niceties and literary conventions and in the face of middle-class conformity flaunted their freewheeling sexuality and consumption of drugs. The Beats produced some memorable prose and poetry, including Allen Ginsberg's angry incantational poem *Howl* (1956) and Jack Kerouac's novel *On the Road* (1957). Although the Beats were largely ignored during the 1950s, millions of young Americans discovered their writings and imitated their lifestyle in the 1960s.

In this cartoon in which Alfred E. Neuman ("What, me worry?") joins the presidential pantheon on Mount Rushmore, *Mad* magazine parodied a venerable icon. Started in 1952, *Mad* was second in popularity only to *Life* magazine among teenagers by the early 1960s. *Mad* mocked suburbia, President Eisenhower, and the smugness of the American middle class.   (*Mad* magazine Mount Rushmore cover used with permission, © 1956, 1984 by E.C. Publications, Inc.)

The Other America

In an age of abundance and rampant consumerism, most Americans dismissed poverty, if they noticed it at all, as the fault of poor people themselves. But by 1961 about 42.5 million Americans (nearly one of every four) were poor—too large a group to ignore much longer. Age, race, gender, education, and marital status were all factors in their poverty. One-fourth of the poor were over age sixty-five. One-fifth were people of color, including almost half of the nation's African American population and more than half of all Native Americans. Two-thirds lived in households headed by a person with an eighth-grade education or less, one-fourth in households headed by a single woman. More

than one-third were under age eighteen. Few of these people had much reason for hope.

A disproportionate number of the poor in postwar America were women. Occupational segregation was pervasive. Men tended to receive the better-paying positions; thus many

Women

women were forced to take low-paying jobs as laundresses, short-order cooks, and janitors. Median annual earnings for full-time women workers stood at 60 percent of men's earnings in 1960. Moreover, many women's jobs were not covered by either the minimum wage or Social Security. And if divorce, desertion, or death did break up a family, the woman was usually left with responsibility for the children. Many divorced fathers evaded their regular child-support payments. Single mothers and

Three generations of the Moreira family gathered for an Easter celebration in Los Angeles in 1960. By the end of the 1950s many Mexican American families had established businesses, bought homes, and entered the middle class.   (Shades of L.A. Archives/Los Angeles Public Library)

their children, dependent on welfare or low wages, more often than not slipped into poverty.

While millions of Americans (most of them white) were settling in the suburbs, the poor were congregating in the inner cities, including African Americans who had migrated from the South. Joining African Americans in the exodus to the cities were poor whites from the southern Appalachians, many of whom moved to Cincinnati, Baltimore, and Detroit. Meanwhile, Latin Americans were arriving in growing numbers from Mexico, the Dominican Republic, Colombia, Ecuador, and Cuba. And New York City's Puerto Rican population exploded from 70,000 to over 600,000 in just twenty years.

Second only to African Americans in numbers of urban newcomers were Mexican Americans. Millions came as farm workers during and after the Second World War, and increasing numbers remained to make their lives in the United States. Despite the initiation in 1953 of Operation Wetback, a federal pro-

The Inner Cities

gram to find and deport illegal aliens, Mexicans continued to enter the country in large numbers, many of them illegally. Most settled in cities. According to the 1960 census, over a half-million Mexican Americans had migrated to the *barrios* of the Los Angeles–Long Beach area since 1940. Estimates of uncounted illegal aliens suggest that the actual total was far higher. The same was true in the *barrios* in southwestern and northern cities.

Native Americans, whose average annual income was barely half of the poverty level, were the country's poorest people. Many Native Americans moved to the cities in the 1950s and 1960s, particularly after Congress in 1953 adopted the termination policy (see page 795). Accustomed to semicommunal rural life on the reservation, many had difficulty adjusting to the urban environment. Like other groups who migrated to the cities in hope of finding a place to prosper, they found only a dumping ground for the poor.

Not all of the poor, however, lived in cities. In 1960, 30 percent of the poor still lived in small towns,

Rural Poverty

15 percent on farms. Tenant farmers and sharecroppers, both black and white, continued to suffer severe economic hardship. Migratory farm workers lived in abject poverty. In postwar America, elderly people tended to be poor regardless of where they lived.

Americans living in poverty were poor in part because federal legislation had shortchanged them. Government-sponsored housing and highways worked largely to improve life for middle-class whites; disadvantaged Americans did not share much in their benefits. For example, the National Housing Act of 1949, passed to make available "a decent home . . . for every American family," failed in several respects. A primary feature of the act was "urban redevelopment" (slum clearance). Unsightly structures were torn down; entire neighborhoods were leveled. They were replaced not with low-income housing but with luxury high-rise buildings, parking lots, and highways. Many poor people lost what little housing they had.

With the publication of Michael Harrington's *The Other America* in 1962, people became aware of the contradiction of poverty in their midst. America's poor, wrote Harrington, were "the strangest poor in the history of mankind," for they "exist within the most powerful and rich society the world has ever known. Their misery has continued while the majority of the nation talked of itself as being 'affluent.'" Whether living in urban obscurity or rural isolation, the poor had "dropped out of sight and out of mind"—particularly the minds of comfortable suburbanites.

The Election of 1960 and the Dawning of a New Decade

The election of 1960 was one of the closest and most hard-fought in the twentieth century. The forty-three-year-old Democratic candidate, Senator John F. Kennedy of Massachusetts, was handsome and intelligent; born to wealth, he injected new vigor and glamour into presidential politics. His running mate in 1960 was Senator Lyndon B. Johnson of Texas, added to the ticket to keep white southerners loyal to the Democratic Party as the civil rights issue heated up. The Republican candidate was Richard M. Nixon, the forty-seven-year-old two-term vice president from California. He and his running mate, Ambassador Henry Cabot Lodge of Massachusetts, expected a rugged campaign.

Kennedy, exploiting the media to great advantage, ran a risky but ultimately brilliant race. Aware that his major liability with voters was his Roman Catholicism, he addressed the issue head-on: he went to the Bible belt to tell a group of Houston ministers that he respected the separation of church and state and would take his orders from the American people, not the pope. Seeing opportunity in the African American vote and calculating that Johnson could keep the white South loyal to the Democrats, Kennedy courted black voters. Foreign policy was another major issue. Nixon claimed that he alone knew how to deal with Communists, but Kennedy countered that Eisenhower and Nixon had let American prestige and power erode, and

John F. Kennedy is surrounded by supporters and the press as he arrives for the 1960 Democratic National Convention in Los Angeles. Young, handsome, and articulate, Kennedy introduced new vitality, and perhaps superficiality, into political campaigning. On television and in person, Kennedy was a popular politician; when he became president, he became a media star as well. (Wide World Photos, Inc.)

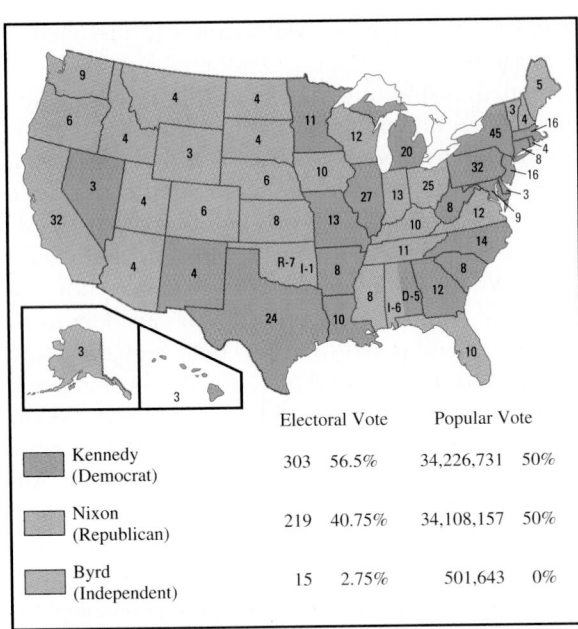

Map 28.3   Presidential Election, 1960   In 1960 John F. Kennedy won the closest presidential election in twentieth-century American history. In fact, Richard M. Nixon won the popular votes of twenty-six states to Kennedy's twenty-four. In the electoral college, fifteen southerners voted for neither Kennedy nor Nixon but cast protest votes for Harry F. Byrd, a conservative senator from Virginia.

	Electoral Vote		Popular Vote	
Kennedy (Democrat)	303	56.5%	34,226,731	50%
Nixon (Republican)	219	40.75%	34,108,157	50%
Byrd (Independent)	15	2.75%	501,643	0%

he promised victory instead of stalemate in the Cold War. Kennedy subscribed to the two fundamental tenets of the postwar consensus—economic growth and anticommunism—and asserted that he could expand the benefits of economic progress and win foreign disputes through more vigorous leadership.

As Kennedy gained momentum, Nixon was saddled with the handicaps of incumbency: he had to answer for the recession of 1960 and the Soviet downing of a U-2 spy plane. Nixon also looked unsavory on TV; in televised debates with Kennedy, he came across as heavy-jowled and surly. Perhaps worse, Eisenhower gave him only a tepid endorsement. Asked to list Nixon's significant decisions as vice president, Eisenhower replied, "If you give me a week, I might think of one."

In an election characterized by the highest voter participation (63 percent) in a half-century, Kennedy defeated Nixon by the razor-slim margin of 118,000 votes. Kennedy's electoral college margin, 303 to 219, was much closer than the numbers suggest (see Map 28.3). Slight shifts in the popular vote in Illinois and Texas—two states where electoral fraud helped produce narrow Democratic majorities—would have made Nixon president. Although Kennedy's Catholicism lost him some votes, religious bigotry did not decide the election, and Kennedy became the first Roman Catholic U.S. president.

Summary

In the fifteen years after the Second World War, Americans focused on their private lives. Those who had served their country either on the battlefield or in defense factories believed they needed to make up for lost time. Millions of veterans used the GI Bill to attend college, buy homes, and start businesses. These Americans also wanted to have babies, and they worked hard to provide a comfortable standard of living for their growing families. And as their level of consumption rose in the 1940s and 1950s, American business boomed.

During the Cold War presidencies of Truman and Eisenhower, the country was engaged in a mortal struggle with communism; and during such a crusade, people believed, citizens should support, not criticize, the government. Much as they might bicker about how to wage the Cold War or how to manage the economy, they were one when it came to anticommunism and faith in economic progress. In the 1940s and 1950s the civil rights movement reminded the country that not all Americans were first-class citizens. But most white Americans believed that the United States was the greatest nation in the world and that its potential was boundless. For middle-class Americans who surrounded themselves with the trappings of economic success—automobiles, televisions, houses in suburbia—the American dream seemed a reality.

Only a few years later, however, comfortable middle-class Americans discovered that millions of poor people were living in their midst and that most of them had been deprived of the civil rights the rest of the nation took for granted. Ironically, it would be the privileged children of suburbia—the generation of the baby boom—who would energize the movement to eradicate not only racism and poverty but the whole value system of the postwar American middle class.

LEGACY FOR A PEOPLE AND A NATION
The Eradication of Polio

No disease was more dreaded by postwar Americans, especially the nation's families with children, than infantile paralysis, or poliomyelitis. Children of all ages knew that polio seemingly struck out of nowhere (it is a water-borne virus), caused intense pain, and could be a lifelong affliction, leaving paralysis. During the Second World War, newspapers and magazines carried alarming stories about polio epidemics and gave advice on how to reduce the risks to children. Although important medical advances occurred then, including the introduction of penicillin and antibiotics, research into polio failed to produce an effective vaccine to ward off the disease.

As frightening as the epidemics during the war had been, polio's most fearsome years came in 1949–1954, when the incidence of polio doubled the rate for the worst of the wartime epidemics. The year 1952 ranked as the worst ever, with 57,900 cases. The nation was in a panic in the early 1950s. Cities closed pools and beaches. Children were told not to jump in puddles or drink from water fountains, or even to make new friends. Polio was terrifying, recalled one girl; it was "a fear that gripped my life."

Year by year, tests for a polio vaccine showed success. Then, in April 1955, the federal government approved a vaccine developed by Dr. Jonas E. Salk at the University of Pittsburgh. In the preceding forty years polio had killed or crippled 357,000 people in the United States alone, not to mention millions of others worldwide. But in spring 1955, American children lined up in schools and clinics, even on street corners, to be injected by needle with the vaccine; and in 1962 an oral vaccine was licensed by the federal government. Between 1969 and 1979 the United States counted only 179 new polio cases. A terrible scourge, as well as a massive source of childhood fears, had been eradicated from the United States; in succeeding years, polio was also eliminated from most of the Western Hemisphere. Finally, in 1999, the World Health Organization announced that polio would be eradicated worldwide by the end of the year 2000—a triumphant legacy of medical research, government activism, and community cooperation.

For Further Reading, see page A-32 of the Appendix. For Web resources, go to http://college.hmco.com.

On July 16, 1945, the "Deer" Team leader parachuted into northern Vietnam, near Kimlung, a village nestled in a valley of rice paddies surrounded by mosquito-infested forests. Colonel Allison Thomas could not know that the end of the Second World War was just weeks away, but he and the other five members of his Office of Strategic Services (OSS) unit knew their mission: to work with the Vietminh, a nationalist Vietnamese organization, to sabotage Japanese forces that in March had seized Vietnam from France. After disentangling himself from the banyan tree into which his parachute had slammed him, Thomas spoke a "few flowery sentences" to two hundred Vietminh soldiers assembled near a banner proclaiming "Welcome to Our American Friends." Ho Chi Minh, head of the Vietminh, ill but speaking in good English, cordially greeted the OSS team and offered supper. The next day Ho denounced the French but remarked that "we welcome 10 million Americans." "Forget the Communist Bogy," Thomas radioed OSS headquarters in China.

A communist who had worked for decades to win his nation's independence from France, Ho helped supply information on Japanese military forces and rescue downed American pilots during the war. He also met in March 1945 with U.S. officials in Kunming, China. There he read the *Encyclopaedia Britannica* and *Time* magazine at an Office of War Information facility. Receiving no aid from his ideological allies in the Soviet Union, Ho hoped that the United States would favor his nation's long quest for liberation from colonialism.

Other OSS personnel soon parachuted into Kimlung, including a male nurse who diagnosed Ho's ailments as malaria and dysentery; quinine and sulfa drugs restored his health, but Ho remained frail. As a sign of friendship, the Americans in Vietnam named Ho "OSS Agent 19." Everywhere the Americans went, impoverished villagers thanked them with gifts of food and clothing, despite the devastating famine of 1944–1945 in which at least a million Vietnamese died. The villagers interpreted the foreigners' presence as a sign of U.S. anticolonial and anti-Japanese sentiments. In early August the "Deer" Team began to give Vietminh

The Vietnamese nationalist Ho Chi Minh (1890–1969) meets with OSS "Deer" team members in 1945. On the right is Colonel Allison Thomas. (Private Collection)

29

THE COLD WAR AND AMERICAN GLOBALISM 1945–1961

soldiers weapons training. During many conversations with the OSS members, Ho said that he hoped young Vietnamese could study in the United States and American technicians could help build an independent Vietnam. Citing history, Ho remarked that "your statesmen make eloquent speeches about . . . self-determination. We are self-determined. Why not help us? Am I any different from . . . your George Washington?"

A second OSS unit, the "Mercy" Team headed by Captain Archimedes Patti, arrived in the city of Hanoi on August 22. When Patti met Ho—"this wisp of a man"—the Vietminh leader applauded America's assistance and called for future "collaboration." But, unbeknownst to these OSS members, who believed that President Franklin D. Roosevelt's general sympathy for eventual Vietnamese independence remained U.S. policy, the new Truman administration in Washington had decided to let France, America's emerging Cold War ally, decide the fate of Vietnam. That change in policy explains why Ho never received answers to the several letters and telegrams he sent to Washington—the first dated August 30, 1945.

On September 2, 1945, amid great fanfare in Hanoi, with OSS personnel present, an emotional Ho Chi Minh read his declaration of independence for the Democratic Republic of Vietnam: "All men are created equal; they are endowed by their Creator with certain unalienable Rights; among these are Life, Liberty, and the pursuit of Happiness." Having borrowed from the internationally renowned 1776 American document, Ho then itemized Vietnamese grievances against France. At one point in the ceremonies, two American P-38 aircraft swooped down over the crowded square. The Vietnamese cheered, interpreting the flyby as U.S. endorsement of their independence. Actually, the pilots had no orders to make a political statement; they just wanted to see what was happening.

By late September both OSS teams had departed Vietnam. In a last meeting with Captain Patti, Ho expressed his sadness that the United States had armed the French to reestablish their colonial rule in Vietnam. Sure, Ho said, U.S. officials in Washington judged him a "Moscow puppet" because he was a communist. But Ho claimed that he drew inspiration from the American struggle for independence and that he was foremost "a free agent," a nationalist. If necessary, Ho insisted, the Vietnamese would go it alone, with or without American or Soviet help. And they did—first against the French and eventually against more than

half a million U.S. troops in what became America's longest war. How different world history would have been had President Harry S Truman responded favorably to Ho Chi Minh's last letter to Washington, dated February 16, 1946, which asked the United States "as guardians and champions of World Justice to take a decisive step in support of our independence."

Because Ho Chi Minh and many of his nationalist followers had declared themselves communists, U.S. leaders rejected their appeal. Endorsing the containment doctrine to draw the line against communism everywhere, American presidents from Truman to George Bush believed that a ruthless Soviet Union was directing a worldwide communist conspiracy against peace, free-market capitalism, and political democracy. Soviet leaders from Joseph Stalin to Mikhail Gorbachev protested that a militarized, economically aggressive United States sought nothing less than world domination. This protracted contest between the United States and the Soviet Union acquired the name Cold War.

The primary feature of world affairs for more than four decades, the Cold War was fundamentally a bipolar contest between the United States and the Soviet Union over spheres of influence, over world power. Decisions made in Moscow and Washington dominated world politics, as the capitalist "West" squared off with the communist "East." Like a glacier, the Cold War began in the 1940s to cut across the global terrain, changing the topography of international relations. The Cold War eventually took the lives of millions, cost trillions of dollars, spawned fears of doomsday, and destabilized one nation after another. On occasion the two superpowers negotiated at summit conferences and signed agreements to temper their dangerous arms race; at other times they went to the brink of war and armed allies to fight vicious wars in the Third World.

Vietnam was part of the Third World, a general term for those nations that during the Cold War era wore neither the "West" (the "First World") nor the "East" (the "Second World") label. Sometimes called developing countries, Third World nations on the whole were nonwhite, nonindustrialized, and located in the southern half of the globe—in Asia, Africa, the Middle East, and Latin America. Many of them had been colonies of European nations or Japan. The great-power Cold War rivalry intruded into the Third World. U.S. leaders often interpreted Third World anticolonialism, political instability, and restrictions on foreign-owned property as Soviet or communist in-

IMPORTANT EVENTS

1945 Yalta Conference charts postwar order
Roosevelt dies; Truman becomes president
OSS cooperates with Vietminh
Potsdam agreements on postwar Germany
Atomic bombings of Japan; Tokyo surrenders
Ho Chi Minh declares Vietnam independent
World Bank and IMF begin operations

1946 U.S. backs shah in contest over Iran
Kennan's "long telegram" criticizes USSR
Churchill's "iron curtain" speech
Philippines gain independence
Baruch Plan to control atomic weapons falters
Truman fires Wallace from cabinet
Vietnamese war against France erupts

1947 Truman Doctrine seeks aid for Greece and Turkey
Communists take power in Hungary
Marshall offers Europe economic assistance
National Security Act reorganizes government
"X" article posits containment doctrine
Lippmann criticizes containment in *The Cold War*

1948 Fulbright Program initiates academic exchanges
Communists take power in Czechoslovakia
OAS founded as alliance in Latin America
Marshall Plan aids European economic recovery
Truman recognizes Israel
U.S. organizes Berlin airlift

1949 Truman calls for Point Four technical assistance
NATO founded as anti-Soviet alliance
Soviet Union explodes atomic bomb
Mao's Communists win power in China

1950 NSC-68 recommends major military buildup
U.S. aids France in Vietnam
Radio Free Europe begins broadcasts
Korean War starts in June; China enters in fall

1951 Truman fires General MacArthur
Armistice talks open in Korea
U.S. signs security treaty with Japan

1952 U.S. explodes first H-bomb

1953 Eisenhower becomes president
Stalin dies
U.S. helps restore shah to power in Iran
USIA created as propaganda agency
Korean War ends

1954 Siege of Dienbienphu in Vietnam
Geneva accords partition Vietnam
CIA overthrows Arbenz in Guatemala
Crisis over islands of Jinmen and Mazu
SEATO alliance formed for Southeast Asia

1955 Formosa Resolution to defend Taiwan
Puerto Rico's Operation Bootstrap expands
U.S.-USSR summit meeting at Geneva
Occupation of Austria ends
Soviets create Warsaw Pact
U.S. backs Diem regime in Vietnam
Bandung Conference of nonaligned nations

1956 Soviets crush uprising in Hungary
Suez crisis sparks war in Middle East

1957 Eisenhower Doctrine for Middle East
Soviets fire first ICBM and launch *Sputnik*
SANE founded

1958 U.S.-USSR cultural exchanges begin
U.S. launches *Explorer I*
NASA created
U.S. troops land in Lebanon
Berlin crisis

1959 Castro ousts Batista in Cuba
Rostow's *Stages of Economic Growth*
Nixon-Khrushchev "kitchen debate" in Moscow

1960 18 African colonies become independent
U.S. begins embargo against Cuba
Soviets shoot down U-2 spy plane
Vietcong organized in South Vietnam

1961 U.S. breaks relations with Cuba

spired or capable of being exploited by Moscow—in short, as Cold War matters rather than as expressions of profound indigenous nationalism. As an example, Vietnam became one among many sites where the Cold War and the Third World intersected, prompting U.S. intervention.

Critics in the United States challenged the architects of the Cold War, questioning their exaggerations of threats from abroad, meddlesome interventions in the Third World, and the expensive militarization of foreign policy. But when leaders such as Truman described the Cold War in extremist terms as a life-and-death struggle against a monstrous enemy, legitimate criticism became suspect and dissenters discredited. The critics' searching questions about America's global, interventionist foreign policy and reliance on nuclear weapons were drowned out by redbaiting charges that they were "soft on communism," if not un-American. Decision makers in the United States successfully cultivated a Cold War consensus that dampened debate (see Chapter 28). ■

Why the Cold War Began

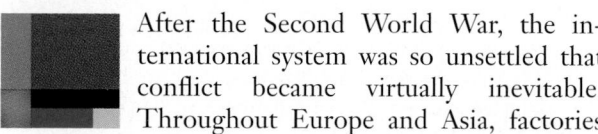 After the Second World War, the international system was so unsettled that conflict became virtually inevitable. Throughout Europe and Asia, factories and transportation and communications links had been reduced to rubble. Agricultural production plummeted, and displaced persons wandered around in search of food and family. How would the devastated economic world be pieced back together? The United States and the Soviet Union offered very different answers and models. The collapse of Germany and Japan, moreover, had created power vacuums that drew the two major powers into collision as they sought influence in countries where the Axis aggressors once had held sway. And the political turmoil that many nations experienced after the war also spurred Soviet-American competition. For example, in Greece and China, where civil wars raged between leftists and conservative regimes, the two powers supported different sides.

The international system also became unstable because empires were disintegrating, creating the new **Decolonization** Third World. Financial constraints and nationalist rebellions forced the European imperial states to set their colonies free. Britain exited India (and Pakistan) in 1947 and Burma and Sri Lanka (Ceylon) in 1948. After four years of battling nationalists in Indonesia, the Dutch left in 1949. In the Middle East, Lebanon (1943), Syria (1946), and Jordan (1946) gained independence. America and the Soviet Union vied to win new Third World states like these as allies that might provide military bases, resources, and markets. Some new nations chose nonalignment in the Cold War. "We do not intend to be the playthings of others," declared India's leader Jawaharlal Nehru.

Driven by different ideologies and different economic and strategic needs in this volatile international climate, the United States and the Soviet Union downgraded diplomacy to build what Secretary of State Dean Acheson called "situations of strength." Finding the Soviets rude and abusive, this conservative diplomat asserted that "it is a mistake to believe that you can, at any time, sit down with the Russians and solve problems." Both nations marched into the Cold War with convictions of righteousness that gave the contest an almost religious character. Each saw the other as the world's bully, itself as the world's savior. While Americans feared "communist aggression," Soviets feared "capitalist encirclement."

U.S. officials vowed never to repeat the experience of the 1930s: they would accept no more Munichs, no more appeasement, and no more depressions that might spawn political extremism and war. To growing numbers of Americans after the Second World War, it seemed that Soviet Russia had simply replaced Nazi Germany, that communism was simply the flip side of the totalitarian coin. The popular term "Red fascism" captured this sentiment.

U.S. leaders also knew that the nation's economic well-being depended on an activist foreign policy. An economic giant at a time when much of the world struggled to overcome **U.S. Economic and Strategic Needs** the devastation of the Second World War, the United States stood as the largest supplier of goods to international markets. But that trade became jeopardized by the postwar economic paralysis of Europe—traditionally America's major customer—and by discriminatory trade practices that violated the Open Door doctrine (see page 624). Europe's economy was so prostrate that it could not earn dollars to buy American products (the "dollar gap"); if the gap were not closed, the United States might face a severe depression once again. U.S. automobile, steel, and machine-tool industries, as well as wheat, cotton, and tobacco farmers, relied heavily on foreign trade. Indeed, exports constituted about 10 percent of the gross national product. And the United States also needed to import essential minerals such as zinc, tin, and manganese. Thus economic expansionism, so much a part of pre–Cold War history, remained a central feature of postwar foreign relations.

New strategic theory also propelled the United States toward an expansionist, globalist diplomacy. The shrinkage of the globe with the advent of the "air age" made the world more compact. Faster travel brought nations closer at the same time that it made them more vulnerable to surprise attack from the air. "As top dog, America becomes target No. 1," warned air force general Carl Spaatz. The Americans and the Soviets collided as they strove to establish defensive positions, sometimes far from home. The United States sought overseas bases and air transit and landing rights to guard the approaches to the Western Hemisphere. These bases also would permit the United States to launch offensive attacks with might and speed. When asked where the U.S. Navy would float, Navy Secretary James Forrestal declared, "Wherever there is a sea."

President Truman, who shared these economic and strategic assumptions, had a personality ill suited

Truman's Get-Tough Style

for diplomacy. Whereas Franklin D. Roosevelt had been ingratiating, patient, and evasive, Truman was brash, impatient, and direct. He often glossed over nuances, ambiguities, and counterevidence; he preferred the simple answer stated in either-or terms. As Winston Churchill, who admired Truman's decisiveness, once observed, the president "takes no notice of delicate ground, he just plants his foot firmly on it." Truman constantly exaggerated, as when he declared in his undelivered farewell address that he had "knocked the socks off the communists" in Korea (see pages 834–838). Shortly after Roosevelt's death in early 1945, Truman met the Soviet commissar of foreign affairs, V. M. Molotov, at the White House. When the president sharply protested that the Soviets were not fulfilling the Yalta agreement on Poland, Molotov stormed out. Truman had self-consciously developed what he called his "tough method," and he bragged after the encounter that "I gave it to him straight 'one-two to the jaw.'" Although the Soviets acted heavy-handedly in Poland, whether they violated the vaguely written Yalta accord remains open to interpretation. Truman's display of toughness nonetheless became a trademark of American Cold War diplomacy.

The Soviets remembered that since the Bolshevik Revolution the hostile West had attempted to defeat and then ostracize them. Fearful of a revived Germany and a resurgent Japan, anticipating that capitalist nations once again would attempt to extinguish the communist flame, facing a monumental task of economic reconstruction in their devastated nation, and embracing Marxist-Leninist doctrine, the Soviets made territorial gains in eastern Poland, the Baltic states of Lithuania, Latvia, and Estonia, and parts of Finland

and Romania—some of these areas having once been part of the Russian Empire. In eastern Europe Soviet officials began to suppress noncommunists and install communist clients. The Americans, the steely premier Joseph Stalin protested, were surrounding the USSR with hostile bases and practicing atomic and dollar diplomacy. He nonetheless knew that the Soviets could not realize many of their goals without cooperation from the United States. That is why, the historian Melvyn Leffler has written, "Stalin's approach to international affairs" was "cautious" and "expedient," lacking a "distinct strategy."

Throughout the Cold War era, Americans debated Soviet intentions and capabilities. Many no doubt agreed with Churchill, who compared

Debate over Soviet Intentions and Behavior

dealing with the Soviet Union to "wooing a crocodile. You do not know whether to tickle it under the chin or to beat it over the head. When it opens its mouth you cannot tell whether it is trying to smile or . . . eat you up." Some diplomats believed that the Soviet Union—well armed, opportunistic, and aggressive—could never be trusted. On the other hand, critics of U.S. policies charged that American officials exaggerated the Soviet/communist threat, imagining a bigger-than-life, monolithic archenemy, finding it at work everywhere, blaming it for troubles it never started, attributing to it accomplishments it never achieved.

In the immediate postwar years, in fact, the Soviet Union suffered a hobbled economy and, like the United States, undertook a major postwar demobilization of its armed forces. The Soviet Union was a regional power in eastern Europe, not a global menace. American leaders feared that the ravaging postwar economic and social unrest abroad would leave American strategic and economic interests vulnerable to political disorders that the Soviets might exploit, perhaps through subversion. In other words, Americans feared Soviet seizure of opportunities to challenge U.S. interests more than they feared a direct Soviet attack on western Europe.

The United States took advantage of the postwar power vacuum and economic supremacy to expand its overseas interests and shape a peace on American terms. The U.S. pursuit of nuclear superiority, outlying bases, raw materials and markets, supremacy in Latin America, and control of the Atlantic and Pacific Oceans aroused many opponents, in particular the Soviet Union. To Americans who thought that vigorous U.S. globalism must and would save the world, Soviet opposition simply confirmed Moscow's wicked obstructionism.

Truman's Cold War: Europe and Global Containment

One of the first Soviet-American clashes came in Poland in 1945, when the Soviets refused to allow conservative Poles from London to join the communist government in Lublin. Truman officials argued that Stalin at the Yalta Conference had agreed to a democratic government for Poland, but the Soviet Union, fearing Western inroads into its sphere of influence, disputed that interpretation and sustained a procommunist regime. The Soviets also snuffed out civil liberties in the former Nazi satellite of Romania, justifying their actions by pointing to what they claimed was an equivalent U.S. manipulation of Italy. Moscow initially allowed free elections in Hungary and Czechoslovakia, but as the Cold War accelerated and U.S. influence in Europe expanded, the Soviets encouraged communist coups in Hungary (1947) and Czechoslovakia (1948). Yugoslavia stood as a unique case: its independent communist government, led by Josip Broz Tito, successfully broke with Stalin in 1948.

To defend their actions, the Soviets pointed out that the United States was reviving their traditional enemy, Germany. The Soviets also protested that the United States was meddling in eastern Europe. They cited clandestine American meetings with anti-Soviet groups, repeated calls for elections likely to produce anti-Soviet regimes, and the use of loans to gain political influence (dollar diplomacy). Moscow charged that the United States was pursuing a double standard—intervening in the affairs of eastern Europe but demanding that the Soviet Union stay out of Latin America and Asia. Americans called for free elections in the Soviet sphere, Moscow noted, but not in the U.S. sphere in Latin America, where several military dictatorships ruled.

The atomic bomb also divided the two major powers. The Soviets believed that the United States was practicing "atomic diplomacy"—maintaining a nuclear monopoly to scare the Soviets into diplomatic concessions. Secretary of State James F. Byrnes thought that the atomic bomb gave the United States bargaining power and could

Atomic Diplomacy

serve as a deterrent to Soviet expansion, but Secretary of War Henry L. Stimson thought otherwise in 1945. If Americans continued to have "this weapon rather ostentatiously on our hip," he warned Truman, the Soviets' "suspicions and their distrust of our purposes and motives will increase."

In this atmosphere of suspicion and distrust, Truman refused to turn over the weapon to an international control authority. In 1946 he backed the Baruch Plan, named after its author, financier Bernard Baruch. Largely a propaganda ploy, this proposal provided for U.S. abandonment of its atomic monopoly only after the world's fissionable materials were brought under the authority of an international agency. The Soviets retorted that this plan would require them to shut down their atomic-bomb development project while the United States continued its own. Washington and Moscow soon became locked into an expensive and frightening nuclear arms race.

Soviets and Americans clashed on every front in 1946. When the United States turned down a Soviet request for a reconstruction loan but gave a loan to Britain, Moscow upbraided Washington for using its dollars to manipulate foreign governments. The two Cold War powers also backed different groups in Iran, where the United States helped bring the pro-West shah to the throne. Unable to agree on the unification of Germany, the Cold War antagonists built up their zones independently.

The new World Bank and International Monetary Fund (IMF), created at the July 1944 Bretton Woods Conference by forty-four nations to stabilize trade and finance, also became tangled in the Cold War. The Soviets refused to join because the United States so dominated both institutions and because their purpose was to promote private investment and open and multilateral international commerce, which Moscow saw as capitalist tools of exploitation. With the United States as its largest donor, the World Bank opened its doors in 1945 and began to make loans to help members finance reconstruction projects; the IMF, also heavily backed by the United States, helped members meet their balance of payments problems through currency loans.

World Bank and International Monetary Fund

After Stalin gave a speech in February 1946 that depicted the world as threatened by capitalist acquisitiveness, the American chargé d'affaires in Moscow, George F. Kennan, sent a pessimistic "long telegram" to Washington. Kennan asserted that Soviet fanati-

Kennan and Churchill Warn Against Soviet Power

cism made even a temporary understanding impossible. His widely circulated report fed a growing belief among American officials that only toughness would work with the Soviets. The following month, Winston Churchill delivered a stirring speech in Fulton, Missouri. The former British prime minister warned that a Soviet-erected "iron curtain" had cut off eastern European countries from the West. With an approving Truman sitting on the stage, Churchill called for Anglo-American partnership to resist the new menace.

Secretary of Commerce Henry A. Wallace charged that Truman's get-tough policy was substituting atomic and economic coercion for diplomacy. Wallace told a Madison Square Garden audience in September 1946 that "'getting tough' never brought anything real and lasting—whether for schoolyard bullies or businessmen or world powers. The tougher we get, the tougher the Russians will get." Truman soon fired Wallace from the cabinet, blasting him privately as "a real Commy and a dangerous man" and boasting that he, Truman, had now "run the crackpots out of the Democratic Party." Such mistaken and extremist words helped kindle the exaggerations so common to the Cold War.

The Cold War escalated further in early 1947, when the British requested American help in Greece to defend their conservative client

Truman Doctrine

government against a leftist insurgency. In his March 12, 1947, speech to Congress, Truman requested $400 million in aid to Greece and Turkey. He had a selling job to do. The Republican Eightieth Congress wanted less, not more, spending, and many of its members had little respect for the Democratic president whose administration the voters had repudiated in the 1946 elections. Republican senator Arthur Vandenberg of Michigan, a bipartisan leader who backed Truman's request, bluntly told the president that he would have to "scare hell out of the American people" to gain congressional approval.

With that advice in mind, the president delivered a speech laced with alarmist language intended to stake out the United States's role in the postwar world. Truman claimed that communism, feeding on economic dislocations, imperiled the world. "If Greece should fall under the control of an armed minority," he gravely concluded in an early version of the domino theory (see page 839), "the effect upon its neighbor, Turkey, would be immediate and serious. Confusion and disor-

On March 5, 1946, former British prime minister Winston S. Churchill (1874–1965) delivered a speech, which he intended for a worldwide audience, at Westminster College in Fulton, Missouri. President Harry S Truman *(right)* had encouraged Churchill *(seated)* to speak on two themes: the need to block Soviet expansion and the need to form an Anglo-American partnership. Always eloquent and provocative, Churchill denounced the Soviets for drawing an "iron curtain" across eastern Europe. This speech became one of the landmark statements of the Cold War. (Harry S Truman Library)

der might well spread throughout the entire Middle East." At the time, civil war in which communists played a prominent role rocked Greece. Turkey bordered the Soviet Union, considered by American leaders to be masterminding global communist expansion. At issue, Truman insisted, was the very security of the United States.

Especially momentous in the dramatic speech were the words, later known as the Truman Doctrine, that would guide American policymakers for almost a half-century: "I believe that it must be the policy of the United States to support free peoples who are resisting attempted subjugation by armed minorities or by outside pressures." Secretary of State George C. Marshall privately questioned the "flamboyant anti-

Communism" of the speech, but two new and young members of the House of Representatives, John F. Kennedy and Richard M. Nixon, applauded Truman's message that day. When they assumed the presidency in the 1960s, the Truman Doctrine still guided their policies.

Critics correctly pointed out that the Soviet Union was little involved in the Greek civil war, that the communists in Greece were more pro-Tito than pro-Stalin, and that the resistance movement had noncommunist as well as communist members. Nor was the Soviet Union threatening Turkey at the time. Others suggested that such aid should be channeled through the United Nations. Truman countered that should communists gain control of Greece, they might open the door to Soviet power in the Mediterranean. After much debate, the Senate approved Truman's request by 67 to 23 votes. Using U.S. dollars and military advisers, the Greek government defeated the insurgents in 1949, and Turkey became a staunch U.S. ally on the Soviets' border.

The "X" Article

Four months after Truman's speech, Kennan, having moved from the U.S. embassy in Moscow to the State Department in Washington, published an influential statement of the containment doctrine. Writing as "Mr. X" in the magazine *Foreign Affairs*, Kennan advocated a "policy of firm containment, designed to confront the Russians with unalterable counterforce at every point where they show signs of encroaching upon the interests of a peaceful and stable world." Such counterforce, Kennan argued, would check Soviet expansion and eventually foster a "mellowing" of Soviet behavior. Along with the Truman Doctrine, Kennan's "X" article became a key manifesto of Cold War policy.

The Containment Doctrine Debated

The veteran journalist Walter Lippmann took issue with the containment doctrine in his book *The Cold War* (1947), calling it a "strategic monstrosity" that failed to distinguish between areas vital and peripheral to U.S. security. If American leaders defined every place on earth as strategically important, Lippmann reasoned, the nation's patience and resources soon would be drained. Nor did Lippmann share Truman's conviction that the Soviet Union was plotting to take over the world. The president, he asserted, put too little emphasis on diplomacy. Lippmann's critique, although prophetic, proved no match for the emerging Cold War mentality of 1947.

Invoking the containment doctrine, the United States in 1947 and 1948 began to build an international economic and defensive network to protect American prosperity and security and to advance U.S. hegemony. In western Europe, the region of primary concern, American diplomats pursued several objectives: partnership with Great Britain; economic reconstruction; ouster of communists from governments, as occurred in 1947 in France and Italy; blockage of "third force" or neutralist tendencies; keeping the decolonization of European empires orderly; creation of a military alliance; and unification of the western zones of Germany. At the same time, American culture—consumer goods, music, consumption ethic, and production techniques—permeated European societies. Some Europeans resisted Americanization, but transatlantic ties strengthened.

Marshall Plan

The first instrument designed to achieve U.S. goals in western Europe was the Marshall Plan. European nations, still reeling economically and unstable politically, lacked the dollars to buy vital American-made goods. Americans, who already had spent billions of dollars on European relief and recovery by 1947, remembered all too well the troubles of the 1930s: global depression, political extremism, and war born of economic discontent. Such cataclysms could not be allowed to happen again; communism must not replace fascism. Western Europe, said one State Department diplomat, was "the keystone in the arch which supports the kind of a world which we have to have in order to conduct our lives."

In June 1947 Secretary of State Marshall announced that the United States would finance a massive European recovery program. Launched in 1948, the Marshall Plan sent $12.4 billion to western Europe before the program ended in 1951 (see Map 29.1). To stimulate business at home, the legislation provided that the foreign-aid dollars must be spent in the United States on American-made products. The Marshall Plan proved a mixed success; some scholars today even argue that Europe could have revived without it. The program caused inflation, failed to solve a balance-of-payments problem, took only tentative steps toward economic integration, and further divided Europe between "East" and "West." But the program spurred impressive western European industrial production and investment and started the region toward self-sustaining economic growth. From the American perspective, moreover, the plan succeeded because it helped contain communism.

Under official postwar relief and recovery programs, including the Marshall Plan, the United States shipped billions of dollars' worth of food and equipment to western European nations struggling to overcome the destruction of the Second World War. Private efforts also succeeded, such as this one in 1950. The people of Jersey City, New Jersey, sent this snowplow to the mountainous village of Capracotta, Italy.   (Corbis-Bettman)

To streamline the administration of U.S. defense, Truman worked with Congress on the National Security Act of July 1947. The act created

National Security Act

the Office of Secretary of Defense (which became the Department of Defense two years later), the National Security Council (NSC) of high-level officials to advise the president, and the Central Intelligence Agency (CIA) to conduct spy operations and information gathering. By the early 1950s the CIA had become a significant member of the national security state and had expanded its functions to include covert (secret) operations aimed at overthrowing unfriendly foreign leaders and, as a high-ranking American official put it, a "Department of Dirty Tricks" to stir up economic trouble in "the camp of the enemy."

In 1948 the United States implemented the Fulbright Program—a "cultural Marshall Plan for the intellectual reconstruction of the West," as the historian Richard Pells has written. The brainchild two years earlier of Democratic senator J. William Fulbright of Arkansas, a former Rhodes scholar and uni-

Fulbright Program and Cultural Expansion

versity president, this example of "public diplomacy" attempted to overcome cultural barriers to reach foreign peoples with a positive message about the United States. The Fulbright Program sponsored educational exchanges; professors and students from the United States went abroad to teach and study, and their counterparts from foreign countries came to the United States. By 1953 influential intellectual elites in twenty-eight nations were participating in the program in Europe, Asia, and the Middle East. In some countries, former Fulbrighters rose to political prominence, keeping their governments allied with the United States. Because considerable anti-Americanism still persisted, some American and European intellectuals in 1950 created a new organization, the Congress for Cultural Freedom, to blunt it; the CIA secretly subsidized this effort to promote America in Europe.

American officials also made military linkages around the world. The United States granted the Philippines independence in 1946 while retaining

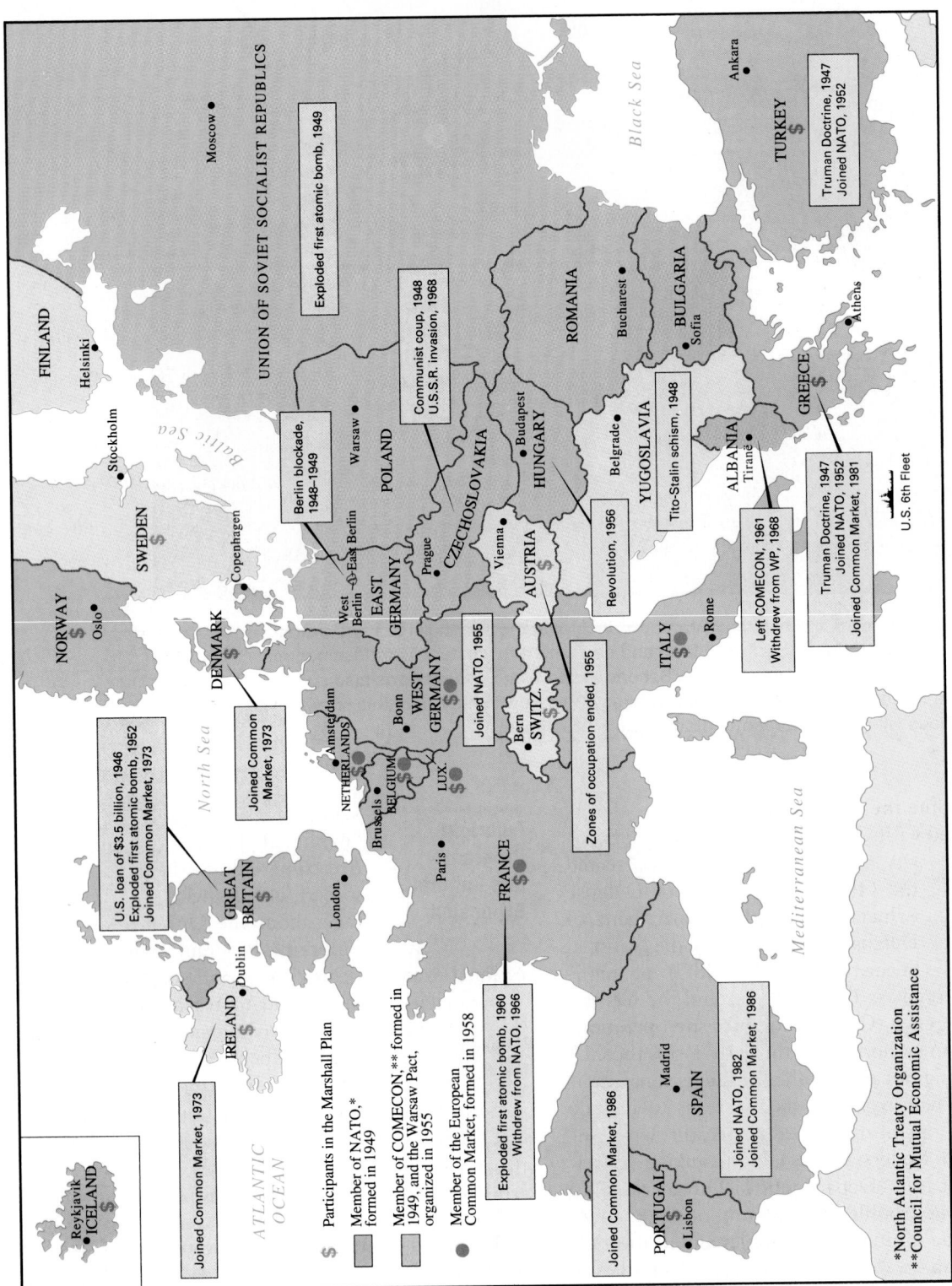

Map 29.1 Divided Europe After the Second World War, Europe broke into two competing camps. When the United States launched the Marshall Plan in 1948, the Soviet Union countered with its own economic plan the following year. When the United States created NATO in 1949, the Soviet Union answered with the Warsaw Pact in 1955. On the whole, these two camps held firm until the late 1980s.

military and economic hegemony there. The following year, American diplomats created the Rio Pact in Latin America. To enforce this hemispheric military alliance, the United States helped found the Organization of American States (OAS) in 1948. Under this and other agreements the Truman administration sent several military missions to Latin America and to Greece, Turkey, Iran, China, and Saudi Arabia to improve the armed forces of those nations.

In May 1948 Truman quickly recognized the newly proclaimed state of Israel, which had been carved out of British-held Palestine after years of Arab-Jewish dispute. Despite State Department objection that recognition would alienate oil-rich Arab nations, Truman made the decision for three reasons: he believed that, after the Holocaust, Jews deserved a homeland; he desired Jewish-American votes in the upcoming election; and he sought another international ally, which Israel became.

Recognition of Israel

In June 1948 the Americans, French, and British agreed to fuse their German zones, including their three sectors of Berlin. They sought to integrate West Germany (the Federal Republic of Germany) into the western European economy, complete with a reformed German currency. Fearing a resurgent Germany tied to the American Cold War camp, the Soviets cut off Western land access to the jointly occupied city of Berlin, located well inside the Soviet zone. In response to this bold move, President Truman ordered a massive airlift of food, fuel, and other supplies to Berlin. Their spoiling effort blunted, the Soviets finally lifted the blockade in May 1949 and founded the German Democratic Republic, or East Germany.

Berlin Blockade and Airlift

In his inaugural address of January 20, 1949, President Truman announced "a bold new program" of technical assistance for "underdeveloped areas." Insisting on self-help by the participants, the Point Four Program began in 1950 with a comparatively meager $35 million to improve food supplies, public health, housing, and private investment in Third World countries that the United States sought to woo to its side in the Cold War. In 1953 fifteen hundred Point Four technicians visited thirty-five countries. They dug compost pits in India, combated a locust plague in Iran, and instructed teachers in Peru. Point Four lost its identity in 1953 when it became part of the Mutual Security Agency and

Point Four Program

America's first ambassador to Israel, James G. MacDonald (1886–1964) *(left)* meets in 1948 with Israel's President Chaim Weizmann (1874–1952) *(center)* and Prime Minister David Ben-Gurion (1886–1973) *(right)*. The historian Michelle Mart has written that "Jews in the postwar world first symbolized a complete lack of masculinity for their role as victims and then masculine resurgence in their survival and construction of a new state"—a change in image that conditioned American leaders to respect the new Israeli leaders.   (National Archives)

increasingly emphasized the flow of strategic raw materials to the United States. Still, the Truman administration championed Point Four as an inexpensive means to thwart communism—"less than the price of one battleship."

The administration gave far more attention to formation of a Western security pact. The United States, Canada, and many western European nations founded the North Atlantic Treaty Organization (NATO) in April 1949 (see Map 29.1). The treaty aroused considerable domestic debate, for not since 1778 had the United States entered a formal European military alliance, and some critics, such as Senator Robert A. Taft, Republican of Ohio, claimed that NATO would provoke rather than deter war. Other critics argued that the Soviets did not pose a military threat. Administration officials themselves did not anticipate a Soviet military thrust against western Europe, but they responded that, should the Soviets ever probe westward, NATO would function as a "tripwire," bringing the full force of the United States

Founding of NATO

to bear on the Soviet Union. Truman officials also hoped that NATO would keep western Europeans from embracing communism or even neutralism in the Cold War. The Senate ratified the treaty by 82 votes to 13, and the United States soon began to spend billions of dollars under the Mutual Defense Assistance Act.

In September 1949 an American reconnaissance aircraft detected unusually high radioactivity in the atmosphere. The news stunned U.S. officials: the Soviets had exploded an atomic bomb. With the American nuclear monopoly erased, western Europe seemed more vulnerable. At the same time, communists had won the civil war in China, and Moscow was scoring propaganda points by advocating "peaceful coexistence" with the West. American leaders did not respond to this changed state of affairs with a call for high-level negotiations but rather, in early 1950, with Truman's secret decision to start production of a hydrogen bomb, the "Super."

After Mao's victory in China and Moscow's acquisition of the atomic bomb, the National Security Council delivered to the president in April 1950 a significant top-secret document tagged NSC-68. Predicting continued tension with expansionistic communists and describing "a shrinking world of polarized power," the report appealed for a much enlarged military budget and the mobilization of public opinion to support such an increase. Officials worried about how to sell this prescription to voters and budget-conscious members of Congress. "We were sweating over it, and then—with regard to NSC-68—thank God Korea came along," recalled one U.S. official.

NSC-68

Asian Acrimony: Japan, China, and Vietnam

Asia, like Europe, became ensnared in the Cold War. The victors in the Second World War dismantled Japan's empire. The United States and the Soviet Union divided Korea into competing spheres of influence. Pacific islands (the Marshalls, Marianas, and Carolines) came under American control, and Formosa (Taiwan) was returned to China.

As for Japan itself, the United States monopolized its reconstruction through a military occupation directed by General Douglas MacArthur, who envisioned turning the Pacific Ocean into "an Anglo-Saxon lake." Truman did not like "Mr. Prima Donna,

Reconstruction of Japan

Brass Hat" MacArthur, but the general initiated "a democratic revolution from above," as the Japanese called it, that reflected Washington's wishes. MacArthur wrote a democratic constitution, gave women voting rights, revitalized the economy, and destroyed the nation's weapons. U.S. authorities also helped Americanize Japan through censorship; films that hinted at criticism of the United States (for the destruction of Hiroshima, for example) or that depicted traditional Japanese customs such as suicide, arranged marriages, and swordplay were banned. In 1951, against Soviet protests, the United States and Japan signed a separate peace that restored Japan's sovereignty and ended the occupation. A Mutual Security Treaty that year provided for the stationing of U.S. forces on Japanese soil, including a base on Okinawa.

Meanwhile, America's Chinese ally was faltering. The United States had long backed the Nationalists of Jiang Jieshi (Chiang Kai-shek) against Mao Zedong's communists. But after the Second World War, Generalissimo Jiang became an unreliable partner who rejected U.S. advice. His government had become corrupt, inefficient, and out of touch with discontented peasants, whom the communists enlisted with promises of land reform. Jiang also subverted American efforts to negotiate a cease-fire and a coalition government. "We picked a bad horse," Truman admitted, privately denouncing the Nationalists as "grafters and crooks." Still, seeing Jiang as the only alternative to Mao, Truman backed him to the end.

Communist Victory in Chinese Civil War

American officials divided on the question of whether Mao was a puppet of the Soviet Union. Some considered him an Asian Tito—communist but independent—but most believed him to be part of an international communist movement that might give the Soviets a springboard into Asia. Thus when the Chinese communists made secret overtures to the United States to begin diplomatic talks in 1945 and again in 1949, American officials rebuffed them. Mao decided to "lean" to the Soviet side in the Cold War. Because China always maintained a fierce independence that rankled the Soviets, before long a Sino-Soviet schism opened. Indeed, Mao deeply resented the Soviets' refusal to aid the communists during the civil war; Stalin offered no help, "not even a fart," Mao once growled.

In fall 1949 Jiang fled to the island of Formosa, and Mao proclaimed the People's Republic of China

U.S. Nonrecognition Policy

(PRC). Truman hesitated to extend diplomatic recognition to the new government. The British prime minister asked the president: "Are we to cut ourselves off from all contact with one-sixth of the inhabitants of the world?" Washington did precisely that. U.S. officials became alarmed by the 1950 Sino-Soviet treaty of friendship and by the harassment of Americans and their property in China. Truman also chose nonrecognition because a vocal group of Republican critics, the so-called China lobby, was winning headlines by charging that the United States had "lost" China. The publisher Henry Luce, Senator William Knowland of California, and Representative Walter Judd of Minnesota pinned Jiang's defeat on Truman. The president stoutly answered that the self-defeating Jiang, despite billions of dollars in American aid, had proven a poor instrument of the containment doctrine. The administration nonetheless took the politically safe route and rejected recognition. (Not until 1979 did official Sino-American relations resume; see page 903.)

Mao's victory in China drew urgent American attention to Indochina (Vietnam, Cambodia, and Laos).

Vietnam's Quest for Independence

Would the PRC attempt to exploit France's troubles with its rebellious colonies, converting them to communism, denying western Europe their raw materials, and closing them to the sale of Japanese goods, which Japan needed in order to reconstruct as a U.S. ally? For decades after the French takeover of Indochina in the late nineteenth century, France exploited Vietnam for its rice, rubber, tin, and tungsten. Although the French beat back recurrent rebellions, Vietnamese nationalists dedicated to independence grew in strength. Their leader Ho Chi Minh, born in 1890, lived in France before the First World War, and at the close of the war he joined the French Communist Party to use it as a vehicle for Vietnamese independence. For the next two decades, living in China, the Soviet Union, and elsewhere, Ho patiently planned and fought to free his nation from French colonialism. During World War II, as we have seen, Ho's Vietminh warriors harassed both French and Japanese forces—near the end of the war with OSS help.

Even though, as Secretary Marshall remarked, the French had a "dangerously outmoded colonial outlook and method," the Truman administration rejected Vietnam's independence in the 1940s in favor of the restoration of French rule. Why? First, Americans

CHILDREN'S CRUSADE AGAINST COMMUNISM

2. MacArthur Heads UN Forces

North Korean Reds attacked South Korea in what is believed to be part of a communist plan gradually to conquer the whole world. The United Nations pitched in to help the South Koreans, like your dad would help the folks next door if some bad men were beating them up. The troops sent to Korea for the UN were put under command of General Douglas MacArthur. "Mac" has a long military record. But you know him best as the general who led the Allied forces to victory in the Pacific during the second world war.

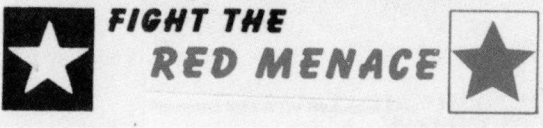

FIGHT THE RED MENACE

Intensely anticommunist groups thrived in the United States during the Cold War. The "Children's Crusade Against Communism" distributed its exaggerated message of a global communist conspiracy in the early 1950s through bubble-gum cards such as this one. (The Michael Barson Collection/Past Perfect)

wanted France's cooperation in the Cold War. Second, Southeast Asia was an economic asset: its rice could feed America's emerging ally Japan; it could provide markets for Japanese exports; and it was the world's largest producer of natural rubber. Third, the area seemed strategically vital to the defense of Japan and the Philippines. Finally, Ho Chi Minh, the State Department declared, was an "agent of international communism," who, it was assumed, would assist Soviet and Chinese expansionism. Overlooking the native roots of the nationalist rebellion against France, and the tenacious Vietnamese resistance to foreign intruders,

Washington officials took a globalist view of Vietnam, interpreting events through a Cold War lens.

In the 1940s Americans saw Vietnam as France's problem, even after the Vietminh and the French went to war in 1946. But when Jiang's regime collapsed in China three years later, the Truman administration made two crucial decisions—both in early 1950, before the Korean War. First, in February, Washington recognized the French puppet government of Bao Dai, a playboy and former emperor who had collaborated with the French and Japanese. In the eyes of the Vietnamese, the United States thus became in essence a colonial power, an ally of the hated French. Second, in May, the administration agreed to send weapons, and ultimately military advisers, to sustain the French in Indochina. From 1945 to 1954, the United States gave $2 billion of the $5 billion that France spent to keep Vietnam within its empire—to no avail, as we shall see (Chapter 31). How Vietnam ultimately became the site of America's longest war, and how the world's most powerful nation failed to subdue a peasant people who suffered enormous losses, is one of the most remarkable and tragic stories of modern history.

U.S. Aid to France in the War Against the Vietminh

The Korean War

In the early morning of June 25, 1950, a large military force of the Democratic People's Republic of Korea (North Korea) moved across the 38th parallel into the Republic of Korea (South Korea). Although the Soviets had armed the North and the Americans had armed the South (U.S. aid had reached $100 million a year), the Korean War began as a civil war. Since August 1945, when U.S. officials hastily cut Korea at the 38th parallel and then gained Soviet acceptance of the division, the two parts had been skirmishing along their supposedly temporary border while antigovernment (and anti-U.S.) guerrilla fighting flared in the South.

Both the North's communist leader Kim Il Sung and the South's president Syngman Rhee sought to reunify their nation. Kim's military especially gained strength when tens of thousands of battle-tested Koreans returned home in 1949 after serving in Mao's army. Displaying the Cold War mentality of the time, however, President Truman claimed that the Soviets had masterminded the North Korean attack. "Com-

munism was acting in Korea just as Hitler, Mussolini, and the Japanese had acted [in the 1930s]," he said.

Actually, Kim had to press a doubting Joseph Stalin, who only reluctantly approved the attack after Kim predicted an easy, early victory and after Mao backed Kim. The three communist leaders might have calculated that the United States would not come to South Korea's defense—indeed, that the United States was in the process of abandoning the Korean peninsula. In a public speech in early 1950, Secretary of State Acheson had drawn the American defense line in Asia through the Aleutians, Japan, and Okinawa to the Philippines. Formosa and Korea clearly lay beyond that line. Acheson did say, however, that those areas could expect U.N. (and hence U.S.) assistance if attacked. Kim, Stalin, and Mao must have missed that point. Two other thoughts probably convinced Stalin to support Kim: first, if he did not back North Korea, Mao might gain influence over Kim; second, if the United States rearmed Japan, South Korea might once again become a beachhead for Japanese (and American) expansion on the Asian continent.

Origins of the War

Whatever Stalin's reasoning, his support for Kim's venture remained lukewarm. When the United Nations Security Council voted to defend South Korea, the Soviet representative was not even present to veto the resolution because the Soviets were boycotting the United Nations to protest its refusal to grant membership to the People's Republic of China. During the war, Moscow gave limited aid to North Korea and China, which grew angry at Stalin for reneging on promised Soviet airpower. Stalin did not want to be dragged into a costly war.

The president first ordered General Douglas MacArthur to send arms and troops to South Korea. Worried that Mao might attempt to take Formosa, Truman also directed the Seventh Fleet to patrol the waters between the Chinese mainland and Jiang's sanctuary on Formosa, thus inserting the United States once again into Chinese politics. After the Security Council voted to assist South Korea, MacArthur became commander of U.N. forces in Korea (90 percent of them American). North Korean tanks and superior firepower sent the South Korean army into chaotic retreat. The first American soldiers, taking heavy casualties, could not stop the North Korean advance. Within weeks, the South Koreans and Americans had

Truman Commits U.S. Forces

How do historians know...

that the Korean War began as a civil war among Koreans, not as a Soviet-inspired thrust to advance an international communist conspiracy, and thus that U.S. officials misinterpreted the war's origins? After the Cold War ended in the late 1980s and early 1990s, especially after the collapse of the Soviet Union in 1991, politicians and records-keepers in the new noncommunist Russia opened previously classified documents to researchers. The Cold War International History Project, established in 1991 at the Woodrow Wilson Center for Scholars in Washington, D.C., has translated many released foreign documents and publishes them in its printed *Bulletin* (also available at http://cwihp.si.edu).

The opening of such documents invites historians to revisit key moments in the Cold War, such as the outbreak of the Korean War. In 1994 Russian President Boris Yeltsin presented to President Kim Young-Sam of South Korea 548 pages of high-level Soviet documents, including telegrams and letters between Moscow and Pyongyang (the capital of North Korea). The documents reveal that during 1949 Kim repeatedly asked Stalin for permission to launch a military attack against the South. Stalin repeatedly rebuffed Kim's requests. The initiative for the North Korean attack on South Korea was Kim's, not Stalin's, and stemmed from Kim's insistence on overthrowing the American-backed southern regime to achieve unification. As Stalin's telegram of January 30, 1950, to the Soviet ambassador in North Korea (reprinted here in its original Russian) indicates, not until early 1950 did Stalin give what might be construed an approval to invasion, and then coolly, noting that "large preparation" was needed first.

Historians use declassified documents—both American and foreign—with caution. The declassification process is often selective and incomplete (for national security reasons some materials remain classified as "Top-Secret" and some records have been lost or destroyed). Some documents are identified for release in the hope of making a political

point. Also, translations and word meanings can vary from interpreter to interpreter. Finally, historians need more than Soviet records; they also need greater access to the archives of South Korea, North Korea, the People's Republic of China, and the Republic of China (Taiwan) in order to understand fully how the Korean War started.

U.S. leaders claimed that the North Korean assault sprang from a Soviet-engineered plot to conquer the world. Scholars see the Korean War no longer as a simple Cold War contest, but rather as a chapter in *Korean* history that reveals how client states or local actors can foment crises that draw the great powers into confrontation. Declassified documents from foreign archives, then, help historians test the accuracy of American assumptions and weigh the terrible consequences of wrong assumptions—in this case, intensification of the Cold War. (Photo: "The Cold War International History Project Bulletin," Spring 1995, Issue 5, p. 9. Courtesy of the Woodrow Wilson Center)

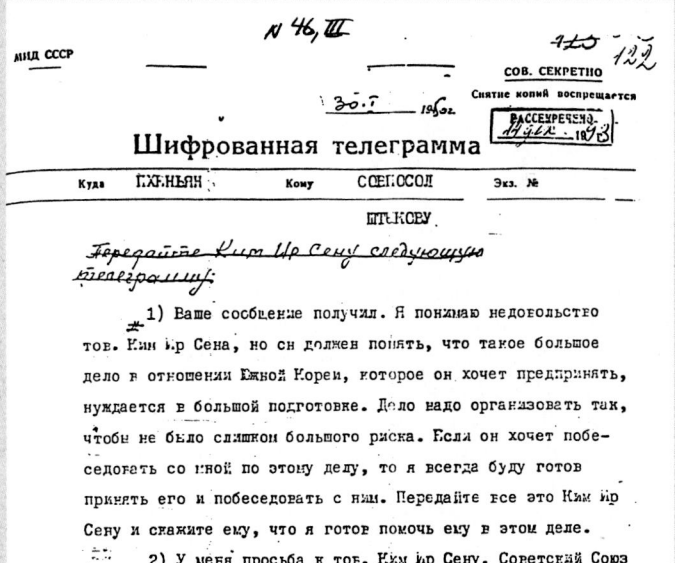

been pushed into the tiny Pusan perimeter at the base of South Korea (see Map 29.2).

General MacArthur planned a daring operation: an amphibious landing at heavily fortified Inchon, several hundred miles behind North Korean lines. After U.S. guns and bombs pounded Inchon, marines sprinted ashore on September 15, 1950. They soon liberated the South Korean capital of Seoul and pushed the North Koreans back to the 38th parallel. Even before Inchon, Truman had redefined the U.S. war goal, changing it from the containment of North Korea to the reunification of Korea by force. Communism not only would be stopped; it would be rolled back.

Map 29.2 The Korean War, 1950–1953 Beginning as a civil war between North and South, this war became international when the United States, under the auspices of the United Nations, and the People's Republic of China intervened with their military forces. (Source: Adapted from Thomas G. Paterson, J. Garry Clifford, and Kenneth J. Hagan, *American Foreign Relations: A History,* vol. 2, 5th ed. Copyright © 2000 by Houghton Mifflin Company.)

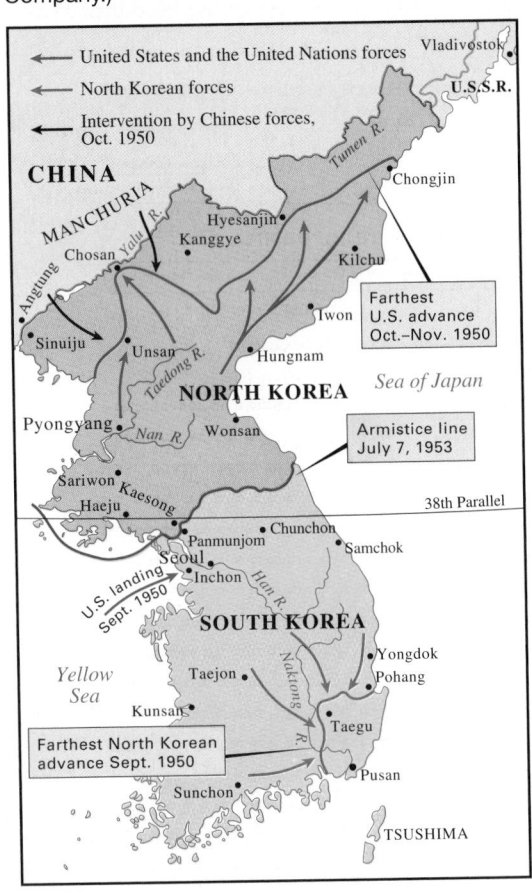

In September Truman authorized U.N. forces to cross the 38th parallel. These troops drove deep into North Korea, and American aircraft began strikes against bridges on the Yalu River, the border between North Korea and China. The Chinese watched warily, fearing that the Americans would next stab at the People's Republic. Mao publicly warned that China could not permit the bombing of its transportation links with Korea and would not accept the annihilation of North Korea itself. MacArthur shrugged off the warnings, and Washington officials agreed with the strong-willed general, drawing further confidence from the fact that the Soviets were not preparing for war.

Chinese Entry into the War

Concluding that the "Americans would run more rampant" unless stopped, Mao, on October 25, sent Chinese soldiers into the war near the Yalu. Perhaps to lure American forces into a trap or to signal willingness to begin negotiations, they pulled back after a brief and successful offensive against South Korean troops. Then, after MacArthur sent the U.S. Eighth Army northward, tens of thousands of Chinese troops counterattacked on November 26, surprising American forces and driving them pell-mell southward.

By early 1951 the front had stabilized around the 38th parallel. Both Washington and Moscow welcomed negotiations, but MacArthur had other ideas. The theatrical general recklessly called for an attack on China and for Jiang's return to the mainland. Now was the time, he insisted, to smash communism by destroying its Asian flank. Denouncing the concept of limited war (war without nuclear weapons, confined to one place), MacArthur hinted that the president was practicing appeasement. In April, backed by the Joint Chiefs of Staff (the heads of the various armed services), Truman fired MacArthur. The general, who had not set foot in the United States for more than a decade, returned home to ticker-tape parades and the lecture circuit but soon faded from the American political scene. Truman's popularity sagged, but he weathered demands for his impeachment.

Truman's Firing of General MacArthur

Armistice talks began in July 1951, but the fighting and dying went on for two more years. The most contentious point in the negotiations was the fate of prisoners of war (POWs). Defying the Geneva Prisoners of War Convention (1949), U.S. officials announced that only

Dispute over POWs

Chinese soldiers guard marching American prisoners of the Korean War during the cold winter of 1950.   (Xinhua, New China News Agency)

those North Korean and Chinese POWs who wished to go home would be returned. Responding to the American statement that there would be no forced repatriation, the North Koreans denounced forced retention. Both sides undertook "reeducation" or "brainwashing" programs to persuade POWs to resist repatriation. Tensions built up in prison camps in South Korea. In early 1952, at the Kobe camp, U.S. troops suppressed a Chinese/North Korean POW riot, killing more than one hundred. In North Korea's camps, murder and illness took the lives of hundreds of POWs.

As the POW issue stalled negotiations, U.S. officials made deliberately vague public statements about

Costs and Consequences of the War

using atomic weapons in Korea. American bombers obliterated dams (whose rushing waters then destroyed rice fields), factories, airfields, and bridges in North Korea. Casualties on all sides mounted. Not until July 1953 was an armistice signed. Stalin's death in March and the coming to power of a more conciliatory Soviet government helped ease the way to a settlement that the Chinese especially welcomed. The combat-

ants agreed to hand over the POW question to a special panel of neutral nations, which later gave prisoners their choice of staying or leaving. (In the end, 70,000 of about 100,000 North Korean and 5,600 of 20,700 Chinese POWs elected to return home; 21 American and 325 South Korean POWs of some 11,000 decided to stay in North Korea.) The North Korean–South Korean borderline was set near the 38th parallel, the prewar boundary, and a demilitarized zone was created between the two Koreas.

American casualties totaled 54,246 dead and 103,284 wounded. Close to 5 million Asians died in the war: 2 million North Korean civilians and 500,000 soldiers; 1 million South Korean civilians and 100,000 soldiers; and at least 1 million Chinese soldiers—ranking Korea as one of the costliest wars of the twentieth century.

The Korean War carried major domestic political consequences. The failure to achieve victory and the public's impatience with a stalemated war undoubtedly helped to elect Eisenhower (see page 795). The powers of the presidency grew as Congress repeatedly deferred to Truman. The president had never asked Congress for a declaration of war, believing that as commander-in-chief he had the authority to send troops wherever he wished. A few dissenters such as Senator Taft disagreed, but Truman saw no need to consult Congress—except when he wanted the $69.5 billion Korean War bill paid.

The implementation of military containment worldwide became entrenched as U.S. policy. In-

Globalization of Containment

creased American aid flowed to the French for their die-hard stand against nationalist insurgents in Vietnam. Because of heightened Sino-American hostility, South Korea and Formosa became major recipients of American foreign aid. The alliance with Japan strengthened as the island's economy boomed after filling large procurement orders from the United States. Australia and New Zealand joined the United States in a mutual defense agreement, the ANZUS Treaty (1951). The U.S. Army sent six divisions to Europe, and the administration initiated plans to rearm West Germany. The Korean War, Acheson cheerfully noted, removed "the recommendations of NSC-68 from the realm of theory and made them immediate budget issues." Indeed, the military budget shot up from $14 billion in 1949 to $44 billion in 1953; it remained between $35 billion and $44 billion a year throughout the 1950s. In sum, Truman's legacy was a highly militarized U.S. foreign policy active on a global scale.

Eisenhower, Dulles, and Unrelenting Cold War

President Dwight D. Eisenhower largely sustained Truman's Cold War policies. Eisenhower brought considerable experience in foreign affairs to his presidency. He had lived and traveled in Europe, Asia, and Latin America and, as a general during the Second World War, had negotiated with world leaders. After the war, he served as army chief of staff and NATO supreme commander. Eisenhower accepted the Cold War consensus about the threat of communism and the need for global vigilance. Partisan Democrats promoted an image of Eisenhower as a bumbling, passive, aging hero. Granted, Eisenhower did not always stay abreast of issues because he chose to delegate authority to others, and he seemed stuck in tired views just when the international system was becoming more fluid. Without doubt, though, the president commanded the policymaking process and tamed the more hawkish

proposals of Vice President Richard Nixon and Secretary of State John Foster Dulles.

Eisenhower questioned Dulles's "practice of becoming a sort of international prosecuting attorney,"

John Foster Dulles

but the president relied heavily on the strong-willed secretary of state. Few Cold Warriors rivaled Dulles's impassioned anticommunism, often expressed in biblical terms. A graduate of Princeton and George Washington Universities, Dulles had assisted Woodrow Wilson at Versailles, and later became a senior partner in a prestigious Wall Street law firm and an officer of the Federal Council of Churches. Though polished and articulate, Dulles impressed people as arrogant, stubborn, and hectoring— and averse to compromise, an essential ingredient in successful diplomacy.

Like the president, Dulles conceded much to the anticommunist McCarthyites, who claimed that the State Department was infested with communists (see page 799). The State Department's chief security officer, a McCarthy follower, targeted homosexuals and other "incompatibles" and made few distinctions between New Dealers and Communists. Dulles thus forced many talented officers out of the Foreign Service with unsubstantiated charges that they were disloyal. Among them were Asia specialists whose expertise was thus denied to the American leaders who later plunged the United States into war in Vietnam. "The wrong done," the journalist Theodore A. White wrote, "was to poke out the eyes and ears of the State Department on Asian affairs, to blind American foreign policy."

Dulles considered containment too defensive a stance toward communism. He called instead for

Eisenhower-Dulles Policies

"liberation," although he never explained precisely how the countries of eastern Europe could be freed from Soviet control. "Massive retaliation" was the administration's phrase for the nuclear obliteration of the Soviet state or its assumed client, the People's Republic of China, if either one took aggressive actions. Eisenhower said it "simply means the ability to blow hell out of them in a hurry if they start anything." The ability of the United States to make such a threat was thought to provide "deterrence," the prevention of hostile Soviet behavior.

In their "New Look" for the American military, Eisenhower and Dulles emphasized airpower and nuclear weaponry. The president's preference for heavy weapons stemmed in part from his desire to trim the

President Eisenhower *(left)* confers with Secretary of State John Foster Dulles (1888–1959), known for his strong anticommunism and his often self-righteous, lecturing style. Dulles once remarked that the United States "is almost the only country strong enough and powerful enough to be moral." (Corbis-Bettmann)

federal budget ("More bang for the buck," as the saying went). The United States's stockpile of nuclear weapons grew during the Eisenhower presidency from 1,200 to 22,229. Backed by its huge military arsenal, the United States practiced "brinkmanship": not backing down in a crisis, even if it meant taking the nation to the brink of war. Eisenhower also popularized the "domino theory": that small, weak, neighboring nations would fall to communism like a row of dominoes if they were not propped up by the United States.

Eisenhower increasingly utilized the Central Intelligence Agency as an instrument of foreign policy.

CIA as Foreign Policy Instrument

Headed by Allen Dulles, brother of the secretary of state, the CIA put foreign leaders (such as King Hussein of Jordan) on its payroll; subsidized foreign labor unions, newspapers, and political parties (such as the conservative Liberal Democratic Party of Japan); planted false stories in newspapers through its "disinformation" projects; and trained foreign military officers in counterrevolutionary methods. The CIA hired American journalists and professors, secretly funded the National Student Association to spur contacts with foreign student leaders, used business executives as "fronts," and conducted experiments on unsuspecting Americans to determine the effects of "mind control" drugs (the MKULTRA program). The CIA also launched covert operations (including assassination schemes) to subvert or destroy governments in the Third World. The CIA helped overthrow the governments of Iran (1953) and Guatemala (1954) but failed in attempts to topple regimes in Indonesia (1958) and Cuba (1961).

The CIA and other components of the American intelligence community followed the principle of plausible deniability: covert operations should be conducted in such a way, and the decisions that launched them concealed so well, that the president could deny any knowledge of them. Thus President Eisenhower disavowed any U.S. role in Guatemala, even though he had ordered the operation. He and his successor Kennedy also denied that they had instructed the CIA to assassinate Cuba's Fidel Castro, whose regime after 1959 became stridently anti-American.

The Eisenhower administration also sought to interject American culture into the Soviet Union and its

Propaganda and Cultural Infiltration

eastern European allies as a means to popularize democratic principles and to stimulate public discontent. The primary propaganda tool was the United States Information Agency

On July 22, 1959, in Moscow, the Soviet capital, Vice President Richard M. Nixon (1913–1994) *(hands clasped)* and Premier Nikita Khrushchev *(finger pointing)* toured the American National Exhibition, sponsored by the U.S. Information Agency. When they stopped at this display of a modern American kitchen, Khrushchev doubted Nixon's claim that average American workers owned such appliances. In the "kitchen debate" that followed, the two leaders sparred over comparative national strengths and over whether capitalism or communism best served people's needs.   (Howard Sochurek, Time-Life Agency © Time Inc.)

(USIA), founded in 1953. One of the USIA's agencies, Voice of America, broadcast news, editorials, and music worldwide. The CIA secretly funded Radio Free Europe, operated since 1950 by anticommunist eastern European émigrés headquartered in Munich, West Germany. Radio Liberty, also CIA-subsidized, began in 1951 and beamed incendiary anti-Soviet messages into the USSR. The Soviets often jammed such broadcasts, but some got through. Did these broadcasts carry influence? Historians disagree. Some claim that they helped cultivate an anticommunism that eventually undermined pro-Soviet regimes. Others argue that they proved counterproductive because they raised hopes—ultimately false—that the United States would back its propaganda calls for liberation with power. In any case, throughout Europe, the popularity of American nonconformists, such as singer Elvis Presley and actors Marlon Brando and James Dean, attracted youth to American culture, including jazz, Coke, and blue jeans.

The United States and the Soviet Union attempted to regularize cultural relations in January 1958 through an agreement that provided for reciprocal exchange of radio and television broadcasts, films, students, professors, athletes, and civic groups. One result was Vice President Richard Nixon's trip in July 1959 to Moscow to open an American products fair, where, in the "kitchen debate," he extolled capitalist consumerism in a model six-room ranch-style house, while Soviet premier Nikita Khrushchev, Stalin's successor, touted the merits of communism. Khrushchev followed in September with an eye-opening tour of the United States.

Such expanded cultural relations did not calm the Cold War or temper the nuclear arms race. In No-

Hydrogen Bomb
vember 1952 the United States detonated the first hydrogen bomb. Then, in early 1954, the largest bomb the United States has ever tested destroyed the Pacific island of Bikini. This H-bomb,

packing the power of 15 million tons of TNT (750 times as powerful as the atomic bomb that leveled Hiroshima), produced a fallout of radioactive dust that showered a Japanese fishing boat in the area. The crew of the *Lucky Dragon* suffered severe nausea, fever, and blisters. When one of the sailors died, international protest bombarded the United States. Anti-American sentiment flared in Japan.

The Soviets tested their first H-bomb in 1953. Four years later, they shocked Americans by firing the world's first intercontinental ballistic missile (ICBM) and then propelling the satellite *Sputnik* into orbit in outer space. Americans felt more vulnerable to air attack and inferior in rocket technology, even though in 1957 the United States had 2,460 strategic weapons and a nuclear stockpile of 5,543, compared to the Soviet Union's 102 and 650. As President Eisenhower said, "If we were to release our nuclear stockpile on the Soviet Union, the main danger would arise not from retaliation but from fallout in the earth's atmosphere."

Sputnik and Missiles

The United States soon tested its own ICBMs, became embarrassed in late 1957 when the rocket for the *Vanguard* satellite caught fire and crashed on its launch pad, and then successfully launched the satellite *Explorer I* in early 1958. The administration also enlarged its fleet of long-range bombers (B-52s) and deployed intermediate-range missiles in Europe, targeted against the Soviet Union. At the end of 1960 the United States began adding Polaris missile–bearing submarines to its navy. To foster future technological advancement, the National Aeronautics and Space Administration (NASA) was created in 1958.

The CIA's U-2 spy planes collected information demonstrating that the Soviets had deployed very few ICBMs. Yet politically partisan critics charged that Eisenhower had allowed the United States to fall behind in the missile race. The much-publicized "missile gap" was actually not in the USSR's favor but rather America's. "Everyone knows," air force general Nathan Twining privately told the president, "we already have a [nuclear] stockpile large enough to obliterate the Soviet Union." As the 1950s closed, the United States enjoyed overwhelming strategic dominance because of its air-sea-land triad of long-range bombers, submarine-launched ballistic missiles (SLBMs), and ICBMs.

President Eisenhower grew uneasy about the arms race and the deterrence policy that became known as "mutual assured destruction," or MAD. He feared nuclear war, and the cost of the new weapons made it

Eisenhower's Critique of Nuclear Arms

difficult to balance the budget. In a 1953 speech, the president noted that "every gun that is made, every warship launched, every rocket fired signifies, in the final sense, a theft from those who hunger and are not fed. . . . The cost of one modern heavy bomber is this: a modern brick school in more than 30 cities." He also doubted the need for more and bigger nuclear weapons. How many times, he once asked, "could [you] kill the same man?" So devastating would be a nuclear war with the Soviet Union, he said, "you might as well go out and shoot everyone you see and then shoot yourself." Spurred by such thoughts, by citizens' groups such as the Committee for a Sane Nuclear Policy (SANE), founded in 1957, and by neutralist and Soviet appeals, the president cautiously initiated arms-control proposals.

Eisenhower's 1953 "atoms for peace" initiative recommended that fissionable materials be contributed to a U.N. agency for use in industrial projects. Two years later, to counter Soviet appeals for disarmament, the Eisenhower administration issued its own propaganda ploy—the "open skies" proposal: aerial surveillance of both Soviet and American military sites to reduce the chances of surprise attacks. In response to worldwide alarm over radioactive fallout, the two powers unilaterally suspended atmospheric testing from 1958 until 1961, when the Soviets resumed it. The United States also began testing again at the same time, but underground. Despite a series of disarmament talks in Geneva, Switzerland, and Eisenhower's meeting there in July 1955 with Khrushchev (the first summit meeting in ten years), neither side could agree on nuclear-testing bans or suitable inspection systems to ensure compliance should they sign arms-control treaties.

In May 1955, in a rare example of Cold War cooperation, the two great powers ended their ten-year occupation of Austria. But events in eastern Europe soon revived the customary acrimony of the Cold War. In 1956 Khrushchev called for "peaceful coexistence" between capitalists and communists, denounced Stalin, and suggested that Moscow would tolerate different brands of communism. Revolts against Soviet power erupted in Poland and Hungary, testing Khrushchev's new permissiveness. After a new Hungarian government in 1956 announced its withdrawal from the Warsaw Pact (the Soviet military alliance formed in 1955 with communist countries of eastern Europe), Soviet troops and

Rebellion in Hungary

tanks battled students and workers in the streets of Budapest and crushed the rebellion.

Although the Eisenhower administration's propaganda had been encouraging liberation efforts, U.S. officials found themselves unable to aid the rebels without igniting a world war. The United States could only welcome Hungarian immigrants in greater numbers than American quota laws allowed. The West could have reaped some propaganda advantage from this display of Soviet brute force had not British, French, and Israeli troops—U.S. allies—invaded Egypt during the Suez crisis just before the Soviets smashed the Hungarian uprising (see pages 848–849).

Hardly had the turmoil subsided in eastern Europe when the divided city of Berlin once again became a Cold War flash point. The Soviets railed against the placement in West Germany of American bombers capable of carrying nuclear warheads, and they complained that West Berlin had become an escape route for disaffected East Germans. In 1958 Khrushchev announced that the Soviet Union would recognize East German control of all of Berlin unless the United States and its allies began talks on German reunification and rearmament. The United States refused to give up its hold on West Berlin or to break West German ties with NATO. Khrushchev backed away from his ultimatum but promised to press the issue again.

Berlin and Germany were on the agenda of a summit meeting planned for Paris in mid-1960. On May

U-2 Incident

1, two weeks before the conference, a U-2 spy plane carrying high-powered cameras crashed 1,200 miles inside the Soviet Union. Moscow claimed credit for shooting down the plane, which it put on display along with Francis Gary Powers, the captured CIA pilot, and the pictures he had been snapping of Soviet military sites. Khrushchev demanded an apology for the U.S. violation of Soviet airspace. When Washington refused, the Soviets walked out of the Paris summit—"a graveyard of lost opportunities," as a Soviet official put it. Eisenhower bemoaned "the stupid U-2 mess." U.S. reconnaissance continued, and with far greater sophistication than that provided by the U-2. In August 1960 the CIA's CORONA project saw its first successful mission when a spy satellite circling the globe ejected to earth a film capsule containing photographic coverage of the USSR. CORONA satellites provided data on Soviet missile bases for top-secret intelligence reports to the president.

While sparring over Europe, both sides kept a wary eye on the People's Republic of China, which

Jinmen-Mazu Crisis

denounced the Soviet call for peaceful coexistence. Despite evidence of a widening Sino-Soviet split, most American officials still treated communism as a unified world movement. The isolation separating Beijing and Washington stymied communication and made continued conflict between China and the United States likely. In a dispute over Jinmen (Quemoy) and Mazu (Matsu), two tiny islands off the Chinese coast, the United States and the People's Republic of China lurched toward the brink. Jiang used these islands as bases from which to raid the mainland. Communist China's guns bombarded the islands in 1954. Thinking that U.S. credibility was at stake, Eisenhower decided to defend the outposts; he even hinted that he might use nuclear weapons. Why massive retaliation over such an insignificant issue? "Let's keep the Reds guessing," advised John Foster Dulles. But what if they guessed wrong? critics replied.

Congress passed the Formosa Resolution (1955), authorizing the president to deploy American forces to defend Formosa and adjoining islands, and two years later the United States installed tactical nuclear weapons on Taiwan. Although diplomats from the People's Republic of China and the United States held secret meetings in Geneva and Warsaw, war loomed again in 1958 over Jinmen and Mazu. But this time, after Washington strongly cautioned him not to use force against the mainland, Jiang withdrew some troops from the islands. China then relaxed its bombardments. One consequence accelerated the arms race: Eisenhower's nuclear threats persuaded the Chinese that they, too, needed nuclear arms. In 1964 China exploded its first nuclear bomb.

As the United States went to the brink with China, it went to the market with Japan, rebuilding the

"Japanese Miracle"

nation with foreign aid as an anticommunist military partner and trader, all the while worrying China, the Soviet Union, and other past victims of Japanese aggression. Huge U.S. purchases in Japan during the Korean War and American assistance in developing an export-oriented economy in the 1950s produced what many called the "Japanese miracle"—double-digit economic growth. Led by the powerful Ministry of International Trade and Industry (MITI), Japan copied American technology (Motorola, for example, helped start the electronics industry), practiced trade protectionism, and gained a reputation for industrial efficiency and quality control. Before long, Japan became a major economic competitor with the United States, stirring measures to curb Japanese goods—such as textiles—in the American marketplace. In Japan labor strikes and student riots against America's reliance on nuclear weapons and the substantial U.S. military presence forced Eisenhower to cancel a goodwill trip to Tokyo in 1960. Japan remained a Cold War ally, but uneasily.

Western Europeans also developed an uneasy relationship with Americans, raising doubts about the "family" the United States was trying to cultivate through NATO. McCarthyite extremism disturbed them. U.S. calls for German rearmament and for fighting in Vietnam alarmed them. They wondered about American credibility: would the United States really defend western Europe against a Soviet attack if such defense triggered a punishing Soviet nuclear assault against the United States itself? As well, NATO countries—especially France—thought that the United States, while championing an "Atlantic community," treated them like dependent clients, too seldom consulting with them.

At Odds with the Third World

A process of decolonization that began during the First World War accelerated after the Second World War, when the economically wracked imperial countries proved incapable of resisting their colonies' demands for freedom. A cavalcade of new nations cast off their colonial bonds (see Map 29.3). In 1960 alone, eighteen new African nations did so. From 1943 to 1994 a total of 125 countries became independent (the figure includes the former Soviet republics that departed the USSR in 1991). The emergence of so many new states in the 1940s and after, and the instability associated with the transfer of authority, shook the foundations of the international system. Power was redistributed, creating "near chaos," said one U.S. government report. In the United States's traditional sphere of influence, Latin America, nationalists once again challenged U.S. hegemony.

By the late 1940s, when Cold War lines were drawn fairly tightly in Europe, Soviet-American rivalry shifted increasingly to the Third World. Much was at stake. The new nations could buy American

Interests in the Third World

goods and technology, supply strategic raw materials, and invite investments (more than one-third of America's private foreign investments were in Third World countries in 1959). And they could build cultural ties with the United States. Both great powers, moreover, looked to these new states for votes in the United Nations and sought sites within their borders for military and intelligence bases. But, often poor and unstable, rife with tribal, ethnic, and class rivalries, many new nations sought to end the economic, military, and cultural hegemony of the West. Many of these new nations learned to play off the two superpowers against each other to garner more aid and arms. U.S. interventions—military and otherwise—in the Third World, American leaders believed, became necessary to impress Moscow with Washington's might and resolve and to counter nationalism and radical anticapitalist social change that threatened American strategic and economic interests.

To thwart nationalist, radical, and communist challenges, the United States directed massive resources—foreign aid, propaganda, development projects—toward the Third World. By 1961 more than 90 percent of U.S. foreign aid was going to developing nations. Washington also allied with native elites and with undemocratic but anticommunist regimes, meddled in civil wars, and unleashed CIA covert operations. Bitter resentments built up in the Third World, where millions of lives were lost in conflicts aggravated by U.S. intervention.

Many Third World states—notably India, Ghana, Egypt, and Indonesia—refused to take sides in the Cold War. To the dismay of both Washington and Moscow, they declared themselves nonaligned, or neutral. Nonalignment became an organized movement in 1955 when twenty-nine Asian and African nations met at the Bandung Conference in Indonesia. Secretary Dulles, alarmed that neutralist tendencies would deprive the United States of potential allies, denounced neutralism as a step on the road to communism. Both he and Eisenhower insisted that every nation should take a side in the life-and-death Cold War struggle. Neutralism had to be contained.

Nonaligned Movement

American leaders argued that technologically "backward" Third World peoples needed Western-induced capitalist development and modernization in

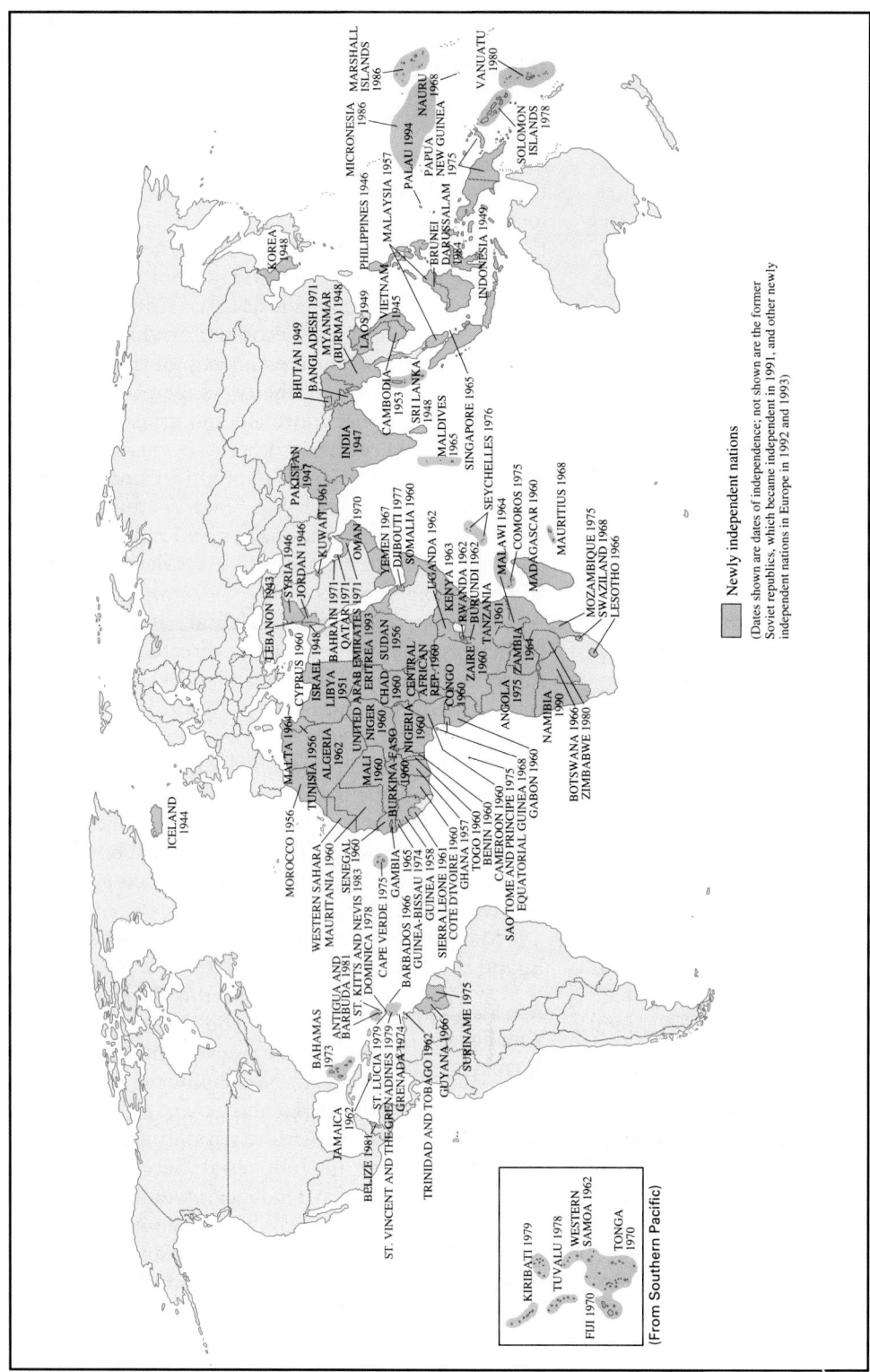

Map 29.3 The Rise of the Third World: Newly Independent Nations Since 1943 Accelerated by the Second World War, decolonization liberated many peoples from imperial rule. New nations emerged in the postwar international system dominated by the Cold War rivalry of the United States and the Soviet Union. Many newly independent states became targets of great-power intrigue but chose nonalignment in the Cold War.

American Images of Third World Peoples

order to enjoy economic growth, social harmony, and political moderation. U.S. policymakers placed Third World peoples low in the hierarchy of power and claimed that they needed fatherly tutelage by the United States. American leaders ascribed stereotyped race-, age-, and gender-based characteristics to Third World peoples, seeing them as dependent, emotional, and irrational. Cubans, CIA director Allen Dulles told the National Security Council in early 1959, "had to be treated more or less like children. They had to be led rather than rebuffed. If they were rebuffed, like children, they were capable of almost anything." American officials also used gendered language, suggesting that Third World countries were weak women—passive and servile, unable to resist the menacing appeals of communists and neutralists. For example, such thinking conditioned U.S. relations with India, a neutralist nation that Americans deemed effeminate and submissive—a place where, said President Eisenhower, "emotion rather than reason seems to dictate policy." Changing images of Israel helped condition U.S. policy in the Middle East. From seeing Jews as pusillani-

mous and passive because of their role as victims to seeing them as masculine and tough in their fight to survive and construct a new state in the midst of violently hostile Arab neighbors, Americans moved toward alliance with a thus admirable Israel.

Race attitudes and segregation practices in the United States especially influenced relations. In 1955

Racism and Segregation as U.S. Handicaps

G. L. Mehta, the Indian ambassador to the United States, was refused service in the whites-only section of a restaurant at Houston International Airport. The insult stung deeply, as did many similar indignities experienced by other Third World diplomats. Fearing damaged relations with India, a large, neutralist nation whose allegiance the United States sought in the Cold War, John Foster Dulles apologized to Mehta. The secretary thought racial segregation in the United States a "major international hazard," spoiling American efforts to win friends in Third World countries and giving the Soviets a propaganda advantage. American practices and ideals did not align.

When the U.S. attorney general appealed to the Supreme Court to strike down segregation in public

In the 1950s, these specially outfitted jeeps (equipped with projectors, screens, and films) served America's overseas information program in what the State Department called "isolated areas." Believing that social modernization and economic progress would counter leftist and communist ideas, U.S. propaganda officials dispatched these "mobile motion picture units" to such places as rural Mexico, seeking to reach people with films on U.S. sports, music, health, and agriculture. (National Archives)

schools, he underlined that the humiliation of dark-skinned diplomats "furnished grist for the Communist propaganda mills." When the Court announced its *Brown* decision in 1954 (see page 802), Voice of America quickly broadcast news of the desegregation order around the world in thirty-five languages. But the problem did not go away. For example, after the 1957 Little Rock crisis (see page 803), Dulles remarked that racial bigotry was "ruining our foreign policy. The effect of this in Asia and Africa will be worse for us than Hungary was for the Russians." Still, when an office of the Department of State decided to counter Soviet propaganda by creating for the 1958 World's Fair in Brussels an exhibit titled "The Unfinished Business," on race relations in the United States and strides taken toward desegregation, southern conservatives kicked up such a furor that the Eisenhower administration closed the display.

The hostility of the United States toward revolution also obstructed its quest for influence in the Third World. In the twentieth century, the United States has openly opposed revolutions in Mexico, China, Russia, Cuba, Vietnam, Nicaragua, and Iran, among other nations. Americans celebrated the Spirit of '76 but grew intolerant of revolutionary disorder because many Third World revolutions arose against America's Cold War allies and threatened American investments, markets, and military bases. Indeed, by midcentury the United States stood as an established power in world affairs, eager for stability and order to protect American prosperity and security. During revolutionary crises, therefore, the United States usually supported its European allies or the conservative, propertied classes in the Third World. In 1960, for example, when forty-three African and Asian states sponsored a U.N. resolution endorsing decolonization, the United States abstained from the vote.

U.S. Hostility to Nationalist Revolution

Believing that Third World peoples craved modernization and that the American economic model of private enterprise and cooperation among business, labor, and government was best for them, American policymakers launched various "development" projects. Such projects held out the promise of sustained economic growth, prosperity, and stability, which the benefactors hoped would undermine radicalism. In the 1950s the Carnegie, Ford, and Rockefeller Foundations worked with the U.S. Agency for International

Development and Modernization

Development (AID) to sponsor a Green Revolution—a dramatic increase in agricultural production, for example, by the use of hybrid seeds. The Rockefeller Foundation supported foreign universities' efforts to train national leaders committed to nonradical development; in Nigeria from 1958 to 1969 the philanthropic agency spent $25 million. Before Dean Rusk became secretary of state in 1961, he served as president of the Rockefeller Foundation.

In the 1950s and 1960s the views of Massachusetts Institute of Technology professor Walt W. Rostow influenced U.S. leaders. Rostow wrote in his popular book, *Stages of Economic Growth: A Non-Communist Manifesto* (1959), that if the United States sponsored development projects in the Third World through capital investment and infusions of Western culture and technology, and U.S. foreign aid, then class conflict, civil war, and revolution would diminish if not disappear. They seldom did either, however.

To persuade Third World peoples to abandon radical doctrines and neutralism, American leaders, often in cooperation with the business-sponsored Advertising Council, directed propaganda at the Third World. The U.S. Information Agency used films, radio broadcasts, the magazine *Free World*, exhibitions, exchange programs, and libraries (in 162 cities worldwide by 1961) to trumpet the theme of "People's Capitalism." Citing America's economic success—contrasted with "slave-labor" conditions in the Soviet Union—the message showcased well-paid American workers, political democracy, and religious freedom. To counter ugly pictures of segregation and white attacks on African Americans and civil rights activists in the South, the USIA applauded success stories of individual African Americans such as the boxers Floyd Patterson and Sugar Ray Robinson. In 1960 alone some 13.8 million people visited U.S. pavilions abroad, including 1 million at the consumer-products exhibit "Tradeways to Peace and Prosperity" in Damascus, Syria. The Fulbright Program (see page 829) and trade fairs also brought America's message before the Third World.

Some Third World peoples did yearn to be like Americans—to enjoy their consumer goods, music, economic status, and educational opportunities. Hollywood movies offered enticing glimpses of middle-class materialism, and North American films dominated the Latin American market. Blue jeans, advertising billboards, and soft drinks flooded foreign societies.

Third World Views of the United States

If foreigners envied Americans, they also resented them for having so much and wasting so much while poorer peoples went without. The popular American novel *The Ugly American* (1958) spotlighted the "golden ghettoes" where American foreign diplomats lived in compounds separated from their poorer surroundings by high walls. The people of many countries, moreover, resented the ample profits that American corporations extracted from them. Americans often received blame for the persistent poverty of the Third World, even though the leaders of those nations made decisions that hindered their own progress, such as pouring millions of dollars into their militaries while their people craved food. Nonetheless, anti-American resentments could be measured in the late 1950s in attacks on USIA libraries in Calcutta (India), Beirut (Lebanon), and Bogotá (Colombia). The American film and television industries were so active abroad that some foreigners protested "cultural imperialism." Third World peoples also rejected unsavory aspects of American life, including racial segregation, political corruption, and drug abuse.

U.S. Interventions in the Third World

Anti-Yankee feelings grew in Latin America, where poverty, class warfare, overpopulation, illiteracy, and foreign exploitation fed discontent, which U.S. leaders feared might be exploited by communists. Two examples spotlighted Latin American hostility toward the United States: in 1958 rioters in Venezuela and elsewhere interrupted Vice President Nixon's goodwill trip to South America and threatened his life; the following year Panamanians rioted after U.S. officials denied them permission to raise the Panamanian flag in the Canal Zone.

In 1951 the leftist Jacobo Arbenz Guzmán was elected president of Guatemala, a poor country whose largest landowner was the American-owned United Fruit Company (UF).

CIA in Guatemala

United Fruit was an economic power throughout Latin America, where it owned 3 million acres of land and operated railroads, ports, ships, and telecommunications facilities. To fulfill his promise of land reform, Arbenz expropriated UF's uncultivated land and offered compensation. UF dismissed the offer and charged that Arbenz posed a communist threat—a charge that CIA officials had already floated because Arbenz employed

some communists in his government. The CIA began a secret plot to overthrow Arbenz. He turned to Moscow for military aid, thus reinforcing American suspicions. The CIA airlifted arms into Guatemala, dropping them at UF facilities, and in mid-1954 CIA-supported Guatemalans struck from Honduras. U.S. planes bombed the capital city, and the invaders drove Arbenz from power. The new pro-American regime returned United Fruit's land, but an ensuing civil war staggered the Central American nation into the 1990s.

The Cuban Revolution soon represented the greatest challenge to U.S. hegemony. In early 1959

The Cuban Revolution and Fidel Castro

Fidel Castro's rebels, or *barbudos* ("bearded ones"), driven by profound anti-American nationalism, had ousted Fulgencio Batista, a long-time U.S. ally who had welcomed North American investors, U.S. military advisers, and tourists to the Caribbean island. Batista's corrupt, dictatorial regime had helped turn Havana into a haven for gambling and prostitution run by organized crime. Cubans had resented U.S. domination ever since the early twentieth century, when the Platt Amendment was imposed on them (see page 627). Curbing U.S. influence became a rallying cry of the Cuban Revolution, all the more after the CIA conspired secretly but futilely to block Castro's rise to power in 1958. From the start Castro sought to roll back the influence of American business, which had invested some $1 billion on the island, and to break the U.S. grasp on Cuban trade.

Castro's increasing authoritarianism, anti-Yankee declarations, and growing popularity in the hemisphere alarmed Washington. In early 1960, after Cuba signed a trade treaty with the Soviet Union, Eisenhower ordered the CIA to organize an invasion force of Cuban exiles to overthrow the Castro government. The agency also began to plot an assassination of the Cuban leader. When the president drastically cut U.S. purchases of Cuban sugar, Castro seized all North American–owned companies that had not yet been nationalized. Threatened by U.S. decisions designed to bring him and his revolution down, Castro appealed to the Soviet Union, which offered loans and expanded trade. Just before leaving office in early 1961, Eisenhower broke diplomatic relations with Cuba and advised President-elect John F. Kennedy to advance plans for the invasion, which came in early 1961 (see page 888).

A different sort of U.S. intervention occurred in Puerto Rico—tourism and industrial development.

Operation Bootstrap in Puerto Rico

Under the leadership of Teodoro Moscoso, Operation Bootstrap attracted investments from U.S. corporations with tempting tax benefits. In 1955 a General Electric (GE) circuit-breaker facility became the four hundredth manufacturing plant to open under Bootstrap. A GE officer remembered that Puerto Rico "offered many of the advantages of the Third World, such as an abundant, relatively low-cost and eager-to-work labor force, but none of the disadvantages," such as political instability and hostility to foreign investment. Tourism

In 1960 Egypt's neutralist leader, Gamal Abdul Nasser (1918–1970), with raised hand, and revolutionary Cuba's Fidel Castro (b. 1926), center with beard, went together to New York City's Harlem area when both were attending a meeting of the United Nations. Often angering U.S. officials and thwarting U.S. foreign policy aims, the two strong-willed, nationalistic Third World leaders issued anti-American declarations and accepted Soviet military assistance. (Corbis-Bettmann)

also expanded greatly in Puerto Rico; the opening of the Caribe Hilton hotel in late 1949 set off a resort-building boom along the island's beautiful beaches. In 1952, 37,000 tourists visited; by 1960 the number had leaped to 145,000. The lush hotels contrasted conspicuously with the squalor of the seaside slum La Perla, in the capital of San Juan, chronicled in the anthropologist Oscar Lewis's book *La Vida* (1966). Critics protested that Puerto Rico had spent millions on luxury hotels for North American tourists but little to combat poverty. At the same time, increasing numbers of Puerto Ricans journeyed to the United States, creating *barrios* in American cities, especially in New York.

In the Middle East, where the Arab-Israeli dispute particularly upended order, the Eisenhower administration confronted challenges to U.S.

U.S. Interests in the Middle East

influence from Arab nationalists (see Map 31.2 on page 904). American interests were conspicuous: survival of the Jewish state of Israel and extensive oil holdings (American companies produced about half of the region's petroleum in the 1950s). Oil-rich Iran had become a special friend. Its ruling shah had granted American oil companies a 40 percent interest in a new petroleum consortium in return for CIA help in the successful overthrow, in 1953, of his rival, Mohammed Mossadegh, who had attempted to nationalize foreign oil interests.

Egypt's Gamal Abdul Nasser became a towering figure in a pan-Arabic movement to reduce Western interests in the Middle East. Nasser vowed to expel the British from the Suez Canal and the Israelis from Palestine. The United States wished neither to anger the Arabs, for fear of losing valuable oil supplies, nor to alienate its ally Israel, which was supported at home by politically active American Jews. But when Nasser declared neutrality in the Cold War, Dulles lost patience.

In 1956 the United States abruptly reneged on its offer to Egypt to help finance the Aswan Dam, a project to provide inexpensive electricity

Suez Crisis

and water for thirsty Nile valley farmland. Secretary Dulles's blunt economic pressure backfired, for Nasser responded by nationalizing the British-owned Suez Canal, intending to use its profits to build the dam. At a mass rally in Alexandria, Nasser expressed the profound nationalism typical of Third World peoples shedding an imperial past: "Tonight our Egyptian canal will be run by Egyptians. Egyptians!" Fully 75 percent of western Europe's oil came from the Middle East, most of it transported through the Suez Canal. Fearing an interruption in this vital trade, the British and French conspired with Israel to bring down Nasser. On October 29, 1956, the Israelis invaded Suez, joined two days later by British and French forces.

Eisenhower fumed. America's allies had not consulted him and the attack had shifted attention from Soviet intervention in Hungary. The president also feared that the invasion would cause Nasser to seek help from the Soviets, inviting them into the Middle East. Eisenhower sternly demanded that London, Paris, and Tel Aviv pull their troops out, and they did. Egypt took possession of the canal, the Soviets built the Aswan Dam, and Nasser became a hero to Third World peoples. To counter Nasser, the United States determined to "build up" as an "Arab rival" the conservative King Ibn Saud of Saudi Arabia. Although the monarch renewed America's lease of an air base, few Arabs respected the notoriously corrupt Saud.

Washington officials worried that a "vacuum" existed in the Middle East—and that the Soviets might fill it. Nasserites insisted that there

Eisenhower Doctrine

was no vacuum but rather a growing Arab nationalism that provided the best defense against communism. In an effort to improve the deteriorating Western position in the Middle East and to protect American interests there, the president proclaimed the Eisenhower Doctrine in 1957. The United States would intervene in the Middle East, he declared, if any government threatened by a communist takeover asked for help. In 1958 fourteen thousand American troops scrambled ashore in Lebanon to quell an internal political dispute that Washington feared might be exploited by pro-Nasser groups or communists. By 1961, most analysts agreed, the Eisenhower administration had deepened Third World hostility toward the United States.

Such was especially true in Vietnam, where nationalists battled the French and Americans for independence. Despite substantial U.S.

Dienbienphu Crisis in Vietnam

aid, the French lost steadily to the Vietminh. Finally, in early 1954, Ho's forces surrounded the French fortress at Dienbienphu in northwest Vietnam (see Map 31.1 on page 892). Although some of Eisenhower's advisers recommended a massive American air strike against Vietminh positions, perhaps even using tactical atomic weapons, the president moved cautiously. The United States had been advising and bankrolling the French,

but it had not committed its own forces to the war. If American airpower did not save the French, would ground troops be required next, and in hostile terrain? As one high-level doubter remarked, "One cannot go over Niagara Falls in a barrel only slightly."

Worrying aloud about a communist victory, Eisenhower compared the weak nations of the world to a row of dominoes, all of which would topple if just one fell. He pressed the British to help form a coalition to address the Indochinese crisis, but they refused. At home, influential members of Congress told the president they wanted "no more Koreas" and warned him to avoid any U.S. military commitment, especially in the absence of cooperation from U.S. allies. Some felt very uneasy about supporting colonialism. The issue became moot on May 7, when the weary French defenders at Dienbienphu surrendered.

To compound the administration's problems, the French wanted out of the war. In April they had entered into peace talks at Geneva with

Geneva Accords

the United States, the Soviet Union, Britain, the People's Republic of China, Laos, Cambodia, and the competing Vietnamese regimes of Bao Dai and Ho Chi Minh. Asked at a press conference if he would meet with Chinese delegates, Dulles retorted, "Not unless our automobiles collide." The 1954 Geneva accords, signed by France and Ho's Democratic Republic of Vietnam, temporarily divided Vietnam at the 17th parallel; Ho's government was confined to the North, Bao Dai's to the South. Only after pressure from the Chinese, who feared U.S. intervention in Vietnam without an agreement, did Ho's government agree to this compromise. The 17th parallel was meant to serve as a military truce line, not a national boundary; the country was scheduled to be unified after national elections in 1956. In the meantime, neither North nor South was to join a military alliance or permit foreign military bases on its soil.

Certain that the Geneva agreements ultimately would mean communist victory, the United States and Bao Dai refused to accept the accords and set about to sabotage them. Soon after the conference, a CIA team entered Vietnam and undertook secret operations against the North, including commando raids across the 17th parallel. In fall 1954 the United States also joined Britain, France, Australia, New Zealand, the Philippines, Thailand, and Pakistan in the anticommunist Southeast Asia Treaty Organization (SEATO), one purpose of which was to protect the southern part of Vietnam.

In the South, the United States helped Ngo Dinh Diem push Bao Dai aside and inaugurate the Republic of Vietnam. A Catholic in a Buddhist nation, Diem had many enemies and no mass support. But he was a nationalist and an anticommunist. With American aid he staged a fraudulent election that gave him 98 percent of the vote. When Ho called for national elections in keeping with the Geneva agreements, Diem and Eisenhower refused, fearing that the popular Vietminh leader would win. From 1955 to 1961, the Diem government received more than $1 billion in American aid, most of it military. American advisers organized and trained Diem's army, and American agriculturalists worked to improve crops. Diem's Saigon regime became dependent on the United States for its very existence, and the culture of southern Vietnam became increasingly Americanized.

Backing the Diem Regime in South Vietnam

Diem proved a difficult ally. He acted dictatorially, abolishing village elections and appointing to public office people beholden to him. He threw dissenters in jail and shut down newspapers that criticized his regime. Noncommunists and communists alike began to strike back at Diem's corrupt and repressive government. Not until early 1959 did Ho's regime in the northern capital of Hanoi begin to send aid to southern insurgents, who embarked on a program of terror, assassinating hundreds of Diem's village officials. In late 1960 southern communists organized the National Liberation Front (NLF), known as the Vietcong. The Vietcong in turn attracted other anti-Diem groups in the South. The war against imperialism had become a two-part civil war: Ho's North versus Diem's South, and NLF guerrillas versus the Diem government. And the United States, perceiving in Ho and the NLF the menace of a monolithic communism—a universal communist conspiracy to take over the world—marched into this multifaceted war certain that superior U.S. firepower and technology could succeed against inferior Asians.

Summary

The United States emerged from the Second World War preeminent in power but fearful that the unstable international system, an unfriendly Soviet Union, and the decolonizing Third World threatened American plans for the postwar world, American economic-strategic interests, and principles such as the Open Door and political democracy. Locked with the Soviet Union in a "Cold War," U.S. leaders marshaled their nation's superior resources to influence and cajole other countries. Foreign economic aid, new international organizations, threats to use atomic weapons again, client states, reconstruction of former enemies Germany and Japan, development of new long-range missiles, military alliances, covert operations, interventions, propaganda, cultural infiltration—these and more became the instruments to wage the Cold War, a global war.

America's claim to international leadership sparked resistance. Communist countries condemned dollar and atomic diplomacy; Third World nations sought to undermine America's European allies and identified the United States as an imperial coconspirator; and even America's allies bristled at a United States that boldly proclaimed itself economic master and global policeman and haughtily touted its hegemonic status. Liberal and radical domestic critics protested that Presidents Truman and Eisenhower exaggerated the communist threat, wasting U.S. assets on immoral foreign ventures, crippled legitimate nationalist aspirations, and displayed racial bias. Still, these presidents and their successors held firm to the mission of creating a nonradical, capitalist, free-trade international order in the mold of domestic America. They seldom hesitated to flex American muscle to enlarge the American sphere of influence and shape the world in an age when the airplane shrank the globe, making the United States forever "de-isolated," as one foreign policy analyst remarked. In their years of nurturing allies and applying the containment doctrine worldwide, Truman and Eisenhower held the line—against the Soviet Union, the People's Republic of China, nonalignment, communism, nationalism, and revolution everywhere.

Putting itself at odds with the Third World, the United States usually stood with its European allies to slow decolonization and preach evolution rather than revolution. The globalist perspective of the United States prompted Americans to interpret many Third World troubles as Cold War conflicts, inspired if not directed by Soviet-backed communists. The intensity of the Cold War obscured for Americans the indigenous roots of most Third World troubles, as the wars in Korea and Vietnam attested. Nor could the United States abide Third World nations' drive for economic independence—for gaining control of their own raw materials and economies. Deeply intertwined in the global economy as importer, exporter, and investor, the

United States read Third World challenges as threats to the American standard of living and way of life characterized by private enterprise. The Third World, in short, challenged the United States's strategic power by forming a third force in the Cold War, and it challenged American economic power by demanding a new economic order of shared interests. Overall, the rise of the Third World introduced new actors to the world stage, challenging the bipolarity of the international system and diffusing power. So alarmed was the Democratic candidate for president in 1960, Senator John F. Kennedy of Massachusetts, that he charged that the United States under President Eisenhower's leadership was losing the Cold War, especially in the Third World.

All the while, the threat of nuclear war unsettled Americans and foreigners alike. In the film *Godzilla* (1956), a prehistoric monster, revived by atomic bomb tests, rampages through Tokyo. Stanley Kramer's popular but disturbing movie *On the Beach* (1959), based on Nevil Shute's bestselling 1957 novel, depicts a nuclear holocaust in which the last humans on earth choose to swallow government-issued poison tablets so that they could die before H-bomb radiation sickness kills them. Such doomsday or Armageddon attitudes contrasted sharply with official U.S. government assurances that Americans would survive a nuclear war. In *On the Beach*, a dying wife asks her husband, "Couldn't anyone have stopped it?" His answer: "Some kinds of silliness you just can't stop." Eisenhower did not halt it, even though he told Khrushchev in 1959 that "we really should come to some sort of agreement in order to stop this fruitless, really wasteful rivalry."

LEGACY FOR A PEOPLE AND A NATION
The National Security State

To build a cathedral, someone has observed, you first need a religion, and a religion needs inspiring texts that command authority. For decades, America's Cold War religion has been national security, its texts the Truman Doctrine, "X" article, and NSC-68, and its cathedral the national security state. The word *state* in this case means "civil government." During the Cold War, embracing preparedness for total war, the U.S. government essentially transformed itself into a huge military headquarters that interlocked with corporations and universities. Preaching the doctrine of na-

tional security, moreover, members of Congress strove to gain lucrative defense contracts for their districts.

Overseen by the president and his advisory body, the National Security Council, the national security state has had as its core what the National Security Act of 1947 called the National Military Establishment; in 1949 it became the Department of Defense. This department ranked as a leading employer; its payroll by 1990 included almost 5 million persons. It operated 1,265 major installations, 375 of them abroad. Spending for national defense and veterans topped $328 billion, a quarter of the federal budget. In 1998, years after the Cold War ended, with the closing of some military facilities and downsizing of staffs, the figure still stood at $300 billion (about 16 percent of the budget). Over time, critics railed against waste, cost overruns, and questionable military "toys," but the national security state continued to figure prominently in the U.S. economy, especially in California, Texas, Virginia, Colorado, and New York.

Joining the Department of Defense as instruments of national security policy were the Joint Chiefs of Staff, Central Intelligence Agency, National Security Agency, U.S. Information Agency, Agency for International Development, and dozens more government bodies. The national security state also built ties to corporations such as General Dynamics, General Electric, and Raytheon, which received much of their income from defense contracts and even shared executives through a revolving military-industrial door. Scientists and engineers also joined the partnership. In the early 1970s, at least 50 percent of America's aeronautical engineers and 30 percent of its physicists worked on military-related projects. MIT scientists and defense contractors turned Boston's Route 128 into a high-technology zone; California's Silicon Valley sprang from Stanford University's research links with defense industries.

In 1961 President Eisenhower warned against a "military-industrial complex," while others feared a "garrison state" or "warfare state." Despite the warnings, by the start of the twenty-first century, the national security state remained vigorous, a lasting legacy of the early Cold War period for a people and a nation.

For Further Reading, see page A-34 of the Appendix. For Web resources, go to http://college.hmco.com.

Reform and Conflict at Home: A Turbulent Era 1961–1974

In 1964 politics and civil rights claimed front-page news, and they were inextricably tied together. When the Democrats convened in Atlantic City, New Jersey, to pick a presidential candidate in that election year, they discovered the volatility of the civil rights issue. Two delegations had arrived from Mississippi demanding to be seated. One was all white; the other was largely African American and called itself the Mississippi Freedom Democratic Party (MFDP). The MFDP asked the convention to honor its credentials instead of those of the state's vehemently segregationist regular Democratic organization.

In Mississippi, as a result of phony literacy tests, economic intimidation, and violence, less than 7 percent of the black population could vote. Civil rights activists had decided in 1963 to conduct their own "freedom vote"—a mock election to prove, as one worker put it, "that politics is not just white folks' business." And in 1964 the MFDP ran candidates for Congress. The same year, more than a thousand northern students traveled south to Mississippi to work for the Freedom Summer Project, registering voters and organizing protests against segregation. But these challenges to white supremacy did not go unanswered. White vigilantes bombed and burned two dozen black churches, and sheriff's deputies murdered three young civil rights workers—one black and two white—in Philadelphia, Mississippi.

The Democratic Party's credentials committee met on August 22, 1964, to hear the contesting delegations. The hearings were nationally televised. Speaking for the MFDP was an inspiring figure, Fannie Lou Hamer, a forty-six-year-old African American organizer for the Student Nonviolent Coordinating Committee (SNCC). Born in 1917, she was the twentieth child of sharecropper parents. At age six, she went to work chopping and picking in the cotton fields, and by the time she was thirteen, she was pick-

Fannie Lou Hamer was an inspirational civil rights leader in Mississippi in the 1960s, and she spoke and sang gospel and freedom songs at numerous rallies for racial equality. In this photograph taken in 1966, Hamer sang at the campsite for a "march against fear" organized by James Meredith, another hero of the civil rights movement who earlier had desegregated the University of Mississippi. During the march Meredith was ambushed and shot in the back by a member of the Ku Klux Klan. (© Charmian Reading, NYC)

ing from three to four hundred pounds a day on a plantation in Sunflower County.

In the early 1960s Fannie Lou Hamer began to envision a better future through the direct action of the civil rights movement. Paraphrasing John F. Kennedy's 1961 inaugural address, she explained, "I am determined to give my part not for what the movement can do for me, but what I can do for the movement to bring about a change in the State of Mississippi." In 1962 she lost her job on the plantation when she attempted to register to vote. Then, fearing violence, she fled to a neighbor's home, which was soon riddled with bullets intended for her. The next year, Hamer was arrested with five other SNCC volunteers in Winona, Mississippi, taken to jail, and brutally assaulted by police swinging blackjacks. By 1964 Hamer had become a field worker for SNCC, known for her courage and refusal to surrender as well as for her inspiring speeches and singing. She began her speeches with a spiritual; often it was her favorite, "This Little Light of Mine."

Sitting before the credentials committee and the television cameras in Atlantic City, Hamer told the country about her experience in the Winona jail. "I was beaten until I was exhausted," she recalled. "I began to scream, and one white man got up and began to beat me on the head and tell me to hush. . . . All of this on account we wanted to register, to become first class citizens." She insisted that the MFDP—those who had fought for freedom—be seated, not those who opposed it. If "the Freedom Party is not seated now, I question America," she said. Emotion filled her voice as she asked, "Is this America, the land of the free and the home of the brave, where we have to sleep with our telephones off the hooks because our lives be threatened daily, because we want to live as decent human beings, in America?"

The MFDP did not receive justice from President Johnson or the Democratic Party. Offered a consolation prize of two seats, the MFDP refused. "We didn't come all this way for no two seats," Hamer said, "when *all* of us is tired." In that election year, Johnson would not alienate powerful southern white politicians by seating the civil rights delegation, but his action threw into question the Democrats' commitment to racial equality. It was already too late, moreover, to placate white southerners who had begun to switch to the more conservative Republican Party. Despite Johnson's capitulation to Mississippi's regular Democrats, the state's whites voted for Senator Barry Goldwater, the Republican candidate, in 1964. Civil rights had be-

come the most important political issue in the country, threatening to destroy the New Deal coalition in the South and the North.

The civil rights movement became a dynamic motive force in American society in the 1960s, helping to give birth in subsequent years to the antiwar movement, the New Left, a resurgent feminist movement, the environmental movement, and equality movements for other minorities. The civil rights movement also energized the presidential politics of John F. Kennedy and Lyndon B. Johnson. Kennedy's call for a New Frontier had inspired liberal Democrats, idealists, and brave young activists to work to eliminate poverty, segregation, and voting rights abuses. But Americans' dreams were shattered on November 22, 1963, when President Kennedy was assassinated in Dallas. For four days Americans wept, prayed, and gazed at their television sets, numbed by the unbelievable. "In retrospect," journalist Godfrey Hodgson has written, "people looked back to Friday, November 22, 1963, as the end of a time of hope, the beginning of a time of troubles."

Lyndon Johnson, who asked for national unity in the wake of the Kennedy assassination, was a strong political leader who knew what he wanted. Johnson presided over what he called the Great Society, a flood of legislation designed to eradicate poverty in the United States and guarantee equal rights to all its citizens. But even during these years of liberal triumph, anger and social tension intermittently flared into violence. Beginning with Kennedy's assassination in 1963, ten years of bloodshed—race riots, the murders of other political and civil rights leaders, and the war in Vietnam—shattered the optimism of the Kennedy and Johnson eras.

Urban blacks were angry that poverty and segregation persisted despite the passage of landmark civil rights laws, and their discontent exploded during the "long hot summers" of the 1960s. This social turbulence added to snowballing white opposition to the civil rights movement, prompting many Americans to shift to the right politically. In 1968 the Republican Richard M. Nixon was elected president, but his presidency polarized the nation still further. The presidencies of Nixon's two immediate predecessors had ended tragically: Dallas and Vietnam were the sites of their undoing. A third location, the Watergate apartment-office complex in Washington, D.C., marked Richard Nixon's downfall. In 1974, the corruption of his administration having been exposed, he resigned from office, the only American president to have done so.

IMPORTANT EVENTS

1960 Sit-ins begin in Greensboro
Birth-control pill approved for use
Kennedy elected president

1961 Freedom Rides protest segregation in transportation
President's Commission on the Status of Women established

1962 Glenn orbits globe in space capsule
Students for a Democratic Society issues Port Huron Statement
Meredith enters University of Mississippi
Baker v. Carr establishes "one person, one vote" principle

1963 Friedan's *The Feminine Mystique* published
Civil rights advocates march on Washington
Baptist church in Birmingham bombed
Kennedy assassinated; Johnson becomes president

1964 Economic Opportunity Act allocates funds to fight poverty
Civil Rights Act outlaws discrimination in jobs and public accommodations
Twenty-fourth Amendment outlaws the poll tax in federal elections
Riots break out in first of the "long hot summers"
Hamer speaks on behalf of Mississippi Freedom Democratic Party at Democratic convention
Free Speech movement begins at Berkeley
Johnson elected president

1965 Malcolm X assassinated
Voting Rights Act allows federal supervision of voting registration
Medicare and Medicaid programs begun
Elementary and Secondary Education Act provides federal aid to education
Watts race riot leaves thirty-four dead
Immigration and Nationality Act lowers barriers to certain ethnic and racial groups

1966 National Organization for Women founded
Miranda v. Arizona requires police to inform suspects of their rights

1967 Race riots erupt in Newark, Detroit, and other cities
Twenty-fifth Amendment establishes the order of presidential succession

1968 U.S.S. *Pueblo* captured by North Korea
Tet offensive causes fear of losing war
King assassinated
African Americans riot in 168 cities and towns
Civil Rights Act bans housing discrimination
Antiwar protests escalate
R. Kennedy assassinated
Violence erupts at Democratic convention
Nixon elected president

1969 Stonewall riot sparked by police harassment of homosexuals
Apollo 11 lands on moon
400,000 gather at Woodstock festival
Moratorium Day calls for end to war

1970 United States invades Cambodia
Students killed at Kent State and Jackson State Universities
First Earth Day celebrated
Environmental Protection Agency created

1971 *Pentagon Papers* published
Twenty-sixth Amendment extends vote to eighteen-year-olds
Inmates revolt at Attica prison
Swann v. Charlotte-Mecklenberg upholds North Carolina desegregation plan

1972 Nixon visits China and Soviet Union
Congress approves ERA
Wallace shot and paralyzed
"Plumbers" break into Watergate
Revenue sharing distributes funds to states
Nixon reelected

1973 Watergate burglars tried
Ervin chairs Watergate hearings
White House aides Ehrlichman and Haldeman resign
Roe v. Wade legalizes abortion
War Powers Act passed
Agnew resigns; Ford named vice president
Saturday Night Massacre provokes outcry

1974 Supreme Court orders Nixon to release White House tapes
House Judiciary Committee votes to impeach Nixon
Nixon resigns; Ford becomes president
Ford pardons Nixon
Freedom of Information Act passed over Ford's veto

Battered by more than a decade of turmoil, many Americans became cynical and ceased to believe in the American Dream. ■

Civil Rights and the New Frontier

President John F. Kennedy was, as the writer Norman Mailer observed, "our leading man." Young, handsome, and vigorous, the new chief executive was the first president born in the twentieth century. Kennedy had a genuinely inquiring mind, and as a patron of the arts he brought wit and sophistication to the White House. Kennedy was born to wealth and politics: his Irish American grandfather had been mayor of Boston, and his millionaire father, Joseph P. Kennedy, had served as ambassador to Great Britain. In 1946 the young Kennedy, having returned from the Second World War a naval hero, perpetuated the family tradition by campaigning to represent Boston in the House of Representatives. He won easily, served three terms in the House, and in 1952 was elected to the Senate.

President John F. Kennedy, his wife Jacqueline, and their two young children, John Jr. and Caroline, symbolized youthful energy and idealism. This photograph was taken at their vacation home at Hyannisport on Cape Cod in July 1963.   (John F. Kennedy Library)

As a Democrat, Kennedy inherited the New Deal commitment to America's social welfare system. He generally cast liberal votes in line with the prolabor sentiments of his low-income, blue-collar constituents. But he avoided controversial issues such as civil rights and the censure of Joseph McCarthy. Kennedy won a Pulitzer Prize for *Profiles in Courage* (1956), a study of politicians who had acted on principle, but he shaded the truth when he claimed sole authorship of the book, which had been written largely by his staff. As one critic put it, he himself showed "too much profile and not enough courage." Kennedy nevertheless enjoyed an enthusiastic following, especially after his landslide reelection to the Senate in 1958.

Kennedy's vitality and style captured the imagination of many Americans. In a departure from the Eisenhower administration's staid, conservative image, the new president surrounded himself with young men of intellectual verve who proclaimed that they had fresh ideas for invigorating the nation; the writer David Halberstam called them "the best and the brightest" (Kennedy appointed only one woman to a significant position). Secretary of Defense Robert McNamara (age forty-four) had been an assistant professor at Harvard at twenty-four and later the whiz-kid president of the Ford Motor Company. Kennedy's special assistant for national security affairs, McGeorge Bundy (age forty-one) had become a Harvard dean at thirty-four with only a bachelor's degree. Kennedy himself was only forty-three, and his brother Robert, the attorney general, was thirty-five.

"The Best and the Brightest"

The New Frontier

Kennedy's ambitious program, the New Frontier, promised more than the president could deliver: an end to racial discrimination, federal aid to education, medical care for the elderly, and government action to halt the recession the country was suffering. Only eight months into his first year, it was evident that Kennedy lacked the ability to move Congress, which was dominated by a conservative coalition of Republicans and southern Democrats.

Struggling to appease conservative southern members of Congress, the new president appointed five die-hard segregationists to the federal bench in the Deep South, and he pursued civil rights with a notable lack of vigor. Kennedy did establish the President's Committee on Equal Employment Opportunity to eliminate racial discrimination in government hiring. But he waited until late 1962 before honoring a 1960 campaign pledge to issue an executive order forbidding segregation in federally subsidized housing. The struggle for racial equality was the most important domestic issue of the time, and Kennedy's performance disheartened civil rights advocates.

Despite President Kennedy's lack of support, African American civil rights activists in the early 1960s continued their struggle through the tactic of nonviolent civil disobedience. Volunteers organized by SNCC and by the Southern Christian Leadership Conference (SCLC), headed by Reverend Martin Luther King, Jr., deliberately violated segregation laws by sitting in at whites-only lunch counters, libraries, and bus stations in the South. The Congress of Racial Equality (CORE) initiated the Freedom Rides in May 1961: an integrated group of thirteen people boarded a bus in Washington, D.C., and traveled into the South, where they braved attacks by white mobs for daring to desegregate interstate transportation.

In the South many black high-school and college students joined SNCC, established in 1960 soon after the sit-ins began in Greensboro, North Carolina (see page 804). These young people walked the dusty back roads of Mississippi and Georgia, encouraging African Americans to resist segregation and register to vote. Some SNCC volunteers were white, and some were from the North; but most were black southerners, and many were from low-income families. These volunteers understood from experience how racism, powerlessness, and poverty intersected in the lives of African Americans.

Student Nonviolent Coordinating Committee

As the civil rights movement gained momentum, President Kennedy gradually made a commitment to first-class citizenship for blacks. In 1962 he ordered U.S. marshals to protect James Meredith, the first African American student to attend the University of Mississippi. The

"I Have a Dream"

A historic moment for the civil rights movement was the March on Washington of August 28, 1963. The Reverend Martin Luther King, Jr. *(center),* joined a quarter of a million black people and white people in their march for racial equality. Addressing civil rights supporters, and the nation, from the steps of the Lincoln Memorial, King delivered his "I Have a Dream" speech.   (R. W. Kelley, LIFE magazine © Time, Inc.)

following spring, under court order, federal officials ignored the defiant governor of Alabama, George C. Wallace, and forced the desegregation of the University of Alabama. And in June 1963 Kennedy finally requested legislation to outlaw racial discrimination in employment and racial segregation in public accommodations. When more than 250,000 people, black and white, gathered at the Lincoln Memorial for a March on Washington that August, they did so with the knowledge that President Kennedy was at last on their side. They also heard a most memorable speech: "I have a dream," the civil rights movement's inspirational leader, Martin Luther King, Jr., told the crowd, "that my four little children will one day live in a nation where they will not be judged by the color of their skin but by the content of their character."

The television nightly news programs brought the civil rights struggles into Americans' homes. The story was sometimes grisly. In 1963 Medgar Evers, director of the NAACP in Mississippi, was gunned down in his own driveway. The same year police in Birmingham, Alabama, under the command of Sheriff "Bull" Connor attacked nonviolent civil rights demonstrators, including children, with snarling dogs, fire hoses, and cattle prods. Then two horrifying events helped to convince reluctant politicians that action on civil rights was long overdue. In September white terrorists exploded a bomb during Sunday morning services at Birmingham's Sixteenth Street Baptist Church. Sunday school was in session, and four black girls were killed. A little more than two months later, John Kennedy was assassinated in Dallas.

The first dreadful flash from Dallas clattered over newsroom Teletype machines across the country at

The Kennedy Assassination

1:34 p.m. Eastern Standard Time, November 22, 1963. Broadcast immediately on radio and television, the news was soon on the streets. Time stopped for Americans, and they experienced what psychologists call flashbulb memory, the freeze-framing of an exceptionally emotional event down to the most incidental detail. For an earlier generation, the indelible memory was of December 7, 1941. Now it was November 22, 1963, the day John Kennedy's promise was snuffed out.

In New York City a driver stopped in the middle of a busy intersection and ran over to a sidewalk luncheonette. "Is it true?" he shouted. Without looking up, the counterman replied, "Yes, he's dead." The man returned to his car and slumped over the wheel, obliv-

ious to the impatient honking around him. Ken Kesey's play *One Flew over the Cuckoo's Nest* had just opened on Broadway, and Kesey and a couple of friends were driving triumphantly back to the West Coast. They heard the news in Pennsylvania. As "we stopped in at service stations and Howard Johnson's and little fast-food places across the United States," Kesey later recalled, "a really profound thing happened to us. We felt like we were seeing the real soul of America with its shirt torn open in grief."

Kennedy's murder still baffles many Americans. Was the accused assassin, Lee Harvey Oswald, acting alone or as part of a conspiracy?

Who Killed President Kennedy?

What was his motive? Two days later, in full view of millions of TV viewers, Oswald himself was shot dead by a nightclub owner and small-time Mafia figure named Jack Ruby. The same questions were asked again: What was Ruby's motive? Was he silencing Oswald to prevent him from implicating others? Two years later, the seven-person Warren Commission, headed by Earl Warren, Chief Justice of the Supreme Court, issued a report that concluded Oswald had acted alone. But many Americans questioned this finding.

Historians have wondered what John Kennedy would have accomplished had he lived. Although his legislative achievements were meager, he inspired genuine idealism in Americans. When Kennedy exhorted Americans in his inaugural address to "Ask not what your country can do for you; ask what you can do for your country," tens of thousands volunteered to spend two years of their lives in the Peace Corps. "We had such faith in what Kennedy was doing," recalled one volunteer, "and we all wanted to be a part of it."

Kennedy also promoted a sense of national purpose through his vigorous support of the space program. America lagged behind the Soviet Union, which sent a missile carrying cosmonaut Yuri Gagarin into orbit around the earth in April 1961. But Americans celebrated a month later when Alan Shepard, one of the seven original astronauts, rode the Mercury 3 missile into space. After marine lieutenant colonel John Glenn orbited the globe in a space capsule in February 1962, the United States accelerated its Apollo program, which developed more powerful rocket boosters and lunar landing vehicles for the first astronauts on the moon. Americans embraced Kennedy's challenge to put a man on the moon before the Soviets did and by the end of the decade. And on July 20, 1969, that challenge was met when Apollo 11's lunar module, with two American astronauts aboard, landed on the moon.

In recent years, writers have drawn attention to Kennedy's recklessness in world events, such as authorizing the Bay of Pigs invasion of 1961 (see page 888) and CIA attempts to assassinate Cuba's leader Fidel Castro. They also have criticized his timidity in civil rights and have pointed to his extramarital sex life as evidence of a serious character flaw. It is clear, however, that Kennedy had begun to grow as president during his last few months in office. He made a moving appeal for racial equality and called for reductions in Cold War tensions. Partly because of the Kennedy aura of glamour and youth and hope, John Kennedy acquired an even loftier reputation in death than he had enjoyed in life. And in a peculiar way he accomplished more in death than in life. In the postassassination atmosphere of grief and remorse, Lyndon Johnson pushed through Congress practically the entire New Frontier agenda.

Kennedy in Retrospect

The Great Society and the Triumph of Liberalism

The new president was a big man and a passionate one. As Senate majority leader from 1954 to 1960, Lyndon Johnson had learned how to manipulate people and power to achieve his ends. "This ponderous . . . Texan knows more about the sources of power in the political world of Washington than any president in this century," wrote columnists Rowland Evans and Robert Novak. "He can be gentle and solicitous as a nurse, but as ruthless and deceptive as a riverboat gambler." In the aftermath of the assassination, Johnson resolved to unite the country behind the unfulfilled legislative program of the martyred president. More than that, he wanted to realize Roosevelt's and Truman's unmet goals. He called his new program the Great Society.

Johnson made civil rights his top legislative priority. "No memorial oration or eulogy," he told a joint session of Congress five days after the assassination, "could more eloquently honor President Kennedy's memory than the earliest passage of the civil rights bill." Within months Johnson had signed into law the Civil Rights Act of

Civil Rights Act of 1964

On July 20, 1969, American astronauts Neil A. Armstrong and Edwin E. (Buzz) Aldrin, Jr. *(shown above),* plant an American flag on the moon, thus fulfilling President John F. Kennedy's pledge to land a man on the moon by the end of the 1960s.   (NASA)

1964, which outlawed discrimination on the basis of race, color, religion, sex, or national origin, not only in public accommodations but also in employment. The act also authorized the government to withhold funds from public agencies that discriminated on the basis of race, and it empowered the attorney general to guarantee voting rights and end school segregation. In 1964 African Americans gained two additional victories. First, President Johnson appointed an Equal Employment Opportunity Commission to investigate and judge complaints of job discrimination. Second, the states ratified the Twenty-fourth Amendment to the Constitution, which outlawed the poll tax as a prerequisite for voting in federal elections.

Surrounded by an illustrious group of civil rights leaders and members of Congress, President Lyndon B. Johnson signs the Civil Rights Act of 1964. Standing behind the president is Reverend Martin Luther King, Jr.   (Corbis-Bettmann)

Johnson enunciated another priority in his first State of the Union address: "The administration today, here and now, declares unconditional war on poverty." Eight months later, he signed into law the Economic Opportunity Act of 1964, which allocated almost $1 billion for programs to assist the poor. The act became the opening salvo in Johnson's War on Poverty.

In the year following Kennedy's death, Johnson sought to govern by appealing to the shared values and aspirations of the majority of the nation for continued economic growth and social justice. His lopsided victory over his conservative Republican opponent in 1964, Senator Barry Goldwater of Arizona, indicates that he succeeded. Johnson garnered 61 percent of the popular vote and the electoral votes of all but six states. Riding on Johnson's coattails, the Democrats won large majorities in both the House (295 to 140) and the Senate (68 to 32). Johnson recognized that the opportunity to push through further reform had arrived. Congress responded in 1965 and 1966 with the most sweeping reform legislation since 1935.

Election of 1964

Three bills enacted in 1965 were legislative milestones: the Medicare and Medicaid programs insured the elderly against medical and hospital bills and assisted the needy and disabled in paying for medical care; the Elementary and Secondary Education Act provided for general federal aid to education for the first time; and the Voting Rights Act of 1965 empowered the attorney general to supervise voter registration in areas where fewer than half of the minority residents of voting age were registered (see Map 30.1). In 1960 only 29 percent of the South's African American population was registered to vote; when Johnson left office in 1969, the proportion was approaching two-thirds. Even in Mississippi, one of the most resistant states, black registration figures grew from 7 percent in 1964 to 59 percent in 1968.

Voting Rights Act of 1965

The flurry of legislation enacted into law during Johnson's presidency was staggering: establishment of the Department of Housing and Urban Development, the Department of Transportation, and the National Endowments for the Arts and Humanities; water- and air-quality improvement acts; and appropriations for

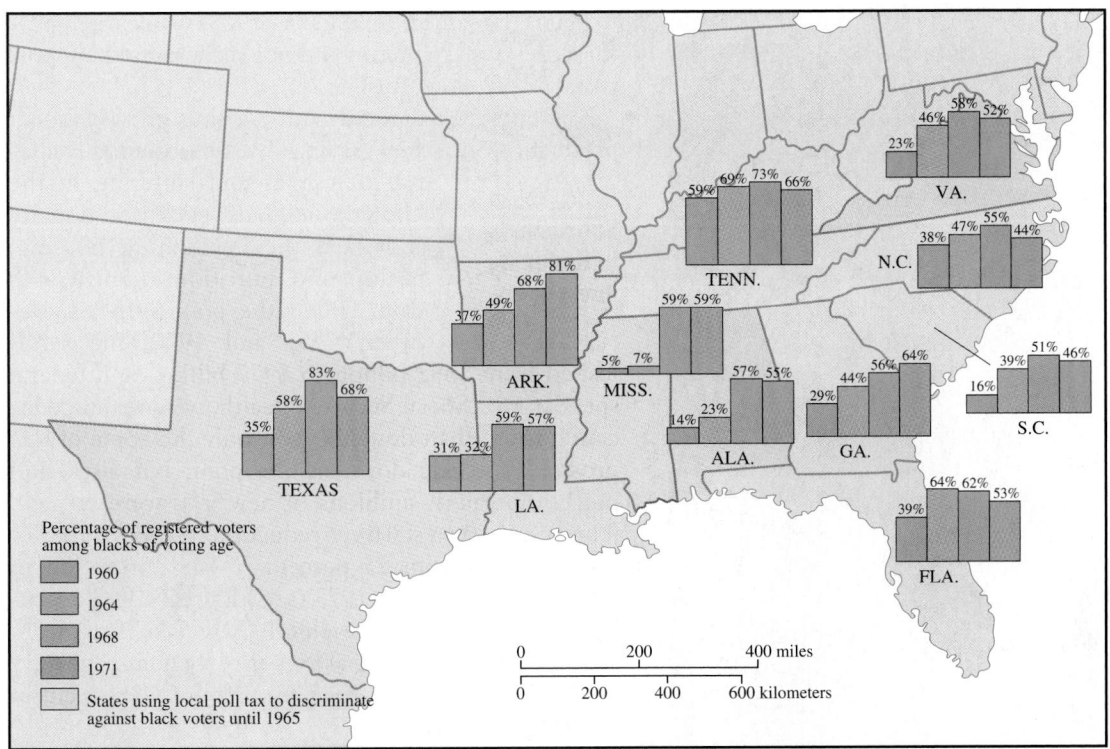

Map 30.1   African American Voting Rights, 1960–1971   After passage of the 1965 Voting Rights Act, African American registration skyrocketed in Mississippi and Alabama and rose substantially in other southern states.   (Source: Harold W. Stanley, *Voter Mobilization and the Politics of Race: The South and Universal Suffrage, 1952–1984* [Praeger Publishers, an imprint of Greenwood Publishing Group, Westport, CT, 1987], p. 97. Copyright © 1987 by Harold W. Stanley. Used with permission.)

the most ambitious federal housing program since 1949, including rent supplements to low-income families. The Immigration and Nationality Act of 1965, the first overhaul of immigration law in forty years, lowered the barriers erected by the national origins quota system, which had severely restricted, or excluded altogether, certain ethnic and racial groups (see page 681). In 1968 Johnson signed another Civil Rights Act—his third—banning racial and religious discrimination in the sale and rental of housing. Another provision of this legislation, known as the Indian Bill of Rights, extended those constitutional protections to Native Americans living under tribal self-government on reservations.

By far the most ambitious of Johnson's initiatives was the War on Poverty. Beginning with a $1 billion appropriation in 1964, the War on Poverty evolved in 1965 and 1966 to include the Job Corps, to provide

War on Poverty

marketable skills, work experience, and remedial education for young people; Project Head Start, to prepare preschoolers from low-income families for grade school; and Upward Bound, to help high-school students from low-income families to prepare for a college education. Other antipoverty programs were Legal Services for the Poor, Volunteers in Service to America (VISTA), and the Model Cities program, which channeled federal funds to upgrade employment, housing, education, and health in targeted urban neighborhoods.

The War on Poverty was a mixed success. For one thing, it was politically volatile because its "community-action programs" angered powerful mayors: it deliberately bypassed them and encouraged "maximum feasible participation" in decision making by the poor themselves, who served on antipoverty governing boards that allocated large sums of money. Furthermore, confusion abounded in the ambitious program.

This three-year-old Hispanic girl learns to read in a Head Start program. One of several programs established by the 1964 Economic Opportunity Act, Head Start prepared preschoolers from low-income families for grade school. (E. Crews/The Image Works)

Not even R. Sargent Shriver, who administered the War on Poverty as head of the Office of Economic Opportunity (OEO), could deny this: "It's like we . . . launched a half-dozen rockets at once," he later conceded. Another failing was that the War on Poverty did little to reduce poverty in rural areas or to discourage the South-to-North migration that was worsening already overwhelming poverty in northern inner cities.

Another group that remained poor despite antipoverty initiatives consisted of women and children living in female-headed families; they constituted 40 percent of the poor in the United States. The economic boom that lasted from 1963 to 1969 lifted 12 million people in male-headed families out of poverty. Left behind were 11 million in families headed by women (the same number as in 1963) who earned pitiful wages and frequently did not receive child-support payments from ex-husbands.

Even so, in tandem with a rising gross national product (GNP), the War on Poverty substantially alleviated hunger and suffering in the United States. Its legislation directly addressed the debilitating housing, health, and nutritional deficiencies from which the poor suffered. Between 1965 and 1970, the GNP leaped from $685 billion to $977 billion, and federal spending for Social Security, health, welfare, and education more than doubled. Not only did some of this prosperity trickle down to the poor, but also—and more important—millions of new jobs were created. The result was a startling reduction in the number of poor people, from 25 percent of the population in 1962 to 11 percent in 1973 (see Figure 30.1). Particularly fortunate were the elderly, who benefited from large increases in Social Security benefits; poverty among the elderly dropped from about 40 percent in 1960 to 16 percent in 1974.

Successes in Reducing Poverty

The period of liberal ascendancy represented by the War on Poverty was short-lived; most of the Great Society's legislative achievements occurred in 1964, 1965, and 1966 (see Table 30.1). Disillusioned with America's deepening involvement in Vietnam (see Chapter 31) and upset by the violence of urban race riots (see page 865), many of Johnson's allies began to reject both him and his liberal consensus.

One branch of government, however, maintained the liberal tradition: the Supreme Court. Under the intellectual and moral leadership of Chief Justice Earl Warren, the Court in the 1960s was disposed by political conviction and a belief in judicial activism to play a central role in the resurgence of liberalism. In 1962 the Court began handing down a series of landmark decisions. *Baker v. Carr* (1962) and subsequent rulings established that the principle of "one person, one vote" must prevail at both the state and the national levels. This decision required the reapportionment of state legislatures by shifting seats from lightly populated rural areas to the burgeoning cities, so that each representative would serve the same number of constituents. The Court also outlawed required prayers and Bible reading in public schools, explaining that such practices imposed an "indirect coercive pressure upon religious minorities."

The Warren Court

The Court also attacked the legal underpinning of the anti-Communist crusade, ruling in 1965 that a person need not register with the government as a member of a subversive organization because doing so would violate constitutional safeguards against self-incrimination. In *Griswold v. Connecticut* (1965), the Court ruled that a state law prohibiting the use of contraceptives by married couples violated "a marital right of privacy" and was unconstitutional. The Court upheld the Civil Rights Act of 1964 and the Voting Rights Act of 1965. In other rulings that particularly upset conservatives, the Court decreed that books, magazines, and films could not be banned as obscene unless they were found to be "utterly without redeeming social value."

Civil Rights Rulings

Perhaps most controversial of all was the Court's transformation of the criminal justice system. Beginning with *Gideon v. Wainwright* (1963), the Court ruled that a poor person charged with a felony had the right to a state-appointed lawyer. In *Escobedo v. Illinois* (1964), it decreed that the accused had a right to counsel during interrogation and a right to remain silent. *Miranda v. Arizona* (1966) established that police had to inform criminal suspects that they had these rights and that any statements they made could be used against them. Critics denounced the decisions as victories for criminals, and the right-wing John Birch Society campaigned to impeach Earl Warren.

Despite conservatives' demands for Warren's removal, constitutional historians consider him one of the two most influential chief justices in the nation's history (the other was John Marshall). Whether or not one approved of the decisions of the Warren Court (which ended with Warren's retirement in 1969), its effect on the American people is undeniable.

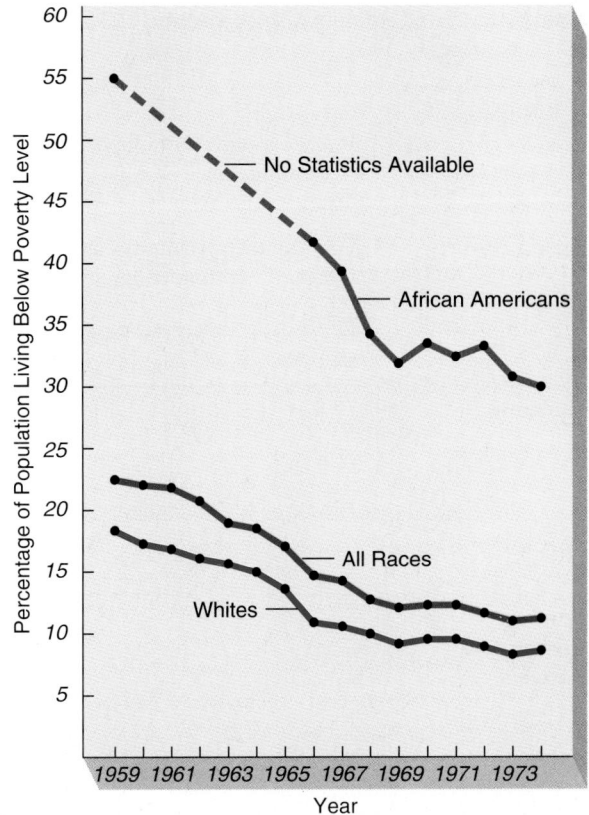

Figure 30.1   Poverty in America for Whites, African Americans, and All Races, 1959–1974   Because of rising levels of economic prosperity, combined with the impact of Great Society programs, the percentage of Americans living in poverty in 1974 was half as high as in 1959. African Americans still were far more likely than white Americans to be poor. In 1959 more than half of all blacks (55.1 percent) were poor; in 1974 the figure remained high (30.3 percent). The government did not record data on African American poverty for the years 1960 through 1965.

Civil Rights Disillusionment, Race Riots, and Black Power

Even while the civil rights movement was winning important victories in the mid-1960s, some activists began to grumble that the federal government was not to be trusted. Fannie Lou Hamer and the Mississippi Freedom Democratic Party felt betrayed by Lyndon Johnson and the Democrats at the 1964 Atlantic City convention, and evidence suggested that the Federal Bureau of Investigation was hostile to the civil rights movement. Indeed, it turned out that at least one FBI informant not only was a member of the Ku Klux Klan but also was a terrorist who instigated violence against volunteers in the civil rights movement. FBI director J. Edgar Hoover was a racist, activists charged, and they were disturbed by rumors (later confirmed) that Hoover had wiretapped and bugged Martin Luther King, Jr.'s hotel rooms and planted allegations in the newspapers about his sexual improprieties.

The year 1964 witnessed the first of the "long hot summers" of race riots in northern cities. In Harlem

Table 30.1   Great Society Achievements, 1964–1966

	1964	1965	1966
Civil Rights	Civil Rights Act Equal Employment Opportunity Commission Twenty-fourth Amendment	Voting Rights Act	
War on Poverty	Economic Opportunity Act Office of Economic Opportunity Job Corps Legal Services for the Poor VISTA		Model Cities
Education		Elementary and Secondary Education Act Head Start Upward Bound	
Environment		Water Quality Act Air Quality Act	Clean Water Restoration Act
New Government Agencies		Department of Housing and Urban Development National Endowments for the Arts and Humanities	Department of Transportation
Miscellaneous		Medicare and Medicaid Immigration and Nationality Act	

The Great Society of the mid-1960s saw the biggest burst of reform legislation since the New Deal of the 1930s.

Explosion of Black Anger

and Rochester in New York, and in several cities in New Jersey, brutal actions by white police officers, including vicious, unprovoked beatings in police stations, sparked riots in black neighborhoods. African Americans deeply resented the unnecessary force that police sometimes used. As the black writer James Baldwin put it, the white officers patrolling black neighborhoods represented "the force of the white world."

Whites wondered why African Americans were venting their frustration violently at a time when they were making real progress in the civil rights struggle. The civil rights movement, however, had focused mostly on the South, aiming to abolish Jim Crow and black disfranchisement. In the North, African Americans could vote, but many were living in dire poverty. The median income of northern blacks was little more than half that of northern whites, and their unemployment rate was twice as high. Many African American families, particularly those headed by women, lived in perpetual poverty. The primary assistance program, Aid to Families with Dependent Children (AFDC), failed to meet the needs of the poor. AFDC payments were inadequate to cover a family's rent, utilities, and household expenses, let alone its food.

Northern blacks, surveying the economic and civil rights gains of the 1960s, wondered when they, too, would benefit from the Great Society. Concentrated in the inner cities, they looked around the ghettos in which they lived and knew their circumstances were deteriorating. Their neighborhoods were more segregated than ever; in increasing numbers during the 1960s, whites had responded to the continuing black migration from the South by fleeing to the suburbs. And as inner-city neighborhoods became all black, so did the neighborhood schools. "It doesn't cost anything to move a few feet along a hamburger counter to make room for a Negro," one writer observed. "But the cost—economic, social, psychological—of abolishing forever a Negro ghetto of half a million souls is only now becoming apparent."

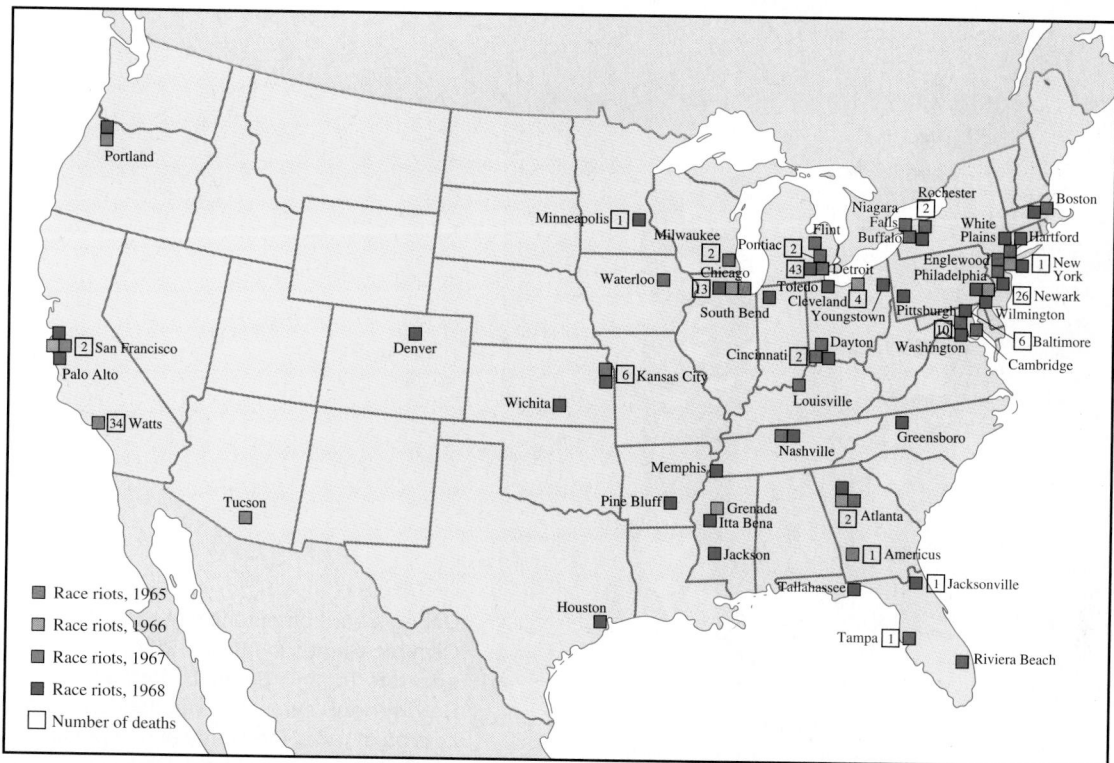

Map 30.2   Race Riots, 1965–1968   The first major race riot of the 1960s exploded in the Los Angeles neighborhood of Watts in 1965. The bloodiest riots of 1967 were in Newark, New Jersey, and Detroit. Scores of riots erupted in the aftermath of Martin Luther King, Jr.'s assassination in 1968.

If 1964 was fiery and violent, 1965 was even more so. In August an altercation between blacks and police sparked rioting in the Watts section of Los Angeles; thirty-four people were killed (see Map 30.2). White mobs did not initiate the violence (as they had done in Chicago in 1919 and Detroit in 1943); instead, blacks exploded in anger over their joblessness and lack of opportunity, as well as police brutality. They looted white-owned stores, set fires, and threw rocks at police and firefighters. The police retaliated, and twenty-eight blacks died in the Watts riot.

Race Riots

Other cities exploded in riots between 1966 and 1968. In July 1967 twenty-six people were killed in street battles between blacks and police and army troops in Newark, New Jersey. A week later a race riot in Detroit led to the deaths of forty-three people. In 1968 the National Advisory Commission on Civil Disorders, chaired by Governor Otto Kerner of Illinois, released a report blaming white racism for the riots: "The nation is rapidly moving toward two increasingly separate Americas . . . a white society principally located in suburbs . . . and a Negro society largely concentrated within large central cities."

Clearly, many blacks, especially in the North, were beginning to question whether the nonviolent civil rights movement was serving their needs. In 1963 Martin Luther King, Jr., had appealed to whites' humanitarian instincts in his "I Have a Dream" speech. Now another voice was beginning to be heard, one that urged blacks to seize their freedom "by any means necessary." It was the voice of Malcolm X, a one-time pimp and street hustler who had converted while in prison to the Nation of Islam faith, whose followers were commonly known as the Black Muslims.

A small sect that espoused black pride and separatism from white society, the Black Muslims condemned the "white devil" as the chief source of evil in the world, and they exhorted blacks to lead sober lives

During award ceremonies at the 1968 Olympic Games in Mexico City, American sprinters Tommie Smith *(center)* and John Carlos *(right)* extend gloved hands skyward to protest racial inequality and express Black Power. In retaliation, Olympic officials suspended Smith and Carlos, but other African American athletes emulated them by repeating the clenched-fist salute on the victory stand. (Wide World Photos, Inc.)

Malcolm X

and practice thrift. By the early 1960s Malcolm X had become the Black Muslims' chief spokesperson, and his advice was straightforward: "If someone puts a hand on you, send him to the cemetery." But Malcolm X was murdered in early 1965. His assassins were Black Muslims who believed he had betrayed their cause because he said he had met whites who were not devils and had expressed cautious support for the nonviolent civil rights movement. Still, for both blacks and whites, Malcolm X symbolized black defiance and self-respect. A compelling figure in life, in death he would become a hero to increasing numbers of black nationalists and proponents of Black Power.

A year after Malcolm X's death, Stokely Carmichael, chairman of SNCC, denounced "the betrayal of black dreams by white America" and called on African Americans to assert "Black Power." To be truly free

Black Power

from white oppression, Carmichael proclaimed, blacks had to elect black candidates, organize their own schools, and control their own institutions. Several influential organizations that previously had been committed to racial integration and nonviolence embraced Black Power. SNCC in 1966 and CORE in 1967 expelled their white members and repudiated integration, arguing that black people needed power, not white friendship.

To many white Americans, one of the most fearsome of the new groups was the Black Panther Party. Blending black nationalism and revolutionary communism, the Panthers dedicated themselves to destroying both capitalism and "the military arm of our oppressors," the police in the ghettos. The Panthers defied authority and carried rifles, but they also instituted free breakfast and healthcare programs for ghetto children, taught courses in African American history, and demanded jobs and decent housing for the poor. What particularly worried white parents was that some of their own children agreed with the Panthers. Called the New Left, this vocal subset of the baby-boom generation set out to "change the system."

The New Left and the Counterculture

 "I'm tired of reading history," Mario Savio, a graduate student at the University of California, complained in a letter to a friend in 1964. "I want to make it." Within a few months Savio realized his ambition as a leader of the campus Free Speech movement. After teaching in SNCC's Mississippi Freedom Summer Project, Savio and others returned to Berkeley convinced that the power structure that dominated blacks' lives also controlled the bureaucratic machinery of the university.

In fact, the University of California was a model university in 1964, with a worldwide reputation for excellence and public service. Its chancellor, the economist Clark Kerr, had written approvingly that higher education had become "a component part of the 'military-industrial complex,'" and he likened the "multiversity" with its many separate colleges and research institutes to a big business. But its strength was also its weakness. The largest single campus in the country, with tens of thousands of students, Berkeley had become hopelessly impersonal by the 1960s. Some students complained that they felt like cogs in a machine.

The struggle at Berkeley began when the university administration yielded to pressure from political conservatives and banned recruitment by civil rights and antiwar organizations in Sproul Plaza, the students' traditional gathering place. Savio denounced the ban, saying that the time had come for students to "put [their] bodies against the gears . . . and make the machine stop until we are free." Militant students defied Kerr's ban; the administration suspended them or had them arrested. In December the Free Speech movement seized and occupied the main administration building. Governor Pat Brown dispatched state police to Berkeley, and more than eight hundred people were arrested. Angry students shut down classes for several days in protest.

Free Speech Movement

The willingness of those in positions of authority to mobilize the police against unruly but not violent students was shocking and radicalizing to many young people. Having grown up comfortable and even indulged, they soon found themselves treated like criminals for questioning authority. By the end of the decade, the activism born at Berkeley would spread to hundreds of other campuses as students actively opposed what they considered a criminal war in Vietnam and racial injustice in their own country.

Two years earlier, another group of students had founded Students for a Democratic Society (SDS). Like their leaders Tom Hayden and Al Haber, most SDS members were white, middle-class college students. In 1962, meeting in Port Huron, Michigan, the SDS adopted a statement of principles. "We are people of this generation," the Port Huron Statement asserted, "bred in at least modest comfort, housed now in the universities, looking uncomfortably to the world we inherit." The statement condemned racism, poverty in the midst of plenty, and the Cold War. SDS sought nothing less than the revitalization of democracy by wresting power from the corporations, the military, and the politicians and returning it to the people.

Students for a Democratic Society and the New Left

Inspired by the Free Speech Movement and SDS, a minority of students identified themselves as members of the "New Left." The New Left was united in its hatred of racism and the Vietnam War, but it divided along philosophical and political lines. Some radicals were Marxists, others black nationalists, anarchists, or pacifists. Some believed in pursuing social change through negotiation; others were revolutionaries who regarded compromise as impossible.

As the slogan "Make Love, Not War" suggests, the New Left and the counterculture discovered a common cause as the war in Vietnam escalated. Drugs and sexuality also were central to the "hippie" experience. Exhorted by Timothy Leary— a former Harvard instructor and advocate of expanded consciousness through use of LSD and other mind-altering drugs—to "turn on, tune in, drop out," millions of students experimented with marijuana and hallucinogenic drugs. Young people's drug experiences and experiments with communal living persuaded them that they lived in a new era unconnected to the past. In fact, in a list of twenty-one academic subjects, students in the sixties ranked history "the most irrelevant."

Countercultural Revolution

Inspired by Ken Kesey and his Merry Pranksters, who traveled in a 1939 International Harvester school bus, hippies seemed drawn to buses. This bus, named "The Road Hog," carries members of the New Buffalo Commune in the 1968 Fourth of July parade in El Rito, Mexico. (Lisa Law/Image Works)

Music more than anything else expressed the countercultural assault on the status quo. Bob Dylan promised revolutionary answers "blowin' in the wind," and young people cheered Janis Joplin, who brought African American blues to white Americans. Like sex and drugs, the music of the 1960s represented a quest to redefine reality and create a more just and joyful society. Rock festivals became cultural watersheds. In 1969 at Woodstock in upstate New York, more than four hundred thousand people ignored or reveled in rain and mud for days, without shelter and without violence. A number of them began to dream of a peaceful "Woodstock nation" based on love, drugs, and rock music.

Rock 'n' Roll

Some young people tried to construct alternative ways of life. In the Haight-Ashbury section of San Francisco, "flower children" created an urban subculture as distinctive as that of any Chinatown or Little Italy. "Hashbury" inspired numerous other communal

living experiments. The counterculture represented only a small proportion of American youth, but to middle-class parents, hippies seemed to be everywhere.

The so-called generation gap was yawning wide, but most disturbing to parents were the casual sexual mores that young people were adopting. In 1960 the government approved the birth-control pill, and use of the pill accelerated among young people. For many young people, living together no longer equaled living in sin; and as attitudes toward premarital sex changed, so did notions about homosexuality and sex roles.

Sexuality

The militancy of the 1960s helped inspire the gay rights movement. Homosexuals had long feared that disclosing their sexual orientation would mean losing not only their jobs but even their friends and families. That attitude began to change in June 1969. In New York's Greenwich

Gay Rights Movement

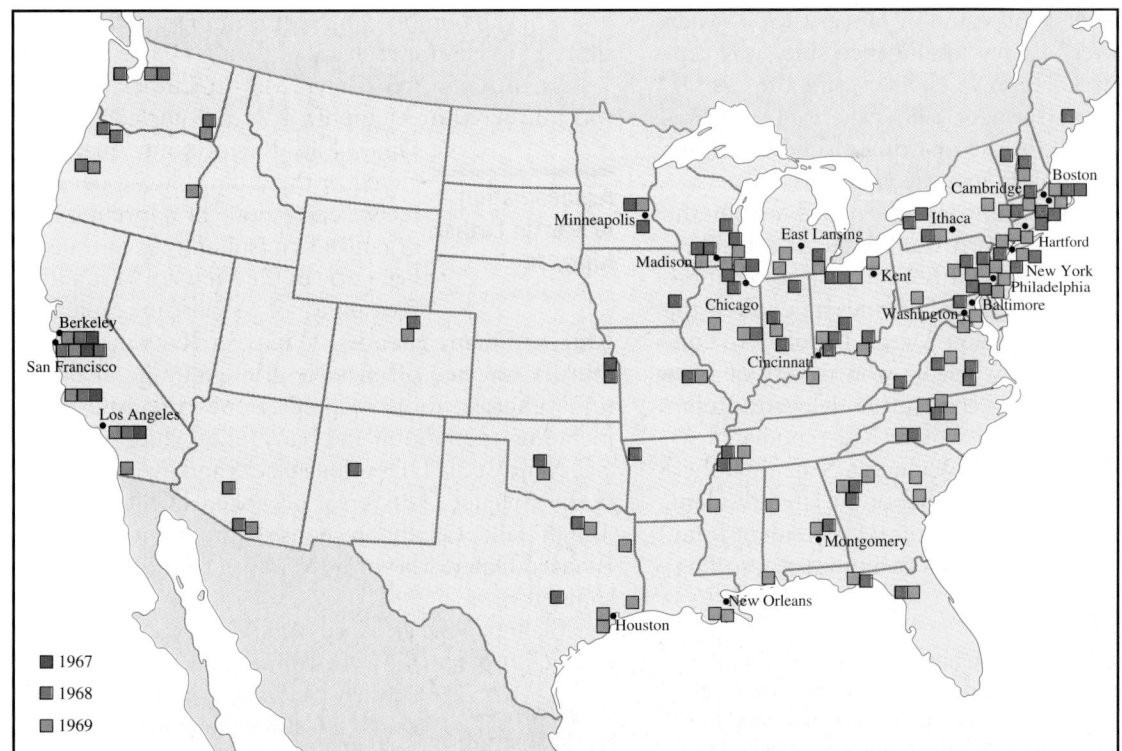

Map 30.3   Disturbances on College and University Campuses, 1967–1969   Students on campuses from coast to coast protested against the Vietnam War. Some protests were peaceful; others erupted into violent confrontations between protesters and police and army troops.

Village, a riot erupted when police raided the Stonewall Inn, a gay bar on Christopher Street, and were greeted with a volley of beer bottles hurled by patrons tired of police harassment. Rioting continued into the night, and graffiti calling for "Gay Power" appeared along Christopher Street. The Stonewall riot, as historian John D'Emilio has written, "marked a critical divide in the politics and consciousness of homosexuals and lesbians. A small, thinly spread reform effort suddenly grew into a large, grass-roots movement for liberation . . . as a furtive subculture moved aggressively into the open."

During Lyndon Johnson's presidency, antiwar marches and demonstrations became a widespread protest tactic (see Map 30.3), and students on campuses across the country held teach-ins—open forums for discussion of the war by students, professors, and guest speakers. Some young men fled the draft by moving abroad—mostly to Canada and Scandinavia—while others protested, violently and nonviolently, at local draft board offices.

Antiwar Protests

The Johnson administration charged that such acts threatened the nation's war-making powers.

By this time, however, growing numbers of Americans, young and old, had quit believing their elected leaders. In 1965, having ordered combat troops to Vietnam, President Johnson claimed the United States was fighting for honorable reasons. But people wondered what goal could justify the murder of Vietnamese women and children. As troop levels increased, many recalled ruefully that in 1964 they had voted for Johnson as the "peace candidate." By 1968 almost a half-million American soldiers were stationed in Vietnam, and Johnson's credibility had evaporated.

1968: A Year of Protest, Violence, and Loss

As stormy and violent as the years from 1963 through 1967 had been, many Americans still tried to downplay the nation's distress in the hope that it would go away. But in 1968 a series of shocks hit them harder than ever. The first jolt came in January 1968, when the U.S.S. *Pueblo*, a navy intelligence ship, was captured by North Korea. A week later came the Tet Offensive in Vietnam (see page 898). American casualties were climbing, and for the first time many Americans believed that they might lose the war.

Controversy over the war deepened within the Democratic Party, and two candidates rose to challenge Johnson for the 1968 presidential nomination. Senator Eugene McCarthy of Minnesota entered the New Hampshire primary on March 12 solely to contest the Vietnam War; when he won twenty of New Hampshire's twenty-four convention delegates, Johnson recognized that these voters had repudiated his war policies. Soon another Democrat, Senator Robert F. Kennedy of New York, brother of the late president, entered the race. Then, on March 31, President Johnson went on national television to announce a scaling-down of the bombing in North Vietnam and his decision not to run for reelection.

Less than a week later, Martin Luther King, Jr., was murdered in Memphis. It is still unclear whether

Assassination of Martin Luther King, Jr.

James Earl Ray, a white man convicted in the killing, was a deranged racist acting alone or a hireling in an organized conspiracy. As an outspoken critic of the Vietnam War and increasingly of American capitalism, King had many enemies. Whatever Ray's motive, the murder touched off massive grief and rage in the nation's ghettos. Riots erupted in 168 cities and towns, including the looting and burning of white businesses (see Map 30.2). Thirty-four blacks and five whites died in the violence. The terror provoked a white backlash. Tough talk was the response from Chicago mayor Richard Daley, who ordered police to shoot to kill arsonists.

Gallup polls in April and May reported Robert Kennedy to be the front-running Democratic presidential candidate, and in June he

Assassination of Robert Kennedy

won the California primary. After addressing his joyous supporters in a Los Angeles hotel, Kennedy took a shortcut through the kitchen to a press conference. A young man stepped forward with a .22-caliber revolver and fired. Sirhan Sirhan, the assassin, was an Arab nationalist who despised Kennedy for his unwavering support of Israel. Many antiwar liberals felt they had lost a friend in Robert Kennedy, who in the wake of his brother's assassination had developed deep empathy with the sufferings of the underprivileged and strong opposition to the Vietnam War.

Violence erupted again in August at the Democratic national convention in Chicago. The Democrats were divided over the war, and thou-

Violence at the Democratic Convention

sands of antiwar protesters and members of the zany and anarchic Youth International Party (Yippies) had traveled to Chicago. The Chicago police force was still in the psychological grip of Mayor Daley's shoot-to-kill directive. Twelve thousand police were assigned to twelve-hour shifts, and another twelve thousand army troops were on call with rifles, bazookas, and flamethrowers. They attacked in front of the Hilton Hotel, wading into the ranks of demonstrators, reporters, and TV camera operators. Throughout the nation, viewers watched as club-swinging police beat protesters to the ground.

To preserve law and order against protesters during the 1968 Democratic National Convention, Chicago Mayor Richard J. Daley *(center)* mobilized twelve thousand police officers. But in what a federal commission called a "police riot," the officers overreacted and used tear gas and clubs to stop protesters from marching to the convention hall.   (Collection of Philip J. and Suzanne Schiller)

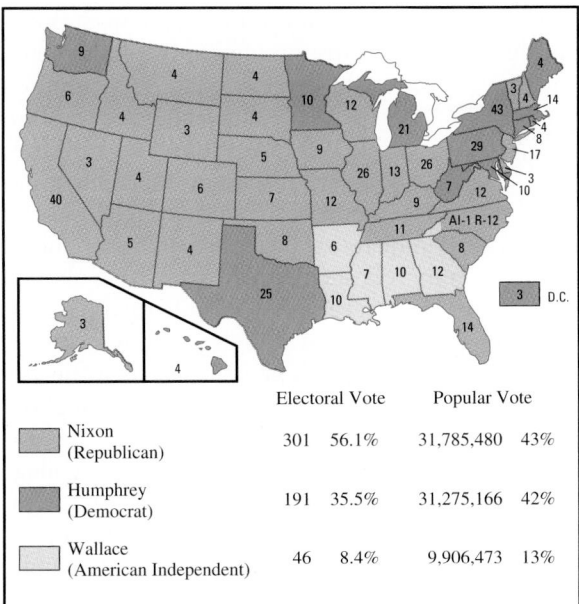

Map 30.4 Presidential Election, 1968 The popular vote was almost evenly split between Richard M. Nixon and Hubert Humphrey, but Nixon won 31 states to Humphrey's 14 and triumphed easily in electoral votes. George Wallace, the American Independent Party candidate, won 5 states in the Deep South.

	Electoral Vote		Popular Vote	
Nixon (Republican)	301	56.1%	31,785,480	43%
Humphrey (Democrat)	191	35.5%	31,275,166	42%
Wallace (American Independent)	46	8.4%	9,906,473	13%

The Democratic convention nominated Vice President Hubert Humphrey for president and Senator Edmund Muskie of Maine for vice president. Like Johnson and Kennedy before him, Humphrey was both an unstinting supporter of the Vietnam War and a political liberal supported throughout his career by big-city bosses, African Americans, and union members. The Republicans selected as their presidential nominee Richard M. Nixon; his running mate was the tough-talking Governor Spiro Agnew of Maryland. Another tough-talking governor, George C. Wallace of Alabama, ran as the nominee of the American Independent Party. Wallace was a segregationist, a proponent of reducing North Vietnam to rubble with nuclear weapons, and an advocate of "law and order."

When the votes were tabulated, Nixon emerged the winner by the slimmest of margins. Wallace collected nearly 10 million votes, or almost 14 percent of the total, the best performance by a third party since 1924. His strong showing made Nixon a minority president, elected with 43 percent of the popular vote (see Map 30.4). Moreover, the Dem-

Election of 1968

ocrats maintained control of the House (245 to 189) and the Senate (57 to 43).

Still, given that the combined vote for Nixon and Wallace was 57 percent, the 1968 election was a triumph for conservatism. The war had hurt the Democrats' appeal, but even more politically damaging was the party's identification with the cause of civil rights and welfare for the poor. In 1968 Humphrey received 97 percent of the black vote but only 35 percent of the white vote. Among the defectors from the New Deal coalition were not only southern whites but also northern blue-collar ethnic voters. "In city after city," one observer noted, "racial conflicts had destroyed the old alliance. The New Deal had unraveled block by block."

Unraveling of the New Deal Coalition

Rebirth of Feminism

Another liberation movement gained momentum during the turbulence of the 1960s, at first quietly and then on the picket line. The women's rights movement had languished after the adoption of the Nineteenth Amendment in 1920. But in the 1960s feminism was reborn. Many women were dissatisfied with their lives, and in 1963 they found a voice with the publication of Betty Friedan's *The Feminine Mystique*. According to Friedan, women across the country were deeply troubled by "the problem that has no name." Most women had grown up believing that "all they had to do was devote their lives from earliest girlhood to finding a husband and bearing children." The problem was that this "mystique of feminine fulfillment" left many wives and mothers feeling empty and incomplete.

President Kennedy appointed only one woman to a policymaking post in his administration, but she proved to be an effective advocate of women's rights. Esther Peterson served as assistant secretary of labor and director of the Women's Bureau. In 1961, at her urging, Kennedy established the first President's Commission on the Status of Women. Its report, *American Women* (1963), urged that every obstacle to women's full participation in society be removed. But little federal action resulted from the release of *American Women*, and the government was failing to enforce the gender-equality provisions of the Civil Rights Act of

National Organization for Women

1964. The need for action inspired the founding in 1966 of the National Organization for Women (NOW). In the reform tradition, NOW battled for "equal rights in partnership with men" by lobbying for legislation and testing laws in the courts.

Not long after NOW's formation, a new generation of radical feminists emerged. Most radical feminists were white and well educated; many were the daughters of working mothers. Most had been raised in the era of sexual liberation, taking for granted liberation from unwanted pregnancy. The intellectual ferment of their movement produced a new feminist literature. Radical feminists focused not only on legal barriers but also on cultural assumptions and traditions. In the process they introduced the term *sexism* to signify a phenomenon far more pervasive and demeaning than lack of legal equality, and they challenged everything from women's economic and political inequality to sexual double standards and sex-role stereotypes.

Radical feminists practiced what they called "personal politics." Charlotte Bunch, a feminist, explained,

"Personal Politics"

"There is no private domain of a person's life that is not political, and there is no political issue that is not ultimately personal." Unlike NOW, the radical feminists practiced direct action, such as picketing the 1968 Miss America contest in Atlantic City. One woman auctioned off an effigy of Miss America: "Gentlemen, I offer you the 1969 model. . . . She walks. She talks. She smiles on cue. *And* she does the housework." Into the "freedom trash can" the pickets dumped false eyelashes, hair curlers, girdles, and *Playboy* magazine to protest the prevailing view of women as domestic servants and sex objects.

Many radical feminists were veterans of the struggles for black civil rights and against the Vietnam War. Even in movements dedicated to equality and peace, however, they often found that they were second-class citizens. Instead of making policy, they were expected to make coffee, take minutes, and even provide sexual favors. Many of these feminists organized consciousness-raising groups to discuss wide-ranging and sensitive matters such as homosexuality, abortion, and power relationships in romance and marriage. The issue of homosexuality caused a split in the women's movement. In 1969 and 1970 NOW forced lesbians to resign from membership and offices in the organization. The rift was healed in 1971, largely because lesbians as well as gay men had begun to fight back.

For working women in the 1960s, the most pressing problems were sex discrimination in employment, meager professional opportunities, low pay, lack of adequate daycare for children, and prohibitions against abortion. Although the Equal Pay Act of 1963 required equal pay for equal work in industries producing goods for commerce, such equality has been slow in coming. In 1963 the average woman earned 63 cents for every dollar a man earned. Ten years later the figure had fallen to 57 cents. The main cause of this pay disparity was "occupational segregation": throughout the labor force, women were concentrated in the low-paying positions. Because many women with college educations earned less than men with eighth-grade educations, it was natural that two of the most important women's goals of the 1960s were equal job opportunity and equal pay for equal work.

Working Women's Burdens

Another goal of working women was child daycare. In 1971 a bill passed Congress that would have set up a national system of daycare facilities for the children of working parents, but President Nixon vetoed it. The bill, Nixon asserted, would have committed government to "communal approaches to child-rearing over against the family-centered approach," thus imperiling the American family. In fact, there was a growing need for childcare: 11 million additional women joined the labor force between 1960 and 1972, and many were mothers of young children.

Despite opposition and setbacks, women were making impressive gains. They entered professional schools in record numbers: from 1969 to 1973, the number of women law students almost quadrupled, and the number of women medical students more than doubled. Under Title IX of the Educational Amendments of 1972, female college athletes gained the right to the same financial support as male athletes. The same year, Congress approved the Equal Rights Amendment (ERA)—"Equality of rights under the law shall not be denied or abridged by the United States or by any State on account of sex"—and sent it to the states for ratification. It fell three states shy of the three-fourths majority needed for adoption.

Women's Educational and Professional Gains

The Supreme Court also ruled on several issues particularly pertinent to women. In 1973, following the lead of some states, the Court struck down laws that made abortion a crime. Justice Harry A. Blackmun

Roe v. Wade

wrote the majority (7–2) opinion in *(Roe v. Wade):* The constitutional "right of privacy . . . is broad enough to encompass a woman's decision whether or not to terminate her pregnancy." Only in the last three months of pregnancy could a state bar abortion. The Court at this time also addressed sex discrimination. In a 1971 ruling *(Reed v. Reed)*, it held that legislation differentiating between the sexes "must be reasonable, not arbitrary," and in 1973 *(Frontiero v. Richardson)* the justices went a step further in declaring that job-related classifications based on sex, like those based on race, were "inherently suspect." These victories gave women new confidence in the 1970s.

Nixon and the Divided Nation

Richard Nixon's presidency was born in chaos. Bloody confrontations occurred at Berkeley, Wisconsin, Cornell, Harvard, and scores of other colleges and universities in 1969. In October three hundred Weathermen (a splinter group of SDS) raced through Chicago's downtown district, smashing windows and attacking police officers in a deluded attempt to incite armed class struggle. Violence was absent a month later, however, when a half-million people assembled peacefully at the Washington Monument on Moratorium Day to call for an end to the Vietnam War.

If 1969 was bloody and turbulent, 1970 proved to be even more so. President Nixon appeared on television on April 30 to announce that the United States had launched an "incursion" into Cambodia (see page 899), a neutral country bordering Vietnam. Antiwar protest escalated. On May 4 national guardsmen in Ohio fired into a crowd of fleeing students at Kent State University, killing four young people. Ten days later, police and state highway patrolmen armed with automatic weapons blasted a women's dormitory at Jackson State, an all-black university in Mississippi, killing two students and wounding nine others. The police claimed they had been shot at, but no evidence of sniping could be found.

Kent State and Jackson State

Calling their movement "Red Power," these American Indian activists dance in 1969 while "reclaiming" Alcatraz Island in San Francisco Bay. Arguing that an 1868 Sioux treaty entitled them to possession of unused federal lands, the group occupied the island until mid-1971.   (Ralph Crane, LIFE Magazine © Time, Inc.)

Many Americans, though disturbed by the increasing ferocity of campus confrontations, felt more personally endangered by street crime than student unrest. Sales of pistols, burglar alarms, and bulletproof vests soared, as did demand for private guards and special police. Conservatives accused liberals and the Supreme Court of causing the crime wave by coddling criminals.

Fear of Crime

Responding to public calls for crackdowns, government officials sometimes overreacted. Governor Nelson Rockefeller of New York did so in September 1971 when more than a thousand inmates of the state prison at Attica seized thirty-eight guards and took over a cellblock. Rather than agree to come to Attica to negotiate, Rockefeller ordered state troopers, sheriff's deputies, and guards to storm the prison. Under a pall of tear gas Rockefeller's army regained control, but at a horrifying cost: twenty-nine inmates and ten hostages were dead.

This new wave of riots, protests, and violent crime convinced Nixon that the nation was plunging into anarchy. Worried like Lyndon Johnson before him that the antiwar movement was communist inspired, he ordered the FBI, the CIA, the National Security Agency, and the Defense Intelligence Agency in mid-1970 to formulate a coordinated attack on "internal threats." Meanwhile, the administration also worked to put the Democratic Party on the defensive. The theme for the upcoming elections was enunciated in a memorandum by Jeb Stuart Magruder, a White House assistant: "The Democrats should be portrayed as being on the fringes: radical liberals who . . . excuse disorder, tolerate crime . . . and undercut the President's foreign policy." But Republican attempts in 1970 to discredit the Democrats failed. The Democrats gained seats in the House, and the Republicans lost eleven state governorships.

Politics of Divisiveness

Nixon's fortunes declined further in 1971. In June the *New York Times* began to publish the *Pentagon Papers*, a top-secret Defense Department study that revealed that the government had repeatedly lied to the American people about the Vietnam War (see page 899). Nixon also had to contend with inflation, a problem not entirely of his making. Lyndon Johnson's policy of "guns and butter"—massive deficit financing to support both the Vietnam War

Stagflation

and the Great Society—had fueled inflation. By early 1971 the United States was suffering from a 5.3 percent inflation rate and a 6 percent unemployment rate. The word *stagflation* soon would be coined to describe this coexistence of economic recession (stagnation) and inflation.

Nixon shocked both critics and allies by declaring in early 1971 that "I am now a Keynesian." (According to the British economist John Maynard Keynes, governments could stimulate economic growth in the private sector by means of "pump priming," even if it necessitated deficit financing.) Nixon's budget for fiscal 1971 would have a built-in deficit of $23 billion, just slightly less than the all-time high of $25 billion (1968 to 1969). Then in August, in an effort to correct the nation's balance-of-payments deficit, Nixon announced that he would devalue the dollar and allow it to "float" in international money markets. Finally, to curb inflation, the president froze prices, wages, and rents for ninety days. Wage and price controls exemplified what surprised observers called Nixon's "great turnabout" from outspoken conservative to pragmatic liberal.

One of Nixon's chief legislative aims was revenue sharing, a program that distributed federal funds to the states to use as they saw fit. In 1972 the president signed a revenue-sharing bill. Invoking the federalism of the nation's founders, he called this effort to shift responsibility back to state and local governments the New Federalism. The historian Stephen E. Ambrose has written that the program had special appeal to "the surburban, small-town, and rural homeowning Silent Majority," who expressed disgust that they had to pay "high taxes to support giveaway programs for the poor." They wanted to control their own tax dollars.

The environmental movement, which gained momentum in the 1960s, bore fruit during Nixon's first term. Alerted in 1962 to ecological hazards by Rachel Carson's *Silent Spring* (see page 810), growing numbers of Americans began to heed warnings of impending disaster due to rapid population growth and rampant development. Gradually, Congress responded, establishing the National Wilderness Preservation System (1964) and giving the federal government the power to set water-quality standards (1967).

Environmental Issues

Environmental tragedies such as a 1969 oil spill that fouled the beaches and killed wildlife in Santa Barbara, California, spurred citizen action. The En-

In 1969 a petroleum rig off the coast of Santa Barbara, California, ruptured, spilling millions of gallons of toxic oil. Fisheries were destroyed, and seabirds, seals, and other wildlife coated with viscous oil struggled to stay alive. The tragedy motivated environmental activists, who lobbied for laws that would protect nature. And in 1970, Americans concerned about pollution of the environment celebrated the first Earth Day.   (J. Eyerman/Black Star)

vironmental Defense Fund (founded in 1967) successfully fought the use of DDT, and Greenpeace (founded in 1969) protested radioactive poisoning from nuclear-bomb testing. In 1970 Americans celebrated the first Earth Day, convinced that the planet's fate hung in the balance. Barry Commoner's *The Closing Circle* (1971) put the issue squarely: "The environment got here first, and it's up to the economic system to adjust to the environment. Any economic system must be compatible with the environment, or it will not survive."

In the 1970s states took action; Oregon, for example, passed the first bottle-recycling act in 1972. And although President Nixon was personally unsympathetic to the environmental movement, some of his subordinates were not. Nixon acknowledged the movement's political appeal by reluctantly agreeing to the establishment of the Environmental Protection Agency in 1970 and by signing into law the Clean Air Act (1970), Clean Water Act (1972), and Pesticide Control Act (1972).

Nixon's Reelection and Resignation

 Political observers believed that President Nixon would have a hard time running for reelection on his contrary first-term record. Having urged Americans to "lower our voices," he had ordered Vice President Agnew to denounce the press and student protesters. Having espoused unity, he had practiced the politics of polarization. Having campaigned as a fiscal conservative, he had authorized near-record budget deficits. And having promised peace, he had widened the war in Southeast Asia.

During Nixon's first term, the Democrats dominated both houses of Congress, and they continued to pursue a liberal agenda. Indeed, Congress's accomplishments were more despite Nixon than because of him. Congress increased Social Security payments and food-stamp funding and established the Occupational Safety and Health Administration to reduce hazards in the workplace. Moreover, in 1971 the states quickly ratified the Twenty-sixth Amendment, which extended the vote to eighteen-year-olds.

Liberal Legislative Victories

In his 1968 presidential campaign, Nixon had echoed George Wallace's appeal for the law and order vote. In his campaign for reelection, Nixon continued to employ a "southern strategy" of political conservatism. A product of the Sunbelt, he was acutely aware of the growing political power of that conservative region. He thus appealed to the Silent Majority. And as in the 1970 congressional elections, Nixon equated the Republican Party with law and order and the Democrats with permissiveness, crime, drugs, pornography, the hippie lifestyle, student radicalism, black militancy, feminism, homosexuality, and dissolution of the family.

Nixon's "Southern Strategy"

In some ways, Nixon had been pursuing a southern strategy all along. A furor had arisen in 1970 when the press published a memorandum by Daniel Moynihan, Nixon's adviser on urban affairs and social welfare, who had recommended that "the issue of race could benefit from a period of benign neglect." Incensed, blacks and white liberals responded that this was another example of how uncaring the Nixon administration was. Moreover, Attorney General John Mitchell had courted southern white voters by trying to delay school desegregation in Mississippi and to prevent extension of the 1965 Voting Rights Act.

The southern strategy also guided Nixon's nomination of Supreme Court justices. After appointing Warren Burger, a conservative federal judge, to succeed Earl Warren as chief justice, Nixon had selected two southerners to serve as associate justices, one of whom was a segregationist. When the Senate declined to confirm either nominee, Nixon protested angrily, "I understand the bitter feelings of millions of Americans who live in the South." By 1972, however, the president had

Nixon and the Supreme Court

managed to appoint three more conservatives to the Supreme Court. Ironically, the new appointees did not always vote as Nixon would have wished: the Court's decisions on abortion, publication of the *Pentagon Papers*, the death sentence, wiretapping, and busing for school desegregation all ran counter to Nixon's views.

The Court was at the center of one of the most emotional issues of the 1972 election: busing of schoolchildren for purposes of integration. In *Swann v. Charlotte-Mecklenberg* (1971), the justices had upheld a desegregation plan that required a school system in North Carolina to work toward racial integration through massive cross-town busing. The decision generated widespread protest. The next year Governor George Wallace of Alabama won the Democratic primary in Florida after taking a strong antibusing stand. Three days later Nixon proposed that Congress pass a busing moratorium, and he appeared on television to denounce busing as a reckless and extreme remedy for segregation. Nixon's opposition to busing was a well-planned aspect of his southern strategy, but it clearly appealed to many northern whites as well.

Besides Governor Wallace, the Democratic candidates for the 1972 presidential nomination were Senators Hubert Humphrey, George McGovern, Edmund Muskie, and Edward Kennedy, the younger brother of John and Robert Kennedy. Wallace fell victim to an assassination attempt: he was shot and paralyzed by a disturbed young man in Maryland and began a long convalescence. After his shooting, the right-wing law-and-order vote had no place to turn but to Nixon. Kennedy had ceased to be a serious contender in 1969; in that year, he left the scene of an accident in which a woman passenger in his car drowned, at Chappaquiddick, an island off the Massachusetts coast near Martha's Vineyard. The other Democratic candidates inspired little enthusiasm. Senator McGovern of South Dakota, who enjoyed the support of many followers of the late Robert F. Kennedy, won several primaries and arrived at the Democratic convention with enough votes to secure the nomination of his party.

Election of 1972

Nixon campaigned by assuming the elevated role of world statesman: in early 1972 he traveled to China and to the Soviet Union. Both trips were elaborately staged and televised for maximum political effect. But it was the inept campaign waged by George McGovern that handed victory to the Republicans. When

McGovern endorsed a $30 billion cut in the defense budget, people began to fear that he was a neo-isolationist who would reduce the United States to a second-rate power. McGovern's proposals split the Democrats between his supporters—antiwar activists, African Americans, feminists, young militants—and old-guard urban bosses, labor leaders, white southerners, and growing numbers of blue-collar workers.

Nixon benefited greatly from the rumor planted by his aides that the Vietnam War was near its end. Troops were being pulled out; by September 1972 the American death rate was almost zero. Then in late October, less than two weeks before the election, Henry Kissinger (then assistant to the president for national security affairs) announced a breakthrough in the peace negotiations. "Peace is at hand," he proclaimed. The announcement proved inaccurate but helped persuade some people to vote for Nixon.

Nixon's victory in November was overwhelming: he polled 47 million votes, more than 60 percent. McGovern received only 29 million

Nixon's Landslide Victory

and won just one state, Massachusetts, and the District of Columbia. Nixon's southern strategy had been supremely successful. He carried the entire Deep South, which once had been solidly Democratic. He also gained the suburbs and won over a majority of the urban vote, including long-time Democrats such as blue-collar workers, Catholics, and white ethnics. Only blacks, Jews, and low-income voters stuck by the Democratic candidate.

Yet the 1972 election had another significant result, one that would recur in subsequent elections. Despite Nixon's landslide victory, his coattails proved to be short, and the Democrats retained control of both houses of Congress. Democratic voters were becoming independent, resorting to ticket-splitting to reject an unacceptable Democratic presidential candidate but support the party's congressional candidates.

Little noticed during the campaign was a break-in at the Watergate apartment-office complex in Washington, D.C., on June 17, 1972. A

Watergate Break-in

watchman telephoned the police to report an illegal late-night entry into the building through an underground garage. At 2:30 A.M., police arrested five men who were attaching listening devices to telephones in the sixth-floor offices of the Democratic National Committee. The men had cameras and had been rifling through files.

One of those arrested was James W. McCord, a former CIA employee who had become security coordinator of the Committee to Re-Elect the President (CREEP). The other four were anti-Castro Cubans from Miami who had worked with the CIA before. Unknown to the police, two other men had been in the Watergate building at the time of the break-in. One was E. Howard Hunt, a one-time CIA agent who had become a White House consultant. The other was G. Gordon Liddy, a former FBI agent serving on CREEP's staff.

The Watergate fiasco actually began in 1971, when the White House established not only CREEP but the Special Investigations Unit,

White House Cover-up

known familiarly as the "Plumbers," to stop the leaking of secret government documents to the press. After publication of the *Pentagon Papers*, the Plumbers burglarized the office of Daniel Ellsberg's psychiatrist in an attempt to discredit Ellsberg, who had leaked the top-secret report to the press. It was the Plumbers who broke into the Democratic National Committee's headquarters to photograph documents and install wiretaps; money raised by CREEP was used to pay the Plumbers' expenses both before and after the break-ins. CREEP's official duty was to solicit campaign contributions, and the committee managed to collect $60 million, much of it donated illegally by corporations, including big oil companies like Gulf Oil and Phillips Petroleum, as well as defense contractors and airlines.

The arrest of the Watergate burglars generated furious activity in the White House. Incriminating documents were shredded; E. Howard Hunt's name was expunged from the White House telephone directory; and President Nixon ordered his chief of staff, H. R. Haldeman, to discourage the FBI's investigation into the burglary on the pretext that it might compromise national security. Nixon also authorized CREEP "hush money" payments in excess of $460,000 to keep Hunt and others from implicating the White House in the crime. And he assured the press that his White House counsel, John W. Dean III, had conducted a "complete investigation" and that no one in the administration "was involved in this very bizarre incident."

Because of successful White House efforts to cover up the scandal, the break-in was almost unnoticed by the electorate. Had it not been for the diligent efforts of reporters, government special prosecutors,

How do historians know...

that President Richard M. Nixon was guilty of obstructing justice in the Watergate affair? What was the evidence—the "smoking gun"—that established his guilt? The so-called smoking gun referred to the tape recording of a White House conversation on June 23, 1972, that proved Nixon had foreknowledge of the Watergate break-in, had instigated a cover-up, and had obstructed justice almost from the outset of the scandal. That day, Nixon ordered his top aide to stop the Federal Bureau of Investigation's inquiry into the Watergate break-in. Tell the Central Intelligence Agency, Nixon thundered, to call the FBI, claim that the break-in was a secret spy operation related to the 1961 Bay of Pigs invasion, and say ". . . that we wish for the country [that you] 'don't go further into this case,' period." In 1973 and 1974 special prosecutors and congressional committees sued for release of this and other tapes, but Nixon resisted. On August 5, 1974, the Supreme Court ruled that executive privilege did not protect the subpoenaed tapes; the next day, the White House turned over a number of tapes, including the smoking gun. Three days later, Richard Nixon resigned the presidency.

Afterward, historians sued for access to the thousands of hours of unreleased tapes; but for twenty-one years, Nixon and his family succeeded in keeping them private. In 1996, however, the Nixon estate, the National Archives and Records Administration, and Stanley I. Kutler, a history professor at the University of Wisconsin, reached an agreement that called for some 3,700 hours of tapes to be made public over the next several years. The first tapes released condemned President Nixon in his own words and shocked the American people. For example, on May 13, 1971, Nixon was recorded growling demands for a commissioner of the Internal Revenue Service, who "is a ruthless son of a bitch, that he will do what he is told, that every income tax return I want to see, I see. That he will go after our enemies and not go after our friends." A month later, Nixon ordered his aides to arrange a break-in at the Brookings Institution, a liberal think tank in Washington: "Goddammit," he swore, "get in and get those files. Blow the safe and get it." In January 2000 some of Watergate tapes became available to the public when the National Archives began to sell cassettes containing the 264 hours of so-called abuse of government power recordings.   (Photo: Nixon Presidential Materials Project)

Watergate Hearings and Investigations

federal judges, and members of Congress, President Nixon might have succeeded in disguising his involvement in Watergate. Slowly, however, the tangle of lies and distortions began to unravel. In early 1973 U.S. District Judge John Sirica tried the burglars, one of whom implicated his superiors in CREEP and at the White House. From May until November, the Senate Select Committee on Campaign Practices, chaired by Senator Sam Ervin of North Carolina, heard testimony from White House aides. John W. Dean III acknowledged not only that there had been a cover-up but that the president had directed it. Another aide shocked the committee and the nation by disclosing that Nixon had had a voice-activated taping system installed in his White House office and that conversations about Watergate had been recorded.

Nixon feigned innocence. In April 1973 he tried to distance himself from the cover-up by announcing the resignations of his two chief White House aides, John Ehrlichman and H. R. Haldeman.

Saturday Night Massacre

The administration then appointed Archibald Cox, a Harvard law professor with a reputation for uncompromising integrity, to fill the new position of special Watergate prosecutor. But when Cox sought in October to obtain the White House tapes by means of a court order, Nixon decided to have him fired. Both Attorney General Elliot Richardson and his deputy resigned rather than carry out the dismissal order. It thus fell to the third-ranking person in the Department of Justice, Solicitor General Robert H. Bork, to fire Cox. The public outcry provoked by the so-called Saturday Night Massacre compelled the president to agree to the appointment of a new special prosecutor, Leon Jaworski. When Nixon still refused to surrender the tapes, Jaworski took him to court.

In the same month as the Saturday Night Massacre, the Nixon administration was stung by another scandal. Vice President Spiro Agnew resigned after pleading no contest to charges of income-tax evasion and acceptance of bribes when he was governor of Maryland. Under the provisions of the Twenty-fifth Amendment, ratified in 1967 after President Kennedy's assassination, Nixon nominated Gerald R. Ford, the House minority leader from Michigan, to replace Agnew. Ford's voting

Agnew's Resignation

record was conservative—he had opposed most of the 1960s reform legislation—but he was popular on Capitol Hill, and his nomination was promptly confirmed by Congress.

Throughout 1973 and 1974, enterprising reporters uncovered more details of the break-in, the hush money, and the various people from Nixon on down who had taken part in the cover-up. White House aides and CREEP subordinates began to go on trial, and Nixon was cited as an "unindicted co-conspirator." *Washington Post* reporters Carl Bernstein and Bob Woodward found an informant, known as Deep Throat, who provided damning information about Nixon and his aides. As Nixon's protestations of innocence became less credible, his hold on the tapes became more tenuous. In late April 1974 the president finally released an edited transcript of the recorded conversations.

The edited transcript, however, had a lot of gaps. It swayed neither the public nor the House Judiciary Committee, which had begun to draft articles of impeachment against the president. Nixon still was trying to hang onto the original tapes when the Supreme Court in July, in *U.S. v. Nixon*, unanimously ordered him to surrender the recordings to Judge Sirica. At about the same time, the Judiciary Committee conducted nationally televised hearings. After several days of testimony, the committee voted for impeachment on three of five counts: obstruction of justice through the payment of hush money to witnesses, lying, and withholding evidence; defiance of a congressional subpoena of the tapes; and use of the CIA, the FBI, and the Internal Revenue Service to deprive Americans of their constitutional rights of privacy and free speech.

On August 6 the president finally handed over the complete tapes, which he knew would condemn him.

Nixon's Resignation

Three days later he became the first president to resign from office. Nixon's successor was Gerald Ford. The first substantive act of the new president was to pardon Nixon. When the pardon was announced, some people concluded that Ford and Nixon had struck a deal.

The Watergate scandal prompted the reform of abuses that predated the Nixon administration. The executive's usurpation of legislative prerogatives, which historian Arthur M. Schlesinger, Jr., called "the imperial presidency," dated from Franklin D. Roosevelt's administration. Roosevelt had signed executive agreements that were in effect treaties with foreign nations, but he never sent them to the Senate for its advice and consent. Presidents Truman and Johnson had led the nation into the Korean and Vietnam Wars without securing a congressional declaration of war as required by the Constitution. And President Nixon had impounded—that is, refused to spend—federal funds appropriated for health, the environment, space exploration, and other programs.

To end the nation's participation in undeclared wars, Congress in 1973 overrode Nixon's veto and passed the War Powers Act, which mandated that "in every possible instance" the president must consult with Congress before sending American troops into foreign wars. Under this law the president could commit American troops abroad for no more than sixty days, after which he had to obtain congressional approval. (The act did not specify what Congress could do if the president refused to comply.) The next year Congress approved the Congressional Budget and Impoundment Control Act, which prohibited the impounding of federal money. Finally, to aid citizens who were victims of dirty-tricks campaigns, in 1974 Congress strengthened the Freedom of Information Act of 1966. The new legislation, which Congress passed over President Ford's veto, permitted access to government documents and provided penalties if the government "arbitrarily or capriciously" withheld such information.

Post-Watergate Restrictions on Executive Power

Summary

The 1960s had begun with high hopes for a more democratic America. Starting with the first sit-ins in 1960, civil rights volunteers spread the quest for racial equality to all parts of the country. And activists in this movement were among the founders of other protest movements, including feminism, the New Left, Black Power, gay rights, and emerging civil rights movements for Native Americans and Mexican Americans. Although these movements achieved notable goals, including landmark civil rights legislation, another legacy was political disenchantment in the United States.

The thirteen years coinciding with the presidencies of John Kennedy, Lyndon Johnson, and Richard Nixon were a period of increasing disillusionment. As historian James T. Patterson observed, the period be-

gan with "grand expectations" about the attainability of "the Good Life." But riots in cities, violence on campus, diminished respect for government leaders, and growing economic uncertainty shattered Americans' illusions and supplanted earlier hopes for peaceful social change. "Americans had gone into the age of Kennedy and Nixon convinced that their government's action . . . could make over the world, at home and abroad," journalist Godfrey Hodgson explained, but "they had been burned." They had learned some hard lessons: how much harder it was to change the world than they thought it would be, and how there often was "little that political action could achieve, however idealistic its intentions, without evoking unforeseen and unwanted reaction."

When John F. Kennedy delivered his inaugural address in 1961, he challenged Americans to "pay any price, bear any burden, meet any hardship" to defend freedom and inspire the world. Twelve years later, Richard M. Nixon echoed that rhetoric: "Let us pledge to make these four years the best four years in America's history, so that on its 200th birthday America will be as young and vital as when it began, and as bright a beacon of hope for all the world." Largely because of his own actions, however, Nixon resigned the presidency before the nation could celebrate its bicentennial in 1976. Rather than young and vital, America seemed bruised and battered.

LEGACY FOR A PEOPLE AND A NATION
Watergate and Political Reforms

The legacy of Watergate has helped to undermine, if not destroy, many Americans' trust in their government. For the past twenty-five years, Watergate has contributed greatly to political cynicism, and it has cast a shadow over the presidencies of all of Nixon's successors, from Gerald Ford to Bill Clinton. Its legacy is evident in the proliferation of special prosecutors, independent counsels, and congressional investigating committees, not to mention TV and newspaper reporters, who have examined political and personal behavior in the White House as never before. Both John F. Kennedy and Lyndon B. Johnson were widely known to be philanderers, yet the press subscribed to an unwritten code that held that such behavior was off-limits to reporters. This hands-off decorum all changed with Watergate. After 1974 Washington became an increasingly paranoiac and cynical place where even the smallest presidential mistakes were scrutinized and vilified.

In 1978 Congress passed the Ethics in Government Act authorizing the appointment of special prosecutors to investigate criminal wrongdoing in the White House. Sometimes, the controversial decisions and behavior were substantive, such as Ronald Reagan's Iran-contra affair and Bill Clinton's host of scandals, including a sexual relationship with a White House intern. The last special prosecutor, known as an independent counsel, was Kenneth Starr, who in more than five years of investigating scandals in the Clinton White House spent $48 million for private investigators, office space, computers, travel, and other expenses. In 1999 the independent counsel law expired and was not extended.

Watergate's legacy, however, is not limited to scandal-mongering. Soon after Nixon's resignation, Congress made a modest attempt to reduce campaign fundraising abuses, setting ceilings on campaign contributions. However, instead of limiting such abuses, this legislation provided new loopholes for electioneers to exploit. To circumvent the ceilings on contributions, special-interest groups established political-action committees (PACs). In 1980 there were 2,765 PACs, more than four times as many as in 1974. Moreover, Capitol Hill was crawling as never before with lobbyists from trade associations, corporations, labor unions, and single-issue groups such as the National Rifle Association. As the influence of money in politics has grown in the aftermath of Watergate, so too has political disillusionment. In the 1998 congressional elections, spending on television advertising, largely negative "attack" ads, reached an all-time high, while voter turnout was the lowest in fifty-six years.

For Further Reading, see page A-36 of the Appendix. For Web resources, go to http://college.hmco.com.

S outh Vietnam was "crumbling fast," Secretary of
Defense Robert McNamara remarked. So the
Joint Chiefs of Staff boldly recommended that
another hundred thousand American troops be added
to the eighty thousand already in Vietnam. In a tense
meeting on July 21, 1965, President Lyndon B. Johnson asked his advisers, "Is there anyone here of the
opinion we should not do what the [JCS] memorandum says?" Only Undersecretary of State George Ball
spoke up: "I can foresee a perilous voyage." Johnson
responded, "What other road can I go?" Ball answered, "Take our losses, let their government fall
apart, negotiate, discuss, knowing full well there will
be a probable takeover by the Communists." The
president, imbued with the Cold War mentality, recoiled from the conclusion that what he once called a
"damn little pissant country" could deny victory to the
United States.

At an afternoon session, Ball again forthrightly argued a case few of his colleagues endorsed. "The war
will be long and protracted. The most we can hope for
is a messy conclusion." Not only did dangers arise
from possible Chinese intervention, negative world
opinion, and domestic political dissent, but "the enemy cannot be seen in Vietnam. He is indigenous to
the country." Ball doubted that "an army of Westerners can successfully fight Orientals in an Asian jungle."
Remember what happened to France. In the long run,
he insisted, "the war will disclose our weakness, not
our strength." Worried about U.S. credibility, Johnson
jumped in: "But, George, wouldn't all these countries
say that Uncle Sam was a paper tiger?" "No sir," Ball
retorted. "The worse blow would be that the mightiest
power on earth is unable to defeat a handful of guerrillas."

The next day Johnson met with top military officials. They told him that more men, more bombings,
and more money were needed to save America's ally
South Vietnam from defeat at the hands of North
Vietnamese and Vietcong forces. "But if we put in
100,000 men," the president asked, "won't they put in
an equal number, and then where will we be?" And
have the bombing raids hurt the enemy? Not really,
the generals answered, but they would if more sites

In Chu Lai, Vietnam, U.S. soldiers of the 1st Cavalry Division (Airmobile) leap from a helicopter during Operation Oregon in 1967. (Sgt. Howard Breedlove, DASPO,
U.S. Army)

31

DISASTER AND DÉTENTE: THE COLD WAR, VIETNAM, AND THE THIRD WORLD 1961–1989

were added to the target list. Johnson wondered: "Isn't this going off the diving board?" When McNamara argued that the United States had a commitment to South Vietnam and that America's credibility was on the line, Johnson shot back: "But, if you make a commitment to jump off a building and you find out how high it is, you may want to withdraw that commitment."

After asking searching questions and even revealing some doubts, Johnson nonetheless rejected a withdrawal strategy and gave the Joint Chiefs of Staff what they wanted. He thought that America could win the war. A turning point in the Vietnam War, this decision meant that the United States was for the first time assuming primary responsibility for fighting the war. Fearing that he might spark a national debate about the deepening U.S. role, Johnson practiced subterfuge, deliberately underplaying the decision's importance when he announced it. He chose to deceive the American people because if the public focused its attention on the war, he argued, his Great Society reform legislation might be derailed: his reform supporters might splinter and conservatives might cut his domestic budget in order to pay for the mounting costs of war.

By the end of 1965, nearly two hundred thousand American combat troops were at war in Vietnam. Yet Congress had not passed a declaration of war, and most of the American people remained ignorant of the venture. Ball later called Johnson's July decision "the greatest single error that America had made in its national history." McNamara, who vigorously challenged Ball's case in 1965, later wrote that he, McNamara, has been "wrong." Indeed, he conceded, "we were sinking into quicksand."

Vietnam bedeviled the United States from 1945, the year Vietnamese nationalists declared independence from France, to well beyond 1975, the year the last Americans withdrew in defeat. Presidents Truman and Eisenhower had taken the Cold War perspective and attempted to roll back the Vietnamese independence movement (see Chapter 29). President John F. Kennedy, sharing the Cold War faith and fearing that Communist China was expanding into Vietnam, greatly enlarged the U.S. presence there. Johnson "Americanized" the war, increasing U.S. troops to more than half a million. Presidents Richard Nixon and Gerald Ford pulled out American soldiers while further punishing the enemy in an attempt not to lose the war. Their successors had to deal with defeat and the anguished aftermath of America's longest war.

While the Vietnam War intensified, the Cold War that Truman and Eisenhower had waged became even more acrimonious, engulfing much of the world. Interventions and dangerous confrontations in the Third World, the nuclear arms race, propagandistic shouting matches, and brinkmanship unsettled people everywhere. The Cuban missile crisis of 1962 brought the Soviet Union and the United States close to nuclear disaster. In its drive to win the Cold War, deter neutralism, and defuse revolutionary nationalism, the United States employed a host of instruments—foreign aid, CIA covert actions, military assaults, cultural penetration, economic sanctions, and diplomacy, among them. But the world did not become a safer place, and the Vietnam War undermined the Cold War consensus in the United States. Other questions, long dwarfed by the superpower contest and global interventionism, began to crowd onto the international agenda, especially the deteriorating natural environment.

Ultimately the two great powers, the United States and the Soviet Union, weakened by the huge costs of their competition and challenged by other nations demanding that the Cold War end, faced an international system in which power became diffused. In an effort to stem their relative decline, the two adversaries began cautiously in the 1970s to embrace a process of détente, which soon sputtered. In the late 1980s, however, they took important steps toward ending the Cold War. ■

Kennedy's Nation Building, Arms Buildup, and the Cuban Missile Crisis

President John F. Kennedy's views owed much to the past. He criticized the appeasement policy of the 1930s for abetting aggressors (see page 742) and praised the containment doctrine of the 1940s for thwarting communists (see page 826). An eloquent speaker and fierce competitor known for his womanizing and cultivated image of manliness, he vowed to rout communism in the 1960s—to win the missile race, the arms race, the space race, and the race for influence in the Third World. "Everyone around him thought he had the Midas touch and could not lose," remarked an assistant, the historian Arthur M. Schlesinger, Jr. Kennedy's arrogant national security affairs adviser, McGeorge Bundy, asserted that "the United States is the engine of mankind, and the rest of the world is the

IMPORTANT EVENTS

1961 Kennedy becomes president
Peace Corps is initiated
Invasion at Cuba's Bay of Pigs fails
Alliance for Progress begins
Berlin Wall is built
Kennedy increases aid to South Vietnam

1962 Agreement on neutralizing Laos
Cuban missile crisis courts nuclear war

1963 Treaty bans atmospheric nuclear testing
U.S. cooperates in removal of Diem
Johnson becomes president

1964 Tonkin Gulf Resolution permits wider war

1965 Operation Rolling Thunder bombs North
Vietnam
Johnson increases troop strength in Vietnam
Antiwar teach-ins and demonstrations begin

1966 Fulbright's Senate hearings on Vietnam

1967 Six-Day War in the Middle East

1968 Tet Offensive sets back U.S. objectives
Dollar/gold crisis threatens U.S. economy
My Lai massacre leaves hundreds dead
U.S. invades Dominican Republic
Vietnam peace talks open in Paris

1969 Nixon becomes president; promotes détente
"Vietnamization" begins exit of U.S. troops
Nixon Doctrine calls for self-help by nations

1970 U.S. ratifies 1968 nuclear nonproliferation
treaty
Invasion of Cambodia sparks demonstrations
Senate repeals Tonkin Gulf Resolution

1971 *Pentagon Papers* reveal lies by U.S. leaders

1972 Nixon's trip to China thaws relations
SALT-I treaty limits nuclear weapons
"Christmas bombing" of North Vietnam

1973 Vietnam cease-fire agreement
Allende ousted in Chile
Arab-Israeli war and oil embargo
War Powers Act restricts president

1974 Ford becomes president
U.N. proposes "New International
Economic Order"

1975 Vietnam reunified under Communist rule
Helsinki accords endorse human rights

1977 Carter becomes president

1978 Senate approves Panama Canal treaties
Mideast peace accord made at Camp David

1979 SALT-II treaty recognizes nuclear parity
Hostages taken in Iran after shah falls
Soviets invade Afghanistan

1980 U.S. grain embargo and Olympics boycott
against USSR
Carter Doctrine for Persian Gulf

1981 Reagan becomes president
American hostages released in Iran
U.S. intervenes in Central America
Nuclear freeze movement grows worldwide

1982 U.S. troops intervene in Lebanon
START talks over nuclear forces begin
Law of the Sea Convention adopted, but not
by U.S.

1983 Reagan introduces SDI
Soviets shoot down Korean airliner
U.S. deploys Pershing missiles in Europe
Terrorists kill U.S. Marines in Lebanon
U.S. invasion of Grenada

1984 Reagan aids contras despite congressional ban

1985 Reagan Doctrine extols "freedom fighters"
Gorbachev promotes reforms in USSR
Geneva summit collapses over SDI

1986 Iran-contra scandal
U.S. economic sanctions against South Africa

1987 INF Treaty bans some missiles in Europe

1988 Negotiated settlement in Namibia

caboose." Kennedy's inaugural address suggested no halfway measures: "Let every nation know that we shall pay any price, bear any burden, meet any hardship, support any friend, oppose any foe to assure the survival and the success of liberty." A skeptical Adlai Stevenson, U.S. ambassador to the United Nations, told a friend that "they've got the damnedest bunch of

boy commandos running around down there [in Washington] you ever saw."

After Khrushchev endorsed "wars of national liberation" such as the one in Vietnam, Kennedy called for "peaceful revolution" based on the concept of nation building. The administration set out to help developing nations through the early stages of nationhood

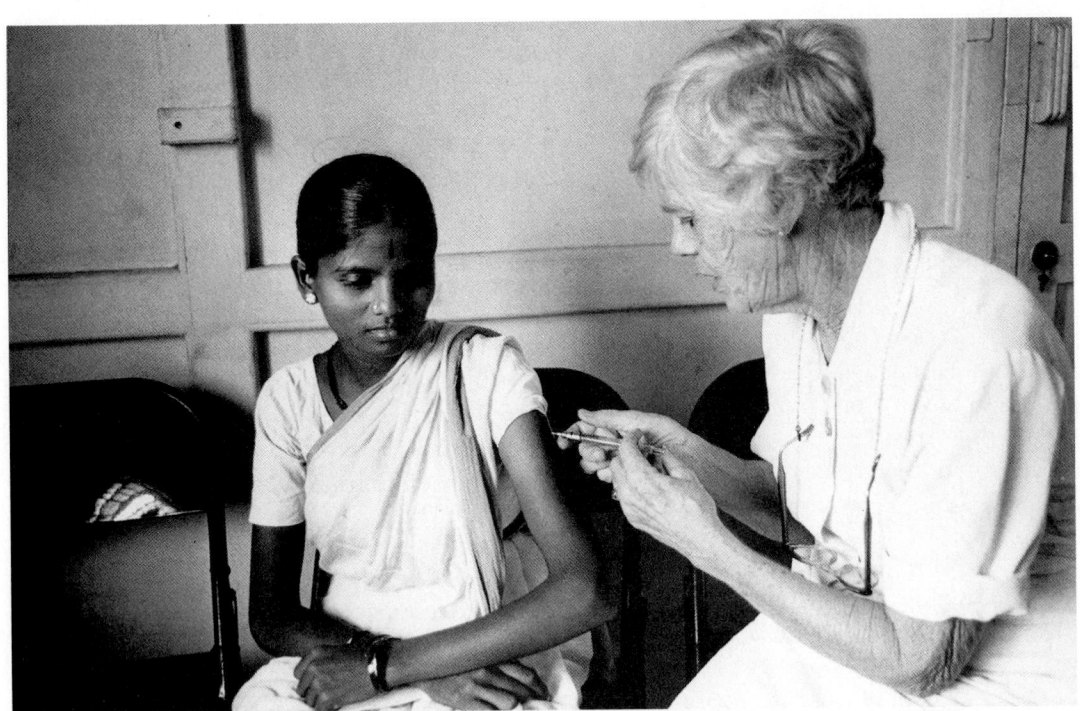

Seventy-year-old Lillian Carter, mother of future president Jimmy Carter, served as a Peace Corps volunteer in India in 1967–1968. Here she treats a tuberculosis patient. Most volunteers were young people better able to withstand difficult conditions, but Lillian Carter seldom shrunk from challenge, even when she became very homesick. "I've forgotten luxuries and most comforts," she wrote home. "I helped Dr. Bhatia today, and gave injections to three hundred and fifty children. I am so tired and REFRESHED!" As she prepared to leave India, she penned another letter: "I didn't dream that in this remote corner of the world . . . I would discover what Life is really all about. Sharing yourself with others, and accepting their love of you, is the most precious gift of all."   (National Archives)

Nation Building and Counterinsurgency

with aid programs aimed at improving agriculture, transportation, and communications. Kennedy thus initiated the multibillion-dollar Alliance for Progress in 1961 to spur economic development in Latin America. That year Kennedy also created the Peace Corps. This agency sent thousands of American teachers, agricultural specialists, and health workers into developing nations. The Peace Corps's humanitarian purpose, however, sometimes competed with the administration's political agenda. Conflicts arose between corps members in the field, many of whom identified with Third World peoples' desire for neutrality in the Cold War, and headquarters in Washington, where the goal was aligning those peoples with U.S. foreign policy. One group of corps volunteers—depicting themselves as "Marines in velvet gloves"—protested their role as instruments of policymakers.

Kennedy also relied on counterinsurgency to defeat revolutionaries who challenged Third World governments friendly with the United States. American military and technical advisers trained native troops and police forces to quell unrest. And American soldiers—especially the Special Forces (Green Berets)—provided a protective shield against insurgents while American civilian personnel worked on economic projects.

Nation building and counterinsurgency seldom worked. The Alliance for Progress stumbled; infant mortality rates improved, but Latin American economies registered unimpressive growth rates and class divisions continued to widen, exacerbating political unrest. Americans assumed that the U.S. model of capitalism and representative government could be transferred successfully to foreign cultures. But, although many foreign peoples welcomed U.S. economic assistance and craved U.S. material culture, they resented meddling by outsiders. And because aid was usually funneled through a self-interested elite, it often failed to reach the very poor. To people who preferred the relatively quick solutions of a managed economy, moreover, the American emphasis on private enterprise seemed inappropriate.

Under Kennedy, the CIA continued its covert operations, including training the Cuban exile brigade and Operation Mongoose against Cuba (see page 888). The agency also plotted in the Congo in 1960 and 1961 to poison Premier Patrice Lumumba with a lethal injection of a virus. A CIA-backed Congolese political faction finally murdered Lumumba, who had turned to the Soviet Union for help during a civil war. In Brazil the CIA spent $20 million to influence the 1962 elections against President João Goulart, who had expropriated the property of the U.S.-based firm International Telephone and Telegraph and had refused to vote to oust Cuba from the Organization of American States. When Goulart's supporters won, the CIA helped organize opposition groups. In 1964, with U.S. complicity, the Brazilian military overthrew Goulart.

In fall 1961 the Soviet Union ended its moratorium on above-ground nuclear testing by exploding a

Military Expansion

giant 50-megaton bomb. Khrushchev also bragged about Soviet ICBMs, raising American anxiety over Soviet capabilities. Intelligence data soon demonstrated that there was no "missile gap"—except the one in America's favor. Kennedy nonetheless sought to fulfill his campaign commitment to a military buildup based on the principle of flexible response: the capability to make any kind of war, from guerrilla combat to nuclear showdown. Thus the United States would be able to contain both the Soviet Union and revolutionary movements in the Third World. In 1961 the military budget shot up 15 percent; by mid-1964, U.S. nuclear weapons had increased by 150 percent. Government advice to citizens to build fallout shelters in their backyards intensified public fear of devastating war. Kennedy inaugurated the Arms Control and Disarmament Agency and signed the Limited Test Ban Treaty with the Soviet Union (1963), which banned nuclear testing in the atmosphere, in outer space, and under water, but his legacy was an accelerated arms race.

Once again, in 1961, the Soviets demanded negotiations to end Western occupation of West Berlin.

Berlin Wall

Calling the city "the great testing place of Western courage and will," Kennedy rejected negotiations and asked Congress for an additional $3.2 billion for defense. In August the Soviets, at the urging of the East German regime, erected a concrete and barbed-wire barricade to halt the exodus of East Germans into the more prosperous and politically free West Berlin. The Berlin Wall inspired protests

When the East Germans first put up the Berlin Wall in 1961, they hastily constructed it of barbed wire. Later they added concrete blocks to the 28-mile barricade that divided East Berlin *(left)* and West Berlin *(right)*. The large building with the chariot on top is the Brandenburg Gate. The ugly wall—symbol of the Cold War—came down in 1989, when the long Soviet-American conflict finally waned.   (Corbis-Bettmann)

throughout the noncommunist world, but Kennedy privately sighed that "a wall is a hell of a lot better than a war." The ugly barrier shut off the flow of refugees, and the crisis passed.

U.S. hostilities with Cuba provoked Kennedy's most serious confrontation with the Soviet Union. As

Bay of Pigs Invasion

in Vietnam, Cold War and Third World issues dramatically intersected in Cuba. Kennedy once acknowledged that most American allies thought the United States had a "fixation" with Cuba. The Eisenhower administration had contested the Cuban Revolution and bequeathed to the Kennedy administration a partially developed CIA plan to overthrow Fidel Castro (see page 847): Cuban exiles would land and secure a beachhead; the Cuban people would rise up against Castro and welcome a new government brought in from the United States. Because he felt uneasy over such a blatant attempt to topple a sovereign government, Kennedy ordered that the U.S. hand be kept hidden—wishful thinking at best given the size of the operation. The president never attempted to negotiate Cuban American troubles with Castro.

On April 17, 1961, directed by the CIA and escorted by U.S. warships, some fourteen hundred commandos scrambled ashore at the Bay of Pigs (*Bahía de Cochinos*). A CIA scheme to assassinate Castro before the invasion had faltered. The Cuban people did not rise up against Castro. Within two days most of the invaders had been captured by Cubans loyal to Castro. Although Kennedy refused to order an air strike to aid the invaders when the landing was failing, the operation from the start never had much chance of success. Boats went aground on coral reefs that the CIA had identified as seaweed, and equipment malfunctioned. If the exiles had managed to move inland, they would have faced Castro's large armed militia. Before the operation was over, 4 Americans, 114 Cuban exile invaders, and 150 Cuban defenders had died. As for Castro, the Bay of Pigs invasion helped him remain popular as a nationalist hero, as did his land reform and improvements in healthcare and education. Concluding that the United States would not take defeat well and might launch another invasion, the Cuban leader looked even more toward the Soviet Union for a military and economic lifeline.

Kennedy vowed to bring Castro down. His brother, Attorney General Robert Kennedy, promised "to stir things up on the island with espionage, sabotage, [and] general disorder." The CIA soon hatched a project called Operation Mongoose to disrupt the island's trade, support raids on Cuba from Miami, and plot with organized-crime bosses to assassinate Castro. The United States also tightened its economic blockade, engineered Cuba's eviction from the Organization of American States, and undertook military maneuvers in the Caribbean. The Joint Chiefs of Staff sketched plans to spark a rebellion in Cuba that would be followed by an invasion of U.S. troops. "If I had been in Moscow or Havana at that time," Defense Secretary Robert McNamara later remarked, "I would have believed the Americans were preparing for an invasion."

Had there been no Bay of Pigs invasion, no Operation Mongoose, no assassination plots, no program of diplomatic and economic isolation,

Cuban Missile Crisis

and no military maneuvers and planning, there would have been no missile crisis. Cuba would have had no urgent need for Soviet military assistance. For Castro, relentless U.S. hostility represented a real threat to Cuba's independence. For the Soviets, American actions challenged the only procommunist regime in Latin America. Premier Khrushchev also saw an opportunity to improve the Soviet position in the nuclear arms race. Castro and Khrushchev devised a risky plan to deter any new U.S. intervention. In mid-1962 they agreed to install in Cuba nuclear armed missiles capable of hitting the United States. The world soon faced brinkmanship at its most frightening.

In mid-October 1962 a U-2 plane flying over Cuba photographed missile sites. The president immediately organized a special Executive Committee of advisers to find a way to force the missiles and their nuclear warheads out of Cuba. Some members advised a surprise air strike. The Joint Chiefs of Staff recommended a full-scale military invasion, an option that risked a prolonged war with Cuba, a Soviet attack against West Berlin, or even nuclear holocaust. The diplomat Charles Bohlen, a U.S. expert on Soviet affairs, unsuccessfully urged quiet, direct negotiations with Moscow. McNamara proposed the formula that the president accepted: a naval quarantine of Cuba.

Kennedy addressed the nation on television on October 22 to demand that the Soviets retreat. U.S. warships began crisscrossing the Caribbean, while B-52s with nuclear bombs took to the skies. Khrushchev replied that the missiles would be withdrawn if Washington pledged never to attack Cuba. And he added that American Jupiter missiles aimed at the Soviet Union must be removed from Turkey. Edgy advisers predicted war, but on October 28 came a Soviet-American compromise. The United States promised

How do historians know...

that, at the outset of the Cuban missile crisis, President John F. Kennedy preferred military action to diplomacy to force out the Soviet missiles? Months before that dangerous October 1962 crisis, Kennedy had ordered the Secret Service to install an audiotape system to record White House meetings. The system recorded its first meeting on July 30, 1962. A Dictabelt system for recording telephone conversations was installed later, in early September. Besides Kennedy himself, only the president's personal secretary, two Secret Service agents, and possibly the president's brother Robert knew about the taping system. Microphones were concealed in light fixtures in the Cabinet Room and in the president's desk in the Oval Office. Kennedy could activate the system by flipping hidden switches. The recording quality proved poor, full of background noise, leaving some words unintelligible.

Whether Kennedy wanted the recordings as an accurate record for future memoirs or as protection against misrepresentations of private discussions, he left historians a rich source on high-level decision making in the White House: 127 audiotapes (248 hours) and 73 Dictabelts (12 hours) on wide-ranging topics. During the missile crisis, Kennedy regularly convened and taped meetings of an advisory Executive Committee. Shown below is an excerpt from the transcript of the committee's first meeting, 11:50 A.M. to 12:57 P.M., October 16, 1962, in which the president emphasizes "taking out" the missiles.

Some three decades after the event, the John F. Kennedy Library in Boston declassified the recordings, making them available to researchers. A Harvard University project headed by Ernest R. May and Philip D. Zelikow transcribed the recordings and published the results as *The Kennedy Tapes* (1997). Because of such tapes, historians can study the minute-by-minute, hour-by-hour handling of significant issues, in this case a crisis that brought the Soviet Union and the United States to the nuclear brink. (Photo: John F. Kennedy Library)

JFK?:   . . . is to figure out what are the minimum number of people that we really have to tell. ▓▓▓▓▓▓▓▓▓▓▓▓▓▓▓▓▓▓▓

Bundy: Right. ▓▓▓▓▓▓▓▓▓▓▓▓▓▓▓▓▓▓▓ You've got to tell, it seems to me you're going to have to tell SACEUR*** . . .

JFK: Uhm.

Bundy: . . . and, uh, and the commandant.

Dillon: I would think this business about the Soviet reaction, that there, that might be helpful, uh, if we could maybe take some, uh, general war preparation type of action that would show them that we're ready if they want to start anything, without what you might, with starting anything.

Bundy: One. . . .

Dillon: You just don't know.

Bundy: On this track, one obvious element on the political side is do we say something simultaneously or, uh, to the Cubans, to the Soviets, or do we let the action speak for itself?

Rusk: This point whether we say something to the Cubans and the Soviets before any, before . . .

JFK: I think we ought to, what we ought to do is, is, uh, after this meeting this afternoon, we ought to meet tonight again at six, consider these various, uh, proposals. In the meanwhile, we'll go ahead with this maximum, whatever is needed from the flights, and, in addition, we will. . . . I don't think we got much time on these missiles. They may be. . . . So it may be that we just have to, we can't wait two weeks while we're getting ready to, to roll. Maybe just have to just take them out, and continue our other preparations if we decide to do that. That may be where we end up. I think we ought to, beginning right now, be preparing to. . . . Because that's what we're going to do anyway. We're certainly going to do number one; we're going to take out these, uh, missiles. Uh, the questions will be whether, which, what I would describe as number two, which would be a general air strike. That we're not ready to say, but we should be in preparation for it. The third is the, is the, uh, the general invasion. At least we're going to do number one, so it seems to me that we don't have to wait very long. We, we ought to be making those preparations.

Bundy: You want to be clear, Mr. President, whether we have definitely decided against a political track. I, myself, think we ought . . .

▓▓▓▓▓▓▓▓▓▓▓▓▓▓▓   ***Supreme Allied Commander, Europe.

not to invade Cuba and secretly pledged to withdraw the Jupiters from Turkey in exchange for the withdrawal of Soviet offensive forces from Cuba. Fearing accidents or some provocative action by Castro that might start a "real fire," Khrushchev decided to settle without consulting the Cubans. The missiles departed Cuba.

"I cut his balls off," Kennedy privately crowed to friends. Forcing Khrushchev to back down, many said, was his finest hour. But critics then and now hold Kennedy responsible in the first place for provoking the crisis through his anti-Cuban projects. These critics also reject the view that Kennedy practiced an exemplary model of crisis management. His handling of the crisis actually courted disaster. Accidents, near misses, and inadequate information caused events to come close to spinning out of control. On October 27, for example, a Soviet commander shot down a U-2 plane over Cuba. The Americans prepared to retaliate, not knowing that Soviet commanders had tactical nuclear weapons to use against an invasion. Robert Kennedy himself feared "a chain reaction will quickly start that will be very hard to stop." That same day, a U.S. military jet mistakenly crossed into Soviet territory, nearly setting off an air war. Finally, critics have argued that the strategic balance of power was not seriously altered by the missiles in Cuba; the United States still enjoyed a tremendous advantage over the Soviets in the nuclear arms race. Did Kennedy risk doomsday unnecessarily?

Kennedy's Handling of the Crisis

The Cuban missile crisis both calmed and accelerated the Cold War. In June 1963 Kennedy spoke at American University in conciliatory terms, urging cautious Soviet-American steps toward disarmament. In August the adversaries signed a treaty banning nuclear tests in the atmosphere. They also installed a coded wire-telegraph "hot line" staffed around the clock by translators and technicians. Both sides refrained from further confrontation in Berlin. Still, humiliated by the missile crisis, the Soviets determined to catch up in the nuclear arms race, sending the Cold War to a more dangerous stage. In mid-1963 Castro, seeking an accommodation with Washington because he was still angry with Moscow for failing to consult him during the missile crisis, directed "feelers" toward U.S. diplomats. Kennedy authorized contacts with Cuban intermediaries, but in June he also approved a new sabotage program against Cuba. The

Aftermath

CIA at the same time revitalized assassination plots, all of which failed. After Kennedy's death, Johnson decided to put the cautious diplomatic contacts "on ice," words that well describe the years of Cuban-U.S. antagonism that followed. Wondering why the United States did not simply overpower his small island nation, Castro later remarked that Cuba was "saved by Vietnam" because "the immense American drive that went into Vietnam" might very well "have been turned against Cuba."

Johnson and Americanization of the War in Vietnam

Kennedy's successor, Lyndon B. Johnson, held firmly to ideas about U.S. superiority and the menace of communism. A supreme can-do politician from Texas—a "flawed giant" of a man, according to one biographer—Johnson saw the world in simple, bipolar terms: them against us, and he saw a lot of "them." A fierce competitor, Johnson once declared that he had sex with more women by accident than Kennedy had on purpose. Invoking macho images of a fight-to-the-last-man Alamo, Johnson often exaggerated, went into rages, and lied. He opened a credibility gap with the American people, many of whom came to wonder if he could tell the difference between truth and falsehood. An old New Dealer and ardent liberal reformer, the president talked about building Tennessee Valley Authorities around the world. "I want them to say, 'This is what Americans left—schools and hospitals and dams.'" The general problem, said Senator J. William Fulbright, chair of the Foreign Relations Committee, was that an "arrogance of power" made Americans such as Johnson believe that they could run the world.

Championing the global containment doctrine and holding a monolithic view of communism, Johnson drew the line not only in Southeast Asia but also in Latin America. In spring 1965, with the president fearing "another Cuba," twenty-three thousand U.S. troops landed in the Dominican Republic to prevent a leftist government from coming to power. Johnson growled, "What the hell can we do in Vietnam if we can't clean up the Dominican Republic?" His disparaging view of Dominicans (they needed "cleaning up") and continued worries about anti-Americanism led to U.S. backing of a dictatorship on the island that lasted some thirty years.

President Lyndon B. Johnson (1908–1973) *(left),* here meeting with Secretary of Defense Robert S. McNamara (b. 1919) at the president's Texas ranch in December 1964, agonized over the Vietnam War. That year, recorded telephone conversations reveal, the president remarked that the war was "just the biggest damn mess I ever saw." Johnson also lamented that "I don't think it's worth fighting for, and I don't think we can get out." Later, McNamara wrote in his memoir, *In Retrospect* (1995), that U.S. officials "acted according to what we thought were the principles and traditions of this nation. We made our [Vietnam] decisions in light of those values. Yet we were wrong, terribly wrong."   (Yoichi R. Okamoto/Lyndon B. Johnson Library)

As both the United States and the Soviet Union grew more alarmed by China's nuclear capability (the Chinese detonated their first atomic bomb in 1964), the Johnson administration in 1968 successfully completed negotiations for the Treaty on the Non-proliferation of Nuclear Weapons (which went into effect in 1970). But many nonnuclear states saw discrimination because they had to renounce nuclear weapons while the nuclear states (United States, Soviet Union, Britain, France, and China) could keep them. The treaty ran into other obstacles. Both France and China refused to sign the agreement and supplied nonnuclear countries with nuclear fuel, and other nations defied the treaty by eventually developing their own nuclear weapons—Israel, South Africa, India, and Pakistan, among them. The Soviet invasion of Czechoslovakia in 1968 to block a nationalist movement caused Johnson to shelve further arms-control talks. With the Soviet Union and

Nuclear Non-proliferation Treaty

the United States backing opposing forces in the Vietnam War, opportunities for relaxing the Cold War diminished even more.

Some observers called it "Johnson's War," but President Kennedy had significantly deepened U.S. engagement in Vietnam, where Ho Chi Minh's North assisted the Vietcong in the South to advance the reunification of his country under a Communist government. Kennedy stepped up aid dollars to the Diem regime in the South, increased the airdropping of raiding teams into North Vietnam, and launched crop destruction by herbicides to starve the Vietcong and expose their hiding places. Under Project Beef-up, he sent more U.S. military personnel to South Vietnam; by late 1963 some 16,000 of these American "advisers" operated in Vietnam, and, that year, 489 of them were killed.

Kennedy's Legacy in Vietnam

Meanwhile, Diem's opponents grew in number. The U.S. Strategic Hamlet Program, which aimed to

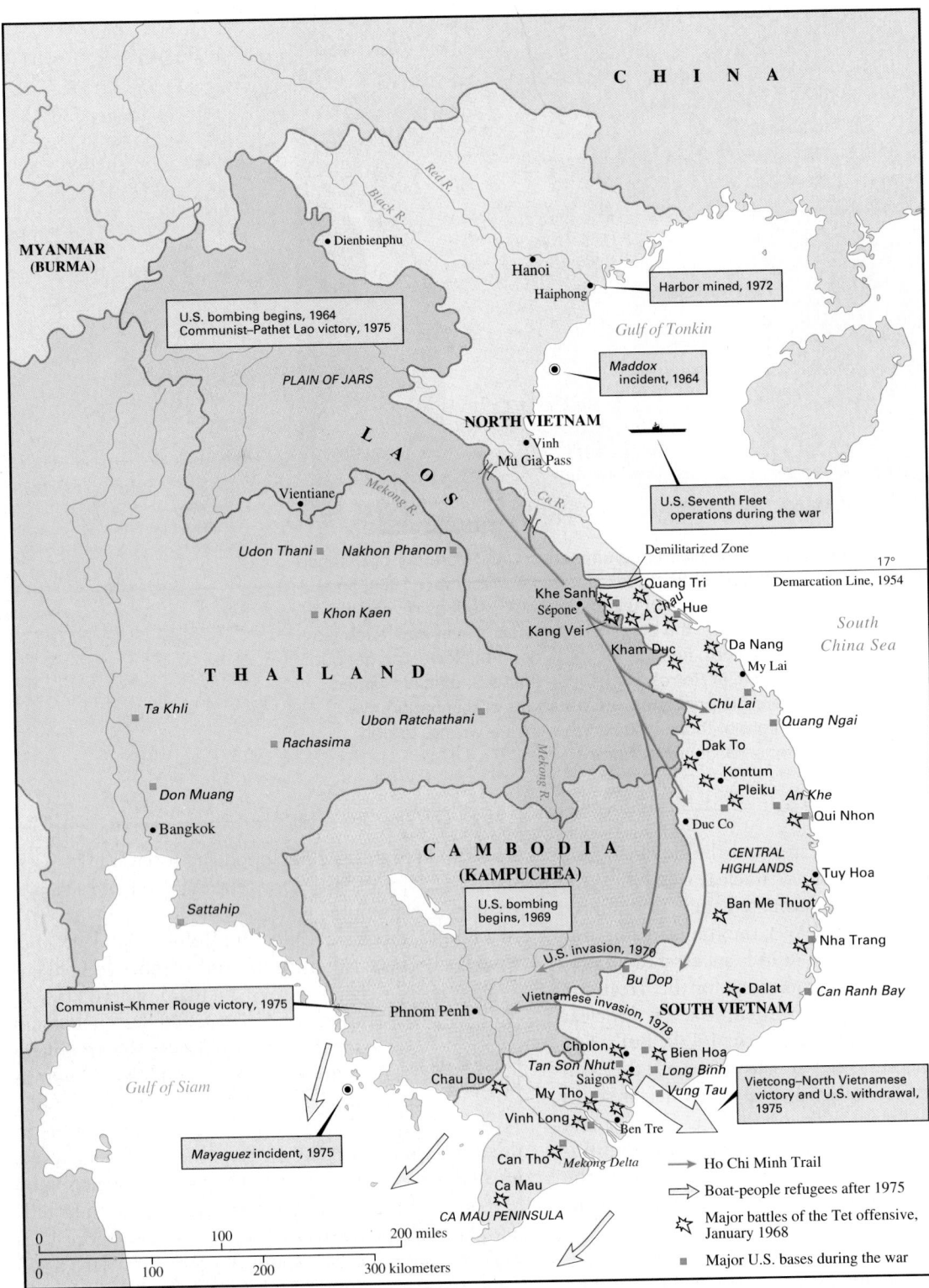

Map 31.1   Southeast Asia and the Vietnam War   To prevent communists from coming to power in Vietnam, Cambodia, and Laos in the 1960s, the United States intervened massively in Southeast Asia. The interventions failed, and the remaining American troops made a hasty exit from Vietnam in 1975, when the victorious Vietcong and North Vietnamese took Saigon and renamed it Ho Chi Minh City.

isolate peasants from the Vietcong by uprooting them into barbed-wire compounds, alienated villagers. Buddhist priests charged Diem with religious persecution. In the streets of Saigon, protesting monks poured gasoline over their robes and ignited themselves. Diem ran a corrupt government that handed out financial favors to family and friends. He jailed critics to silence them. U.S. officials, with Kennedy's approval, encouraged ambitious South Vietnamese generals to remove Diem. Working with a CIA agent, the generals struck on November 1, 1963, capturing and murdering Diem. Worried that the new military junta's reputation would be immediately sullied if the truth became known—that its leader had ordered the assassination of Diem—Kennedy engineered a cover-up. "It ought to be a true story," Kennedy told his aides, "if possible." Just a few weeks later Kennedy himself met death by an assassin's bullet.

With new governments in Saigon and in Washington, some analysts urged a reassessment. United Nations, Vietcong, and French leaders called for a coalition government in South Vietnam. But Lyndon Johnson vowed victory. On August 2, 1964, the U.S.S. *Maddox*, sailing in the Gulf of Tonkin off the coast of North Vietnam on an electronic intelligence–gathering patrol in an area where South Vietnamese commando raids recently had hit North Vietnam, came under attack from northern patrol boats (see Map 31.1). The unharmed *Maddox* inflicted heavy damage on the small craft. Two days later, the *Maddox*, joined by another destroyer, moved toward the North Vietnamese shore once again. In bad weather on a moonless night, sonar technicians reported torpedo attacks; the two destroyers began firing ferociously. Johnson quickly informed his advisers that the United States would retaliate. But then the *Maddox* sent a flash message: "Review of action makes many reported contacts and torpedoes fired appear doubtful." Indeed, no attack occurred on the pitch-black night of August 4; the *Maddox*'s sonar had probably picked up the noise of the destroyer itself. "Those dumb, stupid sailors," Johnson later said, "were just shooting at flying fish!"

President Johnson, aware at the time that the evidence was questionable, nonetheless pulled from his desk a resolution for Congress that he had had drafted months before. He announced on television that the United States would strike back against the "unprovoked" attack in the Tonkin Gulf by bombing North Vietnam. After this presidential deception and only

Tonkin Gulf Incident

brief debate, Congress passed the Tonkin Gulf Resolution, by 466 votes to 0 in the House and by 88 votes to 2 in the Senate. Only Wayne Morse of Oregon and Ernest Gruening of Alaska dissented from the resolution's sweeping language, which authorized the president to "take all necessary measures to repel any armed attack against the forces of the United States and to prevent further aggression." By passing the Tonkin Gulf Resolution—which Johnson considered nearly equivalent to a declaration of war—Congress essentially surrendered its powers in the foreign policy

Senator J. William Fulbright (1905–1995), a Democrat from Arkansas who studied at Oxford as a Rhodes scholar and helped create the Fulbright scholarships, chaired the Foreign Relations Committee from 1959 to 1974. His committee held hearings and published reports to inform the public about the Vietnam War, which Fulbright increasingly saw as immoral and dangerous to U.S. interests. He opposed the bombing campaigns and the deepening U.S. intervention, arguing that the war undermined détente with the Soviet Union, threatened war with China, alienated the Third World, and corrupted American values. An intemperate President Lyndon B. Johnson, who Fulbright believed had misled him in order to gain his vote for the Tonkin Gulf Resolution, fumed against the senator, ridiculously suggesting that he was a communist dupe and tagging him "half-bright." (Library of Congress)

process by giving the president wide latitude to conduct the war as he saw fit. The resolution, McNamara later noted, served "to open the floodgates."

Meanwhile, in Laos, Vietnam's neighbor, American bombers hit the "Ho Chi Minh Trail"—supply routes connecting the Vietcong with the North Vietnamese (see Map 31.1). The bombings were kept secret from Congress and the public. Despite a 1962 agreement among Laotian noncommunists and communists to create a neutralist government, "we ran Laos," Ambassador William H. Sullivan admitted. After winning the presidency in his own right in the fall of 1964, Johnson directed the military to plan stepped-up bombing of both Laos and North

Bombing Campaigns in Laos and Vietnam

Vietnam. Undersecretary Ball urged caution: "Once on the tiger's back we cannot be sure of picking the place to dismount."

In February 1965 the Vietcong, who controlled nearly half of South Vietnam, attacked the American airfield at Pleiku, killing nine Americans. In response, Johnson ordered Operation Rolling Thunder, a sustained bombing program by carrier-based jets that pounded the North (above the 17th parallel). Before the war was over, more bombs would fall on Vietnam than U.S. aircraft had dropped in the Second World War. The North Vietnamese, however, would not give up. They hid in shelters and rebuilt roads and bridges with a perseverance that frustrated and awed American decision makers. The war was not going well for the United States or its ally, the unstable and corrupt South Vietnamese government in Saigon, where hostility festered between Catholics and Buddhists and coups and countercoups by self-serving military leaders undermined U.S. efforts to win the war. "I don't think we ought to take this government seriously," Ambassador Henry Cabot Lodge told a White House meeting. "There is simply no one who can do anything."

Then came Johnson's July decision to increase significantly U.S. ground forces. Month by month the war became Americanized. In 1966 American troops climbed to 385,000. In 1967 alone U.S. warplanes flew 108,000 sorties and dropped 226,000 tons of bombs on North Vietnam. In 1968 U.S. troop strength reached 536,100; in 1969 it peaked at 543,400 before falling by the end of the year to 475,200 (see Figure 31.1). In 1967 the secret CIA-run Phoenix Program began to kill Vietcong leaders; probably 60,000 were assassinated. That year, too, the United States sent $625 million in foreign aid to South Vietnam—25 percent of America's total aid to the entire world. Undeterred, Ho increased the flow of arms and men to the rebels in the South.

Troop Strength

In this seemingly endless war of attrition, each American escalation begot a new Vietnamese escalation. "Vietnam is like being in a plane without a parachute when the engines go out," Johnson remarked. "If you jump, you'll probably be killed, and if you stay in you'll crash and probably burn." Rejecting the Joint Chiefs' view that U.S. reserve forces should be mobilized and a national emergency declared, the president kept thinking that the North Vietnamese and Vietcong, taking heavy casualties, had a breaking point. Johnson also worried that if he did not win that "bitch

Figure 31.1 U.S. Troops in Vietnam, 1960–1972
These numbers show the Americanization of the Vietnam War under President Johnson, who ordered vast increases in troop levels. President Nixon reversed the escalation, so that by the time of the cease-fire in early 1973 fewer than 25,000 American troops remained in Vietnam. Data are for December 31 of each year. (Source: U.S. Department of Defense)

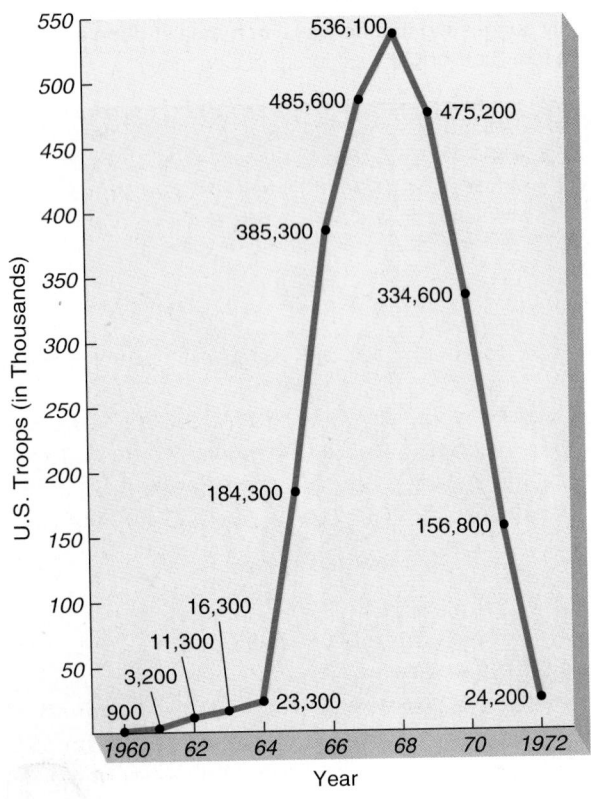

of a war" in Vietnam, members of Congress would cripple his Great Society reform program—"the woman I really loved" (see pages 859–862).

Vietnam: Escalation, Carnage, and Protest

The Americanization of the war under Johnson troubled growing numbers of Americans, especially as television coverage brought the war into their homes every night. Villages went up in flames, innocent civilians were maimed and died, and refugees straggled into "pacification" camps. U.S. planes sprayed chemicals such as Agent Orange to kill crops and forests. This ecological warfare meant that a once-rich agricultural nation became dependent on imports of food. The Vietcong and North Vietnamese contributed to the carnage and destruction, but American guns, bombs, and chemicals took by far the greater toll, and the Vietnamese people knew it. Indeed, America's search-and-destroy missions proved counterproductive; rather than winning the war, they were molding an ever-growing population of anti-American peasants who gave secret aid to the Vietcong. Even U.S. allies among the Vietnamese came to resent their nation's growing dependency. Their politics manipulated and their traditional culture challenged by rock-'n'-roll music, interracial marriages, honky-tonk bars, and prostitution, some anticommunist Vietnamese said that they feared becoming "a little America." One U.S. official later admitted, "It was as if we were trying to build a house with a bulldozer and wrecking crane."

Stories of atrocities made their way home. Most gruesome was the My Lai massacre of March 16, 1968.

My Lai Massacre

The freelance journalist Seymour Hersh broke the story after a military cover-up kept the tragedy out of the news for twenty months. A U.S. army unit led by Lieutenant William Calley entered the hamlet of My Lai and for four hours mutilated, raped, sodomized, and killed unarmed Vietnamese civilians, most of them women and children. Herding shrieking, pleading villagers near a ditch, Calley and his troops shot scores of them. When a two-year-old child, its mother dead, began to crawl out of the mass grave, Calley tossed the infant down the slope and shot it. The army awarded Calley's brigade a Special Commendation for 128 "enemy" killed even though there had been no combat and no

"There's Money Enough To Support Both Of You — Now, Doesn't That Make You Feel Better?"

President Johnson repeatedly claimed that the mounting costs of the war in Vietnam would not drain funds from his domestic reform programs. Others, such as Herblock in this August 1, 1967, cartoon, saw danger. So did Martin Luther King, Jr. He calculated that the United States was spending $500,000 to kill one enemy Vietnamese soldier but only $35 a year to assist one American in poverty. "The promises of the Great Society," King regretted, "have been shot down on the battlefield of Vietnam." (© 1967 by Herblock in *The Washington Post*)

battle at My Lai. The actual death toll numbered some 500.

An army photographer captured the horror in graphic pictures. Why did the massacre occur? Applying a "war is hell" theory, some soldiers explained that they had been trained to kill. Calley fingered anticommunism: "I looked at communism as a southerner looks at a Negro. . . . It's evil." Racism certainly played a role: dehumanizing Vietnamese as "gooks" and "slants," GIs murdered in cold blood people they ranked with animals. A culture of male supremacy, accentuated by the military environment, also influenced these infantrymen: girls and young women suffered gang rapes; some victims had their vaginas ripped

Aftermath of the My Lai massacre, March 16, 1968, photographed by U.S. Army photographer Ronald Haeberle of the 11th Infantry Brigade, American Division.   (Ron Haeberle/*Life Magazine* © Time Inc.)

open with knives and bayonets. Calley and the other rapists and killers had lost their moral bearings. But the aftermath reveals that U.S. officials had lost theirs too. In 1971 Calley was court-martialed, but President Nixon ordered him released from jail; three years later the mass murderer was paroled. Army juries acquitted and army officials dismissed murder and cover-up charges against all other personnel connected with the My Lai massacre. Today in Vietnam a museum and monument stand at the site of the massacre. In 1998 the U.S. government awarded the former pilot Hugh Thompson the prestigious Soldier's Medal for his heroism on March 16, 1968, at My Lai: he stopped some of the bloodletting by placing his helicopter between rampaging American GIs and villagers crowded in a hut.

Many incidents of deliberate shooting of civilians, torturing and killing of prisoners, taking of Vietnamese ears as trophies, and burning of villages have been recorded. Most American soldiers, however, were not committing atrocities. They were trying to save their own young lives (their average age was only nineteen)

American Soldiers in Vietnam

and to serve the U.S. mission of defeating enemy troops. Less than 15 percent actually served in combat units; most made up the important rear-echelon supply and medical services that supported the "grunts" in the field. But wherever they were, the environment was inhospitable, for no place in Vietnam was secure. Well-hidden booby traps blasted away body parts. And the enemy was everywhere yet nowhere, often burrowed into elaborate underground tunnels or melded into the population, where any Vietnamese might be a Vietcong.

Infantrymen on maneuvers carried heavy rucksacks into thick jungle growth, where every step was precarious. Insects swarmed, and leeches sucked at weary bodies. Boots and human skin rotted from the rains, which alternated with withering suns. "It was as if the sun and the land itself were in league with the Vietcong," recalled marine officer Philip Caputo in *A Rumor of War* (1977), "wearing us down, driving us mad, killing us." Wounded GIs shouted for a medic, who in turn might call in a "medevac" (medical evacuation helicopter). A medevac could carry the wounded within minutes to operating tables in MASH (Mobile Army Surgical Hospital) units or on hospital ships

Wounded American soldiers after a battle in Vietnam.   (Larry Burrows/*Life* Magazine © Time Warner, Inc.)

such as the U.S.S. *Sanctuary.* "What I saw were young men coming in, eighteen or nineteen years old . . . and they would be without a leg," remembered Gayle Smith, a nurse at the 3rd Surgical Hospital. She was one of 7,465 women who served in the military in Vietnam, most of them army nurses.

As the war ground on to no discernible conclusion and became increasingly unpopular at home, growing numbers of GIs became cynical, believing either that the administration in Washington restrained them from clobbering the enemy or that the United States had no business being in Vietnam. Leaders kept saying that the war was being won, but the GIs in the field knew better. The then Army captain and later chairman of the Joint Chiefs of Staff, Colin Powell, recalled that a "conspiracy of illusion" fed on "the secure-hamlet nonsense, the search-and-sweep nonsense, the body-count nonsense, all of which we knew was nonsense, even as we did it." Body counts of killed "enemy" forces became a false measure of success. Powell remembered the litany of each night: "'How many did your platoon get?' 'I don't

"Body-count Nonsense"

know. We saw two for sure.' 'Well, if you saw two, there were probably eight. So let's say ten.'" Powell later wrote that "counting bodies became a macabre statistical competition. Companies measured against companies, battalions against battalions, brigades against brigades. Good commanders scored high body counts. And good commanders got promotions."

Given these corrupting conditions and the war against what Powell called a "phantom enemy," morale in the U.S. armed forces sagged, and discipline sometimes lapsed. Disobedience, desertions, and absent-without-official-leave (AWOL) cases steadily increased. Racial tensions between whites and blacks intensified. Drug abuse became serious. Many soldiers smoked plentiful, cheap marijuana; 10 percent of the troops used heroin. "Fragging"—the murder of officers by enlisted men, usually using hand grenades—took at least a thousand lives between 1969 and 1972.

At home some young men were expressing their opposition to the war by fleeing the draft. By the end of 1972 more than thirty thousand draft resisters were living in Canada; thousands more had gone into exile in Sweden or Mexico or were living under false identities in the United States. During the war more than a half-million men committed draft violations, including a quarter-million who never registered and thousands who burned their draft cards. Others legally joined the National Guard to avoid the draft.

As American military engagement in Vietnam escalated, so did protest at home. Teach-ins at universi-

Growing Antiwar Sentiment

ties began in 1965, followed by years of campus and street demonstrations (see pages 867–869). In 1966 Senator Fulbright held televised public hearings on whether the national interest was being served by pursuing the war in Asia. What exactly was the threat? senators asked. To the surprise of some, George F. Kennan testified that his containment doctrine was meant for Europe, not the volatile environment of Southeast Asia. A year later, former Attorney General and then Senator Robert Kennedy pressed the president to try negotiations to end the war. In a White House meeting with Kennedy, an enraged Johnson warned, "I'll destroy you and every one of your dove friends." Not so; Kennedy went on to vie for the Democratic presidential nomination in 1968, but an assassin's bullet ended his life that year. In a direct rebuke of Johnson's policies, antiwar senator Eugene McCarthy of Minnesota announced his candidacy for the Democratic presidential nomination.

Disenchantment also rose in the administration itself. Defense Secretary Robert McNamara, once a vig-

McNamara's Doubts

orous advocate of prosecuting the war, became aghast over the Joint Chiefs' contemplating the use of nuclear weapons in Vietnam and came to believe that continued bombing would not win the war. "The picture of the world's greatest superpower killing or seriously injuring 1,000 noncombatants a week, while trying to pound a tiny backward nation into submission on an issue whose merits are hotly disputed, is not a pretty one," he told Johnson in mid-1967. But, publicly, McNamara endorsed the war until early 1968, when he left office to head the World Bank. Much later, in his 1995 autobiography, he lamented that the decisions of the Kennedy and Johnson administrations on Vietnam "were wrong, terribly wrong."

Cheered by opinion polls that showed Americans favored escalation over withdrawal, Johnson dug in, snapping at "those little shits on the campuses." Though on occasion he halted the bombing to encourage Ho Chi Minh to negotiate and to disarm critics, such pauses often were accompanied by increases

in American troop strength. And the United States sometimes resumed or accelerated the bombing just when a diplomatic breakthrough seemed imminent—as in 1966, when a Polish diplomat's efforts were cut short by a resumption of bombing. The North demanded a complete suspension of bombing raids before sitting down at the conference table. And Ho could not accept American terms: nonrecognition of the Vietcong as a legitimate political organization, withdrawal of northern soldiers from the South, and an end to North Vietnamese military aid to the Vietcong—in short, abandonment of his lifelong dream of an independent, unified Vietnam.

In January 1968 a shocking event forced Johnson to reappraise his position. During Tet, the Vietnamese

Tet Offensive

holiday of the lunar new year, Vietcong and North Vietnamese forces—intending to "deal" the United States "thundering blows"—struck all across South Vietnam, capturing provincial capitals (see Map 31.1). Vietcong raiders even penetrated the American embassy compound in Saigon. U.S. and South Vietnamese units eventually regained much of the ground they lost, including the cities, and inflicted heavy casualties on the enemy. In the process, numerous villages were devastated. As one sober-faced American officer explained about the leveling of Ben Tre to drive the Vietcong out: "It became necessary to destroy the town to save it."

The Tet Offensive jolted Americans. Although Tet ultimately counted as a U.S. military victory, it proved a psychological defeat for the U.S. war effort. Had not the Vietcong and North Vietnamese demonstrated that they could strike when and where they wished? Did they not have the advantage of fighting on home territory? Why did "their Vietnamese" fight harder than "our Vietnamese"? If all of America's airpower and dollars and half a million troops could not defeat the Vietcong once and for all, could anything do so? Had the American public been deceived? The highly respected CBS television anchorman Walter Cronkite went to Vietnam to find out. The military brass in Saigon assured him that "we had the enemy just where we wanted him." The newsman recalled, "Tell that to the Marines, I thought—the Marines in the body bags on that helicopter." When Cronkite somberly raised questions about the war on his evening telecasts, President Johnson sensed political trouble: "If I've lost Cronkite, I've lost middle America."

The new secretary of defense, Clark Clifford, told Johnson that the war—"a sinkhole"—could not be won, even if the 206,000 more soldiers requested by

Dollar/Gold Crisis

the army were sent to Vietnam. The ultimate Cold Warrior, Dean Acheson—one of the "wise men" Johnson brought in to advise him—bluntly told the surprised president that the generals did not know what they were talking about. The wise men were aware that the nation was suffering a financial crisis prompted by rampant deficit spending, largely due to heavy U.S. expenditures abroad to sustain the war and other global commitments. Nervous foreigners were exchanging their U.S. dollars for gold at an alarming rate. On March 14 alone, foreigners—especially Europeans—redeemed $372 million for gold. A post-Tet effort to take the initiative in Vietnam would surely cost billions more and thus further derail the budget, panic foreign owners of dollars, and wreck the economy. Clifford heard from his associates in the business community: "These men now feel we are in a hopeless bog," he told the president. To "maintain public support for the war without the support of these men" was impossible.

Strained by exhausting sessions with skeptical advisers, troubled by the economic implications of escalation, sensing that more soldiers and firepower would not bring victory, meeting protesters wherever he went, and faced with serious opposition within his own party (McCarthy had just made a strong showing in the New Hampshire primary), Johnson changed course. On March 31 he announced that he had stopped the bombing of most of North Vietnam, and he asked Hanoi to begin negotiations. Then he stunned the television audience by dropping out of the presidential race. American leaders, having come reluctantly to the view that they could not win the war, at least would try not to lose it. Peace talks began in May in Paris, but the war ground on.

Johnson's Exit

Nixon, Vietnamization, and the Impact of America's Longest War

"I'm not going to end up like LBJ," Richard Nixon vowed after winning the 1968 presidential election (see page 871). "I'm going to stop that war. Fast." He did not. In July 1969 the new president announced the Nixon Doctrine: the United States will help those nations that help themselves. Washington knew that it no longer could afford to sustain its many overseas commitments and that the United States would have to rely more on regional allies to maintain an anti-

communist world order. In Southeast Asia this doctrine translated into "Vietnamization"—building up South Vietnamese forces to replace U.S. forces. Nixon began to withdraw troops from Vietnam, decreasing their number to 156,800 by the end of 1971. But he also intensified the bombing of the North, hoping to pound Hanoi into concessions. As the death toll mounted in Southeast Asia, antiwar protest in the United States accelerated.

Nixon had been an ardent Cold Warrior before becoming president. Secretive, suspicious, and scowling, he spawned the Watergate political scandal and constitutional crisis that stemmed from his drive to "get" his enemies—especially critics of his Vietnam War policies. He resigned ignobly in 1974, and Gerald Ford succeeded him (see pages 879–880). Nixon believed that leaders earned greatness by acting decisively in "crisis situations" and by creating a "mystique," which "is more important than content." His self-professed "madman theory" was calculated to deter foreign adversaries by making them think that he was unpredictable and irrational—that "I might do *anything*," even use nuclear weapons in Vietnam. His chief foreign policy adviser, Henry A. Kissinger, once observed that Nixon liked the "jugular response" because "there was nothing he feared more than to be thought weak." In relations with China and the Soviet Union, Nixon shifted the Cold War from confrontation to negotiation (see pages 902–903). But in Vietnam, Nixon prolonged the war.

Telling his advisers that withdrawal was "a boy's job," Nixon decided to do a "man's job": in April 1970 South Vietnamese and U.S. forces invaded Cambodia in search of arms depots and enemy forces using the neutral nation as a sanctuary. B-52 raids had been bombing Cambodia for more than a year, although Nixon never informed Congress or the American people. But the conspicuous venture into Cambodia could not be kept secret; it especially provoked angry demonstrations on college campuses (see page 873). In June the Senate joined the outcry against Nixon's broadening of the war by terminating the Tonkin Gulf Resolution of 1964.

Invasion of Cambodia

Nixon's troubles at home mounted in June 1971 when the *New York Times* began to publish the *Pentagon Papers*, a top-secret official study of U.S. decisions in the Vietnam War. Secretary McNamara had initiated the study in 1967 to preserve the war's documentary record. Daniel Ellsberg, a former Defense Department official working at the RAND Corporation (a think tank for analyzing defense policy), leaked the report to the *Times.* Nixon secured an injunction to prevent publication, but the Supreme Court overturned the order. The *Pentagon Papers* revealed that leaders frequently had lied to the American people. President Johnson, for example, had claimed repeatedly in public that the United States increased its forces in South Vietnam only to respond to escalating North Vietnamese infiltration. The classified study, however, showed that after mid-1967 the United States itself escalated the war because American officials believed that more troops would deliver victory.

The Nixon administration continued to expand the war. Johnson had lacked the will to "go to the brink," Nixon told Kissinger. "I have the *will* in spades." In December 1972 the United States launched a massive air strike on the North—the "Christmas bombing." Kissinger called the saturation air terror of 20,000 tons of bombs "brutal unpredictability." At the same time, the United States lost fifteen B-52 bombers. "After B-52s, there doesn't seem to be anything more that they can do," claimed one North Vietnamese. "Apparently they have come to their technological limit."

In Paris, meanwhile, the peace talks begun in 1968 seemed to be going nowhere. The South Vietnamese delegate, who saw defeat coming,

Cease-fire Agreement

purposely stalled the negotiations. But Kissinger was also meeting privately with Le Duc Tho, North Vietnam's chief delegate. Nixon instructed Kissinger to make concessions because the president was eager to improve relations with the Soviet Union and China, to win back the allegiance of America's allies, and to restore stability at home. When President Nguyen Van Thieu of South Vietnam balked at compromise, Nixon decided to "let Thieu paddle his own canoe." On January 27, 1973, Kissinger and Le Duc Tho signed a cease-fire agreement, and Nixon compelled Thieu to accept it by threatening to cut off U.S. aid while at the same time promising to defend the South if the North violated the agreement. In the accord, the United States promised to withdraw all of its troops within sixty days. All Vietnamese troops would stay in place, and a coalition government that included the Vietcong eventually would be formed in the South.

The United States pulled its troops out of Vietnam, leaving behind some advisers. Soon, both North and South violated the cease-fire, and full-scale war erupted once more. The feeble South Vietnamese government—for so long an American puppet—could not hold out. Just before its surrender, hundreds of Americans and Vietnamese who had worked for them were hastily evacuated from Saigon. On April 29, 1975, the South Vietnamese government collapsed. Shortly thereafter Saigon was renamed Ho Chi Minh City for the persevering patriot, who had died in 1969.

The overall costs of the war were immense. More than 58,000 Americans and some 1.5 million Vietnamese had died. Civilian deaths in

Costs of the Vietnam War

Cambodia and Laos numbered in the millions. The war cost the United States at least $170 billion, and billions more would be paid out in veterans' benefits. The vast sums spent on the war became unavailable for investment at home to improve the infrastructure and quality of life. Instead, the nation suffered inflation and retreat from reform programs (see Chapters 30 and 32), as well as political schism, violations of civil liberties, and abuses of executive power. The war also delayed accommodation with the Soviet Union and the People's Republic of China, fueled friction with allies, and alienated Third World nations.

In 1975 communists assumed control and instituted repressive governments in South Vietnam, Cambodia, and Laos, but the domino effect once predicted by U.S. officials never occurred. Acute hunger afflicted the people of those devastated lands. Soon refugees—"boat people"—crowded aboard unsafe vessels in an attempt to escape their battered homelands. Many emigrated to the United States, where they were received with mixed feelings by Americans reluctant to be reminded of defeat in Asia. But many Americans faced the fact that the United States, which had relentlessly bombed, burned, and defoliated once-rich agricultural lands, bore considerable responsibility for the plight of the Southeast Asian peoples.

This sad conclusion prompted an American ambassador to pose a central question about the U.S. defeat: How was it that "so many with so much could achieve so little for so long against so few"? General Maxwell Taylor, summarizing the reasons why Americans could not win the Vietnam War, answered that "we didn't know our ally. Secondly, we knew even less about the enemy. And, the last, most inexcusable of our mistakes, was not knowing our own people."

Debate over the Lessons of Vietnam

Americans seemed both angry and confused about the nation's war experience. For the first time in their history, the historian William Appleman Williams observed, Americans, having had their overseas sphere of influence violently pushed back, were suffering from a serious case of "empire shock." Hawkish leaders claimed that America's failure in Vietnam undermined the nation's credibility and tempted enemies to exploit opportunities at the expense of U.S. interests. They pointed to a "Vietnam syndrome"—a suspicion of foreign entanglements—that they feared would inhibit the exercise of U.S. power. Next time, they said, the military should be permitted to do its job—use nuclear weapons? invade the North? bomb more sites?—free from the constraints of whimsical public opinion, stab-in-the-back journalists, and meddlesome politicians. America lost in Vietnam, they asserted, because Americans lost their guts at home.

Dovish leaders drew different conclusions, denying that the military had suffered undue restrictions. Some blamed the war on an imperial presidency that had permitted strong-willed men to act without restraint, and on pusillanimous Congresses that had conceded too much power to the executive branch. Make the president adhere to the checks-and-balances system—make him go to Congress for a declaration of war—these critics counseled, and America would become less interventionist. This view found expression in the War Powers Act of 1973, which sought to limit the president's war-making freedom.

Other critics claimed that as long as the United States remained a major power with compelling ideological, strategic, economic, and political needs that could be satisfied only through activism abroad, the nation would continue to be interventionist, especially in the Third World. The United States was destined to intervene abroad, they argued, to sustain its hegemonic role as the world's policeman, teacher, social worker, banker, and merchant. Some critics blamed the containment doctrine—that "prison-house" for policymakers, according to the historian George C. Herring—for failing to make distinctions between areas vital and peripheral to the national security and for relying too heavily on military means. Containment could not work, they believed, if there were no political stability and no effective popular government in the country where it was being applied.

Public discussion of the lessons of the Vietnam War also was stimulated by veterans' calls for help in

Vietnam Veterans

dealing with post-traumatic stress disorder, which afflicted thousands of the 2.8 million Vietnam veterans. Once home, they suffered nightmares and extreme nervousness. Doctors reported that the disorder stemmed primarily from the

Dedicated in 1993 in Washington, D.C., the Vietnam Women's Memorial honors the several thousand military women who served in Vietnam, many of them as nurses who volunteered for duty. One nurse, Judy Marron, remembered treating wounded soldiers round the clock: "There were days when the stress and strain and blood and guts almost had to equal the frontlines." This bronze sculpture, by Glenna Goodacre, stands near the long wall on which are etched the names of Americans who died in Vietnam. (Brad Markel/Liaison Agency)

soldiers' having seen so many children, women, and elderly people killed. Some GIs inadvertently killed these people; some killed them vengefully and later felt guilt. Other veterans heightened public awareness of the war by publicizing their deteriorating health from the effects of Agent Orange and other chemicals they had handled or were accidentally sprayed with in Vietnam. Feature films such as *Coming Home* (1978), *The Deer Hunter* (1978), and *Apocalypse Now* (1979), personal accounts such as Philip Caputo's *A Rumor of War* (1977), and novels such as James Webb's *Fields of Fire* (1978), all of which depicted the soldier's Vietnam, hinted that defeat had been inevitable, given the inhospitable environment and an elusive enemy fighting a guerrilla war. The Vietnam Veterans Memorial, erected in Washington, D.C., in 1982, has kept the question alive, as have many oral history projects of veterans conducted by school and college students in classes to this day.

Nixon, Kissinger, and Détente

Nixon's national security affairs adviser (1969–1973) and secretary of state (1973–1977), Henry Kissinger, often gets the credit (or blame) for the Nixon administration's grand strategy to promote a global balance of power. Actually, *Nixinger*—a term coined by the historian Joan Hoff—captures well the shared views of Nixon and Kissinger about the need boldly and repeatedly to demonstrate U.S. power. The first part of the strategy was détente: measured cooperation with the Soviets through negotiations within a general environment of rivalry. Détente's primary purpose, like that of the containment doctrine it resembled, was to check Soviet expansion and limit the Soviet arms buildup. The second part of the strategy sought to curb revolution and radicalism in the Third World so as to quash threats to American interests.

The grand design seemed attractive to its architects: the Cold War and limited wars such as in Vietnam were costing too much; more trade with friendlier Soviets and Chinese might reduce the huge U.S. balance-of-payments deficit; and improving relations with both Communist giants, at a time when a Sino-Soviet split had opened wide, might exacerbate feuding between the two, weakening communism. Skeptics, however, soon faulted the Nixinger posture for its assumption that the United States had the right and the ability to manipulate a disorderly world. The travails of the Vietnam War—which Kissinger insensitively dismissed as a mere "footnote" in history—illustrated the point.

Pros and Cons of Détente

Nixon and Kissinger pursued détente with extraordinary energy and fanfare. They expanded trade with the Soviet Union; a 1972 deal sent $1 billion worth of American grain to the Soviets at bargain prices. To slow the costly arms race, they initiated the Strategic Arms Limitations Talks (SALT). In May 1972 Soviet and American negotiators produced two SALT I agreements. The first treaty limited antiballistic missile (ABM) systems for each nation to just two sites. ABM systems had accelerated the arms race because both sides built more missiles to overcome the ABM protection. In essence, SALT I sustained the Mutual Assured Destruction (MAD) doctrine: by leaving cities and offensive missile bases in both countries vulnerable to nuclear attack by not protecting them with defensive ABMs, it was assumed that war would be deterred because neither Washington nor Moscow would want to trigger its own, assured destruction.

SALT

The other SALT I agreement imposed a five-year freeze on the number of offensive nuclear missiles each side could possess. At the time, the Soviets held an advantage in total strategic forces (ICBMs, SLBMs, and long-range bombers)—2,547 to 2,160. But the United States had more warheads per missile because it could outfit each missile with MIRVs (multiple independently targeted reentry vehicles) that could send warheads to several different targets. In short, the

Henry A. Kissinger (b. 1923) *(right)* walks with President Nixon. An ambitious, knowledgeable, and self-flattering German-born political scientist from Harvard University, Kissinger served as assistant for national security affairs and secretary of state. Although he and the president shared basic assumptions about U.S. foreign relations, especially the need to promote détente and curb revolution, Kissinger judged Nixon an "egomaniac." Critics on the left compared Kissinger to Dr. Strangelove, the fictional Germanic adviser—played by Peter Sellers in the movie of the same name—who was so deranged that he welcomed a nuclear holocaust. Critics on the right thought Kissinger too conciliatory to the communists. (Dennis Brack/Black Star)

United States had a two-to-one advantage in deliverable warheads (5,700 to 2,500). Because SALT did not restrict MIRVs, the nuclear arms buildup actually continued.

In 1975, at the Conference on Security and Cooperation in Helsinki, Finland, the United States, Canada, and most European nations signed several accords that accepted the permanence of existing European boundaries, including adjustments made in Germany and eastern Europe right after the Second World War. The conferees also applauded détente and endorsed human rights for all. Conservatives in the United States excoriated the Ford administration for a sellout to the Soviets, but dozens of "Helsinki groups," including Solidarity in Poland and Charter 77 in Czechoslovakia, sprang up to press Communist regimes to honor the human-rights pledge.

Helsinki Accords

While cultivating détente with the Soviet Union, the United States took dramatic steps to end more than two decades of Sino-American hostility. The Chinese welcomed the change because they wanted to spur trade and hoped that friendlier Sino-American relations would make their onetime ally and now enemy, the Soviet Union, more cautious. Nixon reasoned the same way: "We're using the Chinese thaw to get the Russians shook." In early 1972 Nixon made a historic trip to "Red China," where he and the venerable Chinese leaders Mao Zedong and Zhou Enlai agreed to disagree on a number of issues, except one: the Soviet Union should not be permitted to make gains in Asia. Nixon also hoped that China would press North Vietnam to make peace. Sino-American relations improved slightly, and official diplomatic recognition and the exchange of ambassadors came in 1979.

Opening to China

Events in the Third World—especially in the Middle East—revealed the fragility of the U.S. grand strategy. Israel, using American weapons, had scored victories against Egypt and Syria in the Six-Day War (1967), seizing the West Bank and the ancient city of Jerusalem from Jordan, the Golan Heights from Syria, and the Sinai Peninsula from Egypt (see Map 31.2), and thereby creating the enduring problem of the "occupied territories." Israel's Arab adversaries had used Soviet weapons. Palestinians, many of them expelled from their homes in 1948 when the nation of Israel was created, had organized the Palestine Liberation Organi-

War in the Middle East

zation (PLO) and pledged to destroy Israel. PLO sympathizers made hit-and-run raids on Jewish settlements, hijacked jetliners, and murdered Israeli athletes at the 1972 Olympic Games in Munich, West Germany. The Israelis retaliated by assassinating PLO leaders.

In October 1973 Egypt and Syria attacked Israel. In spite of détente, Moscow (backing Egypt) and Washington (backing Israel) put their armed forces—including their nuclear forces—on alert. In an attempt to push Americans into a pro-Arab stance, the Organization of Petroleum Exporting Countries (OPEC) embargoed shipments of oil to the United States. An energy crisis and dramatically higher oil prices rocked the nation. Soon Kissinger arranged a cease-fire and undertook "shuttle diplomacy," flying repeatedly among Middle Eastern capitals in search of a settlement. In March 1974 OPEC lifted the oil embargo. The next year Kissinger persuaded Egypt and Israel to accept a U.N. peacekeeping force in the Sinai. But peace did not come to the region because Palestinian and other Arabs still vowed to destroy Israel, and Israelis insisted on building Jewish settlements in occupied lands.

In Latin America, meanwhile, the Nixon administration pursued the traditional antiradical course of the United States. In Chile, after voters in 1970 elected a Marxist president, Salvador Allende, the CIA began secret operations to disrupt Chile ("make the economy scream") and encouraged military officers to stage a coup. In 1973 a military junta ousted Allende and installed an authoritarian regime under General Augusto Pinochet. Washington publicly denied any role in the affair that implanted iron-fisted tyranny in Chile for two decades.

Chile

In Africa, from which Americans imported large quantities of oil, chromium, cobalt, and other strategic minerals, Washington preferred the status quo. Slurring black Africans as "jigs" and "niggers," Nixon backed the white-minority regime in Rhodesia (now Zimbabwe); activated the CIA in a failed effort to defeat a Soviet- and Cuban-backed faction in newly independent Angola's civil war; and in South Africa tolerated the white rulers who imposed the segregationist policy of apartheid on blacks (85 percent of the population), keeping them poor, disfranchised, and ghettoized in prison-like townships. After the leftist government came to power in Angola, however, Washington took a keener interest in the rest of Africa, building economic

Containing Radicalism in Africa

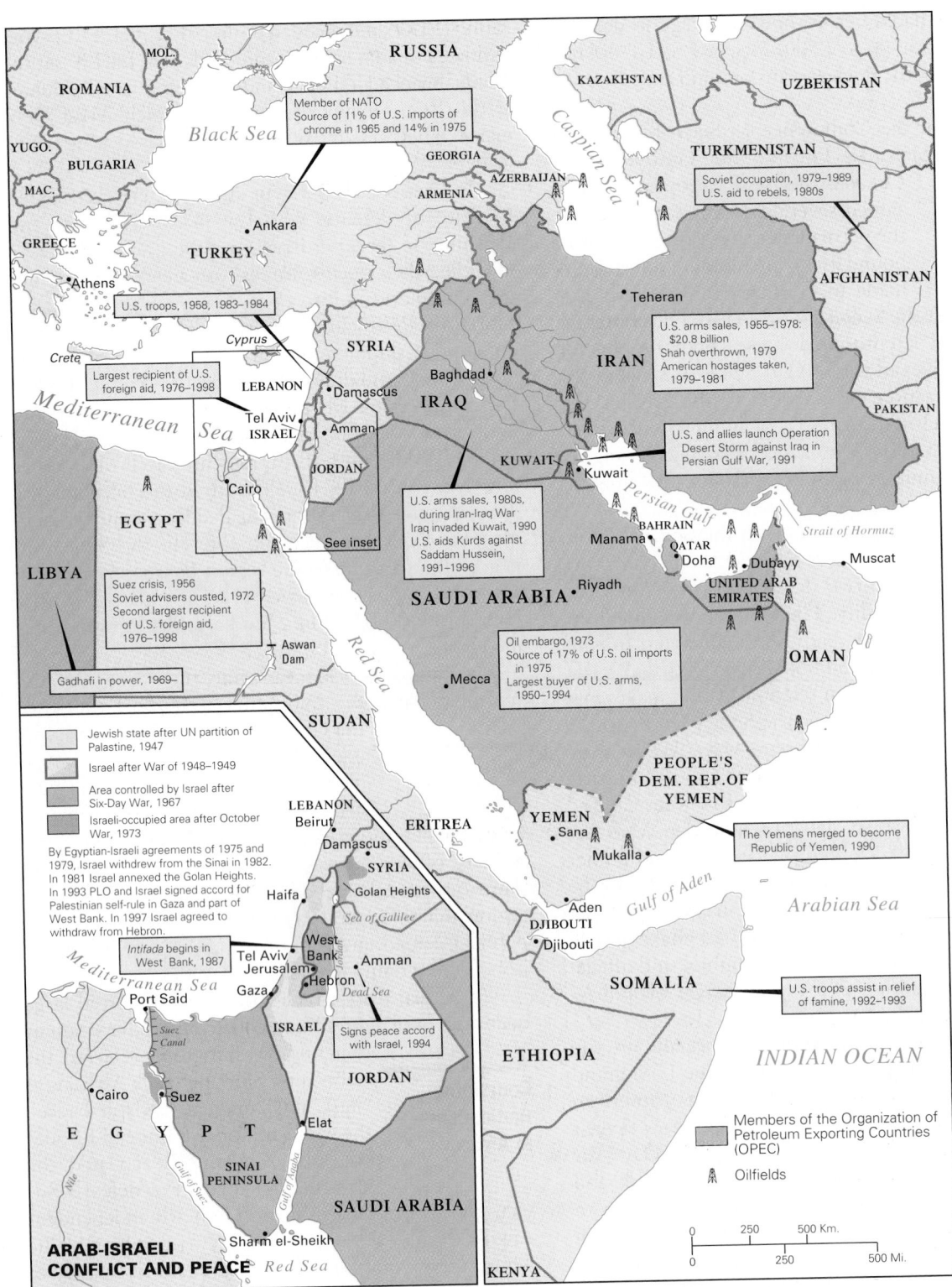

Member of NATO
Source of 11% of U.S. imports of
chrome in 1965 and 14% in 1975

Soviet occupation, 1979–1989
U.S. aid to rebels, 1980s

U.S. troops, 1958, 1983–1984

U.S. arms sales, 1955–1978:
$20.8 billion
Shah overthrown, 1979
American hostages taken,
1979–1981

Largest recipient of U.S.
foreign aid, 1976–1998

U.S. and allies launch Operation
Desert Storm against Iraq in
Persian Gulf War, 1991

U.S. arms sales, 1980s,
during Iran-Iraq War
Iraq invaded Kuwait, 1990
U.S. aids Kurds against
Saddam Hussein,
1991–1996

Suez crisis, 1956
Soviet advisers ousted, 1972
Second largest recipient
of U.S. foreign aid,
1976–1998

Gadhafi in power, 1969–

Oil embargo, 1973
Source of 17% of U.S. oil imports
in 1975
Largest buyer of U.S. arms,
1950–1994

The Yemens merged to become
Republic of Yemen, 1990

U.S. troops assist in relief
of famine, 1992–1993

Members of the Organization of
Petroleum Exporting Countries
(OPEC)

Oilfields

Legend (inset):
Jewish state after UN partition of
Palastine, 1947
Israel after War of 1948–1949
Area controlled by Israel after
Six-Day War, 1967
Israeli-occupied area after October
War, 1973

By Egyptian-Israeli agreements of 1975 and
1979, Israel withdrew from the Sinai in 1982.
In 1981 Israel annexed the Golan Heights.
In 1993 PLO and Israel signed accord for
Palestinian self-rule in Gaza and part of
West Bank. In 1997 Israel agreed to
withdraw from Hebron.

Intifada begins in
West Bank, 1987

Signs peace accord
with Israel, 1994

**ARAB-ISRAELI
CONFLICT AND PEACE**

0   250   500 Km.
0   250   500 Mi.

Map 31.2 The Middle East Extremely volatile and often at war, the nations of the Middle East maintained precarious relations with the United States. To protect its interests, the United States extended large amounts of economic and military aid and sold huge quantities of weapons to the area. At times, Washington ordered American troops to the region. The Arab-Israeli dispute particularly upended order, although the peace process moved forward.

ties and sending arms to friendly black nations such as Kenya and the Congo (then called Zaire). The administration also began to distance the United States from the white governments of Rhodesia and South Africa. America had to "prevent the radicalization of Africa," said Kissinger.

The United States was interventionist in the Third World in part because the American economy was so intertwined with the world economy.

United States in the World Economy

American investments abroad totaled more than $133 billion by the mid-1970s. Coca-Cola, Exxon, and many other American (or, more accurately, multinational) corporations earned at least half of their profits abroad. Furthermore, one-fourth of U.S. agricultural sales came from exports; one out of every nine manufacturing jobs depended on exports. The United States also depended on imports of strategic raw materials such as manganese (by 1980, 97 percent of America's consumption of this metal essential to steel production was imported from such countries as South Africa, Gabon, and Brazil). American leaders read threats to markets, investments, and raw materials as stabs at the high American standard of living, as when Venezuela nationalized American oil properties in 1976, India legislated that its nationals must own a majority of voting shares in industrial firms, and terrorists around the world destroyed American facilities and kidnapped American corporate executives. Particularly alarming was the United Nations' 1974 call for a "New International Economic Order" for the Third World: low-interest loans, lower prices for technology, and higher prices for raw materials. To counter such demands, some multinational corporations sought to influence foreign politics, as when International Telephone and Telegraph helped undermine Allende in Chile and Lockheed Aircraft bribed foreign leaders to promote sales. Multinationals also provided "cover" for CIA agents.

Global economic instability undercut the Nixon-Kissinger grand design. The worldwide economic downturn of the early 1970s was the worst since the 1930s. Inflation and high oil prices pinched rich and poor nations alike. Protectionist tendencies raised tariffs and impeded world trade. And debt-ridden Third World nations—sometimes called the "South"—insisted that countries of the industrial "North" share their wealth. In this turbulent setting, the United States began to suffer a trade deficit—importing more goods than it exported (see Figure 31.2). A "dollar glut" abroad threatened to drain the U.S. gold supply as foreigners exchanged their dollars for the precious metal. In 1971 Nixon shocked foreign capitals when he devalued the dollar, suspended its convertibility into gold, and imposed a surtax on imports, seeking thereby to reduce the influx of Japanese and European goods. All the while, Americans sensed a continued U.S. slippage in the international economy. "I think of what happened to Greece and Rome," Nixon said in reviewing statistics, "and, as you see, what is left? Only the pillars." He insisted that "it's terribly important that we be #1 economically because otherwise we can't be #1 diplomatically or militarily."

Economic relations with Japan soured. Kissinger's derogatory private comment about the Japanese as "little Sony salesmen" reflected American wariness of Japan's economic prowess.

Economic Competition with Japan

U.S. officials bristled that Japan sold plenty but did not buy enough in the world economy and discriminated against American autos in the Japanese marketplace. Nixon's 1971 decisions shocked Japan, which enjoyed a favorable balance of trade with the United States ($3.2 billion in 1971) derived from an increasing share of the American market in motor vehicles and electronics and from sales to U.S. forces in Vietnam and for maintaining the 169 U.S. military bases in Japan. Although the Japanese agreed to limit some exports to the United States (such as color televisions), the two nations were "getting bogged down in economic arm-wrestling," as Kissinger feared. By 1980 the trade balance had jumped even more in Japan's favor to $10.4 billion; by 1989 to $50 billion. Americans increasingly worried that in the contest between the two economic giants, Japan was winning. So it seemed in 1989 when the best-selling car in America was the Honda Accord and Sony bought Columbia Pictures. Still, by most measurements, Americans remained at the top of the economic hill.

Changes in the natural environment also earned a place on America's foreign policy agenda. Public discussion of environmental degradation (the first Earth Day was celebrated in 1970) and of the imbalance between food supplies and burgeoning populations, along with the work of nongovernmental organizations (NGOs) such as Greenpeace, formed in 1969, pressed Washington to act. In 1972 the United States agreed to participate in a U.N.-sponsored environmental conference in Stockholm, Sweden. Attended by 113 nations and 400 NGOs, the conference created an en-

International Environmental Issues

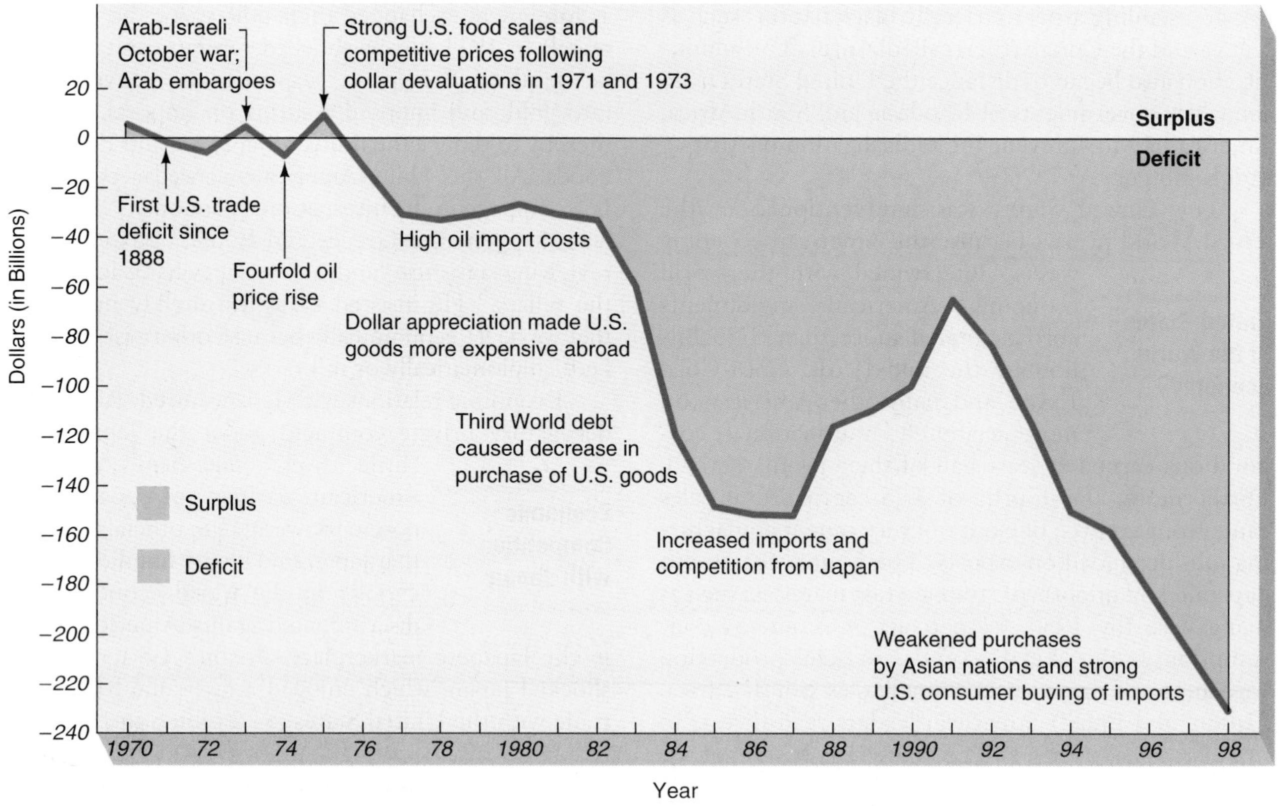

Arab-Israeli October war; Arab embargoes

First U.S. trade deficit since 1888

Fourfold oil price rise

Strong U.S. food sales and competitive prices following dollar devaluations in 1971 and 1973

High oil import costs

Dollar appreciation made U.S. goods more expensive abroad

Third World debt caused decrease in purchase of U.S. goods

Surplus

Deficit

Increased imports and competition from Japan

Weakened purchases by Asian nations and strong U.S. consumer buying of imports

Surplus

Deficit

Dollars (in Billions): 20, 0, −20, −40, −60, −80, −100, −120, −140, −160, −180, −200, −220, −240

Year: 1970, 72, 74, 76, 78, 1980, 82, 84, 86, 88, 1990, 92, 94, 96, 98

Figure 31.2 U.S. Trade Balance, 1970–1998 Importing more than it exports, the United States has suffered trade deficits for years. Foreign political and economic crises, growing competition from Japanese products in the American marketplace, and strong consumer buying have created large trade deficits, which must be financed by borrowing. One result has been a mounting U.S. external debt.   (Source: U.S. Department of State)

vironmental fund, a global monitoring system, and a new coordinating agency, the U.N. Environmental Program. The conferees especially spotlighted trans-border pollution, the overkilling of whales to the point of endangerment, and goals for environmental protection that all nations should seek to meet.

Carter, Preventive Diplomacy, and a Reinvigorated Cold War

When President Jimmy Carter took office in 1977, he asked Americans to put their "inordinate fear of Communism" behind them. With reformist zeal, Carter vowed to reduce the U.S. military presence overseas (by persuading NATO countries to pay a greater share of their own defense), to cut back arms sales (which had reached the unprecedented height of $10 billion per year under Nixon), and to slow the nuclear arms race

(by spurring a new round of SALT talks). At the time, more than four hundred thousand American military personnel were stationed abroad, the United States had military links with ninety-two nations, and the CIA was active on every continent. Carter promised to avoid new Vietnams through an activist preventive diplomacy in the Third World and to give more attention to North-South and environmental issues. He especially determined to improve human rights abroad—the freedom to vote, worship, travel, speak out, and get a fair trial. Like his predecessors, however, Carter identified revolutionary nationalism as a threat to America's prominent global position.

Carter spoke and acted inconsistently, in part because in the post-Vietnam years no consensus existed in foreign policy and in part because his advisers squabbled among themselves. One source of the problem was the stern-faced Zbigniew Brze-

Carter's Divided Administration

zinski, a Polish-born political scientist who became Carter's national security adviser. An old-fashioned Cold Warrior, Brzezinski viewed foreign crises in globalist terms—that is, he blamed them on the Soviet Union. Carter gradually listened more to Brzezinski than to Secretary of State Cyrus Vance, an experienced public servant who advocated quiet diplomacy. Vocal neoconservative intellectuals such as Norman Podhoretz, editor of *Commentary* magazine, and the Committee on the Present Danger, founded in 1976 by Cold War hawks such as Paul Nitze, who had composed NSC-68 in 1950, criticized Carter for any relaxation of the Cold War and demanded that he jettison détente.

Under Carter, détente deteriorated and the Cold War deepened. He at first angered Soviet leaders by insisting that their authoritarian regime respect human rights, including lifting restrictions on Jewish emigration from the USSR—an issue heated up in American politics by the 1974 Jackson-Vanik Amendment. This provision denied most-favored-nation trading status to the Soviet Union until it allowed free Jewish emigration. Moscow rejected Jackson-Vanik as U.S. interference in its domestic affairs and reproached the United States for dictating Soviet policy while playing its "China card"—building up China in order to threaten the Soviet Union.

Despite this rocky start, a new treaty, SALT II, codified Soviet-American nuclear parity in 1979. The

SALT II

agreement placed a ceiling of 2,250 delivery vehicles (long-range bombers, ICBMs, and SLBMs) on each side, capped MIRVed launchers at 1,200 for each, and limited the number of warheads per delivery vehicle. The Soviet Union had to dismantle more than 250 existing delivery vehicles, whereas the United States was permitted to expand from its existing 2,060 to the new ceiling. The treaty did not affect nuclear warheads, which stood at 9,200 for the United States and 5,000 for the Soviet Union. To win votes for the treaty from skeptical conservatives, Carter announced an expensive military expansion program and deployment of Pershing II missiles and cruise missiles in NATO countries.

As Senate ratification of SALT II stalled and Moscow fumed over the Pershings, events in Afghanistan led to Soviet-American confrontation. In late 1979 the Red Army bludgeoned its way into Afghanistan to shore up a faltering Communist government under siege by Muslim rebels. Carter shelved SALT II (the two powers nonetheless unilaterally hon-

ored its terms later), suspended shipments of grain and high-technology equipment to the Soviet Union, and initiated an international boycott of the 1980 Summer Olympics in Moscow. The Soviets did not withdraw their forces from Afghanistan.

The president also announced the Carter Doctrine: the United States would intervene, unilaterally and militarily if necessary, should Soviet aggression threaten the petroleum-rich Persian Gulf. George F. Kennan called Carter's reaction exaggerated and wrongheaded in assuming that the Soviets would attack elsewhere in the Middle East. Kennan noted that in Afghanistan the Soviet Union was dealing with a local crisis in a strategically important client state on its southern border, not with the entire Gulf region. He faulted Carter for not trying diplomacy first.

Carter markedly improved the Mideast peace process. Through tenacious personal diplomacy at a

Camp David Accords

Camp David, Maryland, meeting in September 1978 with Egyptian and Israeli leaders, the president persuaded Israel and Egypt to sign a peace treaty, gained Israel's promise to withdraw from the Sinai Peninsula, and forged an agreement that provided for continued negotiations on the future status of the Palestinian people living in the occupied territories of Jordan's West Bank and Egypt's Gaza Strip (see Map 31.2). Revealing a crack in Arab unity, other Arab states denounced the agreement for not requiring Israel to relinquish all occupied territories and for not guaranteeing a Palestinian homeland. But the treaty at least ended warfare along one frontier in that troubled area of the world.

Carter's toughest foreign policy test came in Iran. Many Iranians had not forgotten that the United

Iranian Hostage Crisis

States had meddled in Iranian affairs by backing the shah in the 1946 crisis and restoring him to his throne in 1953. Iranian revolutionaries led by Ayatollah Ruhollah Khomeini, a bitterly anti-American Muslim cleric, also resented the CIA's training of the shah's ruthless secret police and the huge infusion of U.S. arms into their country— $19 billion worth between 1973 and 1978 alone. When the shah was overthrown in 1979 and then admitted to the United States for medical treatment, mobs stormed the U.S. embassy in Teheran. They took American personnel as hostages, demanding the return of the shah to stand trial. The Iranians eventually released a few American prisoners, but fifty-two others languished more than a year under Iranian

On March 26, 1979, Egypt's president Anwar el-Sadat (1918–1981) on the left, Israel's prime minister Menachem Begin (1913–1992) on the right, and U.S. president Jimmy Carter (b. 1924) signed a peace treaty known as the Camp David accords. Studiously negotiated by Carter, the Egyptian-Israeli peace has held to this day—despite conflict in much of the rest of the Middle East. (Jimmy Carter Presidential Library)

guard. They suffered solitary confinement, beatings, and terrifying mock executions.

Unable to gain the hostages' freedom through diplomatic intermediaries, Carter said that he felt "the same kind of impotence that a powerful person feels when his child is kidnapped." He took steps to isolate Iran economically, freezing Iranian assets in the United States. When the hostage takers paraded their blindfolded captives before television cameras to taunt the United States, Americans seethed in anger. In April 1980, frustrated and at low ebb in public opinion polls, Carter broke diplomatic relations with Iran and ordered a daring rescue mission. But the rescue effort miscarried after equipment failure in the sandy Iranian desert, and during the hasty withdrawal two aircraft collided, killing eight American soldiers. Critics chided Carter for undertaking a risky operation that surely would have cost the lives of many hostages. Secretary Vance, already troubled by the growing militancy of Carter's foreign policy and the president's acceptance of Brzezinski's "visceral anti-Sovietism," resigned in protest. The hostages were not freed until

January 1981, after Carter left office and the United States unfroze Iranian assets and promised not to intervene again in Iran's internal affairs.

In Latin America, Carter sought compromise with nationalists (see Map 31.3), even seeking to reduce tensions with Castro's Cuba by establishing limited diplomatic links. But a crisis in 1980, during which the island regime allowed a hundred thousand Cubans to sail to Florida from the port of Mariel, poisoned relations once again. When it was discovered that many of the migrants were mentally ill or prisoners freed from jail, the mayor of Miami charged that "Fidel has flushed his toilet on us."

In Panama, citizens longed for control over the Canal Zone, which they believed had been wrongfully taken from them in 1903 (see page 629). U.S. officials feared that Panamanians might try to seize the canal by force or damage the vulnerable waterway. Recognizing also that the canal's value had dwindled because of advances in air transportation and because many new, large ships

Panama Canal Treaties

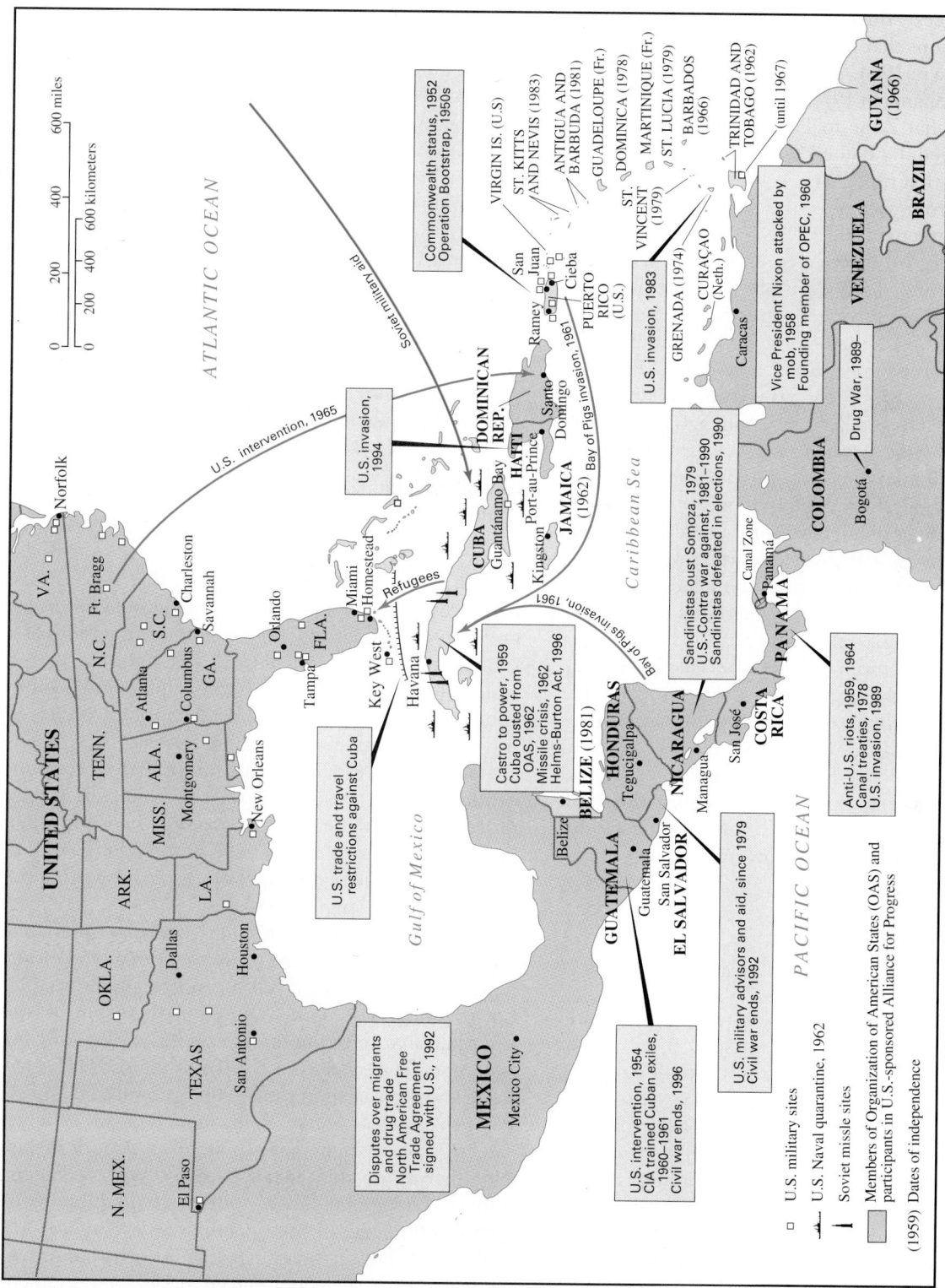

Map 31.3   The United States in the Caribbean and Central America   The United States often has intervened in the Caribbean and Central America. Geographical proximity, economic stakes, political disputes, security links, trade in illicit drugs, and Cuba's alliance with the Soviet Union and defiance of the United States have kept North American eyes fixed on events in the region.

could not squeeze through its locks, Carter reenergized negotiations that had begun after anti-American riots in Panama in 1964. The United States signed two treaties with Panama in 1977. One provided for the return of the Canal Zone to Panama in 2000, and the other guaranteed the United States the right to defend the canal after that time. With conservatives denouncing a retreat from greatness, the Senate narrowly endorsed both agreements in 1978.

Carter's record sparked considerable criticism from both left and right. Contrary to his goals, more American military personnel were stationed overseas in 1980 than in 1976; the defense budget climbed and sales of arms abroad grew to $15.3 billion in 1980. On human rights, the president proved inconsistent. He practiced a double standard by applying the human-rights test to some nations (the Soviet Union, Argentina, and Chile) but not to U.S. allies (South Korea, the shah's Iran, and the Philippines). Still, if inconsistent, Carter's human-rights policy was not unimportant: he gained the release and saved the lives of some political prisoners, and he popularized and institutionalized concern for human rights around the world. Carter did not satisfy Americans who wanted a post-Vietnam restoration of the economic hegemony and military edge the United States once enjoyed. He had earned some diplomatic successes in the Middle East, Africa, and Latin America, but the revived Cold War and the prolonged Iranian hostage crisis had politically hurt the administration. He lost the 1980 election to the hawkish Ronald Reagan, former Hollywood actor and governor of California.

The Ups and Downs of Reagan's World

Reagan did not have a firm grasp of world issues, history, or geography. After returning from his first trip to South America, he commented, "Well, I've learned a lot. . . . You'd be surprised. They're all individual countries." When Reagan told French president François Mitterand, a socialist, that communism and socialism were the same, Mitterand wondered, "What planet is that man living on?" Superficial and often mistaken about elementary facts, Reagan acted more on instinct than on analysis. Expressing the reformist message so common in U.S. foreign policy, he liked to quote Tom Paine of the American Revolution: "We have it in our power to begin the world over again."

Embracing traditional American bipolar thinking, Reagan endorsed a devil theory: a malevolent Soviet Union, the "evil empire," would "commit any crime," "lie," and "cheat" to achieve a communist world. Because he attributed Third World disorders to Soviet intrigue, the president in 1985 declared the Reagan Doctrine: the United States would openly support anticommunist movements—"freedom fighters"—wherever they were battling the Soviets or Soviet-backed governments. Under this doctrine, the CIA funneled aid to insurgents in Afghanistan, Nicaragua, Angola, and elsewhere. In open defiance of the sovereignty of those nations, Reagan worked to overthrow their governments.

Reagan officials also championed free-market capitalism, evident in their enthusiasm for the 1988

Law of the Sea Convention

U.S.-Canada Free Trade Agreement, and in their rejection of the 1982 United Nations' Convention on the Law of the Sea, patiently crafted through compromise over a ten-year period. Third World nations argued that rich sea-bed resources of petroleum and minerals should be shared under international supervision among all nations as a "common heritage of mankind." The industrial states, which alone had the capital and equipment needed to conduct excavating and drilling operations, preferred private exploitation with minimal international management. The Reagan administration shelved the convention on the grounds that it did not adequately protect private American companies. (In 1994, when the treaty went into effect, the Clinton administration sent it to the Senate for approval; as of this writing the convention still languishes there.)

Another Reagan tenet held that a substantial military buildup would thwart the Soviet threat and intimidate Moscow. Tainted CIA reports overestimating Soviet military strength—tainted because some of the information came from double agents working for the Soviet secret service (the KGB), as the Aldrich Ames spy scandal revealed in the 1990s—reassured the president that he was on the right track. Reagan launched the largest peacetime arms buildup in American history, driving up the federal debt. In 1985, when the military budget hit $294.7 billion (a doubling since 1980), the Pentagon was spending an average of $28 million an hour. Assigning low priority to arms-control talks, Reagan announced in 1983 development of an antimissile defense system in space: the Strategic Defense Initiative (SDI). His critics tagged it "Star Wars." As the veteran diplomat George Ball observed when U.S. forces overthrew a leftist, pro-Cuban government on the tiny Caribbean island of Grenada in 1983, once again "we shiver in the icy winds of the Cold War."

Reagan's first decision affecting the Soviets was actually friendly. Fulfilling a campaign pledge to help American farmers, in 1981 he lifted the grain embargo. The Soviet Union soon bought grain worth $3 billion. But bitter hostility soon followed when Poland's pro-Soviet leaders cracked down on the Solidarity labor movement in that nation bordering the USSR. In response, Washington placed restrictions on Soviet-American trade and hurled angry words at Moscow. In 1983 Reagan restricted commercial flights to the Soviet Union after a Soviet fighter pilot mistakenly shot down a South Korean commercial jet that had strayed some 300 miles off course into Soviet airspace. The world was shocked by the death of 269 passengers, and Reagan exploited the tragedy to score Cold War points.

When he came to office, Reagan believed that the Soviets and Castro's Cuba were fomenting disorder in Central America (see Map 31.3). In small, very poor El Salvador, revolutionaries challenged the government, which was dominated by the military and a landed elite. The regime used (or could not control) right-wing death squads, which by the end of the decade had killed forty thousand dissidents and other citizens as well as several American missionaries who had been working with landless peasants. Inheriting Carter's policy of backing the regime and looking the other way on human-rights abuses, Reagan officials hoped for reform but intended to prevent revolution in El Salvador. By 1989 the United States had spent $6 billion there in a counterinsurgency war.

Intervention in El Salvador

The U.S. intervention in the Salvadoran civil war sparked a debate much like the earlier one over Vietnam. Those who urged negotiations thought Reagan wrong to interpret the conflict as a Cold War contest; such civil wars stemmed not from Soviet meddling but from deep-seated economic instability, poverty, and class oppression. Resurrecting the discredited domino theory, Reagan retorted that the "Communists" would soon be at the Texas border if they were not stopped in El Salvador. Reagan also made a strategic argument: Central America hugs the Caribbean Sea, "our lifeline to the outside world." After intense debate, Congress repeatedly gave Reagan the funds he wanted for El Salvador, while the death squads murdered at will,

thwarting the radicals. "The less you know, the better," admitted a U.S. intelligence officer. In January 1992 the Salvadoran combatants finally negotiated a U.N.-sponsored peace.

The Reagan administration also meddled in the Nicaraguan civil war. In 1979 leftist insurgents in Nicaragua overthrew Anastasio Somoza, a long-time ally of the United States and member of the dictatorial family that had ruled the Central American nation since the mid-1930s. The revolutionaries called themselves Sandinistas in honor of the Nicaraguan who had fought U.S. Marines then (see page 740), and they denounced the tradition of U.S. imperialism in their country. When the Sandinistas aided rebels in El Salvador, bought Soviet weapons, and invited Cubans to work in Nicaragua's hospitals and schools and to help reorganize their army, Reagan officials charged that Nicaragua was becoming a Soviet client. In 1981 the CIA began to train, arm, and direct more than ten thousand counterrevolutionaries, called contras, to overthrow the Nicaraguan government. From CIA bases in Honduras and Costa Rica, the contras crossed into Nicaragua to kill officials and destroy oil refineries, transportation facilities, and medical clinics. As the contra attacks multiplied and the death toll mounted, the Nicaraguan government curbed civil liberties and shifted scarce money to its military.

Contra War in Nicaragua

In 1984 Congress voted to stop U.S. military aid to the contras ("humanitarian" aid was soon sent in its place). Secretly, the Reagan administration lined up other countries, including Saudi Arabia, Panama, and Korea, to funnel money and weapons to the contras, and in 1985 Reagan imposed an economic embargo against Nicaragua. The next year, Congress once again voted military aid for the contras after vigorous White House lobbying and apparent Sandinista intransigence. (The Sandinistas refused to accept a peace accord unless the United States halted support for the contras.) During the undeclared U.S. war against Nicaragua, Reagan rejected opportunities for diplomacy, especially the plan proposed by Costa Rica's president Oscar Arias Sánchez in 1987 to obtain a cease-fire in Central America through negotiations and cutbacks in military aid to all rebel forces. (Arias won the 1987 Nobel Peace Prize.) Three years later, under arrangements brokered by the Central American presidents, the Sandinistas lost a national election to a U.S.-funded party. After nearly a decade of civil war, thirty thousand Nicaraguans had died and the ravaged economy had dwindled to one of the poorest in the hemisphere.

Scandal tainted the North American crusade against the Sandinistas. It became known in 1986 that

Iran-Contra Scandal

the president's national security adviser, John M. Poindexter, and an aide, Marine Lieutenant Colonel Oliver North, in collusion with CIA director William J. Casey, had covertly sold weapons to Iran and then diverted the profits to the contras so that they could purchase arms. The diversion occurred after Congress had prohibited military assistance to the contras. During the same period, Washington had been condemning Iran as a terrorist nation and demanding that America's allies not trade with the radical Islamic state. North later admitted that he illegally had destroyed government documents and lied to Congress to keep the operation clandestine. President Reagan lied when he said that he knew nothing of these activities. In late 1992 outgoing president George Bush pardoned several former government officials who had been convicted of lying to Congress. Critics smelled a cover-up, for Bush himself, as vice president, had participated in high-level meetings on Iran-contra deals. As for North, his conviction was overturned on a technicality. The Iran-contra secret network, the scholar William LeoGrande has argued, "posed a greater threat to democracy in the United States than Nicaragua ever did."

Elsewhere in the Third World, the deeply divided Middle East continued to defy American solutions (see

U.S. Interests in the Middle East

Map 31.2). The United States had commitments (Israel, which in 1985 received more American foreign aid—$3 billion—than any other country), political friends (Saudi Arabia, to which the United States sold $8.5 billion worth of military equipment in 1981), and enemies (the Islamic states of Libya, which U.S. planes bombed, and Iran, against which the United States imposed an economic embargo). Mideast oil supplies fueled Western economies. An Iraqi-Iranian war, in which the United States aided Iraq, threatened Persian Gulf shipping. The Middle East was also a major source of the world's terrorism against U.S. citizens and property. In 1985 Shiite Muslim terrorists from Lebanon hijacked an American jetliner, killed one passenger, and held thirty-nine Americans hostage for seventeen days. Three years later, a Pan American passenger plane was destroyed over Scotland, probably by terrorists who concealed the bomb in a cassette player.

Even Israel gave the United States trouble. In retaliation for Palestinian shelling of Israel from

Crisis in Lebanon

Lebanon, the Israelis repeatedly bombed suspected Palestinian camps inside Lebanon, killing hundreds of civilians. And in 1981, without warning, Israel annexed the Syrian territory of the Golan Heights. Many American supporters of Israel, though well aware that the Jewish state faced hostile Arabs, became impatient with Israel's provocative acts toward its neighbors. The following year, Israeli troops invaded civil war–torn Lebanon, reaching the capital Beirut and inflicting massive damage. The beleaguered Palestine Liberation Organization and various Lebanese factions called on Syria to contain the Israelis. Thousands of civilians died in the multifaceted conflict, and a million people became refugees. Soon after Reagan sent U.S. Marines to Lebanon to join a peacekeeping force, the American troops became embroiled in a war between Lebanese factions. In October 1983 terrorist bombs demolished a barracks, killing 241 American servicemen. Four months later, Reagan recognized failure and pulled the remaining marines out.

Washington, which openly sided with Israel, continued to propose peace plans designed to persuade the Israelis to give back occupied territories and the Arabs to give up attempts to push the Jews out of the Middle East (the "land-for-peace" formula). As the peace process stalled in 1987, Palestinians living in the West Bank began an uprising called *intifada* against Israeli forces. Israel refused to negotiate, but the United States decided to reverse its policy and talk with PLO chief Yasir Arafat after he renounced terrorism and accepted Israel's right to live in peace and security.

In South Africa the Reagan administration at first followed a policy called "constructive engagement"—

South Africa

asking the white government to reform its repressive system. But many Americans demanded economic sanctions: cutting off imports from South Africa and pressing some 350 American companies—led by Texaco, General Motors, Ford, and Goodyear—to cease operations there. Some American cities and states passed divestment laws, withdrawing dollars (such as pension funds used to buy stock) from American companies active in South Africa. Public protest and congressional legislation forced the Reagan administration in 1986 to impose economic restrictions against South Africa. Within two years, about half of the American companies in South Africa had pulled out.

On April 18, 1983, a car bomb placed by terrorists demolished the U.S. embassy in Beirut, Lebanon, killing 63 people, 17 of them Americans. An American soldier stands guard near the destroyed building. Then in October of the same year, terrorist bombs leveled a military barracks, killing 241 American personnel. A few months later, President Reagan withdrew U.S. Marines from a multinational peace-keeping force that had been dispatched to Lebanon to calm a war waged there by Israel against PLO and Syrian forces.   (Bill Pierce/Sygma)

Elsewhere in Africa, hunger and famine exacerbated by drought and warfare took a ghastly human toll and contributed to political instability as governments failed to satisfy their people's basic needs. In the early 1980s experts estimated that annual hunger-related deaths numbered between 13 million and 18 million people—twenty-four people per minute, many of them in Africa. In Ethiopia and Sudan, both wracked by civil war, hundreds of thousands starved to death. Almost the only good news to come out of Africa was the 1988 agreement, engineered by U.S. negotiators, among Angola, Cuba, and South Africa: withdrawal of Cuban troops from Angola and black majority rule in Namibia, the former German colony that had come under South Africa's rule after the First World War.

Famine in Africa

The Third World also continued to suffer economic setbacks that endangered American prosperity. Third World nations had sunk into staggering debt.

Having borrowed heavily in the 1970s, they were unable to repay the loans when world prices for sugar, coffee, and other commodities slumped. By 1989 they owed creditors, including American banks, more than $1.2 trillion. Many Third World nations burdened with such debt—Mexico alone owed more than $100 billion—had to cut back on imports of American goods. Hundreds of thousands of jobs in the United States were lost as a result, while economic instability spawned political unrest throughout the Third World. Reagan had intervened repeatedly in the Third World, but intervention served to aggravate not subdue economic crises, civil wars, and ethnic and class conflicts.

Reagan's expansion of the U.S. military, his careless utterances about winning a limited nuclear war, and his quest for nuclear supremacy provoked worldwide debate. In 1981 hundreds of thousands of marchers in London, Rome, Bonn, and other European cities demanded Soviet-

Debate over Nuclear Weapons

In one of several summit meetings, top Soviet leader Mikhail Gorbachev (b. 1932) and President Ronald Reagan (b. 1911) met in Moscow in May 1988 in hopes of signing a Strategic Arms Reduction Talks (START) agreement. The "chemistry" of warm friendship that Reagan later claimed characterized his personal relationship with Gorbachev fell short of producing cuts in dangerous strategic weapons. But their cordial interaction encouraged the diplomatic dialogue that helped end the Cold War.   (Ronald Reagan Presidential Library)

American negotiations to prevent a nuclear holocaust. The evangelist Billy Graham joined peace groups and politicians in appeals for a freeze in the nuclear arms race. In the largest peaceful protest in American history, a million people marched through New York City in June 1982 to support a freeze. Towns across the nation and the House of Representatives passed resolutions to freeze the development, production, and deployment of new weapons. Roman Catholic bishops in the United States issued a pastoral letter in 1983 condemning nuclear weapons as "immoral" and urging an end to the arms race, "which robs the poor and the vulnerable." Meanwhile, scientists described the "nuclear winter" that would follow a nuclear war: the earth, cut off from the sun's rays, would turn cold, and food sources would disappear.

In 1982 Reagan substituted the Strategic Arms Reduction Talks (START) for the inactive SALT talks. At the 1985 Geneva summit meeting, Reagan and the new Soviet leader Mikhail S. Gorbachev agreed in principle that strategic weapons should be substantially reduced, and at the 1986 Reykjavik, Iceland, meeting they came very close to a major reduction agreement. SDI, however, stood in the way: Gorbachev insisted that it be shelved, and Reagan refused to part with it despite widespread scientific opinion that it would cost billions of dollars and never work. But Reagan and Gorbachev warmed toward one another, and the American president, as his more hawkish advisers left the administration in the late 1980s, toned down his strident anti-Soviet rhetoric.

The turnaround in Soviet-American relations stemmed more from changes abroad than from Reagan's decisions. As Reagan said near the end of his presidency, he had been "dropped into a grand historical moment." Under Gorbachev, a younger generation of Soviet leaders came to power in 1985. They began to restructure and modernize the highly bureaucratized, decaying economy (a reform program called *perestroika*) and to liberalize the authoritarian political system (a reform program called *glasnost*). For these reforms to work, Soviet military expenditures had to be reduced and foreign aid decreased.

Gorbachev's Reforms

In 1987 Gorbachev and Reagan signed the Intermediate-range Nuclear Forces (INF) Treaty banning all land-based intermediate-range nuclear missiles in Europe. Soon began the destruction of 2,800 missiles, including Soviet SS-20s targeted at western Europe and NATO Pershing and cruise missiles aimed at the Soviet Union. Gorbachev also unilaterally reduced his nation's armed forces, helped settle regional conflicts, and began the withdrawal of Soviet troops from Afghanistan. After more than forty chilling years, the Cold War was waning.

Summary

Secretary of State Henry Kissinger once observed that the international order was coming apart "politically, economically, and morally." The world, he feared, was "tilting against us." Indeed, the emergence of the Third World in the 1950s and 1960s and growing independent decision making on the part of allies undermined the bipolar Cold War international system the

United States and the Soviet Union had constructed at the end of the Second World War. By the 1980s power had become more diffused: great-power management of world affairs had diminished, and international relations had become more fluid and less predictable as more and more nations demanded a voice and a vote. In this changed setting, the United States and the Soviet Union moved haltingly toward détente and a winding down of the Cold War, as the INF Treaty demonstrated.

But this superpower shift toward diplomacy and cooperation came only after dangerous crises, nuclear brinkmanship that courted doomsday, international economic instability, monumental expenditures, and interventionism in the Third World. Driven by Cold War calculations and fears that the Third World would undermine America's standard of living, Presidents Kennedy, Johnson, Nixon, Ford, Carter, and Reagan sought to sustain U.S. preeminence in the world through a variety of methods, from overt economic and military pressure and weapons programs to covert political manipulation. On the whole, they maintained U.S. supremacy, but at great costs.

For the United States, the Vietnam War proved the most damaging. Determined to contain communism, Washington threw its young armed services personnel and its national wealth into a war it could not and did not win in a country it did not understand. Steeped in the Cold War mentality, American officials wrongheadedly saw the Soviet Union and the People's Republic of China—leaders of a supposed international communist conspiracy—maliciously at work in Vietnam, where the issue was actually more one of independence than of communism. The Vietnam War, as did wars in the 1890s and 1930s, set off a major national debate about the fundamental purposes of American foreign policy—a debate that still resonates today when the United States engages in nation building and dispatches its military forces into foreign disputes.

LEGACY FOR A PEOPLE AND A NATION
The Peace Corps

"How many of you are willing to work in the foreign service and spend your lives traveling around the world?" Democratic presidential candidate John F. Kennedy asked University of Michigan students on October 14, 1960. He was trying out an idea he inherited from others: overseas service "working for freedom." The huge crowd cheered, many inspired to sign up for the "peace race." Some forty years later, a Peace Corps recruitment poster echoed the original challenge: "How far are you willing to go to make a difference?" Since the corps' founding in 1961 to promote world peace through cross-cultural understanding and economic development, more than 155,000 Americans have volunteered for service in 134 countries. Currently, 7,000 volunteers are active in 77 countries. Most volunteers are college educated, female, single, and white, and their average age is twenty-eight (2000 figures; for more recent data, see www.peacecorps.gov). Over the years, volunteers have built fish farms in Togo, water pumps in Kenya, sawmills in Peru, poultry cooperatives in India, and bridges in Sierra Leone. They have served as nurses in Tanganyika and as English teachers in country after country.

Today, many host nations instead want Peace Corps volunteers to run computer workshops, create management models, teach free-market business skills, launch small-business enterprises, and design web pages. In its first decades, volunteers largely went to the Third World, where they were sent not only as goodwill ambassadors but also as foreign policy instruments to win friends to the U.S. side of the Cold War. Today, in the post–Cold War era, increasing numbers serve in eastern Europe and in the former Soviet republics, helping them in the transition to market-oriented economies and political democracy.

From the beginning, not all Peace Corps projects have succeeded, and some volunteers proved ill-suited for corps work. Also, during the Vietnam War, after volunteers protested U.S. intervention, President Nixon demanded that the Peace Corps serve, not question, U.S. Cold War goals and sharply cut its budget. As the Vietnam War and Watergate scandal spawned public cynicism, and as the military-minded era of the Reagan eighties marginalized the volunteers' way of promoting peace, the number of volunteers dropped, hitting an all-time low of 5,219 in 1987.

Today, the Peace Corps is highly respected as an institution where American ideals of humanitarian service, cultural understanding, and self-determination repose, even when U.S. leaders sometimes trample on such principles. In 1999 Congress voted to increase the corps to 10,000 volunteers by 2003, allocating a generous budget of $241 million. With such assistance, a legacy from the 1960s has been secured for a people and a nation—and the world.

For Further Reading, see page A-38 of the Appendix. For Web resources, go to http://college.hmco.com.

32

THE END OF THE POSTWAR BOOM 1974–1989

Nguyet Thu Ha was twenty-two years old when South Vietnam capitulated to North Vietnamese and Vietcong forces in 1975. She had never before spent a night away from her parents; but North Vietnamese soldiers were fighting close to her home, so she fled, taking along her four younger brothers and sisters, all teenagers, and a six-year-old nephew whose distraught parents had entrusted him to Ha for safekeeping. The six found their way onto a fishing ship dangerously overcrowded with refugees. They stopped first at Guam, a Pacific island controlled by the United States; their second stop was a refugee camp in Arkansas; finally, Nguyet Ha and the children went to Kansas City, Missouri. Ha's immediate challenge was to earn enough money to support six people, but her dream was to reunite her family.

Nguyet Ha obtained a job working seven days a week as a hotel housekeeper, and at night she taught herself to sew, making shirts and dresses. She next worked as a waitress, saving her tips to buy a house. "I'm very tough about my budget," Ha explained, "even if I know something I really like to buy. I tell myself, 'Hold it, hold it until you can do it. For now, just forget it.'" Within eight months, she had saved enough for a down payment on a $16,000 house; she paid off the mortgage in three years. She married and had two daughters of her own, and in 1989 she bought a laundromat, five adjoining lots, and a vacant building to house her relatives, should they be allowed to emigrate to the United States. Ha also began to take college courses; she wanted to become a teacher. After earning two associate of arts degrees, she was hired as a paraprofessional at Kansas City's Northeast High School, a magnet school for law and public service.

What sustained Nguyet Thu Ha was her dream of bringing her entire family to Kansas City. Soon after she and the children fled Vietnam, Ha's father died, perhaps of sadness, she thought. Her mother and four older siblings and their families remained in Vietnam. Ha often dreamed about her mother, and sometimes her sobbing woke her daughters. "They wake me up and they wipe my tears and they say, 'Mommy, it's OK.'" For ten years, Ha filled out U.S. government forms and telephoned and visited the offices of the Im-

New immigrants were often eager to become new citizens. In 1996, in a naturalization ceremony held in San Jose, California, a woman from Southeast Asia proudly held an American flag as she took the oath to become a citizen of the United States.   (© David Butow/Saba)

migration and Naturalization Service (INS), but nothing happened. Then she received a call from the INS: Ha's mother, two brothers, a sister-in-law, and a niece would be arriving in a couple of days at Kansas City International Airport. Her mother, the last to leave the airplane, was engulfed by hugs. Ha was overjoyed: "I say, 'Is this real or I still dream?' You wish to have it for long time, and then one moment you have it, and you don't trust it." But it was real. (By 1997, not only Ha's mother but all eight of her siblings, most with their children, were living in the United States.)

Nguyet Thu Ha and her family were part of the "new immigration," which began in the early 1970s, when record numbers of immigrants came to the United States from Asia, Mexico, Central and South America, and the Caribbean. Many of the new immigrants came as families, though some—such as Nguyet Thu Ha's group—arrived a few family members at a time over a period of years. Unlike earlier immigrants, most of the new arrivals were people of color, and race proved to be both a barrier and a spur to success for the new immigrants. Established migration patterns tended to determine where the newcomers, such as Ha's family, went. "People immigrate to where they find connections and a measure of familiarity," explained Alejandro Portes, a sociologist at Johns Hopkins University. Almost 70 percent of the new immigrants settled in six states: California, Florida, Texas, New York, New Jersey, and Illinois. The newcomers redefined urban areas such as Los Angeles, Chicago, and Miami, where nearly three-quarters of city residents spoke a language other than English at home.

Although well-wishers often were on hand to greet the newcomers, the history of the nation's treatment of people of color did not augur well for them. Most found only low-paying jobs, and some suffered hostility and even violence from native-born Americans. Nevertheless, they persevered, pursuing their dreams in a country that was changing racially and ethnically. At Northeast High School, for example, where Nguyet Thu Ha found her first job as a teacher's aide, the student body was richly diverse: white, black, Hispanic, Asian, and American Indian. In their pursuit of both a magnet school and cultural diversity, these teenagers were bused to Northeast from all over Kansas City. Andrea Johnson, a junior and an African American, explained that it was "beneficial going to a school with different races because you learn about different cultures." Rebecca Hernandez, a senior, agreed, saying she believed it would get monotonous going to school "with the same people your whole life.

The world is not separate but equal. I don't want to crawl into my little Hispanic shell."

The American people experienced wrenching economic, political, and social change in the 1970s and 1980s. First, the new immigration touched millions of people's lives, immigrant and nonimmigrant alike. Second, in the 1970s, the twenty-five-year postwar economic boom ended. The rate of economic growth slowed and sometimes stalled, and disquieting signs of inflation materialized. Third, economic inequality and social polarization grew in the 1970s and 1980s, widening the gap between rich and poor, between whites and people of color, and between the suburbs and the inner cities. Fourth, a host of new social problems emerged in the 1980s, notably AIDS and crack cocaine. Finally, although women made significant gains in the 1970s and 1980s, especially in education, the professions, and the job market, they also suffered setbacks, including the emergence of an antifeminist movement that opposed women's aspirations for gender equality.

After Vietnam and Watergate, the American people were cynical about politics and skeptical of their leaders. The presidency of Gerald R. Ford was a time of healing, not activism. Ford's successor as president, Jimmy Carter, scored notable domestic successes, but he was unpopular with the public. Moreover, neither Ford nor Carter was able to restore economic or social health to the nation. But in response to their failures, there was a resurgence of conservatism, particularly among Americans who believed that the 1960s had been a period of immoral excesses, and who doubted that government had the capacity to serve the people, let alone solve major problems. Ronald Reagan became a hero to the conservatives, and after defeating Carter in 1980, he served as president for the next eight years. In 1988, when the voters went to the polls, the nation was at peace, both unemployment and inflation were at low levels, and Reagan was still a political hero to many Americans. ■

Economic Crisis and Ford's Response

 It was evident in the early 1970s that the United States was beginning to suffer economic decline. Recessions—which economists define as at least two consecutive quarters of no growth in the gross national product (GNP)—began to occur more frequently. An

IMPORTANT EVENTS

1974 OPEC increases oil prices

Nixon resigns; Ford becomes president

Ford creates WIN program to fight inflation

Equal Credit Opportunity Act equalizes loan and credit card terms for men and women

1975 Nuclear accident occurs at Brown's Ferry

Antibusing agitation erupts in Louisville and Boston

Economic recession hits nation

1976 Hyde Amendment cuts off Medicaid funds for abortions

Carter elected president

1978 *Bakke v. University of California* outlaws quotas but upholds affirmative action

California voters approve Proposition 13

1979 Three Mile Island nuclear accident raises fears of meltdown

Moral Majority established

Federal Reserve Board tightens money supply

American hostages seized in Iran

1980 Economic recession recurs

Race riots break out in Miami and Chattanooga

Reagan elected president

Republicans gain control of Senate

1981 AIDS first observed in United States

Prime interest rate reaches 21.5 percent

Congress approves Reagan's budget and tax cuts

Reagan breaks air traffic controllers strike

Economic recession; unemployment hits 8 percent

1982 Unemployment reaches 10 percent

Voting Rights Act of 1965 renewed

1983 More than half of adult women work outside the home

ERA dies for lack of ratification

1984 Reagan reelected

1985 Gramm-Rudman bill calls for balanced budget by 1991

1986 Tax Reform Act lowers personal income taxes

Immigration Reform and Control (Simpson-Rodino) Act provides amnesty to undocumented workers

Iran-contra scandal breaks

Republicans lose control of Senate

1987 Stock market prices drop 508 points in one day

1988 *Understanding AIDS* mailed to 107 million households

Bush elected president

---

eleven-month recession struck the country in 1969 and 1970, the first recession in almost a decade. Between 1973 and 1990, there were four more, and two (1973–1975, 1981–1982) were particularly long and harsh. Americans' economic insecurity, which was pronounced in the 1970s, persisted into the 1980s.

America's economic vulnerability was confirmed by the Arab oil embargo of 1973 (see page 903), which debunked the myth that the United States was a fortress that could stand alone. The country, which was importing one-third of its oil supplies, was dependent for its survival on imported oil. Even before the embargo, the United States had suffered occasional shortages of natural gas, heating oil, and gasoline. But the American people, who had grown up on inexpensive and abundant energy, made few efforts to conserve; they drove big cars and lived in poorly insulated homes.

In 1973 the American people also had to deal with the oil price increases ordered by the Organization of Petroleum Exporting Countries (OPEC). Oil prices rose 350 percent that year. As Americans grappled with the economic, social, and political costs of the price hikes, multinational oil companies prospered: their profits jumped 70 percent in 1973 and another 40 percent in 1974. Meanwhile, the steep rises in oil prices reverberated through the entire economy, tending to make everything that had to be shipped cost more. Inflation jumped from 3 percent in 1972 to a frightening 11 percent in 1974. Many Americans were suffering hard times.

OPEC Price Increases Fuel Inflation

In 1973 General Motors laid off 38,000 workers indefinitely—6 percent of its domestic work force—and put another 48,000 on leaves for up to ten days at

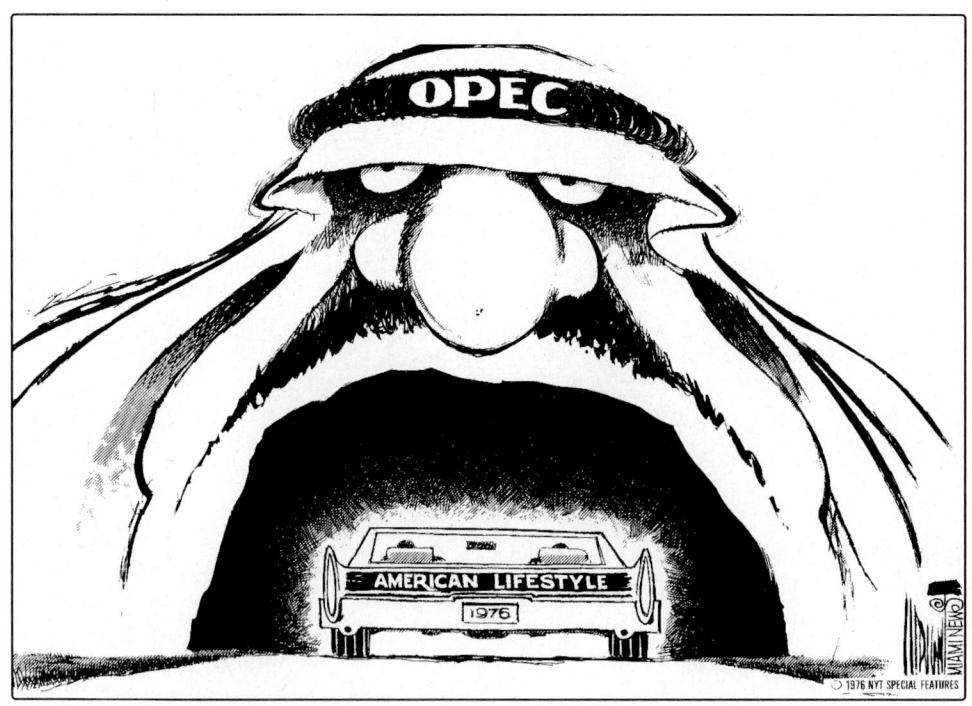

The Organization of Petroleum Exporting Countries (OPEC) raised oil prices several times in the 1970s. Each increase fueled the rise of inflation in the United States; and Americans, who had expected cheap energy to last forever, saw their expectations dashed. Long lines at the gas pumps were a reminder that an era of easy abundance had passed. (Don Wright in the *Miami News,* 1976, Tribune Media Services)

Auto Industry Recession

a time. Sales of gas-guzzling American autos plummeted as consumers rushed to purchase energy-efficient foreign subcompacts from Japan and Europe. Like Ford and Chrysler, GM was stuck with mostly large-car assembly plants. The recession that hit the auto industry in 1973 deepened in 1974. Moreover, there was an accelerator effect because the ailing American auto companies quit buying steel, glass, rubber, and tool-and-die products. And as the recession in the auto industry spread, other manufacturers began laying off experienced employees with seniority.

Unlike earlier postwar recessions, this one did not fade away in a year or two. Americans in the 1970s reeled under the one-two punch of *stagflation*. First, economic *stag*nation produced unemployment, particularly in heavy industry. Americans saw once-proud automobile and steel plants close. As a result of such "deindustrialization," many jobs were jeopardized while others disappeared forever. Second, in*flation* produced soaring prices, which eroded the purchasing power of workers' paychecks and forced them to raid their savings, sacrificing future security to current needs. The 1970s was the first decade since the Great Depression in which Americans' purchasing power declined, and the experience shook people's confidence that they could shape their personal destinies.

Stagflation also presented formidable problems to government policymakers. In earlier recessions, Republican as well as Democratic administrations had held to a policy of Keynesianism. To minimize the swings in the business cycle, they had manipulated federal policies—both fiscal policies (taxes and government spending) and monetary policies (interest rates and the money supply). They hoped by so doing to keep employment up and inflation down. Beginning in the 1970s, however, joblessness and prices both began to rise sharply. Policies designed to correct one problem seemed only to worsen the other.

Even in the best of times, the economy would have been hard-pressed to produce jobs for the millions of baby boomers who joined the labor market in the 1970s. As it was, economic activity created 27 million additional jobs during the decade, a remarkable increase of 32 percent.

The Shifting Occupational Structure

But deindustrialization was causing a shift in the occupational structure. As heavy industries collapsed, laid-off workers took jobs in the service sector, working in fast-food restaurants, all-night gas stations, and convenience stores—but at half of their former wages and without healthcare and other bene-fits. In 1979, 31 percent of households lived on incomes below $25,000; the comparable figure a decade later was 42 percent. Workers who once had held high-paying blue-collar jobs saw their middle-class standards of living slipping away from them.

A central economic problem was a slowing of growth in productivity—the average output of goods

Lagging Productivity

per hour of labor. Between 1947 and 1965, American industrial productivity had increased an average of 3.3 percent a year, raising manufacturers' profits and lowering the cost of prod-ucts to consumers. From 1966 to 1970, annual pro-ductivity growth averaged only 1.5 percent; it fell further between 1971 and 1975 and reached a mere 0.2 percent between 1976 and 1980. Economists blamed lack of business investment in state-of-the-art technol-ogy, declining educational standards, and an alleged erosion of the work ethic. Whatever the causes, Amer-ican goods cost more than those of foreign competi-tors; in the world's increasingly competitive markets, many American products fared poorly. The Joint Eco-nomic Committee of Congress warned, "The average American is likely to see his standard of living drasti-cally decline in the 1980s unless the United States ac-celerates its rate of productivity growth."

The lag in productivity was not matched by a de-crease in workers' expectations. Wage increases regu-larly exceeded production increases, and some economists blamed the raises for inflation. Indeed, wages that went up seldom came down again. Man-agers of the nation's basic industries—steel, autos, rub-ber—complained that the automatic cost-of-living adjustments in their labor contracts left them little margin to restrain price hikes.

Another spur to inflation was easy credit. More people had credit cards; the number of MasterCard

Easy Credit and Inflation

cardholders jumped from 32 million in 1974 to 57 million five years later. And with their credit cards in hand, Americans went on a buying spree; between 1975 and 1979, household and business borrowing more than tripled (from $94 billion to $328 billion). The credit explosion helped bid up the price of everything, from houses to gold. Farmers bought new farmland and expensive machin-ery and irrigation equipment. The nation's farm debt, $55 billion in 1971, had reached $166 billion by 1980. Overburdened with debts, many farmers faced bank-ruptcy in the 1980s.

Every expert had a scapegoat to blame for the na-tion's economic doldrums. Labor leaders cited foreign competition and called for protective tariffs. Some businesspeople and economists blamed the cost of obeying federal health and safety laws and pollution controls. They urged officials to abolish the Environ-mental Protection Agency and the Occupational Safety and Health Administration. They also pressed for deregulation of the oil, airline, and trucking indus-tries on the theory that competition would drive prices down. Above all, critics attacked the federal govern-ment's massive spending programs; the mounting na-tional debt, they said, was the sad result.

By the time Gerald Ford became president after Richard M. Nixon's resignation in 1974, OPEC price

President Ford's Response

increases had pushed the inflation rate to 11 percent. Appalled, Ford created Whip Inflation Now (WIN), a voluntary program that encouraged businesses, consumers, and workers to save energy and organize grassroots anti-inflation efforts. In the 1974 congressional elections, voters re-sponded to WIN, Watergate, and Ford's pardon of Nixon by giving the Democrats fifty-two additional seats in the House and four in the Senate. Ford showed political courage in 1974 when he offered clemency to Vietnam War draft evaders, but he re-ceived blistering criticism from veterans' groups and other conservatives.

Ford's response to inflation was to curb federal spending and encourage the Federal Reserve Board to raise its interest rates to banks, thus tightening credit. Ford was following the tenets of monetary theory, which held that the best way to reduce inflation was to keep the nation's money supply growing at a slow, con-sistent rate. With less money available to "chase" the supply of goods, monetarists contended, price in-creases would gently slow down. But these actions prompted yet another recession—only this time it was the worst in forty years. Unemployment jumped to 8.5 percent in 1975, and because the economy had stag-nated, the federal deficit for fiscal year 1976–1977 hit a record $60 billion.

Ford devised no lasting solutions to the energy crisis, but the crisis seemed to pass when OPEC ended

Nuclear Power

the embargo—and the incentive to prevent future shortages dissolved as well. The energy crisis, however, did intensify public debate over nuclear power. For the sake of energy independence, advo-cates asserted, the United States had to rely more on nuclear energy. Environmental activists countered that the risk of nuclear accident was too great and that there was no safe way to store nuclear waste. Accidents in the nuclear power reactors at Brown's Ferry, Alabama (1975), and Three Mile Island, Pennsylvania (1979), gave credence to the activists' arguments. By 1979, however, ninety-six reactors were under construction throughout the nation, and thirty more were on order.

In the 1970s the combined effects of the energy crisis, stagflation, and the flight of industry and the middle class to the suburbs and the Sunbelt were producing fiscal disaster in the nation's cities (see Chapter 30). Not since 1933, when Detroit defaulted on its debts, had a major American city gone bankrupt. But New York City was near financial collapse by late 1975. President Ford vowed "to veto any bill that has as its purpose a federal bailout of New York City," but he relented after the Senate and House Banking Committees approved loan guarantees, and the city was saved. New York was not alone in its financial problems; other Frostbelt cities were in trouble, saddled with growing welfare rolls, deindustrialization, and a declining tax base. In 1978 Cleveland defaulted on its debts.

Throughout Ford's two-and-a-half-year presidential administration, relatively little was accomplished.

Gerald Ford's Presidency

After Vietnam and Watergate, Congress asserted itself and enjoyed new power. Ford almost routinely vetoed its bills, but Congress often overrode his vetoes. For the first time in the nation's history, furthermore, neither the president nor the vice president had been popularly elected. One of Ford's first acts as president had been to select Nelson Rockefeller, former governor of New York, as his vice president. But Republican prospects for retaining the presidency in the 1976 election seemed gloomy.

While Ford struggled with a Democratic Congress, the Democratic Party geared up for the presidential election of 1976. Against the

Election of 1976

background of Watergate secrecy and corruption, one candidate in particular promised honesty and openness. "I will never lie to you," pledged Jimmy Carter, an obscure former one-term governor of Georgia. Carter presented himself as both a fiscal conservative who would restrain government spending and a social liberal who would fight for the poor, the aged, people of color, workers, urban dwellers, and farmers. When

On inauguration day, President Jimmy Carter (b. 1924) and his wife Rosalyn caught the public's fancy by walking from the Capitol to the White House. Despite this symbolic beginning, Carter became increasingly isolated both from the American people and from Congress. (Jimmy Carter Library)

this born-again Christian promised voters efficiency and decency in government, they believed him. It helped, too, that Carter was a southerner, whose candidacy might block Republican electoral advances in the white South. Carter arrived at the convention with more than enough delegates to win the nomination. His choice of Senator Walter Mondale of Minnesota as his running mate served to cement relations with northern liberals, African Americans, union members, and political bosses.

Neither Carter nor President Ford, the Republican nominee, inspired much interest, and on election day only 54 percent of the electorate bestirred itself to vote. Nevertheless, an analysis of the turnout was instructive. Carter did carry ten of the eleven states in the Deep South. But as one political commentator observed, the vote nationwide was "fractured to a marked degree along the fault line separating the haves and have-nots." Although Carter won nearly 90 percent of the African American and Mexican American vote, he squeaked to victory by a slim 1.7 million votes out of 80 million cast. Ford's appeal was strongest among middle- and upper-middle-class white voters.

Continuing Economic Problems and the Carter Presidency

 Economic troubles got worse, and by 1980 the economy was in a shambles. Inflation had jumped in 1979 to over 13 percent, and traders around the world had lost confidence in the dollar, causing unprecedented increases in the price of gold. To steady the dollar and curb inflation, the Federal Reserve Board took drastic measures. First, the board cut the money supply— partly by selling Treasury securities to take money out of circulation—thus forcing borrowers to bid up interest rates sufficiently to dampen the economy and reduce inflation. Second, it raised the rate at which the Federal Reserve loaned money to banks. As a result, mortgage-interest rates leaped beyond 15 percent, and the prime lending rate (the rate charged to businesses) hit an all-time high of 20 percent. Inflation fell, but only to 12 percent.

Worse still, by 1980 the nation was in a full-fledged recession. The 1980 unemployment rate of 7.5 percent, combined with the 12 percent inflation rate, had produced a staggeringly high "discomfort index" (the unemployment rate plus the inflation rate) of just

Economic Discomfort in 1980

under 20 percent (see Figure 32.1). Yet the government was unable to control the causes of the discomfort. In 1976 Carter had gibed at the incumbent president, Gerald Ford, by saying, "Anything you don't like about Washington, I suggest you blame on him." In 1980 Carter was the incumbent, and many Americans blamed *him* for the problems that beset the country.

Carter failed to inspire Americans, and he alienated Democratic Party members. Elected as an outsider, he remained one throughout his presidency. Moreover, Carter's conservative economic policies disenchanted Democrats who had grown up in the party's

Figure 32.1 "Discomfort Index" (Unemployment Plus Inflation), 1974–1989   Americans' economic discomfort directly determined their political behavior. When the "discomfort index" was high in 1976 and 1980, Americans voted for a change in presidents. When economic discomfort declined in 1984 and 1988, Ronald Reagan and George Bush were the political beneficiaries.   (Source: Adapted from *Economic Report of the President, 1992* [Washington, D.C., 1992], pp. 340, 365.)

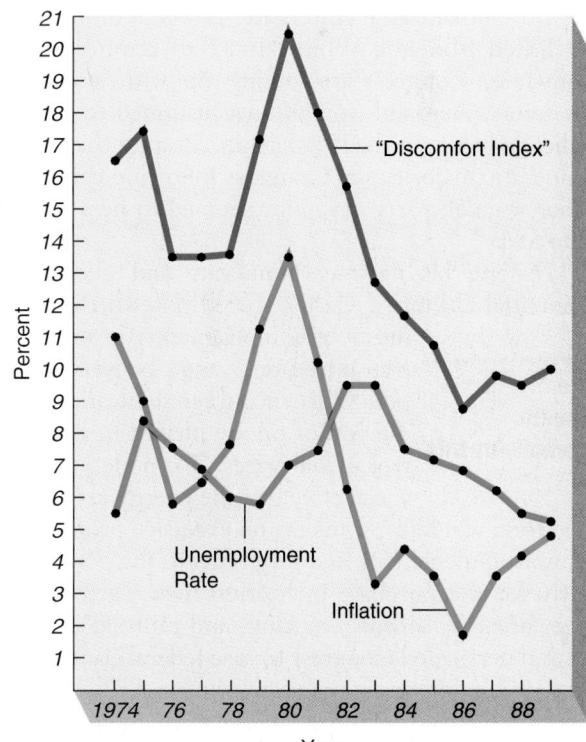

Carter's Flagging Popularity

New Deal liberal tradition. His support of deregulation and his opposition to wage and price controls and gasoline rationing ran counter to liberal Democratic principles. Seeing inflation as a greater threat to the nation's economy than either recession or unemployment, Carter announced that his top priority would be "to discipline the growth of government spending," even though doing so would add to the jobless rolls. But he was unable to gain Congress's cooperation, and both federal expenditures and inflation continued to rise.

Carter's problems were not entirely of his own making. In 1979 the shah of Iran's government fell to revolutionary forces. When Carter admitted the shah to the United States for medical treatment, mobs seized the American embassy in Teheran and held fifty-two Americans as hostages for 444 days (see page 907). The new Iranian government also cut off oil supplies to the United States. The same year OPEC raised its prices again, and the cost of crude oil nearly doubled. As Americans waited in long lines at gasoline pumps, and as they bridled at Carter's inability to free the hostages, public approval of the president reached a new low.

Carter also inherited political problems. In the wake of Vietnam and Watergate, power temporarily had shifted from the White House to Capitol Hill. Meanwhile, Congress was filling up with political newcomers, men and women unaccustomed to reflex obedience to established leadership. Despite the large Democratic majorities in Congress following the Watergate scandal, party discipline seemed to be a thing of the past.

Carter's Domestic Accomplishments

Despite his flagging popularity and declining presidential authority, Carter scored noteworthy domestic accomplishments in energy, transportation, and conservation policy. To encourage domestic production of oil, he phased in decontrol of oil prices. To moderate the social effects of the energy crisis, he called for a windfall-profits tax on excessive profits resulting from decontrol, and for grants to the poor and elderly for the purchase of heating fuel. Carter also deregulated the airline, trucking, and railroad industries and persuaded Congress to ease federal control of banks. His administration established a $1.6 billion "superfund" to clean up abandoned chemical-waste sites and created two free-standing departments—the

Departments of Energy and Education. Finally, he placed more than 100 million acres of Alaskan land under the federal government's protection as national parks, national forests, and wildlife refuges.

Conservative Resurgence and Reagan

Political and economic conservatives had long expressed doubt about whether big government programs can actually serve the people. Critics pointed to stagflation as evidence of the failure of New Deal and Great Society economics. Even some Democrats agreed. Senator Gary Hart, a Colorado Democrat, characterized this mood as "a nonideological skepticism about the old, Rooseveltian solutions to social problems."

In the 1970s conservatives at the state level worked to repeal the social welfare system. California voters approved a 1978 tax-cutting referendum called Proposition 13, which reduced property taxes and put stringent limits on state spending for social programs. Proposition 13 set off shock waves: nearly a score of other states imposed similar ceilings on taxes and expenditures. On the national level, conservatives lobbied for a constitutional amendment to prohibit federal budget deficits. Perhaps most significant, tax revolts became political vehicles for conservative candidates to win elections.

In the 1970s and 1980s political and economic conservatives joined forces with cultural and religious conservatives and thereby changed

Resurgence of Conservatism

the political landscape. In 1979 Reverend Jerry Falwell, a minister from Virginia, helped to found the Moral Majority, which advocated what it called "family values," including opposition to abortion rights and homosexuality. Together with conservative think tanks like the Hoover Institution and the American Enterprise Institute and conservative magazines like *National Review*, the Moral Majority and various church groups formed a flourishing network of potential supporters for conservative candidates. By the late 1970s, conservatism was becoming a potent political force.

Ronald Reagan appealed mightily to both wings of the movement. A proponent of prayer in the public schools and an opponent of abortion, Reagan argued for a return to the morality that he believed had domi-

How do historians know...

that the political influence of Christian conservatives grew significantly in the 1970s and 1980s? Evidence can be found in the nation's media, including television, radio, and newspapers and magazines. References to numerous articles on the Christian right may be found in a number of indexes, including the *Reader's Guide to Periodical Literature* and the *New York Times Index*. The media reported extensively in 1979, for example, that the Reverend Jerry Falwell, a radio-TV preacher whose *Old Time Gospel Hour* reached 15 million Americans, had helped to establish the Moral Majority in support of "family values." The organization quickly registered between 2 and 3 million new voters, started a newspaper, and bought daily time on 140 radio stations. Increasingly, evangelical Christians believed they had a moral obligation to enter politics on the side of "a pro-life, pro-traditional family, pro-moral position." In 1980 the Republicans eagerly sought, and received, the political support of Falwell and his followers. During the 1980s Christian conservatives boosted Pat Robertson, another so-called televangelist, to national political influence. Robertson, a Baptist minister, was host of television's popular *700 Club*, as well as founder of the Christian Coalition, the nation's largest religious-political conservative organization, and, in 1988, a candidate for the Republican presidential nomination.

Evidence of Christian conservatives' growing political activism can also be found in local elections where the issues have frequently involved abortion, gay rights, prayer in the public schools, and the teaching of creationism. Evidence exists, too, in the published platforms of the Republican Party, particularly in 1992, when the party denounced any deviation from "family values." In 1994 the Christian

Coalition reciprocated by endorsing the Republicans' Contract with America. With political success, however, have come divisions within the Christian conservative movement, as well as deep frustrations, especially over Congress's failure, in 1999, to remove Bill Clinton from the presidency. During that year's impeachment hearings, with Clinton enjoying widespread public support, some Christian conservatives withdrew from politics. Having concluded that the Moral Majority had become the moral minority, they vowed not to participate in the elections of 2000. (Photo: Dennis Brack/Black Star)

---

nated American culture before the 1960s. He promised a balanced budget, and he blamed government for fettering American economic creativity. Reagan's 1980 presidential victory revealed that conservatism had become the dominant mood of the nation.

The 1980 federal census provided additional insights into the reasons for conservatism's resurgence in

A Shifting Population

the United States. First, the 1980 census revealed significant growth in the more politically conservative elderly population—up 24 percent since 1970—and a two-year rise in the median age. In addition, the number of retired people increased by more than 50 percent in the

REAGAN

FOR PRESIDENT
Let's make America great again.

Ronald Reagan, the Republican presidential candidate in 1980, campaigned for "family values," an aggressive anti-Soviet foreign and military policy, and tax cuts. He also exuded optimism and appealed to Americans' patriotism. This poster issued by the Republican National Committee included Reagan's favorite campaign slogan, "Let's make America great again." (Collection of David J. and Janice L. Frent)

1970s. Second, the census documented the continuing shift of large numbers of people from the politically liberal Frostbelt states of the Northeast and Midwest to the more conservative Sunbelt states of the South and West (see Map 32.1). The census findings also meant that seventeen seats in the House of Representatives would shift from the Frostbelt to the Sunbelt by the 1982 elections. Florida would gain four seats, Texas three, and California two; New York would lose five.

In 1980 several conservative Republican politicians ran for the White House. Foremost among them was Ronald Reagan, former movie star and two-term governor of California. When he was president of the Screen Actors Guild in Hollywood in the 1940s, his

Reagan's Early Career

politics were those of a New Deal Democrat. But touring the country in the 1950s as host of the television program *General Electric Theatre*, he became increasingly conservative. In 1964 he made a televised appeal for Senator Barry Goldwater, the Republican presidential candidate. Reagan's speech catapulted him to the forefront of conservative politics and became his personal platform for the presidency. America, Reagan said, had come to "a time for choosing" between free enterprise and big government, between individual liberty and "the ant heap of totalitarianism." Two years later he was elected governor of California.

During his two four-year terms as governor, Reagan maintained his conservative rhetoric but displayed a pragmatic approach to governing. While denouncing welfare, he presided over reform of the state's social welfare bureaucracy. While demanding that student radicals at the University of California either obey the rules or face the prospect of a "bloodbath," he endorsed most of the university's budget requests. And he signed one of the nation's most liberal abortion laws.

In the Republican primaries, Reagan triumphed easily over former CIA director George Bush and Representative John Anderson, who

Reagan as the Republican Candidate

ran as an independent. Reagan's appeal to the voters in the presidential campaign was much broader than experts had predicted. He promised economy in government and a balanced budget, and he committed himself to "supply-side" economics, or tax reductions to businesses to encourage capital investment. Although Reagan planned to slash federal spending, he also pledged to cut income taxes and boost the defense budget—a prescription that George Bush ridiculed as "voodoo economics." Reagan declared that he now opposed legalized abortion, and his stand against the Equal Rights Amendment (ERA) recommended him to social conservatives.

The strength of Reagan's candidacy was that it united the old right wing with the new. The old right had never been very interested in social or cultural issues, explained Richard Viguerie, a conservative fundraiser. "But when political conservative leaders began to . . . strike an alliance with social conservatives—the pro-life people, the anti-ERA people, the evangelical and born-again Christians, the people concerned about gay rights, prayer in the schools, sex in

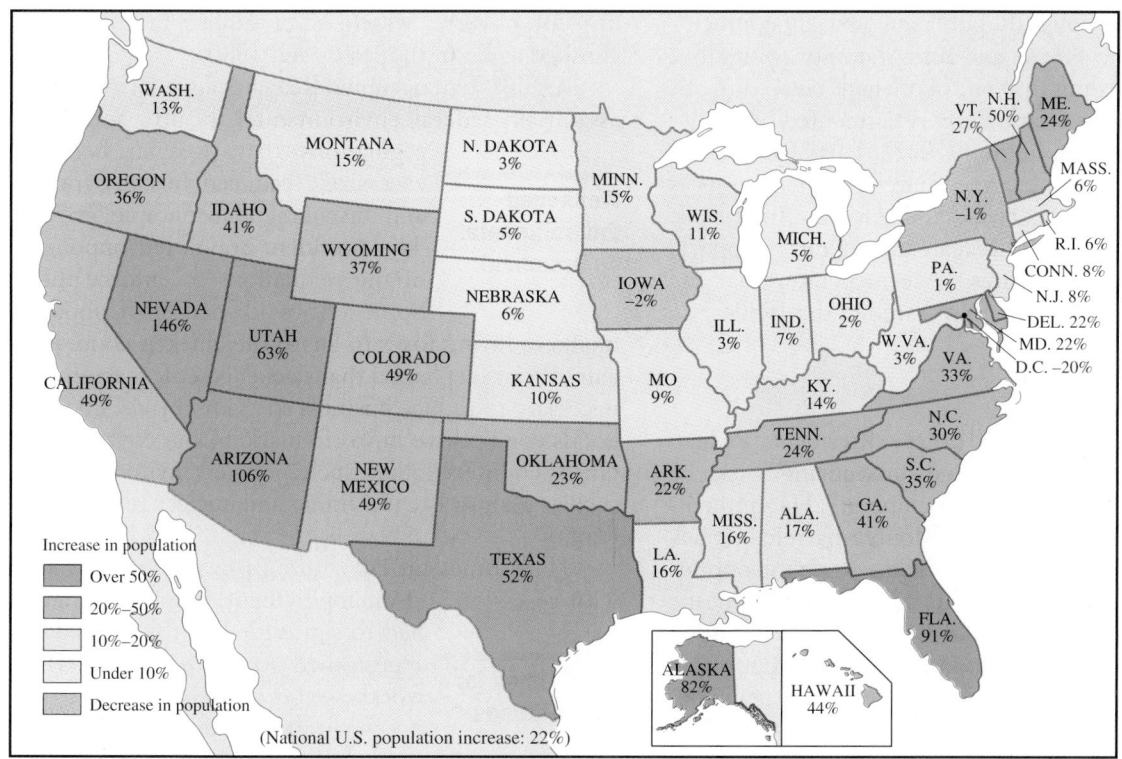

Map 32.1 The Continued Shift to the Sunbelt in the 1970s and 1980s Throughout the 1970s and 1980s, Americans continued to leave economically declining areas of the North and East in pursuit of opportunity in the Sunbelt. States in the Sunbelt and in the West had the largest population increases.

the movies or whatever—that's when this whole movement began to come alive."

In the 1980 election, President Carter faced formidable problems. American hostages were still held captive in Iran, and stagflation beset the economy. Carter's major problem was his abysmal approval rating of 21 percent, even lower than Richard Nixon's 24 percent during the Watergate crisis. And on election day, voters gave Reagan and his running mate George Bush 51 percent of the vote versus 41 percent for Carter and almost 7 percent for Anderson (see Map 32.2). Reagan's sweep was nationwide; Carter carried only six states and the District of Columbia. The vote was not only an affirmation of Reagan's conservatism but also a signal of the nation's deep dissatisfaction with Jimmy Carter's management of both the economy and foreign policy. As startling as Reagan's sweep was the capture of twelve Senate seats by Republican candidates, giving the Republicans a

Election of 1980

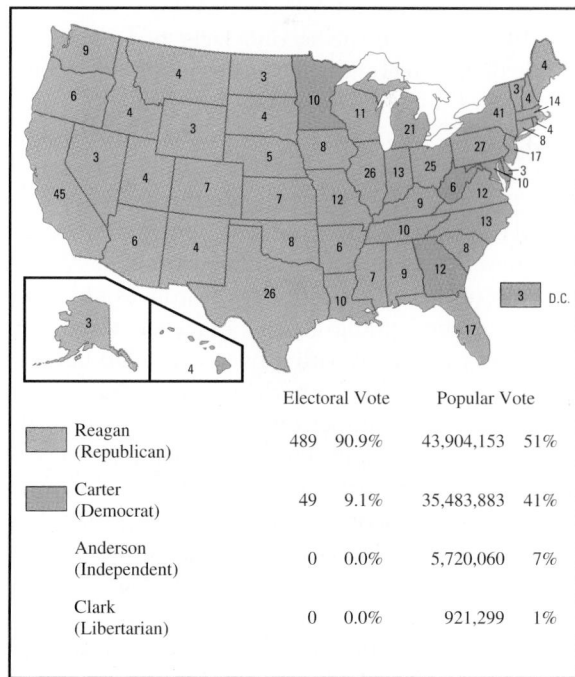

	Electoral Vote		Popular Vote	
Reagan (Republican)	489	90.9%	43,904,153	51%
Carter (Democrat)	49	9.1%	35,483,883	41%
Anderson (Independent)	0	0.0%	5,720,060	7%
Clark (Libertarian)	0	0.0%	921,299	1%

Map 32.2 Presidential Election, 1980 Ronald Reagan scored the first of two political landslides in 1980, when he won forty-four states to Jimmy Carter's six.

majority in that house. Republicans also gained thirty-five seats in the House and four state governorships.

The preceding fifteen years had been difficult ones for the Democratic Party. Fragmented by the issues of race and war, in the 1970s the party had lost the support of many whites, who viewed the Democrats as the party of welfare, taxes, and African Americans. With self-proclaimed "Reagan Democrats" supporting Republican candidates, it seemed clear that the Democrats would be running scared in the 1980s.

"Reaganomics"

 Upon taking office, President Reagan wasted little time announcing what he called "a new beginning." He immediately launched a double-barreled attack called "Reaganomics" on problems in the economy. First, he asked Congress to cut billions from domestic programs, including Medicare and Medicaid, food stamps, welfare subsidies for the working poor, and school meals. Congress endorsed most of Reagan's demands; joining the Republicans in support were conservative southern Democrats. Reagan soon initiated a second round of budget cuts, resulting among other things in the trimming of a million food-stamp recipients from government rolls.

Tax cuts were the second facet of Reagan's economic plan. A fervent believer in supply-side economics, he called for reductions in the

Tax Cuts

income taxes of the affluent and of corporations in order to stimulate savings and investments. New capital would be invested, the argument went, and would produce new plants, new jobs, and new products. As prosperity returned, the profits at the top would "trickle down" to the middle classes and even to the poor. Congress responded with a five-year, $750 billion tax cut, the largest ever in American history, featuring a 25 percent reduction in personal income taxes over three years. Other provisions increased business investment tax credits and depreciation allowances and lowered the maximum tax on income from 70 to 50 percent.

The wealthy gained the most from these tax cuts. In the 1980s, the rich got richer, as poverty deepened for many others. Women and people of color were particularly hard hit, for they usually were the last hired and the first laid off. Even when they had jobs, they were paid less than white men, and experts pointed to the growing "feminization" and "blacken-ing" of poverty, which, after falling in the 1960s, climbed again in the 1970s and 1980s.

A third item occupied Reagan's agenda: a vigorous assault on federal environmental, health, and safety

**Weakened
Environmental
Enforcement**

regulations that, Reagan believed, excessively reduced business profits and discouraged economic growth. The president appointed opponents of the regulations to enforce them. Some critics likened such appointments to hiring foxes to guard the chicken coop. Reagan officials explained that slackened enforcement was necessary to reduce business costs and make American goods competitive in world markets, but environmentalists countered that such policies invited disaster, such as toxic-waste poisoning and nuclear reactor accidents.

Hard times hit labor unions in the 1980s. Faced with recession and unemployment, union negotiators

**Hard Times for
Labor Unions**

had to settle for less than they were accustomed to receiving. American workers who ratified contracts during the first three months of Reagan's term settled for pay increases averaging only 2.2 percent, the biggest drop in wage settlements since the government began collecting such data in 1954. Unions had suffered large membership losses when unemployment hit heavy industry, and their efforts to unionize the high-growth electronics and service sectors of the economy were failing.

Reagan made the unions' hard times worse. He presided over the government's busting of the Professional Air Traffic Controllers Organization (PATCO) during the union's 1981 strike. His appointees to the National Labor Relations Board consistently voted against labor and for management. Although Reagan appeared to be an enemy of labor, an estimated 44 percent of union families had voted for him in 1980, and many still responded positively to his genial personality, espousal of old-fashioned values, and vigorous anticommunist rhetoric.

Reagan enjoyed two notable economic successes during his first two years in office. First, the inflation

Falling Inflation

rate plummeted, falling from 12 percent in 1980 to less than 7 percent in 1982. Oil led the way in price declines; after eight years OPEC had at last increased its oil production, thus lowering prices. In 1981 the United States was awash with oil as world production exceeded demand by 2 million barrels a day. Moreover, as inflation fell, so too did the cost of borrowing money. Interest rates for bank loans, which had stood at a record high of 21.5 percent in early 1981, dropped to 10.5 percent by 1983.

But there was a second, more sobering, explanation for the decline in inflation. By mid-1981 the nation was mired in a recession that not only persisted but deepened. During the last three months of the year, the GNP fell 5 percent, and sales of cars and houses dropped sharply. With declining economic activity, unemployment soared to 8 percent, the highest level in almost six years.

A year later, in late 1982, unemployment had reached 10.8 percent, the highest rate since 1940.

Rising Unemployment

Most of the jobless were adult men, particularly African Americans, who suffered an unemployment rate of 20 percent. Many of the unemployed were blue-collar workers in ailing "smokestack industries" such as autos, steel, and rubber. Reagan and his advisers had promised that supply-side economics would produce demand-side results and that consumers would lift the economy out of the recession by spending their tax cuts. But as late as April 1983, unemployment still stood at 10 percent and people were angry. Heavy industry was in a shambles. Jobless steelworkers paraded through McKeesport, Pennsylvania, carrying a coffin that bore the epitaph "American Dream." Agriculture, too, was faltering and near collapse. Farmers suffered not only from falling crop prices due to overproduction, but also from floods and droughts and from burdensome debts they had incurred at high interest rates. Many lost their property through mortgage foreclosures and farm auctions. Others filed for bankruptcy.

As the recession deepened in 1982, poverty rose to its highest level since 1965. The Bureau of the Census

Resurgence of Poverty

reported that the number of Americans living in poverty increased from 26 million in 1979 to 34 million in 1982. The largest single category of poor families consisted of households headed by women (36 percent). With one exception, poverty continued its rise in 1983, returning to the level that had prevailed before the enactment of President Johnson's Great Society. That exception was the elderly; politicians had begun paying attention to this vocal and rapidly growing population whose needs were ably articulated by the American Association of Retired Persons (AARP) and other groups.

President Reagan had announced that his administration would halt the expansion of social and health programs but would retain a "safety net" for the "truly needy." But he reneged on this promise, and Congress, unwilling to buck the popular president, sustained most of his decisions. Facing a budget deficit in excess of $200 billion in mid-1982, Reagan had three choices. First, he could cut back on his rearmament plans to spend $1.7 trillion over five years. This he refused to do; in fact, the budget he signed raised defense spending another 13 percent. Second, he could suspend or reduce the second installment of his tax cut. This choice, too, he found unacceptable. Third, he could—and did—cut welfare and social programs, pushing through Congress further cuts in Medicare and Medicaid, food stamps, federal pensions, and government-guaranteed home mortgages. Nevertheless, in the absence of budget cuts in other areas, or higher taxes, the federal debt continued to grow.

Democrats predicted victory for their party in the 1982 congressional elections. Just a week before the elections, however, a *New York Times*/CBS News poll reported that the American public was being tugged sharply in different directions: toward the Democrats by unemployment, toward the Republicans by declining inflation and the president's popularity. Nothing revealed Reagan's winning style better than his courageous response to an attempt on his life by a deranged young man in March 1981. John W. Hinckley, Jr., wounded the president, his press secretary, a Secret Service agent, and a police officer. Reagan's grace under fire caused his popularity ratings to soar. In the 1982 elections, 26 House seats swung to the Democrats, giving them a lead of 269 to 166. The Senate remained pro-Reagan, with a continued Republican majority of 54 to 46.

1982 Elections

In another two years, there would be a presidential election. The president had to prove before then that he could restore prosperity to the nation. As it turned out, Reagan's key reelection asset in 1984 was the economy, which was showing strong signs of recovery. In 1984 the GNP rose 7 percent, the sharpest increase since 1951, and midyear unemployment fell to a four-year low of 7 percent. The economy was heating up, but without sparking inflation. Indeed, inflation (4 percent in 1984) fell to its lowest level since 1967. A second factor in Reagan's favor was people's perception of him as

The Election of 1984

In 1984 Geraldine Ferraro, Democratic congresswoman from New York, made history by being the first woman nominated to run for the vice-presidency on a major party's ticket. (Collection of David J. and Janice L. Frent)

a strong leader in foreign as well as national affairs. Many Americans were proud that their nation was confronting the Soviets not only with firm words but with military interventions and a large military buildup (see Chapter 31). Third, Reagan was the enthusiastic choice of political conservatives of all kinds across the country. Patriotism was back in style, and Reagan won the approval of millions of other Americans who agreed with his television ads that it was "Morning in America" after two twilight decades of turmoil and self-doubt.

Aiding Reagan was the Democrats' failure to field a convincing alternative. The Democratic nominee—former vice president Walter Mondale—did not inspire Americans. Even the policies that Mondale espoused seemed timeworn and out of step with the nation's conservatism. Adding to Mondale's woes was the disarray of the Democratic Party; it had fragmented into separate caucuses of union members, African Americans, women, Jews, homosexuals, Hispanics, and other groups. Each caucus had its own agenda. The one bright spot for the Democrats was Mondale's historic selection of Representative Geraldine Ferraro of New York as the first woman vice-presidential candidate of a major political party. Ferraro showed herself to be an intelligent, indefatigable campaigner.

Mondale wanted to debate the federal deficit, but Reagan preferred to invoke the theme of leadership and rely on slogans. Mondale chastised Reagan for the mounting deficit, which had reached $175 billion in fiscal year 1984. But when Mondale announced that he would raise taxes to cut the deficit, he lost votes. Voters in 1984 had a clear choice, and in every state but Minnesota—Mondale's home state—they chose the Republican ticket. The election returns were the most convincing evidence yet that the nation had shifted to the right. The only groups still loyal to the Democratic ticket were African Americans, Hispanics, Jews, and the poor. Reagan scored solid victories with all other voting groups, including young people, whites in both North and South, high-school and college graduates, and Catholics as well as Protestants.

Fifty years earlier, the Democratic Party had gained the allegiance of millions of Americans, including blue-collar workers, who credited President Franklin Roosevelt's New Deal with having saved them during the Great Depression. The New Deal coalition controlled national politics for the next thirty years. But in the 1970s and 1980s, a deep reaction set in against the liberalized moral standards associated with the Democratic Party. Many Democrats held conservative views on welfare, abortion, homosexuality, and other social issues, and they switched their votes to Ronald Reagan and the Republican Party. Whether Reagan had forged a lasting conservative coalition—one that could repeal the New Deal—remained to be seen. What was not debatable was that, during his first term, he had succeeded in his principal aims.

People of Color and New Immigrants

 Poverty was a growing problem in the 1970s and 1980s, particularly for people of color. Joblessness plagued blacks, Native Americans, and Hispanics, as well as many of the new immigrants. Most of America's poor were white, but African Americans made up a disproportionate share of the total. The overall poverty rate was 13 percent by 1980, but among blacks it was 33 percent and among Hispanics 26 percent, compared with 10 percent for whites. These figures had barely changed by the end of Ronald Reagan's presidency in 1989 (see Figure 32.2).

The weight of poverty fell most heavily on children, especially African American children, almost half of whom lived below the poverty line. A 1981 Children's Defense Fund survey reported that black children in the United States were four times more likely than whites to be born into poverty, twice as likely to drop out of school before twelfth grade, three times as likely to be unemployed, and five times as likely to be murdered. "Millions of black children lack self-confidence, feel discouragement, despair, numbness or rage as they try to grow up on islands of poverty, ill health, inadequate education . . . crime and rampant unemployment in a nation of boastful affluence," the report concluded. Many children lived in poor families headed by single women who earned meager incomes as domestic servants, laundresses, and kitchen helpers, supplemented by welfare assistance.

Some whites and even other blacks grumbled that poor blacks were responsible for their own poverty.

Declining Job Opportunities for African Americans

But the job market in the 1970s and 1980s was far different from that of twenty-five, fifty, or seventy-five years before. During periods of rapid industrialization, unskilled European immigrants and black migrants from the South had been able to find blue-collar jobs. Beginning in the 1970s, fewer such jobs were available; demand was greatest for skilled workers such as computer operators, bank tellers, secretaries, and bookkeepers. Most jobless people could not qualify. Moreover, blue-collar jobs in the inner cities were disappearing or moving to the suburbs. New York City alone had 234,000 fewer blue-collar workers in 1980 than it had at the beginning of the 1970s. For young African American men and women who lacked marketable skills, the situation was often tragic. The psychiatrist Alvin Poussaint observed, "A lot of black kids simply feel they don't count. . . . In terms of what makes this society run, they're expendable."

But a historical anomaly was at work. For even as the plight of the African American poor worsened, the black middle class expanded. The

African American Middle Class

number of black college students increased from 282,000 in 1966 to more than 1 million in 1980; by 1980 about one-third of all black high-school graduates were going on to college, the same proportion as among white youths. Some benefited from affirmative-action programs, which sought to compensate for decades of racial dis-

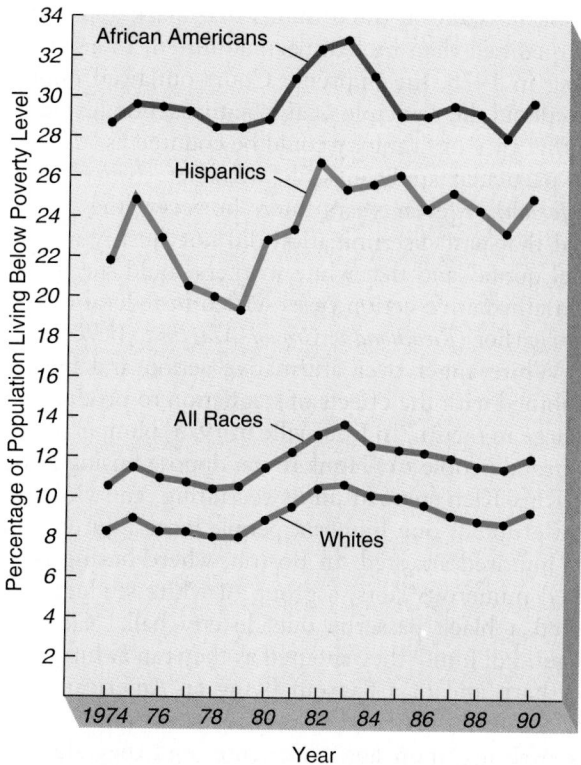

Figure 32.2 Poverty in America by Race, 1974–1990
Poverty in America rose in the early 1980s but subsided afterward. Many people of color, however, experienced little relief during the decade. Notice that the percentage of African Americans living below the poverty level was three times higher than that for whites. It also was much higher for Hispanics. (Source: Adapted from U.S. Bureau of the Census, *Statistical Abstract of the United States* [Washington, D.C., 1992], p. 461.)

crimination by granting African American men and women educational (and employment) opportunities to advance themselves. By 1990 the number of black college students had increased further to 1.3 million. At least at the upper levels of black society, the dream of equality was being realized.

But as middle-class African Americans made gains, resentful whites complained that they were being victimized by "reverse discrimination." To meet federal affirmative-action requirements, some schools and companies had established quotas for minorities and women; in some cases the standards were lower than those for whites. When Allan Bakke, a white man, was denied admission to medical

White Backlash

school, he sued on the grounds that black applicants less qualified than he had been admitted. In a 5-to-4 ruling in 1978, the Supreme Court outlawed quotas but upheld the principle of affirmative action, explaining that race or ethnicity could be counted as "a 'plus' in a particular applicant's file" *(Bakke v. University of California)*. Eleven years later, however, the Court ruled that past discrimination did not "justify a rigid racial quota" and that white workers could sue to reopen affirmative-action cases settled in federal courts years earlier *(Richmond v. Croson, Martin v. Wilks)*.

White anger over affirmative action and busing combined with the effects of stagflation to produce an upsurge in racism. In Louisville in 1975, bumper stickers urged people to "Honk if you oppose busing," the Ku Klux Klan stepped up its recruiting, and violence soon erupted: one hundred people were injured and two hundred arrested. In Boston, where busing provoked numerous riots, a group of white students attacked a black passerby outside city hall. "Get the nigger; kill him!" they shouted as they ran at him with the sharp end of a flagstaff flying an American flag. Racial tension rose in cities across the nation.

African Americans were tense, and they showed their anger more openly than in the past. Charles Silberman wrote in *Criminal Violence, Criminal Justice* (1978) that "black Americans have discovered that fear runs the other way, that whites are intimidated by their very presence. . . . The taboo against expression of antiwhite anger is breaking down, and 350 years of festering hatred has come spilling out." That hatred erupted several times in 1980, most notably in Miami and Chattanooga, after all-white juries acquitted whites in the killings of blacks. Miami's three days of rioting left eighteen dead and four hundred injured.

Black Anger

In the 1980s African American civil rights leaders denounced not only the judicial system but also the executive branch headed by President Ronald Reagan. Appointments were one issue: whereas 12 percent of President Jimmy Carter's high-level appointees had been black and 12 percent women, Reagan's were 4 percent black and 8 percent women. (Reagan did appoint four women to his cabinet and made history by appointing Sandra Day O'Connor the first woman associate justice of the Supreme Court.) Moreover, Reagan's civil rights chief in the Justice Department opposed busing and affirmative action, and he was criticized for lax enforcement of fair housing laws and laws banning sexual and racial discrimination in feder-

ally funded education programs. He also fought against renewing the Voting Rights Act of 1965, but Congress ignored his efforts and renewed the act in 1982.

"The Kerner report warning is coming true," asserted a group of scholars, politicians, and civil rights leaders who met in 1988 to assess race relations on the twentieth anniversary of the publication of the Kerner Commission report (see page 865). "America is again becoming two separate societies," with whites residing in the comfortable suburbs while African Americans in inner cities lived amid poverty, segregation, and crime. "Even the most pessimistic observers of the social scene in the later 1960s," observed a member of the group, "probably did not foresee or anticipate the sharp increases in the rates of social dislocation and massive breakdown of social institutions in ghetto areas."

Every bit as angry as African Americans were Native Americans. For one thing, in the 1970s and 1980s they suffered the worst health of any group in the United States. American Indians suffered the highest incidence of tuberculosis, alcoholism, and suicide of any ethnic group in the country. Four in ten Native Americans were unemployed, and nine out of ten lived in substandard housing. The American Indian population did rise after the Second World War, reaching 1.7 million in 1990—more than half of whom lived in California, Oklahoma, Arizona, New Mexico, and North Carolina—but that was only a fraction of their population when the first Europeans arrived in North America. Faced with deplorable conditions in the 1970s, Native American militants were prepared to struggle to improve the quality of life on the reservations.

Native Americans

In 1973 members of the militant American Indian Movement (AIM) called for "Red Power." Demanding the rights guaranteed Indians in treaties with the United States, they seized eleven hostages and a trading post on the Pine Ridge Reservation at Wounded Knee, South Dakota, where troops of the Seventh Cavalry had massacred three hundred Sioux in 1890 (see page 468). Their seventy-one-day confrontation with federal marshals ended with a government agreement to examine the treaty rights of the Oglala Sioux. Prosecution of AIM leaders for the Wounded Knee occupation was dismissed by a federal court in 1974. And for once, Congress listened to Native America, in 1974 passing

"Red Power": Indian Self-Determination

For nearly 115 years, an Arizona land dispute has divided the Hopi and Navajo tribes. A law passed by Congress in 1974 called for the division of 1.8 million acres between the tribes and ordered the relocation of tribal members living on land given to the other tribe. Hopi and Navajo traditionalists claimed that they had no dispute and that powerful economic interests were using the issue as a cover for seizing the area's rich coal and water rights. In 1986 these Hopis and Navajos joined forces to protest federal law directing the secretary of the interior to "expedite" relocation "without regard to any law or regulation."   (Lawrence Gus/Sygma)

the Indian Self-Determination Law, which provided Indians with greater control over federal programs, including schools, operating on reservations.

Native Americans also accused the federal government of breaking its treaty commitments—by seizing Indian lands, especially when they contained valuable minerals. In 1946 Congress established the Indian Claims Commission to compensate Indians for lands stolen from them. Under the legislation, lawyers for the Native American Rights Fund and other groups scored notable victories. In the 1970s the Chippewas in the upper Midwest, Indians on Washington's Puget Sound, and the Cheyenne-Arapaho tribes in Oklahoma won protection of their hunting and fishing rights and restitution of their land and water. And in 1980 the Supreme Court ordered the government to pay $106 million plus interest to the Sioux nation for the Black Hills of South Dakota, stolen when gold was found there in the 1870s. Nevertheless, corporations and govern-

Indian Suits for Lost Lands

ment agencies continued to covet Indian lands and disregard Indian religious beliefs: a coal company strip-mined a portion of the Hopi Sacred Circle, which according to tribal religion is the source of all life, and the sacred Black Hills of South Dakota are being mined again, this time for uranium.

As Indians fought to regain old rights, Hispanic Americans struggled to make a place for themselves. An inflow of immigrants unequaled since the turn of the century, coupled with a high birth rate, made Hispanic peoples America's fastest-growing minority by the 1970s. Of the more than 20 million Hispanics living in the United States in the 1970s, 8 million were Mexican Americans concentrated in California, Texas, Arizona, New Mexico, and Colorado. Several million Puerto Ricans, Cubans, Dominicans, and other immigrants from the Caribbean also lived in the United States, clustered principally on the East Coast in cities in Florida, New York, and other states.

Hispanic Americans

In 1976, folk singer Joan Baez and César Chávez, leader of the United Farm Workers (UFW), marched with other mourners through vineyards near Delano, California, at the funeral of Juan de la Cruz, a farm worker. De la Cruz had been murdered in a drive-by shotgun attack on a UFW picket line. (Bob Fitch/Take Stock)

These officially acknowledged Hispanic Americans were joined by millions of undocumented workers, or illegal aliens. Beginning in the mid-1960s, large numbers of poverty-stricken Mexicans began to cross the poorly guarded 2,000-mile border. The movement north continued in the 1970s and 1980s. By 1990 one out of three Los Angelenos and Miamians were Hispanic, as were 48 percent of the population of San Antonio and 70 percent of El Paso. Discrimination awaited many of these new immigrants, as it had previous groups of newcomers. And the larger the Hispanic population has become, the more widespread has been the discrimination. "Anglos are afraid," said

California assemblyman Richard Alatorre. "They think they will get to be the minorities and we'll be opposing them."

Most of these new Americans preferred their family-centered culture to Anglo culture and, for that reason, resisted assimilation. "We want to be here," explained Daniel Villanueva, a TV executive in Los Angeles, "but without losing our language and our culture. They are a richness, a treasure that we don't care to lose."

Hispanic Cultural Pride

Like other minorities, Hispanics wanted political power—"brown power." In the 1960s César Chávez's United Farm Workers was the first Hispanic interest group to gain national attention. The militant Brown Berets attracted notice for their efforts to provide meals to preschoolers and courses in Chicano studies and consciousness raising to older students. And throughout the 1970s the Mexican American political party *La Raza Unida* was a potent force in the Southwest and in East Los Angeles.

Still, the group that was becoming the nation's largest minority exercised a disproportionately small share of political power. One reason was that Latin America is tremendously diverse. Although Mexican Americans, Puerto Ricans, Cubans, and other Hispanic groups shared a language and a religion, they differed in countless ways. And the differences were not only in country of origin: economic immigrants such as Mexican Americans crowded into West Coast *barrios* side by side with political refugees from Central American wars. Poverty was most severe where the population was most concentrated. "We need a Spanish Bobby Kennedy or Martin Luther King," observed Daniel Villanueva. "Right now he's just not there."

During the 1970s and 1980s people of color immigrated to the United States in record numbers from Indochina, Mexico, Central and South America, and the Caribbean. Between 1970 and 1980 the United States absorbed more than 4 million immigrants and refugees and uncounted numbers of illegal aliens. High as these figures were, they doubled again during the next decade, with almost 9 million new arrivals. Many of the new immigrants came in family units, and women and children accounted for two-thirds of all legal immigrants. Although the new residents faced a long struggle, they were willing to work hard to succeed. Among the newcomers, Asian Americans seemed to be the most suc-

New Flux of Immigrants

cessful. There had been a burst of Asian immigration; the number of people whose origins were in Asia or the Pacific increased by 385 percent from 1971 to 1990.

The arrival of so many newcomers put pressure on Congress to curtail the flow and perhaps offer amnesty to aliens already living illegally in the United States. In 1978 Congress authorized a comprehensive reexamination of America's immigration policy. The immigration commission completed its study in 1981, but legislative solutions were delayed until 1986, when Congress passed the Immigration Reform and Control (Simpson-Rodino) Act, which provided amnesty to undocumented workers who had arrived before 1982. The act's purpose was to discourage illegal immigration by imposing sanctions on employers who hired undocumented workers, but it failed to stem the flow of people fleeing Mexico's economic woes. In 1988 the number of new immigrants from Mexico approached the record numbers reached before the reform law went into effect.

Immigration Reform

Feminism, Antifeminism, and Women's Lives

Women scored some impressive victories in the 1970s. In 1974 Congress passed the Equal Credit Opportunity Act, which enabled women to get bank loans and obtain credit cards on the same terms as men. In the field of criminal law, many states revised their statutes on rape, prohibiting defense lawyers from discrediting rape victims by revealing their previous sexual experience. Perhaps most significant were women's gains from affirmative action in hiring. As mandated by the Civil Rights Act of 1964 and the establishment of the Equal Employment Opportunity Commission, women and people of color applying for jobs had to receive the same consideration as white males. To take advantage of new opportunities, many women delayed having children until reaching their thirties and establishing themselves in their careers. The number of women enrolled in college rose 45 percent between 1970 and 1975, and numerous women were elected to political offices.

Still, women continued to encounter opposition in their struggle for gender equality. Particularly formidable was the antifeminist or "pro-family" movement, which contended that men should lead and

Antifeminist Movement

women should follow, especially within the family, and that women should stay home and raise children. In defense of the patriarchal, or father-led, family, antifeminists campaigned against the Equal Rights Amendment, the gay rights movement, and abortion on demand. The conservative backlash against feminism became an increasingly powerful political force in the United States, especially in the Republican Party.

Antifeminists blamed the women's movement for the country's spiraling divorce rate; they charged that feminists would jettison their husbands and even their children in their quest for job fulfillment and gender equality. The number of divorces jumped 56 percent from 1960 to 1970, 60 percent from 1970 to 1980, and remained near that level in the 1980s. Often, however, the decision to divorce was made not by the wives but by the husbands. According to Barbara Ehrenreich, a feminist scholar, men started walking out on their families in large numbers in the 1950s and 1960s, well before the rebirth of feminism. Tired of fulfilling the role of husband, father, and financial provider, men responded to the image of carefree bachelorhood presented in the pages of men's magazines such as *Playboy*, which attacked wives as parasites who gobbled up their husbands' salaries but were too sexually repressed to give much in return. Many men came to see their wives as the agents of their entrapment; in "flight from commitment," they chose divorce.

Antifeminists successfully stalled ratification of the Equal Rights Amendment, which after quickly passing thirty-five state legislatures fell three states short of success in the late 1970s. Phyllis Schlafly's "Stop ERA" campaign claimed that the ERA would abolish alimony, legalize homosexual marriages, and subject women to single-sex bathrooms and the draft. The debate was occasionally vicious. Refusing to acknowledge gender-based discrimination, Schlafly derided ERA advocates as "a bunch of bitter women seeking a constitutional cure for their personal problems." The ERA died in 1982 when an extended time limit expired for ratification by the states.

Equal Rights Amendment

Many conservative women also participated in the anti-abortion or "prolife" movement, which sprang up almost overnight in the wake of the Supreme Court's 1973 decision in *Roe v. Wade* (see page 872). People whose opposition to abortion was heartfelt and uncompromising denounced that ruling and called for an

Women entered the space program as astronauts in the 1970s. Several members of the group shown in this poster from the National Aeronautics and Space Administration (NASA) achieved distinction. The two astronauts on the left side are *(above)* Shannon W. Lucid and *(below)* Sally K. Ride. Sally Ride was the first woman in space, spending six days in orbit in 1983. In 1996 Shannon Lucid set a longevity record for American astronauts, female or male: 188 days in orbit. Across from Lucid is Judith Resnik, who died in 1986 in the explosion of the space shuttle *Challenger.*   (Corbis-Bettmann)

amendment to the Constitution defining human life as beginning at conception. Along with Catholics, Mormons, and other religious opponents of abortion, including the Moral Majority, the anti-abortion movement supported the Hyde Amendment, the successful legislative effort of Representative Henry Hyde of Illinois in 1976 to cut off most Medicaid funds for abortions. At the state level, the anti-abortion movement lobbied for restrictions on access to the procedure, such as mandating parental notification. In 1989 the Supreme Court (in *Webster v. Reproductive Health Ser-*

vices) ruled that a Missouri law restricting the right to an abortion was constitutional, thus encouraging further assaults on *Roe v. Wade.*

Feminists fought back. Indeed, Ronald Reagan's most vocal critics were women who mobilized in op-

Women Opponents of Reagan's Conservatism

position to the conservative agenda of the White House. The *New York Times* reported a "gender gap" between men's and women's opinions of Reagan's performance in 1983: far fewer women (38 percent) than men (53 percent) believed Reagan deserved reelection. What accounted most centrally for the gender gap were Reagan's social welfare, health, and education cuts. Many working mothers expressed shock at the Reagan administration's insensitivity to children's welfare. One feminist critic quipped that, for Reagan, "life begins at conception and ends at birth." Children's poverty continued its rise throughout the decade, and by 1989 children accounted for about 40 percent of America's poor people.

Reagan's critics assailed him for failing to reverse "the feminization of poverty" and for approving cuts in food stamps and school meals. The Reagan administration's opposition to federally subsidized childcare and the feminist goal of "comparable worth" also drew their ire. Because of persistent occupational segregation, 80 percent of all working women in 1985 were concentrated in low-paying "female" occupations such as clerking, selling, teaching, and waitressing. Recognizing this, feminists supplemented their earlier rallying cry of "equal pay for equal work" with a call for "equal pay for jobs of comparable worth." Why, women asked, should a grade-school teacher earn less than an electrician, if the two jobs require comparable training and skills and involve comparable responsibilities? In the 1970s female workers still took home only 60 cents to every male worker's dollar; by 1990 the figure had risen to 71 cents.

Activists in the women's struggle had to acknowledge certain harsh realities. One was the tight job mar-

Increased Burdens on Women

ket created by the economic recessions of the 1970s and 1980s. Other problems included a high teenage pregnancy rate and a rising divorce rate that left increasing numbers of women and their children with lower standards of living. The number of single mothers rose to 7.7 million in 1990, up from 5.8 million a decade earlier. The tandem of divorce and teenage pregnancy meant that a progressively smaller proportion of America's children lived with two parents. In 1990, about a quarter of all children, 16 million, lived with only one parent—double the percentage of 1970.

Many mothers thus had to find employment. Still others worked to preserve or improve the living standard of two-parent households that otherwise would have experienced substantial declines. Families were paying a higher percentage of their income to buy houses, and often two wage earners were required to pay the bills. In 1983, for the first time in the nation's history, more than half of all adult American women (51 percent) held jobs outside the home. Another milestone was recorded in 1987: the share of women returning to work or actively seeking jobs within a year after the arrival of a baby exceeded 50 percent for the first time. (By contrast, just ten years earlier, the figure had been 31 percent.) The working mother had become the norm in America.

Such women had to contend with what came to be called "the Superwoman Squeeze." According to a report by the Worldwatch Institute, most working wives and mothers, even those with full-time jobs, "retained an unwilling monopoly on unpaid labor at home." Combining housework and outside employment, wives

worked 71 hours a week; husbands worked 55 hours a week. Women traded stories of "couch-potato" husbands who watched television while their wives did chores. Soon only one in four wives would be a full-time housewife and mother. The remainder would be trying to balance the more-than-full-time demands of a family and a career without shortchanging either— or themselves—in the process.

A Polarized People: American Society in the 1980s

The United States became an increasingly polarized society in the 1980s. The rich got richer, while the poor sank deeper into despair (see Figure 32.3). The incomes of the bottom fifth of American families fell by 13 percent, but the top fifth earned 27 percent more, and the top 1 percent saw their incomes double. Indeed, by 1989 the top 1 percent (834,000 households with $5.7 trillion in net worth) was worth more than the bottom 90 percent (84 million households with $4.8 trillion in net worth). The United States was polarizing not only economically but also socially, and societal divisions were exacerbated by new problems:

Figure 32.3   While the Rich Got Richer in the 1980s, the Poor Got Poorer   Between 1977 and 1989, the richest 1 percent of American families reaped most of the gains from economic growth. In fact, the average pretax income of families in the top percentage rose 77 percent. At the same time, the typical family saw its income edge up only 4 percent. And the bottom 40 percent of families had actual declines in income.   (Source: Data from the *New York Times*, March 5, 1992.)

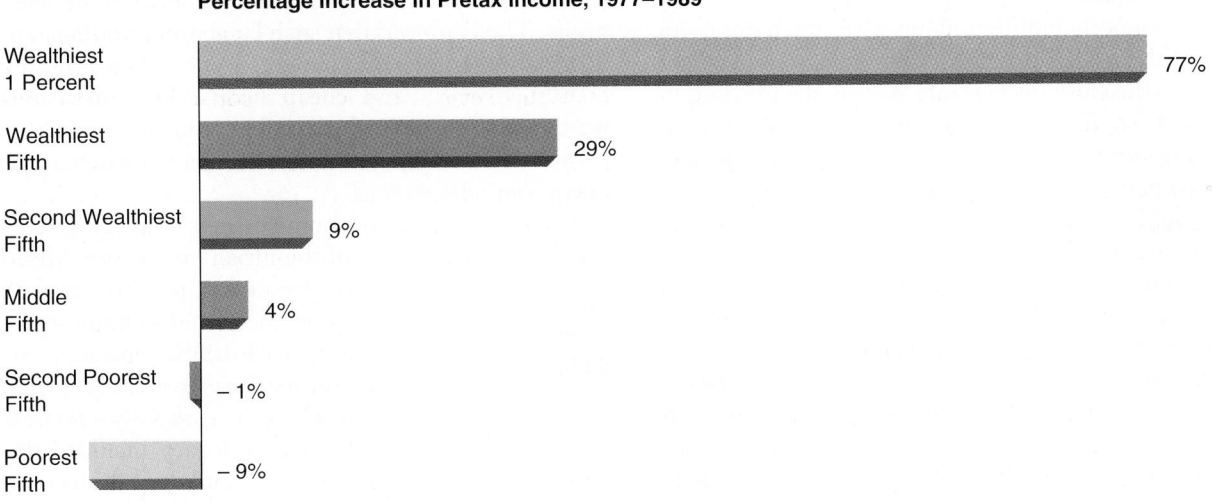

Percentage Increase in Pretax Income, 1977–1989

- Wealthiest 1 Percent — 77%
- Wealthiest Fifth — 29%
- Second Wealthiest Fifth — 9%
- Middle Fifth — 4%
- Second Poorest Fifth — – 1%
- Poorest Fifth — – 9%

A stunned nation watched in 1986 as the space shuttle *Challenger* exploded seventy-three seconds after lifting off. The *Challenger* explosion produces a flashbulb memory for many younger Americans who watched the tragedy on television at school (one of the *Challenger* crew, Christa McAuliffe, was an elementary school teacher).   (Corbis-Bettmann)

AIDS (acquired immune deficiency syndrome) and the cocaine-derived drug known as crack.

By the end of the 1980s, as many Americans were living in poverty as had been in 1964, when 36 million were poor and President Johnson declared a War on Poverty. But the poor themselves were somewhat different. The poverty of the 1980s, explained the authors of a 1988 report of the Social Science Research Council, "is found less among the elderly and people living in nonurban areas and more among children living with one parent—in households headed principally by young women." In the 1970s the child poverty rate increased 6 percent; in the 1980s, it jumped 11 percent, with thirty-three states registering increases. As inequality grew, the gap widened between affluent whites and poor blacks, Indians, and Hispanics, and between the suburbs and the inner cities. And as inequality increased, so too did social pathology. Violent crime, particularly homicides and gang warfare, grew alarmingly, as did school dropout rates, crime rates, and child abuse.

Increasing Inequality

Poverty resulted not only from discrimination based on race and gender, but also from economic recessions and from the changing structure of the labor market. As deindustrialization took hold, the job market shifted from high-paying, unionized, blue-collar jobs to low-paying service jobs. Minimum-wage employment burgeoned in fast-food restaurants, but such jobs meant a substantial drop in workers' standard of living. In 1974 blue-collar jobs accounted for half of the employment of African American males between the ages of twenty and twenty-four. Just ten years later, such jobs accounted for only one-fourth of their employment. North Lawndale, a black neighborhood on Chicago's West Side, exemplified the problem. In prosperous days, the community's economy had depended on the 43,000 jobs at the Hawthorne plant of Western Electric. But the Hawthorne plant closed in 1984. Soon, so did the banks and small stores that depended on the workers' wages.

Changing Job Market

According to sociologist William Julius Wilson, the issue of "the truly disadvantaged" was "one of the most important social issues of the remainder of the 20th century." Life was becoming precarious not only for the underclass but also for the working poor, whose numbers increased by more than one-third during the 1980s. By the end of the decade, 40 percent of the nation's poor were working, but few had full-time, year-round jobs. At the same time, social workers reported that more and more of the nation's homeless were families.

About a third of the homeless were former psychiatric patients who found themselves living on the streets after hospitals emptied their psychiatric wards in a burst of enthusiasm for "deinstitutionalization." By 1985, 80 percent of the total number of beds in state mental hospitals had been eliminated on the premise that small neighborhood programs would be more responsive than large state hospitals to people's needs. The truth was that such local programs failed to materialize, and former patients went to live in unsafe boarding houses and cheap hotels. Few provisions were made for medical treatment, and these troubled people increasingly found that they had nowhere to go except onto the streets.

Another cause of homelessness was drug use, which was the scourge of the urban underclass. Mired in hopelessness, poverty-stricken men and women tried to find forgetfulness in hard drugs, especially cocaine and its derivative crack, which first struck New York City's poorest neighborhoods in 1985. Crack's legacy included destroyed families, abused children, and drug dealers too young for a driver's license but with access to subma-

Drugs and Violence

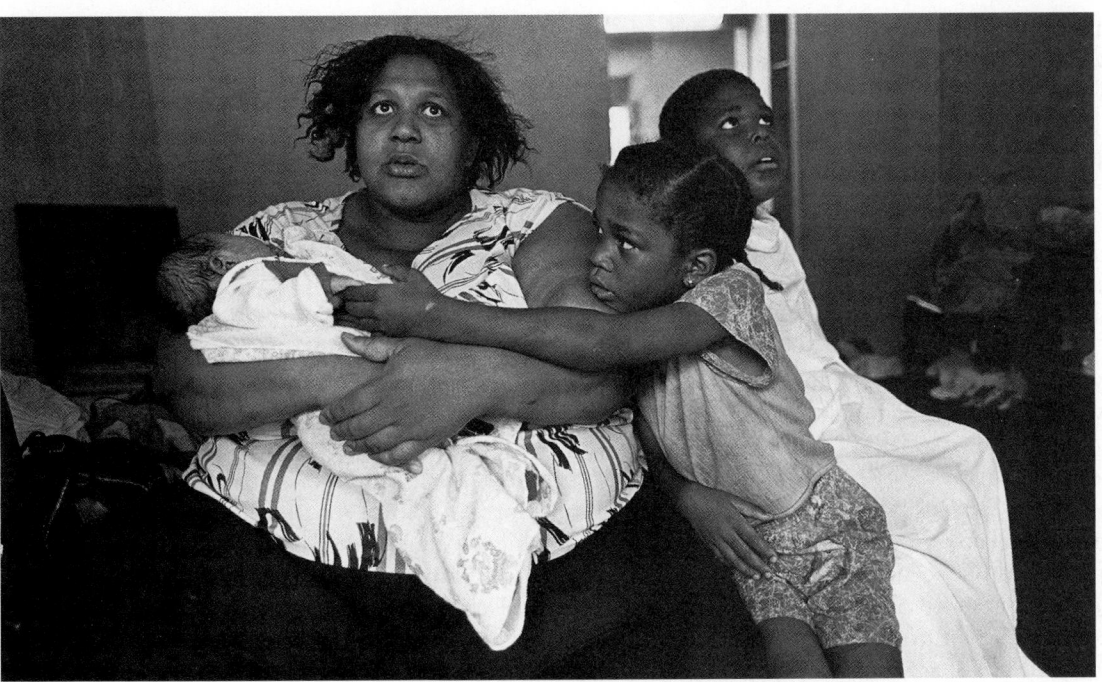

For this family, which includes a one-week-old baby, homelessness came suddenly. Home had been a squalid motor inn in North Bergen, New Jersey, but the board of health condemned the motel and the police put the family out on the street. In 1988 as many as a million people were homeless.   (Eugene Richards/Magnum)

chine guns and other state-of-the-art firearms. Gang shootouts over drugs were deadly: the toll in Los Angeles in 1987 was 387 deaths; more than half of the victims were innocent bystanders. After a bloody drug murder in New York City's Spanish Harlem, a sixteen-year-old girl moaned, "It's frightening. . . . It's crazy. There's no answer to it. And there's no end to it."

Another lethal byproduct of the 1980s drug epidemic was the spread of AIDS. First observed in the

AIDS

United States in 1981, AIDS is a disease transmittable through the sharing of intravenous needles by drug users or through the exchange of infected body fluids, often during sexual contact. Caused by a virus that attacks cells in the immune system, AIDS makes its victims susceptible to deadly infections and cancers. In the United States, AIDS initially was confined to the sexual practices of male homosexuals, but the disease spread to heterosexuals and those receiving transfusions of tainted blood.

Between 1981 and 1988, of the 57,000 AIDS cases reported, nearly 32,000 resulted in death. Public health officials were slow to recognize the enormity of the epidemic, partly because the AIDS virus (HIV) can

In the 1980s there was an alarming spread of sexually transmitted diseases, especially acquired immune deficiency syndrome (AIDS). Campaigns for "Safe Sex," such as this New York City subway ad, urged people to use condoms.   (Reprinted with permission of Saatchi & Saatchi)

lie dormant for several years before presenting symptoms. But the worst had not yet revealed itself. A 1988 study reported that half of the gay men in San Francisco would develop AIDS and another 25 percent would develop the AIDS-related complex within about nine years of infection. Some religious leaders and politicians heartlessly blamed the victims. "A man reaps what he sows," declared the Reverend Jerry Falwell of the Moral Majority. "If he sows seed in the field of his lower nature, he will reap from it a harvest of corruption."

AIDS divided American communities, and AIDS—along with other sexually transmitted diseases such as genital herpes and chlamydia—affected Americans' sexual behavior. In the 1980s caution replaced the sexual revolution. "Safe sex" campaigns urged the use of condoms. But conservative Protestant sects joined the Roman Catholic Church in warning that condom advertising implicitly sanctioned contraception and encouraged promiscuity. Sex education should not be offered in the schools, they contended, citing their deep belief that any sexual activity other than heterosexual matrimonial monogamy was wrong. The Supreme Court struck a blow against gay rights in 1986, when it upheld a Georgia felony statute that punished consensual anal or oral sex between men with up to twenty years in jail *(Bowers v. Hardwick)*. Although gay men expected little assistance from the conservative executive branch, they were partly wrong. In 1988 the federal government mailed a booklet entitled *Understanding AIDS* to 107 million households. Nevertheless, AIDS continued to be one of several unsolved social problems dividing the nation in the late 1980s.

Economic Upturn and the Election of 1988

 Despite Ronald Reagan's overwhelming reelection victory in 1984, for much of 1985 the president was on the defensive. One reason was the mounting fiscal deficit. A fiscal conservative long committed to balanced budgets, Ronald Reagan nonetheless oversaw the accumulation of more new debt than all previous American presidents put together.

Reagan had assailed President Carter's $74 billion deficit during the 1980 campaign, but the deficit exceeded $212 billion in fiscal 1985 and $221 billion in fiscal 1986. Although Republicans blamed the deficit

Mounting Fiscal Deficit

on the Democrats, almost half of the national debt derived from fiscal years 1982 through 1986, when Reagan occupied the White House and the Republicans controlled the Senate. Because of tax reductions, growing entitlement programs such as Social Security, and upwardly spiraling defense budgets, the national debt grew by $955 billion during this five-year period (see Figure 32.4).

In response, Reagan and Congress reluctantly agreed to the 1985 Gramm-Rudman bill, which called for a balanced federal budget by fiscal 1991 through a gradual reduction of the annual deficit. The deficit did drop, but for the three fiscal years from 1987 to 1989, it still totaled $457 billion. Another important bill, the Tax Reform Act of 1986, lowered personal income taxes while closing some flagrant loopholes and eliminating 6 million poor people from the tax rolls. The law represented a compromise between supply-side conservatives, who argued that lower tax rates would act as an incentive to savings, investment, and growth, and liberals whose focus was the unfairness of the tax codes.

During his second term, Reagan realized one of his most important goals: putting more conservative justices on the Supreme Court so as to overthrow liberal rulings made in the 1960s under Chief Justice Earl Warren (see page 862). After Warren Burger's decision to retire from the Supreme Court in 1986, Reagan nominated conservative William Rehnquist to serve as chief justice and conservative Antonin Scalia to fill Rehnquist's seat; the Senate confirmed both choices.

A Conservative Supreme Court

Until late 1986 Reagan's place in history was secure. But the Iran-contra disclosures caused his aura to fade, not only sullying his last two years in office but also endangering his historical reputation and raising the Democrats' hopes for a presidential victory in 1988. Reagan's political troubles began on election day 1986. First, the Republicans lost control of the Senate, stripping the president of a crucial power base. Second, from Lebanon came a bizarre story that the president's national security adviser had traveled to Iran with a Bible, a cake, and a planeload of weapons seeking the release of Americans held hostage in the Middle East. "No comment," Reagan told reporters, but details of the Iran-contra scandal soon began to surface (see page 912).

Iran-Contra Scandal

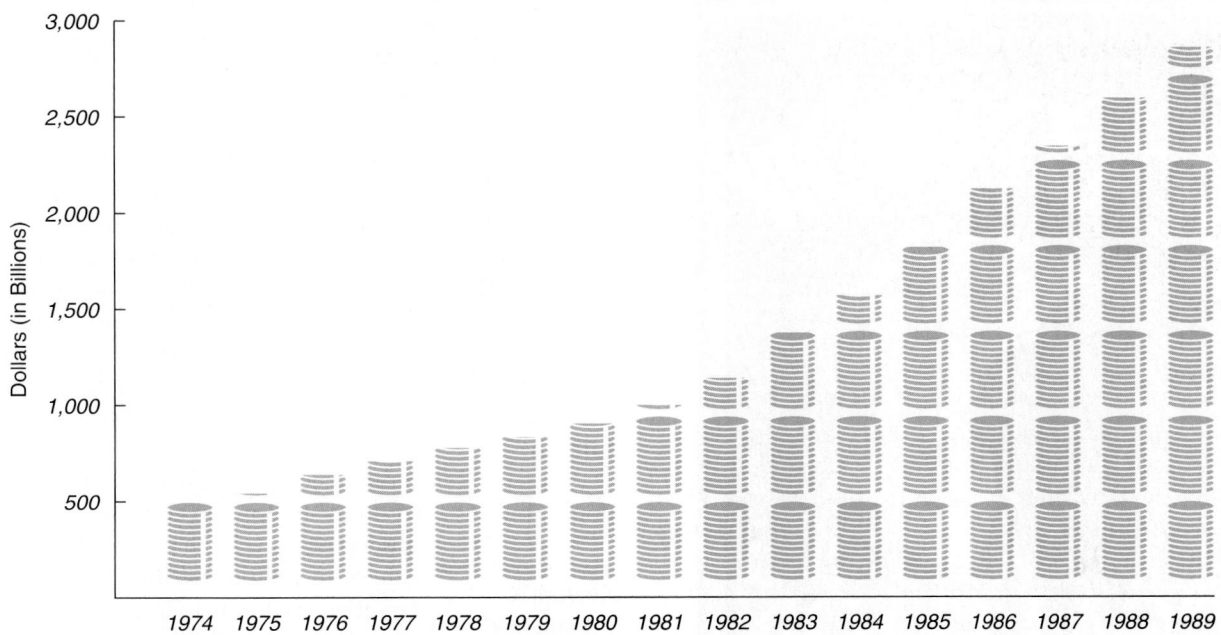

Figure 32.4   America's Rising National Debt, 1974–1989   America's national debt, which rose sporadically throughout the 1970s, soared to record heights during the 1980s. Under President Reagan, large defense expenditures and tax cuts caused the national debt to grow by $1.5 trillion.   (Source: Adapted from U.S. Bureau of the Census, *Statistical Abstract of the United States* [Washington, D.C., 1992], p. 315.)

"An irony of the Reagan era," wrote Senator Daniel Patrick Moynihan, Democrat of New York, "is that having at midpoint reached a crescendo of triumphalism—morning in America—it is closing amid talk of decline." On a personal level, President Reagan had lost his mastery; the Great Communicator had taken on the appearance of a tired, bumbling old man. "Who's in Charge Here?" asked a *Time* magazine headline. The Iran-contra hearings focused attention on President Reagan's hands-off management style. Some observers, both outsiders and insiders, argued that Reagan was unengaged and uninformed. Donald T. Regan described his experience: "In the four years that I served as Secretary of the Treasury I never saw President Reagan alone and never discussed economic philosophy or fiscal and monetary policy with him one-on-one."

Reagan's Decline

Half of the people in the country believed that Reagan was lying about his lack of involvement in the Iran-contra scandal. Doubtless any lame-duck presi-

dent would have suffered a loss of power in his second term, but the scandal encouraged Reagan's opponents. "No one is afraid of him anymore," said one political observer. And the political satirists were in hot pursuit. The real question, went one gibe, was not "what did the President know and when did he know it?" but "what didn't the President know, and why didn't he know it?"

Reagan's problems continued in 1987 and 1988. Congress overrode his veto of a massive highway construction bill, and twice his choices for the Supreme Court failed to win confirmation by the Senate. His first nominee, federal judge Robert Bork, who in 1973 had fired the special Watergate prosecutor during the Saturday Night Massacre (see page 879), failed to convince the Senate that he was not a right-wing ideologue. Reagan's second choice, another federal judge, withdrew his name from consideration after revelations that he had smoked marijuana while a professor at Harvard Law School. Then, on October 19, 1987,

Reagan's Ongoing Political Woes

During the 1984 and 1988 campaigns, Reverend Jesse Jackson won a large following as the first African American to make a serious bid for the presidential nomination of a major party. His multiethnic political organization, the Rainbow Coalition, included people of all colors.   (Smithsonian Institution, Division of Political History, Washington, D.C.)

a decade-low 5.4 percent in April 1988, it did so without refueling inflation (see Figure 32.1).

The Reagan administration pointed to the economy as proof of the success of supply-side economics. Critics retorted that Reagan's policy of pursuing massive tax cuts while greatly increasing the defense budget was just another form of Keynesianism—in this case, massive deficit financing to stimulate the economy. But the average American, caring little about this kind of debate, was content to enjoy the economic recovery. It was true that the poor had little to rejoice over and that Americans viewed the economic future with uncertainty. But it was also true that in the 1980s most Americans had jobs and were living very comfortably.

Ronald Reagan's reelection in 1984 was never in doubt, but his forty-nine-state sweep convinced some

Reagan's Presidency Assessed

observers that he had transformed American politics by forging a conservative coalition that could dominate for years. Still, as popular a president as Reagan was, his programs provoked severe criticism. Liberal opponents lambasted his economic policies as favoring the rich and penalizing the poor. Despite the criticism, Reagan seemed to escape personal blame. Representative Patricia Schroeder, a Colorado Democrat, gave this phenomenon a memorable label: Reagan, she said, was "perfecting a Teflon-coated presidency. . . . He sees to it that nothing sticks to him." Reagan's favorable image was tarnished by the Iran-contra scandal in late 1986 (see page 912), and his influence diminished during his final two years in office. But had Reagan been allowed by the Constitution to run for a third term, he probably would have ridden both his personal popularity and the economic boom to victory.

The 1988 election was for Reagan's successor, and the competition in both parties was intense. On the

George Bush

Republican side the candidates included Vice President George Bush, Senate minority leader Bob Dole, and Pat Robertson, a television evangelist. Bush emerged with the nomination after bitter Republican infighting in state primaries. A native of Connecticut and a Yale graduate whose father had been a U.S. senator, Bush had served heroically as a navy pilot during the Second World War. He had moved to Texas to enter the oil business and had become involved in politics. Bush possessed broad

the stock market went into a nosedive and fell 508 points.

Still, as the 1988 elections approached, Republicans took heart over some excellent political and economic news for their party. First,

Continuing Economic Recovery

Reagan had moderated his anti-Soviet rhetoric and in 1988, to the applause of most Americans, had traveled to the Soviet Union—the first American president to visit Moscow since Richard Nixon in 1972. Second—and of greater importance to voters—after the economic recession of 1981 and 1982, the United States had embarked on a six-year business recovery. The discomfort index, which had risen alarmingly in the 1970s and early 1980s, dropped to more comfortable levels in the later 1980s. And although unemployment dropped to

government experience, including service as a congressman, ambassador to China, and director of the Central Intelligence Agency. He had contested Reagan for the Republican nomination in 1980 and then served as Reagan's two-term vice president.

The Democratic side also saw a scramble for the presidential nomination. Beginning with a half-dozen campaigners, the race narrowed to a two-person contest between Michael Dukakis, under whose governorship Massachusetts had seemed a model of economic recovery and welfare reform, and Jesse Jackson, a former colleague of Reverend Martin Luther King, Jr., who had moved to Chicago to organize economic and educational programs for the poor. An eloquent preacher, Jackson campaigned on his dream of forming a "Rainbow Coalition" of the "rejected"—African Americans, women, Hispanics, the disabled. Jackson was the first African American to win mass support in seeking the presidential nomination of a major political party. But Dukakis won the Democratic nomination in 1988 by emerging victorious in key state presidential primary elections.

Both Bush and Dukakis avoided serious debate of the issues: drugs, environmental collapse, poverty, rising medical and educational costs, childcare, and the fiscal and trade deficits. Despite the gravity of the problems, the candidates relied on clichés and negative attack advertising. Television dominated the presidential election as never before. Bush aimed his appeals at the "Reagan Democrats" by pushing emotional "hot buttons" such as patriotism and the death penalty. A Republican advertisement for television appealed to racism and fear by accusing Dukakis of being soft on crime for furloughing Willie Horton, a black convicted murderer who while on weekend leave had stabbed a white man and raped a white woman. Voters expressed their disgust at the 1988 race. Former president Richard Nixon, no stranger to political combat, called the presidential campaign "trivial, superficial and inane."

Presidential Campaign of 1988

But with America at peace and inflation and unemployment both low, Bush's victory was seldom in doubt. His margin over Dukakis was substantial: 53 percent of the popular vote to 46 percent (see Map 32.3). Significantly, Bush was the beneficiary of the Reagan political legacy. He retained 85 percent of Reagan's supporters by

Bush's Victory in 1988

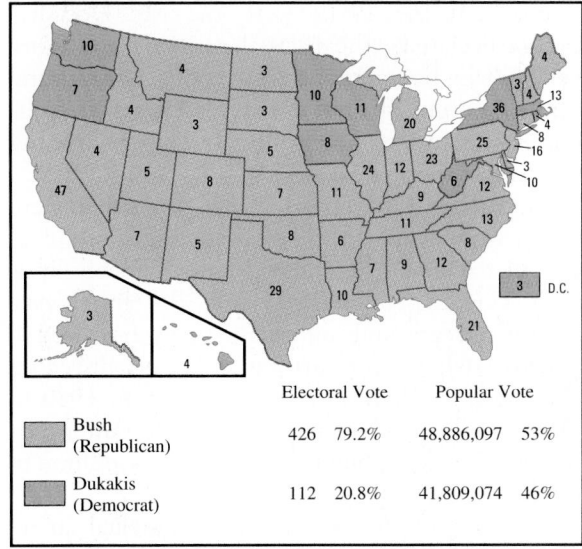

Map 32.3 Presidential Election, 1988   George Bush easily defeated Michael Dukakis in both popular and electoral votes. The key to Bush's victory was his ability to retain the political support that Ronald Reagan had enjoyed in 1980 and 1984.

promising to keep the nation on the course set by his predecessor, and Reagan Democrats again crossed over, this time voting for Bush in sufficient numbers for him to carry Michigan, Pennsylvania, and other key industrial states.

The 1988 election confirmed that the "Solid South," once a Democratic stronghold, had become solidly Republican. Bush won every state in the region. In both South and North, race was a key factor, as it had been in every presidential election since 1964: for twenty-five years, the Republican vote had been almost exclusively white, and almost all blacks had voted Democratic. Another political constant was low voter turnout. Only 50 percent of Americans who were eligible to vote in 1988 voted, compared with 63 percent in 1960. Voter turnout had declined markedly after the 1968 election, but after turning slightly upward in 1984 (53 percent), it fell again in 1988.

Many Americans seemed unconcerned as they confronted the new decade. College students in the 1980s, unlike many of their predecessors in the 1960s, aspired to join the system. Called Yuppies (young urban professionals), they yearned not to save the world but to scramble up the corporate ladder, and many educated young people worked long hours in pursuit of that goal. "If the 1970s were the Me Decade," *Newsweek* declared, "the 1980s have been the Work Decade." Baby boomers and their younger sisters and brothers reported frustration in their efforts to replicate their parents' standard of living, particularly because of high housing costs.

But polls in 1989 reported that Americans were generally happy with their lives. Many expressed pleasure with the new toys and amenities in their lives. Sales of videocassette recorders (VCRs), microwave ovens, camcorders, and compact disc players soared in the 1980s. At-home comfort was an important reason for buying a VCR. In just four years, from 1980 to 1984, the number of videotapes rented by Americans for viewing movies at home jumped from 26 million to 304 million.

Even more impressive was the phenomenal spread of computers, which revolutionized not only communications but also people's workplaces and lifestyles. In 1981 the number of personal computers in use in America numbered 2 million; in 1988 the figure was 45 million. Companies raced to market with ever-speedier technology. In 1985 a new computer was introduced to the public at the Lawrence Livermore Laboratory in California. "What took a year in 1952," explained a scientist, "we can now do in a second." But in the 1990s this, too, would be eclipsed by revolutionary advances in computer technology such as the phenomenal spread of the Internet.

Summary

The United States changed in fundamental ways between 1974 and 1989. The spread of technological developments was part of that change. So too was the new immigration, which in the 1970s and 1980s not only swelled tremendously but shifted in origin. People came from Mexico, Central and South America, and the Caribbean, as well as from the Philippines, Korea, Taiwan, and India. Refugees of the Vietnam War also arrived, and Cubans and Haitians risked their lives in flimsy boats to come to America. The totals of the new immigration exceeded those of the turn-of-the-century immigration of millions of people from southern and eastern Europe.

Another change was the country's shift to the right politically. The champion of this change was President Ronald Reagan, whose supporters included both eco-

nomic and social conservatives and both Republicans and disillusioned Democrats. Moreover, after two presidents, Gerald Ford and Jimmy Carter, who were perceived to be weak or ineffective leaders, Reagan restored the presidency to its central role in politics and the government.

Despite Reagan's successes, when he left office in 1989, the country faced unsolved economic, social, and political issues of great importance. "Ronald Reagan leaves no Vietnam War, no Watergate, no hostage crisis," reported the *New York Times*. "But he leaves huge question marks—and much to do." First, inequality had escalated in the 1980s, as the poor got poorer and the rich got richer. The poorest Americans of all were children, and economics and racism had conspired to widen racial divisions. Second, the rise of the federal debt continued unabated. In 1981 the debt stood at $994 billion; by the time Reagan left office, it had jumped to almost $2.9 trillion. Third, the effects of mismanagement and outright fraud were beginning to show in certain industries, forcing the federal government to consider massive bailouts and threatening greater fiscal deficits. In 1989 Congress debated legislation to rescue insolvent savings-and-loan associations by paying the government's insurance obligations to depositors; the eventual cost was $153 billion.

When George Bush was inaugurated as the forty-first president of the United States on January 20, 1989, the American people prepared to greet not only a new presidency but also a new decade. It was clear that Americans and their leaders would have to make difficult economic, social, and political choices in the 1990s.

LEGACY FOR A PEOPLE AND A NATION
Ethnic America

The legacy of the new immigration of the 1970s and 1980s is evident in cities and towns across America. Mexican newcomers, for example, have opened restaurants, started Spanish-language newspapers and cable television channels, and flocked to the concerts of such Latino superstars as Selena and Ricky Martin. Meanwhile, Mexican culinary culture is being consumed by millions of Americans of all groups. Asian American immigrants constitute a diverse group, including Laotian and Vietnamese refugees drawn to Garden City, Kansas, to work in the world's largest meatpacking plant; Korean greengrocers opening shops on

Manhattan's Upper West Side; and Chinese workers assembling integrated circuits in California's Silicon Valley. Wherever they have settled, America's newcomers have established their own communities with their own distinctive cultures.

The legacy of America's new immigration resembles that of its predecessor one hundred years ago. With almost 9 million immigrants arriving in the 1980s, that decade surpassed the historic high mark set by the 8.7 million immigrants from Russia, Austria-Hungary, Italy, and other countries who had reached American shores between 1900 and 1909. In addition to the approximately 1 million people who move to the United States each year, an additional 300,000 come as undocumented, or illegal, aliens. Like the earlier immigration, the new influx has also provoked a nativist reaction. A *Newsweek* poll in 1993 reported that 60 percent of Americans believed that immigration was "bad for the country."

Immigrants have arrived from all over the world, bringing their cultures not merely from Latin America and Asia, but also from Europe, Africa, and the Middle East. Like the immigrants of a century before, these newcomers crave education and flock to public libraries to learn. The branch library in Flushing, New York, for example, has been inundated with Chinese, Korean, Indian, Russian, Colombian, and Afghan immigrants. "Watch Your Belongings" signs are displayed in several languages, and librarians are available who speak Russian, Hindi, Chinese, Korean, Gujarati, and Spanish. The legacy of the new immigration has permanently altered, and deeply enriched, the United States.

For Further Reading, see page A-40 of the Appendix. For Web resources, go to http://college.hmco.com.

Tuesday, April 20, 1999, began as it always did for some students at Columbine High School in Littleton, Colorado, with a popular early-morning bowling class. On this day, one of the bowlers, Dylan Klebold, wore a shirt that read "SERIAL KILLER." Classmates recalled that when he and his friend Eric Harris would hit strikes or spares, they would shout "Sieg Heil!" in celebration. And, in fact, April 20 was Adolf Hitler's birthday. Later that morning, after donning black trench coats, Harris and Klebold returned to the high school, armed with two shotguns, two semiautomatic rifles, and thirty pipe bombs filled with gunpowder, nails, and broken glass. Walking toward the school, one of the boys pointed a rifle at a seventeen-year-old student and fatally shot her in the head. It was a little after 11 A.M.

That morning, there were some five hundred people in the school cafeteria when Harris and Klebold opened fire and threw pipe bombs, filling the air with smoke. Teacher Dave Sanders ran from the cafeteria to warn students in the library, but Harris and Klebold, encountering him in the hallway, shot him in the chest. Sanders crawled to a nearby room, but bled to death. A teacher phoned 911: "Oh, God! Oh, God! Kids, just stay down. I'm in the library. . . . He's right outside of here." The gunmen then entered the library, laughing and taunting students, and shooting their victims at point-blank range. "All jocks stand up!" one gunman yelled. Isaiah Shoels, eighteen, was both an athlete and an African American. "Hey, I think we got a n——here," one of the killers exclaimed, spotting Shoels. Then they shot him in the head and added two more bullets in the face. "Hey, I always wondered what n——brains looked like," said one of the killers, laughing.

About 12:30 P.M., SWAT teams entered Columbine High School and began a room-by-room sweep of the building. At 4:30, police found Harris and Klebold in the library, both suicides, their bodies surrounded by the corpses of ten of their victims. In all, fifteen people were dead. And the nation was shocked and dumbfounded. What had motivated these two self-proclaimed members of the "Trenchcoat Mafia" to go on a hate-filled shooting spree? Did the massacre mean that guns were too readily available, or that there

On April 20, 1999, students evacuated Columbine High School in Littleton, Colorado, after two schoolmates went on a shooting rampage, killing twelve students and a teacher before killing themselves. (Wide World Photos, Inc.)

Prosperity, Power, and Peril: America in the 1990s

was too much violence on television, or that America's children were troubled, or that American society was sick? The American people wanted answers, but each question only prompted more questions.

In the 1990s, violence of various kinds erupted in the United States. In addition to the Columbine shootings, students in Paducah, Kentucky; Jonesboro, Arkansas; Springfield, Oregon; and elsewhere opened fire on their schoolmates. Hate crimes against African Americans, homosexuals, and Jewish Americans produced gruesome deaths, and in the worst act of terrorism in U.S. history, 168 people were killed in 1995 in a bomb blast in Oklahoma City, Oklahoma.

The 1990s proved to be a decade of political volatility and cultural conflict, and it was not just the far right that was politically disaffected. People of far more moderate beliefs also abjured political participation, denouncing the government for being corrupt, arrogant, and downright stupid. In *Why Americans Hate Politics* (1991), E. J. Dionne, Jr., a columnist, ventured that voters were disgusted with the divisive debate that dominated politics in an era of negative attack advertisements. In the 1990s, moreover, many Americans did not know where to turn to make meaningful political choices in their lives. They rejected the Democratic Party for having lost touch with their cultural and moral values, and they rejected the Republicans for failing to represent their economic and social needs. Some Americans wanted new political parties.

America's president from 1989 to 1993 was George Bush. Victory in the Persian Gulf War in 1991 seemed to guarantee his reelection in 1992. But the economy had stagnated, and the president seemed without a plan to spur recovery. The Cold War was over, but the president seemed to lack vision for a new world order. And Ross Perot, a multibillionaire who vowed he could fix the fiscal deficit, waged a popular third-party campaign. But the winner and president-elect was the Democratic candidate, Governor Bill Clinton of Arkansas.

Politics grew even more volatile during Bill Clinton's two presidential terms in the 1990s, culminating in his impeachment in 1999. Clinton was the first baby boomer to become president, and his opponents argued that his character was severely flawed. In 1994, just two years after Clinton defeated Bush, the "Republican Revolution" led by Representative Newt Gingrich routed the Democrats in congressional elections, winning control of both houses of Congress. In 1996, however, Clinton revealed that he was a battler and still popular; and, running against the House Republicans, he won reelection. Aiding him, too, was

prosperity. The nation's economy began its recovery in 1991, and economic growth—marked by low inflation and a spectacular rise in stock prices—continued throughout the decade and into the new century.

But the president had a formidable enemy: himself, notably his history of philandering and lying. In 1999 Clinton was impeached by the House of Representatives, which alleged that he had committed perjury and obstructed justice. And while the Senate acquitted the president in a subsequent trial presided over by the chief justice of the United States, Clinton had permanently tarnished his historical reputation. Still, Clinton survived this grave crisis; his public approval rating remained high; and angry conservatives reproached the "immoral [American] majority" who supported the president and applauded his presidency. "Let's move on," said Bob Smith, a Republican senator who voted guilty. "He won. He always wins."

For both Bush and Clinton, the 1990s was a decade of power and perils in world affairs. The Bush administration witnessed the dramatic end of the Cold War, symbolized by the collapse of Communist regimes in eastern Europe, the reunification of Germany, and the dissolution of the Soviet Union. Disorder, however—created by ethnic wars, natural disasters, economic crises, and religious conflict—soon followed, disappointing Americans who wanted less overseas activism. The Clinton administration struggled to articulate new doctrines and to clarify U.S. interests in the absence of a Soviet threat. Moreover, some threats, long overshadowed by the Cold War, became more pressing: nuclear proliferation, chemical warfare, population explosion, drug trafficking, the spread of diseases, and pollution of the natural environment.

The decade of the 1990s concluded what some called the "American century." The nation, though basking in prosperity and power, was at the same time cautious about the future, very aware that perils at home and abroad could undermine its purpose and position. ■

Economic and Social Anxieties: The Presidency of George Bush

 As president from 1989 to 1993, George Bush had a rough ride. He and the Democratic Congress seemed unable to work together or agree on anything. Beginning in 1989 with his veto of an increase in the minimum wage, Bush vetoed thirty-seven bills during his presidency, only one of which was overridden by a two-thirds vote of both houses of Congress. Rarely in

IMPORTANT EVENTS

1989 Bush becomes president
Tiananmen Square massacre in China
Bush vetoes increase in minimum wage
World accord controls ozone-killing
chemicals
Berlin Wall opens
U.S. troops invade Panama
Third World debt reaches $1.2 trillion

1990 Communist regimes in eastern Europe
collapse
Sandinistas lose Nicaragua election
Recession begins; personal incomes fall
Americans with Disabilities Act passed
Iraq invades Kuwait
Reunification of Germany
Bush-Congress budget agreement raises
taxes; Bush reneges on "no new taxes"
Clean Air Act reauthorization requires
reduction in emission of pollutants
South Africa begins to dismantle apartheid

1991 Persian Gulf War
START I treaty reduces nuclear warheads
Ethnic wars flare in former Yugoslavia
Hill testifies at Thomas confirmation
hearings; Thomas confirmed
USSR dissolves into independent states
U.N. mediation ends Salvadoran civil war

1992 Los Angeles riots erupt
U.S. in minority at Rio Earth Summit
Federal deficit hits $4 trillion
California pays employees with IOUs
Planned Parenthood v. Casey upholds the
right to an abortion
Clinton elected president
Perot's third-party candidacy wins one-fifth
of the vote
Bush pardons former government officials
indicted in Iran-contra scandal
Twenty-seventh Amendment prohibits
future midterm congressional pay raises
U.S. troops sent to Somalia
Canada, Mexico, and U.S. sign NAFTA

1993 Clinton becomes president
Clinton lifts restrictions on abortion
counseling
START-II treaty reduces warheads and
ICBMs
H. Clinton heads task force on healthcare
Branch Davidian compound burns in Waco
Clinton's proposal to lift ban on homo-
sexuals in the military stirs controversy

Clinton appoints Ginsberg to Court
Congress approves NAFTA
Agreement for Palestinian self-rule
Motor-voter and family-leave acts passed
Gun control laws require waiting period for
handguns and ban sale of assault weapons

1994 Republican candidates for Congress propose
Contract with America
Clinton appoints Breyer to Supreme Court
Genocide in Rwanda
U.S. troops sent to Haiti
Clinton signs crime bill into law
Republicans win House and Senate

1995 Bombing in Oklahoma City kills 168 people
Nuclear nonproliferation treaty renewed
U.S. opens diplomatic relations with
Vietnam
World Conference on Women
U.S. diplomats broker peace for Bosnia

1996 Telecommunications Act allows telephone
and cable companies to compete
Helms-Burton Act tightens Cuba embargo
Freedom to Farm Act mandates phase-out
of federal farm subsidies
Convictions in first Whitewater trials
Clinton signs welfare act eliminating Aid to
Families with Dependent Children
Guatemalan civil war ends
Clinton reelected

1997 Albright is first woman secretary of state
Israeli withdrawal from Hebron
U.S. ratifies Chemical Weapons Convention

1998 Independent counsel investigates Clinton's
relationship with Lewinsky
Independent counsel sends impeachment
report to House
India and Pakistan explode nuclear devices
U.S. signs Global Warming Convention
Republicans lose seats in House
House votes to impeach Clinton

1999 Senate votes to acquit Clinton
NATO bombs Serbia over Kosovo crisis
Senate rejects Comprehensive Test Ban
Treaty

2000 Y2K bug fails to precipitate computer collapse
Gore and Bush score major victories in spring
primaries; Bradley and McCain end
campaigns
Nation records longest economic expansion in
its history

American history had the relationship between Congress and the president been as sour and the legislative results so meager. Among the major issues left unresolved were healthcare, the budget deficit, taxes, crime, and family leave.

Decisive presidential leadership might have broken the gridlock, but Bush was a political chameleon. Once a supporter of family planning and a woman's right to an abortion, he had switched his position and denounced abortion as murder. In the 1980 Republican primaries, he had dismissed Ronald Reagan's supply-side economic ideas as "voodoo economics," but he quickly endorsed these policies when he became Reagan's running mate in 1980. In loyally supporting all of Reagan's policies, even those that he formerly opposed, Bush seemed to lack firm convictions of his own. Still, when he was inaugurated in 1989, the future appeared bright. The Cold War was waning, and Americans looked forward to a "peace dividend" in the form of lower defense expenditures. The country had enjoyed six straight years of economic growth, and both unemployment and inflation were low. Bush hoped the good news would continue; and on inauguration day, when he called for a "kinder, gentler nation," it seemed that a compassionate president would be occupying the White House.

Soon, however, the economy took a nosedive. In late 1989 *Newsweek* detected a "peek-a-boo recession,"

Economic and Social Problems

pointing to slumping car and housing sales and declining orders for manufacturing products. By mid-1990, signs of recession were everywhere. Workers were laid off or furloughed, but Bush took no action, revealing the shallowness of his inaugural promise. The Bush administration, one columnist wrote, was "leading a retreat from social responsibility." He had vetoed an increase in the minimum wage and defended tax breaks for the rich while opposing extended relief payments to the long-term unemployed.

Yet the social ills that had plagued the United States in the 1980s—AIDS, homelessness, drug and alcohol addiction, racism and inequality, poverty among children, the day-to-day struggles of single-parent families—persisted unabated, and even the middle class experienced a decline in the standard of living. Scholars who tracked the "social health" of the nation diagnosed America's well-being as at its lowest level since 1970, when the data were first analyzed. Problems that reached their worst recorded levels in 1990 were child abuse, teen suicide, the gap between rich and poor, and lack of health insurance coverage. "If you look at it as a report card," observed the director of Fordham University's Institute for Innovation in Social Policy, "the country gets an F."

Healthcare, in particular, caused increasing anxiety. With few incentives to control healthcare costs and the spread of expensive technologies, medical expenses were rising rapidly. In 1992 healthcare costs absorbed 12 percent of the national income, appreciably more than in other industrialized nations. Health insurance also had become a leading labor issue in the country, as steeply rising insurance premiums ate into both profits and wages. In 1990, for example, disputes over health insurance sparked 55 percent of the strikes in the United States.

Still worse, some 33 million Americans, about 13 percent of the population, had no health insurance at all. Three-fourths of these people were employed but worked at minimum-wage jobs that did not provide health benefits. Additional tens of millions had such limited coverage that they constantly were at risk of financial devastation. The Price family of Mebane, North Carolina, already $1,000 in debt for medical expenses, was typical. Self-employed, William Price could not afford the family policy available at $350 per month; and at Paula Price's job, there was no group health insurance. As William said, "We just have to hope the family stays healthy."

Also fueling Americans' anxieties were the growing numbers of job layoffs, some temporary but many permanent. In a practice called "outsourcing," companies stopped making their components and began ordering them from factories in other states as well as other countries, where wages were far lower and benefit packages nonexistent. Other businesses replaced workers with computers and other machines to cut costs and increase productivity. Employment in the chemical industry, for example, had been declining for several years. "Companies in our industry," said the chief economist of the Chemical Manufacturers Association, "don't want to hire more people because people cost money." Numerous industries were deciding whether to reduce labor costs by opting for technology, outsourcing, or moving their plants to Mexico, South Korea, and other low-wage countries. Many businesses downsized, eliminating tens of thousands of jobs.

In the face of flat wages and job insecurity caused by downsizing, some Americans blamed their plight on job competition from the new immigrants who had arrived in increasing numbers in the 1970s and 1980s (see page 934). Politicians decried what they called the "flood" or the "invasion" of new immigrants. A *Newsweek* poll in 1993 reported that 60 percent of Americans believed that immigration was "bad for the country." And in 1994 voters in California approved Proposition 187, a ballot initiative to cut off social services to illegal aliens.

One group, however, made real progress in 1990. That year, President Bush signed the Americans with

Americans with Disabilities Act

Disabilities Act, which banned job discrimination, in companies with twenty-five or more employees, against the blind, deaf, mentally retarded, and physically impaired, as well as against those who are HIV-positive or have cancer. The act, which covered 87 percent of all wage earners, also required that "reasonable accommodations," such as wheelchair ramps, be made available to people with disabilities. Many businesses opposed the bill, but the U.S. Chamber of Commerce supported it. As a Chamber official explained, the bill "opens up a huge untapped resource of workers."

Bush's domestic problems were complicated by a pledge he had made at the 1988 Republican convention: "Read my lips: No new taxes."

Failed Promises

But during the 1990 budget summit with Congress, to keep the deficit from rising even higher, he agreed to a tax increase. Bush's press secretary was shocked: "That means we've broken the pledge."

Other campaign pledges were broken, too. As a candidate in 1988, Bush had promised that he would be the "education president" as well as the "environmental president"; but he failed in both areas. He was unable, and perhaps unwilling, to tackle the difficult problem of a nation with thousands of local school systems and much disagreement about education. Other than argue for government vouchers that parents could use to pay tuition at public or private schools of their choice, his administration did little to support educational reform despite his promise that by 2000 American students would lead the world in science and math. Bush got good marks from environmentalists for signing the 1990 reauthorization of the Clean Air Act, which limited emissions of sulfur dioxide and nitrogen oxides, but his Council on Competitiveness gutted enforcement. Headed by Vice President Dan Quayle, the council declared that environmental regulations were unnecessary and should be eliminated because they slowed economic growth and cost jobs. The council halted the enforcement of some regulations

The Americans with Disabilities Act of 1990 was the result of many people's efforts, including activists with disabilities. Daniel Wilkins became a paraplegic in an automobile accident at age twenty-three. An outdoorsman, he was determined not to be isolated from nature, even though he was confined to a wheelchair. Wilkins led efforts to devise trail-accessibility programs in Ohio and, with his mother, founded a chapter of the National Spinal Cord Injury Association. "Physical barriers are easily overcome," said Dan Wilkins, "once attitudinal barriers vanish." (© Junebug Clark)

and weakened others by rewriting them behind closed doors. In addition, the Justice Department overruled the Environmental Protection Agency's move to prosecute large corporate polluters.

Internationally, the Bush administration took the same cautious approach. In 1989 eighty-six nations, including the United States, agreed to phase out use of ozone-destroying chemicals by the year 2000. The following year the United States and twenty-five nations agreed to protect the fragile environment of Antarctica by banning oil exploration and mining there for fifty years. But at the 1992 Earth Summit in Rio de Janeiro, Brazil, Bush rejected key control agreements, including the Biodiversity Treaty designed to slow the loss of endangered species.

As the criticism of President Bush's performance grew, his credibility fell, especially during the confirmation hearings of Clarence Thomas, whom Bush nominated to the Supreme Court in fall 1991. Few believed this inexperienced federal judge was, as Bush put it, the "best man for the job." But Thomas, an African American, was highly conservative; and although he insisted that he had formulated no legal opinions on controversial issues, his writings and speeches made it clear that he opposed affirmative action in hiring, believed in returning prayer to the schools, and opposed abortion.

Clarence Thomas Nomination

Bush's nomination of Thomas was clever but cynical. Eleanor Holmes Norton, the African American congressional delegate from Washington, D.C., denounced the choice as "calculated . . . to mute the expected reaction to yet another conservative nominee." Then, in October, the nation was electrified by the testimony of Anita Hill, an African American law professor at the University of Oklahoma, who charged that Thomas had sexually harassed her when she worked for him in the early 1980s. Republican senators on the Judiciary Committee sought to discredit Hill, but women around the country identified with her story. The Senate confirmed Thomas, but Hill's testimony—and the Senate's disregard of it—so angered women that many thousands vowed to oppose the Republican Party in 1992.

The End of the Cold War and Global Disorder

When Bush became president, the Cold War was waning—the very Cold War that he had helped wage as ambassador to the United Nations, U.S. representative to China, CIA chief, and vice president. A cautious, reactive conservative, Bush seemed to set few long-range goals except to envision the United States as the supreme power in a unipolar world. "People say I'm indecisive," Bush once joked. "Well, I don't know about that."

In the mid-1980s, Communist Party chief Mikhail S. Gorbachev had set loose cascading changes in the Soviet Union (see page 914). He also had encouraged the people of East Germany and eastern Europe to go their own ways. No longer would a financially hobbled Moscow prop up unpopular Communist regimes. In October 1989 East Germans startled the world by repudiating their Communist government, and in November Germans scaled the Berlin Wall and then tore it down. On October 2, 1990, the two Germanys re-

Collapse of Communist Regimes

"CONGRATULATIONS....YOU WON THE COLD WAR!"

The veteran cartoonist Jim Borgman captured the complexity of what many declared a simple matter: American triumph in the Cold War. Borgman reminded his readers that the Cold War had cost the United States itself a great deal—neglect of its domestic problems, deteriorating infrastructure, unemployment, and millions of people defined by the U.S. government as poor and homeless.   (Jim Borgman for the *Cincinnati Enquirer.* Reprinted with special permission of King Features Syndicate)

united. Veteran Communist oligarchs also fell in Poland, Hungary, Czechoslovakia, Romania, and Bulgaria.

The Union of Soviet Socialist Republics itself collapsed: in 1990 the Baltic states of Lithuania, Latvia, and Estonia declared independence; and in 1991 the Soviet Union disintegrated into independent successor states—Russia, Ukraine, Tajikistan, and many others (see Map 33.1). Muscled aside by Russian reformers who thought he was moving too slowly toward democracy and free-market economics, Gorbachev himself lost power. The breakup of the Soviet empire, dismantling of the Warsaw Pact, repudiation of communism by its own leaders, German reunification, and a significantly reduced risk of nuclear war signaled the end of the Cold War.

The Cold War ended because of the relative decline of the United States and the Soviet Union in the international system. Between the 1950s and the

Why the Cold War Ended

1980s, the contest had undermined the power of its two major protagonists. They moved gradually toward a cautious cooperation whose urgent goals were the restoration of their economic well-being and the preservation of their diminishing global positions.

Four influential trends explain this gradual decline and the resulting attractions of détente. First was the burgeoning economic cost of the Cold War—trillions of dollars spent on weapons and interventions such as that in Vietnam rather than on domestic improvements. As early as the 1950s President Eisenhower had pointed out that defense spending was undermining sound economic policy at home. In the 1960s Americans debated "guns versus butter." In the 1970s President Nixon, aware that Americans had grown weary of Cold War costs, appealed to allies for "burden-sharing." According to the historian Paul Kennedy's

Map 33.1 The End of the Cold War in Europe When Mikhail Gorbachev came to power in the Soviet Union in 1985, he initiated reforms that ultimately undermined the communist regimes in eastern Europe and East Germany and led to the breakup of the Soviet Union itself, ensuring an end to the Cold War.

bestseller *The Rise and Fall of the Great Powers* (1987), the United States suffered from "imperial over-stretch." Kennedy argued that the United States, like Spain and Great Britain in earlier centuries, would continue to suffer the erosion of its power unless the nation restored its productive vitality and international marketplace competitiveness, reduced its huge federal debt, and improved its educational system. One way to stem economic decline, he claimed, was to curb America's costly global interventionism. Soviet reformers voiced similar arguments, urging foreign retrenchment from such places as Afghanistan to save money that could be spent to fix the USSR's domestic woes.

Challenges from within their own spheres of influence also help explain why the two major powers welcomed détente. Cuba's anti-American revolution and France's withdrawal from NATO in the 1960s are but two indications that the United States was losing power. The uprisings in Hungary and Czechoslovakia and the Sino-Soviet rift undercut the Soviet Union's hegemony within its network of allies. Détente seemed to offer a means to restore great-power management of unruly states.

Third, the Cold War ended because of the emergence of the Third World, which introduced new players into the international game, further diffused power, and challenged bipolarism. Soviet-American détente represented a means to apply leverage to volatile Third World nations. Finally, the worldwide antinuclear movement of the 1980s pressed leaders, especially in western Europe, to seek détente in order to stop the arms race.

These four elements—economic burden, challenges from sphere members, rise of the Third World, and antinuclearism—combined to weaken the standing of the two adversaries and ultimately to persuade them to halt their nations' declines by ending the Cold War. Gorbachev emerged as the primary agent for change, and Reagan and Bush eventually reacted favorably. Because the Soviet Union fell much harder than the United States, American leaders crowed that they had won the Cold War. But doubters calculated a high price in dollars and deaths for the United States, too.

As the Cold War closed, Bush struggled futilely to explain the dimensions or shape the agenda of a new world order. His administration sustained a large defense budget and continued to use military force abroad, denying Americans the

START Treaties

"peace dividend" they hoped would reduce taxes and free up funds to address domestic problems. Still, in mid-1991 the Soviet Union and the United States signed the START I treaty to reduce their long-range nuclear weapons (warheads and bombs) by one-third. In 1993 Bush signed the START II agreement with Russia's president Boris Yeltsin, who had ousted Gorbachev. This accord provided for a further 50 percent reduction of nuclear weapons and the elimination of all multiple warhead (MIRV) intercontinental missiles (ICBMs). In April 2000 Russia's parliament approved the agreement.

Bush also struggled to define America's policy toward the People's Republic of China. In June 1989 Chinese armed forces stormed into Beijing's Tiananmen Square, slaughtering hundreds—perhaps thousands—of unarmed students and other citizens who for weeks had been holding peaceful prodemocracy rallies. Bush officials initially expressed revulsion, but muted their response in the belief that America's global security and trade needs required friendly Sino-American ties. A symbol of improved relations and of changes within China was the opening in 1992, near Tiananmen Square, of the largest McDonald's restaurant in the world. Some Chinese citizens recoiled from the Golden Arches, charging cultural imperialism. But others embraced America's icon, not for its hamburgers, but for what McDonald's represented to them: modernization, good management, cleanliness, equality.

Tiananmen Square

Such U.S. symbols held appeal elsewhere in the world, too, especially in Latin America, a major source of immigrants who came to the United States searching for economic improvement in their lives. But immigration often disturbed U.S.–Latin American relations; by 1992 probably 2.5 to 4 million "illegal aliens" from around the world lived in the United States, and most of them came from Mexico. Political and economic refugees from Haiti and Cuba also generated anti-immigrant sentiment. When the Cold War ended, Latin America remained staggered by external debt ($431 billion by 1990), poverty (one-third of the region's people were afflicted), and environmental calamities such as deforestation of the Amazon River basin in Brazil and carbon monoxide emissions that threatened the public health of Mexico City and San-

Peace and War in Latin America

tiago de Chile. A positive note was the North American Free Trade Agreement (NAFTA) with Canada and Mexico. Signed in late 1992, the pact created the world's largest tariff-free trade bloc. Critics claimed that the agreement would cost many U.S. workers their jobs because corporations would move south to exploit less expensive Mexican labor and minimal environmental controls. The Clinton administration nonetheless lobbied NAFTA through Congress in 1993; the agreement became operative the following year.

In Central America, the Bush administration cooled the zeal with which Reagan had meddled because the interventions had largely failed and, with the Cold War over, anticommunism seemed irrelevant. The death-dealing, U.S.-financed contra war had not forced the Sandinistas from power in Nicaragua. Instead, in 1989 the Central American presidents devised a workable plan for free elections in Nicaragua (the Sandinista Front lost the 1990 elections) and the disbanding of the contras. In December 1991 U.N. diplomats mediated an agreement in El Salvador ending the civil war. In Guatemala in late 1996 Norwegian and U.N. representatives brokered a peace accord that terminated a civil war that had been raging since 1954. Three years later, after a truth commission in Guatemala issued a detailed report that blamed that country's military for the deaths of at least two hundred thousand people during the civil war, Clinton apologized for U.S. backing of the security forces that "engaged in violent and widespread repression" in that Central American nation.

As the Cold War receded, the drug war accelerated, and Washington attempted to use the U.S. military to quash drug producers and traffickers in Colombia, Bolivia, and Peru, sources of cocaine and crack, both processed from coca leaves. By 1990 the U.S. drug market was probably worth $100 billion. "This is more serious than the Vietnam War," declared Maryland's governor. U.S. officials concentrated on eradication programs and interrupting supply through interdiction. Many Latin Americans resented being blamed for the U.S. drug problem and stressed the need to halt consumer demand inside the United States itself. To this day the drug war has not been won.

Drugs became conspicuous in relations with Panama. Soon after General Manuel Antonio Noriega took power in 1983, he cut deals with Colombia's cocaine barons. Noriega also went on the CIA payroll and helped the United States aid the

Invasion of Panama

contras. Appreciative, Washington turned a blind eye to his drug trafficking. When exposés of Noriega's sordid record provoked protests in Panama, however, Bush decided to dump the dictator. Under Operation Just Cause, launched on December 20, 1989, 22,500 U.S. troops invaded Panama. More than three hundred Panamanians died; twenty-three American soldiers perished. Noriega was captured and taken to Miami, where, in 1992, he was convicted of drug trafficking and imprisoned. The chair of the Republican National Committee called the Panama invasion a "political jackpot" for Bush, whom some had been calling a "wimp." Devastated Panama, meanwhile, like war-torn Nicaragua, became all the more dependent on the United States, which offered little reconstruction aid.

Seeking to end apartheid in South Africa, the United States maintained sanctions against the segregated nation, costing South Africa billions of dollars. Fearing economic disaster and an ultimately successful black revolt, South African president F. W. de Klerk in 1990 lifted restrictions on dissent and legalized the militantly anti-apartheid African National Congress (ANC). De Klerk also released from prison his nation's most celebrated critic, ANC leader Nelson Mandela. In 1994 Mandela became his nation's first black president. When apartheid ended, the U.S. Congress repealed sanctions, and American companies invested once again in South Africa.

End of Apartheid in South Africa

The Middle East became the site of the Bush presidency's major foreign policy venture. When Iraq's dictator, Saddam Hussein, sent troops to invade his peaceful neighbor Kuwait in August 1990, oil-rich Saudi Arabia, long a U.S. ally, felt threatened. In Operation Desert Shield, Bush dispatched more than five hundred thousand U.S. forces to the region. Likening Saddam to Hitler and declaring the moment the first post–Cold War "test of our mettle," Bush rallied a deeply divided Congress to authorize "all necessary means" to oust Iraq from Kuwait (a vote of 250 to 183 in the House and 52 to 47 in the Senate). The United Nations helped organize a coalition of forces. Although many Americans believed that economic sanctions imposed on Iraq should be given more time to work, Bush would not wait. "This will not be another Vietnam," the president said. On the contrary, "Maybe I'll turn out to be a Teddy Roosevelt."

Persian Gulf War

In the Persian Gulf War of early 1991, Operation Desert Storm forced Iraqi troops out of Kuwait. Much of that nation's oil industry was destroyed by bombs and the retreating Iraqis, who torched oil facilities as they left. Oil wells burned for months, darkening the sky over these American forces and causing environmental damage. (Bruno Barbey/Magnum Photos, Inc.)

Operation Desert Storm began on January 16, 1991, with the greatest air armada in history pummeling Iraqi targets. American missiles reinforced round-the-clock bombing raids on Baghdad, Iraq's capital. In late February, coalition forces launched a ground war that quickly routed the Iraqis from Kuwait. Critics called it "a war to make the world safe for gas-guzzlers," but the *Wall Street Journal* welcomed the Gulf War because it "lets America, and above all else its elite, recover a sense of self-confidence and self-worth." When the war ended on March 1, Bush's popularity in the polls soared to 89 percent, tied with the high set by Harry Truman in June 1945 after the surrender of Germany.

The war's toll: at least 40,000 Iraqis dead; 240 coalition soldiers dead, including 148 Americans. But Saddam Hussein remained in power. By 2000, although Saddam's chemical and nuclear weapons had been exposed by U.N. inspections and partially destroyed, U.N. restrictions had diminished Iraq's oil exports, and continued U.S. air attacks had punished violations of "no-fly zones," he remained defiant while his people suffered.

People suffered in Africa, too. In Somalia, strategically located on the Horn of Africa, famine joined political bickering to upend civil order. Jilting its Cold War ally the Soviet Union in the late 1970s, Somalia began to receive great amounts of U.S. foreign aid. That assistance stopped with the end of the Cold War. After Somalia's repressive dictator was driven from power in 1991, public authority broke down as rival clans vied for power. While gun-toting bandits stole international relief supplies, hundreds of thousands of Somalis died. Appalled by television pictures of starving children, President Bush ordered 28,150 American troops to Somalia in December 1992 to ensure the delivery of relief aid. A U.N. peacekeeping force, including 9,000 Americans, took over in mid-1993. After changing the mission from feeding to reforming Somalia, Washington soon admitted defeat and in early 1994 withdrew U.S. troops; U.N. peacekeepers left about a year later. The humanitarian mission had saved lives, but Somalia returned once again to violent politics and dire hunger.

Operation Restore Hope in Somalia

Economic Doldrums, American Voters, and the Election of 1992

Success in the Persian Gulf obscured Bush's mixed success in foreign affairs, and Republicans were confident they would retain the White House in the 1992 presidential election. The Republican coalition was intact, uniting economic conservatives who had always voted Republican, cultural conservatives (the fundamentalist and evangelical Christians who advocated "family values"), "Reagan Democrats" (blue-collar workers and one-time Democrats who had supported Bush as Reagan's heir), white voters in the South, young Americans who had come of age politically during the Reagan years, and conservative voters in America's ever-growing suburbs, which in 1990 were home to almost half of the country's population. There was no denying the sheer size of the suburban vote, which tended to be antitax and antigovernment. In the 1980s what had held the Republican coalition together were economic growth, anticommunism, and Ronald Reagan. In 1992, however, these three factors were absent.

As the 1992 presidential election neared, the stagnant economy pushed the Gulf War into the background. Between 1989 and 1992, the economy had grown slowly or not at all; the gross domestic product averaged an increase of only 0.7 percent a year, the worst showing since the Great Depression of the 1930s. By 1992 several million Americans had joined the unemployment rolls, and factory employment was skidding to its lowest level since the recession of 1982. Even for Americans with jobs, personal income was stagnant. In fact, in 1991 median household incomes fell by 3.5 percent, the most severe decline since the 1973 recession. Mounting annual fiscal deficits and the $4.4 trillion federal debt meant the federal government could afford to do little to stimulate the economy and create jobs. And in 1992 the number of poor people in America reached the highest level since 1964.

A Stagnant Economy

Some city and state governments faced bankruptcy. California, out of money in mid-1992, paid its workers and bills in IOUs. A series of "tax revolts," beginning with Proposition 13 in 1978, had cut property taxes at just the time California's population was booming. But California was not alone; some thirty states were in serious financial difficulty in the 1990s. Businesses, too, were deeply burdened with debt; real-estate, home-building, and insurance companies were all overextended. And as companies tottered, the American people grew anxious about their jobs. "The recession that won't go away," *Newsweek* reported in November 1991, "has average Americans spooked and politicians running scared." And a poll that month showed that for the first time in Bush's presidency, less than a majority of the voters (47 percent) were inclined to reelect him in 1992.

Bush's greatest handicap as president was his inability to reassure Americans that he would take action on the economy. By January 1992 his approval rating had dropped to half of what it had been after the Persian Gulf War just ten months before. He seemed to be out of touch with the American people. He "lacks any fingertip feel," noted one political analyst, "for what it is to be a member of the wage-earning middle class in America."

Bush's inaction gave the Democrats hope, but they had problems of their own, particularly in the 102nd Congress, which they controlled. The most blatant scandal involved the House bank, where members of Congress wrote thousands of bad checks, all of which the bank covered at no fee. In the Senate, several members did favors for Charles Keating, who had plundered a large California savings and loan association, causing many unsuspecting small investors to lose their savings. Many Americans also blamed Congress for the gridlock in Washington. Then, with few accomplishments to their credit, the members of Congress voted themselves a pay raise. Said Representative Leon Panetta, a Democrat from California, "When people look back on the 102nd Congress, they will say, 'Let's never repeat this experience again.'" Anti-incumbent sentiment was on the rise, along with calls for term limits.

Scandals in Congress

Among the Democratic presidential hopefuls in 1992 was Bill Clinton, governor of Arkansas. Born in 1946, this baby boomer had wanted to be president most of his life. As a college student in the 1960s, he had opposed the Vietnam War and pulled strings to avoid being drafted (as had Vice President Dan Quayle, also of the Vietnam generation). After studying in England as a Rhodes scholar and graduating from Yale law school, Clinton returned to Arkansas and dived into politics, becoming governor in 1979 at the age of thirty-two. In the 1992 presidential primaries he slugged it out with Paul Tsongas, former senator from Massachusetts, and Jerry Brown, former governor of California. But by July, when the

Bill Clinton

Democrats met for their convention, Clinton emerged the clear victor.

Clinton's message to the voters was mixed. Calling himself a "New Democrat," Clinton sought to inch his party to the right to make it more attractive to white suburbanites, Reagan Democrats, and members of the business community. Clinton hoped, said an ally, "to modernize liberalism so it could sell again." He emphasized the need to move people off welfare, and he called for more police officers on the streets and for capital punishment. But he also advocated greater public investment in building roads, bridges, and communications infrastructure; universal access to apprenticeship programs and college educations; basic healthcare for all Americans; and a shift of funds from defense to civilian programs. Clinton's running mate, Tennessee senator Albert Gore, came from the same mold. He too was a baby boomer, a white southerner, a Baptist, and a moderate Democrat. Gore also appealed to environmentalists as the author of a best-selling book, *Earth in the Balance: Ecology and the Human Spirit* (1992).

Clinton was not Bush's only opponent in 1992. The case against the president was also being made by Patrick J. Buchanan, a conservative television talk-

Ross Perot

show regular and former Nixon speechwriter, who entered the New Hampshire primary to contest Bush for the Republican nomination. And in April 1992, H. Ross Perot, who had amassed a fortune in the computer industry, announced on a television call-in show that he would run for president if voters in all fifty states put his name on the ballot. Many people responded to Perot's candidacy, convinced that he had the answers and intrigued by the possibility of electing the first president since George Washington who belonged to no party. "He stands for a fresh start," explained one backer. "He doesn't have to answer to anybody but the people."

Still the chameleon, in 1992 Bush reverted to an earlier identity: "I care," he told the voters. He won the New Hampshire presidential pri-

Los Angeles Riots

mary, but just weeks later, during race riots in Los Angeles, he revealed his inability to respond to a domestic crisis. The violence erupted after a California jury had discounted videotaped evidence and acquitted four police officers charged with beating Rodney King, an African American motorist pulled over after a high-speed chase. In the bloodiest urban

The televised presidential debates took on an informal air in 1992. At this debate at the University of Richmond, President George Bush *(left)* talked with independent presidential candidate Ross Perot, while Democratic candidate Bill Clinton responded to a question from the audience.   (Wide World Photos, Inc.)

riot since the 1960s, forty-four people died and two thousand were injured. Entire blocks of houses and stores went up in flames, leaving $1 billion in charred ruins.

President Bush paid a two-day trip to Los Angeles and advocated emergency aid, but he missed an opportunity to take a bold step in addressing the nation's urban and racial problems. He gave no civil rights talks, and he avoided meeting with the nation's mayors. It seemed to increasing numbers of voters that President Bush did not really care after all.

In August, when the Republicans held their national convention, Bush promoted his identity as

Bush's Campaign

guardian of family values but had little new to offer. The "vision thing," Bush once conceded, had eluded him. For a presidential candidate in changing times, this was a fatal flaw. The Bush-Quayle election strategy featured negative campaigning, particularly attacks on Clinton's character. He was caricatured as "Slick Willie," a draft-dodger, and a womanizer. Bush said the issue was trust, and he asked whether the American people could trust Clinton's international leadership.

But on November 3, with the highest voter turnout (55 percent) since 1976, the American people voted to make a change. The Clinton-

Clinton's Victory

Gore ticket swept all of New England and the West Coast and much of the industrial heartland of the Midwest (see Map 33.2). It also made the deepest Democratic inroads into the South since Jimmy Carter's 1976 near-sweep. The Republican coalition had not held. Clinton captured Democrats who earlier had fled to Ronald Reagan, and he ran well in the suburbs and among voters who labeled themselves independents and moderates. Although Perot won no electoral votes, he claimed almost one-fifth of the popular vote, demonstrating the public's dissatisfaction with both major parties. It was the most successful run for the presidency by a candidate unattached to the major parties in eighty years.

Voters also changed Congress. Though party distribution remained about the same, with the Democrats in control of both houses, four more women were sent to the Senate and nineteen more to the House. Voters also elected more African American and Hispanic American representatives. When the 103d Congress met in January 1993, it had 110 new representatives and eleven new senators. Many of the first-term members of Congress were—like Clinton—

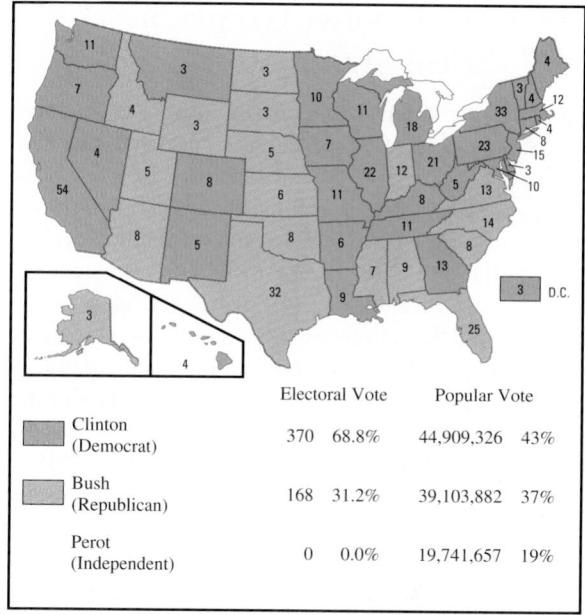

	Electoral Vote		Popular Vote	
Clinton (Democrat)	370	68.8%	44,909,326	43%
Bush (Republican)	168	31.2%	39,103,882	37%
Perot (Independent)	0	0.0%	19,741,657	19%

Map 33.2 Presidential Election, 1992 Although a minority of voters cast ballots for Bill Clinton, he won handily in the electoral college. Clinton's share of the popular vote was the lowest for anyone elected president since Woodrow Wilson won with 42 percent of the popular vote in 1912. Exit polls revealed that the votes cast for Perot would have divided about evenly between Clinton and Bush had Perot not been in the race.

in their forties with advanced degrees, no military service, and considerable experience in politics at the state level. "The baby boomers' generation—or at least some of its most upwardly mobile members—is taking over," observed *Washington Post* columnist David Broder. "It will be different."

One of Bush's last decisions as president smacked of the discredited past. Just before leaving office, the

Bush's Pardon of Iran-Contra Officials

president pardoned Reagan's secretary of defense Caspar Weinberger and other Iran-contra figures who had been indicted on felony counts for lying to Congress and obstructing a congressional inquiry (see page 912). Had elected officials learned nothing from the Watergate scandal, asked David Broder, not even "their duty to obey the law"? The veteran journalist added a grim conclusion: "We have failed as a society to express our contempt and disgust for those who violate their oaths of office with such impunity."

Bill Clinton, Newt Gingrich, and Political Stalemate

 President Bill Clinton was one of the most paradoxical presidents in American history. In a 1996 story for the *New York Times*, the journalist Todd S. Purdum observed that, "one of the biggest, most talented, articulate, intelligent, open, colorful characters ever to inhabit the White House [Clinton] can also be an undisciplined, fumbling, obtuse, defensive, self-justifying rogue. . . . He is essentially sunny, yet capable of black cloudbursts of thundering rage. He is a splendid salesman and tireless storyteller but confesses that he has failed to tell his Administration's story. . . . He is breathtakingly bright while capable of doing really dumb things."

Clinton's immediate goal as president was to mobilize the nation to pull itself out of its economic, social, and political doldrums. He named to his cabinet a mix of seasoned politicos, young politicians, intellectuals, women, and minorities. In his inaugural address, he called on Americans to "take more responsibility, not only for ourselves and our families, but for our communities and our country." One of Clinton's first acts was to overturn Bush's "gag rule," which had prohibited abortion counseling in clinics that received federal funds. And he appointed his wife, Hillary Rodham Clinton, to draft a plan for healthcare reform. He seemed to be off to a fast start but soon ran into trouble over a campaign pledge to lift the ban on homosexuals in the military. Finally accepting a "Don't ask, don't tell" compromise, he alienated both liberals and conservatives, both the gay community and the military. Clinton's honeymoon in office was brief.

In 1993 the unemployment rate stood at 7.2 percent, and IBM, General Motors, AT&T, and other corporations were laying off thousands of workers. The troubled economies of Europe and Japan portended lower U.S. exports and a bigger trade deficit; the trade deficit already had reached $84.3 billion in 1992, a 29 percent jump from 1991. Still reeling from losses on real-estate loans, banks were hesitant to lend to small businesses, although interest rates had begun to drop. Mounting healthcare costs threatened to drive up the federal deficit.

Economic Proposals

Clinton's economic plan, sent to Congress in early 1993, called for higher taxes for the middle class, a 10 percent surtax on individuals with taxable incomes over $250,000, an energy tax, and a higher corporate tax. Clinton promised to end business deductions for expense accounts, such as memberships in country clubs. He also proposed to cut government spending through a smaller defense budget and a downsized bureaucracy, and he offered an immediate stimulus to the economy through public works projects.

Interest-group lobbyists wasted no time in attacking Clinton's economic plan. Republicans protested that Clinton was not cutting back enough on spending, and other critics hammered him for going back on his campaign pledge to provide tax relief for middle-class Americans. The president fought back, arguing that federal indebtedness was graver than anticipated and that all Americans must pay to clean up the mess the deficit-spending Republicans had left them. Intent on avoiding the "trappings of Washington," he crisscrossed the nation to speak directly to people.

With reduced spending and higher taxes, the federal deficit declined by some $83 billion during Clinton's first fiscal year in office. The president touted the accomplishment but could not take credit alone. The economy rebounded in 1993, outperforming estimates, increasing tax revenues, and cutting interest on the federal debt. Spending for healthcare and for Social Security fell below estimates. The decline in the fiscal deficit begun in 1993 continued throughout the Clinton administration.

Clinton broke legislative gridlock. The so-called motor-voter act enabled people to register to vote when they applied for drivers' licenses, and the Family and Medical Leave Act required employers to grant workers unpaid family or medical leave of up to twelve weeks. Clinton also signed into law measures dealing with the sale of firearms. The Brady law (1993) required a short waiting period (to allow for a background check) before the sale of a handgun; a second law banned the sale of assault weapons. And in 1994 Clinton, with the help of three Republican senators who broke with their party, secured the enactment of a $30.2 billion crime bill that provided funds for building prisons and increasing the size of urban police forces. Finally, with considerable opposition from his own party and from organized labor, Clinton secured congressional approval of NAFTA (see page 955).

Legislative Successes

When Byron R. White, a conservative justice, retired in 1993, Clinton altered the outlook of the Supreme Court by appointing Ruth Bader Ginsburg, an experienced women's rights advocate and federal

Supreme Court Appointments

appeals court judge. The next year he named Stephen Breyer, a federal judge from Massachusetts, to succeed Justice Harry Blackmun. The Court would be less conservative, but it was deeply divided over cases involving gay rights, free speech, and voting rights. The right to an abortion had survived a Court challenge in 1992 by a 5-to-4 vote *(Planned Parenthood v. Casey)*, but the issue had not been laid to rest.

The 1994–1995 term produced conservative rulings that placed limits on affirmative action and school desegregation, but a year later the new justices began to speak up. In *U.S. v. Virginia*, the Court held that the Virginia Military Institute could not exclude women because to do so would violate the constitutional guarantee of "equal protection of the laws"; thus separate-but-equal was unconstitutional whether based on race or gender. Also in 1996, in a landmark gay rights case *(Romer v. Evans)*, the Court ruled unconstitutional a Colorado amendment that nullified civil rights protections for homosexuals.

Almost everyone—liberal and conservative, Democrat and Republican—agreed that the nation's health-

Defeat of Healthcare Reform

care system was in crisis and that its welfare system was a failure. Different constituencies, however, had vastly different "solutions" to offer. The result was continued gridlock between Democrats and Republicans, and between the White House and Congress, and eventual defeat for healthcare reforms, which were opposed by powerful business and insurance industry interests. The failure to deliver on healthcare was Clinton's major defeat, and it was one he shared with his wife, who cochaired the president's task force on healthcare reform.

On the stump in 1992, Bill Clinton had praised his wife, Hillary Rodham Clinton, as a major asset, promising the voters, "Buy one, get one

A Controversial Couple

free." A Yale law school graduate, Hillary Clinton had her own career as a partner in a law firm in Little Rock and as a feminist and social activist. Both she and her husband were controversial. Bill Clinton conceded that he had smoked marijuana in the 1960s but insisted that he had not inhaled. Few people, conservative or liberal, believed him. As president, Clinton was the defendant in a civil lawsuit alleging sexual harassment, and he was the most frequent butt of jokes on the Jay Leno and David Letterman late-night television shows. Letterman cracked, for ex-

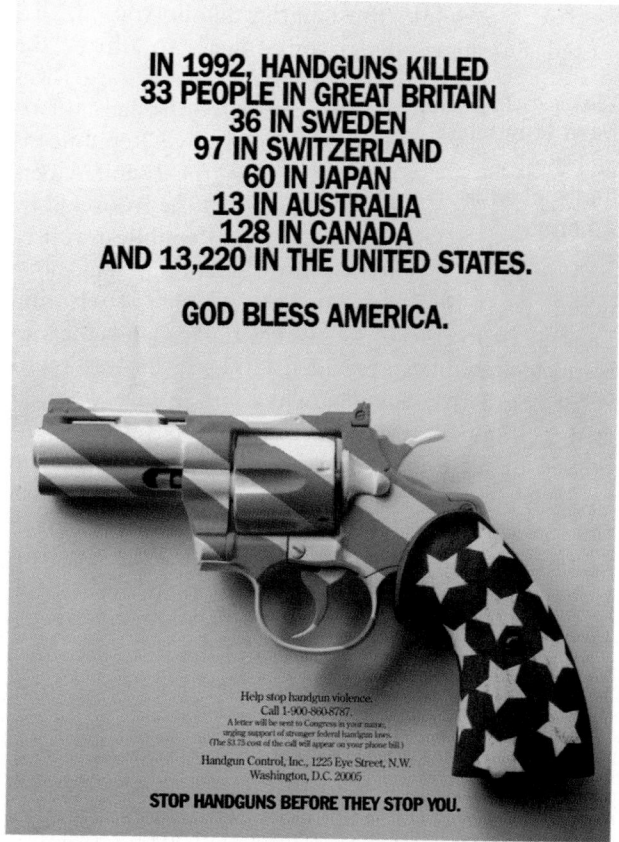

In 1993 Congress took action on gun control, passing the Brady Bill into law. Named for James Brady, paralyzed by a gunshot wound during an assassination attempt on President Ronald Reagan in 1981, the new law mandated a short waiting period before the purchase of a handgun. Brady and his wife Sarah founded Handgun Control, Inc., which sponsored this magazine advertisement. (Handgun Control, Inc.)

ample, that Clinton had agreed to play a cameo role in an upcoming film, but "was disappointed that he didn't have to sleep with anybody to get the part." In addition, a scandal dating back to the mid-1980s began to embarrass the Clintons. It involved the Whitewater Development Company, and in 1994 Kenneth Starr was appointed special prosecutor to investigate the matter.

Hillary Clinton was also a magnet for criticism, having been in the middle of several of the defining controversies of the Clinton administration, including the firing of the White House travel office staff in 1993; the suicide later that year of her friend and former law partner, deputy White House counsel Vincent Foster; and the Whitewater land deal.

Two years into the Clinton administration, disgusted and angry voters vowed again to "throw the rascals out." This time the target was

Newt Gingrich and the Contract with America

the Democratic-controlled Congress, and conservative Republicans stood ready to lead the assault. Meeting in 1989 and 1990, a group led by Newt Gingrich, a Republican representative from Georgia, had pondered ways to break America's habit of electing Democrats to the House even as it gave landslide victories to Republican presidents. The result was a ten-point legislative agenda, which, if events went as Gingrich hoped, would be tested in focus groups, endorsed by all Republican candidates, and enacted in the first one hundred days of the new Congress. Bush rejected the plan in 1992, and he went down to defeat. Gingrich resurrected the plan for the 1994 congressional elections and this time found many takers. Especially drawn to this Republican campaign was a group who felt that its needs and interests had been overlooked in recent political debates—the "angry white men."

Standing on the steps of the U.S. Capitol in September 1994, more than three hundred Republican candidates for the House of Representatives proclaimed their endorsement of the "Contract with America." The document called for a balanced-budget amendment to the Constitution; a presidential line-item veto; the prohibition of welfare payments to unmarried mothers under eighteen and a two-years-and-out limit on welfare benefits; more prisons and longer prison sentences; a $500-per-child tax credit; increased defense spending; a reduced capital gains tax; and congressional term limits. Lobbyists from conservative organizations, including the National Rifle Association, the Christian Coalition, and the National Federation of Independent Business, applauded the contract and gave money to Republican candidates.

In 1994 the Republican Party scored one of the most smashing victories in American political history,

The "Republican Revolution"

winning both houses of Congress for the first time since 1954 and making huge gains in statehouses and legislatures; thirty of fifty governors were Republicans. In the 104th Congress, the Republicans controlled the Senate by 52 seats to 48 and the House by 230 seats to 204, with one Independent. Not a single Republican incumbent lost, and many newcomers were elected, 73 in the House alone. Gingrich became Speaker of the

House, and Bob Dole of Kansas became majority leader of the Senate.

Ideological passions ran high, and Republicans launched a counterrevolution to reverse more than sixty years of federal dominance and to dismantle the welfare state. "It's the Russian Revolution in reverse," gloated Bill Kristol, a Republican strategist. Confronted with the Contract with America, Democrats appeared helpless, and even President Clinton took time at a press conference to insist that he was still "relevant."

Anger, Apathy, and the Election of 1996

On April 19, 1995, 168 children, women, and men were killed in a powerful bomb blast that destroyed the nine-story Alfred P. Murrah Federal Building in downtown Oklahoma City. Americans were dazed, saddened, and incensed. In the aftermath of the tragedy, they called in to radio talk shows to denounce the bombers and express their sorrow for the victims and their families. At first, many thought the bomb had come from abroad, perhaps set off by Middle Eastern terrorists. But a charred piece of truck axle located two blocks from the explosion, with the vehicle identification number still legible, proved otherwise. Arrested and convicted of the crime in 1997 was Timothy McVeigh, a native-born white American and a veteran of the Persian Gulf War. He hated the federal government, which he condemned for betraying the American people and the Constitution.

McVeigh later said he was agitated by a tragedy in Waco, Texas, in 1993, when the FBI led an assault on

Hostility to Government and Political Alienation

the compound of a religious sect known as the Branch Davidians; a fire had broken out, and some eighty people died. He called the attack a deliberate slaughter by the FBI. In the months that followed, reporters and government investigators discovered networks of Militiamen, Patriots, tax resisters, and various Aryan-supremacist groups that thrived on the growing climate of fear and hatred. The Southern Poverty Law Center identified well over four hundred paramilitary groups operating across the country. Computer-literate "patriots" used the Internet to rally support for their view that the federal government was controlled by Zionists, corrupt politicians, cultural elitists, the Russians, the United Nations, and other "sinister" forces.

Internet use skyrocketed in the 1990s, aided by the development of commercial Web "browsers" and by the Telecommunications Act of 1996, which stimulated mergers between telephone companies and cable companies. By 2000 there were two hundred million Internet users worldwide, including these patrons of a cybercafé. (Markus Matzel/Das Fotoarchiv)

While terrorism was relatively new to the American experience, hostility to the government was not. In fact, the American Revolution was an antigovernment movement directed against George III and his rule in the colonies. The Civil War began as a revolt against the federal Union. In the twentieth century, antigovernment ideas ranged from McCarthyism in the 1950s, to the New Left a decade later, to the militias in the 1990s. As the historian Michael Kazin has noted, "Throughout American history groups on the right and the left have seen the Federal Government as an alien force, inimical to their interests." Some antigovernment movements have been bitter and resentful, lashing out at people of color, Jews, and Roman Catholics. Yet, no matter their form, these movements have believed that the government has betrayed the people; its leaders are corrupt; and the Constitution has been subverted. In the 1990s increasing numbers of Americans seemed to share this outlook.

For many Americans, the roots of hostility to government were planted during the Vietnam War. "What happened in the 1960s," stated Gerald Marwell, a sociologist at the University of Wisconsin, "was that the

Government was successfully 'delegitimated.' We had a period from World War II through the 1950s," Marwell explained, "where the Government was seen as having rescued the nation from the Depression and successfully prosecuted the war, and then we were told in the 1960s that the emperor has no clothes and people shouldn't accept what they're told. And rather than going away, that sensibility has grown over the past 30 years."

In the 1960s, leftists had seen government as an instrument of the ruling classes, while libertarians called for freedom from government restraints. Student radicals opposed the draft and demanded the right to smoke marijuana. In the 1990s, conservatives railed against taxes and proclaimed the unfettered right to own handguns and assault weapons. The scandals—Watergate, Iran-contra—of the decades in between had only deepened Americans' distrust of the federal government. And in Clinton's era, scandal undermined the presidency once again.

In quite a different way, President Ronald Reagan had also fueled hostility to the government, in the process shifting American politics to the right. In his inaugural address in 1981, he had asserted that "government is not the solution to our problem; government *is* the problem." Reagan's continuing antigovernment rhetoric drew many devoted listeners. And his compounding of the federal debt (aided by a fiscally irresponsible Congress) from $1 trillion to $3 trillion set severe financial constraints on what the government could afford to do in the future. When George Bush left office in 1993, the federal debt was $4.4 trillion. No wonder many Americans believed government was more a burden than a benefit.

American voters felt deeply alienated. They had had their fill of political "dirty tricks" and negative attack advertisements on television. They were disgusted not only with the presidency and Congress but also with political parties, special-interest groups, and the press, and they found few politicians to admire or even trust. Journalists pointed to a "raw tomato-hurling fury that has characterized and transformed modern American politics."

Soon the Republicans in the 104th Congress, led by Newt Gingrich, proceeded to make the voters even angrier than Bush or Clinton had made them. It turned out that although Americans applauded economy in government, they were resistant to personal sacrifice. And under the Contract with America, most of those whose benefits would be cut were members of the middle class. People worried especially about Medicare and Medicaid, aid to education and college loans, highway construction and farm subsidies, Social Security, and veterans' benefits. When the Republicans attempted to turn over to the states responsibility for child nutrition programs, including school lunches, the Democrats resisted and the public rallied to their side. Republicans later repeated the mistake in pushing to cut spending for education and to repeal decades of environmental and occupational safety legislation. And the Republicans had underestimated Clinton, who frustrated the Republicans by positioning himself as the protector of the federal programs and policies under assault.

The Republicans also made a mistake when they used the threat of a federal government shutdown as a bargaining chip in their quest for a balanced budget by the year 2002. When the government temporarily closed its doors in 1995 and 1996, the public was inconvenienced and angry. Most Americans perceived Congress as ideologically inflexible but tended to see

Failures and Successes of the "Republican Revolution"

Clinton as moderate and reasonable. Speaker of the House Gingrich conceded that "our strategy failed" because Clinton and his allies, instead of surrendering and making a budget deal, "were tougher than I thought they would be."

Republicans in the 104th Congress were clearly frustrated. Their proposed constitutional amendments were defeated, and Clinton vetoed their tax cuts. Their domestic spending decreases were more than offset by defense spending increases. Congress did, however, pass several significant acts, including the line-item veto, which allowed the president to cut specific spending items from the federal budget. It also passed a measure to curb the federal government's practice of imposing programs on the states without paying for them—known as "unfunded mandates." Of far-reaching influence, the Telecommunications Act of 1996 made sweeping changes in federal law, allowing telephone companies and cable companies to compete, deregulating cable rates, and permitting media companies to own more television and radio stations. With the Freedom to Farm Act of 1996, Congress also made historic changes in farm policy, throwing out the 1938 law that established agricultural subsidies and mandating the seven-year phase-out of payments to farmers.

In 1996 Congress hiked the minimum wage and enacted legislation that made all health insurance portable from job to job and curtailed exclusions based on preexisting medical conditions. Most important, it passed a welfare reform act (The Personal Responsibility and Work Opportunity Act), which eliminated the provision in the Social Security Act of 1935 that guaranteed cash assistance for poor children (Aid to Families with Dependent Children). Instead, under the new law each state received a lump sum of federal money to design and run its own "welfare-to-work" programs. In addition to reducing food stamps and restricting welfare eligibility for legal immigrants, the law mandated that the head of every family on welfare must find work within two years, or the family loses benefits. And it decreed that no one can get more than five years of welfare benefits over a lifetime.

While the Republican 104th Congress elected in 1994 under Gingrich's leadership failed to secure most of its legislative goals, it did recast the American political debate. Many Democrats conceded that the government could not solve all problems and needed to be shrunk. Both Congress and the president urged returning power to the states. Sacred cows from the New Deal and the Great Society, such as Social Secu-

President Bill Clinton suffered political repudiation in the Republican sweep of Congress in 1994. But two years later his popularity was on the upswing. Here he and Hillary Clinton and Vice President Al Gore (with wife Tipper) celebrate their renomination at the 1996 Democratic National Convention in Chicago.   (Wide World Photos, Inc.)

rity and Medicare, were under scrutiny as never before. Civil rights issues seemed to be of secondary political importance to both major parties.

The 1996 Election

As the 1996 election neared, some political observers predicted that voters would send Clinton back to Arkansas and put a conservative Republican in the White House. But these pundits overlooked an essential segment of the electorate: women. Women tended to view the 104th Congress as hostile to measures essential to family welfare. For years, political scholars had identified a "gender gap" in voting behavior: women were more likely than men to vote Democratic. In the mid-1990s, that gap threatened to become a chasm.

"Women are still bigger believers in government," explained Andrew Kohut, a veteran pollster, in 1996. "Women are stronger environmentalists, more critical of business and less critical of government. This drives their party preferences." Issues like health insurance, daycare for children, and education were also of keen importance to women, who were more likely than men

to want an activist government. They also were more suspicious of attempts to downsize government, fearing for the future of safety-net programs and believing that the government should do more to help families. Looking to the 1996 elections, Democrats hoped that women could do for them what "angry white men" had done for the Republicans in 1994.

But Republicans remained confident that President Clinton was vulnerable. Among those running in the primaries was Bob Dole of Kansas, the Senate majority leader and an army veteran of the Second World War who had been badly wounded while fighting in Italy. Dole had served in Congress for thirty-five years, and many Republicans, believing that he had earned his party's presidential nomination, cast their votes for him. He chose Jack Kemp, a former congressman, cabinet officer, and professional football player, to be his running mate.

Both the Clinton-Gore and the Dole-Kemp tickets were amply funded by campaign contributors. Candidates running for federal offices spent a total of $2 billion. Businesses and labor unions alike used

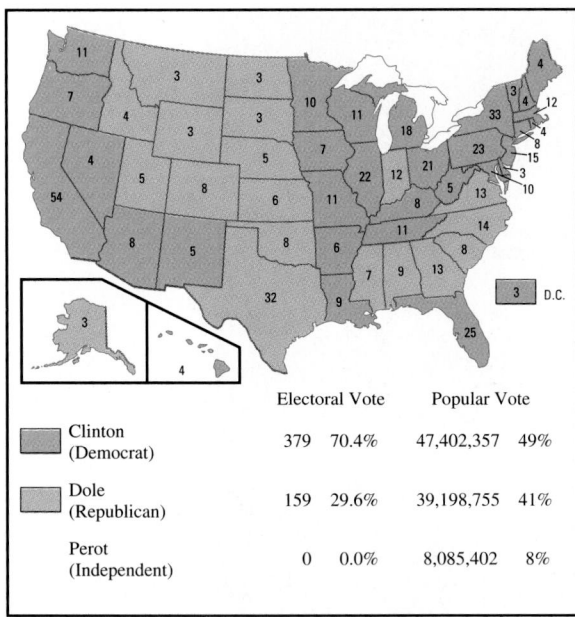

Map 33.3 Presidential Election, 1996 Although Bill Clinton did not win a majority of the vote, he came close at 49 percent, winning thirty-one states to nineteen for Bob Dole. Ross Perot, with 8 percent of the vote, was less of a factor than in 1992, when he had earned 19 percent of the vote. Despite Clinton's victory, the Republicans retained control of both houses of Congress.

loopholes in the campaign-financing laws to donate tens of millions of dollars, much of it used for costly attack advertisements on television. These negative ads offended many voters, and on election day turnout was a mere 49 percent, the lowest rate since before the Second World War.

On the eve of the voting, Clinton's approval rating stood at 56 percent, and in the election he carried thirty-one states. The public had responded to his promise that, if reelected, his administration would build "a bridge to the twenty-first century, wide enough and strong enough to take us to America's best days." But Clinton was reelected with only 49 percent of the popular vote, and he did not achieve his goal of winning a majority. Still, he easily defeated Dole (41 percent) and Ross Perot (8 percent), who ran again, this time as the Reform Party candidate (see Map 33.3). Although the Republicans lost the contest for the White House, they retained control of both houses of Congress.

Clinton had won, in part, because he stole some of the conservatives' thunder. He called for a balanced budget, declared "the era of big government" was over, and invoked family values such as "fighting for the family-leave law or the assault-weapons ban or the Brady Bill or the V-chip for parents or trying to keep tobacco out of the hands of kids." He had cooperated with Republicans in ending agricultural subsidies and ending "welfare as we know it." Bill Clinton, the first Democratic president to be reelected since Franklin D. Roosevelt in 1936, accomplished that feat partly by running against Roosevelt's New Deal. It was evident that the conservative revolution that had germinated in the 1970s, and that had come to fruition during the Reagan years of the 1980s, was very much alive as the United States entered the second half of the 1990s.

The Prospects and Perils of Hegemonic Power: Military Interventions, Peace Diplomacy, Trade, and Culture

 Clinton and his secretaries of state, the veteran diplomat Warren Christopher and Madeleine Albright, the first woman ever to hold that high post, championed domestic themes in their foreign policy agenda—especially the expansion of economic prosperity, democracy, and environmental controls. But the U.S. posture in world affairs seemed at times more reactive than promotional, especially as vicious ethnic rivalries erupted, making intrastate conflict more common than the interstate conflict of the Cold War era. Notwithstanding Clinton's reelection in 1996, moreover, Republicans in Congress derailed his ambassadorial appointments, cut foreign aid, refused to pay America's U.N. dues, and blocked major treaties. Clinton sustained a large military budget ($270 billion in 1999), in part because defense spending served as a federal jobs program, and like presidents before him, he repeatedly deployed U.S. armed forces abroad (see Table 33.1). He oversaw a changing CIA, which increasingly practiced economic espionage on the business activities and weapons contracts of other nations. Although some observers claimed that the United States, at the end of the twentieth century, had become the world's lone global policeman, foreign policy analyst Joseph S. Nye, Jr., identified America as the "sheriff of the posse, leading shifting coalitions of friends and allies."

One consequence of the end of the Cold War proved savage: ethnic wars in Yugoslavia, from which

Table 33.1   U.S. Military Personnel on Active Duty in Foreign Countries, 1996

Country	Personnel	Country	Personnel	Country	Personnel	Country	Personnel
In foreign countries*	240,421	Cote D'Ivoire	19	Japan	42,962	Qatar	43
Ashore	213,467	Croatia	4,007	Jordan	24	Romania	12
Afloat	26,954	Cuba (Guantánamo)	1,886	Kazakhstan	7	Russia	74
Albania	3	Cyprus	50	Kenya	29	Saudi Arabia	1,587
Algeria	8	Czech Republic	10	Korea, Rep. of	36,539	Senegal	11
Angola	3	Denmark	38	Kuwait	5,531	Serbia	8
Antarctica	19	Diego Garcia	878	Kyrgyzstan	1	Sierra Leone	6
Antigua	2	Djibouti	7	Laos	3	Singapore	158
Argentina	25	Dominican Republic	10	Latvia	1	Slovakia	4
Armenia	1	Ecuador	70	Lebanon	2	South Africa	23
Australia	328	Egypt	1,066	Liberia	9	Spain	2,746
Austria	37	El Salvador	26	Lithuania	2	Sri Lanka	7
Azerbaijan	1	Eritrea	1	Luxembourg	9	St. Helena	3
Bahamas, The	53	Estonia	2	Macedonia	501	Suriname	2
Bahrain	598	Ethiopia	10	Madagascar	6	Sweden	13
Bangladesh	10	Fiji	2	Malaysia	19	Switzerland	24
Barbados	11	Finland	17	Mali	6	Syria	11
Belarus	2	France	73	Malta	8	Tanzania, U. Rep. of	5
Belgium	1,646	Georgia	2	Mexico	35	Thailand	242
Belize	2	Germany	48,878	Moldova	1	Togo	6
Bolivia	24	Ghana	7	Morocco	17	Trinidad and Tabago	32
Bosnia and Herzegovina	15,003	Gibraltar	4	Mozambique	5	Tunisia	19
Botswana	7	Greece	507	Nepal	6	Turkey	2,922
Brazil	47	Greenland	141	Netherlands	747	Turkmenistan	1
Bulgaria	14	Guatemala	17	New Zealand	32	Uganda	9
Burma	11	Guinea	6	Nicaragua	15	Ukraine	8
Burundi	5	Haiti	277	Niger	6	United Arab Emirates	23
Cambodia	5	Honduras	865	Nigeria	16	United Kingdom	11,662
Cameroon	9	Hong Kong	29	Norway	104	Uruguay	9
Canada	208	Hungary	6,523	Oman	30	Uzbekistan	1
Chad	9	Iceland	1,893	Pakistan	26	Venezuela	30
Chile	24	India	24	Panama	6,435	Vietnam	6
China	32	Indonesia	43	Paraguay	10	Yemen	11
Colombia	34	Ireland	8	Peru	26	Zaire	9
Congo	5	Israel	44	Philippines	138	Zambia	6
Costa Rica	9	Italy	12,401	Poland	20	Zimbabwe	8
		Jamaica	10	Portugal	1,075		

*Includes areas not shown separately.

Source: U.S. Bureau of the Census, *Statistical Abstract of the United States: 1998* (Washington, D.C., 1998), p. 366.

**Ethnic Wars
in Former
Yugoslavia**

Slovenia, Croatia, and Macedonia seceded in 1991, followed the next year by Bosnia-Herzegovina. Yugoslavia (primarily Serbia but including Montenegro) fought these moves toward independence. Bosnian Muslims, Serbs, and Croats were soon killing one another by the hundreds of thousands. Noting Europe's reluctance to act in its own backyard, Clinton talked tough against Serbian aggression and atrocities in Bosnia-Herzegovina, especially the Serbs' cruel "ethnic cleansing" of Muslims through massacres and rape camps. On occasion he ordered U.S. airpower to strike Serb positions. In late 1995, after American diplomats brokered an agreement in Dayton, Ohio, among the belligerents for a new multiethnic state in Bosnia-Herzegovina, Clinton contributed thousands of U.S. troops to a NATO Implementation Force that continued to keep a fragile peace as the twentieth century closed.

American ideals, declared Clinton, had won the Cold War and were being tested in the Balkans. The president denounced an "isolationist backlash" and called the United States the world's "best peacemaker." "If we've got troops looking for somewhere to help," dissented a nurse in a high-crime district of St. Louis, "send them in here." In contrast, a Missouri trucker saw a moral duty: "You think of the pictures of those poor people, lying in the street, some of them kids, raped, tortured, murdered. That's pretty hard to turn away from." So it seemed in March 1999, when U.S. and NATO forces began to bomb Yugoslavia (Serbia) to stop the ethnic cleansing of its province of Kosovo, whose majority were ethnic Albanians. The bombing at first unleashed even more cruelties as the Serbs massacred, raped, and evicted ethnic Albanians from their homes; a huge refugee exodus burdened NATO, U.N., and international relief agencies in neighboring nations. Yugoslav president Slobodan

In spring 1999, as NATO bombing raids pounded Serbia (Yugoslavia) and Serb military positions in Kosovo to punish Serbia for killing and displacing ethnic Albanians, the number of Kosovar refugees dramatically increased. Desperate and hungry, they fled to neighboring nations. Here, in a NATO-run refugee camp outside Skopje, Macedonia, U.S. Marines distribute food to some of the 850,000 forced to leave their Kosovo homes.   (Wide World Photos, Inc.)

Milošević finally relented in June, withdrawing his brutal military from Kosovo, where U.S. troops joined a U.N. peacekeeping force. The International War Crimes Tribunal indicted Milošević and his top aides for atrocities. The Kosovo war revealed fissures in NATO as some allies, especially France, Greece, and Italy, opposed an aggressive bombing campaign.

Russia strongly protested the bombing of Yugoslavia. Economically hobbled, and led by an ailing and ineffective Boris Yeltsin, Russia found itself increasingly isolated. Just before the Kosovo crisis, Washington had expanded NATO to include Poland, Hungary, and the Czech Republic. Moscow read the expansion as an anti-Russian step. In 1997 Clinton and Yeltsin had negotiated a START-III agreement, cutting strategic nuclear weapons once again, but Moscow bristled against the U.S. decision to move ahead on an antiballistic missile system. When Russia would ratify START III remained a mystery. By 2000 a "Cold Peace" characterized U.S.-Russia relations over this issue as well as over Russia's inability to curb its rampant political and business corruption and refusal to launch effective reforms.

The Middle East also continued to draw intense U.S. interest. As Saudi Arabia punished the Palestine Liberation Organization for its support of Iraq in the Persian Gulf War by trimming financial assistance, and as the *intifada* raised Israel's costs of maintaining control over occupied territories (see Map 31.2 on page 904), the PLO and Israel seemed more willing to settle their differences. U.S. diplomats once again took an active role in the peace process, encouraging Arab and Israeli leaders to attend a peace conference in Madrid in fall 1991. In September 1993 the PLO's Yasir Arafat and Israel's prime minister Yitzhak Rabin signed an agreement for Palestinian self-rule in the Gaza Strip and the West Bank's Jericho. In 1994 Israel signed a peace accord with Jordan, further reducing the chances of another full-scale Arab-Israeli war. Radical anti-Arafat Palestinians, however, continued to stage bloody terrorist attacks on Israelis, while extremist Israelis killed Palestinians and, in November 1995, even Rabin himself. Only after American-conducted negotiations and renewed violence in the West Bank did Israel agree in early 1997 to withdraw its forces from the Palestinian city of Hebron. Thereafter the peace process alternately sagged and spurted.

Arab-Israeli Agreements

Ethnic rivalry also bewildered Africa. In mid-1994, in Rwanda, the majority Hutus butchered eight hundred thousand of the minority Tutsis. The United

Genocide in Rwanda

States and the United Nations responded too late, with Clinton resisting appeals for intervention to stop the killing. In 1998, while visiting Africa to promote trade and democracy, the president apologized for not "calling these crimes by their rightful name: genocide" and vowed never to let such a horror happen again.

Throughout Latin America, the Clinton administration continued to promote liberalized trade, private enterprise economies, orderly immigration, democratization, and the war against drugs (spending some $3 billion a year). In the early 1990s in poverty-wracked and environmentally devastated Haiti, a military coup and political instability provoked U.S. economic sanctions. Tens of thousands of black Haitians fled in boats for U.S. territory, spawning an immigration crisis. After swinging between tough talk against the military junta and indecision, President Clinton sent Jimmy Carter to the Caribbean island nation in September 1994. The former president cut a deal granting amnesty to the generals, who stepped down. Clinton soon ordered U.S. troops to Haiti in Operation Uphold Democracy. In early 1996 American forces departed, their mission to revitalize Haiti unfulfilled.

Pressures Against Haiti and Cuba

As for Cuba, Clinton improved telecommunications and cultural linkages while maintaining the punishing economic embargo. In summer 1995 Cubans set to sea in all forms of craft for Florida, sparking dispute. Clinton decided to admit thousands of detained Cuban refugees while turning away new arrivals. In March 1996, after an airplane manned by a provocative anti-Castro group was shot down by Cuban fighter pilots near Cuba, Clinton, on the eve of the Florida primary, pandered to the politically influential Cuban-American community and signed the Helms-Burton Act. This legislation tightened the economic embargo by allowing American nationals and companies to sue in U.S. courts foreign companies that were using formerly American-owned properties in Cuba. The Castro government had seized these assets in the early days of the Cuban Revolution, and they were valued at $1.8 billion, or $5.5 billion with interest. Canada and the European Union, both of which traded with and invested in Cuba, condemned the measure. Alert to international protest, Clinton suspended the act's provision that permitted the suing of foreign companies. Meanwhile, eager U.S. companies scouted prospects in Cuba, where tourism was becoming big business.

Protesting that the World Trade Organization (WTO) possessed the dangerous power to challenge any nation's environmental laws if the WTO deemed them barriers to trade, chanting demonstrators marched in the streets of Seattle on November 30, 1999. Critics of the WTO have claimed that sea turtles and dolphins have already been victimized by the WTO. Demonstrators identified the WTO as an example of globalization gone wrong. The WTO meeting went on, but the results proved meager because nations could not agree on rules governing dumping, subsidies for farm goods, genetically altered foods, and lower tariffs on high-tech goods. (Paul Joseph Brown/Seattle Post-Intelligencer)

Seeing flourishing foreign trade as essential to U.S. prosperity and to world economic and political stability, the Clinton administration strove to open foreign markets to American products and to close the U.S. trade gap (which in 1998 reached a record deficit of $233.4 billion). "If the past generation tended to produce soldier-statesmen," remarked one diplomat, "the next generation will have to produce economist-statesmen." Besides guiding NAFTA through Congress, Clinton announced in 1994, when granting China most-favored-nation trading status, that the United States was decoupling trade and human-rights issues. While Washington would not ignore human-rights violations in China, human-rights questions would not interfere with trade. In 1999 the United States supported China's membership in the World Trade Organization (WTO) in return for increased U.S. access to the Chinese domestic market.

Trade Expansion and Globalization

The WTO, which in 1994 replaced the General Agreement on Tariffs and Trade, became the main body regulating and settling disputes over international trade. As a symbol of globalization—the greater movement of goods, services, money, and people across national borders—the WTO became a target of environmental and labor groups, such as the Sierra Club and the AFL-CIO. They charged that the powerful organization of 135 nations served corporate interests and had the dangerous authority to overrule national laws protecting labor standards, human rights, and public health, if the WTO judged those laws barriers to trade. When the WTO held a summit meeting in Seattle in late 1999, antiglobalization protesters marched and nongovernmental organizations (NGOs) publicized their case against the WTO.

Economic and financial issues remained high on the administration's agenda. When politically corrupt Mexico's economy neared collapse in 1995, the United States bailed it out with large loans. Elsewhere, such as in Indonesia and Russia, the Clinton administration backed International Monetary Fund (IMF) efforts to rescue faltering economies and force banking and budget reforms that often undercut social welfare programs and stirred political crisis. In 1999, after the European Union banned hormone-treated American beef, the United States imposed 100 percent tariffs on some imported European goods, including Roquefort cheese and mustard. French protesters ransacked a McDonald's restaurant and one French town slapped a 100 percent tax on bottles of Coca-Cola because "it is a symbol of the American multinational that wants to uniformize taste all over the planet."

Trade issues also lay at the center of tense U.S.-Japanese relations. Most nettlesome was the huge trade deficit in Japan's favor (about $50 billion in the mid-1990s). American manufacturers protested that Japan's tariffs, cartels, and government subsidies blocked U.S. goods from Japanese markets. The Japanese countered that obsolete equipment, poor education, and inadequate spending on research and development undercut U.S. competitiveness. Trade talks with Japan proved divisive and produced small gains, but both nations knew that their economies were too interdependent for one to punish or isolate the other. By the late 1990s, as Japan's economy stagnated and America's galloped, "Japan bashing" declined, while McDonald's became Japan's largest restaurant chain.

The question of trade also influenced U.S. policy toward Vietnam. Military veterans and families of missing-in-action (MIA) soldiers berated Clinton's 1994 decision to lift the trade embargo against Vietnam and his 1995 opening of full diplomatic relations. American businesses such as Otis, General Electric, and Pepsico welcomed the new economic opportunities there. "English is the language of money, the language of our future," remarked a Vietnamese diplomat.

Weapons of Mass Destruction

Weapons proliferation alarmed people everywhere. Arms sales, including surface-to-surface missiles, accelerated across the post–Cold War world and the United States continued as the world's largest arms merchant (see Figure 33.1). Nuclear proliferation continued to worry leaders, despite renewal of the nonproliferation treaty in 1995. Argentina, Brazil, and South Africa abandoned nuclear weapons programs, but India and Pakistan exploded nuclear devices in 1998. The United States spent more than a billion dollars to help Russia and other former Soviet republics dismantle their nuclear arsenals. The Comprehensive Nuclear-Test-Ban Treaty of 1996 earned 151 signatories, including the United States. But the Clinton administration seemed lackluster in its advocacy of U.S. ratification. In October 1999 the Republican-dominated Senate rejected the treaty by a vote of 51 to 48 (67 votes needed), causing an awakened Clinton to denounce "reckless partisanship." Secretary Albright soon announced that the United States would honor the treaty anyway. Still, the United States projected a negative image: indulging in narrow partisan politics at home while snubbing collective agreements for global security.

In 1997 the United States finally ratified the Chemical Weapons Convention, which required the destruction of chemical weapons, such as poison gas. Also that year, more than one hundred nations endorsed a treaty banning antipersonnel land mines, but Clinton refused to sign because U.S. troops in South Korea relied on mines along the border with North Korea. Terrorists with access to deadly explosives also threatened danger; in early 1993, for example, Islamic extremists bombed New York's World Trade Center. In 1998 Clinton ordered air attacks against suspected terrorist sites in Afghanistan and Sudan. The CIA paid increasing attention to the possibility that terrorists would use biological weapons, such as viruses, against the American people.

Environmental woes also continued to disturb world order and political stability. Acid rain, toxic

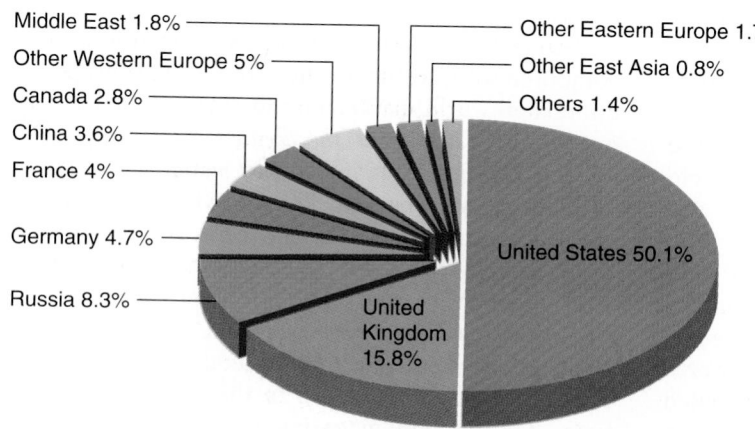

Figure 33.1 Shares of World Arms Exports, 1992–1994 The United States led the world in the 1990s in the export of weapons. In 1992–1994 U.S. arms exports totaled more than $39 billion. Most went to the Middle East (especially Saudi Arabia, Egypt, and Israel), followed by western Europe and East Asia (especially Japan, South Korea, and Taiwan). Americans debated whether these weapons shipments helped keep the peace or helped fuel regional arms races that aggravated conflict. (Source: Thomas G. Paterson, J. Garry Clifford, and Kenneth J. Hagan, *American Foreign Relations: A History,* vol. 2, 5th ed. Copyright © 2000 by Houghton Mifflin Company; Data from U.S. Arms Control and Disarmament Agency.)

Environmental and Population Crises

waste, deterioration of the protective ozone layer (which blocks the sun's carcinogenic ultraviolet rays), soil erosion, water pollution, and destruction of tropical forests spoiled the natural environment, killed wildlife, and poisoned land. Warming of the earth's climate due to the greenhouse effect—the buildup of carbon dioxide and other gases in the atmosphere—threatened a rise in ocean levels, flooding farmland and dislocating millions of people. As the world's population swelled to 6 billion in 1999 (increasing at a rate of some 80 million a year) and droughts unleashed killer famines and massive human migrations, ill-equipped governments struggled to provide welfare for the hungry. Still, analysts noted that women were having fewer babies; the global fertility rate declined from a high of 6 children per woman in the 1950s to 2.9 by 2000.

In contrast to the Bush administration, the Clinton administration, recalled Secretary Christopher, decided "to persuade the American people that a healthy environment is critical to national security." In 1993 Clinton signed the Biodiversity Treaty and sent it to the Senate, where it remains pending. The United States approved the Convention on Desertification (1994) to support land preservation and reclamation and signed the Global Warming Convention (1997) to reduce greenhouse gas emissions (not yet ratified). In fall 1997 Clinton transmitted the 1982 Convention on the Law of the Sea to the Senate. Although 129 nations and the European Union have ratified the accord and activated the International Seabed Authority, the Senate has so far refused to approve this convention.

In the mid-1990s the State Department and the United Nations studied the treatment of women as a worldwide human rights issue. Their reports revealed that 70 percent of the world's poor people were women. Women faced not only job discrimination (women worldwide earned 30 to 40 percent less than their male counterparts for the same work) and political discrimination (women held only 10 percent of national legislative seats) but also forced sterilization and abortion, coerced prostitution, and genital mutilation. Half of the world's people were women, observed one U.S. official, "and until you improve their situation, you're not going to improve human rights around the world." The 1995 Fourth World Conference on Women, held in Beijing, called for the "empowerment of women" through "human rights and fundamental freedoms." Gender issues and international relations became intertwined. The

Human Rights for Women

United States soon made genital mutilation and other gender-based abuses grounds for asylum.

The U.N.'s specialized agency, the World Health Organization (WHO), continued its lifesaving work to combat diseases and promote medical research. The United States has traditionally supplied the largest share of WHO's regular budget and has also volunteered funds for WHO's Global Program on AIDS. The AIDS pandemic by the mid-1990s had taken the lives of millions, especially in sub-Saharan Africa. In 1997 WHO called cancer-causing smoking "a fire in the global village" and denounced the growing popularity in Asia of Western-style cigarettes marketed aggressively by U.S. firms that faced antitobacco sentiment at home.

The export of American popular culture became one of the 1990s' most prominent features. After the Cold War ended, American culture became particularly coveted in eastern Europe and the former Soviet republics. Featuring the "Beeg Mek," McDonald's in 1990 opened a fast-food restaurant in the very heart of Moscow; within five years it had served 80 million customers. Many residents of former Communist countries strove to learn the English language like their counterparts in western Europe, where 70 percent of people between the ages of eighteen and twenty-four spoke English. Interest in American basketball soared everywhere, especially after the American "Dream Team" (made up of National Basketball Association stars) triumphed at the televised 1992 Summer Olympics in Barcelona. Images of the slam-dunking Chicago Bulls hero Michael Jordan adorned T-shirts worldwide, and players from foreign lands, including eastern Europe, increasingly enrolled in U.S. colleges to play hoops.

Globalization of American Culture

American movies, TV programs, music, books, computer software, and other "intellectual property" dominated world markets in the 1990s. The TV soap opera *The Young and the Restless* became popular in New Delhi; people in Warsaw watched *Dr. Quinn, Medicine Woman;* even in Tehran, where anti-Americanism flourished and Muslim censorship prevailed, young people with VCRs watched the movie *Air Force One.* Time Warner, Inc., sold TV programs in 175 countries. *Reader's Digest* circulated in nineteen languages with sales of 28 million (compared to its U.S. circulation of 14.7 million). In thirty-six foreign editions, *Cosmopolitan* magazine touted the glamorous woman. An estimated 90 percent of all global Internet traffic was in English, and through e-mail people who lacked freedom abroad communicated with Americans who had it and wanted to promote it worldwide. The popularity of U.S. culture abroad stemmed in good part from the themes it presented: wealth, individuality, freedom, optimism, sex, violence, mobility, technological progress.

Some world affairs specialists predicted the growth of a single global culture, with the United States at its center. "It's inevitable," declared one Iranian. "I mean, it's happening in France. Do you know how many McDonald's are in France now? And the French are supposed to have the best cooking." The globalization of American culture, however, did not unfold conflict-free: some peoples protested the emasculation of their native ways by U.S. imports that seemed tawdry, unhealthy, and violent. Yet, with power in the world "no longer defined solely by territory or industrial capacity, but increasingly by the development of intellectual capital," the scholar Barry Fulton has suggested, the United States was well positioned to lead the so-called Information Age of the twenty-first century.

With its preeminent high-tech military, moreover, the United States could conduct information warfare,

| **Information Warfare** | using "smart bombs" to target and destroy an enemy's information nerve center, as when in spring 1999 missiles destroyed Serbia's communications network and television system. |

At that time, too, U.S. defense officials considered but rejected hacking into Serbia's computer networks, conducting "cyberwarfare" to derail trains and disrupt electrical services. One reason for not doing so: American officials might be vulnerable to war crimes charges because civilians as much as military targets would be hurt.

At the start of the twenty-first century, the United States held immense power, measured in so many ways. As "globocop" it intervened in other countries. As banker and trader, it pressed other nations to open their markets to U.S. commerce. Accelerated by the World Wide Web and the Internet, American culture spread everywhere. Yet, throughout history, hegemonic powers have had difficulty sustaining their supremacy. Would America, too, falter? By 2000 many nations and peoples had grown wary and critical of the United States. French foreign minister Hubert Vedrine declared, "we cannot accept either a politically unipolar world, not a culturally uniform world, nor the unilateralism of a single hyper-power" like the United States. Clinton's national security adviser Samuel R. Berger acknowledged America's reputation as a "hectoring hegemon." But he did not apologize.

McDonald's restaurants circled the globe by the early twenty-first century, exemplifying the globalization of American culture. This Ukrainian woman in Kiev seems to enjoy both her hamburger and a conversation with the human symbol of the fast-food chain, Ronald McDonald. (Wide World Photos, Inc.)

Instead, in traditional American terms, Clinton's spokesman asserted that the United States put "the greater good" of other nations ahead of its selfish interests. Given such self-congratulatory utterances, the debate over America's global role did not abate.

Clinton's Second Term: Scandal, Impeachment, and Political Survival

 Misconduct and scandals had tainted the Clinton White House from the beginning. Bill Clinton's character was often the issue, and allegations of his marital infidelity abounded. But, as one reporter noted, "If Ronald Reagan was the Teflon President, then Bill Clinton is the Timex President. He takes his lickings, keeps on ticking." Clinton's second term as president would test how durable he really was.

The scandal involving the Whitewater Development Company continued to dog the White House. In

| **Whitewater Indictments and Investigation** | the mid-1980s, the Clintons had been partners in the company with James McDougal, who was later indicted for conspiracy and mail fraud, along with his wife Susan and Governor Jim |

Guy Tucker, Clinton's successor in Arkansas. In 1994 Kenneth Starr, the independent counsel investigating Whitewater, accepted a plea agreement with Webb Hubbell, former managing partner of the law firm in which Hillary Clinton had worked and a close friend whom President Clinton had appointed deputy attorney general. In return for his cooperation in the ongoing investigation, Hubbell was allowed to plead guilty to one count of tax evasion and one count of mail fraud.

During the 1996 elections, independent counsel Starr began to produce indictments and even convictions: the McDougals and Tucker were found guilty. Hillary Clinton, testifying before a Senate committee, could not explain how long-lost law-firm billing records from Little Rock, which had been subpoenaed, disappeared for two years before surfacing in the family quarters of the White House. At a later point, the Clinton administration said it was a mistake that in 1993 and 1994 the FBI had sent over to the White House the confidential records of some nine hundred Republicans. Others thought the manipulation of federal agencies smelled of an earlier scandal, Watergate.

Meanwhile, Starr expanded his investigation of Bill Clinton to matters unrelated to Whitewater, including allegations of illegal campaign contributions, sexual harassment, and lying to a grand jury about the nature of his relationship with a White House intern named Monica S. Lewinsky. In early 1998 Linda Tripp, a former White House employee, informed Starr's office that Clinton had had a sexual affair, and she had tapes of telephone conversations to prove it. A week later, in a sworn deposition to the grand jury investigating sexual harassment, Clinton denied the affair. But in late July, Starr granted Lewinsky and her mother full immunity in exchange for testimony, and the next day Clinton's lawyer announced that the president would also testify. Two weeks later Starr requested that the president provide a fresh sample of his DNA to test for a match with a semen stain on one of Lewinsky's dresses.

Monica Lewinsky

On the night of August 13, 1998, Bill Clinton confessed to his wife that he had had a sexual relationship with Monica Lewinsky. Four days later, Clinton testified, telling the grand jury that he recalled a half-dozen sexual encounters with Lewinsky, beginning in late 1995 and ending by 1997. That evening, he spoke from the Oval Office. "I have sinned," he told the American people, and he expressed "sorrow" for the "hurt" he had caused his family, his staff, Lewinsky and her family, and the American people. "I have asked all for their forgiveness." But Clinton's testimony had been less than complete, and his tribulations were far from over; for at just that time, Starr was preparing a 445-page impeachment report for consideration by Congress.

The Starr report described ten sexual encounters between Clinton and Lewinsky, as well as fifteen phone-sex conversations, and mapped out eleven possible grounds for impeachment of the president, accusing Clinton of lying under oath, obstruction of justice, witness tampering, and abuse of power. On December 19, the House voted on four articles of impeachment against Clinton; largely along party lines, the House passed two of the articles, one alleging that the president had committed perjury in his August 17 grand-jury testimony, the other that he had obstructed justice. With the House vote, Clinton became only the second president—and the first in 130 years—to face a trial in the Senate, which has the constitutional responsibility to decide (by a two-thirds vote) whether to remove a president from office.

Impeachment by the House

But even as the House Republicans voted for Clinton's impeachment, poll after poll showed that the majority of Americans approved of the president's job performance and did not want him removed from office. In the 1998 congressional elections, voters expressed their opposition to the drive for impeachment by reducing the Republican majority in the House to ten seats (222 to 212, and one Independent). Republicans then turned on their leader, Newt Gingrich, blaming his confrontational leadership for the defeat; Gingrich resigned both the speakership and his seat in the House.

The 1998 elections left the Republican majority in the Senate unchanged at 55 to 45, and everyone expected that the Senate vote would generally break along party lines. "It takes two-thirds to get rid of this fella," said Senator Strom Thurmond, a Republican from South Carolina. "We don't have it. Let's get it over." After a five-week trial, during which thirteen House Republicans acted as Clinton's prosecutors, the Senate, by a 55-to-45 vote, found the president not guilty of perjury. And voting 50 to 50, the Senate cleared him of obstructing justice. For his part, Clinton appeared contrite, saying that he was "profoundly sorry . . . for what I did and said to trigger these events and the great burden they have imposed on the Congress and the American people."

Acquittal by the Senate

How do historians know...

that Bill Clinton lied to the American people when he denied having a sexual relationship with former White House intern Monica Lewinsky? The evidence is Clinton's DNA. For the first half of 1998, the president stuck by his adamant denial. But in July 1998, when Lewinsky agreed to cooperate with independent counsel Kenneth Starr, she also turned over to him a critical piece of evidence (see the photo): a navy blue dress stained with Clinton's semen. Two weeks later, the independent counsel requested that the president provide a DNA sample. Realizing that the FBI had analyzed the genetic material on Lewinsky's dress and that Starr was looking for a match, Clinton within days confessed the affair to his wife and later to the American people.

DNA evidence is crucial because each person's genetic makeup is unique. (DNA is the nucleic acid that carries genetic information in cells.) In recent years, DNA tests have helped not only to convict murderers, rapists, and other criminals, but also to establish the innocence of people falsely accused, convicted, and/or imprisoned for violent crimes. Analysis of genetic material can also determine paternity; two hundred years after the fact, DNA evidence established with near certainty that Thomas Jefferson fathered at least one of the children born of his slave Sally Hemings in the 1790s. (Photo: Allan Tannebaum/Sygma)

Throughout 1999 bitter political partisanship impeded the passage of much-needed legislation. Rejected, vetoed, or left unacted upon were proposals to restructure Social Security and Medicare in preparation for the retirement of the baby-boom generation; to safeguard patients' rights in HMOs (health maintenance organizations); to cut taxes; and to reform campaign finance by regulating attack ads and banning unlimited "soft money" contributions to political parties. Even the shootings at Columbine High School could not propel through Congress legislation requiring criminal background checks of purchasers at gun shows. "This was not a session of great initiatives," lamented one senator. "This was a session that was post-impeachment and pre-[2000] election."

As America entered a new century, its people yearned for a president with character and leadership. Some Americans embraced Senator John McCain, a Republican from Arizona who championed campaign finance reform. McCain was also a war hero; as a navy pilot in 1967, he was shot down by a surface-to-air missile over Hanoi, captured by the Vietnamese, and

held as a prisoner of war under brutal conditions for the next five and a half years. The Democratic presidential race also featured a genuine hero; Bill Bradley had been an All-American basketball player at Princeton, a Rhodes scholar at Oxford University, a Hall of Fame basketball player for the New York Knicks, and a former U.S. senator from New Jersey. Bradley joined McCain in demanding campaign finance reform.

The race for the presidency accelerated in 2000 with primary elections, party caucuses, and state party conventions scheduled in thirty-two states during the first three months of the year, beginning in Iowa in January. The front runners were George W. Bush, the Republican governor of Texas, and Al Gore, Jr., Democratic vice president under Clinton. Bush's father, George H. W. Bush, had served as president; Gore's father had been an influential U.S. senator from Tennessee. Loyalists in both parties supported the younger Bush and Gore politically and financially. By 2000 Bush had amassed more than $67 million in political contributions, more than twice Gore's $28 million, but Gore would be receiving an additional $12

Just after midnight on January 1, 2000, these jubilant Americans welcomed the new year, century, and millennium in New York City's Times Square. (Nicole Beniveno/The New York Times)

million in federal matching funds during the year. On Super Tuesday in March, Gore swept the presidential primaries, including California and New York, and Bush won all but a handful of states in New England. McCain and Bradley ended their campaigns, and Gore and Bush squared off for the November election.

Summary

In 2000 the United States was riding a wave of great prosperity. Prior to 2000, the longest economic expansion in American history had lasted for 106 months, from 1961 through 1969. But in February 2000 an expansion that had begun in 1991 eclipsed that record, and it did so without fueling inflation. In 1999 consumer confidence reached its highest level in three decades, and prices on the stock exchanges rose dramatically, establishing all-time highs by the end of the decade.

America at the turn of the twenty-first century was engaged in a technological and scientific revolution. A century earlier, electricity and the internal-combustion engine were transforming communica-

tions and transportation in the United States. And one hundred years before that, the steam engine was poised to initiate America's industrial revolution. But in 2000 it was a digitized revolution in communications and information that generated American prosperity and was transforming life in America and around the globe.

The United States was not only prosperous in 2000, it also was powerful. The 1990s began with challenges to the old world order. Like a retreating glacier, the Cold War left behind a scarred landscape and debris that complicated the shaping of a new world order. Localized conflicts and ethnic rivalries, such as those in the Balkans, Middle East, and Africa, crowded the international agenda, as did human rights, the natural environment, and the proliferation of deadly weapons. In the 1990s Bush and Clinton officials spoke of America's "world responsibilities" to spread democracy and free-market economics abroad and to intervene for humanitarian purposes. In the ensuing national debate, others argued that the United States lacked the cultural sensitivity, funds, or ability to build, reform, or police other societies. Reasserting traditional notions of U.S. world leadership, Clinton dismissed such thinking as a dangerous retreat to isolationism. His military interventions in a host of countries—especially against what Washington officials called "rogue states"—and trade and cultural expansion demonstrated a fervent traditional U.S. activism to make the world more American and to sustain U.S. hegemony against all challengers.

Envious of America's prosperity and power, nations everywhere struggled to adopt American economic and political institutions. But perils also confronted America and the world in the new century. Speaking just minutes before midnight on December 31, 1999, Bill Clinton called on the American people not to fear the future, but to "welcome it, embrace it and create it." Americans, however, were fearful about the future. For one thing, the State Department had warned of terrorist attacks to be launched on New Year's Eve. For another, the arrival of "Y2K" (year 2000) threatened to crash computer systems around the world. In the United States alone an estimated $100 billion was spent to prevent the collapse on January 1, 2000, of banks and automated teller machines, the Internet, financial markets, air traffic control, and the national defense system. But the Y2K catastrophe did not happen, and the few problems that did arise were more humorous than dangerous. In Albany, New York, for example, a customer returning a video was handed a $91,250 late fee after a computer showed the tape was a century overdue.

Just as no Y2K bug precipitated a computer collapse, so too no terrorist attacks marred the arrival of the new millennium. Ironically, however, at this time of apparent triumph, many Americans had lost faith in their own government. Confidence in government, which was expressed by 76 percent of Americans in 1964, plummeted to 19 percent by 1996. In 1996 a majority (51 percent) of voting-age Americans chose not to vote, and 64 percent did not vote in 1998. Americans were deeply skeptical about the political process, and they expressed disgust not only at Bill Clinton's behavior, but also at the Republicans' single-minded determination to destroy the president.

In his first newspaper column in 2000, David Broder observed a paradox in American democracy. In the preceding hundred years, thanks to persevering woman suffrage and civil rights movements, women and African Americans had gained the vote, thus enfranchising well over half the population. But the American voter in 2000 was cynical, having endured too many politicians who "find it easier to denigrate their opponents . . . than to describe their own views or defend their own records." "We begin the new century," Broder concluded, "with a paradox: Democracy is stronger than ever in the United States; representative government, weaker." The challenge of the new century would be to restore Americans' faith in their government.

LEGACY FOR A PEOPLE AND A NATION
The Internet

In the 1990s America—and the world—went online, forever changing the way people communicate (e-mail), do business (e-commerce), and experience life. Although a crude version of the Internet known as ARPANET went online in 1969, when two bulky computers were linked by a 15-foot cable, it was a series of developments in the late 1980s and 1990s that stimulated the Net revolution. First, Tim Berners-Lee, a British physicist, devised the three basic elements of the Web's operation: URL (uniform resource locator), HTML (hypertext markup language), and HTTP (hypertext transfer protocol). Then in 1993 the first commercial "browser" to aid navigation through the Web hit the market. Called Mosaic, it was soon followed by a much more successful product: Netscape. The prospect of millions of computers connected worldwide had become a reality.

By 2000 there were nearly 200 million Internet users worldwide, including 80 million Americans. By 2003 more than 500 million people will be surfing the World Wide Web. For their Christmas shopping in 1999, for example, millions of Americans avoided the malls and clicked through their gift lists. Some bought books from Amazon.com, while others bid on items being auctioned at eBay. Psychologists at Carnegie Mellon University, surveying the lives of Net users, found that people who spend even a few hours a week online suffer higher levels of loneliness and depression. Seemingly nothing, however, can slow down the digitized transformations in communications and information. Indeed, for the American people and nation in the new millennium, there could be no more fitting legacy than the Internet.

For Further Reading, see page A-41 of the Appendix. For Web resources, go to http://college.hmco.com.

APPENDIX

Suggestions for Further Reading

Chapter 1

General

Noble D. Cook, *Born to Die: Disease and New World Conquest, 1492–1650* (1998); Alfred W. Crosby, *The Columbian Exchange: Biological and Cultural Consequences of 1492* (1972); Alfred W. Crosby, *Ecological Imperialism: The Biological Expansion of Europe, 800–1900* (1986); John R. Elliott, *The Old World and the New* (1970); Bernard Lewis, *Cultures in Conflict: Christians, Muslims, and Jews in the Age of Discovery* (1995); D. W. Meinig, *Atlantic America, 1492–1800* (1986); Herman Viola and Carolyn Margolis, eds., *Seeds of Change: Five Hundred Years Since Columbus* (1991); Eric Wolf, *Europe and the People Without History* (1982).

Mesoamerican Civilizations

Inga Clendinnen, *Aztecs: An Interpretation* (1991); Michael Coe, *Mexico from the Olmecs to the Aztecs* (1994); Brian Fagan, *Kingdoms of Gold, Kingdoms of Jade: The Americas Before Columbus* (1991); John S. Henderson, *The World of the Ancient Maya* (1997); Eduardo Matos Moctezuma and David Carrasco, *Moctezuma's Mexico: Visions of the Aztec World* (1992); Linda Schele and David Friedel, *A Forest of Kings* [on the Mayas] (1990).

North American Indians

Kathleen Bragdon, *Native People of Southern New England, 1500–1650* (1996); Brian Fagan, *Ancient North America: The Archaeology of a Continent* (1991); Brian Fagan, *The Great Journey: The Peopling of Ancient America* (1987); Francis Jennings, *The Founders of America: From the Earliest Migrations to the Present* (1993); Alvin Josephy, Jr., ed., *America in 1492* (1992); Mark Mehrer, *Cahokia's Countryside: Household Archaeology, Settlement Patterns, and Social Power* (1995); Elsa Redmond, ed., *Chiefdoms and Chieftaincy in the Americas* (1999); Lynda N. Shaffer, *Native Americans Before 1492: The Moundbuilding Centers of the Eastern Woodlands* (1992); Colin F. Taylor, ed., *The Native Americans: The Indigenous People of North America* (1992); David Hurst Thomas, *Exploring Ancient Native America: An Archaeological Guide* (1999); Bruce Trigger and Wilcomb Washburn, eds., *The Cambridge History of the Native Peoples of the Americas*, vol. 1: *North America* (1996).

Africa

Jacob Ade Ajayi and Michael Crowder, *History of West Africa* (1985); Paul Bohannon and Philip Curtin, *Africa and Africans* (1988); Basil Davidson, *Africa in History*, rev. ed. (1991); Philip Curtin et al., eds., *African History: From Earliest Times to Independence*, rev. ed. (1995); John Iliffe, *Africans: The History of a Continent* (1996); Robert July, *A History of the African People* (1992); Paul Lovejoy, *Transformations in Slavery: A History of Slavery in Africa* (1983); Roland Oliver and J. D. Fage, *A Short History of Africa* (1988); John Thornton, *Africa and Africans in the Making of the Atlantic World, 1400–1680* (1992).

Europe in the Age of Discovery

Christopher Allmand, *The Hundred Years' War: England and France at War, ca. 1300–ca. 1450* (1988); Fernand Braudel, *The Mediterranean and the Mediterranean World in the Age of Philip II*, 2 vols., 2d ed. (1977); Roger Chartier, ed., *A History of Private Life*, vol. 3: *Passions of the Renaissance* (1989); G. R. Elton, ed., *The Reformation* (1990); Anthony Grafton, *New Worlds, Ancient Texts: The Power of Tradition and the Shock of Discovery* (1992); Denys Hay, *Europe in the Fourteenth and Fifteenth Centuries*, 2d ed. (1989); H. G. Koenigsberger et al., *Europe in the Sixteenth Century*, 2d ed. (1989); Robert S. Lopez, *The Commercial Revolution of the Middle Ages, 950–1350* (1971); Anthony Pagden, *Lords of All the World: Ideologies of Empire in Spain, Britain and France, 1500–1800* (1995); J. R. S. Phillips, *The Medieval Expansion of Europe* (1988); Philip Ziegler, *The Black Death* (1982).

Exploration and Discovery

Emerson Baker et al., eds., *American Beginnings: Exploration, Culture, and Cartography in the Land of Norumbega* (1994); Fredi Chiappelli et al., eds., *First Images of America: The Impact of the New World on the Old*, 2 vols. (1976); Felipe Fernández-Armesto, *Before Columbus: Exploration and Colonization from the Mediterranean to the Atlantic, 1229–1492* (1987); Felipe Fernández-Armesto, *Columbus* (1991); Charles Hudson, *Knights of Spain, Warriors of the Sun: Hernando de Soto and the South's Ancient Chiefdoms* (1997); Jerald T. Milanich, *Florida Indians and the Invasion from Europe* (1995); Jerald T. Milanich and Susan Milbrath, eds., *First Encounters: Spanish Explorations in the Caribbean and the United States,*

1492–1570 (1989); Samuel Eliot Morison, *The European Discovery of America: The Northern Voyages*, A.D. 1500–1600 (1971); Samuel Eliot Morison, *The European Discovery of America: The Southern Voyages*, A.D. 1492–1616 (1974); J. H. Parry, *The Age of Reconnaissance* (1963); J. H. Parry, *The Discovery of the Sea* (1974); William and Carla Phillips, *The Worlds of Christopher Columbus* (1992); David B. Quinn, *North America from Earliest Discovery to First Settlements* (1977); Irving Rouse, *The Tainos: Rise and Decline of the People Who Greeted Columbus* (1992); P. E. Russell, *Portugal, Spain, and the African Atlantic* (1995); Kirsten Seaver, *The Frozen Echo: Greenland and the Exploration of North America, ca.* A.D. 1000–1500 (1995); Roger C. Smith, *Vanguard of Empire: Ships of Exploration in the Age of Columbus* (1993).

Early European Conquest and Settlements

Kenneth Andrews, *Trade, Plunder and Settlement: Maritime Enterprise and the Genesis of the British Empire, 1480–1630* (1984); Nancy Farriss, *Maya Society Under Colonial Rule* (1984); Charles Gibson, *Spain in America* (1966); Ross Hassig, *Mexico and the Spanish Conquest* (1994); Paul E. Hoffman, *A New Andalucia and a Way to the Orient: The American Southeast during the Sixteenth Century* (1990); Karen O. Kupperman, *Roanoke, the Abandoned Colony* (1984); Miguel León-Portilla, ed., *The Broken Spears: The Aztec Account of the Conquest of Mexico* (1992); James Lockhart, ed. and trans., *We People Here: Nahuatl Accounts of the Conquest of Mexico* (1993); James Lockhart, *The Nahuas after the Conquest: A Social and Cultural History of the Indians of Central Mexico, Sixteenth Through Eighteenth Centuries* (1992); A. J. R. Russell-Wood, *A World on the Move: The Portuguese in Africa, Asia, and America, 1415–1808* (1993); Hugh Thomas, *Conquest: Montezuma, Cortés, and the Fall of Old Mexico* (1993); David J. Weber, *The Spanish Frontier in North America* (1992).

Chapter 2

General

David Hackett Fischer, *Albion's Seed: Four British Folkways in America* (1989); Karen O. Kupperman, ed., *America in European Consciousness, 1493–1750* (1995); D. W. Meinig, *Atlantic America, 1492–1800* (1986); Gary B. Nash, *Red, White, and Black: The Peoples of Early America*, 4th ed. (2000); Mary Beth Norton, *Founding Mothers & Fathers: Gendered Power and the Forming of American Society* (1996); John E. Pomfret, *Founding the American Colonies, 1583–1660* (1970); Paula Treckel, *To Comfort the Heart: Women in Seventeenth-Century America* (1996); Alden T. Vaughan, *Roots of American Racism* (1994).

New Spain, New Netherland, New France, and the Caribbean

Karen Anderson, *Chain Her by One Foot: The Subjugation of Native Women in Seventeenth-Century New France* (1991);

Charles R. Boxer, *The Dutch Seaborne Empire, 1600–1800* (1965); Denys Delâge, *Bitter Feast: Amerindians and Europeans in Northeastern North America, 1600–64* (1993); Richard S. Dunn, *Sugar and Slaves: The Rise of the Planter Class in the English West Indies, 1624–1713* (1972); William J. Eccles, *France in America*, rev. ed. (1990); Carol Hoffecker et al., eds., *New Sweden in America* (1995); Jonathan Israel, *Dutch Primacy in World Trade, 1585–1740* (1989); Donna Merwick, *Possessing Albany, 1630–1710* (1990); Sidney Mintz, *Sweetness and Power: The Place of Sugar in Modern History* (1985); Marc Simmons, *The Last Conquistador: Juan de Oñate and the Settling of the Far Southwest* (1991); David J. Weber, *The Spanish Frontier in North America* (1992).

England

Susan Dwyer Amussen, *An Ordered Society: Gender and Class in Early Modern England* (1988); Carl Bridenbaugh, *Vexed and Troubled Englishmen, 1590–1642*, rev. ed. (1976); Patrick Collinson, *The Religion of Protestants: The Church in English Society, 1559–1625* (1982); A. G. Dickens, *The English Reformation*, 2d. ed. (1989); Ralph Houlbrooke, *The English Family, 1450–1700* (1984); Peter Laslett, *The World We Have Lost*, 3d ed. (1984); J. P. Sommerville, *Politics and Ideology in England, 1603–1640* (1986); Keith Wrightson, *English Society, 1580–1680* (1982).

Early Contact Between Europeans and Indians

James Axtell, *The Invasion Within: The Contest of Cultures in Colonial North America* (1985); Philip Barbour, *Pocahontas and Her World* (1970); Alfred Cave, *The Pequot War* (1997); William Cronon, *Changes in the Land: Indians, Colonists, and the Ecology of New England* (1983); Frederic W. Gleach, *Powhatan's World and Colonial Virginia: A Conflict of Cultures* (1997); Francis Jennings, *The Invasion of America: Indians, Colonialism, and the Cant of Conquest* (1975); Karen O. Kupperman, *Settling with the Indians: The Meeting of English and Indian Cultures in America, 1580–1640* (1980); Patrick Malone, *The Skulking Way of War: Technology and Tactics Among the Indians of New England* (1991); Kenneth Morrison, *The Embattled Northeast: The Elusive Ideal of Alliance in Abnaki-Euroamerican Relations* (1984); Daniel Richter, *The Ordeal of the Longhouse: The Peoples of the Iroquois League in the Era of European Colonization* (1992); Helen C. Rountree, *Pocahontas's People: The Powhatan Indians of Virginia Through Four Centuries* (1990); Neal Salisbury, *Manitou and Providence: Indians, Europeans, and the Making of New England, 1500–1643* (1982); Bernard Sheehan, *Savagism and Civility: Indians and Englishmen in Colonial Virginia* (1980); Timothy Silver, *A New Face on the Countryside: Indians, Colonists, and Slaves in South Atlantic Forests, 1500–1800* (1990); Alden T. Vaughan, *The New England Frontier: Puritans and Indians, 1620–1675*, rev. ed. (1979); Peter Wood et al., eds., *Powhatan's Mantle: Indians in the Colonial Southeast* (1989).

Chesapeake Society and Politics

Lois Green Carr et al., *Robert Cole's World: Agriculture and Society in Early Maryland* (1991); David Galenson, *White Servitude in Colonial America: An Economic Analysis* (1981); James Horn, *Adapting to a New World: English Society in the Seventeenth-Century Chesapeake* (1994); Ivor Noël Hume, *The Virginia Adventure: Roanoke to James Towne* (1994); A. J. Leo Lemay, *The American Dream of Captain John Smith* (1991); Gloria L. Main, *Tobacco Colony: Life in Early Maryland, 1650–1720* (1983); Edmund S. Morgan, *American Slavery, American Freedom: The Ordeal of Colonial Virginia* (1975); James Perry, *The Formation of a Society on Virginia's Eastern Shore, 1615–1655* (1990); Darrett Rutman and Anita Rutman, *A Place in Time: Middlesex County, Virginia, 1650–1750* (1984); Alden T. Vaughan, *American Genesis: Captain John Smith and the Founding of Virginia* (1975).

New England Communities, Politics, and Religion

David Grayson Allen, *In English Ways: The Movement of Societies and the Transferral of English Law and Custom to Massachusetts Bay in the 17th Century* (1981); Virginia DeJohn Anderson, *New England's Generation: The Great Migration and the Formation of Society and Culture in the 17th Century* (1991); Charles Cohen, *God's Caress: The Psychology of Puritan Religious Experience* (1986); Philip Gura, *A Glimpse of Sion's Glory: Puritan Radicalism in New England, 1620–1660* (1984); David D. Hall, *Worlds of Wonder, Days of Judgment: Popular Religious Belief in Early New England* (1989); Stephen Innes, *Creating the Commonwealth: The Economic Culture of Puritan New England* (1995); Stephen Innes, *Labor in a New Land: Economy and Society in 17th-Century Springfield* (1983); Sydney V. James, *Colonial Rhode Island* (1975); George Langdon, *Pilgrim Colony: A History of New Plymouth, 1620–1691* (1966); Kenneth A. Lockridge, *A New England Town: The First Hundred Years (Dedham, Massachusetts, 1636–1736)* (1970); John Frederick Martin, *Profits in the Wilderness: Entrepreneurship and the Founding of New England Towns in the 17th Century* (1991); Edmund S. Morgan, *The Puritan Dilemma: The Story of John Winthrop* (1958); Darrett Rutman, *Winthrop's Boston* (1965).

New England Women and Family Life

David Cressy, *Coming Over: Migration and Communication Between England and New England in the Seventeenth Century* (1987); John P. Demos, *A Little Commonwealth: Family Life in Plymouth Colony* (1970); Philip J. Greven, Jr., *Four Generations: Population, Land, and Family in Colonial Andover, Massachusetts* (1970); Lyle Koehler, *A Search for Power: The "Weaker Sex" in Seventeenth-Century New England* (1980); Edmund S. Morgan, *The Puritan Family*, rev. ed. (1966); Amanda Porterfield, *Female Piety in Puritan New England* (1992); Roger Thompson, *Sex in Middlesex: Popular Mores in a Massachusetts County, 1649–1699* (1986); Laurel Thatcher Ulrich, *Good Wives: Image and Reality in the Lives of Women in Northern New England, 1650–1750* (1982).

Chapter 3

General

Colin Calloway, *New Worlds for All: Indians, Europeans, and the Remaking of Early America* (1997); Wesley Frank Craven, *The Colonies in Transition, 1660–1713* (1968); W. J. Eccles, *France in America*, rev. ed. (1990); Jack P. Greene and J. R. Pole, eds., *Colonial British America* (1984); John J. McCusker and Russell R. Menard, *The Economy of British America, 1607–1789* (1985).

New Netherland and the Restoration Colonies

Edwin Bronner, *William Penn's "Holy Experiment": The Founding of Pennsylvania, 1681–1701* (1962); Wesley Frank Craven, *New Jersey and the English Colonization of North America* (1964); Joyce Goodfriend, *Before the Melting Pot: Society and Culture in Colonial New York City, 1664–1730* (1992); Donna Merwick, *Death of a Notary: Conquest and Change in Colonial New York* (1999); Donna Merwick, *Possessing Albany, 1630–1710: The Dutch and English Experiences* (1990); Oliver Rink, *Holland on the Hudson: An Economic and Social History of Dutch New York* (1986); Robert C. Ritchie, *The Duke's Province: A Study of Politics and Society in Colonial New York, 1660–1691* (1977); Robert M. Weir, *Colonial South Carolina: A History* (1983).

Imperial Trade and Administration

Robert M. Bliss, *Revolution and Empire: English Politics and the American Colonies in the Seventeenth Century* (1991); Lawrence W. Harper, *The English Navigation Laws: A Seventeenth-Century Experiment in Social Engineering* (1939); Marcus Rediker, *Between the Devil and the Deep Blue Sea: Merchant Seamen, Pirates, and the Anglo-American Maritime World, 1700–1750* (1987); Robert C. Ritchie, *Captain Kidd and the War Against the Pirates* (1986); I. K. Steele, *Politics of Colonial Policy: The Board of Trade in Colonial Administration* (1968); Stephen Saunders Webb, *Lord Churchill's Coup: The Anglo-American Empire and the Glorious Revolution Reconsidered* (1995); Stephen Saunders Webb, *1676: The End of American Independence* (1984); Stephen Saunders Webb, *The Governors-General: The English Army and the Definition of the Empire, 1569–1681* (1979).

Africa and the Slave Trade

Robin Blackburn, *The Making of New World Slavery: From the Baroque to the Modern, 1492–1800* (1997); Jay Coughtry, *The Notorious Triangle: Rhode Island and the African Slave Trade, 1700–1807* (1981); Philip D. Curtin, *The Atlantic Slave Trade: A Census* (1969); Joseph Inikori and Stanley Engerman, eds., *The Atlantic Slave Trade* (1992); Herbert Klein,

The Middle Passage (1978); Robin Law, *The Slave Coast of West Africa, 1550–1750: The Impact of the Atlantic Slave Trade on an African Society* (1991); Daniel C. Littlefield, *Rice and Slaves: Ethnicity and the Slave Trade in Colonial South Carolina* (1981); James Rawley, *The Transatlantic Slave Trade: A History* (1981); Barbara Solow, ed., *Slavery and the Rise of the Atlantic System* (1991).

Africans in America

Ira Berlin, *Many Thousands Gone: The First Two Centuries of Slavery in North America* (1998); T. H. Breen and Stephen Innes, *"Myne Owne Ground": Race and Freedom on Virginia's Eastern Shore, 1640–1676* (1980); Douglas Deal, *Race and Class in Colonial Virginia: Indians, Englishmen, and Africans on the Eastern Shore During the Seventeenth Century* (1993); Michael A. Gomez, *Exchanging Our Country Marks: The Transformation of African Identities in the Colonial and Antebellum South* (1998); Graham R. Hodges, *Root & Branch: African Americans in New York and East Jersey, 1613–1863* (1999); Allan Kulikoff, *Tobacco and Slaves: The Development of Southern Cultures in the Chesapeake, 1680–1800* (1986); Jane Landers, *Black Society in Spanish Florida* (1999); Edgar J. McManus, *Black Bondage in the North* (1973); Edmund S. Morgan, *American Slavery, American Freedom: The Ordeal of Colonial Virginia* (1975); Lorena S. Walsh, *From Calabar to Carter's Grove: The History of a Virginia Slave Community* (1997); Betty Wood, *The Origins of American Slavery* (1997); Peter H. Wood, *Black Majority: Negroes in Colonial South Carolina from 1670 Through the Stono Rebellion* (1974).

European–Native American Relations in the North

Russell Bourne, *The Red King's Rebellion: Racial Politics in New England, 1675–1678* (1991); John Demos, *The Unredeemed Captive: A Family Story from Early America* (1994); Matthew Dennis, *Cultivating a Landscape of Peace: Iroquois-European Encounter in Seventeenth-Century America* (1993); Francis Jennings, *The Ambiguous Iroquois Empire* (1984); Jill Lepore, *The Name of War: King Philip's War and the Origins of American Identity* (1998); Peter Mancall, *Deadly Medicine: Indians and Alcohol in Early America* (1995); Michael Puglisi, *Puritans Beseiged: The Legacies of King Philip's War in the Massachusetts Bay Colony* (1991); Daniel Richter, *The Ordeal of the Longhouse: The Peoples of the Iroquois League in the Era of European Colonization* (1992); Daniel Richter and James Merrell, eds., *Beyond the Covenant Chain: The Iroquois and Their Neighbors in Indian America, 1600–1800* (1987); Richard White, *The Middle Ground: Indians, Empires, and Republics in the Great Lakes Region, 1650–1815* (1991).

European–Native American Relations in the South and West

David H. Corkran, *The Creek Frontier, 1540–1783* (1967); Verner W. Crane, *The Southern Frontier, 1660–1732* (1929);

Carl Ekberg, *French Roots in the Illinois Country: The Mississippi Frontier in Colonial Times* (1998); Ramón Gutiérrez, *When Jesus Came, the Corn Mothers Went Away: Marriage, Sexuality, and Power in New Mexico, 1500–1846* (1991); Elizabeth A. H. John, *Storms Brewed in Other Men's Worlds: The Confrontation of Indians, Spanish, and French in the Southwest, 1540–1795* (1975); Andrew Knaut, *The Pueblo Revolt of 1680* (1995); James Merrell, *The Indians' New World: Catawbas and Their Neighbors from European Contact through the Era of Removal* (1989); Daniel H. Usner, Jr., *Indians, Settlers, and Slaves in a Frontier Exchange Economy: The Lower Mississippi Valley before 1783* (1992).

Colonial Politics

Patricia U. Bonomi, *The Lord Cornbury Scandal: The Politics of Reputation in British America* (1998); Lois Green Carr and David W. Jordan, *Maryland's Revolution of Government, 1689–1692* (1974); Richard P. Johnson, *Adjustment to Empire: The New England Colonies, 1675–1715* (1981); David S. Lovejoy, *The Glorious Revolution in America* (1972); Jack M. Sosin, *English America and Imperial Inconstancy: The Rise of Provincial Autonomy, 1696–1715* (1985); Jack M. Sosin, *English America and the Restoration Monarchy of Charles II* (1980); Jack M. Sosin, *English America and the Revolution of 1688* (1982).

New England

Bernard Bailyn, *The New England Merchants in the Seventeenth Century* (1955); Richard Bushman, *From Puritan to Yankee: Character and the Social Order in Connecticut, 1690–1765* (1967); Christine Heyrman, *Commerce and Culture: The Maritime Communities of Colonial Massachusetts, 1690–1750* (1984); Richard Melvoin, *New England Outpost: War and Society in Colonial Deerfield* (1990); Amanda Porterfield, *Female Piety in Puritan New England* (1991); Laurel Thatcher Ulrich, *Good Wives: Image and Reality in the Lives of Women in Northern New England, 1650–1750* (1982).

New England Witchcraft

Paul Boyer and Stephen Nissenbaum, *Salem Possessed: The Social Origins of Witchcraft* (1974); Elaine Breslaw, *Tituba, Reluctant Witch of Salem: Devilish Indians and Puritan Fantasies* (1996); John Demos, *Entertaining Satan: Witchcraft and the Culture of Early New England* (1982); Richard Godbeer, *The Devil's Dominion: Magic and Religion in Early New England* (1992); Peter Hoffer, *The Devil's Disciples: Makers of the Salem Witchcraft Trials* (1996); Carol Karlsen, *The Devil in the Shape of a Woman: Witchcraft in Early New England* (1987); Bernard Rosenthal, *Salem Story: Reading the Witch Trials of 1692* (1993); Richard Weisman, *Witchcraft, Magic, and Religion in 17th-Century Massachusetts* (1984).

Chapter 4

General

Carol R. Berkin, *First Generations: Women in Colonial America* (1996); Jack P. Greene, *Pursuits of Happiness: The Social Development of the Early Modern British Colonies and the Formation of American Culture* (1988); Richard Hofstadter, *America at 1750: A Social Portrait* (1971); Peter C. Mancall, *Deadly Medicine: Indians and Alcohol in Early America* (1995); D. W. Meinig, *Atlantic America, 1492–1800* (1986); Stephanie G. Wolf, *As Various as Their Land: The Everyday Lives of 18th Century Americans* (1992).

New France and New Spain

Ramón Gutiérrez, *When Jesus Came, the Corn Mothers Went Away: Marriage, Sexuality, and Power in New Mexico, 1500–1846* (1991); Gwendolyn Midlo Hall, *Africans in Colonial Louisiana: The Development of Afro-Creole Culture in the Eighteenth Century* (1992); Dale Miquelon, *New France, 1701–1744* (1987); G. F. G. Stanley, *New France, 1744–1760* (1968); Daniel H. Usner, Jr., *Indians, Settlers, and Slaves in a Frontier Exchange Economy: The Lower Mississippi Valley Before 1783* (1992); David J. Weber, *The Spanish Frontier in North America* (1992); Richard White, *The Middle Ground: Indians, Empires, and Republics in the Great Lakes Region, 1650–1815* (1991).

Anglo-American Society

T. H. Breen, *Tobacco Culture* (1985); Carl Bridenbaugh, *Cities in Revolt: Urban Life in America, 1743–1776* (1955); Lois Green Carr et al., eds., *Colonial Chesapeake Society* (1988); David Conroy, *In Public Houses: Drink and the Revolution of Authority in Colonial Massachusetts* (1995); Rhys Isaac, *The Transformation of Virginia, 1740–1790* (1982); Christopher Jedrey, *The World of John Cleaveland: Family and Community in Eighteenth-Century New England* (1979); Sung Bok Kim, *Landlord and Tenant in Colonial New York: Manorial Society, 1664–1775* (1978); Peter C. Mancall, *Valley of Opportunity: Economic Culture Along the Upper Susquehanna, 1700–1800* (1991); Gary B. Nash, *The Urban Crucible: Social Change, Political Consciousness, and the Origins of the American Revolution* (1979); Michael Rozbicki, *The Complete Colonial Gentleman: Cultural Legitimacy in Plantation America* (1998); David S. Shields, *Civil Tongues and Polite Letters in British America* (1997); Michael Zuckerman, *Peaceable Kingdoms: New England Towns in the Eighteenth Century* (1970).

American Economic Development

Richard Bushman, *The Refinement of America: Persons, Houses, Cities* (1992); Cary Carson et al., eds., *Of Consuming Interests: The Style of Life in the Eighteenth Century* (1994); Marc Egnal, *New World Economies: The Growth of the Thirteen Colonies and Early Canada* (1999); David Hancock, *Citizens of the World: London Merchants and the Integration of the British Atlantic Community, 1735–1785* (1995); Stephen Innes, ed., *Work and Labor in Early America* (1988); Alice Hanson Jones, *Wealth of a Nation to Be: The American Colonies on the Eve of the Revolution* (1980); Cathy Matson, *Merchants and Empire: Trading in Colonial New York* (1998); John J. McCusker and Russell R. Menard, *The Economy of British America, 1607–1789* (1985); Margaret E. Newell, *From Dependency to Independence: Economic Revolution in Colonial New England* (1998); Edwin J. Perkins, *The Economy of Colonial America* (1980); Gary M. Walton and James F. Shepherd, *The Economic Rise of Early America* (1979).

Anglo-American Politics

Bernard Bailyn, *The Origins of American Politics* (1968); Patricia U. Bonomi, *A Factious People: Politics and Society in Colonial New York* (1971); Richard Bushman, *King and People in Provincial Massachusetts* (1985); Edward M. Cook, Jr., *The Fathers of the Towns: Leadership and Community Structure in Eighteenth-Century New England* (1976); Jack P. Greene, *The Quest for Power: The Lower Houses of Assembly in the Southern Royal Colonies, 1689–1776* (1963); John Gilman Kolp, *Gentleman and Freeholders: Electoral Politics in Colonial Virginia* (1998).

Immigration to British America

Bernard Bailyn, *The Peopling of British North America* (1986); Bernard Bailyn, *Voyagers to the West* (1986); Bernard Bailyn and Philip Morgan, eds., *Strangers Within the Realm* (1991); Marilyn Baseler, *"Asylum for Mankind": America 1607–1800* (1998); Jon Butler, *The Huguenots in America* (1983); R. J. Dickson, *Ulster Immigration to Colonial America, 1718–1775* (1966); David Dobson, *Scottish Immigration to Colonial America, 1607–1785* (1994); A. Roger Ekirch, *Bound for America: The Transportation of British Convicts to the Colonies, 1718–1775* (1987); Colin Kidd, *British Identities before Nationalism: Ethnicity and Nationhood in the British Atlantic World, 1600–1800* (1999); Ned Landsman, *Scotland and Its First American Colony* (1985); A. G. Roeber, *Palatines, Liberty, and Property: German Lutherans in Colonial British America* (1993); Marianne Wokeck, *Trade in Strangers: The Beginnings of Mass Migration to North America* (1999).

African Americans

Ira Berlin, *Many Thousands Gone: The First Two Centuries of Slavery in North America* (1998); Ira Berlin and Philip Morgan, eds., *Cultivation and Culture: Labor and the Shaping of Slave Life in the Americas* (1993); Thomas J. Davis, *A Rumor of Revolt: The "Great Negro Plot" in Colonial New York* (1985); Michael A. Gomez, *Exchanging Our Country Marks: The Transformation of African Identities in the Colonial and Ante-*

bellum South (1998); Graham R. Hodges, *Root & Branch: African Americans in New York and East Jersey, 1613–1863* (1999); Marvin L. Michael Kay and Lorin Lee Cary, *Slavery in North Carolina, 1748–1775* (1995); Allan Kulikoff, *Tobacco and Slaves: The Development of Southern Cultures in the Chesapeake, 1680–1800* (1986); Philip D. Morgan, *Slave Counterpoint: Black Culture in the Eighteenth-Century Chesapeake and Low Country* (1998); Gerald [Michael] Mullin, *Flight and Rebellion: Slave Resistance in Eighteenth-Century Virginia* (1972); Michael Mullin, *Africa in America: Slave Acculturation and Resistance in the American South and the British Caribbean, 1736–1834* (1992); William Pierson, *Black Yankees: The Development of an Afro-American Subculture in Eighteenth-Century New England* (1988); Mechal Sobel, *The World They Made Together: Black and White Values in Eighteenth-Century Virginia* (1987); Betty Wood, *Women's Work, Men's Work: The Informal Slave Economies of Low Country Georgia* (1995); Anne Yentsch, *A Chesapeake Family and Their Slaves* (1994).

Anglo-American Women, Men, and Families

Kathleen M. Brown, *Good Wives, Nasty Wenches, and Anxious Patriarchs: Gender, Race, and Power in Colonial Virginia* (1996); Cornelia Hughes Dayton, *Women Before the Bar: Gender, Law, and Society in Connecticut, 1639–1789* (1995); Philip J. Greven, *The Protestant Temperament: Patterns of Child-Rearing, Religious Experience, and the Self in Early America* (1977); Joan Gundersen, *To Be Useful to the World: Women in Eighteenth-Century America* (1996); Barry J. Levy, *Quakers and the American Family* (1988); June Namias, *White Captives: Gender and Ethnicity on the American Frontier* (1993); Marylynn Salmon, *Women and the Law of Property in Early America* (1986); Daniel Blake Smith, *Inside the Great House: Planter Family Life in Eighteenth-Century Chesapeake Society* (1980); Merril D. Smith, *Breaking the Bonds: Marital Discord in Pennsylvania, 1730–1830* (1992); Lisa Wilson, *Ye Heart of a Man: The Domestic Life of Men in Colonial New England* (1999).

Anglo-American Education, Science, and the Enlightenment

Patricia Cline Cohen, *A Calculating People: The Spread of Numeracy in Early America* (1982); Lawrence A. Cremin, *American Education: The Colonial Experience, 1607–1783* (1970); Richard Beale Davis, *Intellectual Life in the Colonial South, 1585–1763* (1978); Brooke Hindle, *The Pursuit of Science in Revolutionary America* (1956); Kenneth Lockridge, *Literacy in Colonial New England* (1974); Henry F. May, *The Enlightenment in America* (1976); Amy R. W. Meyers and Margaret Beck Pritchard, eds., *Nature's Empire: Mark Catesby's New World Vision* (1998); Thomas P. Slaughter, *The Natures of John and William Bartram* (1996); William Sloan and Julie Williams, *The Early American Press, 1690–1783* (1994); Raymond P. Stearns, *Science in the British Colonies of America* (1970).

Religion and the Great Awakening

Catherine Brekus, *Strangers and Pilgrims: Female Preaching in America, 1740–1845* (1998); Patricia U. Bonomi, *Under the Cope of Heaven: Religion, Society, and Politics in Colonial America* (1986); J. M. Bumstead and John E. Van de Wetering, *What Must I Do to Be Saved? The Great Awakening in Colonial America* (1976); Jon Butler, *Awash in a Sea of Faith: Christianizing the American People* (1990); Michael Crawford, *Seasons of Grace: Colonial New England's Revival Tradition in Its British Context* (1991); Alan E. Heimert, *Religion and the American Mind: From the Great Awakening to the Revolution* (1966); Frank Lambert, *Inventing the "Great Awakening"* (1999); David S. Lovejoy, *Religious Enthusiasm in the New World* (1985); Harry S. Stout, *The Divine Dramatist: George Whitefield and the Rise of Modern Evangelicalism* (1991); Patricia Tracy, *Jonathan Edwards, Pastor* (1980).

Chapter 5

General

Ian R. Christie and Benjamin W. Labaree, *Empire or Independence, 1760–1776: A British-American Dialogue on the Coming of the American Revolution* (1976); Barbara DeWolfe, ed., *Discoveries of America: Personal Accounts of British Emigrants to North America during the Revolutionary Era* (1997); Marc Egnal, *A Mighty Empire: The Origins of the American Revolution* (1988); Merrill Jensen, *The Founding of a Nation: A History of the American Revolution, 1763–1776* (1968); John Phillip Reid, *The Constitutional History of the American Revolution* (1995); Robert W. Tucker and David C. Hendrickson, *The Fall of the First British Empire: Origins of the War of American Independence* (1982).

Colonial Warfare and the British Empire

Fred Anderson, *A People's Army: Massachusetts Soldiers and Society in the Seven Years' War* (1984); Frank W. Brecher, *Losing a Continent: France's North American Policy, 1753–1763* (1998); Lawrence Henry Gipson, *The British Empire Before the American Revolution* (1936–1970); Douglas Leach, *Roots of Conflict: British Armed Forces and Colonial Americans, 1677–1763* (1986); Robert C. Newbold, *The Albany Congress and Plan of Union of 1754* (1955); William Pencak, *War, Politics, and Revolution in Provincial Massachusetts* (1981); Alan Rogers, *Empire and Liberty: American Resistance to British Authority, 1755–1763* (1974); John Shy, *Toward Lexington: The Role of the British Army in the Coming of the American Revolution* (1965); Ian K. Steele, *Warpaths: Invasions of North America* (1994); James Titus, *The Old Dominion at War: Society, Politics, and Warfare in Late Colonial Virginia* (1991).

British Politics and Policy

Colin Bonwick, *English Radicals and the American Revolution* (1977); James E. Bradley, *Popular Politics and the American*

Revolution in England (1986); John Brewer, *Party Ideology and Popular Politics at the Accession of George III* (1976); John Brooke, *King George III* (1972); John L. Bullion, *A Great and Necessary Measure: George Grenville and the Genesis of the Stamp Act, 1763–1765* (1981); Michael Kammen, *A Rope of Sand: The Colonial Agents, British Politics, and the American Revolution* (1968); Nancy F. Koehn, *The Power of Commerce: Economy and Governance in the First British Empire* (1994); P. D. G. Thomas, *Tea Party to Independence* (1991); P. D. G. Thomas, *The Townshend Duties Crisis* (1987); P. D. G. Thomas, *British Politics and the Stamp Act Crisis* (1975).

Native Americans and the West

Richard Aquila, *The Iroquois Restoration: Iroquois Diplomacy on the Colonial Frontier, 1701–1754* (1983); Andrew Cayton and Fredrika Teute, eds., *Contact Points: American Frontiers from the Mohawk Valley to the Mississippi, 1750–1830* (1998); David H. Corkran, *The Cherokee Frontier: Conflict and Survival, 1740–1762* (1962); Gregory Dowd, *A Spirited Resistance: The North American Indian Struggle for Unity, 1745–1815* (1992); Tom Hatley, *The Dividing Paths: Cherokees and South Carolinians through the Revolutionary Era* (1995); Francis Jennings, *Empire of Fortune: Crowns, Colonies and Tribes in the Seven Years' War in America* (1988); Howard H. Peckham, *Pontiac and the Indian Uprising* (1947); Jack M. Sosin, *Whitehall and the Wilderness: The Middle West in British Colonial Policy, 1760–1775* (1961); Richard White, *The Middle Ground: Indians, Empires and Republics in the Great Lakes Region, 1650–1815* (1991).

Political and Economic Thought

Bernard Bailyn, *The Ideological Origins of the American Revolution* (1967); J. C. D. Clark, *The Language of Liberty, 1660–1832: Political Discourse and Social Dynamics in the Anglo-American World* (1994); J. E. Crowley, *This Sheba, Self: The Conceptualization of Economic Life in Eighteenth-Century America* (1974); Jay Fliegelman, *Prodigals and Pilgrims: The American Revolution Against Patriarchal Authority, 1750–1800* (1982).

American Resistance

T. H. Breen, *Tobacco Culture: The Mentality of the Great Tidewater Planters on the Eve of the Revolution* (1985); Joseph Albert Ernst, *Money and Politics in America, 1755–1775: A Study in the Currency Act of 1764 and the Political Economy of Revolution* (1973); David Conroy, *Drink and the Revolution of Authority in Colonial Massachusetts* (1995); Dirk Hoerder, *Crowd Action in Revolutionary Massachusetts, 1765–1780* (1977); Woody Holton, *Forced Founders: Indians, Debtors, Slaves, and the Making of the American Revolution in Virginia* (1999); Benjamin W. Labaree, *The Boston Tea Party* (1964); Pauline R. Maier, *The Old Revolutionaries: Political Lives in the Age of Samuel Adams* (1980); Pauline R. Maier, *From Resistance to Revolution: Colonial Radicals and the Development of American*

Opposition to Britain, 1765–1776 (1972); Edmund S. Morgan and Helen M. Morgan, *The Stamp Act Crisis: Prologue to Revolution* (1953); Gary B. Nash, *The Urban Crucible: Social Change, Political Consciousness, and the Origins of the American Revolution* (1979); Bruce A. Ragsdale, *A Planters' Republic: The Search for Economic Independence in Revolutionary Virginia* (1996); Richard Ryerson, *The Revolution Has Now Begun: The Radical Committees of Philadelphia, 1765–1776* (1978); Peter Shaw, *American Patriots and the Rituals of Revolution* (1981); Peter Thompson, *Rum Punch & Revolution: Taverngoing & Public Life in Eighteenth-Century Philadelphia* (1999); Joseph Tiedemann, *Reluctant Revolutionaries: New York City and the Road to Independence, 1763–1776* (1997); John W. Tyler, *Smugglers and Patriots: Boston Merchants and the Advent of the American Revolution* (1986); Richard Walsh, *Charleston's Sons of Liberty: A Study of the Artisans, 1763–1789* (1959); Hiller B. Zobel, *The Boston Massacre* (1970).

Chapter 6

General

Benson Bobrick, *Angel in the Whirlwind: The Triumph of the American Revolution* (1997); Colin Bonwick, *The American Revolution* (1991); Edward Countryman, *The American Revolution* (1985); Theodore Draper, *A Struggle for Power: The American Revolution* (1996); Robert Middlekauff, *The Glorious Cause: The American Revolution, 1763–1783* (1982); Harry M. Ward, *The American Revolution: Nationhood Achieved, 1763–1788* (1995); Alfred F. Young, ed., *Beyond the American Revolution* (1993); Alfred F. Young, ed., *The American Revolution: Explorations in the History of American Radicalism* (1976).

Continental Congress, Committees, and the Declaration of Independence

David Ammerman, *In the Common Cause: American Response to the Coercive Acts of 1774* (1974); Richard D. Brown, *Revolutionary Politics in Massachusetts: The Boston Committee of Correspondence and the Towns, 1772–1774* (1970); Jay Fliegelman, *Declaring Independence: Jefferson, Natural Language, & the Culture of Performance* (1993); Pauline Maier, *American Scripture: Making the Declaration of Independence* (1997); Jerrilyn Marston, *King and Congress: The Transfer of Political Legitimacy, 1774–1776* (1987); Garry Wills, *Inventing America: Jefferson's Declaration of Independence* (1978); Ann Withington, *Toward a More Perfect Union: Virtue and the Formation of American Republics* (1992).

Military Affairs

Jeremy Black, *War for America: The Fight for Independence, 1775–1783* (1991); Richard Buel, *In Irons: Britain's Naval Supremacy and the American Revolutionary Economy* (1999); E. Wayne Carp, *To Starve the Army at Pleasure: Continental Army Administration and American Political Culture, 1775–*

1783 (1984); Stephen Conway, *The War of American Independence, 1775–1783* (1995); Don Higginbotham, *The War of American Independence: Military Attitudes, Policies, and Practice, 1763–1789* (1971); Ronald Hoffman and Peter Albert, eds., *Arms and Independence: The Military Character of the American Revolution* (1984); Richard Ketchum, *Saratoga: Turning Point of America's Revolutionary War* (1997); Piers Mackesy, *The War for America, 1775–1783* (1964); James K. Martin, *Benedict Arnold, Revolutionary Hero* (1997); James K. Martin and Mark Lender, *"A Respectable Army": The Military Origins of the Republic, 1763–1789* (1982); Charles Niemeyer, *America Goes to War: A Social History of the Continental Army* (1997); Charles Royster, *A Revolutionary People at War: The Continental Army and American Character, 1775–1783* (1980); John Shy, *A People Numerous and Armed: Reflections on the Military Struggle for American Independence,* rev. ed. (1990).

Local and Regional Studies

Michael Bellesiles, *Revolutionary Outlaws: Ethan Allen and the Struggle for Independence on the Early American Frontier* (1993); Richard Buel, *Dear Liberty: Connecticut's Mobilization for the Revolutionary War* (1980); Edward Countryman, *A People in Revolution: The American Revolution and Political Society in New York, 1760–1790* (1981); Elaine Crane, *A Dependent People: Newport, Rhode Island, in the Revolutionary Era* (1985); Jeffrey Crow and Larry Tise, eds., *The Southern Experience in the American Revolution* (1978); Thomas Doerflinger, *A Vigorous Spirit of Enterprise: Merchants and Economic Development in Revolutionary Philadelphia* (1986); John Mack Faragher, *Daniel Boone* (1992); David Hackett Fischer, *Paul Revere's Ride* (1994); Craig T. Friend, ed., *The Buzzel about Kentuck: Settling the Promised Land* (1999); Robert A. Gross, *The Minutemen and Their World* (1976); Ronald Hoffman, *A Spirit of Dissension: Economics, Politics, and the Revolution in Maryland* (1973); Ronald Hoffman, Thad W. Tate, and Peter Albert, eds., *An Uncivil War: The Southern Backcountry During the American Revolution* (1985); Jean B. Lee, *The Price of Nationhood: The American Revolution in Charles County* (1994); Stephen Rosswurm, *Arms, Country, and Class: The Philadelphia Militia and the "Lower Sort" During the American Revolution* (1988); John Selby, *The Revolution in Virginia, 1775–1783* (1988).

Indians and African Americans

Colin Calloway, *The American Revolution in Indian Country* (1995); Sylvia Frey, *Water from the Rock: Black Resistance in a Revolutionary Age* (1991); Barbara Graymont, *The Iroquois in the American Revolution* (1972); Isabel T. Kelsey, *Joseph Brant, 1743–1807: Man of Two Worlds* (1984); James H. O'Donnell III, *Southern Indians in the American Revolution* (1973); Anthony F. C. Wallace, *The Death and Rebirth of the Seneca* (1969).

Loyalists

Bernard Bailyn, *The Ordeal of Thomas Hutchinson* (1974); Robert McCluer Calhoon, *The Loyalists in Revolutionary America, 1760–1781* (1973); Mary Beth Norton, *The British-Americans: The Loyalist Exiles in England, 1774–1789* (1972); Janice Potter, *The Liberty We Seek: Loyalist Ideology in Colonial New York and Massachusetts* (1983); Paul H. Smith, *Loyalists and Redcoats: A Study in British Revolutionary Policy* (1964); James W. St. G. Walker, *The Black Loyalists: The Search for a Promised Land in Nova Scotia and Sierra Leone, 1783–1870* (1976).

Women

Richard Buel and Joy Buel, *The Way of Duty: A Woman and Her Family in Revolutionary America* (1984); Ronald Hoffman and Peter Albert, eds., *Women in the Age of the American Revolution* (1989); Linda K. Kerber, *Women of the Republic: Intellect and Ideology in Revolutionary America* (1980); Holly Mayer, *Belonging to the Army: Camp Followers and Community during the American Revolution* (1996); Mary Beth Norton, *Liberty's Daughters: The Revolutionary Experience of American Women, 1750–1800* (1980).

Foreign Policy

Jonathan Dull, *A Diplomatic History of the American Revolution* (1985); Ronald Hoffman and Peter Albert, eds., *Peace and the Peacemakers: The Treaty of 1783* (1986); Ronald Hoffman and Peter Albert, eds., *Diplomacy and Revolution: The Franco-American Alliance of 1778* (1981); Lawrence Kaplan, ed., *The American Revolution and a "Candid World"* (1977); Jan Willem Schulte Nordholt, *The Dutch Republic and American Independence* (1982); Richard W. Van Alstyne, *Empire and Independence: The International History of the American Revolution* (1965).

Patriot Leaders

Fawn M. Brodie, *Thomas Jefferson: An Intimate History* (1974); Richard Brookhiser, *Founding Father: Rediscovering George Washington* (1996); Joseph Ellis, *American Sphinx: The Character of Thomas Jefferson* (1997); John E. Ferling, *The First of Men: A Life of George Washington* (1988); Eric Foner, *Tom Paine and Revolutionary America* (1976); Norman Risjord, *Thomas Jefferson* (1994); John Rhodehamel, *The Great Experiment: George Washington and the American Republic* (1998); Charles Royster, *Light-Horse Harry Lee and the Legacy of the American Revolution* (1981); Peter Shaw, *The Character of John Adams* (1976); Sheila Skemp, *Benjamin and William Franklin: Father and Son, Patriot and Loyalist* (1994); Esmond Wright, *Franklin of Philadelphia* (1986).

Chapter 7

General

Richard Beeman et al., eds., *Beyond Confederation: Origins of the Constitution and American National Identity* (1987); Andrew Burstein, *Sentimental Democracy: The Evolution of America's Romantic Self-Image* (1999); John E. Crowley, *The Privileges of Independence: Neomercantilism and the American Revolution* (1993); Ronald Hoffman et al., eds., *The Economy of Early America: The Revolutionary Period, 1763–1790* (1988); Ronald Hoffman and Peter Albert, eds., *The Transforming Hand of Revolution: Reconsidering the American Revolution as a Social Movement* (1995); Mark E. Kann, *A Republic of Men: The American Founders, Gendered Language, and Patriarchal Politics* (1998); Cathy Matson and Peter S. Onuf, *A Union of Interests: Political and Economic Thought in Revolutionary America* (1990); Forrest McDonald, *Novus Ordo Seclorum: The Intellectual Origins of the Constitution* (1985); Edmund S. Morgan, *Inventing the People: The Rise of Popular Sovereignty in England and America* (1988); David Waldstreicher, *In the Midst of Perpetual Fetes: The Making of American Nationalism, 1776–1820* (1997); Gordon S. Wood, *The Radicalism of the American Revolution* (1992); Gordon S. Wood, *The Creation of the American Republic, 1776–1787* (1969); Alfred F. Young et al., eds., *We the People: Voices and Images of the New Nation* (1993); Rosemarie Zagarri, *The Politics of Size: Representation in the United States, 1776–1850* (1988).

Continental Congress and Articles of Confederation

E. James Ferguson, *The Power of the Purse: A History of American Public Finance, 1776–1790* (1961); H. James Henderson, *Party Politics in the Continental Congress* (1974); Merrill Jensen, *The New Nation: A History of the United States During the Confederation, 1781–1789* (1950); Richard B. Morris, *The Forging of the Union, 1781–1789* (1987); Peter S. Onuf, *Statehood and Union: A History of the Northwest Ordinance* (1987); Jack N. Rakove, *The Beginnings of National Politics: An Interpretive History of the Continental Congress* (1979).

State Politics

Willi Paul Adams, *The First American Constitutions: Republican Ideology and the Making of the State Constitutions in the Revolutionary Era* (1980); Robert Gross, ed., *In Debt to Shays* (1992); Ronald Hoffman and Peter Albert, eds., *Sovereign States in an Age of Uncertainty* (1981); Donald Lutz, *Popular Consent and Popular Control: Whig Political Theory in the Early State Constitutions* (1980); Jackson Turner Main, *Political Parties Before the Constitution* (1973); Jackson Turner Main, *The Sovereign States, 1775–1783* (1973); David P. Szatmary, *Shays' Rebellion: The Making of an Agrarian Insurrection* (1980).

The Constitution

Thornton Anderson, *Creating the Constitution: The Convention of 1787 and the First Congress* (1993); Lance Banning, *The Sacred Fire of Liberty: James Madison and the Founding of the Federal Republic* (1995); Roger H. Brown, *Redeeming the Republic: Federalists, Taxation, and the Origins of the Constitution* (1993); Saul Cornell, *Anti-Federalism & the Dissenting Tradition in America, 1788-1828* (1999); Christopher Duncan, *The Anti-Federalists and Early American Political Thought* (1995); Jackson Turner Main, *The Anti-Federalists: Critics of the Constitution, 1781–1788* (1961); Frederick W. Marks III, *Independence on Trial: Foreign Affairs and the Making of the Constitution* (1973); Jack N. Rakove, *Original Meanings: Politics and Ideas in the Making of the Constitution* (1996); Robert A. Rutland, *The Ordeal of the Constitution: The Antifederalists and the Ratification Struggle of 1787–88* (1966); Abraham Sofaer, *War, Foreign Affairs, and Constitutional Power,* vol. 1: *The Origins* (1976).

Education and Culture

Cathy N. Davidson, *Revolution and the Word: The Rise of the Novel in America* (1987); Joseph M. Ellis, *After the Revolution: Profiles of Early American Culture* (1979); Carl F. Kaestle, *Pillars of the Republic: Common Schools and American Society, 1780–1860* (1983); Russel B. Nye, *The Cultural Life of the New Nation, 1776–1803* (1960); Kenneth Silverman, *A Cultural History of the American Revolution* (1976).

Women

Edith Gelles, *Portia: The World of Abigail Adams* (1992); Ronald Hoffman and Peter Albert, eds., *Women in the Age of the American Revolution* (1989); Susan Juster, *Disorderly Women: Sexual Politics and Evangelicalism in Revolutionary New England* (1994); Linda K. Kerber, *Women of the Republic: Intellect and Ideology in Revolutionary America* (1980); Mary Beth Norton, *Liberty's Daughters: The Revolutionary Experience of American Women, 1750–1800* (1980); Sheila Skemp, *Judith Sargent Murray* (1998); Rosemarie Zagarri, *A Woman's Dilemma: Mercy Otis Warren and the American Revolution* (1995).

African Americans and Slavery

Ira Berlin, *Many Thousands Gone: The First Two Centuries of Slavery in North America* (1998); Ira Berlin and Ronald Hoffman, eds., *Slavery and Freedom in the Age of the American Revolution* (1983); Patricia Bradley, *Slavery, Propaganda, and the American Revolution* (1998); David Brion Davis, *The Problem of Slavery in the Age of Revolution, 1770–1823* (1975); Paul Finkelman, *Slavery and the Founders: Race and Liberty in the Age of Jefferson* (1996); Carol V. R. George, *Segregated Sabbaths: Richard Allen and the Emergence of Independent Black*

Churches, 1760–1840 (1973); Michael A. Gomez, *Exchanging Our Country Marks: The Transformation of African Identities in the Colonial and Antebellum South* (1998); Graham R. Hodges, *Root & Branch: African Americans in New York and East Jersey, 1613–1863* (1999); Winthrop Jordan, *White over Black: American Attitudes Toward the Negro, 1550–1812* (1968); Duncan J. Macleod, *Slavery, Race, and the American Revolution* (1974); Gary Nash, *Forging Freedom: The Formation of Philadelphia's Black Community, 1720–1840* (1988); Donald L. Robinson, *Slavery in the Structure of American Politics, 1765–1820* (1971); Shane White, *Somewhat More Independent: The End of Slavery in New York City, 1770–1810* (1991); Arthur Zilversmit, *The First Emancipation: The Abolition of Slavery in the North* (1967).

Indians

Harvey L. Carter, *The Life and Times of Little Turtle* (1987); Gregory E. Dowd, *A Spirited Resistance: The North American Indian Struggle for Unity, 1745–1815* (1992); Dorothy Jones, *License for Empire: Colonialism by Treaty in Early America* (1982); Wiley Sword, *President Washington's Indian War: The Struggle for the Old Northwest, 1790–1795* (1985); Anthony F. C. Wallace, *The Death and Rebirth of the Seneca* (1969); Richard White, *The Middle Ground: Indians, Empires, and Republics in the Great Lakes Region, 1650–1815* (1991).

Chapter 8

National Government and Administration

Kenneth Bowling, *The Creation of Washington, D.C.* (1991); Ralph Adams Brown, *The Presidency of John Adams* (1975); William Casto, *The Supreme Court in the Early Republic: The Chief Justiceships of John Jay and Oliver Ellsworth* (1995); Stanley Elkins and Eric McKitrick, *The Age of Federalism, 1788–1800* (1993); Morton Frisch, *Alexander Hamilton and the Political Order* (1991); Ronald Hoffman and Peter J. Albert, eds., *Launching the "Extended Republic": The Federalist Era* (1998); Richard Kohn, *Eagle and Sword: The Federalists and the Creation of the Military Establishment in America, 1783–1802* (1975); Tadahisa Kuroda, *The Origins of the Twelfth Amendment: The Electoral College in the Early Republic, 1787–1804* (1994); Forrest McDonald, *Alexander Hamilton* (1979); Forrest McDonald, *The Presidency of George Washington* (1974); John R. Nelson, Jr., *Liberty and Property: Political Economy and Policymaking in the New Nation, 1789–1812* (1987); James R. Sharp, *American Politics in the Early Republic: The New Nation in Crisis* (1993); Garry Wills, *Cincinnatus: George Washington and the Enlightenment* (1984).

Partisan Politics

Lance Banning, *The Jeffersonian Persuasion: Evolution of a Party Ideology* (1978); Richard Buel, *Securing the Revolution: Ideology in American Politics, 1789–1815* (1972); Joseph Charles, *The Origins of the American Party System* (1956); Noble E. Cunningham, *The Jeffersonian Republicans: The Formation of Party Organization, 1789–1801* (1957); Manning J. Dauer, *The Adams Federalists* (1953); Richard Hofstadter, *The Idea of a Party System: The Rise of Legitimate Opposition in the United States, 1780–1840* (1970); Thomas Slaughter, *The Whiskey Rebellion* (1986); John Zvesper, *Political Philosophy and Rhetoric: A Study of the Origins of American Party Politics* (1977).

Economics in Thought and Practice

Joyce Appleby, *Capitalism and a New Social Order: The Republican Vision of the 1790s* (1984); Christopher Clark, *The Roots of Rural Capitalism: Western Massachusetts, 1780–1860* (1990); Paul Gilje, ed., *Wages of Independence: Capitalism in the Early American Republic* (1997); James A. Henretta, *The Origins of American Capitalism* (1991); Allan Kulikoff, *The Agrarian Origins of American Capitalism* (1992); Curtis Nettels, *The Emergence of a National Economy, 1775–1815* (1962); Winifred Rothenberg, *From Market-Places to Market Economy: The Transformation of Rural Massachusetts, 1750–1850* (1992) .

Foreign Relations

Harry Ammon, *The Genêt Mission* (1973); Samuel F. Bemis, *Jay's Treaty*, 2d ed. (1962); Samuel F. Bemis, *Pinckney's Treaty*, 2d ed. (1960); Jerald A. Combs, *The Jay Treaty* (1970); Alexander DeConde, *The Quasi-War: Politics and Diplomacy of the Undeclared War with France, 1797–1801* (1966); Alexander DeConde, *Entangling Alliance: Politics and Diplomacy Under George Washington* (1958); Felix Gilbert, *To the Farewell Address: Ideas of Early American Foreign Policy* (1961); Reginald Horsman, *The Diplomacy of the New Republic, 1776–1815* (1985); Lawrence Kaplan, *"Entangling Alliances with None": American Foreign Policy in the Age of Jefferson* (1987); Conor Cruise O'Brien, *The Long Affair: Thomas Jefferson and the French Revolution, 1785–1800* (1996); Bradford Perkins, *The First Rapprochement: England and the United States, 1795–1805* (1967); Matthew Spalding and Patrick J. Garrity, *A Sacred Union of Citizens: George Washington's Farewell Address and American Character* (1996); William Stinchcombe, *The XYZ Affair* (1981); William E. Weeks, *Building the Continental Empire: American Expansion from the Revolution to the Civil War* (1996).

Civil Liberties

Ronald Hoffman and Peter Albert, eds., *The Bill of Rights: Government Proscribed* (1997); Leonard W. Levy, *Emergence of a Free Press* (1985); Leonard W. Levy, *Origins of the Fifth Amendment* (1968); Robert A. Rutland, *The Birth of the Bill of Rights, 1776–1791*, rev. ed. (1983); James Morton Smith, *Freedom's Fetters: The Alien and Sedition Laws and American Civil Liberties* (1956).

Indians and African Americans

Douglas Egerton, *Gabriel's Rebellion: The Virginia Slave Conspiracies of 1800 and 1802* (1993); Dorothy Jones, *License for Empire: Colonization by Treaty in Early America* (1982); Theda Perdue, *Cherokee Women: Gender and Culture Change, 1700–1835* (1998); Francis Paul Prucha, *American Indian Policy in the Formative Years: The Indian Trade and Intercourse Acts, 1790–1834* (1962); James Sidbury, *Ploughshares into Swords: Race, Rebellion, and Identity in Gabriel's Virginia, 1730–1810* (1997); Mechal Sobel, *The World They Made Together: Black and White Values in Eighteenth-Century Virginia* (1987); Anthony F. C. Wallace, *The Death and Rebirth of the Seneca* (1969).

Chapter 9

General

Henry Adams, *History of the United States of America During the Administration of Thomas Jefferson and of James Madison*, 9 vols. (1889–1891); Noble E. Cunningham, Jr., *The United States in 1800: Henry Adams Revisited* (1988); Jean V. Matthews, *Toward a New Society: American Thought and Culture, 1800–1830* (1991); John Mayfield, *The New Nation, 1800–1845* (1981); Marshall Smelser, *The Democratic Republic, 1801–1815* (1968).

Party Politics

James M. Banner, *To the Hartford Convention: The Federalists and the Origins of Party Politics in the Early Republic, 1789–1815* (1967); Noble E. Cunningham, Jr., *The Jeffersonian Republicans in Power: Party Operations, 1801–1809* (1963); David Hackett Fischer, *The Revolution of American Conservatism: The Federalist Party in the Era of Jeffersonian Democracy* (1965); Linda K. Kerber, *Federalists in Dissent* (1970); Milton Lomask, *Aaron Burr*, 2 vols. (1979, 1983); Richard P. McCormick, *The Presidential Game: The Origins of American Presidential Politics* (1982); Drew McCoy, *The Elusive Republic* (1980); Arnold A. Rogow, *A Fatal Friendship: Alexander Hamilton and Aaron Burr* (1998); James Roger Sharp, *American Politics in the Early Republic: The New Nation in Crisis* (1993); James Sterling Young, *The Washington Community, 1800–1828* (1966).

Jefferson and Madison

Noble E. Cunningham, Jr., *In Pursuit of Reason: The Life of Thomas Jefferson* (1987); Noble E. Cunningham, Jr., *The Process of Government Under Jefferson* (1978); Joseph J. Ellis, *American Sphinx: The Character of Thomas Jefferson* (1996); Annette Gordon-Reed, *Thomas Jefferson and Sally Hemings: An American Controversy* (1997); Ralph Ketcham, *Presidents Above Party: The First American Presidency, 1789–1829* (1984); Drew R. McCoy, *The Last of the Fathers: James Madison and the Republican Legacy* (1989); Peter S. Onuf, ed., *Jeffersonian Legacies* (1993); Merrill D. Peterson, *Thomas Jefferson and the New Nation* (1970); Norman K. Risjord, *Thomas Jefferson* (1994); Robert Allen Rutland, *The Presidency of James Madison* (1990); Robert W. Tucker and David C. Hendrickson, *Empire of Liberty: The Statecraft of Thomas Jefferson* (1990).

The Supreme Court and the Law

Leonard Baker, *John Marshall: A Life in Law* (1974); Robert Lowry Clinton, *Marbury v. Madison and Judicial Review* (1989); Richard E. Ellis, *The Jeffersonian Crisis: Courts and Politics in the Young Republic* (1971); Morton J. Horowitz, *The Transformation of American Law, 1780–1860* (1977); Herbert A. Johnson, *The Chief Justiceship of John Marshall, 1801–1835* (1997); R. Kent Newmyer, *The Supreme Court Under Marshall and Taney* (1968); Thomas C. Shevory, *John Marshall's Law: Interpretation, Ideology, and Interest* (1994); Francis N. Stites, *John Marshall: Defender of the Constitution* (1981).

Louisiana and Lewis and Clark

Stephen E. Ambrose, *Undaunted Courage: Meriwether Lewis, Thomas Jefferson, and the Opening of the American West* (1996); Alexander De Conde, *This Affair of Louisiana* (1976); Donna J. Kessler, *The Making of Sacagawea: A Euro-American Legend* (1996); James P. Ronda, *Lewis and Clark Among the Indians* (1984); James P. Ronda, ed., *Thomas Jefferson and the Changing West* (1997); James P. Ronda, ed., *Voyage of Discovery: Essays on the Lewis and Clark Expedition* (1998).

Expansionism, the War of 1812, and Foreign Relations

Robert J. Allison, *The Crescent Obscured: The United States and the Muslim World, 1776–1815* (1995); Paul Baepler, ed., *White Slaves, African Masters: An Anthology of American Barbary Captivity Narratives* (1999); Roger H. Brown, *The Republic in Peril* (1964); R. David Edmunds, *Tecumseh and the Quest for Indian Leadership* (1984); R. David Edmunds, *The Shawnee Prophet* (1983); Clifford L. Egan, *Neither Peace nor War: Franco-American Relations, 1803–1812* (1983); Kenneth J. Hagan, *This People's Navy* (1991); Donald R. Hickey, *The War of 1812: A Short History* (1995); Frank Lawrence Owsley, Jr., and Gene A. Smith, *Filibusters and Expansionists: Jeffersonian Manifest Destiny, 1800–1821* (1997); Bradford Perkins, *The Creation of a Republican Empire, 1776–1865* (1993); Julius W. Pratt, *Expansionists of 1812* (1925); Robert V. Remini, *The Battle of New Orleans: Andrew Jackson and America's First Military Victory* (1999); J. C. A. Stagg, *Mr. Madison's War: Politics, Diplomacy, and Warfare in the Early Republic, 1783–1830* (1983); Anders Stephanson, *Manifest Destiny: American Expansionism and the Empire of Right* (1995); Steve Watts, *The Republic Reborn: War and the Making of a Liberal America, 1790–1820* (1987); David J. Weber, *The Spanish Frontier in North America* (1992); J. Leitch Wright, Jr., *Creeks and Seminoles* (1986).

Chapter 10

General

Jack Larkin, *The Reshaping of Everyday Life, 1790–1840* (1988); D. W. Meinig, *The Shaping of America: A Geographical Perspective on 500 Years of History*, vol. 2: *Contininental America, 1800–1867* (1993); Charles G. Sellers, Jr., *The Market Revolution: Jacksonian America, 1815–1840* (1991); Melvyn Stokes and Stephen Conway, eds., *The Market Revolution in America: Social, Political, and Religious Expressions, 1800–1860* (1996).

Postwar Nationalism

Harry Ammon, *James Monroe: The Quest for National Identity* (1971); Noble E. Cunningham, *The Presidency of James Monroe* (1996); Mary W. M. Hargreaves, *The Presidency of John Quincy Adams* (1985); Morton J. Horowitz, *The Transformation of American Law, 1780–1860* (1977); Ralph Ketcham, *Presidents Above Party: The First American Presidency, 1789–1829* (1984); Walter LaFeber, ed., *John Quincy Adams and American Continental Empire* (1965); Ernest R. May, *The Making of the Monroe Doctrine* (1976); Paul C. Nagel, *John Quincy Adams: A Public Life, a Private Life* (1997); R. Kent Newmyer, *The Supreme Court Under Marshall and Taney* (1968); Dexter Perkins, *Hands Off: A History of the Monroe Doctrine* (1941); Robert V. Remini, *Henry Clay: Statesman for the Union* (1991); Thomas C. Shevory, *John Marshall's Law: Interpretation, Ideology, and Interest* (1994); William Earl Weeks, *John Quincy Adams and American Global Empire* (1992).

The Market Economy, Manufacturing, and Commerce

Stuart Bruchey, *Enterprise: The Dynamic Economy of a Free People* (1990); Alfred D. Chandler, Jr., *The Visible Hand: Managerial Revolution in American Business* (1977); William Cronon, *Nature's Metropolis: Chicago and the Great West* (1991); Paul A. Gilje, ed., *Wages of Independence: Capitalism in the Early American Republic* (1997); Louis Hartz, *Economic Policy and Democratic Thought: Pennsylvania, 1776–1860* (1954); David A. Hounshell, *From the American System to Mass Production, 1800–1932: The Development of Manufacturing Technology in the United States* (1984); David J. Jeremy, *Transatlantic Industrial Revolution: The Diffusion of Textile Technologies Between Britain and America, 1790s–1830s* (1981); Herbert A. Johnson, *The Chief Justiceship of John Marshall, 1801–1835* (1997); David Klingaman and Richard Vedder, eds., *Essays in Nineteenth-Century History* (1975); Stanley I. Kutler, *Privilege and Creative Destruction: The Charles River Bridge Case* (1971); Walter Licht, *Industrializing America: The Nineteenth Century* (1995); Otto Mayr and Robert C. Post, eds., *Yankee Enterprise: The Rise of the American System of Manufacturers* (1981); Douglass C. North, *Economic Growth of the United States, 1790–1860* (1966); Theodore Steinberg, *Nature Incorporated: Industrialization and the Waters of New England* (1991).

Transportation

Albert Fishlow, *American Railroads and the Transformation of the Ante-Bellum Economy* (1965); Carter Goodrich, *Government Promotion of American Canals and Railroads, 1800–1890* (1960); Louis C. Hunter, *Steamboats on the Western Rivers* (1949); Richard R. John, *Spreading the News: The American Postal System from Franklin to Morse* (1995); Harry N. Scheiber, *Ohio Canal Era: A Case Study of Government and the Economy, 1820–1861* (1969); Ronald E. Shaw, *Canals for a Nation: The Canal Era in the United States, 1790–1860* (1990); Carol Sheriff, *The Artificial River: The Erie Canal and the Paradox of Progress, 1817–1862* (1996); George R. Taylor, *The Transportation Revolution, 1815–1860* (1951); James A. Ward, *Railroads and the Character of America, 1820–1887* (1986).

Commercial Farming

"American Agriculture, 1790–1840, A Symposium," *Agricultural History* 46 (January 1972); Jeremy Atack and Fred Bateman, *To Their Own Soil: Agriculture in the Antebellum North* (1987); Allen G. Bogue, *From Prairie to Corn Belt: Farming on the Illinois and Iowa Prairies in the Nineteenth Century* (1963); Christopher Clark, *The Roots of Rural Capitalism: Western Massachusetts, 1780–1860* (1990); Clarence Danhof, *Change in Agriculture: The Northern United States, 1820–1870* (1969); Paul W. Gates, *The Farmer's Age: Agriculture, 1815–1860* (1962); Benjamin H. Hibbard, *A History of Public Land Policies* (1939); Joan M. Jensen, *Loosening the Bonds: Mid-Atlantic Farm Women, 1750–1850* (1986); Robert Leslie Jones, *History of Agriculture in Ohio to 1880* (1983); Peter D. McClelland, *Sowing Modernity: America's First Agricultural Revolution* (1999); Sally McMurry, *Transforming Rural Life: Dairying Families and Agricultural Change, 1820–1885* (1995); Gavin Wright, *The Political Economy of the Cotton South* (1978).

Workers

Mary H. Blewett, *Men, Women, and Work: Class, Gender, and Protest in the New England Shoe Industry, 1780–1910* (1988); Jeanne Boydston, *Home and Work: Housework, Wages, and the Ideology of Labor in the Early Republic* (1990); Thomas Dublin, *Transforming Women's Work: New England Lives in the Industrial Revolution* (1994); Thomas Dublin, *Women at Work: The Transformation of Work and Community in Lowell, Massachusetts, 1826–1860* (1979); Bruce Laurie, *Artisans into Workers: Labor in Nineteenth-Century America* (1989); Howard B. Rock, Paul A. Gilje, and Robert Asher, eds., *American Artisans: Crafting Social Identity, 1750–1850* (1995); Sean Wilentz, *Chants Democratic: New York City and the Rise of the American Working Class, 1788–1850* (1984); David A. Zonderman, *Aspirations and Anxieties: New England Workers and the Mechanized Factory System, 1815–1850* (1992).

Americans on the Move

Joan Cashin, *A Family Venture: Men and Women on the Southern Frontier* (1991); James E. Davis, *Frontier America 1800–1840: A Comparative Demographic Analysis of the Frontier Process* (1977); Stewart Holbrook, *The Yankee Exodus: An Account of Migration from New England* (1950); Julie Roy Jeffrey, *Frontier Women: The Trans-Mississippi West, 1840–1880* (1979); Peter D. McClelland and Richard J. Zeckhauser, eds., *Demographic Dimensions of the New Republic* (1982); Virginia E. and Robert W. McCormick, *New Englanders on the Ohio Frontier* (1998); Gerald McFarland, *A Scattered People: An American Family Moves West* (1985); James Hebron Moore, *The Emergence of the Cotton Kingdom in the Old Southwest: Mississippi, 1770–1860* (1987); James Oakes, *The Ruling Race: A History of American Slaveholders* (1982); Malcom J. Rohrbough, *The Trans-Appalachian Frontier: People, Societies, and Institutions, 1775–1850* (1978); Russell Thornton, *American Indian Holocaust and Survival: A Population History Since 1492* (1987); David J. Weber, *The Spanish Frontier in North America* (1992); Richard White, *"It's Your Misfortune and None of My Own": A History of the American West* (1991).

Native American Resistance and Removal

Robert F. Berkhofer, Jr., *The White Man's Indian* (1978); Paul H. Carlson, *The Plains Indians* (1998); James W. Covington, *The Seminoles of Florida* (1993); Michael D. Green, *The Politics of Indian Removal: Creek Government and Society in Crisis* (1982); Stanley W. Hoig, *The Cherokees and Their Chiefs in the Wake of Empire* (1998); William G. McLoughlin, *Cherokee Renascence in the New Republic* (1986); Theda Perdue, *Slavery and the Evolution of Cherokee Society, 1540–1866* (1979); Ronald N. Satz, *American Indian Policy in the Jacksonian Era* (1975); Daniel H. Usner, Jr., *American Indians in the Lower Mississippi Valley* (1998); Anthony F. C. Wallace, *The Long, Bitter Trail: Andrew Jackson and the Indians* (1993); Richard White, *The Roots of Dependency: Subsistence, Environment, and Social Change Among the Choctaws, Pawnees, and Navajos* (1983); James Wilson, *The Earth Shall Weep: A History of Native America* (1998); J. Leitch Wright, Jr., *Creeks and Seminoles: The Destruction and Regeneration of the Muscogulge People* (1986).

Chapter 11

General

George Dangerfield, *The Awakening of American Nationalism, 1815–1828* (1965); Daniel Feller, *The Jacksonian Promise: America, 1815–1840* (1995); Jean V. Matthews, *Toward a New Society: American Thought and Culture, 1800–1830* (1991); John Mayfield, *The New Nation, 1800–1845* (1981); Charles Sellers, *The Market Revolution: Jacksonian America, 1815–1846* (1991).

Religion, Revivalism, and Reform

Robert H. Abzug, *Cosmos Crumbling: American Reform and the Religious Imagination* (1994); Michael Barkun, *Crucible of the Millennium: The Burned-over District of New York in the 1840s* (1986); Terry Bilhartz, *Urban Religion and the Second Great Awakening: Church and Society in Early National Baltimore* (1986); Paul K. Conkin, *The Uneasy Center: Reformed Christianity in Antebellum America* (1995); Clifford S. Griffen, *Their Brothers' Keepers: Moral Stewardship in the United States, 1800–1865* (1960); Keith J. Hardman, *Charles Grandison Finney, 1792–1875: Revivalist and Reformer* (1987); Nathan O. Hatch, *The Democratization of American Christianity* (1989); Christine Leigh Heyrman, *Southern Cross: The Beginnings of the Bible Belt* (1997); Curtis D. Johnson, *Islands of Holiness: Rural Religion in Upstate New York, 1790–1860* (1989); Paul E. Johnson, *A Shopkeeper's Millennium: Society and Revivals in Rochester, New York, 1815–1837* (1978); Steven Mintz, *Moralists and Modernizers: America's Pre–Civil War Reformers* (1995); Timothy L. Smith, *Revivalism and Social Reform in Mid-Nineteenth Century America* (1957); Alice Felt Tyler, *Freedom's Ferment* (1944); Ronald G. Walters, *American Reformers, 1815–1860*, rev. ed. (1997).

Temperance, Asylums, and Antimasonry

Thomas J. Brown, *Dorothea Dix: New England Reformer* (1998); David Gollaher, *Voice for the Mad: The Life of Dorothea Dix* (1995); Paul Goodman, *Towards a Christian Republic: Antimasonry and the Great Transition in New England, 1826–1836* (1988); Gerald N. Grob, *Mental Institutions in America: Social Policy to 1875* (1973); Kathleen Smith Kutolowski, "Antimasonry Reexamined: Social Bases of the Grass-Roots Party," *Journal of American History* 71 (September 1984): 269–293; W. J. Rorabaugh, *The Alcoholic Republic: An American Tradition* (1979); David J. Rothman, *The Discovery of the Asylum: Social Order and Disorder in the New Republic* (1971); Ian R. Tyrrell, *Sobering Up: From Temperance to Prohibition in Antebellum America, 1800–1860* (1979); William Preston Vaughn, *The Antimasonic Party in the United States, 1826–1843* (1983).

Women and Reform

Barbara J. Berg, *The Remembered Gate: Origins of American Feminism: The Woman and the City, 1800–1860* (1977); Ellen C. Du Bois, *Feminism and Suffrage: The Emergence of an Independent Woman's Movement in America, 1848–1869* (1978); Barbara Leslie Epstein, *The Politics of Domesticity: Women, Evangelism, and Temperance in Nineteenth-Century America* (1981); Lori D. Ginzberg, *Women and the Work of Benevolence: Morality, Politics, and Class in the Nineteenth-Century United States* (1990); Debra Gold Hansen, *Strained Sisterhood: Gender and Class in the Boston Female Anti-Slavery Society* (1993); Nancy A. Hewitt, *Women's Activism and Social Change: Rochester, New York, 1822–1872* (1984); Sylvia D. Hoffert, *When Hens Crow: The Woman's Rights Movement in*

Antebellum America (1995); Nancy Isenberg, *Sex and Citizenship in Antebellum America* (1998); Gerda Lerner, *The Grimké Sisters of South Carolina* (1967); Amanda Porterfield, *Mary Lyon and the Mount Holyoke Missionaries* (1997); Mary P. Ryan, *Cradle of the Middle Class: The Family in Oneida County, New York, 1790–1865* (1981); Mary P. Ryan, *Women in Public: Between Banners and Ballots, 1825–1880* (1990); Shirley J. Yee, *Black Women Abolitionists: A Study in Activism, 1828–1860* (1992); Jean Fagan Yellin, *Women & Sisters: The Antislavery Feminists in American Culture* (1989).

Antislavery and Abolitionism

James Brewer Stewart, *Holy Warriors: The Abolitionists and American Slavery*, rev. ed. (1996); David Brion Davis, *Slavery and Human Progress* (1984); Frederick Douglass, *Life and Times of Frederick Douglass* (1881); George M. Fredrickson, *The Black Image in the White Mind: The Debate on Afro-American Character and Destiny, 1817–1914* (1971); Lawrence J. Friedman, *Gregarious Saints: Self and Community in American Abolitionism, 1830–1870* (1982); Paul Goodman, *Of One Blood: Abolitionism and the Origins of Racial Equality* (1998); David Grimsted, *American Mobbing, 1828–1861* (1998); Aileen S. Kraditor, *Means and Ends in American Abolitionism: Garrison and His Critics on Strategy and Tactics* (1967); Henry Mayer, *All on Fire: William Lloyd Garrison and the Abolition of Slavery* (1998); William Lee Miller, *Arguing About Slavery: The Great Battle in the United States Congress* (1995); William H. Pease and Jane H. Pease, *They Who Would Be Free: Blacks' Search for Freedom, 1830–1861* (1974); Benjamin Quarles, *Black Abolitionists* (1969); John L. Thomas, *The Liberator: William Lloyd Garrison* (1963); Ronald G. Walters, *The Antislavery Appeal: American Abolitionism After 1830* (1976).

Politics and Diplomacy, 1816–1828

Harry Ammon, *James Monroe: The Quest for National Identity* (1971); Noble E. Cunningham, *The Presidency of James Monroe* (1996); Mary W. M. Hargreaves, *The Presidency of John Quincy Adams* (1985); Morton J. Horowitz, *The Transformation of American Law, 1780–1860* (1977); Ralph Ketcham, *Presidents Above Party: The First American Presidency, 1789–1829* (1984); Walter LaFeber, ed., *John Quincy Adams and American Continental Empire* (1965); Ernest R. May, *The Making of the Monroe Doctrine* (1976); Paul C. Nagel, *John Quincy Adams: A Public Life, a Private Life* (1997); R. Kent Newmyer, *The Supreme Court Under Marshall and Taney* (1968); Dexter Perkins, *Hands Off: A History of the Monroe Doctrine* (1941); Robert V. Remini, *Henry Clay: Statesman for the Union* (1991); Thomas C. Shevory, *John Marshall's Law: Interpretation, Ideology, and Interest* (1994); William Earl Weeks, *John Quincy Adams and American Global Empire* (1992).

Andrew Jackson and the Jacksonians

Donald B. Cole, *Martin Van Buren and the American Political System* (1984); Michael F. Holt, *Political Parties and American Political Development from the Age of Jackson to the Age of Lincoln* (1992); Richard B. Latner, *The Presidency of Andrew Jackson* (1979); John F. Marszalek, *The Petticoat Affair: Manners, Mutiny, and Sex in Andrew Jackson's White House* (1997); Marvin Meyers, *The Jacksonian Persuasion* (1960); John Niven, *Martin Van Buren* (1983); Edward Pessen, *Jacksonian America: Society, Personality, and Politics*, rev. ed. (1979); Robert V. Remini, *The Legacy of Andrew Jackson: Essays on Democracy, Indian Removal, and Slavery* (1988); Robert V. Remini, *The Life of Andrew Jackson* (1988); Harry L. Watson, *Liberty and Power: The Politics of Jacksonian America* (1990).

Democrats and Whigs

William J. Cooper, *The South and the Politics of Slavery, 1828–1856* (1978); Ronald P. Formisano, *The Transformation of Political Culture: Massachusetts Parties, 1790s–1840s* (1983); William W. Freehling, *Prelude to Civil War: The Nullification Controversy in South Carolina* (1966); Daniel Walker Howe, *The Political Culture of the American Whigs* (1979); Lawrence Frederick Kohl, *The Politics of Individualism: Parties and the American Character in the Jacksonian Era* (1989); Richard P. McCormick, *The Second American Party System: Party Formation in the Jacksonian Era* (1966); Merrill D. Peterson, *The Great Triumvirate: Webster, Clay, and Calhoun* (1987); Norman Lois Peterson, *The Presidencies of William Henry Harrison and John Tyler* (1989); James Roger Sharp, *The Jacksonians Versus the Banks: Politics in the States After the Panic of 1837* (1970).

Manifest Destiny and Foreign Policy

John M. Belohlavek, *"Let the Eagle Soar!" The Foreign Policy of Andrew Jackson* (1985); T. R. Fehrenbach, *Lone Star: A History of Texas and the Texans* (1968); Norman B. Graebner, ed., *Manifest Destiny* (1968); Thomas R. Hietala, *Manifest Destiny: Anxious Aggrandizement in Late Jacksonian America* (1985); Reginald Horsman, *Race and Manifest Destiny* (1981); Michael Hunt, *Ideology and U.S. Foreign Policy* (1987); Bradford Perkins, *The Creation of a Republican Empire, 1776–1865* (1993); David M. Pletcher, *The Diplomacy of Annexation: Texas, Oregon, and the Mexican War* (1973); Charles G. Sellers, Jr., *James K. Polk: Continentalist, 1843–1846* (1966); Anders Stephanson, *Manifest Destiny: American Expansionism and the Empire of Right* (1995); Paul A. Varg, *United States Foreign Relations, 1820–1860* (1979); David J. Weber, *The Spanish Frontier in North America* (1992); Albert K. Weinberg, *Manifest Destiny* (1935).

The Supreme Court and the Law

Leonard Baker, *John Marshall: A Life in Law* (1974); Francis N. Stites, *John Marshall: Defender of the Constitution* (1981).

Chapter 12

Rural and Utopian Communities

Leonard J. Arrington and Davis Bitton, *The Mormon Experience: A History of the Latterday Saints* (1979); Priscilla J. Brewer, *Shaker Communities, Shaker Lives* (1986); David B. Danbom, *Born in the Country: A History of Rural America* (1995); John Mack Faragher, *Sugar Creek: Life on the Illinois Prairie* (1986); Laurence Foster, *Religion and Sexuality: Three American Communal Experiments of the Nineteenth Century* (1981); Steven Hahn and Jonathan Prude, eds., *The Countryside in the Age of Capitalist Transformation* (1985); Joan M. Jensen, *Loosening the Bonds: Mid-Atlantic Farm Women, 1750–1850* (1986); Sally McMurry, *Families and Farmhouses in Nineteenth Century America: Vernacular Design and Social Change* (1988); Anthony F. C. Wallace, *Rockdale: The Growth of an American Village in the Early Industrial Revolution* (1978); Kenneth H. Winn, *Exiles in a Land of Liberty: Mormons in America, 1830–1846* (1989).

The West

John Mack Faragher, *Women and Men on the Overland Trail* (1979); Ramón A. Gutiérrez and Richard J. Orsi, eds., *Contested Eden: California Before the Gold Rush* (1998); Julie Roy Jeffrey, *Frontier Women: The Trans-Mississippi West, 1840–1880* (1979); Rudolph M. Lapp, *Blacks in Gold Rush California* (1977); Malcolm J. Rohrbough, *Days of Gold: The California Gold Rush and the American Nation* (1997); Quintard Taylor, *In Search of the Racial Frontier: African Americans in the American West, 1528–1990* (1998); John D. Unruh, Jr., *The Overland Emigrants and the Trans-Mississippi West, 1840–1860* (1979); David J. Weber, *The Spanish Frontier in North America* (1992); Richard White, *"It's Your Misfortune and None of My Own": A History of the American West* (1991).

Urban Communities

Melvin A. Adelman, *A Sporting Time: New York City and the Rise of Modern Athletics, 1820–1870* (1986); Stuart M. Blumin, *The Emergence of the Middle Class: Social Experience in the American City, 1760–1900* (1989); Edwin G. Burrows and Mike Wallace, *Gotham: A History of New York City to 1898* (1999); Susan G. Davis, *Parades and Power: Street Theater in Nineteenth-Century Philadelphia* (1986); Timothy J. Gilfoyle, *City of Eros: New York City, Prostitution, and the Commercialization of Sex, 1790–1920* (1992); Karen V. Hansen, *A Very Social Time: Crafting Community in Antebellum New England* (1994); Carl Kaestle, *Pillars of the Republic: Common Schools and American Society, 1780–1860* (1982); Jack Larkin, *The Reshaping of Everyday Life, 1790–1840* (1988); Timothy R. Mahoney, *Provincial Lives: Middle-Class Experience in the Antebellum Middle West* (1999); Edward Pessen, *Riches, Class and Power Before the Civil War* (1973); Christine Stansell, *City of Women: Sex and Class in New York, 1789–1860* (1986); Richard B. Stott, *Workers in the Metropolis: Class, Ethnicity, and Youth in Antebellum New York City* (1990); Alexis de Tocqueville, *Democracy in America*, 2 vols. (1835, 1840).

Women and American Families

Virginia K. Bartlett, *Keeping House: Women's Lives in Western Pennsylvania, 1790–1850* (1994); Janet Farrell Brodie, *Contraception and Abortion in Nineteenth-Century America* (1994); Lee Virginia Chambers-Schiller, *Liberty, A Better Husband: Single Women in America: The Generations of 1780–1840* (1984); Clifford Edward Clark, Jr., *The American Family Home, 1800–1960* (1986); Nancy F. Cott, *The Bonds of Womanhood: "Woman's Sphere" in New England, 1780–1835* (1977); Linda Gordon, *Woman's Body, Woman's Right: A Social History of Birth Control in America* (1976); Joan Hoff, *Law, Gender and Injustice: A Legal History of U.S. Women* (1991); Suzanne Lebsock, *The Free Women of Petersburg: Status and Culture in a Southern Town, 1784–1860* (1984); Glenda Riley, *Divorce: An American Tradition* (1991); Mary P. Ryan, *Cradle of the Middle Class: The Family in Oneida County, New York, 1790–1865* (1981); Kathryn Kish Sklar, *Catharine Beecher: A Study in American Domesticity* (1973); Maris A. Vinovskis, *Fertility in Massachusetts from the Revolution to the Civil War* (1981); Robert V. Wells, *Revolutions in Americans' Lives* (1982); Barbara Welter, "The Cult of True Womanhood, 1820–1860," *American Quarterly* 18 (Summer 1966): 151–174.

Immigrants and Hispanics

Thomás Almaguer, *Racial Fault Lines: The Historical Origins of White Supremacy in California* (1994); Gunther Barth, *Bitter Strength: A History of Chinese in the United States, 1850–1870* (1964); Kathleen Neils Conzen, *Immigrant Milwaukee: 1836–1860* (1976); Arnoldo De León, *The Tejano Community, 1836–1900* (1982); Hasia R. Diner, *Erin's Daughters in America: Irish Immigrant Women in the Nineteenth Century* (1983); David A. Gerber, *The Making of an American Pluralism: Buffalo, New York, 1825–60* (1989); Noel Ignatiev, *How the Irish Became White* (1995); Matthew Frye Jacobson, *Whiteness of a Different Color: European Immigrants and the Alchemy of Race* (1998); Walter D. Kamphoefner, *The Westfalians: From Germany to Missouri* (1987); Walter D. Kamphoefner et al., eds., *News from the Land of Freedom: German Immigrants Write Home* (1991); Dale T. Knobel, *Paddy and the Republic: Ethnicity and Nationality in Antebellum America* (1986); Timothy M. Matovina, *Tejano Religion and Ethnicity: San Antonio, 1821–1860* (1995); Kerby A. Miller, *Emigrants and Exiles: Ireland and the Irish Exodus to North America* (1985); Stanley Nadel, *Little Germany: Ethnicity, Religion, and Class in New York City, 1845–80* (1990); David Roediger, *The Wages of Whiteness: Race and the Making of the Working Class* (1991); David J. Weber, *The Spanish Frontier in North America* (1992); Mark Wyman, *Immigrants in the Valley: Irish, Germans, and Americans in the Upper Mississippi, 1830–1860* (1984).

Free People of Color and Race

Ira Berlin, *Slaves Without Masters: The Free Negro in the Antebellum South* (1974); Dale Cockrell, *Demons of Disorder: Early Blackface Minstrels and Their World* (1997); Leonard P. Curry, *The Free Black in Urban America, 1800–1850* (1981); Thomas F. Gossett, *Race: The History of an Idea in America* (1963); James O. Horton and Lois E. Horton, *In Hope of Liberty: Culture, Community and Protest Among Northern Free Blacks, 1700–1860* (1996); Luther Porter Jackson, *Free Negro Labor and Property Holding in Virginia, 1830–1860* (1942); David M. Katzman, *Before the Ghetto: Black Detroit in the Nineteenth Century* (1973); W. T. Lhamon, Jr., *Raising Cain: Blackface Performance from Jim Crow to Hip Hop* (1998); Leon Litwack, *North of Slavery: The Negro in the Free States, 1790–1860* (1961); Eric Lott, *Love and Theft: Blackface Minstrelsy and the American Working Class* (1995); Joanne Pope Melish, *Disowning Slavery: Gradual Emancipation and "Race" in New England, 1780–1860* (1998); Floyd J. Miller, *The Search for a Black Nationality: Black Colonization and Emigration, 1787–1863* (1975); Gary B. Nash, *Forging Freedom: The Formation of Philadelphia's Black Community, 1720–1840* (1988); Quintard Taylor, *In Search of the Racial Frontier: African Americans in the American West, 1528–1990* (1998); Arthur Zilversmit, *The First Emancipation: The Abolition of Slavery in the North* (1967).

Chapter 13

The Peculiar South

Wilbur J. Cash, *The Mind of the South* (1939); Carl N. Degler, *Place Over Time* (1977); Drew G. Faust, "The Peculiar South Revisited," in John B. Boles and Evelyn T. Nolen, eds., *Interpreting Southern History* (1987); James Oakes, *Slavery and Freedom* (1990); C. Vann Woodward, *The Burden of Southern History* (1960).

Southern Society

Edward L. Ayers, *Vengeance and Justice* (1984); Bradley G. Bond, *Political Culture in the Nineteenth-Century South* (1995); Randolph B. Campbell, "Planters and Plain Folks," in John B. Boles and Evelyn T. Nolen, eds., *Interpreting Southern History* (1987); William J. Cooper, *The South and the Politics of Slavery, 1828–1856* (1978); Clement Eaton, *The Growth of Southern Civilization, 1790–1860* (1961); William W. Freehling, *Prelude to Civil War* (1965); Eugene D. Genovese, *The Political Economy of Slavery* (1965); Peter Kolchin, *Unfree Labor: American Slavery and Russian Serfdom* (1987); Donald G. Mathews, *Religion in the Old South* (1977); Christine L. Heyrman, *Southern Cross* (1997); James Hebron Moore, *The Emergence of the Cotton Kingdom in the Old Southwest: Mississippi, 1770–1860* (1987); Frederick Law Olmsted, *The Slave States*, ed. Harvey Wish (1959); Charles S. Sydnor, *The Development of Southern Sectionalism, 1819–1848* (1948); Larry E. Tise, *Proslavery* (1987); Ralph A. Wooster, *Politicians, Planters, and Plain Folk* (1975); Gavin Wright, *The Political Economy of the Cotton South* (1978); Bertram Wyatt-Brown, *Southern Honor* (1982).

Slaveholders and Nonslaveholders

Edward L. Ayers and John C. Willis, eds., *The Edge of the South* (1991); Bennet H. Barrow, *Plantation Life in the Florida Parishes of Louisiana*, ed. Edwin Adams Davis (1943); Ira Berlin, *Slaves Without Masters* (1974); Joan E. Cashin, *A Family Venture* (1991); Bill Cecil-Fronsman, *The Common Whites* (1992); Charles B. Dew, *Bond of Iron* (1995); Everett Dick, *The Dixie Frontier* (1948); Clement Eaton, *The Mind of the Old South* (1967); Paul D. Escott, ed., *North Carolina Yeoman* (1996); Drew Faust, *James Henry Hammond and the Old South* (1982); Drew Faust, *A Sacred Circle: The Dilemma of the Intellectual in the Old South* (1977); Drew Faust, ed., *The Ideology of Slavery* (1981); J. Wayne Flynt, *Dixie's Forgotten People* (1979); John Hope Franklin, *The Militant South, 1800–1861* (1956); John Inscoe, *Mountain Masters* (1989); Michael P. Johnson and James L. Roark, *Black Masters* (1984); Kenneth S. Greenberg, *Masters and Statesmen* (1985); Stephanie McCurry, *Masters of Small Worlds* (1995); Robert Manson Myers, ed., *The Children of Pride* (1972); James Oakes, *The Ruling Race* (1982); Frank L. Owsley, *Plain Folk of the Old South* (1949); Loren Schweninger, *Black Property Owners in the South, 1790–1915* (1990); J. Mills Thornton III, *Politics and Power in a Slave Society: Alabama, 1800–1860* (1978).

Southern Women

Carol Bleser, *In Joy and in Sorrow* (1990); Carol Bleser, ed., *Tokens of Affection* (1995); Victoria Bynum, *Unruly Women* (1992); Jane Turner Censer, *North Carolina Planters and Their Children, 1800–1860* (1984); Catherine Clinton, *The Plantation Mistress* (1982); Elizabeth Fox-Genovese, *Within the Plantation Household* (1988); Jean E. Friedman, *The Enclosed Garden* (1985); Harriet Jacobs, *Incidents in the Life of a Slave Girl*, ed. Jean Fagan Yellin (1987); Jacqueline Jones, *Labor of Love, Labor of Sorrow* (1985); Frances Anne Kemble, *Journal of a Residence on a Georgia Plantation in 1838–1839* (1863); Suzanne Lebsock, *Free Women of Petersburg* (1984); Sally McMillen, *Motherhood in the Old South* (1990); Patricia Morton, ed., *Discovering the Women in Slavery* (1995); Elisabeth Muhlenfeld, *Mary Boykin Chesnut* (1981); Mary D. Robertson, ed., *Lucy Breckinridge of Grove Hill* (1979); Deborah G. White, *Ar'n't I a Woman?* (1985); Virginia Ingraham Burr, ed., *The Secret Eye* (1990).

Conditions of Slavery

Larry E. Hudson, Jr., *To Have and to Hold* (1997); Kenneth F. Kiple and Virginia H. Kiple, "Black Tongue and Black Men," *Journal of Southern History* 43 (August 1977): 411–428; Wilma King, *Stolen Childhood* (1995); Peter Kolchin, *American Slavery, 1619–1877* (1993); Ronald L.

Lewis, *Coal, Iron, and Slaves* (1979); Randall M. Miller and John David Smith, eds., *Dictionary of Afro-American Slavery* (1997); Randall M. Miller, ed., *The Afro-American Slaves: Community or Chaos* (1981); Orlando Patterson, *Rituals of Blood* (1998); Todd L. Savitt, *Medicine and Slavery* (1978); Mark M. Smith, *Mastered by the Clock* (1997); Kenneth M. Stampp, *The Peculiar Institution* (1956); Robert S. Starobin, *Industrial Slavery in the Old South* (1970); Brenda E. Stevenson, *Life in Black and White: Family and Community in the Slave South* (1996); Michael Tadman, *Speculators and Slaves* (1989).

Slave Culture and Resistance

Herbert Aptheker, *American Negro Slave Revolts* (1943); William F. Allen, Charles P. Ware, and Lucy McKim, *Slave Songs of the United States* (1867); John W. Blassingame, *The Slave Community* (1979); John Blassingame, ed., *Slave Testimony* (1977); Judith Wragg Chase, *Afro-American Art and Craft* (1971); Frederick Douglass, *Narrative of the Life of Frederick Douglass*, ed. David W. Blight (1993); Dena J. Epstein, *Sinful Tunes and Spirituals* (1977); Paul D. Escott, *Slavery Remembered: A Record of Twentieth-Century Slave Narratives* (1979); Thomas Wentworth Higginson, "Negro Spirituals," *Atlantic Monthly* 19 (June, 1867); John Hope Franklin and Loren Schweninger, *Runaway Slaves* (1999); Eugene D. Genovese, *From Rebellion to Revolution* (1979); Eugene D. Genovese, *Roll, Jordan, Roll* (1974); Michael A. Gomez, *Exchanging Our Country Marks* (1998); Kenneth Greenberg, ed., *The Confessions of Nat Turner and Related Documents* (1996); Herbert G. Gutman, *The Black Family in Slavery and Freedom, 1750–1925* (1976); Vincent Harding, *There Is a River* (1981); Bruce Jackson, ed., *The Negro and His Folklore in Nineteenth Century Periodicals* (1967); Charles Joyner, *Down by the Riverside* (1984); Lawrence W. Levine, *Black Culture and Black Consciousness* (1977); Albert J. Raboteau, *Slave Religion* (1978); James Sidbury, *Plowshares into Swords: Gabriel's Virginia* (1997); Robert S. Starobin, *Denmark Vesey* (1970); Sterling Stuckey, *Slave Culture* (1987).

Chapter 14

General

Thomas B. Alexander, *Sectional Stress and Party Strength* (1967); Tyler Anbinder, *Nativism and Slavery* (1992); Maurice G. Baxter, *One and Inseparable: Daniel Webster and the Union* (1984); Paul Bergeron, *The Presidency of James K. Polk* (1987); Frederick J. Blue, *The Free Soilers: Third Party Politics, 1848–1854* (1973); Stanley W. Campbell, *The Slave Catchers* (1968); Richard J. Carwardine, *Evangelicals and Politics in Antebellum America* (1997); Don E. Fehrenbacher, *The Dred Scott Case* (1978); George M. Fredrickson, *The Black Image in the White Mind* (1971); William W. Freehling and Craig M. Simpson, eds., *Secession Debated* (1992); William W. Freehling, *The Road to Disunion* (1990); Holman Hamilton,

Prologue to Conflict: The Crisis and Compromise of 1850 (1964); Michael F. Holt, *Political Parties and American Political Development* (1992); Michael F. Holt, *The Political Crisis of the 1850s* (1978); Daniel Walker Howe, *The Political Culture of the American Whigs* (1979); Stephen E. Maizlish and John J. Kushma, eds., *Essays on American Antebellum Politics, 1840–1860* (1982); William Lee Miller, *Arguing About Slavery* (1996); Chaplain W. Morrison, *Democratic Politics and Sectionalism: The Wilmot Proviso Controversy* (1967); Paul D. Nagle, *One Nation Indivisible* (1964); Merrill D. Peterson, *The Great Triumvirate: Webster, Clay, and Calhoun* (1987); David M. Potter, *The Impending Crisis, 1848–1861* (1976); James A. Rawley, *Race and Politics* (1969); Robert V. Remini, *Henry Clay: Statesman for the Union* (1991); Richard H. Sewell, *A House Divided: Sectionalism and the Civil War, 1848–1865* (1988); Joel H. Silbey, *The Transformation of American Politics, 1840–1960* (1967); Joel H. Silbey, ed., *The American Party Battle*, 2 vols. (1999); Elbert B. Smith, *The Presidency of James Buchanan* (1975); Kenneth M. Stampp, *America in 1857* (1991); Kenneth M. Stampp, *And the War Came* (1950); Gerald W. Wolff, *The Kansas-Nebraska Bill* (1977).

The South and Slavery

William L. Barney, *The Secessionist Impulse* (1974); Malcolm Bell, Jr., *Major Butler's Legacy: Five Generations of a Slaveholding Family* (1987); Steven A. Channing, *A Crisis of Fear: Secession in South Carolina* (1970); William J. Cooper, Jr., *The South and the Politics of Slavery, 1828–1856* (1978); Avery O. Craven, *The Growth of Southern Nationalism, 1848–1861* (1953); Daniel W. Crofts, *Reluctant Confederates: Upper South Unionists in the Secession Crisis* (1989); Merton L. Dillon, *Slavery Attacked* (1991); Drew G. Faust, *The Ideology of Slavery* (1981); Drew G. Faust, *A Sacred Circle: The Dilemma of the Intellectual in the Old South* (1978); Lacy K. Ford, Jr., *Origins of Southern Radicalism* (1988); Eugene D. Genovese, *The World the Slaveholders Made* (1969); Eugene D. Genovese, *The Political Economy of Slavery* (1967); Michael P. Johnson, *Toward a Patriarchal Republic: The Secession of Georgia* (1977); John Niven, *John C. Calhoun and the Price of Union* (1988); James Oakes, *Slavery and Freedom* (1991); David M. Potter, *The South and the Sectional Conflict* (1968); Thomas E. Schott, *Alexander H. Stephens of Georgia* (1988); William R. Stanton, *The Leopard's Spots* (1960); J. Mills Thornton III, *Politics and Power in a Slave Society* (1978); Larry E. Tise, *Proslavery* (1987); Ralph Wooster, *The Secession Conventions of the South* (1962).

The North and Antislavery

Dale Baum, *The Civil War Party System* (1984); Eugene H. Berwanger, *The Frontier Against Slavery* (1967); Frederick J. Blue, *Salmon P. Chase* (1987); Gary Collison, *Shadrach Minkins: From Fugitive Slave to Citizen* (1997); David Donald, *Charles Sumner and the Coming of the Civil War* (1960); Paul

Finkelman, ed., *His Soul Goes Marching On: Responses to John Brown and the Harpers Ferry Raid* (1995); Eric Foner, *Free Soil, Free Labor, Free Men* (1970); Louis S. Gerteis, *Morality and Utility in American Antislavery Reform* (1987); William E. Gienapp, *The Origins of the Republican Party, 1852–1856* (1986); Joan D. Hedrick, *Harriet Beecher Stowe* (1994); James O. and Lois E. Horton, *In Hope of Liberty* (1997); James O. Horton, *Free People of Color* (1993); Henry V. Jaffa, *Crisis of the House Divided* (1959); Robert W. Johannsen, *Lincoln, the South, and Slavery* (1991); Robert W. Johannsen, *Stephen A. Douglas* (1973); Aileen S. Kraditor, *Means and Ends in American Abolitionism* (1969); Stephen B. Oates, *To Purge This Land with Blood*, 2d ed. (1984); Lewis Perry and Michael Fellman, eds., *Antislavery Reconsidered* (1979); Benjamin Quarles, *Black Abolitionists* (1969); C. Peter Ripley et al., ed., *Witness for Freedom: African American Voices on Race, Slavery and Freedom* (1993); Jeffrey Rossbach, *Ambivalent Conspirators* (1982); Richard Sewell, *Ballots for Freedom: Antislavery Politics in the United States, 1837–1860* (1976); Thomas P. Slaughter, *Bloody Dawn: The Cristiana Riot and Racial Violence* (1991); James B. Stewart, *Holy Warriors: The Abolitionists and American Slavery*, 2d ed. (1996); Albert J. Von Frank, *The Trials of Anthony Burns* (1998).

The War with Mexico and Foreign Policy

K. Jack Bauer, *Zachary Taylor* (1985); Gene M. Brack, *Mexico Views Manifest Destiny, 1821–1846* (1976); Richard Griswold del Castillo, *The Treaty of Guadalupe Hidalgo* (1990); Neal Harlow, *California Conquered* (1982); Reginald Horsman, *Race and Manifest Destiny* (1981); Robert W. Johannsen, *To the Halls of the Montezumas: The Mexican War and the American Imagination* (1985); Ernest M. Lander, Jr., *Reluctant Imperialists: Calhoun, the South Carolinians, and the Mexican War* (1980); Robert E. May, *The Southern Dream of a Caribbean Empire, 1854–1861* (1973); Frederick Merk, *The Monroe Doctrine and American Expansion, 1843–1849* (1966); Frederick Merk, *Manifest Destiny and Mission in American History* (1963); David M. Pletcher, *The Diplomacy of Annexation: Texas, Oregon, and the Mexican War* (1973); Dirk Raat, *Mexico and the United States* (1992); John H. Schroeder, *Mr. Polk's War: American Opposition and Dissent* (1973); Otis A. Singletary, *The Mexican War* (1960); Anders Stephanson, *Manifest Destiny* (1995); David J. Weber, *The Mexican Frontier, 1821–1846* (1982).

Chapter 15

The War and the South

Thomas B. Alexander and Richard E. Beringer, *The Anatomy of the Confederate Congress* (1972); Stephen Ash, *When the Yankees Came* (1995); Richard E. Beringer et al., *Why the South Lost the Civil War* (1986); William A. Blair, *Virginia's Private War: Feeding Body and Soul in the Confederacy* (1998); Gabor S. Boritt, ed., *Why the Confederacy Lost* (1992); Richard N. Current, *Lincoln's Loyalists* (1992); William C. Davis, *Jefferson Davis* (1991); Robert F. Durden, *The Gray and the Black: The Confederate Debate on Emancipation* (1972); Paul D. Escott, *Many Excellent People* (1985); Paul D. Escott, *After Secession: Jefferson Davis and the Failure of Confederate Nationalism* (1978); Eli N. Evans, *Judah P. Benjamin* (1987); Drew Gilpin Faust, *The Creation of Confederate Nationalism* (1988); Mark Grimsley, *The Hard Hand of War* (1995); J. B. Jones, *A Rebel War Clerk's Diary*, 2 vols., ed. Howard Swiggett (1935); Ella Lonn, *Desertion During the Civil War* (1928); Mary Elizabeth Massey, *Refugee Life in the Confederacy* (1964); Larry E. Nelson, *Bullets, Ballots, and Rhetoric: Confederate Policy for the United States Presidential Contest of 1864* (1980); Alan T. Nolan, *Lee Considered* (1991); Harry P. Owens and James J. Cooke, eds., *The Old South in the Crucible of War* (1983); James L. Roark, *Masters Without Slaves* (1977); Daniel Sutherland, *Seasons of War* (1995); Emory M. Thomas, *The Confederate Nation* (1979); Emory M. Thomas, *The Confederacy as a Revolutionary Experience* (1971); William A. Tidwell, *April '65* (1995); Bell Irvin Wiley, *The Life of Johnny Reb* (1943); Bell Irvin Wiley, *The Plain People of the Confederacy* (1943); W. Buck Yearns, ed., *The Confederate Governors* (1985).

The War and the North

Ralph Andreano, ed., *The Economic Impact of the American Civil War* (1962); Iver Bernstein, *The New York City Draft Riots* (1990); Robert Cruden, *The War That Never Ended* (1973); David Donald, ed., *Why the North Won the Civil War* (1960); J. Matthew Gallman, *The North Fights the Civil War* (1994); James W. Geary, *We Need Men* (1991); Wood Gray, *The Hidden Civil War* (1942); Randall C. Jimerson, *The Private Civil War* (1988); Frank L. Klement, *The Copperheads in the Middle West* (1960); Susan Previant Lee and Peter Passell, *A New Economic View of American History* (1979); James M. McPherson, *Battle Cry of Freedom* (1988); James H. Moorhead, *American Apocalypse* (1978); Phillip S. Paludan, *"A People's Contest": The Union and the Civil War, 1861–1865* (1989); Robert Hunt Rhodes, ed., *All for the Union: The Civil War Diary and Letters of Elisha Hunt Rhodes* (1991); Anne C. Rose, *Victorian America and the Civil War* (1992); George Winston Smith and Charles Burnet Judah, *Life in the North During the Civil War* (1966); *George Templeton Strong, Diary*, 4 vols., ed. Allan Nevins and Milton Hasley Thomas (1952); Paul Studenski, *Financial History of the United States* (1952); Maris A. Vinovskis, ed., *Toward a Social History of the American Civil War* (1990); Bell Irvin Wiley, *The Life of Billy Yank* (1952).

Women

John Q. Anderson, ed., *Brokenburn: The Journal of Kate Stone* (1955); John R. Brumgardt, ed., *Civil War Nurse: The Diary and Letters of Hannah Ropes* (1980); Catherine Clinton and

Nina Silber, eds., *Divided Houses: Gender and the Civil War* (1992); Beth Gilbert Crabtree and James W. Patton, eds., *"Journal of a Secesh Lady": The Diary of Catherine Ann Devereux Edmondston, 1860–1866* (1979); Drew Gilpin Faust, *Mothers of Invention* (1996); Jacqueline Jones, *Labor of Love, Labor of Sorrow* (1985); Mary Elizabeth Massey, *Bonnet Brigades* (1966); George C. Rable, *Civil Wars: Women and the Crisis of Southern Nationalism* (1989); Mary D. Robertson, ed., *Lucy Breckinridge of Grove Hill: The Journal of a Virginia Girl, 1862–1864* (1979); Lee Ann Whites, *The Civil War as a Crisis in Gender* (1995); C. Vann Woodward and Elisabeth Muhlenfeld, eds., *Mary Chesnut's Civil War* (1981); Agatha Young, *Women and the Crisis* (1959).

African Americans

Virginia M. Adams, ed., *On the Altar of Freedom: A Black Soldier's Civil War Letters from the Front* (1991); Ira Berlin, ed., *Freedom: A Documentary History of Emancipation, 1861–1867*, Series I, *The Destruction of Slavery* (1979), and Series II, *The Black Military Experience* (1982); Richard M. Blackett, ed., *Thomas Morris Chester: Black Civil War Correspondent* (1989); David W. Blight, *Frederick Douglass' Civil War* (1989); Dudley Cornish, *The Sable Arm* (1956); Barbara Jeanne Fields, *Slavery and Freedom on the Middle Ground* (1985); Joseph T. Glatthaar, *Forged in Battle* (1990); James G. Hollandsworth, *The Louisiana Native Guards* (1995); Leon Litwack, *Been in the Storm So Long* (1979); James M. McPherson, *The Negro's Civil War* (1965); James M. McPherson, *The Struggle for Equality* (1964); Clarence L. Mohr, *On the Threshold of Freedom* (1986); Lynda J. Morgan, *Emancipation in Virginia's Tobacco Belt, 1850–1870* (1992); Benjamin Quarles, *The Negro in the Civil War* (1953); Edwin S. Redkey, ed., *A Grand Army of Black Men* (1992).

Military History

Nancy Scott Anderson and Dwight Anderson, *The Generals: Ulysses S. Grant and Robert E. Lee* (1987); David W. Blight, ed., *When This Cruel War Is Over: The Civil War Letters of Charles Harvey Brewster* (1992); Albert Castel, *Decision in the West* (1992); Bruce Catton, *Grant Takes Command* (1969); Bruce Catton, *A Stillness at Appomattox* (1953); Benjamin Franklin Cooling, *Forts Henry and Donelson* (1988); Peter Cozzens, *This Terrible Sound* (1992); William C. Davis, ed., *The Image of War*, multivolume (1983–1985); Michael Fellman, *Citizen Sherman* (1995); Shelby Foote, *The Civil War, a Narrative*, 3 vols. (1958–1974); Douglas Southall Freeman, *Lee's Lieutenants*, 3 vols. (1942–1944); Douglas Southall Freeman, *R. E. Lee*, 4 vols. (1934–1935); Gary W. Gallagher, *The Confederate War* (1997); Gary W. Gallagher, *Lee and His Generals in War and Memory* (1998); Joseph T. Glatthaar, *The March to the Sea and Beyond* (1985); Herman Hattaway and Archer Jones, *How the North Won* (1983); Laurence M. Hauptman, *Between Two Fires: American Indians in the Civil War* (1995); Archer Jones, *Civil War Command and Strategy*

(1992); Alvin M. Josephy, Jr., *The Civil War in the American West* (1991); Gerald F. Linderman, *Embattled Courage* (1989); Thomas L. Livermore, *Numbers and Losses in the Civil War in America* (1957); Grady McWhiney and Perry D. Jamieson, *Attack and Die* (1982); Reid Mitchell, *Civil War Soldiers* (1988); Reid Mitchell, *The Vacant Chair* (1993); Roy Morris, Jr., *Sheridan* (1992); Charles Royster, *The Destructive War* (1991); Stephen W. Sears, *To the Gates of Richmond* (1992); Stephen W. Sears, *George B. McClellan* (1988); Emory M. Thomas, *Robert E. Lee* (1995); Emory M. Thomas, *Bold Dragoon: The Life of J. E. B. Stuart* (1987); Noah Andre Trudeau, *The Last Citadel* (1991); Steven E. Woodworth, *Jefferson Davis and His Generals* (1990).

Foreign Relations

Stuart L. Bernath, *Squall Across the Atlantic: American Civil War Prize Cases and Diplomacy* (1970); Kinley J. Brauer, "The Slavery Problem in the Diplomacy of the American Civil War," *Pacific Historical Review* 46, no. 3 (1977): 439–469; David P. Crook, *The North, the South, and the Powers, 1861–1865* (1974); Charles P. Cullop, *Confederate Propaganda in Europe* (1969); Norman B. Ferris, *The Trent Affair* (1977); Howard Jones, *Union in Peril* (1992); Frank J. Merli, *Great Britain and the Confederate Navy* (1970); Frank L. Owsley and Harriet Owsley, *King Cotton Diplomacy* (1959); Gordon H. Warren, *Fountain of Discontent: The Trent Affair and Freedom of the Seas* (1981).

Abraham Lincoln and the Union Government

Allan G. Bogue, *The Earnest Men: Republicans of the Civil War Senate* (1981); Gabor S. Borit, ed., *The Historian's Lincoln* (1989); Fawn Brodie, *Thaddeus Stevens* (1959); Richard N. Current, *The Lincoln Nobody Knows* (1958); Leonard P. Curry, *Blueprint for Modern America: Non-Military Legislation of the First Civil War Congress* (1968); Christopher Dell, *Lincoln and the War Democrats* (1975); David Donald, *Charles Sumner and the Rights of Man* (1970); David Donald, *Lincoln* (1995); Ludwell H. Johnson, "Lincoln's Solution to the Problem of Peace Terms, 1864–1865," *Journal of Southern History* 34 (November 1968): 441–447; Peyton McCrary, *Abraham Lincoln and Reconstruction: The Louisiana Experiment* (1978); James M. McPherson, *Abraham Lincoln and the Second American Revolution* (1990); Mark Neely, *The Fate of Liberty* (1991); Stephen B. Oates, *With Malice Toward None* (1977); Philip S. Paludan, *The Presidency of Abraham Lincoln* (1994); Heather Cox Richardson, *The Greatest Nation of the Earth: Republican Economic Policies During the Civil War* (1997); Joel Silbey, *A Respectable Minority: The Democratic Party in the Civil War Era* (1977); Benjamin P. Thomas, *Abraham Lincoln* (1952); Hans L. Trefousse, *The Radical Republicans* (1969); Glyndon G. Van Deusen, *William Henry Seward* (1967); T. Harry Williams, *Lincoln and His Generals* (1952); T. Harry Williams, *Lincoln and the Radicals* (1941).

Chapter 16

National Policy, Politics, and Constitutional Law

Richard H. Abbott, *The Republican Party and the South, 1855–1877* (1986); Herman Belz, *Emancipation and Equal Rights* (1978); Herman Belz, *A New Birth of Freedom* (1976); Michael Les Benedict, *A Compromise of Principle: Congressional Republicans and Reconstruction, 1863–1869* (1974); Michael Les Benedict, *The Impeachment and Trial of Andrew Johnson* (1973); Charles S. Campbell, *The Transformation of American Foreign Relations, 1865–1900* (1976); Adrian Cook, *The Alabama Claims* (1975); Michael Kent Curtis, *No State Shall Abridge* (1987); David Donald, *Charles Sumner and the Rights of Man* (1970); Harold M. Hyman, *A More Perfect Union* (1973); Ronald J. Jensen, *The Alaska Purchase and Russian-American Relations* (1975); William S. McFeely, *Grant* (1981); William S. McFeely, *Yankee Stepfather: General O. O. Howard and the Freedmen* (1968); Eric L. McKitrick, *Andrew Johnson and Reconstruction* (1966); James M. McPherson, *The Abolitionist Legacy* (1975); Joel Silbey, *A Respectable Minority: The Democratic Party in the Civil War Era* (1977); Brooks D. Simpson, *Let Us Have Peace* (1991); Brooks D. Simpson, *The Reconstruction Presidents* (1998); Kenneth M. Stampp, *The Era of Reconstruction* (1965); Hans L. Trefousse, *Andrew Johnson* (1989).

The Freed Slaves

Roberta Sue Alexander, *North Carolina Faces the Freedmen* (1985); Ira Berlin, ed., *Freedom: A Documentary History of Emancipation, 1861–1867* (1984); Elizabeth R. Bethel, *Promiseland* (1981); Orville Vernon Burton, *In My Father's House Are Many Mansions* (1985); Edmund L. Drago, *Black Politicians and Reconstruction in Georgia* (1982); Paul D. Escott, *Slavery Remembered* (1979); Eric Foner, "Reconstruction and the Crisis of Free Labor," in *Politics and Ideology in the Age of the Civil War*, ed. Eric Foner (1980); Gerald Jaynes, *Branches Without Roots: The Genesis of the Black Working Class in the American South, 1862–1882* (1986); Leon Litwack, *Been in the Storm So Long* (1979); Edward Magdol, *A Right to the Land* (1977); Robert Morris, *Reading, 'Riting and Reconstruction* (1981); Howard Rabinowitz, ed., *Southern Black Leaders in Reconstruction* (1982); Emma Lou Thornbrough, ed., *Black Reconstructionists* (1972); Okon Uya, *From Slavery to Public Service* (1971); Clarence Walker, *A Rock in a Weary Land* (1982).

Politics and Reconstruction in the South

Robert W. Coakley, *The Role of Federal Military Forces in Domestic Disorders, 1789–1878* (1988); Richard N. Current, *Those Terrible Carpetbaggers* (1988); Jonathan Daniels, *Prince of Carpetbaggers* (1958); W. E. B. Du Bois, *Black Reconstruction* (1935); Paul D. Escott, *Many Excellent People: Power and Privilege in North Carolina, 1850–1900* (1985); W. McKee Evans, *Ballots and Fence Rails: Reconstruction on the Lower Cape Fear* (1966); Michael W. Fitzgerald, *The Union League Movement in the Deep South* (1989); Eric Foner, *Reconstruction: America's Unfinished Revolution, 1863–1877* (1988); Eric Foner, *Nothing but Freedom* (1983); William C. Harris, *The Day of the Carpetbagger* (1979); Thomas Holt, *Black over White: Negro Political Leadership in South Carolina During Reconstruction* (1977); J. Morgan Kousser and James M. McPherson, eds., *Region, Race and Reconstruction* (1982); Elizabeth Studley Nathans, *Losing the Peace* (1968); Michael Perman, *The Road to Redemption* (1984); Michael Perman, *Reunion Without Compromise* (1973); Lawrence N. Powell, *New Masters* (1980); George C. Rable, *But There Was No Peace* (1984); James Roark, *Masters Without Slaves* (1977); James Sefton, *The United States Army and Reconstruction, 1865–1877* (1967); Mark W. Summers, *Railroads, Reconstruction, and the Gospel of Prosperity* (1984); Allen Trelease, *White Terror* (1967); Ted Tunnell, *Carpetbagger from Vermont* (1989); Ted Tunnell, *Crucible of Reconstruction* (1984); Michael Wayne, *The Reshaping of Plantation Society* (1983); Sarah Woolfolk Wiggins, *The Scalawag in Alabama Politics, 1865–1881* (1977).

Women, Family, and Social History

Virginia I. Burr, ed., *The Secret Eye* (1990); Ellen Carol Dubois, *Feminism and Suffrage* (1978); Herbert G. Gutman, *The Black Family in Slavery and Freedom, 1750–1925* (1976); Elizabeth Jacoway, *Yankee Missionaries in the South* (1979); Jacqueline Jones, *Labor of Love, Labor of Sorrow* (1985); Jacqueline Jones, *Soldiers of Light and Love* (1980); Robert C. Kenzer, *Kinship and Neighborhood in a Southern Community* (1987); Mary P. Ryan, *Women in Public* (1990); Rebecca Scott, "The Battle over the Child," *Prologue* 10 (Summer 1978): 101–113.

The End of Reconstruction

Michael Les Benedict, "Southern Democrats in the Crisis of 1876–1877," *Journal of Southern History* 66 (November 1980): 489–524; William Gillette, *Retreat from Reconstruction, 1869–1879* (1980); William Gillette, *The Right to Vote* (1969); Keith Ian Polakoff, *The Politics of Inertia* (1973); John G. Sproat, *"The Best Men": Liberal Reformers in the Gilded Age* (1968); C. Vann Woodward, *Reunion and Reaction* (1951).

Reconstruction's Legacy for the South and the Nation

Robert G. Athearn, *In Search of Canaan* (1978); Edward L. Ayers, *The Promise of the New South* (1992); David W. Blight, *Race and Reunion: The Civil War in American Memory, 1863–1915* (2000); Norman L. Crockett, *The Black Towns* (1979); Stephen J. DeCanio, *Agriculture in the Postbellum South* (1974); Steven Hahn, *The Roots of Southern Populism* (1983); Jay R. Mandle, *The Roots of Black Poverty* (1978); Nell Irvin Painter, *Exodusters* (1976); Howard Rabinowitz, *Race Relations in the Urban South, 1865–1890* (1978); Roger L. Ransom and Richard Sutch, *One Kind of Freedom* (1977); Laurence Shore, *Southern Capitalists* (1986); Peter Wallenstein, *From Slave South to New South* (1987); Jonathan M. Wiener, *Social Origins of the New South* (1978); C. Vann Woodward, *Origins of the New South* (1951).

Chapter 17

Native Americans

Ralph K. Andrist, *The Long Death: The Last Days of the Plains Indians* (1964); Leonard A. Carlson, *Indians, Bureaucrats, and Land: The Dawes Act and the Decline of Indian Farming* (1981); David Courtwright, *Violent Land* (1996); Frederick E. Hoxie, *A Final Promise: The Campaign to Assimilate the Indians, 1880–1920* (1984); Janet A. McDonnell, *The Dispossession of the American Indian* (1991); Francis Paul Prucha, *The Great Father: The United States Government and the American Indians* (1984); Robert M. Utley, *The Lance and the Shield: The Life and Times of Sitting Bull* (1993); Robert M. Utley, *The Indian Frontier of the American West, 1846–1890* (1984); Philip Weeks, *Farewell, My Nation: The American Indian and the United States* (1990); Richard White, *The Roots of Dependency* (1983).

The Western Frontier

Ray A. Billington and Martin Ridge, *Westward Expansion*, 5th ed. (1982); Sara Deutsch, *No Separate Refuge: Culture, Class, and Gender on an Anglo-Hispanic Frontier in the American Southwest* (1987); James R. Grossman, ed., *The Frontier in American Culture* (1994); Robert V. Hine, *The American West*, 2d ed. (1984); Julie Roy Jeffrey, *Frontier Women* (1979); Patricia Limerick, *The Legacy of Conquest: The Unbroken Past of the American West* (1987); Timothy R. Mahoney, *River Towns in the Great West* (1990); Peggy Pascoe, *Relations of Rescue: The Search for Female Moral Authority in the American West* (1990); Rodman W. Paul, *The Far West and the Great Plains in Transition, 1859–1900* (1988); Robert J. Rosenbaum, *Mexican Resistance in the Southwest* (1981); Lillian Schlissel, *Women's Diaries of the Westward Journey* (1982); Richard White, *"It's Your Misfortune and None of My Own": A New History of the American West* (1991).

Water and the Environment

Roderick Nash, *American Environmentalism*, 3d ed. (1990); Joseph M. Petulla, *American Environmental History* (1977); Thurman Wilkins, *John Muir: Apostle of Nature* (1995); Donald Worster, *Rivers of Empire: Water, Aridity, and the Growth of the American West* (1985); Donald Worster, *An Unsettled Country: Changing Landscapes of the American West* (1994).

Railroads

Alfred D. Chandler, ed., *Railroads* (1965); Edward C. Kirkland, *Men, Cities, and Transportation* (1948); George R. Taylor and Irene Neu, *The American Railroad Network* (1956); Alan Trachtenberg, *The Incorporation of America* (1982); O. O. Winther, *The Transportation Frontier* (1964).

Ranching and Settlement of the Plains

Lewis Atherton, *The Cattle Kings* (1961); William Cronon, *Nature's Metropolis: Chicago and the Great West* (1991); Gilbert C. Fite, *The Farmer's Frontier* (1963); Robert V. Hine, *Community on the American Frontier* (1980); Richard W. Slatta, *Cowboys of the Americas* (1990); Walter Prescott Webb, *The Great Plains* (1931).

Chapter 18

General

Daniel J. Boorstin, *The Americans: The Democratic Experience* (1973); Alan Dawley, *Struggle for Justice: Social Responsibility and the Liberal State* (1991); Stephen Diner, *A Very Different Age* (1998); Ray Ginger, *The Age of Excess* (1965); Samuel P. Hays, *The Response to Industrialism* (1975); Thomas J. Schlereth, *Victorian America: Transformations in Everyday Life* (1991).

Technology and Invention

Robert W. Bruce, *Bell: Alexander Graham Bell and the Conquest of Solitude* (1973); Gary Cross and Rich Szostak, *Technology and American Society* (1995); David Hounshell, *From the American System to Mass Production* (1984); Thomas Parke Hughes, *American Genesis: A Century of Technological Enthusiasm* (1989); John P. Kasson, *Civilizing the Machine: Technology and Republican Values in America* (1976); Leo Marx, *The Machine in the Garden: Technology and the Pastoral Ideal* (1964); Andre Millard, *Edison and the Business of Innovation* (1990); David E. Nye, *Electrifying America* (1990).

Industrialism, Industrialists, and Corporate Growth

W. Eliot Brownlee, *Dynamics of Ascent: A History of the American Economy*, 2d ed. (1979); Stuart Bruchey, *Growth of the Modern Economy* (1973); Vincent P. Carosso, *The Morgans* (1987); Alfred D. Chandler, *The Visible Hand: The Managerial Revolution in American Business* (1977); Thomas C. Cochran, *Business in American Life* (1972); Francis L. Eames, *The New York Stock Exchange* (1968); David F. Hawkes, *John D.: The Founding Father of the Rockefellers* (1980); Robert Higgs, *The Transformation of the American Economy, 1865–1914* (1971); Harold C. Livesay, *Andrew Carnegie and the Rise of Big Business* (1975); Glen Porter, *The Rise of Big Business* (1973); Martin J. Sklar, *The Corporate Reconstruction of American Capitalism* (1988); Richard Tedlow, *The Rise of the American Business Corporation* (1991); Joseph Wall, *Alfred I. du Pont: The Man and His Family* (1990).

Work and Labor Organization

Alan Derickson, *Workers' Health, Workers' Democracy: The Western Miners' Struggle, 1891–1925* (1988); Melvin Dubofsky, *We Shall Be All: A History of the Industrial Workers of the World* (1969); Sarah Eisenstein, *Give Us Bread, Give Us Roses: Working Women's Consciousness in the United States* (1983); Leon Fink, *Workingmen's Democracy: The Knights of Labor and American Politics* (1982); Philip S. Foner, *The Great Labor Uprising of 1877* (1977); Herbert G. Gutman, *Work, Culture and Society in Industrializing America* (1976); Tamara K. Hareven, *Family Time and Industrial Time* (1982); Alice Kessler-Harris,

Out to Work: A History of Wage Earning Women in the United States (1982); Susan Lehrer, *Origins of Protective Labor Legislation for Women* (1987); Harold Livesay, *Samuel Gompers and Organized Labor in America* (1978); Milton Meltzer, *Bread and Roses: The Struggle of American Labor, 1865–1915* (1967); Ruth Milkman, ed., *Women, Work, and Protest* (1985); David Montgomery, *The Fall of the House of Labor: The Workplace, the State, and American Labor Activism, 1865–1925* (1987); Stephen H. Norwood, *Labor's Flaming Youth: Telephone Operators and Worker Militancy* (1990); Elizabeth Ann Payne, *Reform, Labor, and Feminism: Margaret Dreier Robins and the Women's Trade Union League* (1988); Leon J. Wolff, *Lockout: The Story of the Homestead Strike of 1892* (1965).

Living Standards and New Conveniences

Susan Porter Benson, *Counter Cultures: Saleswomen, Managers, and Customers in American Department Stores, 1890–1940* (1986); T. J. Jackson Lears and Richard W. Fox, eds., *The Culture of Consumption* (1983); Godfrey M. Lebhar, *Chain Stores in America* (1962); Harvey A. Levenstein, *Revolution at the Table: The Transformation of the American Diet* (1988); Kathy Peiss, *Hope in a Jar: The Making of America's Beauty Culture* (1998); Daniel Pope, *The Making of Modern Advertising* (1983); Peter R. Shergold, *Working Class Life* (1982); Susan Strasser, *Satisfaction Guaranteed: The Making of the American Mass Market* (1989); Gwendolyn Wright, *Building the Dream: A Social History of Housing in America* (1983).

Attitudes Toward Industrialism

Sidney Fine, *Laissez Faire and the General Welfare State* (1956); Louis Galambos and Barbara Barron Spence, *The Public Image of Big Business in America* (1975); Richard Hofstadter, *Social Darwinism in American Thought*, rev. ed. (1955); T. J. Jackson Lears, *No Place of Grace: Antimodernism and the Transformation of American Culture* (1981); Robert McCloskey, *American Conservatism in the Age of Enterprise* (1951); John L. Thomas, *Alternative America: Henry George, Edward Bellamy, Henry Demarest Lloyd, and the Adversary Tradition* (1983).

Southern Industrialism

Edward Ayers, *The Promise of the New South* (1992); James C. Cobb, *Industrialization and Southern Society, 1877–1984* (1984); Paul M. Gaston, *The New South Creed* (1970); C. Vann Woodward, *Origins of the New South* (1951); Gavin Wright, *Old South, New South* (1986).

Chapter 19

Urban Growth

Howard P. Chudacoff and Judith E. Smith, *The Evolution of American Urban Society*, 5th ed. (1999); David Goldfield, *Cotton Fields and Skyscrapers: Southern City and Region* (1982); Kenneth T. Jackson, *The Crabgrass Frontier: The Suburbanization of the United States* (1985); Harold Platt, *City Building in the New South* (1983); Jon Teaford, *The Unheralded Triumph: City Government in America, 1870–1900* (1984); Sam Bass Warner, Jr., *The Urban Wilderness* (1982).

Immigration, Ethnicity, and Religion

Aaron I. Abell, *American Catholicism and Social Action* (1960); John Bodnar, *The Transplanted* (1985); John Bodnar, Roger Simon, and Michael P. Weber, *Lives of Their Own: Blacks, Italians, and Poles in Pittsburgh, 1900–1960* (1982); Sucheng Chan, ed., *Entry Denied: Exclusion and the Chinese Community in America, 1882–1943* (1990); Elizabeth Ewen, *Immigrant Women in the Land of Dollars* (1985); Donna R. Gabaccia, *From the Other Side: Women, Gender, and Immigrant Life in the United States* (1994); Mario T. Garcia, *Desert Immigrants: The Mexicans of El Paso, 1880–1920* (1981); Oscar Handlin, *The Uprooted*, 2d ed. (1973); John Higham, *Strangers in the Land: Patterns of American Nativism* (1955); Yusi Ichioka, *The Issei: The World of the First Japanese Immigrants, 1885–1924* (1988); Matthew Frye Jacobson, *Whiteness of a Different Color: European Immigrants and the Alchemy of Race* (1998); Matt S. Maier and Felciano Rivera, *The Chicanos* (1972); Henry F. May, *Protestant Churches and Industrial America* (1949); Werner Sollors, *Beyond Ethnicity* (1986); Ron Takaki, *Iron Cages: Race and Culture in Nineteenth-Century America* (1979); Stephan Thernstrom, ed., *Harvard Encyclopedia of American Ethnic Groups* (1980).

Urban Services

Christine Boyer, *Dreaming the Rational City: The Myth of American City Planning* (1983); Charles W. Cheape, *Moving the Masses* (1980); Lawrence A. Cremin, *American Education: The Metropolitan Experience* (1988); David R. Johnson, *American Law Enforcement* (1981); Martin V. Melosi, *Garbage in the Cities* (1981); Eric Monkkonen, *America Becomes Urban* (1988); Mark Rose, *Cities of Light and Heat* (1995); Barbara Gutmann Rosencrantz, *Public Health and the State* (1972); Stanley K. Schultz, *Constructing Urban Culture: American Cities and City Planning* (1989).

Family and Individual Life Cycles

W. Andrew Achenbaum, *Old Age in the New Land* (1979); George Chauncey, *Gay New York* (1995); Howard P. Chudacoff, *The Age of the Bachelor* (1999); Howard P. Chudacoff, *How Old Are You? Age in American Culture* (1989); Carl N. Degler, *At Odds: Women and the Family in America* (1980); John D'Emilio and Estelle B. Freedman, *Intimate Matters: A History of Sexuality in America* (1988); Carole Haber, *Beyond Sixty-five: Dilemmas of Old Age in America's Past* (1983); Joseph Kett, *Rites of Passage: Adolescence in America* (1979); E. Anthony Rotundo, *American Manhood* (1994).

Mass Entertainment and Leisure

Gunther Barth, *City People* (1980); Jessica H. Foy and Thomas J. Schlereth, eds., *American Home Life, 1880–1930* (1992); Donna R. Gabaccia, *We Are What We Eat: Ethnic Food and the Making of Americans* (1998); Allen Guttmann, *A Whole New Ball Game: An Interpretation of American Sports* (1988); Katrina Hazzard-Gordon, *Lookin': The Rise of Social Dance Formulations in African-American Culture* (1990); George Juergens, *Joseph Pulitzer and the New York World* (1966); John F. Kasson, *Amusing the Million: Coney Island at the Turn of the Century* (1978); David Nasaw, *Going Out: The Rise and Fall of Popular Amusements* (1993); Kathy Peiss, *Cheap Amusements: Working Women and Leisure in Turn-of-the-Century New York* (1986); Benjamin G. Rader, *American Sports*, 4th ed. (1999); Steven A. Riess, *City Games* (1989); Roy Rosenzweig, *Eight Hours for What We Will! Workers and Leisure in an Industrial City, 1870–1920* (1983); Robert Sklar, *Movie-Made America* (1976); Ronald A. Smith, *Sports and Freedom: The Rise of Big-Time College Athletics* (1988); Robert V. Snyder, *The Voice of the City: Vaudeville and Popular Culture in New York City, 1880–1920* (1990); Robert C. Toll, *On with the Show: The First Century of Show Business in America* (1976).

Mobility and Race Relations

James Borchert, *Alley Life in Washington* (1980); Howard P. Chudacoff, *Mobile Americans* (1972); Clyde Griffen and Sally Griffen, *Natives and Newcomers* (1977); Jacqueline Jones, *Labor of Love, Labor of Sorrow: Black Women, Work and the Family from Slavery to the Present* (1985); David M. Katzman, *Before the Ghetto* (1973); Kenneth L. Kusmer, *A Ghetto Takes Shape* (1976); Gilbert Osofsky, *Harlem: The Making of a Ghetto* (1966); Elizabeth H. Pleck, *Black Migration and Poverty: Boston, 1865–1900* (1979); Howard N. Rabinowitz, *Race Relations in the Urban South* (1978); Allan H. Spear, *Black Chicago* (1967); Stephan Thernstrom, *The Other Bostonians: Poverty and Progress in the American Metropolis* (1973); Olivier Zunz, *The Changing Face of Inequality* (1982).

Boss Politics

Alexander B. Callow, Jr., ed., *The City Boss in America* (1976); Lyle Dorsett, *The Pendergast Machine* (1968); Leo Hershkowitz, *Tweed's New York: Another Look* (1977); Terrence J. McDonald, *The Parameters of Urban Fiscal Policy* (1986); Zane L. Miller, *Boss Cox's Cincinnati* (1968); Bruce M. Stave and Sondra Stave, eds., *Urban Bosses, Machines, and Progressive Reformers* (1984).

Urban Reform

John D. Buenker, *Urban Liberalism and Progressive Reform* (1973); James B. Crooks, *Politics and Progress* (1968); Doris Groshen Daniels, *Always a Sister: The Feminism of Lillian D. Wald* (1989); Allen F. Davis, *Spearheads for Reform* (1967);

Lori Ginzberg, *Women and the Work of Benevolence* (1991); Rivka Shpak Lissack, *Pluralism and Progressives: Hull House and the New Immigrants, 1890–1919* (1989); Roy M. Lubove, *The Progressives and the Slums* (1962); Clay McShane, *Technology and Reform* (1974); Robyn Muncy, *Creating a Female Dominion in American Reform* (1991); Martin J. Schiesl, *The Politics of Efficiency* (1977); Kathryn Kish Sklar, *Florence Kelley and the Nation's Work* (1995).

Chapter 20

General

Charles W. Calhoun, ed., *The Gilded Age: Essays on the Origins of Modern America* (1995); Sean Denis Cashman, *America in the Gilded Age* (1984); Steven J. Diner, *A Very Different Age* (1998); Ray Ginger, *The Age of Excess*, 2d ed. (1975); H. Wayne Morgan, ed., *The Gilded Age* (1970); Nell Irvin Painter, *Standing at Armageddon* (1987).

Parties and Political Issues

John M. Dobson, *Politics in the Gilded Age* (1972); Ari A. Hoogenboom, *Outlawing the Spoils: The Civil Service Movement* (1961); Morton Keller, *Affairs of State* (1977); Paul Kleppner, *The Third Electoral System, 1853–1892* (1979); Michael E. McGerr, *The Decline of Popular Politics* (1986); Walter T. K. Nugent, *Money and American Society* (1968); A. M. Paul, *Conservative Crisis and the Rule of Law: Attitudes of Bar and Bench, 1887–1895* (1969); John G. Sproat, *The Best Men: Liberal Reformers in the Gilded Age* (1968); Hal R. Williams, *Years of Decision: American Politics in the 1890s* (1978).

The Presidency

Kenneth E. Davison, *The Presidency of Rutherford B. Hayes* (1972); Justus D. Doenecke, *The Presidencies of James A. Garfield and Chester A. Arthur* (1981); Lewis L. Gould, *The Presidency of William McKinley* (1981); Homer E. Socolotsky and Allen B. Spetter, *The Presidency of Benjamin Harrison* (1987); Richard G. Welch, *The Presidency of Grover Cleveland* (1988).

Women's Rights and Disfranchisement of African Americans

Edward L. Ayers, *The Promise of the New South* (1992); Paula Baker, *The Moral Framework of Public Life* (1991); Beverly Beeton, *Women Vote in the West: The Suffrage Movement, 1869–1896* (1986); Fitzhugh Brundage, *Lynching in the New South* (1993); Glenda Elizabeth Gilmore, *Gender & Jim Crow* (1996); Elisabeth Griffith, *In Her Own Right: The Life of Elizabeth Cady Stanton* (1984); Joel Williamson, *The Crucible of Race* (1984); C. Vann Woodward, *The Strange Career of Jim Crow*, 3d rev. ed. (1974).

Protest and Socialism

William M. Dick, *Labor and Socialism in America* (1972); Ray Ginger, *Bending Cross: A Biography of Eugene Victor Debs* (1969); J. Anthony Lukas, *Big Trouble* (1997); Nick Salvatore, *Eugene V. Debs: Citizen and Socialist* (1982); Carlos A. Schwantes, *Coxey's Army* (1985); David Shannon, *The Socialist Party of America* (1955).

Populism and the Election of 1896

Donna A. Barnes, *Farmers in Rebellion: The Rise and Fall of the Southern Farmers Alliance and People's Party in Texas* (1984); Paolo Coletta, *William Jennings Bryan: Political Evangelist* (1964); Paul W. Glad, *McKinley, Bryan, and the People* (1964); Lawrence Goodwyn, *Democratic Promise: The Populist Movement in America* (1976); Steven Hahn, *The Roots of Southern Populism* (1983); J. Morgan Kousser, *The Shaping of Southern Politics* (1974); Robert C. McMath, Jr., *American Populism* (1993); Walter T. K. Nugent, *The Tolerant Populists* (1963); Jeffrey Ostler, *Prairie Populism* (1993); Norman Pollack, *The Populist Response to Industrial America* (1962); Barton C. Shaw, *The Wool-Hat Boys: Georgia's Populist Party* (1984); Allan Weinstein, *Prelude to Populism: Origins of the Silver Issue* (1970).

Chapter 21

General

Paul M. Boyer, *Urban Masses and Moral Order in America, 1820–1920* (1978); Walter M. Brasch, *Forerunners of Revolution: Muckrakers and the American Social Conscience* (1990); John M. Cooper, Jr., *The Pivotal Decades* (1990); Steven J. Diner, *A Very Different Age: Americans of the Progressive Era* (1998); Richard Hofstadter, *The Age of Reform* (1955); William R. Hutchinson, *The Modernist Impulse in American Protestantism* (1976); Morton Keller, *Regulating a New Economy* (1990); Gabriel Kolko, *The Triumph of Conservatism* (1963); Arthur Link and Richard L. McCormick, *Progressivism* (1983); Daniel T. Rodgers, *Atlantic Crossings: Social Politics in a Progressive Age* (1998); Robert Wiebe, *The Search for Order* (1968).

Regional Studies

Dewey Grantham, *Southern Progressivism* (1983); William A. Link, *The Paradox of Southern Progressivism* (1992); David P. Thelen, *Robert La Follette and the Insurgent Spirit* (1976); Richard White, *"It's Your Misfortune and None of My Own": A History of the American West* (1991); C. Vann Woodward, *Origins of the New South* (1951).

Legislative Issues and Reform Groups

Ruth H. Crocker, *Social Work and Social Order* (1992); Robert M. Crunden, *Ministers of Reform: The Progressives' Achievement in American Civilization* (1982); Allen F. Davis, *Spearheads for Reform: The Social Settlements and the Progressive Movement, 1890–1914* (1967); Ruth Rosen, *The Lost Sisterhood: Prostitution in America, 1900–1918* (1982); W. J. Rorabaugh, *The Alcoholic Republic* (1979); Kathryn Kish Sklar, *Florence Kelley and the Nation's Work* (1995); James H. Timberlake, *Prohibition and the Progressive Crusade* (1963); Walter I. Trattner, *Crusade for the Children* (1970); Irwin Yellowitz, *Labor and the Progressive Movement in New York State* (1965); James Harvey Young, *Pure Food* (1989). (For works on socialism, see the listings under "Protest and Socialism," Chapter 20.)

Education, Law, and the Social Sciences

Jerold S. Auerback, *Unequal Justice: Lawyers and Social Change in Modern America* (1976); Lawrence Cremin, *The Transformation of the School: Progressivism in American Education* (1961); Paula S. Fass, *Outside In: Minorities and the Transformation of American Education* (1989); Ellen Fitzpatrick, *Endless Crusade: Women Social Scientists and Progressive Reform* (1990); Lynn D. Gordon, *Gender and Higher Education in the Progressive Era* (1990); Thomas L. Haskell, *The Emergence of Professional Social Science* (1977); Helen Horowitz, *Alma Mater: Design and Experience in Women's Colleges* (1984); David W. Marcell, *Progress and Pragmatism: James, Dewey, Beard, and the American Idea of Progress* (1974); Lawrence Veysey, *The Emergence of the American University* (1970).

Women

Ruth Borden, *Women and Temperance* (1980); Ellen Chesler, *Woman of Valor: The Life of Margaret Sanger* (1992); Nancy F. Cott, *The Grounding of American Feminism* (1987); Carl N. Degler, *At Odds: Women and the Family in America* (1980); Linda Gordon, *Woman's Body, Woman's Right: A Social History of Birth Control in America* (1976); Evelyn Higginbotham, *Righteous Discontent: The Women's Movement in the Black Baptist Church, 1880–1920* (1993); Alice Kessler-Harris, *Out to Work: A History of Wage-Earning Women in the United States* (1982); Robyn Muncy, *Creating a Female Dominion in American Reform* (1991); Rosalind Rosenberg, *Beyond Separate Spheres: Intellectual Roots of Modern Feminism* (1982); Sheila M. Rothman, *Woman's Proper Place* (1978).

African Americans

John Dittmer, *Black Georgia in the Progressive Era* (1977); George Frederickson, *The Black Image in the White Mind* (1971); Glenda Elizabeth Gilmore, *Gender & Jim Crow* (1996); Louis R. Harlan, *Booker T. Washington*, 2 vols. (1972 and 1983); Jacqueline Jones, *Labor of Love, Labor of Sorrow: Black Women, Work and the Family from Slavery to the Present* (1985); David Levering Lewis, *W. E. B. Du Bois* (1993); August Meier, *Negro Thought in America, 1880–1915* (1963).

Roosevelt, Taft, and Wilson

Francis L. Broderick, *Progressivism at Risk: Electing a President in 1912* (1989); Paolo E. Coletta, *The Presidency of William Howard Taft* (1973); John M. Cooper, Jr., *The Warrior and the Priest: Woodrow Wilson and Theodore Roosevelt* (1983); Lewis Gould, *The Presidency of Theodore Roosevelt* (1991); August Hecksher, *Woodrow Wilson* (1991); Edmund Morris, *The Rise of Theodore Roosevelt* (1979); James Pednick, Jr., *Progressive Politics and Conservation: The Ballinger-Pinchot Affair* (1968).

Chapter 22

General

Robert L. Beisner, *From the Old Diplomacy to the New, 1865–1900*, 2d ed. (1986); Manfred F. Boemeke et al., eds., *Anticipating Total War: The German and American Experiences, 1871–1914* (1999); Daniel R. Headrick, *The Invisible Weapon: Telecommunications and International Politics, 1851–1945* (1991); Ronald J. Jensen, *The Alaska Purchase and Russian-American Relations* (1975); Paul Kennedy, *The Rise and Fall of the Great Powers* (1987); Paul A. C. Koistinen, *Mobilizing for Modern War: The Political Economy of American Warfare, 1865–1919* (1997); Walter LaFeber, *The American Search for Opportunity, 1865–1913* (1993); Walter LaFeber, *The New Empire*, anniv. ed. (1998); Ernest R. May, *American Imperialism* (1968); Emily Rosenberg, *Spreading the American Dream* (1982); William Appleman Williams, *The Tragedy of American Diplomacy*, new ed. (1988).

Imperial Promoters

Howard K. Beale, *Theodore Roosevelt and the Rise of America to World Power* (1956); H. W. Brands, *T.R.* (1997); John M. Cooper, Jr., *The Warrior and the Priest* (1983) (on Roosevelt and Wilson); Edward P. Crapol, *James G. Blaine* (1999); Lewis L. Gould, *The Presidency of Theodore Roosevelt* (1991); Lewis L. Gould, *The Presidency of William McKinley* (1981); Frederick Marks III, *Velvet on Iron: The Diplomacy of Theodore Roosevelt* (1979); Edmund Morris, *The Rise of Theodore Roosevelt* (1979); Ernest N. Paolino, *The Foundations of the American Empire: William Henry Seward and U.S. Foreign Policy* (1973); William C. Widenor, *Henry Cabot Lodge and the Search for an American Foreign Policy* (1980).

Economic and Financial Expansion

William H. Becker, *The Dynamics of Business-Government Relations* (1982); Robert B. Davies, *Peacefully Working to Conquer the World: Singer Sewing Machines in Foreign Markets, 1854–1920* (1976); David Pletcher, *The Diplomacy of Trade and Investment* (1998); Emily Rosenberg, *Financial Missionaries to the World: The Politics and Culture of Dollar Diplomacy,* 1900–1930 (1999); Tom Terrill, *The Tariff, Politics, and American Foreign Policy, 1874–1901* (1973); Mira Wilkins, *The Emergence of the Multinational Enterprise* (1970); William Appleman Williams, *The Roots of the Modern American Empire* (1969).

Ideology and Culture

Gail Bederman, *Manliness & Civilization* (1995); Alexander DeConde, *Ethnicity, Race, and American Foreign Policy* (1992); Thomas G. Dyer, *Theodore Roosevelt and the Idea of Race* (1980); Willard B. Gatewood, Jr., *Black Americans and the White Man's Burden* (1975); Michael H. Hunt, *Ideology and U.S. Foreign Policy* (1987); Robert D. Johnson, ed., *On Cultural Ground* (1994); Amy Kaplan and Donald E. Pease, eds., *Cultures of United States Imperialism* (1993); Catherine A. Lutz and Jane L. Collins, *Reading National Geographic* (1993); Robert Rydell, *World of Fairs* (1993); Robert Rydell, *All the World's a Fair* (1985); David Spurr, *The Rhetoric of Empire* (1993).

Religious Missionaries

Nancy Boyd, *Emissaries: The Overseas Work of the American YWCA, 1895–1970* (1986); Wayne Flynt and Gerald W. Berkley, *Taking Christianity to China* (1997); John K. Fairbank, ed., *The Missionary Enterprise in China and America* (1974); Gael Graham, *Gender, Culture, and Christianity: American Protestant Mission Schools in China, 1880-1930* (1995); Patricia R. Hill, *The World Their Household* (1985); Jane Hunter, *The Gospel of Gentility: American Missionaries in Turn-of-the-Century China* (1984); Irwin T. Hyatt, Jr., *Our Ordered Lives Confess* (1976) (on China); Ian Tyrrell, *Woman's World, Woman's Empire: The Woman's Christian Temperance Union in International Perspective, 1880–1930* (1991).

Navalism and the Navy

Benjamin F. Cooling, *Gray Steel and Blue Water Navy* (1979); Frederick C. Drake, *The Empire of the Seas: A Biography of Rear Admiral Robert W. Shufelt* (1984); Kenneth J. Hagan, *This People's Navy* (1991); Peter Karsten, *The Naval Aristocracy* (1972); Mark R. Shulman, *Navalism and the Emergence of American Sea Power* (1995); Robert Seager II, *Alfred Thayer Mahan* (1977); Ronald Spector, *Admiral of the New Empire: The Life and Career of George Dewey* (1974).

The Spanish-American-Cuban-Filipino War

Graham A. Cosmas, *An Army for Empire* (1971); Kristin L. Hoganson, *Fighting for American Manhood* (1998); Gerald F. Linderman, *The Mirror of War* (1974); Joyce Milton, *The Yellow Kids* (1989); John Offner, *An Unwanted War* (1992); Louis A. Pérez, Jr., *The War of 1898* (1998); David F. Trask, *The War with Spain in 1898* (1981).

Anti-Imperialism and the Peace Movement

Robert L. Beisner, *Twelve Against Empire* (1968); Kendrick A. Clements, *William Jennings Bryan* (1983); Charles DeBenedetti, *Peace Reform in American History* (1980); C. Roland Marchand, *The American Peace Movement and Social Reform, 1898–1918* (1973); Thomas J. Osborne, *"Empire Can Wait": American Opposition to Hawaiian Annexation* (1981); David S. Patterson, *Toward a Warless World* (1976).

Cuba, Mexico, Panama, and Latin America

Arturo M. Carrión, *Puerto Rico* (1983); Richard H. Collin, *Theodore Roosevelt's Caribbean* (1990); Judith Ewell, *Venezuela and the United States* (1996); David Healy, *Drive to Hegemony: The United States in the Caribbean, 1898–1917* (1989); Walter LaFeber, *Inevitable Revolutions: The United States in Central America*, 2d rev. ed. (1993); Walter LaFeber, *The Panama Canal*, updated ed. (1990); Lester D. Langley, *Struggle for the American Mediterranean* (1980); Lester D. Langley, *The United States and the Caribbean, 1900–1970* (1980); John Major, *Prize Possession: The United States and the Panama Canal, 1903–1979* (1993); David McCullough, *The Path Between the Seas: The Creation of the Panama Canal, 1870–1914* (1977); Louis A. Pérez, Jr., *Cuba and the United States*, 2d ed. (1997); Louis A. Pérez, Jr., *Cuba Under the Platt Amendment, 1902–1934* (1986); Fredrick B. Pike, *The United States and Latin America* (1992); Brenda G. Plummer, *Haiti and the Great Powers, 1902–1915* (1988); Stephen J. Randall, *Colombia and the United States* (1992); Ramón E. Ruíz, *The People of Sonora and Yankee Capitalists* (1988); Lars Schoultz, *Beneath the United States* (1998); Josefina Vázquez and Lorenzo Meyer, *The United States and Mexico* (1985).

Hawai'i, China, Japan, and the Pacific

Warren I. Cohen, *America's Response to China*, 3d ed. (1989); Michael H. Hunt, *The Making of a Special Relationship* (1983) (on China); Akira Iriye, *Pacific Estrangement* (1972); Paul M. Kennedy, *The Samoan Tangle* (1974); Walter LaFeber, *The Clash: A History of U.S. Japanese Relations* (1997); Brian M. Linn, *Guardians of Empire* (1997); Charles J. McClain, *In Search of Equality: The Chinese Struggle Against Discrimination in Nineteenth-Century America* (1994); Thomas J. McCormick, *China Market* (1967); Craig Storti, *Incident at Bitter Creek: The Story of the Rock Springs Chinese Massacre* (1991); Merze Tate, *Hawaii: Reciprocity or Annexation* (1968); Merze Tate, *The United States and the Hawaiian Kingdom* (1965); Marilyn Blatt Young, *The Rhetoric of Empire* (1968).

The Philippines and the Insurrection

John M. Gates, *Schoolbooks and Krags* (1973) (on the U.S. Army); Stanley Karnow, *In Our Image* (1989); Brian M. Linn, *The Philippine War, 1899–1902* (2000); Brian M. Linn, *The U.S. Army and Counterinsurgency in the Philippine War* (1989); Glenn A. May, *Battle for Batangas* (1991); Glenn A. May, *Social Engineering in the Philippines* (1980); Stuart C. Miller, *"Benevolent Assimilation"* (1982); Peter Stanley, *A Nation in the Making* (1974); Richard E. Welch, *Response to Imperialism: American Resistance to the Philippine War* (1972).

Great Britain and Canada

Robert Bothwell, *Canada and the United States* (1992); Kenneth Bourne, *Britain and the Balance of Power in North America, 1815–1908* (1967); Charles S. Campbell, *From Revolution to Rapprochement* (1974); David Dimbleby and David Reynolds, *An Ocean Apart* (1988); Kurkpatrick Dorsey, *The Dawn of Conservation Diplomacy* (1999); Bradford Perkins, *The Great Rapprochement* (1968); William N. Tilchin, *Theodore Roosevelt and the British Empire* (1997).

Chapter 23

General

John W. Chambers, *The Tyranny of Change* (1992); Steven J. Diner, *A Very Different Age* (1998); Paul Fussell, *The Great War and Modern Memory* (1975); Otis L. Graham, Jr., *The Great Campaigns* (1971); Ellis W. Hawley, *The Great War and the Search for a Modern Order*, 2d ed. (1999); Clayton D. James and Anne S. Wells, *America and the Great War* (1998); Henry F. May, *The End of American Innocence* (1964); Stuart I. Rochester, *American Liberal Disillusionment in the Wake of World War I* (1977); Daniel T. Rodgers, *Atlantic Crossings: Social Politics in a Progressive Age* (1998); John A. Thompson, *Reformers and War* (1987).

Wilson, Wilsonianism, and World War I

Lloyd E. Ambrosius, *Wilsonian Statecraft* (1991); Thomas A. Bailey and Paul B. Ryan, *The Lusitania Disaster* (1975); Frederick S. Calhoun, *Power and Principle* (1986); Kendrick A. Clements, *The Presidency of Woodrow Wilson* (1992); John W. Coogan, *The End of Neutrality* (1981); John M. Cooper, Jr., *The Warrior and the Priest* (1983); Robert H. Ferrell, *Woodrow Wilson and World War I* (1985); Manfred Jonas, *The United States and Germany* (1984); Thomas J. Knock, *To End All Wars* (1992); N. Gordon Levin, Jr., *Woodrow Wilson and World Politics* (1968); Arthur S. Link, ed., *Woodrow Wilson and a Revolutionary World, 1913–1921* (1982); Arthur S. Link, *Woodrow Wilson: Revolution, War and Peace* (1979); Arthur S. Link, *Wilson* (1947–1965); Bert E. Park, *Ailing, Aging, Addicted* (1993) (on Wilson's health); Frank Ninkovich, *Wilsonian Century* (1999); J. W. Schulte Nordholt, *Woodrow Wilson* (1991); Tony Smith, *America's Mission: The United States and the Worldwide Struggle for Democracy in the Twentieth Century* (1994); Edwin A. Weinstein, *Woodrow Wilson: A Medical and Psychological Biography* (1981).

Fighting and Remembering the Great War in Europe

Allan M. Brandt, *No Magic Bullet: A Social History of Venereal Disease in the United States since 1880* (1985); John W. Chambers, *To Raise an Army* (1987); J. Garry Clifford, *The Citizen Soldiers* (1972); Edward M. Coffman *The War to End All Wars* (1968); James J. Cooke, *The U.S. Air Service in the Great War: 1917–1919* (1996); Harvey A. DeWeerd, *President Wilson Fights His War* (1968); Byron Farwell, *Over There* (1999); Martin Gilbert, *The First World War* (1994); Paul G. Halpern, *A Naval History of World War I* (1994); G. Kurt Piehler, *Remembering War the American Way* (1995); Donald Smythe, *Pershing* (1986); Stephen R. Ward, ed., *The War Generation: Veterans of the First World War* (1975); Russell F. Weigley, *The American Way of War* (1973).

The Home Front

William J. Breen, *Labor Market Politics and the Great War* (1997); Thomas A. Britten, *American Indians in World War I* (1997); Craig W. Campbell, *Reel America and World War I* (1985); Valerie Jean Conner, *The National War Labor Board* (1983); Alfred W. Crosby, *America's Forgotten Pandemic: The Influenza of 1918* (1989); Robert D. Cuff, *The War Industries Board* (1973); Leslie M. DeBauche, *Reel Patriotism* (1997); David M. Kennedy, *Over Here* (1980); Paul A. C. Koistinen, *Mobilizing for Modern War* (1997); Seward W. Livermore, *Politics Is Adjourned* (1966); Frederick C. Luebke, *Bonds of Loyalty: German Americans and World War I* (1974); Joseph A. McCartin, *Labor's Great War* (1997); John F. McClymer, *War and Welfare* (1980); George H. Nash, *The Life of Herbert Hoover*, vol. 3 (1996); Ronald Schaffer, *America in the Great War: The Rise of the War Welfare State* (1991); Stephen L. Vaughn, *Holding Fast the Inner Lines: Democracy, Nationalism, and the Committee on Public Information* (1979); Neil A. Wynn, *From Progressivism to Prosperity* (1986).

Women and the War

Frances H. Early, *A World Without War: How U.S. Feminists and Pacifists Resisted World War I* (1997); Lettie Gavin, *American Women in World War I* (1997); Maurine W. Greenwald, *Women, War, and Work* (1980); Kathleen Kennedy, *Disloyal Mothers and Scurrilous Citizens: Women and Subversion During World War I* (1999); Erika A. Kuhlman, *Petticoats and White Feathers* (1997); Dorothy Schneider and Carl J. Schneider, *Into the Breach: American Women Overseas in World War I* (1991); Barbara J. Steinson, *American Women's Activism in World War I* (1982).

African Americans and Migration

Arthur E. Barbeau and Florette Henri, *The Unknown Soldiers* (1974); Marvin E. Fletcher, *The Black Soldier and Officer in the United States Army, 1891–1917* (1974); James B. Grossman, *Land of Hope: Chicago, Black Southerners, and the Great Migration* (1989); Robert V. Haynes, *A Night of Violence: The Houston Riot of 1917* (1976); Carole Marks, *Farewell—We're Good and Gone: The Great Black Migration* (1989); Elliot M. Rudwick, *Race Riot at East St. Louis, July 2, 1917* (1964); Joe William Trotter, Jr., ed., *The Great Migration in Historical Perspective* (1991); William M. Tuttle, Jr., *Race Riot: Chicago in the Red Summer of 1919*, rev. ed. (1996).

Dissenters, Wartime Civil Liberties, and the Red Scare

David Brody, *Labor in Crisis: The Steel Strike of 1919* (1965); Charles Chatfield, *The American Peace Movement* (1992); Stanley Coben, *A. Mitchell Palmer* (1963); Charles DeBenedetti, *Origins of the Modern Peace Movement* (1978); Sondra Herman, *Eleven Against War* (1969); C. Roland Marchand, *The American Peace Movement and Social Reform* (1973); Charles H. McCormick, *Seeing Reds* (1997); Elizabeth McKillen, *Chicago Labor and the Quest for a Democratic Diplomacy* (1995); Paul L. Murphy, *World War I and the Origin of Civil Liberties* (1979); Robert K. Murray, *Red Scare* (1955); William Pencak, *For God and Country: The American Legion, 1919–1941* (1989); H. C. Peterson and Gilbert C. Fite, *Opponents of War, 1917–1918* (1968); Richard Polenberg, *Fighting Faiths: The* Abrams *Case, the Supreme Court, and Free Speech* (1987); William Preston, *Aliens and Dissenters* (1995); Francis Russell, *A City in Terror: 1919, the Boston Police Strike* (1975).

The United States and the Bolshevik Revolution

Peter G. Filene, *Americans and the Soviet Experiment, 1917–1933* (1967); David S. Foglesong, *America's Secret War Against Bolshevism* (1995); John Lewis Gaddis, *Russia, the Soviet Union, and the United States*, 2d ed. (1990); Christopher Lasch, *The American Liberals and the Russian Revolution* (1962); David McFadden, *Alternative Paths* (1993); Betty M. Unterberger, *The United States, Revolutionary Russia, and the Rise of Czechoslovakia* (1989).

Paris Peace Conference, Treaty of Versailles, and League Fight

Manfred F. Boemeke et al., eds., *The Treaty of Versailles* (1998); Lloyd Ambrosius, *Woodrow Wilson and the American Diplomatic Tradition* (1987); Inga Floto, *Colonel House in Paris* (1973); Warren F. Kuehl, *Seeking World Order* (1969); Arno Mayer, *Politics and Diplomacy of Peacemaking* (1967); Keith Nelson, *Victors Divided* (1973); Ralph A. Stone, *The Irreconcilables* (1970); Arthur Walworth, *Wilson and the Peacemakers* (1986); William C. Widenor, *Henry Cabot Lodge and the Search for an American Foreign Policy* (1980).

Chapter 24

Overviews of the 1920s

William E. Akin, *Technocracy and the American Dream* (1977); Paul A. Carter, *Another Part of the Twenties* (1977); Lynn Dumenil, *Modern Temper* (1995); David J. Goldberg, *Discontented America: The United States in the 1920s* (1999); William E. Leuchtenburg, *The Perils of Prosperity* (1958); Robert Lynd and Helen Lynd, *Middletown* (1929); Geoffrey Perrett, *America in the Twenties* (1982).

Business and the Economy

William W. Barber, *Herbert Hoover, the Economists, and American Economic Policy, 1921–1933* (1986); Irving L. Bernstein, *The Lean Years: A History of the American Worker, 1920–1933* (1960); Morton Keller, *Regulating a New Economy* (1990); David Montgomery, *The Fall of the House of Labor* (1987); Allan Nevins, *Ford*, 2 vols. (1954–1957); Emily Rosenberg, *Spreading the American Dream* (1982).

Politics and Law

Christine Bolt, *American Indian Policy and American Reform* (1987); Paula Eldot, *Governor Alfred E. Smith: The Politician as Reformer* (1983); Allan J. Lichtman, *Prejudice and the Old Politics: The Presidential Election of 1928* (1979); Alpheus Mason, *The Supreme Court from Taft to Warren* (1958); Donald R. McCoy, *Calvin Coolidge* (1967); Robert K. Murray, *The Politics of Normalcy* (1973); George Tindall, *The Emergence of the New South* (1967); James Weinstein, *The Decline of Socialism in America, 1912–1925* (1967); Joan Hoff Wilson, *Herbert Hoover: The Forgotten Progressive* (1975).

African-Americans, Asians, and Hispanics

Rodolfo Acuna, *Occupied America: A History of Chicanos* (1980); Roger Daniels, *Asian America* (1988); James R. Grossman, *Land of Hope* (1989); Jacquelyn Jones, *Labor of Love, Labor of Sorrow* (1985); Gilbert Osofsky, *Harlem: The Making of a Ghetto* (1965); Ricardo Romo, *East Los Angeles: History of a Barrio* (1983); George Sanchez, *Becoming Mexican American* (1993); Judith Stein, *The World of Marcus Garvey* (1986); Ronald Takaki, *Strangers from a Different Shore* (1989).

Women, Family, and Lifestyles

W. Andrew Achenbaum, *Shades of Gray: Old Age, American Values, and Federal Policies Since 1920* (1983); Beth Bailey, *From Front Porch to Back Seat: Courtship in Twentieth Century America* (1988); Dorothy M. Brown, *Setting a Course: American Women in the 1920s* (1987); George Chauncey, *Gay New York* (1995); Howard P. Chudacoff, *How Old Are You? Age in American Culture* (1989); Nancy F. Cott, *The Grounding of Modern Feminism* (1987); John D'Emilio and Estelle B. Freedman, *Intimate Matters: A History of Sexuality in America* (1988); Elizabeth Ewen, *Immigrant Women in the Land of Dollars* (1985); Lillian Faderman, *Odd Girls and Twilight Lovers* (1991); Linda Gordon, *Woman's Body, Woman's Right: A Social History of Birth Control in America* (1976); J. Stanley Lemons, *The Woman Citizen: Social Feminism in the 1920s* (1973); Lois Scharf, *To Work and to Wed* (1980); Susan Strasser, *Never Done: A History of American Housework* (1982); Winifred D. Wandersee, *Women's Work and Family Values, 1920–1940* (1981).

Lines of Defense

Paul Avrich, *Sacco and Vanzetti* (1991); Edith L. Blumhofer, *Aimee Semple McPherson* (1993); Norman H. Clark, *Deliver Us From Evil: An Interpretation of American Prohibition* (1976); John Higham, *Strangers in the Land: Patterns of American Nativism* (1955); David A. Horowitz, ed., *Inside the Klavern* (1999); Kenneth T. Jackson, *The Ku Klux Klan and the City* (1967); Edward J. Larson, *Summer for the Gods* (1997); Nancy Maclean, *Behind the Mask of Chivalry: The Making of the Second Ku Klux Klan* (1994); George M. Marsden, *Fundamentalism and American Culture* (1980).

Mass Culture

Stanley Coben, *Rebellion Against Victorianism* (1991); Robert Creamer, *Babe* (1974); Kenneth S. Davis, *The Hero, Charles A. Lindbergh* (1959); Susan J. Douglas, *Inventing American Broadcasting* (1987); Paula Fass, *The Damned and the Beautiful: American Youth in the 1920s* (1977); James J. Flink, *The Car Culture* (1975); Richard Wightman Fox and T. Jackson Lears, eds., *The Culture of Consumption* (1983); William R. Leach, *Land of Desire* (1993); Harvey J. Levenstein, *Revolution at the Table: The Transformation of the American Diet* (1988); Roland Marchand, *Advertising the American Dream* (1985); Randy Roberts, *Jack Dempsey, the Manassa Mauler* (1979); Virgnina Scharff, *Taking the Wheel: Women and the Coming of the Motor Age* (1991); Robert Sklar, *Movie-made America* (1976); Ronald A. Smith, *Sports and Freedom: The Rise of Big-Time College Athletics* (1988); Susan Smulyan, *Selling Radio* (1994).

Literature and Thought

Mary Campbell, *Harlem Renaissance: Art of Black America* (1987); Robert Crunden, *From Self to Society: Transition in American Thought, 1919–1941* (1972); Nathan I. Huggins, *Harlem Renaissance* (1971); David L. Lewis, *When Harlem Was in Vogue* (1981); Cary D. Mintz, *Black Culture and the Harlem Renaissance* (1988); Roderick Nash, *The Nervous Generation: American Thought, 1917–1930* (1969); Kenneth M. Wheller and Virginia L. Lussier, eds., *Women and the Arts and the 1920s in Paris and New York* (1982).

Boom and Bust: The Crash

Peter Fearon, *War, Prosperity, and Depression* (1987); John Kenneth Galbraith, *The Great Crash: 1929* (1989); and Robert T. Patterson, *The Great Boom and Panic, 1921–1929* (1965).

Chapter 25

Hoover and the Worsening Depression

William J. Barber, *Herbert Hoover, the Economists, and American Economic Policy, 1921–1933* (1986); Michael A. Bernstein, *The Great Depression: Delayed Recovery and Economic Change in America, 1929–1939* (1988); David Burner, *Herbert Hoover* (1979); Martin L. Fausold, *The Presidency of Herbert C. Hoover* (1985); John A. Garraty, *The Great Depression* (1986); James S. Olson, *Herbert Hoover and the Reconstruction Finance Corporation, 1931–1933* (1977); Jordan A. Schwarz, *Interregnum of Despair* (1970).

The New Deal

Anthony J. Badger, *The New Deal: The Depression Years, 1933–1940* (1989); William J. Barber, *Designs Within Disorder: Franklin D. Roosevelt, the Economists, and the Shaping of American Economic Policy, 1933–1945* (1996); Alan Brinkley, *Liberalism and Its Discontents* (1998); Alan Brinkley, *The End of Reform: New Deal Liberalism in Recession and War* (1995); Steve Fraser and Gary Gerstle, eds., *The Rise and Fall of the New Deal Order, 1930–1980* (1989); Colin Gordon, *New Deals: Business, Labor, and Politics in America, 1920–1935* (1994); David M. Kennedy, *Freedom from Fear: The American People in Depression and War, 1929–1945* (1999); William E. Leuchtenburg, *Franklin D. Roosevelt and the New Deal* (1963); Albert U. Romasco, *The Politics of Recovery: Roosevelt's New Deal* (1983).

Franklin and Eleanor Roosevelt

James MacGregor Burns, *Roosevelt: The Lion and the Fox* (1956); Blanche Wiesen Cook, *Eleanor Roosevelt: Volume One, 1884–1933* (1992), and *Volume Two, 1933–1938* (1999); Kenneth S. Davis, *FDR: Into the Storm, 1937–1940* (1993); Kenneth S. Davis, *FDR: The New Deal Years, 1933–1937* (1986); Frank Freidel, *Franklin D. Roosevelt: A Rendezvous with Destiny* (1990); Joseph P. Lash, *Eleanor and Franklin* (1971); Arthur M. Schlesinger, Jr., *The Age of Roosevelt*, 3 vols. (1957–1960).

Voices from the Depression

James Agee, *Let Us Now Praise Famous Men* (1941); Federal Writers' Project, *These Are Our Lives* (1939); Robert S. McElvaine, ed., *Down and Out in the Great Depression* (1983); Studs Terkel, *Hard Times: An Oral History of the Great Depression* (1970); Tom E. Terrill and Jerrold Hirsch, eds., *Such as Us: Southern Voices of the Thirties* (1978).

Alternatives to the New Deal

Alan Brinkley, *Voices of Protest: Huey Long, Father Coughlin, and the Great Depression* (1982); William Ivy Hair, *The Kingfish and His Realm: The Life and Times of Huey P. Long* (1992); Robin D. G. Kelley, *Hammer and Hoe: Alabama Communists During the Great Depression* (1991); Fraser M. Ottanelli, *The Communist Party of the United States from the Depression to World War II* (1991); Leo Ribuffo, *The Old Christian Right: The Protestant Far Right from the Great Depression to the Cold War* (1983); Donald Warren, *Radio Priest: Charles Coughlin, the Father of Hate Radio* (1996); Frank A. Warren, *An Alternative Vision: The Socialist Party in the 1930s* (1976); Clyde P. Weed, *The Nemesis of Reform: The Republican Party During the New Deal* (1994).

Workers and Organized Labor

Irving Bernstein, *Turbulent Years: A History of the American Worker, 1933–1941* (1969); Lizabeth Cohen, *Making a New Deal: Industrial Workers in Chicago, 1919–1939* (1991); Melvin Dubofsky and Warren Van Tine, *John L. Lewis* (1977); Sidney Fine, *Sit-Down: The General Motors Strike of 1936–1937* (1969); Gary Gerstle, *Working-Class Americanism: The Politics of Labor in a Textile City, 1914–1960* (1989); Roger Horowitz, *Negro and White, Unite and Fight: A Social History of Unionism in Meatpacking, 1930-1990* (1997); Nelson Lichtenstein, *The Most Dangerous Man in Detroit: Walter Reuther and the Fate of American Labor* (1995); Robert H. Zieger, *The CIO, 1935–1955* (1995).

Agriculture and the Environment

William U. Chandler, *The Myth of TVA: Conservation and Development in the Tennessee Valley, 1933–1983* (1984); David E. Conrad, *The Forgotten Farmers: The Story of Sharecroppers in the New Deal* (1965); James N. Gregory, *American Exodus: The Dust Bowl Migration and Okie Culture in California* (1989); David E. Hamilton, *From New Day to New Deal: American Farm Policy from Hoover to Roosevelt, 1928–1933* (1991); Theodore M. Saloutos, *The American Farmer and the New Deal* (1982); John L. Shover, *Cornbelt Rebellion: The Farmers' Holiday Association* (1965); Donald Worster, *Dust Bowl: The Southern Plains in the 1930s* (1979).

People of Color

Dan T. Carter, *Scottsboro*, rev. ed. (1979); James Goodman, *Stories of Scottsboro* (1994); Camille Guerin-Gonzales, *Mexican Workers and American Dreams: Immigration, Repatriation, and California Farm Labor, 1900–1939* (1994); Laurence C. Kelly, *The Assault on Assimilation: John Collier and the Origins of Indian Policy Reform* (1983); George Lipsitz, *The Possessive Investment in Whiteness: How White People Profit from Identity*

Politics (1998); Donald J. Lisio, *Hoover, Blacks, and Lily-Whites* (1985); Kenneth R. Philp, *Termination Revisited: American Indians on the Trail to Self-Determination, 1933-1953* (1999); George J. Sanchez, *Becoming Mexican American: Ethnicity, Culture and Identity in Chicano Los Angeles, 1900-1945* (1993); Harvard Sitkoff, *A New Deal for Blacks* (1978); Patricia Sullivan, *Days of Hope: Race and Democracy in the New Deal Era* (1996); Mark V. Tushnet, *The NAACP's Legal Strategy against Segregated Education, 1925-1950* (1987); Nancy J. Weiss, *Farewell to the Party of Lincoln: Black Politics in the Age of FDR* (1983).

Women

Glen H. Elder, Jr., *Children of the Great Depression: Social Change in Life Experience* (1974); Linda Gordon, *Pitied but Not Entitled: Single Mothers and the History of Welfare, 1890-1935* (1994); Alice Kessler-Harris, "Designing Women and Old Fools: The Construction of the Social Security Amendments of 1939," pp. 87–106 in Linda K. Kerber et al., eds., *U.S. History as Women's History* (1995); Lois Scharf, *To Work and to Wed: Female Employment, Feminism, and the Great Depression* (1980); Winifred Wandersee, *Women's Work and Family Values, 1920-1940* (1981); Susan Ware, *Holding Their Own: American Women in the 1930s* (1982); Susan Ware, *Beyond Suffrage: Women in the New Deal* (1981).

Cultural and Intellectual History

Daniel Aaron, *Writers on the Left: Episodes in American Literary Communism* (1961); Michael Denning, *The Cultural Front: The Laboring of American Culture in the Twentieth Century* (1997); Jerre Mangione, *The Dream and the Deal: The Federal Writers' Project, 1935-1943* (1972); Barbara Melosh, *Engendering Culture: Manhood and Womanhood in New Deal Public Art and Theater* (1991); Richard H. Pells, *Radical Visions and American Dreams: Culture and Social Thought in the Depression Years* (1973); Warren I. Susman, "The Culture of the Thirties," pp. 150–183 in Warren I. Susman, ed., *Culture as History* (1984).

Chapter 26

General

Warren I. Cohen, *Empire Without Tears* (1987); Justus D. Doenecke and John E. Wilz, *From Isolation to War*, 2d ed. (1991); Karen A. J. Miller, *Populist Nationalism: Republican Insurgency and American Foreign Policy, 1918-1925* (1999); Elting E. Morison, *Turmoil and Tradition* (1964) (on Stimson); Brenda G. Plummer, *Rising Wind: Black Americans and U.S. Foreign Affairs, 1935-1960* (1996); Emily S. Rosenberg, *Spreading the American Dream* (1982); Joan Hoff Wilson, *Herbert Hoover* (1975).

Arms Control and the Military

Thomas H. Buckley, *The United States and the Washington Conference, 1921-1922* (1970); Emily O. Goldman, *Sunken Treaties* (1994); Paul A. C. Koistinen, *Planning War, Pursuing Peace: The Political Economy of American Warfare, 1920-1939* (1998); Brian M. Linn, *Guardians of Empire: The U.S. Army and the Pacific, 1902-1940* (1997); Michael S. Sherry, *The Rise of American Airpower* (1987); Mark A. Stoler, *George Marshall* (1989).

Peace Groups and Leaders

Harriet H. Alonso, *The Women's Peace Union and the Outlawry of War* (1989); Charles Chatfield, *For Peace and Justice* (1971); Charles DeBenedetti, *The Peace Reform in American History* (1980); Charles DeBenedetti, *Origins of the Modern American Peace Movement, 1915-1929* (1978); Carrie A. Foster, *The Women and the Warriors* (1995); Robert D. Johnson, *The Peace Progressives and American Foreign Relations* (1995); Warren F. Kuehl and Lynne K. Dunn, *Keeping the Covenant* (1997); Linda A. Schott, *Reconstructing Women's Thoughts: The Women's International League for Peace and Freedom Before World War II* (1997); Lawrence Wittner, *Rebels Against War* (1984).

Economic and Financial Relations

Frederick Adams, *Economic Diplomacy* (1976); Derek H. Aldcroft, *From Versailles to Wall Street, 1919-1929* (1977); Michael Butler, *Cautious Visionary: Cordell Hull and Trade Reform, 1933-1937* (1998); Michael J. Hogan, *Informal Entente: The Private Structure of Cooperation in Anglo-American Economic Diplomacy* (1977); Charles Kindleberger, *The World in Depression* (1973); Stephen J. Randall, *United States Foreign Oil Policy, 1919-1948* (1986); Emily S. Rosenberg, *Financial Missionaries: The Politics and Culture of Dollar Diplomacy, 1900-1930* (1999); Mira Wilkins, *The Maturing of Multinational Enterprise* (1974); Joan Hoff Wilson, *American Business and Foreign Policy, 1920-1933* (1971).

Cultural Expansion and Philanthropy

Frank Costigliola, *Awkward Dominion* (1984); Marcos Cueto, ed., *Missionaries of Science: The Rockefeller Foundation and Latin America* (1994); Mary Nolan, *Visions of Modernity: American Business and the Modernization of Germany* (1994); Thomas J. Saunders, *Hollywood in Berlin* (1994).

Latin America and the Good Neighbor Policy

G. Pope Atkins and Larman C. Wilson, *The Dominican Republic and the United States* (1998); John A. Britton, *Revolution and Ideology: Images of the Mexican Revolution in the United States* (1995); Bruce J. Calder, *The Impact of Intervention: The Dominican Republic During the U.S. Occupation of 1916-1924* (1984); Arturo Morales Carrión, *Puerto Rico* (1983); Paul J. Dosal, *Doing Business with the Dictators* (1993); Paul W.

Drake, *The Money Doctors in the Andes* (1989); Alton Frye, *Nazi Germany and the American Hemisphere, 1933–1941* (1967); Irwin F. Gellman, *Good Neighbor Diplomacy* (1979); Linda B. Hall, *Oil, Banks, and Politics: The United States and Postrevolutionary Mexico, 1917–1924* (1995); Walter LaFeber, *Inevitable Revolutions: The United States in Central America*, 2d and extended ed. (1993); Lester D. Langley, *The United States and the Caribbean, 1900–1970* (1980); Abraham F. Lowenthal, ed., *Exporting Democracy* (1991); John Major, *Prize Possession: The United States and the Panama Canal, 1903–1979* (1993); Louis A. Pérez, *Cuba and the United States*, 2d ed. (1997); Louis A. Pérez, *Cuba Under the Platt Amendment* (1986); Fredrick B. Pike, *FDR's Good Neighbor Policy* (1995); Brenda G. Plummer, *Haiti and the United States* (1992); W. Dirk Raat, *Mexico and the United States* (1997); Friedrich E. Schuler, *Mexico Between Hitler and Roosevelt* (1998); Bryce Wood, *The Making of the Good Neighbor Policy* (1961).

Isolationists and Isolationism

Wayne S. Cole, *Roosevelt and the Isolationists, 1932–1945* (1983); Manfred Jonas, *Isolationism in America, 1935–1941* (1966); Thomas C. Kennedy, *Charles A. Beard and American Foreign Policy* (1975); Richard C. Lower, *A Bloc of One: The Political Career of Hiram W. Johnson* (1993); Richard Lowitt, *George W. Norris* (1963–1978); John Wiltz, *In Search of Peace: The Senate Munitions Inquiry* (1963).

Europe, Roosevelt's Policies, and the Coming of World War II

J. Garry Clifford and Samuel R. Spencer, Jr., *The First Peacetime Draft* (1986); David H. Culbert, *News for Everyman* (1976) (on radio); Robert Dallek, *Franklin D. Roosevelt and American Foreign Policy* (1995); Robert A. Divine, *Roosevelt and World War II* (1969); Barbara R. Farnham, *Roosevelt and the Munich Crisis* (1997); Frank Freidel, *Franklin D. Roosevelt* (1990); Manfred Jonas, *The United States and Germany* (1984); Warren F. Kimball, *The Juggler* (1991); Warren F. Kimball, *The Most Unsordid Act: Lend-Lease, 1939–1941* (1969); Melvyn P. Leffler, *The Elusive Quest: America's Pursuit of European Stability and French Security, 1919–1933* (1979); Douglas Little, *Malevolent Neutrality: The United States, Great Britain, and the Origins of the Spanish Civil War* (1985); Thomas R. Maddux, *Years of Estrangement: American Relations with the Soviet Union, 1933–1941* (1980); Arnold A. Offner, *American Appeasement* (1969); David Reynolds, *The Creation of the Anglo-American Alliance* (1982); David F. Schmitz, *The United States and Fascist Italy* (1988); James C. Schneider, *Should America Go to War?* (1989); Richard Steele, *Propaganda in an Open Society* (1985); Donald C. Watt, *How War Came* (1989); Theodore A. Wilson, *The First Summit* (1991).

China, Japan, and the Coming of War in Asia

Dorothy Borg and Shumpei Okomoto, eds., *Pearl Harbor as History* (1973); R. J. C. Butow, *Tojo and the Coming of War* (1961); Warren I. Cohen, *America's Response to China*, 3d ed. (1990); Peter Conn, *Pearl S. Buck* (1996); Hilary Conroy and Harry Wray, eds., *Pearl Harbor Reexamined* (1990); Herbert Feis, *The Road to Pearl Harbor* (1950); Waldo H. Heinrichs, Jr., *Threshold of War* (1988); Akira Iriye, *The Origins of the Second World War in Asia and the Pacific* (1987); Akira Iriye, *Across the Pacific* (1967); Akira Iriye, *After Imperialism* (1965); T. Christopher Jespersen, *American Images of China* (1996); Walter LaFeber, *The Clash: A History of U.S.-Japan Relations* (1997); James Morley, ed., *The Final Confrontation* (1994); Jonathan Utley, *Going to War with Japan* (1985).

Attack on Pearl Harbor

David Kahn, *The Codebreakers* (1967); Robert W. Love, Jr., ed., *Pearl Harbor Revisited* (1995); Martin V. Melosi, *The Shadow of Pearl Harbor* (1977); Gordon W. Prange, *Pearl Harbor* (1986); Gordon W. Prange, *At Dawn We Slept* (1981); John Toland, *Infamy* (1982); Roberta Wohlstetter, *Pearl Harbor* (1962).

Chapter 27

The Second World War

John W. Dower, *War Without Mercy: Race and Power in the Pacific War* (1986); John Keegan, *The Second World War* (1989); David M. Kennedy, *Freedom from Fear: The American People in Depression and War, 1929–1945* (1999); Eric Larabee, *Commander in Chief* (1987); Samuel Eliot Morison, *The Two-Ocean War* (1963); Ronald Schaffer, *Wings of Judgment: American Bombing in World War II* (1985); Gordon W. Prange et al., *At Dawn We Slept: The Untold Story of Pearl Harbor* (1981); Ronald H. Spector, *Eagle Against the Sun: The American War with Japan* (1984); Gerhard L. Weinberg, *A World at Arms: A Global History of World War II* (1994).

Fighting the War: Americans in Combat

Robert H. Abzug, *Inside the Vicious Heart: Americans and the Liberation of Nazi Concentration Camps* (1985); Stephen E. Ambrose, *The Victors* (1998); Stephen E. Ambrose, *Citizen Soldiers* (1997); Stephen E. Ambrose, *D-Day, June 6, 1944* (1994); Allan Berube, *Coming Out Under Fire: The History of Gay Men and Women in World War II* (1990); Michael D. Doubler, *Closing with the Enemy: How GIs Fought the War in Europe, 1944–1945* (1994); Paul Fussell, *Wartime* (1989); Gerald F. Linderman, *The World Within the War: America's Combat Experience in World War II* (1997); David Reynolds, *Rich Relations: The American Occupation of Britain, 1942–1945* (1995); E. B. Sledge, *With the Old Breed at Peleliu and Okinawa* (1990).

Wartime Diplomacy

Russell Buhite, *Decisions at Yalta* (1986); Diane Clemens, *Yalta* (1970); Robert Dallek, *Franklin D. Roosevelt and Ameri-*

can Foreign Policy, 1932–1945 (1979); Henry L. Feingold, Bearing Witness: How America and Its Jews Responded to the Holocaust (1995); George C. Herring, Aid to Russia, 1941–1946 (1973); Gary R. Hess, The United States at War, 1941–1945 (1986); Robert C. Hilderbrand, Dumbarton Oaks (1990); Townsend Hoopes and Douglas Brinkley, Franklin D. Roosevelt and the Creation of the United Nations (1997); Akira Iriye, Power and Culture: The Japanese-American War, 1941–1945 (1981); Warren Kimball, Forged in War: Roosevelt, Churchill, and the Second World War (1997); Gabriel Kolko, The Politics of War: The World and United States Foreign Policy, 1943–1945, rev. ed. (1990); Walter LaFeber, The Clash: A History of U.S.-Japan Relations (1997); Verne W. Newton, ed., FDR and the Holocaust (1996); Keith Sainsbury, Churchill and Roosevelt at War (1994); Mark Stoler, The Politics of the Second Front (1977); David S. Wyman, The Abandonment of the Jews (1984).

Mobilizing for War

Amy Bentley, Eating for Victory: Food Rationing and the Politics of Domesticity (1998); George Q. Flynn, The Draft, 1940–1973 (1993); Gregory Hooks, Forging the Military-Industrial Complex: World War II's Battle of the Potomac (1991); Clayton R. Koppes and Gregory D. Black, Hollywood Goes to War (1987); Nelson Lichtenstein, Labor's War at Home: The CIO in World War II (1983); George H. Roeder, Jr., The Censored War: American Visual Experience During World War II (1993); Lawrence R. Samuel, Pledging Allegiance: American Identity and the Bond Drive of World War II (1997); Bartholomew H. Sparrow, From the Outside In: World War II and the American State (1996); Richard W. Steele, Free Speech in America's Good War (1999); Harold G. Vatter, The U.S. Economy in World War II (1985); Allen M. Winkler, The Politics of Propaganda: The Office of War Information, 1942–1945 (1978).

The Home Front

John Morton Blum, V Was for Victory: Politics and American Culture During World War II (1976); John D'Emilio, Sexual Politics, Sexual Communities: The Making of a Homosexual Minority in the United States, 1940–1970 (1983); Doris Kearns Goodwin, No Ordinary Time: Franklin and Eleanor Roosevelt: The Home Front in World War II (1994); Gerald D. Nash, The American West Transformed (1985); William L. O'Neill, A Democracy at War: America's Fight at Home and Abroad in World War II (1993); Studs Terkel, ed., "The Good War": An Oral History of World War Two (1984); William M. Tuttle, Jr., "Daddy's Gone to War": The Second World War in the Lives of America's Children (1993).

The Internment of Japanese-Americans and Enemy Aliens

Roger Daniels, Prisoners Without Trial (1993); Stephen Fox, The Unknown Internment: An Oral History of the Relocation of Italian Americans During World War II (1990); Peter Irons, Justice at War (1983); Arnold Krammer, Undue Process: The Untold Story of America's German Alien Internees (1997); Gary Okihiro, Cane Fires: The Anti-Japanese Movement in Hawaii, 1865–1945 (1991); Page Smith, Democracy on Trial: The Japanese American Evacuation and Relocation in World War II (1995).

African Americans and Wartime Violence

A. Russell Buchanan, Black Americans in World War II (1977); Dominic J. Capeci, Jr., The Harlem Riot of 1943 (1977); Dominic J. Capeci, Jr., and Martha Wilkerson, Layered Violence: The Detroit Rioters of 1943 (1991); Mauricio Mazon, The Zoot-Suit Riots (1984); Patrick S. Washburn, A Question of Sedition: The Federal Government's Investigation of the Black Press During World War II (1986); Neil A. Wynn, The Afro-American and the Second World War, rev. ed. (1993).

Women at War

Karen T. Anderson, Wartime Women (1981); D'Ann Campbell, Women at War with America (1984); Claudia Goldin, Understanding the Gender Gap: An Economic History of American Women (1990); Susan M. Hartmann, The Home Front and Beyond (1982); Leslie Haynsworth and David Toomey, Amelia Earhart's Daughters (1998) (about American women aviators in the war); Judy Barrett Litoff and David C. Smith, eds., We're in This War, Too: World War II Letters from American Women in Uniform (1994); Leisa D. Meyer, Creating GI Jane: Sexuality and Power in the Women's Army Corps During World War II (1996); Ruth Milkman, Gender at Work: The Dynamics of Job Discrimination by Sex During World War II (1987); Leila J. Rupp, Mobilizing Women for War: German and American Propaganda, 1939–1945 (1978).

The Atomic Bomb and Japan's Surrender

Gar Alperovitz, The Decision to Use the Atomic Bomb and the Architecture of an American Myth, 2d ed. (1995); Michael Hogan, ed., Hiroshima in History and Memory (1995); Robert Jay Lifton and Greg Mitchell, Hiroshima in America: Fifty Years of Denial (1995); Richard Rhodes, The Making of the Atomic Bomb (1987); Stephen I. Schwartz, ed., Atomic Audit: The Costs and Consequences of U.S. Nuclear Weapons since 1940 (1998); Martin J. Sherwin, A World Destroyed: The Atomic Bomb and the Grand Alliance (1975); Leon V. Sigal, Fighting to a Finish (1994); Ronald Takaki, Hiroshima: Why America Dropped the Atomic Bomb (1995); J. Samuel Walker, Prompt and Utter Destruction: Truman and the Use of the Atomic Bombs Against Japan (1997).

Chapter 28

An Age of Consensus

John Patrick Diggins, The Proud Decades: America in War and Peace, 1941–1960 (1988); David Halberstam, The Fifties

(1993); Marty Jezer, *The Dark Ages: Life in the United States, 1945–1960* (1982); William L. O'Neill, *American High: The Years of Confidence, 1945–1960* (1986); James T. Patterson, *Grand Expectations: The United States, 1945–1974* (1996).

Cold War Culture

Paul Boyer, *By the Bomb's Early Light: American Thought and Culture at the Dawn of the Atomic Age* (1985); Tom Engel-hardt, *The End of Victory Culture: Cold War America and the Disillusioning of a Generation* (1995); William S. Graebner, *The Age of Doubt: American Thought and Culture in the 1940s* (1991); Margot A. Henriksen, *Dr. Strangelove's America: Society and Culture in the Atomic Age* (1997); Lary May, ed., *Recasting America: Culture and Politics in the Age of Cold War* (1989); Richard H. Pells, *The Liberal Mind in a Conservative Age* (1985); Lisle A. Rose, *The Cold War Comes to Main Street: America in 1950* (1999); Stephen J. Whitfield, *The Culture of the Cold War*, rev. ed. (1996).

The Truman Presidency

Robert J. Donovan, *Tumultuous Years: The Presidency of Harry S. Truman, 1949–1953* (1982); Robert J. Donovan, *Conflict and Crisis: The Presidency of Harry S. Truman, 1945–1948* (1977); Alonzo L. Hamby, *Man of the People: The Life of Harry S. Truman* (1995); Michael J. Hogan, *A Cross of Iron: Harry S. Truman and the Origins of the National Security State* (1998); David McCullough, *Truman* (1992); Paul G. Pierpaoli, Jr., *Truman and Korea: The Political Culture of the Cold War* (1999).

Eisenhower and the Politics of the 1950s

Stephen E. Ambrose, *Eisenhower: The President* (1984); Robert F. Burk, *Dwight D. Eisenhower* (1986); Donald L. Fix-ico, *Termination and Relocation: Federal Indian Policy, 1945–1960* (1986); Fred I. Greenstein, *The Hidden-Hand Presidency* (1982); Chester J. Pach, Jr., and Elmo Richardson, *The Presidency of Dwight D. Eisenhower*, rev. ed. (1991); Geoffrey Perret, *Eisenhower* (1999).

McCarthyism

Richard M. Fried, *Nightmare in Red* (1990); Robert Griffith, *The Politics of Fear: Joseph R. McCarthy and the Senate*, rev. ed. (1987); John Earl Haynes and Harvey Klehr, *Venona: Decoding Soviet Espionage in America* (1999); Harvey Klehr et al., *The Soviet World of American Communism* (1998); David M. Oshinsky, *A Conspiracy So Immense: The World of Joe McCarthy* (1983); Richard Gid Powers, *Not Without Honor: The History of American Anticommunism* (1995); Ellen W. Schrecker, *Many Are the Crimes: McCarthyism in America* (1998); Ellen W. Schrecker, *No Ivory Tower: McCarthyism in the Universities* (1986).

Race Relations and the Civil Rights Movement

Taylor Branch, *Parting the Waters: America in the King Years, 1954–1963* (1988); Robert F. Burk, *The Eisenhower Administration and Black Civil Rights* (1984); William H. Chafe, *Civilities and Civil Rights: Greensboro, North Carolina, and the Black Struggle for Freedom* (1980); David J. Garrow, *Bearing the Cross: Martin Luther King, Jr., and the Southern Christian Leadership Conference* (1986); Arnold R. Hirsch, *Making the Second Ghetto: Race and Housing in Chicago, 1940–1960* (1983); Richard Kluger, *Simple Justice: The History of Brown v. Board of Education and Black America's Struggle for Equality* (1975); Gail Williams O'Brien, *The Color of Law: Race, Violence, and Justice in the Post–World War II South* (1999); Thomas J. Sugrue, *The Origins of the Urban Crisis: Race and Inequality in Postwar Detroit* (1996); Jules Tygiel, *Baseball's Great Experiment: Jackie Robinson and His Legacy*, rev. ed. (1997); Juan Williams, *Thurgood Marshall: American Revolutionary* (1998).

The Baby Boom, Youth Culture, and Cold War Families

James Gilbert, *A Cycle of Outrage: America's Reaction to the Juvenile Delinquent* (1986); Landon Y. Jones, *Great Expectations: America and the Baby Boom Generation* (1980); James H. Jones, *Alfred C. Kinsey* (1997); Paul Leinberger and Bruce Tucker, *The New Individualists: The Generation After the Organization Man* (1991); Elaine Tyler May, *Homeward Bound: American Families in the Cold War Era* (1988); John Modell, *Into One's Own: From Youth to Adulthood in the United States, 1920–1975* (1989); Grace Palladino, *Teenagers* (1996).

Suburbia and the Spread of Education

Robert Fishman, *Bourgeois Utopias* (1987); Mark I. Gelfand, *A Nation of Cities* (1975); Dolores Hayden, *Redesigning the American Dream* (1984); Kenneth T. Jackson, *Crabgrass Frontier: The Suburbanization of the United States* (1985); Zane L. Miller, *Suburb* (1982); Diane Ravitch, *The Troubled Crusade: American Education, 1945–1980* (1983); Joel Spring, *The Sorting Machine: National Educational Policy Since 1945* (1976).

Women's Lives and Women's Rights

Wini Breines, *Young, White, and Miserable: Growing Up Female in the Fifties* (1992); Ruth Schwartz Cowan, *More Work for Mother* (1983); Myra Dinnerstein, *Women Between Two Worlds* (1992); Barbara Ehrenreich, *The Hearts of Men: American Dreams and the Flight from Commitment* (1983); Cynthia Harrison, *On Account of Sex: The Politics of Women's Issues, 1945–1968* (1988); Eugenia Kaledin, *Mothers and More: American Women in the 1950s* (1984); Susan Lynn, *Progressive Women in Conservative Times* (1992); Glenna Matthews, *"Just a Housewife"* (1987); Joanne J. Meyerowitz, ed., *Not June Cleaver: Women and Gender in Postwar America, 1945–1960* (1994); Leila J. Rupp and Verta Taylor, *Survival in the Dol-*

drums: The American Women's Rights Movement, 1945 to the 1960s (1987).

The Affluent Society

Loren Baritz, *The Good Life: The Meaning of Success for the American Middle Class* (1982); Kevin Fernlund, ed., *The Cold War American West* (1998); John Kenneth Galbraith, *The Affluent Society* (1958); Ann Markusen et al., *Rise of the Gunbelt: The Military Remapping of Industrial America* (1991); Kirkpatrick Sale, *Power Shift: The Rise of the Southern Rim and Its Challenge to the Eastern Establishment* (1975); Bruce J. Schulman, *From Cotton Belt to Sunbelt: Federal Policy, Economic Development, and the Transformation of the South, 1938–1980* (1991).

Farmers and Laborers

Gilbert C. Fite, *American Farmers* (1981); James R. Green, *The World of the Worker* (1980); Nelson Lichtenstein, *The Most Dangerous Man in Detroit: Walter Reuther and the Fate of American Labor* (1995); George Lipsitz, *Rainbow at Midnight: Labor and Culture in the 1940s* (1994); John L. Shover, *First Majority—Last Minority: The Transforming of Rural Life in America* (1976).

The Other America

Richard B. Craig, *The Bracero Program* (1971); J. Wayne Flint, *Dixie's Forgotten People: The South's Poor Whites* (1979); Mario T. Garcia, *Mexican Americans: Leadership, Ideology, and Identity, 1930–1960* (1990); Michael Harrington, *The Other America*, rev. ed. (1981); Dorothy K. Newman et al., *Politics and Prosperity: Black Americans and White Institutions, 1940–75* (1978); James T. Patterson, *America's Struggle Against Poverty, 1900–1994*, rev. ed. (1994).

Chapter 29

The Cold War: Overviews

Stephen Ambrose and Allen Brinkley, *Rise to Globalism*, 8th rev. ed. (1997); H. W. Brands, *The Devil We Knew* (1993); Warren Cohen, *America in the Age of Soviet Power, 1945–1991* (1993); Gordon A. Craig and Francis L. Loewenheim, eds., *The Diplomats, 1939–1979* (1994); John Lewis Gaddis, *We Now Know* (1997); John Lewis Gaddis, *The Long Peace* (1987); John Lewis Gaddis, *Strategies of Containment* (1982); Walter Isaacson and Evan Thomas, *The Wise Men* (1986); Robert H. Johnson, *Improbable Dangers: U.S. Perceptions of Threat in the Cold War and After* (1994); Paul Kennedy, *The Rise and Fall of the Great Powers* (1987); Walter LaFeber, *America, Russia, and the Cold War, 1945–1996*, 8th ed. (1996); Deborah Larson, *Anatomy of Distrust* (1997); Ralph Levering, *The Cold War*, 2d ed. (1994); Thomas McCormick, *America's Half-Century*, 2d ed. (1994); Thomas G. Paterson, *On Every Front: The Making and Unmaking of the Cold War*, rev. ed. (1992); Thomas G. Paterson, *Meeting the Communist Threat* (1988); Michael S. Sherry, *In the Shadow of War* (1995).

Relations with the Third World: Overviews

Richard J. Barnet, *Intervention and Revolution* (1972); Edward H. Berman, *The Influence of the Carnegie, Ford, and Rockefeller Foundations on American Foreign Policy* (1983); Scott L. Bills, *Empire and Cold War* (1990); H. W. Brands, *The Specter of Neutralism* (1989); Gabriel Kolko, *Confronting the Third World* (1988); Michael L. Krenn, *Black Diplomacy: African Americans and the State Department, 1945–1969* (1998); Michael L. Krenn, ed., *Race and U.S. Foreign Policy during the Cold War* (1998); Brenda G. Plummer, *Rising Wind: Black Americans and U.S. Foreign Affairs, 1935–1960* (1996); David F. Schmitz, *Thank God They're on Our Side: The U.S. and Right-Wing Dictatorships, 1921–1965* (1999); Penny M. von Eschen, *Race Against Empire: Black Americans and Anticolonialism, 1937–1957* (1996).

Truman, Cold War Origins, Containment, and the National Security State

James Chace, *Acheson* (1998); Carolyn W. Eisenberg, *Drawing the Line: The American Decision to Divide Germany, 1944–1949* (1996); Bruce E. Field, *Harvest of Dissent: The National Farmers Union and the Early Cold War* (1998); Richard M. Fried, *The Russians Are Coming! The Russians Are Coming!* (1998); Frazer Harbutt, *The Iron Curtain* (1986); Walter Hixson, *George F. Kennan* (1990); Michael J. Hogan, *A Cross of Iron: Harry S. Truman and the Origins of the National Security State* (1998); Michael J. Hogan, *The Marshall Plan* (1987); Lawrence S. Kaplan, *The United States and NATO* (1984); Gabriel Kolko and Joyce Kolko, *The Limits of Power* (1972); Bruce R. Kuniholm, *The Origins of the Cold War in the Near East* (1980); Melvyn Leffler, *The Specter of Communism* (1994); Melvyn Leffler, *A Preponderance of Power: National Security, the Truman Administration, and the Cold War* (1992); Alan Milward, *The Reconstruction of Western Europe* (1984); Wilson D. Miscamble, *George F. Kennan and the Making of American Foreign Policy, 1947–1950* (1992); Ann Markusen et al., *The Rise of the Gunbelt* (1991); David Reynolds, ed., *The Origins of the Cold War in Europe* (1994); Thomas A. Schwartz, *America's Germany* (1991); Mark A. Stoler, *George C. Marshall* (1989); Marc Trachtenberg, *A Constructed Peace: The Making of the European Settlement, 1945–1963* (1999); Lawrence S. Wittner, *American Intervention in Greece, 1943–1949* (1982); Vladislav Zubok and Constantine Pleshakov, *Inside the Kremlin's Cold War* (1996); Randall B. Woods, *A Changing of the Guard: Anglo-American Relations, 1941–1946* (1990).

Eisenhower-Dulles Foreign Policy

Stephen E. Ambrose, *Eisenhower*, 2 vols. (1982, 1984); Stephen E. Ambrose, *Ike's Spies* (1981); Michael Beschloss,

MAYDAY: Eisenhower, Khrushchev, and the U-2 Affair (1986); Jeff Broadwater, *Eisenhower and the Anti-Communist Crusade* (1992); Robert A. Divine, *Eisenhower and the Cold War* (1981); Fred Greenstein, *The Hidden-Hand Presidency* (1982); Townsend Hoopes, *The Devil and John Foster Dulles* (1973); Richard Immerman, *John Foster Dulles* (1998); Richard Immerman, ed., *John Foster Dulles* (1990); Burton I. Kaufman, *Trade and Aid* (1982); Frederick W. Marks, *Power and Peace* (1993) (on Dulles); Jack M. Schick, *The Berlin Crisis* (1971).

The CIA and Counterinsurgency

Douglas S. Blaufarb, *The Counterinsurgency Era* (1977); Peter Grose, *Gentleman Spy: The Life of Allen Dulles* (1994); Rhodi Jeffreys-Jones, *The CIA and American Democracy* (1989); Loch K. Johnson, *America's Secret Power* (1989); Mark Lowenthal, *U.S. Intelligence* (1984); John Ranelagh, *The Agency* (1986); Jeffrey T. Richelson, *A Century of Spies* (1995); Jeffrey T. Richelson, *The U.S. Intelligence Community* (1999); Evan Thomas, *The Very Best Men* (1995).

Atomic Diplomacy, Nuclear Arms Race, and Public Attitudes

Howard Ball, *Justice Downwind: America's Atomic Testing Program in the 1950s* (1986); Paul Boyer, *Fallout* (1998); Paul Boyer, *By the Bomb's Early Light* (1986); McGeorge Bundy, *Danger and Survival* (1988); Campbell Craig, *Destroying the Village: Eisenhower and Thermonuclear War* (1998); Robert A. Divine, *The Sputnik Challenge* (1993); Robert A. Divine, *Blowing on the Wind: The Nuclear Test Ban Debate, 1954–1960* (1978); Margot Henriksen, *Dr. Strangelove's America* (1997); Gregg Herken, *Counsels of War* (1985); Gregg Herken, *The Winning Weapon* (1981); James G. Hershberg, *James B. Conant* (1993); Richard G. Hewlett and Jack M. Hall, *Atoms for Peace and War, 1953–1961* (1989); David Holloway, *Stalin and the Bomb* (1994); Robert Jervis, *The Meaning of the Nuclear Revolution* (1989); Fred Kaplan, *The Wizards of Armageddon* (1983); Milton Katz, *Ban the Bomb* (1986); Stuart W. Leslie, *The Cold War and American Science* (1994); John Newhouse, *War and Peace in the Nuclear Age* (1989); Richard Rhodes, *Dark Sun: The Making of the Hydrogen Bomb* (1995); David N. Schwartz, *NATO's Nuclear Dilemmas* (1983); Martin Sherwin, *A World Destroyed* (1975); Spencer Weart, *Nuclear Fear* (1988); Allan M. Winkler, *Life Under a Cloud* (1993); Lawrence S. Wittner, *The Struggle Against the Bomb* (1993, 1998).

Cultural Relations and Expansion

Robert H. Haddow, *Pavilions of Plenty* (1997); Walter L. Hixson, *Parting the Curtain: Propaganda, Culture, and the Cold War* (1997); Frank A. Ninkovich, *The Diplomacy of Ideas* (1981); Richard Pells, *Not Like Us: How Europeans Have Loved, Hated, and Transformed American Culture Since World War II* (1997); Reinhold Wagnleitner, *Coca-Colonization and the Cold War* (1994).

Japan, China, and Asian Issues

H. W. Brands, *India and the United States* (1989); Kenton J. Clymer, *Quest for Freedom: The United States and India's Independence* (1995); Gordon Chang, *Friends and Enemies* (1990); Thomas J. Christensen, *Useful Adversaries* (1996); Warren I. Cohen, *America's Response to China*, 3d ed. (1990); Nick Cullather, *Illusions of Influence: The Political Economy of United States–Philippines Relations, 1942–1960* (1994); Richard B. Finn, *Winners in Peace* (1995); Kyoko Hirano, *Mr. Smith Goes to Tokyo: Japanese Cinema Under the American Occupation, 1945–1952* (1992); E. J. Kahn, Jr., *The China Hands* (1975); Walter LaFeber, *The Clash: A History of U.S.-Japan Relations* (1997); Paul G. Lauren, ed., *The "China Hands" Legacy* (1987); Robert J. McMahon, *The Limits of Empire: The United States and Southeast Asia Since World War II* (1999); Robert J. McMahon, *Colonialism and Cold War: The United States and the Struggle for Indonesian Independence, 1945–49* (1981); Dennis Merrill, *Bread and the Ballot: The United States and India's Economic Development, 1947–1963* (1990); Robert P. Newman, *Owen Lattimore and the "Loss" of China* (1992); Michael Schaller, *Douglas MacArthur* (1989); Michael Schaller, *The American Occupation of Japan* (1985); William W. Stueck, Jr., *The Road to Confrontation* (1981); Nancy B. Tucker, *Taiwan, Hong Kong, and the United States* (1994); Nancy B. Tucker, *Patterns in the Dust: Chinese-American Relations and the Recognition Controversy, 1945–1950* (1983); Philip West et al., eds., *America's Wars in Asia* (1998).

The Korean War

Roy E. Appleman, *Disaster in Korea* (1992); Roy E. Appleman, *Escaping the Trap* (1990); Roy E. Appleman, *Ridgeway Duels for Korea* (1990); Conrad C. Crane, *American Airpower Strategy in Korea* (2000); Bruce Cumings, *Korea's Place in the Sun* (1997); Bruce Cumings, *The Origins of the Korean War* (1980, 1991); Rosemary Foot, *A Substitute for Victory* (1990); Rosemary Foot, *The Wrong War* (1985); Sergei Goncharov et al., *Uncertain Partners: Stalin, Mao, and the Korean War* (1993); John Halliday and Bruce Cumings, *Korea* (1989); Chen Jian, *China's Road to the Korean War* (1995); Burton I. Kaufman, *The Korean War*, 2d ed. (1997); Callum A. MacDonald, *Korea* (1987); John W. Spanier, *The Truman-MacArthur Controversy and the Korean War* (1959); William Stueck, *The Korean War* (1995); Shu Guang Zhang, *Mao's Military Romanticism* (1996).

Vietnam

David L. Anderson, ed., *Shadow on the White House* (1993); David L. Anderson, *Trapped by Success* (1991); Melanie Billings-Yun, *Decision Against War: Eisenhower and Dien Bien Phu, 1954* (1988); William J. Duiker, *U.S. Containment Policy and the Conflict in Indochina* (1994); Lloyd C. Gardner, *Approaching Vietnam* (1988); George C. Herring, *America's Longest War*, 3d ed. (1996); Gary R. Hess, *Vietnam and the United States*, rev. ed. (1998); Gary Hess, *The United States'*

Emergence as a Southeast Asian Power (1987); Lawrence S. Kaplan et al., eds., *Dien Bien Phu and the Crisis of Franco-American Relations* (1990); Gabriel Kolko, *Anatomy of a War* (1986); David G. Marr, *Vietnam 1945* (1995); Joseph G. Morgan, *The Vietnam Lobby: The American Friends of Vietnam, 1955–1975* (1997); Andrew Rotter, *The Path to Vietnam* (1987); Robert D. Schulzinger, *A Time for War* (1997); Anthony Short, *The Origins of the Vietnam War* (1989); Robert R. Tomes, *Apocalypse Then: American Intellectuals and the Vietnam War, 1954–1975* (1998); Stein Tonnesson, *The Vietnamese Revolution of 1945* (1991); Marilyn B. Young, *The Vietnam Wars* (1991).

Latin America

Cole Blasier, *Hovering Giant* (1974); John Coatsworth, *Central America and the United States* (1994); Michael Conniff, *Panama and the United States* (1992); Nick Cullather, *Secret History: The CIA's Classified Account of Its Operations in Guatemala, 1952–1954* (1999); Mark T. Gilderhus, *The Second Century* (2000); Piero Gleijeses, *Shattered Hope: The Guatemalan Revolution and the United States, 1944–1954* (1991); Richard Immerman, *The CIA in Guatemala* (1982); Walter LaFeber, *Inevitable Revolutions: The United States in Central America*, 2d and expanded ed. (1993); Walter LaFeber, *The Panama Canal*, updated ed. (1990); Lester Langley, *America and the Americas* (1989); Abraham F. Lowenthal, ed., *Exporting Democracy* (1991); A. W. Maldonado, *Teodoro Moscoso and Puerto Rico's Operation Bootstrap* (1997); Thomas G. Paterson, *Contesting Castro* (1994); Louis A. Pérez, Jr., *Cuba and the United States*, 2d ed. (1997); W. Dirk Raat, *Mexico and the United States*, 2d ed. (1997); Stephen G. Rabe, *Eisenhower and Latin America* (1988); Stephen G. Rabe, *The Road to OPEC: United States Relations with Venezuela* (1982); Lars Schoultz, *Beneath the United States* (1998); Gaddis Smith, *The Last Years of the Monroe Doctrine* (1994); Peter H. Smith, *Talons of the Eagle* (1996).

Middle East and Africa

Nigel J. Ashton, *Eisenhower, Macmillan, and the Problem of Nasser* (1996); James A. Bill, *The Eagle and the Lion: The Tragedy of American-Iranian Relations* (1988); Thomas Borstelmann, *Apartheid's Reluctant Uncle: The United States and Southern Africa in the Early Cold War* (1993); William J. Burns, *Economic Aid and American Policy Toward Egypt, 1955–1981* (1985); Michael J. Cohen, *Truman and Israel* (1990); Michael J. Cohen, *Palestine and the Great Powers, 1945–1948* (1983); Mark Gasiorowski, *U.S. Foreign Policy and the Shah* (1991); Peter L. Hahn, *The United States, Great Britain, and Egypt, 1945–1956* (1991); Mary Ann Heiss, *Empire and Nationhood: The United States, Great Britain, and Iranian Oil, 1950–1954* (1997); Burton I. Kaufman, *The Arab Middle East and the United States* (1996); Diane Kunz, *The Economic Diplomacy of the Suez Crisis* (1991); Zach Levy, *Israel and the Great Powers* (1998); William Roger Louis and Roger Owen, eds., *Suez 1956* (1989); Aaron D. Miller, *Search for Security* (1980); Donald Neff, *Warriors at Suez* (1981); Thomas J. Noer, *Cold War and Black Liberation* (1985); David Schoenbaum, *The United States and the State of Israel* (1993); Robert W. Stookey, *America and the Arab States* (1975); Daniel Yergin, *The Prize: The Epic Quest for Oil, Money, and Power* (1991).

Chapter 30

The 1960s

David Burner, *Making Peace with the 60s* (1996); Dominick Cavallo, *A Fiction of the Past: The Sixties in American History* (1999); David Chalmers, *And the Crooked Places Made Straight: The Struggle for Social Change in the 1960s* (1991); David Farber, *The Age of Great Dreams* (1994); David Farber, ed., *The Sixties* (1994); James J. Farrell, *The Spirit of the Sixties* (1997); Godfrey Hodgson, *America in Our Time* (1976); Michael Kazin and Maurice Isserman, *America Divided: The Civil War of the 1960s* (2000); Arthur Marwick, *The Sixties* (1998); Allen J. Matusow, *The Unraveling of America: A History of Liberalism in the 1960s* (1984); James T. Patterson, *Grand Expectations: The United States, 1945–1974* (1996).

The Kennedy Presidency

Irving Bernstein, *Promises Kept: John F. Kennedy's New Frontier* (1991); James Giglio, *The Presidency of John F. Kennedy* (1991); David Halberstam, *The Best and the Brightest* (1972); Christopher Matthews, *Kennedy and Nixon: The Rivalry That Shaped Postwar America* (1996); Herbert S. Parmet, *J.F.K.—The Presidency of John F. Kennedy* (1983); Thomas C. Reeves, *A Question of Character* (1991); Arthur M. Schlesinger, Jr., *Robert Kennedy and His Times* (1978); Arthur M. Schlesinger, Jr., *A Thousand Days: John F. Kennedy in the White House* (1965); Ronald Steel, *In Love with Night: The American Romance with Robert Kennedy* (1999); Garry Wills, *The Kennedy Imprisonment* (1982).

The Kennedy Assassination

Edward Jay Epstein, *Legend: The Secret World of Lee Harvey Oswald* (1978); Henry Hurt, *Reasonable Doubt* (1985); Gerald Posner, *Case Closed* (1993); Anthony Summers, *Conspiracy* (1980).

Lyndon B. Johnson and the Great Society

Irving Bernstein, *Guns or Butter: The Presidency of Lyndon Johnson* (1996); Robert Dallek, *Flawed Giant: Lyndon Johnson and His Times, 1961–1973* (1998); Doris Kearns, *Lyndon Johnson and the American Dream* (1976); Sar A. Levitan and Robert Taggart, *The Promise of Greatness* (1976); Charles Murray, *Losing Ground: American Social Policy, 1950–1980* (1983); James T. Patterson, *America's Struggle Against Poverty, 1900–1994*, rev. ed. (1994); John E. Schwarz, *Amer-*

ica's Hidden Success: A Reassessment of Twenty Years of Public Policy (1983); Irwin Unger, *The Best of Intentions: The Triumph and Failure of the Great Society Under Kennedy, Johnson, and Nixon* (1996).

Civil Rights, Black Power, and Urban Riots

Taylor Branch, *Pillar of Fire: America in the King Years, 1963-1965* (1998); Taylor Branch, *Parting the Waters: America in the King Years, 1954–1963* (1988); Clayborne Carson, *In Struggle: SNCC and the Black Awakening of the 1960s* (1981); John Dittmer, *Local People: The Struggle for Civil Rights in Mississippi* (1994); David J. Garrow, *Bearing the Cross: Martin Luther King, Jr., and the Southern Christian Leadership Conference* (1986); David Halberstam, *The Children* (1998); Gerald Horne, *Fire This Time: The Watts Uprising and the 1960s* (1996); Chana Kai Lee, *For Freedom's Sake: The Life of Fannie Lou Hamer* (1999); Malcolm X and Alex Haley, *The Autobiography of Malcolm X* (1965); August Meier and Elliott Rudwick, *CORE* (1973); Charles M. Payne, *I've Got the Light of Freedom: The Organizing Tradition and the Mississippi Freedom Struggle* (1995); David Remmick, *King of the World: Muhammad Ali and the Rise of An American Hero* (1999); Belinda Robnett, *How Long? How Long? African-American Women in the Struggle for Civil Rights* (1997).

The Warren Court

Gerald Dunne, *Hugo Black and the Judicial Revolution* (1977); Morton J. Horwitz, *The Warren Court and the Pursuit of Justice* (1998); Bernard Schwartz, *Super Chief: Earl Warren and His Supreme Court* (1983); G. Edward White, *Earl Warren* (1982).

The New Left and Protest for Peace and Justice

Terry H. Anderson, *The Movement and the Sixties* (1995); Wini Breines, *Community and Organization in the New Left, 1962–1968*, rev. ed. (1989); Dudley Clendinen and Adam Nagourney, *Out for Good: The Struggle to Build a Gay Rights Movement in America* (1998); Charles DeBenedetti, *An American Ordeal: The Antiwar Movement of the Vietnam Era* (1990); John D'Emilio, *Sexual Politics, Sexual Communities: The Making of a Homosexual Minority in the United States, 1940–1970* (1983); Todd Gitlin, *The Sixties* (1987); James Miller, *"Democracy Is in the Streets": From Port Huron to the Siege of Chicago* (1987); Doug Rossinow, *The Politics of Authenticity: Liberalism, Christianity, and the New Left in America* (1998); Kirkpatrick Sale, *The Green Revolution: The American Environmental Movement, 1962–1992* (1993); Tom Wells, *The War Within: America's Battle over Vietnam* (1994).

The Counterculture

Morris Dickstein, *Gates of Eden: American Culture in the Sixties* (1977); James Miller, *Flowers in the Dustbin: The Rise of Rock and Roll, 1947–1977* (1999); Tim Miller, *The Hippies and American Values* (1991); Charles Perry, *The Haight-Ashbury* (1984); Jay Stevens, *Storming Heaven: LSD and the American Dream* (1987); Jon Weiner, *Come Together: John Lennon in His Time* (1984); Tom Wolfe, *The Electric Kool-Aid Acid Test* (1968).

The Rebirth of Feminism

Flora Davis, *Moving the Mountain: The Women's Movement in America Since 1960* (1991); Alice Echols, *Daring to Be Bad: Radical Feminism in America, 1965–1975* (1989); Sara Evans, *Personal Politics* (1978); Jo Freeman, *The Politics of Women's Liberation* (1975); David J. Garrow, *Liberty and Sexuality: The Right to Privacy and the Making of* Roe v. Wade (1994); Cynthia Harrison, *On Account of Sex: The Politics of Women's Issues, 1945–1968* (1988); Judith Hole and Ellen Levine, *Rebirth of Feminism* (1971); Daniel Horowitz, *Betty Friedan and the Making of the "Feminine Mystique"* (1999); Ruth Rosen, *The World Split Open: How the Modern Women's Movement Changed America* (2000).

Year of Shocks: 1968

David Farber, *Chicago '68* (1988); Carole Fink et al., eds., *1968: The World Transformed* (1998); Ronald Fraser et al., *1968: A Student Generation in Revolt* (1988); Charles Kaiser, *1968 in America* (1988); Jules Witcover, *The Year the Dream Died: Revisiting 1968 in America* (1997) .

Richard M. Nixon and the Resurgence of Conservatism

Stephen E. Ambrose, *Nixon*, 3 vols. (1987–1991); William C. Berman, *Right Turn: From Nixon to Bush* (1994); Mary C. Brennan, *Turning Right in the Sixties: The Conservative Capture of the GOP* (1995); Dan T. Carter, *The Politics of Rage: George Wallace, the Origins of the New Conservatism, and the Transformation of American Politics* (1995); Robert Alan Goldberg, *Barry Goldwater* (1995); Allen J. Matusow, *Nixon's Economy: Booms, Busts, Dollars, and Votes* (1998); Herbert S. Parmet, *Richard Nixon and His America* (1990); James A. Reichley, *Conservatives in an Era of Change: The Nixon and Ford Administrations* (1981); Melvin Small, *The Presidency of Richard Nixon* (1999); Tom Wicker, *One of Us* (1991); Garry Wills, *Nixon Agonistes* (1970).

Watergate

Jim Hougan, *Secret Agenda: Watergate, Deep Throat and the CIA* (1984); Stanley I. Kutler, ed., *Abuse of Power: The New Nixon Tapes* (1997); Stanley I. Kutler, *The Wars of Watergate* (1990); J. Anthony Lukas, *Nightmare: The Underside of the Nixon Years* (1976); Kim McQuaid, *The Anxious Years: America in the Vietnam-Watergate Era* (1989); Michael Schudson, *Watergate in American Memory* (1992); Theodore H. White, *Breach of Faith* (1975); Bob Woodward, *Shadow: Five Presidents and the Legacy of Watergate* (1999); Bob Woodward and Carl Bernstein, *All the President's Men* (1974).

Chapter 31

General

See works listed under Chapter 29 and Richard J. Barnet, *Intervention and Revolution* (1972); Edward H. Berman, *The Influence of the Carnegie, Ford, and Rockefeller Foundations on American Foreign Policy* (1983); Alvin Z. Rubenstein and Donald E. Smith, eds., *Anti-Americanism in the Third World* (1985).

Foreign Policy in the 1960s: Kennedy and Johnson

LeRoy Ashby and Rod Gramer, *Fighting the Odds: The Life of Senator Frank Church* (1994); Michael Beschloss, *The Crisis Years* (1991); James A. Bill, *George Ball* (1997); Kai Bird, *The Color of Truth: McGeorge Bundy and William Bundy* (1998); H. W. Brands, ed., *The Foreign Policies of Lyndon Johnson* (1999); H. W. Brands, *The Wages of Globalism* (1995); Warren I. Cohen, *Dean Rusk* (1980); Warren I. Cohen and Nancy B. Tucker, eds., *Lyndon Johnson Confronts the World* (1995); Robert Dallek, *Flawed Giant: Lyndon Johnson and His Times, 1961–1973* (1998); Fritz Fisher, *Making Them Like Us: Peace Corps Volunteers in the 1960s* (1998); James N. Giglio, *The Presidency of John F. Kennedy* (1991); David Halberstam, *The Best and the Brightest* (1972); Seymour Hersh, *The Other Side of Camelot* (1997); Elizabeth Cobbs Hoffman, *All You Need Is Love: The Peace Corps and the Spirit of the 1960s* (1998); Robert D. Johnson, *Ernest Gruening and the American Dissenting Tradition* (1998); Doris Kearns, *Lyndon Johnson and the American Dream* (1976); Montague Kern et al., *The Kennedy Crises* (1984); Diane Kunz, ed., *The Diplomacy of the Crucial Decade* (1994); Herbert S. Parmet, *JFK* (1983); Thomas G. Paterson, ed., *Kennedy's Quest for Victory* (1989); Gerald T. Rice, *The Bold Experiment: JFK's Peace Corps* (1985); Arthur M. Schlesinger, Jr., *Robert Kennedy and His Times* (1978); Thomas J. Schoenbaum, *Waging Peace and War: Dean Rusk in the Truman, Kennedy, and Johnson Years* (1988); Deborah Shapley, *Promise and Power: The Life and Times of Robert McNamara* (1993); Mark J. White, *Kennedy* (1998); Randall Woods, *Fulbright* (1995); Thomas W. Zeiler, *Dean Rusk* (1999).

Cuba and the Missile Crisis

Graham Allison and Philip Zelikow, *Essence of Decision: Explaining the Cuban Missile Crisis*, 2d ed. (1999); James G. Blight, *The Shattered Crystal Ball* (1990); James G. Blight et al., *Cuba on the Brink* (1993); James G. Blight and Peter Kornbluh, eds., *Politics of Illusion: The Bay of Pigs Invasion Reexamined* (1998); James G. Blight and David A. Welch, *On the Brink* (1989); Raymond Garthoff, *Reflections on the Cuban Missile Crisis*, rev. ed. (1989); Trumbull Higgins, *The Perfect Failure: Kennedy, Eisenhower, and the CIA at the Bay of Pigs* (1987); Donna R. Kaplowitz, *Anatomy of a Failed Embargo: U.S. Sanctions Against Cuba* (1998); Richard Ned Lebow and Janice Gross Stein, *We All Lost the Cold War* (1993); Ernest R.

May and Philip Zelikow, eds., *The Kennedy Tapes* (1997); Morris Morley, *Imperial State and Revolution* (1987); James Nathan, ed., *The Cuban Missile Crisis Revisited* (1992); Thomas G. Paterson, *Contesting Castro* (1994); Louis A. Pérez, Jr., *Cuba and the United States*, 2d ed. (1997); Scott D. Sagan, *The Limits of Safety* (1993); Mark J. White, *The Cuban Missile Crisis* (1996).

The Vietnam War

See Duiker, Herring, Hess, Kolko, Morgan, Schulzinger, Tomes, and Young listed under Chapter 29 and David L. Anderson, *Facing My Lai* (1998); Loren Baritz, *Backfire* (1985); David M. Barrett, *Uncertain Warriors* (1993); Eric M. Bergerud, *The Dynamics of Defeat* (1991); Larry Berman, *Lyndon Johnson's War* (1989); Larry Berman, *Planning a Tragedy* (1982); Robert K. Brigham, *Guerilla Diplomacy: The NFL's Foreign Relations and the Viet Nam War* (1999); Robert Buzzanco, *Vietnam and the Transformation of American Life* (1999); Robert Buzzanco, *Masters of War: Military Dissent and Politics in the Vietnam Era* (1996); Larry Cable, *Unholy Grail* (1991); Mark Clodfelter, *The Limits of Power: The American Bombing of North Vietnam* (1989); Phillip B. Davidson, *Vietnam at War* (1988); Charles DeBenedetti and Charles Chatfield, *An American Ordeal: The Antiwar Movement of the Vietnam War* (1990); David L. DiLeo, *George Ball, Vietnam, and the Rethinking of Containment* (1991); Frances FitzGerald, *Fire in the Lake* (1972); Lloyd C. Gardner, *Pay Any Price* (1995); William C. Gibbons, *The U.S. Government and the Vietnam War* (1986–1994); Daniel C. Hallin, *The "Uncensored War"* (1986); George C. Herring, *LBJ and Vietnam* (1994); Michael H. Hunt, *Lyndon Johnson's War* (1996); Rhodri Jeffreys-Jones, *Peace Now!* (1999); Jeffrey Kimball, *Nixon's Vietnam War* (1998); Fredrick Logevall, *Choosing War* (1999); George McT. Kahin, *Intervention* (1986); Robert S. McNamara, James G. Blight, and Robert K. Brigham, *Argument Without End: In Search of Answers to the Vietnam Tragedy* (1999); Edwin E. Moïse, *Tonkin Gulf and the Escalation of the Vietnam War* (1996); William Prochnau, *Once upon a Distant War* (1995) (on journalists); William Shawcross, *Sideshow: Kissinger, Nixon, and the Destruction of Cambodia* (1979); Kevin Sim and Michael Bilton, *Four Hours in My Lai* (1992); Melvin Small, *Johnson, Nixon and the Doves* (1988); Ronald H. Spector, *After Tet: The Bloodiest Year in Vietnam* (1992); Ronald H. Spector, *United States Army in Vietnam* (1983); Brian VanDerMark, *Into the Quagmire* (1991).

Legacy and Lessons of the Vietnam War

Eric T. Dean, Jr., *Shook Over Hell: Post-Traumatic Stress, Vietnam, and the Civil War* (1998); John Hellman, *American Myth and the Legacy of Vietnam* (1986); Herbert Hendin and Ann P. Haas, *Wounds of War: The Psychological Aftermath of Combat in Vietnam* (1984); Ole R. Holsti and James Rosenau, *American Leadership in World Affairs: Vietnam and the Breakdown of Consensus* (1984); David Levy, *The Debate over Vietnam* (1991);

Myra MacPherson, *Long Time Passing* (1984); Norman Podhoretz, *Why We Were in Vietnam* (1982); Earl C. Ravenal, *Never Again* (1978); Harrison E. Salisbury, ed., *Vietnam Reconsidered* (1984); Harry G. Summers, Jr., *On Strategy* (1982); Fred Turner, *Echoes of Combat: The Vietnam War in American Memory* (1996).

Nixon, Kissinger, and Détente

Stephen Ambrose, *Nixon*, 3 vols. (1987–1991); Michael B. Froman, *The Development of the Idea of Détente* (1992); Raymond L. Garthoff, *Détente and Confrontation* (1985); John R. Greene, *The Limits of Power* (1992); Seymour Hersh, *The Price of Power* (1983); Joan Hoff, *Nixon Reconsidered* (1994); Walter Isaacson, *Kissinger* (1992); Allen J. Matusow, *Nixon's Economy* (1998); Keith L. Nelson, *The Making of Détente* (1995); Herbert S. Parmet, *Richard Nixon and His America* (1990); Andrew J. Pierre, *The Global Politics of Arms Sales* (1982); Robert D. Schulzinger, *Henry Kissinger* (1989); Melvin Small, *The Presidency of Richard Nixon* (1999).

Carter Foreign Policy and Human Rights

Anne H. Cahn, *Killing Détente: The Right Attacks the CIA* (1998); Gary M. Fink and Hugh Davis Graham, eds., *The Carter Presidency* (1998); Erwin C. Hargrove, *Jimmy Carter as President* (1988); Charles O. Jones, *The Trusteeship Presidency* (1988); Burton I. Kaufman, *The Presidency of James Earl Carter, Jr.* (1993); David S. McLellan, *Cyrus Vance* (1985); Richard A. Melanson, *Reconstructing Consensus* (1990); A. Glenn Mower, Jr., *Human Rights and American Foreign Policy* (1987); John Newhouse, *Cold Dawn* (1973) (on SALT); Kenneth A. Oye et al., *Eagle Entangled* (1979); Herbert D. Rosenbaum and Alezej Ugrinsky, eds., *Jimmy Carter* (1994); Gaddis Smith, *Morality, Reason, and Power* (1986); Strobe Talbott, *Endgame: The Inside Story of SALT II* (1979); Sandy Vogelsang, *American Dream, Global Nightmare* (1980); Odd Arne Westad, ed., *The Fall of Détente* (1997).

Reagan's Foreign Policy and Military Buildup

Dana H. Allin, *Cold War Illusions* (1995); Michael R. Beschloss and Strobe Talbott, *At the Highest Levels* (1993); Archie Brown, *The Gorbachev Factor* (1996); Lou Cannon, *President Reagan* (1991); Theodore Draper, *A Very Thin Line: The Iran-Contra Affairs* (1991); John Ehrman, *The Rise of Neoconservatism* (1995); Beth A. Fischer, *The Reagan Reversal* (1997); Raymond L. Garthoff, *The Great Transition* (1994); Seymour Hersh, *"The Target Is Destroyed": What Really Happened to Flight 007 and What America Knew About It* (1986); Haynes Johnson, *Sleepwalking Through History* (1991); Robert G. Kaiser, *Why Gorbachev Happened* (1991); Peter Kornbluh and Malcolm Byrne, eds., *The Iran-Contra Scandal* (1993); Michael MccGwire, *Perestroika and Soviet National Security* (1991); Edmund Morris, *Dutch* (1999); Don Oberdorfer, *From the Cold War to a New Era* (1998); Kenneth A. Oye et al., eds., *Eagle Resurgent?* (1987); William E. Pember-

ton, *Exit with Honor* (1997); Michael Schaller, *Reckoning with Reagan* (1992); Strobe Talbott, *The Master of the Game: Paul Nitze and the Nuclear Peace* (1988); Strobe Talbott, *Deadly Gambit* (1984); Daniel Wirls, *Buildup* (1992).

Latin America: General

Cole Blasier, *Hovering Giant* (1974); David W. Dent, ed., *U.S.–Latin American Policymaking* (1995); Guy Gugliotta and Jeff Leen, *Kings of Cocaine* (1989); Eldon Kenworthy, *America/Americas* (1995); Lester Langley, *America and the Americas* (1989); Abraham F. Lowenthal, ed., *Exporting Democracy* (1991); Abraham F. Lowenthal, *Partners in Conflict*, rev. ed. (1990); Donald J. Mabry, ed., *The Latin American Narcotics Trade and U.S. National Security* (1989); W. Dirk Raat, *Mexico and the United States*, 2d ed. (1997); Stephen G. Rabe, *The Most Dangerous Area in the World: John F. Kennedy Confronts Communist Revolution in Latin America* (1999); Stephen G. Rabe, *The Road to OPEC: United States Relations with Venezuela* (1982); William F. Sater, *Chile and the United States* (1990); Lars Schoultz, *Beneath the United States* (1998); Peter H. Smith, *Talons of the Eagle* (1996).

Central America and Panama

Cynthia J. Arnson, *Crossroads* (1989); Morris J. Blachman et al., eds., *Confronting Revolution* (1986); E. Bradford Burns, *At War in Nicaragua* (1987); John Coatsworth, *Central America and the United States* (1994); Kenneth M. Coleman and George C. Herring, eds., *Understanding the Central American Crisis* (1991); Michael L. Conniff, *Panama and the United States* (1992); Piero Gleijeses, Michael Klare and Peter Kornbluh, eds., *Low Intensity Warfare* (1988); Walter LaFeber, *Inevitable Revolutions*, 2d ed. (1993); Walter LaFeber, *The Panama Canal*, updated ed. (1989); William M. LeoGrande, *Our Own Backyard* (1998); John Major, *Prize Possession: The United States and the Panama Canal, 1903–1979* (1994); Robert A. Pastor, *Whirlpool: U.S. Foreign Policy Toward Latin America and the Caribbean* (1992); Robert A. Pastor, *Condemned to Repetition: The United States and Nicaragua* (1987); Peter Dale Scott and Jonathan Marshall, *Cocaine Politics* (1991); Christian Smith, *Resisting Reagan: The U.S.–Central America Peace Movement* (1996); Thomas W. Walker, ed., *Revolution and Counterrevolution in Nicaragua* (1991).

The Middle East and Iranian Hostage Crisis

James A. Bill, *The Eagle and the Lion: The Tragedy of American-Iranian Relations* (1988); William J. Burns and Richard W. Cottam, *Iran and the United States* (1988); Mark Gasiorowski, *U.S. Foreign Policy and the Shah* (1991); James E. Goode, *The United States and Iran* (1997); Burton I. Kaufman, *The Arab Middle East and the United States* (1996); William B. Quandt, *Peace Process* (1993); Cheryl A. Rubenberg, *Israel and the American National Interest* (1986); David Schoenbaum, *The United States and the State of Israel* (1993);

Gary Sick, *October Surprise: America's Hostages in Iran and the Election of Ronald Reagan* (1991); Steven L. Spiegel, *The Other Arab-Israeli Conflict* (1985); Robert W. Stookey, *America and the Arab States* (1975); Daniel Yergin, *The Prize: The Epic Quest for Oil, Money, and Power* (1991).

Africa

Pauline H. Baker, *The United States and South Africa: The Reagan Years* (1989); Christopher Coker, *The United States and South Africa, 1968–1985* (1986); David N. Gibbs, *The Political Economy of Third World Intervention : Mines, Money, and U.S. Policy in the Congo Crises* (1991); Richard D. Mahoney, *JFK: Ordeal in Africa* (1983); Robert K. Massie, *Loosing the Bonds: The United States and South Africa in the Apartheid Years* (1997); Thomas J. Noer, *Cold War and Black Liberation* (1985); Peter J. Schraeder, *United States Policy Toward Africa* (1994).

Asia

Walter LaFeber, *The Clash: A History of U.S.-Japan Relations* (1997); James Mann, *About Face: A History of America's Curious Relationship with China, From Nixon to Clinton* (1999); Robert McMahon, *The Limits of Empire: The United States and Southeast Asia Since World War II* (1999); Robert S. Ross, *Negotiating Cooperation: The United States and China, 1969–1989* (1995); Michael Schaller, *Altered States: The United States and Japan Since the Occupation* (1997); Nancy B. Tucker, *Taiwan, Hong Kong, and the United States* (1994). See above for Vietnam.

The World Economy and the Natural Environment

Richard J. Barnet, *The Lean Years* (1980); Richard J. Barnet and John Cavanaugh, *Global Dreams* (1994); Richard J. Barnet and Ronald Müller, *Global Reach* (1974); Richard E. Benedick, *Ozone Diplomacy* (1991); David P. Calleo, *The Imperious Economy* (1982); Alfred E. Eckes, *The United States and the Global Struggle for Minerals* (1979); David E. Fisher, *Fire & Ice: The Greenhouse Effect, Ozone Depletion, and Nuclear Winter* (1990); Edward M. Graham and Paul R. Krugman, *Foreign Direct Investment in the United States* (1989); Stephen D. Krasner, *Defending the National Interest* (1978); Diane B. Kunz, *Butter and Guns* (1997); John McCormick, *Reclaiming Paradise: The Global Environmental Movement* (1989); Joan E. Spero and Jeffrey A. Hart, *The Politics of International Economic Relations*, 5th ed. (1997); Herman Van Der Wee, *The Search for Prosperity: The World Economy, 1945–1980* (1986).

Chapter 32

Deficits, Deindustrialization, and Other Economic Woes

Barry Bluestone and Bennett Harrison, *The Deindustrialization of America* (1982); Richard Feldman and Michael Bet-zold, *End of the Line: Autoworkers and the American Dream* (1988); Robert Heilbroner and Peter Bernstein, *The Debt and the Deficit* (1989); John P. Hoerr, *And the Wolf Finally Came: The Decline of the American Steel Industry* (1988); Gregory Pappas, *The Magic City: Unemployment in a Working-Class Community* (1989).

The Ford and Carter Administrations

Gary M. Fink and Hugh Davis Graham, eds., *The Carter Presidency* (1998); John Robert Greene, *The Presidency of Gerald R. Ford* (1995); Erwin C. Hargrove, *Jimmy Carter as President* (1989); Charles O. Jones, *The Trusteeship Presidency: Jimmy Carter and the United States Congress* (1988); Burton I. Kaufman, *The Presidency of James Earl Carter, Jr.* (1993).

Women and Children's Struggles

Marian Wright Edelman, *Families in Peril* (1987); Barbara Ehrenreich, *The Hearts of Men: American Dreams and the Flight from Commitment* (1983); David T. Ellwood, *Poor Support: Poverty in the American Family* (1988); Susan Faludi, *Backlash: The Undeclared War Against American Women* (1991); Sylvia Ann Hewlett, *When the Bough Breaks: The Cost of Neglecting Our Children* (1991); Arlie Russell Hochschild, *The Second Shift: Working Parents and the Revolution at Home* (1989); Rebecca E. Klatch, *Women of the New Right* (1987); Kristin Luker, *Abortion and the Politics of Motherhood* (1984); Winifred D. Wandersee, *On the Move: American Women in the 1970s* (1988).

People of Color and New Immigrants

Leslie W. Dunbar, ed., *Minority Report: What Has Happened to Blacks, Hispanics, American Indians, and Other Minorities in the Eighties* (1984); Reynolds Farley and Walter R. Allen, *The Color Line and the Quality of Life in America* (1987); Nancy Foner, ed., *New Immigrants in New York* (1987); Ronald P. Formisano, *Boston Against Busing* (1991); Joane Nagel, *American Indian Ethnic Revival: Red Power and the Resurgence of Identity and Culture* (1996); David M. Reimers, *Still the Golden Door: The Third World Comes to America* (1985); Paul Chaat Smith and Robert Allen Warrior, *Like a Hurricane: The Indian Movement from Alcatraz to Wounded Knee* (1996); Sanford J. Ungar, *Fresh Blood: The New Immigrants* (1995); William Julius Wilson, *The Truly Disadvantaged: The Inner City, the Underclass, and Public Policy* (1987).

The New Conservatism and the Election of 1980

William C. Berman, *America's Right Turn* (1994); Sara Diamond, *Not by Politics Alone: The Enduring Influence of the Christian Right* (1998); Thomas Byrne Edsall, *The New Politics of Inequality* (1984); Lee Edwards, *The Conservative Revolution* (1999); Jack W. Germond and Jules Witcover, *Blue Smoke and Mirrors: How Reagan Won and Why Carter Lost the Election of 1980* (1981); Godfrey Hodgson, *The World Turned*

Right Side Up: A History of the Conservative Ascendancy in America (1996).

Ronald Reagan and His Presidency

Lou Cannon, *President Reagan* (1991); Paul D. Erickson, *Reagan Speaks: The Making of an American Myth* (1985); Mark Hertsgaard, *On Bended Knee: The Press and the Reagan Presidency* (1988); Haynes Johnson, *Sleepwalking Through History: America in the Reagan Years* (1991); Nicholas Laham, *The Reagan Presidency and the Politics of Race* (1998); Jane Mayer and Doyle McManus, *Landslide: The Unmaking of the President, 1984–1988* (1988); William E. Pemberton, *Exit with Honor: The Life and Presidency of Ronald Reagan* (1997); John W. Sloan, *The Reagan Effect: Economics and Presidential Leadership* (1999); Garry Wills, *Reagan's America* (1987).

"Reaganomics"

Joan Claybrook, *Retreat from Safety: Reagan's Attack on America's Health* (1984); Benjamin Friedman, *Day of Reckoning: The Consequences of American Economic Policy Under Reagan and After* (1988); Jonathan Lash, *A Season of Spoils: The Story of the Reagan Administration's Attack on the Environment* (1984); Robert Lekachman, *Greed Is Not Enough: Reaganomics* (1982); William A. Niskanen, *Reaganomics* (1988); Charles Noble, *Liberalism at Work: The Rise and Fall of OSHA* (1986); Kevin Phillips, *The Politics of Rich and Poor* (1990); Kitty Calavita et al., *Big Money Crime: Fraud and Politics in the Savings and Loan Crisis* (1997).

A Polarized Society in the 1980s

Chandler Davidson, *Race and Class in Texas Politics* (1990); Michael Harrington, *The New American Poverty* (1984); Katherine S. Newman, *Declining Fortunes: The Withering of the American Dream* (1993); Randy Shilts, *And the Band Played On: Politics, People and the AIDS Epidemic* (1987); Studs Terkel, *The Great Divide* (1988); Edward N. Wolff, *Top Heavy: A Study of Increasing Inequality in America* (1995).

Presidential Politics: The Elections of 1984 and 1988

Sidney Blumenthal, *Pledging Allegiance: The Last Campaign of the Cold War* (1990); Richard Ben Cramer, *What It Takes* (1992); Thomas Byrne Edsall and Mary D. Edsall, *Chain Reaction: The Impact of Race, Rights, and Taxes on American Politics* (1991); Thomas Ferguson and Joel Rogers, *Right Turn: The Decline of the Democrats and the Future of American Politics* (1986); Marshall Frady, *Jesse: The Life and Pilgrimage of Jesse Jackson* (1996); Jack W. Germond and Jules Witcover, *Wake Us When It's Over: Presidential Politics of 1984* (1985); Peter Goldman and Tom Mathews, *The Quest for the Presidency: The 1988 Campaign* (1989).

Chapter 33

The Bush Administration

Donald L. Bartlett and James B. Steele, *America: What Went Wrong?* (1992); Michael Duffy and Don Goodgame, *Marching in Place: The Status Quo Presidency of George Bush* (1992); John Robert Greene, *The Presidency of George Bush* (2000); Dilys M. Hill and Phil Williams, eds., *The Bush Presidency* (1994); Herbert S. Parmet, *George Bush: The Life of a Lone Star Yankee* (1998).

Politics and the Election of 1992

Alan Ehrenhalt, *The United States of Ambition: Politicians, Power, and the Pursuit of Office* (1991); William Greider, *Who Will Tell the People: The Betrayal of American Democracy* (1992); Kathleen Hall Jamieson, *Dirty Politics* (1992); Kevin Phillips, *The Politics of Rich and Poor* (1990); Gerald Posner, *Citizen Perot* (1996); Ruy A. Teixeira, *The Disappearing American Voter* (1992); George F. Will, *Restoration: Congress, Term Limits and the Recovery of Deliberative Democracy* (1992).

American Society in the 1990s

Sheldon Danziger and Peter Gottschalk, *American Unequal* (1996); Robert H. Frank and Philip J. Cook, *The Winner-Take-All Society* (1995); Herbert J. Gans, *The War Against the Poor* (1995); Barry Glassner, *The Culture of Fear* (1999); David M. Gordon, *Fat and Mean: The Corporate Squeeze of Working Americans and the Myth of Managerial "Downsizing"* (1996); Jennifer L. Hochschild, *Facing Up to the American Dream: Race, Class, and the Soul of the Nation* (1995); Katherine S. Newman, *Declining Fortunes: The Withering of the American Dream* (1993); Robert J. Samuelson, *The Good Life and Its Discontents: The American Dream in an Age of Entitlements* (1995); Michael D. Yates, *Longer Hours, Fewer Jobs* (1994).

Disgruntled Americans: Political Apathy, Antigovernment Movements, and Culture Wars

Stephen Ansolabehere and Shanto Iyengar, *Going Negative: How Attack Ads Shrink and Polarize the Electorate* (1995); Sara Diamond, *Not by Politics Alone: The Enduring Influnce of the Christian Right* (1998); E. J. Dionne, Jr., *Why Americans Hate Politics* (1991); James Fallows, *Breaking the News: How the Media Undermine American Democracy* (1996); Thomas Ferguson, *Golden Rule: The Investment Theory of Party Competition and the Logic of Money-Driven Political Systems* (1995); William Martin, *With God on Our Side: The Rise of the Religious Right in America* (1996); Larry J. Sabato and Glenn R. Simpson, *Dirty Little Secrets: The Persistence of Corruption in American Politics* (1996); Neil J. Smelser and Jeffrey C. Alexander, eds., *Diversity and Its Discontents: Cultural Conflict and Common Ground in Contemporary American Society* (1999);

Kenneth S. Stern, *A Force upon the Plain: The American Militia Movement and the Politics of Hate* (1996).

The Election of 1994: The "Republican Revolution"

Dan Balz and Ronald Brownstein, *Storming the Gates: Protest Politics and the Republican Revival* (1996); Elizabeth Drew, *Showdown: The Struggle Between the Gingrich Congress and the Clinton White House* (1996); David Frum, *Dead Right* (1994); Linda Killian, *The Freshmen: What Happened to the Republican Revolution?* (1998); David Maraniss and Michael Weisskopf, *"Tell Newt to Shut Up!"* (1996).

The 1996 Election and the Future of American Politics

E. J. Dionne, Jr., *They Only Look Dead: Why Progressives Will Dominate the Next Political Era* (1996); Martin Plissner, *The Control Room: How Television Calls the Shots in Presidential Elections* (1999); Jake H. Thompson, *Bob Dole* (1994); Ben J. Wattenberg, *Values Matter Most: How Republicans or Democrats or a Third Party Can Win and Renew the American Way of Life* (1995); Jacob Weisberg, *In Defense of Government: The Fall and Rise of Public Trust* (1996); Bob Woodward, *The Choice* (1996).

Clinton's Presidency, Impeachment, and Survival

Alan M. Dershowitz, *Sexual McCarthyism: Clinton, Starr and the Emerging Constitutional Crisis* (1998); Michael Isikoff, *Uncovering Clinton: A Reporter's Story* (1999); David Maraniss, *First in His Class: A Biography of Bill Clinton* (1995); Roger Morris, *Partners in Power: The Clintons and Their America* (1996); Richard A. Posner, *Affair of State: The Investigation, Impeachment, and Trial of President Clinton* (1999); Richard Reeves, *Running in Place: How Bill Clinton Disappointed America* (1996); Gail Sheehy, *Hillary's Choice* (1999); James B. Stewart, *Blood Sport: The President and His Adversaries* (1996); Jeffrey Toobin, *A Vast Conspiracy: The Real Story of the Sex Scandal That Nearly Brought Down a President* (2000); Bob Woodward, *The Agenda: Inside the Clinton White House* (1994).

The Foreign Policies and Wars of Bush and Clinton

See some works listed under Chapter 31 and Deborah Amos, *Lines in the Sand: Desert Storm and the Remaking of the Arab World* (1992); Michael R. Beschloss and Strobe Talbott, *At the Highest Levels: The Inside Story of the End of the Cold War* (1993); Douglas Brinkley, *The Unfinished Presidency: Jimmy Carter's Journey Beyond the White House* (1998); Archie Brown, *The Gorbachev Factor* (1996); Kevin Buckley, *Panama* (1991); John Coatsworth, *Central America and the United States* (1994); Michael Conniff, *Panama and the United States* (1992); Timothy J. Dunn, *The Militarization of the U.S.-Mexico Border* (1996); Lawrence Freedman and Efraim Karsh, *The Gulf Conflict, 1990–1991* (1993); John Lewis Gaddis, *The United States and the End of the Cold War* (1992); Raymond L. Garthoff, *The Great Transition* (1994); Stephen Graubard, *Mr. Bush's War* (1992); Avigdor Haselkorn, *The Continuing Storm: Iraq, Poisonous Weapons, and Deterrence* (1999); John L. Hirsch and Robert B. Oakley, *Somalia and Operation Restore Hope* (1995); Stanley Hoffmann, *World Disorders* (1999); Michael Hogan, ed., *The End of the Cold War* (1992); William G. Hyland, *Clinton's World* (1999); Burton I. Kaufman, *The Arab Middle East and the United States* (1996); Walter LaFeber, *The Clash: A History of U.S.-Japan Relations* (1997); Robert J. Lieber, ed., *Eagle Adrift* (1997); Robert K. Massie, *Loosing the Bonds: The United States and South Africa in the Apartheid Years* (1998); James Mayall, ed., *The New Interventionism* (1996); Larry Minear and Thomas G. Weiss, *Humanitarian Politics* (1995); John Mueller, *Policy and Opinion in the Gulf War* (1994); Don Oberdorfer, *From the Cold War to the New Era* (1998); Kenneth A. Oye et al., eds., *Eagle in a New World* (1992); W. Dirk Raat, *Mexico and the United States*, 2d ed. (1997); Jeffrey T. Richelson, *The U.S. Intelligence Community*, 4th ed. (1999); Jean Edward Smith, *George Bush's War* (1992); Peter H. Smith, *Talons of the Eagle* (1996) (on U.S.-Latin America); Stephen R. Weissman, *A Culture of Deference: Congress's Failure of Leadership in Foreign Policy* (1995); Susan Woodward, *Balkan Tragedy* (1995).

Global Economic and Cultural Issues

Richard J. Barnet and John Cavangh, *Global Dreams: Imperial Corporations and the New World Order* (1994); Ronald J. Bee, *Nuclear Proliferation* (1995); Thomas L. Friedman, *The Lexus and the Olive Tree* (1999) (on globalization); Laurie Garrett, *Microbes Versus Mankind: The Coming Plague* (1997); George W. Grayson, *The North American Free Trade Agreement* (1995); Frank Ninkovich, *Information Policy and Cultural Diplomacy* (1996); Richard Pells, *Not Like Us: How Europeans Have Loved, Hated, and Transformed American Culture Since World War II* (1997); Peter Dale Scott and Jonathan Marshall, *Cocaine Politics* (1991); Robert Soloman, *Money on the Move: The Revolution in International Finance Since 1980* (1999); Paul B. Stares, *Global Habit: The Drug Problem in a Borderless World* (1996); Jessica Stern, *The Ultimate Terrorists* (1999); James L. Watson, ed., *Golden Arches East: McDonald's in East Asia* (1997).

Historical Reference Books by Subject:
Encyclopedias, Dictionaries, Atlases, Chronologies, and Statistics

American History: General

Gorton Carruth, ed., *The Encyclopedia of American Facts and Dates* (1993); *Dictionary of American History* (1976) and Joan Hoff and Robert H. Ferrell, eds., *Supplement* (1996); John M. Farragher, ed., *The American Heritage Encyclopedia of American History* (1998); Eric Foner and John A. Garraty, eds., *The Reader's Companion to American History* (1991); Bernard Grun, *The Timetables of History* (1991); *International Encyclopedia of the Social Sciences* (1968–); Richard B. Morris and Jeffrey B. Morris, eds., *Encyclopedia of American History* (1996); Harry Ritter, *Dictionary of Concepts in History* (1986); Lawrence Urdang, ed., *The Timetables of American History* (1996); U.S. Bureau of the Census, *Historical Statistics of the United States* (1975).

American History: General, Twentieth Century

John D. Buenker and Edward R. Kantowicz, eds., *Historical Dictionary of the Progressive Era, 1890–1920* (1988); Robert H. Ferrell and John S. Bowman, eds., *The Twentieth Century: An Almanac* (1984); George H. Gallup, *The Gallup Poll: Public Opinion, 1935–1971* (1972), *1972–1977* (1978), and annual reports (1979–); Stanley Hochman, *The Penguin Dictionary of Contemporary American History* (1997); Stanley I. Kutler, ed., *Encyclopedia of the United States in the Twentieth Century* (1995); Peter B. Levy, *Encyclopedia of the Reagan-Bush Years* (1996); James S. Olson, *Historical Dictionary of the 1920s* (1988); Thomas Parker and Douglas Nelson, *Day by Day: The Sixties* (1983).

American History: General Atlases and Gazetteers

Geoffrey Barraclough, ed., *The Times Atlas of World History* (1994); Rodger Doyle, *Atlas of Contemporary America* (1994); Robert H. Ferrell and Richard Natkiel, *Atlas of American History* (1987); Edward W. Fox, *Atlas of American History* (1964); Archie Hobson, *The Cambridge Gazetteer of the United States and Canada* (1996); Eric Homberger, *The Penguin Historical Atlas of North America* (1995); Kenneth T. Jackson and James T. Adams, *Atlas of American History* (1978); National Geographic Society, *Historical Atlas of the United States* (1994); U.S. Department of the Interior, *National Atlas of the United States* (1970). Other atlases are listed under specific categories.

American History: General Biographies

Lucian Boia, ed., *Great Historians of the Modern Age* (1991); John S. Bowman, *The Cambridge Dictionary of American Biography* (1995); *Current Biography* (1940–); *Dictionary of American Biography* (1928–); John A. Garraty and Mark C. Carnes, eds., *American National Biography* (1999); John Garraty and Jerome L. Sternstein, eds., *The Encyclopedia of American Biography* (1996); *National Cyclopedia of American Biography* (1898–). Other biographical works appear under specific categories.

African Americans

Molefi Asante and Mark T. Mattson, *Historical and Cultural Atlas of African-Americans* (1991); John N. Ingham, *African-American Business Leaders* (1993); Rayford W. Logan and Michael R. Winston, eds., *The Dictionary of American Negro Biography* (1983); Sharon Harley, *The Timetables of African-American History* (1995); Darlene C. Hine et al., eds., *Black Women in White America* (1994); Charles D. Lowery and John F. Marszalek, eds., *Encyclopedia of African-American Civil Rights* (1992); Larry G. Murphy et al., eds., *Encyclopedia of African American Religions* (1993); Jack Salzman et al., eds., *Encyclopedia of African-American Culture and History* (1996); Jessie Carney Smith, ed., *Notable Black American Women* (1992). See also "Slavery."

American Revolution and Colonies

Richard Blanco and Paul Sanborn, eds., *The American Revolution* (1993); Lester J. Cappon, ed., *Atlas of Early American History: The Revolutionary Era, 1760–1790* (1976); Jacob E. Cooke, ed., *Encyclopedia of the American Colonies* (1993); John M. Faragher, ed., *The Encyclopedia of Colonial and Revolutionary America* (1990); Jack P. Greene and J. R. Pole, eds., *The*

Blackwell Encyclopedia of the American Revolution (1991); Douglas W. Marshall and Howard H. Peckham, *Campaigns of the American Revolution* (1976); Gregory Palmer, ed., *Biographical Sketches of Loyalists of the American Revolution* (1984); John W. Raimo, ed., *Biographical Directory of American Colonial and Revolutionary Governors, 1607–1789* (1980); *Rand-McNally Atlas of the American Revolution* (1974); Seymour I. Schwartz, *The French and Indian War, 1754–1763* (1995).

Architecture

William D. Hunt, Jr., ed., *Encyclopedia of American Architecture* (1980).

Asian Americans

Hyung-Chan Kim, ed., *Dictionary of Asian American History* (1986); Brian Niiya, ed., *Japanese American History* (1993); Lynn Pan, ed., *The Encyclopedia of the Chinese Overseas* (1999). See also "Immigration and Ethnic Groups."

Business and the Economy

Christine Ammer and Dean S. Ammer, *Dictionary of Business and Economics* (1983); Douglas Auld and Graham Bannock, *The American Dictionary of Economics* (1983); Michael J. Freeman, *Atlas of World Economy* (1991); John N. Ingham, *Biographical Dictionary of American Business Leaders* (1983); John N. Ingham and Lynne B. Feldman, *Contemporary American Business Leaders* (1990); William H. Mulligan, Jr., ed., *A Historical Dictionary of American Industrial Language* (1988); Glenn G. Munn, *Encyclopedia of Banking and Finance* (1973); Paul Paskoff, ed., *Encyclopedia of American Business History and Biography* (1989); Glenn Porter, *Encyclopedia of American Economic History* (1980); Richard Robinson, *United States Business History, 1602–1988* (1990); Malcolm Warner, ed., *International Encyclopedia of Business and Management* (1996). See also "African Americans," "Native Americans and Indian Affairs," and "Transportation."

Cities and Towns

John L. Androit, ed., *Township Atlas of the United States* (1979); David J. Bodenhamer and Robert J. Barrows, eds., *The Encyclopedia of Indianapolis* (1994); Gary A. Goreham, ed., *Encyclopedia of Rural America* (1997); Melvin G. Holli and Peter d'A. Jones, eds., *Biographical Dictionary of American Mayors, 1820–1980: Big City Mayors* (1981); Kenneth T. Jackson, ed., *Encyclopedia of New York City* (1995); George T. Kurian, *World Encyclopedia of Cities* (1994); Ory M. Nergal, ed., *The Encyclopedia of American Cities* (1980); Neil Larry Shumsky, ed., *Encyclopedia of Urban America* (1998); David D. Van Tassel and John J. Grabowski, eds., *The Dictionary of Cleveland Biography* (1996); David D. Van Tassel and John J. Grabowski, eds., *The Encyclopedia of Cleveland History* (1987). See also "Politics and Government."

Civil War and Reconstruction

Mark M. Boatner III, *The Civil War Dictionary* (1988); Richard N. Current, ed., *Encyclopedia of the Confederacy* (1993); John T. Hubbell and James W. Geary, eds., *Biographical Dictionary of the Union* (1995); Kenneth C. Martis, *The Historical Atlas of the Congresses of the Confederate States of America: 1861–1865* (1994); James M. McPherson, ed., *The Atlas of the Civil War* (1994); Mark E. Neely, Jr., *The Abraham Lincoln Encyclopedia* (1982); Craig L. Symonds, *A Battlefield Atlas of the Civil War* (1983); Hans L. Trefousse, *Historical Dictionary of Reconstruction* (1991); U.S. War Department, *The Official Atlas of the Civil War* (1958); Jon L. Wakelyn, ed., *Biographical Dictionary of the Confederacy* (1977); Ezra J. Warner and W. Buck Yearns, *Biographical Register of the Confederate Congress* (1975); Steven E. Woodworth, ed., *The American Civil War* (1996). See also "South" and "Politics and Government."

The Cold War

Thomas S. Arms, *Encyclopedia of the Cold War* (1994); Michael Kort, *The Columbia Guide to the Cold War* (1998); Richard A. Schwartz, *Cold War Culture: The Media and the Arts* (1998). See also "Foreign Relations" and "Military and Wars."

Constitution, Supreme Court, and Judiciary

David Bradley and Shelly F. Fishkin, eds., *The Encyclopedia of Civil Rights* (1997); Congressional Quarterly, *The Supreme Court A to Z* (1994); Kermit L. Hall, ed., *The Oxford Companion to the Supreme Court of the United States* (1992); Kermit L. Hall, ed., *The Oxford Guide to United States Supreme Court Decisions* (1999); Richard F. Hixson, *Mass Media and the Constitution* (1989); Robert J. Janosik, ed., *Encyclopedia of the American Judicial System* (1987); John W. Johnson, ed., *Historic U.S. Court Cases, 1690–1990* (1992); Leonard W. Levy et al., eds., *Encyclopedia of the American Constitution* (1986); Fred R. Shapiro, *The Oxford Dictionary of American Legal Quotations* (1993); Melvin I. Urofsky, ed., *The Supreme Court Justices* (1994). See also "Politics and Government" and "Sexuality."

Crime, Violence, Police, and Prisons

William G. Bailey, *Encyclopedia of Police Science* (1994); Sanford H. Kadish, ed., *Encyclopedia of Crime and Justice* (1983); Marilyn D. McShane and Frank P. Williams III, eds., *Encyclopedia of American Prisons* (1995); Michael Newton and Judy Ann Newton, *Racial and Religious Violence in America* (1991); Michael Newton and Judy Newton, *The Ku Klux Klan* (1990); Carl Sifakis, *Encyclopedia of Assassinations* (1990); Carl Sifakis, *The Encyclopedia of American Crime* (1982).

Culture and Folklore

Hennig Cohen and Tristam Potter Coffin, eds., *The Folklore of American Holidays* (1987); Richard M. Dorson, ed., *Handbook of American Folklore* (1983); Robert L. Gale, *A Cultural Encyclopedia of the 1850s in America* (1993); Robert L. Gale, *The Gay Nineties in America* (1992); M. Thomas Inge, ed., *Handbook of American Popular Culture* (1979–1981); Wolfgang Mieder et al., eds., *A Dictionary of American Proverbs* (1992); J. F. Rooney, Jr., et al., eds., *This Remarkable Continent: An Atlas of United States and Canadian Society and Cultures* (1982); Jane Stern and Michael Stern, *Encyclopedia of Pop Culture* (1992); Justin Wintle, ed., *Makers of Nineteenth Century Culture, 1800–1914* (1982). See also "The Cold War," "Entertainment and the Arts," "Mass Media and Journalism," "Music," and "Sports."

Education and Libraries

Lee C. Deighton, ed., *The Encyclopedia of Education* (1971); Joseph C. Kiger, ed., *Research Institutions and Learned Societies* (1982); John F. Ohles, ed., *Biographical Dictionary of American Educators* (1978); Wayne A. Wiegard and Donald E. Davis, Jr., eds., *Encyclopedia of Library History* (1994).

Entertainment and the Arts

Tim Brooks and Earle Marsh, *The Complete Directory to Prime Time Network and Cable TV Shows, 1946–Present* (1995); Barbara N. Cohen-Stratyner, *Biographical Dictionary of Dance* (1982); John Dunning, *Tune in Yesterday* (radio) (1967); Larry Langman and Edgar Borg, *Encyclopedia of American War Films* (1989); Larry Langman and David Ebner, *Encyclopedia of American Spy Films* (1990); *Notable Names in the American Theater* (1976); Andrew Sarris, *The American Cinema: Directors and Directions, 1929–1968* (1968); Anthony Slide, *The American Film Industry* (1986); Anthony Slide, *The Encyclopedia of Vaudeville* (1994); Evelyn M. Truitt, *Who Was Who on Screen* (1977); Don B. Wilmeth and Tice L. Miller, eds., *The Cambridge Guide to American Theatre* (1993). See also "The Cold War," "Culture and Folklore," "Mass Media and Journalism," "Music," and "Sports."

Environment and Conservation

André R. Cooper, ed., *Cooper's Comprehensive Environmental Desk Reference* (1996); Forest History Society, *Encyclopedia of American Forest and Conservation History* (1983); Irene Franck and David Brownstone, *The Green Encyclopedia* (1992); Robert J. Mason and Mark T. Mattson, *Atlas of United States Environmental Issues* (1990); Robert Paehlke, ed., *Conservation and Environmentalism* (1995); World Resources Institute, *Environmental Almanac* (1992).

Exploration: From Columbus to Space

Silvio A. Bedini, ed., *The Christopher Columbus Encyclopedia* (1992); Michael Cassutt, *Who's Who in Space* (1987); W. P.

Cumming et al., *The Discovery of North America* (1972); William Goetzmann and Glyndwr Williams, *The Atlas of North American Exploration* (1992); Clive Holland, *Arctic Exploration and Development* (1993); Adrian Johnson, *America Explored* (1974); Kenneth Nebenzahl, *Atlas of Columbus and the Great Discoveries* (1990). See also "Science and Technology."

Foreign Relations

Gerard Chaliand and Jean-Pierre Rageau, *Strategic Atlas* (1990); Alexander DeConde, ed., *Encyclopedia of American Foreign Policy* (1978); Margaret B. Denning and J. K. Sweeney, *Handbook of American Diplomacy* (1992); Graham Evans and Jeffrey Newnham, eds., *The Dictionary of World Politics* (1990); John E. Findling, *Dictionary of American Diplomatic History* (1989); Chas. W. Freeman, Jr., *The Diplomat's Dictionary* (1997); Michael Kidron and Ronald Segal, *The State of the World Atlas* (1995); Bruce W. Jentleson and Thomas G. Paterson, eds., *Encyclopedia of U.S. Foreign Relations* (1997); Warren F. Kuehl, ed., *Biographical Dictionary of Internationalists* (1983); Edward Lawson, *Encyclopedia of Human Rights* (1991); Jack C. Plano and Roy Olton, eds., *The International Relations Dictionary* (1988). See also "The Cold War," "Peace Movements and Pacifism," "Politics and Government," "Military and Wars," and specific wars.

Immigration and Ethnic Groups

James P. Allen and Eugene J. Turner, *We the People: An Atlas of America's Ethnic Diversity* (1988); Gerald Chaliand and Jean-Pierre Rageau, *The Penguin Atlas of Diasporas* (1995); Francesco Cordasco, ed., *Dictionary of American Immigration History* (1990); David Levinson and Melvin Ember, eds., *American Immigrant Cultures* (1997); Judy B. Litoff and Judith McDonnell, eds., *European Immigrant Women in the United States* (1994); Sally M. Miller, ed., *The Ethnic Press in the United States* (1987); Stephan Thernstrom, ed., *Harvard Encyclopedia of American Ethnic Groups* (1980); Rudolph J. Vecoli et al., eds., *Gale Encyclopedia of Multicultural America* (1995). See also "Asian Americans," "Jewish Americans," and "Hispanics."

Jewish Americans

American Jewish Yearbook (1899–); Jack Fischel and Sanford Pinsker, eds., *Jewish-American History and Culture* (1992); Geoffrey Wigoder, *Dictionary of Jewish Biography* (1991). See also "Immigration and Ethnic Groups."

Labor

Ronald L. Filippelli, *Labor Conflict in the United States* (1990); Gary M. Fink, ed., *Biographical Dictionary of American Labor* (1984); Gary M. Fink, ed., *Labor Unions* (1977); Philip S. Foner, *First Facts of American Labor* (1984).

Hispanics

Nicolás Kanellos, ed., *The Hispanic-American Almanac* (1993); Nicolás Kanellos, ed., *Reference Library of Hispanic America* (1993); Francisco Lomelí, ed., *Handbook of Hispanic Cultures in the United States* (1993); Matt S. Meier, *Mexican-American Biographies* (1988); Matt S. Meier, *Notable Latino Americans* (1997); Matt S. Meier and Feliciano Rivera, *Dictionary of Mexican American History* (1981); Joseph C. Tardiff and L. Mpho Mabunda, eds., *Dictionary of Hispanic Biography* (1996). See also "Immigration and Ethnic Groups."

Literature

James T. Callow and Robert J. Reilly, *Guide to American Literature* (1976–1977); *Dictionary of Literary Biography* (1978–   ); Eugene Ehrlich and Gorton Carruth, *The Oxford Illustrated Literary Guide to the United States* (1982); Jon Tuska and Vicki Piekarski, *Encyclopedia of Frontier and Western Fiction* (1983). See also "Culture and Folklore," "The South," and "Women."

Mass Media and Journalism

Robert V. Hudson, *Mass Media* (1987); Joseph P. McKerns, ed., *Biographical Dictionary of American Journalism* (1989); William H. Taft, ed., *Encyclopedia of Twentieth-Century Journalists* (1986). See also "The Cold War," "Constitution, Supreme Court, and Judiciary," "Entertainment and the Arts," and "Immigration and Ethnic Groups."

Medicine and Nursing

Rima D. Apple, ed., *Women, Health, and Medicine in America* (1990); Vern L. Bullough et al., eds., *American Nursing: A Biographical Dictionary* (1988); Martin Kaufman et al., eds., *Dictionary of American Nursing Biography* (1988); Martin Kaufman et al., eds., *Dictionary of American Medical Biography* (1984); George L. Maddox, ed., *The Encyclopedia of Aging* (1995).

Military and Wars

William M. Arkin et al., *Encyclopedia of the U.S. Military* (1990); Charles D. Bright, ed., *Historical Dictionary of the U.S. Air Force* (1992); John W. Chambers, ed., *Oxford Companion to United States Military History* (2000); Andre Corvisier, ed., *A Dictionary of Military History* (1994); R. Ernest Dupuy and Trevor N. Dupuy, *The Harper Encyclopedia of Military History* (1993); David S. Frazier, ed., *The United States and Mexico at War* (1998); John E. Jessup, ed., *Encyclopedia of the American Military* (1994); Kenneth Macksey and William Woodhouse, *The Penguin Encyclopedia of Modern Warfare* (1992); Franklin D. Margiotta, ed., *Brassey's Encyclopedia of Naval Forces and Warfare* (1996); David F. Marley, *Pirates and Privateers of the Americas* (1994); James I. Matray, ed., *Historical Dictionary of the Korean War* (1991); Stanley

Sandler, ed., *The Korean War* (1995); Roger J. Spiller and Joseph G. Dawson III, eds., *Dictionary of American Military Biography* (1984); Jerry K. Sweeney, ed., *A Handbook of American Military History* (1996); Peter G. Tsouras et al., *The United States Army* (1991); U.S. Military Academy, *The West Point Atlas of American Wars, 1689–1953* (1959); Bruce W. Watson et al., eds., *United States Intelligence* (1990); Bruce W. Watson and Susan M. Watson, *The United States Air Force* (1992); Bruce W. Watson and Susan M. Watson, *The United States Navy* (1991). See also "American Revolution and Colonies," "Civil War and Reconstruction," "The Cold War," "Vietnam War," and "World War II."

Music

John Chilton, *Who's Who of Jazz* (1972); Donald Clarke et al., eds., *The Penguin Encyclopedia of Popular Music* (1999); Edward Jablonski, *The Encyclopedia of American Music* (1981); Roger Lax and Frederick Smith, *The Great Song Thesaurus* (1984); Philip D. Morehead, *The New International Dictionary of Music* (1993); Austin Sonnier, Jr., *A Guide to the Blues* (1994). See also "Culture and Folklore" and "Entertainment and the Arts."

Native Americans and Indian Affairs

Gretchen M. Bataille, ed., *Native American Women* (1992); Michael Coe et al., *Atlas of Ancient America* (1986); Mary B. Davis, ed., *Native America in the Twentieth Century* (1994); Rayna Green, *The British Museum Encyclopedia of Native North America* (1999); *Handbook of North American Indians* (1978–); Sam D. Gill and Irene F. Sullivan, *Dictionary of Native American Mythology* (1992); J. Norman Heard et al., *Handbook of the American Frontier: Four Centuries of Indian–White Relationships* (1987–); Bruce E. Johansen, ed., *The Encyclopedia of Native American Economic History* (1999); Bruce E. Johansen, ed., *The Encyclopedia of Native American Legal Tradition* (1998); Bruce E. Johansen et al., eds., *The Encyclopedia of Native American Biography* (1997); Barry Klein, ed., *Reference Encyclopedia of the American Indian* (1993); Barry M. Plitzker, *Native Americans* (1998); Francis P. Prucha, *Atlas of American Indian Affairs* (1990); Paul Stuart, *Nation Within a Nation: Historical Statistics of American Indians* (1987); Helen H. Tanner, ed., *Atlas of Great Lakes Indian History* (1987); Carl Waldman, *Encyclopedia of Native American Tribes* (1988); Carl Waldman, *Atlas of the North American Indian* (1985).

The New Deal and Franklin D. Roosevelt

Otis L. Graham, Jr., and Meghan R. Wander, eds., *Franklin D. Roosevelt: His Life and Times* (1985); James S. Olson, ed., *Historical Dictionary of the New Deal* (1985). See also "Politics and Government."

Peace Movements and Pacifism

Harold Josephson et al., eds., *Biographical Dictionary of Modern Peace Leaders* (1985); Ervin Laszlo and Jong Y. Yoo, eds., *World Encyclopedia of Peace* (1986); Robert S. Meyer, *Peace Organizations Past and Present* (1988); Nancy L. Roberts, *American Peace Writers, Editors, and Periodicals* (1991). See also "Foreign Relations," "Military and Wars," and specific wars.

Politics and Government: General

Erik W. Austin and Jerome M. Clubb, *Political Facts of the United States Since 1789* (1986); *The Columbia Dictionary of Political Biography* (1991); Jack P. Greene, ed., *Encyclopedia of American Political History* (1984); Leon Hurwitz, *Historical Dictionary of Censorship in the United States* (1985); George T. Kurian, ed., *A Historical Guide to the U.S. Government* (1998); Philip Rees, *Biographical Dictionary of the Extreme Right Since 1890* (1991); Charles R. Ritter et al., *American Legislative Leaders, 1850–1910* (1989); William Safire, *Safire's Political Dictionary* (1993); Robert Scruton, *A Dictionary of Political Thought* (1982); Jay M. Shafritz, *The HarperCollins Dictionary of American Government and Politics* (1992). See also "Cities and Towns," "Constitution, Supreme Court, and Judiciary," "States," and the following sections.

Politics and Government: Congress

American Enterprise Institute, *Vital Statistics on Congress* (1980–); Donald C. Brown et al., eds., *The Encyclopedia of the United States Congress* (1995); Stephen G. Christianson, *Facts About the Congress* (1996); Congressional Quarterly, *Biographical Directory of the American Congress, 1774–1996* (1997); Congressional Quarterly, *Congress and the Nation* (1965–); Kenneth C. Martis, *Historical Atlas of Political Parties in the United States Congress, 1789–1989* (1989); Kenneth C. Martis, *Historical Atlas of United States Congressional Districts, 1789–1983* (1982); Joel H. Silbey, ed., *Encyclopedia of the American Legislative System* (1994).

Politics and Government: Election Statistics

Congressional Quarterly, *Guide to U.S. Elections* (1994); Congressional Quarterly, *Presidential Elections, 1789–1996* (1997); L. Sandy Maisel, ed., *Political Parties and Elections in the United States* (1991); Svend Petersen and Louis Filler, *A Statistical History of the American Presidential Elections* (1981); Richard M. Scammon et al., eds., *America Votes* (1956–); Harold W. Stanley and Richard G. Niemi, *Vital Statistics on American Politics* (1988–); Lyn Ragsdale, *Vital Statistics on the Presidency* (1998); G. Scott Thomas, *The Pursuit of the White House* (1987).

Politics and Government: Parties

Earl R. Kruschke, *Encyclopedia of Third Parties in the United States* (1991); George T. Kurian, ed., *The Encyclopedia of the Republican Party* and *The Encyclopedia of the Democratic Party* (1996); Edward L. Schapsmeier and Frederick H. Schapsmeier, eds., *Political Parties and Civic Action Groups* (1981). See also other listings for "Politics and Government."

Politics and Government: Presidency and Executive Branch

Alan Brinkley and Davis Dyer, eds., *The Reader's Companion to the Presidency* (2000); Henry F. Graff, *The Presidents* (1996); Bernard S. Katz and C. Daniel Vencill, eds., *Biographical Dictionary of the United States Secretaries of the Treasury, 1789–1995* (1996); Richard S. Kirkendall, ed., *The Harry S Truman Encyclopedia* (1989); Leonard W. Levy and Louis Fisher, eds., *Encyclopedia of the American Presidency* (1993); Merrill D. Peterson, ed., *Thomas Jefferson* (1986); Lyn Ragsdale, *Vital Statistics on the Presidency* (1998); Robert A. Rutland, ed., *James Madison and the American Nation* (1995); Robert Sobel, ed., *Biographical Directory of the United States Executive Branch, 1774–1977* (1977). See other categories for various presidents.

Politics and Government: Radicalism and the Left

Mari Jo Buhle et al., eds., *The American Radical* (1994); Mari Jo Buhle et al., eds., *Encyclopedia of the American Left* (1998); David DeLeon, ed., *Leaders of the 1960s* (1994); Bernard K. Johnpoll and Harvey Klehr, eds., *Biographical Dictionary of the American Left* (1986).

Religion and Cults

Henry Bowden, *Dictionary of American Religious Biography* (1993); S. Kent Brown et al., eds., *Historical Atlas of Mormonism* (1995); Edwin Gaustad and Philip L. Barlow, *New Historical Atlas of Religion in America* (1998); Michael Glazier and Thomas J. Shelley, eds., *The Encyclopedia of American Catholic History* (1997); Bill J. Leonard, *Dictionary of Baptists in America* (1994); Donald Lewis, ed., *A Dictionary of Evangelical Biography* (1995); Charles H. Lippy and Peter W. Williams, eds., *Encyclopedia of the American Religious Experience* (1988); J. Gordon Melton, *The Encyclopedia of American Religions* (1987); J. Gordon Melton, *The Encyclopedic Handbook of Cults in America* (1992); Mark A. Noll and Nathan O. Hatch, eds., *Eerdman's Handbook to Christianity in America* (1983); Stephen R. Prothero et al., *The Encyclopedia of American Religious History* (1996); Paul J. Weber and W. Landis Jones, *U.S. Religious Interest Groups* (1994). See also "African Americans."

Science and Technology

James W. Cortada, *Historical Dictionary of Data Processing* (1987); Clark A. Elliott, *Biographical Index to American Science: The Seventeenth Century to 1920* (1990); Charles C. Gillespie et al., eds., *Dictionary of Scientific Biography* (1970–); National Academy of Sciences, *Biographical Memoirs* (1877–);

Roy Porter, ed., *The Biographical Dictionary of Scientists* (1994). See also "Exploration."

Sexuality

Robert T. Francoeur, ed., *The International Encyclopedia of Sexuality* (1998); Wayne R. Dynes, ed., *Encyclopedia of Homosexuality* (1990); Steve Hogan and Lee Hudson, *Completely Queer: The Gay and Lesbian Encyclopedia* (1998); Arthur S. Leonard, ed., *Sexuality and the Law* (1993); Neil Schlager, ed., *Gay & Lesbian Almanac* (1998); Michael J. Tyrkus, ed., *Gay & Lesbian Biography* (1997); Bonnie Zimmerman and George Haggerty, eds., *Encyclopedia of Lesbian and Gay Histories and Cultures* (1999). See also "Social History and Reform."

Slavery

Seymour Drescher and Stanley L. Engerman, eds., *A Historical Guide to World Slavery* (1998); Paul Finkelman and Joseph C. Miller, eds., *Macmillan Encyclopedia of World Slavery* (1998); Randall M. Miller and John D. Smith, eds., *Dictionary of Afro-American Slavery* (1997); Junius P. Rodriguez, ed., *The Historical Encyclopedia of World Slavery* (1997). See also "African Americans."

Social History and Reform

Mary K. Cayton et al., eds., *Encyclopedia of American Social History* (1993); Louis Filler, *Dictionary of American Social Change* (1982); Robert S. Fogarty, *Dictionary of American Communal and Utopian History* (1980); Joseph M. Hawes and Elizabeth I. Nybakken, eds., *American Families* (1991); David Hey, ed., *The Oxford Companion to Local and Family History* (1996); Harold M. Keele and Joseph C. Kiger, eds., *Foundations* (1984); Mark E. Lender, *Dictionary of American Temperance Biography* (1984); Patricia M. Melvin, ed., *American Community Organizations* (1986); Randall M. Miller and Paul A. Cimbala, eds., *American Reform and Reformers* (1996); Roger S. Powers and William B. Vogele, eds., *Protest, Power, and Change* (1996); Alvin J. Schmidt, *Fraternal Organizations* (1980); Peter N. Stearns, ed., *Encyclopedia of Social History* (1993); Walter I. Trattner, *Biographical Dictionary of Social Welfare in America* (1986). See also "Crime, Violence, Police, and Prisons" and "Sexuality."

South

Edward L. Ayers and Brad Mittendorf, eds., *The Oxford Book of the American South* (1997); Robert Bain et al., eds., *Southern Writers* (1979); Kenneth Coleman and Charles S. Gurr, eds., *Dictionary of Georgia Biography* (1983); William S. Powell, ed., *Dictionary of North Carolina Biography* (1979–1996); David C. Roller and Robert W. Twyman, eds., *The Encyclopedia of Southern History* (1979); Walter P. Webb et al., eds., *The Handbook of Texas* (1952, 1976); Charles R. Wilson and William Ferris, eds., *Encyclopedia of Southern Culture* (1986).

See also "Civil War and Reconstruction," "Politics and Government," and "States."

Sports

Peter C. Bjarkman, ed., *Encyclopedia of Major League Baseball Team Histories* (1991); Ralph Hickok, *A Who's Who of Sports Champions* (1995); Ralph Hickok, *The Encyclopedia of North American Sports History* (1991); David Levinson and Karen Christensen, eds., *Encyclopedia of World Sport* (1996); Jonathan F. Light, *The Cultural Encyclopedia of Baseball* (1997); David L. Porter, *Biographical Dictionary of American Sports: Baseball* (2000), *Basketball and Other Indoor Sports* (1989), *Football* (1987), and *Outdoor Sports* (1988); Victoria Sherrow, *Encyclopedia of Women and Sports* (1996); David Wallechinsky, *The Complete Book of the Summer Olympics* (1996); David Wallechinsky, *The Complete Book of the Winter Olympics* (1993). See also "Culture and Folklore."

States

Gary Alampi, ed., *Gale State Rankings Reporter* (1994); Roy R. Glashan, comp., *American Governors and Gubernatorial Elections, 1775–1978* (1979); John Hoffmann, ed., *A Guide to the History of Illinois* (1991); Edith R. Hornor, *Almanac of the Fifty States* (1997); Joseph E. Kallenback and Jessamine S. Kallenback, *American State Governors, 1776–1976* (1977); Joseph N. Kane et al., eds., *Facts About the States* (1994); John E. Kleber et al., eds., *The Kentucky Encyclopedia* (1992); Thomas A. McMullin and Marie Mullaney, *Biographical Directory of the Governors of the United States, 1983–1987* (1988) and *1988–1993* (1994); Marie Mullaney, *Biographical Directory of the Governors of the United States, 1988–1994* (1994); Thomas J. Noel, *Historical Atlas of Colorado* (1994); John W. Raimo, ed., *Biographical Directory of the Governors of the United States, 1978–1983* (1985); James W. Scott and Ronald L. De Lorme, *Historical Atlas of Washington* (1988); Benjamin F. Shearer and Barbara S. Shearer, *State Names, Seals, Flags, and Symbols* (1994); Robert Sobel and John W. Raimo, eds., *Biographical Directory of the Governors of the United States, 1789–1978* (1978); Richard W. Wilkie and Jack Tager, eds., *Historical Atlas of Massachusetts* (1991). See also "Politics and Government," "South," and "West and Frontier."

Transportation

Keith L. Bryant, ed., *Railroads in the Age of Regulation, 1900–1980* (1988); Rene De La Pedraja, *A Historical Dictionary of the U.S. Merchant Marine and Shipping Industry* (1994); Robert L. Frey, ed., *Railroads in the Nineteenth Century* (1988). See also "Business and the Economy."

Vietnam War

John S. Bowman, ed., *The Vietnam War: An Almanac* (1986); Stanley I. Kutler, ed., *Encyclopedia of the Vietnam War* (1996); James S. Olson, ed., *Dictionary of the Vietnam War* (1988);

Harry G. Summers, Jr., *Vietnam War Almanac* (1985). Also see "Peace Movements and Pacifism" and "Military and Wars."

West and Frontier

William A. Beck and Ynez D. Haase, *Historical Atlas of the American West* (1989); Doris O. Dawdy, *Artists of the American West* (1974–1984); J. Norman Heard, *Handbook of the American Frontier* (1987); Howard R. Lamar, ed., *The New Encyclopedia of the American West* (1998); Clyde A. Milner III et al., eds., *The Oxford History of the American West* (1994); Jay Robert Nash, *Encyclopedia of Western Lawmen and Outlaws* (1992); Doyce B. Nunis, Jr., and Gloria R. Lothrop, eds., *A Guide to the History of California* (1989); Charles Phillips and Alan Axelrod, eds., *Encyclopedia of the American West* (1996); Dan L. Thrapp, *The Encyclopedia of Frontier Biography* (1988–1994); David Walker, *Biographical Directory of American Territorial Governors* (1984). See also "Cities and Towns," "Literature," and "Native Americans and Indian Affairs."

Women

Anne Gibson and Timothy Fast, *The Women's Atlas of the United States* (1986); Karen Greenspan, *The Timetables of Women's History* (1996); Maggie Humm, *The Dictionary of Feminist Theory* (1990); Edward T. James et al., *Notable American Women, 1607–1950* (1971); Lina Mainiero, ed., *American Women Writers* (1979–1982); Wilma Mankiller et al., *The Reader's Companion to U.S. Women's History* (1998); Kirstin Olsen, *Chronology of Women's History* (1994); Barbara G. Shortridge, *Atlas of American Women* (1987); Barbara Sicherman and Carol H. Green, eds., *Notable American Women, The Modern Period* (1980); Helen Tierney, ed., *Women's Studies Encyclopedia* (1991); James Trager, *The Women's Chronology* (1994); Angela H. Zophy and Frances M. Kavenik, eds., *Handbook of American Women's History* (1990). See also "African Americans," "Immigration and Ethnic Groups," "Medicine and Nursing," "Native Americans and Indian Affairs," and "Sports."

World War I

David F. Burg and L. Edward Purcell, *Almanac of World War I* (1998); Martin Gilbert, *Atlas of World War I* (1994); Holger H. Herwig and Neil M. Heyman, *Biographical Dictionary of World War I* (1982); George T. Kurian, *Encyclopedia of the First World War* (1990); Stephen Pope and Elizabeth-Anne Wheal, *The Dictionary of the First World War* (1995); Anne C. Venzon, *The United States in the First World War* (1995). See also "Military and Wars."

World War II

Marcel Baudot et al., eds., *The Historical Encyclopedia of World War II* (1980); David G. Chandler and James Lawton Collins, Jr., eds., *The D-Day Encyclopedia* (1993); I. C. B. Dear and M. R. D. Foot, eds., *The Oxford Companion to World War II* (1995); Simon Goodenough, *War Maps: Great Land Battles of World War II* (1988); Robert Goralski, *World War II Almanac* (1981); John Keegan, ed., *The Times Atlas of the Second World War* (1989); George T. Kurian, *Encyclopedia of the Second World War* (1991); Norman Polmer and Thomas B. Allen, *World War II: America at War* (1991); Louis L. Snyder, *Louis L. Snyder's Historical Guide to World War II* (1982); U.S. Military Academy, *Campaign Atlas to the Second World War: Europe and the Mediterranean* (1980); Peter Young, ed., *The World Almanac Book of World War II* (1981). See also "Military and Wars."

Documents

DECLARATION OF INDEPENDENCE IN CONGRESS, JULY 4, 1776

When, in the course of human events, it becomes necessary for one people to dissolve the political bonds which have connected them with another, and to assume, among the powers of the earth, the separate and equal station to which the laws of nature and of nature's God entitle them, a decent respect to the opinions of mankind requires that they should declare the causes which impel them to the separation.

We hold these truths to be self-evident: That all men are created equal; that they are endowed by their Creator with certain unalienable rights; that among these are life, liberty, and the pursuit of happiness; that, to secure these rights, governments are instituted among men, deriving their just powers from the consent of the governed; that whenever any form of government becomes destructive of these ends, it is the right of the people to alter or to abolish it, and to institute new government, laying its foundation on such principles, and organizing its powers in such form, as to them shall seem most likely to effect their safety and happiness. Prudence, indeed, will dictate that governments long established should not be changed for light and transient causes; and accordingly all experience hath shown that mankind are more disposed to suffer, while evils are sufferable, than to right themselves by abolishing the forms to which they are accustomed. But when a long train of abuses and usurpations, pursuing invariably the same object, evinces a design to reduce them under absolute despotism, it is their right, it is their duty, to throw off such government, and to provide new guards for their future security. Such has been the patient sufferance of these colonies; and such is now the necessity which constrains them to alter their former systems of government. The history of the present King of Great Britain is a history of repeated injuries and usurpations, all having in direct object the establishment of an absolute tyranny over these states. To prove this, let facts be submitted to a candid world.

He has refused his assent to laws, the most wholesome and necessary for the public good.

He has forbidden his governors to pass laws of immediate and pressing importance, unless suspended in their operation till his assent should be obtained; and, when so suspended, he has utterly neglected to attend to them.

He has refused to pass other laws for the accommodation of large districts of people, unless those people would relinquish the right of representation in the legislature, a right inestimable to them, and formidable to tyrants only.

He has called together legislative bodies at places unusual, uncomfortable, and distant from the depository of their public records, for the sole purpose of fatiguing them into compliance with his measures.

He has dissolved representative houses repeatedly, for opposing, with manly firmness, his invasions on the rights of the people.

He has refused for a long time, after such dissolutions, to cause others to be elected; whereby the legislative powers, incapable of annihilation, have returned to the people at large for their exercise; the state remaining, in the mean time, exposed to all the dangers of invasions from without and convulsions within.

He has endeavored to prevent the population of these states; for that purpose obstructing the laws for naturalization of foreigners; refusing to pass others to encourage their migration hither, and raising the conditions of new appropriations of lands.

He has obstructed the administration of justice, by refusing his assent to laws for establishing judiciary powers.

He has made judges dependent on his will alone, for the tenure of their offices, and the amount and payment of their salaries.

He has erected a multitude of new offices, and sent hither swarms of officers to harass our people and eat out their substance.

He has kept among us, in times of peace, standing armies, without the consent of our legislatures.

He has affected to render the military independent of, and superior to, the civil power.

He has combined with others to subject us to a jurisdiction foreign to our constitution, and unacknowledged by our laws, giving his assent to their acts of pretended legislation:

For quartering large bodies of armed troops among us;

For protecting them, by a mock trial, from punishment for any murders which they should commit on the inhabitants of these states;

For cutting off our trade with all parts of the world;

For imposing taxes on us without our consent;

For depriving us, in many cases, of the benefits of trial by jury;

For transporting us beyond seas, to be tried for pretended offenses;

For abolishing the free system of English laws in a

neighboring province, establishing therein an arbitrary government, and enlarging its boundaries, so as to render it at once an example and fit instrument for introducing the same absolute rule into these colonies;

For taking away our charters, abolishing our most valuable laws, and altering fundamentally the forms of our governments;

For suspending our own legislatures, and declaring themselves invested with power to legislate for us in all cases whatsoever.

He has abdicated government here, by declaring us out of his protection and waging war against us.

He has plundered our seas, ravaged our coasts, burned our towns, and destroyed the lives of our people.

He is at this time transporting large armies of foreign mercenaries to complete the works of death, desolation, and tyranny already begun with circumstances of cruelty and perfidy scarcely paralleled in the most barbarous ages, and totally unworthy the head of a civilized nation.

He has constrained our fellow-citizens, taken captive on the high seas, to bear arms against their country, to become the executioners of their friends and brethren, or to fall themselves by their hands.

He has excited domestic insurrection among us, and has endeavored to bring on the inhabitants of our frontiers the merciless Indian savages, whose known rule of warfare is an undistinguished destruction of all ages, sexes, and conditions.

In every stage of these oppressions we have petitioned for redress in the most humble terms; our repeated petitions have been answered only by repeated injury. A prince, whose character is thus marked by every act which may define a tyrant, is unfit to be the ruler of a free people.

Nor have we been wanting in our attentions to our British brethren. We have warned them, from time to time, of attempts by their legislature to extend an unwarrantable jurisdiction over us. We have reminded them of the circumstances of our emigration and settlement here. We have appealed to their native justice and magnanimity; and we have conjured them, by the ties of our common kindred, to disavow these usurpations, which would inevitably interrupt our connections and correspondence. They, too, have been deaf to the voice of justice and of consanguinity. We must, therefore, acquiesce in the necessity which denounces our separation, and hold them, as we hold the rest of mankind, enemies in war, in peace friends.

We, therefore, the representatives of the United States of America, in General Congress assembled, appealing to the Supreme Judge of the world for the rectitude of our intentions, do, in the name and by the authority of the good people of these colonies, solemnly publish and declare, that these United Colonies are, and of right ought to be, FREE AND INDEPENDENT STATES; that they are absolved from all allegiance to the British crown, and that all political connection between them and the state of Great Britain is,

and ought to be, totally dissolved; and that, as free and independent states, they have full power to levy war, conclude peace, contract alliances, establish commerce, and do all other acts and things which independent states may of right do. And for the support of this declaration, with a firm reliance on the protection of Divine Providence, we mutually pledge to each other our lives, our fortunes, and our sacred honor.

———

ARTICLES OF CONFEDERATION

(The text of the Articles of Confederation can be found at http://college.hmco.com.)

———

CONSTITUTION OF THE UNITED STATES OF AMERICA AND AMENDMENTS*

Preamble

We the people of the United States, in order to form a more perfect union, establish justice, insure domestic tranquillity, provide for the common defense, promote the general welfare, and secure the blessings of liberty to ourselves and our posterity, do ordain and establish this Constitution for the United States of America.

Article I

Section 1 All legislative powers herein granted shall be vested in a Congress of the United States, which shall consist of a Senate and a House of Representatives.

Section 2 The House of Representatives shall be composed of members chosen every second year by the people of the several States, and the electors in each State shall have the qualifications requisite for electors of the most numerous branch of the State Legislature.

No person shall be a Representative who shall not have attained to the age of twenty-five years, and been seven years a citizen of the United States, and who shall not, when elected, be an inhabitant of that State in which he shall be chosen.

Representatives and direct taxes shall be apportioned among the several States which may be included within this Union, according to their respective numbers, *which shall be determined by adding to the whole number of free persons, including those bound to service for a term of years and excluding Indians not taxed, three-fifths of all other persons.* The actual enumeration shall be made within three years after the first meeting of the Congress of the United States, and within

---

*Passages no longer in effect are printed in italic type.

every subsequent term of ten years, in such manner as they shall by law direct. The number of Representatives shall not exceed one for every thirty thousand, but each State shall have at least one Representative; *and until such enumeration shall be made, the State of New Hampshire shall be entitled to choose three, Massachusetts eight, Rhode Island and Providence Plantations one, Connecticut five, New York six, New Jersey four, Pennsylvania eight, Delaware one, Maryland six, Virginia ten, North Carolina five, South Carolina five, and Georgia three.*

When vacancies happen in the representation from any State, the Executive authority thereof shall issue writs of election to fill such vacancies.

The House of Representatives shall choose their Speaker and other officers; and shall have the sole power of impeachment.

Section 3　The Senate of the United States shall be composed of two Senators from each State, *chosen by the legislature thereof,* for six years; and each Senator shall have one vote.

Immediately after they shall be assembled in consequence of the first election, they shall be divided as equally as may be into three classes. The seats of the Senators of the first class shall be vacated at the expiration of the second year, of the second class at the expiration of the fourth year, and of the third class at the expiration of the sixth year, so that one-third may be chosen every second year; and if vacancies happen by resignation or otherwise, during the recess of the legislature of any State, the Executive thereof may make temporary appointments until the next meeting of the legislature, which shall then fill such vacancies.

No person shall be a Senator who shall not have attained to the age of thirty years, and been nine years a citizen of the United States, and who shall not, when elected, be an inhabitant of that State for which he shall be chosen.

The Vice-President of the United States shall be President of the Senate, but shall have no vote, unless they be equally divided.

The Senate shall choose their other officers, and also a President *pro tempore,* in the absence of the Vice-President, or when he shall exercise the office of President of the United States.

The Senate shall have the sole power to try all impeachments. When sitting for that purpose, they shall be on oath or affirmation. When the President of the United States is tried, the Chief Justice shall preside: and no person shall be convicted without the concurrence of two-thirds of the members present.

Judgment in cases of impeachment shall not extend further than to removal from the office, and disqualification to hold and enjoy any office of honor, trust or profit under the United States: but the party convicted shall nevertheless be liable and subject to indictment, trial, judgment and punishment, according to law.

Section 4　The times, places and manner of holding elections for Senators and Representatives shall be prescribed in each State by the legislature thereof; but the Congress may at any time by law make or alter such regulations, except as to the places of choosing Senators.

The Congress shall assemble at least once in every year, and such meeting *shall be on the first Monday in December, unless they shall by law appoint a different day.*

Section 5　Each house shall be the judge of the elections, returns and qualifications of its own members, and a majority of each shall constitute a quorum to do business; but a smaller number may adjourn from day to day, and may be authorized to compel the attendance of absent members, in such manner, and under such penalties, as each house may provide.

Each house may determine the rules of its proceedings, punish its members for disorderly behavior, and with the concurrence of two-thirds, expel a member.

Each house shall keep a journal of its proceedings, and from time to time publish the same, excepting such parts as may in their judgment require secrecy; and the yeas and nays of the members of either house on any question shall, at the desire of one-fifth of those present, be entered on the journal.

Neither house, during the session of Congress, shall, without the consent of the other, adjourn for more than three days, nor to any other place than that in which the two houses shall be sitting.

Section 6　The Senators and Representatives shall receive a compensation for their services, to be ascertained by law and paid out of the treasury of the United States. They shall in all cases except treason, felony and breach of the peace, be privileged from arrest during their attendance at the session of their respective houses, and in going to and returning from the same; and for any speech or debate in either house, they shall not be questioned in any other place.

No Senator or Representative shall, during the time for which he was elected, be appointed to any civil office under the authority of the United States, which shall have been created, or the emoluments whereof shall have been increased, during such time; and no person holding any office under the United States shall be a member of either house during his continuance in office.

Section 7　All bills for raising revenue shall originate in the House of Representatives; but the Senate may propose or concur with amendments as on other bills.

Every bill which shall have passed the House of Representatives and the Senate, shall, before it become a law, be presented to the President of the United States; if he approve he shall sign it, but if not he shall return it with objections to that house in which it originated, who shall enter the objections at large on their journal, and proceed to reconsider it. If after such reconsideration two-thirds of that house shall agree to pass the bill, it shall be sent, together with the objections, to the other house, by which it shall likewise be reconsidered, and, if approved by two-thirds of that house, it shall become a law. But in all such cases the votes of both houses shall be determined by yeas and nays, and the names of the persons voting for and against the bill shall be entered on the journal of each house respectively. If any bill shall not be returned by the President within ten days (Sundays excepted) after it shall have been presented to him, the same shall be a law, in like manner as if he had signed it, unless the Congress by their adjournment prevent its return, in which case it shall not be a law.

Every order, resolution, or vote to which the concurrence of the Senate and House of Representatives may be necessary (except on a question of adjournment) shall be presented to the President of the United States; and before the same shall take effect, shall be approved by him, or being disapproved by him, shall be repassed by two-thirds of the Senate and House of Representatives, according to the rules and limitations prescribed in the case of a bill.

Section 8   The Congress shall have power

To lay and collect taxes, duties, imposts, and excises, to pay the debts and provide for the common defense and general welfare of the United States; but all duties, imposts and excises shall be uniform throughout the United States;

To borrow money on the credit of the United States;

To regulate commerce with foreign nations, and among the several States, and with the Indian tribes;

To establish an uniform rule of naturalization, and uniform laws on the subject of bankruptcies throughout the United States;

To coin money, regulate the value thereof, and of foreign coin, and fix the standard of weights and measures;

To provide for the punishment of counterfeiting the securities and current coin of the United States;

To establish post offices and post roads;

To promote the progress of science and useful arts by securing for limited times to authors and inventors the exclusive right to their respective writings and discoveries;

To constitute tribunals inferior to the Supreme Court;

To define and punish piracies and felonies committed on the high seas and offenses against the law of nations;

To declare war, grant letters of marque and reprisal, and make rules concerning captures on land and water;

To raise and support armies, but no appropriation of money to that use shall be for a longer term than two years;

To provide and maintain a navy;

To make rules for the government and regulation of the land and naval forces;

To provide for calling forth the militia to execute the laws of the Union, suppress insurrections, and repel invasions;

To provide for organizing, arming, and disciplining the militia, and for governing such part of them as may be employed in the service of the United States, reserving to the States respectively the appointment of the officers, and the authority of training the militia according to the discipline prescribed by Congress;

To exercise exclusive legislation in all cases whatsoever, over such district (not exceeding ten miles square) as may, by cession of particular States, and the acceptance of Congress, become the seat of government of the United States, and to exercise like authority over all places purchased by the consent of the legislature of the State, in which the same shall be, for erection of forts, magazines, arsenals, dockyards, and other needful buildings; —and

To make all laws which shall be necessary and proper for carrying into execution the foregoing powers, and all other powers vested by this Constitution in the government of the United States, or in any department or officer thereof.

Section 9   *The migration or importation of such persons as any of the States now existing shall think proper to admit shall not be prohibited by the Congress prior to the year 1808; but a tax or duty may be imposed on such importation, not exceeding $10 for each person.*

The privilege of the writ of habeas corpus shall not be suspended, unless when in cases of rebellion or invasion the public safety may require it.

No bill of attainder or ex post facto law shall be passed.

No capitation, or other direct, tax shall be laid, unless in proportion to the census or enumeration herein before directed to be taken.

No tax or duty shall be laid on articles exported from any State.

No preference shall be given by any regulation of commerce or revenue to the ports of one State over those of another; nor shall vessels bound to, or from, one State, be obliged to enter, clear, or pay duties in another.

No money shall be drawn from the treasury, but in consequence of appropriations made by law; and a regular statement and account of the receipts and expenditures of all public money shall be published from time to time.

No title of nobility shall be granted by the United States: and no person holding any office of profit or trust under them, shall, without the consent of the Congress, accept of any present, emolument, office, or title, of any kind whatever, from any king, prince, or foreign state.

Section 10   No State shall enter into any treaty, alliance, or confederation; grant letters of marque and reprisal; coin money; emit bills of credit; make anything but gold and silver coin a tender in payment of debts; pass any bill of attainder, ex post facto law, or law impairing the obligation of contracts, or grant any title of nobility.

No State shall, without the consent of Congress, lay any imposts or duties on imports or exports, except what may be absolutely necessary for executing its inspection laws: and the net produce of all duties and imposts, laid by any State on imports or exports, shall be for the use of the treasury of the United States; and all such laws shall be subject to the revision and control of the Congress.

No State shall, without the consent of Congress, lay any duty of tonnage, keep troops or ships of war in time of peace, enter into any agreement or compact with another State, or with a foreign power, or engage in war, unless actually invaded, or in such imminent danger as will not admit of delay.

Article II

Section 1   The executive power shall be vested in a President of the United States of America. He shall hold his office during the term of four years, and, together with the Vice-President, chosen for the same term, be elected as follows:

Each State shall appoint, in such manner as the legislature thereof may direct, a number of electors, equal to the whole number of Senators and Representatives to which the State may be entitled in the Congress; but no Senator or Representative, or person holding an office of trust or profit under the United States, shall be appointed an elector.

The electors shall meet in their respective States, and vote by ballot for two persons, of whom one at least shall not be an inhabitant of the same State with themselves. And they shall make a list of all the persons voted for, and of the number of votes for each; which list they shall sign and certify, and transmit sealed to the seat of government of the United States, directed to the President of the Senate. The President of the Senate shall, in the presence of the Senate and House of Representatives, open all the certificates, and the votes shall then be counted. The person having the greatest number of votes shall be the President, if such number be a majority of the whole number of electors appointed; and if there be more than one who have such majority, and have an equal number of votes, then the House of Representatives shall immediately choose by ballot one of them for President; and if no person have a majority, then from the five highest on the list said house shall in like manner choose the President. But in choosing the President the votes shall be taken by States, the representation from each State having one vote; a quorum for this purpose shall consist of a member or members from two-thirds of the States, and a majority of all the States shall be necessary to a choice. In every case, after the choice of the President, the person having the greatest number of votes of the electors shall be the Vice-President. But if there should remain two or more who have equal votes, the Senate shall choose from them by ballot the Vice-President.

The Congress may determine the time of choosing the electors and the day on which they shall give their votes; which day shall be the same throughout the United States.

No person except a natural-born citizen, *or a citizen of the United States at the time of the adoption of this Constitution*, shall be eligible to the office of President; neither shall any person be eligible to that office who shall not have attained to the age of thirty-five years, and been fourteen years a resident within the United States.

In cases of the removal of the President from office or of his death, resignation, or inability to discharge the powers and duties of the said office, the same shall devolve on the Vice-President, and the Congress may by law provide for the case of removal, death, resignation, or inability, both of the President and Vice-President, declaring what officer shall then act as President, and such officer shall act accordingly, until the disability be removed, or a President shall be elected.

The President shall, at stated times, receive for his services a compensation, which shall neither be increased nor diminished during the period for which he shall have been elected, and he shall not receive within that period any other emolument from the United States, or any of them.

Before he enter on the execution of his office, he shall take the following oath or affirmation:—"I do solemnly swear (or affirm) that I will faithfully execute the office of the President of the United States, and will to the best of my ability preserve, protect and defend the Constitution of the United States."

Section 2   The President shall be commander in chief of the army and navy of the United States, and of the militia of the several States, when called into the actual service of the United States; he may require the opinion, in writing, of the principal officer in each of the executive departments, upon any subject relating to the duties of their respective offices, and he shall have power to grant reprieves and pardons for offenses against the United States, except in cases of impeachment.

He shall have power, by and with the advice and consent of the Senate, to make treaties, provided two-thirds of the Senators present concur; and he shall nominate, and by and with the advice and consent of the Senate, shall appoint ambassadors, other public ministers and consuls, judges of the Supreme Court, and all other officers of the United States, whose appointments are not herein otherwise provided for, and which shall be established by law: but Congress may by law vest the appointment of such inferior officers, as they think proper, in the President alone, in the courts of law, or in the heads of departments.

The President shall have power to fill up all vacancies that may happen during the recess of the Senate, by granting commissions which shall expire at the end of their next session.

Section 3   He shall from time to time give to the Congress information of the state of the Union, and recommend to their consideration such measures as he shall judge necessary and expedient; he may, on extraordinary occasions, convene both houses, or either of them, and in case of disagreement between them, with respect to the time of adjournment, he may adjourn them to such time as he shall think proper; he shall receive ambassadors and other public ministers; he shall take care that the laws be faithfully executed, and shall commission all the officers of the United States.

Section 4   The President, Vice-President and all civil officers of the United States shall be removed from office on impeachment for, and on conviction of, treason, bribery, or other high crimes and misdemeanors.

Article III

Section 1   The judicial power of the United States shall be vested in one Supreme Court, and in such inferior courts as the Congress may from time to time ordain and establish. The judges, both of the Supreme and inferior courts, shall hold their offices during good behavior, and shall, at stated times, receive for their services a compensation which shall not be diminished during their continuance in office.

Section 2   The judicial power shall extend to all cases, in law and equity, arising under this Constitution, the laws of the United States, and treaties made, or which shall be made, under their authority;—to all cases affecting ambassadors, other public ministers and consuls;—to all cases of admiralty and maritime jurisdiction;—to controversies to which the United States shall be a party;—to controversies between two or more States;—*between a State and citizens of another State;*—between citizens of different States;—between citizens of the same State claiming lands under grants of different States, and between a State, or the citizens thereof, and foreign states, citizens or subjects.

In all cases affecting ambassadors, other public ministers and consuls, and those in which a State shall be party, the Supreme Court shall have original jurisdiction. In all the other cases before mentioned, the Supreme Court shall have appellate jurisdiction, both as to law and fact, with such exceptions, and under such regulations, as the Congress shall make.

The trial of all crimes, except in cases of impeachment, shall be by jury; and such trial shall be held in the State where said crimes shall have been committed; but when not committed within any State, the trial shall be at such place or places as the Congress may by law have directed.

Section 3   Treason against the United States shall consist only in levying war against them, or in adhering to their enemies, giving them aid and comfort. No person shall be convicted of treason unless on the testimony of two witnesses to the same overt act, or on confession in open court.

The Congress shall have power to declare the punishment of treason, but no attainder of treason shall work corruption of blood, or forfeiture except during the life of the person attainted.

Article IV

Section 1   Full faith and credit shall be given in each State to the public acts, records, and judicial proceedings of every other State. And the Congress may by general laws prescribe the manner in which such acts, records, and proceedings shall be proved, and the effect thereof.

Section 2   The citizens of each State shall be entitled to all privileges and immunities of citizens in the several States.

A person charged in any State with treason, felony, or other crime, who shall flee from justice, and be found in another State, shall on demand of the executive authority of the State from which he fled, be delivered up, to be removed to the State having jurisdiction of the crime.

No person held to service or labor in one State, under the laws thereof, escaping into another, shall, in consequence of any law or regulation therein, be discharged from such service or labor, but shall be delivered up on claim of the party to whom such service or labor may be due.

Section 3   New States may be admitted by the Congress into this Union; but no new State shall be formed or erected within the jurisdiction of any other State; nor any State be formed by the junction of two or more States, or parts of States, without the consent of the legislatures of the States concerned as well as of the Congress.

The Congress shall have power to dispose of and make all needful rules and regulations respecting the territory or other property belonging to the United States; and nothing in this Constitution shall be so construed as to prejudice any claims of the United States, or of any particular State.

Section 4   The United States shall guarantee to every State in this Union a republican form of government, and shall protect each of them against invasion; and on application of the legislature, or of the executive (when the legislature cannot be convened), against domestic violence.

Article V

The Congress, whenever two-thirds of both houses shall deem it necessary, shall propose amendments to this Constitution, or, on the application of the legislatures of two-thirds of the several States, shall call a convention for proposing amendments, which, in either case, shall be valid to all intents and purposes, as part of this Constitution, when ratified by the legislatures of three-fourths of the several States, or by conventions in three-fourths thereof, as the one or the other mode of ratification may be proposed by the Congress; provided *that no amendments which may be made prior to the year one thousand eight hundred and eight shall in any manner affect the first and fourth clauses in the ninth section of the first article;* and that no State, without its consent, shall be deprived of its equal suffrage in the Senate.

Article VI

All debts contracted and engagements entered into, before the adoption of this Constitution, shall be as valid against the United States under this Constitution, as under the Confederation.

This Constitution, and the laws of the United States which shall be made in pursuance thereof; and all treaties made, or which shall be made, under the authority of the United States, shall be the supreme law of the land; and the judges in every State shall be bound thereby, anything in the Constitution or laws of any State to the contrary notwithstanding.

The Senators and Representatives before mentioned, and the members of the several State legislatures, and all executive and judicial officers, both of the United States and of the several States, shall be bound by oath or affirmation to support this Constitution; but no religious test shall ever be required as a qualification to any office or public trust under the United States.

Article VII

The ratification of the conventions of nine States shall be sufficient for the establishment of this Constitution between the States so ratifying the same.

Done in Convention by the unanimous consent of the States present, the seventeenth day of September in the year of our Lord one thousand seven hundred and eighty-seven and of the Independence of the United States of America the twelfth. In witness whereof we have hereunto subscribed our names.

AMENDMENTS TO THE CONSTITUTION*

Amendment I

Congress shall make no law respecting an establishment of religion, or prohibiting the free exercise thereof; or abridging the freedom of speech, or of the press; or the right of the people peaceably to assemble, and to petition the government for a redress of grievances.

Amendment II

A well-regulated militia being necessary to the security of a free State, the right of the people to keep and bear arms shall not be infringed.

Amendment III

No soldier shall, in time of peace, be quartered in any house without the consent of the owner, nor in time of war, but in a manner to be prescribed by law.

Amendment IV

The right of the people to be secure in their persons, houses, papers, and effects, against unreasonable searches and seizures, shall not be violated, and no warrants shall issue but upon probable cause, supported by oath or affirmation, and particularly describing the place to be searched, and the persons or things to be seized.

Amendment V

No person shall be held to answer for a capital, or otherwise infamous crime, unless on a presentment or indictment of a grand jury, except in cases arising in the land or naval forces, or in the militia, when in actual service in time of war or public danger; nor shall any person be subject for the same offense to be twice put in jeopardy of life or limb; nor shall be compelled in any criminal case to be a witness against himself, nor be deprived of life, liberty, or property, without due process of law; nor shall private property be taken for public use without just compensation.

Amendment VI

In all criminal prosecutions, the accused shall enjoy the right to a speedy and public trial, by an impartial jury of the State and district wherein the crime shall have been committed, which district shall have been previously ascertained by law, and to be informed of the nature and cause of the accusation; to be confronted with the witnesses against him; to have compulsory process for obtaining witnesses in his favor, and to have the assistance of counsel for his defense.

Amendment VII

In suits at common law, where the value in controversy shall exceed twenty dollars, the right of trial by jury shall be preserved, and no fact tried by a jury shall be otherwise reexamined in any court of the United States, than according to the rules of the common law.

Amendment VIII

Excessive bail shall not be required, nor excessive fines imposed, nor cruel and unusual punishments inflicted.

Amendment IX

The enumeration in the Constitution, of certain rights, shall not be construed to deny or disparage others retained by the people.

Amendment X

The powers not delegated to the United States by the Constitution, nor prohibited by it to the States, are reserved to the States respectively, or to the people.

Amendment XI

[Adopted 1798]

The judicial power of the United States shall not be construed to extend to any suit in law or equity, commenced or prosecuted against one of the United States by citizens of another State, or by citizens or subjects of any foreign state.

Amendment XII

[Adopted 1804]

The electors shall meet in their respective States, and vote by ballot for President and Vice-President, one of whom, at least, shall not be an inhabitant of the same State with themselves; they shall name in their ballots the person voted for as President, and in distinct ballots the person voted for as Vice-

---

*The first ten Amendments (the Bill of Rights) were adopted in 1791.

President, and they shall make distinct lists of all persons voted for as President, and of all persons voted for as Vice-President, and of the number of votes for each, which lists they shall sign and certify, and transmit sealed to the seat of government of the United States, directed to the President of the Senate;—the President of the Senate shall, in the presence of the Senate and House of Representatives, open all the certificates and the votes shall then be counted;—the person having the greatest number of votes for President shall be the President, if such number be a majority of the whole number of electors appointed; and if no person have such majority, then from the persons having the highest numbers not exceeding three on the list of those voted for as President, the House of Representatives shall choose immediately, by ballot, the President. But in choosing the President, the votes shall be taken by States, the representation from each State having one vote; a quorum for this purpose shall consist of a member or members from two-thirds of the States, and a majority of all the States shall be necessary to a choice. And if the House of Representatives shall not choose a President whenever the right of choice shall devolve upon them, before *the fourth day of March* next following, then the Vice-President shall act as President, as in the case of the death or other constitutional disability of the President.

The person having the greatest number of votes as Vice-President shall be the Vice-President, if such number be a majority of the whole number of electors appointed; and if no person have a majority, then from the two highest numbers on the list the Senate shall choose the Vice-President; a quorum for the purpose shall consist of two-thirds of the whole number of Senators, and a majority of the whole number shall be necessary to a choice. But no person constitutionally ineligible to the office of President shall be eligible to that of Vice-President of the United States.

Amendment XIII

[Adopted 1865]

Section 1 Neither slavery nor involuntary servitude, except as a punishment for crime whereof the party shall have been duly convicted, shall exist within the United States, or any place subject to their jurisdiction.

Section 2 Congress shall have power to enforce this article by appropriate legislation.

Amendment XIV

[Adopted 1868]

Section 1 All persons born or naturalized in the United States, and subject to the jurisdiction thereof, are citizens of the United States and of the State wherein they reside. No State shall make or enforce any law which shall abridge the privileges or immunities of citizens of the United States; nor shall any State deprive any person of life, liberty, or property, without due process of law; nor deny to any person within its jurisdiction the equal protection of the laws.

Section 2 Representatives shall be apportioned among the several States according to their respective numbers, counting the whole number of persons in each State, excluding Indians not taxed. But when the right to vote at any election for the choice of Electors for President and Vice-President of the United States, Representatives in Congress, the executive and judicial officers of a State, or the members of the legislature thereof, is denied to any of the male inhabitants of such State, being twenty-one years of age and citizens of the United States, or in any way abridged, except for participation in rebellion, or other crime, the basis of representation therein shall be reduced in the proportion which the number of such male citizens shall bear to the whole number of male citizens twenty-one years of age in such State.

Section 3 No person shall be a Senator or Representative in Congress, or Elector of President and Vice-President, or hold any office, civil or military, under the United States, or under any State, who, having previously taken an oath, as a member of Congress, or as an officer of the United States, or as a member of any State legislature, or as an executive or judicial officer of any State, to support the Constitution of the United States, shall have engaged in insurrection or rebellion against the same, or given aid or comfort to the enemies thereof. Congress may, by a vote of two-thirds of each house, remove such disability.

Section 4 The validity of the public debt of the United States, authorized by law, including debts incurred for payment of pensions and bounties for services in suppressing insurrection or rebellion, shall not be questioned. But neither the United States nor any State shall assume or pay any debt or obligation incurred in aid of insurrection or rebellion against the United States, or any claim for the loss of emancipation of any slave; but all such debts, obligations, and claims shall be held illegal and void.

Section 5 The Congress shall have power to enforce, by appropriate legislation, the provisions of this article.

Amendment XV

[Adopted 1870]

Section 1 The right of citizens of the United States to vote shall not be denied or abridged by the United States or by any State on account of race, color, or previous condition of servitude.

Section 2 The Congress shall have power to enforce this article by appropriate legislation.

Amendment XVI

[Adopted 1913]

The Congress shall have power to lay and collect taxes on incomes, from whatever source derived, without apportionment among the several States, and without regard to any census or enumeration.

Amendment XVII

[Adopted 1913]

Section 1   The Senate of the United States shall be composed of two Senators from each State, elected by the people thereof, for six years; and each Senator shall have one vote. The electors in each State shall have the qualifications requisite for electors of [voters for] the most numerous branch of the State legislatures.

Section 2   When vacancies happen in the representation of any State in the Senate, the executive authority of such State shall issue writs of election to fill such vacancies: Provided, that the Legislature of any State may empower the executive thereof to make temporary appointments until the people fill the vacancies by election as the Legislature may direct.

Section 3   This amendment shall not be so construed as to affect the election or term of any Senator chosen before it becomes valid as part of the Constitution.

Amendment XVIII

[Adopted 1919; Repealed 1933]

Section 1   After one year from the ratification of this article the manufacture, sale, or transportation of intoxicating liquors within, the importation thereof into, or the exportation thereof from the United States and all territory subject to the jurisdiction thereof, for beverage purposes, is hereby prohibited.

Section 2   The Congress and the several States shall have concurrent power to enforce this article by appropriate legislation.

Section 3   This article shall be inoperative unless it shall have been ratified as an amendment to the Constitution by the legislatures of the several States, as provided by the Constitution, within seven years from the date of the submission thereof to the States by the Congress.

Amendment XIX

[Adopted 1920]

Section 1   The right of citizens of the United States to vote shall not be denied or abridged by the United States or by any State on account of sex.

Section 2   The Congress shall have power to enforce this article by appropriate legislation.

Amendment XX

[Adopted 1933]

Section 1   The terms of the President and Vice-President shall end at noon on the 20th day of January, and the terms of Senators and Representatives at noon on the 3rd day of January, of the years in which such terms would have ended if this article had not been ratified; and the terms of their successors shall then begin.

Section 2   The Congress shall assemble at least once in every year, and such meeting shall begin at noon on the 3d day of January, unless they shall by law appoint a different day.

Section 3   If, at the time fixed for the beginning of the term of the President, the President-elect shall have died, the Vice-President–elect shall become President. If a President shall not have been chosen before the time fixed for the beginning of his term, or if the President-elect shall have failed to qualify, then the Vice-President–elect shall act as President until a President shall have qualified; and the Congress may by law provide for the case wherein neither a President-elect nor a Vice-President–elect shall have qualified, declaring who shall then act as President, or the manner in which one who is to act shall be selected, and such persons shall act accordingly until a President or Vice-President shall have qualified.

Section 4   The Congress may by law provide for the case of the death of any of the persons from whom the House of Representatives may choose a President whenever the right of choice shall have devolved upon them, and for the case of the death of any of the persons from whom the Senate may choose a Vice-President whenever the right of choice shall have devolved upon them.

Section 5   Sections 1 and 2 shall take effect on the 15th day of October following the ratification of this article.

Section 6   This article shall be inoperative unless it shall have been ratified as an amendment to the Constitution by the Legislatures of three-fourths of the several States within seven years from the date of its submission.

Amendment XXI

[Adopted 1933]

Section 1   The eighteenth article of amendment to the Constitution of the United States is hereby repealed.

Section 2   The transportation or importation into any State, Territory, or Possession of the United States for delivery or use therein of intoxicating liquors, in violation of the laws thereof, is hereby prohibited.

Section 3   This article shall be inoperative unless it shall have been ratified as an amendment to the Constitution by conventions in the several States, as provided in the Constitution, within seven years from the date of submission thereof to the States by the Congress.

Amendment XXII

[Adopted 1951]

Section 1   No person shall be elected to the office of President more than twice, and no person who has held the office of President, or acted as President, for more than two years of a term to which some other person was elected President shall be elected to the office of President more than once. But this article shall not apply to any person holding the office of President when this article was proposed by the Congress, and shall not prevent any person who may be holding the office of President, or acting as President, during the term within which this article becomes operative from holding the office of President or acting as President during the remainder of such term.

Section 2   This article shall be inoperative unless it shall have been ratified as an amendment to the Constitution by the legislatures of three-fourths of the several States within seven years from the date of its submission to the States by the Congress.

Amendment XXIII

[Adopted 1961]

Section 1   The District constituting the seat of Government of the United States shall appoint in such manner as the Congress may direct:

A number of electors of President and Vice-President equal to the whole number of Senators and Representatives in Congress to which the District would be entitled if it were a State, but in no event more than the least populous State; they shall be in addition to those appointed by the States, but they shall be considered for the purposes of the election of President and Vice-President, to be electors appointed by a State; and they shall meet in the District and perform such duties as provided by the twelfth article of amendment.

Section 2   The Congress shall have the power to enforce this article by appropriate legislation.

Amendment XXIV

[Adopted 1964]

Section 1   The right of citizens of the United States to vote in any primary or other election for President or Vice-President, for electors for President or Vice-President, or for Senator or Representative in Congress, shall not be denied or abridged by the United States or any State by reason of failure to pay any poll tax or other tax.

Section 2   The Congress shall have the power to enforce this article by appropriate legislation.

Amendment XXV

[Adopted 1967]

Section 1   In case of the removal of the President from office or of his death or resignation, the Vice-President shall become President.

Section 2   Whenever there is a vacancy in the office of the Vice-President, the President shall nominate a Vice-President who shall take office upon confirmation by a majority vote of both Houses of Congress.

Section 3   Whenever the President transmits to the President pro tempore of the Senate and the Speaker of the House of Representatives his written declaration that he is unable to discharge the powers and duties of his office, and until he transmits to them a written declaration to the contrary, such powers and duties shall be discharged by the Vice-President as Acting President.

Section 4   Whenever the Vice-President and a majority of either the principal officers of the executive departments or of such other body as Congress may by law provide, transmit to the President pro tempore of the Senate and the Speaker of the House of Representatives their written declaration that the President is unable to discharge the powers and duties of his office, the Vice-President shall immediately assume the powers and duties of the office as Acting President.

Thereafter, when the President transmits to the President pro tempore of the Senate and the Speaker of the House of Representatives his written declaration that no inability exists, he shall resume the powers and duties of his office unless the Vice-President and a majority of either the principal officers of the executive department[s] or of such other body as Congress may by law provide, transmit within four days to the President pro tempore of the Senate and the Speaker of the House of Representatives their written declaration that the President is unable to discharge the powers and duties of his office. Thereupon Congress shall decide the issue, assembling within forty-eight hours for that purpose if not in session. If the Congress, within twenty-one days after receipt of the latter written declaration, or, if Congress is not in session, within twenty-one days after Congress is required to assemble, determines by two-thirds vote of both Houses that the President is unable to discharge the powers and duties of his office, the Vice-President shall continue to discharge the same as Acting President; otherwise, the President shall resume the powers and duties of his office.

Amendment XXVI

[Adopted 1971]

Section 1   The right of citizens of the United States, who are eighteen years of age or older, to vote shall not be denied or abridged by the United States or by any State on account of age.

Section 2   The Congress shall have power to enforce this article by appropriate legislation.

Amendment XXVII

[Adopted 1992]

No law, varying the compensation for the services of the Senators and Representatives, shall take effect, until an election of Representatives shall have intervened.

The American People and Nation: A Statistical Profile

Population of the United States

Year	Number of States	Population	Percent Increase	Population Per Square Mile	Percent Urban/ Rural	Percent Male/ Female	Percent White/ Non-white	Persons Per House-hold	Median Age
1790	13	3,929,214		4.5	5.1/94.9	NA/NA	80.7/19.3	5.79	NA
1800	16	5,308,483	35.1	6.1	6.1/93.9	NA/NA	81.1/18.9	NA	NA
1810	17	7,239,881	36.4	4.3	7.3/92.7	NA/NA	81.0/19.0	NA	NA
1820	23	9,638,453	33.1	5.5	7.2/92.8	50.8/49.2	81.6/18.4	NA	16.7
1830	24	12,866,020	33.5	7.4	8.8/91.2	50.8/49.2	81.9/18.1	NA	17.2
1840	26	17,069,453	32.7	9.8	10.8/89.2	50.9/49.1	83.2/16.8	NA	17.8
1850	31	23,191,876	35.9	7.9	15.3/84.7	51.0/49.0	84.3/15.7	5.55	18.9
1860	33	31,443,321	35.6	10.6	19.8/80.2	51.2/48.8	85.6/14.4	5.28	19.4
1870	37	39,818,449	26.6	13.4	25.7/74.3	50.6/49.4	86.2/13.8	5.09	20.2
1880	38	50,155,783	26.0	16.9	28.2/71.8	50.9/49.1	86.5/13.5	5.04	20.9
1890	44	62,947,714	25.5	21.2	35.1/64.9	51.2/48.8	87.5/12.5	4.93	22.0
1900	45	75,994,575	20.7	25.6	39.6/60.4	51.1/48.9	87.9/12.1	4.76	22.9
1910	46	91,972,266	21.0	31.0	45.6/54.4	51.5/48.5	88.9/11.1	4.54	24.1
1920	48	105,710,620	14.9	35.6	51.2/48.8	51.0/49.0	89.7/10.3	4.34	25.3
1930	48	122,775,046	16.1	41.2	56.1/43.9	50.6/49.4	89.8/10.2	4.11	26.4
1940	48	131,669,275	7.2	44.2	56.5/43.5	50.2/49.8	89.8/10.2	3.67	29.0
1950	48	150,697,361	14.5	50.7	64.0/36.0	49.7/50.3	89.5/10.5	3.37	30.2
1960	50	179,323,175	18.5	50.6	69.9/30.1	49.3/50.7	88.6/11.4	3.33	29.5
1970	50	203,302,031	13.4	57.4	73.6/26.4	48.7/51.3	87.6/12.4	3.14	28.0
1980	50	226,542,199	11.4	64.1	73.7/26.3	48.6/51.4	85.9/14.1	2.75	30.0
1990	50	248,718,301	9.8	70.3	75.2/24.8	48.7/51.3	83.9/16.1	2.63	32.8
1998	50	270,299,000	8.0	76.4	NA	48.9/51.1	82.5/17.5	2.62	35.2

NA = Not available.

Vital Statistics

| Year | Birth Rate* | Death Rate* | Life Expectancy in Years | | | | | Marriage Rate | Divorce Rate |
			Total Population	White Females	Nonwhite Females	White Males	Nonwhite Males		
1790	NA	NA	NA	NA	NA	NA	NA	NA	NA
1800	55.0	NA	NA	NA	NA	NA	NA	NA	NA
1810	54.3	NA	NA	NA	NA	NA	NA	NA	NA
1820	55.2	NA	NA	NA	NA	NA	NA	NA	NA
1830	51.4	NA	NA	NA	NA	NA	NA	NA	NA
1840	51.8	NA	NA	NA	NA	NA	NA	NA	NA
1850	43.3	NA	NA	NA	NA	NA	NA	NA	NA
1860	44.3	NA	NA	NA	NA	NA	NA	NA	NA
1870	38.3	NA	NA	NA	NA	NA	NA	NA	NA
1880	39.8	NA	NA	NA	NA	NA	NA	NA	NA
1890	31.5	NA	NA	NA	NA	NA	NA	NA	NA
1900	32.3	17.2	47.3	48.7	33.5	46.6	32.5	NA	NA
1910	30.1	14.7	50.0	52.0	37.5	48.6	33.8	NA	NA
1920	27.7	13.0	54.1	55.6	45.2	54.4	45.5	12.0	1.6
1930	21.3	11.3	59.7	63.5	49.2	59.7	47.3	9.2	1.6
1940	19.4	10.8	62.9	66.6	54.9	62.1	51.5	12.1	2.0
1950	24.1	9.6	68.2	72.2	62.9	66.5	59.1	11.1	2.6
1960	23.7	9.5	69.7	74.1	66.3	67.4	61.1	8.5	2.2
1970	18.4	9.5	70.8	75.6	69.4	68.0	61.3	10.6	3.5
1980	15.9	8.8	73.7	78.1	73.6	70.7	65.3	10.6	5.2
1990	16.6	8.6	75.4	79.4	75.2	72.7	67.0	9.8	4.7
1998	14.4	8.5	76.5†	73.9†	76.1°	74.3†	68.9°	8.9†	4.3

Note: Data per one thousand for Birth, Death, Marriage, and Divorce Rates.

NA = Not available. *Data for 1800, 1810, 1830, 1850, 1870, and 1890 for whites only. †Data for 1997. °Data for 1996.

Immigrants to the United States

Immigration Totals by Decade			
Years	Number	Years	Number
1820–1830	151,824	1911–1920	5,735,811
1831–1840	599,125	1921–1930	4,107,209
1841–1850	1,713,251	1931–1940	528,431
1851–1860	2,598,214	1941–1950	1,035,039
1861–1870	2,314,824	1951–1960	2,515,479
1871–1880	2,812,191	1961–1970	3,321,677
1881–1890	5,246,613	1971–1980	4,493,314
1891–1900	3,687,546	1981–1990	7,338,062
1901–1910	8,795,386	1991–1997	6,944,591
		Total	63,938,605

Major Sources of Immigrants by Country or Region (in thousands)

Period	Asia[a]	Germany	Mexico	Italy	Great Britain (UK)[b]	Ireland	Canada	Austria and Hungary	Soviet Union (Russia)	Caribbean	Central America and South America	Norway and Sweden
1820–1830	—	8	5	—	27	54	2	—	—	4	—	—
1831–1840	—	152	7	2	76	207	14	—	—	12	—	1
1841–1850	—	435	3	2	267	781	42	—	—	14	4	14
1851–1860	42	952	3	9	424	914	59	—	—	11	2	21
1861–1870	65	787	2	12	607	436	154	8	3	9	1	109
1871–1880	124	718	5	56	548	437	384	73	39	14	1	211
1881–1890	70	1,453	2[c]	307	807	655	393	354	213	29	3	568
1891–1900	75	505	1[c]	652	272	388	3	593	505	33	2	321
1901–1910	324	341	50	2,046	526	339	179	2,145	1,597	108	25	440
1911–1920	247	144	219	1,110	341	146	742	896	921	123	59	161
1921–1930	112	412	459	455	340	211	925	64	62	75	58	166
1931–1940	17	114	22	68	32	11	109	11	1	16	14	9
1941–1950	37	227	61	58	139	20	172	28	—	50	43	21
1951–1960	153	478	300	185	203	48	378	104	—	123	136	45
1961–1970	428	191	454	214	214	33	413	26	2	470	359	33
1971–1980	1,588	74	640	129	137	11	170	16	39	741	430	10
1981–1990	2,738	92	2,336	67	160	32	157	25	58	872	930	15
1991–1997	2,134	66	1,801	56	118	54	143	20	357	750	786	13
Total	8,153	7,149	5,689	5,429	5,238	4,779	4,439	4,363	3,801	3,453	2,856	2,159

Notes: Numbers for periods are rounded. Dash indicates less than 1,000. [a]Includes Middle East. [b]Since 1925, includes England, Scotland, Wales, and Northern Ireland data. [c]No data available for 1886–1894.

The American Worker

Year	Total Number of Workers	Males as Percent of Total Workers	Females as Percent of Total Workers	Married Women as Percent of Female Workers	Female Workers as Percent of Female Population	Percent of Labor Force Unemployed	Percent of Workers in Labor Unions
1870	12,506,000	85	15	NA	NA	NA	
1880	17,392,000	85	15	NA	NA	NA	
1890	23,318,000	83	17	14	19	4 (1894 = 18)	
1900	29,073,000	82	18	15	21	5	
1910	38,167,000	79	21	25	25	6	
1920	41,614,000	79	21	23	24	5 (1921 = 12)	
1930	48,830,000	78	22	29	25	9 (1933 = 25)	
1940	53,011,000	76	24	36	27	15 (1944 = 1)	
1950	62,208,000	72	28	52	31	5.3	
1960	69,628,000	67	33	55	38	5.5	
1970	82,771,000	62	38	59	43	4.9	
1980	106,940,000	58	42	55	52	7.1	
1990	125,840,000	55	45	54	58	5.6	
1998	137,673,000	54	46	53	60	4.5	

NA = Not available.

The American Economy

Year	Gross National Product (GNP) and Gross Domestic Product (GDP)[a] (in $ billions)	Steel Production (in tons)	Corn Production (millions of bushels)	Automobiles Registered	New Housing Starts	Foreign Trade (in $ millions) Exports	Foreign Trade (in $ millions) Imports
1790	NA	NA	NA	NA	NA	20	23
1800	NA	NA	NA	NA	NA	71	91
1810	NA	NA	NA	NA	NA	67	85
1820	NA	NA	NA	NA	NA	70	74
1830	NA	NA	NA	NA	NA	74	71
1840	NA	NA	NA	NA	NA	132	107
1850	NA	NA	592[d]	NA	NA	152	178
1860	NA	13,000	839[e]	NA	NA	400	362
1870	7.4[b]	77,000	1,125	NA	NA	451	462
1880	11.2[c]	1,397,000	1,707	NA	NA	853	761
1890	13.1	4,779,000	1,650	NA	328,000	910	823
1900	18.7	11,227,000	2,662	8,000	189,000	1,499	930
1910	35.3	28,330,000	2,853	458,300	387,000 (1918 = 118,000)	1,919	1,646
1920	91.5	46,183,000	3,071	8,131,500	247,000 (1925 = 937,000)	8,664	5,784
1930	90.7	44,591,000	2,080	23,034,700	330,000 (1933 = 93,000)	4,013	3,500
1940	100.0	66,983,000	2,457	27,465,800	603,000 (1944 = 142,000)	4,030	7,433
1950	286.5	96,836,000	3,075	40,339,000	1,952,000	9,997	8,954
1960	506.5	99,282,000	4,314	61,682,300	1,365,000	19,659	15,093
1970	1,016.0	131,514,000	4,200	89,279,800	1,434,000	42,681	40,356
1980	2,819.5	111,835,000	6,600	121,601,000	1,292,000	220,626	244,871
1990	5,764.9	98,906,000	7,933	143,550,000	1,193,000	394,030	485,453
1998	8,511.0	107,600,000	9,761	129,749,000[f]	1,617,000	682,100	911,900

[a]In December 1991 the Bureau of Economic Analysis of the U.S. government began featuring Gross Domestic Product rather than Gross National Product as the primary measure of U.S. production.

[b]Figure is average for 1869–1878.

[c]Figure is average for 1879–1888.

[d]Figure for 1849.

[e]Figure for 1859.

[f]Figure for 1997.

NA = Not available.

Federal Budget Outlays and Debt

Year	Defense[a]	Veterans Benefits[a]	Income Security[a]	Social Security[a]	Health and Medicare[a]	Education[a,d]	Net Interest Payments[a]	Federal Debt (dollars)
1790	14.9	4.1[b]	NA	NA	NA	NA	55.0	75,463,000[c]
1800	55.7	.6	NA	NA	NA	NA	31.3	82,976,000
1810	48.4 (1814: 79.7)	1.0	NA	NA	NA	NA	34.9	53,173,000
1820	38.4	17.6	NA	NA	NA	NA	28.1	91,016,000
1830	52.9	9.0	NA	NA	NA	NA	12.6	48,565,000
1840	54.3 (1847: 80.7)	10.7	NA	NA	NA	NA	.7	3,573,000
1850	43.8	4.7	NA	NA	NA	NA	1.0	63,453,000
1860	44.2 (1865: 88.9)	1.7	NA	NA	NA	NA	5.0	64,844,000
1870	25.7	9.2	NA	NA	NA	NA	41.7	2,436,453,000
1880	19.3	21.2	NA	NA	NA	NA	35.8	2,090,909,000
1890	20.9 (1899: 48.6)	33.6	NA	NA	NA	NA	11.4	1,222,397,000
1900	36.6	27.0	NA	NA	NA	NA	7.7	1,263,417,000
1910	45.1 (1919: 59.5)	23.2	NA	NA	NA	NA	3.1	1,146,940,000
1920	37.1	3.4	NA	NA	NA	NA	16.0	24,299,321,000
1930	25.3	6.6	NA	NA	NA	NA	19.9	16,185,310,000
1940	17.5 (1945: 89.4)	6.0	16.0	.3	.5	20.8	9.4	42,967,531,000
1950	32.2	20.3	9.6	1.8	.6	.6	11.3	256,853,000,000
1960	52.2	5.9	8.0	12.6	.9	1.0	7.5	290,525,000,000
1970	41.8	4.4	8.0	15.5	6.2	4.4	7.3	308,921,000,000
1980	22.7	3.6	14.6	20.1	9.4	5.4	8.9	909,050,000,000
1990	23.9	2.3	11.7	19.8	12.4	3.1	14.7	3,266,073,000,000
1998	16.2	2.5	14.1	22.9	19.6	3.3	14.7	5,555,565,000,000

[a]Figures represent percentage of total federal spending for each category. Not included are transportation, commerce, housing, and various other categories.

[b]1789–1791 figure.

[c]1791 figure.

[d]Includes training, employment, and social services.

NA = Not available.

The Fifty States, District of Columbia, and Puerto Rico

State	Date of Admission (with Rank)	Capital City	Population (1998) (with Rank)	Racial/Ethnic Distribution (1998)	Per Capita Personal Income (1998) (with Rank)	Total Area in Square Miles (with Rank)
Alabama (AL)	Dec. 14, 1819 (22)	Montgomery	4,352,000 (23)	White: 3,141,000; Black: 1,132,000; Hispanic: 36,000; Asian: 28,000; Native American: 15,000	$21,442 (40)	52,423 (30)
Alaska (AK)	Jan. 3, 1959 (49)	Juneau	614,000 (48)	White: 444,000; Black: 24,000; Hispanic: 19,000; Asian: 28,000; Native American: 100,000	$25,675 (20)	656,424 (1)
Arizona (AZ)	Feb. 14, 1912 (48)	Phoenix	4,669,000 (21)	White: 3,182,000; Black: 169,000; Hispanic: 963,000; Asian: 98,000; Native American: 256,000	$23,060 (35)	114,006 (6)
Arkansas (AR)	June 15, 1836 (25)	Little Rock	2,538,000 (33)	White: 2,055,000; Black: 408,000; Hispanic: 44,000; Asian: 19,000; Native American: 14,000	$20,346 (46)	53,182 (29)
California (CA)	Sept. 9, 1850 (31)	Sacramento	32,667,000 (1)	White: 16,511,000; Black: 2,456,000; Hispanic: 9,454,000; Asian: 3,938,000; Native American: 309,000	$27,503 (1)	163,707 (3)
Colorado (CO)	Aug. 1, 1876 (38)	Denver	3,971,000 (24)	White: 3,125,000; Black: 172,000; Hispanic: 541,000; Asian: 96,000; Native American: 37,000	$28,657 (18)	104,100 (8)
Connecticut (CT)	Jan. 9, 1788 (5)	Hartford	3,274,000 (29)	White: 3,125,000; Black: 172,000; Hispanic: 238,000; Asian: 96,000; Native American: 37,000	$37,598 (1)	5,544 (48)
Delaware (DE)	Dec. 7, 1787 (1)	Dover	744,000 (45)	White: 560,000; Black: 144,000; Hispanic: 22,000; Asian: 15,000; Native American: 2,000	$29,814 (6)	2,489 (49)
District of Columbia (DC)	U.S. Capital, Dec. 1, 1800	Washington (coextensive with DC)	523,000 (not ranked)	White: 149,000; Black: 326,000; Hispanic: 30,000; Asian: 16,000; Native American: 2,000	$33,433 (not ranked)	68 (not ranked)
Florida (FL)	Mar. 3, 1845 (27)	Tallahassee	14,916,000 (4)	White: 10,239,000; Black: 2,268,000; Hispanic: 2,080,000; Asian: 271,000; Native American: 58,000	$25,852 (19)	65,756 (22)
Georgia (GA)	Jan. 2, 1788 (4)	Atlanta	7,642,000 (10)	White: 5,100,000; Black: 2,181,000; Hispanic: 193,000; Asian: 149,000; Native American: 18,000	$25,020 (23)	59,441 (24)
Hawai'i (HI)	Aug. 21, 1959 (50)	Honolulu	1,193,000 (40)	White: 344,000; Black: 35,000; Hispanic: 51,000; Asian: 757,000; Native American: 7,000	$26,137 (17)	10,932 (43)
Idaho (ID)	July 3, 1890 (43)	Boise	1,229,000 (41)	White: 1,109,000; Black: 7,000; Hispanic: 82,000; Asian: 14,000; Native American: 17,000	$21,081 (43)	83,574 (14)
Illinois (IL)	Dec. 3, 1818 (21)	Springfield	12,045,000 (5)	White: 8,630,000; Black: 1,840,000; Hispanic: 1,145,000; Asian: 403,000; Native American: 27,000	$28,873 (8)	57,918 (25)
Indiana (IN)	Dec. 11, 1816 (19)	Indianapolis	5,899,000 (14)	White: 5,206,000; Black: 491,000; Hispanic: 132,000; Asian: 56,000; Native American: 15,000	$24,219 (29)	36,420 (38)

The Fifty States, District of Columbia, and Puerto Rico (continued)

State	Date of Admission (with Rank)	Capital City	Population (1998) (with Rank)	Racial/Ethnic Distribution (1998)	Per Capita Personal Income (1998) (with Rank)	Total Area in Square Miles (with Rank)
Iowa (IA)	Dec. 28, 1846 (29)	Des Moines	2,862,000 (30)	White: 2,709,000; Black: 57,000; Hispanic: 52,000; Asian: 36,000; Native American: 8,000	$23,925 (32)	56,276 (26)
Kansas (KS)	Jan. 29, 1861 (34)	Topeka	2,629,000 (32)	White: 2,278,000; Black: 155,000; Hispanic: 137,000; Asian: 46,000; Native American: 23,000	$24,981 (24)	82,282 (15)
Kentucky (KY)	June 1, 1792 (15)	Frankfort	3,936,000 (25)	White: 3,591,000; Black: 285,000; Hispanic: 28,000; Asian: 27,000; Native American: 6,000	$21,506 (39)	40,411 (37)
Louisiana (LA)	Apr. 30, 1812 (18)	Baton Rouge	4,369,000 (22)	White: 2,787,000; Black: 1,407,000; Hispanic: 100,000; Asian: 55,000; Native American: 19,000	$21,346 (41)	51,843 (31)
Maine (ME)	Mar. 15, 1820 (23)	Augusta	1,244,000 (39)	White: 1,215,000; Black: 6,000; Hispanic: 8,000; Asian: 9,000; Native American: 6,000	$22,952 (36)	35,387 (39)
Maryland (MD)	Apr. 28, 1788 (7)	Annapolis	5,135,000 (19)	White: 3,329,000; Black: 1,428,000; Hispanic: 158,000; Asian: 204,000; Native American: 16,000	$29,943 (5)	12,407 (42)
Massachusetts (MA)	Feb. 6, 1788 (6)	Boston	6,147,000 (13)	White: 5,217,000; Black: 395,000; Hispanic: 298,000; Asian: 223,000; Native American: 15,000	$32,797 (3)	10,555 (44)
Michigan (MI)	Jan. 26, 1837 (26)	Lansing	9,817,000 (8)	White: 7,961,000; Black: 1,405,000; Hispanic: 234,000; Asian: 158,000; Native American: 60,000	$25,857 (18)	96,705 (11)
Minnesota (MN)	May 11, 1858 (32)	Saint Paul	4,725,000 (20)	White: 4,328,000; Black: 141,000; Hispanic: 76,000; Asian: 124,000; Native American: 58,000	$27,510 (11)	86,943 (12)
Mississippi (MS)	Dec. 10, 1817 (20)	Jackson	2,752,000 (31)	White: 1,701,000; Black: 1,003,000; Hispanic: 18,000; Asian: 19,000; Native American: 10,000	$18,958 (50)	48,434 (32)
Missouri (MO)	Aug. 10, 1821 (24)	Jefferson City	5,439,000 (16)	White: 4,668,000; Black: 613,000; Hispanic: 77,000; Asian: 60,000; Native American: 21,000	$24,427 (28)	69,709 (21)
Montana (MT)	Nov. 8, 1889 (41)	Helena	880,000 (44)	White: 803,000; Black: 3,000; Hispanic: 13,000; Asian: 5,000; Native American: 56,000	$20,172 (47)	147,046 (4)
Nebraska (NE)	Mar. 1, 1867 (37)	Lincoln	1,663,000 (38)	White: 1,493,000; Black: 67,000; Hispanic: 66,000; Asian: 22,000; Native American: 15,000	$24,754 (27)	77,358 (16)
Nevada (NV)	Oct. 3, 1864 (36)	Carson City	1,747,000 (36)	White: 1,248,000; Black: 133,000; Hispanic: 253,000; Asian: 81,000; Native American: 31,000	$27,200 (14)	110,567 (7)
New Hampshire (NH)	June 21, 1788 (9)	Concord	1,185,000 (42)	White: 1,109,000; Black: 9,000; Hispanic: 16,000; Asian: 14,000; Native American: 2,000	$29,022 (7)	9,351 (46)
New Jersey (NJ)	Dec. 18, 1787 (3)	Trenton	8,115,000 (9)	White: 5,586,000; Black: 1,188,000; Hispanic: 866,000; Asian: 453,000; Native American: 22,000	$33,937 (2)	8,722 (47)
New Mexico (NM)	Jan. 6, 1912 (47)	Santa Fe	1,737,000 (37)	White: 834,000; Black: 45,000; Hispanic: 669,000; Asian: 26,000; Native American: 163,000	$19,936 (48)	121,598 (5)

The Fifty States, District of Columbia, and Puerto Rico (continued)

State	Date of Admission (with Rank)	Capital City	Population (1998) (with Rank)	Racial/Ethnic Distribution (1998)	Per Capita Personal Income (1998) (with Rank)	Total Area in Square Miles (with Rank)
New York (NY)	July 26, 1788 (11)	Albany	18,175,000 (3)	White: 11,895,000; Black: 3,220,000; Hispanic: 1,990,000; Asian: 995,000; Native American: 76,000	$31,734 (4)	54,471 (27)
North Carolina (NC)	Nov. 21, 1789 (12)	Raleigh	7,546,000 (11)	White: 5,545,000; Black: 1,665,000 Hispanic: 139,000; Asian: 100,000; Native American: 98,000	$24,036 (31)	53,821 (28)
North Dakota (ND)	Nov. 2, 1889 (39)	Bismarck	638,000 (47)	White: 593,000; Black: 4,000; Hispanic: 6,000; Asian: 5,000; Native American: 30,000	$21,675 (38)	70,704 (19)
Ohio (OH)	Mar. 1, 1803 (17)	Columbus	11,209,000 (7)	White: 9,610,000; Black: 1,290,000; Hispanic: 158,000; Asian: 129,000; Native American: 23,000	$25,134 (21)	44,828 (34)
Oklahoma (OK)	Nov. 16, 1907 (46)	Oklahoma City	3,347,000 (27)	White: 2,668,000; Black: 262,000; Hispanic: 109,000; Asian: 45,000; Native American: 263,000	$21,072 (44)	69,903 (20)
Oregon (OR)	Feb. 14, 1859 (33)	Salem	3,282,000 (28)	White: 2,888,000; Black: 61,000; Hispanic: 182,000; Asian: 106,000; Native American: 45,000	$24,766 (26)	98,386 (9)
Pennsylvania (PA)	Dec. 12, 1787 (2)	Harrisburg	12,001,000 (6)	White: 10,354,000; Black: 1,166,000; Hispanic: 265,000; Asian: 198,000; Native American: 18,000	$26,792 (16)	46,058 (33)
Puerto Rico (PR)	Ascession 1898; Common-wealth Status 1952	San Juan	3,860,000 (not ranked)	White: <1,000; Black: <1,000; Hispanic: 3,856,000; Asian: <1,000	$7,882* (not ranked)	3,427*
Rhode Island (RI)	May 29, 1790 (13)	Providence	988,000 (43)	White: 859,000; Black: 49,000; Hispanic: 52,000; Asian: 23,000; Native American: 5,000	$26,797 (15)	1,545 (50)
South Carolina (SC)	May 23, 1788 (8)	Columbia	3,836,000 (26)	White: 2,603,000; Black: 1,147,000; Hispanic: 42,000; Asian: 34,000; Native American: 9,000	$21,309 (42)	32,008 (40)
South Dakota (SD)	Nov. 2, 1889 (40)	Pierre	738,000 (46)	White: 662,000; Black: 5,000; Hispanic: 7,000; Asian: 5,000; Native American: 59,000	$22,114 (37)	77,121 (17)
Tennessee (TN)	June 1, 1796 (16)	Nashville	5,431,000 (17)	White: 4,413,000; Black: 900,000; Hispanic: 54,000; Asian: 53,000; Native American: 12,000	$23,559 (33)	42,149 (36)
Texas (TX)	Dec. 29, 1845 (28)	Austin	18,760,000 (2)	White: 11,038,000; Black: 2,430,000; Hispanic: 5,640,000; Asian: 556,000; Native American: 96,000	$24,957 (25)	268,601 (2)
Utah (UT)	Jan. 4, 1896 (45)	Salt Lake City	2,100,000 (32)	White: 1,866,000; Black: 19,000; Hispanic: 132,000; Asian: 53,000; Native American: 30,000	$21,019 (45)	84,904 (13)
Vermont (VT)	Mar. 4, 1791 (14)	Montpelier	591,000 (49)	White: 577,000; Black: 3,000; Hispanic: 5,000; Asian: 5,000; Native American: 2,000	$24,175 (30)	9,615 (45)
Virginia (VA)	June 25, 1788 (10)	Richmond	6,791,000 (12)	White: 4,943,000; Black: 1,363,000 Hispanic: 220,000; Asian: 247,000; Native American: 19,000	$27,385 (13)	42,777 (35)

The Fifty States, District of Columbia,
and Puerto Rico (continued)

State	Date of Admission (with Rank)	Capital City	Population (1998) (with Rank)	Racial/Ethnic Distribution (1998)	Per Capita Personal Income (1998) (with Rank)	Total Area in Square Miles (with Rank)
Washington (WA)	Nov. 11, 1889 (42)	Olympia	5,689,000 (15)	White: 4,743,000; Black: 198,000; Hispanic: 315,000; Asian: 330,000; Native American: 103,000	$27,961 (11)	71,302 (18)
West Virginia (WV)	June 20, 1863 (35)	Charleston	1,811,000 (35)	White: 1,732,000; Black: 58,000; Hispanic: 9,000; Asian: 9,000; Native American: 3,000	$19,362 (49)	24,231 (41)
Wisconsin (WI)	May 29, 1848 (30)	Madison	5,224,000 (18)	White: 4,687,000; Black: 291,000; Hispanic: 120,000; Asian: 80,000; Native American: 56,000	$25,079 (22)	65,499 (23)
Wyoming (WY)	July 10, 1890 (44)	Cheyenne	481,000 (50)	White: 435,000; Black: 4,000; Hispanic: 27,000; Asian: 4,000; Native American: 11,000	$23,167 (34)	97,818 (10)

*1996 figure.

Presidential Elections

Year	Number of States	Candidates	Parties	Popular Vote	% of Popular Vote	Electoral Vote	% Voter Participation[a]
1789	10	**George Washington**	No party			69	
		John Adams	designations			34	
		Other candidates				35	
1792	15	**George Washington**	No party			132	
		John Adams	designations			77	
		George Clinton				50	
		Other candidates				5	
1796	16	**John Adams**	Federalist			71	
		Thomas Jefferson	Democratic-Republican			68	
		Thomas Pinckney	Federalist			59	
		Aaron Burr	Democratic-Republican			30	
		Other candidates				48	
1800	16	**Thomas Jefferson**	Democratic-Republican			73	
		Aaron Burr	Democratic-Republican			73	
		John Adams	Federalist			65	
		Charles C. Pinckney	Federalist			64	
		John Jay	Federalist			1	
1804	17	**Thomas Jefferson**	Democratic-Republican			162	
		Charles C. Pinckney	Federalist			14	
1808	17	**James Madison**	Democratic-Republican			122	
		Charles C. Pinckney	Federalist			47	
		George Clinton	Democratic-Republican			6	
1812	18	**James Madison**	Democratic-Republican			128	
		DeWitt Clinton	Federalist			89	
1816	19	**James Monroe**	Democratic-Republican			183	
		Rufus King	Federalist			34	
1820	24	**James Monroe**	Democratic-Republican			231	
		John Quincy Adams	Independent Republican			1	

Presidential Elections (continued)

Year	Number of States	Candidates	Parties	Popular Vote	% of Popular Vote	Electoral Vote	% Voter Participation[b]
1824	24	**John Quincy Adams**	Democratic-Republican	108,740	30.5	84	26.9
		Andrew Jackson	Democratic-Republican	153,544	43.1	99	
		Henry Clay	Democratic-Republican	47,136	13.2	37	
		William H. Crawford	Democratic-Republican	46,618	13.1	41	
1828	24	**Andrew Jackson**	Democratic	647,286	56.0	178	57.6
		John Quincy Adams	National Republican	508,064	44.0	83	
1832	24	**Andrew Jackson**	Democratic	701,780	54.2	219	55.4
		Henry Clay	National Republican	484,205	37.4	49	
		Other candidates		107,988	8.0	18	
1836	26	**Martin Van Buren**	Democratic	764,176	50.8	170	57.8
		William H. Harrison	Whig	550,816	36.6	73	
		Hugh L. White	Whig	146,107	9.7	26	
1840	26	**William H. Harrison**	Whig	1,274,624	53.1	234	80.2
		Martin Van Buren	Democratic	1,127,781	46.9	60	
1844	26	**James K. Polk**	Democratic	1,338,464	49.6	170	78.9
		Henry Clay	Whig	1,300,097	48.1	105	
		James G. Birney	Liberty	62,300	2.3		
1848	30	**Zachary Taylor**	Whig	1,360,967	47.4	163	72.7
		Lewis Cass	Democratic	1,222,342	42.5	127	
		Martin Van Buren	Free Soil	291,263	10.1		
1852	31	**Franklin Pierce**	Democratic	1,601,117	50.9	254	69.6
		Winfield Scott	Whig	1,385,453	44.1	42	
		John P. Hale	Free Soil	155,825	5.0		
1856	31	**James Buchanan**	Democratic	1,832,955	45.3	174	78.9
		John C. Frémont	Republican	1,339,932	33.1	114	
		Millard Fillmore	American	871,731	21.6	8	
1860	33	**Abraham Lincoln**	Republican	1,865,593	39.8	180	81.2
		Stephen A. Douglas	Democratic	1,382,713	29.5	12	
		John C. Breckinridge	Democratic	848,356	18.1	72	
		John Bell	Constitutional Union	592,906	12.6	39	
1864	36	**Abraham Lincoln**	Republican	2,206,938	55.0	212	73.8
		George B. McClellan	Democratic	1,803,787	45.0	21	
1868	37	**Ulysses S. Grant**	Republican	3,013,421	52.7	214	78.1
		Horatio Seymour	Democratic	2,706,829	47.3	80	

Presidential Elections (continued)

Year	Number of States	Candidates	Parties	Popular Vote	% of Popular Vote	Electoral Vote	% Voter Participation[b]
1872	37	**Ulysses S. Grant**	Republican	3,596,745	55.6	286	71.3
		Horace Greeley	Democratic	2,843,446	43.9	[b]	
1876	38	**Rutherford B. Hayes**	Republican	4,036,572	48.0	185	81.8
		Samuel J. Tilden	Democratic	4,284,020	51.0	184	
1880	38	**James A. Garfield**	Republican	4,453,295	48.5	214	79.4
		Winfield S. Hancock	Democratic	4,414,082	48.1	155	
		James B. Weaver	Greenback-Labor	308,578	3.4		
1884	38	**Grover Cleveland**	Democratic	4,879,507	48.5	219	77.5
		James G. Blaine	Republican	4,850,293	48.2	182	
		Benjamin F. Butler	Greenback-Labor	175,370	1.8		
		John P. St. John	Prohibition	150,369	1.5		
1888	38	**Benjamin Harrison**	Republican	5,447,129	47.9	233	79.3
		Grover Cleveland	Democratic	5,537,857	48.6	168	
		Clinton B. Fisk	Prohibition	249,506	2.2		
		Anson J. Streeter	Union Labor	146,935	1.3		
1892	44	**Grover Cleveland**	Democratic	5,555,426	46.1	277	74.7
		Benjamin Harrison	Republican	5,182,690	43.0	145	
		James B. Weaver	People's	1,029,846	8.5	22	
		John Bidwell	Prohibition	264,133	2.2		
1896	45	**William McKinley**	Republican	7,102,246	51.1	271	79.3
		William J. Bryan	Democratic	6,492,559	47.7	176	
1900	45	**William McKinley**	Republican	7,218,491	51.7	292	73.2
		William J. Bryan	Democratic; Populist	6,356,734	45.5	155	
		John C. Wooley	Prohibition	208,914	1.5		
1904	45	**Theodore Roosevelt**	Republican	7,628,461	57.4	336	65.2
		Alton B. Parker	Democratic	5,084,223	37.6	140	
		Eugene V. Debs	Socialist	402,283	3.0		
		Silas C. Swallow	Prohibition	258,536	1.9		
1908	46	**William H. Taft**	Republican	7,675,320	51.6	321	65.4
		William J. Bryan	Democratic	6,412,294	43.1	162	
		Eugene V. Debs	Socialist	420,793	2.8		
		Eugene W. Chafin	Prohibition	253,840	1.7		
1912	48	**Woodrow Wilson**	Democratic	6,296,547	41.9	435	58.8
		Theodore Roosevelt	Progressive	4,118,571	27.4	88	
		William H. Taft	Republican	3,486,720	23.2	8	
		Eugene V. Debs	Socialist	900,672	6.0		
		Eugene W. Chafin	Prohibition	206,275	1.4		
1916	48	**Woodrow Wilson**	Democratic	9,127,695	49.4	277	61.6
		Charles E. Hughes	Republican	8,533,507	46.2	254	

Presidential Elections (continued)

Year	Number of States	Candidates	Parties	Popular Vote	% of Popular Vote	Elec-toral Vote	% Voter Partici-pation[b]
		A. L. Benson	Socialist	585,113	3.2		
		J. Frank Hanly	Prohibition	220,506	1.2		
1920	48	**Warren G. Harding**	Republican	16,143,407	60.4	404	49.2
		James M. Cox	Democratic	9,130,328	34.2	127	
		Eugene V. Debs	Socialist	919,799	3.4		
		P. P. Christensen	Farmer-Labor	265,411	1.0		
1924	48	**Calvin Coolidge**	Republican	15,718,211	54.0	382	48.9
		John W. Davis	Democratic	8,385,283	28.8	136	
		Robert M. La Follette	Progressive	4,831,289	16.6	13	
1928	48	**Herbert C. Hoover**	Republican	21,391,993	58.2	444	56.9
		Alfred E. Smith	Democratic	15,016,169	40.9	87	
1932	48	**Franklin D. Roosevelt**	Democratic	22,809,638	57.4	472	56.9
		Herbert C. Hoover	Republican	15,758,901	39.7	59	
		Norman Thomas	Socialist	881,951	2.2		
1936	48	**Franklin D. Roosevelt**	Democratic	27,752,869	60.8	523	61.0
		Alfred M. Landon	Republican	16,674,665	36.5	8	
		William Lemke	Union	882,479	1.9		
1940	48	**Franklin D. Roosevelt**	Democratic	27,307,819	54.8	449	62.5
		Wendell L. Wilkie	Republican	22,321,018	44.8	82	
1944	48	**Franklin D. Roosevelt**	Democratic	25,606,585	53.5	432	55.9
		Thomas E. Dewey	Republican	22,014,745	46.0	99	
1948	48	**Harry S Truman**	Democratic	24,179,345	49.6	303	53.0
		Thomas E. Dewey	Republican	21,991,291	45.1	189	
		J. Strom Thurmond	States' Rights	1,176,125	2.4	39	
		Henry A. Wallace	Progressive	1,157,326	2.4		
1952	48	**Dwight D. Eisenhower**	Republican	33,936,234	55.1	442	63.3
		Adlai E. Stevenson	Democratic	27,314,992	44.4	89	
1956	48	**Dwight D. Eisenhower**	Republican	35,590,472	57.6	457	60.6
		Adlai E. Stevenson	Democratic	26,022,752	42.1	73	
1960	50	**John F. Kennedy**	Democratic	34,226,731	49.7	303	62.8
		Richard M. Nixon	Republican	34,108,157	49.5	219	
1964	50	**Lyndon B. Johnson**	Democratic	43,129,566	61.1	486	61.7
		Barry M. Goldwater	Republican	27,178,188	38.5	52	
1968	50	**Richard M. Nixon**	Republican	31,785,480	43.4	301	60.6
		Hubert H. Humphrey	Democratic	31,275,166	42.7	191	
		George C. Wallace	American Independent	9,906,473	13.5	46	
1972	50	**Richard M. Nixon**	Republican	47,169,911	60.7	520	55.2

Presidential Elections (continued)

Year	Number of States	Candidates	Parties	Popular Vote	% of Popular Vote	Electoral Vote	% Voter Participation[b]
		George S. McGovern	Democratic	29,170,383	37.5	17	
		John G. Schmitz	American	1,099,482	1.4		
1976	50	**James E. Carter**	Democratic	40,830,763	50.1	297	53.5
		Gerald R. Ford	Republican	39,147,793	48.0	240	
1980	50	**Ronald W. Reagan**	Republican	43,904,153	50.7	489	52.6
		James E. Carter	Democratic	35,483,883	41.0	49	
		John B. Anderson	Independent	5,720,060	6.6	0	
		Ed Clark	Libertarian	921,299	1.1	0	
1984	50	**Ronald W. Reagan**	Republican	54,455,075	58.8	525	53.3
		Walter F. Mondale	Democratic	37,577,185	40.6	13	
1988	50	**George H. W. Bush**	Republican	48,886,097	53.4	426	50.1
		Michael S. Dukakis	Democratic	41,809,074	45.6	111[c]	
1992	50	**William J. Clinton**	Democratic	44,909,326	43.0	370	55.2
		George H. W. Bush	Republican	39,103,882	37.4	168	
		H. Ross Perot	Independent	19,741,048	18.9	0	
1996	50	**William J. Clinton**	Democratic	47,402,357	49.2	379	49.1
		Robert J. Dole	Republican	39,196,755	40.7	159	
		H. Ross Perot	Reform	8,085,402	8.4	0	
		Ralph Nader	Green	684,902	0.7	0	

Candidates receiving less than 1 percent of the popular vote have been omitted. Thus the percentage of popular vote given for any election year may not total 100 percent.

Before the passage of the Twelfth Amendment in 1804, the Electoral College voted for two presidential candidates; the runner-up became vice president.

Before 1824, most presidential electors were chosen by state legislatures, not by popular vote.

[a]Percent of voting-age population casting ballots.

[b]Greeley died shortly after the election; the electors supporting him then divided their votes among minor candidates.

[c]One elector from West Virginia cast her Electoral College presidential ballot for Lloyd Bentsen, the Democratic Party's vice-presidential candidate.

Presidents and Vice Presidents

1. President	**George Washington**	1789–1797
Vice President	John Adams	1789–1797
2. President	**John Adams**	1797–1801
Vice President	Thomas Jefferson	1797–1801
3. President	**Thomas Jefferson**	1801–1809
Vice President	Aaron Burr	1801–1805
Vice President	George Clinton	1805–1809
4. President	**James Madison**	1809–1817
Vice President	George Clinton	1809–1813
Vice President	Elbridge Gerry	1813–1817
5. President	**James Monroe**	1817–1825
Vice President	Daniel Tompkins	1817–1825
6. President	**John Quincy Adams**	1825–1829
Vice President	John C. Calhoun	1825–1829
7. President	**Andrew Jackson**	1829–1837
Vice President	John C. Calhoun	1829–1833
Vice President	Martin Van Buren	1833–1837
8. President	**Martin Van Buren**	1837–1841
Vice President	Richard M. Johnson	1837–1841
9. President	**William H. Harrison**	1841
Vice President	John Tyler	1841
10. President	**John Tyler**	1841–1845
Vice President	None	
11. President	**James K. Polk**	1845–1849
Vice President	George M. Dallas	1845–1849
12. President	**Zachary Taylor**	1849–1850
Vice President	Millard Fillmore	1849–1850
13. President	**Millard Fillmore**	1850–1853
Vice President	None	
14. President	**Franklin Pierce**	1853–1857
Vice President	William R. King	1853–1857
15. President	**James Buchanan**	1857–1861
Vice President	John C. Breckinridge	1857–1861
16. President	**Abraham Lincoln**	1861–1865
Vice President	Hannibal Hamlin	1861–1865
Vice President	Andrew Johnson	1865
17. President	**Andrew Johnson**	1865–1869
Vice President	None	
18. President	**Ulysses S. Grant**	1869–1877

Vice President	Schuyler Colfax	1869–1873
Vice President	Henry Wilson	1873–1877
19. President	**Rutherford B. Hayes**	1877–1881
Vice President	William A. Wheeler	1877–1881
20. President	**James A. Garfield**	1881
Vice President	Chester A. Arthur	1881
21. President	**Chester A. Arthur**	1881–1885
Vice President	None	
22. President	**Grover Cleveland**	1885–1889
Vice President	Thomas A. Hendricks	1885–1889
23. President	**Benjamin Harrison**	1889–1893
Vice President	Levi P. Morton	1889–1893
24. President	**Grover Cleveland**	1893–1897
Vice President	Adlai E. Stevenson	1893–1897
25. President	**William McKinley**	1897–1901
Vice President	Garret A. Hobart	1897–1901
Vice President	Theodore Roosevelt	1901
26. President	**Theodore Roosevelt**	1901–1909
Vice President	Charles Fairbanks	1905–1909
27. President	**William H. Taft**	1909–1913
Vice President	James S. Sherman	1909–1913
28. President	**Woodrow Wilson**	1913–1921
Vice President	Thomas R. Marshall	1913–1921
29. President	**Warren G. Harding**	1921–1923
Vice President	Calvin Coolidge	1921–1923
30. President	**Calvin Coolidge**	1923–1929
Vice President	Charles G. Dawes	1925–1929
31. President	**Herbert C. Hoover**	1929–1933
Vice President	Charles Curtis	1929–1933
32. President	**Franklin D. Roosevelt**	1933–1945
Vice President	John N. Garner	1933–1941
Vice President	Henry A. Wallace	1941–1945
Vice President	Harry S Truman	1945
33. President	**Harry S Truman**	1945–1953
Vice President	Alben W. Barkley	1949–1953
34. President	**Dwight D. Eisenhower**	1953–1961
Vice President	Richard M. Nixon	1953–1961
35. President	**John F. Kennedy**	1961–1963
Vice President	Lyndon B. Johnson	1961–1963

Presidents and Vice Presidents (continued)

36. President	**Lyndon B. Johnson**	1963–1969
Vice President	Hubert H. Humphrey	1965–1969
37. President	**Richard M. Nixon**	1969–1974
Vice President	Spiro T. Agnew	1969–1973
Vice President	Gerald R. Ford	1973–1974
38. President	**Gerald R. Ford**	1974–1977
Vice President	Nelson A. Rockefeller	1974–1977
39. President	**James E. Carter**	1977–1981
Vice President	Walter F. Mondale	1977–1981
40. President	**Ronald W. Reagan**	1981–1989
Vice President	George H. W. Bush	1981–1989
41. President	**George H. W. Bush**	1989–1993
Vice President	J. Danforth Quayle	1989–1993
42. President	**William J. Clinton**	1993–2001
Vice President	Albert Gore	1993–2001

For a complete list of Presidents, Vice Presidents, and Cabinet Members, go to http://college.hmco.com.

Party Strength in Congress

Period	Congress	House Majority Party		House Minority Party		House Others	Senate Majority Party		Senate Minority Party		Senate Others	Party of President	
1789–91	1st	Ad	38	Op	26		Ad	17	Op	9		F	Washington
1791–93	2nd	F	37	DR	33		F	16	DR	13		F	Washington
1793–95	3rd	DR	57	F	48		F	17	DR	13		F	Washington
1795–97	4th	F	54	DR	52		F	19	DR	13		F	Washington
1797–99	5th	F	58	DR	48		F	20	DR	12		F	J. Adams
1799–1801	6th	F	64	DR	42		F	19	DR	13		F	J. Adams
1801–03	7th	DR	69	F	36		DR	18	F	13		DR	Jefferson
1803–05	8th	DR	102	F	39		DR	25	F	9		DR	Jefferson
1805–07	9th	DR	116	F	25		DR	27	F	7		DR	Jefferson
1807–09	10th	DR	118	F	24		DR	28	F	6		DR	Jefferson
1809–11	11th	DR	94	F	48		DR	28	F	6		DR	Madison
1811–13	12th	DR	108	F	36		DR	30	F	6		DR	Madison
1813–15	13th	DR	112	F	68		DR	27	F	9		DR	Madison
1815–17	14th	DR	117	F	65		DR	25	F	11		DR	Madison
1817–19	15th	DR	141	F	42		DR	34	F	10		DR	Monroe
1819–21	16th	DR	156	F	27		DR	35	F	7		DR	Monroe
1821–23	17th	DR	158	F	25		DR	44	F	4		DR	Monroe
1823–25	18th	DR	187	F	26		DR	44	F	4		DR	Monroe
1825–27	19th	Ad	105	J	97		Ad	26	J	20		C	J. Q. Adams
1827–29	20th	J	119	Ad	94		J	28	Ad	20		C	J. Q. Adams
1829–31	21st	D	139	NR	74		D	26	NR	22		D	Jackson
1831–33	22nd	D	141	NR	58	14	D	25	NR	21	2	D	Jackson
1833–35	23rd	D	147	AM	53	60	D	20	NR	20	8	D	Jackson
1835–37	24th	D	145	W	98		D	27	W	25		D	Jackson
1837–39	25th	D	108	W	107	24	D	30	W	18	4	D	Van Buren
1839–41	26th	D	124	W	118		D	28	W	22		D	Van Buren
1841–43	27th	W	133	D	102	6	W	28	D	22	2	W	W. Harrison
												W	Tyler
1843–45	28th	D	142	W	79	1	W	28	D	25	1	W	Tyler
1845–47	29th	D	143	W	77	6	D	31	W	25		D	Polk
1847–49	30th	W	115	D	108	4	D	36	W	21	1	D	Polk
1849–51	31st	D	112	W	109	9	D	35	W	25	2	W	Taylor
												W	Fillmore
1851–53	32nd	D	140	W	88	5	D	35	W	24	3	W	Fillmore
1853–55	33rd	D	159	W	71	4	D	38	W	22	2	D	Pierce
1855–57	34th	R	108	D	83	43	D	40	R	15	5	D	Pierce
1857–59	35th	D	118	R	92	26	D	36	R	20	8	D	Buchanan
1859–61	36th	R	114	D	92	31	D	36	R	26	4	D	Buchanan
1861–63	37th	R	105	D	43	30	R	31	D	10	8	R	Lincoln
1863–65	38th	R	102	D	75	9	R	36	D	9	5	R	Lincoln

Party Strength in Congress (continued)

Period	Congress	House Majority Party		House Minority Party		House Others	Senate Majority Party		Senate Minority Party		Senate Others	Party of President	
1865–67	39th	U	149	D	42		U	42	D	10		R	Lincoln
												R	A. Johnson
1867–69	40th	R	143	D	49		R	42	D	11		R	A. Johnson
1869–71	41st	R	149	D	63		R	56	D	11		R	Grant
1871–73	42nd	R	134	D	104	5	R	52	D	17	5	R	Grant
1873–75	43rd	R	194	D	92	14	R	49	D	19	5	R	Grant
1875–77	44th	D	169	R	109	14	R	45	D	29	2	R	Grant
1877–79	45th	D	153	R	140		R	39	D	36	1	R	Hayes
1879–81	46th	D	149	R	130	14	D	42	R	33	1	R	Hayes
1881–83	47th	D	147	R	135	11	R	37	D	37	1	R	Garfield
												R	Arthur
1883–85	48th	D	197	R	118	10	R	38	D	36	2	R	Arthur
1885–87	49th	D	183	R	140	2	R	43	D	34		D	Cleveland
1887–89	50th	D	169	R	152	4	R	39	D	37		D	Cleveland
1889–91	51st	R	166	D	159		R	39	D	37		R	B. Harrison
1891–93	52nd	D	235	R	88	9	R	47	D	39	2	R	B. Harrison
1893–95	53rd	D	218	R	127	11	D	44	R	38	3	D	Cleveland
1895–97	54th	R	244	D	105	7	R	43	D	39	6	D	Cleveland
1897–99	55th	R	204	D	113	40	R	47	D	34	7	R	McKinley
1899–1901	56th	R	185	D	163	9	R	53	D	26	8	R	McKinley
1901–03	57th	R	197	D	151	9	R	55	D	31	4	R	McKinley
												R	T. Roosevelt
1903–05	58th	R	208	D	178		R	57	D	33		R	T. Roosevelt
1905–07	59th	R	250	D	136		R	57	D	33		R	T. Roosevelt
1907–09	60th	R	222	D	164		R	61	D	31		R	T. Roosevelt
1909–11	61st	R	219	D	172		R	61	D	32		R	Taft
1911–13	62nd	D	228	R	161	1	R	51	D	41		R	Taft
1913–15	63rd	D	291	R	127	17	D	51	R	44	1	D	Wilson
1915–17	64th	D	230	R	196	9	D	56	R	40		D	Wilson
1917–19	65th	D	216	R	210	6	D	53	R	42		D	Wilson
1919–21	66th	R	240	D	190	3	R	49	D	47		D	Wilson
1921–23	67th	R	301	D	131	1	R	59	D	37		R	Harding
1923–25	68th	R	225	D	205	5	R	51	D	43	2	R	Coolidge
1925–27	69th	R	247	D	183	4	R	56	D	39	1	R	Coolidge
1927–29	70th	R	237	D	195	3	R	49	D	46	1	R	Coolidge
1929–31	71st	R	267	D	167	1	R	56	D	39	1	R	Hoover
1931–33	72nd	D	220	R	214	1	R	48	D	47	1	R	Hoover
1933–35	73rd	D	310	R	117	5	D	60	R	35	1	D	F. Roosevelt
1935–37	74th	D	319	R	103	10	D	69	R	25	2	D	F. Roosevelt
1937–39	75th	D	331	R	89	13	D	76	R	16	4	D	F. Roosevelt
1939–41	76th	D	261	R	164	4	D	69	R	23	4	D	F. Roosevelt
1941–43	77th	D	268	R	162	5	D	66	R	28	2	D	F. Roosevelt

Party Strength in Congress (continued)

Period	Congress	House Majority Party		House Minority Party		Others	Senate Majority Party		Senate Minority Party		Others	Party of President	
1943–45	78th	D	218	R	208	4	D	58	R	37	1	D	F. Roosevelt
1945–47	79th	D	242	R	190	2	D	56	R	38	1	D	Truman
1947–49	80th	R	245	D	188	1	R	51	D	45		D	Truman
1949–51	81st	D	263	R	171	1	D	54	R	42		D	Truman
1951–53	82nd	D	234	R	199	1	D	49	R	47		D	Truman
1953–55	83rd	R	221	D	211	1	R	48	D	47	1	R	Eisenhower
1955–57	84th	D	232	R	203		D	48	R	47	1	R	Eisenhower
1957–59	85th	D	233	R	200		D	49	R	47		R	Eisenhower
1959–61	86th	D	284	R	153		D	65	R	35		R	Eisenhower
1961–63	87th	D	263	R	174		D	65	R	35		D	Kennedy
1963–65	88th	D	258	R	117		D	67	R	33		D	Kennedy
												D	L. Johnson
1965–67	89th	D	295	R	140		D	68	R	32		D	L. Johnson
1967–69	90th	D	246	R	187		D	64	R	36		D	L. Johnson
1969–71	91st	D	245	R	189		D	57	R	43		R	Nixon
1971–73	92nd	D	254	R	180		D	54	R	44	2	R	Nixon
1973–75	93rd	D	239	R	192	1	D	56	R	42	2	R	Nixon
1975–77	94th	D	291	R	144		D	60	R	37	3	R	Ford
1977–79	95th	D	292	R	143		D	61	R	38	1	D	Carter
1979–81	96th	D	276	R	157		D	58	R	41	1	D	Carter
1981–83	97th	D	243	R	192		R	53	D	46	1	R	Reagan
1983–85	98th	D	269	R	166		R	54	D	46		R	Reagan
1985–87	99th	D	253	R	182		R	53	D	47		R	Reagan
1987–89	100th	D	258	R	177		D	55	R	45		R	Reagan
1989–91	101st	D	259	R	174		D	55	R	45		R	Bush
1991–93	102nd	D	267	R	167	1	D	56	R	44		R	Bush
1993–95	103rd	D	258	R	176	1	D	57	R	43		D	Clinton
1995–97	104th	R	230	D	204	1	R	52	D	48		D	Clinton
1997–99	105th	R	227	D	207	1	R	55	D	45		D	Clinton
1999–2001	106th	R	223	D	211	1	R	55	D	45		D	Clinton

AD = Administration; AM = Anti-Masonic; C = Coalition; D = Democratic; DR = Democratic-Republican; F = Federalist; J = Jacksonian; NR = National Republican; Op = Opposition; R = Republican; U = Unionist; W = Whig. Figures are for the beginning of the first session of each Congress, except the 93rd, which are for the beginning of the second session.

Justices of the Supreme Court

	Term of Service	Years of Service	Life Span		Term of Service	Years of Service	Life Span
John Jay	1789–1795	5	1745–1829	Ward Hunt	1873–1882	9	1810–1886
John Rutledge	1789–1791	1	1739–1800	*Morrison R. Waite*	1874–1888	14	1816–1888
William Cushing	1789–1810	20	1732–1810	John M. Harlan	1877–1911	34	1833–1911
James Wilson	1789–1798	8	1742–1798	William B. Woods	1880–1887	7	1824–1887
John Blair	1789–1796	6	1732–1800	Stanley Mathews	1881–1889	7	1824–1889
Robert H. Harrison	1789–1790	—	1745–1790	Horace Gray	1882–1902	20	1828–1902
James Iredell	1790–1799	9	1951–1799	Samuel Blatchford	1882–1893	11	1820–1893
Thomas Johnson	1791–1793	1	1732–1819	Lucius Q. C. Lamar	1888–1893	5	1825–1893
William Paterson	1793–1806	13	1745–1806	*Melville W. Fuller*	1888–1910	21	1833–1910
*John Rutledge**	1795	—	1739–1800	David J. Brewer	1890–1910	20	1837–1910
Samuel Chase	1796–1811	15	1741–1811	Henry B. Brown	1890–1906	16	1836–1913
Oliver Ellsworth	1796–1800	4	1745–1807	George Shiras, Jr.	1892–1903	10	1832–1924
Bushrod Washington	1798–1829	31	1762–1829	Howell E. Jackson	1893–1895	2	1832–1895
Alfred Moore	1799–1804	4	1755–1810	Edward D. White	1894–1910	16	1845–1921
John Marshall	1801–1835	34	1755–1835	Rufus W. Peckham	1895–1909	14	1838–1909
William Johnson	1804–1834	30	1771–1834	Joseph McKenna	1898–1925	26	1843–1926
H. Brockholst Livingston	1806–1823	16	1757–1823	Oliver W. Holmes	1902–1932	30	1841–1935
Thomas Todd	1807–1826	18	1765–1826	William D. Day	1903–1922	19	1849–1923
Joseph Story	1811–1845	33	1779–1845	William H. Moody	1906–1910	3	1853–1917
Gabriel Duval	1811–1835	24	1752–1844	Horace H. Lurton	1910–1914	4	1844–1914
Smith Thompson	1823–1843	20	1768–1843	Charles E. Hughes	1910–1916	5	1862–1948
Robert Trimble	1826–1828	2	1777–1828	Willis Van Devanter	1911–1937	26	1859–1941
John McLean	1829–1861	32	1785–1861	Joseph R. Lamar	1911–1916	5	1857–1916
Henry Baldwin	1830–1844	14	1780–1844	*Edward D. White*	1910–1921	11	1845–1921
James M. Wayne	1835–1867	32	1790–1867	Mahlon Pitney	1912–1922	10	1858–1924
Roger B. Taney	1836–1864	28	1777–1864	James C. McReynolds	1914–1941	26	1862–1946
Philip P. Barbour	1836–1841	4	1783–1841	Louis D. Brandeis	1916–1939	22	1856–1941
John Catron	1837–1865	28	1786–1865	John H. Clarke	1916–1922	6	1857–1945
John McKinley	1837–1852	15	1780–1852	*William H. Taft*	1921–1930	8	1857–1930
Peter V. Daniel	1841–1860	19	1784–1860	George Sutherland	1922–1938	15	1862–1942
Samuel Nelson	1845–1872	27	1792–1873	Pierce Butler	1922–1939	16	1866–1939
Levi Woodbury	1845–1851	5	1789–1851	Edward T. Sanford	1923–1930	7	1865–1930
Robert C. Grier	1846–1870	23	1794–1870	Harlan F. Stone	1925–1941	16	1872–1946
Benjamin R. Curtis	1851–1857	6	1809–1874	*Charles E. Hughes*	1930–1941	11	1862–1948
John A. Campbell	1853–1861	8	1811–1889	Owen J. Roberts	1930–1945	15	1875–1955
Nathan Clifford	1858–1881	23	1803–1881	Benjamin N. Cardozo	1932–1938	6	1870–1938
Noah H. Swayne	1862–1881	18	1804–1884	Hugo L. Black	1937–1971	34	1886–1971
Samuel F. Miller	1862–1890	28	1816–1890	Stanley F. Reed	1938–1957	19	1884–1980
David Davis	1862–1877	14	1815–1886	Felix Frankfurter	1939–1962	23	1882–1965
Stephen J. Field	1863–1897	34	1816–1899	William O. Douglas	1939–1975	36	1898–1980
Salmon P. Chase	1864–1873	8	1808–1873	Frank Murphy	1940–1949	9	1890–1949
William Strong	1870–1880	10	1808–1895	*Harlan F. Stone*	1941–1946	5	1872–1946
Joseph P. Bradley	1870–1892	22	1813–1892	James F. Byrnes	1941–1942	1	1879–1972

Justices of the Supreme Court (continued)

	Term of Service	Years of Service	Life Span		Term of Service	Years of Service	Life Span
Robert H. Jackson	1941–1954	13	1892–1954	Thurgood Marshall	1967–1991	24	1908–1993
Wiley B. Rutledge	1943–1949	6	1894–1949	*Warren C. Burger*	1969–1986	17	1907–1995
Harold H. Burton	1945–1958	13	1888–1964	Harry A. Blackmun	1970–1994	24	1908–1998
Fred M. Vinson	1946–1953	7	1890–1953	Lewis F. Powell, Jr.	1972–1987	15	1907–1998
Tom C. Clark	1949–1967	18	1899–1977	*William H. Rehnquist*	1972–	—	1924–
Sherman Minton	1949–1956	7	1890–1965	John P. Stevens III	1975–	—	1920–
Earl Warren	1953–1969	16	1891–1974	Sandra Day O'Connor	1981–	—	1930–
John Marshall Harlan	1955–1971	16	1899–1971	Antonin Scalia	1986–	—	1936–
William J. Brennan, Jr.	1956–1990	34	1906–1977	Anthony M. Kennedy	1988–	—	1936–
Charles E. Whittaker	1957–1962	5	1901–1973	David H. Souter	1990–	—	1939–
Potter Stewart	1958–1981	23	1915–1985	Clarence Thomas	1991–	—	1948–
Byron R. White	1962–1993	31	1917–	Ruth Bader Ginsburg	1993–	—	1933–
Arthur J. Goldberg	1962–1965	3	1908–1990	Stephen Breyer	1994–	—	1938–
Abe Fortas	1965–1969	4	1910–1982				

Note: Chief justices are in italics.

*Appointed and served one term, but not confirmed by the Senate.

INDEX

Library and Learning
Resources Center
Bergen Community College
400 Paramus Road
Paramus, N.J. 07652-1595

Return Postage Guaranteed

GREENLAND
(DENMARK)

ICELAND

80°N

60°N

ALASKA
(U.S.)

CANADA

IRELAND

PORTUGAL

40°N

Azores

Bermuda

ATLANTIC OCEAN

MOR

Midway Is.

WESTERN
SAHARA
(MOROCCO)

Hawaiian Is.

UNITED STATES

MEXICO

BAHAMAS

DOMINICAN REP.
Virgin Is.

CUBA

JAMAICA   HAITI

BELIZE

ST. KITTS AND NEVIS
ANTIGUA AND BARBUDA
DOMINICA
BARBADOS
ST. LUCIA
ST. VINCENT AND
THE GRENADINES

Puerto Rico

HONDURAS

GUATEMALA

NICARAGUA

EL SALVADOR

GRENADA

COSTA RICA

PANAMA

VENEZUELA

TRINIDAD AND TOBAGO

GUYANA

FR. GUIANA

COLOMBIA

PACIFIC OCEAN

20°N

MAURITAN

CAPE
VERDE

SENEGAL

GAMBIA

GUINEA-BISSAU   GUINEA

IV
CO

SIERRA
LEONE

LIBERIA

G

EQU

Equator

Galapagos Is.

ECUADOR

SURINAM

0°

SAO TOME

PERU

BRAZIL

WESTERN
SAMOA

BOLIVIA

TONGA

20°S

PARAGUAY

Easter Is.

CHILE

URUGUAY

ARGENTINA

40°S

Falkland Is.

160°W   140°W   120°W   100°W   80°W   60°W   40°W   20°W

60°S

80°S